FICTION CATALOG

EIGHTH EDITION

STANDARD CATALOG SERIES

ESTELLE A. FIDELL, GENERAL EDITOR

CHILDREN'S CATALOG

FICTION CATALOG

JUNIOR HIGH SCHOOL LIBRARY CATALOG

PUBLIC LIBRARY CATALOG

SENIOR HIGH SCHOOL LIBRARY CATALOG

FICTION CATALOG

EIGHTH EDITION

EDITED BY

ESTELLE A. FIDELL

74-538   NEW YORK
THE H. W. WILSON COMPANY
1971

PREFACE

FICTION CATALOG had its beginning in 1908 when The H. W. Wilson Company, then in Minneapolis, published a slight paperback called "English Prose Fiction, a selected list of about 2,000 titles, cataloged by author and title with annotations." Its preface characterized it as comprising "the best fiction of all time." Not all titles were annotated, presumably because a review could not always be found, but a source was cited for each annotation. Sixty-three years and seven editions later, FICTION CATALOG has developed into an important element of the Standard Catalog Series. Intended to be a companion volume to the PUBLIC LIBRARY CATALOG, whose bulk precludes the listing of fiction, the Catalog is primarily a list of adult fiction. Many titles are, however, suitable for young adult reading, and these are designated by a *y*.

New editions of both FICTION CATALOG and PUBLIC LIBRARY CATALOG, formerly published at ten-year intervals, will hereafter appear every five years. Each catalog will include four annual Supplements as a part of its service. This new publishing schedule will place FICTION CATALOG and PUBLIC LIBRARY CATALOG in conformity with the selection aids for school libraries: CHILDREN'S CATALOG, JUNIOR HIGH SCHOOL LIBRARY CATALOG, and SENIOR HIGH SCHOOL LIBRARY CATALOG.

This, the Eighth Edition of FICTION CATALOG, includes 4,315 titles selected by the staffs of a variety of public library systems. The systems are chosen with the advice of two divisions of the American Library Association: the Public Library Association and the Adult Services Division. Since, in most cases, the voting represents the collective opinion of several staff members of a library, the consensus has a relatively broad base.

As in previous editions, out-of-print titles have been included in the belief that good fiction is not superseded, even if, by chance, it goes out of print. The popularity of a title is, of course, not an infallible guide to its quality as a creative work.

During the 1960's the publication of large type books has dramatically increased; consequently, large type versions of titles have been included for the first time in FICTION CATALOG. Titles in this format are listed in the Title and Subject Index under the heading: Large type books.

The practice of starring titles has been discontinued in all Wilson catalogs, and it has been dropped in this edition of FICTION CATALOG. (The reasons for this decision are given in the Preface to the fifth edition of PUBLIC LIBRARY CATALOG, published in 1969.)

Titles, with minor exceptions, have been cataloged under the form of the author's name as it appeared on the title page. References have been made from all known variations of a name. There are 1,954 analytical entries for novelettes and composite works, which include titles previously published independently. Prices quoted have been obtained from the publisher and are as up to date as possible.

The primary purpose of FICTION CATALOG remains that of the first edition in 1908: to serve as a guide to the best fiction in the English language.

The H. W. Wilson Company sincerely thanks those publishers who have supplied copies of their books and provided information on prices and editions. In addition, the editor acknowledges indebtedness to a diligent staff. Finally, to the staffs of the following library systems who participated in the selection of titles, the publisher is most grateful:

Allentown Public Library
Allentown, Pa.

Atlanta Public Library
Atlanta, Ga.

Enoch Pratt Free Library
Baltimore, Md.

Burbank Public Library
Burbank, Calif.

Public Library of Charlotte & Mecklenburg
County
Charlotte, N.C.

Dallas Public Library
Dallas, Texas

Public Library
Dayton, Ohio

Public Library
Denver, Colo.

Public Library
East Cleveland, Ohio

Great Falls Public Library
Great Falls, Mont.

Hawaii State Library
Honolulu, Hawaii

Queens Borough Public Library
Jamaica, N.Y.

Miami Public Library
Miami, Fla.

Minneapolis Public Library
Minneapolis, Minn.

Phoenix Public Library
Phoenix, Ariz.

Library Association of Portland
Portland, Ore.

Providence Public Library
Providence, R.I.

Rochester Public Library
Rochester, N.Y.

Seattle Public Library
Seattle, Wash.

Syracuse Public Library
Syracuse, N.Y.

Public Library
West Allis, Wis.

Public Library
Yonkers, N.Y.

DIRECTIONS FOR USE

This Catalog is arranged in three parts as follows:

Part 1 is an author alphabet of the 4,315 titles with full bibliographical information followed by a brief annotation. Bibliographic data include name of the author as it appears on the title page, title of the book, publisher, date of publication, paging, and latest known price. In some instances several editions of the same work have been elected; these are listed alphabetically by publisher. Titles designated by the symbol y are deemed suitable for young adults.

Part 2 is a title and subject index to Part 1. Each book is entered under title and under the main subject or subjects of the story.

Part 3 is a Directory of Publishers and Distributors of the books listed.

TABLE OF CONTENTS

FICTION CATALOG

EIGHTH EDITION

Abaunza, Virginia

y Sundays from two to six. Bobbs 1956 222p
o.p. 1970

"A novel about the effect of parental separation upon Cody Benson, sixteen years old,
and her younger brothers, when they had to
adjust to seeing their father just on Sundays,
from two to six." Pub W

"This is not a lament but an honest and believable attempt to see an unhappy situation
clearly, in order to deal with it in the most sensible manner. The writing is competent, and
the atmosphere is relieved by the absence of
money worries." New Yorker

Abé, Kobo

The ruined map; tr. from the Japanese by
E. Dale Saunders. Knopf 1969 299p
boards $5.95

Original Japanese edition, 1967

The "non-hero is an overly conscientious private eye who undertakes to search for the missing husband of a quiet, unassuming Japanese
housewife. The lady, Nemuro Haru, proves not
what she seems. Soon he follows his few clues
into the Tokyo underworld—which one suspects is Abé's Tokyo underworld—and the
more deeply he becomes obsessed with the mystery, the more his mind identifies with the
lost man. . . . He winds up jobless, suffering
total amnesia, his mind, like the frightening
city whose most sinister corners he has explored, a ruined map." Pub W

This "is not escape literature for the mystery fan. It is a dramatically violent, instinctively earthy, complex and complicated melodrama, a novel for the man rather than for
the woman. . . . [It is] a novel for the man
who is interested in the intricacies of mental
processes as he follows the detective into the
world of the missing man." Best Sellers

The woman in the dunes; tr. from the
Japanese by E. Dale Saunders. With drawings by Machi Abé. Knopf 1964 239p illus
$4.95

"A symbolical novel about a Japanese en-
tomologist trapped in a strange sanddune village while looking for desert beetles along the
coast. In the village the houses are at the bottom of pits, and the villagers spend their lives
fighting the encroaching sand. The entomo-
logist, left in such a pit with a widow, tries
desperately to escape but in vain." Bk Buyer's
Guide

The author "follows with meticulous precision his hero's constantly shifting physical,
emotional and psychological states. He also
presents the most minute descriptions of the
trivia of everyday existence in a sandpit with
such compelling realism that these passages
serve both to heighten the credibility of the bizarre plot and subtly increase the interior tensions of the novel." N Y Times Bk R

Abrahams, Peter

Mine boy. Knopf 1955 252p o.p. 1970

"Kuma, handsome and strong, came from
the home of his tribe in the north seeking work
in Johannesburg. He had heard tales of the
workers needed in the mines and although
many tried to discourage him, he persisted in
his plan to become a mine worker. For Kuma
the real danger of the city was the sordid negro slum in which he was forced to live, and in
the hatred of the black men for all white people.
But the heroism of a white man and the love
of a negro woman were his salvation." Huntting

"'Mine Boy' should be taken for what it is—
a good story of what happened to one African
country boy who sought the City of Gold."
Christian Science Monitor

A wreath for Udomo. Knopf 1956 356p
o.p. 1970

"A novel of a possible near-future in a hypothetical African country. A successful revolution puts an educated Negro into a position of
power as prime minister. Helped by the whites,
he attempts to modernize the country and so
rouses the antagonisms of his own people and
is killed by them." Book Rev Digest

Abrahams, William

(ed.) Prize stories, 1969: The O. Henry
Awards. See Prize stories, 1969: the O. Henry
Awards

Abramov, Fyodor

One day in the "new life." Tr. by David
Floyd. Praeger 1963 174p o.p. 1970

Events of single day on a collective farm in
Russia. The author shows in a series of conversations between the chairman and various
members of the farm that there can be no reconciliation between the real interests of the
peasants and the instructions that filter down
to them, via their local authorities from the
remote great powers. (Publisher)

"Comment is made on the effectiveness of
the collective farms: the work does not get done
except through capitalistic incitements, namely, more and more money. The book is light,
but revealing reading and the author manages
to keep everything in a fine ironic glow." Best
Sellers

Achebe, Chinua

Arrow of God. Day [1967 c1964] 287p $5.50

First published 1964 in England

"Authenticity and simplicity in the telling
characterize this story of Nigeria where the
age-old tribal customs are in continuous conflict with the thoughts and ways of western-
ization. Ironically it is Ezeulu, Chief Priest of
Ulu, who is the one man of all the tribe to send
his son to missionary school. Ezeulu and his
son are the chief characters, with the English
administrator, Captain Winterbottom playing
a significant, if secondary role. It is the son's
over-zealous conversion to Christianity that
brings the final clash between Ezeulu and Winterbottom, and ends in tragedy for the Chief
Priest." Pub W

Things fall apart. McDowell, Obolensky
1959 215p $4.95

"The setting is a remote Nigerian village in
the late 19th century. The white man and his
civilization have not yet made their impact.
The life of the village still follows the formal, stately rhythm that has come down
through the centuries. For a self-made man
like Okonkwo there was pleasant security in
this old order of things. A stern but upright
man, he lived only to further himself and to
insure an untroubled world for his three wives
and his numerous children. The conversion of
one of his favorite sons to Christianity was
the utmost indignity that could befall him. It
killed him and it killed his world." N Y Her
Trib Books

The story is written in English by a Nigerian.
"No European ethnologist could so intimately
present this medley of mores of the Ibo tribe,
nor detail the intricate formalities of life in
the clan. . . . The flashbacks of the book
are confusing, the narration undisciplined, but
as an objective view of the Ibo customs it is
of both interest and value." Sat R

Acred, Arthur

Passions of the ring. Morrow 1967 289p boards $4.95

The setting is Ireland. In Boonham's small itinerant circus, "Boonham himself is the master hand, but without Jackie, his lovely daughter; or Conka, the wise and compassionate clown; or Sam, doctor to men and animals, he wouldn't be able to survive. His son, however, is a problem, rebellious against his father, yet afraid of him." Publisher's note

The author "captures all the color and excitement of circus life without sacrificing too much in the way of believable characterization and narrative along the way." Pub W

Aczel, Tamas

The ice age; a novel. Simon & Schuster 1965 287p $5.95

"When a Party official dies in the clinic run by honest and forthright Dr. Karolinsky, who hardly takes the trouble to hide his scorn of the Communists, the Party officials seize the opportunity to put on a great trial and show—which involves them as well as Karolinsky. Set in Hungary during the Stalin era." Bk Buyer's Guide

"The author, by burrowing into the lives of such people and by making them vivid to the reader, conjures up a veritable ice age. Personal warmth, freedom, spontaneity, even the seasons are chilled by the coldness of the regime." Book of the Month Club News

Adams, Andy

Log of a cowboy; a narrative of the old trail days; illus. by E. Boyd Smith. Houghton 1903 387p illus o.p. 1970

"The journal of a cattle drive, with a herd of several thousand, from Texas through Arkansas and Wyoming to the Blackfoot Agency in Montana. The account is admitted to be an extremely accurate picture of a bygone phase of existence in the Far West." Baker's Historical

Adams, Clifton

Hell command

In Western Writers of America. A Western boanza p 1-65

Tragg's choice. Doubleday 1969 186p $3.95

"DD western"

"An unusual Western novel of a grease paint hero who had to face real-life, six-gun danger." Book News

Adams, Henry

Democracy; an American novel. Farrar, Straus 1952 246p o.p. 1970

"Published anonymously in 1879, the central theme of this novel is the corruption of individual and political morality in the second administration of Ulysses S. Grant. It presents its picture of Washington society through the story of the relationship of a young hostess and a powerful politician." Huntting

Adams, Samuel Hopkins

Canal town; a novel. Random House 1944 465p o.p. 1970

"Set against an authentic historical background—York State in the 1820's—the plot concerns the problems of a young physician combating ignorance and prejudice, with the pitifully small medical knowledge of the time. The wealth of medical lore . . . and the folkways of the Upstaters make absorbing reading—while the doctor's romance with and marriage to the daughter of one of the town's two wealthiest men—and his involvement in the fateful and illicit love affair of the daughter of the other—provides the romantic background." Huntting

"The novel is highly successful in depicting the conflict of mass interests, the emergence and recession of individual leaders, in short, the whole pattern of social and economic conflict." Springf'd Republican

Tenderloin. Random House 1959 372p o.p. 1970

New York City in the Gay Nineties was in the toils of corrupt police and politicians who battened on the bribes they took from gambling houses and houses of prostitution. Dr Farr, a clergyman, determined to rid the city of this corruption, donned a disguise to gain entrance to places where he hoped to secure evidence. His friends warned him that this would lead to disaster. It nearly did, both for him and for them. (Publisher)

"It is a period piece with a period plot written in period prose. But it has the sentimental lift of a barbershop ballad and the charm of a day when women in hourglasses worshiped men out of mustache cups." Time

Ade, George

The America of George Ade (1866-1944); fables, short stories, essays; ed. with an introduction by Jean Shepherd. Putnam 1960 284p illus o.p. 1970

Analyzed in Short Story Index

Contains some 70 fables, 6 short stories, and 3 essays selected by the editor from George Ade's writings

"Selections from the work of an Indiana humorist whose writings incorporated the speech and mores of early-twentieth-century Midwesterners. Most of this delightfully entertaining book is devoted to gently satiric fables distinguished by a profusion of capital letters, appended morals, and an intuitive understanding of the average person's foibles and frustrations. Ade's America has changed but his humor, drawn as it is from the human condition, is still fresh and relevant." Booklist

Agee, James

y A death in the family. Grosset [1967 c1957] 339p $4.95

Pulitzer Prize, 1958

A reprint of the title first published 1957 by McDowell, Obolensky

"Published posthumously this simply but poetically told novel unfalteringly describes the impact of tragedy upon a close-knit family living in Knoxville, Tennessee in the early years of the present century. Beginning a few hours before Jay Follet's death in a car accident and ending on the day of his funeral the story, inhabited by wonderfully human people, offers a moving, warm, and unsentimental portrayal of love, death, and grief." Booklist

"The novel resolves nothing, answers no questions, solves no problems. But it does pose, with precision of phrase and in particular terms, a universal human situation most affectingly, for our observation and contemplation. To do this is noble achievement." Chicago Sunday Tribune

The morning watch. Houghton 1951 120p $3.50

"Young Richard takes part in the Morning Watch of a Tennessee church school on Good Friday. With remarkable perception and skill the author follows the boy's alternate moments of exaltation and of shame (as his mind wanders to earthly things), his yearning for noble self-sacrifice, and his final return to wholly normality." Retail Bookseller

"Mr. Agee takes full advantage of the power, evocativeness, and unbridled richness of liturgical language to achieve an effect of extreme tension, loneliness, and longing." New Yorker

Agnon, S. Y.

Nobel Prize in literature, 1966

Betrothed

In Agnon, S. Y. Two tales p 1-139

The bridal canopy; tr. by I. M. Lask. Schocken 1967 389p $5.95

Reissue of the title first written 1922 in Hebrew, published 1937 in English by Doubleday

"Reb Yudel, a poor but devout Jew, lived in Galicia in the early years of the nineteenth century. When it came time for his three dowerless daughters to marry the Rabbi commanded Reb Yudel to roam thruout Galicia in his search

Agnon, S. Y.—*Continued*

for dowries. Richly provided for by his neighbors he set out on his journey, accompanied by the teamster Nuta. The account of their wanderings is spiced with stories, and stories within stories which the two told each other on their way." Book Rev Digest

"The book is altogether rewarding, for its vigor and its narrative charm as well as for its fresh and recreative use of Hebrew tradition." Sat R

Edo and Enam

In Agnon, S. Y. Two tales p141-233

A guest for the night; tr. from the Hebrew by Misha Louvish. Schocken 1968 485p $6.95

First published 1939 in Israel

"A visitor from Palestine journeys to his native town in the Polish province of Galicia shortly after World War I. There he settles down at the local inn where he becomes, in a sense, 'a guest for the night' inasmuch as he remains apart from the life of the town itself and is able to observe its activities with some degree of impartiality. . . . Eventually, he is able to reconcile his strong attachment to the lost dead past with the ever changing present and looks to the Land of Israel as the hope of his people." Best Sellers

This book "is partly autobiographical, and it is rich in realistic detail. The precise and sympathetic portrayal of people and places vividly re-creates the world of Eastern European Jewry as it existed in the 1920s." Atlantic

In the heart of the seas; a story of a journey to the land of Israel; tr. from the Hebrew by I. M. Lask; with drawings by T. Herzl Rome. Schocken [1967 c1947] 128p illus $3.95

Reissue of the title first published 1947

"A folk tale in which a group of [pious] Jews journey from Middle Europe to the land of Israel, encountering along the way a miracle. An interesting original story told here as if it were an old legend, this is written in simple though archaic language. For those who know something about Hebrew history and literature. Hasidic mysticism and symbolism, it is a tale with many layers of significance." Pub W

Two tales; Betrothed & Edo and Enam; tr. from the Hebrew by Walter Lever. Schocken 1966 2v in 1 (237p) $4.95

These two short novels were originally published in 1943 and 1950, respectively

"'Betrothed,' the first of these tales, is set in Jaffa in the years before World War I; the second, 'Edo and Enam,' in Jerusalem after World War II." Publisher's note

There is a "kind of mystical, bitter-sweet humor that pervades these stories, the half-real, half-dreamlike quality they convey through a simplistic kind of narrative that is set down, not as allegory but as direct symbol." Library J

Agnon, Samuel Joseph. See Agnon, S. Y.

Aiken, Conrad

The blue voyage

In Aiken, C. The collected novels of Conrad Aiken p15-166

The collected novels of Conrad Aiken; Blue voyage, Great circle, King Coffin, A heart for the gods of Mexico [and] Conversation. Introduction by R. P. Blackmur. Holt 1964 575p o.p. 1970

The blue voyage, published 1927, describes the people and incidents of a transatlantic voyage, written mostly in stream-of-consciousness style. Great circle, published 1933, is a psychological novel also written in stream-of-consciousness style in which the central character, fighting alcoholism, fears his wife is untrue to him and his best friend has betrayed him. King Coffin, published 1935, is a psychological horror story which follows the twisted thinking of an intellectual mind rapidly going insane, as he broods over the idea of a perfect crime, the unmotivated murder of a

stranger. A heart for the gods of Mexico, written 1939 but not published in the United States before, a portrayal of Malcolm Lowry, takes a woman and two men on a mortal journey across a changing American landscape into a heightened awareness of life and finality. Conversation, published 1940, probes the conflict between art and human relationships in a domestic crisis between man and wife

The collected short stories of Conrad Aiken; preface by Mark Schorer. World Pub. 1960 566p $7.95

Contents: Bring! Bring; The last visit; Mr Arcularis; The bachelor supper; Bow down, Isaac; A pair of Vikings; Hey, taxi; Field of flowers; Gehenna; The disciple; Impulse; The anniversary; Hello. Tib; Smith and Jones; By my troth; Nerissa; Silent snow, secret snow; Round by round; Thistledown; State of mind; Strange moonlight; The fish supper; I love you very dearly; The dark city; Life isn't a short story; The night before prohibition; Spider, spider; A man alone at lunch; Farewell! Farewell! Your obituary, well written; A conversation; No. no, go not to Lethe; Pure as the driven snow; All, all wasted; The moment; The woman-hater; The professor's escape; The orange moth; The necktie; O how she laughed; West End; Fly away ladybird

In these stories "the author is mainly concerned with the individual's response to his inner consciousness and unconscious, with reality and appearance, with the line that divides the sane and the insane, tragedy and comedy, life and death." Pub W

Conversation

In Aiken, C. The collected novels of Conrad Aiken p473-575

Great circle

In Aiken, C. The collected novels of Conrad Aiken p167-295

A heart for the gods of Mexico

In Aiken, C. The collected novels of Conrad Aiken p415-72

King Coffin

In Aiken, C. The collected novels of Conrad Aiken p297-414

Ainsworth, W. Harrison

Old Saint Paul's; a tale of the plague & fire. Dutton 476p (Everyman's lib) $3.25

First published 1841; this edition 1911

"History of a London grocer and his family during the years of the Plague and the Fire (1665-6); rich in local and historical colour and in portraits of [contemporary] celebrities." Baker's Best

Aird, Catherine

Henrietta who? Published for the Crime Club by Doubleday 1968 188p o.p. 1970

"Until her widowed mother was killed in a hit-and-run accident, Henrietta thought her last name was Jenkins. And then the post-mortem revealed that Grace Jenkins had never borne a child—that her death was not an accident. . . . Why had Grace Jenkins never told her the truth? Inspector Sloan wanted answers to other questions. Was it a coincidence that the murderer struck just before Henrietta's twenty-first birthday?" Publisher's note

Set in a quiet English village, "this is a shrewdly plotted story, and Miss Aird's telling is entrancingly crisp." N Y Times Bk R

A most contagious game. Published for the Crime Club by Doubleday 1967 192p o.p. 1970

"At 52, Thomas Harding must learn to adapt himself to a quiet life of retirement, and at the same time adjust to the way of life in the country. His dull and placid existence is disrupted when he recognizes the feeling of secret guilt the villagers seem to share with the family that built his home in the days of the first Elizabeth, and their even stranger reaction to the brutal death of Mary Fenny. Two unsolved murders, and a skeleton in the closet are only part of the fun here." Library J

"An entertaining mystery that will appeal to those with a taste for English history." Pub W

Aird, Catherine—*Continued*

The religious body. Published for the Crime Club by Doubleday 1966 191p o.p. 1970

In a convent in a small English town "one of the nuns is found murdered and thrown down the cellar stairs. Inspector C. D. Sloan is unfamiliar with convents and nuns and is further mystified when students at a neighboring agricultural institute attempt to burn a 'Guy' on Bonfire Night and the effigy is dressed in nun's garments with the murdered nun's glasses tied on the face. Later one of the Institute students is strangled." Best Sellers

"A freshly original and impishly humorous English mystery." Bk Buyer's Guide

Airth, Rennie

Snatch. Simon & Schuster 1969 256p $4.95

Harry Brighton, a passport forger, is blackmailed into joining an ex-criminal partner in a plan to "rent a baby, kidnap the son of a wealthy Italian villain, leave the 'rental' in his place, then collect a quarter-million to change them back." N Y Times Bk R

This "is a perfectly charming first crime novel, funny, ingenious and . . . this column's choice for thriller of the year." Times (London) Lit Sup

Akutagawa, Ryūnosuke

Exotic Japanese stories, the beautiful and the grotesque; 16 unusual tales and unforgettable images. Tr. by Takashi Kojima and John McVittie. Introduction by John McVittie. Ed. for Western readers by John McVittie and Arthur Pell. 22 collage illus. in color and black & white by Masakazu Kuwata. Liveright 1964 431p illus $6.95

Analyzed in Short Story Index
Short storis included are: The robbers; The dog, Shiro; The handkerchief; The dolls; Gratitude; The faith of Wei Shêng; The lady, Roku-no-miya; The Kappa; Saigō Takamori; The greeting; Withered fields; Absorbed in letters; The garden; The badger; Heresy

Japanese short stories; tr. by Takashi Kojima; introduction by John McVittie; with very unusual illus. by Masakazu Kuwata. Liveright 1961 224p illus $5.95

Analyzed in Short Story Index
Contents: The hell screen; A clod of soil; "Nezumi-Kozo"—the Japanese Robin Hood; Heichu, the amorous genius; Genkaku-Sanbo; Otomi's virginity; The spider's thread; The nose; The tangerines; The story of Yonosuke

Rashomon, and other stories; tr. by Takashi Kojima; introduction by Howard Hibbert; illus. by M. Kuwata. Liveright 1952 119p illus $5

Analyzed in Short Story Index
Contents: In a grove; Rashomon; Yam gruel; The martyr; Kesa and Morito; The dragon

Alain-Fournier. See Fournier, Alain

Alarcón, Pedro A. de

The three-cornered hat; tr. by H. F. Turner. Dufour 1965 [c1959] 134p $3.50

Original Spanish edition published 1874
Translation of a classic of modern Spanish literature. This Andalusian folk tale is the story "of a miller and his perfect wife, who understood each other so thoroughly that even the wiles of the evil Corregidor [Mayor] in his crimson robe and gorgeous three-cornered hat did not mar their happiness; although indeed they might have, had not two humble donkeys provided an unexpected twist to this Spanish Canterbury tale." Ind

"A witty, mischievous, but inoffensive comedy of errors which skates beautifully over thin ice." Booklist

Albrand, Martha

A call from Austria. Random House 1963 180p boards $3.95

A novel of espionage and mystery "set in Austria, where an American newspaperman comes looking for his missing brother, in a situation that holds danger for them both, and finds instead a pretty girl who bears him an old grudge." Pub W

"The usual amount of suspense, authentic background of a resort in the Austrian Alps, and a romance." Booklist

A day in Monte Carlo. Random House 1959 177p o.p. 1970

"The murder of his best friend, a French politician connected with the Algerian rebellion, starts an American writer [Mark Travers] on a perilous search through Paris and the Riviera for the suspected killer." Chicago

A door fell shut. New Am. Lib. 1966 214p o.p. 1970

This tale of intrigue centers on Bronsky "a world-famous concert violinist suddenly trapped in the deadly game of [defection] murder and espionage in divided Berlin. The plot comes to a climax when the violinist, during an ovation, becomes a prisoner on the stage." McClurg. Book News

Another of the author's "studies of espionage and conflicting personal and political motives. . . . This is musically literate as well as exciting." Library J

Meet me tonight. Random House 1960 184p o.p. 1970

The first person Sarolta saw in Brussels, where she had come to meet her husband, was Farkas, the man responsible for the imprisonment and death of many of her family and friends in Hungary. It soon became evident to her that both Farkas and her husband were involved with the leader of the Hungarian underground, for reasons which drew Sarolta into a life-and-death stuggle to save herself and those she loved. (Publisher)

Nightmare in Copenhagen. Random House 1954 236p o.p. 1970

"If the Russians ever get hold of the secret explosive that a Danish fisherman has recovered from a wrecked German submarine, they will, of course, blow everybody up, and, as it happens, nothing stands in their way except a young American scientist. In addition to bringing in all these nationalities. Miss Albrand's book has quite a lot to say about love, kidnapping, Communism, and various brands of scenery and manners." New Yorker

No surrender
In Haycraft, H. ed. Five spy novels p485-613

Reunion with terror
In The Saturday Evening Post. Danger p 1-106

Rhine replica. Random House 1969 243p $5.95

Andrew Waldron, an American journalist "comes to Cologne for the last five days of carnival to see the treasures of the past and to dance madly in the streets. But instead he meets Bettina van Alten, and they are both caught up in an old terror and a resurgent Nazi group determined to exploit the future." Library J

"In this secret world of neo-Nazi plotters and counterplotters, there is mounting mystery and suspense, adding up to an exciting climax. A modern near-Gothic with a difference: it has a young hero beset by terrors instead of a heroine. A skillful job by an expert in the genre." Pub W

Aldiss, Brian W.

Cryptozoic! Doubleday 1968 [c1967] 240p (Doubleday Science fiction) o.p. 1970

First published 1967 in England
"An experienced mind traveler is assigned to search through time, locate and kill a traitor to the country's new regime." Chicago

"Though slow in spots, this is another fine performance by one of the best [science fiction] writers of the day." Library J

Aldiss, Brian W.—*Continued*

(ed.) Nebula award stories, two. See Nebula award stories, two

Who can replace a man? The best science-fiction stories of Brian W. Aldiss. Harcourt [1966 c1965] 253p o.p. 1970

Analyzed in Short Story Index
First published 1965 in England with title: The best science-fiction stories of Brian W. Aldiss
The author presents 14 stories that "possess much fantasy and humor, although mainly concerned with the impact of science on life." Library J
Contents: Who can replace a man; Not for an age; Psyclops; Outside; Dumb show; The new Father Christmas; Ahead; Poor little warrior; Man on bridge; The impossible star; Basis for negotiation; Old Hundredth; A kind of artistry; Man in his time

Aldrich, Bess Streeter

y The Bess Streeter Aldrich reader. Appleton 1950 467p o.p. 1970

Analyzed for short stories only in Short Story Index
Contains the novels: A lantern in her hand: A white bird flying, both entered separately, and the short stories: The day of retaliation; How far is it to Hollywood; Juno's swans; Will the romance be it to the same; Welcome home, Hal

A Bess Streeter Aldrich treasury; with an introduction by Robert Streeter Aldrich. Appleton 1959 452p o.p. 1970

Analyzed for short stories only in Short Story Index
Contains two complete novels and five short stories, depicting life in the Middle West. The novels are: A lantern in her hand (1928); and Miss Bishop (1933) both entered separately below. The short stories are: The day of retaliation; Will the romance be the same; Star across the tracks; Another brought gifts; I remember

Journey into Christmas, and other stories; illus. by James Aldrich. Appleton 1949 265p illus $4.95

Analyzed in Short Story Index
Contents: Journey into Christmas; Star across the tracks; The drum goes dead; Youth is all of an up-and-coming; The man who caught the weather; Bid the tapers twinkle; Christmas on the prairie; Low lies His bed; Another brought gifts; Suzanne's own might; The silent stars go by; I remember
"For family reading aloud." Wis Lib Bul

y A lantern in her hand
Some editions are:
Appleton $3.50
Grosset $2.50
First published 1928
"The story of a pioneer woman who, as a bride, followed the covered-wagon trail to the Nebraska prairies and lived there the rest of her eighty years. A devoted wife and mother, Abbie Deal brought a large and united family through poverty and hardship. Denying herself that the children might have the advantages her talented youth had coveted, she went through life with 'courage her lode-star and love her guide, a song upon her lips and a lantern in her hand.'" Cleveland
Followed by: A white bird flying

also in Aldrich, B. S. The Bess Streeter Aldrich reader p3-209

also in Aldrich, B. S. A Bess Streeter Aldrich treasury p3-209

y The lieutenant's lady. Appleton 1942 275p o.p. 1970

"The scene: early Omaha and the forts along the Missouri River just after the Civil War. When Cynthia Colsworth jilts Lt. Norman Stafford, he marries her cousin, Linnie, and the novel shows the growth of their love amidst the hardships of frontier life. A terrific journey, down the river in flat boats, tests and develops their affection into great and enduring love —and when circumstance makes it possible

for Norman to leave Linnie for Cynthia, he realizes that it is Linnie, only, that he loves." Huntting

y Miss Bishop. Appleton 1933 337p o.p. 1970

"This portrait of another woman with 'lantern in her hand' is of Ella Bishop, teacher of English in Midwestern College. . . . With indomitable courage and with little bitterness she struggled along caring for her frail little mother, losing two lovers, bringing up other people's children, and seeing her own hopes retreating into the background. And altho she faced old age with practically no money she had the satisfaction of knowing that she had carried the torch worthily." Book Rev Digest
"It is a constructive and inspiring book, but not in the least old-fashioned—courage and unselfishness are not dated." N Y Times Bk R

also in Aldrich, B. S. A Bess Streeter Aldrich treasury p211-379

Song of years. Appleton 1939 490p o.p. 1970

"Story of pioneer Iowa during the years 1854 to 1865. When Wayne Lockwood took up his quarter-section about a hundred miles west of Dubuque, he found his nearest neighbor to be Jeremiah Martin, a sturdy pioneer with a family of seven hearty daughters and two sons. From that time on Wayne's destiny was bound up with the Martins." Book Rev Digest
"The substance of the book—and no one would deny that it has substance—lies . . . in its study of a locale and a period." N Y Times Bk R

Spring came on forever. Appleton 1935 333p $3.95

"In Illinois, in the spring of 1866. Amalia Stolz and Mathias Meier met and fell in love. But a dominating father carried Amalia off to the Nebraska prairies in a covered wagon, and although Mathias followed, he arrived too late. The story follows Mathias and Amalia and their descendants, as spring follows spring, and wagon trails become highways—and ends with Amalia's great grandson and Mathias's granddaughter, caught in the depression of 1933, starting life anew on Amalia's old homestead." Wis Lib Bul
"It is a book of clear characterizations, stirring narrative, insight and savor. It is as clean and refreshing as a strong spring wind." N Y Her Trib Books

y A white bird flying. Appleton 1931 336p $3.50

Sequel to: A lantern in her hand
"Pulled by literary ambitions in one direction and by her heart strings in another, young Laura Deal of Nebraska, tries to ignore her liking for dependable Allan Rinemiller. This tale of the second and third generations of a pioneer family, while perhaps too deliberately patterned, gives careful attention to its setting and has a popular appeal through its sentiment, romance and happy ending." N Y Libraries

also in Aldrich, B. S. A Bess Streeter Aldrich reader p211-392

Aldridge, James

A captive in the land. Doubleday 1963 [c1962] 381p o.p. 1970

Rupert Royce, an Englishman, succeeds in the daring rescue of an injured Russian in the Arctic and is invited to visit the Soviet Union. Although such friendship with the Russians puts him somewhat under the suspicion of British and American security agents, Royce has actually agreed to do some spying for Navy Intelligence and is soon involved in an adventure of intrigue and espionage. (Publisher)
"By and large, the Russians in Mr. Aldridge's book seem to have his sympathy, while too often, he reserves the back of his hand for the West. The Russians are more fully developed than the Britons. Too frequently the West is represented by self-seeking bureaucrats who believe in guilt by association, who use security checks for their own selfish ends, who cannot recognize principle. The simplicity of a 'people to people' program is most idealistic and appealing." Best Sellers

Aldridge, James—*Continued*

The last exile. Doubleday 1961 738p o.p. 1970

A novel set against the background of politics in modern Egypt. "The hero is an Englishman who, feeling that he has been badly treated by his own people, casts in his lot with the Nasser regime. He helps to free a political prisoner, is suspected of complicity in a plot to assassinate Nasser, lives through the Suez [Canal] affair." Pub W

This novel "is sprawling often downright rambling in structure, and its English protagonist remains a cryptic figure right to the last line. But the clarity with which the author portrays the massive and complex Middle East of today [1961] keeps the book moving and believable." Best Sellers

My brother Tom; a love story. Little [1967 c1966] 183p boards $4.95

"Small-town Australia in the 1930's is the setting for a quietly related, understated novel in which the narrator tells of his brother's love for the beautiful Peggy MacGibbon and of the repercussive feud between the fathers in the two families. The ironic ending is in keeping with a story that, despite its air of detachment, holds the reader's interest." Booklist

"Mr. Aldridge has an old-fashioned narrative gift which is good enough—but only just good enough—to make us want to know what happens next." Times (London) Lit Sup

Alegría, Ciro

Broad and alien is the world; tr. from the Spanish by Harriet de Onís. Rinehart 1941 434p o.p. 1970

"For generations the Indians of Rumi, a village high in the Andes, have lived a contented, tranquil community life, loving their land jealously. Suddenly in the 1860's all this is changed when the rich and avaricious Don Alvaro Amenabar decides to cheat them out of their land and to force them to labor in his mines and fields practically as slaves. In a long, leisurely novel, packed with colorful incident illustrative of Indian psychology, superstitions and way of life, the author . . . follows the Indians, helplessly fighting for their rights in corrupt courts, now hopeful, now in despair, until finally resisting gallantly with their very life's blood, they are vanquished." Bookmark

Aleichem, Sholom

The adventures of Menahem-Mendl; tr. from the Yiddish by Tamara Kahana. Putnam 1969 222p $5.95

Original Yiddish edition published 1909 in Russia

The story, told in letters exchanged between the hero, trying his luck in the bigger cities of Czarist Russia, and his wife, who has remained behind in a small town in the hinterlands, describes the adventures of "an incurable optimist, whose every venture ends in disaster." Publisher's note

"Sholom Aleichem's characters are as deeply embedded in their society as Chaucer's, and their language is densely idiomatic. No doubt a good deal gets lost in translation: some of Sheineh-Sheindl's malapropisms, for instance, sound impossibly far-fetched in English. But enough survives in Mrs. Kahana's version to make this a delightful book, full of easy natural humor, and quite free from any taint of folksiness or sentimentality." N Y Rev of Books

The adventures of Mottel, the cantor's son; tr. by Tamara Kahana; illus. by Ilya Schor. Abelard-Schuman 1953 342p illus o.p. 1970

"The lighthearted humor of young Mottel, the narrator, adds a touch of pathos to the stories of an impoverished Jewish family in a European village, its wanderings in Europe en route to America, and finally its arrival and settlement in the U.S." Booklist

"The series has an auto-biographical tinge to it and each sketch etches sharp pictures of Mottel, his family and friends in the immigration phase at the beginning of the 20th century. . . . Recommended as good folk literature." Library J

Inside Kasrilevke; drawings by Ben Shahn. Schocken [c1965, 1948] 222p illus $4.95

Analyzed in Short Story Index

A reissue of the title first published 1948, translated from the Yiddish by Isidore Goldstick

Contents: A guide to Kasrilevke: Transportation; Hotels; Restaurants; Liquor; Theater; Fires; Bandits. The poor and the rich: The delegation; Fishel rouses the world; Disaster; Reb Yozifl challenges the Creator; After the disaster; On the march; Among the nations; Among their own; The man who knows his way around; Chaos; In high places; The miracle

The old country; tr. by Julius and Frances Butwin. Crown 1946 434p $1.98

Analyzed in Short Story Index

Contents: Town of the little people; The inheritors; Tevye wins a fortune; Page from The Song of Songs; Two dead men; Clock that struck thirteen; Home for Passover; Enchanted tailor; Yom Kippur scandal; In haste; Eternal life; Hannukah money; Tit for tat; Modern children; You mustn't weep—it's Yom-Tev; I'm lucky—I'm an orphan; Dreyfus in Kasrilevka; The convoy; The fiddle; Day before Yom Kippur; Three little heads; Country Passover; Lottery ticket; Miracle of Hashono Rabo; Hodel; Daughter's grave; Cnards

Old country tales; selected and tr. with an introduction by Curt Leviant. Putnam 1966 319p $5.95

Analyzed in Short Story Index

"This collection of stories is translated from the Yiddish for the first time and will please the many fans of Sholom Aleichem. . . . A wide variety of shtetl (village) life is covered from malicious and innocent childhood to disasters of the pogroms." Library J

Contents: Tevye reads the Psalms; Final pages from The Song of Songs; Visiting with King Ahasuerus; The Holiday Kiddush; The flag; Methuselah—a Jewish horse; The Great Panic of the little people; Gitl Purishkevitch; A predestined disaster; A white bird; Sticks and stones may break my bones; No luck; It doesn't pay to do favors; The station at Baranovitch; Two anti-Semites; Sixty-six; Ritual fringes; A job as easy as pie; Back from the draft; The first Passover night of the war; Purim sweet-platters; David, King of Israel; The malicious matza; One hundred and one; Burnt out; The village of Habne

Selected stories of Sholom Aleichem; with an introduction by Alfred Kazin. Modern Lib. 1956 432p $2.95

Analyzed in Short Story Index

Contents: On account of a hat; The pair; The town of the little people; Tevye wins a fortune; A page from The Song of Songs; Two dead men; The clock that struck thirteen; Home for Passover; The enchanted tailor; A Yom Kippur scandal; In haste; Eternal life; Hannukah money; Tit for tat; Modern children; You mustn't weep—it's Yom-Tev; I'm lucky—I'm an orphan; Dreyfus in Kasrilevka; The convoy; The fiddle; The day before Yom Kippur; Three little heads; A country Passover; The lottery ticket; The miracle of Hashono Rabo; Hodel; A daughter's grave; Cnards

Some laughter, some tears; tales from the old world and the new; selected and tr. with an introduction by Curt Leviant. Putnam 1968 254p $5.95

Analyzed in Short Story Index

"Stories and sketches typical of Sholom Aleichem's humor, pathos, and mild satire, some of which appear here for the first time in English while others have appeared in earlier volumes but are newly translated." Booklist

Contents: Elijah the Prophet; The esrog; The guest; Pages from The Song of Songs; This night; The dreydl; Robbers; Esther; Pity for living creatures; A lost Lag B'Omer; The penknife; A bit of advice; It's a lie; The tenth man; Boaz the teacher; Velvel Gambetta; Isser the shamesh; The little redheaded Jews; Mr Green has a job; Otherwise, there's nothing new; The story of a greenhorn

Aleichem, Sholom—*Continued*

Stories and satires. Drawings by Arthur Zaidenberg. Tr. by Curt Leviant. Yoseloff 1959 381p illus o.p. 1970

Analyzed for short stories only in Short Story Index

Contents: Progress in Kasrilevke; Summer romances; Birth; Geese; My first love affair; Three calendars; There's no dead; Happy New Year; Someone to envy; At the doctor's; Three windows; The Passover Eve vagabonds; Homesick; On America; 75,000; Agents: a one-act play; The ruined Passover; From the Riviera; A home away from home; To the hot springs

Tevye's daughters; tr. by Frances Butwin. Crown 1949 302p $1.98

Analyzed in Short Story Index

Contents: Bubble bursts; If I were Roths-child; Modern children; Competitors; Another page from The Song of Songs; Hodel; Happiest man in Kodno; Wedding without musicians; What will become of me; Chava; Joys of parenthood; Littlest of kings; Man from Buenos Aires; May God have mercy; Schprintze; The merrymakers; Easy fast; Little pot; Two Shalachmones; Tevye goes to Palestine; Gy-ma-na-sia; Purim feast; From Passover to Succos; Get thee out; Passover expropriation; The German; Third class

Wandering star; tr. by Frances Butwin. Crown 1952 314p o.p. 1970

"Slightly picaresque novel about two groups of wandering Yiddish actors in Europe some fifty or sixty years ago. The two central characters are Reizel and Leibel, who ran away from the same Bessarabian village when they were very young." Book Rev Digest

"One of Sholom Aleichem's minor works, light and amusing and peppered with the cele-brated wit of the humorist, but not memorable for the delineation of character or even good plot construction." N Y Times Bk R

Algren, Nelson

The man with the golden arm; a novel. Doubleday 1949 343p o.p. 1970

"A realistic story of Chicago's underworld. The chief character, the man with the golden arm, is Frankie Machine, a card dealer, an ex-veteran who has brought back from the war a Good Conduct medal and a Purple Heart." Book Rev Digest

"Readers with queasy stomachs may shrink from an environment in which the unbeliev-ably sordid has become a way of life. They will also come away with some of Algren's own tender concern for his wretched, confused and hopelessly degenerate cast of characters. In that, Writer Algren scores a true novelist's triumph." Time

A walk on the wild side. Farrar, Straus 1956 346p o.p. 1970

"A novel about the residents of a slum street in New Orleans during the early years of the Depression." Book Rev Digest

"Algren's vivid writing gives this degen-erate cast the power to shock or appall, and if a glimmer of compassion leaks through occa-sionally it is slapped down before it gets out of hand." Library J

Allen, Don B. See Allen, T. D.

Allen, Henry. See Henry, Will

Allen, Hervey

Anthony Adverse; decorations by Allan McNab. Rinehart 1933 1224p illus $8.50

"This vast romantic novel recounts the story of Anthony—born in 1775, illegitimate, or-phaned, left to die in a Catholic convent, educated by the Church, and apprenticed to a wealthy Italian merchant whose heir he be-came. His business interests were world wide: in early manhood a slave trader, he was later connected with the financial interests of Napoleon in France, England, Spain, and the new world. Anthony carried with him through

life his one link to the past, a beautiful small figure of the Madonna that identified him to others though he himself never learned his identity." Booklist

"Only a scholar could have assembled the enormous knowledge that has gone into the book and only a poet and a critic could have caught so acutely the implications of that knowledge as idea and emotion in human be-ings. The triumph of the book, however, is that this wealth of fact and feeling is fused by the gusto of the true story-teller." N Y Her Trib Books

Bedford Village. Rinehart 1944 305p front o.p. 1970

Sequel to: The forest and the fort

The second in a series of colonial novels called: The disinherited. In 1763 "Salathiel Albine, the strong, handsome hero who was brought up by Indians, moves a hundred miles or so east from the scene of his last exploits, in western Pennsylvania. Here he helps or-ganize relief for refugees from the Indian wars, falls in love with a nice girl, has several fights with rowdies in the town, engages in a massacre of Indians, and finally (having been jilted by the nice girl) takes up with an Irish serving maid whom we met briefly in the first volume. The novel has the admirable docu-mentation for which Mr. Allen can be counted on and the action rolls along smoothly and cheerfully." New Yorker

Followed by: Toward the morning

Bedford Village [abridged]
In Allen, H. The city in the dawn p224-408

The city in the dawn; containing: the forest and the fort, Bedford Village, Toward the morning. Rinehart 1950 696p $5.95

"This volume comprises an abridgement of the first three books [of the Disinherited] plus the part of the fourth that the author left [unfinished] making one complete narra-tive. The editorial work was done by Julie Eidesheim." Book Rev Digest

"The title for the whole comes from this last section in which Salathiel Albine and entou-rage at last reached Philadelphia. The projected novel was to have been much longer and the announced title of the whole was 'The dis-inherited.'" Booklist

The forest and the fort. Rinehart 1943 344p illus o.p. 1970

The first in a series of colonial novels called: The disinherited. "It begins during the French and Indian wars and part one is set in the forests of Pennsylvania and westward. Sala-thiel Albine, stolen by Indians, was brought up as a Shawnee chieftain's son, called Little Turtle; later, a strapping young man, he was returned to white people. Part two relates his life at Fort Pitt, his assimilation into the white man's life, and the successful conclusion of a responsible assignment closing with Salathiel's anticipation of his first sight of a town—Bed-ford." Booklist

"Even the most revolting episodes in the book have no bad after-taste, because they are mitigated by Allen's magnificent and ex-pressive style." Book Week. Chicago Sun

Followed by: Bedford Village

The forest and the fort [abridged]
In Allen, H. The city in the dawn p 1-223

Toward the morning. Rinehart 1948 485p front o.p. 1970

Sequel to: Bedford Village

"This third volume in a series on colonial America [called: The disinherited] is still in the pre-revolutionary period and again Salathiel Al-bine, the rescued Indian captive, is the central figure. Traveling eastward to Philadelphia from Bedford in the winter of 1764-1765 the Al-bine party is caught between the frontier still alert to Indian threats and other frontier perils and the civilized eastern seaboard alive with rumors of strained relations between the colo-nists and the British. There is little plot but good integration of historical incident and scene." Booklist

"While developing Albine's adjustment to civilized ways, the author's accustomed broad sweep and wealth of convincing detail bring the frontier to effective life." Library J

Allen, Hervey—*Continued*

Toward the morning [abridged]
In Allen, H. The city in the dawn p409-677

Allen, T. D.

Doctor in buckskin. Harper 1951 277p o.p. 1970

Based upon the lives of medical missionary Marcus Whitman and his wife Narcissa, this is the story of Oregon when there were few white pioneers there. It also introduces many other real figures from history. A tragic ending when the Indians, suspicious of the doctor's medical powers, massacre his entire family

"The story, if without literary pretense, is readable, because in spite of too many incidents it moves along at a satisfactory pace." Booklist

Allen, Terry D. and Allen, Don B. See Allen, T. D.

Allingham, Margery

The Allingham Case-book. Morrow 1969 221p $5.50

This volume contains a profile of the author written by her husband, P. Y. Carter, and "eighteen short stories featuring such old favorites as Albert Campion, Charlie Luke, Lugg, Amanda Campion." Pub W

Contents: Tall story; Three is a lucky number; The villa Maria Celeste; The psychologist; Little Miss Know-All; One morning they'll hang him; The lieabout; Face value; Evidence in camera; Joke over; The lying-in-state; The pro and the con; Is there a doctor in the house; The borderline case; They never get caught; The mind's eye mystery; Mum knows best; The snapdragon and the C. I. D.

Cargo of eagles. Morrow 1968 233p boards $4.95

"Albert Campion, aided by the ever faithful Lugg and a likable young American professor, ferrets out the secret of a mysterious English village, once the 17th century bolt-hole out of London for the criminals of the day. 20th century Saltey turns out to be quite a rum place itself, with leather jacketed motorcycle rockers adding their own brand of terror to the scene. A hunt for buried treasure, poison pen letters directed against a pretty young lady doctor who has just inherited a house in Saltey, a hint from Mr. Campion's own war time past, all add up to a capital entertainment, atmospheric and tricky." Pub W

The china governess; a novel of suspense. Doubleday 1962 282p o.p. 1970

"Turk Street, 'the wickedest street in London,' had been destroyed in the war and new apartments had been built there. Then someone smashed up everything in one apartment and wrote 'Let the dead past bury its dead' on the mirror. What connection could there be between this, young Tim Kinnit, who might have come from Turk Street as a baby, and the Staffordshire figure of 'Miss Thyrza's chair,' the statuette of a governess charged with murder long ago? It took Albert Campion to find it." Bk Buyer's Guide

"A gripping novel intricately constructed of villains and innocents and a memorable nanny." Library J

Crime and Mr Campion. Published for the Crime Club by Doubleday 1959 575p o.p. 1970

An omnibus volume containing the complete texts of three mystery novels, all starring the British detective, Albert Campion: Death of a ghost (1934); Flowers for the judge (1936) and, Dancers in mourning (1937)

Dancers in mourning
In Allingham, M. Crime and Mr Campion p363-575

Death of a ghost
In Allingham, M. Crime and Mr Campion p7-175

The fashion in shrouds
In Allingham, M. Three cases for Mr Campion p9-255

Flowers for the judge
In Allingham, M. Crime and Mr Campion p177-362

The Gyrth Chalice mystery
In Allingham, M. Three cases for Mr Campion p421-604

The mind readers. Morrow 1965 274p boards $4.50

Albert Campion "is involved in 'a mystic, curling pattern of human adventure' which spreads from his young nephews, Edward and Sam, to Lord Ludor, the enigmatic industrialist and his secret research station on Godley Island, its scientific staff, and on to 'the Daily Paper' and the entire field of extrasensory perception." Library J

Margery Allingham "makes remarkably convincing stuff of a science-fiction sort of plot involving some miniature transistorised amplifiers using a new element, nipponanium, by which two youngsters are able to send messages simply by concentration of thought, even though at considerable distance and, by the same means, to discover what others are thinking or feeling." Best Sellers

Three cases for Mr Campion. Published for the Crime Club by Doubleday 1961 604p o.p. 1970

An omnibus volume of the author's earlier Albert Campion mysteries, set in England containing: The fashion in shrouds (1938); Traitor's purse (1941); and The Gyrth Chalice mystery (1931)

"The Gyrth Chalice mystery" unravels Mr Campion's solution to the secret in the locked room of Gyrth Tower; "The fashion in shrouds" involves the theft of dress designs, sixty cages of canaries, and blackmail, as Albert Campion investigates a three-year-old murder; "Traitor's purse" finds Albert Campion, an amnesia victim haunted by an urgency to do something of immense consequence before time ran out. (Publisher)

Traitor's purse
In Allingham, M. Three cases for Mr Campion p257-420

Almedingen, E. M.

Frossia. Harcourt 1943 358p o.p. 1970

"Laid in Petrograd, in the early 20's, this is the story of a girl of good family, alone in the world, who lives through the transition period, uninterested in politics but convinced of the essential value of Russia and loyal to it. Every variety of person, from aristocrat to peasant, with every sort of reaction to the situation, moves through the story. As fiction often can, it gives a clearer idea of life in Russia, 1914 to 1925, than many a study of the subject." Wis Lib Bul

Almedingen, Martha Edith von. See Almedingen, E. M.

Amado, Jorge

Dona Flor and her two husbands; a moral and amorous tale; tr. from the Portuguese by Harriet de Onís. Knopf 1969 553p $6.95

Original Portuguese edition published 1966

"Dona Flor has such a harridan of a mother (Dona Rozilda) that you would like her to have her cake and eat it, too, and she very nearly does. Dona Flor's first husband, Vadinho, is a scamp, a prevaricator, and a 'shameless lover.' On Carnival Sunday, at the height of the gaiety, filled with rum, he drops dead. Dona Flor is desolate but cuts a handsome figure as a widow. She lives through the wake (a gem of a scene) and her mourning quite well, with memories and her cooking school to sustain her. Then suitors appear. None appeal but Dr. Teodoro Madureira, pharmacist and bassoonist, a pillar of propriety. Dona Rozilda is ecstatic, but the well-rounded Dona Flor

Amado, Jorge—*Continued*

has her troubles, for alas, Dr. Teodoro is no lover. Dreams haunt her and strange things begin to happen. Thanks to a Yoruba charm, Vadinho returns to ravish our bewildered heroine, and then the fun begins. Bahia in Brazil is the setting for this delectable rum cake of a novel." Pub W

"The conclusion with its change to fantasy jars somewhat, but Amado's skill with words soon has the reader believing that this did happen in Bahia. The leisurely pace may deter some readers; the bawdiness others. Those who respond to Amado's qualities, his joy, color, gaiety, and satirical impudence will be delighted. The translation is excellent." Library J

Gabriela, clove and cinnamon; tr. from the Portuguese by James L. Taylor and William L. Grossman. Knopf 1962 425p $5.95

Original Portuguese edition copyright 1958
"Gabriela's romance highlights the picture of a town in the cacao-growing region of Brazil in a year of many changes in the 1920's. The violence of recent frontier days is still resorted to, the town is under the dominance of an old-fashioned autocrat, and a double standard is observed for extramarital love affairs. Coming from the impoverished backlands, the beautiful Gabriela, with the soul of a child and a child's lack of conventional morality, becomes first the cook of the cafe owner Nacib the Arab, then his mistress, and reluctantly his wife. At the end she is again cook and mistress. Robust and realistic, the picture is drawn with humor but genuine understanding of a place and a time and subtle appreciation of individual character." Booklist

"The sensuality of the novel, though marked, is not offensive. The translation reads excellently." Library J

Home is the sailor; the whole truth concerning the redoubtful adventures of Captain Vasco Moscoso de Aragão, master mariner. Tr. from the Portuguese by Harriet de Onís. Knopf 1964 298p $4.95

"Like the Gilbert & Sullivan admiral, Captain Vasco de Aragão had never been to sea, but he kept the people of the Brazilian seaside resort spellbound with his tales of adventure. Pacheco discovered the fake but couldn't convince the people. But when Vasco was persuaded to bring a liner into port it looked as though the game was up." Bk Buyer's Guide

"Mr. Amado's urbane conversational style, humor, and inventiveness compensate for the casual construction of the novel. Some ribald situations and words may limit the book to more sophisticated readers." Library J

Shepherds of the night; tr. from the Portuguese by Harriet de Onís. Knopf 1967 [c1966] 364p $5.95

Originally published 1964 in Brazil
"Three interconnected tales sharing the same cast and the same Brazilian port-town setting tell of a short-lived marriage between a nomadic man and the wily woman who trapped him, the strange circumstances surrounding a christening, and dramatic developments in the local shantytown." Booklist

This book "does not quite reach the superb level of such earlier Amado classics as The Violent Land [entered below] or Gabriela, Clove and Cinnamon [entered above] but it ripples with the special inner music that has made Amado's work popular the world over. Like all Amado's novels, this one is filled with the coppery women of Bahia and the men who chase them through nights of song and stars." Time

The violent land; tr. from the Portuguese (Terras do sem fim) by Samuel Putnam; with a new foreword by the author. Knopf 1965 336p $5.95

First American edition 1945, published by Putnam
"The story of a bloody feud between two landowning Brazilian families for the possession of a tract of virgin forest to which neither has any right. The background is the wild, lush countryside of eastern Brazil during a boom in the rich cocoa-growing district." New Yorker

"Critics have regarded this novel of the Brazilian 'cacao rush' as one of the finest pictures ever drawn of the bloody, turbulent period that was equalled only by the California gold rush of '49." Huntting

Amazing Stories

The best of Amazing; selected by Joseph Ross. Doubleday 1967 222p (Doubleday Science fiction) o.p. 1970

Analyzed in Short Story Index
"These nine stories from the oldest science-fiction magazine cover nearly forty years [i.e. 1926-1962] of horror, fantasy and futuristic writing." Chicago

Contents: The lost machine, by J. B. Harris; The worm, by D. H. Keller; The runaway skyscraper, by M. Leinster; Marooned off Vesta, by I. Asimov; Anniversary, by I. Asimov; The Metal Man, by J. Williamson; Pilgrimage, by N. S. Bond; Sunfire, by E. Hamilton; Try to remember, by F. Herbert

Ambler, Eric

Background to danger
In Ambler, E. Intrigue p467-631

Cause for alarm
In Ambler, E. Intrigue p295-465

A coffin for Dimitrios. Knopf 1939 281p o.p. 1970

Published in England with title: Mask of Dimitrios
"The story of an English writer who sees a corpse in a Turkish morgue, hears a little about the history of the dead man—a nondescript Greek fig-packer who had wandered in and out of criminal records of every country in central Europe for two decades—and decides to track down the man's whole life in order to know how he 'got that way.' The yarn moves quickly and interestingly and is full of grotesque and fascinating characters." Huntting

also in Ambler, E. Intrigue p147-294

Epitaph for a spy; with a footnote by the author. Knopf 1952 259p o.p. 1970

First published 1938 in England
This story "concerns the predicament of Josef Vadassy, harmless language teacher on a vacation in Nice, who picks up the wrong camera, finishes a roll of films, and is suspected of being a spy when the roll is discovered to contain pictures of military installations. To prove his innocence, Vadassy clumsily tries to find the real spy in his hotel." Retail Bookseller

"Vadassy himself is excellently realized and the others in various degrees. Once, before the final pull-up, the whole drags a bit. But this is a tale well worth acquaintance." N Y Her Trib Books

also in Haycraft, H. ed. Five spy novels p343-483

The Intercom conspiracy. Atheneum Pubs. 1969 241p $5.95

In Geneva, two top intelligence officers plot to get paid off—for their silence. "The pawn in their game is a hard-drinking, irascible, but shrewd ex-reporter who is running a newsletter that up to now has been pushing ultra-right wing propaganda. In the hands of the two plotters it is put to a sinister new use that draws down the wrath of Americans, Russians, West Germans alike." Pub W

"The tale is ingenious and expertly told. Not quite the cliff-hanging thriller, but suspenseful enough to carry one to the last page." Best Sellers

Intrigue; four great spy novels. With an introduction by Alfred Hitchcock. Knopf 1960 [c1943] 631p $5.95

First published in this anthology form 1952
Contents: Journey into fear (1940); A coffin for Dimitrios (1939) entered separately; Cause for alarm (1939); Background to danger (1937)

Ambler, Eric—*Continued*

The intriguers; four superb novels of suspense. Knopf 1965 592p $5.95

Contents: Passage of arms (1960) entered separately; State of seige (1956); The Schirmer inheritance (1953) entered separately; Judgment on Deltchev (1951) entered separately

State of seige, published in England with title: The night comers, is "set in a small country in Southeast Asia. Steve Ambler, the British engineer who tells the story . . . [and a Eurasian girl] are unexpectedly caught in the cross fire between insurgents attacking the capital and the defending government forces." Booklist

Journey into fear
In Ambler, E. Intrigue p 1-145
In Haycraft, H. ed. A treasury of great mysteries v 1 p437-576

Judgment on Deltchev. Knopf 1951 247p o.p. 1970

"Foster, English dramatist assigned to the trial of Yordan Deltchev in an Iron Curtain country, knows the trial is fixed and Deltchev is doomed. Accidentally, however, he uncovers clues leading to an amazing and ironic double-cross." Retail Bookseller

"The politically uninformed may find some of Mr. Ambler's book pretty difficult, for the goings on are at least as chaotic and apparently senseless as they unquestionably are in fact behind the Iron Curtain, but there is probably enough genuine excitement to outweigh this confusion." New Yorker

also in Ambler, E. The intriguers p433-592

A kind of anger. Atheneum Pubs. 1964 311p $4.95

"The story is told by an English-educated Dutchman, a reporter for a New York newspaper, but a man who has not made a great success of his life to date. The setting is the French Riviera where the reporter is sent . . . on the key assignment of finding the girl who has been the mistress of an Iraqi colonel who has just been murdered before her eyes." Publisher's note

"The European resort-area background is so well drawn that one has, as the blurb writers say, a tour for the price of the novel." Book of the Month Club News

The light of day. Knopf 1963 [c1962] 243p maps $3.95

First published 1962 in England
The protagonist of his novel of international intrigue is a disreputable adventurer named Arthur Simpson, who leads a perilous existence as, among other things, a petty thief in Athens. He forms an alliance with a man named Harper and agrees to drive a car into Istanbul. But the car is an arsenal of hidden ammunition so that when Arthur reaches Istanbul he finds himself involved in an international conspiracy. (Publisher)

"The operation in question is ingenious and the Middle Eastern setting is picturesque and realistic." Times (London) Lit Sup

Passage of arms. Knopf 1960 [c1959] 246p $4.95

First published 1959 in England
"Taking Southeast Asia for his background, the author . . . has written a first-class suspense story. Its plot centers on a shrewd and ambitous Indian clerk in the Malay jungle, a devious trio of Chinese brothers doing business in Singapore and Manila, and a middle-aged American tourist and his wife who ingenuously agree to assist a passage of arms to anticommunist forces in Indonesia. Despite the intricate chain of events leading to a violent climax, setting and character are as important as the intrigue." Booklist

also in Ambler, E. The intriguers p 1-168

The Schirmer inheritance. Knopf 1953 246p o.p. 1970

The story of "a lawyer searching for the lost heir to an American fortune among the displaced and dispersed peoples of Europe. He succeeds in doing so, going as far back as the Napoleonic wars for the start of his story, and later conducting a crook's tour through Europe, finally to find the missing millionaire, a German sergeant in the occupation forces during the war, living as a bandit chief in the hills of Greece." Times (London) Lit Sup

also in Ambler, E. The intriguers p291-432

State of siege
In Ambler, E. The intriguers p169-290

(ed.) To catch a spy; an anthology of favourite spy stories; ed. and introduced by Eric Ambler. Atheneum Pubs. 1965 [c1964] 224p boards $4.50

Analyzed in Short Story Index
First published 1964 in England
"The editor has selected seven spy stories and prefaced them with an introduction which discusses the . . . arrival of the spy story." Book Rev Digest
Contents: The loathly opposite, by J. Buchan; Giulia Lazzari, by S. Maugham; The first courier, by C. Mackenzie; I spy, by G. Greene; Belgrade 1926, by E. Ambler; From a view to a kill, by I. Fleming; On slay down, by M. Gilbert

American short stories of the nineteenth century. Dutton 1930 372p (Everyman's lib) $2.95

Analyzed in Short Story Index
Edited with an introduction by John Cournos
Contents: Peter Rugg, the missing man, by W. Austin; Rip Van Winkle, by W. Irving; Tell-tale heart, by E. A. Poe; Ethan Brand, by N. Hawthorne; "Town-ho's" story, by H. Melville; Diamond lens, by F. O'Brien; Luck of Roaring Camp, by B. Harte; Marjorie Daw, by T. B. Aldrich; Celebrated jumping frog of Calaveras County, by M. Twain; Griffin and the minor canon, by F. R. Stockton; Horseman in the sky, by A. Bierce; Passionate pilgrim, by H. James; Hiltons' holiday, by S. O. Jewett; 'Sieur George, by G. W. Cable; Madame Célestin's divorce, by K. Chopin; Little room, by M. Y. Wynne; Village Lear, by M. E. Wilkins; Van Bibber's burglar, by R. H. Davis; God of his fathers, by J. London; Furnished room, by O. Henry

Ames, Francis H.
y That Callahan spunk! Doubleday 1965 236p $4.50

A story of John Conway who had "a dogged determination in face of seeming insurmountable obstacles. He needed all of it when, in 1908, with his wife and 12-year-old son, Tom, he took up a homestead in Montana. Tom, the narrator, tells of their first year in their sod shanty. It is an awe-inspiring tale of the terrible hardships of pioneer life on the range where winters are long and blizzards severe. Some amusing incidents relieve the tension momentarily. . . . [The book pictures] the winning of the West. It will be useful in libraries where this subject is in demand, in collections devoted to the local history of Montana and in teenage collections." Library J

Amis, Kingsley
The Anti-Death League. Harcourt 1966 307p $5.95

"A very complicated book—this novel has two major interrelated themes: the inevitability and cruel illogic of death, and some deadly serious exploration of the topical 'God is dead' debate. But along the road of exploration, Amis strings out his ludicrous targets: the Army mind, the spy mania, the psychologists (pro and amateur) with their pat solutions for everything, the padre who avoids an answer to anything, and—most ludicrous of all—the 'ultimate deterrent' approach to a solution of the world's problems." Library J

The author "has a keen ear for English slang, military jargon and linguistic class indicators, which in combination sometimes makes his story harder to follow than he intends. Still, the conversation, even when obscure is amusing, and the whole thing is rather like a film on late TV." Book of the Month Club News

Amis, Kingsley—*Continued*

I want it now. Harcourt [1969 c1968] 255p $5.75

First published 1968 in England
"Ron Appleyard, TV MC, wanted fame, money, and lots of women. When he first met Simon, a thin but beautiful girl with dirty bare feet, he thought her a nymphomaniac. Then he discovered her mother was filthy rich and pursued her around the world—only to discover at last it was Simon he wanted, not her money." Book Buyer's Guide
"In dealing with—the typical young Englishman on the make—the anti-hero . . . Amis has ended up with both an anti-heel and an anti-climax. . . . [This novel] satirizes TV panel discussion programs, great wealth, and —inadvertently—sex." Sat R

Lucky Jim; a novel. Doubleday 1954 256p o.p. 1970

"Jim Dixon, Mr. Amis' protagonist, is an amiable and irreverent opportunist who has found himself, after the war, in the improbable role of an instructor in medieval history in a minor British college. . . . The academic life is sketched in a kind of hilarious hatred through Dixon's eyes." N Y Times Bk R
This "is an extremely interesting . . . novel, and parts of it are very funny indeed: the episodes of the bed-burning and Jim's public lecture, for instance, mount to the complexity and tension of certain passages in the Marx Brothers' films or in the paper-hanging act one still sees from time to time in pantomime. And Mr. Amis has an unwaveringly merciless eye for the bogus." New Statesman & Nation

(ed.) Spectrum [I]-V; a science fiction anthology; ed. by Kingsley Amis and Robert Conquest. Harcourt 1962-1967 5v v I-II, IV-V ea $4.95, v III o.p. 1970

Analyzed in Short Story Index
First published 1961-1966 in England
Contents [I] The Midas plague, by F. Pohl; Limiting factor, by C. D. Simak; The executioner, by A. Budrys; Null-p, by W. Tenn; The homing instinct of Joe Vargo, by S. Barr; Special fight, by J. Berryman; Inanimate objection, by H. C. Elliott; Pilgrimage to earth, by R. Sheckley; Unhuman sacrifice, by K. MacLean; By his bootstraps, by R. A. Heinlein
II: Beyond bedlam, by W. Guin; Bridge, by J. Blish; There is a tide, by B. W. Aldiss; Second variety, by P. K. Dick; The feeling of power, by I. Asimov; Sense from thought divide, by M. Clifton; Resurrection, by A. E. van Vogt; Vintage season, by H. Kuttner
III: Killdozer, by T. Sturgeon; The voices of time, by J. G. Ballard; Call me Joe, by P. Anderson; We would see a sign, by M. Rose; Dreams are sacred, by P. Phillips; Exploration team, by M. Leinster; Fondly Fahrenheit, by A. Bester; The sentinel, by A. C. Clarke
IV: The marching morons, by C. M. Kornbluth; Gadget vs. trend, by C. Anvil; Such stuff, by J. Brunner; The sellers of the dream, by J. Jakes; The large ant, by H. Fast; Barrier, by A. Boucher; The great Nebraska Sea, by A. Danzig; Compassion circuit, by J. Wyndham; A planet named Shayol, by C. Smith; Into the shop, by R. Goulart; The secret songs, by F. Leiber; Stranger Station, by D. Knight; Hot planet, by H. Clement; The choice, by W. Young
V: Student body, by F. L. Wallace; Crucifixus etiam, by W. M. Miller; Noise level, by R. F. Jones; Grandpa, by J. H. Schmitz; Mother of invention, by T. Godwin; The far look, by T. L. Thomas; Big Sword, by P. Ash; Commencement night, by R. Ashby

Analog 1-7; ed. by John W. Campbell. Doubleday 1963-1969 7v o.p. 1970

Volumes 1-6 analyzed in Short Story Index
Contents: 1: Monument, by L. Biggle, Jr; The plague, by T. Keller; Remember the Alamo, by T. R. Fehrenbach; The hunch, by C. Anvil; Barnacle Bull, by W. P. Sanders; Join our gang, by S. E. Lanier; Sleight of wit, by G. R. Dickson; Prologue to an analogue, by L. Richmond
2: The weather man, by T. L. Thomas; Good Indian, by M. Reynolds; Blind man's lantern, by A. K. Lang; Junior achievement, by W. Lee; Novice, by J. H. Schmitz; Ethical

quotient, by J. T. Phillifent; Philosopher's stone, by C. Anvil; The circuit riders, by R. C. FitzPatrick
3: Hilifter, by G. Dickson; Not in the literature, by C. Anvil; Sonny, by R. Raphael; The trouble with Telstar, by J. Berryman; New folks' home, by C. D. Simak; Industrial revolution, by W. P. Sanders; A world by the tale, by S. McKettrig; Thin edge, by J. B. MacKenzie
4: Subjectivity, by N. Spinrad; The permanent implosion, by D. McLaughlin; Sunjammer, by P. Anderson; A day in the life of Kelvin Throop, by R. A. J. Phillips; Genus traitor, by M. Reynolds; A case of identity, by R. Garrett; The Mary Celeste move, by F. Herbert
5: "Scientists are stupid," by J. W. Campbell; Coincidence day, by J. Brunner; The adventure of the extraterrestrial, by M. Reynolds; Fighting division, by R. Garrett; Computers don't argue, by G. R. Dickson; Say it with flowers, by W. P. Sanders; Mission "red clash," by J. Poyer; Countercommandment, by P. Meadows; Balanced ecology, by J. H. Schmitz; Overproof, by J. B. MacKenzie
6: Prototaph, by K. Laumer; Bookworm, run, by V. Vinge; The easy way out, by L. Correy; Giant meteor impact, by J. E. Enever; Early warning, by R. S. Scott; Call him Lord, by G. R. Dickson; CWACC strikes again, by H. Dempsey; Stranglehold, by C. Anvil; The message, by P. Anthony; Light of other days, by R. Shaw; Something to say, by J. Berryman; Letter from a higher critic, by S. Robb; Not a prison make, by J. P. Martino; 10:01 A.M. by A. B. Malec
7: Aim for the heel, by J. T. Phillifent; Fiesta brava, by M. Reynolds; Free vacation, by W. Macfarlane; The featherbedders, by F. Herbert; Weyr search, by A. McCaffrey; Lost calling, by V. Foray; The last command, by K. Laumer; Dead end, by M. Hodous; There is a crooked man, by J. Wodhams; Elementary mistake, by P. Anderson; Burden of proof, by B. Shaw

Anderson, Poul

Brain wave. Walker & Co. [1969 c1954] 164p $4.50

First published 1954 in England
"Imagine what would happen if the intelligence of every living creature in the world were to double overnight. What would become of the economy? What would a farmer do when his pigs rebelled at going to the slaughter —and his intelligent sheep were hunted by wolves of genius? What would happen to politics, to war, to marriage? What would man do in the boredom of problems solved? These are the questions asked and answered in this provocative account of a world gone sane." Am News of Bks

also in Boucher, A. ed. A treasury of great science fiction v2 p7-119

The corridors of time. Doubleday 1965 209p (Doubleday Science fiction) o.p. 1970

"Malcolm Lockridge was awaiting trial for murder when beautiful and imperious Storm Darroway came to his help. Her lawyer had him acquitted; then Lockridge began the strange, often technically lawless, and always dangerous journeying from century to century with Storm in defense of the highest good." Bk Buyer's Guide

Hiding place

In Anderson, P. Trader to the stars p 1-54

The high crusade. Doubleday 1960 192p o.p. 1970

"An innocent and humorous monk tells the story of a crusade to outer space in the fourteenth century. Sir Roger de Tourneville planned to take his knights and archers on a crusade to the Holy Land; instead, they found themselves on a star, and went on to conquer this empire and other stars in the galaxy, and install feudal order and Christianity." Hunting
"This is, of course, excellent s.f., astounding in the detailed plausibility with which Anderson makes you believe in this star-conquest by men of the fourteenth century. It is also a wholly captivating light novel." N Y Her Trib Books

Anderson, Poul—*Continued*

The longest voyage
In Asimov, I. ed. The Hugo winners
p279-310

The master key
In Anderson, P. Trader to the stars
p127-76

(ed.) Nebula award stories, four. See Nebula award stories, four

Satan's world. Doubleday 1969 204p (Doubleday Science fiction) $4.95

"David Falkyn and his space-merchant employer Nicholas van Rijn, a genuinely funny character, contend with mysterious aliens, the Shenna. The immediate prize is the wealth of a new planet, Satan, but the ultimate issue is galactic domination by Man or Shenna. There is a typically bravura ending, with a small band of earthmen whipping the Shenna hordes on the aliens' own planet. But there are a number of interesting twists along the way: the computer-spy techniques employed by the Shenna; The nature of the Shenna, aggressive herbivores; the interplay of the humans and their alien allies; and the offbeat character van Rijn. A rouser; good light reading." Library J

Seven conquests; an adventure in science fiction. Macmillan (N Y) 1969 224p $4.95

"Brilliantly imaginative tales of man caught up in the superagonies of cosmic warfare. The setting of each tale is in the twilight zone of future technologies." Publisher's note
Contents: Kings who die; Wildcat; Cold victory; Inside straight; Details; License; Strange bedfellows

Territory
In Anderson, P. Trader to the stars p55-124

Trader to the stars. Doubleday 1964 176p music (Doubleday Science fiction) o.p. 1970

Analyzed in Short Story Index
"Three novelettes about a swash-buckling merchant prince of the twenty-first century, Nicholas van Rijn, who goes dashing about space dodging Adderkops, solving interstellar riddles, and making love to beautiful space girls." Bk Buyer's Guide
Contents: Hiding place; Territory; The master key

Anderson, Sherwood

Dark laughter; with an introduction by Howard Mumford Jones. Liveright 1960 319p $5.95

A reissue with a new introduction of the title first published 1925 by Boni & Liveright
Bruce Dudley is "the spoiled child of industrialism, longing to create with his brain or with his hands, but balked by a country that asks for neither sound handling of tools nor true worlds. And Bruce leaves his newspaper and his short-story writing wife and goes drifting down the river, scarcely knowing what he wants, unless it is to see what life really is like and put it into poetry." Sat R
"Anderson's prose has a certain rhythm and fluency. His imagery has a natural grandeur, his phraseology is ardent and exuberant, his descriptions have a sincerely poetic note. Typical of these are his impressions of Negro boathands on the Mississippi. He has a feeling for the fulness and color of words that goes beyond mere technical art or accuracy. He combines a rich simplicity with a fervent honesty to create a fineness and nobility of utterance." Int Bk R

Poor white; a novel. Huebsch, B. W. 1920 371p o.p. 1970

The author "tells the story of an Ohio town. It is a story of the transition period of the eighties and nineties between an agricultural and an industrial civilization. . . . The hero of the book, however, is not an Ohioan. He is a poor white who wanders up from Missouri, an indolent, dreaming boy, shaken out of his lethargy by a New England woman who tries

to train his mind to definite channels. The result is the development of an inventive strain which the awakening giant, Industry, takes and uses to its own ends. The author's treatment of Hugh is pathologic. He is attracted to women but is afraid of them. . . . And never, except for fleeting moments, does he find satisfaction, either in his marriage or his work." Book Rev Digest

Sherwood Anderson: Short stories. Ed. and with an introduction by Maxwell Geismar. Hill & Wang 1962 289p (American century ser) $4.95

Partially analyzed in Short Story Index
Stories from "The Triumph of the Egg," "Horses and Men," "Death in the Woods," and "The Sherwood Anderson Reader"
Contents: The dumb man; I want to know why; The other woman; The egg; The man in the brown coat; Brothers; I'm a fool; The triumph of a modern, or, Send for the lawyer; The man who became a woman; Milk bottles; The sad horn blowers; Death in the woods; There she is—she is taking her bath; The lost novel; Like a queen; In a strange town; These mountaineers; A meeting south; Brother death; The corn planting; Nobody laughed; A part of earth; Morning roll call; The yellow gown; Daughters; White spot; A walk in the moonlight; His chest of drawers; Not sixteen

Tar: a midwest childhood; a critical text; ed. with an introduction by Ray Lewis White. Press of Case Western Reserve Univ. 1969 xx, 257p $7.50

SBN 8295-0150-2
First published 1926 by Boni & Liveright
"Tar is one of the many children born to Dick and Mary Moorehead. Dick is a garrulous, idle, affable fellow, and his wife a darkly beautiful woman, silent but not taciturn. Tar has something of both parents. The story begins when Tar is about four and continues up to early adolescence, describing the incidents in the small town life about him that brought his consciousness to a new focus and marked a new stage in his development." Book Rev Digest
"Unforgettable, and so tenderly told! A childhood well remembered—and yet, one feels, the book is not remembrance, but imagination." Boston Transcript

Winesburg, Ohio

Some editions are:
Modern Lib. $2.95 Introduction by Ernest Boyd
Viking $4.50 Introduction by Malcolm Cowley
Modern Library edition is analyzed in Short Story Index
First published 1919
Contents: Hands; Paper pills; Mother; Philosopher; Nobody knows; Godliness; Surrender; Terror; Man of ideas; Adventure; Respectability; Thinker; Tandy; Strength of God; Teacher; Loneliness; Awakening; 'Queer'; Untold lie; Drink; Death; Sophistication; Departure

Andrew, Prudence

A new creature. Putnam 1968 331p $5.95

"Bristol in 1739 was a rich city, rich from the coal and slave trade. One of its most prosperous merchants was Will Beckford, a red-faced, blaspheming slave trader. This novel tells of Beckford's confrontation with the new religion Methodism, and its effect on his life and family. Until he heard John Wesley speak, religion was of little concern to him. His adoption of Methodism separated him from his closest friends, the Harts, as well as causing his business associates to turn against him." Library J

Andrews, Mary Raymond Shipman

The perfect tribute; drawing by Rudolph Ruzicka. Scribner 1956 48p $2.50

First published 1906
"'The perfect tribute' on the Gettysburg speech is rendered directly to Lincoln, in a Washington hospital, by a wounded soldier who had read the address in a morning newspaper. . . . Leaving veracity out of consideration, it must be confessed that the little story is written with a tenderness of touch and a delicacy of diction." Dial

Andreyev, Leonid

The seven who were hanged; a story; illus. by Irving Politzer. Garden City Pub. Co. 190p illus o.p. 1970

First written 1908
"The fear of death. the horror and iniquity of capital punishment, is the theme of this powerful study of the character, thoughts, and feelings of men and women condemned to die. Five of the prisoners are revolutionists who have attempted to assassinate a high official in Russia, two are common peasant murderers. They wait in solitary confinement for seventeen days after the judgment, and are finally summoned to ride in the dark to midnight execution." Keller's Reader's Digest of Books

Andrézel, Pierre

The angelic avengers. Random House 1947 402p o.p. 1970

Original edition published 1944 in Denmark
"Deliberately imitative of early nineteenth-century novels, this story of distressed females at the mercy of a villain is told in mannered prose, and is said to have been accepted as political allegory at its publication in Denmark during German domination. Two homeless English girls accepted the offer of a retired clergyman who, in memory of his daughter, would take them into his home in France and continue their education. It was a trap, for girls had been sold into slavery there, and it took careful planning and daring to escape from the scoundrel to the romantic young men who waited." Booklist

Andrić, Ivo

Nobel Prize in literature, 1961

Anika's times
In Andrić, I. The vizier's elephant p55-130

Bosnian chronicle; tr. from the Serbo-Croatian by Joseph Hitrec. Knopf 1963 429p $6.95

Sequel to: The woman of Sarajevo
Original Serbo-Croatian edition published 1945 in Belgrade; in England, translated by Kenneth Johnstone, 1959 with title: Bosnian story
"The scene is Travnik, administrative capital of Bosnia, during the seven years before the fall of Napoleon. Daville, poetaster and family man, goes to Travnik as Napoleon's consul. The real theme is the clash between enlightened but war-tormented Christian Europe and the savage conservatism of oriental Europe." New Statesman
"Andric is a master of character and he draws each of his people, along with the members of his retinue, marvelously. . . . I don't believe that any writer has given a more fascinating description of his birthplace than this one by Andric. . . . The book is episodic in character, yet so well ordered that it does not fragment." Book Week
Followed by: The bridge on the Drina

The bridge on the Drina; tr. from the Serbo-Croat by Lovett F. Edwards. Macmillan (N Y) 1959 314p o.p. 1970

Sequel to: Bosnian chronicle
Original Serbo-Croatian edition published 1945 in Belgrade
This story "centers on a bridge that was a focal point through the three centuries that the Ottoman Empire drove westward into Europe, and on the efforts of Yugoslavia to stop this encroachment." McClurg. Book News
The book "is not light summer reading: only the tragic and the near-tragic events witnessed by the bridge through three and a half centuries are described. It is not, however, a morbid and forbidding book, for Ivo Andric has faith and hope for the future of mankind intact. This is serious and good reading." Best Sellers

The Pasha's concubine, and other tales; tr. from the Serbo-Croatian by Joseph Hitrec. Knopf 1968 302p $6.95

Analyzed in Short Story Index
Originally published 1963 in Serbo-Croatian as part of a twelve-volume work

"A collection of thirteen short stories set in Yugoslavia which cover a span of three centuries, from the Ottoman empire to the Nazi occupation in World War II." Book Rev Digest
Contents: The bridge on the Žepa; The journey of Ali Djerzilez; Confession; By the brandy still; Mustapha Magyar; In the camp; The Pasha's concubine; Thirst; The snake; The scythe; Woman on the rock; Bar Titanic; A summer in the south

The vizier's elephant; three novellas; tr. from the Serbo-Croat by Drenka Willen. Harcourt 1962 247p boards $4.75

Analyzed in Short Story Index
"In the title story, the whims of the Turkish rulers of Bosnia are epitomized in an elephant brought by the vizier to wreak havoc on the village of Travnik. . . . 'Anika's Times' probes the nature of evil and finds it in communal sin. Using the frame story of a priest gone mad, Andric flashes back to the time of the priest's grandfather, when a beautiful outcast girl held the village in thrall. . . . In 'Zeko,' the final story . . . a man depressed by every aspect of bourgeois life in Belgrade, is driven to the point of suicide. Awakened by the real life of the workers around him . . . he rises to heroism in the resistance movement." N Y Her Trib Books

The vizier's elephant [novelette]
In Andrić, I. The vizier's elephant p 1-54

The woman from Sarajevo. Tr. from the Serbo-Croatian by Joseph Hitrec. Knopf 1965 245p $5.95

Original Serbo-Croation edition published 1945 in Yugoslavia
First volume of trilogy. Followed by: Bosnian chronicle
A novel set in Sarajevo and Belgrade, Yugoslavia in the early 20th century. "The deathbed words of her embittered father took such firm root in Miss Raika's consciousness that she became a miser—almost a monster of thrift in fact. Yet in spite of that, she was still a woman and far from impregnable in her defenses against the world." Huntting
"A small gallery of lively characters swirl around the larger-than-life figure of Miss Raika and lend touches of humor and excitement to a stark portrayal of a mean and humorless woman. The details of the accumulation of wealth are as fascinating as the fresh and vital background." Library J

Zeko
In Andrić, I. The vizier's elephant p131-247

Angoff, Charles

Between day and dark. Yoseloff 1959 620p $5.95

Sequel to: The sun at noon
"Young David Polonsky finds a career in New York City which forces him to leave his home and family, to find happiness with a different breed of people, and to reconcile his strict Jewish past with new manners and customs. The time is the mid-1920's." Pub W
Followed by: The bitter spring

The bitter spring. Yoseloff 1961 730p $5.95

Sequel to: Between day and dark. Followed by: Summer storm

In the morning light. Yoseloff 1952 736p $5.95

Sequel to: Journey to the dawn
This chapter in the saga of the Polonskys "takes them through the tumultuous years of World War I and the subsequent depression." Huntting
Followed by: The sun at noon

Journey to the dawn. Yoseloff 1951 421p $5.95

First volume in a series of eight novels about a Jewish family, the Polonskys, which emigrated from a small village in Czarist Russia to the United States, i.e. Boston. The novels trace the experiences of the family, as individuals and as Jews, in their new country, from the turn of the century to the late 1940's

Angoff, Charles—*Continued*

"The narrative lights up their daily lives, focusing on Great-grandmother Yente and on little David, who loves school and the new country's ways." Bookmark
Followed by: In the morning light

Memory of autumn. Yoseloff 1968 454p $5.95

Seventh in the series, and sequel to: Summer storm. Followed by: Winter twilight

(ed.) Stories from The Literary Review. Fairleigh Dickinson Univ. Press 1969 312p $8

"From the international pages of 'Literary Review' issues, 1957-1968, comes this anthology of reasonably sound absorbing, if rarely brilliant or experimental, stories by 24 authors from as many countries." Booklist
Contents: Two short stories: Stepfield; Sonatina, by H. von Doderer; The broken globe, by H. Kreisel; The last rite, by Lee Yu-Hwa; The eye, by C. Bodker; Still life, by G. Helbemäe; October, by S. Streuvels; Other versions, by A. A. Aidoo; Birth, by M. R. Anand; A boy with a gun, by D. Clarke; The bridge, by T Takeda; Mrs Kimble, by S. Nair; My mother and the roomer, by Chu Yo-Sup; Tale of a return, by A. Irbe; The organ of Kurliskés, by J. Kaupas; The swamp, by A. Alberts; Indoro Bush College, by R. A. Freeman; The yellow shawl, by F. Arcellana; Beside the railroad track, by Z. Nalkowska; Negostina, by A. I. Ghilia; Three sketches: The black something; An inexpensive present for my nephew; Treetops, by N. Narokov; Polluted zone, by L. Ahlin; They stole our cattle, by N. Obudo; The fine white mist of winter, by J. C. Oates; The death of Mr Goluza, by B. Scepanovic

Most of the stories "are written in traditional literary style with little experimentation; however, a spectrum of various views and conflicts is presented. . . . This collection would be especially useful for college and large public libraries." Library J

Summer storm. Yoseloff 1963 569p $5.95

Sequel to: The bitter spring
This volume "follows David Polonsky's career as managing editor of the magazine 'American World' as it founders in the depths of the Depression [1933-1935]. . . . The reader sees the new optimism under Roosevelt, the effect of Father Coughlin's broadcasts; but also such things as the move toward assimilation of second-generation Jews and the return to orthodoxy at times of stress." Library J
Followed by: Memory of autumn

The sun at noon. Yoseloff 1955 572p $5.95

Sequel to: In the morning light
This volume in the series "of novels about a family of Russian-Jewish immigrants who settle in Boston . . . deals with the period 1919-1923, and mainly with a son of the family, a student at Harvard." Pub W
Followed by: Between day and the dark

Winter twilight. Yoseloff 1970 474p $6.95

Sequel to: Memory of autumn
The author describes the life of the Polonskys in the years 1946-1947, years which saw the beginnings of the state of Israel, and the relations of Jews in the United States to this event and to each other. (Publisher)

Anthony, Evelyn

All the Queen's men. Crowell 1960 307p o.p. 1970

"Historical novel about Elizabeth Tudor, with the main emphasis on her relationship, changing through the years, with Robert Dudley, early of Leicester." Book Rev Digest
"All characters are so well drawn and presented that the reader is on the stage all the time, following all events and crisis from the moment Elizabeth took the throne in 1558 to the defeat of the Armada and the death of Leicester in 1588." Library J

Anne Boleyn. Crowell 1957 310p o.p. 1970

"This fictional biography of Anne Boleyn turns upon the story of a king and his subject which was to change the course of history. Handsome, dominating King Henry VIII found a match in the beautiful Anne Boleyn, whose courage, pride and ambition won her a crown and lost her her life. The intrigues and events

of the Reformation in 16th century England furnish the framework of the story." Publisher's note
The author "emphasizes Anne's ambition and her vindictiveness so that Anne is not an especially attractive heroine until she gains the reader's sympathies toward the end of the book. . . . A good, straightforward, but not unusual historical novel." Pub W

The Cardinal and the Queen. Coward-McCann 1968 221p $4.95

"Set against the glittering intrigue-ridden court of Louis the XIII, the drama of proud, beautiful Queen Anne who found fulfillment as a woman and queen in a passionate affair with Cardinal Richelieu, the King's minister." McClurg. Book News
"The Louvre, Luxembourg Palace, and other royal buildings of seventeenth-century Paris provide much of the authentic background for this historical novel." Booklist

Charles, the King. Doubleday 1961 427p o.p. 1970

In this biographical novel the author "portrays Charles Stuart, England's last absolute monarch, as an uncompromisingly honest man, a passionately loving husband, and a firm believer in the divine rights of kings. Devoted equally to Charles's public and personal life, the story covers the period from the young king's first meeting with Henrietta, his French bride, through a 20-year reign filled with intrigue, conflicts with Parliament, and civil war, ending with his execution by Cromwell." Booklist

The legend. Coward-McCann 1969 253p $5.95

"Retired because of pressure from his conformist wife, [Peter Arundsen a former British spy] . . . writhes in his domestic chains. When at a weekend party, he meets a beautiful and sensual divorcée, he is drawn, not only into an agonizing love affair, but back into the spy business, with a vengeance." Pub W
This "is a very contemporary novel in setting and in its blase attitude toward sex, marriage, the Establishment, and living. The love affair between Mary and Peter, although not completely descriptive, seems at first to be an orgy of sex. It is not, because as the story progresses all parts fit together neatly for a fast-moving readable adult mystery story." Best Sellers

Royal intrigue. Crowell 1954 279p o.p. 1970

Published in England with title: Curse not the King
"The relationship between Catherine the Great of Russia and her son, Paul, was not a healthy one. Portraying this unnatural hatred and suspicion with its eventual results on the personality of Paul and in the cruelties and sadism of his brief reign as emperor, this novel takes the reader into the uncivilized Russia of the eighteenth century. With few deviations from historical fact, the author brings to life these two dread monarchs surrounded by their scheming barbaric advisers and courtiers." Cincinnati

Victoria and Albert; a novel. Crowell 1958 312p o.p. 1970

"Dealing only with the period from Victoria's accession to the death of Albert, the writer has written a convincingly human story in which she interprets Victoria as a headstrong, autocratic young queen passionately devoted to a reserved and studious Prince Consort who brought her happiness but never fully returned her love. The fictional reconstruction of their marriage is set against a background of England's domestic and diplomatic affairs and filled with a number of clearly delineated historical figures." Booklist
"Whether the author's estimate of the Queen's personality be right or wrong this volume is a valuable contribution to understanding of the Victorian era. Miss Anthony has a knack of evoking a period and bringing alive the actors in it. . . . Even in a book which cannot be considered buoyant, the story is enthralling to the point of making it difficult to lay aside." Christian Science Monitor

Anthony, Michael

Green days by the river. Houghton 1967 191p $4.50

Set in a Trinidad village the story "follows 15-year-old Shellie, newly come to Mayaro, through his initial shyness and first experiences of love—and death. His father's lingering illness casts the sensitive boy in the role of family breadwinner, most often on the local cocoa plantation, occasionally planting at the side of his solicitous neighbor, Mr. Gidharee. Shellie falls in love . . . with Mr. Gidharee's daughter, Rosalie, but then, just as quickly, he is smitten with the more outgoing Joan. Complications arise, since the observant Mr. Gidharee has tacitly accepted the idea of Shellie as a future husband for Rosalie." Pub W

"The book is a good example of West Indian literature and will be useful in libraries with sophisticated readers." Library J

Aragon, Louis

Holy Week; a novel; tr. by Haakon Chevalier. Putnam 1961 541p o.p. 1970

Original French edition published 1958
The author recreates "the seven days between Palm Sunday and Easter in the year 1815. This week began the most unbelievable episode in French history, the hundred days of Napoleon's reestablished Empire. . . . As Napoleon started his triumphant march from Antibes to Paris, Louis XVII, in spite of his promise not to leave the capital, set out in the opposite direction towards the Belgian frontier. This novel is the story of his flight. It is seen through several eyes . . . but largely through those of a young Royal Musketeer, Théodore Géricault, later to become famous as the leader of the French realistic school of painting." N Y Her Trib Books

"The structure of 'Holy Week' is willfully fragmentary and episodic. . . . What saves 'Holy Week' is Aragon's prose—a marvelously zestful, turbulent stream of language." N Y Times Bk R

Arblay, Frances (Burney) d'. See Burney, Fanny

Arent, Arthur

The laying on of hands. Little 1969 273p $5.95

The story "opens on May 6, 1945, in a specially designed room in Auschwitz, and it ends with a wild fight on a street in Madrid in March of 1968. Between those dates Arthur Arent draws the story of the hunt for an infamous Nazi doctor, a plot to import arms to Haiti to overthrow Papa Doc Duvalier's dictatorship, two beautiful love affairs, one in the past, the other in the present, and a deadly game played between Israelis and ex-Nazis." Publisher's note

"It is purely secular and reminded this reader of a scenario for a rather poor made-for-television movie. On second thought, the sex scenes are much too explicit for viewing in one's living room so we'll have to view it in so called 'art theaters.' " Best Sellers

Arkin, Frieda

The Dorp. Dial Press 1969 360p $6.95

"This is the story of the citizens of Kuyper's Dorp, a small town in upstate New York. In it the reader meets Eunice Dewsnap with her romantic fancies; Evelyn Clancy, the alcoholic, who won an appearance on television; Justin Barrows and his newspaper; Vebber Stevens, the would-be author who is going to revolutionize medicine with his book—an alphabetical listing of all human ailments; the minister and his struggle to get people to admit their doubts and stop being hypocrites; and many more." Library J

"To read this gentle, brilliant novel is actually to be in the town of Kuyper's Dorp—or any other small town in America in the present time. More than that—much more—is to know and understand and be tolerant of the people who live there. There is no one person or theme that dominates the novel, but all the drama of each life is minutely studied and shown as it interweaves with the other lives." Pub W

Armah, Ayi Kwei

The beautiful ones are not yet born; a novel. Houghton 1968 215p $4.95

This novel "presents the case of a poor but honest ('beautyful') man in a rotten world. A middle-class government worker, eager to do right but just managing to feed his wife and three children, is constantly tempted to partake of the petty, common, accepted corruptions of Nkrumaist Ghana. Looming large and wealthy before him is a former schoolmate who has gone the usual route and has thereby become a government Minister. Mr. Armah's hero is greatly bothered, but something within him compels him to refuse to compromise, though he suffers daily for his stand. Then comes the 1966 coup that ousts Nkrumah from office and reorders the seats of power. But what difference does it make to the man? Or indeed to the nation?" Book of the Month Club News

Fragments. Houghton [1970 c1969] 287p $5.95

"A young African returns to his homeland after five years in America, only to find a people too eager to ape Western ways and values, especially the more negative ones. Baako goes to work for Ghanavision as a writer, but finds himself surrounded by inertia, corruption and careerism, with the only bright spot provided by a young Puerto Rican psychiatrist, herself in quest of a purpose in life. Through it all there is the presence of the blind and aging [grandmother] N'aana, troubled by the new nation she senses about her, conscious that in rejecting their old dreams and values, her people have embarked on a present and future that promise only ultimate frustration and decay. All three of these characters inevitably come into conflict with the society around them." Pub W

"One relishes Mr. Armah's sensitivity to words; his concern for the evocatively right word; his use of simple diction and sentences constructed with an ear for rhythm and meaning reveal the talented writer." Best Sellers

Armstrong, Charlotte

The balloon man. Coward-McCann 1968 253p $4.95

Sherry Reynard leaves her husband, a struggling writer who takes LSD, and rents a room in a dingy Los Angeles boardinghouse to be near her hospitalized little boy. She soon begins to find her neighbors strange. then finds her life threatened by the same drug that destroyed her husband. (Publisher)

Dream of fair woman. Coward-McCann 1966 254p o.p. 1970

"Matt Cuneen's search is for the identity of the breathtakingly lovely blonde who falls asleep in his mother's rooming house, and who continues in a coma in spite of the efforts of the staff of the hospital to which she is moved. Newspaper publicity provides three possible answers and Matt assumes the responsibility for determining the correct one. His trail leads to shocking revelations of greed, blackmail, twisted hope, and sudden death. Charlotte Armstrong once more produces masterly plotting, chilling suspense, and sharply focused, living people." Library J

The gift shop. Coward-McCann [1967 c1966] 255p illus o.p. 1970

"A dying detective gets off a plane, staggers to Jean's airport gift shop, and hides a note about a small child's whereabouts in a China piggy bank. The bank leads Jean on a wild chase from California to an Irish castle, with ruthless bad guys in pursuit." Bk Buyer's Guide

"Credibility gap and all, this is a gem of a thriller and the most sheerly enjoyable (and warmly human) Armstrong in some . . . years." N Y Times Bk R

The protégé. Coward-McCann 1970 223p $4.95

"The beautiful and charming young man told old Mrs. Moffat that he was Simon Warren, the boy who had lived next door fifteen years ago. Soon he was established as her guest, gardener, and companion to the uneasiness of her daughter-in-law, Alexandra. Why

Armstrong, Charlotte—*Continued*

had he taken the trouble to ingratiate himself and was he responsible for the strange things that began to happen?" Bk Buyer's Guide

"This is a well-plotted and well-planned mystery which has the reader curious and uncertain until the final pages." Best Sellers

Seven seats to the moon. Coward-McCann 1969 320p $5.95

"While he was in the hospital, J. Middleton Little heard a patient saying something about the end of the world and tickets to the moon. Soon he is offered seven seats to the moon as the price of silence. The man who makes the offer then jumps or is pushed to his death and Little realizes he is in terrible danger." Bk Buyer's Guide

"Any writer as prolific and as good as Charlotte Armstrong is entitled to an occasional lapse, and that is how we'd describe 'Seven Seats to the Moon.' It's not a bad book, but it's just not up to Miss Armstrong's usual standard." Pub W

The witch's house. Coward-McCann 1963 253p o.p. 1970

"A novel of suspense set in a California university town. When young mathematics professor Pat O'Shea accuses a colleague of petty theft, the outcome is more terrible than he could have imagined. He eventually finds himself trapped in a prison that seems inescapable, for his captor is an old woman whose crazed imagination sees in him her own dead son—a son she insists will never leave her again." Huntting

"This is Charlotte Armstrong at her best—violence, action, a touch of zaniness, and even humor." Pub W

Arnold, Elliott

y Blood brother; illus. by Dale Nichols. Duell 1950 558p $6.95

First published 1947. The 1950 edition adds new illustrations

"This long, readable book tells the tragic story of the Chiricahua Apaches and their great chief, Cochise, the only individual Indian for whom an Arizona county is named. Of all the Apaches, the Chiricahuas were fiercest, raiding for centuries into Mexico. But when the Americans took over their country, Cochise with great intelligence saw his people could not fight the invaders. After some sporadic raids, Cochise controlled the majority of his people, a few headed by the notorious Geronimo breaking away. But the American contractors for Army stores wanted conflict, and only the tight-lipped intervention of Tom Jefford, blood brother of Cochise, kept the peace. Filled with authentic lore and the sweep of Arizona's deserts and mountains, this is a book to be read slowly and savored well." Literary Guild

A night of watching. Scribner 1967 441p $5.95

"In the fall of 1943, in the fourth year of the German occupation of Denmark, there occurred one of the most remarkable and successful exoduses of modern times, the rescue of the Jews of Denmark by their fellow countrymen and the smuggling to safety of nearly all of them. This book is a fictionalized account of what happened when a German informed a Danish Underground leader that the 8000-odd Danish Jews were to be rounded up on Yom Kippur for transportation to Germany." Pub W

"A crowded, exciting novel that cannot quite maintain the split-second pace of its early chapters. 'A Night of Watching' is a good reminder that there is more to Denmark than Hans Christian Andersen and Victor Borge." Book of the Month Club News

Arnow, Harriette

y The dollmaker. Macmillan (N Y) 1954 549p $7.50

Also available in a large type edition $8.95

"Gertie Nevels, a courageous and unselfish Kentucky countrywoman who has a talent amounting to a passion for whittling small objects out of wood, is forced by the war to leave the happy, although poverty-stricken, community where she has spent her life and go to Detroit, where her husband has found work in a factory. The meanness, squalor, and lack of privacy of her new surroundings, and the debasing effect of the city on her husband and on some of their children, oppress her, but she maintains her integrity and her faith in her fellow human beings." New Yorker

"It is hard to believe that anyone who opens its pages will soon forget the big woman and her sufferings as traced in Harriette Arnow's long, heavily packed masterwork." N Y Times Bk R

Hunter's horn. Macmillan (N Y) 1949 508p o.p. 1970

"A poor white subsistence farmer, aroused by the depredations of a fox, obsessed by determination to kill it, urged by natural love of the chase . . . handicapped by a weakness for moonshine, almost brings his farm and family to ruin. Unforgettable many-sided picture of family and community life in Kentucky hills." Library J

"It is outstanding in that it is quite grown up, fully mature in its philosophy of life. . . . The underlying philosophy—the willingness to accept and present life as it is—which fits the novel into its fine, strong frame of universality." N Y Her Trib Books

The weedkiller's daughter. Knopf 1970 [c1969] 371p $6.95

The "story of Susie Schnitzer 'outstanding junior girl student' in her affluent Eden Hills high school, in Detroit: her father, whom she called Bismarck with reason; the little stratagems necessary in her closely inspected life; her mother's gentle efforts at peace making; the normal trials and joys of high school life; plus Susie's quick, intelligent, but dreamy search for happiness." Bk Buyer's Guide

"The book is beautifully and skillfully written with insight and understanding on many levels." Best Sellers

Arzhak, Nikolai. See Daniel, Yuli

Asch, Sholem

The Apostle; tr. by Maurice Samuel. Putnam 1943 804p o.p. 1970

Second of a trilogy. Sequel to: The Nazarene

This "story of Paul opens seven weeks after the crucifixion of Christ. From this beginning [the author] portrays . . . the slow spread of Christianity, under the heroic leadership of Paul, the Apostle—the impassioned young man of Tarsus, the Roman citizen equally learned in both the laws of the Jews and the Gentiles, the tortured soul who brought a message of hope to the oppressed throughout the Empire of Rome." Huntting

In "'The Apostle,' Sholem Asch has written a book which should stand beside 'The Nazarene.' Its erudition, its essential reverence for the two faiths concerned, its scholarly and dramatic portrayal of the Jew who spread the gospel to the gentiles will call forth the respect of every civilized and intelligent reader. The story of the life of Paul, as told by Mr. Asch, is one that could be powerfully effective in breaking down the barriers of prejudice and ignorance." N Y Her Trib Books

"The novel is bound to arouse even more controversy than did its predecessor. Its quality as great literature, however, cannot be disputed." Christian Century

Followed by: Mary

East River; a novel; tr. by A. H. Gross. Putnam 1946 438p o.p. 1970

A "complex story of the conflicts arising from the differences in nationality and religious belief among residents of New York City's tenemented East Side at the turn of the century. It is the story of Moshe Wolf Davidowsky, a devout Jew and his two sons—Nathan, crippled by infantile paralysis, and the up-and-coming Irving who defies his father by jilting the brilliant Rachel and marrying Irish Catholic Mary McCarthy. A Catholic grandson is a bitter disappointment to Moshe, but through his understanding heart he takes in the girl and her child when Irving deserts them." Literary Guild

"It is a big, ambitious novel . . . achieving much less than it grasps at, yet rich in the beauty and vigor of its thrust." Sat R

The little town

In Asch, S. Tales of my people

Asch, Sholem—*Continued*

Mary; tr. by Leo Steinberg. Putnam 1949 436p o.p. 1970

"The final volume of the author's trilogy completing the story begun in The Nazarene and The Apostle [entered below and above, respectively]." Book Rev Digest

"The true value of such books lies in their enrichment of the human background of Bible times, which must turn the thoughtful reader back to the Bible records with deeper appreciation of their great beauty and their spiritual import." Christian Science Monitor

Moses; tr. by Maurice Samuel. Putnam 1951 505p o.p. 1970

"A panoramic novel of the Exodus, with Moses the epic hero. From the early identification of Moses with the Egyptian god Horus, through mighty deeds and deep sufferings of soul, to the final assumption of Moses into the heaven of the Hebrew God, the tale has heroic proportions." Library J

The story is "sincere, reverent and, in this translation by Maurice Samuel, at times eloquent. . . . A vast amount of descriptive detail bodies forth the customs, the manners and the occupations of the period—from the bustle and pomp of Egyptian civilization along the banks of the Nile to primitive quiet of life in the desert. It is as though an illuminated scroll were unrolled on which a people are depicted, collectively and individually, playing out their destiny." Book of the Month Club News

The mother; authorized tr. by Elsa Krauch. AMS Press 295p $8.75

First published 1930 by Liveright, translated by Nathan Ausubel. This AMS edition is a reprint of the 1937 Putnam edition

"A Yiddish family, the Zlotniks, emigrates to America, following the success of their eldest son in the new country. Here, as in Poland, Surè, the mother, finds she must fight against poverty, and works herself to death. Dvoyrelè, the eldest daughter, gives her love and encouragement to a despondent young sculptor until he achieves success; then she returns to her own family to care for the younger brothers and sisters, left motherless." Book Rev Digest

"The emotional depths of Jewish womanhood is the theme of this story of two generations, in Poland and on the East Side." Pittsburgh

Mottke, the thief; tr. by Willa and Edwin Muir. Putnam 1935 314p o.p. 1970

First published 1917 with title: Mottke the vagabond

"This novel, translated from the Yiddish, is a story of life in a Jewish village in Russian Poland and in the underworld of Warsaw. . . . At fourteen [Mottke] had experienced all the sensations of life—except murder. And that follows not long after. In turn Mottke is a blower in a glass factory, a member of a troupe of wandering acrobats, and keeper of a brothel. He is torn between his love for two women, is moved to reform himself for the sake of one of them, is betrayed by her, and in the face of the other's efforts to save him gives himself up to defeat." Book Rev Digest

"Filled with astonishing adventures and a wealth of fascinating characters, this novel is a sort of Jewish Beggar's opera." St Louis

The Nazarene; tr. by Maurice Samuel. Putnam 1939 698p o.p. 1970

First volume of a trilogy

"A wealth of incident and historical detail make this novel very long. . . . It is told by three people; an old gentile scholar, haunted by memories of an earlier incarnation, tells how, as a Roman official, he contributed to the persecution of Jesus, and he forces his Jewish assistant to recall his own experiences of that time as a disciple of the Pharisees in Jerusalem. The third part of the narrative is in the form of a gospel by Judas Iscariot." Booklist

"Judged purely as a novel, The Nazarene is a superb achievement. Even on the factual side, a work such as Papini's Life is thin beside it. This is because Mr. Asch has taken an infinite amount of trouble to build up an historical background against which the figure of Jesus may move authentically, with that sense of reality which we should expect of fiction as of life." Atlantic

Followed by: The Apostle

A passage in the night. Putnam 1953 367p o.p. 1970

"The story of a modern [American] Jew's great business success and his atonement for a sin committed early in his career, a small theft from a man he scarcely knew. His atonement appears so quixotic that his family has him confined to a 'rest home.' Here Isaac Grossman finally finds a way to pay his debt and to come to peace with himself, renewing his religious faith." Pub W

"Mr. Asch has written a story both eloquent and inspiring and has employed the simple device of one man's search for peace of soul as a reproof to materialism and a fervent plea for a deeper, more understanding acceptance of spiritual truths." Springf'd Republican

The prophet; tr. by Arthur Saul Super. Putnam 1955 343p o.p. 1970

"The fifth and last in the series of Biblical novels written by this author, beginning with The Nazarene. This volume tells of the second Isaiah, or Deutero-Isaiah, who supposedly lived during the conquest of Babylon by Cyrus the Persian in the fifth century B.C. At the close of the book the first of the Israelites are about to set out for their homeland." Book Rev Digest

"The story unfolds against a lush . . . background of pagan life in Babylon. All the same, it remains high level fiction of biblical background, about one of the strangest but most inspired of the great prophets of Israel, in her time of troubles." Chicago Sunday Tribune

"The English text reads like a literal translation from the Yiddish. . . . Yet, completing as it does Mr. Asch's noble design of the Messiah as the bridge from Judaism to Christianity, [this book] commands respect." Sat R

Salvation; tr. by Willa and Edwin Muir. [2d ed] Schocken [1968 c1962] 343p $7.50

A reissue of the title first published 1934 by Putnam

"The story of the life and religous reactions of Jechiel, a Polish Jew of the period of Napoleon. Jechiel is a conscientious youth brought up by a devoted mother who instills a love for the 'Faith' which bears fruit in an exemplary life and wide influence as a rabbi." Huntting

"A peculiarly fervid religious sense pervades the book, which . . . turns to dramatic use a great deal of Talmudic knowledge." Times (London) Lit Sup

Tales of my people; tr. by Meyer Levin. Putnam 1948 272p o.p. 1970

Analyzed in Short Story Index

A "collection of short stories and one short novel, The Little Town, commemorating the Jewish people, especially the Polish Jews. All treat of Jewish life and customs before, during, and after the rise of the Nazis." Book Rev Digest

Contents: The little town; Tricked; A divorce; The dowry; Yiskadal v' Yiskadash; A child leads the way; The duty to live; Jewish eyes; Eretz Israel; Mama; The finger

The "book is filled with an ironic humor and a simplicity of faith that is moving." Library J

Three cities; a trilogy; tr. by Willa and Edwin Muir. Putnam 1933 899p o.p. 1970

"Three cities, three tense periods in Russia's dramatic, twentieth-century history, and the two classes into which the Industrial Revolution had spilt the Jews are dealt with in this novel. The cities and the periods are St. Petersburg in the commercial and industrial expansion after 1905, Warsaw during the pre-World War [I] years of unrest which probably determined the Czarist decision for war to divert the Russian masses from rebellion, and Moscow during and after the October revolution. The two classes are the fawning Jewish millionaires who intrigued for, married for, and paid for Russification to make themselves safe and powerful in a hostile society, and the Jewish workers, also seeking a secure future, but an honorably unprivileged one in a classless proletarian state." Nation

"Unpleasant at times, it is dramatic throughout." Cincinnati

Ashe, Gordon

A clutch of coppers by John Creasey as Gordon Ashe. Holt [1969 c1967] 183p $3.95

"A Rinehart Suspense novel"
First published 1967 in England
"Police from all over the world have gathered in London for Commissioner Dawlish's Crime Haters conference on methods of criminal identification. One of the policemen is murdered and American Captain Randy Patton barely escapes death. Then Randy's daughter is kidnapped, and Dawlish must act quickly to save the girl and Patton." Bk Buyer's Guide
"Good Creasey-Ashe action." Pub W

For other titles by this author see Creasey, John

Ashton, Winifred. See Dane, Clemence

Ashton-Warner, Sylvia

Bell call. Simon & Schuster 1964 317p boards $5

"The novel is set in New Zealand in the present. Its central character is a genius-mother, Tarl, a young woman totally committed to her belief in freedom—freedom for herself and her children. When the bell calls to summon her six-year-old Bennie to school, Tarl stands by her judgment that he is not ready. . . . She defies the community and the law." Publisher's note
"We as readers grow to admire Tarl for clinging to her principles and to repudiate her inability to see that what she calls principles are really not so and should be abandoned. This is a thoughtful book." Best Sellers

Greenstone. Simon & Schuster 1966 217p $4.50

The author "chronicles ten years in the lives of the Considines of New Zealand: Richard, crippled with arthritis; his wife, energetic, plain, but full of love for her husband; and their twelve children, not to mention a half-Maori granddaugher." Bk Buyer's Guide
"A bit thin and perhaps too mistily poetic sometimes, Greenstone is a happy, lovely, comic novel that touches on the sadness of the streaming away of time." Book of the Month Club News

Spinster; a novel. Simon & Schuster 1959 [c1958] 242p o.p. 1970

First published in England, 1958
"An outpost schoolhouse in New Zealand is the setting in which Anna Vorontosov meets with compassion, humor and brilliance the multiple difficulties of teaching seventy small children, most of whom are Maori, and struggles too with the problems of spinsterhood, a young teacher and an old love." Pub W
"Reminiscent in many ways of Margaret Landon's story of Anna Leonowens and the King of Siam, Mrs. Ashton-Warner's account, set in the present, is as delightful, certainly funnier and, at the same time, deeply poetic and strikingly apropos." N Y Times Bk R

Asimov, Isaac

y Asimov's mysteries. Doubleday 1968 228p (Doubleday Science fiction) $4.50

Analyzed in Short Story Index
"Asimov has brought together stories written throughout his career, the earliest dating from 1939. All have some element of mystery, and several deal with a favorite space-sleuth, Dr. Wendell Orth. There is also a James Bond-like space adventure. . . . There are 14 stories in all, and they're universally good." Pub W
Contents: The singing bell; The talking stone; What's in a name; The dying night; Pâté de foie gras; The dust of death; A loint of paw; I'm in Marsport without Hilda; Marooned off Vesta; Anniversary; Obituary; Star light; The key; The billiard ball

y The caves of steel. Doubleday 1954 217p o.p. 1970

"In an air-conditioned, canopy-covered New York of the future, millions of people hated the efficient robots which they called 'job stealers.' When Dr. Sarton was murdered, police detective Elijah Baley was assigned to work on the case with one Daneel, a robot." Hunting
"Here is an unusually exciting and engrossing detective story set in a science fictional background convincingly worked out." N Y Times Bk R

also in Asimov, I. The rest of the robots p165-362

The currents of space
In Asimov, I. Triangle: The currents of space, Pebble in the sky, The stars, like dust p 1-172

y Fantastic voyage; a novel. Based on the screenplay by Harry Kleiner from the original story by Otto Klement and Jay Lewis Bixby. Houghton 1966 239p $3.95

"Five people are sent on a rescue mission in a submarine, but this is no ordinary submarine moving through an ordinary sea. The people and the submarine are miniaturized. They are moving through a man's blood vessels to reach and break up a blood clot in his brain. The miniaturization will not last—they have only 60 minutes to do the job and leave the man's body, before they return to ordinary size." Pub W
A "highly entertaining fantasy. Nobody dies but the villain. The characters are pretty much the stock types of the gender. Asimov's style is never terribly good and never poor. The book is free of offensive incidents or language. The moral, as always, is that science conquers all. A jolly tale which, fortunately, nobody will take seriously." Best Sellers

y Foundation. Doubleday 1951 255p $4.50

First published by Gnome Press
"A story of a Galactic Empire of the future, and its successor in the government of the Milky Way." Pub W
Followed by: Foundation and empire

y Foundation and empire. Doubleday 1952 247p $4.50

Sequel to: Foundation
First published by Gnome Press
"Two groups struggle for control of the world's destiny in a future time when mankind has settled in the Milky Way. Then a mutant appears bringing with him a new threat for everyone." Chicago
"Too carefully thought out and well written to be labeled simply 'Space opera,' these stories are still recommended only with caution to the general reader; they are so elaborately and coldly contrived that they lose sight of humanity." N Y Her Trib Books
Followed by: Second Foundation

y (ed.) The Hugo winners. Doubleday 1962 318p o.p. 1970

Analyzed in Short Story Index
"A collection of nine science fiction stories which won the Hugo Awards for science fiction writing from 1939-1961." Chicago
Novelettes are: The darfsteller, by W. M. Miller, Jr; Exploration team, by M. Leinster; The big front yard, by C. D. Simak; Flowers for Algernon, by D. Keyes; The longest voyage, by P. Anderson. Short stories are: Allamagoosa, by E. F. Russell; The star, by A. C. Clarke; Or all the seas with oysters, by A. Davidson; The Hellbound train, by R. Bloch

y I, robot. Doubleday 1963 [c1950] 218p $3.95

First published 1950 by Gnome Press, and analyzed in Short Story Index
The book contains nine related science fiction stories about robots: Robbie; Runaround; Reason; Catch that rabbit; Liar; Little lost robot; Escape; Evidence; The evitable conflict
"This is an exciting science thriller. . . . It could be fun for those whose nerves are not already made raw by the potentialities of the atomic age." N Y Times Bk R

The naked sun. Doubleday 1957 187p (Doubleday Science fiction) o.p. 1970

"Detective Elijah Baley's missions to the planet Solaria were to investigate the first murder ever committed among that odd

Asimov, Isaac—*Continued*

population and, secretly, to find out the weakness within Solaria that could help Earth withstand the inevitable future conquest by the 'Outer Worlds.' " McClurg. Book News

also in Asimov, I. The rest of the robots p363-554

Nightfall, and other stories. Doubleday 1969 343p (Doubleday Science fiction) $5.95

"Twenty imaginative stories, each selected and wittily prefaced by the author, will have wide appeal among science-fiction devotees." Booklist

Contents: Nightfall; Green patches; Hostess; Breeds there a man . . .; C-Chute; In a good cause; What if; Sally; Flies; Nobody here but-; It's such a beautiful day; Strikebreaker; Insert knob A in hole B; The up-to-date sorcerer; Unto the fourth generation; What is this thing called love; The machine that won the war; My son, the physicist; Eyes do more than see; Segregationist

y Nine tomorrows; tales of the near future. Doubleday 1959 236p $4.50

Analyzed in Short Story Index
A collection of stories "written with the author's usual verve and skill. Selections range from the frankly humorous 'I'm in Marsport without Hilda' to a startling illustration of the results of heartless experimentation. A must for the science fiction fan." Ontario Lib Rev
Contents: Profession; Feeling of power; Dying night; I'm in Marsport without Hilda; Gentle vultures; All the troubles of the world; Spell my name with an S; Last question; Ugly little boy

Pebble in the sky
In Asimov, I. Triangle: The currents of space, Pebble in the sky, The stars, like dust p173-346

y The rest of the robots. Doubleday 1964 556p (Doubleday Science fiction) $6.50

Analyzed in Short Story Index
Contains two novels: The caves of steel and The naked sun, first published 1954 and 1957 respectively
Short stories included are: Robot AL-76 goes astray; Victory unintentional; First Law; Let's get together; Satisfaction guaranteed; Risk; Lenny; Galley slave
"Unlike some science fiction, this is written with a light touch, and with an active sense of humor." Pub W

y Second Foundation. Doubleday 1953 210p $3.95

First published by Gnome Press
"This volume follows 'Foundation' and 'Foundation and empire' [entered above]. It is the story of the adventures of fourteen-year-old Arkady Darrell, who finds herself caught up in the search for Second Foundation which is secretly attempting to put the Seldon Plan back into effect." Huntting

The stars, like dust
In Asimov, I. Triangle: The currents of space, Pebble in the sky, The stars, like dust p347-516

Triangle: The currents of space, Pebble in the sky, The stars, like dust. Doubleday 1961 516p o.p. 1970

A science fiction anthology of the three titles first published 1952, 1950, and 1951 respectively
In the first novel "The Currents of Space" a man is caught in a galactic web of intrigue; in "Pebble in The Sky," Mr. Schwartz "raises one foot in the 20th-century and lowers it in Galactic Era 827; "The Stars, Like Dust' concerns a University student who becomes a fugitive fleeing an assassin." McClurg. Book News

A whiff of death. Walker & Co. [1968 c1958] 210p o.p. 1970

Originally published 1958 with title: The death dealers
"The police think the death of graduate student Ralph Neufeld in the chemistry lab is an unfortunate accident, but Lou Brade, associate professor of chemistry, has too much respect for Neufeld's ability to agree. He realizes it is up to him, and not Detective Jack Doheny of the local police force, to find the murderer." Library J
"The story that develops appeals more to the intellect than to the emotions. Asimov is too good a writer to do a bad job, but a little more suspense and a little less academic theorizing would have helped this a lot." Pub W

Asquith, Cynthia

(ed.) A book of modern ghosts. Scribner 1953 236p o.p. 1970

Analyzed in Short Story Index
First published 1952 in England under the title: The second ghost book
Contents: Captain Dalgety returns, by L. Whistler; Christmas meeting, by R. Timperley; Danse macabre, by L. A. G. Strong; The bewilderment of Snake McKoy, by N. Spain; A story of Don Juan, by V. S. Pritchett; The guardian, by W. De La Mare; Whitewash, by R. Macaulay; The Chelsea Cat, by C. H. B. Kitchin; W. S., by L. P. Hartley; The amethyst cross, by M. Fitt; Bombers' night, by E. Fabyan; Spooner, by E. Farjeon; Autumn cricket, by Lord Dunsany; The restless rest-house, by J. Curling; Back to the beginning, by J. Connell; Possession on completion, by C. Brooks; Hand in glove, by E. Bowen; The lass with the delicate air, by E. Bigland; One grave too few, by C. Asquith
"Fine collection, with accent on sound plotting, good writing." Sat R

Assis, Joaquim Maria Machado de. See Machado de Assis

Asturias, Miguel Angel

Nobel Prize in literature, 1967
Mulata; tr. from the Spanish by Gregory Rabassa. Delacorte Press 1967 307p boards $7.95

"A Seymour Lawrence book"
Original Spanish edition published 1963 in Argentina

"Celestino, a woodcutter, agrees to give his unfaithful wife to Tazol, the corn-leaf devil, in return for great wealth. He is given a voluptuous mulata to replace his Catalina. There follow wild adventures, often quite Rabelaisian, which mix Maya superstition in a sort of surrealistic fantasy." Bk Buyer's Guide
"The lucidity of the narrative does not diminish even in the extremes of sexual panic experienced by the sexton as he shudders in the slime of snails who crawl over him murmuring 'We want to be born, we want to be born'. The teeming uninhibitedness of the Maya mind becomes a quality of Señor Asturias's Spanish, translated with great skill by Gregory Rabassa. . . . [This] is a very rich and subtle book, even too rich, too kaleidoscopic." Times (London) Lit Sup

Strong wind; tr. from the Spanish by Gregory Rabassa. Delacorte Press 1968 242p $6.95

"A Seymour Lawrence book"
Original Spanish edition published 1962 in Argentina

"The novel's protagonist, Lester Mead, an American entrepreneur, once an official of Tropical Banana, Inc., in an unidentified Central American country . . . becomes absolutely convinced of the need to educate the United States company and the native growers so that they will work together in harmony. . . . [He and his] wife, Leland, who shares his convictions . . . struggle for their ideal but are finally defeated—destroyed by the 'strong wind' or hurricane, which wipes out the good with the bad and is nature's revenge for her violation by man." Sat R
"It is a novel of protest by design and not by natural result. As such, and as a formative novel, it does not achieve the poetic and climatic excellence of 'Mulata.' [entered above]. Still, it is a key novel within the genre of social realism." Best Sellers

Atherton, Gertrude

The conqueror; a dramatized biography of Alexander Hamilton. Lippincott 1943 536p front $6.95

First published 1902 by Macmillan (N Y)
"Told in the manner of fiction, though based on a careful study of the Hamilton family papers and public records of the West India Islands . . . Washington, Lafayette, Laurens, Adams, Madison, Burr, and Hamilton's other friends and enemies are the dramatis personae." Baker's Historical
"Neither fiction nor biography, pure and simple, but a mingling of both, which one critic has called 'dramatized biography.'" Pittsburgh

Atkins, Margaret Elizabeth. See Atkins, Meg Elizabeth

Atkins, Meg Elizabeth

The shadows of the house. Viking 1969 282p boards $5.95

"Jonathan Lister, the famous author, had written his books about and for Mouse; now he was dead, and Mouse, in her thirties, was free. But she didn't know what to do with her freedom until three males entered her life: Dereck, the adoring boy scout; Clancy, the rogue who took her to bed and discovered the secret of the house; and Ernest, the rough diamond who yearned to protect her." Bk Buyer's Guide
This "is a zany fairy tale romance, peopled by mad-cap characters who live in a never-never land all their own. Mouse's ultimate savior-knight is a bit earthy and roughhewn, but he suits the uninhibited lady just fine. Pleasant escape reading for a feminine audience." Pub W

Aucassin et Nicolette

Aucassin and Nicolette, and other mediaeval romances and legends; tr. with an introduction, by Eugene Mason. Dutton 1958 249p (New American Everymans lib) o.p. 1970

Analyzed in Short Story Index
Contents: 'Tis of Aucassin and of Nicolette; The story of King Constant, the emperor; Our Lady's tumbler; The lay of the little bird; The divided horsecloth; Sir Hugh of Tabarie; The story of King Florus and of the fair Jehane; Of the covetous man and of the envious man; Of a Jew who took as surety the image of Our Lady; The lay of Graelent; The three thieves; The friendship of Amis and Amile; Of the knight who prayed whilst Our Lady tourneyed in his stead; The priest and the mulberries; The story of Asenath; The palfrey

Auchincloss, Louis

The embezzler. Houghton 1966 277p $4.95

"The financial and social worlds of New York City are the background for an entertaining novel of manners, centering on Guy Prime—handsome, generous, a man of good will with one fatal flaw in his character—from his gay, promising youth to the scandal of his embezzlements which shook Wall Street in 1936 and sent him to prison and eventual self-exile in Panama. The story unfolds as the three people most closely concerned look upon the same scenes and events—first Guy, then his best friend, Rex Geer, and finally his wife, Angelica—and reveal three conflicting points of view." Booklist
Mr Auchincloss "has a great gift as a writer, one that even the most exotic literary criticism cannot gainsay—the consummate ability to hold on to a reader with the totality of his very civilized art, alone." Best Sellers

The great world and Timothy Colt. Houghton 1956 285p $4.95

"Anne tolerates Timothy's grinding hours at the office and his neglect of his family because she believes in him. Timothy, a tireless, dedicated, young lawyer soon rises in the firm and is involved in the conflict between ethics and ambition. The foundations of his beliefs are shaken and he becomes unfaithful to Anne and a party to actual dishonesty." Huntting
The author's "most distinctive characteristic is his interest in contemporary manners and his belief that small differences in social behavior cannot only reveal character, but affect destinies." N Y Times Bk R

The house of five talents. Houghton 1960 369p boards $6

The novel "traces the history of an enormously rich New York family from the founding of the fortune by a nineteenth-century robber baron to the late 1940's. Through the eyes of the granddaughter of the man who made the money originally, we see the effects of great wealth upon the actions and characters of numerous members of the family and those who marry into it." Pub W
"The author describes with competence, deftness and a wry wit the world of society in Newport and New York—balls, receptions, dinner parties, garden parties and the opera. His plan is elaborate and his cast of characters extensive, so much so that the family tree on the endpapers is a necessity. A finished piece of work in the James-Wharton-Marquand tradition." Library J

Portrait in brownstone. Houghton 1962 371p boards $4.95

"The story of Ida Hartley, a woman of sixty-one in the first chapter, wife of a powerful [New York] financier. . . . The story, which is told partly by Ida and partly in the third person, goes back to the beginning of the century, when Ida [Denison] was a little girl, and then moves forward to 1950. We learn about her relationship with her beautiful cousin Geraldine about her marriage to Derrick Hartley, about the marital difficulties of her daughter Dorcas and the problems of her son Hugh. At last we catch up with the episode that opens the novel—Geraldine's suicide in 1950—and go beyond it to watch the emergence of a new Ida." Sat R
"Derrick, Ida and Geraldine are complex, interesting, if not particularly likable people. Derrick may be cool and ruthless, but what a welcome relief to have a hero of a novel who is not a feckless blob but a man of determination who knows exactly what he wants and goes out to get it. When we come to the Hartley children of the present generation, however, the spark seems to have died out, and Mr. Auchincloss cannot make them nearly so interesting. He is at his best when chronicling a vanished way of life." Atlantic

Powers of attorney. Houghton 1963 280p boards $5.95

Analyzed in Short Story Index
Short stories about "the public and private lives of persons in a large New York City law firm." Booklist
Contents: Power in trust; Power of suggestion; Power of bequest; The single reader; The revenges of Mrs Abercrombie; The mavericks; The power of appointment; From bed and board; The deductible yacht; The 'true story' of Lavinia Todd; The ambassador from Wall Street; The crowning offer
"Mr. Auchincloss is adept at presenting human beings with all their peculiarities and foibles in a most understanding and sympathetic manner." Library J

The Rector of Justin

Some editions are:
Houghton $4.95
Modern Lib. $2.95

First published 1964
"The rector of a New England Episcopal private school, eighty-year-old Dr. Frank Prescott, is seen through the eyes of both admirers and detractors. The principal narrator is Brian Aspinwall, a shy young English master. Others include former students, Prescott's youngest daughter, Cordelia, and his oldest friend, Horace Havistock." Book Rev Digest
"This is not only a passionately interesting, but a spiritually important study of the American character of, and for our time. . . . If Mr. Auchincloss had confided his portrait of Dr. Prescott to the gentle brush strokes of Brian Aspinwall . . . we would never have had the blazing totality of the man that emerges from this book. . . . Had he not fallen heir to the notes and records of five other people who had set down what they remembered about his subject, his account would have made of Dr. Prescott a Mr. Chips instead of an eagle. . . . In revealing both the best and the

Auchincloss, Louis—*Continued*

worst of Dr. Francis Prescott, he has created as inspiring a character as any reader could want." N Y Times Bk R

Tales of Manhattan. Houghton 1967 304p $4.95

Partially analyzed in Short Story Index

"As an acute observer of the social scene the author offers a collection of stories and vignettes about people among the New York uppercrust." Chicago

Contents: Stirling's folly; The question of the existence of Waring Stohl; The moon and six guineas; Collector of innocents; The money juggler; The senior partner's ghosts; Foster Evans on Lewis Bovee; Lloyd Degener on Eric Temple; Cliffe Beach on himself; The landmarker; Sabina and the herd; The club bedroom; The Wagnerians

A world of profit. Houghton 1968 265p $5.95

The Shallcross family "have fallen upon fiscally dark days, and thus find themselves the victims of [Jay Livingstone] an opportunistic real estate sharpshooter who not only buys up their old Long Island estate for a housing complex but moves ominously in upon their anguished [Shallcross] family relationships. . . . A story of grasping parvenu versus old society —that dramatic gift is well displayed, and, as always, [Auchincloss] writes with admirable authority of money, manners and social change." Book of the Month Club News

"Taken on its own terms, this tale works as well as Auchincloss tales always have. Not sex but plot persistently raises its ugly head. . . . Auchincloss's discerning intelligence still moves all around its subject, describing accurately, deftly probing motives, analyzing social forces, but hesitating at the point of final judgment." Sat R

Austen, Jane

y The complete novels of Jane Austen. Modern Lib. 1933 1364p $4.95

Contents: Sense and sensibility; Pride and prejudice; Mansfield Park; Emma; Northanger Abbey [and] Persuasion, all of which are separately entered below

y Emma

Some editions are:
Dodd (Great illustrated classics) $4.50 With illustrations of the author and her environment and pictures from early editions of the book, together with an introduction by Frederic E. Faverty
Dutton $3.95
Dutton (Everyman's lib) $3.25
Harcourt (The Harcourt Lib. of English and American classics) $3.95
Oxford (World's classics) $2.25
Oxford (Oxford Illustrated Jane Austen v4) $5
St Martins $2.25 Illustrated by H. Thomson
First published 1815
"The heroine is a pretty girl with a feminine rage for match-making." Lenrow. Reader's Guide to Prose Fiction

"Less brilliant than 'Pride and Prejudice,' 'Emma' is equally rich in humor, in the vivid portraiture of character, and a never-ending delight in human absurdities, which the fascinated reader shares from chapter to chapter." Keller's Reader's Digest of Books

also in Austen, J. The complete novels of Jane Austen

y Mansfield Park

Some editions are:
Dutton $3.95
Dutton (Everyman's lib) $3.25
Harcourt (The Harcourt Lib. of English and American classics) $3.95
Oxford (World's classics) $2.75
Oxford (Oxford Illustrated Jane Austen v3) $5
St Martins $2.25 Illustrated by H. Thomson
First published 1814
"Presents a houseful of young people in love with the right or the wrong person. Thru the device of marrying off three sisters into different ranks, upper middleclass distinctions

come in for amusing comparisons." Lenrow. Reader's Guide to Prose Fiction

also in Austen, J. The complete novels of Jane Austen

y Northanger Abbey

Some editions are:
Dutton $3.95
Harcourt (The Harcourt Lib. of English and American classics) $3.95
Oxford (World's classics) $2.25
First published 1818
"The heroine is a girl in the first innocent bloom of youth, whose entry into life is attended by the collapse of many illusions." Lenrow. Reader's Guide to Prose Fiction

"The origin of the story is the desire to ridicule tales of romance and terror such as Mrs. Radcliffe's 'Mysteries of Udolpho' and to contrast with these life as it really is." Oxford Companion to English Literature

also in Austen, J. The complete novels of Jane Austen

Northanger Abbey [and] Persuasion

Some editions are:
Dutton (Everyman's lib) $3.25 Introduction by R. Brimley Johnson
Oxford (Oxford Illustrated Jane Austen v5) $5
Combined edition of the two titles entered separately

y Persuasion

Some editions are:
Dutton $3.95
Harcourt (The Harcourt Lib. of English and American classics) $3.95
Oxford (World's classics) $2.75 With an introduction by Forest Reid
First published 1818
"In this, Miss Austen's last work, satire and ridicule take a milder form, the tone is graver and tenderer, and the interest lies in a more subtle interplay of the characters; indeed, it is a matter of tradition that a love-story of Jane's own life is reflected in Anne Elliot's." Oxford Companion to English Literature

also in Austen, J. The complete novels of Jane Austen

also in Austen, J. Northanger Abbey [and] Persuasion

y Pride and prejudice

Some editions are:
Dodd (Great illustrated classics) $4.50 With an introductory sketch of the author and with illustrations of the Jane Austen country
Dutton $3.95 Illustrated by C. E. Brock
Dutton (New American edition. Everyman's lib) $3.45 Introduction by R. B. Johnson
Harcourt (The Harcourt Lib. of English and American classics) $3.95
Harper (Harper's Modern classics) $2.16 With an introduction by Rosemary G. Wilson
Macmillan (N Y) (The Macmillan classics) $3.95 Illustrated by Bernarda Bryson; afterword by Clifton Fadiman
Oxford (World's classics) $2.25
Oxford (Oxford Illustrated Jane Austen v2) $5
St Martins $2.25 Illustrated by C. E. Brock
Watts, F. $8.95 Large type edition complete and unabridged. A Keith Jennison book
Watts, F. Ultra type edition $5.95 With a critical and biographical profile of Jane Austen by John W. Loofbourow
First published 1813
"A history of the gradual union of two people, one held back by unconquerable pride and the other blinded by prejudice; but in spite of little plot, the interest is sustained through the book. The characters are drawn with humor, delicacy, and the intimate knowledge of men and women that Miss Austen always shows." Keller's Reader's Digest of Books

also in Austen, J. The complete novels of Jane Austen

Austen, Jane—*Continued*

y Sense and sensibility

Some editions are:
Dodd (Great illustrated classics) $4.50 With illustrations reproducing drawings for early editions and photographs of historical scenes together with an introductory biographical sketch of the author and anecdotal captions by Basil Davenport
Dutton $3.95 illustrated by C. E. Brock
Dutton (Everyman's lib) $3.25
Harcourt (The Harcourt Lib. of English and American classics) $3.95
Oxford (World's classics) $2.75
Oxford (The Oxford Illustrated Jane Austen v 1) $5
St Martins $2.25 Illustrated by H. Thomson
First published 1811

"The story tells of two sisters: Elinor, who has sense; and Marianne, who has sensibility. Their unfortunate love affairs form the basis of the narrative. Edward Ferrars, with whom Elinor is in love, is entangled with a sly, avaricious girl, Lucy Steele. His mother, upon learning this, disinherits him. Lucy, being without scruple, then jilts him for his younger brother, now the heir. So Edward returns to Elinor, who takes him back. Marianne's lover, the handsome and dashing John Willoughby, is a heartless rascal. He leaves her and goes to London. Romantic by nature, she follows him to the city, but his insolent conduct soon disillusions her. She then sacrifices her childish and absurd romanticism for the joys of a sensible marriage with staid, middle-aged Colonel Brandon." Haydn. Thesaurus of Book Digests

also in Austen, J. The complete novels of Jane Austen

The Watsons; Jane Austen's fragment continued and completed by John Coates. Crowell 1958 318p o.p. 1970

Based on a fragment probably written between 1803 and 1805
The main characters comprising the Watson family are: Emma Watson; her three sisters, Elizabeth, Penelope, and Margaret; her brother Robert and her sister-in-law Jane and her invalid father. The plot revolves around the attempts of the three sisters to get married. Set in England in the early nineteenth century

Ayrton, Michael
The maze maker; a novel. Holt 1967 320p $6.95

"This is a novel written in the form of an autobiography. The speaker is Daedalus, the Greek artificer and labyrinth builder who constructed wings and flew away from a maze in Crete with his son." Best Sellers
"Mr. Ayrton, sculptor turned novelist, makes the world of mythology a superbly real place, with a relevance to our technological society that is inescapable in this beautiful, cruel and fascinating recreation of the Daedalus-Icarus myth." Pub W

Azuela, Mariano
The trials of a respectable family
In Azuela, M. Two novels of the Mexican Revolution: The trials of a respectable family, and The underdogs p 1-59

Two novels of the Mexican Revolution: The trials of a respectable family, and The underdogs; tr. by Frances Kellam Hendricks and Beatrice Berler. Principia Press of Trinity Univ. 1963 xxvii, 267p $6

The first story is set "during the Mexican Revolution [in which] the Vásquez Prados of Zacatecas, a wealthy and substantial family, suffer successive stages of declining fortunes to a condition of degrading poverty. A division in the family, between members who are obtuse in the face of revolutionary changes and time-serving in their own interests and those who are moved by innate honesty and a sense of responsibility, provides the conflict about which the narrative develops." Publisher's note

"The underdogs" penetrates the psychology of the people in crisis. "Forced to take to the mountains by the animosity of the local cacique, Demetrio Macías found himself ranged on the side of the revolutionaries in Mexico without knowing how or why. . . . Through the influence of a townsman who deserted the Federalists to take up with the 'serranos' after deciding that tomorrow would belong to them, Demetrio joined forces with one of Pancho Villa's generals. . . . These 'indomitable men of the indigenous race' were swept along by the revolution through the months and years. Pillaging was their reward; carousing their release. Though they smiled as they robbed and killed, they could smile as they died. Disenchantment and futility; sadness and even horror mark these pages." Publisher's note

The underdogs
In Azuela, M. Two novels of the Mexican Revolution: The trials of a respectable family, and The underdogs p163-261

B

Babel, Isaac
The collected stories; ed. and tr. by Walter Morison; with an introduction by Lionel Trilling. Criterion Bks. 1955 381p o.p. 1970

Partially analyzed in Short Story Index
"The text of this volume follows that of the 1934 Russian edition of Babel's stories, which included 'Red Cavalry' [first published in the United States 1929 by Knopf] 'Tales of Odessa,' and all but the last five of the group called 'Stories.'" Translator's note
Contents: Crossing into Poland; The church at Novograd; A letter; The Remount Officer; Pan Apolek; Italian sunshine; Gedali; My first goose; The Rabbi; The road to Brody; Discourse on the "Tachanka"; The death of Dolgushov; The Brigade Commander; Sandy the Christ; The life and adventures of Matthew Pavlichenko; The cemetery at Kozin; Prishchepa's vengeance; The story of a horse; Konkin's prisoner; Berestechko; Salt; Evening; Afonka Bida; In St Valentine's Church; Squadron Commander Trunov; Two Ivans; The story of a horse, continued; The widow; Zamoste; Treason; Chesniki; After the battle; The song; The Rabbi's son; Argamak; The King; How it was done in Odessa; The father; Lyubka the Cossack; The sin of Jesus; The story of my dovecot; First love; The end of St Hypatius; With Old Man Makhno; You were too trusting, Captain; Karl-Yankel; In the basement; Awakening; The S. S. "Cow-Wheat;" Guy de Maupassant; Oil; Dante Street; The end of the old folks' home; Through the fanlight; The kiss; Line and color; Di Grasso
These "tales, brief vignettes of life among Odessa Jews under the Communists and with General Budenny's Red Cossack cavalry during the bloody Russian civil war, are ironical, realistic, and filled with a fresh, honest vigor." Library J

Red cavalry
In Babel, I. The collected stories p41-200

You must know everything; stories, 1915-1937; tr. from the Russian by Max Hayward; ed. and with notes, by Nathalie Babel. Farrar, Straus 1969 283p $5.95

In addition to nineteen stories never translated previously, this volume includes six of the author's journalistic pieces, written in 1918, which reflect his views of the new Bolshevik regime. An interview with Babel, as well as reflections on his life and work by Ehrenburg, Paustovsky, and others, are also included. (Publisher)
Stories included are: The public library; The nine; Odessa; Inspiration; Shabos Nahamu; On the field of honor; The deserter; Old Marescot's family; The quaker; An evening at the Empress's; The Chinaman; Bagrat-Ogly and the eyes of his bull; Grishchuk; And then there were none; Sunset; **A hard-working woman;** The Jewess; Sulak

Bacchelli, Riccardo

The mill on the Po; tr. by Frances Frenaye. Pantheon Bks. 1950 590p o.p. 1970

Combines the first two volumes of a trilogy, the third of which is Nothing new under the sun

"Spanning the period from 1812 to 1872, from Napoleonic times to the unification of Italy, it traces, fully and in detail, the fortunes of a miner, his family, and his floating mill on the River Po . . . describing historical events as they affect the lives of little people of Italy." Huntting

Bagley, Desmond

y The golden keel. Doubleday 1964 [c1963] 281p $4.95

First published 1963 in England.
"Years after WW II three British adventurers, determined to find out what happened to Mussolini's booty—moved north by the Nazis—and to recover it. An adventure tale with English smugglers, former partisans, and other dangers." Bk Buyer's Guide
"This is a well-told adventure story, no more and no less, with plenty of action on both land and sea. It belongs in those collections which purchase Hammond Innes and Alistair MacLean.' Library J

Landslide. Doubleday 1967 252p $4.95

"Ten years after the car accident that had destroyed his memory and had given him a new face, Bob was back in British Columbia doing a surveying job for a lumber tycoon. It was the tycoon's partner and son who had supposedly been killed in the accident; Bob believed he was a criminal who alone had survived. But could he really be the partner's son, Frank, and might the accident have been really murder?" Bk Buyer's Guide

The spoilers. Doubleday 1970 [c1969] 259p $5.95

First published 1969 in England
"A wealthy young girl dies from an overdose of heroin, legally administered by Dr. Nick Warren [who works with drug addicts]. The girl's enraged father enlists the doctor's help, and they succeed in uncovering the Middle Eastern source of the drugs. Exciting adventure and suspense." Cincinnati

The Vivero letter. Doubleday 1968 278p $4.95

"A fascinating historical jigsaw puzzle which moves from the present-day English countryside to Yucatán. The solution involves Cortes and the conquest of Mexico and the discovery of a lost city of the Mayas." MClurg. Book News
"Bagley drops his cast [of characters] into the adventure by helicopter and then proceeds to make life exceedingly miserable and dangerous for them—exactly what a thriller should be." Book World

Wyatt's hurricane. Doubleday 1966 301p $4.95

"Dave Wyatt was a West Indian meteorologist stationed with the U.S. Navy hurricane hunters on a Caribbean Island. He predicted a hurricane, but no one paid attention because a revolution was imminent. As the rebels' guns hammered one end of town, the storm threatened the other. In between was Wyatt's little party [who believed in his prediction]." Pub W
"The book suffers from a lack of distinct characterization and from excessive melodrama. But there are some descriptive scenes and scenes of violence which are well written for the most part." Best Sellers

Bagnold, Enid

National Velvet

In Costain, T. B. ed. Stories to remember v2 p339-504

Bailey, Charles W.

(jt. auth.) Knebel, F. Seven days in May

Bailey, Robeson

(jt. ed.) Canby, H. S. ed. The book of the short story

Baker, Carlos

A friend in power. Scribner 1958 312p o.p. 1970

"The president of Enfield University has retired and a successor must be chosen. Among the faculty advisory committee is Professor Tyler, in his forties. Chiefly through his eyes we follow the search for an able executive, watch the university year, and see some of the personal problems of the faculty members." Retail Bookseller
"Most meaningful to readers with academic background." Bookmark

Baker, Dorothy

Young man with a horn. Houghton 1938 243p $2.75

"Story of a young American jazz artist who had begun by 'fooling around with pianos' but soon changed to brass because he had what it takes to make music with the horn. The underlying theme of the story is the tragedy of a man's life when he is unable to reconcile his art with acceptance of the world at large. In a preliminary note the author says the book had its inspiration in the music of Leon (Bix) Beiderbecke, but that it is not based on his life." Book Rev Digest
"Mrs. Baker is vastly informed about her subject, and she is brilliant in reproducing the spoken words of people whose real language is music. Careful observation occasionally illuminates her cold, flat style. And, indeed, the book reads more like a good magazine article than a novel; it is valuable for its information rather than for its story." N Y Times Bk R

Baker, Elliott

A fine madness. Putnam 1964 319p $4.95

"Samson Shillitoe cares about nothing but poetry. . . . The book's action takes Samson through the crisis of his struggle for life; fighting with his fingernails every inch of the way, thieving, wriggling, cheating to make elbow-room for himself in the world to do what he cares about—write poetry. . . . At the end he has triumphed. He is on his way back to the Indiana home left to him by his father, accompanied by his dumb but somehow comforting wife (now pregnant), having paid for his freedom with a piece of his brain." New Repub
"This clever, ribald novel is a wonderful lampoon on psychiatry and on over-literary literature (the latter in just one episode). It has a large quota of down-to-earth laughs, and a lot of perceptive comment on the American scene." Pub W

The penny wars. Putnam 1968 255p $5.95

"The setting is the [upper New York State] small-town lower middle class of the 1930s, with everyone listening to The Major Bowes Amateur Hour on this side of the Atlantic, while Hitler is marching into Poland on the other. Tyler [aged sixteen and a half] feels that he ought to be fighting for democracy at the head of a squadron of Spitfires, but first there are battles to win at home—his endless struggle to unburden himself of his aching virginity; his ignominious attempt to get the best of an anti-British, professionally Irish teacher-bully; and his guerrilla war with the only person who is even more of a misfit than he, a German refugee dentist named Axelrod." Sat R
"The events of the story, though set in [the] frightening ambience [of 1939], are seemingly the trivia of any adolescence. But Baker has made every sequence a bland-looking pellet that explodes and reverberates." New Repub

Baker, William Howard. See Ballinger, W. A.

Balchin, Nigel

Kings of infinite space. Doubleday 1968 [c1967] 264p $4.95

First published 1967 in England
"An American-manned spaceship has landed on the moon [and] . . . an English physiologist is asked to join NASA, to conduct studies

Balchin, Nigel—*Continued*

in fatigue deterioration. . . . [Here is Frank Lewis] looking with cool, amused English eyes at the American space program, at Texas and Texans, at the games scientists play, and at the lives and loves of astronauts and their wives." Pub W

"The personal and emotional entanglements of the characters are skillfully interwoven with the scientific and technical matter to produce an entertaining, revealing . . . story. Recommended for large fiction collections." Library J

Baldwin, Faith

The velvet hammer. Holt 1969 213p $4.95

"When widowed Meg Brand comes to live with her strong-willed mother-in-law, Cornelia Brand, she discovers that Cornelia is determined to bring up Meg's baby son. Cornelia opposes Meg's re-marriage [to a doctor] because of a feud between the two families but Meg's future mother-in-law gives the girl a new weapon." Bk Buyer's Guide

Baldwin, James

Another country. Dial Press 1962 436p $5.95

A "novel of sex and blacks and whites in New York, from Greenwich Village to Harlem, with mixed love, drugs, and violence commonplaces. The chief characters are Rufus Scott, Negro musician; Leona, his Southern poor white love; Ida, his beautiful sister, who hates the whites; Vivaldo Moore, 'Irish wop' friend of Rufus and Ida; and others—actors, writers, and musicians." Bk Buyer's Guide

This book "represents an extreme mood of outrage against whatever demeans the black man in a predominantly white society—and thereby demeans the white. To the degree that this mood is growing . . . Mr. Baldwin's new novel becomes important as a harsh textbook to feelings seldom disclosed." Christian Science Monitor

Giovanni's room; a novel. Dial Press 1956 248p $4.50

"We meet the narrator, known to us only as David, in the south of France, but most of the story is laid in Paris. It develops as the story of a young American involved both with a woman and with another man, the man being the Giovanni of the title. When a choice has to be made, David chooses the woman, Hella." N Y Times Bk R

"Mr. Baldwin has taken a very special theme and treated it with great artistry and restraint." Sat R

y Go tell it on the mountain. Dial Press 1963 [c1953] 253p $4.95

A reissue of the title first published 1953 by Knopf

"A story of religious experience among Harlem Negroes. The account of young John's conversion on his fourteenth birthday, is set against the story of his forefathers, told in flashbacks covering the lives and sins of three generations." Book Rev Digest

"His people have an enormous capacity for sin, but their capacity for suffering and repentance is even greater. I think that is the outstanding quality of this work, a sometimes majestic sense of the failings of men and their ability to work through their misery to some kind of peaceful salvation." Commonweal

Going to meet the man. Dial Press 1965 294p $4.95

Analyzed in Short Story Index

"Eight stories that, with the exception of an expatriate's experiences, focus on American Negroes in their home environment." Booklist

Contents: The rockpile; The outing; The man child; Previous condition; Sonny's blues; This morning, this evening, so soon; Come out the wilderness; Going to meet the man

Tell me how long the train's been gone; a novel. Dial Press 1968 484p $5.95

"Leo Proudhammer, a successful Negro actor, has a serious heart attack on stage. Barbara King, his leading lady, to the manner born in Kentucky and in a strange way his

inamorata, stays by his side. In a series of flashbacks, in his dressingroom, in the ambulance on the way to the hospital, and as he convalesces, Leo relives his past from his Harlem boyhood on. Although he learned early to hate 'the man.' Leo's own betrayal as a man and as a human being is not limited to the white man's corruption." Pub W

"No one evokes the Harlem of the Thirties and Forties more convincingly than Baldwin—never mind the occasion. . . . But something seems to go wrong when he moves downtown. Baldwin's tone changes, he becomes shrill. . . . When he gets back to the family, he dispenses with this nonsense and really writes. . . . [However,] I think he has . . . batted out a careless book, alive where it touches his own interests, borrowed and mechanical where it doesn't." Book World

Ball, Doris Bell (Collier) See Bell, Josephine

Ball, John

In the heat of the night. Harper 1965 184p boards $5.95

A novel "introducing a Negro detective, Virgil Tibbs, a homicide expert, a clever, sophisticated man from Pasadena, California. Tibbs uses unusual methods to find information, but he does succeed in pinning down a murderer who has killed a distinguished musician. . . . The scene is a small town in the Carolinas where Tibbs, innocently waiting for a train, is brought in as a murder suspect and then, on request, assists the unhappy, baffled local police, who don't really want him, but do need him." Pub W

"This book combines humor with an understanding both of social problems and of detection." Library J

Johnny get your gun; a novel. Little 1969 227p boards $5.95

In Pasadena, "nine-year-old Johnny McGuire's greatest treasure was a transistor radio. When bullying Billy Hotchkiss snatched it away and accidently broke it, Johnny got his father's gun and set out to kill Billy. Black policeman Virgil Tibbs was called in and eventually saved Johnny from a Negro mob." Bk Buyer's Guide

"Sympathetic to the problems of the police, for a change, it is possible the author goes too far. . . . The story is engrossing and touching!" Best Sellers

Ballard, Todhunter

(ed.) Western Writers of America. A Western bonanza

Ballinger, W. A.

The men that God made mad; a novel of Ireland's Easter rising. Putnam [1969 c1966] 319p $5.95

First published 1966 in England with title: Rebellion

"This is the story of Declan O'Donovan, the brawling giant, whose bouts of fighting, drinking, and lovemaking were legendary. He was one of the little band of rebels brought to Dublin that Easter from Kilcroom by the schoolmaster Terrence McKeon. Before the day was out, Declan was broken and dead. But Declan's cowardly end was known only to the Lady Kingston who loved him and McKeon. The latter, knowing the rebels' need for a hero, made a martyr of Declan." Library J

"What's appealing about Ballinger's book, apart from its desperate, bittersweet love story, is the way in which it brings to life Ireland, the Irish, and those desperate days. Mr. Ballinger breathes life into his people." Pub W

Balmer, Edwin

After worlds collide

In Balmer, E. When worlds collide v2

y When worlds collide, by Edwin Balmer and Philip Wylie. Lippincott 1950 2v in 1 $6.50

Bound with their "After worlds collide"

An "omnibus edition of 'When Worlds Collide' and 'After Worlds Collide' [first published

Balmer, Edwin—*Continued*

1933 and 1934, respectively]. The former describes the earthly crisis which followed the discovery that this planet was about to be destroyed by collision with another body approaching through space, and the design and launching of an atomic space ship in which a few humans were able to make their escape. 'After Worlds Collide' continues the story of the intrepid pioneers on a new planet." Hunting

Balzac, Honoré de

The bachelor's house. Juniper Press, distributed by Criterion Bks. 1956 319p o.p. 1970

First published in France 1842
Translated by Frances Frenaye
"The bachelor is a rich old uncle of the Bridau family, the eldest son of which contrives to marry his uncle to a pretty housekeeper, then marries her himself & inherits the property, & after a disreputable career ends his life miserably." Baker's Best

The Chouans. Dutton 370p (Everyman's lib) o.p. 1970

First French edition 1829, rearranged 1846. This edition first published 1908, translated by Miss Ellen Marriage
The heroine of this historical novel which is part of "The human comedy" series, is "the beautiful spy, Marie de Verneuil and the hero the Marquis de Montauran, a Royalist leader. The Chouans were French insurgents of the Royalist party during the Revolution. Jean Cottereau was their leader, nicknamed Chouan (a corruption of French 'chathuant,' a screech owl) because he was accustomed to warm his companions of danger by imitating the screech of an owl." University Handbook for Readers and Writers
"An essay in the historical romance as written by Scott. Deals with the Royalist struggle in Brittany in 1799, is full of historical and local colour, and adds strong personal interest to the national issues involved." Baker's Historical

The country doctor. Dutton 287p (Everyman's lib) $3.25

Original French edition 1833. This edition, first published 1911, is translated by Miss Ellen Marriage. Introduction by Marcel Girard
The device with which this character study is held together concerns the visit of Pierre Joseph Genastas, an ex-soldier, who is searching for the saintly doctor Benassis. "A minute description of country life in the hilly region about Grenoble; the agricultural doings, the wretchedness of the peasantry, and M. Benassis' persevering attempts to ameliorate their condition, furnish a good example of Balzac's indefatigable realism. In this practical philanthropist, the reformed sinner who becomes a public benefactor, an ideal figure is created, a great soul, unselfish, full of love for man, unconquerably patient." Bkaer's Best

Cousin Bette; tr. from the French by Kathleen Raine. Modern Lib. 1958 432p o.p. 1970

First appeared 1846. "This powerful story is a vivid picture of the tastes and vices of Parisian life in the middle of last century. Lisbeth Fischer, commonly called Cousin Bette is an eccentric poor relation, a worker in gold and silver lace. The keynote of her character is jealousy, the special object of it her beautiful and nobleminded cousin Adeline, wife of Baron Hector Hulot. The chief interest of the story lies in the development of her character, of that of the unscrupulous beauty Madame Marneffe, and the base and empty voluptuary Hulot. . . . Gloomy and despairing . . . [it is] yet terribly powerful." Keller's Reader's Digest of Books

Cousin Pons. Dutton 345p (Everyman's lib) o.p. 1970

Written in 1847. Belongs to the series of "Scenes from Parisian life." This translation by Ellen Marriage, first published in this edition 1910
"Exposes the selfishness, vanity, and corruption of Parisian life with the same relentless realism, in the lower social world of the minor theatres, lodging-house keepers, curiosity shops, poor artists and bohemians. Over against this sordid section of society is set the friendship of two old musicians, the sentimental Schmucke and Cousin Pons. . . . Pons is a virtuoso who, in spite of poverty, has collected a treasury of beautiful things." Baker's Best

Droll stories

Some editions are:
Dufour (Masterpiece of world literature) $5.95 Translated into modern English by Alec Brown. With engravings by Gustave Doré. Has title: Droll stories, collected in the monasteries of Touraine and given to the light
Liveright (Black and gold lib) $6.95 Translated and revised by Ernest Boyd
Liveright edition analyzed in Short Story Index
Written between 1832-1833
Contents: Fair Imperia; Venial sin; King's sweetheart; Devil's heir; Merry jests of King Louis the eleventh; High constable's wife; Maid of Thilouse; Brother-in-arms; Vicar of Azayle-Rideau; Reproach; Three clerks of St Nicholas; Continence of King Francis the first; Merry tattle of the nuns of Poissy; How the Chateau d'Azay came to be built; False courtesan; Danger of being too innocent; Dear night of love; Sermon of the merry vicar of Meudon; Succubus; Despair in love; Perseverance in love; Concerning a provost who did not recognize things; About the Monk Amador, who was a glorious Abbot of Turpenay; Bertha the penitent; How the pretty maid of Portillon convinced her judge; In which it is demonstrated that fortune is always feminine; Concerning a poor man who was called Le Vieux par-Chemins; Odd sayings of three pilgrims; Innocence; Fair Imperia married

Eugénie Grandet; introduction by Marcel Girard. Dutton 1956 235p (Everyman's lib) $2.95

First appeared 1833. One of the "Scenes of provincial life" series
Published in this edition 1907, translated by Ellen Marriage
"Grandet, a rich miser has an only child. Eugénie. She falls is love with her charming but spoiled young cousin Charles. When she learns he is financially ruined, she lends him her savings. But her father will never consent to her marrying a bankrupt's son. Charles goes to the West Indies, secretly engaged to marry Eugénie on his return. Years go by, Grandet dies and Eugénie becomes an heiress. But Charles, ignorant of her wealth, writes her to ask for his freedom: he wants to marry a rich girl. Eugénie releases him, pays his father's debts, and marries without love an old friend of the family." Haydn. Thesaurus of Book Digests

Lost illusions; tr. from the French by Kathleen Raine; illus. by Philippe Jullian. Modern Lib. [1967 c1951] 695p illus o.p. 1970

First written in three parts, 1837-1839; published in this edition 1961 in England
"Lucien de Rubenpré, a weak and dandified young author, is the central figure throughout. After scandalizing the people of Angoulême by his platonic relations with a great lady, he goes to Paris as her protegé, full of confidence about the sensation he is to make. His disillusionment begins without delay. First taken up by the Cénacle, a coterie of literary men, he is soon dropped by them, and enters upon journalism. Parisian journalism is abominably corrupt, and Lucien, after a meteoric career, goes back to his native city ruined in money, morals, and health. His calamities also involve his blameless relatives, the young married people. Eve and David, two quiet and industrious trades-people, a model of conjugal fidelity." Baker's Best

The old maid
In Dupee, F. W. ed. Great French short novels p195-339

Père Goriot

Some editions are:
Dodd (Great illustrated classics) $4.50 Translated by Jane Minot Sedgwick. With illustrations of the author and his environment and reproductions of drawings from early editions of the book together with an introduction and descriptive captions by Allen Klots, Jr.

Balzac, Honoré de—*Continued*

Dutton (Everyman's lib) $3.25 Translated by Ellen Marriage. Introduction by Marcel Girard. Has title: Old Goriot

First published in France 1835. Another in the "Scenes of Parisian life" series

"Goriot, a retired manufacturer of vermicelli, is a good man and a weak father. He has given away his money in order to ensure the marriage of his two daughters, Anastasie and Delphine. Because of his love for them, he has to accept all kinds of humiliations from his sons-in-law, one a 'gentilhomme,' M. de Restaud, and the other a financier, M. de Nucingen. Both young women are ungrateful. They gradually abandon him. He dies without seeing them at his bedside, cared for only by young Rastignac, a law student who lives at the same boarding house, the pension Vauquer." Haydn. Thesaurus of Book Digests

The rise and fall of César Birotteau. Dutton 345p (Everyman's lib) o.p. 1970

First published in France 1837; first issued in this edition, 1912

"A reprint of the translation made by Miss Ellen Marriage"

"A novel about shopkeepers and bourgeois life in Paris during the Restoration. César Birotteau, wearing peasant sabots comes from his native Vendée to Paris. He works his way up, becomes the owner of a perfume shop. He is rich, a knight of the Legion of Honor. But this distinction goes to his head. He dreams of enlarging his shop and of pushing himself into society. He speculates and loses everything. He takes a little job in an office, and in misfortune becomes a noble figure. Finally he dies, having regained his self-respect and overcome with joy at his rehabilitation." Haydn. Thesaurus of Book Digests

The short novels of Balzac; with an introduction by Jules Romains. Dial Press 1948 503p (Permanent lib. ser) o.p. 1970

Analyzed in Short Story Index
Contents: Gobseck; At the sign of the Cat and Racket; Maître Cornélius; Colonel Chabert; The vicar of Tours; Louis Lambert; Juana; A commission in lunacy; The secrets of the Princess de Cadignan; Paz

The wild ass's skin. Dutton 238p (Everyman's lib) $3.25

First written 1831. Published in this edition 1906; translated by Ellen Marriage
Variant title: The magic skin

"A young man becomes possessed of a magic piece of leather, which enables him to gratify any wish, but at the expense of its size, which measures his life span. He dies of self-indulgence. His sweethearts, an evil and good genius, typify, one, Illusion, the other, Society." Miller

Banerjee, Bibhutibhushan. See Banerji, Bibhutibhushan

Banerji, Bibhutibhushan

Pather Panchali: Song of the road; a Bengali novel. Tr. into English by T. W. Clark and Tarapada Mukherji. Ind. Univ. Press 1968 326p (UNESCO Collection of representative works: Indian ser) $6.95

"Anyone who reads accounts of life in Indian villages may wonder why 80 percent of India's population lives in them. Mr. Banerji shows why in this story of the small boy Opu and his experiences of growing up in a village. It is true that hunger is a constant concern of Opu, his sister Durga, and his parents; yet the simple life of a villager and Opu's childhood joys show us that village life is not so bleak for people who know no other way of life." Library J

Banks, Lynne Reid

Children at the gate; a novel. Simon & Schuster 1968 287p $5.95

The setting of this novel is in Israel, and is written in form of a journal. "Gerda—in her thirties, Jewish, divorced, torments herself with guilt for the death of her adored small son [and] for the wreck of her marriage. . . . She is saved by the patient, persistent care of an Arab friend who finds for her—virtually thrusts into her arms against her will—the two starving, terrified Arab children [Peretz and Ella] whose desperation calls to her own, and whom she illegally adopts." Publisher's note

"Lynne Banks writes well and has a firm grasp of her material. Women readers will find it hard to put this book down." Library J

Barbusse, Henri

Under fire; the story of a squad; tr. by Fitzwater Wray. Dutton 358p (Everyman's lib) $2.95

Original French edition published 1916; this English translation published 1917

"An epic of . . . [World War I] ranked as the greatest piece of imaginative war literature produced in France and awarded the Goncourt Prize of 1916. A grimly realistic picture of the dull misery and nastiness of trench warfare." Cleveland

Barker, Elsa

Marshall for Las Moras
In Western Writers of America. A Western bonanza p66-123

Barker, S. Omar

(ed.) Western Writers of America. Frontiers West

Barker, Shirley

Peace, my daughters. Crown 1949 248p o.p. 1970

A "novel about that curious chapter in Salem Village history when witchcraft obsessed its godly settlers. In 1691, young Remember Winster, married eleven years to old Jonathan, felt the Devil's full power in the person of the handsome newcomer John Horne. Their eerie love story unfolds against the background of witch trials and executions." Library J

"Finely conceived and, on the whole, finely executed, it not only tells an absorbing story but illuminates one of the most violent, disturbing and perplexing episodes of the American past." N Y Her Trib Books

Strange wives. Crown 1963 377p o.p. 1970

"The Jewish families of Lisbon had to practice their religion in secret, until they heard of Roger Williams' declaration that the people of Rhode Island could believe what they would. The Bravos and the Touros came to the New World, built a synagogue, and almost inevitably young Reuben Bravo married a Christian girl, who had to learn a new faith and its ways." Bk Buyer's Guide

"'Strange Wives' is rich in Jewish lore and customs and, while the style of storytelling is suited more for feminine readers, it offers an honest and wholesome picture of a mixed marriage and of the difficulties that have to be overcome." Best Sellers

Barnes, Djuna

Nightwood; introduction by T. S. Eliot. New Directions 1937 211p (New classics ser) $5

"Psychological study of five people enduring their tortured existences in Paris. They are a half-mad doctor from the Barbary coast, who serves as a sort of Greek chorus for the other characters; a fantastic baron, whose main idea was to provide an heir for his shaky title; his wife, who bore him one sickly child and then left him; and the two women who loved the baroness." Book Rev Digest

"The story is told swifty and with immense vigour, while commonplace incidents and the repartee of salon or café are absorbed into the style with perfect aptness. . . . One cannot recommend Nightwood indiscriminately to the novel-reading public any more than one can describe it plainly as a novel." Spec

Barnes, Margaret Ayer

Years of grace. Norman S. Berg by arrangement with Houghton. 581p $7.95

Pulitzer Prize, 1931
A reissue of the title first published 1930
"A chronicle of the life of a charming and well-balanced woman, Jane Ward, who was born in Chicago in the later years of the last century. Thru all the great experiences of her life, from her girlhood engagement to the lovable André, the years of her marriage to Stephen Carver of Boston, and her love for the husband of a friend, Jane maintained the even tenor of her way and emerged gracefully into middle age." Book Rev Digest
"A detached and clear picture of the great changes of the past fifty years and a faithful mature rendition of an ordinary life and its setting of people and things, give this novel solidity. Vivid descriptions and excellent dialogue give it sparkle." Outlook

Barnes, Margaret Campbell

Brief gaudy hour; a novel of Anne Boleyn. Macrae Smith Co. 1949 335p o.p. 1970

"Historical novel based on the life of Anne Boleyn, from her eighteenth year until the hour of her death. The author stresses the importance of her love for Harry Percy of Northumberland, whom she was not allowed to marry, and her hatred for Cardinal Wolsey." Book Rev Digest
"Ranks as light fiction despite a sturdy historical background and almost exclusive use of historical characters. Anne is presented sympathetically, but not always as an admirable person. . . . A well-written, romantic novel." Library J

Isabel the Fair. Macrae Smith Co. 1957 349p o.p. 1970

In this "realistic but compassionate portrait of Isabel, the French consort of Edward II. Isabel, first glimpsed as an eager sixteen-year-old bride wholeheartedly bent on being an excellent wife and queen, is [later] seen as an increasingly embittered woman, as she takes in the extent of her adored husband's shortcomings as a king, and the scandal of his private life. Even at the end, when Isabel's misguided choice of Roger Mortimer as a lover has brought destruction upon Edward, Mortimer, and herself, the reader feels not condemnation, but regret for capabilities wasted." Booklist
"The situations that Isabel faced have compelling human interest in any period; in this novel, interest is heightened by the actuality of history and the contrasts in ways of life six hundred years ago." N Y Her Trib Books

The King's bed. Macrae Smith Co. [1962 c1961] 286p o.p. 1970

First published 1961 in England
This novel "takes its title from the magnificent traveling bed left at the inn where richard III slept the night before he was killed in battle. Viewed through the eyes of his illegitimate son Dickon Broome, the innkeeper's young daughter Tansy, and others who knew him, Richard is presented here as a sad, kindly and doomed man, while Henry VII emerges an unpleasant but competent king. The romance between Dickon and Tansy provides most of the action and introduces a likable pair." Booklist
"The author has done her research carefully and there is considerable detail as to the confusing political situation in England during that time." Best Sellers

y King's fool. Macrae Smith Co. 1959 286p o.p. 1970

"A revealing picture of the lavish Tudor court of Henry VIII is presented through the eyes and ears of William Somers, King's Jester, who is always a step [away] from the intrigues and passions that surround him." McClurg. Book News
"The book is probably less exciting than some that Mrs. Barnes has written but it is no less worth reading. Some readers may prefer the love story, which is a sympathetic one, to the background material, or vice versa. All should be warned that, despite the title, they will not encounter the traditional fool." Chicago Sunday Tribune

Mary of Carisbrooke. Macrae Smith Co. 1956 [c1955] 319p o.p. 1970

"The tragic story of Charles I during the period of his imprisonment in Carisbrooke Castle on the Isle of Wight, as seen through the loyal, alluring eyes of Mary, the Housekeeper's niece." McClurg. Book News
"Margaret Campbell Barnes is an experienced hand at a historical novel, but the subject of this book must be of peculiar interest to her. She lives on the Isle of Wight herself and has based her story on local records of Charles' imprisonment. Perhaps because of this she writes with a warmth and a detail which free her book from the cardboard quality of the standard historical romance." N Y Her Trib Books

y My lady of Cleves; a novel. Macrae Smith Co. 1946 351p o.p. 1970

"Anne of Cleves, the fourth wife of Henry VIII, has the most remarkable record of any of his many queens. Divorced after six months of marriage, she continued to live in England, remained Henry's friend and advisor and retained the affection of his three children. She is presented here as a warm-hearted and intelligent woman, respected by the King and loved by Hans Holbein who painted her portrait." Wis Lib Bul
"A dramatic story, full of color and good characters, great people made more human than romantic. And Anne, its center, is lifted from her historical obscurity, and made a new and fully realized character type for English historical fiction." Book of the Month Club News

The passionate brood; a novel. Macrae Smith Co. 1945 308p o.p. 1970

"They live again in the pages of this book—lusty Henry II, first scion of the Plantagenet brood, lovely Eleanor of Aquitaine, and their four quarrelsome children: Henry, John, Johanna, and Richard, the Lion Hearted. Here, once more, are the loves, intrigues unbridled passions and gaiety of England's Angevin rulers. Here also are Robin Hood, Berengaria, Blondel de Cahaignes, little blond Yvette, Barbe of Chalus, Ida Comnenos, the Cyprian hostage, whose beauty cost England a queen . . . saints as well as sinners." Huntting
"Well-written historical novel. . . . Should be liked by young people as well as by adults who enjoy romanticized history." Wis Lib Bul

y The Tudor rose. Macrae Smith Co. 1953 313p $4.95

A portrait "of the gentle Elizabeth of York, daughter of Edward IV, wife of the first Tudor king, and mother of Henry VIII. Elizabeth, a loyal and warmhearted girl, agreed to marry the Lancastrian heir for the good of England; hoping to find in him an upright man and a loving husband, she was disillusioned to learn that he was morally, if not actually, a murderer and that he was interested only in good administration and cheese-paring economies." Booklist
"As a picture of people, its colors are bright and true. It is a tale that, in addition to picturing the past, casts light on some of the eddies of nationalism and political intrigue in our time." N Y Her Trib Books

Barnsley, Alan Gabriel. See Fielding, Gabriel

Baroja y Nessi, Pio

The tree of knowledge; tr. from the Spanish by Aubrey F. G. Bell. Knopf 1928 329p o.p. 1970

"A story of student life in Madrid. Andrés Hurtado is one of a large ill-conducted household, full of dissensions and antagonisms. He is intelligent, moody, and his experiences as a medical student and later as a doctor only deepen his conviction of the cruelty and bitterness of life. He falls in love at last with his only friend, a girl who has loved him for a long time, and marries her. Even thus, his happiness is short-lived. Lulu dies in childbirth, and Andrés has no wish to survive her." Book Rev Digest
"The terse descriptions of student life in Madrid and small-town existence in the provinces are probably the best things in the book. . . . The author seems to write with unusual sincerity and integrity." New Repub

Baron, Alexander

The golden princess. Washburn 1954 378p o.p. 1970

"Through the eyes of an Indian princess, the reader follows the long struggle of the Spaniards to conquer the Aztec empire. Marina, beautiful, intelligent and courageous, became the mistress of Cortes, and the mother of his son. She was his adviser, but only as long as he had need of her in his conquest." Huntting

The author "has created a cast of characters so real that the reader becomes convinced that these are actually the people who lived and loved and fought in that period of North American discovery, change and conflict." N Y Times Bk R

Barr, Stringfellow

Purely academic; a novel. Simon & Schuster 1958 304p o.p. 1970

"Heartily sick of low salaries, debts, campus politics, feuds among faculty wives, slippery diplomacy of college presidents, indifferent students, and curricula designed to please donors rather than to educate, Henry Schneider head of the history departmant in a Midwestern college, begins to feel that the academic life has lost its dignity and savor. At that moment fortune smiles on Schneider, his life is brightened by a brief romantic passage with the pretty wife of a colleague, his reputation is enhanced by hoax, and his escape is assured by the offer of a job with the Winthrop Foundation, headed by a like-minded refugee from the university world. A satire that will especially delight other members of the profession." Booklist

Barrett, B. L.

Love in Atlantis; a novel. Houghton 1969 182p $4.95

"14-year-old Virginia comes to San Soleo a pretty, virtuous, 'well brought up' girl who looks super in Tangee lipstick and the new satin-Lastex bathing suits. She is quickly caught up in a delicious popularity. With the rectitude of the very young, Virginia views with candid disapproval the sexual goings-on of the adult world. But when she dates Dwayne Skinner—doomed, serious and grown-up beyond his years—she is forced to face head-on more than she can handle." Am News of Bks

This novel "sustains an honest and absorbing level of reader interest until its abrupt disapointing ending. The book relies on, and justly so, the subtle occurrences of adolescence with which the reader can easily identify." Best Sellers

Barrett, William E.

The glory tent. Doubleday 1967 72p boards $2.95

"Homer Smith of 'The Lilies of the Field' [entered below] sees the posters announcing a series of revival meetings in a Missouri town, decides to visit them, and is talked into replacing the preacher for one night. To his confusion a white girl in a wheel chair gets up, walks to him, and at once he becomes a 'miracle worker' with all the troubles it brings." Bk Buyer's Guide

"It is a pleasure to welcome back Homer, but it is a pity that Mr. Barrett doesn't have a story of more substance or a character confrontation as memorable as that between Homer and the Mother Superior in 'Lilies' to offer us this time." Pub W

The left hand of God. Doubleday 1951 275p $3.95

"In a remote corner of China a young American flyer manages to escape from the local war lord by assuming the guise of a Roman Catholic priest. In the mission where he seeks refuge his problems multiply rapidly when he finds himself taking Mass, hearing confession and with every move reluctantly taking advantage of the faith of a simple people. His moral struggle, his love affair, and the manner in which he extricates himself from his difficult situation make an interesting though far fetched story." Ontario Lib Rev

The author "has persuasively depicted the doubts and gropings of an honest man forced by unusual circumstances to revalue his approach to religion and to his fellow man. . . .

And he has betrayed an occasional superior attitude toward the Chinese, which does not sit well with his Christian approach. But in general he has ably constructed an inspirational romance which is highly readable and should not offend readers of Catholic or other religious persuasion." Sat R

y The lilies of the field; drawings by Burt Silverman. Doubleday 1962 92p illus $3.50

"An amiable southern Negro, driving through the Southwest after getting out of the Army, stops to help four German refugee nuns build a church, stays to finish the job, with one spell of restless wandering away, and then disappears, leaving behind him the legend of his faithful help." Pub W

"This refreshing and haunting novelette projects a situation which the reader would like to believe. There are moments of humor and pathos. . . . A story for reading aloud." Wis Lib Bul

The wine and the music. . . . Doubleday 1968 381p $5.95

"Book 1 Portrait of a celibate; book 2 Portrait of a woman; book 3 Tomorrow and tomorrow." Title page

This is a "novel about a dedicated Catholic priest—a man of strong character and religious belief—who, against his will, falls in love with a divorcée, has an affair with her, resigns from the priesthood and marries her. As the story unfolds, the reader is caught up in a tale of two mature, likable people, very much in love, who are trying desperately to make a life for themselves." Am News of Bks

"One puts the book down with reluctance. Mr. Barrett obviously knows the Church, her practices and problems, and he presents them in a novel touched with compassion for the human souls who must make difficult decisions. . . . In 'The Wine and the Music' he has given us a mature, readable and thoughtful novel." Best Sellers

Barrie, J. M.

y Little minister. Scribner 1921 510p front $5.95

First published 1891

"A romantic fantasia on the Thrums motive: the love affairs of the Auld Licht minister and a beautiful and sprightly 'Egyptian,' who is a lady in disguise. . . . The sketches of character and of Scottish manners and religious sentiments are very humorous, and there are passages of concentrated pathos." Baker's Best

"Aside from its intrinsic interest, there is much skilful portrayal of the complexities of Scotch character, and much sympathy with the homely lives of the poverty-stricken weavers, whose narrow creed may make them cruel, but never dishonorable." Keller's Reader's Digest of Books

Sentimental Tommy. Scribner 503p front $5.95

First published in England 1895; in this edition, 1896

"A study of a sensitive mobile boy, who passes his life in cloud-castles where he always dramatizes himself as the hero, who has no continuity of purpose and no capacity of self-sacrifice except in spasms of impulse, and in emotional feeling." Pratt Alcove

Barry, Jane

Grass roots. Doubleday 1968 327p $5.95

"Barney Condon is a PR man who specializes in managing political campaigns. This is his story—and that of his non-machine candidate for a Congressional seat. Republican Jefferson Fairfax, an attractive, well-bred, well-to-do, bland young man. Under Condon's expert guidance, Fairfax wins the primary, but loses in November to the incumbent Democrat. Paralleling the ups and downs of the campaign is Barney's love affair with Grace, a successful painter." Pub W

"A major interest of the story is the strain the political campaign imposes on Barney's and Grace's relationship. . . . Many of the political issues [of 1968] are the issues of the novel—the war in Viet Nam, big government versus the individual, the rights of minority groups. The questions asked are significant

Barry, Jane—*Continued*

and, if the resolution is unsatisfactory, it might be because the novel is a realistic picture of contemporary American politics." Best Sellers

Maximilian's gold. Doubleday 1966 281p $4.95

"An old legend of treasure hidden in a Mexican cave is the core of this story of hardbitten adventure in post-Civil War days. Six Southerners, three of them Confederate veterans, ride south to the Mexican border, guided by an old mountain man and beating their way through brigands, Comanches, and a sandstorm. This novel is raised far above the level of the usual western by its dramatic style of writing and by the portrait of the mountain man as one of the last to know the great wild West in its primeval state." Pub W

A shadow of eagles. Doubleday 1964 424p $5.95

"It was 1875, during the last of the free, wild days of the Texas cattle barons. Ben was driving two herds northward, for Don Ramon and for the widowed Avis, whose hotheaded stepson, Frankie, came along. Ben put up with Frankie for the sake of Avis, but realized that the two would [never] marry. Then he was able to console Don Ramon's daughter, Cayetana, and grew to love her." Bk Buyer's Guide

"Mrs Barry is an excellent writer, with a strong sense of the time and place of which she writes. Even though an odor of soap opera mingles with the smells of sweaty horses and cattle, this is a superior Western yarn." Book of the Month Club News

Bart, André Schwarz- See Schwarz-Bart, André

Barth, John

The end of the road. [Rev. ed] Doubleday 1967 188p $4.95

First published 1958

"In the story, at once comic, tragic and satirical, Barth made a frontal attack on the excesses of Sartrean existentialism and existential philosophy popular in the 1950's. The hero is Jacob Horner, a Kafkaesque character, whose quack therapist advises him to teach prescriptive grammar as an antidote to his fits of manic depression. Horner takes a job at a small teachers' college in Maryland and meets Joe Morgan, history teacher and Boy Scout troop leader, and his wife, Rennie. Joe and Rennie believe in the perfect existential love relationship, involving endless intellectual probing and analysis." Pub W

"The plot sounds absurd, but beneath the comic surface, questions are being raised regarding choice and meaning in life. The writing is very good, but may occasionally shock some readers. Otherwise, highly recommended." Library J

The floating opera. [Rev. ed] Doubleday 1967 252p $4.95

First published 1956 by Appleton

"A 50-year-old bachelor relives the day 10 years before when he decided to commit suicide. He had changed his mind (in true existentialist fashion) only because suicide, just like every other action in his life, would have been without meaning. In retracing the day he fills in the main events of his life as child, student, and lawyer in a sleepy backwater Maryland town." Library J

"Just as Voltaire's Candide decides to contentedly cultivate his garden after a disillusioning journey, so does Barth's Todd come to terms with life by discovering in time that it is best to choose among the relative values that life offers rather than cynically rejecting all values by way of suicide." N Y Times Bk R

"If prizes were offered for strangely constructed novels, this one would win hands down. . . . It jumps around in time and wanders off into digressions at the least excuse. It is unique—but fascinating in its uniqueness." Chicago Sunday Tribune

Giles goat-boy; or, The revised new syllabus. Doubleday 1966 xxxi, 710p $6.95

The plot "is extremely difficult to delineate. It concerns George, who was brought up as a goat until his formative years, when he was thrust upon the society of man, which in this context takes the form of a university campus. Here begins the chronicles of George's strange encounters and adventures, which in sum are meant to represent the total fabric of human existence and interplay." Best Sellers

"This allegory is worked out in great detail, with dozens of ingenious parallels, many of them blasphemous to Christian readers although inoffensive to Jews and Moslems. There are many telling hits at modern intellectual fashions in statistics and cybernetics and pseudologics; there are many orgies and copulation explosions, as though Cecil B. De Mille were staging a new superdrama called 'incontinence.' Satire is meant to shock and to amuse. This book does both." Book of the Month Club News

Lost in the funhouse; fiction for print, tape, live voice. Doubleday 1968 201p $4.95

Partially analyzed in Short Story Index

"Stories written at various times but meant to be read or heard as one narrative (some were meant to print, some to be heard rather than read). They record the conception and naming of Ambrose (a wildly farcical tale) and others of his thoughts and adventures." Bk Buyer's Guide

Contents: Night-sea journey; Ambrose his mark; Autobiography; Water-message; Petition; Lost in the funhouse; Echo; Two meditations; Title; Glossolalia; Life-story; Menelaiad; Anonymiad

The sot-weed factor. [Rev. ed] Doubleday 1967 756p $7.95

First published 1960

"Picaresque novel about [Ebenezer Cooke], a young man, scholar and poetaster his twin sister and their young tutor. Set in late 17th century England and Maryland." Pub W

" 'The Sot-Weed Factor' ostensibly is an historical novel about the early years of the Maryland colony. But it is an historical novel to end all historical novels. . . . It so completely spoofs and satirizes the typical historical novel that no self-respecting historical novelist should ever be able to take himself seriously again. . . . A further delight is that the novel can be read on many levels. Read it deadpan, if you must, as a straight historical novel. . . . Read it as a satire on all historical novels. . . . Or, best, read it as a novel in the great 18th century tradition." Chicago Sunday Tribune

Barthelme, Donald

Unspeakable practices, unnatural acts. Farrar, Straus 1968 170p $4.95

Analyzed in Short Story Index

"Fifteen very short surrealistic stories on war, love, suburbia, technology, and related subjects written with humor and satire." Booklist

Contents: The Indian uprising; The balloon; This newspaper here; Robert Kennedy saved from drowning; Report; The dolt; The police band; Edward and Pia; A few moments of sleeping and waking; Can we talk; Game; Alice; A picture history of the war; The President; See the moon

Barzun, Jacques

(ed.) The delights of detection; ed. with an introduction by Jacques Barzun. Criterion Bks. 1961 381p o.p. 1970

Analyzed in Short Story Index

Seventeen "classic, modern and historic tales of detection." Pub W

Contents: The tragedy at Brookbend Cottage, by E. Bramah; The bottomless well, by G. K. Chesterton; The log case, by K. Livingston; The professor's manuscript, by D. Sayers; The unknown peer, by E. C. Bentley; The Greek play, by H. G. Bailey; A case of premeditation, by R. A. Freeman; The nine-mile walk, by H. Kemelman; The weir, by F. Pettiward; The homesick Buick, by J. D. MacDonald; Otherwhere, by E. Crispin; One word at a time, by B. Wendell; The oyster catcher,

Barzun, Jacques—*Continued*

by M. Gilbert; Murder is no joke, by R. Stout; Cloak without dagger, by P. C. de Beaumarchais; The rifle, by W. Legget; The king's private eye. by A. Dumas

"A collection remarkable above all for the infrequency with which these stories have been anthologized." San Francisco Chronicle

Bass, Milton R.

Jory. Putnam 1969 255p $5.95

"At 14, Jory sees his alcoholic father kicked to death on a barroom floor, and a few nights later, avenges his death. Not long thereafter he joins up with a group of trail herders heading for Texas. . . . When the herd arrives at its destination, he is made bodyguard for the ranch owner's daughter, and this leads to still more notches on Jory's gun, and tentative hint at romance." Pub W

In this novel of the West in the 1870's, the author "has given us a memorable character who is a sort of Huckleberry Finn, John Wesley Hardin, and Holden Caulfield rolled into one. Jory's natural talent with guns provides an obvious device for an action-packed story and at the same time allows Bass to pose some questions about violence and its responsibilities." Library J

Bassani, Giorgio

The garden of the Finzi-Continis; tr. from the Italian by Isabel Quigly. Atheneum Pubs. 1965 293p $4.95

Original Italian edition 1962

"When racist rulings isolate the Jewish community of the ducal town of Ferrara in Fascist Italy, two adolescents, the narrator and Micol of the rich Finzi-Contini family find a tentative, hesitant love." McClurg. Book News

"Nuances of period, place, and personal relationships are caught in this subtle remembrance-of-things-past novel of an aristocratic Italian-Jewish family during the early days of World War II. . . . This brooding loving portrait . . . gives individuality to the characters yet the overriding impression is one of seeming familial unity intensified by the encroaching shadow of war." Booklist

Bassett, James

Harm's way. World Pub. 1962 510p o.p. 1970

A World War II novel "covering the first year after the attack on Pearl Harbor, specifically the battles and adventures of Navy men and their women." Bk Buyer's Guide

"A long, exciting, authentic-sounding novel about Navy brass in the first year of the Pacific war. The battle action is tense, swiftmoving, and thundering. . . . The story only slows down in the naval politics and maneuverings ashore in Pearl Harbor; most of the time the action is swift and absorbing, with good crisp dialog and strong drama." Pub W

Bassing, Eileen

Home before dark. Random House 1957 335p o.p. 1970

"After two years in an inadequate state mental hospital Charlotte Bronn [wife of a professor] is sufficiently recovered to be released. Terrified of recommittment, for three months Charlotte fights a losing battle for self-control and self-understanding, until a Christmas Eve debacle opens her eyes to the cause of her trouble—her marriage, and in fact the whole of her life, has been an attempt to compete with her beautiful, admired, and selfish stepsister." Booklist

"It reads like a psychiatric case history which has been miraculously transformed, by a more than competent writer, into a novel of distinction. This is not a happy book—but it is a moving and compassionate study of human relationships of a more than unusual kind." N Y Times Bk R

Basso, Hamilton

The Light Infantry Ball. Doubleday 1959 476p o.p. 1970

"A romantic historical novel about a Carolina planter and his experiences during the Civil War. Some of the characters are ancestors of those in the earlier book [The view from Pompey's Head, entered below] and the setting is the town of Pompey's Head. . . . The hero has various difficulties with love and politics. . . . On the political front, he works as assistant to a cabinet member in the Confederate government and exposes a smuggling scandal." Pub W

"Like its predecessor this long detailed novel examines and dissects Southern traditions and their consequences." Booklist

A touch of the dragon; a novel. Viking 1964 241p $4.95

"The narrator, Sebastian Venables, talks indirectly of his two marriages and career but sooner or later the plot drifts back to Edwina Deydier, a woman whose unscrupulous activities complicate more than one life. A literary hoax in which Edwina and her husband, a self-styled critic are entangled is a major element in [this] story." Booklist

"A highly enjoyable comedy of manners in which the author looks at moneyed society in the Middle West, Washington, Virginia, and a Caribbean island. . . . The conversations in the book are skillfully written and biting in tone." Pub W

The view from Pompey's Head. Doubleday 1954 409p o.p. 1970

"Anson Paige, a young New York lawyer employed by a large publishing house, returns after fifteen years to the small Southern city where he grew up. He is investigating what happened to the $20,000 which the wife of the firm's most celebrated author accuses the firm of stealing from her husband. Anson not only finds out what became of the money, but also learns a few things about himself." Hunting

"A long, mildly ironic, and deliberately discursive work, it weaves two of his favorite subjects, the subtle social distinctions of a small Southern city and the subtle questions of reputation and standing in New York literary and publishing circles. . . . There is nothing like the authority behind the picture of the literary world that there is behind the picture of the society of Pompey's Head." Sat R

Bataille, Michel

y The Christmas tree; tr. from the French by Harold J. Salemson. Morrow 1969 255p boards $5.95

Original French edition 1967

"Pascal, a 10-year-old French boy, has been exposed to radiation from an unexploded bomb that dropped near him in the sea. He is given three months to live, and his father takes the boy from Paris to an ancient chateau in the Auvergne. There, the pair live out the waning days together: Pascal with his blue tractor, and a pair of wolves, a boyish obsession that the father satisfies by stealing them for him from a Paris zoo. The boy dies, alone with the wolves, on Christmas Eve." Pub W

Bates, H. E.

The best of H. E. Bates; with a preface by Henry Miller. Little 1963 454p o.p. 1970

"An Atlantic Monthly Press book"

Analyzed in Short Story Index

Published in England with title: Seven by five

Includes the following 35 stories, covering the period 1926-1961: The flame; A flower piece; The mower; Time; The mill; The station; The kimono; Breeze Anstey; The ox; Colonel Julian; The lighthouse; The flag; The frontier; A Christmas song; The Major of Hussars; Elaine; The daffodil sky; The good corn; Country society; Across the bay; Chaff in the wind; The evolution of Saxby; Go lovely rose; The maker of coffins; Love in a wych elm; Let's play soldiers; The watercress girl; The cowslip field; Great Uncle Crow; The enchantress; Now sleeps the crimson petal; Where the cloud breaks; Lost ball; Thelma; Mrs Eglantine

A breath of French air. Little 1959 209p o.p. 1970

"An Atlantic Monthly Press book"

Continues the adventures of the Larkin family of The darling buds of May, entered below

Bates, H. E.—*Continued*

"The unconventional vacationing Larkin family—ten strong—descends on a quiet French hotel and proceeds to stir things up in hilarious fashion." Chicago

"Despite the fact that some of the characters seem to be thoroughly amoral, this reviewer found the novel a breath of fresh air as well as French air, following in the wake of so many tired stories, reeking with biology. Recommended for all fiction collections." Library J

The darling buds of May. Little 1958 219p o.p. 1970

Set in rural England. "Pop and Ma Larkin and their happy-go-lucky brood are, when necessity urges, fruit pickers and junk dealers. Their farm is a hodgepodge of geese, scrap iron, and pigs. They pay no taxes, work only occasionally; they live to eat, and the meals are engrossing. The story begins with the attempt of young Mr. Charlton to get Pop into the books of the Bureau of Inland Revenue and to withstand the charms of Mariette, their seductive older daughter; a dried-up young tax collector, he instinctively resists the blandishments of the family, but in the end he is overwhelmed and spellbound." Atlantic

The book "is a switch on Bates' usually tense bucolics. It offers gusto instead of agony; Rabelais (adapted to English propriety) rather than Webster. The result is a delightful conte which, if it has no great future, at least has an entertaining present." Commonweal

Fair stood the wind for France. Little 1944 270p o.p. 1970

In this story of World War II an "English bomber en route from Italy is grounded by an engine defect somewhere in occupied France, near a farm and a mill. Franklin, the pilot, is badly wounded in the arm and nearly bleeds to death. A girl finds the crew, hides them, gets Franklin, at great peril to herself and her family, to a doctor, and helps them escape." Book of the Month Club News

"An almost unbearable suspense, the romance of the two young people and a true portrait of the little people of France, defenseless but possessed of an enduring power, all these go to make an unforgettable story, beautifully told." Bookmark

Bates, Herbert Ernest. See Bates, H. E.

Bates, Ralph

The olive field. Washington Sq. Press 1966 439p o.p. 1970

First published 1936 by Dutton

"A novel of Spain in the revolutionary years of 1931 to 1934. The two chief characters are the friends, Caro and Mudarra, workers in the olive groves, who are separated because of their love for the same woman, then reunited by their political passions." Book Rev Digest

This "analysis of Spanish political emotions in the 1930s stands up very well to the test of historical perspective. . . . Bates must have studied Los Olivares with all the care of a scientific field worker. . . . [His] great strength lies in his authentic characterization of the villagers and their way of life. He respects and understands the viewpoint of all his characters. Some weaknesses would seem to be inevitable. . . . [The] ambiguity [of the end of the novel] perhaps reflects the author's honest uncertainty as to the ultimate meaning for the survivors of the events preceding the Spanish Civil War which he has so powerfully described." Nation

Baum, Vicki

Grand Hotel; tr. by Basil Creighton. Doubleday 1931 309p o.p. 1970

Original German edition published 1929

"The story takes up the many things that happen within the course of two days to some of the people who are stopping at a large hotel in post-war [I] Germany. Among the characters who receive, thru their contact with fellow-guests such a 'coup de grâce' from life are the timid political clerk, Kringelein, the ballet-dancer, Grusinskaya, and the charming Baron Gaigern. In contrast to these beneficiaries of fate are the selfish and scheming capitalist, Herr Preysing, and the disillusioned Dr Otternschlag,

whose cynicism negates the beauty and significance of those who live life fully." Book Rev Digest

"The people who are shovelled in through the hotel's revolving door are a fascinating collection, and all sharply and eagerly visualised. . . . They are drawn in with the quick clear lines that mark the artist. The translation is excellent." New Statesman

Bawden, Nina

Devil by the sea. Lippincott 1959 [c1957] 224p o.p. 1970

First published 1957 in England

"A hair-raising suspense story about a little girl who is able to identify a murderer. She knows that he knows this and that he will kill her, too, if he can. Meanwhile, none of the adults believe her story that she saw him with his victim." Pub W

"The quality of Miss Bawden's writing and her acute psychological perception distinguish the novel from other high-class thrillers." Spec

The grain of truth. Harper 1968 206p boards $4.95

"Emma and Henry are neighbors and best friends of Holly and Felix. All seems placid until Henry's father dies, which causes Emma's facade to crack. A collection of unsent letters to a lover is found. Then Emma disappears and is later found at the police station, where she has 'confessed' to killing the old man. The others rally around to protect her from her 'confession' and life resumes as before, but with a grain of truth, perhaps, added to the mixture." Library J

"The fine etchings of the human experience—this is the stuff of which Nina Bawden's novels are fashioned. Her cameo study of two couples working out their inter- and intrapersonal relationships in a rather ordinary setting fraught with shades of tragedy is brilliant. Not as intense as in Albee, nevertheless the involvement of Emma and Henry, and of Holly and Felix deepens as the novel moves on until the reader is quite caught up." Best Sellers

A little love, a little learning. Harper 1966 233p o.p. 1970

"The story is told by the protagonist, 12-year-old Kate, . . . the middle daughter in a family of three girls, who live with their mother and stepfather (a doctor) in the goldfishbowl community of an English village. Circumstances and some deliberate careless talk on Kate's part nearly involve the family in a bad scandal. But just as the situation seems too complicated to be bearable, things are straightened out. And the point is clear—even to a 12-year old: calamity is never total." Christian Science Monitor

"The novel is a commentary on an adult society in which seemingly mature grownups can be as firmly convinced as immature children that abortion is wrong, that prolonging a life of suffering by drugs is right, and that living together outside of holy wedlock is sin. The children's growth toward a more compassionate morality is sympathetically portrayed." Library J

Tortoise by candlelight. Harper 1963 238p o.p. 1970

"This is the story of [British] fourteen-year-old Emmie Bean and the family she cherishes when her mother deserts them: her well-meaning, hard-drinking father; her older sister; and especially her angelic-looking kleptomaniac small brother, who brings about a dramatic crisis." Bk Buyer's Guide

The story is "both charming and chilling . . . because children can also be both. At its most charming, it is an intimate portrait of children growing up, of a child's mind without any barriers between fact and fantasy. At its most chilling, it is horror at the realization of a child's capacity for evil, whether done deliberately or from ignorance." Best Sellers

Under the skin. Harper 1964 250p o.p. 1970

"Tom Grant tells with a sort of wry humor how he and Louise, his wife, welcome Jay Nbola of Kenya at the airport. They have invited Jay to stay with them while he studies in London. They really like Jay, try to like his friends, but find that friends and relatives are not always as 'liberal' as they and at length learn much about themselves and about color prejudice." Bk Buyer's Guide

Bawden, Nina—*Continued*

"Before everyone more or less accepts the message that people are people, no matter what their color, the ripples of reaction have reached far into the white man's family and the black man's friends. The dialog is a joy—sharp, revealing, very true to the emotions and to the natures of the characters." Pub W

A woman of my age. Harper 1967 159p o.p. 1970

"The tale is one of a group of travelers, a middle-aged English professor, his wife, and their companions, who take their holiday in Morocco. Richard and his wife, Elizabeth, have achieved a surface peace in their marriage. The Hobbses, a wealthy and devoted couple present a picture of latter years of contentment and mutual understanding. Flora, an old friend of Richard's and a successful career woman joins the group with the latest of her 'young men.' The story is told episodically, with Elizabeth narrating, alternately, events of the present and of the past." Pub W

"A clever dissection of the bored, neurotic middle-aged housewife who resents the world. Writing in the first person from Elizabeth's point of view limits the author's exploration of her other characters, but in flashbacks she fills out Elizabeth's background as that self-centered woman sees it." Sat R

Baxt, George

"I!" said the demon. Random House 1969 179p boards $4.50

Sylvia Plotkin, high school teacher, and Max Van Larsen, Missing Persons Bureau detective collaborate on a case which involves the disappearance of a crooked judge

"Brilliant technique in dialog and narrative devoted to a warm and loving portrayal of people in all their improbable variety. There is a wonderful zany atmosphere to this case which rests for its final resolution on the solution of many old crimes." Book News

Beach, Edward L.

y Run silent, run deep; illus. with line drawings. Holt 1955 364p $4.95

"Ingeniously framed as a first person account tape recorded by one Commander Richardson, the narrative combines simple, accurate, and detailed description of submarine training, patrolling, and fighting with clear portraits of the commander and his crew, and a tensely dramatic story of revenge on a deadly Japanese sub hunter. A grippingly realistic novel of submarine activity in the Pacific during World War II." Booklist

"The adventures of the hero and his shipmates are enthralling from the first page to last and are often charged with high excitement. . . . Anyone young or old who enjoys adventure and appreciates good atmosphere and good storytelling cannot fail to admire this book." Book of the Month Club News

Beagle, Peter S.

A fine and private place; a novel. Viking 1960 272p illus o.p. 1970

A fantasy "set in a cemetery, and the characters include an eccentric gentleman who lives there. He spends his time conversing with a raven, with a Bronx widow who comes to visit her husband's grave and with various ghosts. They all have interesting and often witty things to say about life and love." Pub W

"If you are willing to shelve your aversion to the subject and suspend your disbelief, you will find yourself succumbing to Peter Beagle's jokes and poignancies, to his sensibility and his unquestionable charm. . . . This book, more than a ghost story and less than a sermon, is oddly haunting. It leaves you with considerable admiration for its young author." N Y Her Trib Books

y The last unicorn. Viking 1968 218p boards $4.95

"The story of a search by the Unicorn, Schmendrick the Magician and Molly Grue. The search reaches its climax at the castle of King Haggard, where the terrifying Red Bull is encountered and where Prince Lir plays his predestined role." McClurg. Book News

This "is a fable, of course, as well as a fantasy. The unicorn is a symbol of the imagination, and King Haggard's country is an image of a world in which the imagination has been destroyed, a wasteland. . . . Beagle is a true magician magician with worlds, a master of prose and a deft practitioner in verse." He has been compared, not unreasonably with Lewis Carroll and J. R. R. Tolkien, but he stands squarely and triumphantly on his own feet." Sat R

Bean, Amelia

Time for outrage. Doubleday 1967 445p $5.95

This novel "deals with violence, rapine and lawlessnesses, and the corruption of government officials in . . . Lincoln County in the New Mexico Territory in the late 1870's." Library J

"There are so many characters here who have interesting stories that it is often difficult to remember who is on what side, but for real-life excitement nothing beats this story of greed and the lust for power." Pub W

Beauvoir, Simone de

The age of discretion
In Beauvoir, S. de. The woman destroyed p9-85

All men are mortal; a novel. Tr. by Leonard M. Freedman. World Pub. 1955 345p o.p. 1970

"The book opens upon the realistic world of Parisian actors and producers, that of Regina, an ambitious actress, and her friends who are also her enemies. . . . Regina is just another woman in the life of a dark man of mystery named Fosca whom Regina has encountered while on tour and whose story now proceeds to unfold. Rendered immortal through an elixir drunk five centuries ago, Fosca has been in the thick of history ever since. . . . It is packed with problems of politics, economics, and metaphysics." Sat R

"The reader may gain an insight into Existentialism and, simultaneously, be entertained by a pretty good yarn. Large public and college libraries will want this." Library J

Les belles images; tr. by Patrick O'Brian. Putnam 1968 224p $4.95

Original French edition, 1966

"The focus of the novel is Laurence, a wealthy advertising executive [married] and mother of two daughters. The action consists of her gradual realization of the meaninglessness of her life and her decision to keep from imposing her own hollow values on her daughters." Library J

"At first glance, this book has all been done before, and more intensely. But its final effect is cumulative and peculiarly moving. . . . Simone de Beauvoir has the true novelist's gifts of selecting detail and creating individuals whilst refusing to sum up situations." New Statesman

The mandarins; a novel. World Pub. 1956 610p o.p. 1970

Set in Paris, France, after the German occupation, this is "a group portrait of the Existentialist clique, its fellow travelers, and its adversaries and a chronicle of the political role played by the leading Existentialists from the Liberation to the late nineteen-forties." Atlantic

"This work must be judged a formally poor novel—too rambling, too redundant, too loosely constructed. But Mme. de Beauvoir's ability to recreate a time, a feeling, her perceptive facility with interpersonal relations, her wonderful analysis of the wellsprings of art, make it a remarkable book. Recommended for general collections." Library J

The monologue
In Beauvoir, S. de. The woman destroyed p87-120

Beauvoir, Simone de—*Continued*

The woman destroyed; tr. by Patrick O'Brian. Putnam 1969 254p $5.95

"The title story describes the heartjolting experience of a betrayed wife, and her gradual descent into the abyss of absolute estrangement from her husband. In a grimly revealing 'Monologue,' about another lady in deep distress, Mme. de Beauvoir permits her to speak for herself in a shattering rage against the world that has cast her out for her crimes against it. The third story, 'Age of Discretion,' has overtones of autobiography as it takes the reader on a voyage of discovery between the heroine, a writer, and her scientist husband, as they come to share, at last, the bitter knowledge of their son's reputation." Pub W

"There are no traces of humor, few pleasures of style, and no characters one would willingly remember. Relentless readers of Simone de Beauvoir will want to read it—but they should be forewarned that its intellectual interest is small indeed. . . . [The auhor] expresses those moments of despair we must fight against when we fear that after all it is no fun to grow old." Christian Science Monitor

The woman destroyed [novelette]

In Beauvoir, S. de. The woman destroyed p121-254

Becker, Stephen

A covenant with death. Atheneum Pubs. 1964 240p $4.50

Set in the American Southwest of the 1920's, the narrator of this novel "tells of the trial at which he presided long ago as a twenty-nine-year-old judge, [Bryan] Talbot was convicted of the murder of his wife: then he killed his executioner, pleading self-defense. It was this trial that helped the judge to maturity." Bk Buyer's Guide

"This is a skillful flavorful novel with excellent characterization which raises it well above categorization either as a 'western' or a 'mystery.' " Best Sellers

The outcasts. Atheneum Pubs. 1967 240p $4.95

"Morrison, a middle-aged engineer whose two marriages had ended unhappily, was sent to the tropics to build a bridge and fell in love with the hot country, his bridge, and the primitive native village at the other end of it. He did not foresee what the bridge would mean to these people until the end." Bk Buyer's Guide

This is a "fine, ironic novel. . . . It enables Mr. Becker to make a sardonic commentary on 'civilization' vs. 'savagery,' white vs. black, idealism foundering under the harsh realities of life." Pub W

When the War is over. Random House 1969 240p $5.95

"Max Catto, a lieutenant in the Army of the United States, is shot in the shoulder by Thomas Martin, a boy of 16 or so who said he was in the Confederate Army. The time is May 11, 1865, 32 days after Lee's surrender, and the incident on which this novel is based really took place. Catto recovers, but the boy is courtmartialed and sentenced to death. The execution is put off, however. Then comes Lincoln's assassination and the death sentence is carried out relentlessly in the wave of hysteria that sweeps the country." Pub W

"The irony, horror, and useless deaths of war are epitomized . . . in this novel of character sensitively delineated through dialog. . . . The implications of the events related are stated with subtlety; an epilog covers developments after the war concerning fictional and actual persons." Booklist

Beckett, Samuel

Malone dies

In Beckett, S. Molloy, Malone dies, and The unnamable p241-398

Molloy, Malone dies, and The unnamable; three novels. Grove 1959 577p o.p. 1970

Original French editions of Molloy and Malone dies published 1951; The unnamable, 1953. These translations published separately 1955, 1956 and 1958, respectively

The trilogy "is concerned with the search for identity, for the true self which can rest from self-caricature; and as a parallel it is concerned with the true silence which is the end of speech. Molloy, Malone and their final unnamable incarnation are paradigms of humanity in general and of the artist in particular. . . . The trilogy seen as a whole composes one of the most remarkable, most original and most haunting prose-works of the century." Times (London) Lit Sup

Murphy. Grove 1957 282p o.p. 1970

First published 1938 in England

This is "a character study of one Murphy, an Irishman living in squalor in London. He passes from one species of despair to the next, finally taking a job in an insane asylum." Book Rev Digest

"The humor and tragedy of Murphy's search for his own self has been set down in the brilliant, highly individual style that also distinguishes Beckett's more recent work. The dialogue is pungent, often ribald, and the London and Dublin backgrounds are deftly drawn. Recommended for discriminating readers of contemporary fiction and for larger library collections." Library J

Stories & Texts for nothing. Grove 1967 140p illus $5.00

Partially analyzed in Short Story Index

Original French edition published 1958

Contents: The expelled; The calmative; The end; Texts for nothing

"Three major Beckett short stories & [a group of] thirteen shorter pieces of fiction. In each of the three stories, old men displaced or expelled from the modest corners where they have been living, bestir themselves in search of a new corner, where they can find relative peace once more, usually without much success." Publisher's note

These "are all fragments of the single epic of which all Beckett writings are ultimately a part: the epic of man's last days on earth, of each man's last days, which in their bareness and desiccation become those of everyman. . . . This book belongs in public and college libraries and will be useful in high school libraries as an introduction to Beckett." Library J

The unnamable

In Beckett, S. Molloy, Malone dies, and The unnamable p400-577

Beckford, William

Vathek; with an introduction by Ben Ray Redman; illus. by Mahlon Blaine. Day 1928 xx, 229p illus. o.p. 1970

Written in French, 1782. Published in England 1784

Variant title: History of the Caliph Vathek

"A brilliant medley of Oriental magic and Western comedy. The sultan Vathek, a despot of portentous attributes, whose Court and courtiers are depicted with a mingling of burlesque and Eastern magnificence, commits a series of detestable crimes at the instance of a diabolical Giaour, who leads him at length to the Hall of Eblis, an inferno whose torments are pictured with Dantesque imagination. Beckford hated women, and his female personages are etched in with vitrolic satire." Baker's Best

Beckham, Barry

My main mother. Walker & Co. 1969 214p $5.95

"The story of a young [Black] boy growing up in a small Maine town under the control of his [selfish, insensitive] mother, who constantly betrays him and tramples on the things he loves." Chicago

"The mood of this novel wavers between black irony and nostalgic Southern-gothic decadence. Although individual scenes have vitality and even power, the cumulated impressions do not give dramatic validity to Mitchell's actions. This is Beckham's first novel; he is a writer to watch, and libraries may want to consider this." Library J

Bedford, Sybille

A compass error. Knopf 1969 270p $5.95

The author "focuses on Flavia Herbert as she recalls her seventeenth summer, spent on the Riviera just prior to World War II. Left alone by Constanza, her dynamic, mercurial mother, Flavia promises to study for her entrance to Oxford, but gradually becomes involved with a wealthy set, especially Therese, wife of an artist. Later Flavia meets Andrée and is further implicated in a relationship, again with lesbian overtones, that threatens her mother's remarriage." Booklist

"Miss Bedford's success lies in her portraiture of this half girl, half woman, poised on the threshold of maturity, and in her adroit sketches of the French dwellers in the coastal village; less plausible, it seems to me, are the highly colored adventures of Flavia's elders." Atlantic

A favourite of the gods. Simon & Schuster 1963 287p boards $4.50

A picture of a sophisticated European society and a "portrait of a family and a period. It is divided between physical and moral settings as far apart as aristocratic Rome and unconventional London before and during World War I. The young narrator tells the story of a beautiful and gifted mother, Constanza, child of an Italian father and a New England mother, who through much of her life was a British subject with no place of residence and no settled emotional commitment." Library J

The novel "seems artlessly and arbitrarily put together but is actually shaped with great skill and assurance. . . . Miss Bedford writes with originality, precision, wit and grace." Sat R

Beebe, Elswyth Thane Ricker. See Thane, Elswyth

Beecroft, John

(jt. ed.) Costain, T. B. ed. More Stories to remember

(jt. ed.) Costain, T. B. ed. Stories to remember

(jt. ed.) Haycraft, H. ed. Ten great mysteries

(jt. ed.) Haycraft, H. ed. Three times three

(jt. ed.) Haycraft, H. ed. A treasury of great mysteries

Beerbohm, Max

A Christmas garland. Dutton 1913 197p o.p. 1970

Analyzed in Short Story Index

Imitations of well known authors. The titles and authors imitated are: Mote in the middle distance, by H. J*m*s; P. C., X, 36, by R. K*pl*ng; Out of harm's way, by A. C. B*ns*n; Perkins and mankind, by H. G. W.*lls; Some damnable errors about Christmas, by G. K. Ch*st*rt*n; Sequelula to "The dynasts", by T. H*rdy; Shakespeare and Christmas, by F. H*rr*s; Scruts, by A. B*nn*tt; Endeavor, by J. G*lsw*rthy; Christmas, by G. S. Str**t; Feast, by J. C*nr*d; Recollection, by E. G*sse; Of Christmas, by H. B*ll*c; Straight talk, by G. B. Sh*w; Fond hearts askew, by M. H*w*l*tt; Dickens, by G. M**re, Euphemia Clashthought, by G. M*r*d*th

Zuleika Dobson; or, An Oxford love story. Dodd 1965 252p o.p. 1970

First published 1911 by Lane

"This is the wittiest and most amusing of extravaganzas. Auleika Dobson descends upon Oxford during Eights week, as guest of her grandfather, the Warden of Judas, being herself a performer of conjuring tricks, and worldwide in renown—not, indeed, for skill or originality, but for irresistible beauty. The Duke of Dorset . . . falls in love with her so desperately that the white pearls of his shirtstuds turn, the one pink and the other black, to match the black and pink pearls of Zuleika's earrings. What happens to him, what happens to the whole undergraduate population of Oxford, it would be unfair to divulge." Ath

Behan, Brendan

The Scarperer. Doubleday 1964 158p o.p. 1970

This novel was first published in 1953 as a serial in the Irish Times. It appeared under the pen-name Emmet Street. The "plot has to do with an Irish criminal mastermind who arranges the escape of an English prisoner from a Dublin jail. The prisoner is under the mistaken impression that he is being helped to cross to London. Actually, he is a Judas goat, chosen because he is the double of a ranking French gangster who is anxious to arrange a false demise. The Judas goat is taken to the Aran Islands, fitted out with the gangster's clothes and drowned off the French coast." Book Week

"This Behan yarn has the springy, immoral zest of an early Alec Guinness movie, strengthened by Behan's first-hand acquaintance with the British jail-world. There is enough foreign crook slang to warrant a glossary, but the characters who mouth it are drawn into wonderfully petrifying portraits." Book of the Month Club News

Behn, Noel

The shadowboxer. Simon & Schuster 1969 317p boards $5.95

The background of this book "is Europe in 1944. Its hero is Erik Spangler 'The Shadowboxer,' a lone wolf—so well disguised that nobody knows what he looks like—who smuggles prisoners out of concentration camps and manages to elude every trap. It is the story of a three-way duel, fought out across an occupied continent—Spangler's aim to outwit the Germans and preserve his independence from the Allies; the Nazis' plans to identify and eliminate him; the Americans' attempts to make him their agent in the biggest and most secret conspiracy of the war." Am News of Bks

Behrman, S. N.

The burning glass; a novel. Little 1968 396p boards $6.95

This is "a novel about the world of the theater, laid in Salzburg, Hollywood, and New York, in the years from 1937 to 1940. It is . . . about the love affairs of a young [Jewish dramatist from Ohio] on the way up. Stanley Grant. . . . [It is also concerned with] the effect that the triumph of Nazism has on Grant and on his world." Sat R

"The finale suits a novel whose ring of truth derives from Mr. Behrman's thorough knowledge of his field based on long experience as a successful dramatist, screen playwright, and biographer." Christian Science Monitor

Bekessy, Emery

Barabbas; a novel of the time of Jesus, by Emery Bekessy, with the collaboration of Andreas Hemberger; tr. from the German by Richard and Clara Winston. Prentice-Hall 1946 324p o.p. 1970

"In this interpretation of Biblical figures and events, Barabbas is portrayed in contrast to Jesus as the materialistic man of action who believed only in violence as a means of defending his people against foreign rulers. Usual fictional liberties are taken with interpretation of other characters. The novel reads smoothly and has modern parallels." Booklist

"The best of the novel is the web of intrigue spun between Pilate, Herod and the High Priest, Caiaphas; but there is also a philosophic interest in the contrast between Barabbas and Jesus, the one who would compel men by fear, the other who would win them by love." Book of the Month Club News

Bekessy, Jean. See Habe, Hans

Bell, Josephine

The catalyst. Macmillan (N Y) [1967 c1966] 190p $4.50

"A Cock Robin mystery"

"'The catalyst' of the title is nothing less than glorious Greece, which has such a profoundly unsettling effect on a trio of visiting

Bell, Josephine—*Continued*

English all of whom are caught up in a vicious love-hate relationship to begin with, that they are whirled to their doom as if pursued by the furies. The trio are a middle-aged man, his weepy, whining wife and her sharp-tongued sister. There is also a lovely but not very bright English movie star who plays a catalytic role of her own, heedless of the damage she does. This is good, if on the grim side." Pub W

The upfold witch. Macmillan (N Y) 1964 190p o.p. 1970

"A Cock Robin mystery"
"The discovery of human bones buried in the garden of their home in a small English village leads Dr. Frost and his wife into a mystery involving witchcraft and an evil old woman." Bk Buyer's Guide
"Good chiller." Am News of Bks

The Wilberforce legacy. Walker & Co. 1969 189p boards $4.50

"A fictional Caribbean island makes a colorful setting for a trim little English mystery in which a reclusive old man holds the key to murder. A macabre touch is added to the deaths because the victims are all found wearing a mask that exactly duplicates the old man's face. Some sympathetic characterizations of local islanders, including a couple of black detectives, a touch of romance, and a plot that puzzles nicely." Pub W

Bellairs, John

The face in the frost; illus. by Marilyn Fitschen. Macmillan (N Y) 1969 174p illus $4.95

"Take two wizards named Prospero and Roger Bacon, place in a land that never was involve several types of men with which wizards would have truck, and set them out to fight Melichus—another wizard who is evil incarnate! These are the ingredients of a fantasy invented by John Bellairs." Library J
"There are secret tunnels and trolls and weird happenings enough to impart a chill to the reader. Marvelous is the collection of comets and galaxies and constellations of King Gorm, and marvelous, too, the plants the green-thumb monk has grown. The illustrations . . . are appropriately blurry and eerie." Pest Sellers

Bellamann, Henry

Kings Row. Simon & Schuster 1940 674p o.p. 1970

"Beginning with a classroom of children in a typical midwestern town of the late '90's (probably Fulton, Missouri), the story, follows their lives as they grow up and later widens to include other town characters. Parris Mitchell is the sensitive young boy who becomes a psychiatrist and observes the hidden horrors of the town. The abnormalities, snobbishness, and degenerative tendencies of the town's citizens are presented." Booklist
"The 'Dracula' elements in 'Kings Row' are at times subordinated to a less sensational picture of the life of the town. In the person of Parris Mitchell, who has idealism and integrity, Mr. Bellamann projects his indictment of small-town vulgarity, meanness, and plain criminality. We've had the situation before; but Mr. Bellamann gives new life to a familiar thesis by a heightening of incident and an operatic conception of character. I don't think his novel a sound one, but it's interesting enough as melodrama." New Yorker

Bellamy, Edward

Looking backward: 2000-1887

Some editions are:
Harvard Univ. Press (The John Harvard lib) $5.95 A Belknap Press book. Edited by John L. Thomas
Hendricks House $3 Edited by Frederic R. White
Modern Lib. $2.95

First published 1888
"Julian West, a wealthy Bostonian, after spending the evening with his fiancée Edith Bartlett, finds that he cannot fall asleep. Hypnotized by Dr. Pillsbury, he awakens to find that it is 113 years later. Still retaining the vigor and appearance of his youth in 2000 A.D., he falls in love with another Edith, the great-granddaughter of his first fiancée. She guides him on a tour of the cooperative commonwealth which has come into existence. Labor is the cornerstone of society; all work and share alike. The State is the Great Trust. Economic security and a healthy moral environment have reduced crime. The cultural level has risen. Julian dreams that he is again in the old society, which now appalls him as ruthless, greedy, and unjust. To his relief, however, he awakens and finds himself still in the new Utopia." Haydn

Bellow, Saul

The adventures of Augie March; a novel. Viking 1953 536p $6

"An admirable essay into the picaresque; a narrative that describes in terms of what-happened-next the development of Augie March from child to man: The son of poor but honest Russian-Jewish immigrants settled in Chicago, he grows up, and at last achieves facile dishonesty, a film-star wife, residence in Paris, and even a certain understanding of himself and other people." New Yorker
"If 'The Adventures of Augie March' is great it is great because of its comprehensive, not-naturalistic survey of the modern world, its wisely inconclusive presentation of its problems; because its author dares to let go; because the style of its telling makes the sequence of events seem real even when one knows they couldn't be; because the novel is intelligently and ambitiously conceived as a whole that esthetically comprehends its parts." Sat R

Dangling man. Vanguard 1944 191p $5.95

"Purports to be the journal of a young man living in Chicago, who gives up his job, expecting to be inducted into the army. Owing to technicalities Joseph is left dangling for almost a year. His journal explains his psychological reactions to idleness how he passes his time, his growing unrest, and finally the relief when his call comes." Book Rev Digest
"The book is an excellent document on the experience of the non-combatant in time of war. It is well written and never dull—in spite of the dismalness of the Chicago background and the undramatic character of the subject. It is also one of the most honest pieces of testimony on the psychology of a whole generation who have grown up during the depression and the war." New Yorker

Henderson the rain king; a novel. Viking 1959 341p $6

"Eugene Henderson is an intensely self-concerned Connecticut millionaire of 55, whose violent efforts to 'burst the spirit's sleep' drive him to the remotest parts of Africa. . . . A big, profane, roaring bull of a man nagged by an inner voice that cries 'I want, I want, I want,' he marches to his retreat with the irresistible energy of an American go-getter who has never understood where he was going or what he hoped to get. Before he is through, he has blown up a tribal village's reservoir, befriended a lion, and lifted a mammoth wooden goddess, thereby becoming rain king of the Wariri." Christian Science Monitor
"No brief sketch of Henderson's quest will remotely do, but nothing else can suggest the originality and unforced invention of the book. It is a highly sophisticated effort to work with materials of myth, and its most notable achievement is the fine modulation of the traditionally ironic 'imaginery voyage,' the great comic force of the narrator, and the poetic symbolism Bellow makes of the familiar stuff of anthropologists' reports. . . . At its worst the novel drifts into loose talk about high matters, a 'mazy dance' of great ideas; at its best, as in the rain ritual or the fine scenes in the lion's den ('It stank radiantly'), the novel has the concentration, sensuous brilliance, and depth of meaning that we might expect of a fine poem." Yale R

Herzog. Viking 1964 341p $5.75

National Book Award for 1965
"A novel which is a vehicle for the outpourings of the hero, a Jewish scholar, about himself, about his friends, about the state of the country and of life in general. Moses Herzog is in a great state of emotional confusion after

Bellow, Saul—*Continued*

his humiliating second divorce. He vents frustration and irritation in visualizing frank, sarcastic letters—letters to the N. Y. Times,' to his psychiatrist, to his son, to his second mother-in-law. He is on the verge of a nervous breakdown. His predicament has pathos, humor, silliness, and, oddly enough, a Rabelaisian humor, too, but readers should not expect a dramatic entity, a novel with developing plot. What they will find instead is a sequence of pointed satirical comment—on modern women, marriage, politics, philosophy—and a characterization of a present-day American Jewish intellectual." Pub W

"There is nothing in any novel I have read quite like these letters Herzog writes. In no sense formal in tone, they represent at once a fictional device and a prodigiously productive aggression of the mind. . . . Among the elements back of [Bellow's style] is, no doubt, a deep sense of humor specifically derived from his Jewish background and thoroughly assimilated to his sensibility. This style is sensibility in action." Book Week

Mr Sammler's planet. Viking 1970 313p boards $6.95

"Although he is in his seventies, in the concluding years of a life that has known more than its share of adventure and tragedy, Arthur Sammler's planet extends far beyond the upper West Side of New York, where he lives with his widowed niece. It encompasses both his memories—the prewar years as a Polish journalist in London, where he knew many of the best minds and talents of the period, the terrible time in a Nazi prison camp—and the events of the present. It is a present that includes such things as a bizarre encounter with a debonair black pickpocket, and the theft of an esoteric manuscript by Mr. Sammler's daughter. In between, Mr. Sammler finds time for a metaphysical musing on the state of mankind, the world, America, his own self." Pub W

"Masterful in its artistry. . . . [The novel] has to do with sexual primitivism, the breakup of the family, the craving for violence, the bastardization of art, the death of manners, the upsurge of crime, madness, and every other current obscenity—in sum, with the full modern catastrophe." Book World

Mosby's memoirs, and other stories. Viking 1968 184p boards $5

Analyzed in Short Story Index
Contents: Leaving the yellow house; The old system; Looking for Mr Green; The Gonzaga manuscripts; A father-to-be; Mosby's memoirs

"Three of these leisurely, free-flowing stories should add to Mr. Bellow's deservedly high reputation. The remaining three, if less successful, will not diminish it. . . . Beside Mr. Bellow's extraordinary acquaintance with varied universes of character one must set his energy, his ease of manner, his unsentimental compassion, and finally his humor, which, however ironical, is never bitter." Book of the Month Club News

Seize the day; with three short stories and a one-act play. Viking 1956 211p $3.95

Partially analyzed in Short Story Index
Contents: Seize the day: A father-to-be; Looking for Mr Green; The Gonzaga manuscripts; The wrecker (a one-act play)

"Seize the Day, the long title story, is a great one. . . . The other work in the book is much lighter. . . . Seize the Day gives contemporary literature a story which will be explained, expounded, and argued, but about which a final reckoning can be made only after it ripples out in the imagination of the generations of readers to come. I suspect that it is one of the central stories of our day." Nation

The victim. Vanguard 1947 294p $5.95

"Asa Leventhal held a position on a New York trade journal, and had won a certain security, but a few sultry weeks while his wife was away almost wrecked him. The remembrance of his insane mother, and the constant harrying of a Gentile friend, who insisted that Asa had ruined his career, brought him to the verge of insanity." Book Rev Digest

" 'The Victim' rates as a subtle and thoughtful contribution to the literature of twentieth century anti-Semitism." N Y Her Trib Books

Bemelmans, Ludwig

The Blue Danube; illus. by the author. Viking 1945 153p illus o.p. 1970

"Fanciful story about a group of kindly people living on an island in the Danube. Since the island was inundated yearly and its inhabitants disappeared during that time, and since they had no money whatsoever—only a crop of radishes—the people were of little interest to the Nazis. Then one day a beautiful pig floated down the Danube, past the hungry diners at an open-air cafe, and landed on the island. Then the poor people began to have their troubles." Book Rev Digest

"The story has a fairytale quality but it deftly satirizes Nazis and German officialdom in general, and sentimentalizes the more agreeable and decent German people." Booklist

Benchley, Nathaniel

The off-islanders. McGraw 1961 238p o.p. 1970

"A comic novel about what supposedly happens when a Russian submarine, assigned to secretly chart New England coastal waters, goes aground on a sandbar near one of the islands south of Cape Cod. The Soviet captain sends some of his men ashore, at night, to seize a motorboat . . . but before they can carry out this assignment the Russian seamen run afoul of the native islanders, who assume that a full-scale Russian invasion is under way. . . . The Russians finally sail away, sadder but wiser men, leaving behind one of the crew who has decided that he wants to become an American." Springf'd Republican

"A stylish, amusing piece of escape fiction, told with charm and wit at a breakneck pace." N Y Her Tirb Books

The visitors. McGraw 1965 248p o.p. 1970

"Everybody in the New England coast town knew that the old Twitchell house was haunted, and was very curious about the reaction of the Powells, who had rented it for the summer. Stephen and Kathryn Powell were disturbed by the pranks of the poltergeist (or their son Steve), but it was Stephen who felt something evil in the air. Then Uncle George's boat was wrecked, the naked woman appeared and vanished, and Captain Pedersen vanished too." Bk Buyer's Guide

"The story, even at its creepiest, is so mocking and witty that it is very good fun." Pub W

The wake of the Icarus. Atheneum Pubs. 1969 308p $6.95

Icarus, an intelligence ship of the U.S. Navy patrolling the Caribbean area "hits a mine in the dark, sinks with much loss of life, and the 15 survivors reach a small island. There they become involved in a gun-running plot by Castro-style agents. The U.S. Navy men find themselves in possession of guns meant for the Liberation Army. . . . The main character is the captain of the 'Icarus,' [Lt.] Commander Harry Evers, whose admirable and at times heartrending goal is to do the right thing, the decent thing. In the end he is court-martialled for poor leadership even though he was motivated by concern for other humans." Pub W

The author "very deftly mixes tears, horror, laughter, suspense as he gives us a macabre dance of fools. . . . [This] is an exciting and highly readable tale that grips one in disbelief from start to finish." Library J

Welcome to Xanadu. Atheneum Pubs. 1968 304p boards $5.95

"Doris Mae Winter, a young, bored, overworked farm girl, is kidnaped by Leonard Hatch, who offers her a ride in his pickup truck and then proceeds to take her to his hideaway in the New Mexico desert. Hatch, an escaped mental patient, takes the opportunity of the abduction to prove his own intellectual superiority while he introduces Doris Mae to classical poetry and literature before she unwittingly causes his capture and death." Booklist

Benchley, Nathaniel—*Continued*

"The author treads—not always successfully —a tightrope between melodrama and sentimentality but he keeps the thrills coming to the very end." Harper

A winter's tale. McGraw 1964 214p o.p. 1970

"A New York theater director is hired to direct a series of plays to provide much-needed winter entertainment on Nantucket Island. Although he would like to try Ibsen's 'Ghosts,' a 'safer' play (like 'You Can't Take It With You') seems more appropriate. This is the story of the play and the players, the island and the island people." Huntting

"The author delineates his characters with wit and perception, relying on dialogue rather than description to sketch the type of character intended." Best Sellers

Benedetti, Mario

The truce; tr. from the Spanish by Benjamin Graham. Harper 1969 184p $5.95

Original Spanish edition, 1963

"This moving story is the journal of a cost accountant in Montevideo, Uruguay. His wife Isabelle died five years after their marriage, soon after giving birth to Jaime, who becomes his favorite son. For twenty years, Martin has concentrated on his job and his children, having given up becoming the man he thinks he might have been. A little while before he is to retire, he is assigned three young assistants. Among them is Avellaneda, a 23-year-old girl whom he comes to love. Martin's journal reflects his memories of his wife, his concern for his children, the progress and illumination of his love for Avellaneda, his happiness when she tells him that she loves him." News of Bks

"Graham's translation conveys the evident poetic style of the original. Although unlikely to become a popular success, this novel deserves a place in larger public libraries and all collections of contemporary Latin American writing." Library J

Beneš, Jan

Second breath; tr. from the Czech by Michael Montgomery. Orion 1969 161p $6

"The time is the 1950's. The place, a labor camp in Czechoslovakia. . . . [The author] details the life of a group of prisoners—men who band together in a fight for justice and decency. 'The story,' he says in the preface, 'has no guilty parties—only people with whom one can agree or disagree.' The book ends with the prisoners' . . . ideological triumph over the bureaucratic escort guards and the warden." Publisher's note

"The concept of loyalty for loyalty's sake is not the only critically important concept dealt with. . . . Benes is concerned for instance, with the hideous irony familiar to Americans, that so many law breakers come out of prison far more damaged or dangerous than they were going in. He is concerned also, in his philosophically intelligent way, with the humanness of prisoners and guards equally." N Y Times Bk R

Benét, Stephen Vincent

y The Devil and Daniel Webster; illus. by Harold Denison. Rinehart 1937 61p illus $3

"The story is of a poor New Hampshire farmer, the devil in new guise and New Hampshire's famous native son, Daniel Webster. . . . A twentieth century version of the familiar Faust legend." Boston Transcript

"It is slight only in length, for it is rare to find so much natural humor and true characterization in so short a space. The author has long excelled in his ability to recapture in brief, graphic word pictures scenes and heroes of the past and makes these a part of our present. It is to be doubted if, even in his acknowledged masterpiece, 'John Brown's Body,' he has surpassed this short prose portrait of Daniel Webster." Christian Science Monitor

The last circle; stories and poems. Farrar, Straus 1946 309p o.p. 1970

Partially analyzed in Short Story Index
Contains the following 15 stories which have never before appeared in book form: Bishop's beggar; The captives; Minister's books; The angel was a Yankee; As it was in the beginning; Three fates; Gentleman of fortune; Famous; Good picker; Prodigal children; This bright dream; William Riley and the fates; Danger of shadows; Gold dress; Land where there is no death

"The stories all have the stamp of the serious and expert craftsman who has something to say. . . . They are all worth reading. . . . [The book] is a collection of its writer's minor work, but a collection which echoes the strong affection for humanity that is the dominant note in all his writings." Sat R

Selected works. Volume two: Prose. Rinehart 1942 483p o.p. 1970

Analyzed in Short Story Index
Contents: Jacob and the Indians; Tooth for Paul Revere; Devil and Daniel Webster; Freedom's a hard-bought thing; O'Halloran's luck; Die-hard; Johnny Pye and the fool-killer; Spanish bayonet; Too early spring; Story about the Anteater; Schooner Fairchild's class; Everybody was very nice; All around the town; Glamour; No visitors; Death in the country; The curfew tolls; King of the cats; Doc Mellhorn and the pearly gates; Last of the legions; Blood of the martyrs; Into Egypt: By the waters of Babylon

Thirteen o'clock; stories of several worlds. Farrar 1937 305p o.p. 1970

Analyzed in Short Story Index
Contents: By the waters of Babylon: The blood of the martyrs; The king of the cats; A story by Angela Poe; The treasure of Vasco Gomez; The curfew tolls; The sobbin' women; The Devil and Daniel Webster; Daniel Webster and the sea serpent; Glamour; Everybody was very nice; A death in the country; Blossom and fruit

Twenty-five short stories. Garden City Pub. Co. 1943 2v in 1 o.p. 1970

Analyzed in Short Story Index
Formerly published in 2 volumes under titles: "Thirteen o'clock" (1937) entered above and "Tales before midnight" (1939)

Bengtsson, Frans G.

The long ships; a saga of the Viking age; tr. from the Swedish by Michael Meyer. Knopf 1954 503p illus $6.95

"Originally published in Sweden in two volumes. . . . An English translation by Barrows Mussey of Volume I was published in the United States in 1942 under the title Red Orm." Publisher's note

"Red Orm of Danish Skania is the hero of a long narrative of adventures which take place from approximately 980 to 1010. Captured during a pillaging voyage westward, Orm becomes the slave of a Spanish Moor until he is able to escape. Later he becomes a Christian so that he can marry one of King Harald's daughters. In his last voyage he crosses eastern Europe by boat to retrieve a horde of gold and silver." Booklist

"Under the merriment and the fighting there is a great deal of scholarship as sound as it is imperceptible. Reading this marvelously good-humored ale-broth of a book, you say: this is how it must have been to be a Viking chief a thousand years ago." N Y Times Bk R

Bennett, Arnold

Buried alive; a tale of these days. Doubleday 1908 253p $4.50

"Here is entertaining farce extracted from the old device of the master changing places with his servant. It all comes about from a more or less natural misunderstanding when the valet catches cold and dies, and Priam Faril, the greatest of modern painters . . . too shy to take the trouble to correct the misunderstanding, steps forth into London, a discharged middle-aged valet. Priam Faril is dead. Unknown in England save as a signature on sundry much-talked-of masterpieces and equally unknown in the big continental hotels where his shyness has led him to find solitude, buried alive, in fact, he enjoys the by no means unique experience of reading his own obituaries. With some agitation, however, he attends his own funeral in Westminster Abbey

Bennett, Arnold—*Continued*

and learns that his large fortune is to be applied to the foundation of a gallery of great masters. Then it was that Mrs. Alice Chalice proved balm to him." Nation

Clayhanger. Doubleday 1910 698p o.p. 1970

"A story of the Five towns, describing with amplitude of realistic detail and almost uncanny psychological insight, the life of Edwin Clayhanger from his school days to his marriage." N Y State Lib

Imperial Palace. Doubleday 1930 796p o.p. 1970

"The central figure of the book is the imperial Palace a super-luxury hotel, 'the kind of hotel whose directors are gods, whose managers are archangels, whose myriad head-waiters and staff are the choir of cherubim and seraphim.' This vast and splendidly organized hotel is the creation of that artist among hotel-managers, Evelyn Orcham, and like every one else on its staff he is enslaved to it. Just for a moment he is deflected by the heady charms of Gracie Savott, who deliberately vamps him, but he returns to the more soberly satisfying Violet Powler, head housekeeper of the Imperial Palace, whose allegiance to the hotel is as strong as his own." Book Rev Digest

"It is a magnificent tour de force. The writing is a little hard in its detachment. There are no lovable characters." Christian Science Monitor

The old wives' tale. Modern Lib. 640p $2.95

A reprint of the title first published 1908

The author describes "the separate histories of two sisters, who in the first chapters of the book are in their later teens, while the curtain does not fall till they have both died as elderly women. . . . The other characters in the book are grouped round these two salient figures, and though they stand out from the canvas, yet do so in due subordination to the two heroines." Spec

"A faithful piece of realism describing the commonplace, sordid life of a small English industrial town with keen observation, convincing psychology, and a somewhat grim humor." Pratt Alcove

Bennett, Enoch Arnold. See Bennett, Arnold

Bennett, Jack

y Jamie. Little 1963 245p $4.95

A "story of a boy growing in the drought-ridden farm country of South Africa. He lives in friendship with a Xhosa boy, and grows in courage and independence [after his father is killed by a thirst-crazed buffalo]." Pub W

"The author maintains his valid drama, follows it skillfully, and avoids plot stencils. His writing is clean and hard and sharp, vivid but never florid. . . . The book is notable for two things, the African background and the sense of boyhood, inner boyhood with its inevitable hurts and triumphs. . . . The relationship between Jamie and [the Xhosa boy] Kiewiet is memorable, particularly in view of Africa's racial troubles." N Y Times Bk R

Benson, Robert Hugh

Come rack! Come rope! Ed. and with a foreword by Philip Caraman. Kenedy 1957 377p o.p. 1970

First published 1913 by Dodd

This novel "deals with the persecution of Catholics during the reign of Elizabeth I, and though it is very sympathetic towards the Catholic cause, it is not polemic in tome. The excitement of life in time of persecution, the mental anguish involved in reconciling conflicting loyalties, the inner psychological experiences of those tortured on the rack are superbly portrayed." Library J

"Derbyshire, London, etc., 1579-88. Illustrates the religious position . . . as viewed by the able Roman Catholic author. The Jesuit martyr, Campion, is prominent, and Mary Queen of Scots' later period of captivity is an important background to the story." Nield

Bentley, E. C.

Trent intervenes

In Bentley, E. C. Trent's case book v3

Trent's case book [comprising] Trent's last case, Trent's own case, with H. Warner Allen [and] Trent intervenes. With an introduction by Ben Ray Redman. Knopf 1953 3v in 1 $5.95

Omnibus collection of detective stories including two novels, Trent's last case (1913) entered below, and Trent's own case (1936), and a collection of short stories, Trent intervenes (1938). Volume three, which is analyzed in Short Story Index, contains the following stories: Clever cockatoo; Genuine tabard; Inoffensive captain; Little mystery: Ministering angel; Ordinary hairpins; Public benefactor; Sweet shot; Trent and the bad dog; Trent and the fool-proof lift; Unknown peer; Vanishing lawyer

These tales of Detective Trent's adventures represent "the perfect writing of a detective story—prose as impeccable, humor as absurd and unexpected as have ever graced the field. This omnibus is not for renting, but for your permanent library." N Y Times Bk R

Trent's last case. Knopf 1930 237p o.p. 1970

First published 1913 with title: Woman in black

"Trent is a dilettante and artist who occasionally is requisitioned to solve murder problems by the editor of a London newspaper. This last case concerns the mysterious death of an American multi-millionaire living in England and married to a young and beautiful wife." Washington D.C. Pub Lib

"The plot of 'Trent's last case' is at once unorthodox and cunningly contrived. . . . The style is adept, light, and entertaining." Howard Haycraft

also in Bentley, E. C. Trent's case book v 1

Trent's own case

In Bentley, E. C. Trent's case book v2

Bentley, Phyllis

Inheritance. Macmillan (N Y) 1932 592p o.p. 1970

"With the struggle between capital and labor in the Yorkshire weaving trade between 1812 and 1931 as her background the author has told a story of six generations of the Oldroyd family, one branch of which were mill owners and men of wealth, the other champions of the oppressed mill workers. The book is long . . . [but the] discriminating reader will find it well worth reading." Wis Lib Bul

Berckman, Evelyn

The heir of Starvelings; a novel of innocence and evil. Doubleday 1967 235p $4.50

"The scene is 19th century England, the setting a vast, moldering manor house presided over by an evil, lustful old [noble] man. To it comes a courageous and innocent maiden, the vicar's daughter, assigned as nurse, friend, protectress of the young heir, who has been brought up in brute ignorance and abject poverty by his vile old father. They play out an exciting melodrama with a poignant epilog showing what happened to the little boy many years later." Pub W

"The difficult child is . . . one of the most original character creations I have met for quite awhile. This is a treasure for all regular readers of such [Gothic] romances and for many who usually shun them." N Y Times Bk R

She asked for it. Doubleday 1969 212p $4.95

"Not a murder mystery, but a modest little novel . . . with some elements of suspense. The story is told by the embittered and [crippled] ugly secretary to an actress, who is past her prime but very comfortably well off in Hollywood. When the actress marries a much younger man, her secretary is sure he is after her money, and takes to spying on them

Berckman, Evelyn—*Continued*

and even bugging their bedroom. She devises a cruel plot to steal the man's idea for a play from him and in doing so brings down ruin on all of them. The kicker, only revealed at the end, lies in the real relationship between the actress and the secretary." Pub W

Stalemate. Published for the Crime Club by Doubleday 1966 240p o.p. 1970

In this novel "set in England two men [both financiers] are led into a hideous trap when they plan a desperate scheme to lose their wives." Bk Buyer's Guide

"This ironic novel of murder and strong passions is not based on a new plot idea: yet the author is so proficient and so imaginative that she sustains a high level of suspense." Pub W

Berger, Thomas

Little Big Man. Dial Press 1964 xxii, 440p boards $5.95

This story "purports to be the reminiscences —dictated at the ripe age of 111—of one Jack Crabb—plainsman, Indian scout, gunfighter, buffalo hunter, bunco schemer and renegade squaw man. Cynical and unscrupulous, yet also a sentimental idealist, Jack Crabb alternates between life with the Cheyenne Indians, to whom he is a blood-brother, and the white company of such friends and enemies as Wild Bill Hickok, Wyatt Earp, Calamity Jane, and George Armstrong Custer. With a mixture of courage and cowardice, luck and guile, he survives the major events of the most exciting quarter century on the frontier—from the days of the Oregon Trail to the Little Big-horn Battle, in which he is General Custer's confidant." Publisher's note

"In about the same way that Faulkner delivers the old South to the ken of a jaded but renewable imagination, Berger delivers the West. He took on an apparently impossible task and made the dead bones live. . . . And oh, [the] Wild West dream is funny, magically and marvelously funny as Berger recreates it, like an embarrassment and a rapture we never quite knew how to confess." Book Week

Berlin, Ellin

The best of families. Doubleday 1970 330p $5.95

A story of the four Cameron sisters who are "wealthy, pretty, motherless and spirited. Esther, the oldest sister, marries an older man, and creates a scandal by her affair and child by Augie Wenger. Maud upsets the applecart by becoming a Catholic and eventually marrying a artist. Julia marries properly, and Nell, the narrator, marries her childhood sweetheart, Bertie, after he comes home from World War I. It's the leisurely story of the four girls, [and] their beautiful, safe world in which it seemed as if nothing could change." Pub W

This is "a charming, conversational reminiscence of New York City society prior to World War I. . . . Nell, now a grandmother, tells the story of past past which spans the generations to the present with graceful discernment, and an eye for the fashions, the religious prejudices, and the social manners of the era in a novel of especial appeal to women." Booklist

Bermant, Chaim

Diary of an old man. Holt [1967 c1966] 191p $3.95

First published 1966 in England

"A subdued first-person novel in which a cantankerous old man records his visits to the local library, unsuccessful struggles against illness, inability to communicate with another lodger, and other facets of his lonely life in an English rooming house." Booklist

"A daring venture into a realm of human experience most of us would prefer not to think too much about—what happens to old people—but it is a stunning success. Guaranteed to make you feel a bit creaky at the knees, but warmer and wiser." Pub W

Bernanos, Georges

The diary of a country priest; tr. from the French by Pamela Morris. Macmillan (N Y) 1937 398p o.p. 1970

First published 1936 in France

"Assigned to a country parish in northern France, a young priest finds himself isolated among ignorant, malicious peasants. Bewildered by the general indifference to Christian principles, and humbled by his own inadequacy, he confides to his diary the rebuffs, the spiritual strivings, and the physical pain that fill his days, and records long conversations on the religious life, poverty, and social injustice. The book is quite without plot or action—a self-portrait of a naive, saintly person with little worldly wisdom and no sentimentality, who faced failure and death with great simplicity. Serious reading, of limited appeal." Booklist

Under the sun of Satan; a novel. Tr. by Harry L. Binsse. Pantheon Bks. 1949 252p o.p. 1970

First published 1926 in French. English translation by Pamela Morris first published by Macmillan 1940 with title: The star of Satan

"The story is roughly in two parts—the first dealing with the girl Mouchette, and her fall, the second, with the life and death of a Catholic priest who becomes a saint." Book Rev Digest

"However great its qualities may be, it is obvious that this book is not for everyone. Indeed, it may be safely recommended to only two classes of readers: those whose faith obviates the need of an imaginative effort; and those whose powers of imaginative sympathy are sufficient to enable them to feel and understand—at least partially—even in the absence of belief." Sat R

Bernanos, Michel

The other side of the mountain; tr. by Elaine P. Halperin. Houghton 1968 107p $4.95

Original French edition 1967

This novel is a first person narrative by "a youth on a French galleon under Spanish rule supposedly on its way to Peru for gold. There is a shipwreck. After . . . storms, madness of the crew and . . . cannibalism, there are only two survivors, the youth and the ship's cook [Toine], an old man, who has been his protector against the rest of the crew. They awaken in a mysterious land, without human or animal life—only lifelike statues of men and beasts, with trees and vegetation that possessed strange powers at night. The pair decide to push on to the highest mountain and their inevitable fate." America

"This posthumous tale, a gripping and deeply disturbing story of adventure, laden with symbols of evil forces which engulf paralyzed human creatures, reveals an extraordinary talent, with a streak of Melville, of Poe, even of Dostoevsky." N Y Times Bk R

Bernkopf, Jeanne F.

(comp.) Boucher's choicest; a collection of Anthony Boucher's favorites from Best detective stories of the year. Introduction by Allen J. Hubin. Dutton 1969 320p $5.95

"Contains four short stories from each of the annual volumes of 'Best Detective Stories of the Year,' which . . . Anthony Boucher edited for the six years from 1962 to 1968." Pub W

Contents: H as in homicide, by L. Treat; Justice, inc. by R. Phillips; The adventure of the double-bogey man, by R. L. Fish; File 1: the Mayfield case, by J. Gores; A humanist, by R. Gary; A case for the U. N., by M. A. deFord; A soliloquy in tongues, by W. Wiser; I will please come to order, by W. N. Jayme; His brother's keeper, by J. McKimmey; The opposite number, by J. Hay; The right man for the right job, by J. C. Thompson; The adventure of Abraham Lincoln's clue, by E. Queen; The chosen one, by R. Davies; The adventure of the red leech, by A. Derleth; The two kings and the two labyrinths, by J. L. Borges; Papa Tral's harvest, by B. Perowne; Good man, bad man, by J. Weidman; The Stollmeyer sonnets, by J. Powell; The Dr Sherrock

Bernkopf, Jeanne F.—*Continued*

commission, by F. McAuliffe; The oblong room, by E. D. Hoch; The peppermint-striped goodby, by R. Goulart; The gracious, pleasant life of Mrs Afton, by P. Highsmith; By child undone, by J. Ritchie; The possibility of evil, by S. Jackson

Berri, Claude

y   The two of us; drawings by Lydia Rosier; tr. from the French by Helen Weaver. Morrow 1968 156p illus $4.95

Originally published in French

"The Langmann boy's parents, in constant fear of being picked up by the Germans, find their mischievous nine-year-old son constantly gets into trouble and brings them all into terrible danger. They send him to the home of a friend's family for the duration. Provided with false papers, he gives up his Jewish identity. . . . 'The Two of Us' is the record of his farm years and the growing affection between the boy and the violently anti-Semitic but loving old man who shelters him. Berri's simple, unpretentious style is well suited to the melancholy and very human tale he tells. He does especially well with the boy's gradual recognition and understanding of his Jewishness, blending the more serious theme all the while with the child's irrepressible penchant for boyish pranks." Pub W

Berry, Don

Moontrap; a novel. Viking 1962 339p o.p. 1970

John Monday, "trapper and hunter, couldn't settle down as a farmer. The people of Oregon City [of the 1850's] hated his Indian wife, driving her to murder [of her child] and suicide. An old mountain man takes a savage revenge, this bringing about his own death and that of [Monday]." Bk Buyer's Guide

"The author is on the side of the Indians and the mountain men. . . . It is, because of its inevitably hopeless conclusions, a more somber book [than Trask]." Pub W

"The narrative is almost classic in its simplicity and directness. . . . It is a tough, stark story; and its raucous humor and brutal, earthy language are intrinsic to it." N Y Times Bk R

Trask; a novel. Viking 1960 373p o.p. 1970

Adventures in Oregon Territory in the 1840's of "the first homesteaders and their treaties and troubles with the various native Indian tribes such as the Clatsops and the Killamooks form the historical background of a novel based on the story of an actual pioneer, Elbridge Trask. . . . [The book has] some rough backwoods language and events." Booklist

This "novel is one of the few about the American west . . . that attempt to deal with the quality, character, and motives of the Indian. . . . There is a certain amount of real ordinariness in the description of the people and the country. Yet the final effect is one of a hard, new, uncompromising look at the dramatic corner of the continent where these actions occur, where these vigorous people move." Chicago Sunday Tribune

Berto, Giuseppe

The sky is red; tr. from the Italian by Angus Davidson. New Directions 1948 397p o.p. 1970

"It is the story of four teen-aged children living in a bombed city in Italy. In order to exist they are forced into strange ways: Tullio is the leader of a black market gang; Carla, becomes a prostitute; Giulia who kept house for the others dies of tuberculosis; and Daniele, who loved Giulia, commits suicide. The essential goodness of the children is brought out, in the midst of the ugliness of life in wartime." Book Rev Digest

"Written with unflinching realism and a deeply tragic sense of life, [the story] has a heartbreaking sadness, an intensely human appeal." Atlantic

The **Best** American short stories, 1915-1969; and the Yearbook of the American short story. . . . Houghton 1915-1969 55v 1915-1966 o.p. 1970; 1967 $6; 1968 $6.50; 1969 $6.95

Editors: 1915-1941, Edward J. O'Brien; 1942-1958, Martha Foley; 1958-1969, Martha Foley and David Burnett

1915-1941 volumes had title: Best short stories

Analyzed in Short Story Index

Contents: 1967: The promise of heat, by E. Ayer; A place not on the map, by G. Blake; The wild horses, by K. Boyle; Will you please be quiet, please, by R. Carver; One of the boys, by H. E. Francis; Trepleff, by M. Harris; White Anglo-Saxon Protestant, by R. Hazel; Acme rooms and sweet Marjorie Russell, by H. A. Hunt; The heroic journey, by L. Lee; Search for a future, by A. Miller; The apartment hunter, by B. Moore; Andrew, by B. Morgan; Where are you going, where have you been, by J. C. Oates; Song of the simidor, by D. Radcliffe; The surveyor, by H. Roth; Longing for America, by D. Rubin; The accident, by J. Stuart; The kid who fractioned, by C. Sturm; The big brown trout, by R. Travers; House of the blues, by W. Wiser

1968: Tell me how long the train's been gone, by J. Baldwin; Greased samba, by J. Deck; An American student in Paris, by J. T. Farrell; An old man and his hat, by G. H. Freitag; Who is Harry Kellerman and why is he saying those terrible things about me, by H. Gardner; In the heart of the heart of the country, by W. H. Gass; The rotifer, by M. L. Gavell; The heart of this or that man, by D. Gropman; The snooker shark, by W. Harrison; The only people, by J. Higgins; The tenant, by H. Hudson; In shock, by L. E. Litwak; The sons of Martha, by R. McKenna; The preacher and Margery Scott, by W. Moseley; Celtic twilight, by J. Ostrow; Early morning, lonely ride, by N. H. Parker; Bleat Blodgette, by J. Phillips; The Ambassador, by L. P. Spingarn; The games that we played, by W. Weathers; Dried rose petals in a silver bowl, by J. Bruce

1969: The eldest child, by M. Brennan; Play like I'm sheriff, by J. Cady; Murphy's Xmas, by M. Costello; Walking wounded, by J. B. Gerald; The foreigner in the blood, by M. G. Hughes; The boy in the green hat, by N. Klein; Happiness, by M. Lavin; The boat, by A. MacLeod; The day the flowers came, by D. Madden; Pictures of Fidelman, by B. Malamud; Porkchops with whiskey and ice cream, by M. W. McGregor; Gold coast, by J. A. McPherson; The inheritance of Emmy One Horse, by J. R. Milton; By the river, by J. C. Oates; The visitation, by N. P. Pansing; Johnny Panic and the Bible of Dreams, by S. Plath; Paper poppy, by M. Rugel; The tea bowl of Ninsei Nomura, by M. Shipley; The colony, by I. B. Singer; Benjamen burning, by J. M. Winslow

Best British short stories, 1922-1940 & The yearbook of the British and Irish short story; ed. by Edward J. O'Brien. Houghton 1922-1940 19v o.p. 1970

Analyzed in Short Story Index

Selections of short stories from representative British and Irish authors

Best detective stories of the year, 1946-1959/ 1961-1968; ([1st]-23d annual collection) Dutton 1946-1968 23v 1946-1965 o.p. 1970; 1966-1968 ea $4.50

Analyzed in Short Story Index

Editors: 1946-1959, David C. Cooke; 1961-1962, Brett Halliday; 1963-1968, Anthony Boucher

Contents: 1966: The hypothetical arsonist, by R. Phillips; The adventure of Abraham Lincoln's clue, by E. Queen; The poison necklace, by M. A. deFord; Package deal, by J. Ritchie; Queasy does it not, by J. Ritchie; Foxer, by B. Cleeve; The locked house, by S. Barr; The big job, by T. B. Dewey; A as in accident, by L. Treat; The Dr Sherrock Commission, by F. McAuliffe; Blood brothers, by C. Brand; The lesson, by H. Cecil; Grandfather and the pair of knaves, by L. Biggle, Jr.; The long way down, by E. D. Hoch; Sleeping dog, by R. Macdonald; The peppermint-striped goodby, by R. Goulart; The possibility of evil, by S. Jackson

Best detective stories of the year, 1946-1959/1961-1968—*Continued*

1967: The yellow brick road, by G. Williams; The theft of the clouded tiger, by E. D. Hoch; The adventure of the red leech, by A. Derleth; Miss Phipps and the invisible murderer, by P. Bentley; Speaking of murder, by J. Ritchie; The opposite number, by J. Hay; The delinquent account, by A. Wright; Murder is a gas, by A. K. Lang; They do not always remember, by W. Burroughs; K as in knife, by L. Treat; The tin ear, by R. Goulart; The Stollmeyer sonnets, by J. Powell; The chosen one, by R. Davies

1968: By child undone, by J. Ritchie; Kessler, the inside man, by G. Fox; Good man, bad man, by J. Weidman; Long way up, short way down, by K. W. Purdy; The Beddoes scheme, by J. Powell; The dead man, by J. L. Borges; B as in burglary, by L. Treat; Rink: a 1001st precinct mystery, by R. Goulart; File 1: the Mayfield case, by J. Gores; Through time and space with Ferdinand Feghoot, by G. Briarton; A delicate balance, by J. McKimmey; The road to Damascus, by M. Gilbert; The best driver in the county, by J. Ritchie; The oblong room, by E. D. Hoch

The Best from Fantasy and Science Fiction; 1st-18th ser. Doubleday 1952-1969 18v 1st-17th ser. o.p. 1970; 18th ser. $4.95

Analyzed in Short Story Index
Editors: 1st-4th series, Anthony Boucher and J. Francis McComas; 5th-8th series, Anthony Boucher; 9th-11th series Robert P. Mills; 12th-14th series, Avram Davidson; 15th-18th series, Edward L. Ferman

Contents for 18th series: The cloud-sculptors of Coral D, by J. G. Ballard; The people trap, by R. Sheckley; In his own image, by L. Biggle; Ogre, by E. Jesby; Lunatic assignment, by S. Dorman; Gifts from the universe, by L. Tushnet; Sundown, by D. Redd; Beyond the game, by V. Aandahl; Sea home, by W. M. Lee; That high-up blue day that saw the black sky-train come spinning, by D. R. Bunch; Muscadine, by R. Goulart; Final war, by K. M. O'Donnell; I have my vigil, by H. Harrison; The egg of the Glak, by H. Jacobs

Best of the Best American short stories, 1915-1950; ed. by Martha Foley. Houghton 1952 369p $5.95

Analyzed in Short Story Index
Contents: How the devil came down Division Street, by N. Algren; I'm a fool, by S. Anderson; The blue sash, by W. Beck; Nothing ever breaks except the heart, by K. Boyle; Horse thief, by E. Caldwell; Sex education, by D. Canfield; The enormous radio, by J. Cheever; The wind and the snow of winter, by W. V. Clark; Boys will be boys, by I. S. Cobb; Christ in concrete, by P. Di Donato; Hand upon the waters, by W. Faulkner; My old man, by E. Hemingway; The peach stone, by P. Horgan; Haircut, by R. Lardner; Man on a road, by A. Maltz; Prince of darkness, by J. F. Powers; Resurrection of a life, by W. Saroyan; Search through the streets of the city, by I. Shaw; The interior castle, by J. Stafford; How beautiful with shoes, by W. D. Steele; The women on the wall, by W. Stegner; Dawn of remembered spring, by J. Stuart; A wife of Nashville, by P. Taylor; The catbird seat, by J. Thurber; A curtain of green, by E. Welty

Best of the Best detective stories; ed. by David C. Cooke. Dutton 1960 279p o.p. 1970

Analyzed in Short Story Index
To celebrate the fifteenth anniversary in 1960, of this annual series the editor chose from 200 selections, the best stories of each year from 1946 to 1959. This is in effect the 15th annual volume of: Best detective stories of the year. (Publisher)
Contents: Body in the barn, by M. Manners; The perfectionist, by M. St Clair; Revenge, by S. Blas; Being a murderer myself, by A. Williams; Blackmail, by A. V. Elston; A boy's will, by Q. Patrick; The kiss-off, by J. P. Foran; For value received, by R. Deming; The killer is loose, by J. Hawkins; Chinese puzzle, by R. Marsten; First offense, by E. Hunter; Three wives too many, by K. Fearing; The day of the execution, by H. Slesar; Over there—darkness, by W. O'Farrell; Bottle of death, by G. Ralston

Best SF: 1968; ed. by Harry Harrison and Brian W. Aldiss. Putnam 1969 245p $4.95

"Four reviews of the motion picture '2001: a space odyssey' and a poem along with 12 well-selected and varied tales, all previously published, most in various magazines, during 1968 in the U.S. or Britain. An afterword by Aldiss takes a synoptic look at the science fiction of 1968." Booklist
Short stories included are: Budget planet, by R. Sheckley; Appointment on Prila, by B. Shaw; Lost ground, by D. I. Masson; The annex, by J. D. MacDonald; Segregationist, by I. Asimov; Final war, by K. M. O'Donnell; The serpent of Kundalini, by B. W. Aldiss; Golden acres, by K. Reed; Criminal in Utopia, by M. Reynolds; One station of the way, by F. Leiber; Sweet dreams, Melissa, by S. Goldin; To the dark star, by R. Silverberg

The Best science fiction stories and novels: 1949-1958; ed. by T. E. Dikty. Fell 1949-1958 9v o.p. 1970

Analyzed in Short Story Index
Title varies, 1949-1954: The Best science fiction stories
Editors: 1949-1954: Everett F. Bleiler and T. E. Dikty; 1955-1956, 1958: T. E. Dikty
Volume for 1958, called 9th series, published by Advent
No volume published for 1957
Selections from the annual outputs of science fiction

Beyle, Marie Henri. See Stendhal

Biderman, Sol
Bring me to the banqueting house. Viking 1969 284p $5.95

"Young David, bereft of mother, lives in the Denver Jewish Foundling House, where he is visited only rarely by his impoverished father. An eccentric child, he grows from a six-year-old who threads stars on pine needles, to the militant defender of the tomatoes in his portion of the orphanage's victory garden, to the 14-year-old with an itch in his private parts that is diagnosed differently by the rabbi, the doctor, and the social worker." Library J
"On the whole characterizations are good and the setting realistic, but the abundance of lavatory humor may be detracting for some readers." Booklist

Bierce, Ambrose
Can such things be? Boni & Liveright 1918 427p o.p. 1970

Analyzed in Short Story Index
First published 1893 by Cassell
Contents: The death of Halpin Frayser; The secret of Macarger's Gulch; One summer night; The moonlit road; A diagnosis of death; Moxon's master; A tough tussle; One of twins; The haunted valley; A jug of sirup; Staley Fleming's hallucination; A resumed identity; A baby tramp; The night-doings at "Deadman's"; Beyond the wall; A psychological shipwreck; The middle toe of the right foot; John Mortonson's funeral; The realm of the unreal; John Bartine's watch; The damned thing; Haita the shepherd; An inhabitant of Carcosa; The stranger; Present at a hanging; A cold greeting; A wireless message; An arrest; A man with two lives; Three and one are one; A baffled ambuscade; Two military executions; The Isle of Pines; A fruitless assignment; A vine on a house; At Old Man Eckert's; The spook house; The other lodgers; The thing at Nolan; The difficulty of crossing a field; An unfinished race; Charles Ashmore's trail

In the midst of life; tales of soldiers and civilians. Chatto & Windus [distributed by Dufour] 1964 244p $2.95

Modern Library edition analyzed in Short Story Index
Published in 1891 by Boni & Liveright with title; Tales of soldiers and civilians
Contents: A horseman in the sky; An occurrence at Owl Creek Bridge; Chickamauga; A son of the gods; One of the missing; Killed at Resaca; The affair at Coulter's Notch; The coup de grâce; Parker Adderson, Philosopher;

Bierce, Ambrose—*Continued*

An affair of outposts; The story of a conscience; One kind of officer; One officer, one man; George Thurston; The mocking-bird; The man out of the nose; An adventure at Brownville; The famous Gilson bequest; The applicant; A watcher by the dead; The man and the snake; A holy terror; The suitable surroundings; The boarded window; A lady from Red Horse; The eyes of the panther

Biggers, Earl Derr

Seven keys to Baldpate. Bobbs 1913 408p o.p. 1970

"Baldpate is an inn, perched high and lonely on a mountain side. In summer it is a scene of gayety; in winter it stands desolate and deserted. But there are seven keys opening seven of the Baldpate doors which, in various ways, come into the possession of seven people who, for various reasons, desire solitude; and they all seek it, by means of the keys in their possession, during the same week in December. First among these solitude-seekers is the young novelist, who, having won a popular reputation by the writing of melodrama, desires to escape from all thought of the adventurous, only to find himself plunged into real melodrama of the most exciting order." Book Rev Digest

The "characters are not characters at all, but cleverly invented little mannikins so far as their speech is concerned. . . . Yet they seem alive, because they are well described. The plot is of course impossible, but it is no less amusing." Boston Transcript

Billing, Graham

Forbush and the penguins. Holt [1966 c1965] 191p $3.95

"A novel based partly on the actual work of scientists stationed at Cape Royds, Antarctica, to observe the Adélie penguins. The fictional observer, Richard John Forbush, a New Zealand ornithologist, comes to feel protective and possessive of the Cape and the penguins. In the Antarctic spring, the penguins laboriously plod south for miles across the ice to reach their old rookery at Cape Royds, in order to mate, nest and bring up their chicks and then leave. Meanwhile they confront all the hazards of Antarctic life, the greatest of them the voracious skua." Pub W

Forbush's "reaction to solitary life, reflected in his letters, daydreams, philosophizing, reminiscences, strange methods of amusement, and particularly in his involvement in the welfare of the penguins is made extremely vivid, but the most impressive writing in this unusual novel is that describing the awesome silence and loneliness of the Antarctic and the survival struggle of the penguins." Booklist

Birmingham, Stephen

Heart troubles; short stories. Harper 1968 213p $4.95

Analyzed in Short Story Index

"Fourteen stories of love in the U.S. and abroad arranged under the headings The young in heart, The partly joined, and The partly parted. . . . These [are] brief tales for women readers." Booklist

Contents: "She ate grass"; Call before dinner; "Do you believe in change"; Between the maples; The backgammon table; Race day; We lucky geniuses; Bright, young faces; Blighted cedar; Dorothy, Dorothy; Lydia; The snows of youth; Water won't quench fire; Storm

Bissell, Richard

7 ½ cents. Little 1953 245p o.p. 1970

"An Atlantic Monthly Press book"

"What goes on in the Sleep Tite pajama factory before, during, and after a strike." McClurg. Book News

Bittle, Camilla R.

A Sunday world. Coward-McCann 1966 224p $4.50

"Set in a small university town in the South this is the story of a woman's desperate attempt to hold on to the pleasant, gentle world she grew up in where no one agitated for civil rights and there were always plenty of willing Negro domestics. Rosemarie Storie is a young matron living in the present but refusing to accept it; Flashbacks contrast her childhood with the present and help show her reluctant awareness of the changes taking place in her life. A nostalgic but effective picture of a rapidly changing society." Booklist

Bjarnhof, Karl

The good light; tr. from the Danish by Naomi Walford. Knopf 1960 [c1959] 272p $4

First published in Denmark 1957. Sequel to: The stars grow pale

Continues the story of a sensitive nearly blind boy growing up in pre-World War I Denmark. Following its narrator through adolescence and into manhood, it evokes his life at the Blind Institute in Copenhagen, his contacts with the sighted world, his introduction to sex and first love affair, his discovery of literature, art, and more particularly music, and his acceptance of the total blindness which finally comes." Booklist

"For its detailed account of institutional life in the early 1900's and as an inspiring narrative of a youth who accepts and transcends his handicap, this novel is generally recommended." Library J

The stars grow pale; tr. from the Danish by Naomi Walford. Knopf 1958 310p boards $5.95

First published 1956 in Denmark

"Acute observation, told in the form of a novel, of the world of a sensitive, young Danish boy who is going blind. As his vision decreases, the child realizes he must bid farewell to the security of home and childhood, to go to an Institute for the Blind, in Copenhagen." Pub W

"A haunting and evocative reminiscence for appreciative readers." Booklist

Followed by: The good light

Bjorn, Thyra Ferré

Dear papa. Holt 1963 191p boards $3.95

Cast in fiction form, this title is a continuation of the author's stories about her life as the daughter of a Swedish-American clergyman, Mama, now "an elderly widow, reminisces in simple, homely, humorous anecdotes about her large family and tells what her children, now grown, are doing." Pub W

"This is a sentimental, humorous, and, above all, loving tribute to both parents. Recommended for public libraries, especially for young people. Also possible for church libraries." Library J

y Mama's way. Rinehart 1959 214p $3.50

This novel "is an inspirational collection of powerful little sermons, woven into the story of [the author's] Mama's handling of the problems that beset [her]." Springf'd Republican

"The author states that her aim is to devote her book 'to writing about the power of prayer' and that it 'would carry a message to those who were too busy or too tired to read deeper books on religion.' It shows a childlike faith in God's concern for the individual, has many samples of answered prayers, but is rather thin in content. Should be useful in young adult and senior citizen collections." Library J

also in Bjorn, T. F. Papa's wife, Papa's daughter, Mama's way v3

y Papa's daughter. Rinehart 1958 238p boards $3.95

Sequel to: Papa's wife

This autobiographical novel presents "the life story of a minister's daughter who came to America as a child with her family in the early 1900's from Swedish Lapland. The theme is her lifelong ambition to be a writer." Pub W

It is "sentimental and episodic but sincere and pervaded by a sense of deep religious faith." Booklist

also in Bjorn, T. F. Papa's wife, Papa's daughter, Mama's way v2

y Papa's wife. Rinehart 1955 305p $4.50

The "story of a Swedish housemaid who married her pastor, raised and ruled eight children, and led a happy, useful life. Most of the setting is a New England town though it begins in [Swedish] Lapland." Pub W

Bjorn, Thyra F.—*Continued*

This "novel emphasizes kindliness, piety, family affections and noble character. . . . It may be our young people are too sophisticated to enjoy this story, but surely older women viewing their own families in retrospect will be touched by [it]." Library J

Followed by: Papa's daughter, entered above

also in Bjorn, T. F. Papa's wife, Papa's daughter, Mama's way v 1

y Papa's wife, Papa's daughter, Mama's way; a trilogy. Holt 1961 3v in 1 boards $6.95

For descriptive notes see entries under the individual titles

Black, Gavin
The cold jungle. Harper 1969 226p boards $4.95

"A Joan Kahn-Harper Novel of suspense" Paul Harris, a Scottish businessman based in Malaysia, comes "to England to have a ship built by a former friend of his. Pressure is put on him, his friend killed, and Harris is threatened in various ways." Best Sellers

Harris's "boat buying leads to adventure as thrilling, as tense, and as unsentimental as any he has hitherto encountered in South-East Asia. Gavin Black's thrillers really deserve the highest praise, and not least for an attitude of moderation and good sense that pervades them." Times (London) Lit Sup

Blackburn, John
Children of the night. Putnam 1969 [c1966] 192p $4.50

"Red mask mystery"
First published 1966 in England

Only a series of frightful tragedies, each more baffling than its predecessor, brings Dunstonholme to the attention of the world's press. Reporters find a village trembling before terror that only the local doctor, the vicar, and a visiting writer can begin to comprehend. The horror they discover rooted in Dunstonholme's medieval past erupts in a grisly climax." Am News of Bks

Blackburn, Tom W.
(ed.) Western Writers of America. They opened the West

Blacker, Irwin R.
(ed.) The Old West in fiction. Astor-Honor 1961 471p boards $7.50

Partially analyzed in Short Story Index
Contains one novel, excerpts from three other novels, and twelve short stories (including a television script from "Gunsmoke") listed under the following categories: The mountain men; Settlers and Indians: The miners; Badmen and cattlemen

Contents: Grant of kindom, by H. Fergusson (A complete novel first published 1950); The buffalo, by S. E. White (from The long rifle); Rendezvous, by A. B. Guthrie (from The big sky); The raid, by A. LeMay (from The searchers); Flame on the frontier, by D. Johnson; The bride comes to Yellow Sky, by S. Crane; The wind and the snow of winter, by W. V. Clark; Early marriage, by C. Richter; The Iliad of Sandy Bar, by B. Harte; An odyssey of the North, by J. London; The fool's heart, by E. M. Rhodes; The Lone Star ranger, by Z. Grey; Gunsmoke, by J. Meston; Stage to Lordsburg, by E. Haycox; Open winter, by H. L. Davis; The leader of the people, by J. Steinbeck

Blackmore, R. D.
y Lorna Doone

Some editions are:
Dodd (Great illustrated classics) $4.50 With illustrations from photographs of the Doone country, together with an introductory biographical sketch of the author by Basil Davenport
Dutton $3.50 Illustrated by Lionel Edwards
Dutton (Everyman's lib) $3.25
Oxford (World's classics) $3.50

First published 1869
A romantic love-story of Exmoor and the North Devon Coast of England, telling of the outlaw Doones, the maid brought up in the midst of them, and plain John Ridd's herculean power and his service to James II during Monmouth's Rebellion

"The scenic descriptions of the lovely region befits the tale, and many local worthies have their lineaments preserved here. Though 'Lorna Doone' made little stir at the time of its appearance, it has had innumerable imitations since, and it initiated a return to . . . romanticism in historical fiction." Baker's Best

Blackmur, R. P.
(ed.) American short novels. Crowell 1960 398p (Reader's bookshelf of American literature) $6.95

Analyzed in Short Story Index
Contents: Billy Budd, by H. Melville; The man that corrupted Hadleyburg, by M. Twain; Maggie: a girl of the streets, by S. Crane; Washington Square by H. James (1881); Melanctha, by G. Stein; The great American novel, by W. C. Williams; The Venetian glass nephew, by E. Wylie (1925)

Most of these seven titles illustrate the use of symbolism or allegory

Blackstock, Charity
A house possessed. Lippincott 1962 [c1961] 222p o.p. 1970

First published in England 1961 with title: The exorcism

The setting is "a guest home on the banks of Loch Ness. . . . The proprietor of the establishment, Miss Murphy, engages the local priest to exorcise the spirits of a disowned daughter of the house and her soldier husband, who fell at Waterloo. The priest obliges, but the night-bumpings continue, and are eventually . . . satisfactorily explained and forever silenced." Sat R

The knock at midnight. Coward-McCann [1967 c1966] 254p o.p. 1970

"The scene is Hungary in the summer of 1938, the year of Munich. . . . The heroine is [Maggie] a spunky Scottish spinster of 35 who has come to Hungary on a romantic impulse and who stays to help rescue a terrified Jewish girl with the aid of another equally intrepid Scot, a man [to whom Maggie had once been engaged]. A . . . blend of love story and thriller that paints a frighteningly vivid picture of Nazi evil just coming into power." Pub W

The lemmings. Coward-McCann 1969 255p $5.95

"Miss Diya Audu, a brilliant and beautiful Nigerian, had been admitted to Timperley Commercial College without question, but now Graham Timperley, its founder, said she must go. Todd Murray was one of those who defended her against the insults and even violence that Timperley had set in train. Then he found he was falling in love with her while his own wife lay dying. And in the end Diya was defeated by fear, not of the fiery cross and the jeers, but of humiliation at being called a 'colored girl.' " Bk Buyer's Guide

"These people and others in and out of the college are brought to life in a realistic, absorbing, well-cast novel that speaks more effectively against bigotry than would a solemn polemic." Booklist

Blackwood, Algernon
In the realm of terror; 8 haunting tales. Pantheon Bks. 1957 312p o.p. 1970

Analyzed in Short Story Index
Contents: The willows; The man whom the trees loved; The Wendigo; A haunted island; A psychical invasion; Smith: an episode in a lodging house; The empty house; The strange adventures of a private secretary in New York

These light "examples of [Blackwood's] elaborately detailed style, evoke a very real consciousness of forces and beings unseen and unknowable. . . . Most of the collections from which the selection was made appeared around 1910, so now they are available, if at all, only as second hand items in archaic and unattractive formats." Library J

Blackwood, Algernon—*Continued*

Tales of the uncanny and supernatural. British Bk. Centre 1949 426p front o.p. 1970

Analyzed in Short Story Index
Contents: The doll; Running Wolf; The little beggar; The occupant of the room; The man whom the trees loved; The Valley of the Beasts; The south wind; The man who was Milligan; The trod; The terror of the twins; The deferred appointment; Accessory before the fact; The glamour of the snow; The house of the past; The decoy; The tradition; The touch of Pan; Entrance and exit; The Pikestaffe case; The empty sleeve; Violence; The Lost Valley

Blair, Clay

The board room; a novel, by Clay Blair, Jr. Dutton 1969 352p boards $6.95

"A brilliant young journalist is hired to put 'The Weekly Tribune' on its feet. Lee Crawford moves it from Washington to New York, revitalizes it, but soon runs into George Cooper, controller and hatchet man. There is an incipient editorial rebellion, especially when it comes out that the Marshall Publishing Company plans a merger with Florida Broadcasting. In the end the cold money men win." Bk Buyer's Guide

"Mr. Blair who uses a staccato style, builds to quite a peak of tension in his final board room confrontation between the good guys and the bad guys. His people are stock cardboard figures, but his story has enough bite to do well in the inside business novels category." Pub W

Blais, Marie-Claire

A season in the life of Emmanuel; tr. from the French by Derek Coltman; introduction by Edmund Wilson. Farrar, Straus 1966 145p boards $4.50

"This is the story of the struggle for survival of a poor French Canadian family. The father is an illiterate farmer; the mother simply bears children. There are perhaps sixteen of them, including Emmanuel, who is in the first season of his life and through whose eyes the reader sees the people who surround him. One of the most affecting of the swarm of children is Jean-Le Maigre, a precocious adolescent wracked by tuberculosis. . . . His sister Héloïse seems to have a religious vocation, but she . . . will drift docilely into a brothel. Dominating the tribe is Grand-mère Antoinette, an indestructible old Frenchwoman." Publisher's note

The book "has come to grips with the reality of French Canada, and it is a dark grey piece of literature. It has been said that great poverty, disease and ignorance breed great artists. And it cannot be denied that Mlle. Blais is a gifted writer." Best Sellers

Blasco Ibáñez, Vicente

Blood and sand. Ungar 1958 319p $4.50

First published 1919 by Dutton. This edition translated from the Spanish by Frances Partridge

"For one who has the hardihood to read it thru to the end this is a powerful and terrible novel of the Spanish bull ring. No detail of the professional career of Juan Gallardo, who has risen from the lowest ranks of poverty to unprecedented heights of riches and popular favor, is spared. His vanities, his superstitions, his sufferings from fear, his daring attacks, the technique of his killings, his wounds and recoveries, and the final accident that brings his death, as well as the tortures of the beasts and the joyous delight of the populace in this national sport, are related with stoical calm, that breaks down and blazes into anger only in the final sentence." Book Rev Digest

The four horsemen of the Apocalypse; tr. from the Spanish by Charlotte Brewster Jordan. Dutton 1918 489p $6.95

"An interpretation of German and French psychology [during World War I] through the reactions of the two branches of a wealthy Argentinian family, who settle respectively in France and Germany before the war. A powerful and well-written novel, giving detailed pictures of French mobilization, the German occupation of Northern France, trench fighting, etc., and enlarging on contrasting views of humanity, liberty, culture and international relations. . . . [The] 'four horsemen' are War, Pestilence, Famine and Death." Cleveland

"The most impressive scenes of the story are the careful, and painful though restrained descriptions of German brutal methods against French civilians at the Battle of the Marne. The translation is inadequate." N Y Best Books

"The novel is very interesting both because of its presentation of the war from a new viewpoint and its graphic narrative and virile character portrayal." N Y Times Bk R

Mare nostrum (Our sea); a novel. Authorized translation from the Spanish by Charlotte Brewster Jordan. Dutton 1919 518p o.p. 1970

"The mythology and history of the Mediterranean form the rich background for a [World War I] novel whose main character, a [Spanish] sea captain, supplies petrol to the German submarines at the instigation of an alluring woman [spy]. Thereby he loses his son voyaging to meet him [and dedicates himself to vengeance]." Booklist

"With not a little that is sincere and powerful in the work, there is also much that, like this, points to a desire by the author to 'make copy' of the awful scenes of the war. . . . The book nowhere lacks interest or color." N Y Evening Post

Bleeck, Oliver

The brass go-between. Morrow 1969 256p boards $5.95

"Philip St. Ives is a top go-between who mediates between the owner of the stolen goods and the thieves who stole them. In this novel of suspense and adventure, his assignment is to recover a rare and politically important brass shield stolen from a Washington, D. C. museum." News of Bks

"It is "the work of an accomplished writer—every character has individuality. . . . There's a terrific climax at, of all places, Bull Run. Highly recommended for . . . [readers of] intelligent suspense novels." Pub W

For another story by this author see Thomas, Ross

Bleiler, Everett F.

(ed.) The Best science fiction stories and novels: 1949-1958. See The Best science fiction stories and novels: 1949-1958

Blish, James

A case of conscience. Walker & Co. [1969 c1958] 188p boards $4.50

"This semi-religious, science fiction novel tells of one man's encounter with the seemingly sinless natives of Lithia, an Eden-like paradise." Bk Buyer's Guide

We all die naked
In Three for tomorrow p153-204

Blixen, Karen. See Andrézel, Pierre; Dinesen, Isak

Blocker, Joel

(ed.) Israeli stories; a selection of the best contemporary Hebrew writing; introduction by Robert Alter. Schocken 1962 256p $3.95

Analyzed in Short Story Index
"Nine contemporary short stories with critical introductions and biographical sketches of the Israeli authors." Pub W

Contents: Tehilah, by S. Y. Agnon; The sermon, by H. Hazaz; The name, by A. Megged; The parched earth, by Y. Kaniuk; A roll of canvas, by B. Tammuz; The prisoner, by S. Yizhar; Next of kin, by M. Shamir; Battle for the hill, by Y. Amihai; Forevermore, by S. Y. Agnon

Boccaccio, Giovanni

The Decameron

Some editions are:
Doubleday $5.95 Illustrated in black and white and four-color by Rockwell Kent; translated by Richard Aldington
Dutton (Everyman's lib) 2v ea $3.25 Introduction by Edward Hutton
Liveright (Black and gold lib) $6.95 Translated by John Payne; with an introduction by Sir Walter Raleigh
Modern Lib. $2.95 Translated from the Italian by Frances Winwar

During the pestilence of 1348, seven ladies and three gentlemen of Florence took refuge in the Italian countryside, where they spent ten days traveling from one luxurious country house to another, idling away the hours by talking, reading, making love, and telling stories. The stories which the ladies and gentlemen told during the ten days constitute the major portion of the book. These stories cover almost every phase of human life

Bodelsen, Anders

Think of a number; tr. from the Danish by David Hohnen. Harper 1969 186p boards $4.95

"A Joan Kahn-Harper Novel of suspense"
Original Danish edition 1968
"This Danish suspense novel is a real find, inventive, exciting, psychologically probing. We couldn't put it down, it's that good. A rather mousey 37-year-old bank clerk stumbles on advance notice of a stick-up that may be pulled off in his suburban bank. Instead of going to the police, he begins to dream, with mounting intensity, of how he can turn the robbery to his own advantage. And this is just what he does in a plot as daring as it is simple. The one thing he does not count on in advance is the reaction of the thief when he discovers he has been had." Pub W

Bodsworth, Fred

The sparrow's fall. Doubleday 1967 255p o.p. 1970

In the wilderness of the Hudson Bay tundra "'live Jacob Atook and his' bride, Niska primitive Atihk-anishini Indians. When subzero cold and snow force the caribou to migrate for food, Jacob sets out in grim pursuit to find game to save his wife from starvation. . . . [During his long trek] flashbacks reveal [his] inner conflicts between Christian concepts and native ways." Library J
"Mr. Bodsworth blends all his ingredients to make this much more than a man-against-nature tale. Skillful flashbacks give a good picture of Indian life. Jacob works out his religious conflict during his long trek, and the animal and nature lore of the country are all worked in without diminishing the very real suspense." Pub W

The strange one. Dodd 1959 400p $6.95

A "heavily symbolic nature story. A barnacle goose from the Outer Hebrides reaches Canada instead of its original goat mates with a Canada goose, goes home to Barra, but in the end returns to Canada to rejoin its strange mate. A young man from the bleak island of Barra escapes to get an education as an ornithologist, falls in love with [a Cree] Indian girl around James Bay, leaves her because of prejudice, but, inspired by the example of the barnacle goose, returns to claim her." Library J
"This is a sentimental, old-fashioned and somewhat clumsily written book. . . . But even those who find Bodsworth's characterization awkward and his prose pedestrian may well find other rewards in 'The Strange One.' Its quantities of information about wild geese . . . and about the Cree Indians of the James Bay region are thoroughly interesting." San Francisco Chronicle

Bojer, Johan

The emigrants; tr. from the Norwegian by A. G. Jayne. Appleton 1925 351p o.p. 1970

"The story of Erik Foss's colony of Norwegians, who, land-hungry and impoverished at home, came to take up sections in Red River valley, North Dakota, only to fight drought, frost, poverty and isolation in this country.

The book is the first to describe from the Norwegian point of view the operations of that pioneer army of Scandinavians who settled so much of the Middle West from Wisconsin to North Dakota. In its zest, vitality and pungent native flavors, 'The emigrants' is happily free from the sogginess of some of our own novels of the soil." Cleveland

The great hunger; tr. from the Norwegian by W. J. Alexander Worster and C. Archer. Moffat 1919 327p o.p. 1970

"Story of Peer Holm, whose soul's hunger for the divine on earth attains its goal, not through his fight for education, his success as a master engineer, his happiness in love, but through disaster, suffering and sacrifice." Pittsburgh
"Told with the simplicity and directness which carry conviction and hold the interest from beginning to end. It will always find some readers in any library." Booklist

Böll, Heinrich

Absent without leave: two novellas; tr. from the German by Leila Vennewitz. McGraw 1965 148p boards $3.95

"Two narratives set in Germany and dealing with the disasters of war. The individual stories, 'Absent without leave' and 'Enter and exit,' were originally published in Germany in 1964 and 1962 respectively." Pub W
"Both have as narrator-protagonists irreverent, compassionate Germans whose preference for individuals rather than nations and peace for war estrange them from most of their World War II countrymen. Experiences as a sharer-in-our-national-destiny, one narrator's ironic term for military service, are at the core of these strong, supple stories veined with a satire that has universal application." Booklist

Billiards at half-past nine; tr. from the German. McGraw 1962 280p boards $4.95

First published 1959 in Germany
This is "the story of a family—the Faehmels, father, son, and grandson—of a city, unnamed, but most likely Cologne, and of Germany between about 1880 and 1958. None of the leading figures of these years is mentioned. . . . What they did for and to Germany is shown in the changes occurring in the city, the Faehmel family and the people who enter into their circle and disappear from it. The plot of the novel can be compressed into a single sentence: What father Faehmel, a highly successful architect has built, his son Robert, also an architect, but working as a demolition expert in World War II, destroys. The action moves along in a series of recollections, each of which sheds light on another feature of the main characters." Christian Science Monitor
"Böll reminds one of Heinrich Mann at his peak as an uncompromising foe of conventionality and political faddism, as well as a writer who in many respects courts the label of 'old-fashioned' by putting narrative ahead of experimentation." N Y Times Bk R

Children are civilians too; tr. from the German by Leila Vennewitz. McGraw 1970 189p $5.95

These stories were originally part of a volume entitled: 1947 bis 1951
Contents: Across the bridge; My pal with the long hair; The man with the knives; Rise, my love, rise; That time we were in Odessa; "Stranger, bear word to the Spartans we . . ."; Drinking in Petöcki; Dear old Renée; Children are civilians too; What a racket; At the bridge; Parting; Breaking the news; Between trains in X; Reunion with Drüng; The ration runners; Reunion in the avenue; In the darkness; Broommakers; My expensive leg; Lohengrin's death; Business is business; On the book; My sad face; Candles for the Madonna; Black sheep

The clown; tr. from the German by Leila Vennewitz. McGraw 1965 247p boards $5

First published 1963 in Germany
"Hans Schnier, clown and mime, is an artist, who specializes in capturing revealing incidents in peoples' lives and re-creating them in pantomime. Through flashbacks in his own life a

Böll, Heinrich—*Continued*
portrait of German society under Hitler [and] in the postwar period is revealed." McClurg. Books News

"What Schnier (and the author) seem to be asking is: How can an honest man profess Christianity when Christian culture in the West failed to stop the rise of Nazism . . . and when the Church thrives in a society that worships nothing but the values of the market-place? Hard questions but embodied in a bitter and brilliant book." N Y Times Bk R

18 stories; tr. from the German by Leila Vennewitz. McGraw 1966 243p $5.50

Analyzed in Short Story Index
Contents: Like a bad dream; The thrower-away; The Balek scales; My Uncle Fred; Daniel the just; The post card; Unexpected guests; The death of Elsa Baskoleit; A case for Kop; This is Tibten; And there was the evening and the morning . . .; The adventure; Murke's collected silences; Bonn diary; Action will be taken; The laughter; In the valley of the thundering hooves; The seventh trunk

The writing is tight and the stories move rapidly. Although the milieu which Böll describes is different from our American society, it is no less interesting to read these stories and compare their contents with similar happenings." Best Sellers

End of a mission; tr. from the German by Leila Vennewitz. McGraw [1967 c1968] 207p $5.95

First published 1966 in Germany
"When a young German soldier and his carpenter father set fire to an Army jeep at the side of a road near a Rhineland village, they are arrested, jailed for six weeks, then brought to trial before Judge Alois Stollfuss, who will close his career with their case. The novel covers the proceedings of the one-day trial, which opens early in the morning and concludes with the judge's verdict delivered shortly after midnight. . . . Both young Gruhl and his father plead guilty but claim that their action was not a criminal one but an artistic 'happening' not subject to the conventional laws of the Federal Republic." America

"The book contains satire of contemporary German life, politics, and economics, and raises some serious questions about values and justice. It reveals once again Boll's skill and insight in portraying human beings of all types, and perhaps better than ever before his sense of humor. It is probably his most delightful and provocative novel to date." Choice

Enter and exit
In Böll, H. Absent without leave: two novellas p91-148

Bond, Raymond T.
(ed.) Doyle, Sir A. C. Sherlock Holmes: detective

Bonnet, Theodore
y The mudlark. Doubleday 1949 305p o.p. 1970

"An interesting and amusing account of a small event during the reign of Victoria at a time when her popularity was at its lowest. A seven-year-old boy almost miraculously managed to enter Windsor Castle and surprised the Queen and her guests at dinner. This mole hill developed into a mountain as Disraeli, Scotland Yard and the House of Commons became involved. The 'Wheeler Case' assumed national proportions. Perhaps, because of it, important legislation was passed and England maintained her world position." Library J

"Anyone who enjoys Victorian vignettes will find that The Mudlark has plenty of wit and charm, based on a very intelligent understanding of the period and the people. It also has one of the most graphic descriptions of the old House of Commons that I have ever read." Commonweal

Bor, Josef
The Terezín Requiem; tr. from the Czech by Edith Pargeter. Knopf 1963 112p boards $3.50

During World War II Raphael Schachter trained the inmates of the concentration camp at Terezin, Czechoslovakia "to play Verdi's 'Requiem' and gave a performance in the presence of Eichmann himself, only to have the Nazi betray them to death." Bk Buyer's Guide
"Throughout the novel [the author] displays great intimacy with the score of the 'Requiem' and achieves the difficult task of relating its emotional content to the anguish of Jews about to be subjected to Hitler's final solution. Readers with a knowledge of music may find this unusual novel especially interesting, but it is for any reader who enjoys fine fiction." Library J

Borgenicht, Miriam
Margin for doubt. Published for the Crime Club by Doubleday 1968 [c1967] 209p o.p. 1970

"Jane and Tony Bassett have trouble making Tony's salary as a high school teacher cover expenses in the posh Connecticut suburb where they live. When another teacher commits suicide because Tony gets the job as head of the English department that the other had expected, Tony is so remorseful he goes all out to help the widow, Doreen. Then the Bassetts' troubles really begin." Pub W

The tomorrow trap. Published for the Crime Club by Doubleday 1969 214p $3.95

"Ralph Thornton was a model citizen but Claire, his wife, thought he spent altogether too much time on duties outside the home and not enough on his wife and sons. She left for California and Ralph's putting things off to tomorrow got the two boys into trouble with some tough teenagers." Bk Buyer's Guide

Borges, Jorge Luis
Ficciones; ed. and with an introduction by Anthony Kerrigan. Grove 1962 174p o.p. 1970

Analyzed in Short Story Index
First Spanish edition 1944
Contents: Tlön, Uqbar, Orbis tertius; The approach to Al-Mu'tasim; Pierre Menard, author of Don Quixote; The circular ruins; The Babylon lottery; An examination of the work of Herbert Quain; The library of Babel; The garden of Forking Paths; Funes, the Memorious; The form of the sword; Theme of the traitor and hero; Death and the compass; The secret miracle; Three versions of Judas; The end; The sect of the Phoenix; The south
"Borges himself calls most of the 17 stories in 'Ficciones' fantasies. They are that and a great deal more. For one thing, they are vehicles for his ideas. In most of these short tales, a literary Everyman races through centuries of world literature." Library J

Borland, Hal
The amulet. Lippincott 1957 224p $4.95

"As a young man, Quincy Scott felt the need to join a contingent of Confederate sympathizers and take a man's part in the world. He left his Denver home and his girl Rhoda, who gave him an amulet as a token for his safe return. The little band lived on the land and in the open as it crept ahead, avoiding a brush with the enemy. Quincy had time for reflection on the meaning of war, and as he buried his comrades after the battle of Wilson Creek, he decided to turn back. This story portrays a little known segment of life in that period, and it presents a young man's problems in growing up." Wis Lib Bul

y When the legends die. Lippincott 1963 288p $4.95

A story "about a Ute Indian boy, child of outlaws, brought up in the Colorado wilderness in the old ways and in friendship with a bear cub. His boyhood—when he is torn away from his mountains and 'civilized' against his will—and his young manhood are harsh and brutal: he becomes a bronc-buster with a reputation for a murderous riding style. The time is from 1910 up into the 1920's." Pub W

Borland, Hal—*Continued*

"The moral of the tale (and Mr. Borland is not averse to some explicit moralizing) is that it is good for a people to change but not good for them to forget their past. A good book for adults and a very fine book for young adults." Library J

Bottome, Phyllis

The mortal storm. Little 1938 357p o.p. 1970

A "portrayal of the tragedy that the early Nazi regime brings to the happy, ordered, peaceful home of the Roths. The author has created in this family a perfectly plausible situation fraught with potential danger since the father, a world-famous doctor has some Jewish blood, while his two Gentile stepsons are blindly dedicated to the Nazi cause, and Freya, the doctor's own child, is independent enough to follow the dictates of her eager young heart when she falls in love with a fine, simple peasant, idealistically Communistic, who lives in the mountains above Munich. The few menacing months before doom implacably descends upon the Roths are tense with emotion and marked by the author's psychological and imaginative insight and adherence to historical verity." N Y Libraries

"The author's method is laborious in places, and a shade sentimental: her dialogue is often windy and untrue; but she has a marked sense of character and of values, and she knows Germany." Spec

Private worlds. Houghton 1934 342p o.p. 1970

"The scene of the story is a British hospital for the insane, and three of the principal characters are psychiatrists; one is the superintendent of the hospital and the other two, a man and a woman doctor, are his coworkers. Living under the same roof, the insane with their strange fantasies and the sane with their emotional problems inwardly upsetting if outwardly controlled, are revealed as souls alike withdrawn into their 'private worlds.' " Book Rev Digest

The author "has here an unusual background which she handles expertly, and she has a situation with all the elements of tragedy. She takes all these elements, and because she weaves through them one of the most charming and idealistic love stories of recent days, she gives us a novel whose essential atmosphere is a happy one." Boston Transcript

Boucher, Anthony

Best detective stories of the year, 1963-1968. See Best detective stories of the year, 1963-1968

The case of the Baker Street Irregulars. Simon & Schuster 1940 336p illus. o.p. 1970

"An Inner sanctum mystery"

"A group of Sherlock Holmes fans get together in Hollywood to keep tabs on the filming of 'Adventure of the Speckled Band,' and to check up on the elainous script-writer, who hasn't the proper respect for the Holmes tradition." New Yorker

"If you know your Sherlock Holmes—and even if you don't—you will enjoy this delightfully farcical narrative, which offers a surprise on nearly every page. There is a good mystery plot, too, and the solution is the biggest surprise of all." N Y Times Bk R

The compleat werewolf, and other stories of fantasy and science fiction. Simon & Schuster 1969 256p boards $6.50

"This excellent collection presents ten short stories [including novelettes] varying in mood from serious to funny to horrifying, and proving the late Mr. Boucher a master storyteller." Cincinnati

Contents: The compleat werewolf [novelette]; The pink caterpillar; Q. U. R.; Robnic; Snulbug; Mr Lupescu; The bite; Expedition; We print the truth [novelette]; The ghost of me

(ed.) A treasury of great science fiction. Doubleday 1959 2v $5.95

Partially analyzed in Short Story Index

Contents: v 1 Re-birth, by J. Wyndham; Shape of things that came, by R. Deming; Pillar of fire, by R. Bradbury; Waldo, by R. A. Heinlein; Father-thing, by P. K. Dick; Children's hour, by H. Kuttner; Gomez, by C. M. Kornbluth; The (Widget), the (Wadget), and Baff, by T. Sturgeon; Sandra, by G. P. Elliott; Beyond space and time, by J. T. Rogers; Martian crown jewels, by P. Anderson; The Weapon shops of Isher, by A. E. van Vogt

v2 Brain wave, by P. Anderson; Bullard reflects, by M. Jameson; Lost years, by O. Lewis; Dead center, by J. Merrill; Lost art, by G. O. Smith; Other side of the sky, by A. C. Clarke; Man who sold the moon, by R. A. Heinlein; Magic city, by N. S. Bond; Morning of the day they did it, by E. B. White; Piggy bank, by H. Kuttner; Letters from Laura, by M. Clingerman; The stars my destination, by A. Bester

We print the truth

In Boucher, A. The compleat werewolf, and other stories of fantasy and science fiction p170-239

Bernkopf, J. F. comp. Boucher's choicest

(comp.) Ellery Queen's Mystery Magazine. The quintessence of Queen

Boulle, Pierre

y The bridge over the River Kwai; tr. by Xan Fielding

Some editions are:
Vanguard $5.95
Watts, F. $7.95 Large type edition complete and unabridged. A Keith Jennison book
First published 1952 in France

A satire "on a certain type of British officer, a colonel who, even in a Japanese prison camp, [during World War II] keeps a stiff upper lip and clings to discipline. Put in charge of building a bridge with prison labor he carries out the job so satisfactorily that when a team of commandos arrives to blow up his handiwork he indignantly exposes them to the Japanese." Pub W

"This is a stirring and imaginative book. Whatever Monsieur Boulle may think of Kipling standards he has, to his advantage, soaked in the Master's atmosphere. Ably seconded by an excellent translation he has achieved something of the brisk yet laconic style, the unforgettable character sketches, the technical details, the storytelling magic, which were part of The Day's Work and Many inventions." New Statesman & Nation

The executioner. Vanguard 1961 186p boards $4.95

"Chong, born in Yi-Ping of an honorable and respected family of executioners, returns home after 10 years' banishment to resume his hereditary role as executioner. Not long after, he is found guilty of poisoning seven criminals fifteen minutes prior to decapitation. His breach of duty is viewed as murder and results in a death sentence. Tribunal judges probe Chong's motive for murder; they find none. The question of whether it is criminal perversity or mercy is raised but left unanswered. A skillfully contrived, ironical story . . . is written in dialog between an old Chinese doctor and a Western writer (presumably Boulle himself)." Booklist

Face of a hero; tr. from the French by Xan Fielding. Vanguard 1956 221p boards $4.95

First published in France, 1953. Published in England, 1956, with title: Saving face

An "ironic story in which the hero, the public prosecutor in a French town, convinces himself that an accused man is guilty of murder even though he knows the man to be innocent." Pub W

" 'Face of a Hero' should have a peculiar fascination for the analytically minded reader as well as for the lover of paradox." Sat R

Boulle, Pierre—*Continued*

y Garden on the moon; tr. by Xan Fielding. Vanguard 1965 315p boards $5.95

First published 1964 in France
"The race to the moon, novelized from the time of the Peenemünde rocket base to the final conquest of the moon, estimated here for 1970. The story begins as the rocket experts work at Peenemünde; it continues as the German defeat scatters the scientists to America, to Russia, to France, to Japan." Pub W
"The protagonist, Dr. Stern, more than strongly suggests Werner Von Braun. . . There is effective suspense as Russians and Americans vie in their achievements. A competent piece of writing which men and teenage boys will admire, this is technical enough to be thought-provoking, but not bewildering." Library J

y Planet of the Apes; tr. by Xan Fielding. Vanguard 1963 246p boards $5.95

The time in this science fiction novel "is the year 2052. Ulysse Méron, a journalist, is one of a small party from earth which lands on a planet in the 300-light-year-distant constellation of Betelgeuse. They find to their horror that man is in a wild state and that apes—gorillas, chimpanzees, and orangutans—run the planet, in some ways better than civilized man runs his own planet. Their cities, vehicles, clothes, even, are much like what people have on earth, and they have eliminated war. They keep men in zoos and use them for biological experiments, because of all creatures men are physically closest to the simian. In this Swiftian fable Boulle gives full play to his not inconsiderable gift for irony and satire." Library J

Bourjaily, Vance

The end of my life. Dial Press 1961 [c1947] 278p o.p. 1970

First published 1947 by Scribner
"The adventures of a cynical American college boy, as an ambulance driver for the British Field Service in the Levant and in Italy, parallel his search for values—emblemized by his projected football game between the 'Yes' team (Lincoln, Lenin, D. H. Lawrence, Christ, and others) against the 'No' team (including Swift, Hemingway, Eliot, Voltaire, and Freud)." Good Reading
"It is indeed possible that many of the attitudes to life as expressed will horrify some and that scenes described and expressions used may send an eyebrow or two upward. On the other hand, there is certainly no intention to shock, and the tone of the book as a whole is astonishingly civilized, earnest and illuminating." N Y Her Trib Books

Bourne, Peter

Drums of destiny. Putnam 1947 570p o.p. 1970

Published in England with title: Black saga
"Historical novel about the revolt of the slaves in Haiti against their French masters. It is essentially a fitionized biography of Christophe, and is told from the viewpoint of a Scottish doctor who sought refuge on the island during the last years of the struggle." Book Rev Digest
"Mr. Bourne writes skillfully and sympathetically of the social and political conflict between Negro and white, between Negro and mulatto, between Negro and Negro. He has dug deeply into Haitian history and produced a fine novel of a gaudy, dramatic era." N Y Times Bk R

Bowen, Elizabeth

The death of the heart. Knopf 1939 418p $5.95

"Psychological study of a young girl, whose innocence and honesty are brought into conflict with the sophisticated futility of life in her half-brother's home in Regency Park, London." Book Rev Digest
"Miss Bowen writes with both art and skillful artifice; the passages from Portia's diary, in which she recaptures the ingenuousness, the clarity of insight and emotion of a child: her ability to animate a house, a landscape and make them illustrative of her characters. But, foremost, Miss Bowen has a sharp sense of the urbanities and subtleties of present-day society, of the interplay of almost imperceptible shades of feeling. This quality of restraint, of the unsaid, gives her novel its curious tautness and intensity." N Y Times Bk R

Eva Trout; or, Changing scenes. Knopf 1968 302p $5.95

"Eva Trout [24 years of age] a great, tall girl, is something of an oddity . . . a 'natural,' an original . . . and her devastating simplicity makes her an enigma to those around her. Motherless, she has spent her childhood with a father whose obsessive, absorbing love for another man left him with little to spare for his only child. Disappointed by reality, Eva is dangerously half-enmeshed in a world of fantasy and steers in her imperious way an erratic course." Publisher's note
"There is something about Eva that suggests one of Henry Moore's monumental women, a hugeness, a strength (like a 'dedicated discus thrower'), and a rooted stability combined with the instinctive wisdom of an E. M. Forster character." Christian Science Monitor

The heat of the day. Knopf 1949 [c1948] 372p $4.95

"Character studies of Stella Rodney, and the two men who loved her. The background is London after Dunkirk, a London of blitzes and buzz bombs; and peaceful Ireland. The two men are Robert Kelway, Stella's lover, and the mysterious Harrison, who betrays Kelway's secret in order to gain Stella for himself." Book Rev Digest
"Miss Bowen's novel expertly flicks the rawness of several unsolved queries concerning loyalty and love and ponders the degree to which human beings are strangers to each other. More densely written than her earlier work, this study of behavior is a soberly shocking, compassionate baring of the confused and vulnerable human heart." N Y Her Trib Books

The little girls. Knopf 1964 [c1963] 306p $4.95

"Can a friendship take up where it left off? It is fifty years since the three principal characters last met. Hand-in-glove confederates at St. Agatha's school on the South Coast of England, they had been aged eleven in 1914. Diana, a beauty to whom time has so far done little; Clare, a career woman; and Sheila, a matron, cool and collect—these are the three who find themselves jerked back into an ancient net." Huntting
"The details of their lives, their beliefs and interests, are sufficient to flesh out the vision of relationship that is the pretext for the story. But a sure compensation is offered: the author so thoroughly knows the world she is writing about that she contrives to appear to convey it to use whole." N Y Times Bk R

Bowles, Jane

The collected works of Jane Bowles; with an introduction by Truman Capote. Farrar, Straus 1966 431p $6.95

Contents: Two serious ladies [novel]; In the summer house [play]; Plain pleasures; Everything is nice; A Guatemalan idyll; Camp Cataract; A day in the open; A quarreling pair; A stick of green candy
The "almost monotonous presentation and lack of emphasis, of course, will limit this to readers interested in unusual modern works. But for them it is effective writing, well handled for its purpose." Library J

Two serious ladies
In Bowles, J. The collected works of Jane Bowles p 1-201

Bowles, Paul

The sheltering sky. New Directions 1949 318p o.p. 1970

"Three Park Avenue candidates for the lost generation, man and wife and male hanger on, travel into North Africa seeking and escaping things unclear to themselves. . . . Husband dies of typhoid. Wife gets lost in deep Sahara and ends up in a harem." Library J

Bowles, Paul—*Continued*

"Disintegration of personality is the theme of 'The Sheltering Sky.' An ugly theme at best, it is developed here with the hideous urgency of nightmare, each episode more macabre and imperative than the last, until the whole mad dream is consciously exorcized." Christian Science Monitor

Boyce, Burke

Man from Mt Vernon. Harper 1961 338p boards $6.95

"The historic figure of George Washington is humanized and at least partially brought to life in a biographical novel. . . . Spanning the crucial years between Washington's appointment as commander of the Continental army and the surrender of the British at Yorktown, the story concentrates on his personal and family life, interpreting political and military events largely in terms of his development as a man and leader." Booklist

"The dialog, from the historical point of view, is credible. The characterization generally squares with what historians know of Washington. The descriptive passages bear the stamp of authenticity, and the episodes that loom large in the narrative have a sound basis in historical scholarship." Chicago Sunday Tribune

Boyd, James

y Drums; with pictures by N. C. Wyeth. Scribner 1928 409p illus $6

First published 1925

"A story of North Carolina and the Scotch who dwelled there and who had not forgot Culloden. It is the story of John Fraser Sr. and Fraser Jr. and a most lovable mother, Caroline. . . . John Fraser is Elder, Justice of the Peace and respected squire of the community. Through the eyes of his son Johnny, a sensitive boy, unrolls the spectacle of the struggle for freedom in North Carolina." N Y Times Bk R

"It is not fiction: it is history—history in its most vital form; history told with all the thrill and feeling of actuality; history treated with creative imagination as Crane treated the Civil war in 'The red badge of courage'; history that leaves with the reader the atmosphere and the soul of a vanished era." N Y Her Trib Books

Marching on. Scribner 1927 426p o.p. 1970

James Fraser the hero, is a descendant of the Frasers of Revolutionary times who appeared in the author's "Drums" entered above

"Though this is a story of the South during the Civil War with the hero a soldier in the Confederate Army, it is written with a noticeable lack of rancour even in the mention of Sherman's march to the sea. James Fraser is the son of a poor farmer. He loves at first sight the daughter of a wealthy planter, and has just reached the point of confessing his love when the war carries him away. The story follows him on the march, into battle and to a Federal prison from which after two years he is released to return to the broken South and the girl he left behind." Book Rev Digest

Boyle, Kay

Generation without farewell. Knopf 1960 [c1959] 300p boards $3.95

"A tale about Germany in the immediate post-war period. Its characters are in a sense the conquerors and the conquered. . . . There is a gentle German newspaper man, in love with America, where he had spent two years as a prisoner of war, and also in love with the mistily beautiful wife of the American colonel who heads the local occupation unit. The colonel is a stupid brute who wants his daughter to marry a career minded lieutenant. But his daughter . . . is in love with a young German trainer of Lipizzaner horses." Chicago Sunday Tribune

"In the complex relationships and events involving a group of Americans and Germans in the Occupied Hessian town of Fahrbach, Miss Boyle has constructed a series of parables of the human condition. . . . Several pointed stories are told, many levels of meaning are discovered within the framework of this book.

The plot is perhaps the merest excuse, a means that allows the characters to reveal themselves . . . . Miss Boyle demands of her language descriptive precision but also depth of feeling; attempting to fuse complexly the denotive and affective functions of language, she sometimes fails. Some passages seem overwritten, but many more impress with their beauty, skill, and taste." N Y Her Trib Books

Boyle, Patrick

At night all cats are grey, and other stories. Grove [1969 c1966] 256p $4.95

First published 1966 in England

Contents: Oh death where is thy sting-aling-aling; Go away, old man, go away; The port wine stain; The metal man; The window; Myko; Odorous perfume her harbinger; Meles vulgaris; The pishogue; The betrayers; Square dance; At night all cats are grey; Suburban idyll; The lake

"This collection of 14 stories about the people, places, farm and suburban life of Ireland has the racy language, the robust style, the penetrating and devastating view of man's (particulary the Irishman's) inability to control his most destructive impulses." Pub W

Brace, Gerald Warner

The department; a novel. Norton 1968 289p boards $4.95

This is "the story of Robert Sanderling, Professor of English at a Boston University. As he is about to retire, Professor Sanderling considers his apparently successful life, his marriage to vivacious, sardonic Harriet, his parents and his younger years, the people and institutions who have made him what he is, and the future of man in an increasingly chaotic world." Bk Buyer's Guide

"The book is well written though not densely plotted, rather leisurely in pace, somewhat old-fashioned as befits its narrator, who feels himself inadequate beside his ambitious younger colleagues and left behind by undergraduates who sneer at most things he has always thought worthwhile. Neither notably comic nor truly tragic, his story nevertheless has moments capable of moving us to tears or laughter." Sat R

The Garretson chronicle. Norton 1947 383p o.p. 1970

"A chronicle of three generations of a New England family living in a beautiful old village not far from Boston. The stories of his grandfather's life, briefly; his father's life more extensively; and his own life in detail, are set down by young Ralph Garretson in an attempt to explain how his father came to choose his way of life and why Ralph rebelled against it and chose a different life." Book Rev Digest

"There are times when the work almost has the essence of biography and autobiography rather than fiction, a persuasion artfully intended by the author. Concerned with the conflict of ideas, it is a rich and thoughtful book, written with maturity of understanding that holds satire as well as sympathy." N Y Her Trib Books

Bradbury, Ray

y Dandelion wine; a novel. Doubleday 1957 281p o.p. 1970

"A novel about one summer in the life of a twelve-year-old boy, Douglas Spaulding: the summer of 1928. The place is Green Town, Illinois, and Doug and his brother Tom wander in and out among their elders, living and dreaming, sometimes aware of things, again just having a wonderful time. Doug's big discovery that summer was that he was alive." Book Rev Digest

"The writing is beautiful and the characters are wonderful living people. A rare reading experience—highly recommended to all libraries." Library J

y Fahrenheit 451. Simon & Schuster 1967 192p boards $4.95

Analyzed in Short Story Index

First published 1953 by Ballantine

Contents: Fahrenheit 451; The playground; And the rock cried out

Bradbury, Ray—*Continued*

The title story concerns "the book-burner of the future who found out that books are living things, too, reissued for the appearance of the movie." Bk Buyer's Guide

"Here is a different, off-trail book, filled with intimations of a time to come, of regimented men and women, of a complex atomic age which looms ahead. It is an ideal book for that reader whose appetite is in danger of becoming jaded, as well as for him who yearns for something new, some strange adventure in print." Chicago Sunday Tribune

The golden apples of the sun; drawings by Joe Mugnaini. Doubleday 1953 250p o.p. 1970

Analyzed in Short Story Index
Contents: Fog horn; The pedestrian; April witch; The wilderness; Fruit at the bottom of the bowl; Invisible boy; Flying machine; The murderer; Golden Kite, the Silver Wind; I see you never; Embroidery; Big black and white game; Sound of thunder; Great wide world over there; Powerhouse; En la noche; Sun and shadow; The meadow; Garbage collector; Great fire; Hall and farewell; The golden apples of the sun

"Mr. Bradbury's fantastic tales, which are mostly concerned with flights into the distant future, are his most successful. . . . The more everyday stories, in which we observe the frustrations, regrets, and occasional surges of hope in the lives of a few pathetic, faintly drawn people, are vaporish and sad, and without much core." New Yorker

also in Bradbury, R. Twice twenty-two: The golden apples of the sun; A medicine for melancholy p7-209

I sing the Body Electric! Stories. Knopf 1969 305p $6.95

In these eighteen stories, the author "conducts the reader on a tour through time and space—into the unbounded dimensions of the future, and through remapped patterns of the past—as he intermingles the bizzare with the familiar and brings tomorrow and yesterday closer to today." Publisher's note

Contents: The Kilimanjaro device; The terrible conflagration up at the place; Tomorrow's child; The women; The inspired chicken motel; Downwind from Gettysburg; Yes, we'll gather at the river; The cold wind and the warm; Night call, collect; The haunting of the new; I sing the Body Electric; The Tombling day; Any friend of Nicholas Nickleby's is a friend of mine; Heavyset; The man in the Rorschach shirt; Henry the Ninth; The lost city of Mars; Christus Apollo

y The illustrated man. Doubleday 1951 251p $4.50

Analyzed in Short Story Index
Contents: The veldt; Kaleidoscope; The other foot; The highway; The man; The long rain; The rocket man; The fire balloons; The last night of the world; The exiles; No particular night or morning; The fox and the forest; The visitor; The concrete mixer; Marionettes, inc.; The city; Zero hour; The rocket

"As almost every science fiction fan knows, there is no writer quite like Ray Bradbury. Deftly plotted, beautifully written, characterized by protagonists who are intensely real, this book of eighteen stories makes for very good news to SF aficionados." N Y Times Bk R

The machineries of joy; short stories. Simon & Schuster 1964 255p boards $4.50

Analyzed in Short Story Index
Contents: The machineries of joy; The one who waits; Tyrannosaurus Rex; The vacation; The drummer boy of Shiloh; Boys! raise giant mushrooms in your cellar; Almost the end of the world; Perhaps we are going away; And the sailor, home from the sea; El día de muerte; The illustrated woman; Some live like Lazarus; A miracle of rare device; And so died Riabouchinska; The beggar on O'Connell Bridge; Death and the maiden; A flight of ravens; The best of all possible worlds; The lifework of Juan Díaz; To the Chicago abyss; The anthem sprinters

"The stories themselves run the gamut from science fiction to comedy. Several depend on weird and fantastic happenings; a couple are rather depressing. The care that was taken in selecting the titles has resulted in a pleasant variety instead of the sameness that often occurs in collections such as this." Library J

y The Martian chronicles; prefatory note by Clifton Fadiman. Doubleday 1958 222p $4.50

Analyzed in Short Story Index
First published 1950
"Connected episodes on the settlement and abandonment of Mars during the 21st century." Retail Bookseller

Contents: January 1999: rocket summer; February 1999: Ylla; August 1999: the summer night; August 1999: the earth men; March 2000: the taxpayer; April 2000: the third expedition; June 2001: —and the moon be still as bright; August 2001: the settlers; December 2001: the green morning; February 2002: the locusts; August 2002: night meeting; October 2002: the shore; February 2003: interim; April 2003: the musicians; June 2003: way in the middle of the air; 2004-2005: the naming of names; April 2005: Usher II; August 2005: the old ones; September 2005: the Martian; November 2005: the luggage store; November 2005: the off season; November 2005: the watchers; December 2005: the silent towns; April 2026: the long years; August 2026: there will come soft rains; October 2026: the million-year picnic

"Earth people will find the 'Chronicles' suspenseful and, at times, funny." N Y Times Bk R

A medicine for melancholy. Doubleday 1959 240p o.p. 1970

Analyzed in Short Story Index
Contents: In a season of calm weather; The dragon; A medicine for melancholy; The end of the beginning; The wonderful ice cream suit; Fever dream; The marriage mender; The town where no one got off; The scent of sarsaparilla; Icarus Montgolfier Wright; The headpiece; Dark they were, and golden-eyed; The smile; The first night of Lent; The time of going away; All summer in a day; The gift; The great collision of Monday last; Little mice; The shore line at sunset; The strawberry window; The day it rained forever

"Twenty-two imaginative tales which range from science fiction and fantasy to allegory and stories of the supernatural and will appeal most to readers who appreciate the development of setting and atmosphere." Booklist

also in Bradbury, R. Twice twenty-two: The golden apples of the sun; A medicine for melancholy p213-406

The October country. Knopf 1970 [c1954] 272p illus $6.95

First published 1955 by Ballantine and analyzed in Short Story Index
Contents: The Dwarf; The next in line; The watchful poker chip of H. Matisse; Skeleton; The jar; The lake; The emissary; Touched with fire; The small assassin; The crowd; Jack-in-the-box; The scythe; Uncle Einar; The wind; The man upstairs; There was an old woman; The cistern; Homecoming; The wonderful death of Dudley Stone

Something wicked this way comes; a novel. Simon & Schuster 1962 317p $5.95

"A story of terror and the supernatural. Two boys are fascinated by the carnival that visits their small town, perhaps even the more because there is something sinister about its owner and about its pleasures." Bk Buyer's Guide

"A night-marish allegory which can stand on its own merits as a suspense tale and still make a significant comment on the human situation." Christian Science Monitor

y Twice twenty-two: The golden apples of the sun; A medicine for melancholy. Drawings by Joe Mugnaini. Doubleday 1966 406p $5.95

Analyzed in Short Story Index
A combination of two earlier books published in 1959 and entered separately above. Each contains 22 fantasy and science fiction short stories

Contents: The golden apples of the sun: The fog horn; The pedestrian; The April witch; The wilderness; The fruit at the bottom of the bowl; Invisible boy; The flying machine; The murderer; The golden kite, the silver wind; I

Bradbury, Ray—*Continued*

see you never; Embroidery; The big black and white game; A sound of thunder; The great wide world over there; Powerhouse; En la noche; Sun and shadow; The meadow; The garbage collector; The great fire; Hail and farewell; The golden apples of the sun

A medicine for melancholy: In a season of calm weather; The dragon; A medicine for melancholy; The end of the beginning; The wonderful ice cream suit; Fever dream; The marriage mender; The town where no one got off; A scent of sarsaparilla; Icarus Montgolfier Wright; The headpiece; Dark they were, and golden-eyed; The smile; The first night of Lent; The time of going away; All summer in a day; The gift; The great collision of Monday last; The little mice; The shore line at sunset; The strawberry window; The day it rained forever

The Vintage Bradbury; Ray Bradbury's own selection of his best stories; with an introduction by Gilbert Highet. Vintage 1965 329p lib. bdg. $2.29

Analyzed in Short Story Index
Contents: The watchful poker chip of H. Matisse; The veldt; Hail and farewell; A medicine for melancholy; The fruit at the bottom of the bowl; Yila; The little mice; The small assassin; The anthem sprinters; And the rock cried out; Invisible boy; Night meeting; The fox and the forest; Skeleton; Illumination; Dandelion wine; Statues; Green wine for dreaming; Kaleidoscope; Sun and shadow; The illustrated man; The fog horn; The dwarf; Fever dream; The wonderful ice cream suit; There will come soft rains

Braddon, Russell

y When the enemy is tired. Viking 1969 251p boards $5.95

Also available in large type edition $7.95
First published 1968 in England
"It is 1975. The United States is now totally isolationist. Asian countries are falling to China as fast as they can capitulate. Only Australia still puts up resistance, and an Australian colonel and his men have been captured by the Chinese, who set out to break the Colonel and force him to make propaganda broadcasts for them. Physical torture having failed, the Chinese force him to put down in writing all he can remember of his life to age 20." Pub W
"Some novels defy classification. After reading a chapter or two of Mr. Braddon's book, one might be tempted to consign it to the now-familiar prisoner-of-war-brainwashing niche, but that would be a serious mistake. The novel has much suspense and drama . . . but its principal appeal is the skillful and original way it develops a 'formula' situation." Book of the Month Club News

Bradford, Richard

y Red sky at morning; a novel. Lippincott 1968 256p $4.95

"When World War II begins Josh Arnold's father Frank joins the Navy and sends his wife and son from Mobile, Alabama to tiny Sagrado, New Mexico where the family had spent previous summers. Josh's observations of life among the motley Mexican and Anglo inhabitants of Sagrado and his disarming schoolmates and his concern for his Southern mother and for the nearly permanent house guest Jimbob Buel result in a humorous, honest, and affirmative portrayal of a teen-ager's seventeenth summer." Booklist
This novel "is warm and funny and yet has a sharp bite to it, like the snap of fangs crunching through corn pone. The genteel Old South hasn't taken such a beating since Sherman's day. . . . But what makes the book a true delight is the dead-pan, irreverent humor with which Josh tells the story." Book World

Bradford, Roark

Ol' man Adam an' his chillun. . . . With drawings by A. B. Walker. Harper 1928 264p illus $4.95

Analyzed in Short Story Index
"Being the tales they tell about the time when the Lord walked the earth like a natural man." Subtitle

Contents: Eve and that snake; Populating the earth; Sin; Steamboat days; Romance and marriage of Abraham; Little Isaac; Mrs Lot; Esau; Wrestling Jacob; Fortune-teller; All about the Potiphar scandal; Old King Pharaoh's daughter; Romance and education of Moses; Trick boys; Manna of the Lord; Understanding; Big lodge; Crossing Jordan; Stratagem of Joshua; Sun trick; Younger generation; Battling with Baal; Balaam and his talking mule; Samson, strong boy; Old man Job; Little David; Mantle of Saul; Adulteration of Old King David; Wisdom of King Solomon; Green pastures; Preliminary motion in Judge Pilate's court; Nigger Deemus

These stories formed the basis for Marc Connelly's Pulitzer Prize play "Green pastures"

Brady, Charles A.

Stage of fools. Dutton 1953 381p o.p. 1970

This novel "parades across the Henrican stage of kaleidoscopic 16th century English history, the 'fools': Henry VIII, Thomas Cromwell, Anne Boleyn, Wolsey Cranmer and company, and the 'wise man' St. Thomas More. The theme is the Chancellor's martyrdom for placing Christ before Caesar." Library J
"This novel never relies on the sex and melodrama of much historical fiction, and incorporates a wealth of literary and historical scholarship without becoming too weighted down with factual detail." Booklist

Braider, Donald

Color from a light within; a novel based on the life of El Greco. Putnam 1967 379p $6.95

"With the skeletal chronology of Domenikos Theotokopoulos' stay in Crete, Venice, Rome and Spain as his basis (evidently supplemented by considerable research) Donald Braider has reconstructed from fact and fancy El Greco's personal and artistic life. The result is an absorbing historical novel of the 16th century. Set in relief against vivid portraits of the cities he chose and the times in which he lived, the hero comes alive as man and artist." Pub W

Rage in silence; a novel based on the life of Goya. Putnam 1969 318p $6.95

"Picking up the story of Goya's life at midpoint, after his reputation as Spain's greatest portrait painter had been established and an illness had left him deaf and discouraged, Braider describes the restorative love affair with the Duchess of Alba and, after her death, the liaison with the youthful but mercenary Leocadia. Goya's involvement in Spain's political troubles, together with his personal and family life, receive more emphasis than his artistic reputation and achievement." Booklist
The novel "is an interesting, wholly absorbing, if stylistically pedestrian work. If it is repetitious, it is the characterization of Goya which activates the reader's curiosity. Unfortunately, there are long stretches of purely expository history to set the scenes, to fill the gaps, and then we are plunged again into 'novelized' encounters." Best Sellers

Braine, John

The crying game. Houghton 1968 302p $5.95

"Integrity versus corruption, both personal and professional, is the theme of a novel set in London in the near future. Varying in credibility, the characters move through an intricate plot, focused on and related by Frank Batcombe, a young, aspiring, Catholic journalist caught for a season in a web of intrigue until rescued by his own morality." Booklist
"The book, which is readable and sometimes amusing, has too much sham sex and sham politics. . . . Braine is adroit when he deals with the politics of religion." Sat R

Life at the top. Houghton 1962 308p o.p. 1970

Sequel to: Room at the top
"The young man who clawed his relentless way upward from working-class origins is now ensconced in relative luxury, married to a rich and beautiful young woman, working for his powerful father-in-law, elected (as a conservative, of course) to the local council. He

Braine, John—*Continued*

finds he has traded more than the rigors of poverty for his present moneyed comfort: his personal freedom has been exchanged for a form of elegant slavery. Still angry, still unhappy, he now lacks the will power to break loose. The energy which drove him upward has been sapped, and he knows that he must remain in his self-attained captivity. The characterization and the writing are just as sharp and good as in the earlier book, but something of Joe's own disenchantment seems to have rubbed off on this sequel." Library J

Room at the top; a novel. Houghton 1957 301p $4.95

The hero of this novel "is a rising public official in the new governmental machine which is rapidly taking over Britain. He belongs to the Brave New World so completely that he and his friends even classify the women they know in administrative terms, as Grade Three, Grade Six and so on. Yet beneath his lower-middle-class ambition and his slightly vulgar manners, he is a human being, and very much of a man. He falls in love with two women: one just wrong for him, being married and some years older; one just too right, being rich and Grade Two. The result is not a romantic excitement but something like a bitter little tragedy, deeply felt and well told. Room at the Top is recommended to those who can understand a good deal of English slang and technical phrasing, and for those readers who can feel pathos even in squalor." Book of the Month Club News
Followed by: Life at the top

Brand, Max

Max Brand's Best stories; ed. by Robert Easton. Dodd 1967 255p front $5
Analyzed in Short Story Index
Contents: The king; Honor bright; Wine on the desert; Our daily bread; The wolf pack and the kill; Internes can't take money; The claws of the tigress; The silent witness; The Kinsale; A life for a life; The luck of Pringle; A special occasion; The sun stood still

The Stingaree. Dodd [1968 c1930] 216p $3.95
"Silver star westerns"
First copyright 1930
The "story of a man of many names and many skills who found that his ordeal had just begun when he met his enemy. Ahead of him lay the perils of hired guns, of wilderness traps and a bitter conflict with his own code of honor." Am News of Bks

Thunder Moon. Dodd [1969 c1955] 180p $3.95
"Dodd Mead Silver star westerns"
First copyright 1927
"Thunder Moon had been stolen from the whites by the Cheyenne. Because he fainted in the ritual test of courage by torture, he went into battle against the Pawnees prepared to die [and] covered himself with glory—but couldn't scalp his enemies." Bk Buyer's Guide

Brand, Millen

The outward room. Simon & Schuster 1937 309p o.p. 1970
"When the story opens Harriet Demuth has been in a hospital for the insane for seven years, ever since the death of her brother. Partially cured but yet unwilling to return to her home, she runs away to New York. After several days of vain searching for work, she accepts the friendly offer of a working man and goes to live with him. Thru the months that follow she gradually finds her place and when sorrow comes to the man, she knows that her love can help him and that it has worked her own cure." Book Rev Digest

Savage sleep; a novel. Crown 1968 465p $6.95
"The time is the 1940's, when psychotherapy for excited catatonics consisted of electric shock treatments and insulin. Dr. Marks, the young psychiatrist hero of the novel, battles to introduce psychoanalysis as a method of treatment, and the novel proceeds on three

levels: his scrupulous, patient persistent treatment of his patients, with emphasis on two case histories; his own psychoanalysis; his battles with hospitals and other doctors bitterly opposed to his methods." Pub W
"Readers must walk warily through the argument of this tract disguised as a novel. It is, essentially, an attack on accepted techniques of handling psychotics and, on occasion, it generates tremendous dramatic power as the psychiatrist-hero rescues suffering patients from disintegration and death. . . . Of topical interest only." Choice

Brandt, E. N.

(ed.) The Saturday Evening Post. The Saturday Evening Post Reader of western stories

Braun, Lilian Jackson

The cat who ate Danish modern. Dutton 1967 192p $4.50
The "adventures of Koko, The Siamese, and his Watson, Jim Qwilleran. The 'Daily Fluxion' assigns Jim to mastermind a new Sunday supplement called, of all things, 'Gracious Abodes.' But the shocking consequences of the first few issues make Jim realize that he is back in his own field, crime reporting, and that only [the cat] Koko, can help with the answers." Library J

The cat who turned on and off. Dutton 1968 186p $4.50
"Qwilleran had an idea for a Christmas feature for 'The Daily Fluxion,' the Holiday in Junktown—but Junktown turned out to be the antiques center of the city. A short time [before] Andy Glang had fallen off a ladder and was impaled on a finial. Qwilleran got the idea it was no accident, and Koko, his Siamese that could turn lights on and off, helped him [delve]." Bk Buyer's Guide
"Miss Braun knows about cats, journalism and antiques, and has used them all in this thriller, just as the blurb claims. Her stories about aging journalist Qwilleran and his detective Siamese are a bit girly, but likable by anyone who likes rather old-fashioned American lady-written detection." Times (London) Lit Sup

Bray, Christopher

The scarecrow man. Viking 1968 122p boards $3.95
"Two derelicts meet on a parapet near Marble Arch in London, during the Christmas season. Each is pursued by—or pursuing—his private god—or his private demon. Gonlag tells of his underground friend, Surzo, a Brooklyn-accented voice, which urges him to communicate a message to the world; Mason . . . [is haunted by] the Scarecrow Man he first encountered in his youth, then in a dream, and in a church. The two wind up painting Surzo's message on the wall of the Royal College of Art. Mason's mission is more complicated and ends in a mixture of fulfillment and somewhat contrived tragedy." Pub W
"Many first novels fail by attempting too much, but Christopher Bray has attempted just enough, and within his own terms has succeeded perfectly." Sat R

Brecht, Bertolt

Threepenny novel; tr. from the German by Desmond I. Vesey; verses tr. by Christopher Isherwood. Grove 1956 369p o.p. 1970
Published in England, 1937 with title: A penny for the poor
"Satire, not unlike the Beggar's Opera, translated from the German. The scene is Victorian London, and the main characters are three scamps: Peachum, the proprietor of a beggar's supply house; MacHeath, whose line is supplying stolen goods to second-rate shops; and Coax, who has a plan for selling rotten transports to the government to use in sending soldiers to the Boer War." Book Rev Digest

Brennan, Maeve

In and out of never-never land; 22 stories. Scribner 1969 274p $5.95

A collection of short stories grouped under four sections: stories of animals and people in New York; stories which draw on the author's childhood in Dublin; a group centering around a Mrs Bagot in Dublin; and several about Rose and Hubert Derdan who have an unhappy marriage

Contents: The door on West Tenth Street; A large bee; The children are very quiet when they are away; In and out of never-never land; The children are there, trying not to laugh; I see you, Bianca; The morning after the big fire; The old man of the sea; The barrel of rumors; The day we got our own back; The clever one; The lie; The devil in us; The twelfth wedding anniversary; The carpet with the big pink roses on it; The sofa; The shadow of kindness; The eldest child; Stories of Africa; A young girl can spoil her chances; The drowned man; A free choice

Breslin, Jimmy

The gang that couldn't shoot straight. Viking 1969 249p $5.95

This is the columnist's first novel. It concerns a Mafia family in Brooklyn. "There is Papa Baccala; he is very big in a number of enterprises. Then there is Kid Sally Palumbo, a revisionist, who would like to be very big; his grandmother, . . . named Big Mama Ferrara [who] will go to extravagant lengths to see her boy make his mark [and Sally's sister Angela who] tumbles for an artistic type who is a six-day bike-rider." Publisher's note

Brick, John

y Jubilee. Doubleday 1956 320p o.p. 1970

"The story of Sherman's March to the Sea is told from the Northern point of view. The hero is Jeff Barnes to whom the army means more than anything else in life—including his marriage. Jeff drives himself and his men mercilessly and soon becomes known as Ramrod Barnes. The Battle of Lookout Mountain and the burning of . . . Atlanta are well portrayed." Huntting

"The tragedy of young Captain Jeff Barnes, obsessed with his sense of duty, is . . . complete in itself. Ballads and marching songs of the period and effective leitmotifs, and the talk of the soldiers is accurately recorded. Recommended to all libraries." Library J

The Richmond raid; a novel. Doubleday 1963 279p o.p. 1970

This "is novel about one of the most fantastic episodes of the Civil War. Under the leadership of Colonel Dahlgren an advance force of Union Cavalry set out on the mission of burning Richmond, freeing the prisoners on Belle Isle, and [capturing or] killing Jefferson Davis." Publisher's note

"Author Brick utilizes all the tools of good historical writing. He tells of the personal lives of the leading men, and in true Homeric fashion delves deeply into the all-too-human reasons that really explain success and failure. His realism sometimes becomes ironically effective also." Best Sellers

The rifleman; a novel. Doubleday 1953 349p o.p. 1970

"Tim Murphy, a little-known hero of the American Revolution, is the principal character in this novel. . . . Tim was a woodsrunner and Indian fighter who enlisted with the Pennsylvania riflemen to fight the British. He fought through the entire war, and is credited with turning the tide at Saratoga. After the final victory of the Colonial Army he settled at Schoharie with Peggy whom he had married before the campaign that ended at Yorktown." Huntting

Rogues' kingdom. Doubleday 1965 301p o.p. 1970

"This novel is based on the exploits of a notorious family of horse thieves and robbers who preyed on the towns of Upper New York state just before the Civil War. A tale of zestful people with both a swagger of contempt for law and a poignant love story when one of them fell in love with a law abiding, respected, school teacher." Huntting

"A fast, often humorous adventure yarn." Bk Buyer's Guide

Bridge, Ann

The dangerous island. McGraw 1963 275p o.p. 1970

"A novel in which Julia Probyn, the heroine, and Colonel Philip Jamieson of the British Secret Service search for Russian satellite tracking stations in the Hebrides, the Isles of Scilly and the West Coast of Ireland." Book Rev Digest

"The Dangerous Islands is a must for all Julia Probyn fans, for here at last our Julia finds true love, with marriage waiting shortly after the last page. It is also quite an enchanting travelogue of remote islands . . . rich in local lore." N Y Times Bk R

The dark moment. Macmillan (N Y) 1952 337p o.p. 1970

"Mustapha Kemal's revolution in Turkey, soon after World War I, is the setting for the story of Feride, young Turkish wife, and Fanny, an English girl. Feride and her friend Nilufer escape to Ankara in disguise to join their husbands, take their part in the toil and danger of the revolution, and become two of Turkey's emancipated women. Meanwhile Fanny feels the pull of the new Turkey and a much more specific attachment." Retail Bookseller

"The Turkish scene is rendered with fidelity and feeling. Turkish characters and the family relationships in an aristocratic household are described with real skill and sensitive perception. Plot and characterization are secondary to the scenic and political background." Library J

Emergency in the Pyrenees. McGraw 1965 271p boards $5.50

"Julia Probyn, has now married Colonel Philip Jamieson of the British Secret Service. When Philip is sent to the Middle East, Julia spends the latter part of her first pregnancy at Philip's boyhood summer home, a remote spot in the Pyrenees, with a former pupil, Luzia, as her companion. Julia's involvement in an international sabotage plot, the premature arrival of her baby, and Luzia's matrimonial choice between twin suitors provide the elements of danger and romance in a pleasing women's novel which seems somewhat more matronly in tone than its predecessors." Booklist

The episode at Toledo. McGraw 1966 249p boards $5.95

"Julia Probyn, who has dabbled in international espionage through many of Ann Bridge's novels, is now married. . . . But she has a suitable substitute, Hetta, wife of a British diplomat in Spain. She handles admirably two cases of communist conspiracy against important visitors from America. . . . As always, the author supplies an authentic attractive background, this time, a country estate in Portugal." Pub W

"The new reader of Ann Bridge is reminded of John Buchan and the secret service of a generation ago. Even if this type of refined novel is dated, it has its use in fiction collections and will be read with pleasure by many older men and women who find the James Bond tales too tough." Library J

Illyrian spring. Little 1935 384p o.p. 1970

"A delightful tale . . . of an English-woman, a talented painter, who, puzzled and hurt by the attitude toward her of husband and children, runs away to Dalmatia to think things over. Introduced into the story which the author holds skilfully in suspense, are a friendly psychologist and a young artist protege, both of whom contribute to her understanding of herself and her family. The loveliness of Dalmatian flowers, villages and mountains so faithfully depicted here, reflects doubtless the author's own enchantment with the scene." N Y Libraries

y The malady in Madeira. McGraw 1969 300p $6.95

"The last thing recently widowed Julia Probyn expects to find on the lush and charming island of Madeira is a clue to her husband's mysterious death, for he perished somewhere in

Bridge, Ann—*Continued*

the wilds of Central Asia, while on a top-secret mission for British Intelligence. No sooner does Julia arrive at Madeira with her infant son and his devoted Nanny, however, when a series of strange, sinister, but apparently unconnected events begin thrusting themselves upon her." News of Books

"This is an old-fashioned, unsophisticated novel combining a mild suspense with a colorful travelogue of Madeira, especially suitable for YA collections." Library J

Peking picnic. Little 1932 354p o.p. 1970

"Despite disquieting rumors and unsettled conditions around Peking, a group of English, French and Americans set out for a week-end picnic at an old monastery. The center of the group is Laura Leroy, whose undeniable charm and art of living influences each one in the party to consult her about the hopes, fears, or love affairs that beset him. Thus, the way each person reacts to the difficulties that attend the picnic and the consequent capture by bandits is brought out. An excellent picture is drawn of the intricacies and delights of legation life in China." Wis Lib Bul

The Portuguese escape; a novel. Macmillan (N Y) 1958 278p o.p. 1970

"Julia Probyn, British reporter, arrives in Portugal to cover a wedding and becomes involved in the escape of a Hungarian priest, his Communist pursuers, and a Hungarian countess recently released from behind the Iron Curtain." McClurg. Book News

"An excellent romantic novel in the strict sense of the word. . . . Some young Americans may take exception to the extremely British point of view which makes the American characters in the book vulgar and/or stupid, but, otherwise, there are some delightful characterizations." Library J

The tightening string; a novel. McGraw 1962 250p map o.p. 1970

A "picture of a lovely aristocratic old world, the Hungary of big estates and a cultured elite, giving way before the onslaught of World War II. The story is about the adventures of a lady in a task of mercy. The heroine is the gentle, middle-aged wife of a British diplomat in Budapest. She devotes herself to prisoner-of-war relief. The story has a background of bad war news, the heroine's daughter's unhappy love affairs, and her husband's serious illness." Pub W

"The stream of consciousness in 'The Tightening String' isn't dirty or turgid or depressing or even monumentally dull. The story doesn't unroll in symbols to reveal essential nothing. It is a well constructed, fast paced, moving, quietly heroic story about human beings, told in distinguished English. How new fashioned, how exciting!" Chicago Sunday Tribune

Brinkley, William

Don't go near the water. Random House 1956 373p $5.95

The adventures in World War II, of a U.S. Navy Public Relations unit of landlocked mariners for whom the naval watchword "Don't give up the ship" became "Don't go near the water." By 1945 this unit managed inspite of wartime adversities to convert the island of Tulura into a Radio City of the Pacific. (Publisher)

"Profanity, bald references to sex, and broad humor make this a book with more appeal for men than women." Booklist

The ninety and nine. Doubleday 1966 393p $5.95

"In a more romantic and more tragic tale than his 'Don't go near the water' [entered above] Brinkley tells the story of the crew of a landing ship tank plying between Naples and Anzio during World War II. Episodic in form and skirting sentimentality the novel nevertheless gives a convincing picture of the interaction of servicemen and civilian population in a war." Booklist

"The crew members are the usual ones, no real original creations in the lot, but they are always interesting. Most of the book is lighthearted fun with the escapades, feuds, and love affairs of men who have been thrown together by the accident of war. When the end comes, it is grim and tragic, but in a realistic sense and not a fictional one. Even readers who do not like the usual war novel find this one a real surprise." Library J

Bristow, Gwen

y **Celia Garth.** Crowell 1959 406p $6.95

This story "takes its background from South Carolina during the Revolutionary War. Its heroine is Celia Garth, a spirited orphan girl working as an apprentice dressmaker in Charleston, who witnesses the British siege of the city and returns during the occupation to become a spy for the rebels." Booklist

"Celia Garth's story is adventurous and romantic, patriotic and sentimental. Miss Bristow's historical novel presents abundant terror, but it is the terror endured by civilians more than the terror of bloody battle. The general public will find no trace of the realistic, detailed description of love and war that so often characterizes this variety of fiction. Nevertheless, the book successfully brings to life the patriotic Revolutionary fighters." Best Sellers

y **Deep summer.** Crowell [1964 c1937] 258p $5.95

A reissue of the original edition published 1937

"A story of Louisiana in the last quarter of the eighteenth century. The heroine is Judith Sheramy, daughter of Puritan Connecticut farmer folk who migrate to the South when bad times strike their northern country. On the way they encounter Philip Larne, scion of an aristocratic South Carolina family, and these two, so different in temperament and upbringing, fall in love and marry. The novel covers the course of their married life thru calm days and turbulent ones." Book Rev Digest

Followed by: The handsome road

also in Bristow, G. Gwen Bristow's Plantation trilogy p 1-258

y **Gwen Bristow's Plantation trilogy; Deep summer, The handsome road [and] This side of glory.** . . . Crowell 1962 812p $8.95

An omnibus volume of the three titles published originally 1937, 1938 and 1940, respectively and entered separately

"The historical background material for each book was supplied by the author especially for this volume." Title page

y **The handsome road.** Crowell 1968 [c1938] 268p $5.95

A reissue of the title first published 1938

Some of the families portrayed in the author's "Deep summer", entered above, appear again in this story

"Uneducated but ambitious, Corrie May, a pretty, poor white girl, envies the ample life of the Larnes, rich Louisiana plantation owners, in whose home she sometimes works. The story, colorful and dramatic, though somewhat biased in its concern with a social problem, contrasts the lives of Corrie May, disillusioned and hardened by injustice, and the aristocratic Mrs Denis Larne, and follows them into the Civil War and the Reconstruction period. Corrie May, after a brief hour of triumph in which she takes her turn 'walking up the handsome road' with a thieving carpetbagger, decides at long last that her little illegitimate son, sturdily earning his own way is better off, with his strength to make new traditions, than the Larne boy, 'perfect embodiment of a tradition that no longer has any reason for existence.'" N Y Libraries

Followed by: This side of glory

also in Bristow, G. Gwen Bristow's Plantation trilogy p263-530

y **Jubilee Trail.** Crowell 1950 564p $7.50

"The story of Garnet Cameron who, in 1844, exchanges wealth and position for an adventurous pioneer life with Oliver Hale. After a glamorous honeymoon in New Orleans, where they meet the beautiful and mysterious Florinda, they travel via St. Louis to Santa Fe, and then start in the difficult trek over the Jubilee Trail to Los Angeles. There she learned, tragically, of her young husband's

Bristow, Gwen—*Continued*

weakness, and faced treachery and despair. And there, too, she learned how to meet life without compromise and, finally, with the help of John Ives, found the real meaning of love." Huntting

"A long but colorful novel which recreates vividly the arduous journey over the Santa Fe trail and the crudeness of the early California settlements." Booklist

y This side of glory. Crowell 1940 400p $5.95

Sequel to: Deep summer and The handsome road

The third of Miss Bristow's novels placed in Louisiana continues with the Larnes and the Upjohns and the old plantation of Ardeth. In this book the story is brought down to the period following the first World war

"It is strongest in its reconstruction of a period and its sidelights on local history, though its romance if hackneyed, is interesting." Book of the Month Club News

also in Bristow, G. Gwen Bristow's Plantation trilogy p535-812

y Tomorrow is forever. Crowell 1943 259p o.p. 1970

"The story of Elizabeth Heriong who knew war as only a woman can know it—her husband had been killed in the first World War. A clean break from the town where they had lived was Elizabeth's only salvation—she went to California and began life anew—and her second marriage, her children, and their home kept her busy and made her forget . . . until the day she came face to face with her first husband—reclaimed from the dead. The author reveals—with understanding and sympathy—Elizabeth's courageous solution to a situation as strange as it was intolerable.' Huntting

"It will appeal to a universal audience of woman who are seeing their own sons going off to 'another war', but strangely enough it will add to their fund of inner strength in the acceptance of these things." Book Week

Bromfield, Louis

A Bromfield galaxy: The green bay tree, Early autumn, A good woman. Harper 1957 639p o.p. 1970

Published 1924, 1926, and 1927, respectively. "these three panels of American life immediately aroused the enthusiasm of the critics and achieved very wide readership both here and abroad. Early Autumn was awarded the Pulitzer Prize." Foreword

"The green bay tree" is entered separately below

"Early autumn" concerns "the Pentland family and the Pentland tradition [which] are made alive in this story of life in a small New England town. The atmosphere and environment in which Olivia lived because she had married a Pentland are portrayed." Booklist

"A good woman" has for its central character a domineering woman who bends others to her will, with tragic consequences, especially on her son who is only partially successful in freeing himself from her domination

Early autumn

In Bromfield, L. Bromfield galaxy: The green bay tree, Early autumn, A good woman p217-403

A good woman

In Bromfield, L. Bromfield galaxy: The green bay tree, Early autumn, A good woman p405-639

The green bay tree. Stokes 1924 341p o.p. 1970

First in the tetralogy called "Escape"

The action of this story begins in one of the huge steel towns of the Middle West, where the mills had surrounded the ornate house and park known as Shane's Castle. John Shane had died ten years before the story opens but his widow still kept up a sort of feudal state, clothing her own arrogant pride with a semblance of aristocracy. The two daughters approaching womanhood, are in complete contrast to each other: Lily, voluptuous in her beauty, pleasure-loving, generous, ardent; Irene, repressed and neurotic, her tense gaze set even in girlhood toward the only possible life for her—that of a religious recluse. Lily at twenty realizes that she is no more monogamous than her father's son would probably have been. She has money enough to choose her own way of life, and she chooses to return to France where her school days had been spent. It is with her life there during the following twenty years—her home, her friendships, her loves, that the story is chiefly concerned." Book Rev Digest

also in Bromfield, L. Bromfield galaxy: The green bay tree, Early autumn, A good woman p5-216

Mrs Parkington. Harper 1943 330p o.p. 1970

"The story of a fabulously rich . . . old woman, worldly and indomitable. The daughter of a Nevada mining-town hotel-keeper, she married a robber baron and became famous and infamous on two continents. Now, at eighty-four, she has more zest and energy than any of her descendants. This is their story and hers—and the telling makes a multicolored exciting and richly crowded novel." Huntting

The rains came; a novel of modern India. Harper 1937 597p o.p. 1970

"A long novel dealing with life in a modern native Indian state. A group of people—Indians, Europeans and Americans, are working, some more, some less consciously and eagerly, to raise the state to a way of living equal to Occidental standards. Disaster, earthquake, flood, and plague wipe out many of their achievements, bring tragedy and death to some, but leave a remnant ready to go on." Book Rev Digest

Brontë, Anne

Agnes Grey

Some editions are:
Dufour $2.75
Oxford (World's classics) $2.75

"Anne Bronte's first novel, was published in December, 1847, a year and a half before her death, when she was twenty-seven years old. . . . The heroine, Agnes Grey, the daughter of a clergyman in the North of England, becomes, through reverses of fortune, a governess. Her experiences are those of Anne Brontë herself, the unpleasant side of such a position being set forth. The book, however, ends happily in the marriage of Agnes to a clergyman. Although well written, it lacks the elements of strength and warmth. It lives by the name of the author rather than by its intrinsic merit." Keller's Reader's Digest of Books

The tenant of Wildfell Hall

Some editions are:
Harcourt (The Harcourt Lib. of English and American classics) $3.95
Oxford (World's classics) $3.50

First published 1848

"Chiefly of biographical interest, giving the mournful story of Branwell Bronte's debased life, and meant as a warning example to young people." Baker's Best

Brontë, Charlotte

y Jane Eyre

Some editions are:
Dodd (Great illustrated classics) $4.50 With illustrations made up of drawings by contemporary artists and photographs from the Jane Eyre country, together with an introductory biographical sketch of the author and anecdotal captions by Basil Davenport
Dutton (Everyman's lib) $3.25
Harcourt (The Harcourt Lib. of English and American classics) $3.95
Macmillan (N Y) (The Macmillan classics) $3.95 Illustrated by Ati Forberg; afterword by Clifton Fadiman
Modern Lib. $2.95
Oxford (World's classics) $2.25
Watts, F. $8.95 Large type edition complete and unabridged. A Keith Jennison book
Watts, F. Ultratype edition $5.95 With a critical and biographical profile of Charlotte Brontë by Inga-Stina Ewbank
First published 1847

Brontë, Charlotte—*Continued*

An autobiographical novel of a strong woman who rebelled against the narrow social and religious conventions of her day. As a heroine, she is described as a plain faced creature, who loved the ugly but forceful Rochester. Many dramatic episodes occur before a tragedy finally reunites them

"A tale with an extraordinary atmosphere of passion and a 'Byronic hero with a sinful past,' Mr Rochester, it has remained the most popular of Charlotte's novels." The Reader's Guide to Everyman's Library

The professor

Some editions are:
Dutton (Everyman's lib) $2.95
Oxford (World's classics) $2.75

First published 1857
"A first study for [her later] Villette. Scene: the same pensionnat at Brussels, where a pair of unworldly characters . . . advance from sympathy to love." Baker's Best

Shirley

Some editions are:
Dutton (Everyman's lib) $2.95
Oxford (World classics) $3.50

First published 1849
"Against the background of a changing world at the beginning of the nineteenth century, the story of a spirited heiress, Shirley Keeldar, is told. The author patterned her after her own sister, Emily. Robert Moore, millowner in Yorkshire, introduces labor-saving devices which cause workmen's riots. He persists, in spite of financial and physical hazards, and wins his point with a promise to give more jobs, and provide better housing. Caroline Helstone, his gentle cousin, is seeking a meaning to her life. Dissatisfied with doing nothing, she marries Robert, whom she adores, and finds direction in her decision to help him. Shirley also is a new type of woman. She marries Robert's brother, Louis a tutor, who has as much spirit as she." Haydn. Thesaurus of Book Digests

Villette

Some editions are:
Dutton (Everyman's lib) $2.95
Harcourt (The Harcourt Lib. of English and American classics) $3.95
Oxford (World's classics) $2.75

First published 1853
Based on the author's experiences as a teacher in a school at Brussels
In Villette "Lucy Snowe, makes her way by teaching, as she watches unhappily John Bretton's infatuation for the flirt Ginevra Fanshawe, then falls in love herself with and transforms the professor, Monsieur Paul Emanuel." Haydn. Thesaurus of Book Digests

Brontë, Emily

y Wuthering Heights

Some editions are:
Dodd (Great illustrated classics) $4.50 With illustrations from paintings by contemporary artists and photographs from the Wuthering Heights country together with an introductory biographical sketch of the author and anecdotal captions by Basil Davenport
Harcourt (The Harcourt Lib. of English and American classics) $3.95
Macmillan (N Y) (The Macmillan classics) lib. bdg. $4.24 Illustrated by Bernarda Bryson. Afterword by Clifton Fadiman
Modern Lib $2.95
Oxford (World's classics) $2.25 With a preface and memoir of Emily and Anna Brontë by Charlotte Brontë and introduction by H. W. Garrod
Watts, F. $8.95 Large type edition complete and unabridged. A Keith Jennison book

First published 1847
Set against a somber background of the moorlands, this novel about Catherine Earnshaw and Heathcliff starts at Wuthering Heights, Catherine's childhood home
"A wild tale of terror and hatred among the rough people of the Yorkshire moors. The solitary novel of the sister of Charlotte Brontë. It is a work of true genius, and is considered by many critics the most brilliant contribution of the gifted Brontë sisters." Pratt Alcove

Brooks, Gwendolyn

Maud Martha; a novel. Harper 1953 180p o.p. 1970

"Maud Martha is a young colored girl growing up on Chicago's South Side, who yearns for no more than the common decencies, but who finds her way toward accomplishing them blocked in every direction by the restrictions of the white race. Her life, as viewed in a series of short episodes from childhood to motherhood, is an unremitting effort to find some kind of status and prestige in an environment which gives her nothing but shabbiness, second-class citizenship, and the subtler forms of race discrimination. Her plight is told in prose which has the rhythmic beauty of free verse." Booklist

Brown, Charles Brockden

Wieland; or, The transformation, together with Memoirs of Carwin the biloquist, a fragment; ed. with an introduction by Fred Lewis Pattee. Harcourt 1926 xlix, 351p (American authors ser) o.p. 1970

First published 1798
"Brown was the first American novelist to count in literary history. . . . A mysterious voice bids Wieland sacrifice his wife and children to show his obedience to Heaven; but this oracle is only another fanatic who happens to be a ventriloquist." Baker's Best

Brown, Harry

A walk in the sun. Knopf 1944 187p $3.95

"An American platoon, landing on the beach in Italy, loses its lieutenant, and then, in fairly quick succession, three sergeants. Finally a corporal takes over and leads the men toward a vaguely sensed objective—a farmhouse six miles inland—and there they accomplish the mission they were sent to perform." Book Rev Digest

"It is a gripping little tale, albeit unrestrained in spots, which the reader does not want to lay down having once begun it." Christian Science Monitor

Brown, Joe David

Kings go forth. Morrow 1956 256p o.p. 1970

"A story about two American artillery observers in action against the Germans during World War II. Italy and Southern France are the scenes in which Lieutenant Sam Loggins, recipient of a battlefield commission, nurses hatred for Sergeant Britt Harris after Harris has stolen Sam's girl with honeyed tactics and then drives the jilted girl to suicide. A hairraising reconnaissance mission brings with it a rout of the enemy and a fiendish personal revenge for Harris." Sat R

Brown, Morna Doris. See Ferrars, E. X.

Brunner, John

The devil's work. Norton 1970 365p $5.95

"Stephen Green has just left his English public school to come to live with his father in a boring little country town. He has previously been in the custody of his mother, an elegant and sophisticated woman, recently killed in a car crash. Stephen's father is a second-rate insurance salesman with pitiful social pretentions, living in a dreary house, occasionally sleeping with his housekeeper. Poor Stephen tries to adjust to this anti-intellectual atmosphere and to the double loss of his mother and the security of school. His gentle, cultivated ways make people, including his father, begin to suspect him of homosexuality, and he begins to doubt himself. It is at this crucial moment that the real corrupters arrive on the scene." Pub W

Stand on Zanzibar. Doubleday 1968 505p (Doubleday Science fiction) $6.95

"A massive novel of the world some forty years from now, when General Technics' famed computer Shalameser knows all, when Georgette Tallon Buckfast rules the great corporation, although she is 90 and about half prosthetics and half herself, and young Norman N. House, a junior V.P., who believes he is on the way to the top." Bk Buyer's Guide

Brunner, John—*Continued*

The publisher "classifies the whole thing as science fiction, but its far from the conventional science fiction-fantasy category of writing." Pub W

Bryan, C. D. B.

P. S. Wilkinson. Harper 1965 441p o.p. 1970

"The probably largely autobiographical story of Lt. P. S. Wilkinson, who acquits himself well in Korea, is rather unhappy at home, partly because his girl has married someone else, partly because he is a bit self-satisfied and selfish and can't fit in anywhere. The novel ends with his being recalled to the Army during the Berlin crisis." Bk Buyer's Guide

"P. S. is a very real person and this is a very good novel. His 'adventures,' seen against the background of world events, actually are appropriate and even mirror the muddled spirit of these years. P. S. is well-intentioned, but weak, confused and blundering; but he is occasionally strong enough to make a decision that is good, brave and meaningful." Library J

Bryan, Courtlandt Dixon Barnes. See Bryan, C. D. B.

Bryan, J. Y.

Come to the bower; a novel. Viking 1963 496p o.p. 1970

In 1835 Perry Allan, a young lawyer, leaves New Orleans and Camilla, the young widow he loves, to aid in the Texan war for independence. The novel details the events of the war from the Alamo to the final struggle at San Jacinto where the Texans defeated the Mexican general Santa Anna. It is also the story of Camilla's long journey into Texas seeking Perry in a wilderness of ragged armies and fleeing refugees. (Publisher)

"Bryan's pioneer and battle scenes are not pretty but are encompassing and compassionate. He uses dialect extensively, spelled by ear, a flavorful and poetic evocation of speech and thought. Crowds of characters and their dirty, vital life are crammed into the novel whose theme is that love is the only answer to death and destruction." Booklist

Bryan, Jack Yeaman. See Bryan, J. Y.

Bryher

Beowulf; a novel. Pantheon Bks. 1956 201p $4.50

"Originally published in French to acquaint the British author's friends on the continent with wartime conditions in London, this novel now appears in its first English edition. It is a series of impressions of two elderly British ladies who run a tea shop, their staff, customers, and the assorted roomers who occupy the upper floors of the building. Their reactions, before and after the Warming Pan [tea shop] is blitzed, are homely lifelike exemplifications of the English spirit in adversity, as symbolize by the life-sized plaster bulldog which one of the ladies brings home for a mascot." Booklist

"The traces of sentimentality in the book are more the result of embarrassment in the face of great feeling than they are evidence of softness in the writer or in any of her many appealing people. It is a touching work, with a splendidly characteristic last line." New Yorker

y The coin of Carthage. Harcourt 1963 240p boards $4.50

"A Helen and Kurt Wolff book"

A novel about "the ancient world of Rome and Carthage [at the time of the Second Punic War] the ordinary ways of life in rural Italy and northern Africa—farming, sheepherding, trading, festivals—and their cruel dislocation by the endless warfare. One thread weaves together the stories of the people, Roman or Carthaginian—the lives of two Greek traders who adapt themselves ingeniously to fortune, wherever they are." Pub W

"The novel is constructed like a mosaic: the interactions of lives of several major and a number of minor characters present finally a delicate, somber picture of the wasteful and needless war between two great powers." Booklist

The colors of Vaud. Harcourt 1969 136p $4.75

"A Helen and Kurt Wolff book"

"In the late eighteenth century, the canton of Vaud in Switzerland was struggling for independence from Berne. Young Sophie, half English and half Swiss, took a part in this revolutionary activity, hoping to win her own freedom too, from the restraints imposed by her elders." Bk Buyer's Guide

"The little group of men and women, boys and girls about whom Bryher writes are very real, but nothing very dramatic or exciting happens to them, even under the impact of impending revolution." Pub W

The fourteenth of October; a novel. Pantheon Bks. 1952 223p $3

"A Saxon youth taken as a hostage by marauding Danes is sold to a Norman lord, only to make his escape and return to England to fight for his country under Harald at the Battle of Hastings. As the Normans conquer he knows that he can never accept their rule and must choose the life of a sea raider rather than submit." Pub W

Gate to the sea. Pantheon Bks. 1958 128p illus boards $3.95

Set in the ancient Greek city of Paestum, south of Naples, in the fourth century B.C. this novel tells the story of Harmonia, the priestess and guardian of the Poseidonian relics as she faces the increasing power of the Lucanian conquerors. How Harmonia is saved at a moment of utter peril and leads a little band of exiles to the rescue ship is told here. (Publisher)

"Tense as is the plot, it is but secondary to the picture which the author draws of a conquered city and of the varying spirits of ancient times. This is done with superb scholarship and unusual literary skill." Christian Science Monitor

The player's boy; a novel. Pantheon Bks. 1953 201p $3.50

"A novel that re-creates the atmosphere of the Elizabethan and Jacobean theater through the life and death of one James Sands, actor's apprentice. His loyalty to the great age that is passing, symbolized by the heroic figure of Sir Walter Raleigh, is the center of Sands' existence and he comes to a tragic end himself because he cannot compromise with honor." Pub W

"It catches the spirit of the 17th century English stage." Library J

y Roman wall; a novel. Pantheon Bks. 1954 219p $3.95

"A historical novel of the third century which is set at a military outpost near Lake Geneva. The great Roman empire is crumbling, soon to be over-run by hordes of barbarians and three men—Valerious, the good soldier; Demetrius, the migrant trader; and Vinodius, the Roman governor—face the danger in entirely different ways." Retail Bookseller

"Bryher notes with perception the break-up of the outer reaches of Rome and draws a parallel (by inference) to modern conditions of politics and aggrandizement. Her writing, as usual, is deft and impressive, as exemplified in her treatment of the major characters, all of whom knew (however mutely or eloquently) that the old order was changing." Wis Lib Bul

y Ruan. Pantheon Bks. 1960 190p map boards $3.50

"The novel is set in Sixth Century Britain, Cornwall, the Sicily islands, Ireland and Wales. It follows the adventures of a young man who prefers to hunt for unknown distant isles rather than to take his inherited position of Druid priest. Its theme is man's aspiration to be himself, to escape to that kind of life which to him is freedom—'The promise of the far isles.'" San Francisco Chronicle

Bryher—*Continued*

"Unobtrusive details give Bryher's books their distinctive flavor, their ability to so perfectly evoke the past. . . . The ceremony of the King's burial and the voyage to the Islands of the Dead seen through the boy Ruan's eyes . . . the descriptions of the flowers, the woods, and the sea are all Bryher-like and lovely." Sat R

This January tale. Harcourt 1966 181p $4.50

"Set mostly in Exeter, England, in 1068, when Duke William of Normandy laid siege to the city and vanquished it, the plot follows the fortunes of a Saxon blacksmith's family which fled by sea from Exeter in that black January. The family's adventures, their trials and homesickness are individual and poignant and true in detail to the historical background. Yet they have a timeless quality: the emotions might be those of many of the displaced persons of our own times. The slow, deliberate near-poetry of Bryher's style perfectly fits her tale." Pub W

The novel "is spare and lean, but alive with color, with sound and smell, with people who must suffer from the ambitions of others." Best Sellers

Buchan, John

Adventurers all. . . . Houghton [1942] 3v in 1 $6.95

"Sir Richard Hannay, Sir Edward Leithen [and others] . . . containing Huntingtower. John Macnab [and] The three hostages." Subtitle

Originally published separately 1922, 1925 and 1924, respectively

y Adventures of Richard Hannay. . . . Houghton 1939 3v in 1 $10

Contents: The thirty-nine steps; Greenmantle; Mr Standfast

A series of good adventure stories dealing with the work of the British Intelligence Service before and during the first European War. The first two titles are entered separately below

Greenmantle. Nelson 1957 376p (Nelson classics) $1.75

First published 1916 by Houghton

"A good adventure story of the European war dealing with the work of English secret service agents in Constantinople. The object of their mission is to foil an attempt of the Germans to stir up a holy war in the East." Pittsburgh

"The fact that the author wrote it while in active service accounts for the vividness of some of its details." Cleveland

also in Buchan, J. Adventures of Richard Hannay v2

also in Haycraft, H. ed. Five spy novels p163-342

Huntingtower
In Buchan, J. Adventurers all v 1

John Macnab
In Buchan, J. Adventurers all v2

Mr Standfast
In Buchan, J. Adventures of Richard Hannay v3

Mountain meadow; with an introduction by Howard Swiggett. Houghton 1941 xlviii, 276p o.p. 1970

Published in England under title: Sick heart river

"The story of Sir Edward Leithen's last adventure. Warned by his physician that he has but a year to live, he resolves that, come what may, he will 'die on his feet.' At that moment, along comes Blenkiron, his old American comrade of the First World War, with a new quest to be undertaken—Francis Gaillard, an important New York banker, has disappeared. It is a chance to die standing and Leithen takes it, and his adventures, as he follows his man to the frozen north, make a moving and memorable book." Ontario Lib Rev

"The book's philosophical tone will limit its appeal somewhat. The introduction by Howard Swiggett gives interesting comments on the author's complete series of novels." Booklist

y The thirty-nine steps. Nelson 170p (Nelson classics) $1.75

First published in this edition 1922, combined with "The power-house." This edition is reset and reprinted 1960

"An ante-bellum mystery story in which the English hero, in order to foil an international conspiracy, incurs the suspicion of murder and exposes himself to the double risk of capture by the police and assassination by the members of a powerful and relentless secret society." Cleveland

"Modeled on the 'shilling shocker' but distinguished by just that quality of literary amenity which the shocker conspicuously lacks." Spec

also in Buchan, J. Adventures of Richard Hannay v 1

The three hostages
In Buchan, J. Adventurers all v3

Buchard, Robert

Thirty seconds over New York; tr. from the French by June P. Wilson and Walter B. Michaels. Morrow 1970 218p $5.95

Original French edition published 1969

This novel "explores the fatal possibility of undeclared nuclear war. Brilliantly plotted, the novel moves breathlessly between Paris and China, the White House and Omaha, and finally the mid-Atlantic and New York to chronicle, step by agonizing step, the plot of a deranged Chinese colonel to provoke total war by dropping a nuclear bomb on America's largest city." News of Books

"The most interesting parts concern the non-adventures of a solitary Chinese agent in Paris and the moments when the Red Alert is on in the U.S." Pub W

Buck, Pearl S.
Nobel Prize in literature, 1938

Command the morning; a novel. Day 1959 317p $6.95

"This stars fictitious characters but traces actual events in its portrayal of the group of scientists who, in Chicago on December 2, 1942, ushered in the atomic age by producing the first self-sustaining chain reaction. Ranging from Chicago to Oak Ridge and from Washington to Los Alamos the novel emphasizes the changes in the private and professional lives of persons burdened with awesome responsibility and gnawing guilt. The author has diligently explored the background of her story, and, although the characterizations are commonplace, the novel sustains interest." Booklist

Dragon seed. Day 1942 378p $7.95

The story of the farmer Ling Tan, and his wife and sons and daughters. The scene is outside and inside the walls of Nanking just before the Japanese assault and the fall of the city

"As war propaganda, the message which this book brings is terrific. And, to Mrs. Buck's honor, be it recorded that it is not so much anti-Japanese propaganda as a wider and deeper propaganda which becomes antibestiality and antidictatorship wherever that monster lifts its head." Christian Science Monitor

Followed by: The promise

East wind: west wind. Day 1930 277p $5.95

"The conflict between the old China and the new is the theme of this absorbing, delicately written chronicle. The daughter of a noble family, trained for wifehood in the old customs and traditions and betrothed since childhood, is married to a Chinese of the new era who has received his medical training in America. It is only by adopting the Western habits which her husband esteems, that the little bride finds love and happiness. Her brother's love for an American girl is another phase of the conflict." Cleveland

Buck, Pearl S.—*Continued*

First wife, and other stories. Day 1933 312p
o.p. 1970

Analyzed in Short Story Index
Contents: First wife; Old mother; The frill;
The quarrel; Repatriated; Rainy day; Wang
Lung; Communist; Father Andrea; New road;
Barren spring; The refugees; Fathers and
mothers; Good river

y Fourteen stories. Day 1961 250p $5.95

Analyzed in Short Story Index
"A collection of short stories written by the
author from 1943 to the present. In these, the
author writes of the nature and customs of
Asian people, the relationships of East to
West, universal family life, and the interplay
between man and woman." McClurg. Book
News
Contents: A certain star; The beauty; Enchantment; With a delicate air; Beyond language; Parable of plain people; The Commander and the Commissar; Begin to live; The engagement; Melissa; Gift of laughter; Death and
the dawn; The silver butterfly; Francesca

God's men. Day 1951 375p $7.95

"Out of their childhood background as sons
of missionaries to China two men derive opposite beliefs in man's needs. Kindly, poor, uneducated Clem spends his life providing cheap
food for everyone, believing that it will cure
their ills. William, arrogant, college bred scorns
the masses whom he thinks are sheep, providing them with mental pablum through his chain
of tabloid newspapers. Their lives are linked
through marriages; their viewpoints never
meet. An absorbing story with appeal for men
and women. For public libraries." Library J

The good deed, and other stories of Asia,
past and present. Day 1969 254p $5.95

This collection "includes ten delightful stories, all warm and humorous glimpses of Asian
life and culture." Cincinnati
Contents: The courtyards of peace; Letter
home; Dagger in the dark; The green sari; The
sacred skull; Sunrise at Juhu; The cockfight;
Duet in Asia; Going home; The good deed
"Six of these ten short stories have never
been published before. Many have World War
II settings in China and Korea and reflect wartime emotions and predicaments. . . . The stories are simply told, old-fashioned yet with an
understanding of the 1960's." Library J

y The good earth

Some editions are:
Day $5.95
Watts, F. $9.95 Large type edition complete and
unabridged. A Keith Jennison book
First published 1931
Pulitzer Prize, 1932
This first volume of a trilogy of Chinese life
in pre-war days tells the "story of a Chinese
peasant and his passionate, dogged accumulation of land and more land, while weathering
famine and drought and revolution. Authentic
in its portrayal of Chinese life and character,
and of universal appeal." N Y Libraries
"There is simple dignity of style, easy flow
of narrative, firmness of character drawing,
above all wealth of detail in The Good Earth,
detail which builds up solidly and securely a
scene in which men and women move and grow
and meet and act upon one another as in life."
Outlook
Followed by: Sons

also in Buck, P. S. The house of earth:
The good earth; Sons; A house
divided v 1

The hidden flower. Day 1952 308p $6.95

A "novel about a mixed marriage. The heroine is a beautiful, aristocratic Japanese girl;
her husband, who met her in Japan during the
Occupation, is a member of a prominent Virginia family. The marriage, resented by both
families, came to an end when Josui, realizing
the impossibility of her situation, went back
to her life as a Japanese. She entrusts her son
to a woman doctor to be raised." Book Rev
Digest
"Though the descriptions of Japanese landscape and customs are interesting, the characters are not presented with enough force to
arouse our sympathy." Library J

A house divided. Day 1935 353p $6.95

This concludes the trilogy which opened with
The Good Earth and continued with Sons.
China in revolution is its scene, the dilemma
of the modern, educated young men and
women its theme. Yuan, son of Wang the Tiger,
grandson of Wang Lung spends some years in
America as a student. He returns to find his
country greatly changed and torn by the conflict between Eastern and Western forces, with
the latter in ascendancy. Yuan marries a girl of
his own race and class and resolves to forward the cause of the New China by teaching
students modern methods of agriculture."
Book Rev Digest
"Mrs. Buck has made China live for a reader,
but her theme outstretches locality—it is humanity, anywhere,—and we notice its universality particularly in this last volume." Cath
World

also in Buck, P. S. The house of earth:
The good earth; Sons; A house
divided v3

The house of earth: The good earth; Sons;
A house divided. Day 1935 3v in 1 o.p. 1970

A trilogy of Chinese life in pre-war days
"Good earth" was first published 1931,
"Sons" in 1932, "A house divided" in 1935, all
entered separately. The publishers state that the
author revised "Good earth' and that it has
been completely reset

y Imperial woman; a novel. Day 1956 376p
$7.95

"A biographical novel about Tzu-hsi, last
Empress of China, known as Old Buddha. Her
life is pictured from the day she received the
Imperial summons to appear before the Emperor, to her death in 1908." Book Rev Digest
"The accuracy or lack of accuracy will probably be of no particular concern to the readers of 'Imperial Woman.' . . . The details of the
secluded life in the Forbidden City, the political jugglings of the court, and the increasing
pressure from the Western powers as the Manchu Dynasty breaks up—these contribute to
the novel's movement." N Y Times Bk R

Kinfolk. Day 1949 406p $7.95

" 'Kinfolk' presents a provocative paradox:
Dr. Liang Wen Hua, distinguished scholar and
champion of an ancient culture, has reared his
children in New York, center of the modern,
materialistic civilization he despises. But all
except one of his four children, though products of Western education, return to their ancestral home when they become adult. It is
the elder son, idealistic young Dr. James
Liang, who sacrifices his love for beautiful
Lili Li and a promising career in New York, in
order to discover the heart of old China and to
serve his countrymen." N Y Times Bk R

y Letter from Peking; a novel. Day 1957
252p $5.95

This novel "deals largely with the devotion
of an American wife of a part-Chinese university president, living in Vermont with her
teen-aged son while her husband remains at his
post in Peking. Even when her husband asks
her permission to take another wife, the
heroine's love for him does not falter. There
is also the story of the son's problems in
growing up." Pub W
"Mrs. Buck has brought to this East-West
story all the sensitive empathy and warm-heart-
edness that have so generally characterized her
creative work, plus a dependable skill in saying, graciously and finely, precisely what she
wants to say." N Y Her Trib Books

y The living reed; a novel. Day 1963 478p
$7.95

"Pearl Buck tells the history of Korea
through the story of four generations of the
remarkable and patriotic Kim family. Kim Il-
han, adviser to the ill-fated Queen of Korea,
as his father was to the King, lived to see his
sons and his grandsons driven from power as
aristocrats and become engrossed in new
causes and ideas in the struggle for Korean
independence. Il-han sees his elder son, Yul-
chun, go underground because of the Japanese
occupation, join the revolutionary forces in
China, suffer disillusionment, and return to
Korea with his communist-reared son, Sasha.

Buck, Pearl S.—*Continued*

II-han sees his younger son marry a Christian and be killed with his wife and daughter during the Japanese persecution. It is through his two grandsons, Sasha, the Russian-influenced North Korean, and Liang, the Western-oriented South Korean, that II-han recognizes the forces at work in Korea today. Specifically, the novel traces the events from 1881 to the Korean War in 1952." Best Sellers

"Actual historical personages, including Woodrow Wilson and several of our consuls and other emissaries, are introduced, somewhat in the style of Upton Sinclair's Lanny Budd series. Miss Buck's admirers will surely want to read the book, which reflects once more her humanity and sympathy for the weak and powerless." Book of the Month Club News

The mother. Day 1934 302p $6.95

This "novel centers about one woman, a full-blooded, passionate peasant and her small patch of land. Cheated, by her husband's desertion, of the normal life and the many children she had anticipated, she slaves to support the three she has, with a blind, dogged devotion that achieves its reward at last in a grandchild. The characters are types, without names; the story is somber and extremely frank about physical facts; its appeal lies in its somewhat sentimental picturization of the universality of mother love." Booklist

"It is written in the same biblical style as 'The Good Earth.' It has the same tragic overtones, the same calm melody. It has not the cosmic power that was in the pages of 'The Good Earth,' but it has the same deep and rich and rooted reality." Chicago Daily Tribune

The new year; a novel. Day 1968 255p $5.95

Kim "the half-Korean 12-year-old son of an American. [Christopher Winters]. who sired him during the Korean War, is brought to this country and is taken into his father's household at the insistence of the man's understanding wife. The father is campaigning for Governor [of Pennsylvania] at the start of the story and wins the election. The climax comes when he and his wife give a New Year's Eve party and introduce their son to the assembled guests." Pub W

The book "is pure propaganda. yet Miss Buck. with her passionate concern for all neglected children, makes it effective in an obvious way. Anyone criticizing the novel harshly may be at as much disadvantage as an avowed enemy of motherhood and monogamy. [The author's] status is too high, her good will too pervasive to fault her for style." Book of the Month Club News

Pavilion of women. Day 1946 316p $6.95

"The Pavilion of the title is the great house of the wealthy Wu family, oldest and most powerful of a provincial Chinese city, over which presides, in the weakness of her amiable husband, Madame Wu. The story is of her acquisition of true wisdom and understanding after her 40th birthday, largely through the agency of a saintlike foreign priest." Am News of Bks

"It is a searching, adult study of women written with high seriousness and sympathy, which should find a multitude of women readers. Mrs Buck's grave unaccented prose is well suited to the delicate matters at hand." N Y Times Bk R

Peony. Day 1948 312p $6.95

The story of Peony, sold as a child into a rich Jewish home in China [of 100 years ago] brought up as a bondmaid, one who is more than a servant, less than a daughter. She grows into a provocative and lovely girl and falls in love with the only son of the house. But tradition forbids her to be his wife. How she deals with her love, how she controls her destiny— and his too—make the story

The promise. Day 1943 248p $5.95

This book "carries the story begun in 'Dragon Seed' through the tragedy of North Burma in the Spring of 1942. The setting is southwestern China, Burma and India, and the tale takes in the complex relations between Chinese, Burmese, British and Americans [and] the meaning of the war for the people of China and the world." Huntting

"Sometimes the plot is sacrificed to the theme of racial equality and justice which has been the burden of perhaps most of the author's . . . work. But obtrusive as this may seem to some, this novel is a gripping and thrilling tale of daring adventure, heroic sacrifice and reckless devotion to a great cause, and of elemental romance." Book Week

Sons. Day 1932 467p $8.50

This second volume of a trilogy, which begins with The good earth, tells the story of Wang Lung's three sons who after the death of their father "are in great haste to divide the many fields he had spent his lifetime accumulating. It is with the third son, fierce, haughty and hungry-eyed, and the use he makes of his patrimony, that the story is mainly concerned. His rise and fall as a petty warlord, and his molding of his son to succeed him, only to have him revert to the land of his grandfather, make interesting reading though less gripping than the earlier novel." N Y Libraries

Followed by: A house divided

also in Buck, P. S. The house of earth: The good earth; Sons; A house divided v2

y The three daughters of Madame Liang; a novel. Day 1969 315p $6.95

"Madame Liang is the owner of the most exclusive and fashionable restaurant in Shanghai. In spite of Communist scrutiny . . . she manages to provide gourmet foods and elegant service to her customers. . . . Madame Liang had three daughters (Grace, Mercy, Joy) who were all sent to America to be educated. [They] all come into the story and show the conflicting aspects and dimensions of the new China emerging from the old." Best Sellers

(tr.) Shui hu chuan. All men are brothers

Buckmaster, Henrietta

All the living; a novel of one year in the life of William Shakespeare. Random House 1962 523p o.p. 1970

This is the story of Shakespeare's love for two women and a re-creation of Elizabethan England with the Globe Theatre at its center. It is against this background that Will Shakespeare lives his most crucial year; the mysterious Dark Lady of the Sonnets is seen as both beautiful and malign; Anne Hathaway, his wife, is described as a vivid human being. (Publisher)

"The author does not really reveal the nature of genius, but the picture of a decent and tormented man is cumulatively impressive. The novel's style, a compound of literary Elizabethan speech and quotations from Shakespeare's writings, will disturb all but the tenacious, seasoned reader of historical fiction. The novel is uneven, but its theatrical color, evidence of solid research, and enigmatic hero commend it." Booklist

The lion in the stone; a novel. Harcourt 1968 464p $6.95

"The year is 1969, at the opening of the 25th Session of the General Assembly. The UN, having resolved the Vietnam War, must now take action on an alarming confrontation between Russia and China over Mongolia. It is a period of tense and weary trial for Devar Morogoda, Ceylonese Secretary-General of the UN, who rejects nuclear-power politics. . . . During the same weeks, he also has a personal crisis, the discovery of his love for Senta, his brother's estranged Norwegian wife." Library J

"Essentially, [it] is a political tract in fictional form arguing the case for subordination of national interests to an international authority." N Y Times Bk R

Budd, Lillian

y April harvest. Duell 1959 309p o.p. 1970

The final novel of a trilogy including April snow, entered below and Land of strangers

This novel "tells a sentimental story about a Swedish-American girl's triumph over poverty and her romance with a doctor with whom she finds true love at last." Pub W

Budd, Lillian—*Continued*

April snow. Lippincott 1951 317p $4.50

"A story of a peasant woman's life in Sweden in the later years of the nineteenth century. Sigrid, married early to a fanatic, domineering, selfish man, bears a child every year, and works incessantly but faces life courageously and even joyously. Tragedy enters her life because of one or two of her children but finally the tale ends happily for Sigrid and those she loved best." Book Rev Digest

"'April Snow,' despite its privations, its bitterness, its cruelties of man and nature, is actually an idyll." Chicago Sunday Tribune

Buechner, Frederick

The entrance to Porlock. Atheneum Pubs. 1970 [c1969] 270p $5.95

"Peter Ringkoping, owner of a second-hand bookshop in New England, sets out with his two sons and a grandson to visit a community for retarded adults. Peter, now in his eighties, plans to turn over to the leader, an old friend, a substantial tract of land. But the physical facts of the journey are accompanied by mysticism and an almost dreamlike discovery of identities." Bk Buyer's Guide

"There appears every now and again a lyrical, dreamlike novel that is more poem than prose, more parable than story. Such novels incapacitate conventional critical faculties; we do not understand and evaluate them rationally but rather are immersed, lulled, and transported, as in listening to music, into an obscure, shadowy world where feelings are evoked and nothing is explained. 'The Entrance to Porlock' is that kind of novel. One is not sure after reading it whether one has read or imagined it. . . . Beyond his originality of characters and mood . . . Buechner is further distinguished by his use of language." Christian Science Monitor

The return of Ansel Gibbs. Knopf 1958 [c1957] 308p o.p. 1970

Ansel Gibbs, summoned from retirement to a post in the President's cabinet, stops in New York en route to Washington. There he learns that his daughter, Anne, may be in love with Robin Tripp, a television interviewer. Gibbs agrees to appear on Tripp's program with Senator Farwell who is opposed to the Senate's confirming Gibb's appointment. The result of their confrontation makes up the story. (Publisher)

"Mr. Buechner has written sympathetically and perceptively about the emotional blind spots of the highly civilized egghead, and about the dilemmas that face the critical and self-critical mind, constantly in modulation, when it is challenged by demagoguery." Atlantic

Bulgakov, Mikhail

Black snow; a theatrical novel; tr. from the Russian by Michael Glenny. Simon & Schuster [1968 c1967] 190p $4.50

First published in the August 1965 issue of a Russian literary monthly under the title: A theatrical novel

An autobiographical novel "based on Bulgakov's experiences with his novel The White Guard which was dramatized as The Days of the Turbins and produced in 1926. 'Sergi Leontievich Maxudov' is a struggling author when a producer at the Independent Theater approaches him with the possibility of adapting his unsuccessful novel for the stage. Caught up in the . . . theatrical whirl, Maxudov is enchanted at first, until even his . . . naïveté is shaken by the constant feuds among the personnel." Pub W

"Bulgakov's most savage barbs are reserved for the generally respected Moscow Art Theater and its universally revered genius, Konstantin Stanislavsky, flimsily disguised as the 'Independent Theater' and 'Ivan Vasilievich.' . . . Bulgakov does recognize Stanislavsky's mastery as actor, but in every other respect he debunks him mercilessly as a vain, eccentric autocrat devoid of taste. . . . There are many marvelous vignettes in this witty novel. . . . Bulgakov's power of satirical observation and his ability to write natural dialogue [make this book with its smooth translation] a delight to read and a delectable inside view of the Soviet theater and intelligentsia." Sat R

The heart of a dog

Some editions are:
Grove $3.95 Translated by Mirra Ginsburg
Harcourt $3.95 Translated with an introduction by Michael Glenny. A Helen and Kurt Wolff book

First published 1968

This book is a satire on Soviet man and Soviet society. "A world-famous Russian surgeon specializing in rejuvenation techniques transplants human glands into a dog and turns him into a man—of sorts. Idle, slovenly, foulmouthed, he ends up as a Commissar 'for the elimination of vagrant quadrupeds,' and a menace to men and women as well." Publisher's note

This work "firmly establishes Bulgakov as one of the few truly great writers produced by the Soviet Union during the half-century of its existence, and also as that nation's most accomplished satirist." Sat R

The Master and Margarita

Some editions are:
Grove $5.95 Translated from the Russian by Mirra Ginsburg
Harper $5.95 Translated from the Russian by Michael Glenny

First appeared in Russian in the magazine Moskva in late 1966 and early 1967

A mysterious stranger arrives in Moscow in the 1930's and describes the Crucifixion. He is Satan. "The Master of the title is an inmate of a lunatic asylum, driven there by critics and publishers who scorned his masterpiece, a novel about the Crucifixion. His mistress, Margarita, wins her freedom by her dealings with Satan. It is through the intervention of Christ that the two lovers at last find peace." Pub W

"Since there is no doubt that every library in the land should acquire at least one copy, the problem arises: which edition? This is not easy to answer, because this time the competition between the publishers succeeded only too well. Both translations are excellent. Miss Ginsburg's 'forte' seems to be her Russian, while Mr. Glenny's is his command of the English language. Thus her translation is on the balance more faithful, but occasionally more awkward. Mr. Glenny takes more liberties with his Russian, but achieves a smoothly flowing, poetic and perceptive English text. Thus, the Grove edition may be more suitable for the academic, and the Harper one for the public libraries." Library J

Bulwer-Lytton, Sir Edward

y The last days of Pompeii

Some editions are:
Dodd (Great illustrated classics) $4.50 Illustrated with a portrait of the author and photographs and drawings of Pompeii. With an introduction by Curtis Dahl
Dutton (Everyman's lib) $3.25 Introduction by the Earl of Lytton

First published 1834

"The simple story relates principally to two young people of Grecian origin, Glaucus and Ione, who are deeply attached to each other. The former is a handsome young Athenian, impetuous, high-minded, and brilliant, while Ione is a pure and lofty-minded woman. Arbaces, her guardian, the villain of the story, under a cloak of sanctity and religion, indulges in low and criminal designs. His character is strongly drawn; and his passion for Ione, and the struggle between him and Glaucus, form the chief part of the plot. . . . The book, full of learning and spirit, is not only a charming novel, but contains many minute and interesting descriptions of ancient customs; among which, those relating to the gladiatorial combat, the banquet, the bath, are most noteworthy." Keller's Reader's Digest of Books

Bunin, Ivan

Nobel Prize in literature, 1933

The gentleman from San Francisco; authorized tr. from the Russian by Bernard Guilbert Guerney. Knopf 313p o.p. 1970

First published in 1923 by Seltzer, and analyzed in Short Story Index

Contents: Dreams of Chang; Compatriot; Brethren; Gautami; The son; Light breathing; An evening in spring; Sacrifice; Aglaia; Grammar of love; Night conversation; Goodly life; "I say nothing"; Death; Gentleman from San Francisco

Bunyan, John

y The Pilgrim's progress

Some editions are:
Dodd (Great illustrated classics) $4.50 Including an introduction to the book and a note on the William Blake designs by A. K. Adams, together with an essay on John Bunyan by Thomas Babington Macaulay. 16 pages of illustrations, including reproductions of the frontispiece and 8 designs for the first part, by William Blake
Dutton $3.50 Illustrated by Frank C. Papé
Dutton $3.25 (Everyman's lib) Introduction and notes by G. B. Harrison
Grosset $2.95 Illustrated by Leonard Vosburgh. Has title: The Pilgrim's progress from this world to that which is to come
Nelson (Nelson classics) $1.75
Oxford (World's classics) $2.25
Zondervan $3.95
Zondervan (Great religious books ser) $2.95

First published 1678
"The 'immortal allegory,' next to the Bible the most widely known book in religious literature. It was written in Bedford jail, where Bunyan was for twelve years a prisoner for his convictions. It describes the troubled journey of Christian and his companions through this life to a triumphal entrance into the Celestial city. Bunyan 'wrote with virgin purity utterly free from mannerisms and affectations; and without knowing himself for a writer of fine English, produced it.'" Pratt Alcove

Burdick, Eugene

y Fail-safe, by Eugene Burdick & Harvey Wheeler. McGraw 1962 286p boards $6.95

"What might happen, sometime in the future, if in a missile raid warning which proved a false alarm, one group of bombers was by fateful accident, not given its recall and flew on towards Moscow with nuclear bombs. The scene is, mostly Washington, the President's air raid shelter, where he has a private telephone wire to Khrushchev." Pub W

"This book is both a novel and an essay on the end of man. . . . As a novel, it is a swiftly paced, ingeniously constructed suspense story —in many ways the most unusual suspense story ever written. What makes it unique is that the ingredients that have gone into it have never existed until now. . . . The novel is less about an ultimate war between one nation and another than it is about the ultimate war between man and his machines. It is in this sense that the book becomes an essay on man—and a powerful one. It indicates that as man has gone up in the order of power he has gone down in the order of control. . . . Any book that gives people a glimpse of reality in our time is a precious commodity in the world." Sat R

The ninth wave. Houghton 1956 332p o.p. 1970

"Traces the rise from poverty of Mike Freesmith, a California politician. Early in his nefarious career Mike learned that fear plus hate equal power, and he played his knowledge for all it was worth. Just as he was on the point of gaining complete control of the state, he was met by disaster." Book Rev Digest

(jt. auth.) Lederer, W. J. The ugly American

Burgess, Alan

The word for love. Dutton 1968 319p boards $5.95

"Love, marriage, and personal fulfillment concern Burgess in a novel of modern Southern Rhodesia. William Field, inspector of police, caught in an unrewarding marriage and accused of the rape of an African housemaid relates his search for love in flashbacks. . . . Field's love for the daughter of a wealthy colonist is returned and the novel closes with a measure of happiness and honor." Booklist

"The picture of a beautiful land torn by racism and of the violent, divergent people who keep it in turbulence, is compelling and not to be forgotten. In fact, the background is more effective than the story itself, which has a rather contrived ending." Pub W

Burgess, Anthony

A clockwork orange. Norton [1963 c1962] 184p boards $3.95

First published 1962 in England
"In Mr. Burgess's Slav-oriented state of the future, the Lower Orders are in ascendence and happy hooligans roam the London streets, bashing senior citizens in the eyes with bicycle chains. The protagonist is a 15-year-old psychopath named Alex who undergoes a corrective brainwashing that makes him allergic to violence." N Y Times Bk R

"'A Clockwork Orange' is a gruesome fable. Its poisonous culture has obvious roots in our own. It is a nightmare world, made terrifyingly real through Burgess' extraordinary use of language." N Y Her Trib Books

A clockwork orange, and Honey for the bears. Modern Lib. [1968] 436p $2.95

First published 1962 and 1963, respectively, in England and entered separately

Enderby. Norton 1968 412p boards $5.95

An expanded version of a novel first published 1963 in England under the pseudonym Joseph Kell, with title: Inside Mr Enderby

"The trials of a minor poet caught up by commercialism and unwanted fame. . . . Enderby writes his poetry in the lavatory, filling the bathtub with drafts of his work, examples of which appear at the end of the book. Enderby's recluse existence is interrupted by Vesta, editor of a woman's magazine, whom he marries unsuccessfully. Further vicissitudes involve Enderby, after psychoanalysis, as a bartender called Hogg, before he finally regains his poetic ability and his identity." Booklist

"Enderby is an appealing figure, a reticent but independent soul not so much against the world as ignoring it completely, a world far more comic than he realizes. Mr. Burgess' novel has its long bleak voids, and few books can boast of more bathroom scenes—both private and public—but when everything is going well it is outrageously funny." Book of the Month Club News

Honey for the bears. Norton [1964 c1963] 255p boards $3.95

First published 1963 in England
This is "a novel about an English antique dealer who hopes to enrich a trip to Leningrad by illegally selling dresses to the natives. Problems becloud the voyage and continue to flourish throughout a stay in Russia which is sometimes farcical, sometimes frightening. Paul's involvements with his wife's new medical friends, the secret police, and a group of bohemians thicken the plot and complicate the climax of a satiric story shaped with comic artistry but weakened by the author's preoccupation with male and female homosexuality." Booklist

also in Burgess, A. A clockwork orange, and Honey for the bears p187-436

Tremor of intent. Norton 1966 239p boards $4.95

"Denis Hillier, a British agent in Yugoslavia, is given his last assignment: he has got to bring back from Russia his old school-friend, the scientist Roper, who has defected. After a flashback to the schooldays of Hillier and Roper the central bulk of the novel deals with Hillier's . . . adventures on a cruise to a Black Sea port where he jumps ship, disguised as a Soviet policeman, and makes his bid to bring his man back alive." Times (London) Lit Sup

"There is an underlay of somewhat cynical humor, some very violent action, and intricate plots and counterplots to entice readers through a recondite suspense story—readers who might be put off at first by Hillier's intense analysis of his own motives and those of Roper." Pub W

(ed.) Joyce, J. A shorter Finnegans wake

Burnett, David

(ed.) The Best American short stories, 1915-1969. See The Best American short stories, 1915-1969

Burnett, Hallie
(jt. ed.) Burnett, W. ed. The modern short story in the making

Burnett, Ivy Compton- See Compton-Burnett, Ivy

Burnett, W. R.
The asphalt jungle. Knopf 1949 271p o.p. 1970

"Newspapers in a large Midwestern city were riding the police department for its general ineffectiveness in dealing with crime wave. A new honest and industrious commissioner was appointed and conditions began to improve, until a spectacular, million-dollar jewel robbery took place. How the police, with the cooperation of the press, solved the case makes fast, light reading." Library J

Little Caesar. Dial Press 1929 308p o.p. 1970

"This is the inside story of a Chicago gang, told from the gangster's point of view and in his language. Rico and Sam Vettori fight for leadership and Rico wins. He is little Caesar to the gunmen who obey his orders without question. During a night-club hold-up Rico kills a policeman. The gang is broken up—one turns state's evidence, another is shot as a squealer—and Rico himself becomes one of the hunted, until a policeman's bullet cancels the score against him." Book Rev Digest

"The book is full of sordid details of gang life which make it unpleasant but exciting reading." Booklist

Burnett, Whit
(ed.) The modern short story in the making [by] Whit and Hallie Burnett. Hawthorn Bks. 1964 405p $6.95

Analyzed in Short Story Index

"Editors and some twenty modern writers present a discussion of the art of short-story writing explaining why they wrote certain works, how these fit into their artistic development, and what they think of them in retrospect." McClurg. Book News

Contents: The greatest thing in the world, by N. Mailer; Clothes make the man, by J. Stuart; A casual incident, by J. T. Farrell; Two bottles of relish, by Lord Dunsany; My friend Flicka, by M. O'Hara; Sherrel, by W. Burnett; The house divided, by G. Schmitt; The important thing, by T. Williams; Winter, by D. McCleary; The windfall, by E. Caldwell; Rest cure, by K. Boyle; My side of the matter, by T. Capote; Seventy thousand Assyrians, by W. Saroyan; The thief of the Champs Elysees, by H. Burnett; A morning drive, by G. Hitchcock; The top, by G. S. Albee; Address unknown, by K. Taylor; Exchange of men, by H. Nemerov; A turn with the sun, by J. Knowles; The dream of Angelo Zara, by G. D'Agostino; The captive, by L. Pirandello; Noon wine, by K. A. Porter

(ed.) Story Magazine. Story jubilee

(ed.) Story: the yearbook of discovery, 1968-1969. See Story: the yearbook of discovery, 1968-1969

Burney, Fanny
Evelina; or, A young lady's entrance into the world; introduction by Lewis Gibbs. Dutton 1958 378p (Everyman's lib) $2.95

First published 1778; in this edition 1909

"Pictures of the pleasures and pursuits of the gay social set of London in the latter part of the 18th century. Written in the form of letters." Pratt Alcove

Burnford, Sheila
y The incredible journey

Some editions are:
Little boards $4.50 An Atlantic Monthly Press book
Watts, F. $7.95. Large type edition. A Keith Jennison book. With illustrations by Carl Burger

First published 1961

The adventures of "two dogs and a cat [who] set out to cross three hundred rugged miles of northern Ontario. The English bull terrier is old and not in condition for a trip. The cat is a Siamese, a breed noted for being unable to stand cold weather. Only the large Labrador retriever is suited to strenuous fall conditions, but not even he is used to dealing with lynxes, bears, porcupines, rushing rivers, or angry human beings." Library J

"How [the animals] look after one another, sharing the scarce food they manage to catch, defending and, yes, encouraging one another, is heartwarming and convincing. . . . Throughout this lovingly told account of intense drama and suspense, is the keynote of courage and devotion. . . . All ages will love this book, a fine one for family reading out loud." Christian Science Monitor

Burns, John Horne
The gallery. Harper 1947 342p o.p. 1970

"Series of portraits of Americans and Italians who met in an arcade called the Galleria Umberto in Naples in 1944. There is very little plot; the sketches of the various characters carry on this study of the lonely, the unhappy and the frustrated. The author is a former army officer." Book Rev Digest

"A novel of extraordinary skill and power. . . . Mr. Burns writes unevenly, perhaps deliberately so, sometimes using the shock technique of photographic realism, sometimes employing a kind of stylzed symbology, but always with telling effect. In this, his first novel, Mr. Burns shows a brilliant understanding of people, a compassion for their frailties and an urge to discover what inner strength or weakness may lie beneath the surface." N Y Her Trib Books

Burrell, Angus
(ed.) An anthology of famous American stories, ed. by Angus Burrell and Bennett Cerf. Modern Lib. 1953 1340p (Modern Lib. giant) $4.95

Analyzed in Short Story Index

First published in 1936 by Random House under title: The bedside book of famous American stories. The 1953 edition has included eight new stories and omitted seven stories included in the 1936 edition. Both editions analyzed in Short Story Index

Contents: Legend of Sleepy Hollow, by W. Irving; Rip Van Winkle, by W. Irving; Great Stone Face, by N. Hawthorne; Rappaccini's daughter, by N. Hawthorne; Murders in the Rue Morgue, by E. A. Poe; Pit and the pendulum, by E. A. Poe; Purloined letter, by E. A. Poe; Billy Budd, foretopman, by H. Melville; Man without a country, by E. E. Hale; Diamond lens, by F. J. O'Brien; Lady or the tiger, by F. R. Stockton; Celebrated jumping frog of Calaveras County, by M. Twain; Man that corrupted Hadleyburg, by M. Twain; Marjorie Daw, by T. B. Aldrich; Editha, by W. D. Howells; Outcasts of Poker Flat, by F. B. Harte; Occurrence at Owl Creek Bridge, by A. Bierce; Boarded window, by A. Bierce; Real thing, by H. James; Author of Beltraffio, by H. James; Brer Rabbit, Brer Fox, and Tar Baby, by J. C. Harris; Courting of Sister Wisby, by S. O. Jewett; Boy who drew cats, by L. Hearn; Pearls of Loreto, by G. Atherton; Return of a private, by H. Garland; New England nun, by M. E. Wilkins; Mission of Jane, by E. Wharton; Furnished room, by O. Henry; Blackjack bargainer, by O. Henry; Municipal report, by O. Henry; Bar sinister, by R. H. Davis; Effie Whittlesy, by G. Ade; "Little gentleman," by B. Tarkington; Deal in wheat, by F. Norris; Open boat, by S. Crane; Lost Phoebe, by T. Dreiser; Big Dan Reilly, by H. O'Higgins; Good Anna, by G. Stein; Paul's case, by W. Cather; To build a fire, by J. London; I'm a fool, by S. Anderson; I want to know why, by S. Anderson; Great pancacke record, by O. Johnson; Porcelain cups, by J. B. Cabell; Wild oranges, by J. Hergesheimer; Jury of her peers, by S. Glaspell; Afternoon of a faun, by E. Ferber; Some like them cold, by R. Lardner; Golden honeymoon, by R. Lardner; Man who saw though heaven, by W. D. Steele; Tact, by T. Beer; Silent snow, secret snow, by C. Aiken; Big blonde, by D. Parker; The arrow, by C. Morley; Cycle of Manhattan, by T. S. Winslow; Maria Concepciòn, by K. A. Porter; Secret life of Walter Mitty, by J. Thurber; Rich boy, by F. S. Fitzgerald; Body of an American, by J. Dos Passos; Rose for Emily, by W. Faulkner; The

Burrell, Angus—*Continued*

killers, by E. Hemingway; The gambler, the nun, and the radio, by E. Hemingway; Red pony, by J. Steinbeck; Portrait of Bascom Hawke, by T. Wolfe; Night club, by K. Brush; Kneel to the rising sun, by E. Caldwell; Do you like it here, by J. O'Hara; Daring young man on the flying trapeze, by W. Saroyan; The hitch-hikers, by E. Welty; Portable phonograph, by W. Van T. Clark; Act of faith, by I. Shaw; My Christmas carol, by B. Schulberg; Pretty mouth and green my eyes, by J. D. Salinger

Burrell, John Angus. See Burrell, Angus

Burroway, Janet

The buzzards. Little 1969 303p boards $5.95

"This is a novel of a contemporary American conservative politician [Alex] who becomes trapped, and therefore traps his family and associates, in the crossfire of a heated senatorial campaign in Arizona." News of Bks
"In 'The Buzzards' politics is not a game, even a dirty game; it is a pathology and the people intimately involved with it are diseased and ultimately destroyed. . . . This is a book with a lot of suspense and complex, convoluted characters. It displays a frightening sense of veracity." Pub W

Busch, Niven

The San Franciscans; a novel. Simon & Schuster 1962 349p o.p. 1970

"Both sides of Market Street are well represented in this novel about a family-owned San Francisco bank involved in a lawsuit that could besmirch its reputation as well as deplete its treasury. The bank president dies before the trial, so his widow must fight the opposition lawyer who is as attractive in a masculine way as she is in a feminine one. She has mixed success: she loses the case, but wins him." Library J

Bush, Christopher

The case of the deadly diamonds. Macmillan (N Y) [1969 c1967] 159p boards $4.50

"A Cock Robin mystery"
First published 1967 in England
"Another of Mr. Bush's tidy and well-plotted English mysteries featuring that most respectable private investigator, Ludovic Travers . . . [in which he and] his old friend Inspector Jewle . . . investigate a diamond robbery that may tie in with a seemingly unimportant theft from a jeweler's home safe some months before. The conclusion sees a once happy family caught up in murder and suicide." Pub W

Butler, Ellis Parker

Pigs is pigs. Doubleday 37p o.p. 1970

First published 1906
In serio-comic style the author relates the trials of a freight agent with a pair of guinea-pigs

Butler, Samuel

Erewhon, and Erewhon revisited. Dutton 389p (Everyman's lib) $2.95

First published 1872 and 1901 respectively
"By projecting his satirical imagination into a land peopled by extraordinary creatures with exasperating ideas, Butler attempted to lampoon English society, its customs and manners. The hero, George Higgs, seeks his fortune abroad. On a sheep farm, apparently in New Zealand, he meets with a native, who tells him about Erewhon ('nowhere' spelled backward), a fabulous country where monsters dwell, and leads him there. Higgs finds the citizens of Erewhon principally preoccupied with keeping healthy and pretty. . . . Visiting the College of Unreason, the School of Inconsistency, and the School of Evasion, he discovers that 'consistency is a vice which degrades human nature, and levels man with the brute.'" Haydn. Thesaurus of Book Digests

"Erewhon revisited" is a sequel to Erewhon. This work "brings George Higgs back to the land of the strange people after an absence of twenty years." Haydn. Thesaurus of Book Digests

y The way of all flesh

Some editions are:
Dodd (Great illustrated classics) $4.50 With illustrations of the author, his environment and the setting of the book, together with an introduction and captions by Louis B. Salomon
Dufour $4.50 With drawings by Donna Nachshen
Dutton (Everyman's lib) $3.25 Introduction by A. J. Hoppé
Published posthumously 1903
"The theme is the hypocrisy and smug complacency of English middle-class life, and particularly the relationship between parents and children, which is traced through several generations of the Pontifex family. . . . 'The Way of All Flesh' is generally regarded as a very original work; it exercised considerable influence on later English writers. 'It contains records of the things I saw happening rather than imaginary incidents,' said the author. Undoubtedly this novel has a strong vein of autobiography." Haydn. Thesaurus of Book Digests

Butler, William

The house at Akiya. Scribner 1969 139p $4.95

This "is the story of an American businessman, Ephraim Rome, who with wife and two children, moves into a house where the previous occupants had committted suicide. Soon a succession of tragedies begins—the death of his son and daughter, the despairing illness of his wife—and Rome's normal life gradually and inexorably slips away as he becomes more and more absorbed by the country." Publisher's note
"Mr. Butler has written a very sensitive story and has not found it essential to spell out in intricate detail every gory or sensuous movement and action. . . . It is quite slim in volume, but its value lies in its content and style of writing and in its subtle undertones." Best Sellers

Byrd, Elizabeth

Immortal queen. Ballantine 1956 591p o.p. 1970

This fictional biography of Mary Queen of Scots tells of her girlhood and her three marriages; first to the Dauphin Francis, second to Lord Darnley, and third to Bothwell. Against the drama of her personal life her political career is outlined as it highlights her conflict with Elizabeth I of England. (Publisher)

Byrne, Donn

Messer Marco Polo; illus. by C. B. Falls. Century 1921 147p illus o.p. 1970

"Story of Marco Polo of Venice as it should have been and his love for Golden Bells, the beautiful daughter of Kubla Khan. . . . He is appointed by the pope to go to China at the request of Kubla Khan to explain the mysteries of Christianity, but his only convert is Golden Bells." Booklist

C

Cabell, James Branch

Jurgen: a comedy of justice; with twelve illus. by Ray F. Coyle. McBride Co. 1923 368p illus o.p. 1970

First published 1919
"The tale, which tells how Jurgen, a poet and pawnbroker, entering the cave on Anneran Heath in search of his wife, Dame Lisa, meets a centaur named Nessus who transports him to the garden between dawn and sunrise, finds his lost love, is permitted to relive a year

Cabell, James B.—*Continued*

of his youth and has other adventures, is made up of chapters with such titles as: Why Jurgen did the manly thing; Showing that Sereda is feminine; Old toys and a new shadow; Why Merlin talked in twilight, etc." Book Rev Digest

"As blithely fantastic, as shrewdly pointed and launched with as impudent a flourish of spurious erudition as any of its predecessors." Dial

Cadell, Elizabeth

Canary yellow. Morrow 1965 [c1964] 256p boards $4.95

"Having won a magazine contest trip for two to the Canary Islands just before breaking her engagement, London secretary Elaine Tracy decides to take the holiday cruise by herself. Her adventures with a peculiar pair of cabin mates, two attractive young men, and a former acquaintance on shipboard lead to dangerous consequences in the deceptively idyllic setting of Las Palmas." Booklist

"In reading this short . . . tight novel we are reminded that pleasure is still in importance in reading. Even though we hear some cliches . . . it is pleasant to know that in this best of all story book worlds, all's well that ends well." Best Sellers

y The golden collar. Morrow [1969 c1968] 221p boards $4.95

"Henry Eliot, engaged to the beautiful and wealthy daughter of his employer, is sent to Portugal to purchase land for his architectural firm and falls in love with the landowner's niece." Cincinnati

This novel "has a happy ending, a bit of a moral, a nice love story and some delightful and colorful characters. Good, right, and love triumph, as you always know they will, but 'The Golden Collar' will while away some undemanding hours for ladies who like this untaxing fiction genre and its inherently relaxing qualities." Pub W

The lark shall sing. Morrow 1955 224p $4.95

"The six orphaned Waynes had been dispersed after their parents death by Lucille, the eldest, and their lovely old home in the English New Forest was rented. . . . When Lucille announced her engagement, she also told her younger brothers and sisters that their home was to be sold. Five protesting young Waynes arrived in wrath and despair and the home was saved." Book Rev Digest

"Mrs. Cadell has created another of her charmingly topsy-turvy microcosms, and her readers will be well content. For junior members of the family, too." Library J

Followed by: Six impossible things

Six impossible things. Morrow 1961 253p $4.95

This sequel to: The lark shall sing, "finds the scattered members of the Wayne family returning to Wood Mount some ten years later for the forthcoming wedding of their childhood friend Miriam Arkwright. Nicholas, the still unattached older brother who has maintained the family home, and dreamy twenty-one-year-old Julia, just back from her music studies in Italy, hold the center of attention." Booklist

The yellow brick road. Morrow 1960 224p boards $4.95

"Jody was visiting a beauty-treatment customer in London when she fell down a flight of stone steps. Her sister believed it must have been the concussion that made Jody see a man leading a goat. But the goatman turned out to be real, and he and Jody set out to discover what was behind a lot of queer happenings." Bk Buyer's Guide

"Although essentially a mystery [this story] is full of startling psychological insights into human nature and is peopled with an assortment of intriguing characters." Best Sellers

Caidin, Martin

Four came back; a novel. McKay 1968 275p $5.50

"The story of eight astronauts orbiting in the internationally sponsored space station 'Epsilon.' They are stricken by a mysterious, and apparently fatal, disease. The plot revolves around their attempts to discover the cause and the cure for the affliction, and their decision whether to sacrifice themselves rather than bring a 'plague from space' to a panic-stricken world. . . . The authenticity of the space technology, and the breathless pace of action, make the novel a thoroughly enjoyable adventure story, one which makes the reader forget any short-comings of style. Only those offended by fairly explicit sexual scenes are likely to find this story anything but exciting and highly entertaining." Library J

Marooned; a novel. Dutton 1964 378p boards $5.95

"Set in the near future, America's fifth astronaut Pruett [of Project Mercury] develops mechanical trouble which prevents his reentry into the earth's atmosphere within the time limit set by his oxygen supply. Our space experts work frantically to save his life, while Pruett recalls the events leading up to this fatal moment. Mr. Caidin incorporates highly technical information into the story." Library J

"The colorful description of the attempted rescue of a man hurtling through space at 300 miles per minute forms a gripping story of what can happen in our man-in-space program." Huntting

The Mendelov conspiracy. Meredith 1969 274p $5.95

"Flying disks begin to appear over America and elsewhere and although a conspiracy of silence sets out to pretend they never happened, the truth involves a vast conspiracy to destroy nuclear power before the nations that wield it can destroy the world." Pub W

Caillou, Alan

Bichu the jaguar; illus. by Alex Tsao. World Pub. 1969 216p illus $4.95

"Suffering from a bullet wound and pursued by an Indian and his daughter, Bichu begins a perilous journey through the Brazilian desert and jungle toward her lair in the mountains, where she must go to die." Cincinnati

"This classic novel of survival reveals the deep emotions felt by an animal and the humans pursuing it. It captures the drama of man and beast in their most elemental relationship to each other, and to the changeless order of nature." Book News

Cain, James M.

Cain x 3; three novels. . . . With a new introduction by Tom Wolfe. Knopf 1969 465p $6.95

Contents: The postman always rings twice (1934); Mildred Pierce (1934); Double indemnity (1943)

The first story concerns a young vagrant and a restaurant keeper's wife who plan to murder the latter's husband; the second is a picture of a grass widow, her husband and a daughter who becomes a monster; the last deals with an insurance salesman who plots the perfect murder

Double indemnity
In Cain, J. M. Cain x 3 p363-465

Mildred Pierce
In Cain, J. M. Cain x 3 p103-362

The postman always rings twice
In Cain, J. M. Cain x 3 p 1-101

Caird, Janet

In a glass darkly. Morrow 1966 251p o.p. 1970

First published 1965 in England with title: Murder reflected

"Marble statues, a hidden camera, and a murder all figure in Margaret Maclean's first day in the little town of Inverbane. The police and her cousin Robert were pleasantly unbelieving. Determined to solve the mysteries herself, Margaret moved further and further into danger." Am News of Bks

"Here is a Gothic tale of modern Scotland equipped with living characters with a realistic approach to life and love, a good detective story." Library J

Caird, Janet—*Continued*

The Loch. Published for the Crime Club by Doubleday 1969 [c1968] 209p $4.50

First published 1968 in England

"The little Scottish [Highland] town of Lochy had nestled for centuries beside the placid lake for which it was named, until one February afternoon the waters rose up in a mammoth crystalline wall and descended on the town. The next day the waters receded, and the survivors went about the task of burying the dead, cleaning up and rebuilding. But they labored with a growing sense of uneasiness, for it soon became clear that the Loch was drying up. As it disappeared, relics of other ages were uncovered. Old happenings and older tragedies came to light; in the Lochside cliffs a series of caves appeared." Publisher's note

Calder-Marshall, Arthur

The Scarlet boy. Harper 1962 212p o.p. 1970

"George Grantley, the narrator, is a scholarly biographer whose quiet life is excitingly disturbed when an old friend buys Anglesey House nearby and moves in with his artist wife, his young daughter, and a Hungarian cook. Midway in the negotiations for the house Grantley becomes convinced that the house is haunted, but he cannot dissuade the Evernesses from completing the purchase. In the ensuing pages they come to believe in God and ghosts." Booklist

Caldwell, Erskine

Complete stories of Erskine Caldwell. Little 1953 664p $8.95

Analyzed in Short Story Index

In substance and setting these ninety-three stories range familiarly from New England to the deep South, from violence to broad humor, from pathos to a frank treatment of man's baser drives from crisp little monologues to full scale studies of character under stress

Contents: After-image; August afternoon; Automobile that wouldn't run; Autumn courtship; Back on the road; Balm of Gilead; Big Buck; Blue Boy; Candy-man Beechum; Carnival; Cold winter; Corduroy pants; Country full of Swedes; Courting of Susie Brown; Crownfire; Daughter; Day the presidential candidate came to Ciudad Tamaulipas; Day's wooing; Dorothy; The dream; Empty room; End of Christy Tucker; Evelyn and the rest of us; Evening in Nuevo Leon; First autumn; Fly in the coffin; Girl Ellen; Grass fire; Growing season; Hamrick's polar bear; Handy; Here and today; Honeymoon; Horse thief; Indian summer; It happened like this; Joe Craddock's old woman; John the Indian and George Hopkins; Kneel to the rising sun; Knife to cut the corn bread with; Lonely day; Mama's little girl; Man and woman; Man who looked like himself; Martha Jean; Masses of men; Mating of Marjorie; Maud Island; Meddlesome Jack; Medicine man; Memorandum; Midsummer passion; Mid-winter guest; Molly Cotton-tail; Negro in the well; New cabin; Nine dollars' worth of mumble; Over the Green Mountain; People v. Abe Lathan, colored; People's choice; Picking cotton; The picture; Priming the well; Rachel; Return to Lavinia; The rumor; Runaway; Saturday afternoon; Savannah River payday; The shooting; Sick horse; Slow death; Small day; Snacker; Squire Dinwiddy; Strawberry season; Summer accident; The Sunfield; Swell-looking girl; Ten thousand blueberry crates; Thunderstorm; Uncle Henry's love nest; Uncle Jeff; Very late spring; The visitor; Walnut hunt; Warm river; We are looking at you, Agnes; Where the girls were different; Wild flowers; The wildfall; Woman in the house; Yellow girl

"Caldwell's short stories are notable for social significance, a frequently subtle technique, and some fairly good folk humor. . . . No fictionist has written more strikingly of the modern south's problems, or depicted more arrestingly the exploitation of the share cropper and the intimidation of the Negro, even by the law itself." Chicago Sunday Tribune

God's little acre; illus. by Milton Glaser. Farrar, Straus [1962 c1960] 218p illus $6.50

First published 1933

"Concerns the Georgia mountaineer Ty Ty Walden, who has been digging for gold for fifteen years, but always retains the proceeds of one acre for the church. In his family are daughter Darling Jill, who invites the advances of all men; and daugher Rosamund, whose husband Will Thompson is enamored of Griselda, wife of Buck Walden. Will dies in a miners' strike, and Buck commits suicide after shooting his brother Jim, also enamored of Griselda. Ty Ty is grief-stricken, but primarily concerned with his prospecting." Haydn. Thesaurus of Book Digests

"A novel that will lift the noses of the sensitive, Erskine Caldwell's 'God's Little Acre,' is nevertheless a beautifully integrated story of the barren Southern farm and the shut Southern mill, and one of the finest studies of the Southern poor white which has ever come into our literature. Writing in the brutal images of the life of his poor white people, Mr. Caldwell has caught in poetic quality the debased and futile aspiration of men and women restless in a world of long hungers which must be satisfied quickly, if at all." Sat R

Tobacco road. Modern Lib. 1947 241p $2.95

First published 1932 by Scribner

"Story of a degraded poor-white Georgia family living in a tumble-down shack on worn out land which had once been the prosperous tobacco plantation of Jeeter Lester's grandfather. The story carries this family some steps further in their progressive degeneration." Book Rev Digest

"Mr. Caldwell's humor, like Mark Twain's has at its source an imagination that stirs the emotions of the reader. The adolescent, almost idiotic gravity of Mr. Caldwell's characters produces instantaneous laughter and their sexual adventures are treated with an irreverence that verges upon the robust ribaldry of a burlesque show." N Y Her Trib Books

Caldwell, Janet Taylor. See Caldwell, Taylor

Caldwell, Taylor

Dear and glorious physician. Doubleday 1959 574p $5.95

This novel about Lucanus, or Luke, "physician and author of one of the Gospels, depicts him as an individual apart plainly marked out for the service of God in spite of his almost lifelong protest against a deity who inflicted pain on men. Antioch, scene of his boyhood; Rome where he visited his family in the intervals between his restless travels; Alexandria; where he was educated; and Judaea, where he learned the story of Jesus from his mother Mary and acknowledged him as the Christ, provide a background." Booklist

"In spite of its great length and wealth of detail, this fictional biography of St. Luke will be read by good readers of mature interests. Miss Caldwell says she has been working on this since she was twelve years old, and her re-creation of New Testament times has a feeling of personal experience." Library J

Dynasty of death. Doubleday [1970 c1938] 851p $7.95

A reissue of the title first published 1938 by Scribner

"A long novel dealing with a family of munition makers who come from England, settle in Pennsylvania and start a small firearms factory in partnership with a Frenchman, the firm becoming Barbour and Bouchard. Chiefly it is the story of Ernest, met first as a boy of 12, but even then cold, calculating and ruthless. Contrasted with Ernest is Martin, gentle and shy, who becomes an inevitable abolitionist and pacifist. The novel is long and powerful, embracing three generations, taking in the Civil War and ending with the rumblings of trouble in Europe, for which, it is intimated, the munition makers are largely responsible." Wis Lib Bul

"The armaments industry is a subject which fiction does well to take up; and [the author's] attack is handled with the patience and skill of a prosecuting attorney." Sat R

Followed by: The eagles gather

The eagles gather. Scribner 1940 498p o.p. 1970

Sequel to: Dynasty of death

"Continues through the 1920's the story of the Bouchard family of munitions manufacturers, begun in 'Dynasty of death.' All of the

Caldwell, Taylor—*Continued*

male relatives hate each other and spend their lives scheming for supremacy in the huge industry. They oppose anything in national and international affairs which might hinder their interests. Peter alone is interested in decency; his love for his cousin Celeste provides romantic relief. Though melodramatic and overwritten, with too many characters, the book is often impressive." Booklist

Followed by: The final hour

The final hour. Scribner 1944 563p o.p. 1970

Sequel to: The eagles gather

"From summer of 1939 through the early months of 1942, the Bouchard family's bickerings, feuds, and struggle for power among individual members are sharpened by the political division of the family between those who want to do business with Hitler and the fascists and the more powerful bloc that develops a conscience about the United States. Occupying the personal entanglements is the relationship between Henri, the most hated but most influential, and Celeste, wife of the invalid Peter whose awareness of political movements makes him a family oddity." Booklist

Grandmother and the priests. Doubleday 1963 469p $4.95

"At the turn of the century in the city of Leeds a small girl was permitted by her fascinatingly irreligious Irish grandmother to sit in the drawing room and listen to the absorbing tales told by Grandmother's dinner guests. That these guests were all priests was a source of wonder to little Rose's Presbyterian heart and even more so were the tales told in lilting Celtic voices." Library J

The book "technically a novel, is actually a collection of tales set within a frame: a device not unknown in literature. . . . Readable enough, frequently exciting, and never particularly demanding on the reader, 'Grandmother and the Priests' could prove just the book for those who want to 'get away from it all'—from reality, that is." Best Sellers

A pillar of iron. Doubleday 1964 649p $6.95

This novel "goes back to the period when decadence was destroying the Roman Empire. Here is Caesar, quite unlike any previous characterization, an affectionate, shrewd and deceitful man with great humor and charm. Here is Catiline, handsome and degenerate, an aristocrat who taunts Cicero and marries the love of Cicero's life. And here, most of all, is Cicero, born of a middle-class family, but who very early in life established a friendship with Caesar that was to save his life many times later. This is Rome in its greatest glory." Am News of Bks

A prologue to love. Doubleday 1961 614p boards $5.95

"The story of Caroline Ames' rise from a poverty-ridden childhood in Massachusetts to financial success. The financial teachings of her father helped her to amass a fortune, but the lack of teaching in regard to love was Caroline's tragedy. Much of the novel is set in and around Boston in the period of 1880 to 1914." Huntting

"Essentially 'A Prologue to Love' serves up a rich distillation of evil deeds flowering out of the deep roots of fear. As always, Miss Caldwell creates a lively world in which her characters pursue their troubled ways. . . . Authentic Caldwell, for Taylor Caldwell fans." N Y Her Trib Books

Testimony of two men. Doubleday 1968 605p $6.95

"Jonathan Ferrier is the central character. He is dedicated to perfection—to perfect asepsis when few doctors yet acknowledged or even knew the need for it in 1901, and to perfect truth in human relations. Ironically, he himself has been tried for the murder of his wife and justly acquitted. The verdict was not acceptable to his community. Since they are incapable of the perfection he vocally demands, the people around him hate him and are delighted by an apparent opportunity to condemn him." Library J

"Caldwell combines incisive characterization with an absorbing description of nineteenth-century medical practices. Chiefly for women readers." Booklist

This side of innocence. Scribner 1946 499p o.p. 1970

"History of a town and a family. In 1868, the Lindseys of up-state New York were a peaceful, contented group until beautiful Amalie Maxwell decided to marry Alfred, the adopted son, for his money—and promptly fell in love with his dashing brother. The household soon seethed with passion, bitterness and hatred, a situation which was not resolved for twenty years. Yet, because of it, agrarian Riversend grew into an industrial Utopia." Library J

Calisher, Hortense

Extreme magic; a novella and other stories. Little 1964 260p $5

Analyzed in Short Story Index

"Eight short stories and a novella by a skillful observer of modern life from Greenwich Village to Paris, Miss Calisher understands people and writes of them with sensitivity and compassion." Cincinnati

Contents: Il ploe:r dã mõ koe:r; Two colonials; A Christmas carillon; The rabbi's daughter; Little did I know; The gulf between; Songs my mother taught me; If you don't want to live I can't help you; Extreme magic

False entry; a novel. Little 1961 484p boards $6.95

The "story of a kind of 'Doppelgänger,' a voyeur whose phenomenal memory seems destined to rob him of his own identity and force him to effect false entry into the lives of others through knowledge of their past. In form a journal, the book details the life of 'Pierre Goodman' (we never know his real name) from his birth in London on the first Armistice Day, through his early youth as a seamstress' son in the Goodman household, his boyhood in the little southern town of Tuscana, Alabama, a trial during which he assumes the identity of another to give testimony against a chapter of the KKK for the murder of a Negro, and, after numerous other incidents, a love affair which promises finally to release him from his burdens and allow him to become himself." Library J

The New Yorkers. Little 1969 559p $7.95

The author's earlier novel False entry "dealt in part with a wealthy New York Jewish family, the Mannixes. 'The New Yorkers' circles back on the Mannixes, their family connections, friends and acquaintances, during an eventful 12-year-period, 1943-1955, in which the life of each member of the family [the Judge, his unfaithful wife, their deaf son, and their daughter Ruth] is overshadowed by a dark and violent secret having to do with the death of the mother. The Mannixes move in a charmed and cosmopolitan circle—there are some fine side glimpses of London and one memorable vignette of Paris society pre-World War I—but it is New York that is the focus of their story and have been drawn into their orbit." Pub W

"Some of the secondary characters seem more real than the judge. Presences, living and dead, are felt throughout, especially in the judge's old house on New York's East Side. Long, complex descriptions of physical and psychological states are interrupted by startling events. . . . The author's physical and social evocation of the city is most perceptive. Recommended for most public libraries, especially where a novel combining old-fashioned family chronicle and modern awareness of change would find an audience." Library J

Textures of life; a novel. Little 1963 249p $4.95

"A story of a difficult, rebellious, but highly sympathetic young couple who build their marriage in a bare, uncluttered domestic world of cold-water lofts in New York City. Running parallel to their story is the wiser, more serene marriage of the boy's father and the girl's mother, drawn together by loneliness and mutual need after their children's wedding." Pub W

"The novel is full of the author's particular magic of illuminating the ordinary, her way of examining the progress of love and understanding, of observing the agony of parents watching a stricken child, of limning her characters, both major and minor, deftly and exactly.

Calisher, Hortense—*Continued*

Each new book increases Miss Calisher's stature as a novelist. This one belongs in every respectable collection of modern fiction." Library J

Calvino, Italo

Cosmicomics; tr. from the Italian by William Weaver. Harcourt 1968 153p $3.95

Analyzed in Short Story Index
"A Helen and Kurt Wolff book"
First published 1965 in Italy
These twelve "imaginative and deeply philosophical stories, escape classification into a genre—mathematical formulas, gases, and man's evolutionary ancestors are among the characters; the plot is the creation of the universe." Library J
Contents: The distance of the moon; At daybreak; A sign in space; All at one point; Without colors; Games without end; The aquatic uncle; How much shall we bet; The dinosaurs; The form of space; The light-years; The spiral

Camp, L. Sprague de. See De Camp, L. Sprague

Campbell, John W.

(ed.) Analog 1-7. See Analog 1-7

Campbell, Michael

Lord dismiss us. Putnam [1968 c1967] 384p $5.95

First published 1967 in England
"Carleton, the gifted and popular second prefect of Weatherhill School [an English public school] is shaken from his aloof insensibility by the discovery that he is in love with a junior boy, while he in turn is loved by Ashley, his eccentric teacher. Ashley is destroyed by the strength of his forbidden desires, but Carleton, with youthful resilience, emerges unharmed." Library J
"It is funny and tragic, extravagant and yet controlled. . . . The tone, a little strident, a little hysterical, lifted just clear of realism yet never allowed to bolt into fantasy, is held confidently and without faltering throughout." Times (London) Lit Sup

Campbell, William Edward March. See March, William

Camus, Albert

Nobel prize in literature, 1957

Exile and the kingdom; tr. from the French by Justin O'Brien. Knopf 1958 213p boards $3.95

Analyzed in Short Story Index
Original French edition published 1957
"Discipline of thought and style characterize six short stories by a noted French author-philosopher. The distinguishing marks of locales ranging from North Africa to Brazil are etched with telling detail, but it is the landscape of man's inner life which is most important here. The diverse protagonists—and it is intimated all men—are exiled from themselves, others, and the life of the spirit, but now and again a word or an action renews their courage to continue the pilgrimage. For discerning readers." Booklist
Contents: The adulterous woman; The renegade; The silent men; The guest; The artist at work; The growing stone

also in Camus, A. The fall & Exile and the kingdom p149-361

The fall; tr. from the French by Justin O'Brien. Knopf 1957 [c1956] 147p boards $3.95

Original French edition published 1956
"The hero of this novel tells his story to a stranger whom he has picked up in a sailors' bar in Amsterdam. He was once a successful Parisian lawyer noted for his modesty and kindly thoughtfulness for the poor and the defeated. At heart, however, he despised all but himself. Two insignificant experiences cause him to be revealed to himself in all his insincerity, sham, and shameless immorality. He sets about to reveal his true self to all which soon brings about his calamitous descent to disgrace. In him, Camus mirrors the vices and the despair of his generation." Library J
"Though 'The Fall' seems at times a meditation rather than a novel, it is an irresistibly brilliant examination of the modern conscience. Only a very obdurate reader could finish it without finding himself much more honest about the character of his motives and the contradictions in his values. Despite its external ambiguity and apparent negations, the book has a positive effect of a uniquely personal kind. This is existentialism in practice." N Y Times Bk R

The fall & Exile and the kingdom; tr. from the French by Justin O'Brien. Modern Lib. [1964] 361p $2.95

A combination of two titles which have been published separately 1956 and 1958 respectively in this country by Knopf, and are entered separately

The plague; tr. by Stuart Gilbert

Some editions are:
Knopf $4.95
Modern Lib. $2.95
Original French edition, 1947
"A coastal city in Algeria is struck by bubonic plague and shut off from the world while the pestilence rages for months. The impact on a small group of people and their ways of meeting the catastrophe make the story." Booklist
"Sober, tautly written . . . it creates a situation of soul-revealing crisis, and peoples that situation with very real and well differentiated characters. . . . In telling their story of brave resistance, Albert Camus has accomplished a perfect achievement which, despite the unrelieved grimness of the theme, contains great variety, gay humor and stimulating philosophy." New Repub

y The stranger; tr. from the French by Stuart Gilbert. Knopf 1946 154p $3.95, lib. bdg. $2.29

First French edition published 1942. Published in England with title: The outsider
"An ordinary little clerk living in Algiers is the subject of this novel. . . . The little man lives quietly and for the most part unemotionally until he becomes involved in another man's folly. He shoots an Arab, is tried for murder, and condemned to die. As he contemplates his fate he does seem on the verge of a bit of human emotion." Book Rev Digest
"This is an excellent piece of short fiction, in the classic French tradition. Like many French novelists before him, Camus excels in delineating the narrowness of French provincial life. . . . The trial itself is reported with a detached irony which makes the underlying horror only the more noticeable. Stuart Gilbert's translation merits unreserved praise. Camus emerges as a master craftsman who never wastes a word." Sat R

Canby, Henry Seidel

(ed.) The book of the short story; ed. by Henry Seidel Canby and Robeson Bailey. New and enl ed. Appleton 1948 406p text ed. $4.50

Analyzed in Short Story Index
First published 1903 under the authorship of Alexander Jessup and H. S. Canby. The 1948 edition contains nine more stories
These 27 short stories are selected to illustrate short story writing from 2500 B.C. to modern times. Arranged chronologically
Contents: The shipwrecked sailor, from an Egyptian papyrus of the XIIth dynasty; The Book of Ruth, from the Bible; The story of Cupid and Psyche, by Apuleis; Frederick of the Alberighi and his falcon, by Boccaccio; The nun's priest's tale, by G. Chaucer; The story of Ali Baba and the forty robbers destroyed by a slave, from the Thousand and one nights; The apparition of Mrs Veal, by D. Defoe; Jeannot and Colin, by Voltaire; Rip Van Winkle, by W. Irving; Wandering Willie's tale, by Sir W. Scott; The taking of the Redoubt, by P. Mérimée; La Grande Bretéche,

Canby, Henry S.—*Continued*

by H. de Balzac; The cask of Amontillado, by E. A. Poe; Ethan Brand, by N. Hawthorne; Markheim, by R. L. Stevenson; A coward, by G. de Maupassant; Without benefit of clergy, by R. Kipling; The blue hotel, by S. Crane; The darling, by A. Chekhov; Mrs Medwin, by H. James; The secret sharer, by J. Conrad; A little cloud, by J. Joyce; A dill pickle, by K. Mansfield; Haircut, by R. Lardner; The killers, by E. Hemingway; Brother Death, by S. Anderson; The Devil and Daniel Webster, by S. V. Benet

Canfield, Dorothy

y The bent twig; with an introduction and notes by Marian W. Skinner. Holt 1926 497p o.p. 1970

First published 1915
The bent twig "is a social-psychological study of American middle-class family life, in a midwestern university town. Sylvia Marshall has been raised by genial, easy-going parents. When she enters college, she is slighted socially because of the contempt in which they are held by the conventionally-minded. The Marshalls are regarded as 'peculiar,' their home a rendezvous for all the college 'freaks' or intellectuals. Sylvia, an impetuous young lady, becomes involved with a gay, popular man. Then, tiring of him, she falls in love with Austin Fling, a serious-minded radical determined to improve the conditions of the miners. The 'bent twig' is finally straightened out." Haydn. Thesaurus of Book Digests

The deepening stream. Modern Lib. 393p o.p. 1970

First published 1930 by Harcourt
"A serious and conscientious piece of writing, telling a story that begins with Matey Gilbert's childhood in a middle western college town, carries her to other college towns, to Europe on Sabbatical leaves, and finally to the little village on the Hudson where her family has its roots. Here she finds love and marriage and a simple, satisfying life, broken by a period of war work in France, and resumed afterwards, with a realization that life goes on, that there is never any going back." Wis Lib Bul

A harvest of stories; from a half century of writing. Harcourt 1956 352p $5.95

Analyzed in Short Story Index
Contents: Nothing ever happens; Flint and fire; Old Man Warner; Uncle Giles; Ann Story; The bedquilt; Almera Hawley Canfield; The heyday of the blood; The forgotten mother; Scylla and Charybdis; The rainy day, the good mother, and the brown suit; "Vive Guignol"; The Saint of the Old Seminary; Gold from Argentina; The apprentice; The murder on Jefferson Street; The biologist and his son; Sex education; A family alliance; As ye sow—; Married children; The washed windows; "Through pity and terror . . ."; In the eye of the storm; The knot-hole; Memorial Day; The old soldier
"A few of the stories in this section seem contrived in an old-fashioned way; one, in fact, has a twist that would have pleased O. Henry; but even in the weakest of them there is a core of shrewdness and a generosity of common sense and goodwill." N Y Times Bk R

Canning, John

(ed.) 50 great horror stories. Taplinger 1969 494p $5.95

"Strange, strange horror stories of this and other ages—werewolves, Apazauca spiders, vampires, mournful spirits of walled-up-monks, hideous cries of zombies, a Cambridge scholar sung to his own death by his dead colleagues, etc." Book News
Contents: The ruff, by M. Hardwick; The werewolf of St-Claude, by R. Seth; The band of Father Arrowsmith, by M. Hardwick; The man who turned into a cat, by J. W. Day; The dead killed him in his own grave, by J. W. Day; The devil in the flesh, by R. Seth; The bo'sun's body, by M. Hardwick; A warning to sceptics, by M. Hardwick; Doubled damnation, by M. Hardwick; The tongueless woman of Glamis Castle, by J. W. Day; Trapped in a flooded tunnel, by G. Williamson; The girl in the

flame-red dress, by I. Fellowes-Gordon; With this ring, by M. Hardwick; The vampire of Croglin, by M. Hardwick; Donovan's drop, by I. Fellowes-Gordon; The beaked horror which sank a ship, by J. W. Day; The dog-man horror of the valley, by J. W. Day; They ate their young shipmate, by G. Williamson; The mate of the Squando, by M. Hardwick; Ripe Stilton, by M. Hardwick; The princess of Thebes, by M. Hardwick; Death takes vengeance, by V. Derry; A date with a spider, by V. Derry; Ole rockin' chair, by M. Hardwick; The frightened corpse, by V. Derry; The vampire of Castle Furstenstein, by J. W. Day; The great white bat, by F. Usher; Let sleeping bones lie, by M. Hardwick; Sung to his death by dead men, by J. W. Day; The man who hated cats, by M. Hardwick; Accusing eyes of vengeance, by G. Williamson; The walking dead, by F. Usher; Visit from a vampire, by R. Seth; The exorcising of the restless monk, by R. Seth; The recluse of Kotka Veski, by R. Seth; The secret agents and the corpse, by R. Seth; The bath of acid, by F. Usher; The girl in the train, by I. Fellowes-Gordon; The Black Dahlia, by F. Usher; Scent of death, by R. Seth; The face of Mrs Cartwright, by I. Fellowes-Gordon; The events of Schloss Heidiger, by I. Fellowes-Gordon; The birthday gift, by I. Fellowes-Gordon; The attic room, by I. Fellowes-Gordon; Footprints in the dust, by R. Seth; Amazonian horrors, by F. Usher; The image of fear, by V. Derry; Lullaby for the dead, by M. Hardwick; Rose: a Gothick tale, by M. Hardwick; The eyes of Thomas Bolter, by M. Hardwick

Canning, Victor

The melting man. Morrow 1969 286p boards $5.95

"A suspenseful tale, which involves Rex Carver in a search for a millionaire's stolen car, about which he is suspiciously concerned. Carter encounters numerous situations involving dead bodies and very lively ones." Book News
"Canning is always urbane and such weaknesses as several dangling loose ends can be forgiven him in the thrills of the chase." Pub W

The Scorpio letters. Sloane 1964 256p boards $3.95

"When Luigi Fettoni was killed by a London bus the police found four stamped and addressed letters in his pocket. They were all signed Scorpio and were levying blackmail. One of those letters, however, was to Professor Dean, who had been almost a father to George Constantine. He thought that Scorpio had been killed, but George soon found out that Scorpio had still to be caught and silenced." Bk Buyer's Guide

Cannon, LeGrand

y Look to the mountain

Some editions are:
Holt $1.95
Watts, F. $9.95 Large type edition. A Keith Jennison book
First published 1942
"Long novel about pioneering in the New Hampshire Grants from 1769 to 1777. The chief characters are a young bride and groom who left the settlements to make their home in the wilderness of the Grants." Book Rev Digest
There is "an understanding of primitive courage and simplicity, a sense of the free and lovely wilderness from which they carved a spare living with heroic fortitude of soul and muscle. There is also an intricate knowledge of the details of living in those times which shows that Mr. Cannon has read long and sympathetically of their records." Yale R

Čapek, Karel

The absolute at large
In Knight, D. ed. A century of great short science fiction novels p169-229

Capote, Truman

Breakfast at Tiffany's; a short novel and three stories. Random House 1958 179p $3.95

Analyzed in Short Story Index
" 'Breakfast at Tiffany's' tells the story of haunting and neurotic Holiday Golightly, Texan child-bride, girl-about-New York and

Capote, Truman—*Continued*

friend of gangster czar, Sally Tomato, in a remarkable novelette that bears the Capote trademark of neat prose, multiple dimensions and unusual atmosphere. The three other shorter stories in the collection corroborate a new maturity of insight and control of materials." Ontario Lib Rev

Short stories included are: House of flowers; A diamond guitar; A Christmas memory

A Christmas memory. Random House [1966 c1956] 45p $5

Appeared originally in Mademoiselle, and later in the author's "Breakfast at Tiffany's"

"This beautiful, bittersweet story evokes Alabama 'coming-of-winter' mornings, 'fruitcake weather' and the special joys of Christmas preparations shared by a small boy and his best friend [an elderly cousin]." McClurg. Book News

also in Capote, T. Breakfast at Tiffany's

The grass harp. Random House 1951 181p o.p. 1970

"Collin, the sixteen-year-old narrator, is an orphan who lives with his aunts, shrewish, miserly Verena, and sweet, addled Dolly; his story deals principally with Dolly's great rebellion. When Verena and a sharpster tried to capitalize on Dolly's dropsy remedy, the much put-upon sister ran away, taking refuge with Collin and a devoted servant in a tree house, where they withstood Verena's siege with the aid of an elderly genteman who was smitten with Dolly, and a traveling female evangelist and her 15 children." Booklist

"This is a situation which is obviously hard to handle, but Mr. Capote's art endows it with life and poetic beauty and, what is more, with meaning, and his prose style, which has great depth and texture, is a splendid vehicle for his tale and never obtrudes itself in a way that confuses his sharp and sympathetic delineation of character. In the end, he makes his tree house and all its peculiar denizens as understandable and actual as his panorama of a Southern town and of the more stable characters within it." Book of the Month Club News

Other voices, other rooms. Random House 1968 231p $4.95

First published 1948

A "novel describing the abnormal maturing of a loveless thirteen-year-old boy who goes to live with his father in a run-down Louisiana mansion peopled with eccentric characters." Book Rev Digest

"Much may still be desired in this tale of a pilgrimage through adolescence whose sources appear to be first-hand and autobiographical despite the apparent influences of McCullers, Barnes, Faulkner and Proust. 'Other Voices, Other Rooms' must be reckoned with as a fascinating experiment in symbols and images . . . notwithstanding the immediate reservations made by those who prefer obscure substance to definite shadow." Commonweal

y The Thanksgiving visitor. Random House [1968 c1967] 63p boards $4.95

"Odd [a bully] picked especially on a polite, neat, tiny boy named Buddy, who was 8 years old and lived with four elderly unmarried cousins in a big house on the edge of town. As a result Buddy hated Odd almost as much as he feared him, so who would have dreamed that Odd Henderson in the flesh, his hair combed and an embarrassed look on his face, would turn up at Buddy's house . . . on Thanksgiving Day? Truman Capote's brief story is as wispy as Buddy himself must have been at the age of 8, but it has that peculiar Capote blend of energy and whimsy." Book of the Month Club News

A tree of night, and other stories. Random House 1949 209p o.p. 1970

Analyzed in Short Story Index

Eight short stories with psychic or supernatural backgrounds

Contents: Master Misery; Children on their birthdays; Shut a final door; Jug of silver; Mirian; The headless hawk; My side of the matter; A tree of night

Capps, Benjamin

The white man's road. Harper 1969 309p $6.95

This is a "portrait of a young Comanche and his quest for the adventures, and the pride, of his ancestors. Son of an Indian mother and a white father he has not seen since childhood, Joe Cowbone has arrived at the age of 27 with far more questions than answers. Principal among them is how one can become, or remain, a man in the midst of the conditions resulting from the white man's takeover of the Indians' land and challenge to his heritage. The vehicle for Joe's self-discovery is a dramatic horse-stealing raid he devises and carries out with the aid of three friends." Pub W

"The book suffers from a trite ending in which everyone lives happily ever after according to the white man's laws, but that is not enough to reject this otherwise interesting book of Indian life in the 1890's." Library J

A woman of the people; a novel. Duell 1966 242p boards $5.95

Captured in 1854 by Comanche Indians, nine-year-old Helen Morrison "yearned to escape, but over the years the tribe absorbed her into their ways, and the love of her adopted family and, later of her husband, tied emotional bonds. Her slow change from white to Indian, the nomadic way of life, the tribe's pursuit of the buffaloes, and the tragic last years of the tribe as the white men raided, killed, and destroyed are . . . portrayed." Pub W

"'A Woman of the People' tells a dramatic story of the Morrison girl's captivity, but it tells also in copious and apparently authentic detail about 19th-century Comanche life: how 'the people' dressed, what they ate, how they hunted, traded, sang, tended their sick and wounded, buried their dead." Book of the Month Club News

Carleton, Jetta

The moonflower vine. Simon & Schuster 1962 352p boards $4.95

"Matt and Callie moved to a remote Missouri farm about 1899, and Matt farmed and worked his way up from teaching in the country to being principal of the town school. Each summer the family returned to the farm. The moonflower vine bloomed at dusk—a miracle of fragile white beauty with bittersweet scent. Fifty years later the girls return for their annual visit. Mary Jo, the youngest, recalls the family story: Matt's struggle for success; Callie's love and loyalty; Jessica's elopement; Leonie, beautiful, prim and ambitious, whose life was full of frustrations; Mathy, for 15 years the youngest—gay, unpredictable, different—whose short marriage ended in death; and relatives and friends whose lives touched theirs." Library J

Carpenter, Don

The murder of the frogs, and other stories. Harcourt 1969 242p $5.95

"The High Sierras, the Oregon back country, Hollywood, San Francisco and its environs provide settings for the two novellas and eight shorter pieces brought together in this . . . volume." Publisher's note

Contents: Road show; The crossroader; Blue eyes; New York to Los Angeles; Silver lamé; Limbo; The murder of the frogs [novella]; Hollywood heart; Hollywood whore; One of those big-city girls [novella]

One of those big-city girls

In Carpenter, D. The murder of the frogs, and other stories p199-242

Carpentier, Alejo

The kingdom of this world. Tr. from the Spanish by Harriet de Onís. Knopf 1957 150p o.p. 1970

This short work "re-creates the eighteenth-century era of foreign misrule in Haiti, the subsequent native uprising, and the travesty of government by the new conquerors who turned out to be more tyrannical than their former

Carpentier, Alejo—*Continued*

masters. Historic figures, notably Toussaint L' Ouverture, Henri Christophe, and Pauline Bonaparte, mingle with fictitious characters in a picaresque tale narrated by Ti Nöel, a slave who lived through the successive dynasties. A story with an implied moral—that violence breeds violence—marked by a distinguished style." Booklist

Carr, John Dickson

The Arabian nights murder

In Carr, J. D. Three detective novels p3-195

The bride of Newgate. Harper 1950 308p o.p. 1970

"Historical novel of England in 1815. Dick Darwent, a condemned felon, marries Lady Caroline Ross, one hour before he is to die. Lady Caroline wanted a marriage in name only to preserve her inheritance, and Dick wanted the fifty pounds she offered to leave to his mistress. But owing to his cousins' deaths at the battle of Waterloo Dick becomes Marquess of Darwent and is saved just in time. The long battle which ensues between the ex-felon and his unwilling-to-willing wife completes the story." Booklist

"Fast and entertaining reading. . . . There is an abundance of accurate detail on the social life of London at the time of Bonaparte's final defeat, when the laws of etiquet were regarded as more binding than the laws of parliament. And there is continuous action and suspense." Chicago Sunday Tribune

The burning court

In Carr, J. D. Three detective novels p197-355

The case of the constant suicides

In Carr, J. D. A John Dickson Carr trio p339-472

The crooked hinge

In Carr, J. D. A John Dickson Carr trio p175-338

The ghosts' high noon; a detective novel. Harper 1969 255p $5.95

"Col. George Harvey, the editor of Harper's Weekly, has sent Jim Blake to New Orleans to do a story on the congressional election. Jim found New Orleans a town of rumors and enchantment, anonymous letters, odd phone calls and sudden death." News of Bks

"The politician, it develops, is threatened owing to sexual peccadilloes, both real and imaginary. Then comes impossible murder. If the verbal posturing seems too heavily laid on here, if Mr. Carr's tale has a mite less vitality than in times past—still its charm and intricacy easily make it worthwhile." N Y Times Bk R

The house at Satan's Elbow. Harper 1965 249p o.p. 1970

"Dr. Fell is back to explain another locked room mystery. A 'ghost' has attempted to shoot elderly Pen Barclay, there have been mysterious women about, but a clever trap catches the villain." Bk Buyer's Guide

A John Dickson Carr trio. . . . Harper 1957 472p o.p. 1970

"Including The three coffins; The crooked hinge; The case of the constant suicides." Subtitle

Dr Gideon Fell is the detective in all three

" 'The Crooked Hinge' deals with the claimants to a huge estate; 'The Three Coffins' tells of the murder of Professor Grimaud; 'The Case of the Constant Suicides' revolves around a Highland ghost and a drink called 'the Doom of the Campbells.' " Huntting

Papa Là-bas. Harper 1968 277p $5.95

The scene is "New Orleans in the spring of 1858. There strong men, lovely women, and dark magic and violence swirl around Senator Judah P. Benjamin, a wise man who can solve any problem by logical analysis, and around Richard Macrae, Her Majesty's Consul. Together they witness the first death at the home of their friends the de Sancerres." Library J

Carr's New Orleans is "vividly constructed out of diligent research and peopled, in part, with historical characters. On his stage he has put murder, and concealed the killer with devilish cleverness; as before, he has the effrontery to sprinkle the proceedings with clues (you won't spot them!) to the murderer's identity. And as side attraction, there's a strong howdunit aspect as well." N Y Times Bk R

The problem of the wire cage

In Carr, J. D. Three detective novels p357-508

Scandal at High Chimneys; a Victorian melodrama. Harper 1959 230p o.p. 1970

"Victorian London, on the surface stuffy and proper, but beneath the surface bawdy and dangerous, is the brilliant background for a. [mystery] period novel—with two beautiful sisters, a detective drawn from history, and an impossible murder." McClurg. Book News

The three coffins

In Carr, J. D. A John Dickson Carr trio p 1-173

Three detective novels; including the Arabian nights murder, The burning court, The problem of the wire cage. Harper 1959 508p o.p. 1970

In this anthology of Carr's earlier books, Arabian nights murder, first published 1936, and The problem of the wire cage, first published 1939, feature the beloved detective Dr Gideon Fell. The third title, The burning court, first published 1937, deals with supernatural phenomena in a suspenseful, haunting mystery

(jt. auth.) Doyle, A. C. Exploits of Sherlock Holmes

Carr, Terry

(ed.) Science fiction for people who hate science fiction. Doubleday 1966 190p (Doubleday Science fiction) o.p. 1970

Analyzed in Short Story Index

"Space and time travel, mutations, nuclear disaster, aliens, dark and light humor, social satire—the major themes and approaches are all represented." Library J

Contents: The star, by A. C. Clarke; A sound of thunder, by R. Bradbury; The year of the jackpot, by R. A. Heinlein; The man with English, by H. L. Gold; In hiding, by W. H. Shiras; Not with a bang, by D. Knight; Love called this thing, by A. Davidson; The weapon, by F. Brown; What's it like out there, by E. Hamilton

Carroll, Gladys Hasty

y As the earth turns

Some editions are:

Macmillan (N Y) $3.95

Watts, F. $9.95 Large type edition complete and unabridged. A Keith Jennison book

First published 1933

"A chronicle of the events of one year in the lives of the family of Mark Shaw, a Maine farmer of the present day. Winter chores, spring plowing, summer work, fall harvesting; a wedding, a death, and a birth are all recorded 'as the earth turns.' The principal character is the oldest daughter, Jen, about whom all the family life revolves." Book Rev Digest

"Mrs. Carroll has caught the atmosphere just as she has mirrored the character of these people with humor and real understanding." Boston Transcript

Come with me home. Little 1960 308p boards $5.95

A "story of an elderly Maine spinster. Rosamond Lacey lives alone in her remote family home and has few friends except for a local college boy who does her chores. As the result of a Minnesota newspaper article, her entire way of living changes and her influence spreads far and wide, helping everyone it touches through her innate humor and sturdy philosophy of life founded on two salient precepts—'to live well and without fear of anyone or anything.' " Library J

"Even though contrived, discursive, and didactic the book, by virtue of its regional setting and meaningful theme, will please conservative women readers." Booklist

Carroll, Gordon
(ed.) The Saturday Evening Post. The Post Reader of Civil War stories

Carroll, Lewis
The annotated Alice; Alice's adventures in Wonderland & Through the looking glass. Illus. by John Tenniel; with an introduction and notes by Martin Gardner. Bramhall House 1960 352p illus $10

Classic stories for all ages, first published 1865 and 1871 respectively

Through the looking glass

In Carroll, L. The annotated Alice p175-352

Carse, Robert
Great circle. Scribner 1956 243p o.p. 1970

A tale of a whaling voyage in the 1840's. The "Obis," out of Salem, is commanded by young Jered Naish on a long, cruel voyage into the South Atlantic, around the Horn, eventually to an atoll in the South Pacific. (Publisher)

"Paradoxically Robert Carse has written a lusty and vigorous novel with fastidious restraint. There are episodes which, in a less gifted author, would be treated with salacious luridness, but which Mr. Carse has chosen not to ignore, but to portray in a fashion calm, almost detached." N Y Her Trib Books

Carter, Youngman
Mr Campion's farthing; from an idea by Margery Allingham. Morrow 1969 219p boards $4.95

The book "concerns a missing Russian scientist whose whereabouts are of considerable interest to several governments, and, of course, to that eminent detective, Mr. Albert Campion. Campion's chief concern is for his friend, Lottie Cambric, for it was at her estate, Inglewood Turrets, the scientist last had been seen. But that utterly charming, theatrical and quick-witted lady shrugs off all questions, saying 'He was here, he left, and that's it.' Mr. Campion doesn't believe her. Neither do the Russians." Publisher's note

Carvic, Heron
Miss Seeton draws the line. Harper 1970 200p boards $4.95

"A Joan Kahn-Harper Novel of suspense"

Miss Seeton, an "elderly drawing-mistress who is on vacation in the little village of Plummergen, England and whose talent for catching in her drawings of people the clues that lead to discovery of hidden qualities, finds herself somewhat beset by an unidentified strangler who has killed six children, a pair of bandits on bikes, and an absconding cashier. Sergeant Delphick of Scotland Yard has faith in the little old lady's extraordinary skill." Best Sellers

Picture Miss Seeton. Harper 1968 209p boards $4.95

"A Joan Kahn-Harper Novel of suspense"

"On her way back from the opera Miss Seeton witnesses a murder. Although the police try to protect her by secluding her in the country, the gang responsible trails her there and some rum encounters ensue, with several other deaths, before Miss Seeton nails the master mind of a dope ring. Amusing dialog, a pleasant atmosphere of rather bumbling British country high society, and a heroine we hope to see more of." Pub W

Cary, Joyce
The African witch. Harper 313p o.p. 1970

A reprint of the title first published 1936 by Morrow

"Compellingly engrossing novel, portraying with satire, humor and terrific realism a tensely critical situation in a British protectorate in Africa. Aladai, a young native, educated at Oxford, returns home, aspiring to become chief of his people. He finds other aspirants, and the English Resident wavering in his support. The native political pot boils over into strife and bloodshed, a powerful 'ju-ju' priestess performs violent and horrifying deeds, there is a native women's war, and there is bad feeling, even tragedy among the English, muddling along with their usual ineptitude. Brilliant in interpretation of native psychology, and striking for its color, suspense, and atmosphere. Gruesome scenes may repel some readers." N Y Libraries

Charley is my darling. Harper [1960] 342p o.p. 1970

First published 1940 in England

"The story of a small boy evacuated to the West Country from a London slum [in World War II]. He overcomes his initial unpopularity among his fellow evacuees to become the leader of a gang." Pub W

"'Charley Is My Darling' is authentic Cary, and for those new to him it is the perfect introduction to his work. One finds the humor, wild at times almost to the point of farce and yet never departing from credibility, and the poignancy. . . . There are extraordinarily vivid character sketches of men, women, and children caught, it seems, in the very moment of living. There are also exquisite passages." Sat R

Except the Lord; a novel. Harper 1953 276p o.p. 1970

Sequel to: Prisoner of grace

"Chester Nimmo of the author's 'Prisoner of grace' writes an account of his childhood and young manhood in Devonshire of the 1870's, he reveals the conditions and people that determined his life as preacher, labor leader, and politician. The characterizations are particularly well done, especially of the fiery tempered older sister who kept the poor family together after the mother's death, and of the father, a self-educated farm helper and preacher who firmly believed in the Second Coming." Booklist

"The story is a rich and spirited piece of work, but it lacks the excitement of a natural rise, or climax, and of a natural ending." New Yorker

Followed by: Not honour more

A fearful joy; a novel. Harper 1950 343p o.p. 1970

First published 1949 in England

"The story of Tabitha Baskett's stormy and fitful romance with Dick Bonser. Though she ran off with him in early youth, Tabitha was long past middle age and a grandmother before he at last fulfilled his promise to marry her. By that timet, she had been twice married and twice widowed and as wife of one of England's great industrialists, had helped wage and win a war. On the whole, her life had been busy and rewarding, but it was Bonser, by the power of his imagination—an imagination he used for lies and crookery—who touched it with a kind of glory." Huntting

"Through Tabitha's associates, the author comments freely on art, literature, war profiteering, and changing morals in England during the 50 year period covered by the novel." Booklist

First trilogy. Harper 1958 3v in 1 $7.95

Contains: Herself surprised; To be a pilgrim; The horse's mouth, all entered separately

Herself surprised; a novel. Harper 1948 275p o.p. 1970

First published in England 1941

"The life story, in the first person singular, of one of the most engaging and most realized heroines of recent fiction. Here is a saga of the downward path which has robust reality and intense feeling, and which is richly humorous in the telling." Atlantic

The author's "light-hearted yet shrewd story of this buxom daughter out of Moll Flanders by Rubens may not be what is sometimes referred to as 'good clean fun,' but it is fun indeed and subtly, tangily, somewhat more: it is social satire of the sort that Mrs. Gaskell, say, was perfect mistress of a hundred-odd years ago." N Y Her Trib Books

The horse's mouth; a novel. Harper 1950 311p o.p. 1970

Followed by: To be a pilgrim

First published in England

Sequel to: To be a pilgrim

"Once quite famous, Gulley Jimson, 67-year-old English artist, reveals his reflections, his

Cary, Joyce—*Continued*

ideas for pictures, hi sefforts to cadge a dinner or the price of a canvas, his interlude in jail (for smashing windows), his reunion with his old love, Sara Monday. The story of an engaging, if unprincipled, Bohemian." Retail Bookseller

"His story is inspired, hilarious, alive and somewhat bawdy. It's an impressive job of portraiture and wonderful entertainment." Library J

Mister Johnson; a novel. Harper 1951 261p o.p. 1970

First published 1939 in England

"A black Walter Mittee, in Nigeria, lets his dreams of grandeur ruin him. Johnson is a very minor government clerk, hardly more than a boy. Friendly and happy, he buys a bride he cannot afford, gets deeper and deeper into debt, and finally is caught at the government till and kills his captor." Retail Bookseller

"Cary knows what he is writing about. During World War I he fought through the Cameroons campaign as a officer in a Nigerian regiment, later became magistrate of a district deep in the bush. Of the four novels that have come out of his African experience, Mister Johnson is the best, at once humorous and sympathetic, fresh and exuberant." Time

Not honour more; a novel. Harper 1955 309p o.p. 1970

Third novel in a trilogy about Chester Nimmo of which the first two were: Prisoner of grace, and Except the Lord

Chester Nimmo "is presented here in the narration of Captain Latter, childhood sweetheart and second husband of Nina. The time is that of the General Strike in England when the aging Nimmo tries to reassert himself as a labor leader and also continues a hold over Nina, still his secretary although no longer his wife. The political disparity of Nimmo and Latter and their rivalry for Nina lead to the violent ending foreshadowed throughout the book." Booklist

"It may be the work suffers from having as its central figure a character who would ordinarily be playing a supporting part. However, Cary's characterization of the Captain is excellent. In any case the importance of the book rests in its completion of the trilogy. Cary fans will be interested in reading it." Library J

Prisoner of grace; a novel. Harper 1952 301p o.p. 1970

The author's story "beginning in the late Victorian era, is told in the first person by an English gentlewoman in love with a quite worthless cousin, by whom she contrives to have two children, although she is married to a parvenu who in the First World War achieves Cabinet rank and leadership in his party. . . . It is a woman's version of the perpetual battle of the sexes and of her domination by a man whom she partly admires and partly despises. . . . It is also a devastating account of the developing ambition and egotism of a politician, a type which seems about the same in England and America." Book of the Month Club News

"It is hard to praise adequately the power, the understanding, and the degree of organisation with which this rich, full story is told." Spec

Followed by: Except the Lord

To be a pilgrim; a novel. Harper 1949 343p o.p. 1970

First published 1942 in England

Sequel to: Herself surprised

"A retired English lawyer is the narrator. Tom Wilcher is taken by Ann, his plain young doctor niece to the family's country house, where she plans to attend him in his last years. A nephew arrives and takes over the farm and marries Ann. The stories of the present and the past intermingle as Tom Wilcher relives his life in memory, and proves to Ann and her husband that he is not so crazy as the family consider him." Book Rev Digest

"Mr. Cary is incapable of plot or profundity. Instead, he has actuality like Defoe, humor and energy like Dickens, hand-made prose and improvisation like both these great writers. After your few hours with Tom Wilcher's memories, life won't look very different, but you will

probably see it more clearly, and like it better —that is, you will have read a classic." N Y Times Bk R

Followed by: The horse's mouth

Case, David

The cell; three tales of horror. Hill & Wang 1969 269p $5

Contents: The cell; The hunter; The dead end

These three tales "are chilling examples of fantastic terror involving lycanthropy, paranoia, and a mad scientist." Library J

Caskoden, Edwin. See Major, Charles

Castillo, Michel del. See Del Castillo, Michel

Cather, Willa

y Death comes for the archbishop. Knopf 1927 303p $4.95

"Miss Cather tells the story of a French priest who in the middle years of the last century went to New Mexico, as vicar apostolic and became archbishop of Santa Fe. With him went also Father Joseph Vaillant, friend of his seminary days in France. The two labored together devotedly and by their love and wisdom won the Southwest for the Catholic church. It was after nearly forty years of good works in his diocese that death came for the archbishop and he lay before the high alter in the church he had built. He died 'of having lived.' " Book Rev Digest

"A mature and beautiful novel by one of our great living prose writers. Serene and contemplative in manner, it is typical of Miss Cather's best work, symbolizing the fruition of her literary artistry." Ind

Early stories of Willa Cather; selected with commentary by Mildred R. Bennett. Dodd 1957 275p o.p. 1970

Analyzed in Short Story Index

Nineteen "stories published in newspapers and magazines between 1892-1901, annotated throughout to point out literary or personal influences and possible seeds of themes, plots and characters which germinated in her later larger works." Pub W

Contents: Peter; Lou, the prophet; A tale of the white pyramid; A son of the Celestial: a character; The clemency of the court; "The fear that walks by noonday"; On the divide; A night at Greenway Court; Nanette: an aside; Tommy, the unsentimental; The Count of Crow's Nest; A resurrection; The prodigies; Eric Hermannson's soul; The dance at Chevalier's; The sentimentality of William Tavener; The affair at Grover Station; A singer's romance; The conversion of Sum Loo

"A portrait of the artist as a young lady, a curiosity piece, this is a book less to be read and enjoyed than to be studied and enjoyed." San Francisco Chronicle

y A lost lady. Knopf 1923 173p $4.50

"The story of Marian Forrester is told by Niel Herbert, a Midwestern youth. Married to rugged old empire-builder Captain Forrester, Marian's graciousness sets her much above her commonplace neighbors. She becomes the lover of his friend, Frank Ellinger, however; and after the Captain's death due to a stroke, the lover of Ivy Peters, the man who acquires her home. Peters marries, and the impoverished Marian returns to the West, a 'lost lady' in the eyes of her youthful admirer, Niel. He later hears that Marian, married to a wealthy Englishman, won the respect and admiration of all in her new surroundings." Haydn. Thesaurus of Book Digests

"There would be no excuse for calling it a great novel—it is not that; but there would be equally little excuse for not recognizing the fact that it is that very rare thing in contemporary literature, a nearly perfect one." Nation

Lucy Gayheart. Knopf 1935 231p o.p. 1970

"The story of a frustrated life ending in double tragedy. At the turn of the century, eighteen-year-old Lucy Gayheart leaves her small-town western home to study music in Chicago. After three years, an opportunity comes to play for rehearsals for a noted concert singer whom she has idolized since first she heard

Cather, Willa—*Continued*

him sing. Love follows, and tragedy ensues. A concluding chapter brings the story up to the present [1930's] . . . and traces the effect of circumstances on the life of the man Lucy might have married." Huntting

"A short tale whose charm lies in the beauty of the writing rather than in the events of the story." Pratt Q

y My Ántonia

Some editions are:
Houghton $6.95 With illustrations by W. T. Benda
Watts, F. $9.95 Large type edition. A Keith Jennison book

First published 1918
"Story is told by a New York lawyer who reviews his Nebraska boyhood days and his friendship with a young Bohemian girl, the strong and simple Antonia Shimerda, who is the central figure the novel. A convincing picture of pioneering conditions and of America's assimilation of the immigrant, and a fine portrayal of character." N Y State Lib

"The story is simply and faithfully told with appreciation of character and a strong feeling for the stubborn country and the rich rewards of its final yielding." Cleveland

My mortal enemy. Knopf 1926 122p illus $4.50

This is a "portrait of a lady seen . . . thru the eyes of an admiring yet clear-sighted friend of a younger generation. Myra Driscoll was an orphan brought up by her rich great-uncle in the fine old Driscoll home in Parthia, Illinois. The price the wilful, high-spirited girl paid for her runaway marriage was the omission of her name in her uncle's will and a life-long discontent. Love was not enough. Myra was, by her own confession, a greedy, selfish, worldly woman who wanted success and a place in the world. The young girl who narrates the story saw her on three occasions, once when Myra was visiting in Parthia, a woman of forty-five with a strange fascination about her, again in New York and finally, ten years later, in a shabby West Coast hotel where, ministered to by her devoted, if ineffectual husband, she was dying alone with her 'mortal enemy,' her inescapable, turbulent self." Book Rev Digest

y O pioneers!

Some editions are:
Houghton $4
Watts, F. $9.95 Large type edition. A Keith Jennison book

First published 1913
"The heroic battle for survival of simple pioneer folk in the Nebraska country of the 1880's. John Bergson, a Swedish farmer, struggles desperately with the soil but dies unsatisfied. His daughter Alexandra resolves to vindicate his faith, and her strong character carries her weak older brothers and her mother along to a new zest for life. Years of privation are rewarded on the farm. But when Alexandra falls in love with Carl Linstrum, and her family objects because he is poor, he leaves to seek a different career. After Alexandra's younger brother Emil is killed by the jealous husband of the French girl Marie Shabata, however, Carl gives up his plans to go to the Klondike, returns to marry Alexandra and take up the life of the farm." Haydn. Thesaurus of Book Digests

"The land itself, 'the Divide,' is made almost a character in the narrative and supplies that sense of conflict with the elemental forces of life which is essential to real tragedy. It is written with sympathy and power, compactly and with perfect restraint." Pittsburgh

Obscure destinies. Knopf 1932 229p $4.50

Analyzed in Short Story Index
"Three long short stories of the West. Neighbour Rosicky is the narrative of a Bohemian immigrant whose hunger for the earth drove him from New York to a Nebraska prairie farm; Old Mrs Harris, a character study of a fine old woman who tried to keep up the traditions of her comfortable life in Tennessee when she was transplanted to a Colorado town; Two Friends, the story of two well-to-do business men in a small Kansas town whose long friendship was broken up by their disagreement over politics." Book Rev Digest

The old beauty, and others. Knopf 1948 166p $4.50

Analyzed in Short Story Index
Three short stories
" 'The Old Beauty' is the story of a woman's life, done in brief compass through the power of suggestion and the use of telling and dramatic incident. . . . In 'The Best Years,' Miss Cather returns to the country of her heart, telling a story of youth in the Nebraska farm country. . . . 'Before Breakfast,' the final story in the collection, is the study of a man's success and failure, the setting of which is the Canadian island where Miss Cather often worked in the summer." Huntting

One of ours. Knopf 1922 459p $5.95

Pulitzer Prize 1923
"A spiritual biography of a young American brought up on a Nebraska farm, with a mediocre education, married to a prim and passionless wife, living a life which he could not make seem real until [the First World War] saved him and gave him something big to do that seemed worth doing." Pittsburgh

"A fine achievement. The first portion dealing with a farm life in Nebraska could not be matched by any one else now writing. The second part, in France and at the war, is more removed, but has its poignant beauty." Int Bk R

The professor's house. Knopf 1925 283p $4.50

"This novel concerns Professor Godfrey St. Peter, whose middle age in a university town in the 1920's is made interesting by completion of a work on Spanish explorers in America. Another theme is the Professor's gradual adjustment to personal loneliness. His wife Lillian has bought a new house, but he prefers to work in his old study; his daughters have married; his favorite student, Tom Outland (who had explored an old New Mexican cliff city) has died in the first World War. Rosamond and her husband Louie Marsellus are wealthy from a patent willed to her by Tom, her former fiancé. Kathleen is married to Scott McGregor, a writer who makes money by producing commercial pieces. One summer the Professor is about to commit suicide when the friendship and sympathy of old Augusta, a sewing woman, give him courage to face life again." Haydn. Thesaurus of Book Digests

This "is a disturbingly beautiful book, full of meanings, full of intentions. . . . Professor St. Peter is rather a spirit than a man. He is a spirit saying goodby to something much larger than the ugly old square domicile in which his life work was accomplished. He is a spirit reluctantly bidding farewell to a generation of American life, to a vanishing order of civilization." N Y Her Trib Books

Sapphira and the slave girl. Knopf 1940 295p $4.50

"Having married below her social rank, Sapphira Colbert, before the Civil War, exiled herself to a backwoods Virginia farm, with her husband, a miller, and her family slaves, and now aging and dropsical she puts an erroneous construction on her husband's interest in Nancy, a golden-skinned slave, once her own favorite. How Sapphira not only spoils a sweet companionship but sets about to persecute the once happy and devoted girl and even to bring about her downfall by keeping a rakish young nephew about the house is related." Bookmark

"It shows in its central character the tangible passion and struggle, in its secondary characters the honest virtue and credible humility, and in its general atmosphere of fear and obsession a dramatic force that lift the tale out of its exaggerated moralism and dramatic simplicity into its own kind of truth and power. Its people rise above the flat dimensions of moral humors." Nation

y Shadows on the rock. Knopf 1931 280p $4.95

"In this charming idyll of the French colony at Quebec in the time of Frontenac and Bishop Laval, Willa Cather has again chosen a background of Roman Catholic civilization. It is hardly a novel—rather a series of pictures and anecdotes of the homes, the marketplace, the Ursuline convent, the hunters, and the missionary priests of old Canada." Booklist

Cather, Willa—*Continued*

"In this quiet book, one steps back three and a half centuries, and shares, through the glowing magic of a deeply understanding prose, the life of the French colony, dwelling on the gray mountain rock, 'Kebec.' Characters, historic or imagined, are finely created, and the aspect of the rock itself, with its fortifications and churches, its convents and gardens, the mighty St Lawrence glittering at its base, is lovingly portrayed through the changing seasons." N Y Libraries

y The song of the lark. Houghton 1915 580p $5

"The story of the development of a great American singer. The old broken down music master in Moonstone, Colorado, told Mrs. Kronborg, wife of the Swedish minister, that the little girl, Thea, had talent. From that moment Thea's career was determined on. She must practice four hours a day and become a piano teacher. It is not until she goes to Chicago to continue her studies that she learns that her future lies in her voice. Three men believe in Thea, Ray Kennedy, the freight train conductor, Howard Archie, the Moonstone doctor, and Fred Ottenburg, the millionaire brewer. Each in his way helps her, and she justifies their faith. She leaves Moonstone far behind her, but she never gets away from its influence." Book Rev Digest

"It is not so much the feeling of life that I get here, as the sense of something less common than life; namely, art as it exists in life, —a very curious and elusive thing, but so beautiful, when one gets at it, that one forgets all else." Dial

The troll garden
In Cather, W. Willa Cather's Collected short fiction, 1892-1912 p147-261

Willa Cather's Collected short fiction, 1892-1912. Introduction by Mildred R. Bennett. Univ. of Neb. Press 1965 3v in 1 (xli, 594p) $8.50

Analyzed in Short Story Index
An anthology of Willa Cather's early writings
Contents: v 1 The Bohemian girl; v2 The troll garden [published separately, 1905]; v3 On the divide
Short stories included are: v 1: The Bohemian girl; Behind the Singer Tower; The joy of Nelly Deane; The enchanted bluff; On the gulls' road; Eleanor's house; The willing muse; The profile; The namesake; v2: Flavia and her artists; The sculptor's funeral; The garden lodge; "A death in the desert"; The marriage of Phaedra; A Wagner matinee; Paul's case; v3: The treasure of Far Island; The professor's commencement; El Dorado: A Kansas recessional; Jack-a-Boy; The conversion of Sum Loo; A singer's romance; The affair at Grove Station; The sentimentality of William Tavener; Eric Hermannson's soul; The westbound train; The way of the world; Nanette: an aside; The prodigies; A resurrection; The strategy of the Were-Wolf Dog: The Count of Crow's Nest; Tommy, the unsentimental; A night at Greenway Court; On the divide; "The fear that walks by noonday"; The clemency of the court; A son of the Celestial; A tale of the white pyramid; Lou, the prophet; Peter
"These early magazine stories . . . tend to be a pat and dreary lot, written in what young Miss Cather believed to be a style of international sophistication. . . . [But] 'On the Gulls' Road' is a beauty, and several others are interesting for one reason or another, and well worth having, The editing, with scrupulous bibliographical appendices, meets the highest standards of scholarship." New Yorker

Youth and the bright Medusa. Knopf 1920 303p $4.50

Analyzed in Short Story Index
Contents: Coming, Aphrodite; Diamond mine; Gold slipper; Scandal; Paul's case; Wagner matinee; Sculptor's funeral; "Death in the desert"

"The stories have the radiance of perfect cleanliness, like the radiance of burnished glass. Miss Cather's book is more than a random collection of excellent tales. It constitutes

as a whole one of the truest as well as, in a sober and earnest sense, one of the most poetical interpretations of American life that we possess." Nation

Catto, Max
Murphy's war. Simon & Schuster [1969 c1968] 284p boards $5.95

Murphy, an Australian seaman, "is the sole survivor of an armed merchantman torpedoed by [German submarine] U-482. Cast up on a reef at the mouth of a great African river, he witnesses the ruthless sinking of a helpless hospital ship by the same submarine. Struggling for his own survival, he sees . . . the submarine making its way into hiding far up the estuary of the winding jungle river. Even after he finds safety at a missionary hospital, Murphy is driven to pursue the submarine that now represents for him all the evils of war." Publisher's note

"Catto describes the milieu of this struggle vividly. The noises and smells of the estuary, the slithering animals as they come and go in the water, the torpid heat and Murphy's relentless revenge are contrasted and skillfully related. This is a don't-stop-till-you-finish story, swiftly told and believable." Best Sellers

Cecil, Henry
Friends at court. Harper 1957 [c1956] 178p o.p. 1970

First published 1956 in England
"After 12 successful years, Roger Thursby, naive junior barrister of 'Brothers in law' (1955) is about to be appointed a Queen's Counsel and this is the entertaining tale of his unorthodox handling of a police bribery case and his courtship of the Chief Constable's daughter." Bookmark

Cela, Camilo José
Mrs Caldwell speaks to her son. Mrs Caldwell habla con su hijo, in the authorized English translation and with an introduction by J. S. Bernstein. Cornell Univ. Press 1968 xxvi, 206p $5.95

Original Spanish edition published 1953
"Mrs. Caldwell, an elderly English widow, is eccentric at the beginning of the story and grows progressively more alienated from reality as she recalls her past and brings forth memories of Eliacim, her dead son. The book consists of her reminiscences, which are addressed to him." Publishtr's note

"The atmosphere of [this novel] is euphuistic and rarefied [and it is] avant-garde in technique. . . . In spite of its occasional strange beauty, the novel finally seems just that irrelevant: a madwoman interminably addressing a dead person who was never very real to her in the first place." N Y Times Bk R

Céline, Louis Ferdinand
Castle to castle; tr. by Ralph Manheim. Delacorte Press 1968 xx, 359p boards $7.50

"A Seymour Lawrence book"
Original French edition 1957; National Book Award, 1969
"Human deterioration from age and under persecution depicted in the character of a Frenchman who collaborated with the Germans in World War II and whose mind and body were destroyed." Chicago
"Céline's style pretends to complete cynicism, but the richness of his writing is built on his intense sympathy with individual human beings and his disgust with the laws and values and ambitions that destroy them. Which is greatly to oversimplify a difficult and excellent book." Book World

Journey to the end of the night; tr. from the French by John H. P. Marks. Little 1934 509p o.p. 1970

First published 1932 in France
"The story follows the adventures of Bardamu, the narrator, from the outbreak of the war to the present. Bardamu escapes from the front and lands in a hospital for the mentally deranged. Later he embarks for French Colonial Africa, and then for America. He winds up as a doctor in a squalid suburb of Paris.

Céline, Louis F.—*Continued*

The book is an outlet for the expression of his disgust for everything in life." Book Rev Digest

"A vast, sardonic, lyrical, obscene phantasmagoria in which one sees the whole modern world go marching to its doom. War, business, industry, cities, crowds, soldiers, tropical forests, colonial outposts, whore houses, factories, the slums and backwaters of civilization flash before the reader. . . . Creates the effect of extraordinary scope, the mood of the endlessness of suffering and defeat." Nation

Cerf, Bennett

(ed.) An anthology of famous British stories; ed. by Bennett Cerf and Henry C. Moriarty. Modern Lib. 1952 xxii, 1233p $4.95

First published in 1940 with title: The bedside book of famous British stories, and analyzed in Short Story Index

Contents: Pardoner's tale, by G. Chaucer; Marvellous adventure of the sword, by Sir T. Malory; Apparition of Mrs Veal, by D. Defoe; Vision of Mirza, by J. Addison; Asem, an Eastern tale, by O. Goldsmith; Two drovers, by Sir W. Scott; Iron shroud, by W. Mudford; The gridiron, by S. Lover; House and the brain, by E. Bulwer-Lytton; Con Cregan's legacy, by C. Lever; Rab and his friends, by J. Brown; Half-brothers, by E. C. Gaskell; Sultan stork, by W. M. Thackeray; Christmas carol, by C. Dickens; Malachi's Cove, by A. Trollope; Punishment of Shahpesh, the Persian, on Khipil, the builder, by G. Meredith; Three strangers, by T. Hardy; Story of a piebald horse, by W. H. Hudson; Sire de Malétroit's door, by R. L. Stevenson; Lodging for the night, by R. L. Stevenson; Story of Dr MacLure, by J. Watson; Faith, by R. C. Graham; Clerk's quest, by G. Moore; Birthday of the Infanta, by O. Wilde; Youth, by J. Conrad; Captain of the "Ullswater" by M. Roberts; Adventure of the speckled band, by A. C. Doyle; Courting of T'nowhead's Bell, by Sir J. M. Barrie; Babus of Nayanjore, by Sir R. Tagore; Philippa's fox-hunt, by E. Somerville; The mezzotint, by M. R. James; "Hey diddle diddle, the cat . . ." by E. Phillpotts; Adventure of the kind Mr Smith, by W. J. Locke; Roll-call on the reef, by Sir A. T. Quiller-Couch; That brute Simmons, by A. Morrison; Monkey's paw, by W. W. Jacobs; Doll in the pink silk dress, by L. Merrick; Drums of the fore and aft, by R. Kipling; Man who would be king, by R. Kipling; Red Hanrahan, by W. B. Yeats; Country of the blind, by H. G. Wells; Mary with the high hand, by A. Bennett; Appletree, by J. Galsworthy; Action, by C. E. Montague; Valley of beasts, by A. Blackwood; Mrs Packletide's tiger, by Saki; Happy hypocrite, by M. Beerbohm; The derelict, by H. M. Tomlinson; Red, by W. S. Maugham; Hammer of God, by G. K. Chesterton; Kings of Orion, by J. Buchan; Stranger in the village, by Sir P. Gibbs; The higgler, by A. E. Coppard; Western islands, by J. Masefield; Sword of Welleran, by Lord Dunsany; Celestial omnibus, by E. M. Forster; Log of the "Evening Star," by A. Noyes; Jeeves and the song of songs, by P. G. Wodehouse; Three lovers who lost, by J. Stephens; The dead, by J. Joyce; Purple and fine linen, by M. Edginton; Mr Oddy, by Sir H. Walpole; Busman's holiday, by F. B. Young; Sleeping draft, by W. Martyr; Prussian officer, by D. H. Lawrence; Fish are such liars, by R. Pertwee; Source of irritation, by S. Aumonier; Chink and the child, by T. Burke; Life of Ma Parker, by K. Mansfield; Day in a woman's life, by Kaye-Smith; Rivers of Damascus, by D. Byrne; Gioconda smile, by A. Huxley; Cavalier of the streets, by M. Arlen; Old hunter, by L. O'Flaherty; White cottage, by L. A. G. Strong; Trapper's mates, by H. Williamson; Forty-third division, by R. Bates; The eyes, by T. O. Beachcroft; Betting Scotchman; Bella Fleace gave a party, by E. Waugh

(ed.) Famous ghost stories; comp. and with an introductory note by Bennett A. Cerf. Modern Lib. 1944 361p $2.95

Analyzed in Short Story Index
First published in this edition 1919 with title: The best ghost stories
Contents: The haunted and the haunters, by E. Bulwer-Lytton; The damned thing, by A. Bierce; The monkey's paw, by W. Jacobs;

The phantom, 'rickshaw, by R. Kipling; The willows, by A. Blackwood; The rival ghosts, by B. Matthews; The man who went too far, by E. F. Benson; The mezzotint, by M. R. James; The open window, by "Saki"; The beckoning fair one, by O. Onions; On the Brighton Road, by R. Middleton; The considerate hosts, by T. McClusky; August heat, by W. F. Harvey; The return of Andrew Bentley, by A. W. Derleth; The supper at Elsinore, by I. Dinesen; The current crop of ghost stories. by B. A. Cerf

(ed.) Great German short novels and stories. Modern Lib. 1933 475p $2.95

Analyzed in Short Story Index
Contents: Sorrows of Werther, by J. W. von Goethe; Sport of destiny, by J. von Schiller; History of Krakatuck, by E. T. W. Hoffmann; Hansel and Gretel, by J. L. Grimm; Cinderella, by J. L. Grimm; Gods in exile, by H. Heine; Immensee, by T. W. Storm; Naughty Saint Vitalis, by G. Keller; New Year's Eve confession, by H. Sudermann; Fate of the baron, by A. Schnitzler; Flagman Thiel, by G. Hauptmann; Lukardis by J. Wassermann; Death in Venice, by T. Mann; Amok, by S. Zweig; The parcel, by A. Zweig

(ed.) Great modern short stories; an anthology of twelve famous stories and novelettes, selected, and with a foreword and biographical notes by Bennett A. Cerf. Modern Lib. 1942 480p $2.95

Analyzed in Short Story Index
Contents: Heart of darkness, by J. Conrad; The apple-tree, by J. Galsworthy; The Prussian officer, by D. H. Lawrence; Miss Brill, by K. Mansfield; The letter, by W. S. Maugham; The snows of Kilimanjaro, by E. Hemingway; Paul's case, by W. Cather; I'm a fool, by S. Anderson; Haircut, by R. Lardner; Turn about, by W. Faulkner; The old demon, by P. S. Buck; The red pony, by J. Steinbeck

(jt. ed.) Burrell, A. ed. An anthology of famous American stories

Cervantes, Miguel de

The colloquy of the dogs

In Cervantes, M. de. Three exemplary novels p125-217

y Don Quixote de la Mancha

Some editions are:
Dodd (Great illustrated classics. Titan eds) $5.50 Introduction by John Kenneth Leslie. Has title: The adventures of Don Quixote de la Mancha
Dutton (The Children's illustrated classics) $3.50 Illustrated with eight pages of colour plates and drawings in the text by W. Heath Robinson. Has title: The adventures of Don Quixote de la Mancha
Dutton (Everyman's lib) 2v ea $3.25 Introduction by J. G. Lockhart. Translated by Motteux
Grosset $4.95 Has title: The adventures of Don Quixote, man of la Mancha
Modern Lib. $4.95 Ozell's revision of the translation of Peter Motteux; introduction by Herschel Brickell
Modern Lib. $2.95 Complete in two parts. A new translation from the Spanish, with a critical text based upon the first editions of 1605 and 1615, and with variant readings, variorum notes, and an introduction by Samuel Putnam. Has title: The ingenious gentleman Don Quixote de la Mancha
Viking $7.95 Complete in two parts. A new translation from the Spanish, with a critical text based upon the first editions of 1605 and 1615, and with variant readings, variorum notes, and an introduction by Samuel Putnam. Has title: The ingenious gentleman Don Quixote de la Mancha

"Treats of the pleasant manner of the knighting of that famous gentleman, Don Quixote, of the dreadful and never-to-be imagined adventure of the windmills, of the extraordinary battle he waged with what he took to be a giant, and of divers other rare and notable adventures and strange enchantments which befell this valorous and witty knight-errant." Pittsburgh

Cervantes, Miguel de—*Continued*

"By the time of the death of the Knight, Sancho Panza [his squire] has become an altogether lovable, quixotic character, so that the reader parts from them and their exciting world of marvels with deeply felt regret. The novel which obviously had for its genesis the satire of romances of chivalry, gradually grew into a vast panorama of Spanish life and into a most entertaining work of fiction, the first modern novel, read and admired to this day as one of the world's great literary achievements." Haydn. Thesaurus of Book Digests

Don Quixote de la Mancha; abridged

In Cervantes, M. de. The portable Cervantes p39-702

Man of glass

In Cervantes, M. de. The portable Cervantes p760-96

In Cervantes, M. de. Three exemplary novels p75-121

The portable Cervantes; tr. and ed. with an introduction and notes by Samuel Putnam. Viking 1951 854p $5.95

The "Putnam translation of 'Don Quixote' has been made available in this edition by omission of digressions, extraneous matter, etc., which have been intelligently summarized. Plus two 'Exemplary Novels,' the author's farewell to life, and a biographical and critical introduction." Retail Bookseller

Rinconete and Cortadillo

In Cervantes, M. de. The portable Cervantes p705-59

In Cervantes, M. de. Three exemplary novels p9-71

Three exemplary novels; tr. by Samuel Putnam; illus. by Luis Quintanilla. Viking 1950 xxi, 232p illus o.p. 1970

"Contains three novellas. 'Rinconete and Cortadillo,' a tale of Seville at the turn of the 17th century; 'Man of Glass,' the story of a truth teller who goes forth to reveal the lie upon which most human existence is based; and 'The Colloquy of the Dogs,' a source of information on life in Cervantes' time. With 20 full-page and 4 smaller illustrations." Huntting

Chandler, Raymond

The big sleep. Knopf 1939 277p o.p. 1970

"A tale of degeneracy in southern California, in which two Hollywood heiresses become mixed up in blackmail and murder; and Philip Marlowe is the private detective, who tells the story." Washington. D.C. Pub Lib

also in Chandler, R. The Raymond Chandler omnibus p 1-139

also in Haycraft, H. ed. A treasury of great mysteries v2 p3-130

Farewell, my lovely

In Chandler, R. The Raymond Chandler omnibus p141-315

The high window

In Chandler, R. The Raymond Chandler omnibus p317-468

The lady in the lake. Knopf 1943 216p o.p. 1970

"A woman disappears and her husband, who hates her, hires a detective to find her. It is the beginning of a most extraordinary case, and the detective, Philip Marlowe, soon understands that what is important is the character of the vanished woman. His investigation leads him to a world of evil—and he gradually begins to realize what she might have done and what might have been done to her. An above average crime story hard to match in sinister atmosphere and dangerous events." Huntting

also in Chandler, R. The Raymond Chandler omnibus p469-625

also in Haycraft, H. ed. Three times three p11-188

The long goodbye. Houghton 1953 316p $3

"Philip Marlowe is back, this time with a client named Terry Lennox who has just undergone plastic surgery. Marlowe could understand Terry's eagerness to flee to Mexico, for his client was quite sure he had murdered somebody." McClurg. Book News

"This is Mr. Chandler's longest novel to date, one of his most meticulously plotted and by some stretches his most corrosive. What he gives us here is painful if exciting pleasure." N Y Her Trib Books

The Raymond Chandler omnibus; four famous classics. Foreword by Lawrence Clark Powell. Knopf 1964 625p $5.95

Contents: The big sleep (1939); Farewell, my lovely (1940); The high window (1942); The lady in the lake (1943)

An anthology of the author's mysteries, in which Philip Marlowe is the sleuth. The first and last mentioned titles are entered separately

In "Farewell, my lovely" Philip Marlowe agrees to help Mike Mizurki hunt down the girl he loved before he was sent to jail. In "The high window" Marlowe is hired by Mrs Elizabeth Murdock to find her missing early American doubloon

The simple art of murder; with an editor's introduction by James Nelson. Norton 1968 533p $6.95

Analyzed in Short Story Index

"Twelve detective stories by the acknowledged master of the hard-boiled school. It includes Mr. Chandler's essay on detective fiction." McClurg. Book News

Contents: Finger man; Smart-aleck kill; Guns at Cyrano's; Pick-up on Noon Street; Goldfish; The King in yellow; Pearls are a nuisance; I'll be waiting; Red wind; Nevada gas; Spanish blood; Trouble is my business

Chapman, Hester W.

Fear no more. Reynal & Co. 1968 349p boards $6.95

This historical novel "is based upon the brief life of the young Dauphin of France, son of Louis XVI and Marie Antoinette. With the seeds of the Revolution already sown, Charles was the hope of the people. When he was only five, he started the rigorous training that was to prepare him for the throne. Though he was to live only five more years, much was crammed into them: imprisonment, the execution of his father, the trial of his mother for incest, as a result of which she was sent to the guillotine, the treachery of Charles' tutor, and his own innocence and aspirations corrupted." Pub W

The story is told "by a woman who knows the dreadful history of the Revolution well. It is a moving tale. But it is told exclusively from the little boy's point of view and within his necessarily limited horizon." Book of the Month Club News

Chapman, Margaret Storm Jameson. See Jameson, Storm

Charles, Gerda

(ed.) Modern Jewish stories. Prentice-Hall 1965 [c1963] 276p o.p. 1970

Analyzed in Short Story Index

First published 1963 in England

Contents: The conversion of the Jews, by P. Roth; The judgment of Solomon, by Y. Yaari; Face from Atlantis, by N. Gordimer; First love, by I. Babel; Gimpel the fool, by I. B. Singer; Act of faith, by I. Shaw; The Czecho-Slovakian chandelier, by G. Charles; Mr Kaplan and the Magi, by L. Q. Ross; The Zulu and the Zeide, by D. Jacobson; The prisoner, by S. Yizhar; My grandmother's hands, by A. Baron; Angel Levine, by B. Malamud; A betting man, by B. Glanville; The hand that fed me, by I. Rosenfeld; Pools, by A. Wesker

Charles-Roux, Edmonde

To forget Palermo; tr. by Helen Eustis. Delacorte Press 1968 304p boards $5.95

Original French edition published 1966

"Gianna Meri, travel writer for one of America's most popular women's fashion magazine,

Charles-Roux, Edmonde—*Continued*

is haunted by her memories of Sicily . . . and her own youthful and tragic love affair there. She is appalled by the emotionally impoverished landscape of New York. . . . Then she discovers Mulberry Street, the heart of New York's Italian community. American-born Rocco Bonavia, the local political leader, and his neighbors seem to have been transplanted intact from the old country. This renewed contact with her past only sharpens Gianna's nostalgia, which she communicates to the successful but strangely restless Rocco, who becomes the victim of fateful and violent consequences." Publisher's note

"The stories of New York and Sicily are interwoven, back and forth, vital and exciting and sometimes satirically funny, and come to a strange and violent climax." Harper

Charques, Dorothy

The dark stranger. Coward-McCann 1957 352p o.p. 1970

An historical novel set in the period of the English Civil War. "Elizabeth Devize, daughter of a Parliament man, discovers that her aunt and guardian, Dame Alys Cuttler, is both a Royalist plotter and an active member of a witch cult. . . . Elizabeth seeks and finds refuge with Parliamentary sympathizers, but, on learning that her aunt has been arrested, returns to offer help and is herself accused of witchcraft. All ends well when Dame Alys' sins bring retribution and Elizabeth is rescued by her ardent admirer, young Captain Swallow of Cromwell's staff." Booklist

"A first-rate novel that conforms to the pattern of historical events and is impregnated in plot and character with the mood, the motives, and the mentality of the generation involved." N Y Her Trib Books

The nunnery. Coward-McCann [1960 c1959] 354p o.p. 1970

First published in England 1959

"An historical novel of the court and time of Henry VIII. The King has moved to close the convents and monasteries and to seize the property for the crown. The extensive property of beautiful, sixteen-year-old Jane Ingham is to go to Cokehill Priory, when and if she takes the vows of a nun. Jane however, is undecided about the religious life, and shows great strength and courage as she seeks to find the answer for herself." Huntting

"Much research has gone into the making of this excellent historical novel of court intrigue. . . . All the characters are well drawn and live out their parts in the plot with a perfection of reality that makes of this novel a work of art." Library J

Charteris, Hugo

The coat. Harcourt [1970 c1966] 224p $5.50

First published 1966 in England

"The story concerns the departure of Tim Loxley, 14-year-old son of the Earl of Bewick, from England to America in 1941. Tim wears a special coat in which the earl has secreted a fortune in jewels he wants taken out of the country against the possibility of a German invasion. Accompanying the boy to the ship in Liverpool is his young but overripe stepmother. While waiting for the ship to leave, the two are overtaken by a series of serio-comic adventures involving his stepmother's lover and a family in a Liverpool slum." Library J

"Tim predictably loses his innocence along with the coat. . . . The tale of the loss of illusions moves at a great pace; The characters are fascinating, if somewhat shopworn, and the whole experience of the novel is engrossing." Best Sellers

Charteris, Leslie

The first Saint omnibus; an anthology of Saintly adventures. Doubleday 1939 639p o.p. 1970

Analyzed in Short Story Index
Contents: Man who was clever; Wonderful war; Story of a dead man; Unblemished bootlegger; Appalling politician; Million pound day; Death penalty; Simon Templar Foundation; Unfortunate financier; Sleepless knight; High fence; Unlicensed victuallers; Affair of Hogsbotham; Last word

The second Saint omnibus. Doubleday 1951 336p o.p. 1970

Analyzed in Short Story Index
Contents: Star producers; Wicked cousins; Man who liked ants; Palm Springs; Sizzling saboteur; Masked angle; Judith; Jeannine; Teresa; Dawn

Charyn, Jerome

American scrapbook. Viking 1969 177p boards $4.95

"During World War II, large numbers of Japanese-Americans . . . were herded into detention camps in the West. . . . Charyn charts [the effects of this internment on] six members of one family, the Tanakas. Each one narrates a chapter, documenting the daily routine of the camp from his own perspective." Newsweek

"The impact of the fresh subject matter alone is considerable. [The author] possesses both a gift for the comically grotesque and a sensitivity for the wide range of reactions evoked among internees of concentration camps. . . . The language and explicitness of some scenes do seem unnecessarily obscene. Nonetheless, this is a book that will be read and probably should be as a reminder of one of the less publicized horrors of war." Library J

Going to Jerusalem; a novel. Viking 1967 180p boards $4.95

"The Admiral (whose wife is insane) and his epileptic son Ivan operate an 'Academy' for chess prodigies. Six-year-old Van is the champion. Ivan and Van plan to bedevil a world chess champion, a former Nazi, as he tours the United States. They travel with a circus of freaks, later joined by Van's nymphomaniac mother. Such an assemblage of bizarre characters invites comic extravaganza, but the humor is grim and black. As they travel, a pernicious impression of the country emerges. . . . Jerome Charyn, like other younger novelists, writes in terms so depressing, that the reader cannot enjoy his obvious talents. Rather, readers are shocked into sharp questionings." Library J

(ed.) The single voice; an anthology of contemporary fiction. Collier Bks. 1969 516p pa $2.95

This volume "captures the particular voice of our time in all of its agony, uncertainty, and nervous vitality. Along with its 32 selections from the most outstanding writers on the contemporary scene, the book provides a thorough and perceptive critical introduction to the modern world of fiction." Publisher's note

Short stories included are: The guest, by S. Elkin; Parker's back, by F. O'Connor; The potato-elf, by V. Nabokov; Charles Axis, by L. Cohen; Smolak, by S. Bellow; Snowden, by J. Heller; V. in love, by T. Pynchon; In time which made a monkey of us all, by G. Paley; Hencher, by J. Hawkes; Novotny's pain, by P. Roth; In the heart of the heart of the country, by W. H. Gass; A change of air, by I. Gold; The law, by J. Barth; City boy by L. Michaels; Gogol's wife, by T. Landolfi; The man who grew younger, by J. Charyn; The Indian uprising, by D. Barthelme; The solitary life of man, by L. E. Litwak; This way for the gas, ladies and gentlemen, by T. Borowski; White days and red nights, by F. Conroy; Where they burn the dead, by C. T. Miller; The incubus, by A. J. Guerard; Simcha by M. Mirsky; Luther, by J. Neugeboren; Wobbilobby Mobbays, by I. Faust; Randolf's party, by J. Lennon

Chase, Mary Ellen

The edge of darkness. Norton 1957 235p $4.95

"The death of Sarah Holt, ninety-year-old matriarch of an unnamed fishing village on the northern coast of Maine, is the focal point for a virtually plotless story in the tradition of the author's earlier novels. Portraying the reactions of the small group of coastal and backwater neighbors and acquaintances who gather for Sarah's funeral, the writer conveys their individual stories and characters and interprets the meaning of their lives." Booklist

Chase, Mary E.—*Continued*

"Miss Chase's quiet authority and felicity of style combine to provide here a warm and accurate portrait of a Down East Our Town." Book of the Month Club News

The lovely ambition; a novel. Norton 1960 288p $5.95

"This narrative of an English Methodist minister and his family who emigrate to New England around 1900 seems to be about actual people, so real are their experiences and characters. . . . The Reverend John Tillyard rejoices equally in the life of a small farmer and in his scholarly and ministerial activities. His 'lively ambition' is to bring to a normal state of being the inmates of a mental hospital in Augusta where he also acts as Chaplain. Several of these people visit the Tillyards during the summers and the experiments succeed because of the healing quality of living in the serene little village of Pepperell, Maine, and the devotion of each of the Tillyards and their housekeeper, Mrs. Baxter, the mainspring of the family." Library J

Mary Peters. Macmillan (N Y) 1934 377p $4.95

"A lovely book to read. It is peopled by normally odd persons, with not a psychotic in sight, a pleasant family, close and affectionate though somewhat less than perfect, not troubled with frustrations, libido and the whole mess of modern isms, with a first class fatherly father and motherly mother. This is a rare book in this era of psychopathic literary excavations." Best Sellers

"The story follows the life of Mary Peters through her childhood on board her father's ship, school days in a Maine sea coast village, years of marriage to a charming man of unstable character, and leaves her approaching old age, feeling that life had been complete, glad of the seafaring heritage that had given her a broad outlook and the memory of far places. Throughout the story this seafaring heritage is shown as the influence for stability for Maine coast dwellers during the changing forces of the last 50 years." Wis Lib Bul

"Beautifully written in a minor key, it is notable for two elements: its effective rendition of the atmosphere of time and place—particularly of shipboard life and of the coast where pine and rock meet the salt marshes; and its delicate analysis of psychological states of a quite normal type." Sat R

The plum tree. Macmillan (N Y) 1949 98p o.p. 1970

"The plum tree stood on the lawn of The Home For Aged Women. It happened to be in full bloom on a day when three of the old ladies, all over eighty, were to be transferred to an insane asylum. The story is of the loving understanding of the matron and nurse who had presided over the home for thirty years. They turned the day into a gala occasion with a special dinner and a tea party, so that what had promised to be a nightmare ended well for all of them." Book Rev Digest

"Told with a tenderness that never descends to the mawkish, with a poignancy that never asks the reader's pity, with a depth of feeling and compassionate understanding which leaves that reader stirred as though by a genuine experience." Best Sellers

y Silas Crockett. Macmillan (N Y) 1935 404p $5.50

"The stirring story of four generations of a New England family: Silas, captain of a clipper, who took his wife with him on his voyages; his son Nicholas, lost at sea in a storm; his grandson Reuben, who was captain of a passenger coast-steamer, and when that stopped running, of a ferryboat; and his great-grandson Silas, who had to leave college to work in a herring-factory." Book Rev Digest

"A saga, written in well nigh perfect form and diction. . . . 'Silas Crockett' is well balanced, with a maximum of characterization and atmosphere and a minimum of dialog. Sympathy and humor, convictions about life and practical religion . . . are blended with a few pictorial scenes." Springf'd Republican

y Windswept. Macmillan (N Y) 1941 440p $6.95

"On a high, bare and windswept Maine promontory, hitherto shunned by man, Philip Marston, in the eighties, decides to build a home for himself and John, his 14-year-old son. Dead in a hunting accident before the consummation of his dream, Philip is buried near the site of Windswept, leaving John to carry out the plan. And John and his children and grandchildren put down their roots in the sturdy old soil of Windswept, a beneficient place where they, and those they draw into their intimate circle, discover life's realities and values." Bookmark

"One is caught and held by the fine penetration and analysis of spirit, the sensitive capture of the sounds and odors and moods of a Maine seacoast during every season of the year." N Y Her Trib Books

Chaze, Elliott

Wettermark. Scribner 1969 159p $4.95

"The story of Cliff Wettermark, a newspaperman in a small Mississippi town, who turns to crime out of boredom and frustration with his life." Bk Buyer's Guide

"Mr. Chaze does such a good job of evoking the atmosphere of small town Mississippi life, and etching in interesting and believable characters, whose failings are all too human, that it is a pity he hasn't more of a story to tell. . . . What this novel does add up to is a rather touching study of a man who fails at everything, including a try at crime." Pub W

Cheever, John

The brigadier and the golf widow. Harper 1964 275p $5.95

Analyzed in Short Story Index
Contents: The brigadier and the golf widow; The angel of the bridge; An educated American woman; The swimmer; Metamorphoses; The bella lingua; Clementina; A woman without a country; Reunion; The chaste Clarissa; The music teacher; The seaside houses; Just one more time; Marito in città; A vision of the world; The ocean

"Cheever's incisive style and masterful techniques make this collection very engrossing reading matter." Best Sellers

Bullet Park; a novel. Knopf 1969 245p $5.95

"The interplay between [suburban] Eliot Nailles, Paul Hammer, and Nailles's son Tony forms the structure of a novel superbly embodying many contemporary issues and problems. Using the third person, Cheever depicts Nailles as an open-faced, conscientious man, driven to desperation when his son is ill. Hammer, in a first-person account, is revealed as criminally insane beneath his [middle-class] neighborly exterior. The third part portrays Hammer's attempt to murder Tony Nailles, an act narrowly averted by his father." Booklist

The author "mixes compassion and high comedy brilliantly, holding up to view an [affluent] America that is fatally schizoid in many of its manifestations. The confrontation that finally comes between Hammer and Nailles is a horrifying, dark allegory of our times." Pub W

The housebreaker of Shady Hill, and other stories. Harper 1958 185p o.p. 1970

Analyzed in Short Story Index
"Seven stories provide wall to wall suburbia-cum-nightmare for this collection." Kirkus
Contents: The housebreaker of Shady Hill; O youth and beauty; The country husband; The sorrows of gin; The worm in the apple; The five-forty-eight; Just tell me who it was; The trouble of Marcie Flint

The Wapshot chronicle. Harper 1957 307p boards $5.95

"A picture of life in an old New England town during the first half of the twentieth century, this is also a family chronicle of the Wapshots. Leander, his wife Sarah, and their two sons, Moses and Coverly." Book Rev Digest

"An episodic, but cleverly written, narative . . . can be enjoyed for its affectionate analysis of small-town personalities, its atmosphere, and its spicy anecdotes." Booklist

Cheever, John—*Continued*

The Wapshot scandal. Harper 1964 309p $4.95

This sequel to: The Wapshot chronicle "continues the tale of the decline of the fortunes of the Wapshot family and of the mythical New England town of St. Botolphs. The 'scandal' is the discovery that Aunt Honora has never paid her income taxes, and the principal disaster stems from the long-standing oversight. The novel also traces the misfortunes of two Wapshot nephews. Coverly a public relations man at a missile site, and Moses, an alcoholic." Library J

"There are values that range from grim realism and scornful satire to benign good humor and gentle humanity. The steady succession of mistakes, triumphs, shocks, whimsies defeats, and engaging portraits will provide plentiful interest and fruitful reflection for the mature reader disposed to do the thinking that Cheever provokes without incurring an inartistic didacticism." Best Sellers

Chekhov, Anton

The best known works of Anton Chekhov. Blue Ribbon Bks. 1936 678p o.p. 1970

Analyzed in Short Story Index
Contains the following stories: The kiss; Chorus girl; La cigale; Verotchka; Match; Excellent people; Black monk; Family council; Woe; Women; A husk; Anna round the neck; The incubus; Miss N. N's story; Young wife; The peasants; Shooting party; Terrible night; In exile; The proposal; Who to blame; Rothschild's fiddle; Sleepyhead; Princess; Fish; Mass for the sinner; The lament; Oysters; Vanka Zinotchka; Privy councillor; The wager; Cossack; At the manor; Event; Art; Birds; Ward no. 6: At home; An adventure; A father; Two tragedies; Rook; On the way; Children; Head gardener's tale; The runaway; The reed; In the ravine

The darling, and other stories; from the Russian by Constance Garnett, with an introduction by Edward Garnett. Macmillan (N Y) 1916 329p (The Tales of Chekhov v1) o.p. 1970

On cover: The tales of Chekhov
Analyzed in Short Story Index
Contains the following stories: The darling; Ariadne; Polinka; Anyuta; The two Volodyas; The trousseau; The helpmate; Talent; An artist's story; Three years

The duel, and other stories; from the Russian by Constance Garnett. Macmillan (N Y) 1916 323p (The Tales of Chekhov v2) o.p. 1970

Analyzed in Short Story Index
Contents: The duel; Excellent people; Mire; Neighbours; At home; Expensive lessons; The princess; The chemist's wife

The image of Chekhov; forty stories in the order in which they were written. Newly tr. and with an introduction, by Robert Payne. Knopf 1963 xxxvii, 344p front $5.95

Partially analyzed in Short Story Index
These translations have been made from the twelve-volume edition of Chekhov's Collected works, edited by W. W. Yermilov and published in Moscow. 1950

"Payne has written an introductory essay on Chekhov's life and writings, including critical comments on many of the stories included in this volume. As a translator Payne has had his difficulties with Chekhov's idiomatic nineteenth-century Russian, but the effect is generally fresh and has a comparatively modern tone." Booklist

Contents: The little apples; St Peter's Day; Green Scythe; Joy; The ninny; The highest heights; Death of a government clerk; At the post office; Surgery; In the cemetery; Where there's a will, there's a way; A report; The threat; The huntsman; The malefactor; A dead body; Sergeant Prishibeyev; A blunder; Heartache; Anyuta; The proposal; Vanka; Who is to blame; Typhus; Sleepyhead; The Princess; Gusev; The peasant women; After the theater; A fragment; In exile; Big Volodya and Little Volodya; The student; Anna round the neck;

The house with the mezzanine; In the horse-cart; On love; The lady with the pet dog; The Bishop; The bride

Late-blooming flowers, and other stories; tr. by I. C. Chertok & Jean Gardner. McGraw 1964 xx, 252p o.p. 1970

Analyzed in Short Story Index
"A collection of eight Chekhov stories, ranging from 1882 to 1903, most of which have not been translated into English for more than 40 years. The title story, a tale of a tragically delayed marriage, has never been published in the U.S. Not all of the selections equal in depth and range the Russian writer's better-known works." Booklist

Contains the following stories: Late-blooming flowers; The little trick; Verochka; The beauties; Big Volodya and Little Volodya; A visit to friends; A reward denied; The fiancée

The Oxford Chekhov; v8: stories, 1895-1897. Tr. and ed. by Ronald Hingley. Oxford 1965 325p $5.60

Analyzed in Short Story Index
This is the fiction selection of the set; volumes 1-3 are collected plays

Stories included are: His wife; Patch; The Order of St Anne; Murder; Ariadne; The artist's story; My life; Peasants; The savage; Home; In the cart

In addition to extensive explanatory material "this volume contains Chekhov's entire output of fiction first published during the years 1895-7 inclusive, with the exception of the story 'Three Years'. . . . The present volume also includes four fragments not published in Chekhov's lifetime, but probably written during the period." Preface

St Peter's Day, and other tales; tr. with an introduction, by Frances H. Jones. Capricorn Bks. 1959 191p o.p. 1970

Analyzed in Short Story Index
"A hilarious collection of early Chekhov stories and sketches available for the first time in English." McClurg. Book News

Contains the following stories: The willow; The liberal; The woman who had no prejudices; Marriage for money; Appropriate measures; The mask; Civil service exam; Trifon; The delegate; Tears the world sees not; Reading; 75,000; The conqueror's triumph; The flying islands; The lady the manor; The reporter; A revolting story; The village of Green Scythe; St Peter's Day

Select tales of Tchehov; tr. from the Russian by Constance Garnett. Barnes & Noble [1963 c1949] 2v ea $4

Analyzed in Short Shory Index
First published in this edition 1949 in England

Contents: v 1: The lady with the dog; The horse-stealers; The bishop; In the ravine; Sleepy; Ionitch; At Christmas time; My life; The chorus girl; The new villa; The teacher of literature; The witch; An anonymous story; The beauties; A transgression; Gusev; A woman's kingdom; Mire; Easter Eve; A dreary story; An incident; An artist's story; A misfortune; Happiness; The darling

v2: The kiss; Anyuta; The grasshopper; The bet; The duel; Zinotchka; Kashtanka: a story; In passion week; The schoolmistress; The huntsman; The marshal's widow; The steppe: the story of a journey; a daughter of Albion; The old house; The black monk

The stories of Anton Tchekov; ed. with an introduction by Robert N. Linscott. Modern Lib. [1959 c1932] 448p $2.95

A reissue of a title first published 1932, and analyzed in Short Story Index

Contents: A day in the country; Old age; Kashtanka; Enemies; On the way; Vanka; La cigale; Grief; Inadvertence; The black monk; The kiss; In exile; A work of art; Dreams; A woman's kingdom; The doctor; A trifling occurrence; The hollow; After the theatre; The runaway; Vierochka; The steppe; Rothschild's fiddle

Chekhov, Anton—*Continued*

The unknown Chekhov; stories and other writings; tr. and with an introduction by Avrahm Yarmolinsky. Funk [1969 c1954] 316p boards $6.95

A reprint of a collection first published 1954 by Noonday Press, and analyzed in Short Story Index

The twenty stories, four fragments and an excerpt "are translated into English for the first time. They most certainly make a valuable contribution towards a fuller and better understanding of Chekhov's artistic genius." Sat R

Short stories included are: Because of little apples; Two in one; Perpetuum mobile; The skit; Worse and worse; Vint; Two of a kind; Drowning; The village elder; Saintly simplicity; Hydrophobia; Other people's misfortune; Women make trouble; The lodger; Boa constrictor and rabbit; An unpleasantness; A fragment; Peasants; A visit to friends; Decompensation

Ward no. 6
In Neider, C. ed. Short novels of the masters p386-438

Cheshire, Giff

Ambush at Bedrock. Doubleday 1969 189p $4.50

"Doubleday western"
"Someone was out to get Pace Larrabee—someone who wanted his ranch—someone who had tried to kill him once and would try again." Book News

Chesnoff, Richard Z.

If Israel lost the war, by Richard Z. Chesnoff, Edward Klein [and] Robert Littell. Coward-McCann 1969 253p $5.95

This "documentary novel recreates the 1967 Arab-Israeli war in exact reverse. . . . As Israel's air force is suddenly destroyed by Arab jets, sounding the death knell for the Jewish state, Nasser proclaims the second coming of Islam. World reaction is violent. America is racked by mass guilt, mass protest, and the resignation of the President and the UN Ambassador, among others. The balance of power in the Near East—and in the world—shifts dramatically and ominously." Publisher's note

Chesterton, G. K.

Father Brown mystery stories; selected and ed. with an introduction by Raymond T. Bond. Dodd 1962 246p $3.50

Analyzed in Short Story Index

Contents: The blue cross; The queer feet; The flying stars; The invisible man; The sins of Prince Saradine; The absence of Mr Glass; The dagger with wings; The oracle of the dog; The insoluble problem

All the stories centering around the detective-priest "appear exactly as they were originally written, except for the omission here and there of such alien matters as a discussion of British political parties or reference to people and events now largely forgotten." Publisher's note

y The Father Brown omnibus. . . . [New and rev. ed] Dodd 1951 993p $6

First edition of this omnibus was published 1933

Fifty separate stories published in five volumes, with an additional story; analyzed in Short Story Index

"Including The innocence of Father Brown; The incredulity of Father-Brown; The scandal of Father Brown; The wisdom of Father Brown; The vampire of the village [short story]" Subtitle

Contents: Absence of Mr Glass; Actor and Alibi; Arrow of heaven; Blast of the book; Blue cross; Chief mourner of Marne; Crime of the Communist; Curse of the golden cross; Dagger with wings; Doom of the Darnaways; Duel of Dr Hirsch; Eye of Apollo; Fairy tale of Father Brown; Flying stars; Ghost of Gideon Wise;

God of the Gongs; Green man; Hammer of God; Head of Cæsar; Honour of Israel Gow; Insoluble problem; Invisible Man; Man in the passage; Man with two beards; Miracle of Moon Crescent; Mirror of the magistrate; Mistake of the machine; Oracle of the dog; Paradise of thieves; Perishing of the Pendragons; Point of a pin; Purple wig; Pursuit of Mr Blue; Queer feet; Quick one; Red Moon of Meru; Resurrection of Father Brown; Salad of Colonel Cray; Scandal of Father Brown; Secret garden; Secret of Father Brown; Secret of Flambeau; Sign of the broken sword; Sins of Prince Saradine; Song of the flying fish; Strange crime of John Boulnois; Three tools of death; Vampire of the village; Vanishing of Vaudrey; Worst crime in the world; Wrong shape

The incredulity of Father Brown
In Chesterton, G. K. The Father Brown omnibus p433-630

The innocence of Father Brown
In Chesterton, G. K. The Father Brown omnibus p 1-226

The man who was Thursday; a nightmare. Dodd 1908 281p $3.50

"Here the Rabelaisian fun is fast and furious. The oracles are masquerading as clowns and harlequins: wisdom flashes out in starshowers. The story seems as empty and preposterous as a nightmare; then, suddenly, it has a meaning. A club of seven anarchists are in a plot to destroy the world; six of them, after terrific efforts to run each other to earth and foil the deadly scheme, turn out to be police officers in disguise. But narrative and talk are a form of dialectic. The chief detective sitting in the darkness had given each man his commission. It is all an allegory of human life, the everlasting struggle in which man finds it so hard to distinguish friend from foe, right from wrong; Where the whole basis and ultimate sanction of his faith must be an enigma." Baker's Best

The scandal of Father Brown
In Chesterton, G. K. The Father Brown omnibus p815-974

The secret of Father Brown
In Chesterton, G. K. The Father Brown omnibus p631-811

The wisdom of Father Brown
In Chesterton, G. K. The Father Brown omnibus p227-431

Christie, Agatha

The A.B.C. murders
In Christie, A. Surprise endings by Hercule Poirot p 1-135

And then there were none. Dodd 1940 264p o.p. 1970

Published in England with title: Ten little niggers

"An island off the Devon coast; a group of ten oddly assorted people cut off from mainland communication; successive demises weirdly symphonized by an old nursery rhyme; even, for full luxury, a manuscript set adrift in a bottle—Mrs. Christie certainly had fun. The reader, who need not be too scrupulous, will have it too. The best of it is that murder so wholesale need not be taken too bitterly; and all ten victims had been culled for offenses of their own which the law could not reach." Book of the Month Club News

No detective

also in Christie, A. Christie classics p169-318

Appointment with death
In Christie, A. Make mine murder! p9-155

At Bertram's Hotel. Dodd [1966 c1965] 272p o.p. 1970

First published 1965 in England

"A solid, comfortable, respectable London hotel where Miss Jane Marple is spending a

FICTION CATALOG
EIGHTH EDITION

Christie, Agatha—*Continued*

two weeks' vacation is suddenly of intense interest to the police. An elderly absent-minded clergyman has vanished from the hotel, and one or two other things seem very odd about the establishment. This London crime tale, complete with a clever Chief Inspector who cooperates with Miss Marple is neatly constructed, psychologically interesting, and brought to an end with a surprising stroke of horror." Pub W

"The book is a joy to read from beginning to end, especially in its acute sensitivity to the contrasts between this era and that of Miss Marple's youth." N Y Times Bk R

The body in the library
In Christie, A. Murder in our midst p9-130

By the pricking of my thumbs. Dodd 1968 275p boards $4.95

The ingredients of this mystery plot "run all the way from the fancies of some old ladies in a home for the elderly, to dark hints at child murder, the machinations of a clever criminal gang, and the secret life of a supposedly peaceful English village. . . . [Solved by] the husband-and-wife team of Tuppence and Tommy [Beresford]." Pub W

"'A pleasant, unremarkable couple' now, the Beresfords are wonderfully revived in this [mystery]. . . . Smooth, beautifully paced and effortlessly convincing." N Y Times Bk R

Cards on the table
In Christie, A. Surprise endings by Hercule Poirot p275-405

A Caribbean mystery. Dodd [1965 c1964] 245p o.p. 1970

First published 1964 in England
"Miss Jane Marple, vacationing at a pleasant sunlit island resort in the Caribbean, is thoroughly bored—until someone dies in mysterious circumstances, and it becomes plain that a murderer is stalking the island." Pub W

"The plot is conventional . . . but the details are handled with that exquisitely smooth technique that is uniquely Mrs. Christie's." N Y Times Bk R

Christie classics: The murder of Roger Ackroyd; And then there were none; The witness for the prosecution; Philomel Cottage [and] Three blind mice. Dodd 1957 410p illus o.p.

The first two titles are full-length novels and entered separately, the third and fourth are two of the author's most famous short stories, and the last is a novelette based on the play called; The mousetrap

y The clocks. Dodd [1964 c1963] 276p o.p. 1970

First published 1963 in England
"A public stenographer, sent to a private home and instructed before hand to wait in a certain room, finds the room lavishly decorated with clocks, and the body of a dead man on the floor. The local detective inspector, assisted by a young man from a special branch and by Hercule Poirot . . . investigates the private lives and aberrations of a more than usually odd neighborhood." Pub W

"The tone of this latest of the long Christie line is cheerful, not to say cozy." Book of the Month Club News

Dead man's mirror
In Haycraft, H. ed. Three times three p479-543

Death on the Nile. Dodd [1970 c1965] 317p $3.95

"The Greenway edition"
First published 1937
"Hercule Poirot was aboard a Nile steamer when the tragedy occurred. At first it seemed obvious who the murderer was, but almost at once the complications multiplied." Publisher's note

"Slightly transparent plot, plethora of action, but all is handled with customary Christie expertness. Very good." Sat R

also in Christie, A. Perilous journeys of Hercule Poirot v2

Endless night. Dodd [1968 c1967] 248p o.p. 1970

First published 1967 in England
"A young man with a dream meets the girl he is to marry at an auction of a piece of land known as Gipsy's Acre. The story concludes in the revelation of a monstrous crime, complete with all the paraphernalia that had been required to effect it." McClurg. Book News

"Use of the two-way clue is dazzling. And, more than ever, the rigorous Christie epistemology-psychology invades every page of the book; her characters are normal people whose own free will essentially decides their courses." N Y Times Bk R

y Hallowe'en party. Dodd 1969 248p $5.95

This Hercule Poirot mystery brings "the mustachioed old master out of his retirement in England to find the murderer of a 13-year-old girl at a children's Halloween party. The unknown had taken the means at hand, holding Joyce's head under water in an apple-bobbing pail. There was no apparent motive. Most people in Woodleigh Common decided that [it] was a pathological killer until Poirot began probing into the past lives of both children and adults in the town." Pub W

"If you are familiar with Miss Christie's works and her methods you may suspect the correct criminal half-way through; but even then you will not be sure until the end." Best Sellers

Lord Edgware dies. . . . Dodd [1970 c1960] 255p $3.95

"The Greenway edition"
"Originally published [1933] in the United States as Thirteen at dinner." Title page

"Hercule Poirot, the famous detective, was enjoying a pleasant little supper party as the guest of Lady Edgware. . . . During the conversation Lady Edgware spoke of the desirability of getting rid of her husband, Lord Edgware, since he refused to divorce her, and she wanted to marry the Duke of Merton. Poirot jocularly replied that getting rid of husbands was not his speciality. Within twenty-four hours, however, Lord Edgware died!" Publisher's note

"This story presents a most ingenious crime puzzle and a still more ingenious solution, all set forth with the consummate skill of which Agatha Christie is mistress." N Y Times Bk R

Make mine murder! Including: Appointment with death; Peril at End House; Sad cypress. Dodd 1962 473p o.p. 1970

The three novels reprinted here were published 1938, 1932 and 1940 respectively. In each story Hercule Poirot, the Belgian detective, is the sleuth

The mirror crack'd. Dodd [1963 c1962] 246p o.p. 1970

First published 1962 in England with title: The mirror crack'd from side to side

Miss Jane Marple, whose house in St Mary Mead is close to the scene of the crime "gives Scotland Yard her gracious cooperation in solving a poisoning that takes place at a village reception where the hostess is a lovely film star. The murder puzzle is a good one, the village people and their gossip are acute and interesting, and Miss Christie's fans will be pleased." Pub W

The moving finger
In Christie, A. Murder in our midst p319-444

The murder at the vicarage
In Christie, A. Murder in our midst p131-317

Murder in Mesopotamia
In Christie, A. Perilous journey of Hercule Poirot v3

Murder in our midst; including: The body in the library; The murder at the vicarage; The moving finger. Dodd 1967 444p illus o.p. 1970

The three titles included in this omnibus volume were first published 1942, 1930 and 1942, respectively. Each is set in a small English village and features Jane Marple as sleuth

Christie, Agatha—*Continued*

Murder in the Calais coach
In Haycraft, H. ed. A treasury of great
mysteries v 1 p9-146

Murder in three acts
In Christie, A. Surprise endings by Hercule Poirot p139-272

The murder of Roger Ackroyd. Dodd [1967
c1926] 288p $3.95

"The Greenway edition"
First published 1926
"Roger Ackroyd, a retired business man, is
found dead in his study shortly after the suicide of the woman he was to have married.
Suspicion and the police point to Ackroyd's
adopted son as the murderer, but the outcome
of the story is a complete surprise. As in others of Miss Christie's tales, the mystery is
solved by the quaint Frenchman, M. Poirot."
Booklist
"Miss Christie's dedication of the book is to
one 'who likes an orthodox detective story,
murder, inquest, and suspicion falling on every
one in turn!' So she set herself to write such
an orthodox story, with the strange result
that she has succeeded in producing one of
the few notable for originality." Sat R

also in Christie, A. Christie classics p 1-
167

also in Costain, T. B. ed. More Stories to
remember v2 p281-438

Murder on the Orient Express. . . . Dodd
[1968 c1960] 254p $3.95

"The Greenway edition"
"Originally published [1934] in the United
States as 'Murder in the Calais coach.' " Title
page
"A man is murdered on a through train from
Stamboul to Calais. He was stabbed twelve
times and this number was one of the clues
that enabled the famous French detective, M.
Hercule Poirot, who happened to be on board,
to unravel the mystery. The plot has the advantage of being something different, and the
story is swiftly moving and entertaining."
Huntting

The mystery of the blue train
In Christie, A. Perilous journeys of Hercule Poirot v 1

Ordeal by innocence. Dodd 1959 [c1958]
247p o.p. 1970

When Jack Argyle, deceased, was absolved
of the murder of his mother, "suspicion was
shifted to the other [surviving] members of
the household, Mrs Argyle had been a peculiarly domineering woman with a considerable
fortune at her disposal, and motives were not
difficult for Superintendent Huish to discover.
But who in the little family circle was the
guilt one? And which were the innocent?"
Publisher's note

The pale horse. Dodd 1962 [c1961] 242p
o.p. 1970

First published 1961 in England
A story of a Catholic priest who was murdered after hearing a dying woman's confession. "On his body was discovered a list of
names, mysterious in that the people had
nothing in common; yet, when Mark Easterbrook came to inquire into the circumstances
of the people named, he began to discover a
connection between them, and an ominous pattern." Publisher's note
"A 'tour de force' in mystery stories, an
extraordinary story in which the author goes
deep into the human mind and dips into occult knowledge, and does this with no lessen-
ing of her skill at writing dramatic scenes and
interspersing very effective humor." Pub W

Peril at End House
In Christie, A. Make mine murder! p157-
297

Perilous journeys of Hercule Poirot. . . .
Dodd 1954 3v in 1 o.p. 1970

"Including The mystery of the blue train,
Death on the Nile [entered separately] and
Murder in Mesopotamia." Subtitle
The three novels reprinted here were published 1928, 1937 and 1936 respectively
"In the Blue Train a girl has been murdered and a ruby stolen. In Mesopotamia, a
woman is murdered under circumstances that
rival a sealed room mystery." Huntting

Sad cypress
In Christie, A. Make mine murder! p299-
473

Surprise endings by Hercule Poirot; including The A.B.C. murders, Murder in three acts,
and Cards on the table. Dodd 1956 405p
o.p. 1970

"Hercule Poirot, the lively Belgian detective
of the 'little grey cells' was the master of
dramatic surprises. Here in one volume are
three of his outstanding triumphs [originally
published 1934, 1935, 1936 respectively]." Mc-
Clurg. Book News

They do it with mirrors. . . . Dodd [1970
c1952] 223p $3.95

"The Greenway edition"
"Originally published [1952] in the United
States as Murder with mirrors." Title page
Inspector Curry of Scotland Yard and Jane
Marple investigate a murder at Stonygates, a
rehabilitation center for delinquent boys
The author "is, here as before, a content-
ing craftsman. Her capacities for legitimate
misdirection are meticulously founded upon
incident and upon what she has chosen to suggest of character. And she has a sharp ear for
the diversities of tongue and tone to mark her
creatures out neatly." N Y Her Trib Books

Third girl. Dodd [1967 c1966] 248p $4.50

First published 1966 in England
This mystery "puts Poirot in touch with
modern youth, with shattering impact on his
ego. The girl came to consult him about 'a
murder she might have committed,' but decided
that he was too old to be of any help to her.
His pride had to be resurrected and refur-
bished before he and his mystery writer friend,
Ariadne Oliver, could embark on the chase
through Norma Restarick's mind, and her
strange friendships before the unusual things
that happened to her could be explained." Library J
"Miss Christie is in top form, satirizing the
far-out younger set with a cool eye, and weaving a clever mystery in which the incomparable
M. Poirot is both hampered and helped delightfully by an old friend, Mrs. Oliver, a writer of detective stories." Pub W

13 clues for Miss Marple; a collection of
mystery stories. Dodd 1966 241p $3.50

Analyzed in Short Story Index
"A representative collection of 13 short
stories about Miss Jane Marple [who lives in
the little English village of St. Mary Mead]
selected from Christie's 'Three blind mice, and
other stories, Double sin, and other stories,'
and 'The Tuesday Club murders.' Christie fans
may be familiar with the stories, but they will
serve as a good introduction to the genre for
the uninitiated." Booklist
Contents: Tape-measure murder; Strange
jest; Sanctuary; Greenshaw's Folly; The case
of the perfect maid; The case of the caretaker;
The blue geranium; The companion; The four
suspects; Motive v. opportunity; The thumb-
mark of St Peter; The bloodstained pavement; The herb of death

Three blind mice
In Christie, A. Christie classics p357-410

What Mrs McGillicuddy saw! Dodd 1957
192p o.p. 1970

"Red Badge detective"
"Her fleeting view of a strangling aboard a
passing train leaves Mrs McGillicuddy quite
shaken. She reports her shattering experience
to her friend Miss Marple who, after some
false starts, is able to trap the culprit." Pub W

Christie, Kate

Child's play. Harcourt [1969 c1968] 156p $3.95

"Jessica and her brother Dave live in a conservative British village. Jessica is engaged to the local clergyman, Dave may go to sea; but at the moment they most enjoy a game left over from their childhood. An innocent game of let's pretend it is—but leading unobtrusively, into unspeakable horror." N Y Times Bk R

"From a rather quiet beginning, this brief English novel builds to a chilling climax as it delineates an incestuous relationship between a brother and sister. . . . A carefully understated horror tale." Pub W

Christopher, John

The little people. Simon & Schuster [1967 c1966] 224p $4.95

A "strange union of Irish legend and Nazi persecution. . . . When Bridget Chauncey learns of her unexpected inheritance from an unknown uncle, she and her British fiance go . . . to see Killabeg Castle, with the strange and beautifully furnished doll houses in the tower room. Once there, Bridget decides to stay for a few months and try to turn the castle into a successful hotel. She and her small staff work hard, but are rewarded when guests began to come. Then they discover the first of the little people. Strange things happen and people began to know themselves and gain and lose by that knowledge." Library J

"The author's specialty is carefully laid-on horror, and that's what we find in Killabeg Castle." N Y Times Bk R

Pendulum. Simon & Schuster 1968 254p $4.95

"Told by a master of science fiction, Christopher's new novel takes us into the not-too-distant future when England has succumbed to rule by motorcycle gangs, the yobs. They terrorize the Gawfrey family after invading their home, but opposition slowly emerges and the pendulum swings back—perhaps too far." Cincinnati

The author "manages to hew to a peak of sustained horror that is almost unbearable. And in between he provides glimpses of sweetness and gentleness that make the climax all the more chilling." Pub W

The ragged edge. Simon & Schuster [1966 c1965] 254p $4.50

"When a series of earthquakes dry up the English Channel—and destroy much of the world—Matthew sets out from the island of Guernsey to find his daughter, taking ten-year-old Billy with him. They encounter wild bands, a mad sea captain (who refuses to leave his ship), but eventually are able to return to Guernsey, where a small band of survivors has gathered." Bk Buyer's Guide

"Out of . . . horror and a soupcon of hope Mr. Christopher whips up a marrow-chilling entertainment." N Y Times Bk R

Churchill, Winston

The crisis. Macmillan (N Y) 1901 516p $6.50

Sequel to: Richard Carvel

Deals "with the South's problems at the time of the Civil War. Among fictional characters are Eliphalt Hopper, the carpetbagger, Judge Whipple, the idealistic abolitionist, and Colonel Carver, a true Southern gentleman. The hero is Stephen Brice, an anti-slavery New Englander who accepts a job in the judge's law office and meets Virginia Carvel, descendant of Richard Carvel. The young people fall in love, but Virginia, because of her Southern convictions, renounces Stephen's affection and becomes engaged to her cousin, Clarence Colfax, a Confederate cavalier. Stephen is wounded with the Union Army, and becomes an aide to Lincoln. Virginia finally breaks with Clarence, who is taken as a spy, and while visiting Lincoln to seek his pardon, is reunited with Stephen." Haydn. Thesaurus of Book Digests

The crossing; with illus. by Sydney Adamson and Lillian Bayliss. Literature House 508p illus $12

A reprint of the title first published 1904 by Macmillan (N Y)

The crossing "tells of the Kentucky frontier's part in the Revolution. David Ritchie lives in North Carolina. His father, a dour Scotchman, joins the American Army, and the youth is left with the Temple family in Charleston. When Mr. Ritchie is killed, David returns to the farm as a worker. Later he accompanies Tom McChesney in George Rogers Clark's wilderness campaign. After the fighting at Vincennes and Kaskaskia he studies law, joined by Nick Temple, who turns out to be his cousin. In New Orleans he marries a French refugee Hélène d'Ivry-le-Tour, and takes her back to the Kentucky frontier." Haydn. Thesaurus of Book Digests

Richard Carvel. Macmillan (N Y) 1899 538p $6.95

"Richard Carvel spends his early life in Maryland, brought up by his grandfather, a supporter of the English King George. He loves Dorothy Manners, but she is taken to London and expected to marry a wealthy Englishman. An uncle arranges to have pirates kidnap Richard, but he is rescued by John Paul Jones. Their experiences together follow, including Richard's imprisonment in London and eventual rescue by Dorothy. Richard then lives among such Englishmen of distinction as Fox and Walpole. He prevents Dorothy's marriage; then, learning of the loss of his inheritance, he returns to America, and becomes a real estate lawyer. At the outbreak of the Revolution he enlists with John Paul Jones. The famous victory of the 'Bonhomme Richard' over the 'Serapis' takes place. Richard is able to go to England and marry Dorothy, who has always loved him. They return to America, and live happily." Haydn. Thesaurus of Book Digests

Followed by: The crisis

Chute, B. J.

y Greenwillow; drawings by Erik Blegvad. Dutton 1956 237p illus boards $5.95

"An enigmatic novel describing life in a small English village where for a time two pastors seek to save the souls of the inhabitants. The Reverend Lapp preached hell fire, but the mysterious Reverend Birdsong was more gentle, and it was doubtless the latter who was responsible for breaking the curse of the Briggs family." Book Rev Digest

"Creating its own reality as it goes along, conjuring up a pastoral microcosm that exists outside space and time, eloquently celebrating the natural world, 'Greenwillow' is a work of sheer, happy imagination—one of those small brave books that defy literary fashions and so add variety, freshness and delight to a publishing season." N Y Her Trib Books

The moon and the thorn. Dutton 1961 190p o.p. 1970

"A woman who has 'sinned'—who has gone away with a married man and lived with him in Paris for thirty glorious years—returns to the American island where her wealthy family maintains a summer home and where her sister now lives. The sinner is a woman of great charm and warmth; the thirty years of ecstatic happiness shine through her entire being. But to most of the island she is the Scarlet Woman, and to her sister she is an object of bitter hatred. How this situation is changed is the story." Book of the Month Club News

Chute, Beatrice Joy. See Chute, B. J.

Clark, Barrett H.

(comp.) Great short novels of the world; a collection of complete short novels chosen from the literature of all periods and countries. McBride Co. 1927 1304p o.p. 1970

Analyzed in Short Story Index

Contents: Judith; Daphnis and Chloe, by Longus; Cupid and Psyche, by Apuleius; Apaharavarman's adventure, by Dandin; Voyages

Clark, Barrett H.—*Continued*

of Sinbad, from Arabian nights; Sir Galahad, by T. Malory; Apolonius and Silla, by B. Riche; Incognita, by W. Congreve; Rosanna, by M. Edgeworth; Bedford-Row Conspiracy, by W. M. Thackeray; Rain, by W. S. Maugham; Apple tree, by J. Galsworthy; Poor Heinrich, by H. von Aue; Peter Schlemihl, by A. von Chamisso; Inmensee, by T. Storm; Aucassin and Nicolette; Zadig, by Voltaire; Carmen, by P. Mérimee; Pastoral symphony, by A. Gide; Romeo and Giulietta, by M. Bandello; In silence, by L. Pirandello; Test of friendship, by J. Perez de Montalván: Their son, by E. Zamacois; Miraculous portrait, from Marvelous Tales; Old bamboo-hewer's story; Outlawed, by J. Aho; Lear of the steppes, by I. Turgenev; Sky-blue life, by M. Gorky; Tomek Baran, by W. S. Reymont; Dream of Doctor Misić, by L. Babic-Gjalski; Childless, by L. Hermann; Bridal march, by B. Björnson; Four devils, by H. Bang; Rip Van Winkle, by W. Irving; Daisy Miller, by H. James; Youma, by L. Hearn; Evelina's Garden, by M. E. W. Freeman; Tubal Cain, by J. Hergesheimer

(comp.) Great short stories of the world; a collection of complete short stories chosen from the literatures of all periods and countries, by Barrett H. Clark and Maxim Lieber. World Pub. 1925 1072p $9.95

First published by Robert M. McBride Company

Contents: Two brothers (Anpu and Bata); Setna and the magic book; Eumæus' tale, by Homer; Country mouse and the town mouse, by Æsop; King Rhampsinitus and the thief, by Herodotus; Phineus and the harpies, by Apollonius of Rhodes; Robbers of Egypt, by Heliodorus; Horatius at the bridge, by Livy; Orpheus and Eurydice, by Ovid; Shipwreck of Simonides, by Phædrus; Matron of Ephesus, by Petronius; Haunted house, by Pliny the younger; Dream, by Apuleius; Book of Ruth, from the Old Testament; History of Susanna, from the Apocrypha; Prodigal son, from the New Testament; Raising of Lazarus, from the New Testament; Rabbi Akiva, from the Talmud; Jewish mother, from the Talmud; Ass in the lion's skin, from the Jatakas; Dove and the crow, from the Panchatantra; Story of Devadatta, by Somadeva; Jackal, from the Hitopadesa; Jamshid and Zuhak, by Firdawsi; Sailor and the pearl merchant; Khaled and Djaida, by Al-Asma'I; Abou Hassan the wag, from the Thousand and one nights; Grendel's raid, by Beowulf; Esyllt and Sabrina, by Geoffrey of Monmouth; Humbling of Jovinian, from the Gesta Romanorum; Lludd and Llevelys, from the Mabinogion; Launcelot's tourney, by T. Malory; Roberto's tale, by R. Greene; True relation of the apparition of one Mrs Veal, by D. Defoe; Story of an heir, by J. Addison; Disabled soldier, by O. Goldsmith. Bridal of Janet Dalrymple, by W. Scott; White trout, by S. Lover; Queer client, by C. Dickens; Terribly strange bed, by W. Collins; Squire Petrick's lady, by T. Hardy; Thrawn Janet, by R. L. Stevenson; Selfish giant, by O. Wilde; Julia Cahill's curse, by G. Moore; That brute Simmons, by A. Morrison; Lay of Hildebrand; Siegfried and Kriemhild, from The Lay of the Nibelungs; Coming of Gandin, by G. von Strassburg; Bruin the bear and Reynard the fox, from Reynard the fox; Eulenspiegel and the merchant, from Eulenspiegel; Doctor Faust and the usurer; from the history of Dr. J. Faust; Sick wife, by C. Gellert; Little Briar-rose, by the Brothers Grimm; Story of Serapion, by E. T. A. Hoffmann; Legend of the dance, by G. Keller; Fury, by P. Heyse; Triple warning, by A. Schnitzler; New-Year's Eve confession, by H. Sudermann; Divided horsecloth, by Bernier; Priest and the mulberries; Lay of the two lovers, by M. de France; Pious lady and the gray friar, by M. de Navarre; He who married a dumb wife, by F. Rabelais; Roast-meat seller, by F. Rabelais; Little Red Riding-Hood, by C. Perrault; Four friends, by J. de LaFontaine; Memnon the philosopher, by Voltaire; Lausus and Lydia, by J. F. Marmontel; Mysterious mansion, by H. de Balzac; Mateo Falcone, by P. Mérimée; Mummy's foot, by T. Gautier; Torture of hope, by V. de L'Isle Adam; Last lesson, by A. Daudet; Fairy amoureuse, by É. Coppée; Our lady's juggler, by A. France; Necklace, by G. de Maupassant; Bell of Atri, from the Hundred ancient tales; Falcon, by Boccaccio Galgano, by S. Giovanni; Two ambassadors, by F. Sacchetti; Cavalier of Toledo,

by Masuccio (Guardato); Belphagor, by N. Macchiavelli; King in disguise, by M. Bandello; Friar of Novara, by A. Firenzuola; Greek merchant, by G. G. Cinthio; Venetian silk-mercer, by C. Gozzi; Cavaleria Rusticana, by G. Verga; Peasant's will, by A. Fogazzaro; Mendicant melody, by E. de Amicis; Lulu's triumph, by M. Serao; Hero, by G. d'Annunzio; Two miracles by G. Deledda; Miracle of the Jew, from Chronicle of the Cid; Son and his friends, by J. Manuel; How Lazaro served a bulero, by D. Hurtado de Mandoza; Guzman and my Lord Cardinal, by M. Alemán; Rinconete and Cortadillo, by M. Cervantes; Tall woman, by P. A. de Alarcón; Maese Perez, the organist, by G. A. Bécquer; Adios, Cordera! by L. Alas; Story of Ming-Y, from Marvelous tales; Fickle widow, from Marvelous tales Virtuous daughter-in-law, by P'u Sung-Ling; Forty-seven Rônins; Pier, by M. Ogwai; Domestic animal, by S. Toson; Higher the flight the lower the fall, by J. Cats; Story of Saïdjah, by E. D. Dekker; Grandfather's birthday present, by H. Heijermans; Invisible wound, by Kisfaludi; Ball, by M. Jokai; Green fly, by K. Mikszath; Silver hilt, by F. Molnar; Snow storm by A. Pushkin; St John's eve, by N. Gogol; District doctor, by I. Turgenev; Christmas tree and the wedding, by F. Dostoievsky; Long exile, by L. Tolstoy; Old bell-ringer, by V. Korolenko; Signal, by V. Garshin; The bet, by A. Chekhov; One autumn night, by M. Gorky; Silence, by L. Andreyev; Lighthouse keeper of Aspinwall, by H. Sienkiewicz; Human telegraph, by B. Prus; Forebodings, by S. Zeromski; Woman's wrath, by I. L. Peretz; Passover guest, by S. Aleichem; Picnic, by S. Libin; Kaddish, by A. Raisin; Abandoned, by S. Asch; In the storm, by D. Pinski; Balder's bale, by S. Sturluson; Regin's tale, from Volsunga Saga; Shepherdess and the sweep, by H. C. Andersen; Henrik and Rosalie, by M. A. Goldschmidt; Two worlds, by J. P. Jacobsen; Smith who could not get into hell, by P. C. Asbjörnsen; Father, by B. Björnson; Skobelef, by J. Bojer; Love and bread, by A. Strindberg; Eclipse, by S. Lagerlöf; The falcon, by P. Hallström; Mysterious picture, by C. de Coster; Massacre of the innocents, by M. Maeterlinck; Soul of Veere, by C. Lemonnier; One night, by E. Verhaeren; Neighbor, by A. Matoš; Children and old folk, by I. Cankar; At the well, by L. K Lazarevich; Vampire, by J. Neruda; Foltýn's drum, by S. Cech; Priest's tale, by D. Bikelas; Easter torch, by I. L. Caragiale; What Vasile saw, by Marie, Queen of Roumania; Commissioner's Christmas, by D. Ivanov; Chivalry, by R. Fernández-Garcia; Attendant's confession, by J. M. Machado de Assis; Legend of Pygmalion, by V. García-Calderón; Creole democracy, by R. Bianco-Fombóna; Deaf satyr, by R. Darío; Specter bridegroom, by W. Irving; Mrs Bullfrog, by N. Hawthorne; Tell-tale heart, by E. A. Poe; Journalism in Tennessee, by M. Twain; Man and the snake, by A. Bierce; Outcasts of Poker Flat, by B. Harte; Story in it, by H. James; King Solomon of Kentucky, by J. L. Allen; Miss Tempy's watchers, by S. O. Jewett; Letter and a paragraph, by H. C. Bunner; Supply and demand, by O. Henry; Darkbrown dog, by S. Crane; Lost Phoebe, by T. Dreiser; Sophistication, by S. Anderson; Wagner matinée, by W. Cather; Brown woman, by J. B. Cabell

Clark, Walter Van Tilburg
y The Ox-bow incident. Random House 1940 309p o.p. 1970

The scene is Nevada in 1885. A group of citizens of the town of Bridger's Gulch learn that one of their members has been murdered by cattle rustlers. They form an illegal posse, pursue the murderers and lynch them

"A cowboy story but much more than a run-of-the-mill western, for both the writing and the psychological insight set it apart. It is an expert narrative, with sharp, effective dialog." Booklist

The track of the cat; a novel. Random House 1949 404p o.p. 1970

"Symbolic novel depicting the struggle between good and evil. The action takes place in three days on a remote Nevada ranch. Only one family lives in the secluded valley. The first snowfall of the season brings the knowledge that a panther has been killing the cattle. Two of the Bridges brothers go out to track down the panther and both meet death. The story of

Clark, Walter V.—*Continued*

the effects of this upon the other members of the family is on two levels: the realistic and the symbolic." Book Rev Digest

"There is artistic unity and simplicity in 'The Track of the Cat,' but there is also some of the looseness and apparent capriciousness of events which are in life. The actions have implications that go far beyond their limited context. It is masterful, consistently sustained story telling, and it purges with pity and terror." Sat R

Clarke, Arthur C.

y Across the sea of stars; an omnibus containing the complete novels, Childhood's end, and Earthlight and eighteen short stories. Introduction by Clifton Fadiman. Harcourt 1959 584p $5.75

Partially analyzed in Short Story Index
The novels included first published 1953 and 1955, respectively, are entered separately
The short stories are: The sentinel; Inheritance; Encounter at dawn; Superiority; Hide and seek; History lesson; "If I forget thee, oh Earth. . ."; Breaking strain; Silence please; Armaments race; The pacifist; The next tenants; The reluctant orchid; Rescue party; Technical error; The fires within; Time's arrow; Jupiter Five

Against the fall of night
In Clarke, A. C. The lion of Comarre & Against the fall of night p63-214

Childhood's end. Harcourt [1963 c1953] 216p boards $4.50

A reissue of the title published 1953 by Ballantine
"A futurama projects changes in human society when the inhabitants of Earth discover that there is a super-intelligence in the universe which has a greater destiny in store for mankind than mere existence on this planet." Chicago

also in Clarke, A. C. Across the sea of stars p247-434

y The city and the stars. Harcourt 1956 310p boards $4.95

"A story of the remote future, when civilization sleeps in a solitary city lost in the sands of an age-worn earth—until one man arises who challenges the boundaries of time and space." McClurg. Book News
"Expansion of the story in the Author's 'Against the fall of night.' published in 1953." Booklist

also in Clarke, A. C. From the ocean, from the stars p321-515

y The deep range. Harcourt 1957 238p $4.95

A science fiction set in the deep sea one hundred years in the future when the earth's population is fed principally from the sea either on whale products or from plankton farms. The hero is a grounded spaceship engineer assigned to a submarine patrol tending the whale herds. His adventures include the capture of a giant squid and an encounter with a sea serpent. (Publisher)
"Clarke writes with such grace, verve and scientific authority that even readers who shy from science-fiction as such might respond favorably to 'The Deep Range.' It is superior adventure fiction." San Francisco Chronicle

also in Clarke, A. C. From the ocean, from the stars p 1-165

y Earthlight. Ballantine 1955 155p o.p. 1970

"Sadler was sent to the Moon to find a spy —someone was telling Earth's secrets to the Federation—but he was powerless to stop the war of the worlds." Retail Bookseller

also in Clarke, A. C. Across the sea of stars p435-584

Expedition to earth. Harcourt 1970 181p boards $5.75

First published 1953 by Ballantine, and analyzed in Short Story Index

Contents: Second dawn; "If I forget thee, oh earth"; Breaking strain; History lesson; Superiority; Exile of the eons; Hide and seek; Expedition to earth; Loophole; Inheritance; The sentinel

"Genuine space fiction, in which the probabiblities of natural science are respected, rather than space fantasy, in which imagination is given free play." Christian Science Monitor

y A fall of moondust. Harcourt 1961 248p $4.95

A science fiction novel set far enough into the future for man to have been long established on the Moon. One of the high points on the conducted tours for vacationers is a cruise around the Sea of Thirst, a body of fine volcanic dust, in a specially designed vessel called the "Selene." One day the "Selene" became imbedded in the dust. This story tells of the complicated and perilous rescue operation that ensued. (Publisher)

"The fascination of this simple tale lies in its transferring a universal predicament to surroundings at once alien and possessed of verisimilitude. Mr. Clarke has thought out his Moon; he has thought it out with such thoroughness, consistency and care that we simply must believe him; and believing him, we are engrossed." Times (London) Lit Sup

y From the ocean, from the stars; an omnibus containing the complete novels: The deep range and The city and the stars, and twenty-four short stories. Harcourt 1962 515p $5.75

The deep range and The city and the stars are entered separately above. Fourteen of the twenty-four short stories are from The other side of the sky, entered separately; analyzed in Short Story Index
Short stories included are: The nine billion names of God; Refugee; Special delivery; Feathered friend; Take a deep breath; Freedom of space; Passer-by; The call of the stars; The wall of darkness; Security check; No morning after; The starting line; Robin Hood, F.R.S.; Green fingers; All that glitters; Watch this space; A question of residence; Publicity campaign; All the time in the world; Cosmic Casanova; The star; Out of the sun; Transience; The songs of distant earth

The lion of Comarre & Against the fall of night. Harcourt 1968 214p $4.75

"'The Lion of Comarre', a novella written in 1946 appeared in a magazine in 1949, but has not previously been available in book form. 'Against the Fall of Night,' a novel completed in 1946, was published in a magazine in 1948 and as a book in 1953." Publisher's note

"Clarke's subject in both tales is the leveling effect of time on civilization and the emergence of basic values fater the superficial forces of that civilization were wiped out. . . . [Both] are entertaining and well-constructed works of science fiction." Pub W

y The nine billion names of God; the best short stories of Arthur C. Clarke. Harcourt 1967 277p $4.75

Analyzed in Short Story Index
"The author has made his own selection of the twenty-five stories he likes best of more than one hundred he has written." Bk Buyer's Guide
Contents: The nine billion names of God; I remember Babylon; Trouble with time; Rescue party; The curse; Summertime on Icarus; Dog star; Hide and seek; Out of the sun; The wall of darkness; No morning after; The possessed; Death and the Senator; Who's there; Before Eden; Superiority; A walk in the dark; The call of the stars; The reluctant orchid; Encounter at dawn; "If I forget thee, oh earth . . ."; Patent pending; The sentinel; Transience; The star

y The other side of the sky. Harcourt 1958 245p boards $4.95

Analyzed in Short Story Index
A collection of "science fiction stories, including 'The Star,' selected as a best science fiction story of 1956." Library J
Contents: The nine billion names of God; Refugee; The other side of the sky; The wall of darkness; Security check; No morning after; Venture to the moon; Publicity campaign; All the time in the world; Cosmic Casanova; The star; Out of the sun; Transience; The songs of distant earth

Clarke, Arthur C.—*Continued*

y Prelude to Mars. . . . Harcourt 1965 497p $5.75

Partially analyzed in Short Story Index
"An omnibus containing the complete novels: Prelude to space and The sands of Mars [first published 1954 and 1952 respectively, and entered separately] and sixteen short stories." Title page
Short stories included are: Big game hunt; Critical mass; The ultimate melody; Moving spirit; The man who ploughed the sea; Cold war; What goes up; Trouble with the natives; A walk in the dark; The forgotten enemy; The awakening; Exile of the eons; Second dawn

y Prelude to space. Harcourt 1970 209p $5.75

First published 1952 by Gnome Press
Written more than twenty years ago while the author was a student, this novel, set in London and in Australia, tells of the events which culminated in man's first landing on the moon. (Publisher)
"Equally absorbing to the novice reader and to the most ingrained aficionado." N Y Her Trib Books

also in Clarke, A. C. Prelude to Mars p 1-143

y The sands of Mars. Harcourt 1967 218p $4.95

First published 1954 by Grome Press
"A neatly plotted tale of interplanetary travel which seems more realistic than many in this genre. Martin Gibson, author of science fiction stories, tells of his participation in the maiden voyage of the new spaceship 'Ares' and the establishment of a colony on Mars. Especially interesting is the description of Space Station One." Booklist

also in Clarke, A. C. Prelude to Mars p315-497

Tales of ten worlds. Harcourt 1962 245p $4.50

Analyzed in Short Story Index
Contents: I remember Babylon; Summertime on Icarus; Out of the cradle, endlessly orbiting; Who's there; Hate; Into the comet; An ape about the house; Saturn rising; Let there be light; Death and the senator; Trouble with time; Before Eden; A slight case of sunstroke; Dog star; The road to the sea

y (ed.) Time probe: the sciences in science fiction; collected and with an introduction by Arthur C. Clarke. Delacorte Press 1966 242p $4.95

Analyzed in Short Story Index
These stories "illustrate some particular aspect of science or technology." Introduction
Contents:—And he built a crooked house, by R. A. Heinlein; The Wabbler, by M. Leinster; The weather man, by T. L. Thomas; The artifact business, by R. Silverberg; Grandpa, by J. H. Schmitz; Not final, by I. Asimov; The little black bag, by C. Kornbluth; The Blindness, by P. Latham; Take a deep breath, by A. C. Clarke; The Potters of Firsk, by J. Vance; The tissue-culture king, by J. Huxley

y 2001: a space odyssey. . . . New Am. Lib. 1968 221p boards $4.95

"Based on a screenplay by Stanley Kubrick and Arthur C. Clarke." Title page
The novel depicts the interplanetary voyage "of the spacecraft 'Discovery,' hurtling its human voyagers . . . toward a confrontation with an unknown Intelligence." Publisher's note
"By standing the universe on its head, he makes us see the ordinary universe in a different light. . . . [This novel becomes] a complex allegory about the history of the world." New Yorker

Clarke, John Henrik

(ed.) American Negro short stories. Hill & Wang 1966 355p $5.95

Analyzed in Short Story Index
Contents: The lynching of Jube Benson, by P. L. Dunbar; On being crazy, by W. E. B. Du Bois; The goophered grapevine, by C. W. Chesnutt; The city of refuge, by R. Fisher; The overcoat, by J. P. Davis; Truant, by C. McKay; A summer tragedy, by A. Bontemps; The gilded six-bits, by Z. N. Hurston; Bright and morning star, by R. Wright; The boy who painted Christ black, by J. H. Clarke; One Friday morning, by L. Hughes; So peaceful in the country, by C. R. Offord; And/or, by S. Brown; Fighter, by J. C. Smith; The homecoming, by F. Yerby; How John Boscoe outsung the devil, by A. P. Davis; Solo on the drums, by A. Petry; Mama's missionary money, by C. Himes; See how they run, by M. E. Vroman; Exodus, by J. Baldwin; God bless America, by J. O. Killens; Train whistle guitar, by A. Murray; The Senegalese, by H. W. Fuller; A matter of time, by F. L. Brown; Cry for me, by W. M. Kelley; Reena; by P. Marshall; The convert, by L. Bennett; The winds of change, by L. Hairston; The screamers, by L. Jones; Sarah, by M. J. Hamer; The sky is gray, by E. J. Gaines

Clarkson, Ewan

y Syla, the mink; drawings by David Carl Forbes. Dutton 1968 126p boards $3.95

Published in England with title: Break for freedom
"The life story, from birth to death, of Syla, a mink who escapes from the fur farm where she was born. Syla makes her new home in a remote, wild valley where she must learn the laws of survival." Bk Buyer's Guide
"It is as much a lyric recital of the moods of nature and the habits of small animals, their ecology, and description of the countryside as it is the story of Syla. It will captivate animal lovers, although a mink, like a weasel, does not seem a likely heroine for a story." Best Sellers

Clavel, Bernard

The fruits of winter; tr. by Patsy Southgate. Coward-McCann [1969 c1968] 382p boards $6.95

Original French edition published 1968
"This novel explores two relevant areas: the psychology of old age and the effect of war on people. Provincial France during the last year of World War II provides the setting. Père Dubois sees the little world he has created threatened by the war and by the feuding of his two sons who reflect conflicting political views." Library J
"The book will have undoubted appeal to the public library patron, especially those women who like to shed a tear over the fate of fictional heroes and heroines." Best Sellers

Clavell, James

King Rat; a novel. Little 1962 406p $6.95

"A novel about corruption, fear and despair among the prisoners in a Singapore prison camp in World War II. 'King Rat,' so called because he breeds the prison rats and sells them for food, is an American corporal turned gambler and black marketeer. He has bribed his way into a position as real though unofficial ruler of the camp." Pub W
This novel "is strong in narrative detail, penetrating in observation of human nature under stress, and thought-provoking in its analysis of right and wrong." Cincinnati

Tai-Pan; a novel of Hong Kong. Atheneum Pubs. 1966 590p $6.95

A panoramic "massive novel about the conflict between Struan, 'Tai-Pan' or top man of Hong Kong in 1841, and the Manchu Government on the one hand and next-in-line Flint. . . . The opium trade, Chinese politics, lovely Chinese concubines, and a typhoon all play their part in the story." Bk Buyer's Guide
The author "has a first rate command of dialogue; the story, in fact, is told almost completely in dialogue. The little narration that does occur is quietly effective. . . . The theme of the novel, if it can be said to have a theme other than that of excellent entertainment, is man and the uses he makes of power." Best Sellers
"The backgrounds—Hong Kong, is sailing ships, the trading preserve in Canton—surge with life, and the plot is neatly dovetailed with history. Superb storytelling; an utterly absorbing book." Pub W

Clayton, Richard. See Haggard, William

Cleary, Jon

The High Commissioner; a novel. Morrow 1966 284p boards $4.95

"Detective Sergeant Scobie Malone was told to bring High Commissioner John Quentin back from England to Australia to face an old murder charge. But Quentin was involved in high level Conferences to bring peace to Vietnam, in spite of the efforts of Saigon's vice queen to sabotage his mission. He needed five days, and Malone got them for him." Bk Buyer's Guide

Malone "falls into a surprising relationship of friendship and mutual admiration with the man he supposed to arrest. . . . Though the plot creaks in a few places, it offers a moving picture of a great man's fall from greatness, an acid and entertaining view of diplomatic cocktail parties, some sequences of tingling suspense and drama, and a good detective whom one would like to see again." Pub W

The long pursuit; a novel. Morrow 1967 282p boards $4.50

"This takes place in wartime Sumatra during 1942. A small group of men and one woman are trying to fight their way out of the crossfire of Southeast Asia, down through Sumatra to link up with a guerrilla force in contact with Australia. . . . Predictable maybe, but still a sound professional job with lots of excitement and a touch of love interest." Pub W

North from Thursday. Morrow 1961 [c1960] 373p o.p. 1970

First published 1960 in England
"A story of the primitive New Guinea backcountry jungles among the still cannibalistic tribesmen. Police officer Roy Narvo has his job complicated by a pair of Iron Curtain fugitives, including a woman." Am News of Bks

"It necessitates the skill of a master to recreate the gorgeous colors, the vastness and opulence, the exotic magnificence which is New Guinea. . . . Suffice it to say that all of these things are present in abundance, the work of a master craftsman." Best Sellers

Season of doubt. Morrow 1968 285p boards $4.95

"A tense, actionful novel of political intrigue set in Lebanon at the beginning of the Middle East crisis of late spring, 1967. Paul Tancred, economic secretary in the American embassy, discovers that the man who had been his protector in a North Korean prison camp is in Beirut to sell arms to the highest bidder. Committed to American noninvolvement and also morally committed Tancred tries to stop the sale and save his friend's life." Booklist

"As a spy story it is a mild one though competently enough written, and rather lacking in excitement until the last few pages." Pub W

The sundowners. Scribner 1952 290p o.p. 1970

"A story of one year in the life of a nomadic family in Australia. The chief characters are Paddy Carmody and his wife, Ida, and their fourteen year old son, Sean. The year saw ups and downs in their fortunes, hard times and good times, and the growth to maturity and understanding of the young boy." Book Rev Digest

"A warmhearted feeling pervades the story but [it has] occasional earthy humor." Booklist

Cleeve, Roger

The last, long journey. Scribner 1969 271p $4.95

"The protagonist, an Indian civil servant in the grips of disillusionment with his country and himself, is sent on a government mission to capture a gunrunner between Kashmir and Pakistan. The gunrunner, a British national, was a childhood friend and Cambridge classmate of the pursuer. The story alternates between the present and the past where double standards and color and class prejudice left many scars and unhealed wounds." Library J

"A well-written blend of physical action and emotional insight." Pub W

Clemens, Samuel Langhorne. See Twain, Mark

Clézio, J. M. G. le. See Le Clézio, J. M. G.

Clifford, Francis

All men are lonely now. Coward-McCann 1967 251p $4.95

"David Lancaster, a security officer in a very secret Ministry of Defense Department in London, has safely passed much classified information to the other side, and when leaks are discovered he has had no hesitation in planting fatal evidence on a coworker who is then held responsible. When he falls in love, the picture changes [and] faking evidence and planning cover-up moves becomes more difficult and dangerous for him. And there is a final twist in the last assignment." Library J

"Mr. Clifford can hold us immovable without using violence (that enters in only at the end and then from a distance). None of his characters is particularly attractive yet we become desperately involved with them." Christian Science Monitor

Another way of dying. Coward-McCann [1969 c1968] 220p $4.95

First published 1968 in England
"Neal Forrester, head of a British demolition company, is vacationing in Sicily, and lends a hand to Inger Lindeman, whose companion has died a suicide. While traveling to Palermo they are kidnapped by peasants looking for ransom. It's a case of mistaken identity, but their captors decide to use Neal's expertise with dynamite to accomplish their main objective: the springing of one of their number from prison." N Y Times Bk R

The naked runner. Coward-McCann 1966 255p $4.95

"Sam Laker, British businessman, agrees to run an errand for British Secret Operations in Leipzig, where he and his son are going for a trade fair. Something goes wrong: Laker is trapped by the East German police. They use a weapon of special terror, a threat to kill his son, in order to force Laker to shoot a man for them in Copenhagen. Agonized about his son and unskilled at cold-war intrigue, Laker has to make up his mind between murdering a stranger and leaving his son to die." Pub W

"A grand, strong thriller. . . . The rules of the game forbid me to explain why I find the ending ingenious but irritating, though I guess I may say I miss the uncompromising integrity of earlier Clifford novels; but ending and all, this is one of the season's more exciting intrigue-adventures." N Y Times Bk R

Cloete, Stuart

The fiercest heart. Houghton 1960 435p o.p. 1970

"This big book tells the story of the great Boer trek of the 1830's. During this time nearly 10,000 men, women and children left their homes in the Cape Colony to free themselves of the British. They traveled north and east several hundred miles there to found state of the Transvaal. It was a time of hardship, daring, and danger." Library J

Rags of glory. Doubleday 1963 631p o.p. 1970

A long novel about the Boer War in South Africa in which the author depicts Boers, British soldiers, women and children moving over plains and mountains in battles among burning farms. The principal characters are Turnbull, the English captain, Moolman, the ivory hunter, and a lovely Dutch girl who betrays her country. Many historic persons such as Lord Roberts, Cecil Rhodes, De Wet and Smuts appear. (Publisher)

"It is a rousing, lusty story full of violence, bloodshed, battle scenes, passionate love, sex, handsome hussars, and beautiful women. Altogether pretty strong stuff, and some of the scenes will haunt you for days after. Cloete is a consummate storyteller, skillfully weaving several subsidiary plots into an integrated, swiftly paced whole. His many characters are sharply detailed and believable." Library J

Cloete, Stuart—*Continued*

The turning wheels. Houghton 1937 434p map o.p. 1970

"A powerful story of the Dutch pioneers in South Africa. Resenting the freedom of the slaves in the midst of the harvest, the Boers turned from their homes in the Cape Colony, which they had founded, and headed for the North, braving hardships and hostility of Kaffir and Zulu to found the Orange Free States and to penetrate even farther North into the Transvaal. In writing this story, the author drew on the personal records of the great trek of 1836 left by his great grandfather." N Y Libraries

"It is told in heroic vein; the land, the men and women, and their loves and hates are all violent and untamed, and they are described realistically." Booklist

Closs, Hannah

Deep are the valleys. Vanguard 1960 261p boards $4.95

Sequel to: High are the mountains

This novel of 13th century France centers on idealistic Wolf of Foix and "his determination to avenge the death of his good friend, Trencavel, his hazardous adventures and continued search for inward, spiritual guidance." Bookmark

Followed by: The silent Tarn

High are the mountains; a novel. Vanguard 1959 342p illus boards $4.95

"A richly detailed and well-plotted tale, set in thirteenth-century southern France, envisions a feudal world torn by social, political, and religious conflict. The action centers on the struggle between the Albigensian heretics and the Church, a struggle finally resolved by a crusade against the Albigensians proclaimed by Pope Innocent III. Lifelike people and excellent descriptive passages distinguish this substantial historical novel." Booklist

Followed by: Deep are the valleys

The silent Tarn. Vanguard 1963 219p boards $4.95

"The last volume of a trilogy, concerning the thirteenth-century Albigensian heresy, the first two volumes of which were 'High are the mountains' and 'Deep are the valleys.' The hero of the earlier novels, Wolf of Foix, is also the chief protagonist of this one. Grown now and married to a Cathar woman. Wolf, after many vicissitudes, is reunited with his child love, Esclarmonde." Booklist

"But even as it stands, not quite finished and not finally hardened. 'The Silent Tarn' remains a gripping and thoughtful tale of a great crisis in medieval history." N Y Her Trib Books

Cockrell, Marian

The revolt of Sarah Perkins. McKay 1965 310p boards $4.95

A novel set in the Colorado Territory in 1869-1870. "Schoolteacher Sarah Perkins, chosen for her plainness by a Colorado school board tired of losing its teachers to matrimony, proves herself an unexpectedly valuable addition to the frontier community. A predictable yet entertaining woman's novel." Booklist.

Cocteau, Jean

The holy terrors; with illus. by the author. Tr. by Rosamond Lehmann. New Directions 1957 193p illus o.p. 1970

Original French edition 1929. First English translation published 1930 by Bewer and Warren with title: Enfants terrible

"After their mother's death, Paul and Elizabeth live in a room which is to them like an island in the midst of Paris. They are wild, poetic, original children, with a deep-rooted attachment to each other, whose destiny is to live and die together. Each draws a single friend into the circle of their life, a friend more normal, more worldly, than themselves, and soon overwhelmed with the hopelessness of love for such precocious beings. The spiritual flow between brother and sister is an active and dangerous force. When Elizabeth steps outside the circle to take a husband, the husband is immediately killed in an accident. When her friend, Agatha, confesses her love for Paul, Elizabeth treacherously prevents their union. Her insane stratagems to preserve the ideal world of their childhood end with the suicides of both Paul and herself." Book Rev Digest

The imposter; tr. from the French by Dorothy Williams. Noonday 1957 132p o.p. 1970

Original French edition 1923; first English translation published 1925 by Appleton with title: Thomas the imposter

The setting of M. Cocteau's short novel "is the First World War; his imposter, a French youth, too young for the services, who in a borrowed uniform and under a borrowed name succeeds in obtaining a post in a curious nursing unit run by a Polish princess and her daughter. He plays the part he has adopted so well that in the end he succeeds in convincing even himself of his authenticity, and having finally been adopted as their mascot by a unit of Marines dies in the end a gallant death." Times (London) Lit Sup

Coe, Tucker

Murder among children. Random House [1968 c1967] 177p $4.50

Ex-cop Mitch Tobin "tells how he becomes involved in knife-murders of young Terry Wilford and a Negro prostitute because his own pretty cousin, Robin Kenney seems to be the only possible suspect. Much against his will and the advice of unfriendly police, he promises to do what he can for Robin." Bk Buyer's Guide

"His search into the backgrounds of the boy who was killed and the Negro girl who died with him, takes Mitch into danger and into some strange places in New York's slums and byways. All of which makes this topnotch in realistic excitement." Pub W

Wax apple. Random House 1970 179p $4.95

Mitchell Tobin, former New York cop, "takes up residence in the Midway House, where patients discharged from mental institutions may spend six-month readjustment periods before re-entering their normal environments. His job is to discover who is responsible for disturbing accidents that have so far caused only broken limbs and bruises. . . . When one of the 'accidents' causes death, the police have to be called in. They quickly secure a false confession, but Tobin, by deduction, finds the real culprits." Pub W

For other titles by this author see Westlake, Donald E.

Cole, Burt

The funco file. Doubleday 1969 282p $4.95

"The government's monolithic, central computer refuses to believe that four freaks like the ones the FDI (Federal Deviation Investigation) has uncovered can exist. When the machine demands that the freaks be brought in for examination and trial, a . . . search begins for an Indian goddess of love, an elite robot-killer AWOL from M corps, an Ozark Mountain boy as wise as Daniel Boone and able to cause the Poltergeist phenomenon, and a shy corporation accountant who finds he can write indelible blue letters in the air with the tip of his nose." Am News of Bks

This "is clever, light summer satire. When you're all through you may decide you've only been dining on a trifle after all, but it is palatable one, with a certain bubbly zest." Pub W

Coles, Cyril Henry. See Coles, Manning

Coles, Manning

Alias Uncle Hugo

In Coles, M. The exploits of Tommy Hambledon p349-480

Coles, Manning—*Continued*

Drink to yesterday; with an introduction by James Nelson. Norton 1967 270p (The Seagull lib. of mystery and suspense) $4.50

A reissue of the title published 1941 by Knopf
"Story of an English spy in Germany during the last war. He so impresses a German intelligence officer with his hatred of England and devotion to the German cause that he is sent to England as a spy, thus making it easy for him to convey information to the War Office but compelling him to live a double life. When he returns to England after the war he is so changed by the experiences he has undergone that he is unable to take up his old life." Book Rev Digest

> *also in* Coles, M. Exploits of Tommy Hambledon p7-162

Exploits of Tommy Hambledon. Doubleday 1959 480p o.p. 1970

The adventures of Thomas Elphinstone Hambledon of British Intelligence in Germany during World War II and in a small country in Europe after the war. Contains these three novels previously published: Drink to yesterday (1941) and its sequel: Toast to tomorrow (1941) both entered separately and, Alias Uncle Hugo (1952)

No entry

> *In* Haycraft, H. ed. Five spy novels p615-758

A toast to tomorrow. Doubleday 1941 310p o.p. 1970

Sequel to: Drink to yesterday
The story "of a man who lost his memory and wandered through Germany after the War [of 1914-1918] was over seeking to pick up the threads of his earlier life. He became an intimate of Hitler and rose high in the inner circles of the Nazi party. When Hitler burned the Reichstag he became Chief of Police for the Nazi party—and remembered who he really was." Literary Guild

> *also in* Coles, M. The exploits of Tommy Hambledon p163-347

Colette

The blue lantern
> *In* Colette. Break of day v2

Break of day; tr. by Enid McLeod; introduction by Glenway Wescott; and, The blue lantern, tr. by Roger Senhouse. Farrar, Straus [1966 c1963] 2v in 1 boards $5.95

Original French edition published in Paris 1928. This translation first published 1961. Reissued with the author's "The blue lantern" which is half journal, half reminiscenes
"A novel based on her own life just after her second marriage had ended and she was ready to begin another life." Bk Buyer's Guide

The cat
> *In* Colette. 7 by Colette v 1 p69-193

Chance acquaintances
> *In* Collette. Gigi. Julie de Carneilhan. Chance acquaintances p225-315
> *In* Colette. 7 by Colette v3 p139-230

Chéri
> *In* Colette. Chéri, and The last of Chéri
> *In* Colette. 7 by Colette v2 p 1-154
> *In* Colette. Six novels p411-534

Chéri, and The last of Chéri. [Tr. by Roger Senhouse] Farrar, Straus 1953 [c1951] 296p o.p. 1970

Original French editions published 1920 and 1926 respectively. This translation first published 1951 in England

"These two short novels tell the story of a young Frenchman, beautiful, charming and irresponsible, whose mistress is Léa de Lonval, a middle-aged courtesan of considerable fame and wealth. When Chéri makes a 'fortunate' marriage his liaison with Léa breaks off. Years, after the marriage proves emotionally unsatisfactory, Chéri returns to Léa only to find her an ugly, old woman, ostensibly satisfied with her lot— and that is the last of Chéri." Book Rev Digest

"The tragicomedy of the boy who will not grow up and the woman who cannot stay young is worked out with wit, a fine assortment of supporting characters, perfectly chosen detail, and a detachment that has in it an almost feline quality." Atlantic

Claudine at school; tr. by Antonia White. Farrar, Straus 1957 286p o.p. 1970

"A translation of Colette's first novel, written when she was twenty-two, and published in 1900. In it a precocious school girl, by peeping and spying on both her contemporaries and her boarding school teachers, discovers all the secrets of the people around her, and describes them." Book Rev Digest

"Like most restless and intelligent adolescents, Claudine seeks knowledge for its own sake. For her, adult behavior is neither good nor evil. It is just continuously absorbing, as the sex life of a lemming might be to a biologist." Time

> *also in* Colette. Six novels p 1-234

Gigi
> *In* Colette, Gigi. Julie de Carneilhan. Chance acquaintances p9-74
> *In* Colette. 7 by Colette v 1 p 1-67
> *In* Colette. Six novels p649-97

Gigi. Julie de Carneilhan. Chance acquaintances. Farrar, Straus 1952 315p o.p. 1970

"Three novellas; one of them already famous in this country as a play; the others less renowned but equally piquant. Especially Julie de Carneilhan which tells of a much married aristocrat down on her luck, who agrees with an ex-husband to blackmail his present wife and split the gain. The other story concerns Madame Colette at a country lodge, and her part in the amorous schemes of the visitors." Library J

"These three short novels do not represent Colette at her best, but they all bear distinct traces of her wisdom, her incomparable style, and her humor." New Yorker

Julie de Carneilhan
> *In* Colette. Gigi. Julie de Carneilhan. Chance acquaintances p77-222

The last of Chéri
> *In* Colette. Chéri, and The last of Chéri p155-296
> *In* Colette. 7 by Colette v2 p155-296
> *In* Colette. Six novels p535-648

Mitsou
> *In* Colette. Six novels p339-410

Music-hall sidelights
> *In* Colette. Six novels p237-337

My mother's house
> *In* Colette. 7 by Colette v3 p 1-138

The ripening seed. (Le blé enherbe) Farrar, Straus 1956 [c1955] 186p o.p. 1970

Original French edition 1923. This translation by Roger Senhouse was first published 1955 in England

"The love story of an adolescent boy and girl, complicated when an older woman seduces the boy, but teaches him manhood." Book Rev Digest

"A luminous and sensuously intuitive study of adolescent awakening." Time

Colette—*Continued*

7 by Colette. Farrar, Straus 1955 4v in 1 o.p. 1970

Contents: Gigi; The cat; Chéri; The last of Chéri; My mother's house; Chance acquaintances; The vagabond

Six novels. Modern Lib. 697p $2.45

Contents: Claudine at school; Music-hall sidelights; Mitsou; Chéri; The last of Chéri; Gigi

The vagabond

In Colette. 7 by Colette v4 p 1-223

Colette, Sidonie Gabrielle. See Colette

Collier, John

Fancies and goodnights. Doubleday 1951 364p o.p. 1970

Analyzed in Short Story Index
"The author has selected the best stories from his two previous collections ('Presenting Moonshine' and 'A Touch of Nutmeg'), and has added seventeen stories which have never before appeared in book form, making [fifty] weird and fantastic stories in this omnibus volume." Huntting
Contents: Bottle party; De mortuis; Evening primrose; Witches money; Are you too late or was I too early; Fallen star; Touch of nutmeg makes it; Three bears cottage; Pictures in the fire; Wet Saturday; Squirrels have bright eyes; Halfway to hell; Lady on the grey; Incident on a lake; Over insurance; Old acquaintance; Frog prince; Season of mists; Great possibilities; Without benefit of Galsworthy; Devil George and Rosie; Ah the university; Back for Christmas; Another American tragedy; Collaboration; Midnight blue; Gavin O'Leary; If youth knew, if age could; This I refute Beelzy; Special delivery; Rope enough; Little Memento; Green thoughts; Romance lingers, adventure lives; Bird of prey; Variation on a theme; Night youth, Paris and the moon; Steel cat; Sleeping beauty; Interpretation of a dream; Mary; Hell hath no fury; In the cards; Invisible dove dancer of Strathpheen Island; Right side; Spring fever; Youth from Vienna; Possession of Angela Bradshaw; Cancel all I said; The chaser

Collins, Norman

The Governor's lady. Simon & Schuster [1969 c1968] 381p $6.95

"Amimbo, a small British colony in West Africa, in the 1930's is the setting for a skillful tale of death and danger on a leopard hunt. Here Harold Stebbs comes on his first foreign office assignment as special assistant to the governor, and here the governor's lady helps him set in motion a train of events that will haunt him for 30 years. The underlying motive that brings the characters together and that separates them in the end is loyalty, but loyalty to different things and for different reasons." Library J
"Readers searching for any profound moral significance are advised to look elsewhere or endure disappointment with this book. It is highly recommended, however, for leisurely and entertaining reading on the basis of its gripping suspense, dimensional characterization, and the sheer adventure and romanticism of the imperialist African setting." Best Sellers

Collins, Wilkie

y The moonstone

Some editions are:
Dodd (Great illustrated classics) $4.50. With illustrations of the author and the setting of the book together with an introduction and descriptive captions by Basil Davenport
Dutton (Everyman's lib) $3.25
Oxford (World's classics) $3.50
Watts, F. $9.95 Large type edition, complete and unabridged. A Keith Jennison book

First edition 1868
This novel "concerns the disappearance of the Moonstone, an enormous diamond that once adorned a Hindu idol and came into the possession of an English officer. The heroine, Miss Verinder, believes her lover, Franklin Blake, to be the thief; other suspects are

Blake's rival and three mysterious Brahmins. The mystery is solved by Sergeant Cuff, possibly the first detective in English fiction." Benét. The Reader's Encyclopedia

Short stories [selected by J. I. Rodale]. With wood engravings by Fritz Eichenberg. Story Classics 1950 167p illus. o.p. 1970

Contents: A terribly stange bed; The caldron of oil; The fatal cradle; Mr Captain and the nymph; "Blow up with the brig"

y The woman in white. Dutton 569p (Everyman's lib) $2.95

First published 1873; in this edition, 1910
"Practically the first English novel to deal with the detection of crime. The plot is based on the resemblance between the heroine and a mysterious woman in white, and involves an infamous attempt to obtain the heroine's money." Lenrow. Reader's Guide to Prose Fiction

Colver, Anne

Mr Lincoln's wife. Holt 1965 363p $5.95

A reissue in new format, of the title first published 1943 by Farrar, Straus
"She was the most gossiped about woman in Washington. She was written about, photographed, interviewed and criticized. She married Mr. Lincoln because she loved him and because she felt he needed her—and, in spite of everything, she never stopped loving him. Though presented in the form of a novel, the story is based pretty close to fact. It is an understanding and sympathetic portrayal of Mary Todd as she really was—her mistakes, good intentions, impatience, tenderness, happiness and disillusions." Huntting

Comber, Elizabeth. See Han, Suyin

Compton-Burnett, Ivy

Darkness and day. Int. Publications 298p $6.25

Reprint of title published 1951 by Knopf
"In brief, the plot of this novel centers in a retelling of the Oedipus story of incest set in a modern—i.e. a Victorian England scene. However the interest lies mainly in the author's satirical probing of life and character set forth in lengthy conversations among the members of two neighboring households, including children and servants as well as adults." Book Rev Digest

Mother and son. Int. Publications [1967 c1955] 256p $5.25

A reprint of the edition first published 1955 by Messner
"In a subtle English story conveyed through seemingly casual conversations, the author introduces a family in which a mother and grown son are linked in a relationship that excludes the husband and three younger children. The children, a precocious but likable lot, sense the mystery of a situation later clarfied by a confession, a death, and discovery of a hidden letter. While neither minor characters nor members of the family react or talk in an ordinary manner, in retrospect both characters and situation remain convincing." Booklist

Conan Doyle, Sir Arthur. See Doyle, Sir Arthur Conan

Condon, Richard

Mile high. Dial Press 1969 364p $6.95

"Three generations of the Wests, from Paddy the Irish immigrant who laid the base of the family fortune by forging a link between politics and crime, through Edward Courance West, unscrupulous wheeler-dealer who invented Prohibition for the money to be made in bootleg liquor, down to architect Walt and Mayra his Negro wife, who at last are to visit Edward's mile-high castle in upstate New York." Bk Buyer's Guide
"One of the large weaknesses of the book, as fiction, is that we never feel anything about Eddie West himself, not even loathing. . . . Condon has a mania for absolute detail that reminds you frequently of Ian Fleming. . . .

Condon, Richard—*Continued*

[His precision] adds believability to the [novel's] fictional structure. . . . Despite the cult that has grown up around Condon, he is not really a great novelist. . . . But as a practitioner of the fiction of information, no one else comes close to him. [Condon] has written with brilliance and style an indictment that forgives nothing." N Y Times Bk R

Conklin, Edward Groff. See Conklin, Groff

Conklin, Groff

(ed.) The best of science fiction; ed. with an introduction by Groff Conklin. Preface by John W. Campbell, Jr. Crown 1946 xxviii, 785p o.p. 1970

Analyzed in Short Story Index

Contents: Solution unsatisfactory, by A. MacDonald; Great war syndicate, by F. R. Stockton; Piper's son, by L. Padgett; Deadline, by C. Cartmill; Lobby, by C. D. Simak; Blowups happen, by R. Heinlein; Atomic power, by D. A. Stuart; Killdozer, by T. Sturgeon; Davy Jones' ambassador, by R. Z. Gallun; Giant in the earth, by M. Colladay; Goldfish bowl, by A. MacDonald; Ivy war, by D. H. Keller; Liquid life, by R. M. Farley; Tale of the Ragged Mountains, by E. A. Poe; Great Keinplatz experiment, by A. C. Doyle; Remarkable case of Davidson's eyes, by H. G. Wells; Tissue-culture king, by J. Huxley; Ultimate catalyst, by J. Taine; Terrible sense, by C. Peregoy; Scientist divides, by D. Wandrei; Trickytonnage, by M. Jameson; Lanson screen, by A. L. Zagat; Ultimate metal, by N. Schachner; The machine, by D. A. Stuart; Short-circuited probability, by N. L. Knight; The search, by A. E. van Vogt; Upper level road, by W. van Lorne; 32nd of May, by P. Ernst; Monster from nowhere, by D. Wandrei; First contact, by M. Leinster; Universe, by R. Heinlein; Blind alley, by I. Asimov; En route to Pluto, by W. West; Retreat to Mars, by C. B. White; Man who saved the earth, by A. Hall; Spawn of the stars, by C. W. Diffin; Flame midget, by F. B. Lond. Jr. Expedition, by A. Boucher; Conquest of Gola, by L. F. Stone; Jackson, by R. Rocklynne

y (ed.) Giants unleashed. Grosset 1965 248p $2.95

Analyzed in Short Story Index

Twelve science fiction tales "based on the theme of infinite might of intelligence unleashed on earth and in the universe." McClurg. Book News

Contents: Microcosmic god, by T. Sturgeon; Commencement night, by R. Ashby; Deep range, by A. C. Clarke; Machine made, by J. T. McIntosh; Trip one, by R. Grendon; Venus is a man's world, by W. Tenn; Good-bye, Ilha, by L. Manning; Misbegotten missionary, by I. Asimov; The ethical equations, by M. Leinster; Misfit, by R. Heinlein; Genius, by P. Anderson; Basic right, by E. F. Russell

(ed.) Invaders of Earth. Vanguard 1952 333p $5.95

Analyzed in Short Story Index

"Twenty-one science-fiction stories, all of invasions of this planet from outer space . . . [including] the full script of the sensational Orson Welles' broadcast of 'Invasion from Mars.'" Retail Bookseller

Contents: This star shall be free, by M. Leinster; Castaway, by R. M. Williams; Impulse, by E. F. Russell; Top secret, by D. Grinnell; Eel by the tail, by A. K. Lang; Date to remember, by W. F. Temple; Storm warning, by D. Wollheim; Child of void, by M. St Clair; Tiny and the monster, by T. Sturgeon; Discord makers, by M. Reynolds; Pen pal, by M. Lesser; Not only dead men, by A. E. Van Vogt; Enemies in space, by K. Grunert; Invasion from Mars, by H. Koch; Minister without portfolio, by M. Clingerman; The waveries by F. Brown; Crisis, by E. Grendon; Angel's egg, by E. Pangborn; "Will you walk a little faster." by W. Tenn; Man in the moon, by H. Norton; Pictures don't lie, by K. MacLean; Greatest Tertian, by A. Boucher

(ed.) Possible worlds of science fiction. Vanguard 1951 372p $4.95

Analyzed in Short Story Index

Twenty-two "stories which depict a very possible program for the conquest of the solar and stellar systems." Chicago

Contents: Operation Pumice, by R. Z. Gallun; Black pits of Luna, by R. A. Heinlein; Enchanted village, by A. E. Van Vogt; Lillies of life, by M. Jameson; Asleep in Armageddon, by R. Bradbury; Not final, by I. Asimov; Cones, by F. B. Long; Moon of delirium, by D. L. James; Completely automatic, by T. Sturgeon; The day we celebrate, by N. S. Bond; The pillows, by M. St Clair; Proof, by H. Clement; Propagandist, by M. Leinster; In value deceived, by H. B. Fyfe; Hard-luck diggings, by J. Vance; Space rating, by J. Berryman; Contagion, by K. MacLean; Limiting factor, by C. D. Simak; Exit line, by S. Merwin, Jr.; Second night of summer, by J. H. Schmitz; A walk in the dark, by A. C. Clarke; Helping hand, by P. Anderson

(ed.) Science-fiction adventures in dimension. Vanguard 1953 354p $4.95

Analyzed in Short Story Index

A "collection of short stories concerned with travels in the fourth dimension, or space-time travel." Booklist

Contents: Yesterday was Monday, by T. Sturgeon; Ambition, by W. L. Bade; Middle of the week after next, by M. Leinster; And it comes out here, by L. Del Rey; Castaway, by A. B. Chandler; Good provider, by M. Gross; Reverse phylogeny, by A. R. Long; Other tracks, by W. Sell; "What so proudly we hail . . .", by D. Keene; Night meeting, by R. Bradbury; Perfect murder, by H. L. Gold; Flight that failed, by E. M. Hull; Endowment policy, by L. Padgett; Pete can fix it, by R. F. Jones; The mist, by P. Cartur; The gostak and the doshes, by M. J. Breuer; What if . . ." by I. Asimov; Ring around the redhead, by J. D. MacDonald; Tiger by the tail, by A. E. Nourse; Way of escape, by W. F. Temple; Suburban frontiers, by R. F. Young; Business of killing, by F. Leiber, Jr; To follow knowledge, by F. B. Long

(ed.) Science-fiction thinking machines: robots, androids, computers. Vanguard 1954 367p $5.95

Analyzed in Short Story Index

This collection "has most of the classics in the genre, including [the play] 'R.U.R.' which first gave the word robot to the language, and ends with a . . . bibliography of robot stories." San Francisco Chronicle

Contents: Automata: I, by S. F. Wright; Moxon's master, by A. Bierce; Robbie, by I. Asimov; The scarab, by R. Z. Gallun; Mechanical bride, by F. Leiber; Virtuoso, by H. Goldstone; Automata:II, by S. F. Wright; Boomerang, by E. F. Russell; The jester, by W. Tenn; R.U.R., by K. Capek; Skirmish, by C. Simak; Soldier boy, by M. Shaara; Automata:III, by S. F. Wright; Men are different, by A. Bloch; Letter to Ellen, by C. Davis; Sculptors of life, by W. West; Golden egg, by T. Sturgeon; Dead end, by W. MacFarlane; Answer, by H. Clement; Sam Hall, by P. Anderson; Dumb waiter, by W. M. Miller, Jr.; Problem for Emmy, by R. S. Townes

Connell, Evan S.

Mr Bridge [by] Evan S. Connell, Jr. Knopf 1969 369p $5.95

This companion volume to the author's Mrs Bridge, is made up "of fragments of experience from the life of a middle-aged suburban couple between the world wars. Brief episodes are juxtaposed to reveal the stereotyped values and emotional and spiritual aridity of the prosperous, proper Bridges." Library J

It "is a sensitive novel, moving, funny, deeply nostalgic, at once ironic and compassionate as it searches among the parts of a man's life. And, despite being about a time thirty years ago, it tells a good deal about the way we live now." Book of the Month Club News

Mrs Bridge. Viking 1959 254p o.p. 1970

"A story about Mrs Bridge who is married to a Kansas City lawyer. A series of very short chapters depict in understated, realistic prose.

Connell, Evan S.—*Continued*

the everyday incidents of marriage: the gradual achievement of a workable adjustment,
visits with friends, the bringing-up of two
daughters and a son, and later the unsuccessful
attempts to alleviate the loneliness and boredom of middle age. The cumulative effect of
these episodic snapshots is a discerning full-
length portrait. For a feminine audience."
Booklist
"This must have been a difficult novel to
write, lacking height, depth and forward progress—as Mrs. Bridge's life did—but Mr. Connell has been most successful in his dissection
of one life of quiet desperation which stands
for many such lives. Written in classic prose,
illuminated by wit and compassion." Library J

Connolly, Cyril
(ed.) Great English short novels. Dial
Press 1953 879p $7.50
Partially analyzed in Short Story Index
This collection "presents the entire range
of the English short novel from the eighteenth
century to the present with particular em-
phasis on earlier fiction." McClurg. Book News
Contents: The simplest forms: Life of Rich-
ard Savage, by S. Johnson; Castle Rackrent. by
M. Edgeworth; The room in the Dragon Volant,
by J. S. Le Fanu; The expanding psyche:
Cousin Phillis, by Mrs Gaskell; The lifted veil,
by G. Eliot; The secret sharer, by J. Conrad;
The farcical history of Richard Greenow, by
A. Huxley; The limits of the form: The case of
General Ople and Lady Camper, by G. Meredith; Nightmare Abbey, by T. L. Peacock;
Liber amoris, by W. Hazlitt; Between the acts,
by V. Woolf.

Conquest, Robert
(jt. ed.) Amis, K. ed. Spectrum [I]-V

Conrad, Barnaby
Matador; illus. by the author. Houghton
1952 213p o.p. 1970
"Pacote, a famous matador, is goaded into
making one more appearance, altho he has announced his retirement. For some time he has
been bolstering his courage with alcohol, and
the early part of his last fight shows it. Then a
newcomer enters the ring to show up the master and, stung into action, Pacote makes a marvelous comeback. The scene is Seville." Book
Rev Digest
"The emphasis here is on fear. The novel has
a pulsing drive and I feel communicates the
raw drama and the brutal beauty of the bullfight to a greater extent than The Brave Bulls
[by Tom Lea] though the writing is not as distinguished. It builds up a crescendo of excitement to a peak which is almost unbearable.
Highly recommended for all fiction collections."
Library J

Conrad, Joseph
Almayer's folly. Macmillan (N Y) 1895
276p o.p. 1970
"The history of a European married to a
Malayan wife, who reverts to her ancestral savagery. He lives a miserable life among the
fierce Malays and Dyaks of Borneo, and the
tragedy culminates when his beloved daughter
forsakes him to marry a savage. The awful effect on the mental and moral nature of the
solitude and the contact with savagery is
brought out with intense imaginative skill."
Baker's Best

> *also in* Conrad, J. Tales of the East and
> West p 1-128

The arrow of gold. Doubleday 1919 385p
o.p. 1970
"A curious, absorbing tale, set in the seventies and concerned with the love of an English sea captain carrying Carlist munitions
along the Spanish coast, and the beautiful
sphinx-like Dona Rita who is financing the
project. Romantic possibilities of intrigues,
gun-running adventures and the sinister pic-
turesqueness of nature are all slighted in favor
of the beautiful but love idyll." Cleveland
"A love story that is one of the big love
stories of the world of books." F. T. Cooper

Chance; a tale in two parts. Doubleday 1913
468p o.p. 1970
"Romance of simple plot and excellent workmanship, but involved in effect, because told
in the first person by several characters. Shows
the dealings of chance in the life of the
daughter of a convicted swindler, who, taught
to believe that no one can love her, is saved
from suicide by a chivalrous sea captain."
N.Y. State Lib

The duel
> *In* Conrad, J. Tales of land and sea p441-
> 504
> *In* Costain, T. B. comp. Twelve short
> novels p171-234

The end of the tether
> *In* Conrad, J. Tales of land and sea p505-
> 610
> *In* Conrad, J. Youth, and two other
> stories

Great short works of Joseph Conrad. Har-
per 1966 378p o.p. 1970
"A Harper Perennial classic"
Analyzed in Short Story Index
Contents: The lagoon [short story]; The
Nigger of the Narcissus (1914); Youth (1903);
Heart of darkness (1899); Typhoon (1902); The
secret sharer [short story]

Heart of darkness
> *In* Conrad, J. Great short works of
> Joseph Conrad p175-256
> *In* Conrad, J. The portable Conrad p490-
> 603
> *In* Conrad, J. Stories and tales of Joseph
> Conrad
> *In* Conrad, J. Tales of land and sea p33-
> 104
> *In* Conrad, J. Typhoon, and other tales
> of the sea p273-371
> *In* Conrad, J. Youth, and two other
> stories

y Lord Jim
Some editions are:
Dodd (Great illustrated classics) $4.50. With
pictures of the author and his environment
and illustrations of the setting of the book
together with an introduction by Edward Ells-
berg
Doubleday $4.95
Modern Lib. $2.95
Watts, F. $8.85 Large type edition. A Keith
Jennison book
First published 1899

"A merciless analysis of a man who, branded
as a coward among his fellows, found himself
ultimately a demi-god among the Malay savages. Much of the incident of the Orient is
drawn from scenes in the life of Rajah Brooke
of Sarawak." Pratt Alcove

y The Nigger of the Narcissus
Some editions are:
Doubleday $3.95
Heritage $6.95. With an introduction by How-
ard Mumford Jones and illustrated by Mil-
lard Sheets
First published 1897 with title: Children of
the sea

"An account of a voyage home from India
in an old-fashioned sailing ship. A wonderfully
realistic description of rough seafaring life, by
one who has been a seaman, and has moreover a poetic imagination. The description of
a storm rivals the finest performances of Loti.
The unfortunate negro and the rest of the
ship's crew are striking characters portrayed

Conrad, Joseph—*Continued*

with a deep sense of humanity and not without strokes of saturnine comedy." Baker's Best

also in Conrad, J. Great short works of Joseph Conrad p21-140

also in Conrad, J. The portable Conrad p292-453

also in Conrad, J. Tales of land and sea p106-210

also in Conrad, J. Typhoon, and other tales of the sea p91-236

y Nostromo; a tale of the seaboard. With an introduction by Rupert Croft-Cooke, and illus. by Lima de Freitas. Heritage 1961 xxiii, 376p illus $6.95

First published 1904
"Episodes of adventure and daring exploit in the revolutionary broils of the American republic of Costaguana, loosely connected into a long story, in which the man of action, Nostromo, a rich Englishman and his admirable wife, an old Garibaldian, brigand, politicians, adventurers, and others make a motley crowd of personages. The narrative is straightforward, for Conrad, and not made up of impressions gathered from different quarters." Baker's Best

The portable Conrad. Ed. and with an introduction and notes by Morton Dauwen Zabel. Viking [1968 c1947] 762p (Viking Portable lib) $6.50

This collection first published 1947 and partially analyzed in Short Story Index
Contains two novels: The Nigger of the 'Narcissus,' and Typhoon: three long stories; six shorter stories; and a selection from Conrad's prefaces, letters and autobiographical writings." Book Rev Digest
Short stories included are: Prince Roman; Warrior's soul; Youth; Amy Foster; Outpost of progress; Heart of darkness; Il Conde; The lagoon; The secret sharer

The rescue; a romance of the shallows. Doubleday 1920 404p o.p. 1970

An island in the Malay archipelago is the hiding place of an alliance of island chiefs and an English sea captain dedicated to the restoration of a young prince as ruler of his people. When their yacht founders on the island's shore, a party of Europeans becomes a threat to the alliance's plans. In a chain of events full of suspense and adventure this strangely assorted group of people, each distrusting the other, gradually drive one another to the edge of disaster

The rover. Doubleday 1923 286p o.p. 1970

"The scenes are laid in the Mediterranean during the period of the Napoleonic wars. Peyrol, the rover, has left the lawless sea to end his days in peace in the quiet village of his birth. But even that obscure section of the French coast has felt the pressure of Napoleon's naval wars with England. Swiftly but reluctantly, Peyrol is involved in a romance and a secret operation which rises to the great adventure of his life, eclipsing in dramatic force all the anxious contents of his roving career." Publisher's note

Secret agent
In Conrad, J. Tales of the East and West p353-544

Stories and tales of Joseph Conrad. Funk 1968 437p pa $2.50

Analyzed in Short Story Index
This volume includes three short works: Youth (1903); Heart of darkness (1899); Typhoon (1902) and five short stories: The duel; The brute: an indignant tale; An outpost of progress; Karain; a memory; Falk: a reminiscence

Tales of land and sea; introduction by William McFee; illus. by Richard M. Powers. Hanover House 1953 695p $4.95

Analyzed in Short Story Index
Contents: Youth; Heart of darkness; The Nigger of the Narcissus; Il Conde; Gaspar Ruiz; The brute; Typhoon; The secret sharer; Freya of the Seven Isles; The duel; The end of the tether; The shadow-line

Tales of the East and West; ed. and with an introduction by Morton Dauwen Zabel. Hanover House 1958 xxx, 544p o.p. 1970

Analyzed in Short Story Index
Companion volume to: Tales of land and sea, listed above
"It contains short stories, novelettes and short novels, with settings varying from the South Seas to central Europe." Huntting
Contents: Almayer's folly; Karain; a memory; The planter of Malata; An outpost of progress; Falk; Prince Roman; The warrior's soul; Amy Foster; The secret agent

Typhoon
In Conrad, J. Great short works of Joseph Conrad p259-328

In Conrad, J. The portable Conrad p192-287

In Conrad, J. Stories and tales of Joseph Conrad

In Conrad, J. Tales of land and sea p287-347

y Typhoon, and other tales of the sea. . . . Dodd 1963 371p illus (Great illustrated classics) $4.50

Analyzed in Short Story Index
"With photographs of the author and his environment as well as illustrations from early editions, together with an introduction by Edouard A. Stackpole." Subtitle
Contents: Typhoon; The Nigger of the Narcissus; Youth, a narrative; Heart of darkness

Under Western eyes; a novel. Harper 1911 377p o.p. 1970

"A somber but powerful psychological study dealing with a pathology of crime, fear, distrust and treachery, as exemplified by a circle of Russian political refugees and plotters. The central figure is Razumov, young student of philosophy, who, involved against his will in a revolutionist murder, first becomes an informer and police agent, and then confesses to the revolutionist in an effort to clear his conscience." Lenrow. Reader's Guide to Prose Fiction

Victory. Modern Lib. 385p $2.95

First published 1915 by Doubleday
" 'Enchanted Heyst,' a detached, introspective Swedish nobleman, lives alone on an island in the South seas. Pity obliges him to rescue a girl from a travelling 'ladies orchestra' and to take her to his retreat upon which exciting and tragic happenings follow. There is more of action than in most of his books." N Y State Lib

Youth
In Conrad, J. Great short works of Joseph Conrad p21-140

In Conrad, J. Stories and tales of Joseph Conrad

In Conrad, J. Tales of land and sea p7-32

In Conrad, J. Typhoon, and other tales of the sea p237-72

Youth, and two other stories. McClure 1903 381p o.p. 1970

Analyzed in Short Story Index
Contents: Youth, a narrative; Heart of darkness; The end of the tether

Cooke, David C.

(ed.) Best detective stories of the year, 1946-1959. See Best detective stories of the year, 1946-1959

(ed.) Best of the Best detective stories. See Best of the Best detective stories

Cooper, Brian

Monsoon murder. Vanguard [1968 c1967] 266p $5.95

First published 1967 in England under title: A mission for Betty Smith

"In post-war India an Armenian had been murdered and John Harrington, of the Ranital police, had to find a Eurasian girl seen visiting the dead man. So he followed Betty Smith's trail through love, sorrow, and pain to a final peace." Bk Buyer's Guide

"The reader is drawn along into a series of adventurous tales involving Calcutta brothels, a Catholic orphanage and an Anglican clergyman, with the vast countryside of India as backdrop. The detail is authentic and the story never lags." Pub W

Cooper, James Fenimore

y The Deerslayer

Some editions are:
Dodd (Great illustrated classics) $4.50 Biographical sketch by Basil Davenport. Illustrations reproducing drawings for early editions and photographs of historical scenes
Scribner (The Scribner illustrated classics) $6 With pictures by N. C. Wyeth

First published 1841. First of the Leatherstocking tales

"A rousing tale of warfare between the Iroquois Indians and the white settlers about Lake Otsego before 1745. The chief characters are Hawkeye, Uncas, and the two sisters, Judith and Hetty, who defy the Indians in an attempt to rescue Hawkeye." Toronto
Followed by: The last of the Mohicans

The Deerslayer [abridged]
In Cooper, J. F. The Leatherstocking saga p39-274

y The last of the Mohicans

Some editions are:
Collins $1.95
Dodd (Great illustrated classics) $4.50 Introduction and captions by Basil Davenport with illustrations from contemporary artists
Dutton (Everyman's lib) $3.25
Scribner (The Scribner Illustrated classics) $5 Illustrated by N. C. Wyeth
Watts, F. $7.95 Large type edition, complete and unabridged. A Keith Jennison book

Sequel to: The Deerslayer
First published 1826

A swiftly moving story of pursuit and capture in the wilderness around Lake George during the French and Indian Wars, the second in the series of Leatherstocking tales and one of the most popular
Followed by: The Pathfinder

The last of the Mohicans [abridged]
In Cooper, J. F. The Leatherstocking saga p275-462

y The Leatherstocking saga. . . . Ed. by Allan Nevins; illus. by Reginald Marsh. Pantheon Bks. 1954 833p illus maps $6.99

"Being those parts of The Deerslayer, The last of the Mohicans, The Pathfinder, The pioneers, and The prairie which specially pertain to Natty Bumppo, otherwise known as Pathfinder, Deerslayer, or Hawkeye; the whole arranged in chronological order from Hawkeye's youth on the New York frontier in King George's War until his death on the western prairies in Jefferson's administration." Subtitle

"Not a condensation or simplification in the usual use of those terms, but rather a narrative reorganization of five of Cooper's novels into one complete chronicle of the hero, with digressive sections removed." Booklist

The Pathfinder

Some editions are:
Dodd (Great illustrated classics) $4.50 With illustrations of the author and his environment and reproductions of drawings for early editions of the book together with an introduction and descriptive captions by Allen Klots, Jr.
Dutton (Everyman's lib) $3.25

Sequel to: The last of the Mohicans
The third of the Leatherstocking tales, published 1840

Considered the best of Cooper's novels from a literary point of view. The scene is laid in the vicinity of Lake Ontario during the French and Indian War
Followed by: The pioneers

The Pathfinder [abridged]
In Cooper, J. F. The Leatherstocking saga p463-613

y The pilot; with illustrations of contemporary scenes and a foreword by Basil Davenport. Dodd 1947 339p illus (Great illustrated classics) $4.50

First published 1824
"[John] Paul Jones's adventures suggested the plot; which is, in brief, an attempt during the Revolutionary War to abduct some prominent Englishmen for exchange against American prisoners." Keller's Reader's Digest of Books

y The pioneers. . . . Dodd 1958 477p illus (Great illustrated classics) $4.50

Sequel to: The Pathfinder
First published 1822
"With illustrations of the author and his environment and reproductions of pictures for early editions of the book, together with a foreword and descriptive captions by Allen Klots, Jr." Subtitle
"Story of pioneer life on the banks of Lake Otsego. Fourth in the series of 'Leatherstocking tales.'" Pittsburgh
Followed by The prairie

The pioneers [abridged]
In Cooper, J. F. The Leatherstocking saga p615-762

y The prairie; introduction by Basil Davenport. Dodd 1954 453p (Great illustrated classics) $4.50

The last of the Leatherstocking tales, published 1827, being a sequel to: The pioneers
"It relates the story of the last days of Leatherstocking, now an exile whom civilization has driven westward to the great prairies beyond the Mississippi. Here the old scout becomes a trapper, and here as everywhere, there are captives for him to rescue and numerous adventures for him to undertake. Finally, the old trapper dies in the arms of friends. Much of the action is taken up with the concerns of the rough, crude squatter Ishmael Buch and his family." Benét. The Reader's Encyclopedia

The prairie [abridged]
In Cooper, J. F. The Leatherstocking saga p763-829

The Red Rover; ed. with an introduction by Warren S. Walker. Univ. of Neb. Press [distributed by Smith, P.] 1963 xx, 532p illus $3.85

First published 1827
"A tale of adventure on the deep, with racy characterization and lively episodes, the hero a former pirate who fights for his country in the War of Independence." Baker's Best

y The spy

Some editions are:
Dial Press (A Heritage Press bk) $6.95
Dodd (Great illustrated classics) $4.50 With illustrations of contemporary scenes and a foreword by Curtis Dahl

Written in 1821-1822
A story of the American Revolution. The hero, the spy, is a cool, shrewd, fearless man, who is employed by General Washington in service which involves great personal danger and little glory

Cooper, James F.—*Continued*

Covers "the locality 'between the royal barracks in New York City and the American outposts on the Hudson' where a mixed population of loyalists and British sympathisers mistrusted one another. Not many historic figures or events are introduced . . . but the tale well illustrates the later Revolution period, and is full of allusions to such men as Burgoyne, Gates, Tarleton, Sumter, etc." Nield

Cooper, Page

(ed.) Famous dog stories; illus. by Diana Thorne. Doubleday 1948 336p illus o.p. 1970

Partially analyzed in Short Story Index

"The heroes of these tales and sketches include mongrels as well as the finest-bred show dogs . . . and the backgrounds range from America to Scotland, from Moscow to the Pearly Gates. There are twenty-five pieces in all." Huntting

The stories included are: Mumú, by I. Turgeniev; Moses, by W. D. Edmonds; Rex, by D. H. Lawrence; To him who waits, by R. G. Kirk; Short and merry, by M. de la Roche; Hooded man, by V. Woolf: B from Bull's foot, by C. Gordon; The professionals, by C. Aldin; Gettin rid of Fluff, by E. P. Butler; Memories, by J. Galsworthy; Minda, by K. Capek; Jupiter, by S. Zweig; Hot dog, by S. E. White; Seegar and Cigareet, by J. Hines; Bump, by R. S. Spears; Man and dog, by L. Housman; Canny canines, by E. Roarck; Kentucky code, by N. B. Williams; Eight-dollar pup, by P. Curtiss; Dog named Joe, by N. Paige; Tailless tyke at bay, by A. Ollivant

(ed.) Great horse stories; drawings by Paul Brown. Doubleday 1946 366p illus o.p. 1970

Partially analyzed in Short Story Index

"Twenty-one stories and four poems. Some of the stories are true, such as Phil Stong's account of the Morgan horse, and in each the horse is definitely the leading character. All of the pieces are by modern writers, English, Irish, American, and European." Booklist

Includes the following stories: Breakneck hill, by E. Forbes; The begats, by P. Stong; Grand filly, by E. OE. Somerville; Seeing eye, by W. James; Ghost horse, by Chief Buffalo Child Long Lance; Maltese cat, by R. Kipling; Ride of his life, by D. Gray; Red terror, by M. O. Knott; Florian, by F. Salten; Cristano, by W. H. Hudson; Highboy rings down the curtain, by G. A. Chamberlain; Black kettle, by F. M. Lockard; Tzagan, by C. Wood; Horse of Hurricane Reef, by C. T. Jackson; Royal cream horses and ponies, by Sir H. G. Tyrwhitt-Drake; Dark child; by E. N. Robinson; Cinderella and warrior, by Lord Mottistone; Look of eagles, by J. T. Foote; Skipper, by S. Ford; It happened at Aintree, by P. Brown; Strider, by L. Tolstoi

Coppard, A. E.

The collected tales of A. E. Coppard. Knopf 1948 532p o.p. 1970

Analyzed in Short Story Index

Contents: The higgler; Cherry tree; Poor man; Ballet girl; Arabesque—the mouse; Alas, poor Bollington; Dusky Ruth; Old Venerable; Adam and Eve and Pinch Me; The presser; Green drake; Abel Staple disapproves; Purl and plain Broadsheet ballad; Silver circus; Luxury; The fair young willowy tree; My hundredth tale; Ring the bells of heaven; Nixey's harlequin; Judith; Father Raven; Man from Kilsheelan; Olive and Camilla; Clorinda walks in heaven; Doe; Fine feathers; Christine's letter; Ahoy, sailor boy; Ninepenny flute; Little boy lost; Little mistress; Fishmonger's fiddle; Hurly burly; Field of mustard; Third prize; Watercress girl; Fifty pounds

A collection of 38 of the author's tales written in the 1920's and 1930's. "His strength lies mainly in tender fantasy, an oblique kind of light fingered satire, and an ingratiating (not saccharine) whimsy. Several of these tales, however, handle near-tragic themes with considerable effect. . . . He is a true artist, as sound and delicate as the ring of good glass." Book of the Month Club News

Cordell, Alexander

The rape of the fair country. Doubleday 1959 335p o.p. 1970

This is a "family chronicle set in the Wales of the 1830's. The ironmasters own the land and virtually own the people. . . . The novel begins in 1826 when the narrator, at the age of eight, goes to work in the furnaces; and ends thirteen years later when, a Chartist, he takes part in John Frost's pathetic march on Newport." New Statesman

"The terrible conditions at the iron furnaces are grimly described: child labor, frequent fatal or mutilating accidents and abject poverty of the debt-ridden families of the mining areas. . . . But Cordell writes in the haunting minor key of Welsh idiom. With marvellous wizardry he brings to life the people." Library J

Followed by: Robe of honour

Robe of honour. Doubleday 1960 384p o.p. 1970

Continues the story begun in: The rape of the fair country

Published in England with title: The hosts of Rebecca

Set in 19th century Wales during the period of the Rebecca Riots, this is the story of young Jethro Mortymer, his mother, his sister, and his sister-in-law, Mari, the widow of his exiled older brother. The story of Jethro's growing from boyhood to manhood and of the love between him and Mari is told against the background of the poverty and violence of the times and the unrest of the miners and the farmers which brought about the Rebecca Riots. (Publisher)

"The book is rich in the sights and sounds of the countryside and in Cordell's curious, fascinating, inverted style." Chicago Sunday Tribune

Corley, Edwin

Siege; a novel. Stein & Day 1969 384p $6.95

This novel "depicts, step-by-step, the progress of a black militant plot to train an undercover army and seize control of Manhattan one Labor Day weekend and hold the island, its inhabitants, its wealth, as hostages until the United States agrees to yield the state of New Jersey to become a separate black nation. Some mighty evil and villainous blacks are behind it all, and they trick a black Marine Corps general into being their military leader." Pub W

"This is a very well constructed first novel, far more convincing than most in its genre—resulting largely from excellent characterization; it is also a bit of a 'roman à clef' of actual black activists and political figures." Library J

Corrington, John William

The lonesome traveler, and other stories. Putnam 1968 286p $5.95

Analyzed in Short Story Index

Nine "stories centering on the South and the effects of the Civil War, from 1864 to the present." Chicago

Contents: If time were not a moving thing, New Orleans: 1868-1968; First blood, Atlanta: 1864; Reunion, Gettysburg: 1913; A time to embrace, Shreveport: 1929; The retrievers, Shreveport: 1933; The lonesome traveler, Mississippi: 1935; The dark corner, Shreveport: 1946; The arrangement, Shreveport: 1958; The night school, New Orleans: 1965

Cortázar, Julio

Cronopios and famas; tr. from the Spanish by Paul Blackburn. Pantheon Bks. 1969 161p $4.95

Originally published 1962 in Argentina

Interspersed throughout this collection of fictional prose pieces "are surrealistic juxtapositions and allegorical fantasies. . . . Warm, life-loving 'cronopios' and practical, conventional 'famas' are imaginary but typical personages between whom communication is usually impossible and always ridiculous." Library J

The author "has a rare gift for isolating the absurd in everyday life, for depicting the foibles in human behavior with an unerring thrust that is satiric yet compassionate. . . . Each page sparkles with vivid satire that goes to the heart of human character and, in his best pieces, to the essence of the human condition." Sat R

Cortázar, Julio—*Continued*

End of the game, and other stories; tr. from the Spanish by Paul Blackburn. Pantheon Bks. 1967 277p boards $4.95

Analyzed in Short Story Index
"The stories in the current volume have been selected from three separate Spanish collections." Publisher's note
Contents: Axolotl; House taken over; The distances; The idol of the Cyclades; Letter to a young lady in Paris; A yellow flower; Continuity of parks; The night face up; Bestiary; The gates of heaven; Blow-up; End of the game; At your service; The pursuer; Secret weapons
"Almost all of [the stories] occur in one form or another in a world of dreams, fantasy and hallucination. While several of the stories are little more than literary fragments, there is an eerie, hypnotic fascination to some of them." Pub W

Hopscotch. Tr. from the Spanish by Gregory Rabassa. Pantheon Bks. 1966 564p $6.95

Originally published 1963 in Argentina
"Opening in Paris, with a love affair, the novel moves gradually to Buenos Aires, where Oliveira is employed first as a salesman, then as the keeper of a calculating circus cat which can truly count, and finally as an attendant in a mental asylum owned by his friends. [Here is] one man's exasperated search for what life is really about." McClurg. Book News
"Two-thirds of the way through this odd, experimental novel, the story breaks off. There follows a sequence of 'expendable chapters' to be interpolated in a rereading of the story in a skipping-back-and-forth which the author likens to a child's game of hopscotch. The book is a composition of odd dialog, odder-still psychology, a touch of bawdiness, mocking humor, and shifting patterns of human relationships. . . . The Parisian scenes are high-spirited, fey, and rather wonderful in their exotic mixture of low-life, nonsense, literary allusions, love and tragedy." Pub W

Cost. March

I, Rachel; a biographical novel. Vanguard 1957 477p $4.95

A "romantic novel based on the life of the glamorous mid-nineteenth century French actress, [Elisa Felix known as] Rachel. The author handles Rachel's many love affairs, including one with Louis Napoleon, with great delicacy. . . . The picture of Paris in the 1830's and 1840's is very interesting." Pub W
"The author's imagination has been fed and verified abundantly by excerpts from newspapers, diaries, letters. Some of these she quotes verbatim, fitting them smoothly into a narrative that is sumptuous in detail." N Y Her Trib Books

Jubilee of a ghost. Vanguard [1969 c1968] 183p $4.95

The story "relates the efforts of Dinah Hogarth to vindicate her childhood idol, the ballerina La Ferdel, when a biography attacking La Ferdel's character is published. Dinah's search for the truth involves mystery, suspense, and romance. This is straight narrative with an English setting and eccentric characters; its lucid and polished style adds greatly to its reading pleasure." Library J

Costain, Thomas B.

Below the salt; a novel. Doubleday 1957 480p $5.95

"Convinced that citizens of the modern free world take their hard-won liberties too much for granted, an elderly U.S. senator reveals a closely guarded secret: he believes he is the reincarnation of a Sapon freedman who was present when the Magna Charta was signed. In the role of Tostig he tells how he accompanied his onetime master throughout England and the continent, assisted in the rescue of the Lost Princess, Eleanor of Brittany, and found asylum in Ireland." Booklist
"In spite of an artificial modern frame this story of the events leading up to Magna Carta finally turns into first rate historical romance." Ontario Lib Rev

y The black rose. Doubleday 1945 403p $5.95

This novel laid in the 13th century, is the story of a young English nobleman who fights his way to the heart of the Mongol empire and returns to find that he must choose between an English heiress and a girl of the East
"Its background of history is richly furnished with information and local color. . . . [It is] a story that, in spite of the attention given to the romance, derives its major interest from the remarkable tapestry of history against which it is enacted." Christian Science Monitor

The darkness and the dawn; a novel. Doubleday 1959 478p $5.95

An historical novel of the 5th century Europe when Attila the Hun, determined to conquer the world, set forth to capture Rome. Chief protagonists in the story are: Attila, the Scourge of God; Aetius, the dictator of Rome; Honoria, the love-minded imperial princess; Leo, the courageous pope; and, Nicolan the hero of the story. (Publisher)
"The color and liveliness that characterize the works of this author are [here] present in abundance." Christian Science Monitor

For my great folly; a novel. Putnam 1942 504p o.p. 1970

"John Ward, the hero of this swashbuckling tale of the 17th century, was a man born out of his time. For the great days of the Elizabethan sea dogs is over and, with James I on the throne, freebooting is banned. So it is against the will of his sovereign that Ward (who was a real historic personage) continues his piratical career. The story is told by young Roger Blaise, who deserts his books to join Ward's enterprise, only to learn that a life on the high seas is not all glamour." Wis Lib Bul

High Towers. Doubleday 1949 403p $5.95

An historical romance chronicling the adventures of the fabulous Le Moyne family of Montreal who became the heroes of French Canada and founded the storied city of New Orleans. Time: early 18th century
"Contains plenty of color; action is played against an absorbing historical background. Characters are dashing but convincing and book can be recommended to the readers of popularly written historical fiction." Library J

The last love. Doubleday 1963 434p music $5.95

"In three parts: 'A guest in the house,' 'Betsy grows up,' and 'The twilight falls' telling of Napoleon's stay with the Balcombes on the island of St. Helena while his living quarters were being prepared and of fifteen-year-old Betsy's romantic admiration." Bk Buyer's Guide
"Costain's skill at giving intimate insights into a great historical character has never been better shown." Christian Science Monitor

y The moneyman. Doubleday 1947 434p $6.50

"France in the middle ages forms the elaborate tapestry against which this story is enacted. In Jacques Coeur, the central character, Mr. Costain presents a business tycoon with ideas on finance far in advance of his time. The beautiful Agnes Sorel, mistress of Charles VII, moves as a shadowy figure through the scene but her young counterpart, Valerie, is very much in the foreground and a lively and loveable heroine she is. The passages descriptive of women's clothes in this lush period are breathtaking highlights in a very readable historical romance." Ontario Lib Rev
"Historical background is authentic, characters perform as real men and women, fascinating details are unobtrusively introduced, and plot interweaving is skilfully contrived. The siege of Rouen, where cannon were effectively employed as a prelude to chivalry's doom at Ravenna nearly a century later, is superbly described." N Y Her Trib Books

(ed.) More Stories to remember; selected by Thomas B. Costain and John Beecroft; illus. by Frederick E. Banbery. Doubleday 1958 2v illus o.p. 1970

Analyzed in Short Story Index
Companion volume to: Stories to remember
Contains the following short novels in entirety: Lost horizon, by J. Hilton; The call of

Costain, Thomas B.—*Continued*

the wild, by J. London; The lady, by C. Richter; Good morning, Miss Dove, by F. Patton; The Croxley master, by Sir A. C. Doyle; The murder of Roger Ackroyd, by A. Christie

Short stories and excerpts from novels included are: v 1 Neighbor Rosicky, by W. Cather; The verger, by W. S. Maugham; Jack Still, by J. Marquand; The silver mask, by H. Walpole; The return of the rangers, by K. Roberts; Old man at the bridge, by E. Hemingway; The Cyprian cat, by D. Sayers; The jukebox and the Kallikaks, by B. Chute; The strange ride of Morrowbie Jukes, by R. Kipling; She went by gently, by P. Carroll; Tale of my aunt Jenepher's wooing, by D. Byrne; Through the veil, by A. C. Doyle; The three strangers, by T. Hardy; The old man, by H. Horn; The rollicking god, by N. Johnson; Was it a dream, by G. de Maupassant

v2 Turn about, by W. Faulkner; Mary Smith, by B. Tarkington; Clerical error, by J. Cozzens; The suicide club, by R. Stevenson; Eighteen oak ties, by T. Pridgen; Ultima Thule, by J. Galsworthy; Anty Bligh, by J. Masefield; Sam Weller makes his bow, by C. Dickens; François Villon meets a woman, by J. Erskine; Father and the cook, by C. Day; The grave grass quivers, by M. Kantor; The king waits, by C. Dane; Babylon revisited, by F. S. Fitzgerald; The bowmen, by A. Machen

y The silver chalice; a novel; illus. by Burt Silverman. Doubleday [1964 c1952] 533p illus $5.95

A reissue of the title first published 1952. The illustrations are new with this edition

"The silver chalice was a frame meant to hold the sacred cup from which Christ drank at the Last Supper. This novel, based on legends of the years following Christ's crucifixion, describes the life of Basil, the artisan, who fashioned the silver chalice. The scenes are laid in Antioch, Rome and Jerusalem." Book Rev Digest

Costain paints a tremendous canvas filled with warm color and life. . . . As those know who have read his many vigorous re-creations of the past, Costain has a magnificent talent for breaking life into history. . . . But over and above this the novel does something else. It will make real for thousands, perhaps for the first time, the whole world of the New Testament." Chicago Sunday Tribune

(ed.) Stories to remember; selected by Thomas B. Costain and John Beecroft; illus. by Martha Sawyers and William Reusswig. Doubleday 1956 2v illus o.p. 1970

Analyzed in Short Story Index

Contains the following short novels in entirety: The general's ring, by S. Lagerlöf; Portrait of Jennie, by R. Nathan; Voice of Bugle Ann, by M. Kantor; Bridge of San Luis Rey, by T. Wilder; Sea of grass, by C. Richter; "National Velvet," by E. Bagnold

Short stories and excerpts from novels included are: v 1 Mowgli's brothers, by R. Kipling; Gift of the Magi, by O. Henry; Lord Mountdrago, by W. S. Maugham; Music on the Muscatatuck, by J. West; Pacing goose, by J. West; The birds, by D. du Maurier; Man who lived four thousand years, by A. Dumas; Pope's mule, by A. Daudet; Story of the late Mr Elvesham, by H. G. Wells; Blue cross, by G. K. Chesterton; La Grande Bretéche, by H. de Balzac; Love's conundrum, by A. Hope; Great Stone Face, by N. Hawthorne; Germelshausen, by F. Gerstäcker; I am born, by C. Dickens; Legend of Sleepy Hollow, by W. Irving; Age of miracles, by M. D. Post; Long rifle, by S. E. White; Fall of the house of Usher, by E. A. Poe

v2 Basquerie, by E. M. Kelly; Judith, by A. E. Coppard; Mother in Mannville, by M. K. Rawlings; Kerfol, by E. Wharton; Last leaf, by O. Henry; The bloodhound, by A. Train; What the old man does is always right, by H. C. Andersen; Sire de Malétroit's door, by R. L. Stevenson; The necklace, by G. de Maupassant; By the waters of Babylon, by S. V. Benét; A. V. Laider, by M. Beerbohm; Pillar of fire, by P. Wilde; Strange will, by E. About; Hand at the window, by E. Brontë

The tontine; a novel; illus. by Herbert Ryman. Doubleday 1955 2v illus o.p. 1970

"Chronicles the lives of three generations of two English families living in early nineteenth century England. The novel begins at the time of the Napoleonic wars and the action is based on the results of buying into a kind of insurance lottery called the Great Waterloo Tontine. The last book is almost a mystery thriller when the Tontine becomes the subject of nationwide gambling." Book Rev Digest

"A richly loaded, very readable, honorably managed big novel. It is not a work of high stylistic distinction, nor one of the most profound insight. Yet it has the virtue of good craftsmanship, and the power to project living characters moving in time and making, individually and collectively, their stretch of history." N Y Times Bk R

(comp.) Twelve short novels. Doubleday 1961 798p o.p. 1970

Analyzed in Short Story Index

"The compiler introduces each novel with a note on its author, the place of the work in its author's career, or its influence on other writers." Booklist

Contents: Young Joseph, by T. Mann (1935); The bridge of San Luis Rey, by T. Wilder (1927); The duel, by J. Conrad (1908); The old maid, by E. Wharton (1924); Father Sergius, by L. Tolstoy (1912); The turn of the screw, by H. James (1898); Good-bye, Mr Chips, by J. Hilton (1934); Prisoner of the sand [excerpt from Wind, sand stars] by A. de Saint Exupéry; Portrait of Jennie, by R. Nathan (1939); The lost sea, by J. de Hartog (1951); Father of the bride, by E. Streeter (1949); The short reign of Pippin IV, by J. Steinbeck (1957)

Couch, Arthur Quiller- See Quiller-Couch, Arthur

Courlander, Harold

The African; a novel. Crown 1967 311p $5.95

In 1802 Hwesuhunu, a young African in Dahomey, is captured and sold into slavery in Georgia. This novel follows his experiences in the New World until he plans to run away to Ohio, still in search of his fate

"Courlander, an expert on African history and folklore, emphasizes the influence of their cultural heritage on American Negroes and in a suspenseful, moving story without excessive emotion or sentimentality, depicts the effect on both Negroes and whites." Booklist

Cournos, Helen Sybil Norton. See Norton, Sybil

Cournos, John

(ed.) American short stories of the nineteenth century. See American short stories of the nineteenth century

(ed.) Best world short stories: 1947; ed. by John Cournos and Sybil Norton. Appleton 1947 258p o.p. 1970

Analyzed in Short Story Index

Contents: The mother, by C. Alegría; The cat, by G. N. Biggs; Benefit concert, by R. Davies; Flying highwayman, by L. de la Torre; The actress, by I. Ehrenburg; Golden stallion, by E. Hardwick; The miracle, by C. Hughes; The musicians, by G. Kersh; I had to go sick, by I. Maclaren-Ross; Cynthia, by E. Mallea; Lion's den, by V. S. Pritchett; Jazz player, by M. Roelants; Age of reason, by I. Shaw; Portrait of a traitor by Lao She; Innocent bystander, by M. Shedd; Sometimes you break even, by V. Ullman; There'll come a day, by J. West; As the fur flies, by T. S. Winslow; Purge by fire, by Yang Shuo

(jt. ed.) Haydn, H. ed. A world of great stories

Coward, Noel

Bon voyage. Doubleday 1968 [c1967] 212p $4.95

Analyzed in Short Story Index

First published 1967 in England with title: Bon voyage, and other stories

"Four witty and perceptive short stories, set in the glittering world of fashionable society, that probe the ambiguities of lust and death, of longing and despair." Publisher's note

Contents: Solali; Mrs Ebony; Penny dreadful; Bon voyage

Coward, Noel—*Continued*

Pomp and circumstance. Doubleday 1960 308p o.p. 1970

A "hilarious novel with an inconsequential story of the frantic life on an island paradise where the populace is getting ready for a visit from Queen Elizabeth and Prince Philip." Pub W

"The story is absurd and noisy, and so complicated that it is occasionally difficult to tell whether the plot is evolving or revolving. The people are also absurd; but likable and amusing and pleasantly self-possessed." New Yorker

Cowley, Joy

Nest in a falling tree. Doubleday 1967 336p o.p. 1970

Set in New Zealand. "For the last twenty years Maura Prince, the narrator, has spent herself on the care of her mother, who has a bad heart and who has within the last year become blind. . . . Into this static, dreary world comes eighteen-year-old Red (whom Mrs. Prince insists on calling Percy) to tend the garden in exchange for room and board. . . . Maura finds release for her emotions in an affair with Red that is partly sexual, partly maternal. . . . Inevitably Mrs. Prince's return from the hospital precipitates a crisis." Sat R

The "affair is convincing and unsentimental . . . . Mrs. Cowley knows what she is about; her style is clipped and unelaborate; the first-person narrative is engrossing. If anything, she should avoid occasional magazine slickness. Recommended for general reading shelves in larger and public libraries." Library J

Cox, Maxwell E.

The point of the game. Dodd 1969 283p $5.95

"The latter-day world of mergers and acquisitions comes startlingly to life as the key character Jake, a hatchetman for a large legal firm in Manhattan, goes through the trauma and the triumph of making a successful acuisition for one of his firm's clients." Library J

"This first novel by a New York lawyer presents a nadvocate at sea with himself and his profession. If the people seem predictable, maybe that's the way they might be in real life. Mr. Cox writes tersely and well about the law. His people are less successful." Pub W

Cox, William R.

(ed.) Western Writers of America. Rivers to cross

Coxe, George Harmon

The candid impostor. Knopf 1968 [c1967] 177p boards $4.50

"A New York newspaper man who agrees to impersonate a friend to collect a debt becomes implicated in smuggling and murder." Chicago

"A neatly tied plot that will please readers who follow the author's usual suave news photographer-detective." Pub W

Double identity. Knopf 1970 213p boards $4.95

"Plagued by deep personal problems Alan Carlisle flies to Surinam in South America to help operate a bush-pilot airline. On board the flight there is a man who looks very familiar —in fact, he is a dead ringer for Carlisle himself. This coincidental resemblance leads to an intricate and dangerous case of mistaken identity, in which a man who wants to change his will charts an implausible course in order to checkmate a killer." Publisher's note

An easy way to go. Knopf [1969 c1968] 213p boards $4.50

"When Lloyd Farnsworth saw his ex-wife with Kent Murdock at a night club, he punched Kent in the mouth and Kent floored him. The next night someone roughed up Kent and Lloyd called to taunt him. 'Come on up and finish it,' he jibed. Kent went—and walked right into a pretty frame for murder." Bk Buyer's Guide

"A deftly plotted thriller. The pace is slow but gathers momentum as the plot unravels. . . . In that at least one particular clue is highly significant, the author gives the reader a fighting chance to match wits with him in resolving the puzzle. Good reading!" Best Sellers

The fifth key
In Coxe, G. H. Triple exposure p321-466

The glass triangle
In Coxe, G. H. Triple exposure p3-161

The jade Venus
In Coxe, G. H. Triple exposure p165-318

Triple exposure; a George Harmon Coxe omnibus. Knopf 1959 466p $3.95

"Three mysteries starring Kent Murdock, the photographer: 'The Glass Triangle' (1939) 'The Jade Venus' (1945); 'The Fifth Key' (1947). Three of his best." The Bookseller

Cozzens, James Gould

Ask me tomorrow; or, The pleasant comedy of Young Fortunatus. Harcourt [1969 c1968] 342p $6.95

"Uniform edition"
First published 1940

Set in "the Italy, France, and Switzerland of the well-to-do American expatriate. . . . A bemused young New Englander, a writer unconvinced of his vocation who has published two books in which he has no pride [is] condemned as he fells, to maintain himself by tutoring the twelve-year-old son of a widowed friend of his mother's. This recital of his journeyings with his charge lays bare his mental and emotional instability as he becomes involved in a series of social situations. The plot is tenuous." Library J

By love possessed. Harcourt 1957 570p $5

This novel concerns "49 hours in the life of Arthur Winner, present-day New England lawyer. The stability of Arthur's private and professional worlds is suddenly shaken both by repercussions of unhappy and indiscreet episodes from his supposedly well-ordered past and by present events involving himself and those close to him. . . . Emerging from the period of crisis with a greater knowledge of himself and others Arthur realizes as never before that without compassion man is nothing." Booklist

"All of this has been plotted with such skill that the tantalizing question arises why this good novel never becomes the great novel it intermittently promises to be. One drawback is the style. Cozzens has always favored a glass-pane purity that does not intrude between reader and story. This time the glass is frosted with parenthetical clauses, humpbacked syntax, Jamesian involutions, Faulknerian meanderings. . . . None of these shortcomings will keep By Love Possessed from being . . . well worth reading. It is an education to know Arthur Winner, an education into which Novelist Cozzens has poured everything that 54 years of life have taught and made of him." Time

Castaway. Harcourt [1967 c1962] 115p $3.50

"Uniform edition"
First published 1934

"The imaginative part of the tale is a variation of the Robinson Crusoe theme; a catastrophe, unspecified, has overtaken New York and the sole survivor finds himself in a great store which, like himself, has escaped destruction. Here there is all that a human being would need, not only to support existence, but to afford him luxury and comfort. But there is the mental side of the picture and here the truly frightening realism of Mr. Cozzens develops as the . . . story proceeds." Sat R

Children and others. Harcourt 1964 343p $5.95

Analyzed in Short Story Index
Contents: King Midas has ass's ears; Child's play; Whose broad stripes and bright stars; The animals' fair; Total stranger; Something about a dollar; Someday you'll be sorry; We'll recall it with affection; The guns of the enemy; Candida, by B. Shaw; Men running; One hundred ladies; My love to Marcia; The way to go home; Every day's a holiday; Farewell to Cuba; Eyes to see

Cozzens, James G.—*Continued*

"A mixed bag of tales, these are textured studies rifled of fantasy, but featuring the deft skills of the craftsman, a self-conscious style and a sensible narrative. Mr Cozzens, an urbane and sophisticated writer, is a master of commonplace dimensions. Sometimes epigrammatic and often reminding one of a grammarian. Cozzens's writing is, nonetheless, well endowed with texture, timing and technique." Library J

Guard of honor. Harcourt 1948 631p $5.95

Pulitzer Prize, 1949
This story reviews "three days at an air base in Florida in 1943, where one small incident leads to another, with the complications of conflicting authority, personalities and racial animosities, until real trouble threatens, resolved finally by that loyalty to each other, even in spite of personal dislikes, that makes every officer a guard of the honor of the others." Wis Lib Bul
"As is his custom, Mr. Cozzens looks at his characters with warm understanding, with humor and with tolerance for their failings. Several passages of 'Guard of Honor' are exciting as a story and—again this is usual—the author's style is easy and flowing, with the underemphasis that makes for drama." N Y Times Bk R

The just and the unjust. Harcourt 1960 [c1942] 434p (Harbrace modern classics) $2.95

First published 1942
"The progress of a murder trial in a small eastern city is the background, and most of the substance, of this novel. Other minor cases as they fall to the lot of a district attorney's office intrude at times. The personal affairs of the lawyers and others involved enter somewhat into the plot, and there is a mild love story. There is no question of crime detection involved, for the case is clear from the beginning and such interest as the book has—and it will be very great for some readers—lies in watching the processes of a law court at work and in the reflections on the nature of law and justice." Wis Lib Bul
"In 'The Just and the Unjust' Mr. Cozzens has not only dealt with his most ambitious theme; he has handled it in such a manner as to leave no doubt of his stature as a major novelist. . . . Abner Coates's story carries a suspense and a significance that are bigger than all the communites in the country. Because that is so 'The Just and the Unjust' reaches major dimensions." N Y Times Bk R

Men and brethren. Harcourt 1958 [c1936] 282p $4

Also available in a Uniform edition for $5.95
"First published 1936
"Portrays a young, successful clergyman in charge of a New York parish. In the space of one summer weekend, he is involved in the lives of a score of people and is forced to decide—and act—upon a number of problems that have become urgent in the extreme. His solutions are often unorthodox, and the struggle between his beliefs and the conclusions he draws from his experiences of men and the world makes for a deep, persistent conflict." Publisher's note
"It's a perfect gem and should be a 'must' on the list of everyone interested in the church and in the modern novel at its best." Churchman

Morning, noon, and night. Harcourt 1968 408p $5.95

This novel "is a past-middle-aged man's review of his life. Henry Worthington, the extremely successful founder and director of a management consultant firm, drifts back through his life and times in an attempt to find out what it and he were all about. . . . In Henry's mind the stage is set and swept clean half a dozen times to reveal gradually his career—business, marital, and military. We see his New England entrenchment unfold with ivy covered walls and ivy covered people. The summer resorts, the childhood experiences, the war, the personal crises. We meet his family, his friends, his times." Best Sellers

"This novel is a tour de force of complex structure and challenging insights. . . . There is an overwhelming sense of the power of life to be found here and of the vast richness that even the quietest individuals experience. The novel . . . becomes a memoir of a good part of middle class American society. The major events of the last several decades are seen only dimly, as they affect Worthington's life, and thus Cozzens suggests how gigantic events are microscopically reflected in individual problems." America

Craig, Philip

Gate of ivory, Gate of Horn. Published for the Crime Club by Doubleday 1969 191p $4.50

The elements of this adventure story are "a college drop-out, the professor who won't let him return to graduate, the professor's niece, and a descendant of the Vikings who makes off with the niece. These four leave Boston harbor in a cruising boat to seek Beowulf's burial place off the coast of Sweden." Pub W

Crane, Stephen

Active service
In Crane, S. The complete novels of Stephen Crane p429-592

The complete novels of Stephen Crane; ed. with an introduction by Thomas A. Gullason. Doubleday 1967 821p $5.95

Partially analyzed in Short Story Index
Includes: Maggie: a girl of the streets [1893]; The red badge of courage [1895]; George's mother [1896]; The third violet [1897]; Active service [1899]; The O'Ruddy [1903]

The complete short stories & sketches of Stephen Crane; ed. with an introduction by Thomas A. Gullason. Doubleday 1963 790p boards $6.95

Partially analyzed in Short Story Index
"Contains in one volume all of Stephen Crane's 112 sketches and short stories. . . . The chronological collection begins with a brief but enlightening introduction that comments on the difficulties of compilation as well as on Crane's life and writings." Booklist
Contains the following short stories: The king's favor; The camel; Dan Emmonds; Four men in a cave; Travels in New York: the broken-down van; The octopush; A ghoul's accountant; The black dog; Killing his bear; The Captain; A tent in agony; The cry of a huckleberry pudding; An explosion of seven babies; The mesmeric mountain; The holler tree; Why did the young clerk swear? or, The unsatisfactory French; The pace of youth; The reluctant voyagers; A desertion; An experiment in misery; An experiment in luxury; An ominous baby; A dark brown dog; Billie Atkins went to Omaha; Mr Binks' day off; The men in the storm; Coney Island's failing days; In a Park Row restaurant; Stories told by an artist; When every one is panic stricken; When a man falls a crowd gathers; The duel that was not fought; A Christmas dinner won in battle; A lovely jag in a crowded car; A mystery of heroism; A gray sleeve; One dash —horses; A tale of mere chance; Three miraculous soldiers; A freight car incident; The little regiment; The veteran; The snake; Raft story; An Indiana campaign; In the Tenderloin; The voice of the mountain; Yen-Nock Bill and his sweetheart; Diamonds and diamonds; The auction; A poker game; A man and some others; The open boat; How the donkey lifted the hills; The victory of the moon; Flanagan and his short filibustering adventure; An old man goes wooing; A fishing village; The bride comes to Yellow Sky; Death and the child; The five white mice; The wise men; The monster; His new mittens; The blue hotel; The price of the harness; A self-made man; The clan of no-name; God rest ye, merry gentlemen; The lone charge of William B. Perkins; The angel child; Lynx-hunting; The revenge of the 'Adolphus'; The sergeant's private madhouse; The battle of Forty Fort; The surrender of Forty Fort; "Ol' Bennet" and the Indians; The lover and the telltale: "Showin' off"; Virtue in war; Making an orator; Twelve o'clock; The second generation; An episode of war; Shame; The carriage-lamps; The Kicking Twelfth; The shrapnel of

Crane, Stephen—*Continued*

their friends; "And if he wills, we must die"; The upturned face; The knife; The stove; Moonlight on the snow; The trial, execution, and burial of Homer Phelps; An illusion in red and white; The fight; This majestic lie; The city urchin and the chaste villagers; Manacled; A little pilgrimage; At the pit door; The squire's madness; The man from Duluth; A man by the name of Mud

George's mother
In Crane, S. The complete novels of Stephen Crane p301-47

In Crane, S. The portable Stephen Crane p89-146

In Crane, S. The red badge of courage, and selected prose and poetry p204-58

Maggie: a girl of the streets
In Blackmur, R. P. ed. American short novels p97-133

In Crane, S. The complete novels of Stephen Crane p99-154

In Crane, S. The portable Stephen Crane p3-74

In Crane, S. The red badge of courage, and other stories. Ultratype ed. p184-266

In Crane, S. The red badge of courage, and selected prose and poetry p136-200

In Phillips, W. ed. Great American short novels p237-94

Maggie, together with George's mother and The blue hotel; with an introduction by Henry Hazlitt. Knopf 1931 218p o.p. 1970
Analyzed in Short Story Index
Three of the author's earlier stories Maggie, George's Mother and The blue hotel
"Because of Maggie's historical importance—Beer calls it the first ironic novel ever written by an American—its intrinsic importance has been somewhat overemphasized. The irony, to adapt Disraeli's phase about flattery, has been laid on with a trowel. In a less famous story, 'The Blue Hotel,' included here, Crane's irony may be seen to better advantage—although even here his tendency to underscoring the ironic lesson of his art is apparent. 'The Blue Hotel,' however, remains one of the most exciting short stories ever written in America." N Y Times Bk R

The O'Ruddy
In Crane, S. The complete novels of Stephen Crane p593-790

The portable Stephen Crane; ed. with an introduction and notes, by Joseph Katz. Viking 1969 xxvi, 550p $6.50
"Viking Portable library"
Contains sixteen short stories, plus sketches, letters, pieces of journalism, some poetry and three novels: Maggie: a girl of the streets (1893); George's mother (1896); and The red badge of courage (1895)
Short stories included are: A great mistake; An ominous baby; A dark-brown dog; The men in the storm; An experiment in misery; An experiment in luxury

y The red badge of courage
Some editions are:
Macmillan (N Y) (The Macmillan classics) $3.95 Afterword by Clifton Fadiman; illustrated by Herschel Levit
Modern Lib $2.95
Watts, F. $7.95 Large type edition. A Keith Jennison book
First published 1895
"A young Union soldier, Henry Fleming, tells of his feelings when he is under fire for the first time during the battle of Chancellorsville. He is overcome by fear and runs from

the field. Later he returns to lead a charge that re-establishes his own reputation as well as that of his company. One of the great novels of the Civil War." Cincinnati

also in Crane, S. The complete novels of Stephen Crane p197-299

The red badge of courage, and other stories; with a critical and biographical profile of Stephen Cane. [Ultratype ed. complete and unabridged]. Watts, F. [1969] 356p $4.95
Contents: The red badge of courage; Maggie: a girl of the streets; The open boat; The bride comes to Yellow Sky; The blue hotel

The red badge of courage, and other stories; with an introduction by V. S. Pritchett and a note on the texts by R. W. Stallman. Oxford 1960 366p (The World's classics) $2.75
Partially analyzed in Short Story Index
Contents: Maggie, a girl of the streets; The open boat; The bride comes to Yellow Sky; The blue hotel; His new mittens; The upturned face

The third violet
In Crane, S. The complete novels of Stephen Crane p349-428

Creasey, John
The case of the innocent victims. Scribner [1966 c1959] 191p o.p. 1970
First published 1959 in England
This novel "sends Handsome West on the track of a psychopathic baby killer and through the curious confines of a carpet warehouse. Roger needed not only his own staff for this one, but also the help and understanding of Spendlove of the Globe to supply background information, and to keep his mouth shut, before he reached the end of the long dangerous trail." Library J
"I'm not sure how much I believe the psychopathology of the solution [of the story]; but it's a steadily fascinating baffler, with good action and a credible picture of the Yard at work." N Y Times Bk R

The executioners. Scribner 1967 217p o.p. 1970
"The Scotland Yard man [Roger West] and his able assistants are pitted against a gang of fanatical vigilantes who are harassing nine men, each a convicted murderer but each now released from prison after serving his sentence. The self appointed 'executioners,' however, will be satisfied with nothing less than the death of each by hanging. One of the released prisoners teams up with the police to break the case." Pub W

Murder, London-Australia. Scribner 1965 188p o.p. 1970
An Australian girl is strangled in a London boarding house. Soon Chief Inspector Roger West and his New Scotland Yard colleagues realize that the passengers who were aboard the S.S. Kookaburra with the murdered girl are all threatened by death. Then the entire fleet of the Blue Flag Line is endangered, and the case takes West to Hong Kong and Australia. (Publisher)

Murder, London-Miami. Scribner 1969 160p $3.95
"When Sir David Marshall's wife is murdered in a mental home and his beautiful secretary smuggles out papers to take to him in Miami, Roger West gives chase." Bk Buyer's Guide
"Creasey places his special stamp on [this novel] as on the others in this series: uncluttered plotting, and emphasis on the humanity —or, as Creasey would have it, on the basic goodness of most of the people involved." N Y Times Bk R

Murder, London-South Africa. Scribner 1966 187p o.p. 1970
"Superintendent Roger West takes charge when a South African industrialst and reporter Nightingale disappear after arriving at London

Creasey, John—Continued

Airport. The industrialist has been kidnapped and beaten up by diamond smuggler Bradshaw. So West follows the clues to Africa." Bk Buyer's Guide

For other titles by this author see Ashe, Gordon; Marric, J. J.

Crichton, Michael

y The Andromeda strain. Knopf 1969 295p illus boards $5.95

"An American unmanned space satellite lands on the edge of a small Arizona town. Almost at once it becomes clear that something has gone terribly wrong. All of the town's inhabitants but two, and the first investigators, die suddenly and grotesquely. When a rescue team arrives they find alive only a squalling two-month old baby and an old man who has been quieting his ulcer with massive doses of aspirin and drinking Sterno. . . . Their job: to find out what the contaminating agent from outer space is, and how to fight it." Pub W

The author "reveals his ability to conceive an imaginative idea and construct a plot that is commendable for its scientific and medical verisimilitude. Although, like most science-fiction writers, he fails to create characters of human dimension, he is concerned with moral values, and makes graphic the dangers of exploiting science for such goals as the perfection of chemical- and biological-warfare techniques." Newsweek

Crichton, Robert

The secret of Santa Vittoria; a novel. Simon & Schuster 1966 447p boards $5.95

"A small Italian hill town, Santa Vittoria, endeavors to protect its sole wealth one million bottles of vermouth, from an occupying force of Nazis. The town's new mayor, Bombolini, uses the methods of Machiavelli to deceive and confound the Germans." Bk Buyer's Guide

"It takes a lot of courage—and no little craft—to blend the diverse and exotic ingredients that Robert Crichton has brought together in this heady brew of a novel, a mélange of allegory, symbolism, several kinds of comedy including comedies of error and opéra bouffe, traces of Don Quixote and John Hershey's Major Joppolo, and a plot involving barely credible incidents of blind fate. In Mr. Crichton's hands the result is that most welcome rarity, a novel that is a joy to read, its hallmark something impossible to fake: a rollicking narrative drive that never lets up. . . . [This] is a picaresque novel tinged with black humor, and its flaws seem somehow unimportant when one is under the spell of its runaway zest for life and living." N Y Times Bk R

Crofts, Freeman Wills

The cask; with an introduction by James Nelson. Norton 1967 319p (The Seagull lib. of mystery and suspense) $4.50

First published 1924 in the United States by Seltzer

A woman corpse is found in a cask shipped from Paris to London. "Scotland Yard takes the case immediately but the combined ingenuity of London and Paris detectives fails to break down the wall of circumstantial evidence which encloses Léon Felix, the man to whom the cask is addressed. The quest is finally taken up by London's most skillful detective, Georges La Touche, who discovers the real clue which leads to the discovery of the criminal." Book Rev Digest

"Were the story shorter it would gain in strength. Of the craftsmanship, however, one cannot speak too highly." Boston Transcript

Cronin, A. J.

Beyond this place. Little 1953 361p $5.95

"Prompted by the miscarriages of justice in our time, the novelist tells the story of Paul Mathry, who seeks for his father Rees Mathry a release from Stone-heath prison where he has been sent for life for a murder he did not commit. In the provincial Irish town of Wortley, Paul explores the past in order to piece together the details of the crime; gradually he comes to realize that his father was a victim of entrenched interests which could not allow the facts of the case to come to light. Before restitution is made, Paul, like his father, is reduced to degradation and despair. What might have been a routine detective story becomes an absorbing novel, with convincing characterization and sensitivity to ethical values." Booklist

y The citadel

Some editions are:
Grosset $2.50
Little $5.95

First published 1937

"Story of the career of a conscientious brilliant young doctor, from his start in a mining town in Wales, to the realization of his ambition for a London practice. After years of struggle against mediocrity and indifference, he decided to capitalize on personal charm and make money. But success meant forgetting honor and ideals, and brought estrangement from a gallant wife, until a tragic error brought him to his senses. A restrained, but scathing expose of certain aspects of the British medical profession, which makes a moving and absorbing novel." Wis Lib Bul

y The green years. Little 1944 347p $4.95

"This is a much simpler and less ambitious work than the author's other novels. A story of adolescence, it covers ten years in the life of Robert Shannon, who after the death of his parents in Ireland comes to Scotland to live with his mother's people. There is no room for Robie in the crowded household where every penny is counted with miserly thrift. There isn't even a place for him to sleep. But to compensate for his miseries there is Grandpa. Grandpa (great grandfather really) is a memorable character, vain and boastful and intemperate, but one who understands small boys, and who, in the end, with one magnificent gesture, settles the problem of Robert's future." Wis Lib Bul

"This splendidly written story will delight Dr. Cronin's admirers. It will open their eyes, as all his books have done, to pleasant as well as to unpleasant possibilities of life, with a strong accent on courage and cheerfulness." Book Week

Followed by: Shannon's way

Hatter's castle. Little 1931 605p $6.95

"A long novel, the first by this English doctor, concerning one James Brodie, hatter of Levenford, a small Scottish town. Brodie is a man of virile, domineering character, obsessed with the idea of his possible noble birth and an overweaning desire for eminence. The story relates the cumulating tragedies caused by his cruelty to his family, his own disintegration of character, and the eventual collapse of all his hopes and ambitions." Book Rev Digest

"This is an old-fashioned type of story of which there is more than one example, but which succeeds because it is written with just the qualities that the type requires—force of description, strong human sympathy and deep knowledge of the persons and scenes from which it is drawn." Times (London) Lit Sup

y The keys of the kingdom

Some editions are:
Grosset $1.95
Little $5.95

First published 1941

"Character study of Francis Chisholm, a lovable Scottish Catholic priest. It begins with his boyhood attempts to earn a living after the death of his father and mother, and follows his career thru his years of training for the priesthood at Holywell and in Spain, and his early struggles in getting adjusted to his life work. After working in several difficult parishes, Father Chisholm was sent to a mission in the interior of China, where his brave fight to help humanity thru famine, flood, and pestilence, lasted for over thirty years. When his place was taken by two young priests, Father Chisholm—old, lame, and weary, but still indomitable, came home to spend his remaining years in his native Scotland." Book Rev Digest

Cronin, A. J.—*Continued*

"For a book based specifically on a spiritual theme, 'The Keys of the Kingdom' is oddly superficial. But as an adventure and travel story, packed with melodramatic action, it is, as Father Francis says of something else, 'as clean and sound as a good apple'—that, and nothing more." New Repub

A pocketful of rye. Little 1969 245p $5.95

Sequel to: A song of sixpence

"Lawrence Carrol, young British doctor with a background of completely selfish living, tired of medical work in poor districts, has with some fraud secured for himself a pleasant job in a clinic in Switzerland. To the clinic comes widowed Cathy with her ill son Daniel. Cathy had been Lawrence's first love, abandoned with his usual disregard, and only gradually does he learn the story of her wretched marriage and that Daniel is his son." Library J

"It is a happy ending kind of thing which tends to make good soap opera; yet the author is a man of style and the novel can stand on its own as a good, tight little tale which encourages all of us to face ourselves a bit more honestly. I think most adult readers will enjoy it for solid entertainment." Best Sellers

Shannon's way. Little 1948 313p $4.95

Sequel to: The green years
First published 1948

The story of a doctor in his twenties who put his keen interest in medical research ahead of everything else in life. But he had to face many obstacles, some of which were of his own making

"This new work does not advance Cronin's literary stature, but it does maintain the status quo." Library J

A song of sixpence. Little 1964 344p boards $5.95

This novel depicts "the despair and joy of a Dickensonian childhood in Scotland at the turn of the century. . . . Its hero Laurence Carroll, is a Catholic and so an outcast in a Protestant Scottish community, but secure in his loving family circle, until his father dies of tuberculosis. After that, life is a struggle . . . but a struggle relieved by some rollicking good times, love for his mother and a pretty cousin, and help and sympathy from unexpected sources." Pub W

"Much of the interest of this sympathy-evoking story of a Catholic boyhood lies in the many and varied adult characters who either helped or exploited Laurence. It is told with Cronin's expert professional skill." Library J

The stars look down. Little 1935 626p o.p. 1970

"The background of this novel is an English coal mining town; the span of the story, thirty years from 1903 to 1933. The two chief figures are Arthur Barras, son of the mine owner, and David Fenwick, son of a miner. It is a deep reading of characters, Kaleidoscopic in its changes." Ontario Lib Rev

"Much of this novel is outside the scope of Dr Cronin's capacity. Where he is successful is in the portrayal of the miners' family life, manners and speech, in the vigour and imagination with which he describes a mine disaster, a riot, or an operation and in other passages where he can display his intimate knowledge of the seamy side of things; but his bent for melodrama weakens all his effects." Times (London) Lit Sup

A thing of beauty. Little 1956 440p $6.95

"Character study of a man obsessed with a desire to paint. Stephen Desmonde was destined by his English family for the church, but the call of art was too strong. After ten years of wandering in France and Spain, starving, contracting tuberculosis, and always painting, he returned to England. There he married beneath him, depending on his wife for both spiritual and material sustenance." Book Rev Digest

"For its sympathetic insight into the life of an artist, along with the good story it tells, 'A Thing of Beauty' belongs in the company of 'Lust for Life.'" N Y Her Trib Books

Cross, Amanda

The James Joyce murder. Macmillan (N Y) 1967 176p boards $4.50

"A Cock Robin mystery"

"Kate Fansler, a pretty professor and amateur sleuth, becomes involved in a mystery at her summer home in the Berkshires when an unpleasant local lady is found murdered practically on Kate's doorstep." Bk Buyer's Guide

The author has "written a highly attractive specimen of the leisurely and witty academic mystery novel. . . . Not for action enthusiasts, but a happy souvenir of a once more popular school, which I still find delightful." N Y Times Bk R

Crumley, James

One to count cadence. Random House 1969 338p $6.95

This first novel is "set on a U.S. Air Force Base in the Philippines and in Vietnam. . . . Its hero, Slag Krummel . . . arrives at the base in 1962 as the new sergeant of a drinking, whoring company of enlistees. . . . The novel revolves around Krummel's relationship with his friend, hero and conscience, one Joe Morning, whom he loves, fears and betrays in a moment that will haunt him for the rest of his life." Book World

The author "has a faultless ear for filthy speech . . . and those who do not care to see the unprintable printed had best leave his book alone. . . . [Nevertheless this] is a compelling study of the gratuitous violence in men—and how it is unleashed by the frustrations of military life. It is a story of bars, brawls and brothels—and I don't know of any writer who has done it better." N Y Times Bk R

Cullinan, Elizabeth

House of gold. Houghton 1970 [c1969] 328p $6.95

"A Houghton Mifflin Literary fellowship novel"

This novel "focuses on an Irish-American Catholic family, living in a suburb of New York, at the moment when the elderly mother is dying. As the grown children and grandchildren and in-laws gather, the reader comes to know them intimately and to understand what has made of the Devlins the very special—and flawed—family that they are." Pub W

"A thoughtful evocation of personality in crisis of especial appeal to women." Booklist

Culp, John H.

The bright feathers. Holt 1965 283p $4.95

This "novel, laid in the old West, treats the adventures of three young cowboys as they return to Texas after a cattle drive to Kansas. Against the background of the true West with its Friendly Nations' Indians, renegades, outlaws, and settlers, our heroes get into one difficulty after another, usually accompanied by the goat, Leviticus." Library J

The book "makes excellent use of dialogue and characteristic modes of speech to capture the sights, smells and (almost) the sense of feeling the various objects and scenes described. . . . The list of vividly portrayed characters—Stanley Hightower, a Cherokee undertaker; Booger Red, who is affectionately called a cook; Miss Lockwood who marries an Indian; and the tragic life of the Five Civilized Tribes, as they try to live like their white brethren—all are excellently described and narrated." Best Sellers

The restless land. Sloane 1962 438p o.p. 1970

This novel "has the hardy, sensible, fifteen-year-old Kid, orphaned Martin Cameron, as its hero. He is the inheritor of the Tail End Ranch in northwest Texas in the unsettled 1870's. Comanches, Comancheros, cattle drives, and the cowboys who form his lusty crew combine to make a man of him. Drawing on this strength and maturity the Kid rescues from Indian captivity a girl whom he realizes he loves. The novel at first relies on anecdote and humor for background but becomes a more serious study of Indian and Texas relationships." Booklist

Cummings, E. E.

The enormous room; with a new introduction by the author. Modern Lib. 1934 332p $2.95

First published 1922 by Boni and Liveright
"The enormous room is a French prison camp in which the author, a young American of the Norton-Harjes Ambulance Corps, was confined on an entirely groundless suspicion and without trial. In narrating the horrors and the unsanitary condition of the camp and the needless brutality of the officials and guards, the author veils his bitterness under humorous and somewhat unrestrained language. Much of the book is devoted to skillfully drawn pen-pictures of the officials and guards and the author's fellow-prisoners." Book Rev Digest
Some libraries classify this as non-fiction

Cunningham, E. V.

Penelope; an entertainment. Doubleday 1965 210p o.p. 1970

The Penelope of the title "is a wealthy New York banker's wife who relieves her boredom and tests her ingenuity by robbing her husband's bank: as a sideline she steals her rich friends' jewels and returns them after the insurance money has been collected and spent." New Statesman
"Penelope has a thoroughly delightful time as the law rolls into high-powered action and people such as the Police Commissioner and the handsome young Assistant D.A. fall under her guileless spell, with husband James fuming in the background. The complex of events cascades into an ever frothier farce climaxed by a consistently improbable finale." Book Week

For other titles by this author see Fast, Howard

Cuomo, George

Among thieves. Doubleday 1968 480p $6.95

"Three men, from three very different worlds, are drawn together. . . . Young Mel Simmons, husband, father and ex-con, tried to go straight and failed. Found guilty . . . he is in prison for the second time. Johnny Mancino is a popular television personality who becomes intimately and dangerously involved in Mel's case. Dr Samuel 'Flash' Fleishman, Ph.D., is the Assistant Warden of the prison: self-mocking, courageous and compassionate." Literary Guild
The author "has exceptional insight into the problems of convicts on parole and into the social structure and subculture of the contemporary American prison. He has a fine sense of control over the pacing of plot development, and as a consequence he is able to hold the reader's interest throughout this relatively long novel. . . . Probably few of the readers of this novel will ever experience the problems of prisoners, wardens, and ex-convicts. The average middle-class American knows little about the lives of these people. Thus, for most persons 'Among Thieves' should provide an enlightening and an enjoyable reading experience." Library J

Cuthrell, Faith (Baldwin) See Baldwin, Faith

D

Dahl, Roald

Kiss, kiss. Knopf 1960 [c1959] 308p $4.95

Analyzed in Short Story Index
"Eleven unusual stories (seven of which have appeared in 'The New Yorker,' 'Esquire,' and other magazines). . . . Tension is Mr. Dahl's trademark and his stories are tightly written, fast-paced, and suspenseful. He has a penchant for the fantastic, and is a master of the macabre tale with a surprising and usually shocking twist at the end." Library J
Contents: The landlady; William and Mary; The way up to heaven; Parson's pleasure; Mrs Bixby and the Colonel's coat; Royal jelly; Georgy Porgy; Genesis and catastrophe; Edward the conqueror; Pig; The champion of the world

Selected stories of Roald Dahl. Modern Lib. [1968] 302p $2.45

Analyzed in Short Story Index
These stories were selected by the author from two of his previous collections: Someone like you, published 1953 and, Kiss, kiss, published 1960
Contents: Lamb to the slaughter; Dip in the pool; The landlady; Taste; Parson's pleasure; Georgy Porgy; Royal jelly; Genesis and catastrophe; Mrs Bixby and the Colonel's coat; Skin; The ratcatcher; Rummins; Mr Hoddy; Mr Feasey; The champion of the world

Dale, Celia

Act of love. Walker & Co. 1969 256p $5.95

"Headlong passion, jealousy that spins a malicious web of suspicion, and in the end murder—all grow out of the love affair between a sensitive, weak-natured young tutor and the aristocratic, beautiful, sadly mismated wife of the master of Bulmer Hall, a manly but coarse, hard-drinking person. The two children of the nineteenth-century English household and the family doctor play significant supporting roles in this adroit period piece in which psychological motivation and a thrust of 'deus ex machina' smoothly mesh." Booklist

Daley, Robert

A priest and a girl. World Pub. 1969 415p $6.95

"Father McCabe, one of three curates in a Manhattan parish is mid-thirtyish, caught by the currents of change in both the world and the Catholic Church. His life of traditional priestly duties, prescribed by ancient ritual and edicts from the ecclesiastical hierarchy, distresses him. The ferment inside him intensifies as he concludes that his church operates and survives, not by love, but by threat of punishment. McCabe takes a European vacation in the hope that his doubts will subside. Out of priestly dress, he meets a girl, Michele. The affair progresses to the point that when he returns to New York, he knows he must leave the priesthood and marry. He does, but is shunned cruelly by his family, the church, and the working world where employment comes hard." Pub W
"To be appreciated, . . . the book has to be read as an entertaining topical novel. It aspires neither to complexity in its psychology nor to artfulness in fictional technique. . . . The book will disturb and anger many [Catholics] . . . but it is honest, accurate and fair. It breaks no new ground in fiction, but for many of its readers the sympathetic portrayal of a Catholic priest's lust as a noble, rather than shameful, thing will be remarkable enough." Book World

Daly, Elizabeth

The book of the dead
In Daly, E. An Elizabeth Daly Mystery omnibus v3

An Elizabeth Daly Mystery omnibus. . . . Complete and unabridged. Rinehart 1960 3v in 1 o.p. 1970

"Three Henry Gamadge novels: Murders in volume 2 [1941], Evidence of things seen [1943], [and] The book of the dead [1944]." Title page
Evidence of things seen
In Daly, E. An Elizabeth Daly Mystery omnibus v2

Murders in volume 2
In Daly, E. An Elizabeth Daly Mystery omnibus v 1

Dane, Clemence

Broome stages. Doubleday 1931 703p o.p. 1970

"The first Richard Broome was born in 1715 and hobnobbed with a witch. When he fell

Dane, Clemence—*Continued*

from the loft of a barn into a group of strolling players who were rehearsing a Mid-Summer Night's Dream, he unwittingly committed his descendants to the theater. For more than two hundred years the Broomes, gifted, spectacular, and charming, ornamented the English stage, and then the last of the family went over to the movies." Booklist

"A long, leisurely book, veracious in background, convincing in its deploying of family trait and individual idiosyncrasy, and achieving a moving and dramatic reality of emotion." Sat R

Daniel, Īūlii Markov. See Daniel, Yuli

Daniel, Yuli

This is Moscow speaking, and other stories [by] Yuli Daniel (Nikolai Arzhak) Tr. by Stuart Hood, Harold Shukman [and] John Richardson; with a foreword by Max Hayward. Dutton 1969 [c1968] 159p front $4.95

Original French edition published 1965; first English translation 1968

Contents: This is Moscow speaking; Hands; Atonement; The man from MINAP

"When one reads Daniel in the superb English of these translations, what strikes one . . . is the loving care that goes into his phrases and images. . . . Although [his] stories are political, there is in the writing an old love for private language as well as a new love for public freedom. . . . Daniel is a really gifted writer and something more than a political freak." New Statesman

Daniels, Lucy

Caleb, my son; a novel. Lippincott 1956 125p o.p. 1970

"The effect of segregation upon a family of southern Negroes is the theme of . . . [this] novel in which Asa Blake and his son Caleb are the principal figures. Embittered by his family's unquestioning acceptance of the nature of Negro-white relationships Caleb quits his job and as part of his crusade for equality defies the town's social code by repeatedly dating a white girl. Realizing that Caleb's actions jeopardize the entire Blake family Asa, as a last recourse, kills the son he can no longer understand." Booklist

"Her book is remarkable for its insight into the life of such a family as the Blakes, their anxieties both as Negroes and as human beings, and the expression of those anxieties in speech and gesture." N Y Her Trib Books

Dannay, Frederic. See Queen, Ellery

Dark, Eleanor

The timeless land. Macmillan (N Y) 1941 499p o.p. 1970

"The few boatloads of convicts who landed in Sydney Harbor in 1788 made poor pioneer stock indeed. That they survived at all was due to the courage and wisdom of their Captain Phillip. His story is told here, as is that of a fictional character, Andrew Prentice, a redheaded convict who escaped. The settlement's first five years—and the fate of the black natives whose life and culture were so quickly and cruelly destroyed—make a dramatic, competently told story." Huntting

Daudet, Alphonse

Tartarin of Tarascon; Tartarin on the Alps. Dutton 230p (Everyman's lib) $3.25

"Tartarin of Tarascon" first published 1872 in France, "Tartarin of the Alps in 1885

"Extravaganza satirizing Daudet's Provencal compatriots with a geniality and an irresistible gusto that remove any offence. Tartarin [is] . . . a caricature of the imaginative and unveracious Meridional, with his incorrigible propensity for exaggeration and bragging. He sets out on an expedition to Algeria to prove his reputation for valour and resource, and meets with adventures as monstrous as those of Don Quixote." Baker's Best

Tartarin on the Alps

In Daudet, A. Tartarin of Tarascon

D'Aurevilly, Jules Barbey

Happiness in crime

In Dupee, F. W. ed. Great French short novels p341-90

Davenport, Basil

y (comp.) Famous monster tales; foreword by Clifton Fadiman. Van Nostrand 1967 201p $4.95

Analyzed in Short Story Index

Contents: Smoke ghost, by F. Leiber; The phantom farmhouse, by S. Quinn; The horror of the heights, by A. C. Doyle; The thing on Outer Shoal, by P. S. Miller; The outsider, by H. P. Lovecraft; Second night out, by F. B. Long; It, by T. Sturgeon; The dancing partner, by J. K. Jerome; The damned thing, by A. Bierce; Skeleton, by R. Bradbury; The thing in the pond, by P. Ernst; Negotium perambulans, by E. F. Benson; The fifty-first dragon, by H. Broun

The stories "tell of werewolves, almost-humans, robots, vampires, and awesome survivors from some remote past. These tales do not foretell the future, comment on the past, or bear a message for today. They have no intent other than to entertain." Publisher's note

(ed.) Ghostly tales to be told; a collection of stories from the great masters, arranged for reading and telling aloud. Dodd 1950 317p o.p. 1970

Analyzed in Short Story Index

"An experienced teller of tales, who has been telling and collecting stories for 20 years, includes 16 of his favorites with instructions for adapting each of them." Booklist

Contents: The Wendigo, by A. Blackwood; August heat, by W. F. Harvey; Count Magnus, by M. R. James; Where angels fear, by M. W. Wellman; House of the nightmare, by E. L. White; Screaming skull, by F. M. Crawford; Monkey's paw, by W. W. Jacobs; Gentleman from America, by M. Arlen; White powder, by A. Machen; Couching at the door, by D. K. Broster; Yellow wall-paper, by C. P. Gilman; Johnson look back, by T. Burke; Where their fire is not quenched, by M. Sinclair; Moonlight sonata, by A. Woollcott; Captain murderer, by C. Dickens; The refugee, by J. Rice

(ed.) Tales to be told in the dark; a selection of stories from the great authors, arranged for reading and telling aloud. Dodd 1953 335p $4

Analyzed in Short Story Index

"The editor gives comments and suggestions for telling [these stories] with the largest effects of mystery, horror, and suspense." Huntting

Contents: The beast with five fingers, by W. F. Harvey; By one, by two, and by three, by S. Hall; Sredni Bashtar, by Saki; The black seal, by A. Machen; The two bottles of relish, by Lord Dunsany; The book, by M. Irwin; Thus I refute Beelzy, by J. Collier; The whippoor-will, by J. Thurber; The white people, by A. Machen; Mujina, by L. Hearn; The open window, by Saki; Two anecdotes; Closed cabinet; Closed cabinet, retold

(ed.) 13 ways to dispose of a body; an anthology. Dodd 1966 277p o.p. 1970

Analyzed in Short Story Index

"A collection with commentaries, showing many of the ways of getting rid of your victim's body." Bk Buyer's Guide

Contents: Being a murderer myself, by A. Williams; The best of everything, by S. Ellin; The corpus delicti, by M. D. Post; De mortuis, by J. Collier; Earth to earth, by R. Graves; The Duchess at prayer, by E. Wharton; The hole in the wall, by G. K. Chesterton; The man with copper fingers, by D. Sayers; The night I died, by C. Woolrich; The October game, by R. Bradbury; Out of this nettle, by R. Twohy; The two bottles of relish, by Lord Dunsany; Love lies bleeding, by P. MacDonald

Davenport, Basil—*Continued*

(ed.) 13 ways to kill a man; an anthology; comp. and ed. by Basil Davenport. Dodd 1965 xx, 239p o.p. 1970

Analyzed in Short Story Index
Contents: The candidate, by H. Slesar; Lamb to the slaughter, by R. Dahl; The turn of the tide, by C. S. Forester; The tea leaf, by E. Jepson; The adopted daughter, by M. D. Post: The liqueur glass, by P. Bottome; Hop-Frog, by R. A. Knox; The kennel, by M. Level; The policeman only taps once, by A. Berkeley; Weapon, motive, method—, by R. Arthur; The question my son asked, by S. Ellin; Back for Christmas, by J. Collier

Davenport, Marcia

East side, west side. Scribner 1947 376p o.p. 1970

A "novel of luxury living in New York.... Jessie Bourne, whose mother had been a distinguished, widely loved Jewish actress, is married to a faithless husband belonging to an old, conventional family, and she preserves the fiction of their marriage in the midst of a group who made a sport of divorce and infidelity. When her husband's family is threatened with a devastating scandal of murder and blackmail, Jessie engineers their escape, knows she has no further obligation to her husband, and takes for a lover an idealistic patriot just returned from the Czech underground. Popular appeal, but not a pretty picture of New York life." Booklist

My brother's keeper. Scribner 1954 457p o.p. 1970

"In an old house in a once acceptable, but now run-down neighborhood, two old men lived amidst a collection of useless objects—furniture, junk, newspapers, and a dissembled automobile. Now one is dead, and the other missing. The story of what caused these two educated, well-to-do men to live in such squalor ranges from New York's countryside at the turn of the century, to Vienna and its opera, to Italy's lake region, and back to New York." Huntting

The book "may not be literature but it lives in spite of its contrivances; it remains dramatic rather than clinical. It achieves both pathos and horror, realities of feeling in the midst of fantasies of behavior. There are profounder, richer novels, to be sure, but few are as hypnotic in their content and their narrative flow." Sat R

Of Lena Geyer. Scribner 1936 473p o.p. 1970

"A devotee of Lena Geyer, one of the world's great prima donnas, sets down what he has been able to learn of her life and temperament, either directly or from those closest to her. Thus Lena is seen being transformed from an awkward and struggling peasant girl into an artist, and in her relations with a wealthy and aristocratic lover; her first teacher; a great conductor; Lilli Lehmann; and with the eccentric woman, who watches over her after Lena has shut romantic love out of her life, as deadening to her art. A convincing portrait of a genius against the lovingly painted background of opera in Germany, Paris, Vienna and New York." N Y Libraries

"A novel that successfully combines biographical narrative and musical interest is rather rare, though the subject is frequently attempted. 'Lena Geyer' will be ardently read by those who have deep knowledge of music and also by many who have only an amateur's appreciation." Springf'd Republican

The valley of decision. Scribner 1942 790p o.p. 1970

The "life story of a fifteen-year-old Irish girl who started as a housemaid in the home of a Pittsburgh steel family in the late 1870's—a lovable and powerful figure who stayed on to become its ruling spirit—both at home and in its business development. Though vast in scope, in respect to time and scene, and in the number and variety of its characters, the story is, primarily, a moving and dramatic portrait of a loyal and noble woman who kept a temperamental family together—during numerous crises—through three generations." Huntting

"Author Davenport has packed her book with descriptions of the unfeminine workings of Bessemers, open-hearth furnaces, skiphoists, cast-houses. The men who pump lifeblood through the heart of Pittsburgh come alive in her pages—Irish steelworkers of the 1870s. Slovaks and 'Hunkies' pouring in from the mills of Europe. Novelist Davenport's description of this hard, world-transforming valley of steel and furnaces is the most memorable part of her impressive work." Time

Davidson, Avram

The phoenix and the mirror. Doubleday 1969 209p (Doubleday Science fiction) $4.95

"The setting [of this tale] is ancient Rome, and the story steeped in mythology, combined with the medieval mixture of philosophy and sorcery. An author's note advises that during the Middle Ages many legends became associated with Vergil, author of 'The Aeneid,' attributing to him magical and scientific powers. First in a projected series entitled 'Vergil Magus,' 'The Phoenix and the Mirror' describes the adventures of Vergil when he is set the impossible task of forging a 'speculum majorum'—a virgin mirror that enables the first viewer to see whatever he or she wishes. The tale is fascinating and Mr. Davidson's craft while interweaving such elements as a cyclops and alchemy is evident." Library J

Davidson, Diane

Feversham; a novel. Crown 1969 376p $6.50

A "fictional account of an actual event relates the circumstances surrounding the murder in 1550 of Thomas Arden in the rural village of Feversham, a deed done at the instigation of his wife Alice. Drawn from thorough research and written with candor and incisive characterization the novel includes testimony from all the condemned as given to Sir Thomas Cheyney, the Lord Lieutenant in Kent. A lifelong acquaintance of Alice's family, Cheyney sought to save Alice but was ultimately unsuccessful." Booklist

"Based on a tale in Holinshed's 'Chronicles' and made into a scandalous contemporary play, 'Arden of Feversham,' it is recreated here as a sensational Tudor tale and good historical entertainment." Pub W

Davidson, Lionel

The Menorah men. Harper 1966 277p $5.95

A young English philologist gets "a chance to use a newly discovered Dead Sea scroll in a hunt for buried treasure. The treasure is the true Menorah, the seven branched lamp, symbol of Judaism. There is all-too-evident menace in the Arabs who also know of the menorah; there is the professor's dalliance with his pretty chauffeur (she is a lieutenant in the Israeli army); and there is comic relief in the professor's sardonic sense of humor." Pub W

"The author's account of Laing's adventures is a supple delight in which learning wit and style are beautifully integrated into a rousing chase across the Negev and into a housing project. Mr. Davidson's talents include a flair for crisp characterization." N Y Times Bk R

The rose of Tibet. Harper 1962 330p o.p. 1970

"When Charles Houston leaves England to discover the fate of his brother, who has disappeared in Tibet, he has little inkling of the bizarre adventures that await him and his Sherpa guide—adventures that involve a passionate goddess, barbaric priestesses, a monastery honeycombed with secret passages, a fortune in emeralds, and a perilous flight across towering, snow-capped mountains, beset by blizzards, starvation, and menacing bands of Chinese Communists." Publisher's note

"With the possible exception of a throat-cutting chapter (almost too graphic), [this book] adds up to first-class entertainment." Library J

Davies, L. P.

y The artificial man. Published for the Crime Club by Doubleday 1967 [c1965] 191p o.p. 1970

First published 1965 in England
"In the United Britain of 2016, physicists restore life to a dead man and unknowingly

Davies, L. P.—*Continued*

create a superior being who may rule the world. Alan Fraser's search for identity and his growing mental powers occur amid a struggle for power within an Orwellian Britain and a cold war with Sinoasia. Intrigue and suspicion rip away the rustic facade of Alan's Bewdey town, as strange events threaten his life and the experiment which revolves around him." Library J

This "combines the elements of science fiction and suspense. The story begins very quietly . . . but that is 'just' the beginning." McClurg. Book News

A grave matter. Published for the Crime Club by Doubleday 1968 [c1967] 190p $3.95

First published 1967 in England

"John Morton, idly skimming through a newspaper, reads a brief item about the discovery of two children's skeletons beside a quiet country road. He recalls that the town is Ashmead, where he lived as a boy. He also has a memory, almost buried by time, of having trespassed into a country estate long ago, of having played with a boy and girl and never seen them again. Impelled to investigate on his own, he encounters plenty of trouble before he uncovers the full truth about what happened in the past." Pub W

"Well plotted, well written, it takes one back to the famous British mystery writers. No overtones of sex, no extreme of violence; it is a professional piece of suspense writing." Best Sellers

The Lampton dreamers. Published for the Crime Club by Doubleday 1967 [c1966] 188p o.p. 1970

"A group of Yorkshire villagers suddenly begins to have, each of them, the same recurring dream. From this it is only one step to mass somnambulism. It is clear that someone in the village have acquired such intense powers over other people's minds that they can be manipulated to do anything the control wants. Who is causing the increasingly dangerous and ruthless things that occur? A crippled little girl? Her Romany grandmother? The young doctor who is an 'outsider'? It all mounts to quite a peak of suspense, but the ending is too hurried, too insufficiently explained to fully satisfy the reader." Pub W

y The paper dolls. Published for the Crime Club by Doubleday 1966 [c1964] 216p o.p. 1970

First published 1964 in England

"At Cookley School, in England [schoolboy] Thorne had been bullying twelve-year-old Roddy Blake, and suddenly climbed to a rood and threw himself to his death. Three years [before] . . . a boy at Roddy's school had flung himself through a window. Teachers Gordon Seacombe and Joan Grey began to look into Roddy's background—and discovered there were other facsimiles of Roddy and all with strange and terrifying powers." Bk Buyer's Guide

"Despite the Crime Club imprint, this is a science-fiction novel. . . . There are echoes of many other novels here, and some of the developments may strain one's credulity; but it's a vigorous man-against-the-unknown adventure story, with touches of horror all the more effective for their being underplayed." N Y Times Bk R

The reluctant medium. Published for the Crime Club by Doubleday 1967 [c1966] 191p o.p. 1970

First published 1966 in England with title: Tell it to the dead

A mystery story in which "because Matthew Rawson has confidence in him, David Conway, business consultant, feels that he will be able to take an objective view of the strange happenings at Rawson's home, Butchart House, and that he can prove that the ghostly sounds and sights are the work of a warped but very human mind in the house itself. But he lets himself get emotionally involved, and murder steps in and almost strikes him down." Library J

"A moderately entertaining English thriller . . . blends modern chicanery with a touch of the supernatural." Pub W

Stranger to town. Published for the Crime Club by Doubleday 1969 189p $3.95

"Julian Midwinter lands, apparently by chance, in the British hamlet of Harmsley Cosset, and finds himself beset by memories of places he's never been and people he's never met. One of the latter is a deceased local resident, whose wife (a believer in reincarnation) sets Midwinter up in her husband's old business and invites him into the circle of his old friends." N Y Times Bk R

"A cunning first thriller by a science fiction writer with a long, elusive explanation and good presentation of a provincial-Town society." Times (London) Lit Sup

Twilight journey. Doubleday 1968 [c1967] 191p $4.50

First published 1967 in England

"Set in the year 2123, this is the story of Doctor Clayton Solan, distinguished scientist, who becomes the victim himself of the hallucinatory brain test called Pandect that he had developed. Sentenced to die as a nonconformist, it is only with the help of the girl, Moira, and his loyal assistant that Solan fights his way through hallucinatory terrors back to reality and life. Science fiction buffs will like this complex fantasy. The characters are well drawn and the scenes excitingly different." Pub W

The white room. Published for the Crime Club by Doubleday 1969 189p $4.50

Axel Champlee "a well-to-do industrialist, faced with imminent ruin, tries to find out who has tricked him out of a day of consciousness, and then is horrified to discover it is not one day, but 10 years, that are missing." Pub W

This is "a compelling, well-constructed psychological suspense story set in England." Booklist

Davies, Leslie Purnell. See Davies, L. P.

Davies, Valentine

y It happens every spring. Farrar, Straus 1949 224p o.p. 1970

"Concerns a young chemistry instructor, too poor to marry, who stumbles on a formula that makes a baseball repellent to wood. The college suddenly loses an instructor and the St. Louis baseball team gains a miraculous new pitcher who floats balls over the plate and gives up an enormous amount of walks, but who almost pitches a no-hit season. Complications of a double life plus the loss of the formula on the eve of the World Series add to the plot." Huntting

"It has romance, sport, surprise and suspense—saturated with an irresistible humor. A first class evening's entertainment." Library J

y Miracle on 34th Street. Harcourt 1947 120p $3.95

The "story of an old man who thinks he is Santa Claus. There is plenty of evidence to support his claim; his name is Kris Kringle . . . the reindeer in the zoo eat out of his hand . . . the children who came to Macy's to see him, of course, are convinced . . . and so are their parents. Unfortunately there are, as always, certain practical souls who refuse to believe and, who, unmoved by any Christmas spirit, take steps to have Kris put away. How he ends up in court and tries to prove that he is both sane and Santa Claus, too, makes a tale that will appeal to young and old alike." Huntting

"An amusing mixture of sentiment and fantasy likely to live a long time as a popular Christmas classic." Wis Lib Bul

Daviot, Gordon. See Tey, Josephine

Davis, Christopher

First family. Coward-McCann 1961 253p o.p. 1970

"A family of Negro intellectuals moves into an 'all-white' middle class suburban neighborhood near a large northern city. They are befriended by a young couple who encourage the

Davis, Christopher—*Continued*

friendship between their daughter and the son of the negro college professor and his wife. Soon 'For Sale' signs appear, and the liberal white family come to see that they have promised more than they can give." Huntting

This novel "seems at times to place belligerent emphasis upon the atypical, hypertensive, even unlovable personality. But it thus points up the more subtly how 'gentlemanly' non-violent prejudice aggravates ordinary anxieties, multiplies day-to-day pressures undermines casual friendships, and forces life increasingly out of focus. And it is this insight that makes Mr. Davis's novel a stimulating contemporary study." Best Sellers

Davis, Dorothy Salisbury
Where the dark streets go. Scribner 1969 190p $4.95

"Young Father McMahon, who serves in a Puerto Rican-Irish parish in New York, is very much a priest of today, with all that means in terms of inner turmoil. Called to tend a dying man who has been stabbed, he is drawn into finding out all he can about the victim. The more he discovers—in the East Village, in art circles, among his own parishioners—the closer he comes to the killer. Parallel to this story is the young priest's growing awareness that he is falling deeply in love with the dead man's girl, and that he may have to leave the church." Pub W

"Tragic and compassionate and perhaps not for conservative Catholic readers." Library J

Davis, H. L.
Beulah Land. Morrow 1949 314p o.p. 1970

"Historical novel of the American frontier. Starting out in the Cherokee country of western North Carolina, two young people—an impulsive, trigger-tempered half-Indian girl named Ruhama and a devoted, superstitious, Indian-bred foundling white boy called Askwani—go cross-country to the Mississippi, down it to Natchez, up in to Illinois, then westward across Missouri and Kansas, and south to their own Beulah Land, in what was the Indian Territory. They are accompanied for part of the journey by Ruhama's father, Ewen Warne, to whom Askwani is deeply attached and by an Indian woman, Sedaya. Mr. Davis's novel is essentially the story of the two young people and their long, hazardous journey." New Yorker

Honey in the horn. Harper 1935 380p o.p. 1970

Pulitzer Prize, 1936
"This Harper prize novel is a story of Oregon in the homesteading period at the beginning of the century. As central characters it has the boy, Clay Calvert, and the girl, Luce, whose path crosses his in his life of casual wandering and with whom he strikes up a partnership; but the real interest of the book lies in the many types of characters, and wide range of country, and in the picture of a restless, crude, and lusty civilization." Wis Lib Bul

"Not one of the early pioneers whom the author presents to us may be skipped over, whether he is presented as a type, as a unit in the mass or as an extreme individual. They are all gnarled with uncouthness, colorful with marked peculiarities, more or less plastered over with sin of one sort or another, sturdy with sincerity (whether their sincerity is worth while or not). . . . The book sparkles with humor often of the rough sort." Springf'd Republican

Davis, Harold Lenoir. See Davis, H. L.

Davis, Paxton
The seasons of heroes; a novel. Morrow 1967 276p o.p. 1970

This is the story of three generations of the Gibboneys of Virginia. "Matt, a West Pointer and a career soldier, recalls the totality of his experiences as he makes the painful decision to accept a commission in the Confederate Army; his young son Robert participates in Colonel McNaught's disastrous foray into Pennsylvania in 1864; and finally Robert's son, Will, first seen in 1914 finds in his confrontation of a lynch mob the opportunity for heroism he had thought his times denied him." Publisher's note

"The three narratives combine to define certain ideas, attitudes, and articles of faith which these men embody in their different ways. These are old-fashioned: . . . duty, honor, country. . . . Rather than any unity of action it is the continuity of these ideas (plus family and place) that gives unity to the novel." N Y Times Bk R

Davis, William Stearns
y A friend of Caesar; a tale of the fall of the Roman republic, time, 50-47 B.C. Macmillan (N Y) 1919 501p $7.95

First published 1900
"Adventures of a friend of Julius Caesar in the period 51-40 B.C. Caesar and Antony and Cleopatra are introduced, together with the crossing of the Rubicon and the battle of Pharsalia." Baker's Best

Day, A. Grove
(ed.) Best South Sea stories; selected and ed. by A. Grove Day and Carl Stroven. Appleton 1964 313p boards $5.95

Analyzed in Short Story Index
Contents: Red, by W. S. Maugham; The fourth man, by J. Russell; The forgotten one, by J. N. Hall; The seed of McCoy, by J. London; Mutiny, by J. A. Michener; The black and the white, by E. Burdick; The ghost of Alexander Perks, A. B., by R. D. Frisbie; The beach of Falesá, by R. L. Stevenson; A son of empire, by L. Osbourne; A prodigal in Tahiti, by C. W. Stoddard; Assignment with an octopus, by Sir A. Grimble; A stinking ghost, by Sir A. Grimble; The whale in the cave, by F. T. Bullen; At a kava-drinking, by L. Becke; Norfolk Isle and the Chola widow, by H. Melville

(ed.) Greatest American short stories; twenty classics of our heritage. McGraw 1953 359p $4.75

Analyzed in Short Story Index
Contents: Rip Van Winkle, by W. Irving; Ambitious guest, by N. Hawthorne; Cask of Amontillado, by E. A. Poe; Purloined letter, by E. A. Poe; Celebrated jumping frog of Calaveras County, by M. Twain; Outcasts of Poker Flat, by B. Harte; Wonderful Tar-Baby story, by J. C. Harris; Lady or the tiger, by F. R. Stockton; Occurrence at Owl Creek Bridge, by A. Bierce; Open boat, by S. Crane; Gift of the Magi, by O. Henry; Paul's case, by W. Cather; Lost Phoebe, by T. Dreiser; Fourth man, by J. Russell; I'm a fool, by S. Anderson; Haircut, by R. Lardner; Devil and Daniel Webster, by S. V. Benét; Leader of the people, by J. Steinbeck; Secret life of Walter Mitty, by J. Thurber; The bear, by W. Faulkner

Dayan, Yael
Death has two sons; a novel. McGraw 1967 191p $4.95

"The terrible memory that haunts . . . [Daniel Kalinsky] is that of his father choosing between him and his brother, under Nazi directive, as to which should live. Ironically, Daniel, the son he did not choose, is the only one to survive and now the old man, dying of cancer, and with a second family, has come to Israel where Daniel is trying to come to terms with his feelings about his father." Pub W

Miss Dayan "is writing about the horrors of war, the conflict of generations, the riddle of love. She is also writing of human beings—the father a good if ordinary man forced into an inhuman decision and unable to atone for it; the son a 'child of death' who cannot escape war (his best friend is killed in the Sinai) or the bitterness of his existence." Book of the Month Club News

Deal, Babs H.
High lonesome world; the death and life of a country music singer. Doubleday 1969 300p $5.95

"Anyone familiar with the short, colorful, tragic life of the late Hank Williams, the country music singer and songwriter who died of 'too much living, too much sorrow, too much love, too much alcohol and drugs,' will recognize him as the prototype of the hero of

Deal, Babs H.—*Continued*

this engrossing novel. The story is told in a series of flashbacks in the form of interior monologues by his manager, his two wives, his mother, and some of the people in his hometown." Library J

"Your reaction to this book is going to be very much a matter of your reaction to country music. If you like it, fine. If not, no. For certain people it may be the only book they read this year." Pub W

Deal, Borden

The advocate. Doubleday 1968 257p $5.95

A novel of a small Mississippi town "and its people—honorable and dishonorable, gentle and cruel, loving and hating, and the story of a quiet man in crisis, a lawyer torn by disturbing conflicts between professional ethics and conscience; and a father yearning for the son whose very existence threatens his marriage and his career." Publisher's note

"The plot, well contrived and skillfully unfolded, makes the book hard to put down, despite inequalities, despite its occasional bathos, or 'corn.' Not merely a good picture of an attorney's daily struggles and problems, it also mirrors the mores of this decade, and is seasoned with interesting if caustic observations on the American character, both men and women." Best Sellers

Dunbar's Cove. Scribner 1957 433p illus o.p. 1970

"Matthew Dunbar's determination to preserve his cove for his family in the face of the T.V.A.'s condemnation of his land for a dam site is further complicated by his daughter's love for the young T.V.A. representative. The story of the Dunbars, who have lived on the cove since the days of the Indians, is told with deep sympathy." Cincinnati

"There is much to be said in the author's favor and without reservation: his characters with few exceptions are people of dignity and simple worth; there are no depraved poor whites and no degenerates. He has written a clean and serious book." N Y Her Trib Books

The least one. Doubleday 1967 360p $5.95

"The story of one depression period year in the life of the proud, previously independent Sword family. Told from the viewpoint of 12-year-old 'Boy' . . . it follows the family through the loss of its farm and its acceptance of tenant farmer status in a tiny southern community, presided over by one 'Senator' Clayton. Their stay is a reluctant one, with Mrs. Sword providing constant reminders of the family's loss of self-reliance, and her husband struggling against hard times to feed and clothe his family. . . . But life isn't all trials and unhappiness for the Swords. There is for Boy the pleasure of romping with his first dog, . . . [and] a beginning appreciation of the ways and needs of other people." Pub W

"The mother and father [are] big, stalwart, kindhearted, and very much alive, thanks to Mr. Deal's sensible and observant spirit. The story tells of poverty, struggle, and innocent triumph, and is full of animals and neighbors and the daily adventures and occasional accidents that make each life separately remarkable." New Yorker

De Balzac, Honoré. See Balzac, Honoré de

De Beauvoir, Simone. See Beauvoir, Simone de

De Camp, L. Sprague

The arrows of Hercules. Doubleday 1965 297p o.p. 1970

This novel is "set in the 4th century B.C. and it is based on the account of Dionysios the Great in 'Diodoros of Sicily.' . . . The adventures of the principal character, Zopyros, are vividly traced from Cumae to Velia and then to Syracuse where he becomes Dionysios's ordnance expert. His further adventures take him to Carthage, Utica, Ortygia, Messana, Motya and Panormos." Library J

"The entire story is told in modern language and is intriguingly woven together to make a most readable novel. Based on historical fact, the author's imagination gives itself free rein to fill in the details, but always with consistency." Best Sellers

The bronze god of Rhodes. Doubleday 1960 406p o.p. 1970

"Chares, a sculptor, tells the story of the plans for erecting the famous Colossus of Rhodes, the siege of the island of Rhodes, [by the Macedonians] and his own mission to Egypt where he meets a dark and fiery maiden. The time is the fourth century B.C." Bk Buyer's Guide

This novel "is a brisk entertainment and an impressively learned one. Chares . . . is an appealing protagonist, but the real hero of the book is the wonderful, exploding ancient world itself, in all its wild vigor and bright splendor." N Y Her Trib Books

De Cervantes, Miguel. See Cervantes, Miguel de

Deeping, Warwick

Sorrell and son. Dufour 1966 408p $3.95

First published 1925 by Knopf

"Beggared by the war and deserted by his wife, Stephen Sorrell, in order to give his son a gentleman's opportunities, humbles his own pride and begins life over as a hotel porter. He climbs from one position to another and ends rich. . . . The book covers twenty years with ease and naturalness; it takes Kit from childhood to a responsible place in medicine, and Sorrell from poverty to rather complacent comfort. . . . The significant problem of the book is the relations between father and son. The pair are human because of the warmth and intimacy of their association, because of its frankness and love, because of the spirit of devotion in the boy." Sat R

Defoe, Daniel

The fortunes and misfortunes of the famous Moll Flanders

Some editions are:
Dutton (Everyman's lib) $2.95
Harcourt (The Harcourt Library of English and American classics) $3.95
Oxford (The World's classics) $2.75 With an introduction by Bonamy Dobrée and a note on the text by Herbert Davis

First published 1722

"Moll went to the bad in early life, was five times married (bigamously or legitimately she little cared), a thief and a harlot, and eventually a penitent. She tells her story with a plain sincerity that both captivates and appals." Bakers's Best

The life, adventures & piracies of the famous Captain Singleton. Dutton 244p (Everyman's lib) $3.25

First published 1720; in this edition, 1906

"The boy Singleton was kidnapped and sold to gipsies, headed a band of mutineers, crossed Africa from Madagascar, and became a successful pirate. This part is made up from authentic tales of travellers, and the detailed account of Central Africa has often been taken as far in advance of the best geographical knowledge of that day." Baker's Best

Roxana, the fortunate mistress. . . . Ed. with an introduction by Jane Jack. Oxford 1964 333p (Oxford English novels) $4.80

"Or, A history of the life and vast variety of fortunes of Mademoiselle de Beleau, afterwards called the Countess de Winselsheim in Germany, being the person known by the name of the Lady Roxana in the time of Charles II." Subtitle

First published 1724

This story "traces autobiographically the rise and fall of a woman led morally astray by circumstance. In the time of Charles II, Roxana, of French origin, married in England 'a fool' of a husband, who leaves her destitute after eight years with five children. Her only friend and ally is Amy, her maid. She becomes the mistress of her landlord, and her maid each has a child by him. This benefactor is set upon by

FICTION CATALOG
EIGHTH EDITION

Defoe, Daniel—*Continued*

robbers in France, however, and slain. Roxana takes up with a French prince and is richly rewarded. She tours Italy with him. This connection is followed by other amours in Holland and in England. At last Roxana married a kindly Dutch merchant who had formerly been her lover and their first son is legitimized." Haydn. Thesaurus of Book Digests

De Hartog, Jan. See Hartog, Jan de

Deighton, Len

The billion dollar brain; a novel. Putnam 1966 312p $5.95

A British secret agent reports in an "offhand, jocular manner how he was sent to Finland, found the body of a murdered commentator, and became a part of the computer based organization of a wealthy Texan who planned to start a new Russian revolution." Bk Buyer's Guide

"The book is superb for several reasons: the fertile plot—you begin by being amused at the preposterous capabilities of the Brain, then stop to wonder if it is not merely heralding tomorrow's standard equipment. Then, aside from the plot, which has settings in London, Helsinki, Leningrad, New York and Texas, the characters are drawn with classical craftsmanship and the dialogue keeps pace. Here's a tale that will grip you from beginning to end." Best Sellers

An expensive place to die; a novel. Putnam 1967 252p boards $5.95

First published 1966 in Germany

An English agent investigates Monsieur Datt's clinic in Paris which is the center of an international drama, involving Chinese hydrogen bombs, hallucinogenic drugs, institutes for sex research, blackmail, murder and diplomacy. (Publisher)

The author "offers crisp prose, fast action, vivid scenes and an anonymous agent-narrator whose attitude is cynical, professional and completely of the 1960's." N Y Times Bk R

Funeral in Berlin; a novel

Some editions are:
Putnam $5.95
Watts, F. Large type edition $7.95 A Keith Jennison book

First published 1964

"A cocky and humorous British agent is sent to Berlin to expedite the defection of a Communist-held scientist and enters the bizarre world of double and triple cross with a German contact man and a Russian colonel. The story even has footnotes and needs them." Bk Buyer's Guide

The author "writes well of the circles within circles at international crossroads where enemies can be closer than friends, and where horror and humor follow the agent." Library J

The Ipcress file. Simon & Schuster 1963 [c1962] 287p boards $3.95

First published 1962 in England

In this spy novel, a British secret agent tells "of his mission to capture and return a defecting bio-chemist, a job that takes him across the world into very rough company." Bk Buyer's Guide

"The action, brutality, deaths and the slight bit of romance which is allowed to seep into such stories, are all present; but so are the weaknesses of our C.I.A., Scotland Yard and various other agencies. No one is spared the needle of subtle ridicule, but the author still tells a plausible story which holds your attention throughout." Best Sellers

De La Mare, Colin

(comp.) They walk again; an anthology of ghost stories; with an introduction by Walter De La Mare. Foreword by William Lyon Phelps. Dutton 1931 469p o.p. 1970

Analyzed in Short Story Index

Contents: Keeping his promise, by A. Blackwood; Electric king, by Lord Dunsany; Ghost ship, by R. Middleton; Tough tussle, by A. Bierce; Afterward, by E. Wharton; Powers of the air, by J. D. Beresford; Father Girdlestone's tale, by R. H. Benson; Magic formula,

by L. P. Jacks; Visitor from down under, by L. P. Hartley; Caterpillars, by E. F. Benson; Voice in the night, by W. H. Hodgson; Beckoning fair one, by O. Onions; On the Brighton Road, by R. Middleton; Story of a disappearance and an appearance, by M. R. James; All Hallows, by W. De La Mare; Monkey's paw, by W. W. Jacobs; Green tea, by J. S. Le Fanu; Wood of the dead, by A. Blackwood

De La Mare, Walter

Collected tales; chosen, and with an introduction by Edward Wagenknecht. Knopf 1950 xxi, 467p o.p. 1970

Analyzed in Short Story Index

"Allegories, spectral romances, and introspective narratives written for adults." Library J

Contents: The riddle; The almond tree; In the forest; The talisman; Miss Duveen; The bowl; The tree; Ideal craftsman; Seaton's aunt; Lispet, Lispett and Vaine; Three friends; Willows; Missing; The connoisseur; The nap; All Hallows; The wharf; The orgy; Cape Race; Physic; The trumpet; The creatures; The vats; Strangers and pilgrims

Memoirs of a midget. Knopf 1922 436p o.p. 1970

"The recollections and impressions of Miss M., a perfectly formed little creature so small that the domestic cat knocks her down in brushing past her, but possessed of an incisive wit, and the most delicate and sensitive appreciation of beauty." Cleveland

"She will live in criticism as a masterpiece of characterization." Sat R

De La Motte-Fouque, Friedrich. See La Motte-Fouque, F. H. K. de

De La Roche, Mazo

The building of Jalna. Little 1944 366p $5.50

"In this—the first volume, chronologically, in the Jalna series—Miss de la Roche goes back to the year 1850. She shows us Adeline, the impulsive young bride with her Irish temper and her blazing loyalty—and handsome Captain Whiteoak who sold his comission in order to migrate to the virgin country on the shore of Lake Ontario. She shows us, also, the building of Jalna itself—the skating parties and the swimming—the jealousies, the fierce attachments and the humor." Huntting

Followed chronologically by: Morning at Jalna

Centenary at Jalna. Little 1958 342p $5.50

Sequel chronologically: Variable winds at Jalna

"Traces the activities of the Whiteoak clan in the mid-fifties, a period climaxed by the one-hundredth anniversary celebration of Jalna, the oldest of the family residences. An alienated brother, a neurotic child, and a reluctant bride-to-be play stellar roles in an agreeably related though episodic tale of people to whom family ties and traditions are all-important." Booklist

Finch's fortune. Little 1931 443p $5.95

Sequel chronologically to: Whiteoaks of Jalna

"Young Finch, having come of age, begins the spending of the fortune left him by his malicious old grandmother and Alayne continues her efforts to make a place for herself in the clan life." Booklist

Followed by: Master of Jalna

Jalna. Little 1927 347p $5.95

Sequel chronologically to: Whiteoak brothers

"Jalna is the family home of the Whiteoaks. Gathered under its roof are representatives of each generation from the time the grandparents drifted to Canada via England from India and there built their homestead on a lavish scale. Rennie, 37, is the present head of the household which includes Gran—a formidable old lady of 99—two uncles, an aunt, an elderly sister, and four half-brothers. An affectionate, warring group of strong personalities from the old lady down to Wakefield, the youngest, aged nine. Two of the boys marry and bring their wives home. The coming of the second bride, an

110

De La Roche, Mazo—*Continued*

American, affects each one of the clan for happiness or pain; and conversely, for Alayne the months at Jalna are crowded with sharp experiences of bitterness or delight and when she goes, the problem of her love for Rennie and his for her is only partially solved." Book Rev Digest

Followed chronologically by: Whiteoaks of Jalna

Mary Wakefield. Little 1949 337p $5.95

Sequel, chronologically, to: Morning at Jalna
"This eleventh volume in the Jalna series is the second in point of time. The setting is Jalna in 1893, and the heroine is Mary Wakefield, the beautiful English girl engaged by Ernest Whiteoak to be governess for Philip's motherless children. Adeline in her sixties is still able to put on a good show, and does it when Philip wants to marry Mary. When Philip stands out against his mother, Adeline gives in gracefully, for once. The book ends with the wedding." Book Rev Digest

Followed chronologically by: Young Renny

The master of Jalna. Little 1933 379p $5.50

Sequel to: Finch's fortune
This book in the Whiteoaks saga "takes up the story after the death of Gran in 1932 and carries it to the summer of 1933. Renny, as head of the house, attempts to carry on the traditions of Captain Philip Whiteoak, his grandfather, even tho there is practically no money left. When the book closes Renny has, by an almost superhuman effort, managed to keep the estate intact, and he, Alayne and young Adeline are alone at Jalna." Book Rev Digest

Followed chronologically by: Whiteoak harvest

Morning at Jalna. Little 1960 298p $5.50

A sequel, chronologically, to: The building of Jalna
"This book is set in the time of the Civil War, when Adeline, who was a grandmother in the first book in the series [to appear] was a handsome young matron with four small children. The book is largely concerned with the effect upon her [Canadian] household of a family of Southerners, members of an underground Confederate resistance movement, who came to stay in the household." Pub W

Followed chronologically by: Mary Wakefield

Renny's daughter. Little 1951 376p $5.95

A sequel, chronologically, to: Return to Jalna
This Jalna story "concerns: Renny's eighteen year old daughter Adeline, her trip to Ireland and first, frustrated romance. . . . Renny's resentment at encroaching suburban developments, and his indignant fight to stave them off; and old Uncle Ernest's death. . . . It will be welcomed by Jalna enthusiasts, but perhaps unappreciated by others." Library J

Followed chronologically by: Variable winds at Jalna

Return to Jalna. Little 1946 462p $5.50

A sequel, chronologically, to: Wakefield's course
The tenth book of the Jalna series celebrates the return to Jalna of the Whiteoaks who had been off to World War II

Followed chronologically by: Renny's daughter

Variable winds at Jalna. Little 1954 359p $5.95

A sequel, chronologically, to: Renny's daughter
"Adeline's Irish lover arrives and she plans a double wedding with her cousin; old Nicholas dies, leaving various legacies; TV comes to Jalna; Finch and Meg find new loves; and Renny emerges triumphantly from the danger of losing his daughter to an uncomfortably alien son-in-law." Booklist

Followed chronologically by: Centenary at Jalna

Wakefield's course. Little 1941 406p $5.95

A sequel, chronologically, to: Whiteoak harvest
"The eighth book in the saga of the Whiteoaks of Jalna covers about a year and a half, from the spring of 1939 to the fall of 1940. Renny is prosperous again and wins the Grand National with his horse, Johnny the Bird. Wakefield is a successful actor, and it is his love

story and its bitter ending, which holds the center of the stage. The book closes with Wakefield's winning of the Distinguished Flying Cross for distinguished service in the R.A.F." Book Rev Digest

Followed chronologically by: Return to Jalna

Whiteoak brothers: Jalna—1923. Little 1953 307p $5.50

A sequel, chronologically, to: Whiteoak heritage
"The year is 1923, just a year earlier than the events which took place in the first novel of the series, Jalna. In the new book there is the same spaciousness of outdoor life, the same concentration on family relations within the old house. One after another, the members of the family are caught up in the fever of speculation, while serenely in the midst of all this the young love of Piers and Pheasant unfolds." McClurg. Book News

Followed chronologically by: Jalna

Whiteoak harvest. Little 1936 378p $5.50

"This follows chronologically on the heels of 'The Master of Jalna,' but it can be read as a complete story in itself. Renny and his wife figure as the principal characters. There are marital rearrangements; the old uncles come back to the family home; and young Wakefield, after a trial at monastery life, also returns to Jalna." Lenrow. Reader's Guide to Prose Fiction

Followed chronologically by: Wakefield's course

Whiteoak heritage. Little 1940 325p $5.95

A sequel, chronologically, to: Young Renny
"The fortunes of the Whiteoak family are followed during post-war days. Renny returns from the war to take over the estate and to raise his young brothers. He finds Meg still single and unforgiving. Pheasant a sensitive child, and Eden indulging in his first romance with an older woman, whose frustrations bring about a melodramatic end to the book. His own love affair is unfortunate." Booklist

Followed chronologically by: The Whiteoak brothers

Whiteoaks of Jalna. Little 1929 423p $5.95

"A continuation of 'Jalna,' the novel about the Whiteoaks family. In this story young Finch, the awkward, misunderstood, but musical genius of the family, is the center of interest. A climax is reached when the eccentric old grandmother leaves, at her death, all her fortune to Finch." Book Rev Digest

Followed by: Finch's fortune

Young Renny (Jalna-1906) Little 1935 324p $5.95

A sequel, chronologically, to: Mary Wakefield
"The continuity of the Jalna chronicle is broken in this story to hark back to the time when Renny is yet a boy and old Adeline, formidable, full of vitality, a mere eighty. The customary Whiteoak quarrels flare with more than usual violence because of the presence of Malahide Court who ingratiates himself with his cousin Adeline, and antagonizes everyone else. Renny's efforts to make life unpleasant for their guest afford some amusing incidents, and no story of Jalna is ever lacking in drama." N Y Libraries

Followed chronologically by: Whiteoak heritage

Del Castillo, Michel

Child of our time; tr. from the French by Peter Green. Knopf 1958 281p boards $4.95

Originally published 1957 in France
Like the author, Tanguy, the boy in this story, is half-Spanish, half-French. His mother's republicanism during the Spanish Civil War forces them into exile in France. There his father betrays his mother to the police and later Tanguy is interned in a Nazi concentration camp during World War II. After the war Tanguy eventually finds kindness and help in a Jesuit institution in Spain. (Publisher)

"Eloquently portrays a boy's great courage and strength in the face of man's inhumanity. It warrants inclusion in large fiction collections despite its limited appeal." Library J

Del Castillo, Michel—*Continued*

The disinherited; tr. from the French by Humphrey Hare. Knopf 1960 [c1959] 273p o.p. 1970

Originally published 1958 in France. This translation first published in England 1959 with title: The billsticker
"Novel about the Spanish civil war and the shattering effect which it had on many Spaniards regardless of what part they had in it. The story centers around Olny, a young man brought up in the squalid surroundings of Madrid's poorest section. Drawn to the Communist party as the result of his own experiences and in the belief that it holds out the best hope of a better life for underprivileged people, Olny is disillusioned as the war goes on, with increasing savagery on both sides." Springf'd Republican

The seminarian. Tr. by George Robinson. Holt [1970 c1969] 134p boards $4.95

SBN 03-072505-4
First published 1967 in French
A novel set in a Spanish seminary. "Its protagonist, Gerardo is an introspective youth who suffers a spiritual crisis brought on from doubts stimulated by the death of a brother seminarian, and by homosexual infatuation." Library J
"There is compassion in this novella, a sensitive, honest and moving story of young people's doubts and fears in a rigid, authoritarian society." Pub W

Delderfield, R. F.

The Avenue. Simon & Schuster [1969 c1964] 1032p $8.50

Contains: The dreaming suburb and The Avenue goes to war, originally published in 1958. First published 1964 in England as a double novel with title: The Avenue story
It "is the story of some 20 people who lived in a South London suburb from 1919 to 1947. While the experiences of each during the war and the horrors of the blitz, rationing and the general strike are described, the central focus is on Jim Carver, a man determined that the sacrifices of the Great War will not have been made in vain, that his country will not make the same mistakes again." Library J
"Mr. Delderfield's observation of his fellow-countrymen is incisive but respectful. He . . . recounts their lives with insight, never sentimental sympathy, and perfect grammar. The characters are as individualistic as the author himself, and just as life-size. . . . However irritating and irrelevant jingoism may seem today, it was the true temper of the war years. Mr. Delderfield has captured this atmosphere so convincingly that the reader is led to wonder if the author might not still subscribe to it himself. . . . 'The Avenue' is a masterpiece of intelligent observation and articulate expression, a mildly dated British Manifesto." Christian Science Monitor

The Avenue goes to war
In Delderfield, R. F. The Avenue p451-1032

The dreaming suburb
In Delderfield, R. F. The Avenue p13-446

The green gauntlet. Simon & Schuster 1968 475p $5.95

A sequel to: A horseman riding by
This story "distills the essence of the English experience of the last three decades as it returns to the valley of Shallowford and to Squire Paul Craddock as he confronts the devastations of the war and the crises and uncertanties of the post war years with the moral values inherited from a more self-confident past." Am News of Bks
"The author handles narrative and descriptive writing very well and the reader watches as if he were a spectator, the activities of the characters in their everyday life as well as in the various crises. . . . He watches the events, he sees the Valley; but, best of all, he knows the characters, because this skillfull writer understands how to put flesh on their bones and thoughts into their heads and how to make them grow and develop over the years." Best Sellers

A horseman riding by. Simon & Schuster [1967 c1966] 1150p $7.50

First published 1966 in England
"In 1902, a wounded young soldier back from the Boer War, comes into a substantial inheritance and purchases a rundown Devonshire estate, consisting of seven tenancies. The story concerns the revitalization of the property by the new owner, the vicissitudes of the seven families that are his tenants and the richly fulfilled life of the Squire, himself, and his family." Pub W
"A full-bodied and satisfyingly romantic, nostalgic story for readers of well-crafted escapist fiction. . . . Delderfield vividly sketches a vast cast and their interrelationships and evokes countryside and moors, all in semi-realistic, semi-idyllic vein." Booklist
Followed by: The green gauntlet

Mr Sermon; a novel. Simon & Schuster [1970 c1963] 318p $5.95

SBN 671-20371-1
First published 1963 in England with title: The Spring madness of Mr Sermon
"A middle-aged English school teacher, a little stuffy and comfortably settled in a second-rate school and a placid marriage, suddenly breaks out of his shell one spring day and sets out to wander over England, tasting the long repressed joys of freedom." News of Bks
"Here are just the right ingredients for a tried and true adult love story with more substance than usual. . . . People and places are ones readers will find convincing, amusing, and wholesome. Heartily recommended for public libraries." Library J

De Maupassant, Guy. See Maupassant, Guy de

De Montherlant, Henry. See Montherlant, Henry de

Dennis, Nigel

Cards of identity. Vanguard 1955 369p $4.95

"The story of an Identity Club, which was founded in order to create and define new personalities for its members, and which went so far as to take in strangers, destroy their faint and inadequate characters, and impose new and more suitable identities upon them. . . . At the annual meeting of the Club, these transformations are much admired. Its leading members read autobiographical documents telling of similar metamorphoses, and finally witness a play on the same topic: disguise, deception, transmogrification." Book of the Month Club News
"The most considerable attempt at a serious and sizeable satire that we have had for some years. It is witty, full of comic invention—not all of it on the same level, and its is packed with fundamental brain-work." New Statesman & Nation

Dennis, Patrick

Around the world with Auntie Mame. Harcourt 1958 286p o.p. 1970

Sequel to: Auntie Mame
Auntie Mame's adventures around the world in 1937 are recorded by her irreverent nephew Patrick. Here she is [engaged in such activities as] starring in the Folies-Bergère in Paris and being presented at Court in London." Huntting
"There are a few authentic laughs, but the spontaneous and sustained lunacy of 'Auntie Mame' is conspicuously lacking. Instead, the straining for effect is more noticeable than the effect. This will not, however, influence the initial demand. All fiction collections will want." Library J

Auntie Mame; an irreverent escapade. Vanguard 1955 280p $4.95

"A series of extravagant adventures in the life of a flagrantly capricious but charming madcap of precocious personality, parodying the Most Unforgettable Character sketches in 'Readers' Digest.' Auntie Mame had a [chameleonic] . . . propensity to adapt herself to a variety of difficult situations with enchanting insouciance. The escapades are related in hilarious strain, clever style and ready wit. The humor, broad at times, is coupled with satire

Dennis, Patrick—*Continued*

on phony 'avant garde' intellectuals, racial prejudices as evident in suburban communities, and snobism in general. Highly entertaining for adult readers." Library J

Followed by: Around the world with Auntie Mame

Denniston, Elinore. See Foley, Rae

De Onís, Harriet

(ed.) Spanish stories and tales. Knopf 1954 270p o.p. 1970

Analyzed in Short Story Index

"Twenty-three fictional pieces translated from the Spanish. They were written in the Old World and the New, and cover in time a period from the thirteenth century to the present. Contains a historical introduction and paragraphs about each of the entries." Book Rev Digest

Contents: My sister Antonia, by R. del Valle-Inclan; The secret miracle, by J. L. Borges; The call of the blood, by M. de Cervantes; The cock of Socrates, by L. Alas; Saint Manuel Bueno, Martyr, by M. de Unamuno; The honor of his house, by C. W. Ospina; Sister Aparicion, by E. Pardo Bazan; Life and death of a hero, by A. Cancela; The fatherland, by H. Quiroga; The man who married an ill-tempered wife, by D. J. Manuel; The dark plight of Ramon Yendia, by L. Novas Calvo; The old ranch, by R. Güiraldes; The cabbages of the cemetery, by P. Baroja; The heart's reason, by E. Mallea; Two cooing doves, by R. Palma; The prophecy, by P. A. de Alarcon; I Puritani, by A. Palacio Valdes, A man of character, by R. Gallegos; Coyote 13, by A. Souto Alabarce; Ashes for the wind, by H. Tellez; The salt sea, by B. Subercaseaux

Derleth, August

The casebook of Solar Pons; with a foreword by Vincent Starrett and a monograph by Michael Harrison. Mycroft & Moran 1965 281p maps $5

Analyzed in Short Story Index

"A collection of 12 tales . . . which reverently imitates the adventures of Sherlock Holmes." Pub W

Contents: The adventure of the Sussex Archers; The adventure of the haunted library; The adventure of the fatal glance; The adventure of the intarsia box; The adventure of the spurious Tamerlane; The adventure of the china cottage; The adventure of the Ascot scandal; The adventure of the crouching dog; The adventure of the missing huntsman; The adventure of the amateur philologist; The adventure of the whispering knights; The adventure of the innkeeper's clerk

Mr Fairlie's final journey. Mycroft & Moran 1968 131p $3.50

"Jonas Fairlie set out from Frome, Somerset for London—but he never reached there. When his body was found not far out of Frome, Solar Pons's address was discovered concealed in the lining of his hat. What was the problem he intended to lay before Pons? And who had killed him? These were the related puzzles laid before Solar Pons within hours of the discovery that Fairlie had been murdered." Publisher's note

(ed.) The other side of the moon; selected and with an introduction. Pellegrini & Cudahy 1949 461p o.p. 1970

Partially analyzed in Short Story Index

Contents: The appearance of man, by J. D. Beresford [a play]; The star, by H. G. Wells; The thing on Outer Shoal, by P. S. Miller; The strange drug of Dr Caber, by Lord Dunsany; The world of Wulkins, by F. B. Long; The city of the Singing Flame, by C. A. Smith; Beyond the wall of sleep, by H. P. Lovecraft; The devil of East Lupton, by M. Leinster; Conquerors' isle, by N. Bond; Something from above, by D. Wandrei; Pillar of fire, by R. Bradbury; The monster, by G. Kersh; Symbiosis, by W. F. Jenkins; The cure, by L. Padgett; Vault of the beast, by A. E. Van Vogt; The earth men, by R. Bradbury; Original sin, by S. F. Wright; Spiro, by E. F. Russell; Memorial, by T. Sturgeon; Resurrection, by A. E. Van Vogt

(ed.) Strange ports of call; selected and with an introduction. Pellegrini & Cudahy 1948 393p o.p. 1970

Analyzed in Short Story Index

"Twenty good stories reprinted from books and magazines with accent on the weird tale rather than on what the avid reader calls straight science-fiction." Booklist

Contents: The cunning of he beast, by N. Bond; The worm, by D. H. Keller; Crystal bullet, oy D. Wandrei; Thing from outside, by G. A. England; At the mountains of madness, by H. P. Lovecraft; Mars on the ether, by Lord Dunsany; The God-box, by H. Wandrei; Mr Bauer and the atoms, by F. Leiber; The crystal egg, by H. G. Wells; John Jones' dollar, by H. S. Keeler; Call him demon, by H. Kuttner; Master of the asteroid, by C. A. Smith; Guest in the house, by F. B. Long; The lost street, by C. Jacobi; Forgotten, by P. S. Miller; Far centaurus, by A. E. Van Vogt; Thunder and roses, by T. Sturgeon; The green hills of earth, by R. A. Heinlein; Blunder, by P. Wylie; The million year picnic, by R. Bradbury

Dermoût, Maria

The ten thousand things; a novel. Tr. from the Dutch by Hans Koningsberger. Simon & Schuster 1958 244p o.p. 1970

Original Dutch edition published 1956

"Deals largely with the family history of an aging Dutch woman who seeks refuge from the sorrows of her unhappy marriage by returning to the scene of her childhood, a remote garden on a small estate in the Spice Islands." Pub W

"The book seems no more to tell a story than do a mountain, a wilderness, the sea, a flower in a deep wood. It is more like a mood that comes without warning, wrapped in mystery. But violence is no stranger in its pages." Chicago Sunday Tribune

Der Post, Laurens van. See Van der Post, Laurens

Der Zee, John van. See Van der Zee, John

De Saint Exupéry, Antoine de. See Saint Exupéry, Antoine de

Destuches, Louis Ferdinand. See Céline, Louis Ferdinand

De Unamuno y Jugo, Miguel. See Unamuno y Jugo, Miguel de

De Vigny, Alfred. See Vigny, Alfred de

De Vries, Peter

The blood of the lamb. Little 1961 246p boards $4.95

This novel "traces the life of a rebellious young man who searches for a belief in religion but finds that he can only rely upon human strength and human courage when his life is shattered by grief. In making his point, Mr. DeVries has drawn his hero's life as unusually hard. When he is a child, his beloved brother dies. He is unlucky in love. His father goes mad. His wife commits suicide. Finally, in scenes that are really very painful to read, his daughter dies a miserable death." Pub W

"A story told with such mastery over the resources of English it would be an event in any season. Moreover De Vries writes of people with such love and insight no reader could withhold for long the impulse to involve himself fully with them. This book will trouble many readers but it is a book that should be read and pondered by everyone who recognizes in a forthright challenge to the easy assumptions and affirmations men live by, the substance of great literature." Best Sellers

De Vries, Peter—*Continued*

The cat's pajamas & Witch's milk; two novels. Little 1968 303p boards $5.95

Two novels "about human unhappiness. "The Cat's Pajamas' concerns Hank Tattersall, college professor who rebels against the hypocrisy of his world, gets one job after another, each one worse than its predecessor, with a sort of wry satisfaction with his downfall. In 'Witch's Milk' Tillie Shilepsky marries Peter Seltzer, in spite of her first decision, 'He's out,' and suffers for a while from his compulsion to clown, but eventually finds fulfillment in being needed." Bk Buyer's Guide

"Into Peter DeVries' unique world of idiosyncrasy have come some more inimitable eccentrics with unbelievable names to perpetuate a tradition of pseudo-humor and pseudo-pathos. Readers of DeVries' books who have learned to relish the bizarre will not be disappointed in his two short novels." Best Sellers

Comfort me with apples. Little 1956 280p $5.75

"Marriage and family responsibilites force young Chick Swallow, former cynic and rebel, to accept a job as lovelorn editor on a small-town newspaper. Involvement with some of his less inhibited correspondents leads to threats of blackmail and lawsuits. Written in the tradition of the French bedroom farce, the tale ends on a commendable moral note." Booklist

Let me count the ways. Little 1965 307p boards $5

"A story of a Polish-American family in the midwest. The first narrator is the father, a furniture mover, married to a religious fanatic. He endures a 12-year hangover when he thinks he has disgraced the family. The second narrator is the son, whose story revolves around a split personality caused by a religious mother and an anti-religious father. Mr. De Vries is actually writing a serious commentary on the foibles of man." Library J

"It is when things run away from Mr. De Vries' studied control that his genius, almost against his will, makes itself felt. For his humor has a kind of headlong compulsiveness to it. . . . Farce snowballing with a certain attendant horror-Kafka crossed with the Keystone Kops—this is what one reads Mr. De Vries for." Christian Science Monitor

Reuben, Reuben. Little 1964 435p $5.95

A satirical novel set in suburban Connecticut. The author "tells his story through three separate characters. . . . The first is Spofford, an old chicken-farmer of literary bent who breaks into the arty-party crowd of the rich and the bored and loses his substance to veneer. The second is the poet McGland, an alcoholic, wenching Welshman who bases his life on his sexuality, hinges his sexuality to his four remaining upper teeth and crumbles into disaster when he loses one of them. The third is the writer-actor Mopworth, who has a hard time keeping his sanity and his manhood because of the women—masculine in their thinking and furiously jealous because of the inescapable physical proof of his sex—who keep telling him he is really a homosexual." America

"By turns satirical and somber as it makes its low-keyed commentary on love, sex, the arts and an area of America in transition from old Yankee to new exurbanite, this is good if not superior De Vries—intelligent, spirited, individual as a signature, even when, as it seems to one reader, it tends to diffuseness." Book of the Month Club News

The tents of wickedness. Little 1959 276p o.p. 1970

A "farce in which a number of misguided residents of New York and Connecticut struggle to live like characters in various twentieth century novels. . . . Mr DeVries treats his readers to a barrage of clever parodies of the styles and ideas of D. H. Lawrence, Marquand, Faulkner, Joyce and other writers. The story [line concerns] . . . a conservative newspaper editior pursued by a romantic creature called Sweetie Appleyard." Pub W

Some of the characters have previously appeared in: Comfort me with apples

The tunnel of love. Little 1954 246p $4.95

"A satirical account of the complications that ensue in the lives of two couples when one sets out to adopt a baby and the other pair is called upon to vouch for their suitability as parents." Pub W

In "one of the funniest novels to come along in any season, [the author] uses his puns and fantasies to mask a sometimes frighteningly keen observation of suburban and creative mores in one of those southern Connecticut communities populated by the Babbitts of Bohemia. . . . About the only beef I have with the book is its totally unnecessary use of a flashback technique when it could have been told just as amusingly and more simply for the reader in chronological sequence." Sat R

The vale of laughter. Little 1967 352p boards $5.95

Joe Sandwich, "the hero of the piece, is a clown, a card, a comedian, the life of the party, an impractical joker. . . . Part One, narrated by Sandwich, takes us through his marriage and his life as a stockbroker who requires Dramamine at the sight of the tape. Part Two, narrated by Wally Hines, a philosophy professor who once had Sandwich in a class, takes the Sandwiches through summers on Lake Superior to Joe's bizarre death on a bicycle. . . . The interesting lives of Sandwich and Hines provide the novel with its special kind of cut." N Y Times Bk R

Witch's milk

In De Vries, P. The cat's pajamas & Witch's milk p187-303

De Water, Frederic F. van. See Van de Water, Frederic F.

Dewey, Thomas B.

(ed.) Mystery Writers of America. Sleuths and consequences

De Wohl, Louis

Citadel of God; a novel of Saint Benedict. Lippincott 1959 352p $4.50

This novel "follows Benedictus from his student days in turbulent sixth-century Rome through his years as a hermit and his work in establishing religious communities which were truly citadels of God in the Dark Ages. Interwoven with Benedictus's story is that of his former pupil, Peter, a rich and ambitious politician who becomes tragically involved in a fierce battle for power among Romans, Goths and Byzantines." Publisher's note

The glorious folly; a novel of the time of St Paul. Lippincott 1957 384p o.p. 1970

This novel "begins in the year 36, A.D. and covers some 25 years. With two exceptions, the author notes, all the main characters and events are historical. . . . He uses biblical sources and develops the story mainly through a fictional version of Cassius Longinus and his daughter Acte. The story begins with Saul's zeal for the Law, his role in the stoning of Stephen, and his conversion. These events, as well as his appeal to Caesar at the end of the book, are told in some detail. However, the major part of the story concerns political intrigue in Rome and in Palestine." Library J

The joyful beggar; a novel of St Francis of Assisi. Lippincott 1958 315p o.p. 1970

This is the story of Francis Bernardone, the joyful beggar and founder of the Franciscan Order, and of Roger, Count of Vandria who saved the life of Francis in the war between Assisi and Perugia. Roger learned almost too late that all his acts of courage and years of loyalty to a royal master counted as nothing against the rescue of that boy. (Publisher)

The last crusader. Lippincott 1956 448p o.p. 1970

"A novel based on the life of Don Juan [John] of Austria, who spent his childhood unaware that he was the son of Emperor Charles V of Spain. Recognized in his father's will, he became a favorite at the court of Philip II, and

De Wohl, Louis—*Continued*

won lasting, world-wide fame for his piety, courage, and his tremendous victories over the Moors and the Turks." Retail Bookseller

"A well-patterned, many-charactered novel not limited in appeal to Catholic readers." Booklist

Lay siege to heaven; a novel of Saint Catherine of Siena. Lippincott 1961 [c1960] 315p boards $4.50

A fictional biography of Catherine Benincasa, later St Catherine of Siena, the daughter of a 14th century Siena dyer, who entered a Dominican order at an early age despite parental opposition. This story emphasizes the prominent role Catherine played in bringing an end to the civil war between the Italian city-states and in persuading Pope Gregory XI, the seventh of the Avignon popes, to return to Rome

The quiet light. Lippincott 1956 [c1950] 317p $3.95

A reprint of the title first published 1950

"Historical novel based on the life of St Thomas Aquinas. The Emperor Frederick II is one of the chief characters and the life in castle and monastery in the thirteenth century forms the background." Book Rev Digest

"The attempt to give a compendious account of St. Thomas's philosophy in the course of a novel is an ambitious one; but the author has reached a compromise whereby the average reader will probably be edified without too great a strain." Times (London) Lit Sup

Set all afire; a novel of St Francis Xavier. Lippincott 1953 280p o.p. 1970

"A fictionalized biography of the Roman Catholic priest St. Francis Xavier who . . . became a follower of St. Ignatius Loyola. . . . Recognizing the unusual devotion and power of the young priest, Loyola sent him to the Orient to spread Christianity in India, Japan, and China. The novel describes his travels from Portugal to India and Japan and his attempt to reach China, and portrays the mighty spirit of this simple man as he ministered to the sick and the poor, teaching his message through actions as well as words. Inspirational reading with special Roman Catholic appeal." Booklist

The spear. Lippincott 1955 383p o.p. 1970

"Set in the days of the Crucifixion and centered upon the Roman soldier who thrust his spear into Jesus' side at Golgotha, this religious novel begins in Rome, where the young centurion Cassius Longinus, victimized by political corruption, loses belief in everything except revenge upon his enemies. It ends in Jerusalem when, after witnessing the resurrection, Cassius surrenders the spear, symbol of his unbelief and hatred, to the power of Christ's compassionate love." Booklist

"A story similar in subject to 'The Robe.' Filled with bitterness, brutality, romance, and redemption, this story will appeal to readers of historical fiction with a religious flavor." Library J

Dick, R. A.

The ghost and Mrs Muir. Ziff-Davis 1945 174p o.p. 1970

"Whimsical tale of an English family in which a benevolent ghost plays a starring role. Lucy Muir, with her two small children, moves to Gull Cottage, which is haunted by the voice of Captain Gregg, its former sea-captain owner. Through thick and thin, the ghost watches over Lucy and helps her solve her most difficult problems—and, with his salty humor and down-to-earth wisdom, finally rescues Lucy from her life of seclusion and shows her the way to happiness." Huntting

"In her first novel, Mrs. R. A. Dick . . . writes readable, frolicsome fantasy. She succeeds in maintaining the illusion of a 'human' ghost, and life in a haunted house follows a lively course." N Y Times Bk R

Dickens, Charles

y Barnaby Rudge

Some editions are:
Collins $1.95
Dodd (Great illustrated classics) $5.50 Foreword by May Lamberton Becker

Dutton (Everyman's lib) $2.95
Oxford (The New Oxford Illustrated Dickens) $5 With 76 illustrations by George Cattermole and Hablot K. Browne 'Phiz' and an introduction by Kathleen Tillotson
St Martins $4.25 With illustrations by Phiz; and an introduction by Charles Dickens the younger

First published in 1841

"An historical novel giving a lurid tableau of the orgies and incendiarism of the 'No Popery' riots in 1780. Lord George Gordon is an actor, and the principal events are founded on fact. Inter-twined is a private story with some characteristic traits, e.g. in the Vardens, the Willets, Miggs, and Simon Tappertit." Baker's Best

y Best short stories; collected, with an introduction by Edwin Valentine Mitchell. Scribner 1947 620p illus o.p. 1970

Analyzed in Short Story Index

"Nineteen of Dickens' best short stories—profusely illustrated with the original drawings of Cruikshank, Maclise, Leech and Phiz." Huntting

Contents: The Great Winglebury duel; The wreck of the "Golden Mary"; The story of the pagman's uncle; The perils of certain English prisoners; The holly-tree; Mr Pickwick's tale; Mugby Junction; The haunted house; Holiday romance; Horatio Sparkins; Hunted down; The seven poor travellers; The battle of life; Going into society; Mrs Lirriper's lodgings; Mrs Lirriper's legacy; A Christmas carol; The chimes; The cricket on the hearth

y Bleak House

Some editions are:
Collins $1.95
Dodd (Great illustrated classics) $5.50 Introduction by John Cournos
Dutton (Everyman's lib) $2.95
Oxford (The New Oxford Illustrated Dickens) $5 With 40 illustrations by 'Phiz' and an introduction by Sir Osbert Sitwell
St Martins $4.25

First published 1853

"The heroine is Esther Summerson or rather Esther Hawdon, the illegitimate child of Lady Dedlock and Captain Hawdon. Esther, whom Lady Dedlock believes dead, is the ward of Mr. Jarndyce of the interminable case of Jarndyce and Jarndyce in Chancery Court, and lives with him at Bleak House. Lord Dedlock's lawyer, Mr. Tulkinghorn, gets wind of Lady Dedlock's secret past; and when Tulkinghorn is murdered, Lady Dedlock is suspected, disappears and is later found dead." University Handbook for Readers and Writers

Charles Dickens' Best stories; ed and with an introduction by Morton Dauwen Zabel. Hanover House 1959 669p front o.p. 1970

Partially analyzed in Short Story Index

Contents: The streets—morning; The streets—night; Shops and their tenants; Scotland Yard; London recreations; The river; Early coaches; Omnibuses; Ginshops; Criminal courts; Christmas dinner; Christmas carol (1843); The chimes; Cricket on the hearth (1846); Battle of life; Haunted man and the ghost's bargain; Holly-tree; Somebody's luggage; Mrs Lirriper's lodgings; Doctor Marigold; Mugby Junction; Hunted down; George Silverman's explanation; Detective police; Three "detective" anecdotes; Pair of gloves; Artful touch, The sofa; To be read at dusk; Child's dream of a star

y A Christmas carol

Some editions are:
Doubleday $3.95 Facsimile copy of the first edition published in 1843. Illustrated by John Leech
Lippincott $3.50 Illustrated by Arthur Rackham
Macmillan (N Y) $2.95
Watts, F. (Illustrated editions) $2.95
Watts, F. $7.95 Large type edition complete and unabridged. A Keith Jennison book

Written in 1843

"This Christmas story of nineteenth century England has delighted young and old for generations. In it, a miser, Scrooge, through a series of dreams, finds the true Christmas spirit. . . . The story ends with the much-quoted cry of

Dickens, Charles—*Continued*

Tiny Tim, the crippled son of Bob Cratchit, whom Scrooge now aids: 'God bless us, every-one!' " Haydn. Thesaurus of Book Digests

> *also in* Dickens, C. Best short stories p422-84
>
> *also in* Dickens, C. Charles Dickens' Best stories p83-142
>
> *also in* Dickens, C. Christmas tales p11-77

y Christmas stories; with thirteen illus. by E. G. Dalziel, Townley Green, Charles Green and others, and an introduction by Margaret Lane. Oxford 1956 758p illus (New Oxford Illustrated Dickens) $5

Analyzed in Short Story Index
"Contains 21 of the shorter, less frequently reprinted stories which originally appeared in 'Household Words' and 'All the Year Round' from 1850-1867. Illustrations are taken from the 1871 and 1874 editions of Dickens' works." Booklist

Contents: A Christmas tree; What Christmas is as we grow older; The poor relation's story; The child's story; The schoolboy's story; Nobody's story; The seven poor travellers; The holly-tree; The wreck of the Golden Mary; The perils of certain English prisoners; Going into society; The haunted house; A message from the sea; Tom Tiddler's ground; Somebody's luggage; Mrs Lirriper's lodgings; Mrs Lirriper's legacy; Doctor Marigold; Mugby Junction; No thoroughfare; The lazy tour of two idle apprentices

y Christmas tales; with illus. by contemporary artists and a foreword by May Lamberton Becker. Dodd 1947 [c1941] 414p illus (Great illustrated classics) $4.50

Analyzed in Short Story Index
Contents: A Christmas carol; The chimes; Cricket on the hearth; The haunted man; A Christmas-tree; What Christmas is as we grow older; The poor relation's story; The seven poor traveller's; The holly-tree; Doctor Marigold

y The cricket on the hearth; a fairy tale of home; illus. by Francis D. Bedford. Warne 1956 182p illus $2.95

First published 1846
"In this short Christmas fairy tale of a happy English home, the cricket chirps when all is well, and is silent when sorrow enters. Mr. and Mrs. Perrybingle (John and Dot) give refuge to an old stranger, Edward Plummer. John sees the stranger, as a young man, without his disguise, put his arm around Dot. The cricket takes the form of a fairy and counsels him. John does not judge his young wife and is ready to forgive her. However, Edward bursts in with his bride, May Fielding, and explains everything." Haydn. Thesaurus of Book Digests

> *also in* Dickens, C. Best short stories p553-620
>
> *also in* Dickens, C. Charles Dickens' Best stories p206-70
>
> *also in* Dickens, C. Christmas tales p147-215

y David Copperfield

Some editions are:
Collins, $1.95
Dial Press $6.95 Illustrated by John Austin
Dodd (Great illustrated classics) $4.50 With reproductions of the original illustrations by Cruikshank, Phiz, Gilbert and Darley and with an introduction by May Lamberton Becker
Dutton (Everyman's lib) $3.25
Macmillan (N Y) (The Macmillan Classics) $3.95 Illustrated by N. B. Bodecker; afterword by Clifton Fadiman
Modern Lib. $2.95
Oxford (The New Oxford Illustrated Dickens) $5 With 40 illustrations by 'Phiz'. Has title: The personal history of David Copperfield

St Martins $4.25
First published 1850
A novel that is "admittedly largely autobiographical. As a mere boy, after his mother's death David is sent by his harsh stepfather, Mr. Murdstone to London, where he pastes labels on bottles in a warehouse by day and is the single lodger of the poverty stricken hopeful Micawbers. He finally runs away to his great-aunt Betsy Trotwood at Dover, where he finds a genuine welcome. After a period of school life, he settles down to work with Mr. Wickfield, a lawyer, and finds a warm friend in Wickfield's daughter Agnes. He marries Dora Spenlow, a 'child-wife,' but after her death he marries Agnes Wickfield." Benét. The Reader's Encyclopedia

y Dombey and son

Some editions are:
Dodd (Great illustrated classics) $5.50 Introduction by John Cournos. With illustrations by contemporary artists
Dutton (Everyman's lib) $2.95
First published 1848 in book form; in monthly parts from 1846-1848
"The moral purpose is to anatomize pride and illustrate its strength and weakness. Slenderly attached to the main story developing this idea is the pathetic episode of little Paul Dombey's invalid life and death. Then the history of Mr. Dombey moves on to his business failure and the chastening of his pride." Baker's Best

y Great expectations

Some editions are:
Collins $1.95
Dodd (Great illustrated classics) $4.50 With illustrations from drawings by Frederic W. Pailthorpe together with an introduction by May Lamberton Becker
Dutton (Everyman's lib) $3.25
Oxford (The New Oxford Illustrated Dickens) $5 With 21 illustrations by F. W. Pailthorpe and an introduction by Frederick Page
Watts, F. $9.95 Large type edition complete and unabridged. A Keith Jennison book
First published 1861
"The hero is Pip, who is reared by his sister and her husband, Joe Gargery, the blacksmith. Later he is informed that he is to be reared as a gentleman of 'great expectations,' as an unknown person has provided money for his education and expects to make him his heir. This patron is Magwitch, a runaway convict to whom the boy Pip had once been of great assistance, Magwitch has made a fortune in New South Wales, but when he secretly returns to England, he is arrested as a returned convict and all his money is confiscated. Pip's love affair is a similar 'great expectation.' He falls in love with Estella, the adopted daughter of the rich Miss Havisham, but Estella marries Bentley Drummle." Benét. The Reader's Encyclopedia

y Hard times

Some editions are:
Collins $1.95
Dial Press $6.95 Illustrated by Charles Raymond
Dutton (Everyman's lib) $2.95 Introduction by G. K. Chesterton
Oxford (The New Oxford Illustrated Dickens) $5 With 4 illustrations by F. Walker and Maurice Greiffenhagen and an introduction by Dingle Foot. Has title: Hard times for the times
First published 1854
"A tract-novel inspired by Carlyle's Philosophical Radicalism—a protest against tyrannous utilitarianism and political economy divorced from human feeling. The stage is a hideous manufacturing town created by the two apostles of fact, Gradgrind and Bounderby, and the drama is chiefly enacted by Gradgrind's children brought up on facts, and ruined spiritually by the complete neglect of sympathy and sentiment." Baker's Best

y Little Dorrit

Some editions are:
Collins $1.95
Dodd (Great illustrated classics) $5.50 With sixteen full-page illustrations including reproductions of drawings for early editions, together with an introduction and captions by John Cournos

Dickens, Charles—*Continued*

Dutton (Everyman's lib) $2.95
Oxford (New Oxford Illustrated Dickens) $4
  With 40 illustrations by Phiz
St Martins $4

First published 1857
"Little Dorrit was born and brought up in the Marshalsea prison, Bermondsey, where her father was confined for debt; and when about fourteen years of age she used to do needlework, to earn a subsistence for herself and her father. . . . Her father, coming into a property, was set free at length, and Little Dorrit married Arthur Clennam, the marriage service being celebrated in the Marshalsea, by the prison chaplain." University Handbook for Readers and Writers
"Satirizes the Civil Service under the style of the Circumlocution Office. Also pictures prison life, Little Dorrit's father being Father of the Marshalsea. The melodramatic element appears in the history of the House of Clennam; with the usual complement of originals: Mr. F.'s Aunt, the Meagles, Pancks, Mr. Nanby, Mr Casby, Flora Finching, Miss Wade, Tallycoram." Baker's Best

y Martin Chuzzlewit

Some editions are:
Collins $1.95
Dodd (Great illustrated classics) $5.50 Introduction by May Lamberton Becker. With illustrations by Cruikshank, Leech and 'Phiz'
Dutton (Everyman's lib) $2.95 Introduction by G. K. Chesterton
Oxford (The New Oxford Illustrated Dickens) $5 With 40 illustrations by 'Phiz' and an introduction by Geoffrey Russell. Has title: The life and adventures of Martin Chuzzlewit

First published 1844
"Because of his love for Mary Graham, the titular hero is forced by his old grandfather to leave home and emigrates to America. He has some sadly disillusioning experiences with real estate in an over-advertised swamp named Eden, and returns to England with little love for anything American. The hypocrite, Pecksniff, is a prominent character, as are the various members of the Chuzzlewit family." Benét. The Reader's Encyclopedia

The mystery of Edwin Drood; with 12 illus. by Luke Fildes and 2 by Charles Collins, and an introduction by S. C. Roberts. Oxford 1956 278p illus (New Oxford Illustrated classics) $5

First published 1870
"An unfinished melodrama centering in a mysterious murder and enacted amid the picturesque closes and cathedral buildings of old Rochester (Cloisterham), with scenes in an opium den in Shadwell. The scenic elements create a deep impression of gloom and tragedy, and the plot is an excellent piece of construction. Contains some characteristic types of villainy and passion and some grotesquely humorous figures, who at least reflect the creations of his best period, e.g., Canon Crisparkle, John Jasper, Mr. Sapsea." Baker's Best

y Nicholas Nickleby

Some editions are:
Collins $1.95
Dodd (Great illustrated classics) $5.50 With illustrations by Cruikshank, "Phiz", and others
Dutton (Everyman's lib) $2.95
Nelson (Nelson classics) $1.75
Oxford (The New Oxford Illustrated Dickens) $5 With 39 illustrations by "Phiz" and an introduction by Dame Sybil Thorndike. Has title: The life & adventures of Nicholas Nickleby

First published 1839
"Nicholas Nickleby is the son of a poor country gentleman, and has to make his own way in the world. He first goes as usher to Mr. Squeers, schoolmaster at Dotheboys Hall, in Yorkshire, but leaves in disgust with the tyranny of Squeers and his wife, especially to a poor boy named Smike. Smike runs away from the school to follow Nicholas, and remains his humble follower till death. At Portsmouth, Nicholas joins the theatrical company of Mr. Crummles, but leaves the profession for other adventures. He falls in with the brothers Cheeryble, who make him their clerk;

in this post he rises to success as a merchant, and ultimately marries Madeline Bray." Benét. The Reader's Encyclopedia

y The old curiosity shop

Some editions are:
Dodd (Great illustrated classics) $5.50 With reproductions of the original illustrations by Cruikshank, Phiz, Gilbert and Darley and with an introductory sketch by May Lamberton Becker
Dutton (Everyman's lib) $3.25
Oxford (New Oxford Illustrated Dickens) $5 With 75 illustrations by Cattermole and Phiz

First published 1841
"The heroine, Nell Trent, better known as Little Nell, lives with her grandfather, an old man who keeps a 'curiosity shop.' He adores her, but loses what little he has by gambling and they roam about the country as beggars until finally Little Nell dies. The book relates also the adventures of a boy named Kit Nubles, employed for a time in the curiosity shop. Later, the hunchback, Daniel Quilp, contrives to have him convicted of theft and sentenced to transportation, but he is saved from this fate by the good offices of a girl-of-all-work, nicknamed the Marchioness.'" Benét. The Reader's Encyclopedia

y Oliver Twist

Some editions are:
Collins $1.95
Dial Press $6.95 Illustrated by Barnett Freedman
Dodd (Great illustrated classics) $4.50 With illustrations from drawings by George Cruikshank together with an introduction by May Lamberton Becker
Dutton (Everyman's lib) $3.25 Introduction by G. K. Chesterton
Oxford (The World's classics) $2.75 Has title: The adventures of Oliver Twist
Oxford (The New Oxford Illustrated Dickens) $5 With twenty-four illustrations by George Cruikshank and an introduction by Humphrey House. Has title: The adventures of Oliver Twist
St Martins $4

First published 1837-1838
"A boy from an English workhouse falls into the hands of rogues who train him to be a pickpocket. The story of his struggles to escape from an environment of crime is one of hardship, danger, and the severe obstacles overcome." National Council of Teachers of English

y Our mutual friend

Some editions are:
Collins $1.95
Dodd (Great illustrated classics) $5.50 With sixteen full-page illustrations including reproductions of drawings for early editions, together with an introduction and captions by Allen Klots
Dutton (Everyman's lib) $2.95
Oxford (The New Oxford Illustrated Dickens) $5 With 40 illustrations by Marcus Stone and an introduction by E. Salter Davies

First published 1865
"John Harmon, 'our mutual friend,' will inherit a fortune if he marries Bella Wilfer. He assumes the names of Julius Handford and later John Rokesmith, and his supposed death helps him conceal his identity. John's father's foreman, Nicodemus Boffin, and his wife, Henrietta, help him with the ruse. He enters the employ of Boffin, who has adopted Bella. Bella has had her head turned by wealth, but reforms when her eyes are opened to its evils; she marries Harmon. Other characters are: Jesse Hexam; his son Charley, and daughter, Lizzie; Bradley Headstone, schoolmaster, who is jealous of Eugene Wrayburn's love for Lizzie Hexam; Fanny Cleaver (Jenny Wren), a doll's dressmaker; one-legged Silas Wegg, the villain in the main plot, as Headstone is in the secondary one. Here again Dickens protests against the poor laws through the character Betty Hidgen, who fears the workhouse." Haydn. Thesaurus of Book Digests

y The posthumous papers of the Pickwick Club

Some editions are:
Collins $1.95
Dodd (Great illustrated classics) $5.50 With a foreword by May Lamberton Becker and illustrations by Phiz and others

Dickens, Charles—*Continued*

Dutton (Everyman's lib) $3.25
Oxford (The New Oxford Illustrated Dickens) $5. With forty-three illustrations by Seymour and 'Phiz' and an introduction by Bernard Darwin
St Martins $4.25

First published 1837
"Episodes of the doings and foibles of the Pickwick Club. . . . The book is made up of letters and manuscripts about the club's actions. Among the incidents are: the army parade; trip to Manor Farm; the saving of Rachel Wardle from the villain, Alfred Jingle; trip to Eatonswill; Mrs Leo Hunter's party of authors, including Count Smorltork and Charles Fitz-Marshall; ice skating. Pickwick's landlady, Mrs. Bardell, faints in his arms and compromises the unsophisticated gentleman. She sues him for breach of promise and an amusing court trial follows. Pickwick refuses to pay damages and is put in Fleet prison. Sam Weller, his faithful servant, accompanies him. Mrs. Bardell is also incarcerated for not paying the costs of the trial. When Pickwick is released he retires to a house outside London, with Weller, and the latter's new bride, Mary, as housekeeper. He dissolves the club and spends his time arranging its memoranda." Haydn. Thesaurus of Book Digests

Sketches by Boz; illustrative of every-day life and every-day people. With 55 illus. by George Cruickshank and "Phiz" and an introduction by Thea Holme. Oxford 1957 xxii, 688p illus (New Oxford Illustrated Dickens) $5

The chapters are arranged under the following headings: Our parish; Scenes; Characters; Tales; Sketches of young gentlemen; Sketches of young couples; The Mudfog and other sketches

Sketches by Boz; with illus. by George Cruickshank and an introduction by Charles Dickens the younger. St Martin's [1958 c1892] 464p boards $4.25

This is a reprint of the title first published 1892 in England by Macmillan
The chapters are arranged under the following headings: Our parish; Scenes; Characters; Tales

y A tale of two cities

Some editions are:
Collins $1.95
Dial Press $6.95 Illustrated by René Ben Sussan
Dodd (Great illustrated classics) $4.50 With illustrations from drawings by "Phiz" (Hablot K. Brown) and Fred Barnard together with an introductory sketch by May Lamberton Becker
Dutton (Everyman's lib) $3.25
Macmillan (N Y) (The Macmillan classics) $3.95
Modern Lib. $2.95
Oxford (The World's classics) $2.75
Oxford (The New Oxford Illustrated Dickens) $5 With an introduction by Sir John Schuckburgh and 16 illustrations by Phiz
St Martins $4.25
Watts, F. Ultra type edition. $5.95, lib. bdg. $3.97
Watts, F. $8.95 Large type edition complete and unabridged A Keith Jennison book

First published 1859
A novel of the French Revolution. "The two cities are London and Paris. The plot hinges on the physical likeness of Charles Darnay and Sidney Carton, both of whom are in love with Lucie Manette. Lucie loves Darnay, and Sydney Carton, who is a dissipated ne'er-do-well, never pleads his devotion, but it leads him to go to the guillotine in place of Darnay for the sake of Lucie's happiness." Benét. The Reader's Encyclopedia

Dickens, Monica

The landlord's daughter. Doubleday 1968 329p $5.95

A "40-year chronicle of an Englishwoman's life, her one great love and one great mystery. Charlotte, whose family and friends have begun to despair of her ever marrying, is assisted when her car breaks down by a young man who tells her he is a member of the crew of a new British dirigible (it is 1930), which is about to undertake its maiden flight. When the airship crashes in flames, she is desolate, though she has only met the man once, and seeks out his family, with whom she becomes deeply involved. Somewhat later, a local paper breaks a story about a murder that occurred on the night she met her love, Peter. Charlotte begins to suspect he was probably the murderer. Later on, Peter appears. He hides out in her cottage, they have an affair and a relationship that is a blend of mutual fear and passion, ending tragically. Running through all this is a subplot concerning an unpredictable young pop musician who becomes involved with Charlotte's husband, the chronicler of the tale." Pub W
"Here is satire nonpareil, a massive indictment of a crippling world, giving way, in its breakup of values, to shabby philosophies." Best Sellers

The room upstairs. Doubleday 1966 208p o.p. 1970

"Sybil was in her eighties and lived in a yellow house in—or just out of—a New England town. Here she fretted at her dissolution, tried to put up with her 'companions,' and was joined in the old house by her grandson's English wife. Jess, the young English girl, became gradually aware of something strange and menacing in the old house." Bk Buyer's Guide
"Miss Dickens has written penetrating character sketches of the two female companions. . . . More in the Mary Roberts Rinehart than the James Bond milieu, this book will appeal to women readers who like mystery novels." Best Sellers

Dickinson, Peter

The glass-sided ants' nest. Harper 1968 186p boards $4.95

SBN 06-011027-9
"A Joan Kahn-Harper Novel of suspense" Ku, the chief of a nearly extinct New Guinea tribe that has been transplanted to London by an anthropologist is murdered, and Pibble of Scotland Yard is assigned to solve the case

The old English peep show. Harper 1969 216p boards $4.95

"A Joan Kahn-Harper Novel of suspense"
"Mr. Dickinson turns an irreverent eye toward a pair of doddering British war heroes, brothers who have transformed the family estate into a streamlined, tradition-encrusted, atmosphere-at-8-bob-a-pint tourist trap, complete with a zoo, a scale-model railway, duels on the green, busloads of Americans determined to revive the exchequer—and a disarmingly ordinary suicide. [Superintendent] Pibble is sent down to take care of the formalities surrounding this regrettable latter incident, but Pibble is a trifle too observant. . . . Read this tale carefully. It's a jewel." N Y Times Bk R

Dickson, Gordon R.

None but man. Doubleday 1969 253p (Doubleday Science fiction) $4.95

This fast-moving story "concerns war between the galaxies and an ex-space ship pirate's discovery that outer space destroys human beings, mind, body and soul. Only a certain type of aliens can survive there." Pub W

Diderot, Denis

Rameau's nephew

In Dupee, F. W. ed. Great French short novels p 1-90

Di Donato, Pietro

Christ in concrete; a novel. Bobbs 1939 311p o.p. 1970

An Italian bricklayer pictures "the hazards of the work in which his fellows are engaged; of the sadness, longing and tragedy which are their all-too-familiar lot and of the eagerness with which they seize upon the good things of life which come their way. . . . The narrative consists of five chapters which give revealing episodes in the life of one family and its immediate circle." Baldwin

Di Donato, Pietro—*Continued*

"The characters who vividly people the story are drawn from poverty-ridden New York construction workers and their families, transplanted Italians whom Pietro di Donato knows from his fourteen years as a bricklayer. . . . His own terse style, made telegraphic by personification and frequent omission of the article, throbs with reality, with the feel of brick and mortar, the smells of labor, the tang of sour wine and olive oil and red peppers. Only a man whose muscles and stomach have felt the fatigue and the hunger of hard manual labor can paint them with such blunt, convincing strokes." Nation

Dikty, T. E.

(ed.) The Best science fiction stories and novels: 1949-1958. See The Best science fiction stories and novels: 1949-1958

Di Lampedusa, Giuseppe. See Lampedusa, Giuseppe di

Dinesen, Isak

Ehrengard. Random House 1963 111p o.p. 1970

A "tale laid in a German principality in the early nineteenth century. The heir of the reigning house and his wife are in seclusion in order to conceal the evidence of premarital indiscretion. Ehrengard, the daughter of a general, is chosen as the young wife's companion at the instigation of Herr Cazotte, who understanding Ehrengard's absolute loyalty and innocence, plans her seduction. The irony below the story's seemingly playful surface is revealed when those qualities of Ehrengard which Cazotte intends to utilize bring about his own destruction." Booklist

"The late Isak Dinesen's last story is a sophisticated, rococo fairy tale for grownups. It has the substance of melodrama." Book of the Month Club News

Last tales. Random House 1957 341p $4.95

Analyzed in Short Story Index
Contents: The Cardinal's first tale; The cloak; Night walk; Of hidden thoughts and of heaven; Tales of two old gentlemen; The Cardinal's third tale; The blank page; The Caryatids, an unfinished tale; Echoes; A country tale; Copenhagen season; Converse at night in Copenhagen

Seven Gothic tales; wtih an introduction by Dorothy Canfield. Modern Lib. 402p $2.95

Analyzed in Short Story Index
First published 1934 by H. Smith and R. Haas
Contents: The deluge at Norderney; The old chevalier; The monkey; The roads round Pisa; The supper at Elsinore; The dreamers; The poet

Shadows on the grass. Random House 1961 [c1960] illus $3.95

Analyzed in Short Story Index
Includes four stories based on the author's experiences in Africa's Kenya Colony from 1914 to 1931
Contents: Farah; Barua a Soldani; The great gesture; Echoes from the hills
"These finely drawn autobiographical stories not only re-create the Africans with whom she shared those years, but also convey, in every description and episode, the quality and texture of a past era in Kenya and in the author's life. A memorable book not limited to the Dinesen admirer." Booklist

Winter's tales. Random House 1942 313p o.p. 1970

Analyzed in Short Story Index
Contents: The sailor-boy's tale; The young man with the carnation; The pearls; The invincible slaveowners; The heroine; The dreaming child; Alkmene; The fish; Peter and Rosa; Sorrow-acre; A consolatory tale
"Like strange, exotic gems, these 11 stories, under the brilliant play of the author's richly creative imagination, now strike fantastic fire, now emit a cold foreboding light, now glow with quiet serenity. The subtlety of Isak Dinesen's character delineation, the filuid rhythm of her prose, the originality and ironic implications of her themes, the sensitivity of her feeling for the lovely Danish landscape (background for most of the tales), makes this collection as notable for the discriminating reader as was her 'Seven Gothic tales.'" Bookmark

For another title by this author see Andrézel, Pierre

Disney, Doris Miles

At some forgotten door. Published for the Crime Club by Doubleday 1966 284p o.p. 1970

Set in New England in 1886. "Hetty had scarcely known her father, but when he died he left her the bulk of his estate instead of willing it to her pretty cousin Emily, wife of Hetty's step-brother. Then the widow and her son and Hetty heard that Emily was dead and strange things began to happen." Bk Buyer's Guide
"A leisurely and unsurprising story but uncommonly smooth and readable and with a welcome touch of grisly shock in its finale." N Y Times Bk R

Here lies. Published for the Crime Club by Doubleday 1963 182p o.p. 1970

Detective story concerning "the efforts of young private detective Griff Hughes to learn from yellowed newspaper files and musty municipal records, why an unidentified grave should contain a 44-year-buried skeleton with a bullet in its skull." N Y Times Bk R

Voice from the grave. Published for the Crime Club by Doubleday 1968 190p $3.95

"The story of a vicious youngster and the adoring mother who can see no evil in her son. The scene is an exclusive summer colony in Maine. Before Howie starts tutoring in order to stay in the only prep school that hasn't kicked him out yet, he and his friend Dennis go off on a few days' fishing trip. The boys don't return on time, and the search turns up their wrecked canoe but no bodies." Pub W
The writer "demonstrates a keen eye for rebellious teens and overindulgent motherhood. . . . You may not be entirely shocked at the outcome, but Miss Disney handles her situations with smooth confidence." N Y Times Bk R

Ditzen, Rudolf. See Fallada, Hans

Doderer, Heimito von

The demons; tr. from the German by Richard and Clara Winston. Knopf 1961 2v (1334p) $13.50

Originally published 1956 in Germany
"Ranging through all segments of Viennese society from the fall of 1926 to July 1927, [this novel] leads an enormous cast of characters through comic, tragic, inspiring, and dispiriting encounters to a catastrophe they are unable to foresee or avoid." Publisher's note
This huge novel "is sure to be compared with Proust. It has a host of characters, meticulous detail, and through the narrator, provides a picture of the emotions and ideas be hind their actions." Bk Buyer's Guide

Dodgson, Charles Lutwidge. See Carroll, Lewis

Dodson, Kenneth

Away all boats; a novel. Little 1954 508p $6.50

A novel dealing with U.S. naval operations in the Pacific during World War II. It describes the details of life aboard the attack transport "Belinda," and the stages by which amphibious operations grew in efficiency from the Gilberts to Okinawa
"There are no cursewords, no sex anecdotes or incidents. And despite its length: 45 chapters, the novel moves quickly, and interest is sustained. Women may tire of it, but men will like it." Library J

Dolan, Mary

Hannibal of Carthage. Macmillan (N Y) 1955 308p o.p. 1970

"Hannibal's amazing March on Imperial Rome is recreated. . . . The narrator, Greek

Dolan, Mary—*Continued*

slave who became Hannibal's tutor, actually
lived and wrote a record of Hannibal's exploits,
but his account has long been lost. This is an
imaginary version of what he set down." Hunting

"Admittedly sympathetic to the Carthaginian
viewpoint, this novel, in a modern manner, recreates a stirring historical period with more
than ordinary success. Recommended for school,
college and public libraries." Library J

Dolson, Hildegarde

Heat lightning. Lippincott 1970 [c1969]
246p boards $5.95

"The cheerful and amusing story of a Liberty
Pole Festival planned for the Fourth of July
in a Connecticut town. Cassie Murdoch, one
of the planners offers the services of her musician-beau to supply the music for the play;
wealthy Chester Humboldt, politically ambitious, contributes the money; and much married author Alicia Thorne does the rest." Bk
Buyer's Guide

"The characters are themselves the fireworks
for this novel and they provide a glorious delight for the reader. A well written and plotted
story." Book News

Donato, Pietro di. See Di Donato, Pietro

Donleavy, J. P.

The beastly beatitudes of Balthazar B.
Delacorte Press 1968 403p $6.95

"A Seymour Lawrence book"
"The story involves Balthazar, son of an
inexhaustibly rich French family, who is
sent to England for his early schooling, then
further educated—not altogether academically
—at Trinity College in Dublin. Balthazar becomes the lover of many appreciative women,
the unhappy husband of a shrew, and the
friend, benefactor and partner in sexual fracases of a genially satanic rake out of his
schoolboy past." Book of the Month Club
News

The author's "prose is honed to a fine edge
of humor and tenderness that stops . . . just
short of poetry. . . . Donleavy seeks with short
fragmented sentences to do justice to sensations and moods. . . . The familiar sensations
of food and sex and weather are offered to
us as if for the first time. . . . [And] though
Donleavy presents sex with a virtually unique
charm and gaiety, he is really more interested
in the tenderness that goes with it. . . . In
laughing or weeping over this poor little rich
boy . . . we really laugh and weep not for Balthazar but for ourselves." Sat R

The ginger man. The complete and unexpurgated ed. Delacorte Press 1965 347p $5.75

Originally published 1955 in Paris. First American expurgated edition published 1958 by McDowell, Obolensky

Set in Dublin and London are "the adventures of Sebastian Dangerfield, a scrounger, a
betrayer of [wife] women and friends." Bk
Buyer's Guide

"The zany hero—the rogue, the comic roisterer—for all his low adventures still makes
a comment on the human condition that is serious if banal. It is that despite its sordidness
life has strength. Much of the strength comes
from sex, and this is what the novel dwells upon." N Y Times Bk R

A singular man. Delacorte Press 1967
[c1963] 402p $6.95

"A Seymour Laurence book"
Reprint of the title first published 1963 by
Little

"A modern fantasy about one George Smith,
a city man, an apartment man, with money
from mysterious sources that might be in Wall
Street, with a divorced wife, with four hateful children, and with an earnest desire for
women, especially his secretary. Another thing
about George: he is haunted by fear and pursued by anonymous letters. His salvation is
in bitter, strong humor, a curious private life
in his apartment, 'Merry Mansions,' and the
wherewithal to flee when things get too much
for him." Pub W

"While style, language, and incident are unconventional and often shocking and some
portions of the text need explication, this roguish consideration of sex and death is strongly
recommended to those collections which include
contemporary fiction of consequence." Library
J

Dored, Elisabeth

I loved Tiberius; tr. from the Norwegian by
Naomi Walford. Pantheon Bks. 1963 302p
o.p. 1970

Original Norwegian edition 1959
"Julia, daughter of Augustus and step-sister
of Tiberius, was forced by her father's ambition and her step-mother Livia's greed into a
first, unhappy marriage; a second and happy
marriage to Agrippa; and at last became the
wife of Tiberius, doomed to tragedy because of
Livia's ruthless schemes." Bk Buyer's Guide

"The story of her [Julia's] life through adolescence, marriage, and misfortune against the
background of Imperial Rome civilized in certain aspects and barbarous in others makes
fascinating reading, particularly for women."
Booklist

Dos Passos, John

Adventures of a young man
In Dos Passos, J. District of Columbia
v 1

The big money
In Dos Passos, J. U.S.A. v3

Chosen country. Houghton 1951 485p $5

"Many segments of the American scene from
mid-nineteenth century to the late 1920's are
highlighted in the story of Jay Pignatelli and
Lulie Harringon who meet briefly in childhood, forget each other, but meet again and
marry when they are mature. The Pignatelli
background carries an appreciation of European culture. . . . Lulie's background is
wholly American and the narration of her early
life in the Middle West with brothers and
friends at a summer resort is idyllic. It is when
Jay returns from abroad after World War I and
experience in relief work in the Near East that
he chooses America." Booklist

District of Columbia. Houghton 1952 3v in
1 $14

The publication in one volume of: Adventures of a young man. Number one, and The
grand design, originally published 1938, 1943
and 1949 respectively. This anthology is neither romance, tragedy nor political tract, but
the most serious kind of satiric comedy

In the first story of the Spottswood family,
the hero, Glenn Spottswood grows up, adopts
communism, and becomes disillusioned after
fighting in the Spanish Civil War. The second
story is a character study of a southern politician resembling Huey Long of Louisiana. The
third is treated separately

"Amorphous but interesting and occasionally
brilliant." Book of the Month Club News

The 42nd parallel. Houghton 426p $3.50

A reprint of the title first published 1930 by
Harper

"This novel is an achievement in form. It is
as kaleidoscopic as 'Manhattan transfer' with
less continuity and is forceful, full of color, uneven, sordid, and brilliant. The time is from
1900 to 1914. It contains five distinct narratives
of commonplace characters, separated by nineteen 'News reels' and twenty-seven entries of
'The camera eye,' made up of newspaper headlines and quotations which fix the period. These
are followed by clever biographical sketches of
prominent American figures of the time. . . .
The first section of a long novel satirizing
American life." Booklist

Followed by: 1919

also in Dos Passos, J. U.S.A. v 1

The grand design. Houghton 1949 440p
$7.95

"The author's reportorial sense creates the
sights and sounds, the talk and tension, the
parties and, above all, the people of New Deal

Dos Passos, John—*Continued*

Washington. With Millard Carroll and his wife, Lucille, who left the informal freedom of their Southwest town to join the brain trust, the reader meets the other 'trusters' and their wives. This world is shown as part of a larger whole—a vast and complex machine—and the novel forms a picture of an epoch whose death Dos Passos believes was deliberately concealed by the diversion of popular attention from domestic failure to international chaos." Hunting

also in Dos Passos, J. District of Columbia v3

Manhattan transfer. Houghton 404p $6

A reprint of the title first published 1925 by Harper

"A novel in which thirty or forty characters disappear and reappear, the story adapted in its syncopated rhythms and shifting form and color to the author's conception of New York, the city of intense living." Cleveland

"A thread of continuity in incidents and character binds together these vivid vignettes into a brilliant composite, as impressive as it is depressing." Booklist

Midcentury. Houghton 1961 496p $5.95

This novel constitutes a panoramic view of the 20th century American scene with emphasis upon the labor movement. The author quotes "newspaper and magazine headings and stories, and . . . provides interspersed thumbnail biographies of Bridges, Lewis, MacArthur, Eleanor Roosevelt, Sam Goldwyn, Walter Reuther, Young Bob La Follette, and James Dean, among others. There are [also] . . . narrative segments concerning individuals under pressure from labor racketeers." Library J

"The villain of Dos Passos' latest novel, Midcentury is big unions. This is certainly the most fascinating fact about the book and possibly the most significant. . . . The basic premise of Midcentury is that labor won privileges and power but the individual laborer lost his freedom. . . . Dos Passos has lost much of the freshness, originality and compelling force he had in U.S.A." Time

1919. Harcourt 1932 473p o.p. 1970

Sequel to: The 42nd parallel
"The author continues his chronicle of life in America thru the war years, giving glimpses of the lives and characters of five young Americans—a low caste sailor, the daughter of a Chicago minister, a young girl from Texas, a radical Jew, a young poet." Book Rev Digest

" '1919' is literally what so many books are erroneously called, 'a slice of life.' With infinite skill that slicing is done by the author, and the raw surface which meets the reader's eye is the actual living, breathing record of a period in its most intense manifestation." Chicago Daily Tribune

also in Dos Passos, J. U.S.A. v2

Number one

In Dos Passos, J. District of Columbia v2

Three soldiers. Houghton 1947 [c1921] 433p $6.95

First published 1921 by Doran
"A novel in which the author presents a bitter invective against what he conceived as the tyranny, misery, and degradation of life in the American army during the great [first World] war." Pittsburgh

U.S.A; illus. by Reginald Marsh. Houghton 1937 3v illus $10

Contents: The 42nd parallel, first published 1930; 1919, first published 1932; The big money, first published 1936. The first two titles are entered separately

A chronicle of American life with a unique structure, each novel containing several distinct "narratives separated by 'News reels' and 'The camera eye' made up of quotations from newspapers of the period. Interspersed are short biographical sketches of prominent men of the time

The novels exhibit "the keenness of the author's observation—not only of colors, noises, and odors but, even more important, of human behavior and of American speech." Nation

Dostoevskiĭ, Fedor Mikhaĭlovich. See Dostoevsky, Fyodor

Dostoevsky, Fyodor

The best short stories of Dostoevsky; tr. with an introduction by David Magarshack. Modern Lib. 1955 xxiii, 322p $2.95

Contents: White nights; The honest thief; The Christmas tree and a wedding; The peasant Marey; Notes from the underground; A gentle creature; The dream of a ridiculous man

The brothers Karamazov

Some editions are:
Dutton (Everyman's lib) 2v ea $3.25 Translated by Constance Garnett. Introduction by Edward Garnett
Modern Lib. (Modern Lib giants) $4.95 Translated from the Russian by Constance Garnett
First appeared as a serial 1879-1880

"A story which was to have been Dostoevskii's masterpiece but only the first part of which was completed at his death. The brothers Karamazov are the three sons of an old drunkard and sensualist: Ivan, the materialist, Alyosha, the very human and lovable young mystic, and dissolute, impecunious Mitya, tried and convicted for murdering his father. A remarkable work, showing at the worst the author's faults of style and construction, and at their best his profound understanding of human nature and power to depict Russian character." Cleveland

Crime and punishment; tr. from the Russian by Constance Garnett

Some editions are:
Dutton (Everyman's lib) $2.95 Introduction by Nikolay Andreyev
Modern Lib. $2.95 With an introduction by Ernest J. Simmons
Watts, F. $6.95 Watts Ultratype edition complete and unabridged. With a critical and biographical profile of Fyodor Dostoevsky by Janko Lavrin
Written 1866; translated 1886

A "psychological study, revolving about one incident,—the murder of an old woman, a money-lender, and her sister, by a student in St. Petersburg, Raskolnikoff. The circumstances leading to the murder are extreme poverty, and the resultant physical and mental depletion." Keller's Reader's Digest of Books

The double

In Dostoevsky, F. The short novels of Dostoevsky p475-615

The eternal husband

In Dostoevsky, F. The short novels of Dostoevsky p343-473

The eternal husband, and other stories; from the Russian by Constance Garnett. Macmillan (N Y) 323p o.p. 1970

Analyzed in Short Story Index
First published 1917
Contents: The eternal husband; The double; A gentle spirit

The friend of the family; tr. from the Russian by Constance Garnett. Macmillan (N Y) 1949 358p o.p. 1970

Originally published 1884
"Dostoevsky's first novel after his Siberian exile. The chief figure is a repulsive companion who worms his way into the confidence of his employer, and succeeds in dominating him and his womenfolk—a picture of petty egoism carried almost to the point of insanity." Baker's Best

Includes the novel "Nyetochka Nyezvanov" written 1849. "In this appears for the first time that type of 'proud girl' which was to play such a prominent part in the great novels of his maturity." Encyclopedia Britannica

also in Dostoevsky, F. The short novels of Dostoevsky p617-811

The gambler

In Dostoevsky, F. The short novels of Dostoevsky p 1-126

Dostoevsky, Fyodor—*Continued*

The gambler, and other stories; tr. from the Russian by Constance Garnett. Macmillan (N Y) 318p o.p. 1970

Analyzed in Short Story Index
First published 1914
Contents: The gambler; Poor people; The landlady

An honest thief, and other stories; tr. from the Russian by Constance Garnett. Macmillan (N Y) 325p o.p. 1970

Analyzed in Short Story Index
First published 1919
Contents: An honest thief; Uncle's dream; Novel in nine letters; Unpleasant predicament; Another man's wife; Heavenly Christmas tree; Peasant Marey; Crocodile; Bobok; Dream of a ridiculous man

The house of the dead; a novel in two parts. [Tr.] from the Russian by Constance Garnett. Macmillan (N Y) 1915 284p o.p. 1970

First published in Russian in 1861-62; in English in 1881 under title: "Buried alive." Variant titles: "Prison life in Siberia," "Memorials of a dead house," and "Memoirs from the house of the dead"
"In this autobiography of a Russian landowner condemned to penal servitude in Siberia, Dostoevsky hardly troubles to disguise his own experiences. He traces the different effects of imprisonment on the moral nature, in the life-stories of a group of criminals. It is a terrible record of the anguish of the prisoner's lot." Baker's Best

The idiot

Some editions are:
Modern Lib. (Modern Lib. giants) $4.95. Translated from the Russian by Constance Garnett. Illustrated by Boardman Rabrusin
Dutton (Everyman's lib) $2.95. Translated by Eva M. Martin. Introduction by Richard Curle

Written 1868; translated 1887
"Dostoevsky puts into a world of foolishness, vice, pretence, and sordid ambitions, a being who in childhood had suffered from mental disease, and who with an intellect of more than ordinary power retains the simplicity and clear insight of a child. In the 'Idiot,' he tried to realize his idea of 'a truly perfect and noble man'; this Prince Myshkin of his, an epileptic like himself, is the champion of humanity. The deeply absorbing drama in which he is a protagonist turns on the salvation of a woman, Nasyasya Filipovna who had been corrupted in young girlhood." Baker's Best

Letters from the underworld; The gentle maiden; The landlady; tr. with an introduction by C. J. Hogarth. Dutton 1913 308p (Everyman's lib) $3.25

Letters from the underworld, published 1864, has variant titles: Notes from underground, and Memoirs from underground
Through the actions of a young man, this narrator of the story, the author explores the theme that a perverse human quality, which resists completion, leads individuals to find pleasure in the pain of humiliating experiences
"A terrifying analysis of psychic alienation and impotence. In many ways the protagonist is archetypal 'anti-hero' of 20th century existential fiction." Good Reading

Notes from underground
In Dostoevsky, F. The short novels of Dostoevsky p127-222
In Neider, C. ed. Short novels of the masters p125-219

Nyetochka Nyezvanov
In Dostoevsky, F. The friend of the family p206-358

The possessed; tr. from the Russian by Constance Garnett

Some editions are:
Dutton (Everyman's lib) 2v ea $3.25 Introduction by Nikolay Andreyev

Modern Lib. $2.95 with a foreward by Avrahm Yarmolinsky and a translation of the hitherto suppressed chapter "At Tihon's"

Written 1871; English translation 1914
"Traces with infinite and almost wearisome detail yet with undefinable power the development of a Nihilist conspiracy in a Russian provincial town." Pittsburgh
"The criticism of socialism and godlessness, interrelated by Dostoevsky, are implicit in this novel, which is a sort of exposition of the Parable of the Swine. It is also in this novel that the author propounds his famous exposition of the man-god, i.e., man as god unto himself, the antithesis of the God-man of Christianity." Haydn. Thesaurus of Book Digests

A raw youth. Tr. from the Russian by Constance Garnett. Macmillan (N Y) 1916 560p o.p. 1970

Original Russian edition, 1875
The author "has here drawn a character who is a frank exponent of the Nietzschean 'will to power'; perhaps he has portrayed a phase of his own immaturity, and shown the foolishness of it without . . . satire. The raw youth, poor and illegitimate though he is, determines to be a Rothschild; and to that end starves himself, shuns and decries women, and so on; he is a romantic, with a romantic deficiency of balance, but, at any rate, without any sentimental self-pity." Baker's Best

The short novels of Dostoevsky; with an introduction by Thomas Mann. Dial Press 1945 xx, 811p o.p. 1970

Partially analyzed in Short Story Index
Contents: The gambler; Notes from underground; Uncle's dream; The eternal husband; The double; The friend of the family

The short stories of Dostoevsky; ed. with an introduction by William Phillips. Dial Press 1946 614p $7.50

Analyzed in Short Story Index
Translated by Constance Garnett
Contents: Mr Prohartchin; Novel in nine letters; The landlady; Polzunkov; Faint heart; Another man's wife; An honest thief; Christmas tree and a wedding; White nights; Little hero; Unpleasant predicament; The crocodile; Bobok; Peasant Marey; Heavenly Christmas tree; Gentle spirit; Dream of a ridiculous man
"No single volume could better prove its author's tremendous literary range. 'Another Man's Wife or the Husband Under the Bed' is pure farce; 'An Honest Thief' is a work of unabashed sentiment; 'The Crocodile' is a strange and wonderful mixture of farce, satire, and allegory; in 'The Heavenly Christmas Tree' only the surest hand could have avoided mawkishness; and 'An Unpleasant Predicament,' in which absurdity and tragedy mingle inextricably, is a small masterpiece of characterization, atmosphere, and construction." Sat R

Uncle's dream
In Dostoevsky, F. The short novels of Dostoevsky p223-342

Douglas, Lloyd C.

y The Big Fisherman. Houghton 1948 581p $5.95

"The two-fold story of Simon Peter, the fisherman, chosen by Christ to be the leader of his disciples, and the girl Fara, daughter of the Jewish Herod Antipas and an Arabian princess, whose hatred for her father vanishes when she meets Christ." Retail Bookseller
"With the exception of the Arabian scenes, the story follows the biblical account of Peter, necessarily much condensed. The personalities of Peter and others of the disciples receive interesting and plausible interpretations; the modern idiom is used with somewhat startling effect, and frequent references are made to many persons actual and fictitious who appeared in 'The Robe' [entered separately]." Booklist

Doctor Hudson's secret journal. Grosset 295p $2.95

First published 1939 by Houghton
"After the success of his novel, Magnificent Obsession, the author received thousands of letters about the journal of Dr. Hudson. The

Douglas, Lloyd C.—*Continued*

present book purports to be that journal in full, decoded by Robert Merrick. In it is the explanation of the origin of Dr. Hudson's philosophy of life and its application." Book Rev Digest

The author "feels that this book should be regarded, not as a sequel to 'Magnificent Obsession,' but as a kind of overture. It can be read without bewilderment by those unfamiliar with the earlier volume." N Y Times Bk R

Magnificent obsession

Some editions are:
Grosset $2.95
Houghton $5.95

First published 1929

"The 'magnificent obsession' that was the secret of the famous Dr Hudson's success—a newly interpreted Christian teaching—was put into practice at Dr Hudson's death by the young man who became his successor as a brain-specialist, Bobby Merrick. Bobby, by continuing his 'personality-investments' in the way of secret philanthropies, as advocated by Dr Hudson's formula, miraculously succeeds, and makes a famous surgical invention with which he is able to save the life of the woman he loves." Book Rev Digest

The author "can create characters who seem as real as anyone you know. He can create situations of dramatic intensity, and he can weave his people and incidents into a plot which is a going concern right up to the last page. . . . Above all, he can write dialogue with more skill than any but a very few of the first rank novelists." Christian Century

y The robe. Houghton 508p $6.95

First published 1942

"The story of a young Roman soldier who, on the night of Jesus' crucifixion, wins the robe left at the foot of the cross in a throw at dice. What its possession does to him and its influence on both his character and after life is the theme of [the] story." Wis Lib Bul

A "portrayal of the impact of Jesus upon an age of such widespread tyranny and terror and despair that even the privileged minority wondered whether a world so constituted had a right to survive. While it is a religious book—in the deepest and most moving sense—it is also a novel impressive in its power and reader interest." Huntting

Dourado, Autran

A hidden life; tr. from the Portuguese by Edgar H. Miller, Jr. Knopf 1969 150p boards $4.50

Original Portuguese edition 1964

"The story of an orphaned country girl brought from her remote home in the backlands to life in the city with the prosperous, fashionable cousins who are her only relatives. For a brief moment the trappings of her new life fascinate her but soon they prove alien to her temperament and upbringing. Her quiet determination to live her life on her own terms despite bitter opposition from her 'elegant' cousins—and her final humble success are . . . told." Am News of Bks

"Biela's story; though old-fashioned, should furnish a few hours of enjoyable reading for those who still like a good story well told." Book World

Dourado, Waldomiro Autran. See Dourado, Autran

Dowling, Jennette. See Letton, Jennette

Doyle, Adrian C.

Exploits of Sherlock Holmes, by Adrian C. Doyle and John Dickson Carr. Random House 1954 338p $5.95

Analyzed in Short Story Index

"Twelve reconstructions of Sherlock Holmes tales, each of which takes its beginning from a reference to the case in an old Sherlock Holmes." Book Rev Digest

The following stories are by A. C. Doyle and J. D. Carr: Adventure of the seven clocks; Adventure of the gold hunter; Adventure of the wax gamblers; Adventure of the Highgate miracle; Adventure of the black baronet; Adventure of the sealed room

The following stories are by A. C. Doyle: Adventure of Foulkes Rath; Adventure of the Abbas Ruby; Adventure of the Dark Angels; Adventure of the two women; Adventure of the Deptford horror; Adventure of the red widow

Doyle, Sir Arthur Conan

Adventures and Memoirs of Sherlock Holmes. Modern Lib 1946 612p $2.95

First published 1892 and 1894 respectively

Contents: Adventures of Sherlock Holmes: Scandal in Bohemia; The Red-headed League; Case of identity; Boscombe Valley mystery; Five orange pips; Man with the twisted lip; Adventure of the Blue Carbuncle; Adventure of the speckled band; Adventure of the engineer's thumb; Adventure of the noble bachelor; Adventure of the Beryl Coronet; Adventure of the copper beeches. Memoirs of Sherlock Holmes: Silver Blaze; Yellow face; Stockbroker's clerk; The Gloria Scott; Musgrave ritual; Reigate puzzle; Crooked man; Resident patient; Greek interpreter; Naval treaty; Final problem

y Adventures of Sherlock Holmes. Harper 1892 307p illus $4.95

Analyzed in Short Story Index

Contains the following stories: Scandal in Bohemia; Red-headed League; Case of identity; Boscombe Valley mystery; Five orange pips; Man with the twisted lip; Adventure of the Blue Carbuncle; Adventure of the speckled band; Adventure of the engineer's thumb; Adventure of the noble bachelor; Adventure of the Beryl Coronet; Adventure of the copper beeches

also in Doyle, Sir A. C. Adventures and Memoirs of Sherlock Holmes

also in Doyle, Sir A. C. The complete Sherlock Holmes v 1 p177-380

The case book of Sherlock Holmes
In Doyle, Sir A. C. The complete Sherlock Holmes v2 p1160-1323

y The complete Sherlock Holmes. With a preface by Christopher Morley. Doubleday 1953 [c1930] 2v (1323p) $9.95

Also available in a one-volume edition for $6.95

First published 1930; analyzed in Short Story Index

Contents: Study in scarlet (1887); Sign of the four (1890); Adventures of Sherlock Holmes (1892); Memoirs of Sherlock Holmes (1894); Return of Sherlock Holmes (1905); Hound of the Baskervilles (1902); Valley of fear (1915); His last bow (1917); Case book of Sherlock Holmes (1927)

Contents for the short story volumes included in the above are as follows:

Adventures of Sherlock Holmes: Scandal in Bohemia; Red-headed League; Case of identity; Boscombe Valley mystery; Five orange pips; Man with the twisted lip; Adventure of the Blue Carbuncle; Adventure of the speckled band; Adventure of the noble bachelor; Adventure of the Beryl Coronet; Adventure of the copper beeches

Memoirs of Sherlock Holmes: Silver Blaze; Yellow face; Stockbroker's clerk; The "Gloria Scott"; Musgrave ritual; Reigate puzzle; Crooked man; Resident patient; Greek interpreter; Naval treaty; Final problem

Return of Sherlock Holmes: Adventure of the empty house; Adventure of the Norwood builder; Adventure of the dancing men; Adventure of the solitary cyclist; Adventure of the priory school; Adventure of Black Peter; Adventure of Charles Augustus Milverton; Adventure of the six Napoleons; Adventure of the three students; Adventure of the golden pince-nez; Adventure of the missing three-quarter; Adventure of the Abbey Grange; Adventure of the second stain

His last bow: Adventure of Wisteria Lodge; Adventure of the cardboard box; Adventure of the red circle; Adventure of the Bruce-Parting-

Doyle, Sir Arthur C.—*Continued*

ton plans; Adventure of the dying detective; Disappearance of Lady Frances Carfax; Adventure of the devil's foot; His last bow

Case book of Sherlock Holmes: Adventure of the illustrious client; Adventure of the blanched soldier; Adventure of the Mazarin stone; Adventure of the Three Gables; Adventure of the Sussex vampire; Adventure of the three Garridebs; Problem of Thor Bridge; Adventure of the creeping man; Adventure of the lion's mane; Adventure of the veiled lodger; Adventure of Shoscombe Old Place; Adventure of the retired colourman

The Croxley master

    In Costain, T. B. ed. More Stories to remember v2 p189-221

y Famous tales of Sherlock Holmes. . . . Dodd 1958 339p illus (Great illustrated classics) $4.50

Analyzed in Short Story Index

"With biographical illustrations and pictures from early editions of the stories, together with an introduction by William C. Weber." Title page

Contents: A study in scarlet (1887); A scandal in Bohemia; The Red-headed League; The sign of the four (1890); The Boscombe Valley mystery

His last bow

    In Doyle, Sir A. C. The complete Sherlock Holmes v2 p1021-1155

y The hound of the Baskervilles; another adventure of Sherlock Holmes. With biographical illus. and pictures from early editions of the novel, together with an introduction by James Nelson. Dodd 1968 204p illus (Great illustrated classics) $4.50

First published 1902

This is the "case of the eerie howling on the moor and strange deaths at Baskerville. Sir Charles Baskerville is murdered, and Holmes and Watson move in to solve the crime." Haydn. Thesaurus of Book Digests

    also in Doyle, Sir A. C. The complete Sherlock Holmes v2 p783-899

    also in Doyle, Sir A. C. The later adventures of Sherlock Holmes p1071-1222

    also in Doyle, Sir A. C. Sherlock Holmes' greatest cases. Large type ed. p17-253

    also in Doyle, Sir A. C. Tales of Sherlock Holmes p431-605

The later adventures of Sherlock Holmes; a definitive text, corrected and ed. by Edgar W. Smith; illus. with a selective collation of the original illustrations by Frederic Dorr Steele, Sidney Paget & others. Heritage 1957 p767-1222 o.p. 1970

The second volume of: Sherlock Holmes, the three volume Heritage edition

Comprises the thirteen adventures originally published as "The return of Sherlock Holmes" and "The hound of the Baskervilles"

Contents for The return of Sherlock Holmes: The adventure of the empty house; The adventure of the Norwood builder; The adventure of the dancing men; The adventure of the solitary cyclist; The adventure of the Priory School; The adventure of Black Peter; The adventure of Charles Augustus Milverton; The adventure of the six Napoleons; The adventure of the three students; The adventure of the golden pince-nez; The adventure of the missing three-quarter; The adventure of the Abbey Grange; The adventure of the second stain

The lost world; being an account of the recent amazing adventures of Professor E. Challenger, Lord John Roxton, Professor Summerlee and Mr Ed. Malone of the 'Daily Gazette.' Murray, J. [distributed by Transatlantic] 240p $3.25

First published 1912, this edition first reprinted 1914

"Two professors and two other Englishmen come across a region in the Amazon valley where the Jurassic period still persists, with its flora and fauna, pterodactyls, dinosaurs, iguanodons, and other beasts that we know only in fossil form, still flourishing. The scientific squabbles of Challenger and the other professor provide incidental comedy." Baker's Best

y The Maracot Deep; with an introduction by John Dickson Carr. Norton 1968 119p (The Seagull lib. of mystery and suspense) $4.95

Originally appeared 1929

"Professor Maracot and his crew [in search of the lost civilization of Atlantis] meet a strange and dangerous people at the bottom of the Atlantic Ocean." McClurg. Book News

This story "must rank high among [Doyle's] fiction of mingled romance and science and does not suffer, at least in most of its phases, by comparison with Jules Verne's imaginary trip beneath the sea." N Y Times Bk R

The memoirs of Sherlock Holmes. New and rev. ed. Harper 1894 259p illus o.p. 1970

Analyzed in Short Story Index

First published 1893

Contents: Silver Blaze; Yellow face; Stock broker's clerk; The Gloria Scott; Musgrave ritual; Reigate puzzle; Crooked man; Resident patient; Greek interpreter; Naval treaty; Final problem

    also in Doyle, Sir A. C. Adventures and Memoirs of Sherlock Holmes

    also in Doyle, Sir A. C. The complete Sherlock Holmes v 1 p383-555

Micah Clarke; his statement as made to his three grandchildren Joseph, Gervas and Reuben during the hard winter of 1734. Murray, J. [distributed by Transatlantic] 1950 [c1912] 343p $3.25

First published 1889

A "narrative" romance, beginning in Hampshire at the time of "the hero's birth, 1664, but mainly dealing with Somerset in the year 1685. Essentially a story of the Monmouth Rebellion, telling of doings at Taunton, Keynsham Bridge, and Wells. There is a full account of the Battle of Sedgemoor. Monmouth himself is prominent, while Judge Jeffreys is vividly presented." Nield

The Professor Challenger stories. . . . Murray, J. [distributed by Transatlantic] 1952 577p $7.50

Contents: The lost world; The poison belt; Then land of mist; The disintegration machine; When the world screamed

The return of Sherlock Holmes

    In Doyle, Sir A. C. The complete Sherlock Holmes v2 p559-780

    In Doyle, Sir A. C. The later adventures of Sherlock Holmes p767-1069

y Sherlock Holmes: detective; eight of his famous adventures; arranged for young readers with a preface by Raymond T. Bond; with adventure of the engineer's thumb; The photographs and illus. from the original editions. Dodd 1965 240p illus $2.75

Analyzed in Short Story Index

Contents: The man with the twisted lip; The venture of the speckled band; The adventure of the Beryl Coronet; The adventure of the Copper Beeches; The Boscombe Valley mystery; The final problem; The adventure of the empty house

Doyle, Sir Arthur C.—*Continued*

Sherlock Holmes' greatest cases; introduction by Howard Haycraft. Large type ed. complete and unabridged. Watts, F. [1967] 463p o.p. 1970

Analyzed in Short Story Index
"A Keith Jennison book"
Contents: The hound of the Baskervilles [novel] and selected short stories; The Red-headed League; The adventure of the speckled band; A scandal in Bohemia; The Musgrave ritual; Silver Blaze; The adventure of the Blue Carbuncle

The sign of the four

In Doyle, Sir A. C. The complete Sherlock Holmes v 1 p91-173

In Doyle, Sir A. C. Famous tales of Sherlock Holmes p187-311

In Doyle, Sir A. C. Tales of Sherlock Holmes p131-255

A study in scarlet; a novel, by A. Conan Doyle. Burt 365p o.p. 1970

On cover: The home library
First published 1887 in England
A sensational story in two parts: the first deals with adventures in Utah and the wrong committed by two brutal Mormons on a girl and her lover; the second is the history of a mysterious double murder committed in London and, by the agency of Sherlock Holmes, shown to be the work of the wronged lover, who thus, after many years, attains his revenge." Baker's Best

also in Doyle, Sir A. C. The complete Sherlock Holmes v 1 p3-88

also in Doyle, Sir A. C. Faomus tales of Sherlock Holmes p 1-131

also in Doyle, Sir A. C. Tales of Sherlock Holmes p 1-129

Tales of Sherlock Holmes. Illus. by Harvey Dinnerstein. Afterword by Clifton Fadiman. Macmillan (N Y) 1963 608p (The Macmillan classics) $4.98

Partially analyzed in Short Story Index
Includes three complete novels: A study in scarlet; The sign of four; The hound of the Baskervilles, and the following short stories; The adventure of the Blue Carbuncle; A scandal in Bohemia; A case of identity; The adventure of the speckled band; Silver Blaze; The Red-headed League; The Musgrave ritual

In Doyle, Sir A. C. The complete Sher-

The valley of fear
In Doyle, Sir A. C. The complete Sherlock Holmes v2 p903-1018

y The White Company; with biographical illus. and pictures of the setting of the story, together with an introduction by Donald J. Harvey. Dodd 1962 363p illus (Great illustrated classics) $4.50

First published 1891
"The Hampshire hero joins an English Free Company, and, in the course of much wandering through France and the Pyrenees, meets with stirring adventures and performs many a deed of valour. The historical situation is that arising out of the Black Prince's decision to espouse the cause of Pedro the Cruel of Castile. Edward III, the Black Prince, Chandos, Sir William Felton, Bertrand du Guesclin, Don Pedro and others appear." Nield

Drabble, Margaret

The waterfall. Knopf 1969 290p $5.95

The book "tells the story of a young wife and mother, newly deserted by her weak husband, whom she has driven away from her, and falling impetuously into an affair with her cousin's dashing husband. The progress of the affair is contrasted with all that has gone before in Jane's life, her ugly middle-class girlhood and the frigidity she knew in her marriage." Pub W
"Filled with the brooding thoughts and emotions of a girl and woman who has been unable to adjust to her world, the story details her development of self-understanding through true communication with her lover. . . . Backgrounds of other characters serve to sketch in varying modes and manners of English middle-class life." Library J

Dreiser, Theodore

y An American tragedy; illus. by Grant Reynard; introduction by H. L. Mencken. World Pub. 1948 874p illus $6.95

First published 1925
"The tragedy of a young man brought up in simple Salvation Army piety who comes East to find success: money and social acceptance. Clyde Griffiths loves and is loved by his co-worker in the collar factory, Roberta, but he is dazzled by Sondra of the country clubs. Pregnant, Roberta becomes a threat to the rise Clyde dreams of. . . . He lacks the cruel strength to drop the socially inferior girl for the one who will help him succeed. Instead, madly, ineptly, uncertainly, he plans to resolve his dilemma by drowning Roberta. He is caught easily and easily convicted." College and Adult Reading List
"By making his protagonist a typical American youth, and his opponent the complex and unconquerable forces of heredity and environment (the modern equivalent of the Fates of Greek tragedy), he has translated this story . . . into an American epic." Atlantic

The best short stories of Theodore Dreiser; with an introduction by James T. Farrell. World Pub. 1956 349p $4.95

Analyzed in Short Story Index
First published 1947 with an introduction by Howard Fast
Contents: Khat; Free; St Columba and the river; McEwen of the shining slave makers; The shadow; A doer of the word; Nigger Jeff; The old neighborhood; Phantom gold; My brother Paul; The lost Phoebe; Convention; Marriage—for one; The prince who was a thief

The bulwark; a novel. Doubleday 1946 337p o.p. 1970

"The story of Solon Barnes, a Quaker who devoutly followed the tenets of his faith only to have his life shattered in the conflict with the materialism of twentieth century America. It is also the story of how he became reconciled to his worldly failure and the tragedy of his children's lives by turning to the spiritual core of his religion and finding a renewal of faith." Huntting
"'The Bulwark' is a major novel, a substantial piece of work, well conceived and carefully executed, representing its author in his full creative power. If it may also be taken as a last will and testament, it presents an interesting biographical problem, for here is an answer in faith to the spiritual doubt of his best work." Sat R

The financier; a novel. World Pub. 1946 503p $6.50

First published 1912 by Harper
First volume of a trilogy about the nineteenth century American dream of material power
"An effect of power and magnitude is achieved in this story of the love affairs and business career of a Philadelphia financier whose successive enterprises lead finally to his arrest and conviction for embezzlement." Booklist
Followed by: The titan

Jennie Gerhardt. World Pub. 430p $4.95

First published 1911 by Harper
"The fortunes of two families, German and Irish immigrants. Jennie, child of an unsuccessful German, falls a prey to the pleasure-loving son of the enterprising Irishman. Whether of deep-laid purpose or not, the book illustrates the rottenness of a complex social fabric resting on materialism." Baker's Best

Dreiser, Theodore—*Continued*

"Full of rugged sincerity, a fearless devotion to the truth, and undisguised pity for the impotence of human nature under its double handicap of heredity and environment." Bookman's Manual

Sister Carrie

Some editions are:
Bobbs (The Library of literature) $8 Edited with an introduction by Jack Salzman
Modern Lib. $2.95
World Pub. $6.50
First published 1900
"Plain, unaffected, and unconventional story of the actual life of the lower middle-classes of New York and Chicago. Its chief interest is its exhaustive record of the career of a young woman led into vice by her love of pleasure, and the careful study of a man's moral deterioration." Baker's Best

The stoic. Doubleday 1947 310p o.p. 1970
Sequel to: The titan
Continues the career of Frank Cowperwood in London

The titan. World Pub. 1946 551p $6.50
Sequel to: The financier
First published 1914 by Lane
Continues the career of Frank Cowperwood in Chicago of the 1870's
Followed by: The stoic

Druon, Maurice

The Iron King; a novel; tr. from the French by Humphrey Hare. Scribner 1956 269p (The Accursed kings) $4.50
Original French edition published 1955 as volume one of "Les rois maudits" or "The accursed kings"
The first of a series of novels dealing with King Philip IV of France and his descendants
"Pictures the last years of the 'Iron King,' Philip IV of France—cursed by Jacques de Molay, who was burned at the stake by Philip. This curse applied to 13 generations of the ill-fated House of Valois." McClurg. Book News
"Tightly written and technically admirable in its sustained focus on the central character, this Goncourt Prize-winner should appeal to the jaded reader of historicals. The author is unsentimental about the players in the tragedy and his realism reflects his respect for history rather than his audience indulgence." N Y Times Bk R
Followed by: The strangled queen

The Lily and the Lion; a novel; tr. from the French by Humphrey Hare. Scribner 1961 313p (The Accursed kings) o.p. 1970
Sequel to: The She-Wolf of France; the sixth and final volume of the author's "The accursed kings" series
Original French edition, 1960
"It's setting is fourteenth century England and France, when Edward III as one of his first acts as monarch had arrested the country's former Regent, and Philippe VI in France had become embroiled in the war between Robert of Artois and Countess Mahaut." Bk Buyer's Guide
"While each of the novels is complete in itself the whole forms a dramatic unity. . . . As the reader closes the last of these grim but vivid evocations of the late Middle Ages, perspectives deepen and proportions hitherto unnoticed strike the eye. . . . M. Druon and his translator Mr. Humphrey Hare are to be congratulated on the triumphant achievement of a brilliant and ambitious design." Times (London) Lit Sup

The poisoned crown; a novel; tr. from the French by Humphrey Hare. Scribner 1957 224p (The Accursed kings) o.p. 1970
Sequel to: The strangled queen
"The third in a series of historical novels dealing with the kings of fourteenth-century France, has Louis X as its focal figure. His marriage to his second wife, Clémence of Hungary, the rebellions throughout his kingdom, the intrigues against him, and his fatal poisoning are described in a brisk story which, like the author's previous novels, contains sharply

etched characterizations, realistic dialog, and a wealth of historically accurate details." Booklist
Followed by: The royal succession

The royal succession; a novel; tr. from the French by Humphrey Hare. Scribner 1958 254p (The Accursed kings) o.p. 1970
Sequel to: The poisoned crown
This "novel in an authoritative series on the kings of fourteenth-century France describes the interval after Louis X's murder in which the country was torn by various groups seeking to gain power. When Queen Clémence gives birth to a son shortly after her husband's death various enemies of the king attempt to poison the rightful heir to the throne but are tricked into killing another child. The unlawful ascent of Louis' brother to the throne rounds out a colorful and meticulously detailed story." Booklist
Followed by: The She-Wolf of France

The She-Wolf of France; tr. from the French by Humphrey Hare. Scribner 1960 335p (The Accursed kings) o.p. 1970
Sequel to: The royal succession
Original French edition published 1959
Set in 14th century France and England, this is a fictional account of Isabella, sister of Charles IV of France and wife of Edward II of England. The story centers around the love affair of Isabella and Sir Roger Mortimer and their plot to depose King Edward
"A vivid re-creation of the later Middle Ages in which savagery and courtliness, legalism and barbarity exist in strange contrast." New Statesman
Followed by: The Lily and the Lion

The strangled queen; tr. from the French by Humphrey Hare. Scribner 1957 213p (The Accursed kings) o.p. 1970
Sequel to: The Iron King
First published in England 1956
"A novel about Louis X of France and his attempts to remarry when his wife is convicted of adultery. A dilemma is created by the fact that a new Pope has not yet been elected and so Louis' first marriage cannot be annulled." Pub W
"Not so colorful as 'The Iron King,' this second volume is nonetheless written with close adherence to the historicity of the middle ages and provides an interesting reading experience." Chicago Sunday Tribune
Followed by: The poisoned crown

Drury, Allen

Advise and consent; drawings by Arthur Shilstone. Doubleday 1959 616p illus $6.95
Pulitzer Prize, 1960
"This novel tells of political machinations and personal conflicts which are set in motion when the Senate is called upon to confirm the President's nomination to a Cabinet post. The story is centered on five men who are vitally concerned with the appointment of a new Secretary of State." McClurg. Book News
"Although the narration dwells on the conflict of personal ambitions and the human frailties of the leaders of the defense and the opposition, it gives a graphic picture of the workings of the Senate and innumerable thumbnail sketches of individuals in Washington who figure in the complex political scene. Attempts to identify the fictional characters with real persons will no doubt give added interest to the exciting and suspenseful story." Booklist

Capable of honor; a novel. Doubleday 1966 531p $5.95
"Most of the characters in this novel, and the background of most of the events in it, have appeared in its predecessors, 'Advise and Consent' and 'A Shade of Difference.'" Note to the reader
"The time is late in this century. A Presidential Convention is getting under way. Arch villain Washington columnist Walter Dobius and the lily-livered crew of 'liberals' who support him are trying to force a Convention take over until . . . . President Hudson, steps in to manipulate events." Pub W

Drury, Allen—*Continued*

"As may easily be seen, the basic tone of 'Capable of Honor' is conservative. As such, it will probably be attacked by liberal-minded critics and defended by those of a conservative bent. Its value as a novel will very likely be ignored. But whatever the political implications, Mr. Drury has succeeded in bringing forth an always exciting story. In fact, there is no doubt that it is the political implications that give importance to the novel." Best Sellers

Preserve and protect; a novel. Doubleday 1968 394p $6.95

"Most of the characters in this novel, and the background of most of the events in it, have appeared in its predecessors, 'Advise and Consent,' 'A Shade of Difference' and 'Capable of Honor'." Note to the reader

"Describes the chaos that overtakes America and the world when the suspicious death of the President—just after his renomination—leaves the incumbent party without a candidate or a clear-cut way of selecting one." Publisher's note

The author "knows the political climate of the Savage Seventies, he has infinitely more than the requisite imagination, and he knows how to hold on to a reader. He knows people and he knows political people—the two are not the same: that's what makes politics and apparently it's also what makes fiction." Best Sellers

A shade of difference; a novel. Doubleday 1962 603p illus $7.95

"A novel about the United Nations, as 'Advise and Consent' was a novel about the government in Washington, and some of the same characters. Again, personalities clash in a public arena, the drama is ever-present and growing, and people's motives are stripped bare to the last, often nasty layers. The villain here is the Harvard-and-Oxford-educated potentate of a small African country, who makes trouble for the U.S. when he is the center of a racial incident in Charleston, S.C. The Afro-Asian and the Communist blocs in the U.N. encourage him in an anti-U.S. resolution. One of the few opposing him is a Negro Congressman shown as a responsible American leader." Pub W

Dudintsev, Vladimir

Not by bread alone; tr. from the Russian by Edith Bone. Dutton 1957 512p boards $6.95

In this story of modern Russia "the central character, Lopatkin, is an engineer and inventor of genius—an idealistic man who pits himself against an ambitious, ruthless bureaucrat, Drozdov. Though arrested and deported to Siberia, he refuses to give up his belief in his invention and in himself." Publisher's note

Duerrenmatt, Friedrich

The judge and his hangman; tr. from the German by Therese Pol. Harper 1955 152p o.p. 1970

Original German edition published 1952

"Police Commissioner Barlach, of Switzerland, was dying, but he still has his wits and his daring to pit against the killer of one of his own policemen." Retail Bookseller

"A clever plot, adorned with a little amusing satire on Swiss culture and politics, but laid out so simply that the reader is always a couple of jumps ahead." N Y Times Bk R

The pledge; tr. from the German by Richard and Clara Winston. Knopf 1959 183p boards $3.95

Original German edition published 1958

"A story within a story. A Swiss police commissioner tells a novelist the tale of Captain Matthai, of the police who promised Gritli's mother that he would find the murderer of the little girl. The unceasing, futile search for the murderer proved to be Matthai's undoing as a man. With an ironic ending." The Bookseller

The quarry. N.Y. Graphic 1962 [c1961] 162p o.p. 1970

"Translated from the German by Eva H. Morreale"

"The hero, Hans Barlach, is a retired Swiss police commissioner, convalescing from an operation for cancer. He comes to suspect that a notorious doctor who performed experimental operations without anesthetic in Nazi concentration camps may be the same surgeon who is running a swank sanitarium near Zurich. Barlach commits himself to the sanitarium in the hope of exposing the evil M.D., but finds himself trapped and helpless in Dr. Emmenberger's grisly suite of torture chambers. . . . Salvation [comes] in the mysterious appearance of a wandering Jew called Gulliver who has somehow survived his own torture and 'execution' by the Nazis." Time

" 'The Quarry' has a Police Commissioner as its hero and the plot seems to be the conventional one of clever detection. Yet, it is not a detective story. . . . The Gothic novel has come into its own again. . . . This swift-moving, exciting story demands to be read in one sitting." N Y Her Trib Books

Duggan, Alfred

Children of the wolf. Coward-McCann 1959 283p o.p. 1970

Published in England with title: Founding fathers

In this novel of the founding of the Eternal City, Alfred Duggan brings to life the legendary children of the wolf, Romulus and Remus. Through the eyes of Marcus, a young soldier of fortune, the reader sees the struggle for power between the twin brothers, and witnesses the triumph of Romulus over Remus. As the city grows and the citizens prosper, King Romulus exploits every gambit of politics to insure Rome's strength and his own authority. (Publisher)

Conscience of the king. Coward-McCann 1951 250p o.p. 1970

"Derived from legends, chronicles, and the author's imagination, this is the first-person story of the fifth-century founder of the West Saxon kingdom. Summing up his career at the age of eighty, Cerdic, the third, unwanted son of a petty Roman ruler in Britain, congratulates himself on being a self made man; it does not trouble him at all that his rise was accomplished by all manner of treachery and evil-doing, including the murders of his brothers and wife. . . . A tale of violence and intrigue, notable mainly as a credible recreation of a long-past age." Booklist

The cunning of the dove. Pantheon Bks. 1960 254p map boards $4.95

"A fictional treatment of the reign of Edward the Confessor, [the dove] narrated as the reminiscences of Edgar, chief chamberlain to the king. Along with his fellow-Englishmen, Edgar regards the king's monkish vow of continence, his visions, miracles of healing, and preoccupation with heaven as the marks of a saint; in the chamberlain's matter-of-fact view it is only to be expected that so un-worldly a ruler will leave matters of war and statecraft to his earls, so that Harold Godwinsson, the most capable and ambitious of them, comes to see himself as Edward's natural successor." Booklist

"The book is packed full of the authentic background material characteristic of Mr. Duggan's historical works, and, as everyone who knows his earlier books will expect, is a thoroughly enjoyable reading experience." Spring'd Republican

Lord Geoffrey's fancy. Pantheon Bks. 1962 254p map $3.95

Set in 13th century Greece and Turkey after the Fourth Crusade, this historical novel recreates the court life of the Frankish knights who were defending the Greek lands they had seized from attacks by the Byzantines. The story follows the career of Lord Geoffrey de Bruyere of Romanie, an arrogant knight, through several battles, including Pelagonie, imprisonment in Constantinople, and two trials by his fellow knights. (Publisher)

"It is a good story, one which should not merely please confirmed Dugganites, but a mort of others too. It is laid at a time and in a place that provide ample material for two of this author's most notable gifts, that of not always too subtle irony and that of colorful reconstruction." N Y Times Bk R

Duggan, Alfred—*Continued*

My life for my sheep. Coward-McCann 1955 341p o.p. 1970

Published in England with title: God and my right

This is a "biography, somewhat fictionalized, of the statesman, martyr and saint, of 12th century England, Thomas à Becket." Book Rev Digest

"A fascinating and a valuable book, fascinating both because of its subject and its manner of treatment, valuable because of the exciting way in which it portrays a figure familiar even to high school students of history. . . . One misses, I think, however, the thoughts and the motives both of Becket and of Henry II, the protagonists of this ill-fated drama. . . . One misses, too, any mention of sources." N Y Her Trib Books

Three's company. Coward-McCann 1958 286p o.p. 1970

Imperial Rome during the struggle between Mark Anthony and Octavius Caesar, as seen by Lepidus—the comic, bewildered and least remembered third part of that famous Triumvirate. This is the story of Lepidus who, guided only by his deep-grained instinct for doing the Right Thing, became a pawn in a game far larger and more risky than he could understand (Publisher)

"In spite of all his follies and his pomposity, Lepidus is an engaging figure in Mr. Duggan's vivid pages. Through the eyes of Lepidus the reader sees a new and somehow lesser Rome developing from the old Rome of old-fashioned forms and virtues." Cath Lib World

Dulles, Allen

y (ed.) Great spy stories from fiction. Harper 1969 433p $6.95

"A Giniger book"

A collection of thirty-two examples of spy stories from novels by such writers as Leon Uris, Joseph Conrad, A. Conan Doyle, Vladimir Nabokov, John Le Carré and Ian Fleming. Some of the stories are based on historical fact or persons; others demonstrate current practices in spying

"It is not an essential purchase but would be useful in browsing and YA collections." Library J

Dumas, Alexandre, 1802-1870

The black tulip. Dutton 248p (Everyman's lib) $2.95

First published 1891 by Little
Written in 1850

"Love-romance associated with the Haarlem tulip craze and intertwined with scenes from Dutch history (1672-5), when William of Orange lent himself to the agitation against the brothers De Witt, the patriotic defenders of Dutch liberty." Baker's Best

y The Count of Monte Cristo

Some editions are:
Dutton (Everyman's lib.) 2v ea. $3.25 Introduction by Marcel Girard
Grosset $4.95

First French edition 1844

"Edmond Dantés, a young sailor unjustly accused of helping the exiled Napoleon in 1815, has been arrested and imprisoned in the Cheateau d'IF, near Marseille. After fifteen years, he finally escapes by taking the place of his dead companion, the Abbé Faria, enclosed in a sack, he is thrown into the sea. He cuts the sack with his knife, swims to safety, is taken to Italy on a fisherman's boat. From Genoa, he goes to the cavern of Monte Cristo and digs up the fabulous treasures of which the dying Faria had told. He then uses the money to punish his enemies and reward his friends." Hadyn. Thesaurus of Book Digests

y The man in the iron mask. . . . Dodd 1944 280p illus (Great illustrated classics) $4.50

Forms a part of: The Vicomte de Bragelonne, published frequently as a separate novel

"With illustrations by J. A. Beauce, Philippoteaux, and others, and a foreword by Emile Van Vliet." Title page

Identity of the Man in the iron mask—is an unsolved mystery. Dumas' "iron mask episode is found toward the end . . . of the third volume of 'The Vicomte De Bragelonne.' . . . The present volume remains essentially the story of the . . . closing years of those four men who had performed such prodigies—attacking armies, assaulting castles, terrifying death itself—Athos, Porthos, Aramis, and their captain, D'Artagnan." Preface for the reader

Marguerite de Valois. Dutton (Everyman's lib) 477p $3.25

Written in 1845; first published in this edition 1908. First of the Valois romances (1560-89)

"A novel of love, adventure and political conspiracy in France during the years 1572-1575. It begins shortly before the massacre of St. Bartholomew and ends with the death of Charles IX and the accession of Henry III." Nield

The queen's necklace. Little 2v o.p. 1970

Written 1849-50

"An account of the scandalous affair of the Diamond Necklace in accordance with the known facts, though Dalsams's connection with the intrigue is taken for granted. The period (1784-5) is the beginning of the ill-fated reign of Louis XVI, and Marie Antoinette makes her first appearance." Baker's Best

Short stories. Black 1927 10v in 1 (1003p) o.p. 1970

Analyzed in Short Story Index

Contents: v 1: Courtship of Josephine and Napoleon; Drowner; Blood union; Lady Hamilton and Admiral Nelson; Honor of Von Bulow; Gaetano the gorger; Provisional government; Cannibals; Confession of the district attorney; Vindication; Mme Dubarry; Storming of the Bastile; Aurora; Branded; Tragedy of Nantes; Cripple and giant; Louis XIII; Death of Mirabeau; Anne of Austria; Black pearl

v2: Female defender; Great Copt; Scarlet sphynx; Real Bonaparte; Corneille; Wedding night; Bouquet; Tactics of love; Pipe and a man; Marat and Rousseau; Fate of a regicide; Scar of de Guise; Hollow voice; King and courtiers; Frankfort-on-Main; Bitter cup; Smuggler's inn; Prodigal's favor; Sword of the Swiss; French breed

v3: Vive le roi; Mademoiselle; Uninvited visitors; Death of Richelieu; Vicomte's breakfast; Drum-head marriage; Sword and pistol; It rains; Melancholy tale; Isabella; Ransom of Isabella; Bridals; On to Rome; His oath; Legend; Some Prussian history; Count von Bismarck; Chalice; Avalanche; Little dog Jet

v4: King cobbler; Sweet smell; Citizen Bonaparte; Grecian slave-girl; Glove of Conde; Luisa San Felice; Chevalier San Felice; Martyr San Felice; Mad method; Historic fete; D'Orsay; Chimney-back; Modern Aspasia; Royal criminologist; Tenth muse; Ball of the victims—a sketch; Conquest of Circe; Inscription; Statistics; Bird of prey

v5: Caracciolo's capture; Wild boar hunt; Historic Banquo; Daughter of the Caesars; Three madames—a portrait; Vertigo; La Fontaine's first fable; Glimpse of Paris; Odoardo, the prisoner; Odoardo, the gentleman; Marseillaise; D'Artagnan, the Gascon; D'Artagnan meets the musketeers; Musketeers meet D'Artagnan; Voice of liberty; Dowry; Black tulip; Perennial Venus; Straw; Carnot and conspiracy

v6: Burgomaster; Sack of the Tuileries; Murat; Diana de Castro; Champion of beauty; Glory of love; D'Artagnan, detective; Narcotic dream; Instinct; Moliere; Moreau; View of the terror; Bismarck—his offer; Spanish surprise; Prison; Madam; Substitute; Man in the iron mask; Lame mendicant; Andre Chenier

v7: Career of a courtesan; Strange ending; People; Crossing the Alps; Battle of Langensalza; Diana de Meridor; Assassination; Fruit, a torch and a bouquet; Gourmand; Surprise; Cabaret; Picture; Bastard of Waldeck; Word of a king; Marie Touchet; Remember; Queen's perfumer; Madame de Sauve's chamber; Boxes; To Rusconise

v8: Saint Jean d'Acre; Men from Marseilles; Regent's letter; Regent's revenge; Marengo; Byron sees Kean; Son of a courtesan; Destiny; Call; Dock fight; Regal love; Bal-masque; Chateau d'If; Story of no. 27; Story of no. 34; Cemetery of Chateau d'If; Madness; Paradise for hell; Battle of Charenton; Mercedes

Dumas, Alexandre, 1802-1870—*Continued*

v9: Death of the king's mistress; Theory of war; Two fugitives; Chastelard; Big spider; Count of Monte-Cristo; Slaughter; Italian lover; Dormice; First consul; Death of Hercules; Act of faith; Bernadotte; Pilgrimage; Conscience's dream; Mariettes dream; Vision of Athos; Le terrain de Dieu; Weird costume; Three against three

v10: Goddess of reason; Portrait; Thief; Jean Ouillier—a study; Eight long days; Gay prince; Remark; Augereau; Sacrifice of beauty; D'Artagnan-Marechal; Duel; Corsican mother; Corsican son; Corsican brother; Printing house—a sketch; Milan; Source of money; Hannibal; Brigand's faith; Mercy and Brigand; Reverses

y **The three musketeers**

Some editions are:
Dodd (Great illustrated classics) $4.50 With illustrations from drawings by the French illustrator Maurice Lelor together with an introductory biographical sketch of the author and anecdotal captions by Basil Davenport
Dutton (Everyman's lib) $3.25
Macmillan (N Y) (The Macmillan classics) $3.95 Illustrated by James Daugherty. Afterword by Clifton Fadiman

Written 1844. Published also under title: The three guardsmen
"D'Artagnan arrives in Paris one day in 1625 and manages to be involved in three duels with three musketeers . . . Athos, Porthos, and Aramis. They become d'Artagnan's best friends. The account of their adventures from 1626 on develops against the rich historical background of the reign of Louis XII and early part of that of Louis XIV, the main plot being furnished by the antagonism between Cardinal de Richelieu and Queen Anne d'Autriche." Haydn. Thesaurus of Book Digests
Followed by: Twenty years after

y **Twenty years after;** with illus. from drawings by contemporary French artists together with an introductory sketch of the author and anecdotal captions by Basil Davenport. Dodd 1942 781p illus (Great illustrated classics. Titan eds) $5.50

Sequel to: The three musketeers
Written in 1845
"Anne of Austria's regency, the insurrection of the Fronde, and the execution of Charles I of England mark out the period (1648-9)." Baker's Best

The Vicomte de Bragelonne; or, Ten years later. Little 6v o.p. 1970

Sequel to: The three musketeers
Written 1848-50. Also published in three parts: Louise de la Vallière; The man in the iron mask; Bragelonne, son of Athos
"The great closing scenes in the lives of the four musketeers. . . . Court life, the great personages of this epoch, and state affairs are described with fair accuracy, although facts and fiction are mingled. Mazarin and the king are prominent, and romantic interest attaches to Mlle de la Vallière, the tenderhearted mistress of Louis XIV; Madame de Montespan, Fouquet and Colbert, the great rival ministers of finance, the Man in the Iron Mask, and other famous persons figure among the characters." Baker's Best

Dumas, Alexandre, 1824-1895

Camille; introduction by Edmund Gosse. Modern Lib. 270p o.p. 1970

Written 1848. Also published with title: Lady with the camellias
"Pathetic story of a courtesan, who conceives a pure passion; founded on a true story, and obviously patterned after Manon Lescaut. The subject is treated with all the delicacy possible, where the vices and follies of a great city are to be described realistically." Baker's Best

Du Maurier, Daphne

The flight of the falcon. Doubleday 1965 311p $5.95

"The story grows out of the accidental involvement of young Armino Fabbio in a murder. Reluctantly he returns to his birthplace in Italy where he comes to feel that he is haunted both by the spirit of his beloved elder brother and the demoniacal Duke Claudio who five hundred years before, as the Falcon, had victimized the people of the village." Huntting
"An atmoshpheric, suspenseful, and romantic tale of postwar . . . Italy." Booklist

Frenchman's Creek. Doubleday 1942 310p o.p. 1970

The setting is the coast of Cornwall during the reign of Charles II. The novel recounts the story of rebellious Lady Dona St Columb, darling of the Court of St James's and Jean-Benoit Aubery, pirate, and of their love

also in Du Maurier, D. Three romantic novels of Cornwall: Rebecca, Frenchman's Creek and Jamaica Inn p317-495

The glass-blowers. Doubleday 1963 348p $5.50

The story of a family of master craftsmen, glass-blowers, in France from 1747 to 1845. The author touches on a little known aspect of the French Revolution, the Civil War originating in the Vendée. She reveals how the lives of the Busson family were permanently altered by the Revolution and the Civil War which followed; how it affected Mathurin, the father, and the lives of his five sons and daughters. (Publisher)
"While not so dramatic as some of Daphne Du Maurier's novels this has excellent characterization and presents a strikingly vivid picture of the Reign of Terror as it affected the communities outside Paris." Booklist

y **The house on the strand.** Doubleday 1969 298p $5.95

"Richard Young, a British publisher with marital problems . . . borrows a picturesque house in Cornwall from his friend Professor Magnus Lane [a biochemist] with the promise that he will experiment with a drug on which Magnus is working. Magnus warns him only that although the world of the past will seem very real after he takes the drug, he himself will be invisible and must touch only inanimate objects, not people, or he will awaken instantly to the present with nausea and shock. Richard experiments and discovers, after consultation with Magnus, that he has met the very group of 14th-century gentlefolk and servants whom Magnus had seen in previous experiments. But with Richard there is a difference: in the course of repeated 'trips' he falls in love with Isolda, one of the medieval ladies—a development which, among other things, further complicates his already unhappy marriage." Book of the Month Club News

This "is a gripping and suspenseful double novel from the expert pen of Daphne du Maurier. The realism and authenticity of her work is, no doubt enhanced by the fact that Miss du Maurier is mistress of Kilmarth, the house whose 600-year-old past was the inspiration for and the setting of this tale-within-a-tale." Best Sellers

Hungry hill. Doubleday 1943 402p o.p. 1970

In this novel, the author "depicts the bitter struggle between the proud, semi-aristocratic, land-owning [Irish] Brodericks attempting to escape the destiny inherent in their way of life—and their feud with their sly, improvident and vicious neighbors, the Donovans. . . . A large work covering five stormy generations, starting in 1820 and continuing for a hundred years." Huntting

y **Jamaica Inn.** Doubleday 1960 243p $4.95

A reissue in new format of the title first published 1936

"A stirring tale of an old inn on the desolate moors of Cornwall, where Mary Yellan, left alone in the world at her mother's death took refuge with her aunt. Her uncle the landlord, directed smugglers who wrecked ships on the nearby coast, and the inn was a place of horror and mystery. Mary's hope of rescuing her aunt, and escaping, was soon complicated by her unwilling interest in the landlord's brother, who stole horses but drew the line at murder." Booklist

Du Maurier, Daphne—*Continued*

"In spite of the conventionality of the ingredients, the author has concocted an exciting brew, reminiscent of Stevenson and some of Masefield, and just the thing for late-evening reading. If it adds nothing to the author's reputation, it does provide first-rate entertainment of its 'genre.'" Sat R

also in Du Maurier, D. Three romantic novels of Cornwall: Rebecca, Frenchman's Creek and Jamaica Inn p497-704

The King's general. Doubleday 1946 371p $4.95

The story begins in Devon, England in 1631 when the heroine, Honor Harris celebrates her eighteenth birthday. She meets and falls in love with Sir Richard Grenville, Charles I's general in the West, who shares her tumultuous life during the stress and strife of England's civil wars

"A clever blend of fact and fiction, with fewer than usual of the swashbuckling appurtenances of the historical novel, and somewhat more emphasis on the emotional experiences of these hard-living Cornish aristocrats. And the continuity in English life, the persistence of family names and the old castles still standing, adds to the sense of the tale's authenticity." Book of the Month Club News

Kiss me again, stranger; a collection of eight stories, long and short; drawings by Margot Tomes. Doubleday 1952 319p illus o.p. 1970

Analyzed in Short Story Index

First published in England with title: The apple tree

"In this collection of eight stories (of which all but two are very long) Daphne du Maurier explores horror in a variety of forms; in the macabre, in the psychologically deranged, in the supernatural, in the fantastic [and] most painfully of all, in the sheer cruelty of human beings in interrelationship. Yet on the whole the volume offers absorbing rather than oppressive reading." N Y Her Trib Books

Contents: Kiss me again, stranger; The birds; The little photographer; Monte Verita; The apple tree; The old man; The split second; No motive

My cousin Rachel. Doubleday 1952 348p o.p. 1970

"Philip Ashley and his beloved uncle, Ambrose, lived happily together in their Cornish home, but illness drove Ambrose to Italy. There he married Rachel. After his unexpected death Rachel came to England and stayed with Philip, ten years her junior. Her charms attracted, baffled and finally outraged him. He permitted an accident, without having proof of her guilt. Suspense, suspicion, sharp characterization and not a little strain on the reader's credulity sustain the plot." Library J

y Rebecca

Some editions are:
Doubleday $4.95
Modern Lib. $2.95

First published 1938

"Against the setting of a great English estate unfolds the story of Rebecca, its glamorous mistress, who had been dead for eight months. Maxim de Winter's young and frightened second wife gradually realizes that there is some mystery surrounding her death, but it is not until the night of the big costume ball that her suspicions are confirmed and, with an ever-increasing atmosphere of impending disaster, the real story becomes known." Huntting

"Although this is first and last and always a thrilling story, the novel keeps a genuine human value in the person and problem of its heroine, and rises, thus, above the level of the theatrical. . . . Miss du Maurier's style in telling her story is exactly suited to her plot and her background, and creates the exact spirit and atmosphere of the novel. The rhythm quickens with the story, is always in measure with the story's beat. And the writing has an

intensity, a heady beauty, which is itself the utterance of the story's mood." Books

also in Du Maurier, D. Three romantic novels of Cornwall: Rebecca, Frenchman's Creek and Jamaica Inn p7-316

also in Haycraft, H. ed. A treasury of great mysteries v2 p301-576

The scapegoat. Doubleday 1957 348p $4.50

John, an English professor, on holiday in France, meets his double, Jean, Comte de Gue, who is contemplating flight from his family and business problems. After a drinking bout John awakens to find that Jean has effected an exchange of identities by an exchange of personal possessions. The story centers around John's efforts to solve Jean's problems. (Publisher)

The author's "pictures of the old château and of its disintegrating little glass foundry are warm with life and acute in their perception of French character. With wizardry Miss du Maurier makes the book believable and compelling to unravel." Atlantic

Three romantic novels of Cornwall: Rebecca, Frenchman's Creek and Jamaica Inn. Doubleday 1961 704p o.p. 1970

An anthology of the three complete novels reprinted here, first published in 1938, 1942, and 1936 respectively, all entered separately

(jt. auth.) Quiller-Couch, A. Castle Dor

Du Maurier, George

Peter Ibbetson; with a preface by Daphne du Maurier; illus. by the author. Heritage [1964 c1963] 344p illus boards $7.95

"A melancholy, dreamy book on the idea of a supernatural gift enabling the hero to meet his lost love in the dreamland of the past. Reminiscences of a happy childhood at Passy [France] are the real basis." Baker's Best

Trilby

Some editions are:
Collins $1.95
Dutton (Everyman's lib) $2.95

First published 1894

"Trilby O'Farral, a young artist's model in Paris, is beloved by three English art students. Her engagement to one of them, William Bagot, known as Little Billee, is broken off and she falls into the hands of a sinister Hungarian musician, Svengali. She becomes a great singer under his mesmeric influence, but loses her voice when he suddenly dies of heart failure. She sickens and dies soon after." Benét. The Reader's Encyclopedia

Dumitriu, Petru

The extreme Occident; tr. from the French by Peter Wiles. Holt 1966 378p $6.95

First published 1964 in France

The author's "hero and narrator is a Rumanian exile, a writer, now living in the affluent West as a public relations man for a northern shipping concern in an unnamed country. Behind the glittering opulence, the exotic women, the frantic prosperity, the exile is led to see the shabby and poor, the cheapness of sex and the horrors of sadism, the approach of inflation, strikes, and business catastrophe. A saint, not wholly saintly, and a devil, not entirely evil, move through this profound, thoughtful, allegorical novel." Pub W

Family jewels; tr. from the French by Edward Hyams in consultation with Princess Anne-Marie Callimachi. Pantheon Bks. 1961 437p o.p. 1970

This novel describes "the powerful dynasty of the Coziano's, a family of Rumanian boyar-aristocrats whose wealth is based on huge, semifeudal estates and whose destiny, is intimately linked with that of Rumania's arrogant ruling class. . . . Starting in 1862, in an epoch of lush extravagance and langorous cruelty inherited from centuries of Turkish domination, and ending in 1907 against a background of peasant revolt, Dumitriu tells the story of four generations of Coziano's—their loves and hates, their ruthless political ambi-

Dumitriu, Petru—*Continued*

tions and financial maneuvers, their triumphs and defeats." Publisher's note

"With savage anger and bitterness Dumitriu writes of a social order that accepted corruption and debauchery among the rich and drove the starving poor to extremes of violence in rebellion. . . . He succeeds in painting a vivid canvas of corrupt feudal society." N Y Her Trib Books

The prodigals; tr. from the French by Norman Denny. Pantheon Bks [1963 c1962] 446p o.p. 1970

Original French edition 1960. First published 1962 in England

The second volume of the author's trilogy, The boyars, the first of which is: Family jewels

"The story of the fortunes of the Coziano family is told against the background of Bucharest society from 1915 to 1944. These people are the lineal and spiritual descendants of the great Rumanian boyar aristocrats who amassed large estates and suppressed peasant revolts during the previous century. Their lives portend with clarity the dissolution of the entire ruling class and the end of an era." Huntting

"Here is the blueprint of the communist climb to power in so many countries, a blueprint drafted not by Communists themselves but by spineless men who betray the responsibilities given into their hands because they would sooner wallow in the sick ecstasy of aggravated passions." Best Sellers

Dunbar, Paul Laurence

The strength of Gideon, and other stories. Arno Press 1969 362p (The American Negro, his history and literature) $11.50

A reprint of the collection first published 1900 by Dodd, and analyzed in Short Story Index

Contents: Strength of Gideon; Mammy Peggy's pride; Viney's free papers; The fruitful sleeping of the Rev Elisha Edwards; The ingrate; The case of 'Ca'line'; The finish of Patsy Barnes; One man's fortunes; Jim's probation; Uncle Simon's Sundays out; Mr Cornelius Johnson, office seeker; An old-time Christmas; A mess of pottage; The trustfulness of Polly; The tragedy at Three Forks; The finding of Zach; Johnsonham, Junior; The faith cure man; A council of state; Silas Jackson

Dunnett, Dorothy

The disorderly knights. Putnam 1966 503p maps $6.95

"A duel of personalities and purpose between the seemingly saintly Graham Reid Malett of the Knights of Malta, assisted by his supposedly virginal sister Joleta, and the complex, daring, and dark-of-mood Francis Crawford of Lymond dominates a richly plotted and populated melodramatic historical romance. The year is 1551. The scene shifts back and forth from Malta and Tripoli to Scotland. The onslaught of the Turks, corruption among the Knights of Malta, French intrigue, and feuding between the Scotts and the Kerrs serve as historical counterpoint to fictionalized events. This is Lymond's third appearance, his first having taken place in Dunnett's 'The game of kings'." Booklist

The game of kings. Putnam 1961 543p o.p. 1970

"In the year (1547) preceding the departure of the five-year-old Mary, Queen of Scots for France much of the intrigue and fighting to determine her future and that of Scotland centered, according to this romance, in the controversial figure of Lymond, supposedly a traitor and renegade. Organized to conform to the analogy of a chess game, the story follows Lymond through a series of swashbuckling adventures and perils that further blacken his already evil reputation and nearly cost him his life before he is proved a loyal Scot." Booklist

"The plot, woven at many levels, is devious and complicatedly misleading but, strangely enough, falls into proper order as the story approaches its climax. . . . The style is sparkling and lively with elegant phrase and quotation in abundance and with little Scottish dialect. In brief, this is a slight cut above the usual historical novel." Best Sellers

Pawn in frankincense. Putnam 1969 486p $6.95

The story "begins in the year 1552 with the sailing of the royal galley Dauphine from Marseilles, bound for Algiers and Constantinople. Her commander is Francis Crawford of Lymond, a less than conscientious Special Envoy who is pleased to conduct his pressing personal business under the sancrosanct flag of France. Officially, his mission is to deliver to the Sultan Suleiman France's assurances of her continuing devotion. Privately, it is to arrange the deliverance from slavery of a child named Khaireddin, Lymond's illegitimate son, and the killing of a man named Gabriel, or Sir Graham Reid Malett." Publisher's note

"For those who yearn for adventure-romance with all the trappings: pirates, intrigue, a novel hero, danger, mystery, plus exotic settings—the Mediterranean in the 16th century, when a crucial confrontation was taking place between the Holy Roman and Ottoman Empires. . . . This is the fourth interlocking but independent novel in a series that includes: 'The Game of Kings,' 'Queen's Play,' [and] 'The Disorderly Knights.'" Pub W

Queen's play. Putnam 1964 432p map o.p. 1970

"The decadent court of the French Renaissance supplies the background for this novel of intrigue and romance. Francis Crawford of Lymond sails to France on a secret mission to save the life of his future monarch, Mary Queen of Scots, who is then a child of seven. He becomes involved in a terrifying game to save both the princess and his own life." Huntting

Dupee, F. W.

(ed.) Great French short novels; ed. with an introduction. Dial Press 1952 717p o.p. 1970

Analyzed in Short Story Index

"A praiseworthy anthology including stories of intensity and wit, representing nine novelists. . . . Editor has supplied a perceptive introduction, notes, and another special translation (for Flaubert's 'Legend of Saint Julian')." Library J

Contents: Rameau's nephew, by D. Diderot; Vanina Vanini, by Stendhal; The Malacca cane, by A. De Vigny; The old maid, by H. De Balzac; Happiness in crime, by J. B. D'Aurevilly; The legend of Saint Julian the hospitaller, by G. Flaubert; Captain Burle, by E. Zola; Open all night, by P. Morand; The conquerors, by A. Malraux

Duras, Marguerite

Four novels. . . . Introduction by Germaine Brée. Grove 1965 303p $3.95

Analyzed in Short Story Index

Original French editions published 1955, 1958, 1962 and 1965 respectively

"The square; Moderato cantabile; Ten-thirty on a summer night; The afternoon of Mr Andesmas." Title page

The sea wall. Tr. by Herma Briffault. With a preface by Germaine Brée. Farrar, Straus 1967 288p $4.95

Original French edition, 1950. First published 1952 by Pellegrini & Cudahy

"The scene is the coast of French Indo-China. A French widow who had come here with her schoolmaster-husband takes up land and endeavors to support herself and her two children. The land proves worthless, and the story traces the widow's descent into poverty and madness." Book Rev Digest

The book "is full of realistic detail, from the most humble to the most sordid furniture of poverty. The reader touches and, indeed, is touched by these tangible details at each moment. . . . Yet Suzanne, Joseph and their mother brush past these realities as in sleepwalking or, rather, as in madness. Mlle. Duras—and this is the substance of her gift—compels the reader to share the folly of her characters by making their unreason more reasonable than all the brutal facts of life. Here true reality reposes in the hallucination itself." N Y Times Bk R

Durrell, Gerald

Rosy is my relative. Viking 1968 239p boards $4.95

"The setting is Edwardian England, and a lad named Adrian Rookwhistle . . . inherits Rosy [an elephant], as sweet a beast as one would want to meet until she downs her first barrel or so of beer, from an eccentric uncle. Before long, Adrian and Rosy head for the seashore, where Adrian is sure he will find a circus that will take Rosy off his hands. But in the course of things, the pair become involved in a fox hunt, a disastrous birthday party and a totally outlandish performance of 'Ali Baba.'" Book of the Month Club News

"Picaresque in structure, splendidly comic, and at times splendidly satirical, [it] is a descendant of the traditional rambling, good-natured British novel which goes back at least as far as Smollett, and it is encouraging to see signs that the tradition is being revived." Best Sellers

Durrell, Lawrence

The Alexandria quartet: Justine; Balthazar; Mountolive [and] Clea. Dutton 1962 884p $12.50

An anthology of the four volumes first published 1957, 1958, 1958 and 1960 respectively, all entered separately

Balthazar; a novel. Dutton 1958 250p boards $5.95

Sequel to: Justine

"Once again he writes of Justine, Melissa, Clea, Nessim, Pursewarden, Scobie, Pombal—but from a fresh point of view. The new insights are provided by the psychiatrist, Balthazar, who convinces the narrator that the first volume of the story was almost wholly inaccurate. . . . So this second volume is a correction and an expansion of the first." N Y Times Bk R

"Supposedly Balthazar can be read as a discrete unit without Justine, but it does not have as complete and compelling a forward movement as that remarkable novel did. What it does have are brightly etched sketches of modern Alexandrian life. . . . This is not a book for all readers, but does belong in collections of better modern fiction." Library J

Followed by: Mountolive

also in Durrell, L. The Alexandria quartet: Justine; Balthazar; Mountolive [and] Clea p205-390

Clea; a novel. Dutton 1960 287p $5.95

Sequel to: Mountolive. The final volume of: The Alexandria quartet

"In this novel events are seen from the point of view of the Englishman Darley who, returning to Alexandria to see old friends and lovers, has a passionate affair with Clea, one of the women in the circle of friends. Again, the tone is philosophic, the language frequently overripe, and the characters, though individualistic, are symbolic. Heterosexual and homosexual affairs are prominent in each of the novels." Booklist

"'The Alexandria Quartet' is one of the major achievements of fiction in our time, distinguished not only by its power of language, by its evocation of a place, by its creation of character, by the drama of many of its incidents, but also by its boldly original design. 'Clea' perfects the work, as a spire crowns a cathedral, but the spire is not to be judged in isolation." Sat R

also in Durrell, L. The Alexandria quartet: Justine; Balthazar; Mountolive [and] Clea p653-884

The dark labyrinth. Dutton 1962 266p $4.95

Originally published in England 1947 with title: Cefalû

"A modern-day parable which . . . tells the story of a rather motley collection of people who, as counterparts of lost souls wandering round in a postwar vacuum, seek their separate destinies on a Mediterranean cruise that lands them in the labyrinth said to be once inhabited by the legendary Minotaur. . . . Cut off

from the outside world by a landslide, only a few are able to return to everyday existence. The others either die or remain behind in a sort of Shangri La world from which there is no return from its valley of eternal plenty." Springf'd Republican

"Devious and subtle in the telling, it is written in a spare, sophisticated, witty, amusing, and brilliant style." Pub W

Justine. Dutton 1957 253p $5.95

First volume of: The Alexandria quartet

This novel, set against the background of the modern city of Alexandria in Egypt follows the destinies of four principal characters: Justine, the passionate, tormented Jewess; Melissa, a Greek cabaret dancer; Nessim, the millionaire Coptic financier; and the "I" of the narrative, an Irish schoolmaster. (Publisher)

"The setting of the novel is fiercely real, the intellectual anguish of the characters is real, but the characters themselves are never quite flesh and blood. . . . This defect —if it is a defect rather than a deliberate device—permits Mr. Durrell to be remarkably outspoken without becoming offensive." Atlantic

Followed by: Balthazar

also in Durrell, L. The Alexandria quartet: Justine; Balthazar; Mountolive [and] Clea p653-884

Mountolive; a novel. Dutton 1959 [c1958] 318p $5.95

Sequel to: Balthazar

First published 1958 in England

The perspective is "that of David Mountolive, the British ambassador; and what appeared to be 'the intrigues of desire' are shown to be intrigues motivated by politics. We learn that the beautiful Jewess, Justine, and her Coptic (Christian) husband, Nessim, are passionately united by a common cause: he believes that the formation of a Jewish state will save other minorities in the Arab world from Muslim domination and he is the leader of a group which is smuggling arms to the Jews of Palestine. The discovery of this conspiracy by Nessim's loyal English friends, Pursewarden and the ambassador, and their reactions to it form the plot line of Mountolive." Atlantic

"Durrell's rich and exotic novel is deeply informed by his intimate knowledge of the middle east and of diplomatic life. . . . He succeeds brilliantly in showing how the moral obliquity of each kind of life is mirrored in the other." Chicago Sunday Tribune

Followed by: Clea

also in Durrell, L. The Alexandria quartet: Justine; Balthazar; Mountolive [and] Clea p391-652

Tunc; a novel. Dutton 1968 359p $6.95

First of a projected series of stories

This story is set in Athens, Istanbul and London. It "is told by scientist Felix Charlock: a 'thinking weed' he calls himself. He has created a computer named Abel, a giant memory-bank that can recall or predict just about everything. Abel, and Felix's other inventions, attract the attention of Merlin's, an international firm with holdings in all industries, and it soon adds Felix to its assets. . . . [Other] personalities [include] Benedicta, the girl who so bemused Felix by her strangeness that he married her; Iolanthe, the green-eyed prostitute who later became a movie star; Hippolyta, political maneuverer; Caradoc, the architect; Sipple, clown of the brothel; and Julian, Merlin's . . . elusive chief." Publisher's note

"Mr. Durrell perceives and conveys echoes, resonances, old values and old rottenness. The book is often bawdy and amoral but never seductive: the language is matter-of-factly coarse at times, but tolerable. And Athens with its ancient prototypes made contemporaneous to us is vividly with us in this book, even when the action flits off to London or Turkey." Best Sellers

White eagles over Serbia. Criterion Bks. 1957 200p boards $4.95

"A British agent is murdered in the mountains of Southern Serbia and Special Operations in London assigns Colonel Methuen to find out what actually happened. Disguised as

Durrell, Lawrence—*Continued*

a peasant, he is infiltrated into the area, where intrigue and danger turn his mission into a nightmare." Huntting

"An extremely well-written story of espionage with a conventional hero but some delightful secondary characters." N Y Her Trib Books

Dutourd, Jean

The horrors of love; tr. from the French by Robin Chancellor. Doubleday 1967 665p o.p. 1970

Original French edition published 1963

"The story is that of a sort of contemporary, French Faust figure, a deputy, who, in late middle age, at the end of a not undistinguished career, and after many years as a good 'family man,' ruins himself in a sordid crime of passion. The story is told under the guise of a conversation between two highly cultivated Frenchmen taking a long walk through Paris." Choice

"The theme of the book is the banality and the dreariness of adultery." Sat R

Dutton, Mary

y Thorpe. World Pub. 1967 343p $5.95

"Thorpe relives in thought her Southern childhood and her brother's during a period in which intense pleasure and pain, tenderness and violence, family ties and stress, and Negro friendships left their impress. Troubled times befell them as a family in 1935 with their father's dismissal as school principal because of his unpopular concern for the community's Negro children. Their dilemma was further complicated by their otherwise gentle mother's refusal to leave the place and ways to which she was born." Booklist

The author "handles the color problem skillfully, sympathetically and sensitively. And while the climax derives from the conflict in this local problem, its significance is universal." Library J

Dyke, Henry van. See Van Dyke, Henry

Dykeman, Wilma

The far family. Holt 1966 372p $5.95

"The brothers and sisters of the Thurston family, separated by the paths their various lives have taken, return to their home county in a Southern mountain region to aid one of the brothers suspected of the murder of a Negro. Included in the group is Phil, a son and a recently appointed U.S. Senator, who is facing the compromises and important decisions that such a career requires. From the family crisis and his encounter with a former fiancée he returns to Washington at the end of the novel with a new understanding of personal integrity. Alternating between the past, in the early part of this century . . . and the present, Miss Dykeman depicts the strength of the family roots." Library J

"A modest novel primarily appealing to women readers. . . . Told in alternate present-day happenings and flashbacks a generation and more back, with a dignified but surface skimming of the complex questions of race relations and understanding." Booklist

The tall woman. Holt 1962 315p $5.50

"The story of Lydia McQueen, North Carolina mountain woman, from the time of her marriage during the Civil War to her death some thirty years later. . . . Lydia's husband, Mark, fought in the Union army against her father and brother and, captured, was imprisoned at Andersonville. Her mother . . . died as a result of a brutal assault by wartime plunderers. Her oldest son suffered the mentally crippling effects of a birth improperly managed. Grief and want . . . strengthened rather than destroyed her. A church, a school for the remote community, an education for a younger brother, for her own children and for others, these were the things she fought for with stubborn courage." N Y Her Trib Books

"Lack of narrative artistry is offset by the book's authentic tone and solid regional background." Booklist

E

EQMM annual, 1946-1969. New Am. Lib. 1946-1967 24v 1946-1967 o.p. 1970; World Pub. 1968-1969 1968 boards $5.95, 1969 $6.95

Analyzed in Short Story Index

Annual. First published 1946 by Random House with title: The Queen's awards

Titles vary: 1954-1957: Ellery Queen's awards; 1958: Ellery Queen's annual; 1959-1961: Ellery Queen's Mystery annual; 1962: To be read before midnight; 1963: Ellery Queen's Mystery mix; 1964: Ellery Queen's Double dozen; 1965: Ellery Queen's 20th anniversary annual; 1966: Ellery Queen's Crime carousel; 1967: Ellery Queen's All-star lineup; 1968: Ellery Queen's Mystery parade; 1969: Ellery Queen's Murder menu

Contents for 23rd EQMM annual: The cool ones, by C. Armstrong; The salad maker, by R. McNear; Mom and the haunted mink, by J. Yaffe; Twist for twist [novelette], by C. Brand; P as in payoff, by L. Treat; Mr Strang performs an experiment, by W. Brittain; Divorce—New York style [novelette], by C. Woolrich; The special gift, by C. Fremlin; The justice boy, by H. R. F. Keating; The adventure of the missing three-quarters, by R. L. Fish; The terrorists, by M. Gilbert; The main chance, by J. Symons; The Austin murder case, by J. L. Breen; The intruders, by A. Gilbert; Inspector Maigret pursues, by G. Simenon; The name of the game, by J. Hay; Line of communication, by A. Garve; Change of climate, by U. Curtiss; The twelfth statue [novelette], by S. Ellin

24th EQMM annual: File no. 2: stakeout on Page Street, by J. Gores; The second nail, by S. Cloete; The last bottle in the world, by S. Ellin; From out of the garden, by C. Armstrong; The secret, by P. Bentley; The impossible 'impossible crime', by E. D. Hoch; Frank Merriswell's greatest case, by J. L. Breen; For the rest of her life, by C. Woolrich; Inspector Maigret's war of nerves, by G. Simenon; King of the air; The wicked ghost, by C. Brand; Moment of power, by P. D. James; Maze in the elevator, by J. Powell; A theme for Hyacinth, by J. Symons; The man who read Sir Arthur Conan Doyle, by W. Brittain; Eyes that miss nothing, by M. Gilbert; The betrayal, by C. Fremlin; The sisterhood, by G. Butler; The Pettifer collection, by G. Kersh; Who cares about an old woman, by A. Gilbert; T as in threat, by L. Treat; Match point in Berlin, by P. McGeer

Earley, George W.

(ed.) Encounters with aliens; UFO's and alien beings in science fiction; comp. and ed. by George W. Earley; with an introduction by Ivan T. Sanderson. Sherbourne Press 1968 244p boards $4.95

A "selection of tales about beings and machines from other worlds, ranging from the comic to the terrifying." Pub W

Contents: The four-faced visitors of Ezekiel, by A. W. Orton; The cave of history, by T. Sturgeon; The uninvited guest, by C. Anvil; Something in the sky, by L. Correy; Albatross, by M. Reynolds; The other kids, by R. F. Young; The Grantha Sighting, by A. Davidson; The tie that binds, by G. Whitley; The Venus Papers, by R. Wilson; Minister without portfolio, by M. Clingerman; Fear is a business, by T. Sturgeon; Ringer, by G. C. Edmondson

Eastlake, William

Castle keep. Simon & Schuster 1965 382p $5.95

A "novel about a tenth-century castle located almost at the German-Allied front in World War II. The castle guards, Americans, are split in opinion about what should be the fate of the castle. A captain, an art historian, wants it preserved for its art treasures. A major wants the site held at all costs. The owner, a count, wants to keep his castle safe, at all costs, and, because he is impotent, he wants his young countess to become pregnant, preferably by the major, and thus give him an heir." Pub W

Eastlake, William—*Continued*

"Strong interplay of idealism and realism, fantasy and reality, character and setting are skillfully handled. Some high humor between the bouts of military action, some free-swinging philosophizing, sometimes in smoothly written prose and sometimes in pretty coarse, cross-grained, salty barracks language." Library J

Portrait of an artist with twenty-six horses. Simon & Schuster 1963 221p boards $3.95

"Twenty-six Horses, a young Navaho weaver returning from a look at [the] spectacular sights in the White Man's reservation, pauses by a spring to listen to his native land and hears [a cry] rising from an arroyo. . . . The Indian moves on without knowing that this cry comes not from a spirit, but from Ring Bowman, son of the white trader and a childhood friend, sinking slowly into a quicksand grave at the bottom of that arroyo. The book, largely memories, anecdotes and flashbacks, is mortared together by this inexorable sand, and the trader's search for his trapped son and the trapped boy's search for himself." N Y Her Trib Books

"The plot is developed into a masterpiece of the kind of suspense that makes the reader want to reach into the story and yell at the oblivious characters on whom the outcome depends." N Y Times Bk R

Eaton, Evelyn

Go ask the river. Harcourt 1969 280p $5.95

A "novel based upon the existence, in the eighth century, of a Chinese girl called Hung Tu, who was sold to the Blue House and was trained in the arts of poetry as well as the arts of love. For years she served as the hostess of one governor after another until she was sent into exile by a ruthless emissary of the Emperor. With adaptations by Mary Kennedy of 37 of Hung Tu's poems." Bk Buyer's Guide

"The novel is quietly written as is fitting its character, and its effect is to give the spirit of a time and place—which it does successfully. However, when Miss Eaton attempts to inundate the story with characters who pass in a page or two, the reading becomes difficult and the book is unsuccessful. Libraries which have Miss Eaton's other books will want to purchase this one." Library J

Eberhart, Mignon G.

The cup, the blade or the gun. Random House 1961 241p o.p. 1970

"Sarah, the Yankee bride of Confederate officer Lucien Hugot, awaits the end of the war at his Mississippi plantation. Living under the constant threat of Yankee patrols, the family regards Sarah with mixed emotions. Two murders are committed, attempts are made on Sarah's life, and even Lucien behaves oddly when he returns." Huntting

In essence this is Mrs. Eberhart's standard Brontë-and-water suspense-romance. . . . Neither the love story nor the murder plot contains many surprises for the experienced reader—but it is all told with a nice sense of the woman's view of 1863." N Y Times Bk R

Enemy in the house. Random House 1962 216p o.p. 1970

"On the night that Amity Mallan married her childhood sweetheart Simon, two strange deaths occurred: the parson, who performed the ceremony, was found, neck broken, in a ravine; The family lawyer, who was also present, was shot dead in his doorway. Who wanted to destroy these key witnesses and why? The newlyweds left Amity's Savannah plantation immediately, and she sailed for Jamaica to join her Tory father while Simon returned to his duties as an officer in Washington's army. . . . Frustrated island authorities turn to the obeah woman [to investigate the mystery]." Publisher's note

Message from Hong Kong. Random House [1969 c1968] 212p boards $4.50

"Just a week before Dick Blake and Marcia Lowry are to get married, Marcia receives a message from Hong Kong claiming that Dino, her former husband, is still alive." Bk Buyer's Guide

"The reader knows that all [their misadventures] could have been avoided if Marcia and Richard had only behaved like sensible human beings, but just the same their plight [i.e. involvement in an international smuggling ring] offers sustained suspense that will keep Eberhart devotees glued to the pages." Pub W

Witness at large. Random House 1966 174p boards $3.95

"The proposed sale of a publishing house leads to murder of two of the family concerned and near murder of a third, the narrator, an adopted daughter of the elderly publisher. The setting is an estate on Long Island." Booklist

Woman on the roof. Random House [1968 c1967] 213p boards $4.50

"Some years after Marcus Desort's young wife, Rose, had been murdered on the terrace of their penthouse, he married Sue. She, too, had a tragedy in her life, the loss of Jim Locke in Vietnam. Then Marcus was murdered and Jim Locke, returned from death, was suspected—until the real murderer trapped Sue in the penthouse." Bk Buyer's Guide

Eça de Queiroz

Cousin Bazilio; tr. by Roy Campbell; with an introduction by Federico de Onís. Noonday 1953 343p o.p. 1970

First published 1878

"A new translation of a nineteenth century novel hitherto published in English in a bowdlerized version only. The story, laid in Lisbon in the 1860s, concerns the illicit love affair of a young married woman and her cousin, a childhood sweetheart." Book Rev Digest

"This is a civilized book, and the author treats both his readers and his characters with civility." Times (London) Lit Sup

The Maias; tr. by Patricia McGowen Pinheiro and Ann Stevens. St Martins 1965 633p boards $7.95

Carlos Eduardo "the sole heir of a noble [Portuguese] family culminates the history of the family's fading repute by mistakingly falling in love with his sister. Set against a background of corrupt Lisbon society in the last years of a doomed monarchy." Pub W

"With both the strengths and shortcomings of the naturalist school, a prominent writer of nineteenth-century Portugal mirrors 'the ugly reality of things and society stripped bare.' " Booklist

The mandarin, and other stories; tr. from the Portuguese by Richard Franko Goldman. Ohio Univ. Press 1965 176p $5

Analyzed in Short Story Index

Contains a novelette, The mandarin, first published 1880 in Portugal and three short stories: Peculiarities of a fair-haired girl; A lyric poet; José Matias

Eckert, Allan W.

The crossbreed; with illus. by Karl E. Karalus. Little 1968 242p illus boards $4.95

His mother was a housecat gone wild; his father was a bobcat; "the crossbreed" himself was their largest offspring. His intelligence and ability and the combination of the better attributes of both breeds enabled him to survive in a world of enemies and to undergo an incredible odyssey of over two thousand miles in four years. (Publisher)

"The writing is never sentimental, although the anthropomorphism comes in heavy doses, with a touch of Disney here and there. This remains, however, an absorbing tale, well suited to the young adult. . . . Keep in mind, though, the fact that all adult humans come off badly." Pub W

The great auk; a novel. Little 1963 202p boards $4.95

A "book about the life and death of the last great auk of the thousands of these large, flightless, swimming penguin-like birds that annually migrated from their breeding places in the North Atlantic to Cape Hatteras. Natural calamities—storms, killer whales—and

Eckert, Allan W.—*Continued*

massacres by feather-and-meat hunters and by scientists collecting specimens decimated the species till the last of its kind was slaughtered in 1844." Pub W

"Eckert is masterful when describing incidents and places, some purely imaginative: the life of the bird inside the egg and the fledgling immediately after birth; the undersea scenes when the auks, like diminutive submarines, dive for food or for safety; the storms at sea and on land; the predatory actions of the whales; the massacre of the birds by human hunters. These descriptions are vivid, palpable, intensely real. Amazingly he seems most effective when seeing and assessing these things through the eyes and minds of his 'characters,' a tribute to his imaginative genius." Best Sellers

The silent sky; the incredible extinction of the passenger pigeon; a novel. Little 1965 243p front $4.95

In this fictional account of how an entire species whose greatest menace was man was wiped off the face of the earth, Eckert pinpoints a particular unnamed bird and follows the family line until the very end—Martha, the last known passenger pigeon, who did die in 1914 at the Cincinnati Zoo. (Publisher)

"Written in the form of a novel, the book tells us a great deal about an interesting species. . . . Especially for public libraries." Library J

Edelman, Maurice

The Prime Minister's daughter. Random House [1965 c1964] 246p front boards $4.95

First published 1964 in England

This book centers on Melville, a British prime minister "who has attained his position only after bitter conflict within his party. . . . Melville faces the most serious crisis of his career when a personal scandal involving his daughter serves as an excuse for a new struggle for power within his own party, and is used by the Opposition to try to bring down the Government." Publisher's note

"Sylvia evokes the reader's compassion, although the psychiatric overtones of her story are somewhat obvious and clumsy. The atmosphere of politics and jockeying for position, on the other hand, are conveyed with sophistication." Booklist

Eden, Dorothy

Darkwater. Coward-McCann [1964 c1963] 254p o.p. 1970

First published 1963 in England

"Fanny had been brought up by Uncle Edgar and Aunt Louisa at Darkwater [in Devon]. She had always felt like a poor relation—as she was—and had even planned to run away and become a nurse in the Crimean War, in which handsome Cousin George had received his head injury. But the arrival of two very small cousins stopped that. Then the terrifying things began to happen in Darkwater." Bk Buyer's Guide

Set in Victorian England

Lady of Mallow; a novel. Coward-McCann [1962 c1960] 256p o.p. 1970

Published 1960 in England with title: Samantha

Victorian romance in which "the inheritance of a magnificent country estate, Mallow Hall, is in question. Sarah Mildmay, fiancee of the rightful owner, defies danger to masquerade as a governess in the home of the pretender, a dark adventurer from the West Indies. There is a terrified child, a strange, depraved woman, and a climax of madness, blood and violence." Chicago Sunday Tribune

A "melodrama that parallels the sensational Tichborne imposture; will appeal to women who like romance in a period dress." Booklist

Ravenscroft. Coward-McCann [1965 c1964] 253p o.p. 1970

First published 1964 in England with title: Bella

In a "romantic novel of Victorian England, two orphaned sisters find themselves trapped by procurers in London. A handsome nobleman interested in social reform rescues the girls, marries one in order to quiet gossip, and later has to outwit the vengeful abductors again." Booklist

"The romantic complications that ensue run the gamut from a marriage in name only between our hero and the spunkier of the two sisters and the sinister plotting of a gang of white slavers. Miss Eden has a nice way with the period atmosphere." Pub W

The shadow wife. Coward-McCann 1968 286p $5.95

"In a suspenseful, contemporary Gothic romance Luise Amberley, an impulsive English girl traveling in Majorca, meets and, after a whirlwind courtship, marries Otto Winther, a charming Danish widower. Otto, an epileptic, waits until Luise is pregnant before taking her to his ancestral home Maaneborg, a somber but elegant castle, where his mother and children greet Louise with an inexplicable animosity. . . . Will appeal to women readers of the genre." Booklist

y The vines of Yarrabee. Coward-McCann 1969 381p $6.95

"The story centers on Gilbert Massingham who leaves Suffolk, England, and with a small inheritance establishes a vineyard in New South Wales. His fiancée, Eugenia Lichfield, joins him in three years at his estate Yarrabee and the developing narrative portrays their marriage, their family, and the interweaving of their lives with those of Molly Jarvis, their attractive housekeeper, Colm O'Connor, a portrait painter, and others of their neighbors and friends." Booklist

"The story is plausible. The atmosphere of Australia authentic. The background of wine-growing and wine-making is interesting. These ingredients make for a satisfactory bouquet for the imbibers of light recreational historical novels." Best Sellers

Waiting for Willa. Coward-McCann 1970 254p $5.95

" 'Wilhelmina'—a simple signature at the bottom of a letter from Willa Bedford, but to Grace Asherton it spelled danger. It was the long-standing signal for alarm agreed upon when her cousin Willa had gone to Stockholm to work in the embassy there. Grace flies to Stockholm, where she finds that Willa has disappeared, leaving a trail of ominous clues." News of Bks

"Suspense and romance are combined in a contemporary novel with appeal for women readers." Booklist

Edgar, Day

(ed.) The Saturday Evening Post. The Saturday Evening Post Reader of sea stories

Edgeworth, Maria

Castle Rackrent; ed. with an introduction by George Watson. Oxford 1964 xxxv, 130p (Oxford English novels) $2.60

First published anonymously in 1800

A novel which illustrated the evils of absenteeism. "The annals of an Irish house, an immortal picture of the broken-down gentry. The character-portraits of Sir Patrick, Sir Murtagh, Sir Kit, Sir Condy, and the other squireens and their retainers, and the anecdotes of boisterous, irresponsible life, put into the mouth of an old servitor who is himself a character, are manifestly the work of a great novelist." Baker's Best

Edmonds, Walter D.

The Boyds of Black River. Dodd 1953 248p o.p. 1970

"Upstate New York at the very beginning of the automobile age, upon which the Boyds looked with the disgust of horse lovers. Teddy tells the story—of his Uncle Ledyard, big and volcanic; the Admiral and his daughter Kath, welcome visitors no matter how Uncle Ledyard groused; Teddy's cousin Doone, who loved the great trotter, Blue Dandy; and the friends and retainers of the Boyds. An atmospheric story, entirely different from the author's historical novels but as good." Retail Bookseller

Edmonds, Walter D.—*Continued*

y Chad Hanna. Little 1940 548p o.p. 1970

"The opening chapter finds Chad Hanna, a husky orphan, working as an hostler at a tavern in Canastota, New York, in the year 1836. An attempt to help a runaway slave to escape made the town too hot for Chad and he left hurriedly under the protection of A. D. Huguenine's 'Great and Only International Circus' which had been playing in Canastota that day. And here, this engrossing narrative—that vividly recreates the people and places of the Mohawk Valley in the 1830's—really gets under way." Huntting

"Chad is well done; the minor figures are clearly and vividly conceived; and if some of the major ones are not wholly consistent, it is no great matter in a story that moves along with the interest and vitality of this one. . . . But, after all, the circus is the thing, and the circus makes the story what it is—an extremely good yarn with a faint Dickensian flavor, handled with skill and assurance." Boston Transcript

y Drums along the Mohawk. Little 1936 592p $5.95

"The Mohawk Valley from 1776 to 1784 is the scene. It is a story of the American revolution as it affected the farmers in that frontier section, when unaided they withstood the raids of British regulars from Canada, and the Iroquois from the surrounding country. The battle of Oriskany in 1777 plays an important part in the book." Book Rev Digest

"Mr. Edmonds' history is partly fiction and his fiction is partly history, but the prospective reader need not worry—the truth is in the book, as it is in any first-rate novel. . . . Possibly no competent writer could have wholly failed with this material. But Mr. Edmonds has gone beyond the material and produced a book historic in theme, modern in point of view. His is a novel without dull moments, of drama, poetry and understanding." N Y Times Bk R

Erie water. Little 1933 506p o.p. 1970

"A story of the Erie Canal covering the years of its building from 1817-1825. The work of building and the people who lived along the route of the canal are pictured thru the eyes of a young carpenter, Jerry Fowler, and the main thread of the tale is concerned with his romance with Mary, a girl whom he 'bought' as a redemptioner at Albany." Book Rev Digest

In the hands of the Senecas. Little 1947 213p illus $4.95

"In 1778 the Senecas raided the settlement of Dygartsbush, killed most of the men and carried the women and children into captivity. Among them were two thirteen-year-olds, Ellen Mitchell and Peter Kelly; Caty Breen, hired drudge who found courage when an unknown man had to run the gauntlet; and Delia Borst, bride of a month. . . . But out of this sorrowful situation, these people built toward victory with patience and tenacity." Literary Guild

"There are some especially interesting vignettes of Indian life and custom, some illuminating sidelights on Indian character. Finally, though the narrative, moving as it does from heroine to heroine, lacks cumulative effect, Mr. Edmonds has in store for each of his heroines a climactic episode of A-Grade suspense or nerve-wracking intensity." N Y Times Bk R

Rome haul. Little 1929 347p o.p. 1970

"The Erie canal in the days when it was the important artery of travel is the scene of this novel. Dan, a slow-witted farm boy, comes first as a driver on the canal, but later acquires a boat of his own and experiences to the full the rich and varied life. A distinct contribution to novels of local color." Wis Lib Bul

"It is a segment of life itself, showing on the side a young empire suffering from growing pains and an old industry beginning to feel the withering process of outworn usefulness." Boston Transcript

The wedding journey; drawings by Alan Tompkins. Little 1947 118p illus $3.95

"A short novel describing a wedding journey via Erie Canal boat packet in 1835. During the trip and in the days following both bride and groom learned valuable lessons: the husband gambled and lost the honeymoon money; but the bride had strength of character enough to stand the blow." Book Rev Digest

Young Ames. Little 1942 350p o.p. 1970

"Young Ames, sandy-haired, freckle-faced, 18 years old, comes to New York City to make his fortune. Answering an ad, Boy Wanted, he starts at the bottom in a mercantile house and with dash and effrontery makes his way to the top, marries the boss's niece, and becomes partner in the firm. The time is 1834. The place New York and the picture of the bustling, growing commercial city, with its Five Points gangs, its volunteer fire companies, its high-handed business methods, is vivid and real. Episodic, some of the chapters having appeared as short stories." Wis Lib Bul

Edwards, Anne

The survivors. Holt 1968 253p $5.95

"After ten years in a nursing home, Luanne Woodrow is convinced the time has come for her to face the tragedy that struck when she was 20 years old, when she found her entire family dead of arsenic poisoning. Even her acquittal in the murder trial that followed had not removed her deep feelings of guilt and responsibility. On a winter vacation she goes to a small Swiss village, and is delighted to meet Hans Aldik, a handsome writer who seems more interested in her than in her background, or is he?" Library J

"The tale unfolds past and present relationships, charged emotions, and finally the cause and culprit of the ugly deed in a highly mood-invoking, suspenseful way, all unshockingly traditional barring a diversionary hint of incest." Booklist

Egan, Lesley

A serious investigation. Harper 1968 213p $4.95

"A Joan Kahn-Harper Novel of suspense" Jesse Falkenstein's "latest client is a medium, who leaves the world entirely after one of her seances. It's when Sergeant Clock and the local police decide that murder is involved that Jesse lends a hand, finding himself up to his neck in various nasty matters." McClurg. Book News

The wine of violence. Harper 1969 231p boards $4.95

"The Glendale cops are matched against a murderer, kid drug addicts, and especially one Conway, an escaped killer who has sworn vengeance upon [policeman] O'Connor." Bk Buyer's Guide

The story "hurtles along at a fast clip, expertly juggling several secondary stories, while concentrating especially on an escaped convict's grim vendetta. . . . It builds to a climactic confrontation in a most ironic setting—Forest Lawn Cemetery." Pub W

For other titles by this author see Linington, Elizabeth; Shannon, Dell

Eggleston, Edward

The Hoosier school-boy. Smith, P. 1966 [c1883] 261p front $3.75

Based on memories of the author's own boyhood this is the "story of boy life in Indiana and Ohio about 1840, giving a vivid picture of the difficulties which beset a boy seeking an education in the early days." Mathiews

The Hoosier schoolmaster; a novel. Judd [1871] 226p illus o.p. 1970

Sequel to: The Hoosier schoolmaster
First published 1883 by Scribner

"The lawless and homely pioneer life of Indiana (ca. 1830-5), described by a man who was an itinerant preacher in the West, and knew that life intimately. The schoolmaster boards round among the farmers, and the story is about his love for a servant-girl whose mistress wants him for her daughter." Baker's Best

Followed by: The Hoosier school-boy

Ehrenburg, Ilya

A change of season. Knopf 1962 [c1961] 299p $4.50

Contains: The thaw, first published in the United Sates 1955 and translated by Manya

Ehrenburg, Ilya—*Continued*

Harari. The spring, translated by Humphrey Higgins

These two short novels "are joined to complete the picture of a group of characters in a Russian factory town. The love stories are resolved, an opportunist painter comes to self-realization, and an engineer has his reprimand rescinded. As in 'The thaw', the action in the completed work is minor and the importance of the book lies in its picture of the restlessness and apprehensiveness of Russians in the post-Stalin period." Booklist

The spring

In Ehrenburg, I. A change of season p157-299

The thaw. Regnery 1955 230p o.p. 1970

Translated by Manya Harari

"The story of ordinary people in a provincial town in Russia, doctors, school teachers, artists, engineers—the pillars of Soviet society. Almost all of them are well-meaning little people, concerned with their local problems, but gently critical at times of the Regime." McClurg. Book News

"As a novel, The Thaw is good journalese, in the genre of the 'slick' magazine story, with a fast-moving, formularized plot. But although its significance as literature is slight, as social commentary it is outstanding." New Repub

Followed by: The Spring, included in A change of season

also in Ehrenburg, I. A change of season p 1-155

Ehrlich, Leonard

God's angry man. Simon & Schuster 1932 401p o.p. 1970

" 'God's angry man' is John Brown of Osawatomie, fanatic leader of a forelorn hope, regarded by some as a martyr, by others as a criminal who justly died on the gallows. In this young novelist's powerful portrayal he stands as a man of biblical stature and fiber who believed himself called of God to wipe out that thing which he called the 'sum of all villainies'—slavery." Book Rev Digest

"A personality and a meaning in history are sharpened and deepened in this surefooted, rhythmic and penetrating book." Books

Elder, Joseph

(ed.) The farthest reaches. Trident Press 1968 217p $4.95

Analyzed in Short Story Index

"Set in distant galaxies these 12 science-fiction stories appeal to the reader's sense of wonder and excitement." Booklist

Contents: The worm that flies, by B. W. Aldiss; Kyrie, by P. Anderson; Tomorrow is a million years, by J. G. Ballard; Pond water, by J. Brunner; The dance of the changer and the three, by T. Carr; Crusade, by A. C. Clarke; Ranging, by J. Jakes: Mind out of time, by K. Laumer; The inspector, by J. McKimmey; To the dark star, by R. Silverberg; A night in elf hill, by N. Spinrad; Sulwen's planet, by J. Vance

Elgin, Mary

Highland masquerade. Mill 1966 [c1965] 255p boards $4.95

First published 1965 in England with title: Return to Glenshael

"At the age of sixteen Allie Rannoch had left Glenshael [in northern Scotland] in a despairing fury, vanished in London, and became later a glamorous actress under another name. Then an accident ended her career. She determined to go home again, in disguise. She acted her role of dowdy secretary with great success until her sense of mischief led her one moonlit night to play the part of the ghost of Mad Margaret of bygone times. The consequences were amazing." Am News of Bks

y A man from the mist. Mill 1965 [c1963] 221p boards $4.95

First published 1963 in England with title: Visibility nil

Young, widowed "Catherine Lennox became the housekeeper for a retired Major living in the far northwest of Scotland. In the remote Scottish Lochs she found complete escape until a man from the mist appeared on the scene." McClurg. Book News

"This is high romance in the great tradition, full of conflict and understanding, with growing characters, and overtones of ancient lore." Library J

Eliades, David, and Webb, Robert Forrest.
See Forrest, David

Eliot, George

Adam Bede

Some editions are:

Dodd (Great illustrated classics) $4.50 With illustrations of contemporary scenes and a foreword by Curtis Dahl

Dutton (Everyman's lib) $3.25 Introduction by Robert Speaight

Harcourt (The Harcourt Lib. of English and American classics) $3.95

First published in 1859. A story of English village life in the nineteenth century. Two of George Eliot's best known portraits, Mrs Poyser and Diana Morris, are among the characters

" 'Adam Bede' goes into the dark places of human nature, and sets forth a coherent philosophy of conduct and retribution. An innocent country lass is seduced by the young squire and crime, remorse, suffering . . . are the tragic consequences. . . . All the ordinary aspects of country life a hundred years ago are presented with the minute strokes of a Dutch painter." Baker's Best

also in Eliot, G. The best-known novels of George Eliot p5-390

The best-known novels of George Eliot. Modern Lib. 1350p (Modern Lib. giants) o.p. 1970

Omnibus volume of four titles entered separately

Contents: Adam Bede; The mill on the Floss: Silas Marner; Romola

Daniel Deronda. Introduction by Emrys Jones. Dutton 1964 2v (Everyman's lib) ea $3.25

"Sets forth a grave, spiritual conflict. The chief actors are a gay and accomplished girl, and her husband, a selfish tyrant who exemplifies the blighting influences of purely material civilization in the modern world. Closely connected is the story of the unselfish Deronda and Mordecai, Jewish leaders [who believe in Zionism]." Baker's Best

Middlemarch; a study of provincial life

Some editions are:

Dutton (Everyman's lib) 2v ea $3.25 Introduction by Gerald Bullitt

Harcourt (The Harcourt Lib. of English and American classics) $3.95

Oxford (The World's classics) $3.50 With an introduction by R. W. Hewitt

First published 1872

"Tells two separate stories, that of Dorothea Brooke and her two marriages, and that of Dr. Lydgate and the Vincy family, loosely knit together by the fact that they are acted on the same stage and before the same detailed background of middle-class life in and near an English provincial town." Mudge and Sears' George Eliot dictionary

"A novel almost destitute of plot yet unified by the dominant idea of moral causation into a tragic drama of deserted ideals and failure. Dorothea's unfulfilled aspirations, Casaubon's barren pedantry, Bulstrode's hypocrisy, Lydgate's ambition quenched by an unsuitable marriage; all illustrate the fundamental theorem; the happier lives of Caleb . . . and Mary Garth enforce the moral." Baker's Best

y The mill on the Floss

Some editions are:

Dodd (Great illustrated classics) $4.50 With photographs of the author and her environment as well as drawings from early editions of the book, and an introduction by Louis B. Salomon

Eliot, George—*Continued*

Dutton (Everyman's lib) $3.25 Introduction by W. Robertson Nicoll

Harcourt (The Harcourt Lib. of English and American classics) $3.95

Heritage (Distributed by Dial Press) $7.50 With an introduction by David Daiches. Illustrated with paintings by Wray Manning

Oxford (The World's classics) $3

First published 1860

"Deeply significant tragedy of the inner life, enacted amidst the quaint folk and old-fashioned surrondings of a country town (St. Ogg's is Gainsborough). The conflict of affection and antipathy between a brother and sister, and again in the family relations of their father, is a dominant motive; but the emotional tension rises to a climax in Maggie's unpremeditated yielding to an unworthy lover and betrayal of her finer nature. Brother and sister . . . are purified and reconciled only in death." Baker's Best

> *also in* Eliot, G. The best-known novels of George Eliot p395-784

Romola

Some editions are:

Dutton (Everyman's lib) $2.95 Introduction by Rudolph Dircks

Oxford (The World's classics) $3.50 With an introduction by Viola Meynell

First published in book form in 1863

"Based on a special study of Florentine history in the epoch 1492-1509, the days of Lorenzo de' Medici, and the saintliness and all-conquering energy of Savonarola are finely portrayed. 'Romola' is a sternly tragic novel of temptation, crime and retribution." Baker's Best

> *also in* Eliot, G. The best-known novels of George Eliot p925-1350

y Silas Marner

Some editions are:

Dodd (Great illustrated classics) $4.50 With illustrations of contemporary scenes and a foreword by Basil Davenport

Dutton (Everyman's lib) $3.25 Introduction by John Holloway

Harcourt (The Harcourt Lib. of English and American classics) $3.95

Watts, F. $7.95 LLarge type edition complete and unabridged. A Keith Jennison book

First published 1861

"Silas Marner is a handloom weaver, a good man, whose life has been wrecked by a false accusation of theft, which cannot be disproved. For years he lives a lonely life, with the sole companionship of his loom; and he is saved from his own despair by the chance finding of a little child. On this baby girl he lavishes the whole passion of his thwarted nature, and her filial affection makes him a kindly man again. After sixteen years the real thief is discovered, and Silas's good name is restored. On this slight framework are hung the richest pictures of middle and low class life that George Eliot has painted." Keller's Reader's Digest of Books

> *also in* Eliot, G. The best-known novels of George Eliot p787-917

Ellerman, Winifred. See Bryher

Ellery Queen's Mystery Magazine

The quintessence of Queen. . . . Selected and with an introduction by Anthony Boucher. Random House 1962 560p o.p. 1970

Analyzed in Short Story Index

"Best prize stories from 12 years of Ellery Queen's Mystery Magazine." Title page

Contents: An error in chemistry, by Faulkner; Love comes to Miss Lucy, by Q. Patrick; The house-in-your-hand murder, by R. Vickers; The other side of the curtain, by H. McCloy; From another world, by C. Rawson; The specialty of the house, by S. Ellin; The garden of forking paths, by J. L. Borges; A study in white, by N. Blake; The arrow of God, by L. Charteris; Beyond the sea of death, by M. A. de Ford; The gentleman from Paris, by J. D. Carr; Love lies bleeding, by P. MacDonald; The trial of John Nobody, by A. H. Z. Carr; The

lady-killer, by W. D. Steele; The enemy, by C. Armstrong; The contradictory case, by H. Pentecost; Woman hunt no good, by O. La Farge; Homecoming, by V. P. Johns; The singing stick, by E. Pangborn; The challenge, by J. W. Vandercook; The quality of mercy, by E. Lipsky; You know what, teacher, by Z. Henderson; Tall story, by M. Allingham; Mom in the spring, by J. Yaffe; Dodie and the boogerman, by V. Williams; The man who went to Taltavul's, by D. Alexander; The customs of the country, by T. Flanagan; Only on rainy nights, by M. Van Doren; The necessity of his condition, by A. Davidson; Lilith, stay away from the door, by B. J. R. Stolper; The Gettysburg bugle, by E. Queen

Ellin, Stanley

The Blessington Method, and other strange tales. Random House 1964 185p boards $3.95

Analyzed in Short Story Index

Contents: The Blessington Method: The faith of Aaron Menefee; You can't be a little girl all your life; Robert; Unreasonable doubt; The day of the bullet; Beidenbauer's flea; The seven deadly virtues; The nine-to-five man; The question

"Superbly executed stories with a touch of the malevolent and the macabre. Ellin searches for the unremarkable and discovers the startling." Cincinnati

The Valentine estate. Random House 1968 274p $5.95

"Chris Monte, once bright star of international tennis, but dead broke and out of the game at 28 . . . is startled the sultry night mousy Elizabeth Jones walks into his shop and asks him to marry her because an old family friend in England left her his entire estate if she comes to London quickly with an acceptable husband. Although the request doesn't make sense to Chris, he needs the $50,000 she offers. Thus, he is involved in a long and violent chase in Miami and in Boston before they both face more danger in London. Well written and smoothly plotted." Library J

Elliot, John

(jt. auth.) Hoyle, F. A for Andromeda

(jt. auth.) Hoyle, F. Andromeda breakthrough

Elliott, David W.

y Listen to the silence. Holt 1969 279p $5.95

This is the "story of a 14-year-old orphan [Timmy] and what he discovers about himself and the world during several months in a mental institution. . . . His encounters [with the inmates] are at times chilling and at others profoundly touching, and Elliott . . . writes of them with compassion, occasional humor and flashes of genuine lyricism." Pub W

"Daily particulars, detailed with painful awareness, not only make the place unbearably real but give substance to the contention that society itself is deranged, not its individual members." Booklist

Elliott, Janice

Angels falling. Knopf 1969 409p $6.95

"Lily Garland is dying and the children have gathered round. . . . Lily, born in 1901, on the day of Queen Victoria's funeral, has married a writer, Andrew, and borne him five children, one of whom dies in infancy. . . . [This novel] is the family tale of Lily and Andrew through some 60 years of marital and professional life in England: the wars (Andrew goes to Spain in the '30's), the changing moralities, the changing politics." Pub W

Elliott, Sumner Locke. See Locke Elliott, Sumner

Ellis, A. E.

The rack. Little 1959 [c1958] 414p o.p. 1970

First published 1958 in England

"The story of a young English student, Paul Davenant, who is forced to spend two and a half years in a TB sanatorium. Set in the French Alps, it evokes with love, comedy

Ellis, A. E.—*Continued*

and despair Paul's dreadful race against the disease, his touching and hopeless love affair with a young Belgian girl, and the doctors, patients and nurses who share in his almost superhuman struggle against suffering." Publisher's note

"The detailed descriptions of tuberculosis symptoms and the treatment of the disease are balanced by the graphic portrayals of doctors and patients. . . . For discriminating readers." Booklist

Ellis, Mel

Softly roars the lion. Holt 1968 147p boards $3.95

A blizzard in Arrowhead Forest leaves a puma cub and a deer orphans. They are rescued by the Gallagher family and nursed back to health on their farm. But they cannot resist the call of the wild and run away only to return again to raid the ranches for food. Local people demand their destruction and in the end the Gallaghers come up with an idea that saves cattle, mountain lion and deer. (Publisher)

The author "knows the ways and habits of wild animals and writes with authority about them." Library J

Ellis, William Donahue

The bounty lands. World Pub. 1952 492p o.p. 1970

"Alone in a cabin clearing with his wife and child, Tom Woodbridge was a law unto himself, as rugged and self-centered as only a frontiersman could afford to be. When the town of Hosmer's Village [Ohio] began to grow around him, he fought all improvements: the court, the school, the church and even the town government, each a threat to his own continuing independence." McClurg. Book News

"It is apparent that the author has gone to a great deal of trouble to make sure just how the people lived in that day and that land." Chicago Sunday Tribune

Ellison, Ralph

y Invisible man

Some editions are:
Modern Lib. $2.95
Random House $5:95

First published 1952

In this "first novel, the author dramatizes an interesting theme by telling the story of a Negro going in progressive stages from youthful affirmation, in a small southern town, to total rejection after a Harlem race riot. Striving to be himself, he finds that he must not only contend with the whites but with the powerful members of his own race." Library J

"A book that is a valuable addition to our native literature and a valuable source of information for future historians of Negro-white relations in the depression decade." N Y Her Trib Books

Ellsberg, Edward

Captain Paul. Dodd 1941 607p o.p. 1970

The author recreates the life of John Paul Jones in the form of fictional biography. The story is told in the words of Tom Folger of Nantucket, whose admiration for Captain Paul leads him to throw in his lot with the great fighter from his early days as a privateer to the fatal engagement with the "Serapis"

Elman, Richard M.

Lilo's diary. Scribner 1968 155p $4.95

Sequel to: The 28th day of Elul

The "diary of the thoughts and growing despair of Lilo, beautiful young Hungarian Jewess, a ward in her uncle's household. Puzzled enough by her own uncertain heart in a love affair with Alex Yagodah, her cousin-fiancé, she feels even more perplexed and threatened as she watches the family blindly ignore the surrounding Nazi menace except for securing their material possessions and then senses the length they will go to save themselves in ultimate crisis. The fundamental question of individual guilt underlies Lilo's version of events and betrayal." Booklist

Followed by: The reckoning

The reckoning; the daily ledgers of Newman Yagodah, advokat and factor. Scribner 1969 184p $5.95

The third volume of a trilogy, the first volume being The 28th day of Elul and the second Lilo's diary

"The central figure is Newman Yagodah, a man of substances living in Hungary in 1944. He is a complex man—intelligent, duplicitous, concerned with his family and his position in the town of Clig, and finding human closeness only with his mistress. Newman Yagodah speaks of his political and financial theories; he looks back on his life, to the young wife he married for money and yet with love; and he movingly recounts his affair with his mistress Ileana. While his days move toward disaster, he reveals himself in this reckoning of accounts, his maneuvers and deceptions and his suffering." News of Bks

"The incisive prose, the extraordinary characterization and, most importantly, the compassion of the author realize the intent of the work." Library J

The 28th day of Elul. Scribner 1967 279p $4.95

The second volume in the trilogy of titles listed above

This "is one man's examination of Jewish life in Eastern Europe before and during the war years as he lived through it, and his analysis of himself as a survivor of the experience. Alex, currently living in Israel, can inherit $40,000 from his uncle Bela who emigrated to the United States before the war. The will, dated September 12, 1939 (the 28th day of Elul, 5700 by the Hebrew calendar) imposes conditions, however. Alex must attest that he is a practicing Jew and will raise his descendants according to Jewish law. . . . As he reflects on his own idyllic prewar world and traces its final destruction, he attempts to explain what he and the world have become." Pub W

Elston, Allan Vaughan

Mutiny on the Box Cross

In Western Writers of America. A Western bonanza p124-89

Ely, David

Seconds; a novel. Pantheon Bks 1963 181p o.p. 1970

The author "offers a highly original novel, a fantasy in realistic terms wherein a middle-aged bank official is drawn into an elaborately ingenious organization which fakes his death convincingly, predates a trust indenture preserving his assets, and with surgical alterations releases him 'reborn.'" Am News of Books

"This is a satiric shocker that has its moments of chilling horror and is a cold commentary on the superficiality of American life." Pub W

Time out. Delacorte Press 1968 209p boards $4.95

Analyzed in Short Story Index

"This unusual collection of short stories in a variety of moods displays a thorough command of the form, skill in characterization, and a vivid, lively imaginative style." Library J

Contents: The academy; Creatures of the sea; The Sailing Club; An angel of mercy; The interview; Countdown; Time out; Neighbors; The glory of G. O'D; The persecution of the Colonel; The evening guests; Dolly Madison in Peru; Living in sin; One Sunday after church; The human factor

Endore, Guy

King of Paris; a novel. Simon & Schuster 1956 504p o.p. 1970

A biographical novel about Alexandre Dumas, the author of "The Count of Monte Cristo" and "The three musketeers." The narrative teems with romance, adventure, sex, sentiment, and a throng of lovable and unlovable characters. Interwoven into the account is the story of the conflict between Dumas and his son. (Publisher)

Endore, Guy—*Continued*

This novel "has many things to recommend it: color, warmth, wit, and, that rarest of qualities in the historical novel, an ability to communicate a period tolerably remote from the reader's." Sat R

Erdman, Loula Grace

Another spring. Dodd 1966 305p $4.95

"A Civil War novel set in the western border of Missouri in 1863, a good hunting ground for raiders from both Union and Confederate sides, raiders who looted and burned homes, shot men and evicted families without regard to their politics. The story tells of a group of wealthy whites, poor whites, and some loyal Negroes, all burned out of their homes and thrown together for a winter of exile south of their home county." Pub W

"The writer has told an interesting story and told it well. Characterization is one of her strong points; her people all ring true and there is a balance among them of strength and weakness, of good and evil, and this balance lends life to the entire group." Best Sellers

y   The edge of time. Dodd 1950 275p $4.50

"In 1885, Bethany and Wade Cameron married and left Missouri to become homesteaders in the Texas Panhandle—cow country, where farming was next to sheep raising. They met the challenge of primitive living—built a soddy, hauled water, fought grass fires—and adjusted to the desperate loneliness because of their sturdy independence and faith in a new country. A poignant story of a young woman's acceptance of life and her proficiency in making her home one of love and security." Booklist

y   The far journey. Dodd 1955 282p boards $3.75

Set in the late nineteenth century this is "the story of a brave woman who made the covered wagon journey from Missouri to Texas with her little boy. She faces the hazards of the long trek, the dangers of Indians, river crossings and floods to join her husband in town of Mobeeti." McClurg. Book News

"This unassuming story, like Miss Erdman's earlier books, should help to keep alive traditions that are an exciting and authentic part of the American heritage." N Y Her Trib Books

Estridge, Robin. See Loraine, Philip

Etcherelli, Claire

Elise; or, The real life. Tr. from the French by June P. Wilson and Walter Benn Michaels. Morrow 1969 286p $5.95

Original French edition published 1967

"This novel tells the deeply moving story of a young woman's experiences in Paris during the time of the Algerian war. As she drifts among the revolutionary young and the poor and dispirited outcasts of society with whom she works on an automobile assembly line, Elise falls in love with an Algerian—and her eyes are opened to the destructive hell of racism." Am News of Bks

"This first novel makes its point tellingly: racism is an evil with effects so vicious that society cannot imagine the harm perpetrated on its victims. The story, however, is basically a personal tragedy." Library J

Ettinger, Elżbieta

Kindergarten. Houghton 1970 310p $5.95

" 'Elli Rostow is 13, a Polish Jew, when the Nazis force her family into hiding. Her grandfather's foresight enables the family to escape the ghetto, and her mother's sharp worldliness turns her into Ellie Barska, Polish Catholic.' She learns in this terribly painful kindergarten, how to survive. . . . Elli's participation in Nazi life inures her to her own suffering and leaves her with such strong, automatic defenses that her guilt for the simple act of living is harder to bear than torture in a concentration camp. A fine and sensitive book that avoids the pitfall of sentimentality." Pub W

Every, Dale van. See Van Every, Dale

Exupéry, Antoine de Saint. See Saint Exupéry, Antoine de

Eyre, Katherine Wigmore

The lute and the glove. Appleton 1955 313p o.p. 1970

"Anne Carey, an American girl, after her father's death, returns to the home of her ancestors in . . . England. There, living alone in the old Tudor mansion, she becomes entangled in the mystery concerning the unknown A.C. whose grave she finds in a lonely, isolated part of the grounds." Book Rev Digest

"Mrs. Eyre effectively [combines] an atmosphere of clear reason with the fantastic world of ghosts and spirits." N YTimes Bk R

The sandalwood fan; a novel of suspense. Meredith 1968 279p boards $4.95

"Piqued by the secret her dying amah tried to reveal Nan Allen flies to Hawaii to visit her only living relative, a beautiful, rich, and aloof woman who has never encouraged a close relationship but has supported Nan since her parents' deaths in a Japanese prison camp. Strange and frightening circumstances somehow bound up in a mystery surrounding the deaths of Nan's parents culminate in an attempt on Nan's life." Booklist

Eysselinck, Janet Burroway. See Burroway, Janet

F

Fabricant, Noah

(comp.) A treasury of doctor stories by the world's great authors; comp. by Noah D. Fabricant and Heinz Werner. Fell 1946 493p o.p. 1970

Analyzed in Short Story Index

Contents: Doc Mellhorn and the pearly gates, by S. V. Benét; The nurse, by B. A. Williams; The enemy, by P. Buck; Lord Mountdrago, by W. S. Maugham; Zone of quiet, by R. W. Lardner; Movie scenario, by B. Hecht; She walks in beauty, by N. Foley; A work of art, by A. Chekhov; Who lived and died believing, by N. Hale; Dr Mahony, by H. H. Richardson; Silent snow, secret snow, by C. Aiken; Indian camp, by E. Hemingway; Missis Flinders, by T. Slesinger; The district doctor, by I. Turgeniev; The witch doctor of Rosy Ridge, by M. Kantor; Father is firm with his ailments, by C. Day; Death of a bachelor, by A. Schnitzler; Negro doctor in the South, by W. White; Martha's vacation, by V. Fisher; The scarlet plague, by J. London; "Speaking of operations" by I. S. Cobb; Birth, by A. J. Cronin; The operation, by R. M. Du Gard; Allergies and the man-eating carp, by H. V. O'Brien; The country doctor, by I. Beede; Morton, by L. F. Cooper; Medicine man, by E. Caldwell; Other room, by D. Marquis; Last equation, by R. Burlingame; Surgeon and the nun, by P. Horgan; Three veterans, by L. Zugsmith; Testimony of Dr Farnsworth, by F. L. Golden; The bedchamber mystery, by C. S. Forester; A day's wait, by E. Hemingway; Family in the wind, by F. S. Fitzgerald

Fairbairn, Ann

Five smooth stones; a novel. Crown 1966 756p $6.95

A story of race conflict. "The author follows a Negro hero, David Champlin, from his birth in New Orleans in 1933 to his death by a sniper's bullet thirty years later, after he has become something of a national figure for his part in riots leading out of civil rights demonstrations in a small Southern town. He goes to a liberal Midwestern college, later to Harvard and Oxford (he is a brilliant scholarship student); he makes early friendships which are to last his short lifetime; he marries Sara, who is white. The book ends symbolically enough with the birth of David's son, another David." Book of the Month Club News

Fairbairn, Ann—*Continued*

"He is not a psychological case history. . . . He is not a dope addict with a heart of gold. David Champlin is a man of dignity. . . . [He] is an old-fashioned hero, and his story has many old-fashioned plot ingredients. Miss Fairbairn . . . uses melodrama at times to drive home her points, David's and Sara's romance is perhaps the least convincing part of the novel—though even here there are scenes that blaze with bitter truth. . . . Negro or white, Southern or Northern, illiterate or scholarly, noble or conniving, the numerous people characterized so clearly in this novel are, with few exceptions, 'mortal humans.' That is rare enough in any fiction dealing with one of the bone-deep issues of our time." N Y Times Bk R

Fallada, Hans

Little man, what now? Simon & Schuster 1933 383p o.p. 1970

"Translated from the German by Eric Sutton" "How the years of the depression affect a little German couple, darkening their skies, taking laughter from their lips, as they struggle inarticulately and pathetically to keep their heads above water and to retain their self-respect. German in setting, this record, authentic and individual, is yet significantly representative of thousands in like case everywhere." N Y Libraries

Farge, Christopher la. See La Farge, Christopher

Farge, Oliver la. See La Farge, Oliver

Farrell, Cliff

Westward—to blood and glory
In Western Writers of America. A Western bonanza p190-246

Farrell, James T.

Judgement day. Vanguard 1935 465p o.p. 1970

"This last volume of a trilogy brings to its conclusion the life story of Studs Lonigan, the boy of the Chicago streets, the youth who aspired to be a 'big shot,' the young man beaten down by the depression, dying of pneumonia brought on by excesses and exposure." Book Rev Digest

also in Farrell, J. T. Studs Lonigan v3

The life adventurous
In Farrell, J. T. An omnibus of short stories v3

An omnibus of short stories. Vanguard 1956 3v in 1 $7.50

Analyzed in Short Story Index
Comprises all the stories from: $1000 a week; To whom it may concern; and The life adventurous
$1000 a week; The sport of Kings; Sorel; Monday is another day; After the sun has risen; The fate of a hero; Whoopee for the New Deal; The bride of Christ; A jazz-age clerk; Getting out the vote for the working class; The fall off Machine-Gun McGurk; Yesterday's love; Counting the waves; Accident; A short story; The only son; Baby Mike
To whom it may concern: Mr Gremmer; Patsy Gilbride; A teamster's payday; Street scene; The Hyland family; High-school star; Omar James; Autumn afternoon; A Sunday in April; Tommy Gallagher's crusade
The life adventurous: The philosopher; Young artist; The triumph of Willie Collins; Father Timothy Joyce; Joe Eliot; Scrambled eggs and toast; Saturday night; A love story of our time; Olsen; The dialectic; Young convicts; Pat McGee; Lunch hour: 1923; Called on the carpet; Comrade Stanley; Episode in a dentist's office; Quest; Boyhood

$1000 a week
In Farrell, J. T. An omnibus of short stories v 1

Studs Lonigan; a trilogy. Vanguard 1935 3v in 1 $7.50

An omnibus volume containing the complete life history of Studs Lonigan. The volumes included are: Young Lonigan, first published 1932; The young manhood of Studs Lonigan, first published 1934; Judgment day, first published 1935

A sordid and distressing story. "Mr. Farrell is an excellent story teller. He is a first rate artist in current speech. His descriptions of the cheap squalid streets of Chicago, the poolroom bums, the smells and sounds of the animal life of vicious children trying to be sports are vivid and convincing." Sat R

To whom it may concern
In Farrell, J. T. An omnibus of short stories v2

A world I never made. Vanguard 1936 516p o.p. 1970

A novel of life among the poor-class Irish in Chicago. Some of the characters in the Studs Lonigan trilogy reappear here. "The book begins in August 1911 when sly, timid, little Danny O'Neill has been taken into his grandmother's home because his own parents are too poor to bring him up properly. Pampered by his pipe-smoking old grandmother, Danny suffers from loneliness, becomes a passionate student of big-league batting records, slowly learns a few of the facts of life from the brutal disclosures of his big brother Bill. He starts school, gets sick, snitches on Bill, get beaten up, is becoming a moody, evasive, introspective child, ill at ease both in his own home and at his grandmother's, when the book ends." Time

Young Lonigan; a boyhood in Chicago streets; introduction by Federic M. Thrasher. Vanguard 1932 308p o.p. 1970

"A study of a boy's adolescent years in the Chicago streets. A realistic novel, which is an essay in the stream of consciousness, of a tough little Irish boy from the time he graduates from grade school until he enters high school the following Fall." Washington, D.C. Pub Lib

"It is painfully realistic and frank in its descriptions and written with sufficient skill to seem much more than a case history." Sat R

Followed by: The young manhood of Studs Lonigan

also in Farrell, J. T. Studs Lonigan v 1

The young manhood of Studs Lonigan. Vanguard 1934 412p o.p. 1970

Sequel to: Young Lonigan
"This story of Studs Lonigan's young manhood extends from 1917—while he is still in high school—to 1929, and depicts his gradual disintegration and final degradation." Book Rev Digest

also in Farrell, J. T. Studs Lonigan v2

Farrell, Michael

Thy tears might cease; introduction by Monk Gibbon. Knopf 1964 [c1963] xxv, 577p $6.95

First published 1963 in England
"The story traces the moral and spiritual development of a young Irishman, Martin Reilly, during the early years of this century. Martin's entrance into adolescence coincides with the first stirrings of political rebellion in Ireland, and just as he is striving to come to terms with a newfound land of adult experience, his country is plunged into civil war." Publisher's note

"The beauty of the opening chapters which deal with Martin's generally happy home life in a small village, contrasts sharply with the book's later sections which deal with the fury of war." Huntting

Farris, John

When Michael calls. Trident Press 1967 184p $4.95

"A woman whose nephew disappeared at the age of 10 in a blizzard and was presumed killed, although his body was never found, suddenly begins to receive eerie telephone calls. They

Farris, John—*Continued*

purport to come from the dead boy, Michael, and they touch upon things only the real boy could have known about. Before the ghostly masquerade is over, two men die, a woman is driven to the verge of madness and a whole town is gripped in superstitious terror. The story is handled with terse skill." Pub W

Fast, Howard

y April morning; a novel

Some editions are:
Crown $3.95
Watts, F. $7.95 Large type edition complete and unabridged. A Keith Jennison book
First published 1961

"A brief fictional account of the events in Lexington and Concord on April 19, 1775, as observed by 15-year-old Adam Cooper, son of Moses Cooper, one of the leaders in the Committee of Safety in Lexington. . . . [The story] is recounted within the framework of the homely details of family life." Library J

"A veteran at this sort of historical recreation, Howard Fast has admirably recaptured the sights and sounds, the religious and political idioms, the simple military tactics and strategies of that day." N Y Times Bk R

y Citizen Tom Paine. Duell 1943 341p o.p. 1970

"Tom Paine's life was as heroic as his vision of a better world. Born in poverty in England, he was helped to America by Franklin and became an editor in Philadelphia. With the news of the Battle of Lexington came the crystallization of ideas that had formed as he had watched and worked in the embryonic democracy of the new world. Paine wrote 'Common Sense.' It swept the colonies and finally left its imprint on the shape and on the very words of the Constitution." Huntting

"Whether this portrait is the whole of Paine is questionable; but, granting Mr. Fast's clearly avowed sympathy with this strange and twisted character, it is both a provocative and impressive one. Not all saint or all sinner was Paine, but there was enough of each in him to make him kin to both." N Y Her Trib Books

Freedom road. Crown 263p $3.95

A reprint of the title first published 1944 by Duell

"Historical novel based on the reconstruction period in the South following the Civil War, when for a few years Negroes and whites worked together in harmony. Gideon Jackson, the Negro leader, who rose from illiteracy to be a member of Congress, is the central character. The rise of Gideon, his efforts to help his people, the little settlement over which he presided is pictured. Then the Northern troops are withdrawn from the South, and disaster for the Negroes follows." Book Rev Digest

"This portrayal of a period in our history and of a man who learned the true meaning of freedom and the vigilance necessary to keep it, may not be Howard Fast's best book, and I say this only because of the high caliber of his other works, but it certainly is his most timely novel, for Gideon Jackson is as much a symbol of today and tomorrow as he was of yesterday." N Y Times Bk R

The general zapped an angel; new stories of fantasy and science fiction. Morrow 1970 159p boards $5

Contents: The general zapped an angel; The mouse; The vision of Milty Boil; The Mohawk; The wound; Tomorrow's Wall Street Journal; The interval; The movie house; The insects

Moses, Prince of Egypt. Crown 1958 303p o.p. 1970

This novel about the Biblical patriarch "deals with Moses' childhood and youth and takes him up to his flight from Egypt into the wilderness of Sinai." Pub W

" 'Moses' is a romantic and popularized recreation of the legend. . . . The present interpretation is definite, 'factual' and rather literal. . . . Yet if the present version of the Moses story is open to question and if the central figures in the novel never quite achieve reality

even on their own terms, it is still true that the narrative is interesting and colorful." N Y Times Bk R

For another title by this author see Cunningham, E. V.

Faulkner, William

Nobel Prize in literature 1949

Absalom, Absalom!

Some editions are:
Modern Lib. $2.95 Introduction by Harvey Breit
Random House $4.95
First published 1936

"Strange story of an old Southern tragedy, which is revived and pieced together by a Harvard freshman who came from the same locality and was only indirectly concerned in the matter. The main story deals with Thomas Sutpen, an ambitious planter who settled near Jefferson, Mississippi in 1833." Book Rev Digest

"Occasionally there are passages of great power and beauty in this book, passages which remind us that Faulkner is still a writer with a unique gift of illuminating dark corners of the human soul. There are other passages which, while hardly communicative, drop into a pure blank verse and are estimable for their sheer verbal music." N Y Times Bk R

As I lay dying

Some editions are:
Modern Lib. $2.95
Random House $4.95
First published 1930

"Enclosing their dead mother, Addie Bundren, in a home-made coffin, Cash, Darl, Jewel, Dewey Dell and Vardaman—accompanied by the dazed father Anse—load her on a wagon and travel for several days across a rain-swept country to Jefferson, where Addie wants to be buried with her folks. Flooding rivers, a decaying corpse, buzzards, and a demented small boy are forced upon the reader's senses thru the subjective medium of the minds of this family of poor whites, and thru the more lucid, objective medium of the reflections of their acquaintances concerning their actions." Book Rev Digest

"The whole affair is a psychological jigsaw puzzle, the pieces of which are represented by the distorted mentalities of half a dozen characters. The fascination of the story lies in the manner in which the phosphorescent rottenness of the family gradually reveals itself to the reader." Nation

Big woods; decorations by Edward Shenton. Random House 1955 198p illus $4.95

Analyzed in Short Story Index

"Four of Faulkner's hunting stories from those of the Yoknapatawpha country. . . . They are joined with explanatory passages by the author. The first three stories have been published previously; Race at morning is new." Book Rev Digest

Contents: The bear; The old people; A bear hunt; Race at morning

Collected stories of William Faulkner. Random House 1950 900p $6.95

Analyzed in Short Story Index

Contents: Barn burning; Shingles for the Lord; Tall men; A bear hunt; Two soliders; Shall not perish; Rose for Emily; Hair; Centaur in brass; Dry September; Death drag; Elly; Uncle Willy; Mule in the yard; That will be fine; That evening sun; Red leaves; A justice; A courtship; Lo; Ad astra; Victory; Crevasse; Turnabout; All the dead pilots; Wash; Honor; Dr Martino; Fox hunt; Pennsylvania Station; Artist at home; The brooch; My Grandmother Millard; Golden land; There was a queen; Mountain victory; Beyond; Black music; The leg; Mistral; Divorce in Naples; Carcassonne

"The final impression left by Faulkner's work is that he is a writer of incomparable talents who has used and misused those talents superbly and recklessly. But his book has the excitement that comes from never knowing when, amidst pages of failure, there will come a masterpiece." Time

Faulkner, William—*Continued*

A fable

Some editions are:
Modern Lib. $2.95
Random House $4.95

Pulitzer Prize 1955

First published 1954

"A religious allegory, paralleling the events of Passion Week, a bitter denunciation of war, a novel characterized by the same inspiring philosophy and excellent writing we have come to expect from Faulkner. The background is the week of the false armistice of 1918, the main plot centers in a French corporal and his twelve followers who have brought front action to a standstill by their work to spread the gospel of man's brotherhood to man." Cincinnati

"The prose is sometimes impenetrable, the backtrackings in time and changing points of view confusing to the untrained reader. But the brilliant flights of rhetoric, the spiritual integrity, and the exalted emotional level make the novel something of a landmark in modern literature." Booklist

The Faulkner reader; selections from the works of William Faulkner. Modern Lib. 1959 682p (Modern Lib. giant) $4.95

A reprint of the title first published 1954 by Random House, and partially analyzed in Short Story Index

Contains the following stories: The sound and the fury (1929); The bear, excerpt from Go down, Moses; Old man, excerpt from The wild palms; Spotted horses, excerpt from The hamlet; A rose for Emily; Barn burning; Dry September; That evening sun; Turabout; Shingles for the Lord; A justice; Wash; An odor of verbena, excerpt from The unvanquished; Percy Grimm, excerpt from Light in August; The courthouse, excerpt from Requiem for a nun

Go down, Moses, and other stories

Some recommended editions are:
Random House $4.95
Modern Lib. $2.95

Random House edition analyzed in Short Story Index

First published 1942

"A volume of short stories all dealing directly or indirectly with one family living in Jefferson, Mississippi." Book Rev Digest

Contents: Was: The fire and the hearth; Pantaloon in black; The old people; The bear; Delta autumn; Go down, Moses

The hamlet. [3d ed] Random House 1964 366p $4.95

The first volume of the author's trilogy; Snopes, originally published 1940, the second of which is The town, and the third, The mansion, both entered separately

Set in the 19th century in Yoknapatawpha County, Mississippi, with the principal characters being members of the rapacious Snopes family. Deals alternately with horse-trading and love

"The book's sly, perverse humor is undeniable: yet it is a humor which, for the very reason that it moderates the horrors it plays upon, somehow robs those horrors of the dignity and importance which alone would justify them. The book's imaginativeness has enabled Faulkner to create something like a world of his own; yet that world is too artificially lighted and too demoniacally propelled to mean anything as revelation." Nation

Intruder in the dust

Some editions are:
Modern Lib. $2.95
Random House $4.95

First published 1948

"A Negro is held in a Mississippi jail, charged with murder of a white man; while a mob assembles, evidence proving his innocence is gathered by two 16-year-old boys, one white and one Negro, and their assistant, an elderly spinster of aristocratic family. Faulkner presents this chivalrous exploit as a parable for the South and for hostile 'outlanders.'" Library J

"Intruder in the Dust makes the reader work, it is not easy reading. But the reward is worth the trouble. It can be read as a detective story, a humorous idyl (a kind of second cousin to Huckleberry Finn), an outraged, descriptive exhortation to Southern society, a parable of modern life. It is also a triumphant work of art." Time

Knight's gambit. Random House 1949 246p $4.95

Analyzed in Short Story Index

"Six stories, all stories of violence. In each of them Gavin Stevens, a county attorney, appears." Book Rev Digest

Contents: Smoke; Monk; Hand upon the waters; Tomorrow; An error in chemistry; Knight's gambit

Light in August

Some editions are:
Modern Lib $2.95
Random House $5.95

First published 1932

"A country girl, well advanced in pregnancy, is seeking the lover who has promised to marry her. She walks shoeless in the warm dust, or rides in friendly wagons, or stays in half willing houses, confidently, because the life force within her makes her confident. And in all this story of murder, rape, lynching, insanity, and remorse, no one hurts her, no one is anything but kind to her, no misadventure comes near her, and even when she learns that her lover is worthless, a husband and father for her child, who is not worthless, is provided." Sat R

"The book is no light novel by any stretch of the imagination, but it has more than a little of Faulkner's humor, which is a rare and precious humor, and it shows that he can be tender when he likes." No Am

The mansion. Random House 1959 436p $4.95

The final novel in the trilogy about the Snopes family of Jefferson, Mississippi

"The reader familiar with the chronicle of Flem Snopes's insidious infiltration into the affairs of Jefferson, Mississippi as told in 'The hamlet' and 'The town' will note that even though the narrators and the monolog technique are the same, the characters in this third volume are more concrete, more fully human in their goodness and badness, and the plot gains strength as retribution finally overtakes Snopes." Booklist

The portable Faulkner; rev. and expanded edition. Ed. by Malcolm Cowley. Viking 1967 xxxvii, 724p map (The Viking Portable lib) $6.50

Analyzed in Short story index

First published 1946

Contents: A justice; The courthouse (A name for the city) Red leaves; Was; Wash; An odor of verbena; The bear; Spotted horses; That evening sun; Ad astra; A rose for Emily; Dilsey; Old man; Death drag; Uncle Bud and the three madams; Percy Grimm; Delta autumn; The jail

Pylon. Random House [1965 c1962] 315p $6.95

A reissue of the title first published 1935 by Harrison Smith & Robert Haas, Inc. and recopyrighted 1962

"The scene is a Southern city where a Mardi Gras celebration is in progress. The action covers four days in the lives of a strange set of people, all of them connected in some way with the airplane contests, which are being held in celebration of the opening of a new airport. The main characters are: Shumann, an airplane pilot; Jiggs, his mechanic; Jackson, a parachute jumper; Laverne, Shumann's wife; and a nameless reporter who adopts the group for the time being." Book Rev Digest

"Apart from his difficult style, combination of words, obscurity and his lightninglike changes from one scene to another, the story, in all its tragedy and sordidness, is plausible and authentic. True, it is not a pretty story." Boston Transcript

Faulkner, William—*Continued*

The reivers; a reminiscence. Random House 1962 305p $4.95

Pulitzer Prize 1963

"On a summer day in 1905 Lucius Priest, eleven, is persuaded by Boon Hogganbeck to 'borrow' his grandfather's car and make a trip to Memphis. Ned McCaslin, Negro, stows away and the three are off on a heroic odyssey which ends at Miss Reba's bordello. When Ned turns up in the night with a horse for which he has traded the car, the action accelerates wildly and draws Miss Reba, Boon's friend, Miss Corrie, Lucius, Ned, trainmen, and deputies into a mad melee of smuggling a horse across country, planning a bizarre race, and ending in jail. The use of the archaic term 'reivers' for stealing and destruction carries a double meaning, for Lucius' innocence is destroyed and Ned consummately destroys the old pattern of subservience to his white relatives." Booklist

"'The Reivers' is not 'serious' Faulkner, though the style is as involved as ever. Rather, it has at its surface the rich strain of earthy humor which has always underlaid Faulkner's best work. The result is a funny, universal—and salable—tale." Pub W

Requiem for a nun. Random House 1951 286p $4.95

"A sequel to the author's Sanctuary. It tells partly in prose, partly in play form, the story of Temple Drake, eight years after the time of Sanctuary. The action begins with the death sentence pronounced on Nancy, Temple's nursemaid, for the murder of Temple and Gowan Stevens' child. Temple's effort to have the death sentence commuted involves a night visit to the governor, with a long explanation of her own guilt in the affair." Book Rev Digest

"Among the most successful of Faulkner's many experiments in narrative form. . . . By writing the three narratives, Faulkner translates the past into present and gives his action a sense of historical depth, like a fourth dimension. A book that might otherwise be merely a printed play, without actors or setting, now reads like a thoughtful novel." N Y Her Trib Books

Sanctuary

Some editions are:
Modern Lib. $2.95
Random House $4.95

First published 1931

"Horace Benbow, an ineffectual intellectual, becomes involved in the violent events centering around Temple Drake, a young coed. Temple is raped by Popeye, who murders a man trying to protect the girl. Carried off to a Memphis brothel by Popeye, Temple later protects him and testifies against Lee Goodwin, who is accused of the murder. Benbow defends Goodwin at the trial and unsuccessfully tries to give shelter to his common-law wife. Temple's testimony ends all hope for Goodwin, who is lynched by the townspeople." Benét. The Reader's Encyclopedia

"A brooding atmosphere of obscene and bestial decadence hangs over Mr Faulkner's latest novel, with its Mississippi hills setting and its poor-white moonshiners, halfwits and prostitutes. Mr Faulkner's technique is similar in this novel to that which he employed in As I Lay Dying." Book Rev Digest

Followed by: Requiem for a nun

Sartoris. Random House 380p $4.95

A reprint of the title first published 1929 by Harcourt

"The first of his novels which constitute a bitter panorama of the decadent Sartoris and Compson families of Jefferson, Mississippi. The genteel society of the old Civil War South decays, during three generations, and is replaced during the post-World War I period of disillusion, by such families as the unscrupulous Snopes." Haydn. Thesaurus of Book Digests

Selected short stories of William Faulkner. Modern Lib. 1961 306p $2.95

Analyzed in Short Story Index

A variety of the author's output, diverse in method and subject matter, ranging in original publication dates from 1930 to 1955

Contents: Barn burning; Two soldiers; A rose for Emily; Dry September; That evening sun; Red leaves; Lo; Turnabout; Honor; There was a queen; Mountain victory; Beyond; Race at morning

Soldiers pay. Liveright 1926 319p $5.50

"Concerns Donald Mahon, a wounded aviator of World War I and his homecoming in Georgia. His family and friends misunderstand the compassion of his nurse, the attractive young widow Margaret Powers; and by the time Donald dies his ordeal has revealed the lives of many characters, and changed some." Haydn. Thesaurus of Book Digests

The sound and the fury

Some editions are:
Modern Lib. $2.95
Random House $4.95

First published 1929

"A southern family of gentle blood is shown in decay, its members petty failures, drunkards, suicides, pathological perverts and idiots. Part One presents the tragedy as seen through the eyes of Benjy, the idiot son, a grown man thrown back into childhood by any chance sight or smell. Through his broken thoughts we learn of Caddy, a beloved sister, who has run away from the hideous home and sent back an illegitimate daughter. In Part Two, we move back eighteen years and witness, through the workings of his mind, the last day in the life of Quentin, brother of Benjy and Caddy. Part Three brings us again into the present, where we look through the mean eyes of Jason, the third brother. And in the final part of the novel, in the author's direct narrative, the spectacle of white disintegration is shown and sharpened by the emphasis thrown upon Negro solidity." Outlook

also in Faulkner, W. The Faulkner reader p5-251

The town. Random House 1957 371p $5.95

"'The Town,' the second part of a Snopes trilogy . . . brings Flem and his tribe to Jefferson, the Yoknapatawpha County seat, where his rise at the expense of the Sartorises and their kind continues unabated. The protagonist of this novel is the idealistic, sensitive, vulnerable lawyer, Gavin Stevens. . . . The events of 'The Town' are given a startling precision by being recounted and analyzed in turn from the complementary viewpoints of Stevens, V. K. Ratliff (the shrewd, ironic sewing machine salesman), and Charles Mallison (the innocent yet wise youngster of 'Intruder in the Dust') . . . . It can be read quite profitably by the reader who is not familiar with the earlier works." Library J

"The style is still a series of unoriented episodes that gives us an extraordinary lifelike sensation of groping our own way through each experience, but the world here is much closer to the outside one, and by so much the more accessible to our sympathies." N Y Her Trib Books

The unvanquished; drawings by Edward Shenton. Random House [1965 c1938] 293p illus $4.95

First published 1938 and analyzed in Short Story Index

"Seven short stories, six of which originally appeared in magazines, are here rewritten in novel form. Seen thru the eyes of Bayard Sartoris, twelve-year-old boy, the story depicts the life of the unvanquished Sartoris family on their Mississippi plantation during the latter days of the Civil war and the period of reconstruction." Book Rev Digest

Contents: Ambuscade; Retreat; Raid; Riposte in tertio; Vendée; Skirmish at Sartoris; An odor of verbena

"The motivation is not devious, not psychopathic. There is still violence and rebellion, but it springs directly from a firm moral vision. That is the justification for [Faulkner's] abandonment of difficult stylistic mechanisms." N Y Times Bk R

Faust, Frederick. See Brand, Max

Fearing, Kenneth

The big clock. With an introduction by James Nelson. Norton 1968 175p $4.95

"The Seagull library of mystery and suspense"

First published 1946 by Harcourt

"George Stroud, executive editor of 'Crimeways', a small piece of the huge magazine complex known as Janoth Enterprises, is suddenly confronted with the strange assignment of locating the man seen on 48th Street the night Pauline Delos, the dazzling friend of Earl Janoth, was murdered, and the one woman in the city George should have had enough sense to stay away from. But he let the big clock move him closer and closer to her, just as he later let it move him toward the completion of this assignment that could mean either the end of his career or the end of his life." Library J

Fenton, Charles A.

(ed.) The best short stories of World War II; an American anthology. Viking 1957 428p o.p. 1970

Analyzed in Short Story Index

Contents: A judgment in the mountains, by S. V. Benét; Two soldiers, by W. Faulkner; The thirty-year man, by J. Jones; Layover in El Paso, by R. Lowry; Night flight, by J. W. Johnson; Health card, by F. Yerby; Blockbuster, by M. Schorer; A short wait between trains, by R. McLaughlin; The birthmark, by T. Heggen; Flying home, by R. Ellison; Leipzig, by B. Stiles; The airstrip at Konora, by J. A. Michener; Flesh and blood, by L. Critchell; Queen Penicillin, by J. H. Burns; The women on the wall, by W. Stegner; The four freedoms, by E. Newhouse; Act of faith, by I. Shaw; The paper house, by N. Mailer; School days, by S. Wilson; The long march, by W. Styron

Fenwick, Elizabeth

Disturbance on Berry Hill. Atheneum Pubs. 1968 [c1967] 176p map $4.50

In Berry Hill, a private community near New York, middle-aged Susan "is frightened one day by someone entering her bedroom while she is taking a bath in the adjoining room. The intruder simply looks around, disorders things a bit, and leaves. Several other strange and seemingly innocuous happenings disturb other families on Berry Hill—innocuous until the night when one of the wives is killed." Pub W

"Great economy and subtlety, fine full-fleshed creation of characters, and the usual Fenwick conviction in delicately portraying an abberrant mind in what seems to be a perfectly ordinary person." N Y Times Bk R

Goodbye, Aunt Elva. Atheneum Pubs. 1968 179p boards $4.95

"There is no mystery writer writing today who is more chilling in her perusal of quiet horror in a supposedly normal domestic setting than Elizabeth Fenwick. An elderly woman . . . suddenly finds herself at the heart and center of a criminal conspiracy. She will be used by an ugly and not too bright criminal mother-and-son team to take the place of another old woman, senile and drugged, in an attempt to fool the lawyer in an estate case. Violet Besserman, however . . . is a brave woman and when a curious young man, a distant relative of the old lady she is being forced to impersonate, happens on the scene, tension mounts and you become so involved you can hardly put down the book." Pub W

Ferber, Edna

y Cimarron

Some editions are:
Doubleday $4.95
Grosset $2.50

First published 1930

"Oklahoma, from the run of 1889, through pioneer days, problems of bad-men and Indians and discovery of oil, down to its sophisticated present, is the ever-changing background which makes an epic of the story of Yancey Cravat, dreamer, windmill-tilter, adventurer and gun-man, and Sabra, his wife,

descendant of languid Southern gentlefolk but with enough iron in her blood to be a sturdy pioneer wife and mother, to foster the spirit of feminism in the women of Osage, to build up from infancy a territorial newspaper, and to serve as congresswoman from Oklahoma." Cleveland

"It is a superb example of massing, of selecting and arranging the most effective details out of the greatest number that must have caught the author's fancy. The style fits the material: not beautiful or distinguished, but picturesque." Christian Science Monitor

y Giant

Some editions are:
Doubleday $4.50
Grosset $3.95

First published 1952

"Texas and the Texans are subjected to some unfavorable criticism in the story of a Virginia reared woman who marries a Texan. Bick Benedict, who manages the Benedict family's two and a half million acre ranch, and his friends, who have made their money in cattle, cotton, or oil, have a chance to speak for themselves and defend their brash grandscale way of living but the final word rests with Bick's wife Leslie. Coming fresh from Virginia as a bookish but spirited young woman. Leslie is shocked by the life she finds and is never reconciled to it although her love for her husband holds her to the ranch." Booklist

Ice Palace. Doubleday 1958 411p $5.95

This novel "concerns the lives of two very different men who pioneered in Alaska, their children and their mutual grand-daughter. There is a good deal of interesting material about Alaska, past and present." Pub W

"In spite of a dated style and stock characters the author makes her point and provides eye-opening glimpses of . . . Alaska." Booklist

One basket; thirty-one short stories. Doubleday 1957 [c1947] 581p $3.95

Analyzed in Short Story Index

First published 1947

Contents: The woman who tried to be good; The gay old dog; That's marriage; Farmer in the dell; Un morso doo pang; Long distance; The maternal feminine; Old Man Minick; The afternoon of a faun; Old Lady Mandle; Gigolo; Home girl; The sudden sixties; Classified; Holiday; Our very best people; Mother knows best; Every other Thursday; Blue blood; Hey! Taxi; The light touch; They brought their woman; Glamour; Keep it holy; Blue glasses; Trees die at the top; Nobody's in town; No room at the inn; You're not the type; Grandma isn't playing; The barn cuts off the view

Saratoga trunk. Doubleday 1941 352p $4.95

"Life in New Orleans and Saratoga in the 1880s, as seen thru the lives of Clint Maroon, once a Texas cowboy, and his beloved Clio, the daughter of a New Orleans aristocrat and his mistress, a beautiful adventuress. Driven from New Orleans because she killed her lover, Clio's mother fled to France and there brought up her daughter. After her mother's death Clio, devastatingly beautiful and outrageously clever, returned to New Orleans, determined to marry a wealthy man. There she met and loved Clint Maroon. In Saratoga, where Clint went to play the races, and where Clio joined him, they met the Morgans and Vanderbilts and other railroad barons, and Clint decided he would make his fortune in railroads rather than horses. Sixty years later, when Clint was eighty-nine and had given away most of his enormous wealth he tried to tell his life story to the press, but nobody believed him—nobody but his still lovely Clio." Book Rev Digest

This title "recreates the fabulous Saratoga of the eighties, when fashion was king and robber barons ruled the land. . . . This expertly written, absorbingly entertaining satire likewise adroitly contrasts the ideals of a plutocratic America gradually emerging into a true democracy." Library J

y Show boat

Some editions are:
Doubleday $4.95
Grosset $2.50

First published 1926

"Follows the fortunes of the Hawks-Ravenal family from the 1870's. . . . The main part of

Ferber, Edna—*Continued*

the story takes place on the 'Cotton Blossom floating palace theatre.' a show boat that is towed up and down the Mississippi and its tributaries from New Orleans to St Louis and the coal fields of Pennsylvania." Pittsburgh

"'Show Boat' is a gorgeous thing to read for the reading's sake alone. Some, perhaps, will conscientiously refer to it as a document which reanimates a part of the American scene that once existed and does no more. But this writer cannot believe it is that; rather it is a glorification of that scene, a heightening, an expression of its full romantic possibilities." N Y Times Bk R

y So Big. Doubleday 1924 360p $5.50

Pulitzer Prize. 1925

"Selina DeJong would look up from her work and say, 'How big is my man.' Then little Dirk DeJong would answer in the time-worn way. 'So-o-o big!' And he was so nicknamed. Tho So Big gives the book its title his mother is the outstanding figure. Until Selina was nineteen she traveled with her gambler-father. At his sudden death she secured a teacher's post in the Dutch settlement of High Prairie, a community of hardworking farmers and their thrifty, slaving wives—narrow-minded people indifferent to natural beauty. Soon Selina married Pervus DeJong, a plodding, good-natured boy. With her marriage the never-ending drudgery of a farmer's wife began. Thru all the years of hardship she never lost her gay indomitable spirt. Unfortunately, she was unable to transmit these qualities to her son." Book Rev Digest

"It is a thoughtful book, clean and strong, dramatic at times, interesting always, clear-sighted, sympathetic, a novel to read and to remember." N Y Times Bk R

Fergusson, Harvey

Grant of kingdom

In Blacker, I. R. ed. The Old West in fiction p3-198

Ferrars, E. X.

The swaying pillars. Walker & Co. [1969 c1968] 192p boards $4.50

The setting "is Tondola, capital of the new African country Uyowa, where Helena Sebright brings young Jean Forest from London to her grandparents' spacious home. There she is involved with native uprisings, disappearing former presidents, and the pillars of the pergola Mr. Forest is building in the garden that refuse to stay upright." Library J

"A satisfying thriller with some shrewd if not always flattering observations on the travail of newly emerging nations." Pub W

Feuchtwanger, Lion

The Jew of Rome; tr. by Willa and Edwin Muir. Viking 1936 565p o.p. 1970

Sequel to: Josephus

"A continuation of the story of the Jewish historian, begun in 'Josephus'. Now a favorite of the emperor, Josephus wants to consolidate his position in the Roman world, and still be a loyal Jew; reason shows him the necessity of compromise and at the end he accepts humiliation as a Jew by passing in procession under the arch celebrating the destruction of Jerusalem." Booklist

Josephus; tr. by Willa and Edwin Muir. Viking 1932 504p o.p. 1970

"A long historical and biographical novel based on the life of the Jewish historian. The period covered is from the time of Josephus' visit to Rome in 64 A.D. to the fall of Jerusalem and his return to Rome to take up the life of a writer." Book Rev Digest

"While, considered as 'fictionized' history and even as biography, 'Josephus' is remarkably well done and effective, as a novel it is too overcrowded with people and details of diverging interest." N Y Times Bk R

Followed by: The Jew of Rome

Josephus and the Emperor; tr. by Caroline Oram. Viking 1942 446p o.p. 1970

Published in England with title: The day will come

"The third volume in a trilogy about the Jewish historian, Josephus, of which the earlier volumes were Josephus and The Jew of Rome. The historian, after finishing his Universal History of the Jews is no longer in favor with the Roman emperor, Domitian. His attempts to be both a Jewish teacher and a Roman knight are unsuccessful. He is killed by Roman troops in Judea, as he is trying to reach a band of Jewish rebels." Book Rev Digest

"As a picture of life in Domitian's Rome it conveys a mood of reality vibrant with life." N Y Times Bk R

Proud destiny; a novel. Viking 1947 625p o.p. 1970

Translated by Moray Firth, from the German ms. entitled Waffen für Amerika

"The scene is France, and especially its court, at the time of Louis XVI and Antoinette; the subject is French support of the American revolution, and the central character is Beaumarchais, who schemed and worked for arms and support for the revolutionary Americans but never won the confidence of Benjamin Franklin, although their aim was the same. Through Beaumarchais' authorship of 'The Barber of Seville,' and through an actress, the theater also is brought into the story." Booklist

"In and out of the court of Louis XVI and Marie Antoinette move the tremendous figures of Franklin and Voltaire, making history and foreshadowing the fate of France. The skillful pen of the author does justice to such epoch making figures and events and gives us a rich satisfying novel that is little short of an epic." Ontario Lib Rev

Fiedler, Leslie A.

Nude croquet; the stories of Leslie A. Fiedler. Stein & Day 1969 288p boards $5.95

Contents: Nude croquet [novelette]; The teeth; Let nothing you dismay; Dirty Ralphy; The fear of innocence; An expense of spirit; Nobody ever died from it; Pull down vanity; The stain; Bad scene at Buffalo Jump; The girl in the black raincoat; The dancing of Reb Hershl and the withered hand

Field, Rachel

y All this, and heaven too. Macmillan (N Y) 1938 596p $6.95

"In fiction form the author tells the life story of her great-aunt by marriage, the French governess who in 1847 became involved in a famous murder trial, in which she was known as Mademoiselle D. Altho she was acquitted, life became so difficult for her in France that Mademoiselle came to America, where she married an American and presided over a Gramercy Park salon, frequented by William Cullen Bryant, Harriet Beecher Stowe, Samuel Morse, and Fanny Kemble among others." Book Rev Digest

"The author has projected herself into the mind and being of the woman whose life has long fascinated her, and, in giving us the story she has 'always wanted to tell,' she has given us her best and richest fiction." Sat R

And now tomorrow. Macmillan (N Y) 1942 350p $5.50

"A New England mill town, with its sharp division between the mill workers who live on one side of the river and the owning families who live on the other, is the scene of Miss Field's new story. Emily Blair, is one of the Blairs who have controlled the Peace-Pipe mills for generations. Happily engaged to marry Harry Collins, life looks to her smooth and fair, when an illness, which strikes suddenly, deprives her of her hearing. Forced to adjust herself to a new world of deafness she must also see her lover turn from her to her attractive younger sister. A series of treatments by a young doctor . . . restores her hearing and brings a new love into her life." Wis Lib Bul

Time out of mind. Macmillan (N Y) 1935 462p $4.50

"Kate Fernald, daughter of the Fortune's house-keeper, tells the story of the Fortunes—the Major, whose forebears had been notable

Field, Rachel—*Continued*

shipbuilders and who stubbornly refused to believe that steam would crowd out canvas, his pretty daughter Rissa, and his son Nat, whose love of music won his father's contempt. Kate grew up with Nat and Rissa and remained loyal to them through the years of the decline of the family's fortunes, which came with the passing of the sailing ship and the coming of the summer colonists. Kate's chief devotion is to Nat, and for a brief time, near the end, they are lovers." Wis Lib Bul

"A good story, frank in its romanticism, told with a freshness and honesty that lifts any suspicion of a neo-Victorianism from its attitude and manner." Sat R

Fielding, Gabriel

In the time of Greenbloom. Morrow 1957 [c1956] 407p $4.95

"Events in a richly textured English novel center on John Blaydon, a sensitive, introspective, and highly intelligent adolescent, and on the two most important people in his life—Victoria Blount and Horab Greenbloom. After Victoria is tragically murdered while on a summer outing John withdraws almost completely into the past until his meeting and ensuing friendship with Horab Greenbloom, an eccentric and magnetic Oxford student whose credo is that life, the greatest of gifts, must be lived rather than observed. John's painful achieving of maturity and his final acceptance of Greenbloom's belief are vividly delineated in an absorbing story marked by masterful craftsmanship, tangible characterizations, and depth of insight." Booklist

Fielding, Henry

Amelia. Dutton 2v (Everyman's lib) ea $2.95

First published 1751. Variant title: The history of Amelia

"This comes closest of all Fielding's novels to actuality, for he was drawing upon his personal experiences as a London Magistrate, and was anxious to show up the disorders of society in his pictures of licentious pleasures, depravity and crime, and the horrors of Newgate. Amelia, 'the perfect model of an English wife,' he drew from his own first wife. It is the touching story of a married couple in an uphill struggle with adversity." Baker's Best

The history of the adventures of Joseph Andrews and of his friend Mr Abraham Adams

Some editions are:
Dutton (Everyman's lib) $2.95 Introduction by A. R. Humphreys
Modern Lib. $2.95 With an introduction by Howard Mumford Jones

First published 1742

The author's intention was "to satirize Richardson's 'Pamela.' This novel, given to the world two years before, had depicted the struggle of an honest serving-maid to escape from the snares laid for her by her master. Andrews, the hero of Fielding's story, is a brother of Pamela, like her in service; and the narrative details the trials he endures in the performance of his duty." Keller's Reader's Digest of Books

The history of Tom Jones, a foundling

Some editions are:
Dodd (Great illustrated classics: Titan editions) $5.50 With eight pages of illustrations and an introduction by Arthur Sherbo
Dutton (Everyman's lib) 2v ea $3.25 Introduction by A. R. Humphreys
Heritage $7.95
Modern Lib. $2.95
Random House boxed $10 Illustrated by Lawrence Beall Smith

First published 1749

"The complete and unexpurgated history of a young man of strong natural impulses, a good disposition, and no overpowering sense of morality. Fielding planned it as a 'Comic Epic,' and built the plot with care, a plot turning on the recognition of Jones's birth and on the fortunes of his love for an adorable girl. Life in country and town in the year 1745; with a great crowd of characters of all sorts and conditions. . . . Of the highest importance in the history of literature, as indicating the lines on which the modern novel of manners was to be written." Baker's Best

Firbank, Arthur Annesley Ronald. See Firbank, Ronald

Firbank, Ronald

The artificial princess
In Firbank, R. The complete Ronald Firbank p27-73

Caprice
In Firbank, R. The complete Ronald Firbank p319-86

The complete Ronald Firbank; with a preface by Anthony Powell. Duckworth [distributed by New Directions] 1961 766p o.p. 1970

The output of this English author includes eight novels, two short stories and a play. Introduced by a new biographical and critical introduction

Contents: Odette: a fairy tale for weary people [short story]; The artificial princess (1915); Vainglory (1915); Inclinations (1916); Caprice (1917); Valmouth (1918); Santal [short story]; The flower beneath the foot (1923); Prancing nigger (1924); Concerning the eccentricities of Cardinal Pirelli (1926); The Princess Zoubaroff [a play]

Concerning the eccentricities of Cardinal Pirelli
In Firbank, R. The complete Ronald Firbank p645-98

The flower beneath the foot
In Firbank, R. The complete Ronald Firbank p499-592

Inclinations
In Firbank, R. The complete Ronald Firbank p223-317

Prancing nigger
In Firbank, R. The complete Ronald Firbank p593-643

Vainglory
In Firbank, R. The complete Ronald Firbank p75-222

Valmouth
In Firbank, R. The complete Ronald Firbank p387-477

First-prize stories, 1919-1966: from the O. Henry Memorial Awards; introduction by Harry Hansen. Doubleday 1966 735p $5.95

Analyzed in Short Story Index

Supersedes: First-prize stories, 1919-1963, and includes the annual awards for 1964-1966. Contains 46 stories all of which have been first-prize winners of the annual O. Henry Memorial Awards

Contents: England to America, by M. P. Montague; Each in his generation, by M. S. Burt; The heart of Little Shikara, by E. Marshall; Snake doctor, by I. S. Cobb; Prelude, by E. V. Smith; The spring flight, by I. H. Irwin; Mr Bisbee's princess, by J. Street; Bubbles, by W. D. Steele; Child of God, by R. Bradford; The parrot, by W. Duranty; Big blonde, by D. Parker; Dressing-up, by W. R. Burnett; Can't cross Jordan by myself, by W. D. Steele; An end to dreams, by S. V. Benét; Gal young un, by M. K. Rawlings; No more trouble for Jedwick, by L. Paul; The white horses of Vienna, by K. Boyle; Total stranger, by J. G. Cozzens; The Devil and Daniel Webster, by S. V. Benét; The happiest man on earth, by A. Maltz; Barn burning, by W. Faulkner; Freedom's a hard-bought thing, by S. V. Benét; Defeat, by K. Boyle; The wide net, by E. Welty; Livvie is back, by E. Welty; Walking wounded, by I. Shaw; The wind and the snow of winter, by W. V. Clark; Bird song, by J. M. Goss; The white circle, by J. B. Clayton; Shut a final door, by T. Capote; A courtship, by W. Faulkner; The blue-winged teal, by W. Stegner; The hunters, by H. Downey; The Indian feather, by T. Mabry; In the zoo, by J. Stafford; The country husband, by J. Cheever; Greenleaf, by F.

First-prize stories, 1919-1966—*Continued*

O'Connor; In sickness as in health, by M. Gellhorn; Venus, cupid, folly and time, by P. Taylor; The ledge, by L. S. Hall; Tell me a riddle, by T. Olsen; Holiday, by K. A. Porter; Everything that rises must converge, by F. O'Connor; The embarkment for Cythera, by J. Cheever; Revelation, by F. O'Connor; The Bulgarian poetess, by J. Updike

Fish, Robert L.

The murder league. Simon & Schuster 1968 208p boards $4.50

"An Inner Sanctum mystery"
"Carruthers, Simpson and Briggs, three old duffers who are ex-mystery writers and who have fallen on sad days, decide to marry wit with money by putting their still formidable talents to actual use; they set up their own version of Murder, Inc. . . . They perform their services with dispatch and admirable 'sang froid.' Until . . . finally hoist upon their own roguery, they must need be rescued by Sir Percival Pugh, Barrister, who turns out to be the cleverest rogue of them all." Publisher's note

The Xavier affair; a José da Silva novel. Putnam 1969 191p boards $4.50

"Red mask mystery"
"When Chico Xavier, two other bored rich kids, and Chico's girl friend 'kidnapped' Chico and demanded half a million dollars in ransom from Chico's father, Captain Jose Da Silva was put on the case, which involved both the wealthiest people in Brazil and some of the poorest and soon turned from simple kidnapping to murder." Bk Buyer's Guide
"The story has a colorful hero and locale and some nice action bits, but it is a little too stereotyped." Pub W

(ed.) Mystery Writers of America. With malice toward all

Fisher, Clay

The skinning of Black Coyote
In Western Writers of America. A Western bonanza p247-69

For other titles by this author see Henry, Will

Fisher, Dorothea Canfield. See Canfield, Dorothy

Fisher, Edward

The best house in Stratford. Abelard-Schuman 1965 220p (The Silver Falcon) o.p. 1970

The third volume of the author's trilogy: The Silver Falcon; The first, Shakespeare & Son, 1962, and the second, Love's labour's won, 1963
This novel beginning in 1596 "depicts Shakespeare's life as bon vivant, playwright, and actor in London; his encounter, sportive rivalry, and eventual friendship with Ben Jonson; his feelings of inadequacy as husband and father; and his purchase of the old run-down house in Stratford." Publisher's note

Love's labour's won; a novel about Shakespeare's lost years. Abelard-Schuman 1963 224p o.p. 1970

Sequel to: Shakespeare & son, second in the trilogy, The Silver Falcon
"Covers the decade from 1583 to 1593, when, after failing at other professions, the future Bard succumbs to his theatrical ambitions, competes for recognition among the established playwrights and actors of London, and is honored by the Queen herself." Bk Buyer's Guide

Shakespeare & Son; a novel. Abelard-Schuman 1962 214p o.p. 1970

First in a trilogy: The Silver Falcon
"A fictional account of William Shakespeare's three years between the ages of fifteen and eighteen, years of rebellion against his father, of his growing up in the quiet Stratford, and of his courtship of Anne Hathaway." Bk Buyer's Guide

"It is a happy combination of fact and imagination. . . . This volume, studded with quotations from the plays and sonnets, is a delight to read." Ontario Lib Rev

Fisher, Vardis

Children of God; an American epic. Vanguard 1939 796p $7.50

"Cast in the form of a novel, this is essentially an epic picture of the amazing inception and growth of the Mormon church under two great leaders, Joseph Smith, the prophet and founder, and Brigham Young, the organizer. The author, of Mormon descent, glosses over neither misdeeds of the Mormons nor the brutality of their enemies, as he depicts with sweeping strokes the trek west, or minutely envisages domestic conflicts resulting from plural marriage." Bookmark
"Important as a dramatization of a colorful chapter of our past history and as a well-developed narrative and delineation of character." Baldwin

The mothers; an American saga of courage. Vanguard 1943 334p o.p. 1970

"Story of the Donner Party's almost unbelievable journey in 1846 to California. Without strong leadership, the individual families distrustful of one another, this group crossed the salt marshes and arrived in the Sierras at the beginning of winter. Only the indomitable courage and planning of the mothers brought some of the party through that winter of starvation. Much of story is grim, some seems incredible, but Fisher has followed closely the known facts." Library J

Mountain man; a novel of male and female in the early American West. Morrow 1965 372p boards $5.95

The author delves into the story "of Kate Bowden, whose family has been massacred by Indians, and into the life of the trapper Sam Minard who compassionately builds a cabin for Kate and rides on to take and dearly love a Flathead bride. Sam . . . declares war against the Crow nation after the Crows murder his wife and unborn child." Pub W
"Superb backgrounds, fascinating detail, and consistency of tone elevate this beyond the adventure story; as a picture of a mountain man, his love of nature and struggle to survive, it is a stirring piece of Americana." Library J

Fitzgerald, F. Scott

Babylon revisited, and other stories. Scribner 1960 253p $3.50

Contents: The ice palace; May Day; The diamond as big as the Ritz; Winter dreams; Absolution; The rich boy; The freshest boy; Babylon revisited; Crazy Sunday; The long way out

The beautiful and damned. Scribner 1958 [c1950] 449p $5.95

First published 1922
"A story of the roaring twenties. Anthony Patch grandson and heir-apparent of a multi-millionaire, is an idle and aimless youth, when at twenty-five he meets Gloria Gilbert of Kansas City. With nothing else on which to build their married life than their delight in each other's physical perfection they start at a rapid pace, which is greatly accelerated when Grandfather Patch decides to leave his millions elsewhere. The book leaves them after six years of marriage, damned by their excesses, sunk deep in debauchery and degradation, with Anthony a mental and physical wreck and Gloria's beauty waning." Book Rev Digest

The Fitzgerald reader; ed. by Arthur Mizener. Scribner 1963 xxvii, 509p boards $7.50

Partially analyzed in Short Story Index
This representative selection of Scott Fitzgerald's work "includes the whole of his best novel, 'The Great Gatsby,' and considerable parts of his other two important novels, 'Tender Is the Night' and 'The Last Tycoon.' It also includes two novelettes ('May Day' and 'The Rich Boy'), the four or five best short stories from each period of his career, and his four most famous essays." Foreword

Fitzgerald, F. S.—*Continued*

The short stories are: Winter dreams; Absolution; "The sensible thing"; Basil and Cleopatra; Outside the cabinet-maker's; Babylon revisited; Crazy Sunday; Family in the wind; Afternoon of an author; "I didn't get over"; The long way out; Financing Finnegan; The lost decade

"Mizener's penetrating introduction reveals four distinct periods in Fitzgerald's writing, periods around which the selections are organized. Of particular value as an overview or introduction to Fitzgerald." Booklist

y The Great Gatsby. Scribner 1958 [c1953] 182p $3.50

First published 1925. Copyright renewed 1953
"The mysterious Jay Gatsby lives in a luxurious mansion on the wealthy Long Island shore. . . . Nick Carraway, the narrator, lives next-door to Gatsby, and Nick's cousin Daisy and her crude but wealthy husband Tom Buchanan live in the house directly across the harbor from Gatsby's. Gatsby reveals to Nick that he and Daisy had a brief affair before the war and her marriage to Tom. . . . He persuades Nick to bring him and Daisy together again, but ultimately he is unable to win her from her husband. Daisy, driving Gatsby's car, runs over and kills Tom's mistress Myrtle, unaware of the woman's identity. Myrtle's husband traces the car and shoots Gatsby, who has remained silent in order to protect Daisy. Gatsby's friends and business associates all desert him, and only Nick, Gatsby's father, and one habitué of the parties attend the funeral." Benét. The Reader's Encyclopedia

"The power of the novel derives from its sharp and antagonistic portrayal of wealthy society in America, specifically in New York and Long Island. . . . The 'Jazz Age,' Fitzgerald's constant subject, is exposed here in terms of its false glamor and cultural barrenness." Herzberg. The Reader's Encyclopedia of Am Lit

also in Fitzgerald, F. S. The Fitzgerald reader p105-238

also in Fitzgerald, F. S. The portable F. Scott Fitzgerald p 1-168

also in Fitzgerald, F. S. Three novels of F. Scott Fitzgerald v 1

also in Phillips, W. ed. Great American short novels p451-575

The last tycoon; an unfinished novel. Scribner 1958 [c1941] 163p $3.95

First published with The Great Gatsby, and selected stories in 1941
A revelation of "the inner nature of the movie world and its far-reaching impact on the whole fabric of American life. . . . In addition to providing an illuminating Foreword, Edmund Wilson has assembled a tentative outline of the rest of the story as Fitzgerald intended to develop it, and has appended passages from the author's notes dealing with the characters and scenes." Publisher's note

May Day
In Fitzgerald, F. S. The Fitzgerald reader p3-53

The Pat Hobby stories; with an introduction by Arnold Gingrich. Scribner 1962 xxiii, 159p $3.95

Analyzed in Short Story Index
"The seventeen stories in this volume are short . . . but they are the work of a master hand. The prose is lean, swift and deadly accurate. The tone is typical of Fitzgerald after his crack-up: utterly detached, stripped of all illusion, yet compassionate enough to win sympathy for a protagonist who is essentially a rat. . . . If these aren't the greatest stories Fitzgerald ever wrote, they are important to an understanding of his career, and they belong to the small company of works that genuinely evoke Hollywood." N Y Times Bk R
Contents: Pat Hobby's Christmas wish; A man in the way; "Boil some water—lots of it"; Teamed with genius; Pat Hobby and Orson Welles; Pat Hobby's secret; Pat Hobby, putative father; The homes of the stars; Pat Hobby does his bit; Pat Hobby's preview; No harm trying; A patriotic short; On the trail of Pat Hobby; Fun in an artist's studio; Two old-timers; Mightier than the sword; Pat Hobby's college days

The portable F. Scott Fitzgerald; selected by Dorothy Parker; introduction by John O'Hara. Viking 1945 835p (Viking Portable lib) o.p. 1970

Analyzed in Short Story Index
Contents: Novels: The Great Gatsby; Tender is the night. Stories: Absolution; The baby party; The rich boy; May Day; The cut-glass bowl; The offshore pirate; The freshest boy; Crazy Sunday; Babylon revisited

The rich boy
In Fitzgerald, F. S. The Fitzgerald reader p239-75

Six tales of the jazz age, and other stories. Scribner 1960 192p $3.50

Analyzed in Short Story Index
Contents: The jelly-bean; The camel's back; The curious case of Benjamin Button; Tarquin of Cheapside; "O Russet witch"; The lees of happiness; The adjuster; Hot and cold blood; Gretchen's forty winks

The stories of F. Scott Fitzgerald; a selection of 28 stories; with an introduction by Malcolm Cowley. Scribner 1951 xxv, 473p $5.95

Analyzed in Short Story Index
"The editor has attempted to make the best selection from all stages of Fitzgerald's career; the stories are arranged in chronological groups." Booklist
Contents: Diamond as big as the Ritz; Bernice bobs her hair; Ice palace; May Day; Winter dreams; "The sensible thing"; Absolution; Rich boy; Baby party; Magnetism; Last of the belles; Rough crossing; Bridal party; Two wrongs; Scandal detectives; Freshest boy; Captured shadow; Woman with a past; Babylon revisited; Crazy Sunday; Family in the wind; Alcoholic case; Long way out; Financing Finnegan; Pat Hobby himself; Three hours between planes; Lost decade

Taps at reveille. Scribner 1960 341p $4.95
A reissue of the title first published 1935, and analyzed in Short Story Index
"This volume represents the last of Fitzgerald's work: the last book he published and his last short story collection. Ten of the stories here are unavailable in any other volume. These eighteen stories were written between 1928 and 1932." Best Sellers
Contents: Basil: The scandal detectives; The freshest boy; He thinks he's wonderful; The captured shadow; The perfect life; Josephine; First blood; A nice quiet place; A woman with a past. Crazy Sunday; Two wrongs; The night of Chancellorsville; The last of the belles; Majesty; Family in the wind; A short trip home; One interne; The fiends; Babylon revisited

Tender is the night; a romance; with the author's final revisions; preface by Malcolm Cowley. Scribner 1951 356p $4.95

First published 1934
"The final version of 'Tender is the Night' prepared by Fitzgerald two years before his death. The section 'Case History' which originally came about the middle of the book has been rearranged so as now to form its beginning and other small revisions and corrections have been made throughout as indicated by Fitzgerald in his personal copy of the novel." Pub W

The story of Dick Diver, a young psychiatrist whose career was thwarted and his genius numbed through his marriage to the exquisite and wealthy Nicole Warren. On the outside their life was all glitter and glamour, but beneath the smooth, beautiful surface lay the corroding falseness of their social values and the tragedy of her disturbed mind. Against the opulent background of the Riviera peopled with rich Americans and "intellectuals," Fitzgerald tells of Dick Diver's progress from obscurity to obscurity

Fitzgerald, F. S.—Continued

"Despite the book's many terrifying scenes, the warm tenderness of its writing lifts it into the realm of genuine tragedy." Benét. The Reader's Encyclopedia

also in Fitzgerald, F. S. The portable F. Scott Fitzgerald p169-545

also in Fitzgerald, F. S. Three novels of F. Scott Fitzgerald v2

This side of paradise. Scribner 1920 305p $4.95

"It isn't a story in the regular sense: There's no beginning, except the beginning of Amory Blaine, born healthy, wealthy and extraordinarily good-looking, and by way of being spoiled by a restless mother whom he quaintly calls by her first name, Beatrice. There's no middle to the story, except the closing picture of this same handsome boy, proud, clean-minded, born to conquer yet fumbling at college and in love with Isabelle, then Clara, then Rosalind, then Eleanor. No end to the story except the closing picture of this same boy in his early twenties, a bit less confident about life . . . and yet 'determined to use to the utmost himself and his heritage from the personality he had passed.' " Pub W

Three novels of F. Scott Fitzgerald. . . . Scribner 1953 3v in 1 (Modern standard authors) $5.25

Omnibus volume of three titles, all entered separately

"The great Gatsby; with an introduction by Malcolm Cowley. Tender is the night, with the author's final revisions; edited by Malcolm Cowley. The last tycoon, an unfinished novel; edited by Edmund Wilson." Title page

Flaubert, Gustave

Bouvard and Pécuchet; tr. by Earp and Stonier; introduction by Lionel Trilling. New Directions $4.25

Original French edition 1881

"During the last eight years of his life Flaubert was engaged in writing this fictional attack on the French bourgeoisie. In it two retired clerks set out to educate themselves; but whatever they touch seems to fall to pieces. Their story is told with a blend of satire and sympathy." Book Rev Digest

The legend of Saint Julian the hospitaller

In Dupee, F. W. ed. Great French short novels p391-421

Madame Bovary

Some editions are:
Dodd (Great illustrated classics) $4.50
Dutton (Everyman's lib) $2.95 Translated by Eleanor Marx-Aveling. Introduction by George Saintsbury
Modern Lib. $2.95 A new translation by Francis Steegmuller
Wats, F. $4.95 A Watts Ultratype edition
First appeared in French 1857
"Perhaps the most perfect work . . . of realistic art in any language: a faithful and infinitely painstaking interpretation of actual life. . . . It is a plain history of the slow but inevitable moral degeneration of a weak woman. . . . The passionless candour of the narrative, the patient rendering of the squalor and narrowness of provincial life and of its effect on the woman's mind, make this a landmark in the history of naturalism." Baker's Best

Salammbo; tr. by J. S. Chartres. Dutton 319p (Everyman's lib) $3.25

First published in French 1862

"Flaubert's famous archaeological novel is a tale of ancient Carthage, in which archaeology is perhaps more important than fiction. The plot revolves around Salammbo, the daughter of Hamilcar, and her anxiety to possess and assure the safety of the Tanite, a veil of extremely occult religious significance. Salammbo finally attains possession—and then dies." Haydn. Thesaurus of Book Digests

"The scenes testify to the great erudition of the author, but critics complain that the picture has too little perspective. All is painted with equal brilliance—matter essential and unessential." Keller's Reader's Digest of Books

Sentimental education. Dutton 401p (Everyman's lib) $2.95

First published 1869; in this edition 1941

"The background of this novel is the decline and fall of the Monarchy of Louis Philippe and the Revolution of 1848. . . . The hero, Frederic Moreau, has many of the traits of young Flaubert. Madame Arnous, with whom he falls in love, is very like a Madame Schlesinger whom Flaubert had admired at Trouville as early as 1836. The subject of the novel is really the futility of existence." Haydn. Thesaurus of Book Digests

"A veritable encyclopedia of manners and morals in mid-nineteenth century Paris." Baker's Best

Simple heart

In Neider, C. ed. Short novels of the masters p220-48

Fleming, Ian

Bonded Fleming. Viking [1965] 439p boards $5.75

Partially analyzed in Short Story Index

At head of title: A James Bond omnibus

This volume featuring British Secret Service agent James Bond contains: For your eyes only, a collection of five novelettes: From a view to a kill; For your eyes only; Quantum of Solace; Risico; The Hildebrand rarity, first published 1960, and two novels: Thunderball and The spy who loved me, published 1961 and 1962 respectively

The five stories in For your eyes only, are about dope-smuggling, an assassination, spying and rampaging human emotion. In Thunderball, Bond faces his most dangerous assignment and confronts S.P.E.C.T.R.E. The spy who loved me, is the first-person story of a young woman involved with James Bond both romantically and perilously

Casino Royale. Macmillan (N Y) [1966 c1953] 187p boards $3.95

First published 1953 in England

British Secret Service agent James Bond, addicted to good food, good women, and good spying, faces a challenging assignment—to beat the Communist agent Le Chiffre at baccarat. Gambling always has been a risky business, but when you mix it with a man who has no prejudices about murder, a violent group of foreigners who will stop at nothing to acquire information, and a beautiful but suspiciously vague young woman, you have a menacing situation." Publisher's note

"A Secret Service thriller, lively, most ingenious in detail, on the surface as tough as they are made and charmingly well-bred beneath, nicely written and . . . very entertaining reading." Spec

also in Fleming, I. Gilt-edged Bonds v 1

Diamonds are forever. Macmillan (N Y) [1966 c1956] 215p boards $3.95

A reissue in a new format of the title first published 1956

In this suspense story, secret agent James Bond infiltrates the Spangled Mob, the world's largest group of diamond smugglers and there meets Tiffany Case, as hard and as beautiful as a twenty-four-carat diamond. (Publisher)

also in Fleming, I. More Gilt-edged Bonds p443-661

Doctor No. Macmillan (N Y) [1966 c1958] 188p boards $3.95

A reissue in a new format of the title first published 1958

"James Bond, off on what appears to be a routine investigation and report, meets murder and Doctor No, a half-Chinese and half-German with two pairs of steel pincers for hands and his heart on the right side of his chest." Publisher's note

"Mr. Fleming, despite pandering now and then to low tastes, writes extremely well. He knows how to keep his reader's hair literally standing on end." Springf'd Republican

also in Fleming, I. Gilt-edged Bonds v3

Fleming, Ian—*Continued*

For your eyes only
In Fleming, I. Bonded Fleming p189-328

For your eyes only [novelette]
In Fleming, I. Bonded Fleming p214-47

From a view to kill
In Fleming, I. Bonded Fleming p191-213

From Russia, with love. Macmillan (N Y) [1966 c1957] 191p boards $3.95

A reissue in a new format of the title first published 1957
"James Bond, the British secret agent, here meets the Soviet murder organization SMERSH, once more. His execution has been ordered but Bond's counter activities seem successful—until the last page." Book Rev Digest

also in Fleming, I. Gilt-edged Bonds v2

Gilt-edged Bonds. . . . With an introduction by Paul Gallico. Macmillan (N Y) 1961 2v in 1 $6.95

An anthology of three novels featuring British Secret Service Agent James Bond: Casino Royale (1954); From Russia, with love (1957); Doctor No (1958)

Goldfinger. Macmillan (N Y) [1966 c1959] 191p boards $3.95

A reissue in a new format of the title first published 1959
"James Bond, British Secret Service Agent 007, must retrieve British gold from a Mr. Auric Goldfinger whose ruthless obsession is suggested in his goal—personal possession of half the supply of mined gold in the world." Pub W

The Hildebrand rarity
In Fleming, I. Bonded Fleming p298-328

Live and let die
In Fleming, I. More Gilt-edged Bonds p 1-218

The man with the golden gun. New Am. Lib. 1965 183p o.p. 1970

James Bond, agent 007, has been brainwashed by Soviet captors into becoming the tool of Russia's K.G.B. to perpetrate an act of treachery—against the British Secret Service. In this adventure, he and his adversary, Francisco Scaramanga, meet in mortal combat in that pleasure paradise, the island of Jamaica. (Publisher)
"This is fast, sometimes funny, with the now-classic Fleming touch of self-parody mixed with high-powered action and suspense. But also, alas, it is a stripped-down model, and so short as to be easily polished off in about an hour." Book of the Mouth Club News

Moonraker
In Fleming, I. More Gilt-edged Bonds p219-441

More Gilt-edged Bonds. Macmillan (N Y) [1965] 661p $5.95

An anthology of three novels featuring British Secret Service Agent James Bond: Live and let die, first published 1954 in England: Moonraker, and Diamonds are forever, first published 1955 and 1956, respectively
Includes " 'Live and let die' in which Operator 007 (James Bond) is assigned to annihilate the world's most powerful criminal—Mr. Big, of the infamous SMERSH. 'Moonraker' in which James Bond investigates the motives behind an enigmatic millionaire who is financing a new superrocket that could destroy the world, 'Diamonds are forever' in which, to expose the Spangled Mob, the greatest diamond smugglers, James Bond joins them." Publisher's note

On Her Majesty's Secret Service. New Am. Lib. 1963 299p o.p. 1970

James Bond, British secret service agent, rescues a beautiful woman from disaster and before the afternoon is over, finds himself involved in a dangerous adventure. He is pitted against a crime syndicate which has engineered an atomic blackmail scheme. The action moves from Britain to the ski trails of the Swiss Alps where Bond becomes both quarry and pursuer and in the end knows both victory and defeat. (Publisher)

Quantum of solace
In Fleming, I. Bonded Fleming p248-66

Risico
In Fleming, I. Bonded Fleming p267-97

The spy who loved me
In Fleming, I. Bonded Fleming p329-439

Thunderball
In Fleming, I. Bonded Fleming p 1-188

You only live twice. New Am. Lib. 1964 240p o.p. 1970

"Bond, near-prostrate from his bride's death, is given a Japanese assignment to snap him out of his torpor. . . . [The story] involves Bond's making up as a Japanese and venturing into the den of a foreign 'death collector,' a madman who has set up a poisonous garden complete with noxious plants, volcanic geysers, snakes, and, in a lake, piranha fish. Very grisly and chilling. The ending is an epitome of horror." Pub W

Fleming, Joan

No bones about it. Washburn 1967 253p o.p. 1970

"Old Grandad, who may be getting a bit senile, starts bestowing cold cash on each and every one. No one really believes his tale of having sold off a bit of property up North, but the money is so lovely no one except the practical-minded housekeeper wants to investigate further. Then a chilling note intrudes. The police are looking for the loot from a big robbery stashed somewhere nearby." Pub W
This is "a shrewd domestic comedy of pretty observations and insights and an irony that goes deeper than the situation itself to touch the roots of our affluent society; and the crime-plot and puzzle are admiraly devised." N Y Times Bk R

Fletcher, Inglis

Lusty wind for Carolina. Bobbs 1944 509p o.p. 1970

Sequel to: Men of Albemarle
"Inglis Fletcher's trilogy—'Raleigh's Eden,' 'Men of Albemarle' and 'Lusty Wind for Carolina'—has for a central theme the struggle for freedom in the Carolina colonies that led directly to the Revolution. This third book tells the story of the fight for the freedom of the seas —for trade made safe from interference by English officials and the menace of pirate ships. The love of the bondsman, David Moray, for lovely Gabrielle Fontaine—and the conflict between Anne Bonney, woman leader of a pirate crew, and Captain Woodes Rogers—are interwoven." Huntting
"Both as history and pure entertainment, this book rates high. One exciting incident follows another, and there are no dull pages, particularly not for those who like historical minutiae. And lovers of happy endings will reap a rich and uninterrupted harvest." Book Week

Men of Albemarle. Bobbs 1942 566p o.p. 1970

Sequel to: Raleigh's Eden
A story laid in "the years from 1710 to 1712, a turbulent period during which three governors competed for dominance in North Carolina. . . . For romance, [the author] gives us the love affairs of two women—one a girl enchanted by first love; the other an experienced, alluring woman." Huntting
Followed by: Lusty wind for Carolina

Raleigh's Eden; a novel. Bobbs 1940 662p o.p. 1970

"Raleigh's Eden was the rich fertile land along the coast of North Carolina. This historical novel develops the story of plantation life in that section from 1765, until about the end of the Revolution. Altho more than a hundred characters appear in the book, Adam Rutledge and Mary Warden, representing two of the upper class families, are the leading characters." Book Rev Digest

Fletcher, Inglis—*Continued*

"In spite of its color and occasional violence, 'Raleigh's Eden' remains closer to history than to fiction. Mrs. Fletcher has laid her color on with a lavish hand—for it belongs here rightly enough." N Y Times Bk R

Followed by: Men of Albemarle

Roanoke hundred; a novel. Bobbs 1948 492p o.p. 1970

"Historical novel based on the Grenville expedition to Roanoke, Virginia. It pictures the court life of the days of Queen Elizabeth, and the manners and customs of the people of Devon and Cornwall. The title is taken from the hundred and eight Englishmen who settled on Roanoke island in 1585. The climax of the novel is the famous fight of the Revenge at The Azores, where Grenville lost his life." Book Rev Digest

"Excellent blood-and-thunder reading. . . . Also a good picture of Elizabethan England." Cincinnati

The Scotswoman. Bobbs 1954 480p o.p. 1970

"This American story of Flora MacDonald, who saved Bonnie Prince Charlie, is a novel of the American Revolution. There is action, adventure and romance as the Scots clansmen are torn by conflicting loyalties in an alien land. Sword play, a storm at sea, an attack by pirates, and political intrigue contribute to this narrative which combines fiction and history." Huntting

Toil of the brave. Bobbs 1946 547p o.p. 1970

"The fourth of her historical novels of the colonial and Revolutionary scene in the Albemarle district of North Carolina is set in the late years of the war 1779-1780 with a young Britisher and a young Continental [vying for the affections of the heroine]." Am News of Bks

"Several characters from earlier books in the [Albemarle] series reappear; many new ones are introduced." N Y Her Trib Books

The wind in the forest. Bobbs 1957 448p o.p. 1970

"Letters written by Governor Tryon of the Royal Province of North Carolina, tracts by his Quaker opponent Harmon Husband and the memoirs of an eighteenth-century lady are the principal sources on which the author bases a tale which expands on an incident in her 'Raleigh's Eden'. The pre-Revolutionary disturbances in North Carolina, brought on by unjust taxes and abuse of power and culminating in the Battle of Alamance, are seen from the point of view of Hillary Caswell, a young member of the Governor's staff who is in sympathy with the rebellious colonists. A serious historical novel enlivened by romance and scenes of violent action." Booklist

Fletcher, Lucille

Sorry, wrong number

In Hitchcock, A. ed. Alfred Hitchcock presents: Stories not for the nervous

Flood, Charles Bracelen

Love is a bridge. Houghton 1953 436p $4.50

"A youthful first marriage which ends in divorce leaves its mark on Henry Cobb and Susan Pemmerton. In the years which follow each moves towards a greater maturity and understanding, their lives touching occasionally despite Henry's second marriage. At the book's close each is ready to try again since Henry has left his second wife. A Houghton Mifflin Literary Fellowship Award novel with a background of well-to-do New York and Boston society." Pub W

Flora, Fletcher

(jt. auth.) Palmer, S. Hildegarde Withers makes the scene

Flores, Angel

(ed.) Great Spanish stories; ed. with an introduction. Modern Lib. 1956 490p o.p. 1970

Analyzed in Short Story Index

Contents: Master Perez the organist, by G. A. Bécquer; The three-cornered hat, by P. A. de Alarcón; Torquemada in the flames, by B. P. Galdós; Doña Berta, by L. Alas; Sonata of autumn, by R. M. del Valle-Inclán; Prometheus, by R. P. de Ayala; Saint Manuel Bueno, Martyr, by M. de Unamuno; Saint Alexis, by B. Jarnés; The village idiot, by C. J. Cela; The bewitched, by F. Ayala; Twilight in extremadura, by R. Chacel; The stuffed parrot, by R. Dieste; The return, by C. Laforet; In the trenches, by A. S. Barbudo; The launch, by M. Aub; The cathedral of hearts, by J. M. Gironella

Flynn, Robert

In the house of the Lord. Knopf 1969 270p boards $5.95

"This is a day in the life of Reverend Shahan, a Protestant minister, trying to make sense of his faith and his work. Crowded with incident, with people, with emotion, the novel comes directly to grips with its subject as it follows Shahan through encounters with his parishoners, his fellow clergy, his family—and his doubts—in the course of a typical and tumultuous day in the House of the Lord." Am News of Bks

"A kaleidoscope of images and [the hero's] silent dialogue with God add touches of humor and modernity to this absorbing and thoughtful, though not unique, story which is recommended to general fiction collections in college, public, high school, and theology libraries." Library J

North to yesterday. Knopf 1967 338p $5.95

At the end of the Civil War, Lampassas, a kind of American Don Quixote living in the past, assembles a miscellaneous assortment of misfits and dreamers. His aim is a belated drive of longhorn cattle from Texas to the railhead in Kansas. (Publisher)

This "has to be one of the funniest books of the year. But it is also a thoughtful, tragicomic parable of all America." Sat R

Foley, Martha

(ed.) The Best American short stories, 1915-1969. See The Best American short stories, 1915-1969

(ed.) Best of the Best American short stories, 1915-1950. See Best of the Best American short stories, 1915-1950

(ed.) Fifty best American short stories, 1915-1965. Houghton 1965 814p $6.95

Supersedes the collection: Best of the Best American short stories; analyzed in Short Story Index

A chronological collection "selected from the outstanding hundreds which have appeared in the annual volumes of 'The Best American Short Stories' [anthologies] from 1915 to 1965." McClurg. Book News

Contents: The survivors, by E. Singmaster; The lost Phoebe, by T. Dreiser; The Golden Honeymoon, by R. W. Lardner; I'm a fool, by S. Anderson; My old man, by E. Hemingway; A telephone call, by D. Parker; Double birthday, by W. Cather; The faithful wife, by M. Callaghan; The little wife, by W. March; Babylon revisited, by F. S. Fitzgerald; How beautiful with shoes, by W. D. Steele; Resurrection of a life, by W. Saroyan; Only the dead know Brooklyn, by T. Wolfe; A life in the day of a writer, by T. Slesinger; The Iron City, by L. Thompson; Christ in concrete, by P. Di Donato; The chrysanthemums, by J. Steinbeck; Bright and Morning Star, by R. Wright; Hand upon the waters, by W. Faulkner; The net, by R. M. Coates; Nothing ever breaks except the heart, by K. Boyle; Search through the streets of the city, by I. Shaw; Who lived and died believing, by N. Hale; The peach stone, by P. Horgan; Dawn of remembered spring, by J. Stuart; The catbird seat, by J. Thurber; Of this time, of that place, by

Foley, Martha—*Continued*

L. Trilling; The wind and the snow of winter, by W. Van T. Clark; The enormous radio, by J. Cheever; Children are bored on Sunday, by J. Stafford; The NRACP, by G. P. Elliott; In Greenwich there are many gravelled walks, by H. Calisher; The other foot, by R. Bradbury; Three players of a summer game, by T. Williams; A mother's tale, by J. Agee; The magic barrel, by B. Malamud; A circle in the fire, by F. O'Connor; The first flower, by A. W. Lyons; The contest for Aaron Gold, by P. Roth; One ordinary day, with peanuts, by S. Jackson; To the wilderness I wander, by F. Butler; The ledge, by L. S. Hall; This morning, this evening, so soon, by J. Baldwin; Tell me a riddle, by T. Olsen; The old Army game, by G. Garrett; Pigeon feathers, by J. Updike; Sound of a drunken drummer, by H. W. Blattner; The keyhole eye, by J. S. Carter; A long day's dying, by W. Eastlake; Upon the sweeping flood, by J. C. Oates

(ed.) U.S. stories; regional stories from the forty-eight states; selected with a foreword by Martha Foley and Abraham Rothberg. Farrar, Straus 1949 683p o.p. 1970

Analyzed in Short Story Index
"A collection of forty nine stories, one for each state in the Union, and the District of Columbia, and each by a writer from that region. Brief biographical notes on contributors." Book Rev Digest
Contents: Offending eye, by E. M. Tybout; Doctor's son, by J. O'Hara; Christ in concrete, by P. di Donato; The people vs. Abe Lathan, colored, by E. Caldwell; Secret life of Walter Mitty, by J. Thurber; Revolt of mother, by M. W. Freeman; The manor, by S. Haardt; The halfpint flask, by D. Heyward; Death and transfiguration, by A. Marshall; That woman, by N. Hale; Search through the streets of the city, by I. Shaw; A tempered fellow, by P. Green; Embarkation point, by V. Lincoln; Murder on Jefferson Street, by D. Canfield; Dawn of remembered spring, by J. Stuart; Bright and morning star, by R. Wright; Strength of God and the teacher, by S. Anderson; Cold death, by R. Bradford; First day finish, by J. West; That evening sun go down, by W. Faulkner; How the Devil came down Division Street, by N. Algren; Alabama sketches, by R. P. Tarrt; So Clyde was born, by G. H. Carroll; Weed sack, by J. Johnson; A woman like Dilsie, by D. Thibault; This town and Salamanca, by A. Seager; Benny and the bird-dogs, by M. K. Rawlings; "—Neber said a mumblin' word," by V. Loggins; Jury of her peers by S. Glaspell; The cobweb, by Z. Gale; Red pony, by J. Steinbeck; God made little apples, by M. le Sueur; The bulldogger, by J. Stevens; Kansas afternoon, by S. Babb; If only, by J. P. Bishop; The wind and the snow of winter, by W. van T. Clark; A Jeeter wedding, by D. Thomas; Neither Jew nor Greek, by W. John; Coffin for Anna, by E. Rushfeldt; Chip off the old block, by W. Stegner; Happiness by M. Foster; The scarecrow, by V. Fisher; Wine of Wyoming, by E. Hemingway; Ike and us Moons, by N. Shumway; Happiest man on earth, by A. Maltz; Love charm by O. La Farge; Papago Kid, by M. Austin; The neat Mexicans, by J. Weidman

Foley, Rae

Girl on a high wire. Dodd 1969 218p boards $3.95

"A Red badge mystery"
"Cathy Briggs [a librarian] had inherited $15 million and the Old Mill, where three women had died under suspicious circumstances. Cathy knew that one of the people who hoped to inherit her aunt's fortune was out to kill her, but she refused to run, even when the murderer struck again." Bk Buyer's Guide

No hiding place. Dodd 1969 188p $3.95

"A Red badge mystery"
"If Judy had not borrowed her roommate's briefcase and hadn't switched briefcases with the terrified redheaded woman in the subway and then disposed of the stranger's case in panic, her life would not be in jeopardy." Book News

Foote, Shelby

Follow me down
In Foote, S. Three novels v 1

Jordan County
In Foote, S. Three novels v2

Love in a dry season
In Foote, S. Three novels v3

Three novels; Follow me down; Jordan County; Love in a dry season. Dial Press 1964 3v in 1 $7.50

An omnibus volume of three novels first published separately 1950, 1954 and 1951 respectively
" 'Follow me down' [is] a stark novel of a crime of passion. Racy and brooding, lit by flashes of insight and dry wit, it is the account of Luther Eustis who ran off with a pretty girl of eighteen and, after a three-week idyll, brutally killed her. 'Jordan County' [is] a novel with Place for its hero and Time for its plot. Its seven narratives lead downward through Time from 1950 to 1797. The characters do not reappear, but the scene itself is constant. 'Love in a dry season' [is] set in Bristol, Mississippi, in the 'dry season' that started with the Depression and ended with World War II; it describes the subtle disintegration of an intruder who pitted himself against a town." Publisher's note

Forbes, Esther

The running of the tide. Houghton 1948 632p $7.95

"Chronicles the life of Salem, Massachusetts, from 1795 until after the War of 1812. During those years Salem reached the peak of her golden age, with her ships sailing to all quarters of the globe and returning with rich cargoes. The novel describes principally the lives of the various Inmans, a family of Salem ship owners, tracing their rise to wealth, and their decline as ship owners. Two of the four Inman brothers made fortunes, but Captain Dash remained loyal to his two loves: the sea and Polly Mompesson, the spoiled beauty whom he was never allowed to marry." Book Rev Digest
"Miss Forbes reconstructs the old port with a care that is admirable, if at times overloving. The drawing rooms there occasionally get somewhat wearisome, but there's a minimum of swashbuckling, no hussy worth mentioning, and some good characterization. Put together with nice nautical precision." New Yorker

Ford, Ford Madox

The fifth queen. Vanguard [1963] 592p illus o.p. 1970

Contents: The fifth queen, The fifth queen crowned, and Privy Seal, first published in England 1906, 1910, and 1917 respectively
"The period of the stories is 16th century England, the setting, the court of Henry VIII, the chief characters, the King, Thomas Cromwell, and Katharine Howard, the King's fifth wife, who is portrayed here as virtuous, devout and almost successful in bringing the King back to the Catholic Church." Pub W
"A masterful combination of realism, psychology, and plain literary skill are more than evident, although Ford (1873-1939) alive was less appreciated." Library J

The fifth queen crowned
In Ford, F. M. The fifth queen p419-592

The last post
In Ford, F. M. Parade's end p677-836

A man could stand up
In Ford, F. M. Parade's end p503-674

No more parades
In Ford, F. M. Parade's end p291-500

Parade's end. With an introduction by Robie Macauley. Knopf 1950 xxii, 836p $7.95

"Four out-of-print novels brought together in one volume. They are: Some do not (1924): No more parades (1925); A man could stand up (1926); and The last post (1928). "They concern the personal history of one man, and the social history of Tory England, in World War I and after." Library J

Ford, Ford M.—*Continued*

"Although it has dull stretches and is occasionally confusing in its abrupt changes of time and place. Parade's End has a driving power and a richness of content which are seldom encountered in the novels of today." Atlantic

Privy Seal
In Ford, F. M. The fifth queen p237-413

Some do not
In Ford, F. M. Parade's end p3-288

Ford, Jesse Hill

The feast of Saint Barnabas. Little 1969 308p $6.95

"An Atlantic Monthly Press book"
"On a Sunday morning in June, 1966 as Father Ned, the Negro pastor, was about to preach a sermon on Saint Barnabas to his small congregation, the sweltering little seaport of Ormund City, Florida, was on the brink of a race riot. The trouble was started by a white racist who lost his temper. It is brought to a boil by the wealthiest, most powerful black in town who demands revenge. This is the story of those who found themselves caught up in the turmoil." Publisher's note
"The frankness tends to deliver the action, dialogue, and character portrayal too easily into the road of cliché and truism: the characters act and talk as if they were straight from today's headlines. . . . Despite weaknesses in structure and tone, the novel is an absolute must for contemporary fiction collections." Choice

The liberation of Lord Byron Jones. Little 1965 364p $5.95

"An Atlantic Monthly Press book"
A narrative of racial crisis. "A Negro seeking vengeance, another Negro suing for divorce, a white southerner turning into a reformer, his lawyer uncle resisting change—these are the elements in a drama set in a small Tennessee town, in a few tense days." Pub W
"This is a violent novel, grim at times, and frightening because of the verisimilitude. A shifting viewpoint permits each character to speak from his inner self, a technique which permits the reader to see the conflict in detail. . . . This is one of the best of the current [1965] group of novels on the Southern race problem." Library J

Ford, Norman R.

The black, the gray, and the gold. Doubleday 1961 450p o.p. 1970

"The story centers about the mass violations of the honor code at West Point in 1951, but the plot is merely a background for the portrayal of the opposition of personal integrity and military ethics, and of vanity and honor on both sides. The story is worked out in the events of one day, with an effective use of flashbacks, and the question to be resolved by the reader is whether men and institutions can be right even when they are wrong." Library J

Ford, Paul Leicester

Janice Meredith; a story of the American Revolution. Dodd 1899 536p $3.95

"Presents with realistic accuracy the most dramatic episodes of the American Revolution . . . and offers the reader a striking sketch of George Washington. The opening scene is laid near Brunswick in the province of New Jersey in the year 1774." Keller's Reader's Digest of Books

Forester, C. S.

Admiral Hornblower in the West Indies. Little 1958 329p $4.95

"Hornblower sails again as the hero of six West Indian sea adventures. The first belongs chronologically with 'Lieutenant Hornblower.' The rest are set nearly 15 years later when, as rear admiral in command of His Majesty's fleet in the West Indies, he faces a new Bonapartist uprising, suppresses the slave trade, stamps out piracy, and maintains British diplomacy during the South American revolutions." Booklist
"Recounted with taste, with psychological insight, and with a sure sense of story. This is top grade adventure fiction." N Y Her Trib Books

also in Forester, C. S. The indomitable Hornblower p415-640

y The African Queen; with a new foreword by the author. Modern Lib. 1940 307p $2.95
First published 1935 by Little
"After the death of her brother in an African mission, Rose Sayer, English spinster, resolves to carry on against the German commander who has rounded up her brother's black converts. A gallant little Cockney, Allnutt, comes to her aid with a dilapidated steam launch. They scheme together to blow up the German boat down the lake—but first the long and perilous trip on the river must be made. It is this journey, with many hardships and a constant fight against malaria, which brings out all that is brave and admirable in these two persons so strangely unlike in character and walk of life." Book Rev Digest

y Beat to quarters. Little 1937 324p o.p. 1970
"A sea story of the British navy in the early nineteenth century. Essentially it is a portrait of a man, captain of an English frigate. Hornblower, son of a country doctor, is a man uncertain of his own powers, of his technical skill and of the admiration of his men, yet when he is sent under sealed orders to the Pacific coast of Central America, he accomplishes his mission brilliantly, and fights two successful battles with the same Spanish warship." Book Rev Digest
"There is plenty of action. But there is also an unusual character study." N Y Times Bk R
Followed by: Ship of the line

also in Forester, C. S. Captain Horatio Hornblower p 1-220

The captain from Connecticut. Little 1941 344p $4.95

The adventures of Captain Josiah Peabody of the frigate "Delaware" during the War of 1812. The hazardous voyage of the "Delaware" takes her to the Caribbean. Off Haiti she breaks up a British convoy crippling a frigate and an armed brig and is cornered by a British squadron in French Martinique
"As an adventure story 'The Captain From Connecticut' has everything—the thunder of naval battles, tropic skies and green West Indies Islands, gallant officers and beautiful women and even a satisfactory villain or two." Spring'd Republican

y Captain Horatio Hornblower; with drawings by N. C. Wyeth. Little 1929 662p illus o.p. 1970

A trilogy containing the following: Beat to quarters, first published 1937; Ship of the line, first published 1938; Flying colours, first published 1939

"Everyone is bound to enjoy the saga of Horatio Hornblower, the self-contained but lovable captain of H.M.S. frigate Lydia. . . . When we meet him he's captain of the British frigate Lydia, in the time of the Napoleonic wars, at sea in the Pacific and making for a landfall on the Nicaraguan coast. . . . He is to foment and assist an uprising by Don Julian Alvarado—El Supremo—against the Spanish. . . . He outwits the Spanish man-of-war Natividad, captures her without losing a man, and turns her over to El Supremo. But then when belated news comes in from Europe, he finds that he has to reattack the Natividad. . . . In volume two we find Hornblower helping to blockade the coast of Spain. . . . In the third part we have all the satisfactions of suspense rewarded." Book of the Month Club News

Commodore Hornblower. Little 1945 384p $4.95

Another story of the exploits of Captain Horatio Hornblower. He now "returns to command a squadron on a mission of such delicacy

Forester, C. S.—*Continued*

that the fate of Europe hangs on the outcome. Because Napoleon stands against both Russia and Sweden, it is Hornblower's task to see that these countries maintain their shaky friendship with Britain and to out-maneuver his old enemy." Huntting

"It is a spirited piece of work, and full of interesting detail where matters naval, military, and diplomatic in that year of decision are concerned." Times (London) Lit Sup
Followed by: Lord Hornblower

also in Forester, C. S. The indomitable Hornblower p5-227

Flying colours. Little 1939 294p o.p. 1970
Sequel to: Ship of the line

"Third book in a series which includes Beat to Quarters and Ship of the Line. Captain Hornblower, his crippled first mate, Bush, and his servant, Brown, escape from their escort on the way to Paris to be tried for piracy. The story is of their recapture of an English vessel and return to England, where they are covered with honors." Book Rev Digest

"'Flying Colours' lacks some of the breathless pace of the two previous books, but it remains a worthy successor to them." Springf'd Republican

also in Forester, C. S. Captain Horatio Hornblower p459-662

y **The good shepherd.** Little 1955 310p $5.95

"An Atlantic convoy in 1942 is the scene of the novel. Captain Krause, of the Keeling, had just four ships with which to protect the thirty-seven merchantmen in the convoy. The captain's personal struggle, plus his efforts to do an almost impossible job, are depicted during forty-eight desperate hours." Book Rev Digest

"Out of his expert knowledge of his subject and his technical ability which is miles ahead of any other novelist of sea-battles I can think of, Mr Forester has here spun a yarn that will keep readers on the edge of their chairs until the last gun is fired." San Francisco Chronicle

Hornblower and the Atropos. Little 1953 325p $4.95

"Fills in the three-year period between 'Lieutenant Hornblower' and 'Captain Horatio Hornblower'." Huntting

"It is a series of episodes in the early life of the Captain: a journey across England from Gloucester to London by canal; his part in the funeral of Nelson; and his battles on the coast of Turkey, where he recovers a huge treasure from a sunken English ship." Book Rev Digest

"Although he cuts down on rousing sea action in order to concentrate more on his hero's personal life, the author still tells a good story." Booklist

also in Forester, C. S. Young Hornblower p431-672

Hornblower and the Hotspur. Little 1962 344p $4.95

"From the standpoint of sequence, this new title in the Hornblower saga follows 'Lieutenant Hornblower'." Wis Lib Bul

The novel begins with Commander Hornblower's marriage in England. Soon afterward he sails for duty off the French coast. War breaks out with France, involving Hornblower not only in a land raid which destroys a French signal station, but several sea battles. There is a final encounter with Spanish ships laden with treasure for Napoleon, and Hornblower, after defeating them, becomes Captain Hornblower. (Publisher)

"Mr. Forester has succeeded in humanizing the conventional . . . naval officer of countless novels in much the same way as Simenon has humanized the police inspector of detective fiction." Times (London) Lit Sup

Hornblower during the crisis, and two stories: Hornblower's temptation and The last encounter. Little 1967 174p $4.95

"Posthumous novel fragment and two slender stories. The former concerns Hornblower's eventful voyage to London on another man's ship for reassignment on a spy mission to Spain. . . . In one story Mr. Hornblower is almost taken in by a seemingly harmless mission entrusted to him by a young Irishman before his shipboard execution. In the other tale

a stranded traveler in distress, helped by Admiral Hornblower and wife, proves to be Napoleon Bonaparte." Booklist

"Because Forester died before completing this novel, the reader is left with a summary sketch and his own imagination for final details of the plot. For Forester devotees, this will not detract from the essential verve and dash of Hornblower's last chase." Christian Science Monitor

The indomitable Hornblower; Commodore Hornblower, Lord Hornblower, Admiral Hornblower in the West Indies (complete novels) Little [1963] 640p boards $8.95

An omnibus volume of the three titles published 1945, 1946 and 1958 respectively, and entered separately

y **The last nine days of the Bismarck;** illus. with maps. Little 1959 138p maps $4.95

"A brilliant and exciting account of the nine days when the 'Bismarck,' the supership to which Germany had pinned its hopes, came out proudly, sank the 'Hood' and turned back the 'Prince of Wales,' and at last was pounded to pieces and sunk by British ships as the whole western world listened to news broadcasts." The Bookseller

y **Lieutenant Hornblower.** Little 1952 306p $4.95

"This is the seventh novel in the saga of Horatio Hornblower, in which the central character emerges from his apprenticeship as midshipman to assume the responsibilities thrust upon him by the fortunes of war between Napoleon and Spain. It follows the career of the young lieutenant from his arrival aboard H.M.S. Renown to his promotion to captain." Publisher's note

"'Lieutenant Hornblower' is a good novel to begin the series with. . . . The action of this novel is various and absorbing." Chicago Sunday Tribune

also in Forester, C. S. Young Hornblower p209-430

Lord Hornblower
Some editions are:
Little $4.95
Watts, F. $9.95 **Large type edition.** A Keith Jennison book
Sequel to: Commodore Hornblower
First published 1946
The fifth of the Hornblower series, Sir Horatio again leaves Lady Barbara, "concludes his private war with Napoleon, quells a mutiny, finds his old love, and is made a peer of the realm by his grateful sovereign." Huntting

also in Forester, C. S. The indomitable Hornblower p229-413

y **The man in the yellow raft.** Little 1969 190p boards $5.95

"A fast moving and rich group of [8] short stories written after World War II covering the exploits of an American Destroyer called the 'Boon' and her crew in the Pacific theater of operations." Book News

Contents: The man in the yellow raft; Triumph of the Boon; The boy stood on the burning deck; Dr Blanke's first command; Counterpunch; U.S.S. Cornucopia; December 6th; Rendezvous

"Written in the effortless free-flowing narrative style so characteristic of Forester, these stories with their keen insight into human character and their emphasis on the worth of the individual in cooperative efforts are worthwhile reading for everyone." Best Sellers

Mr Midshipman Hornblower. Little 1950 310p $4.95

Analyzed in Short Story Index

"A sixth Hornblower story (the first chronologically) which tells, in ten adventurous episodes, how this English fictional hero rose from midshipman to naval lieutenant." Book Rev Digest

Contents: Hornblower and the even chance; Hornblower and the cargo of rice; Hornblower and the penalty of failure; Hornblower and the man who felt queer; Hornblower and the

Forester, C. S.—*Continued*

man who saw God; Hornblower, the frogs, and the lobsters; Hornblower and the Spanish galleys; Hornblower and the examination for lieutenant; Hornblower and Noah's Ark; Hornblower, the duchess, and the devil

"The story is told as a series of incidents . . . with only a thin thread of continuity connecting them." Best Sellers

also in Forester, C. S. Young Hornblower p9-208

The ship. Little 1943 281p $4.95

"The story of a naval action in World War II "in the Mediterranean in which a British escort of a Malta convoy engages a major Italian fleet vastly superior in everything but trained personnel. The novel projects the picture of the action from aboard H.M.S. Artemis, a light six-inch gun cruiser, and the reader is taken from the bridge to the engine rooms, fire control rooms, turrets—all over the ship throughout, and made aware of the personalities of officers and men." Am News of Bks

Ship of the line. Little 1938 323p o.p. 1970

Sequel to: Beat to quarters
"In this story Captain Hornblower is given command of the ship Sutherland and sent to join the forces blockading the Spanish coast in the war with Napoleon." Book Rev Digest
Followed by: Flying colours

also in Forester, C. S. Captain Horatio Hornblower p221-458

The sky and the forest. Little 1948 313p o.p. 1970

"In mid-nineteenth century, the vast Congo rain forest contained many villages so isolated that one hardly knew of another. Chief and god of one of these was Loa to whom all his subjects bowed except his first wife, Musini, and his twelve-year-old son, Lanu. When Arab slavers raid the village and drag god-Loa away captive, it is Musini and Lanu who follow to rescue him. The crux of this novel is the gradual evolution into a thinking being of one who never in his life had thought before." Literary Guild

"Narrative skill and anthropological appreciation of the primitive point of view make an absorbing story of an unusual and perhaps not generally appealing subject." Library J

To the Indies. Little 1940 298p o.p. 1970

"The story of Narciso Rich, another of Mr. Forester's inimitable character creations, who is lifted suddenly out of his sedentary life as a successful lawyer to join the swaggering, gold-hungry hidalgos who went with Columbus on his third voyage. He helps fight Indians at San Domingo, is kidnapped by renegades who want to start a gold-hunting expedition of their own, shipwrecked off the coast of Cuba, and finally makes his way back to the settlement in time to return on the boat which carries Columbus in chains." Huntting

Young Hornblower; three complete novels. Little [1960] 672p o.p. 1970

Contents: Mr. Midshipman Hornblower (1950); Lieutenant Hornblower (1952); Hornblower and the 'Atropos' (1953)
This "omnibus volume takes Horatio Hornblower from Midshipman to Lieutenant and finally to Captain in His Majesty's Navy." Publisher's note

Forrest, David

And to my nephew Albert I leave the island what I won off Fatty Hagan in a poker game. . . . Morrow 1969 222p boards $4.95

"Albert's island is just a tiny speck seventy-five yards wide and one-hundred-fifty yards long off the coast of England. It has nothing except, Albert discovers, the frequent presence of Victoria, a nubile young girl in search of a suntan. As they are getting to know each other better, a Russian fishing trawler (translate as spy ship) runs aground on half the island. The other half is soon invaded by the United States Marines. Then the fun begins." Am News of Bks

"Witty satire, hilarious jinks, a fantastic plot, and a wild, idiotically long title, all make this a fun book that I recommend to those libraries feeling this is the kind of novel many of their readers would love." Library J

Forster, E. M.

The collected tales of E. M. Forster. Knopf 1947 308p $4.95

Analyzed in Short Story Index
Originally published separately as two distinct collections: Celestial omnibus, 1923 and Eternal moment, 1928 by Knopf and Harcourt respectively
The celestial omnibus: The story of a panic; The other side of the hedge; The celestial omnibus; Other kingdom; The curate's friend; The road from Colonus
The eternal moment: The machine stops; The point of it; Mr Andrews; Co-ordination; The story of the siren; The eternal moment

Howards End. Putnam 1910 442p o.p. 1970

"An unusual novel wholly outside conventional lines which deals with the Wilcox family, English and not unusual, and with the Schlegels, two sisters and a brother quite unconventional, impractical and out of the ordinary. The story proceeds in a leisurely fashion and even such an amazing thing as murder and disgrace is introduced in a casual fashion. Howards End belongs to Mr Wilcox. The story circles round it, it is here that the family are living when the story opens and it is this place that Mr Wilcox leaves to Margaret Schlegel, his second wife, in the closing pages of the book. There is much interesting character drawing, much human nature and many strange complications when the various personalities cross each other's paths and mar or make each other's lives." Book Rev Digest

A passage to India. Harcourt 1949 320p (Harbrace Modern classics) $2.95

First published 1924
"The story concerns the reactions of two newcomers—Adela Quested and Mrs. Moore, a young and an old woman—to Chandrapore or to as much of Chandrapore as holds India. In the background play the vague colors—romantic and unromantic—of India and Anglo-India., and the gross misunderstandings, and the subtler misunderstandings that must arise when two races live together—rather apart than together—conscious of an urge to transplant a 'civilization' and of as vigorous an urge to keep one's own. The conflict of these several points of view, in the novel, wells up into a noisy tempest when Miss Quested believes she has been wantonly attacked by a heretofore respectful Indian. Dr. Aziz, in one of the Marabar Caves." Literary Rev

"It is a book abundantly worth reading as a story, but it is even more potent in significance as we realize the subtlety and power with which Mr. Forster has revealed to us the Moslem and the Hindu mind and that strange anomaly, the mind of the Anglo-Indian." Boston Transcript

A room with a view. Knopf 1923 318p $4.50

First published 1911 by Putnam
"Scenes laid in England and Italy. The plot concerns the changes wrought in a girl's life by a chance meeting in an Italian pension with two men, father and son. Demands careful reading." Cur Ref Bks

Forster, Margaret

Miss Owen-Owen. Simon & Schuster 1969 255p $5.95

"A concomitance of circumstances permit talented, well-educated, domineering, and unliked Miss Lettice Owen-Owen to become headmistress of Seacrill County High School for Girls. Her ideas for the school are modern and innovative if controversial but her dictatorial, insensitive personality is dated in the extreme. It leads her at school as in her personal life to trample both potential friend and foe and results in the ignominious defeat of herself and her plans." Booklist

"Although the ending is a bit of a let-down —one keeps expecting 'something' more to happen—Miss Owen-Owen is such a memorable personality you won't soon forget her." Pub W

Forster, Margaret—*Continued*

The travels of Maudie Tipstaff. Stein & Day 1967 251p boards $5.95

The "central character is freshly widowed, lonely Maudie Tipstaff, a carping, crusty, constantly criticizing Scotswoman, who journeys from Glasgow to visit in turn and at some length with two married daughters and her bachelor son. As each reunion takes place, familiar and unfortunate interactions are set off recalling the difficult relationships of the past and arousing fresh tensions." Booklist

"Maudie's resemblance to all the other indomitable British old ladies with their rebarbative exteriors and hearts of gold is unmistakable. But the cliché is skilfully elaborated; and Maudie becomes an autonomous character capable on occasion of quite unexpected observations and behaviour." Times (London) Lit Sup

Fournier, Alain

The wanderer; tr. from the French by Françoise Delisle. Houghton 1928 306p o.p. 1970

Original French edition 1912

"This quiet story of rural French life was written just before the [First World] war, in which the young author was killed. It is a charming tale of schoolboy life, of sensitive, imaginative adolescence, of friendship, and love, with enough mystery to catch the fancy of young readers as well as old. There is, indeed, throughout the book a fascinating and delicate elusiveness." Booklist

Fowler, Kenneth

(ed.) Western Writers of America. Rawhide men

Fowles, John

The collector. Little 1963 305p $4.95

Frederick Clegg an obscure little clerk and collector of butterflies "becomes obsessed by a pretty art student he has never met. When he wins a fortune in the football pools, he buys a remote cottage in the country, kidnaps the girl and installs her in a prison in the cellar, determined to make her love him. . . . [The author tells] his story first from the demented viewpoint of the man and then from that of the increasingly desperate girl." Pub W

"Mr. Fowles is a powerful writer; this story has a nightmarish reality and immediacy. Both Miranda and Clegg are completely developed characters; the book is at once horrifying and fascinating. . . . Only for adults with strong nerves." Best Sellers

The French lieutenant's woman. Little 1969 467p $7.95

"An engrossing love story set in [19th century] Lyme Regis, England, is told in the Victorian manner but is influenced by modern psychology and recent experiments in the composition of the novel. Charles Smithson, a young gentleman of traditional values redeemed by intelligence and a measure of irony is betrothed to Ernestina Freeman, the wealthy, shallow daughter of the proprietor of a London dry goods emporium. Haunting Charles' destiny, however, is the enigmatic, independent Sarah Woodruff whom the citizens of Lyme have castigated for her brief affair with a French sailor." Booklist

"The narrative conventions of the Victorian novel—excursive exposition, incidental comment (some of it in Mr. Fowles's mid-20th-century voice), dramatic confrontations, impossible coincidences—are strikingly employed in a mordant examination of Victorian society and psychopathology. The entire novel resounds with the rich and strangled music of an age of paradox and staggering social and intellectual revolution." Book of the Month Club News

The magus. Little [1966 c1965] 582p $7.95

"This novel follows the harrowing misadventures of Nicholas Urfe, a young British schoolmaster who takes a teaching post on a remote Greek island, Phraxos, where he is drawn into an emotional maelstrom of high intrigue. . . . The story moves from a mundane beginning (Nick's sad affair with a mixed-up Australian girl, Alison) to the Phraxos villa of the rich, reclusive Conchis, a sinister old man devoted to enigmatic, spiritualistic poses. Conchis believes that man 'needs the existence of mysteries. Not their solutions.' " Newsweek

"With the narrative skill and literary sleight of hand . . . Fowles again provides hours of engrossing entertainment for an audience susceptible to a massive blend of sensuous realism, suspenseful romanticism, hypertheatrical mystification, psychic intervention, and a gallery of unusual or exotic characters in the vivid setting of the golden, craggy, threatening beauty of an isolated Greek island." Booklist

Frame, Janet

Faces in the water. Braziller 1961 254p boards $4.95

"An account of a frightened young woman's experiences in various mental institutions, in which she is confined as her insanity grows progressively worse. At last, however, responding to better care, she begins to approach normality." Pub W

"An affecting account of mental illness that constitutes not only a remarkable reading experience but also an enlightened view of the responsibility borne by society's more fortunate members. This is a novel of impression rather than action, but it is a major achievement in its class." Best Sellers

Yellow flowers in the antipodean room. Braziller 1969 248p $5.95

"Godfrey Rainbird, a 30-year-old British-born emigrant to New Zealand, is pronounced dead after a traffic accident. . . . A monogrammed casket is purchased, a cemetery plot arranged for. But there is no funeral. Thirty-six hours after his 'death,' Godfrey rises from a deep coma, a little shaky but quite ready to resume his life. Life, however, rejects his resurrection. He is fired from his job as a travel clerk . . . branded an anathema by society . . . resented by his family for the inconvenience of his miracle. . . . His life after death . . . becomes a downhill slide." Time

The book "has all the inevitability and awfulness of a Greek tragedy. . . . Moreover Miss Frame has an ability to keep the sense of everyday ordinariness operating even as the tragedy mounts. The result is masterly writing but hardly comfortable reading." Christian Science Monitor

France, Anatole

Nobel Prize in literature, 1921

The crime of Sylvestre Bonnard. Dodd 310p $3

Original French edition, 1881

"Sylvestre Bonnard is a kind-hearted, absent-minded old archeologist. The aged scholar's crime is the kidnapping of Jeanne Alexandre, the orphaned daughter of his former love, from a school in which she is abused and unhappy. Threatening complications results, but when it is discovered that Jeanne's guardian is an embezzler, she is made the legal ward of M. Bonnard." Benét. The Reader's Encyclopedia

Penguin Island; with an introduction by H. R. Steeves. Modern Lib. 1933 295p o.p. 1970

First published in French 1908; in English 1909

A volume "dealing with French history in satiric vein. The old Breton monk Saint Maël lands on an island and in his semi-blindness fails to perceive that the inhabitants whom he baptizes are penguins and not men. They are, however, changed to men in the course of time and he carefully tows the island back to the Breton shore. Its subsequent history is given at some length." University Handbook for Readers and Writers

The revolt of the angels; tr. by Mrs Wilfrid Jackson; with illus. & decorations by Frank C. Papé. Dodd 1927 357p illus o.p. 1970

First published 1914

"The guardian angels in Paris throw up their job, and joining hands with the seraphim, cherubim, and lower orders of the fallen

France, Anatole—*Continued*

host prepare a modern scientific campaign against Jahveh. The love affairs and general goings on, troubles with the police, and disturbances of various households are all very funny." Baker's Best

Thaïs; a translation by Robert B. Douglas. Lane [distributed by Dodd] 1909 324p o.p. 1970

Original French edition, 1890
Half-title: The works of Anatole France in an English translation, edited by F. Chapman
"Thaïs was a famous courtesan in Alexandria about the fourth century. Paphnutius, a holy man, who has retired to the desert to live the monastic life, has a vision of the beautiful actress and is inspired to convert her and save her from sin." Keller's Reader's Digest of Books

Francis, Dick

Blood sport. Harper 1967 241p boards $4.95

"Gene Hawkins decides to spend his three weeks vacation from the secret security agency in helping Dave Teller, an old friend of his boss, find the vanished Chrysalis, a stallion Dave and his colleagues had paid over a million dollars for, and the third to disappear in the States." Library J
"This is, like all of Francis's work, the thriller 'in excelsis,' beautifully plotted and substantially characterized. There's a splendid quality of absolute professionalism here: in the portrait of an agent at work, and in Mr. Francis's skills as a novelist." N Y Times Bk R

Dead cert
In Francis, D. Three to show p3-216

Flying finish. Harper [1967 c1966] 249p boards $4.95

"The young hero, heir to a title although he insists on working for a living, is both a private plane enthusiast and head groom in a busy operation that flies race horses and brood mares all over the world by cargo plane. There's more behind the operation than meets the eye and he is soon plunged into a terrifying race against time and sure death. The heroine is delightful, an Italian girl whom he meets along the way, who is a very special kind of smuggler. She smuggles birth control pills into Catholic Italy." Pub W
"The reader's interest is caught before he becomes vaguely aware that something is not right and that something dangerous and deadly threatens. This is a fine piece of suspenseful writing." Best Sellers

For kicks. Harper 1965 244p o.p. 1970

This is a "story about an undercover detective who is hired to find out how certain English steeplechase race horses have been doped. . . . He is determined to finish the job in spite of beastly living conditions (he has to masquerade as a stable boy), very real danger, and another kind of trouble from the very enticing promiscuous daughter of a lord." Pub W

Forfeit. Harper 1969 247p boards $4.95

"A Joan-Kahn Harper Novel of suspense"
"James Tyrone was a newspaperman who always needed extra money: his wife was an invalid, ninety per cent paralyzed, unable to breathe without the help of an electric pump. So when Tally magazine asked Ty to do a background story on the famous Lamplighter race, offering a decent fee, Ty accepted. Then the troubzle began." Am News of Bks
"Smoothly written, fast-galloping suspense novel. . . . Good entertainment, with plot and characters skillfully developed and interesting—including a race horse which likes (warm) beer." Book of the Month Club News

Nerve. Harper 1964 273p o.p. 1970

"Rob Finn, like Francis a professional jockey, watched 'an ebbing and flowing undercurrent of resentment and distrust' among trainers, jockeys, and owners. One jockey shot himself in the paddock, one collapsed after a race, one lost his job. Then it began to happen to Rob as he lost a string of races he should have won and mounts became difficult to get. How he found the cause of the disintegration of the jockeys and what he did to stop it are exciting.

The musical overtones are a surprising addition to this authentic account of the steeplechase world and the people connected with it." Library J

also in Francis, D. Three to show p219-491

Odds against. Harper [1966 c1965] 280p o.p. 1970

First published 1965 in England
In England "Sid Halley, former steeplechase champion turned detective-of-sorts, tells how his father-in-law Admiral Charles Roland, sets him at work to keep Seabury Race course out of the greedy hands of [housing developer] Howard Kraye." Bk Buyer's Guide
This is "just like a tight race on a fast track. For horse lovers as well as for . . . mystery fans." Library J

also in Francis, D. Three to show p495-774

Three to show; a trilogy. Harper 1969 774p $8.95

"A Joan Kahn-Harper Novel of suspense"
An anthology of three titles first published 1962, 1964 and 1965 respectively. The second and third titles are entered separately
Contents: Dead cert; Nerve; Odds against
Three stories of horse racing in present-day England. When, in: Dead cert, the author's first novel "Admiral, the favorite to win at Maidenhall, fell and killed his rider, Alan York suspected murder, not accident. He uncovered some unsavory facts about horse races and ran into danger himself." Bk Buyer's Guide

Frank, Pat

y Alas, Babylon; a novel. Lippincott 1959 253p $5.95

"When a defective missile triggers off World War III and the major cities of the U.S. are demolished by nuclear bombing, the inhabitants of Fort Repose, a small town in central Florida, find themselves cut off from the rest of the world and thrown from machine-age society back into a primitive way of living. Young Randy Bragg accepts the challenge imposed by responsibility for his brother's family and becomes a community leader in the fight for survival against panic and lawlessness, disease, and starvation." Booklist
"This is an extraordinarily real picture of human beings numbed by catastrophe but still driven by the unconquerable determination of living creatures to keep on being alive. The writing is simple and straightforward and practical." New Yorker

Frankau, Pamela

Colonel Blessington; ed. [completed] and with an introduction by Diana Raymond. Delacorte Press 1969 207p boards $4.50

This story involves "a suave but enigmatic man with a war record as a commando who has inherited a huge fortune from his parents, but who, in spite of his American beginnings, has opted for British citizenship and has settled down in Minster House, a handsome mansion in the North Royal section of London. A tall and beautiful TV star Anita Gilroy, has fallen deeply in love with him; somehow, too her father Matthew, living alone in a Yorkshire village, becomes involved because of a remembered phrase from his war-time experience as a commando. Then there is the mysterious Mrs. Jane Rolf, the not at all mysterious Anthony Price, numerous walk-ons and extras, many of them sharply realized. When Colonel Blessington disappears on what was supposed to be a weekend trip to a printing business he owned in Bristol and when, later, it is learned that Mrs. Jane Rolf, with whom he had been friendly, has also disappeared, Anita and Price are baffled." Best Sellers

Over the mountains. Random House 1967 340p o.p. 1970

Concluding volume of the trilogy: Clothes of a king's son. Sequel to: Sing for your supper and Slaves of the lamp

Frankau, Pamela—*Continued*

"Thomas Weston, the young hero, is captured at Dunkirk, escapes, and is seized and interned by the Spanish as he is trying to cross the border. His family thinks him dead. Rab, his childhood sweetheart, is an ambulance driver to whom the war years bring a tragic Lesbian love affair. In the end Thomas and Rab are reunited safely in England." Pub W

"This intricate, sophisticated novel [contains] . . . pictures of occupied France, wartime London, the flight of refugees through Lisbon, and some remarkable characterizations . . . told with the superb skill of a master storyteller. The three volumes should be read as a unit." Library J

Sing for your supper. Random House [1964 c1963] 311p o.p. 1970

First published 1963 in England
This first volume of a trilogy called: Clothes of a king's son, concerns an "English theatrical household headed by a charming but impecunious young widower with three children. Various family crises ensue in the course of one summer in the 1920's when a group of rich Americans invades their theatrical circle and the father of the family marries a rich American woman. The period setting, a seaside English town in 1926, is beautifully done. The author has marvelous insight into the children's minds, hearts, and fears." Pub W

Slaves of the lamp. Random House 1965 405p o.p. 1970

Follows: Sing for your supper, entered above, as the second volume of the trilogy: Clothes of a king's son
Young Tom Weston, who has healing powers, is the narrator. "Brother Gerald, actor, and sister Sarah, writer, long residents of the U.S., rugged Nanny, and Grandmother are among the supporting cast in scenes, dilemmas, mystery, and romance complicated by and also largely resolved through Tom's unsuppressible gift of second sight." Booklist
Set against a "London background of the theater, advertising world, and spiritual healers (1937-1939). . . . A sophisticated, tragic tale, written by an expert story teller." Library J

Franken, Rose

Claudia; the story of a marriage. Farrar, Straus 1939 305p o.p. 1970

"Episodes in the first years of the married life of David and Claudia, two young people so much in love that differences of opinion—as to Claudia's health, living in the country, handsome actresses, etc.—seemed very minor and unimportant, except as source material for the story of their lives." Book Rev Digest

Fraser, George Macdonald

Flashman; from the Flashman papers, 1839-1842; ed. and arranged by George Macdonald Fraser. World Pub. 1969 256p $5.95

"An NAL book"
The bounder of Thomas Hughes's Tom Brown's schooldays "left some memoirs, it appears, of which this is the first installment. After a true account of the circumstances of his expulsion from school we learn that he obtained a commission in the 11th Light Dragoons, under the Earl of Cardigan. . . . [Sent to fight in India and Afghanistan] he manages by undeviating cowardice and lack of principle to get himself acclaimed a hero." New Statesman

"Mr. Fraser, whose first novel this is, has achieved a fine blend of several styles. His battle scenes are as exciting as they come, his bedroom bits lusty and funny, and all the while he is satirizing the starchy virtues and inflated snobbery of the Victorian Raj with superb aplomb. . . . Real figures of the time and real battle incidents are cleverly interwoven with the fictional aspects of the tale." Pub W

Fraser, Phyllis

(jt. ed.) Wise, H. A. ed. Great tales of terror and the supernatural

Frayn, Michael

A very private life. Viking 1968 132p boards $4.50

A "novel set in the far distant future, when the world's population is divided into those who live inside and those who live outside. Uncumber, the girl heroine, learns that food and babies are delivered by tube, the holovision supplies news and entertainment, and the inside people never venture outside (where there are friendly and unfriendly people and animals). But it is with an outsider that Uncumber falls in love." Bk Buyer's Guide

"A parody of the middle class's obsessive concern with privacy. . . . The author is telling us that Uncumber—a representative of our future selves—must choose between utter privacy and communal bestiality. But those are not real options, and Frayn manipulates his characters and technology in his attempt to prove they are. . . . [He] has ignored the fact that modern men must solve their problems communally, or there will be no further men, private or communal." N Y Times Bk R

Frederic, Harold

The damnation of Theron Ware. Ed. by Everett Carter. The Belknap Press of Harvard Univ. Press 1960 [c1896] xxiv, 355p (The John Harvard lib) $4.50

First published in England 1896
"A critical edition of the epochal late nineteenth century novel which tells of the downfall of a Methodist minister who is seduced by new thinking about science, art, and sex which were beginning to be current at the time. A landmark both in religious thought and in literary style, its importance is analysed by the editor, Everett Carter, though without any moralizing." Rel Bk Club Bul

Freedman, Benedict

y Mrs Mike; the story of Katherine Mary Flannigan, by Benedict and Nancy Freedman; drawings by Ruth D. McCrea. Coward-McCann 1947 312p illus $5.95

"Katherine Mary O'Fallon was 16 years old when she was sent out from Boston to her uncle's ranch in Alberta. Shortly after, she met and married Sergeant Mike Flannigan of the Canadian Mounted Police and went with him to live in the far north. The story of their life together is one of youth and happiness, hardship, disaster, tragedy and courage. The book reads like a personal narrative and proves to be based on real-life experiences." Wis Lib Bul

"Primarily a love story, but much Indian and nature lore is woven into the narrative. Excellent characterizations." Booklist

Freedman, Nancy

(jt. auth.) Freedman, B. Mrs Mike

Freeling, Nicolas

Criminal conversation. Harper 1966 213p o.p. 1970

Inspector Van der Valk of the Amsterdam police "believes that the fashionable nerve specialist, Dr. Van der Post, has murdered the shabby painter, Cabestan. As the detective acts on his belief, he exerts no pressure except his persistent probing into the other's character. The result is a literate mental drama at the other pole from the violent-action school." Pub W

Double barrel. Harper [1965 c1964] 217p o.p. 1970

First published 1964 in England
The "Dutch police detective, Van der Valk . . . is in this mystery unraveling a messy skein of blackmail and poison-pen letters in a provincial Dutch town. Van der Valk is helped by his French wife, who rather unwillingly but effectively collects town gossip for him." Pub W

Freeling, Nicolas—*Continued*

The Dresden Green. Harper [1967 c1966] 240p boards $4.95

First published 1966 in England

"Louis Schweitzer has made a new life for himself, deliberately choosing the role of a nonentity in which the simplest daily routines make up his entire existence. Everything died for him the night that Dresden was mercilessly bombed by the Allies and his wife and child killed. Suddenly, 20 years later, he is caught up again, by chance, in the horror of the past in a struggle for possession of a symbol of Dresden, the city's famed green diamond. He is forced to face love and life and death once more." Pub W

This is the castle. Harper 1968 218p boards $4.95

"Dutheil, a very successful if second-rate novelist, lived in a Fontainebleau sort of castle with a horde of Spanish servants; his insolent teenage daughter; Nora, his secretary-mistress; and Laure, his gentle wife. When the American Robert Carlsen came to interview him, the day started badly. Bit by bit we learn more about Dutheil and the irritations, in spite of his prosperity, that lead to an explosion." Bk Buyer's Guide

Tsing-boom! Harper 1969 245p boards $4.95

"A Joan Kahn-Harper Novel of suspense"

Esther Marx, "the French wife of a Dutch soldier is murdered in her suburban apartment by an assassin armed with a machine gun, and Amsterdam Police Commissaire Van der Valk, learning that the victim had served as an Army nurse in Vietnam at the time of Dien Bien Phu, trudges thoughtfully off to France in search of a link between her violent past and her violent end." New Yorker

"Freeling is back on the beam with Inspector Van der Valk. . . . The case is all Van der Valk's, listening and peering into dark corners of human motivation, and himself displaying his brusque compassion by adopting [Ruth Marx] the illegitimate daughter of the murder victim." N Y Times Bk R

Valparaiso. Harper [1965 c1964] 216p o.p. 1970

First published 1964 in England

A novel set on the Cote d'Azur. "World weary and broke, Raymond Kapitan had only one dream left—to sail his boat around Cape Horn and drop anchor in sunny Valparaiso. The equally world weary—but not broke—actress, Nathalie Servaz's entrance into his life can bring only tragedy." Huntting

"Sophisticated escape fiction in which melodramatic situations become credible through taut handling of psychological motivations and responses." Booklist

Fremlin, Celia

Possession. Lippincott 1969 190p boards $4.95

When Clare Erskine's daughter becomes engaged to a much older man, Clare's delight is mixed with doubts. Is Mervyn such a catch? Or a "mother's boy?" Driven by fear for her daughter's safety, Clare exposes herself to a generation gap gone crazy, a possessive mother's torment, and a danger greater than she knows, to find the terrifying answer. (Publisher)

"Another one of those chilling exercises in horror in a deceptively quiet English domestic setting at which Celia Fremlin is so expert. It builds to a terrifying and totally unexpected climax." Pub W

Freuchen, Peter

Eskimo; tr. by A. P. Maerker-Branden and Elsa Branden. Liveright 1931 504p o.p. 1970

"A novel of Eskimo life within the Arctic Circle. It is the saga of Mala, a great hero among his people because of his prowess as a hunter. Mala flees with his family after a murder has been committed, is imprisoned by white men, escapes, and finally perishes with the last of his family, his aged wife." Book Rev Digest

White man. Rinehart 1946 275p o.p. 1970

A "story of Norwegian-Danish attempts at colonization in Greenland in the early eighteenth century. The leading character is a hotheaded, stubborn, but intelligent Danish soldier, Peter, who is imprisoned for desertion and sent to Greenland as one of a group of convicts shipped out by the government to help form a settlement. Peter wins the respect of the Eskimos and learns their way of life by living with them. The first part of the book gives a realistic picture of contemporary prison conditions in Denmark." Booklist

Friedman, Bruce Jay

Black angels; stories. Simon & Schuster 1966 188p $4.50

Analyzed in Short Story Index

Contents: Black angels; The punch; The investor; The operator; Brazzaville teen-ager; A change of plan; The interview; Show biz connections; The enemy; The death table; The night boxing ended; The neighbors; The hero; Let me see faces; The mission; The humiliation

Far from the city of class, and other stories. Frommer-Pasmantier 1963 217p o.p. 1970

Analyzed in Short Story Index

Contents: For your viewing entertainment; Far from the city of class; When you're excused you're excused; The trip; A foot in the door; The subversive; The little ball; Mr Prinzo's breakthrough; The good time; The man they threw out of jets; Wonderful golden rule days; The holiday celebrators; Yes, we have no Ritchard; The Big Six; The canning of Mother Dean; 23 Pat O'Brien movies

A mother's kisses; a novel. Simon & Schuster 1964 286p $4.95

A "satiric novel that pits a 17-year-old Brooklyn boy against the world and even against his mother, who is a great manager, supremely confident of her own abilities. The boy sees life straight: what he sees, the adults around him, by and large, is revolting and hypocritical. His mother is one of the most nauseating characters of recent fiction. The boy's hardest problem is to find a college that will admit him; before that, he has to extricate himself from a dreadful summer camp; and when he does get into college his mother, incredibly, comes along with him." Pub W

"Meanwhile, the author has given us humor, pathos, love, vulgarity and, above all, life in a fast-moving vivid style that is full of verbal pyrotechnics. It is a book to read and enjoy and then say to one's self, 'What will Friedman think of next?'" Best Sellers

Frison-Roche, Roger

The raid; tr. from the French, Le rapt, by J. F. Newcombe. Harper 1964 244p boards $4.95

"Paavi warned Kristina and her father that a rival clan of Lapps was about to raid their herd of reindeer—and, sure enough, once Kristina had been sent away to school, the raiders struck and stole more than a thousand of the animals. But teenage Kristina was no one to take robbery lightly, so she and Paavi set out to guard the great herd." Bk Buyer's Guide

"The plot, which turns on a blood-feud and on the love between a young Lapp girl and a half-Lapp, half-Finnish fur-trapper, is not as important here as are the setting, in the harsh but starkly beautiful sub Arctic, and the graphically described folkways." Pub W

Fuentes, Carlos

A change of skin; tr. by Sam Hileman. Farrar, Straus 1968 462p $6.95

Original Spanish edition published 1967

Told by a character identified as the narrator, the novel takes place on a drive from Mexico City to Vera Cruz during Holy Week and concerns "a former Nazi and his Mexican mistress and a talented but unsuccessful writer and his embittered wife. All four are searching for some true value in life." Pub W

"The narrator serves to transform this expedition into an intricate subtle journey back and forth in time through Mexico's history

Fuentes, Carlos—*Continued*

but particularly through the lives of the story's principals, revealing each one's central needs, hopes, and disappointments. Fuentes has absorbed and fused the foreign influences . . . to achieve a richly graphic, ironic, if occasionally unduly complex, narrative that probes souls and society." Booklist

The death of Artemio Cruz; tr. from the Spanish by Sam Hileman. Farrar, Straus 1964 306p boards $4.95

The novel "opens with Artemio Cruz in a dying coma, with the voices of his wife Catalina, his daughter Teresa, and his close associates in his ears. He is a very rich man, a great power in Mexico, owner of much land, proprietor of a powerful newspaper. At 71, returning from a meeting with some government officials he has bribed and coerced, he collapses with a fatal illness. Lying on his deathbed, he begins to remember. What Artemio Cruz remembers—his whole life—is also in essence the story of the tragedy of Mexico." Publisher's note

Where the air is clear; a novel. Tr. by Sam Hileman. Farrar, Straus 1960 376p o.p. 1970

"A novel, set in modern Mexico City. Among the characters are a novelist, a successful but dissatisfied movie writer, a passionate and ambitious woman, members of a decaying aristocracy, newly arrived intellectuals, a prostitute, a cab driver, aging men and women and confused younger people. Wealth and poverty are often counterpointed, as are age and youth, and the style is somewhat impressionistic." Pub W

"Lusty, profane (although not, in any technical sense, obscene) these pages of power cry out a love like death." Cath World

Fuks, Ladislav

Mr Theodore Mundstock; tr. from the Czech by Iris Urwin. Orion 1968 214p $4.95

Originally published in Czechoslovakia

"Prague, 1942: the Germans occupy the country and the Jews await the dreaded summons to concentration camps. Among them is Mr. Theodore Mundstock. . . . Each day his panic mounts, goading him to the brink of insanity. But one day, as he repeats, in his mind the awful ritual of his friends being herded into cattle trucks, he suddenly realizes what is wrong: they are not prepared for the camps. He resolves to prepare; in his little apartment he will simulate the camp. . . . With this revelation, a sudden calm descends upon Mr. Mundstock. Pride, almost joy in anticipation of his fate helps him to strengthen his remaining friends." Publisher's note

"Here a simple tale, told without sentimentality, illuminates the situation of human beings under stress. At the start Mundstock . . . is totally disorganized. Brief staccato passages convey his utter sense of bewilderment and also evoke the memories of his former life. . . . A subtle change in the author's style reflects the growing coherence of the protagonist's activities. The people and places around Mundstock come into focus." Atlantic

Fuller, Iola

y The loon feather. Harcourt 1940 419p $4.75

"A story of life on Mackinac island during the busiest fur-trading years of the early 1800's, related by Oneta, an Ojibway girl, whose father was Tecumseh, chief of the loon tribe. Although Oneta was sent to Quebec to a convent school, education and fashionable clothes did not alter the Indian girl's natural love of the island, of forests and water, and of Indian ways. She returns to them with pleasure and later finds romance with a doctor at the fort. An unusually good Indian story, sympathetic and appealing, yet having a fine and vigorous spirit." Booklist

"A clear and honest picture of the slow retreat of an old civilization before the advance of a new one." Springf'd Republican

y The shining trail; illus. by Dale Nichols. Duell 1951 442p $6.50

First published 1943

"How the great and wise Black Hawk, aging chief of the Sauk Indians, valiantly tries to save for his people their vast, fair homeland and how the Indians, divided among themselves, are forced by the encroaching white men to desperate flight is related in a warmly-sympathetic narrative, revealing the ways of the Sauks, their customs and rites and depicting the course of the Black Hawk War, always emphasizing the treachery of the white men. Among the characters most lovingly portrayed are Black Hawk, his faithful friend Tomah, and Chaske, the Sioux boy Black Hawk has adopted and trained to such good purpose that he can set out on the shining trail of the spirits sure the boy will be a worthy successor and leader of the Indians." Bookmark

G

Gadda, Carlo Emilio

Acquainted with grief; tr. from the Italian by William Weaver. Braziller 1969 244p $6.95

Original Italian edition, 1963

"Set in the mythical province of Néa Keltiké (Lombardi) in the equally mythical country of Maradagàl (Italy), this autobiographical novel . . . is a little like an obstacle course, especially in its diversionary, almost comic-opera opening section. . . . The novel was written between 1938 and 1941 and never completed by the author. This edition contains an unfinished third section, thus far not published in Italy." Pub W

The story "focuses on the almost insane misanthropy of a certain 'hidalgo,' who is actually Mr. Gadda himself portrayed in caricature. He rages wildly against bureaucratic regulations, charity, peasant vulgarity, even certain personal pronouns, and especially the subscription efforts of a provincial guard service." Library J

"This oblique novel is as slippery and clever as a fish. . . . In short, this is a hard nut to crack, and it is a question whether the meat inside is worth it. The answer is probably that it is; for some. The reader who succeeds in simply tracing out the story will get a pleasing sense of accomplishment." Christian Science Monitor

Gaines, Ernest J.

Bloodline. Dial Press 1968 249p boards $4.95

Analyzed in Short Story Index

The five stories included deal with contemporary Negro life in the agrarian South. (Publisher)

Contents: A long day in November; The sky is gray; Three men; Bloodline; Just like a tree

Gainham, Sarah

Night falls on the city. Holt 1967 572p $6.95

When the Nazis arrive in Austria, Julia Homburg, a Viennese actress married to a Jewish Socialist politician, maneuvers to keep her husband safe. In addition to describing the lives of Julia and her husband, the book also depicts Vienna during the last War. (Publisher)

"Miss Gainham, a charming and interesting writer, has forced so much into her novel . . . that action takes over . . . so that the characters, in their increasing helplessness and increasingly courageous endurance, become passive mechanical objects reacting mechanically to mounting pressure. In other words, this book is too long. . . . [Julia, Franz] and their heroic maid, Fina, all so brightly alive at the start of the story, are soon lost to view in events, explanations, and expositions. As a panoramic picture of what took place in Vienna from March, 1938, to May, 1945, this book is entirely successful and convincing, and Miss Gainham's concluding paragraphs are superb." New Yorker

Followed by: A place in the country

A place in the country. Holt 1969 371p $6.95

Sequel to: Night falls on the city

Original German edition published 1968 in Switzerland

"Still featured is Julia Homburg, lovely and renowned Viennese actress; prominent billing

Gainham, Sarah—*Continued*

goes also to familiar Georg Kerenyi, new-comer-narrator Robert Inglis of England, and Julia's deeply troubled niece whom Robert comes to love. Once more current events affect personal relationships, responsibilities, and responses in the world of theater, politics, and intellect in which these people move. Now, however, it is postwar Vienna of the 1940's and 1950's, and Cold War complications and intrigue cast their shadow." Booklist

" 'Sarah Gainham' writes elegantly; she has a fine sense of atmosphere; she is good at intelligent conversations between rather complicated characters; and her stories are distinctive, with no trace of routine or imitation. . . . Although I did not enjoy [this] quite as much as the previous novel, I did enjoy it and took pleasure in rereading it a couple of weeks later." Book of the Month Club News

Galaxy Magazine

The [first]-tenth Galaxy reader. Doubleday 1952-1967 10v o.p. 1970

Analyzed in Short Story Index
The first-fourth volumes entered under Galaxy Science Fiction Magazine. Titles vary; The first-second volumes had title: Galaxy Reader of science fiction and were published by Crown

Editors: First-sixth Galaxy reader: H. L. Gold; Seventh-tenth Galaxy reader: Frederick Pohl

Galbraith, John Kenneth

The triumph; a novel of modern diplomacy. Houghton 1968 239p $4.95

The story of "a political crisis in Puerto Santos—a small Caribbean-like country—where an aging dictator tries to remain in power with United States aid by posing as a bastion of anti-Communism." Library J

"What Galbraith is concerned to demonstrate is the system of interlocking stupidity in which, he believes, the makers of foreign policy are hopelessly imprisoned. . . . It is all quite devastating but, in spite of the author's detailed knowledge of the scene, somewhat tedious and not altogether convincing. Not that one would care to argue at any given point . . . . What works against any 'emergent truth' and, finally, against one's enjoyment of this clever book is the tone in which the enterprise is conducted. It is all loftily condescending and relentlessly witty." New Repub

Galdos, Benito Perez. See Perez Galdos, Benito

Gale, John

The family man. Coward-McCann [1969 c1968] 188p $4.95

First published 1968 in England
"Andy Minuss had moments when he thought he was losing his mind and once his wife did have to put him in a mental hospital. Then they used a small legacy for a year in Provence with their children, and there Claire's brief flirtation with another man gave Andy a surer grip on life." Bk Buyer's Guide

"What John Gale offers the reader is a style of observation, rather than insight into his narrator. . . . The narrator hears men discussing trade union affairs: fascinating dialogue, but he is making no effort to understand the content, merely to record the notes and tones. . . . [These] vignettes seem to be set down at random, prose-poems with no apparent form or discipline." Times (London) Lit Sup

Gale, Zona

Miss Lulu Bett. Appleton 1920 264p o.p. 1970

"The evolution of spunk and gumption in the character of Miss Lula, the trod-upon, is the chief interest in this story of middle western folk. Almost an old maid, she is a sort of Cinderella with a bitter-tongued tyrannical brother and his family in lieu of the traditional stepmother and step-sisters. [This story tells] how she seeks escape in marriage only to find that she has jumped from the fryingpan into the fire, but finally wins through to happiness. Open Shelf

Gallico, Paul

The abandoned. Knopf 1950 307p $3.95

"Peter, a lonely little English boy who longed for a cat as a pet, was knocked down by a lorry as he rushed out to rescue a stray kitten. In his delirium Peter finds himself changed into a cat, with a companion, Jenny, who teaches him the lore of the cat world. Peter and Jenny have some lively experiences before Peter returns to consciousness and a repentant family." Book Rev Digest

The hand of Mary Constable. Doubleday 1964 279p $4.95

A novel of suspense. "Cyberneticist Constable, grieving for the death of his 10-year-old daughter is caught by a slick pair of mediums when they produce a wax hand bearing the fingerprints of the dead child during a seance as proof of the materialization of the girl; they then work on him to betray the secrets of a new missile defense or to defect to the enemy. Alexander Hero of the British Psychical research Society is called in to save the situation." Best Sellers

"This neatly plotted thriller, with plenty of action, is good (if not the best) Gallico, and his fans will appreciate it." Pub W

Ludmila
In Gallico, P. Three legends: The snow goose; The small miracle; Ludmila p77-126

y Mrs 'Arris goes to Paris; drawings by Gioia Fiammenghi. Doubleday 1958 157p illus boards $2.95

"A middle-aged London charwoman, fascinated by one of her employer's gowns, determines to own one, and this . . . tells of her resolute invasion of Christian Dior's salon and its happy effect on three young French people." Bookmark

"Improbable but amusing: its sentimentality will be a recommendation rather than a deterrent to the author's following." Booklist

Mrs 'Arris goes to Parliament; drawings by Gioia Fiammenghi. Doubleday 1965 152p illus $2.95

Companion volume to the author's: Mrs 'Arris goes to Paris

"Cozened into running for the House of Commons as the unknowing victim of unscrupulous politicians, Mrs. Harris is saved from defeat through the ingenious campaign strategy of several loyal supporters, including her chauffeur friend John Bayswater, and takes her seat in Parliament—only to find her troubles just begun." Booklist

y The Poseidon adventure. Coward-McCann 1969 347p $6.95

"It was the beginning of the end—seven o'clock in the morning of December 26. The Poseidon was home-ward-bound for Lisbon after a Christmas cruise to African and South American ports. It was to be a final appalling voyage: a physical and spiritual nightmare endured by fifteen ordinary, yet eventually extraordinary people. Trapped in a sinking ship for ten dark hours of love, hate, and desperation, they face obstacles known only to adventurers who have conquered the far corners of the earth. At the end of their harrowing experience they emerge wholly different persons from what they were before." Am News of Bks

"Back comes the ship-of-fools idea, but with, to use a dreadful pun, a twist. Paul Gallico's new slant to the idea, and the fact that gives him his crises, is that the ship is upside down. Moreover, Mr. Gallico's roster of fools is not only individualized but highly distinctive." Best Sellers

y The small miracle; illus. by Reisie Lonette. Doubleday 1952 58p illus $2.50

"A brief story of a little Italian boy and his beloved donkey, Violetta. When Violetta became very ill Pepino asked permission to take

Gallico, Paul—*Continued*

her into the crypt of St Francis' church in Assisi, and he persisted until permission was granted by the Pope himself." Book Rev Digest

also in Gallico, P. Three legends: The snow goose; The small miracle; Ludmila p47-75

y **The snow goose.** Knopf 1940 57p $2

The tale of a lonely man, a little girl and a wild goose driven by a storm to the coast of England. The story tells how the man came to the aid of his country in its moment of desperate need and how the bird became a symbol of hope and safety to the lost armies on the beach at Dunkirk

also in Gallico, P. Three legends: The snow goose; The small miracle; Ludmila p21-45

y **Thomasina, the cat who thought she was God.** Doubleday 1957 288p illus $4.95

"Thomasina is the pet cat of Mary Ruadh, the motherless daughter of the veterinary surgeon in a Scottish town near the sea. This is really the story of Mary's father, whose thwarted ambition to become a doctor twisted his outlook on life into a bitterness which his kindly, long-time friend, Mr. Peddie, man of God, worked to dispel. The main thread of the story, the setting in the Highlands, the veterinarian's waiting room filled with sick pets and their anxious masters are believable, whereas the red witch, Lori, and Thomasina give the eerie touch of fantasy. Although the plot shows its bones, there is enough story to sustain interest because the reader can identify himself with this man's struggle for peace. Those who are fond of cats will like the story because of the vanity that is Thomasina." Wis Lib Bul

y **Three legends: The snow goose; The small miracle; Ludmila;** illus. by Reisie Lonette. Doubleday 1966 126p illus $3.95

First published 1940, 1952, and 1959 respectively

The snow goose tells the stories of the evacuation of Dunkirk in World War II. The small miracle concerns the cure of a donkey in Assisi. The third story tells about a cow in Liechtenstein who wants to be beautiful

Too many ghosts. Doubleday 1959 288p o.p. 1970

A suspense story which "concerns a detective engaged in uncovering the causes of weird sights and sounds that appear in an Old English country house, terrifying the paying guests who believe the place to be haunted." Pub W

Galsworthy, John

Nobel Prize in literature, 1932

Caravan; the assembled tales. Scribner 1925 760p o.p. 1970

Analyzed in Short Story Index

Contents: Salvation of a Forsyte; A stoic; A portrait; The grey angel; Quality; The man who kept his form; The Japanese Quince; The broken boot; The choice; Ultima Thule; Courage; The bright side; The black godmother; Philanthropy; A man of Devon; The apple tree; The prisoner; A simple tale; The consummation; Acme; Defeat; Virtue; The neighbours; Stroke of lightning; Spindleberries; Salta pro nobis; The pack; "The dog it was that died"; A knight; The juryman; Timber; Santa Lucia; The mother stone; Peace meeting; A strange thing; The nightmare child; A reversion to type; Expectations; A woman; A hedonist; A miller of Dee; Late—299; The silence; A feud: A fisher of men; Manna; "Cafard"; The recruit; Compensation; Conscience; Once more; Blackmail; Two looks; A long-ago affair; The first and the last; Had a horse

End of the chapter. Scribner 1934 897p front o.p. 1970

An omnibus volume containing: Maid in waiting, 1931; Flowering wilderness, 1932 and Over the river (published as One more river, 1933)

"In 'Maid in waiting' Dinny Cherrell was concerned mainly with her brother Hubert's troubles; in 'Flowering wilderness' with her own love for the almost ostracized Wilfred Desert. This last novel of the trilogy, which chronicles the affairs of the Cherrells family connections of the Forsytes, was completed some months before Mr. Galsworthy's death. In it Dinny's chief interest is with her young sister Clare's divorce from a sadistic husband and her eventual acceptance, temporarily at least, of an irregular love affair. Dinny herself, after news of Wilfred's drowning in Siam, finally makes her decision to marry Dornford." Booklist

Flowering wilderness
In Galsworthy, J. End of the chapter p331-592

The Forsyte saga; with a preface by Ada Galsworthy. Scribner 1933 xx, 921p front $8.95

A reissue of the title first published in this edition 1922 brings together in one volume the chronicles of the Forsyte family: Man of property (1906) In chancery (1920) and To let (1921) and two interludes: Indian summer of a Forsyte and Awakening

"Within these pages John Galsworthy has collected his best work as a novelist. It is a compendium of the Victorian epoch and of the first twenty years of the twentieth century. Its characters are verifiably true, and the history of this typical English family is told not only by a first-rate literary artist, but by a thinker who is fundamentally honest and sincere." Lit R

The Galsworthy reader; ed. by Anthony West. Scribner [1968 c1967] xxi, 702p boards $7.95

This omnibus volume includes: The man of property, first published 1906; Indian summer of a Forsyte; excerpts from three other novels; four short stories and two plays

Short stories included are: The consummation; The meeting; A stoic; Virtue

In chancery
In Galsworthy, J. The Forsyte saga

Indian summer of a Forsyte
In Galsworthy, J. The Galsworthy reader p543-86

Maid in waiting
In Galsworthy, J. End of the chapter p 1-330

The man of property
Some editions are:
Heritage $7.50 With an introduction by Evelyn Waugh. Illustrations by Charles Mozley
Scribner $4.95 With an introduction by Lionel Stevenson

First published 1906 by Heinemann

"Main theme [is] the sense of property, or possessive instinct, as embodied to an exaggerated degree in Soames Forsyte. . . . Thru a long series of carefully finished pictures the author conveys the narrowness of upper middle-class London society several generations ago." Lenrow. Reader's Guide to Prose Fiction

also in Galsworthy, J. The Forsyte saga p3-309
also in Galsworthy, J. The Galsworthy reader p15-294

A modern comedy. Scribner 889p front $10

First published 1929

The second part of the Forsyte chronicles containing: The white monkey (1924) The silver spoon (1926) Swan song (1928) and the two interludes: A silent wooing and Passers by. "A modern comedy" closes with the England of 1926

One more river
In Galsworthy, J. End of the chapter p593-897

The silver spoon
In Galsworthy, J. A modern comedy p295-504

Galsworthy, John—*Continued*

Swan song
In Galsworthy, J. A modern comedy p578-889

To let
In Galsworthy, J. The Forsyte saga p665-921

The white monkey
In Galsworthy, J. A modern comedy p3-248

Gann, Ernest K.

Blaze of noon. Holt 1946 298p o.p. 1970

"The early days of airmail transportation forms the background of this novel. It begins with the four MacDonald brothers and their stunt flying at country fairs, sometime after World war I. Then it describes their breakover into the business of flying the mail, their lives in the air in those difficult flying days, the deaths of two of the brothers, and the crippling of the third. Only one of the flying MacDonalds is left on his feet at the end." Book Rev Digest

The high and the mighty. Morrow 342p $5.95

First published 1953 under the imprint of Sloane

"A group of people, casual travelling companions, approach the critical period in their lives as their plane flies from Hawaii to San Francisco. Love, hate, jealousy, tenderness and faith are revealed as the suspense builds to a climax." Huntting

Mr. Gann's examination of character under stress, coupled with the superbly sustained suspense of the plane's fight for survival, makes a dramatic novel which is likely to catch and hold the attention of almost any reader. 'The High and the Mighty' is first-rate intertainment." N Y Her Trib Books

In the company of eagles. Simon & Schuster 1966 342p $5.95

This novel set in 1917 "recreates the frantic pace of bi-plane battles during World War I. A young French aviator swears vengeance on the German ace who flies without fault and kills without mercy." Cincinnati

This "account of [the combatants'] exhilaration, fatigue, pity, fear, and of the corruptive effect of power, represents faithfully what men have experienced in combat since long before the days of Gideon, Samson or David. Ernest Gann handles his material skillfully. . . . Tension builds honestly, imperceptibly, but steadily to a startling climax. . . . The airman's daily battle for objective control of himself, to sustain life in the midst of death, gives Gann's 'In the Company of Eagles' an enduring quality." America

Soldier of fortune. Sloane 1954 314p o.p. 1970

"A story of present day Hong Kong. The heroine is an American girl who goes there in search of her husband, a photographer who has disappeared into Red China. She meets and gains the help of another American, the middle-age adventurer, Hank Lee, and together they accomplish her mission." Book Rev Digest

"Mr. Gann has produced an exotic derring-do, a swashbuckling love story, and a vivid picture of Communist China, all rolled into one." Sat R

Twilight for the gods. Sloane 1956 306p o.p. 1970

This novel "charts the final voyage of the ancient barquentine 'Cannibal,' which sails for Mexico from the South Seas port of Suva under Captain Bell, carrying a cargo of copra and a few passengers seeking to escape the failures of the past. Each of the oddly assorted group finds individual salvation through the common struggle against disaster when the forces of time and the sea threaten to overwhelm the 'Cannibal.' " Booklist

"The best parts of this book remain those in which Mr. Gann gives us all the details of the day-to-day working of a ship under sail. He has written a good sea story." Times (London) Lit Sup

García Márquez, Gabriel

Big Mama's funeral
In García Márquez, G. No one writes to the colonel, and other stories p153-70

No one writes to the colonel, and other stories; tr. from the Spanish by J. S. Bernstein. Harper 1968 170p boards $5.95

Analyzed in Short Story Index

The volume contains one novella, No one writes to the Colonel, originally published 1961 in Columbia, and a collection of short stories, Big Mama's funeral, originally published 1962 in Mexico. The subject matter deals with town and village life in South America, among the very poor or very rich. (Publisher)

Short stories included in Big Mama's funeral are: Tuesday siesta; One of these days; There are no thieves in this town; Balthazar's marvelous afternoon; Montiel's widow; One day after Saturday; Artificial roses; Big Mama's funeral

"With a solid reputation in Latin America and a growing one in Europe, García Márquez confirms the new vitality in Latin American literature and the revolutionary independence of style and content in the works of the younger generation." Am News of Bks

One hundred years of solitude; tr. from the Spanish by Gregory Rabassa. Harper 1970 422p $7.95

First published 1967 in the Argentine Republic

"Tells the story of the rise and fall, birth and death, of the mythical town of Macondo through the history of the Buendía family. . . . Love and lust, war and revolution, riches and poverty, youth and senility—the variety of life, the endlessness of death, the search for peace and truth—these, the universal themes, dominate the novel." Publisher's note

"Macondo may be regarded as a microcosm of the development of much of the Latin American continent: a strange, pristine, fecund, doomed land. . . . In the end, 'progress' is seen as merely the middle phase of a continuous three-phase cycle: primal nature-civilization-primal nature. Although it is first and always a story, the novel also has value as a social and historical document." Sat R

Gardner, Erle Stanley

The case of the crimson kiss
In Haycraft, H. ed. A treasury of great mysteries v 1 p147-87

The case of the fabulous fake. Morrow 1969 222p $4.95

"She was trying to disappear—to help her brother against a blackmailer—and she wouldn't even tell Perry Mason her name. So Perry called her 36-24-36 and when she was suspected of murder he acted in her defense." Bk Buyer's Guide

The case of the worried waitress. Morrow 1966 212p boards $3.95

It was against the rules for a waitress to beleaguer customers for advice, but Katherine Ellis was deeply worried . . . so when Perry Mason finished lunch, he left her a note: 'My usual fee for an office consultation is ten dollars. The tip under the plate is eleven dollars,' . . . and in no time at all, Perry discovered that Katherine had full cause for worry—in fact, she was in serious trouble." Am News of Bks

Gardner, John

A complete state of death. Viking 1969 255p boards $4.95

"The story has to do with a masterminded transatlantic syndicate that operates a finishing school for talented would-be criminals on a big estate near London. . . . The hero

Gardner, John—*Continued*

[Derek Torry]. . . . is a Scotland Yard inspector who . . . grew up in the United States as a wartime evacuee, and served on the New York Police Department." New Yorker

This is the author's "attempt at the serious thriller, which here entails a guilt-ridden Anglo American Roman Catholic policeman trying to discover whether a man of a given name is a crook on an unprecedented scale. The detailed sex puts this book well out of court for the modest." Times (London) Lit Sup

Gardner, Leonard

Fat city. Farrar, Straus 1969 183p boards $5.50

The book "tells the story of two young boxers out of Stockton, California; Ernie Munger and Billy Tully, one in his late teens, the other just turning thirty, whose seemingly parallel lives intersect for a time. . . . [It describes] the two fighters' struggles to escape the confinements of their existence, and . . . the men and women in their world." Publisher's note

This "is a calm, thin little novel (180 pages) tough but tender, painstakingly written, superficially inconclusive, blessed with great vitality and a strong comic strain. . . . Mr. Gardner has a special way with the kind of compliment usually exchanged in barrooms and locker rooms, a gratifyingly cold-blooded view of what used to be called life's little ironies, an honest and affectionate understanding of the Billy Tullys and Ernie Mungers of this world, and no taste at all for the sentimental custard sauce with which Steinbeck flavored some of his California underdog stories. A first novel and a solid achievement." Book of the Month Club News

Garland, Hamlin

Main-travelled roads; with a new preface by B. R. McElderry, Jr. and the 1893 introduction by William Dean Howells. Harper 1956 247p $3.50

Analyzed in Short Story Index
First published 1891
Short stories set in 19th century Middle West
Contents: A branch road; Up the cooly; Among the corn-rows; The return of a private; Under the lion's paw; The creamery man; A days's pleasure; Mrs Ripley's trip; Uncle Ethan Ripley; God's ravens; A "good fellow's" wife

Garner, William

The us or them war. Putnam 1969 285p $5.95

"A brilliant but naive British scientist has seemingly crossed a laser beam with an X-ray to produce the ultimate weapon. News of his invention leaks. . . . The Russians are at first convinced that the British are on the side of the Americans but soon realize that this is not the case—Britain decides to go it alone. With this threat to the balance of power, America and Russia cooperate to nullify the danger. [British intelligence agent Michael Jagger] is called in to protect Britain's interests. There is much action, double-crossing, and some violence before the situation is resolved." Library j

Garnett, David

Lady into fox; with an author's note to the present edition and introduction by Vincent Starrett; illus. with wood engravings by R. A. Garnett. Norton 1966 90p illus (The Seagull lib. of mystery and suspense) $4.50

First published 1922 in England
"A year after her marriage, as Silvia Tebrick was walking with her husband in a wood near their Oxfordshire home, she was suddenly changed into a small red fox. As her nature rapidly became that of the animal into which she had been changed [her husband] continued to love her and deal gently with her vixenish ways. Finally, hunted down by the hounds, she died in his arms where she had sprung for protection." Book Rev Digest

"The book is quick with a deep poetic emotion which comes of a rare sensibility to the English countryside and recalls something of Hudson, something, too, of Edward Thomas." Literary Rev

Two by two; a story of survival. Atheneum Pubs. 1964 [c1963] 143p boards $3.50

First published 1963 in England
A fantasy "of what might have happened on Noah's ark when the animals marched on and animals and people lived amicably, if uncomfortably, until the flood waters receded. As his heroines, Garnett invents stowaways, twin young girls." Pub W

"This playful and inoffensive piece combines imaginativeness, humor, and earthiness to express an intense delight in the animal kindom and an inherent appreciation of the worth and the folly that meet in the human race." Booklist

Garrity, Devin A.

(ed.) 44 Irish short stories; an anthology of Irish short fiction from Yeats to Frank O'Connor. Devin-Adair 1955 500p boards $6.50

Analyzed in Short Story Index
Contents: She went by gently, by P. V. Carroll; The Islandman, by D. Clarke; The lady on the grey, by J. Collier; The awakening, by D. Corkery; The return, by D. Corkery; Saint Bakeoven, by E. Cross; The kith of the Elf-folk, by Lord Dunsany; The burial, by St J. Ervine; Something in a boat, by P. Fallon; Miss Gillespie and the Micks, by A. Hill; The leaping trout, by D. Hogan; Araby, by J. Joyce; Counterparts, by J. Joyce; Football, by P. Kavanagh; The story of the widow's son, by M. Lavin; "All the sweet butter-milk . . .", by D. MacDonagh; Duet for organ and strings, by D. MacDonagh; Myself and a rabbit, by M. MacGrian; The wild duck's nest, by M. McLaverty; Father Christmas, by M. McLaverty; The plain people of England, by B. MacMahon; The cat and the cornfield, by B. MacMahon; Julia Cahill's curse, by G. Moore; The world outside, by V. Mulkerns; The devil and O'Flaherty, by P. O. Conaire; The drunkard, by F. O'Connor; The majesty of the law, by F. O'Connor; Teresa, by S. O'Faolain; Persecution mania, by S. O'Faolain; The hawk, by L. O'Flaherty; The tent, by L. O'Flaherty; Michael and Mary, by S. O'Kelly; Nan Hogan's house, by S. O'Kelly; The Martyr's crown, by B. O'Nolan; Bell Wethers, by J. Phelan; Weep for our pride, by J. Plunkett; The miraculous revenge, by G. B. Shaw; The black mare, by E Sheehy; Schoolfellows, by J. Stephens; A rhinoceros, some ladies and a horse, by J. Stephens; Come back, my love, by M. Walsh; The happy Prince, by O. Wilde; Red Hanrahan, by W. B. Yeats; Where there is nothing, there is God, by W. B. Yeats

Garth, David

Watch on the bridge; a novel. Putnam 1959 320p o.p. 1970

"The factual basis for this carefully plotted, smoothly narrated war story is the Allied capture of the Rhine bridge at Remagen in March, 1945. The author gives meaning and emotional impact to the military action by reconstructing it fictionally, in terms of people ranging from the commanding generals of both sides to the slave laborers employed on the bridge. He focuses particularly on Ilse Margraven, a crippled German girl to whom the bridge has become a symbol of faith and hope, and Doke Stanton, a demoralized American soldier who, through Ilse, regains his courage and discovers what he is fighting for." Bookist

Garve, Andrew

The ascent of D-13. Harper 1968 187p boards $4.95

"A Joan Kahn-Harper Novel of suspense"
"An attempted hijacking by a Russian agent of a plane carrying a new detection device ends with a crash into the summit of D-13, a precipitous peak on [the Soviet-Turkish] border. The Russians send a team to recover the device; the Allies are led by Bill Royce, one of England's best mountain scalers." N Y Times Bk R

Garve, Andrew—*Continued*

"Not only does the account of a long, hazardous climb up an inaccessible mountain peak . . . exert an unbreakable grip, but we are held just as immovable for the equally long climb down again. Somehow Mr. Garve convinces us that if our concentration lapses for a second the climbers will be lost. He adds love interest too, and the unusual background of tourist Turkey." Christian Science Monitor

The ashes of Loda. Large type ed. Harper [1967 c1965] 174p $6.95

A large type edition of a title first published 1965 by Harper

News correspondent Lord Tim Quainton "returns to Moscow determined to unravel the strangely ambiguous past of his fiancée's father—a Polish chemist now employed in England. But the web proves perilously tangled, and Quainton finds himself fleeing for his life across the frozen wastes of rural Russia." Publisher's note

"Garve, who was once a Moscow correspondent himself, embellishes a fine fast adventure story with a more credible picture of the U.S.S.R. than is offered in most thriller." N Y Times Bk R

The far sands. Harper 1960 186p o.p. 1970

"James Renisen thought it rather romantic that Carol, his bride, had an identical twin—until Fay and her husband died under suspicious circumstances. Then he began to wonder about Carol, who set out obstinately to clear her sister's name." Bk Buyer's Guide

The long short cut. Harper 1968 166p boards $4.95

"A Joan Kahn-Harper Novel of suspense"
"A heartstopping story about England's top confidence man, who sets off on his biggest, wildest and most rewarding project, involving a luscious blonde and a gullible financier." McClurg. Book News

"Nobody is better than Andrew Garve at telling a fundamentally simple story and making it absorbing from first to last." San Francisco Chronicle

A very quiet place. Harper 1967 184p boards $4.50

A "girl photographer witnesses part of a London jewel robbery and snaps a picture of the getaway car. The thieves filch both photograph and negative, but her life is in danger because she can identify the driver of the car. Trapped on a remote country road, she is rescued by a passing motorist, a nice young writer. He, too, has seen some of the gang, so the police set them both up in a stakeout in a remote seaside house." Pub W

Gary, Romain

The dance of Genghis Cohn; [tr. from the French by Romain Gary with the assistance of Camilla Sykes]. World Pub. 1968 244p $5

"An NAL book"
Originally published in France

"The spirit of Genghis Cohn, a Jewish actor murdered in a German concentration camp, has possessed a former Nazi—now a high police official investigating a series of weird murders." McClurg. Book News

"It will help if the reader knows enough German and Yiddish to interpret some of the meaning implicit in the names of the characters and some of the expressions which a third-rate comedian of the Yiddish burlesque circuit would naturally use. . . . It is Cohn himself who tells this outrageous tale, which has some deep if not profound symbolism under its mythic skin. It is a comic novel, but the comedy is cosmic. Some may call it black comedy." Best Sellers

Lady L.; a novel. Simon & Schuster 1959 [c1958] 215p o.p. 1970

"Treated with deference by her staid family and hailed as one of England's most famous blue bloods, the still beautiful Lady L. on her eightieth birthday reveals the secrets of her past life to a puritanical and increasingly dismayed friend. A Paris prostitute after her parents' death, she entered the world of wealth and nobility when a group of anarchists selected her to camouflage their activities by playing the role of an impeccably aristocratic young matron. In love with the idealistic leader of the group, she finally betrayed him when she realized that the cause was more important to him than her love. A surprise ending is an additional fillip in a novelette told with irony, wit and sophistication." Booklist

The roots of heaven; tr. from the French by Jonathan Griffin. Simon & Schuster 1958 372p o.p. 1970

Original French edition published 1956

"To Morel, a tough, embittered Frenchman, the most important thing in he world is protecting the elephants of Africa. He believes they are necessary to him and to the world because they live for themselves alone and represent freedom. At first Morel works alone, but soon a strange assortment of people come to his aid." Huntting

"A novel that not only entertains with a suspenseful story in which the action moves across a wonderfully wide and wild and beautiful landscape in which men move and are moved in response to their inner selves rather than at the behest of their inventor; but also a novel that dares to plunge into some of the perplexities that disturb the deepest parts of our minds and hearts, that confronts us with and makes us face up to some of the most profound and important problems men ponder when they look into themselves and at the world about them and ask 'Why?'" Best Sellers

Gaskell, Elizabeth Cleghorn
Cranford

Some editions are:
Dutton (Everyman's lib) $2.95
Nelson (Nelson classics) $1.75

First published 1853

"A pleasing and pathetic story of quiet life in a secluded English village among well-bred and sheltered women of limited opportunities. Supremely typical of the literature chronicling small-community life. The original of Cranford is the peaceful village of Knutsford in Cheshire England." Pratt Alcove

Gaskin, Catherine

Edge of glass. Doubleday 1967 272p $4.95

"Maura D'Arcy, a London model, was winding up the business of her dead mother's antique shop, when a mysterious and romantic Irishman walked in and stole a glass cup, which was of historic as well as artistic importance. This curious event was to lead Maura back to a past she had never dreamed of, and to an eccentric grandmother of whose existence she had been unaware. It was to take her to a moldering Irish manor, to the acient glassworks that should have been her inheritance, to the mystery of some unexplained deaths, and to two men between whom she must choose." Pub W

Sara Dane. Lippincott 1954 448p illus o.p. 1970

"A novel set in Australia during the late 18th and the early 19th centuries. In 1792 young Sara Dane was sentenced in England on a trumped-up charge and sent to Australia. The story follows her through her struggles as she built an empire and returned to London triumphantly wealthy and prominent. This is also the story of the men who loved Sara." McClurg. Book News

Gass, William H.

In the heart of the heart of the country, and other stories. Harper 1968 206p $4.95

Analyzed in Short Story Index
Contents: The Pedersen kid; Mrs Mean; Icicles; Order of insects; In the heart of the heart of the country

"Gass is 'old-fashioned' in his insistence that language is an immediate extension of human feeling and cognition. But what makes him modern is how much he knows—like John Barth, Thomas Pynchon and Walker Percy he is one of the philosopher-novelists who bring a new intellectual power to the basically transcendental American sensibility. It is writing like this that will achieve if it is at all

Gass, William H.—*Continued*

possible, a saving continuity with traditon as it attempts to save human feeling and individuality for art." Newsweek

Omensetter's luck; a novel. New Am. Lib. 1966 304p boards $5.95

Negro "Brackett Omensetter's arrival in Gilean had a profound effect upon the town. To some his force and freedom of spirit was an encouragement. To minister Jethro Furber. Omensetter was a rival, with more power over Furber's people than the minister had. And to Doc Orcutt he was a revelation of how effective a man could be." Bk Buyer's Guide

"An unusual poeticophilosophical novel concerned with good and evil, not easily followed but richly rewarding for the patient, perceptive reader." Booklist

Gautier, Théophile

Mademoiselle de Maupin. Knopf 1920 410p o.p. 1970

First published 1835 in France; in English 1893

"The heroine of this novel, Mademoiselle de Maupin, is an adventurous girl who has disguised herself as a man in order to move about more freely and to be able to study the men she meets. For most of them she has only contempt, but she does come to respect, if not love, young d'Albert, an aesthete who is very fond of 'gold, marble and royal purple.' He sees through the disguise and falls in love with Madelaine. His mistress, deceived by the disguise, falls in love with her also. Eventually Madelaine gives herself to d'Albert for one night and then leaves him forever." Haydn. Thesaurus of Book Digests

"A free glorification of the sensuous side of love, unrestrained and even monotonous in its repetition of erotic scenes, redeemed only by the writer's devotion to the cult of beauty and by his magnificent prose, though he was not uninfluenced by the joy of flouting bourgeois philistinism." Baker's Best

Gavin, Catherine

The cactus and the crown. Doubleday 1962 472p o.p. 1970

"Historical novel set in Mexico in the days of Maximilian and Carlota. Dr. Andrew Lorimer inherits a medical practice and his sister Sally, a sugar plantation in Mexico. There Sally falls in love with Pierre Franchet, a soldier in the French Army sent to insure Maximilian's throne. Sally's love and her experiences in the turbulent time force an early maturity. Andrew's tragic love affair with a Mexican girl turns him back to his early ambitions in medicine." Booklist

"The history, which is sound, seems too obtrusive at times, but for the most part the romantic story moves rapidly, creating some suspense." Library J

Geist, Stanley

(ed.) French stories and tales. Knopf 1954 326p o.p. 1970

Analyzed in Short Story Index
Contents: Mina de Vanghel, by Stendhal; The other Diane, by H. de Balzac; Death of a hero, by C. Baudelaire; The rope, by C. Baudelaire; The red handkerchief, by A. de Gobineau; A simple heart, by G. Flaubert; Julian, by E. Zola; Monsieur Folantin, by J. K. Huysmans; The desire to be man, by V. de l'Isle-Adam; At sea, by G. de Maupassant; Minuet, by G. de Maupassant; A romance, by J. Renard; The spoiled cake, by J. Renard; Crates, by M. Schwob; Paolo Uccello, by M. Schwob; Theseus, by A. Gide

Geld, Ellen Bromfield

The garlic tree. Doubleday 1970 432p $6.95

"Annie Bancroft, New England bred and very proper, meets Jacinto Madureira, son of a Brazilian cattle rancher. She marries and goes back with him to Brazil's remote Mato Grosso. Ellen Bromfield tells the tale of that marriage. According to legend, the Garlic Tree blesses with rich beauty the land where it grows, and he who seeks out its secret truths and is unafraid

to live by them will prosper. Annie's roots go down deep; the land and her marriage succor her and become her strength. It is when the threat of the outside world—a move to force land distribution—intrudes that the idyllic life is shattered and tragedy comes." Pub W

The author "has the countryman's eye and ear for nature, for the changing of the seasons, the movement of birds in the trees, the long shadow that heralds dusk. She has the novelist's eye and ear for dialogue, or character development, for the complex interrelationships among friends and families, between masters and men." Nat R

Gellhorn, Martha

The lowest trees have tops. Dodd [1969 c1967] 215p $4.95

An "excursion into the bizarre world of a group of expatriates in a Mexican mountain village. Raquel de Castana, Spanish aristocrat and misguided good samaritan, falls in love with the local Indian silversmith, Bantolo. The residents sit back to savour this latest and astonishing affair. Susanna, the humorous and affectionate observer of it all, tells the story of this Shangri-la; a sort of place which does not exist, but for most of us is sadly far away." Am News of Bks

This "is a genial novel. . . . It shows how a bit of common sense can sort out the most farfetched muddles. . . . The novel runs along very cheerily; and within its burbling microcosm all manner of nasty problems like snobbery, prejudice and unrequited love are resolved with a sensible smile." Times (London) Lit Sup

Genêt, Jean

Funeral rites; tr. by Bernard Frechtman. Grove [1969 c1953] 256p $7.50

Original French edition, 1953

"Genet laments the tragic death of Jean Decarnin in 1944 during the street-fighting in Paris. His grief sends him into a severe depression and his mental state causes him to transfer his love from Decarnin to an unknown enemy and as the story proceeds, he becomes unable to distinguish between the two." Bk Buyer's Guide

"The novel possesses many homosexual relationships in which love and hate, life and death constantly intermingle. Although the homosexual love scenes are very explicit, there is a great deal that is lyrical and quite touching here, and the novel is almost unquestionably one of Genet's major works." Pub W

Our Lady of the Flowers; tr. by Bernard Frechtman; introduction by Jean-Paul Sartre. Grove 1963 318p $6.50

"The trial and execution of an eighteen-year-old boy called Our Lady of the Flowers is the starting point for a prison revery full of memories of homosexuals called Darling and Devine, philosophical observations, memories from the past, obscenities, bits of poetic imagination. Not the conventional novel but hailed as a masterpiece by Jean-Paul Sartre and likely to shock all but the 'avant garde.'" Bk Buyer's Guide

The thief's journal; foreword by Jean-Paul Sartre; tr. from the French by Bernard Frechtman. Grove 1964 268p $6

Published 1949 in France

It "tells of the years [from 1930 to 1940] that Genet spent among beggars, prostitutes, thieves, and homosexuals in the jails and streets of Spain, Poland, Czechoslovakia, Belgium, Yugoslavia, and France. Since Genet himself was a young beggar, male prostitute, thief, and homosexual, the book is mostly about its author, and the writing falls into two broad categories: autobiographical episodes and philosophical commentary." New Yorker

"The Thief's Journal is a good example of [Genet's] confusing and confused qualities. . . . Though there are flashes of genius in horrible vivid images and scenes, the narrative as a whole is a jumble of fragments without sequence or structure. . . . Genet does not spare us any detail in this account of his degraded past." Atlantic

Gerber, Merrill Joan

An antique man; a novel. Houghton 1967 278p $4.95

A narrative set in Los Angeles "of the relationships of a family, father, mother and two grown daughters, centered around the father's death by leukemia. . . . Abram Goldman had been an antique dealer, or junkman. His life had been spent buying and selling everything. As the father moves toward death, the younger daughter, Carol, moves toward life." Library J

"This is a painful book to read, but there is a great deal of love in it—one is left with the feeling that this is what it is really like to go through such a shattering experience." Pub W

Gerson, Noel B.

The anthem. Evans, M.&Co. 1967 512p boards $6.95

"The great historical conflicts, persecutions, intrigues, issues, and acts and the historical personalities involved through four centuries, from the time of Henry of Navarre, in the erratic march toward religious toleration and freedom are vivified and personalized in a fictitious family chronicle. Successive generations of De Montaubans, eventually on both sides of the Atlantic Ocean, are caught up in the religious struggle of their time." Booklist

Give me liberty; a novel of Patrick Henry. Doubleday 1966 347p $4.95

"The life of a great American patriot—a man whose matchless oratory literally made him the voice of rebellion against England. Until he found his true calling in the law, Patrick Henry had been a failure in the businesses his father had provided for him. By 1773, however, he was the most able and successful trial lawyer in Virginia; he then became a delegate to the Continental Congress and the first Governor of Virginia." Publisher's note

"His words still ring out of these pages today in the orotund but effective style of his time. The book can be recommended to schools, though it is probable that it will not get many readers. Time, changing styles, and other men have combined to thrust Patrick Henry into the shadows." Best Sellers

The land is bright. Doubleday 1961 356p o.p. 1970

An historical "novel about the first three years of the Plymouth Colony and William Bradford, the man responsible for its success. From his early years as a young farmer in Yorkshire . . . [the reader follows] Bradford through the years of his exile in Holland, his unhappy marriage, and the difficult days after the landing of the 'Mayflower' in Plymouth." Publisher's note

"A large bibliography is appended which testifies to the author's interest in historical accuracy, and this together with his skill as a writer has produced a novel of clarity and exciting adventure. For all libraries." Library J

Old Hickory. Doubleday 1964 372p $4.95

Andrew Jackson's three abiding passions were his hatred of the English, his love for Rachel Donelson Robards whom he married and his devotion to Tennessee. In this historical novel, the author describes both Jackson's military and political careers including his campaign against the Creeks and defeat of the British at New Orleans during the War of 1812 and election to the presidency of the United States. (Publisher)

"There is sufficient action and authentic background to hold men readers of light historical fiction, while most women will enjoy more the details of the romance and devotion between Jackson and his wife Rachel." Booklist

The slender reed; a biographical novel of James Knox Polk, eleventh President of the United States. Doubleday 1965 394p $5.95

"A lively, readable chronicle, based on original and secondary sources, of national affairs from Andrew Jackson's administration to Polk's death a few months after his single term in the White House ended. All the characters are real people and the action is concerned almost entirely with Polk's political career. Webster, Van Buren, Tyler, cabinet members, and Congressional leaders are shown in action during the crises over the annexation of Texas, the Mexican War, and the Oregon boundary dispute, with Polk portrayed as an independent, courageous politician and a President distinguished for his integrity and intellect, whose greatest accomplishment was the westward extension of U.S. territory." Booklist

"'The Slender Reed' may not be a great novel . . . but it is certainly a well written volume about a President whose name and accomplishments should be better known." Best Sellers

The Yankee from Tennessee. Doubleday 1960 382p o.p. 1970

This biographical novel dramatizes Johnson's "stormy political years climaxed by near impeachment. Here is told Johnson's remarkable climb to the Presidency, beginning as alderman of Greenville, Tennessee, rising to the position of governor of Tennessee, and winning a seat in the Twenty-Eighth Congress. Mr. Gerson . . . depicts Johnson's tenure as Lincoln's Vice-President, his ascension to the highest office upon Lincoln's assassination, and the attempted impeachment of him by a radical Republican Congress. Here, too, are recreated the early years of Johnson's life—his struggle against poverty, his self-education with the help of his patient and understanding wife, Eliza." Publisher's note

For another title by this author see Vaughan, Carter A.

Gheorghiu, C. Virgil

The twenty-fifth hour; tr. from the Romanian by Rita Eldon. Regnery [1966 c1950] 404p $6.50

First published 1949 in France

"'The twenty-fifth hour is the hour when mankind is beyond salvation.' This is the hour that Johann, a Romanian, finds himself living from the day that he is sent to a Nazi labor camp as a Jew, through the days that he is imprisoned by the Romanians, tortured by the Hungarians, sold to the Germans, and interned by the Allies." Bk Buyer's Guide

"Its plot is heavily propped with coincidence, the characters are undeveloped and its message is spelled out with 'petitions' that bring the story to repeated full stops. Gheorghiu's villain, machine-age power, is neither an original nor a persuasive one. What gives the book its impact is its assembly of evidence of man's inhumanity to man, by no means peculiar to the machine age." Time

Ghose, Zulfikar

The murder of Aziz Khan; a novel. Day [1969 c1967] 315p $6.50

First published 1967 in England

The "characters range from the unthinking Muslim cotton farmer, Aziz Khan, to the rich young Afaq [Shah], whose brothers save him from the consequences of rape and murder, and send him to live it up in England, complete with an E-type Jaguar. The plot centres on the attempts of the Shah brothers to dispossess Aziz Khan of his small cotton farm, in order that their industrial empire, which aims both to grow and manufacture cotton, shall finally control the town of Kalapur. Afaq's excesses are used to further this design." Times (London) Lit Sup

"No 'murder' of Aziz technically occurs during the novel; but the title is brutally justified by the hounding to death of Khan's two sons and wife and the final bulldozing of his land." Library J

Gibbons, Stella

Cold Comfort Farm; illus. by Charles Saxon. Dial Press 1964 254p o.p. 1970

"A Delacorte Press book"

First edition published 1932 in England

"The story of Flora Poste, an English orphan who takes it upon herself to rearrange the lives of the relatives who live at Cold Comfort Farm." Bk Buyer's Guide

Gibbons, Stella—*Continued*

"Perhaps [the book] most resembles a genial nightmare brought on by intensive reading of current fiction; for while it is first and foremost a parody of those great grim novels of life on Sussex farms, it also contains innumerable telling shots at D. H. Lawrence, Brontë biographers, novels of London's Bohemia, and the stream-of-consciousness school. You will find in it overtones of Hardy, Sheila Kaye-Smith, May Sinclair, Julian Green, V. Sackville-West, Eden Phillpotts, and the brothers Powys." Bookman

Gide, André

Nobel Prize in literature, 1947

The counterfeiters; with Journal of "The counterfeiters." The novel tr. from the French by Dorothy Bussy; the Journal tr. from the French and annotated by Justin O'Brian. Modern Lib. [1962 c1955] 432p $2.95

First published 1927

"By the term novel Gide understands a narrative work in which there exists a conflict of characters and a conflict of ideas. This is his initial material; what happens thereafter is determined not so much by the shaping hand and brain of the creator as by the volitional force which seems to be generated by those characters themselves and by those ideas themselves. . . . It is not only a desire to portray in unsentimental terms an increasingly obvious revolutionary tendency in sex morals that has led him to examine the young Olivier and his delicate lover Edouard, the vigorous heterosexual Bernard, the depraved 'raffine' Count Passavant; he is drawn to youth and to boyhood because that is the age which presents the hardest and most fruitful problems to an adult novelist." N Y Evening Post

"In an age of experimentation Gide has produced a novel which is original without being experimental, which is large without being unwieldy, and which is intellectual without being dialectic. . . . 'The Counterfeiters' restores the novel to us in all its creative freshness. It is an advance, but a logical advance, in the great tradition." N Y Times Bk R

Geneviève

In Gide, A. The school for wives, Robert, Geneviève p145-241

The immoralist; a new translation by Richard Howard. Knopf 1970 171p $5

Original French edition, 1902

"A somber psychological study of the disintegration of a man's character under the influences of illness and a tropical climate. Michel, formerly an ascetic young scholar, tells his story to his friends, explaining the change in his attitude toward life, and relating the steps of his moral degeneration." Booklist

"Gide, interested between the conflict of puritan and pagan, examines every oblique angle of human behavior, turns his clear eyes into the obscure corners of the soul. In The Immoralist, he illustrates the conflicting pulls of self-development and self-sacrifice. The moral of the story seems to be that he who loseth his life shall find it, for Michel, having found his life, does not know what to do with it. The Immoralist, like all of Gide's books, is rewarding and provocative reading." Outlook

Isabelle

In Gide, A. Two symphonies p 1-137

Lafcadio's adventures. [Les caves du Vatican] Tr. from the French of André Gide by Dorothy Bussy. Knopf 1928 278p o.p. 1970

Original French edition, 1914

"The book caricatures various types in society by means of the three brothers-in-law and their many relations who comprise its major characters. The plot concerns the confusion resulting from a swindler's scheme to extort money by falsely reporting that the pope has been kidnapped and organizing a conspiracy to liberate him. The interest of the book, however, focuses on the apparently unmotivated murder of one of the brothers by Lafcadio, a bastard relative." Benét. The Reader's Encyclopedia

The pastoral symphony

In Gide, A. Two symphonies p139-233

Robert

In Gide, A. The school for wives, Robert, Geneviève p95-143

The school for wives, Robert, Geneviève; or, The unfinished confidence. Tr. from the French by Dorothy Bussy. Knopf 1949 241p o.p. 1970

Original French editions 1929, 1930, and 1936, respectively. The school for wives was published separately in the United States in 1929

"A probing dissection of an unhappy marriage—of the conflict between love, emotion, passion on the one side and custom, tradition, morality on the other—told through the device of three stories . . . each from a different point of view. . . . 'The School for Wives' shows the wife's side. . . . 'Robert,' the husband's . . . and 'Geneviève' throws new light on the situation from the daughter's point of view." Huntting

Strait is the gate (La porte étroit) tr. from the French by Dorothy Bussy. Knopf 1924 231p $3.95

Original French edition published 1907

"Jerome Palissier and Alissa Bucolin, cousins who have known and loved each other from infancy, find the unquestioning devotion of years ripening into a love whose mysterious force leaves them embarrassed in each other's presence, each doubtful of the other's love. For Jerome, marriage seems the natural fulfilment of this new relation, but Alissa, whose love for her cousin has in it an element of religious ecstasy, dares not risk in marriage the diminution of this love which is the whole of life to her. Torn between her longing for Jerome and her determination to sacrifice her happiness in leaving him free, she only succeeds in convincing him that she does not care for him as he cares for her. Physically unable to bear the pain of their separation, her life ebbs away. After her death, a diary which she has left reveals to Jerome a love which unites them at last beyond all possibility of separation." Book Rev Digest

"Sincere, moving and haunting it is the story of a spiritual martyrdom, self-inflicted and inescapable." Literary Rev

Two symphonies [Isabelle and The pastoral symphony]. Tr. from the French by Dorothy Bussy. Knopf 1931 233p $4.95

"New edition (originally published by Knopf in 1931) reset and printed from new plates, of 'Isabelle' (1911) and 'The Pastoral Symphony' (1919)." Library J

"'Isabelle, the first of these Two Symphonies, is a mystery story. The second story, The Pastoral Symphony, is a modern version of the parable of the lost sheep, in which an elderly Protestant pastor attempts to help a destitute blind girl and succeeds only in bringing her more unhappiness." Book Rev Digest

"These are among Gide's early works, and, in this reviewer's opinion they have not been surpassed as examples of the 'récit,' that form of first-person narrative at which the French excel. They disclose Gide's style in its purity and clarity, and, as stories, they are so direct and vivid that he is a dullard indeed who, having begun to read one, can lay it aside unfinished. The stories balance each other nicely." Outlook

Gilbert, Anthony

The looking glass murder. Random House [1967 c1966] 215p boards $3.95

First published 1966 in England

"A disastrous experience ended Solange Peters' nursing career in Rome, but an airplane crash brought her a new identity as Australian Julie Taylor, and a comfortable job as companion to Bianca Duncan. When she begins to realize the mirror-like qualities of the new situation and the one in Rome, she knows she needs [Arthur] Crook's help." Library J

Gilbert, Anthony—*Continued*

Missing from her home. Random House 1969 184p boards $4.50

"One of the best Arthur Crook mysteries in some time, a well constructed and consistently interesting tale that begins with the disappearance of a 10-year-old child one rainy evening. The missing girl, who has a most formidable Italian mother hell-bent on finding her lost chick, may have been witness to a murder. Arthur Crook comes to the rescue and we encounter along the way a galaxy of muddled but well-meaning witnesses and clever evil-doers, all of whom play key roles in the case." Pub W

The visitor. Random House 1967 182p boards $4.50

"Will Arthur Crook, criminal lawyer, come to the aid of a lady in danger? This time the lady is an attractive divorcee who yields to blackmail because she fears that her young son is involved with an unsuitable woman. In the course of making the arrangements, she finds the blackmailer's body and becomes hopelessly enmeshed as a suspect." McClurg. Book News

"There is a good deal of tension, some hysteria, and considerable plausible action. Good reading, even for the jaded mystery fan." Best Sellers

Gilbert, Stephen

Ratman's notebooks. Viking [1969 c1968] 184p boards $4.95

The protagonist of this novel is an anonymous young man seeking revenge on his employer, Mr. Jones. He develops "skill in training rats to do his bidding—first in chewing through all four of Jones' tires—then on to distracting shopkeepers so that he could make off with money, leaving behind evidence, well chewed by rats. . . . The ultimate crime leaves nothing of Jones but his skull and a little hair." Library J

"Gilbert deftly entices the reader's faith from the mildly unusual to the highly improbable to the wildly outlandish and then, as so often happens with these malevolent Gothic whimsies, decays into a piously proper ending. But while it lasts, the rat ride is entertaining." Atlantic

Giles, Janice Holt

The believers. Houghton 1957 302p boards $5.95

Sequel to: Hannah Fowler
"Rebecca Fowler, daughter of Hannah Fowler followed her beloved husband Richard to a Shaker colony in Kentucky in the early 1800's. Richard became a fanatical 'Believer' but Rebecca did not. Eventually she left the colony, got her divorce, and married the man she had come to love while they were both at the Shaker colony." Book Rev Digest

"Her story, simply and skillfully told, is absorbing reading for those who are interested in off-brand religious sects and their influence on American life." N Y Times Bk R

The great adventure; a novel. Houghton 1966 370p map $4.95

"A young Kentuckian named Joe Fowler (grandson of the principal character of an earlier novel, Hannah Fowler) . . . striking out on his own as a lone trapper, arrives in Santa Fe, acquires an Indian partner (and an agreeable Indian squaw, too), joins a party headed by a mysterious, dying Frenchman, and eventually finds his way to Oregon. The man with whom he joins forces is . . . Captain Benjamin Bonneville, soldier and explorer, secretly assigned by the United States Government to pry into British activities in the Pacific Northwest. Using Bonneville's journals, Mrs. Giles vividly reconstructs his adventures, skillfully works her hero Joe Fowler into them, and, all in all, brings off in good style an episodic story certain to appeal to all who relish this kind of return to romance, responsible history and plausible melodrama." Book of the Month Club News

Hannah Fowler. Houghton 1956 312p $4.95

Hannah Moore, a young woman whose father had died while they were on their way to the Kentucky wilderness with a party of settlers, married Tice Fowler sometime after

her arrival there. This is the story of that marriage and of how Hannah and Tice withstood such vicissitudes of pioneer life as a blizzard, attacks of hungry wolves and Hannah's capture in an Indian raid. (Publisher)

"Devotees of early Americana will be fascinated with accounts of life in the Kentucky country in the days of Daniel Boone." N Y Times Bk R

Followed by: The believers

Johnny Osage. Houghton 1960 313p $4.95

"Readers of the author's earlier 'Hannah Fowler' and 'The believers' will find Johnny Fowler, Hannah's son and the brother of Rebecca, the hero of this new frontier novel. Set in Oklahoma territory during the 1820's the story tells how Johnny, a young trader who admires the Osage Indians and has accepted many of their ways, joins in their struggle against the Cherokees—and how he eventually wins the love of Judith Lowell, a missionary-teacher from Chapman's Union Mission. Solid historical background and a vivid portrayal of Indian life compensate for a somewhat hackneyed subject." Booklist

The land beyond the mountains. Houghton 1958 308p $4.95

This story of the association between Cass Cartwright and General James Wilkinson "is interwoven with the stories of the fight for Kentucky, of the settling of Cass's land grant, and of the two women he loved—Rachel, the gentle and inflexible Quakeress, and Tattie, the waif he rescued from the Philadelphia slums." Publisher's note

"An entertaining book, as well as an historically valid statement of the author's faith in the essential decency and worth of man." Sat R

Savanna. Houghton 1961 397p $5.95

This "novel of frontier life from the woman's point of view revolves about the character and activities of Hannah Fowler's granddaughter, Savanna, who learned early to depend on herself." Wis Lib Bul

"A novel of the American frontier, set in the Arkansas Territory, now the state of Oklahoma, where the author grew up. Widowed at nineteen, Savanna faced life alone, and determined to prove herself the equal of any man. In the five years that followed her lust for living brought her passion, violence, tragedy and despair." Huntting

Shady Grove; a novel. Houghton 1968 [c1967] 260p $4.95

"The setting of this novel is Broke Neck, Kentucky in the heart of the Appalachian Mountains. It centers around the daily life of the Fowler family and its patriarchal head, Sudley. 'Bible Christians,' they are against all denominations and particularly the latest minister sent by the ministerial association. The involvement of this zealous and sincere man with the Fowlers sets off a chain of farcical situations ending with his arrest in the raid of a still." Library J

This novel "achieves a humorful, unpatronizing picture of the proud, individualistic ways of a corner of Appalachia. . . . The dialog of this pleasurable piece of regional writing and regional antics catches the idiom and lilt of Appalachian dialect." Booklist

Six-horse hitch; a novel. Houghton 1969 436p $6.95

"Events and characters from American history provide the background for a novel which carries forward the saga of the Fowler family from 'The great adventure'. Joe Fowler's son, Starr, nineteen years old and a Yankee style reinsman, tells of his adventures during 10 years, beginning in 1859, when he was driving an Overland stage west from Missouri. Starr tells of his unhappy love for Bernie Buchanan and of her abduction by a Ute chieftain, Popo, whom she later marries and who, unknown to Starr, is his own half-brother. Starr concludes the eventful narrative with his witnessing of the ceremonies marking the completion of the transcontinental railroad which ended the decade of the overland stage." Booklist

The definitive book on the Overland Stage has now been written. "It is hard to believe that anyone would want or need to know more about it than appears in 'Six-Horse Hitch.'

Giles, Janice H.—*Continued*

The author has created a romantic plot to accompany it and has dwelled at some length on the Indian wars, producing a western that is interesting and undoubtedly factually accurate. . . . It reads easily and the details of stage-coaching are very well done. . . . And the story is plausible and not romanticized; it is almost a homey chronicle of someone's family. The country and its vastness is authentically described in unsentimental passages." Best Sellers

Voyage to Santa Fe. Houghton 1962 327p $5.95

Further adventures of Johnny Fowler of: Johnny Osage, entered above

"In the spring of 1823, Judith and Johnny Fowler (known as 'Johnny Osage' because of his friendship with the Osage Indians) had been married a year. Johnny had staked everything on his ability to guide a mule train over the dangerous route from the Arkansas Territory to Santa Fe. With the wagons loaded with trade goods they began the long journey which was to test and eventually strengthen their marriage." Huntting

"There is good description of the country and the daily events of the successful three months' trip that ends in a proud entry into Santa Fe. For this reader, the book was even more satisfying reading than other stories of the Fowlers." Library J

Giles, Kenneth

Death in diamonds. Simon & Schuster [1968 c1967] 224p boards $4.50

"An Inner sanctum mystery"

"A Miss Olga Hadden, a zany but nice American tourist in London, whose father is a big wheel in Washington, misplaces both her apartment and her suitcase. An unpleasant gentleman has moved in and taken over while she was out shopping. When Olga and the police (Inspector James and Sergeant Honeybody) regain the flat, they find it contains a decapitated body. A cast of English eccentrics lead into a diamond smuggling operation complete with more motives for murder than there are sparkles in a diamond." Pub W

"Only a rather bulky coincidence mars [these] . . . shenanigans, which are fairly clued and related in a saucy fashion." N Y Times Bk R

Gilford, C. B.

The crooked shamrock. Doubleday 1969 251p $5.95

In this fantasy "about Ireland ruling England, the plot is carried along by Matt O'Quinn at Boyle's bar in Ballydoon. Because of a seduction of the crown prince's governess, O'Quinn succeeds in kidnaping the future king. Whisked away to a remote bog in Ireland, the prince grows up as Kevin O'Quinn. Eighteen years later just as his real father is dying, Kevin's true identity is made known." Library J

The book demonstrates "author Gilford's considerable if not consistent comic humor and fantasy, [and is] entertaining for men, and women too." Library J

Gilliatt, Penelope

Come back if it doesn't get better. Random House 1969 212p $5.95

First published 1968 in England with title: What's it like out?

Contents: Fred and Arthur; Living on the box; Come back if it doesn't get better; Albert; Known for her frankness; The redhead; Was I asleep; The tactics of hunger; What's it like out?

This collection "is a feast; each of the [stories] strikes shockingly close to the heart of emotions and experiences so familiar yet so intensely personal that we might despair of articulating them if they were our own. . . ; All of the work here rings absolutely true." Book World

Gillott, Jacky. See Gillott, Jacqueline

Gillott, Jacqueline

Salvage. Doubleday 1969 [1968] 285p $4.95

First published 1968 in England

"Helena Peake Pascal was thirty-two when she thumbed a ride on the highway—in an emergency, she told the man who picked her up and was kind but couldn't understand her. She couldn't understand herself. So piece by piece we learn about her youth, her working for a magazine while she supported Pope, her marriage to James and the birth of her children, and her growing dissatisfaction with a life that seemed to her incomplete." Bk Buyer's Guide

Gilman, Dorothy

The amazing Mrs. Pollifax. Doubleday 1970 234p $4.95

"An adventure suspense novel featuring the popular Mrs. Emily Pollifax, whose first adventure in international espionage in 'The Unexpected Mrs. Pollifax,' was entirely accidental. This time the talented lady from New Jersey is asked by the C.I.A. to take on a new assignment in Turkey, where she is to aid in the escape of a famous double agent. And once again the irresistible Mrs. Pollifax is involved in an incredibly crazy situation in which she outwits the enemy with her own special brand of logic and wins the admiration of all around her." News of Books

The book will have "more appeal for women readers in general than for hard-core espionage buffs." Booklist

The unexpected Mrs Pollifax. Published for the Crime Club by Doubleday 1966 216p $3.95

"The wealthy Mrs. Pollifax, a widow, wanted to do something for her country, became a secret agent [for the Central Intelligence Agency] and soon had more excitement in Mexico and Albania than she had believed possible." Bk Buyer's Guide

"Mrs. Gilman steers an adroit course between comedy and melodrama, which should delight [the mature reader]." N Y Times Bk R

Gilpatric, Guy

The best of Glencannon; twenty-two stories. Dodd 1968 341p $6.95

Analyzed in Short Story Index

"Here are twenty-two adventures of Chief Engineer Glencannon and his boat, the Inchcliffe Castle. Collected from seven of the author's original volumes." Bk Buyer's Guide

Contents: Mary, Queen of Scots; The lost limerick; He might have been a Rooshan; The snyke in the grass; Cock o' the North; The Flaming Chariot; Odds and ends; Scones upon the waters; The fountain of youth; Just between shipmates; The rolling stone; Star dust and corn; Three lovesick swains of Gibraltar; The ladies of Catmeat Yard; Broilers of the sea; Hams across the sea; One good tern; Gabriel's trumpet; Captain Snooty-off-the-Yacht; The Monte Carlo Massacre; The hunting of the haggis; Monkey business at Gibraltar

The Glencannon omnibus; including Scotch and water, Half-seas over [and] Three sheets in the wind. Dodd 1938 3v in 1 o.p. 1970

Three books formerly published separately 1931; 1932; 1936 respectively, and analyzed in Short Story Index. Contains stories dealing with the humorous adventures of "Muster" Glencannon, engineer on the S.S. Inchcliffe Castle

Contents: Scotch and water: Scotch and water; Mary, Queen of Scots; The last limerick; The missing link; He might have been a Rooshan; The snyke in the grass; The bold man of Dunvegan; Cock o' the North; The Flaming Chariot; The genii of Gibraltar

Half-seas over: Ash cat; Barking dog; Crafty Jerko-Slovaks; Fountain of youth; Glasgow masher; Just between shipmates; Knavery at Naples; Loathsome Captain Skinkly; Odds and ends; Scones upon the water

Three sheets in the wind: The rolling stone; A nosegay for Mr Montgomery; Chinaman's chance; Champagne Charlie; The pearl of Panama; Star dust and corn; The toothless hag of Cadez; Three lovesick swains of Gibraltar; Mud Bottom Mulligan

Gilpatric, Guy—*Continued*

Half-seas over
  In Gilpatric, G. The Glencannon omnibus v2

Scotch and water
  In Gilpatric, G. The Glencannon omnibus v 1

Three sheets in the wind
  Gilpatric, G. The Glencannon omnibus v3

Giovannitti, Len

The prisoners of Combine D. Holt 1957 541p o.p. 1970

"A psychological drama that bares the heart and soul of six men who were shot down over Germany, and, by chance, drifted into the same six-man combine. It is the story of a disastrous attempt to escape, of the incredible hardships of winter, of the Nazi order to segregate Jewish prisoners and of Combine D's conspiracy to defy the order." Huntting

"Mr. Giovannitti's book has the ring of authenticity, written very much as though he had smuggled a tape recorder into his barracks, tuned in on the innumerable conversations of his fellow prisoners, and then edited out nearly all of the profanity." Sat R

Gipson, Fred

y Hound-dog man. Harper 1949 247p $4.95

"Chronicles the adventures of two boys on a Texas hunting trip with the carefree Blackie and his two hound dogs. Blackie wasn't married because he would rather hunt than assume any responsibilities, but several events of the hunting expedition added together ended in a wedding for Blackie. Altho told from the viewpoint of one of the boys, the novel is for adults." Book Rev Digest

"The good old theme of a boy and a dog (a one-man dog with the voice of an army bugle), tall talk and horseplay, fine feeling and clear, beautiful writing make up this book." Christian Science Monitor

y Old Yeller; drawings by Carl Burger. Harper 1956 158p illus $3.50

Also available in a large type edition $7.95
"The story of a few months in the life of a fourteen-year-old boy, Travis, who lives with his father and mother and small brother in a log cabin in the Texas hill country in the eighteen-sixties. When his father departs to drive his cattle to the market in Abilene, six hundred miles away, Travis is left in charge of the family and the farm. Old Yeller is the name of a stray dog who wanders in to help him." New Yorker

"At home in the Texas background and with deep understanding of the heart of a boy faced with decisions that lift him from the world of childhood to manhood, Mr. Gipson tells his story with a deeply moving simplicity." N Y Her Trib Books

y Savage Sam; decorations by Carl Burger. Harper 1962 214p illus $3.95

Savage Sam is the son of Old Yeller, the dog hero of the author's earlier book "Old Yeller" listed above. Set in East Texas in the 1870's, this story tells of Sam's pursuit of a band of Apaches who have seized Travis, Little Arliss, and Lisbeth. (Publisher)

"Although the story is more contrived than its predecessor and overemphasizes the savagery of the Indians, there is good regional background of East Texas during the 1870's and readers will enjoy the fast-paced, sometimes humorous adventure." Booklist

Gironella, José María

The cypresses believe in God; tr. from the Spanish by Harriet de Onís. Knopf 1955 2v (1010p) $10

First published 1953 in Spain
"The first comprehensible portrait of Spain in the years preceding the Civil War of 1936-9. This is only the first part of [an historical series]. . . . It is the story of a single middle-class family: the father a post office worker,

one son a bank employee studying law in night school, the other preparing for the priesthood; and all around them it is the story of the city of Gerona in northeastern Spain, with its business and labor problems, its political divisions, its social conflicts and its typically Spanish extremes of religious feeling." Book of the Month Club News

Followed by: One million dead

One million dead; tr. from the Spanish by Joan MacLean. Doubleday 1963 684p $7.50

Sequel to: The cypresses believe in God
This volume "embraces the entire period of the [Spanish Civil] war. The Alvear family remains in its leading role with a vast supporting cast of characters representing the heterogeneous political parties." Booklist

"The same protagonists appear as in the earlier work, although, like the nation itself, they are divided against each other. Here the canvas is so broad that the breadth and depth of familial and social relationships so well depicted in the earlier book are muted. The author's undisguised hostility toward the Republicans and his propagandizing for the Rebels colors his choice of incident and depiction of character to an inordinate degree. Still, to a marvelous degree one gets the feeling of movement, of things happening, of people living." Library J

Followed by: Peace after war

Peace after war; tr. from the Spanish by Joan MacLean. Knopf [1969 c1966] 774p $10

Sequel to: One million dead
Original Spanish edition 1966
"This is the third novel in a series which is concerned with . . . the history of a family. The first two novels, 'The Cypreses Believe in God' and 'One Million Dead' presented the events immediately preceding and including the Spanish Civil War and concentrated on the Alvear family. In the present novel the background is post-Civil War Spain but the principal subject is still the Alvear family, now together in their home city, Gerona. Actually the city is a microcosm of Spain as it attempts to function again as an integrated nation confronted with food shortages, black markets, industrial and governmental corruption, leveled cities, animosities still alive from the Civil War." Best Sellers

"The novel is long, leisurely paced, and in low key. . . . The book reads more like factual social history than creative literature and will be useful as such." Library J

Gissing, George

New Grub Street; ed. with an introduction by Bernard Bergonzi. Penguin [Hardbound ed. distributed by Smith, P.] 1968 556p $3.50

First published 1891
"Edwin Reardon, a sincere artist, is contrasted with Jasper Milvain, who is frankly basing his career on opportunistic standards. Jasper wins fame and Edwin finally dies of ill health caused by poverty and heartbreak. Writers of artistic integrity starve in garrets while the superficial eat and live well. Amy, Edwin's wife, and their son, Willie, leave him. When Amy inherits a fortune and Edwin dies, Jasper gives up his fiancée, Marian Yule, to marry Amy and her money. Harold Biffen, another struggling writer, is in love with Amy. When he finds he can neither win her nor make a living, he commits suicide. . . . The novel is a realistic picture of the effects of poverty on artistic endeavors and the easy success of the materialist and opportunist conditions which exist in every age. It is laid in London in the 1880's." Haydn. Thesaurus of Book Digests

Glanville, Brian

The Olympian. Coward-McCann 1969 287p boards $5.95

"Ike Low is Britain's new wonder miler; his coach is Sam Dee, a fascinating figure who, vain, eccentric and part devil, discovers Ike as a raw London youth and nurses him toward world championship on a vegetarian diet and a semi-mystical training program. But athlete and coach need each other as son needs father and father needs son, which means that one day (and as happens in this case) the

Glanville, Brian—*Continued*

athlete will resent his 'father' from whom his self-confidence ultimately derives and the coach will demand of his 'son' more loyalty than he can give. . . . At the Tokyo Olympics the many tensions of a tense book finally break." Book of the Month Club News

"Most novels about the athletic world have little appeal to anyone who has achieved a reasonable degree of intellectual maturity, but 'The Olympian' (the 1969 Thomas R. Coward Memorial Award novel) is an exception to that generalization. By concentrating on two major characters, Ike Low and Sam Dee, Glanville reveals some interesting aspects of the special psychology and dedication necessary to produce championship athletes." Best Sellers

Glasgow, Ellen

The collected stories of Ellen Glasgow; ed. by Richard K. Meeker. La. State Univ. Press 1963 254p $5

Analyzed in Short Story Index

Contents: Between two shores; A point in morals; The shadowy third; Thinking makes it so; Dare's gift; The past; Whispering leaves; The difference; The artless age; Jordan's end; Romance and Sally Byrd; The professional instinct

"It is valuable to have these stories back in print and especially with the editor's introduction which relates the stories to the author's life and to her major novels. Recommended for college and large public libraries." Library J

In this our life. Harcourt 1941 467p o.p. 1970

Awarded the Pulitzer Prize, 1942

"This novel is an analytical study of the feeling of kinship as it is manifested in the Timberlake family, decayed aristocrats living in a southern city. The story of how two marriages are wrecked and a great wrong done to an innocent Negro boy, is told largely as it is viewed by Asa Timberlake, sixty years of age, husband of a hypochondriac wife, father of two daughters, one utterly selfish and feminine, the other courageous and gallant but confused and unhappy." Book Rev Digest

"It is a story that deals, as Miss Glasgow's novels habitually do, with individual human relationships, for her interest has always been in the individual's reaction to life, not in the problems and conflicts of the group. Believing, as she does, that the novelist's primary concern is with character, she could not write otherwise." N Y Times Bk R

Vein of iron. Harcourt 1950 462p (Harbrace Modern classics) $2.95

First published 1935

"The Fincastle family are old Scotch Presbyterian stock who have lived for five generations in the mountain region of Virginia. An iron vein of strength and resolution in their characters has carried them through difficulties of all kinds, from the hardships of pioneering to those of the depression. The story is concerned primarily with Ada Fincastle and her love for Ralph McBride. The post-war years take the family to the city, where a few years of prosperity are followed by hard times and the familiar struggle with poverty, finally leading them back to their old home in the valley. Life brings them much trouble and sorrow, but through it all they attain a quiet happiness." Booklist

"A thoughtful, searching study of character under the stress of both immemorial and modern problems." N Y Libraries

Gloag, Julian

Our mother's house. Simon & Schuster 1963 286p boards $4.95

A macabre novel set in England. "When Mrs. Hook died, her seven children, fearing to be put in a 'home,' did not tell any adults. They buried their mother at night in the garden, built a shed over her grave, and kept her memory alive in an unhealthy ritual of which two of the oldest took advantage to terrorize the smaller ones. This is the story of their strange, secret lives." Pub W

"Julian Gloag has achieved a memorable, unsentimental portrait of seven highly individual children. He raises some speculation about the world of childhood and what happens to that world without adult supervision. He traces with amazing delicacy the intricate inter-mingling of innocence and evil. He provokes some questions about the apparent force of evil." Best Sellers

A sentence of life; a novel. Simon & Schuster 1966 380p $5.95

"A charge of murder is brought against a gentle man whose loving impulses have always been frustrated. He is an English publisher accused of murdering his secretary. He reacts first in panicky wooly-mindedness in answering police questions. Then he desperately searches his memories, making a lonely attempt at understanding himself." Pub W

The author's goal is "the dramatization in terms of a man of our time of Pilate's crime—the refusal to accept responsibility. This ethical dilemma is explored within the framework of a suspenseful murder case and taut trial scenes." Sat R

Glyn, Caroline

Don't knock the corners off. Coward-McCann [1964 c1963] 256p o.p. 1970

First published 1963 in England

"A precocious nine-year-old, whose doting parents treat her as an equal, is rudely awakened when she enters the rough-and-tumble world of the English elementary school." Pub W

"Antonia's first-person narrative, describing these schools from a child's point of view, presents a humorous, sometimes shocking picture of the English educational system. Being a determined individualist, she is bewildered and frustrated but never defeated by it. In spite of an overabundance of incidents involving childish violence and adolescent stresses, this is a refreshing, lighthearted story that will appeal to many, though not all, readers." Booklist

Godden, Jon

In the sun. Knopf 1965 236p $4.95

A Spanish villa on the Mediterranean "should have been a refuge for Janey Parrish, middle-aged Englishwoman, well-to-do after her father's and sister's deaths back in England. Instead, the villa became a place of horror when her blackmailing young nephew arrived, accused her of murdering the father and sister, and sponged off her." Pub W

A winter's tale. Knopf 1961 [c1960] 274p boards $3.95

"Jerome Holt, novelist and playwright, retreated to his house in the country where his manservant Peter and his dog Sylvie waited for him. He wanted seclusion from London's attractions so that he could finish his novel; he also was escaping a flirtation that threatened to become serious. But the girl Una followed Jerome, and the next week, when all were snowbound, was marked by passion and jealousies." Booklist

"It is beautifully subtle, sometimes ironic, sometimes deeply tender. . . . It is a crafty satire on human passion, on the urgencies and demands of the born writer, and in it there is a deep understanding of the interdependence between a dog and its humans." Chicago Sunday Tribune

Godden, Rumer

The battle of the Villa Fiorita. Viking 1963 312p boards $5

"Hugh, 14, and Caddie, 11, trek by train, ship, and bus from England to Italy to try to prevent their divorced mother's marriage to a movie director. Their invasion of the villa where the couple is enjoying a pre-marital honeymoon starts a complex conflict, intensified by the arrival of the movie director's 10-year-old daughter, Pia. Characterization is good; the setting seems very real; and the plot becomes more gripping as the narrative proceeds and the reader becomes accustomed to the author's technique of shifting tenses to mid-scene." Library J

Godden, Rumer—*Continued*

"An enjoyable novel, even if one cannot quite accept the central situation. Its plot is full of surprises, and its evocation of the Italian setting is vivid." N Y Times Bk R

Black Narcissus. Little 1939 294p o.p. 1970

A "story of a small group of Anglican nuns newly settled in a convent, formerly a general's pleasure palace, on a high ledge facing Himalayan winds and snows. How the strange pagan environment and unusual experiences affect each of the Sisters, and how a year's efforts to teach and heal the natives come to naught is related in a portrayal impressive for its beauty, poignancy and insight." Bookmark

Breakfast with the Nikolides. Viking 1964 [c1942] 291p $4.50

First published 1942 by Little

"An unusual novel, elusive in treatment, and not easy to read; it is limited in appeal to a few readers. Much of the plot is suggested only indirectly, through dreams, conversations, and memories of the past. Absorbed in his work in an Indian agricultural school, an Englishman is still estranged from his wife who has returned after years of separation. His sympathies are for Emily, the awkward, adolescent child, who is disliked by her mother. Strangely enough, it is the death of the child's dog that brings to the surface the conflicting, seething emotions of the family, the child, and the Indian natives." Booklist

A breath of air. Viking 1951 [c1950] 280p o.p. 1970

The author spins a tale "this time a 'Tempest' in modern dress. When a Scottish peer renounced his earldom on his wife's death, he took his infant daughter to a South Sea island. There they lived an idyllic life for twenty years, until a plane was forced down which carried a world-famous playwright. What happened when the beautiful daughter, who knew the world only through the carefully selected library her father had brought from civilization, met the sophisticated visitor makes an absorbing and provocative story." Literary Guild

y A candle for St Jude. Viking 1948 252p $5

"Madame Holbein is an aging dancer who now runs a ballet school in London. It is the fiftieth anniversary of Madame's debut, and there is to be a gala commemorative program in the little private theater where Madame's pupils perform. Madame's star pupil is the fiery Hilda, doomed to trouble because Madame hates her not only for being young, but especially for possessing something which she did not teach her—genius and vision. On this day when Madame is remembering her past and longing to be young again, she is more than ever resentful of Hilda in whom she sees her lost youth. Wildly jealous of Hilda, too, is Caroline, prima ballerina who expects to star in the show. And when Madame realizes that Hilda has fallen madly in love with Lion, Caroline's dancing partner, there is almost unbearable tension all around." Literary Guild

The author "has a way of making you feel the presence of her characters constantly; like the recurring themes in a piece of music, one looks for them all." N Y Times Bk R

y China Court; the hours of a country house; a novel. Viking 1961 304p boards $5

"When young Tracy returns from the United States to England to attend her beloved grandmother's funeral, the family country house, China Court, yields up its past in kaleidoscopic chapters patterned after the medieval Book of Hours." Bookmark

"All the peace that comes from uninterrupted order, from a sense of continuity and service, fills the pages of this book. This is a measure of Miss Godden's success, since she has juggled the time-sequence of the five generations who lived in China Court. . . . Yet the threads stay untangled and the reader unmuddled, his interest unflagging." Christian Science Monitor

y An episode of sparrows; a novel. Viking 1955 247p boards $5

Also available in a large type edition. $7.95

This is the story of how two London slum children made a garden from a packet of cornflower seeds dropped on the pavement and how it changed several people's lives; not only the children's, but those of Vincent the restaurant-keeper and the rich Misses Chesney who lived in the Square." (Publisher)

"It is a deft, amusing, and touching story of a London neighborhood where wealth adjoins poverty. . . . It is a novel which rests lightly on the yearnings of childhood and the dreams of the unworldly. A false touch would tip it over, but Miss Godden stays this side of sentiment and of undue irony." Sat R

Gone; a thread of stories. Viking 1968 213p boards $4.95

Analyzed in Short Story Index

A collection of the author's stories each preceded by an introduction setting it in its place in her actual life and writing

Contents: No more Indians; Down under the Thames; The little fishes; Why not live sweetly; Telling the time by the starlings; Lily and the sparrows; To Uncle, with love; Fireworks for Elspeth; You need to go upstairs; L'Élégance; Whither the swans and turtles go; Time is a stream

y The greengage summer; a novel. Viking 1958 218p $5.75

"The story tells of the summer adventures of a group of English children, in somewhat shadowed circumstances, at a second-rate hotel on the Marne, near the forest of Compiègne. . . . Their mother is taken seriously ill as they are enroute to the hotel Les Oeillets, at Vieux-Moutiers. Upon arrival, she is rushed to the hospital for a long stay. The disconcerted children are stranded at the hotel where neither the proprietress, Mademoiselle Zizi, nor her henchwoman, Mme. Corbet, want them. It is the somewhat mysterious Englishman, Eliot, apparently romantically involved with Mlle. Zizi, who takes them under his wing and casually superintends their stay." N Y Times Bk R

"There is real evil in Miss Godden's novel as well as real good: sex and theft and even murder intrude upon her dewy world as baldly as on the daily papers. But even violence she handles with consummate delicacy. If she allows a moral to creep in, it is that we lose something valuable in gaining maturity." N Y Her Trib Books

In this house of Brede. Viking 1969 376p $6.95

The author writes "about a cloistered order of English Benedictine nuns (Roman Catholic), the way of life they follow in the 20th century, the very real problems, human and spiritual, with which they must grapple, and above all, the intense inner faith that infuses everything they do. . . . Her story centers on a successful career woman in her forties who renounces the world to enter Brede monastery, and what happens to her thereafter." Pub W

"The reader gets an excellent insight into the daily life, rules, and rituals of a religious order. Miss Godden has maintained her high level of writing; as usual her characters are very much alive. Her six-page description of nature around the abbey as a year passes is a little gem that can be reread time and again. For all fiction collections for Catholic and non-Catholic readers alike." Library J

The kitchen Madonna; illus. by Carol Barker. Viking 1967 89p illus boards $3.75

"Withdrawn and living in himself, a little boy begins to communicate through his efforts to make a Ukranian housekeeper feel at home in England." Minnesota

"The humour of the characterization of nine-year-old Gregory will appeal less to his contemporaries than to those who delightedly recognize in him younger brothers and sisters. He is a sensitive withdrawn child with a disconcertingly adult understanding of situations. His mother's despair with this apparently unnatural child is amusingly real." Times (London) Lit Sup

y The river. Little 1946 176p $3.50

This story, set in India, tells of a child growing up. During a brief Indian winter, as inevitably as the river that flowed past the house of her family in Bengal, Harriet knew death, birth, cruelty, kindness, retribution, and the shadow of love

Godden, Rumer—*Continued*

"A flawless account of two children on the brink of girlhood, that must owe at least as much to the author's present power of listening as to her remembrance of her own past." Commonweal

Take three tenses; a fugue in time. Little 1945 252p o.p. 1970

"An interweaving of the lives and loves of three generations of an English family. The lease on the old house in a London square where the family had lived for ninety-nine years is about to expire. As the old general, the last inhabitant of the house, relives his own life and that of his long-dead parents, two young offshots of the family arrive, brought to England by the war. And a new life begins as the old general dies in England, shortly after the news of the death of his beloved in Italy." Book Rev Digest

Goethe, Johann Wolfgang von

Elective affinities; tr. by Elizabeth Mayer and Louise Bogan; introduction by Victor Lange. Regnery 1963 305p $5.95

First German edition 1809
This novel "concerns four people whose personalities combine and conflict, as in a chemical experiment, in curious but inevitable ways. Charlotte and Eduard are living an idyllic life on their great country estate: the Captain, an old friend of Eduard, is invited to help with the managing of the grounds; Charlotte's lovely foster-daughter, Ottilie, joins the trio as companion to her stepmother. The cross-currents of the shifting relationships among them provide the unfolding action of the story." Publisher's note

The sufferings of young Werther

Some edition are:
Norton $6. Translated by Harry Steinhauer
Ungar $4. Translated by Bayard Quincy Morgan
First published in German in 1774; in English in 1779. Variant title: The sorrows of young Werther
"Certain passages between Goethe himself and some friends and the suicide of a disappointed young man gave him the outline of a story that reflected a phase of his own emotional history. An ardent idealist falls hopelessly in love, and dies rather than face the anguish of renunciation. Written in the form of a journal (1771-2), it is an intimate and poignant study of a mind diseased and therewithal a dramatic picture of the people and the society among whom his lot was cast." Baker's Best

Wilhelm Meister's apprenticeship; tr. by Thomas Carlyle; new introduction by Franz Schoenberner; illus. by William Sharp. Heritage 1965 567p $6.95

First published 1924 in English
"The hero, the son of a well-to-do German merchant, leaves his comfortable bourgeois surroundings to roam about with a company of strolling players, whose bohemian life has great attractions for him. He falls in love with Marianne, one of the group, and the lovers have a child named Felix, but Wilhelm leaves both mother and son in a foolish mood of jealousy. He rescues Mignon, a charming elf-like Italian girl, from some abusive rope dancers, and his kindness awakens in her a passionate love that he does not return and that brings about her death. In the course of time Wilhelm becomes disillusioned with stage life and settles down into a more conventional existence. He assumes the responsibilities of a father toward young Felix and eventually marries a lady of position and becomes proprietor of an estate." University Handbook for Readers and Writers

Gogol, Nikolai

Dead souls

Some editions are:
Modern Lib. $2.95. Translated by B. G. Guerney
Oxford (World classics) $3.50. Translated from the Russian by George Reavey; with an introduction by Maurice Bowra

Published in Russia in 1842. Also published with title: Tchitchikoff's journeys
"A tale of the old days of serfdom, when the peasants were registered and counted as 'souls' and those who died between the registrations were denominated 'dead souls.' An adventurer buys up a large number of these at nominal prices, and then raises money on the certificates. This farcical proceeding gives opportunity for numerous and often bitterly satirical pictures of the Russian landowning class." Baker's Best

The overcoat, and other stories; [tr. by Constance Garnett]. Knopf 1923 262p o.p. 1970

Analyzed in Short Story Index
"The rise of the Russian realistic school of fiction is generally ascribed to the title-story of this collection, written when Gogol was in his early twenties. 'We all,' wrote Dostoevsky, 'come out from under Gogol's "Overcoat."' The overcoat belonged to Akaky Akakyevitch, a poor government clerk whom it had cost a good part of his yearly salary and untold privations to buy. He had owned it but a day when it was stolen from him, and within a few days more he had died from exposure. His ghost haunted the neighborhood that had known him and stripped overcoats from the shoulders of passers-by. That is all. But there is infinite pathos and richness of imagination in the telling." Book Rev Digest
Contents: The overcoat; The carriage; The Nevsky prospect; A madman's diary; The prisoner; The nose; The portrait

Taras Bulba, a tale of the Cossacks; tr. from the Russian by I. F. Hapgood; illus. by Zhenya Gay. Knopf 284p illus o.p. 1970

Original Russian edition 1834. First translated in 1915
"An epic in poetic prose which gives a glowing picture of the Cossack struggle with the Catholic Poles and the Mohammedan Tartars in the sixteenth century. 'It stands equally with his other volumes in the first rank in poetry, dramatic power, and truth to life' and in the portrayal of national types." Pratt Alcove

Gold, H. L.

(ed.) Galaxy Magazine. The [first]-tenth Galaxy reader

Gold, Herbert

Fathers; a novel in the form of a memoir. Random House [1967 c1966] 308p $4.95

"The story of the persecution of Jews in Czarist Russia . . . the determined flight of Mr. Gold's father to the United States when only thirteen years old, his struggle against poverty and harassment by racketeers, and his eventual success. It is also a story of the conflict between immigrant parents and first generation Americans." Library J
"His approach is tender and warmhearted and lyrical. He charms rather than probes. He etches in vignettes as he edges away from dramatics. The result is a book that is often eloquently and deeply moving, because it is constantly informed with a search for love—father love: so hard to describe, so difficult to understand, yet so impossible to live without." N Y Times Bk R

(ed.) Fiction of the fifties; a decade of American writing; stories selected and with an introduction, by Herbert Gold. Doubleday 1959 383p o.p. 1970

Analyzed in Short Story Index
Contains the following stories: Sonny's blues, by J. Baldwin; Sermon by Doctor Pep, by S. Bellow; What the cystoscope said, by A. Broyard; The prize, by R. V. Cassill; Country husband, by J. Cheever; The condor and the guests, by E. S. Connell, Jr; In a while crocodile, by W. Eastlake; Among the Dangs, by G. P. Elliott; Love and like, by H. Gold; Solitary life of man, by L. E. Litwak; Magic barrel, by B. Malamud; Artificial nigger, by F. O'Connor; Devil was the joker, by J. F. Powers; Cyclist's raid, by F. Rooney; The dancer, by H. Swados

Gold, Herbert—*Continued*

The man who was not with it. Little 1956 314p o.p. 1970

"An Atlantic Monthly Press book"
"The hero of this story of carnivals, narcotics, sexual perversion, and near patricide is with it when the story opens. He is an apprentice 'talker' or cheater of marks, and has a heroin habit. He eventually discovers that the values of the outside world—marriage, family, constructive work, in brief, normality—are more desirable than being with it. The writing is at times almost poetic and some of the author's comments on adjustment are extremely perceptive. But all in all this is a not very pleasant book about not very pleasant people." Library J

Golding, William

The inheritors. Harcourt [1962 c1955] 233p $4.95

First published 1955 in England
This novel is "an inspection of man's defenses under testing circumstances. . . . The beleaguered are the last remnants of a prehistoric tribe of mild-mannered food-gatherers . . . who live hard by an immense waterfall. They are eight in number, one of them an infant. . . . Into their innocent's life of ease and contentment . . . comes a more advanced breed of man, a tribe portaging two canoes up and around the falls. These travelers are the 'inheritors,' 'homo sapiens.' . . . Against these visitors with their relatively advanced technology, the primitive Neanderthal have neither the temperament nor the capacity for evil to endure. The book describes their extermination." N Y Times Bk R
"One is tempted to call 'The Inheritors' science-fiction in reverse, an imaginative exploration of an unknown past, more remote from us now than space travel is in our future." Best Sellers

y Lord of the Flies; introduction by E. M. Forster. Coward-McCann 1962 243p $5.95

First published 1954 in England, 1955 in the United States
It is the "story of a group of boys, evacuated from an atomic holocaust and marooned on a desert island where they try to establish something they can call civilization." Library J
"The hideous accidents that promote the reversion to savagery fill most of the book, and the reader must be left to endure them—and also to embrace them, for somehow or other they are entangled with beauty." Introduction

The pyramid. Harcourt 1967 183p $4.50

"Three episodes in the life of Oliver, who tells about his adolescent fling in the quiet village of Stillbourne [England] while he is in love with an older girl, Imogen; about his part in an operatic society in which he has a glimpse of homosexuality; and of his later memory of Miss Dawlish, 'driven frantic by her love for her married driving teacher.'" Bk Buyer's Guide
"Each episode is part of a subtle process of maturation, and each is described with unusual perception and wry humor." Pub W
"Mr. Golding's theme of love, revealed by Oliver as he applies adult perceptions to memories of his naïve youth, blends these separate recollections into a warm, funny, sad, richly symbolic and highly readable novel." Book of the Month Club News

The spire. Harcourt 1964 215p $4.50

An allegorical story "in which a vision of glory comes to the dean of a medieval cathedral. He dreams of a cathedral spire built higher than anyone has built before. Money comes from a dubious source; the work is started by swarms of worldly craftsmen; there are deaths and warnings; the church is empty because it is unsafe for services; but pride and obsession drive the dean on with the building." Pub W
"It is a stunning show, a capital performance, a fiendish disclosure of Pride in all its naked terror. Mature readers will be entranced by the sure, deep literary lines of this master stylist's carefully charting the psychological progression into the depths of Man's most destructive sin, Pride." Best Sellers
"Will appeal to the reader who appreciates the exploration of ideas rather than one who enjoys historical narrative." Wis Lib Bul

Goldsmith, Oliver

The Vicar of Wakefield

Some editions are:
Dutton (Everyman's lib) $2.95
Oxford (The World's classics) $2.25
First published 1776
"The Vicar is a lovable mixture of virtue and foible, shrewdness and simplicity, unselfishness and vanity; a blameless and pathetic figure, who is tried like Job by undeserved misfortune. He and his family, a group of simple, rustic characters, drawn with delicate touches of eccentricity, make an Arcadian picture of affectionate family concord—a picture tinged with a regretful longing that often breaks out into poetry. The idyll is rudely disturbed by the villainy of a seducer; troubles come thick and fast, but after sounding the depths of affliction all are restored to happiness and prosperity. . . . Goldsmith's style is the perfection of classical English." Baker's Best

Goncharov, Ivan

Oblomov; tr. by Natalie Duddington. Dutton 1932 517p (Everyman's lib) o.p. 1970

First published 1858
Oblomov is "a Russian landowner brought up to do nothing for himself. He, like his parents, only eats and sleeps. He barely graduates from college and cannot force himself to do any kind of work, feeling that work is too much trouble for a gentleman. His indolence results finally in his living in filth and being cheated consistently. Even love cannot stir him. Though he realizes his trouble and dubs it 'Oblomovism,' he can do nothing about it. Eventually his indolence kills him, as his doctors tell him it will." Magill. Cyclopedia of Literary Characters

Gordimer, Nadine

The lying days; a novel. Simon & Schuster 1953 340p o.p. 1970

The scene of this story is "South Africa with Helen Shaw the mine secretary's daughter reliving the first 24 years of her life. In the first person she vividly portrays her memories of her early days and at the same time points out the development of a social consciousness in a period when one accepted segregation and cruelty to South African minorities as the normal thing. This is also a love story of a sensitive person who at 24 enters the world with her eyes open to all the things she had overlooked in the past." Library J

Not for publication, and other stories. Viking 1965 248p boards $4.95

Analyzed in Short Story Index
"Poignant without bathos, sensitive without precocity, these stories of South Africa answer no questions but paint honest portraits and landscapes of a troubled country." Cincinnati
Contents: Not for publication; Son-in-law; A company of laughing faces; Through time and distance; The worst thing of all; The pet; One whole year, and even more; A chip of glass ruby; The African magician; Tenants of the last treehouse; Good climate, friendly inhabitants; Vital statistics; Something for the time being; Message in a bottle; Native country; Some Monday for sure

Occasion for loving; a novel. Viking 1963 308p boards $5

A story "about a middle-class English family living outside of Johannesburg. The husband is a lecturer in history at the university and his wife is secretary to an association of African musicians and entertainers. A Jewish musicologist, friend of the husband, and his pretty young English wife come to stay with them. . . . The young wife falls deeply in love with an African artist. This illicit and dangerous affair in time affects everyone in the household and, since they are all good people, liberal and well-intentioned, the effects are anything but simple." Harper
"The social taboos against fraternization of Negroes and whites in South Africa and the psychological tensions which result from crossing the color bar are set down in a penetrating novel." Booklist

Gordon, Caroline

(ed.) The house of fiction; an anthology of the short story with commentary by Caroline Gordon and Allen Tate. Scribner 1950 649p o.p. 1970

Analyzed in Short Story Index
Contents: A simple heart, by G. Flaubert; Young Goodman Brown, by N. Hawthorne; Benito Cereno, by H. Melville; The fall of the House of Usher, by E. A. Poe; Three deaths, by L. Tolstoy; Byézhin Meadow, by I. Turgenev; Old-world landowners, by N. Gogol; On the road, by A. Chekhov; The story of a farm girl by G. de Maupassant; The beast in the jungle, by H. James; On Greenhow Hill, by R. Kipling; The dead, by J. Joyce; The hunter Gracchus, by F. Kafka; The open boat, by S. Crane; Disorder and early sorrow, by T. Mann; The rocking-horse winner, by D. H. Lawrence; Rain, by W. S. Maugham; The sick child, by Colette; The snows of Kilimanjaro, by E. Hemingway; Haircut, by R. Lardner; Guests of the nation, by F. O'Connor; Old Mortality, by K. A. Porter; The demon lover, by E. Bowen; Spotted horses, by W. Faulkner; The bombshop, by S. O'Faolain; The guide, by A. Lytle; When the light gets green, by R. P. Warren; Why I live at the P.O., by E. Welty; Lions, harts, leaping does, by J. F. Powers; Sky line, by P. Taylor

Gordon, Gordon. See The Gordons

Gordon, Mildred. See The Gordons

Gordon, Noah

The death committee. McGraw 1969 361p $6.95

A novel about the professional and personal lives of three doctors of varied ethnic backgrounds who "take up a year's surgical residency in an old hospital in a shabby section of Boston. . . . Moving through the seasons of the year, the story line . . . [concentrates on] doctor-patient and doctor-doctor relationships. The focal point of each period of time is the meeting of the Death Committee, a monthly surgical board which gathers to judge if the deaths were warranted or occurred through errors made by the attending surgeon." Library J

This novel "could serve as a prototype for the big, fat best-seller. It is written with professional polish, peopled with shallow predictable and ultimately admirable heroes and heroines, and it portrays its milieu . . . with the meticulous attention to detail that characterizes such novels." Sat R

The rabbi. McGraw 1965 389p $5.95

A novel set in such locales as Brooklyn, Georgia, San Francisco, Philadelphia. "The author has portrayed the life of an American rabbi married to a gentile woman who is a convert to Judaism. Mr. Gordon takes them at a crisis in their marriage when the wife is suffering severe mental disturbance (touched off by her menopause) based on sorrow at her father's anger when she became converted." Pub W

"The story evolves according to a set pattern; each of its four parts opens with a contemporary scene and closes with a flashback. Thus the climactic present runs parallel with its build-up. . . . The personal contacts touch us deeply." N Y Times Bk R

It is a "picture of a modern marriage based on love and understanding (in which, however, the sensual side is not neglected) and a picture, which seems extremely truthful, of the various Reform Jewish congregations the Rabbi encounters. These features make this attractive for general collections and obviously for those with a strong Jewish readership." Library J

The Gordons

y Night before the wedding. Doubleday 1969 215p $4.95

"Gail Rogers, young, pretty, and to be married in a few days, is caught in a web of terror when she is forced by a sadistic stranger to act as a go-between in a $200,000 extortion plot. Never seeing her tormentor and constantly in fear of her life Gail, her husband-to-be, and the ultra-modern Heavy Squad of the Los Angeles Police, helplessly await instructions for the payoff. A gripping, edge-of-the-chair mystery . . . this is a welcome addition to the mystery section of any young adult collection." Library J

y Undercover cat. Doubleday 1963 180p $3.95

A mystery in which "the prime clue is brought to light by a typically independent cat, who returns from a nocturnal stroll with a flexible-banded wristwatch around his neck. The wristwatch belongs to a woman bank teller, kidnapped by bank robbers. It's a new problem for the FBI, to follow that cat and to prevail upon the uncooperative animal to lead them to the woman." Pub W

y Undercover cat prowls again. Doubleday 1966 216p $4.50

The Darn Cat Randall, a black cat belonging to the Randall family who solved a kidnapping case in "Undercover cat," is now used by the FBI to unmask a handler of stolen gems. (Publisher)

Gores, Joe

A time of predators. Random House 1969 211p boards $4.95

"Paula Halstead witnessed the attack of four young men on another man and to discourage her from identifying them she was subjected to a gang-rape that resulted in her committing suicide. Her husband, a former commando, began to hunt down her attackers and kill them one by one." Bk Buyer's Guide

"This is more than an engrossing story of a hunter and the hunted, however. It is a serious effort to probe something of the nature of man's aggressive behavior. There are no pat answers here, but some solid storytelling and mature thought." Pub W

Gorky, Maxim

A book of short stories; ed. by Avrahm Yarmolinsky and Baroness Moura Budberg. Holt 1939 403p o.p. 1970

Analyzed in Short Story Index
"Fifteen short stories, six of them here translated into English for the first time. They are arranged chronologically, and range in time from 1894-1924." Book Rev Digest
Contents: Chelkash; One autumn evening; The affair of the clasps; Creatures that once were men; Notch; Chums; Twenty-six men and a girl; Cain and Artyom; Red; Evil-doers; Birth of a man; Going home; Lullaby; The hermit; Karamora

Mother. Appleton 1907 499p o.p. 1970

"An intimate picture of the lives and work of a group of socialists in Russia, who face danger and death for the sake of their ideal, the liberation of the working people from 'the narrow dark cage' of ignorance and oppression. Until the death of her brutal husband, the mother lives in fear, 'in anxious expectation of blows.' She is described as a dazed cowed creature, beaten into a dumb acceptance of her lot. Her son Pavel begins to drink like his father and the other factory workers, but by some hidden way the 'forbidden' socialist books get to him, and change his life. When he tells his mother, his purpose to 'study and then teach others,' to help his fellow-workers to understand why life is so hard for them and to fight with them against its injustice, she is at first terrified for his safety. Gradually her mind stirs in response to his, and she grows in courage and understanding." Keller's Reader's Digest of Books

Selected short stories; with an introductory essay by Stefan Zweig. Ungar 1959 348p $5

Partially analyzed in Short Story Index
Contents: Makar Chudra; Old Izergil; Chelkash; Afloat: an Easter story; Twenty-six men and a girl; Malva; Comrade; The ninth of January; Tales of Italy; The romancer; The Mordvinian girl; A man is born; The breakup; How a song was composed; The philanderer

Gorky, Maxim—*Continued*

Through Russia; tr. by C. J. Hogarth. Dutton 1921 276p (Everyman's lib) $3.25

Analyzed in Short Story Index
Contents: The birth of a man; The icebreaker; Gubin; Nilushka; The cemetery; On a river steamer; A woman; In a mountain defile; Kalinin; The dead man

Goudge, Elizabeth

The bird in the tree. Coward-McCann 1940 339p o.p. 1970

"Like most of Miss Goudge's novels, the action centers around a charming old house and a delightful group of children, but this time the scene is New Hampshire and the time is 1938." Library J
Followed by: Pilgrim's inn

y A city of bells. Coward-McCann 1936 380p $5.95

"Jocelyn Irvin, dispirited because of a wound received in the Boer War, traveled down to the peaceful little English cathedral city of Torminster, there to visit his saintly old grandfather, Canon Fordyce. Practically forced to open a bookshop in a tiny house in the city, Jocelyn became interested in the writings of a former occupant, Ferranti, who had disappeared. In the finishing and producing of a play of Ferranti's, Jocelyn helped himself and others, especially the charming child Henrietta, Cannon Fordyce's adopted grandchild." Book Rev Digest
"A charming story, very English, told in gay style, with lovely word pictures of Torminster, with its Cathedral, cobbled streets and tiny shops." Wis Lib Bul

The Dean's watch; illus. by A. R. Whitear. Coward-McCann 1960 383p illus $6.95

Set like the author's much earlier 'A city of bells' in a mid-nineteenth-century English cathedral town, this is a richly textured, idealistic, and warmly human story of the transforming power of love. It centers on old Isaac Peabody, a simple but talented clockmaker, and Adam Ayscough, respected and feared dean of the cathedral. Through their chance meeting and subsequent friendship, Isaac discovers faith in God; the dean, overcoming his shyness and formidable appearance, wins the affection of those whom he serves; and the lives of a great many people in the city are changed." Booklist
"The stuff of this book is beautiful craftsmanship . . . and warm human affection. . . . There is comparatively little story. Thru the first half, the book rarely moves forward . . but for this reader, at least, there was a quiet, savoring of delight, every inch of the way." Chicago Sunday Tribune

Gentian Hill. Coward-McCann 1949 402p o.p. 1970

"The setting is the Devonshire coast of England in the years when a Napoleonic invasion of England was feared. The heroine is a little girl rescued from a shipwreck and adopted by a farm couple; the hero, an orphan who deserted the navy, who met and loved Stella when they were children. After the battle of Trafalgar the tangled threads of the plot are straightened out." Book Rev Digest
"The medieval legend that gave rise to the story and the still older lore of the countryside, running back through the Romans to and beyond the Saxons, give the book the mood of almost mystic innocence and childlike gayety and gravity so often associated with Miss Goudge's writing." N Y Her Trib Books

y Green Dolphin Street; a novel. Coward-McCann 1944 502p o.p. 1970

"Long romantic novel scened in the Channel Islands and New Zealand. Two beautiful, but wholly unlike sister, daughters of an Island aristocrat, fell in love with the same man. After he joined the navy the sisters waited ten years before William made his decision, and then thru a slip of the pen, he sent for the wrong sister to join him in New Zealand. Nearly forty years later, when William and his wife returned to the island, the truth came out, and the three were reconciled." Book Rev Digest

"The prize-winning novel lacks the sterner virtues of good literature, but it is tasty as a marshmallow, and practically written in Technicolor." Time

The heart of the family. Coward-McCann 1953 337p o.p. 1970

Continues the story begun in The bird in the tree (1940) and Pilgrim's inn (1948)
"Sebastian Weber, an Austrian refugee, once a famous pianist, is the mysterious character in this novel about the Eliot family. By sharing their daily lives, pervaded with a rare religious mysticism, he is purged of the hatred and despair caused by the loss of his family and years of incarceration in a concentration camp. The story is a simple one, yet the author's exquisite portrayal of children, grownups, animals, and the English countryside gives it the refreshing charm for which she is famous." Library J

Pilgrim's inn. Coward-McCann 1948 346p o.p. 1970

Published in England with title: The Herb of Grace
Continues the story of the Eliot's begun in The bird in the tree
"In all the large and charming Eliot connection, Grandmother Lucilla was easily the dominant figure. The end of the war had left nearly every one of her children and grandchildren with some problem, and Lucilla saw a way to a wholesale solution. Because of her benevolent scheming one branch of the family bought an old pilgrim's inn, and before the year was out the benign atmosphere of the place had straightened out the tangles of both the Eliots and the strangers who came under its influence." Booklist
Followed by: The heart of the family

The rosemary tree. Coward-McCann 1956 381p o.p. 1970

This novel, set in an English village "has two plots, one involving a young man who, following a prison term, is rehabilitated, and the other revolving around the household of a gentle, dreamy minister and his ex-actress wife." Pub W
"Mrs. Goudge has a real gift in evoking atmosphere and in expressing her Franciscan love of birds and nature." N Y Times Bk R

The scent of water. Coward-McCann 1963 348p boards $5.95

"A quiet novel of a woman's spiritual regeneration and rebuilding of her life in middle age. The heroine retires at age 50 to an inherited house and garden in the English countryside. With the inheritance comes a set of the private journals of the elderly cousin who once owned the property. Reading these journals and helping her neighbors in their problems, the heroine finds serene happiness and wisdom." Pub W
"Long-time admirers of this author are sure of finding the customary rural-English setting, the poetic writing, the quiet charm and nostalgia, the fairy-tale plot, the touch of enchantment and a mysticism that combine to make a glimmering weft of fantasy for the gentle shuttling of the story's pastel threads. What is unpredictable about this latest novel is its more than usually frequent flashes of human insight, its remarkable devotional eloquence, its spiritual evocations." Christian Science Monitor

y The white witch. Coward-McCann 1958 439p o.p. 1970

Set in 17th century England during the Civil Wars. "Francis Leyland, posing as an itinerant painter, is in reality a nobleman and a Royalist spy. He is befriended by a half-gypsy girl named Froniga, and a series of strange dangerous, and romantic adventures begin. Figures great and small emerge from the pages as great battles and individual skirmishes take place." Huntting

Goytisolo, Juan

Marks of identity. Tr. from the Spanish by Gregory Rabassa. Grove 1969 352p $7.95

First published 1966 in Mexico
"Through fractionated meanderings of memory ailing Alvaro now living in France looks

Goytisolo, Juan—*Continued*

back over his 25 years in and out of his Spanish homeland since revolution overtook his childhood in 1936. In run-together sentences and soliloquies, stage dialog, phrases in free association, or conventional narrative he reviews tumultuous past events, family background, amorous and other experiences, people's ready return to customary ways and outworn values after Spain's bloodbath and suffering, and his own persistent detachment." Booklist

Goytisolo's technical artistry suits his content admirably. For example, the abandonment of temporal sequence, though it makes for difficult reading, echoes random memories stimulated by pictures in an album, newspaper clippings, or maps in an atlas. All in all, a superior achievement." Library J

Graber, George Alexander. See Cordell, Alexander

Graff, Polly Anne (Colver) See Colver, Anne

Graham, John Alexander

Arthur. Harper 1969 179p $4.95

"A Joan Kahn-Harper Novel of suspense"

Arthur Silverman, perpetual graduate student at Harvard, has a chance meeting with one Charlie Hoad while photographing the sea near Gloucester. Upon returning to the same place the next week, Arthur finds Hoad with a lovely girl—obviously not his wife—who is later found dead—and decides to play detective. (Publisher)

"This deft, and slightly daft, chase through the Boston area, urban and suburban, well written and carefully plotted will be a welcome addition to any mystery collection." Library J

Graham, Stephen

(ed.) Great Russian short stories. Liveright 1960 [c1959] 1021p $6.95

Analyzed in Short Story Index
First published in England 1959
Contents: Three girdles, by V. Zhukovsky; Pistol-shot, by A. Pushkin; Postmaster, by A. Pushkin; Cloak, by N. Gogol; Night of Christmas Eve, by N. Gogol; Song of love triumphant, by I. Turgenief; Dream, by I. Turgenief; Bezhin meadow, by I. Turgenief; Death and the soldier, by A. Afanasief; Grand inquisitor, by F. Dostoievsky; Gentle spirit, by F. Dostoievsky; Father Sergius, by L. Tolstoy; Where love is, God is, by L. Tolstoy; Three hermits, by L. Tolstoy; Sentry, by N. Leskov; Archive of Countess D—, by A. Apukhine; Two hermits, by V. Solovyof; Makar's Dream, by V. Korolenko; Four days, by V. Garshin; Crimson flower, by V. Garshin; Specialist, by A. Ertel; Greedy peasant, by A. Ertel; Dushechka, by A. Chekhov; On the way, by A. Chekhov; Rothschild's fiddle, by A. Chekhov; Turandina, by F. Sologub; Herald of the beast, by F. Sologub; Adventures of a cobble-stone, by F. Sologub; Equality, by F. Sologub; Bound over, by E. Chirikof; Magician, by E. Chirikof; How Hassan lost his trousers, by V. Doroshevitch; Twenty-six and one, by M. Gorky; Creatures that once were men, by M. Gorky; Psyche, by A. Kuprin; Tempting providence, by A. Kuprin; Song and the dance, by A. Kuprin; Mechanical justice, by A. Kuprin; Never-ending spring, by I. Bunin; Sunstroke, by I. Bunin; Little angel, by L. Andreyef; Rhea Silvia, by V. Brusof; Marble bust, by V. Brusof; Without cherry blossom, by P. Romanof; His Majesty, Kneeb Piter Komondor, by B. Pilniak; Life and adventures of Matvey Pavlitchenko, by I. Babel; Old rat, by M. Zoschenko; Diphtheria, by G. Alexeyef; Unexpected meeting, by A. Okulof; "Things," by V. Kataey

Graham, Winston

Angell, Pearl and Little God. Doubleday 1970 479p $6.95

"Angell is a middle-aged solicitor, Pearl a young shop-girl, and Little God a would-be boxer and part-time chauffeur. The 46-year-old Angell, a bachelor, successful lawyer and collector of paintings and furniture, meets Pearl on a business trip to Switzerland, where she is on a skiing holiday. He is taken with her, and after a few months, they marry. Little God, as flashy and pushy as his name, has known Pearl before her marriage, and he sees to it that they meet again, with the inevitable result that Pearl betrays Angell, who plots a clever, cruel revenge." Pub W

"Graham has given us a great big glittery entertainment about life among the affluent and the would-be affluent. . . . The scene is very London: shops, theatres, restaurants, everything." New Yorker

The grove of eagles. Doubleday 1964 [c1963] 498p $6.95

First published 1963 in England
In this novel of Elizabethan times and of the Second Armada, "Maugan Killigrew, illegitimate son of John Killigrew, of Pendennis Castle [Cornwall] tells the story of his adventurous life, his service under Sir Walter Raleigh, his capture by the Spanish, and, at long last, his marriage to his boyhood sweetheart, Sue." Bk Buyer's Guide

"There are rather too many historical personages among the minor characters, but this is a convincing picture of a past not so glorious as some suppose." Times (London) Lit Sup

Night journey. Doubleday 1968 [c1966] 237p $4.95

Originally published 1941 in England
"Dr. Mencken, Austrian refugee in England, tells how he is persuaded to attend a scientific meeting in Milan to discover what he can about a new poison gas—and of his frightening adventures there. The time is 1940." Bk Buyer's Guide

"Graham has polished an early and forgotten novel . . . and I'm glad he did. Fair warning: this isn't the subtle and complex novel of character that Graham is capable of in the 1960's, but simply a straightforward spy story of World War II, quietly understated and effective. Graham has rarely touched on espionage, but he has the gifts for it." N Y Times Bk R

The walking stick. Doubleday 1967 278p $4.95

"Deborah, one leg crippled by childhood polio, always overshadowed by her unfeeling parents and popular sisters . . . succumbs to an affair with a rakish artist. . . . [She] is persuaded by her lover and his criminal friends to help them rob the elegant London auction house for which she works." Pub W

"This is a suspense novel—and, indeed, a superbly plotted variant on one of the great classic forms. But it starts out, and continues so long, in such a different manner that you must be left to discover its criminal element for yourself. What you begin with is a delicate and persuasive study of the sexual awakening of a highly intelligent girl, hitherto trapped into introversion by a withered leg. Almost a satisfactory novella in itself, this situation expands into a moving tragedy that represents one of those rare instances . . . in which formal suspense, technique and serious psychological novel reinforce each other." N Y Times Bk R

Grass, Günter

Cat and mouse; tr. by Ralph Manheim. Harcourt 1963 189p $3.95

Original German edition 1961
A novel about Mahlke, a teenager growing up in a Baltic port city during World War II who is set apart from his fellows by his huge Adam's apple. When a classmate attracts a cat to this "mouse" he launches Mahlke on his career. Mahlke becomes an excellent swimmer and athlete, and later a hero to his nation. But the symbolic cat watching him is a society of petty men and Mahlke is eventually doomed. (Publisher)

"The inventive virtuosity that marks Mr. Grass' style seems less distracting in this study than in 'The Tin Drum'. But here, too, the reader will mark an allegory for our times, but at his own risk. Mature readers will appreciate Mahlke's story and the way in which it is told." Best Sellers

Grass, Günther—*Continued*

Dog years; tr. by Ralph Manheim. Harcourt 1965 570p $6.95

Original German edition 1963
A satire on Germany "set in the 1920's to 50's. Three people narrate the story. The first [a maker of scarecrows] is Jewish; the second one is an Aryan who writes his story as love letters to his cousin; and the third is a blood brother to the first and becomes his persecutor and avenger both." Huntting
"A monumental parable on 'mass man, materialism, and transcendence' written in the richly encrusted, playful, brutal, ironic, subtle, sensitive, surrealist, erudite, unique modern baroque of the masterful creator of 'The tin drum'. . . . The cast is large; the canvas is chiefly Danzig and villages along the Vistula; and the scarecrow prevails as dominant symbol." Booklist

The tin drum; tr. from the German by Ralph Manheim. Pantheon Bks. [1963 c1962] 591p $6.95

Original German edition 1959, this translation first published 1962 in England
A novel of twentieth century Germany. The author "tells the story of that epoch as seen through the eyes of Oskar Matzerath, a dwarf who deliberately stopped growing when he was three years old and three feet tall. Yet his intellect developed normally—even faster and sharper than normal. . . . From his third year on, Oskar keeps playing on a tin drum. He becomes a virtuoso on the instrument, using it to stimulate his total recall of the past, the histories of his Kashubian ancestors and the city of Danzig, his birthplace; of the outbreak and course of World War II; the defeat; and, finally, the early years of the economic comeback known as the 'Wirtschaftswunder.' " Christian Science Monitor
"Resembling a confessional, this is the autobiography of a strange, deformed figure, embodying the essence of both innocence and evil, hovering at the edge of a world that is absurd and cruel. The myriad of recollections, the jumble of scenes from daily life, and the patches of heightened emotion are molded by varied techniques into a frightening study of modern society made meaningless by the loneliness of its members. In language, description, symbol, and poetic beauty, this is a modern Pilgrim's Progress; a grim, fascinating, depressing, beautiful book." Library J

Grau, Shirley Ann

The black prince, and other stories. Knopf 1955 [c1954] 293p boards $4.95

Analyzed in Short Story Index
Nine stories, mainly of Negro life in Louisiana
Contents: White girl, fine girl: The black prince; Miss Yellow Eyes; The girl with the flaxen hair; The bright day; Fever flower; The way of a man; One summer; Joshua

The hard blue sky. Knopf 1958 466p $5.95

"One hot, eventful summer on the Isle aux Chiens, a small, wind-swept island off the Louisiana coast, describing the joys and problems of its backward, in-bred inhabitants who have no illusions about the hazards of life or fortune." Chicago
This "is a book rich in incidents, many of them superbly told, and with a multiplicity of characters, all of them firmly drawn. But above all else we have the sense of the community, as it carries on its usual tasks, as it faces the various crisis that are the book's themes, and as it braces itself for the annual ordeal of the hurricane season." Sat R

The keepers of the house. Knopf 1964 309p $5.95

Pulitzer Prize, 1965
In this novel, set in the deep South, "Will Howland, a widower, meets a young Negro who becomes his housekeeper and mistress and bears him children. Years later, Abigail, his only white granddaughter, who has grown up in this mixed-blooded family, marries a segregationist politician, and the Howland past is exposed. The brutal response of the bigoted white community and Abigail's devasting reprisal provide a . . . climax." Publisher's note

"Though the book is permeated with the two primary southern concerns, blood and birth, there isn't the least portrayal of sex. The author seems to be telling the story of not just one southern family; she seems to be telling the story of the South." Best Sellers
"A novel of considerable dramatic force. Miss Grau makes her point—the absurdities as well as the cruelties to which prejudice leads—sharply enough, but this is a story, not a tract." Sat R

Graves, Robert

Claudius, the god and his wife Messalina. . . . Smith, H. 1935 583p illus map o.p. 1970

Sequel to: I, Claudius
"The troublesome reign of Tiberius Claudius Caesar, Emperor of the Romans (born B.C. 10, died A.D. 54) as described by himself; also his murder at the hands of the notorious Agrippina (mother of the Emperor Nero) and his subsequent deification, as described by others." Subtitle
"A vivid picture of profligate Rome during the years in which Claudius conquered Britain and instituted many reforms at home. A story complete in itself, though a continuation of 'I, Claudius.' " Booklist

Collected short stories. Doubleday 1964 323p o.p. 1970

Analyzed in Short Story Index
"These stories are arranged under three main headings: English Stories; Roman Stories; and Majorcan Stories. According to Mr. Graves, 'Most of them, including the more improbable ones, are true, though occasional names and references have been changed." Huntting
Contents: The shout; Old Papa Johnson; Treacle tart; The full length; Earth to earth; Period piece; Week-end at Cwm Tatws; He went out to buy a rhine; Kill them! Kill them; The French thing; A man may not marry his; An appointment for Candlemas; The abominable Mr Gunn; Harold Vesey at the gates of Hell; Christmas truce; You win, Houdini; Epics are out of fashion; The apartment house; The Myconian; They say . . . they say; 6 valiant bulls 6; A bicycle in Majorca; The five godfathers; Evidence of affluence; God grant your honour many years; The Viscountess and the short-haired girl; A toast to Ava Gardner; The lost Chinese; She landed yesterday; The Whitaker Negroes
"For the sophisticated palate." Booklist

Hercules, my shipmate; a novel. Creative Age 1945 464p maps o.p. 1970

"Hinging on the famous voyage of the Argo by Jason and his heroic comrades in their pursuit of the Golden Fleece, the novel widens to embrace the household gossip of all Greece at a time when gods and humans were neighbors, the humans creating the gods in their own image." Literary Guild

I, Claudius; from the autobiography of Tiberius Claudius, born B.C. 10, murdered and deified A.D. 54. Modern Lib. 427p o.p. 1970

First published 1934 by Smith & Haas
"This realistic story purports to be the famous lost autobiography of Emperor Claudius, the historian. The background—imperial Rome, with its political conspiracy murderous citizens, superstitions, bestial orgies, and incest—is vividly pictured. The most fascinating figure is Livia, grandmother of Claudius, whose passion for power is unbounded. The author sustains his illusion so well that this work of imagination has the effect of history. It is full of drama and excitement." Booklist
Followed by: Claudius, the god and his wife Messalina

Gray, Elizabeth Janet. *See* Vining, Elizabeth Gray

Green, Gerald

The last angry man; a novel. Scribner 1957 [c1956] 494p boards $5.95

First published 1956 in England
"The last angry man was a Brooklyn doctor, who for forty years had lived in the slums, angry at all injustice, carrying on his profession

Green, Gerald—*Continued*

as a general practitioner, believing in medical ethics and living up to his beliefs. A TV studio decided to do the story of his life for a new program, and in the process of setting up the program the story of the life and death of Dr Samuel Abelman is told." Book Rev Digest

"The story of the advertising executive is knowledgeable and brightly written, but it proves less than Mr. Green thinks it does. . . . Dr. Abelman's story is considerably better. We get it in large chunks, and it is quite a tale, not altogether fresh to be sure but solid and credible." N Y Times Bk R

To Brooklyn with love. Trident Press [1968 c1967] 305p $5.95

Albert Abrams "takes his suburban children to show them Longview Avenue, the Brownsville street in Brooklyn where he grew up. . . . The main body of the novel is a throwback to Albert's youth [during the depression]; his love of the street and his love-hate relationship with his friends, the Raiders, who bully him because he gets 100s in school, wears glasses, and has weak ankles; his despair over his parents who overprotect him for the same reasons, and over his doctor-father's poverty and rages, his mother's too-fancy manners and diction." Harper

"A sad and yet hopeful novel of yesterday's and today's cities." Library J

Green, Hannah

y I never promised you a rose garden; a novel. Holt 1964 300p $4.95

"The 16-year-old girl who is ill, Deborah, is sick of rebelling against the lies she hears, the hatred she feels, and, at a summer camp, the anti-Semitism she suffers. She is schizophrenic: she has invented for herself a mythical kingdom into which she retreats and only when her parents reluctantly commit her to an asylum does she begin with difficulty to face reality." Pub W

"The hospital world and Deborah's fantasy world are strikingly portrayed, as is the girl's violent struggle between sickness and health, a struggle given added poignancy by youth, wit, and courage. 'I never promised you a rose garden,' she is told. 'I never promised you perfect justice. . . . The only reality I offer is challenge'; and those are the terms Deborah finally accepts." Library J

Green, Henry

Loving; a novel. Dufour 229p $3.95

A reissue of the title first published 1945 in England by Hogarth

"Psychologically sound portrayal of the lives and loves of servants in a wealthy woman's Irish castle during World War II. Style often poetic, is always interesting except for occasional lack of punctuation. Keen sense of drama and astute craftsmanship." Library J

"The novel consists almost entirely of trivial incident and dialogue—incomparable dialogue; into them Mr Green packs all of the magic by which art enlarges our experience, wrests new truths from the familiar." Atlantic

Greenan, Russell H.

It happened in Boston? Random House [1969 c1968] 273p $5.95

Against authentic Boston background, the author "spins a spellbinding tale involving the art world, madness, murder, and, just 'possibly,' the supernatural. . . . The story concerns three painters, friends since art school days, whose lives remain strangely interwoven, and what happens when one of them begins to go mad." Pub W

"Murder and immortality mingle in this powerful, occasionally black comedy about a gifted artist's deception and his search for a god to remedy his betrayal. The book's power lies in the fact that as the deceived artist begins to go mad, the reader begins to go mad with him, until both have reached the point of no return. In this exceptional story there is hatred and love, savagery and kindness, genius and stupidity, greed and betrayal." Am News of Bks

Greenbaum, Leonard

Out of shape. Harper 1969 247p illus boards $5.95

"A Joan Kahn-Harper Novel of suspense"

This suspense novel "records strange extra-curricular activity at Milton University in Michigan where the body of Rudolph Reichert, an unpopular English professor, is found in his office, the face shot away by a gun blast. When Tommy Larkin, Reichert's graduate student assistant, tells Lieutenant Gold of the local police force that he had a phone call from the professor an hour after the shooting, they work together on a search through Reichert's past to find some answers, and the deeper they delve the more terror they uncover. . . . It is a tense, complicated tale lit by concern for the state of the world. For discriminating readers." Library J

Greenberg, Eliezer

(jt. ed.) A treasury of Yiddish stories

Greenberg, Joanne

The Monday voices; a novel. Holt 1965 286p $4.95

"The day-to-day routine of Ralph Oakland, a dedicated social worker who specializes in cases of the physically handicapped and mentally deficent at the Department of Rehabilitation is the subject of this novel." McClurg. Book News

"For those who want sociological fiction, this should be useful in large public library collections and for students in the scholls of the various 'helping' professions." Library J

Greene, Graham

A burnt-out case. Viking 1961 [c1960] 248p $3.95

"Altho 'A Burnt-Out Case' is set in an African leprosarium, run by priests, nuns, and an atheist doctor, its subject is not physical but spiritual disease. Its central character is a world famous architect named Querry, who, having gone thru a wife and a long succession of mistresses, flees the glory of the wide world to retire among the lepers. . . . He is, of course, the 'burntout case'—the man in whom Greene suggests that sin must run its mutilating course until a cure may come, requiring later therapy. . . . World weary, he is rediscovered by the world, and called a saint, because he is exercising his craft to build some modest better facilities for the lepers." Chicago Sunday Tribune

"To be converted to any dogma, as Greene was converted to Catholicism . . . can mean the end of creativity. If you have all the answers, there is nothing to do but to exhort the infidels. Greene, however, in novel after novel, has seemed to be testing his faith by applying it to a series of extreme situations. Thus he has maintained the kind of tension that gives birth to literature. . . . The conflict between faith and doubt is moving because Greene knows so well the difficulties of faith and feels so deeply the agonies of doubt." Sat R

The comedians. Viking 1966 309p boards $5.75

Also available in a large type edition for $8.95

This "book concerns a back-slidden Catholic, a native of Monaco and owner of a run-down tourist hotel in Haiti; his affair with the German wife of a Latin American ambassador; and his involvement with a rascally British con man and an American Presidential candidate and his wife, in Haiti to propagate the cult of vegetarianism—most of them in varying degrees comedians on the stage of life, running a bluff, playing a role, substituting sham for sincerity. And there are the native Haitians, enduring or rebelling against the brutal dictatorship of 'Papa Doc' and his secret police, the dreaded, Tontons Macoute, or bogey-men." Library J

"If we look closer at . . . the familiar goings-on, there is something new; a humility and perseverance, a magnanimity and fortitude . . . [which the characters] show in accepting, with sad good humour, their miserable destiny. A stronger current of optimism runs

Greene, Graham—*Continued*

through the book. . . . Mr. Greene has made golden atonement for the bitter ferocity of his jokes about the other, younger, quiet American. . . . [He] has shaken off the pessimist shadow of Conrad for good and all. . . . There are, too, . . . the characteristic virtues. . . . The comedians are not only strolling players, in the French sense of the word; they are also very, very funny." Times (London) Lit Sup

The confidential agent

In Greene, G. 3: This gun for hire, The confidential agent, The ministry of fear v2

The end of the affair. Viking 1951 240p $4

"The story of a love affair in wartime England and of a woman's reluctant turning to religion is told with the air of suspense of a mystery story. The narrator describes rather bitterly his passionate affair with a beautiful married woman and the puzzling break after a bombing in which he is almost killed. Much later he learns why she left him and how she turned to God." Booklist

"An absorbing piece of work, passionately felt and stirringly written. There are exceedingly few novelists who can match Greene's superb command of language, mood, and suspense." Atlantic

The heart of the matter. Viking 1948 306p $3.95

The corruption of one man in a group of civil servants and natives in a West African colony is the subject of this novel. Scobie, an assistant police commissioner, had maintained his position with integrity for fifteen years. His intense pity for his wife led him to borrow money to send her on a trip. Dring her absence he fell in love with a young widow. The discovery of his indiscretions by a blackmailer and the sudden return of his wife led Scobie to take the only way out compatible with his conscience." Onatario Lib Rev

"The white (and dark) man's burden must always be heavy. And man's debt to man will be forever in arrears—from West Africa to the West End, from Brooklyn to Bucharest. Generations of novelists have wrestled with these melancholy truisms. It is a pleasure to report that Graham Greene, in 'The Heart of the Matter,' has wrestled brilliantly with all three—and scored three clean falls." N Y Times Bk R

The ministry of fear; an entertainment. Viking 1943 239p o.p. 1970

"Sinister story of espionage in England during the early stages of the [Second World] war. The hero is a middle-aged man haunted by the knowledge that he has murdered his wife to keep her from suffering. He falls into the clutches of a band of fifth columnists, and there follows a series of incidents—half way between horror and insanity, before he escapes." Book Rev Digest

"Sensitive and mystifying story, unusual for its artistic style and polish. Public library readers who enjoy macabre and psychological approach to crime and murder will be pleased with Poe-like atmosphere created here." Library J

also in Greene, G. 3: This gun for hire, The confidential agent, The ministry of fear v3

Our man in Havana; an entertainment. Viking 1958 247p o.p. 1970

A "spy adventure story about an impecunious Englishman who accepts a job as a secret agent with no intention of actually doing the job. When the reports that he makes up suddenly begin to come true, he is precipitated into ugly intrigue." Pub W

"A cold, thin, generally fascinating story. . . . The end, which takes place in London, is in keeping with the plot, which is ironic, fantastic, and, in Mr. Greene's talented and contemptuous hands, plausible." New Yorker

The power and the glory. Viking 1946 301p $4.50

Also available in a large type edition at $8.50

First published 1940 with title: The labyrinthine ways

"A man fleeing for his life, a Mexican Catholic priest, is the central character. Profoundly religious, yet too weak to resist whiskey, the priest alternately runs from the military authorities, and risks his life to bring the comfort of the church to the fearful, browbeaten Mexican peasants." Book Rev Digest

"I have never been in Mexico, but the atmosphere and detail of this book are convincing. So are the variegated people. So are the squalor and the heat and the venality of man, the sloth and the violence . . . he [Greene] has now proved himself one of the finest craftsmen of story-telling in our time." Sat R

The quiet American

Some editions are:
Modern Lib $2.95
Viking $4.50

First published in England 1955

The scene is Saigon. The principal characters are a skeptical British journalist, his attractive Vietnamese mistress, and an eager young American sent out by Washington on a mysterious mission. Local intrigue, a night in a beleaguered outpost, a perilous venture behind the Communist lines are the main ingredients of the story. (Publisher)

"Mr. Greene has always been a master of suspense, and the particular excellence of 'The Quiet American' lies in the way in which he builds up the situation finally to explode the moral problem which for him lies at the heart of the matter." Times (London) Lit Sup

The third man. Viking 1950 157p o.p. 1970

"A master hand at suspense and tension. Mr. Greene spins his web in postwar Vienna where a search for a man said to have witnessed the death of a friend ends in a harrowing chase through the sewers." Cincinnati

"The atmosphere of the book, like that of the movie, is one of high suspense and fast action, against a realistic background of postwar Vienna with its occupation zones, its military police, its racketeers, its hotels and cafés." Huntting

This gun for hire

In Greene, G. 3: This gun for hire, The confidential agent, The ministry of fear v 1

3: This gun for hire, The confidential agent, The ministry of fear. Viking 1952 3v in 1 $5.95

A one-volume edition of three suspense stories, the last of which is entered separately. The titles were first published 1936; 1939 and 1943, respectively

Travels with my aunt; a novel. Viking 1969 244p boards $5.95

SBN 670-72524-2

"The plot, which is exuberantly melodramatic, has to do with a stuffy, middle-aged retired London banker, taken in hand by his lively 'Aunt Augusta' (a more lubricious sister of 'Auntie Mame') and whirled away to a life of crime and great good fun that takes him from Turkey to Paraguay and involves a wild cast of characters, from a dope-peddling West African to an American girl hippie whose father is with the CIA." Pub W

21 stories. Viking 1962 245p $4

Analyzed in Short Story Index

First published with title: Nineteen stories. This 1962 collection adds "three stories published in book form in the U.S. for the first time. The story from the earlier collection omitted here is 'Other side of the border.' " Booklist

Contents: The basement room; The end of the party; I spy; The innocent; A drive in the country; Across the bridge; Jubilee; Brother; Proof positive; A chance for Mr Lever; The hint of an explanation; The second death; A day saved; A little place off the Edgware Road; The case for the defence; When Greek meets Greek; Men at work; Alas, poor Maling; The blue film; Special duties; The destructors

Greenlee, Sam

The spook who sat by the door; a novel. Richard W. Baron Pub. Co. 1969 248p $4.95

"It is the story of Dan Freeman, a black James Bond but much more believable, an ex-gang leader who lets the CIA teach him everything it knows about judo, guns, women, and strategy. With the single-mindedness of man who has outgrown despair, he turns his knowledge into an arsenal for subversion on a staggering scale. He organizes the gangs of Chicago into a crack guerrilla force, sends his lieutenants out to train the fighting gangs of every other ghetto city in the country, and turns snipers into marksmen, rioters into combat troops." Publisher's note

"Greenlee successfully portrays the authentic voice of the ghetto activist through his protagonist and will arouse sympathy and recognition in the concerned readers to whom he directs his novel." Booklist

Grey, Zane

The Arizona clan
Some edition are:
Grosset $2.50
Watts, F. $7.95 Large type edition. A Keith Jennison book
First published 1958 by Harper
In the Tonto Basin, land of feuds and Arizona, "white mule," Dodge Mercer meets Nan Lilley, lovely daughter of old Rock, head of the Lilley clan. Dodge learns that much of the sorghum is being stolen at night. He solves the mystery but it is a solution that almost costs him his life. (Publisher)

Riders of the purple sage; a novel; illus. by Douglas Duer. Grosset 334p illus $2.50

First published 1913 by Harper
"Well handled melodramatic story of hairbreadth escapes from Mormon vengeance in southwestern Utah in 1871." Booklist

The vanishing American. Grosset 308p $2.50

First published 1925 by Harper
"A young Nopah Indian, stolen from his tribe and educated in an eastern college where he distinguishes himself both in studies and in athletics, returns to help his people. His romance with the girl who comes from the East to share his struggles is set against a background which reflects the tragedy of the Indian people, despoiled by government agent and missionary." Pittsburgh

Griffin, Gwyn

A last lamp burning; a novel. Putnam [1966 c1965] 512p boards $6.95

Property owner Ercole Sanbrenedetto's death sets in motion this story "about postwar Neapolitan poor people, middle class, 'nouveaux riches,' and degenerate nobility. A slum boy is the book's hero—a part-Italian, part-Chinese boy, clever, quick, and resourceful. . . . What happens to the people is tragic, pathetic, too much for them to bear in several cases." Pub W

This "is a strong novel with a complicated but clear plot. . . . [I] recommend it strongly to readers who are prepared to take it for what it is—a rather melodramatic tale about a highly melodramatic society. . . . [The author] shows us the men and women of the corrupt old aristocracy, the brutal Communist-led mob, the humble emotional artisans; he ties them together in a story of Dickensian intricacy, and, although to us they sometimes seem both irresponsible and irrational, he makes their destinies as real as though we ourselves shared them." Book of the Month Club News

Master of this vessel. Holt 1961 398p o.p. 1970

"A young ship's officer suddenly finds himself in the role of Acting Captain, and, in the midst of a hurricane, is forced to fight both the elements and a hostile ship's company. Among the characters are a group of migrant laborers, a predatory female, a British submarine commander, and the ship's first officer who lets his hate for the 'Captain' smother his nautical judgment." Huntting

"Mr. Griffin has a sharp eye for the phony and his characters, as drab as most of them are, do ring true. Moreover, the characterization of Serafino Ciccolanti, the overburdened young ship's master with the lame foot, is extremely well done." Library J

The occupying power. Putnam 1968 318p $6.95

First published 1956 in England
"In August, 1940, the British take over the Italian colony on the Mediterranean island of Baressa and Major Euan Lemonfield becomes the first British governor. Determined to raise standards of living and stamp out corruption Lemonfield embarks on a career of benevolent dictatorship in which he revels unhindered until the chance arrival of a British general in 1945 sets off a series of events that culminate in tragedy and the expulsion of the British occupiers." Booklist

"The story ridicules the conquest by the English authorities, the subtle ways in which they are seduced or opposed by their Italian captives, and how they are finally ejected; in short, this is a comic opera book about the war, and a good one." Atlantic

An operational necessity. Putnam 1967 477p $6.95

"After torpedoing an unarmed freighter, the captain of a U-boat ordered all survivors destroyed. Technically described as 'an operational necessity,' the act and its moral issues, as well as the captain, go on trial at the end of the war." Cincinnati

"The skill with which the author depicts the alternating hope and despair in [an] open raft under the blazing sun reminds me of that long torture which [Charles] Nordhoff and [J. N.] Hall wrote about in Men Against the Sea. Episodically, [this novel] is a brilliant performance. But there is one serious drawback in a book with as many people and as many casualties as this: one looks in vain for a central character in whom one can repose one's sympathies." Atlantic

Grubb, Davis

y Fools' parade. World Pub. 1969 306p boards $6.95

"An NAL book"
"When three convicts are released from Glory Prison on an April day in 1935, they provoke more than casual interest among the townspeople of Glory, West Virginia, for one of them, Mattie Appleyard, who had served 47 years on a double murder charge, is being released with a check for $25,452.32 which represents his honest savings plus interest accumulated over the years. Mattie and his old friend, Lee Cottrill, plan to open a general store in a small town downstate. . . . But their plans to 'go straight' are disrupted by a trio of 'respectable' citizens: a vengeful prison guard, a jealous banker, and a malicious sheriff who conspire with a couple of professional killers to wipe out the trio at a railroad station." Best Sellers

"The extraordinary thing about [Grubb's] old-fashioned romance is that he makes it fairly believable, consistently engaging and entertaining. . . . It's human interest—how men become what they are, how they look, what they do under stress, what they want—that holds one to his story." N Y Times Bk R

The night of the hunter. Harper 1953 273p o.p. 1970

"Ben Harper hangs for murder but the ten thousand dollars he has stolen remains safely hidden, with only his young children knowing its whereabouts. When the Preacher appears, masquerading in his evil behind a religious guise, only Ben's little boy recognizes him for what he is and fights to keep the secret his father bequeathed to him.' Pub W

"The almost unbearable suspense occasioned by the boy's increasing and well-founded terror is relieved by the author's deft characterization and poetic handling of the tragic atmosphere, as well as by a satisfactory ending to John's nightmarish experience." Booklist

Grubb, Davis—*Continued*

Shadow of my brother. Holt 1966 317p $5.95

"Two young people necking in a car on a country road witness a lynching, three white men killing a Negro. The sight is horrible enough in itself, but made even more horrible because one of the murderers is the father of the girl in the car. The couple's fear and indecision are counterpointed by a tracing of the father's early life and his sick hatred for Negroes. A like hatred, the novelist shows, runs through the community." Pub W

This "masterful narrative of crime without punishment in a small Southern town illuminates the monumental good as well as the monumental evil in the nature of man." Am News of Bks

Gruber, Frank

The Etruscan bull. Dutton 1969 191p $4.50

"Detective Logan is persuaded by Dominick Porsena, an Army buddy, to go to Italy and collect an inheritance. He is to carry an Etruscan statuette as identification and soon learns that his friend Dominick's estate is coveted by people ready to kill to get it." Bk Buyer's Guide

"There are too many coincidences, and too involved personal relations, but the final scenes at a dig in Tuscany are physically and mentally exciting enough to make up for them." Library J

Guareschi, Giovanni

y Comrade Don Camillo; tr. by Frances Frenaye. Farrar, Straus 1964 212p illus boards $3.95

First published 1963 in Italy

Peppone, the Communist mayor of the town, persuades his constant adversary, the Parish priest, to deposit sweepstake winnings for him secretly. However, the mayor continues his anti-clerical statements. The priest retaliates once more by threatening to disclose Peppone's secret unless the mayor permits Don Camillo to join a group of Party members on a trip to Russia. The wily priest sets off with his prayer book bound in a cover stamped: Maxims of Lenin. (Publisher)

"The fifth volume of the Don Camillo series is, as the author remarks in a rather bitter little note, already a period piece. . . . It may be guessed that Mr. Guareschi's good nature as a writer is wearing rather thin, and so in fact it proves in the book itself. . . . This time [Don Camillo] is not permitted by the author to undergo even the smallest setback; Peppone, a shadow of his former self, can hardly manage to do anything except wring his hands on the sidelines while Camillo undermines one after another of the travelers. . . . This may be all very well as propaganda, but lacks much of the rich humanity and comic zest of the earlier books." Times (London) Lit Sup

y Don Camillo and his flock; tr. by Frances Frenaye. Pellegrini & Cudahy 1952 250p o.p. 1970

"More episodes in the lives of the Italian priest Don Camillo and his adversary the Communist Mayor Peppone. A companion volume to: The Little World of Don Camillo." Book Rev Digest

The stories "are what good hot weather stories should be. Unsubtle: no sophisticated, involved arguments, but good, solid kicks in the pants; no wailing, spiraling monologues, but curt, direct." Sat R

Don Camillo meets the flower children; tr. by L. K. Conrad. Farrar, Straus 1969 247p illus $5.95

Further "episodes in the lives of Don Camillo and his arch enemy, the Communist mayor, Peppone. Here are Peppone's long-haired son called Venom, whose motorcycle proves to be his Delilah; Flora, Don Camillo's Flower Child niece; Don Chichi, the assistant to demonstrate to Don Camillo that it was 1969 not 1669; and the leaders of the La Rocca Maoist cell, Dr. Bognoni and his wife." Bk Buyer's Guide

"He writes with affectionate humor colored by a mild satire. Because he does, many readers are likely to make the mistake Peppone makes—just how seriously can one take an 'old parish priest' who debates the crucified Christ?" America

Don Camillo takes the Devil by the tail; tr. by Frances Frenaye. Farrar, Straus 1957 218p illus o.p. 1970

"The amusing rivalry of the hulking parish priest, Don Camille, and his first opponent and friend, the communist mayor, Peppone continued in 23 more episodes, beginning with the rescue of the atrocious statue of forgotten Saint Babila from the river depths where the Don had dumped it one night, and ending with what may well be Peppone's final disillusionment with communism as a result of the Hungarian tragedy of November, 1956." Best Sellers

Don Camillo's dilemma; tr. from the Italian by Frances Frenaye. Farrar, Straus 1954 255p o.p. 1970

"The third series of anecdotes about the priest Don Camillo, his friend Peppone, the Communist mayor, and other inhabitants of a village in the Po River valley. Again the characters are drawn with compassionate understanding and humor, and the series maintains its freshness and interest." Booklist

y The little world of Don Camillo; tr. from the Italian by Una Vincenzo Troubridge. Pellegrini & Cudahy 1950 205p illus $3

In post-war Italy, in the Po Valley, there is a small country village that is a stronghold of Communism. The head of the local unit is Peppone, the Mayor. His favorite adversary is Don Camillo, the parish priest, and vice versa. Peppone cannot be a thorough-going Communist because he is a man of conscience. Don Camillo cannot be a thorough-going Christian because he is all too human. Out of this situation the author has woven a series of anecdotes." Rel Bk Club Bul

"Giovanni Guareschi has performed a rather remarkable feat. He has managed to write a delightfully humorous book with a warm, human and tolerant pen, about some of the main issues in the struggle that confronts the world today—Christian principles as opposed to Communist-totalitarian dogmas." N Y Times Bk R

Guimarães, Rosa João. See Rosa, João Guimarães

Gulbranssen, Trygve

Beyond sing the woods; tr. by Naomi Walford. Putnam 1936 313p $5.75

"Chronicle of fifty years in a Norwegian family living on their huge estate in the hills. The Björndal bred strong men, but they came to tragic ends until one of them, Dag, married a wife from the fertile valley lands, and spent his energies in piling up wealth for himself and his descendants. The tale ends with the engagement of the remaining son of Old Dag, and a beautiful girl from the town." Book Rev Digest

Followed by: The wind from the mountains

The wind from the mountains. Putnam 1937 412p o.p. 1970

Sequel to: Beyond sing the woods

"This book takes up the story in 1809, with the marriage of Adelaide Barr to Young Dag. Altho she loved Young Dag, it was to his staunch father that Adelaide looked for strength and understanding, thus creating a psychological tangle which was not straightened out until the death of Old Dag. Thruout the years she grew more lenient with others, and when a tragic death claimed her husband, Adelaide stepped naturally into the role of head of the house of Björndal, to rule there until her sons came of age." Book Rev Digest

Gulick, Bill

The hallelujah trail; originally titled Hallelujah train. Doubleday 1965 [c1963] 192p maps $3.95

In this story "Colonel Gearheart has to protect a wagon train load of champagne and

Gulick, Bill—*Continued*
whiskey from female temperance fans, marauding Indians, and some Denver hijackers."
Bk Buyer's Guide
"Swashbuckling in its spectacle and action, broad in its humor, superficial and wooden in its characterization, it is calculated to delight the eye without taxing the mind. Based on an actual historical incident in the post-Civil War American West, it recounts the misadventures of the Walsingham train." Best Sellers

The hexed rifle
In Western Writers of America. A Western bonanza p270-308

Liveliest town in the West. Doubleday 1969 258p $4.95
The author describes "what happens when an enterprising newspaper editor decides to build up the sleepy town of Dustville as a place full of glamorous western heroes, villainous desperados and savage western Indian battles. All of it is faked, of course, but until the bubble bursts Dustville does flourish as the 'liveliest town in the West.' " Pub W
A "highly entertaining spoof on Western fiction, legends of folk heroes, and Wild West shows." Booklist

Gulick, Grover C. See Gulick, Bill

Gulik, Robert van
The Chinese bell murders; three cases solved by Judge Dee. A Chinese detective story suggested by three original Chinese plots. With 15 plates drawn by the author in Chinese style. Harper 1958 262p illus o.p. 1970
"A rape murder case based on original ancient Chinese plots and centering around a famous seventh-century Chinese master detective, Judge Dee." Pub W

The emperor's pearl, a Chinese detective story; with eight illus. drawn by the author in Chinese style. Scribner [1964 c1963] 184p illus o.p. 1970
A new story about Judge Dee and his faithful Sergeant Hoong. "Clues ae scarce and elusive in 7th-centruy China, but the deductive reasoning power of the Judge brings together neatly the death of the drummer in the dragon boat race, a missing imperial jewel, an ancient goddess, and a savage murder, and completes the jigsaw puzzle." Library J

The haunted monastery; a Chinese detective story; with eight illus. drawn by the author in Chinese style. Scribner 1969 159p illus $3.95
This story "finds the judge stranded during a violent rainstorm in an extremely strange Taoist cloister, high in a desolate mountain region. During the night he solves no less than three gruesome crimes." Am News of Bks

The monkey and the tiger; two Chinese detective stories; with eight illus. drawn by the author in Chinese style. Scribner [1966 c1965] 143p illus $3.50
Contents: The morning of the monkey; The night of the tiger
"Judge Dee, ancient Chinese detective . . . stars in two stories. 'The Morning of the Monkey' covers a day in 666 A.D. when a gibbon revealed a murder; in 'The Night of the Tiger' set on a night ten years later, the Judge solves the brutal murder of a young girl." Bk Buyer's Guide
These two episodes evoke "an ancient civilization by means of first-rate modern puzzle-entertainment." N Y Times Bk R

The morning of the monkey
In Gulik, R. van. The monkey and the tiger p 1-69

Murder in Canton; a Chinese detective story; with 12 illus. drawn by the author in Chinese style. Scribner [1967 c1966] 207p illus map $3.95
"A baffling web of high political intrigue and vicious murder in the city where Arab assassins and Chinese thugs lurk for hire. Judge Dee stakes his all in a brilliant battle of wits. The time is 680 A.D. and its aura is wonderfully evoked." Publisher's note

The night of the tiger
In Gulik, R. van. The monkey and the tiger p71-141

The phantom of the temple; a Chinese detective story; with nine illus. drawn by the author in Chinese style. Scribner [1967 c1966] 203p illus $3.95
This Judge Dee mystery "is set in the 7th century A.D. in which this most famous magistrate of the Tang dynasty solves the horrors and mysterious rites of a phantom-ridden holy temple. A most unusual and satisfying book for those who savor the eerie." Publisher's note

The Red Pavilion; a Chinese detective story; with six illus. drawn by the author in Chinese style. Scribner [1968 c1964] 173p illus o.p. 1970
First published 1964 in England
Judge Dee, famous detective of ancient China "solves more than one knotty criminal problem, all of them stemming out of the fact that he elects to stay in the infamous Red Pavilion on Paradise Island, not knowing it has been the scene of several mysterious deaths in the past. The Chinese atmosphere is suitably exotic and there is a lovely, mistreated courtesan for the judge to protect." Pub W

The willow pattern; a Chinese detective story; with fifteen illus. drawn by the author in Chinese style. Scribner 1965 183p illus o.p. 1970
"This adventure of the legendary Judge Dee, of Seventh Century China, is a strange, brooding tale of crime, cholera, and corruption, and an example of modern imagination at work in the past. The emperor and his court have fled the plague-ridden city and left the judge and his Colonels, Ma Joong and Chiao Tai, in charge of affairs. They quickly become involved in three murders: 'The Case of the Willow Pattern', 'The Case of the Steep Stairs', and 'The Case of the Murdered Bond-Maid.' " Library J
"The note on Willow Pattern at the end is of interest." Times (London) Lit Sup

Gunga Din, Ali Mirdrekvandi. See Mirdrekvandi, Gunga Din, Ali

Gunnarsson, Gunnar
The black cliffs; Svartfugl; tr. from the Danish by Cecil Wood; with an introduction by Richard N. Ringler. Univ. of Wis. Press 1967 xxxviii, 222p (The Nordic translation ser) $4.95
Original Danish edition published 1929 in Copenhagen
"This is a stirring psychological novel based on an actual murder that occurred in Iceland in the early 1800's. From the first page there is a sense of foreboding as the story, told by the parish curate, follows the trial of the accused man and woman, delving deeply into the characters of the accused, the accusers, and the narrator. . . . Modern jargon in the translation jarred this reader at times. . . . Otherwise the translation reads smoothly." Library J

The good shepherd; tr. by Kenneth C. Kaufman; illus. by Marsha Simkovitch. Bobbs 1940 84p illus o.p. 1970
Published in England under title: Advent
"The simple tale of an Icelandic shepherd. With his two comrades, Leo, the dog, and Gnarly, the wether, Benedikt performs feats of

Gunnarsson, Gunnar—*Continued*
endurance, patience and persistence as he
makes his twenty-seventh annual journey into
the bleak and stormy wastes of the mountains to rescue the sheep that have been missed
in the yearly gathering." Huntting

Guthrie, A. B.
y The big sky
Some editions are:
Houghton $6.95
Watts, F. $9.95 Large type edition. A Keith
Jennison book
First published 1947 by Sloane
"A novel of the west, period 1830-43, with a
strong historical background. It is the story of
the development of the mountain country by
the white man, fur trapping, Indian fights, but
particularly the story of mountain men—how
they lived and worked, fought and loved, their
rise and fall." Library J
"It is a strong and savory tale of adventure
with the first white hunters in the West. Honestly imagined and true to history, it is also a
parable of the way the pioneers, as immoderate
as children, took their measureless paradise
and spoiled it." Time

These thousand hills. Houghton 1956 346p
o.p. 1970
"Lat Evans, son of characters in 'The Way
West,' leaves his home in Oregon to help drive
a herd of cattle to Montana. There he decides
to stay and get a ranch of his own. His adventures, his love for the loving parlor house girl
Callie, and his marriage to respectable Joyce
make a novel more conventional than the
author's previous successes." Retail Bookseller

y The way west
Some editions are:
Houghton $4.95
Watts, F. $9.95 Large type edition complete and
unabridged. A Keith Jennison book
Pulitzer Prize 1950
First published 1949 by Sloane
"A story of an emigrant trek from Independence, Missouri, to Oregon in the 1840s. Dick
Summers, one of the principal characters of
the author's earlier novel, 'The Big Sky' reappears in this." Book Rev Digest
"Where most writers of Western fiction concentrate on what their characters do, Mr. Guthrie concentrates on how they think and feel. It
is this emphasis which gives his books depth
and sense of reality." Christian Science Monitor

Guthrie, Alfred Bertram. See Guthrie, A. B.

H

Haas, Ben
Look away, look away; a novel. Simon &
Schuster 1964 509p boards $5.95
"Cary Bradham is white, Houston Whitley is
Negro. As youngsters the boys had been deeply attached but now, returning to the south
from World War II, Cary is dedicated to the
preservation of a society that offers him power
and an assured career in law and politics. While
Houston takes the first steps that lead him to
the creation of a vast civil rights movement
and Cary moves toward the governorship and
becomes increasingly involved with the last-
ditch segregationists, the two men confront
each other in a series of explosive encounters."
Huntting
"The incidents, the humiliation of Negroes,
the terror, the bombings are familiar. Things
like these have happened, but in this extraordinarily graphic novel they seem to happen to
people one knows well." Pub W

Habe, Hans
The mission; a novel. Tr. from the German
by Michael Bullock. Coward-McCann [1966
c1965] 319p $6
Originally published 1965 in Germany

"In 1938 Roosevelt called a Conference on
Refugees at Evian [France]. Thirty-two nations agreed to attend. Unofficially the Germans sent Dr. Heinrich von Benda, world-
famous urologist and Jew, to transmit Hitler's
offer to 'sell' the Jews of Germany and Austria
at $250 a head. The author presents this fic-
tionalized account of Heinrich von Benda's
desperate but unavailing efforts to win the
ransom of the Jews." Bk Buyer's Guide
"Within the scope of Habe's intention to
point a finger at those who were guilty of
the complicity of silence, the book succeeds
well enough. But as fiction it fails. . . . Yet
because of its extraordinary subject matter,
The Mission ought not to be judged as a work
of fiction alone; what the author wanted to
say is, perhaps, more urgent than art.'" Sat R

The poisoned stream; tr. by J. Maxwell-
Brownjohn. McGraw 1969 366p boards $6.95
Translated from the German manuscript
This "novel of contemporary morality takes
in many levels of society as it tells a story of
murder and greed. A call girl is murdered, and
Emilio Bossi, an unscrupulous reporter, discovers that unsuccessful novelist Aurelio
Morelli is the killer. Bossi and Carlo Vanetti,
publisher of Rome's most sensational tabloid,
plan to buy Morelli's memoirs and serialize
them, beginning in the Christmas issue, after
turning him into the police on Christmas
Eve. As the deadline approaches more and
more people learn this dangerous secret but do
nothing; the police get closer to solving the
crime, and Morelli meets a beautiful young
girl." Library J

Haggard, H. Rider
Allan Quatermain
In Haggard, H. R. Five adventure novels
of H. Rider Haggard p417-636

Allan's wife
In Haggard, H. R. Five adventure novels
of H. Rider Haggard p638-744

Five adventure novels of H. Rider Haggard.
Dover 1951 821p o.p. 1970
Contents: She; King Solomon's mines; Allan
Quatermain; Allan's wife; Maiwa's revenge

King Solomon's mines
Some editions are:
Collins $1.95
Nelson (Nelson classics) $1.75
First published 1885
"Highly coloured romance of adventure in
the wilds of Central Africa in quest of King
Solomon's Ophir; full of sensational fights,
blood-curdling perils and extraordinary escapes." Baker's Best
also in Haggard, H. R. Five adventure
novels of H. Rider Haggard p240-
415

Maiwa's revenge
In Haggard, H. R. Five adventure novels
of H. Rider Haggard p746-819

She; a history of adventure. With an introduction by Stuart Cloete; illus. by Will
Nickless. Collins 319p $1.95
First published 1887; in this edition 1957
" 'She,' or Ayesha, is an African sorceress
whom death apparently cannot touch. The
young English hero, Leo Vincey, sets out to
avenge her murder of his ancestor, an ancient
priest of Isis. The setting of this weird romance is an extinct volcano." University
Handbook for Readers and Writers
also in Haggard, H. R. Five adventure
novels of H. Rider Haggard p 1-238

Haggard, William
A cool day for killing. Walker & Co. 1968
185p boards $3.95
"In a far-off Malay kingdom that had been
a British protectorate a political assassination and military coup have taken place. Colonel Russell, that admirable officer of the Security Executive, is working behind the scenes

Haggard, William—*Continued*

to restore Britain's interests. It is, however, a superbly cool Muslim princess of English blood, and her half caste half-cousin, who really save the day, not stopping at blowing up a safe in the process, with all the aplomb of professional cracksmen." Pub W

Hailey, Arthur

Airport. Doubleday 1968 440p $5.95

"In the space of a single night at the . . . Lincoln International Airport, nearly every imaginable man, machine or function goes wrong. One of the worst snowstorms in history has been raging over the airport for three days. The longest and widest runway is blocked by a mired Boeing 707. A traffic controller is suicidally depressed. And a Rome-bound flight lifts off with a man carrying a bomb in his briefcase. How Airport Manager Mel Bakersfeld and a score of other characters cope provides the [plot of this novel]." Time

"Here are many minor conflicts—of love, sex, business, and psychological problems—all building up to the tremendously exciting scenes of a shattered transoceanic plane trying to make its way back to the airport, and a runway that can't, but must, be cleared." Pub W

The final diagnosis. Doubleday [1969 c1959] 348p $5.95

First published 1959

A "novel of the complex world of modern medicine. It deals mainly with the struggle of Dr. Kent O'Donnell to raise the standards of the Three County Hospital—among the elements of the story are the conflict between a stubborn pathologist who refuses to use modern methods, a tragic love affair between a lovely nurse and an intern, and the antagonism of certain staff and board members." Hunting

"This is the very dramatic story of the wide influence of one man who was too proud to be flexible, and it might very truly be written about any area in life where people are severely tested. . . . A very fast and interesting story for those who can take medical and surgical details impersonally." San Francisco Chronicle

Hotel. Doubleday 1965 376p $5.95

A "novel about a climactic week in the history of a great New Orleans hotel. Written from the viewpoint of a young-acting-manager who must deal with a succession of problems ranging from a near rape by a quartet of fraternity boys, a blackmailing house dick, a clever sneak thief, a vital discrimination case and an elevator disaster, this constitutes an introductory course in hotel management." Am News of Bks

The author "takes pains with his background details but skims the surface of numerous plots and personalities. . . . Geared to the casual reader of popular fiction." Booklist

In high places; a novel. Doubleday 1962 415p o.p. 1970

In this political novel "the theme is a plan to unify Canada and the United States against a possible nuclear war. The Canadian Prime Minister, whose dream is unification, is tripped up by his own imperfect past and by the situation created by the plight of a stateless refugee, whose helplessness has spurred a newspaper crusade to gain him entry into Canada." Pub W

"A long but extremely readable story, it is set in the future. . . . This unlikely story [is] well told." San Francisco Chronicle

Halberstam, David

One very hot day; a novel. Houghton 1968 [c1967] 216p $4.95

The author "focuses here on one ordinary combat infantry mission carried out by Vietnamese soldiers under combined American and Vietnamese command, from the briefing the night before until about 2 P.M. the next day when everything is over and the dead and wounded are being counted. . . . Although there is no direct discussion of whether or not we should be in Vietnam, the sheer bloody futility of it all, the stupidity of much that happens, the agony the war is bringing to both the Americans and Vietnamese are made so abundantly clear that in this sense 'One Very Hot Day' is a profoundly anti-war book. It also makes some telling points about the relations between the Americans and the Vietnamese." Pub W

Hale, Edward Everett

y The man without a country. New ed. with an introduction in the year of the war with Spain. Little 1898 59p o.p. 1970

First published 1863

"This long short-story concerns Philip Nolan, a young officer of the United States Army who is tried for the Aaron Burr conspiracy. During the court-martial he exclaims, 'Damn the United States! I wish I may never hear of the United States again!' The court thereupon sentences him to live out his life on a naval vessel, and never hear news of the United States. The story recounts the mental torments of the countryless prisoner, who after fifty-seven years finally learns that his nation is thriving, and dies happy." Haydn. Thesaurus of Book Digests

Hale, Nancy

Black summer; a novel. Little 1963 312p o.p. 1970

"Seven-year-old Robert Kean is sent by his estranged parents to spend the summer with his 'Yankee Kin' in an upper-class New York suburb. Soon a state of war exists between Robert and his Uncle Malcolm who is determined to teach his nephew some manners. As the battle of wills approaches its denoument, the bystanders find themselves drawn into the conflict." Huntting

"Black Summer is really a long short story, dealing as it does with a single mood and a set of characters who end up more or less as they began, but it is truly a virtuoso performance." Book of the Month Club News

Halévy, Ludovic

Abbé Constantin; with a brief introduction by James Kendrick. Translation Pub. 212p illus o.p. 1970

First published 1882 in France

A tale in which a genial old Abbe assists the love affairs of a rich American girl in France

"A charming story, simply and skillfully told, which will be remembered longest for the lovable character of the old French curé." Pratt Alcove

Hall, Adam

The 9th directive. Simon & Schuster [1967 c1966] 256p $4.95

"Quiller of 'The Quiller Memorandum,' which won the MWA award as best mystery of 1965 appears again. . . . The scene is Bangkok, where Quiller of The Bureau is summoned to prevent the assassination of an English personage, never named, who is visiting the East on an informal goodwill tour. Agents, spies, professional killers of many nationalities plot and counterplot through a few days crammed with danger." Pub W

The Quiller memorandum. Simon & Schuster 1965 224p o.p. 1970

A "spy thriller set in West Berlin where Englishmen and Germans are cooperating to flush out dangerous Nazis who are still at large years after World War II. The English hero, Quiller, is tough, skillful, personally vengeful against the Nazis for what he saw of their concentration camps. Several climaxes and narrow escapes and a chilling session where the Germans use drugs and psychoanalytic methods on Quiller punctuate the plot." Pub W

"The spy machinery is all there: the codes, the tags, the elliptical chatter, the psyche tampering and the suspense. Unlike other espionage thrillers, however, no casual reading will do. The plot is so controlled in its complications that the intellect as well as the emotions are titillated in a quite satisfying way." Best Sellers

Hall, Adam—*Continued*

The Striker portfolio. Simon & Schuster [1969 c1968] 191p boards $4.95

The hero of the author's The Quiller memorandum, and The ninth directive, has for his mission "to find out why thirty-six 'Striker' swing-wing aircraft have crashed, killing their pilots—and destroying any evidence of sabotage." Publisher's note

"Full of oblique dialogue and the wintry chill of cold war intrigue." Book World

For other titles by this author see Trevor, Elleston

Hall, James Norman

(jt. auth.) Nordhoff, C. Botany Bay

(jt. auth.) Nordhoff, C. The Bounty trilogy

(jt. auth.) Nordhoff, C. Falcons of France

(jt. auth.) Nordhoff, C. The hurricane

(jt. auth.) Nordhoff, C. Men against the sea

(jt. auth.) Nordhoff, C. Mutiny on the Bounty

(jt. auth.) Nordhoff, C. Pitcairn's Island

Hall, Oakley

Warlock. Viking 1958 471p o.p. 1970

On the Southwest frontier of the 1880's, Warlock, a territorial mining settlement, is at the mercy of a gang of cattle rustlers led by a wanton killer. A Citizens Committee hires a peace officer, Clay Blaisedell, a renowned gunman. The novel's action spans the year during which he acts as Warlock's marshall—a year of fear, desperation and violence. (Publisher)

Hall, Radclyffe

The well of loneliness; with a commentary by Havelock Ellis. Covici 1928 506p o.p. 1970

"A serious novel that is a plea for greater understanding of the problem of lesbianism "Inflated and sentimental and diffuse as it sometimes is, one cannot deny the earnestness and sincerity which animate 'The Well of Loneliness.' Miss Hall's appeal is a powerful one, and it is supported by passages of great force and beauty." Sat R

Halliday, Brett

(ed.) Best detective stories of year, 1961-1962. See Best detective stories of the year, 1961-1962

Hamalian, Leo

(ed.) Great stories by Nobel Prize winners, ed. by Leo Hamalian and Edmond L. Volpe. Noonday 1959 367p o.p. 1970

Analyzed in Short Story Index
Contents: The father, by B. Björnsen; Man who was, by R. Kipling; The outlaws, by S. Lagerlof; Massacre of the innocents, by M. Maeterlinck; Flagman Thiel, by G. Hauptmann; Saved, by Sir R. Tagore; A fisher nest, by H. Pontoppidan; Call of life, by K. Hamsun; Procurator of Judea, by A. France; Crucifixion of the outcast, by W. B. Yeats; Death, by W. Reymont; Miraculous revenge, by G. B. Shaw; Sardinian fox, by G. Deledda; Little Lizzy, by T. Mann; What that kind of mush gets you, by S. Lewis; Sunstroke, by I. Bunin; War, by L. Pirandello; The operation by R. M. Du Gard; Lost forests, by J. V. Jensen; Within and without, by H. Hesse; That evening sun, by W. Faulkner; The lift that went down into hell, by P. Lagerkvist; Man of letters, by F. Mauriac; Lily, by H. Laxness; The guest, by A. Camus; Il tratto de Apelle, by B. Pasternak

(ed.) Short fiction of the masters; ed. by Leo Hamalian and Frederick R. Karl. Putnam 1963 447p o.p. 1970

Thirty-one "stories by Europeans and Americans and one Japanese story, chronologically arranged, from Balzac to Samuel Beckett [and Alberto Moravia]. . . . Short critical biographies of the writers and study questions for each story are included." Booklist

Contents: A passion in the desert, by H. de Balzac; My kinsman, Major Molineux, by N. Hawthorne; The district doctor, by I. Turgenev; The Grand Inquisitor, by F. Dostoyevsky; Alesha the Pot, by L. Tolstoy; Midnight mass, by M. de Assis; The orphans, by G. Verga; The death of the lion, by H. James; Little Louise Roque, by G. de Maupassant; Il Conde, by J. Conrad; Tit for tat, by S. Aleichem; The bet, by A. Chekhov; The madness of Dr Montarco, by M. de Unamuno y Jugo; The soft touch of grass, by L. Pirandello, Twenty-six men and a girl, by M. Gorki; The melancholy summer of Madame de Breyves, by M. Proust; Little Lizzy, by T. Mann; Within and without, by H. Hesse; A man without character, by R. Musil; Counterparts, by J. Joyce; The judgment, by F. Kafka; The man who loved islands, by D. H. Lawrence; The children's campaign, by P. Lagerkvist; In a grove, by R. Akutagawa; My first goose, by I. Babel; A clean, well-lighted place, by E. Hemingway; The trap, by I. Silone; Brother, by G. Greene; The wall, by J. P. Sartre; Yellow, by S. Beckett; The ruin of humanity, by A. Moravia

Hamilton, Alex

(ed.) Splinters; a new anthology of modern macabre fiction. Walker & Co. [1969 c1968] 237p $5.95

First published 1968 in England
"Fourteen stories especially written for this anthology. The results should delight lovers of spooks and the spooky." Pub W

Contents: Jane, by J. Gaskell; The ice palace, by M. Baldwin; The language of flowers, by H. Atkinson; Grace note, by D. May; Miss Smith, by W. Trevor; An American organ, by A. Burgess; The biggest game, by J. Brunner; The way the ladies walk, by R. Nettell; Home again, home again, jigetty-jig, by P. Boyle; Indoor life, by M. Haltrecht; Don't you dare, by J. Burke; Isabo, by J. A. Cuddon; Mewed up, by P. Brent; Under the eildon tree, by A. Hamilton

Hammett, Dashiell

The big knockover; selected stories and short novels of Dashiell Hammett; ed. and with an introduction by Lillian Hellman. Random House 1966 xxi, 355p $5.95

Analyzed in Short Story Index
"A vintage collection of nine . . . short stories and an unfinished novel." McClurg. Book News

Contents: The gutting of Couffignal; Fly paper; The scorched face; This king business; The Gatewood caper; Dead yellow women; Corkscrew; Tulip [unfinished novel]; The big knockover; $106,000 blood money

The Dain curse
In Hammett, D. The novels of Dashiell Hammett p143-292

The glass key. Knopf 1931 282p o.p. 1970

"One of the two best [mystery] novels by the man who is generally regarded as the creator and still the acknowledged master of the 'hard-boiled' school of detective fiction. Brutal in its subject matter but excellently written." Howard Haycraft

Detective: Ned Beaumont

also in Hammett, D. The novels of Dashiell Hammett p441-588

The Maltese falcon. Knopf 1930 276p (Black widow thrillers) o.p. 1970

"The Maltese Falcon is about a detective, Sam Spade, whose partner is murdered while shadowing a man for a client. In finding the murderer, Spade runs afoul of the police, as well as of several people who are all after a mysterious statuette." Outlook

also in Hammett, D. The novels of Dashiell Hammett p293-440

also in Haycraft, H. ed. Ten great mysteries p11-159

Hammett, Dashiell—*Continued*

The novels of Dashiell Hammett. Knopf 1965 726p $6.95

Includes five novels: Red harvest (1929); The Dain curse (1929); The Maltese falcon (1930); The glass key (1931); The thin man (1934); the last three titles are entered separately

In Red harvest, a hard-boiled detective, Henry F. Neill, arrives in the corrupt town of Personville to find his client murdered. He stays to clean up the town. "The Dain curse" starts with the trivial theft of eight small diamonds only to introduce the detective-narrator, Sam Spade, and the events that follow

Red harvest

In Hammett, D. The novels of Dashiell Hammett p 1-142

The thin man. Knopf 1934 259p o.p. 1970

Story of disappearance, murder and robbery as told by "Nick" Charles the detective who solves the case

"One of the first works to bring humor, and of a distinctly native brand, to the detective story in this country." Howard Haycraft

also in Hammett, D. The novels of Dashiell Hammett p589-726

Tulip

In Hammett, D. The big knockover p238-74

Hammond, Ralph. See Innes, Hammond

Hammond-Innes, Ralph. See Innes, Hammond

Hammond-Innes, William. See Innes, Hammond

Hamner, Earl

y Spencer's Mountain, by Earl Hamner, Jr. Dial Press 1961 247p $4.50

An "account of a boy's growing up in a large and impoverished family in the Blue Ridge Mountains of Virginia. . . . His chief problems are love and the fact that his father feels that a college education is a waste of money." Pub W

"A novel filled with joie de vivre, frank simplicity, a little sinning, and much human goodness." Library J

Hamsun, Knut

Nobel Prize in literature, 1920

Growth of the soil; tr. from the Norwegian by W. W. Worster. Knopf 1968 [c1949] 435p $6.95

Original Norwegian edition, 1917

"A realistic novel of rude peasant life in an out-of-the-way corner of Norway. It has vivid, well-differentiated characters and is of interest as a record of the development of a self-conscious community from a widely separated collection of isolated farms. It makes its deepest human appeal, however, as a story of man making a place for himself under primitive conditions and subject to the ordering of nature, rather than to the feverish demands of civilization; in so far as Isak and Inger, their children and neighbors, live close to the soil, there is wholesome growth and simple happiness. The story is told in a slow, simple style suited to its material." Cleveland

Hunger; newly tr. from the Norwegian by Robert Bly. With introductions by Robert Bly and Isaac Bashevis Singer. Farrar, Straus 1967 xxii, 231p $4.95

Original Norwegian edition appeared 1890. First published in the United States 1920 by Knopf

"A stream-of-consciousness narrative about a young man, a writer, who is literally starving, giddy with light-headed fancies, and occasionally able to sell an essay for a few kroner —and thus to prolong his suffering. The novel seems entirely modern until one realizes that it was first published in 1890 and is hence the grandfather of a whole range of modern novels, both because of its technique and also because of its fancifulness and humor, which are considerable. Only then does Hamsun's radical originality come clear. 'Hunger' was considered in its day, and must still be considered . . . a great book." Book of the Month Club News

Pan; from Lieutenant Thomas Glahn's papers; tr. from the Norwegian by James W. McFarlane. Farrar, Straus 1956 192p $5.50

Original Norwegian edition 1894; English translation, 1920

"The story of a game of love played between a young lieutenant, summering in the wilds with his dog and gun, and a tradesman's daughter. She exasperates him with her incalculable moods which he repays in kind. She ends by marrying a count while for him the aftermath is a ruined life." Book Rev Digest

"A strange and beautiful book. It is also a book which requires a good deal from the reader, both of sympathy with its mood, and of a definite type of visualization." N Y Times Bk R

Victoria; a love story. Newly tr. from the Norwegian by Oliver Stallybrass. Farrar, Straus 1969 170p $4.95

Original Norwegian edition published 1898

A novel about "a Norwegian writer and a girl who loved him but never became his. The young man, Johannes, is the son of a miller; in the Norway of his time . . . he could not aspire to the hand of the daughter of an important land owner. Yet it is just such a girl, the Victoria of the title with whom [he] falls in love. . . . The lovers torment each other, they fall repeatedly just short of agreement, and they end by unwittingly destroying each other." Best Sellers

This novel "superficially a touching idyll of young love, is deceptively simple. It is a passionately lyrical tale deeply saturated with the brooding melancholy so characteristic of Hamsun's fiction." Library J

Han, Suyin

The mountain is young. Putnam 1958 511p o.p. 1970

"Nepal—the Himalayan kingdom just recently linked with India and the West through modern transportation—is really the central force of this novel, coloring and affecting the romance that forms its plot. The excitement of life in its rarefied atmosphere (at 4000 feet), the drama of its historic traditions, the passion of its mingling religious beliefs, all contributing to the strength of living, are the forces that stir its central character, Anne Ford, out of her frigid marriage to a self-centered Englishman and turn her to realization of herself in an ardent love affair with a dynamic native engineer, Unni Menon." Library J

Hanley, Clifford

The red-haired bitch. Houghton 1969 248p $4.95

The novel begins in Majorca "where a self-made millionaire is hooked by the idea of producing a successful Scottish musical. He and several insiders agree that a script entitled 'The Red-Haired Bitch' has possibilities and before long the project is off the ground and moving smartly ahead, into serious trouble. For the director fires the star before walking out himself, and the show is near collapse when the co-producer takes over with a vengeance, shifting parts and players like a crazed juggler and making over the book and music." Am News of Bks

"With fast-moving dialog and narrative that frequently echo the theater, Scottish author Hanley's light, capricious, sophisticated, behind-the-scenes tale conveys the crisscrossing temperament, motives, antics, amorous relations and violent ex-relations among members of a Scottish cast, their hangers-on, and the good sprinkling of humorful satire on Scotproducer, writer, and backer of a play. . . . A land is present throughout." Booklist

Hanley, Gerald
Gilligan's last elephant. World Pub. 1962
262p o.p. 1970

"Obsessed with their individual compulsions,
a professional hunter and a wealthy American
adventurer put each other to inhuman tests
of body and will, while they probe each other's
personalities [on a hunt for a huge rogue elephant in East Africa]." McClurg. Book News

"Read purely as an adventure story this tale
of a grueling East African safari moves swiftly
along in an atmosphere of high-tension suspense." N Y Her Trib Books

Hardy, Thomas
Far from the madding crowd

Some editions are:
Dodd (Great illustrated classics) $4.50 With
photographs of the author, his environment
and the setting of the book, together with
an introduction by E. P. Lawrence
Harper $6.95
St Martins $7.50

First published 1874

"Bathsheba Everdene is courted by Gabriel
Oak, a young farmer who becomes bailiff of
the farm she inherits, by William Boldwood,
who owns the neighboring farm, and by Sergeant Troy, a handsome young adventurer.
She marries Troy, who spends her money
freely. Troy now accidentally meets his old
love Fanny Robin and her child in pitiful condition on the way to the workhouse and the
next day finds them both dead. The incident
brings about a quarrel with Bathsheba and his
departure; and he is swept out to sea. Bathsheba, who believes him drowned, becomes
engaged to William Boldwood. When Troy reappears in blustering mood, Boldwood kills
him and is sentenced to penal servitude for
life. Bathsheba now marries Gabriel Oak."
Benét. The Reader's Encyclopedia

"The tragi-comedy of country life. The title
is ironical, several deaths chequering the
story, though Oak and Bathsheba are wedded
at the end. A harrowing episode of seduction,
desertion and death, is attached to the main
story. . . . Outdoor life on the farm and the
natural scenery make a fine setting, often
colored with the richest poetic imagination."
Baker's Best

Jude the obscure

Some editions are:
Modern Lib. $2.95
St Martins $7.50

First published 1895

A novel which deals "with the mutual love
of Jude Fawley and his cousin, Sue Bridehead.
They both marry outsiders, but finally secure
divorces to live with each other. After some
years, young Jude, the son of Jude's former
wife Arabella, murders Jude's two younger
children and hangs himself to escape from
misery. Broken by this tragedy, Sue returns
to her husband and Jude to Arabella. Soon
afterward Jude dies." Benét. The Reader's Encyclopedia

"Mr. Hardy's rebellious views of life and
religion, and leanings towards naturalistic
methods, are given full play in this story of a
peasant scholar's foiled ambition, which from
beginning to end is sombre and in many of the
incidents extremely painful." Baker's Best

y The mayor of Casterbridge

Some editions are:
Dial Press $6.95 Illustrated with wood engrav-
ings by Agnes Miller Parker. Introduction by
Frank Swinnerton
Modern Lib $2.95
St Martins $7.50

First published 1886

"Michael Henchard, a young hay trusser,
while intoxicated at a fair sells his wife and
child at auction for five pounds to a man
named Newson. Eighteen years afterward when
Henchard has become the Mayor of Casterbridge, they reappear, and most of the novel
deals with the problems and embitterments of
his later life. The girl, Elizabeth Jane, who, he
finally learns, is not his own daughter but
Newson's, marries his business rival, Farfrae."
Benét. The Reader's Encyclopedia

A pair of blue eyes. St Martins 1960 434p
$7.50

First published 1872-1873

"Two friends are in love with the same
Cornish girl, who loves both and marries
neither, the end poignant tragedy. The story
turns on the mutual misunderstandings of the
friends and similar sins of innocence on the
maiden's part." Baker's Best

y The return of the native

Some editions are:
Dodd (Great illustrated classics) $4.50 With
illustrations reproducing drawings for early
editions and photographs of contemporary
scenes together with an introductory biographical sketch of the author and anecdotal captions by Basil Davenport
Harper $5.95
St Martins $7.50
Watts, F. $8.95 Large type edition complete
and unabridged. A Keith Jennison book
Watts, F. $5.95 Ultra type edition

First published 1878

"A drama of passion and nemesis, enacted
amidst the wild and solemn scenery of an
imaginary heath, and animated profoundly by
the author's philosophy of revolt. . . . Fatal
misunderstandings between dear relatives, and
the subtle and imperceptible yielding to temptation which leads to crime and death, are the
determining motives. Clym Yeobright and his
mother and the exotic Eustacia Vye are among
his finest impersonations of human longing
and disillusionment, anguish, and endurance."
Baker's Best

y Tess of the D'Urbervilles

Some editions are:
Dodd (Great illustrated classics) $4.50 With
photographs of the author, his environment,
and the setting of the book, together with
an introduction by Carl J. Weber
Modern Lib. $2.95

First published in complete form 1891

"The tragic history of a woman betrayed.
. . . Tess, the author contends, is sinned
against, but not a sinner; her tragedy is the
work of tyrannical circumstances and of the
evil deeds of others in the past and the present,
and more particularly of two men's baseness,
the seducer, and the well-meaning intellectual
who married her. . . . The pastoral surroundings, the varying aspects of field, river, sky,
serve to deepen the pathos of stage in the
heroine's calamities, or to add beauty and dignity to her tragic personality." Baker's Best

Two on a tower. St Martins 1960 313p
$7.50

First published in 1882

A novel "dealing with the mutual love of
the young astronomer Swithin St. Cleve and
Lady Viviette Constantine. An early secret marriage between them is set aside by later developments, and when St. Cleve finally returns
from South Africa to the familiar observatory
tower to propose marriage, Viviette falls dead
in his arms." Benét. The Reader's Encyclopedia

Under the greenwood tree; or, The Mell-
stock quire; a rural painting of the Dutch
school. St Martins 1957 204p $7.50

First published in England 1872; in this edition 1949

"The first of the Wessex novels proper, the
common groundwork of which is a very vivid
delineation of the people of Dorset and the
neighbouring counties, and of the natural life
and scenery. . . . An idyll of village life, in
which the members of a carrier's family and the
village choir, a gathering of rustic oddities, furnish a sort of comic chorus to the love-affairs
of a rustic boy and girl." Baker's Best

The well-beloved; a sketch of a temperament. St Martins 1964 217p $7.50

First published 1897

"A fantastic jeu d'esprit about an artist in
pursuit of his ideal woman. He sees his vision
embodied successively in three generations and
last of all woos the granddaughter of his
first love. Portland is the principal scene, but
there is less local colour than usual." Baker's
Best

Hardy, Thomas—*Continued*

Wessex tales. . . . St Martins 1960 285p $7.50

First published in two volumes in 1888; Harper edition o.p. 1970, analyzed in Short Story Index

"That is to say: The three strangers. A tradition of eighteen hundred and four, The melancholy Hussar, The withered arm, Fellowtownsmen, Interlopers at the Knap, The distracted preacher." Title page

The woodlanders; with an introduction by Carl J. Weber. St Martins 1958 443p $7.50

First published 1887
A tragic romance set in seventeenth century rural England. On returning to her home village after a year at school, Grace Melbury seemed too cultured for marriage with her childhood friend, an itinerant farmer. She marries a doctor who eventually is convinced he has married beneath his class. After several affairs he leaves her. Grace renews her friendship with her childhood sweetheart, but he dies. In the end she resumes marriage with her husband

Hardy, William M.

U.S.S. Mudskipper; the submarine that wrecked a train; a novel. Dodd 1967 216p $4.50

"Captain Tolliver and crew of the World War II combat submarine U.S.S. 'Mudskipper' plan an irregular enterprise, to send a landing force to blow up the gleaming little locomotive and its bedraggled freight cars that affront their eyes daily on the train's coastal run between Nemuro and Kushiro. The story turns on those who love the little locomotive personally or are involved in its protection, those who plot its destruction, and the unwarlike personal dreams and aspirations their inner musings reveal. An entertaining action-adventure story." Booklist

Harrington, Joseph

The last doorbell; a Lieutenant Kerrigan mystery. Lippincott 1969 192p $4.50

"When Ernie Detweiler died, Jane Boardman inherited the kidnapping case on which he had been working, off and on, for eleven years. A gentle-voiced elderly man had taken little Elsie Gebhart away for a visit and never brought her back. But he was a compulsive letter writer, and it was his letters that gave Lt. Frank Kerrigan and Jane a clue to follow up." Bk Buyer's Guide

Harris, John

The jade wind. Doubleday 1969 283p $5.95

Published in England with title: The mercenaries

"General Tsu, foe to Chinese Nationalism and the growing power of Chiang Kai-shek, hires Ira Penaluma and his mechanic, Sammy Shapiro, to build up an air force to challenge Chiang. The time is the mid-twenties and flying is still full of danger, but there's romance as well as tragedy in this novel." Bk Buyer's Guide

"A fairly routine but exciting air-war adventure yarn set in China. . . . It does have some good material about flying and old planes, however, that buffs will enjoy." Pub W

Harris, John Beynon. See Wyndham, John

Harris, MacDonald

Trepleff. Holt [1969 c1968] 256p $5.95

First published 1968 in England
"The main character, identified with Chekhov's tragic antihero Trepleff in 'The Sea Gull,' is a successful psychiatrist who loses family and career by seducing a patient out of compassion rather than lust. He goes on to a companionship with a dangerous neurotic, accepting her support and watching dumbly as she destroys herself. The predetermined failure of human love to be selfless is a central theme in this expertly written, heartbreaking comedy. A really fine new novel." Library J

Harris, Mark

Bang the drum slowly, by Henry W. Wiggen; certain of his enthusiasms restrained by Mark Harris. Knopf 1956 243p boards $3.95

"A baseball novel which centers on Bruce, a Negro catcher, who is slowly dying of Hodgkin's disease. The narrator tries to keep the matter a secret, but eventually it comes out. The rest of the book concerns the loyalty of Bruce's teammates to their doomed member." Book Rev Digest

"Narrated by 'Author' in the raucous speech of the ball park, yet with an elegiac dignity." Booklist

The southpaw, by Henry W. Wiggen; punctuation freely inserted and spelling greatly improved by Mark Harris. Bobbs 1953 350p o.p. 1970

"A novel based on big league baseball, related in the first person by a young pitcher on the New York Mammoths team." Book Rev Digest

"Even those whose knowledge of baseball is elemental will find the book worth reading." N Y Times Bk R

Harrison, Harry

(ed.) Best SF: 1968. See Best SF: 1968

Captive universe. Putnam 1969 185p boards $4.50

Set in an Aztec village, apparently pre-Columbian in date. "Young Chimal had angered the priests of the walled-in valley, where the serpent-headed goddess, Coatlicue, walked by night. Desperately he fled to the cliffs that surrounded the valley and found a passage that led him from a primitive world to a strange world of the future." Bk Buyer's Guide

"You will either enjoy this fantastic story very much indeed or be unable to finish it." Book of the Month Club News

(ed.) Nova I; an anthology of original science fiction stories. Delacorte Press 1970 222p $4.95

Contents: The big connection, by R. Scott; A happy day in 2381, by R. Silverberg; Terminus est, by B. N. Malzberg; Hexamnion, by C. Davis; The higher things, by J. R. Pierce; Swastika, by B. W. Aldiss; The HORARS of war, by G. Wolfe; Love story in three acts, by D. Gerrold; Jean Duprès, by G. R. Dickson; In the pocket, by K. M. O'Donnell; Mary and Joe, by N. Mitchison; Faces & hands, by J. Sallis; The winner, by D. E. Westlake; The whole truth, by P. Anthony

Harrison, William

In a wild sanctuary. Morrow 1969 320p $6.95

"Almost as a joke, four bright young graduate students at a large Chicago university enter into a suicide pact. They are to kill themselves one by one. But none of them knows the precise order of their deaths, for each has drawn his own number by secret lot. One boy is found dead at the foot of a tall building. Another drowns himself. And the two remaining make their plans, with no one to thwart them but the father of the first dead boy, who gropes for meaning in the midst of meaningless acts." News of Bks

"For insight into today's youth, a book of probing personal-social characterization that, despite noticeable narrative awkwardness as it moves to its disturbing climax, meshes the turmoil of maturing, the overriding sickness of one young man, and the sickness of society." Booklist

Harsányi, Zsolt de

The star-gazer; tr. from the Hungarian by Paul Tabor. Putnam 1939 572p o.p. 1970

"The life story of the scientist, Galileo, from manhood to death: his scientific experiments while teaching at Pisa and at Padua, where he spent the happiest years of his life—his invention of the telescope—his interest in heavenly bodies and his banishment to Arcetri by the Inquisition at Rome whose disapproval he had incurred. Although written like a novel, the story adheres to facts." Huntting

Harsányi, Zsolt de—*Continued*

"The book is a long one, but not too long for the story of a great man who lived amid the gorgeous color, the indescribable squalor, the bravery and the cruelty that was Italy of 300 to 350 years ago." Springf'd Republican

Harte, Bret

The best of Bret Harte; selected by Wilhelmina Harper and Aimée M. Peters; illus. by Paul Brown. Houghton 1947 434p illus $5.95

Analyzed in Short Story Index
Contents: The Luck of Roaring Camp; Tennessee's partner; Brown of Calaveras; How Santa Claus came to Simpson's Bar; The idyl of Red Gulch; Mrs Skagg's husbands; Highwater mark; Protégée of Jack Hamlin's; Wan Lee, the pagan; The post-mistress of Laurel Run; Ingénue of the Sierras; The bell-ringer of Angel's; A passage in the life of Mr John Oakhurst; Miggles; Colonel Starbottle for the plaintiff; The outcasts of Poker Flat; Dick Boyle's business card; Left out on Lone Star Mountain; Plain language from truthful James

The best short stories of Bret Harte; ed. and with an introduction by Robert N. Linscott. Modern Lib. 1947 517p $2.95

Analyzed in Short Story Index
Contents: The Luck of Roaring Camp; The outcasts of Poker Flat; Tennessee's partner; Brown of Calaveras; Iliad of Sandy Bar; Poet of Sierra Flat; How Santa Claus came to Simpson's Bar; Passage in the life of Mr John Oakhurst; Heiress of Red Dog; Ingénue of the Sierras; Chu Chu; Devotion of Enriquez; Yellow dog; Salomy Jane's kiss; Uncle Jim and Uncle Billy; Dick Spindler's family Christmas; Esmeralda of Rocky Canon; Boom in the "Calaveras Clarion"; Youngest Miss Piper; Colonel Starbottle for the plaintiff; Lanty Foster's mistake; Four guardians of LaGrange; Ward of Colonel Starbottle's; Convalescence of Jack Hamlin; Gentleman of La Porte

The Luck of Roaring Camp, and other sketches. Houghton 256p front (Riverside lib) $3.95

Partially analyzed in Short Story Index
First published 1870
Contents: The Luck of Roaring Camp; The outcasts of Poker Flat; Miggles; Tennessee's partner; Idyl of Red Gulch; Brown of Calaveras; High-water mark; Lonely ride; Man of no account; M'Liss; Right eye of the Commander; Notes by flood and field; Mission Dolores; John Chinaman; From a back window; Boonder

The Luck of Roaring Camp, and other tales; with pictures of the author and his environment and illustrations of the setting of the book together with an introduction by Louis B. Salomon. Dodd 1961 309p illus (Great illustrated classics) $4.50

Analyzed in Short Story Index
Contents: The Luck of Roaring Camp; The outcasts of Poker Flat; Miggles; Tennessee's partner; The idyl of Red Gulch; Brown of Calaveras; High-water mark; A lonely ride; The man of no account; Miss; The right eye of the Commander; Notes by flood and field; The Mission Dolores; John Chinaman; From a back window; Boonder; How Santa Claus came to Simpson's Bar; Wan Lee, the pagan; Two Saints of the foothills; The fool of Five Forks; A ghost of the Sierras; My friend the tramp; The office-seeker

Tales of the Argonauts. Houghton 440p o.p. 1970

Analyzed in Short Story Index
First published 1875
Contents: Iliad of Sandy Bar; Mr Thompson's prodigal; Romance of Madroño Hollow; Poet of Sierra Flat; Princess Bob and her friends; How Santa Claus came to Simpson's Bar; Mrs Skagg's husbands; Episode of Fiddletown; Passage in the life of Mr John Oakhurst; Rose of Tuolumne; Monte Flat pastoral; How old man Plunkett went home; Baby Sylvester; Wan Lee, the pagan; Heiress of Red Dog; Man on the beach; Roger Catron's friend; "Jinny"; Two saints of the foot-hills; "Who was my quiet friend"; "Tourist from Injianny"; Fool of Five Forks; Man from Solano; Ghost of the Sierras

y Tales of the gold rush; illus. by Fletcher Martin; with an introduction by Oscar Lewis. Heritage 1944 223p illus $6.95

Analyzed in Short Story Index
Contents: The Luck of Roaring Camp; The outcasts of Poker Flat; Miggles; Tennessee's partner; Brown of Calaveras; The idyl of Red Gulch; The Iliad of Sandy Bar; The poet of Sierra Flat; How Santa Claus came to Simpson's Bar; An apostle of the Tules; An ingenue of the Sierras; A protegee of Jack Hamlin's; Prosper's "old mother"

Harte, Francis Bret. See Harte, Bret

Hartog, Jan de

The artist; drawings by Joseph Low. Atheneum Pubs. 1963 167p illus boards $5

A "story of the unexpected ending of a dream. A lifetime of saving has preceded old [Dutch seaman] Joost Jansen's purchase of a houseboat on the Seine, and settling down to a career as a painter. Then he is disappointed in his talents, but finds a new spirit and hope when he befriends a dying dog." Pub W
" 'The Artist' can be read as a study of the sense of failure which is the universal human experience. . . . On another level, 'The Artist' can be read as a psychological study of the needs of artistic temperament, or a study of the evolution of the religious spirit in a man." Best Sellers

The call of the sea. . . . Atheneum Pubs. 1966 556p $6.95

"Including: The lost sea, The distant shore, and A sailor's life." Title page
The first two books are sea novels. The third one is an autobiographical account of life at sea, "story in form and a novel in effect." Publisher's note

The captain. Atheneum Pubs. 1966 434p $5.95

"In 1942 Captain Martinus Harinxma, a Hollander escaped from the Nazis, is given command of a Dutch tugboat slated for convoy duty on the Iceland-Murmansk run. After the death of his liaison officer, complications pile up for the captain who becomes emotionally involved with the officer's widow. He also discovers that his ideas on war and heroism have changed drastically." Library J
This sea story "is one of those rarities in contemporary fiction, a real spellbinder, a heman story, full of action, in which the hero is brave and likable. . . . The exposure and terror of that long and punishing convoy have never been so powerfully depicted. The art of this book lies in its unforced masculinity, for these men are real." Atlantic

The distant shore
In Hartog, J. de. The call of the sea p89-395

The inspector. Atheneum Pubs. 1960 312p $4

"Story, set in 1946, of a heroic, middle-aged Dutch policeman, Peter Jongman, and a twenty-one-year old Dutch Jewish girl, Anna Held, who is dying of tuberculosis and of injuries inflicted on her in the medical-research laboratory of the concentration camp from which she has recently been freed, and whose one wish is to see Israel before she dies. The policeman, an Inspector of the Criminal Investigation Division in Amsterdam, undertakes to get the girl to Israel, although he knows that his action will probably cost him his career and may cost him his life." New Yorker
"More, it is the story of Peter Jongman's self-immolation and fulfillment as a man. The characters are memorable; even minor ones are distinctive and vivid. The action is dramatic and suspenseful. The almost mystical theme of forgiveness is poignantly and beautifully wrought." Library J

Hartog, Jan de—*Continued*

The little ark; illus. by Joseph Low. Atheneum Pubs. 1970 [c1953] 213p illus boards $5.95

Reprint of title first published 1953 by Harper
"The great hurricane of 1953 swept away the dikes of Holland, drowned thousands of farmers, and left others homeless, but it also brought in a tidal wave of human kindness from all over the world. Among the flood survivors were ten-year-old Jan Brink, a war orphan, and the half-caste little Indonesian girl, Adinda, both of them foster children of Parson Grijpma. Stranded first in a houseboat and then in a hospital ship, the waifs learned that disaster makes all men brothers, and that adults treat children more kindly than usual." Booklist

The lost sea
In Costain, T. B. comp. Twelve short novels p559-616
In Hartog, J. de. The call of the sea p3-85

A sailor's life
In Hartog, J. de. The call of the sea p396-556

The spiral road. Harper 1957 465p o.p. 1970
"A self-assured, smug young doctor goes to the Dutch East Indies. There, helped by a veteran physician and two Salvation Army members, he learns of tragedy and pain while he loses his brashness and is vouchsafed an agonizing glimpse into truth." Cincinnati
"To the confusion of the reader, the narrative shifts between past and present, developing lengthy background incidents that would make complete novels in themselves. However, the story abounds in action and exotic color, and contains a large cast of characters among whom are many striking and fully realized personalities." Booklist

Harwood, Alice

The lily and the leopards. Bobbs 1949 508p o.p. 1970

Published in England with title: She had to be queen
"The tragic story of Lady Jane Grey, nineday Queen of England made into a sweeping novel without manufactured plot or fripperies. The young girl, whom even her enemies loved, is portrayed as the lily among the leopards, a trusting child betrothed to one man, married to another, and at last the victim of the greedy ambitions of others." Retail Bookseller

Merchant of the ruby. Bobbs 1950 447p o.p. 1970

The author "writes of an earlier period of the Tudor dynasty when as an aftermath of the War of the Roses, came a claimant to the throne of England believed by his followers to be Richard of York, escaped from the Tower where his uncle Richard III had ordered his murder with his elder brother Young Edward V. The love story of Richard—or Perkin Warbeck as he came to be known—and Catharine Gordon, cousin of the King of Scotland is told with sympathy and charm." Library J

So merciful a queen, so cruel a woman. Bobbs 1958 380p o.p. 1970

"An off-focus picture of Elizabeth Tudor's reign allows the reader full awareness of the forceful queen, but actually centers on Katheryn and Mary Grey, younger sisters of the ill-fated Lady Jane and heirs presumptive to the throne after Elizabeth. Although neither sister had any desire to be queen, they were regarded with great suspicion by Elizabeth." Booklist

Harwood, Ronald

The girl in Melanie Klein. Holt 1969 184p $4.95

"When Niobe joined the inmates of The Nest [a posh asylum located in suburban London] (she had the Melanie Klein room), she insisted that she was all right, that she had really seen a crime committed. Hugo, Nora, and Wassler, the other three inmates, decide to protect her by stealing and rearranging her interview tapes, with surprising results." Bk Buyer's Guide
"The novel maunders a bit, and when it tries to show that life outside The Nest is batty too it is less funny than the author hopes, but parts of it are delightful and there is a nice, flippant line in throw-away humour." New Statesman

Hasek, Jaroslav

The good soldier: Schweik. Ungar [1962 c1930] 447p illus $6.50

First published 1930 by Doubleday. Translated from the Czechoslovakian by Paul Selver
This is the story "of the good soldier Schweik, the fat dogcatcher from the streets of Prague, who is drafted into the Czech army and sent to the Russian front. . . . Schweik's absurd pranks, the ludicrous situations in which he is involved, his hilarious scenes with the outraged and grotesquely caricatured Austrian military, are all interspersed with Schweik's own naive and immensely funny reflections upon life." Publisher's note
"Schweik is more than the hero of a somewhat Rabelaisian satire. He typifies the Czech resistance to the Austrian domination, and he is admirably drawn—even if the drawing is a caricature. Mr. Jaroslav Hasek has written both an epic and a satire." Spec

Havighurst, Walter

(ed.) Masters of the modern short story. A new ed. Harcourt 1955 453p o.p. 1970

Analyzed in Short Story Index
First published 1945
Contents: Youth, by J. Conrad; Livvie, by E. Welty; Brother death, by S. Anderson; Barn burning, by W. Faulkner; The road from Colonus, by E. M. Forster; Uprooted, by F. O'Connor; A little cloud, by J. Joyce; The madonna of the future, by H. James; The undefeated, by E. Hemingway; He don't plant cotton, by J. F. Powers; The new dress, by V. Woolf; The stranger, by K. Mansfield; The jilting of Granny Weatherall, by K. A. Porter; Odor of chrysanthemums, by D. H. Lawrence; Across the bridge, by G. Greene; The Claxtons, by A. Huxley; The open boat, by S. Crane; Flight, by J. Steinbeck; Mr Cornelius, I love you, by J. West; The girl on the bus, by W. Sansom; The door of opportunity, by W. S. Maugham; The man who invented sin, by S. O'Faolain; Main currents of American thought, by I. Shaw; A summer day, by J. Stafford

Hawkes, John

Charivari
In Hawkes, J. Lunar landscapes p51-136

The goose on the grave
In Hawkes, J. Lunar landscapes p200-75

Lunar landscapes; stories & short novels, 1949-1963: Charivari; The owl; The goose on the grave. New Directions 1969 275p $5.95

The goose on the grave and The owl first published 1954
Short stories included are: The traveler; The grandmother; A little bit of the old slap and tickle; Death of an airman; A song outside; The nearest cemetery
"These are short but major works; each brings us more of the [author's] unique prose style and . . . extraordinary qualities of imagination." News of Bks

The owl
In Hawkes, J. Lunar landscapes p137-99

Hawkins, Sir Anthony Hope. See Hope, Anthony

Hawley, Cameron

Cash McCall; a novel. Houghton 1955 444p $3.95

"Cash McCall is the most spectacular of the merger men to whom 'capital gains' and 'tax

Hawley, Cameron—*Continued*

loss' are sacred words. When Grant Austen decides to sell Suffolk Moulding Co., a small business into which he has poured his life. McCall buys it and quickly realizes he has acquired a lever by which he can gain control of a huge electronics plant. McCall's falling in love with Lory, Grant's daughter, complicates the picture." Library J

"The questions that [the author] raises about those methods, ethics and ends, and the answers he finds, add up to a provocative and interesting picture of an important factor in American business life today." N Y Her Trib Books

Executive suite. Houghton 1952 344p $3.95

"Avery Bullard, head of a large manufacturing concern, had neglected to appoint an executive vice-president and when he died suddenly the Directors were called to elect a new president. This is the story of the twenty-four hours following Avery's death, and of the people—department heads, salesmen, district managers, lawyers, secretaries, taxi drivers and others—who were affected by it." Huntting

"So subtly and seriously has Cameron Hawley written his satire on American big business that he almost persuades you that his tongue has never touched his cheek as he unfolds his plot and characters. While reminiscent of John Marquand and Sinclair Lewis, his work is completely individual not only in content but in style and treatment." N Y Her Trib Books

The hurricane years. Little 1968 567p $7.50

The author "dwells on the often self-inflicted pressures with which businessmen in their forties bring on premature heart attacks. Judd Wilder, carpet corporation executive, is the stricken man. Aaron Kharr is the physician who makes Judd face up to his past and the reasons for his driving himself unmercifully." Booklist

"Are Americans more vulnerable than other people to heart attacks? . . . This is the inquiry which led Cameron Hawley to the writing of [this novel] . . . and he is as deeply concerned with the causes which prompt a man to knock himself out for a corporation as he is with the aftermath. . . . This story may be regarded by some as too didactic and too long; I think it is saved from both charges by its humane and compassionate qualities, and by its characterization." Atlantic

The Lincoln Lords; a novel. Little 1960 556p $5.95

"The role of the top executive is examined in the person of Lincoln Lord who, as new president of a small food-canning plant that had lost its major outlet, has a chance to show whether he is a 'stuffed shirt', a personable front man using other people's ideas, or a man of substance. Lincoln's faithful wife Maggie and Brick, an old associate . . . and numerous other characters afford opportunity for observations on the business world and executives in general." Booklist

"The book gallops along at a fine pace from one long chapter to another, and it succeeds at being good entertainment without ever having to resort to cheap shock." Sat R

Hawthorne, Nathaniel

The best of Hawthorne; ed. with introduction and notes by Mark Van Doren. Ronald 1951 436p $4

Analyzed for short stories only in Short Story Index

"The volume contains all 'The scarlet letter' ten tales and sketches, and selections from 'The American Notebooks.' " Cur Ref Bks

Partial contents: Young Goodman Brown; Roger Malvin's burial; Gray champion; Wives of the dead; Ambitious guest; Minister's black veil; Sunday at home; Celestial railroad; Rappaccini's daughter; Ethan Brand; The scarlet letter

The Blithedale romance. Dutton 250p (Everyman's lib) o.p. 1970

First published 1852

"A novel based on the Brook Farm socialistic experiment which George Ripley started in 1841 with the assistance of certain fellow-Transcendentalists (Emerson, Margaret Fuller and others). Hawthorne himself joined this group, though hardly as an enthusiast, and the romance partially reflects his experiences." Nield

also in Hawthorne, N. The complete novels and selected tales of Nathaniel Hawthorne p439-585

The complete novels and selected tales of Nathaniel Hawthorne; ed. with an introduction, by Norman Holmes Pearson. Modern Lib. 1965 1223p (Modern Lib. giants) $4.95

Partially analyzed in Short Story Index

First published 1937; copyright renewed 1965

Novels included are: Fanshawe; The scarlet letter; The House of the Seven Gables; The Blithedale romance; The marble Faun

Includes short stories from Twice-told tales and Mosses from an old manse, both entered separately. Short stories included from The snow image are: The snow image: a childish miracle; The Great Stone Face; Ethen Brand; The Canterbury pilgrims; The Devil in manuscript; My kinsman, Major Molineux

Complete short stories of Nathaniel Hawthorne. Hanover House 1959 615p front boards $4.95

Analyzed in Short Story Index

"Contains 72 stories from Twice-told tales, Mosses from an old manse, The snow-image, and a few scattered sources. None of the juvenile stories are included. There are also introductory biographical and critical sketches by Henry James, Edgar A. Poe, Anthony Trollope, and Oliver Wendell Holmes." Booklist

Contains the following stories: Gray champion; Wedding knell; Minister's black veil; Maypole of Merry Mount; Gentle boy; Mr. Higginbotham's catastrophe; Wakefield; Great Carbuncle; Prophetic pictures; David Swan; Hollow of the three hills; Vision of the fountain; Fancy's show box; Dr Heidegger's experiment; Howe's masquerade; Edward Randolph's portrait; Lady Eleanore's mantle; Old Esther Dudley; Village uncle; Ambitious guest; Sister years; Seven vagabonds; White old maid; Peter Goldthwaite's treasure; Shaker bridal; Endicott and the Red Cross; Lily's quest; Edward Fane's rosebud; Threefold destiny; The birthmark; Select party; Young Goodman Brown; Rappaccini's daughter; Mrs Bullfrog; Monsieur du Miroir; Hall of fantasy; Celestial railroad; Procession of life; Feathertop: a moralized legend; New Adam and Eve; Egotism; Christmas banquet; Drowne's wooden image; Intelligence office; Roger Malvin's burial; P.'s correspondence; Earth's holocaust; Passages from a relinquished work; Artist of the beautiful virtuoso's collection; Snow-Image: a childish miracle; Great Stone Face; Ethan Brand; Sylph Etherege; Canterbury Pilgrims; Man of Adamant; Devil in manuscript; John Inglefield's Thanksgiving; Wives of the dead; Little Daffydowndilly; My kinsman, Major Molineux; Antique ring; Graves and goblins; Dr Bullivant; Old woman's tale; Alice Doane's appeal; Ghost of Doctor Harris; Young provincial; Haunted quack; New England village; My wife's novel; Bald Eagle

Doctor Grimshawe's secret; ed. with an introduction and notes by Edward H. Davidson. Harvard Univ. Press 1954 305p illus $5

Written 1883

"The first complete publication of this unfinished novel; Hawthorne's six preliminary sketches, his first draft, and his second and final draft after a period of anguished self-criticisms and plans for revision." Bookman's Manual

Fanshawe
In Hawthorne, N. The complete novels and selected tales of Nathaniel Hawthorne p3-80

The Great Stone Face, and other tales of the White Mountains. Houghton 1935 78p $3.95

Contents: The Great Stone Face; The ambitious guest; The great carbuncle; Sketches from memory

Hawthorne, Nathaniel—*Continued*

Hawthorne's Short stories; ed. and with an introduction by Newton Arvin. Knopf 1946 xxii, 422p front $5.95

Analyzed in Short Story Index
Contents: Gray Champion; Minister's black veil; May-pole of Merry Mount; Gentle boy; Wakefield; Great carbuncle; Prophetic pictures; Dr Heidegger's experiment; Lady Eleanore's mantle; Old Esther Dudley; Ambitious guest; White old maid; Peter Goldthwaite's treasure; Endicott and the Red Cross; The birthmark; Young Goodman Brown; Rappaccini's daughter; Celestial railroad; Feathertop: a moralized legend; Egotism; Christmas banquet; Drowne's wooden image; Earth's holocaust; Artist of the beautiful; Great Stone Face; Ethan Brand; Wives of the dead; Antique ring; Alice Doane's appeal

y The House of the Seven Gables

Some editions are:
Dodd (Great illustrated classics) $4.50 Biographical introduction by Basil Davenport with contemporary illustrations
Houghton (Riverside bookshelf) $4.25 With illustrations by Helen Mason Grose
Watts, F. $8.95 Large type edition complete and unabridged. A Keith Jennison book

First published 1851
"Follows the fortunes of a decayed New England family, consisting of four members—Hephzibah Pyncheon, her brother Clifford, their cousin Judge Pyncheon, and other cousin Phoebe, a country girl. At the time the story opens Hephzibah is living in great poverty at the old homestead, the House of the Seven Gables. With her is [her brother] Clifford, just released from prison, where he had served a term of thirty years for the supposed murder of a rich uncle. Judge Pyncheon, who was influential in obtaining the innocent Clifford's arrest, that he might hide his own wrongdoing, now seeks to confine him in an asylum on the charge of insanity. Hephzibah's pitiful efforts to shield this brother, to support him and herself by keeping a centshop, to circumvent the machinations of the judge, are described through the greater portion of the novel. The sudden death of the malevolent cousin frees them and makes them possessors of his wealth." Keller's Reader's Digest of Books
"The analysis of character is stern and uncompromising, and the writer dwells, as is his wont, upon the endless and incalculable consequences of past mistakes and misdeeds. . . . A picture unsurpassed as a symphony in which background and atmosphere play a dominant part." Baker's Best

also in Hawthorne, N. The complete novels and selected tales of Nathaniel Hawthorne p243-436

The Marble Faun; or, The romance of Monte Beni. Ohio State Univ. Press 1968 cxxx, 610p (The Centenary ed. of the works of Nathaniel Hawthorne) $10

"A Publication of the Ohio State University Center for Textual Studies"
First published 1860
"A tale of tragedy and mystery in an Italian setting, and at the same time a brilliant introduction to the art and fascination of modern Rome. The book was first published in England [under the title Transformation] while Hawthorne was U. S. consul at Liverpool." Pratt Alcove

also in Hawthorne, N. The complete novels and selected tales of Nathaniel Hawthorne p589-858

Mosses from an old manse. Houghton 1883 559p (Riverside ed) o.p. 1970

Analyzed in Short Story Index
First published 1846
Contents: Old manse; Birthmark; Select party; Young Goodman Brown; Rappaccini's daughter; Mrs Bullfrog; Fire worship; Buds and bird voices; Monsieur du Miroir; Hall of fantasy; Celestial railroad; Procession of life; Feathertop: a moralized legend; New Adam and Eve; Egotism; Christmas banquet; Drowne's wooden image; Intelligence office; Roger Malvin's burial; P.'s correspondence; Earth's holocaust; Passages from a relinquished work; Sketches from memory; Old apple dealer; Artist of the beautiful; Virtuoso's collection

The portable Hawthorne; ed. with an introduction and notes by Malcolm Cowley. Viking 1948 634p $6

"Viking Portable library"
Partially analyzed in Short Story Index
A collection of Hawthorne's "various manners." It contains The Scarlet Letter; selections from The House of the Seven Gables, The Marble Faun, and The Dolliver Romance; twelve short stories; passages from his notebooks; and eleven letters
Short stories included are: An old woman's tale; My kinsman, Major Molineux; Gray champion; Young Goodman Brown; Golden touch; Feathertop; Wakefield; Egotism; The birthmark; Earth's holocaust; Artist of the beautiful; Ethan Brand

y The scarlet letter

Some editions are:
Dodd (Great illustrated classics) $4.50 With contemporary illustrations and a foreword by Basil Davenport
Dutton (Everyman's lib) $3.25 Introduction by Roy Harvey Pierce
Houghton (Riverside lib) $4.95
Modern Lib. $2.95
Watts, F. $7.95 Large type edition. A Keith Jennison book
Watts, F. $4.95, lib. bdg. $3.30 Ultra type edition complete and unabridged. With a critical and biographical profile of Nathaniel Hawthorne by Norman Holmes Pearson

First published 1850
A classic of American literature—a searching study of the workings of conscience in the human heart, and of the atmosphere of Puritan life
"The scene is Boston, two hundred years ago: the chief characters are Hester Prynne, her lover, Arthur Dimmesdale, the young but revered minister of the town; their child, Pearl; and her husband, Roger Chillingworth, an aged scholar." Keller's Reader's Digest of Books

also in Hawthorne, N. The best of Hawthorne p182-392
also in Hawthorne, N. The complete novels and selected tales of Nathaniel Hawthorne p85-240
also in Hawthorne, N. The portable Hawthorne p269-489

Twice-told tales; selected and introduced by Wallace Stegner; and illus. by Valenti Angelo. Heritage [distributed by Dial Press] 1966 411p illus $7.50

This edition analyzed in Short Story Index
First published 1837
Contents: The snow-image: a childish miracle; The Great Stone Face; Ethan Brand; My kinsman, Major Molineux; Alice Doane's appeal; Young Goodman Brown; Rappaccini's daughter; Celestial railroad; The birth mark; Egotism; Earth's holocaust; The artist of the beautiful; The wedding knell; The minister's black veil; The maypole of Merry Mount; Mr Higginbotham's catastrophe; The hollow of the three hills; Dr Heidegger's experiment; Lady Eleanore's mantle; Old Esther Dudley; The ambitious guest; Feathertop: a moralized legend; The prophetic pictures; Peter Goldthwaite's treasure

Hay, Jacob

Autopsy for a cosmonaut; a novel by Jacob Hay and John M. Keshishian. Little 1969 242p boards $5.95

"Sam Stonebreaker, M.D., a young pathologist, is chosen by a vast computer network as the man in America best suited to become the first doctor in space. His assignment is to find out what killed the Russian cosmonauts in a marooned space vehicle. Naturally, it's a hush-hush proposition for this country, so Dr. Sam is fitted out with a new name, a new face, and identity . . . and finally completes his mission successfully." Pub W
"The book should be read by everyone and is highly recommended simply because it tells a believable story." Library J

FICTION CATALOG
EIGHTH EDITION

Haycraft, Howard

(ed.) Five spy novels; selected and introduced by Howard Haycraft. Doubleday 1962 758p o.p. 1970

Contents: The great impersonation, by E. P. Oppenheim; Greenmantle, by J. Buchan; Epitaph for a spy, by E. Ambler; No surrender, by M. Albrand; No entry, by M. Coles

(ed.) Fourteen great detective stories. Rev. ed. Edited with an introduction by Howard Haycraft. Modern Lib. 1949 464p o.p. 1970

Analyzed in Short Story Index

First collected 1928 under the title: Fourteen great detective stories ed. by Vincent Starrett. Only six of the original selection have been kept, eight being entirely new

Contents: The purloined letter, by E. A. Poe; The Red-headed League, by A. C. Doyle; The problem of cell 13, by J. Futrelle; The case of Oscar Brodski, by R. A. Freeman; The blue cross, by G. K. Chesterton; The age of miracles, by M. D. Post; The little mystery, by E. C. Bentley; The third-floor flat, by A. Christie; The yellow slugs, by H. C. Bailey; The bone of contention, by D. L. Sayers; The adventure of the African traveler, by E. Queen; Instead of evidence, by R. Stout; The house in Goblin Wood, by C. Dickson; The dancing detective, by C. Woolrich

(ed.) Ten great mysteries, ed. by Howard Haycraft and John Beecroft. Doubleday 1959 640p o.p. 1970

Partially analyzed in Short Story Index

Contains two novels: The Maltese falcon, by Dashiell Hammett (1930) and, The franchise affair, by Josephine Tey (1948) and three novelettes and five short stories: The learned adventure of the dragon's head, by D. L. Sayers; The case of the crying swallow, by E. S. Gardner; The witness for the prosecution, by A. Christie; The adventure of the President's half disme, by E. Queen; The case of the late pig, by M. Allingham; No motive, by D. du Maurier; Die like a dog, by R. Stout; The dancing detective, by W. Irish

(ed.) Three times three; mystery omnibus; ed. by Howard Haycraft and John Beecroft. Doubleday 1964 3v (830p) o.p. 1970

Partially analyzed in Short Story Index

Includes three novels: The lady in the lake, by R. Chandler, first published 1943 by Knopf; Rogue male, by G. Household, first published 1939 by Little; Night at the Vulcan, by N. Marsh, first published 1951 by Little. Three novelettes: The empty hours; an 87th Precinct mystery, by E. McBain; Dead man's mirror, by A. Christie; Murder is no joke, by R. Stout. Nine short stories: In the teeth of the evidence, by D. L. Sayers; The case of the irate witness, by E. S. Gardner; Pattern for murder, by F. Lockridge; Silent night, by B. Kendrick; Death by invisible hands, by J. D. Carr; After-dinner story, by W. Irish; Is Betsey Blake still alive, by R. Bloch; The adventure of the Gettysburg bugle, by E. Queen; The orderly world of Mr Appleby, by S. Ellin

(ed.) A treasury of great mysteries; ed. by Howard Haycraft and John Beecroft. Doubleday [1969 c1957] 2v $7.95

First published 1957 by Simon & Schuster

Novels included are: Murder in the Calais coach, by A. Christie; Journey into fear, by E. Ambler; The big sleep, by R. Chandler; Rebecca, by D. du Maurier

Novelettes included are: The case of the crimson kiss, by E. S. Gardner; The secret, by M. R. Rinehart; The lamp of God, by E. Queen; The bone of contention, by D. L. Sayers; Instead of evidence, by R. Stout

Short stories included are: The treasure hunt, by E. Wallace; Maigret's Christmas, by G. Simenon; Puzzle for poppy, by P. Quentin; The incautious burglar, by J. D. Carr; The case of the white elephant, by M. Allingham; Rear window, by W. Irish; The arrow of God, by L. Charteris; I can find my way out, by N. Marsh; Rift in the loot, by S. Palmer; The man who explained miracles, by C. Dickson

Haycraft, Molly Costain

The Lady Royal. Lippincott 1964 253p boards $5.50

"Set during the fourteenth-century reign of England's Edward III. Isabel, the Princess Royal of England, is just fifteen when her father sends for her to join him on the Continent, where he is fighting the French. There she meets two men who are to change her life: haughty Louis, Count of Flanders, and lovable Bernard d'Albert of Gascony." Publisher's note

"The Hundred Years' War rages in the background, the English annihilate the French with their long bows at Crécy, England abounds in French hostages, noble and willing; there is tilting, hawking, music and dancing. Isabel looks the medieval princess, but her reactions are those of any modern girl you know. . . . The story is authentic, and after all, who is to define the mid-14th-century feminine mystique?" Book of the Month Club News

My lord brother the Lion Heart. Lippincott 1968 320p boards $5.95

"Joan, Queen of Sicily, sister of Richard the Lion Heart, daughter of Eleanor of Aquitaine and Henry of England, narrates this historical novel. The story opens in 1148 with the beginnings of the Third Crusade. Richard has just ascended the throne of England. Joan, widowed before the Crusade starts, goes along anyway, as companion for Richard's bride, Berengaria. The unsuccessful Crusade becomes the background for romance—the love of Joan and Raimond of St. Gilles." Pub W

"For readers young or old who like romance in their history, this is a tasty dish." Book of the Month Club News

The reluctant queen. Lippincott 1962 256p boards $5.95

An historical novel about Mary Tudor, sister of Henry VIII of England. Forced into marriage by her brother to the aging king of France, in order to insure peace between the two countries, Mary drives a shrewd bargain and a promise that she may marry Charles Brandon, the commoner she really loves when the king dies

"Henry the King is shown at the height of his youth and good looks. . . . The relationship between brother and sister is amusing, often argumentative, but always affectionate. A rousing tale of 16th-century England and France recommended to adults, both young and otherwise." Library J

Haydn, Hiram

(ed.) A world of great stories; ed. by Hiram Haydn [and] John Cournos [and] Board of Editors. Crown 1947 950p $2.98

Partially analyzed in Short Story Index

Contents: Love-philtre of Ikey Schoenstein, by O. Henry; Hands, by S. Anderson; Ten indians, by E. Hemingway; Rose for Emily, by W. Faulkner; Man who saw through heaven, by W. D. Steele; Baby party, by F. S. Fitzgerald; Ex parte, by R. Lardner; Circus at dawn, by T. Wolfe; Flight, by J. Steinbeck; Snowfall in childhood, by B. Hecht; Day's work, by K. A. Porter; Petrified man, by E. Welty; Act of faith, by I. Shaw; Blue cross, by G. K. Chesterton; Eye of Allah, by R. Kipling; Red, by S. Maugham; Open window, by Saki; Rocking-horse winner, by D. H. Lawrence; Fanfare for Elizabeth, by E. Sitwell; Sunday afternoon, by E. Bowen; Desire, by J. Stephens; Boarding house, by J. Joyce; The sniper, by L. O'Flaherty; Old wife, by M. Jamieson; Keep up appearances, by R. Roberts; Miss Brill, by K. Mansfield; Gray horse, by K. S. Prichard; Sick call, by M. Callaghan; Madame de Luzy, by A. France; Deliverance, by R. Rolland; Overture, by M. Proust; Gentle libertine, by Colette; Crime without a motive, by A. Gide; May on Lake Asquam, by J. Giraudoux'; Man's fate, by A. Malraux; The wall, by J. P. Sartre; The funeral, by A. Camus; Hiep-Hioup, by G. Eekhoud; An unbeliever, by Azorin; Blasa's tavern, by P. Baroja; Woman of Samaria, by G. Miro; Horse in the moon, by L. Pirandello; The travelers, by I. Silone; Story of my death, by L. de Bosis; Last faun, by A. Riberiro; Disorder and early sorrow, by T. Mann; Tale of the hands of God, by R. M. Rilke; Married couple, by F. Kafka; Moonbeam alley, by S. Zweig; Kong at the seaside,

Haydn, Hiram—*Continued*

by A. Zweig; Dead are silent, by A. Schnitzler; Darkness at noon, by A. Koestler; Harry's loves, by H. Hesse; Bluebeard's daughter, by L. Couperus; The suspicion, by J. L. Walch; Birds of passage, by M. A. Nexo; Sailor-boy's tale, by I. Dinesen; Death of Kristin Lavransdatter, by S. Undset; The shark, by J. Bojer; The outlaws, by S. Lagerlöf; In spite of everything, by S. Siwertz; Burning city, by H. Söderberg; In exile, by A. Chekhov; One autumn night, by M. Gorky; Tevye wins a fortune, by S. Aleichem; Hide and seek. by F. Sologub; The abyss; by L. Andreyev; Gentleman from San Francisco, by I. Bunin; Vasily Suchkov, by A. Tolstoy; His only son, by K. Simonov; Death, by W. S. Reymont; Emperor and the Devil, by J. Wittlin; Selma Koljas, by F. E. Sillanpaa; Money, by K. Capek; Vertigo, by E. Hostovsky; Silver hilt, by F. Molnar; Green fly, by K. Mikszath; Children and old folk, by I. Cankor; The neighbor, by A. G. Motos; Easter torch, by I. L. Caragiale; Little coin, by A. Karalitcheff; Maternity, by L. Nakos; Medicine, by L. Hsun; Spring silkworms, by M. Tun; Mr Hua Wei, by C. T'len-i; Ah Ao, by S. Hsi-chen; Growth of hate, by W. Hsiyen; Dog-meat general, by L. Yutang; Doomsday, by Y. Kang; The handkerchief, by R. Akutagawa; My lord, the baby, by R. Tafore; Drought, by S. R. Ratnam; Jealous wife, by H. Davidian; Deserted street, by T. Al-Hakim; Hillbride, by A. El-Khoury; The pig, by C. Zarian; Gray donkey, by R. Halid; Tales of a Burmese soothsayer, by S. Tun; The cock, by T. K. Hai; My Thai cat, by P. Zeng; Horse of the sword, by M. Buaken; Woman of mystery, by M. Latorre; Lucero, by O. Castro Z; Valley heat, by J. de la Cuadra; The well by A. Cespedes; Cross over, Sawyer, by J. del Corral; The failure, by J. Ferretis; Lottery ticket, by V. G. Calderón; Adultery, by E. L. Albújar; Sorrel colt, by B. Lynch; Servant girl, by A. Hernández-Catá; Three letters . . . and a footnote, by H. Quiroga; Ovegon, by L. M. U. Achelpohl; Funny-man who repented, by M. Lobato

Hayes, Alfred

The girl on the Via Flaminia. Harper 1949 215p o.p. 1970

"This novel of the last year of the Second World War in Italy presents a symbolic picture of the relations between conquered and conqueror in a story about an affair between an American GI and a Roman girl." Book Rev Digest

"In the main, Mr. Hayes suggests rather than states his conflicts, through expert dialogue inevitably reminiscent of Hemingway. With its brilliant economy of detail, its dramatic rise and fall, and its wealth of interior suggestiveness, the story is close to the pattern of stage drama. As such it is essentially tragedy—a minor tragedy in the major tragedy of war and human separateness." Christian Science Monitor

Hayes, Joseph

The desperate hours; a novel. Random House 1954 302p o.p. 1970

"A novel of suspense. A trio of escaping convicts select a house in the suburbs of Indianapolis and move in on the occupants. The convicts hold the family of four in their power until they think the time is right for another break. The horror of the members of the family is depicted in detail." Book Rev Digest

"The diabolical ingenuity with which the convicts enforce their control and prevent the family from seeking help from the police or friends, and the unknown qualities of temperament in both the criminals and the family produce a situation tense with the kind of suspense enjoyed by mystery and crime story fans." Booklist

Hazzard, Shirley

People in glass houses; portraits from organization life. Knopf 1967 179p boards $4.95

"Connected episodes focusing on and picturing the Organization, like the UN, an organization aiming at the good of humanity but with its aims often frustrated by pomposity, red-tape, and the unimaginative regulations like those of business and government

which reward mediocrity and conformity at the expense of imaginative intelligence." Bk Buyer's Guide

"Anyone who has known an International Organization at first hand will derive a good deal of wicked satisfaction from this crisp collection of sketches of Organization life. . . . [The author] specializes in the laconic puncturing of pretension. . . . While appreciating the mockery and acknowledging the force of the attack on cowardice and wrongheadedness, we would be rash to take Miss Hazzard's as the last word on the United Nations Organization." Times (London) Lit Sup

Head, Ann

y Mr and Mrs Bo Jo Jones. Putnam 1967 253p $4.95

"A marriage of necessity between two pleasant high school youngsters led astray by their emotions barely holds up against unreadiness for love or marriage and differences in family background and families. After their premature baby's death, Bo Jo and young wife July find their separation, schooling, and return to opposite sides of town assumed and arranged for by their parents. They momentarily yield to seeming reasonableness but, gradually realizing the bonds that have grown between them during a year of marriage, pregnancy, and bereavement, decide to work out their destiny and education together." Booklist

"The appeal of this story is so universal and the problems it deals with so pertinent to modern family life, that it could easily find a wide audience, from teenagers on up to grandparents. The relations between the youngsters and their parents are well handled and made painfully real." Pub W

Head, Bessie

y When rain clouds gather; a novel. Simon & Schuster [1969 c1968] 188p boards $4.95

Makhaya Maseko, a black from South Africa flees Botswana. Here "an old man, Dinorego, befriends him and introduces him to Gilbert Balfour, an Englishman who has set up cooperatives in [the village of] Golema Mmidi. Makhaya is not a farmer, but he is an intelligent man, and so . . . he undertakes the task of teaching methods of farming to the women of the village." Best Sellers

"There is too much undilated sociological and agricultural textbook language, but the book is justified by loving and humorous descriptions of African land and people, by powerful, generous feeling and passionate analysis of the situation of the black African. [The writer] is especially moving on the position of women, . . . and she is coolly humorous about British colonial administrators, reserving rancorous irony for the newly-emergent twopenny-halfpenny revolutionaries." New Statesman

Healy, Raymond J.

(ed.) Famous science fiction stories; adventures in time and space, ed. by Raymond J. Healy and J. Francis McComas. Modern Lib. 1957 997p $4.95

Analyzed in Short Story Index under original title

A reprint of the volume first published 1946 by Random House with title: Adventures in time and space. This edition adds a new introduction

Contents: Requiem, by R. A. Heinlein; Forgetfulness, by D. A. Stuart; Nerves, by L. Del Rey; Sands of time, by P. S. Miller; Proud robot, by L. Padgett; Black destroyer, by A. E. Van Vogt; Symbiotica, by E. F. Russell; Seeds of the dusk, by R. Z. Gullun; Heavy planet, by L. Gregor; Time locker, by L. Padgett; The link, by C. Cartmill; Mechanical mice, by M. A. Hugi; V-2 rocket cargo ship, by W. Ley; Adam and no Eve, by A. Bester; Nightfall, by I. Asimov; Matter of size, by H. Bates; As never was, by P. S. Miller; Q.U.R. by A. Boucher; Who goes there, by D. A. Stuart; Roads must roll, by R. A. Heinlein; Asylum, by A. E. Van Vogt; Quietus, by R. Rocklynne; The twonky, by L. Padgett; Time-travel happens, by A. M. Phillips; Robot's return, by R. M. Williams; Blue giraffe, by L. S. de Camp; Flight into darkness, by W. Marlowe; Weapons shop, by

Healy, Raymond J.—*Continued*
A. E. Van Vogt; Farewell to the master, by
H. Bates; Within the pyramid, by R. D. Miller;
He who shrank, by H. Hasse; By his boot-
straps, by A. MacDonald; Star mouse, by F.
Brown; Correspondence course, by R. F. Jones;
Brain, by S. F. Wright

Hecht, Ben
The collected stories of Ben Hecht; prefaced
by Some introductory thoughts by the author.
Crown 1945 524p o.p. 1970

Analyzed in Short Story Index
Contents: Concerning a woman of sin; Mira-
cle of the fifteen murderers; Remember thy
creator; Mystery of the fabulous laundryman;
Adventures of Professor Emmett; Cafe sinister;
Champion from far away; Death of Eleazer;
Pink hussar; The shadow; God is good to a
Jew; Wistful blackguard; Specter of the rose;
Bull that won; Actor's blood; Crime without
passion; Rival dummy; In the midst of death;
The ax; Lost soul; Heavenly choir
Hecht "loves to write with a flourish, he
loves to write with a swagger, but he can also
write with sobriety and restraint when he
chooses. His passion for word-play, for similes
in particular, often leads him into excess, but
even his excesses are effective, while his best
similes serve, as such figures should, to illuminate or extend the significance of their objects." Sat R

Heckelmann, Charles N.
Death trap for an iron horse
In Western Writers of America. A West-
ern bonanza p309-65

Heggen, Thomas
Mister Roberts. Illus. by Samuel Hanks
Byrant

Some editions are:
Houghton $3.95
Watts, F. $8.95 Large type edition. A Keith
Jennison book
First published 1946 by Houghton
The story of a man who found himself playing guardian angel, referee, and diplomat without portfolio to the men on the U.S.S. Reluctant, a cargo ship, crossing and recrossing
the Pacific during World War II
"The leisurely narrative is told in a very few
incidents, all centering about an admirable
young lieutenant miserably defeated in his
desire to get into the fighting. A quiet, credible story of the corroding effects of apathy
and boredom on men who, in battle, might
have been heroes." New Yorker

Heiney, Donald W. See Harris, MacDonald

Heinlein, Robert A.
The door into summer. Doubleday 1957
188p $3.50
"The story of an inventor who is projected
some 30 years into the future by means of
'cold sleep' and, seeing the results of human
error, takes the opportunity to go back and
correct them." Booklist
"A playful inventory of scientific gadgits-
to-be." Sat R

Double star. Doubleday 1956 186p o.p. 1970
"When Lawrence Smith, an actor, meets a
spaceman, he is obliged to play the most terrifying role of his career. He finds himself disposing of two Earthmen and one Martian,
then embarking on a space ship for Mars. It
is too late to turn back when he learns that he
is acting as 'stand-in' for the most loved—and
most hated—man in the solar system!"
Huntting
"This is a lively adventure story told with
vigorous readability." N Y Her Trib Books

Glory Road; a novel. Putnam 1963 288p
$5.95
Scar Gordon answers a want ad and his
beautiful employer sends him on a dangerous
mission "against weird foes on planets weird-
er still. Ultimately he comes to [the planet]
Center . . . and there finds—or thinks he finds
—the end of his own personal quest." Publisher's note

The green hills of earth; Rhysling and the
adventures of the entire solar system! With
an appreciation by Mark Reinsberg. Shasta
Pubs. 1951 256p o.p. 1970

Analyzed in Short Story Index
Contents: Delilah and the space-rigger; Space
jockey; Long watch; Gentlemen, be seated;
Black pits of Luna; It's great to be back; "—
we also walk dogs"; Ordeal in space; Green
hills of earth; Logic of empire

Gulf
In Knight, D. ed. A century of great
short science fiction novels p231-93

Magic, inc.
In Heinlein, R. A. Three by Heinlein
p327-426
In Heinlein, R. A. Waldo and Magic,
inc.

The menace from earth. Gnome Press 1959
255p o.p. 1970

Analyzed in Short Story Index
Contents: Year of the jackpot; By his bootstraps; Columbus was a dope; Menace from
earth; Sky lift; Goldfish bowl; Project nightmare; Water is for washing

The moon is a harsh mistress. Putnam 1966
383p $5.95
"Luna in the 21st century is a penal colony,
but, since no one can stand earth gravity
after being on the moon for a few weeks, all
who are sent must stay. When the freed people,
both natives and those whose sentences have
been completed, rise against the authority and
its warden, they receive unexpected help from
a computer with a personality. . . . The description of family life in a community of several
wives and husbands where each new person
marries all the individuals of the opposite sex
may bother some people." Library J
"The author draws on revolutionary techniques of the past modified to fit current technology; he spoofs them, parodies them, treats
them with a touch of whimsy and an occasionally distorted sense of humor; he weaves in human foible and stupidity; in brief, he tells a
fascinatingly readable story of an almost incredible revolution." Best Sellers

The past through tomorrow; "future history" stories. Putnam 1967 667p $6.95

Analyzed in Short Story Index
"The collection brings together 21 stories
published at various times from 1939 to 1962
that reveal Heinlein's ideas of possible technological and social developments." Booklist
Contents: Life-line; The roads must roll;
Blowups happen; The man who sold the Moon;
Delilah and the space-rigger; Space jockey;
Requiem; The long watch; Gentlemen, be
seated; The black pits of Luna; "It's great to
be back!"; "—We also walk dogs"; Searchlight; Ordeal in space; The green hills of Earth;
Logic of empire; The menace from Earth; "If
this goes on—"; Coventry; Misfit; Methuselah's children

The puppet masters. Doubleday 1951 219p
o.p. 1970
"The space ship seemed harmless enough,
at first, but something seemed to be corrupting
the farmers and the officials in the Midwest
where it had fallen. Sam and Mary, super secret operatives, soon learned that the 'slugs'
from the space ship dominated completely
anyone on whom they could fasten their parasitic grip." Retail Bookseller
"The taut melodramatic plotting, the skillful
indirect exposition, the careful thinking
through of details make for a nuclear-reactor-
propelled thriller with a deeper conviction of
reality than the average spy or detective story."
N Y Her Trib Books

also in Heinlein, R. A. Three by Heinlein p 1-215

Three by Heinlein. Doubleday 1965 426p
$6.50
An omnibus volume of three science fiction
novels, entered separately
Contents: The puppet masters; Waldo; Magic,
inc.

Heinlein, Robert A.—*Continued*

Waldo

In Heinlein, A. A. Three by Heinlein p217-326

Waldo and Magic, inc. Doubleday 1950 219p o.p. 1970

"'Two short, humorous science fiction novels. 'Waldo' is the story of a power monopoly whose mastery of the radio waves challenged by a weird inventor and a Pennsylvania-Dutch farmer who knew the uses of outer space. 'Magic, Inc.' is the tale of a protection racket whose techniques were magic but whose methods dated back to the early 20th century." Retail Bookseller

"Parts of both may be rather heavy going—especially if you're vague about such matters as turbo-jets, the time-and-space continuum, and the precise use made of ectoplasm by a poltergeist. But they are rewarding experiments in a field of writing that too often becomes both static and sterile." N Y Times Bk R

Heinrich, Willi

The cross of iron; tr. from the German by Richard and Clara Winston. Bobbs 1956 456p map o.p. 1970

"A big dramatic war novel with vivid combat scenes, a tense story line, and a hero of unforgettable quality. The scene is Russia in World War II and the hero, a German corporal, who leads a platoon to safety through Russian territory, and then comes into conflict with his superior officer." Pub W

"The author has caught to perfection the ominous Russian landscape, the atmosphere of defeat slowly enveloping a company so absorbed by its own struggles that major problems of the Wehrmacht soldier, such as the rivalry with the S. S. Troops, or the amateurish strategy of Hitler, never enter their vision. . . . [He has written] a chronicle of ravage, rape and doom, conjuring up before us a bullet-showered moonscape from Mars." N Y Times Bk R

Heller, Joseph

Catch-22; a novel

Some editions are:
Modern Lib. $2.95
Simon & Schuster $6.95
Simon & Schuster $10.95 A large type edition

First published 1961 by Simon & Schuster

"A broad comedy about a bombardier based in Italy during World War II and his efforts to avoid flying bombing missions while his colonel tries to get him killed by demanding that he fly more and more missions. There is some wonderfully funny dialog and some entertaining zany action. Mr. Heller takes up just about every aspect of World War II as seen by the comic as well as the cynical novelists who have come before him: pompous officers, malingering soldiers, faking, trading with the enemy and, of course, the pursuit of the local trollops. Eventually the hero deserts." Pub W

"Through the agency of grotesque comedy, Heller has found a way to confront the humbug, hypocrisy, cruelty, and sheer stupidity of our mass society . . . and through some miracle of prestidigitation, Pianosa has become a satirical microcosm for many of the microcosmic idiocies of our time. . . . Catch-22, despite some of the most outrageous sequences since A Night at the Opera, is an intensely serious work." New Repub

Hemingway, Ernest

Nobel Prize in literature, 1954

Across the river and into the trees. Scribner 1950 308p $3.95

A postwar story of an American colonel, whose fifty years and heart condition weigh heavily upon him, as he spends a weekend in Venice, the city he loves, and sees the 18-year-old Italian contessa who is his "only, last and true love"

y A farewell to arms. Scribner 1929 355p $5.95

"An American ambulance officer serving on the Austro-Italian front becomes entangled with an English nurse and deserts to join her after the retreat of Caparetto. Their affair, casual and tawdry at first, becomes a moving and beautiful love story at the tragic end. Using only the minimum of description, Mr. Hemingway achieves his effects, many of them highly dramatic, by means of conversations in the staccato repetitive style of average human intercourse." Cleveland

"Farewell to Arms has as you read it that quality of warmth, of actuality, of closeness that only your own personal experiences have for you. . . . This book enriches you." Outlook

also in Hemingway, E. Three novels of Ernest Hemingway v2

y For whom the bell tolls. Scribner 1940 471p $5.95

"The story of four days preceding a minor action in the Spanish [Civil] war. An American college professor, working for the Loyalists, was sent to blow up a bridge held by the enemy. Living in a mountain cave, he persuaded a group of guerrillas to accept his plan, saw it ruined by a peasent's malice and went on nevertheless, knowing it was certain death. His sudden love for a refugee girl brought tenderness and a great happiness, but no weakening. The whole tragedy of the war is implicit here. . . . Beneath the brutal realism there is genuine compassion for a people driven to the wall." Booklist

Hemingway; ed. by Malcolm Cowley. Viking 1944 xxiv, 642p (Viking Portable lib) o.p. 1970

Partially analyzed in Short Story Index

Contains 25 short stories, the complete novel The sun also rises, and excerpts from A farewell to arms, from To have and have not, and from For whom the bell tolls

The stories included are: Indian camp; Doctor and the doctor's wife; End of something; Three day blow; The battler; Very short story; Soldier's home; The revolutionist; Mr and Mrs Elliot; Cat in the rain; Out of season; Cross country snow; My old man; Big two-hearted river; In another country; Hills like white elephants; The killers; Today is Friday; A clean, well-lighted place; Light of the world; Way you'll never be; The short happy life of Francis Macomber; The snows of Kilimanjaro

The Hemingway reader; selected with a foreword and twelve brief prefaces by Charles Poore. Scribner 1953 xx, 652p $7.50

Partially analyzed in Short Story Index

This one volume selection includes two complete novels: The sun also rises and The torrents of spring; excerpts from A farewell to arms; Death in the afternoon; Green hills of Africa; To have and have not; For whom the bell tolls; Over the river and into the trees; The old man and the sea; and eleven short stories

The stories included are; In our time; A way you'll never be; Fifty grand; A clean well-lighted place; Light of the world; After the storm; The short happy life of Francis Macomber; Capital of the world; The snows of Kilimanjaro; Old man at the bridge; Fable of the good lion

In our time; stories. Scribner 1930 214p $4.50

Analyzed in Short Story Index

Contents: Indian camp; Doctor and the doctor's wife; End of something; Three day blow; The battler; Very short story; Soldier's home; The revolutionist; Mr and Mrs Elliot; Cat in the rain; Out of season; Cross country snow; My old man; Big two-hearted river

(ed.) Men at war; the best war stories of all time; ed. with an introduction by Ernest Hemingway; based on a plan by William Kozlenko. Crown 1942 xxxi, 1072p o.p. 1970

Analyzed in Short Story Index

Contents: Invasion of Britain, by J. Caesar; Battle of Hastings, by C. Oman; French crusade, 1249-1250 A.D. by J. de Joinville; The

Hemingway, Ernest—*Continued*

battle of Arsouf, by C. Oman; The death of Montezuma, by W. H. Prescott; Who called you here, by E. J. Petersen; The invaders, by R. Hillary; Massacre at Matanzas Inlet, by P. M. de Avilés; Red badge of courage, by S. Crane; The blocking of Zeebrugge, by A. Hurd; Horatius at the bridge, by Livy; Shiloh, bloody Shiloh, by L. Lewis; How David slew Goliath, from The Bible; Fight on the hilltop, by E. Hemingway; Last battle of King Arthur, by Sir T. Malory; At all costs, by R. Aldington; The pass of Thermopylae, by C. Yonge; Sword of the Lord and of Gideon, by T. Roosevelt; Deguelo, by M. James; Torture, by T. E. Lawrence; Tsushima, by F. Thiess; The Parisian, by A. Brooks; March to the sea, by Xenophon; Vale of tears, by L. Stallings; Odyssey of three Slavs, by A. Brooks; Gold from Crete, by C. S. Forester; Harper's Ferry, by L. Ehrlich; Custer, by F. F. Van de Water; An egg for the major, by C. S. Forester; The Merrimac and the Monitor, by M. Johnston; Manila Bay, by G. Dewey; Tank fighting in Libya, by A. Moorehead; Blowing up a train, by T. E. Lawrence; Lisette at Eylau, by General Marbot; The stolen railroad train, by M. James; Turn about, by W. Faulkner; Trojan horse, by Virgil; Air battle, by C. Nordhoff; The people's war, by L. Tolstoy; The wrong road, by M. James; Corvette Claymore, by V. Hugo; Miracle at Dunkirk, by A. D. Divine; Gallipoli, by J. F. C. Fuller; Stars in their courses, by J. W. Thomason, Jr; Waterloo, by V. Hugo; Retreat from Caporetto, by E. Hemingway; Battle of Cannae, by Livy; Victory of the Americans at Saratoga, by E. S. Creasy; Lost battalion, by T. M. Johnson; Bagration's rearguard action, by L. Tolstoy; After the final victory, by A. Smedley; Her privates we, by Private 19022; Borodina, by L. Tolstoy; Trafalgar, by R. Southey; Battle of Atlanta, by L. Lewis; Cavalry charge at Omdurman, by W. Churchill; The sun of Austerlitz, by General Marbot; Oriskany: 1777, by W. D. Edmonds; Marines at Soissons, by J. W. Thomason, Jr; Battle of Ypres, by F. Richards; Occurrence at Owl Creek Bridge, by A. Bierce; Joshua's conquest of Jericho, from The Bible; Taking of Lungtungpen, by R. Kipling; Ball-of-fat, by G. de Maupassant; Hands across the sea, by A. Woollcott; I bombed the barges, by the captain of a Blenheim bomber; Italian debacle at Guadalajara, by F. G. Tinker, Jr; Buchmendel, by S. Zweig; I take Vladivostok, by F. Hunt; UP periscope, by an officer of H. M. submarine Sturgeon; Father Duffy, by A. Woollcott; The war years, by J. Hilton; Soldiers of the republic, by D. Parker; The chauffeurs of Madrid, by E. Hemingway; A man's bound to fight, by J. W. Thomason, Jr; Squadron scramble, by B. Kennerly; A name and a flag, by J. W. Thomason, Jr; A personal view of Waterloo, by Stendhal; Falling through space, by R. Hillary; Pearl Harbor, by B. Clarke; Three men on a raft, by H. F. Dixon; Midway, by W. B. Clausen

Men without women. Scribner 1927 232p $4.95

Analyzed in Short Story Index
Contents: The undefeated; In another country; Hills like white elephants; The killers; Che ti dice la patria; Fifty grand; A simple enquiry; Ten Indians; A canary for one; An Alpine idyll; A pursuit race; Today is Friday; Banal story; Now I lay me

y **The old man and the sea**

Some editions are:
Scribner $3.95
Scribner $5 Illustrated edition

Pulitzer Prize, 1953
First published 1952
"A brief novel about supreme courage. An old Gulf fisherman, overtaken by hard luck, proves his tenacity and courage when he hooks a monster marlin. He kills his catch but is towed out to sea, and then brings what the sharks leave of it back to Havana." Book Rev Digest

"The admirable Santiago, Hemingway's ancient mariner and protagonist of this triumphant short novel, enters the gallery of permanent heroes effortlessly, as if he had belonged there from the beginning. . . . 'The Old Man and The Sea' is a great short novel, told with consummate artistry and destined to become a classic in its field." Sat R

also in Hemingway, E. Three novels of Ernest Hemingway v3

The short stories of Ernest Hemingway. Scribner 1953 499p $6.95

Analyzed in Short Story Index
Originally published 1938 containing play: The fifth column; the collection is entered separately with title: The fifth column and the first forty-nine stories
Contents: The short happy life of Francis Macomber; The capital of the world; The snows of Kilimanjaro; Old man at the bridge; Up in Michigan; On the quai at Smyrna; Indian camp; The doctor and the doctor's wife; The end of something; The three-day blow; The battler; A very short story; Soldier's home; The revolutionist; Mr and Mrs Elliot; Cat in the rain; Out of season; Cross-country snow; My old man; Big two-hearted river; The undefeated; In another country; Hills like white elephants; The killers; Che ti dice la patria; Fifty grand; A simple enquiry; Ten Indians; A canary for one; An Alpine idyll; A pursuit race; Today is Friday; Banal story; Now I lay me; After the storm; A clean, well-lighted place; The light of the world; God rest you merry, gentlemen; The sea change; A way you'll never be; The mother of a queen; One reader writes; Homage to Switzerland; A day's wait; A natural history of the dead; Wine of Wyoming: The gambler, the nun, and the radio; Fathers and sons

The snows of Kilimanjaro, and other stories. Scribner 1961 154p $4.95

First copyright 1927
A sampling of the work of an author whose prose style influenced and continues to influence generations of American writers
Contents: The snows of Kilimanjaro; A clean, well-lighted place; A day's wait; The gambler, the nun, and the radio; Fathers and sons; In another country; The killers; A way you'll never be; Fifty grand; The short happy life of Francis Macomber

The sun also rises. Scribner 1926 259p $5.95

"We are introduced to a group of English and American drifters on the continent who have the money and the time to blow where they list from the boulevards of Paris to the bull-fights of Spain, bathing, eating and drinking the while. . . . Yet the book is by no means a bit of sophisticated fluff. It is the hard, acid truth about this group of ineffectuals and conveys the tragedy of their lives. . . . Conversation is the method chiefly used, and it is real talk, not writing." Book Rev Digest

also in Hemingway, E. Hemingway p5-245

also in Hemingway, E. The Hemingway reader p89-289

also in Hemingway, E. Three novels of Ernest Hemingway v 1

Three novels of Ernest Hemingway. . . . Scribner 1962 3v in 1 (Modern standard authors) o.p. 1970

"The sun also rises, with an introduction by Malcolm Cowley; A farewell to arms, with an introduction by Robert Penn Warren; The old man and the sea, with an introduction by Carlos Baker." Title page
The three novels reprinted here were first published 1926, 1929, and 1952 respectively, and are entered separately

To have and have not. Scribner 1937 262p $5.95

"The hero, Harry Morgan, owned a boat in Key West. When swindled by a wealthy sportsman who had chartered his boat, he turned to smuggling to and from Havana—liquor, Chinamen, revolutionists—rather than go on relief. The separate incidents are told in fast moving, dramatic narrative, full of excitement, brutality, murder. Morgan's toughness and courage, and his satisfaction in his wife are contrasted with the lives of various effete literary people and wealthy yachtsmen in the neighborhood." Booklist

The torrents of spring

In Hemingway, E. The Hemingway reader p25-86

Hemingway, Ernest—*Continued*

Winner take nothing. Scribner 1933 244p $4.95

Analyzed in Short Story Index
Contents: After the storm; A clean well-lighted place; The light of the world; God rest you merry, gentlemen; The sea change; A way you'll never be; A mother of a queen; One reader writes; Homage to Switzerland; A day's wait; A natural history of the dead; Wine of Wyoming; The gambler, the nun, and the radio; Fathers and sons

Hempstone, Smith

In the midst of lions. Harper 1968 308p $5.95

An "attempt to tell the story of [the Arab-Israeli War of 1967] . . . from many points of view. Everyone is there, from Abba Eban and Moshe Dayan to a Bedouin too intent on robbing and killing other Arabs to know there is a war on. Men and women, cowards and heroes, victims and opportunists, politicians and patriots, farmers and soldiers, lovers and killers—the entire panorama of modern Israel at war is presented in anecdotal narrative. The central character is an American news photographer, tough, cynical, war weary, devastating to women—almost too Heminwayesque to be believed. Still, it's a model well chosen for this kind of story and this kind of war, and it works well. There is good background material on the various warring factions, and the result is a well-written action story for which there should be a large public." Pub W

Henderson, Zenna

The people: no different flesh. Doubleday 1967 236p (Doubleday Science fiction) o.p. 1970

Analyzed in Short Story Index
Mixing magic with real life these six fantasy and science fiction "stories are about individuals in a group of benign creatures who look just like people but have fallen from another world. . . . Most of the stories are set in the canyons and mountains of the far West, from pioneer to modern times." Pub W
Contents: No different flesh; Deluge; Angels unawares; Troubling of the water; Return; Shadow on the moon

Henkle, Henrietta. See Buckmaster, Henrietta

Henry, O.

y   The best short stories of O. Henry; selected and with an introduction by Bennett A. Cerf and Van H. Cartmell. Modern Lib. 1945 338p $2.95

Analyzed in Short Story Index under: W. S. Porter
Contents: The gift of the Magi; A cosmopolite in a café; Man about town; The cop and the anthem; The love-philtre of Ikey Shoenstein; Mammon and the archer; Springtime à la carte; From the cabby's seat; An unfinished story; The romance of a busy broker; The furnished room; Roads of destiny; The enchanted profile; The passing of Black Eagle; A retrieved reformation; The Renaissance at Charleroi; Shoes; Ships; The hiding of Black Bill; The duplicity of Hargraves; The ransom of Red Chief; The marry month of May; The whirligig of life; A blackjack bargainer; A lickpenny lover; The defeat of the city; Squaring the circle; Transients in Arcadia; The trimmed lamp; The pendulum; Two Thanksgiving Day gentlemen; The making of a New Yorker; The lost blend; A Harlem tragedy; A midsummer knight's dream; The last leaf; The count and the wedding guest; A municipal report

Cabbages and kings
In Henry, O. The complete works of O. Henry p551-679

y   The complete works of O. Henry; foreword by Harry Hansen. Doubleday 1953 1692p front $8.50, 2v ed $10

Analyzed in Short Story Index under: W. S. Porter

"All of O. Henry's short stories together with selected and random pieces, are contained [in these volumes]. Included are unabridged versions of [previously published volumes] 'The Four Million,' 'The Heart of the West,' 'The Gentle Grafter,' 'Roads of Destiny,' 'Cabbages and Kings,' 'Options,' 'Sixes and sevens,' 'Rolling Stones,' 'Whirligigs,' 'The Voice of the City,' 'Trimmed Lamp,' 'Strictly Business' and 'Waifs and Strays.' " Huntting

Contents: The four million: Tobin's palm; The gift of the Magi; A cosmopolite in a café; Between rounds; The skylight room; A service of love; The coming-out of Maggie; Man about town; The cop and the anthem; An adjustment of nature; Memoirs of a yellow dog; The love philtre of Ikey Schoenstein; Mammon and the archer; Springtime à la carte; The green door; From the cabby's seat; An unfinished story; The caliph, Cupid and the clock; Sisters of the golden circle; The romance of a busy broker; After twenty years; Lost on dress parade; By courtier; The furnished room; The brief début of Tildy

Heart of the West: Hearts and crosses; The ransom of Mack; Telemachus, friend; The handbook of Hymen; The pimienta pancakes; Seats of the haughty; Hygeia at the Solito; An afternoon miracle; The higher abdication; Cupid à la carte; The caballero's way; The sphinx apple; The missing chord; A call loan; The princess and the puma; The Indian summer of Dry Valley Johnson; Christmas by injunction; A chaparral prince; The reformation of Calliope

The gentle grafter: The octopus marooned; Jeff Peters as a personal magnet; Modern rural sports; The chair of philanthromathematics; The hand that riles the world; The exact science of matrimony; A midsummer masquerade; Shearing the wolf; Innocents of Broadway; Conscience in art; The man higher up; A tempered wind; Hostages to Momus; The ethics of pig

Roads of destiny: Roads of destiny; The guardian of the Accolade; The discounters of money; The enchanted profile; "Next reading matter"; Art and the bronco; Phoebe; A double-dyed deceiver; The passing of Black Eagle; A retrieved reformation; Cherchez la femme; Friends in San Rosario; The fourth in Salvador; The emancipation of Billy; The enchanted kiss; A departmental case; The renaissance at Charleroi; On behalf of the management; Whistling Dick's Christmas stocking; The halberdier of the little Rheinschloss; Two renegades; The lonesome road

Cabbages and Kings; The proem: by the carpenter; "Fox-in-the-morning"; The lotus and the bottle; Smith; Caught; Cupid's exile number two; The phonograph and the graft; Money maze; The admiral; The flag paramount; The shamrock and the palm; The remnants of the code; Shoes; Ships; Masters of arts; Dicky; Rouge et noir; Two recalls; The vitagraphoscope

Options: "Rose of Dixie"; The third ingredient; The hiding of Black Bill; Schools and school; Thimble, thimble; Supply and demand; Buried treasure; To him who waits; He also serves; The moment of victory; The head-hunter; No story; The higher pragmatism; Best-seller; Rus in Urbe; A poor rule

Sixes and sevens: The last of the troubadours; The sleuths; Witches' loaves; The pride of the cities; holding up a train; Ulysses and the dogman; The champion of the weather; Makes the whole world kin; At arms with Morpheus; A ghost of a chance; Jimmy Hayes and Muriel; The door of unrest; The duplicity of Hargraves; Let me feel your pulse; October and June; The church with an overshot-wheel; New York by camp fire light; The adventures of Shamrock Jolnes; The lady higher up; The Greater Coney; Law and order; Transformation of Martin Burney; The caliph and the cad; The diamond of Kali; The day we celebrate

Rolling stones: The dream; A ruler of men; The atavism of John Tom Little Bear; Helping the other fellow; The marionettes; The Marquis and Miss Sally; A fog in Santone; The friendly call; A dinner at—; Sound and fury; Tictocq; Tracked to doom; A snap-shot at the President; An unfinished Christmas story; The unprofitable servant; Aristocracy versus hash; The prisoner of Zembla; A strange story; Fickle fortune or how Gladys hustled; An apology; Lord Oakhurst's curse; Bexar scrip no. 2692; Queries and answers

Whirligigs: The world and the door; The theory and the hound; The hypotheses of failure; Calloway's code; A matter of mean

Henry, O.—*Continued*

elevation; "Girl"; Sociology in serge and straw; The ransom of Red Chief; The marry month of May; A technical error; Suite homes and their romance; The whirligig of life; A sacrifice hit; The roads we take; A blackjack bargainer; The song and the sergeant; One dollar's worth; A newspaper story; Tommy's burglar; A chaparral Christmas gift; A little local color; Georgia's ruling; Blind man's holiday; Madame Bo-Peep, of the ranches

The voice of the city: The voice of the city; The complete life of John Hopkins; A lickpenny lover; Dougherty's eye-opener; "Little speck in garnered fruit"; The harbinger; While the auto waits; A comedy in rubber; One thousand dollars; The defeat of the city; The shocks of doom; The Plutonian fire; Nemesis and the candy man; Squaring the circle; Roses, ruses and romance; The city of dreadful night; The Easter of the soul; The fool-killer; Transients in Arcadia; The rathskeller and the roses; The clarion call; Extradited from Bohemia; A philistine in Bohemia; From each according to his ability; The memento

The trimmed lamp: The trimmed lamp; A Madison Square Arabian night; The rubaiyat of a Scotch highball; The pendulum; Two Thanksgiving Day gentlemen; The assessor of success; The buyer from Cactus City; The badge of policeman O'Roon; Brickdust row; The making of a New Yorker; Vanity and some sables; The social triangle; The purple dress; The foreign policy of Company 99; The lost blend; A Harlem tragedy; "The guilty party"; According to their lights; A midsummer knight's dream; The last leaf; The count and the wedding guest; The country of elusion; The ferry of unfulfilment; The tale of a tainted tenner; Elsie in New York

Strictly business: Strictly business; The gold that glittered; Babes in the jungle; The day resurgent; The fifth wheel; The poet and the peasant; The robe of peace; The girl and the graft; The call of the tame; The unknown quantity; The thing's the play; A ramble in Aphasia; A municipal report; Psyche and the skyscraper; A bird of Bagdad; Compliments of the season; A night in New Arabia; The girl and the habit; Proof of the pudding; Past one at Rooney's; The venturers; The duel; "What you want"

Waifs and strays; The red roses of Tonia; Round the circle; The rubber plant's story; Out of Nazareth; Confessions of a humorist; The sparrows in Madison Square; Hearts and hands; The cactus; The detective detector; The dog and the playlet; A little talk about mobs; The snow man

y The four million. Doubleday 1906 261p $3.95

Contents: Tobin's palm; Gift of the Magi; Cosmopolite in a café; Between rounds; Skylight room; Service of love; Coming-out of Maggie; Man about town; Cop on the anthem; Adjustment of nature; Memoirs of a yellow dog; Love-philtre of Ikey Schoenstein; Mammon and the archer; Springtime à la carte; Green door; From the cabby's seat; Unfinished story; Caliph, cupid and the clock; Sisters of the golden circle; Romance of a busy broker; After twenty years; Lost on dress parade; By courier; Furnished room; Brief début of Tildy

also in Henry, O. The complete works of O. Henry p 1-108

The gentle grafter
In Henry, O. The complete works of O. Henry p267-354

Heart of the West
In Henry, O. The complete works of O. Henry p109-266

Options
In Henry, O. The complete works of O. Henry p680-810

Roads of destiny
In Henry, O. The complete works of O. Henry p355-550

Rolling stones
In Henry, O. The complete works of O. Henry p941-1060

Sixes and sevens
In Henry, O. The complete works of O. Henry p811-940

Strictly business
In Henry, O. The complete works of O. Henry p1484-1631

Tales of O. Henry. Doubleday 1969 565p $6.95

"This collection includes tales of New York, the Southwest, and Latin America, covering the full range of O. Henry's humor, irony, and sense of tragedy. Although the decade of which he wrote is long past, his unique talent has made his stories timeless and this volume will provide hours of rare reading entertainment." News of Bks

Contents: The gift of the Magi; A cosmopolite in a café; The skylight room; Man about town; The cop and the anthem; The love-philtre of Ikey Schoenstein; Mammon and the archer; Springtime à la carte; From the cabby's seat; An unfinished story; The romance of a busy broker; After twenty years; The furnished room; Hearts and crosses; The ransom of Mack; Telemachus, friend; The handbook of Hymen; Hygeia at the Solito; The hand that riles the world; The exact science of matrimony; Conscience in art; Roads of destiny; The enchanted profile; The passing of Black Eagle; A retrieved reformation; Friends in San Rosario; The renaissance at Charleroi; Whistling Dick's Christmas stocking; The lotus and the bottle; Shoes; Ships; Masters of arts; "The rose of Dixie"; A poor rule; The last of the troubadours; Makes the whole world kin; Jimmy Hayes and Muriel; The adventures of Shamrock Jolnes; The friendly call; Sound and fury; The theory and the hound; The ransom of Red Chief; The whirligig of life; A blackjack bargainer; One dollar's worth; A lickpenny lover; Dougherty's eye-opener; The defeat of the city; The shocks of doom; Squaring the circle; The memento; The trimmed lamp; Two Thanksgiving Day gentlemen; The making of a New Yorker; A Harlem tragedy; The last leaf; The count and the wedding guest; The robe of peace; A ramble in Aphasia; A night in New Arabia; Proof of the Pudding; Hearts and hands

The trimmed lamp
In Henry, O. The complete works of O. Henry p1365-1483

The voice of the city
In Henry, O. The complete works of O. Henry p1253-1364

Waifs and strays
In Henry, O. The complete works of O. Henry p1632-92

Whirligigs
In Henry, O. The complete works of O. Henry p1094-1252

Henry, Will

Alias Butch Cassidy. Random House [1968 c1967] 209p boards $4.95

"In this well researched, better than average western novel [the author] displays gusto, humor, and plenty of drama. This is the saga of Butch Cassidy, later to become famous as one of the Wild Bunch of outlaws, from the time he was 16 until he was 21. Born George Le Roy Parker, son of a strait-laced Mormon father, he teams up with a raffish old rustler, Mike Cassidy, and flees with him to Robbers' Roost, notorious Utah outlaw hideout." Pub W

The last warpath. Random House 1966 242p boards $4.95

The author chronicles the Cheyenne Indians' forty-year struggle for survival. He reveals the strife between U.S. officers and policy struggles among Indian chiefs. He pictures "the infamous Sand Creek Massacre, the battles of the Washita, Rosebud, Little Big Horn and Powder rivers, all leading to the final blow at Wounded Knee." Publisher's note

"The inexorable steps of decline and fall are narrated from individual viewpoints, showing the mounting daily emotions which characterized each campaign." Am News of Bks

Henry, Will—*Continued*

Mackenna's gold. Random House 1963 276p o.p. 1970

A "Western melodrama with a touch of mystery and superstition. Set in Arizona in 1897, it tells of a tough young prospector who learns from a dying Apache of a valley filled with gold, and is then forced to lead a band of outlaws to the hidden treasure." Pub W

"The novel will never win a Pulitzer prize, but it is still an interesting book for a rainy afternoon." Best Sellers

Herbert, Frank

Dune. Chilton Bks. 1965 xxvi, 422p illus $5.95

"In an extremely detailed, esoteric space fantasy for readers of sociological science fiction, Duke Leto Atreides and his family are forced by the all-powerful Emperor of the known universe to exchange their rich lands for the barren planet Dune, sole producer of a unique narcotic drug. Trained from birth by his mother, a member of a strange religious matriarchy, the Duke's son Paul becomes the prophet Maud'Dib who leads the savage Fremen of Dune against the Empire." Booklist

Followed by: Dune messiah

Dune messiah. Putnam 1969 256p boards $4.95

Sequel to: Dune

This novel "completes the story of Paul Atreides and the worlds and factions that surround him. . . . The destiny which had been indicated for Paul, the product of endless genetic experiments, is finally realized, and with considerable excitement." Pub W

Hergesheimer, Joseph

Java Head. Knopf 1946 320p illus $5.95

First published 1919

"A story of Salem in the days of the sailing vessels in which the un-emphasized but dramatic plot centers about the marriage of the erratic sea-going son of a family of ship owners, to a Chinese lady who brings all the refinements of her Manchu rank into an environment ill-adapted to appreciate her subtle character or assimilate her alien splendors. Remarkable chiefly as a satisfying series of pictures of a port of commerce of the forties with its typical New England village life and its surprising glimpses of Oriental color and mystery." Open Shelf

The three black Pennys; illus. by David Hendrickson. Knopf 1930 319p illus $5.95

First published 1917

"Tale of three men of successive generations of the 'Penny' family, in each of whom a Welch strain reasserts itself and creates the family type of rebellious and restless individualism. Pictured against the background of the development of the steel industry in Pennsylvania." Pittsburgh

Herlihy, James Leo

All fall down; a novel. Dutton 1960 272p o.p. 1970

This first novel "concerns an eccentric family of Clevelanders, the Williamses: father Ralph, a sentimental socialist declining into alcoholism and inaction; mother Annabel, nearly but not quite as helpless as she seems; elder son, Berry-Berry, who as the story begins, is away from home, heard from occasionally from jails in various localities; and younger son Clinton, who at 16 has left school and dreams of joining Berry-Berry, whom he imagines as an heroic rebel against family and convention. . . . Echo O'Brien, an incredible woman of 31, enters the story about midway and acts as the catalyst who first reunites Berry-Berry with the family and apparently redeems him as a person, then reveals his tragic flaw and sends him away, morally, if not legally as a murderer. This climactic revelation also reverses the moral relationship between the two brothers and frees Clinton from the dual domination of his family and his imagination." Library J

Herrick, William

¡Hermanos! A novel. Simon & Schuster 1969 379p $6.95

SBN 671-20356-8

"Jake Starr is sent by the Communist Party to organize and to fight in the Spanish Civil War. While overseas, he meets and falls in love with the wife of a fellow Communist. He comes to grips with the cruelties of his Party, of war, and perhaps of the human animal itself." Best Sellers

"When it is good, this novel about the men and women who fought with the International Brigade during the Spanish Civil War is very good. The battle scenes are particularly well done; they are terrifying! Equally terrifying are the cynicism and brutality with which the idealism of the rank and file and the very survival of the Republic are exploited and subverted by the novel's protagonists—party-line Communists—to the party's own ends." Library J

Herron, Shaun

Miro. Random House 1969 213p $4.95

"Tough, tired Miro, who works for the Firm, is assigned to find out who is behind a number of murders and the case takes him to Canada and a narcotics ring, and lots of action and excitement." Bk Buyer's Guide

"There is a strange, nightmare intensity about this novel that makes for considerable suspense and is strong enough to minimize the fact that several of the plot ingredients are hard to believe." Pub W

Hersey, John

y A bell for Adano

Some editions are:
Knopf $4.95
Watts, F. $8.95 Large type edition. A Keith Jennison book
Pulitzer Prize, 1945
First published 1944

A novel about Americans in Italy which tells of the Italian American major who tried to rebuild an occupied town along the lines of his own good instincts and democratic upbringing

"Makes very good reading for in its capable and wholly unpretentious fashion . . . [it] is an entertaining story, a candid report from behind the line and an effective tract." New Repub

The child buyer. . . . Knopf 1960 257p $4

"A novel in the form of hearings before the Standing Committee on Education, Welfare, & Public Morality of a certain State Senate, investigating the conspiracy of Mr. Wissey Jones, with others, to purchase a male child." Title page

The story "of a poor boy of exceptional intelligence and of a representative of a large corporation who seeks to 'buy' him that he may be trained to use his brains for the benefit of the company." Pub W

"In this harsh, satiric, sometimes shocking and profane book, Mr. Hersey is obviously indicting aspects of American education—and other things—with which he disagrees. . . . He lays down a basic irony in having hardly anyone display outrage, or even overwhelming surprise, at the child buyer's proposal. This is all a kind of a tour de force, sometimes entertaining, sometimes sickening. . . . To a reader concerned about educational shortcomings, materialism, mental manipulation, misguided patriotism, the absurdity is uncomfortable, the questions are pressing, the loud clothing of the parable is less important than the thoughts behind it." Christian Science Monitor

The marmot drive. Knopf 1953 273p $4.95

"The tale concerns a community drive to rid a New England town of a threatening colony of woodchucks. The village is named Tunxis, and the drive is reported to us through the sensibilities of a girl from New York. The climax of the story is an intentional anti-climax—the selectman who incited the drive is flogged for a crime he did not commit, after which he tries futilely to slaughter the few woodchucks that were captured." Sat R

Hersey, John—*Continued*

y A single pebble. Knopf 1956 181p $3.95

A young American engineer travels up the Yangtze River on a junk to find a possible location for a great dam. He is drawn into the settled, ancient way of life of the people on the junk. The interplay of their lives comes to a dramatic climax at the cliff-hemmed depths of the Wind-Box Gorge. (Publisher)

"Author Hersey conjures up the flowering mists, brooding mountain masses and gorge-shadowed surfaces of the Yangtze as if from a child's vivid book of memories. Equally vivid and enlightening is the image of two cultures once fingertip-close in friendship, destined by later history to draw back and ball their fists in sad and bitter enmity." Time

Too far to walk. Knopf 1966 246p $4.95

"John Fist is a sophomore in an Eastern college, there because it is his father's school, but really lost because his parents never accepted him in any sense as their son. He bargains with the Devil for his own soul and seeks, like Faust, the fine adventures of love. But John finds life tasteless, and turns to LSD-induced dreams." Library J

"This is a neat literary device to catalog and satirize aspects of present-day civilization which could correctly be called hellish. The satire is the book's main point. There is a minimal plot." Pub W

Under the eye of the storm. Knopf 1967 244p $4.95

"A noted novelist-moralist has his say about hypocrisy and moral failure as well as the unsuspected moral strength lurking under the veneer and pretense of modern existence. He compresses his story in time and space into hours at sea in a yawl with violent storm overtaking two vacationing married couples. Their emotions and responses to one another under stress take unlooked-for turns. It is through the eyes and mind of Tom Medlar, owner of the boat, disenchanted liver specialist, and would-be decent man and spouse, that the reader views what transpires. The crisis arrives as the boat's flawed keelson, inexcusably neglected by Tom, threatens disaster and in the process briefly exposes the neglected rot at the core of Tom's being. Proficient, pointed writing that touches the mind far more than the emotions." Booklist

y The wall. Knopf 1950 632p $5.95

On the surface this is the story of the systematic extermination of the Jews of the Warsaw ghetto, and of the heroic resistance of defenseless men and women against the full force of the Germans. But the plot of the story concerns the growth in spirit of a group of friends, so that they emerge undismayed and triumphant in the face of physical annihilation

"Only a true novelist could breathe warmth, compassion, humor, into what a historian would necessarily have pictured as a stark, hopeless, tragic series of events. Only a sensitive novelist could compel us to embark upon such a fearful adventure as this and remain until the end; you do not 'read' 'The Wall'—you live it—and if the experience is shattering it is infinitely rewarding." N Y Times Bk R

The war lover. Knopf 1959 404p $5

"This suspenseful novel shows what secret hidden fear can do to one of those seeming heroes, a war lover. The scene is an American bomber-base in England; the characters are the crew of a Flying Fortress. The co-pilot, Borman, tells the story of his worship of the pilot, Marrow, and of how Marrow succumbed, on their final mission, to the fatal weakness with which he camouflaged his fear. Boman also tells the story of the English girl he loved." Huntting

"Some of the language and several of the explicit scenes will be offensive to the fastidious, but the questions raised by the theme of the book will recommend it to the serious reader." Wis Lib Bul

Hesse, Hermann

Nobel Prize in literature, 1946

Beneath the wheel; tr. by Michael Roloff. Farrar, Straus 1968 187p $4.95

Originally published 1906 in Germany

Hans Giebenrath, the sensitive, gifted son of a prosaic German family wins admittance to a regimented, state-supported prep school after competing in a torturous entrance exam. Unable to fulfill his potential and on the verge of a mental breakdown, Hans seeks relief in friendship with a liberated and rebellious fellow-student. However, failing as a scholar and too inhibited to emulate his friend, his end is inevitable. (Publisher)

"This short novel . . . can be read for sheer pleasure. Hesse's peculiarly supple lyricism, his brittle irony, and his stunning descriptions of nature are marvelously carried over into English." Sat R

y Demian, the story of Emil Sinclair's youth; introduction by Thomas Mann; tr. from the German by Michael Roloff and Michael Lebeck. Harper 1965 171p $4.95

Original German edition, 1919. First published 1923 in the United States by Boni and Liveright

This novel "is the story of the boy Arthur Sinclair and his growth into young manhood. At school, Arthur is terrified by a bully until a new boy, Max Demian, who has some unusual and hidden power, appears. . . . Demian . . . fascinates but mystifies Arthur. They are separated when Arthur goes off to boarding school, but years later come together as young men. . . . Demian's secret, which marks him off from the run of mankind, is simply that he is one of those rare ones who have found themselves." Atlantic

"Psychological insight into the problems of growth to adulthood combines with the symbolic picture of an age, which through inwardness, tries to replace the lost moral and social order." Library J

Gertrude; tr. by Hilda Rosner. [Rev. translation] Farrar, Straus 1969 237p $4.95

Original German edition 1910; this translation first published in England

The crippled "narrator, Kuhn, is uncertain, eager to write great music but not sure that he can. The singer, Muoth, becomes his friend though both are in love with Gertrude. Muoth and the beautiful, assured Gertrude help Kuhn to success, but their own marriage ends in unhappiness." Bk Buyer's Guide

"No doubt the models for [Hesse] are Franz Schubert, small, unprepossessing, short-sighted and yet filled with tender romantic passions, and Ludwig van Beethoven, squat, course, combative and yet longing for the Immortal Beloved. Hesse's book . . . describes the growth of a composer not so great as these, but at least of the same type and the same romantic era." Book of the Month Club News

The glass bead game (Magister Ludi); tr. from the German Das Glasperlenspiel by Richard and Clara Winston; with a foreword by Theodore Ziolkowski. Holt 1969 558p $7.95

SBN 03-081851-6

Original German edition published 1943. First published 1949 in the United States with title: Magister Ludi

"Set 5000 years in the future in a utopian European province inhabited by a non-religious, erudite order, [this novel] traces the mental and spiritual maturation of one of its most talented members. At an early age, Knecht attains the role of master of the Glass Bead Game, the most intellectual activity of the order. . . . After intense self-examination, he resigns and returns to the natural world to be a teacher." Pub W

"The book is part romance, part philosophical tract, part utopian Hesse fantasy. Its theme is one that preoccupied Hesse earlier: the conflict between, and the need to synthesize, thought and action, intellect and the flesh. . . . Hesse writes of [Knecht] in an ironic style that seems exactly right: mock-pompous, witty, occasionally even moving. Knecht is a memorable character, and, even though he acts as symbol and mouthpiece for his creator's ideas, it is his human qualities that make the book work. A fascinating novel, well translated at last." Book of the Month Club News

Hesse, Hermann—*Continued*

The journey to the East; tr. by Hilda Rosner. Farrar, Straus [1968 c1956] 118p $4.50

First published 1932 in Germany

"Dealing with the ultimate questions of human life, this is the account of a pilgrimage which apparently failed and of the narrator's despair. It is only as the chronicle unfolds that he learns that it is he who has failed and that the 'journey' continues all about him." McClurg. Book News

"Hesse's somewhat ethereal style lacks some of its original beauty in this translation. . . . Recommended for libraries with representative collections of European literature." Library J

Narcissus and Goldmund; tr. by Ursule Molinaro. Farrar, Straus 1968 315p $5.95

Original German edition published 1930. English translation published 1932 with title: Death and the lover; also 1959 in England, with title: Goldmund

"The setting is Germany in the late Middle Ages—dark forests, wandering scholars, sheltered monasteries, flourishing imperial cities, the plague. The problem is the conflict of the intellectual and the sensual, the scholar and the artist. The device is the biographical novel, half picaresque, half philosophical." Choice

"Hesse's prose, ranging from lyricism to allegory, and from unabashed sentimentality to an intellectuality of a high order, is not easily rendered into another language. . . . The present version . . . is close to perfection. . . . The weighty symbolism exemplified by the title [is] characteristic of the novel and yet, by the alchemy of narration, does not detract from its charm. The panoramic sweep and pervasively lyrical atmosphere gives Narcissus and Goldmund a unity that absorbs its technical flaws. Oedipal situations, homosexuality, hermaphroditism, and necrophilia lurk skin-deep under the pages, but Hesse lifts the contrapuntal play of conflicting forces onto a plane as close to music as words will come. What lingers in the reader's mind is a melancholy melody, a romantic 'lied' full of wanderlust for a trip into the id." Sat R

Peter Camenzind; tr. by Michael Roloff. Farrar, Straus 1969 201p $5.50

First published 1904 in Germany

Born into a tiny isolated Alpine village, the hero "receives a fine basic education because a local monk recognizes his superior intelligence and then continues his studies at the university in Zurich. Peter Camenzind remains a loner, fails to win the affection of two women he romantically idealizes, and never realizes his dream of becoming a poet. Yet his life is not a failure, for he gradually learns to give of himself to others and to relate to nature in an almost mystical sense." Pub W

"Simultaneously spare and lyrical and not out of touch with youthful yearnings today. For comprehensive collections of Hesse's fiction." Booklist

Rosshalde. Tr. by Ralph Manheim. Farrar, Straus 1970 213p $5.50

Original German edition published 1914

The story "concentrates thematically on the inner tensions of the creative artist in the person of famed painter Veraguth. He and his wife live separate lives on their estate Rosshalde tolerating a dead marriage without recourse to divorce largely because of Veraguth's passionate attachment to young son Pierre. Friend Burkhardt perceiving the effect of this essentially sterile existence on Veraguth's creativity holds forth the meaningful release of India, an escape made tragically possible when Pierre sickens and dies." Booklist

"Hesse tells it gently, with compassion for all the members of the troubled family. His portraits of the young son and the artist are especially warm and sensitive." Pub W

y Siddhartha; tr. by Hilda Rosner. New Directions 1951 153p $5

Originally published 1923 in Germany

"It is a moral allegory, based on Indian mysticism, which tries to solve the enigma of human loneliness and discontent. The hero, Siddhartha, endowed with all the virtues, goes through the fire of various experiences to emerge to a state of peace and holiness. Before he has achieved this beatitude he has tasted the pleasure of being a mendicant wanderer, then consort to a courtesan, then wealthy man of business, and finally companion to a humble ferryman, whose wisdom comes from the endlessly murmuring river." Sat R

"The cool and strangely simple story makes a beautiful little book, classic in proportion and style." Nation

y Steppenwolf; tr. from the German by Basil Creighton

Some editions are:
Holt $3.95
Modern Lib. $2.95 Revised by Walter Sorell

Originally published 1927 in German

It is the story of Harry Haller, a man of 50 who considers himself half man, half wolf of the steppes. In Harry Haller, as in intellectual Germany, and as in civilized man of all ages, there is the conflict between nature and spirit

Heyer, Georgette

Bath tangle. Putnam 1955 312p o.p. 1970

"Serena, daughter of the Earl of Spenborough, was left a fortune by her father, contingent upon her marriage to a man of whom the Marquis of Rotherham approved. Serena had just jilted the Marquis, so [she] dashed off to Bath with her young stepmother as a chaperone." Retail Bookseller

"Miss Heyer keeps all of her strands of plot thoroughly ensnarled until the last page. As entertaining as her complicated story is the detail of Regency Bath that she provides." N Y Her Trib Books

Beauvallet. Dutton 1968 243p $4.95

First published 1929 in England

The author "narrates the adventures on land and sea of Sir Nicholas Beauvallet, a gallant super-pirate, scourge of the Spanish Main, a friend of Drake, and a favorite of Queen Elizabeth. On one of his exploits he captures a fiery Spanish girl and her father, falls in love with the girl, lands her in Spain, and returns in disguise to woo her and carry her off once more, this time to England." Booklist

The Black Moth. Dutton 1968 326p $4.95

First published 1921 in England

"John Carstares, heir to the Earl of Wyncham, had been accused of cheating at cards and merely walked out of the room, leaving his intended bride for his younger brother, Richard. It was then that Lord John became a highwayman, but the death of his father and the Duke of Andover's unwanted attention to the beautiful Diana brought him out of hiding." Bk Buyer's Guide

"It is a well filled story which keeps the reader pleased." Times (London) Lit Sup

Black sheep. Dutton 1967 [c1966] 255p boards $4.95

First published 1966 in England

"Miss Heyer has never been in better form than in this very funny Regency romance set in Bath, wherein a seemingly sedate maiden lady who is all of 'eight and twenty' undertakes to save her young neice from a 'ramshackle youth' who is a fortune hunter. In doing so she, herself, falls victim, very prettily, to the young man's 'black sheep' uncle. The conversation is delightful, full of all sorts of quizzical period slang, and the hero and heroine (older style) make a most spirited Beatrice and Benedict." Pub W

A civil contract. Putnam 1961 393p o.p. 1970

"On succeeding to the Lynton title Adam Deveril learns that he lacks funds to maintain the estate and provide for his mother and sisters. At first he indignantly rejects the suggestion that he marry money, but when the Oversleys make it plain that their exquisite Julia is reserved for a rich man he agrees to marry plain, comfortable Jenny, sole heiress of the uncouth but goodhearted Jonathan Chawleigh. How the marriage weathers its first difficult year, bringing to Adam and Jenny the realization their lives will not be lived on mountain peaks of romance but in shared enjoyment of ordinary, everyday things is the substance of the latest lightly humorous novel of Regency England." Booklist

Heyer, Georgette—*Continued*

The Conqueror. Dutton 1966 376p $4.95

First published 1931 in England

"William the Conqueror's story from his birth as the bastard son of Count Robert the Magnificent . . . to the dramatic events that led up to the Battle of Hastings; and, finally . . . the battle itself. The epilogue tells briefly of William's coronation in Westminster Abbey." Publisher's note

"Georgette Heyer catches [William's] complexity. Her novel is primarily valuable, however, not so much as a portrait of a man, as it is a portrait of a period in the history of Western Europe." Best Sellers

The convenient marriage. Dutton 1966 279p $4.95

First published 1934 in England

In Regency England, seventeen-year-old Horatia Winwood takes it upon herself to rescue her sister from an undesired marriage. The author describes what happens, in a story filled with duels, abductions, and misunderstandings. (Publisher)

"Light entertainment for women, especially Heyer devotees." Booklist

The Corinthian. Dutton 1966 [c1940] 244p $4.50

First published 1940 in England. This is a reissue of the title first published 1941 in the United States with title: Beau Wyndham

An early Regency novel which "tells of teenage Penelope Creed, who runs away to avoid an unwelcome marriage and involves the resolutely single Sir Richard Wyndham in her fight." Bk Buyer's Guide

Cousin Kate. Dutton 1968 317p boards $4.95

In this Regency novel "Cousin Kate, a poor relation [is] brought into the aristocratic English Broome household with a very nasty fate indeed planned for her. . . . Kate, aided by a dashing cavalier and the earthy family of her old nurse, wins out. The Gothic gloom and doom is nicely leavened with wit, romance and wonderful period slang." Pub W

"For Heyer fans and women who enjoy period Gothic romances." Booklist

Detection unlimited. Dutton 1969 [c1961] 287p $4.95

First published 1953 in England

Chief Inspector Hemingway is sent to the English village of Thornden "after the body of solicitor Sampson Warrenby is found in his garden. No one in the village liked Warrenby, and everyone has his own solution for the crime." Library J

"This is agreeable escapism, light summer fare for those who enjoy reading about the English country gentry, tennis and lawn parties, genteel murder. . . . A period piece in a way, but a pleasantly engaging one." Pub W

Devil's cub. Dutton 1966 265p $4.95

First published 1932 in England

"The Marquis of Vidal (son of the Duke of Avon) as much of a devil as his father was in his youth, and with his red-headed French mother's quick temper, is forced to flee to France after a duel in a London gambling house. He plans to take a girl with him, without benefit of clergy. Instead, the girl's older sister substitutes and proves to be more than a match for Vidal." Am News of Bks

Duplicate death. Dutton 1969 271p $4.95

First published 1951 in England

"London is the scene for a duplicate bridge party that is given a social climbing hostess who is looking for a good match for her beautiful but silly daughter. The party is interrupted by murder, and there is 'duplicate death' before Inspector Hemingway manages to sort out all the clues." Am News of Bks

Envious Casca. Dutton 1969 [c1941] 320p $4.95

A reprint of a book first published 1941

Set in provincial England, this is a "detective story about the Christmas party that went wrong when the host was found stabbed in a locked bedroom on Christmas Eve." Publisher's note

"Rarely have we seen humor and mystery so perfectly blended as they are in this story.

Some of the humorous episodes which seem least relevant actually contain the clues which lead [Inspector] Hemingway to the correct solution of a very difficult problem." N Y Times Bk R

False colours. Dutton 1964 [c1963] 317p $4.95

First published 1963 in England

"A Regency novel which tells of the 'series of misadventures which occur when the gay and dashing Earl of Denville and his twin brother, Kit, attempt to straighten out their charming mother's chaotic finances following their father's death. Not wishing to inform his stodgy uncle of Lady Denville's dire needs, the young Earl conveniently proposes marriage to a highly eligible and suitable young lady, Miss Cressida Stavely, though neither Denville or Cressy are in love with each other. When the Earl fails to return home in time for a meeting with Cressy's formidable grandmother at a Stavely family party, Kit unwillingly substitutes for his brother. And once having begun the impersonation, he must keep it up until his brother returns, even though he finds that he himself is falling in love with Cressy." Publisher's note

"This novel cannot be dismissed as just another historical novel. It is excellent in its genre. Miss Heyer has the ability to transport the reader back to the early 19th Century and actually sense the elegant mode of living during that time. . . . It is also interesting that Miss Heyer's style of writing is indigenous to the period of which she writes." Best Sellers

Faro's daughter. Dutton 1967 [c1942] 277p $4.95

First published 1941 in England

"Romantic tale of England in Regency days. The heroine is a beautiful young woman who runs a faro table in her aunt's gaming house in London. Two of the contestants for the hand of the fair Deb are young Lord Mablethorpe, and his older, more worldly cousin, Ravenscar." Book Rev Digest

"Altogether, this is a gay and dashing story which should not be taken too seriously." Christian Science Monitor

The foundling. Putnam 1948 380p o.p. 1970

"A light novel of Regency days in which the sheltered young Duke of Sale eludes his protectors, sets out on an adventure, incognito, and has many harrowing experiences for which he had not bargained. In order to get out of numerous scrapes he makes use of a hitherto dormant ingenuity and show of authority; he rescues a beautiful but dumb female, saves a lad from life with a boring tutor, frees himself from kidnapers, falls in love with his fiancée, and has a most enjoyable time." Booklist

Frederica. Dutton 1965 384p boards $4.95

"A 37-year-old bachelor, wealthy, imperious, much the man-about-Regency-London, falls irresistibly for a pretty but not beautiful young woman who, at 24, considers herself put on the shelf and wants only to find a good husband for her younger sister. The girl's two impetuous young brothers and their large friendly dog add hilarious complications." Pub W

Friday's child. Putnam 1946 311p o.p. 1970

England of the Regency period is the setting for this historical novel revolving around the character of Hero Wantage, her marriage to Viscount Sheringham and their social life in the London society of that era

"It is a relief to find a gay, lighthearted historical novel for a change, that is amusing to read, instead of the usual solemn, heavy-handed approach." Sat R

The grand Sophy. Putnam 1950 307p o.p. 1970

"A novel set in the Regency days in London. The Grand Sophy, educated on the Continent, is given a home with her conservative cousins in London. To their surprise and horror Sophy is almost six feet tall, and very forthright, managing, and beautiful. However, her managing turned out to be the best thing that had ever happened to several people." Book Rev Digest

Heyer, Georgette—*Continued*

An infamous army. Dutton 1965 [c1937]
424p $4.95

A reissue of a title first published 1937
"Around the battle of Waterloo and Wellington's defeat of Napoleon Miss Heyer has written a novel . . . with much less emphasis on the battle than on the English and their ladies in nearby Brussels, and on one particular romance. This love affair is between one of Wellington's staff, an attractive but not wealthy man, and a very beautiful young widow with a 'fast' reputation. The backstage astonishingly polite preliminaries to a war of that era included many social events and balls. These give the author occasion for an amusing picture of the clever, crotchety Duke of Wellington and for a revealing description of Empire dresses." Pub W

The masqueraders. Dutton 1967 288p $4.95

First published 1928 in England
"A romance of eighteenth century London in which the two young Merriots, brother and sister, find themselves implicated in the Stuart rebellion and take to masquerade to save their heads. Their father, known as 'the old gentleman,' is an inveterate masquerader and amply accounts for his children's success in that line." Book Rev Digest
"The tale is told rapidly and wittily with events bombarding events and one encounter invariably leading to another. The characters are gaily bedight and they manage to be clever or dull just as each occasion demands for the furtherance of the good-natured, swashbuckling plot." Sat R

The Nonesuch. Dutton 1963 [c1962] 300p $4.95

"Known as the Nonesuch for his athletic prowess, Sir Waldo Hawkridge is the most discussed man in London Society. When he inherits an estate in Yorkshire, he causes quite a stir in the village of Oversett. The unexpected train of events that follow lead to Sir Waldo's surprising choice of a bride." Huntting

Power and patch; (the transformation of Philip Jettan); a comedy of manners. Dutton 1968 233p $4.95

First published 1923 in England with title: The transformation of Philip Jettan
This story "is an unabashed romance about a country girl coming into London to enter its social life and a young dandy who, to woo and win her, adopts extremes of the current fashions of the Regency period, only to find that his tactic repels the object of his affections. She, Cleone, becomes so confused that she gets herself engaged to two other men, neither of whom she likes enough to marry. Of course, it is Philip Jettan who finally straightens things out and all ends happily as anyone could have predicted. . . . This is still skillfully done and makes pleasant and chucklesome reading." Best Sellers

Regency buck. Dutton 1966 332p $4.95

First published 1935 in England
A romance set in Regency England. When the young heiress, Miss Taverner, and her brother, Sir Peregrine, travel from Yorkshire to London to meet their guardian, a number of surprising events occur. Someone seems to be trying to poison Peregrine, and their guardian turns away Miss Taverner's suitors. (Publisher)

Royal escape. Dutton 1967 429p $4.95

First published 1938 in England
This "is a very well-written historical novel dealing with Charles II's escape after the Battle of Worcester. Those gallant, doomed Cavaliers and ladies who gave their all for the Stuart cause are re-created with great charm, and the King, himself, emerges as an appealing and tragic human being." Pub W

The Spanish bride. Dutton 1965 [c1940] 390p $5.95

A reissue of the title first published 1940
"The adventures of a young Spanish bride who follows her soldier husband to war during the Peninsular War of 1812." Chicago
"Soundly based on historical fact, 'The Spanish Bride' is a superb blend of breathtaking description of actual events and vivid portrayals of real people . . . of drama and romance, love and war in the heroic days of the Napoleonic era." Publisher's note

Sprig muslin. Putnam 1956 276p o.p. 1970

In Regency England "Sir Gareth Ludlow's proposal to Lady Hester is rejected because she demands love, not esteem. And a little later Sir Gareth finds himself with the runaway Amanda on his hands, and his reputation if not his life endangered by her irate family." Retail Bookseller

The talisman ring. Dutton 1967 [c1964] 297p $5.95

First published 1936 in England
"A gay, mad adventure story of England in the 1790s, in which an unsolved murder mystery, a band of smugglers, and a lost ring, are inextricably mixed with the love affairs of a pretty young French girl and her English cousins." Book Rev Digest

These old shades. Dutton 1966 [c1926] 362p $4.95

First published 1926 in England
"The Duke of Avon makes a Paris guttersnipe his page, only to have the child turn out to be a girl, no guttersnipe at all, but the disinherited daughter of a French count. How Leon, or more properly Leone, finally achieves her proper status and a most distinguished husband makes a very spirited story. The novel is set in the time of Louis XV." Am News of Bks

The toll-gate. Putnam 1954 310p o.p. 1970

"Captain John Staple returns from the Napoleonic wars, loses his way near a tollhouse and stays in the town to marry the local squire's daughter, clear her family's name, and solve the mystery of a stolen cargo of government gold." Retail Bookseller

Heyward, Du Bose

Mamba's daughters. Doubleday 1929 311p o.p. 1970

"To protect her childlike, giant daughter, and Lissa, her talented granddaughter, both 'bo'n fuh trouble,' Mamba, a wily old Negress of the Charleston waterfront, skillfully campaigns to acquire some 'white folks' of her own who will stand back of her in time of trouble. A penetrating study of Negro character, and psychology which has more plot than 'Porgy.'" Cleveland

Porgy; foreword by Dorothy Heyward. Doubleday 1953 158p o.p. 1970

First published 1925 by Doran
"The story of a crippled Negro beggar in Charleston, the story of his skill with the dice, of his goat wagon, of his love for black Bess, who quits the 'happy dust' under the shining influence of his love and faith; of their ultimate tragedy. . . . Mr Heyward is writing about distinctly drawn individuals, who are important for their own sakes rather than as racial representatives, however true to type they may be." Literary Rev

Hibbert, Eleanor. See Holt, Victoria; Plaidy, Jean

Hichens, Robert

The Paradine case; a novel. Doubleday 1933 525p o.p. 1970

"The elements in this murder story are psychological rather than detective. Mrs Paradine, a beautiful and mysterious Dane, is accused of the murder of her husband, a war hero. The famous criminal lawyer who undertakes her defence is profoundly influenced by the personality of the prisoner, the prejudices of the judge are aroused, the lawyers' families and friends, and London society are drawn into the deep undercurrents of the case. The climax of the story is the sensational trial scene." Book Rev Digest

Higgins, Jack
East of desolation. Published for the Crime Club by Doubleday [1969 c1968] 192p $3.95

"Joe Martin, ex-alcoholic, had made a new life for himself as a charter pilot on Greenland's rugged arctic coast. Now he finds it all threatened by the discovery of an old plane wreck. Concealed identities, a fortune in emeralds, murder, and the struggle to survive in a barren wasteland make this adventure tale something special." Am News of Bks

Highet, Helen MacInnes. See MacInnes, Helen

Highsmith, Patricia
The tremor of forgery. Doubleday 1969 254p $4.95

"A mystery story, in which Howard Ingham, an American writer, finds himself becoming more and more uprooted from his own past, by the impact of Tunisia. In self-defense he attacks an Arab intruder bent on theft and is never quite sure thereafter if he killed the man." Book Rev Digest
"Miss Highsmith's hero is detective and suspect, accused and accuser. . . . Nothing here is as it seems. Miss Highsmith's dry simplicity conceals a labyrinthine complexity it is a challenge and a pleasure to untangle." New Statesman

Hill, Donna
Catch a brass canary. Lippincott 1965 [c1964] 224p $4.50

This story centers on Miguel, a teen-aged Puerto Rican page at an Upper West-Side branch of the New York Public Library. "Because of him, a love affair changes tempo and a Negro boy reveals the true fierceness of his feelings; a young librarian who professes to want no involvement with the others is drawn into a major conflict; and a cruel and callous gang leader is challenged in his own territory." Publisher's note

Hilton, James
y   Good-bye Mr Chips

Some editions are:
Little $3.95 Illustrated by H. M. Brock
Watts, F. $7.95 Large type edition. A Keith Jennison book
First published 1934
"Gentle, humorous Mr Chipping had been known familiarly to three generations of English schollboys at Brookfield, as Mr Chips. As he sat in his pleasant room across from the entrance to the school Mr Chips recalled his life there, the jokes he had made which had become classics, the thousands he had known and regarded as his boys. And just as gently as he lived he faded smilingly out of life." Book Rev Digest
"Not only does 'Good-bye, Mr. Chips' stand very high, intrinsically, as a fine piece of fiction, but I should think that Mr. Hilton's little book might well find a place in writing courses, alongside Edith Wharton's novelettes, as an outstanding example of perfect finesse in the handling of the long short story and as a first-class specimen of the methods of that subtler, yet still somewhat technical matter, literary 'charm.'" N Y Her Trib Books
    also in Costain, T. B. comp. Twelve short novels p417-55

y   Lost horizon. Morrow 1933 277p $5
"Four persons, two Englishmen in Consular service, a woman missionary, and an American fleeing the consequences of shady financial deals, believe they are setting out on an ordinary aeroplane journey in India. They are, however, spirited away to a secret lamasery, a place dominated by a single tremendous idea. This idea, incredible as it is, is made delicately plausible through the consistent reactions of the characters to their strange situation, and through artistic handling of the mysterious." N Y Libraries
    also in Costain, T. B. ed. More Stories to remember v 1 p 1-119

y   Random harvest. Little 1941 326p $4.95
"Set on the eve of the outbreak of a second European war, Mr. Hilton's story is built around a case of lost memory dating from the previous [World] war. Charles Rainier, industrialist, and member of parliament, married to a brilliant and social ambitious wife, is accounted a successful man of affairs. But in his life there is a blank corridor, those years from 1917-1919 of which he has no recollection. The uncovering of this past is the theme which holds the reader to the end." Wis Lib Bul
"Those who are interested in any one of a half dozen war problems, 'shell-shock,' the changing social order, and a good love story will like this book immensely. Above all, it is a good story just for the joy of it." Churchman

So well remembered. Little 1945 309p o.p. 1970
"This story of George Boswell who became Mayor of the small English city where he was born and grew up, spans the twenty years between two world wars. When the story opens George is about to learn that his wife wants to divorce him; twenty years later he learns what that strange woman has done to the career of the man she married after the divorce, and to the son of that marriage." Book Rev Digest

Hingley, Ronald
(ed.) Chekhov, A. The Oxford Chekhov v8

Hintze, Naomi A.
You'll like my mother. Putnam 1969 191p $4.50

"Red mask mystery"
"Another modern Gothic [this suspense-horror tale] has a haunted house in Always, a small town on the Ohio, where Francesca Kinsolving [in her ninth month of pregnancy] comes to meet for the first time the mother of her dead husband." Library J
"Francesca herself is immediately endearing, a vibrant, completely convincing young woman who turns what might have been an ordinary story into a compelling novel to be read at one sitting. Admirers of 'Rosemary's Baby' should attend this birth." Book of the Month Club News

Hiraoka, Kimitake. See Mishima, Yukio

Hitchcock, Alfred
(ed.) Alfred Hitchcock presents: A month of mystery. Random House 1969 428p $6.95 $6.95

A collection of thirty-one mystery and horror stories, arranged under these headings: A week of crime; A week of suspense; A week of detection; A week of the macabre; and A short week of long ones
Contents: The dusty drawer, by H. Muheim; Drum beat, by S. Marlowe; South of the market, by J. Gores; The uses of intelligence, by M. Gant; Love will find a way, by D. Alexander; Retribution, by M. Zuroy; The Queen's jewel, by J. Holding; Pool party, by A. Benedict; That touch of genius, by W. Sambrot; The crooked road, by A. Gaby; A taste for murder, by J. Ritchie; The twelve-hour caper, by M. Marmer; The amateur, by M. Gilbert; Death wish, by L. Block; The singing pigeon, by R. Macdonald; Justice Magnifique, by L. Treat; The white hat, by S. Rohmer; Hard sell, by C. Rice; Greedy night, by E. C. Bentley; A twilight adventure, by M. D. Post; Murder matinee, by H. Q. Masur; A humanist, by R. Gary; The oblong room, by E. D. Hoch; Love me, love me, love me, by M. S. Waddell; Special handling, by J. Keefauver; Dead man's story, by H. Rigsby; The legend of Joe Lee, by J. D. MacDonald; Crooked bone, by G. Kersh; The janissaries of Emilion, by B. Copper; Chinoiserie, by H. McCloy; Soldier Key, by S. E. Lanier

y   (ed.) Alfred Hitchcock presents: My favorites in suspense. Random House 1959 502p $6.95

Partially analyzed in Short Story Index
Contains 20 short stories and the complete novel: The blank wall, by Elizabeth Sanxay Holding

Hitchcock, Alfred—*Continued*

Short stories included: The birds, by D. du Maurier; Man with a problem, by D. Honig; They bite, by A. Boucher; The enemy, by C. Armstrong; Inexperienced ghost, by H. G. Wells; Sentence of death, by T. Walsh; Spring fever, by D. S. Davis; Crate at Outpost I, by M. Gant; My unfair lady, by G. Cullingford; New murders for old, by C. Dickson; Terrified, by C. B. Gilford; The duel, by J. Vatsek; Four o'clock, by P. Day; Too many coincidences, by P. Eiden; Of missing persons, by J. Finney; Island of Fear, by W. Sambrot; Getting rid of George, by R. Arthur; Treasure trove, by F. T. Jesse; The body of the crime, by W. D. Steele; A nice touch, by M. Rubin

(ed.) Alfred Hitchcock presents: Stories for late at night. Random House 1961 469p $6.95

Analyzed in Short Story Index
This collection of eerie tales includes 21 short stories, 2 novelettes: The vintage season, by C. L. Moore, and The fly, by G. Langelaan; and the complete text of the novel: The iron gates, by M. Millar, published 1945

Short stories included: Death is a dream, by R. Arthur; It's a good life, by J. Bixby; The whole town's sleeping, by R. Bradbury; Lady's man, by R. Chatterton; Evening primrose, by J. Collier; The sound machine, by R. Dahl; The cocoon, by J. B. L. Goodwin; Pieces of silver, by B. Halliday; The whistling room, by W. H. Hodgson; Told for the truth, by C. Hume; The ash tree, by M. R. James; Side bet, by W. F. Jenkins; Second night out, by F. B. Long; Our feathered friends, by P. MacDonald; Back there in the grass, by G. Morris; The mugging, by E. L. Perry; Finger! Finger, by M. Ronan; A cry from the penthouse, by H. Slesar; The people next door, by P. C. Smith; D-Day, by R. Trout; The man who liked Dickens, by E. Waugh

(ed.) Alfred Hitchcock presents: Stories my mother never told me. Random House 1963 401p o.p. 1970

Analyzed in Short Story Index
Contains a complete novel: Some of your blood, by T. Sturgeon and two novelettes: The secret of the bottle, by G. Kersh; The idol of the flies, by J. Rice

Short stories included are: The child who believed, by G. Amundson; Just a dreamer, by R. Arthur; The wall-to-wall grave, by A. Benedict; The wind, by R Bradbury; Congo, by S. Cloete; Witch's money, by J. Collier; Dip in the pool, by R. Dahl; I do not hear you. Sir, by A. Davidson; The arbutus collar, by J. Digges; A short trip home, by F. S. Fitzgerald; An invitation to the hunt, by G. Hitchcock; The man who was everywhere, by E. D. Hoch; The summer people, by S. Jackson; Adjustments, by G. Mandel; The children of Noah, by R. Matheson; Courtesy of the road, by M. Morriss; Remains to be seen, by J. Ritchie; The man who sold rope to the Gnoles, by I. Seabright; Lost dog, by H. Slesar; Hostage, by D. Stanford; Natural selection, by G. Thomas; Simone, by J. Vatsek; Smart sucker, by R. Wormser

(ed.) Alfred Hitchcock presents: Stories not for the nerves. Random House 1965 363p $6.95

Analyzed in Short Story Index
This collection of macabre tales includes 20 short stories, 3 novelettes and the complete text of: Sorry, wrong number, a novelization by Allan Ullman from the screen play by Lucille Fletcher, published 1958

Contents: To the future, by R. Bradbury; Rivers of riches, by G. Kersh; Levitation, by J. P. Brennan; Miss Winters and the wind, by C. N. Govan; View from the terrace, by M. Marmer; The man with copper fingers, by D. L. Sayers; The twenty friends of William Shaw, by R. E. Banks; The other hangman, by C. Dickson; Don't look behind you, by F. Brown; No bath for the Browns, by M. Bennet; The uninvited, by M. Gilbert; Dune roller, by J. May; Something short of murder, by H. Slesar; The golden girl, by E. Peters; The boy who predicted earthquakes, by M. St Clair; Walking alone, by M. A. deFord; For all the rude people, by J. Ritchie; The dog died first, by B. Fischer; Room with a view, by H. Dresner; Lemmings, by R. Mathieson; White goddess, by I. Seabright; The substance of martyrs, by W. Sambrot; Call for help, by R. Arthur; Sorry, wrong number, by L. Fletcher

y (ed.) Alfred Hitchcock presents: Stories that scared even me. Random House 1967 463p $6.95

Analyzed in Short Story Index
This collection includes: It, by T. Sturgeon (a novelette); Out of the deeps, by J. Wyndham (a novel, first published 1953) and twenty-three short stories

Short stories included are: Fishhead, by L. S. Cobb; Camera obscura, by B. Copper; A death in the family, by M. A. deFord; Men without bones, by G. Kersh; Not with a bang, by D. Knight; Party games, by J. Burke; X marks the pedwalk, by F. Leiber; Curious adventure of Mr Bond, by N. Barker; Two spinsters, by E. P. Oppenheim; The knife, by R. Arthur; The cage, by R. Russell; Casablanca, by T. M. Disch; The road to Mictlantecutli, by A. James; Guide to doom, by E. Peters; The estuary, by M. St Clair; Tough town, by W. Sambrot; The troll, by T. H. White; Evening at the black house, by R. Somerlott; One of the dead, by W. Wood; The real thing, by R. Specht; Journey to death, by D. E. Westlake; Masters of the hounds, by A. Budrys; The candidate, by H. Slesar

(ed.) Alfred Hitchcock presents: Stories they wouldn't let me do on TV. Simon & Schuster 1957 372p $4.50

Analyzed in Short Story Index
In these twenty-five tales the reader will find cannibalism, devil-possession, filicide, and other subjects too horrible to mention. (Publisher)

Contents: Being a murderer myself, by A. Williams; Lukundoo, by E. L. White; A woman seldom found, by W. Sansom; The perfectionist, by M. St Clair; The price of the head, by J. Russell; Love comes to Miss Lucy, by Q. Patrick; Sredni Vashtar, by "Saki"; Love lies bleeding, by P. MacDonald; The dancing partner, by J. K. Jerome; Casting the runes, by M. R. James; The voice in the night, by W. H. Hodgson; How love came to Professor Guildea, by R. S. Hichens; The moment of decision, by S. Ellin; A jungle graduate, by J. F. Dwyer; Recipe for murder, by C. P. Donnel, Jr.; Nunc dimittis, by R. Dahl; The most dangerous game, by R. Connell; The lady on the grey, by J Collier; The waxwork, by A. M. Burrage; The dumb wife, by T. Burke; Couching at the door, by D. K. Broster; The October game, by A. Bradbury; Water's edge, by R. Block; The jokester, by R. Arthur; The abyss, by L. Andreyev

(ed.) Alfred Hitchcock's Fireside book of suspense; ed. and with introductory notes by Mr Hitchcock. Simon & Schuster 1947 367p o.p. 1970

Analyzed in Short Story Index
Contents: Quality of suspense, by A. Hitchcock; Second-class passenger, by P. Gibbon; News in English, by G. Greene; Leiningen versus the ants, by C. Stephenson; If you don't get excited, by E. Corle; Fire in the galley stove, by W. Outerson; Liqueur glass, by P. Bottome; Alarm bell, by D. Henderson; Room on the fourth floor, by R. Straus; With bated breath, by R. Santee; Flood on the Goodwins, by A. D. Divine; Sunset, by S. H. Small; House of ecstasy, by R. M. Farley; Hangman won't wait, by J. D. Carr; Second step, by M. Sharp; After-dinner story, by W. Irish; The tunnel, by J. Metcalfe; Triggers in leash, by A. V. Elston; Blue paper, by A. P. Terhune; Three good witnesses, by H. Lamb; R. M. S. Titanic, by H. Baldwin; Ringed word, by T. O. Beachcroft; Yours truly, Jack the Ripper, by R. Bloch; Baby in the icebox, by J. M. Cain; Two bottles of relish, by Lord Dunsany; Smee, by "Ex-private X"; His brother's keeper, by W. W. Jacobs; Elementals, by S. V. Benét

Hitchens, Dolores

A collection of strangers. Putnam 1969 253p $5.95

"The Stoddards were a close family once, tightly knit, warm, loving. But the baby was killed accidently while in his grandmother's care, and the family relationship broke down completely. Each person's isolation in no way prepares the family for the demands of an extortioner. Only when it is much too late to

Hitchens, Dolores—*Continued*

make amends for the family rift do they become at last aware of the extent to which a lonely, brokenhearted old woman will go to redeem herself in her family's eyes. And then they must face the tragic consequences of their own acts—the brutal, senseless violence of murder." Publisher's note

The events "add up to a somewhat routine suspense story. The motivation for extortion seems rather weak, although the setting is well drawn." Pub W

Hlasko, Marek

The eighth day of the week; tr. from the Polish by Norbert Guterman. Dutton 1958 128p o.p. 1970

"The cast of 'The Eighth Day of the Week' (set in Warsaw in 1956) includes a father, his daughter Agnieszka, who is working for her master's degree, his son Grzegorz, who wants to become a writer, a young man, Piotr, who is in love with Agnieszka—all wanting to free themselves from the nightmare of their dreadfull everyday life, all waiting for that eighth day of the week which will liberate them, but waiting in vain since the day never comes." Sat R

"Apart from its purely literary merits, the book's content presents illuminating insights into the social and personal problems that beset the Poles; and the controversy which Hlasko's writings arouse points up the widespread discussion of the respective merits of artistic freedom and of 'literature engagée' that agitates Polish intellectuals today." Library J

Hobart, Alice Tisdale

Oil for the lamps of China. Bobbs 1933 403p o.p. 1970

"Working for an American oil company in China, Stephen Chase makes himself increasingly valuable, as he learns to feel out the Chinese merchant mind, and to understand the intricacies of Oriental life. The story of Stephen's rise in the business and of his subsequent undeserved fall is made more absorbing by the penetrating analysis of several relationships: that of Stephen and his wife with Kin, their servant, that of Stephen and his Chinese adviser, Ho, and of the employe with the ruthless corporation." N Y Libraries

"Mrs. Hobart, who has lived in China since 1910 is able to view Western civilization with the eyes of a detached observer. In China she has seen the end of the Manchu Empire, the lords, and the advance of communism. She is thus peculiarly well equipped to set one civilization against the other for the illumination of both. She has done so with a richness and integrity difficult to convey in outline." N Y Times Bk R

The peacock sheds his tail. Bobbs 1945 360p o.p. 1970

"A story of Mexico in the period just preceding the [second world] war. All classes of society enter into it and all the complicated problems of religion, class distinctions, land, oil, foreign concessions, diplomatic relations, are deftly woven into the narrative. A young American, Jim Buchanan, connected with the embassy, marries into one of the old conservative Spanish families. Personal adjustments growing out of the marriage are paralleled by his efforts at mediation in the economic field. Ends in personal tragedy but on a note of hopefulness for better understanding between the two countries." Wis Lib Bul

Hobson, Laura Z.

First papers. Random House 1964 502p $6.95

A "novel that dramatizes the socialist liberal movement in the USA, 1911-1920, by showing the lives of two families, close friends, both families on the fighting lines of the movement. One, headed by an eloquent Russian-Jewish emigré editor, is suffering the stresses and strains of the second generation's urge towards conformity. The other is an old New England family of Unitarians." Pub W

"The central quality of the book is a kind of non-flag-waving patriotism, a sentiment which has nothing in common with the chauvinist extremism of our time. It recreates with affection, but without sentimentality, a period and a family, plus an attitude of mind grounded on respect for ideas, particularly the idea of freedom. The pace, proper to the time it recalls, contrasts pleasantly with the jerky accelerations of the 'modern' novel." Book of the Month Club News

y Gentleman's agreement; a novel. Simon & Schuster 1947 275p o.p. 1970

"Veteran newspaperman, Schuyler Green, a newcomer to New York, is given his first assignment there—a series on anti-Semitism. Endeavoring to expose this menace to democracy, he passes himself off as Jewish. Subjected to hitherto unsuspected everyday humiliations he gains grievous insight into the problem. Green is even more dismayed when he finds a core of prejudice in Kathy, the woman he loves. There is a rift between them when he finds that by refusing to sublet to his Jewish friend, she honors the fascist 'gentleman's agreement' which restricts her lease to Aryans. Then Kathy undergoes a change of heart; explains to all her neighbors she is breaking the agreement." Literary Guild

"It is a good job of story telling. Mrs. Hobson had to choose her characters by types—that is inevitable in a propaganda novel—but, having picked them and named them, she put something much more human than synthetic sawdust inside their skins and pumped in real blood." N Y Her Trib Books

Hodge, Jane Aiken

The adventurers. Doubleday 1965 283p $4.95

"Sonia, a 17-year-old half-English, half-German girl and her slightly older English governess flee when their home is sacked by French and Russian troops during the retreat of Napoleon from Leipzig to Paris (1813-14). In desperation they attach themselves to Charles, a mysterious but chivalrous French-monarchist spy. They all support themselves by winning at cards (quite honestly)!" Library J

"There is just enough of all the basic ingredients—adventure, excitement, love, suspense, and even a surprise ending." Best Sellers

Marry in haste. Doubleday 1970 [c1969] 205p $4.95

First published 1969 in England

Set in Regency England and Portugal "this is a colorful romantic adventure novel for women readers of the genre. After agreeing to a marriage in name only Camilla Forest falls in love with her handsome, enigmatic husband, Lord Leominster, who as special assistant to England's minister at the court of Portugal takes his bride and his young sister to Portugal. The part Leominster plays in trying to save Portugal from Napoleon's forces causes his separation from Camilla, and she and her sister-in-law have to flee in peasant disguises by mule and foot across country to reach safety." Booklist

Maulever Hall. Doubleday 1964 306p o.p. 1970

"A fast-moving adventure-romance of 19th century England. The charming, bright heroine suffers amnesia after a stagecoach upset. Part of the story is taken up with discovering her true identity. She and a little boy whom she mysteriously has in her charge find refuge in a mansion on the moors, and she falls in love with its master, until dangers somehow connected with her past life menace her present life and love. In spite of a contrived ending, this is excellent light reading." Pub W

The winding stair. Doubleday 1969 [c1968] 328p $5.95

"A suspenseful Gothic romance set in early nineteenth-century Portugal under threat from Napoleonic France features a likable half-English, half-Portuguese heroine. Juana Brett returns from England to the ancestral Portuguese castle to care for her ailing but formidable grandmother who wants Juana to assume her position as handmaiden to a dangerous secret society dedicated to gaining control of

Hodge, Jane A.—*Continued*

Portugal by any means, a position the grandmother has used to spy on the group for the English." Booklist
"Colorful background, strange family relationships, and haunting picture of a girl reaching maturity." Library J

Hodgins, Eric

Mr Blandings builds his dream house; illus. by William Steig. Simon & Schuster 1946 237p illus o.p. 1970

"Expanded from a 'Fortune' short story, this book is an amusing story of a New York advertiser who found his apartment much too small and bought 50 acres and a farmhouse in the country. Mr. Blandings' trials and tribulations from the time when the architect, after spending a great deal of time and money, decided that the farmhouse should be torn down instead of remodelled until the new home was finished at a cost of $45,000 more than they expected make hilarious reading. The book contains pointers for would-be home builders, but will probably be read chiefly for sheer entertainment." Ontario Lib Rev

Hoffman, Nicholas von. *See* Von Hoffman, Nicholas

Holding, Elizabeth Sanxay

The blank wall
In Hitchcock, A. ed. Alfred Hitchcock presents: My favorites in suspense p354-502

Holland, Cecelia

Antichrist; a novel of the Emperor Frederick II. Atheneum Pubs. 1970 299p boards $6.95

Emperor Frederick II, "German ruler, raised in Sicily, was a prodigious lover, fighter, politician, patron of the arts, jurist. [This novel] focuses on him during a period of blazing glory in which, although under papal excommunication, he went on Crusade to the Holy Land, and by wily diplomatic maneuvering with the Muslims received the city of Jerusalem for the Christians and had himself crowned king there." Pub W

The firedrake. Atheneum Pubs. 1966 [c1965] 243p boards $5

A "picaresque tale set in 11th century Germany Flanders, Normandy and England. The Irish hero, named Laeghaire, the Gaelic spelling of Lear, is a brave, hard-fighting mercenary in the forces of William of Normandy. He is impetuous, brawling, very proud, with a plain and cutting tongue. Laeghaire kills men in battle with no hesitation, but he is haunted with nightmares about an ugly future. He is a restless adventurer, he is briefly a man in love, he is a violent man of action. This vital central character is placed against a colorful medieval background of castles and wild countryside and in the middle of one fight after another." Pub W
The author's "terse narrative style and accurate historical documentation make her first novel rewarding reading." Cincinnati

The kings in winter. Atheneum Pubs. 1968 [c1967] 208p map boards $5.75

"This is an historical novel . . . which concerns an Irish hero, Brian Boru of the Irish royal house of Munster, and his conquests. The book follows Boru's career and his attempts to unite Ireland." Pub W
"Although some geographical confusion and a spattering of Gaelic words and names are mildly distracting, the tale drives ahead with many a grim episode and many a fine evocation of contemporary thought, emotion and codes of conduct. . . . In Muirtagh The O'Cullinane, the author has created a more complex character than any of those in her first two books. Her knowledge of the ways of primitive, violent men is impressive." N Y Times Bk R

Rakóssy. Atheneum Pubs. [1967 c1966] 243p $5.75

A "novel of historical background dramatizing the harshness of life among ambitious, embattled, and battling men, this time in sixteenth-century Hungary during Turkish incursions. The characters are mainly fictional, among them the protagonist, János Rakóssy, Magyar man of action, his scholarly brother Denis, Catharine the woman János woos and wins from the Austrian court, and his worthy Turkish enemy Mustafa. Terse if not always probable dialog and swift action mark a book likely to hold readers who care more for colorfulness, romance, and pace than historicity." Booklist

Until the sun falls. Atheneum Pubs. [1969 c1968] 491p maps boards $7.95

This novel about the thirteenth-century Mongol invasion of Europe "is told from the points of view of two imaginary generals in the army of Batu, Khan of the Golden Horde. Psin was a veteran of the campaigns of the great Genghis, a crafty commander, fierce, feared and respected. His son Tshant was equally able, but explosively bad-tempered and arrogant. When the two weren't busy fighting their foreign foes, they fought each other." N Y Times Bk R

Holland, Isabelle

y Cecily; a novel. Lippincott 1967 189p $4.50

"Set in an English boarding school for girls. . . . Awkward, overweight Cecily, a thirteen-year-old misfit at the school, is the butt of the other girls' cruelties and disliked by her English teacher, Elizabeth Marks. Elizabeth's fiance, an American Rhodes scholar teaching at a nearby boys' school, sympathizes with Cecily, and his and Elizabeth's conflicting views cause a rift in their romance." Booklist
"The characterization is sharply perceptive; Cecily is painfully real. And the author is particularly adept in describing the power structure in the school, both among the girls and the mistresses." Sat R

Holt, Victoria

Bride of Pendorric. Doubleday 1963 288p boards $4.95

"Favel tells how the darkly handsome Roc Pendorric married her after a whirlwind courtship on Capri, took her to the centuries old Pendorric mansion in Cornwall, and aroused her dark suspicions after she learned of his old loves, of the curse upon the Brides of Pendorric, and of one Bride who still haunted an empty room." Bk Buyer's Guide
"A fine novel in every sense of the word. It has a fast-moving suspenseful storyline and appealing, believable characters, Miss Holt writes in a manner reminiscent of the Bronte sisters and of Daphne du Maurier. As the tale unfolds, the reader is completely caught up in the spell of a master storyteller." Best Sellers

y The king of the castle. Doubleday 1967 310p $5.50

A Gothic novel with a turn-of-the-century setting in France's chateau country, Dallas Lawson has "been hired by the sardonic but attractive Comte de la Talle to restore his art collection. He has a cousin, Philippe, and a headstrong daughter, Genevieve. There is a rumor that he murdered his wife. Dallas finds herself in the midst of romance and danger." Bk Buyer's Guide
"The spooky air of the chateau, interesting details about vineyards and winemaking, the ins and outs of art restoration and French country life contribute to the fun, and there are enough surprising family skeletons to keep things moving at a pace that will delight Miss Holt's fans." Pub W

y Kirkland Revels. Doubleday 1962 312p boards $5.50

"Kirkland Revels, a magnificent manor house, standing grand and aloof on the Yorkshire moors, hides many secrets from Catherine Rockwell, its newest resident. The strange suicide of her young husband prompts Catherine to try to prove his death murder despite certain danger." Cincinnati

Holt, Victoria—*Continued*

"It is pure romantic fiction but well-paced and suspenseful, good for an evening's diversion. The evocation of mood and atmosphere is good." Best Sellers

y The legend of the Seventh Virgin. Doubleday 1965 326p $5.50

"Kerensa Carlee's dream of owning St. Larnston Abbas, the famous convent now the home of Cornwall's leading family, had seemed to be coming true when she married Johnny St. Larnston, but soon her world crumbled as Johnny disappeared and the sinister legendary past of the house enveloped her." McClurg. Book News

This title "has all the ingredients of superior gothic fiction. . . . The Cornish dialect with which Victoria Holt spices her story is a constant delight and a tribute to her skill as a novelist." Best Sellers

y Menfreya in the morning. Doubleday 1966 256p $4.95

"Harriet Delvaney, a poor little rich girl who is afflicted with a limp . . . is despised by her father because her mother died at her birth. She marries Bevil Menfrey, the handsome, tawney-haired scion of a high-spirited but impoverished family, and goes to live at Menfreya, a fortresslike mansion on the Cornish coast. Once installed, Harriet is deliriously happy—but . . . what about the beautiful, coolly poised governess. . . . And what about the legend of the tower clock, which stops when somebody is about to die?" Time

"It's hard to say, objectively, just why . . . [this] is so intensely readable and enjoyable. . . . [It] is Holt's weakest and slightest plot to date, and equally certain nothing much happens in the way of either action of character development for long stretches. But somehow the magic . . . is still there. . . . [It] made me perfectly happy for 110,000 words, and . . . may very well satisfy you too." N Y Times Bk R

y Mistress of Mellyn. Doubleday 1960 334p $5.50

In this romantic novel set in late 19th century England, the heroine is an attractive, young English governess. "She takes charge of the motherless child of a handsome, arrogant gentleman who lives in a large creepy mansion in Cornwall. The plot is lively and complicated. Eventually, our bright heroine discovers that her little pupil's mother was murdered and she narrowly escapes being murdered herself." Pub W

"Victoria Holt writes expertly and with great suspense. It would be quibbling to complain that her novel is patently derivative of 'Jane Eyre.' After all it couldn't follow a better pattern." N Y Her Trib Books

The Queen's confession. Doubleday 1968 430p $5.95

This biographical novel, in the form of a memoir written by herself, describes the life of Marie Antoinette as a young Austrian Archduchess; a spoiled Dauphine in the Versailles court; a misunderstood Queen; and as a woman who achieved tragic nobility. (Publisher)

The author "does her work well. Her story is based on hardcore fact and she provides an excellent bibliography, rich in primary sources. Her imagination embroiders the story delicately and makes the entire work believable." Best Sellers

The shivering sands. Doubleday 1969 305p $5.95

"This book describes a young girl's search for the cause of her sister's mysterious disappearance—a search that takes her to a foreboding old mansion near the cliffs of Dover and the infamous 'shivering sands,' quicksands dotted with the masts of ships they have trapped." News of Bks

"Atmosphere and suspense are well maintained in this Gothic romance with wide appeal for women readers of the genre." Booklist

Hooker, Richard

MASH. Morrow 1968 219p boards $4.95

"Captains Hawkeye Pierce, Duke Forrest, and 'Trapper' John McIntyre, all M.D.'s, are stationed in Korea with the 4077th MASH (Mobile Army Surgical Hospital). The reader is soon involved in many operations and medical jargon. It is, however, the off-duty activities of these three that engages one's attention and laughter. Full of martinis, or bored, or tired, or all three, the men soon start raising hell. . . . Hilarious, occasionally very serious, full of warm, appealing eccentric characters, one could enjoy a very pleasant evening with this sMASHing novel. Recommended for public libraries." Library J

"This is lusty, uninhibited man-stuff with no holds barred. It is also extremely funny. Men, particularly ex-G.I.s, are going to like this book a lot." Pub W

Hope, Anthony

y The prisoner of Zenda; with an introduction by S. C. Roberts; illus. by Donald Spencer. Heritage 1966 188p $6.95

First published 1894

"The extraordinary adventures of Rudolf Rassendyll in an imaginary kingdom in Austrian Tyrol. Duels and hairbreadth escapes, palace intrigues and conspiracies, and two episodes in which the hero takes advantage of his likeness to impersonate the king, fill the [story] with romantic incident." Baker's Best

Horgan, Paul

The common heart

In Horgan, P. Mountain standard time: Main line west, Far from Cibola [and] The common heart p279-595

The devil in the desert

In The Saturday Evening Post. The Saturday Evening Post Reader of Western stories p306-32

y A distant trumpet. Farrar, Straus 1960 629p $6.95

A novel of the Southwest in the 1870's and 1880's. The chief scene of action is at a U.S. Army outpost in Arizona during the Apache Indian Wars. Chief protagonists in the story are Lieutenant Matthew Hazard and his wife, Laura; Major General Alexander Upton Quait, Laura's resourceful eccentric uncle; Colonel and Mrs Prescott and the other officers and their wives; and, White Horn, an Apache scout. (Publisher)

"The author evokes the arid landscape of the Southwest with his usual great skill and feeling; in the characterization of a general officer Mr. Horgan appears to have accomplished a real tour de force!" Library J

Everything to live for. Farrar, Straus 1968 215p $4.95

"Seventeen-year-old Richard [who appeared in the author's Things as they are, entered below] receives an invitation to visit his fabulously wealthy relatives, the Chittendons. His 20-year-old cousin, Max, crown prince of the family, is a stereotype poor little rich boy with an ineffectual father, a physically and emotionally crippled mother, and a fiancée who tried to murder him when they were children. The elder Chittendons approve of the effect young Richard has on his high-strung cousin, and Richard himself is enchanted with the aura of gloom, doom, and money that surrounds Max and his fiancée." Am News of Bks

"In a format almost as tightly disciplined as a Greek tragedy, Horgan has developed a story both modern in its psychological penetration and its exemplification of the new social mores, and classical in its deliberate, chiseled phrasing and the simple directness of its plotting." Book World

Far from Cibola

In Horgan, P. Mountain standard time: Main line west, Far from Cibola [and] The common heart p203-78

Horgan, Paul—*Continued*

Main line west

In Horgan, P. Mountain standard time: Main line west, Far from Cibola [and] The common heart p 1-201

Mountain standard time: Main line west, Far from Cibola [and] The common heart. Introduction by D. W. Brogan. Farrar, Straus 1962 595p $5.95

These novels, first published 1936, 1936, and 1942, respectively have their setting in the American west and southwest

"'Main Line West' is a hymn to the faithfulness of love and the power of the human spirit, even though these conspire to bring bitter tragedy upon a woman and child who embody them. 'Far from Cibola', in both form and content, is a parable of the inescapable effect of men and women upon each other in desire, hunger, joy and sorrow, as these are expressed, now for good, again for evil, by human society. 'The common heart' is an interweaving of four flowing narratives about people of different ages and natures in all of whom can be felt the warmth and glow of life which, even at its humblest, reaches toward creation." Publisher's note

The peach stone; stories from four decades. Farrar, Straus [1967 c1965] 470p $5.95

Analyzed in Short Story Index
Contents: To the mountains; The one who wouldn't dance; Winners and losers; Black snowflakes; A start in life; In summer's name; So little freedom; The huntsmen; The treasure; National honeymoon; The surgeon and the nun; The other side of the street; Tribute; The small rain; The peach stone; The hacienda; Old Army; The head of the House of Wattleman; The devil in the desert; The candy colonel

"The author has selected twenty of his short stories for this collection, written between 1930 and 1966. They are grouped in four sections: childhood, youth, maturity, and age." Book Rev Digest

Things as they are. Farrar, Straus 1964 239p $4.50

"This fictionalized autobiographical reconstruction of boyhood captures with sensitivity the singular purities and guilts the joys and terrors, the understandings and misapprehensions of a youngster growing up amid parents, grandparents, and friends in New York State some years after the turn of the twentieth century." Booklist

"Poorly blurbed, this could be called the story of the phenomenal growth and most critical transition of human life: the loss of childhood and the attainment of manhood. Horgan enriches this appealing story line with a delicacy of style and unhurried pace that gleams with the crystal sparkle of a master. Had he spun the familiar rune of childhood with the attendant recital of longing for return, his story would escape mediocrity by the sheer precision and glow of his prose. . . . The publishers have honored this fine novel with an exceptional achievement in bookmaking at reasonable cost." Library J

Horia, Vintila

God was born in exile; a novel. With a preface by Daniel-Rops. Tr. from the French by A. Lytton Sells. St Martins 1961 301p o.p. 1970

Original French edition published in Paris, 1960

"Ovid the Roman poet was exiled for the last eight years of his life (9-17 A.D.) by the Emperor Augustus partly because his work, especially the 'Ars Amatoria' was considered a bad influence on the younger Romans. Horia . . . has constructed this novel in the form of a journal kept by Ovid during his exile in a garrison town in Dacia, which is roughly modern Rumania. At first Ovid finds life there almost unsupportable, but soon he discovers Zamolxis, the God of the local people, who in some ways prefigures the Christian God. His thought is transformed after visiting the Dacian priests and the Holy places. Ovid also meets Theodore, a Greek physician who has news of Christ's birth." Library J

Hough, Emerson

y The covered wagon. Grosset 386p front $2.50

Reprint of a title first published 1922 by Appleton

"Story of a great migration, the movement of a wagon train of two thousand men, women and children from Missouri to Oregon in 1848. Midway across the continent comes the news of gold in California to disrupt the train and draw many of the adventurous to the southward. An interesting love story holds the tale together." Wis Lib Bul

Household, Geoffrey

The courtesy of death; a novel. Little 1967 214p boards $4.95

"An Atlantic Monthly Press book"
"A lone man chances, in the English countryside, upon a band of dedicated men and women who have revived a primitive cult. They perform their strange ceremonies in secret limestone caves which riddle the green and pleasant landscape of the Mendip Hills. Yarrow, the narrator, a mining engineer in search of a peaceful country location for his early retirement, stumbles into a ritual of the hunt in which he himself will be the victim. The chase . . . takes Yarrow all over the southwest country and into one of the most eerie imprisonments in modern fiction; it introduces characters whose prosaic appearances mask the most sinister and bloody intentions." Publisher's note

Dance of the dwarfs. Little 1968 257p $5.95

"An Atlantic Monthly Press book"
A young Englishman runs an experimental agricultural station in a remote part of South America on the edge of the jungle. When a young Indian girl becomes his mistress, his happiness is complete. Then he discovers the "dwarfs" who dance on moonlight nights. (Publisher)

"The author is particularly daring in choosing to present the 'I' narration by means of a diary rather than through the customary continuous narrative. Though in the early stages of this novel the method operates slowly, the wisdom of the choice and the efficiency of its use become apparent when the events drive the narrator-major character deeper and deeper into an investigation of the impact of events on his emotions." Best Sellers

Rogue male. Little 1939 280p o.p. 1970

"Having been caught with his gun trained on the terrace of the mountain retreat of a certain foreign dictator, a wealthy English big game hunter escapes, more dead than alive, only to be pursued by the dictator's secret agents back to England where he attempts to disappear forever. More thrilling than a detective story, this 'tour de force' traces in his own words, every motive, every ingenious plan, every cunning move and every change in the mental and physical condition of the Englishman, as he turns into a solitary, hunted animal, 'a rogue' attempting to elude the pursuit of the pack." Bookmark

"As a work of the imagination 'Rogue Male' is an almost overpowering 'tour de force'. And in its spare, tense, desperately alive narrative it will keep, long after the last page is finished, its hold from the first page upon the reader's mind. Its deepest and broadest suggestion the reader must find for himself, if he will." N Y Times Bk R

also in Haycraft, H. ed. Three times three p295-419

Run from the hangman

In The Saturday Evening Post. Danger p296-368

Watcher in the shadows; a novel. Little 1960 248p map $5.95

"An Atlantic Monthly Press book"
"The hero, a Viennese who had served in British intelligence during the war, finds himself hunted down by an old enemy who had, naturally, believed him to be a Nazi at the time when he was posing as one in the line of duty. The two finally settle their differences in hand-to-hand combat in a peaceful country setting in England." Pub W

Household, Geoffrey—*Continued*

"It's a thrilling tale that Mr. Household weaves, enriched beyond the ordinary suspense story. For besides giving it a deeply emotional motive, bound to hold universal appeal, he brings to it a strong feeling for the English countryside, its wild life and its people, a knowledge of horses and horsemanship that focuses humorously on a highly engaging animal, and a gift for gently introducing a romantic note which contributes to his hero's character and action." N Y Her Trib Books

Housepian, Marjorie

A houseful of love. Random House 1957 222p o.p. 1970

"Purportedly fiction though autobiographical in tone and written from the viewpoint of a ten-year-old girl, this delightful family story describes growing up in the Armenian-American settlement in New York City during the early thirties. The narrator tells mainly about the problems and fortunes of her large group of relatives, among whom are the volatile restaurant owner Uncle Pousant, tenacious ninety-seven-year-old Marta-mama, and Uncle Kelesh, who dreams of building yogurt factories." Booklist

"The author has combined the richness of adult insight with the innocence and love of the first generation child who tells the story, and the result is a charming and interesting book." Commonweal

Howard, Elizabeth Jane

Something in disguise. Viking [1970 c1969] 280p boards $5.95

First published 1969 in England

"Modern-day England is the setting for a tale of love, dependence, and compromise. Stepsisters Alice and Elizabeth leave home to follow their own bents in love and marriage, and brother Oliver pursues nonproductive forms of dilettantism. Left at home is May, the bewildered mother who seeks religion as a substitute for the daily realities of life with a seemingly innocuous but deadly second husband." Library J

"Miss Howard is a talented Englishwoman who writes with great clarity and ease. Her style is crisp, to the point, and readable, her dialogue rings true to life. She is an experienced author and her polish is evident on every page. This book is by no means the novel of the year or even of the month, but it is a good story and one that reading members of the distaff side of society should enjoy." Best Sellers

Howe, George

y Call it treason; a novel. Viking 1949 344p $5.95

World War II is the background for this author's "story of the Army's G-2, the intelligence section, which chose and trained captured Germans as spies. He expatiates on the motives that led these men to volunteer for this dangerous work. Mr. Howe concerns himself with three particular spies: the Tiger, a Communist with a lust for power and money; Paluka, an adventure seeker; and Happy, a convinced anti-Nazi." Literary Guild

"Aside from presenting a fascinating story, author attempts to explain why people in these circumstances become spies, and he generally succeeds. Awarded the Christophers prize." Library J

Howe, Irving

(ed.) A treasury of Yiddish stories, ed. by Irving Howe & Eliezer Greenberg. With drawings by Ben Shahn. Viking 1954 630p illus $6.95

Analyzed in Short Story Index

Contents: The calf, by M. M. Sforim; On account of a hat, by S. Aleichem; Devotion without end, by I. L. Peretz; Eternal life, by S.

Aleichem; Hodel, by S. Aleichem; The search, by S. Aleichem; Dreyfus in Kasrilevke, by S. Aleichem; The pair, by S. Aleichem; The dead town, by I. L. Peretz; Ne'ilah in Gehenna, by I. L. Peretz; Cabalists, by I. L. Peretz; Bontsha the silent, by I. L. Peretz; If not higher, by I. L. Peretz; The mad talmudist, by I. L. Peretz; Rabbi Yochanan the warden, by I. L. Peretz; The Golem, by I. L. Peretz; And then he wept, by D. Pinski; A meal for the poor, by M. Spector; Sanctification of the name (a legend), by S. Asch; Kola Street, by S. Asch; The poor community, by A. Reisen; The big Succeh, by A. Reisen; Tuition for the Rebbe, by A. Reisen; The recluse, by A. Reisen; Mazel tov, by I. M. Weissenberg; Father and the boys, by I. M. Weissenberg; Revenge (extracts from a Student's diary) by Z. Schneour; The girl, by Z. Schneour; White chalah, by L. Shapiro; Smoke, by L. Shapiro; The rebbe and the rebbetsin; by L. Shapiro; Munie the bird dealer, by M. Kulbak; Repentance, by I. J. Singer; Sand, by I. J. Singer; Competitors, by J. Rosenfeld; Gimpel the fool, by I. B. Singer; May the temple be restored, by J. Opatoshu; A page from the Song of Songs, by S. Aleichem; My first love, by M. Nadir; The adventures of Hershel Summerwind, by I. Manger; Eating days, by L. Shapiro; In a backwoods town, by D. Bergelson; To the new world, by I. Metzker; a quiet garden spot, by S. Asch; The little shoemakers, by I. B. Singer; Higher and higher, by P. Marcus; The eternal wedding gown, by J. Opatoshu; The return, by J. Glatstein; The man who slept through the end of the world, by M. Nadir; A ghetto dog, by I. Spiegel; My quarrel with Hersh Rasseyner, by C. Grade; A tale of a candelabrum, by Rabbi Nachman of Bratzlav; Stories of Hershel Ostropolier; Tales of Chelm

Howells, William D.

A hazard of new fortunes; a novel. Harper 1890 171p illus o.p. 1970

"The 19th century New York streetcar strike furnished the central theme for this novel violently condemning the unionization of industry and the exploitation of labor." Retail Bookseller

"The most realistic and the most modern of all his novels, in its grasp upon the conditions of metropolitan life, especially as these are illustrated in the extremes of poverty and wealth." Keller's Reader's Digest of Books

Indian summer. Ticknor 1886 395p o.p. 1970

A youth-and-age theme is the basis for a story about cultured Americans living in nineteenth century Florence. Theodore Colville, a middle-aged bachelor, in Florence to resume his study of architecture, found his interest diverted by Imogene Graham, a twenty-year-old being chaperoned by an old friend, a widow of his own age. Realistic complications, dramatic and humorous, involve these three and other members of the American colony

A modern instance; a novel. Osgood, J.R. 1882 514p o.p. 1970

"A dissolute journalist, Bartley Hubbard, and his jealous wife are the leading characters of this grim psychological novel. Their unhappy marriage, leading to attempted divorce and tragedy, realistically typifies many cases of incompatibility." English and Pope's What to read

The rise of Silas Lapham. With biographical illus. and pictures of the setting of the book, together with an introduction by C. David Mead. Dodd 1964 367p illus (Great illustrated classics) $4.50

First published 1885

"Silas is a crude, uneducated man, who makes his fortune by methods not above criticism, but manly and capable of better things when his conscience is awakened—a compendium of human virtues and vices, drawn with insight, tenderness and humour. The efforts of the prosperous Laphams to get into Boston society, with their mistakes and disillusionments, the sentimental tragi-comedy of the two daughters, in love with the same young man; and Lapham's business troubles, are more or less neatly woven in to make the plot." Baker's Best

Howells, William D.—*Continued*

Their wedding journey; ed. by John K. Reeves. Ind. Univ. Press 1968 xxxiii, 240p illus (A Selected edition of W. D. Howells) $10

First published 1872 by J. R. Osgood
"His first novel decorously discusses things seen, heard, and experienced by two Bostonians on their wedding trip to Canada and back." Dickinson

Hoyle, Fred

A for Andromeda; a novel of tomorrow [by] Fred Hoyle [and] John Elliot. Harper 1962 206p o.p. 1970

This novel is "based on the BBC Television serial of the same name, the book is published by arrangement with the British Broadcasting Corporation." Pub W
A science fiction novel in which the scene is set ten years from now. A new radio-telescope picks up a complex series of signals from the constellation Andromeda, which proves to be knowledge previously unknown to man, knowledge of such a nature that the security of human life itself is threatened. (Publisher)
"This is a well-paced and credible story of the events which might logically occur as a result of radio-astronomical investigation" Best Sellers
Followed by: Andromeda breakthrough

Andromeda breakthrough [by] Fred Hoyle and John Elliot. Harper [1965 c1964] 192p o.p. 1970

Sequel to: A for Andromeda
"British physicist John Fleming thought he had destroyed the center, an outerspace computer being used against earth, but when he and Andromeda, a computer-designed girl, were kidnapped he discovered the fight had just begun." Bk Buyer's Guide
"The tale is definitely bizarre but well written and is suitable for entertainment reading for adults." Best Sellers

Fifth planet [by] Fred Hoyle and Geoffrey Hoyle. Harper 1963 217p o.p. 1970

"A satiric yet suspenseful science-fiction novel about the race between the Communist block and the Euro-Americans to reach Achilles, Earth-like fifth planet approaching our world in 2087." Bk Buyer's Guide
"This book is well written and is extremely interesting in some sections. It can not be classified as light escape reading since it must be carefully read if any understanding of the author's justification of events is to be had." Best Sellers

October the first is too late. Harper 1966 200p boards $4.95

"A transmission of solar beams plays havoc with time on earth. England is in the 1960's but World War I is still raging in western Europe. Greece is in the golden age of Pericles, America some thousands of years in the future; while Russia and Asia are a glass-like plain, its surface fused together by the burnt-out sun of a far distant future. The central themes are time and the meaning of consciousness, and the heroes are a pianist-composer and his friend, a scientist." Publisher's note
"Fred Hoyle is an astronomer. His science fiction has much basis in modern theories of physics, and appeals to scientists as well as laymen. A serious discussion of the meaning of time is woven through this story." Pub W

Ossian's ride. Harper 1959 207p map o.p. 1970

"The Industrial Corporation of Eire had built a chain of thermonuclear reactors in Ireland, and Thomas Sherwood was sent to discover the most closely guarded secret in the world of 1970, what made the I. C. E. tick. He tells of his own wild adventures with guards, espionage agents, the purveyors of sudden death, and others." The Bookseller

Hoyle, Geoffrey
(jt. auth.) Hoyle, F. Fifth planet

Hubbard, P. M.

Cold waters. Atheneum Pubs. 1969 180p $4.95

"Attracted by the idea of 'getting away from it all,' Giffard takes a job as general handyman to Callander on a lovely island. Here life seems idyllic, with Callander's wife to console during his absences, and a pretty French maid to bed with. But gradually Giffard becomes aware of a deadly menace beneath the cold waters." Bk Buyer's Guide

A hive of glass. Atheneum Pubs. 1965 184p $3.95

"Johnnie Slade, a collector of old glass, tells how he was put on the trail of the Verzelini tazza, a Venetian glass stand some four centuries old. The clues led to a strange ring, a lovely girl and to others who wanted the priceless glass even more than he did, enough to kill for it." Bk Buyer's Guide

Hubbard, Philip Maitland. See Hubbard, P. M.

Hudson, Helen

Meyer, Meyer. Dutton 1967 189p boards $4.50

"The mildly ironic tale of two middle-aged New Yorkers, Meyer Meyer, who refuses to become committed to life and love, and Mendel, emotional and lachrymose. The crisis comes when these two meet red-haired and sensual Lena and the embittered Josie." Bk Buyer's Guide
"Helen Hudson has drawn a very effective portrait of a seemingly sensitive Jewish intellectual who is, in reality, a man able to live only by his own brand of self-pity. There are a lot of Meyers around, but they have seldom been pinned to the drawing board so brilliantly as here." Pub W

Hudson, Jeffery

A case of need; a novel. World Pub. 1968 309p $5.95

"Dr. John Berry, a pathologist in a Boston hospital, is advised that a close friend and colleague has been arrested for performing an illegal abortion that led to the death of the 18-year-old daughter of a prominent surgeon. Believing his friend to be innocent in this case, although he has been known to perform abortions in accord with his conscience in the past, Berry begins a round of the dead girl's family, friends and favorite haunts in an effort to clear the doctor's name." Pub W
The author "has managed to tell a fine story and at the same time comment deftly on some severe contemporary social problems." Best Sellers

Hudson, Lois Phillips

The bones of plenty; a novel. Little 1962 439p $6.95

"An Atlantic Monthly Press book"
This first novel tells "how it was to be a tenant farm family in North Dakota during the early months of the New Deal, when the grave consequences of the Wall Street crash finally reached the wheatlands west of the Mississippi. [The] story spans slightly more than a year—from February 1933, when the local bank closes and the banker leaves town, to May 1934, when the impoverished Custer family packs its pitiful belongings into a trailer and heads for California." Sat R
The story "is documented with facts of the Depression. It reveals the terrible time, the sorrow and tragedy of the '30's." Wis Lib Bul

Hudson, W. H.
y Green mansions

Some editions are:
Collins $1.95
Dodd (Great illustrated classics) $4.50 With illustrations reproducing drawings for early editions and photographs of contemporary scenes together with an introductory biographical sketch of the author and anecdotal captions by Edwin Way Teale

Hudson, W. H.—*Continued*

Knopf $10 Paintings and drawings by Horacio Butler
Watts, F. $7.95 Large type edition complete and unabridged. A Keith Jennison book
First published 1904
"Based on the naturalist-author's extensive travels in South America. A young man making his way over the Andes falls in with a tribe of savage Indians, discovers in the forest and becomes enamored of a mysterious being, part woman and part bird, and in seeking to unravel her mystery, passes through extreme peril of body and soul." Wis Lib Bul
"'Green Mansions,' the romance of the bird girl Rima, a story actual yet fantastic, immortalizes, I think, as passionate a love of all beautiful things as ever was in the heart of man. In form and spirit the book is unique." John Galsworthy

The purple land; being the narrative of one Richard Lamb's adventures in the Banda Oriental in South America as told by himself; illus. by Keith Henderson. AMS Press 368p illus $15

First published 1885
"The land that lies between Buenos Aires and Montevideo is the exotic setting for Hudson's first novel. This beautiful country, called the Banda Oriental, was inhabited by half-sophisticated, half-wild Spaniards and Indians. Richard Lamb, an Englishman traveling through this dangerous country, is the hero of a pseudo-Gothic story of mystery and romance. Narrow escapes, both in love and in battle, provide the suspense. Besides his beautiful wife, seven other lovely women provide diversion for the lone traveler, as do also some villains. More important than the story of Richard Lamb, however, is Hudson's portrayal of the beauty of nature and the romance of native customs in a strange land." Haydn. Thesaurus of Book Digests

Tales of the gauchos; stories by W. H. Hudson; comp. and ed. by Elizabeth Coatsworth; illus. by Henry C. Pitz. Knopf 1946 251p illus lib. bdg. $3.94

Analyzed in Short Story Index
Contents: Niño Diablo; Boy's life on the pampas; Friend of man; Birds and beasts; Purple land; Individuals; Don Gregorio Gandara; Fight in the dark; Old man of the sea; Voice in the forest; Troop of wild horses; Manuel, also called the fox; Serpent with the cross; Plains of Patagonia; Grand archaic ostrich; Meditations on insects; Liberty and dirt; Story of a piebald horse

W. H. Hudson's Tales of the pampas. Knopf 1939 245p illus o.p. 1970

Analyzed in Short Story Index
Reprint of a title published 1916
Contents: El Ombú; Story of a piebald horse; Pelino Viera's confessions; Niño Diablo; Marta Riquelme; Tecla and the little men

Hudson, William Henry. See Hudson, W. H.

Huffman, Laurie

A house behind the mint. Doubleday 1969 304p $5.95

A "novel based upon the actual exploits of Black Bart, the debonair highwayman who made a practice of robbing the Wells Fargo stage and leaving a bit of doggerel to taunt his victims. And all the time that James Hume, special agent of the company, was searching for Black Bart that gentleman was living in a house behind the San Francisco mint—and Hume was one of his friends." Bk Buyer's Guide
"A thoroughly delightful tale of the Olde West. . . . This is the first novel of Laurie Huffman and we hope she will be a prolific writer. She exercises a clever sense of wording without being obvious. This book provides a pleasant interlude." Best Sellers

Hughes, Langston

The best of Simple; illus. by Bernhard Nast. Hill & Wang 1961 245p illus (American century ser) $3.95

Analyzed in Short Story Index
Contains 70 short stories selected by the author from three previously published books: Simple speaks his mind (1950); Simple stakes a claim (1959); and, Simple takes a wife (1960) all entered separately. All of the stories center around a Harlem Negro named Simple and his friends. (Publisher)

(ed.) The best short stories by Negro writers; an anthology from 1899 to the present; ed. and with an introduction by Langston Hughes. Little 1967 508p $7.95

Analyzed in Short Story Index
Contents: The sheriff's children, by C. W. Chesnutt; The scapegoat, by P. L. Dunbar; Fern, by J. Toomer; Miss Cynthie, by R. Fisher; The wharf rats, by E. Walrond; A summer tragedy, by A. Bontemps; Thank you, m'am, by L. Hughes; The gilded six-bits, by Z. N. Hurston; The revolt of the evil fairies, by T. Poston; Almos' a man, by R. Wright; Marihuana and a pistol, by C. B. Himes; The beach umbrella, by C. Colter; The richer, the poorer, by D. West; The almost white boy, by W. Motley; Afternoon into night, by K. Dunham; Flying home, by R. Ellison; Come home early, chile, by O. Dodson; Santa Claus is a white man, by J. H. Clarke; The stick up, by J. O. Killens; Health card, by F. Yerby; We're the only colored people here, by G. Brooks; The pocketbook game, by A. Childress; The checkerboard, by A. Anderson; This morning, this evening, so soon, by J. Baldwin; See how they run, by M. E. Vroman; The blues begins, by S. Leaks; Son in the afternoon, by J. A. Williams; Singing Dinah's song, by F. L. Brown; Duel with the clock, by J. Edwards; Barbados, by P. Marshall; The day the world almost came to an end, by P. Crayton; An interesting social study, by K. Hunter; A new day, by C. Wright; Quietus, by C. Russell; Mother to son, by C. K. Rivers; A long day in November, by E. J. Gaines; Miss Luhester gives a party, by R. Fair; The death of Tommy Grimes, by R. J. Meaddough; Old blues singers never die, by C. V. Johnson; The only man on Liberty Street, by W. M. Kelley; Beautiful light and black our dreams, by W. King; Red Bonnet, by L. Patterson; The burglar, by L. Bethune; Junkie-Joe had some money, by R. Milner; Direct action, by Thelwell; The engagement party, by R. Boles; To Hell with dying, by A. Walker

Laughing to keep from crying. Holt 1952 206p o.p. 1970

Analyzed in Short Story Index
"Realistic short stories and sketches concerning the Negro, and other minority groups in their relationships among themselves and with the dominant whites." Chicago
Contents: Who's passing for who; Something in common; African morning; Pushcart man; Why, you reckon; Saratoga rain; Spanish blood; Heaven to hell; Sailor ashore; Slice him down; Tain't so; One Friday morning; Professor; Name in the papers; Powder-white faces; Rouge high; On the way home; Mysterious Madame Shanghai; Never room with a couple; Little old spy; Tragedy at the Baths; Trouble with the angels; On the road; Big meeting

Not without laughter. Knopf 1930 324p $4.95

"About Sandy, son of Anjeeline, an honest, hardworking cook, and of Jim-boy, a gay mulatto wanderer, the lad growing up under the wing of Hagar, his grandmother, in a small Kansas town. The charm of this first novel by the young Negro poet lies in its simplicity and in its tender, tolerant understanding." Cleveland

Simple speaks his mind. Simon & Schuster 1950 231p o.p. 1970

"A series of conversations and anecdotes by and about a Harlem Negro named Simple who delivers some pithy comments on race relations, jobs, life down South and his troubles with his girl. The articles originated in the pages of a Negro newspaper 'The Chicago Defender.'" Pub W

Hughes, Langston—*Continued*

"Simple is completely frank in his opinions about white people: he dislikes them intensely. The race problem is never absent, but the flow of the book is light-hearted and easy." N Y Times Bk R

Simple stakes a claim. Rinehart 1957 191p o.p. 1970

"A companion volume to 'Simple Speaks His Mind' and 'Simple Takes a Wife' comprised of philosophic or humorous (or both) stories and sketches of Harlem Negroes and their reactions to segregation, the atomic bomb, etc." Retail Bookseller

"As in the earlier conversations of Jess Semple, the last of which was 'Simple takes a wife' there are touches of humor; the tone here, however, is generally more serious except in the sketches about a parasitic cousin Minnie." Booklist

Simple takes a wife. Simon & Schuster 1953 240p o.p. 1970

"Continuing the episodic dialogues begun in 'Simple Speaks His Mind' the Harlem character now embarks on a matrimonial career despite difficulties." Am News of Bks

Simple's Uncle Sam

Some editions are:
Hill & Wang $3.95
Watts, F. $7.95 Large type edition complete and unabridged. A Keith Jennison book
Partially analyzed in Short Story Index
First published 1965
The protagonist of these stories "Jesse B. Semple (Simple) is the author's Harlem-dwelling commentator on the problems, hopes, frustrations and diversions of the contemporary Negro." Cincinnati
Contents: Census; Swinging high; Contest; Empty houses; The blues; God's other side; Color problems; The moon; Domesticated; Bomb shelters; Gospel singers; Nothing but a dog; Roots and trees; For President; Atomic dream; Lost wife; Self-protection; Haircuts and Paris; Adventure; Minnie's hype; Yachts; Ladyhood; Coffee break; Lynn Clarisse; Interview; Simply Simple; Golden Gate; Junkies; Dog days; Pose-outs; Soul food; Flay or pray; Not colored; Cracker prayer; Rude awakening; Miss Boss; Dr Sidesaddle; Wigs for freedom; Concernment; Statues and statues; American dilemma; Promulgations; How old is old; Weight in gold; Sympathy; Uncle Sam

Hughes, Richard

The fox in the attic. Harper 1961 352p boards $6.50

First published in England 1961
This "is the first of a group of novels, 'The Human Predicament,' which is conceived as a long historical novel of my own times culminating in the Second World War." The author
The story centers around Augustine, a young man who left his village to visit some relatives, the Kessens, in Germany at the time Hitler was coming to power. Through all the events of that period and their effects upon the Kessen family, Augustine maintained his chosen role of noncommitment
"Hughes' sketches of the young Hitler are brought off brilliantly. So are the scenes and characterizations that represent the festering Germany of that time. . . . There is a sinister air about this novel that may remind you of that in a superior spy thriller. Yet it is a far more profound and serious fictional investigation of recent history than, say, a Graham Greene entertainment. It is a polished and exciting piece of work once it moves beyond its talky opening stages, and a remarkable 'comeback.' " San Francisco Chronicle

y A high wind in Jamaica

Some editions are:
Harper $5.95
Watts, F. $7.95 Large type edition complete and unabridged. A Keith Jennison book
First published 1929 with title: The innocent voyage
"After the hurricane that razes the Thornton home in the West Indies, the children are sent to England. Word reaches the parents that the children have been captured by pirates and drowned. Actually they continue the voyage on the 'pirate' ship, a voyage that has the

quality of a nightmare wherein the most fantastic events are mixed with the natural and real. These events involve both children and crew, yet the minds of the two groups never meet in understanding, either of each other, or of the terrible things that happen." Book Rev Digest

Hugo, Victor

y The hunchback of Notre Dame

Some editions are:
Collins $1.95
Dodd (Great illustrated classics) $4.50 With illustrations of contemporary scenes and a foreword by Curtis Dahl
First published in France 1830
The hidden force of fate is symbolized by the super-human grandeur and multitudinous imageries of the cathedral. "The first part . . . is a panorama of medieval life—religious, civic, popular, and criminal—drawn with immense learning and an amazing command of spectacular effect. These elements are then set in motion in a fantastic and grandiose drama, of which the personages are romantic sublimations of human virtues and passions—Quasimodo the hunchback, faithful unto death; Esmeralda, incarnation of innocence and steadfastness; Claude Frollo, Faust-like type of the antagonism between religion and appetite. Splendors and absurdities, the sublime and the grotesque are inextricably mingled in this strange romance. The date is fixed at the year 1482." Baker's Best

y Les misérables

Some editions are:
Collins $3.50
Dodd $5.50 Illustrated in color by Mead Schaeffer
Modern Lib. (Modern Lib. giants) $4.95
First published 1862
"A panorama of French life in the first half of the [ninteenth] century, aiming to exhibit the fabric of civilization in all its details, and to reveal the cruelty of its pressure on the poor, the outcast, and the criminal. Jean Valjean, a man intrinsically noble, thru the tyranny of society becomes a criminal. His conscience is reawakened by the ministrations of the saintly Bishop Myriel . . . and Valjean, reformed and prosperous, follows in the good bishop's footsteps as an apostle of benevolence, only to be doomed again by the law to slavery and shame. The 'demi-mondaine' Fantine, another victim of society; her daughter Cosette one of those whom suffering makes sublime; Marius, an ideal of youth and love; Myriel, incarnation of Christian charity, are the leading characters of this huge morality, which is thronged with representatives of the good in man and the cruelty of society. Magnificent descriptions . . . scenes invested with terror, awe, repulsion, alternate with tedious rhapsodies. Realism mingles with the incredible." Baker's Best

"One of the most powerful and absorbing romances in literature dealing with the unfortunate and criminal classes of Paris. The central figure, Jean Valjean, is a conception of great impressiveness and nobility of character." Pratt Alcove

Ninety-three. Little 524p illus o.p. 1970

First published in France 1873
"A grandiose, rhetorical romance of the Revolution . . . the incidents centering in a Breton district, where the Royalists attempt an insurrection." Baker's Best

Toilers of the sea. Dutton 368p (Everyman's lib) $2.95

First published 1866; in this edition 1911, translated by W. Moy Thomas
"A prose-poem of the sea, representing the eternal conflict of the elemental powers of nature against the will of man. Guernsey and the neighbouring seas are the theatre of the struggle, and the life of the mariner, the flora and fauna of the ocean and its isles, the infinite aspects of the sea in storm and calm, are depicted with a characteristic mixture of minute realism and rhapsodical eloquence. The interest is focussed on Gilliatt's superhuman combat with the waves, out of which he issues triumphant, only to be worsted in the hour of victory by a woman's caprice." Baker's Best

Huie, William Bradford

The Klansman. Delacorte Press 1967 303p boards $5.95

A novel set in Alabama in 1965. Sheriff Big Track Bascomb, winner of the Congressional Medal of Honor in Korea, is caught between the rabid Ku Klux Klan and his desire to send his son to West Point. An innocent Negro girl has been jailed 'for investigation,' and has been turned over to a deranged Negro for rape. The crime leads to the destruction of everything Big Track holds dear." Bk Buyer's Guide

"Without question it is a brutal story, brutally told, but along with this, it has the authentic ring of a documentary. . . . Strong, powerful stuff, not for the faint of heart." Pub W

Hulme, Kathryn

y   The nun's story

Some editions are:
Little $5.95
Watts, F. $9.95 Large type edition. A Keith Jennison book
First published 1956

"The story, truly based, it is claimed, of the life of a Belgian girl who became a nun, learned tropical nursing and practiced in a hospital much like Dr Schweitzer's deep in the Belgian Congo. In Europe after the Nazi invasion her hospital became a sanctuary for the Underground and it was then that she realized the lack of humility which made it impossible for her to continue in the Order." Am News of Bks

"Some enlightening vignettes of the disciplines of nursing and missionary orders. Occasional clinical reporting of violent scenes which take place in a mental hospital and a mission station in the jungle may limit the appeal of this semidocumentary." Booklist

Humphrey, William

Home from the hill. Knopf 1957 312p $3.95

"A memorable family—Wade and Harriet Hunnicutt, mismated and unhappy Texas aristocrats, and their only child, Theron, naive and unusual—disintegrates in a melodramatic and holding story. Hunting, small-town life and customs, love interest—all contribute to a well written tale of the 1930's." Wis Lib Bul

"The structure of the novel is rather involved, but the style is very readable and the characters are beautifully portrayed. There are many hunting scenes which will probably appeal especially to men." Pub W

The Ordways. Knopf 1965 [c1964] 362p $5.95

A "novel about rural East Texas, years ago. There are two connected stories, the first a . . . tale of a crippled man's desperation and his wife's heroism in a migration from Tennessee to Texas near the end of the Civil War. . . . Years later, the infant grandson of the first man is kidnapped and the boy's father sets out on a long, eventful search for his son." Pub W

An atmospheric novel "that catches the Southern and Western mystiques. . . . With humor, insight, and poetic style Humphrey introduces characters of great originality and shows their clannishness, a family feeling in which the dead have as much importance as the living." Booklist

A time and a place; stories. Knopf 1968 208p $4.95

Analyzed in Short Story Index
These ten stories about life in Texas and Oklahoma recall "the realities, the dreams, the feelings of the now almost legendary 1930's in the American heartland." Publisher's note

Contents: The ballad of Jesse Neighbours; A good Indian; A job of the plains; Mouth of brass; A home away from home; The rainmaker; The pump; A voice from the woods; The human fly; The last of the Caddoes

"Mr. Humphrey's collection should not be read all of a piece, as a novel is, but savored at intervals, as one suspects the author meant it to be." Book of the Month Club News

Hunt, John

The Grey Horse legacy. Knopf 1968 427p $6.95

"The novel is set in Grey Horse, Oklahoma, during the 1920's and 1950's, and in Paris, France, during the 1960's. The story begins in Oklahoma where, for some time, someone has been systematically killing off an oil-rich Chetopa Indian family [the Red Hawks]. Andrews Thayer comes from the Indian Bureau to gather evidence and is killed in a compromising position with the wife of his chief suspect. The effect of these events, which are related in flashbacks, on Emily, Andrews's wife, and Amory, his son, are chronicled." Library J

This "is in both style and conception, a fine work. Mr. Hunt has given us not only an absorbing and unpredictable thriller but a sensitive and thoughtful portrait of the past as it shapes the future." N Y Times Bk R

Hunter, Evan

The blackboard jungle; a novel. Simon & Schuster 1954 309p o.p. 1970

An "interesting but uneven first novel, timely in its story of an idealistic young man, facing the bitter realities of being a teacher in the frighteningly brutal world of a big city vocational high school. A near-rape, student sluggings, a knifing—all these plus a strong indictment of the inadequacies of routine teachers college preparation in helping teachers to learn how to discipline near-morons and prospective or actual delinquents." Library J

"The author has not used his shocking material merely to appall. With a superb ear for conversation, with competence as a storyteller, and with a tolerant and tough-minded sympathy for his subject, he has built an extremely good novel." N Y Her Trib Books

Last summer. Doubleday 1968 256p $4.95

"During a summer holiday on an Atlantic island. . . . Peter, the narrator, his friend David, and Sandy . . . sail, explore the island [and] tell the 'truth' to each other. . . . Peter discovers the shape of evil and finds cruelty and violence in himself. There are two symbols which pervade the action: the capturing and taming of an injured seagull Sandy finds; and the trio's domination of Rhoda, a shy girl. Both incidents erupt in violence." Library J

The author "effectively portrays the moral degeneracy of our times, the irresponsibility of parents, and the callousness thus induced among those engaged in the serious business of growing up in a world without recognizable ethics or ideals." Va Q R

Sons. Doubleday 1969 396p $6.95

The author "follows three generations of the Tyler family, showing in a series of parallel situations what happened when grandfather, son and grandson, each went off to his own war. Bert, the grandfather, a lumberjack who later becomes a millionaire in the paper business, goes to the Great War . . . and comes home with a loathing for the trenches that he cannot transmit to his son. Will, the son, who later becomes a successful book publisher, goes to World War II as eager as his father but returns with an enthusiasm for all that happened that borders on perversion. Wat, the grandson—high school football player, amateur pop musician, peace and civil rights activist—is drafted and sent to Vietnam, where he dies in mud much like that his grandfather hated in France." Book of the Month Club News

"Hunter's three-pronged novel does contrast, with commendable perceptiveness, the changing attitudes of young Americans toward war, prejudice, sex, personal commitment, and social hypocrisy." Choice

For another title by this author see Mc-Bain, Ed.

Huré, Anne

The two nuns; tr. from the French by Emma Craufurd. Sheed 1964 220p boards $4

Original French edition, 1962
A "dissection of life in a French Benedictine convent where hate and unyielding severity burden the atmosphere. The abbess, a nun of fixed, narrow views close to Jansenism, is opposed by a scholarly nun who had once been her friend. To a large extent it is up to the nuns to settle their discord, as the ruling Catholic powers look on in distress." Pub W

"Though infused with delicate emotional warmth, this tale of convent life makes decidedly intellectual demands on its readers but will reward the efforts of Catholic and non-Catholic alike." Booklist

Hutchinson, R. C.

A child possessed; a novel. Harper 1964 350p o.p. 1970

"Against all advice Stephan Lopuchine, Russian aristocrat turned Marseilles truck driver, takes to live with him his appallingly retarded, deformed daughter whom his world-famed estranged actress-wife had allowed him for many years to believe dead. The father's devotion to and need of the child is used narratively to bring into focus the marriage of two forceful individualists separated through almost total lack of mutual insight. New understanding opens up as crisis overtakes the child." Booklist

"The child is a heartrending character and so is the father." Pub W

The inheritor. Harper 1961 431p o.p. 1970

Published in England with title: Image of my father

"Vincent Levesque returns to his home in Belgium after spending the war in a German army labor batallion. His hold on sanity is seriously shaken by his near-bestial experience and the discovery of his wife's infidelity. He learns that he is the son and sole heir of a wealthy Englishman. The novel details his hunt for his true identity. In the course of the search he opens a new conflict between his moral commitment to his wife and his desire for a new life with a woman he loves." Library J

"Mr. Hutchinson's quiet style may seem a bit old-fashioned now, but there will be many readers who will welcome such a solid, readable novel and be interested in the values that he presents through his well-developed characters." Pub W

Johanna at daybreak. Harper 1969 313p boards $6.95

"A study of a woman living under the burden of guilt for past actions which she cannot and does not want to remember. Set in Holland and Germany in the years following the Second World War and based on a real case history originally found in a Dutch journal, it traces the progression of the narrator from a stage of amnesia . . . to a final acceptance of her past and the responsibilities it brings. . . . The basic predicament is that of a Prussian woman [Johanna] who has married into a Jewish family; her sense of estrangement from the Jews in the early days of Hitler is made worse by the failure of her marriage." New Statesman

The stepmother; a novel. Rinehart 1955 310p o.p. 1970

"Catherine de Lauzun, from Quebec, at age 46, marries a nicely rendered Deputy Under Secretary in the British civil service, a gentle, repressed and earnest widower aged 57. He has, this Lawrence Ashland, a pair of grown children and a reverent memory of Josie, his dead wife. The problem of the second wife is, of course, to fit into the established family and to make everybody, including herself, happy." N Y Times Bk R

Hutchinson, Ray Coryton. See Hutchinson, R. C.

Huxley, Aldous

After many a summer dies the swan. Harper 1939 356p o.p. 1970

"Satiric novel about an American multimillionaire with a terror of death. He lives surrounded by priceless works of art incongruously placed, and waited on by a flock of servants, scholars, and others dependent upon his money. His personal physician is working on a theory of longevity, which ties up with some priceless old documents just purchased. In pursuit of evidence of his theory the doctor goes to England, where in a subterranean den under an English country house, the book closes on a note of horror." Book Rev Digest

"Mr. Huxley's elegant mockery, his cruel aptness of phrase, the revelations and the ingenious surprises he springs on the reader are those of a master craftsman. Mr. Huxley is at the top of his form in this respect. In the cynicism of his view of personal relationships he excels himself; the brutality of his human disgust here is unrelieved." Times (London) Lit Sup

Antic hay. Harper 1948 248p o.p. 1970

First published 1923 by Doran

The title of the book is explained by a couplet of Marlowe found on the title page. 'My men like satyrs grazing on the lawn, Shall with their goat feet dance the antic hay.' With the opening chapter the dance begins when Theodore Gumbril, Jr., Oxford tutor, wearied of his daily round, decided to taste life and become the 'Complete Man.' Across the pages of the book, Gumbril and his fellow satyrs dance from one adventure into another and since there is no lack of women companions, the effect of the whole is that of some bacchanalian revel at which the author is an amused onlooker." Book Rev Digest

Antic hay, and The Gioconda smile; with an introduction by Charles J. Rolo. Harper 1957 280p (Harper's Modern classics) $2

The title story was first published 1923, and is entered separately. This edition is combined with one of the short stories from Mortal coils, a collection first published 1922

y Brave new world; a novel; with a foreword for this edition. Harper 1946 xx, 311p $4.95

First published 1932

"A satirical novel describing a scientific and industrialized utopia in which Ford and his standardized Model T are worshiped." Book Rev Digest

"Dignity, beyond all else, has attended the creation of the classic Utopias, from that of Plato on down to Edward Bellamy's perfectly geared industrial machine. . . . It has remained for Aldous Huxley to build the Utopia to end Utopias. He has satirized the imminent spiritual trustification of mankind, and has made rowdy and impertinent sport of the World State whose motto shall be Community, Identity, Stability." N Y Times Bk R

Collected short stories. Harper 1957 397p o.p. 1970

Analyzed in Short Story Index

"The 21 tales in this collection, represent the greater part of 'Limbo, Mortal coils, Little Mexican, Two or three Graces, and Brief candles': novellas and plays account for most of the omissions. Also included is an excerpt from 'Crome yellow' here entitled 'Sir Hercules.'" Booklist

Contents: Happily ever after; Eupompus gave splendour to art by numbers; Cynthia; The bookshop; The death of Lully; Sir Hercules; The Gioconda smile; The Tillotson banquet; Green tunnels; Nuns at luncheon; Little Mexican; Hubert and Minnie; Fard; The portrait; Young Archimedes; Half holiday; The monocle; Fairy godmother; Chawdron; The rest cure; The Claxtons

Crome yellow. Harper 1922 307p o.p. 1970

"Crome is an English country house to which Denis, an intensely self-conscious youth and would-be poet, goes to join a house party. Priscilla Wimbush, his hostess, dallies with the occult. Her husband has a passion for ancestral history and for the Italian primitives. The other members of the heterogeneous group of people there gathered are the host's niece Anne, with a doll-like beauty and a gift of irony; Mary, a girl of twenty-three who babbles about psycho-analysis and is worried about repressions; Gombauld the artist; Scogan who talks endlessly about the universe; and the engaging Ivor. There is no action—only talk, the most modern kind of talk. The formless fabric of the story is somehow held together by poor lovable Denis, who is hopelessly and inarticulately in love with Anne." Book Rev Digest

Eyeless in Gaza. Harper 1936 473p o.p. 1970

"Thru a series of flash backs in time and place, interspersed with chapters on the present, the writer tells the story of the English boy Anthony Beavis from the death of his mother in 1902, to his early forties in 1934. It is the study of an intellectual youth growing to manhood in a period of war and economic turmoil. He is beset by doubts and vacillations in his attempt to find an acceptable way of living until he meets an indomitable Scotch doctor in Mexico. Thereafter he fashions his life according to the doctor's pattern and finds a new freedom." Book Rev Digest

Huxley, Aldous—*Continued*

"In this book Aldous Huxley emerges a moralist, a believer in the efficacy of the spiritual life, in the necessity that one demand of oneself the achievement of the impossible. Peace for the individual, peace for the world itself, only through the individual exercise of love and compassion. That, in essence, is what Aldous Huxley has to say in this novel." N Y Times Bk R

The Gioconda smile

In Huxley, A. Antic hay, and The Gioconda smile

Island; a novel. Harper 1962 335p $7.95

"The Paradisical island of Pala, where modern science and intelligent attitudes toward education and sex are carrying its people closer to their goal of freedom and enlightenment, is discovered to be rich in oil. Immediately the forces of greed plan to exploit it, making journalist Will Farnaby their agent to the island's dictator, its covetous Rani, and her son. Will is won to the right side by beautiful Susila but Pala is doomed." Bk Buyer's Guide

"Considered as a commentary upon today's [1962] world, this book deserves a wide circulation. It is a mirror in which modern man can see all that is rotten in his society and in himself." Sat R

Point counter point. Harper 432p $5.95

A reprint of the title first published 1928 by Doubleday

The book "presents a satiric picture of London intellectuals and members of English upper-class society during the 1920's. Frequent allusions to literature, painting, music, and contemporary British politics occur throughout the book, and much scientific information is embodied in its background. The story is long and involved, with many characters; it concerns a series of broken marriages and love affairs, and a political assassination. The construction is elaborate, supposedly based on Bach's 'Suite No. 2 in B Minor.' It is also a novel within a novel. Philip Quarles a leading character . . . is himself planning a novel, which echoes or 'counterpoints' the events going on around him." Benét. The Reader's Encyclopedia

Time must have a stop. Harper 1944 311p o.p. 1970

"The story of Sebastian Barnack, a precocious 17-year-old poet who looked 'like a Della Robbia angel aged 13,' and of his Uncle Eustace, an urbane, tolerant, clever, selfish and self-indulgent hedonist of 53. . . . Mr. Huxley alternates his attention between Uncle Eustace's dimly aware consciousness in the hereafter and Sebastian's education on earth." N Y Times Bk R

"Like most of the author's works this is a book for larger libraries. . . . Fundamentally, its purpose is religious." Wis Lib Bul

Hyman, Mac

No time for sergeants. Random House 1954 214p $3.95

"After sundry belligerent maneuverings by Pa, Georgia cracker Will Stockdale is drafted, jailed, sent to camp. There with buddy Ben he finds himself in the Air Force, nearly becoming permanent latrine orderly. Assigned to a daffy air crew, he and Ben narrowly miss a plane crash, claim a medal for Ben, thus bumbling ill-fated Sergeant King out of his stripes and, with them, into an infantry transfer." Library J

"All this is preposterous but pretty funny. And Mr. Hyman does it well enough so that even the most implausible episodes have a kind of inner plausibility about them—which is the test of this kind of thing." San Francisco Chronicle

I

Ibáñez, Vincente Blasco. See Blasco Ibáñez, Vincente

Ibuse, Masuji

Black rain; a novel; tr. by John Bester. Kodansha 1969 300p $6.95

This translation of the Japanese original first appeared in installment form in the Japan Quarterly

This novel "centered around the story of a young woman who was caught in the radioactive 'black rain' that fell after the bombing [of Hiroshima] is based largely on actual accounts written or related by survivors of the holocaust." Publisher's note

"The author avoids the emotional political overtones which could so easily dominate; instead he portrays a group of people living through a period of utmost difficulty. Because he is ultimately concerned with life rather than death, he has been successful where other novelists have failed." Library J

Idell, Albert E.

Centennial summer. Holt 1943 426p o.p. 1970

"The author re-creates the atmosphere of the Philadelphia Centennial of 1876 and against this background tells the story of as miscellaneous a family group as could be gathered under one roof. Jesse Rogers, of sturdy Quaker stock, had married hot-tempered Augustina Borelli, daughter of an impecunious Italian count. Their children are as varied in temperament as might be expected from such a marriage. Add to these Zena, the Parisian sister-in-law, with her two 'dash-hunds,' and Philippe, her handsome nephew come to attend the centennial, and there is plenty of material for comedy." Wis Lib Bul

If

The If Reader of science fiction; ed. by Frederick Pohl. Doubleday 1966 252p o.p. 1970

Analyzed in Short Story Index

Contents: When time was new, by R. F. Young; Father of the stars, by F. Pohl; The life hater, by F. Saberhagen; Old Testament, by J. Bixby; The silkie, by A. E. Van Vogt; A better mousetrap, by J. Brunner; Long day in court, by J. Brand; Trick or treaty, by K. Laumer; The 64-square madhouse, by F. Leiber

Ikor, Roger

The sons of Avrom. Tr. by Leonard M. Friedman and Maxwill Singer. Putnam 1958 383p o.p. 1970

"A translation of the 1955 winner of the Prix Goncourt. Concerning four generations of Russian Jewish immigrants in France, it is a richly detailed family epic. . . . Its major theme is the assimilation into national life of differing alien strains." Library J

"A master of characterization rather than caricature. Mr. Ikor makes Yankel's multifarious family into a rich cavalcade of humanity, authentic and unstereotyped. Unlike the usual epic of assimilation, which concerns itself with the dissolution of folkways under the impact of modernity, 'The Sons of Avrom' is less concerned with parochialism than with the human spirit." N Y Times Bk R

Ilf

The golden calf

In Ilf. Ilf & Petrov's The complete adventures of Ostap Bender v 1

Ilf & Petrov's The complete adventures of Ostap Bender; consisting of the two novels: The twelve chairs and The golden calf. Tr. from the Russian by John H. C. Richardson. Random House [1963 c1962] 2v in 1 o.p. 1970

First combined American printing "of the two comic novels in which the roguish adventurer Ostap makes his precarious way in the Russia of the early days of the Soviet Union." Booklist

Ilf—*Continued*

In the first story "he cavorts around the Soviet Union searching for a hoard of jewels concealed in a set of dining-room chairs . . . and [in the second story] later attempts to unmask an unscrupulous Soviet speculator who has amassed a considerable fortune." Library J

The twelve chairs
In Ilf. Ilf & Petrov's The complete adventures of Ostap Bender v2

Innes, Hammond

Atlantic fury. Knopf 1962 308p $4.95

"'Atlantic Fury' is the story of the evacuation of a British guided weapons unit from Laerg, an island in the Outer Hebrides. . . . It is a tale of men battling the elemental forces of nature as a polar storm rages unchecked, taking its terrifying toll of men and equipment. Underlying the ordeal is the suspenseful mystery of the identity of Major Braddock, hero or murderer, a man 'missing' since his harrowing experience on the same island 22 years before, during World War II." Library J

"It has some beautiful, evocative writing about the fierce Atlantic weather and the terrible danger of rescuing shipwrecked men in gales and bitter cold. . . . It is slow in getting under way and then it ends in a weak anticlimax, but the center part of the book, with the cold menace of the Atlantic storm, is Innes at his taut, exciting best." Pub W

Campbell's kingdom. Knopf 1952 308p o.p. 1970

"This well-written novel of suspense is laid in the Canadian Rockies on oil land belonging to 'Old Campbell' who is labelled a swindler when no oil appears. His grandson attempts to redeem his grandfather's reputation. Opposition, a strike, and floods increase the excitement." Cincinnati

"The Canadian part of the book, which is, indeed, the bulk of it, is unceasingly thrilling. With a girl, a ghost-town, a bursting dam, dynamiting in the mountains and swinging up and down in precarious cable-cars, here's riches indeed, and as good an adventure story to take on holiday as any man could wish." Spec

The doomed oasis. Knopf 1960 341p $4.95

At head of title: A novel of Arabia
This is the story of a quiet solicitor who goes to the Middle East on business and finds himself plunged into the violence and intrigue of a great struggle for oil. The struggle takes him deep into the little-known heart of the Arabian desert, to the middle of a desert war, and to Saraifa, the oasis doomed to obliteration by the shifting sands, that plays a pivotal part in the conflict. (Publisher)

The novel "moves briskly along. Its many characters—Arab chiefs, British oil men and others—are all neatly and believably portrayed. What will happen next is always a matter of lively interest." San Francisco Chronicle

y The land God gave to Cain; a novel of Labrador. Knopf 1958 307p $4.95

"A mysterious radio message received by a ham operator in London, from a man reported killed in an airplane crash in the wilderness of Labrador, sets off a search by the grandson of a prospector who had been murdered at the same spot. The search involves incredible hardship in portaging through the wilderness, complicated by human elements. The denouement is as sudden and unexpected as it is convincing. A thrilling yarn for adults and young people." Library J

The Strode venturer. Knopf 1965 338p $4.95

"Peter Strode, the youngest brother in a family that controls a failing London shipping company, discovers an unknown volcanic isle rich in manganese and proposes to restore the glory of the firm by helping the people of the isle to independence. But opposition from his two greedy brothers causes the venture to end in near-disaster." Bk Buyer's Guide

"Mr. Innes can make exact business details clear and interesting while telling a goood yarn, and he does wonders with a crashing tropical storm, disaster at sea and the eruption of a new volcanic island." Book of the Month Club News

y The wreck of the Mary Deare. Knopf 1956 296p map $4.95

"John Sands saw the 'Mary Deare' briefly that night from the deck of his sailing vessel, the 'Sea Witch'. He saw her again the following morning, abandoned and drifting close to the great reef areas of the Channel Islands. And in boarding her and attempting to satisfy his curiosity, he became involved in the mystery of the 'Mary Deare.'" Publisher's note

"Compounded of mystery, action, and suspense and filled with the drama of man's struggle against storm and tide, this is a first-rate adventure story of the sea." Booklist

Innes, Michael

Appleby intervenes; three tales from Scotland Yard. Dodd 1965 442p boards $4.95

Contains in one volume: One-man show; A comedy of terrors; The secret vanguard; first published 1940, 1952 and 1958 respectively

These tales feature Inspector John Appleby of Scotland Yard "who is as adept in running to earth a classical quotation as a criminal." Publisher's note

The bloody wood. Dodd 1966 217p $3.50

"Red badge detective"
"Sir John Appleby of Scotland Yard and his wife, Lady Judith, become involved in murder at the country estate of Charne where they are guests." Bk Buyer's Guide

The opening scene is "allusive with an added undercurrent of the sinister. The sudden deaths by fire and water are as melodramatic as they are grimly inevitable." Am News of Bks

A change of heir. Dodd 1966 216p boards $3.50

"Red badge mystery"
George Gadberry, an unsuccessful actor agrees "to Nicholas Comberford's proposition that he should go to Bruton Abbey in Yorkshire and put on an impersonation act . . . [as] heir to a great fortune. He could have worked out the complications if the real heir had not come back and threatened him." Library J

A comedy of terrors
In Innes, M. Appleby intervenes p157-304

Death at the chase. Dodd 1970 175p $4.50

"Red badge novel of suspense"
"Retired Chief Commissioner Sir John Appleby thought old Martyn Ashmore was suffering from the delusions of senility when he charged that someone tried to murder him on the anniversary of a Nazi massacre brought about by Ashmore's breaking under torture. Then Sir John was almost killed himself and realized the danger was real." Bk Buyer's Guide

Death by water. Dodd 1968 214p boards $3.95

"Red badge mystery"
This mystery begins when "Sir John Appleby, retired Chief Commissioner of Metropolitan Police, was visiting Allington Park, a partially restored estate dating back to Charles First. While exploring a specially built gazebo with the owner, Sir John noticed a bundle of stuff in a corner of the room. Stopping to examine it, he said grimly, 'It is a man and I think he is dead.'" Am News of Bks

"An old castle, a gay village charity fete, a unique assembly of human oddments among the characters—these and a legendary lost treasure add up to what, in Sir John's words, 'that chap in Baker Street called a two-pipe mystery.'" Publisher's note

One-man show
In Innes, M. Appleby intervenes p 1-156

Picture of guilt. Dodd 1969 219p boards $3.95

"Red badge mystery"
"A series of strange art thefts has occurred over the years, all linked by two bits of curiosa: the 'theft' in each case seems to have started out as a practical joke, and the individuals robbed have been reluctant to publicize their losses too much because of some special aura of embarrassment surrounding the missing object. The climax comes during an Oxford 'rag' on the Isis." Pub W

Innes, Michael—*Continued*

The secret vanguard

In Innes, M. Appleby intervenes p305-442

For another title by this author see Stewart, J. I. M.

Inoue, Yasushi

The counterfeiter, and other stories; tr. with an introduction by Leon Picon. Tuttle 1965 124p (Lib. of Japanese literature) $3.50

Analyzed in Short Story Index
"UNESCO Collection of representative works: Japanese series"
Contents: The counterfeiter; Obasute; The full moon

Iron, Ralph. See Schreiner, Olive

Irving, John

Setting free the bears. Random House [1969 c1968] 335p boards $5.95

Siggy, who works in a motorcycle shop, and Graff, a student who has just failed his exams, are two aimless young men who meet one spring day in Vienna. That afternoon their odyssey begins. Living off the land and traveling aimlessly, playing pranks, meeting and abandoning an assortment of odd characters, they lead a seemingly picaresque existence; but this existence has deeper meanings. (Publisher)
"Not just another book about the alienated young, because the author has considerably more wit than one usually finds in that genre of novels. Still, that is where its strongest reader appeal will probably lie." Pub W

Irving, Washington

Tales; selected and ed. with an introduction by Carl Van Doren. Oxford 1918 452p front o.p. 1970

Analyzed in Short Story Index
Contents: Rip Van Winkle; Spectre bridegroom; Legend of Sleepy Hollow; Stout gentleman; Haunted house; Dolph Heyliger; Stormship; Inn at Terracina; Adventure of the little antiquary; Belated travellers; Adventure of the Popkins family; Painter's adventure; Story of the bandit chieftain; Story of the young robber; Adventure of the Englishman; Hellgate; Kidd the pirate; Devil and Tom Walker; Wolfert Webber; Adventure of the black fisherman; Legend of the Arabian astrologer; Legend of Prince Ahmed Al Kamel; Legend of the Moor's legacy; Legend of the three beautiful princesses; Governor Manco and the soldier; Legend of the two discreet statues; Legend of the enchanted soldier; Widow's ordeal; Guests from Gibbet-Island

Irwin, Margaret

The bride; the story of Louise and Montrose. Chatto & Windus [distributed by Dufour] 1957 431p $3.95

First published 1939
"This novel continues and perhaps completes the author's series of historical romances centering around the family of Charles I and the English civil war. It ties up most closely with 'The proud servant' for it is a story of Montrose, hero of that novel, and of his love for Louise, sister of Prince Rupert. . . . Louise is a fine, spirited heroine for a novel of any time or period and those who have not read the previous books will be tempted to go back to them on finishing this one." Wis Lib Bul

Elizabeth and the Prince of Spain. Chatto & Windus [distributed by Dufour] 1962 255p $3.95

First published 1953
Sequel to: Elizabeth, captive princess
"Deals with the brief rule of Mary Tudor, her marriage to Philip of Spain, his stormy relationship with Elizabeth as protector and would-be lover, and Elizabeth's coronation. Although the story moves more slowly than the earlier books, it gives a reasonably accurate picture of this turbulent period when struggle for political power in Europe was intense." Booklist

Elizabeth, captive princess. Harcourt 1948 246p illus $3.95

Sequel to: Young Bess
"Beginning in 1553 with the death of young Edward VI, this novel presents two tempestuous years in the life of Princess Elizabeth and ends with Mary Tudor's long-sought marriage to Philip of Spain." Cleveland
Followed by: Elizabeth and the Prince of Spain

The Gay Galliard; the love story of Mary, Queen of Scots. Chatto & Windus [distributed by Dufour] 1956 423p $3.95

First published 1941
A novel dealing with the story of Mary Stuart, Queen of Scots. "The facts and incidents in this book are drawn from contemporary records, and so are much of the conversations. Practically everything John Knox says is in his own words, as he himself recorded them." Foreword
"It has exquisite vignettes, little pictures that glow like stained glass, and longer passages of rapid action or of description." Manchester Guardian

Royal flush; the story of Minette. Chatto & Windus [distributed by Dufour] 1966 [c1932] 370p $4.50

First published 1932 by Harcourt
"The fortunes of the family of Charles I, after the king's execution by Cromwell, are the subject of this historical novel. The central figure is Minette, youngest sister of Charles II, who, by her marriage, united the courts of England and France. In spite of occasional stretches of dull reading, the book is unusually successful; it is historically truthful and vivid, and it tells a fascinating story." Booklist

y Young Bess. Harcourt 1945 274p $3.95

"Historical novel based on the childhood and young womanhood of Elizabeth Tudor, later Queen of England. The time covered is from Elizabeth's twelfth year, to the death of her brother Edward VI, in 1553." Book Rev Digest
Followed by: Elizabeth, captive princess

Isherwood, Christopher

The Berlin stories: The last of Mr Norris; Goodbye to Berlin. With a new preface by the author. New Directions 1954 2v in 1 o.p. 1970

The first volume is a "story of a strange friendship that grows up between two Englishmen, one, the narrator, a young university graduate, the other a middle aged, insignificant, moral derelict who has been living for years on his wits in various European and American capitals. The scene of the story is Berlin in the early 1930's." Book Rev Digest
The second volume includes "six short stories or sketches of life in Berlin in the last years before Hitler came to power. Tho written in first person by one calling himself Christopher Isherwood, according to the author's statement, the material is not to be regarded as autobiographical." Book Rev Digest
Contents for volume two: A Berlin diary (Autumn 1930); Sally Bowles; On Ruegan Island (Summer 1931); The Nowaks; The Landauers; A Berlin diary (Winter 1932-3)

Down there on a visit. Simon & Schuster 1962 [c1961] 318p o.p. 1970

This "novel relates, in the first person of Isherwood himself, four distinct long stories: one when the narrator is a very young man in Germany; one five years later on a Greek island with an . . . assortment of characters; one in London during the Munich crisis; and one in California during World War II. Each describes the author's relationship to another person: an aging man who commits suicide, a homosexual Englishman, a young German in England, and a handsome American who has led a debauched life in Europe. The stories

Isherwood, Christopher—*Continued*

are joined not only by the part which the narrator plays in each, but by their common preoccupation with the worst of each individual. Essentially, this is the account of a world in which all decent values save occasional personal loyalties, are shattered." Chicago Sunday Tribune

"Mr. Isherwood is concerned with the souls of his people, and their sexual abnormality is treated only as a manifestation of a universal human loneliness and despair." Atlantic

Goodbye to Berlin

In Isherwood, C. The Berlin stories v2

The last of Mr Norris

In Isherwood, C. The Berlin stories v 1

Israel, Charles E.

Rizpah; a novel. Simon & Schuster 1961 534p o.p. 1970

Although Rizpah is mentioned only in passing in the Biblical narrative of the second Book of Samuel, the author "has built his story about the kind of person she might have been and the kind of life she might have led. She was a Hebrew girl, captured by the Philistines, who escaped [to return] to her people, became the concubine of Saul and eventually was caught in the conflict between the aging monarch and the coming king, David." Pub W

"Although long the novel sustains interest with its geographical and period detail, clearcut character portrayal, and unorthodox interpretation of the personalities of Saul, David, and Samuel." Booklist

J

Jackson, Charles

The lost weekend. Farrar 1940 244p o.p. 1970

"Psychological study of a drunkard. The actual time covered is five days, but in those five days the story of a man's life is told. Don Birnam, a sensitive, charming, and wellread man, left alone for a few days by his brother, struggles with his overwhelming desire for alcohol, succumbs to it, and in the resulting prolonged agony, goes over much of his life up to and including the long weekend." Book Rev Digest

"It's written with complete lack of literary pretensions; yet Jackson's sheer ability to lick the problems of flashback, stream of consciousness, mind wandering, twisted recollection and alcoholic delirium is spectacular. . . . Its frankness is sometimes shocking but never aimed to shock. The aim, and it is unerring, is always for accuracy and the complete truth." Book Week

Jackson, D. V. S.

Walk with peril. Putnam 1959 287p o.p. 1970

"A carefully plotted, richly detailed and skillfully written historical novel about the days of Henry V takes as its hero young Robert Fairfield. Swearing fealty to Henry, Fairfield accompanies the army to France in order to serve his king and fulfill his ambitions of knighthood, even though he has not only gained the enmity of Henry's brother York but also belongs to the Lolards, a group condemned as heretics to persecution and death. There is a subordinate romance, but the main interest stems from Fairfield's perilous position, the intrigue and treachery surrounding Henry, and the climactic battle of Agincourt with which the book ends." Booklist

Jackson, Shirley

The bird's nest. Farrar, Straus 1954 276p o.p. 1970

"Miss Jackson sets forth the predicament of Elizabeth Richmond, a pallid young woman who lives with her aunt in a small New England town. A series of disquieting incidents leads this girl to a psychiatrist, who discovers that her mind is divided among, and tortured by, four separate, strong-willed personalities, each struggling for dominance. These four personalities, which are visible by turns, according to which one is in control, are designated by the doctor as Elizabeth, Betsy, Bess and Beth. Some terrifying experiences and her doctor's patient guidance bring the girl to a state resembling peace." New Yorker

Come along with me: part of a novel, sixteen stories, and three lectures; ed. by Stanley Edgar Hyman. Viking 1968 243p boards $5.95

Partially analyzed in Short Story Index

This "posthumous book contains a section of the novel on which she was working at the time of her death in 1965, plus 14 short stories, three lectures on authorship and two stories . . . illustrating points in the lectures." Library J

Short stories inclded are: Janice; Tootie in peonage; A cauliflower in her hair; I know who I love; The beautiful stranger; The summer people; Island; A visit; The rock; A day in the jungle; Pajama party; Louisa, please come home; The little house; The bus; The night we all had grippe; The lottery

"Mr. Hyman wisely demonstrates the range of Shirley Jackson's imagination in his choice of stories. There are domestic comedies on the one hand and pure fantasies on the other. There are clinical penetrations into madness and senility, and allegories of fairly portentous philosophical weight. Yet everything this author wrote, no matter how innocent the surface, had in it the dignity and plausibility of myth." N Y Times Bk R

y The haunting of Hill House. Viking 1959 246p $5

Also available in large type edition $7.95

"Dr. Montague, a scientific investigator of ghostly phenomena, chose to live for several weeks at Hill House, by repute a place of horror that brooked no human habitation. Ghosts, or the fear thereof, became so much in evidence that for a time the very ultimate in terror was produced." McClurg. Book News

"We have what we ought always to have in ghost stories but so rarely get: a brooding, claustrophobic atmosphere which thickens overpoweringly as we go along. . . . A novel which has distinctiveness and genuine power." Times (London) Lit Sup

The lottery; or, The adventures of James Harris. Farrar, Straus 1949 306p o.p. 1970

Analyzed in Short Story Index

"The twenty-five stories in this volume represent a selection of Shirley Jackson's work. Through some of them wanders James Harris, the daemon lover, in many guises, his veneer of the ordinary covering his elusive, satanic nature." Publisher's note

Contents: The intoxicated; Daemon lover; Like mother used to make; Trial by combat; The villager; My life with R. H. Macy; The witch; The renegade; After you, my dear Alphonse Charles; Afternoon in linen; Flower garden; Dorothy and my grandmother and the sailors; Colloquy; Elizabeth; Fine old firm; The dummy; Seven types of ambiguity; Come dance with me in Ireland; Of course; Pillar of salt; Men with their big shoes; The tooth; Got a letter from Jimmy; The lottery

"Few of the sketches in The Lottery are pleasant stories, but Miss Jackson uses the trick ending device adroitly. She can twist a seemingly normal situation into something that leaves you squirming. . . . Miss Jackson's prose is deft and readable." Library J

The sundial. Farrar, Straus 1958 245p o.p. 1970

"The Halloran clan waits in their well-equipped mansion for the world to end. Influenced by their Aunt Fanny's visions, they are convinced that they will be the only survivors of this catastrophic event." Pub W

"Miss Jackson's technique is flawless throughout and her allegory a disturbing one. Let us say this is another interesting tour de force." San Francisco Chronicle

Jackson, Shirley—*Continued*

y We have always lived in the castle. Viking 1962 214p $3.95

Also available in large type edition $6.95
"Though acquitted by a jury of the arsenic poisoning of four members of her family six years earlier, Constance Blackwood has never been judged anything but guilty by her townspeople and because of their taunts and cruelty she no longer leaves home at all. But this story, told in the first person, is primarily that of her younger sister, Mary Katherine, now 18: an imaginative, poetic, whimsical and ruthless girl—so ruthless, so strong that she is able to turn aside all inroads . . . made against their house" Library J

"The effect of the book does not only depend on mystery or suspense; nor on the casual intimations of evil that Miss Jackson can put in a phrase. . . . The effect depends rather on her ability to specify a real world which is at once more sane and more mad than the world we see. . . . The havoc [Cousin Charles] wreaks, and the unsuspected dénouement of the action, bring into soft focus the human ambivalences of guilt and atonement, love and hate, health and psychosis. . . . Shirley Jackson has once again effected a marvelous elucidation of life in the ageless form of a story full of craft and full of mystery." N Y Times Bk R

Jacobs, Harvey

The egg of the Glak, and other stories. Harper 1969 276p $5.95

Contents: Epilogue; Reasons of health; The girl who drew the Gods; In seclusion; A musical education; The voyage of the peanut; The lion's share; A disturbance of the peace; A break in the weather; The toy; The egg of the Glak

"Although he has good ideas presented with some wryness and irony, the stories suffer mainly from predictability. . . . His work is the kind that enlivens the magazine read on the bus or subway to and from work." Library J

Jacobson, Dan

The beginners. Macmillan (N Y) 1966 469p o.p. 1970

"The grandchildren of Avrom Glickman, a Lithuanian Jew who emigrated to South Africa, are the central characters in this inclusive saga. Joel, Rachel and David pursue different ideals and careers as the setting moves from South Africa to Europe and Israel. Jacobson makes subtle use of several issues of contemporary life: alienation, racism and nationalism." Cincinnati

"Intricate family relationships and recurring characters pull together the series of sketches. . . . Subtleties of character and the Jewish psyche in relation to its environment are given more importance than local color." Library J

Through the wilderness, and other stories. Macmillan (N Y) 1968 214p $5.95

Analyzed in Short Story Index
A collection of stories "centered around the Jewish community in the small town of Lyndhurst in South Africa. . . . His subject is the human condition, black or white, and the sometimes startling confrontation between the two different communities." Pub W

Contents: Through the wilderness; Beggar my neighbor; The example of Lipi Lippmann; An apprenticeship; A way of life; Another day; Poker; Sonia; Trial and error; Only the best; The pretenders; Fresh fields; Led astray

James, Henry

The ambassadors

Some editions are:
Harper $4.95
Heritage $7.50 With illustrations by Leslie Saalburg and a preface by the author
Scribner (The Novels and tales of Henry James. New York editions v21-22) 2v ea $6
First published 1903
Chadwick Newsome, expected to return home and take over his family's New England mills, remains in Paris. His mother, a widow, requests her fiance, Lambert Strether (the chief

ambassador) to go to Europe to rescue her son. Strether finds Paris, its people and culture, as delightful as does Chad. He persuades Chad to remain, even though, by remaining, Chad loses the opportunity to become a rich man. Strether, having failed in his mission, knows he will never marry Mrs Newsome, but decides to return since the journey was financed by her. The struggle between the old-fashioned New England conscience and the cultured maturity of Paris, is told with subtle irony in the novel James considered his best

The American. Scribner (The Novels and tales of Henry James. New York editions v2) 539p $6

First published 1877
"A self-made American goes to Europe to enjoy his 'pile,' and becomes engaged to a French widow of noble family. The match is a good one for both parties, but at length the powers that rule this exclusive social world deliver their verdict: the engagement must be annulled. The American's pluck and good nature are happily contrasted with the colossal pride and essential meanness of the old noblesse." Baker's Best

The American novels and stories of Henry James; ed. and with an introduction by F. O. Matthiessen. Knopf 1947 xxvi, 993p $7.95

Partially analyzed in Short Story Index
Contains the following novels: The Europeans; Washington Square; The Bostonians; The ivory tower. Also the following short stories: The story of a year; The point of view; A New England winter; Pandora; "Europe"; Julia Bride; The jolly corner; Crapy Cornelia; A round of visits

The editor "has collected nearly all the novels and stories with an American setting. . . . For a writer who, as the legend goes, was enamored of old-world privilege and by no means aglow with belligerent fervor in dealing with the national ideals, the work collected in this volume is astonishing in that it shows us to what an extent James was able to express creatively the meaning and quality of American life." N Y Times Bk R

The Aspern papers
In James, H. The Henry James reader p165-254
In James, H. Short novels of Henry James p257-354
In Neider, C. ed. Short novels of the masters p301-85

The Aspern papers, The turn of the screw, The liar, The two faces. Scribner 1936 (The Novels and tales of Henry James. New York editions v12) xxiii, 412p $6

Analyzed in Short Story Index
A collection of stories first published 1888, 1898, 1888 and 1900 respectively
The turn of the screw is entered separately. The Aspern papers is the story of a writer anxious to secure certain material on the poet Aspern. In The liar "James sketches the disintegration of an army officer's character, caught only too clearly by a portrait painter who once loved the officer's wife. 'The Two Faces' . . . tells of the cruelty practiced by Lord Gwyther on his new wife. He takes her to call on his old love Mrs. Grantham, who sees to it that her clothes are a copy of her own." Publisher's note

The awkward age. Scribner 1936 xxiii, 544p (The Novels and tales of Henry James. New York editions v9) $6

A reissue of the title first published 1899
"The story of a girl's emergence out of 'the awkward age' into modernity and understanding. Nanda and her mother are in love with the same man; the mother wants her to marry Mitchett, but the Duchess, her friend, wants Mitchett to marry her niece, Aggie. Hence a social battle, complicated by the appearance of the wealthy Mr. Longdon, who sees in Nanda a close resemblance to her grandmother, with whom he had once been in love. However, Nanda is at last freed from any subservience to social conventions she does not like." Herzberg. The Reader's Encyclopedia of Am Lit

James, Henry—*Continued*

The beast in the jungle
In James, H. The complete tales of Henry James v11 p351-402
In James, H. The Henry James reader p357-400
In James, H. The portable Henry James p270-326

The bench of desolation
In James, H. The portable Henry James p326-87

The Bostonians; a novel. Macmillan (N Y) 1886 449p o.p. 1970
"The story concerns itself primarily with the struggle of Verena Tarrant to decide between Basil Ransom a young Southern lawyer who loves her . . . and the tortured demands of her domineering patroness, a determined Boston feminist who dislikes 'men as a class.' " Huntting

also in James, H. The American novels and stories of Henry James p424-746

A bundle of letters
In James, H. Lady Barbarina, The siege of London, An international episode, and other tales p477-533

The complete tales of Henry James; ed. with an introduction by Leon Edel. Lippincott 1962-[1965 c1964] 12v ea $6.95
Analyzed in Short Story Index
Contents: v 1: 1864-1868: A tragedy of errors; The story of a year; A landscape painter; A day of days; My friend Bingham; Poor Richard; The story of a masterpiece; The romance of certain old clothes; A most extraordinary case; A problem; De Grey: A romance
v2: 1868-1872: Osborne's revenge; A light man; Gabrielle de Bergerac; Travelling companions; A passionate pilgrim; At Isella; Master Eustace; Guest's confession
v3: 1873-1875: The Madonna of the future; The sweetheart of M. Briseux; The last of the Valerii; Madame de Mauves; Adina; Professor Fargo; Eugene Pickering; Benvolio
v4: 1876-1882: Crawford's consistency; The ghostly rental; Four meetings; Rose-Agathe; Daisy Miller: a study; Longstaff's marriage; An international episode; The Pension Beaurepas; The diary of a man of fifty; A bundle of letters; The point of view
v5: 1883-1884: The siege of London; The impressions of a cousin; Lady Barbarina; The author of "Beltraffio"; Pandora
v6: 1884-1888: Georgina's reasons; A New England winter; The path of duty; Mrs Temperly; Louisa Pallant; The Aspern papers; The liar
v7: 1888-1891: The modern warning; A London life; The lesson of the master; The Patagonia; The solution; The pupil
v8: 1891-1892: Brooksmith; The marriages; The chaperon; Sir Edmund Orme; Nona Vincent; The private life; The real thing; Lord Beaupré; The visits; Sir Dominick Ferrand; Collaboration; Greville Fane; The wheel of time
v9: 1892-1898: Owen Wingrave; The middle years; The death of the lion; The Coxon Fund; The next time; The altar of the dead; The figure in the carpet; Glasses; The way it came (The friends of the friends); John Delavoy
v10: 1898-1899: The turn of the screw (novelette); In the cage; Covering end; The given case; The great condition; "Europe"; Paste; The real right thing
v11: 1900-1903: The great good place; Maud-Evelyn; Miss Gunton of Poughkeepsie; The tree of knowledge; The abasement of the Northmores; The third person; The special type; The tone of time; Broken wings; The two faces (novelette); Mrs Medwin; The Beldonald Holbein; The story in it; Flickerbridge; The beast in the jungle (novelette); The birthplace
v12: 1903-1910: The Papers; Fordham Castle; Julia Bride; The jolly corner; The Velvet Glove; Mora Montravers; Crapy Cornelia; The bench of desolation; A round of visits

Daisy Miller; [and An international episode]; illus. from drawings by Harry W. McVickar. Harper 2v in 1 illus o.p. 1970
"Daisy Miller" was first published 1878; "An international episode," 1879
"Daisy Miller" is one of the earliest examples of the type of story known as the 'International novel.' A delicate and subtle study of 'a strange, beautiful, dainty, innocent and very foolish little American girl with her ignorant defiance of all rules.' " Pratt Alcove
"International episode" turns on the problem of whether an English nobleman will marry an American girl

also in James, H. The great short novels of Henry James p85-144
also in James, H. The Henry James reader p403-61
also in James, H. Short novels of Henry James p 1-58
also in James, H. Washington Square, and Daisy Miller p193-258

The Europeans
In James, H. The American novels and stories of Henry James p37-161

The ghostly tales of Henry James; ed. with an introduction by Leon Edel. Rutgers Univ. Press 1949 xxxiv, 765p o.p. 1970
New edition, with title: Henry James: Stories of the supernatural, published by Taplinger, in preparation
Analyzed in Short Story Index
Contents: The romance of certain old clothes; De Grey: a romance; The last of the Valerii; The ghostly rental; Sir Edmund Orme; Nona Vincent; The private life; Sir Dominick Ferrand; Owen Wingrave; The altar of the dead; The friends of the friends; The turn of the screw; The real right thing; The great good place; Maud-Evelyn; The third person; The beast in the jungle; The jolly corner
"Mr. Edel's introductory essay takes up, very ably indeed, the psychoanalytical implications of the stories, as well as the James family traits responsible for the author's particular brand of the shudders. A long-term reading project for connoisseurs of the otherworldly." New Yorker

The golden bowl. Scribner [1965 c1937] 2v (The Novels and tales of Henry James. New York editions v23-24) ea $6
First published 1904
"American millionaire's daughter marries an indigent Italian prince. All is well until first one and then another 'eternal triangle' materializes." Dickinson
"It is not the scriptural golden bowl about which the story moves, but an antique of crystal and gilt which has a fatal flaw, and to which a symbolic meaning is attached." Pittsburgh

The great short novels of Henry James; ed with an introduction & comments by Philip Rahv. Dial Press 1944 799p o.p. 1970
Analyzed in Short Story Index
Contents: Madame de Mauves; Daisy Miller; An international episode; The siege of London; Lady Barberina; The author of Beltraffio; The Aspern papers; The pupil; The turn of the screw; The beast in the jungle

The Henry James reader; selected with a foreword and headnotes by Leon Edel. Scribner 1965 626p boards $7.50
Analyzed in Short Story Index
Contains the short novels: Washington Square (1881); The Aspern papers (1888); The turn of the screw (1898); The beast of the jungle (1903); Daisy Miller (1878); also the following short stories: The author of Beltraffio; Pandora; Owen Wingrave; The real thing; The two faces

James, Henry—*Continued*

In the cage
> *In* James, H. The complete tales of Henry James v10 p139-242
> *In* James, H. What Maisie knew, In the cage, The pupil p365-507

An international episode
> *In* James, H. Daisy Miller v2
> *In* James, H. The great short novels of Henry James p145-222
> *In* James, H. Lady Barbarina, The siege of London, An international episode, and other tales p273-389

The ivory tower
> *In* James, H. The American novels and stories of Henry James p867-993

Lady Barbarina, The siege of London, An international episode, and other tales. Scribner 1936 xxi, 606p (The Novels and tales of Henry James. New York editions v14) $6

Analyzed in Short Story Index
A reissue of the collection first copyrighted 1908 and renewed 1936
Contents: Lady Barbarina; The siege of London; An international episode; The Pension Beaurepas; A bundle of letters; The point of view

The liar
> *In* James, H. The Aspern papers, The turn of the screw, The liar, The two faces p311-88

A London life. Grove 1957 158p o.p. 1970
First published 1889
"A magnificent tale of the English aristocracy and its corrupting power over the people caught in its web." McClurg. Book News

The other house; with an introduction by Leon Edel. New Directions xxi, 228p o.p. 1970
First published in England 1896; in this edition 1924
"One of the novels of James's middle period. The story, which centers around the murder of a little girl, has something in common with 'The Turn of the Screw' and 'What Maisie Knew.' The book is a novelized version of an unproduced play, and there is an introduction by Leon Edel, the chief authority on James's dramatic work, who believes that in drawing the figure of the murderess, James was influenced by the heroines of Ibsen." New Yorker

The Pension Beaurepas
> *In* James, H. Lady Barbarina, The siege of London, An international episode, and other tales p391-476

The point of view
> *In* James, H. Lady Barbarina, The siege of London, An international episode, and other tales p535-[607]

The portable Henry James. Edited, and with an introduction [by] Morton Dauwen Zabel. Rev. in 1968 by Lyall H. P. Powers. Viking 1968 696p (The Viking Portable lib) $5.50
First published 1951
Included are three complete novelettes (The pupil, The beast in the jungle, and The bench of desolation) as well as a number of short stories. There is also a selection of essays, critical writings, letters, and passages from James' autobiographical writings

The portrait of a lady
Some editions are:
Heritage $7.50 Illustrations by Colleen Browning. Introduction by R. W. Stallman
Modern Lib. $2.95 Introduction by Fred B. Millett

Oxford (The World's classics) $3.50 With an introduction by Graham Greene
Scribner (The Novels and tales of Henry James. New York editions v3-4) 2v ea $6
First published 1881
"The motives that led Isabel Archer, a romantic New England girl who inherits an English fortune, to refuse other suitors and marry Gilbert Osmond are skillfully analyzed, and her subsequent disillusionment is traced in devastating detail. . . . After Isabel's marriage she discovers that she has only served the purposes of her quasi-friend, Madame Merle, who, as Osmond's mistress and the mother of Pansy, brought the two together for the sake of Isabel's fortune. Osmond's fine sensibilities are likewise seen to be but the expression of an intensely egocentric, unpleasant nature. The novel has been generally considered one of James's finest works." Benét. The Reader's Encyclopedia

The Princess Casamassima. Scribner [1962 c1936] 2v (The Novels and tales of Henry James. New York edition v5-6) ea $6
First published 1890
"The Princess Casamassima is the former Christina Light, who appears in 'Roderick Hudson' [entered separately]; now, unhappily married, she decides to make a first-hand study of poverty and radicalism in London. The hero of the book is Hyacinth Robinson, the illegitimate son of an English nobleman and a Frenchwoman; though brought up in the London slums and a member of a radical underground movement, he makes his way into upper-class society, meets the princess, and is selected by the revolutionaries to commit an assassination." Benét. The Reader's Encyclopedia

The pupil
> *In* James, H. The portable Henry James p214-70
> *In* James, H. Short novels of Henry James p355-405
> *In* James, H. What Maisie knew, In the cage, The pupil p509-[77]

Roderick Hudson
Some editions are:
Dufour $5 With an introduction by Leon Edel
Scribner (The Novels and tales of Henry James. New York editions v 1) $6
First published serially 1875 in the Atlantic Monthly; in book form 1907
"Undertakes to trace the degeneration of a man of genius, a young American sculptor, when given the freedom of the artistic life in Rome." J. W. Beach

The sense of the past. Scribner [1965 c1945] 358p (The Novels and tales of Henry James. New York editions v26) $6
First published 1917
This novel, incomplete at the author's death, includes his notes for the final chapters
"The central character is a young American who, from the English branch of the family, inherits an old London house. He goes to England, seeks out his new possession, and shuts himself away from the world for a night while he wanders from room to room, yielding to the spell of the past that is cast about him. He sees himself in an old portrait of 1820. A compelling sense of the past slips him out of the year 1910 back into 1820. Comfortably at first, and then uneasily he reacts to the people and conditions of the world into which he is projected." Book Rev Digest

Short novels of Henry James. . . . With eight full-page illustrations. Introduction by E. Hudson Long. Dodd 1961 530p illus (Great illustrated classics: Titan editions) $5.50
Contents: Daisy Miller (1878); Washington Square (1881); The Aspern papers (1888); The pupil (1892); The turn of the screw (1898)

The short stories of Henry James; selected and ed. with an introduction by Clifton Fadiman. Modern Lib. xx, 644p (Modern Lib. giant) $4.95
First published 1945 by Random House and analyzed in Short Story Index

James, Henry—*Continued*

Contents: Four meetings; A bundle of letters; Louisa Pallant; The liar; The real thing; The pupil; Brooksmith; The middle years; The altar of the dead; "Europe"; The great good place; The tree of knowledge; The tone of time; Mrs Medwin; The birthplace; The beast in the jungle; The jolly corner

"These 17 short stories are arranged chronologically, showing James's progress from simplicity to complexity, and to subtlety of thought and style. The editor provides notes on the stories, and a short critical essay." Booklist

The siege of London
In James, H. Lady Barbarina, The siege of London, An international episode, and other tales p143-271

The spoils of Poynton; with a preface by the author. Dufour 1962 224p $1.95

"Owen Gareth, heir to the great house at Poynton, spurns his mother's favorite, Fleda Vetch, to marry Mona Brigstock. Old Mrs. Gareth thereupon removes her art treasures from Poynton. Owen was in fact in love with Fleda, and offers her any object she may desire at Poynton, but suddenly the house is ruined by an accidental fire, which ruins the spoils that have warped so many lives." Haydn. Thesaurus of Book Digests

The tragic muse. Scribner [1963 c1936] 2v (xxi, 373, 440p) (The Novels and tales of Henry James. New York editions v7-8) ea $6
First published in book form 1908
Cover title: New York edition of Henry James

"The 'Tragic Muse' of the title is the startlingly objective Miss Miriam Rooth, a young girl with more ambition than talent who becomes a star of the London stage. But far more important . . . than Miriam's success, is the story of the disappointments to which Nick Dormer and his cousin Peter Sherringham are condemned. Nick, a would-be portrait painter, and Peter, a diplomat, are the victims of a duel between talent and integrity, a duel which forms the real theme of the novel." Publisher's note

y The turn of the screw. Large type ed. complete and unabridged. Watts, F. [1967] 182p $6.95
"A Keith Jennison book"
First published 1898

A haunting terror story "is told in diary form by an inexperienced young governess in love with her employer on a lonely British estate. She gradually realizes that her precocious young charges, Miles and Flora, are under the evil influence of two ghosts, Peter Quint, the ex-steward, and Miss Jessel, their former governess. As the horror mounts the narrator can turn to nobody but the housekeeper for moral support in her attempt at a sort of spiritual battle for the children's souls. At the climax of the story she enters into open conflict with the children alienating Flora and causing Miles to die of fright." Herzberg. The Reader's Encyclopedia of Am Lit

also in Costain, T. B. comp. Twelve short novels p329-412
also in James, H. The Aspern papers, The turn of the screw, The liar, The two faces p145-309
also in James, H. The complete tales of Henry James v10 p15-138
also in James, H. The great short novels of Henry James p621-748
also in James, H. The Henry James reader p255-356
also in James, H. Short novels of Henry James p407-530

The two faces
In James, H. The Aspern papers, The turn of the screw, The liar, The two faces p388-[413]
In James, H. The complete tales of Henry James v10

Washington Square; illus by George du Maurier. Harper 1881 266p illus o.p. 1970

A short novel which portrays the relations between a simple, honest girl and her romantic aunt, her worldly wise father and a suitor who is interested in her income. The story takes place in New York City during the early part of the 19th century

also in Blackmur, R. P. ed. American short novels p134-235
also in James, H. The American novels and stories of Henry James p162-295
also in James, H. The Henry James reader p 1-163
also in James, H. Short novels of Henry James p59-256
also in Phillips, W. ed. Great American short novels p79-236

Washington Square, and Daisy Miller. With an introduction by Oscar Cargill. Harper 1956 xxv, 259p (Harper's Modern classics) o.p. 1970
A combined edition of two titles entered separately

What Maisie knew, In the cage, The pupil. Scribner 1936 xxi, 576p (The Novels and tales of Henry James. New York editions v11) $6

A collection of three titles first published 1897, 1898, and 1891 respectively

In the cage is "the pathetic tale of a girl who lives for the glimpse of the great world she catches while doling out stamps and counting the words in telegrams in an office in a Mayfair grocery. Her tragedy comes when she senses that her marriage to Mr. Mudge (of her very own world) can no longer be postponed. 'The Pupil' . . . sketches the harrowing existence of Pemberton, tutor to young Morgan Moreen, whose parents have forsaken the United States for shabby gentile exile in France and Italy, Pemberton cannot escape the charm of Morgan Moreen, who bravely faces the fact that his father and mother are not above lying and cheating his tutor of his wages." Publisher's note

In: What Maisie knew, Maisie "is the child of divorced parents who have married other people, and she is the innocent and uncomprehending witness of an intrigue between the step-parents." Baker's Best

The wings of the dove
Some editions are:
Dufour $1.75 Introduction by Sir Herbert Read
Modern Lib. $2.95
Scribner (The Novels and tales of Henry James. New York editions v19-20) 2v ea $6
First published 1902

"Three minds become each in turn the stage on which we are shown what is going on: Kate Croy's, Densher's, and Milly Theale's. Kate and Densher are pledged to each other, and Kate persuades her lover to pay attentions to Milly, so that the pair may subsequently enjoy the fortune which would almost certainly be left to Densher when the dying girl is gone. Milly, 'the Dove,' is one of his most delicate creations—shadowed by Fate, marked down for extinction before her splendid chances of joy can be realized, pathetically sure that the will to live might be recreated if she loved and were loved in return." Baker's Best

James, Will

y The American cowboy; illus. by the author. Scribner 1942 273p illus $5.95

"This narrative has three heroes and each one is the father of the next. . . . Three Bills. The story begins in the Southwest when most

James, Will—*Continued*

of the men were away fighting with Sam Houston. After an Apache raid, the first Bill found himself on his own . . . and though he didn't know it, became the first cowboy. And his grandson, Bill, is still a boy when the saga ends." Huntting

y Sand. Scribner 1929 328p o.p. 1970

"The story of a young man's regeneration parallels that of the capture and 'gentling' of a black stallion of the plains. An outgrowth of the author's familiarity with western life, it is written graphically in the cowboy vernacular." Booklist

y Will James' Book of cowboy stories. Scribner 1951 242p illus o.p. 1970

Analyzed in Short Story Index
"A selection of the cowboy-author's best stories and sketches, with his illustrations arranged to give a picture of year-round life on the ranch." Retail Bookseller
Contents: Best riding and roping; Cattle rustlers; Chapo—the faker; For a horse; For the sake of freedom; Lone cowboy; Making of a cowhorse; Narrow escape; On the dodge; On the drift; Once a cowboy; Silver mounted; Smoky, the range colt; When in Rome—; Winter months in a cow camp

Jameson, Storm

The blind heart. Harper 1964 217p o.p. 1970

This philosophical story tells how the impulse of a kind man brings bad luck to himself. "The hero is a southern France restaurant proprietor who is at last about to pay, in cash, for ownership of his restaurant. While he is away on a helpful errand for a former prisoner of war, his foster son steals the money." Pub W
"In her protagonist the author celebrates a warm acceptance of life and a willingness to create new pathways of existence in the face of disaster and disillusionment." Booklist

The early life of Stephen Hind. Harper 1966 283p o.p. 1970

The "story of Stephen Hind, a young Englishman in the first stages of a carefully calculated climb to success. Acting as typist to Sir Henry Chatteney, the fate of whose constantly revised memoirs is the focus of suspense, Stephen manipulates persons and events until he receives a sharp check, but not one that deflects him from his course." Booklist
"A clever story, the surface elegance of which covers a surprising range of human passion, ambition, love and hate. . . . Is this a 'roman à clef?' The memoirs which the old statesman is writing and the glimpses of the London publishing world make one wonder." Pub W

The white crow. Harper 1968 313p $5.95

"John Antigua, misshapen bastard son of a poor Portuguese peasant woman who died in childbirth, is a man whose grotesque frame contains a body of great strength and energy, a highly intelligent mind, a prodigious memory, and a gentle, sensitive spirit. It is his story from 1890 to World War II London that we follow and with him the story of those he befriends and on whom he bestows all the force of his strange charisma." Pub W
"The story is not always clear but always intense, and its permeating tone is corrosive anger with the modern world, mitigated by the picture of John's saintly 'mad love' for mankind. Unsettling, uneven, not entirely controlled, this is nevertheless the work of an unusual mind and of a craftsman." Book of the Month Club News

Janney, Russell

The miracle of the bells. Prentice-Hall 1946 497p o.p. 1970

"When as a dying request she had asked her friend Bill Dunnegan to take her back to Coaltown, Pennsylvania, for burial, Olga Treskovna, Hollywood actress, had asked also that he have the church bells rung for the funeral. But Bill, who is a high-powered press agent, doesn't stop with one bell. There are five churches in Coaltown. He has all of their bells rung, and not one day only but for four days, continuously. What happened to Coaltown as

a result and how the influence spread outward, is the substance of a story which is deeply religious, flippant, and serious, and sentimental all at once. Readers will either like it very much or not at all." Wis Lib Bul

Jarrell, Randall

Pictures from an institution. Farrar, Straus 277p $5.95

A reprint of a title first published 1954 by Knopf
"A satirical account of life for faculty and students in a proudly 'progressive' American college for women, and the events that take place after a celebrated novelist takes her place on the campus as a teacher of creative writing." Pub W
"Mr Jarrell's quiet comedy of ideas and people is a welcome gift. While it laughs at much of our intellectual pride and pomposity, it also develops a breadth of warm sympathy for the angelic touch that may visit the most foolish of us." Sat R

Jeffries, Graham Montague. See Bourne, Peter

Jenkins, Elizabeth

Honey. Coward-McCann 1968 287p $4.95

"From childhood on, Honey Harper couldn't see why she shouldn't have whatever she wanted, and she was beautiful enough to get what she wanted—men and money. She was married for a while, took a succession of lovers, and then married Rolly Ismay. When Rolly's sixteen-year-old son Brian came to live with them, Honey decided she wanted him, too, but Brian was merely embarrassed and resentful." Bk Buyer's Guide
"It is very diverting to take up a novel as charming, as quietly perceptive, and as free from violence as [this]. . . . Miss Jenkins writes with poise and style; she knows human nature." Atlantic

Jennings, John

The raider; a novel of World War I; the chronicle of a gallant ship. Morrow 1963 272p $4.95

This story, based on the exploits of the German light cruiser Emden, "covers the span of time from the outbreak of war in the summer of 1914 until the British Navy tracked the [ship] down and outfought the 'Emden' in a stirring single combat. The tale is told from the point of view of the German officers." Library J
"Although cast in fictional form . . . the real story of the dashing career of the German raider, the punctilious observance of the rules of war, the courtesy and code of honor of the officers is factual enough." Best Sellers

River to the West; a novel of the Astor adventure. Doubleday 1948 368p o.p. 1970

"An historical adventure tale of John Jacob Astor's establishing a trading post in the Pacific Northwest during the months following the Louisiana Purchase. Told through the hazardous adventures of Rory O'Rourke, a clerk in the company and Astor's eyes on the expedition, the venture takes Rory around the Horn under a brutal captain, to the eventual settling of a post and the long trek overland brings him back to his true love. Essentially for masculine tastes." Cincinnati

The Salem frigate; a novel. Doubleday 1946 500p front o.p. 1970

"The frigate Essex, gift of Salem to the United States in 1799, is the scene of much of this novel. Two men, Dr Tisdall, ship's surgeon, and Ben Price, carpenter, sail on each trip of the Essex, fight against the Barbary pirates, are captured and return to Salem several times until the day when Ben Price is killed in battle. Then the doctor returns to Salem, and to the woman he really loves—Ben's wife." Book Rev Digest
"Written in a style deliberately and successfully patterned after journals of those years, the book provides a graphic and realistic picture of naval life afloat and ashore, mixed with romance, human hatreds and a little politics." N Y Her Trib Books

Jennings, John—*Continued*

The sea eagles. . . . Doubleday 1950 299p o.p. 1970

"A story of the American Navy during the Revolution; of the men who fought and the ships they sailed and the women who stood behind them." Subtitle

"While awaiting passage home, Joshua Barney of Baltimore meets Kenny Boyle in Dublin; each helps the other out of a tight spot and they become fast friends. Together they enter the new American Navy, but the first engagement at sea sends them separate ways, and between them the two young men participate in practically every major naval event of the war. Between voyages and experiences in naval prisons, Joshua finds happiness with his lovely bride Ann, but Kenny's love for Barbary suffers many obstacles and delays." Booklist

The tall ships. McGraw 1958 299p o.p. 1970

"This historical sea tale of a Maryland midshipman torn between love and duty is also a rousing adventure story set in the year 1812, the year of 'the tall ships.' " Chicago

Jensen, Johannes V.

Nobel Prize in literature, 1944

Christopher Columbus

In Jensen, J. V. The long journey p491-677

The Cimbrians

In Jensen, J. V. The long journey p227-487

Fire and ice

In Jensen, J. V. The long journey p3-224

The long journey; tr. from the Danish by A. G. Chater; with an introduction by Frances Hackett. Nobel Prize ed. Knopf 1945 xxi, 677p $6.95

First published 1923-1924
Contents: Fire and ice; The Cimbrians; Christopher Columbus

Jerome, Jerome K.

Three men in a boat. Large type ed. complete and unabridged. Watts, F. [1968] 294p $7.95

"A Keith Jennison book"
First published 1889 in Great Britain
This is the lighthearted story of what happened when three friends embarked in a small boat for a holiday, and came up against the river, the weather and the contrariness of hu-nan beings. (Publisher)
This "is a slight tale with only a thin thread of plot. The humor lies in the digressions, which make up the bulk of the book, and in some of the incidents. . . . In this novel [the author] captures much of the charm of boating on the Thames. The characters are delightfully human." Magill. Masterpieces

Jessup, Alexander

The best American humorous short stories. Modern Lib. 1920 xxx, 276p o.p. 1970

Analyzed in Short Story Index
Contents: The little Frenchman and his water lots, by G. P. Morris; The angel of the odd, by E. A. Poe; The schoolmaster's progress, by C. M. S. Kirkland; The Watkinson evening, by E. Leslie; Titbottom's spectacles, by G. W. Curtis; My double, and how he undid me, by E. E. Hale; A visit to the asylum for aged and decayed punsters, by O. W. Holmes; The celebrated jumping frog of Calaveras County, by M. Twain; Elder Brown's backslide, by H. S. Edwards; The hotel experience of Mr Pink Fluker, by R. M. Johnston; The nice people, by H. C. Bunner; The Buller-Podington compact, by F. R. Stockton; Colonel Starbottle for the plaintiff, by B. Harte; The duplicity of Hargraves, by O. Henry; Bargain day at Tutt House, by G. R. Chester; A call, by G. M. Cooke; How the widow won the deacon, by W. J. Lampton; Gideon, by W. Hastings

Jessup, Richard

Sailor; a novel of the sea. Little 1969 471p boards $6.95

This novel "tells how Howard Cadiz left Savannah for the sea at fourteeen, saw the ports of the world, enjoyed the women of the world, and fought his way up, only to find out after twenty-five years that he could not give up the sea, even for Veronica, his bedmate of the day." Bk Buyer's Guide

"The bars, the brothels, the drunks, the degenerates, the fights, the profanity, the monotony, are all here. But there is far more. One feels the tug of the sea, the lure, and one learns that the sea strengthens the strong and mercilessly breaks the weak." Library J

Jewett, Sarah Orne

The best stories of Sarah Orne Jewett; selected and arranged with preface by Willa Cather. Smith, P. 2v in 1 $6.75

Analyzed in Short Story Index
This collection published 1925 in two volumes by Houghton
Volume 1 with running title: The country of the pointed firs was first published 1896; v2 contains stories published at various dates from 1886-1923
Contents: v 1: Return; Mrs Todd; Schoolhouse; At the schoolhouse window; Captain Littlepage; Waiting place; Outer island; Green island; William; Where penny-royal grew; Old singers; Strange sail; Poor Joanna; Hermitage; On Shell-heap island; Great expedition; Country road; Bowden reunion; Feast's end; Along shore; Dunnett shepherdess; Queen's twin; William's wedding; Backward view
v2 A white heron: The flight of Betsy Lane; The Dulham ladies; Going to Shrewsbury; The only rose; Miss Tempy's watchers; Martha's lady; The guests of Mrs Timms; The town poor; The Hilton's holiday; Aunt Cynthy Dallett

The country of the pointed firs. Large type ed. complete and unabridged. Watts, F. [1968] 247p $7.95

"A Keith Jennison book"
First published 1896 by Houghton
Studies of life and character in a Maine seacoast village

also in Jewett, S. O. The best stories of Sarah Orne Jewett v 1

The country of the pointed firs, and other stories; selected and introduced by Mary Ellen Chase; illus. by Shirley Burke. Norton 1968 296p illus $6.50

Analyzed in Short Story Index
The title story, first published 1896, concerns a small Maine coastal town and its people. Included are four related short stories: A Dunnett shepherdess; The foreigner; The queen's twin; William's wedding. Additional short stories are: A white heron; Miss Tempy's watchers; Martha's lady; Aunt Cynthy Dallett

Jhabvala, R. Prawer

The householder. Norton 1960 191p boards $4.50

"A story set in modern India, about a young householder, a teacher, confronting responsibilities and problems he did not know existed in the days of his carefree youth. How Prem and his young, pregnant wife deal with their material affairs, with the worldly wise Mr. Khanna and his wife, and with their own families provides humorous and poignant reading." Pub W

"A delightfully lively and mobile story. . . . Mrs Jhabvala has much talent. The detail of Prem's daily round, school and domestic, is beautifully done. There are some delicious little comic scenes between Prem and his headmaster, Mr Khanna, and his absurd wife, characters who almost suggest an Indian Dickens. This is a short slight novel but everybody in it is a character in his own right." New Statesman

FICTION CATALOG
EIGHTH EDITION

Jhabvala, R. P.—*Continued*

A stronger climate; 9 stories. Norton [1969 c1968] 214p boards $4.95

A collection of stories, most of which were previously published in periodicals, "about Europeans in India. The first section is called The Seekers, and is primarily about people who look to India for something that Europe has failed to give them. . . . The second section, The Sufferers, is about the Europeans who have stayed too long. Everything they once found beautiful and fascinating has turned sour." Publisher's note

Contents: In love with a beautiful girl; The biography; The young couple; Passion; A spiritual call; A young man of good family; An Indian citizen; Miss Sahib; The man with the dog

"The pleasures to be found in [the book] are dry, intellectualized, matters of insight and understanding; not of dramatic interest and vicarious participation." N Y Times Bk R

Jiménez, Juan Ramón

Nobel Prize in literature, 1956

Platero and I; tr. by Eloïse Roach; drawings by Jo Alys Downs. Univ. of Tex. Press 1957 218p illus $3.75

First published 1914 in Spain

"This translation includes all 138 chapters of the poetic musings of a Spaniard that have gained widespread popularity since their publication in Spanish over 40 years ago. In the person of a Spanish villager the writer sings the praises of his soft, small donkey, Platero, and builds a picture of life in an Andalusian village. Though charming in themselves the pieces seem slight when read individually and acquire more depth when taken together. Translation and illustrations in this edition well convey the mood of the pieces." Booklist

Johnson, Dorothy M.

The hanging tree. Ballantine 1957 272p o.p. 1970

Analyzed in Short Story Index

"A collection of nine short stories and novelette set in the old West of the 60's and 70's." Library J

Contents: Lost sister; Last boast; I woke up wicked; Man who knew the Buckskin Kid; Gift by the wagon; Time of greatness; Journal of adventure; Story of Charley; Blanket squaw; The hanging tree [novelette]

Johnson, E. Richard

The inside man. Harper 1969 179p $4.95

"A Joan Kahn-Harper Novel of suspense"

The author "returns to Tony Lonto, detective of the homicide squad of the River Street Station, and gives him the double-edged problem of finding the killer of the man who wore a robe and carried a sign saying 'The End Is Near' and at the same time being an 'internal stoolie' and uncovering the crooked cop who works with Al Pegasus, the boss of Silver Street." Library J

Johnson, Josephine W.

Now in November. Simon & Schuster [1970 c1962] 231p $5.95

SBN 671-20489-0

Pulitzer Prize, 1935

First published 1934

"A realistic story of farm life in the Middle West told in poetic prose. Marget, second of the three daughters of the Haldmarnes, tells the story 'in November' looking back over the ten years of the family's life on the farm, and particularly the last year, when drought, debt, and the knowledge of coming madness, all fed the growing fear of imminent disaster." Book Rev Digest

Johnson, Pamela Hansford

Cork Street, next to the hatter's; a novel in bad taste. Scribner 1965 274p boards $4.95

"Young academician Tom Hariot protests against the excesses and stupidities of current theater and the submissiveness of audiences by writing a despicable, degenerate,

unproducible play to prove there must be limits, only to find the play in production to his horror and consternation. Main plot and satirical subplots all emanate from or lead back to Cork Street and its bookstore." Booklist

"There is much humor in this novel; but there is also a serious, calculated attack on certain contemporary literary and moral standards. College instructors who teach courses in the present day theatre should make 'Cork Street' required reading, along with the texts of the plays." Best Sellers

An error of judgement. Harcourt 1962 251p o.p. 1970

Although William Setter, a London physician, is successful, he is a tormented man since he believes he is fated to harm his fellows, no matter how he struggles against an appalling warp in his nature. Harm does come, in one form or another, to those with whom Setter has dealings: Emily, his ambitious American wife; Jenny Hendry, a guilt-haunted woman; and, Sammy Underwood, a delinquent youth. (Publisher)

"A tricky psychological melodrama, brimming with bitter modern insights and wry commentary on the precarious morality of our day." Book of the Month Club News

Night and silence, who is here? An American comedy. Scribner 1963 246p o.p. 1970

A "humorous novel about some visiting scholars cast adrift in the glacial regions of a New Hampshire liberal arts college which is cold in both climate and welcome. The central character is an English dilettante scholar who likes a de luxe life and schemes to arrange it for himself." Pub W

"The satire is of the mildest sort—nothing like that to be found in Mary McCarthy's The Groves of Academe or Randall Jarrell's Pictures from an Institution—but it is a gay and entertaining book. Miss Johnson has a light touch, and her prose is a pleasure. Perhaps it is not in any very strict sense an American comedy, since it deals so seldom with what one can feel to be representative situations, but it is a comedy." Sat R

The survival of the fittest. Scribner 1968 468p $6.95

This novel describes "the activities of a small group of English writers from Munich through and beyond the time of the Kennedy assassination. The central story is that of Jo, the unsuccessful [woman] novelist, coupled with that of Kit, internationally acclaimed [inclining to alcoholism à la Dylan Thomas] and those of their tight literary group." Library J

"Reading the book is a curious experience; vague and casual from moment to moment, it is nevertheless compulsive and cumulatively gripping. Its mood is elegiac: characters, places, periods, history, are evoked, suggested, rather than solidly dramatic [although] there are moments of drama. . . . But events are subordinated to a sense of the long emotional shifts and structures of whole lives, and the group's corporate life." New Statesman

The unspeakable Skipton. Harcourt 1959 249p o.p. 1970

"A swift-moving, witty, wicked comedy of a self-exiled English novelist who kept up a front in his attic in Bruges while he worked on his jewel-like manuscripts and connived to make small profits out of the British tourists." Chicago

Johnson, Samuel

The history of Rasselas, Prince of Abyssinia. Ed. with introduction and notes by G. B. Hill. Oxford 1898 203p o.p. 1970

First published 1759

"A lay sermon on 'the Vanity of Human Wishes,' written when Johnson was in profound sorrow for the death of his mother; the most majestic example of his prose. Belongs to the philosophic meditations on human destiny, in the form of allegory, dialogue, or fable in which the periodical writers loved to indulge. The prince escapes from his happy valley in quest of a satisfactory object in life, but returns to his paradise again with a sager acceptance of man's limitations." Baker's Best

230

Johnson, Uwe

The third book about Achim. Harcourt 1967 246p $5.75

"A Helen and Kurt Wolff book"
Original German edition, 1961
"A West German journalist goes to East Berlin and gets the idea of writing a book about Achim, a champion bicycle rider. . . . He is faced with great patches where he and Achim see truth from different vantage points. It finally boils down to a battle between the ideologies of East and West Berlin. The two cannot be reconciled, the writing project is abandoned." Pub W
"A book to be undertaken by readers keyed to complex thought and composition." Booklist

Johnston, Mary

y To have and to hold; with illus. by F. C. Schoonover. Houghton 1931 331p illus $4

First published 1900
"A beautiful maid-of-honour, ward of the king, escapes a libertine nobleman, the king's favourite, by fleeing to Virginia with the cargo of brides sent out by the Company (1621). She marries a rough, stanch settler, a famous swordsman, who defends his wife against the favourite, and they meet with strange adventures. Daringly and dazzlingly unreal, full of vigorous movement, characters boldly outlined." Baker's Best

Jones, James

From here to eternity. Scribner 1951 861p $7.95

"A story of Army life in Hawaii in the last months before Pearl Harbor. The chief characters are two soldiers—Pfc Robert Prewitt and First Sergeant Milton Warden—and the women they loved." Book Rev Digest
"Mr. Jones has grappled with a variety of materials and handles some of them less successfully than others. There is a good deal of weak stuff in the two love affairs and the characterizations of the women, and the sorties into the field of general ideas are unimpressive. The book as a whole, however, is a spectacular achievement: it has tremendous vitality and driving power and graphic authenticity." Atlantic

The ice-cream headache, and other stories; the short fiction of James Jones. Delacorte Press 1968 238p $5

Analyzed in Short Story Index
"A collection of twelve short stories and one novella. The author provides a general introduction and brief individual prefatory remarks." Book Rev Digest
Contents: The temper of steel; Just like the girl; The way it is; Two legs for the two of us; Secondhand man; None sing so wildly; Greater love; The King; The valentine; A bottle of cream; Sunday allergy; The tennis game; The ice-cream headache [novella]

The pistol. Scribner 1958 158p o.p. 1970

"This is the account of Pfc. Richard Mast who accidentally comes into possession of a pistol on Pearl Harbor day. It becomes a salvation-symbol to Mast and the center of a sequence of plots to wrest it from him on the part of his peers and military superiors." Book Rev Digest

The thin red line. Scribner 1962 495p $6.95

The story of an Army rifle company named C-for-Charlie during several months of the campaign on Guadalcanal in World War II. It is a detailed account of the battle from the moment of landing on the island, through the bloody battle for a complex of hills, the jungle patrol and respite in bivouac and in the hospital. (Publisher)
"The novel's strength is its depiction of the ordinary American soldier in combat." Booklist

Jones, LeRoi

Tales. Grove 1967 132p $4.50

Analyzed in Short Story Index
"The 16 tales comprising Jones' latest volume are a mixture of wit and terror projected like a missile against the white establishment. Not just another 'hate whitey' volume, Jones' book of snapshots of the Negro is presented with considerable skill. . . . Through it all one is aware of a clever artist at work. . . . This volume belongs in the college library along with Jones' other books. . . . His is a unique expression of the complicated and desperate world of the American Negro." Choice
Contents: A chase (Alighieri's dream); The alternative; The largest ocean in the world; Uncle Tom's cabin: alternate ending; The death of Horatio Alger; Going down slow; Heroes are gang leaders; The screamers; Salute; Words; New-sense; Unfinished; New spirit; No body no place; Now and then; Answers in progress

Jordan, Mildred

One red rose forever. Knopf 1941 550p o.p. 1970

"Using the few authenticated facts now known concerning the life of 'Baron' Henry William Stiegel, the famous early American glass-maker, Miss Jordan has woven them into a stirring tale of early American life. By adding a poignant love story, the author has convincingly portrayed the dynamic 'Baron,' lover of music and beauty in all forms, reckless and daring, and thoroughly convinced of his own lucky star. This is a story that sorely needed telling, and because of the paucity of facts finds its best form in fiction." Library J

Joris, Françoise Mallet-. See Mallet-Joris, Françoise

Joseph, Michael

(ed.) Best cat stories; illus. by Eileen Mayo. Bentley 1953 270p illus o.p. 1970

Partially analyzed in Short Story Index
Contents: Little white cat, by D. Baker; Fine place for the cat, by M. Bonham; Smith, by A. Chadwick; "When in doubt—wash," by P. Gallico; Blue flag, by K. Hill; God and the little cat, by S. Jepson; Fat of the cat, by G. Keller; Broomsticks, by W. De La Mare; New conquest of the Matterhorn, by T. S. Blakeney; Johnnie Poothers, by C. Odger; Fat cat, by Q. Patrick; Kitty, Kitty, Kitty, by J. Pudney; Mr Carmody's safari, by K. Rolland; Cat up a tree, by W. Sansom; Feathers, by C. Van Vechten; Calvin the cat, by C. D. Warner; Traveller from the west and the traveller from the east, by S. T. Warner; Story of Webster, by P. G. Wodehouse; Addressing of cats [a poem], by T. S. Eliot

Joyce, James

The dead
In Neider, C. ed. Short novels of the masters p499-536

Dubliners

Some editions are:
Modern Lib. $2.95 Introduction by Padraic Colum
Viking (The Viking Critical lib) $5.95 Text, criticism, and notes edited by Robert Scholes and A. Walton Litz

Analyzed in Short Story Index
First published 1914
Contents: The sisters; An encounter; Araby; Eveline; After the race; Two gallants; The boarding house; A little child; Counterparts; Clay; A painful case; Ivy day in the committee room; A mother; Grace; The dead

also in Joyce, J. The portable James Joyce p17-242

Finnegans wake. Viking 1939 628p $10

"As 'Ulysses' was the complete record of a life during the day, this is the exploration of the stream of unconsciousness of an individual during the night. In presenting it Mr Joyce has coined what is in considerable part of a new vocabulary composed of familiar syllables yoked in strange fashion and words bearing a strange resemblance to usual ones but twisted from the regular form." Book of the Month Club News
"An experiment in the use of language." Pratt Quarterly

Joyce, James—*Continued*

The portable James Joyce; with an introduction & notes by Harry Levin. [Rev. ed]
Viking 1966 762p (The Viking Portable lib)
$6.50

First published 1947; copyright renewed 1965
Contains the short story collection, Dubliners; A portrait of the artist as a young
man; selections from Ulysses and Finnegans
wake; a collection of poems and Exiles, a play
in three acts

A portrait of the artist as a young man

Some editions are:
Dial Press $8.50 Introduction by Hugh Ken-
ner, illustrated by Brian Keogh
Viking $3.95
Watts, F. $8.95 Large type edition complete
and unabridged. A Keith Jennison book
First published in the United States 1916
This autobiographical novel "portrays the
childhood, school days, adolescence, and early
manhood of Stephen Dedalus, later one of the
leading characters in Ulysses. Stephen's growing self-awareness as an artist forces him to
reject the whole narrow world in which he has
been brought up, including family ties, nationalism, and the Catholic religion. The novel
ends when, having decided to become a writer, he is about to leave Dublin for Paris.
Rather than following a clear narrative progression, the book revolves around experiences
that are crucial to Stephen's development as
an artist; at the end of each chapter Stephen
makes some assertion of identity. Through his
use of the stream-of-consciousness technique,
Joyce reveals the actual materials of his hero's
world, the components of his thought processes." Benét. The Reader's Encyclopedia

also in Joyce, J. The portable James Joyce
p243-526

A shorter Finnegans wake; ed. by Anthony
Burgess. Viking 1967 xxviii, 256p illus $6

An abridgement of the work listed above
The editor has reduced the text of the novel
to something over a third of its original length,
retaining the essential passages, linking them
by a commentary, and adding an introduction.
(Publisher)

Stephen Hero. . . . New Directions 1955
251p illus $5.50

,"Edited from the manuscript in the Harvard
College Library by Theodore Spencer. A new
edition incorporating the additional manuscript pages in the Yale University Library;
edited by John J. Slocum and Herbert Cahoon."
Title page
"Written in about 1904 and published posthumously. [This first version of The portrait
of the artist as a young man, entered above].
It is longer and more conventional in form."
Benét. The Reader's Encyclopedia

Ulysses

Some editions are:
Modern Lib. (Modern Library giants) $4.95
Random House $7.95
First published 1922
"A record of the thoughts and actions of a
group of people in Dublin through a single day,
presented with no reticences, frank, coarse,
often humorous, uninhibited in vocabulary,
obscure, sometimes unpunctuated, and in parts
almost unintelligible without the help of a
key." Booklist
"Joyce's masterpiece, although it has certainly been the most reviled, the most admired, and the most generally discussed work
of our generation, has been at the same time
one of the least read—in the sense of a patient,
conscientious, and thoughtful examination of
its contents. Of course there has never been
any reason to expect that it should be widely
read by the popular reading public: it makes
too many demands on the intellect, the sensibility, and the experience of the average
reader. . . . Even as an intellectual game, a
substitute for the crossword puzzle, the book
must remain an exercise for more or less
superior wits." Nation

K

Kafka, Franz

Amerika; tr. by Edwin Muir, preface by
Klaus Mann; afterword by Max Brod; illus.
by Emlen Etting. Schocken 1962 299p illus
$4.50

Original German edition, 1927. This translation first published 1938 in England
An unfinished novel. "The story concerns
the adventures in America of a younb boy,
Karl Rossmann, who has been driven out of
his home in Prague by his parents after he was
seduced by a servant girl. Karl's America is a
strange land; his adventures border on the
fantastic or the farcical, but at the end there
is a hint that Karl will find a happiness
denied Kafka's other heroes." Book Rev Digest
"Amerika is more hopeful in mood than
Kafka's other efforts. His writing, too, combines dreamlike romanticism and the most
exact realism. It is subtle and intense." Living
Age

The castle; tr. from the German by Willa
and Edwin Muir, with additional materials
tr. by Eithne Wilkins and Ernst Kaiser. With
an homage by Thomas Mann. Definitive ed.

Some editions are:
Knopf $4.95
Modern Lib. $2.95

First published 1926
"In its bare essentials, [this] is the story
of a man against a bureaucracy. . . . The hero,
a land surveyor known only as K., is constantly frustrated in his efforts to gain entrance into a mysterious castle, which is administered by an extraordinarily complicated
and inaccessible bureaucratic hierarchy. The
book invites allegorical interpretation; K.'s
striving has been seen as the human quest for
comprehension of the ways of an incompre-
hensible God and his frustration when he has
seen as symbolic of the actual human condition. But apart from any exact interpretation,
the novel clearly reflects Kafka's convictions
about the problematic nature of human existence, as well as his stylistic mastery and frequent ironic humor." Benét. The Reader's Encyclopedia

Metamorphosis. Vanguard 1946 98p illus
$4.95

Written in 1915 this is "often regarded as
Kafka's most perfect finished work. 'The Metamorphosis' begins as its hero, Gregor Samsa,
awakens one morning to find himself changed
into a huge insect; the story proceeds to develop the effects of this change upon Gregor's
business and family life, and ends with his
death. It has been read as everything from a
religious allegory to a psychoanalytic case history; but its really attractive qualities are its
clarity of depiction and attention to significant
detail, which give its completely fantastic occurrences an aura of indisputable truth, so
that no allegorical interpretation is necessary
to demonstrate its greatness." Benét. The
Reader's Encyclopedia

also in Kafka, F. The penal colony

also in Kafka, F. Selected short stories

also in Neider, C. ed. Short novels of the
masters p537-79

also in Pick, R. ed. German stories and
tales p247-95

The penal colony: stories and short pieces;
tr. by Willa and Edwin Muir. Schocken 1948
320p illus $4.50

Analyzed in Short Story Index
Contents: Conversation with the supplicant;
Medication; The judgment; The metamorphosis;
A country doctor; In the penal colony: A
hunger artist

Selected short stories; tr. by Willa and
Edwin Muir; introduction by Philip Rahv.
Modern Lib. 1952 328p $2.95

Analyzed in Short Story Index
Contents: The judgment; The metamorphosis;
In the penal colony; Great Wall of China;

Kafka, Franz—*Continued*

Country doctor; Common confusion; New advocate; Old manuscript; A fratricide; Report to an academy; Hunter Gracchus; Hunger artist; Investigations of a dog; The burrow; Josephine the singer

The trial

Some editions are:

Knopf Definitive edition $4.95 Translated from the German by Willa and Edwin Muir; revised and with additional materials translated by E. M. Butler. Illustrated by George Salter

Modern Lib. Definitive edition $2.95 Translated from the German by Willa and Edwin Muir; revised and with additional materials translated by E. M. Butler

Original edition published 1924. This translation first published 1937

Insofar as [this unfinished novel] depicts the confrontation of an individual and a baffling bureaucracy, it is similar to Kafka's "The Castle' [entered above]. The hero of 'The Trial', a bank assessor named Joseph K., is accused, by a mysterious legal authority whose headquarters are in a rundown tenement, of an unnamed crime of which he knows nothing. The novel treats his many fruitless attempts to obtain justice from an authority with which he cannot even effectively communicate, and culminates in his utter frustration, his complete loss of human dignity, and his death like a dog." Benét. The Reader's Encyclopedia

Kahn, Joan

(ed.) Hanging by a thread. Houghton 1969 604p $7.95

"Here is a fine new collection of unfamiliar fact and fiction, (mostly fiction), that will please any reader. The editor . . . supplies biographies-in-brief of the authors represented and a great deal of know-how in the way she has arranged these tales to follow one another." Best Sellers

Stories included are: The scorched face, by D. Hammett; The splintered Monday, by C. Armstrong; The mysterious occurrence in Lambeth, by G. P. R. James; The guest, by A. Camus; The grandstand complex, by H. McCoy; The other place, by R. Borger; The blue hotel, by S. Crane; The hashish man, by Lord Dunsany; The true story, by D. Thomas; The Manhattan well murder, by E. S. Gould; The way up to heaven, by R. Dahl; The haunted and the haunters, by E. Bulwer-Lytton; The peasant girl, by A. Budrys; A strange murderer, by M. Gorky; Lost hearts, by M. R. James; A marriage tragedy, by W. Collins; The sea raiders, by H. G. Wells; The waste land, by A. Paton; Beheaded in error, from Ching-pen t'ung-hsu hsiao-shuo; A manner of legacy, by D. Byrne; Funny the way things work out, by J. D. MacDonald; The end, by J. L. Borges; Operation enticement, by H. Cecil; Cambric tea, by M. Bowen; A ghost of a head; A winter's tale, by H. Eustis; The murder at The Towers, by E. V. Knox

Kamarck, Lawrence

The bell ringer. Random House 1969 173p boards $4.50

"Charlie Skragg, Negro chief of police in a small New England town, is called in to investigate the murder of Tom Carew, the town psychiatrist. Among the curious facts surrounding the murder is Carew's toast at the dinner party preceding it, to his murderer-to-be. Skragg's investigation is somewhat hampered by the fact that he suspects he may have committed the murder himself in a mental blackout." Pub W

Kane, Harnett T.

y The amazing Mrs Bonaparte; a novel based on the life of Betsy Patterson. Doubleday 1963 301p o.p. 1970

A novel about the life of Betsy Patterson Bonaparte, wife of Napoleon's youngest brother, Jerome. Soon after their marriage in America Napoleon ordered Jerome to return home alone. During the rest of her long life Betsy attempted to get her son and grandson recognized as Bonapartes. The author has recreated

the society of the Napoleonic era and of early 19th century America along with many notables of the day. (Publisher)

"As is true of his earlier biographical novels Mr. Kane's intensive background research makes this novel as much a study of the era as of the central character." Best Sellers

y Bride of fortune; a novel based on the life of Mrs Jefferson Davis. Doubleday 1948 301p $4.95

"The human story of the Natchez belle who became First Lady of the Confederacy and rescued her husband from death and oblivion. Exciting, dramatic, poignant—these words best describe the extraordinary life of Varina Howell Davis, a woman who had an unshakable faith in her husband, Jefferson Davis, and the lost cause he represented. In telling her extraordinary story, the author of 'New Orleans Woman' has pictured . . . the rise and fall of the Confederacy." Huntting

"The great fault of the book is its excessively romantic quality. . . . Yet the book has merits which leave a distinct impression upon the reader: a vivid apprehension of time and place, a real grasp of the complex politics of the era, and above all an understanding of the unusual woman who always holds the center of the piece." Sat R

y The gallant Mrs Stonewall; a novel based on the lives of General and Mrs Stonewall Jackson. Doubleday 1957 320p illus $4.95

"The story of the brief and poignant married life of Anna Morrison Jackson and her husband, the Confederate leader 'Stonewall' Jackson, who died of pneumonia after battle wounds." Pub W

"There is far more documentation than fiction, and with this particular subject, a lot more history than romance. . . . Of the Civil War. Mr. Kane shows events almost wholly through Anna's eyes, but giving enough through the talk of her contemporaries, and in brief visits to the general's headquarters, to refresh the record." N Y Times Bk R

y The lady of Arlington; a novel based on the life of Mrs Robert E. Lee. Doubleday 1953 288p $4.95

"Beginning with her girlhood it tells the story of this great-granddaughter of Martha Washington who defied her adoring parents to marry into the impoverished Lee family, and takes her thru all the vicissitudes of her married life, ending with Robert E. Lee's death." Book Rev Digest

This book "will undoubtedly stimulate in the reader admiration for the courageous woman who was Robert E. Lee's wife, and arouse a desire to learn more about the great general who loved the United States yet fought against it, and who freed his own few slaves and yet fought on the side of the South." Best Sellers

y The smiling rebel; a novel based on the life of Belle Boyd. Doubleday 1955 314p $4.95

At seventeen, Belle Boyd became a heroine when she shot a Yankee soldier who was trying to raise the Union flag over her family's house in Martinsburg, Virginia. Later she started spying for Stonewall Jackson, was captured by the Northerners but charmed her way out of captivity and lived to marry a Yankee officer. (Publisher)

"Mr. Kane, as always, manages his background with skill . . . but the cheerful Belle is always at stage center, and always in motion. . . . Mr. Kane might have spelled out more fully the details of Belle's 'work,' but he couldn't have made the girl whose avowed colors were 'blood red' more spiritedly convincing." N Y Times Bk R

Kane, Henry

The narrowing list

In Santesson, H. S. ed. The locked room reader p331-464

Kaniuk, Yoram

Himmo, King of Jerusalem; tr. from the Hebrew by Yosef Shachter. Atheneum Pubs. [1969 c1968] 246p $5.75

Original Hebrew edition 1968

Kaniuk, Yoram—*Continued*

"This novel is set within a monastery-hospital for wounded Jewish soldiers during the siege of 1948. To its shelter comes the Jewish nurse Hamotal, attractive, serene and efficient. Her betrothed having been killed, she cares impersonally for those who remain. Suddenly, however, the most hopeless patient of all becomes her special obsession. This growing involvement produces a strange ambience of love, pity, hatred and revulsion throughout the ward." Am News of Bks

Kantor, MacKinlay

y   Andersonville. World Pub. 1955 767p map $8.95

Pulitzer Prize 1956
"A lovely woodland in southwestern Georgia was transformed into the Confederacy's largest prison camp administered by a senile general who derived savage satisfaction from watching Yankees die of exposure, starvation, and disease. Individual stories merge to create an indelible impression of sublimity amidst degradation within the prison, and of the shamed helplessness of cultured Southerners unable to counter the inhumanity of the dregs of their armies." Booklist

"This book may repel the squeamish, for sometimes it is hideous, as war itself is hideous, and the language is frequently soldiers' language. But there are glory and grandeur in it, too. It is a great war novel." N Y Her Trib Books

y   The daughter of Bugle Ann. Random House 1953 122p o.p. 1970

Sequel to: The voice of Bugle Ann
"The background is the fox-hunting country of Missouri, and the story continues from the point where the first story ended. It tells of the marriage between the son and daughter of feuding families, and the part played in the romance by the daughter of that famous hound, Bugle Ann." Book Rev Digest

Long remember; decorations by Will Crawford. Coward-McCann 1934 411p illus o.p. 1970

"The town of Gettysburg, Pennsylvania, is going about its daily life on a day in July, 1863. Daniel Bale has just come home from the West to bury his grandfather, and has fallen in love with his neighbor's wife. Troops are drilling on the village green, but war is far away—something to be talked about. And than suddenly, with little warning, they are overwhelmed, engulfed in a battle. A powerful novel that makes it all very real." Wis Lib Bul

"Unlike most novels of war, Mr. Kantor's is impartial. The southern army as well as the northern army is only a groping group of men blindly doing the bidding of an elemental force." Chicago Daily Tribune

Spirit Lake. World Pub. 1961 957p map o.p. 1970

Based on historical research, this is a fictional account of the 1857 massacre of white settlers by the Wahpekute Indians, a tribe of the Dakotas, at Spirit Lake and the Okoboji lakes in Iowa. The account includes a description of the arrival and the life of the white settlers and their contacts with the Indians before the massacre

"It is, as I have noted, a shocking story and one that will, at times, revolt the reader of sensitivity. But it should also be added that, though this story is suitable only for strong-stomached adults, the near and actual depravities are not glamorized and seem at least in part, necessary to contrast the victims and their murderers. The problem a reader will have to face is similar to that he was confronted with in the same author's 'Andersonville.'" Best Sellers

Story teller; preface by Ben Hibbs. Doubleday 1967 462p $5.95

Partially analyzed in Short Story Index
A collection of stories, each of which is followed by a comment in which the author "tells where he got his ideas, where he found the characters, how hard or easy it was to sell the stories, and what he himself, candidly, feels about them." Pub W

Contents: Again the bugle; The light at three o'clock; A Count now due; Material witness; The fear of Kelly; Blue eyes far away; The wrath of the raped; Blaze of glory; Write me a letter; How happy we could be; Honey on the border; Papa Pierre's pipe; If the South had won the Civil War; The Moon-Caller; All night with my darling; Saturday afternoon; Lilacs for Mr Lace; We'll all feel gay; The star of Prickly Orange; O Tannenbaum; Bringing in the may; The return of the Eagle; In Xanadu

y   The voice of Bugle Ann

Some editions are:
Coward-McCann $3.95
Watts, F. $6.95 Large type edition complete and unabridged. A Keith Jennison book
"Eighty-two-year-old 'Spring' Davis and his neighbors spent thrilling evenings listening to their fox hunting dogs on the hillsides of rural Missouri, but it was the beautiful trumpetlike voice of his own dog, Bugle Ann, that filled the old man with special pride and joy. This short dramatic tale of how 'Spring' was led to commit murder holds the reader in suspense and comes to a surprising and sentimental conclusion." N Y Libraries
"This little story of primitive passions is a marvel of condensation. Characters are rounded out in a sentence, and minute incidents carry far-reaching implications." Boston Transcript
Followed by: The daughter of Bugle Ann
also in Costain, T. B. ed. Stories to remember v 1 p465-505

Karl, Frederick R.

(jt. ed.) Hamalian, L. ed. Short fiction of the masters

Karmel, Ilona

An estate of memory; a novel. Houghton 1969 444p $6.95

"Four women, all Jewish, although one is so Aryan-looking she can 'pass' and has voluntarily declared herself a Jew, are inmates of a concentration camp in Poland in the days when the war was beginning to turn against the Germans. One of the women, the oldest and the most innately selfish, is secretly pregnant. The others band together with the connivance of the camp doctor to help her bear her child and then smuggle it out of the camp to safety with an old Polish couple." Pub W

Karp, David

All honorable men. Knopf 1956 311p o.p. 1970

"A thesis novel which points out the negative consequences of loyalty investigations. Here it is not the government, but a conservative foundation that looks into the private lives of its personnel. The liberal head of the foundation, a superior type of man, seemingly without fear, clashes with rightwing trustees over the hiring of a former government economist accused of having had pro-Communist leanings. Both innocent and some not-so-innocent outsiders become involved, many lives are ruined, and the foundation disintegrates." Library J

"Mr. Karp has written a vigorous defense of freedom to read, to think and to make mistakes. His book is remarkably objective and free from sentimentality, though there is a strong undercurrent of compassion for those who have made, some time in their past, honest if ill-advised mistakes." N Y Times Bk R

Kauffmann, Lane

An honorable estate. Lippincott 1964 424p boards $5.95

The author tells "the interlocking stories of the members of two well-to-do New York families, one part Jewish, who are brought together by the impending marriage of the daughter of one household to the son of the other. . . . [Mr Kauffmann] includes excursions into the world of a successful playwright, a big businessman with a guilty past, a homosexual songwriter, a lonely mistress, a professor married to a rich wife, an autocratic old dowager." Pub W

Kauffmann, Lane—*Continued*

"Lane Kauffmann has done his work well. He writes with skill, with searching character feeling, with lively imagination. The plot unfolds easily and credibly so that people move and take life from the situations presented to us." Best Sellers

Kaufman, Bel

y Up the down staircase. Prentice-Hall 1964 340p illus $5.95

A loosely constructed "novel about a New York City high school. The school is overcrowded, chaotic; the students, disorderly, underprivileged, but some of them very promising; the teachers, inspired, good, bad, or neurotic; their paperwork, mountainous. Frantic . . . notes between two excellent teachers, friends and fellow sufferers (one is deciding whether to quit), excerpts from students' compositions, and bureaucratic school announcements tell the story." Pub W

"'Up the Down Staircase' may not be 'classicle' but it should be read by anyone interested in children and education. The teacher who is trying to get through to the pupil succeeds in communicating to us all. Bel Kaufman has an especially good recollection of dialect and dialogue. She is a woman with a forceful message. She may slip and write the same letter twice but what she says can bear repeating." N Y Times Bk R

Kaufman, Sue

Diary of a mad housewife. Random House 1967 311p $4.95

A novel in form of a diary. Tina Balser is apparently lucky. She has two children; a successful but ambitious and insensitive husband; an apartment on Central Park West, and a housekeeper. But she begins to feel that she is going out of her mind, and starts a secret diary as an escape valve and self-therapy. (Publisher)

"Miss Kaufman brilliantly conveys Tina's malaise, and the portraits of the two daughters Liz and Sylvie, as observed by their harassed mother almost peripherally, will charm your heart away." Book of the Month Club News

Kaufmann, Myron S.

Remember me to God. Lippincott 1957 640p $5.95

"Richard Amsterdam, son of a Boston judge, is the hero. Richard is a Harvard undergraduate who wants to deny his Jewish heritage, and join a Protestant church. His struggle is hampered by his upright father's absolute integrity and by his teen-aged sister's naive ways. The time is the early years of World war II." Book Rev Digest

"The Boston-Cambridge environment and the traditions and customs of Judaism are handled with a deft and familiar touch." Booklist

Kawabata, Yasunari

Nobel Prize in literature, 1968

House of the sleeping beauties, and other stories; with an introduction by Yukio Mishima; tr. by Edward G. Seidensticker. Kodansha 1969 149p $4.50

Stories included are: House of the sleeping beauties [novella]; One arm; Of birds and beasts

"The title 'novella' has been rightfully haled as Kawabata's greatest work. Written on what might seem to certain conservative Western readers a sordid subject—the passion of an old man for sleeping with beautiful young girls who have been drugged—it is told with a quiet simple restraint that gives the reader a notable insight into the mind of the old man. . . . The other two stories, 'One Arm' and 'Of Birds and Beasts,' are odd little psychological studies that are more clever than great." Library J

Snow country and Thousand cranes; the Nobel Prize edition of two novels; tr. from the Japanese by Edward G. Seidensticker. Knopf 1969 2v in 1 $5.95

First American editions 1957 and 1959, respectively

"Snow Country is the story of a geisha, Komako, who gives herself, without illusion and with undismayed directness, to a love affair foredoomed to transience." Publisher's note

The second title is entered separately

Thousand cranes; tr. by Edward G. Seidensticker. Knopf 1959 [c1958] 147p illus boards $3

First published in Japan

"A Japanese writer places the events of his story against the rites and symbols of the tea ceremony. The young man Kikuji becomes unwillingly involved with the middle-aged Mrs. Ota, a teacher of the tea ritual, who had for many years been his late father's mistress. Kikuji's ambivalent feelings of hostility and infatuation cause him much anguish and culminate in Mrs. Ota's suicide. The situation is further complicated by the match-making efforts of another of his father's ex-mistresses, and by Fumiko, Mrs. Ota's beautiful daughter." Booklist

"This novel has many meanings, the kind of rich suggestibility that is demanded of the Japanese novel of quality. The writing is swiftly paced and spare, and a story is told that is human, vivid and moving. It is a novel of exquisite artistry." N Y Her Trib Books

also in Kawabata, Y. Snow country and Thousand cranes v2 p3-147

Kayira, Legson

Jingala. Doubleday 1969 160p $4.95

The author, a young Malawian, "writes about Jingala, an elderly African widower whose son Gregory, at a mission school, has decided to become a priest. In describing Jingala's unsuccessful efforts to keep the boy home and to instill in him respect for his small native village and its way of life, Kayria tells us a good deal not only about African folkways and mores but also about the effect of outside influences on traditional society, the universality of man's hope for his offspring, and the conflict between generations." Library J

Kazan, Elia

America, America; with an introduction by S. N. Behrman. Stein & Day 1962 190p boards $4.95

Copyrighted 1961 as an unpublished dramatic work with title: Hamal

The "story of Stavros, a Greek boy from Anatolia where [in 1896] the Turks slaughter and humiliate at any excuse. Stavros and his Armenian friend and idol, Vartan, dream of going to America and freedom. Vartan is butchered by the Turks but at last Stavros achieves his goal." Bk Buyer's Guide

"Elia Kazan's book is a scenario, with the spareness, emphasis on the concrete, the appeal to eye and ear of the film story. It has a rugged simplicity, vividly sketched characters, and a strong story line. . . . Though marred by an occasional cliché or an infelicity of phrasing, Kazan's story of a latter-day Candide, his loss of innocence and his monomaniacal dream is compelling reading." Library J

Kazantzakēs, Nikos. See Kazantzakis, Nikos

Kazantzakis, Nikos

The fratricides; tr. from the Greek by Athena Gianakas Dallas. Simon & Schuster 1964 254p boards $5

Original Greek edition published 1963

This "novel of an elderly priest, struggling to mediate between Greek loyalists and pro-Communist rebels during the civil wars of the 1940's, is suffused with spiritual passion and ultimate suffering. The novel is a modern parable, with Father Yanaros as the immolated Christ, rejected by his own people and betrayed by the partisan leader, Captain Drakós." Library J

Kazantzakis, Nikos—*Continued*

"The stilted dignity of the style, in this translation . . . is mellowed by rich imagery, but 'The Fratricides' is in a sense classic Greek tragedy and, like its great predecessors, aloof from everyday life." Book of the Month Club News

Freedom or death; a novel; tr. by Jonathan Griffin. Preface by A. Den Doolaard. Simon & Schuster 1956 433p boards $6

"Tells the story of the revolt of 1889 by the suppressed Cretans against their Turkish oppressors, as well as a love intrigue in which the two Cretan heroes, the captains Michales and Polyxigis, fight with each other and with the noble Turk Nuri Bey about the same Circassian woman." Preface

"The reader who attempts to penetrate this strange world will be bewildered and excited by the color, rawness, violence, primitive passions, and superabundant energy of its people." Booklist

The Greek passion; tr. by Jonathan Griffin. Simon & Schuster 1953 432p $6

Published in England with title: Christ recrucified

This story "shows how the suffering and crucifixion of Christ in Roman Judea might be re-enacted in a modern setting—a Greek-inhabited Turkish town, circa 1920." Time

"Some readers will find this novel a refreshingly different product from most contemporary fiction, and some will find it a bit old-fashioned for their taste. For better or for worse. The Greek Passion has the flavor of a parable enlarged to epic dimensions." Atlantic

The last temptation of Christ; tr. from the Greek by P. A. Bien. Simon & Schuster 1960 506p boards $6

"Christ and his disciples are treated as men in this novel, with Christ sometimes depressed, sometimes afraid, sometimes ready to give up his mission and find earthly happiness with Mary Magdalena. Judas is portrayed not as a traitor but as a bold man 'betraying' Christ at his Leader's command." Bk Buyer's Guide

The author "was excommunicated from the Greek Orthodox Church because of the present novel. It has been placed on the Index of the Roman Catholic Church, and it will undoubtedly be controversial material for other groups than these, including linguists and literary purists. The style is difficult to judge in translation as Kazantzakis used the demotic Greek, 'the audacious metaphorical language of the peasants'; but the rich and racy, loose, extravagant, sometimes coarse vocabulary comes through all right in the English, at times in lyric passages, most frequently in sounding, dramatic realism. All the characters are people of this earth, and, while the period and locale are true to history, the story of Christ on earth only outwardly follows the Bible story. In the deepest sense, the novel celebrates the spiritual struggles of mankind and man's passion, power and courage. . . . Philosophically, this is the controversial root of the whole novel—the necessity of the struggle between flesh and spirit. Recommended as an important and meaningful novel." Library J

The rock garden; a novel. Tr. from the French by Richard Howard. Passages from The saviors of God tr. by Kimon Friar. Simon & Schuster 1963 251p boards $4.50

Original French edition 1936

"In a strangely haunting tale of a white man's visit to Japan and China, the author mirrors through his unique combination of the earthy, the exotic, and the exalted his own profound reactions to these two lands during his trip there in the 1930's. The tragic story of love and hate between two Oriental friends of the narrator deftly suggests the growing bitterness between Japan and China." Booklist

Saint Francis; a novel; tr. from the Greek by P. A. Bien. Simon & Schuster 1962 379p boards $5.95

Published in England with title: God's pauper

"The story barely touches on Francis' early life as a soldier and student, beginning really when he meets Leo, who becomes his faithful apostle and constant companion. Leo, who is the narrator, has been wandering in Italy as a mendicant in search of God, and Francis is suddenly converted in his quest. Calling himself God's fool, he starts his complex pilgrimage toward sainthood by singing and dancing in the public square of Assisi to express faith. Through the eyes and ears of Leo, Kazantzakis traces the wanderings of the Poor Man of Assisi through the medieval scene, describing in detail his passionate commitment to privation and humiliation." Book of the Month Club News

"Kazantzakis makes the saint's life seem terribly real, impassioned, and fanatic, a thing of constant struggle with sin and possession by God. In doing so, he loses some of the more peaceful beauty of the Saint's dedication and the legends about him." Pub W

Zorba the Greek; tr. by Carl Wildman. Simon & Schuster 1952 311p $6

"An old Greek workman who is philosopher and hedonist, raconteur and roué, Zorba goes to Crete with the narrator, a rich and cultivated dilettante, who has been stung into activity by being called a 'bookworm' as a parting shot from his closest friend, en route to fight in the Caucasus. He buys a mine and puts Zorba in charge of the workmen. . . . Zorba accomplishes fantastic feats of physical prowess, he tells wild stories of his erotic adventures, he misbehaves badly with his patron's money, he dances, and sings, and talks." Times (London) Lit Sup

"Zorba the Greek is a novel sweet and elate with sunlight, friendship and happiness, with a life full of both sensations and thoughts; it is, in every sense, a minor classic, and Zorba, one feels, is among the significant and permanent characters in modern fiction." New Statesman & Nation

Keating, H. R. F.

Inspector Ghote caught in meshes. Dutton 1968 215p $4.50

"When the famous Professor Gregory Strongbow's brother was killed on the road to Poona [in India], by three men who had waited all morning for him, Inspector Ghote knew he'd have trouble—with an impatient American on one hand and an apparently motiveless murder." Bk Buyer's Guide

"Keating's stories of Inspector Ghote of the Bombay C.I.D. steadily improve, and this present one, about apparent dacoity and possible politicking, is very good. Mr Keating manages to convey a convincing India without falling into patronage, contempt or Indian chauvinism." Times (London) Lit Sup

Inspector Ghote hunts the peacock. Dutton 1968 224p $4.50

Indian detective, Inspector Ganesh Ghote arrives in London "armed with his long-nurtured impressions of what England is like. . . . He has come on a most dignified mission: to attend the Emergency Conference on the Smuggling of Dangerous Drugs. . . . Very much against his will, the Inspector is forced to divide his time in London between official notetaking at the conference and unofficial hunting for the provocative teen-ager known as The Peacock." Publisher's note

Keefe, Frederick L.

The investigating officer. Delacorte Press 1966 406p $5.95

"Did a young American Army officer murder two German prisoners-of-war, SS men, in cold blood while transporting them to a camp at the end of World War II, or did he shoot them when they attempted to escape? Two German civilians witnessed the shooting, and claim it was murder. An investigating officer is appointed to make a report on the matter that will help the commanding officer decide whether to hold a court martial." Pub W

"The writing is skilful, the suspense sustained, the typing and the interplay of the characters, and the moral issues involved are masterfully portrayed." Best Sellers

Kell, Joseph. See Burgess, Anthony

Kelley, William Melvin

A different drummer. Doubleday 1962 223p
o.p. 1970

"Parable of the sudden, spontaneous exodus of every Negro from a nameless Southern state, set in the timeless present of a small town. A quiet Negro, Tucker Caliban, kills his land by sowing it with salt, burns his house and possessions, and leaves, and all other Negroes begin to leave forever, without organization or leadership. The Southerners, dimly realizing some loss, ironically lynch an educated Northern Negro preacher, as ignorant as they of what is happening." Booklist

The author "has hit on an unbeatable idea and couldn't have worked it out more smartly. But this is infinitely more than smart. It's as timely as today's page one. It is radical, and idealistic, and wonderfully fresh—people, action, thought, love, brutality and hate all in the right proportions." N Y Her Trib Books

A drop of patience. Doubleday 1965 237p
o.p. 1970

The "story of Ludlow Washington, born blind, who found in a state school that he was colored but never fully understood why that was bad. But he did learn that just as one of the other Negro boys made him 'a slave,' he would continue to be a slave, to a Negro band leader, to the wife he didn't want, to a world that bewildered and destroyed him." Bk Buyer's Guide

The author "gives us real insight into the Negro artist's obsession with a white world that seems (to him) as perverse as a roulette wheel." Best Sellers

Kellogg, Marjorie

y Tell me that you love me, Junie Moon. Farrar, Straus 1968 216p boards $4.95

This novel concerns "three patients who meet in a hospital [and] decide to live together because they have no other place to go. The first is Warren, a paraplegic. The second is Arthur, victim of a progressive, undiagnosed neurological disease. The third is Junie Moon, who had been beaten half to death and then had acid poured over her face." Pub W

"It is difficult to convey the humor and humanness of . . . [this] novel. . . . Miss Kellogg is not concerned with picturing the possible psychological crippling which might accompany such physical distortions, but rather in stating the universal importance of love and mutual tolerance in human relationships." Library J

Kelly, Michael

Assault. Harcourt [1969 c1967] 190p $4.50

First published 1967 in England

"This exciting World War II episode features the bravery, sacrifice and daring of hunted men. 'Knightsbridge' is the code name for British Special Operations' number one target, a factory near Copenhagen. Four men are parachuted into a field near the city where they are met by members of the Danish underground. Their adventures in the city, where the Germans are on an intense alert, are as thrilling as any espionage novel. Characterizations of the British saboteurs, the men of the Danish underground, and the German commander of the fortress area are good. One is carried swiftly from first page to last in this excellent first novel." Pub W

Kemal, Yashar

Anatolian tales; tr. from the Turkish by Thilda Kemal. Dodd [1969 c1968] 160p $4

Original edition published in Turkey. This translation published 1968 in England

Contents: A dirty story; The white trousers; The drumming-out; On the road; The baby; Green onions; The shopkeeper

"These seven short stories will enhance Kemal's reputation as 'the greatest living Turkish writer.' The stories are poignant and dramatic episodes in the lives of the desperately poor, abysmally ignorant, lustful peasants of Anatolia." Library J

Memed, my hawk; tr. by Edouard Roditi. Pantheon Bks. 1961 371p $4.95

Originally published 1955 in Istanbul

This novel "is a romantic account of the life of a young Turkish peasant, who is driven from his native village because he defies the local Agha, a kind of twentieth century feudal lord. The hero then takes to the hills where he becomes a celebrated brigand, and eventually a kind of local hero." Pub W

"Yashar Kemal is a powerful storyteller: the constant danger, the elemental struggle against fate mercilessly pull the reader along. His mountains, towns, tents, battles, people are superbly described. He re-creates for us not only Memed's thoughts and feelings, but an age-old way of life still to be found in odd corners of the world. Anyone thinking of living or working in the Near East, indeed in a primitive society anywhere, should read this novel. As should anyone interested in a good, strong story." Book of the Month Club News

Kemelman, Harry

Friday the rabbi slept late. Crown 1964 224p $3.95

"Friday, as every day, Rabbi Small ordinarily participated in morning services. But on this particular Friday, the rabbi did not appear: on this morning the body of a dead girl, strangled in the rabbi's own car, was discovered on the Temple grounds. But Rabbi Small—Police Chief Lannigan's prime suspect—proves a master of detection. It is only when the two men come fully to know and understand each other, that the criminal is found." Huntting

"Characters are fresh and true, background material cherishable, and the solution delightfully apt." Book Week

The nine mile walk; the Nicky Welt stories. Putnam 1967 186p $4.50

"Red mask mystery"

Analyzed in Short Story Index

"These tales are very much in the Sherlock Holmes tradition, with Nicky Welt in the Holmes role, and the narrator, a district attorney, a somewhat reluctant Watson." Pub W

Contents: The nine mile walk; The straw man; The ten o'clock scholar; End play; Time and time again; The whistling tea kettle; The bread and butter case; The man on the ladder

Saturday the rabbi went hungry. Crown 1966 249p $3.95

"The absent-minded knowledgeable young Rabbi, leader of a Conservative congregation, collaborates with his friend the Irish Catholic police chief in solving a mystery, this time deciding whether a death is murder or suicide and, if it is murder, who did it. The story is a good mixture of Jewish folk wisdom with modern community problems and with a murder mystery all nicely seasoned with humor." Pub W

"Filled with wonderful characterizations, and probes deeply into comparative religious attitudes toward suicide, drunkenness—even how to name a baby." McClurg. Book News

Sunday the rabbi stayed home

Some editions are:
Lanewood Press $7.50 Large type edition complete and unabridged
Putnam $5.95

First published 1969

"In this third encounter with a murder case, the New England rabbi detective is faced with pot being pushed locally to tempt the young people of the temple; a feud among the mid-dleaged lay leaders that threatens to tear the temple apart; and—in one brisk encounter with an antagonistic Negro—a touch of black anti-Semitism." Pub W

"In addition to the wide ranging philosophical excursions, and the unexpected contacts, this book reaches out to the poblems of drugs and integration. To say it is the Rabbi's best adventure yet, is too faint praise." Library J

Keneally, Thomas

Three cheers for the Paraclete. Viking [1969 c1968] 240p boards $4.95

"The scene is Australia, where the older clergy are conservative off-shoots of their

Keneally, Thomas—*Continued*

Irish forebears. Young Father James Maitland, an intellectual and an honest man, who has had a brief taste of freedom during a sojourn in Louvain, comes home to a House of Studies for the priesthood. Almost everything that he does, says or thinks brings him into conflict with his superiors or brings home to him the plight of other Catholics." Pub W

This novel "succeeds both in underscoring the turmoil within the Catholic Church and portraying the doubts that assail even the most highly committed priests. . . . What is refreshing about this novel is that priests and bishops are seen in the fullness of their humanity and that . . . [Maitland does not] desert the Church." Best Sellers

Kennaway, James

The cost of living like this. Atheneum Pubs. 1969 199p $5.95

"A young English economist who knows without being informed that his cancer is far advanced clings both to his unsophisticated mistress whose extreme youth and warmth seem an affirmation of life and hope and to Christine his wife who loves him in her own strange fashion. Though the two women literally vie for him, in his dying hours each helps the other ease his way." Booklist

"Mr. Kennaway, who was killed in an automobile accident before publication of this novel, wrote with sensitivity, humanity and a sharp perception of contemporary dilemmas, shuttling back and forth in time as he fitted together pieces of the human puzzles, building the suspense as he answered some questions and raised others. An engrossing tale of our time, exceedingly well written." Pub W

Kennedy, Lucy

Mr Audubon's Lucy. Crown 1957 343p o.p. 1970

"Although Lucy Bakewell knew that life would not be easy when she married John James Audubon, she was happy to dedicate herself to helping him achieve success in painting. After years of incredible hardships, the 'impossible dream' came true, but almost cost her the man she loved. To present this portrait the author has searched through journals, records, and other writings of the Audubon family." Huntting

"This is a sympathetic portrait of a remarkable understanding and loving woman. . . . It is also an authentic period piece of nineteenth-century America, when success was always down river, always westward and always ahead." N Y Times Bk R

Kennedy, Margaret

The constant nymph. Doubleday 1925 344p o.p. 1970

"Here is a picture of genius and the children of genius. The genius is Herbert Sanger, musician extraordinary. His children, collectively known as Sanger's circus, are not quite so musical as their father but fully as extraordinary. . . . The book chronicles their joyous and other adventures, concerning itself chiefly with Teresa, the constant nymph." Book Rev Digest

A night in Cold Harbor. Macmillan (N Y) 1960 230p o.p. 1970

This "novel of the early nineteenth century is set in England, mainly among people of good circumstance, and describes the events that lead up to the sudden disappearance of an unlikely pair of companions—a small, poor, illegitimate boy and the distinguished, persecuted man who has appointed himself the child's guardian, protector, and guide." New Yorker

"An unpretentious, well-flavored historical novel that blends good storytelling with vivid social background. . . . There are glimpses of the appalling conditions under which children of 8 and younger were forced to work in the early 19th century." Book of the Month Club News

Kennelly, Ardyth

The peaceable kingdom. Houghton 1949 375p o.p. 1970

"A first novel portraying life among the Mormons in Utah during the years after Brigham Young's death, when the government was beginning to outlaw plural marriages. The central character is Linnea, second wife of Olaf Ecklund. Linnea with her five children, envied Sigrid, the first wife, but her indomitable courage and good sense carried her thru all her troubles. The book closes with the day of days when Olaf promised her a home of her own." Book Rev Digest

"That she has found out how to create one magnificent character and how to give life to a series of amusing and dramatic episodes in that character's life is undeniable. And that both the author and her earthy, rich-hearted Linnea will give pleasure to countless thousands of readers is also undeniable." Chicago Sunday Tribune

Kent, Alexander

Form line of battle! Putnam 1969 320p $5.95

"The author of 'To glory we steer' tells of the further stirring exploits at sea of valiant Captain Richard Bolitho of the Royal Navy. In command of 'Hyperion,' 74-gun ship of the line, Bolitho sails from Gibraltar in 1793 to join Lord Hood who is in charge of British naval operations against French revolutionary forces at Toulon. Bolitho's activities are climaxed by a victory over the French. The novel ends happily with the wedding near his estate at Falmouth of Captain Bolitho and Cheney Seton, sister of a midshipman on the 'Hyperion.'" Booklist

"Action is frequent and intense, and the color and excitement of 18th-Century sea battles are vividly depicted. Best of all, Bolitho will be remembered as a hero who is both human and humane." Library J

To glory we steer. Putnam 1968 328p $5.95

"A taut, actionful sea drama set in 1782 recommended as recreational reading for men who enjoy the genre. Young Captain Richard Bolitho assumes command of the frigate 'Phalarope' with orders to the Caribbean where the royal squadron is threatened by the combined fleets of France and Spain and the American privateers. The previous captain's avoidance of battle and the crew's near mutinous attitude make the 'Phalarope' a marked vessel, and the story centers on Bolitho's efforts to gain the loyalty of the crew and redeem the ship's reputation in battle." Booklist

For other titles by this author see Reeman, Douglas

Kenyon, F. W.

Marie Antoinette; a novel. Crowell 1956 371p o.p. 1970

This novel tells the "story of Marie Antoinette from the time she arrived in France a 14-year-old girl. The main emphasis is on the Queen's development from a wilful girl into a mature and noble woman caught by circumstances not of her own devising." Pub W

"Mr. Kenyon captures the restless mood of the period; the characterizations if not profound are, for the most part, convincing. Should appeal to the readers of historical fiction." Booklist

Mary of Scotland. Crowell 1957 344p o.p. 1970

"A competently written historical romance which tells the ever-popular story of Mary, Queen of Scots. . . . It covers only the years that followed Mary's return to Scotland from France at the age of 19. There is considerable emphasis on court intrigue, [and religious bickering] and Mary's third husband, Bothwell, is a somewhat less romantic figure than he appears in many of the plays and novels that have been written about Mary." Pub W

"The author's affinity for his subject lends his novel the intimacy of a memoir." N Y Times Bk R

Kenyon, F. W.—*Continued*

That Spanish woman. Dodd [1963 c1962] 342p o.p. 1970

First published 1962 in England with title: I, Eugenia

A first-person novel based on the life of Empress Eugénie, the wife of Napoleon III. A woman of charm and energy, Eugénie became a leader of fashion. "As Napoleon's wife she not only bore France a Prince Regent but proved herself an adept politician. And at eighty she found climbing Mt. Vesuvius mere child's play." Publisher's note

"The book reads easily, and should lure the reader to a continued interest in this most fascinating woman, who, for a little while, stood in the spotlight of fickle History." Best Sellers

The Kenyon Review

Gallery of modern fiction; stories from The Kenyon Review; ed. by Robie Macauley; asssociate editors: George Lanning, David Madden. Salem Press 1966 396p $6

Analyzed in Short Story Index

"Twenty-four stories of solid substance and style from 27 years of the 'Kenyon Review.' . . . Certain stories were later used as parts of novels." Booklist

Contents: Aerial ways, by B. Pasternak; The award, by R. P. Jhabvala; Distances from Berlin, by T. Cassity; The dragon skin drum, by A. Davidson; Entropy, by T. Pynchon; A few drinks with Alcock and Brown, by J. Wain; Fifty-fifty, by L. Wolf; Greenleaf, by F. O'Connor; Haboob, by V. G. Dethier; The keyhole eye, by J. S. Carter; Letters never mailed, by J. B. Hall; Message in a bottle, by N. Gordimer; One off the short list, by D. Lessing; The picknickers, by J. West; The safe place, by W. Morris; Sailing against the wind, by J. F. Powers; The short rope, by G. McKinley; A shorter history of the Irish people, by B. Corke; Two recent travelers, by E. Hardwick; Venus, Cupid, folly and time, by P. Taylor; We have seen the best of our times, by N. Potter; A wet day, by M. Lavin; What nice hands held, by W. Eastlake

Kerouac, Jack

The Dharma bums. Viking 1958 244p o.p. 1970

The story "of two young rucksack wanderers of the West Coast making an effort to find a new way of life. The quest for Dharma (roughly the equivalent of Truth) leads Japhy Ryder—poet, mountaineer, dedicated Zen Buddhist—and his freight-hopping friend on a strange odyssey." Book News

"The novel, for all its coarseness and crudity, often attains a beautiful dignity, and builds toward a moving climax in which the hero actually goes up a mountain top to meditate until he finds his Dharma." Chicago Sunday Tribune

On the road. Viking 1957 310p $3.95

"The protagonist Sal Paradise, his friend Dean Moriarty, and various male and female companions all of whom swear, drink, love, and despair with grandiose intensity spend their days and years crossing and recrossing the country in search of new sights, new romances, new adventures, new selves." Booklist

"Quite apart from its characterizations, which are given and illustrated rather than developed, the chief distinction of this novel is its sentimental emotion. Certainly, 'On the Road' is a romantic treatment of delinquency, and, as such, is of considerable interest." N Y Her Trib Books

The subterraneans. Grove 1958 111p o.p. 1970

"This novel is the story of a brief passion between Leo Percepied, a writer, and Mardou Fox, a Negro girl ten years his junior. Leo describes himself as a bum, an egomaniac, a Baudelaire, and a continual sufferer from 'beer-mares,' hangovers and dope. . . . The novel consists mainly of Leo's tortured realization of his inability to live without Mardou just at the moment when she is calmly dropping him for another man." N Y Her Trib Books

Visions of Gerard. Farrar, Straus 1963 151p illus $3.95

"The narrator Jean Duluoz, tells of his brother Gerard, who died at the age of nine when Jean was four. The French Canadian family lived in Lowell, Massachusetts." Book Rev Digest

Kersh, Gerald

The secret of the bottle

In Hitchcock, A. ed. Alfred Hitchcock presents: Stories my mother never told me p85-109

Kesey, Ken

One flew over the cuckoo's nest; a novel. Viking 1962 311p $6

"Novel about events in a mental institution, centering around a struggle for power between the head nurse and one of the men patients that leads up to a . . . climax of hate, violence and death. The story is told as if by a long-term inmate, a half-Indian." Springf'd Republican

"This is at times a boisterous, ribald book (some may object to the language), at times touching and pathetic. The characters are real. Their world, seen as sometimes foggy, sometimes painfully clear through the eyes of the narrator, is unforgettable." Library J

Sometimes a great notion. Viking 1964 628p o.p. 1970

In this novel, set in the Oregon timber country, Hank Stamper "is trying to fill a huge logging contract despite pressure to default. Desperate for help since all the loggers are on strike he asks his half-brother [Lee] to return from Yale. The frame of the story is the Oedipal-like enmity of the weak and the strong brother." Library J

Keshishian, John M.

(jt. auth.) Hay, J. Autopsy for a cosmonaut

Kessel, Joseph

The horsemen; tr. by Patrick O'Brian. Farrar, Straus 1968 469p $6.95

Original French edition published 1967

"Set in Afghanistan—the story of Uraz, the son of Tursen, Master-of-the-Horse, who takes his father's place in the savage buzkaski, a tournament of horsemen. When Uraz is defeated he hurriedly leaves the king's capitol in anticipation of his father's scorn and sets out on the most difficult road back to the Steppes. But only Tursen himself can free Uraz from his self-torment and humiliation." Bk Buyer's Guide

Kessel "has conceived a brilliant novel of epic grandeur, while including a three-track story line so subtly interwoven that its shattering impact is a shimmering, glistening delight. . . . The careful reader will delight in the intricacies of the conflicts; man against nature, in the best traditions of our literary stronghold's mountain sagas; man against self and world, with the darkest labyrinthine ways; and a father-son relationship that is searchingly beautiful in its extremities. Or again, read it for the haunting poetry of description of geographic locales and customs, making it a thing of wonder and awe, and easily the best of similar novels since they invented the National Geographic Magazine!" Best Sellers

The lion; tr. from the French by Peter Green. Knopf 1959 244p boards $4.95

First published in France 1958

"On a great game preserve in Kenya, the warden, once a great hunter, his ten-year-old daughter Patricia, Oriunga, a primitive Masai warrior, and King, the gorgeous lion the small girl loves and knows so well—these are the characters in a . . . suspenseful novel in which love and hate and savagery clash inevitably and then explode." Publisher's note

"An odd, moody novel. . . . Is this a symbolic novel, an allegory, a fantasy overladen with the atmophere of 'The Roots of Heaven.' Romain Gary's elephant story? Or is it sheer narrative? . . . In any event, this is a fascinating jungle tale that leaves one haunted by Patricia." San Francisco Chronicle

Keyes, Daniel

y Flowers for Algernon. Harcourt 1966 274p
$5.75

"A novel which consists of the poignant
journal of a mentally retarded adult, who in
the course of the story changes from an amiable, likeable dull man with a yearning to be
smart, into a genius. The book is really science
fiction in the field of psychology: scientists
operate on the brain of Charlie Gordon, I.O.
68, and raise his I.Q. to 185. He is brilliant but
miserable—he can't completely reject his old
retarded personality and he is tormented by
memories of his earlier life, when people were
cruel to him and his family rejected him. . . .
'The Algernon' of the title is the name of a
mouse who had been subjected to the first such
operation." Pub W
The author "has made a penetrating study
on the mentally retarded. . . . It will make
parents realize that a mentally-deficient child
can be helped more by sympathetic understanding than by medical science." Best Sellers

also in Asimov, I. ed. The Hugo winners
p245-73

Keyes, Frances Parkinson

Blue camellia. Messner 1957 432p illus
o.p. 1970

"In the 1880's Brent Winslow lured by the
advertisements of cheap land, moved with his
wife and small daughter, from Illinois to the
Cajun country of southwestern Louisiana.
This novel is the story of their life in a pioneer
community, of Brent's experiments in growing rice, and of the daughter, Lavinia's, growth
to womanhood." Book Rev Digest
"The setting is authentic, the dates accurate,
and the record of rice breeding factual." Huntting

Came a cavalier. Messner 1947 xxvi, 577p
illus o.p. 1970

"A long and colorful story of a reserved and
beautiful American Red Cross girl who was attached to a Base Hospital in France during the
first world war and as the wife of a French
cavalry officer, maintained her home through
the German occupation of the second war. The
picture of a Red Cross worker's experiences
is particularly interesting." Ontario Lib Rev

The chess players. Farrar, Straus 1960 533p
illus o.p. 1970

"This is a novel about Paul Morphy, one
time world chess champion. Born in New Orleans, he fell in love with a beautiful girl, followed her to Europe when she married a prince,
and during the Civil War acted as a Confederate
secret agent in France. Then the girl he had
loved was murdered by her husband and Paul's
life was empty." Bk Buyer's Guide
"There is a great deal of detail about dress,
decor and other aspects of high [New Orleans]
life." Pub W

Crescent carnival. Messner 1942 807p illus
o.p. 1970

"Long historical novel, chronicling three generations of two New Orleans families. There are
the Breckenridges—Andy, Breck, and Drew,
father, son, and grandson, and their beautiful
plantation Splendida, which eventually succumbs to the devastation of the Mississippi.
There are also three generations of Lenoirs
—Estelle, belle of the carnival in the nineties;
Marie Céleste, who lost the Breckenridge she
loved and found solace in a convent; and Stella,
carnival queen in 1940. Around these characters
are woven fifty years of New Orleans history."
Book Rev Digest

Dinner at Antoine's. Simon & Schuster 1948
422p illus $5.95

First published by Messner
"When Ruth Avery came from New York to
visit her fabulously wealthy uncle, Orson Fox-
worth, the shipping magnate, Orson arranged
a superb dinner at Antoine's world-famous
fashionable restaurant [in New Orleans]. It
was there that she first met the beautiful and
fated Odile St. Amant, victim of a strange illness. It was apparent at this first social event
that Leonce St. Amant was paying far more
attention than was proper to Odile's vivacious

younger sister. But little did any of those present at this exclusive dinner party guess that
before the night was out tragedy would strike,
engulfing them all in a whirlpool of horror
and grief." Literary Guild

The heritage. McGraw 1968 xx, 389p illus
boards $6.95

"Ireland in the 1880's with its anti-English
activities is the scene of [this] romance. . . .
It is Peter Bradford's landed inheritance in
Ireland that takes him away from Boston to a
country, situation, and courtship that challenges him with undreamed of responsibilities,
customs, and complications." Booklist
"Elements of surprise will continue to hold
the reader's interest throughout the story. An
added feature is Mrs. Keyes's account of her
travel experiences while researching and writing this novel. Her engaging narrative and a
selected bibliography are included at the end."
Library J

I, the King. McGraw 1966 351p illus maps
boards $5.95

"The main theme of this historical novel
centering around the life of Philip IV of Spain
is Philip's great desire for an heir. His wife,
Isabel, for whom he deeply cared, had miscarriage after miscarriage until one resulted in her
death. The one son that survived infancy died
in his teen years and although Philip's second
wife, Mariana of Austria, was able to
provide him with heirs, they were weak and
sickly and Philip died uncertain of the future
of the Hapsburg line." Bk Buyer's Guide

Joy Street. Messner 1950 490p illus o.p. 1970

"Emily Thayer, daughter of Beacon Hill
aristocrats, defied them to marry Roger Field,
whose law firm was too democratic for conservative Bostonians. Only Emily's grandmother approved: she gave the young couple
a house on Joy Street that was to become the
haunt of brilliant Jews, Italians, and Irish,
and to provide both tragedy and love." Retail Bookseller

Madame Castel's lodger. Farrar, Straus
1962 471p illus maps o.p. 1970

"A biographical novel about a colorful Civil
War general of Creole background, Pierre Gustave Toutant-Beauregard. . . . The story is told
as if General Beauregard, after the Civil War,
were remembering his past life, his army career
and his love for his two wives, whom he has
outlived." Pub W
"Scrupulously documented with family portraits, genealogies, maps and charts, and a bibliography." Booklist

The River Road. Messner 1945 747p o.p. 1970

"A story of the bayou country of Louisiana
whose people and traditions [the author]
knows so well . . . [and] of the people who
live along the River Road—planters, peddlers,
politicians, field hands, and poor whites. She
tells, too, the story of Belle Heloise, the great
sugar plantation owned by the d'Avery family
for generations—and of how, with the changing world of [1916 to 1941] alien elements crept
into the circle of plantation life." Huntting
"This is a well informed picture of political,
financial and social conditions prevailing [in
Louisiana] from World War I through II."
Library J

Steamboat Gothic. Messner 1952 562p
o.p. 1970

"The chronicle of a family thru three generations beginning with the romance of a
wealthy reformed professional gambler and a
well-born Southern belle. The great plantation
house on the Mississippi River in Louisiana, is
the scene of much of the novel. The time is
from Civil War days until 1930, when the beautiful house called Cindy Lou becomes a Community Center in memory of the man who made
it great." Book Rev Digest

Kielty, Bernardine

(ed.) Treasury of short stories. . . . Simon
& Schuster 1947 849p $6

Analyzed in Short Story Index
"Favorites of the past hundred years from
Turgenev to Thurber, from Balzac to Heming-
way with biographical sketches of the authors."
Title page

FICTION CATALOG
EIGHTH EDITION

Kielty, Bernardine—*Continued*

Contents: Yermolaï and the miller's wife, by I. S. Turgenev; The death of Ivan Ilyich, by L. N. Tolstoi; A day in the country, by A. P. Chekhov; Passion in the desert, by H. de Balzac; A simple heart, by G. Flaubert; Two little soldiers, by G. de Maupassant; Last lesson, by A. Daudet; Our Lady's juggler, by A. France; The steadfast tin soldier, by H. C. Andersen; Germelshausen, by F. Gerstäcker; Saint Joseph's ass, by G. Verga; A lodging for the night, by R. L. Stevenson; Quattrocentisteria, by M. Hewlett; Red-headed League, by Sir A. C. Doyle; Without benefit of clergy, by R. Kipling; Tragedy of a comic song, by L. Merrick; Money box, by W. W. Jacobs; Secret sharer, by J. Conrad; The cask of Amontillado, by E. A. Poe; Horseman in the sky, by A. Bierce; The Hilton's holiday, by S. O. Jewett; The griffin and the minor canon, by F. Stockton; Pace of youth, by S. Crane; To build a fire, by J. London; Coming-out of Maggie, by O. Henry; Altar of the dead, by H. James; Afterward, by E. Wharton; Sorrow-Acre, by I. Dinesen; The storyteller, by F. O'Connor; Old hunter, by L. O'Flaherty; Sinners, by S. O'Faoláin; The rocking-horse winner, by D. H. Lawrence; Doll's house, by K. Mansfield; Mackintosh, by W. S. Maugham; Young Archimedes, by A. Huxley; Bella Fleace gave a party, by E. Waugh; Joining Charles, by E. Bowen; Beware of the dog, by R. Dahl; The mezzotint, by M. R. James; The story of a panic, by E. M. Forster; The open window, by "Saki"; Beckoning fair one, by O. Onions; Haunted house, by V. Woolf; Adam and Eve and Pinch Me, by A. E. Coppard; Voice in the night, by W. H. Hodgson; Bird of prey, by J. Collier; I'm a fool, by S. Anderson; Some like them cold, by R. Lardner; Blood pressure, by D. Runyon; Babylon revisited, by F. S. Fitzgerald; Night club, by K. Brush; A telephone call, by D. Parker; The snows of Kilimanjaro, by E. Hemingway; The leader of the people, by J. Steinbeck; Price's always open, by J. O'Hara; The tuxedos, by J. Weidman; Act of faith, by I. Shaw; Secret life of Walter Mitty, by J. Thurber; Sacre du printemps, by L. Bemelmans; Seventy thousand Assyrians, by W. Saroyan; O'Halloran's luck, by S. V. Benét; Tom Whipple, by W. D. Edmonds; Silent snow, secret snow, by C. Aiken; Sex education, by D. Canfield; Petrified man, by E. Welty; The hound, by W. Faulkner; No door, by T. Wolfe; Saturday afternoon, by E. Caldwell; Almos' a man, by R. Wright; Old order, by K. A. Porter.

Killens, John Oliver

And then we heard the thunder. Knopf 1963 [c1962] 485p $6.95

Novel "about a Negro amphibious regiment in World War II. Solly Saunders, a New York law student, enters Fort Dix determined to be 'the best damn soldier in the Army of the United States of North America.' But the pressures of Jim Crow force upon him the role of a 'race man'—a militant battler for equality. From the red clay country of Georgia, where he is beaten by white police, to the Pacific theater where he is thrown out of a restricted Red Cross Club, Saunders is forced to make common cause with his race rather than with his army. In Australia, the hostilities that have been smouldering throughout the book finally erupt in a bloody race riot." N Y Times Bk R

"The author's earnestness and the obvious justice of his analysis and warning are particularly compelling and sobering. . . . Readers who are not easily offended by unusual frankness of language might find it worth their while to reflect on the problems American Negro soldiers faced in World War II." Best Sellers

Youngblood. Dial Press 1954 566p o.p. 1970

"'How do you live in a white man's world?' asks Joe Youngblood. 'Do you live on your knees—do you live with your shoulders bent and your hat in your hand? Or do you live like a man is supposed to live—with your head straight up?' 'Youngblood' tells how a Negro family, living in a small town in Georgia in the 1920's responded to this challenging and deeply human question." McClurg. Book News

"The characterizations are unusually vivid and true. . . . The style is rough-hewn, phrased in language that sounds like Negro speech. . . Not-withstanding the sensibility-dulling repetition of scenes of violence and brutality . . . 'Youngblood' remains an arresting novel." Best Sellers

Kim, Richard E.

The martyred; a novel. Braziller 1964 316p $4.50

Although set during the Korean War, this "novel is not about the war on the battlefield but the war in the hearts and minds of men. Specifically the story concerns a Korean minister whose life was spared when other Christian ministers, imprisoned by the Communists at the same time, were shot." Huntting

"Despite the war setting, this quest involves little action but rather the baring of profound spiritual questions and conflicts in the human soul. For the contemplative reader there is mounting tension and suspense in this essentially moving excursion by a native Korean into crises of the Christian spirit." Booklist

Kimitake, Hiraoka. See Mishima, Yukio

Kingsley, Charles

y Westward ho!

Some editions are:
Dodd (Great illustrated classics. Titan ed) $5.50 With illustrations from sixteenth century originals and from photographs of the "Westward ho!" country together with an introductory biographical sketch of the author and anecdotal captions
Dutton (Everyman's lib) $3.25 Introduction by J. A. Williamson
Scribner (Scribner Illustrated classics) $6 Pictures by N. C. Wyeth

First published 1855

"Story of adventure and sea fights with the Spaniards in the time of Queen Elizabeth. Gives an account of the Great Armada, and introduces Hawkins, Drake and other British naval heroes." N Y Pub Lib

Kipling, Rudyard

Nobel Prize in literature, 1907

The best short stories of Rudyard Kipling; ed. by Randall Jarrell. Hanover House 1961 693p $7.50

Analyzed in Short Story Index

Contains 50 stories including many of the author's stories about India under British rule as well as several animal and adventure tales

Contents: Lispeth; At the pit's mouth; A wayside comedy; The story of Muhammad Din; A bank fraud; At the end of the passage; Without benefit of clergy; Jews in Sushan; The return of Imray; The phantom 'rickshaw; Moti Guj—mutineer; The drums of the fore and aft; On Greenhow Hill; The man who would be king; Baa baa black sheep; In the rukh; A matter of fact; The disturber of traffic; "The finest story in the world"; "Brugglesmith"; The children of the Zodiac: The Maltese Cat; The miracle of Purun Bhagat; The undertakers; Kaa's hunting; The King's ankus; Red Dog; A Centurion of the Thirtieth; On the great Wall; The Winged Hats; Marklake witches; "Wireless"; A Sahib's war; As easy as A.B.C.; "They"; An habitation enforced; The village that voted the earth was flat; Regulus; The propagation of knowledge; "My son's wife"; Friendly brook; Mary Postgate; "In the interests of the brethren"; A Madonna of the trenches; Dayspring mishandled; The Janeites; The Wish House; The manner of men; Unprofessional; The eye of Allah

The complete Stalky & Co. Illus. by L. Raven-Hill. Doubleday 1930 368p illus o.p. 1970

Analyzed in Short Story Index

Contents: "Stalky"; "In ambush"; Slaves of the lamp pt 1; Unsavoury interlude; Impressionists; Moral reformers; United idolaters; Regulus; Little prep; Flag of their country; Propagation of knowledge; Satisfaction of a gentleman; Last term; Slaves of the lamp pt 2

y The light that failed. Doubleday 1936 289p $3.95

First published 1890

"Through his experience as an illustrator in the Sudan, the hero, Dick Heldar, wins both professional success and a firm friend in the

Kipling, Rudyard—*Continued*

war correspondent Torpenhow. He is in love with his foster sister Maisie, now also an artist, but Maisie is shallow and selfish and does not appreciate his devotion. Dick gradually goes blind from a sword cut received in the Sudan, working courageously against time on his painting. 'Melancholia.' Although Maisie is summoned by Torpenhow, she heartlessly leaves Dick to his fate, and he carries out his plan of dying at the front." Benét. The Reader's Encyclopedia

y Maugham's choice of Kipling's best; sixteen stories selected and with an introductory essay by W. Somerset Maugham. Doubleday 1953 xxviii, 324p $5.50

Analyzed in Short Story Index

First published 1952 in England with title: A choice of Kipling's prose

Contents: 'The finest story in the world'; The man who was; The tomb of his ancestors; At the end of the passage; 'Wireless'; On Greenhow Hill; 'Love-o'-women'; The brush-wood boy; The man who would be king; William the Conqueror; 'They'; Tods' Amendment; Mowgli's brothers; The miracle of Purun Bhagat; Without benefit of clergy; The village that voted the earth was flat

Plain tales from the hills. Doubleday 1899 302p o.p. 1970

Analyzed in Short Story Index

Contents: Lispeth; Three and — an extra; Thrown away; Miss Youghal's Sais; 'Yoked with an unbeliever'; False dawn; The rescue of Pluffles; Cupid's arrows; The three musketeers; His chance in life; Watchers of the night; The other man; Consequences; Conversion of Aurelian McGoggin; Taking of Lungtungpen; Germ destroyer; Kidnapped; Arrest of Lieutenant Golightly; In the house of Suddhoo; His wedded wife; Broken-link handicap; Beyond the pale: In error; Bank fraud: Tods' Amendment; The daughter of the regiment; In the pride of his youth; Pig; Rout of the White Hussars; The Bronckhorst divorce-case; Venus Annodomini; Bisara of Pooree; A friend's friend; Gate of the hundred sorrows; Madness of Private Ortheris; Story of Muhammad Din; On the strength of a likeness; Wressley of the foreign office; By word of mouth; To be filed for reference

Puck of Pook's Hill. Doubleday 1906 253p o.p. 1970

Analyzed in Short Story Index

Contents: Weland's sword; Young men at the manor; The knights of the joyous venture; Old men at Pevensey; A Centurion of the Thirtieth; On the great wall; The winged hats; Hal o' the draft; 'Dymchurch Flit'; The treasure and the law

Kirk, Lydia

The man on the Raffles verandah. Doubleday 1969 184p $4.95

Major Malcolm Gordon, long retired from the Intelligence Service and living in Singapore, is summoned back into service to uncover an espionage scheme

Kirkwood, James

Good times/bad times; a novel. Simon & Schuster 1968 347p $5.95

"Peter Kilburn and Jordan Legier are the twin heroes in this story of a friendship that grows mightily in a boarding prep school. . . . The story is actually worked out as a series of memoirs that Peter writes in jail. When Jordan dies of a heart attack and Mr. Hoyt [the headmaster] persuades himself that Jordan and Peter have been having an affair, he takes out after Peter for himself. . . . In desperation Peter strikes out to save himself and his fine memories of Jordan. The resultant death of Mr. Hoyt at Peter's hands is taken by society to be the brutal murder of a noble, self-sacrificing teacher by a degenerate scholar. . . . 'Good Times/Bad Times' is a major work by an important and talented young author." Best Sellers

Kirst, Hans Hellmut

Brothers in arms; tr. from the German by J. Maxwell Brownjohn. Harper [1967 c1965] 383p o.p. 1970

Original German edition published 1961. This translation first published 1965 in England

"A German officially reported killed in combat at the close of World War II suddenly makes a ghostly reappearance 16 years later in a West German town. To six members of a local veterans' group, who had been his comrades in arms, this comes as a severe shock, not merely because they supposed him to be long dead, but because the true facts surrounding the incident of his 'death'—cowardice, desertion, rape and a civilian murder—are known only to them." Pub W

"Kirst introduces a retired police officer, a wise humanitarian, who eventually uncovers the sordid events of 1945. So much for a very good whodunit, but this same detective expresses Mr. Kirst's views on modern Germany, with its smug prosperity, rising nationalism, and lack of guilt for the past. He doesn't stop even there; the whole book can be considered a plea to all mankind to eschew complacency and stupidity." Library J

Forward, Gunner Asch! Tr. from the German by Robert Kee. Little 1956 368p o.p. 1970

Sequel to: Revolt of Gunner Asch

Originally published 1954 in Germany. English edition has title: Gunner Asch goes to war

"The realistic Asch is quite satisfied with a war of watchful waiting on the Russian front but an [overzealous] officer spoils things." Retail Bookseller

"It is perhaps a bit late in the day for such a satire on the military habits of Germans to take full effect, but Herr Kirst writes with splendid gusto, and the adventures of Asch, Vierbein, Schulz and the rest of them on the Russian front are often very funny indeed. Herr Kirst writes pithily and well, and 'Gunner Asch Goes to War', in Mr. Kee's fluent idiomatic translation, is excellent entertainment." Times (London) Lit Sup

Followed by: The return of Gunner Asch

Last stop Camp 7; tr. by J. Maxwell Brownjohn. Coward-McCann 1969 319p $5.95

Original German edition published 1966. This translation published in England with title: Camp 7 last stop

The novel is set in an internment camp for former Nazis, where the responsibility for determining the fate of the prisoners brings the American commandant, Keller, and his second-in-command, a German Jewish émigré, into conflict. The former is willing to decide a man's guilt on the basis of insufficient evidence; his second-in-command argues that guilt must be substantially proved

The night of the generals; a novel; tr. from the German by J. Maxwell Brownjohn. Harper 1963 319p $5.95

Original German edition 1962

This novel concerns the hunt for the murderer of a Polish prostitute in 1942 in German-occupied Warsaw. The crime is unusual in that evidence points to one of three German generals. Two more murders of a similar type occur before the evidence becomes conclusive. (Publisher)

The author "deftly takes every opportunity for ribald and incisive mockery of militarism, Hitlerism, and high-level hypocrisy. The translation, by J. Maxwell Brownjohn, is very well done." Pub W

The officer factory; tr. by Robert Kee. Doubleday 1963 [c1962] 512p o.p. 1970

Original German edition 1960; this translation first published 1962 in England

A "novel which dissects a German officers' training school early in 1944. This outwardly stiff establishment is laxly conducted, corrupt in small and large ways, and rife with black-mail. Cadets, officers, and women civilians stationed at the post indulge in various kinds of sexual relationships. And, as the story

Kirst, Hans H.—*Continued*

starts, an officer, a good man, has been murdered. The murder investigation boils down to conflict between out-and-out Nazis and anti-Nazis, who include some officers and some cadets." Pub W

Return of Gunner Asch; tr. from the German by Robert Kee. Little 1957 310p o.p. 1970

Sequel to: Forward, Gunner Asch!

The third volume in the author's series about the adventures of a German army sergeant in World War II. The preceding volumes were: The revolt of Gunner Asch; and, Forward, Gunner Asch!

In Germany at the end of World War II, Gunner Asch and his comrades track down the two Nazi officers who bought their own safety by ordering Asch's unit to make a final doomed stand. (Publisher)

"A racy, episodic, sometimes funny but essentially grim novel." Library J

Followed by: What became of Gunner Asch

Revolt of Gunner Asch; tr. from the German by Robert Kee. Little 1955 311p $5.95

First in a series of four novels about Gunner Asch

Published in England with title: Zero eight fifteen

This is "a German novel poking fun at the more idiotic aspects of Army discipline. Set in a garrison town just before the last war, it tells of a one-man battle fought by Gunner Asch, a nice young man with a capacity for indignation, against the bullying N.C.O.'s of his company." Manchester Guardian

"A tale in which elements of drama and suspense are skillfully fused with high comedy—a tale which the author brings to a startling and altogether delightful conclusion. . . . Kirst has succeeded in distilling robust fun out of brutal realities without ever suggesting that the realities were other than brutal." Atlantic

Followed by: Forward, Gunner Asch!

Soldiers' revolt; tr. from the German by J. Maxwell Brownjohn. Harper 1966 416p o.p. 1970

Originally published 1965 in Germany

"A novel based on the attempt of German officers to assassinate Hitler on July 20, 1944. The hero of the novel, Count von Brackwede, is a fictional counterpart of a real man. But the picture is a dark one, of the Reich breakup and the efforts of some men to consolidate their power while others try to save Germany. As a matter of history the attempt failed and the conspirators were killed." Bk Buyer's Guide

"Though documentary aspects and details dominate and sometimes impede the narrative unduly, Von Brackwede and his naive brother emerge with increasing emotional impact. A story particularly likely to be relished by men for its military setting and politico-military plotting and counterplotting." Booklist

What became of Gunner Asch; tr. from the German by J. Maxwell Brownjohn. Harper 1964 275p o.p. 1970

Sequel to: Return of Gunner Asch

Original German edition published 1963 in Austria

Gunner Asch, hotel owner and mayor "has become involved in the rivalry between a Luftwaffe unit and a Bundeswehr regiment, both garrisoned in his [West German] town. The plot concerns the efforts of Asch; Captain Ahlers, an honorable Air Force officer marked for tragedy at the court-martial climax of the novel; and Grenadier Lance-Corporal Kamnitzer, a brash deflator of the military reminiscent of Asch in his youth, to protect Grenadier Martin Recht from his sadistic sergeant-major and a lieutenant of the old-style Prussian type." Library J

"Along with the overlay of fun and the satire on the pettiness and chicanery of service commanders, the story offers a shrewd and intimate view of the manners of the new German army. . . . They are all brightly displayed with wit and very real characters." Best Sellers

The wolves; tr. from the German by J. Maxwell Brownjohn. Coward-McCann 1968 447p $6.95

Original German edition, 1967; this translation published in England with title: The fox of Maulen

"A farm village in East Prussia is the setting for this wartime novel. Alfons Materna plans his act of vengeance for the death of his son by the Nazis. His plans, however, eventually attract support from the other villagers which enables him to destroy all the local Nazi wolves." Bk Buyer's Guide

"Kirst's actional narrative and its almost frantic dramatization of the readily corrupted and brutalized villagers in contrast with the few proven humanitarians incorporates bitter, satirical commentary on Germans and Germany in recent decades." Booklist

Kjelgaard, James Arthur. See Kjelgaard, Jim

Kjelgaard, Jim

y The lost wagon. Dodd 1955 305p $4

"When disaster strikes, Joe Tower knows that he must leave his Missouri farm and travel to Oregon. With his wife and six children, he starts out in a cramped and overburdened wagon. Far behind the other emigrants, a lost wagon, they make their difficult and dangerous way along the endless plains [of the Oregon Trail]. In the end the Towers not only survive, but grow in strength and mutual understanding." Huntting

Klamm, Allis McKay. See McKay, Allis

Klass, Philip. See Tenn, William

Klein, Edward

(jt. auth.) Chesnoff, R. Z. If Israel lost the war

Klinger, Henry

Essence of murder

In Klinger, H. The three cases of Shomri Shomar p305-448

Murder Off-Broadway

In Klinger, H. The three cases of Shomri Shomar p157-303

The three cases of Shomri Shomar. Trident Press 1968 448p boards $6.50

"This volume includes Wanton for Murder—in which Lieutenant Shomri Shomar [of the Tel Aviv police force] befriends the victim of a questionable accident and his young ambulance attendant. They lead Shomri into a nest of diamond smugglers. . . . [In] Murder off-Broadway a playwright is poisoned before he can write the third act of his controversial drama. Shomri travels from New York to Texas and back to Connecticut before he realizes that the only way to catch the murderer is to complete the third act himself. [In] Essence of Murder—a perfume essence stolen from a factory in Haifa causes the deaths of a petty gangster and a perfume expert in New York." Publisher's note

These stories "were originally published in paperback in the early 1960's, and were received favorably. . . . Shomar's taut adventures never let up, even though Biblical scholarship is interwoven into the structure of the trio of tales. . . . The stories can be universally appreciated by mystery fans everywhere." Christian Science Monitor

Wanton for murder

In Klinger, H. The three cases of Shomri Shomar p5-155

Knebel, Fletcher

Night of Camp David. Harper 1965 336p $5.95

"A junior Senator, one of those tapped by the dynamic President of the United States as a possible running-mate for the President's

Knebel, Fletcher—*Continued*

second-term campaign, spends hours talking politics, personalities and international relations with the President. Slowly and with horror, he realizes that the President is a dangerous paranoiac, and that very little can be done about it." Pub W

"The story is swift-moving, and the characters, though not studies in depth, seem plausible enough. There is even a certain poignancy in the unexpected nobility of the President when he donates the surprise ending. For a political thriller—which does indeed dramatize the awesome problems surrounding the office of President—this is distinctly above average." Book Week

y Seven days in May, by Fletcher Knebel and Charles W. Bailey II. Harper 1962 341p $5.95

Also available in a large type edition for $8.95
"The story, set against a . . . political Washington background, is about a military plot to take over the government. Its hero is a President of the U.S. in the 1970's, who with six men he trusts, sets out to prove the plot exists and to foil it." Pub W

"The reporter-authors, inquisitively familiar with the Washington scene, have made character and incident so satisfyingly genuine, the drama of action at the high ramparts of power is so vivid, and the odds against quietly smashing the plot are so severe, that the reader is as anxious to know the outcome as if this were a well-plotted whodunit. . . . The concern which grips the reader, beyond the adventure, is the question whether the United States Government as we know it, could survive a well-laid plot." Christian Science Monitor

Trespass. Doubleday 1969 371p $6.95

"Liz and Tim Crawford return to their elegant estate near Princeton one night to find themselves captives of a contingent of militant Negroes. . . . A story of mysterious Black Power, set in the future and involving even the President of the United States, the FBI and the Joint Chiefs of Staff." Book of the Month Club News

"The reader will keep reading, but the pace and superficial characterizations close the door on depth. Certain to be popular, possibly controversial, hopefully not prophetic, this is a necessary purchase for public libraries." Library J

Vanished. Doubleday 1968 407p $5.95

"The plot revolves around the disappearance of a prominent Washington attorney, the confidential advisor of the President of the United States. There are hints of a scandal when the director of the CIA learns that his organization is being kept off the case and it looks as though the President is trying to protect his image until after the election." Pub W

"A long novel of political intrigue that has for much of the way the pace and tension of a thriller. . . . [Mr. Knebel's] settings are designed with taste and understanding. The result, though a little heavy at the end—like so many fictions of its kind—is a satisfactory work of entertainment." New Yorker

The Zinzin Road. Doubleday 1966 443p o.p. 1970

"The subject matter of the book is contemporary West Africa. Or to be more specific, the adventures of Peace Corps Volunteer Lew Corleigh as he travels the 300 miles from St. Paul in Kalya to the village of Zinzin. . . . As a member of the Peace Corps [Lew] should not be meddling in the internal politics of another country; but he does. . . . Lincoln Beach [his friend] is charged with the attempted assassination of Prime Minister Vining. Lew is convinced that [Beach] has been framed and he is determined to speak the truth." Best Sellers

Knight, Damon

(ed.) Beyond tomorrow; ten science fiction adventures. Harper 1965 332p boards $4.95

Analyzed in Short Story Index
"An anthology of 10 outstanding writers of science fiction in this collection of stories drawn from a 20-year period, from the mid-1930's to the 1950's. He has used the simple idea of futurity to tie the collection together." Library J

Contents: **Brightside Crossing,** by A. E. Nourse; The deep range, by A. C. Clarke; Coventry, by R. A. Heinlein; The mile-long spaceship, by K. Wilhelm; The seesaw, by A. E. van Vogt; Nightfall, by I. Asimov; The million-year picnic, by R. Bradbury; Desertion, by C. D. Simak; Twilight, by D. A. Stuart; Happy ending, by H. Kuttner

(ed.) A century of great short science fiction novels. Delacorte Press distributed by Dial Press 1964 379p o.p. 1970

Analyzed in Short Story Index
Contents: Strange case of Dr Jekyll and Mr Hyde, by R. L. Stevenson (1886); The Invisible Man, by H. G. Wells (1887); The absolute at large, by K. Capek; Gulf, by R. A. Heinlein; E for effort, by T. L. Sherred; Hunter, come home, by R. McKenna

(ed.) A century of science fiction; ed. with an introduction and notes by Damon Knight. Simon & Schuster 1962 352p o.p. 1970

Analyzed in Short Story Index
A collection of 26 stories grouped under the following headings: Robots; Time travel; Space; Other worlds and people; Aliens among us; Superman; and, Marvelous inventions

Contains excerpts from the following novels: The ideal, by S. G. Weinbaum; The time machine, by H. G. Wells; Worlds of the imperium, by K. Laumer; Odd John, by O. Stapledon; Twenty thousand leagues under the sea, by J. Verne

The short stories are: Moxon's master, by A. Bierce; Reason, by I. Asimov; But who can replace a man, by B. W. Aldiss; Of time and Third Avenue, by A. Bester; Sail on! sail on, by P. J. Farmer; The business, as usual, by M. Reynolds; What's it like out there, by E. Hamilton; Sky lift, by R. A. Heinlein; The star, by A. C. Clarke; The crystal egg, by H. G. Wells; The wind people, by M. Z. Bradley; Unhuman sacrifice, by K. Maclean; What was it, by F-J. O'Brien; The first days of May, by C. Veillot; Day of succession, by T. L. Thomas; Angel's egg, by E. Pangborn; Another world, by J-H. R. Aïné; Call me Joe, by P. Anderson; [Story] From the London Times of 1904, by M. Twain; You are with it, by W. Stanton; Cease fire, by F. Herbert

(ed.) Cities of wonder. Doubleday 1966 252p o.p. 1970

Analyzed in Short Story Index
Science fiction stories concerned with cities of the future
Contents: Single combat, by R. Abernathy; Dumb waiter, by W. M. Miller, Jr; Jesting pilot, by H. Kuttner; "It's great to be back," by R. A. Heinlein; Billenium, by J. G. Ballard Okie, by J. Blish; The luckiest man in Denv, by C. M. Kornbluth; The machine stops, by E. M. Forster; The underprivileged, by B. Aldiss; By the waters of Babylon, by S. V. Benét; Forgetfulness, by D. A. Stuart

(ed.) The dark side. Doubleday 1965 241p o.p. 1970

Analyzed in Short Story Index
Contents: The black Ferris, by R. Bradbury; They, by R. A. Heinlein; Mistake inside, by J. Blish; Trouble with water, by H. L. Gold; C/o Mr Makepeace, by P. Phillips; The golem, by A. Davidson; The story of the late Mr Elvesham, by H. G. Wells; It, by T. Sturgeon; Nellthu, by A. Boucher; Casey Agonistes, by R. McKenna; Eye for iniquity, by T. L. Sherred; The man who never grew young, by F. Leiber

The dying man
In Knight, D. Three novels p151-89

Natural state
In Knight, D. Three novels p82-150

(ed.) Nebula award stories, 1965. See Nebula award stories, 1965

(ed.) One hundred years of science fiction. Simon & Schuster 1968 384p $6.50

Analyzed in Short Story Index
"Science fiction is by no means new, science fiction short stories having been published all through the 19th century, and it is gratifying to see some of the best of them represented here." Pub W

FICTION CATALOG
EIGHTH EDITION

Knight, Damon—*Continued*

Contents: With the night mail, by R. Kipling; Mr Murphy of New York, by T. McMorrow; New apples in the garden, by K. Neville; Sanity, by F. Leiber; The snapes, by J. H. Rosny Aîné; The other Celia, by T. Sturgeon; Black Charlie, by G. R. Dickson; A subway named Mobius, by A. J. Deutsch; The man who came early, by P. Anderson; The other now, by M. Leinster; Whatever happened to Corporal Cuckoo, by G. Kersh; The mindworm, by C. M. Kornbluth; Nobody bothers Gus, by A. Budrys; The ingenious patriot, by A. Bierce; The equalizer, by N. Spinrad; Splice of life, by S. Dorman; Business as usual, during alterations, by R. Williams; The man who could work miracles, by H. G. Wells; The quest for St Aquin, by A. Boucher; The nine billion names of God, by A. C. Clarke; The voices of time, by J. G. Ballard

(ed.) Orbit 1-6. See Orbit 1-6

Rule golden
In Knight, D. Three novels p7-81

Three novels. Doubleday 1967 189p (Doubleday Science fiction) o.p. 1970

Contents: Rule golden; Natural state; The dying man
"Science fiction with an unusual twist: it is satiric about modern civilization and nostalgic for the older, simpler ways. Collected from their first appearance in magazines in the 1950's." Pub W

ed.) Toward infinity; 9 science fiction tales. Simon & Schuster 1968 319p $4.95

Analyzed in Short Story Index
"This varied collection contains nine well-selected, imaginitive science-fiction tales." Booklist
Contents: The man who lost the sea, by T. Sturgeon; March hare mission, by F. McCormack; The earth men, by R. Bradbury; Who goes there, by D. A. Stuart; In hiding, by W. H. Shiras; Not final, by I. Asimov; And be merry . . . by K. MacLean; The witches of Karres, by J. H. Schmitz; Resurrection, by A. E. van Vogt

Knight, Eric

This above all. Harper 1941 473p o.p. 1970

"A story of England in the fall of 1940. The protagonist is Clive Briggs, an Englishman of the lower classes, self-educated and thoughtful. Clive has fought and fought well for England but doubts have arisen in his mind as to whether England is worth fighting for. Then he meets Prue Cathaway, daughter of well-to-do parents, and as their love affair develops she attempts to win him over to her point of view. Clive is fatally injured in an air raid but not before Prue has won her battle." Book Rev Digest
" 'This Above All' is a passionate and moving story and, although in many ways pronouncedly British, capable of rising above nationality, of talking finely in terms of human beings as well as nations." N Y Her Trib Books

Knowles, John

Indian summer. Random House 1966 242p $4.95

Without prospects after his Air Force discharge in 1946, Cleet Kinsolving is drawn back by his domineering friend to their hometown in Connecticut and to Neil Reardon's rich and powerful family. There Cleet sees the shallowness of their lives, and finally breaks away to live on his own terms. (Publisher)
"The theme of individualism is explored with great energy and charm; and the commentaries on the rich, the poor, success, failure, and politics are dipped in truth and rolled in humor." Library J

Morning in Antibes; a novel. Macmillan (N Y) 1962 186p boards $3.95

Set 'in the south of France during the French-Algerian disorders that preceded de Gaulle's coming to power in 1958. . . . The story is told by a young American who has been driven by his wife's unfaithfulness to spend a solitary season near Antibes. Here he encounters a sophisticated, highly civilized . . French family—as well as a penniless Algerian from whom he learns the meaning of moral courage." Publisher's note
"Mr. Knowles is telling us the fight for love and reality is worth making, even in so artificial a context as the Riviera." N Y Times Bk R

Phineas; six stories. Random House 1968 147p boards $4.95

Analyzed in Short Story Index
The six stories in this collection are concerned with youth and growing up. The title story, Phineas, served as a basis for the author's: A separate peace, entered separately
Contents: A turn with the sun; Summer street; The Peeping Tom; Martin the fisherman; Phineas; The reading of the will

y A separate peace; a novel. Macmillan (N Y) 1960 [c1959] 186p $4.95

Also availabe in large print edition $6.95
First published 1959 in England
"The narrator-protagonist Gene Forrester looks back 15 years to a World War II year in which he and his best friend Phineas were roommates in a New Hampshire boarding school. The element of rivalry in their friendship is dramatized by Finny's crippling fall, an event for which Gene is responsible and one that eventually leads to tragedy. Without sentimentality and with moving perceptiveness the novel deftly re-creates a personal relationship and a campus increasingly touched by the restiveness of war." Booklist

Koestler, Arthur

The age of longing. Macmillan (N Y) 1951 362p o.p. 1970

The setting is "Paris in the 1950s. His theme is one that concerns everybody alive today; an analysis of the will to resist totalitarian aggression and an appraisal of how much this will is dissipated by fear, disinterest, and hatred. The principal characters are an American girl named Hydie, who is looking for some Absolute in which to have faith, and a Russian official named Nikitin, who is Koestler's symbol of the Soviet threat to Western civilization. For a time Hydie thinks she's found the faith she's searching for in Nikitin. This is a powerful, disturbing novel that should interest all thinking people who are concerned with the overwhelming problem of our time." Literary Guild

Arrival and departure. With a new postscript by the author. Danube ed. Macmillan (N Y) [1967 c1966] 192p $5.95

First published 1943. Reissued 1967
"Psychological study of a European communist, captured and tortured by the Nazis. He escapes and seeks refuge in an unnamed city, presumably Lisbon. Here he is treated by a woman psychoanalyst, who finds that some of his childhood traumas provide the background for the man who is Peter Slavek. On the eve of his planned escape to America, Peter turns back, to live or die in Europe." Book Rev Digest

Darkness at noon. Tr. by Daphne Hardy. Macmillan (N Y) 1941 267p $6.95

"This novel, fruit of [the author's] own experiences is a tale of the imprisonment, confession and death of one of the Old Bolsheviks, a composite picture having resemblances to both Bukharin and Trotsky. The events in it follow the normal course. Rubashov, one of the last survivors of the original Central Committee of the Communist Party, is arrested, is charged with incredible crimes, denies everything, is tortured by means of deprivation of sleep, etc., confesses everything, and is shot in the back of the neck. The story ends with a young girl in whose house Rubashov has once lodged wondering whether to denounce her father to the Secret Police as a way of securing a flat for herself and her future husband." New Statesman & Nation
" 'Darkness at Noon' is, in its way, a remarkable book, a grimly fascinating interpretation of the logic of the Russian Revolution, indeed of all revolutionary dictatorships, and at the same time a tense and subtly intellectualized drama of prison psychology." Times (London) Lit Sup

245

Koestler, Arthur—*Continued*

The gladiators. Tr. by Edith Simon. With a new postscript by the author. Danube ed. Macmillan (N Y) [1967 c1966] 319p $5.95

First published 1939. Reissued 1967
"Excellent fictionalization of the events of the Slave War (73-71 B.C.), led by Spartacus. The style and method remind one of the early Feuchtwanger." New Yorker
"The gladiators in the finest stable outside Rome were beginning to resent the new spirit of sport which demanded group combat and more and more bloodshed. When seventy of them break loose in rebellion, malcontents quickly swell their ranks. The movement grows; the forces sent against it are defeated, and the intelligent young Thracian, Spartacus, suggests establishing a brotherhood of towns, a Sun State. The dilemmas which follow combine to make an exciting and ironic story at an attempt at Utopia." Huntting

Thieves in the night; chronicle of an experiment. With a new postscript by the author. Danube ed. Macmillan (N Y) [1967 c1965] 336p $5.95

First published 1946. Reissued 1967
"Depicting Palestine today, from the viewpoints of established Jews, unhappy would-be immigrants, Arabs and British officials. The mind through which the events filter is that of a young man half Jew, half English, who, before the book closes, has lost his critical semi-aloofness and become deeply involved. The novel brings to life statistics and newspaper headlines." Library J
"Without belaboring the point, the story gives an insight into the desperation and yet careful consideration that lies behind Jewish acts of terrorism in Palestine." Booklist

Kolpacoff, Victor

The prisoners of Quai Dong. New Am. Lib. 1967 214p o.p. 1970

A seventeen-year-old Vietcong suspect is being interrogated in an American military stockade in Vietnam. Kreuger, an infantry lieutenant stripped of rank because he refused to carry out his part in the war, is offered a chance to redeem himself by aiding in the interrogation. His silence passes for acceptance, and involves him in savagery, cowardice, and death. (Publisher)
"Too gruesome for many readers, but a credible account of men under stress." Library J

Komroff, Manuel

Coronet. Coward-McCann 1930 677p o.p. 1970

"An epic romance, extending from 1600 to 1919, the theme of which is the decay of aristocracy, symbolized by a jewelled coronet which passes from one generation to another of the Burin family. The novel is made up of a series of episodes beginning with the Italian renaissance. Following the passing of the artistic aristocracy represented by this period, the author presents, in Napoleon's invasion of Russia and the Moscow retreat, the downfall of military aristocracy. In the chapters entitled The ants bow low, we find Chopin dying in France, and the disintegration of Balzac. The last part of the book deals with the collapse of intellectual aristocracy, reaching its climax with the War and the Russian revolution. With the effect of anticlimax, the coronet finally passes from the hands of the last of the original Senlis family to Chicago, where it is purchased by a hog-butcher millionaire, Mallet, as a gift for his daughter." Book Rev Digest

Kops, Bernard

The dissent of Dominick Shapiro. Coward-McCann [1967 c1966] 207p o.p. 1970

First published 1966 in England
"Sixteen-year-old Dominick Shapiro wants to escape his comfortable ordinary Jewish home in Golders Green. Then, after creating a scene at a wedding and quarreling with his father, he goes to London, becomes a beatnik, and at last gets into trouble with the law, and decides to return to the 'nice' world." Bk Buyer's Guide

"The writing is witty and sympathetic, the characters, sharply drawn, the situations lively. Dominick, himself, becomes a touching and believable representative of his generation. This is a book both parents and teen-agers can enjoy." Pub W

Kornbluth, C. M.

(jt. auth.) Pohl, F. The space merchants

Kosinski, Jerzy

The painted bird. Modern Library [1970 c1965] 234p $2.95

First published 1965 by Houghton
"The wanderings of a stray child in eastern Poland in World War II. The child, dark-haired and dark-eyed, is unlike the fair-haired Polish villagers with whom he tries to take shelter. They are unspeakably cruel to him—he is the stranger, the gypsy, the 'painted bird' in their midst. Their world is one of superstition, ignorance, sadism, hunger, murder, rape." Pub W

Steps. Random House 1968 147p boards $4.95

National Book Award winner, 1968
The author studies evil and "in a series of episodes connected only by fragments of autobiography he recounts acts of violence, perversion, and macabre retribution. . . . 'Steps' is . . . [an] experimetal work subtle and structurally sophisticated, a surrealistic study of absurdity rather than of morality." Library J
"Every picturable aberration in human sexual behavior is experienced by Kosinski's protagonist either directly or vicariously. . . . [These illustrate] the author's repeated suggestion that nothing is impermissible if it brings understanding between two human beings." Best Sellers

Kundera, Milan

The joke; tr. by David Hamblyn and Oliver Stallybrass. Coward-McCann [1969 c1967] 288p boards $5.95

Original Czech edition published 1967
"When Ludvik Jahn sends his relentlessly serious sweetheart a postcard parodying party slogans—'Optimism is the opium of the people! . . . Long live Trotsky'—he learns that Marxist axioms are no laughing matter. Party vengeance is swift in coming. Ludvik is expelled from the university and, worse, from the party. Years at voluntary hard labor offer his only hope of reinstatement. Then a chance encounter with the wife of his adversary, the careerist Zemanek, presents the longed-for opportunity for revenge." Publisher's note

Kuniczak, W. S.

The Sempinski affairs. Doubleday 1969 302p $5.95

"An antiquities expert suddenly finds himself an unwilling secret agent, Oliver Hazard Shippe travels behind the Iron Curtain in search of the Pontic 'Tribunals—the official records of the trial and death of Jesus—and almost instantly is matching brain and brawn with clever killers bent on a world-shattering assassination." Am News of Bks
"Well, credible or not, the story is very well written. If any criticism can be offered in this respect, the author does tend to overwrite: the style is most vivid, the choice of figures of speech most colorful and apt." Best Sellers

The thousand hour day. Dial Press [1967 c1966] 628p $7.95

"The time of this novel is 1939; the setting, Poland. Mr. Kuniczak covers the first 1000 hours of World War II when the small, ill-equipped Polish army made a magnificent holding action before the final surrender to the attacking Germans. Against the speeding background of the war evolves the story of General Janusz Prus, a gentle man of strong character, and his influence on his government and on the men and women around him." Library J
The story "usually sustains its interest. The few flat scenes are more than overbalanced by compelling episodes. . . . There are the vivid battle scenes. . . . We also see a good deal of the countryside, with its peasants and hunters and wandering armies." Sat R

Kuznetsov, Anatoly

y Babi Yar; a documentary novel; tr. by
Jacob Guralsky; illus. by S. Brodsky. Dial
Press 1967 399p illus $5.95

A story concerning the period from 1941 to
1943 in which the Germans systematically murdered some 200,000 people, including 50,000
Jews, at the ravine on the outskirts of Kiev
known as Babi Yar. The author, who was
twelve years old at the time, based his work
on interviews, newspaper clippings, diaries and
other documents of the time. (Publisher)
"Here is a real book. And not just because
its author claims an authentic purpose for it,
nor because its pubication in Moscow last fall
was the first open recognition of the existence
of this death camp on Russian soil. . . . And
it's not real just because 'everything in this
book is the truth,' because Kuznetsov experienced most of these things himself. Not because
he was 'there' but because he is 'here,' in this
book. You feel his presence. . . . Words used
by a man of spirit are mysteriously tinctured,
and it is the spirit of a decent, loving, and
sane human being that makes this a fine book,
not the ghastly revelations of its contents nor
any clever emotional engineering." Book Week

L

La Farge, Christopher

The sudden guest. Coward-McCann 1946
250p o.p. 1970

"This novel has three aspects: it is first a
story of how a New England spinster lived
thru two violent storms, the hurricane of 1938
and the lesser storm of 1944; secondly, it is a
character study of Carrel Leckton, a typical
product of her age and environment; and finally, it is a parable for our times." Book Rev
Digest

La Farge, Oliver

The door in the wall; stories; with a foreword by William Maxwell. Houghton 1965
303p $5.50

Analyzed in Short Story Index
Contents: The creation of John Manderville;
Independent research; The senior assistant; No
Rosetta Stone; Journey in remembering; The
ancient strength; The pot and the cup; The
little stone man; The timely death of Wallace
Caswell; The real thing; Caviar remembered;
The door in the wall
These "reflect Oliver La Farge's intimate
knowledge of archeological and ethnological
techniques." Publisher's note

y Laughing Boy. Houghton 1929 302p $5.95

Pulitzer Prize. 1930
An "idyll of the Navajo country. Laughing
Boy, cunning artificer of silver and maker of
songs, loves Slim Girl who, tainted and embittered as the result of her American schooling, is trying to find her way back into the
heart of her people. The story tells how together they fared along the Trail of Beauty,
the final tragedy leaving Laughing Boy bereft
but not despairing." Cleveland

Lafayette, Mme de

The Princess of Cleves; tr. by Nancy Mitford. New Directions 1951 xxviii, 210p (New
classics ser) o.p. 1970

"First published anonymously in 1678. One of
the earliest of the French novels, it displays
unusual psychological realism unlike the pretentious fiction of its age. It is a clear study
of the 17th century 'grand passion,' the conflict between duty and love." Retail Bookseller

La Fayette, Marie Madeleine (Pioche de la
Vergne) Comtesse. See Lafayette; Mme
de

Lagerkvist, Pär
Nobel Prize in literature, 1951

Barabbas; tr. by Alan Blair; with a preface
by Lucien Maury and a letter by André Gide.
Random House 1951 180p o.p. 1970

Original Swedish edition published 1950
"Lagerkvist's dry-point style, sacrificing sensual coloring so that the lines of a spiritual
dilemma stand out more clearly, suggests the
prose in which Gide wrote his own early
philosophical novels. Barabbas never quite involves a reader in the day-to-day realities of
its hero's gaudy, gaudy, gory times. Its power
is the power of a parable, with the same timeless echo." N Y Times Bk R
"The portrayal of the influence of Christ
Jesus upon the thief who saw him crucified.
Barabbas embodies the author's religious devotion, his emphasis on the humanistic theme
and his use of symbolism." Huntting

The death of Ahasuerus; tr. from the
Swedish by Naomi Walford; drawings by
Emil Antonucci. Random House 1962 118p
illus $3.75

Original Swedish edition published 1960
Another story by Ahasuerus: The sibyl
"This is the apocryphal legend of Ahasuerus,
the Wandering Jew condemned by Christ to
homeless immortality. . . . As the novel opens,
centuries after the curse, the stranger (for
the novel names him only in its title) appears
suddenly out of a storm, seeking refuge in an
inn for medieval pilgrims to the Holy Land.
. . . Among them is Tobias, an unbeliever, who
has felt himself somehow impelled to embark
upon a pilgrimage to Jerusalem on behalf of
an unknown woman whom he had found dead
with the stigmata—the marks of the Crucifixion. Attached to Tobias is Diana, a once
beautiful woman turned promiscuous slattern,
who ridicules the idea of the pilgrimage. . . .
Ahasuerus joins them, and the three unbeliev-
ers set out . . . several days' journey behind
the other pilgrims." Time

The eternal smile, and other stories; tr. by
Alan Blair [and others]. Random House 1954
389p o.p. 1970

Partially analyzed in Short Story Index
Contents: The eternal smile; Father and I;
The adventure; A hero's death; Venerated
bones; Saviour John; Experimental world; Lift
that went down into Hell; Love and death;
The basement; Evil angel; Princess and all the
Kingdom; The hangman; Paradise; Children's
campaign; Guest of reality; Marriage feast;
God's little traveling salesman; Masquerade of
souls; Myth of mankind; Wave of Osiris

Herod and Mariamne; tr. from the Swedish by Naomi Walford. Knopf 1968 115p
$4.95

A "love-hate story that reveals the essence
of that cruel and power-mad King of the Jews,
who was his own worst enemy. Only once in
his life was Herod able to love another human being, Mariamne, the Maccabeean princess
who consented to marry him because she believed she could curb his violence and sooth
his restless spirit." Pub W

The Holy Land; tr. from the Swedish by
Naomi Walford; illus. by Emil Antonucci.
Random House 1966 85p illus $3.95

First published 1964 in Sweden
Shipmates Tobias and Giovanni continue the
journey begun in: Pilgrim at Sea. "Now old
and blind, Giovanni has been cast ashore by
the pirate skipper, and Tobias joins him. On a
bleak and desolate coast they take shelter in
the ruins of an ancient temple, where their
only companions are herdsmen—simple, kind,
ageless men. In this atmosphere they play out
their lives, each surrendering at death the precious empty locket once given Giovanni. Tobias, the eternal wanderer, pursues a god in
whose existence he cannot believe; and a holy
land which, if it be true cannot be reached. In
the end his search becomes his belief; his answer within himself." Publisher's note

Lagerkvist, Pär—*Continued*

Pilgrim at sea; tr. from the Swedish by
Naomi Walford; drawings by Emil Antonucci. Random House 1964 116p illus $3.95

Original Swedish edition, 1962
"This novel opens aboard the pirate ship in
which Tobias, passenger and pilgrim [and the
hero of The death of Ahasuerus] hopes to
reach the Holy Land. Tobias strikes up an acquaintance with Giovanni, one of the pirates
and an unfrocked priest. After a day in which
the pirates massacre the captain and passengers of a wrecked ship, Giovanni tells Tobias
the story of his passion for a woman he had
met in the confessional, his eventual disgrace
and loss of faith. The novel ends with the
pirate ship and Tobias still at sea." Book
Rev Digest
"It is the tale of a man who, though he is
without hope, cannot shake the feeling that
there is meaning beyond the cruelty and lust
and frequent stupidity of the world." Best Sellers

The sibyl; tr. by Naomi Walford. Random
House 1958 154p o.p. 1970

Companion volume to: The death of Ahasuerus
Original Swedish edition published 1956
"A man, condemned to wander forever because he denied a god's son the right to rest on
his way to crucifixion, comes to consult the
Delphic oracle about his fate. The oracle has
no answer, but a beggar directs the seeker to
an aged, outcast sibyl who replies with a
lengthy recital of her own story." Booklist

Lagerlöf, Selma

Nobel Prize in literature, 1909

Charlotte Lowenskold; tr. from the Swedish by Velma Swanston Howard. Doubleday
1927 328p o.p. 1970

A 19th century Swedish romance about
"Charlotte Löwensköld, who loved Karl Arthur
Ekenstedt, the fanatical young minister. In
her loyalty and unselfishness Charlotte took all
the blame for the quarrel between herself and
Karl Arthur, and suffered the censure of the
village in silence until Karl Arthur himself
killed her love by talking about it from the
pulpit. Then Charlotte married the rich widower Schagerström and surprisingly found happiness." Book Rev Digest

The general's ring; tr. from the Swedish by
Francesca Martin. Doubleday 1928 212p
o.p. 1970

"A ring given by Charles XII of Sweden to
one of his officers is stolen from the dead general's hand and, through three generations,
brings disaster and death to whomever possesses it, whether innocently or nefariously."
Cleveland

also in Costain, T. B. ed. Stories to remember v 1 p 1-64

The story of Gösta Berling. Heinman 1959
393p boards $6

Translated from Swedish by Pauline Bancroft Flach and W. H. Hilton-Brown
"It relates the adventures of the impulsive
and temperamental young hero, whose magnetic personality inevitably draws people, particularly women, to him, and whose turbulent
passions just as inevitably involve him and
them in misfortune. Eventually he marries the
Countess Elizabeth, whose husband, Hendrik
Dohna, has divorced her, and through Elizabeth's influence and his own efforts enters
upon a life that more nearly approximates his
own ideals." Benét. The Reader's Encyclopedia

Lamb, Harold

The curved saber; the adventures of Khlit
the Cossack. Doubleday 1964 568p o.p. 1970

"Although Khlit is brave and rugged, the
Cossack leaders have told him that he is too
old to march with his fellows in the army of
the Ukraine. The shrewd old soldier does not
retire; he continues to seek adventure, but now
he rides alone. . . . [This book covers nine tales
of his] exploits ranging from fierce battle to
the chivalrous rescue of fair ladies." Publisher's
note
"Told in the somber, romantic tradition, the
tales project the proud wanderer's heroic deeds
against a tapestrylike setting of sixteenth-century Asia." Booklist

Theodora and the Emperor; the drama of
Justinian. Doubleday 1952 336p o.p. 1970

"Beginning with the appearance in Constantinople about 500 A.D. of eighteen year old Peter Sabbatius, a barbarian peasant from Macedonia, full details of life in this Eastern capital
of the Roman Empire are given down to the
deaths of Justinian and Theodora and the end
of the Ancient World." Library J
"Mr. Lamb's book brings vividly before us
the background and mores of the epoch." Atlantic

Lambert, Derek

Angels in the snow. Coward-McCann 1969
447p $6.95

Through this "story move three major characters, a young British diplomat on his first
mission who becomes involved with an attractive Russian girl, his language teacher; an
American CIA agent, experienced, blasé in the
main but occasionally touched by buried emotions; and a British defector—shades of Philby,
Burgess, and Maclean—who still harbors a
dream of revisiting his homeland." Library
"The theme is sad, and the picture is grimly
significant, but all in all this is a jolly novel,
and long enough to take up the slack of a week
of winter nights." New Yorker

La Motte Fouque, F. H. K. de

Undine; ed. by W. Walker Chambers.
Rinehart 1959 97p $2.65

First published by H. Mitford, 1932
The story is "one of the most beautiful of
modern imitations of the primitive folktale.
Based on a legend from Paracelsus. A water-
nymph, by marrying a mortal gains a soul, but
with it all the pains and penalties that are the
lot of mortality." Baker's Best

Lampedusa, Giuseppe di

The Leopard; tr. from the Italian by Archibald Colquhoun. Pantheon Bks. 1960 319p
o.p. 1970

Originally published posthumously in Italy
1958
Set in Italy in the last half of the 19th century, this novel is based on the life of the author's great grandfather, Don Fabrizio, Prince
of Salina. The "Leopard" of the title, he was a
tolerant despot who ruled over a large domain
in Sicily. The story traces the effect upon Don
Fabrizio of the crumbling of this feudal domain
after Garibaldi's overthrow of the Bourbon
monarchy in Naples. (Publisher)
"Don Fabrizio is a major fictional character
creation. Equally vivid are the evocation of the
author's home soil and the wit with which
Novelist Lampedusa can describe the single-
minded gluttony of hungry rustics or the lethal
chagrin of a jilted woman. . . . But Lampedusa's subtlest effect is to write prose that
seems to be aged in marble and encrusted with
the patina of antiquity. Like a statue or a ruin,
the book congeals a moment of time past and
makes it timeless." Time

Two stories and a memory; tr. from the
Italian by Archibald Colquhoun; with an introduction by E. M. Forster. Pantheon Bks.
1962 189p illus o.p. 1970

Original Italian edition 1961
"Contains three pieces of varying character:
the first and most important, an autobiographical memoir, describes the places which influenced the author's childhood profoundly
and directly inspired his writings; the second,
a story, concerns the unfortunate love of a
Greek scholar for a mermaid; and the third,
the opening chapter of an uncompleted novel,
deals with newly rich Sicilians of 1900 in the
persons of the rapacious Ibba family." Booklist

Lancaster, Bruce

y The big knives; with a historical epilogue by Edward P. Hamilton. Little 1964 371p boards $5.95

"An Atlantic Monthly Press book"
In this novel set during the American Revolution, "Markham Cape was trying to get back from New Orleans to Boston in 1778 when he met George Rogers Clark, who was winning Illinois from the British and the Indians with a couple of hundred fighting men and not much else." Bk Buyer's Guide
"Lively action, vivid characterization, and sound background blend in a posthumous tale by a skilled writer of historical fiction. . . . A stirring yet dignified addition to fictionalized Americana." Booklist

Blind journey. Little 1953 303p $5.95

"History is incidental to mystery in this tale of Revolutionary War days in which Benjamin Franklin's confidential agent, Lieutenant Ward Gratwick, intrusted with important government documents, sails on a French ship transporting gold and supplies to Washington's army. Ward experiences several narrow escapes aboard ship, but lands near Yorktown, delivers his messages, and takes part in the campaign which ends with Cornwallis' surrender." Booklist

Guns of Burgoyne. Stokes 1939 424p map o.p. 1970

Burgoyne's campaign in the American wilderness is the background for an exciting story of Kurt Ahrens, a young Hessian in command of some of Burgoyne's guns
"The book is important for its portrait of 'Gentleman Johnny' Burgoyne and for its account of the part played by the 'mercenaries' from the Rhine, many of whom settled in America and became the founders of staunch, American families." Baldwin

y Night march. Little 1958 341p maps $5.95

This story about the Civil War in the winter of 1863-64 follows the careers of two cavalry captains, Kirk Stedman and his friend Jake Pitler from Virginia's Rappahannock to far-off Nashville. Captured in the skirmishes which marked the failure of the raid on Richmond, Kirk and Jake are thrown into Libby Prison. The nightmarish scenes of prison life are succeeded by their escape, and then by the chronicle of their long march south and west, far behind enemy lines. (Publisher)
"Students of the period may question this or that minor detail, and at points the writer is not entirely convincing in his motivations. Nevertheless he is a superior storyteller, who can make his people and his chapters advance at a fine clip; his book has vigor and an overall conviction." Sat R

No bugles tonight. Little 1948 325p $5.95

"Picture of the Civil war in the South, especially in Tennessee, during the critical period of 1862 and 1863. The hero is a dashing Northern officer, a secret agent, and the heroine is a beautiful Southern widow, who aids the Union." Book Rev Digest

y Roll Shenandoah. Little 1956 316p maps $5.95

It was July, 1864. In the Shenandoah Valley of Virginia there would shortly begin a struggle which would give the advantage in the Civil War to either side. As seen through the eyes of Ellery Starr, a war correspondent, this is the story of how the Union troops under the leadership of General Philip Sheridan won that advantage. (Publisher)
"It is the drama of Phil Sheridan, 'The destroyer with a system,' that dominates the novel. Mr. Lancaster is at his best in the fluid blaze of action that helped make our history what it is." N Y Times Bk R

y The secret road. Little 1952 259p o.p. 1970

"Historical novel about the Revolutionary war. It deals with the activities of General Washington's secret service on and around Long Island Sound in the year 1780." Book Rev Digest
The author's "pictures of Townsend and Andre—real men—are careful and convincing, and the finest things in the book. He is not so interested in his fictional characters. . . . But the book has value because it brings authentic history to the impatient reader who will never take it a slower way." Sat R

Land, Myrick

Quicksand. Harper 1969 217p boards $4.95

"A Joan Kahn-Harper Novel of suspense"
"Fred Donley, a staff writer for a national magazine, had written an article on Congressman Spencer Grayson which might provoke the Congressman to sue the magazine. The story was ready to go; the front cover featuring it was already printed. Then Donley, among others, began to worry about some of the facts he'd collected. The article referred to a Mrs. Harold Burns, member of a national group called Housewives, Inc.; an odd bank account; a disappearance; a midwestern businessman; some stocks . . . and Donley wound up in more trouble than the Congressman." Am News of Bks

Lane, Rose Wilder

y Let the hurricane roar

Some editions are:
McKay $3.95
Watts, F. $7.95 Large type edition. A Keith Jennison book
First published by Longmans
"A short and graphic story of early days in Dakota in which two young people, Caroline and Charles, living in a dug-out, meet the stern realities of life—crop failure, fierce winter storms, and loneliness of separation—with a steadfastness and gallantry that has come to seem typical of pioneer life. As is fitting, the story is told with simplicity and is without sentimentality." Booklist

Langelaan, George

The fly
In Hitchcock, A. ed. Alfred Hitchcock presents: Stories for late at night p225-55

Langley, Adria Locke

A lion is in the streets; a novel. McGraw 1945 482p (Whittlesey House publications) o.p. 1970

"The story of Hank Martin, illiterate boy from the swamplands with a genius for oratory and a passion for power—who becomes Governor Hank Martin—and of his wife, Verity, who watches his ambition outgrow his principles." Huntting
"It is both an intensely readable tale and a social document for it reveals how mass ignorance and legalized injustice becomes grist for the mill of the clever demogogue." N Y Her Trib Books

Lanning, George

Green corn moon. Viking 1968 250p boards $5.95

The author "is writing about a nice couple (not so young as they might be, mid-thirties) on the verge of matrimony, and the problems that beset them in the month beforehand (August, the month of the green-corn moon). Those problems range all the way from the predictable ones involved in fixing up an old house, to Henry's fantasy-life in his new role as part of a ghost-writing team replacing a best selling lady novelist of the Emilie Loring school, now dead, and quixotic goings-on among the members of the local Episcopal church, divided into two implacably warring camps." Pub W

Lardner, Ring

The best short stories of Ring Lardner. Scribner 1957 346p $4.50

Analyzed in Short Story Index
"The publisher states that this replaces the earlier volume 'Round up.' It contains 24 stories from this earlier collection, plus 'Champion.'" Booklist

Lardner, Ring—*Continued*

Contents: The Maysville minstrel; I can't breathe; Haircut; Alibi Ike; Liberty Hall; Zone of quiet; Mr Frisbie; Hurry Kane; Champion; A day with Conrad Green; Old folks' Christmas; Harmony; The love nest; Ex Parte; The golden honeymoon; Horseshoes; There are smiles; Anniversary

Haircut, and other stories. Scribner 1962 190p $3.50

Analyzed in Short Story Index
Contents: Haircut; I can't breathe; Alibi Ike; Zone of quiet; Champion; A day with Conrad Green; The love nest; The golden honeymoon; Horseshoes; Some like them cold

You know me, Al; a busher's letters. Scribner 1960 218p $4.50

Experiences of a professional baseball player told in his humorously illiterate letters to a "pal"

La Roche, Mazo de. See De La Roche, Mazo

Laski, Audrey

The dominant fifth. Norton 1969 192p $4.95

"The Burney Quartet, after playing together for eighteen years, are not simply a string quartet, but a kind of family. Then suddenly their solidarity, their deep rapport, is threatened. For Stewart Gillis, the viola player, finds that he has less than a year to live." Publisher's note

"Undeniably well put together—chamber work fashion—'The Dominant Fifth' has all the niceties and unities and technicalities of string quartet music, but none of its passion." Pub W

Lasswell, Mary

High time; with frontispiece by George Price. Houghton 1947 174p front $3.95

Sequel to: Suds in your eye
"The trio of hearty old ladies from 'Suds in your eye' engage in an all out war effort wherein they have a hilarious . . . time with warboarders, straighten out some love tangles and organize the Four Freedoms Bar and Social Club." Literary Guild
Followed by: One on the house

Let's go for broke; illus. by George Price. Houghton 1962 276p illus $3.95

Sequel to: Tooner Schooner
"The strangely assorted quartet who figured in earlier Lasswell novels reappears after several quiet and relatively affluent years when a startlingly large tax bill and a distaste for the encroaching city strike simultaneously. Mrs. Feeley, Mrs. Rasmussen, Miss Tinkham, and Old-Timer fall in love with a dilapidated Victorian dwelling, and soon after taking possession add to their number a middle-aged Mexican widow in distress and a trio of ingenious young men who appreciate Mrs. Rasmussen's cooking. Mrs. Feeley's malapropisms Miss Tinkham's inventiveness, and Old-Timer's mechanical genius. How this offbeat household with a phenomenal thirst for beer contrives to do more than make ends meet makes a tale as warmhearted and laughable as its predecessors." Booklist

One on the house; with illus. by George Price. Houghton 1949 263p illus $4.95

Sequel to: High time
"The three beer-drinking friends—Mrs. Feeley, Mrs Rasmussen, and Miss Tinkham—who have figured in the author's earlier books spend some time in New York, and finally reach Newark practically broke. They take over a bankrupt barroom while the proprietor is in the hospital, and make so much money for him that there is enough left to finance their own return to California." Book Rev Digest
Followed by: Wait for the wagon

Suds in your eye; with illus. by George Price. Houghton [1959 c1942] 183p illus $3.50

Reprint of the title first published 1942, reset in a new format
Mrs. Feeley had inherited her husband's junk yard, and when financial and domestic afflictions struck her friends she was able to make room for them by putting up partitions, supplemented by secondhand velvet curtains, in

her barnlike one-room house. The three old girls liked their beer; Mrs. Rasmussen, who did the cooking, allotted a generous slice of the budget to beer, in cases. Miss Tinkham, a former music teacher of excessive refinement, sold the flowers Mrs. Feeley grew among her junk, to sailors in taverns. In their leisure time the three rowdies attended a Spanish class and connived at a romance for their teacher." Booklist
Followed by: High time

Tooner Schooner; with illus. by George Price. Houghton 1953 218p illus o.p. 1970

Sequel to: Wait for the wagon
"The further adventures of that hilarious trio, Mrs. Rasmussen, Mrs. Feeley and Miss Tinkham—still fond of their beer, competent cooks and skillful at intrigue. . . . This time, after creating a motel out of five old buses, and acting as crew of a chartered ex-tuna schooner, they secretly, with the best of good will aid the captain to unravel his extremely tangled love affairs." Library J
Followed by: Let's go for broke

Wait for the wagon; with illus. by George Price. Houghton 1951 185p illus $2.75

Sequel to: One on the house
The "unique trio of likable harridans—Mrs. Feeley (unrefined), Miss Tinkham (semi-genteel) and Mrs. Rasmussen (marvelous cook)—take a transcontinental motor trip to California. On the way they meet Dave, a pleasant young truck driver; Miss Uremia De Brie, an ecdysiast; and Dr. Freemartin, a psychiatrist of sorts who also dabbles in narcotics. Good rowdy Americana." Library J
Followed by: Tooner Schooner

Lathen, Emma

Come to dust. Simon & Schuster 1968 251p boards $4.95

"An Inner sanctum mystery"
John Putnam Thatcher, the formidable vice-president of Sloan Guaranty Trust "is torn, grudgingly, from his Wall Street eyrie to search for a stolen $50,000 bearer bond and to track down the puzzling Elliot Patterson, model suburban husband, father and thief." Publisher's note

Death shall overcome. Macmillan (N Y) 1966 190p boards $3.95

"A Cock Robin mystery"
"When a wealthy broker is murdered, and a candidate for the stock exchange is shot at, John Putnam Thatcher finds himself joining civil rights picket lines in pursuit of a blue-chip murderer and the exposure of some slippery under-the-counter hi-jinks." McClurg. Book News
This "attempt to integrate the New York Stock Exchange leads to an unexpectedly hilarious murder story." Chicago

Murder against the grain. Macmillan (N Y) 1967 184p boards $4.50

"A Cock Robin mystery"
"The Russian-American Trade Treaty, an important step toward ending the Cold War, was suddenly imperiled when $985,000 was stolen from the Sloan Guaranty Trust. State officials, Russian V.I.P.'s and others all put pressure on John Putnam Thatcher, boss of the Sloan to get that money back—and in a hurry." Bk Buyer's Guide

Murder makes the wheels go 'round. Macmillan (N Y) 1966 183p boards $3.95

When John Putnam Thatcher, "a New York banker, goes to Detroit to weigh the possibilities of underwriting Michigan Motors' new stock issue, he finds that Jensen, who has just finished a jail term for price-fixing, is demanding reinstatement and making threats to the man who betrayed him. But it is Jensen who is murdered." Bk Buyer's Guide
It is "witty, literate, complicated." Library J

Murder to go. Simon & Schuster 1969 256p $4.95

"An Inner sanctum mystery"
"One of the most entertaining Lathen mysteries yet, featuring as usual John Putnam Thatcher of the Sloan Guaranty Trust. The

Lathen, Emma—*Continued*

Sloan has, unwisely, Thatcher believes, extended 12 million dollars credit to a franchise food service called Chicken Tonight, which delivers some 25 varieties of chicken ready for home consumption. All seems to be going well, however, until, at one blow, some 200 customers throughout the Northeast are laid low with food poisoning. . . . The Public Health Service steps in, with the police, but it's not until Thatcher puts his mind on the problem that the real plotter is found." Pub W

A stitch in time. Macmillan (N Y) 1968 185p boards $4.50

"A Cock Robin mystery"
John Putnam Thatcher, bank vice-president "has problems in settling the estate of the late Pemberton Freebody because Atlantic Mutual Insurance says Freebody was a suicide, and therefore refuses to pay the $100,000 policy on his life to Hanover University. The university takes the case to court, and the trial of the century begins when the company calls Dr. Wendell Martin of Southport Memorial Hospital to the stand." Library J
"A nice puzzle in a most interesting setting—and Miss Lathen's witty, beautifully-controlled writing is a particular pleasure." N Y Times Bk R

When in Greece. Simon & Schuster 1969 256p boards $4.95

"An Inner sanctum mystery"
Another of the author's novels concerning Wall Street's Sloan Guaranty Trust, whose thirty-million-dollar investment in Greece is threatened by a military junta. Ken Nicolls, the company's representative, disappears, as do several others who are sent to resolve the situation but find themselves caught up in adventurous political intrigues of the country
The climax "is both amusing and quite exciting. The confrontation between dramatic Greeks and stuffy but shrewd Wall Streeters is a sight to behold." Pub W

Laumer, Keith

The long twilight. Putnam [1969] 222p $4.95

Originally published in a shorter version as 'And now they wake' in 'Galaxy' magazine." Booklist
"When an experimental power station apparently creates a totally destructive storm, a century-imprisoned man and a Civil War veteran set out for the power station. They have met and fought before, but now the two, born ages ago on another planet, must join forces to save Earth." Bk Buyer's Guide

Nine by Laumer. Doubleday 1967 222p (Doubleday Science fiction) $3.95

Analyzed in Short Story Index
Short stories included as: Hybrid; End as a hero; The walls; Dinochrome; Placement test; Doorstep; The long remembered thunder; Cocoon; A trip to the city

Retief and the warlords. Doubleday 1968 188p (Doubleday Science fiction) $4.50

"An action-packed, humor-filled adventure set in the twenty-seventh century features James Retief, the extraordinary diplomat called in to negotiate with the alien Haterakans who are implementing plans for raising humans for food." Booklist

Laurence, Margaret

A bird in the house; stories. Knopf 1970 207p $5.95

Contents: The sound of the singing; To set our house in order; Mask of the bear; A bird in the house; The loons; Horses of the night; The half-husky; Jericho's brick battlements
"Excellent job of portraying small-town Canadian life and a girl growing into womanhood in a closely-knit family. Each of the short stories that make up the book deal with a stage in the life of Vanessa MacLeod during the depression years. All of the characterizations are beautifully developed with no overwriting." Pub W

The fire-dwellers. Knopf 1969 308p $5.95

This novel tells the story of Stacey MacAindra, who appears in the author's A jest of God. At thirty-nine, Stacey is "Everywoman, Married, at the stage when she is making a last desperate attempt to find something more in life than she has yet had. She drinks a little too much, worries about her weight, makes frantic efforts to talk to her husband, wonders about an affair, has one brief happy experience with a much younger man—and somehow along the way she grows up and accepts the fact that her life is what it is." Pub W
"This book contains flaws enough to sink half a dozen books by lesser novelists. It survives because of the vitality of its central character. . . . It has to be a tribute to Margaret Laurence's talent that we get caught up in Stacey's experience, find her needs and her weaknesses and her curiously innocent infidelities charming and troubling, and in the end learn to care about her and come to believe that what she thinks and feels and tries to do matters." Canadian Forum

A jest of God. Knopf 1966 240p $4.95

"Rachel Mackensie is a provincial spinster schoolteacher trapped between a shallow mother and young children from whom she can expect no more than enforced attention. This novel is the story of her release through baffling pain and abandoned joyousness, in which her knowledge of herself as a woman capable of using the thwarted sexual energies of her nature provides her quite unexpectedly with the strength to take her first steps toward self-liberation." Am News of Bks
"Mrs. Laurence is not writing of a typical woman but of an individual whose life patterns are common to many, and she does so with great insight and poetic emotion. Of necessity, the telling involves a certain explicitness which may offend some women to whom the actions discussed are natural enough but who do not like to read about them. Many others will find it a moving story of distinction." Library J

The stone angel. Knopf 1964 308p $4.95

"Hagar Shipley is proud and independent, and now, at ninety, is suffering the infirmities of age. Through her memories, the reader comes to know her intimately—as a proud young girl in a Canadian prairie town; as a farmer's wife; as a woman separated from her husband and supporting her child; as a dominating mother; and finally as an old woman." Huntting
As Hagar Shipley "daydreams and chatters and lurches through the novel, she traces one of the most convincing—and the most touching —portraits of an unregenerate sinner declining into senility." Time

The tomorrow-tamer; stories. Knopf 1964 [c1963] 236p $4.95

Analyzed in Short Story Index
First published 1963 in England
"A collection of short stories with the central theme of West Africa today." Pub W
Contents: The Drummer of all the world; The perfume sea; The merchant of heaven; The tomorrow-tamer; The rain child; Godman's master; A fetish for love; The pure diamond man; The voices of Adamo; A gourdful of glory

Lauritzen, Jonreed

The cross and the sword. Doubleday 1965 275p o.p. 1970

"Eighteenth-century California is now the setting for another story-biography related to California history. . . . Two personalities dominate the book, Father Junipero Serra and General Juan Bautista de Anza, each engaged in conquest of California for Spain, but one dedicated to military achievement, the other to spiritual victories. Inevitably these goals are at cross-purposes particularly where the fate of the Indians is concerned. In recapitulating Father Serra's establishment of a mission system, this more quiet than dramatic popular presentation adds a significant note of religious interest to a regional piece of fictional Americana." Booklist

Lavin, Mary
In the middle of the fields, and other stories. Macmillan (N Y) [1969 c1967] 215p $4.95

First published 1967 in England

Contents: In the middle of the fields; The lucky pair; Heart of gold; The cuckoo-spit; One summer; The mock auction

"The six stories gathered here are like genre painting whose setting is the rural Ireland which Miss Lavin knows so well. She writes, as Faulkner said a writer should, of 'the old verities and truths of the heart, the old universal truths lacking which any story is ephemeral and doomed.'" Library J

Lawrence, D. H.
Aaron's rod. Seltzer, T. 1922 347p o.p. 1970

"More inchoate than most of Lawrence's novels, it is on the standing subject, the chaos of impulses and incoherent aspirations in the break-up of established moral standards—life in a state of revolution with no terminus in sight. The miner, Aaron Sisson, with his passion for music, who after various adventures wanders off to Italy, is evidently Lawrence himself. There is some vivid character-drawing, and, life in Florence is charmingly pictured." Baker's Best

The complete short stories. Viking 1961 3v (853p) o.p. 1970

"Compass book edition"

First copyright 1922

Contents: v 1 A modern lover; The old Adam; Her turn; Strike-pay; The witch à la mode; New Eve and old Adam; The Prussian officer; The thorn in the flesh; Daughters of the vicar; A fragment of stained glass; The shades of spring; Second best; The shadow in the rose garden; Goose fair; The white stocking; A sick collier; The Christening v2 Odour of chrysanthemums; England, my England; Tickets, please; The blind man; Monkey nuts; Wintry peacock; You touched me; Samson and Delilah; The primrose path; The horse-dealer's daughter; Fannie and Annie; The princess; Two blue birds; Sun; The woman who rode away; Smile v3 The border line; Jimmy and the desperate woman; The last laugh; In love; Glad ghosts; None of that; The man who loved islands; The overtone; The lovely lady; Rawdon's roof; The rocking-horse winner; Mother and daughter; The blue moccasins; Things

The fox

In Neider, C. ed. Short novels of the masters p580-643

Lady Chatterley's lover; with an introduction by Mark Schorer. Modern Lib. 1959 376p $2.95

First published 1928

A novel "presenting the author's mystical theories of sex in the story of Constance, or Connie, the wife of an English aristocrat who runs away with her gamekeeper. Her husband, Sir Clifford, is a physical and emotional cripple. The gamekeeper, Mellors, is a forthright, individualistic man, uncontaminated by industrial society. Because of the frank language and detailed descriptions of love-making, the book was banned in England and the U.S. as obscene. After historic court cases the ban was lifted in the U.S. in 1959 and in England in 1960." Benét. The Reader's Encyclopedia

The plumed serpent <Quetzalcoatl>. Introduction by William York Tindall. Knopf 445p $5.95

First published 1926

"A remarkable attempt to penetrate to the essential spirit of modern Mexico as it reveals itself to a lovely world-weary Irishwoman resident there. The Plumed Serpent is the English name of one of the old Aztec gods, Quetzalcoatl, and the action of the story is based upon a semi-mystical, semi-political movement to revive the cult of the ancient deities. The strange philosophy of the author, the legends interspersed, the rich sensuousness of the style aid in holding the interest to the end of a long volume." Cleveland

The rainbow

Some editions are
Modern Lib. $2.95
Viking $6

First published, 1915

A chronicle of three generations of the Brangwen family, farmers and craftsmen of Nottinghamshire in the nineteenth and early twentieth centuries. It is a study in basic human relations, particularly the sexual aspects of marriage and love

Followed by: Women in love

Sons and lovers

Some editions are
Modern Lib. $2.95 With an introduction by Alfred Kazin
Viking (The Viking Critical lib) lib. bdg. $4.75 Text, background, and criticism edited by Julian Moynahan

First published 1913

"An intense and realistic story in which the relationship of mother and son is the predominating theme. There are two other women in Paul Morel's life; Miriam, highly sensitive and spiritual, who appeals only to his higher nature; and Clara, a woman of fire and passion, who draws him with the lure of the senses. Neither satisfies him; and neither can wean him from devotion to his mother." Book Rev Digest

"This is not merely a story of English cottage life—there is in it something of that universality, that flowering of basic human emotions among very simple folk, that distinguishes some of the Russian stories of peasant life." Ind

The white peacock. Southern Ill. Univ. Press 1966 386p (Crosscurrents: modern fiction) $6.95

First published 1911

"A story of rural England, its characters being farmers and sons of farmers, and its scenes all enacted in the midst of crops and harvests, woods and country lanes. Everywhere we come in close contact with the life of the open, free out-of-doors; everywhere we get the scent of the soil. The tragedy of a rabbit mangled by the steel teeth of a trap, a nest of field-mice dug up and crushed remorselessly, one by one; the sordid wretchedness of a hovel swarming with dirty, quarrelling, half-clad children, mismanaged by a slatternly, overworked drudge of a woman who occasionally relieves her feelings by hitting them over the head with a battered saucepan—such scenes as these are done with a relentless skill that makes them actually hurt as you read them." Bookman's Manual

The woman who rode away, and other stories. Knopf 1928 307p o.p. 1970

Analyzed in Short Story Index

"The theme of most of these short stories is the sexual or conjugal relations of men and women and the intense inner drama that arises from their attraction or repulsion." Book Rev Digest

Contents: Two blue birds; Sun; The woman who rode away; Smile; The border line; Jimmy and the desperate woman; The last laugh; In love; The man who loved islands; Glad ghosts; None of that

Women in love

Some editions are:
Modern Lib. $2.95
Viking $5.75

Sequel to: The rainbow

First published 1920

"This sums up the author's mystical theories of sex, still tentative . . . obscure . . . and by no means stated in a way to conciliate criticism. There are three women . . . and two men of opposite natures, one of whom, almost the author's direct mouthpiece, craves something 'beyond love, beyond any emotional relationship.'" Baker's Best

Lawrence, David Herbert. See Lawrence, D. H.

Lawrence, Hilda
Composition for four hands

In Hitchcock, A. ed. Alfred Hitchcock presents: My favorites in suspense p130-227

Laxalt, Robert

A man in the wheatfield. Harper 1964 178p o.p. 1970

"A short allegorical novel about the strange, lone American in a remote community of Italians in the Southwest whose fascination with rattlesnakes obsesses the local priest." Am News of Bks

The story probes "deeply into the nature of evil, man's reaction to it and man's growing consciousness of himself in relation to it. . . . Because of two incidents one more violent and outspoken than the other, this is a novel for mature readers. But it is a story for everyman, one not lightly put aside nor soon forgotten. It could be called a parable concealing and revealing fear and prejudice which corrupt innocence and separate brothers. Emotionally, this is an intense story." Best Sellers

Laxness, Halldór

Nobel Prize in literature, 1955

Independent people; an epic; tr. from the Icelandic by J. A. Thompson. Knopf 1946 470p o.p. 1970

A story of contemporary Iceland which tells of Bjartur, the crabbed, obstinate sheep raiser, who has bought his own land at last, and is going to hold it against all odds. The valley he names Summerhouses is cursed by an old spell, and gales, snow, ice and semi-starvation are his lot

"The story is told with compassion for the people although the tone is often bitterly ironic." Booklist

Paradise reclaimed; tr. by Magnus Magnusson. Crowell 1962 253p o.p. 1970

First published 1960 in Iceland

The author's "hero, a small farmer named Steinar Steinsson, is persuaded by a Mormon missionary in Iceland to make the long pilgrimage to the land of the Latter-Day Saints. In the pattern of many American immigrants, he changes his name, to Stone P. Stanford, and eventually brings the rest of his family to settle here. At the end we see him revisiting Iceland gazing at the ruins of his farm and wondering whether paradise might not be found in Iceland as much, or as little, as in Utah." Atlantic

World light (Heimsljós); tr. from the Icelandic by Magnus Magnusson. Univ. of Wis. Press 1969 521p (The Nordic translation ser) $7.95

Original 4-volume Icelandic edition, 1937-1940

The novel "is based loosely on the biography of Magnus Hjaltason Magnusson (1873-1916), a mediocre poet even in the folk tradition, but endowed with a deep yearning for a better life than that of a stumblebum in a remote Icelandic fishing village. Magnus, here Olaf Karason, was trapped by a society he did not understand; his life ends as an archetype of the antihero of the 20th Century. Here in psychological insight and character portrayal Laxness reaches the height of his creative power." Library J

Lea, Tom

The brave bulls; a novel. Little 1949 270p illus $5.95

Title page painting and decorative drawings by the author

"The action of this novel about bullfighters takes place in Mexico. The central figure is Luis Bello, a famous fighter. Luis' past life is reviewed in passing, but the focus is on one special fight. There for the first time Luis knows fear and shows it; but when the final moment comes he and his younger brother are conquerors. The author, who is a painter, was born in El Paso, and saw his first bull fight at the age of eight." Book Rev Digest

"Read as a straight story, this is a vivid, intense, colorful narrative, with its technical details impressively accurate. It is bullfighting from the inside, the way it looks to the people who make it a profession, and not even Ernest Hemingway at his best has ever done a better job of getting the whole thing on paper, including the lingo." N Y Times Bk R

The wonderful country; a novel; with drawings by the author. Little 1952 387p illus $6.95

The author "tells of the many people who helped build the frontier town of Puerto in Texas during 1880. He writes of Major Colton and his wife Ellen; of the Texas Rangers; the Negro troops; the railroad promoter; the newspapermen; the Mexicans and Indians." Huntting

"It may be that this is a man's book chiefly. There is a love story, but it is no more than suggested—a concession, perhaps, to tradition in story telling. But there is marvelous action throughout. . . . What it amounts to, really, is an extraordinarily well written costume-piece of 'Western' in essence, but far and away past what one has come to think of as a 'Western.'" San Francisco Chronicle

Leacock, Stephen

Happy stories just to laugh at. Dodd 1943 240p o.p. 1970

Analyzed in Short Story Index

Contents: Mr McCoy sails for Fiji; Pawn to King's Four; Impervious to women; Jones's enchanted castle; Mr Alcron improves himself; Clouds that rolled by; Angel Pond, lure of the north; Cooking for victory; Good news! A new party; Life of Lea and Perrins; Morning off; Mr Plumter, B.A., revisits the old shop; Allegory island; Damon and Pythias, barristers, solicitors, etc; Boom times; Mariposa moves on

Leasor, James

Passport for a pilgrim. Doubleday [1969 c1968] 208p $4.95

First published 1968 in England

Dr Jason Love is sent "to a medical conference in Damascus where he also hopes to find information about Clarissa Head, the daughter of a patient in Somerset who was killed in a car accident there. McGillivray of M.I. 6 also has his man Parkington working on the disappearance of neurosurgical experts in the same area. Inadvertently Love and Parkington find themselves working together toward a wild climax in the Monastery of the Sacred Flame at Maloula." Library J

Leblanc, Maurice

The confessions of Arsène Lupin; tr. by Joachim Neugroschel. Walker & Co. 1967 222p o.p. 1970

Analyzed in Short Story Index

Originally published 1913 in France. This is a new translation

"These nine short stories tell of the adventures of Arsene Lupin, a sophisticated French crook who will often help Inspector Ganimard of the Paris Police to solve an especially baffling crime." Bk Buyer's Guide

Contents: The flashes of sunlight; The wedding ring; The sign of the shadow; The infernal trap; The red silk scarf; Death on the prowl; Edith of the Swan-neck; The straw: The marriage of Arsène Lupin

Extraordinary adventures of Arsène Lupin, gentleman burglar; tr. from the French by George Morehead. Donohue 1910 308p o.p. 1970

Analyzed in Short Story Index

The first story about Arsène Lupin appeared in 1907 in French

"Arsène is a super-criminal, with all the resources of modern civilization at his disposal, who plays the part of a Robin Hood, preying on plutocratic society. Eventually he turns over a new leaf and becomes head of the detective service." Baker's Best

Le Carré, John

Call for the dead

In Le Carré, J. The incongruous spy v 1

The incongruous spy; two novels of suspense. Walker & Co. [1964] 2v o.p. 1970

Contents: Call for the dead; A murder of quality, first published in England 1961 and 1962 respectively

Le Carré, John—*Continued*

In "Call for the dead," George Smiley, an incongruous spy, conducts a duel of wits with a devilish former pupil. In "A murder of quality," Smiley hunts down a ruthless, clever killer. (Publisher)

The looking glass war. Coward-McCann 1965 320p $4.95

A "portrayal of a team of third-rate British agents, living on dreams of war-time glory and itching to get 'operational' again. . . . A poor Anglicized Pole is put over the border into East Germany as a spy. He is caught and the same British agents who groomed him so lovingly for the job sacrifice him." Pub W

The author's "new story concentrates its attention not so much in intrigues in East Germany as on backbiting and petty rivalry within various British intelligence agencies—and bureaucratic madness in London is necessarily less exciting to read about than secret operations behind the Iron Curtain. Le Carré admirers will nevertheless find the same deft touches and tight plot construction they enjoyed in the earlier novel, and the implications this time—if British intelligence workers are really as inept as most of these characters—are even more chilling." Book of the Month Club News

A murder of quality

In Le Carré, J. The incongruous spy v2

A small town in Germany

Some editions are:
Coward-McCann $6.95
Lanewood Press $7.95 Large type edition complete and unabridged
First published 1968
"The scene is Bonn, a small provincial town elevated by the cold war to the artificial status of a capital city. The protagonists are British diplomats, their wives, and aspiring German politicians. The time is the recent future. While the Foreign Office is locked in a last desperate battle to enter the Common market, while the new Germany is being carried away on a rising tide of student-bourgeois nationalism, an aging Second Secretary has vanished from the British Embassy. His name is Leo Harting. . . . And he has taken with him, apparently, official files whose disclosure could ruin Britain's chances at the negotiating table. Alan Turner, a tough investigator from London, is sent to find him." Publisher's note

"The plot is ingeniously constructed with ever-mounting suspense and it is related with the deftness of a writer who possesses an enviable command of description and narration." Best Sellers

The spy who came in from the cold

Some editions are:
Coward-McCann boards $4.95
Watts, F. $8.95 Large type edition. A Keith Jennison book
First published 1963 in England
In this spy novel "Mundt, of the East German Abteilung, had just killed off the last effective agent British Alec Leamas had behind the Iron Curtain. So the British had Leamas apparently become a defector 'to trap Mundt and destroy him.'" Bk Buyer's Guide

"A topnotch spy story, up-to-the-minute and coldly realistic. This was the third of this author's novels to be published in this country, and the best yet." Pub W

Leckie, Robert

Ordained. Doubleday 1969 493p $6.95

"The novel is basically the story of Robert Emmet Cullen and his . . . journey from a north Jersey seminary [via a small poor New Jersey parish, the World War II Pacific war theater, and a fund-raising assignment] to the high altar of the Cathedral as a prothonotary apostolic." Best Sellers

Le Clézio, J. M. G.

The flood; tr. from the French by Peter Greene. Atheneum Pubs. 1968 300p $5.95

"François Besson, a 27-year-old former teacher, sees, or hallucinates, an unknown girl riding by on a motorbike and from that moment 'sees death everywhere.' The unnamed city is Nice, . . . but actually it is the city of dread. . . . In that dying and dead city, emblematic of the world's death by fire and ice, Besson undertakes his voyage to the end of night—a pilgrimage, not toward salvation, but damnation." Newsweek

In this novel "psychedelic images of horror and of vast cosmic animation alternate with conventional pieces of narrative and dialogue, everything dotted with bits of black humor. . . . The feat of pushing us into a schizophrenic world and keeping our nose in the filth of life for 300 pages is, after all, a linguistic accomplishment. Doubtless this is the main reason why Le Clézio is so special." Sat R

Terra amata; tr. from the French by Barbara Bray. Atheneum Pubs. 1969 217p $5.95

Original French edition 1967
Episodes portray the anti-hero, Chancelade, as "a young boy killing potato bugs and playing games, moving on to his first experience of love and his first encounter with death; then growing up, marrying, becoming a father, beginning to question and to challenge the meaning of it all, seeing himself reflected and continued in his son; finally growing old and dying." Pub W

"While presented in the guise of psychological analysis and illustration, [this novel's] basic appeal is sentimental. . . . [Terra Amata] is all paradox from beginning to end—the structuralism of Lévi-Strauss linked to the existentialism of Sartre and the absurdity so dear to the authors of the nouveau roman." Atlantic

Lederer, William J.

y The ugly American [by] William J. Lederer and Eugene Burdick. Norton 1958 285p boards $4.95

Analyzed in Short Story Index
"In this series of related stories, the authors condemn both our policies and our diplomatic personnel in Southeastern Asia." Cincinnati

Contents: Lucky, Lucky Lou #1; Lucky, Lucky Lou #2; Nine friends; Everybody loves Joe Bing; Confidential and personal; Employment opportunities abroad; The girl who got recruited; The ambassador and the working press; Everyone has ears; The ragtime kid; The iron of war; The lessons of war; What would you do if you were President; How to buy an American junior grade; The six-foot swami from Savannah; Captain Boning, USN; The ugly American; The ugly American and the ugly Sarkhanese; The bent backs of Chang 'Dong; Senator, Sir; The sum of tiny things

Lee, C. Y.

Flower drum song. Farrar, Straus 1957 244p o.p. 1970

A "novel with a life-with-father story. The setting is San Francisco's Chinatown, and most of the characters are members of a Chinese household ruled by a wealthy, old-fashioned father, who despairs of keeping his sons to the old Chinese traditions." Pub W

"A first novel that is always fascinating, and by turns amusing and pathetic—a novel written with grace and decorum in the even, unimpassioned narrative style that is characteristic of classical Chinese fiction." Chicago Sunday Tribune

Lee, Harper

y To kill a mockingbird

Some editions are:
Lippincott $4.95
Watts, F. $9.95 Large type edition complete and unabridged. A Keith Jennison book
Pulitzer Prize 1961
First published 1960
In this Southern novel "eight-year-old Jean Louise, nicknamed Scout, tells about growing up as the daughter of a widowed lawyer. Atticus Finch, in the small town of Maycomb, Alabama during the 1930's. She and her older brother Jem happily occupy themselves with resisting 'progressive education,' bedeviling the neighbors, and stalking the local bogeyman—until their father's courageous defense of a Negro falsely accused of rape introduces them to the problems of race prejudice and brings adult injustice and violence into their childhood world." Booklist

Lee, Harper—*Continued*

"A first novel of such rare excellence that it will no doubt make a great many readers slow down to relish the more fully its simple distinction. . . . The style is bright and straightforward; the unaffected young narrator uses adult language to render the matter she deals with, but the point of view is cunningly restricted to that of a perceptive, independent child, who doesn't always understand fully what's happening, but who conveys completely, by implication, the weight and burden of the story. There is wit, grace, and skill in the telling." Chicago Sunday Tribune

Lee, Manfred Bennington. See Queen, Ellery

Leggett, John

Who took the gold away. Random House 1969 468p $6.95

This novel "moves from New Haven to Newport to Cambridge, and the story which unfolds before it is of a deep and complex friendship between two men, Pierce Jay and Benjamin Moseley. They meet at Yale in 1938 as freshmen. . . . Their friendship is founded on their separate strengths and failings rather than on a common bond, although for more than twenty years, through their loves, marriages and business endeavors there is a mutual admiration between them, a wish to serve each other's ambitions; but also there is envy, and even a will to destroy. . . . In the climactic scene, when the differences between them and their changed world can no longer be avoided, the two men confront each other with a savagery which the friendship cannot survive." Publisher's note

Lehmann, Rosamond

The ballad and the source. Harcourt 1945 250p $4.50

"A long psychological novel in which a woman's character is revealed and the story of her past pieced together as a precocious and romance-loving little girl works it all out. The gradual growth and reluctant disillusionment of the child are also brought out as the story advances." Wis Lib Bul

"Told with the skill and the sensitivity that have marked Miss Lehmann's writings, this is a novel out of the ordinary, for the author has created a fictional character that holds the attention in spite of the reader's lack of sympathy for her." Literary Guild

Dusty answer. Harcourt 375p $3

A reissue of the title first published 1927 by Holt

"The story of an English girl, an only child, whose playmates are the children next door. The story follows the group from childhood to early maturity. As they grow up the three boys fall in love with Judith, each in his fashion, but she wants only the middle one, Roddy, whom she idealizes out of all semblance to his real self. Her disillusionment is sudden, jarring. A college friendship . . . ends in much the same way. And then death takes from Judith the proffered security of marriage to Martin, the youngest of the boys—so that to all her eager questionings life gives a 'dusty answer.'" Book Rev Digest

Invitation to the waltz. Harcourt 1932 309p $3.50

"The heroine of this study of youth's tragicomedies is a girl awakening, on the first page, to her seventeenth birthday with a much-anticipated dance just one week away. Most of the book is occupied with the preparations for that important event, with the evening itself, and the emotions it roused in Olivia's young heart." Book Rev Digest

"A thoroughly charming book—slight, but full of sensitive observation and humor." Forum

Leiber, Fritz

Gonna roll the bones

In Nebula award stories, three p89-120

Leinster, Murray

Exploration team

In Asimov, I. ed. The Hugo winners p95-142

Le May, Alan

The unforgiven. Harper 1957 245p o.p. 1970

Texas territory of the 1870's is the setting for this story. "Rachel Zachary's three brothers and her mother had long protected her from the knowledge that she was a foundling, quite possibly an Indian as spiteful people said. Now, at last, the secret came out as the Kiowas attacked 'to take back their own.'" Retail Bookseller

L'Engle, Madeleine

The love letters. Farrar, Straus 1966 365p boards $5.75

A "counterpoint tale of two young women, three centuries apart in time, tormented by their experience of love, each needing to understand love in its deepest sense for her salvation. One is Mariana, long-ago Portuguese nun, won from her vow and soon deserted by a French soldier. The other is Charlotte Napier whose disintegrating marriage, built on an emotionally insecure childhood, has sent her in flight to Beja, Portugal. Learning about Mariana, lingering over her published letters, and pondering her fate, Charlotte comes to understand what love demands of her. Strictly a woman's book, one that gently skims the surface of emotional situations and profundities." Booklist

Lenski, Branko

(ed.) Death of a simple giant, and other modern Yugoslav stories. Vanguard 1965 306p $5.95

Analyzed in Short Story Index

Contents: The story of a bridge, by I. Andrić; Miracle at Olovo, by I. Andrić; Neighbors, by I. Andrić; Hodorlahomor the Great, by M. Krleža; The love of Marcel Faber-Fabriczy for Miss Laura Warronigg, by M. Krleža; The birdman, by P. Voranc; Luck, by C. Kosmač; Death of a simple giant, by C. Kosmač; The shepherdess, by M. Lalić; An awkward companion, by B. Ćopić; The hands, by R. Marinković; Ashes, by R. Marinković; The insect collector, by I. Dončević; Mr Pink's soliloquey, by V. Desnica; The tale of the friar with the green beard, by V. Desnica; The lovers, by M. Bulatović

Lermontov, Mikhail Yurevich

A hero of our own times; tr. from the Russian by Eden and Cedar Paul; with an introduction by Maurice Bowra. Oxford 1958 284p (The World's classics) $3

First published in 1839; variant English translations published in 1854 with title: A hero of our time; in 1912 with title: The heart of a Russian

Setting is in the Caucasus and the episodes take place in the isolated mountain fortresses and garrison towns. "The novel portrays the vices of the modern Russian of rank, fashion, and adventure, and his utter selfishness, and want of principle and conscience. The story takes the form of a series of tales, of which the libertine Petchorin, and his unhappy victims, mostly confiding women, are the subject. Lermontof was a great admirer of Byron; and the fascinating Petchorin, the rascal of the stories, with his mysterious attractiveness, strongly resembles Don Juan. . . . Many people claimed that Petchorin was a portrait; but the author distinctly states that he is not the portrait of any person, but personifies the vices of the whole generation. The author does not set himself up as a reformer, his idea being simply to denounce evil." Keller's Reader's Digest of Books

Le Sage, Alain René

Adventures of Gil Blas of Santillane. Dutton 2v (Everyman's lib) o.p. 1970

"The chief English translation is that based on Smollett's, 1749, and still called after him.

Le Sage, Alain R.—*Continued*

though freely revised and much improved by B. H. Malkin, whose text is followed in this edition"

"Both the form of this masterpiece of picaresque romance and the characters and incidents were borrowed from Spain. It portrays all sides of life and all classes of people, in a series of changing scenes, incident to the hero's adventurous career as he rises stage by stage from the condition of valet to that of confidant of the prime minister of Spain. A 'comedy in a hundred acts,' it has been justly called, the humour being too good-natured and tolerant to be described as satire." Baker's Best

Leskov, Nikolai

The enchanted wanderer

In Leskov, N. Selected tales p51-211

Selected tales; tr. by David Magarshack. With an introduction by V. S. Pritchett. Farrar, Straus 1961 300p $5

Analyzed in Short Story Index
Contents: Lady Macbeth of the Mtsensk District; The enchanted wanderer; The left-handed craftsman; The sentry; The white eagle

"The stories vary considerably in length, one 'The enchanted wanderer,' being over 150 pages long. They represent the author's skill in several genres: the picaresque tale, the allegory, and the ghost story. A strong sense of the supernatural permeates all five stories." Booklist

Leslie, Doris

The Prime Minister's wife. Doubleday 1961 [c1960] 319p o.p. 1970

First published in England 1960
A biographical "novel about a British milliner, Mary Anne Evans, who became the wife of Disraeli [the Prime Minister]. In her first steps upward in Society, the beautiful Mary Anne pleases her relatives by marrying the wealthy Wyndham Lewis. Later, however, she meets and comes to love the elegant, dramatic 'Dizzy.'" Huntting

"This book is accurate historical writing, as far as history is involved. But primarily, it is a popularly written novel, picturing the Prime Minister's wife as she might have been." Library J

Leslie, Josephine A. C. See Dick, R. A.

Lesser, Milton. See Marlowe, Stephen

Lessing, Doris

African stories. Simon & Schuster 1965 636p boards $7.95

Analyzed in Short Story Index
"This book includes every story written by Doris Lessing about Africa: all of her first collection, 'This Was the Old Chief's Country' (unavailable in America); the four long tales about Africa from 'Five' (also unavailable); the African stories from 'The Habit of Loving' and 'A Man and Two Women'; and four stories never before collected." Publisher's note

Contents: The black Madonna; The trinket box; The pig; Traitors; The old Chief Mshlanga; A sunrise on the veld; No witchcraft for sale; The second hut; The nuisance; The De Wets come to Kloof Grange; Little Tembi; Old John's place; "Leopard" George; Winter in July; A home for the highland cattle; Eldorado; The antheap; Hunger; The words he said; Lucy Grange; A mild attack of locusts; Flavours of exile; Getting off the altitude; A road to the big city; Flight; Plants and girls; The sun between their feet; A letter from home; The new man; The story of two dogs

Children of violence v 1-5. Simon & Schuster 1964-1969 5v v 1 $7.50, v2 $6.95, v3-4 o.p. 1970, v5 $7.50

A five novel saga of the troubled journey of self-discovery of Martha Quest, rebellious middle-class daughter of English colonists in South Africa. The final episode deals with her life in postwar London

Contents: v 1: Martha Quest, first published 1952 in England; v2: A proper marriage, first published 1954 in England; v3: A ripple from the storm, first published 1958 in England; v4: Landlocked; v5: The four-gated city

The four-gated city

In Lessing, D. Children of violence v5

The golden notebook. Simon & Schuster 1962 567p $5.95

In this novel "the literary device used is the keeping of five notebooks, journals of major parts of her life, by the main character, pictured as an English novelist who has been a convinced Communist but is now disillusioned by the Party. She is also quite disillusioned by her life of 'free love,' which has brought her no enduring attachment." Pub W

"A valuable treatise on the art of writing is threaded through this novel of a British writer's unsparing analysis of herself and her inability to write, of her political beliefs, and of the relationships of men and women, which she sees as the real revolution of our times. Complex in form, the book is for mature, thoughtful readers." Booklist

Landlocked

In Lessing, D. Children of violence v4

A man and two women; stories. Simon & Schuster 1963 316p boards $5

Analyzed in Short Story Index
Contents: One off the short lift; The story of two dogs; The sun between their feet; A woman on a roof; How I finally lost my heart; A man and two women; A room; England versus England; Two potters; Between men; A letter from home; Our friend Judith; Each other; Homage for Isaac Babel; Outside the ministry; Dialogue; Notes for a case history; The new man; To room nineteen

Martha Quest

In Lessing, D. Children of violence v 1

A proper marriage

In Lessing, D. Children of violence v2

A ripple from the storm

In Lessing, D. Children of violence v3

Letton, Francis

(jt. auth.) Letton, J. The young Elizabeth

Letton, Jennette

Allegra's child. Macrae Smith Co. 1969 216p $4.50

"Maggie, young wife of Hank Farber, has developed the unfortunate habit of drinking until she blacks out. Her condition seems connected with her inability to have a child and also with her longing for her childhood home and the uncle with whom she has a compulsive rapport. Nothing will do, when Maggie is released from her latest detention, but that Hank take her to Medford [to exorcise her fears]. . . . In the dilapidated old Medford house, Maggie becomes disillusioned with her worthless, alcoholic uncle and worried over by her austere aunt, who leaves the house every night for her duty as night nurse at the local hospital; both Maggie and Boy [the dog] frightened by the cold blue mist that pervades the upper floors of the house. A satisfying Gothic." Pub W

The young Elizabeth [by] Jennette and Francis Letton. Harper 1953 277p o.p. 1970

A novel which deals with Elizabeth's presence in the home of Katherine Parr and her new husband, Thomas Seymour, soon after the death of Henry VIII and the romantic attachment between the girl and Seymour." Retail Bookseller

Levin, Ira

A kiss before dying. Simon & Schuster 1953 244p boards $4.95

"An Inner sanctum mystery"
"The story of a man very much on the make and completely immoral in the way he makes it, including diabolical murders." Book News

Levin, Ira—*Continued*

"The book is a succession of solid and quite legitimate surprises, the suspense is admirably sustained, the detail is thorough and convincing, and the writing is considerably above the level usually associated with fictional crime and passion." New Yorker

y Rosemary's baby; a novel. Random House 1967 245p boards $4.95

"Ignoring the warnings of an old friend who cautions them against a move they are considering. Rosemary and Guy Woodhouse rent an apartment in the Bramford, an old plush apartment building in Manhattan, [which] had been the scene of a distressing number of unholy practices ranging from witchcraft to cannibalism to suicide. . . . A strange couple in a nearby apartment, Mr. and Mrs. George Castevet, introduce themselves to Rosemary and Guy; gradually they retain an inexplicable hold on Rosemary's husband. Rosemary becomes pregnant under strange dream-like circumstances . . . [and] becomes a suspecting but practically helpless victim of the Castevets." Best Sellers

"It may be inappropriate to compare Mr. Levin with Shirley Jackson, but the veneer of normality with hideous evil forces busy just beneath the surface is reminiscent of her work. . . . Mr. Levin suspends disbelief so effectively that the unwary reader may well be converted to belief in the supernatural." Library J

Levin, Meyer

Compulsion. Simon & Schuster 1956 495p o.p. 1970

A novel suggested by the Leopold-Loeb murder case, using different names. Leopold and Loeb were brilliant, immensely wealthy eighteen-year-old university graduates from Chicago who together kidnapped and murdered a little boy and then tried to collect ransom. Meyer Levin, in retelling the story of their crime as a novel, has tried to discover the true psychology behind it. (Publisher)

"Well and powerfully written, but the case remains one of the most repulsive on record." Pub W

Eva. Simon & Schuster 1959 311p o.p. 1970

"A compelling World War II novel focuses on Eva Korngold, a young Jewish woman who effects an escape from occupied Poland by assuming the identity of Katya, a Ukrainian peasant girl. Her jobs and her friendships in Austria, her disclosure as a Jewess, experiences in a German concentration camp, and her escape from the Auschwitz death march in the final days of the war are eloquently and convincingly described. Horror and suffering are not glossed over but Eva's struggle to preserve her personal identity lies at the heart of the story and endows it with hope." Booklist

My father's house. Viking 1947 192p o.p. 1970

"A boatload of 'illegals' successfully land in Palestine, among them the boy David expecting a family reunion, for when the Germans herded the family into the square at Cracow and David escaped, didn't his father say to meet him in Palestine? In spite of the poignancy of the boy's lonely and unrealized search the story is not a sad one and gives an optimistic picture of social and economic life in the Jewish settlements." Library J

The old bunch. Viking 1937 964p o.p. 1970

This novel "tells the story of a group of Jewish children growing up in Chicago." McClurg. Book News

Levy, Barbara

The missing Matisse. Doubleday 1969 255p $4.95

"Jacqueline Perrault [comes] home . . . after the death of Uncle Edward to the lovely house on the Côte d'Azur she has inherited from him. But she must also face the disturbing story of the forged paintings found in the boathouse. Jacqueline's determination to vindicate her uncle has a stormy course that takes her to Corsica where she finds she doesn't know who is with her and who is against." Library J

Lewis, C. S.

y Out of the silent planet. Macmillan (N Y) 1943 174p $4.95

Also available in large print edition $6.95

First published in England 1938

"A philologist, kidnapped by a physicist and a promoter is taken via space-ship from England to Malacandra (Mars). There he escapes and goes on the run. Philological, philosophical, social and religious overtones, plus human-interest detail on the Malacandrians make this a credible and stimulating 'tour de force.'" Library J

Followed by: Perelandra

y Perelandra; a novel. Macmillan (N Y) [1968 c1944] 222p $4.95

Sequel to: Out of the silent planet
A reissue of the title first published 1944

"Continues the planetary journeying of Ransom, the English visitor to Malacandra (Mars). . . . He is ordered to Perelandra (Venus) by the supreme being and finds there a paradise threatened by the villainous scientist Weston, who becomes the devil incarnate. There are some pleasantly imaginative descriptions of physical appearances and properties, but the development of theological and ethical ideas definitely predominates." Booklist

Followed by: That hideous strength

That hideous strength; a modern fairy-tale for grown-ups. Macmillan (N Y) 1946 459p $5.95

"Concluding the trilogy begun in 'Out of the silent planet' and 'Perelandra.'" Booklist

"A satirical tale in which Ransom and Weston of the author's earlier stories again represent the struggle between good and evil, this time on Earth, in a college community. Mark Studdock learns the error of his attempts to play faculty politics, and his wife discovers the footlessness of modern theories of love and life." Washington, D.C. Pub Lib

Till we have faces; a myth retold. Harcourt 1957 [c1956] 313p illus $5.75

First published in England 1956

"Introducing his own version of the myth of Psyche and Cupid the author weaves it into a fantasy in which he gives expression to some of his persisting ideas on the forces at work in the soul of man. Orual, queen of a fictional kingdom of the Near East in ancient times, tells the story." Booklist

"The religious allegory is plain to read. In Mr. Lewis's sensitive hands the ancient myth retains its fascination, while being endowed with new meanings, new depths, new terrors." Sat R

Lewis, Clive Staples. See Lewis, C. S.

Lewis, Gogo

(jt. ed.) Manley, S. ed. Shapes of the supernatural

Lewis, Robert

Michel, Michel; a novel. Simon & Schuster 1967 735p $7.50

"An interesting, emotion-charged and highly controversial novel . . . which has its basis in several actual cases, has to do with the protracted custody battle over a Jewish child whose Austrian-born parents died in the Nazi holocaust and who was rescued by a French Catholic woman and, finally, in defiance of canon law, baptized as a Catholic. A surviving Jewish relative, now in Israel, has managed to trace the boy, who is seven when the story opens. Thus begins a harrowing tale of Michel, racked and torn as his case passes through the French courts and becomes a 'cause célèbre.' Michel is awarded to his Jewish relatives but spirited away by Roman Catholic adherents, winding up in the Basque country of Spain where his sad little fate is finally decided. Michel is a pitiable pawn, his Catholic foster mother a fascinatingly repellent character, stubborn, possessive, 'loving' the boy in her own warped way." Pub W

Lewis, Robert—*Continued*

"An honest and researched exposure of traditional and modern anti-Semitism in the Church. . . . Lewis follows step by step the court proceedings, settings, plots and counterplots of real life. . . . This is a profound, soul-searching and moving book. Long and repetitious, it yet fascinates the reader with its unfolding vision of power in high places and in the human heart." America

Lewis, Sinclair

Nobel Prize in literature, 1930

Ann Vickers. Doubleday 1933 562p o.p. 1970

"Ann Vickers is of the host of young women who came out of college in the years just before the war, eager to have a part in the work of the world, somewhat self-consciously hopeful of doing something to make it a better place. Like too many others she finds it hard to make the adjustment between her desire to count as an individual and the insistent demand of her emotional needs as a woman." Ontario Lib Rev

y Arrowsmith. Harcourt 1925 448p $2.95

Pulitzer Prize, 1926
The author "has drawn a full-length figure of a physician, a born seeker and experimentalist. He follows Martin Arrowsmith from medical school thru experiences as general country practitioner, as health officer and clinician, as fighter of the plague on a West Indian island and finally as director of a medical institute." Book Rev Digest
"One does not gallop through 'Arrowsmith.' It is absolutely an interesting story, but one goes slowly to the end, with no temptation to turn a few pages and come to some more dialogue. It is an effective and interesting novel, judged by the standards of mere writing. Beyond this, it is deeply understanding and unflinchingly honest." Boston Transcript

y Babbitt. Harcourt 1949 401p (Harbrace Modern classics) $2.95

First published 1922
"Satire on American middle-class life in a good-sized city. George F. Babbitt is a successful real estate man, a regular fellow, booster, rotarian, Elk, Republican, who uses all the current catchwords, molds his opinions on those of the Zenith Advocate-Times and believes in 'a sound business administration in Washington.'" Book Rev Digest
"The story, though intensely American in its setting and the language in which it is told, is a drama of something universal—the tyranny of conventions." Times (London) Lit Sup

Cass Timberlane; a novel of husbands and wives. Random House 1945 390p o.p. 1970

"Cass Timberlane at forty-one was sober, thoughtful, and respected by the Minnesota town in which he was a judge. This story of Cass's second marriage to a girl in her early twenties is punctuated by stories of the married lives of many of his friends." Book Rev Digest

y Dodsworth; a novel. Harcourt 1929 377p o.p. 1970

Samuel Dodsworth, a rich automobile manufacturer in the Midwestern city of Zenith, retires and goes to Europe with his frivolous wife, Fran. Fran becomes involved in several love affairs with European adventurers, and Dodsworth, lonely and unhappy, meets Edith Cortwright, an American widow, who teaches him to appreciate the traditions of Europe. He eventually leaves his wife for the more mature companionship of Edith." Benét. The Reader's Encyclopedia
"Of more interest, even, than Dodsworth's story, is the commentary on the differences between European and American civilization, conveyed on the thread of his travels." Book Rev Digest

Elmer Gantry. Harcourt 1927 432p o.p. 1970

This novel "deals with a brazen ex-football player who enters the ministry and, through his half-plagiarized sermons, his physical attractiveness, and his unerring instinct for promotion, becomes a successful evangelist and later the leader of a large Middle Western church. Carefully researched, the novel was realistic enough to shock both the faithful and unfaithful." Benét. The Reader's Encyclopedia

"This novel is, in my opinion, the greatest, most vital and most penetrating study of religious hypocrisy that has been written since Voltaire." Literary Rev

It can't happen here; a novel. Doubleday 1935 458p o.p. 1970

This novel "presents a fancied fascist dictatorship in the U.S., set up by Berzelius Windrip, a New England demagogue who is elected to the presidency. Doremus Jessup, a Vermont editor, fights Windrip, is arrested, escapes, and joins an underground movement in Canada headed by Walt Trowbridge, Windrip's opponent in the election." Benét. The Reader's Encyclopedia

Kingsblood royal. Random House 1947 348p o.p. 1970

"Neil Kingsblood, a promising young banker back from the war, uncovers, while tracing his mother's family tree, an ancestor who was a full-blooded Negro. Neil then starts out to discover for himself what it is to be a Negro in a world of prejudice." Cleveland

y Main Street. Harcourt 1950 451p (Harbrace Modern classics) $2.95

First published 1920
"Carol, college-bred girl with a liking for 'high-brow' drama and a hobby for town planning, marries a small-town doctor and tries to uplift the natives of Gopher Prairie, Minnesota." Cleveland
"A remarkable book. A novel, yes, but so unusual as not to fall easily into a class. There is practically no plot, yet the book is absorbing. It is so much like life itself, so extraordinarily real. These people are actual folk, and there was never better dialogue written than their revealing talk." N Y Times Bk R

Lewisohn, Ludwig

The island within; with an introduction by Stanley F. Chyet. Jewish Pub. 1968 266p (The JPS Library of contemporary American Jewish fiction) $4.50

First published 1928 by Harper
"This saga of a Jewish family begins in 1840, in Poland, where Reb Mendel ben Reb Jizchock taught children their Hebrew letters. Mendel's grandson, Jacob, emigrated to New York in the 70's and here the family rises to affluence. Jacob's son Arthur, graduates at Columbia, studies medicine, marries a Gentile and becomes a practising psychiatrist. But he cannot become an Americanized Jew and fuse himself with our civilization. He cannot disown his heritage and tradition. Finally, after an intense struggle within himself Arthur leaves his Christian-born wife and his children and goes on a Jewish mission to the Balkans." Book Rev Digest

Lieber, Maxim

(ed.) Great stories of all nations; one hundred sixty complete short stories; from the literature of all periods and countries, ed. by Maxim Lieber & Blanche Colton Williams. Brentano's 1927 1121p o.p. 1970

Analyzed in Short Story Index
Contents: Doomed prince, Ares and Aphrodite, by Homer; Candaules' folly, by Herodotus; Cnemon's story, by Heliodorus; Talkative tortoise; Butter-blinded Brahman; Devasmita, by Somadeva; Book of Esther, from Old Testament; Bel and the dragon, from the Apocrypha; Pyramus and Thisbe, by Ovid; Trimalchio's dinner, by Petronius; Three robbers, by Apuleius; Feridun and his three sons, by Firdawsi; Treasure of Manseur; Jar of olives and the boy Kazi; Our lady's tumbler; Husband who was blind of an eye, by M. de Navarre; Blue Beard, by C. Perrault; Jeannot and Colin, by Voltaire; Soliman II, by J. F. Marmontel; Executioner, by H. de Balzac; Taking of the Redoubt, by P. Merimee; Omphale: A rococo story, by T. Gautier; Heroism of Dr Hallidonhill, by V. de L'Isle Adam; Ensign, by A.

Lieber, Maxim—*Continued*

Daudet; Maid of the Dauber, by E. Zola; Lost stars, by C. Mendès; Constant Guinard, by J. Richepin; Dowry, by G. de Maupassant; Horse of Genghis Khan, by P. Morand; Man who tamed the shrew, by J. Manuel; How Lazaro served a priest, by D. Hurtado de Mendoza; Mock aunt, by M. Cervantes; Paul turns beggar, by F. de Quevedo; Bella-flor, by F. Caballero; Cordovans in Crete, by J. Valera; Stubbook, by P. A. Alarcón; First prize, by E. Bazan; Stone of invisibility, by G. Boccaccio; Usurer's will, by G. F. Straparola; Jealous wife, by A. F. Grazzini; Love triumphant, by G. G. Cinthio; Story of the Saint Joseph's ass, by G. Verga; Orderly, by E. de Amicis; Turlendana returns, by G. d'Annunzio; Mere formality, by L. Pirandello; Mirrors, by M. Bontempelli; Slap, by R. Calzini; Pardoner's tale, by G. Chaucer; Sir Simon Eyer, by T. Deloney; In defence of his right, by D. Defoe; Tom Varnish, by R. Steele; Wandering Willie's tale, by Sir W. Scott; Paddy at sea, by S. Lover; Half-brothers, by E. C. Gaskell; Convict's return, by C. Dickens; "Blow up with the brig!", by W. Collins; Markheim, by R. L. Stevenson; Clerk's quest, by G. Moore; Sphinx without a secret, by O. Wilde; Il conde, by J. Conrad; Stolen bacillus, by H. G. Wells; Mary with the high hand, by A. Bennett; Quality, by J. Galsworthy; Two blue birds, by D. H. Lawrence; Mrs Beelbrow's lions, by S. Aumonier; Apple-tree, by K. Mansfield; Hubert and Minnie, by A. Huxley; Eulenspiegel carries off the parson's horse; Dr Faust arranges a marriage; New-Year's night of an unhappy man, by J. P. Richter; Broken pitcher, by H. Zschokke; Friends, by J. L. Tieck; Rumpelstiltskin, by J. Grimm; Virgin and the nun, by G. Keller; Victim, by H. Sudermann; Flowers, by A. Schnitzler; Beast, by J. Wassermann; Railway accident, by T. Mann; Peter Rugg, the missing man, by W. Austin; Stout gentleman, by W. Irving; Rappaccini's daughter, by N. Hawthorne; Cask of Amontillado, by E. A. Poe; What was it, by F. J. O'Brien; Tale of negative gravity, by F. R. Stockton; Celebrated jumping frog of Calaveras County, by M. Twain; Postmistress of Laurel Run, by F. B. Harte; Occurrence at Owl Creek Bridge, by A. Bierce; Zenobia's infidelity, by H. C. Bunner; Drifting crane, by H. Garland; New England nun, by M. W. Freeman; Municipal report, by O. Henry; Debt, by E. Wharton; Papago wedding, by M. H. Austin; One hundred dollar bill, by B. Tarkington; Doomdorf mystery, by M. D. Post; Death in the woods, by S. Anderson; Blue murder, by W. D. Steele; Coffin-maker, by A. Pushkin; Raspberry water, by I. Turgenev; Beggar boy at Christ's Christmas tree, by F. Dostoievsky; Empty drum, by L. Tolstoy; Darling, by A. Chekhov; White dog, by F. Sologub; Her lover, by M. Gorky; Caprice, by A. Kuprin; Lie, by L. Andreyev; Legend, by Z. Krasinsky; Do you remember, by E. Orzeszkowa; Twilight, by W. Reymont; Assignation, by K. Kisfaludi; Room with forty-eight stars, by M. Jokai; Grass of Lohina, by K. Mikszath; Dancing bear, by E. Bársony; Darkening shadows, by L. Biro; Reincarnated melody, by I. L. Peretz; Eva, by S. Aleichem; Livelihood, by J. Steinberg; Military service, by M. J. Berdyczewski; Black cat, by D. Pinski; Jewish child, by S. Asch; Winter wolves, by J. Opatoshu; Glass house, by C. Lemmonier; City hunter, by G. Rodenbach; Horse fair at Opdorp, by E. Verhaeren; Johannes attends a party, by F. W. Van Eeden; About myself and others, by L. Couperus; Chicken, by H. Heijermans; Farm magnate, by M. Lobato; Healer, by M. Ugarte; Rip-Rip, by M. Gutierrez-Nájera; Marble bust, by F. Fiallo; Nights in Talca, by A. Zegri; Lodger for the night, by J. Neruda; Apple-tree, by S. Cech; Island, by K. Capek; Happiness, by T. Panov; Vouya goes a-wooing, by M. Glishich; Ferid, by V. Trescec; Man with the ragged soul, by F. X. Mesko; Sacrifice of Yang Chioa-Ai; Donkey's revenge, by P'u Sung-Ling; Of a dancing girl, by I. Hearn; Tsugaru Strait, by S. Toson; Bill-collecting, by N. Kafu; Birth of Sinfjotli, the son of Sigmund; What the old man does is always right, by H. C. Andersen; Plague at Bergamo, by J. P. Jacobsen; Irene Holm, by H. J. Bang; Fidelity, by B. Björnson; Story of a chicken, by J. Lie; At the fair, by A. Kielland; Funeral, by A. Strindberg; Outlaws, by S. Lagerlöf; Fig-tree, by V. von Heidenstam; Bear Solomon, by P. Molin; Great invention, by I. L. Caragiale; Wanderers, by M. Sadoveanu

(jt. comp.) Clark, B. H. comp. Great short stories of the world

Lin, Yutang

(ed.) Famous Chinese short stories; retold. Day 1952 299p o.p. 1970

Analyzed in Short Story Index
Contents: Curly-beard, by Tu Kwang-t'ing; White Monkey; The stranger's note, by "Ch'ing-p'ingshan T'ang"; Jade goddess, by "Chingpen T'ungshu"; Chastity; Passion, by Yuan Chen; Chienniang, by Chen Hsuanyu; Madame D. by Lien Pu; Jealousy, by "Chingpen T'ungshu"; Jojo, by P'u Sung-ling; Cinderella, by Tuan Ch'eng-shih; Cricket boy, by P'u Sung-ling; Poets' club, by Wang Chu; The bookworm, by P'u Sung-ling; Wolf of Chungshan, by Hsieh Liang; Lodging for the night, by Li Fu-yen; Who became a fish, by Li Fu-yen; The tiger, by Li Fu-yen; Matrimony Inn, by Li Fu-yen; Drunkard's dream, by Li Kung-tso

Lady Wu; a novel. Putnam 1965 255p boards $4.95

This novel is based on the "life of Lady Wu, the cruel and pleasure-loving queen who created an empire of unparalleled despotism in seventh-century China. Lady Wu was a unique character who combined criminality with enormous intelligence [and] . . . rose from obscurity to become 'Female Emperor.'" Publisher's note
"The tale adheres strictly to the Tangshua (official Tang histories), even to minor incidents and dialogues. This is authentic history." Library J

Moment in Peking; a novel of contemporary Chinese life. Day 1939 815p o.p. 1970

A story of family life among the upper middle class of China, covering forty years from the time of the Boxer Rebellion to the Japanese invasion
"There are many scenes and passages of great beauty in the book, excerpts from the classics, poetry and philosophy. There are also incidents of humor, delicate and subtle. Equally skillful is the author in depicting scenes of dramatic intensity, stark tragedy of war and acts of heroism." Springf'd Republican

The vermilion gate; a novel of a far land. Day 1953 438p o.p. 1970

"A novel of China in the 1930's, when many educated young Chinese were beginning to question the traditional authority of their elders and to act independently. The courtship of Li Fei, a roving correspondent, and Jo-an Tu, daughter of a liberal-minded scholar, was regarded by both families with benign approval, but before a marriage could be solemnized Li Fei was obliged to flee from an offended war lord. Realizing that she was pregnant, and that this was an unpardonable offense against both families, Jo-an followed Li Fei into exile, and was reunited with him after displaying such loyalty amid hardships that she won the forgiveness of the elders. Background material is good, and the characters have individuality." Booklist

Lincoln, Victoria

Charles; a novel. Little 1962 438p boards $5.75

This novel, based on certain events in the life of Charles Dickens, presents the man himself, the people around him, his family and friends, and a picture of London society before and during the reign of Victoria, from the squalor of debtor's prison to the flamboyant moneyed classes. (Publisher)
"A conducted tour through the intimate and public life and times of one of the most absurd and interesting of men. That he was also the most popular good novelist who ever lived adds a special interest to all that [the author] tells us. . . . Perhaps the time has come for us to rediscover Dickens. . . . I recommend this book for a most pleasant way to meet a great author who still has much to say to our nail-chewing age." Sat R

A dangerous innocence. Rinehart 1958 310p o.p. 1970

Set in 17th century Massachusetts at the time of the witchcraft trials. "Narrated by a young matron of Salem, the story describes

Lincoln, Victoria—*Continued*

the trial and conviction of this woman and her husband and the wife's affair with another man." Pub W

"Both the love story and the spine-chilling suspicion-of-witchcraft theme are well managed. A good period piece." Book of the Month Club News

Lind, Jakov

Landscape in concrete; a novel; tr. from the German by Ralph Manheim. Grove 1966 190p o.p. 1970

First published 1963 in Germany

A tragi-comedy which sketches "the odyssey of Gauthier Bachmann in the closing days of World War II. The huge Wehrmacht sergeant discharged as mentally unfit, has wandered from the Russian front, where he had lost his regiment and his sanity, to the Ardennes, Norway, and back into Germany in search of a unit with which he can fight and re-establish his manhood." Library J

Lindbergh, Anne Morrow

y Dearly beloved; a theme and variations. Harcourt 1962 202p $3.95

"A Helen and Kurt Wolff book"

A novel which "acts out a philosophy of the meaning of marriage. It portrays a New England family's reactions to the wedding ceremony of a first grandchild. For each of the friends and kinsmen, the ceremony crystallizes some fear, love, hate, or unhappiness and sharpens awareness of the enduring quality of perfect love." Pub W

"Mrs. Lindbergh writes with style and distinction; her chiseled, cadenced, almost classic prose delights the eye, the ear and the tongue. . . . 'Dearly Beloved' is for everyone: the young will respond to its affirmation; men will be stimulated, possibly disturbed, by its courageous honesty; women will welcome its revealing wisdom; all will enjoy its refreshing approach to simple verities." Best Sellers

Lindop, Audrey Erskine

I start counting. Doubleday 1966 310p o.p. 1970

"Although there is a busy strangler of women at work in the English village of Dalstead, this story is more a family comedy than one of suspense. It's told by 14-year-old Wynne Kinch as she waits in a Remand Home, charged with obstructing police investigation of [several] murders. The Kinch family is composed of unique characters: Grandad, who breeds mice; teen-age twins and their mother; Aunt Rene, whose greatest bliss is describing the intimate details of her friends' illnesses; a remarkably intelligent cat; and Wynne's stepcousin, George, upon whom she dotes. But she also suspects that he is the strangler. Her efforts to protect him result in madly funny scenes—worth wading through some of Wynne's puerile imaginings to reach." Pub W

Sight unseen. Doubleday 1969 304p $5.95

"A talented but alcoholic young artist [who paints eerie pictures] becomes the guest of Colonel Hawkins in a lonely old house on the Romney Marshes—only to discover that he's really a prisoner; that two other artists have died under mysterious circumstances." Am News of Bks

The author's "modern-day Gothic novel has some entertaining touches. There's plenty of suspense, some good cat-and-mousing with the reader, and, best of all, a spicy, tongue-in-cheek style that makes the most of some highly comic yet spooky situations." Pub W

Linington, Elizabeth

Greenmask! Harper 1964 217p o.p. 1970

"The only thing that connects the four Hollywood murders . . . is the county guide books tied with green ribbon and the notes signed 'Greenmask' that were found beside each. Sergeant Ivor Maddox, with the improbable middle name, can find no way to connect the victims, nor can he find any private motive for the first two. While the Sergeant and his assistants interview friends and relatives, track

down leads, and find new clues, he remembers an old Agatha Christie and sees a ray of light." Library J

The long watch; a novel. Viking 1956 377p o.p. 1970

Set in New York City during the Revolution this is the story of James Bethune, a runaway orphan who "found his lifework at sixteen when he became clerk to MacDonald, editor of the 'New York Courier.' Their mutual, inarticulate devotion, and their passionate belief in freedom of information are two aspects of a . . . tale rounded out by the love story of shy Bethune and lovable Margaret Thurstan." Booklist

"It's a charming tale, strengthened with some excellent background, in an area, the newspaper of the 1770s, too little known." Chicago Sunday Tribune

Policeman's lot. Harper 1968 232p boards $4.95

"A Joan Kahn-Harper Novel of suspense"

"Sergeant Ivor Maddox, Policewoman Sue Carstairs, and their colleagues of Hollywood's Wilcox Street precinct confront a brand-new assortment of puzzles and dramas, including a surprise romance for Sue." McClurg. Book News

"A Policeman's Lot may not always be a happy one, but in Elizabeth Linington's hand the game seems worth the candle. . . . The Queen of the Procedurals has never been better." N Y Times Bk R

For other titles by this author see Egan, Lesley; Shannon, Dell

Linney, Romulus

Slowly, by thy hand unfurled. Harcourt 1965 214p $4.50

Ths story is told through "the journal of an ignorant and near-illiterate woman who struggles to understand the good and evil in her own life by writing it all down. The evil is all too apparent to everyone except the diarist. Against her own image of herself as a devoted wife and mother, a pillar of the church, a leader of society in her small southern town, a gracious employer to her Negro girls, slowly, by one disastrous unfurling after another, she is revealed to the reader (and to herself) as an evil and stupid woman." Best Sellers

Linscott, Robert N.

(ed.) The best American humorous short stories; ed. with an introductory note. Modern Lib. 436p $2.95

Analyzed in Short Story Index

First published by Random House 1945

Contents: Swallowing an oyster alive, by J. S. Robb; How daddy played hoss, by G. W. Harris; The Shakers, by A. Ward; Mrs McWilliams and the lightning, by M. Twain; Journalism in Tennessee, by M. Twain; Brother Rabbit takes some exercise, by J. C. Harris; How Brother Rabbit frightened his neighbors, by J. C. Harris; How Mr Rooster lost his dinner, by J. C. Harris; Colonel Starbottle for the plaintiff, by B. Harte; Piece of red calico, by F. R. Stockton; Mr Dooley on the game of football, by F. P. Dunne; Pigs is pigs, by E. P. Butler; Ransom of Red Chief, by O. Henry; Little gentleman, by B. Tarkington; Three without doubled, by R. Lardner; Mr and Mrs Fix-it, by R. Lardner; Death of Red Peril, by W. D. Edmonds; Travel is so broadening, by S. Lewis; Crazy fool, by D. O. Stewart; Mr and Mrs Haddock abroad, by D. O. Stewart; Benny and the bird-dogs, by M. K. Rawlings; The legislature, by J. M. Cain; Little hours, by D. Parker; But the one on the right, by D. Parker; Snatching of Bookie Bob, by D. Runyon; Interesting cure, by F. Sullivan; Gendarmes and the man, by D. Moffat; Carnival days in sunny Las Los, by R. Benchley; The guest, by M. Connelly; Primrose path, by S. Benson; Secret life of Walter Mitty, by J. Thurber; Night the bed fell, by J. Thurber; Night the ghost got in, by J. Thurber; University days, by J. Thurber; Man who hated Moonbaum, by J. Thurber; Father and his hard-rocking ship, by C. Day; The prince, by R. McKenney; Chocolate for the woodwork, by A. Kober; Terrible vengeance of

Linscott, Robert N.—*Continued*

H*Y*M*A*N K*A*P*L*A*N, by L. Q. Ross; Hand in Nub, by St C. McKelway; Down with the restoration, by S. J. Perelman; Kitchen bouquet, by S. J. Perelman; Dental or mental, I say it's spinach, by S. J. Perelman

Lipsky, Eleazar

The Devil's daughter. Meredith 1969 633p $8.95

"California in the eighties was a lusty, brawling empire ruled by self-made multimillionaires who bought and sold politicians, women's virtue, railroads and justice. This novel recreates this era and its most famous trial. Pitted against each other in a fight for principle and power were Mark Trumbull a former judge and a symbol of honor, and the 'Silver King' Lew Hagerman, libertine, unscrupulous, oppressor of the weak and friend of the mighty. Between them stood Trumbull's client, beautiful, well-born, enigmatic Jessica Roux, called 'The Devil's Daughter,' who swore that her scandalous relationship with Hagerman was in reality a secret marriage. As the case moved from court to court, with suits and countersuits, dozens of minor figures became involved, including servants, society women, fortune tellers and labor leaders." Am News of Bks

The Literary Review

Angoff, C. ed. Stories from The Literary Review

Littell, Robert

(jt. auth.) Chesnoff, R. Z. If Israel lost the war

Llewellyn Lloyd, Richard David Vivian. See Llewellyn, Richard

Llewellyn, Richard

Chez Pavan. Doubleday 1958 527p o.p. 1970

A novel "about the manager of a top rank Paris hotel whose dedication to his profession is complete. The guests, known by their room or suite numbers usually, and the large staff furnish the daily problems he handles with efficiency, and his personal concern with amor is kept properly subordinated." Am News of Bks

y How green was my valley. Macmillan (N Y) 1940 495p $5.95

In this "novel of the Welsh mining country the story is told by Huw Morgan, youngest son of a miner's family. In his boyhood, in the '80's, the valley was green and beautiful, the people were prosperous and law abiding; gradually the countryside was changed to a place of desolation as slag-heaps of mine refuse covered the mountain slopes; hard times, with strikes and layoffs, brought suffering, and a wholesome way of life was destroyed." Booklist

"A remarkably beautiful novel of Wales. And although it follows stirringly in the romantic traditions, there is the resonance of a profound and noble realism in its evocation, its intensity and reach of truth." N Y Times Bk R

Followed by: Up, into the singing mountain

None but the lonely heart. Macmillan (N Y) 1969 518p $6.95

"First published in 1943, this novel of London low-life has been revised and finished—author Llewellyn was called into the armed services before the work was completed." Best Sellers

This "is the story of Ernest Mott, a boy growing up in the rough and tumble section of London, who becomes a soldier and saves himself from a life of delinquency." Bk Buyer's Guide

"The [new] additional chapters make it a stronger book. For the first time the career and character of Ernie Verdun Mott are rounded out and the Cockney adolescent becomes a man. Nineteen-year-old Ernie, his 'Ma,' Ada, and the London East End are made very real. When Ernie is fired, the reader feels what it is like to be out of work and can understand how a young man can turn to petty crime; he rejoices when the army gives Ernie a second chance. Vitality, realistic dialogue, and dramatic moments give this story a new impact now that crime is news." Library J

Up, into the singing mountain. Doubleday 1960 378p o.p. 1970

Sequel to: How green was my valley

"Huw Morgan, the narrator of the author's How green was my valley, tells here of the life he found in Patagonia after he left Wales to avoid the unhappiness of sharing a house with Bronwen, his widowed sister-in-law, whom he loved but could not marry. As a skilled cabinetmaker he quickly made a place for himself in the Welsh community he joined but a stubborn independence and individuality put him at odds with some of the leading citizens." Booklist

White horse to Banbury Cross. Doubleday 1970 353p $5.95

The hero of this story is Edmund Trothe, former M.I. 5 agent. "Trothe discovers that two of his former friends in M.I. 5 have penetrated his Anglo-Arabian oil empire, have killed some of his employees, and are out to get him." News of Bks

Llosa, Mario Vargas. See Vargas Llosa, Mario

Locke Elliott, Sumner

Careful, he might hear you. Harper 1963 339p o.p. 1970

This first novel, "set in Australia, deals with a six-year-old boy [named P. S.] and his four maternal aunts, all of whom are directly or peripherally engaged in a battle for his custody." Book Week

"The novel derives its distinction mainly from the author's impressive skill in weaving into a coherent narrative the curiously assorted collection of forgotten times, distorted memories, false sentiments, fantastic imaginings, and a bit of lunacy. The descriptive writing is superb, and, overall, it is an engrossing, promising novel." Library J

Edens lost. Harper 1969 279p $5.95

"It begins in Australia, but a fascinatingly different Australia, a beautiful and remote mountain resort area to which a lonely 17-year-old boy has come as the guest of a remarkable family, the St. Jameses. To Angus, everything about the St. Jameses, and especially the lovely mother, Eve, is so perfect and right that he feels he is in paradise. It is only gradually that we begin to see how Eve's possessive love for her husband is warping and distorting the lives of her children and all those who come into her orbit." Pub W

"This is a subtle, realistic novel which explores, in expert fashion and on several levels, the melancholy of falling out of childhood." Best Sellers

Lockridge, Richard

Die laughing. Lippincott 1969 192p boards $4.50

"A policeman saw Roy Baker running from Jennifer Singleton's house and stopped him. The teen-ager told him that the famous actress had been shot or stabbed. Roy was the natural suspect but Rose Shapiro was firm in her denial that he could be guilty, she 'knew' him. So Nate, her detective husband, had to look for another suspect." Bk Buyer's Guide

"Standard Richard Lockridge is always diverting fare. [This] is all of that in its solid and uncomplicated fashion." N Y Times Bk R

Murder for art's sake. Lippincott 1967 190p $3.95

"They said artist Shack Jones had shot himself and when lieutenant Nate Shapiro looked at Shack's paintings he could believe it. Shack's agent said Shack was painted out and discouraged but why would a man planning suicide plan, as well, for a squab dinner afterward?" Bk Buyer's Guide

"A professional job, easily readable, with much local New York color, ranging from the wilds of Greenwich Village to smart apartments on the upper East Side." Pub W

Lockridge, Richard—*Continued*

A risky way to kill; an Inspector Heimrich mystery. Lippincott 1969 192p $4.95

"Someone put an ad in the 'Van Brunt Citizen' offering a bay stallion and a size 10 wedding dress for sale—obviously a vicious blow at the Wainwrights, whose daughter had been thrown by her bay stallion and killed some months before she was to be married. The 'Citizen's' owner spoke to Inspector Heimrich about it, and Heimrich followed what few clues there were—to murder." Bk Buyer's Guide

Troubled journey. Lippincott 1970 [c1969] 192p boards $4.95

"A young widow, whose husband had recently committed suicide, takes a nightmare four-day trip in her car with her Siamese cat from New York to her home in the family compound in Vero Beach, Florida." Pub W

With option to die; a Captain Heimrich mystery. Lippincott 1967 192p $3.95

"A race issue disrupts a quiet, conservative, wealthy village in northern Westchester. Vandalism and threatening phone calls are followed by warning rifle shots, and finally there is murder. The local newspaper office is dynamited, and hand grenades are thrown at some new residents. With all this are the pleasantly familiar figures of Inspector Heimrich of the State Police, his wife, and their huge dog, Colonel. There are all the nice background touches and entertaining sidelights that one expects from this popular mystery writer." Pub W

Lockridge, Ross

Raintree County. Houghton 1948 1066p maps $12.50

"The events of July 4, 1892, when Raintree county, Indiana, with the rest of the U.S. was celebrating the Fourth with fitting ceremonies, furnish the frame for a story of the county from 1844 to 1892 and particularly of the schoolteacher, John Wickliff Shawnessy. Johnny was a dreamer and poet and everyone thought the boy was destined to be a great writer known to all the world. But Johnny always came back, from the Civil war and from adventures in the east, because his dream had its roots in his home county and he felt inseparably bound to it. One girl personified his dream yet he married another. . . . A second marriage brought more happiness and stability." Booklist

"The weaving of the long flashbacks, the history, the poetry, anecdotes, plays, oratory, into the fabric of a single day's events represents a monumental tour de force. More than one critic will compare the author to Thomas Wolfe, and with justice." Literary Guild

Lodge, David

The British Museum is falling down. Holt [1967 c1965] 176p boards $3.95

First published 1965 in England

This novel "takes place on one frantic, muddled day in the lives of Adam Appleby, impoverished English Catholic graduate student, father of three, and a man laboring under the horrible thought that he may soon be the father of four, and [of] his just possibly pregnant wife, Barbara. Their efforts to cope with the incredibly unworkable nuances of the rhythm method of birth control are [related] . . . but Mr. Lodge is also satirizing the scholarly world, Catholics, intellectual and otherwise, and sex itself." Pub W

"A certain kind of filial respect and kindliness permeates Lodge's satire so that his laughter is that of a member of the family rather than the attack of a defector." Best Sellers

Loewengard, Heide Huberta (Freybe) See Albrand, Martha

Lofts, Norah

Bless this house. Doubleday 1954 285p o.p. 1970

"The chronicle of a house and its inmates over a period of more than three hundred and fifty years. The house was called Merravay, a handsome E-shaped building, which was erected in East Anglia in 1577 and went thru many hands until 1953 when it came back to the Rowhedges." Book Rev Digest

"To span four centuries in a normal-sized book requires some fast footwork on the part of the writer. Miss Lofts covers the distance by weaving together eight separate episodes, each of a different generation." N Y Times Bk R

The Concubine. . . . Doubleday 1963 310p o.p. 1970

"A novel based upon the life of Anne Boleyn, Henry VIII's second wife, whom the Spanish Ambassador most often referred to as 'the Concubine' in his dispatches." Title page

Story of Anne Boleyn, "commoner, sixteen-year-old lady-in-waiting at the court of King Henry VIII, dark-haired slip of a girl [for whom] . . . the powerful monarch of sixteenth-century England was to remain celibate for nine long years, shed his queen, Catherine of Aragon, bastardize his one legitimate child, Mary and destroy scores of men, including Sir Thomas Wolsey, his oldest and truest friend. Norah Lofts has constructed this . . . novel of Anne Boleyn's life—from her first acquaintance with Henry, through her coronation and ultimate execution." Publisher's note

"Each chapter of the novel begins with a brief excerpt from an historical source. The excerpt is then augmented; a device which Miss Lofts uses well and one which adds to her realistic treatment of the oft-told tale." Best Sellers

Esther. Macmillan (N Y) 1950 163p o.p. 1970

"An interpretation of Esther in the form of colorful fiction. The essential points in the Biblical narrative are fully preserved, emphasizing the devotion of the Jewish girl at the Persian court of Artaxerxes to her people. The brief book of the Old Testament, however, is expanded and embellished with a great amount of imaginative detail. The result is a good picture of the times and a fascinating story. The significance of the volume is more on the literary than the religious side." Rel Bk Club Bul

The house at Old Vine. Doubleday 1961 408p o.p. 1970

Set in England between 1496 and 1679, this story tells of the descendants of Martin Reed, the hero of the author's "The town house," a serf who became a man of property. Reed's descendants inherited his ambition and the house at Old Vine serves as a background for their struggles to maintain their hard-won position in a time of great religious, political, and economic ferment. (Publisher)

"This is not an 'historical' novel in the usual sense but a story of individuals against a vivid and changing background that Mrs. Lofts has made distinctively her own. Here, as in her earlier books, her gifts as a storyteller give life and meaning to her wealth of lore of the past." N Y Her Trib Books

The house at sunset. Doubleday 1962 370p o.p. 1970

"The last part of the trilogy which began with 'Town house' and 'The house at Old Vine' relates episodes from the lives of the people who lived in an English mansion from the eighteenth century to the present." Chicago

"The trilogy, scanning nearly five centuries of English social history, will appeal mostly to historically minded readers." Booklist

How far to Bethlehem? A novel. Doubleday 1965 353p $5.95

A "retelling, as a novel, of the Bible story of Mary and the birth of Jesus. The story begins with Mary's vision of the angel [follows the journey to Bethlehem] and ends with the three wise men (whose lives, as Miss Lofts has viewed them, make engrossing dramas) in the stable paying homage to Jesus." Pub W

The author presents "some of the characters involved in a different light. The imagination is teased, and the reader wonders if perhaps this might be a better picture than that given us by tradition. The characters are carefully drawn, and the background is authentic. The culture and life of several different countries is introduced into the story as it moves toward its climax." Library J

Lofts, Norah—*Continued*

The King's pleasure. Doubleday 1969 372p
$5.95

"Henry the Eighth's first wife, the proud and pious Katherine of Aragon is the subject of . . . [this] historical novel. Rejected by Henry because she could not bear him a son and would not submit to a divorce unrecognized by Rome, Katherine was left to a tormented and lonely life. While her husband openly courted Anne Boleyn, the Queen waited in vain for vindication from Rome—and whie she waited England teetered on the brink of a schism that would change the course of world history." News of Bks

"The book is well written in [the author's] delightful simplicity of style, the conversation is credible, the characters and events are as freshly appealing in new interest in spite of the thousands of books on the subject and period that for four centuries have poured from the press." Best Sellers

y The lost queen. Doubleday 1969 302p
$5.95

"Caroline Matilda, sister of George III of England, is married off to Christian, Crown Prince of Denmark, while both are in their teens. It is not a happy marriage. Christian, who becomes king, is egocentric, sadistic, plagued by syphilis, and dominated by power-hungry courtiers. Caroline is accused of adultery, her children taken from her, and imprisoned at Elsinore until George III sends a warship for her." Pub W

"The book is rich in the atmosphere of the 18th century. Both extremes of the economic scale are revealed and the great social cruelties and injustices of the time come to light in the author's skillful weaving of the plot. The characters are vividly drawn and Mrs. Lofts is extremely sympathetic to her heroine." Best Sellers

The lute player. Doubleday 1951 465p
o.p. 1970

"A plausible explanation of the peculiar marriage of Richard the Lionhearted is given by the three persons closest to Richard and his wife Berengaria. Eleanor of Aquitaine, Blondel the minstrel, and the fictional Duchess Anna, a hunchbacked, illegitimate sister of Berengaria, reluctantly reveal the cruel trick fate played on the beautiful, self-willed princess, who broke through all obstacles to marry the man of her choice, only to learn that he was an unabashed homosexual, who had married her to obtain money for his crusade. An excellent portrayal of the times and a sympathetic presentation of the people involved." Booklist

Scent of cloves. Doubleday 1957 320p
o.p. 1970

Julia, the daughter of Irish nobility, murdered by Cromwell was glad to leave her orphanage, even to marry by proxy some planter in the Spice Islands. When she found her unknown husband was an idiot, she felt free—until she learned her father-in-law's plan for acquiring an heir. (Publisher)

"Mrs Lofts's writing is marked by romance, abundance—a piling up of plot, color, romance, sentiment, and suspense. 'Scent of Cloves' is a fruitcake full of exotic surprises prepared to delight the appetites of those readers who search for rich literary fare." Sat R

Silver nutmeg. Doubleday 1947 368p
o.p. 1970

"The three-cornered rivalry for the nutmeg monopoly of the Dutch East Indies serves as a background for a tale of love and violence in the 17th century. Evert sends to Holland for a beautiful wife, plans her murder when he sees her stricken by disease, and loses her love to Christy, an English dealer in black-market nutmegs. English, Dutch, and natives finish the novel in a bloody climax." Retail Bookseller

The town house; the building of the house. Doubleday 1959 403p o.p. 1970

Set in England in the late Middle Ages this is the story of Martin Reed who "escapes from serfdom to become a wealthy merchant. Kate, the wife of his youth, perishes with their two

children in a fire. . . . His second wife, a gypsy, deserts him shortly after the birth of their son Richard. The events of Richard's life carry the narrative to the third generation [that] of Martin's grandchildren." Library J

"A novel related by five persons speaking in turn spans the lifetime of the first speaker, Martin Reed. . . . A richly mounted tale, plentifully endowed with vivid pictures of the period." Booklist

Winter harvest; a novel. Introduction by Stewart H. Holbrook. Doubleday 1955 347p o.p. 1970

First published 1941 in England with title: Road to revelation

"A parallel, in fiction form, to the terrible story of the hapless people who tried to cross the Donner Pass in 1846. The author follows the dire sufferings of a similar party, led by the visionary Keven Furmage, who tried a new trail, were caught by winter, and endured unspeakable hardships." Retail Bookseller

"The four brief, fictitious biographies are works of real imagination. So the reader believes the series of events that leads the party towards tragedy, victory, or mere defeat. Here even the treatment of cannibalism, which occurs in other fiction of the early West, is unique and plausible, and all in all this is a superior novel." Sat R

London, Jack

Best short stories. Garden City Bks. 1945 311p o.p. 1970

Analyzed in Short Story Index
Contents: White silence; To build a fire; Odyssey of the North; League of the old men; Lost face; Piece of steak; The heathen; Samuel; On the Makaloa mat; Daughter of the Aurora Law of life; Story of Jees Uck; To the man on trail; Story of Keesh; Wit of Porportuk; Love of life; The Mexican; All gold canyon; Wisdom of the trail; House of Mapuhi; Pearls of Parlay

y The call of the wild

Some editions are:
Grosset (Famous dog stories) $2.50
Macmillan (N Y) $3.95 Illustrated by Robert Todd
Watts, F. $7.95 Large type edition. A Keith Jennison book

First published 1903
"The dog hero, Buck, is stolen from his comfortable home and pressed into service as a sledge dog in the Klondike. At first he is abused by both men and dogs, but he learns to fight ruthlessly and finally finds in John Thornton a master whom he can respect and love. When Thornton is murdered, he breaks away to the wilds and becomes the leader of a pack of wolves." Benét. The Reader's Encyclopedia

also in Costain, T. B. ed. More Stories to remember v 1 p205-63

y The call of the wild, and other stories. With biographical illus. and pictures of contemporary scenes, together with an introduction and captions by Louis B. Salomon. Dodd 1960 242p illus (Great illustrated classics) $4.50

Analyzed in Short Story Index
"The 'north country' with its cruelty and heroism is the background of the nine stories in this book." Publisher's note
Contents: The call of the wild; The man with the gash; Jan, the unrepentant; The white silence; To the man on trail; The wisdom of the trail; An odyssey of the north; The law of life; A daughter of the aurora

The iron heel; introduction by Max Lerner. Macmillan (N Y) 1958 303p o.p. 1970

First published 1908
"A 'prophetic' novel of 1912-1918 narrating the advent of a great capitalistic fascist dictatorship, with its treacherous liquidation of the middle class and the power of labor. The hero is Ernest Everhard, a socialist revolutionary of the group which finally overthrows 'The Iron Heel.'" Haydn. Thesaurus of Book Digests

London, Jack—*Continued*

Jack London: short stories; ed. with an introduction by Maxwell Geismar. Hill & Wang 1960 xx, 228p o.p. 1970

Analyzed in Short Story Index
"Eighteen of London's later short stories, most of which express his bitter disillusion with the nature of life." Pub W
Contents: Love of life; To build a fire; The apostate; The Chinago; Make westing; Semper Idem; A curious fragment; The whale tooth; Mauki; Yah! Yah! Yah; Good-by, Jack; Aloha oe; The eternity of forms; Told in the drooling ward; The strength of the strong; South of the Slot; The unparalleled invasion; The sea farmer

Jack London's Tales of adventure. Ed. by Irving Shepard. Doubleday 1956 531p illus $5.95

"A collection of over fifty pieces written by Jack London between 1893 and 1916, including articles and war dispatches, short stories and selections from his novels. Some of the material has not been published before in book form." Book Rev Digest
There are selections from the following novels: The Sea Wolf; The iron heel; Martin Eden; Burning daylight; The valley of the moon; The mutiny of the Elsinore; The Star Rover
Short stories: To the man on trail; The white silence; An odyssey of the North; Jan, the unrepentant; The man with the gash; The law of life; The one thousand dozen; Bâtard; All Gold Canyon; The apostate; Love of life; The passing of Marcus O'Brien; To build a fire; Flush of gold; Lost face; A piece of steak; The seed of McCoy; The Mexican; The strength of the strong; War; The pearls of Parlay; The race for number three; Samuel; Told in the drooling ward; The princess

Martin Eden. Library ed. Macmillan (N Y) 1957 381p $5.95

First published 1909, recopyrighted 1936
"Eden has had a knockabout life as a sailor, and falling in love with a girl used to middle-class refinement and luxuries, tries to write. He is rejected by editors, and the girl jilts him. The abysmal contrast between the genius of this man, his vital ideals and the big realities of life, and, on the other hand, the narrow, unintelligent mediocrity of the 'cultured classes' is brought out with characteristic force." Baker's Historical

y The Sea-Wolf

Some editions are:
Grosset $2.50
Macmillan (N Y) $4.95, large print edition $7.95
First published 1904
"Wolf Larsen, ruthless captain of the tramp steamer 'Ghost,' receives as unexpected passenger on the high seas Humphrey Van Weyden, a wealthy ne'er-do-well. In spite of his selfish brutality, Larsen becomes an instrument for good. The treatment he gives to the dilettante Van Weyden teaches the latter to stand on his own legs. He and the poet Maude Brewster, whom the 'Sea-Wolf' loves also escape to an island as the 'Ghost' sinks and Larsen, mortally sick, is deserted. The lovers later return to civilization." Haydn. Thesaurus of Book Digests

South sea tales. Macmillan (N Y) 1961 [c1939] 327p $3.95

Analyzed in Short Story Index
A reissue of a title first published 1911
Contents: The house of Mapuhi; The whale tooth; Mauki; "Yah! Yah! Yah"; The heathen; The terrible Solomons; The inevitable white man; The seed of McCoy

The star rover. Autobiographical introduction. Epilogue by Gardner Murphy. Illus. by Leonard Everett Fisher. Macmillan (N Y) 1963 336p illus $4.50

"A science-fiction novel, originally published in 1915, based on the theory of the transmigration of souls." Booklist
"The hero, condemned to solitary confinement in a corrupt prison, discovers how to free his soul from his body. He escapes through space and time to relive experiences of the past stored in his 'racial memory.'" Huntting

Stories of Hawaii; ed. by A. Grove Day. Appleton 1965 282p boards $5.95

Analyzed in Short Story Index
Contents: The house of pride; Koolau the leper; Good-by, Jack; Aloha oe; Chun Ah Chun; The sheriff of Kona; On the makaloa mat; The bones of Kahekili; When Alice told her soul; Shin bones; The water baby; The tears of Ah Kim; The Kanaka surf; A royal sport: surfing at Waikiki; From "My Hawaiian aloha"
"These are stories written when London was living in Hawaii. . . . With a wide range of themes he covers many superstitions, beliefs, problems, and pleasures of those glamorous and fascinating islands and captures the flavor of life there at the turn of the century." Library J

y White Fang

Some editions are:
Grosset (Famous dog stories) $2.50
Macmillan (N Y) $5.95
Watts, F. $7.95 Large type edition. A Keith Jennison book
First published 1906
White Fang "is about a dog, a crossbreed, sold to Beauty Smith. This owner tortures the dog to increase his ferocity and value as a fighter. A new owner, Weedon Scott, brings the dog to California and, by kind treatment, domesticates him. White Fang later sacrifices his life to save Scott." Haydn. Thesaurus of Book Digests

y White Fang, and other stories. . . . Dodd 1963 308p illus (Great illustrated classics) $4.50

Analyzed in Short Story Index
"With photographs of the author and his environment as well as illustrations from early editions, together with an introduction by A. K. Adams." Subtitle
Stories included are: The one thousand dozen; All gold canyon; The son of the wolf; In a far country

Longo, Lucas

The family on vendetta street. Doubleday 1968 240p $4.95

A story of immigrant life in the Italian community of Brooklyn. "Young Marco recalls the day when he heard shots and learned that his father had killed his mother. After that he went to live, very happily, with Nonna, his grandmother, and his Aunt Rose and bit by bit through the years learned the reasons for the feud between his father's and his mother's families." Bk Buyer's Guide

Longstreet, Stephen

Pedlock & Sons; a novel. Delacorte Press 1966 370p o.p. 1970

"Rich, elegant, an international socialite, Judith, now past 80, decides to remarry, an act which begins a chain of events. Judith, a stern-willed, strong-minded, perceptive 'bubba', has created a fantastic but now increasingly empty life for herself at her family's emotional expense. Her new husband, Jacob Ellenbogan, a European Jewish scholar of the Talmud and the Cabala, becomes her hope for redemption. His arrival in the New World rattles the wealthy Pedlock family out of their secure little ruts of business, art, and Protestant names. . . . It is Jacob who stirs the family into a painful awareness of themselves as members of a people that has survived transplantings, pogroms, and holocausts." Library J
"The pungent Jewish dialog, the picture of a wealthy and slightly decadent family and the department store empire it has controlled for three generations, and the mad dynamics of the Pedlocks under stress made interesting reading." Pub W

Pedlock saint, Pedlock sinner. Delacorte Press 1969 469p $6.95

This "is the story of two rabbis, Stephen Pedlock and his nephew, David Mendoza. The decadent, hypocritical older rabbi, who has succumbed to all the evils of the flesh and has successfully wheeled and dealed his way to fortune and fame, is sharply contrasted with the young, idealistic chaplain, now a civilian, seeking his first rabbinical post, and

Longstreet, Stephen—*Continued*

intent on becoming a 'real' rabbi concerned with the souls and not the contributions of his congregation." Pub W

Loraine, Philip

A Mafia kiss. Random House [1969 c1968] 248p boards $4.95

"When Ben Lister attempts to get the key to a strong box left him by his father, he finds out the legend his father became in his old hometown in Italy—and he finds out also that the Mafia would rather have him dead than [let him] carry on the work of his father." Bk Buyer's Guide

"This is a dramatic, absorbing story that conveys the poignant reality of Sicilian peasant life under the heel of the Mafia." Pub W

Loti, Pierre

y Iceland fisherman. Dutton 1935 242p (Everyman's lib) $2.95

Original French edition, 1806. This edition translated by W. P. Baines

"The most popular and poetic novel of this original French writer. It is a story of the hardships and danger of his own Breton fisherfolk in their perilous life on the northern seas." Pratt Alcove

Lott, Milton

The last hunt. Houghton 1954 399p o.p. 1970

"The main currents of this story center upon the buffalo-hunter turned hide-collector, Sandy MacKenzie, and upon two of the men who join him in his first expedition to kill for profit. . . . The two are Charley Gilson, a young hot-head remarkably handy with a rifle or revolver; and Jimmy, part Indian part whiteman, who hires out to Sandy as a skinner. . . . The lives of all are interwoven, and the separate threads are, eventually, followed each in its end, with Sandy promised a peaceful old age with the Indian squaw he had helped escape from Charley; and Jimmy presumably winning his Letty from the jealous ward of Thimmes, the faro-dealer. But Charley dies after killing his last buffalo in a heavy snowstorm." Best Sellers

"The writing is simple, clear, and at times acidulous; the movement is inevitable, and the characterizations, while overdrawn, are mainly good. Here are suspense, rawness, and even ecstasy." Wis Lib Bul

Lovecraft, H. P.

The Dunwich horror, and others; the best supernatural stories of H. P. Lovecraft. Selected and with an introduction by August Derleth. Arkham House 1963 xx, 431p $6.50

Analyzed in Short Story Index

Contents: In the vault; Pickman's model; The rats in the walls; The outsider; The colour out of space; The music of Erich Zann; The haunter of the dark; The picture in the house; The call of Cthulhu; The Dunwich horror; Cool air; The whisperer in darkness; The terrible old man; The thing on the doorstep; The shadow over Innsmouth; The shadow out of time

Lovelace, Earl

The schoolmaster. Regnery 1968 224p $4.95

"Set in a remote village on Trinidad, Earl Lovelace's second novel chronicles the corruption of native innocence by modern civilization. Ironically, the villagers bring about their own fall by seeking the education necessary to become like the outside world. They hire a schoolmaster who perverts that knowledge and wisdom he is supposed to have. . . . Slowly at first, then with accelerated tempo, all the old values are swept away until a village girl, the daughter of one of the leaders who recruited the schoolmaster, drowns herself after the schoolmaster has made her pregnant. Mr. Lovelace's style is spare and understated, and he is content to present his characters in their own context with no commentary on the events set forth. The result is prose endowed with a certain haunting and primitive beauty." Pub W

Lowry, Clarence Malcolm. See Lowry, Malcolm

Lowry, Malcolm

Dark as the grave wherein my friend is laid; ed. by Douglas Day & Margerie Lowry. New Am. Lib. 1968 xxiii, 255p $5.95

"In this novel about the trip of Sigbjorn Wilderness and his wife, Primrose, to Mexico, the author is really telling the story of his own trip with his wife to look up his old friend, Fernando, but Fernando is already dead, and at last Sigbjorn (a fear-ridden writer) realizes that Fernando had really symbolized the death Sigbjorn (and Lowry) craved." Bk Buyer's Guide

This book "is full of movement; it begins with a long airplane flight and goes on to include several bus journeys through wild Mexican country, alternately uplifting and terrifying, all of which is described very well. This constant change of locale is needed to balance the fact that from another point of view it is an entirely stationary book, immovably fixed in one spot: the consciousness of the hero." Atlantic

The forest path to the spring

In Lowry, M. Hear us O Lord from heaven thy dwelling place p215-83

Hear us O Lord from heaven thy dwelling place. Lippincott 1961 283p $4.95

Partially analyzed in Short Story Index

A posthumous collection of five short stories and two novellas or novelettes

Contents: The bravest boat; Through the Panama [novelette]; Strange comfort afforded by the profession; Elephant and colosseum; Present estate of Pompeii; Gin and goldenrod; The forest path to the spring [novelette]

Through the Panama

In Lowry, M. Hear us O Lord from heaven thy dwelling place p29-98

Under the volcano. With an introduction by Stephen Spender. Lippincott 1965 xxvi, 375p boards $6.50

A reissue of a title first published 1947 by Reynal & Hitchcock

Set in Mexico, this is "the story of Geoffrey Firmin—formerly a British consul but now with no occupation except his fabulous drinking—and of his efforts to rise to the occasion of the unexpected return, on the Day of the Dead, of his estranged wife Yvonne." Am News of Bks

"So strong is the light which the author directs upon his central character that the shadow it casts is one of tragic dimensions." Times (London) Lit Sup

Lurie, Alison

Imaginary friends. Coward-McCann 1967 277p boards $4.95

"The scene is upstate New York where a group of townspeople, who call themselves the Truth Seekers, are convinced they have been receiving messages from Ro of the planet Varna. Two sociologists, one famous, one a young assistant, move in to study the phenomenon, with the younger one falling for Verena, spiritual leader and medium of the cult. Before long the two big city intellectuals begin subtly to influence the Truth Seekers and to be affected by them." Pub W

The author "continues to produce satiric novels of a very high order. . . . Miss Lurie is aware that no sane person can give himself to religious flummery, but she is equally aware that the religious instincts of the Seekers, however grotesque the form they take, are a valid response to the pressures of life, and that science is, if anything, an even less adequate way out." Book World

Real people. Random House 1969 180p $4.95

"Janet Belle Smith, 42, is a minor short-story writer who is appreciated for her cultivated prose and sensitivity. . . . [She comes] for a stay at Illyria [a northern New England

Lurie, Alison—*Continued*

artists' colony, and] . . . settles down to [write] only to be distracted by a long over-due awareness of her own insubstantiality. She is also distracted by other guests: an old pla-tonic friend who she discovers is a homo-sexual, an alcoholic has-been novelist, a pro-fessional East Village poet . . . and a sexy, uncouth junk-sculptor. . . . Janet [comes to] realize that she has been denying her impulses as a writer." Time

Lyle-Smythe, Alan. See Caillou, Alan

Lytton, Edward George Earle Lytton Bulwer-Lytton, 1st Baron. See Bulwer-Lytton, Sir Edward

M

Macardle, Dorothy

The uninvited. Doubleday 1942 342p o.p. 1970

Published in England under title: Uneasy freehold

"A beautiful old English house, situated on the Devon cliffs, is reputed to be haunted. Rod-erick Fitzgerald, a London journalist, and his sister, buy the house, and convert it into a thing of beauty. Almost immediately psychic manifestations occur which grow stronger after every visit of the lovely Stella, who was born in the house, and whose mother has died there. Roderick's growing love for Stella nerves him to a terrible ordeal, and the hauntings cease." Book Rev Digest

"This is the ideal ghost story and the au-thor writes with such conviction as to make the story quite credible; above all, she writes with a curious understanding of and pity for the ghosts who are, quite obviously, as real to her as the flesh and blood people in her tale." Times (London) Lit Sup

Macaulay, Rose

The towers of Trebizond. Farrar, Straus 1957 [c1956] 277p o.p. 1970

First published 1956 in England

"Travelog and commentary on a multiplicity of situations and problems both modern and ancient are combined in the story of an in-destructible little English widow who goes to Turkey to observe the condition of women, ac-companied by her niece, who is to illustrate her aunt's book; an English cleric, who is explor-ing the possibilities of establishing an Anglican mission in Turkey; and her white racing camel.' Booklist

"The early part of the book is pure fantasy and fun, a kind of conversational amble." Spec

The world my wilderness. Little 1950 244p o.p. 1970

This novel is "concerned with the bewilder-ment of Barbary Deniston, who grew up in the moral and social chaos of occupied France. Living in England with her father and step-mother, her only escape was to a real but fan-tastic world she created for herself in the wrecked and flowering wastes around St. Paul's. In this characterization of a young girl, in her portrayal of the mature woman, her hus-bands, her lover and her older son, the author has set the unformed groping spirit of the post-war world against the essences of the prewar world." Huntting

Macauley, Robie

(ed.) The Kenyon Review. Gallery of mod-ern fiction

McBain, Ed

The empty hours: an 87th Precinct mystery *In* Haycraft, H. ed. Three times three p233-88

Fuzz; an 87th Precinct mystery. Doubleday 1968 240p $4.95

"Steve Carella and the other detectives of the 87th Precinct are handling such routine affairs as a bomb scare, teen-agers who like to set drunken bums alight, and similar problems, when the blond extortioner begins his deadly work." Bk Buyer's Guide

"The blazing climax rises above the long arm of coincidence that pulls it together." Library J

Shotgun; an 87th Precinct mystery. Double-day 1969 192p $4.95

"Detectives Carella and Kling are in charge of the investigation into the murders of Rose and Andrew Leyden, both killed by a shotgun fired full in their faces. Far from the Leydens' comfortable apartment is Margie Ryder's pad, where her body is found several days after she has been stabbed." Pub W

"An ingenious puzzler which concerns three murders. This 87th precinct novel is a laugh-packed labyrinth of crime and detection." Book News

For another title by this author see Hun-ter, Ed

McCarthy, Mary

A charmed life. Harcourt 1955 313p $3.95

"John and Martha Sinnott encounter an amaz-ing assortment of would-be bohemians when, in the hope of gaining a new lease on their mar-riage, they move to the artistic community of New Leeds. They long for privacy but cock-tail parties, drama groups, and Martha's first husband Miles keep breaking in. Even Martha's pregnancy brings unforeseen problems for due to one after-the-party interlude the question of fatherhood broadens to two possibilities: John or Miles. The author is at her brilliant best in this comic tragedy of modern man's dilemma: the fluctuation between belief and unbelief, courage and despair." Booklist

The company she keeps. Harcourt [1960 c1942] 304p $4.95

First published 1942 by Simon & Schuster

"The six episodes that tell of the experiences of a girl, in her twenties and on her own in New York, fuse into both a portrait of an in-dividual and a revelation of a distinct social milieu." Publisher's note

The group. Harcourt 1963 378p $5.95

The Group is made up of "eight Vassar girls of the class of '33 who had lived to-gether during their upperclass years, in the South Tower of Main. We see them first at the wedding of Kay Strong to Harald Petersen a week after Commencement. . . . We see them last at Kay's funeral seven years later. . . . Libby MacAusland, is a romantic snob who thinks of herself as 'a gentlewoman'; she be-comes a successful literary agent and marries a famous writer. Polly Andrews, after a love affair with a man helplessly—and needlessly—in the clutches of an analyst, marries a psy-chiatrist who is glad to have her divorced father live with them (The Group is horrified), Priss Hartshorn marries a pediatrician and struggles anxiously to raise her child according to his theories. . . . Together with Kay and Dottie [Renfrew, a girl from Boston], these are the prominent members of The Group. In the background are Pokey Prothero, the in-nocently insensitive rich girl, Helena Davison, the ugly intelligent one, and Elinor Eastlake, the cultivated Lesbian." N Y Times Bk R

"It is perhaps as social history that the novel will chiefly be remembered; but over and above its sensitive observations it has a quality that one has not come to expect from this particu-lar author, and that is compassion." Sat R

The groves of Academe. Harcourt 1952 302p $4.75

"An intelligent and sophisticated dissection of faculty life at Jocelyn, a small progressive college in Pennsylvania. The impending dis-missal of self-styled liberal, Henry Mulcahy, Joycean scholar and instructor in literature, and the spring Poetry Conference are the main incidents in the narrative; but woven around them and even tying them together quite neat-ly is the probing, satirical and often deadly ac-curate account of college administration and personalities. A few of America's leading poets seem to appear pseudonymously during the conference." Library J

McCarthy, Mary—*Continued*

"Miss McCarthy's satiric manner is based on a stunning, narrowly aimed accuracy rather than on exaggeration. While she provides her specimens of men and mores with few softening extra-curriculum features, neither does she deny them their humanity by making caricatures of them. Miss McCarthy's report on the Joyceans . . . is fierce and faithful. And, for anyone interested in the conduct of our least orthodox campuses, mortally entertaining." N Y Times Bk R

McComas, J. Francis
(jt. ed.) Healy, R. J. ed. Famous science fiction stories

McCullers, Carson
The ballad of the sad café; the novels and stories of Carson McCullers. Houghton 1951 791p $6.50

Analyzed in Short Story Index
An omnibus volume of three novels all entered separately, including: The heart is a lonely hunter, The member of the wedding, Reflections in a golden eye; a novelette (the title story) and six short stories
Stories included are: The ballad of the sad café: Wunderkind; The jockey; Madame Zilensky and the King of Finland; The sojourner; A domestic dilemma; A tree, a rock, a cloud

Clock without hands. Houghton 1961 241p $4.95

A "study of the change in Southern mores as seen in the actions and thoughts of two men and two adolescents—one a Negro. The local druggist is awaiting an inexorable but imprecise death from leukemia; old Judge Clane, reft of his beloved son and his wife, partially incapacitated by a stroke, is clinging to a wild idea of forcing at least partial redemption of Confederate money on the Federal Government; his grandson, Jester, is lost in the limbo of his teens; and Sherman, a blue-eyed young Negro taken on as the Judge's 'amanuensis,' is searching for racial justice and the truth about his parentage. . . . To say that this is a book about miscegenation, incipient homosexuality, racial violence, suicide, and murder would be true but far from the whole truth. A thoughtful, intermittently brilliant book." Library J

The heart is a lonely hunter. Houghton 1940 356p $4.95

"The story has for its scene a southern town and covers in time about a year in the recent past. Its chief character is one John Singer, a deaf mute, who, when the story opens loses his only friend, another mute, committed to an insane hospital. Forced to listen and not to 'talk,' Singer becomes the recipient of the confidences of several other residents of the town—the proprietor of a quick-lunch counter, a little girl, an intellectual Negro doctor, a half-crazy, drunken radical." Book Rev Digest

"There is real beauty, poetry, and power, as well as heartbreak in this strange, authentic story about people who work grimly for their living, uncomplaining, each one shut up with his own secret trouble and pain, each one longing for more serenity, more peace, more harmony." Book of the Month Club News

also in McCullers, C. The ballad of the sad café p141-498

y The member of the wedding. Houghton 1946 195p $3.95

"A fictional study of child psychology. Twelve-year-old Frankie is utterly bored until she hears about her older brother's wedding. He returns from Alaska to his Georgia home, and Frankie decides she will go, uninvited, on the honeymoon. The few days of excitement of the wedding are pictured in terms of Frankie's reactions, with her six-year-old cousin, and the Negro cook as chorus." Book Rev Digest

"The tremendous feeling of the world lost, and meaning lost; of life recovered and meaning recovered; the merciful power of the young

to forget, and thus be healed of fractures, is one of the realest things about this fine book." Commonweal

also in McCullers, C. The ballad of the sad café p595-791

Reflections in a golden eye. Houghton 1941 182p $4.50

"The scene is a Southern army camp in peacetime. The characters are a group of society misfits, whose strange psychological turmoils lead them a wretched existence. The culmination is a murder." Book Rev Digest

"The situations in which the characters are placed are too weird for belief, and the actions of some of the characters, notably Capt Penderton and Alison, are those of insanity. The novel is written in the simplest form of narration, with terse sentences containing a wealth of detail in characterization. This language of realism is in sharp contrast to the fantastic situations which it creates." Springf'd Republican

also in McCullers, C. The ballad of the sad café p499-567

MacDonald, John D.
The deep blue good-by
In MacDonald, J. D. Three for McGee p149-297

Nightmare in pink
In MacDonald, J. D. Three for McGee p5-148

A purple place for dying
In MacDonald, J. D. Three for McGee p299-452

Three for McGee. Doubleday 1967 [c1964] 452p o.p. 1970

Originally published 1964 by Fawcett
Contents: Nightmare in pink; The deep blue good-by; A purple place for dying

MacDonald, Philip
Escape
In MacDonald, P. Triple jeopardy p205-337

The list of Adrian Messenger. Published for the Crime Club by Doubleday 1959 224p o.p. 1970

"Adrian Messenger wrote the names and occupations of ten men on a slip and gave it to Scotland Yard. The next day Messenger was dead and further investigation revealed that nine out of the ten men on the list were also dead." McClurg. Book News

"If some readers find Mr. MacDonald's style a bit stiff and old-fashioned, they will also find that he provides such other old-fashioned elements as honest clues, characters who stick in the mind from page to page, an original idea, and, in Anthony Gethryn, a detective who inspires utter confidence." New Yorker

The Polferry riddle
In MacDonald, P. Triple jeopardy p339-446

Triple jeopardy; three novels. Published for the Crime Club by Doubleday 1962 446p o.p. 1970

Contains the complete text of: The Polferry riddle and Warrant for X published 1931 and 1938, respectively, both featuring Colonel Anthony Gethryn; and Escape, published 1932, has Superintendent Dudley Allwright as the detective

Warrant for X
In MacDonald, P. Triple jeopardy p5-204

Macdonald, Ross

Archer in Hollywood. . . . With a foreword by the author. Knopf 1967 528p $6.95

"Three exciting novels: The moving target, The way some people die [and] The barbarous coast." Title page

A combination of three titles published separately 1949, 1951 and 1956 respectively, starring Lew Archer, private detective

The barbarous coast

In Macdonald, R. Archer in Hollywood p171-346

Black money. Knopf 1966 238p boards $3.95

Private detective Lew Archer "explores the secret life of a rich California residential community. A beautiful young woman has jilted her fiancé and taken up with a mysterious character who represents himself as a French political refugee. Hired to investigate this man, Archer becomes involved in several murders and a gigantic swindle." Publisher's note

"The interplay of people is so strong here that it sustains the novel for almost half its length without a murder." N Y Times Bk R

The goodbye look. Knopf 1969 243p boards $4.95

"Irene Chalmers had hired Lew Archer to discover who had rifled the big, old-fashioned safe and stolen a Florentine gold box from it. It was clear that she was afraid that her son Nick might have taken it—but why? He was given plenty of money and had no involvements." Bk Buyer's Guide

The instant enemy. Knopf 1968 227p boards $4.50

"Lew Archer is hired by Keith Sebastian, a Los Angeles business executive, to find his daughter Sandy, a highschool senior who has run off with a homeless boy. . . . Archer finds the runaways easily enough, but before he can return Sandy to her parents, she has participated in a violent crime. Archer's efforts to save the girl from the consequences of her actions, and to understand those actions, involve him in a . . . plot twisting deep into the past." Publisher's note

"You may feel, at first, that there is one death too many in the book. But I have a strong hunch that this is what [Macdonald] is getting at—there is always one death too many." Book World

The moving target

In Macdonald, R. Archer in Hollywood p3-169

The way some people die

In Macdonald, R. Archer in Hollywood p347-528

The zebra-striped hearse. Knopf 1962 278p o.p. 1970

Lew Archer, a private detective, is engaged by Colonel Blackwell to look into the background of Burke Damis, the fiancé of Harriet, the Colonel's daughter. Almost at once Archer discovers the body of a man stabbed to death with an ice pick. Meanwhile Harriet and Damis have disappeared. Archer's investigation of the mystery leads eventually to a group of gamblers and their girls. Set in California and Mexico. (Publisher)

"This is completely and formally a detective novel, but with more meat on its bones than nine out of ten novels in the main-stream." N Y Times Bk R

McFee, William

(ed.) Great sea stories of modern times; ed. with original material and with an introduction. McBride Co. 1953 346p o.p. 1970

Analyzed in Short Story Index

Contents: Log the man dead, by E. Burdick; R. M. S. Titanic, by H. W. Baldwin; The raft, by E. V. Rickenbacker; Alone in shark waters, by J. Kruse; Archerfish, by E. L. Beach; Cheerful tortoise, by J. N. Hall; Reluctant hero, by W. McFee; Some "Q" ships, by "Bartimeus"; Boat journey, by Sir E. Shackleton; Three Skeleton Key, by G. G. Toudouze; Rescuer extraordinary, by J. C. Bruce; Secret sharer, by J. Conrad

The harbourmaster; a novel. Doubleday 1932 439p o.p. 1970

"This author, who is often compared with Conrad, tells his story in Conradian manner, at second hand, through the lips of one who has been a more or less impartial observer of events. Mr. Spenlove, the chief engineer on a cruising steamer, is in the habit of entertaining the passengers at his table with bits of adventure drawn from his long experience at sea. An event on shore in a Caribbean port—the death of Mrs. Fraley and the suicide of her husband, the harbormaster,—starts him off on the long narrative of the strange life of this storm-tossed pair as he had known it. Long, but of absorbing interest to those who like the method." Wis Lib Bul

(ed.) World's great tales of the sea; ed. with an introduction. World Pub. 1944 446p o.p. 1970

Analyzed in Short Story Index

Contents: Typhoon, by J. Conrad; Night stalk, by C. S. Forester; Rule Britannia, by J. N. Hall; Make westing, by J. London; The open boat, by S. Crane; The ship that found herself, by R. Kipling; Mutiny on the brig Somers, by H. Baldwin; The last battle of the Revenge, by Sir W. Raleigh; S. S. San Pedro, by J. G. Cozzens; Bowleg Bill and the mermaid, by J. Digges; Blow up with the brig, by W. Collins; Engine-room stuff, by W. McFee; The leopard of the sea, by H. G. Dwight; Privilege, by B. Gill; Shovels and bricks, by M. Robertson; Ms. found in a bottle, by E. A. Poe; A voyage to the East Indies, by R. Hakluyt; The derelict, by H. M. Tomlinson; The mandarin's bell, by E. Noble; The ultimate factor, by Bartimeus; Benito Cereno, by H. Melville; Legends of the sea, by J. Masefield

Machado de Assis

Dom Casmurro; tr. and with an introduction by Helen Caldwell. Univ. of Calif. Press 1966 269p $5.50

Original Portuguese edition published 1900. This translation first published 1953 by Noonday

"Relates the life of Bento Santiago of Brazil whose mother wishes him to become a priest. In the seminary he makes a life-long friendship with Escobar. Both soon desert theology: Escobar for commerce, Bento for law. Bento then marries a childhood sweetheart. How his friend and his wife deceive him—(or does it only 'seem to him' that they do?)—is the key to a tragedy with a striking dénouement." Library J

Epitaph of a small winner; tr. from the Portuguese by William L. Grossman. Drawings by Shari Frisch. Noonday 1952 223p illus o.p. 1970

"An ironic and humorous novel by the nineteenth-century Brazilian, Machado de Assis, a mulatto who rose to be the friend of statesmen and president of the Brazilian Academy of Letters. . . . The present novel is presented as the irreverent memoirs of a ghost—Braz Cubas was his name on earth, and although he rose to be a deputy he owed his comfortable life to the invention of the Braz Cubas Plaster. Wealthy and successful enough, he was also blessed—if blessing it was—with the love of his best friend's wife. . . . When, after his own death, he balanced the books of his life he found that the good and the bad mostly canceled each other except for one item—'I had no progeny, I transmitted to no one the legacy of our misery.'" Nation

Esau and Jacob; tr. with an introduction by Helen Caldwell. Univ. of Calif. Press 1965 xx, 287p $5

First published 1904 in Brazil

"This tale is set in the last days of the old Brazilian Empire and concerns the rivalry in love and politics of the twin sons of beautiful, ambitious Natividade, wife of a Rio banker. Narrated by one of Natividade's admirers." Cincinnati

The book "is social criticism done with wit and depth. . . . The novel is full of allusions to classical literature, Dante, and the Bible." Library J

Machado de Assis, Joaquim Maria. See Machado de Assis

Machen, Arthur

Tales of horror and the supernatural; introduction by Philip Van Doren Stern. Dufour 1964 427p illus $6

First published 1948 by Knopf and analyzed in Short Story Index. This edition originally published 1949 in England

Contents: The novel of the black seal; The novel of the white powder; The great god Pan; The white people; The inmost light; The shining pyramid; The bowmen; The great return; The happy children; The bright boy; Out of the earth; N; Children of the pool; The terror

MacInnes, Colin

Absolute beginners

In MacInnes, C. The London novels of Colin MacInnes p249-449

City of spades

In MacInnes, C. The London novels of Colin MacInnes p 1-248

The London novels of Colin MacInnes; City of spades, Absolute beginners, Mr Love and justice. With an introduction by Nat Hentoff. Farrar, Straus 1969 626p $7.50

The three novels were "published from 1957 to 1960. . . . The first takes up the problems of Negroes in London and the misunderstanding they meet, the second is about the generation gap, the third about the relationship between a lawbreaker and a plainclothes policeman." Bk Buyer's Guide

Mr Love and justice

In MacInnes, C. The London novels of Colin MacInnes p451-626

Westward to Laughter. Farrar, Straus [1970 c1969] 237p $5.95

First published 1969 in England

A story concerned "with the relations of blacks and whites . . . [in] the West Indies of the 1750's, where there were white as well as black slaves. The novel is the memoir of Alexander Nairn, a young Scotsman forced into slavery on the island of Laughter. His attempts to liberate himself and his eventual involvement in a slave uprising form the substance of his story." Publisher's note

The author "has written an 18th-century adventure novel for a contemporary audience. On its own merits, the book is morally provocative and entertaining; as a literary imitation, it is quite extraordinary. MacInnes has done his homework in Defoe and Smollett. . . . In keeping with the 18th-century mood, morality, sex and physical suffering are treated by the narrator in an open, explicit and almost offhand manner. It is a novel of brilliant and gruesome surfaces, not one of intellectual subtlety or psychological depth." N Y Times Bk R

MacInnes, Helen

y Above suspicion. Harcourt 1954 333p $5.95

A reissue of the title first published 1941 by Little

"An Oxford don and his very attractive young wife are chosen for a dangerous mission in Germany, in the summer of 1939. They are selected just because they are taking their usual summer vacation on the continent, and can act like ordinary tourists, while following out their work. Their mission is to discover the whereabouts of an anti-Nazi agent. The summer is exciting, nearly ending in tragedy several times, but they come thru successfully." Book Rev Digest

also in MacInnes, H. Assignment: suspense p 1-194

y Assignment in Brittany. Little 1942 373p o.p. 1970

"A young British officer is sent to France after the debacle of Dunkirk, in the guise of a wounded French soldier, to find out what the Nazis planned to do with the coast of France. His was a dangerous mission at best . . . and it became nerve-racking in the extreme when he discovered, almost too late, that there had been important omissions in his information. A fully developed love story, counter-espionage, and touch-and-go situations provide suspense and excitement in a superior tale." Huntting

also in MacInnes, H. Assignment: suspense p315-561

y Assignment: suspense; a three novel omnibus: Above suspicion, Horizon, Assignment in Brittany. Harcourt 1961 561p $7.50

Reprint of three novels of intrigue set in the period of Nazi terror, first published separately 1941, 1946 and 1942 respectively, and entered separately

y Decision at Delphi

Some editions are:
Harcourt $5.95
Watts, F. $9.95 Large type edition complete and unabridged. A Keith Jennison book

First published 1960

"Kenneth Strang and his Greek-American friend Steve Kladas are to meet in Greece for a magazine assignment, but Steve disappears en route, leaving clues that point to his family's activities in World War II. Cecilia Hillard is sent to take Steve's place, and fortunately proves to be as resourceful as she is charming, for she promptly gets involved in Kenneth's dangerous hunt for Steve." Booklist

Miss MacInnes "has added a glamorous gratuity: landscapes from Taormina to Sparta, all freshly observed and deftly sketched into the background, so that, for instance, we get a proposal on the Acropolis, a thrilling midnight chase through the precipitous streets of Athens, and a panoramic finale on the noble heights of Delphi." N Y Her Trib Books

The double image. Harcourt 1966 309p map $5.95

"John Craig stopped in Paris to see his sister before he went to the Mediterranean to research his projected book on trade routes as motives for war. Before he could meet her, he ran into an old friend, Dr. Sussman, and learned of his fear of Heinrich Berg, a Nazi war criminal, alive in Paris, not resting quietly in his Berlin grave. John, too, saw Berg, and after Sussman's suicide, was the only person who could identify him. Security forces felt that an intelligent amateur with good cover and essential information was invaluable, so John became part of the mixed crew of agents, double agents, and innocent bystanders who were involved in Operation Pear Tree on the Greek island of Mykonos." Library J

Horizon

In MacInnes, H. Assignment: suspense p195-313

North from Rome. Harcourt 1958 307p boards $5.95

"In Rome to try to persuade his former fiancée to resume their engagement, American playwright Bill Lammiter goes to the rescue of an Italian girl who is being abducted and straightway finds himself embroiled in intrigue and violence centering in a narcotics ring set up by Moscow with political ends in view. A pursuit leading north out of Rome, the rescue of Bill's Eleanor, who is innocently involved, and the break-up of the ring are recounted." Booklist

y Pray for a brave heart. Harcourt 1955 311p $5.95

"Arrayed against the ruthless brains of an international Communist gang are the ill-fated Max Meyer, of U. S. Counter-Intelligence; Captain William Denning, on terminal leave in Switzerland; Le Brun of the French Intelligence; Keppler of Swiss Security; and the appealing Francesca Vivenzio, involved in the perilous business of rescuing anti-Communist intellectuals from the grip of the Soviets. The background is relatively fresh, the dialogue neat and believable, and there's enough action to satisfy the most hardened reader of thrillers." Book of the Month Club News

MacInnes, Helen—*Continued*

Rest and Be Thankful. Little 1949 368p
o.p. 1970

"Mrs. Peel, a wealthy widow, and Sally Bly, exploring America after many years spent in Europe, get caught in a rainstorm in Wyoming and eventually find their way to the nearest ranch. Here they fall in love with and buy the beautiful ranch house. The whole point of the story is how this peaceful way of life benefits the most sophisticated of their Eastern visitors. Pleasantly written and above the usual type of 'Western'." Library J

y The Salzburg connection. Harcourt 1968
406p $5.95

"In a deep, forbidding lake surrounded by the silent Austrian Alps, the Nazis hid a sealed chest. Now, more than twenty years later, only a handful of people know that the chest exists. Certainly Bill Mathison, a young attorney representing a New York book publisher and arriving in Switzerland on that firm's business, has no such knowledge. He considers his trip little more than routine. Yet, unwittingly, he makes a connection." Am News of Bks

"A fascinating exercise in wide-screen spymanship. . . . The appeal [of the author's books]. I think, lies in [her] unfailing eye for vivid backgrounds; in her deft control of complex story-lines; in her clean-cut presentation of each important member of her casts. These combined qualities have given her fiction a kind of grandeur." N Y Times Bk R

The Venetian affair. Harcourt 1963 405p
$5.95

This "suspense novel is set in Paris and Venice in 1961. An American newspaperman on vacation picks up the wrong raincoat on arrival at Orly airport, and finds himself involved in a Communist plot to assassinate De Gaulle and implicate the United States. American agents enlist his help to thwart the plotters and to unmask the mysterious and ruthless spymaster." Pub W

"Miss MacInnes' (Mrs. Gilbert Highet's) usual skillful plotting, excellent style and happily authentic background make this wonderful reading." Best Sellers

McKay, Allis

y They came to a river. Binfords 651p $5.95

First published 1941 by Macmillan (N Y)

"Although the book is about pioneer life from 1900 to 1920 along the upper Columbia river in Washington, when the now world famous apple orchards were planted, it is Chris Hollowell's development which dominates. The historical and regional material is subordinated to the characters in a well-written story which will please many readers. The daughter of a minister who was also ferryman and postmaster, Chris grew up loving the river and the country. She married a young rancher, brought up her children and managed the orchard after his death, and met both disaster and success with intelligence and common sense. The book closes with Chris at thirty happily beginning a new married life." Booklist

The women at Pine Creek; a novel. Macmillan (N Y) 1966 374p $5.95

Early in the twentieth century "Althea and Mary Hollister inherited from their father an 82-acre tract of land at Pine Creek, Washington. Still in deep mourning and with new luggage and stout hearts, the sisters traveled by train and steamboat to Pine Creek to claim their inheritance. Their courage carried them through the first hard winter and in the spring they planted their own apple orchard. While they dreamed of the apple blossoms and the fruit to come, love and marriage came first to one and then to the other. . . . A good story well told." Library J

Macken, Walter

Rain on the wind. Macmillan (N Y) 1950
312p o.p. 1970

"The life of the poor fishermen of the west coast of Ireland, near Galway, provides the background of this story. The hero is Mico, an honest man, giant in stature, who has a

badly disfigured face, which makes him imagine he will never win the girl he loves. His story is told from the age of five until he really wins the girl." Book Rev Digest

Mr Macken "creates characters as naturally and memorably as he does the savage and the kinder moods of the sea. In its vigour, its humour and poignancy, this is an admirable novel of Irish life." Manchester Guardian

The scorching wind. Macmillan (N Y) 1964
308p $5.95

"This is the story of two brothers, Dominic and Dualta, who grow up in the Ireland of the Anglo-Irish and Civil Wars, a study of the impact of the Troubles on them and of the Troubles themselves. More specifically, it is a study of the effect of these wars on the people of Galway, in the west of Ireland, which is the author's province. In the Civil War it is brother against brother." N Y Times Bk R

Seek the fair land. Macmillan (N Y) 1959
308p map o.p. 1970

An "historical novel about three men whose lives were intertwined during the years when Ireland was under the rule of Oliver Cromwell's armies. One of them is a priest who dies for his faith. Another is a young merchant who succeeds in saving his children from destruction. [The third is a giant from the west highlands where clan wars keep the unrest alive]." Pub W

"Adventure, romance, history all woven into a tight little tale." Library J

The silent people. Macmillan (N Y) 1962
371p illus $5.95

"Irish history in the first half of the 19th century provides the background for this latest work of an Irish actor-novelist. . . . The struggles of tenant farmers against rack-renting, tithes, and eviction; Daniel O'Connell's election as M.P. for Clare; Catholic emancipation: the attempt to repeal the Union with England; and finally the tragedy of the Great Famine are reflected in the lives of Dualta Duane and Una Wilcocks, which provide the narrative's central thread." Library J

McKenna, Richard

Hunter, come home

In Knight, D. ed. A century of great short science fiction novels p343-79

The Sand Pebbles: a novel. Harper 1962
597p $7.95

A "novel with two main, intertwined threads: the titanic struggle of a man trying to find himself and the Chinese rebellion of the 1920's. The man is Jake Holman, machinist assigned to the U.S. gunboat 'San Pablo,' patrolling Chinese waters. Misanthropic with good reason and a determined nonconformist, Jake is beginning to resolve some of his perplexities and rebellions when China erupts. Ordered to refrain from battle for diplomatic reasons 'San Pablo' remains passive under fire and insult until the crew's morale is shattered and the shamed captain takes 'ash, fatal action. Life in engine room, forecastle, and brothel is recreated forthrightly, and the characters, including missionaries and coolies as well as sailors, are individuals to be remembered." Booklist

Mackenzie, Compton

Whisky galore. Dufour 1964 255p $3.50

First published 1947 in England. Published 1959 by Houghton with title: Tight little island

"The diverting story of two beautiful, misty islands in the Outer Hebrides. The war is drawing to a close . . . but not the whiskey shortage. The islanders have had about all the drought they can stand, as they see every drop of Scotch whiskey exported to America—boatload by boatload. Finally, one midnight, they act." Huntting

Mackintosh, Elizabeth. See Tey, Josephine

MacIntosh, Kim Hamilton. See Aird, Catherine

MacLean, Alistair

Fear is the key. Doubleday 1961 264p
o.p. 1970

"This intrigue-adventure story starts in a
courtroom in a town near Clearwater, Florida.
A British soldier, being tried for illegal entry,
suddenly pulls a gun, shoots a police officer,
kidnaps a girl, and escapes. A gang of thugs
who are operating a mysterious salvage operation from an oil rig several miles off shore in
the Gulf of Mexico features in the events which
follow." Huntting

"Like parts of a fine watch, the ingredients
of the story fit together to make an absorbing narrative that moves swiftly to an almost
fantastic climax." Chicago Sunday Tribune

y Force 10 from Navarone. Doubleday 1968
274p map $4.95

The three heroes of The guns of Navarone,
Mallory, Miller and Stavros are assigned a new
mission during World War II. "They are dropped into Yugoslavia to join the Partisans, prevent a German attack, blow up a dam, and provide a diversion to draw German troops out of
Italy." Pub W

"This is a typical Alistair MacLean rapid-
fire, thrill-on-every-page suspense story. . . .
It is escape literature, guaranteed—to hold the
reader to the last page." Library J

The golden rendezvous. Doubleday 1962
301p $4.95

"When an American scientist vanished with
the country's newest nuclear missile, it looked
as though he must have stowed away on the
'Campari,' tramp cargo and passenger ship
favored by millionaires. Then the mysterious
cargo from the dictator-ruled Caribbean island
arrived—apparently bringing with it two more
disappearances and murder. Chief Officer Carter
tells the story." Bk Buyer's Guide

"Readers of adventure-suspense will find the
author up to his usual form in this improbable
but holding yarn." Booklist

y The guns of Navarone. Doubleday 1957
320p $5.95

"Derring-do in the grand tradition, this recounts the exploits of a five-man British army
team chosen to knock out the guns of Navarone, which control the approaches to the
eastern Mediterranean islands." Cincinnati

"The book is literally a cliff-hanger, but it
offers readers the finest kind of vicarious adventure." Sat R

y H.M.S. Ulysses. Doubleday 1956 [c1955]
316p illus map $5.95

First published 1955 in England

"The murderous and tragic World War II
sea route to Murmansk, in Arctic Russia, is the
subject. . . . A blend of naval tactics and high
powered dramatics 'HMS Ulysses' tells of the
week-long disintegration of a British light
cruiser and its overworked 'zombie' crew while
shepherding a convoy in gale-lashed Arctic
waters between Iceland and Sweden's North
Cape." San Francisco Chronicle

The book "is more a legend than a novel of
real flesh and blood people. Like most legends,
it is larger than life. This does not gainsay the
truth of its elements. . . . And despite one's
foreboding of the denouement, despite even
theatrical, sometimes melodramatic touches,
the Ulysses and her officers and men come to
have personal meaning. The result is a moving
and thrilling book." N Y Her Trib Books

y Ice Station Zebra. Doubleday 1963 276p
$4.50

A novel of suspense and intrigue that begins
on "a bitter-cold morning in Holy Loch, Scotland, when a British doctor with top-level en-
dorsements from the American and British
military forces seeks admission to an American
nuclear submarine. The submarine is slated for
a perilous trip to rescue the starving, freezing
British crew of a meteorological station situated on an ice floe in the Arctic." Pub W

"The rescue and the return trip, when the
answers to all mysteries are cleared up, put a
fitting climax to a new class of novel, adventure and mystery. This is not history, but a
fast-moving tale of fiction, which can be and
is 'recommended' to all readers searching for
light diversion." Best Sellers

Night without end. Doubleday 1960 287p
$4.95

"An airliner crash lands on the Greenland
icecap near a small I.G.Y. observation station.
It soon becomes clear that the landing was
planned and certain of the passengers and crew
murdered for reasons unknown, while at least
eight of the 10 survivors were drugged into insensibility—the other two of course, being the
killers. But which two? . . . A sometimes barely credible, but always absorbing, thriller that
combines elements of the espionage story and
murder mystery with those of the 'castaways'
adventure tale." Library J

Puppet on a chain. Doubleday 1969 281p
$5.95

"Maj. Paul Sherman, London chief of Interpol, [is sent] to Amsterdam to collect information on narcotics too valuable to be for-
warded by diplomatic pouch. At Schipol Airport he sees the messenger shot down before
he can reach him. Then problems are compounded by barrel organs, beautiful puppets
exquisitely dressed in traditional Dutch costumes, a picture-book town in the Zuider Zee,
the clocks of Kasteel Linden, and the giant
crane of urban renewal." Library J

"A tightly plotted story with a good deal of
mayhem and an excellent chase sequence."
Book News

The secret ways. Doubleday 1959 286p
o.p. 1970

"Michael Reynolds [a British agent] went
to Hungary to get Professor Jennings [a sci-
entist] away from the communists, but he soon
found he was going to have trouble getting
out himself. And he had fallen in love with the
daughter of the Resistance leader." The Bookseller

South by Java Head. Doubleday 1958 319p
o.p. 1970

In World War II several survivors of the fall
of Singapore to the Japanese in 1942 escape
across the China Seas in an old slave ship.
"Despite the Japanese bombers they keep afloat
long enough to be rescued by a British tanker.
The tanker, too, becomes a Japanese target,
and eventually the members of the group . . .
again find themselves adrift, this time in small
lifeboats." Huntting

"The fact that the characters are rather pat
and the hairbreadth escapes predictable will
probably not disturb [the readers] much, for
they are all made believable through the superb
telling of the story." Library J

When eight bells toll. Doubleday 1966 288p
$5.50

Philip Calvert, the hero-narrator of this action tale of British Intelligence, is concerned
with "the hijacking along the Scottish coast
of a number of small ships carrying extremely
valuble cargo, heavily insured. Slipping aboard
one such ship, the freighter 'Nantesville,' Calvert discovers that the two agents he had
placed on board have been stabbed, and that
he himself is faced with imminent extinction.
But he manages to stay alive as the corpses
pile up. Finally Calvert's chief, Rear Admiral
Sir Arthur Arnford-Jason, K.C.B. (known to
underlings as Uncle Arthur), arrives on the
scene, and it becomes clear that the problem
is to locate the hijackers' hideout and identify
the brains behind the gang." Book of the
Month Club News

"The descriptions—both at sea and of the
technical gadgetry—are realistic and there are
sufficient twists in the plot to maintain interest
until the end." Library J

y Where eagles dare. Doubleday 1967 312p
$4.95

"Secrecy and stealth are essential to the mission of an assorted crew from MI 6 who must
rescue an American general, the coordinator
of Overlord, from Schloss Adler, a castle built
by a mad Bavarian prince, which is the combined HQ of the German Secret Service and
the Gestapo of South Germany in the bitter
winter of 1943-44. And if that isn't enough,
there is Major Smith's second assignment to
bring out the pyrotechnic display of excitement
and suspense." Library J

McLeish, Dougal

The valentine victim. Houghton 1969 201p $4.95

"On her way to a Valentine party [in the little village of Farnham, Ontario] Lori Weston stopped off at the police station to report a prowler outside her house. Hardly had she left the station when the police received a call that one of Lori's stepdaughters had been murdered. Inspector Rodericks solves the case in time to save the other daughter." Book News

A "highly satisfactorily and credibly resolved [novel] with enough side plots and love interest to keep the mind pleasantly diverted from the corpse who started it all." Harper

MacLennan, Hugh

Return of the sphinx. Scribner 1967 303p 5.95

Set in Ottawa and Montreal, this is the "story of a struggle in two dimensions, the separatists against the English and the Canadian establishment and the personalizing of that struggle in the tension between a father and son. Alan Ainslie, a government official, and his son, a hotheaded and immature youth, almost destroy each other in their support of opposite ideals for their country." Booklist

"Presents a penetrating cross-section of the temper of modern society." McClurg. Book News

Two solitudes. Duell 1945 370p o.p. 1970

A novel based upon the lack of understanding between French and English in Canada. It is told in terms of two families, one, French landowners from a small, old world Quebec village, the other, English businessmen from Montreal. Through the years from 1916 to the beginning of the present second world war, Pierre Tallard and Heather Methuen of the younger generation fare better in strength of mind and spirit than their elders—Pierre's father who died of his tragic indecision and Heather's mother who lived by her grief and other people's safe opinions. (Publisher)

"A novel of great warmth and skill, well characterized with people whose lives are interwoven with racial and religious problems of their homeland." Ontario Lib Rev

Macleod, Alison

City of light. Houghton 1969 287p $4.95

Sequel to: The hireling

Continues the story of "Tom Vaughan, an exile from England, [who] leaves 16th century Venice for Geneva, to see his [illegitimate] son, Timothy. He finds Geneva clean, orderly, but ruled by Calvin and his bigoted followers. Becoming friendly with Dr. Bologna and his wife, Constanza, Tom has a near escape from death: the doctor dies of natural causes, and Tom eventually marries Constanza." Bk Buyer's Guide

"While a previous reading of 'The Hireling' is not required, there are often references to events which occurred in it, and this is sometimes confusing. However, this exciting Tudor story has more than enough attributes to overcome this fault and will carry the reader back into an age we read about in history but rarely find captured with such detail, precision, and finesse." Library J

The heretic; a novel. Houghton 1966 [1965] 243p $5.95

First published 1965 in England with title: The heretics

"In 16th-century England a heretic was anyone who dared question the beliefs held by the reigning sovereign. Anne Askew disagreed with Henry VIII, who was himself a heretic in the eyes of the Catholic Church. Her real crime seems to have been her insistence that her marriage was a nullity. She had been forced, while still a child, to marry Thomas Kyne, who later turned her out of his house." Am News of Bks

"This absorbing 16th-century novel . . . is written as if told 15 years later by Nancy Scarlett, Anne's personal maid, to a chronicler of the Protestant Martyrs. It shows the changes —religious and some social—that had come about in England. . . . The book is well written." Library J

The hireling. Houghton 1968 256p $4.95

"How Tom Vaughan is selected by Thomas Cromwell to spy on Katherine of Aragon for Henry VIII and is later assigned to spy on Cardinal Pole in Italy. But when Cromwell loses Henry VIII's favor, Tom Vaughan changes sides and wins back his self respect." Bk Buyers Guide

Followed by: City of light

Macpherson, Annie Winifred (Ellerman) See Bryher

McPherson, James Alan

Hue and cry; short stories. Little 1969 275p boards $5.95

"An Atlantic Monthly Press book"

A collection of ten "stories about Negroes— Pullman porters, students, intellectuals, jazz musicians, Black Power leaders—and about whites as well." N Y Times Bk R

Contents: A matter of vocabulary; On trains; A solo song: for Doc; Gold coast; Of cabbages and kings; All the lonely people; An act of prostitution; Private domain; A new place; Hue and cry

Macpherson, Winifred (Ellerman) See Bryher

McWhirter, Millie

Hushed were the hills. Abingdon 1969 176p boards $3.95

"The author here has set down reminiscences of her stay in Willow Creek, Tennessee. Her mother, recently widowed, brought Millie and Polly to this remote corner of the hills to ta : a post as teacher in the two-room school. Although the period was that of the Depression and they were from The Town, they became part of a community where people knew each other well and lived by a common standard. Their lives were close to the soil and the surrounding harsh but beautiful hills. All of this spiced with superstition and deep religious belief. . . . Although by any standard this is a slight book, it has charm. The spare use of country language makes for easy reading while still retaining the flavor of authenticity. In all, a pleasant diversion for a few hours of rest and relaxation." Best Sellers

The Magazine of Fantasy and Science Fiction

The Best from Fantasy and Science Fiction; 1st-18th ser. See The Best from Fantasy and Science Fiction; 1st-18th ser.

A decade of Fantasy and Science Fiction; selected by Robert P. Mills. Doubleday 1960 406p o.p. 1970

Analyzed in Short Story Index

Twenty-five "stories range from the wryly humorous to the deadly serious, from the purely ingenious to the downright sinister." Publisher's note

Contents: The Martian shop, by H. Fast; Walk like a mountain, by M. W. Wellman; Men of iron, by G. Endore; Rabbits to the moon, by R. E. Banks; The certificate, by A. Davidson; The sealman, by J. Masefield; The Sky People, by P. Anderson; The causes, by I. Seabright; The hypnoglyph by J. Anthony; A tale of the thirteenth floor, by O. Nash; Spud and Cochise, by O. La Farge; Unto the fourth generation, by I. Asimov; Jordan, by Z. Henderson; Will you wait, by A. Bester; Proof positive, by G. Greene; Shock treatment, by J. F. McComas; Gandolphus, by A. Boucher; The last shall be first, by R. P. Mills; A trick or two, by J. Novotny; Lot's daughter, by W. Moore; Saturnian Celia, by H. Walpole; Fear is a business, by T. Sturgeon; Meeting of relations, by J. Collier; First lesson, by M. Clingerman; To fell a tree, by R. F. Young

Magidoff, Robert

(ed.) Russian science fiction, 1968-1969; an anthology. Comp. and ed. by Robert Magidoff. N.Y. Univ. Press 1968-1969 2v 1968 $6.50, 1969 $6.95

1968 volume translated by Helen Jacobson, and Analyzed in Short Story Index

Magidoff, Robert—*Continued*

Contents: 1968: A dweller in two worlds, by G. Gor; Desert encounter, by I. Rosokhvatsky; Tales of the distant past, by R. Podolny; The heroic feat, by A. Dnieprov; Formula for the impossible, by E. Voisunsky; Life is so dull for little girls, by K. Bulichev; Thread of life, by Y. Safronov; The mystery of Green Crossing, by M. Emtsov; Storm, by V. Zhuravleva; In man's own image, by I. Varshavsky; The founding of civilization, by R. Yarov; The robotniks, by V. Bakhnov; Mutiny, by V. Bakhnov
1969: In the land of science fiction (essay) by Y. Brandis; Journey into the future (essay) by D. Granin; Unique, by V. Bakhnov; Speaking of demonology, by V. Bakhnov; Crabs take over the island, by A. Dnieprov; The garden, by G. Gor; Human frailty, by A. Xlebnikov; A modest genius: a fairy-tale for grown-ups, by V. Shefner; A raid takes place at midnight, by I. Varshavsky; A farewell on the shore, by Y. Voiskunsky; Robot humor, by E. Zubkov; The minotaur, by G. Gor

Mahoney, William

Black Jacob; a novel. Macmillan (N Y) 1969 247p $5.95

The story "of Jacob Blue, a successful Negro doctor in 'Matchez,' Mississippi, who had the naive daring to run for Congress. What makes Jacob unique is that he had rarely before personally encountered either the overt and overpowering hostility of the white world or the degrading poverty and repressed hatred of the poor blacks. As his campaign progresses, Jacob relies increasingly on the organizational help of civil rights workers who rally the exploited laborers and farmers to his support. Intimidation and coercion inevitably change to open violence." Pub W

Mailer, Norman

An American dream. Dial Press 1965 270p $4.95

"A satiric novel replete with some very rough sex; a novel in the tradition Mailer has set for himself, a nightmare vision of life. The central character is a hard-drinking TV figure who has fought in World War II, dabbled in politics, married a rich wife, and taught in a university. He has schizophrenic tendencies. He realizes he could murder someone: then he chokes his wife to death, not without provocation. This is only the beginning of the deliberately fantastic plot. The action skips all over New York City from Harlem to the Waldorf Towers." Pub W

"It is an American Dream as Oedipus the King is a Greek dream: not the fantasying of a personal or communal ideal but the acting out of personal and communal guilt. . . . Though the idiom of the novel is perfectly, and often brilliantly, realistic . . . the atmosphere is mythic. . . . The states of mind are extreme, not rendered by psychological explanation but with an extraordinary, almost unbearable immediacy." Harper

The naked and the dead

Some editions are:
Holt $6
Modern Lib. $2.95
First published 1948

"A long novel based on the reactions of the members of an American platoon to their part of the invasion and occupation of a Japanese-held island—presumably in 1944. The action is divided into three dramatic stories: the landing on the island; a Japanese counter-attack by night; and a daring patrol of the platoon behind the enemy lines." Book Rev Digest

"It is distinguished primarily for simple realism, a forthright, almost childlike honesty, a command of ordinary speech, a cool and effortless narrative style, quickened here & there with a mild, understated humor. The battle scenes are so vivid as to suggest Tolstoy's War and Peace, the common soldiers as clearly visualized as Tolstoy's peasants." Time

Major, Charles

When knighthood was in flower. . . . AMS Press [1970 c1898] 295p illus $7.50

A reprint of the title first published 1898 by Bowen-Merrill

"The love story of Charles Brandon and Mary Tudor, the King's sister, and happening in the reign of Henry VIII; rewritten and rendered into modern English from Sir Edwin Caskoden's memoir, by Edwin Caskoden <Charles Major>." Subtitle

Malamud, Bernard

The assistant; a novel. Farrar, Straus 1957 246p boards $4.50

"Novel about a poverty-stricken Jewish family living in New York City. Bad luck seems to follow the footsteps of the Bobers in every thing and in every way. The only son dies, their grocery store is a failure, the daughter cannot achieve her desire to go to college, the assistant at the store steals from the Bobers. After the death of the grocer, the assistant takes over." Book Rev Digest

"'The Assistant' will reaffirm his talent as a writer about simple people struggling to make their lives better in a world of bad luck. The clarity and concreteness of his style, the warm humanity over his people, the tender wit that keeps them firm and compassionate, will delight many." N Y Times Bk R

also in Malamud, B. A Malamud reader

The fixer. Farrar, Straus 1966 335p $5.75

Pulitzer Prize. 1967

In Kiev "a handy man becomes a hero in spite of himself when he is unjustly accused of a murder as part of an anti-Semitic movement. Set in Czarist Russia." Pub W

"What Mr. Malamud has done in this novel, his fourth, is to present a study of human suffering in which the sufferer, a common ordinary man, manages to rise above his suffering and to remain alive when death seems easier, simply as a symbol of truth. . . . The Christian reads these pages with a sense of shocked outrage as the worst accusations of the Middle Ages are hurled against the Jews in the present century, including, most horribly, that of ritualistic blood-murder." Best Sellers

"The prose is transparently simple, like that of an old legend. The atmosphere of the long-ago period is remarkably conveyed." Book of the Month Club News

Idiots first. Farrar, Straus 1963 212p boards $4.50

Analyzed in Short Story Index

"Powerful, bitter short stories about men and women defeated by life. Malamud's main characters, trapped in desperately tragic circumstances, are mostly American Jews, and the settings are mostly New York City or Italy. The writer's insight is painfully accurate, and the writing, as to be expected of Malamud, is superb." Pub W

Contents: Idiots first; Black is my favorite color; Still life; The death of me; A choice of profession; Life is better than death; The Jewbird; Naked nude; The cost of living; The maid's shoes; Suppose a wedding [a scene from a play]; The German refugee

The magic barrel. Farrar, Straus 1958 214p boards $5.50

Analyzed in Short Story Index

"A collection of short stories with a strong folk flavor. Each tale reveals some facet or characteristic of the Jewish tradition." Booklist

Contents: The first seven years; The mourners; The girl of my dreams; Angel Levine; Behold the key; Take pity; The prison; The lady of the lake; A summer's reading; The bill; The last Mohican; The loan; The magic barrel

"They all are quietly, thoroly done stories. There are no flourishes of fancy words, no sensational exploitations of shock or melodrama. This is gentle work, with a curious, almost magical charm. And perhaps the charm lies, really, in the profound concern shown in every story for people, for human existence itself, for what might even be called the holiness of life." Chicago Sunday Tribune

A Malamud reader. Farrar, Straus 1967 528p boards $6.95

Analyzed in Short Story Index

Contains ten short stories from: Idiots first, and The magic barrel, and selections from the novels: A new life, The natural, and The fixer. This book also includes the complete text of: The assistant, first published 1957

Malamud, Bernard—*Continued*

Short stories included: The mourners; Idiots first; The first seven years; Take pity; The maid's shoes; Black is my favorite color; The Jewbird; The magic barrel; The German refugee; The last Mohican

The natural. Farrar, Straus 1961 237p $4.95

First published 1952 by Harcourt

"The story follows Roy Hobbs and his record-shattering baseball career, and the bizarre company: Pop, the canny manager of the Knights; Otto Zipp, the monomaniacal midget; the Judge, owner of the Knights; and Max Mercy, the coolly suspicious sportswriter." Publisher's note

"What he has done is to contrive a sustained and elaborate allegory in which the 'natural' player—who operates with ease and the greatest skill, without having been taught—is equated with the natural man who, left alone by, say, politicians and advertising agencies, might achieve his real fulfillment. . . . A brilliant and unusual book." N Y Times Bk R

A new life. Farrar, Straus 1961 367p $5.95

"Thirty-year-old Seymour Levin, late of New York City, takes a college teaching job in the Pacific Northwest in the hopes of creating a completely new life for himself. He finds the conservatism and intellectual apathy of the college and community deeply disturbing but seeks solace in an affair with a colleague's wife whom he later marries. Some of the people and situations seem contrived but the college and the town, as seen through a newcomer's eyes, take on reality. The time is 1950." Booklist

What the author "has attempted in the book, I think, is a rather special kind of realism, disregarding all the familiar categories of fiction. This is basically a serious novel about the difficulties of leading the good life, and in the end, because he will not abandon his struggle, Levin emerges as a hero. . . . [Malamud] has taken most unpromising materials and, by virtue of insight, technical mastery, and a kind of heroic quality in himself, has made out of them an exciting and memorable novel." Sat R

Pictures of Fidelman; an exhibition. Farrar, Straus 1969 208p boards $5.95

"Six picaresque episodes in the life of Fidelman, 'artiste manqué' from the Bronx, who has come to Italy to find himself. . . . [The stories] form a caustic whole, sometimes richly comic, sometimes terrifying, as they depict Fidelman's fall from New World naiveté and hope, his ferocious attempts to hang onto the idea of being an artist even though it is clear he will never make it, and his equally ill-fated grapplings with love. . . . He is a memorable human being." Pub W

Contents: Last Mohican; Still life; Naked nude; A pimp's revenge; Pictures of the artist; Glass blower of Venice

Mallea, Eduardo

All green shall perish, and other novellas and stories; ed. with an introduction, by John B. Hughes; tr. from the Spanish by the editor and others. Knopf 1966 xxiii, 431p $7.95

Analyzed in Short Story Index

Includes three short novels: Fiesta in November; All green shall perish; Chaves; and the following short stories, Anguish; The lost cause of Jacob Uber; The heart's reason; The shoes

"The translations, each by a different person, are excellent. The introduction is long and incisive. Highly recommended for all serious fiction collections." Library J

Chaves

In Mallea, E. All green shall perish, and other novellas and stories p253-303

Fiesta in November

In Mallea, E. All green shall perish, and other novellas and stories p 1-108

Malleson, Lucy Beatrice. See Gilbert, Anthony

Mallet-Joris, Françoise

The favourite; tr. from the French by Herma Briffault. Farrar, Straus 1962 282p o.p. 1970

"A novel based on the character of Louise de La Fayette, maid of honor to Queen Anne and a favorite of King Louis XIII. . . . The purity of the friendship between the king and the girl set against the cynicism and intrigue of the court arouses the jealousy of the factions of both Richelieu and the queen. This fact combined with Louise's refusal to become part of either clique leads to her banishment to a convent. Against this backdrop the author uses reverie, impressionistic conversation, letters, and chronicles to show Louise's gradual realization that she has taken the right course for the wrong reason. A grave and dramatic novel for the reader of serious fiction." Booklist

The witches; three tales of sorcery. Tr. by Herma Briffault. Farrar, Straus 1969 391p $6.95

Contents: Anne, or Theater; Elizabeth, or Demonic love; Jeanne, or Revolt

"These three stories about 'witches' are really stories about exceptional girls acting in unusual ways. One 'witch' is Anne, daughter of a drunkard, who is easily persuaded to turn from 'pure' religion to the black arts and who suffers accordingly. The second is Elizabeth, a strictly brought-up young girl whose sexual longings, long repressed, lead her to 'unnatural acts.' The third is Jeanne, a particularly brilliant girl who, when brought to trial as a witch, demonstrates the remarkable powers of insight (even into the character of her judge) which caused her to be tried in the first place." Book of the Month Club News

Malraux, André

The conquerors

In Dupee, F. W. ed. Great French short novels p535-717

Days of wrath; tr. by Haakon M. Chevalier; with a foreword by Waldo Frank. Random House 1936 174p o.p. 1970

"A short novel which tells a story of a Communist's imprisonment in a Nazi concentration camp, his release when an unknown comrade takes his place, and his reunion with his wife and child." Book Rev Digest

"André Malraux's vivid prose is well suited to his subject; he utilizes all his sharpest weapons—logic, brutality, fantasy, beauty—to make this brief story of Kassner's incarceration and triumph a burning commentary on contemporary conditions." Christian Science Monitor

Man's fate (La condition humaine)

Some editions are:

Modern Lib. $2.95 Translated by Haakon M. Chevalier

Random House boards $4.95

"First published in the United States by Smith & Haas in 1934. Published in England under title: Storm in Shanghai

"Out of the conspiracy, the bombing, and the bloodshed of the Shanghai insurrection of 1927, and against a background of Oriental vice, emerges a small group of revolutionaries. They are French, Russian, Japanese, and Chinese, but are all engaged in the same social struggle to free the Chinese workers. . . . The problem of the novel is the dilemma with which these men find themselves abruptly confronted—namely, the determination of the value of human life." Booklist

"Undoubtedly one can learn a great deal about the Chinese revolution in particular and about revolutionary tactics in general from this work, but it is not so much a record or a manual of revolution that Malraux has written as a profound study of universal human psychology under the pressure of a particular set of conditions." Nation

Man's hope; tr. from the French by Stuart Gilbert and Alastair Macdonald. Random House 1938 511p o.p. 1970

Published in England under title: Days of hope

Malraux, André—*Continued*

"The story of the first eight months of the Civil War in Spain. The author has himself served in Spain as commander of the Loyalist government's International air force." Book Rev Digest

"Vividly realistic as it is, the book is remarkably free from that senseless dwelling upon physical injuries which often weakens the effect of war novels. M. Malraux has concentrated upon the essential rather than the incidental horrors of war, of civil war in particular." Manchester Guardian

Mandel, Paul

The Black Ship [by] Paul and Sheila Mandel. Random House [1969 c1968] 371p $5.95

"Lieutenant Craig is part of an untried American torpedo boat squadron assigned to Britain in the spring of 1943 and reluctantly allowed by the British to participate in a battle against the elusive SS German destroyer nicknamed the Black Ship. Craig's boat is sunk, but he manages to reach shore in Holland where reunited with several shipmates he joins with the Dutch underground in a daring and hazardous plan to destroy the Black Ship in the harbor." Booklist

Mandel, Sheila

(jt. auth.) Mandel, P. The Black Ship

Mankiewicz, Don M.

Trial. Harper 1955 306p o.p. 1970

"A realistic picture of Communist exploration of the trial of a young Mexican for rape and murder. The place is a West Coast city where racial prejudice makes a verdict of guilt highly probable, a situation seized on by the Communists. The novel presents quite clearly the helplessness of the innocent defendant, the ruthless moving in of the front name defense lawyer, the innocent involvement of a law professor, and the far from objective motivations and conduct of others connected with the case." Booklist

Mankowitz, Wolf

A kid for two farthings; illus. by James Boswell. Dutton 1954 [c1953] 120p illus o.p. 1970

First published 1953 in England
"In London's East Side Jewish community there lived a number of people who each wanted something very badly—Mr. Kadinsky a steam presser, the apprentice boy money to buy his girl a ring, little Joe the return of his father from Africa. So little Joe buys a unicorn [goat] in the animal market, and with faith and love, quite a few people win their hearts' desires." Book Rev Digest

"In this enchanting story, so brief in length, so rich in content, London's East End is drawn in all its stark realism and immense sociability through the haze of a 6-year-old boy's fantasy." N Y Times Bk R

Manley, Seon

(ed.) Shapes of the supernatural; ed. by Seon Manley and Gogo Lewis. Doubleday 1969 370p illus $5.95

In this collection the editors have selected ten pairs of stories "each pair containing one story from the nineteenth century and one from the twentieth, in order to show the continuing pattern and strange new shapes of a world just beyond the frontiers of human understanding." Publisher's note

Contents: The werewolf, by H. B. Marryat; The ghost-eater, by C. M. Eddy; The secret of Goresthorpe Grange, by Sir A. C. Doyle; The crown Derby plate, by M. Bowen; William Wilson, by E. A. Poe; The statement of Randolph Carter, by H. P. Lovecraft; On the river, by G. de Maupassant; The uncharted isle, by C. A. Smith; The bagman's story, by C. Dickens; A warning to the curious, by M. R. James; Rappaccini's daughter, by N. Hawthorne; The flowering of the strange orchid, by H. G. Wells; Mad Monkton, by W. Collins; The hound of death, by A. Christie; The banshee; The albatross, by H. Bolitho; The old nurse's story, by E. Gaskell; The rocking-horse winner, by D. H. Lawrence; The diamond lens, by F. O'Brien; The fly, by G. Langelaan

Mann, Heinrich

Henry, King of France; tr. from the German by Eric Sutton. Knopf 1939 786p o.p. 1970

Published in England under title: Henri quatre, king of France

A sequel to: Young Henry of Navarre. The present volume begins after the battle of Arques and carries the story on to the assassination of King Henry

"Has a breadth, vigour and scholarship that makes one forgive its shortcomings." New Statesman & Nation

Young Henry of Navarre; tr. from the German by Eric Sutton. Knopf 1937 585p o.p. 1970

Published in England with title: King Wren; the youth of Henry II

"A long, exciting historical novel, done with great verisimilitude of scene and with excellent visualization of character development, the whole centering in the fascinating person of Henry of Navarre, from his childhood until he became king of France as Henry IV in 1589. The machinations and deadly intrigues, the fleeting sensuous adventures exotic glamour and dissoluteness of the court, and the turbulent clashes in state and religion, all are caught in the surging flood of the engrossing narrative." N Y Libraries

Mann, Thomas

Nobel Prize in literature, 1929

The beloved returns. Lotte in Weimar, tr. from the German by H. T. Lowe-Porter. Knopf 1940 453p $4.95

Originally published 1939 in Sweden with title: Lotte in Weimar

"An acute, erudite and sometimes humorous presentation of Goethe, his creative power and weaknesses. The novel is centered around Charlotte Kestner's return to Weimar after many years to see again the Goethe who immortalized her as Lotte in his 'Sorrows of Werther.' In her long conversations with the inn's head waiter and prominent citizens, Goethe's character is partially delineated." Booklist

"Exquisitely written study of what achieving genius does to a human being. An unforgettable contrast is drawn between the aging poet, now a public figure, and the finely natural woman who has lived life humanly, not as material for poetry." Book of the Month Club News

The black swan; tr. from the German by Willard R. Trask. Knopf 1954 141p $3.95

"A short novel about the infatuation of a middle-aged widow in Düsseldorf for the young American tutor of her son. Frau Rosalie von Tümmler had always worshipped nature; when she suddenly returned to the sexual vigor of her youth in the middle of her menopause she thanked nature for this miracle, and set about to consummate her affair. It was never to take place, for in a few weeks Frau Rosalie lay dead from cancer of the uterus." Booklist

"None of the characters is developed with enough amplitude to make them very interesting, and Mann lavishes all his attention on the invention of symbolic detail. What determines the pattern of symbolism, of course, is the special quality of Rosalie's experience—the deceptive flowering of life and joy from death and corruption." New Repub

Buddenbrooks; tr. from the German by H. T. Lowe-Porter. Together with Lubeck as a way of life and thought; a lecture by the author on June 5, 1926, on the 700 anniversary of its founding; tr. from the German by Richard and Clara Winston. Knopf 1964 xxiv, 604p $6.95

Original German edition 1901; first published 1924 in America in a two volume edition

"This novel is already one of the classics of modern German literature. . . . It is the chronicle of the Buddenbrook family through four generations. In the first generation of 1830, we see Johann Buddenbrook the respected head of a prosperous family of Lübeck's merchant nobility; in the next, with

Mann, Thomas—*Continued*

Consul Buddenbrook, all the appearances of prosperity and success are still there, but in the third generation of Thomas and Christian, a decline is noticeable, the firm is sinking, and not even the election of Thomas as Senator can conceal the fact that the Buddenbrooks are on the downward grade. After his death the business is sold, and in the last generation, Hanno, the weak, dreamy, ineffectual artist, symbolizes the extinction of a great family through over-refinement." Publisher's note

Confessions of Felix Krull, confidence man; the early years. Tr. from the German by Denver Lindley

Some editions are:
Knopf $4.95
Modern Lib. $2.95

Originally written as a short story in 1921. This novel was first published 1954 in Germany "On the surface 'Felix Krull' is a light-hearted study of an artistic rogue who makes a career out of chicanery and considers himself an eminent citizen of the modern world." N Y Times Bk R

"In its adventurous and episodic quality it is . . . [Mann's] closest approach to the picaresque novel. Krull, like many of Mann's characters, represents the artist, and his profession indicates the symbolic connection in Mann's mind between the artist and the actor or charlatan." Benét. The Reader's Encyclopedia

Death in Venice; tr. from the German by Kenneth Burke. Knopf 1965 118p $6

Original German edition 1913
"Gustav von Aschenbach, the hero, is a successful author, proud of the self-discipline with which he has ordered his life and work. On a trip to Venice, however, he becomes aware of mysterious decadent potentialities in himself, and he finally succumbs to a consuming love for a frail but beautiful Polish boy named Tadzio. Though he learns that there is danger of a cholera epidemic in Venice, he finds he cannot leave the city, and eventually dies of the disease. The story is permeated by a rich and varied symbolism with frequent overtones from Greek literature and mythology." Benét. The Reader's Encyclopedia

also in Mann, T. The Thomas Mann reader

also in Neider, C. ed. Short novels of the masters p439-98

also in Pick, R. ed. German stories and tales p302-68

Doctor Faustus; the life of the German composer, Adrian Leverkühn, as told by a friend; tr. from the German by H. T. Lowe-Porter

Some editions are:
Knopf $4.95
Modern Lib. $2.95

Original German edition, 1947
In this novel "the intense and tragic career of the hero Adrian Leverkühn, a composer is made to parallel the collapse of Germany in World War II. To achieve this end, Mann employs the device of having another character, Serenus Zeitblom, narrate Leverkühn's story from memory, while the war is going on, and intersperse his narrative with remarks about the present situation. In this way, it is implied that it is the same demonic and always potentially destructive energy inherent in Leverkühn's music that is also, on a larger scale, behind the outburst of Nazism. Mann thus suggests that the violent 'Faustian' drive, when it is not diverted into art, or when there is no single artistic genius to harness it into creative process, will be perverted and result in grossly sub-human degradation." Benét. The Reader's Encyclopedia

Joseph and his brothers; tr. from the German by H. T. Lowe-Porter; with an introduction by the author. Knopf 1948 xxi, 1207p $12.50

An omnibus edition of four titles published separately, now all out of print
Contents: The tales of Jacob; Young Joseph; Joseph in Egypt; Joseph the provider

Joseph in Egypt
In Mann, T. Joseph and his brothers p447-840

Joseph the provider
In Mann, T. Joseph and his brothers p843-1207

The magic mountain (Der Zauberberg); tr. from the German by H. T. Lowe-Porter. Knopf 1927 900p $6.95

"Hans Castorp, a young German, goes to the International Sanitorium of Berghof to visit a tubercular cousin for three weeks, but, discovering that he too is diseased, stays on for seven years, only released by his call to the Great [first world] War." Open Shelf
"The novel is much more than a discussion of the effects of disease in an isolated group; it is a tremendous philosophical and prophetic treatise on contemporary society, and all the issues and ideas of the 20th century western world enter into it. The sanatorium itself, as a community organized with exclusive reference to ill health, stands as a symbol of the diseased capitalistic society of prewar Europe —the world which made war inevitable. This outer world is seen thru the diseased minds of the patients, and the book ends in fact with society plunged into the maelstrom of the World War. Similarly the ostensible hero, a young engineer of no great importance in himself, assumes profound importance as a representative of humanity subjected to the stress of primal experiences." Lenrow. Reader's Guide to Prose Fiction

Stories of three decades; tr. from the German by H. T. Lowe-Porter

Some editions are:
Knopf $6.75
Modern Lib. $4.95

Analyzed in Short Story Index
First published 1936
Contents: Little Herr Friedemann; Disillusionment; Dilettante; Tobias Mindernickel; Little Lizzy; Wardrobe; Way to the churchyard; Tonio Kröger; Tristan; Hungry; Infant prodigy; Gladius Dei; Fiorenza; Gleam; At the prophet's; Weary hour; Blood of the Walsungs; Railway accident; Fight between Jappe and Do Escobar; Felix Krull; Death in Venice; Man and his dog; Disorder and early sorrow; Mario and the magician

The tales of Jacob
In Mann, T. Joseph and his brothers p3-258

The Thomas Mann reader; selected, arranged, and ed. by Joseph Warner Angell. Knopf 1950 xx, 754p o.p. 1970

Includes short novels: Tonio Kröger; Death in Venice. Excerpts from Buddenbrooks, The magic mountain and Joseph and his brothers and Dr Faustus; Essays and character portraits; Political essays and credo. Also the following four short stories: Disillusionment; The wardrobe; The way to the churchyard; At the prophets

Tonio Kröger
In Mann, T. The Thomas Mann reader

Young Joseph
In Costain, T. B. comp. Twelve short novels p 1-105

In Mann, T. Joseph and his brothers p261-444

Mannes, Marya

They; a novel. Doubleday 1968 215p $4.95
"As chilling a little exercise in futuristic horror as you are likely to encounter, this first novel by the talented commentator on the American scene so unrelievedly grim that it makes painful, if provocative, reading. In the computerized America of the not-so-distant future the printed word is obsolete. . . . 'They' are in complete power, and 'They' are the ruthless young. At age 50 everyone is forcibly

Mannes, Marya—*Continued*

retired, 'put-away' to live in special communities. . . . At 65, if death has not occurred under these repressive conditions, life is ended, voluntarily or involuntarily. Miss Mannes focuses on five people living together for some years in a lonely house by the sea, all of them now nearing the dread cut-off year of 65. They philosophize endlessly. . . . The philosophizing, however, makes this more of a tract than a novel, and the strange figure of a deaf mute young man washed up from the sea to accompany the five in their last days adds a touch of symbolism more mystifying than anything else." Pub W

Manning, Adelaide Frances Oke. See Coles, Manning

Mannix, Daniel P.

The killers; illus. by George Ford. Dutton 1968 255p $5.95

The author tells the story of a life-long duel between two birds—Whitehackle, a fighting cock, and Ishmael, a female Cooper's hawk. The setting is a Pennsylvania Dutch farm and the surrounding woods. (Publisher)

"Mr. Mannix has romanticized both the fighting cock and the wild hawk in this account of a life-long struggle: of the cock to maintain his farmyard dominance, of the hawk to survive. . . . In all, one's sympathies are aroused for both protagonists; and it is of interest to report that in spite of the title, both killers survived." Best Sellers

Mano, D. Keith

Bishop's progress; a novel. Houghton 1968 356p $5.95

"Whitney Belknap, Episcopal Bishop of Queens, author of the best-selling 'A God for Our Time,' is a man who preaches 'Love' without knowing its meaning. He discovers he has a serious heart condition requiring immediate surgery. One of the few who can perform it is Dr. Terrence Snow, self-described as 'one of the three or four greatest surgeons in America.' He is in many ways the Bishop's own reflection. . . . In Belknap he is hoping to find someone who 'can help me—vindicate me, condemn me.' Employing a day-by-day chronicle as a framework, Mr. Mano follows the proud, egocentric Bishop from the time of his arrival in the hospital through his spiritual testing by Snow, his reaction to his fellow patients, and his realization that he 'wasn't prepared for death.'" Pub W

Horn. Houghton 1969 337p $5.95

Set in the early 1970's this is the "story of Negro George Horn Smith, from whose forehead an eleven inch horn thrust outward and upward. Using his freakishness, Horn became many things and ultimately a sort of king in Harlem until one of his co-leaders turned against him. The Rev. C. B. Pratt of St. Bart's in Harlem, who becomes Horn's victim and friend, tells this story of hate and a strange love." Bk Buyer's Guide

"Although it has its weaknesses, 'Horn' successfully blends symbolism, realism and fantasy in an ominous and not altogether far-fetched picture." Pub W

Mansfield, Katherine

Bliss, and other stories. Knopf 1923 277p o.p. 1970

Analyzed in Short Story Index

Contents: Prelude; Je ne parle pas français; Bliss; The wind blows; Psychology; Pictures; The man without a temperament; Mr Reginald Peacock's day; Sun and Moon; Feuille d'album; A dill pickle; The little governess; Revelations; The escape

The garden party, and other stories. Knopf 1923 255p o.p. 1970

Analyzed in Short Story Index

Contents: At the bay; The garden party; The daughters of the late colonel; Mr and Mrs Dove; The young girl; Life of Ma Parker; Marriage à la mode; The voyage; Miss Brill; Her first ball; The singing lesson; The stranger; Bank holiday; An ideal family; The lady's maid

The short stories of Katherine Mansfield. Knopf 1937 688p $6.95

Analyzed in Short Story Index

Contents: Tiredness of Rosabel; How Pearl Button was kidnapped; Journey to Bruges; Truthful adventure; New dresses; Germans at meat; Baron; Sister of the baroness; Frau Fischer; Frau Brechenmacher attends a wedding; Modern soul; At Lehmann's; Luft bad; Birthday; Child-who-was-tired; Advanced lady; Swing of the pendulum; Blaze; Woman at the store; Ole Underwood; Little girl; Millie; Pension Séguin; Violet; Bains Turcs; Something childish but very natural; Indiscreet journey; Spring pictures; Little governess; Wind blows; Prelude; At the bay; Late at night; Two tuppenny ones, please; Black cap; Suburban fairy tale; Psychology; Carnation; Feuille d'album; Dill pickle; Bliss; Je ne parle pas francais; Sun and Moon; Mr Reginald Peacock's day; Pictures; Sea-saw; This flower; Wrong house; Man without a temperament; Revelations; Escape; Bank holiday; Young girl; Stranger; Lady's maid; Daughters of the late colonel; Life of Ma Parker; Singing lesson; Mr and Mrs Dove; Ideal family; Her first ball; Sixpence; Voyage; Garden-party; Miss Brill; Marriage à la mode; Poison; Doll's house; Honeymoon; Cup of tea; Taking the veil; Fly; Canary; Married man's story; Doves' nest; Six years after; Daphne; Father and the girls; All serene; Bad idea; Man and his dog; Such a sweet old lady; Honesty; Susannah; Second violin; Mr and Mrs Williams; Weak heart; Widowed

Manzoni, Alessandro

The betrothed, "I promessi sposi"; a tale of XVII century Milan. Tr. with a preface by Archibald Colquhoun. Dutton 1956 xxvi, 535p (Everyman's lib) $2.95

Original Italian edition published 1824

"The story tells of Renzo and Lucia, peasant lovers. They are about to be married when Father Abbondino, the priest who is to officiate at the ceremony, is threatened with death by Don Rodrigo and his bandits, for Don Rodrigo is desirous of claiming Lucia for himself. Lucia thereupon enters a convent and prepares to become a nun but relinquishes her vows when a pestilence attacks the city, killing Don Rodrigo and restoring Renzo to her." Book Rev Digest

March, William

y The bad seed. Rinehart 1954 247p o.p. 1970

"Rhoda Penmark at 8 years of age had a mind of her own and a will to match. Aged people doted on her splendid manners, but rogues knew her as one of themselves while other children were afraid of her. Christine, her mother suddenly discovers her daughter's horrible tendencies and also finds out that she is the murderess of two people who stood in her way. Christine resolves to check back and finds that she had been adopted and that the mother she had never known had also been a successful killer. Christine tries to stop the pattern in her daughter but in the process dies herself." Library J

"By making the dilemma of an ordinary mother with a psychopathic child both interesting and plausible, the writer raises some important questions on heredity, training, and environment." Booklist

Company K

In March, W. A William March omnibus p 1-132

October Island

In March, W. A William March omnibus p369-96

A William March omnibus; with an introduction by Alistair Cooke. Rinehart 1956 397p o.p. 1970

Partially analyzed in Short Story Index

Includes the complete novel, Company K, a roundup of Fables, twenty-one short stories, and the novelette, October Island. (Publisher)

March, William—*Continued*

Short stories included are: Little wife; Mist on the meadow; Miss Daisy; Shop in St Louis, Missouri; Happy Jack; Heavy load: Arrogant shoat; Personal letter; Toy bank; Bill's eyes; Not worthy of a Wentworth; Memorial to the slain; Female of the fruit fly; The funeral; Cinderella's slipper; First sunset; The slate; Willow fields; I broke my back on a rosebud; Dirty Emma; She talks good now

Margolies, Joseph A.

(ed.) Strange and fantastic stories; fifty tales of terror, horror and fantasy; introduction by Christopher Morley. McGraw 1946 762p o.p. 1970

Analyzed in Short Story Index
Contents: Ancient sin, by M. Arlen; The executioner, by H. de Balzac; Enoch Soames, by M. Beerbohm; Daniel Webster and the sea serpent, by S. V. Benét; Caterpillars, by E. F. Benson; The criminal, by J. D. Beresford; Middle toe of the right foot, by A. Bierce; Occupant of the room, by A. Blackwood; In the mirror, by V. Brussof; Jean-ah Poquelin, by G. W. Cable; Variation on a theme, by J. Collier; Trial for murder, by C. Collins; "Blow up with the brig," by W. Collins; The brute, by J. Conrad; Upper berth, by F. M. Crawford; True relation of the apparition of one Mrs Veal, by D. Defoe; No. 1 branch line: the signal man, by C. Dickens; Three infernal jokes, by Lord Dunsany; Other side of the hedge, by E. M. Forster; Elixir of life, by R. Garnett; President Lincoln's dream, by Lord Halifax; August heat, by W. F. Harvey; Wakefield, by N. Hawthorne; Story of Serapion, by E. T. A. Hoffmann; The ghost, by R. Hughes; Romance of certain old clothes, by H. James; The mezzotint, by M. R. James; Mrs Drainger's veil, by H. M. Jones; "Wireless", by R. Kipling; Woman who rode away, by D. H. Lawrence; Carmilla, by J. S. Le Fanu; The kennel, by M. Level; Novel of the white powder, by A. Machen; Lord Mountdrago, by W. S. Maugham; The specter, by G. de Maupassant; Bartleby the scrivener, by H. Melville; Ghost ship, by R. Middleton; Diamond lens, by F. J. O'Brien; Ligeia, by E. A. Poe; Laura, by Saki; Cyprian cat, by D. L. Sayers; Wandering Willie's tale, by Sir W. Scott; The victim, by M. Sinclair; Desire, by J. Stephens; Thrawn Janet, by R. L. Stevenson; Torture of hope, by V. De L'Isle-Adam; Tarnhelm, by H. Walpole; Door in the wall, by H. G. Wells; Kerfol, by E. Wharton; Vanishing lady, by A. Woollcott

Marius, Richard

The coming of rain. Knopf 1969 437p $6.95

A first novel. "The place is Bourbonville, Tennessee, in the 1880's—in the grip of unbearable drought, just after a horrifying murder. . . . But the real mystery and violence that hang over Bourbonville have to do with the past—with the War and its terrible, dividing aftermath. They center on the family of young Sam Beckwith: on his aristocratic mother [Sarah], who is, for the town, a symbol of the purest Southern womanhood; on his father [and] . . . on young Sam himself and the beautiful German girl, Emily, whose 'unsuitable' presence in the Beckwith pantheon his mother is determined to exorcise." Publisher's note

Mark Twain. See Clemens, Samuel L.; Twain, Mark

Markandaya, Kamala

The coffer dams; a novel. Day 1969 256p $5.95

"The novel deals with men who love machines and what they build, and a woman who is regenerated as she comes to understand the old ways of India and the people who live by them. Clinton, a British contractor, has come to southern India to build a dam. His wife joins him, and as time goes on, she begins to acquaint herself with the local villagers and their customs. Her guide in this is Bashiam, a self-made Indian, a crane operator, who works for her husband, and whom she comes to love. Slowly, work on the dam progresses, but not without a chain of tragedy that includes violent death and the peril of the monsoon." Pub W

A handful of rice; a novel. Day 1966 297p $6.95

"The story of one individual and the family into which he marries serves to convey the condition of the mass and does so clearly and simply. Ravi, the young man, has run away from his village home [in India] to escape its poverty and the lack of opportunity. In the city he first finds outlet for his ambitions and rebelliousness with a gang of street thieves but then is sucked into the poverty mill when he falls in love with a pretty girl and becomes assistant to her father, a poor tailor with an innate dignity but a long heritage of servility." Booklist

"There are curious echoes of Western proletarian novels here, without the revolutionary hope which relieved their somber gloom. . . . Recommended as a depressing but honest portrayal of a culture with too many people and scarcely the material means to satisfy their barest needs." Library J

y Nectar in a sieve. Day 1955 [c1954] 248p $5.50

First published 1954 in England
"The story of a peasant family in rural India and of the resignation and ingenuity with which they met economic changes and natural disasters. Dignity of character, self-reliance, and unselfish love are portrayed with a skill and charm that mitigate the baser human attributes and the somber succession of tragedies that followed industrialization in their village." Booklist

"A simple, unaffected story of human suffering [which] does more than a shelf of books on history and economics to explain the people of India." Time

Possession. Day 1963 249p o.p. 1970

"Lady Caroline Bell, a wealthy and arrogant English [divorcee], discovers a young artist of great promise during a chance visit to a village [in India]. He is an illiterate shepherd boy called Valmiki. Impressed by his extraordinary natural talent, Caroline decides to take him under her wing and ship him off to England, where he will presumably be given every opportunity to develop and mature as an artist. What happens next is narrated by Anasuya, a friend of Valmiki's and Caroline's. . . . Under [Caroline's] tutelage he begins to exhibit a taste for success; just as inevitably he becomes her lover. . . . The situation reaches its climax when Valmiki falls in love with a girl of his own age and Caroline's plans for him grind to a sudden, wrenching halt." N Y Times Bk R

A silence of desire. Day 1960 253p o.p. 1970

A story "of old and new ways in conflict in modern India. An Indian civil servant finds his ordered life disturbed as his wife develops a tumor, and begins to drain their substance—physical and mental—into the hands of a Swami faith healer." Library J

Some inner fury. Day 1956 [c1955] 255p o.p. 1970

First published 1955 in England
Mira, the young daughter of an upper class Hindu family, the central character and narrator reveals the conflict of the modern Indian during the time of India's struggle for independence by telling of her relations with her family and of the effects of the political strife upon her romance with a young British government official. (Publisher)

"The book is excellently written, with a rare understanding of both psychologies, Indian and Western." Library J

Marlowe, Stephen

The search for Bruno Heidler. Macmillan (N Y) 1966 246p o.p. 1970

"The adventures of an amateur sleuth, who makes mistakes but atones for them, working on an emergency job for American counter-intelligence in France. This story has sustained excitement, a little humor, lots of fast and furious action, and an admirable hero, an Army employee jolted into a chase after a Nazi war criminal because the criminal was once connected with his wife. Very good reading; the Gallic background adds a great fillip." Pub W

Marquand, John P.

B. F.'s daughter. Little 1946 439p o.p. 1970

"Character study of the beautiful daughter of a very wealthy industrialist, known to his friends as B. F. All her early life was dominated by B. F., so when Polly married a young professor, she started running his life for him. That time it did not work. The war gave her husband an excuse to make a getaway, and Polly, failing to capture the man she really wanted, was adrift." Book Rev Digest

"A modern, sophisticated novel depicting the bewilderment and confusion of a woman whose background and inheritance limit her life and character." Booklist

H. M. Pulham, esquire. Little 1941 431p $5.95

"The story opens when Harry Pulham is talked into collecting class biographies for his 25th reunion. He starts to write his own and begins to tell the reader of his life—boyhood, school, college, war, the advertising job in New York, and the girl he met and fell in love with. . . . Like the 'Late George Apley' it is a story of a man whose life is shaped by his surroundings." Huntting

"The right school, Harvard College, the right club were guaranty of a correct job, a correct marriage and an accepted life. Mr. Marquand has produced a superlative picture of this life and of the forces behind it. He has created living men and women, not photographs. Their problems and emotions and adjustments will be interesting and familiar to any one, regardless of habitat." N Y Her Trib Books

The late George Apley; a novel in the form of a memoir. Little 1937 354p $6.95

Pulitzer Prize, 1938

"The story is told by Horatio Willing, a staid and polished annotator, who manages to satirize himself as he recounts the life of the recently deceased George Apley, a conventional, tradition-bound, but somewhat pathetic Bostonian." Benét. The Reader's Encyclopedia

Melville Goodwin, USA. Little 1951 596p o.p. 1970

"Melville Goodwin, a General through the ambitious efforts of Muriel, his wife, knew a great deal about combat, not so much about ordinary living. When he became a publicized hero, he suddenly found himself wooed by attractive Dottie Peale and confronted by problems which terrified him more than enemy guns. Once more it was Muriel who came to his rescue." Retail Bookseller

"An engrossing novel with many virtues. . . . Like every other novel by a deservedly popular novelist, 'Melville Goodwin, USA' reflects something of the emotional climate of its time." N Y Her Trib Books

Mr Moto is so sorry

In Marquand, J. P. Mr Moto's three aces p291-447

Mr Moto's three aces; a John P. Marquand omnibus. Little 1956 447p o.p. 1970

"An omnibus edition including 'Thank You, Mr. Moto,' 'Think Fast, Mr. Moto,' and 'Mr. Moto Is So Sorry,' three novels about the Japanese detective with whom the author won his first success." Retail Bookseller

Published 1936, 1937 and 1938 respectively

Point of no return. Little 1949 559p $5.95

The first and third parts of this new novel "deal with a few days in April, 1947, in the life of Charles Gray, an assistant vice-president in the conservative Stuyvesant Bank in New York. But the main and perhaps the more significant scenes, as related in the much longer second part of the novel, lie in the town where Charles was born and brought up—Clyde, Massachusetts, some thirty miles north of Boston. A combination of present and of retrospect gives a vivid picture of the vicissitudes of small-town and middle-class life in the twentieth century." Huntting

"John P. Marquand's . . . novel is the shrewdest picture of American middleclass life that has appeared since Sinclair Lewis' 'Main Street.'" Chicago Sun

also in Marquand, J. P. So little time, and Point of no return p403-792

Sincerely, Willis Wayde. Little 1955 511p $6.95

"Biographies of American industrial leaders praised Willis Wayde for having reached the top the hard way. What they failed to include were the more important facts, readily obtainable from the people whom Wayde had used and discarded to get there. Prominent among them were the Harcourts whose textile mill in Clyde, Massachusetts, was Wayde's first stepping stone to power and money. One of the most acute satires on small minds engaged in big business since Sinclair Lewis' 'Babbitt,' and a faithful portrayal of the impact of economic changes on Americans during the last half-century." Booklist

So little time. Little 1943 594p o.p. 1970

"So little time to live one's life according to one's deepest desires and abilities, beset by social convention, custom, and sophisticated, unimportant incidentals, Jeffrey Wilson was a small-town boy who had been an aviator in the first World war. Now the second war, already begun in Europe, colors all his thoughts, as his oldest and dearest son Jim nears and finally reaches enlistment age. As Jeffrey looks back over his own life, he determines that Jim shall not be managed by others and that he shall marry the girl he loves. There is so little time, especially for Jim and the other boys who will fight. The contemporary scene is beautifully satirized in a succession of scenes. The foreign correspondent, the publishing field, the theatrical and the literary groups, Hollywood, the city dweller in the country. No actual plot, but the interest is constant and real, for this is a familiar world." Booklist

So little time, and Point of no return; two complete novels. Little [1961] 792p o.p. 1970

The two novels included here were first published 1943 and 1947 respectively and are entered separately

Thank you, Mr Moto

In Marquand, J. P. Mr Moto's three aces p7-147

Think fast, Mr Moto

In Marquand, J. P. Mr Moto's three aces p149-289

Wickford Point. Smith, P. 458p $4

A reprint of the title first published 1939 by title

"The flavor of New England of this generation as well as of the one before is in this story of the Brill family of Wickford Point, an hour north of Boston, and their friends. Told by one of its characters, the period of the story, so far as the straight narrative is concerned, is but a few days, but about thirty years are covered by flashbacks." Huntting

"The narrative, skilfully woven of memories and the more tangible present, while touching with satiric nicety upon the vagaries of this ingrown New England family, leads up to the escape of one man, a cousin, from the group, though he has long been held in thrall by the charms of Wickford Point, and by the beauty of two of its women, and their seeming dependence upon his constant presence." N Y Libraries

Women and Thomas Harrow. Little 1958 497p o.p. 1970

"The author focuses on a New England setting and on an introspective leading character who views his past with mingled happiness and regret. The reflections of Thomas Harrow, a once successful playwright, center on his first wife Rhoda who divorced him while he was serving in World War II. His [current marriage to Emily], held together by habit rather than harmony, and problems relating to financial losses represent the pallid present, but it is the old days that hold the greatest interest for Harrow." Booklist

"Much of the novel is told in flashbacks which bring back to vivid life the social and theatrical life of New York of the 1920's. Very readable." Library J

Márquez, Gabriel García. See García Márquez, Gabriel

Marric, J. J.

Gideon's day. Harper 1955 216p o.p. 1970

In this novel of Scotland Yard "Superintendent Gideon starts his day by suspending a detective accused of taking bribes. From then on, he hardly has time for a cup of tea as he directs investigations of the day's quota of underworld crimes and of sudden, unplanned burglaries, assaults, sex offenses, and murders or suspected murder." Booklist

Gideon's fire. Harper 1961 210p o.p. 1970

"Gideon has plenty to cope with—a strangled child, tight-lipped thief, a wayward son, and three bodies in a grave. And, to make matters worse, a mad arsonist starts burning one tenement after another, threatening London with another Great Fire." Huntting

Gideon's power. Harper 1969 197p $4.95

"A Joan Kahn-Harper Novel of suspense"

"Commander George Gideon of Scotland Yard believes that the power failures that have blacked out London have been planned. He is also disturbed by a wave of child murders and a fire that may have been set deliberately." Bk Buyer's Guide

"One of the better Gideons in some time, probably because the pace is much swifter than in some of the recent ones." Pub W

Gideon's ride. Harper 1963 209p o.p. 1970

Gideon conducts Scotland Yard's investigation of London's transportation system as crimes move back and forth through the huge city, a number of people begin plunging to their deaths in subways, while others are attacked in buses. Gideon is helped by a courageous young woman bus conductor who believes that she can identify the criminals. (Publisher)

Gideon's river. Harper 1968 213p boards $4.95

"A Joan Kahn-Harper Novel of suspense"

"Another top-of-the-list challenger, when the usually unflappable Gideon finds himself in the midst of a spectacular festival on the Thames, featuring a fortune in jewels and furs just ripe for the taking. There's also the disappearance of a young girl, and Gideon is plunged into one of the most exasperating and challenging cases of his career." Am News of Bks

"Gideon at his best, and the Thames at its most diversified." Library J

Gideon's wrath. Harper 1967 205p boards $4.50

"A man who has just killed his mistress in a fit of passion is trying to calm himself in the darkness of a London church when he sees a burglar stealing the altar plate. Outraged at this affront to propriety, he turns in an alarm secretly and starts Gideon of Scotland Yard on one of the most bizarre cases he has yet encountered. . . . This is the most interesting of the three cases Gideon and his staff are juggling here—the others involve the murderer mentioned before and a lurid drug and sex ring preying on young girls. . . . A good workmanlike job of building suspense by John Creasey." Pub W

For other works by this author see Creasey, John

Marryat, Frederick

Mr Midshipman Easy. Dutton 406p (Everyman's lib) $2.95

First published 1836; in this edition 1906

Founded "on Marryat's personal experiences of active service round the coasts of France and Spain during the [Peninsular] war; full of horseplay, absurd incident and miscellaneous jocosity, as well as thrilling nautical adventure; rich in saltwater and other characters, such as the philosophic father and the silly mother; full also of yarns which Munchausen might have fathered." Baker's Best

Marsh, Ngaio

Another Three-act special; 3 complete mystery novels; False scent; Scales of justice [and] Singing in the shrouds. Little [1962] 541p o.p. 1970

The three mystery novels reprinted here were first published 1959, 1955, and 1958 respectively, and are entered separately. In each of them Inspector Roderick Alleyn is the sleuth

Clutch of constables. Little 1969 244p boards $4.95

"Ngaio Marsh gives art forgery colorful and wholly enchanting treatment in [this novel]. While Superintendent Roderick Alleyn is in America working out cooperative details for dealing with a singularly successful art forger known as the Jampot, wife Troy takes a peaceful five-day riverboat trip through rural England. With, it should be added, an odd lot of companions, one of whom is murdered and another of whom buys what might be a valuable painting at a riverside junk shop. With devilish cunning Miss Marsh hides the identity of the master miscreant until virtually the last page. Don't miss this one." N Y Times Bk R

Colour scheme. Little 1943 314p o.p. 1970

"Set in New Zealand at a second-rate bath establishment with an ill assorted group of New Zealanders, Britishers, and Maoris, this is a novel of character and atmosphere. There is murder to be reckoned with and the famous inspector, Roderick Alleyn, plays his usual important role. Somewhat sinister, part international spy story and part detective story, the whole is a strange and intriguing novel of suspense." Huntting

Dead water. Little 1963 244p o.p. 1970

"The threat to close a lucrative tourist attraction angers a village and hostility is evinced even to the extent of a murder. A Superintendent Alleyn mystery set [on an island, off the coast of England]." Pub W

False scent. Little 1959 273p o.p. 1970

This mystery "story takes place in the opulent London home of a famous—and temperamental—actress on her 50th birthday anniversary. The flamboyant people surrounding Mary Bellamy are properly subdued only when the polished Roderick Alleyn of Scotland Yard and his capable assistant, Inspector Fox, enter the scene and uncover the ugly secrets that led to murder." Library J

also in Marsh, N. Another three-act special p5-175

Hand in glove. Little 1962 243p o.p. 1970

"In a little English village, a man is shoved into an excavation and a piece of pipe is rolled in after him. The investigators, Superintendent Roderick Alleyn and his assistant Fox, find that most of the man's acquaintances would willingly have done him in." McClurg. Book News

Killer dolphin. Little 1966 304p $4.95

"Ngaio Marsh is in her element when writing about the theater and the production of plays, as she does here. Violent death occurs in a newly restored dockside theater in London where a young playwright-director is staging his own play about Shakespeare. A publicity prop, real and immensely valuable, is a glove which once belonged to Shakespeare's son, Hamnet. Civilized and near-telepathic detecting by Superintendent Roderick Alleyn and Inspector Fox solves a puzzle which has more humor than Miss Marsh's usual mysteries." Pub W

Night at the Vulcan

In Haycraft, H. ed. Three times three p639-830

also in Marsh, N. Three-act special p381-541

Scales of justice. Little 1955 303p o.p. 1970

"Inspector Roderick Alleyn appears on the scene quickly to solve a village murder in which friends of his are involved." McClurg. Book News

also in Marsh, N. Another Three-act special p177-368

Singing in the shrouds. Little 1958 272p o.p. 1970

Seeking the killer of a girl delivering flowers to a departing freighter-cruise ship, Inspector Alleyn of Scotland Yard boards the ship as it leaves London. His first problem is to discover whether the murderer is actually on board but there are no clues, though each of his oddly assorted shipmates seems suspect. To solve the mystery Alleyn sets the stage for the slayer to kill again. (Publisher)

also in Marsh, N. Another Three-act special p269-541

Spinsters in jeopardy. Little 1953 278p o.p. 1970

"Except for Inspector Alleyn, his wife, and their son, almost everybody . . . is either sinister or foreign or both. Most of the action takes place in a chateau in the Maritime Alps, the headquarters of a gang of dope peddlers whose activities include religious rites of a singularly degraded nature, the kidnapping of the Alleyn's little boy, and a murder in which the identity of the victim remains a mystery until the final chapter." New Yorker

also in Marsh, N. Three-act special p193-380

Three-act special; 3 complete mystery novels. Little [1960] 541p o.p. 1970

Contents: A wreath for Rivera (1949); Spinsters in jeopardy (1953); Night at the Vulcan (1951)

A wreath for Rivera
In Marsh, N. Three-act special p5-192

Marshall, Arthur Calder- See Calder-Marshall, Arthur

Marshall, Bruce

Father Hilary's holiday. Doubleday 1965 177p o.p. 1970

This novel tells how Father Hilary attends a sort of ecumenical congress convened by the Liberator of Tomasio in Latin America and relates the adventures and misadventures which befall the priest when he criticizes the sentiments voiced by the Liberator. (Publisher)

The author "manages also to sling several satiric stones at various ecclesiastical pomps and circumlocutions. . . . There's a lot of fun in the whacky plot as well as some common sense." Best Sellers

The world, the flesh, and Father Smith. Houghton 1945 191p o.p. 1970

"A very human and endearing portrait study of a simple yet wise, devout yet mellow Catholic priest in his relations to his parishioners and to his bishop and other ecclesiastical associates in a Scottish city that spurns their faith. In a succession of telling vignettes, some comic, some tragic, some significant for depth of religious feeling, Father Smith, who 'has knocked about with his Lord in all corners of the vineyard.' is followed down the years from the days when he cycles to say Mass in a rented, ramshackle fruit market to the time in the second World War, when, as an old man he sees his new church bombed and carries the Blessed Sacrament to safety. The author's satiric wit, flashing in and out of the narrative, may offend some readers." Bookmark

Marshall, Catherine

y Christy. McGraw 1967 496p map boards $6.95

This novel is based on the life of the author's "mother. Christy, who at 19 in 1912 joined an interdenominational mission in Cutter Gap, Ky. The transition from a genteel home to rugged life in the Kentucky backwoods is major, but Christy meets it with courage and enthusiasm. In her first year of teaching in a makeshift school she learns much about herself, and even more about the feuding, primitive, clannish folk she ministers to." Pub W

"The novel is honest and seems to catch the flavor of Appalachia in the period immediately before World War I. Mrs. Marshall does a convincing job of following a young girl's search for maturity, which, as she sees it, means coming to a confident, active faith in God. 'Christy' is a religious (Christian but nondenominational) novel which those who like inspirational stories will enjoy, although even the most devout readers may find the sentimental ending hard to take." Book of the Month Club News

Marshall, James Vance

y A river ran out of Eden; illus. by Maurice Wilson. Morrow 1963 [1962] 127p illus boards $4

First published in England, 1962

Unak, a small island in the Aleutians held only four people, Jim, his wife and two small children. Then came Howard Crawford and soon a rare golden seal. To Jim, the capture of the rare pelt was an ambition, to Crawford she was simply prey and to Jim's young son she was something to be cherished. Out of this conflict came violence and even death before Unak returned to its state of innocence. (Publisher)

"Beautifully told, with a spare economy and with a vein of poetic feeling, this story is worth a score of turgid novels. The reader is transported to the Aleutian islands almost immediately, the characters are briefly but deeply etched and the narrative never falters. It is a story one reads with rapt attention and it will linger long in the reader's memory." Best Sellers

A walk to the hills of the Dreamtime; illus. by Lydia Rosier. Morrow 1970 150p illus $5.50

"Set in the Australian Outback, this is most interesting for what it reveals of the aborigines' age-old tribal way of life, still persisting into the 20th century. A young brother and sister, half-aborigine, half-Japanese, and mission-educated, are stranded alone in the vast desert at the onset of the dry season. They are befriended by a tribe of aborigines, on walkabout. Sarah and Joey survive only because they are helped by these Stone Age people. Joey reverts happily to ancestral ways. Sarah, who is 14 and older, is torn between the white culture and civilization she has known and atavistic longings." Pub W

Walkabout. [Rev. ed] Morrow 123p illus $5.95

First published in England 1959; in the U.S. by Doubleday 1961

"A short novel about two children from Barbados who are the only survivors of an aeroplane crash in the Australian bush. With the aid of a bush boy they survived, learning a great deal about the strange animals and birds, the fruits and vegetables of the country. In the end it is the Aborigine who dies while Mary and Peter live." Huntting

"Written in an effectively simple style, showing keen psychological insight, interesting glimpses of aboriginal customs, and vivid pictures of the flora, fauna, and terrain of the Australian bush, this short novel has much more to offer than its plot indicates." Booklist

Marshall, Paule

Barbados
In Marshall, P. Soul clap hands and sing p3-28

Brazil
In Marshall, P. Soul clap hands and sing p131-77

British Guiana
In Marshall, P. Soul clap hands and sing p67-127

Brooklyn
In Marshall, P. Soul clap hands and sing p31-64

Marshall, Paule—*Continued*

Soul clap hands and sing. Atheneum Pubs. 1961 177p o.p. 1970

"A collection of four novellas with locales as varied as the titles would indicate: 'Barbados,' 'Brooklyn,' 'British Guiana,' 'Brazil.' Each background seems authentic. . . . The men are as varied as the locales, but each is frustrated and bewildered and has denied life in some way. Mr. Watford, a retired coconut grower in Barbados; Max Beman, Jewish teacher in Brooklyn; Gerald Motley, a creole in British Guiana; Heitor Guimares, a Brazilian night-club entertainer—all have their problems." Book of the Month Club News

Martin, Sylvia

I, Madame Tussaud. Harper 1957 370p o.p. 1970

"A portrait of the 18th century Swiss modeler in wax. Madame Tussaud, founder of the famous London waxworks which bears her name. Written in the form of a fictional autobiography, based principally on the 'Memoirs,' published in 1838, the narrative moves from Versailles to a revolutionary prison and then to Madame Tussaud's new start in England." Pub W

Martin du Gard, Roger

Nobel Prize in literature, 1937

Summer 1914; tr. by Stuart Gilbert. Viking 1941 1008p o.p. 1970

This volume comprises the three French volumes entitled: L'été 1914 (Part VII of Les Thibaults) and a fourth volume entitled Epilogue (Part VIII)

"This gigantic continuation of 'The Thibaults' follows the fortunes of the Thibault sons, with Jacques living and dying a Socialist, and Antoine, a doctor, dying from lung disease contracted in the war. Important contributions of the book, which is sometimes powerful, sometimes boring, are a painstakingly detailed account of the Socialist collapse, and an unusually complete picture of Paris just before the first World war. All characters are analyzed minutely." Booklist

The Thibaults; tr. by Stuart Gilbert. Viking 1939 871p o.p. 1970

"The original work was published in France in separate volumes from 1922 to 1936. This omnibus volume contains the first six parts of the work." Ontario Lib Rev

The Thibaults are a French family in prewar Paris, the father a pillar of society, the older son a rising young doctor, the younger, a romantic adventurer who wants to be a writer. Thru the gradual unfolding of their story, from the sons' adolescence to the father's death, the author brings to life a whole world of aspirations and human behavior

Followed by: Summer 1914

Marttin, Paul

Heartsblood; a novel. Delacorte Press 1970 312p $5.95

"A Seymour Lawrence book"

"Matthew Kraft, professor of medicine, brilliant cardiologist, and Nobel Prize nominee . . . is passionate in his involvement with the only thing that has any meaning for him—his work as a heart specialist. After being forced to abandon a career in laboratory research, he rises to the top of his field through a combination of genius and ruthless dedication. . . . The crisis in Kraft's life comes when he suffers a heart attack and becomes aware of the fact that he is living under the shadow of death. . . . When his heart disease recurs, Kraft . . . conceives a plan which will at once ensure his longevity and win him an immortal place in medical history." Publisher's note

Masefield, John

The Bird of Dawning; or, The fortune of the sea. Macmillan (N Y) 1933 310p $4.95

"This story of a sailing ship race from the Pagoda Anchorage to the Thames, in the early '60's of the last century in the closing years of the romantic era of the clippers, hums with the salt spume of the sea, cracks with the straining of spars and gears, the tight drumming of canvas, and is alive with the salty talk of ways of clipper ship sailor men. Cold fact. records of knots logged under canvas across the farthest seas attest the truth of this existence, but few have been the written words capable of recreating these seamen. John Masefield, poet and sailor, has added a vivid scene to the small gallery in which we find the pictures of the sea." N Y Her Trib Books

Mason, A. E. W.

Four feathers. Macmillan (N Y) 1902 400p o.p. 1970

"Painful story, worked out with power and beauty, of the restoration of a brave man, who, in morbid fear of showing cowardice, becomes a coward in the eyes of friends." N Y State Lib

Scene is laid partly in the Sudan

Mason, Alfred Edward Woodley. See Mason, A. E. W.

Mason, F. Van Wyck

(ed.) American men at arms; selected and introduced by F. Van Wyck Mason. Little 1964 619p $6.95

An anthology containing 56 extracts from American fiction about the two world wars and the war in Korea, with World War II selections predominating. James Michener is the most quoted author: John Dos Passos, James Jones, Norman Mailer, John Horne Burns, Quentin Reynolds, and Glen Ross are a sampling of the other authors represented." Booklist

Eagle in the sky. Lippincott 1948 500p o.p. 1970

"The fourth in the author's tetralogy of American Revolutionary novels, the others being Three Harbours, Stars on the Sea, and Rivers of Glory [entered separately]. The time covered is 1780 to 1781. It follows the adventures of three doctors: Asa Peabody, Peter Burnham, and Lucius Devoe, and ends with Peter Burnham's winning of Sabra Stanton." Book Rev Digest

The author "gives a vivid picture of medicine and surgery at sea and on land in those early days." Wis Lib Bul

Golden Admiral. Doubleday 1953 435p o.p. 1970

"Biographical novel of Sir Francis Drake and his defeat of the Spanish Armada. Book covers only one year in his life but includes a multitude of facts about his earlier accomplishments, gives a sharp picture of English life and customs of that day, and parades author's knowledge of nautical terms and affairs." Library J

"Gaudy as a Chinese pheasant and noisy as a kindergarten recess, 'Golden Admiral' is entertainment at its best." N Y Times Bk R

Harpoon in Eden. Doubleday 1969 430p $6.95

"A Nantucket whaling captain and his adventuresome sea-going sister, cast loose by their father's death, undertake a far from routine whaling expedition that unexpectedly leads them to a completely new life in New Zealand." Booklist

The author's "creative vigor is as marked as ever. . . . Tall adventure, but told with a kind of robust innocence and with—one may insist on the apparently contradictory terms—romance and realism." Book of the Month Club News

Manila Galleon; illus. by John Alan Maxwell. Little 1961 495p illus o.p. 1970

A "sea tale based upon fact. in which the central figure is Commodore George Anson, 18th century British seaman who is given the assignment of raiding Spanish galleons off South America and in the Pacific. His greatest prize is the capture of a treasure ship, the 'Manila Galleon.'" Pub W

Mason, F. V.—*Continued*

"Mason's novel recreates the voyage in vivid, robust, and sometimes harrowing detail. . . . The novel paints a memorable portrait of Admiral Anson in the midst of the perils of seamanship and war. It is history and adventure on a grand scale." Chicago Sunday Tribune

Maracaibo mission. Doubleday 1965 230p o.p. 1970

This adventure story takes Colonel Hugh North of U.S. Army Intelligence "to the shores of Lake Maracaibo [in Venezuela]. Here . . . [he] must outwit Russian agents who plan to financially cripple and politically ruin the village in order to establish a base in the Western hemisphere." McClurg. Book News

Our valiant few; illus. by John Alan Maxwell. Little 1956 436p illus map o.p. 1970

This historical novel about the South's struggle to break the Union naval blockade around southern ports "is set in Charleston during the Civil War. The hero is a fearless newspaper editor who seeks to expose Southern war profiteers." Pub W

Proud new flags. Lippincott 1951 493p o.p. 1970

"Historical novel about the Confederate Navy in the Civil War, in the year 1861 to 1862. The hero is Sam Seymour who followed his father Captain Felix Seymour, U.S.N. into the navy but left it for the Confederacy." Book Rev Digest

Rivers of glory. Lippincott 1942 572p o.p. 1970

"Third of Mr. Mason's historical tetralogy of which the second was 'Stars on the sea.' Time 1778-1779." Time

" 'Proud New Flags' has the distinction of being a historical novel about the Lost Cause in which the accent is upon boilers and armor plate and the slogging labor of building a fleet, rather than upon magnolia and roses—and which yet manages to be dramatic and colorful." N Y Her Trib Books

"The adventurous career of Andrew Warren an American naval officer, told against the colourful pageantry of the colonies' fight for a place among nations. Throughout the story runs the theme of his romance with a beautiful Loyalist refugee." Ontrario Lib Rev

The Sea 'Venture. Doubleday 1961 349p maps o.p. 1970

"In 1609, Admiral George Somers set out for Jamestown. Two thirds of the way across the Atlantic, a storm struck and forced him to run his sinking ship onto a reef near the uninhabited Bermuda Islands. He and his passengers made their way to safety and discovered a semitropical paradise. This is the story of how the Virginia Colony almost failed, how Bermuda came to be settled, and what life in the young colony was like." Huntting

Stars on the sea. Lippincott 1940 720p o.p. 1970

The second in the author's tetralogy of American Revolutionary novels the "story is of privateering in the early days of the American revolution, the backgrounds being Newport, Rhode Island; South Carolina; and the Bahamas. The hero is Timothy Bennett; the heroine is Lucy, the girl he loves, who remains faithful to him thru any number of vicissitudes. The period covered is the two years beginning with the siege of the British in Boston by the Colonial army." Book Rev Digest

Three harbours. Lippincott 1938 694p o.p. 1970

"Determined to keep on trading despite all obstacles, when the start of the American Revolution completely ruins the shipping business in Norfolk (Virginia), young Robert Ashton sails for Bermuda in his last brig. He helps loot the British fort on the island and sails north with the powder, arriving just in time to encourage Washington to maintain his siege of Boston." Huntting

"The book makes a distinct contribution, . . . in presenting to its readers two unstressed aspects of Revolutionary history, the attitude of the American merchant, and Bermuda's assistance in the early days." Boston Transcript

Wild horizon; drawings by Samuel H. Bryant. Little 1966 390p maps $6.95

A "Revolutionary War novel about a year in the embattled life of American patriot settlers in the mountains of the Middle Tennessee. The story culminates in the American victory of King's Mountain, October, 1780. The principal episode is a winter trek west by a column of pioneers and soldiers into the Indians' hunting grounds. Men, women, and children cross icy rivers, suffer with cold and hunger, beat off Indians in order to take up land and set up forts for the colonists expected to follow them. A subplot deals with the bloody raids of dragoons led by the English Lt.-Col. Banastre Tarleton in South Carolina." Pub W

"Mason describes the battle scenes realistically, especially the struggle at King's Mountain, one of the turning points in the Revolutionary War." Best Sellers

Young titan. Doubleday 1959 621p o.p. 1970

"The plot traces the lives of various English settlers who suffer at the hands of the enemy in the [early] French and Indian wars. The climax of the novel comes with the capture of the French fortress of Louisburg in Canada [in 1745]." Pub W

"This panoramic novel is full of the harsh beauty of the seacoast and the somber spell of the forest primeval. If it contains no memorable character portrayal, its pages are alive with vigorous woodsmen, soldiers and seamen, with Indians and halfbreeds and with women, old and young, who are equal to the rigors and promises of frontier life." Chicago Sunday Tribune

Mason, Francis Van Wyck. See Mason, F. Van Wyck

Mason, Richard

The world of Suzie Wong. World Pub. 1957 344p o.p. 1970

"The love story of an inpecunious English painter and a charming little Chinese prostitute. Robert, not understanding Chinese, takes a room in a Hong Kong hotel thinking he has found a cheap boarding house. When it becomes apparent to him that it is a house of assignation he stays on, partly to paint the girls, and partly because he cannot afford anything better. And here he meets Suzie, who is charming and has good principles despite her trade. The novel ends with their marriage." Book Rev Digest

"Though the book may be a little distasteful to some readers it is never sordid nor unwholesome. Suzie and the other girls have a high moral code—in their fashion." Library J

Masters, Dexter

The accident; new ed. with a foreword by Milton Mayer. Knopf 1965 406p $5.75

First published 1955

"Set against the desert background of Los Alamos, where the first A-bombs were assembled, this long novel has a theme as hot as tomorrow's headlines—the death of a man from radiation poisoning. The time is 1946, and the victim is a brilliant young scientist (Louis Saxl), who is fatally exposed while conducting an outmoded experiment with a small atomic pile. He saves the lives of his assistants but succumbs after a week of increasing agony. . . . The clinical details are agonizing but never superfluous, and the sense of time and place is sure. A score of minor characters, from doctors to chauffeurs, are skillfully handled, and the 'edgy' atmosphere of such towns as Los Alamos is expertly conveyed." Book of the Month Club News

Masters, Hilary

An American marriage. Macmillan (N Y) 1969 338p $6.95

"Having taught an unscheduled lesson to a 19-year-old student named Patricia, Professor Hamilton Phillips of the faculty of a junior college somewhere in New England marries Patricia and hastens to accept a teaching post overseas in the renowned old capital city of Alclair [Dublin]. Hamilton and poor pretty Pat . . . cross the Atlantic and try to settle

Masters, Hilary—*Continued*

down. About half of Hilary Masters' meandering but entertaining novel tells how the newly-weds managed to become such good friends in the first place. The other half details their Alclair experience, beset as they are with domestic problems." Book of the Month Club News

"Masters' skills are evident everywhere here, in characterization, dialog, pace, construction and style. But his wit always rests on a sense of real life and humanity and perhaps that's where his special talent lies. 'An American Marriage' casually mirrors us all, while it delights, amuses, sometimes jabs home ruefully." Pub W

Masters, John

Bhowani Junction; a novel. Viking 1954 394p o.p. 1970

"A modern story of the violence, misunderstanding, and terror preceding the coming of Indian independence, that tells of the beautiful Victoria Jones, daughter of two heritages and two bloods, and of Patrick Taylor, whose mixed blood matches hers; of Col. Rodney Savage, whose love offered one solution to her dilemma; or the Sikh Ranjit, who offered a different answer altogether." McClurg. Book News

"It is refreshing to come upon a man like Mr. Masters who is really interested in the old-fashioned business of telling a story frankly intended to hold the reader from the first page to the very last. On the whole he has succeeded." Book of the Month Club News

Far, far the mountain peak; a novel. Viking 1957 471p o.p. 1970

"This book opens with a gay party at Cambridge University in the Edwardian era, and ends in the 1920s with a dramatic account of an attempt to climb one of the almost inaccessible Himalayan mountain peaks. But between the sunlit, optimistic 1900s and the final effort of Mr. Masters' heroes, there intervenes the First World War; and in that his heroes and heroines lose the simple standards by which they once judged their friends and themselves, lose some of their money and influence, and begin to abandon the belief that the world was made to be ruled by the English." Book the Month Club News

"'Far, Far the Mountain Peak,' like Mr Masters' earlier novels, is a superb and absorbing narrative, exciting in its moments of action, strongly plotted, and furnished with a vigorous, full-blooded cast of characters. Few novelists can describe an emergency, a catastrophe, or a crisis with the power that John Masters brings to bear, and in this novel he allows himself full rein." N Y Her Trib Books

Nightrunners of Bengal; a novel. Viking 1951 339p o.p. 1970

"The Sepoy mutiny of 1857 in Bengal is the backdrop for the colorful story of Captain Rodney Savage, his socially ambitious wife, the Rani who offered him untold wealth, and Caroline Langford, serious young woman who outraged English garrison wives by her intellect and honesty." Cincinnati

To the coral strand; a novel. Harper 1962 305p o.p. 1970

"The violence in this novel of India simmers and bursts around the figure of an English soldier who loses his vocation when the Indians, newly independent, cast out the English. ... Scraping up work as a white hunter ... and then an an Indian ruler's aide, he contrives to stay on, with the help of three women all of whom are in love with him." Pub W

Mather, Melissa

y One summer in between. Harper 1967 213p boards $5.95

"Harriet Brown, a nineteen-year-old Negro student at Jacob's Ladder Teachers College in South Carolina, comes north to Vermont to spend a summer working for the Daley family, which includes six active and uninhibited children. Her personal journal, kept as part of a research project ... not only records the summer's frenetic farm activities but also reveals Harriet's impressions of Northern whites, her own prejudices, and her gradual acceptance of the Daleys as friends." Booklist

"This is a woman's book, brim full of children, preserves, vegetable gardening, the building of a new house, beautiful rural Vermont. It would be a mistake to read this book for a message, the last word about Negro-white relations; better to enjoy it for Harriet Brown's cross-grained humor and for a record of the growth of a friendship between Harriet and the Daleys." Pub W

Matthews, Jack

Hanger Stout, awake! Harcourt 1967 151p $3.95

"This tale revolves about Clyde Stout, a high school dropout who soon acquires the nickname Hanger through his special capacity for 'free-hanging,' an exercise in endurance. ... Hanger's character is revealed through his home life, his love for an unattainable girl, his naive acceptance of the free-hanging exercise, and his complete absorption in the mechanics of automobiles." Library J

"Mr. Matthews' deceptively naïve novel is Hanger's vaguely ungrammatical diary, and if the style at times comes dangerously close to cuteness, the book is a vibrant portrait—sometimes sad but more often a truly funny one—of a pivotal summer in a young man's life." Book of the Month Club News

Matthiessen, Peter

At play in the fields of the Lord. Random House 1965 373p $5.95

An adventure tale set in the South American "jungle, at once majestic and malevolent: the principal characters are four fundamentalist missionaries and [Lewis Moon] a soldier of fortune; and the plot concerns their fanatical conflict over the fate of a primitive and dangerous tribe of jungle Indians." Publisher's note

"Both the political dreams of Moon and the religious dreams of the missionaries fail. ... But it is always Moon's personal saga which dominates the novel. In the last pages, as Moon flees alone down the jungle rivers, Mr. Matthiessen makes his point implicitly: one has to lose his life in order to gain it. Over all lies the author's vivid and knowledgeable presentation of the jungle as a dark, threatening force filled with violence and mystery." Book of the Month Club News

"The language is often strong and may offend some readers, as may also the portrayal of the missionaries. Yet, the work is not sacrilegious. It is a compassionate and perceptive picture of persons under stress." Library J

Maugham, Robin

The link; a Victorian mystery; a novel. McGraw 1969 262p $6.95

"The bizarre and licentious life of James Steede, a young baronet, unfolds within a ... portrayal of Victorian society and among a group of colorful and vivid characters, moving from Public School and great estates in England, to lurid bars and brothels of Mexico's West Coast, Australia's rugged gold fields and, finally, to Sessions Court at Westminster. It is when James Steede meets another man who totally and uncannily resembles him that the story takes a fantastic and dramatic turn." Publisher's note

Maugham, W. Somerset

Ashenden; or, The British agent. Doubleday 1928 304p o.p. 1970

Analyzed in Short Story Index

"Stories of the British secret service during the first World War." Booklist

Contents: R; Domiciliary visit; Miss King; Hairless Mexican; Dark woman; The Greek; Trip to Paris; Giulia Lazzari; Gustav; The traitor; Behind the scenes; His Excellency; Flip of a coin; Chance acquaintance; Love and Russian literature; Mr. Harrington's washing

Maugham, W. S.—*Continued*

The best short stories of W. Somerset Maugham. Selected, and with an introduction by John Beecroft. Modern Lib. 1957 489p $2.95

Analyzed in Short Story Index
Contents: The letter; The verger; The vessel of wrath; The hairless Mexican; Mr Harrington's washing; Red; Mr Know-All? The alien corn; The book-bag; The round dozen; The voice of the turtle; The facts of life; Lord Mountdrago; The colonel's lady; The treasure; Rain; P. & O.

Cakes and ale; or, The skeleton in the cupboard. Doubleday 1930 308p o.p. 1970

"Clever, satiric tale of the hypothetical last of the Victorian novelists, who, born the son of a bailiff, marries first a too-generous barmaid and later—after her defection—a nurse who boosts him into fame." Pittsburgh

Cakes and ale, and twelve short stories; selected and with an introduction by Angus Wilson. Doubleday 1967 512p front o.p. 1970

Partially analyzed in Short Story Index
The title story was first published 1930
Contents: The three fat women of Antibes; Mackintosh; The lotus eater: The yellowstreak; Before the party; Rain; Mr Harrington's washing; The force of circumstances; Footprints in the jungle; A man with a conscience; P. & O.; Virtue; Cakes and ale [novel]

Complete short stories. Doubleday 1952 2v $15

Analyzed in Short Story Index
Ninety-one stories are included in this collection. "The first volume includes all those previously published in 'East and West.' The second volume. 'The World Over,' contains the rest of Maugham's short stories." Retail Bookseller

Contents: v 1: Rain; Fall of Edward Barnard; Mackintosh; Red; Honolulu; The pool; The letter; Before the party; Force of circumstance; The outstation; Yellow streak; P. & O.; Jane; Round dozen; Creative impulse; Miss King; Hairless Mexican; Giulia Lazzari; The traitor; His Excellency; Mr Harrington's washing; Footprints in the jungle; Human element; Virtue; Alien corn; Book-bag; Vessel of wrath; Door of opportunity; Back of beyond; Neil MacAdam

v2: Woman of fifty; Man with the scar; The bum; Closed shop; Official position; Man with a conscience; French Joe; German Harry; Four Dutchmen; End of the flight; Flotsam and jetsam; Casual affair; Mr Know-All; Straight flush; Portrait of a gentleman; Raw material; Friend in need; The dream; The taipan; The consul; Mirage; Mabel Masterson; Marriage of convenience; Princess September; In a strange land; Lotus eater; Salvatore; Washtub; Mayhew; Happy man; Point of honour; The mother; Romantic young lady; The poet; Man from Glasgow; Lion's skin; Three fat women of Antibes; Happy couple; Voice of the turtle; Facts of life; Gigolo and gigolette; Appearance and reality; The luncheon; The unconquered; Ant and the grasshopper; Home; The escape; Judgment seat; Sanatorium; Louise; Lord Mountdrago; String of beads; The promise; The verger; Social sense; Colonel's lady; Episode; The kite; The treasure; Winter cruise

East and West
In Maugham, W. S. Complete short stories v 1

The moon and sixpence. Modern Lib. 1935 314p $2.95

First published 1919 by Doran
"Based closely on the life of the French painter Paul Gauguin. It tells of Charles Strickland, a conventional London stock broker, who in middle life becomes interested in painting, changes completely in character, and deserts his wife, family, and business in order to live and paint in Tahiti, where he takes a native mistress and eventually dies of leprosy." Benét. The Reader's Encyclopedia

"The painter, in this novel, is an incarnate example of the 'divine tyranny of art' in his quest of the moon, in which the sixpence in every conventional form—home, family, food, the opinion of mankind, fame, decency itself—is contemptuously thrown aside." Booklist

y Of human bondage

Some editions are:
Doubleday $4.50 Illustrated by Randolph Schwabe
Modern Lib. $2.95
First published 1915
"Portrayal of the life of a youth handicapped by deformity, whose early life was a process of self-torture. When he escapes from the cruelty of his school-fellows and the uncongenial atmosphere of his hypocritical and selfish uncle it is only to plunge deeper into gloom as a lonely lad in London, as a student at Heidelberg, and as a would-be artist in the Latin quarter in Paris." Pittsburgh
"The novel is written with a carefulness and conscientiousness which are entirely praiseworthy. The very leisurely method gives opportunity for any quantity of pictures, pictures in which each minute detail is elaborated and finished. His book is one of those novels which deserve and should receive the attention of all those who care for what is worth while in contemporary fiction." N Y Times Bk R

Quartet; stories by W. Somerset Maugham; screen-plays by R. C. Sherriff. Doubleday 1949 189p o.p. 1970

Analyzed in Short Story Index
"Four of Maugham's published short stories: 'The Facts of Life,' 'The Alien Corn,' 'The Kite,' and 'The Colonel's Lady.' With them are the screen plays made from these stories by R. C. Sherriff. Maugham has linked them up by dialogue and Sherriff has done a foreword." Retail Bookseller

The razor's edge; a novel. Doubleday 1944 343p $4.95

"Character study of a young American, a flyer in World War I, who returns to his home in Chicago in 1919, vaguely conscious that he is missing something. To the horror of the girl who wants to marry him, he will not take a job; he wants to 'loaf.' He goes to Paris and then to India in search of his ideal, and finds a certain measure of personal peace, but succeeds in making life even more difficult for those who have tried to make him lead a conventional life." Book Rev Digest
"This is a sophisticated, mature novel, and satisfying reading." Booklist

Seventeen lost stories; comp. and with an introduction by Craig V. Showalter. Doubleday 1969 273p $5.95

"Early stories written between 1898 and 1908 and never republished during Maugham's lifetime occasionally presage some character types and ironic twists of his later writing but otherwise their literary quality and interest are minimal. As indicated in the introduction Maugham himself once described these selections as 'immature,' yet the devotee may want even these first attempts." Booklist
Contents: The punctiliousness of Don Sebastian; A bad example; De amicitia; Faith; The choice of Amyntas; Daisy; Cupid and the vicar of Swale; Lady Habart; Pro patria; A point of law; An Irish gentleman; Flirtation; The fortunate painter; A marriage of convenience; Good manners; Cousin Amy; The happy couple

(ed.) Tellers of tales; 100 short stories from the United States, England, France, Russia and Germany. Doubleday 1939 xxxix, 1526p o.p. 1970

Analyzed in Short Story Index
"I do not claim that these are the best stories that have been written during the last century; they are the stories amongst all those that I have read that have interested me most. . . . I have inserted nothing that does not seem to me to have a living interest. That is why I have chosen mostly stories that are contemporary, or almost so,

Maugham, W. S.—Continued

. . . I have chosen more stories from England and America than from France and Russia and Germany." Introduction

Contents: Two drovers, by Sir W. Scott; Rip Van Winkle, by W. Irving; Stout gentleman, by W. Irving; La Grande Bretèche, by H. de Balzac; Gray champion, by N. Hawthorne; Crimson curtain, by J. B. d'Aurevilly; Gold-bug, by E. A. Poe; Simple heart, by G. Flaubert; Krambambuli, by M. von Ebner-Eschenbach; Outcasts of Poker Flat, by F. B. Harte; Olympe and Henriette, by V. de l'Isle Adam; Three strangers, by T. Hardy; Jolly corner, by H. James; Procurator of Judaea, by A. France; Youth, by K. E. Franzos; Markheim, by R. L. Stevenson; Necklace, by G. de Maupassant; Legacy, by G. de Maupassant; Useless mouths, by O. Mirbeau; Happy prince, by O. Wilde; Adventure of the Bruce-Partington plans, by A. C. Doyle; Typhoon, by J. Conrad; Fate of the Baron, by A. Schnitzler; Whirligig of life, by O. Henry; Without visible means, by A. Morrison; Stricken doe, by P. Mille; Monkey's paw, by W. W. Jacobs; Coach, by V. Hunt; Last visit, by T. Bernard; Man who would be king, by R. Kipling; Without benefit of clergy, by R. Kipling; Papago wedding, by M. Austin; Uncle Franz, by L. Thoma; Door in the wall, by H. G. Wells; Experiment in misery, by S. Crane; Tobermory, by Saki; To build a fire, by J. London; Death of Iván Ilých, by L. Tolstoi; Toupee artist, by N. Lyeskov; Mouzhiks, by A. Chekhov; Twenty-six and one, by M. Gorky; Sunstroke, by I. Bunin; Captain Ribnikov, by A. Kuprin; Hydromel, by V. Iretsky; Without cherry blossom, by P. Romanof; In the town of Berdichev, by V. Grossman; Hunger, by A. Neweroff; Romance, by V. Inber; Earth on the hands, by V. Pilnjak; Letter, by I. Babel; Child, by V. Ivanov; Customer, by G. Peskov; Knives, by V. Katayev; Pippo Spano, by H. Mann; Old Rogaum and his Theresa, by T. Dreiser; A. V. Laider, by M. Beerbohm; Amulet, by J. Wassermann; Cavalry patrol, by H. von Hofmannsthal; Seeds, by S. Anderson; Other woman, by S. Anderson; Early sorrow, by T. Mann; Mr and Mrs Abbey's difficulties, by E. M. Forster; Invisible collection, by S. Zweig; Uncle Fred flits by, by P. G. Wodehouse; In the last coach, by L. Frank; Counterparts, by J. Joyce; Tragedy of Goupil, by L. Pergaud; Odour of chrysanthemums, by D. H. Lawrence; Ching, by A. Arnoux; Haircut, by R. Lardner; Champion, by R. Lardner; A Balaam, by A. Zweig; Old man Minick; by E. Ferber; Golden beetle, by B. Frank; Catalan night, by P. Morand; Silent snow, secret snow, by C. Aiken; Lovely day, by J. de Lacretelle; On the farm, by H. F. Blunck; Killers, by E. Hemingway; Stranger, by K. Mansfield; House of mourning, by F. Werfel; Start in life, by R. Suckow; Desert islander, by S. Benson; Big blonde, by D. Parker; Orphant Annie, by T. S. Winslow; Nuns at luncheon, by A. Huxley; Rich boy, by F. S. Fitzgerald; Imposition, by L. A. G. Strong; Turn about, by W. Faulkner; Doll, by J. Kessel; Reduced, by E. Bowen; María Concepción, by K. A. Porter; Cherry feast, by E. Glaeser; No more trouble for Jedwick, by L. Paul; If you can't be good, be cautious, by T. O. Beachcroft; The ball, by I. Némirovsky; Kneel to the rising sun, by E. Caldwell; Nowaks, by C. Isherwood; Convalescence, by K. Boyle; Station, by H. E. Bates; Oklahoma race riot, by F. W. Prentice

Then and now; a novel. Doubleday 1946 278p o.p. 1970

"The scene is Italy at the dawn of the sixteenth century, and the not entirely heroic hero is Niccolo Machiavelli, best known to posterity as author of 'The Prince.' The main action runs from October 1502 into January of the following year; the principal elements of this action being diplomacy and love, nicely mingled in almost equal parts. Thanks to the diplomatic element, we witness the education of a political philosopher. Thanks to the amorous element, we witness the aspiration and frustration of a practised lecher." Sat R

The trembling of a leaf; little stories of the South Sea Islands. Doran 1921 302p o.p. 1970

Analyzed in Short Story Index
Contents: The Pacific; Mackintosh; The fall of Edward Barnard; Red; The pool; Honolulu; Rain; Envoi

Trio; original stories. Screen-plays by W. Somerset Maugham, R. C. Sherriff [and] Noel Langley. Doubleday 1950 156p o.p. 1970

Analyzed in Short Story Index
Includes " 'Sanitorium,' the story of doomed patients who fell in love; 'The Verger,' which describes the ironic failure and success of an illiterate; and 'Mr. Know-All,' about a jewel expert who [chivalrously] declared Mrs. Ramsay's fabulous pearls were worth only $18." Retail Bookseller

World over
In Maugham, W. S. Complete short stories v2

Maughan, A. M.

Harry of Monmouth. Sloane 1956 440p $6.95

"The story has a spectacular hero. Henry V, Shakespeare's Prince Hal, one of the most dashing figures of history. Maughan tells with great literary éclat the story of Henry's reign, his battles and his marriage, for love, to Lady Katherine of France." Pub W

"Harry's life contains material enough for several books but this is a unified and plausible account of a complex figure projected against a background which is one of the best reconstructions of early fifteenth-century Britain. The result should interest the historian, fascinate the confirmed lover of period pieces, and provide an exciting introduction to this 'star of England.' " N Y Times Bk R

Maupassant, Guy de

Bel-Ami; tr. from the French by Eric Sutton. Pantheon Bks. 369p (Novel lib) o.p. 1970

First French edition 1885
"The subtitle of Bel-Ami, or The history of a Scoundrel, is not inappropriate for the story of an intriguer who climbs to a position of wealth and power by publishing the story of his first wife's disgrace and later cheating her of part of her fortune. The unscrupulous parvenu and the women he dupes are among the masterpieces of characterization produced by the French realistic school to which de Maupassant belonged." Magill. Masterpieces

Best stories of Guy de Maupassant; selected, and with an introduction by Saxe Commins. Modern Lib. 1945 551p $2.95

Contents: Mademoiselle Fifi; Vain beauty; The Horla; Madame Tellier's excursion; Piece of string; The story of a farm girl; That pig of a Morin; The umbrella; Was it a dream; False gems; Hautot Senior & Hautot Junior; A family affair; A Normandy joke; The diamond necklace; In the moonlight; Love; The little cask; Clochette; A fishing excursion; Humiliation; Julie Romain; The specter; My Uncle Sosthenes; The duel; A vagabond; Madame Parisse; One phase of love; Simon's papa; The vendetta; Farmer's wife; A matter of business; The signal; Love's awakening; The olive grove; Saved; A country excursion; The diary of a madman; Two little soldiers; The white wolf; The devil; A lucky burglar; Moonlight; The mad woman; A costly outing; Ball-of-fat

The complete short stories of Guy de Maupassant; introduction by Professor Artine Artinian. Doubleday 1339p $8.95

Analyzed in Short Story Index
First published 1955 by Hanover House
Contents: Ball of fat; The secret; The shepherd's leap; Mouche—a boating man's reminiscence; On a spring evening; The legacy; Madame Tellier's establishment; A crisis; An idyl; The prisoners; Châli; The story of a farm girl; At the Spa—Diary of the Marquis de Roseveyre; Madame Hermet; For sale; Yvette; The piece of string; The funeral pile; An old man; A surprise; In the moonlight; Love—three pages from a sportsman's book; On the river; The necklace; Father Judas; The inn; A humble drama; A vagabond; A little

Maupassant, Guy de—*Continued*

walk; The Sisters Rondoli; The dancers; Checkmate; The accursed bread; Mademoiselle Fifi; A sale; An affair of state; The mask; A cock crowed; That drowned man; Mad; The revenge; The father; A Normandy joke; Monsieur Parent; Fear; The hole—cuts and wounds which caused death; Caresses; Bellflower; Simon's papa; That pig of a Morin; The christening; Miss Harriet; Misti—recollections of a bachelor; In the wood; Our friends the English; A family; Roger's method; The Marquis de Fumerol; The castaway; Saved; The confession; The Devil; The mother of monsters; The rabbit; The keeper; The madwoman; A bad error; Coco; Epiphany; Happiness; The unknown; The double pins; The signal; Graveyard sirens; A madman; Growing old; M. Belhomme's beast; A French Enoch Arden; The little one; Julie Romain; A memory; Confessing; Rosalie Prudent; A parricide; The olive orchard; Hippolyte's claim; Guillemot Rock; Benoist; A true story; Fecundity; Alexander; A way to wealth; The putter-to-sleep; Am I insane; A wife's confession; A divorce case; Madame Parisse; Duchoux; The Mother Superior's twenty-five francs; Forbidden fruit; The peddler; Old objects; The old man; The coconut-drink vendor; The charm dispelled; Making a convert; The cake; A dead woman's secret; Love's awakening; Dreams; Bed no. 29; Marroca; Old Milon; A philosopher; A mistake; Florentine; The orphan; Consideration; Woman's wiles; A cry of alarm; Moonlight; Doubtful happiness; In a railway carriage; Humiliation; The wedding night; The noncommissioned officers; In the courtroom; A peculiar case; A practical joke; The wreck; A strange fancy; After death; On cats; Old Amable; One phase of love; Good reasons; A fair exchange; A traveler's notes; The tobacco shop; A poor girl; The substitute; the hermit; A passion; The orderly; Feminine men; Joseph; Regret; The deaf-mute; At the church door; Magnetism; The false gems; The colonel's ideas; Was it a dream; Mademoiselle Pearl; Two little soldiers; The will; A country excursion; Bertha; Walter Schnaffs' adventure; The log; Bric-a-brac; The tomb; The artist's wife; In the spring; Night: a nightmare; The rendezvous; An artifice; Solitude; A Norman; The specter; The relic In the country; The bed; The awakening; Words of love; The legend of Mont-Saint-Michel; Christmas Eve; Madame Baptiste; Revenge; Queen Hortense; Complication; Forgiveness; The white wolf; The father; Toine; An enthusiast; The traveler's story; A jolly fellow; Room no. 11; A lively friend; The patron; The impolite sex; The blind man; The Corsican bandit; The duel; Mother Savage; The love of long ago; The farmer's wife; Beside a dead man; The lock; A queer night in Paris; A duel; The kiss; Old Mongilet; The umbrella; Denis; The donkey; The question of Latin; Mother and son; He; Monsieur Jocaste; The avenger; The conservatory; My wife; Letter found on a corpse; The little cask; Rust; Poor Andrew; A fishing excursion; After; An adventure in Paris; The spasm; A meeting; A New Year's gift; A family affair; My uncle Sosthenes; All over; My landlady; Paul's mistress; The horrible; The first snowfall; The legacy; The wooden shoes; Boitelle; Selfishness; Of Doctor Heraclius Gloss; The watchdog; Christening; A costly outing; A king's son; Walter, a bock; Mohammed Fripouli; "Bell"; Hautot and his son; The victim; The Englishman; One evening; Sentiment; Traveling; Francis; The assassin; Our letters; The cripple; Semillante; In port; Suicides; A portrait; A miracle; My twenty-five days; Allouma; A lucky burglar; An odd feast; Who knows; A traveler's tale; Little Louise Roque; The Orient; How he got the Legion of Honor; My Uncle Jules; The horla; Useless beauty

Pierre and Jean; tr. from the French by Clara Bell; with a critical introduction by the Earl of Crewe. Appleton lxvii, 237p illus o.p. 1970

First published in French in 1888

"A sombre and tragic study of bourgeois life, the tale of two brothers, one of whom is suddenly led to suspect that the other is the child of his mother's adultery. With infinite reluctance he compels himself to follow up the inquiry, while the mother, impassive and remorseful, awaits the discovery of her guilt. A superb example of Maupassant's faculty for observing the infinite details of life and reproducing them with unerring artistic fidelity." Baker's Best

The portable Maupassant; ed. and with an introduction by Lewis Galantiere. Viking 1947 756p (Viking Portable lib) $5.50

Analyzed in Short Story Index
Contains 23 short stories; one complete novel, A woman's life; a collection of letters including the correspondence with Marie Bashkirtseff; and his Essay on the novel
The stories included are: Story of a farm girl; Théodule Sabot's confession; Rosalie Prudent; The Devil; Martin's girl; Toine; Confessing; The return; The string; In port; A million; Chair mender; Adventure in Paris; Little fellow; The necklace; Saved; Duchoux; Yvette; Walter, a bock; Old Milon; Coup d'état; Boule de suif; The horla; A woman's life

Selected short stories; with a critical and biographical profile of Guy de Maupassant by Jean-Albert Bédé. [Ultratype ed. complete and unabridged] Watts, F. 1969 312p $4.95

"A Watts Ultratype edition"
This volume presents most of Guy de Maupassant's best known stories. (Publisher)
Contents: Ball-of-Fat; The diamond necklace; A piece of string; The story of a farm-girl; Mme Tellier's excursion; A vagabond; A Normandy joke; The father; Miss Harriet; Bellflower; Simon's papa; Waiter, a bock; Châli; How he got the Legion of Honor; A crisis; Am I insane; A little walk; Moonlight; A practical joke; Room no. eleven; The false gems; A country excursion

Tales of Guy de Maupassant. Tr. by Lafcadio Hearn and others, chosen & with an introduction by Justin O'Brien. Illus. from watercolors by Gunter Bohmer. Heritage 1964 472p illus o.p. 1970

Analyzed in Short Story Index
Contains the following stories: The adopted child; The adventures of Walter Schnaffs; Am I insane; The artist; At the spa; The baptism; The chair-mender; Chali; The child; Clochette; The colonel's ideas; The confession; A coward; A crisis; Denis; The dowry; The fare; Graveyard sirens; The hand; Happiness; He; In the wood; The jewelry; Joseph; The little cask; Madame Tellier's establishment; A madman; La Mère Sauvage; Miss Harriet; My Uncle Jules; The necklace; The old man; The olive grove; On a spring evening; A parricide; The piece of string; The prisoners; The return; A revelation; Roly-Poly (Boule de suif); Saint Anthony; The sheperd's leaf; The signal; Simon's papa; The story of a farm girl; That pig of a Morin; Toine; Two friends; A vendetta; Waiter, a bock

A woman's life
In Maupassant, G. de. The portable Maupassant p377-631

Mauriac, François

Nobel Prize for literature, 1952

The desert of love
In Mauriac, F. A Mauriac reader p133-269

Genetrix
In Mauriac, F. A Mauriac reader p63-130

A kiss for the leper
In Mauriac, F. A Mauriac reader p3-60

The knot of vipers
In Mauriac, F. A Mauriac reader p273-430

The lamb (L'agneau) Tr. by Gerard Hopkins. Farrar, Straus 1955 156p o.p. 1970

First published in France, 1954
Another story about the de Mirbel family of: Woman of the Pharisees
"On the way to the seminary, Xavier encounters Jean de Mirbel and, shaken by the man's need, is persuaded to cancel his own plans and accompany him home, a step that drastically alters the lives of several persons." Booklist

Mauriac, François—*Continued*

The mask of innocence; tr. by Gerard Hopkins. Farrar, Straus 1953 206p o.p. 1970

First French edition, 1936
"As in other works of Mauriac, the scene is provincial France, and the characters are middle-class people all but lost in greed and sensuality. Selfishness isolates them and they sink variously into despair; yet beyond sin they find repentance. The typically complex plot centers upon the chief sinner, Gabriel." Chicago Sunday Tribune

A Mauriac reader; tr. by Gerard Hopkins; introduction by Wallace Fowlie. Farrar, Straus 1968 xx, 610p $7.95

Contents: A kiss for the leper; Genetrix; The desert of love; The knot of vipers; Woman of the Pharisees
Original French editions published 1922, 1923, 1925, 1932 and 1941 respectively. English translations first published 1950, 1950, 1951, 1949 and 1946 respectively
"This volume presents five novels, selected as some of his greatest, by the notable modern French writer who was awarded the Nobel Prize in literature in 1952 for his work as novelist, dramatist, critic and journalist. Like all his fiction, these five novels reveal the often inbred bourgeois, provincial, Christian scene of Bordeaux and its environs." Pub W

Questions of precedence (Préséances) Tr. by Gerard Hopkins. Farrar, Straus 1959 [c1958] 158p o.p. 1970

Original French edition published in 1921. This translation published 1958 in England
"An incisive short novel explores the moral consequences of using another human being for an unworthy purpose, then discarding him when this seems well accomplished. The author demonstrates the unhappy effects on the guilty schoolboy-narrator, his sister Florence, and the unlucky Augustin, whom they first befriended and flattered to gain an entree into the ruling society of Bordeaux, then dropped when they were accepted into the fashionable clique and the girl has married into one of the first families. An ironic tale for the discerning reader." Booklist

Thérèse; a portrait in four parts; tr. by Gerard Hopkins. Holt 1947 383p o.p. 1970

First American edition published separately by Boni & Liveright 1928
"Portrait of a mentally confused woman, Thérèse Desqueyroux. Four aspects of her character are studied to form the whole picture. In the first she is Thérèse, the poisoner, the intelligent woman; in the second more of her experiences are related in Paris; in the third she is middle-aged; and in the final section is the story of Thérèse and her daughter and her daughter's fiancé." Book Rev Digest

Vipers' tangle; tr. by Warre B. Wells. Sheed 1947 288p o.p. 1970

First published 1933 in England
"A study of covetousness. . . . Mauriac presents an unfortunate millionaire whose drama is that the fatter his purse the leaner his humaneness. He hates, and in turn is hated by, his wife, his children, his grandchildren. He has no friends, no sentimental attachments. . . . There is, too, in this novel an exhaustive study of the family . . . a family thoroughly eaten up, gangrened, by hatred." N Y Her Trib Books

Woman of the Pharisees (La pharisienne) tr. by Gerard Hopkins. Holt 1946 241p o.p. 1970

The author introduces Brigitte Pian, a virtuous but oppressively righteous character. "She molds the lives of others—unconsciously she tyrannizes over them—but it is not until she has brought disaster to those over whom she has power, and whom she loves, that she is brought to realize she is indeed a woman of the Pharisees." Hunting
"The book is imbued with Catholic thought and will appeal to the introspective reader." Booklist

also in Mauriac, F. A Mauriac reader
p433-610

Maurier, Daphne du. See Du Maurier, Daphne

Maurois, André

Bernard Quesnay
In Maurois, A. Maurois reader

The collected stories of André Maurois; tr. by Adrienne Foulke. Washington Sq. Press 1967 396p o.p. 1970

Analyzed in Short Story Index
Contents: Reality transposed; Darling, good evening; Lord of the shadows; Ariane, my sister . . .; Home port; Myrrhine; Biography; Thanatos Palace Hotel; Friends; Dinner under the chestnut trees; Bodies and souls; The curse of gold; For piano alone; The departure; The fault of M. Balzac; Love in exile; Wednesday's violets; A career; Ten years later; Tidal wave; Transference; Flowers in season; The will; The campaign; The life of man; The Corinthian porch; The Cathedral; The ants; The postcard; Poor Maman; The green belt; The Neuilly Fair; The birth of a master; Black masks; Irene; The letters; The cuckoo; The house
These stories offer the reader "a chance to eavesdrop on the lives and loves of a brilliant world of artists, actresses, playwrights, diplomats, industrialists, wives, lovers, and mistresses." Publisher's note

The family circle; tr. by Hamish Miles. Appleton 1932 330p o.p. 1970

"The theme of the story is the warping of a girl's personality thru her knowledge of her mother's infidelity to her husband. Denise Herpain develops into a beautiful and keenly intelligent, but neurotic woman. She loves, marries, and herself turns faithless to her husband. After much emotional torment and bafflement Denise finds her bearings, tests the security of her marriage and French family solidarity, linking herself finally to the family circle. The scene is a small textile manufacturing town in [Northern France]." Book Rev Digest

Maurois reader; novels, novelettes and short stories. Introduction by Anne Fremantle. Didier Pubs. 1949 448p o.p. 1970

Analyzed in Short Story Index
Contents: Novels: The silence of Colonel Bramble; The weigher of souls; Bernard Quesnay. Novelettes and short stories: Harpies on the shore; After ten years; The guardian angel; Bonsoir, chérie; The unexpected always happens; The earth dwellers; The role of Myrrhine; The schoolboy's return; Chelsea way; Proust in England; If Louis XVI had had an atom of firmness; Fragment from a universal history published in 1992

The silence of Colonel Bramble
In Maurois, A. Maurois reader

The weigher of souls
In Maurois, A. Maurois reader

Maxtone, Graham Joyce Anstruther. See Struther, Jan

Maxwell, William

The château. Knopf 1961 401p $4.95

To the France of 1948 "come two young Americans, Barbara and Harold Rhodes. . . . As paying guests at the decaying chateau of Madame Vienot, they seek to come to grips with France and the French. . . . France and the French people prove elusive, even treacherous, and their hungry pursuit of understanding and friendship leads both everywhere and nowhere. . . . The last forty-odd pages of the book, titled 'Some Explanations,' is a . . . question-and-answer session in which the author unravels mysteries, fills in details, and lets the reader in on things that Barbara and Harold didn't understand." San Francisco Chronicle
"This is a beguilingly old-fashioned novel, almost Jamesian in its restraint and in its delineation of subtle shifts in consciousness. . . . In the end, the reader comes away with an enhanced sense of what Europe can mean to sensitive and kindly Americans." N Y Times Bk R

Maxwell, William—*Continued*

They came like swallows. Harper 1937 267p o.p. 1970

"The intimate family life of a Midwest, middle-class family about 1918 is presented through the thoughts and feelings of three people—a boy of eight, his brother of twelve, and the father. Although practically without plot, it achieves a sensitive characterization of the mother whose understanding, humor, and graciousness smoothed their lives until she died. The characterization is unusually successful, but the book, will interest chiefly cultivated readers." Booklist

Maybury, Anne

The Minerva stone. Holt 1968 276p boards $5.95

In this novel "the stone stands by the lily pond at Guinever Court, a stately home built around the remains of a 13th-Century castle in Dorset. There Sarah Rhodes relaxes with her talented, affectionate family while she tries to understand what is happening to her year-old marriage to Niall Rhodes, a famous, self-centered TV personality whose attempts to change her into the kind of robot wife he wants have been unsuccessful. Niall's return from a trip brings her more problems. There are mysterious messages, a car that almost runs her down, and the threatening shot at Niall in the dark garden. And then there is much more." Library J

For another title by this author see Troy, Katherine

Meaker, Marijane. See Packer, Vin

Meeker, Richard K.

(ed.) Glasgow, E. The collected stories of Ellen Glasgow

Meisels, Andrew

Son of a star. Putnam 1969 383p boards $6.95

This is the "story of the bitter struggle of a handful of Jews against overwhelming odds—in this case, the formidable might of Rome. The time is A.D. 132 when a simple warrior named Simon Bar Kochba (son of a Star) unites the hill tribes of Judah, and for an incredible three years the Jewish rebellion rages unchecked against everything the Romans can muster. When as is inevitable —it is finally crushed, the Jewish state comes to an end [for 1800 years]." Am News of Bks

The novel "is hardly first rate historical fiction but it does do much to restore the memory of a dramatic revolt that shook the Roman Empire but has been overlooked by history." Best Sellers

Melville, Herman

Bartleby the scrivener

In Melville, H. Five tales p 1-44

In Melville, H. Shorter novels of Herman Melville p107-55

Benito Cereno

In Melville, H. Five tales p45-137

In Melville, H. Shorter novels of Herman Melville p 1-106

In Neider, C. ed. Short novels of the masters p52-124

In Phillips, W. ed. Great American short novels p 1-78

Billy Budd

In Blackmur, R. P. ed. American short novels p18-67

y Billy Budd, foretopman

Some editions are:

Univ. of Chicago Press $8.95 Edited by Harrison Hayford and Merton Sealts, Jr. Has title: Billy Budd, sailor

Watts, F. $3.95 Illustrated by Robert Quackenbush

Watts, F. $7.95 Large type editon complete and unabridged. A Keith Jennison Book

Written in 1891 but in a still "unfinished" manuscript stage when Melville died. First publication 1924 in England, as part of the Standard edition of Melville's complete works

"Narrates the hatred of petty officer Claggart for Billy, handsome Spanish sailor. Billy strikes and kills Claggart, and is condemned by Captain Vere even though the latter senses Billy's spiritual innocence." Haydn. Thesaurus of Book Digests

also in Melville, H. Five tales p183-274

also in Melville, H. Shorter novels of Herman Melville p227-328

The complete stories of Herman Melville; ed. with an introduction and notes by Jay Leyda. Random House 1949 xxxiv, 472p o.p. 1970

Analyzed in Short Story Index

"Fifteen short stories written after Melville completed 'Moby Dick;' six were published in 'Piazza Tales' (1856), eight were published in magazines of the 1850's, one was never printed in Melville's lifetime." Library J

Contents: Bartleby; The Encantadas; or, Enchanted Isles; Cock-a-doodle-doo! or, The crowning of the noble cock Beneventano; The two temples; Poor man's pudding and rich man's crumbs; The paradise of bachelors and the Tartarus of maids; The lightning-rod man; The happy failure: a story of the River Hudson; The fiddler; Jimmy Rose; Benito Cereno; The bell-tower; I and my chimney; The apple-tree table; The piazza

The Encantadas

In Melville, H. Shorter novels of Herman Melville p157-225

Five tales; with illus. of the author and his environment, together with an introduction by James H. Pickering. Dodd 1967 274p illus (Great illustrated classics) $4.50

Analyzed in Short Story Index

Contents: Bartleby the scrivener; Benito Cereno; I and my chimney; The lightening-rod man; Billy Budd, foretopman

"'Five Tales' presents a selection of . . . short fiction that attests to the rich complexity of Melville's vision." Publisher's note

Israel Potter: his fifty years of exile. Putnam 1855 276p o.p. 1970

Also published with titles: The refugee; His fifty years of exile

"From the Life of Potter published in 1824, Melville refashioned this congenial record of human effort and endurance ending in hopeless misery. Potter fought at Bunker Hill (1775), served as messenger from Horne Tooke and other sympathizers to Dr. Franklin at Paris, fought under Paul Jones—the duel of the 'Bon Homme Richard' and the 'Serapis' is a tremendous battlepiece—but fell again into English hands and lived in toil and penury in London for forty-five years—'a long life still rolling in early mishap.' " Baker's Best

y Moby Dick; or, The white whale

Some editions are:

Dodd $5.50 Illustrated by Mead Shaeffer

Hendricks House $6.50 Edited by Luther S. Mansfield and Howard P. Vincent

Macmillan (N Y) $3.95 Illustrated by Robert Shore; afterword by Clifton Fadiman

Modern Lib. $3.25

Watts, F. $9.95 Large type edition complete and unabridged, A Keith Jennison book

Watts, F. $6.95 Ultratype edition complete and unabridged. With a critical and biographical profile of Herman Melville by Tyrus Hillway

First published 1851

A classic of the sea, telling of the pursuit of Moby Dick, the white whale who defied capture

"In that wild, beautiful romance, Melville seems to have spoken the very secret of the sea, and to have drawn into his tale all the magic, all the sadness, all the wild joy of many waters." John Masefield

Melville, Herman—*Continued*

Omoo

Some editions are:
Heritage $7.50 Introduction by Van Wyck
Brooks; wood engravings by Ronald Stone
Hendricks House $5.50 Edited by Harrison Hayford and Walter Blair
Northwestern Univ. Press $10

Sequel to: Typee
First published 1847
"A romance of the South Seas [mainly the Marquesas]. . . . 'Omoo' is Polynesian for 'rover.' The scene is laid largely in Tahiti; and sailors, natives, beach-combers and missionaries are portrayed in lively manner. The book occasioned much criticism because of its treatment of missionaries." Gerwig. University Handbook for Readers and Writers
"The pictures of nautical life, of fights with savages, narrow escapes and tropical scenery have often been mistaken for statements of fact." Baker's Historical

Piazza tales; ed. by Egbert S. Oliver. Hendricks House 1948 256p $4.50

This collection first published in 1856 by Dix and Edwards
Farrar, Straus edition analyzed in Short Story Index
Contents: The piazza; Bartleby; Benito Cereno; The lightning-rod man; The Enchantadas; The bell-tower

Pierre; or, The ambiguities; ed. by Henry A. Murray. Farrar, Straus 1949 504p $6.50

"Hendricks House publication"
First published 1852 by Harper
A "strange novel, semi-autobiograhical, which Melville wrote immediately after 'Moby Dick' (and published a year later, in 1852). It bears little resemblance to the great demonic story of Ahab and his whale. . . . [In his introduction] Mr. Murray chooses to ignore many of the esthetic questions the book inevitably raises, and to concentrate on psychological analysis." N Y Times Bk R

Selected writings of Herman Melville: complete short stories, Typee [and] Billy Budd, foretopman. Modern Lib. 1952 903p $4.95

Analyzed in Short Story Index
Contents: Bartleby; Encantadas; or, Enchanted Isles; Cock-a-doodle-doo! or The crowing of the noble cock Benevantano; The two temples; Poor man's pudding and rich man's crumbs; The paradise of bachelors and the Tartarus of maids; The lightning-rod man; The happy failure: a story of the river Hudson; The fiddler; Jimmie Rose; Benito Cereno; The bell-tower; I and my chimney; The apple-tree table; The piazza; Typee; The story of Toby; Billy Budd, foretopman

Shorter novels of Herman Melville; with an introduction by Raymond Weaver. Liveright 1956 li, 328p $6.95

"Black and gold library"
Benito Cereno, first published anonymously in 1855 is a story of piracy on the high seas. Bartleby the scrivener, published anonymously in 1853 is an allegorical tale of an eccentric copyist working in a Wall Street office, who refuses to do any work except copying. The Encantadas which first appeared 1854, is set in the Galapagos islands, and "evokes the loneliness and the savage beauty of Oceania and the intrinsic majesty of human suffering." Baker's Best

Typee

Some editions are:
Dodd $5 Illustrated by Mead Schaeffer
Dufour $3.50 Edited by Herbert V. Thal
Northwestern Univ. Press $10 Edited by Harrison Hayford, Herschell Parker and G. Thomas Tanselle
Oxford $2.75

First published 1846
A romance of the South Seas by Herman Melville "recording the adventures of a whaling voyage in the Pacific. 'Typee' (Taipi) is a valley in one of the Marquesas where Melville was kept captive by the natives. The book gives a vivid picture of a civilized man in contact with the exotic dreamlike life of the tropics. Its popularity was revived by the South Sea furor of the 1920's." Benét. The Reader's Encyclopedia
Followed by: Omoo

also in Melville, H. Selected writings of Herman Melville p465-784

White-jacket; or, The world in a man-of-war. Harper 1850 465p o.p. 1970

"The voyage from Hawaii around Cape Horn to the Atlantic Coast [on a United States frigate] returning from Japan is described in realistic detail. Melville reveals his distaste for bruital and inhumane practices of the officer aboard a U.S. Navy man-of-war. Some of the flogging scenes later convinced Congressmen to abolish that punishment." Benét. The Reader's Encyclopedia

Menen, Aubrey

The prevalence of witches; a novel. Scribner 1948 271p o.p. 1970

"In a fictional section of India, called Limbo, the British authorities imprison a chieftain accused of murder, though the chieftain has thought himself quite justified in disposing of a witch. The pro-Limbodian investigation that follows satirizes certain aspects of western civilization." Pub W

Mercer, Charles

The minister. Putnam 1969 347p $6.95

This novel portrays "the lives of two deeply committed clergymen, Martin Judson and his son-in-law, David Murchison, who is very much of the new school of social action. Though they see their calling differently, they both confront the common problems and quotidian details of the minister's life: the difficulties of living on a minister's salary in today's affluent society, the politics of a deacons' meeting, the need to keep a minister's wife slightly less well dressed than the wives of congregational leaders, the presence of unchristian bigotry in the 'best' Christians, and the 'dangerous years' for any minister—when he reaches the age of 40." Publisher's note
"Since Mr. Mercer writes from first-hand experience, presumably the details he supplies of a Protestant minister's existence are authentic. . . . If one wishes to fault this novel, it would probably be on the ground of episodicity: panoramic in scope, it moves on from city to city, church to church, deriving its interest from the varying problems its protagonists encounter." Best Sellers

Meredith, George

Diana of the crossways; a novel. Rev. ed. Scribner 1919 415p o.p. 1970

First published 1885
"A study of character and emotion in which a beautiful and gifted woman comes through varied experiences of love and matrimony to happiness at the end. It is full of both comedy and passion and is direct, dramatic and vivacious. The character of Diana was modeled from the Hon. Caroline Norton, a poet and beauty who was conspicuous in London society in the early part of the nineteenth century." Pratt Alcove

The egoist; a comedy in narrative. Oxford 1956 547p (The World's classics) $1.75

First published 1879
"A psychological comedy, mercilessly laying bare the soul of a spoiled child of fortune, outwardly a pattern of conventional virtue, inwardly a thrall to selfishness; tragical in its exposure of the secret egoism that is in all men. . . . Clara Middleton, whose engagement to the hero [Sir Willoughby Patterne] and its rupture are the pith of the story, is a charming personification of [Meredith's] refined ideas of women; and the genial epicure, her father, the boy Crossjay, and Vernon Whitford . . . are all intensely Meredithian creations. The novel is very long, the time of the action very brief, each act in the drama being developed with huge elaboration." Baker's Best

Meredith, George—_Continued_

The ordeal of Richard Feverel; introduction by Robert Sencourt. Dutton 1967 [c1935] 493p (Everyman's lib) $2.95

First published 1859
"Primarily a story of father and son. The father, though a man of fine intelligence and noble aims, through his fatal pedantry brings ruin and misery to the son he loves." Pratt Alcove

Merejkowski, Dmitri

The death of the gods; tr. by Herbert Trench. Authorised English version. Putnam 1901 414p o.p. 1970

"The first of a trilogy of historical novels the theme of which is the eternal antagonism between the Christian and pagan elements in our nature. In this volume Julian the Apostate is the central figure; in the two following volumes the role is filled by Leonardo da Vinci and Peter the Great." Pittsburgh
Followed by: Romance of Leonardo da Vinci

Peter and Alexis; the romance of Peter the Great; authorized translation from the Russian. Putnam 1906 556p o.p. 1970

Sequel to: The romance of Leonardo da Vinci
"Peter the Great and his imbecile son Alexis are but the protagonists in a vast and crowded drama representing the whole life of Russia at the epoch (1715-18)." Baker's Best

The romance of Leonardo da Vinci; the forerunner; exclusively authorized translation from the Russian of The resurrection of the gods by Herbert Trench. Putnam 1902 463p illus o.p. 1970

Sequel to: The death of the gods
Published in Russia as: The resurrection of the gods and in England, 1902, as: The forerunner
"A eulogy of individualism in the character and career of Leonardo, and an elaborate study of the artistic temperament. The action takes place in and about Florence at the end of the 15th century. Pictures Savonarola, Italian officials and rulers, and Raphael, Michelangelo, and other artist contemporaries. Stresses Leonardo's inventive and scientific curiosity." Lenrow. Readers' Guide to Prose Fiction
Followed by: Peter and Alexis

Merezhkovskiĭ, Dmitriĭ Sergeevich. See Merejkowski, Dmitri

Merimée, Prosper

Carmen; tr. from the French and illus. by Edmund H. Garrett, with a memoir of the author by Louise Imogen Guiney. Little 1896 xxx, 117p illus o.p. 1970

Original French edition 1845
"The tale so well known from Bizet's opera, which is founded on it. . . . The story of a Spanish gipsy, in whose nature are concentrated the primitive instincts of the savage, chief among them a passion for freedom. The tale is pure romance, the method calmly realistic, and it is a masterpiece of pure objective art. The scenery and costumes of Spain add to its picturesque qualities." Baker's Best

Colomba; tr. from the French by Rose Sherman. Crowell 1897 223p illus o.p. 1970

Original French edition 1840
A "drama of Corsican life, into which is precipitated the sense of beauty and strangeness that seems to belong to this land, where assassination is still a recognized means of settling differences. Colomba is a young Corsican in whom the vendetta spirit is incarnate, while her brother, who ought to avenge his father's death, is Parisianized and emancipated from ancestral barbarism. The touches of local colour, the outlined under-characters, and the romantic scenery combine into a perfect artistic whole." Baker's Best

Merle, Robert

The day of the dolphin; a novel; tr. from the French by Helen Weaver. Simon & Schuster 1969 320p $5.95

Original French edition 1967
"In 1971 Professor Henry Sevilla shows off his two dolphins, Bi and Fa, whom he has taught to communicate with humans and even to read. But the CIA sees a military value in the dolphins, there's a plot to start WW III, and it is the dolphins who at last carry Sevilla to safety in Cuba, proving their superiority to the humans they love." Bk Buyer's Guide
"The plot, rather fantastic in its bare outlines, moves credibly and swiftly to its conclusion, offering along the way forceful political and social satire in tones that range from the apocalyptic to the maudlin. It is an ambitious novel, a full and absorbing book which explores the corruption of man and his institutions." Best Sellers

Merril, Judith

Daughters of Earth; three novels. Doubleday 1969 [c1968] 255p (Doubleday Science fiction) $4.95

These novels tell "of the generations of women who push back the frontiers of exploration." Am News of Bks
Contents: Project Nursemaid; Daughters of Earth; Homecalling

Homecalling
_In_ Merril, J. Daughters of Earth p166-[256]

Project Nursemaid
_In_ Merril, J. Daughters of Earth p7-96

(ed.) SF: the best of the best. Delacorte Press 1967 438p $6.50

Analyzed in Short Story Index
This anthology contains twenty-nine vintage science fiction stories from the first five annuals (1955-1960) of The year's best S-F. (Publisher)
Contents: The hoofer, by W. M. Miller; Bulkhead, by T. Sturgeon; The anything box, by Z. Henderson; Prima Belladonna, by J. G. Ballard; Casey Agonistes, by R. M. McKenna; A death in the house, by C. D. Simak; Spacetime for springers, by F. Leiber; Pelt, by C. Emshwiller; Stranger Station, by D. Knight; Satellite passage, by T. L. Thomas; No, no, not Rogov, by C. Smith; Compounded interest, by M. Reynolds; Junior, by R. Abernathy; Sense from thought divide, by M. Clifton; Mariana, by F. Leiber; Plenitude, by W. Worthington; Day at the beach, by C. Emshwiller; Let's be Frank, by B. W. Aldiss; The wonder horse, by G. Byram; Nobody bothers Gus, by A. Budrys; The prize of peril, by R. Sheckley; The handler, by D. Knight; The golem, by A. Davidson; The sound sweep, by J. G. Ballard; Hickory, dickory, Kerouac, by R. Gehman; Dreaming is a private thing, by I. Asimov; The public hating, by S. Allen; You know Willie, by T. R. Cogswell; One ordinary day, with peanuts, by S. Jackson

(ed.) The 6th-12th annual of the year's best SF. Delacorte Press 1961-1968 7v illus 1961 $3.95, available from Simon & Schuster, 1962-1966 o.p. 1970, 1968 $5.95

Volumes 6-9 published by Simon & Schuster. No volume published in 1967
Titles vary
Analyzed in Short Story Index
Preceded by annual volumes for 1956-1959 with title: SF: the year's greatest science fiction and fantasy, published by Gnome Press
Contains the following stories: v6: Double, double, toil and trouble, by H. Cantine; The never ending penny, by B. Wolfe; The fellow who married the Maxill girl, by W. Moore; Something invented me, by R. C. Phelan; A sign for cybernetics, by F. Lamport; Obvious, by M. Ffolkes; I remember Babyon, by A. C. Clarke; The lagging profession, by L. Lockhard; Report on the nature of the lunar surface, by J. Brunner; J.G. by R. Price; Chief, by H. Slesar; The large ant, by H. Fast; A rose by other name, by

Merril, Judith—*Continued*

C. Anvil; Enchantment, by E. Emmett; Thiotimoline and the space age, by I. Asimov; Beach scene, by M. King; Creature of the snows, by W. Sambrot; Adominable by F. Brown; The man on top, by R. Bretnor; David's daddy, by R. G. Brown; Something bright, by Z. Henderson; In the house, another, by J. Whitehill; A serious search for weird worlds, by R. Bradbury; Instructor, by Thelwell; The brotherhood of keepers, by D. McLaughlin; Hemingway in space, by K. Amis; Mine own ways, by R. McKenna; Old Hundredth, by B. W. Aldiss

v7: A passage from the stars, by K. Hurlbut; Among the Dangs, by G. P. Elliot; Immediately yours, by R. B. Hale; Parky, by D. Rome; The fastest gun dead, by J. F. Grow; All the tea in China, by R. Bretnor; The Portobello Road, by M. Spark; Ottmar Balleau X 2, by G. Bamber; The dandelion girl, by R. F. Young; It becomes necessary, by W. Moore; My trial as a war criminal, by L. Szilard; A prize for Edie, by J. F. Bone; Freedom, by M. Reynolds; High barbery, by L. Durrell; The Quaker cannon, by F. Pohl and C. M. Kornbluth; Judas bomb, by K. Reed; A small miracle of fishhooks and straight pins, by D. R. Bunch; The tunnel ahead, by A. Glaser; The countdown, by J. Haase; The beat cluster, by F. Leiber; The ship who sang, by A. MacCaffrey; A planet named Shayol, by C. Smith; The Asteroids, by J. Wyndham; The long night, by R. Russell

v8: The unsafe deposit box, by G. Kersh; Seven-day terror, by R. A. Lafferty; The toy shop, by H. Harrison; The face in the photo, by J. Finney; The circuit riders, by R. C. FitzPatrick; Such stuff, by J. Brunner; The man who made friends with electricity, by F. Leiber; Kings who die, by P. Anderson; The unfortunate Mr Morky, by V. Aandahl; Christmas treason, by J. White; A miracle of rare device, by R. Bradbury; All the sounds of fear, by H. Ellison; One of those days, by W. F. Nolan; The day Rembrandt went public, by A. M. Auerbach; Ms. found in a bus, by R. Baker; The insane ones, by J. G. Ballard; Leprechaun, by W. Sambrot; Change of heart, by G. Whitley; Angela's satyr, by B. Cleeve; Puppet show, by F. Brown; Hang head, vandal, by M. Clifton; Earthlings go home, by M. Reynolds; The Martian stargazers, by F. Pohl; Planetary effulgence, by B. Russell; Deadly game, by E. Wellen; Subcommittee, by Z. Henderson; The piebald hippogriff, by K. Anderson; Home from the shore, by G. R. Dickson

v9: Bernie the Faust, by W. Tenn; Fortress ship, by F. Saberhagen; Mr Waterman, by P. Redgrove; Mrs Pigafetta swims well, by R. Bretnor; They don't make life like they used to, by A. Bester; The great Nebraska Sea, by A. Danzig; The Faces outside, by B. McAllister; A slight case of limbo, by L. Biggle; 237 talking statutes, etc. by F. Leiber; The jazz machine, by R. Matheson; Mourning Song, by C. Beaumont; The Jewbird, by B. Malamud; On the fourth planet, by J. F. Bone; Poppa needs shorts, by W. Richmond; Double standard, by F. Brown; Interview, by F. A. Javor; Eight o'clock in the morning, by R. Nelson; Where is everybody, by B. Bova; The Earth Dwellers, by A. Maurois; The Nobel Prize winners, by W. J. J. Gordon; Hot planet, by H. Clement; Confessions of the first number, by C. Owsley; The Ming vase, by E. C. Tubb; A bargain with Cashel, by G. Kersh; Drunkboat, by C. Smith

v10: Automatic tiger, by K. Reed; The Carson effect, by R. Wilson; The shining ones, by A. C. Clarke; Pacifist, by M. Reynolds; The new encyclopaedist, by S. Becker; The legend of Joe Lee, by J. D. MacDonald; Gas mask, by J. D. Houston; A sinister metamorphosis, by R. Baker; Sonny, by R. Raphael; The last secret weapon of the Third Reich, by J. Nesvadba; Descending, by T. M. Disch; Decadence, by R. Gary; Be of good cheer, by F. Leiber; It could be you, by F. Roberts; A benefactor of humanity, by J. T. Farrell; Synchromocracy, by H. Cawood; The search, by B. Simonds; The Pirokin effect, by L. Eisenberg; The twerlik, by J. Sharkey; A rose for Ecclesiastes, by R. Zelazny; The terminal beach, by J. G. Ballard; Problem child, by A. Porges; The wonderful dog suit, by D. Hall; The mathenauts, by N. Kagan; Family portrait, by M. Kent; The red egg, by J. M. Gironella; The power of positive thinking, by M. E. White; A

living doll, by R. Wallace; Training talk, by D. R. Bunch; A Miracle too many, by P. H. Smith; The last lonely man, by J. Brunner; The man who found Proteus, by R. Rohrer; Yachid and Yechida, by I. B. Singer

v11: Something else, by R. J. Tilley; The volcano dances, by J. G. Ballard; Slow Tuesday night, by R. A. Lafferty; Better than ever, by A. Kirs; Coming-of-age day, by A. K. Jorgensson; The wall, by J. Saxton; The survivor, by W. F. Moudy; Moon duel, by F. Leiber; Project inhumane, by A. B. Malec; Those who can, do, by B. Kurosaka; Susan, by A. Bevan; Yesterdays' gardens, by J. Byrne; The roaches, by T. M. Disch; Game, by D. Barthelme; J is for Jeanne, by E. C. Tubb; Terminal, by R. Goulart; The plot, by T. Herzog; Investigating the Bidwell endeavors, by D. R. Bunch; The case, by P. Redgrove; There's a starman in ward 7, by D. Rome; Eyes do more than see, by I. Asimov; Maelstrom II, by A. C. Clarke; Two letters to Lord Kelvin, by A. Jarry; Warrior, by G. R. Dickson; Mars is "ours", by A. Buchwald; Scarfe's world, by B. W. Aldiss; A singular case of extreme electrolyte balance associated with folie a deux, by R. D. Tschirgi; A magus, by J. Ciardi; The circular ruins, by J. L. Borges; The girl who drew the gods, by H. Jacobs; The drowned giant, by J. G. Ballard; Circe undersea, by G. MacBeth; Somewhere not far from here, by G. Kersh; In the ruins, by R. Dahl; Traveller's rest, by D. I. Masson; Ado about nothing, by B. Ottum

v12: In seclusion, by H. Jacobs; The food farm, by K. Reed; Gogol's wife, by T. Landolfi; The balloon, by D. Barthelme; The cloud-sculptors of Coral D, by J. G. Ballard; Luana, by G. Thomas; During the Jurassic, by J. Updike; The fall of Frenchy Steiner, by H. Bailey; Light of other days, by B. Shaw; Beyond the weeds, by P. Tate; The primary education of the Camiroi, by R. A. Lafferty; When I was Miss Dow, by S. Dorman; Confluence, by B. W. Aldiss; An ornament to his profession, by C. L. Harness; Narrow valley, by R. A. Lafferty; They do not always remember, by W. Burroughs; The winter flies, by F. Leiber; And more changes still, by H. Michaux; The other, by K. MacLean; Chicken Icarus, by C. Emshwiller; The star-pit, by S. R. Delany

Merton, Thomas

My argument with the Gestapo; a macaronic journal. Doubleday 1969 259p $4.95

"A young American's stay in World War II England and, very briefly, France is recorded in an autobiographical novel that closely observes the appearance of besieged London and effectively conveys that curious sense of disorientation and heightened awarness experienced by civilians in time of war." Booklist

"The book offers a fascinating insight into the evolution of a profoundly committed writer." Pub W

Mertz, Barbara. See Michaels, Barbara; Peters, Elizabeth

Michaels, Barbara

y Ammie, come home. Meredith 1968 252p $4.95

"Ruth Bennett, an attractive widow, her niece Sara, Pat MacDougal, Sara's anthropology Professor, and Sara's boyfriend Bruce find themselves in the midst of a modern-day ghost hunt when Sara becomes 'possessed' by the spirit of the long-dead Amanda Campbell." Bk Buyer's Guide

"The search for answer to the mystery leads to research in Georgetown history, into philosophical speculation, theology, superstition, and much more. . . . The author writes well enough to bring her characters into a focus of identification." Best Sellers

Prince of darkness. Meredith 1969 230p $4.95

"For those who like the Gothic bit, this is pleasant mystery fare. The [Maryland] hunt country setting is well handled and Miss Michaels leaves you with more than a suggestion that she had her tongue in her cheek throughout. It all has to do with black magic and a witchs' coven in the middle of the hunt country, with a congregation including a senator and a general and a melodramatic finale in which a baby is rescued from being a human sacrifice." Pub W

Michener, James A.

y The bridges at Toko-ri. Random House 1953 146p $2.95

A story of the men of a naval task force operating in the icy waters off the Korean shore with a vital mission to perform: to destroy with jet bombers the heavily guarded bridges at Toko-ri and thus to stop essential supplies from moving to the Communist front lines

"A tense and exciting book, enthralling in its picture of life aboard an aircraft carrier and of the valor, the judgment and the skill which such service entails. Though focused about the figure of a pilot named Brubaker, its interest lies not only in his individual fortunes but also in the life aboard ship.' Book of the Month Club News

Caravans; a novel. Random House 1963 341p $5.95

The story, set in Afghanistan in the year 1946, "of Ellen Jasper, an American bored with her native land, who flees to Afghanistan to become the second wife of a man named Nazrullah. Her parents haven't heard from her in 13 months and Mark Miller, of the U.S. Embassy in that country, is sent to investigate. The search takes Miller into unknown territory. He joins a nomad tribe and experiences a love affair of rare beauty with Mira, daughter of the Great Zulfiqar, chieftain of all the nomadic peoples scattered around Afghanistan. [The novel describes] Ellen's degeneration into a sensualist, [and] the encounter of Miller (a Jew) with an ex-Nazi who tortured Jews." America

"The story cannot be said to dominate this novel. What dominates it—indeed, frequently shoulders the action right off stage—is information, facts, explanation." Newsweek

The fires of spring. Random House 1949 495p $6.95

"A character study of David Harper, from his boyhood in the Pennsylvania poorhouse where his aunt was superintendent, to his marriage to his childhood sweetheart in New York. Along the way he worked summers in an amusement park, where he had his first sex experience; he went to a Quaker college near Philadelphia; and travelled for a time with a Chautauqua group. When he settled in New York he finally discovered his vocation: he was to become a writer." Book Rev Digest

y Hawaii. Random House 1959 937p $7.95

A fictional history of the Hawaiian Islands from the faraway time when the volcanic islands rose from the sea to their present status as our fiftieth state. The author has told this story in terms of the personal triumphs and tragedies of some highly individual characters, men and women of the many peoples of Hawaii, the Polynesians, American missionaries, Chinese, Japanese, and Filipinos. (Publisher)

"James Michener, the Pepys of the Pacific, has gone behind the image as far as historical fact, reasonable supposition, and the limits of his imagination have permitted him. 'Hawaii' is a long, long, look and a fascinating one. . . . High-domed, long-haired 'littérateurs' may argue that Michener's characters are often as paper-thin as the colorad image in which 'Hawaii' is held by mainland tourists, but 'Hawaii' is still a masterful job of research, an absorbing performance of story telling, and a monumental account of the islands from geologic birth to sociological emergence as the newest, and perhaps the most interesting of the United States." Sat R

Sayonara. Random House 1954 243p $4.95

"The love story of an American Air Corps major and a beautiful Japanese girl. When Major Gruver sets up housekeeping with Hanaogi there is consternation among the Americans, for Gruver is engaged to an American general's daughter. Contrary to the course of Madame Butterfly, in this instance it is the Japanese girl who says Sayonara (farewell) to the American." Book Rev Digest

"The graphic love passages are not likely to offend the mature reader because they are described with delicacy and restraint. Highly recommended for public libraries." Library J

The source; a novel. Random House 1965 909p illus maps $7.95

An archeological dig in Israel is the focal point of this novel. "John Cullinane, an American Catholic archaeologist, educated at Harvard and Grenoble, heads the dig. Jemail Tabari, an Arab scientific archaeologist has the task of maintaining scientific accuracy and keeping both the workers and the American Jewish financial backer happy. Ilan Eliav, a Jewish soldier and scholar is the administrator. The feminine element is provided in the person of Dr. Bar-El, an Israeli educated pottery expert whose presence is an absolute necessity for identification of pottery found in the lowest levels. However, this work does not concern itself with just the lives of these four people; as the dig proceeds and the objects found at various levels are identified and accurately recorded, Michener attempts to recreate the history of the people who occupied Makor—a history which takes the reader from 10,000 BCE to the present state of Israel." Best Sellers

"The shaping of the Jewish religion has a special fascination for the author (a gentile), and for the average reader the book throws much light on . . . key chapters in the history of Judaism. . . . Told with remarkable erudition and moving human detail, The Source is a monumental and imaginative study in depth of the old-new nation Israel." Sat R

Tales of the South Pacific. Macmillan (N Y) 1947 326p $4.95

Also available in large type edition for $7.95
Pulitzer Prize, 1948
Analyzed in Short Story Index

Describes "the strain and the boredom, the careful planning and heroic action, the color and beauty of the islands, and all that made up life during the critical days of the war in the Pacific." Wis Lib Bul

Contents: South Pacific; Coral Sea; Mutiny; Officer and a gentleman; The cave; Milk run; Alligator; Our heroine; Dry rot; Fo'dolla'; Passion; Boar's tooth; Wine for the mess at Segi; Airstrip at Konora; Those who fraternize; The strike; Frisco Landing on Kuralei; Cemetery at Hoga Point

Millar, Kenneth. See Macdonald, Ross

Millar, Margaret

The fiend. Random House 1964 244p o.p. 1970

Novel of suspense. "The 'fiend' is a borderline case who has served time for assaulting a little girl but who might yet be able to adjust himself to a normal life—if it were not for his obsessed attraction to 9-year-old Jessie. We come to know . . . poor Charlie and his problems, and Jessie . . . and the adults who surround her. . . . A crime finally occurs." N Y Times Bk R

The iron gates

In Hitchcock, A. ed. Alfred Hitchcock presents: Stories for late at night p315-469

Miller, Arthur

I don't need you any more; stories. Viking 1967 240p $5

Analyzed in Short Story Index

Contents: I don't need you any more; Monte Sant' Angelo; Please don't kill anything; The misfits; Glimpse at a jockey; The prophecy; Fame; Fitter's night; A search for a future

"These stories represent change of pace or viewpoint, an opportunity not found in drama to hold characters and events frozen and to see them isolated in stillness. Many selections contain echoes of Miller's plays, but the characters are distinct individuals in their own right." Booklist

Miller, Caroline

Lamb in his bosom. Berg [1966 c1933] 345p $7.50

Pulitzer Prize, 1934
First published 1933 by Harper

"A quiet chronicle of isolated, hardworking people on a Georgia farm in the years preceding the Civil war, it is the story of Cean Carver from girlhood to old age, and it is concerned with elemental things—weather, hard time, births and deaths—all accepted with the matter-of-fact realism of the pioneer, but related with a warmth that surmounts the deliberately slow-moving style of the prose." Booklist

Miller, Henry

Tropic of Cancer. Grove 1961 318p $7.50

First published 1934 in France

"An autobiographical first novel recounting the experiences, sensations, thoughts of Miller, a penniless American in the Paris of the early thirties. It is not so much a novel as an intense journal, written daily about what was happening to him daily . . . as he scrounged for food, devoured books, conversed volubly, and flung himself into numerous beds." New Repub

"It must be granted that parts of 'Tropic of Cancer' will hammer away at some of the strongest of stomachs, even in this epoch in which so many books are really scabrous. However, in the present volume, among other things, Miller projects with gusto some of the great comic scenes of modern literature. . . . If literary quality is a criterion, these passages run far ahead of any considerations of obscenity; in themselves they guarantee that Henry Miller is an authentic, a significant author whose ripest work has been too long forbidden in his homeland." N Y Times Bk R

Followed by: Tropic of Capricorn

Tropic of Capricorn. Grove [1962 c1961] 348p $7.50

Sequel to: Tropic of Cancer

First published 1939 in France

"Covers Miller's early years in New York and Brooklyn, the twenties, the Cosmodemonic Telegraph Company, for which he worked, and the flow of life in a great city." Bk Buyer's Guide

"Like Whitman, who also sent his barbaric yawp over the roof-tops of the world, Miller has blasted the very foundations of human hypocrisy—moral, social and political. . . . The story, of course, is nothing. The style—which is alternately naturalistic and surrealistic—is all. The fact remains that the greatest passages in this book are the scenes of love-making. . . . They join in a grand paean to all that is still joyous, healthy, happy and affirmative in this age of atomic bombs." Nation

Miller, Walter M.

y A canticle for Leibowitz; a novel by Walter M. Miller, Jr. Lippincott 1960 [c1959] 320p o.p. 1970

"Some decades after the atomic war, a monastery, founded by the scientist Leibowitz to preserve such knowledge as could be buried, memorized, or otherwise saved from destruction by the new barbarian hordes, still survived. The first part of Mr. Miller's novel is concerned with a novice in this monastery. The second part is set in a new Renaissance, when scholars exist again and seek out the old learning. The last section is projected into Earth's second atomic era, with neither man's feckless proneness to disaster nor his capacity for blind hope impaired." Library J

"It has elements in common with science fiction, yet it would be quite impossile to classify it narrowly as such. It is fanciful yet as deeply true as any book I've read. it brilliantly combines several qualities: It is prodigiously imaginative and original, richly comic, terrifyingly grim, profound both intellectually and morally, and, above all, is simply such a memorable story as to stay with a reader for years." Chicago Sunday Tribune

The darfsteller

In Asimov, I. ed. The Hugo winners p5-71

Miller, Warren

The cool world; a novel. Little 1959 241p $4.95

"Duke, one of the leaders of a teen-age gang, [in New York City's Harlem] and old for his fourteen years, is convinced that the purchase of a $15 gun will convince everyone that 'he is cool. he has heart.' Although he sells dope in order to raise the money Duke's plans go awry and his life changes when the consequences of a gang 'rumble' send him to reform school. Dope addicts, prostitutes, homosexuals, and delinquents crowd these pages but the keynote is one of tragedy. not sensationalism." Booklist

Mills, Robert P.

(ed.) Magazine of Fantasy and Science Fiction. A decade of Fantasy and Science Fiction

Milne, A. A.

Mr Pim. Dutton 1930 315p o.p. 1970

A pleasant novelization of the delightful English comedy of manners, Mr. Pim passes by. "Old Mr. Pim, in his gentle way, shuffled into the charming English household composed of Mr. Marden, typical conservative land owner, his adorable wife, his young ward and her would-be fiancé. Mr. Pim said a few words and went away leaving Mr. Marden with the devastating knowledge that his wife's first husband instead of lying in his grave in Australia has just landed in England." Publisher's note

The red house mystery; with an introduction by the author. Dutton 1936 [c1922] 211p $3.95

First printing 1922; reissued (reset) in a popular edition, 1936

"A murder mystery unravelled in clever dialogue, and based upon mistaken identity and the diabolical machinations of the victim's private secretary. The scene is an old English manor house." Cleveland

Mirdrekvandi Gunga Din, Ali

No heaven for Gunga Din; consisting of the British and American officers' book, by Ali Mirdrekvandi Gunga Din. Ed. and with an introduction by John Hemming; with a foreword by R. C. Zaehner. Dutton 1965 128p o.p. 1970

"Written by a Persian peasant for the amusement of British and American officers for whom he worked, this fable recounts their journey or Pilgrim's Progress heavenward after World War III." Pub W

"Only a highly original talent could have lampooned earthly vices—drinking and swearing, especially—as 'Gunga Din' has, or conceived such amusing and exasperating red tape for admission into heaven." Pub W

Mishima, Yukio

Nobel Prize in literature, 1969

After the banquet; tr. from the Japanese by Donald Keene. Knopf 1963 [c1960] 270p $4

Original Japanese edition 1960

"Kazu, a middle-aged woman who believes that love has long since been put out of her life, is proprietress of a highly successful restaurant in Tokyo that is much frequented by retired diplomats and politicians. One of the latter is Noguchi, a slightly threadbare but haughty aristocrat. Kazu . . . is a woman of the people who harbors a very romantic heart beneath the veneer of a successful professional woman. The opposites attract each other, fall in love, and get married. . . . When ¡Noguchi attempts a comeback in politics, Kazu throws herself into the campaign; but her methods in going directly to the people scandalize her husband, and the marriage breaks up." Atlantic

"Although this novel differs in setting and subject from Mishima's earlier 'The Temple of the Golden Pavilion' both deal with the conflict between idealism and the real world. This is an excellent translation of an important Japanese novel and should be added to most collections." Library J

Forbidden colors; tr. from the Japanese by Alfred H. Marks. Knopf 1968 403p $6.95

Original Japanese edition 1951

An elderly novelist "Shunsuke, who has been embittered by his experiences with women, is attracted to Yuichi. Because of Yuichi's great beauty and his inability to love a woman, Shunsuke suggests a plan to avenge the wrongs which he feels he himself has experienced. Three of the women in Shunsuke's past are introduced to Yuichi and led into relationships which cause them much difficulty. At the same time Mishima analyzes and describes the relationships which Yuichi develops with a number of male companions in his attempt to satisfy his own needs for love and affection." Library J

Mishima, Yukio—*Continued*

"Only a writer with Mishima's artistic delicacy could take readers into a world they long considered anathema and give them an intuitive sympathy for the characters who populate [it]. . . . The subject matter of 'Forbidden Colors' will probably frighten away many readers. They are missing an outstanding introduction to a forbidden world and a fine example of sustained writing skill." Best Sellers

The sailor who fell from grace with the sea; tr. from the Japanese by John Nathan. Knopf 1965 181p boards $3.95

Original Japanese edition published 1963
Set in present day Japan, this is a story of "a love affair between an attractive widow and Ryuji, a naval officer—and its shattering effect on the widow's son. The boy, Noboru, is part of a grisly group of 13-year-old nihilists who dissect kittens and think 'a father is . . . a machine for dishing up lies to kids.' When Ryuji proposes to Noboru's mother and is accepted, the sailor loses his status in the boy's eyes and becomes another of the gang's hated objects." Newsweek

The sound of waves; tr. by Meredith Weatherby; drawings by Yoshinori Kinoshita. Knopf 1956 182p illus $4.50

"The scene of this novel is a Japanese fishing village. The hero, Shinji, a young fisherman, falls in love with the daughter of the wealthiest man of the village. The story is of the hazards which had to be overcome before the young people could be married." Book Rev Digest
"'The Sound of Waves' is a simple and satisfying story, concerned with human relationships as timeless as the sea, and far removed from the complexities and strife of urban industrial society." N Y Her Trib Books

The temple of the golden pavilion; tr. by Ivan Morris. Introduction by Nancy Wilson Ross. Drawings by Fumi Komatsu. Knopf 1959 262p illus $4.50

"Based on an actual incident in 1950, when a Zen Buddhist acolyte burned down a temple which was a national shrine. Like the real arsonist, the fictional Mizoguchi is ugly and a pathological stutterer, and long before his hostility becomes overt, has developed a compulsion to destroy whatever is morally or physically beautiful. As told by the young acolyte, this is a masterly description of the growth of an obsession and an acute interpretation of the deliberate symbolism underlying Mizoguchi's irrational, perverse behavior." Booklist

Thirst for love; tr. from the Japanese by Alfred H. Marks; introduction by Donald Keene. Knopf 1969 200p $4.95

Original Japanese edition published 1950
"The story concerns a young widow named Etsuko, who lives on a large farm with her father-in-law and other members of his family. She falls in love with Saburo, a handsome servant, and her love for him, which is unrequited, becomes an obsession. . . . Mishima's writing is simple but sensitive; yet this novel's effect is uneven. Several passages are extremely poetic and effecting; other sections of the book are flat and, essentially, pedestrian." Best Sellers

Mitchell, Margaret

y **Gone with the wind.** Macmillan (N Y) 1936 1037p $6.95

Also available in a large type edition $13.95
Pulitzer Prize, 1937
"A story of the years before, during and after the Civil war, in [Georgia]. Its heroine, Scarlett O'Hara, is anything but the usual Southern belle, and once freed from the shackles of ladyhood in which she has been bred, she emerges as a forceful and ruthless woman. Matching her is Rhett Butler, the blockade runner, as engaging a scoundrel as has appeared in fiction for many a day. There are dozens of other characters representing the old and the new forces in the South. A long novel but one in which interest never falters." Wis Lib Bul

"For sheer story value this is one of the finest Civil War epics of all time. . . . Miss Mitchell has shown amazing restraint in dealing with two characters as dramatic and colorful as Scarlett and Rhett. That restraint has strengthened every fiber of her story. She is never for a moment guilty of sentimentalizing or of explaining and inviting sympathy." America
"Margaret Mitchell gives us our Civil War through Southern eyes exclusively, and no tolerant philosophy illumines the crimes of the invaders; she writes with the bias of passionate regionalism, but the verifiable happenings described eloquently justify prejudice." Nation

Mitford, Nancy

The blessing. Random House 1951 305p o.p. 1970

"Grace, a beautiful dull English smart blonde . . . marries a madly glamorous French marquis and gets swept into the network of Parisian society, with its peculiar contemporary complexities. They have a child—The Blessing—named Sigismond. . . . Grace, on a specially guided tour of the private houses of Paris, finds her husband making love to his mistress, and returns in tears to England. There she oscillates for a while between members of White's and the literary 'intelligentsia,' until the book ends with a reconciliation with the marquis." Times (London) Lit Sup
"Her analysis of the characteristic French and English virtues and faults is, on the whole, shrewd and just." Sat R

Mizener, Arthur

(ed.) Fitzgerald, F. S. The Fitzgerald reader

Moberg, Carl Arthur Vilhelm. See Moberg, Vilhelm

Moberg, Vilhelm

The emigrants; a novel; tr. from the Swedish by Gustaf Lannestock. Simon & Schuster 1951 366p o.p. 1970

"This is the first volume of a trilogy which tells the story of a band of Swedish emigrants to the United States. This volume tells the story in particular of one family, Karl Oskar Nilsson, his wife and children, and his young brother Robert, of their life in Sweden and of the long, arduous journey across the Atlantic in the summer of 1850." Book Rev Digest
"A novel of peasant life, drawn to the last homely and superstitious detail. It is a story of poverty and heartbreak over which human faith has its will. And it is filled with an earthy humor, the unpredictable flash of human malice and emotion which bring Mr. Moberg's characters sharply into focus." N Y Times Bk R

Followed by: Unto a good land

The last letter home; a novel; tr. from the Swedish by Gustaf Lannestock. Simon & Schuster 1961 383p o.p. 1970

Originally published in Sweden 1956 and 1959. Parts 3 and 4 of the author's cycle, the first of which is The emigrants and the second, Unto a good land
"The final volume in a trilogy about a family of Swedish immigrants living in Minnesota in the middle of the 19th century. The reader follows the lives of a man and his wife as they change from pioneers in the wilderness to established citizens in a township with neighbors, shops and gossip." Huntting

A time on earth; tr. from the Swedish by Naomi Walford. Simon & Schuster 1965 252p boards $4.50

Original Swedish edition published 1963
"Albert Carlson, resident of California for over 40 years, twice divorced, unneeded by grown sons, and retired from disappointing work, contemplates life and death with a sense of futility until reviewing family and early years in Sweden he comes to an understanding of the tensions between the generations and an acceptance of the significance of life and death in the cyclic scheme of nature." Booklist

Moberg, Vilhelm—*Continued*

"It is Mr. Moberg's special achievement that he can make this contrast of past and present so meaningful—the juxtaposition of the rural Scandinavia of another era with the frightful implications beneath the restless, prosperous surfaces of American urban life today, specifically in a California setting." N Y Times Bk R

Unto a good land; a novel; tr. from the Swedish by Gustaf Lannestock. Simon & Schuster 1954 371p o.p. 1970

Sequel to: The emigrants
"It tells how farmer Karl Oskar Nilsson, his wife and children, and ten other peasants from his own parish in the province of Smaland, sailed in the brig Charlotta in the spring of 1850 to North America, landing ten weeks later at the East River Pier in New York on a sweltering June day and how, by river-boat and steam-wagon, on foot and in an ox-drawn cart, Karl Oskar and his family reach at last the shore of the Minnesota lake where out of the great trees he finds there he hews himself a home." N Y Her Trib Books
Followed by: The last letter home

Moll, Elick

Mr Seidman and the geisha; drawings by Fred Banbery. Simon & Schuster 1962 186p illus o.p. 1970

Mr Seidman the hero of: Seidman and Son reappears, this time on a business trip to Japan. At a party in his honor he meets the gentle geisha, O-yuki, for which nothing in his experience in the garment trade on Seventh Avenue had ever prepared him. This is the humorous story of what happens when O-yuki offers him her hospitality, and two people try to communicate through the barriers of age and custom. (Publisher)
"The story is related by Seidman in a seemingly casual tone but it dramatizes one of the vexing problems of our shrunken world—the difficulty of perceiving a foreign culture in its own terms." Library J

Seidman and son. Putnam 1958 288p o.p. 1970

"Morris Seidman, a New York garment manufacturer, unfolds the fabric of his ghetto-to-Easy-Street career through two integrated stories (one about his former partner, the other about his relationship to his son). Full of the wry sarcasm and head-on approach to life found in many other stories of Jewish families, the tale succeeds in engraving the likeness of an impatient, warmhearted, blundering figure. First-person technique helps in developing Morris' color and vitality." Wis Lib Bul

Molloy, Paul

A pennant for the Kremlin. Doubleday 1964 185p $3.95

The story of what happens "when the Soviet Union inherits (!) the Chicago White Sox and Goes All Out to garner a Major League gonfalon [pennant]. . . . The team's player representative urges his mates not to play for those Reds; sign-stealing is declared decadent and un-Russian; and the Baseball Commissar's pretty daughter is placed under secret surveillance when she begins dating the players." Publisher's note

Momaday, N. Scott

House made of dawn. Harper 1968 212p boards $4.95

Pulitzer Prize, 1969
Abel is a young American Indian who had been living in the pueblo of San Ysidro with his grandfather until he was drafted into the army. This novel "spans the seven years from 1945 to 1952 [during which he lived as] an unassimilated Indian [unable] either to adapt to the white world or to find himself among the vestiges of his dying culture. [It] reflects the plight of the American Indian. Abel's contacts with the white world often erupted into violence—once in murder. . . . The first and last sections of this four-part novel present Abel in relation to reservation life while the midsection portrays the Indian in relation to the white man's civilization." Library J

"N. Scott Momaday's book is superb in its own right. . . . There is a quality of revelation here as the author presents the heartbreaking effort of his hero to live in two worlds. . . . There is plenty of haze in the telling of this tale—but that is one reason why it rings so true." N Y Times Bk R

Monsarrat, Nicholas

y The cruel sea. Knopf 1951 509p $5.95

"This is a compelling novel of contemporary history—of convoy, duty abroad the corvette, 'Compass Ross,' during the Battle of the North Atlantic from 1939-1945. Old sea dogs, young officers, the captain—all are pitted against a relentless and merciless sea in a never-to-be-forgotten struggle." Huntting
"'The Cruel Sea' is an impressive work of fiction, portraying the war at sea with great emotion and restraint, with drama, tenderness, and terror, and with deep humanity. It is a somber and compassionate novel." Chicago Sunday Tribune

Richer than all his tribe. Morrow 1969 [c1968] 372p $6.95

Sequel to: The tribe that lost its head
First published 1968 in Great Britain
This story "opens with the celebration of the island [of Pharamaul's] Independence Day. Former Paramount Chief Dinamaula, once exiled by the British, is now Prime Minister; next to him sits David Bracken, the Chief Secretary, who has worked for this day for many years. . . . From such a beginning Monsarrat traces the subsequent story of the nation, and [the corruption of its leaders]." Publisher's note
"Like the earlier book, this is highly competent, ingeniously slanted, middlebrow documentary, likely to be popular more for the received opinions it confirms than for detailed insights into politics or people, which it altogether lacks. . . . Sex and violence, both handled crudely, are added to give pace and interest." Times (London) Lit Sup

The tribe that lost its head. Sloane 1956 598p map $5.95

"On the same plane that carried David Bracken, an idealistic British civil servant, to his post as government secretary there went two other men who were to change Pharamaul's [an imaginary British colony off the coast of Africa] history. One was a sober young Negro, Oxford educated, who was going home to claim his inheritance as native chief of the island. The other was a cynical, muckraking London journalist who knew just how to pervert and inflate a news dispatch so as to create scare headlines back in England." Book of the Month Club News
"Mr. Monsarrat's sympathy with the colonial problems of this age is resolved in a plea for more understanding and patience, and this is tempered with a strong admiration for the luckless few who have to live with them and cope with them." Sat R

Montherlant, Henry de

Chaos and night; a novel; tr. from the French by Terence Kilmartin. Macmillan (N Y) 1964 240p boards $4.95

First published 1963 in France
"Story of an old exile's dream of home—and his confrontation with reality after more than 20 years. The 67-year-old hero, a Spanish Anarchist, has been trapped in Paris becoming more eccentric each year. Now, with the thought of his own extinction, he becomes romantic about his youth." McClurg. Book News
"Social criticism, symbolism, philosophy and realism are woven into the fabric of the novel. The most vivid and ironic chapter is the bullfight scene (anti-Hemingwayesque). . . . It is a funny, mad, bitter commentary on 'the terrain of truth.'" Library J

The girls; a tetralogy of novels. . . . Tr. from the French by Terence Kilmartin. Introduction by Peter Quennell. Harper 1968 639p $8.95

Original French edition 1954
"The girls; Pity for women; The hippogriff; The lepers." Title page

Montherlant, Henry de—*Continued*

Original French editions published separately in 1936, 1936, 1937 and 1939 respectively. American edition of The girls and Pity for women first published 1938 by Knopf. The hippogriff, and The lepers were first published 1940 with title: Costals & The hippogriff. First French one-volume edition published 1954

"The tetralogy's central figure is a famous French novelist and poet named Pierre Costals. Women write adoring fan letters to him and declare their love as the protagonist takes every advantage to move from mistress to mistress. Besides writing, the only interest Costals has is womanizing. . . . A bitter skeptic, he mocks marriage, religion, the middle class, France—in fact little escapes his devastating satire." Best Sellers

"This translation of 'Les Jeunes Filles' is superb. It preserves the elegance, the freedom, and the wit of the original. Rereading this novel in translation, one realizes that it is just as fresh as when it was first published in the 1930's. The unconventional structure and the great variety of tones of this tetralogy may explain its lasting novelty." Choice

The hippogriff
In Montherlant, H. de. The girls p321-460

The lepers
In Montherlant, H. de. The girls p461-626

Pity for women
In Montherlant, H. de. The girls p178-319

Moorcock, Michael
Behold the man
In Nebula award stories, three p121-92

Moore, Brian
The emperor of ice-cream; a novel. Viking 1965 250p boards $4.95

At odds with both his Catholic family and Protestant Belfast, a frustrated sensualist, and unsuccessful in his college entrance examinations, Gavin Burke considers himself a failure at seventeen. Then with the outbreak of World War II, he joins the Air Raid Precautions, and new encounters change Gavin's relationships with both his family and his girl. (Publisher)

"By being very Irish and very individual 'The Emperor of Ice-Cream' succeeds in touching on Everyman's youth. And it does so in a most welcome manner: no sentimentality, much wit and an astringent charm on every page." N Y Times Bk R

I am Mary Dunne; a novel. Viking 1968 217p boards $4.95

A portrait of a sexually emancipated modern woman. "Mary Dunne, twice-divorced, three times married, Canadian-Irish Catholic by birth, is, on the surface, a sophisticated, even glamorous, New Yorker. In the course of the one day in which her story unfolds, however . . . we catch her at her most vulnerable, tormented by pre-menstrual tension, brought face to face with truths about herself and the men in her life." Pub W

"The sexual passages are frankly erotic but honestly related to the narrative; only the prudish would find them offensive. Mary Dunne can take her place beside Judith Hearne as one of Brian Moore's marvelously human and perceptive character studies." Library J

The lonely passion of Judith Hearne. Little [1956 c1955] 223p $4.95

"An Atlantic Monthly Press book"
First published 1955 in England with title: Judith Hearne

"The story of a lonely, middle-aged spinster living in a Belfast boarding house where she sees her last hope for love and domesticity destroyed." Book Rev Digest

"Dry on a tearful subject, this book is at once so astringent and so compassionate that it manages (that rare feat) to be sad without being depressing." Spec

The luck of Ginger Coffey; a novel. Little 1960 243p $4.95

"An Atlantic Monthly Press book"
"Ginger Coffey, an Irishman of almost forty, has not made what he could of his new life in present-day Montreal. He has lost his job, his wife is attracted to a younger man, and his money is rapidly dwindling. He finally gets work but, in the face of his wife's departure this provides little comfort. In the final scene the Coffeys—husband, wife and teen-age daughter—are reunited after a series of events that have matured them all and given them a new understanding of each other. Lifelike characterizations and episodes distinguish this compassionate, highly perceptive novel." Booklist

Moore, C. L.
The vintage season
In Hitchcock, A. ed. Alfred Hitchcock presents: Stories for late at night p100-40

Moore, George
Esther Waters

Some editions are:
Dutton (Everyman's lib) $3.25 With an introduction by Walter Allen
Liveright (Black and gold lib) $6.95
Oxford (World's classics) $3.00 With an introduction by Graham Hough
First published 1894

"A study of low life in England, especially of people connected with horseracing. The household of a racing squire, described as it appears to Esther the scullery-maid, is broken up on the squire's bankruptcy, and the crowd of servants, jockeys, and stablemen disperse, most of them to get a living on the race-course or in shady business in London. . . . After many troubles . . . [Esther] marries her old lover, who now keeps a low public-house and is a book-maker." Baker's Best

Heloise and Abelard. Liveright 1921 2v in 1 $6.95

"Black and gold library"
A fictionalized version of the twelfth century's classic and tragic love affair between Heloise, a beautiful and learned woman, and Pierre Abelard, the brilliant philosopher who served as her tutor. The author ends the story after Heloise returns to the convent and Abelard to the monastery, and prior to the exchange of the famous love letters.

Moore, John
The waters under the earth. Lippincott 1965 464p $6.95

"Doddington Manor was old and stately, with oaks centuries old. The Seldons, who live there, are Father, who drinks to forget how his world is changing; Mother, who still rides to the hounds and considers Fenton, the new gardener, somewhat of a revolutionary because he votes for Labour; and Susan, seventeen in 1950 when the novel opens. The story is of Susan and the three men in her life, courtly Stephen Le Mesurier, her hearty and eventually to be rich cousin Tony, and young Ben Fenton, the gardener's son." Bk Buyer's Guide

"This fine book fits into the old grand tradition of the Victorian novel, and it has the same fascination for the reader." Pub W

Moore, Robin
The green berets. Crown 1965 341p $4.95

Analyzed in Short Story Index
"The men who wear the green berets may be paratroopers, medics, pilots, even women; the chief point is that they have to be especially picked and trained. The author went through their tough hardening course, and went with them to Vietnam. He tells stories of their . . . courage, their ingenuity, their frustrations, their tragedies—all based on actual fact." Bk Buyer's Guide

Contents: A green beret—all the way; The immortal Sergeant Hanks; The Cao-Dai pagoda; Two birds with one stone; Coup de grace; Home to Nanette; Fourteen VC POW's; The immodest Mr Pomfret; Hit 'em where they live

Moore, Ruth

Candlemas Bay. Morrow 1950 341p o.p. 1970

"Novel of family life in a Maine coast town during 1947 and 1948. The Ellis family had lived at Candlemas Bay for almost two hundred years. The head of the family, Grampie, was trying to take care of his three grown daughters as well as his daughter-in-law and her six children, after Jen's husband was drowned. The story is of Jen's valiant struggle to help Grampie." Book Rev Digest

"A regional novel with universal appeal; a fine example of man's (and woman's!) indomitable spirit when faced by almost insuperable difficulties." Library J

The gold and silver hooks. Morrow 1969 330p $5.95

"Abby Randall Plummer is a staunch New Englander, a woman of integrity and unflinching principles. Her lot is a life of family troubles, starting in the early 1900's and continuing through the rum-running prohibition years, when her irresponsible husband succumbs to the lure of easy money." Pub W

The Sea Flower. Morrow [1965 c1964] 282p boards $4.50

Orphaned Marney is left alone after his uncle dies in a motorcycle crash. The youth "meets another waif . . . Liz. The two are in a houseboat [the Sea Flower] when a hurricane strikes; they are blown to a Maine island, where amiable Arvid and Philomela, his niece, want to adopt the two and Toughy, their cat." Bk Buyer's Guide

"The storm is fantastic, so are some of the happenings, but the people are individuals, and the reader is carried along almost as fast as the winds." Cincinnati

Second growth. Morrow 1962 407p boards $4.95

This novel "dramatizes the events of six months in the lives of the men and women of Hillville [Maine]. . . . The events include the birth of an illegitimate child in peculiarly humiliating circumstances, a murder . . . and many kinds of contemptible and appalling betrayals of helplessness. . . . It is . . . [an] account of a way of life that is critically in need of rehabilitation, but where an unyielding will to survive still confers an impressive dignity on many." Sat R

Speak to the winds. Morrow 1956 309p o.p. 1970

Chin Island, near Passamaquoddy, Maine, beginning in 1855 is the setting. "The island had been the scene of a flourishing granite industry, but at that time had passed, and the descendants of the original settlers and the people who had worked for them, lived by fishing. A thoughtless prank at a Christmas party started a full-fledged feud which threatened to disrupt the whole life of the island, until tragedy brought them together again." Book Rev Digest

Spoonhandle. Morrow 1946 377p o.p. 1970

A Maine coastal village provides the locale for the story "of the Stilwells—of Pete and his sister Agnes, who wanted money and thought they could get it by cheating their neighbors—of their brothers, Hod and Willie, who as fishermen kept the dignity and the proud individuality which was their heritage—and of the love story of Hod and Ann Freeman." Hunting

"There is generally an authentic feeling for place, for the true and ordinary values of every day, the meaningfulness of independence, of work, of honesty and kindness." N Y Times Bk R

Morand, Paul

Open all night

In Dupee, F. W. ed. Great French short novels p463-533

Moravia, Alberto

Command, and I will obey you; tr. from the Italian by Angus Davidson. Farrar, Straus 1969 190p $5.50

Original Italian edition published 1967

A collection of 27 tales. "All are first-person narratives and the tellers are mostly ordinary people, husbands, students, bank messengers. One is told by a dog." Pub W

Contents: Command, and I will obey you; Celestina; A middling type; All-seeing; Wake up; Exactly; The sister-in-law; The chase; Down and out; Signs; You know me, Carlos; The Judas tree; Don't let's be dramatic; Enrica Baile; Why, who said so; A thing is a thing; Ambiguities; Words are sheep; Doubles; A disengaged conscience; The things that grow; The monster; Reconciliation; The stammerer; Man of power; Proto; Smells and the bone

More Roman tales; selected and tr. by Angus Davidson. Farrar, Straus [1964 c1963] 254p boards $4.75

Analyzed in Short Story Index

Original Italian edition, 1959; this translation first published 1963 in England

Contents: The chimpanzee; The spell; The uncle; The vow; He and I; All for the family; Dancing is life; Overtaking; Golden hair; A double game; The Chinese vase; Silvano and Romildo; Operation Pasqualino; Reparation; Good-for-nothing; The bite; A tough nut; Naturally; Not one but five; The loveliest thing of all; The pearwood table; Mother's boy; Ah, women, women; The red waterproof; The dimple; You old harpy . . .; Furniture-legs; A policy of silence; Eye-witness; The small hours; Slave-driver

Roman tales; selected and tr. by Angus Davidson. Farrar, Straus 1957 229p o.p. 1970

Analyzed in Short Story Index

Contents: The fanatic; Rain in May; Don't delve too deeply; Hot weather jokes; The clown; The lorry-driver; Poor fish; The go-between; The baby; The perfect crime; The strawberry mark; Jewellery; Taboo; I don't say no; The film test; The girl from Ciociaria; The terror of Rome; Friendship; The ruin of Humanity; Silly old fool; Pair of spectacles; Mario; Appetite; The nurse; The treasure; The caretaker; The nose

Two women; tr. from the Italian by Angus Davidson. Farrar, Straus 1958 339p o.p. 1970

"The two women are Cesira, a country born widowed shopkeeper, and her adored daughter, Rosetta, a lovely innocent girl nearing womanhood. As the Allies and Germans battle in Italy, Cesira flees with Rosetta to the country, taking money to buy provisions and shelter. Their prolonged hardships and Rosetta's shameful fate just when peace and safety seemed near are recounted by Cesira herself." Chicago Sunday Tribune

"A troubling and powerful novel of total war. . . . Although the reader is forewarned and there is no suspense in the ordinary sense, there is a dread that the reader can allay only by reading on. Moravia prepares the climax with masterly deliberation. . . . There will, I am sure, be many novels of the war more sensational and harrowing than 'Two Women,' but I doubt whether any will probe more disturbingly its effects on those who seem farthest from the heart of the fury." N Y Her Trib Books

Morgan, Charles

The fountain. Knopf 1932 451p $5.95

"The scene of this excellent story is laid in Holland, at the castle of the van Leydens, a Dutch family of ancient lineage. To it comes Lewis Alison, a British officer interned for the duration of the . . . [first World War]. Here he writes his history of the comtemplative life, but here he finds Julie, stepdaughter of his host. She is the English wife of a Prussian nobleman, an officer at the front. First an interloper, then an interlude, Julie finally becomes the whole meaning in Alison's life. Then suddenly the husband returns—a very wraith of a man.' Ontario Lib Rev

Morgan, Charles—*Continued*

"It is not everybody's book. That it demands useful attention is of little consequence, since it deserves it. If you like literature that is almost architecture, 'The Fountain' however, will be accepted by you without question." Sat R

Moriarty, Henry C.

(jt. ed.) Cerf, B. ed. An anthology of famous British stories

Morley, Christopher

The haunted bookshop; illus. by Douglas Gorsline. Lippincott 1955 253p illus $4.95

Sequel to: Parnassus on wheels
First published in 1919 by Doubleday. Reset in 1955 with added illustrations
"Roger Mifflin, whom we met in the author's 'Parnassus on wheels', here keeps a secondhand bookshop in Brooklyn, N.Y. He takes in the young daughter of a friend to learn the book trade, and immediately a mystery develops. There is much good discussion of books and reading sandwiched with the plot." Wis Lib Bul

Kitty Foyle. Lippincott 1939 339p o.p. 1970

"Kitty Foyle is the daughter of a retired Philadelphia night watchman, a Londonderry Irishman with a taste for cricket. In this autobiographical novel Kitty's story from childhood to the age of twenty-eight is told in the stream-of-consciousness method. Her language is frank and open, her reactions completely modern. The scene is successively Philadelphia, Illinois, and New York; the time is from about 1918 on." Book Rev Digest
"Those who have been afraid of Mr. Morley because they figure his whimsy will come off on them should not on that account steer clear of 'Kitty Foyle.' It has the Morley touch, all right, but the fancifulness is retrained, and somehow the book seems pretty close to certain realities of the twenties and early thirties." New Yorker

Parnassus on wheels; illus. by Douglas Gorsline. Lippincott 1955 160p illus $4.95

First published by Doubleday in 1917. Reset 1955 with an introduction by John T. Winterich and added illustrations
"Breezy and thoroughly enjoyable story of a spinster of thirty-nine, who impulsively buys a wagon van of books, and coached by its former owner, a shy middle-aged author starts out on the country roads for an adventure. The selling of the books proves a subordinate issue." N Y State Lib
Followed by: The haunted bookshop

Morris, Edita

y The flowers of Hiroshima. Viking 1959 187p $4.95

"Sam Willoughby visits Hiroshima 13 years after the black rain fell on that city and finds the tragedy of that day still alive. He sees beautiful Ohatsu run away from her home because, with her tainted blood she dare not marry and bear children to the man she loves; he sees Fumio's once strong body succumb to internal injuries; he sees poverty, loss and the scars, both physical and psychic. He also sees the beauty of these people, their childish gaiety, their sensitivity and their kindness. This story, the pathos of which escapes being mawkish, should help to keep alive the memory of the tragedy of Hiroshima and, by reducing it to simple human terms, should confirm the resolve that it shall not happen again." Library J

Morris, Ivan

(ed.) Modern Japanese stories; an anthology. With translations by Edward Seidensticker [and others] and woodcuts by Masakazu Kuwata. Tuttle 1962 512p illus (UNESCO Collection of representative works: Japanese ser) $6.50

Analyzed in Short Story Index
"Selection of short stories by 25 twentieth-century writers, one story from each writer.

The stories were selected as representative of various types of fiction writing developed in modern times." Booklist
Contents: Under reconstruction by Mori Ōgai; Order of the White Paulownia, by Tokuda Shūsei; Hydrangea, by Nagai Kafū; Seibei's gourds, by Shiga Naoya; Tatto, by Tanizaki Junichirō; On the conduct of Lord Tadanao, by Kikuchi Kan; The Camellia, by Satomi Ton; Brother and sister, by Murō Saisei; The house of a Spanish dog, by Satō Haruo; "Autumn mountain", by Akutagawa Ryūnosuké; The handstand, by Ogawa Mimei; Letter found in a cement-barrel, by Hayama Yoshiki; The charcoal bus, by Ibusé Masuji; Machine, by Yokomitsu Riichi; The moon on the water, by Kawabata Yasunari; Nightingale, by Itō Einosuké; Morning mist, by Nagai Tatsuo; The hateful age, by Niwa Fumio; Downtown, by Hayyashi Fumiko; A man's life, by Hirabayashi Taiko; The idiot, by Sakaguchi Ango; Shotgun, by Inoué Yasushi; Tiger-poet, by Nakajima Ton; The courtesy call, by Dazai Osamu; The priest and his love, by Mishima Yukio
"The book is supplied by its editor with a very helpful and interesting introduction and is enlivened by 25 woodcuts by the Japanese expressionist illustrator Masakazu Kuwata. This anthology is a major bridge to present-day Japan and its literature. The quality of all the translations makes it eminently readable." Library J

Morris, Wright

Ceremony in Lone Tree. Atheneum Pubs. 1960 304p $4

Another novel about the Scanlon family of: Field of vision, entered below
"Old Tom Scanlon's kinfolk and well-wishers decide to assemble in the Nebraska ghost-town where Scanlon is now the only inhabitant, and celebrate his ninetieth birthday. All else in this book is a background and preparation for this, and the coming together of the clan brings about the final revelation of past and present inextricably wedded in individual and collective lives." N Y Her Trib Books

The field of vision. Harcourt 1956 251p o.p. 1970

"The lives of seven oddly-assorted people attending a bullfight in Mexico are dissected in this new novel. . . . Mr. Morris makes full use of symbolism and the stream-of-consciousness technique as he tells the stories of his characters who include a Bohemian-playwright, a psychiatrist, a middle-class family from Nebraska and a young man who firmly believes himself to be a woman." Pub W
"The search for time past leads to a well-trodden literary path. But Mr. Morris travels it with high purpose and uncompromising standards. These, along with an imaginative grasp of his theme and technical skill, combine to produce a distinguished novel whose power and resonance commend it to all serious readers." Commonweal

also in Morris, W. Wright Morris: a reader p365-584

In orbit. New Am. Lib. 1967 153p o.p. 1970

"In the space of one day, Jubal E. Gainer, high school dropout and draft dodger, manages to rack up an impressive array of crimes, moral and felonious. He steals a friend's motorcycle, rapes a simple-minded spinster, mugs a pixyish professor, and stabs an obese visionary who runs a surplus store. He then waits out an Indiana twister and goes on his way, leaving as much wreckage in his path as the twister itself." Library J
"There is . . . a muscular quality to Mr. Morris's writing that makes it a suitable instrument for conveying harsher things; and there is his sense of the comic, which springs up constantly." N Y Times Bk R

Love among the cannibals. Harcourt 1957 253p o.p. 1970

"The story of a middle-aged member of a Hollywood song writing team, and his searing love affair with a wildly passionate, yet curiously detached young woman whose background never becomes quite clear. Included in the cast is the hero's partner, complete with a nubile seductress. The ill-assorted quartet warms beds from Malibu to Acapulco, on whose fabled strand the story peters out." Library J

Morris, Wright—*Continued*

"A swift-paced, readable story, written with zest and humor. . . . Some readers may be puzzled by the author's philosophy of love but they will probably be willing to read about it anyway." Pub W

What a way to go. Atheneum Pubs. 1962 310p o.p. 1970

This comic novel follows "the Odyssey of lanky, pipe-smoking, middle-aged Professor Arnold Soby, on a sabbatical voyage to Italy and Greece, and his shipboard companions, Miss Winifred Throop, retired headmistress of the Winnetka Country Day School, Miss Mathilde Kollwitz, teacher of French and German, and Miss Throop's niece, Cynthia, the eternal teenager—studiously vulgar, sensual, scatterbrained, yet with an inner wisdom. It relates Soby's unconscious pursuit of youth, in the person of Cynthia." Library J

"A piece of caustic writing that ought to give pause to the travel agents. Morris may intend this novel partly as a takeoff on 'Lolita,' but its strongest feature, aside from some ribald humor, is the long and devastating description of a tourist cruise." Pub W

The works of love
In Morris, W. Wright Morris: a reader p53-192

Wright Morris: a reader; introduction by Granville Hicks. Harper 1970 648p $12.95

In addition to two complete novels, The field of vision (entered separately) and The works of love, the book includes "nine excerpts from the other novels, two short stories, 'The Safe Place' and 'The Ram in the Thicket,' and two excerpts from Morris' essay on literary criticism 'The Territory Ahead.'" Library J

Morrison, Lucile

y The lost queen of Egypt; decorations by Franz Geritz. Lippincott 1937 367p illus $4.75

"A vivid portrayal of the life of Princess Ankhsenomon, Egyptian princess, from her earliest childhood until the death of her husband, Tutankhamon. Old Egypt and its customs come to life in this story of love, politics and intrigue, accurately presented and wholly absorbing. For older high school students and adults." Wis Lib Bul

Morrison, Margaret Mackie. See Cost, March

Morrison, Peggy. See Cost, March

Morrison, Theodore

The stones of the house. Viking 1953 375p o.p. 1970

"Character study of Andrew Aiken, acting president of a small college called Rowley. The novel covers one year in Andrew's life, describing his difficulties with staff, trustees or would-be trustees, and academic freedom, among many other things. At the end of the year his appointment as president comes as a surprise to him." Book Rev Digest

"Although the book is full of details of academic life, closely observed and justly recorded, in an important sense it is not an academic novel at all. It is a study of an experienced, conscientious, introspective man of 50 at a turning point in his career, which happens to be in the college world." N Y Times Bk R

Morrow, Honoré Willsie

Forever free. Morrow [1958 c1927] 405p o.p. 1970

A reissue of the title first published 1927

"The chief figure and hero is Lincoln himself—Lincoln torn between patriotic duty and human tenderness—Lincoln going through the spiritual struggle culminating in the Emancipation proclamation, the struggle to master himself, to compel true cooperation in his Cabinet and effective warfare by his generals—all against the background of domestic life and social intrigue, with Mary Lincoln and the beautiful Miss Ford, Confederate spy, taking active parts." Publisher's note

Followed by: With malice toward none, entered below

The last full measue. Morrow [1958 c1930] 337p o.p. 1970

Sequel to: With malice toward none

A reissue of the title first published 1930

"The final novel of Abraham Lincoln, covering the last dramatic period of his life and telling the extraordinary story of the whole Booth conspiracy." Publisher's note

"It is a better novel than either of the others, having this advantage over them, that the historical material with which it has to do is more dramatic and of a more personal nature." N Y Her Trib Books

With malice toward none. Morrow [1958 c1928] 342p o.p. 1970

Sequel to: Forever free

A reissue of the title first published 1928

"A novel of the last two years of the Civil War preceding the fall of Richmond—a period vibrant with the grim drama of desperate warfare and the bitter political struggle over reconstruction plans between Lincoln and the man he loved—Senator Charles Sumner." Publisher's note

Followed by: The last full measure

Mortimer, Penelope

The pumpkin eater. McGraw 1962 222p o.p. 1970

A "novel about an Englishwoman who, in four marriages, has had an enormous brood of children. Her fourth marriage, to a man she deeply loves, is going wrong because of her husband's unfaithfulness, and she is reluctantly telling her troubles to an analyst." Pub W

"A subtle, fascinating, unhackneyed novel. . . . Mrs. Mortimer is toughminded, in touch with human realities and frailties, unsentimental and amused. Her prose is deft and precise. A fine book, and one to be greatly enjoyed." N Y Times Bk R

Moskowitz, Sam

(ed.) Masterpieces of science fiction. World Pub. [1967 c1966] 552p $6.50

Analyzed in Short Story Index

"A treasury of science-fiction writing from 1650 to 1935." McClurg. Book News

Contents: Voyage to the moon, by C. de Bergerac; The mortal immortal, by M. W. Shelley; Hans Phaall—a tale, by E. A. Poe; The Wondersmith, by F. J. O'Brien; Eternal Adam, by J. Verne; The brick moon, by E. E. Hale; Lost in a comet's tail, by L. P. Senarens; The country of the blind, by H. G. Wells; The place of pain, by M. P. Shiel; The Los Amigos fiasco, by A. C. Doyle; The resurrection of Jimber-Jaw, by E. R. Burroughs; The people of the pit, by A. Merritt; System, by J. Capek; Extra sensory perception, by H. Gernsback; The colour out of space, by H. P. Lovecraft; Humanity on Venus, by O. Stapledon; Jungle journey, by P. Wylie; The Lotus Eaters, by S. G. Winbaum

(ed.) Modern masterpieces of science fiction. World Pub. 1965 518p $6.50

Analyzed in Short Story Index

Contents: The vortex blaster, by E. E. Smith; Night, by J. W. Campbell; A logic named Joe, by M. Leinster; Requiem, by E. Hamilton; With folded hands, by J. Williamson; Adaptation, by J. Wyndham; The witness, by E. F. Russell; The command, by L. S. de Camp; Kindness, by L. del Rey; ". . . we also walk dogs", by R. A. Heinlein; The enchanted village, by A. E. van Vogt; Liar, by I. Asimov; Microcosmic god, by T. Sturgeon; Huddling place, by C. D. Simak; Coming attraction, by F. Leiber; Doorway into time, by C. L. Moore; We guard the Black Planet, by H. Kuttner; The strange flight of Richard Clayton, by R. Bloch; Wake for the living, by R. Bradbury; Before Eden, by A. C. Clarke; Mother, by P. J. Farmer

Mosley, Nicholas

Impossible object. Coward-McCann [1969 c1968] 219p boards $4.95

First published 1968 in England

This novel "is made up of eight episodes. The nameless characters are the same in each segment: the locale varies from England to

Moseley, Nicholas—*Continued*

Italy to North Africa. The man and the woman are lovers, each married to another, each with children. The stories, separate but united by character, theme, and an omniscient writer-narrator, depict eight incidents in the love affair. Each probes a new dimension of the prismatic, elusive, illicit relationship, while the narrator's recitative relates the intimate scene to our larger and public world." Pub W

"Interpolated among the eight stories, and standing as prologue and epilogue to the larger sequence, are nine little fables or parables on related themes. These are brilliant prose constructions.... The scenes they present are grotesque and bizarre, but always rooted in life and returning to life." Sat R

Motley, Willard

Knock on any door. Appleton 1947 503p o.p. 1970

"Realistic story of a Chicago boy whose early tendencies towards decency were slowly beaten down by his contacts with life along Chicago's streets—among the poolrooms and honky-tonks. Nick Romano had good friends who tried to help him, but fate and sometimes the law were against him. He turned killer and died in the electric chair." Book Rev Digest

"Here is a book to jolt and shock you, to impress you with its mightiness and power, a book that will reach out for your heart and your mind and your emotions and grip them tightly until you have read every last one of its 240,000 smashing words." Chicago Sun Book Week

Followed by: Let no man write my epitaph

Let no man write my epitaph. Random House 1958 467p $5.95

Sequel to: Knock on any door

This novel, set in the Chicago slums "is the story of the brutal education of young Nick Romano, illegitimate son of a gangster executed for murder and Nellie Watkins, a dope addict. Young Nick hasn't much of a chance. There is little hope for the boy until a well-intentioned policeman, a free-lance writer and a group of neighbors urge him to give up narcotics. How long Nick can stay away from them will be anyone's guess." Library J

"A stark, sordid tale of society's dregs, told with an unsentimental compassion that is extremely moving." Booklist

Moyes, Patricia

Dead men don't ski
In Moyes, P. Murder by 3's p3-288

Down among the dead men
In Moyes, P. Murder by 3's p289-540

Falling star
In Moyes, P. Murder by 3's p542-789

Murder by 3's.... With an introduction by Anthony Boucher. Holt [1965] 789p o.p. 1970

Three suspense novels "including Dead men don't ski [1960]; Down among the dead men [1961]; and Falling star [1964]." Title page

In the first story, Scotland Yard Inspector Henry Tibbett on vacation at a ski resort tries to prove it is a drug smugglers station. In the second story, the Inspector's sailing holiday is upset by an "accidental" drowning. In the last story, Inspector Tibbett tackles one of his toughest cases when an aging British film star falls under the wheels of a train

Moynahan, Julian

Pairing off. Morrow 1969 251p boards $5.95

"Meet Myles McCormick, the smash with women. The stacks of the Boston Free Library, where Miles spends his days cataloguing books of odd alphabets, are fairly littered with female bodies—all of them nubile. Yes, Myles has a way with the ladies but he does have trouble relating to them on any but the most superficial level. It's symptomatic of his whole approach to life, which is to laugh a lot." Am News of Bks

"The adventures of a rare book librarian are a new subject for contemporary fiction, although in fact Myles McCormick's adventures in outline bear a striking resemblance to those of other literary heroes. ... Moynahan lacks full literary control. Sometimes he thinks he is James Joyce, sometimes Kingsley Amis. He takes potshots at business efficiency, at psychiatry, at romanticism; he resolves his novel with a happy ending so wildly inappropriate that it seems to have strayed in." Choice

Munchausen

The adventures of Baron Munchausen, by R. E. Raspe and others; profusely illus. by Ronald Searle; with an introduction by S. J. Perelman. Pantheon Bks. 1969 138p illus $7.95

First published in England 1785

"A mock-serious recital of absurdly impossible feats and adventures—now a byword for extravagant braggadocio—originally intended as a satire on the 'Memoirs' of Baron de Trenck. The authorship is attributed to Raspe, a German emigrant to London." Baker's Best

"Searle competes well with such celebrated previous illustrators as Gustave Doré and Rowlandson." Time

Munro, Hector Hugh. See Saki

Muntz, Hope

The golden warrior; the story of Harold and William. With a foreword by G. M. Trevelyan. Scribner 1949 354p $5.95

"An historical novel depicting the events culminating in the defeat of Harold by William the Conqueror. A scholarly work, keeping close to the historical record. Conflicting claims and ambitions of William and Harold, and their devious subtleties to gain the Crown are the main theme. Playing their part are the internecine strifes and jealousies of the English nobility, a picture of Normandy, and the power of the Church." Library J

Murasaki Shikibu. See Murasaki, Lady

Murasaki, Lady

The tale of Genji; a novel in six parts; tr. from the Japanese by Arthur Waley. Modern Lib. 1960 1135p $4.95

"Tells of the gallantries and love adventures of Prince Genji, son of an emperor. It is a Japanese classic written by a lady-in-waiting to the Japanese empress and probably appeared in the early part of the 11th century." Pittsburgh

"The success of this work as a modern novel is due very greatly to the creative artistry of the translator. The English is a poet's, flexible, sensitive, and full of color." Ind

Murdoch, Iris

The bell; a novel. Viking 1958 342p o.p. 1970

"An interesting, wicked, and witty plot around a heterogeneous group of characters who populate a model Utopian community attached to a convent. Led by a young intellectual whose fondness for other men eventually results in destroying the community, the group entertains strange happenings—a legend confirmed, a marriage destroyed, a new bell for the convent, and a bishop embarrassed." The Bookseller

"The development hinges too much, perhaps, on such devices as the overheard conversation, the dropped letter, the too-chancy meeting and the marvelous rescue. ... But what is more important is that Miss Murdoch is writing a highly charged story and is not afraid to use the extreme means she needs. The melodramatic qualities in her novel are an aspect of her vitality. ... Miss Murdoch, in short, has written a rare kind of book that is both absorbing story and novel of ideas." Commonweal

Bruno's dream. Viking 1969 311p boards $5.75

In this novel, the author examines "the nature of love, of forgiveness, and of the impact

Murdoch, Iris—*Continued*

of impending death. . . . The setting is London, and old house close by the Thames which . . . becomes a scene of flood disaster. Bruno, the dying old man, who possesses a fortune in rare stamps, [Danby] his son-in-law and [Miles,] his estranged son, and the women in their lives, living and dead, move through a ritual pavane in which love takes many forms and relationships shift and reverse themselves." Pub W

The author "has made her point about the ebb and flow of human folly. Her novel sometimes seems to veer dangerously close to the edge of slapstick and silliness, but on the whole it is well-designed, delightful entertainment." Book of the Month Club News

A fairly honourable defeat. Viking 1970 436p boards $6.95

SBN 670-30533-2

This novel is concerned with a "happily married couple, a dropout son, a sister who has 'a compulsive genius for muddles,' her estranged husband, and a homosexual younger brother living . . . with an older man. The sister's former lover . . . sets out to show how . . . [both] loving couples can be detached from their loyalties. In his role as puppet master, he manipulates their vanities to ends which he had not quite intended." Publisher's note

"As is usual with a Murdoch novel, the action in summary seems preposterous. But given her inventiveness, her Gothic imagination, her gift for melodrama and suspense, she creates a world that becomes an effective vehicle for her moral vision. The action, much of which is erotic, takes place during a spell of excessively hot London weather. Some of the scenes are wildly contrived and comic. There are long stretches of dialogue . . . some of which are run through with the philosophic subtlety readers have come to expect of Murdoch." Choice

The flight from the enchanter. Viking 1956 316p o.p. 1970

Uninhibited portrayal of some people in present-day London whose lives become entangled. The characters include a teenage girl who runs away from boarding school; a government bureaucrat of cautiously amatory impulses; a charming, unworldly woman, and a wealthy cosmopolite with a secret source of power over people's lives. (Publisher)

"It is never heavily metaphysical or slavishly Existentialist. It can be read as a comic novel about a 'wayward segment of humanity,' but it can, and I think should, be read also as a philosophical novel with almost as many levels of meaning as Joyce's 'Ulysses.' " Sat R

The Italian girl; a novel. Viking 1964 213p $4.50

"An engraver by profession, Edmund Narraway considered himself a very superior person—almost a saint. But life was lying in wait for Edmund and eventually the would-be saint collapsed. In his brother Otto he no longer saw his antithesis but himself and, in the place of his mother's hated memory, he discerned two figures—one of them the Italian girl." Huntting

"In her latest novel, Miss Murdoch gives us another of her incredible sexual, psychological and philosophical menageries, skillfully presented, and viewed with a classical tolerance and freedom which she dares us to equal." Library J

The nice and the good. Viking 1968 378p boards $5.75

"Presumably Joseph Radeechy, brilliant, interested in black magic, had shot himself in the mouth, but he was left-handed and the gun was near his right hand. The death involved everyone in the British Foreign Office and most of their families." Bk Buyer's Guide

What the author is really discussing in this book "is love in various forms: puppy love, married love, the love of a mistress for a man who is tired of her—even homosexual love. Her subtly drawn and intellectually interesting characters act out their drama not only against such conventional backgrounds as an English

country house and various London drawing rooms, but in secret vaults below Whitehall and a death-trap cave along the Dorset coast, with Black Masses and an occasional flying saucer involved." Book of the Month Club News

The red and the green. Viking 1965 311p o.p. 1970

The novel "treats in time the week or so preceding the Easter Rising in Ireland in 1916, and concerns the tensions within a family, part English, part Irish, caught up in the events culminating in the dramatic but ineffectual rebellion; a love affair taken for granted which does not follow its predicted path; an aging, beautiful, selfish and ruthless woman whose unbridled sexual appetites tangle the skein of family relationships; and the struggle for communication, understanding, and love between members of the family." Library J

The sandcastle; a novel. Viking 1957 342p o.p. 1970

"A tragicomic story of a middle-aged [married] teacher at a British boys' school who falls in love with a charming but rather fey young woman." Pub W

"The expected triangular conflict which ensues is resolved with finesse and a sense of the inevitable. . . . Humorous episodes of school life lighten the tension in a story primarily for women readers." Booklist

A severed head; a novel. Viking 1961 248p o.p. 1970

"A comic novel set in a London society—an artificial world ruled over by a modern magician, the half-American psychoanalyst, Palmer Anderson. The narrator, married to an older woman and having an affair with a younger one, falls under the spell of Honor Klein, the analyst's half-sister, and knows genuine passion for the first time." Huntting

"Author Murdoch's intelligence, both as critic and novelist, is above question. But this sophisticated shocker seems to have little point beyond the homely moral that those who think life would be simpler without moral rules are very simple indeed." Time

The unicorn; a novel. Viking 1963 311p o.p. 1970

This fantasy-novel explores "variations of action, inactivity, love, and guilt. Marian Taylor undertakes a mysterious assignment as governess at a weird, remote seacoast castle, the odd inmates of which are presided over by a pale 'belle dame sans merci.' After this romantic Victorian opening, the author displays her usual brilliant legerdemain in a succession of revelations about the inhabitants of Castle Gaze and involves them in her habitual series of permutations and combinations of search for possession of each other. While explicators will make much of the novel's profuse symbolism, the fascination of the bizarre story about the efforts of Marian and ineffectual Effingham Cooper to rescue the lady of the castle from the strange domination of Gerald Scottow may well attract readers from outside Miss Murdoch's usual coterie." Library J

"The style of this odd story is sensitive and graceful, with particular beauty in the descriptions of houses and landscapes. The characters are curious but credible." Book of the Month Club News

An unofficial rose; a novel. Viking 1962 344p boards $4.95

An "existential novel about love, this time examining the multileveled relationships between the members of two English country families. Hugh Peronett, his wife recently dead, is pursuing Emma, his old mistress. Hugh's son Randall, a rose grower, is about to leave his wife Ann and go away with 'his' mistress, curiously a companion of Emma's. Ann is coveted by Felix Meecham, whose sister Mildred wants Hugh." Library J

"Miss Murdoch never loses one great gift, her power to make us feel exactly what it is like to be each of her characters." Guardian

Murphy, Robert

y A certain island; drawings by John Pimlott. Evans, M.&Co. 1967 239p illus boards $4.95

A story about Geordie, a sixteen-year-old boy who was more interested in wildlife than his father's profession of law. He "joined an expedition to Laysan Island, an atoll in the Pacific, where five species of oceanic birds unique to that island were threatened with extinction. . . . Geordie learned that life is full of cruelty as well as beauty, and that no man can stand aside from involvement with both these forces." Publisher's note

"Based on an actual incident, the novel is . . . notable chiefly for its accurate and vivid descriptions of nature and wildlife." Booklist

y The mountain lion; illus. by Theodore A. Xaras. Dutton 1969 128p illus $3.95

This nature novel is about Seeta who is a "young and inexperienced cat, unprotected because her mother and brother are dead. She travels and lives in northern Arizona, a land of canyons, mountains, mesas and desert. Murphy describes Seeta's haunts and habits and what happens, when, driven by her mating instinct, she moves out of her usual territory and exposes herself to new dangers." Pub W

"Sympathetic but unsentimental in tone. . . . For the conservation-minded wildlife enthusiast." Booklist

y The peregrine falcon; illus. by Teco Slagboom. Houghton 1964 [c1963] 157p illus $4.95

The story of the first year in the life of a falcon and of a perilous journey, "the first migration of Varda, the peregrine, from her birthplace in northern Canada to the Florida Keys. . . . [There are] background facts about hawks and the training of the falcon." Library J

"There is true suspense in the story, a great deal to fascinate bird-lovers about the falcon, her prey, and her equals among birds, and some sharp comments on the ways in which man may mistreat or sometimes aid the birds in their passage. . . . The illustrations, by Teco Slagboom, are very special. They are majestic, soaring pictures of the hawks and other birds and of the wild lands they love." Pub W

y The Pond; illus. by Teco Slagboom. Dutton 1964 254p illus $5.50

Winner of the Dutton Animal book award, 1964

"Fourteen-year-old Joey and his friend Bud drove to the Pond in a Model-T in 1917 to fish and hunt. But the great cypresses, the Pond, old Mr. Ben the caretaker, and even Charley, Sam White's dog, woke in Joey a protective understanding for all wild life." Bk Buyer's Guide

"There is little or no plot to 'The Pond': just the day-by-day adventures of a boy in the woods who is learning to understand dogs, coon hunting, camping techniques—and human beings. Simple—deceptively simple—and appealing." Book of the Month Club News

Murray, A. A.

The blanket; a novel. Vanguard [1958] 192p $4.95

In this novel which gives a view of the customs of the Basuto tribe, "violence, murder, and the ironic course of justice force an African youth, the son of a tribal chieftain, to assume, almost overnight, the responsibilities of a leader of men." Pub W

"The story is tragic and beautiful and extraordinarily dramatic. It is a novel of suspense, as hard to put down as any mystery story, in spite of its apparent simplicity and dignity." Library J

Musil, Robert

The man without qualities; tr. from the German by Eithne Wilkins and Ernest Kaiser. Coward-McCann 1953-1954 2v o.p. 1970

A projected four volume work left unfinished at the time of the author's death in 1942

The events in volume one occur in Vienna in 1913. "It chronicles the philosophizing, emotions, and desultory adventures of Ulrich (probably the author) with friends, a mistress, and the people planning a Franz-Joseph Jubilee." Retail Bookseller

"The second volume of the English edition takes us up to the critical turning-point of Musil's great novel, his hero's departure from the capital after being informed of his father's death." Times (London) Lit Sup

Mydans, Shelley Smith

The open city. Doubleday 1945 245p o.p. 1970

This novel tells what happened to a group of American civilians who were interned when the Japanese invaded the Philippines. Based on the author's personal experiences

"'The Open City' leaves one with a sense of pride in the steadfastness and courage of the men and women who lived through their three-year ordeal. They weakened, but never despaired." N Y Her Trib Books

Thomas; a novel of the life, passions, and miracles of Becket. Doubleday 1965 439p $5.95

A re-creation of the life of Thomas à Becket. Archbishop of Canterbury, diplomat, politician, and soldier. This book follows the 12th century figure from youth through his murder by knights of King Henry II. (Publisher)

"By paralleling Becket's steady rise to power with the story of a family of Saxon coiners, Mrs. Mydans not only introduces life outside the Norman court of Henry II but also shows how Christianity and paganism were combined into a dramatic, workable religion. Politics, be it church or state, forms the background for fully three-quarters of Thomas. . . . Characterizations are sound—both historically and artistically—and the backgrounds are brilliant. It is a good story, well told, with enough plot to fill a trilogy." Book of the Month Club News

Myrer, Anton

Once an eagle. Holt 1968 817p $7.95

"This novel concerns the conflict between Sam Damon, an American who serves in several military campaigns and wars, rises from private to general, but never forgets that soldiers are human, and Courtney Massengale, a West Point graduate who allies himself with the sources of political power and considers war a game." Book Rev Digest

This is "as good a story as one will find of the American Army and fighting men and that mystical thing that seems to happen to men who have fought together, and of the dreadful responsibility of the man in command. It is an even more vivid depiction of the horrors of war. . . . The mind boggles at the amount of well-digested research that must have gone into this work to come out in such easy, compelling narrative." Harper

Mystery Writers of America

Masters of mayhem; the 1965 Mystery Writers of America anthology; ed. by Edward D. Radin. Morrow 1965 287p o.p. 1970

Analyzed in Short Story Index

"Examples of the many forms of the mystery: the tale of suspense, the thriller, the chase, mood, fantasy and crime stories, the police procedure and many others." Publisher's note

Contents: A woman has been murdered, by M. Manners; Merry-go-round, by R. L. Fish; Keep away from my wife, by J. Barry; He was frightened, by M. A. deFord; The solid gold brick, by R. M. Gordon; Direct hit, by J. Buchanan; Family affair, by R. Hardwick; A great day coming, by M. Avallone; Time and tide, by L. Treat; Man with a hobby, by R. Bloch; Ripe for plucking, by J. M. Ullman; An exercise in insurance, by J. Holding; I, said the sparrow, by C. Cluff; The truck that went nowhere, by C. Norman; The fatal diary, by W. T. Brannon; The gentle touch, by A. S. Reach; Joke on a nice old lady, by H. Slesar; The secret secret secret, by De Forbes; A little honest stud, by A. Boucher; She fell among thieves, by R. E. Alter; When are people going to learn, by J. F. Suter; Touch and blow, by C. H. Rathjen; Cops dont have wings, by M. Hershman; Wild goose chase, by R. Macdonald

Mystery Writers of America—*Continued*

Merchants of menace; an anthology of mystery stories, by the Mystery Writers of America; ed. by Hillary Waugh. Doubleday 1969 298p $5.95

"A balanced collection, ranging from police procedure to a Westlake 'cutesy,' from the almost-gothic to a Goulart take-off and a Queen puzzle. A must for every whodunit fan and a good Christmas item for all others." Pub W

Contents: H as in homicide, by L. Treat; Domestic intrigue, by D. E. Westlake; The front room, by M. Butterworth; The real bad friend, by R. Bloch; Wide O-, by E. A. Gardner; Death on Christmas Eve, by S. Ellin; Gone girl, by R. MacDonald; The President's half disme, by E. Queen; Amateur standing, by S. Blanc; The peppermint-striped goodbye, by R. Goulart; Marmalade wine, by J. Aiken; Counter intelligence, by R. L. Fish; The man who played too well, by D. V. Elsmer; Never hit a lady, by F. S. Tobey; Farewell to the Faulkners, by M. A. deFord; The dead past, by A. Nussbaum; The cries of love, by P. Highsmith; Something evil in the house, by C. Fremlin; The tilt of death, by R. Amateau; The moon of Montezuma, by C. Woolrich

Murder in mind; an anthology of mystery stories by the Mystery Writers of America; ed. by Lawrence Treat. Dutton 1967 220p $3.95

Analyzed in Short Story Index
Contents: The sailing club, by D. Ely; Thicker than water, by H. Slesar; The chase, by J. A. Kirch; H. as in heist, by L. Treat; The dinner party, by J. M. Ullman; Quetzalcoatl, by De Forbes; Assignment: marriage, by C. M. Macleod; The second coming, by J. Gores; The magic tree, by J. McKimmey; Who's afraid of Katherine Mansfield? by W. Snow; What's the answer, lady, by J. Reach; The way home, by R. M. Gordon; A fair share for Sadie, by F. S. Tobey; Mary—Mary—, by B. Kendrick; Unseen alibi, by B. Graeme; The breakdown, by A. Loring; The little spy, by E. Queen

Sleuths and consequences; an anthology of mystery stories by the Mystery Writers of America; ed. by Thomas B. Dewey. Simon & Schuster 1966 311p $4.95

Analyzed in Short Story Index
Contents: The Hochmann miniatures, by R. L. Fish; Ask a stupid question, by L. Treat; The specialist, by J. Reach; Squeeze play, by A. K. Lang; Twelve and a half cents, by C. Norman; The five-minute millionaire, by J. Cross; Pretty Polly Perkins, by G. Cluff; The scent of terror, by R. Bloch; A choice of witnesses, by H. Slesar; End game, by P. Podolsky; Game of skill, by E. D. Hoch; The journeymen, by J. Buchanan; The impossible theft, by J. F. Suter; A tired Romeo, by J. Johnson; Guessing game, by R. M. Healey; The $2,000,000 defense, by H. W. Masur; The perfectionist, by D. M. Douglass; By the scruff of the soul, by D. S. Davis; "Puddin' and Pie", by De Forbes; The crime of Ezechiele Coen, by S. Ellin

With malice toward all; an anthology of mystery stories by the Mystery Writers of America; ed. and with a foreword by Robert L. Fish. Putnam 1968 256p boards $4.95

"Red mask mystery"
Analyzed in Short Story Index
Contents: The merciful, by C. L. Sweeney; Long shot, by H. Slesar; The letter of the law, by D. Knowlton; Every litter bit hurts, by M. Avallone; Strictly diplomatic, by J. D. Carr; The impersonation murder case, by M. A. deFord; Always a motive, by D. Ross; The orderly world of Mr Appleby, by S. Ellin; Number one, by J. Holt; The release, by C. Woolrich; The house at the end of the lane, by B. Norton; Command performance, by A. Boucher; End of the day, by J. Speed; The reference room, by J. D. MacDonald; Sauce for the gander, by M. Hershman; Mr Wickwire's widow, by M. Eberhart; Death by the numbers, by E. Lacy; The accident, by J. Symons; String of pearls, by R. Bloch; E=murder, by E. Queen; Darl I luv U, by J. Gores; The inquisitive butcher of Nice, by J. Holding; The ring with the velvet ropes, by E. D. Hoch; Angelica is still alive, by W. Snow

N

Nabokov, Vladimir

Ada; or, Ardor: a family chronicle. McGraw 1969 589p $8.95

"The memoir of Dr. Ivan (Van) Veen, psychologist, professor of philosophy and student of time, who chronicles his life-long love for [his half-sister] Ada Veen. . . . [Part One] details Van's youth, travels and incestuous romance with Ada at Arcadian Ardis Hall, the opulent country-estate of his uncle. Part Two ends with Van forsaking Ada, following his father's implorations. In Part Three, after many amorous vicissitudes, Ada gets married and Van loses her for 17 years, finally regaining her in 1922 in Part Four, while he is working on his book, 'The Texture of Time. Part Five . . . finds them together, with a small entourage, celebrating Van's 97th birthday and the virtual completion of the memoir at hand, which is to be published posthumously.'' N Y Times Bk R

" 'Ada' can be reveled in for its archly magnificent prose. . . [Nabokov] has found an entirely new way of putting a novel together and as original a way of dealing with duration in fiction as Proust did. On the other hand, there has never been a more cerebrally constructed, less emotionally involving book that this geometric study of lifelong illicit passion. But that irony was also intended." Newsweek

The defense; a novel; tr. by Michael Scammell in collaboration with the author. Putnam 1964 256p o.p. 1970

First published in book form 1930 in Germany
"The game's the thing, the only thing in the life of Luzhin, an expatriate Russian Chess Master. The story traces his life from his introverted childhood to the moment in middle age when he stands at the point of crisis. Engaged in the major match of his career, he suffers a breakdown, and, in the care of his loving but uncomprehending wife, tries to live his life devoid of chess. Inevitably, he is bound to fail, and suicide ends the stalemate." Library J

"It is an oddly fascinating work, for neither Luzhin nor his wife are particulary attractive if even credible people. Yet one reads along wondering why one continues to read. It must be Nabokov's charm and his stylistic approach to this novel." Best Sellers

Despair; a novel. Putnam 1966 222p $5.95
Original Russian edition written 1932, published 1936 in Berlin

"An eerie tale about an incipient schizophrenic who concocts a criminal plot based on the existence of a man greatly resembling him. The scenes and people materialize foggily in the plotter's memory: his double, whom he encounters on a trip away from his home in Berlin; his vacuous but pretty wife (does he love her or despise her?); his failing business." Pub W

"The whole value of the novel lies in the method of revelation of the anti-hero's character. . . . We see him clearly, but we look on him much as we would look at a laboratory specimen. The method of revelation, however, is something else again; it is clever, literate. Mr. Nabokov has once more shown that he is a skillful narrator." Best Sellers

The gift; a novel; tr. from the Russian by Michael Scammell with the collaboration of the author. Putnam 1963 378p $6.95

First English translation of the orginal Russian edition written in Berlin, 1935-1937
A "book with a Slavic flavor, it concerns the life of young Fyodor Godunov-Cherdyntzev, poet and writer, in the 'émigré' colony of Berlin following World War I. Interwoven with Fyodor's hand-to-mouth existence among the chattering intellectuals who had fled the Bolshevik revolution to Germany, his love affair with Zena, and his literary endeavors are a Proustian remembrance of childhood and a memorable portrait of his father, explorer and lepidopterist, who vanished into the Siberian wastes during the revolution." Library J

"This English version, which was supervised by Nabokov, has those qualities of freshness combined with highly original and detailed observation that make the best Russian books in English seem not so much translations as a special branch of English literature with a peculiarly strong flavor. For many readers this

Nabokov, Vladimir—*Continued*

novel will be put on their book shelves beside the stories of Tolstoy and Chekhov. . . . What one values in 'The Gift' are passages of great power sustained over many pages." N Y Times Bk R

Invitation to a beheading; tr. by Dmitri Nabokov in collaboration with the author. Putnam 1959 223p boards $5.95

Original Russian edition first published 1938 in Paris

"Cincinnatus has been sentenced to death by beheading. His crime, that of being the only one really alive in a world of sham, pretense and disintegration. Only he can cope with reality and for this he must die. His imprisonment a strange one, his time of death unknown, his executioner, a disguised prisoner. A meaningful and beautifully written [surrealistic] fantasy." Cincinnati

"The weird, dream-like quality of the book will not please the general public, but the volume has great merit as a subtle allegory of our times." Library J

King, queen, knave; a novel; tr. by Dmitri Nabokov in collaboration with the author. McGraw 1968 272p $5.95

Original Russian edition 1928

The author has set this novel "in Berlin in 1928, the Berlin of complacent suburbs, acquisitive wealthy businessmen, their pampered, materialistic women, Dreyer and his bored wife, Martha, return from a vacation. Unbeknown to all concerned, their compartmentmate on the return railway journey is Franz, a second cousin whom Dreyer has not met. The coincidence is, of course, discovered when Franz, the country bumpkin, arrives at the Dreyers' chic suburban home to call. Dreyer gets Franz a job, Martha enters into a casual affair with him that soon becomes a grand passion. The lovers plot to kill the unsuspecting, heavy-humored Dreyer but are defeated by their own greed." Pub W

"Here, as in [his] more sophisticated novels, an important theme is the nature of fiction itself. By putting his comic trio through a series of abstract stances . . . he never allows the reader to forget that fiction is essentially artifice. In [this novel] the artifice may be a little too obvious, but intelligence and wit keep it working smoothly to the end." Time

Laughter in the dark. Bobbs [1960 c1938] 292p o.p. 1970

Another version published in England has title: Camera obscura

"On the first page the author outlines his story thus: 'Once upon a time there lived in Berlin, Germany, a man called Albinus. He was rich, respectable, happy; one day he abandoned his wife for the sake of a youthful mistress; he loved; he was not loved; and his life ended in disaster.' The novel itself fills in the details of the story, emphasizing the psychological aspects." Book Rev Digest

Lolita. Putnam 1958 [c1955] 319p $6

First edition published in France 1955

"This story seems to be a travesty on the dignity of man and on his fellow men. The story centers on a handsome, pathological character who has a lust for certain girls from 9 to 12 years of age, and follows his journey with Lolita, his stepdaughter, until he is avenged for her departure. During the telling, there are grotesquely humorous scenes, satiric comments on the tourist scene of the American countryside, and a play on words to amuse the narrator. There is a literary quality that lures the serious reader, while those searching for pornography will be disappointed." Wis Lib Bul

Nabokov's dozen; a collection of thirteen stories. Doubleday 1958 214p o.p. 1970

Analyzed in Short Story Index

Contents: Spring in Fialta; A forgotten poet; First love; Signs and symbols; The assistant producer; The Aurelian; Cloud, castle, lake; Conversation piece, 1945; "That in Aleppo once. . ."; Time and Ebb; Scenes from the life of a double monster; Mademoiselle O; Lance

Nabokov's quartet. Phaedra Pubs. 1966 104p $3.95

Analyzed in Short Story Index

Four stories in which the author handles dream as reality and reality as dream

Contents: An affair of honor; Lik; The Vane sisters; The visit to the museum

"Three of the stories were written in the 1930's in Russian and have been excellently translated into English by the author's son, Dmitri. The fourth, 'The Vane Sisters,' was written in England in 1959. . . . A pleasant collection for all public and college library collections." Library J

Pale fire; a novel. Putnam 1962 315p $6.95

"The story is told in the form of a poem and a commentary on the poem and deals with the escapades of a deposed Balkan King in a New England college town. . . . The poem itself . . . a thousand lines long, divided into four cantos, . . . purports to be the composition of John Shade, a white-thatched and venerable poet in residence at a New England university. . . . The commentator—hence, the first person singular of the novel—is revealed in the beginning as Charles Kinbote, a queer 'émigré teaching at Shade's university. . . . He is, in fact, the deposed King of Zembla, identified only as 'a distant northern land.' . . . A secret agent, Gradus, is dispatched from Zembla to kill the King, and his progress across continents is followed step by step in Kinbote's commentary until he arrives. . . . By mistake, Gradus kills John Shade. Modern dictatorships spare the buffoon (Kinbote) but kill the poet (Shade)." Atlantic

"That the novel is intended as a kind of spoof of scholarly textual criticism and its apparatus, something of a satire on cloak and dagger tales, and a mild swipe at academic life seems apparent. That the poem is frequently lyric and touching, even reminiscent of Conrad Aiken in spots, is not surprising. The whole thing is perhaps caviar for the general, but it is delectable, too." Best Sellers

Pnin. Doubleday 1957 191p o.p. 1970

"Not a novel, not really a collection of short stories, but rather a series of sketches, all of them dealing with Timofey Pnin, professor of Russian in a small American university. Each one finds Pnin valiantly trying to cope with the daily crises of American society—Pnin on the wrong train, Pnin learning to drive, Pnin giving a party, Pnin and the washing machine. They are all gently amusing, affectionate portraits of a Russian expatriate of the old school caught up in the inexplicable complexities of daily life. Diverting, but limited in appeal." Library J

"It is a satiric book with many a knowing jab at some vulnerable part of our collegiate practices. And, as the campus is in no alien country, the points scored are at least partly at the expense of all of us. But fun and satire are just the beginning of the rewards of this novel. Generous, bewildered Pnin, that most kindly and impractical of men, wins our affection and respect." Chicago Sunday Tribune

The real life of Sebastian Knight. New Directions 1959 205p $5

A reissue of the novel first published in this country 1941

"The 'story' here is the record of the attempt of the narrator to discover the personality of his [half] brother, a novelist who has recently died, from his books and the traces his personality has left on the people whom he knew. Except for the eye-rolling prose of the new introduction by Conrad Brenner, this is highly recommended for all collections of adult fiction." Library J

Naipaul, V. S.

A house for Mr Biswas. McGraw 1961 531p o.p. 1970

"A satiric novel about meek little Mr. Biswas, coerced into marriage and taken into Hanuman House under the rule of the matriarch of his new family, Mrs. Tulsi. But with all his mildness Mr. Biswas was obstinate, and he wanted a house of his own. The characters are Hindus in the West Indies." Bk Buyer's Guide

Naipaul, V. S.—*Continued*

The author "is particularly sensitive to the subtle changes which enduring relationships undergo beneath their surface continuity, particularly within a family. His style is precise and assured. In short, he gives every indication of being an important addition to the international literary scene. This novel is funny, it is compassionate. It has more than 500 pages and not one of them is superfluous." N Y Her Trib Books

Narayan, R. K.

The guide; a novel. Viking 1958 220p o.p. 1970

"A province in southern India is the locale for the story of a rogue who accidentally becomes a holy man. Resting on his way back to his native town after release from prison Raju is mistaken by a simple peasant for a holy man. Cared for by a growing and respectful group of villagers he is reluctant to tell them the truth of his past." Booklist

"A delightful picture of human frailties, described with a sympathetic twinkle of the eye. The heart-warming quality of all of Narayan's stories is his belief in the basic goodness of man." Library J

A horse and two goats; stories; with decorations by R. K. Laxman. Viking 1970 148p $5.75

SBN 670-37885-2

These short stories written by an Indian novelist blend humor and characterizations to interpret native customs and traits. All five have previously been published in magazines. (Publisher)

Contents: A horse and two goats; Uncle; Annamalai; A breath of Lucifer; Seventh House

The man-eater of Malgudi. Viking 1961 250p o.p. 1970

The narrator, Nataraj, "is a printer in a small Indian town who bats out jobs on an ancient press but finds his real pleasure in running a kind of literary salon whose major figures are an unpublished poet and a jobless journalist. Slam-bang into his nerveless world crashes a huge, careless taxidermist [Vasu], a man who is physically powerful and morally indifferent. He moves in on the printer, pays no rent, entertains the town whores, and laughs his unpaid, gentle landlord into inconsequence. Just when the reader is beginning to ask why the mild printer has to take all this, Author Narayan . . . shows that the meek have their own kind of strength." Time

"Ironic, amusing, the portrayal of people and scene is presented, however, with the air of documentary realism." Booklist

The vendor of sweets. Viking 1967 184p boards $4.95

Also available in large type edition, $6.95

"Jagan is an elderly sweetshop keeper caught in a crisis of fatherhood and personal dignity. Jagan's troubles begin when his son Mali returns from the United States accompanied by an American-Korean girl and tries to persuade his father to finance the manufacture of a story-writing machine." Book Rev Digest

"At first glance, Jagan appears to be a simple village shopkeeper, but essentially he is a far more complex personage. He is a merchant but he is also a patriot. . . . However, at the same time he earnestly counts the daily take, plus a little portion he puts aside and does not report for tax purposes. . . . Narayan also gives valuable insight into the Indian culture and its timeless rituals that, for a Westerner, cloak the East in fascinating mystery." Best Sellers

Waiting for the Mahatma. Mich. State Univ. Press 1955 241p illus $3.50

"Tale of a wealthy young Indian who falls in love with a beautiful follower of Mahatma Ghandi. He becomes a follower himself, out of love for the girl, but has to wait months for the Mahatma's blessing on the wedding." Book Rev Digest

Nathan, Robert

The adventure of Tapiola. Knopf 1950 2v in 1 illus $4.50

A combined volume of: Journey of Tapiola and Tapiola's brave regiment, first published 1938 and 1941 respectively

"Tales of the adventuring Yorkshire terrier and his friends." Am News of Bks

The color of evening. Knopf 1960 219p boards $4.50

One star-blown night Halys, a wisp of a girl, unexpectedly entered the life of the painter, Max Loeb. Drawn by the fragile beauty of her face and touched by her loneliness Max brought Halys to his studio in Santa Monica. This story tells of the effects of this strange girl upon the lives of Max's landlady, a widow; Jon, his talented young pupil; and, on Max, himself. (Publisher)

"Mr. Nathan treats, with compassionate understanding, the interlocking problems of age and youth, and demonstrates the need for affection and sympathy in both periods of life." Springf'd Republican

The devil with love. Knopf 1963 200p boards $4.50

"Alfred Sneeden, a repairer of electrical devices in the town of Parish, develops a wild longing for shiny-haired, 17-year-old Gladys Milhouser, daughter of a local tycoon. . . . He invokes the devil to aid him. Lucifer hears Alfred Sneeden and takes note of the offer. He does not want Alfred's soul. (There are too many souls in hell as it is.) On the other hand, there is a dearth of human hearts. . . . He decides to leave Alfred's soul alone and dispatches an emissary to take his heart instead. Two days later, when a new doctor comes to town and sets up as a specialist in rejuvenating processes, Sneeden has already forgotten what he told the devil. It is the other people in the town—the old general practitioner, the druggist, the postmistress, and above all the parish priest, Father Deener—who look with suspicion upon Dr. Samuel Hod [Samael of Hod]." N Y Times Bk R

"In passing, Nathan has a few caustic comments to make on man's behavior in the present day. We find Lucifer telling Samael that this great mission to the world may very well be his last since man may blow himself off the earth at any moment. . . . A delightful excursion into the fantastic with not a few philosophical and sociological implications. An important buy for all libraries." Library J

The enchanted voyage. Knopf 1936 187p $4.50

"Mr Hector Pecket was an unsuccessful carpenter somewhere in the Bronx. His wife, Sarah Pecket, was a managing woman, capable of facing facts, even tho her husband was not. In his dreams Mr Pecket sailed the seven seas in the little boat which he had built and kept in the back yard. When Mrs Pecket had wheels put under the boat and sold it to the butcher to use for a lunch wagon it was just too much. Mr Pecket hoisted his sail, and with Mary Kelly, a weary little Fordham Road waitress for crew, sailed south. On the way they picked up a traveling dentist who was also a knife-grinder, and the way was paved for romance and adventure." Book Rev Digest

The fair. Knopf 1964 208p boards $4.50

"Allegory about a very young noble lady, Penrhyd (niece of King Arthur), her awkward but well-meaning young lover, Thomas of Glen Daur, and her guardian angel, Azael, who appears as a black man with magic powers over animals. With an abbot, a chaperone, and Arthur's grandson, young mischievous Godwin, a demon with a singshot, the party flees the invading Saxons." Pub W

"Robert Nathan again tells a charming story, woven of fantasy and innocence that has its subtle overtones for the older reader and wonder enough for the younger folk." Best Sellers

One more spring

Some editions are:
Knopf $4.50
Watts, F. $7.95 Large type edition. A Keith Jennison book
First published 1933

"In this charming, gentle, and ironic story Mr. Nathan offers subtle and wise reflections

Nathan, Robert—*Continued*

on the depression [of 1929]. A dealer in antiques, who had lost everything except a huge bed carved with cupids, and an impecunious, but ambitious, violinist spend the winter in a tool shed in Central Park. Reluctantly they take in a homeless prostitute who proves to be of considerably better caliber than the ruined banker whom they add later. The four viewed life from quite different angles, but they all wished to live to see 'one more spring.' Written in beautiful and simple prose with tenderness and quiet humor." Booklist

y Portrait of Jennie

Some editions are:

Knopf $4.50

Watts, F. $7.95 Large type edition. A Keith Jennison book

First published 1939

"A young artist, his courage gone and desperate at the world's indifference, meets a little girl in an old-fashioned dress one night, playing alone on a New York street, who asks him to wait for her to grow up. How in the following months, Jennie, transcending time and space, and on each visit several years older comes to him, waiting and longing, and how he paints her portrait which is to make him famous, and through Jennie finds meaning in life and love and beauty is delicately revealed in a fantasy whose gossamer threads are as real as the realities with which they are interwoven." Bookmark

> *also in* Costain, T. B. ed. Stories to remember v 1 p229-96
> *also in* Costain, T. B. comp. Twelve short novels p491-558

Road of ages. Knopf 1935 232p o.p. 1970

"Mr Nathan has imagined a final exile of all Jews from all countries and this is the story of their slow march eastward across Europe toward Asia to the Gobi desert, offered by the Mongols as a haven. With gentle but convincing irony the heterogeneous mass of humanity is presented—all nationalities, many creeds, rich, poor, communists, musicians, scientists, bankers, traders, and many others. Through a few characters of very different backgrounds the story is told; love, death, birth, and strife go on as ever; hardships are endured; seasons change. A distinguished work which, because more serious in conception than 'One more spring', . . . will have a somewhat more limited appeal." Booklist

The sea-gull cry. Knopf 1942 214p $4.50

"Weary of a world at war, middle-aged, lonely Mr Smith, a schoolteacher, decides for just one summer to free himself from all problems and responsibilities. So he buys a boat, only to pile it up on the coast of Cape Cod near Truro. Here in the weeks that follow, Mr Smith becomes more and more interested in two penniless young refugees, the lovely courageous Louisa, and her dauntless little brother Jeri, temporarily safe in the haven of an old scow. What becomes of Mr Smith's determination to rid himself of responsibilities is related with quiet artistry in an unpretentious little story whose romance is balanced by clever characterization of native Cape Cod types." Bookmark

So love returns. Knopf 1958 214p boards $4.50

In this fantasy, "a writer, bereft of a beloved wife, left with the responsibility of bringing up his daughter Trisha and the younger son, Chris, is doing his best to earn and be a good father in a scantily furnished house by the sea. A strange young woman saves Chris from the sea and disappears before the distracted father, who tells this story, can thank her. Eventually he finds her. . . . An idyll ensues. But it ends, with a bitter-sweet note that seems to indicate that the lady from the sea, Kathleen, is a representative of the dead Trina; that love extends beyond the beyond into the here." Best Sellers

A star in the wind. Knopf 1962 [c1961] 302p $4.50

After a brief stay in Rome, Joseph Victor, an American Jewish correspondent, is sent to Palestine in 1948 to cover the Israel-Arab War. Enroute, aboard a refugee ship, he meets Anna

Muhlmann, a widow haunted by the memory of her husband's brutal death. Through his love for her and her tragic death in the war, as well as, his own experiences on the battlefront, Joseph finally realizes what it means to be a Jew." (Publisher)

Stonecliff. Knopf 1967 176p boards $4.50

"There is a subtle blending of illusion and reality in this well-written story about a young writer commissioned to write the biography of the aging novelist Edward Granville, whose private life is shrouded in secrecy. At Stonecliff, Granville's remote California mountain home, the mystery is heightened by the absence of Granville's wife and the presence of the beautiful young girl whose exact relationship to Granville is an enigma." Booklist

"It is delightful to come again upon prose that sings and images that shimmer in fresh, clear beauty. Mr. Nathan is subtle master of the seafoam world of half illusion." Library J

The wilderness-stone. Knopf 1961 204p boards $4.50

"Into the fictional fabric Robert Nathan has woven people and events from his own past, as Edward the narrator looks back to a time when youth was less cautious. It is the story of Miranda, who comes to live with her small daughter in an apartment next to Edward in Los Angeles. As the wilderness-stone represents the dream of freedom, so Nathan's tale of Miranda illuminates his belief that love is immortal." Huntting

Winter in April. Knopf 1938 228p $4.50

"An elderly man of fine feeling and perception is keenly sensitive to the emotions of his 15-year-old granddaughter and through his awareness the author draws a charming and authentic portrait of an adolescent girl in love, for the first time, with her grandfather's secretary, a scholarly young German exile. In the background of this quiet story which is related with tenderness and whimsical humor, are the noise of New York City and the conflicts engaging the world today." N Y Libraries

Nathanson, E. M.

The dirty dozen. Random House 1965 498p $5.95

Twelve assorted soldier-prisoners "are offered a more honorable death and possibly a pardon if they train for a dangerous mission behind the lines in Europe before D-Day. It is the task of Captain Reisman to use the violent tendencies of these men for the job at hand." McClurg. Book News

Natsume, Kinnosuke. See Natsume, Soseki

Natsume, Soseki

Botchan; tr. by Umeji Sasaki. Tuttle [1967 c1968] 188p illus $2.50

Original Japanese edition 1906

This "is the story of a simple, honest, and direct young man from Tokyo who goes to the provinces to teach high school. Because he is uncompromising and always sees things as black and white, he is immediately and constantly embroiled in misunderstandings and difficulties with his fellow teachers and his students. He is an attractive character, sometimes amusing and sometimes pathetic, but always enjoyable. . . . This reissue of a translation first printed in 1922 is very readable." Library J

Natwar-Singh, K.

(ed.) Tales from modern India; ed. with an introduction and notes by K. Natwar-Singh. Macmillan (N Y) 1966 274p $6.95

Analyzed in Short Story Index

"The major themes of contemporary Indian life and literature are presented in these twenty short stories." Bk Buyer's Guide

Contents: The Cabuliwallah, by R. Tagore; The hungry stones, by R. Tagore; Drought, by S. C. Chatterjee; Ardhanari, by C. Rajagopalachari; The shroud, by P. Chand; Resignation, by P. Chand; The barber's trade union, by M. R. Anand; The informer, by M. R. Anand; An astrologer's day, by R. K. Narayan; The blind dog, by R. K. Narayan; The little gram shop,

Natwar-Singh, K.—*Continued*

by Raja Rao; Nimka, by Raja Rao; The mystery, by P. B. Bhave; The soldier, by K. Chandar; Kalu Bhangi, by K. Chandar; Father and son, by T. S. Pillai; Karma, by K. Singh; The rape, by K. Singh; On the boat, by P. Padmaraju; Who cares, by S. Rama Rau

Nebula award stories [1]-4. Doubleday 1966-1969 4v (Doubleday Science fiction) v 1-2 o.p. 1970, v3 $4.95, v4 $5.95

Analyzed in Short Story Index
Editors vary: 1965 [v 1] by Damon Knight; v2 by Brian W. Aldiss and Harry Harrison; v3 by Roger Zelazny; v4 by Poul Anderson
Anthologies of stories chosen for publication by the Science Fiction Writers of America
Contents: v 1 The doors of his face, the lamps of his mouth, by R. Zelazny; Balanced ecology, by J. H. Schmitz; "Repent, Harlequin!" said the Ticktockman, by H. Ellison; He who shapes, by R. Zelazny; Computers don't argue, by G. R. Dickson; Becalmed in hell, by L. Niven; The saliva tree, by B. W. Aldiss; The drowned giant, by J. G. Ballard
v2 The secret place, by R. McKenna; Light of other days, by B. Shaw; Who needs insurance, by R. A. Lafferty; The last castle, by J. Vance; Day million, by F. Pohl; When I was Miss Dow, by S. Dorman; Call him Lord, by G. R. Dickson; In the Imapicon, by G. H. Smith; We can remember it for you wholesale, by P. K. Dick; Man in his time, by B. W. Aldiss
v3 The cloud-sculptors of Coral D, by J. G. Ballard; Pretty Maggie Moneyeyes, by H. Ellison; Mirror of ice, by G. Wright; Aye, and Gomorrah, by S. R. Delany; Gonna roll the bones, F. Leiber; Behold the man, by M. Moorcock; Weyr search, by A. McCaffrey
v4 Mother to the world, by R. Wilson; The dance of the changer and the three, by T. Carr; The planners, by K. Wilhelm; Sword game, by H. H. Hollis; The listeners, by J. E. Gunn; Dragonrider, by A. McCaffrey

Neider, Charles

(ed.) Great short stories from the world's literature. Rinehart 1950 502p o.p. 1970

Analyzed in Short Story Index
Contents: Passover guest, by S. Aleichem: Passion in the desert, by H. de Balzac; Evening in spring, by I. Bunin; Vanka, by A. P. Chekhov; True relation of the apparition of one Mrs Veal, by D. Defoe; Savannah-la-mar, by T. De Quincey; Heavenly Christmas tree, by F. M. Dostoyevsky; That evening sun go down, by W. Faulkner; Legend of St Julian the Hospitaller, by G. Flaubert; My mother, by A. Gide; Disabled soldier, by O. Goldsmith; Gray champion, by N. Hawthorne; Tale of olden time, by H. Heine; Snows of Kilimanjaro, by E. Hemingway; History of Krakatuk, by E. T. A. Hoffmann; Stout gentleman, by W. Irving; Great good place, by H. James; Araby, by J. Joyce; Country doctor, by F. Kafka; Beggar-woman of Locarno, by H. von Kleist; The outlaws, by S. Lagerlöf; Two blue birds, by D. H. Lawrence; Benediction, by L. Hsun; Massacre of the innocents, by M. Maeterlinck; Weary hour, by T. Mann; The piazza, by H. Melville; Birds of passage, by M. A. Nexo; Horse in the moon, by L. Pirandello; Imp of the perverse, by E. A. Poe; Flowering Judas, by K. A. Porter; Filial sentiments of a parricide, by M. Proust; The undertaker, by A. Pushkin; Twilight, by W. S. Reymont; The stranger, by R. M. Rilke; Letter to a hostage, by A. de Saint Exupéry; The wall, by J. P. Sartre; Mr Aristotle, by I. Silone; Markheim, by R. L. Stevenson; Generous wine, by I. Svevo; Hungry stones, by R. Tagore; Three hermits, by L. N. Tolstoy; District doctor, by I. Turgenev; Dog's tale, by M. Twain; Solitude, by M. de Unamuno; Duchess and the jeweller, by V. Woolf

(ed.) Short novels of the masters. Rinehart 1948 643p $6.95

Contents: Benito Cereno, by H. Melville; Notes from underground, by F. M. Dostoyevsky; A simple heart, by G. Flaubert; The death of Iván Ilých, by L. N. Tolstoy; The Aspern papers, by H. James; Ward no. 6, by A. P. Chekhov; Death in Venice, by T. Mann; The dead, by J. Joyce; The metamorphosis, by F. Kafka; The fox, by D. H. Lawrence

(ed.) Tolstoy, L. Tolstoy's Tales of courage and conflict

Nessi, Pio Baroja y. See Baroja y Nessi, Pio

Neugeboren, Jay

Corky's brother. Farrar, Straus 1969 261p $5.95

"There is no young writer today who catches as successfully as Jay Neugeboren the wild, grim subculture of our ghettos. Corky's Brother ... is a collection of twelve stories and one novella." News of Bks
Contents: Luther; Joe; The application; The Zodiacs; Finkel; A family trip; Ebbets Field; The campaign of Hector Rodriguez; Something is rotten in the borough of Brooklyn; The child; Elijah; The pass; Corky's brother [novella]

Corky's brother [novelette]
In Neugeboren, J. Corky's brother p213-61

The New Yorker

55 short stories from The New Yorker. Simon & Schuster 1949 480p o.p. 1970

Analyzed in Short Story Index
Covers the decade 1940-1950
Contents: (Stories only) Enormous radio, by J. Cheever; Defeat, by K. Boyle; Man here keeps getting arrested all the time, by J. McNulty; Down in the reeds by the river, by V. Lincoln; Winter in the country, by R. M. Coates; Catbird seat, by J. Thurber; Lady with a lamp, by S. Benson; Act of faith, by I. Shaw; Ballet visits the Splendide's magician, by L. Bemelmans; Middle draw, by H. Calisher; Dilemma of Catherine Fuchsias, by R. Davies; Nightingales sing, by E. Parsons; Second tree from the corner, by E. B. White; Pleasures of travel, by W. Wilcox; Content with the station, by J. A. Rice; Perfect day for bananafish, by J. D. Salinger; Patterns of love, by W. Maxwell; The lottery, by S. Jackson; The decision, by J. O'Hara; Her bed is India, by C. Weston; Inflexible logic, by R. Maloney; Falling leaves, by F. G. Patton; My Da, by F. O'Connor; Four freedoms, by E. Newhouse; View of Exmoor, by S. T. Warner; Children are bored on Sunday, by J. Stafford; Mr Skidmore's gift, by O. La Farge; Short wait between trains, by R. McLaughlin; Party at the Williamsons', by A. Peters; Monsoon, by J. Weidman; Song at twilight, by W. Gibbs; Run, run, run, run, by A. J. Liebling; The jockey, by C. McCullers; Pigeons en casserole, by B. Breuer; A killing, by R. Angell; Goodbye, my love, by M. Panter-Downes; Colette, by V. Nabokov; Clean, quiet house, by D. Fuchs; Village incident, by J. A. Maxwell; De mortuis, by J. Collier; Then we'll set it right, by R. G. Davis; Mysteries of life in an orderly manner, by J. West; Porte-cochere, by P. Taylor; Evolution of knowledge, by N. Tucci; Continued humid, by M. Shorer; The baby-amah, by E. Hahn; Truth and consequences, by B. Gill; Between the dark and the daylight, by N. Hale; Judgment of Paris, by J. R. Parker; Mary Mulcahy, by C. La Farge; The bummers, by J. Powell; Under Gemini, by I. Bolton; Improvement in Mr Gaynor's technique; by S. N. Behrman; Black secret, by M. K. Rawlings

Short stories from The New Yorker. Simon & Schuster 1940 438p o.p. 1970

Analyzed in Short Story Index
"Sixty-eight stories, representing the selected best of fifteen and a half years—February 1925 to September 1940." Huntting
Contents: Girls in their summer dresses, by I. Shaw; Over the river and through the wood, by J. O'Hara; Secret life of Walter Mitty, by J. Thurber; Net, by R. M. Coates; Home atmosphere, by S. Benson; Toast to captain Jerk, by R. Maloney; Kroy Wen, by K. Boyle; Nice girl, by S. Anderson; H*Y*M*A*N K*A*P*L*A*N, samaritan, by L. Q. Ross; Prelude to reunion, by O. La Farge; Small day, by E. Caldwell; Midsummer, by N. Hale; Door, by E. B. White; Tourist home, by B. Thielen; Arrangement in black and white, by D. Parker; Courtship of Milton Barker, by W. Gibbs; Homecoming, by W. Maxwell; Only the dead know Brooklyn, by T. Wolfe; Works, by N. Asch; Do you like it here? by J. O'Hara; Conversation piece, by L. Bogan; Fury, by R. M. Coates; Venetian perspective, by J. Flanner; Ping-pong, by S. McKelway; Three veterans, by L. Zugsmith; Wet Saturday, by J. Collier; Soldiers of

The New Yorker—*Continued*

the republic, by D. Parker; Houseparty, by W. Bernstein; All the years of her life, by M. Callaghan; Explorers, by J. Weidman; Old lady, by T. S. Winslow; Matter of pride, by C. La Farge; Love in the snow, by J. Sayre; Profession: housewife, by S. Benson; Great Manta, by E. Corle; My sister Frances, by E. Hahn; Accident near Charlottesburg, by W. A. Krauss; In honor of their daughter, by J. Mosher; Test, by A. Gibbs; Goodbye, Shirley Temple, by J. Mitchell; Honors and awards, by J. R. Parker; Pastoral at Mr Piper's, by M. Panter-Downs; Man and woman, by E. Caldwell; Main currents of American thought, by I. Shaw; Knife, by B. Gill; Pelican's shadow, by M. K. Rawlings; Incident on a street corner, by A. Maltz; Such a pretty day, by D. Powell; Portrait of ladies, by M. Schorer; Parochial school, by P. Horgan; I am waiting, by C. Isherwood; Letter from the Bronx, by A. Kober; Little woman, by S. Benson; Apostate, by G. Milburn; Sailor off the Bremen, by I. Shaw; Barmecide's feast, by M. Connelly; Fish story, by D. Moffat; I've got an anchor on my chest, by R. H. Newman; Happiest days, by J. Cheever; Black boy, by K. Boyle; Nice judge Trowbridge, by R. Lockridge; Love in Brooklyn, by D. Fuchs; Great-grandmother, by N. Hale; Chutzbah, by J. Weidman; Mr Palmer's party, by T. Slesinger; Different world, by R. M. Coates; Are we leaving tomorrow? by J. O'Hara; Getaway, by D. Thomas

Stories from The New Yorker, 1950-1960. Simon & Schuster 1960 780p $7.50

Analyzed in Short Story Index
Contents: The man of the world, by F. O'Connor; Lance, by V. Nabokov; The golden west, by D. Fuchs; Just a little more, by V. S. Pritchett; Raise high the roof beam, carpenters, by J. D. Salinger; Bernadette, by M. Gallant; The bell of charity, by C. Kentfield; Chopin, by N. Stewart; Immortality, by R. Henderson; The happiest I've been, by J. Updike; The French scarecrow, by W. Maxwell; The code, by R. T. Gill; What you hear from 'em, by P. Taylor; Sentimental education, by H. Brodkey; Death of a favorite, by J. F. Powers; In a café, by M. Lavin; Defender of the faith, by P. Roth; In the village, by E. Bishop; A father-to-be, by S. Bellow; Three players of a summer game, by T. Williams; Can't you get me out of here, by J. Strachey; Ask me no questions, by M. McCarthy; A game of catch, by R. Wilbur; Elegant economy, by E. Templeton; First dark, by E. Spencer; Wedding at Rociada, by O. La Farge; Côte d'azur, by R. Angell; The white wild bronco, by B. Kiely; The champion of the world, by R. Dahl; Terror and grief, by N. Tucci; The parson, by P. Mortimer; I live on your visits, by D. Parker; The rose, the mauve, the white, by E. Taylor; Reason not the need, by W. Stone; The stream, by A. Vivante; The interview, by R. P. Jhabvala; In the zoo, by J. Stafford; The rose garden, by M. Brennan; The bubble, by N. Hale; More friend than lodger, by A. Wilson; Return, by R. M. Coates; The children's grandmother, by S. T. Warner; Six feet of the country, by N. Gordimer; Kin, by E. Welty; The classless society, by E. Hardwick; First marriage, by St C. McKelway; The country husband, by J. Cheever

"The stories in this collection are, of course, the best The New Yorker has published in the last decade, but apart from that they are representative of its editors' judgment. By limiting most of the fiction they publish to a verisimilar representative of contemporary life and to an unobtrusive voice, they have bridged the gap between the high culture of the intellectuals and the urban culture of a large section of the popular audience." N Y Times Bk R

Newby, P. H.

Something to answer for; a novel. Lippincott 1969 [c1968] 285p boards $5.95

First published 1968 in England
"Jack Townrow, returns to Port Said as the 1956 Suez crisis is burgeoning. He decides to help the widow of an old friend settle her affairs and in the process finds that strange things happen to a man as he struggles toward self-discovery. He finds that in his search for identity, a man must answer for himself." Book News

"The novel is superficially confusing, supposedly because life for Townrow and particularly life for Townrow in Suez in those days was confusing." Best Sellers

Nexo, Martin Andersen

Pelle the conqueror.... Smith, P. 4v in 1 $10

First published separately 1906-1917. Volumes 1-3 translated by Jessie Muir; v4 translated by Bernard Miall
Contents: Boyhood; Apprenticeship; The great struggle; Daybreak
"Reared on an isolated Danish dairy farm, Pelle, the son of a poor unskilled Swedish laborer, is apprenticed to a shoemaker in a small provincial town. There he learns the value of love and a hatred of vice and tyranny. His social consciousness wakes when he goes to Copenhagen and lives in a squalid tenement. On his release from the prison where he is thrown for leading a strike, his vision is broadened and he achieves greatness by laying the foundation for a co-operative workmen's village. An important social novel." Enoch Pratt

Pelle the conqueror: Apprenticeship
In Nexo, M. A. Pelle the conqueror v2

Pelle the conqueror: Boyhood
In Nexo, M. A. Pelle the conqueror v 1

Pell the conqueror: Daybreak
In Nexo, M. A. Pelle the conqueror v4

Pelle the conqueror: The great struggle
In Nexo, M. A. Pelle the conqueror v3

Nichols, John

The sterile cuckoo. McKay 1965 210p $4.50

"Pookie Adams, an odd, cross-grained teenage girl with an unending stream of good conversation, is a heroine to remember. The author has written a . . . story of the beginning and end of a rapturous love affair between two crazy college kids. The college and the high school crowds should love it for its sexiness and its mood of wild rebellion." Pub W

Nielsen, Helen

Darkest hour. Morrow 1969 281p boards $5.95

"Sam Godard had a fatal car accident, Dr. Kwan was murdered; and former movie actor Monte Monterey was off and running from the vengeance of Max Berlin. He ran into Hannah Lee's car in his desperation and that brought Simon Drake into the puzzling case because Simon had had only two loves in his life: the girl he was engaged to and Hannah Lee, now in her sixties." Bk Buver's Guide

Nin, Anais

The four-chambered heart. Swallow Press 1959 187p illus $3.50

First published 1950 by Duell
"A novel of the lovers, Djuna and Rango, who live on a barge in the Seine. Rango's wife pretends to accept the situation, but thru her feigning of illness and subsequent insanity she nearly wrecks Djuna's life." Book Rev Digest

A spy in the house of love. Swallow Press 1959 140p illus $3.50

First published 1954 by The British Book Centre
"The story's structure and rhythms are somehow suggestive of a ballet in which the heroine, Sabina, acts out her relationships with five very different men—her husband and four lovers—seeking all the while to understand why mobility in love is the condition of her existence: to understand what it is in each man that she so deeply needs and what makes her eventually reject him." Atlantic

Noble, Hollister

Woman with a sword; the biographical novel of Anna Ella Carroll of Maryland. Doubleday 1948 395p o.p. 1970

"Based on 'long buried historical facts,' this is the story of Anna Ella Carroll (of the Maryland Carrolls), journalist, lawyer, and Abe Lincoln's personal investigator. It was Anne who planned an attack upon the rebellious South by way of the Tennessee River, though she was never to receive official recognition for it." Retail Bookseller

Nordhoff, Charles

y Botany Bay, by Charles Nordhoff and James Norman Hall. Little 1941 374p $4.95

"The story of the Australian penal colony at Botany Bay, and especially of Hugh Tallant, an American. who had been stranded in England turned highwayman, and was one of the first criminals shipped to Botany Bay, where life was bitterly hard and adventurous." Ontario Lib Rev

"While this drama of life has its depressing pages, romance triumphs in the end. A lesser tale than Mutiny on the Bounty, but a worthy addition to the fiction section." Library J

y The Bounty trilogy . . . by Charles Nordhoff and James Norman Hall; illus. by N. C. Wyeth. Little 1946 691p illus $7.95

"An Atlantic Monthly Press book"
"Comprising the three volumes: Mutiny on the Bounty, Men against the sea & Pitcairn's Island." Title page
A reissue of the combined volume first published in 1936

y Falcons of France; a tale of youth and the air, by Charles Nordhoff and James Norman Hall; with illus. by A. Vimnèra. Little 1929 332p illus $4.95

"A story of the Lafayette flying corps which portrays the allied aviator as a knight 'without fear and without reproach' and the German aviator as an honorable enemy. A war story which fosters the spirit of peace." Cleveland

y The hurricane, by Charles Nordhoff and James Norman Hall. Little 1936 257p $4.95

"On a South Sea island live some hundred and fifty souls in amiable community. There is a priest who has labored lovingly there for fifty years, a French administrator, and his sympathetic wife. And Terangi, a superb native who, because he could not endure the jail to which a saloon brawl had sent him, becomes a fugitive from justice, a murderer with a price on his head. It takes a hurricane to solve Terangi's problem, a hurricane that wipes out the smiling island and most of the inhabitants." New Yorker

"The convincing tale depicts the life of the native and the several white inhabitants, and both the beauty and desolation of their surroundings." N Y Libraries

y Men against the sea, by Charles Nordhoff and James Norman Hall. Little 1934 251p $5.95

Sequel to: Mutiny on the Bounty
"This volume tells the story of Captain Bligh and the eighteen loyal men, who under his leadership sailed in an open boat thirty-six hundred miles from the Friendly Islands in the South Pacific to the Dutch colony of Timor in the East Indies. The story is told as if by Ledward, the surgeon, but the events, the wind and the weather of the narrative are those recorded in Captain Bligh's log." Book Rev Digest

Followed by: Pitcairn's Island

also in Nordhoff, C. The Bounty trilogy p297-438

y Mutiny on the Bounty

Some editions are:
Little $5.95 An Atlantic Monthly Press book
Watts, F. $9.95 Large type edition. A Keith Jennison book
First published 1932
"This vivid narrative is based on the famous mutiny which members of the crew of the 'Bounty', a British war vessel, carried out in 1787 against their cruel commander, Captain William Bligh. The authors kept the actual historical characters and background, using as narrator an elderly man, Captain Roger Byam, who had been a midshipman on the 'Bounty.' The story tells how the mate of the ship, Fletcher Christian, and a number of the crew rebel and set Captain Bligh adrift in an open boat with the loyal men of the crew. The book was followed by two others, forming a trilogy: 'Men Against the Sea' (1934), which tells of Bligh and his men in the open boat,

and 'Pitcairn's Island' (1934), which describes the mutineers' life on a tiny Pacific island for 20 years." Benét. The Reader's Encyclopedia

also in Nordhoff, C. The Bounty trilogy p 1-295

y Pitcairn's Island, by Charles Nordhoff and James Norman Hall. Little 1934 333p $5.95

Sequel to: Men against the sea
"This final volume [of the triology] is the history of those mutineers who, with eighteen Polynesian men and women, reached Pitcairn's Island and there destroyed the 'Bounty.' Unvisited for eighteen years, the community fought over women and possessions, and all but one of the men died violent deaths. A blood-curdling story, not for the squeamish reader." Booklist

also in Nordhoff, C. The Bounty trilogy p441-691

Norris, Frank

McTeague; a story of San Francisco. Smith, P. 442p $3.75

First published 1899 by Doubleday
"Forbidden to practice dentistry when Marcus Schouler informs the authorities that he lacks both license and diploma, McTeague grows brutish and surly, while his wife, Trina, who had won $5,000 in a lottery, becomes a miser. He eventually murders Trina, steals her money, and is pursued into Death Valley by Schouler. McTeague kills Schouler, but the latter manages to handcuff their wrists. Tied to the corpse, McTeague is doomed to die of thirst in the desert." Benét. The Reader's Encyclopedia

y The octopus; a story of California. Doubleday 1901 361p $5.95

This story of social protest describes the war between California wheat growers and the railroads
"One cannot read it without a thrill at the breadth of purpose, the earnestness, the astonishing verbal power of its author. The characters are rather dwarfed by the main conception. 'The pit' has a stronger appeal as a human story." F. T. Cooper
Followed by: The pit

The pit; a story of Chicago. Smith, P. 403p $4.25

First published 1903 by Doubleday
Sequel to: The octopus
A novel "dealing with the wheat market of Chicago. The hero is Curtis Jadwin, whose winning of Laura Dearborn and subsequent growing prosperity mark him as a successful man. He is ruined in the Pit, but his misfortune wins back for him the love and devotion of his wife." Benét. The Reader's Encyclopedia

Norton, Sybil

(jt. ed.) Cournos, J. ed. Best world short stories: 1947

Norway, Nevil Shute. See Shute, Nevil

Novak, Joseph. See Kosinski, J.

O

Oates, Joyce Carol

Expensive people. Vanguard 1968 308p $5.95

"The journal of a self-styled 18-year-old madman, looking back at his childhood in one affluent American suburb after another, always precociously aware of what his parents demanded of him and how cruelly they misunderstood his needs. Father is a philistine with a talent for making money and a longing for a son who will play in the Little League. Mother, perhaps the most fascinating character in the novel, is a writer whose

Oates, Joyce C.—*Continued*

work appears in 'little magazines' and who is periodically driven to desert her family and babbitry for a life of sexual and artistic freedom. . . . It is the narrator-son's desperate oedipal love for his mother that precipitates a final crisis of horror, of the 'nice boy suddenly runs amok' variety." Pub W

"The author so well documents the logical stages in the boy's pathological development that a reader accepts the inevitable outcome with little if any skepticism. . . . This writer is to be congratulated for a new twist in plot, but the characters hardly enlist sympathy. . . . This fictionalized documentary may for the thoughtful reader be more sobering than mere chilling entertainment." Best Sellers

A garden of earthly delights. Vanguard 1967 440p $5.95

The book describes the early life of Clara Walpole, the daughter of a migrant farm worker; her life after she leaves her father; her romance with a rum-runner; and her marriage to a rich man, whom she convinces is the father of her illegitimate baby. The final part of the novel deals with the childhood and adolescence of Swan, the son

"The book has much to say of society's indifference to the plight of the disadvantaged, and of the shallowness of a way of life based entirely on getting and spending." Library J

Them. Vanguard 1969 508p $6.95

National book award, 1969
"Loretta Wendall, her daughter Maureen, and her son Jules are 'them'—three characters held together by corroding hatred and mute love. . . . [Set in] Detroit and its environs between 1937 and 1967—the three Wendalls experience their everydays in the midst of ominous history, trying by almost any means to cope with the 'thems' they cannot understand." Publisher's note

The author shows "marvelous talent in this . . . book—insight into people, ability to control a narrative, remarkable command of language, and a fine sense for the right detail. She puts a slight strain on credibility by having three of her characters psychologically strained, practically capable of sitting beside themselves—but the story is so utterly real that one can only conclude that such people exist and Miss Oates knows them." Best Sellers

Upon the sweeping flood, and other stories. Vanguard 1966 250p boards $4.95

Analyzed in Short Story Index
Contents: Stigmata; The survival of childhood; The death of Mrs Sheer; First views of the enemy; At the seminary; Norman and the killer; "The man that turned into a statue"; Archways; Dying; What death with love should have to do; Upon the sweeping flood

"Even though at times the death and violence becomes almost sickening, one cannot ignore Miss Oates' mastery of her art." Library J

O'Brian, Patrick

Master and commander. Lippincott 1969 384p map $6.95

"This historical sea tale chronicles the adventures of Jack Aubrey of the Royal Navy, master and commander of the brig 'Sophie,' and his crew as they battle the French and Spanish in the Mediterranean during the [Napoleonic wars of] early 1800s." Cincinnati

"There is a rich atmosphere of salt spray and close quarters aboard the sailing ships and all the blood-and-thunder and derring-do of the last battles ever fought under sail." Pub W

O'Brien, Edward J.

(ed.) The Best American short stories, 1915-1969. See The Best American short stories, 1915-1969

(ed.) Best British short stories, 1922-1940. See Best British short stories, 1922-1940

(ed.) The great modern English stories; an anthology. Liveright 1919 366p (Great modern stories ser) o.p. 1970

Analyzed in Short Story Index
Contents: Three strangers, by T. Hardy; Lodging for the night, by R. L. Stevenson; Star-child, by O. Wilde; Dying of Francis Donne, by E. Dowson; To Nancy, by F. Wedmore; Empty frame, by G. Egerton; Three musketeers, by R. Kipling; Wee Willie Winkie, by R. Kipling; How Gavin Birse put it to Mag Lownie, by J. M. Barrie; Fisher of men, by F. Macleod; Quattrocentisteria, by M. Hewlett; Stolen bacillus, by H. G. Wells; Old Aeson, by A. T. Quiller-Couch; Fire of Prometheus, by H. W. Nevinson; Man who played upon the leaf, by A. Blackwood; Old Thorn, by W. H. Hudson; Fourth Magus, by R. B. C. Graham; Ghost ship, by R. Middleton; Business is business, by J. Trevena; Chink and the child, by T. Burke; Monsieur Félicité, by H. Walpole; Red and white, by R. Pertwee; Man and brute, by E. L. G. Watson; Lost suburb, by J. D. Beresford; Birth of an artist, by H. de Sélincourt; Sick collier, by D. H. Lawrence; Greater than love, by C. Evans; Birth, by G. Cannan

O'Connor, Edwin

All in the family. Little 1966 434p $6.95

"An Atlantic Monthly Press book"
"The Kinsellas, like the Kennedys, were Irish-Catholic immigrants; they became powerful in New England through the manipulations of millionaire Uncle Jimmy. Jack, nephew of Uncle Jimmy, tells how Charles was pushed into the mayoralty and the governorship, but eventually ruined the Family Unity by turning against his conscientious brother." Bk Buyer's Guide

"This is an intensely interesting story that illuminates some dark patches of present-day politics." Library J

The edge of sadness. Little 1961 460p $6.95

Pulitzer Prize 1962
"An Atlantic Monthly Press book"
This story concerns "members of the Irish-American community of a large Massachusetts city. The narrator is Father Hugh Kennedy, a man who discloses the problems and decisions in his life as he talks of his lifelong connection with the Carmody family dominated by the wily old miser Charlie Carmody who, in a moment of weakness, bares his soul to Father Kennedy." Booklist

"These reflections, woven among the alternate lively jigs and melancholy fears of the Carmody family warfare, make a rich, dark novel exclusively Roman Catholic in atmosphere but often catholic with a small 'c' in its view of human relations and aspirations." Christian Science Monitor

I was dancing. Little 1964 242p $4.95

"An Atlantic Monthly Press book"
Waltzing Daniel Considine, retired after years in vaudeville, "wants chiefly to spend the rest of his days in the home of his son—whom he has not seen for twenty years—and his son's wife—whom he has never seen at all. The two young people accept him into their home as a temporary guest; it is only when they discover his intention to stay that the conflict begins." Publisher's note

"This book is basically a drama of old age and its eccentricities. It has some great farcical moments and some rousing vinegary conversations between the old man and his sister." Pub W

y The last hurrah. Little 1956 427p $6.95

"Typical of the old style political boss Frank Skeffington had kept his power as mayor of a large eastern U.S. city for almost 40 years. During the course of his last campaign . . . he is seen not only as the corrupt grafter ruthless with his enemies but also as a man of infinite charm who truly loved his city. . . . Some [high lights of the story are] the descriptions of the Irish groups who were Skeffington's chief supporters." Booklist

"A revealing study of a benevolent dictator at work. More, it is a genuine portrait of all the ebullience and rascality, loyalty and duplicity that enliven the typical Irish-American community." Christian Science Monitor

O'Connor, Flannery

Everything that rises must converge. Farrar, Straus 1965 xxxiv, 269p front boards $5.50

Analyzed in Short Story Index
"Nine stories of the fierceness and struggle of life among white people in the new South. Buyer's Guide Judgement day
The pathos and bitterness of the characters and the truths about themselves which they are made to face unwillingly could almost be placed in any setting." Pub W
Contents: Everything that rises must converge; Greenleaf; A view of the woods; The enduring chill; The comforts of home; The lame shall enter first; Revelation; Parker's back; Judgement day

A good man is hard to find, and other stories. Harcourt 1955 251p $4.50

Analyzed in Short Story Index
Contents: A good man is hard to find; The river; The life you save may be your own; A stroke of good fortune; A temple of the Holy Ghost; The artificial nigger; A circle in the fire; A late encounter with the enemy; Good country people; The displaced person

The violent bear it away. Farrar, Straus 1960 243p boards $3.75

"His fanatical great-uncle, in dying had impressed it on fifteen-year old Francis Marion Tarwater that the Lord would call him—and in the meantime he must baptize his atheist uncle Rayber's idiot child. And eventually Tarwater baptizes and drowns the boy at the same time. The setting is backwoods Tennessee; the story is largely allegorical." Bk Buyer's Guide
"The book is one of grotesques, but this does not mean that the characters are fantastic or incredible. On the contrary, it becomes impossible not to believe in them. . . . Miss O'Connor is thoroughly in control of her world; she knows it and she knows where she stands in relation to it. Her prose is strong, supple, at times full of beauty, never pretentious." Sat R

Wise blood. Farrar, Straus 1962 232p $4.50

A reissue of a title first published 1952 by Harcourt
"A novel of religious fanaticism. It centers around Hazel Motes, a young war veteran, who attempts to found a new religion, the Church Without Christ. Only when he blinds himself with quicklime and dies a slow death does he find his own salvation. The scene is a Tennessee mountain town." Book Rev Digest
"Though there is very little actual life going on the people live and speak authentically. A good solid work more concerned with people and moods than story." Library J

O'Connor, Frank

More stories. Knopf 1954 385p $5.95

Analyzed in Short Story Index
Contents: The lady of the sagas; Guests of the nation; Eternal triangle; Orpheus and his lute; The face of evil; Masculine protest; The man of the house; Judas; My first Protestant; The sorcerer's apprentice; Don Juan (retired); A romantic; The custom of the country; The little mother; The mad Lomasneys; A sense of responsibility; Council for Oedipus; A torrent damned; The shepherds; The old faith; The miracle; The frying-pan; Vanity; Darcy in the land of youth; The sentry; Father and son; Jerome; Unapproved route; Lonely rock

A set of variations; twenty-seven stories. Knopf 1969 338p $6.95

A collection of stories written between 1957 and 1966 on the themes of "manhood, love, faith, and the infinite web of relationships to family, to church, and to country by which men and women are sustained or entrapped." Publisher's note
Contents: A set of variations on a borrowed theme; The American wife; The impossible marriage; The cheat; The weeping children; The saint; A minority; An out-and-out free gift; Anchors; Sue; Music when soft voices die; A life of your own; The Corkerys; A story by Maupassant; A great man; The school for wives; Androcles and the Army; Public opinion; The party; Achilles' heel; Lost fatherlands; The wreath; The teacher's mass; The martyr; Requiem; An act of charity; The Mass Island

"This fine collection of short stories . . . testifies conclusively to Frank O'Connor's mastery of that essential element of the successful short story, namely, design. Each story has perfect structure, proportion, climax, and elements. And in addition, the tenderness and perceptiveness characteristic of Mr. O'Connor's writings make each story, however sad it may be, a celebration of life." Library J

The stories of Frank O'Connor. Knopf 1952 367p $5.95

Analyzed in Short Story Index
Contents: My Oedipus complex; Old fellows; The drunkard; Christmas morning; The idealist; First confession; My da; The pretender; First love; Freedom; News for the church; Don Juan's temptation; The long road to Ummera; The bridal night; Legal aid; Peasants; In the train; The majesty of the law; Song without words; Uprooted; The babes in the wood; The miser; The house that Johnny built; The cheapjack; The masculine principle; The Luceys; The Holy door

O'Connor, Mrs Frank. See Rand, Ayn

O'Donnell, Peter

A taste for death. Doubleday 1969 284p $4.95

"Modesty Blaise and Willie Garvin are back in action again. This time, the caper involves an innocent blind girl whose special talents mark her as the victim of an almost superhuman freak, and an organization of evil men who turn an archeological expedition into a nightmare." Book News

O'Donovan, Michael. See O'Connor, Frank

O'Faolain, Sean

The finest stories of Sean O'Faolain. Little 1957 385p boards $5.95

Analyzed in Short Story Index
Contents: Midsummer night madness; Fugue; The patriot; A broken world; The old master; Sinners; Admiring the scenery; A born genius; Discord; The confessional; Mother Matilda's book; One true friend; The man who invented sin; Teresa; Unholy living and half dying; Up the bare stairs; The Judas touch; The trout; The fur coat; The end of a good man; The silence of the valley; The end of the record; Lord and master; Persecution Mania; An enduring friendship; Childybawn; Lovers of the lake
"He is saturated with a sense of Ireland, but he is not parochial. . . . In this age of literary deadness and pretense, the re-publication of these stories of Sean O'Faolain takes on the character of a literary event. The word 'finest' is not at all misplaced in the title of this book. These are some of the finest stories written in English during the last quarter century." New Repub

The heat of the sun; stories and tales. Little 1966 243p boards $5.95

"An Atlantic Monthly Press book"
Analyzed in Short Story Index
Eleven stories of the Irish and Ireland. Each is concerned with some aspect of love
Contents: In the bosom of the country; Dividends; The heat of the sun; The human thing; One man, one boat, one girl; Charlie's Greek; Billy Billee; Before the daystar; £1000 for Rosebud; A sweet colleen; Passion

I remember! I remember! Stories by Sean O'Faolain. Little 1961 240p boards $4.95

Analyzed in Short Story Index
"An Atlantic Monthly Press book"
"Short stories concerned with the uneasily muted lives of some of the modern Irish. In Ireland and in other countries." New Yorker
Contents: I remember! I remember!; The sugawn chair; A shadow, silent as a cloud; A touch of autumn in the air; The younger

A nest of simple folk. Viking 1934 398p o.p. 1970

"A novel of sustained power and real vitality which tells the story of three generations of Irish people living, between 1854 and 1916, in southwestern Ireland. Their simple, poverty-stricken existence was punctuated with violence

O'Faolain, Sean—*Continued*

of revolutions and family dissension. The central figure, who is the link connecting the dozens of characters, is Leo Foxe-Donnel, who spent a large part of his life in prison for Fenian activities, and wasted the other part in various ways. In spite of the sordidness of many scenes, the book as a whole is lifted above its frequent somber tone by touches of idealism and excellent descriptive passages." Booklist

O'Flaherty, Liam

Famine. Random House 1937 466p o.p. 1970

"A story of Irish peasant life during the 1840s, when a potato blight brought widespread suffering that reached the proportions of a national calamity. It is a bitterly realistic picture of prolonged poverty, misgovernment, and ineffectual relief measures that resulted in mass emigration to America." Booklist

"The book is filled in with a wealth of native color, speech, and manner of living. . . . There are a dozen first-rate characterizations the author has built up with ease." Sat R

The informer. Knopf 1925 312p o.p. 1970

"Gypo Nolan, a gigantic brutal type, an ex-policeman who has even been expelled from the 'Revolutionary Organization,' a secret Communistic society, after months of semi-starvation, betrays, on sudden impulse, a comrade to the police. . . . Cautious in mind, yet careless, he squanders the 'bloodmoney' in low public-houses and dens of vice, with a growing sense of exaltation caused by sudden wealth, intoxication and danger. In a last harrowing scene, Gallagher, the revolutionary leader, tortures the giant intellectually in cross-examination, and watches the struggles of that inarticulate mind dulled by drink. However, sordid the scenes may be, Mr. O'Flaherty shows us the pitiable humanity of the unfortunate informer, and sees, awed by his own creation, beneath the brutality and stupidity, the childlike soul of the man." Times (London) Lit Sup

"Mr. O'Flaherty handles this nightmare stuff with consummate skill and fervor. We are under the spell of his inventions from first page to last." N Y Times Bk R

Insurrection. Little 1951 248p o.p. 1970

An account of the 1916 Easter Rebellion in Ireland. "A tale of how it linked together a few unusual people—a Dublin slum mother and her colorless son, a poet teacher, a mystic and a rough Connemara man who fought only because he adored his captain." Library J

"'Insurrection' remains a notable novel, its tale of violence curbed by an austere spirit." N Y Her Trib Books

The stories of Liam O'Flaherty. Introduction by Vivian Mercier. Devin-Adair 1956 419p boards $7.50

Analyzed in Short Story Index

Contents: Spring sowing; The cow's death; The tramp; The rockfish; The landing; The blackbird; His first flight; A shilling; The black mare;; The fight; Going into exile; The tent; Milking time; The conger eel; The wild goat's kid; The wounded cormorant; A red petticoat; Mother and son; The wing three-quarter; Birth; The oar; The mountain tavern; The fairy goose; The child of God; Red Barbara; Two lovely beasts; The touch; The water hen; Life; The tide; The new suit; The wedding; The parting; The old woman; The beggars; Galway Bay; The hawk; The blow; The mirror; Desire; The post office; The wild swan

"Most of these forty-two brief, slight episodes of Irish life are set in the west of Ireland, and they are all either painful or full of the premonition of pain. . . . The writing is clear and sharp and hard, each sentence marked with its author's furiously alive individuality." New Yorker

Ogilvie, Elisabeth

y Bellwood. McGraw 1969 278p $5.95

"Caroline went to the Maine coast estate of Rees Morgan to care for his small son, a retarded cripple. Soon she found that there was something menacing in the atmosphere of Bellwood and something mysterious about Mrs. Morgan's fall from the cliffs. But by that time Caroline was in love with her employer. The author's first Gothic romance." Bk Buyer's Guide

"Miss Ogilvie writes with ease and skill. Her characters, while not distinguished, are credible. Her descriptions of the Maine setting are pleasing and form an attractive contrast to the dark story of Rees Morgan. The story line moves briskly and logically. 'Bellwood' will be popular with the woman reader." Best Sellers

The seasons hereafter. McGraw 1966 308p boards $3.50

"One of the author's novels with Bennett's Island, Maine for a setting describes the transformation of a newcomer from a slovenly, bookish, antisocial escapist into a mature young housewife. An abandoned child and state ward, Vanessa had always taken a perverse pride in being free, different, and disdainful of conventional people like her long-suffering husband, but the combination of the islanders' unaffected friendliness, an abortive love affair with a reformed rake who elects to remain with his wife and children, and her husband's unexpected assertion of manhood brings about the long-awaited day when Vanessa achieves a sense of identity." Booklist

"Woven throughout the plot of the novel are beautiful scenes of Maine and glimpses of the demanding lives of the Maine fishermen." McClurg. Book News

Waters on a starry night. McGraw 1968 309p boards $5.95

"Jethro's Island is the setting for the story of Lyle and Thora Ritchie, who married very young and now find themselves with children, debts, and Lyle's infatuation with a younger woman." Bk Buyer's Guide

A "regional novel in which, though the plot is predictable, the characters and locale are well realized." Pub W

O'Hara, John

And other stories. Random House 1968 336p $5.95

Analyzed in Short Story Index

"Most of the eleven stories and one novella of this collection are set in the town of Gibbsville in the 1920's and 1930's and provide glimpses into the lives of the town's wealthier citizens." Book Rev Digest

Contents: Barred; The broken giraffe; The farmer; A few trips and some poetry [novella]; The gangster; The gunboat and Madge; How old, how young; A man on a porch; Papa Gibraltar; The private people; The strong man; We'll have fun

Appointment in Samarra

Some editions are:
Modern Lib. $2.95
Random House $3.95

First published 1934

"Julian English is an aristocratic drunkard. He is neither malicious, nor degenerate, but a victim of psychological and moral flabbiness. He outrageously mistreats his wife Caroline, although he loves her; he becomes concerned in needless altercations with strangers, and even with friends toward whom he feels a moral obligation. His tragedy begins on Christmas Eve, after a drinking bout. By the next day, he is so overwhelmed by his grossness and futility that he commits suicide. The only seemingly normal people in the story are Luther Fliegler, a salesman, and his wife. But they, too, are condemned to suffer from Julian's acts, as are Al Grecco, a bootlegger, the inoffensive Harry Reilly and many others whose lives become involved in a casual way with Julian's. The novel is written episodically, but achieves integration by its hard-boiled theme of the destructive effects of fast living." Haydn. Thesaurus of Book Digests

Assembly. Random House 1961 429p $6.95

Analyzed in Short Story Index

"Twenty-four stories and two novellas. . . . In most of them he deals, as he has so often in the past, with middle-aged people coping with fears or regrets that they have lived with for a long time." Pub W

Contents: Mrs Stratton of Oak Knoll [novelette]; The weakness; The man with the broken arm; The lighter when needed; The pioneer hep-cat; The sharks; The girl from California; A cold calculating thing; You can always tell Newark; The high point; Call me, call me; It's mental work; In the silence; First day in town;

O'Hara, John—*Continued*

Exactly eight thousand dollars exactly; Mary and Norma; The cellar domain; The properties of love; Reassurance; The free; The compliment; Sterling silver; The trip; In a grove; The old folks; A case history [novelette]

also in O'Hara, J. 49 stories v 1

Butterfield 8. Modern Lib. [1961 c1935] 310p $2.95

First published 1935 by Harcourt
"Realistic story of a young girl who lived a fast life in New York city during the early 1930's. The title is the telephone exchange of the Park avenue region in which many of the characters lived. The story is similar in outline to one which caused a stir in the New York papers of about that time." Book Rev Digest
"Stemming, all too obviously, from the Starr Faithfull case. . . . Mr. O'Hara describes her career with a cruel detachment which makes his book doubly effective." Forum

The Cape Cod lighter. Random House 1962 425p $5.95

Analyzed in Short Story Index
"A collection of 23 short stories and novellas, some not previously published and some reprinted from the 'New Yorker.' Most are vignettes of imaginary citizens representing all ranks of society in the author's fictional home town of Gibbsville, Pennsylvania." Booklist
Contents: Appearances; The Bucket of Blood; The butterfly; Claude Emerson, reporter; The engineer; The father; The first day; Jurge Dulrumple; Justice; The lesson; Money; The nothing machine; Pat Collins; The professors; A short walk from the station; Sunday morning; The sun-dodgers; Things you really want; Two turtledoves; Winter dance; The women of Madison Avenue; You don't remember me; Your fah neefah neeface

also in O'Hara, J. 49 stories v2

A case of history
In O'Hara, J. Assembly p382-429
In O'Hara, J. 49 stories v 1 p382-429

Elizabeth Appleton; a novel. Random House 1963 310p $4.95

"By background and temperament an outsider in the academic world, Elizabeth Appleton fills the role of faculty wife capably, yet with unconscious snobbery. A five-year affair with Porter Ditson, a fellow sophisticate and the real love of her life, carries Elizabeth through some difficult years, but when he proposes marriage Elizabeth decides that for everyday living she prefers the marriage she has. She then turns her energies to winning the presidency of Spring Valley College for her husband and fails." Booklist
"Mr. O'Hara's art is by now perfect. It has always been a master's style, tough, alert to detail, and spare in its drawing. . . . The impact of the novel comes from the authenticity of its perfectly real scenes, living room after living room. Mr. O'Hara's ear misses nothing. His eye, however, is severely selective. . . . But to write that life, John O'Hara has imagined so real a story that we can only guess that he knows life in Pennsylvania as no one before, and is not likely to be surpassed .His compassion moves us with its honesty. His moral insight and patience in analyzing confused motives constitute a triumph of the novelist's art." Nat R

A few trips and some poetry
In O'Hara, J. And other stories p42-165

49 stories. Modern Lib. [1963 c1962] 2v in 1 $4.95

Analyzed in Short Story Index
"This collection contains all the stories that were published in two separate volumes [by Random House] 'Assembly' (1961) and 'The Cape Cod Lighter' (1962) [entered separately]" Publisher's note

From the terrace; a novel. Random House 1958 897p $6.95

This novel is the story of Alfred Eaton through boyhood and prep school, his stay at Princeton (interrupted and terminated by

World War I) his career in the early aviation business and in Wall Street, as a sub-Cabinet officer during World War II, and his return to private life. (Publisher)
"Indeed the novel's central achievement is surely the impression it conveys of the morality—or amorality, or immorality—of this [social register] class. . . . It is difficult to do justice to the keenness of his ear for people talking, the acid wit with which he endows many of his characters, or the variety of his narrative techniques." N Y Her Trib Books

The girl on the baggage truck
In O'Hara, J. Sermons and soda water v 1

The hat on the bed. Random House 1963 405p $5.95

Analyzed in Short Story Index
Contents: Agatha; Aunt Anna; Eminent domain; Exterior: with figure; The flatted saxophone; The friends of Miss Julia; The Glendale people; The Golden; How can I tell you; I know that, Roy; John Barton Rosedale, actors' actor; The locomobile; The manager; The man on the tractor; The mayor; Ninety minutes away; Our friend the sea; The public Dorothy; The ride from Mauch Chunk; Saturday lunch; Teddy and the special friends; The twinkle in his eye; The windowpane check; Yucca Knolls
"This vital and prolific reporter of the American scene once again shows his mastery of the short-story form, his gift for dialogue, his ability to reproduce flawlessly familiar people in convincing situations. Never surprising, never wildly humorous or imaginative, but also never dull." Cincinnati

The horse knows the way. Random House 1964 429p $5.95

Analyzed in Short Story Index
"Twenty-eight short stories, all slick, competent, bound to be popular. As usual, they concern the upper middle class for the most part, the upper middle-aged (though not especially mature). Some are sharply satirical, and most of them are more concerned with ideas than action." Bk Buyer's Guide
Contents: All tied up; The answer depends; Arnold Stone; At the window; Aunt Fran; The bonfire; The brain; Can I stay here; Clayton Bunter; The clear track; The gun; The hardware man; His Excellency; The house on the corner; I can't thank you enough; In the mist; I spend my days in longing; The jet set; The lawbreaker; The Madeline Wherry case; Mrs Allanson; The pig; School; The staring game; The victim; What's the good of knowing; The whole cherry pie; Zero

Imagine kissing Pete
In O'Hara, J. Sermons and soda water v2

The instrument; a novel. Random House 1967 297p $5.95

The author "presents a dedicated playwright who uses people to feed his talent. Yank Lucas has written a great play and leading actress Zena Gollum accepts it as her next vehicle. It becomes a Broadway success. Yank and Zena become lovers. He leaves her to work on his new play. After a few more affairs in the small Vermont town he has escaped to, he finishes the play that was written unconsciously for Zena. But she had committed suicide, and with her death went Yank's talent." Library J
The novel "succeeds for all the old reasons. O'Hara eavesdrops on speech like an electronic listening device. His authentication—buttons on clothes, furnishings in rooms—creates reality." Time

The Lockwood concern; a novel. Random House 1965 407p $5.95

"Through his grandfather and his father, George Lockwood had inherited great wealth and a tainted mind. He built himself a mansion with a secret staircase and a spiked wall. But his brother shot and killed himself and his mistress. His son ran off to California. His insatiable daughter married a New Englander with homosexual tendencies and George's insane schemes ended in a plunge down his secret staircase." Bk Buyer's Guide

O'Hara, John—*Continued*

"It has the usual O'Hara embellishments of brief shocking episodes told deadpan . . . plenty of sex, reams of clipped conversation and devious intrigues of a business or social character, sometimes both." Pub W

Lovey Childs: a Philadelphian's story; a novel. Random House 1969 249p $5.95

This "piece is all about the vicissitudes in the young life of a girl from a Main Line family in the 1920s. One traumatic experience after another hits Lovey—first her father's death and then a mother who has to be 'put away' because of her infatuation with girls of Lovey's own age. Lovey marries on impulse and, for a while, the escapades of 'Lovey and Sky,' typical of the '20s, make them tabloid favorites. But fate steps in with more blows—a messy divorce, Lovey's own introduction to lesbianism, then the murder of one man who seems to interest her, and the suicide of a priest whom she has seduced. But there's a happy ending for Lovey—marriage to a distant cousin and a return to her suburban estate with the prospect of 40 less eventful years." Pub W

Mrs Stratton of Oak Knoll
In O'Hara, J. Assembly p3-63
In O'Hara, J. 49 stories v 1 p3-63

The O'Hara generation. Random House 1969 491p $6.95

"A collection of 22 of John O'Hara's stories from previously published volumes illustrates the various aspects of his writing talents." Bk Buyer's Guide

Contents: The doctor's son; Over the river and through the wood; Do you like it here; Summer's day; The decision; Drawing room B; Mrs Stratton of Oak Knoll; Mary and Norma; You can always tell Newark; Pat Collins; The first day; Your fah neefah neeface; The friends of Miss Julia; The manager; The Madeline Wherry case; The bonfire; The hardware man; Andrea; Flight; The General; Afternoon waltz; Fatimas and kisses

This anthology "is a well-rounded sampling of John O'Hara's prolific talents and an excellent introduction to his imposing body of work." Literary Guild

Ourselves to know; a novel. Random House 1960 408p $4.95

"The story of Robert Millhouser, prominent citizen of Lyons, Pa., who shot and killed his young wife in 1908. The narrator is Gerald Higgins, who first became aware of the mystery connected with Millhouser when he was a small boy. With his subject's help, Gerald reconstructed his life and crime, seeking to determine the inner forces that motivated him." Pub W

"The murder and other melodramatic elements are recounted with a dispassionate objectivity that precludes sensationalism." Booklist

A rage to live. Random House 1949 590p $5.95

"Novel describing a wealthy woman who had 'a rage to live.' Eventually it destroyed her marriage and made her an exile from her Pennsylvania town." Book Rev Digest

Selected short stories of John O'Hara; with an introduction by Lionel Trilling. Modern Lib. 1956 303p $2.95

Analyzed in Short Story Index

Contents: The decision; Everything satisfactory; The moccasins; Doctor and Mrs Parsons; Pardner; A phase of life; Walter T. Carriman; Now we know; Too young; Summer's day; The king of the desert; Bread alone; Graven image; The next-to last dance of the season; Where's the game; Mrs Whitman; Price's always open; The cold house; Are we leaving tomorrow; No mistakes; The ideal man; Do you like it here; The Doctor's son; Hotel kid; The public career of Mr Seymour Harrisburg; In the morning sun; War aims; Secret meeting; Other women's households; Over the river and through the wood; I could have had a yacht; A respectable place

Sermons and soda water. Random House 1960 3v $5.95

Contents: v 1 The girl on the baggage truck; v2 Imagine kissing Pete; v3 We're friends again

These three short novels "deal with people observed by a young man from Gibbsville, Pa., over a period of years from 1930 to the present. . . . The most vivid characters are an aging movie star, who appears in the first book, and the miserable mismatched Gibbsville husband and wife whose wretched marriage provides the plot for the second book." Pub W

"Good staple O'Hara, full of sex and sharp observation of New York and Pennsylvania 'mores,' social and theatrical, of 30 years ago." Library J

Ten North Frederick. Random House 1955 408p $6.95

A character study of one of the "first citizens" of a Pennsylvania town, Gibbsville. "In the first quarter of a crowded, eventful narrative, Joe Chapin is seen only through the eyes of some of those at [his] funeral. Then [O'Hara] . . . switches back to Joe's parents, who established the home at Ten North Frederick Street, where Joe lived all his life. He tells Joe's story from the beginning, and the stories of those whose lives have touched Joe's at some significant point." N Y Times Bk R

"We are persuaded that these pages tell us all any one could know of Joseph Chapin. We understand him better than he understood himself—better, I dare say, than we understand ourselves. And that is about as significant an experience as fiction can afford us." N Y Her Trib Books

Waiting for winter. Random House 1966 466p $5.95

Analyzed in Short Story Index

"Twenty-one short stories mainly about lonely people set in Pennsylvania, Hollywood and East Hampton." Chicago

Contents: Afternoon waltz; Andrea; The assistant; Fatimas and kisses; Flight; The gambler; The General; A good location; The Jama; James Francis and The Star; Late, late show; Leonard; Natica Jackson; The neighborhood; The pomeranian; The portly gentleman; The skeletons; The tackle; The way to Majorca; The weakling; Yostie

We're friends again
In O'Hara, J. Sermons and soda water v3

Oldenbourg, Zoé

The awakened; tr. by Edward Hyams. Pantheon Bks. 1957 o.p. 1970

Original French edition published 1956

"Stephanie, daughter of a highly intellectual, rather arrogant Jew turned Catholic, and Ilya, son of a white Russian officer who has fallen on evil days, join in a passionate love affair while France moves toward World War II." Retail Bookseller

The author's "book is a truly distinguished work of a generation thrown helplessly into chaos, yet strong enough to measure up to its inhuman pressures." San Francisco Chronicle

The chains of love; tr. from the French by Michael Bullock. Pantheon Bks. 1959 327p o.p. 1970

Original French edition published 1958

"'The Chains of Love' continues the story of the star-crossed lovers, Elie and Stephanie, begun in her earlier 'The Awakened.' The scene is Paris, among the White Russian exiles and the artists colony from 1947 to 1951. Elie, returning from seven years' imprisonment in Russia, tries to pick up the strands of a broken life. Stephanie, and their daughter, do what they can to help but after four years Elie is a suicide. The mood of the book is fatalistic, frustrated, unredeeming, and offers a sharply perceptive and touching insight into the lives of the truly displaced persons." Library J

Cities of the flesh; or, The story of Roger de Montbrun. Tr. from the French by Anne Carter. Pantheon Bks. 1963 503p o.p. 1970

Set in twelfth-century France at the time of the Albigensian Crusade this is "a tale of

Oldenbourg, Zoé—Continued

the love and lust of Roger de Montbrun, a Catholic knight of Toulouse, with his lady Gentian, Cartharist wife of the noble Bérenger d'Aspremont. The passion which awakes in their hearts begins the story; it is followed by an awakening of conscience in Gentian, who is true to her faith; and it ends with her final repudiation of her love. Roger, on the other hand, loves his lady until death. While they still possess one another, he is already excommunicated, suspected of aiding the heretics. Yet not until they are apart is the prophecy of his destruction fulfilled." N Y Times Bk R

"In describing the horrors of thirteenth-century life Zoé Oldenbourg writes as powerfully as ever. She enters into the minds of her characters so that we are convinced they acted as she says they did; though they remain so strange to the modern world that we cannot ever say what they will do next." Times (London) Lit Sup

The cornerstone; tr. by Edward Hyams. Pantheon Bks. 1955 482p o.p. 1970

"Like author's 'The World Is Not Enough' this novel of 13th century France is beautifully written and absorbing, and carries on the story begun in the earlier book. Here are knights and ladies, cruel and ruthless lords, devotees of superstition and witchcraft, and men whose great faith in the honor and goodness of spiritual man has made them the corner-stone of civilization. In the fashion of a beautiful tapestry the author weaves a picture of 13th century life, especially the religious and chivalrous side." Library J

"Lacking the subtle but unfaltering faith of the thirteenth century, we may find this a grim book. The author does not lighten the horrors with pageantry, flashing sword blades or specious consolations. . . . But out of the earnest intent and the grimness of truth a terrible beauty is born." N Y Her Trib Books

Destiny of fire; tr. from the French by Peter Green. Pantheon Bks. 1961 378p $4.95

Originally published in France 1960

The novel "describes the fate and misfortunes of the noble Seigneur of Montgeil and his family, who, as vassals of the Count of Toulouse and as devout adherents of the Albigensian heresy, were victims of the fantastically cruel 'Fourth Crusade' at the beginning of the thirteenth century [in France]." Publisher's note

"Lengthy disquisitions on Cathar theology and way of life and minute, graphic descriptions of death at the stake and other inhuman methods will limit this to readers who share the author's passion for knowledge and understanding of past times and issues." Booklist

The world is not enough; a novel; tr. from the French by Willard A. Trask. Pantheon Bks. 1948 509p maps $6.95

"This novel of the middle ages, at the time of the Crusades, pictures men preoccupied with hunting, fighting and lust, most of them brutal, and still capable of being sincerely moved by religion and emotion. Practically without plot, it follows the career of Ansiau of Linnieres and his wife Alis, married at 16 and 14, for forty years, through three Crusades, and the birth of 17 children, Alis struggling with the mortgaged land while Ansiau follows his pleasures, until almost blind and helpless, he sits with the wife who has always been the stable point in his world." Wis Lib Bul

"It is a refreshingly unsentimental re-creation of medieval life, which makes that remote period and the people in it come alive as if they were our contemporaries. . . . The book would have been very greatly improved by a good deal of cutting." Commonweal

Oliver, Jane

Candleshine no more. Putnam 1967 316p $5.95

A novel about "Bonnie Prince Charlie and the ill-fated Rebellion of 1745. Charles Edward's dramatic attempt to reclaim the throne of England and Scotland for the House of Stuart is truly history's gift to romance, as is the tragedy of his annihilating military defeat and the bitter intrigue of royalty in exile." Huntting

Olsen, Paul

The Virgin of San Gil; a novel. Holt 1965 189p $4.95

"In a remote mountain village of Mexico the statue of the Virgin is stolen from the church and denuded of its jewels and gold decorations. Joaquin, an Indian charcoal seller who is probably the lowliest person in San Gil, finds the statue, is accused of the theft, and is subjected to inquisitorial questioning by the ruling triumvirate of San Gil consisting of the chief of police, the civil authority, and the local priest, who has kept the church going by compromising with paganism. The only protest comes from the new young priest who suffers martyrdom as a consequence, but not before he has set in motion the forces of retribution." Booklist

O'Malley, Mary Dolling (Sanders) Lady. See Bridge, Ann

Onís, Harriet de. See De Onís, Harriet

Oppenheim, E. Phillips

The great impersonation; with illus. by Nana French Bickford. Little 1920 322p illus o.p. 1970

"Baron Leopold von Ragastein had been educated in England, at Eton and Oxford. While there he had had a double in a school mate, Sir Everard Dominey. Later they meet again in a German colony in East Africa. . . . They exchange confidences and when the German receives sudden orders to go to England on a secret mission he resolves to go as Sir Everard Dominey after first making away with the real Sir Everard. . . . When the [First World] war breaks out he out-does himself by enlisting in the Norfolk yeomanry and at the very end comes the startling disclosure that it is after all the real Sir Everard, who had not been so drunk in Africa 'but that he was able to pull himself up when the great incentive came.' Book Rev Digest

also in Haycraft, H. ed. Five spy novels p 1-161

Orbit 1-6; a science fiction anthology; ed. by Damon Knight. Putnam 1966-1970 6v v 1 o.p. 1970, v2-6 ea $4.95

Analyzed in Short Story Index
Subtitles vary

Anthologies, published annually, of hitherto unpublished science fiction

Contents: v 1 Staras Flonderans, by K. Wilhelm; The secret place, by R. McKenna; How beautiful with banners, by J. Blish; The disinherited, by P. Anderson; The loolies are here, by A. Rice; Kangaroo court, by V. Kidd; Splice of life, by S. Dorman; 5 eggs, by T. M. Disch; The deeps, by K. Roberts

v2: The doctor, by T. Thomas; Baby, you were great, by K. Wilhelm; Fiddler's green, by R. McKenna; Trip, trap, by G. Wolfe; The dimple in Draco, by P. Latham; I gave her sack and sherry, by J. Russ; The adventuress, by J. Russ; The hole on the corner, by R. A. Lafferty; The food farm, by K. Reed; Full sun, by B. W. Aldiss

v3: Mother to the world, by R. Wilson; Bramble bush, by R. McKenna; The barbarian, by J. Russ; The changeling, by G. Wolfe; Why they mobbed the White House, by D. P. Buck; The planners, by K. Wilhelm; Don't wash the carats, by P. J. Farmer; Letter to a young poet, by J. Sallis; Here is thy sting, by J. Jakes

v4: Windsong, by K. Wilhelm; Probable cause, by C. L. Harness; Shattered like a glass goblin, by H. Ellison: This corruptible, by J. Transue; Animal, by C. Emshwiller; One at a time, by R. A. Lafferty; Passengers, by R. Silverberg; Grimm's story, by V. Vinge; A few last words, by J. Sallis

v5: Somerset dreams, by K. Wilhelm; The roads, the roads, the beautiful roads, by A. Davidson; Look, you think you've got troubles, by C. Carr; Winter's king, by U. K. LeGuin; The time machine, by L. Jones; Configuration of the north shore, by R. A. Lafferty: Paul's treehouse, by G. Wolfe; The price, by

Orbit 1-6—*Continued*

C. D. Belcher; The Rose Bowl-Pluto hypothesis, by P. Latham; Winston, by K. Reed; The history makers, by J. Sallis; The big flash, by N. Spinrad

v6: The second inquisition, by J. Russ; Remembrance to come, by G. Wolfe; How the whip came back, by G. Wolfe; Goslin Day, by A. Davidson; Maybe Jean-Baptiste Pierre Antoine De Monet, Chevalier De LaMarck, was a little bit right, by R. Scott; The chosen, by K. Wilhelm; Entire and perfect chrysolite, by R. A. Lafferty; Sunburst, by R. Thorp; The creation of Bennie Good, by J. Sallis; The end, by U. K. LeGuin; A cold dark night with snow, by K. Wilhelm; Fame, by J. Cox; Debut, by C. Emshwiller; Where no sun shines, by G. R. Dozois; The Asian shore, by T. M. Disch

Orczy, Baroness

y Adventures of the Scarlet Pimpernel. Doubleday 1929 302p o.p. 1970

"New exploits of the Scarlet Pimpernel, Sir Percy Blakeney, the daring Englishman, who, with his loyal friends and helpers, rescues aristocrats from the guillotine during the French Revolution. Each chapter records a separate adventure." Cleveland

y The elusive Pimpernel; with frontispiece by John Rae. Dodd 1908 344p front o.p. 1970

Another chapter in the adventurous life of The Scarlet Pimpernel, that thorn in the side of the terrorists of the French Revolution, & a delivering angel to condemned aristocrats. In an increasingly tense situation, this languid, Englishman deliberately enters the French trap in an attempt to rescue his wife, the beautiful Marguerite Blakeney

y The Scarlet Pimpernel

Some editions are:
Dodd (Great illustrated classics) $4.50 With photographs of the author and her environment as well as illustrations from early editions, together with an introduction by Howard Breslin
Macmillan (N Y) (The Macmillan classics) $3.95 Illustrated by John Falter
Putnam $3.75

First published 1905
"The Scarlet Pimpernel is the leader of a little band of titled Englishmen, who during the reign of terror, assist condemned or suspected emigrés to escape to England." Public Opinion

"Melodramatic, but picturesque and well told tale." Sat R

Orczy, Emmuska, Baroness. See Orczy, Baroness

O'Rourke, Frank

The bright morning; a novel. Morrow 1963 219p o.p. 1970

"A pleasant, bucolic story of life and love in a small Midwestern town in the 1930's. Wholesome, capable Meta Odlum, newly graduated from normal school, bicycling back and forth from her first teaching job in a rural school, and shyly in love with the unattainable, is the likable central character whose yearlong passage from girlhood to womanhood makes the framework for a tale most memorable for its re-creation of time and place." Booklist

The far mountains. Morrow 1959 474p o.p. 1970

"The book's setting is in the Southwest, primarily New Mexico, 1800-1845. Young John O'Brien enlists in an American filibustering expedition headed into the Spanish Southwest. Surviving a Spanish attack, O'Brien attaches himself to a Blas Pelletier, adventurer and renegade from Old Mexico, and decides to live the rest of his life in New Mexico. O'Brien quickly discovers there is much more to adapting to his new environment than the changing of his name to Juan Obregon. After four decades, however. Obregon has become sufficiently assimilated to have risen to grandee status in the Spanish-dominated society." Library J

The characters "all seem real, believable and fascinating. They epitomize the author's ability to transmute historic significance into human dimensions. Frank O'Rourke . . . has a special way with words, too, which frequently lends touches of beauty to what is always a fast-paced narrative." Christian Science Monitor

Instant gold. Morrow 1964 155p o.p. 1970

This title "describes what happens when a remarkable trio of twentieth-century alchemists put on the market a product that actually does become gold when sea water is added. Having outwitted gangsters, entrepreneurs, the U.S. Treasury Department, and the FBI, all of whom want to take control, the three broadcast their formula, close their shops, and disappear, leaving the public a moral and economic lesson which is promptly forgotten." Booklist

The swift runner. Lippincott 1969 352p $6.95

"Doc Neely, once the best horse thief in the country, sly as a fox, cunning as a coyote, inventor of the finest tricks, sets out to right the wrong done him and to pull the pieces of his life together after serving a seven-year prison sentence for horse stealing. Knowing that all men are exiles from their youth and that for the weak the dream of paradise exists only through faith in legend, Doc assembles his cast and lays his plans for a chase that covers a wide sweep of the West in the early days of this century." Library J

"A grand and glorious western. . . . Comedy, marvelously exciting chase sequences, a genuine feeling for the land and for horses, and a nice touch of romance, all make this great fun. Doc's team—an orphan boy, an ex-bum, a retired Mississippi riverboat man, a con artist, a former actress and a retired madam—could have come straight out of Bret Harte or Mark Twain." Pub W

Orwell, George

y Animal farm; illus. by Joy Batchelor and John Halas. Harcourt 155p illus $3.75

First published 1945 in England
"A stinging, allegorical satire directed at communism and its ramifications. It all happens on Farmer Jones's farm where one day the animals rise up against . . . [his] cruelty, drive all human beings away and set up a supposedly Utopian government. How the clever, unscrupulous pigs gradually gain ascendancy over the other creatures is related with effective and devastating wit." Bookmark

"It is absolutely first-rate. . . . Mr. Orwell has worked out his theme with a simplicity, a wit, and a dryness that are closer to La Fontaine and Gay, and has written in a prose so plain and spare, so admirably proportioned to his purpose, that 'Animal Farm' even seems very creditable if we compare it with Voltaire and Swift." New Yorker

A clergyman's daughter. Harcourt 1960 320p $4.95

First published 1935 in England
The central figure of this satirical novel is Dorothy Hare, daughter of a tyrannical rector. She loses her memory and finds herself in London, penniless and unable to make her living. She gets a job for a time in the hopfields and later in a horrible girls' school. When the scandal over her departure from home has died down, Dorothy returns once more to her arduous duties of running the parish." Book Rev Digest

"A minor novel in Gissing's tradition, a shade more lively as to tone, rendered in a quiet fluent texture which has a way of making detail count, and garnished with modest incidental ironies." Books

Coming up for air. Harcourt 1950 278p $4.95

First published in England 1939
"George Bowling won seventeen pounds on a horse one day and, utterly disheartened by the machine-made urban world at home, and by his wife's narrow outlook, decided to blow the money on a visit to the small village where he spent his childhood, in search of a way of life that he remembered as natural and sane. But complete disillusionment awaited him . . .

Orwell, George—*Continued*

for the modern world he tried so hard to escape pursued him without remorse . . . and his attempt to 'come up for air' was a complete failure." Huntting

Keep the aspidistra flying. Harcourt 1956 248p $4.95

First published in England 1936

"Gordon Comstock, part-time poet and bookstore assistant, believes that Britain's coat of arms should be the aspidistra plant—the symbol of the middle-class 'money world' that he despises. The author turns his satirical guns on a variety of types and characters, including Gordon himself with stunning effect." McClurg. Book News

"Not pretty, but powerful, accurate, and fair. This book projects as do few others the desperate expedients and blind rage of the educated moneyless. And Orwell's power is wielded responsibly. Neither the rebels nor the hucksters are romanticized, nor is life—which wins in the end." Chicago Sunday Tribune

y Nineteen eighty-four. Harcourt 1949 314p $5.75

"A satirical novel about a future time when people living in a collectivist society are persuaded by Thought Police into thinking that ignorance is strength and war is peace. The chief character is an average man, Winston Smith, whose work in the Ministry of Truth consists of falsifying records when state policy changes." Book Rev Digest

It "is a profound, terrifying, and wholly fascinating book. . . . Orwell's theory of power is developed brilliantly, at considerable length. And the social system that it postulates is described with magnificent circumstantiality." New Yorker

Osborne, Helena

The yellow gold of Tiryns. Coward-McCann 1969 221p $5.95

"A young English schoolmarm, Lydia Barnett, is hired by a rich American woman, Mrs. Erskine to give her a guided tour of Greece. Visiting a fabled isle, Lydia becomes enmeshed in a plot to steal priceless Greek treasures, buried by a German archaeologist and missing for years. At first the police suspect Lydia, but, aided by a romantically-inclined Oxford professor, they zero in on a group of on-location movie makers instead." Pub W

The author "wastes very little time on ruminations and the build-up of suspense, she jumps right into the story and races it along. . . . She has told us a story with directness and skill. Women readers will love it." Best Sellers

Osbourne, Lloyd

(jt. auth.) Stevenson, R. L. The wrecker

Ott, Wolfgang

Sharks and little fish. [Tr. by Ralph Manheim] Pantheon Bks. 1958 431p o.p. 1970

Original German edition published 1956.

A translation by Oliver Coburn was published in England in 1957

"This sea novel of World War II depicts naval warfare from the German side. The central figure is a young man. Teichmann, thrown at the age of seventeen into the horror and cruelty of modern war." McClurg. Book News

This novel "provides a powerfully grim picture of naval warfare from the German viewpoint. . . . It is a searing indictment of war. It is quite understandable that this novel should have raised a considerable storm of controversy in the author's native Germany." Springf'd Republican

Ouida

Under two flags; a novel. Stein & Day [1967 c1966] 537p (Doughty lib) $6.95

First published 1867

The Honorable Bertie Cecil "a young nobleman and an officer in the Life Guards . . . travels in fashionable circles. Though deep in debt, he is a gallant young man ,loved by the ladies and admired by the men. When he is accused of forgery he lets the accusation stand in order to save a woman's honor. He flees to Africa and joins the Foreign Legion, serving

gallantly. He is condemned to death for striking a superior officer who insulted a noblewoman, but he is saved from a firing squad by a camp follower who loves him and takes the bullets in her own body." Magill. Cyclopedia of Literary Characters

"The numerous episodes of exciting action, foxhunts in the shires, battles of French and Kabyles in Algeria, are well described, and the book is full of imagination of an Oriental kind. The characters are all idealizations of good or bad and stand out well." Baker's Best

Ousmane, Sembene

God's bits of wood; tr. by Francis Price. Doubleday 1962 333p o.p. 1970

A "novel, based on fact, about a strike in 1947 by native African workers on the railroad running through French West Africa, from Dakar on the coast to the distant Niger River in the center of the continent. . . . [The author] a native of what is now the Senegal Republic . . . shows how the native African people were affected by the impact of European technological developments, and the strains and stresses which resulted. . . . The title comes from a native saying that people are 'God's bits of wood.' " Springf'd Republican

"A proletarian novel whose vigor arises not from its characters and situations but rather from the African background which is its real hero." N Y Her Trib Books

Owens, William A.

Look to the river. Atheneum Pubs. 1963 185p boards $3.95

A novel about the adventures of a runaway boy "who in part of the story runs off in company with a Negro from a chain gang. The time is 1910, the place is the Red River plains of Texas, and the special strength of the story, besides its fine, unpretentious picture of the farm lands and the people, is the boy's integrity, in keeping to the bargains he makes, helping the unfortunate, oppressed Negro, and sticking to his friends." Pub W

P

Packer, Vin

Don't rely on Gemini. Delacorte Press 1969 209p $4.95

"A TV writer, who thinks astrology is a lot of bunk, is working with an irascible and bossy lady astrologer on a program about the subject. The hunt for an 'astral twin,' someone born at the same moment in the same latitude and longitude, turns up the writer's exact opposite number in a psychologist who is having marital troubles. The two men's lives and marriages get mixed up together and since the psychologist is very soon revealed as at least a potential murderer an element of danger enters in. Nice little touches of local Gramercy Park and Nyack-Sneden's Landing atmosphere, some believable husband-and-wife dialogue and just enough astrological lore to make you wonder a little." Pub W

Page, Elizabeth

y The tree of liberty. Farrar, Straus 1939 985p $7.50

"Matthew Howard, frontiersman, and his wife Jane Peyton, of Tidewater Virginia, are the central figures in this long novel of the making of the nation. Matthew was a friend and follower of Jefferson. Jane was an aristocrat who feared and distrusted Jefferson and his ideas. From their marriage just before the Revolution, to the time their grandson, another frontiersman established his home in Ohio in 1806, their family circle and its widespread affiliations epitomized the political history of the country, the conflicting loyalties to different leaders, the economic differences, and the regional partisanships as a nation was fused from colonies." Booklist

Page, Elizabeth—*Continued*

"It is all very old-fashioned, and a little un-real. . . . Yet this is not to disparage either the historical authenticity or the sincerity of Miss Page's performance. An immense amount of research is skillfully concealed in the nar-rative and it cannot be said that the book does injustice to any of the important characters or episodes of our history. And the story it-self—clear, straight-forward, skillfully contrived and gracefully told has a vitality that sustains it to the end." N Y Times bk R

Wilderness adventure. Rinehart 1946 309p map o.p. 1970

"A girl is carried off by the Indians, and John Howard and his son, who loves the girl, with her father and a French woodsman start in pursuit. The chase takes them from Virginia to the Mississippi, through country where the French are fighting the English, to New Or-leans where they are thrown in prison. All ends happily, after they have travelled to France and England." Booklist

"Miss Page is adept at describing the life and resourcefulness of the American pioneer and her novel is a good historical adventure despite some monotony in the narrative." On-tario Lib Rev

Paley, Grace

The little disturbances of man. Viking [1968 c1959] 189p $4.50

Analyzed in Short Story Index
First published 1959 by Doubleday
"A superb group of stories about sexy little girls, loving and bickering couples, enven-omed suburbanites, yowling job-hunters in an America that is nutty but so recognizable that it hurts." McClurg. Book News

Contents: Goodbye and good luck; A wom-an, young and old; The pale pink roast; The loudest voice; The contest; An interest in life; An irrevocable diameter; The used-boy raisers; A subject of childhood; In time which made a monkey of us all; The floating truth

Palmer, Marian

The white boar. Doubleday 1968 373p $6.95

"A major historical novel about loyalty and treason in the court of the brilliant, contro-versial King who was Richard III, last of the Plantagenets. 'The White Boar' is the story of the Lovell cousins—Francis, who became Rich-ard's Lord Chamberlain, and Phillip, a shad-owy figure behind the throne who served as a secret ambassador. The author presents an his-torically accurate view of feudalism in the pro-cess of destroying itself. This is a beautifully written, excellently researched 'first' novel." Am News of Bks

"Mrs. Palmer must be commended for her extensive research which provides the reader with an excellent sketch of English life in the 15th century. Her description of life at the great manor houses, like the household of the Earl of Warwick at Middleham, and the royal court, are indeed magnificent." Best Sellers

Palmer, Stuart

Hildegarde Withers makes the scene, by Stuart Palmer and Fletcher Flora. Random House 1969 182p boards $4.50

Hildegarde Withers is called out of her Flor-ida retirement by her old friend, Oscar Piper, Captain of the NYPD. She traces Lenore Greg-ory, a VIP's missing daughter, to San Fran-cisco and finds the girl is going on a "pilgrim-age" aboard the yacht Karma with fifteen or twenty pilgrims. A dead body upsets the plans as Hildegarde has to find the real murderer amongst the hippies in order to clear Lenore of the charge

Pargeter, Edith. See Peters, Ellis

Parker, Dorothy

The collected stories of Dorothy Parker; with a foreword by Franklin P. Adams. Mod-ern Lib. 1942 362p $2.95

Analyzed in Short Story Index
A reprint of the title first published by Vik-ing, 1939 with title: Here lies

Contents: Arrangement in black and white; Sexes: Wonderful old gentleman; Telephone call; Here we are: Lady with a lamp; Too bad; Mr Durant; Just a little one; Horsie; Clothe the naked; Waltz; Little Curtis; Little hours; Big blonde; From the diary of a New York lady; Soldiers of the republic; Dusk before fireworks; New York to Detroit; Glory in the daytime; Last tea; Sentiment; You were perfectly fine; Custard heart

Dorothy Parker; with an introduction by W. Somerset Maugham. Viking 1944 544p (Viking Portable lib) $5.95

Partially analyzed in Short Story Index
A collection of poems and stories
Stories included are: Lovely leave; Arrange-ment in black and white; The sexes; Standard of living; Mr Durant; The waltz; Wonderful old gentleman; Song of the shirt, 1941; Telephone call; Here we are; Dusk before fireworks; You were perfectly fine; Mrs Hofstadter on Jose-phine Street; Soldiers of the republic; Too bad; Last tea; Big blonde; Just a little one; Lady with a lamp; Little hours; Horsie; Glory in the daytime; New York to Detroit; Custard heart; From the diary of a New York lady; Cousin Larry; Little Curtis; Sentiment; Clothe the naked

Parks, Gordon

y   The learning tree. Harper 1963 303p $5.95

"A small town in Kansas in the 1920's is set-ting for the story of a year in the life of a teen-age boy. The usual personal and family crises, degrees of understanding and misunderstand-ing between children and adults, first experi-ence of sex, and a touching first experience of love are parts of Newt's growing up. But also part of his experience is consciousness of being a Negro in a community where the behavior of the individual Negro affects the community's reaction to all Negroes." Booklist

"This first novel by versatile (sometime mu-sician, renowned photographer) Gordon Parks is not written with resentment, but rather with rueful reminiscence, even humor. It is an un-assuming and thoroughly conventional book, but it has freshness, sincerity, and charm." Library J

Parrish, Anne

A clouded star. Harper 1948 242p $5.95

"A very old Negro, Samuel, tells in retrospect his experiences with Harriet Tubman, the ex-slave who acted as guide on the underground railroad. As a small boy Samuel accompanied Harriet and eight others on a journey to Can-ada." Book Rev Digest

Pasinetti, P. M.

Venetian red. Random House 1960 503p $4.95

This novel has been rewritten in English by the author from the original Italian edition published in Rome 1959

"Set in Italy just before World War II, this is the story of two families—one direct and ruthless, the other concerned with things of the mind and spirit—and their personal and poli-tical conflicts." Bk Buyer's Guide

"The feeling of the times is re-created. But this is not only the story of political differ-ences; a much larger struggle is depicted—the struggle between good and evil, freedom and tyranny. The combination of the subtly drawn characters, the carefully delineated scenes and the ever-critical theme results in an absorbing book." Library J

Passos, John dos. See Dos Passos, John

Pasternak, Boris

Nobel Prize in literature, 1958

Doctor Zhivago [Tr. from the Russian by Max Hayward and Manya Harari]

Some editions are:
Modern Lib. $4.95
Pantheon Bks. $5

First published 1957 in Italy
A "long novel, which traces the life of a Rus-sian from 1900 to 1929. . . . It is a powerful and enormously interesting work, which, while perhaps not on a par with 'War and Peace,'

Pasternak, Boris—*Continued*

with which it has frequently been compared, gives a vivid picture of what it was like to be a Russian in those years and to feel the impact of the tremendous events of the times. There are dozens of characters. The hero [Zhivago, physician and poet] his wife, from whom he is separated by the Bolsheviks, and another woman whom he loves are especially fine creations." Pub W

"By its sweep, its understanding of man's fate, its deep humanity and religious feeling, its sense of tragedy and joyous love of life, [this novel] is in the tradition of the great Russian novels of the nineteenth century." N Y Her Trib Books

Pater, Walter

Marius the Epicurean. Dutton 1934 267p (Everyman's lib) $2.95

First published 1885
A philosophic romance. "The hero is a young Roman noble of the time of Marcus Aurelius, and the book records his 'sensations and ideas' rather than outward events. Though he makes no formal profession of Christianity, Marius is greatly drawn to it through his friend Cornelius and his own high principles and deeply religious nature. His death is of such a nature that the Christian Church looks upon him as a martyr." Benét. The Reader's Encyclopedia

Paton, Alan

y   Cry, the beloved country

Some editions are:
Scribner $3.95 Has subtitle: A story of comfort in desolation
Watts, F. $9.95 Large type edition. A Keith Jennison book

First published 1948
This "widely read and influential novel [tells the moving story of a Zulu country parson who comes to Johannesburg to find that the environment has forced his sister to become a prostitute and his son a murderer. The language is Biblical and poetic." Benét. The Reader's Encyclopedia

"As it stands, 'Cry, the Beloved Country' commends itself to readers as an outstanding example of a creative effort embodying social comment. The story, the characters, and the problems are all memorable. The book suggests that there are men of good intentions everywhere, but not enough of them to rebuild society in terms of justice, equality, and generosity." Survey G

Tales from a troubled land. Scribner 1961 128p $3.95

Analyzed in Short Story Index
Contents: Life for a life; Sponono; Ha'penny; The waste land; The worst thing of his life; The elephant shooter; Debbie go home; Death of a tsotsi; The divided house; A drink in the passage

"Most of the tales are told from the point of view of a compassionate white director of a boys' reformatory; however, one of the most moving concerns a native shepherd who, though innocent, becomes a victim when his employer is robbed. A small but significant book by an author eminently qualified to write on an important theme." Booklist

Too late the phalarope. Scribner 1953 276p $4.95

"The story is basically that of a well loved white police lieutenant who in his need turns to a native girl. He is betrayed, reported and thus brings shame on himself and his family. The narrator of the story is an aunt who fills in the entire picture of family pride, righteous disdain, unbending adherence to an imposed restriction, and the falsity of many basic customs in parts of South Africa." Library J

"The book is written with superb simplicity. It is cadenced but unaffected; it will inevitably be called Biblical and yet there is no conscious parodying of scriptural prose. It flows relentlessly to its crisis, and sometimes we cry out at its power. The people are all clear and real, the South African backgrounds are colorfully and deeply etched. The conflicts are diverse but they all contribute to the basic struggle: father and son, races, languages, prejudices." Christian Science Monitor

Patton, Frances Gray

y   Good morning, Miss Dove; illus. by Garrett Price. Dodd 1954 218p illus $3.95

"Miss Dove had taught geography in the same school for thirty-five years: some people in town thought that was too long. Miss Dove was a stern disciplinarian with old-fashioned ideas and ideals, but on the April day when she was stricken in the classroom the whole town came to realize how much Miss Dove had meant in their lives." Book Rev Digest

"If sentiment as well as selection has been at work here, it is sentiment of a highly superior variety. Leavened with wit and sound common sense, written with an unerring rightness of touch, the whole book rings with the truth about human nature in its nicer aspects." N Y Her Trib Books

also in Costain, T. B. ed. More Stories to remember v2 p 1-95

Twenty-eight stories. Dodd 1969 375p $7.50

"This collection of short stories appears to be based on the experiences of a college faculty wife. . . . The reader meets stock characters from a small, Southern college town setting. . . . Descriptions, language, and style seem to come out of the late 1940's." Library J

Contents: Grade 5B and the well-fed rat; The music of the spheres; The educated classes; Elinor and the normal life; Remold it nearer; A friend of the court; In a Philadelphia park; And hearts in heaven; The representative ham; First principles; The terrible Miss Dove; The falling leaves; A nice name; An honored guest; Apricot pie; The finer things of life; Mothers and daughters; A little obvious; The second-grade mind; A spring motif; The homunculus; The house below the street; As man to man; Loving hands at home; The mimosa blight; The game; The man Jones; A piece of luck

Pavese, Cesare

Among women only

In Pavese, C. The selected works of Cesare Pavese p175-275

The beach

In Pavese, C. The selected works of Cesare Pavese p3-56

The Devil in the hills

In Pavese, C. The selected works of Cesare Pavese p279-390

The house on the hill

In Pavese, C. The selected works of Cesare Pavese p59-171

The selected works of Cesare Pavese; tr. from the Italian and with an introduction by R. W. Flint. Farrar, Straus 1968 xxiii, 390p $6.95

This translation contains four short novels: The beach (published 1942); The house on the hill; The Devil in the hills; Among women only (all published 1949)

"Postwar Turin figures in these novel as background for middle-class characters who act out melancholy tales of loneliness and alienation." Pub W

Pearson, Diane

The marigold field. Lippincott 1969 315p boards $6.50

"From the turn of the century to the end of World War I, this novel follows the fortunes of two families in that transitional period when the English rural poor began to set their sights on the world beyond the squire's domain. The central characters are Jonathan Whitman, who educates himself from books borrowed from the library of the estate on which he works, and Anne-Louise Pritchard, whose obsession is to marry Jonathan. She goes off to service in London when he marries another, and samples the wicked life of music halls and mashers. Eventually, she returns home to trap Jonathan into marrying her when he comes back from the Boer War and finds his first wife dead." Pub W

Pearson, Drew

The senator. Doubleday 1968 447p $6.95

"A provocative novel about a corrupt Senator—the kind who passes legislation to promote his own financial interests—and the behind-the-scenes political, fiscal, and sexual activities he dabbles in." McClurg. Book News

"Disclosures about abuses of power and double-dealings . . . are given fictional form in this novel. . . . Overextended and weak as a novel, the story is interesting for its disclosures of practices and traditions in the U.S. Senate, and portrayal of senators, both bad and good, many of whom are evidently drawn in full or in part from actual persons." Booklist

Peebles, Melvin van. See Van Peebles, Melvin

Pentecost, Hugh

Dead woman of the year; a John Jericho mystery novel. Dodd 1967 183p o.p. 1970

"A Red badge mystery"

"Lydia Trask has been named Woman of the Year and a reporter scheduled to do a feature article on her arrives at her apartment [at the same time] as a beautiful model, a stand-in for Lydia's TV appearances. Some one throws acid . . . in her face and she dies in agony. Was the acid meant for Lydia? The police seek valiantly for the perpetrator of the most vicious of crimes. Then John Jericho, a painter and former lover of Lydia's is asked to help." Best Sellers

"This is a whodunit for readers who like them both urbane and romantic." Pub W

The gilded nightmare; a Pierre Chambrun mystery novel. Dodd 1968 214p boards $3.95

"Red badge mystery"

"Two highly sophisticated and complex killers prowl the plush corridors of New York City's top luxury hotel, the Beaumont, while two intended victims dine and dance and sleep without anxiety because they haven't the remotest idea that they are marked for murder." McClurg. Books News

Girl watcher's funeral; a Pierre Chambrun mystery novel. Dodd 1969 184p $3.95

"Red badge mystery"

"Nikos was murdered in the bar of New York's plush Hotel Beaumont, surrounded by the people who had the most to lose by his death. Possessing a fortune astronomical even for a Greek tycoon, he was noted for his generosity as well as for his ruthlessness. Pierre Chambrun, the resident manager of the Beaumont, knew that among the beautiful women and the ambitious men was a murderer, hiding behind a mask of shock and grief. Before he could penetrate the killer's disguise there was a second victim, and the hotel had become a bloody testing ground between the forces of good and evil." Am News of Bks

The golden trap. Dodd 1967 183p o.p. 1970

"Red badge mystery"

"Even after he had retired from his job as espionage agent, Lovelace was threatened with death. At least he would run no more. He went to his old friend, manager of one of New York's most expensive hotels, and together they set a trap. Was it to catch Lovelace, or his hunter?" Bk Buyer's Guide

"The mystery itself, however romantic and unrealistic, is a good one." Pub W

Percy, Walker

The moviegoer. Knopf 1961 241p boards $4.95

"National Book Award, 1961"

"Binx Bolling is an intelligent, successful young New Orleans businessman, who goes to the movies avidly. He goes because the world has become actually more real to him on the screen than in life. Action takes place in one week—Carnival Week—during which Binx's dreamlike existence is disrupted, and he re-discovers his strength and his capacity to love." Huntting

"Actually, Mr. Percy has done a remarkably skillful job in pointing up the despair and meaninglessness in so much of our modern-day life. In terms of a young New Orleans businessman's addiction to the movies, he has drawn an indelible picture of one man's escape into fantasy." Springf'd Republican

Perez Galdos, Benito

Doña Perfecta; tr. by Mary J. Serrano, introduction by William Dean Howells. Harper 1896 319p o.p. 1970

Original Spanish edition published 1876

"The social problem which engrosses so much of the author's interest, the struggle between scientific and social enlightenment and the tyrannous obscurantism of the church, is here set forth in the domestic conflict of a group of characters and the political strife agitating a provincial town. Dona Perfecta is a devout lady whose daughter is sought by a promising young man, a representative of modernism. A wily priest is her chief ally, and eventually the rival intrigues drag in a host of forces on either side, the anarchic elements that exist beneath the surface in modern Spain being strikingly revealed." Baker's Best

The spendthrifts; with illus. by Charles Mozley, introduction by Gerald Brenan. Farrar, Straus 1952 282p illus (The Illustrated novel lib) o.p. 1970

Translated from the Spanish by Gamel Woolsey

"This comic novel takes place during 1868, just before an uprising against a corrupt government, and relates the trials of the Bringas family. Francisco Bringas, a government employee residing in the Royal Palace, has a wife, Rosalia, who is so fond of good clothes that she cannot help borrowing money to satisfy her desires. How she finds herself being dragged down by the whirlpool of debt, how she endeavors to keep knowledge of her condition from Francisco, and how she finally rescues herself from a perilous situation form the central story." Library J

Peterkin, Julia

Scarlet Sister Mary. Berg 345p $7.50

Pulitzer Prize, 1929

A reprint of the title first published 1928 by Bobbs

"A slender, darting, high-spirited girl married at 15 to the wildest young buck on the plantation' and deserted within a year is the Scarlet 'Si Maye' of the story, who keeps her high spirits as she fills her house with a new child year after year. A sympathetic, colorful tale, with mingled humor and pathos, revealing the fineness as well as the weaknesses and superstitions of the Gullah Negro of South Carolina." N Y Libraries

Peters, Elizabeth

The Camelot caper. Meredith 1969 247p boards $4.95

"An American girl on her first visit to England is pursued by dark villains and rescued by a young man who writes paperback Gothics. The settings, Salisbury, Wells, Glastonbury and Bath, are rendered with fidelity, and make a romantic backdrop for the story. Most intriguingly of all, the motive, when it is uncovered, has little to do with stolen gems or anything so mundane. It is, we may say without giving too much away, a brilliant and scholarly ploy based on the latest archaeological findings." Pub W

"Fun all the way, and delightfully preceptive on the Arthurian legends." Library J

The jackal's head. Meredith 1968 244p $4.95

"Althea Tomlinson arrives in Luxor traveling incognito in order to clear the name of her late father, falsely accused of forging antiquities. Althea makes a series of startling discoveries, but finds herself a prisoner within some dark tomb walls. Modern Egypt is the setting for this swiftly moving Gothic tale." McClurg. Book News

"Well-maintained suspense and atmosphere add to this entertaining Gothic romance set in the present but bound up in the past through a search for Nefertiti's tomb." Booklist

Peters, Ellis

The grass-widow's tale. Morrow 1968 205p boards $5.95

"Bunty Felse feels like a grass widow when her police inspector husband goes off to London on a case and her college-age son seems too preoccupied to come home for her birthday. Feeling lonely, she visits a pub by herself for the first time and accepts a drink and a drive home from a distraught young man who says he has just been jilted. Bunty's compassion turns to horror when she discovers a girl's corpse in the trunk of the young man's car." Library J

"A compassionate and suspenseful story, written with great insight." N Y Times Bk R

y The house of green turf. Morrow 1969 220p $5.50

"A car crash on the way to her concert in Liverpool sends Maggie Tressider, a gifted, dedicated, and famous soprano, into shock, and makes her feel that a dead man is pressing on her heels. At her surgeon's suggestion she hires Francis Killian, a respected private inquiry agent, to search through her past to find the answer. His research leads him to Bunty Felse, and her memories of the European tour ten years before when Maggie's genius was first recognized, and when a member of the group on the tour vanished in Scheidenau in the Volburg." Library J

"A very good mystery with some eerie touches, an alternatively attractive but threatening Austrian atmosphere, and a plot that sees Ellis Peters' detective husband and wife team of George and Bunty Felse playing key, if lookers-on roles." Pub W

The piper on the mountain. Morrow 1966 248p o.p. 1970

"Did British agent Terrell die by accident or was he killed because he had found a trail to [Karol] Alda, vanished with hush-hush plane secrets? His step-daughter Tossa decided to find out, and set off for Czechoslovakia with three Oxford classmates [and Dominic Felse]. A spy story with too many detectives and lots of action." Bk Buyer's Guide

Who lies here? Morrow 1965 [c1964] 265p boards $3.95

"Detective Inspector George Felse with Bunty and their eighteen-year-old son, Dominic, was vacationing in Cornwall when Dominic 'rescued' young Paddy Rossall from the dangerous water. Paddy thought he had seen a body but there was no body—until that of a villager was found in the two centuries old stone coffin of Jan Treverra." Bk Buyer's Guide

Petrakis, Harry Mark

A dream of kings. McKay 1966 180p $4.50

Leonidas Matsoukas, a Greek in the United States "operates a counseling service that supplements his winnings at gambling. Affirmative in his outlook, Matsoukas believes if he can get enough money to take his retarded, dying son back to Greece, the sun will rejuvenate him. An affair with a widow, a first futile attempt at cheating in gambling, and a series of relapses in his son's health culminate in Matsoukas and his son boarding an airplane for Greece." Library J

Matsoukas "tackles life vigorously, with gusto and with imposing and eloquent invective for his creditors and enemies. He is a magnificent hero, however pursued by the Furies, and his Greek-American big-city neighborhood is a picturesque, boisterous, intensely human environment for him." Pub W

The waves of night, and other stories. McKay 1969 230p $5.95

Contents: Rosemary; The sweet life; The shearing of Samson; The witness; The bastards of Thanos; End of winter; The victim; Chrisoula; Homecoming; Dark eye; The waves of night [novella]

"There aren't many short-story writers left these days like Harry Mark Petrakis, who declines to fall into a pattern. . . . For him, material dictates form and tone, as witness this collection of tales, some of them with a traditionally solid beginning-middle-end, others

that are more in the nature of character studies, and all of them, in this reader's view, touched with a humane observer's concern for the lot of his fellowman." Book of the Month Club News

Petrov

(jt. auth.) Ilf. Ilf & Petrov's The complete adventures of Ostap Bender

Petry, Ann

The street. Houghton 1946 435p o.p. 1970

"The story of a Negro mother's struggle to protect her nine year old son from the debasing influences of the mean street in Harlem on which she is forced to live. Her hard-won civil service job doesn't pay enough to provide better living quarters, even if such were open to colored tenants. A night club promises a way out but results in tragedy." Wis Lib Bul

"Fine piece of realistic writing conveying what it means to be a Negro in this white world. Comparable to An American Tragedy in stature and execution." Library J

Peyrefitte, Roger

Knights of Malta; tr. from the French by Edward Hyams. Criterion Bks. [distributed by Phillips] 1959 317p $5.95

Original French edition 1957

"A novel of intrigue, based upon the attempt, in the early 1950's, by an ambitious cardinal to bring the powerful, wealthy, international Order of Malta under the control of the Vatican." Book Rev Digest

"The book is not only continuously interesting, it is also extremely funny, especially when familiar figures from the real world of Vatican politics appear in the story. . . . But along with the sharply told gossip and the harsh clatter of M. Peyrefitte's often cruel laughter there is a solider element. A true nobility resides in the Knights' loyalty to each other and to their lost and anachronistic cause." New Yorker

The prince's person; tr. by Peter Fryer. Farrar, Straus [1965 c1964] 212p $4.95

Original French edition 1963. This translation first published 1964 in England

This book "tells of a marriage contract between [Vincenzo I Gonzaga, Prince of Mantua] and a daughter of the Medici. Because of a rumored doubt of the prince's virility, one clause of this contract, required a public test prior to the marriage." Library J

"To tell a tale of bawdy Peyrefitte deploys all the graces of his style. Nuance, delicate thrust, allusion, humorous understatement, and the strictest propriety of language keep the story from foundering in its offensiveness. He is an artist, not a pornographer. A historian, too, if you will, of impressive erudition—but still an artist, who makes fact and document cast their own spell within a most terse narration." Sat R

Pharr, Robert Deane

The book of numbers. Doubleday 1969 374p $5.95

This first novel is set in a Southern city in the 1930s. "Two itinerant Negro waiters named Dave Greene and Blueboy Harris make themselves rich by setting up a thriving numbers bank in the city's ghetto. . . . [The racket brings Dave] power only at the cost of respectability, and even that power is sharply circumscribed. The plot springs from his search for moral equilibrium. . . . His mistress Kelly Sims, a college-educated chemist . . . banks her hopes for Negro progress on intellect. His eventual wife, Lila, a . . . country girl, has the 'black granite' endurance that was once popularly thought to be the essential quality of the Negro race. . . . [All of the] characters are destroyed in one way or another, even Blueboy." Newsweek

Philips, Judson Pentecost. See Pentecost, Hugh

Phillips, William

(ed.) Great American short novels. Dial Press 1946 682p o.p. 1970

Analyzed in Short Story Index
"Each novel is accompanied by a critical introduction by William Phillips which relates it to American writing and to American life as a whole." Huntting
Contents: Benito Cereno, by H. Melville; Washington Square, by H. James; Maggie, by S. Crane; Melanctha, by G. Stein; False dawn, by E. Wharton; The great Gatsby, by F. S. Fitzgerald; Pale horse, pale rider, by K. A. Porter; The pilgrim hawk, by G. Wescott

Pick, Robert

(ed.) German stories and tales. Knopf 1954 371p o.p. 1970

Analyzed in Short Story Index
Contents: Youth, beautiful youth by H. Hesse; Kannitverstan, by J. P. Hebel; An episode in the life of the Marshal de Bassompierre, by H. von Hofmannsthal; Lukardis, by J. Wassermann; Krambambuli, by M. von Ebner-Eschenbach; Cardiac suture, by E. Weiss; The message that failed, by M. Heimann; Rock crystal, by A. Stifter; The bachelor's death, by A. Schnitzler; Unexpected reunion, by J. P. Hebel; Mona Lisa, by A. Lernet-Holenia; The picnic of Mores the cat, by C. Brentano; Zerline, the old servant girl, by H. Kesten; The metamorphosis, by F. Kafka; A little legend of the dance, by G. Keller; Death in Venice, by T. Mann; The hussar, by J. P. Hebel

Pincherle, Alberto. See Moravia, Alberto

Pirandello, Luigi

Nobel Prize in literature, 1934

Horse in the moon; twelve short stories; tr. from the Italian and with an introduction by Samuel Putnam. Dutton 1932 238p o.p. 1970

Analyzed in Short Story Index
Contents: Horse in the moon; Adriana takes a trip; Cat, a goldfinch and the stars; Schoolmistress's romance; Dinner guest; Sunlight and shadow; Goy; Imbecile; Miss Holloway's goat; Light across the way; Wee sma' drop; Sicilian limes

The late Mattia Pascal; tr. by William Weaver. Doubleday 1964 252p o.p. 1970

Original Italian edition published 1904; first English edition 1923
"A comedy which points the moral, that it is vain for a man to seek reality outside the circle wherein his own character and mode of life have circumscribed him. A librarian, weary of his monotonous existence and of harassing relatives, takes advantage of an accident to assume a new personality and a more colourful life in Rome. All goes well until he falls in love; he realizes then that he is a living lie with no place in the scheme of things. But when he decides to fake another accident, throw off his assumed character and return home, he finds that his wife re-married and his old existence too is closed to him." Baker's Best

The outcast; authorized tr. from the Italian by Leo Ongley. Dutton 1925 334p o.p. 1970

"For three generations the wife of the head of the house of Pentagora had been false to her husband. Marta, also, the innocent young wife of Rocco of the fourth generation, was hastily judged, condemned and cast out to be harried by the outside world. A masterly, moving story." Cleveland

Short stories; selected, tr. and introduced by Frederick May. Oxford 1965 xxxvi, 260p (Oxford Lib. of Italian classics) $5.75

Analyzed in Short Story Index
This "collection contains twenty-one stories, carefully edited, which show the breadth of [Pirandello's] unique talent." Cincinnati
Contents: The little hut; The cooper's cockerels; A dream of Christmas; Twelve letters; Fear; The best of friends; Bitter waters; The jar; The tragedy of a character; A call to duty; In the abyss; The black kid; Signora Frola and her son-in-law, Signor Ponza; The man with the flower in his mouth; Destruction of the man; Puberty; Cinci; All passion spent; The visit; The tortoise; A day goes by

Plagemann, Bentz

The best is yet to be. Morrow 1966 288p $4.95

Sequel to: Father to the man
Now that their son "Cameron is married, the Wallaces decide to go vacationing, but find in Italy that they still have problems with the young, in this case an American girl who tries to dodge a too-attentive Italian." Bk Buyer's Guide
"An amusing story of a couple's adjustment to the marriage of their only son, this novel also gives insight into the relationships between the generations from the point of view of the parents. . . . [The author] wears rose-colored glasses and writes slickly, so that the book is not as realistic as it might be but, in spite of these drawbacks, it makes good reading, particularly for those in the same stage of life as the protagonists." Library J
Followed by: A world of difference

Father to the man. Morrow 1964 223p o.p. 1970

A father pictures the passage from adolescence to manhood of his son "Goggle," also known as Cameron. The novel starts in the summer before Cam's "entrance into Princeton, looks in a bit on that disaster, follows him through a tour with the Coast Guard, and ends in the winter of his confrontation with his parents over a matter of marriage." Publisher's note
"All in all, this is a pleasant, worldly-wise little novel that should provide middle-aged parents with some enjoyable hammock reading." America
Followed by: The best is yet to be

A world of difference. Morrow 1969 219p boards $4.95

Sequel to: The best is yet to be
"With his son married and far flown from the family nest, Bill Wallace thought he had it made. Not so! Not only was he forced to come to grips with the facts of his own life—including several . . . struggles with Broadway and Hollywood producers—but there was the matter of the new family next door. Tim Bailey introduced him to the world of social protest, and in that challenging arena Bill and his . . . wife Kate were forced to reexamine all their old values—for better or for worse." Am News of Bks
"This book was not written for the jet-set, not for kooks, hippies, SDS'ers, not any others who are in the headlines. It was written for ninety-five percent of humanity, the average person who enjoys life, is thankful for what he or she has, and is only too willing to share it with his neighbor. In other words, this is a wholesome, true to life story to be enjoyed by everyone except those included in the first sentence, and those of similar tendencies." Best Sellers

Plaidy, Jean

The sixth wife. Putnam [1969 c1953] 252p $5.95

First published 1953 in England
"It is the spring of 1543 and Henry VIII is 52 years old. Having put his fifth wife, Catharine Howard, to death, he wants to take a sixth, and his choice is Lady Latimer, Katharine Parr, fiancee of his brother-in-law, Sir Thomas Seymour. This is Katharine Parr's story, from the time she became Henry VIII's queen until her death." Publisher's note
"All the figures of history are here: Mary Tudor and Elizabeth, the young frail Edward VI, Lady Jane Grey, the Herberts and the Suffolks and the Seymours, the Tower of London, the torture chambers, the heretics and heretic-baiting—all the persons and the panoply and the cruelty of the Tudor era—and the story of Katharine Parr appears to be authentic. If this seems to me to lack the intensity, the roar and gusto that properly belongs to this period in history, it is an entertaining and even absorbing novel and should draw a wide woman audience." Best Sellers

Playboy

The Playboy Book of horror and the supernatural; selected by the editors of Playboy. Playboy Press 1967 391p $5.95

Analyzed in Short Story Index
Contents: Softly walks the beetle, by J. Collier; Heavy set, by R. Bradbury; Nasty, by F. Brown; Sardonicus, by R. Russell; Sorcerer's moon, by C. Beaumont; First anniversary, by R. Matheson; The jam, by H. Slesar; Beelzebub, by R. Bloch; The machine in Ward Eleven, by C. Willeford; The Academy, by D. Ely; The manuscript of Dr Arness, by G. Wilson; The party, by W. F. Nolan; Burnt toast, by M. Reynolds; Rendezvous, by J. Christopher; Side by side, by J. Tomerlin; The sea was wet as wet could be, by G. Wilson; Hey, look at me, by J. Finney; For the rich they sing—sometimes, by K. W. Purdy; I'm yours, by C. Schafhauser; Double exposure, by J. Reese; The taste of fear, by H. G. Foster; No such thing as a vampire, by R. Matheson; Virginia, by C. Tomkins; Black country, by C. Beaumont; The traveling salesman, by R. Bloch; Weird show, by H. Gold; The life work of Juan Diaz, by R. Bradbury; Comet wine, by R. Russell

"Some people will turn away from this book under the assumption that since it bears the 'Playboy' imprint it must contain salacious material. If they do, they are certainly the losers, for the stories 'Playboy' prints are well written, well plotted, and by reputable authors . . . and the book is certainly recommended for those who like well-written horror or parapsychic stories." Library J

The Playboy Book of science fiction and fantasy; selected by the editors of Playboy. Playboy Press 1966 403p $5.95

Analyzed in Short Story Index
"The best s-f and fantasy from 'Playboy' . . . twenty-five in all." Bk Buyer's Guide
Contents: The fly, by G. Langelaan; Blood brother, by C. Beaumont; Love, Incorporated, by R. Sheckley; A foot in the door, by B. J. Friedman; The vacation, by R. Bradbury; The never ending penny, by B. Wolfe; Bernie the Faust, by W. Tenn; A man for the moon, by L. Webb; The noise, by K. W. Purdy; The killer in the TV set, by B. J. Friedman; I remember Babylon, by A. C. Clarke; Word of honor, by R. Bloch; John Grant's little angel, by W. Grove; The fiend, by F. Pohl; Hard bargain, by A. E. Nourse; The nail and the oracle, by T. Sturgeon; After, by H. Slesar; December 28th, by T. L. Thomas; Spy story, by R. Sheckley; Punch, by F. Pohl; The crooked man, by C. Beaumont; Who shall dwell, by H. C. Neal; Double take, by J. Finney; Examination day, by H. Slesar; The mission, by H. Nissenson; Waste not, want not, by J. Atherton; The dot and dash bird, by B. Wolfe; The sensible man, by A. Davidson; Souvenir, by J. G. Ballard; Puppet show, by F. Brown; The room, by R. Russell; Dial "F" for Frankenstein, by A. C. Clarke

Plievier, Theodor

Berlin; a novel; tr. by Louis Hagen and Vivian Milroy. Doubleday 1957 446p map o.p. 1970

Original German edition published 1954. This translation first published 1956 in England

Completes the trilogy begun in Stalingrad and Moscow, entered separately

This World War II novel about the conquest of Berlin in 1945 describes the fall of Nazi Germany's queen city and the chaotic period following the fall. It tells among other things of the Soviet annexation of important assets, the redrawing of allegiances, and the anxiety and fright of a divided land. (Publisher)

"With this novel Plievier added the final, flaming centerpiece to his grim and terrible triptych on the horrors of war." N Y Her Trib Books

Moscow; tr. from the German by Stuart Hood. Doubleday 1954 [c1953] 318p o.p. 1970

English edition first published 1953
This panoramic novel "depicts early stages of Hitler's attack on Russia very vividly [and] tells in a sequence of remarkable chapters how the horrors of the campaign affected high officers and common soldiers on both sides. A grim story, but well worth reading." Library J

"Moscow, no novel in the ordinary sense of plot and character, is a stunning documentary of victory, defeat, brutality and horror." Time

Stalingrad; tr. from the German by Richard and Clara Winston. Appleton 1948 357p o.p. 1970

"A fictionalized recital of the siege of Stalingrad, this book tells the story from the standpoint of the German troops who took part in that horror. Starting with a description of a penal battalion engaged in burying corpses, the complete encirclement of the German Sixth Army follows. The retreat toward the center of the city, disintegration of units and men, complete collapse of morale and final surrender succeed each other in deadly progression. A brutal, realistic book, it is not light reading, but contains some very fine writing." Library J

Plunkett, James

Strumpet city; a novel. Delacorte Press 1969 533p $6.95

Set in Dublin, Ireland. "The background of the story is the stormy labor movement of the early 20th century, and in its depiction of the agonizing struggles of Irish working men against the power of the Establishment. . . . Many men and women move through these pages, playing out their personal dramas, and they come to life all the more believably because they are as fallibly human as we are: a slum landlord, a priggish young priest and a drunken older one, an Anglo-Irish Protestant who is moved to join his cause with that of the workers and the laboring men themselves, and their women." Pub W

"The author has a nice sense of period and the gentle pomposities of Edwardian Dublin are carefully evoked. . . . He has, for example, a good eye for the physical atrocity of extreme poverty. . . . He also has a keen anti-clerical sense. . . . [This novel] will satisfy a large number of readers, both inside Ireland and elsewhere." New Statesman

Poe, Edgar Allan

The best tales of Edgar Allan Poe; ed. with an introduction by Sherwin Cody. Boni & Liveright 1924 476p o.p. 1970

Analyzed in Short Story Index
Contents: Ms. found in a bottle; Descent into the Maelstrom; Thousand-and-second tale of Scheherazade; Mellonta Tauta; Devil in the belfry; X-ing a paragrab; The sphinx; Imp of the perverse; The assignation; Ligeia; Fall of the House of Usher; Masque of the Red Death; Murders in the Rue Morgue; Purloined letter; Gold-bug; William Wilson; Black cat; Man of the crowd; Berenice; Tell-tale heart; Cask of Amontillado; Hop-Frog; Pit and the pendulum; Facts in the case of M. Valdemar; Prose poems; Studies in landscape

y Complete stories and poems of Edgar Allan Poe. Doubleday 1966 819p $5.95

Partially analyzed in Short Story Index
This volume contains five sections: Tales of mystery and horror; Humor and satire; Flights and fantasies; The narrative of A. Gordon Pym of Nantucket [novelette, published 1838] and The poems

Short stories included are: The murders in the Rue Morgue; The mystery of Marie Rogêt; The black cat; The gold-bug; Ligeia; A descent into the Maelstrom; The tell-tale heart; The purloined letter; The assignation; Ms. found in a bottle; William Wilson; Berenice; The fall of the House of Usher; The cask of Amontillado; The pit and the pendulum; A tale of the ragged mountains; The man of the crowd; Morella; "Thou art the man"; The oblong box; The conversation of Eiros and Charmion; Metzengerstein; The masque of the Red Death; The premature burial; The imp of the perverse; The facts in the case of M. Valdemar; Hop-Frog; The system of Doctor Tarr and Professor Fether; The literary life of Thingum Bob, Esq.; How to write a Blackwood article; A predicament; Mystification; Loss of breath; The man that was used up; Diddling;

Poe, Edgar A.—*Continued*

The angle of the odd; Mellonta Tauta; The thousand-and-second tale of Scheherazade; X-ing a paragrab; The business man; A tale of Jerusalem; The sphinx; Why the little French-man wears his hand in a sling; Bon-Bon; The Duc De l'Omelette; Three Sundays in a week; The Devil in the belfry; Lionizing; Some words with a mummy; The spectacles; Four beasts in one; Never bet the Devil your head; The balloon-hoax; Mesmeric revelation; Eleanora; The unparalleled adventure of one Hans Pfaall; King Pest; The island of the Fay; The oval portrait; The domain of Arnheim; Landor's cottage; The power of words; The colloquy of Monos and Una; Von Kempelen and his discovery

The complete tales and poems of Edgar Allan Poe; with an introduction by Hervey Allen. Modern Lib. 1938 1026p (Modern Lib. giants) $4.95

Partially analyzed in Short Story Index
Stories included are: Unparalleled adventure of one Hans Pfaall; The gold-bug; The balloon-hoax; Von Kempelen and his discovery; Mesmeric revelation; Facts in the case of M. Valdemar; Thousand-and-second tale of Scheherazade; Ms. found in a bottle; Descent into the Maelström; Murders in the Rue Morgue; Mystery of Marie Roget; Purloined letter; The black cat; Fall of the House of Usher; Pit and the pendulum; Premature burial; Masque of the Red Death, Cask of Amontillado; Imp of the perverse; Island of the Fay; Oval portrait; The assignation; Tell-tale heart; System of Doctor Tarr and Professor Fether; Literary life of Thingum Bob, Esq.; How to write a Blackwood article; A predicament; Mystification; X-ing a paragrab; Diddling; Angel of the odd; Mellonta Tauta; Loss of breath; Man that was used up; The business man; Maelzel's chessplayer; Power of words; Colloquy of Monos and Una; Conversation of Eiros and Charmion; Shadow—a parable; Silence—a fable; Philosophy of furniture; Tale of Jerusalem; The sphinx; Man of the crowd; Never bet the Devil your head; "Thou art the man"; Hop-Frog; Four beasts in one; The homocameleopard; Why the little French-man wears his hand in a sling; Bon-Bon; Some words with a mummy; Magazine-writing—Peter Snook; The quacks of Helicon—a satire; Astoria; Domain of Arnheim; Landor's cottage; William Wilson; Berenice; Eleonora; Ligeia; Morella; Metzengerstein; Tale of the Ragged Mountains; The spectacles; Duc De l'Omelette; Oblong box; King Pest; Three Sundays in a week; Devil in the belfry; Lionizing; Narrative of A. Gordon Pym

Edgar Allan Poe; selected and ed. with an introduction and notes, by Philip Van Doren Stern. Viking 1945 xxxviii, 664p (Viking Portable lib) o.p. 1970

Partially analyzed in Short Story Index
In six parts: Letters, Tales, Articles, Criticism, Poems and Opinions
The tales included are: William Wilson; Tale of the Ragged Mountains; Eleonora; Oval portrait; Man of the crowd; Ms. found in a bottle; Descent into the Maelström; Pit and the pendulum; Premature burial; The assignation; Berenice; Morella; Ligeia; Fall of the House of Usher; Facts in the case of M. Valdemar; Masque of the Red Death; Tell-tale heart; Black cat; Cask of Amontillado; Hop-Frog; Murders in the Rue Morgue; Mystery of Marie Roget; Purloined letter; The gold-bug

The murders in the Rue Morgue
In Poe, E. A. The purloined letter [and] The murders in the Rue Morgue p 1-55

Narrative of A. Gordon Pym of Nantucket
In Poe, E. A. Complete stories and poems of Edgar Allan Poe p611-736

The narrative of Arthur Gordon Pym; with design by René Clark. Heritage 1955 267p o.p. 1970

First published 1838; introduction by Joseph Wood Krutch
A Gothic tale of horror type of story presented as the journal of Pym, a young man who was smuggled aboard a ship owned by the father

of a friend. Mutiny, cannibalism, fantastic animals and natives of the Antarctica, and supernatural happenings comprise a tale of adventure in the South Seas. The story has been considered a celebrated literary hoax by some and by others a profound symbolic enactment of man's search for logic and meaning

The purloined letter [and] The murders in the Rue Morgue; illus. by Rick Schreiter. Watts, F. 1966 85p illus $3.95

Two short stories featuring Poe's detective, Monsieur C. Auguste Dupin. In "The murders in the Rue Morgue," Dupin solves a particularly horrible murder to which there is apparently no clue. "The purloined letter" sets 'a different sort of problem, but again Monsieur Dupin, drawing on his deep knowledge of human nature, finds the answer." Publisher's note

Selected stories and poems
Some editions are:
Watts, F. $7.95 Large type edition, complete and unabridged. A. Keith Jennison book. Selected and with an introduction by Floyd Zulli
Watts, F. $4.95 A Watts Ultratype edition, complete and unabridged. With a critical and biographical profile of Edgar Allan Poe by Joseph Wood Krutch

Contents: The murders in the Rue Morgue; The mystery of Marie Roget; The black cat; The gold-bug; A descent into the Maelström; The tell-tale heart; The purloined letter; The cask of Amontillado; The pit and the pendulum; The masque of the Red Death; Annabel Lee; To Helen; The city in the sea; The raven; Ulalume; Eldorado; The bells; A dream within a dream; Sonnet: To science; Alone; To one in Paradise; A poean

Short stories; selected short stories and poems; ed. by Floyd Zulli. Large type ed. complete and unabridged. Watts, F. [1967] 363p $8.95

"A Keith Jennison book"
Partially analyzed in Short Story Index
Stories included are: The murders in the Rue Morgue; The mystery of Marie Roget; The black cat; The gold-bug; A descent in the Maelström; The tell-tale heart; The purloined letter; The cask of Amontillado; The pit and the pendulum; The masque of the Red Death

y Tales
Some editions are:
Dodd (Great illustrated classics) 4$.50 With 16 full-page illustrations of the author, his family and environment, and reproductions from previous editions, together with an introductory biographical sketch and captions by Laura Benét
Dutton (Everyman's lib) $2.95 Has title: Poe's Tales of mystery and imagination; introduction by Padraic Colum

Analyzed in Short Story Index
Contents: William Wilson; A tale of the Ragged Mountains; The domain of Arnheim; Landor's cottage; The elk; The Island of the Fay; The Sphinx; The gold-bug; The man of the crowd; Shadow; Silence; The colloquy of Monos and Una; The conversation of Eiros and Charmion; The fall of the House of Usher; The assignation; Ligeia; Eleonora; Berenice; Morella; The oval portrait; King Pest; The masque of the Red Death; The cask of Amontillado; Metzengerstein; The pit and the pendulum; Hop-Frog; A descent in the Maelström; Ms. found in a bottle; The premature burial; The facts in the case of M. Valdemar; The tell-tale heart; Mellonta Tauta; The thousand-and-second tale of Scheherazade; The oblong box; The spectacles; X-ing a paragrab; The imp of the perverse; The balloon hoax; The murders in the Rue Morgue; The mystery of Marie Roget; The purloined letter; "Thou art the man"; Loss of breath; Bon-Bon; The Devil in the belfry; The black cat

y Tales and poems of Edgar Allan Poe; illus. by Russell Hoban; afterword by Clifton Fadiman. Macmillan (N Y) 1963 338p (The Macmillan classics) $4.95

Contains the following stories: The murders in the Rue Morgue; A descent into the Maelström; Ms. found in a bottle; The balloon-hoax; The purloined letter; The fall of the House of

Poe, Edgar A.—*Continued*

Usher; The pit and the pendulum; The black cat; The cask of Amontillado; Some words with a mummy; The man that was used up; The Sphinx; The system of Doctor Tarr and Professor Fether; The tell-tale heart; The masque of the Red Death; The gold-bug; The premature burial

Tales of mystery and imagination. Oxford [1964] 419p $2.75

Analyzed in Short Story Index
Contents: The gold bug; The facts in the case of M. Valdemar; Ms. found in a bottle; A descent into the Maelström; The murders in the Rue Morgue; The mystery of Marie Rogêt; The purloined letter; The fall of the House of Usher; The pit and the pendulum; The premature burial; The black cat; The masque of the Red Death; The cask of Amontillado; The oval portrait; The oblong box; The tell-tale heart; Ligeia; Loss of breath; Shadow—a parable; Silence—a fable; The man of the crowd; Some words with a mummy

Pohl, Frederik

The age of the pussyfoot. Trident Press 1969 191p boards $4.95

In this science fiction novel "the hero is Forrester, and he had been burned to death. But not permanently—for the medical science of six centuries of progress had learned how to freeze a man at the instant of dying, hold him in the slow dreamless calm of the liquid helium chambers and bring him back to life with all his mortal ills healed." Am New of Bks
"Should a stylist of satirical science fiction underscore his prophecies of warning by use of foreword and afterword comments? . . . In the afterward, Pohl supports his futuristic society as being, chillingly, 'maybe not even five decades away' rather than five centuries." Library J

The space merchants, by Frederick Pohl and C. M. Kornbluth. Ballantine 1953 179p o.p. 1970

"In a future world where Congress is made up of senators from large corporations, and armed warfare occurs between advertising agencies, Mitch Courtney is assigned by his advertising company to sell people the idea of emigrating to Venus. He is opposed by a rival agency, an underground organization, and his wife." Huntting
Here is "integration of melodramatic plot with an infinitely detailed depiction of a logically developed world. Whether you want entertainment or sharp social criticism don't miss this!" N Y Her Trib Books

(ed.) Galaxy Magazine. The [first]-tenth Galaxy reader

(ed.) If. The If Reader of science fiction

Poldermans, Joost

Vincent; a novel based on the life of Van Gogh. Holt 1962 317p o.p. 1970

In this novel based on "letters, excerpts from diaries, and other biographical records, the author tells of Vincent's unhappy home life, his hunger for love, his dependence on the affection of his brother Theo, his dedication to his art, and at last the madness that destroyed him." Bk Buyer's Guide
"This is not the Vincent of romantic legend or the artist in a mythical world, but a man of flesh and blood in a real world not too distant from our own. Sympathy, with Poldermans, is shown by the constraint of understatement." Library J

Pope, Dudley

Drumbeat. Doubleday 1968 279p $4.95

Sequel to: Ramage
First published 1967 with title: Ramage and the drumbeat. Sequel to: Ramage
"Lieutenant Nicholas Ramage continues his naval career by rescuing his marchioness. On the way he captures a Spanish frigate, loses his ship, 'Kathleen,' is taken prisoner, but escapes to warn England of an invasion." Cincinnati

y Ramage; a novel. Lippincott 1965 302p boards $5.95

During the Napoleonic Wars, Lieutenant Ramage of His Majesty's Royal Navy carries through a secret mission to rescue Italian noblemen sympathetic to the British cause, faces a court-martial, completes a mission which Lord Nelson assigned hoping to disprove the accusations, and wins a marchesa. (Publisher)
"We have been waiting too long for a thoroughly good post-Forester story of naval adventure; here it is." Book of the Month Club News
Followed by: Drumbeat

The Triton brig. Doubleday 1969 378p $5.95

A sea adventure set in 18th century England and the West Indies as well as on the high seas
"In the third of the author's series about the adventures of Lieutenant Lord Ramage of the British Navy, Ramage is again issued a challenging order. Assigned to the brig 'Triton,' Ramage must stop an incipient mutiny and solve the mystery of the disappearing trading schooners." Cincinnati
The author's "expert but simply related knowledge of naval lore lends so much authenticity that, if one closes his eyes, one can almost taste salt and feel the sting of sea spray. Pope's characters are real people, his vignettes of sea life in the British Navy and his account of the Spitshead Mutiny are the work of a naval historian." Best Sellers

Popkin, Zelda

Herman had two daughters. Lippincott 1968 382p $6.95

"Through the stories of Celia and Jessie Weiss told by their friend Sam Rosenbaum, we watch the change in Jewish life from the strongly religious ghetto people of Grady's Mills, Pennsylvania, to the prosperous, less committed Celia Sloan (ex-Slomowitz) the pretty girl who married well; clever Jessie who exploited her people in her plays; and Sam, the journalist." Bk Buyer's Guide
"Undoubtedly, there is an attempt to record the changing view which the Jewish people are taking toward their role in society." Best Sellers

Porter, Katherine Anne

The collected stories of Katherine Anne Porter. Harcourt 1965 495p $6.95

Pulitzer Prize, 1966
Analyzed in Short Sory Index
Contains three collections: Flowering Judas, and other stories (1935); The leaning tower, and other stories (1944); Pale horse, pale rider (1939), and four additional short stories: Virgin Violeta; The martyr; The fig tree, and Holiday

Flowering Judas and other stories: María Concepción; Virgin Violeta; The martyr; Magic; Rope; He; Theft; That tree; The jilting of Granny Weatherall; Flowering Judas; The cracked looking-glass; Hacienda
Pale horse, pale rider: Old mortality; Noon wine; Pale horse, pale rider
The leaning tower, and other stories: The old order; The downward path to wisdom; A day's work; Holiday; The leaning tower

Flowering Judas, and other stories. Harcourt 1935 285p (Harbrace Modern classics) $2.95

Analyzed in Short Story Index
Contents: María Concepción; Magic; Rope; He; Theft; That tree; Jilting of Granny Weatherall; Flowering Judas; Cracked looking-glass; Hacienda

also in Porter, K. A. The collected stories of Katherine Anne Porter p3-170

The leaning tower, and other stories. Harcourt 1944 246p o.p. 1970

Analyzed in Short Story Index
"Nine pieces; six of them give further glimpses of Miranda and the Southern family portrayed in the author's 'Pale horse, pale rider.' " Booklist

Porter, Katherine A.—*Continued*

Contents: The source; The witness; The circus; The old order; The last leaf; The grave; The downward path to wisdom; A day's work; The leaning tower

also in Porter, K. A. The collected stories of Katherine Anne Porter p321-495

Noon wine

In Porter, K. A. The collected stories of Katherine Anne Porter p222-68

In Porter, K. A. Pale horse, pale rider p93-176

Old mortality

In Porter, K. A. The collected stories of Katherine Anne Porter p173-221

In Porter, K. A. Pale horse, pale rider p3-89

Pale horse, pale rider; three short novels. Harcourt 1939 264p $5.75

Analyzed in Short Story Index
Contents: Old mortality; Noon wine; Pale horse, pale rider

also in Phillips, W. ed. Great American short novels p577-624

also in Porter, K. A. The collected stories of Katherine Anne Porter p173-317

Pale horse, pale rider [story]

In Porter, K. A. The collected stories of Katherine Anne Porter p269-317

In Porter, K. A. Pale horse, pale rider p179-264

Ships of fools. Little 1962 497p $6.95

"An Atlantic Monthly Press book"
Taking the title from a fifteenth-century German allegory Miss Porter presents a modern allegory in describing the microcosm of a ship sailing from Mexico to Germany in 1931. Aboard the passenger-freight carrier are 46 first-class passengers and almost 900 Spaniards in the steerage, the latter a poverty-stricken, almost faceless lot being returned to their native land because of a drop in the Cuban sugar market. Each of the first-class passengers and some of the crew and the steerage passengers are subjected to a dispassionate scrutiny and most are seen as fools if not knaves; a few enlist sympathy but seldom respect." Booklist
"Miss Porter's image, as she points out, is the simple, universal one of the 'ship of this world on its voyage to eternity'; her theme is human folly—the evil done by innocence, the destructiveness of love; further irony derives from the voyage's time and destination. A rich, complex novel of rare distinction in both aim and execution; for all fiction collections." Library J

Porter, William Sydney. See Henry, O.

Portis, Charles

Norwood. Simon & Schuster 1966 190p $3.95

"Norwood is a decent country boy, just out of the Marines, who makes a crazy journey from Texas to New York to get $70 owed him by an old pal—and ends up on the road back, by bus, with a midget friend, a trained chicken, and a girl just as quietly beat, yet as full of hope, as he is. This is more like early Steinbeck than Kerouac and should find appreciative readers." Pub W

y True grit; a novel. Simon & Schuster 1968 215p $4.95

Also available in a large type edition for $6.95
"Mattie Rose tells soberly of her amazing—and funny—adventures as a fourteen-year-old, when she set out into the wilds of the Indian Territory with Rooster Gogburn, a fast gun marshal, to punish the miscreant who had shot her father." Bk Buyer's Guide

"You will find here a most agreeable little novel, told in the mock-serious style the author attributes to a woman looking back upon the great adventure of her life.... The atmosphere seems genuine and the events she takes part in have the ring of truth. . . . The tone is low-keyed and light even while the doings recounted are chiefly dark. This could, one suspects, turn out to be a pioneering work in a new school of storytelling about old-time adventures in the American West." Book of the Month Club News

Post, Laurens van der. See Van der Post, Laurens

Potok, Chaim

y The chosen; a novel. Simon & Schuster 1967 284p $4.95

Also available in large type edition at $7.95
"Danny and Reuven grew up in the Williamsburg section of Brooklyn, but lived in entirely different worlds. They met at a baseball game between their two Jewish parochial schools, which turned into a holy war. This is a story of friendship; of fathers and sons; and a fine portrayal of Orthodox and Hasidic beliefs." English Speaking Union
"The writing is warm and natural, the characterization well developed. The propounding of the Talmud, which is central to this story, may very well put off many readers, Jewish and non-Jewish. However, the novel has much to offer and should please many readers." Library J

y The promise. Knopf 1969 358p $6.95

"Reuven Malter and Danny Saunders, the two close friends encountered in the author's earlier novel 'The chosen' are, in this sequel, young men whose lives are beginning to take shape around their chosen vocations: for Reuven, the rabbinate, for David, clinical psychology. Their two worlds, increasingly separated by occupational and personal involvements, are brought in touch again through a complex situation centering on Michael Gordon, a brilliant adolescent heading toward complete breakdown." Booklist
"The somewhat mechanical writing exhibited in 'The Chosen' shows up again. Yet, the characters continue to be recognizable and moving, not literary abstractions. The message seems to be that there is slightly more good than evil in the world, so those who keep plugging away serving their conscience are likely to come out on the plus side of life's ledger. That kind of guarded optimism is pleasant to encounter in these days when most novelists are saying it's all hopeless and meaningless." Best Sellers

Potter, Nancy A. J.

We have seen the best of our times; short stories. Knopf [1969 c1968] 242p boards $4.95

Date on title page: 1968
"A collection of [12] short stories examining the loneliness of the human condition in twentieth century America." Chicago
Contents: We have seen the best of our times; Just tell me all your troubles; The crooked man; In union sweet; The old gardener's daughter-in-law; The saved man; Sunday's children; There won't be any scars at all; Divorcing the dead husband; The happiest you've ever been; The collection; Somewhere between the sky and the ground we try to live

Potts, Jean

The little lie. Scribner 1968 159p $3.95

"It begins quietly enough, with a strong-willed woman telling 'a little lie' out of hurt pride. She hides from her family and friends the fact that she has been suddenly jilted and pretends her lover has just gone out of town looking for a new job. . . . Jean Potts builds up an altogether plausible tale of some ordinary people increasingly entangled in deception, torn by a family fight and getting nearer and nearer to violence every minute. Little Mr. Fly, the schoolteacher, quite unwittingly becomes the 'deus ex machina' that brings a whole elaborate structure of lies toppling down in a murderous finale. 'The Little Lie' is very well told." Pub W

Powell, Anthony

The acceptance world

In Powell, A. A dance to the music of time v3

At Lady Molly's

In Powell, A. A dance to the music of time: second movement v 1

A buyer's market

In Powell, A. A dance to the music of time v2

Casanova's Chinese restaurant

In Powell, A. A dance to the music of time: second movement v2

A dance to the music of time. A question of upbringing; A buyer's market [and] The acceptance world. Little 1962 3v in 1 $6.95

An omnibus volume of three titles published separately 1951, 1953 and 1955 respectively. In the author's "The Music of time" series

"'A Question of Upbringing' introduces Nick Jenkins in 1921 as a student at Eton, takes him to France for a summer, and shows him at Oxford. We meet several of his schoolfellows. . . . There is Widmerpool, for example, who is noted for wearing the wrong kind of overcoat. . . . With 'A Buyer's Market' we move into the later Twenties. . . . 'The Acceptance World' brings us to the early Thirties. . . . The climax is a dinner . . . that Nick and other old boys give in honor of Le Bas, master of their house at Eton." Sat R

A dance to the music of time: second movement. Little [1964] 3v in 1 $6.95

An omnibus edition of three novels, the fourth through sixth, published separately in the author's: The Music of time series and available at $4.95 each

Contents: At Lady Molly's; Casanova's Chinese restaurant; The kindly ones

At Lady Molly's, first published 1957, is a satiric picture of London society in pre-World War II era, personified by a group of characters who turn up for an evening at Lady Molly's "at homes"

Casanova's Chinese restaurant, first published 1960 takes place in "England during the Spanish Civil War and the Abdication. The theme: the interrelationships between 'smart' society and the poverty-stricken Bohemianism of the time. The characters are the people who frequent Casanova's Chinese restaurant." Hunting

The kindly ones, first published 1962, is a portrait of English society between World Wars I and II. The novel opens with the last summer of Nicholas Jenkins' childhood at the old mansion of Stonehurst. Among the inhabitants are Bilson, the neurotic maid, and Dr Trelawney, high priest of a mystic cult. In the following section which continues to the outbreak of World War II, the emotions and actions of all the characters are intensified as England moves through an atmosphere of impending calamity. (Publisher)

The kindly ones

In Powell, A. A dance to the music of time: second movement v3

The military philosophers. Little [1969 c1968] 243p (The Music of time) boards $4.95

First published 1968 in England

The ninth volume of the authors series entitled, The Music of time and the third volume of a trilogy within the series dealing with the Second World War

In this novel "the time span is 1942, from the fall of Singapore, through the years of the V-2 bombs and increasing Allied triumphs, to the great victory celebration in St. Paul's Cathedral. Nicholas Jenkins, the narrator and central figure in each of the books, is now part of a London War Office Section working closely with officers of the Allied forces, including certain proud exile groups. . . . Focusing on individuals, many of them old friends and acquaintances from earlier novels in the series, others lively newcomers . . . [the author describes] the war years as they were lived by a certain class of Englishman." Pub W

"Powell characteristically writes about men who happen to be in uniform, fundamentally unchanged, rather than about soldiers. . . . [His] readers will find themselves on familiar ground, running into old acquaintances, picking up allusions from earlier books, breathing an atmosphere that is as distinct as Jane Austen's or Proust's, its slightly old-fashioned air fully redeemed by Mr. Powell's humor and sophistication. But this is no place for a new reader to join in. The three wartime books are far more interdependent than any of the others and, in any case, the whole sequence should be read from the beginning, leisurely and with relish." Christian Science Monitor

A question of upbringing

In Powell, A. A dance to the music of time v 1

The soldier's art. Little [1967 c1966] 227p (The Music of time) boards $4.95

The eighth volume of the author's series entitled, The Music of time and the second volume of a trilogy within the series dealing with the Second World War

In this book "narrator Jenkins records the workings of a British training camp in 1940-1941. Personal interests and petty power struggles among officers are in the foreground with only faint echoes of the war on the Continent and an undemonstrative attitude toward German bombings of England, but a change in tone is foreshadowed in the last pages as the German invasion of Russia is announced." Booklist

The valley of bones. Little 1964 242p (The Music of time) $4.95

The seventh volume of the author's series entitled, The Music of time and the first volume within the series dealing with the Second World War

"Nicholas Jenkins, the narrator, now in his thirties, is second lieutenant in the Welsh infantry, installed in backwater posts of Ireland and Wales. The tediousness and insignificance of military duty on the home front is . . . portrayed." Publisher's note

What's become of Waring. Little 1963 236p boards $4.95

First published 1939 in England

A humorous novel about "the delicate, jealous maneuverings inside an English publishing house and the sad fate of the publisher's best-selling author . . . a very glamorous, very expensive young woman who drifts in and out of the story." Pub W

"The quest for the historical Waring becomes the wildly entangled pursuit and exposure of a literary charlatan, and involves a gallery of British comic types, on the whole rather broadly sketched. . . . The action moves from the center, in London, to an archetypal English country house, to the French Riviera. There is laughter all the way." N Y Times Bk R

Powell, Richard

The Philadelphian. Scribner 1956 376p o.p. 1970

"Covering four generations of a Philadelphia family . . . this novel begins with an untutored Irish immigrant girl in 1857, and ends with her great-grandson—a successful Philadelphia lawyer astride the very top of the social ladder." Publisher's note

"It lays bare the customs, habit patterns and state of mind that have been functioning independently from the rest of the Republic for 250 years." San Francisco Chronicle

Pioneer, go home! Scribner 1959 320p $4.95

The story of the Kwimper family and how they fared when the government stopped "providing . . . Relief and Unemployment Compensation and aid to Dependent Children. . . . Stalled on an untravelled road in a southern state, the Kwimpers claim squatter's rights to a bit of unclaimed land and try to hold it against the massed onslaught of the Government, of social workers, of gangsters, of hunger and poverty, and of Mother Nature herself." Publisher's note

"Mr. Powell's book is a free-wheeling farce with a certain amount of real satiric bite." Book of the Month Club News

Power, Richard

The hungry grass. Dial Press 1969 288p $5.95

This is "the story of [the last days of] an ordinary Irish country parish priest, a man beset by very human failings and weaknesses, who seems never to have done anything remarkable, and is painfully aware of his own failings, his own submerged longings for another kind of life than the priesthood." Pub W

This novel "is an intimate account, undramatic on the surface but roiling underneath with self-confrontation, digging inward to bare various bleak truths about the clerical life. . . . Mr. Power's achievement is to transcend the banality of this life without sentimentalizing or condemning it. [This] is a sad book but not a bitter one." Sat R

Powers, J. F.

Morte d'Urban. Doubleday 1962 336p $4.50

Winner of the 14th annual National Book Awards

The author "writes about a priest belonging to an impoverished religious order who just can't help being quite an operator—for the good of the order. Under his skillful manipulations the tottering order flourishes. But Father Urban is really a good man and a good priest and when the chips are down he makes a series of small decisions involving principle that cost him his popularity and his rich benefactors. He winds up, an aging failure even to his fellow priests.' Pub W

Powers' "novel presents a delightful catalogue of characters and originals comparable to that of the 'Canterbury Tales,' and like Chaucer, Powers writes from an honest Catholic point of view. Despite its satire on clerical types, petty jealousies of the religious orders, and frailties of the religious. . . . 'Morte d'Urban' never questions the Faith. Powers uses corrosive irony to expose the problems of religion and the religious life in modern society." N Y Her Trib Books

Prince of Darkness, and other stories. Doubleday 1947 277p o.p. 1970

Analyzed in Short Story Index
Contents: The Lord's day; The trouble; Lions, harts, leaping does; Jamesie; He don't plant cotton; The forks; Renner; The valiant woman; The eye; The old bird. a love story; Prince of Darkness

Poyer, Joe

North Cape. Doubleday 1969 231p (Doubleday Science fiction) $4.95

"The time is the mid-1970's. A lone pilot is flying the latest supersonic spy plane over the Russo-Chinese border, recording border incidents for American propaganda purposes. Rushing to meet him at a refueling rendezvous, the nuclear powered destroyer, RFK, is fighting its way through the worst Atlantic storm of the century. The pilot of the spy plane discovers that the Russians are out to get him at all costs." Pub W

Prebble, John

The buffalo soldiers. Harcourt 1959 256p o.p. 1970

"Lieutenant Byrne. Irish-born former Union Army sergeant, with a small detachment of Negro troops [detailed to escort a band of Comanches on their last buffalo hunt before confinement to a reservation] goes after the Comanche Quasia, who has fled the reservation and killed one child and kidnapped another. The chase crosses the Staked Plains, where thirst and hardship take a toll of the troops and Indians. This is a fine adventure story, but in addition it is an excellent character study. The three-color racial issue is an important element. Here are no heroes, just people." Library J

Premchand

The gift of a cow; a translation of the Hindi novel, Godaan; tr. by Gordon C. Roadarmel. Ind. Univ. Press 1968 442p (UNESCO Collection of representative works: Indian ser) $7.95

First published 1936 in India

Set in India, "the story concerns a poor farmer and his dream of owning a cow. Through Hori Ram's devious, sometimes foolish, sometimes humiliating experiences and those of one of his sons who goes to the city a cross-section of the life of India's poor in village and city is clearly drawn. The compassionate portrayal of characters makes them real." Booklist

Prescott, H. F. M.

The man on a donkey; a chronicle. Macmillan (N Y) 1952 631p illus o.p. 1970

"Forming the background for this story is the tragic North Country rebellion in 1536 when the commons and their captains tried to save the monasteries from suppression, and to resist the attacks of Henry VIII on the church. It is the chronicle of the lives of five main persons whose stories portray the life in 16th-century England from the Royal Court to the peasant's hovel." Huntting

"A unique achievement. It blends fine scholarship with great literary imagination and it has sweep and a breadth that one had forgotten could belong to the historical novel." New Statesman & Nation

Son of dust. Macmillan (N Y) 1956 288p illus o.p. 1970

First published in England 1932

"Except for its comparative brevity, this romance set in eleventh-century Normandy is strongly reminiscent of Zoé Oldenbourg's tales of medieval France. Fulcum Geroy and Alde of Fervacques elope believing that Alde's husband is dead: when he appears, battered, but alive Alde's conscience compels her to return to him. Fulcum, indoctrinated with a monastic relative's belief that God demands the whole of one's love, endeavors to put Alde out of his mind, but a wise and understanding abbot paves the way for an eventual reunion by convincing Fulcan that God is not the enemy, but the giver of all love." Booklist

Prévost, Abbé

Manon Lescaut; tr. from the edition of 1731 by Helen Waddell, and with an introduction by George Saintsbury. Dutton 262p o.p. 1970

First published 1731

"Manon is a young harlot with whom the Chevalier des Grieux falls madly in love. He gives up his studies to follow her. They elope. Manon shortly proves faithless. The rest of the story details Manon's infidelities and des Grieux' inability to give her up. In a way Manon loves him, but not as much as she loves the luxuries other lovers provide. When finally she is arrested as a common prostitute and transported to the colony of Louisiana, des Grieux, who has already given up fortune, family and friends, goes with her. He almost commits murder for her sake. After her death he is unable to pick up the pieces of a ruined life." Haydn. Thesaurus of Book Digests

Prévost, Antoine François. See Prévost, Abbé

Price, Eugenia

The beloved invader; a novel. Lippincott 1965 284p $5.95

"A fictionalized account of the life's work of Anson Dodge, an actual person, in rebuilding a St Simons Island church that had been vandalized during the Civil War. The narrative begins with young Dodge, a Northerner, coming to the Georgia island to help look after his wealthy family's business and his discovery of the neglected church that aroused his compassion. Although a sentimental tone pervades the telling this is interesting, especially to women, as the story of a dedicated man." Booklist

Followed by: New moon rising

y New moon rising. Lippincott 1969 281p $5.95

"This second novel in a proposed trilogy about St. Simon's Island, Georgia, follows 'The Beloved Invader.' . . . Based upon actual history, the new story, of pre-Civil War life and strife and Civil War days, has been researched with . . . care. The central character is Horace Bunch Gould. His story starts, amusingly

Price, Eugenia—*Continued*

enough, when he is dismissed from Yale in [1830] for his part in a student rebellion. He returns to St. Simon's during the uneasy days of Nat Turner's uprising. Before Horace eventually goes off to war, he works the family plantation, marries, produces nine children, and develops a troubled conscience about slavery." Pub W

"The novel is well out of the mainstream of current writing with its almost mercifully prim approach to sex, birth, and death. Certainly no one can complain if this book were to fall into the hands of an innocent child; but the literate child would find it wearisome." Best Sellers

Price, Reynolds

A generous man. Atheneum Pubs. 1966 275p $4.95

Set in North Carolina "young Milo Mustian (15, going on 16) is the central figure of this narrative which concentrates on some kind of change in him (boy to man) in the period of three days. He has no father: a mother, Emma, is as ineffectual as her name is vapid: a brother Rato and a younger sister Rosacoke. Rato has a sick dog, Phillip, and before long we are involved with Lois Privo, the snake girl, a python, and a hunt in the woods for the mad dog Phillip, the python Death, and good old Rato." Best Sellers

"The story of a three-days' quest after life, [sex] and love combines, in the telling, elements of magic, mystery, broad rural humor, and tragedy. . . . Full of life and emotion, written in a spare and artful style, this is a good story that goes far beyond simple realism. The Mustian family also appeared in Reynolds Price's first book. 'A long and happy life' [entered below]." Pub W

A long and happy life. Atheneum Pubs. 1962 [c1961] 195p $4.95

Laid in a North Carolina small town, this story is "about a girl who loves a young man who does not love her in return. If he has any to share, his love is directed toward his motorcycle, and his energies toward a variety of other young women. . . . [Rosacoke] gives herself to Wesley, but that accomplishes nothing, as Wesley then seems to be even more indifferent to her. All Rosa wants is a long and happy life with her young man. The prospects are not promising, especially when Rosa finds herself pregnant. Yet could this be the beginning of the long and happy life? . . . The reader is left to decide." San Francisco Chronicle

"It is a love story, and one of the simplest and most poignant I have ever read. . . . The last scene, the scene of the pageant, is full of echoes, and one realizes how carefully conceived this apparently artless narrative is. All the author's skills, however, are tools in the service of this insight, which is phenomenal. To have created Rosacoke Mustian is an achievement that the most mature novelist might envy." Sat R

The names and faces of heroes. Atheneum Pubs. 1963 178p $4.95

Analyzed in Short Story Index

"Stories which are drawn closely from the author's rural North Carolina family and neighborhood." Pub W

Contents: A chain of love; The Warrior Princess Ozimba; Michael Egerton; The anniversary; Troubled sleep; Uncle Grant; The names and faces of heroes

"In a way Mr. Price tends to be a 'local colorist' as he reflects his Southern background but at the same time he becomes universal in his treatment of his heroes as their hopes, aspirations, and apparently small problems are unfolded." Best Sellers

Priestley, J. B.

Angel Pavement. Little 1967 608p $6.95

"An Atlantic Monthly Press book"

First published 1930 by Harper

"In Angel Pavement, one of the many backwaters of London's office districts is the decaying firm of Twigg and Dersingham, dealers in veneers and inlays, to whom one memorable day comes Mr. Golspie, loud-voiced and jovial, newly arrived from the Baltic states, with the offer of an agency which will bring wealth and power to them all. But somehow through it a storm is brewing—it comes in a rush. Golspie sails away for the Argentine, with pockets well lined and a beautiful disturbing daughter in tow, leaving Angel Pavement considerably torn up, but Angel Pavement like London itself, can stand many a shock, and life there will go on, changed, but undefeated. A great and delightful novel, and a worthy successor to 'Good Companions' [entered below]." Ontario

The good companions. Harper 1929 640p $7.95

"Three people, set forth to solitary high adventure: Oakroyd, a Yorkshire factory hand with a nagging wife; the gentle lady of a Cotswold manor, with a small legacy in hand and thirty-seven monotonous years behind her, and Inigo Jollifant, a Cambridge man with a distaste for teaching small boys and a talent for airy improvisation on the piano. These amateur vagabonds unite in taking over a traveling dramatic company which has gone on the rocks." Cleveland

"It is possible to recommend it heartily without calling in any comparisons to Dickens or Thackeray to strengthen one's opinion. It is long enough to have suited either of them, and to suit readers who still like meaty books. . . . It suffices to call The Good Companions a robust and diverting tale, told in meandering fashion, lit by rich humor and warm sentiment and centered about a group of perennially engaging characters." Outlook

The image men. Little 1969 2v in 1 (492p) $8.95

"An Atlantic Monthly Press book"

"Published originally [1968] in England in two volumes entitled 'Out of Town' and 'London End.' . . . This American edition in one volume has been slightly abridged." Verso of title page

Contents: V 1: Out of town; v 2: London End

This novel follows the career of two impecunious highbrow rascals—Cosmo Saltana and Owen Tuby, who "have retired early from careers as professors in South America and Singapore. . . . Styling themselves sociologists, they instantly establish The Institute of Social Imagistics with the assistance of a . . . wealthy widow. The 'image men' first tie their organization to the new University of Brockshire. . . . Next they graduate to London. . . . Finally they become renowned enough to be invited to shape the identity of the next Prime Minister." Publisher's note

Priestley has written "a very funny story, with occasional digs at British politics, business, or the scholastic field, and an occasional mildly anti-American passage. . . . The book is a complaint against the sobriety of modern life, against its predictability, against its lack of flair. . . . Take the book for what it is: a thing to read and enjoy, a volume to restore your slipping faith in the comic novel." Book World

It's an old country; a novel. Little 1967 276p $5.95

"An Atlantic Monthly Press book"

"Concerns Tom Adamson, 36, professor of colonial economic history in Sydney, Australia. Fulfilling his mother's dying request, he flies to England to try and find his father, Charles, a one-time actor and painter, who deserted his family when Tom was three. In the course of his search Tom encounters family, England itself, and a marvelous assortment of colorful spivs and campy characters. Travelling all over England, he gets into amusing, improbable and very British situations as he tracks down every lead. Of course, he finds his father, and as a little extra fillip, the girl he will marry. Mr. Priestley keeps the reader on his toes, includes engaging dialog and amusing asides, takes some measured pot shots at 'modern Britain.' " Pub W

Lost Empires; being Richard Herncastle's account of his life on the variety stage from November 1913 to August 1941, together with a prologue and epilogue. Little 1965 364p boards $5.95

"An Atlantic Monthly Press book"

"Narrated 50 years later by a successful water-color painter who served as his uncle's assistant in a top ranking magician act for

Priestley, J. B.—*Continued*

the year reviewed, the story conveys the backstage life of an assorted lot of characters—some grotesque, some amoral, some half-mad—and more specifically follows the narrator's sexual maturing and development as a person." Booklist

"The characters are real and absorbing, and the evocation of joy in life and in art as contrasted to the more logical despair is vivid. . . . The reader gets a good picture of life in pre-war England at many levels of society." Library J

Saturn over the water. . . . Doubleday 1961 284p o.p. 1970

"An account of his adventures in London, New York, South America and Australia by Tim Bedford, painter; edited—with some preliminary and concluding remarks—by Henry Sulgrave; and here presented to the reading public." Title page

"Tim Bedford, a young painter, undertakes a search for a cousin's husband, a scientist who has disappeared somewhere in South America. This [quest] . . . involves him in an international plot." McClurg. Book News

"Part of the fun of Mr. Priestley's tale lies in the rapidly changing scenes. . . . Part of the fun lies in the author's minor characters, a vast collection of businessmen, bohemians, scientists, and international big-wigs. Part of the fun lies in the slow unraveling of a mystery, with all the attendant delays, false clues, and dead ends." Sat R

Priestley, John Boynton. See Priestley, J. B.

Prior, Allan

The loving cup; a novel. Simon & Schuster [1969 c1968] 380p boards $5.95

First published 1968 in England

"April and Tom Winter have money, fame, and a loving, happy marriage. Although the idyll they inhabit rests on Tom's skill and luck as an internationally famous auto racing driver, they have come to feel invulnerable against the deceits and misfortunes which befall less adulated mortals. The shattering end to this dream comes suddenly when Tom kills a woman in a highway accident and goes to prison, bankrupt and disgraced." Library J

The prison "scenes, together with the descriptions of April's hopeless existence with both breakdown and poverty threatening, are as shocking as they are meant to be." Times (London) Lit Sup

Pritchett, V. S.

Blind love, and other stories. Random House 1969 246p boards $5.95

Contents: Blind love; The nest builder; A debt of honor; The cage birds; The skeleton; The speech; The liars; Our oldest friend; The Honeymoon; The chain-smoker

The author "explores the depths and facets of human nature with apparent ease and a faultless eye for detail." Pub W

The key to my heart; a comedy in three parts; illus. by Paul Hogarth. Random House [1964 c1963] 107p illus boards $3.95

First published 1963 in England

"The social structure in a small English town is neatly reflected in an amusing narrative about a young baker who becomes enamored of the richest woman in the county. Bob Fraser, the baker, has his first real encounter with Mrs. Brackett when he tries to collect a long-overdue bill and is, in part, responsible for the charming but irresponsible Noisy Brackett's temporary desertion of his wife." Booklist

"A surprise ending climaxes this brief but wonderful bit of purely English fun." Library J

Prize stories from Latin America; winners of the Life en español literary contest. Doubleday 1963 398p o.p. 1970

Analyzed in Short Story Index

"Though these stories have been chosen for their literary merit, they also give valuable insights into the social, economic, and political problems of South America. Their characters are taken from almost every stratum of Latin American society." Publisher's note

Contents: Secret ceremony, by M. Denevi; The aborigines, by C. M. Moreno; Nausicaa, by A. Echeverría; The harp, by T. Mojarro; A plum for Coco, by L. del Castillo; The yoke, by F. González-Aller; The black ship, by C. R. Larrain; The cause, by H. P. Conti; Jacob and the other, by J. C. Onetti; Dream with no name, by R. F. López; Sunday for an architect, by R. Venturini

Prize stories, 1919-1966. See First-prize stories, 1919-1966

Prize stories, 1919-1970: The O. Henry Awards. . . . Doubleday 1920-1970 50v v 1-48 o.p. 1970, v49-50 ea $5.95

Analyzed in Short Story Index

Editors: 1919-1932, Blanche C. Williams; 1933-1940, Harry Hansen; 1941-1951, Herschel Brickell; 1954-1956, Paul Engle and Hansford Martin; 1957, Paul Engle assisted by Constance Urdang; 1958, Paul Engle assisted by Curt Harnack; 1959, Paul Engle assisted by Curt Harnack and Constance Urdang; 1961-1964, Richard Poirier; 1965-1966, Richard Poirier and William Abrahams; 1967-1970, William Abrahams

Title varies: 1919-1946, O. Henry Memorial Award prize stories; 1947-1959, Prize stories The stories for 1919-1927 were "chosen by the Society of Arts and Sciences"

No volumes issued for 1952-1953

Contents: v49 Man in the drawer, by B. Malamud; Accomplished desires, by J. C. Oates; Lost in the funhouse, by J. Barth; Early morning, lonely ride, by N. H. Packer; In shock, by Litwak; Manikin, by L. Michaels; The common courtesies, by A. Tyler; The invitations, by E. Shefner; To be an athlete, by E. L. Corfman; First heat, by P. Taylor; Bedlam's rent, by T. Sterling; Service, by M. Rubin; Distance, by G. Paley; You, Johann Sebastian Bach, by B. Maddow; Color the daydream yellow, by M. Steele; The empire of things, by H. L. Mountzoures; Lambs of God, by S. Engberg

v50: The girl who sang with the Beatles, by R. Hemenway; The biggest thing since Custer, by W. Eastlake; A cliff of fall, by N. Rindfleisch; It's cold out there, by P. Buchan; A modern development, by G. Blake; Patients, by J. Strong; Joe College, by H. E. F. Donohue; Am strande von tanger, by J. Salter; My son the murderer, by B. Malamud; Nights at O'Rear's, by P. B. Griffith; Saint John of the Hershey Kisses: 1964, by T. Cole; Bech takes pot luck, by J. Updike; A day in operations, by D. Grinstead; Theo's girl, by N. Willard; Of cabbages and kings, by J. A. McPherson

Procter, Maurice

Exercise Hoodwink. Harper 1967 185p boards $4.50

"It started when an Aston-Martin crashed on a dangerous curve. The front seat was covered with blood but there was no body—until it was found miles away. But ultimately the wrecked car was to lead to evidence of a clever and ruthless gang of jewel thieves. And the Grantchester police organized Exercise Hoodwink to trap the gang's leader." Bk Buyer's Guide

"Procter's manner is as beguiling and as businesslike as ever, and his present story, about gangs of cruel thieves who show no honor even among themselves, proves once again what a thoroughgoing craftsman he is." New Yorker

Protter, Eric

(ed.) Monster festival; illus. by Edward Gorey. Vanguard 1965 286p illus $4.95

"An Edward Ernest book"

Analyzed in Short Story Index

A collection eighteen classic tales. "Each story deals with a different monster, or a monstrous happening, the eerie, the fantastic that occur both within the mind and outside it." Library J

Contents: What was it, by F. J. O'Brien; Impulse, by E. F. Russell; Podolo, by L. P. Hartley; Moonlight sonata, by A. Woollcott; Revelations in black, by C. Jacobi; The thing in the cellar, by D. H. Keller; The novel of the

Protter, Eric—*Continued*

white powder, by A. Machen; Thirteen at table, by Lord Dunsany; The facts in the case of M. Valdemar, by E. A. Poe; The refugee, by J. Rice; The squaw, by B. Stoker; Caterpillars, by E. F. Benson; The tell-tale heart, by E. A. Poe; The judge's house, by B. Stoker; A diagnosis of death, by A. Bierce; Brenda, by M. St Clair; The deferred appointment, by A. Blackwood; The lost room, by F. J. O'Brien

Proust, Marcel

The captive; tr. by C. K. Scott Moncrieff. Modern Lib. 1929 563p $2.95

Sequel to: Cities of the plain

"In this [fifth] part of the monumental novel 'Remembrance of things past,' Albertine is living with the narrator under his own roof. He has tired of her, yet is held to her by the torturing bonds of suspicion and jealousy of her relations with other women. The long novel is an analysis of the narrator's soul upon the rack of jealousy. At the end comes the anticipated break between the lovers." Book Rev Digest

Followed by: The sweet cheat gone

also in Proust, M. Remembrance of things past v2

Cities of the plain; tr. by C. K. Scott Moncrieff. Modern Lib. 1938 384p $2.95

Sequel to: The Guermantes way

The fourth part of "Remembrance of things past"

"Marcel again meets Swann at a reception given by the Princesse de Guermantes, a cousin of the Duchesse. Swann is now suffering from a deadly ailment. He is an ardent adherent of Alfred Dreyfus. Swann urges Marcel to write to Gilberte, since she speaks of him frequently. But Gilberte no longer has any enchantment for Marcel; Albertine again holds his affections. She offers herself to him, but distracted by physical attachments for other women, he desires her company only at intervals to titillate his jaded senses. Eventually he is drawn closer to her, but now his suspicion that she is a Lesbian causes him jealousy and endless torment." Haydn. Thesaurus of Book Digests

Followed by: The captive

also in Proust, M. Remembrance of things past v2

The Guermantes way; tr. by C. K. Scott Moncrieff. Modern Lib 1933 395p $2.95

Sequel to: Within a budding grove

"Book III of 'Remembrance of Things Past' by Marcel Proust, published 1920-1921. It deals exhaustively with personalities, places, balls, dinners, and entertainments, gossip and conversation, family history, jealousies and animosities, social and political intrigue, duplicity, adultery, and sexual inversion in the aristocratic circle of the de 'Guermantes' family. The subject matter is continued in 'Cities of the Plain.' The title, 'The Guermantes Way,' refers to one of the two paths usually taken by the narrator Marcel during childhood walks at 'Combray'—the one which led past the Guermantes property." Benét. The Reader's Encyclopedia

Followed by: Cities of the plain

also in Proust, M. Remembrance of things past v1

Jean Santeuil; tr. by Gerard Hopkins; with a preface by André Maurois. Simon & Schuster 1955 xxiv, 744p $5.95

Original French edition 1952

"An unrevised unfinished work discovered after World War II that tells of Jean Santeuil's development from youth to maturity in the turn-of-the-century period. The reader is confronted by the Proustian phenomenon of total recall and the probing introspection that recreates the essence of an experience. The autobiographical element, the alternating moods of happiness and despair, the magic evoked by the long, leisurely spun out sentences are all foreshadowings of the more mature genius of 'Remembrance of things past.' " Booklist

The past recaptured; tr. from the French by Andreas Mayor. Random House 1970 272p $7.95

Sequel to: The sweet cheat gone

This translation published in England with title: Time regained

"The final volume of Marcel Proust's long novel 'Remembrance of Things Past', published in 1928. It carries the narrator and the various characters down to the time of World War I, showing the effect of the war on their lives and thoughts, and presents generalizations by the author on the subject of time and memory." Benét. The Reader's Encyclopedia

also in Proust, M. Remembrance of things past v2

Remembrance of things past. . . . Random House v 1, 1934; v2, 1932 2v $17.50

Includes the seven volumes, published separately and entered in this catalog. Translated by C. K. Scott Moncrieff and Frederick A. Blossom

Contents: v 1: Swann's way; Within a budding grove; The Guermantes way. v2: Cities of the plain; The captive; The sweet cheat gone; The past recaptured

"Into this long and complex psychological study and panorama of an epoch in social history there has been introduced some of the finest writing of our time on the subject of art in general, painting, music, acting, literature, architecture, and the like, as well as on our reaction to these arts. . . . And the long series as a whole is really an experiment—remarkably successful—in making the author's past live again in the eternity of art." Lenrow. Reader's Guide to Prose Fiction

Swann's way; tr. by C. K. Scott Moncrieff; introduction by Lewis Galantière. Modern Lib. 1928 551p $2.95

First French edition, 1918; English edition 1923

"This, the first volume of the . . . series, 'Remembrance of Things Past,' describes in an involved parenthetical style, with a multitude of details, the brilliant society in which the author moved. The 'Marcel' of the story is Proust's own counterpart, and it is through his hypersensitive and critical eye that we examine the tastes, feelings, motives and actions of the characters, most of whom can be identified as real people." Enoch Pratt

Followed by: Within a budding grove

also in Proust, M. Remembrance of things past v 1

The sweet cheat gone; tr. by C. K. Scott Moncrieff. Modern Lib. 1930 379p $2.95

Sequel to: The captive

"This volume forms the [sixth] and the penultimate part of the famous and many-thousand-pages-long novel. The central event of 'The Sweet Cheat Gone' is the flight from the hero, from the 'I' narrating the whole novel, of Albertine, his mistress. Exasperated by his constant suspicious jealousy which made of her literally a 'captive,' she left him; but separation was more than both of them could stand; and they were about to become united again when he received the telegram informing him that she was killed in an accident during a horse-back ride." N Y Times Bk R

Followed by: The past recaptured

also in Proust, M. Remembrance of things past v2

Within a budding grove; tr. by C. K. Scott Moncrieff. Modern Lib. 1930 356p $2.95

Sequel to: Swann's way

"As he grows up, Marcel falls in love with Swann's daughter, Gilberte. It is a deep and poetic attachment, but she gradually tires of him; his ardent nature and his attentions begin to irritate her. Out of wounded pride he avoids her, although he continues his friendly relations with the Swanns. Two years later he feels he is thoroughly cured of his hopeless passion, when he becomes involved with Albertine, a beautiful brunette he meets in Balbec.

Proust, Marcel—*Continued*

But he eventually discovers that she is interested only in platonic relations with men, and so he suffers another disappointment." Haydn. Thesaurus of Book Digests

Followed by: The Gulimantes way.

also in Proust, M. Remembrance of things past v 1

Purdy, James

Malcolm. Farrar, Straus 1959 215p $3.95

A "surrealist story set in the present about a 15-year-old boy named Malcolm who lives in a hotel waiting for his father, who never appears. Malcolm sits on a bench in front of the hotel all day, all the time, till a Mr. Cox, who is an astrologer, gives him several addresses of people to look up to get him out of himself. He meets a colored undertaker, a midget and a millionaire, artists, jazz musicians, and a girl whom he marries." Library J

"A very good novel indeed. . . . Call it a comic fantasy, and you must add that it is also wise and sad. Indicate its candour, its sharp surface innocence, and you might fail to recognise the depths of its underlying worldliness. . . . Praise its fresh, individual, 'contemporary' voice and you must also say that it has the oldest fictional virtue of all, the immediate establishment of its strange bunch of characters as people, or creatures, you have known for a lifetime." Guardian

Pushkin, Alexander

The captain's daughter, and other stories; tr. with an introduction by Natalie Duddington. Dutton 1961 280p (Everyman's lib) $3.25

Analyzed in Short Story Index
The title story was first published 1832
This translation by Natalie Duddington of Pushkin's historical novel [The captain's daughter] is hailed by many as the first complete and adequate English version. The book, described by Edward Garnett as 'the first pure example of Russian realism,' deals with the adventures of young Grinyov who, detailed to service in distant Orenburg, finds both love and excitement during the unexpected horror of the Pugatchov wars." Wis Lib Bul

Contents: The captain's daughter; The Queen of Spades; Dubrovsky; Peter the Great's Negro; The station-master; The snowstorm

The complete prose tales of Alexandr Sergeyevitch Pushkin; tr. from the Russian by Gillon R. Aitken. Norton 1966 495p illus $6.95

Analyzed in Short Story Index
"Tales of Pushkin arranged chronologically and introduced by the translator's very brief comments on Pushkin's life and writing." Booklist

Contents: The Moor of Peter the Great; A novel in letters; The tales of the late Ivan Petrovitch Belkin; The history of the village of Gorukhino; Roslavlev; Dubrovsky; The Queen of Spades; Kirdjali; Egyptian nights; The captain's daughter

Putnam, Samuel

(ed.) Cervantes, M. de. The portable Cervantes

Puzo, Mario

The fortunate pilgrim. Atheneum Pubs. 1965 [c1964] 301p o.p. 1970

A novel set on Manhattan's West Side portraying "the hard, full life of an Italian family poor for so many generations that it was enough to survive; Lucia Santa, whose first husband had died in an accident and whose second was to go insane, and her six children, whom she loved so fiercely that they rebelled against her domination." Bk Buyer's Guide

"This is a turbulent and loving chronicle." Book of the Month Club News

The godfather. Putnam 1969 446p $6.95

This novel of the violence-infested society of the Mafia and its gang wars focuses on Vito, the head of the Corleone family, and his ambitious sons who preside over their vast underground empire from a fortress on Long Island. (Publisher)

"Puzo has wrought his prose so skillfully that the most outrageous episodes seem totally natural. All the blood, all the slaughter, all the raw sex are in consonance with the people about whom he is writing. Yet at the same time he makes his frightening cast of characters seem human and possible. . . . The book pulses with movement, giving the reader scarcely a pause for reflection. Within its genre, which is action rather than philosophy, it is a staggering triumph." Sat R

Pynchon, Thomas

V; a novel

Some editions are:
Lippincott $5.95
Modern Lib. $2.95

First published 1963
" 'V' has two main characters. One of them is Benny Profane—on the loose in New York City following a Navy hitch and a spell as a road-laborer. . . . His function in the novel is to perfect his state of 'schlemihlhood'—that is to say being the victim. . . . His friends are called the Whole Sick Crew. . . . He joins a patrol in the sewers to kill alligators. . . . Set in contrast to Profane is a young adventurer named Stencil. He is . . . obsessed by a self-imposed duty which he follows, somewhat joylessly—a Quest to discover the identity of V., a woman's initial which occurs in the journals of his father, a British Foreign Office man, drowned in a waterspout off Malta. . . . V. turning up first as a young girl in Cairo at the start of the century, reappears under various names and guises . . . in Florence, Paris, Malta, South America." N Y Times Bk R

"This maze-like novel . . . is first rate. Pitched at the highest level of farce, at times, it seems, going too high for the human ear to hear, the novel is at once a frantic comedy, a tough puzzle, a spectacular cavalcade of Western life in the past 75 years, and a melancholy comment on the way things are now (not that they ever were, on balance, any better). One of the remarkable things about the novel is that each of its wildly dissimilar parts is as good as the rest." Newsweek

Q

Queen, Ellery

And on the eighth day. Random House 1964 191p o.p. 1970

"It all happened in a few days in April, 1944. Ellery lost himself somewhere in California or Nevada, found a small religious community in the valley of Quenan and was told by the Teacher that Elroi's coming had been foretold: he was to help them in a disaster. But what disaster could come to these saintly people living in a sinless world of their own?" Bk Buyer's Guide

The bizarre murders; three mysteries in one volume, complete and unabridged: The Siamese twin mystery; The Chinese orange mystery; The Spanish cape mystery. Lippincott 1962 510p illus o.p. 1970

An omnibus volume of three titles first published 1933, 1934 and 1935 respectively

The Siamese twin mystery is "a story in which, after two false starts, due to the subtlety of the faked clues, Ellery finally wrings confession from the guilty person at a time when the whole party are in greatest danger of their lives." Booklist

The second story is a mystery which begins with the discovery of a murdered stranger locked in an empty room, with his clothes and every movable object turned back to front

In the Spanish cape mystery, John Marco, a handsome ladies' man is found murdered, and likely prospects are Stella Godfrey one of society's prettiest matrons, her wronged husband, and their eighteen-year-old daughter

Calamity town
In Queen, E. Wrightsville murders p7-204

The case against Carroll
In Queen, E. Queens full p117-73

Queen, Ellery—*Continued*

The Chinese orange mystery
In Queen, E. The bizarre murders p175-327

Cop out; a novel. World Pub. 1969 180p $4.95

"An NAL book"
"Payroll robbers, prevented from leaving town by roadblocks decide to cache their loot with a local small-town policeman and take his young daughter as security." N Y Times Bk R
The policeman's "desperate attempts to get his daughter back . . . and the solution are handled in taut, believable fashion." Library J

The death of Don Juan
In Queen, E. Queens full p 1-62

(ed.) EQMM annual, 1946-1968. See EQMM annual, 1946-1968

(ed.) Ellery Queen's Minimysteries; 70 short-short stories of crime, mystery, and detection. World Pub. 1969 298p boards $6.95
A collection of stories by such authors as Jack London, Thomas B. Costain, Ogden Nash, and Charlotte Armstrong. Arranged under the headings: The first minimystery; Minicrimes; Minimysteries; Miniclassics; Minisherlockiana; Minidetection; The last minimystery

The fourth side of the triangle. Random House 1965 183p o.p. 1970
"Ellery Queen is called upon to find out who really killed a New York dress designer when one of the city's wealthiest families seems to be involved." Bk Buyer's Guide

The house of brass. New Am. Lib. 1968 210p o.p. 1970
"Not Ellery, but his father Richard Queen, former New York Police Inspector, is the chief sleuth. Richard, with his new wife Jessie, obeys a strange summons to an even stranger ménage on the Hudson, the House of Brass. The owner, blind Hendrik Brass, has supposedly hidden a six million dollar fortune in his mansion. Here, with Hendrik and his only servant, misshapen Hugo, are gathered the six heirs to the fortune. When Hendrik is murdered, Richard finds several false solutions to the case. It is not until Ellery's arrival in the last chapter that the truth about this typically bizarre Queen mystery is deduced." Pub W

Inspector Queen's own case: November song. Simon & Schuster 1956 312p o.p. 1970
"The attempt to kidnap multi-millionaire Alton Humffrey's adopted baby sends Inspector Richard Queen, retired, on the trail to help personable Nurse Sherwood clear her own name." Retail Bookseller

The lamp of God
In Haycraft, H. ed. A treasury of great mysteries v 1 p345-98

Mum is the word
In Queen. E. Q.E.D. Queen's experiments in detection p3-63

The murderer is a fox
In Queen, E. Wrightsville murders p205-378

(ed.) 101 years' entertainment; the great detective stories, 1841-1941. Modern Lib. 1946 995p illus $4.95
First published 1941 by title
1941 edition analyzed in Short Story Index
Contents: Purloined letter, by E. A. Poe; Mystery of Mrs Dickinson, by N. Carter; Lenton Croft robberies. by A. Morrison; The S.S. by M. P. Shiel; Dublin mystery, by Baroness Orczy; Problem of cell 13, by J. Futrelle; Absent-minded coterie, by R. Barr; Red silk scarf, by M. Leblanc; Puzzle lock, by R. A. Freeman; Secret garden, by G. K. Chesterton; Man who

spoke Latin, by S. H. Adams; Doomdorf mystery, by M. D. Post; Sweet shot, by E. C. Bentley; Tragedy at Brookbend cottage, by E. Bramah; Pink edge, by F. Froest; Long dinner, by H. C. Bailey; Chess problem, by A. Christie; Owl at the window, by G. D. H. Cole; Matter of taste, by D. L. Sayers; Cyprian bees, by A. Wynne; Solved by inspection, by R. A. Knox; Avenging chance, by A. Berkeley; Border-line case, by M. Allingham; Two bottles of relish, by Lord Dunsany; Man called Spade, by D. Hammett; Resurrection of Chin Lee, by T. S. Stribling; Mad tea party, by E. Queen; Crime in nobody's room, by C. Dickson; Tea leaf, by E. Jepson; Mackenzie case, by V. B. Shore; Introducing Susan Dare, by M. Eberhart; Treasure hunt, by M. R. Rinehart; Disappearance of Mrs Leigh Gordon, by A. Christie; Mystery of the missing wash, by O. R. Cohen; Criminologists' club, by E. W. Hornung; Arsene Lupin in prison, by M. Leblanc; Blind man's buff, by F. I. Anderson; Stolen Romney, by E. Wallace; Paris adventure, by L. Charteris; The clock, by A. E. W. Mason; Most dangerous game, by R. Connell; Eleventh juror, by V. Starrett; Philomel cottage, by A. Christie; Faith, hope and charity, by I. S. Cobb; Hands of Mr Ottermole, by T. Burke; Treasure trove, by F. T. Jesse; Suspicion, by D. L. Sayers; Silver mask, by H. Walpole. Ransom, by P. S. Buck; Perfect crime, by R. B. Redman

The origin of evil. Little 1951 245p o.p. 1970
"Ellery's intentions of writing a book in Hollywood are disrupted by appeals from two lovely women to solve mystery of strange death and fantastic warnings." Sat R

Q.E.D. Queen's experiments in detection. World Pub. 1968 240p $5.50
"An NAL book"
Analyzed in Short Story Index
Contents: Mum is the word; Object lesson; No parking; No place to live; Miracles do happen; The lonely bride; Mystery at the Library of Congress; The broken T; Half a clue; Eve of the wedding; Last man to die; Payoff; The little spy; The President regrets; Abraham Lincoln's clue

Queen's Bureau of Investigation. Little 1954 228p o.p. 1970
Contents: Money talks; Matter of seconds; Three widows; "My queer dean!"; Driver's seat; Lump of sugar; Cold money; Myna birds; Question of honor; Robber of Wrightsville; Double your money; Miser's gold; Snowball in July; Witch of Times Square; Gambler's Club; GI story; Black ledger; Child missing!

Queens full; 3 novelets and a pair of short shorts. Random House 1965 173p o.p. 1970
Analyzed in Short Story Index
Contents: The death of Don Juan; The Wrightsville heirs; The case against Carroll, and two short stories: E=murder; Diamonds in Paradise

The Siamese twin mystery
In Queen, E. The bizarre murders p7-173

The Spanish cape mystery
In Queen, E. The bizarre murders p329-510

Ten days' wonder
In Queen, E. Wrightsville murders p379-575

The tragedy of X
In Queen, E. The XYZ murders p7-216

The tragedy of Y
In Queen, E. The XYZ murders p217-419

The tragedy of Z
In Queen, E. The XYZ murders p421-575

The Wrightsville heirs
In Queen, E. Queens full p73-105

Queen, Ellery—*Continued*

Wrightsville murders; an Ellery Queen omnibus. Little 1956 575p o.p. 1970

An omnibus volume of three Ellery Queen novels: Calamity town; The murderer is a fox; Ten days' wonder: originally published 1942, 1945 and 1948 respectively

"The town of Wrightsville, New York, is the setting for all three." McClurg. Book News

The XYZ murders; three mysteries in one volume complete and unabridged: The tragedy of X; The tragedy of Y; The tragedy of Z. Lippincott [1961] 575p o.p. 1970

These books were originally published under the name of Barnaby Ross in 1932, 1932 and 1933 respectively

Drury Lane, retired Shakespearean actor and brilliant connoisseur of crime, helps New York City's District Attorney Bruno and Inspector Thumm solve the mysteries. (Publisher)

Quiller-Couch, Arthur

Castle Dor, by Arthur Quiller-Couch and Daphne du Maurier. Doubleday 1962 274p o.p. 1970

This unfinished novel was continued and finished by Miss Du Maurier at the request of the author's daughter. No notes were left as to his plan for its conclusion. (Publisher)

"A modern version of the Tristan and Iseult legend. . . . The action of 'Castle Dor'—the title comes from one of the Cornish settings of the Tristan tales—is pushed up into the 1860s. Its hero is a young Breton sailor. Amyot Trestane, a reincarnation of the famous warrior-lover. When Amyot jumps ship near Castle Dor, he meets a girl with the Arthurian-romance name of Linnet who is . . . married to an aging man called Mark. The three of them carry the story to its inevitably fatal conclusion." Sat R

Quoirez, Françoise. See Sagan, Françoise

R

Rabie, Jan

A man apart; tr. by the author from the original Afrikaans. Macmillan (N Y) 1969 286p $6.95

Original Afrikaans edition published 1966

"The story is set in the closing year of the 18th Century when the tensions between the Dutch and the black Kaffirs coming down from the northeast broke into open conflict. . . . The hero is the half-breed Hottentot Douw Prins who fiercely desired, above all else, that he be free and independent—a man. For a while he was succeeding in his search for independence with help from Ruth, the dark-skinned girl who loved him, and from Tielman Roux, his white friend. But in the end, Prins lost even his life, destroyed by the unreasoning hatred bred of racial prejudice." Library J

The author "provides a fascinating picture of a little known time and culture whose implications remain valid and meaningful after nearly three centuries." Pub W

Rabinowitz, Shalom. See Aleichem, Sholom

Radcliffe, Ann

The mysteries of Udolpho; a romance interspersed with some pieces of poetry; ed. with an introduction by Bonamy Dobrée. Oxford 1966 xxii, 672p illus (Oxford English novels) $5.60

First published 1794

"Centres in a gloomy castle in the Apennines, the haunt of brigands, where the heroine is immured by a sinister Italian. Haunted chambers and a mystic veil play blood-curdling parts among the horrors. The idyllic scenes interspersed might have been imagined by Rousseau. The Pyrenees, the Alps, Venice, and the Apennines supply an harmonious background. Date about 1580-90." Baker's Best

Raddall, Thomas H.

The Governor's lady. Doubleday 1960 474p o.p. 1970

"A biographical novel about the frivolous but charming Frances, who had fallen in love with John Wentworth, governor of the New Hampshire colony, even before the death of her first husband and married him ten days later. In spite of her or because of her he became governor of Nova Scotia [and acquired a title]." Bk Buyer's Guide

"This lively and well-told story of an actual eighteenth-century marriage reflects both the refinements and the hardships of life in the colonies. Told by a Canadian who is an historian as well as a novelist. 'The Governor's Lady' gives an unaccustomed view of our Revolution as a civil war that brought sorrow to some who loved the new land but upheld the side of the King as a matter of principle and conscience." N Y Her Trib Books

Radin, Edward D.

(ed.) Mystery Writers of America. Masters of mayhem

Rae, Hugh C.

The house at Balnesmoor. Coward-McCann [1969 c1968] 236p $4.95

First published 1968 in England

"The bodies of two teenage girls were found in moorland graves near Glasgow. Inspector McCaig has to find the killer—[expecting that] a lecherous real estate agent [is] marked as the possible next victim." Bk Buyer's Guide

The novel "is well written, well plotted and well presented. Rae develops his characters fully, even down to their Scottish dialect. He is able to take the many diverse people and many different situations and weave them effectively into a suspenseful mystery which holds the reader to the last. Rae uses psychology plausibly and intricately to present a story which is as entertaining as it is intriguing." Best Sellers

Rahv, Philip

(ed.) Great Russian short novels [by] Gogol [and others]. Dial Press 1951 774p (Permanent library bk) o.p. 1970

Analyzed in Short Story Index

Contents: The overcoat, by Gogol; First love, by Turgenev; The Amazon, by Leskov; The eternal husband, by Dostoevsky; Ward No. 6, by Chekhov; Hadji Murad, by Tolstoy; Dry valley, by Bunin; Envy, by Olyesha

Rai, Dhanpat. See Premchand

Raja Rao

The serpent and the rope. Pantheon Bks. [1963 c1960] 407p o.p. 1970

First published 1960 in England

A "novel about a Brahmin studying in Europe. . . . The student Rama, loves his native India and makes two visits to it during the course of the narrative; but he is much attached to France, where he resides with his French wife (Madeleine), and to England, where he goes to pursue both his studies and his love affair with a compatriot, Savithri. Madeleine bears Rama two children but neither survives infancy. Savithri marries the husband chosen for her by her father. Rama is divorced from Madeleine and settles down into bewildered bachelorhood." Best Sellers

"Rao does not merely confront East and West; he shows them working together and apart at the same instant. Yet the symbolism is easily apparent. Either one believes in the serpent or one believes in the rope. The serpent is the imagination; the rope is reality. Either the world is real and each man a part of it; or each man creates the world in his own image." Commonweal

Rama Rau, Santha

Remember the house. Harper 1956 241p
$4.50

This novel of modern India "is a story of
a young Indian girl, daughter of a wealthy
aristocratic family, who samples the influence
of the western world (it is the last year of the
British occupation) and then finds peace and
fulfillment in her own people's traditions and
moral values." Pub W

"The understanding that comes to Baba will
come to many American young people as they
read this book filled with the authentic flavor
of India and offering, as it does, a key to the
philosophy of Indian life." Library J

Ramuz, C. F.

When the mountain fell. Pantheon Bks.
1947 221p o.p. 1970

First published 1936 in French with the title:
Derborence. This English translation is by
Sarah Fisher Scott

"Based on tremendous 1749 landslide in Canton of Valais, Switzerland, when the Devil's
Tower fell on grazing valley of Derborence
during the night of June 22, destroying 40
chalets and checking the Lizerne torrent to
the present lake. Of nineteen men and several
hundred animals buried, one man escaped. . . .
Story is built out of the impact of sole survivor's return on his wife and friends." Library
J

Rand, Ayn

Anthem. Caxton Ptrs. 1953 105p $3.25

First published 1946 by Pamphleteers
A story which contrasts a completely collectivized society with the principles of individualism. (Publisher)

Atlas shrugged. Random House 1957 1168p
$7.95

"A long, complicated novel about what the
author believes to be the outcome of today's
world. She pictures America as ruined by false
leaders who persecute the doers and builders
for earning large amounts of money. . . . Her
heroes are a copper tycoon, a great steel maker and an inventor. Her heroine is vice-president of a trans-continental railroad system."
Pub W

"Miss Rand's sincerity is beyond question,
but her passionate protest is weakened by her
tendency to mistake prejudices and opinions
for facts and to see all things and people in
terms of black and white." Booklist

"Miss Rand is as convinced as is Nietzsche
that to help the weak or to live for others is
a betrayal of the soul of man. Many readers
will reject her views with fury. Few will deny
the narrative power and cunning construction
of 'Atlas Shrugged.'" Book of the Month Club
News

The fountainhead. Bobbs 1943 754p $8

"Unusual story of struggle for success
among New York architects. Careers of Keating and Roark are followed up, from day one
graduates with honors from his alma mater
and other is expelled because of unruliness,
although he is real genius. Interesting insights
into methods by which, for a while, people
may gain glory and money, but creative artist
wins out. No lack of romance, but amorous
ways of Dominique Francon may not appeal
to all." Library J

"A dramatic, action-filled book, set against
a fascinating background, and based on an
uncompromising belief in the importance of
the individual—and on the provocative idea
that man's ego is the fountainhead of progress." Huntting

We the living. Random House 1959 433p
$5.95

A republication of the title first published
1936 by Macmillan, with a new foreword reviewing the plight of the individual in Russia
since 1936

Russia in 1922 is the scene of this story
which "tells of the impact of the Russian revolution on a woman and the two men who loved
her—one a communist, the other an aristocrat." McClurg. Book News

Randall, Florence Engel

The place of sapphires. Harcourt 1969 248p
$4.95

"The story is modern—about the good sister
and the bad sister who, with Maggie, the family retainer, are recovering from the death of
their parents in an auto accident, caused by
whoever of the sisters was driving the car. Elizabeth and Gabrielle retreat to an old New England house where their sister-prototypes had
lived, suffered and died many years before. In
this haunted house, Gabrielle assumes the
identity of Alarice who had been the bad sister
of the past. Trouble ensues for Elizabeth for
Maggie, and for the doctor whom Elizabeth
loves." Pub W

Rascovich, Mark

The Bedford incident. Atheneum Pubs.
1963 337p $5.95

A sea novel in which "the Bedford, a destroyer on duty in the North Atlantic [for NATO] is
engaged in hunting out Russian ships, submarines particularly, that are trying to pry into
our radar defenses. Though she cannot fire on
these vessels, she can dog them enough to
make their spying difficult. This hunt builds
up all the aggressions of warfare, but, unlike a
shooting war, does not permit their release in
the act of destroying the enemy. Hence, an unbearable tension builds up within the Bedford's crew." Atlantic

"The Moby Dick symbolism doesn't quite
come off, nor does the philosophizing about the
cold war, but the picture of a ship in action
and the suspenseful narration are excellent,
and the book is an important, very salable novel, with special appeal to men." Pub W

Raspe, R. E.

Munchausen. The adventures of Baron
Munchausen

Rau, Santha Rama. See Rama Rau, Santha

Rawlings, Marjorie Kinnan

The Marjorie Rawlings reader; selected
and ed. with an introduction by Julia Scribner
Bigham. Scribner 1956 504p boards $5

Includes the novel: South moon under, entered separately; selections from: Cross Creek,
The yearling and When the whippoorwill; and
the following short stories: Jessamine Springs;
The Pelican's shadow; The shell

The sojourner. Scribner 1953 327p o.p. 1970

"Here is the story of Asahel Linden, a simple
and good man who, in his inarticulate fashion,
loved his family and his land. He was betrayed
by his wastrel brother and by his unnatural
mother. Nor was he fortunate in his children
whose moral fibre was so inferior to his own.
The character who prevents the tale from being
gloomy is Asa's wholesome and cheerful wife,
Nellie, who makes his lonely life a joy. The
changing seasons and the satisfaction of farming are enjoyable aspects of a novel deeply
rooted in the land." Ontario Lib Rev

"It is a moving story of the conflict between
good and evil and final triumph of the good
man." Wis Lib Bul

South moon under. Scribner 1933 334p
o.p. 1970

"A simple story of life in the Florida backwoods, in the scrub country where the hard
conditions of pioneer life still exist. Lant Jack-
lin, the hero of 'South Moon Under,' is a modern descendant of Deerslayer and the Indian
fighters, a keen hunter, a solitary unable to adjust himself to the social requirements of the
community. . . . There is surprisingly little to
the story aside from the long accounts of
Lant's lift in the woods. . . Mrs. Rawlings
brings her fullest powers of observation to bear
upon the scrub itself, on Lant's long hunting
trips, his trapping and logging expeditions, his
encyclopedic knowledge of the woods." New
Outlook

also in Rawlings, M. K. The Marjorie
Rawlings reader p3-270

Rayner, D. A.

The long haul; a novel. McGraw 1960 194p
o.p. 1970

Published in England with title: The crippled tanker

An account of a World War II maritime ma-
neuver "in which a torpedoed British tanker is
towed into port by a destroyer despite stormy
seas and the presence of enemy planes and submarines." Pub W

Rayner, Denys Arthur. See Rayner, D. A.

Rayner, William

The last days. Morrow 1969 [c1968] 298p
boards $5.95

"To the Jews revolting against the Romans
in A.D. 66-73, the Last Days meant that at the
moment of crisis when their defeat seemed imminent, the Messiah would appear and usher in
a new world of justice and peace. After the fall
of Jerusalem, the Jews still in revolt—nearly
a thousand of them in the fortress of Masada—
committed suicide when this prophecy was not
fulfilled. This dramatic novel tells the story of
the events leading up to that terrible climax, as
experienced by a holy man and a young Alexandrian." Am News of Bks

Read, Miss

The Fairacre Festival; illus. by J. S. Goodall. Houghton 1969 [c1968] 103p illus
boards $4

First published 1968 in England

"In 'The Fairacre Festival,' Miss Read tells
the story of how the villagers go about the task
of raising the money needed to repair the roof
of St. Patrick's Church by a whist drive, a food
sale, a Christmas Bazaar, and finally by the
Festival itself." Book News

"A delightful hour in the village of Fairacre;
like most charming villages, it is inhabited by
people who are not always charming and one
of the pleasures of Miss Read's stories is that
she sometimes shows her character when they
are not at their best. This honesty results in the
balance which makes her books so delightful."
Best Sellers

Fresh from the country; illus. by J. S.
Goodall. Houghton 1961 [c1960] 221p illus
o.p. 1970

First published in England 1960

"Anna Lacey, who has lived all her life on
an Essex farm with a large and loving family,
takes a new teaching post in a London suburb.
Adjusting to drab and confining living quarters, learning to handle an over crowded classroom, making new friends, and a blossoming
romance make up Anna's first year of teaching.
A wholesome story for any library where its
decidedly British vocabulary will not deter the
reader." Library J

The Howards of Caxley; drawings by
Harry Grimley. Houghton 1968 [c1967] 223p
illus $4

First published 1967 in England

The author continues the story of the Howard and North families of "The Market
Square," entered below, who live in Caxley,
near Salisbury. "The central role in this novel
belongs to Edward Howard, 21 in 1939, a flier
in World War II, and the victim of a broken
war-time marriage. He slowly forges his way
back to happiness in a challenging business and
in another marriage." Pub W

The market square; drawings by Harry
Grimley. Houghton 1967 [c1966] 223p illus $4

First published 1966 in England

Two friends and their families who had
grown up together in an English country town
maintain a bond through the years despite misunderstandings and different economic circumstances. (Publisher)

"There may be a little less humor in this story than in the others, but the characterizations are deeper and stronger and the book
doesn't lose any of Miss Read's special brand
of warm, never-sticky sentiment." Pub W

Miss Clare remembers; illus. by J. S. Goodall. Houghton 1963 [c1962] 216p illus
boards $3.75

First published 1962 in England

Another of the author's novels about the English countryside. This one tells the life of a
village schoolteacher from the 1880's to a few
years after World War II. Miss Clare's long life
is shown to be a life of outward serenity but
one with much personal drama. (Publisher)

"Quiet, rarely sentimental, sometimes touching never condescending either to its subject
or its audience, Miss Clare Remembers is a reminder that any writer who can give an honest,
uncluttered account of how something happened will be worth reading." Harper

Over the gate; illus. by J. S. Goodall.
Houghton 1965 [c1964] 236p illus boards $4

First published 1964 in England

"Gently gossipy tales of Miss Read's small
English village of Fairacre, where she teaches
school. These are quiet stories of happy children, pleasant or crotchety neighbors, and a
bit of fantasy and magic." Pub W

"As before, the rural atmosphere and season-
al festivities of the West Country are described
with loving felicity." Booklist

Thrush Green; illus. by J. S. Goodall.
Houghton 1960 [c1959] 226p illus o.p. 1970

First published in England 1959

For three generations May Day in the small
English village of Thrush Green had meant the
fair and Curdle's Caravans, now ruled by the
widow Curdle, a fierce old matriarch. Before
the day is over life and love touch the peace
of the village, the lives of Mrs Curdle; her
grandson, Ben; Ruth Bassett, returned home
after a broken engagement; and, young Dr
Lovell, come to help old Dr Bailey. (Publisher)

"This is a gentle novel which honestly reflects the manners and mores of rural life."
Pub W

Village Christmas. Houghton 1966 45p $2.95

A story about a "family, newly moved from
London to a quiet country village, who are
accepted by the unfriendly townfolk only after
a newborn baby boy is added to their three
little daughters at Christmas." Pub W

"With deft touches Miss Read brings out
the contrasts in this little English community:
conventionality and sobriety, on the one hand,
and gay bohemian laxity, on the other. The
birth, so embarrassingly inapropos on Christmas Day, serves as a welder of the two divergent ways of life." Book of the Month Club
News

Winter in Thrush Green; illus. by J. S.
Goodall. Houghton 1962 [c1961] 226p illus
boards $3.75

First published 1961 in England

"Here are the people of peaceful Thrush
Green once more: the widower rector, Miss
Ella and Miss Dimity, Dr. Lovell and Ruth
(now expecting a baby). And Harold Shoo-
smith, a newcomer, adds a mild excitement to
life in the English village." Bk Buyer's Guide

" 'Miss Read' unquestionably is a romantic,
but, thankfully, she is not a sentimentalist. . . .
Her humor is kindly rather than acid. It is a
genuine humor and it is delightful." Chicago
Sunday Tribune

Reade, Charles

The cloister and the hearth

Some editions are:
Dodd (Great illustrated classics) $5.50 With il-
lustrations by Charles Keene from old prints,
and a foreword
Dutton (Everyman's lib) $2.95
Harper (Harper Modern classics) $2.40
Modern Lib. $2.95

First published 1861

"The action takes place on the Continent in
the latter years of the 15th century; and among
the historical characters of note introduced are
Froissart, Gringoire, Deschamps, Luther, Villon and the child Erasmus. The interest centers in the love story of Erasmus' parents—
Gerard, a talented young writer, and the red-
haired Margaret, daughter of Peter Brandt. A
forged letter convinces Gerard of Margaret's

Reade, Charles—*Continued*

death and he becomes a monk, but after many misadventures, the pair meet again at last." Benét. The Reader's Encyclopedia

"As a piece of historical narrative, crowded with characters, brilliantly pictorial, and based on indefatigable study, this is one of our finest novels of the Middle Ages, taking the hero from the Netherlands through Germany and France to Italy and Rome, and depicting the state of all these countries (1465-85). Attempts with amazing success to reconstruct the whole life of the time. The hero is said to be the father of Erasmus, and his story to be true in the main." Baker's Best

Reback, Marcus, and Reback, Janet Taylor Caldwell. See Caldwell, Taylor

Redgate, John

Barlow's kingdom. Trident Press 1969 160p boards $4.50

SBN 671-27020-6

"It is a classic story, relentless and remorseless, of love and betrayal, death and revenge, and it captures, without frills, the flavor of the lusty and aggressive frontier West. The . . . hero is Roy Barlow, who returns to Montana after the Civil War, to find his father dead, his mother married to his father's brother, and a sense of unrest hanging over the valley settlement. While it is true that the story often parallels 'Hamlet,' . . . Roy Barlow, unlike the Danish prince, knows so exactly where his duty lies, that one follows the story to its tragic end inexorably." Pub W

Reeman, Douglas

The deep silence. Putnam [1968 c1967] 303p $5.95

First published 1967 in England

".HM.S. 'Temeraire,' latest and best of Britain's nuclear attack submarines, is ordered on a top secret mission to the Far East to oppose a new Red Chinese threat to the beleaguered American fleet. Personal and political intrigue enter into the plot, with the staunch commander of the 'Temeraire' having to fight not only underseas danger but a conspiracy against himself from high places. His ultimate mission is to find, at all costs, a damaged American nuclear sub, rescue her if possible, but destroy her and her crew without a trace if there is a chance of her secrets falling into Chinese Communist hands." Pub W

H.M.S. Saracen. Putnam [1966 c1965] 320p $5.95

"A young naval officer who felt a strange affinity for the ship in which he served in World War I finds himself in command of her when he rejoins the navy in the Second World War. Set in Britain." Pub W

"His story of identification with the awkward ship of the monitor class, their shared sea fights, and ultimate vindication has stereotyped characters but lots of action for lovers of marine battles." Booklist

The pride and the anguish. Putnam [1969 c1968] 320p $5.95

First published 1968 in England

"Lieutenant Ralph Trewin of Britain's Royal Navy is sent to Singapore to recover from battle wounds and the death of his wife in the bombing of London. What is to be an easy assignment, second in command of the gunboat, H.M.S. 'Porcupine,' turns into something very different when Trewin must rouse his crew and persuade his doubting captain that Singapore is vulnerable to attack. The city, is, indeed, captured, but in the midst of a bloody and hopeless campaign, Trewin, 'Commander Corbett and their men make the 'Porcupine' a symbol of Britain's stubborn resistance against impossible odds." Pub W

"Although this is a novel filled with the conflict and bloody action of war, its underlying theme is the triumph of the human spirit over misery and despair." Library J

With blood and iron. Putnam [1965 c1964] 288p o.p. 1970

First published 1964 in England

When World War II "was going badly for the Germans, Captain Rudolph Steiger set out to lead a U-boat wolf pack based at St. Pierre. But one by one the U-boats were destroyed and at last Steiger was forced to surrender." Bk Buyer's Guide

"The book is filled with the scream and burst of shells, the rending of steel, the suspense of the chase, the awesome boom of torpedoes and the disintegration of ships and men, the atmosphere of sabotage and treachery and hatred, the brief shore leaves with their passionate affairs, and the dogged courage of losers who fought to the end 'by the Code.' " Best Sellers

For other titles by this author see Kent, Alexander

Rees, Barbara

Mrs Wall, Mrs Wall

In Rees, B. Try another country p55-120

Poor Margaret

In Rees, B. Try another country p121-78

Sidney, oh Sidney

In Rees, B. Try another country p 1-53

Try another country; three short novels. Harcourt 1969 178p $4.95

Contents: Sidney, oh Sidney; Mrs Wall, Mrs Wall; Poor Margaret

The author "explores the lives of people who are looking for the proverbial fulfillment: symbolically, they need to 'try another country.' In 'Sidney, Oh Sidney' she presents a selfish, neurotic young man who makes a victim of a young girl whom he pretends to befriend. In 'Mrs. Wall' a mother vicariously enjoys her naïve daughter's affair with a young Italian. The much-too-often-portrayed spinster school teacher is the subject of 'Poor Margaret.' . . . Miss Rees has a marvelous depth and sensitivity. However, she lacks the essential dramatic skill the novelist needs. Her characters do not act on their own; Miss Rees manipulates them—and the reader." Library J

Remarque, Erich Maria

y All quiet on the western front; tr. from the German by A. W. Wheen. Little 1929 291p $4.95

"The narrator of this apparently autobiographical story is a young German private who with three of his classmates is snatched away from school at the age of nineteen to serve in the trenches. Tho the author is a German, the book transcends nationality. A simply written life of the common soldier, told without anger or passion, and with an almost unendurable realism and pathos, the book is a powerful indictment of war. When the Armistice comes Paul is the sole survivor of his group of comrades, but it is his flesh only that has escaped. His spirit is destroyed." Book Rev Digest.

"It is difficult to think of any significant experience of a man at the front which is not represented; everything is there—horror, coarseness, lewdness, humour, pathos, comradeship, even the unexpected beauty of nature. Gradually death takes toll of it all." Nation and Ath

Followed by: The road back

Arch of triumph; tr. from the German by Walter Sorell and Denver Lindley. Appleton 1945 455p o.p. 1970

"A story of Paris in the period preceding the [second World] war. The central character is a German doctor who, having escaped from the Nazis, is living illegally in France, subject to deportation if the police discover his presence. Without a passport and identification papers he is not allowed to practice, but in secret performs difficult operations for a well-known society doctor. Other refugees, figures from the underworld, outcasts and derelicts are the characters in a book which pictures a society nearing its doom." Wis Lib Bul

Remarque, Erich M.—*Continued*

The black obelisk; tr. from the German by Denver Lindley. Harcourt 1957 434p $4.50

"Long and short philosophical discussions on religion, love, death, the meaning of life and other eternally unsettled topics are scattered throughout a novel set in inflation-ridden Germany of the 1920's. The narrator, an employee of a tombstone and coffin company, is a questing soul who wrings all he can from every experience be it a visit to a night club, a talk with a schizophrenic friend, or a fight with an unsavory neighbor." Booklist

"Remarque has written a brilliant satirical novel, witty, often very funny, picaresque and serious at the same time, filled with sadness, as it would have to be." N Y Her Trib Books

Heaven has no favorites; tr. by Richard and Clara Winston. Harcourt 1961 302p $4.50

"A novel about the all-consuming love of an attractive European racing car driver and a lovely young invalid, each facing imminent disaster. The sequence of events takes place during a spring and summer,, in Paris, Sicily, Venice, and on the Riviera." Pub W

"The dialogue is full of delicate ironies and paradoxical reflections on the brevity of life, the enigmatic inevitability of death, the emptiness of material possessions." Best Sellers

The night in Lisbon; tr. by Ralph Manheim. Harcourt 1964 244p $4.95

"One night in Lisbon in 1942 a German refugee offers passage to the U.S. and his passport to another refugee on condition that he be kept company through the night and that he be permitted to tell his story. The narration reveals the first refugee's flight from Germany in the 1930's, his hazardous return after five years to see his wife, his second escape in which his wife joins him, and their subsequent flight from place to place in Europe during which, in spite of dangers, they achieved moments of intense happiness because of their mutual love and understanding. The suspense of the beautifully told, ironic idyll is climaxed in the tragic end and is echoed in the framing story of the second refugee who is given the passage to America." Booklist

The road back; tr. from the German by A. W. Wheen. Little 1931 343p o.p. 1970

Sequel to: All quiet on the western front

Containing some of the characters of: All quiet on the western front, this story is about a "little group of war-weary, disillusioned German soldiers [who] return to their homes and find that adjustment to peace in a Fatherland which is a rioting, cynical republic is impossible. The book is . . . poignant and tragic . . . stressing as it does the sense of futility, the lack of initiative, and the inability ever again to look on life as others do, which embitter the days and nights of the returned soldier." Cleveland

Three comrades; tr. from the German by A. W. Wheen. Little 1937 479p $6.95

"Three German ex-soldiers, none of them over thirty, in the year 1928 made a precarious living from a garage and car repair business. They were comrades and shared their resources, and the advantages of their beloved car, Karl. On one of their excursions in Karl they met the girl Pat, and all fell in love with her. But it was Robby who was completely her slave, and the story of their love and Pat's struggle with tuberculosis and her death complete the story." Book Rev Digest

A time to love and a time to die; tr. from the German by Denver Lindley. Harcourt 1954 378p o.p. 1970

"Ernst, a young German soldier, gets a furlough in the closing days of World War II. He marries Elizabeth, a neighbor girl, who grew up while he was away. Their brief but touching honeymoon helps them discover love and each other—a time to love. Upon his return from a furlough, Ernst is set to guard four Russian prisoners. In a generous gesture, he releases them, but one of them turns on him and kills him—a time to die." Wis Lib Bul

"The whole story is told with great restraint, with little sentimentality for those in misery and with little open rage at those who caused it." Chicago Sunday Tribune

Renault, Mary

y The bull from the sea

Some editions are:
Modern Lib. $2.95
Pantheon Bks. $4.95

Sequel to: The king must die
First published 1962

A "tale that continues the adventures of Theseus. . . . It is about Theseus as King of Athens, as lover of the Amazon Hippolyta (there is great dramatic intensity in this long episode), and as husband of the Cretan princess, Phaedra." Pub W

"A superb historical novel. It is brilliantly and convincingly imagined, artistically presented, at once mind-stretching and deeply moving. . . . Miss Renault has not only integrated what can be known of Theseus' life and time and contemporaries into her story, but has made the elements intelligible and coherent." N Y Her Trib Books

The charioteer. Pantheon Bks. 1959 346p o.p. 1970

"A modern-day allegorical story of a young Englishman whose inclination toward homosexuality reaches a critical point when he is wounded at Dunkirk and under treatment in a military hospital in England during World War II." Pub W

"This unusual novel, told with artistry and skill, is compelling and haunting. Slowly the life of these men who love men emerges into reality—a life of sordidness, greatness, pain and joy." Wis Lib Bul

Fire from heaven. Pantheon Bks. 1969 375p $7.95

The author tells the story of Alexander's life from childhood to the age of twenty when he succeeded his murdered father, King Philip of Macedon. The book also describes the court and peasant life, the military and political events of the time, as well as the impact of such figures as Aristotle and Demosthenes. (Publisher)

"Miss Renault suggests but does not depict Alexander's homosexual relation with Hephaiston [and] suggests but does not detail Philip's lusting. . . . The whole novel is rich and expertly controlled." Best Sellers

y The king must die. Pantheon Bks. 1958 338p $4.50

This novel, based on history and legend, tells of Theseus, slayer of monsters, abductor of princesses, King of Athens, sent to destroy the matriarchal pattern of Eleusis and Crete. The core and climax of the novel is the Cretan adventure. (Publisher)

"Author Renault ably dramatizes the cultural clash between Mycenean Greece (masculine, simple-souled and semiprimitive), and Minoan Crete (effeminate, sophisticated and decadent). She has obviously lived her period, which is the closest a historical novelist can ever come to making a period live." Time

Followed by: The bull from the sea

The last of the wine

Some editions are:
Modern Lib. $2.95
Pantheon Bks. $4.95

First published 1956

"In this re-creation of ancient Greece, the author tells the story of Alexias, a young Athenian of good family, who reaches manhood in the last phase of the Peloponnesian War. Against this background develops the friendship of Alexias and Lysis, both of whom have fallen under the spell of Socrates. In their relationship the author shows the impact of Socrates' teaching on the ethics of his time." McClurg. Book News

"This canvas is rich in battles by land and sea, in the starvation of siege and the disaster of defeat, in a description that you will not forget of a wrestling match and almost to the death at the Isthmian Games, and in sensitively poised emotional bonds between both man and woman, and man and man. Miss Renault moves through all aspects of Athenian relationships with disarming candor and flawless taste." N Y Times Bk R

Renault, Mary—*Continued*

The mask of Apollo. Pantheon Bks. 1966
371p $5.95

"A novel set in Syracuse and Athens in the
fourth century B.C. which concerns Nikeratos,
the actor, who carries an antique mask of Apollo with him on his travels. The mask becomes
by degrees his artistic conscience. Niko narrates the struggle for power between Dion,
philosopher and soldier, the friend of Plato, and
the tyrant Dionysios the Younger." Book Rev
Digest

"The story is masterfully told, one gets the
feel of the era, hears great heroes talk, learns
how backstage life in the Greek theater went
on, what ingenious devices were used for the
production of the dramatic effects. One also is
aware throughout of the acceptance of a kind
of homosexuality which, however, insofar as
Miss Renault handles it in her story, might
have been quite Platonic ,for there is none of
the need for anatomical 'realism' in this novel."
Best Sellers

Rendell, Ruth

The secret house of death. Published for
the Crime Club by Doubleday 1969 [c1968]
179p $4.50

First published 1968 in England
"The deaths of Louise North and Vernard
Heller were at first assumed to have resulted
from the suicide pact of adulterous lovers. But
then next-door neighbor Susan Townsend and
Bob North began to put various facts together."
Bk Buyer's Guide
"Very good characterizations here, and a
plot that, although it leans a bit too heavily on
coincidence, is genuinely puzzling." Pub W

Reymont, Ladislas

Nobel Prize in literature, 1924

The peasants; a tale of our own times.
Knopf 1924-1925 4v o.p. 1970

Contents: v 1 Autumn; v2 Winter; v3 Spring;
v4 Summer. Translated by M. H. Dziewicki
"The chronicle of a Polish village under the
old Rusian rule. It follows the daily rounds
of peasant life through the circle of the year
—toils and pleasures and customs and the
drama of human loves and hates. Tragedy centers in the person of the heroine who comes
between father and son, rivals for her love."
Book Rev Digest

Rhodes, Eugene Manlove

The best novels and stories of Eugene Manlove Rhodes; ed. by Frank V. Dearing. Introduction by J. Frank Dobie. Houghton 1949
xxii, 551p $6.95

Partially analyzed in Short Story Index
Contents: Novels: Pasó por aqui [1927]; Good
men and true [1910]; Bransford of Rainbow
Range [1914 with title] Bransford in Arcadia];
The trusty knaves [1933]; Novelettes: The
desire of the moth [1916]; Hit the line hard
[1920]; Short stories: Consider the lizard; The
perfect day; Beyond the desert; Maid most
dear; Narrative: Penalosa; Essay: Say now
shibboleth; Poem: The hired man on horseback

Bransford of Rainbow Range
In Rhodes, E. M. The best novels and
stories of Eugene Manlove Rhodes
p105-212

The desire of the moth
In Rhodes, E. M. The best novels and
stories of Eugene Manlove Rhodes
p299-351

Good men and true
In Rhodes, E. M. The best novels and
stories of Eugene Manlove Rhodes
p45-104

Hit the line hard
In Rhodes, E. M. The best novels and
stories of Eugene Manlove Rhodes
p353-98

Pasó por aqui
In Rhodes, E. M. The best novels and
stories of Eugene Manlove Rhodes
p 1-44

The trusty knaves
In Rhodes, E. M. The best novels and
stories of Eugene Manlove Rhodes
p213-98

Ribalow, Harold U.

(ed.) Treasury of American Jewish stories;
ed. with an introduction by Harold U. Ribalow. Yoseloff 1958 724p o.p. 1970

Analyzed in Short Story Index
Contents: Where are your guns, by H. Fast;
Red necktie, by J. Sinclair; With the aid of the
one above, by Y. Suhl; Alte Bobbe, by C. Angoff; Lady of my own, by M. Seide; Old man
had four wives, by F. Scheiner; Death of an
actor, by D. Bernstein; Under the dome; Aleph,
by W. Frank; Mr K*A*P*L*A*N the magnificent, by L. Q. Ross; The minyan, by A. Klein;
The Kinnehorrah, by J. Weidman; Nasty Kup-
perman and The Ku Klux Klan, by L. Berg;
Writ of divorcement, by L. Lewisohn; Yisgadal,
by J. M.. Klein; Maurie finds his medium, by
M. Levin; Return to the Bronx, by R. Marke-
wich; Nobody can beat Freidkin's meats, by A.
Kober; Purification of Thelma Augenstern, by
V. Wolfson; Resurgam, by L. Zara; Message
for Harold, by V. Ullman; Night my brother
came home, by R. Kaplan; Bitter farce, by D.
Schwartz; Memorial Synagogue, by P. Goodman; Act of faith, by I. Shaw; Americanisation
of Shadrach Cohen, by B. Lessing; Hunger, by
A. Yezierska; Cycle of Manhattan, by T. S.
Winslow; God is good to a Jew, by B. Hecht;
My mother's love story, by A. Halper; God's
agents have beards, by E. Winters; Mrs Riv-
kin grapples with the drama, by E. Rosenberg;
Man in Israel, by P. Perl; Bond, by S. Karch-
mer; So help me, by N. Algren; Ph.D. by W.
Markfield; Mr Feldman, by J. Yaffe; Shock
treatment, by I. Stark; One of the chosen,
by H. Calisher; Passport to nowhere, by B.
Schulberg; The victory, by M. Schwartz; The
plan, by S. Sulkin; The bride, by S. Wohl;
Second Lieutenant, U.S.A. Res. by S. Katz;
Adam and I, by I. Kristol; Carmi, by D. B.
Karp; Not with our fathers, by A. Rothberg;
After all I did for Israel, by M. Levin; The
prophet, by N. Appet; Monte Saint Angelo,
by A. Miller

Rice, Jane

The idol of the flies
In Hitchcock, A. ed. Alfred Hitchcock
presents: Stories my mother never
told me p207-28

Richardson, Henry Handel

Australia Felix
In Richardson, H. H. The fortunes of
Richard Mahony v 1

The fortunes of Richard Mahony. Norton
3v in 1 o.p. 1970

A one-volume edition of the trilogy containing: Australia Felix (first published 1917 with
the title: The fortunes of Richard Mahony);
The way home (first published 1930); Ultima
Thule (first published 1929). It traces the life
story of Richard Mahony from his early days
in the gold fields of Australia thru prosperity
in middle age and the tragedy of his deterioration in later life

Ultima Thule
In Richardson, H. H. The fortunes of
Richard Mahony v3

The way home
In Richardson, H. H. The fortunes of
Richard Mahony v2

Richardson, Samuel

Clarissa Harlowe; or, The history of a young lady. Ed. with an introduction by John Angus Burrell. Modern Lib. 1950 786p $2.95

First published 1749
This novel "is constructed as a series of letters to Clarissa's friend, Miss Howe. To avoid a marriage to which her heart cannot consent, but to which she is urged by her parents, Clarissa cast herself on the protection of a lover, named Lovelace, who abuses the confidence reposed in him. He afterwards proposes marriage; but she refuses his proposal, and retires to a solitary dwelling, where she pines to death with grief and shame." Benét. The Reader's Encyclopedia

Pamela. Dutton [1914] 2v (Everyman's lib) ea $2.95

First published 1740-1742
"A didactic novel written in letters of great prolixity and minuteness. . . . The story of a maid-servant of good and prudent unbringing whose virtue is pertinaciously assailed by her master. Epoch-making in literature as a study of the female heart." Baker's Best

Richter, Conrad

The aristocrat. Knopf 1968 180p $4.50

The heroine of the book set in Pennsylvania "Miss Alexandria Morley, is an octogenarian spinster lady, the last member of the town's first family, living still in its great house, never forgetting her old-fashioned sense of noblesse oblige or losing her serene composure. The story of her struggle against an encroaching modern world in the last years of her life is told by the fifteen-year-old son of [her] handyman." Harper

"Miss Morley is one of Richter's saltier characters. Yet 'The Aristocrat' is not one of his major works, and one might question whether it should be called a novel at all. I like to think of it as comparable in a small way to those evenings with Mark Twain or Oscar Wilde, in which the central character is delivered over to us as a theatrical tour de force. Miss Morley also overwhelms her milieu, but because of this she gives the impression of existing in a rather one-dimensional world. We get a portrait rather than a novel, but it is an affectionate and entertaining one, for above all, Miss Morley knows how to pose." N Y Times Bk R

y The awakening land. I The trees; II The fields; III The town. Knopf 1966 3v in 1 (630p) $7.95

An anthology of the author's three novels published 1940, 1946 and 1950, respectively, and entered separately

y A country of strangers. Knopf 1966 169p map $3.95

Companion volume to: The light in the forest, entered separately
This is a "story about a white girl, child of Pennsylvania pioneers, who was kidnapped by Indians when she was five. She grew up to love her adopted Indian family, and had a child by an Indian brave. When still in her teens, she was traded, through various hands, with her baby son, back to her white father—who disowned her. An impostor had claimed her place in the white family. An outcast neither white nor Indian, the girl chose to return to the Indians." Pub W

"The author's sympathy is with the Indians as he defends their way of living and thinking and their hatred of the white settlers who took over their lands and scattered their tribes. Indian lore and legends are interwoven in the narrative. The characters are well drawn especially Stone Girl, torn between her real identity and her loyalty to her Indian upbringing. Absorbing reading in Mr. Richter's impeccable style." Library J

y The fields. Knopf 1946 288p $4.95

Sequel to: The trees
"Sayward, the 'woodsy girl,' is the central figure of this inspiriting, authentic pioneer story of southern Ohio in the early 19th century. How Sayward, unlettered but 'cam,' steady and independent, undertakes, with the help of her grist of children, the back-breaking job of making a farm out of her clearing in the endless wilderness, is instrumental in bringing a church and a school to the scattered settlement and refuses, in spite of her lawyer-husband's desire to leave, to run away and be licked by the encroaching trees, is related in the vigorous speech of the period." Bookmark

Followed by: The town

also in Richter, C. The awakening land p169-329

The grandfathers. Knopf 1964 179p $4.50

The core of this "story is a big, casual, not to say slatternly family of western Maryland hill folk, close in family feeling though the women seldom go through the formality of marriage and the newest generation of children is illegitimate. The 15-year-old heroine is a very direct, wise and clear-eyed girl who is curious about the identity of her father and badgers her mother about it, in vain." Pub W

"As usual, the author writes his story in the simple, colloquial, and idiomatic tone that attracts and beguiles the reader. Not only is there broad comedy here, but there is poignancy too, the poignancy of place and innocence." Sat R

The lady. Knopf 1957 191p $3.95

"Northern New Mexico in the 1880's is the scene of this tale of violence and revenge. The lady is Ellen Sessions, wife of a district judge and a member of a wealthy English-Spanish family. The narrator is the boy Jud, a relative of Judge Sessions, who went to live with The Lady and her husband, after the death of his own father. When the feud between The Lady and her sister's wicked husband finally culminated in the latter's death, Jud is all the man Ellen has left, for her husband and son had vanished mysteriously." Book Rev Digest

"This short novel is bathed in the light and the legends of territorial New Mexico. Doña Ellen is the only fully developed character, but she is enough. With her vitality, her charm, her sparkling spirit, and her power of endurance, she easily dominates this story of malice and retribution." Sat R

also in Costain, T. B. ed. More Stories to remember v 1 p364-440

y The light in the forest. Knopf 1953 179p $3.95

Companion volume to: A country of strangers
"Novel about a fifteen-year-old boy who finds himself irrevocably divided in heart between the people who adopted him as a child and the people among whom he was born. The boy, John Butler, kidnapped by Delaware Indians at the age of four and brought up by them as their own son, is forcibly returned to his family after eleven years, under a truce agreement made between the Colonial's and the Indians. This is the story of what happened to him during the first year after his return." New Yorker

"It is more evident here than in the earlier books that Mr. Richter's aim is less, as he says, to tell a story than to give an impression of frontier life—and a philosophy of 'civilization' as well. In his philosophy 'civilization' presents a sorry contrast to the Indians' oneness with nature. Possibly he tips the scales a little, but it is impossible to doubt the detailed if one-sided accuracy of the picture." N Y Her Trib Books

y The sea of grass

Some editions are:
Knopf $3.50
Watts, F. $7.95 Large type edition. A Keith Jennison book

First published 1937
"A story reminiscent in some degree of Willa Cather's 'A lost lady.' The heroine, a delicate refined, lovely lady, leaves her husband and children and the life on a huge cattle ranch to return to the city. Twenty years later, her youngest son, who is not, according to the whispers of the country, her husband's child, is killed as a desperado, and Lutie Brewton comes back to the man who has loved her in spite of everything." Book Rev Digest

"The story is deftly written in the spirit of romance and creates an authentic atmosphere." Springf'd Republican

also in Costain, T. B. ed. Stories to remember v2 p185-244

Richter, Conrad—*Continued*

A simple honorable man. Knopf 1962 309p $4.95

Harry Donner (the father in the author's "The Waters of Kronos" (entered separately) is the central figure of this novel. The day-to-day activities of the kindly storekeeper turned Lutheran preacher in rural early twentieth century Pennsylvania is depicted. He is seen as son, husband, father, friend, and counselor in an age when home and family exerted moral conviction and social authority. (Publisher)

"A quiet, slow-moving story that has a fine regional feeling for the Pennsylvania farming and mining country, some wonderful, sturdy, likable characters and a strong theme of integrity and human sympathy." Pub W

Smoke over the prairie
In The Saturday Evening Post. The Saturday Evening Post Reader of Western stories p333-58

y The town. Knopf 1950 434p $4.95

Pulitzer Prize, 1951
Last of the trilogy of which The trees, and The fields, are the first parts

"In this novel the town grows and even changes its name. Sayward Wheeler and her husband move from the old cabin into a mansion, and one by one the children set up their own homes. Chancey, the youngest, delicate and spoiled by his mother, is one of the central characters. The book closes with Sayward's death." Book Rev Digest

"Even in its drier passages The Town is always readable, full of a sweet nostalgia that only occasionally spills over into sentimentality. . . . A good bit of fictional Americana." Time

also in Richter, C. The awakening land p331-630

y The trees
Some editions are:
Knopf $4.95
Watts, F. $8.95 Large type edition complete and unabridged. A Keith Jennison book

First published 1940
First in a trilogy of American pioneer life
"The Lucketts were the first family to cross the Ohio into the new territory so soon to be opened up to settlement. It was a land of untouched virgin forest in which Worth Luckett, his rifle in the crook of his elbow, felt at home, but Jary, his wife, looked up thru the all but impenetrable branches and longed for the sun. Sayward, the eldest daughter, could take it, and make the best of it, while to the young ones it was a paradise. The trees shape the destinies of all of them, and shape them differently. Only Sayward remains at the end, strong and serene, and ready to take up the new ways of clearing and cultivation." Wis Lib Bul

"It's a period piece, with no great pretensions to exciting storytelling, but craftily done, with all the detail convincing and quite without the usual pioneer-hero sentimentality." New Yorker

Followed by: The fields
also in Richter, C. The awakening land p 1-167

The waters of Kronos. Knopf 1960 175p $3.50

National Book Award, 1960
"Unionville, a Pennsylvania Dutch mining village, home of John Donner and his forbears, long since had been completely submerged in the waters of a power project. Nevertheless John, now subject to the frailties of old age, felt an irresistible impulse to visit the locality. Arriving there, he is overcome by a 'stroke' and passes 'as in a dream' into a phantasy in which he, as an old man, re-enters the scenes of his boyhood." Library J

"An evocative story which may be appreciated for its symbolic meanings or simply for its recreation of the past." Booklist

Rinehart, Mary Roberts

The case of Jennie Brice
In Rinehart, M. R. Mary Roberts Rinehart's Mystery book p349-442

y The circular staircase; with illus. by Lester Ralph. Bobbs 1908 362p o.p. 1970

Entertaining detective story. A maiden aunt, her nephew and niece take a country house for the summer, and are plunged into a series of mysterious crimes

Detective: Mr Jamieson
also in Rinehart, M. R. Mary Roberts Rinehart's Mystery book p3-178

The confession
In Rinehart, M. R. Mary Roberts Rinehart Crime book p227-91

The door
In Rinehart, M. R. Mary Roberts Rinehart Crime book p 1-226

Haunted lady
In Rinehart, M. R. Miss Pinkerton p249-403

The man in lower ten
In Rinehart, M. R. Mary Roberts Rinehart's Mystery book p181-345

Mary Roberts Rinehart Crime book; The door, The confession [and] The red lamp. Rinehart 1957 505p o.p. 1970

" 'The Door' [1930] was the best-selling mystery of its time; 'The Confession,' [1922] a shorter novel, is a perfect baffler; 'The Red Lamp' [1925] is one of the few Rinehart books written from the point of view of a man." Huntting

Mary Roberts Rinehart's Mystery book; The circular staircase, The man in lower ten [and] The case of Jennie Brice. Rinehart 1947 442p $4.95

A reissue of the titles first published 1908, 1909, and 1913 respectively. The circular staircase is entered separately

"If you have never read these stories, now is your chance. If you read them years ago, you will find that they have lost nothing of their power to thrill and entertain." N Y Times Bk R

Miss Pinkerton; adventures of a nurse detective. Rinehart 1959 403p o.p. 1970

Two short stories and two novels in which "Nurse Pinkerton", that is Hilda Adams, figures

Contents: The buckled bag; Locked doors; Miss Pinkerton (1932); Haunted lady (1942)

The red lamp
In Rinehart, M. R. Mary Roberts Rinehart Crime book p293-505

The secret
In Haycraft, H. ed. A treasury of great mysteries v 1 p253-332

The swimming pool. Rinehart 1952 312p o.p. 1970

"The plot begins with the return of the newly-divorced, terror-stricken Judith Maynard to the old Westchester mansion, followed by complications such as a body in the swimming pool, a suicide attempt, more murder, and romance." Retail Bookseller

The author "displays undiminished skill at weaving romance, family skeletons, heinous villainy, and situations of emotional terror into a tale of puzzling murder involving the upper social strata." Chicago Sunday Tribune

Ríos, Tere

y The fifteenth pelican; illus. by Arthur King. Doubleday 1965 118p illus o.p. 1970

"Tiny Sister Bertrille feels uproarious when the wind lifts her high into the air. It isn't a miracle, it's just that the Daughters of Charity atop the highest hill in San Juan, Puerto Rico, wear folded cornettes like big white birds in flight. When Sister Bertrille willy-nilly becomes part of a flight of pelicans one day,

Ríos, Tere—*Continued*

and finds herself dropped into the middle of a U.S. Army security area, she has much to explain and to prove." Pub W

"Children and adult readers who enjoy naïveté and an unsophisticated approach in their reading will certainly enjoy the Mary Poppins world of Sister Bertrille." Library J

Rioseco, Arturo Torres- See Torres-Rioseco, Arturo

Roberts, Dorothy James

y The enchanted cup. Appleton 1953 368p o.p. 1970

"The story of Tristan and Isolde has been recreated in novel form for the modern reader. Against the background of medieval pageantry, tournaments, and the splendor of the Court of King Arthur, this story of a great love is told." Huntting

"Based on Malory's 'Morte d'Arthur,' a book to delight all but the most serious students who prefer the legend in its older form." Booklist

Fire in the ice. Little 1961 342p o.p. 1970

Set in Medieval Iceland, this story is based on the Laxdaela and Njal sagas

"The narrative centers in Hallgerda, a beautiful troublemaker whose behavior reflects her rebellion against her womanhood and its accompaniment, subordinate status. From her tenth year until the final chapter, when her half brother and grandson pronounce her epitaph, Hallgerda displays wilfulness, spite, lust for power and wealth, and a ruthless disregard of consequences that cost the lives of many men, including three husbands and the foster father whose influence in her life made something of a scandal." Booklist

"Hallgerda is not a true heroine but an evil fate, beautiful and appealing, pursuing her husbands to their death. The handling of a complex narrative, the building of tragedy and the psychological understanding of Hallgerda make this historical novel an excellent example of its genre." Library J

y Kinsmen of the Grail. Little 1963 367p o.p. 1970

"Set in twelfth-century Wales, this is the story of the quest for the Holy Grail by Sir Perceval and Sir Gawin. Gawin is torn between his duty to King Arthur and his desire to find the Grail. The author recounts his attempt and failure to match the exploits of the young and spiritual Perceval." Book Rev Digest

"The story is derived not from Thomas Malory but from the 12th-century legend of Perceval le Galois. The knights, ladies, priests and peasants are made very believable, the background is a fascinating mixture of paganism and Christianity, and the story moves fast and smoothly, with much rousing action." Pub W

Launcelot, my brother. Appleton 1954 373p o.p. 1970

"A retelling of the Arthurian legend in which the narrator is Bors de Ganis, brother of Sir Launcelot. In this tale the liaison between Launcelot and the Queen brings about the destruction of the Round Table because of the search for the Grail, which Sir Gawaine insisted upon." Book Rev Digest

"Written eloquently, with great attention to detail, this account certainly surpasses certain other attempts to bring to life the archaic language and the outmoded feelings of that bygone era." Wis Lib Bul

Roberts, James Hall

The Q document. Morrow 1964 289p o.p. 1970

"After the tragic death of his wife and child, Cooper went to Tokyo to translate old documents for the villainous Victor Hawkins, who had the Q document, supposedly revealing that the Christ story was fraudulent. Victor blackmailed Cooper into passing on its authenticity, hoping to sell it to the Chinese Reds." Bk Buyer's Guide

"No plot summation could really capture the 'can't stop reading' quality of this book. It is fascinating in its wealth of scholarly detail concerning the deciphering of ancient manuscripts and has a story line that intrigues to the end." Library J

Roberts, Kenneth

y Arundel; a chronicle of the province of Maine and of the secret expedition led by Benedict Arnold against Quebec. Doubleday 1933 632p $4.95

A revised shortened version of a novel published 1930

"An historical novel of the Revolutionary period, the setting of which is the garrison house at Arundel in southern Maine. Steven Nason, the hero of the story, goes with his friend Benedict Arnold on a hazardous expedition against Quebec. Young Nason has a very personal interest in the success of the enterprise, since Mary Mallinson, the girl he loves, has been taken by the Indians and is a captive in Quebec. Steven's recollections of the hardships, and dangers of the expedition, and its blunders and failure in spite of individual acts of heroism, make up the bulk of the narrative." Book Rev Digest

"As a full-blooded, human, heroic chronicle of a gallant adventure, and as a memorial of Revolutionary days in Maine, and as a fascinating story, this is a book of special importance." Christian Science Monitor

Followed by: Rabble in arms

Boon Island. Doubleday 1956 [c1955] 275p $4.95

This "novel is built around the wreck of the 'Nottingham Galley' on Boon Island, in the vicinity of Portsmouth, New Hampshire, December 11, 1710. The vessel is bound from England and the Maine shore has been sighted. During a snow storm the vessel goes on the rocks but the crew manages to leave the boat and climb the ledges which make up Boon Island." Huntting

"Offers a somber study in merciless hunger and pitiless cold—and in the greed and endurance, the treachery and loyalty that emerge in men under stress." Chicago Sunday Tribune

y Captain Caution; a chronicle of Arundel. Doubleday 1934 310p $4.95

Sequel to: The Lively Lady

"Unaware that the United States is at war with England, the merchant barque 'Olive Branch' of Arundel, Maine, is captured early in the War of 1812. Thereafter the fortunes of war, and the dead Captain's lovely but wrongheaded daughter keep Dan Marvin, the cautious first mate, in hot water as he strives to save the girl from a villain whose duplicity long prevents the Yankees from sailing home. Full of action and romance." N Y Libraries

The Kenneth Roberts reader; introduction by Ben Ames Williams. Doubleday 1945 460p o.p. 1970

Twenty-five excerpts from "Trending in Maine," "For authors only" and from the novels "Northwest passage," "Oliver Wiswell" and "Arundel." The essay, "Experiments with a forked twig" is published here for the first time

Contents: This is how it was; Roads of remembrance; Grandma's kitchen; Hot buttered rum; Lure of the great north woods; Frustration; Inquiry into diets; Glories of war; Education; An American looks at Oxford; Oxford oddities; British mysteries; Men in a swamp; Little home in the country; Palace, Italian style; Doing as Romans do; Country life in Italy; Truth about a novel; It takes all kinds to make an army; Dog days; Death of a lady; Prison hulks at Chatham; It must be your tonsils; Dissolution of a hero; Christmas in the depot at Dartmoor; Experiments with a forked twig

y The Lively Lady. Doubleday 1959 346p $4.95

Sequel to: Rabble in arms

A reprint in new format of the title first published 1931

"Satisfying both as a spirited adventure story ad as an authentic historical novel of the War of 1812. Richard Nason, captain of the

Roberts, Kenneth—*Continued*

armed sloop, the 'Lively Lady' and son of Steven Nason of 'Arundel' experiences the fortunes of war on the high seas, and later as prisoner in the terrible English prison at Dartmoor. A gallant and lively English lady furnishes the bright note of romance." N Y Libraries

Followed by: Captain Caution

Lydia Bailey. Doubleday 1947 488p $4.95

"A susceptible young Maine lawyer who has fallen in love with the portrait of a girl he believes to be in Haiti reaches the island just as Napoleon's attempt to take over the government sets off the bloody Negro uprising under Toussaint. The hero finds the girl, and from that point the extremely elaborate plot carries them through an encounter with Tobias Lear, the pig-headed evil genius of Jefferson's State Department: spirited engagements against the French; capture by Barbary pirates and slavery in Tripoli; and, finally, the Tripolitan War and its intrigues and political jealousies." New Yorker

"The story avoids finely phrased philosophies, but identifies itself with the present through its declaration for the freedom of nations and individuals. Here is vigorous, effective writing coming nearer the narrative gusto of Dumas." San Francisco Chronicle

y Northwest Passage. Doubleday 1937 709p $5.95

"The central figure of this historical novel is Major Robert Rogers, American ranger commander who led the expedition against the Indian town of St Francis in 1759, and whose dream was to find an overland passage to the Pacific. The narrator is one Langdon Towne, from Kittery, Maine, whose two ambitions were to paint the Indians as they really looked, and to follow Rogers. The book falls into three sections, the first dealing with the St Francis expedition; the second with the interlude in London, when Rogers was attempting to gain influential friends and money and Towne was learning to paint; and the third dealing with Rogers' career as governor of Michilimackinac, his court martial, and Towne's success as a painter." Book Rev Digest

"There are love and humor in this magnificent book and flavor in the full sensory meaning of the word. Best of all, after the first impetuous pleasure of the story itself, there remains the satisfying knowledge of a shrewd and fresh approach to pre-Revolutionary American history." Forum

y Oliver Wiswell. Doubleday 1940 836p $6.95

The background for this novel of the American Revolution is Boston, New York, Paris, Kentucky, and South Carolina. The story is told by Oliver Wiswell, New Englander, who is loyal to the mother country

"The present novel, which is history for all its fictional form, will startle every man, woman and child who has been taught to believe that the American Revolution was fought and won by bands of angels. It is, in short, the Revolution as seen by men whom the Revolutionary fathers called Tories and who called themselves Loyalists. In it all the bitterness of a horrible civil war is powerfully and dramatically brought back to life." N Y Times Bk R

y Rabble in arms; portraits by Esta Cosgrove. Doubleday 1947 622p illus $5.95

Sequel to: Arundel

First published 1933. The 1947 edition contains eight portraits in color of the characters of the story

"The principal villain of this realistic, unromantic tale of the American Revolution is the American Congress, the real hero is Benedict Arnold. The story relates the adventures of a group of men from Arundel, Maine, who fight with the American forces in the campaign ending with the battle of Saratoga. Men and events, politics and battles are seen thru the eyes of one Peter Merrill, mariner, who tells the story." Book Rev Digest

"Benedict Arnold, the misjudged, is the book's true hero, and though an ill-fated attempt is made to whitewash him completely at the end, he looms big and real, and when he captains a ship or rips into a council of generals with his high, penetrating voice, you get the power behind it, somehow." Books

Followed by: The Lively Lady

Robertson, Don

By Antietam Creek. Prentice-Hall 1960 268p maps o.p. 1970

"Mr. Robertson uses an interesting device, prefacing each chapter of his Civil War novel with a terse, exciting summary of the military action taking place within the same time span as that covered by the chapter. . . . This novel of the terrible battle of Antietam, where nearly 5000 lives were lost and some of the fiercest fighting of the War took place, weaves together the personal stories of a number of soldiers, Yankee and Rebel, and civilians. The descriptions of the battlefield are genuinely exciting and convincing." Pub W

The greatest thing since sliced bread; a novel. Putnam 1965 255p $4.50

This novel concerns nine-year-old Morris Bird, "a resolute little boy who is determined to see his old friend, Stanley Chaloupka, and in the course of his crosstown excursion incidentally becomes a hero in the East Ohio Gas Company explosion that rocked Cleveland's east side in October of 1944." Best Sellers

"The boy is a marvelous character. So is his humorous, understanding grandmother. A good story, with a very salable combination of humor, sentiment and suspense." Pub W

The sum and total of now; a novel. Putnam 1966 251p $4.95

Morris Bird III who appeared in the author's " 'The greatest thing since sliced bread' is now 13 and suffering the pangs of growing up. It is 1948; his beloved grandmother is dying. Morris finds this fact difficult to accept, especially since all his aunts and uncles, and his mother, too, spend most of their time arguing over his grandmother's possessions. Morris, ever the sensitive thinker, finds a perfect solution to the problem of distributing the relics. Robertson has expert control of his subject matter in this novel; he doesn't permit the adult outlook to mar any of Morris' story as he did in the earlier book. Morris' classification of women and the description of the ball game are, in my opinion, fine examples of sustained good writing." Library J

Robinson, Henry Morton

The cardinal. Simon & Schuster 1950 579p o.p. 1970

"A story of a Catholic priest born and bred in Boston, son of an Irish-American street-car motorman, and his brilliant rise from priest to cardinal. The reader is taken literally behind the scenes. Rectory, sacristy, confessional, bishop's offices, the various secretariats, and the innermost rooms of the Vatican are thrown open. No punches are pulled; no apologies are given. The Catholic Church is seen vividly in its social, juridical and mystical aspects through the eyes of the protagonist, Stephen Fermoyle. The book is sprinkled judiciously with pertinent quotations from the encyclicals, St. Augustine and St. Thomas Aquinas, canon law and the litanies." Library J

Robinson, Rose

y Eagle in the air; a novel. Crown 1969 159p $4.95

"Jeanie, expelled from college for joining a sit-in, finds refuge for a time with her older, working-class boy friend, then flees his bad temper and instability. When her family can't help her, in desperation she sets out to hitchhike to the West Coast and a chance at a new life. Her experiences on the road are sad and frightening, including near rape, from which she is rescued by two unlikely but colorful cavaliers, white Hoosiers. It is in the last part of the trip with one-armed Johnny, a strong and honest man, and his companion, the Kid, a smart aleck, illiterate teen-ager, that Jeanie comes to a new understanding of herself, her relations with whites, and her ability to offer and receive friendship. There's no maudlin sentimentality here, just a simple, honest story with believable dialog." Pub W

Roche, Roger Frison- See Frison-Roche, Roger

Roffman, Jan

A daze of fears. Published for the Crime Club by Doubleday 1968 190p $3.95

"After the morning when Clare Finch found the body of her best friend [Alexandra Shaw] on the back stairs of Shellgrave Manor, she went abroad, sold the house, and went to live in a penthouse apartment with Giles, her husband. She knew that Superintendent Worsley had suspected her of the murder because she was supposed to have been alone in the house with Alexandra. And now Alexandra's husband had hired a detective to reopen the case." Bk Buyer's Guide

"Jan Roffman writes with competence about interesting people in emotionally charged circumstances." Pub W

Rolland, Romain

Nobel Prize in literature, 1915

Jean-Christophe; tr. from the French by Gilbert Cannan. Holt 1927 3v o.p. 1970

Consists of: Jean Christophe; Jean Christophe in Paris; Jean Christophe: journey's end

"Biographical novel . . . relating the infancy, growth and career of a musical genius born in a small German ducal town. The scale of the book makes it a sort of social treatise illuminating the history of society, art, and ideas, both in Germany and France. The life of Beethoven (1770-1827) has inspired the work to a large extent." Baker's Best

"Acknowledged the greatest novel of the early 20th century, this life study of a musical genius has profoundly influenced the fiction of both England and America." Pratt Alcove

Rolvaag, O. E.

y Giants in the earth; a saga of the prairie; tr. from the Norwegian. Harper 1927 465p $5.95

"The Norwegian immigrant as a pioneer in America is finely viewed through the characterization of Per Hansa, to whom the Dakota prairie meant life, exhilarating struggle, and freedom, and through the characterization of Beret, his well-loved wife, to whom it brought loneliness, terror, and despair. Professor Rolvaag, a Norwegian who has lived in the United States . . . first wrote his story in his native language and then translated it into English." Pittsburgh

"It is half an adventure story, a realistic description of the physical facts of the homesteader's life 50 miles from anywhere on the Dakota plains, and half a penetrating study of pioneer psychology; and it is hard to say which is better done." Sat R

Followed by: Peder Victorious

Peder Victorious; a novel; tr. from the Norwegian; English text by N. O. Solum and the author. Harper 1929 350p o.p. 1970

Sequel to: Giants in the earth

"Carries on the characters of 'Giants in the earth,' the interest centering in Peder Victorious and Beret, the boy's mother, against the background of a community no longer intensely struggling with the soil, but adapting itself to the ways of the new country, or resisting adaptation as Beret continues to do. The boy Peder, with his changing ideas and his ardent pursuit of girls is a foil for the character of Beret, perhaps the most finely conceived personality in the book." N Y Libraries

Romains, Jules

Aftermath; tr. from the French by Gerard Hopkins. Knopf 1941 435, xxviii p (Men of good will v9) o.p. 1970

Contents: bk.17 Vorge against Quinette; bk.18 Sweets of life

"Concerns characters already introduced and their adjustments to the post-war period. The first part has some of the fascination of a horror tale; it continues the story of Quinette, bookseller and murderer of women, whose past is beginning to catch up with him, and who is partly tortured, partly befriended by the poet Vorge, morbidly captivated by his 'master's' sinister character. Part two affords moderate relief in the more normal journal of Jallez, a young newspaperman who observes the world and describes his mild love for a young working girl. Both parts are unresolved and dependent on future treatment. The author's ability to analyze character, to create suspense, and to evoke moods is evident." Booklist

The battle
    In Romains, J. Verdun

Black flag
    In Romains, J. Death of a world

Childhood's loves
    In Romains, J. Passion's pilgrims

Death of a world; tr. from the French for the first time, by Gerard Hopkins. Knopf 1938 551p (Men of good will v7) o.p. 1970

Contents: bk.13 Mission to Rome; bk.14 Black flag

"The first half concerns Abbé Mionnet's secret mission to Rome on behalf of the French government to discover what the papacy's foreign policy is. . . . The second half traces Europe's precipitate course toward war, chiefly as seen by that astute and mysterious observer Maykosen, and reaches its peak in the portrait of Lenin as an exile in Cracow." Nation

The depths and the heights; tr. from the French for the first time by Gerard Hopkins. Knopf 1937 546p (Men of good will v6) o.p. 1970

Contents: bk.11 To the gutter; bk.12 To the stars

"Here the politics of Europe, rushing headlong toward war in 1912, are in the background as a rumbling undertone of catastrophe, while the author concentrates on the intellectual and cultural life of Paris." Lenrow. Reader's Guide to Prose Fiction

The earth trembles; tr. from the French for the first time by Gerard Hopkins. Knopf 1936 582, xxx p (Men of good will v5) o.p. 1970

Contents: bk.9 Flood warning; bk.10 The powers that be

"Concerns the social, political, and industrial life of France during 1910-1911. The lives of some of the officials and the intricacies of governmental affairs are related realistically, with occasonal possible offense to some. Dramatic and involved." Booklist

Eros in Paris
    In Romains, J. Passion's pilgrims

Escape in passion; tr. from the French by Gerard Hopkins. Knopf 1946 557p (Men of good will v13) o.p. 1970

Contents: bk.25 The magic carpet; bk.26 Françoise

"Covers the fateful year 1933. Of the chief characters, Jallez pursues his amorous adventures in London, Nazi Berlin, Warsaw, Budapest and Paris; Jerphanion serves briefly as Foreign Minister, and resigns in despair; Haverkamp Bonds crash and Haverkamp dramatically disappears." Huntting

Flood warning
    In Romains, J. The earth trembles

Françoise
    In Romains, J. Escape in passion

The gathering of the gangs
    In Romains, J. The wind is rising

The lonely
    In Romains, J. The world from below

The magic carpet
    In Romains, J. Escape in passion

The meek
    In Romains, J. The proud, and The meek

Men of good will; tr. from the French for the first time by Warre B. Wells. Knopf 1933 457p (Men of good will v 1) $5

Contents: bk. 1 The sixth of October; bk.2 Quinette's crime

Romains, Jules—*Continued*

"This story, tho apparently complete in itself, is but the opening chapter of a novel which promises to reach considerable dimensions—a Comedie Humaine having for its background the world of Paris. The first part of the present volume deals with the detached episodes of a single day—October the sixth, 1908. In the second part of the volume the various themes converge and attention centers upon Quinette, the bookbinder, who out of pure curiosity had allowed himself to become dangerously involved in the affairs of a murderer. The story here becomes a psychological study of murder." Book Rev Digest

Mission to Rome
In Romains, J. Death of a world

Mountain days
In Romains, J. Work and play

The new day; tr. from the French by Gerard Hopkins. Knopf 1942 553, xxxv p (Men of good will v10) o.p. 1970

Contents: bk.19 Promise of dawn; bk.20 The world is your adventure
"In this new addition to 'Men of Good Will' (and the end is not yet), society is still demoralized, but men are turning their faces toward a new light, a light which comes from the east, from Russia. 'It may be the dawn; it may be a conflagration. But whether we believe it to be the one or the other, we are all agog to get there.'" Sat R

Offered in evidence
In Romains, J. The wind is rising

Passion's pilgrims; tr. from the French for the first time by Warre B. Wells. Knopf 1934 503p (Men of good will v2) o.p. 1970

Contents: bk.3 Childhood's loves; bk.4 Eros in Paris
"'Childhood's loves,' dealing largely with student life; and 'Eros in Paris,' which treats 'the eroticism of the great city to the point of torture and frenzy.' Quinette and other figures presented in the first volume reappear and their stories are carried forward." Book Rev Digest

The powers that be
In Romains, J. The earth trembles

The prelude
In Romains, J. Verdun

Promise of dawn
In Romains, J. The new day

The proud, and The meek; tr. from the French for the first time by Warre B. Wells. Knopf 1934 569p (Men of good will v3) o.p. 1970

Contents: bk.5 The proud; bk.6 The meek
"Book Five, 'The Proud,' is devoted largely to the intricate manoeuverings of the sly Haverkamp in his dangerous and daring real estate deals, and to the final stages of Sammécaud's long and arduous seduction of the coy and giddy Marie de Chamcenais. . . . We see, in Book Six ['The Meek'], the Bastide family plunging toward the lower depths when Monsieur Bastide loses the job he has held for twenty years. . . . Romains tells the story of the Bastides largely through the naïve, imaginative mind of Louis, the boy with the hoop. Slowly and painfully he learns the meaning of money, which society has made the material measure of life." N Y Times Bk R

Provincial interlude
In Romains, J. The world from below

Quinette's crime
In Romains, J. Men of good will

The seventh of October; tr. from the French by Gerard Hopkins. Knopf 1946 295, xvci p (Men of good will v14) o.p. 1970

Book 27 and final volume
"The action takes place between dawn and midnight of October 7th, 1933—and through it we are given a kaleidoscopic picture of France in crisis, and a final glimpse of most of the people, great and small, who have appeared from time to time in the vast cavalcade of the work." Huntting
Index of characters to all fourteen volumes: p i-xcvi

The sixth of October
In Romains, J. Men of good will

Sweets of life
In Romains, J. Aftermath

To the gutter
In Romains, J. The depths and the heights

To the stars
In Romains, J. The depths and the heights

Verdun; tr. from the French by Gerard Hopkins. Knopf 1939 500, xxii p (Men of good will v8) o.p. 1970

Contents: bk.15 The prelude; bk.16 The battle
This volume brings the "story of modern France down to the second winter of the first World War. The battle of Verdun is examined in minute detail both as to matters of military strategy and action and as it is seen thru the minds of a group of soldiers." Book Rev Digest
"The true greatness of this book lies in its simple picture of the agony and humiliation of man before the crime of modern war." Boston Transcript

Vorge against Quinette
In Romains, J. Aftermath

The wind is rising; tr. from the French by Gerard Hopkins. Knopf 1945 588, xxi p (Men of good will v12) o.p. 1970

Contents: bk.1 The gathering of the gangs; bk.2 Offered in evidence
The "theme of this volume . . . is the rise of gangs and the gang spirit in the Europe of 1927 and 1928. . . . Though Jerphanion and his friend, Jallez [introduced in earlier volumes] figure prominently, there are also many new characters." Huntting

Work and play; tr. from the French by Gerard Hopkins. Knopf 1944 562p (Men of good will v11) o.p. 1970

Contents: bk.21 Mountain days; bk.22 Work and play
The scene of this novel is France during the second decade of the twentieth century. Jerphanion, one of the central figures, and his friends are greatly concerned with the shadows of coming events that were to immerse Europe in chaos

The world from below; tr. from the French for the first time, by Gerard Hopkins. Knopf 1935 560, xxii p (Men of good will v4) o.p. 1970

Contents: bk.7 The lonely; bk.8 Provincial interlude
The lonely "deals principally with the young students and intellectuals of Paris who in that time of restlessness and spiritual indecision felt themselves homeless and without roots. They were searching for something to believe in for a faith, a church, an ideal. . . . [Provincial interlude] takes us to the French countryside, into the lives of the squires, and into the society and the politics of the provincial aristocracy." Lenrow. Reader's Guide to Prose Fiction

The world is your adventure
In Romains, J. The new day

Rooke, Daphne
Beti. Houghton 1959 146p o.p. 1970

"A romantic tale of modern India. The plot revolves around Larki, gentlehearted daughter of a quietly respectable Indian family, her cruel and beautiful cousin Beti, who was kidnapped when a child and reared as a pirate

Rooke, Daphne—*Continued*

queen, and Rammohun, the clever conjurer who brings them together in an exotic and perilous Arabian Nights adventure." Booklist

Mittee. Houghton 1952 [c1951] 312p o.p. 1970

"Selina, Mittee's comely colored companion and maid, narrates the story of the hot passions surrounding her mistress in the Africa of the Kaffir uprising and the Boer War. Paul, later General Du Plessis, began a clandestine affair with Selina when Mittee was cool to him. The protection of his guilty secret led from one violence to another." Retail Bookseller

Rosa, João Guimarães

The devil to pay in the Backlands. "The Devil in the street, in the middle of the whirlwind." Tr. from the Portuguese by James L. Taylor and Harriet de Onis. Knopf 1963 494p $5.95

Original Portuguese edition published 1956
"An old man, once an outlaw in the backlands of Brazil, tells of his life-long search to prove that the Devil doesn't exist so that he could not have signed a compact with him long ago." Bk Buyer's Guide
"Because of its realism, which at times is crude, it might be distasteful to fastidious readers. The book is recommended primarily to those who like manly, action-type books." Library J

The third bank of the river, and other stories (Primeriras estorias) Tr. from the Portuguese, with an introduction, by Barbara Shelby. Knopf 1968 238p $5.95

Analyzed in Short Story Index
Originally published 1962 in Brazil
"Posthumous short stories of a distinguished Brazilian writer. . . . The stories are laid in the Brazilian state of Minas Gerais and contain a rich range of character and situation." Booklist
Contents: The thin edge of happiness: Tantarum, my boss; Substance; Much ado; A woman of good works; The aldacious navigator; Honeymoons; A young man, gleaming, white; The horse that drank beer; Nothingness and the human; Condition; The mirror; Cause and effect; My friend the fatalist; No man, no woman; Hocus psychocus; The third bank of the river; The Dagobé brothers; The girl from beyond; Soroco, his mother, his daughter; Notorious; Treetops

Ross, Barnaby. See Queen, Ellery

Ross, Joseph

(ed.) Amazing Stories. The best of Amazing

Rosten, Leo

Captain Newman, M.D. Harper 1961 331p $6.95

"The story of the chief of the psychiatric ward of an Air Force hospital in the Southwest. Captain Newman is a compassionate doctor who conducts a private war against the Brass and their formalities on behalf of his patients. He has the help of some highly individualistic and zany assistants." Huntting
"A book of great insight, warmth and humor. . . . It is a tremendously impressive piece of verbal tight-rope walking. There are the expected flashes of GI humor, the much-documented war of rank, there are also moments of great tenderness and understanding in this chronicle of that most delicate of explorations, the exploration into the shattered minds that are the common responsibilities of all of us." N Y Her Trib Books

A most private intrigue. Atheneum Pubs. 1967 270p $5.95

"When Peter Hazlett Galton goes to Istanbul to aid in the escape of three Western scientists who have been detained behind the Iron Curtain, he becomes involved in more adventures than he has bargained for. He falls in love with a beautiful English actress who has come to the city seeking her father, who had defected to the enemy; he arouses the ire of secret agents who try to kill him, and he ends up by going into Russia to effect an escape. Although this reads as pure fiction, a forward implies that this is all based on a true incident.' Library J

Under the boardwalk. Prentice-Hall 1968 131p boards $4.95

"This book tells the story of fifteen aspects of a Coney Island [Jewish] boyhood. All the chapters have the same setting: a boarding house near the boardwalk amusement area in Coney Island; all have the same characters: the young boy learning about the world from the people around him, his mother the matriarch who knows all the answers, his unhappy father who asks all the questions, his demented dying grandmother, concessioneers, sailors on leave, swimmers, lovers, cops, lost children—all the people of a summer at the beach." Am News of Bks

Roth, Henry

Call it sleep; a novel. With a history by Harold U. Ribalow; a critical introduction by Maxwell Geismar, and a personal appreciation by Meyer Levin. Cooper Sq. [1965 c1962] 599p $5.95

First published 1934; recopyrighted 1962
"The story of a New York childhood in Brownsville and Jewish East Side Manhattan. David's father, Albert, is a hard-working man of violent temper. The boy fears him, and turns always to his gentle and comforting mother for protection. More sensitive and imaginative than most of his little Jewish playmates, David goes thru a number of childhood experiences that strike him harshly, others that are pure terror." Book Rev Digest

Roth, Philip

Goodbye, Columbus, and five short stories
Some editions are:
Houghton $5.95
Modern Lib. $2.95

Analyzed in Short Story Index
First published 1959
"The title story in this collection is about a young Radcliffe girl and a Rutgers boy who learn that there is more to love than exuberance and passion. All of the stories dramatize the dilemma of modern American Jews, torn between two worlds." Pub W
Contents: Goodbye, Columbus; Conversion of the Jews; Defender of the faith; Epstein; You can't tell a man by the songs he sings; Eli, the fanatic

Letting go. Random House 1962 630p $5.95

The author "continues to investigate the American Jewish community and cultural scene. [This] novel of the young academic crowd of the 1950s . . . focuses on three main characters. Gabe Wallach, a young instructor in the humanities, has an independent income. . . . He lives a good life, but is forever plagued by a vague guilt. Then there are the Herzes, Libby and Paul. They represent the disaster-bent among Roth's generation. They are forever plagued by money and domestic crises, including an unwanted pregnancy. Roth treats their problems . . . as the story shifts from the University of Chicago to New York City and points on the road." San Francisco Chronicle

Portnoy's complaint. Random House 1969 274p $6.95

Alex Portnoy "fumbles at meanings for his fantasied life as he pours out his story to his analyst. A brilliant lawyer on Mayor Lindsay's staff, he is the product of a dominant Yiddish mama, and an overdemanding, overindulgent, and overworked, constipated father. His main goal in life is the seduction of as many 'shiksas' as possible for revenge on the goyim." Library J
This is "a novel that is playfully and painfully moving, but also a work that is certainly catholic in appeal, potentially monumental in effect—and, perhaps more important, a deliciously funny book, absurd and exuberant, wild and uproarious. . . . On one level . . . Portnoy's

Roth, Philip—*Continued*

past comes off as a kind of universal pop boyhood of the forties, with a Jewish accent and comic twist. On another level . . . Portnoy's adolescence is revealed with a rare candor: not only is his gnawing special sense of Jewishness —and guilt—completely detailed, but also his compulsive nonstop masturbatory rites of puberty and his first vain attempts to enter the adult world of heterosexuality are fully annotated." N Y Time Bk R

When she was good. Random House 1967 306p $5.95

A story set in the small town of Liberty Center which recounts the life of "Lucy Nelson, a Midwestern girl who believes herself to be the moral superior of her family and friends, and of how she and those around her are destroyed when she sets out to prove that in matters of right and wrong she is the ultimate authority. Lucy's special mission is to make men do their duty by their wives and children. She begins her feverish crusade by attempting to reform her alcoholic father, and ends it, and her life, in an . . . attempt to convert into 'a good man' her boyish young husband, Roy Bassart . . . who never quite gets the drift of what is wanted of him." Publisher's note

Rothberg, Abraham

The song of David Freed; a novel. Putnam 1968 252p $4.95

David Freed is an Orthodox Jewish boy who lives in a lower middle class neighborhood in Brooklyn. This is the story of his growth from innocence to maturity, when his illusions are stripped away and he must reevaluate the faith he lives by. (Publisher)

"For many readers wearied by the shredding of the Jewish ego . . . this novel will come as balm. . . . It sings (with the pure voice of the boy cantor) of a touching and trying time in Jewish life in America." N Y Times Bk R

(jt. ed.) Foley, M. ed. U.S. stories

Roux, Edmonde Charles- See Charles- Roux, Edmonde

Rowson, Susanna Haswell

Charlotte Temple, a tale of truth

Some editions are:
Garrett Press $7.50
College and Univ. Press (Masterworks of literature series) $4 Edited by Clara M. and Rudolf Kirk

First published 1791 in England; 1794 in the United States

"The heroine is lured from her English home and deserted in New York by a British officer named Montraville, who later repents." Benét. The Reader's Encyclopedia

Roy, Gabrielle

Street of riches; tr. by Harry Binsse. Harcourt 1957 246p $3.95

Though presented by the author as fiction, "these episodic stories about a large French-Canadian family, living on the Rue Deschambault or Street of Riches in a small Manitoba town a generation ago, have the nostalgic quality of personal reminiscence. Christine, the narrator, portrays her volatile Maman and her brooding Papa who worked with the Dukhobors and Ruthenian settlers on the desolate prairie, together with other relatives and neighbors, in a series of sketches which vary in tone from humor to pathos." Booklist

The tin flute. Harcourt 1947 315p o.p. 1970

Translated from the French by Hannah Josephson

"A tale of a French-Canadian family which each day faces the problem of going on relief, but manages to survive because of the daughter's job in a Montreal dime store. Father eventually gives his family security by joining the army and daughter finds hope for future happiness by marrying a soldier. Without being sordid author portrays the problems of these people who were victims of the depression." Library J

Ruark, Robert

Something of value; drawings by Daniel Schwartz. Doubleday 1955 566p illus $5.95

Set in present day Africa this novel "follows the fortunes of two boys, a white Englishman and his native friend. . . . [Interwoven in the plot] are accounts of safaris; of life in Kenya and the mores of the British colony; of the growth and spreading of the Mau Mau (native terrorist) movement." Library J

"This is a bloody, violent, horrible story, in many respects; it shocks and revolts, but it also has beauty and love and a warm appreciation of friendship, bravery, and courage. And it is not a tract." Chicago Sunday Tribune

Uhuru; a novel of Africa today. McGraw 1962 555p o.p. 1970

"The central motif in [this novel] . . . is the gradual loosening of the grip of the whites on the land, symbolized in the disintegration of the white hunter Brian Dermott. A decorated hunter of Mau-Maus, a dedicated game warden, now a hugely successful safari operator and heir to a substantial farm. Dermott seems to have everything. But he is haunted by the failure of his marriage, and even more by the shadow of doom that hangs over Kenya. He bitterly opposes a scheme to foster a co-operative farm on his family's land, on the grounds that the black politicians will never let it succeed. . . . The final situation is in part pessimistic—a bitter-ender OAS-type organization of whites, loss of land values, failure of well-intentioned efforts—but in larger part optimistic, in that it recognizes a capacity for responsiblity in the Negro body politic." N Y Her Trib Books

Rubens, Bernice

Chosen people. Atheneum Pubs. 1969 275p $5.95

Published in England with title: The elected member

"The scene is London and the family in question is lower middle class Jewish, the elderly father an Orthodox rabbi, who loves his grown children but is powerless to help them. It is Norman, the once brilliant barrister son, who is now a drug addict and madman, beset by hallucinations, periodically taken off for longer and longer stays in a mental hospital. Miss Rubens explores the agony of Norman's multiple breakdowns, his brief moments of lucidity in which he is overwhelmed by guilt feelings, his desperate cravings as an addict. On another level, weaving back into the past, she shows how each member of the family has contributed his or her own share of neurosis to the burden." Pub W

Runyon, Damon

Best of Runyon; E. C. Bentley selected these stories; Nicolas Bentley drew the pictures. Stokes 1938 xxv, 318p illus o.p. 1970

Analyzed in Short Story Index

"Contents: Breach of promise; Romance in the roaring forties; Dream street Rose; Old doll's house; Blood pressure; Bloodhounds of Broadway; Tobias the terrible; Snatching of Bookie Bob; Lily of St Pierre; Hold 'em Yale; Earthquake; "Gentlemen, the King"; Nice price; Broadway financier; Brain goes home

Blue plate special

In Runyon, D. Guys and dolls p345-505

Guys and dolls. Lippincott 1950 505p o.p. 1970

An omnibus volume of three titles first published 1931, 1935 and 1934 respectively

Contents: Guys and dolls: Bloodhounds of Broadway; Social error; Lily of St. Pierre; Butch minds the baby; Lillian; Romance in the roaring forties; Very honorable guy; Madame La Gimp; Dark Dolores; "Gentlemen, the King!"; Hottest guy in the world; Brain goes home; Blood pressure

Money from home: Earthquake; Bred for battle; Breach of promise; Story goes with it; Sense of humor; Broadway financier; Broadway complex. It comes up mud; Nice price; Pick the winner; Undertaker song; Tobias the terrible

Runyon, Damon—*Continued*

Blue plate special: Hold 'em, Yale; That everloving wife of Hymie's; What, no butler; Brakeman's daughter; Snatching of Bookie Bob; Dream street Rose; Little Miss Marker; Dancing Dan's Christmas; Old doll's house; Lemon drop kid; Three wise guys; Princess O'Hara; For a pal

Money from home
In Runyon, D. Guys and dolls p167-337

Runyon first and last; foreword by Clark Kinnaird. Lippincott 1949 255p o.p. 1970

Analyzed in Short Story Index
A collection of 39 short stories hitherto unpublished in book form, including a selection of short-shorts from the author's earliest and latest efforts
Contents: Blonde mink; Big boy blues; Defense of Strikerville; Fat Fallon; Two men named Collins; As between friends; informal execution of Soupbone Pew; My father; Dangerous guy indeed; Old New Year's; Story without a moral; Old men of the mountain; At Dead Mule crossing; Right good-looking gal; As far as a man possibly can; In one ear; Dumb Dan, the wooden Indian; Very married man; Very touching story to some; What do you think they see; Big strong man six feet two; Nellie Morgan; Great man for playing jokes; Slight hitch in Uncle Tom's cabin; Bad Bud and the Reverend; Old Simp; 100 percent man; Samson and Delilah all over; Sure thing named Marmaduke James; Wooing of Nosey Gillespie; Highpockets; No use whatever for banks; Elopement of Missus Camp; Christmas revenge; Rawhide for short; Halloweve spirits; No fun for Lee Sing; Women are very strange; Just a young squirt

S

Sabatini, Rafael

y Captain Blood; his odyssey. Houghton 1927 437p illus (Riverside bookshelf) $4.95

First published 1922
"Peter Blood was many things in his time—soldier, country doctor, slave, pirate, and finally Governor of Jamaica. Incidently, he was an Irishman. Round his humorous-heroic figure Mr Sabatini has written an exciting romance of the Spanish Main, the facts of which he alleges to have been found in the diary and log-books of one Jeremiah Pitt, a follower of Monmouth in 1685 and Blood's faithful companion in adventure." Times (London) Lit Sup

y Scaramouche, the king-maker. Houghton 1931 420p $4.95

"The story, primarily of love and adventure, is woven around a hero who devoted himself to furthering the republican cause during the first years of the French Revolution (1788-1792). The title character, successively a lawyer, politician, swordsman, and buffoon, crosses paths repeatedly with his sworn enemy, in the end attaining love and happiness." Lenrow. Reader's Guide to Prose Fiction

y The Sea-hawk. Houghton 1923 366p front o.p. 1970

First published 1915
"Elemental in its record of unrepressed loves and hates is the story of how Sir Oliver Tressilian, Cornish gentleman and sometime commander of one of her majesty's ships which dispersed the Spanish Armada, became a follower of Mahmud—and a Barbary-corsair, winning for himself the title of Sakr-el-Bahr—Hawk of the sea." Boston Transcript

Sackville-West, Victoria

All passion spent. Doubleday 1931 294p o.p. 1970

"When Lady Slane, after the death of her famous husband, shocks her family by going to live by herself in a little house in Hempstead, she is for the first time in her eighty-eight years asserting her right to live her own life. The year of quiet reminiscences there is not wthout exciting moments, for a man who has loved her silently for sixty years renews his friendship, tells her of his love then suddenly dies, and leaves her his enormous fortune. What she does with this fortune is another instance of her self-assertion. Gentle, charming Lady Slane, her family, and her friends, drawn with wit and skill in this tale of graceful old age, create an impression of subtlety and beauty." Booklist

The Edwardians. Doubleday 1930 314p o.p. 1970

"The setting of this story of Edwardian England is the beautiful old manor-house of Chevron. The characters are grouped around Sebastian, the young heir to the dukedom, and his mother, a famous hostess of the day. Individuals count for less in the novel than the beautiful old house and all that it represents—a decadent but decorative society. The close of the story, marked by King George's coronation, finds the young duke breaking with the traditions that have bound him, not unwillingly, and starting a new era for himself." Book Rev Digest

Sagan, Françoise

Bonjour tristesse. Tr. from the French by Irene Ash. Dutton 1955 128p $4.50

"It is written in the first person by the young heroine and tells the story of her attempt to block her widowed father's marriage, an attempt that destroyed her would-be stepmother, revealed to her the world of love, lost her the last vestiges of her girlhood innocence, and gained her a sense of corruption and sadness that she could neither lose nor comprehend." Library J
"Of course the 'untroubled artistic amorality' of her story is typically French; it may as a result, particularly for Anglo-Saxon readers, rob Francoise Sagan's novel of the essential nobility which a tragi-comic work of this sort demands." Springf'd Republican

A certain smile; tr. from the French by Anne Green. Dutton 1956 128p boards $3.95

The story "concerns the love affair of a 20 year old Sorbonne student and a married man twice her age. After spending two blissful weeks on the Riviera, they return to Paris where their affair simmers down to a some-time thing. Slight though the story is, it is told with style, and the emotional development of the girl is well done." Library J

La chamade; tr. from the French by Robert Westhoff. Dutton 1966 156p boards $4.50

Original French edition published 1965
"Lucile, a beautiful woman of thirty, shares the luxurious apartment of her wealthy protector, Charles. Lucile may occasionally betray Charles, yet she is really fond of him. In their Paris milieu where amoral enjoyment depends on expensive luxuries, Lucile lives for the pleasures of each day until she meets the young editor Antoine, who is the . . . companion of a fashionable older woman. . . . Lucile and Antoine become lovers." Publisher's note

Saint, Dora Jessie. See Read, Miss

Saint Exupery, Antoine de

y Night flight; preface by André Gide; tr. by Stuart Gilbert. Appleton 1932 198p o.p. 1970

"Rivière, chief of the airport at Buenos Aires, is a ruthless adherent to duty. His motto is 'Love the men under your orders, but do not let them know it.' As he waits for the arrival of the night mail planes from Patagonia, Chile and Paraguay he is busy overseeing the preliminaries of the departure of the European mail plane. Two of the planes arrive safely; the third encounters a storm over the Andes. The pilot battles bravely, but the plane crashes, and news of the accident reaches Buenos Aires. But Rivière does not hesitate; if he holds up even one departure he knows it means the end of night flights. The European mail plane departs as planned." Book Rev Digest
"Fashioned with artistic restraint, the story fuses details of reality with dramatic suspense and a current of underlying psychology." N Y Libraries

Saint Exupery, Antoine de—*Continued*

Prisoner of the sand

In Costain, T. B. comp. Twelve short novels p457-90

St Johns, Adela Rogers

Tell no man. Doubleday 1966 444p $6.95

"After the suicide of his friend, prosperous Hank Gavin turned to religion. Rather to the dismay of his skeptic wife he left everything to follow Jesus, becoming a minister in a California town and preaching a return to the basic Christian ideals." Bk Buyer's Guide

Saki

The short stories of Saki; with an introduction by Christopher Morley. Modern Lib. 718p $2.95

First published 1930 by Viking, and analyzed in Short Story Index

Contents: Reginald; Reginald on Christmas presents; Reginald on the academy; Reginald at the theatre; Reginald's peace poem; Reginald's choir treat; Reginald on worries; Reginald on house-parties; Reginald at the Carlton; Reginald on besetting sins; Reginald's drama; Reginald on tariffs; Reginald's Christmas revel; Reginald's Rubaiyat; Innocence of Reginald; Reginald in Russia; Reticence of Lady Anne; Lost Sanjak; Sex that doesn't shop; Blood-feud of Toad-water; Young Turkish catastrophe; Judkin of the parcels; Gabriel-Ernest; Saint and the goblin; Soul of Laploshka; Bag; Strategist; Cross currents; Baker's dozen; Mouse; Esmé; Match-maker; Tobermory; Mrs Packletide's tiger; Stampeding of Lady Bastable; Background; Hermann the Irascible—a story of the great weep; Unrest-cure; Jesting of Arlington Stringham; Sredni Vashtar; Adrian; Chaplet; Quest; Wratislav; Easter egg; Filboid Studge, the story of a mouse that helped; Music on the hill; Story of St Vespaluus; Way to the dairy; Peace offering; Peace of Mowsie Barton; Talking-out of Tarrington; Hounds of fate; Recessional; Matter of sentiment; Secret sin of Septimus Brope; "Ministers of grace"; Remoulding of Groby Lington; She-wolf; Laura; Boar-pig; Brogue; Hen; Open window; Treasureship; Cobweb; Lull; Unkindest blow; Romancers; Schwartz-Metterklume method; Seventh pullet; Blind spot; Dusk; Touch of realism; Cousin Teresa; Yarkand manner; Byzantine omelette; Feast of Nemesis; Dreamer; Quince tree; Forbidden buzzards; Stake; Clovis on parental responsibilities; Holiday task; Stalled ox; Storyteller; Defensive diamond; Elk; "Down pens"; Name-day; Lumber-room; Fur; Philanthropist and the happy cat; On approval; Toys of peace; Louise; Tea; Disappearance of Crispina Umberleigh; Wolves of Cernogratz; Louis; Guests; Penance; Phantom luncheon; Bread and butter miss; Bertie's Christmas Eve; Forewarned; Interlopers; Quail seed; Canossa; Threat; Excepting Mrs Pentherby; Mark; Hedgehog; Mappined life; Fate; Bull; Morlvera; Shock tactics; Seven cream jugs; Occasional garden; Sheep; Oversight; Hyacinth; Image of the lost soul; Purple of the Balkan kings; Cupboard of the yesterdays; For the duration of the war; Square egg; Birds on the western front; Gala programme; Infernal parliament; Achievement of the cat; Old town of Pskoff; Clovis on the alleged romance of business; Comments of Moung Ka

The unbearable Bassington; with an introduction by Maurice Baring. Viking 244p o.p. 1970

First published 1913

"The character study of Comus Bassington, a witty, handsome, lovable yet exasperating youth, with just that lack in character which predicated failure. His mother is a selfishly ambitious woman to whom Comus's failures are torture. Mother and son are drawn to the life. Their friends and enemies, members of the aritocratic set in which they move, are summed up in a paragraph, set off in a phrase, in 'Saki's' inimitable style. The story moves toward tragedy, when the spiritual breach between mother and son becomes irremediable." Book Rev Digest

Salamanca, J. R.

Lilith. Simon & Schuster 1961 381p o.p. 1970

"Vincent Bruce, a devoted and able attendant in a mental hospital, is drawn into the mad world of the beautiful schizophrenic, Lilith, who seduces him and then leads him into bizarre sin and servitude." Bk Buyer's Guide

"Beautiful prose combined with a depth of feeling that not only illuminates characters but the shadowy borderlines of good and evil, sanity and insanity. Not to every taste but haunting to its admirers." Booklist

Salinger, J. D.

y The catcher in the rye

Some editions are:
Little $4.95
Watts, F. $8.95 Large type edition. A Keith Jennison Book

First published 1951

"Just before Christmas young Holden Caulfield, knowing that he is to be dropped by his school, decides to leave early and not report home until he has to. He spends three days and nights in New York City and this is the story in his own words, of what he did and saw and suffered." Book Rev Digest

"The author presents an understanding and sincere account of the mental gropings and disillusionment of a sensitive and precocious adolescent boy. . . . The dangers he encounters are terrifying to the adult mind; the language he uses to describe his adventures is downright bad; but the soul of the boy is pure and innocent and wholly honest. He rejects the unwholesome and the evil, not heroically but in a very matter of fact manner and because he is fundamentally decent. He gains knowledge but without sacrifice of his integrity." Ontario Lib Rev

y Franny and Zooey. Little 1961 201p $4.95

Contains two stories: Franny, and Zooey. Both stories belong to a series of stories about the Glass family of twentieth century New York. In the first story "college girl Franny has a date spoiled by her conversion through a religious book, and [in the second] Zooey, her older brother, tries to make her see that it is her job to become an actress." Bk Buyer's Guide

"The dialog is expert. Still, it is a rather wandering, sometimes maddening book, less effective or meaningful than 'The Catcher in the Rye.' However, it seems certain to be successful, especially with readers who are young, and perhaps confused themselves." Pub W

y Nine stories. Little 1953 302p $4.95

Analyzed in Short Story Index

Contents: A perfect day for bananafish; Uncle Wiggily in Connecticut; Just before the war with the Eskimos; The laughing man; Down at the dinghy; For Esmé—with love and squalor; Pretty mouth and green my eyes; De Daumier-Smith's blue period; Teddy

"They are penetrating in insight, moving in their quiet indirectness, and polished in their craft." Wis Lib Bul

Raise high the roof beam, carpenters, and Seymour: an introduction. Little [1963] 248p $4.95

Two long stories originally written 1955 and 1959 respectively, for the New Yorker containing episodes from the life of the Glass family with Seymour Glass, the oldest child, as the central character. Since Seymour never appears the episodes are recounted by his brother Buddy, an English teacher at a girls' college

"The reader should appreciate the artistry in Salinger's deftness of diction, sureness of touch, clearness of tone. This is particularly important for the latter piece, 'the long, agonizing prose poem,' sounding observations on Life, Character, and the Vocation of the literary artist. The style may get in the way of a reader who mistakes an essay for a short story. The tone may puzzle many. . . . Mature readers will marvel at the brilliant performance that marks the unmistakable Salinger style in presenting his unmistakable Glass Family." Best Sellers

Salinger, J. D.—*Continued*
Seymour: an introduction
In Salinger, J. D. Raise high the roof beam, carpenters, and Seymour: an introduction

Sandburg, Carl
Remembrance Rock. Harcourt 1948 1067p $6.75
"Taking as its starting point the exciting period just after VE Day, the story moves backward in time to early 17th century England, then to America with the Pilgrims. The reader follows the new country as it struggles and grows during the Revolution . . . during the Civil War . . . and the great movement, Westward . . . while an epilogue brings the story back to the present time." Huntting

Sanders, Joan
Baneful sorceries; or, The countess bewitched. Houghton 1969 352p $6.95
"The affair of the poisons during Louis XIV's time involved people in high places, witchcraft, all kinds of skulduggery. Joan Sanders' novel tells of Margot Renard, daughter of a rich jeweler who was married off to the Comte du Rocsur-Bresbre, a penniless nobleman. It is in his ancient, crumbling country estate where all the dangerous, eerie happenings occur." Pub W
"The book is well within the girl-meets-boy-meets-castle gothic tradition." Library J

Sanders, Lawrence
The Anderson tapes; a novel. Putnam 1970 254p $5.95
"In this novel tapes are the medium for describing a burglary involving the looting of an entire apartment building. Several government agencies . . . have planted 'bugs' over most of the island of Manhattan, and from the . . . transcriptions of the tapes . . . we follow the plot. John 'Duke' Anderson, the central figure and brains of the caper, recruits and organizes a gang, with Mafia backing. Their nemesis is a . . . crippled 14-year-old, who uses a hidden short-wave transmitter to halt the crime." Library J

Sandoz, Mari
Miss Morissa, doctor of the gold trail; a novel. McGraw 1955 249p o.p. 1970
"The story of a pioneer woman doctor who sets up practice and struggles for existence on the Nebraska frontier in the 1870's." Pub W
y Winter thunder. Westminster Press 1954 61p boards $2.50
"The story of a school bus lost in a Nebraska blizzard, and how the valiant young teacher fought to save the lives of the driver and the children when the bus burned up." Book Rev Digest

Sansom, William
The stories of William Sansom; with an introduction by Elizabeth Bowen. Little 1963 421p o.p. 1970
"An Atlantic Monthly Press book"
Analyzed in Short Story Index
Contents: The wall; Difficulty with a bouquet; Something terrible, something lovely; Displaced persons; The vertical ladder; How Claeys died; A saving grace; Various temptations; Building alive; Three dogs of Siena; Pastorale; My little robins; Gliding gulls and going people; Time and place; A world of glass; The girl on the bus; A waning moon; A game of billiards; On stony ground; Impatience; Episode at Gastein; Life, death; A contest of ladies; An interlude; Question and answer; A country walk; A last word; A woman seldom found; A Among the dahlias; Outburst; To the rescue; Eventide; Cat up a tree.

Santayana, George
The last Puritan; a memoir in the form of a novel. Scribner 1936 602p o.p. 1970
"A picture of American life, especially in New England, from the 1890's to the close of the World War, as seen through the eyes of a young man who 'convinced himself on Puritan grounds that it was wrong to be a Puritan . . . and remained a Puritan notwithstanding.' Full of ironic wisdom and poetic tenderness, of long views and exact pictorial details. The book is more than a novel, it is the commentary of a philosopher upon the blind confusions of modernity." Ontario Lib Rev
"This book provides a brilliant picture of New England life in that epoch which the war brought to a close. . . . It is perhaps because his own tradition and his own likings are so different that Mr. Santayana can write with such revealing understanding, such wit and humor, of the Puritan tradition as it appeared in the twentieth century." Boston Transcript

Santesson, Hans Stefan
(ed.) The locked room reader; stories of impossible crimes and escapes. Random House 1968 464p $6.95
Analyzed in Short Story Index
This collection includes fourteen short stories and two complete novels: The big bow mystery, by Israel Zangwill, first published 1895; and The narrowing list, by Henry Kane, first published 1955 with title: Too French and too deadly
Short stories included are: The locked room, by J. D. Carr; The Dauphin's Doll, by E. Queen; Nothing is impossible, by C. Rawson; His heart could break, by C. Rice; The oracle of the dog, by G. K. Chesterton; When a felon needs a friend, by M. Hershman; The Doomdorf mystery, by M. D. Post; The man who read John Dickson Carr, by W. Brittain; The long way down, by E. D. Hoch; Time trammel, by M. A. deFord; Reprieve, by L. G. Blochman; The smoke-filled locked room, by A. Boucher; Bones for Davy Jones, by J. Commings; The fine Italian hand, by T. Flanagan

Saroyan, William
After thirty years: The daring young man on the flying trapeze. Harcourt [1964] 312p $5.95
Previous edition had title: The daring young man on the flying trapeze, and other stories, and was analyzed in Short Story Index
Contents: The daring young man on the flying trapeze; Seventy thousand Assyrians; Among the lost; Myself upon the earth; Love, death sacrifice and so forth; 1, 2, 3, 4, 5, 6, 7, 8; And man; Curved line; Snake; Big valley vineyard; Aspirin is a member of the N.R.A.; Seventeen; Cold day; Earth, day, night, self; Harry; Laughter; Big tree coming; Dear Greta Garbo; Man with the French post cards; Three stories; Love; War; Sleep in unheavenly peace; Fight your own war; Common prayer; Shepherd's daughter

y The human comedy; illus. by Don Freeman; ed. by Marion C. Sheridan. Harcourt 1944 299p illus $4.95
"The setting is the California town of Ithaca, the time the present and the cast of characters dominated by the Macauley family depicted by the author with loving and meticulous care. The father, Matthew, has died before the story begins, leaving a gracious and understanding wife to watch over four children; Marcus, off in the army; Bess, just turned eighteen and ready for love; Homer (Saroyan himself), messenger for the local Postal Telegraph office; and four-year-old Ulysses." Books
"Mr. Saroyan is a complete romantic. His fancifulness, his ecstatic love and admiration for children and even half-wits, his enthusiasm, his delight, his wonder at everything and anything, his faith in the promptings of the heart over those of the head . . . his conviction that good always drives out sickness and evil and that love conquers all, make him difficult to argue with. One can only disagree." N Y Times Bk R

Saroyan, William—*Continued*

Mama, I love you. Little 1956 245p o.p. 1970

Nine year old Twink tells how she and her mother "secure complementary roles in an allegorical Broadway production that exploits Twink's elfin charm. Mama Girl proves that she has the makings of an actress, and her achievement releases Twink, who really wants an ordinary childhood with her father and brother in Paris." Booklist

y My name is Aram; illus. by Don Freeman. Harcourt 1940 220p illus $2.95

Analyzed in Short Story Index

Sketches concerning Aram, an American-born Armenian boy and his mad cousin, his sad uncle, his reckless uncle, etc.

Contents: Summer of the beautiful white horse; Journey to Hanford; Pomegranate trees; One of our future poets, you might say; Fifty-yard dash; Nice old-fashioned romance, with love lyrics and everything; My cousin Dikran, the orator; Presbyterian choir singers; Circus; Three swimmers and the grocer from Yale; Locomotive 38, the Ojibway; Old country advice to the American traveler; Poor and burning Arab; Word to scoffers

One day in the afternoon of the world. Harcourt 1964 245p o.p. 1970

A "novel about a writer flat broke and in trouble with the tax collector. He is visiting New York City to sell some of his plays and to visit his two children by his divorced wife. Though down on his luck, he still has much of the charm and joy of his youth, and people remember his best books." Pub W

"The whole is pervaded by a warmly human, but unsentimental, and comic imagination. In trying 'to help men to be men,' he does more than merely advertize himself.' . . . He helps the reader to realize the essential beauty of life in love and the importance and dignity of human beings." Best Sellers

The Saroyan special; selected short stories; illus. by Don Freeman. Harcourt 1948 368p illus o.p. 1970

Analyzed in Short Story Index

Contents: Myself upon the earth; Seventy thousand Assyrians; Aspirin; Curved line; 1, 2, 3, 4, 5, 6, 7, 8; Laughter; Shepherd's daughter; Daring young man on the flying trapeze; Five ripe pears; The oranges; Two days wasted in Kansas City; Going home; Horses and the sea; World wilderness of time lost; Fresno; Broken wheel; The war; Death of children; Barber whose uncle has his head bitten off by a circus tiger; Antranik of Armenia; Little Miss Universe; Our little brown brothers the Filipinos; Dark sea; Malenka Manon; Proletarian at the trap drum; Black Tartars; Little dog laughed to see such sport; Train going; The whistle Finlandia; The Armenian and the Armenian; Man with the heart in the Highland; Bitlis; Baby; The beggers; Quarter, half, three-quarter, and whole notes; Living and the dead; Laughing Sam; Sunday Zeppelin; Corduroy pants; First day of school; Man who got fat; The messenger; My uncle and the Mexicans; Countryman, how do you like America; Where I come from people are polite; The trains; One of the least famous of the great love affairs of history; La Salle Hotel in Chicago; Ah life, ah death, ah music, ah France, ah everything; The genius; The fire; Filipino and the drunkard; Jim Pemberton and his boy Trigger; Insurance salesman, the peasant, the rug merchant, and the potted plant; Year of heaven; 1924 Cadillac for sale; Love kick; Warm quiet valley of home; Number of the poor; Peace, it's wonderful; Piano; Sweet singer of Omsk; Russian writer; Journey and the dream; The tiger; Sweetheart sweetheart sweetheart; Brothers and sisters; The ants; Great leapfrog contest; The acrobats; Citizens of the third grade; Prayer for the living; Memories of Paris; The job; The vision; We want a touchdown; Saroyan's fables, IX; Saroyan's fables, XXIV; Dear baby; Hummingbird that lived through winter; Stolen bicycle; Story of the young man and the mouse; Struggle of Jim Patros with death; Sailing down the Chesapeake; I know you good; How it is to be; Declaration of war; Highway America; My home, my home; The grapes; My witnesseth

Sarraute, Nathalie

The golden fruits; a novel; tr. by Maria Jolas. Braziller 1964 177p $4.95

Originally published in France 1963

"This novel centers about the criticism of a novel and reflects the different attitudes or schools of literary thought in Paris. Especially of interest to the reader who follows the new literary forms and asks, what is taste and what relationship does it bear to time?" Wis Lib Bul

"The whole book is built of the most elusive and ephemeral materials, but it is a success both in involving the reader intimately in the passing tide of comment and in creating a vivid sense of the precariousness of reputation. For all collections of fine experimental writing." Library J

Tropisms; tr. from the French by Maria Jolas. Braziller [1967 c1963] 59p $3.50

Original French edition, 1939; revised and enlarged 1957. This translation first published 1963 in England

The book "consists of 24 brief descriptions of moments of inner movement or change. These movements Mme. Sarraute calls tropisms 'because of their spontaneous, irresistible, instinctive nature, similar to that of the movements made by certain organisms under the influence of outside stimuli, such as light or heat." Library J

"Since they are stripped of their narrative context, Mme. Sarraute's tropists are more often character-traits than characters, pieces of people rather than people. . . . [But the book] displays an outstanding prose talent with crystalline reminders of Jane Austen and Virginia Woolf." Christian Science Monitor

Sarton, May

The birth of a grandfather. Rinehart 1957 277p o.p. 1970

The story of Boston bred Sprig Wyeth's struggle to overcome a sense of failure as a husband, father and friend is bound up with the problems precipitated for both Sprig and his wife by their daughter's marriage to a young man of Irish descent. By helping a dying friend, however, Sprig gains a more workable outlook on life just in time to welcome his first grandchild

"Perhaps the finest thing about Miss Sarton's book is its revelation that, as human beings worthy of the name, we never stop learning; never cease to explore the mysteries of this life in which human relationships are undoubtedly the greatest mystery of all." N Y Her Trib Books

The fur person. Illus. by Barbara Knox. Norton [1968 c1957] 106p illus $4.95

First published 1957 by Rinehart

This "story is drawn from the barely concealed true adventures of May Sarton's own cat, and recounts his evolution from Cat-about-Town, with no place to lay his head, to a Gentleman Cat, and finally his emergence as a genuine Fur person." McClurg. Book News

"What a joy it is to collect the fine creative geniuses of the world who can write delightful books about fine animals. Limited in interest but important." Library J

y Joanna and Ulysses; a tale; illus. by James J. Spanfeller. Norton 1963 127p illus boards $3.95

A "story about an idyllic holiday on a Greek island. The heroine, Joanna, a good-looking 30-year-old, is taking her first holiday in ten years after a harrowing decade of family troubles. Her companion, whom she rescues from ill treatment, is a little gray donkey named Ulysses. It is a wonderful escape for Joanna, who enjoys nursing Ulysses back to health and loves plunging into the painting that has been her dream of a life work." Pub W

"This gently realistic, mildly plaintive story is told in Miss Sarton's quiet, pretty manner and might be a good one for young adults, or even for younger girls." Library J

Sarton, May—*Continued*

Miss Pickthorn and Mr Hare; a fable. Norton 1966 92p illus boards $3.50

Miss Jane Pickthorn (the "Maiden Porcupine") is annoyed when someone moves into the tumbledown henhouse across the road. The story of how Miss Pickthorn and Mr Hare (the new neighbor) resolve their difficulties is an allegory of love, neighbors, and independence. (Publisher)

"With porcupine and hare hovering faintly behind the characters, this 'fable' would be interesting to students of literature and creative writing. . . . [This] book, close to poetry, manages to both 'mean' and 'be.' " Choice

y The poet and the donkey; illus. by Stefan Martin. Norton 1969 126p boards $4.50

This is an "account of the events in the life of Andy Lightfoot, an aging poet who suffers moments of depression because his talent seems to be waning. Whiffenpoof, the donkey, experiences cataclysmic moments because arthritis impedes her liberty. They achieve some consolation through knowledge and understanding of each other. This association cultivates a healthy relationship and both Lightfoot and Whiffenpoof identify with reality and manage to forget the problems which threatened to bring them to ruin." Best Sellers

"A gentle, sunny little tale. . . . The whimsey works because it is not overdone and because May Sarton has such a very nice way of writing about animals." Pub W

The small room; a novel. Norton 1961 249p o.p. 1970

"Lucy Winter, professor and seeker of refuge in the kingdom of a progressive [New England] woman's college, becomes involved when a top student is caught in a case of plagiarism, and peace dissolves. The faculty must face the guilt of having pushed for intellectual attainment with inadequate knowledge and consideration for emotional factors, i.e. the crime of not teaching 'the whole child.' Each person reacts to crisis differently—sometimes disastrously, but all can meet finally in the small room to evaluate the past and to agree on the college's proposed plan for the future." Library J

"May Sarton writes with a clarity akin to sunlight after a rain. She presents her cast of faculty types with scrupulous respect. There is no villain among them. . . . The essence of this novel is not so much in the conflict of characters as in the conflict in ideas—and ideas about teaching." N Y Her Trib Books

Sartre, Jean-Paul

Nobel Prize in literature, 1964

The age of reason; tr. from the French by Eric Sutton. Modern Lib. 1947 397p (The Roads to freedom, v 1) $2.95

Original French edition, 1945. First published 1947 by Knopf

First of a series of three novels by the French philosopher, exponent of existentialism. The scene of this novel is Paris in 1938

"The central character is Mathieu, a professor to philosophy who writes one short story a year. . . . The problem that obsesses Mathieu, that of freedom, how to remain free, is worked out in the story and exemplified in the lives of the characters. . . . Mathieu differs from your ordinary character of fiction in that he is motivated by this abstract ethical ideal to keep his freedom. It is assailed as soon as the novel opens, for he learns that his mistress is pregnant; the action consists largely of his attempts to raise by borrowing—in the end, by stealing—the five thousand francs required to procure an abortion; unnecessarily, as it turns out, for Marcelle decides to marry someone else and have the child." Spec

Followed by: The reprieve

Intimacy, and other stories; tr. by Lloyd Alexander. New Directions 1952 [c1948] 270p o.p. 1970

Analyzed in Short Story Index

First published 1948 with title: The wall, and other stories

Contents: The wall; The room; Erostratus; Intimacy; The childhood of a leader

"His characters and situations mirror the unpleasantness, oppression, sensuality and neurosis of the Twentieth Century. His intellectual underworld includes a modern Erostratus who is compelled to murder, a psychotic who lives in a dark room, a marriage gone to seed, a boy's metamorphosis into a fascist, and the fate of a political prisoner." Publisher's note

Nausea; tr. from the French by Lloyd Alexander. New Directions 1949 238p (Modern French lit) o.p. 1970

"Sartre's first novel, published in France in the middle thirties, deals with a mysterious inner crisis in the life of Antoine Roquentin, who, after some years of travel, has buried himself in the dismal provincial town of Bouville. Roquentin has lately been subject to shattering attacks of 'nausea'—a species of d.t.'s without alcoholic cause—and he starts to keep a journal in the hope it will lead him to their source." Atlantic

"A brilliant, disturbing, sometimes bracing portrait of Sartre's wasteland." Good Reading

The reprieve; tr. from the French by Eric Sutton (The Roads to freedom, v2)

Some editions are:
Knopf $5.95
Modern Lib. $2.95

Sequel to: The age of reason

Original French edition 1945. First published 1947

"The second novel, ironically titled The Reprieve, confines itself to the eight frenetic days that led to the Munich Pact and the rape of Czechoslovakia. The original characters reappear merging now with many others as a shocked France mobilizes for war. Sartre, the leading exponent of Existentialism manages in this kaleidoscopic novel to recreate the confusion, even the odor of the fear that gripped Europe in September, 1938." Library J

Followed by: Troubled sleep

Troubled sleep; tr. from the French by Gerard Hopkins. Knopf 1950 421p (The Roads to freedom, v3) $5.95

Sequel to: The reprieve

First published in France, 1949; English edition has title: Iron in the soul

"A story of the French people after the fall of Paris in World War II, of many individuals of different walks of life and their reactions to defeat." Pub W

"No other book gives such insight into the anguished feelings of the French as they passed from apathy to consciousness of their dignity as men revolting against fate, accepting their solidarity with other men—wretched, but lucid and free fighters." Sat R

The Saturday Evening Post

Best modern short stories; selected from The Saturday Evening Post. Curtis Bks. [distributed by Doubleday] 1965 494p $5.95

Contents: Power in trust, by L. Auchincloss; A story for Teddy, by H. Swados; A tough nut, by A. Moravia; A humanist, by R. Gary; The refugee, by B. Malamud; One hundred ladies, by J. G. Cozzens; The inhabitants of Venus, by I. Shaw; The root of all evil, by G. Greene; The lucid eye in Silver Town, by J. Updike; Sucker, by C. McCullers; Boys and girls together, by W. Saroyan; Esther Kreindel the second, by I. B. Singer; Perlmutter at the East Pole, by S. Elkin; No more roses, by A. Seager; Walker's peak, by R. White; The ballet of Central Park, by K. Boyle; John Sobieski runs, by J. Buechler; Dance of the divorced, by H. Gold; The suicide, by E. S. Connell; Chaos, disorder and the late show, by W. Miller; Figure over the town, by W. Goyen; Little did I know, by H. Calisher; Center of gravity, by L. J. Amster; A life of your own, by F. O'Connor; The appraiser, by M. Wood; The moon of the arfy darfy, by N. Algren; One man, one boat, one girl, by S. O'Faolain; The birthday party, by G. Berriault; The old dancers, by T. Williams; The secret integration, by T. Pynchon

The Saturday Evening Post—_Continued_

Danger; great stories of mystery and suspense; selected by the editors of The Saturday Evening Post. Curtis Bks. distributed by Doubleday 1967 368p o.p. 1970

Analyzed in Short Story Index
Contents: Reunion with terror [novelette] by M. Albrand; The dream, by A. Christie; Set up for murder, by R. Stern; The mystery of the master safe-cracker, by R. Standish; Dead man in the water, by P. Wylie; One of the dead, by W. Wood; Hand upon the waters, by W. Faulkner; The possibility of evil, by S. Jackson; The woman who wouldn't stay dead, by G. Kersh; Motive for murder, by R. Stern; The black cat, by E. A. Poe; Run from the hangman [novelette] by G. Household

The Post Reader of Civil War stories; ed. by Gordon Carroll; with an introduction by E. B. Long. Illus. by Ray Houlihan. Doubleday 1958 331p illus o.p. 1970

Analyzed in Short Story Index
Contents: First blood at Harper's Ferry, by J. W. Bellah; The secret of the seven days, by J. W. Bellah; How Stonewall came back, by J. W. Bellah; The lost soldier, by J. Brick; The crystal chandelier, by J. Hergesheimer; Weep not for them, by C. Dowdey; Gentleman in blue, by L. Stallings; Jack Still, by J. P. Marquand; High tide, by J. P. Marquand; The Rebel Trace, by J. Hergesheimer; A mountain victory, by W. Faulkner; The duke's brigade, by C. Dowdey; Beautiful rebel, by P. Jones; No enemy, by M. Kantor; Ambuscade, by W. Faulkner; A preacher goes to war, by J. W. Thomason, Jr; The stars in their courses, by J. W. Thomason, Jr; The preacher calls the dance, by J. W. Thomason, Jr; The die-hard, by S. V. Benét

The Post Reader of fantasy and science fiction; selected by the editors of The Saturday Evening Post. Doubleday 1964 311p o.p. 1970

Analyzed in Short Story Index
The editors "have selected nineteen short stories and one novelette as the best they have published since 1937." Bk Buyer's Guide
Contents: Doctor Hanray's second chance, by C. Richter; Fallout island, by R. Murphy; The green hills of earth, by R. A. Heinlein; Doomsday deferred, by W. F. Jenkins; Test-tube terror, by R. Standish; Island of fear, by W. Sambrot; Sinister journey, by C. Richter; The place of the gods, by S. V. Benét; The phantom setter, by R. Murphy; The big wheel, by F. McMorrow; The death dust, by F. Harvey; The lost continent, by G. Household; The trap, by K. Bennett; Space secret, by W. Sambrot; The unsafe deposit box, by G. Kersh; The second trip to Mars, by W. Moore; The voice in the earphones, by W. Schramm; Moon crazy, by W. R. Shelton; The little terror, by W. F. Jenkins; The answer [novelette] by P. Wylie

The Saturday Evening Post Reader of sea stories; ed. by Day Edgar. Doubleday 1962 310p o.p. 1970

Analyzed in Short Story Index
Contents: Under the deck-awnings, by J. London; The beast from 20,000 fathoms, by R. Bradbury; Vengeance reef, by D. Waters; The snowflake and the starfish, by R. Nathan; Hornblower and the man who felt queer, by C. S. Forester; The capture of the Swordray, by C. Blair, Jr; Jarge makes in, by C. Rawlings; The living torpedo, by T. Yates; A sailor to the wheel, by B. Adams; Cargo of gold, by C. Rawlings; The ransom of Peter Drake, by J. Marmur; Port of call, by B. Hutton; The sea devil, by A. Gordon; The kid in command, by J. Marmur; Troubled voyage, by W. Holder; Captive captain, by J. P. Heffernan; Without warning, by R. Murphy; Treachery's wake, by O. Ruhen; Dr. Blanke's first command, by C. S. Forester; The cruise of the Breadwinner, by H. E. Bates

The Saturday Evening Post Reader of Western stories; ed. by E. N. Brandt. Doubleday 1960 358p o.p. 1970

Analyzed in Short Story Index

Contains 18 stories and two novelettes published in The Saturday Evening Post during the past sixty years
Contents: Outlaw Trail, by S. O. Barker; May the land be bright, by S. Byrd; Law of the lash, by P. Combs; Stage to Yuma, by M. DeVries; Fiddle-footed, by C. Farrell; The lady from Red Gulch, by M. Fessier; Test by torture, by W. Forrest; The marriage of Moon Wind, by W. Gulick; A widow of the Santa Ana Valley, by B. Harte; Dead-man trail, by E. Haycox; Dakotahs coming, by M. Kantor; How Mr Hickok came to Cheyenne, by A. H. Lewis; The hasty hanging, by M. Lewis; The fool's heart, by E. M. Rhodes; Top hand, by L. Short; Guest's gold, by S. E. White; Fast gun, by R. P. Wilmot; The gift horse, by O. Wister; The devil in the desert [novelette] by P. Horgan (1950) Smoke over the prairie [novelette] by C. Richter

The Saturday Evening Post Sports stories; selected and with an introduction by "Red" Smith. Barnes, A.S. 1949 307p o.p. 1970

Analyzed in Short Story Index
Contents: One hit, one error, one left, by R. Lardner; Ides of June, by R. Lardner; My kingdom for Jones, by W. Schramm; Greatest victory, by F. O'Rourke; You could look it up, by J. Thurber; Name of the game, by S. Frank; Ten rounds for baby, by J. Reeve; Brooklyn Mick, by E. Orcutt; Hello, Joe, by W. Fay; Russian dressing, by S. Hellman; Champion's due, by C. F. Coe; Second wind, by T. Josselyn; Taming of Tiger Meraz, by H. M. Alexander; Man who sank the navy, by W. Fay; Gravy game, by H. Stuhldreher; You can't win with women, by B. Stiles; Ninety and nine, by S. Hellman; Golf is a nice friendly game, by P. Gallico; Tennis racket, by C. Ford; Amateur spirit, by R. Macauley; See how they run, by G. H. Coxe; What's it get you, by J. P. Marquand

Savage, Mildred

Parrish; a novel. Simon & Schuster 1958 470p o.p. 1970

"This novel concerns America's gigantic tobacco business and the men and women who live by it—from lowly farm hands to the rich owners and their families. When Ellen married the most powerful planter of the [Connecticut] tobacco country, she did not forsee the tensions that would arise between her new husband and her 18-year-old son, Parrish." McClurg. Book News

Savage, Thomas

The liar; a novel. Little 1969 311p boards $5.95

"Hal Sawyer meant well, but his wife left him after a brief marriage and he had never seen his son. Hal sent the boy letters and pictures that shored up his fatherly pride with lies about his own success. But at last there was a confrontation between the son, who had done well to prove his worth to the father who, he thought, had deserted him. Now, the son saw through his father's anxious deceptions and understood them." Bk Buyer's Guide

Saxton, Mark

The Islar, a narrative of Lang III. Houghton 1969 308p map $5.95

"Lang III is grandson of the fictional hero of 'Islandia' by Austin Wright, edited by Mark Saxton in 1942. 'The Islar' is a fable in the form of a suspense story concerning a mythical country in the South Pacific. Islandia, whose culture and government the author describes in detail, existed in splendid isolation until valuable mineral resources were located. Promptly Russian agents infiltrate, and an exciting tale of treachery and intrigue develops. The fable advocates an enlightened United States foreign policy in regard to underdeveloped countries." Library J

Sayers, Dorothy L.

The bone of contention
_In_ Haycraft, H. ed. A treasury of great mysteries v2 p131-70

Sayers, Dorothy L.—*Continued*

Busman's honeymoon; a love story with detective interruptions. Harper [1960 c1937] 381p $5.95

A reissue of the title first published 1937 by Harcourt

"Lord Peter and Harriet consider Miss Twitterton's isolated cottage ideal for their honeymoon, until Miss Twitterton's missing uncle turns up murdered." McClurg. Book News

Dorothy L. Sayers omnibus. . . . Harcourt 3v in 1 o.p. 1970

Published as follows: Whose body (1923); Unpleasantness at the Bellona Club (1928); Suspicious characters (1931) This last title was published in England with title: The five red herrings and is entered separately. They are all stories of Lord Peter Wimsey

The five red herrings (Suspicious characters) Harper [1958 c1931] 306p map boards $5.95

First published in 1931 by Harcourt with title: Suspicious characters

"When Lord Peter Wimsey first saw her, Harriet Vane was standing trial for her life, accused of murdering her lover. So begins one of Lord Peter's most brilliant jobs of sleuthing and the start of a most romantic love story." McClurg. Book News

Gaudy Night. Harper [1960 c1936] 469p $5.95

A reissue of the title first published 1936 by Harcourt

"Harriet's return to Oxford for the Gaudy Dinner is welcomed by poison-pen letters and attempted blackmail. Lord Peter, of course, summons all his skill to detect the blackmailer . . . and win Harriet." McClurg. Book News

"Aside from the mystery, the psychological problem of what happens to the ordinarily sensible minds of a group of women who become suspicious of each other, is excellently handled. Characterization is good and the descriptions of life in a women's college in England are extremely interesting. Oxford town itself stands out clearly." Wis Lib Bul

Have his carcase. Harper [1959 c1932] 448p boards $5.95

A reissue of the title first published 1932 by Harcourt

"A murdered man, an ivory-handled razor, three hundred pounds in gold coins and a coded message are among the ingredients of this Lord Peter Wimsey mystery." Huntting

Murder must advertise. Harper [1959 c1933] 344p boards $5.95

A reissue of the title first published 1933 by Harcourt

"A copywriter plunges to his death down an iron staircase, and his replacement snoops among private papers and practices with a catapult on the roof. A Lord Wimsey novel." Huntting

"One of the most famous in the . . . series, this is also a funny spoof of the advertising business." McClurg. Book News

The nine tailors; changes rung on an old theme in two short touches and two full peals. Harcourt 1934 331p o.p. 1970

"One New Year's Eve, Lord Peter Wimsey, driving through a snowstorm, goes off the road near Fenchurch St Paul, and is the chance guest of the rector. A providential visit all around, for Peter, acquainted with the ancient art of bell-ringing, acts that night as a substitute, but further than that, he finds use for his versatile mind later, upon the shocking discovery of a mutilated corpse in another man's grave. The unusual plot is developed with dexterity and ingenuity." N Y Libraries

Strong poison

Some editions are:
Harper $5.95
Watts, F. $7.95 Large type edition. A Keith Jennison book
First published 1930 by Brewer

"Kirkcudbright, a proud Scottish village, was not ordinarily tolerant of outsiders, but Lord Peter had always found himself welcome. The came the day when Kirkcudbright offered him an occupation right in his own line—a corpse." McClurg. Book News

Suspicious characters
In Sayers, D. L. Dorothy L. Sayers omnibus v3

The unpleasantness at the Bellona Club. Harper [1956? c1928] 345p boards $5.95

A reprint of the title first published 1928 by Harcourt

"There was no reason to suspect causes other than natural ones in the death of a frail man of ninety. But matters of money developed which depended on exactly when the old man had died and it took all of Lord Peter Wimsey's skill to unravel the mystery." McClurg. Book News

also in Sayers, D. L. Dorothy L. Sayers omnibus v2

Whose body?
In Sayers, D. L. Dorothy L. Sayers omnibus v 1

Schaefer, Jack

The canyon
In Schaefer, J. The short novels of Jack Schaefer p221-316

The collected stories of Jack Schaefer; with an introduction by Winfield Townley Scott. Houghton 1966 520p $6

Analyzed in Short Story Index

The stories "trace the story of the frontier from its lawless beginnings to the present day and give us a living gallery of some of the men and women whose lives shaped the old West." Publisher's note

Contents: Major Burl; Miley Bennett; Emmet Dutrow; Sergeant Houck; Jeremy Rodock; Cooter James; Kittura Remsberg; General Pingley; Elvie Burdette; Josiah Willett; Something lost; Leander Frailey; Jacob; My town; Old Anse; That Mark horse; Ghost town; Takes a real man; Out of the past; Hugo Kertchak, builder; Prudence by name; Harvey Kendall; Cat nipped; Stalemate; Nate Bartlett's store; Salt of the earth; One man's honor; The old man; The coup of Long Lance; Enos Carr; The fifth man; Stubby Pringle's Christmas

"The author's mastery of narrative technique, his excellent character development, and his consistently concise description combine in avoiding the unfortunate aspects of typical 'Western' fiction and melodrama." Library J

Company of cowards. Houghton 1957 203p o.p. 1970

A novel based on a little-known episode of the Civil War. Eight men, seven of them former union officers who have been convicted of cowardice and reduced in rank to privates, form Company Q in the hope that they may redeem themselves. Led by Sergeant Jared Heath, former captain of a Massachusetts company of infantry, the men of Company Q must depend on their own resources to get the equipment they need, and when they are assigned to the frontier in New Mexico they must find their own way." Library J

also in Schaefer, J. The short novels of Jack Schaefer p317-460

First blood
In Schaefer, J. The short novels of Jack Schaefer p113-220

The Kean land
In Schaefer, J. The short novels of Jack Schaefer p461-525

FICTION CATALOG
EIGHTH EDITION

Schaefer, Jack—*Continued*

The Kean land, and other stories. Houghton 1959 309p boards $3.75

Analyzed in Short Story Index
Contents: The Kean land; Stalemate; Nate Bartlett's store; Old man; in harmony; Trail crew; Fifth man; Enos Carr; Coup of Long Lance; Salt of the earth; One man's honor

Monte Walsh. Houghton 1963 501p boards $5.95

This novel of the old West follows "Monte from runaway boy to trail hand, to topnotch cowhand and bronc buster, to aging saddle bum . . . [and encompasses] the rise, the peak and the eventual collapse of the open range." Publisher's note

"His characters seem real, and, according to the author, the characters and the episodes are based upon historical accounts. This is not just another 'Western.' It is worthy of a place alongside the writing of Will James and Eugene Manlove Rhodes." Library J

(ed.) Out West; an anthology of stories. Houghton 1955 331p o.p. 1970

Analyzed in Short Story Index
Contents: An Indian divorce, by F. G. Applegate; Tricks in all trades, by F. G. Applegate; The vengeance of Padre Arroyo, by G. Atherton; The walking woman, by M. Austin; Stewed beans, by M. Austin; Papago wedding, by M. Austin; The coroner story, by W. A. Baillie-Grohman; Ba'tiste's story of the medicine bag, by G. Catlin; The buck in the hills, by W. Van T. Clark; Bank holiday, by E. Corle; The bride comes to Yellow Sky, by S. Crane; The cloud puncher, by W. Cunningham; Old man Isbell's wife, by H. L. Davis; Death in October, by R. Easton; Mister Death and the redheaded woman, by H. Eustis; Spoil the child, by H. Fast; The scarecrow, by V. Fisher; Lone wolf's old guard, by H. Garland; Tennessee's partner, by B. Harte; A question of blood, by E. Haycox; Scars of honor, by D. Johnson; All the young men, by O. La Farge; Oh, once in my saddle, by D. Lamson; Jake Hoover's pig, by F. B. Linderman; The postoffice at Wolftail, by F. B. Linderman; All Gold Canyon, by J. London; The last thunder song, by J. G. Neihardt; A sketch by MacNeil, by E. Remington; Beyond the desert, by E. M. Rhodes; Early marriage, by C. Richter; Dog eater, by C. M. Russel; The girl in the Humbert, by M. Sandoz; The colt, by W. Stegner; The honk-honk breed, by S. E. White; At the sign of the Last Chance, by O. Wister

y Shane. Houghton 1949 214p o.p. 1970

"A vivid story of Wyoming in 1889, when homesteaders were battling with the cattlemen, as told by Bob Starrett, a fifteen-year-old boy. Basically this is the story of Shane, the stranger who rode into the valley, into the hearts of the Starrett family, and when his work was done rode out, alone and unfollowed." Booklist

"Many readers will enjoy its restrained and sensitive treatment of a theme usually embroidered with gunsmoke and punctuated with bullets." Literary Guild

also in Schaefer, J. The short novels of Jack Schaefer p 1-111

The short novels of Jack Schaefer; with an introduction by Dorothy M. Johnson. Houghton 1967 525p $6.95

Analyzed in Short Story Index
These five novels depict the West from the Civil War to the present century
Content: Shane [1949]; First blood [1953]; The canyon [1953]; Company of cowards [1957]; and The Kean land [1959]

Schmitt, Gladys

David the king; engravings by Cathal O'Toole. Dial Press 1946 631p illus o.p. 1970

"David, a shepherd boy, comes to the court of Saul to soothe a mad king with his songs. He becomes the friend of Jonathan and son-in-law to the king. But Saul, fearing for his crown, drives him forth to wander in the wilderness. David, after becoming a friend of the Philistines, is recalled and is crowned king of Israel. He sinks deeper into iniquity in his desire for Bath-sheba and his killing of Uriah, but finally wins victory over his selfishness and depravity to become a wise and understanding ruler." Booklist

"Because there have been many so-called 'biblical' novels whose main appeal has been rather mawkish, it is perhaps important to stress first of all the point that 'David the King' is serious, profound and creative fiction. As a piece of writing, an achievement in words, it is a stalwart and beautiful contribution to the literature of our times." N Y Times Bk R

Electra. Harcourt 1965 313p $4.95

In this retelling of the mythical tragedy of the House of Aulis "Agamemnon is more barbaric than heroic, the love of Clytemnestra and Aegisthus is a febrile passion of unlovely middle age, and Electra's hatred for her mother and Aegisthus and her love for Orestes are based on a morbid hatred of sex. In Miss Schmitt's version the story ends before Orestes' murder of Clytemnestra and with the hint of a love affair for Electra." Booklist

Apart from the ending "'Electra' is a fine historical novel, infused with primitive energy and breathing the passions and violences of the Bronze Age. The characters (particularly Agamemnon, Cassandra and Electra herself) are remarkably vivid, strange but wholly credible; and the harsh Mycenaean scenery is finely described." Book of the month Club News

Rembrandt; a novel. Random House 1961 657p $6.95

A fictional biography of the famous 17th century Dutch painter. It follows Rembrandt's life "from his birth as the son of a mill owner, through his marriage to Saskia and his great success as an artist, his spendthrift ways and his rudeness, to the death of Saskia, his affair with his housekeeper, and his declining success." Bk Buyer's Guide

Obviously, an enormous amount of research has gone into the writing of this book, and the period atmosphere is excellent. The characters, especially Rembrandt himself, come alive through the masses of detail that Miss Schmitt has so carefully assembled and imparted about them." Pub W

Schmitz, Ettore. See Svevo, Italo

Schoonover, Lawrence

The burnished blade. Macmillan (N Y) 1948 371p o.p. 1970

"A first novel which is a combination of history, romance, and adventure. The scene is mainly fifteenth century France. The orphaned Pierre, adopted by a famous armorer, witnesses the death of Joan of Arc; enters the service of Jacques Coeur, the renowned financier; rescues a titled lady in plague-stricken Paris; and travels to Byzantium and Trebizond, where he is kidnapped and tortured. But he renders a great service to the ruler of Trebizond and so returns to France a wealthy man, in time to marry his beloved, who had been about to become a nun." Book Rev Digest

"Three years research preceded the novel's writing, and no small measure of Mr. Schoonover's ability lies in the skill with which that research into the politics and history of half a dozen nations, into arms and the armorer's art, into customs ecclesiastical and secular, into chirurgery and navigation, is woven into the fabric of the tale." N Y Times Bk R

Central passage. Sloane 1962 246p o.p. 1970

"When the atomic holocaust comes, the target is the Panama Canal. As the last remnants of the isthmus sink below the water, the Gulf Stream changes its course and a modern ice age begins. The theme of destruction and survival is told from the point of view of two families: an American Navy man's household and a Gaspé fisherman's. Each family produces in the period of the Twenty Minute War an 'intruder,' a boy and girl endowed with superior intellect and extra-sensory power, who are fated to come together and die together." Library J

"Frightening but credible novel of survival." Cincinnati

The gentle infidel. Macmillan (N Y) 1950 304p o.p. 1970

"A historical novel of medieval Turkey, culminating in the capture of Constantinople

356

Schoonover, Lawrence—*Continued*

by Mohammed II, in 1453. . . . A Christian orphan, kidnapped by Turks, trained as Moslem janissary, opposes his unknown Italian guardian arms smuggler. After high adventure he is dramatically reconverted to Christianity, and regains wealth and love. Packed with historic detail depicting Turkish military life and Levantine affairs. Interest sustained by lively incidents, graphic descriptions, rather than by too convenient plot." Library J

Key of gold; a novel. Little 1968 279p boards $5.95

"Three doctors from the House of Baruch, from Granada in 1492, to New Amsterdam in 1663 had the doubtful honor of ministering to those in power. Dr. Benedict of Seville was physician to the dreaded Torquemada and suffered for it. Later Jan van Benedict was doctor to Spinoza, and his son Benedict had charge of Peter Stuyvesant—all dedicated medical men despite their persecution." Bk Buyer's Guide

"The novel is necessarily episodic because of its wide coverage of time and place. However, the theme, the persistent thread of devotion to the healing profession, makes for a smoothly worked, whole cloth." Library J

The prisoner of Tordesillas. Little 1959 309p o.p. 1970

"Juana of Castile was the daughter of Ferdinand and Isabella of Spain, the wife of Philip 'the Handsome,' Archduke of Austria; the mother of Charles V. . . . The iron rod of her power was broken by her father's cruelty, her husband's infidelity and her son's indifference. . . . She spent the last part of her life almost half a century, imprisoned in the grim fortress of Tordesillas." Publisher's note

The Queen's cross; a biographical romance of Queen Isabella of Spain. Sloane 1955 377p o.p. 1970

"A biographical novel based on the life of Isabelle I, Queen of Spain. It begins in her girlhood and follows the course of her marriage to Ferdinand, their wars before Spain became a united country, and ends with the pawning of the queen's jewels to finance Columbus." Book Rev Digest

The revolutionary. Little 1958 495p o.p. 1970

"In this fictional treatment of John Paul Jones over three fifths of the account is given to his life and affairs preceding his naval action in the American Revolution. His dealings in the slave trade as a very young sailor from Scotland, and escapee from a British prison, are described in detail and his service in an ungrateful Russia in the 1780's is reviewed with equal candor." Booklist

The Spider King; a biographical novel of Louis XI of France. Macmillan (N Y) 1954 403p o.p. 1970

"The ghosts of his forebears gather at the birth of Louis XI of France to endow him with fateful gifts; he will excel as a general, diplomat, statesman, financier, codifier of laws, and patron of the arts and sciences, he will break the power of feudalism and thus bring peace and order to his kingdom—but he will also be an epileptic. Even the epilepsy becomes an asset in its way, because it forces Louis to live an exemplary life for a ruler of his times, and causes him to develop his manifold good gifts in compensation." Booklist

Schorer, Mark

(ed.) The story; a critical anthology. Prentice-Hall 1950 606p o.p. 1970

Analyzed in Short Story Index

"Twenty-four short stories designed to assist the reader in appreciation and critical evaluation of the short story as a literary form. The author offers a more than technical analysis . . . he encourages the reader to be a critic . . . and explores short fiction from the simplest forms through forms more complex in plot, symbolism and style." Huntting

Contents: Railway accident, by T. Mann; Bride comes to Yellow Sky, by S. Crane; Use of force, by W. C. Williams; Do you like it here, by J. O'Hara; Gooseberries, by A. Chekhov; The egg, by S. Anderson; Freshest boy, by F. S. Fitzgerald; Catbird seat, by J. Thurber; Old hard, by T. O. Beachcroft; Valiant woman, by J. F. Powers; Basement room, by G. Greene; Silent snow, secret snow, by C. Aiken; Amy Foster, by J. Conrad; The grave, by K. A. Porter; Love—three pages from a hunter's diary, by G. de Maupassant; Portable phonograph, by W. Van T. Clark; Little cloud, by J. Joyce; Horse dealer's daughter, by D. H. Lawrence; Death of a travelling salesman, by E. Welty; In dreams begin responsibilities, by D. Schwartz; Gentleman from San Francisco, by I. Bunin; Old people, by W. Faulkner; A clean, well-lighted place, by E. Hemingway; Turn of the screw, by H. James

Schreiner, Olive

The story of an African farm; with an introduction by S. C. Cronwright Schreiner. Collins 1959 283p (Collins classics) $1.95

First published 1883

"Most of the action takes place on a Boer farm in South Africa in the late 19th century. The principal characters are three childhood playmates: Waldo, son of the kindly, pious German overseer; Em, the good-hearted stepdaughter of Tant' Sannie, owner of the farm; and Lyndall, Em's talented orphan cousin. Lyndall grows into a woman of great beauty and power, but her life is unhappy. She separates Em from her lover, has a child by a man whom she refuses to marry, and soon afterward dies. Waldo, who has always loved her, outlives her only a short while." Benét. The Reader's Encyclopedia

Schulberg, Budd

The disenchanted. Random House 1950 388p o.p. 1970

"Manley Halliday, has-been literary genius of the 20's is given a last chance by Hollywood: to co-author a college musical. A trip East to pick up atmosphere serves as catalyst to bring about Halliday's complete physical and spiritual disintegration. As Fitzgeraldian as Fitzgerald, Halliday is the very essence of 'the lost generation,' and the novel contrasts effectively the manners and ideology of that period with our own." Library J

Sanctuary V. World Pub. 1969 415p $6.95

"An NAL book"

"Justo Moreno Suarez, figurehead president of a Latin country recently taken over by a socialist revolution, has a falling out with the revolutionary leader, Angel Bello. About to be arrested, Justo flees with his wife and daughter into an embassy in his country's capital. As Justo becomes acclimated to his refuge, he perceives his rescuers as polite, hypocritical jailers and sanctuary as cruel incarceration. . . . [This] is an intelligent, humanistic examination of Cuban-style revolution as well as a vivid portrayal of deterioration in captivity." Book World

Waterfront; a novel. Random House 1955 320p o.p. 1970

"Though the basic facts are those of his hit movie, 'On the Waterfront,' the ending has been changed and the story has been given substance impossible to a movie. It is his tough, sometimes horrifying story of young Father Barry's quixotic fight against the criminal rulers of New York harbor, a warfare that brought death to two men." Retail Bookseller

"The more leisurely framework of the novel form permits the author to document to the full the abuses in longshoremen's unions, without sacrificing the explosive force of the film." Booklist

What makes Sammy run? Random House 1941 303p o.p. 1970

"Portrait of a volatile, cruel, grasping little live wire, Sammy Glick, whose ambition to get to the top of the heap is finally realized in Hollywood. He begins as copy boy in a New York newspaper office, and by means of cheating, double crossing his friends, and behaving like a heel generally, he finally gets what he wants." Book Rev Digest

Schulberg, Budd—*Continued*

"Although it is a novel of hard surface, in which nobody speaks without wise-cracking, it is not hard-boiled. Under the satire there is a sound sense of values, and not a little pity." Atlantic

Schulman, L. M.

y (ed.) The loners; short stories about the young and alienated. Macmillan (N Y) 1970 279p $4.95

Contents: What every boy should know, by W. Maxwell; Awakening, by I. Babel; Bad characters, by J. Stafford; Philco baby, by I. Faust; Barn burning, by W. Faulkner; The loneliness of the long-distance runner, by A. Sillitoe; Sonny's blues, by J. Baldwin; Soldier's home, by E. Hemingway; The secret sharer, by J. Conrad; A tree, a rock, a cloud, by C. McCullers

Schwarz, Leo W.

(ed.) The Jewish caravan; great stories of twenty-five centuries; selected and ed. by Leo W. Schwarz. Rev. and enl. Holt 1965 829p o.p. 1970

Partially analyzed in Short Story Index
First published 1935 by Rinehart
"An anthology of Jewish stories from all the major languages in which the Jews have written, arranged as a sort of cultural history of the Jewish people." Bk Buyer's Guide
The arrangement is under the following headings: The making of a people: Beginnings; The alien world; Torah: law and legend; Under the crescent and the cross: Medieval times; Ghetto lights and shadows; The world of Hasidism. The modern world: To be or not to be; America; Soviet Russia; The holocaust; Israel

Schwarz-Bart, André

The last of the Just; tr. from the French by Stephen Becker. Atheneum Pubs. 1960 374p $4.95

Originally published 1959 in France. Winner of the Prix Goncourt
"It starts with the [Jewish] pogrom at York, England, in 1185 and ends in the Auschwitz gas chambers some 760 years later. In between are more pogroms and persecutions in Germany, Spain, and Poland. . . . Interwoven with the tale of the Levy family is the legend of the 'thirty-six just men.' According to Jewish tradition, these thirty-six 'are the hearts of the world multiplied, and into them as into one receptacle, pour all our griefs.' . . . In each generation, the Levy family produced one of those 'just men.' How they bore the burden placed upon them is . . . told by the author." Christian Science Monitor
"A moving book, one very nearly adequate—there is no higher praise—to its dreadful theme." New Statesman

Science Fiction Writers of America

Nebula award stories, 1965 [1]-4. See Nebula award stories, 1965 [1]-4

Scott, J. M.

Heather Mary. Dutton 1953 224p o.p. 1970
"The story of a perilous trip across the Atlantic from England to Bermuda in a sailing yacht. The Heather Mary is named after the skipper's dead wife, and her spirit hovers over the whole trip. Charrington, the [egotistic] skipper, is the only one of the five men aboard who has any knowledge of sailing; the other four are supposed to be his guests. Gradually it appears that there was a purpose in gathering the group together; each of the four had known Heather Mary." Book Rev Digest
"His descriptions of foul weather as seen from the rolling deck of [the] yacht, are painted with broad, confident strokes, and delicate navigational problems are solved with the deft touch of a Melville." N Y Times Bk R

Sea-Wyf. Dutton 1956 [c1955] 255p o.p. 1970

First published in England, 1955 with title: Sea-Wyf and Biscuit
"A mysterious woman, a lawyer, a drifter and a one-legged black man are cast away on a tropic island. Eventually, out of their fears, loves and hates comes murder. The story is based on a series of personal ads which actually appeared in a London newspaper." Huntting
"A seaworthy adventure novel with probably the most ingeniously constructed plot in the whole castaways-on-a-raft class." Time

Scott, Jack Denton

Elephant grass. Harcourt 1969 312p $5.95
"Story of a shikar, a hunt for big game in the foothills of the Himalayas, told from the point of view of Ram Kumar, the Shikari, who loved the land and its creatures. The party consists of the raja, owner of Shikars and Shooting, Inc, two young women, a doctor, and the bullying, strutting Tain, who kills for love of it. The stunning climax comes when the party must hunt down a tiger Tain has wounded—the moment of truth." Bk Buyer's Guide

Scott, Paul

The day of the scorpion; a novel. Morrow 1968 483p boards $6.95
"A long and substantial novel of India when the Congress Party had adopted a resolution 'as good as a call to, nation-wide insurrection' with the Japanese threatening all Asia. Almost a sequel to 'The Jewel in the Crown,' [listed below] it tells of the lives of Sarah and Susan Layton; Lady Manners and Parvati (daughter born of the rape of Daphne); Kasim; Captain Merrick; and Kasim's two sons, all caught up in the violence of war and civil strife." Bk Buyer's Guide
This "is a moderately good novel of a classic type, but hardly a leader. . . . [Scott] writes honestly, carefully, occasionally memorable. The sense of a community running down is conveyed by unexpected turns. . . . The book is fearfully long, however, and diffuse in a way that suggests not so much breadth of view as inability to select and discard." New Statesman

The jewel in the crown; a novel. Morrow 1966 462p boards $5.95
"Around a central incident of the rape of a young Englishwoman in an Indian garden in August, 1942, the author has woven a . . . picture of India before independence. The two main threads of plot are the fate of the raped girl and the tragic end of an elderly English schoolteacher who is a very brave woman. There are other stories within the story. . . . This is a masterly narrative, a leisurely and skillful depiction of a wide Indian landscape and a large canvas showing people who are made very real. It is also a dissection of Anglo-British [educated Indian] animosities." Pub W

Scott, Sir Walter

The bride of Lammermoor. Dutton 1906 342p (Everyman's lib) $2.95
First published 1819
"The most tragic of Scott's romances, on which Donizetti's opera 'Lucia di Lammermoor' is based. The last scion of a ruined family and the daughter of his ancestral enemy in possession of the estates fall in love. For a while there is a glimpse of hope and happiness; but the ambitious mother opposes the match, prophecies and apparitions prognosticate tragedy, and the romance closes in death and sorrow. . . . Caleb Balderstone, the faithful retainer, is one of Scott's humorous creations, whose obstinate care for his unhappy master relieves the overpowering tragedy." Baker's Best

The heart of Midlothian

Some editions are:
Collins $1.95 With an introduction by Sir H. J. C. Grierson
Dutton (Everyman's lib) $2.95 Preface and glossary by W. M. Parker
First published 1818

Scott, Sir Walter—*Continued*

"Eighteenth century Scotland and England form the background of this novel, and many views of the island are presented as Jeannie Deans trudges from Edinburgh to London to obtain a pardon for her sister Effie, who is falsely charged with the murder of her son. She obtains the pardon, but already Effie has escaped with her lover, and before the sisters are reunited, many adventures befall them. Although the novel contains fewer historical events than most of Scott's, the reader's interest is always held by such living characters as Ratcliffe, the jailer, and Black George, the vagabond leader." English and Pope's What's to Read

y **Kenilworth**

Some editions are:
Dodd (Great illustrated classics) $4.50 with a portrait of the author, pictures of contemporary scenes and drawings reproduced from early editions together with an introduction and captions by Basil Davenport
Dutton (Everyman's lib) $2.95 Preface and glossary by W. M. Parker
First published 1821

A novel "famous for its portrayal of Queen Elizabeth. Aside from Her Majesty, the chief characters are the Earl of Leicester, who entertains ambitions of becoming king-consort, and his beautiful, unhappy wife, Amy Robsart. She suffers neglect, insult and finally death at his hands." Benét. The Reader's Encyclopedia

y **Quentin Durward**

Some editions are:
Dodd (Great illustrated classics) $4.50 with illustrations in color by Percy Tarrant
Dutton (Everyman's lib) $3.25 Preface and glossary by W. M. Parker
Scribner (Scribner Illustrated classics) $5
First published 1823

"A story of French history. In this novel are introduced Louis XI and his Scottish Guards, Oliver le Dane and Tristan l'Hermite, Cardinal Balue, De la Marck (The 'Wild Boar of Ardennes') Charles the Bold, Philip des Comines, Le Glorieux (the court jester), and other well-known historic characters. The main plot has to do with the love of the gallant young Quentin Durward, a member of the Scottish Guards, and Isabelle, Countess of Croye. The hero saves the King's life in a boar hunt and later wins the hand of the Countess from his rival, the Duke of Orleans." Benét. The Reader's Encyclopedia

y **Rob Roy**

Some editions are:
Collins $1.95
Dutton (Everyman's lib) $2.95 Preface and glossary by W. M. Parker
First published 1817

"The scenes are laid in Northumberland, Glasgow, and the Highlands about Loch Lomond. . . . Jacobite intrigues among the English gentry have a good deal to do with the evolution of the story. A young Englishman unwittingly becomes mixed up with these affairs, has to escape into Scotland, and journeys into Rob Roy's territory in search of a missing document on which depends the credit of his father's firm. Diana Vernon is one of the most romantic and captivating of Scott's heroines. . . . Rob Roy plays an unobtrusive part in the action." Baker's Historical

y **The talisman**

Some editions are:
Dodd (Great illustrated classics) $4.50 With illustrations from drawings by Rowland Wheelwright, together with an introductory sketch of the author by Basil Davenport
Dutton (Everyman's lib) $3.25 Preface and glossary by W. M. Parker
First published 1829

"Relating the adventures of Sir Kenneth, Prince Royal of Scotland, as a knight in disguise in the Holy Land [during the third Crusade] under Richard Coeur De Lion. Richard and his noble enemy, Saladin, are leading characters. Hearing of Richard's illness, Saladin assumes the disguise of the physician Adonbec al Hakim and gives his patient a healing drink of spring water into which he has dipped his 'talisman.' At the end of the novel, Sir Kenneth marries his kinswoman, Lady Edith **Plantagenet**." Benét. The Reader's Encyclopedia

Waverley; or, 'Tis sixty years since. Dutton 1906 496p (Everyman's lib) $3.25
First published 1814

"This celebrated romance of the '45 [Jacobite] Rebellion depicts more especially its earlier stages . . . the later period of the Derby retreat being rapidly sketched, while the disaster of Culloden is introduced only in the shape of news. The book, even apart from its own special merits, must always hold a position of great importance as being Scott's first venture in fiction." Nield

Searls, Hank

The crowded sky. Harper 1960 274p o.p. 1970

"Dramatic novel of flying, suspense-loaded, traces the human factors underlying an air collision in the Southwest between a Navy jet and a passenger plane, such as has been in the news in recent years." Am News of Bks

The hero ship. World Pub. 1969 304p $5.95
"An NAL book"

"A story of the U.S. Navy in World War II in which a personal enmity based on the hero's shock at discovering his wife's affair with a popular officer is set against the horrors of the Pacific combat aboard an aircraft carrier. Based on the actual tragedy of the destruction of the U.S.S. 'Franklin.' " Booklist

"Hank Searls has a fondness for flashbacks. He interrupts the narrative repeatedly to tell us about Ben's courtship and marriage, how he won his wings as a pilot, what happened when he suddenly arrived at Pearl Harbor on Dec. 7, 1941, and so on. All these things are interesting but they weaken the unity of the story and certainly slow up the action." Best Sellers

Searls, Henry. See Searls, Hank

Sedges, John. See Buck, Pearl S.

Segal, Erich W.

Love story. Harper 1970 131p boards $4.95

"Oliver is Harvard, rich, a big campus athlete. Jenny is a Radcliffe scholarship student in music from a poor Italian Catholic background. They meet, fall in love, and marry, even though the boy's father wants him to go to law school first. Jenny gives up a chance to study in Paris and works to put her young husband through law school—and they win out to the beginnings of a great life and promising career for him. Then tragedy steps in." Pub W

"A very professionally crafted short first novel. . . . The story is all on the surface. But it is funny and sad and generally recommended." Library J

Selinko, Annemarie

y **Désirée.** Morrow 1953 594p $7.50

"Eugénie Désirée Clary, the daughter of a rich silk merchant of Marseille, records in her diary the history of her two love affairs, first with Napoleon Bonaparte, who jilted her to marry Josephine, and the second with General Bernadotte, who married her and ended his career as the first of a new line of Swedish kings. Since Eugénie's two loves happen to be famous in history, the diary Miss Selinko has written for her naturally reads like a chronicle of the period between 1794 and 1829." New Yorker

"It is detailed but very readable and gives the Republican viewpoint with emphasis on the Rights of Man. Characters live, plot moves, fine style." Library J

Seltzer, Thomas

(comp.) Best Russian short stories; comp. and ed. by Thomas Seltzer. Modern Lib. [1970 c1925] 556p $2.95

A reissue of a title first published 1917 by Liveright, and analyzed in Short Story Index
Contents: The queen of spades, by A. S. Pushkin; The cloak, by N. V. Gogol; The district doctor, by I. S. Turgenev; The Christmas tree and the wedding, by F. M. Dostoyevsky; God sees the truth, but waits, by L. N. Tolstoy; How a Muzhik fed two officials, by M. Y.

Seltzer, Thomas—*Continued*

Saltykov; The shades, a phantasy by V. G. Korolenko; The signal, by V. M. Garshin; The darling, by A. P. Chekhov; The bet, by A. P. Chekhov; Vanka, by A. P. Chekhov; Hide and seek, by F. Sologub; Dethroned, by I. N. Potapenko; The servant, by S. T. Semyonov; One autumn night, by M. Gorky; Her lover, by M. Gorky; The revolutionist, by M. P. Artzybashev; The outrage, by A. I. Kuprin; Lazarus, by L. N. Andreyev; The seven that were hanged, by L. N. Andreyev; The red laugh, by L. N. Andreyev; The gentleman from San Francisco, by I. Bunin

Serling, Robert J.

The President's plane is missing. Doubleday 1967 297p $4.95

"President Jeremy Haines' plane went down on the way to Palm Springs, just when China was being especially belligerent. The nation was in the hands of Vice President Madigan, 'platitudinous and pompous' mediocrity. The whole world waited in breathless suspense, except for the few people who realized there were many odd features about the plane trip, not the least of which was the fact that the President's body could not be found." Bk Buyer's Guide

Seton, Anya

Avalon. Houghton 1965 440p $5.95

"The romance is a deep lifelong attachment between a wandering French prince, an idealistic, poetic man, and a Cornish girl of peasant and Viking blood. The story opens in a courtly, gentle mood which changes to fury, lust and murderous greed when the scene shifts to the English court, and to adventure and exploration when the girl is captured by her father's people and the Vikings take the center of the stage." Pub W

"Late tenth- and early eleventh-century life in England and in the lands colonized by the Norsemen is re-created from early Anglo-Saxon chronicles, French manuscripts, and secondary sources. . . . The action and milieu are vivid and though the characterization is not strong the psychological and historical motivations are believable. An honest historical novel for enthusiasts of the genre. An epilog sketches events between the end of the story and the Norman Conquest of 1066 and lists sources." Booklist

Devil Water. Houghton 1962 526p maps $6.95

"In this biographical novel about England and Virginia in the early eighteenth century, about the two Jacobite rebellions, the Radcliffe family and that of William Byrd of Westover, I have adhered scrupulously to facts, when they can be found." Author's note

The action centers around "Charles Radcliffe, who escaped from Newgate prison after his brother's execution, of Jenny, his daughter by a secret marriage, and of the strong affection between them, which endured through years of separation and despite conflicting beliefs and loyalties." Publisher's note

"Devil Water contains many moving pictures of eighteenth-century high life in Northumberland, London, and Virginia, with copious descriptions of manners and customs." Times (London) Lit Sup

Dragonwyck. Houghton [1968 c1944] 336p $5.95

This is a reissue of a title first published 1944

"In the early 1800's the daughter of a poor New England farmer was invited to live with her wealthy cousins in their baronially splendid Hudson Valley house. She made the mistake of falling in love with her handsome cousin, eventually married him and then found that aristocratic patron families held skeletons that couldn't be kept in closets." Library Guild

"For all its trappings and devices—and they are good, spine-chilling trappings, handled with considerable skill—the novel manages to have life and substance. The character of Nicholas, in spite of its exaggeration for the purposes of romance, emerges with a timely vividness." N Y Her Trib Books

Foxfire. Houghton 1950 346p o.p. 1970

"An engrossing story about foxfire—that luminous glow as false as any desert mirage. . . . Amanda Lawrence, the sheltered product of New York and the best schools, was on her way home from Europe when she met and fell in love with Jonathan Dartland, one-fourth Apache. She had no ritual to guide her, no certainty of faith, when she followed her husband to the grim town of Lodestone. Then, in Dart's old trunk, she found a map to a lost mine. She dreamed of the gold which the Apaches would not touch because of legendary bans . . . and three people are caught in the shimmer of the ancient curse." Huntting

The Hearth and Eagle. Houghton 1948 464p $6.95

"Back in the 17th century, Mark Honeywood had built the house in Marblehead for Phebe, his gentle bride. When Mark was crippled by a fall, Phebe wanted to go back to her soft life in England, yet she turned the house into a tavern and stuck it out. Some 200 years later red-haired Hesper was to know the love of three men and heartbreak, but she, too, learned to endure, and somehow the solid old Hearth and Eagle helped her. A long story of fisher folk, the Civil War, and the next half century." Retail Bookseller

"A substantial and well-told story that makes real one of the longest and most vigorous strands in the making of our country. The story of the woman is interesting and convincing, but stronger will be the appeal of the town to those who know and love that rocky coast." NY Her Trib Books

Katherine. Houghton 1954 588p $6.95

"In telling the love story of John of Gaunt and Katherine Swynford, the author re-creates the England of the fourteenth century. This was the England of Geoffrey Chaucer and John Wyclif, of the Black Death and of the Peasant's Revolt. Here John of Gaunt fought for power and lost his heart to Katherine who was his mistress for twenty years and his wife for three." Huntting

"The novelist's scrupulous use of findings based on careful research, combined with her own interpretations, produces a warm, alive picture of the fourteenth century, convincing characterizations, and a touching romance." Booklist

The Winthrop woman. Houghton 1958 586p $5.95

"The heroine is an attractive, high-spirited woman who dared to flout the conventions of her day. Elizabeth Fones was the niece of John Winthrop, governor of Massachusetts Bay, and wife of his son. Widowed at twenty, she came to Boston and managed to survive tragedy, disease, famine, childbirth, and Indian hostilities. This is the story of her three marriages and her hopeless love for her cousin John. It is also an authoritative account of the Massachusetts Bay and Connecticut Colonies." Huntting

"This is all an amazing story, too little known before. Anya Seton has not distorted or trifled with it, or sought to embellish it. She has clothed the name of Elizabeth, and those about her, with flesh and blood to make them real to us. The novel is noteworthy for its insights into the Puritan 'Bible Commonwealth.'" Sat R

Settle, Mary Lee

O Beulah Land; a novel. Viking 1956 368p o.p. 1970

"A pre-revolutionary war novel covering the years 1754-1774 that describes the valiant lives of a handful of men and women who settle the Virginia lands beyond the Alleghenies. The story centers around Jonathan Lacey, a Captain in the French and Indian wars, who after surviving Braddock's dismal Battle of the Wilderness, claims his bounty of acreage and brings his family to live in Beulah. It is the story too of his wife Sal, a gently bred English girl, who feels herself to be better than the hard-bitten pioneers among whom she is forced to dwell. But it is the people like Hannah, former London guttersnipe, who in the prologue, escapes from her Indian captors and beats her

Settle, Mary L.—*Continued*

way alone through forest and mountain toward Beulah, and Jarcey Pentacost, ex-felon, printer and schoolmaster who give the book its unusual flavor." Library J

Shadbolt, Maurice

This summer's dolphin. Atheneum Pubs. 1969 166p $4.95

"Gathered on a New Zealand resort island, an assortment of misfits and dropouts, who display most of the soul-sickness modern man is heir to, are for a few days charmed out of themselves by a dolphin whose luminous presence gives a piscine benediction to believers crowding the shore. Inevitably the dolphin is destroyed, thus restoring normal human unregeneracy." Choice

Shannon, Dell

Coffin corner. Morrow 1966 254p o.p. 1970

"Lieutenant Luis Mendoza, of Los Angeles' homicide division, was called on to investigate what seemed to be the death-from heart failure of the proprietor of a second-hand shop —and this led into the case of a cop hit by a car and the presumable suicide of a girl." Bk Buyer's Guide

Crime on their hands. Morrow 1969 223p boards $5.95

"Mendoza's Homicide Squad at L.A.P.D. becomes as overburdened as ever with cases of youthful snipers, suicides, the driver of a stolen Maserati wanted for murder, even the death of a witch woman. Most puzzling of all, and the case on which Mendoza concentrates, is the shooting of a small-time con man and charmer of women. Adding quite an amusing touch is the injured mockingbird which has found shelter with the Mendoza family, and refuses to leave when its wings are healed because it has become addicted to the Mendoza rye." Pub W

Kill with kindness. Morrow 1968 250p o.p. 1970

While recovering from the measles Lieutenant Luis Mendoza of the Los Angeles Police Department investigates the case "of a practical nurse caring for [a] widow who charges only $25.00 a week and who seems to be keeping the neighbors from seeing old Mrs. Weaver who has nothing but the house she lives in and a pension." Best Sellers

Schooled to kill. Morrow 1969 220p $5.50

"Lt. Luis Mendoza and the Los Angeles police are up to their necks in crime, but their chief compulsion is to find the rape-murderer of two school girls. This book introduces a welcome new character in the Mendoza stories, a sheepdog named Cedric who adopts the family." Bk Buyer's Guide

For other titles by this author see Egan, Lesley; Linington, Elizabeth

Sharp, Margery

Britannia Mews. Little 1946 377p o.p. 1970

"A long chronicle of English life and customs over a period from 1865 to the 1940's, in which the central character is Adelaide Culver. Adelaide rebelled against her Victorian family, eloped with her drunken drawing master, and went to live with him in Britannia Mews, where once her father's coachman had lived. Thru the years while the Mews were undergoing their change from slums, to fashionable quarters, Adelaide continued to live there, and in time achieved the very Victorian virtues against which she had once rebelled." Book Rev Digest

Cluny Brown. Little 1944 270p o.p. 1970

"Because her uncle, a rather unusual plumber, thought orphaned Cluny Brown had better go into service, she was shipped off to Devon to a job in a big 'county' house owned by Sir Henry Carmel. But life could never be simple when Cluny was around—it was still less simple when Sir Henry's son Andrew visited his parents there—and the beautiful Betty Cream, loved by Andrew, didn't help matters when she arrived. Then more complications are added

by the famous Polish writer, Mr. Belinski . . . though in the end it is he and Cluny who suddenly startle the reader and solve the plot." Huntting

"Miss Sharp's characters are always amusing and whimsically drawn, but Cluny is probably the most startling of them all. Wherever Cluny appears life takes on an Alice-in-Wonderland quality, people and things behave in the strangest fashion, and through it all Cluny moves unselfconsciously, unaware of the disorderly fairy tale she is making of life." N Y Times Bk R

In pious memory. Little 1967 184p boards $4.95

The story arises from "the sudden passing of a famous economist, whose ample legacies cushion family grief. . . . The late Arthur Prelude's wife, in spite of a deep sense of loss, is discreetly auditioning a successor. Or two. Son William is going to wait a decent three months to get married. Daughter Elizabeth finances a holiday in Greece with her lover. But 16-year-old Lydia, the deceased's youngest, persists in believing that her father has survived a Swiss plane crash and is alive somewhere in the Alps. When she and her first cousin Toby set out on bicycles to find Mr. Prelude, the balance of funeral bliss is . . . altered." N Y Times Bk R

"Light as meringue but twice as satisfying for anyone who feels like tucking up for an hour or two with a book that will transport him to the lovely never-never land of a good story well told." Pub W

The nutmeg tree. Little 1938 313p o.p. 1970

"Julia Packett had not seen her young daughter for more than a decade when, one day, the girl wrote to her mother an appeal for help in a love affair. As love affairs were Julia's forte, she responded with alacrity, left England —and some pressing debts—behind her, and traveled to southern France. There she quickly found herself on the wrong side in her daughter's affair, and falling rapidly in love herself. Eventually all is settled to everybody's satisfaction." Book Rev Digest

"It is the author's triumph that through her brilliant characterization and insight into life she elicits affection and respect for the dramatic mother, a light o'love, almost amoral, yet with inherently fine qualities." N Y Libraries

Rosa. Little 1970 249p boards $5.95

"Rosa, the 'by-blow' of a groomsman, formerly employed by Sir Charles Ramillies of Yorkshire, and his common-law Latin wife, is eventually returned to England to the custody of Ramillies, who accepts her charge as a bawdy good joke. The setting is England during the 1890's and Miss Sharp's delineation of the period is absolutely without flaw. Hardy Yorkshire nobility is contrasted with vainglorious London aristocracy with great sensitivity and insight. Sir Charles weds Rosa in a last-ditch effort to provide heirs to his estate and thus keep the Hall out of the grasp of the London Ramillies. No children brighten the marriage, but Rosa herself lives out her long life in noble comfort at the Hall in Yorkshire, entertaining each new generation of Ramillies youngsters with ever-more-fictive accounts of her romantic youth." Best Sellers

Something light. Little 1960 247p o.p. 1970

"Louise Mary Datchett was indiscriminately-fond of men and men took advantage of her. She was always being sent for when their prescriptions needed filling, socks washed, suits fetched from the cleaners. So, in her thirtieth year, still unmarried, she suddenly decided the situation must be changed. This is the story of what happened in her search for a husband." Huntting

Shaw, Irwin

Love on a dark street, and other stories. Delacorte Press 1965 285p o.p. 1970

Here are ten "stories of love . . . of violence . . . of passion . . . of folly. Some of them are witty, others romantic or tragic—but all are written with an intimacy that is richly human." Publisher's note

Contents: The man who married a French wife; The inhabitants of Venus; Noises in the city; A year to learn the language; Love on a dark street; Once, in Aleppo; Circle of light; Wistful, delicately gay; Tune every heart and every voice; Goldilocks at graveside

Shaw, Irwin—*Continued*

Selected short stories of Irwin Shaw; with a preface by the author. Modern Lib. 1961 426p o.p. 1970

Analyzed in Short Story Index
Contents: The eighty-yard run; Main currents of American thought; The girls in their summer dresses; Sailor off the Bremen; Welcome to the city; Weep in years to come; Search through the streets of the city; Night birth and opinion; The city was in total darkness; Hamlets of the world; Walking wounded; Gunners' passage; Medal from Jerusalem; Act of faith; Age of reason; Mixed doubles; The climate of insomnia; The green nude; Tip on a dead jockey; In the French style; Voyage out, voyage home; The sunny banks of the River Lethe; Then we were three

The young lions. Modern Lib. 1958 689p $2.95

First published 1948 by Random House
"This is a long novel about World War II. . . . Shaw has told his story through three main characters: Christian Deistl, a Nazi; Michael Whitacre, successful Broadway producer; and Noah Ackerman, a twenty-one-year-old American Jew who grew up in homeless poverty. We are given in each instance the backgrounds of these men, including the women they loved." Literary Guild
"Shaw has turned out a fine, full, intelligent book, packed with wonderful talk and crackling writing. . . . He reveals in even greater stature the delicious wit, the dramatic sense of scene-making, and the full hearted compassion of his short stories." Sat R

Shaw, Robert

A card from Morocco. Harcourt 1969 182p $4.95

"In Madrid two middle-aged men meet and become drinking and yarning friends: Lewis, a retired British major who worries about the satisfaction he gives his much younger wife, and Slattery, an artist, a liar, and a violent drunk with a desire to stamp people. Lewis wants to provide a younger bedmate for his wife; Slattery wants revenge upon the father he hates—and each tries to save the other from himself." Bk Buyer's Guide
"The novel is virtually a dialogue between the two men, filled with dramatic nuance, obscenities, and down-to-earth humor." Library J

The man in the glass booth. Harcourt 1967 180p $4.50

"Prompted by the news of the Vatican Council's document repudiating Jewish guilt, New York real estate magnate Arthur Goldman begins his own quest for justice which takes him back to his internment in a Nazi concentration camp. Goldman's confession that he is really former S.S. colonel Adolf Dorff leads to his arrest and trial by Israeli authorities." Library J
This book "is often as baffling as it is original—a pop-art novel of the absurd that ranges with astonishing vitality from braying comic vulgarities to subtly and scrupulously weighing political guilt and atonement." Christian Science Monitor

Sheed, Wilfrid

The blacking factory & Pennsylvania gothic; a short novel and a long story. Farrar, Straus 1968 246p boards $5.50

"The novel, The Blacking Factory, concerns the boyhood experiences of an American radio commentator when a student at Sopworth, a boarding-school in England. The story, Pennsylvania Gothic, describes Charlie Trimble's boyhood in a suburb of Philadelphia, his father's suicide, the visits he makes to Miss Skinner, an elderly neighbor, at age twelve and his last visit when he is thirty-two years old." Book Rev Digest
"Of the two, I much prefer the short novel, but both are pure Sheed of the finest quality. In both, a young teen-ager stands at a crossroad in his life, one that will be indelibly impressed upon the matured adult and the direction he takes. . . . This volume is an important literary work, one that librarians may well mark for first purchase." Best Sellers

The hack. Macmillan (N Y) 1963 279p boards $4.95

"The story of the disintegration of Bert Flax, a hack writer, who specializes in the most glib and superficial sort of pious Catholic writing. On the eve of Christmas, with the grim necessity of supporting a wife and five children uppermost in his mind, Bert is suddenly faced with gnawing doubts about the value of his writing and the very essence of his faith as a Catholic. In increasing desperation he searches for help from his wife, his old friends, from the priests most responsible for his 'career.'" Pub W
"Like all good satire, this novel applies its wit to a serious base. It is a well-put-together work showing a striking use of sharp, epithetic description and effective caricature of certain pro- and anti-Catholic types." Library J

Office politics; a novel. Farrar, Straus 1966 339p boards $4.95

"The much-disliked editor of a liberal 'little magazine,' which has seen better days, is felled by a heart attack. The oh so carefully contrived jockeying for position, the delicate little knifings in the back, the suddenly resurgent egos that flourish among the colleagues he has bullied into submission for years (and one nice young newcomer, who is not without his own twinges of ambition) are beautifully portrayed. In the end the Great Man returns, with a diabolically clever offer designed to seduce the one person who has seen through him and is strong enough to make it on his own. Along the way Mr. Sheed gets in some lovely thrusts at 20th century marriage, the neurotic intellectual and the office manager type who is secretly convinced she puts out the whole magazine single-handed." Pub W

Pennsylvania gothic

In Sheed, W. The blacking factory & Pennsylvania gothic p3-63

Square's progress; a novel. Farrar, Straus 1965 309p $4.95

The story of a "marriage in a New Jersey setting. Fred Cope's culturally pretentious wife leaves him, and her expectation that he will follow is disappointed when he leaves suburbia, his job, and her to seek life as she extols it first in Greenwich Village and then in an artist's colony in Spain. . . . The eventual reunion of the Copes finds Fred more aware, Alison wary of him, and the marriage tentatively reestablished." Booklist
"Sheed is a very perceptive person, a shrewd judge of character traits, and an exceedingly honest writer. Probably only an equally honest and mature reader will accept his portraits without feeling either argumentative or uncomfortable. But agree or not, every thoughtful reader will respond at least with amusement." Best Sellers

Shellabarger, Samuel

y Captain from Castile. Little 1945 632p $5.95

A long historical romance of Mexico and Spain centering on Pedro de Vargas, who "found himself a fugitive in Cuba because of an old family enemy whose weapon was the Inquisition. With an eye to the main chance, De Vargas joined the forces of Cortes and became a Captain with the Conquistadors. The author has successfully interwoven the passions of love and hate, of war and intrigue, of action and suspense, against the vivid background of the early 16th century, rich in the spirit of the modern man, irrevocably changed by the Renaissance, but closely tied to a feudal past." Huntting

The King's cavalier. Little 1950 377p illus $5.95

"The conflict between Francis I of France and the Duke of Bourbon furnishes the background for a tale of picaresque adventure and love involving Blaise, loyal to the King, and lovely Anne Russell, British agent, who befuddles and tricks Blaise but in the end fights on his side to save Francis." Retail Bookseller
"Mr. Shellabarger is a scholar. Not only does he contrive vivid scenes and live characters—often all good or all bad—but his detailed knowledge of those times cloaks this tale of olden days with authenticity. . . . Tops of its kind." Spring'f'd Republican

Shellabarger, Samuel—*Continued*

Lord Vanity. Little 1953 467p $5.95

Set against a background of lavish aristocratic entertainments and political intrigues of eighteenth century Venice, Bath, London, and Paris, this novel begins in the Venice of 1757. "Richard Morandi, extra violin, bit player in the theater, illegitimate son of Lord Marny and a seamstress, meets there the lovely dancer, Maritza, and sees Tromba, the adventurer who is to be his benefactor, and Sagredo, who is at once his enemy. There follows an adventurous chronicle of a duel, sentence to the galleys, rescue by Lord Marny, and a military career [in Quebec and Paris]." Retail Bookseller

"A superior historical romance which draws on meticulous scholarship, and adroitly balances melodrama with ideas." Booklist

y Prince of foxes. Little 1947 433p $6.95

"A romantic novel of the Renaissance period in Italy, particularly of the years during which Cesare Borgia rose to power—and fell. At the beginning of the tale, the chief character, a mysterious soldier of fortune, is a protege of the Borgias. Andrea Orsini falls in love with one of the Cesare's intended victims, changes sides, and eventually defeats his master's purposes in one small city state in Italy." Book Rev Digest

"With all its fast-paced gait—and there is something doing on every page the novel still has room for character development and for genuine historical background." N Y Her Trib Books

Tolbecken. Little 1956 370p $4.95

This posthumous novel is concerned with the Tolbeckens, an old American family noted for its high ideals and public service. Above all it is the story of Jared Tolbecken, the young grandson of the house, struggling to find his roots in a world of change brought about by the encroachment of a modern business center upon the old family mansion and his own experiences in World War I. (Publisher)

"Some readers will not approve of the author's summary disposal of plot, but nearly all will be impressed by his fictionalized treatment of earlier social patterns which helped to shape us. Dr. Shellabarger has used his final novel as a vehicle to bring us what he understands about idealism, faith, despair and cynicism in American life." N Y Times Bk R

Shelley, Mary W.

y Frankenstein; or, The modern Prometheus. Dutton 242p (Everyman's lib) $2.95

First published 1818; in this edition 1912

"The best of the tales of mystery and horror written in friendly competition by Shelley, Byron, Polidori, and Mrs. Shelley at Geneva. . . . It is ghastly extravaganza, built up on the idea of a monster created on pseudo-scientific principles, and endowed with life, by a young German, whom the monster forthwith turns upon and keeps in anxiety and torment." Baker's Best

"The story is one of unrelieved gloom, but in its invention and conduct exhibits unquestioned genius. It is unique in English fiction." Keller's Reader's Digest of Books

"The German student's name has come, erroneously, into use as a term applied to any dominating mechanical creation." Lenrow. Reader's Guide to Prose Fiction

Sherman, D. R.

Brothers of the sea. Little 1966 247p boards $4.95

A "story of Roger, a Seychelles Island fisherman; Paul, the boy left on Roger's doorstep fifteen years ago; and Marsouin, Paul's dolphin playmate. Roger has a broken leg, has been unable to go fishing, and is threatened with . . . [eviction] from his home, and Paul has fallen in love with Danielle. If Paul can bring himself to kill the dolphin, Roger can pay the back rent and Paul can still see his Danielle." Bk Buyer's Guide

This novel "is built on the legends of the boy who plays with a dolphin and rides on the back of the giant friendly 'fish.' . . . Episodes of undersea swimming and spearfishing, the happy cavorting of boy and dolphin, and the tragic resolution of the story are all equally convincing and moving." Pub W

Into the noonday sun. Little [1967 c1966] 159p $4.50

First published 1966 in England

"Lions attack the livestock of Alan, a farmer of Africa, and in tracking down the lions he brings his young son. The boy makes his first kill; but the story moves inevitably to tragedy as they continue the hunt and through carelessness both father and son are killed. The story has much of the fatalistic in it, with echoes of a primitive code. And the earthy realism of some of the story might be too much for the very young. But the tale also has strength in its realism, reflecting as it does the tension of the situation and the savagery of the land." Best Sellers

y Old Mali and the boy. Little 1964 144p boards $4.50

"A timeless story of a boy growing into manhood. The boy is 12 and lives with his widowed mother in India. Mali is their gardener. A wise and humble man, he teaches the boy wood lore and tells him stories. After he has learned to shoot Mali's bow, and to make arrows, the boy coaxes his mother to allow them to go on a hunting trip to the deer forest. It is a long journey, but Mali assures the boy's mother 'On the third day I will return him.' He keeps this promise, and gives the boy an unforgettable lesson in courage." Library J

"Written by a young Rhodesian, the brief novel is memorable for its compelling simplicity of style and universality of theme." Booklist

Sherred, T. L.

E for effort

In Knight, D. ed. A century of great short science fiction novels p295-341

Shipway, George

The Imperial Governor. Doubleday 1968 446p $6.95

"Paulinus, an honored military commander, tells how Nero sent him to Britain to conquer that land, not for military glory but to find some new source of revenue for Rome. Paulinus tells of the intrigues and corruption that beset him, of Nero's Hitler-like fluctuations, and finally of the Emperor's decision to evacuate Britain and recall its governor in disgrace." Bk Buyer's Guide

"Mr. Shipway uses imagination and scholarship in reconstructing the personality of the great Roman general, and while this novel may seem to be clotted with factual minutiae and the deadly details of the forced march, it will delight the historical fiction fans who frequent public libraries." Library J

Sholokhov, Mikhail

Nobel Prize in literature, 1965

And quiet flows the Don; tr. from the Russian by Stephen Garry. Knopf 1934 755p o.p. 1970

Available as first volume of: The silent Don, entered separately

"The story of a group of Cossacks, living along the Don River—a primitive, virile, and unbelievably brutal people—centers about Gregor Melekhov, a young Cossack with Turkish blood in his veins. His home life, his unhappy marriage and impassioned love affair, and his military adventures and experiences in the Revolution are told with frank naturalism, from a Bolshevik point of view, and a host of other characters crowd the pages of a powerful but unpleasant novel of war and revolution." Booklist

This book "is one of the best translations from Russian that I have ever come across. In its English version it keeps all the atmosphere, spontaneity, and color of the original." Sat R

Followed by: The Don flows home to the sea

also in Sholokhov, M. The silent Don v 1

The Don flows home to the sea; tr. from the Russian by Stephen Garry. Knopf 1941 777p o.p. 1970

Available as second volume of: The silent Don, entered separately

Sholokhov, Mikhail—*Continued*

Sequel to: And quiet flows the Don, entered above

First published in English 1940

"Begins with the period immediately after the Revolution of 1917 and carries on to the end of the civil war in 1921, when peace was finally established. It follows the fortunes of a group of Cossacks and their women as now they fight with the Reds and now with the Whites—as they fluctuate between the intense individualism of their Cossack tradition and the socialism of the new society." Publisher's note

"It is a tale of misfortunes multiplied, yet a broad and earthy humor and the hearty Cossack gaiety break continuously over the grim surface. At the end the Cossack, with his intense individualism, his passionate love of the land, and his primitive pride, stands revealed." Nation

Followed by: Seeds of tomorrow

also in Sholokhov, M. The silent Don v2

y Fierce and gentle warriors; three stories. Tr. by Miriam Morton; illus. by Milton Glaser. Doubleday 1967 109p illus $3.95

Analyzed in Short Story Index

Three stories about life on the Don during the First and Second World Wars. (Publisher)

Contents: The colt; The rascal; The fate of a man

Harvest on the Don; tr. from the Russian by H. C. Stevens. Knopf 1961 [c1960] 367p $5.95

Sequel to: Seeds of tomorrow with which it was published under title: Virgin soil upturned

Original Russian edition published 1960. This translation first published in England 1960

This story describes the effects of collectivism upon the Don village. "Davidov, a party member sent by the central government to direct the newly organized collectivized farms in the area, meets obstacles arising from country revolutionaries hiding in the village . . . and from his . . . attachment to the woman, Lushka." Booklist

"In general, 'Harvest on the Don' carries the narrative forward with vigor; those who like the earlier volumes will like this one. They will relish its old-fashioned virtues . . . they will enjoy its touches of peasant earthiness, shrewdness, and bawdiness, its uncomplicated emotion, and its utterly pre-Freudian view of human motivation." N Y Her Trib Books

Seeds of tomorrow; tr. from the Russian by Stephen Garry. Knopf 1959 [c1935] 404p (Virgin soil upturned, v 1) $5.95

Sequel to: The Don flows home to the sea

First published in English 1935 with title: Virgin soil upturned

"Picture of a Cossack community on the Don during the Communists' difficult attempt in 1930 to organize a complete collectivization of farming. As the peasants respond variously with enthusiasm, antagonism, duplicity or open hostility to the orders of the mild-mannered, ex-locksmith Davidov, there unfolds before the reader a vivid revelation of the kind of men these Cossacks are, of the characteristics of the land itself, as well as of the problems of Communism. Scenes which are sometimes brutal or coarse intermingle with amusing incidents and all are expressive of character and conditions." N Y Libraries

Followed by: Harvest on the Don

The silent Don. . . . Tr. from the Russian by Stephen Garry. Knopf 2v in 1 $14.95

Also available separately at $7.95

Contents: And quiet flow the Don (1934); The Don flows home to the sea (1941) Both are entered separately

Tales of the Don; tr. from the Russian by H. C. Stephens. Knopf 1962 [c1961] 310p $4.50

Analyzed in Short Story Index

"A collection of sixteen short stories written by the Soviet novelist between 1924 and 1926. The tales are concerned with peasant life along the river Don, and this volume makes the fifth book in the author's Don cycle." Book Rev Digest

Contents: The birthmark; The herdsman; Shibalok's family; The food commissar; Chairman of the Revolutionary Military Committee of the Republic; The watchman in the vegetable plots; A family man; The shamechild; The diehard; The way and the road; The foal; The azure steppe; Alien blood; A mortal enemy; The farm labourer; Dry rot

Sholom Aleichem. See Aleichem, Sholom

Short, Luke

Danger hole

In Western Writers of America. A Western bonanza p366-419

Shui hu chuan

All men are brothers; tr. from the Chinese by Pearl S. Buck. [Day 1933] 2v illus o.p. 1970

"The translator says of this famous Chinese novel: 'I think it is one of the most magnificent pageants ever made of any people. Before your eyes upon the pages of this book march the people of China—all the people. . . . They are a host living and vivid beyond belief.' The story is long and involved; packed with details of a decadent period in which oppression by officials forced a group of brigands to take refuge in the mountains, and made up chiefly of loosely connected picaresque tales of the activities of these rebels against the social order. It belongs to the thirteenth century but was not written down in its present form until about two hundred years later, when the incidents were familiar to the people through frequent retelling. For the student of Chinese literature and history it is richly rewarding." Booklist

Shulman, Max

Anyone got a match? Harper 1964 278p o.p. 1970

"This novel has to do with the four greatest threats of all—cigarettes, food, TV, and love. The main characters are Jefferson Tatum, mighty cigarette tycoon; Ira Shapian, TV magnate, more self-loathing than self-made; and a fascinating female who is important to both their worlds, but in different ways." Huntting

"Several subplots manage to ring in for spoofing most current topics from civil rights to surfing as well as providing the necessary dollops of sex. None of this is very incisive, but most of it is amusing and occasionally downright funny." Library J

Barefoot boy with cheek

In Shulman, M. Max Shulman's Large economy size v 1

The feather merchants

In Shulman, M. Max Shulman's Large economy size v2

y I was a teen-age dwarf; introduction by Art Linkletter. Geis; distributed by Random House 1959 204p o.p. 1970

More episodes in the life of Dobie Gillis who appeared in The many loves of Dobie Gillis, entered below

This book centers around Dobie's "problems with girls from his high school days, when he was shorter than most of his feminine classmates, through his thirtieth year when he has grown up and married." Pub W

"Mr. Shulman fills out Dobie's dossier with good humor, a touch of satire, and his customary ebullience." Sat R

y The many loves of Dobie Gillis; eleven campus stories. Doubleday 1951 223p o.p. 1970

Analyzed in Short Story Index

"Here are 11 short stories dealing with Dobie Gillis, of the crew cut set, and his adventures and misadventures on the Golden Gopher's campus. The stories appeared individually in the Saturday Evening Post, American Magazine and other periodicals. Most of the time Dobie is becoming infatuated with or disinfatuated with one fair coed or another, and the woes and worries which these damsels

Shulman, Max—*Continued*

bring with them supply obstacles for the nimble-witted freckled Casanova." San Francisco Chronicle

Contents: Unlucky winner; She shall have music; Love is a fallacy; Sugar bowl; Everybody loves my baby; Love of two chemists; Face is familiar but—; Mock governor; Boy bites man; King's English; You think you got trouble

Max Shulman's Large economy size; illus. by Bill Crawford. Doubleday 1948 3v in 1 illus $4.95

Contents: Barefoot boy with cheek; The feather merchants; The zebra derby. Published separately in 1943, 1944, and 1946, respectively

Rally round the flag, boys! Doubleday 1957 278p o.p. 1970

"The setting is a small Connecticut town where three ethnic groups struggle for dominance—the Commuters, the Italians, and the Yankee Natives. The establishment of a Nike base in the town leads to no end of hilarious complications." Library J

"A bit of lusty fun at the expense of commuters, exurban manners and mores, teen-age cults, Army red tape, progressive education, and whatever else catches the author's satiric eye." Booklist

The zebra derby
In Shulman, M. Max Shulman's Large economy size v3

Shute, Nevil

The breaking wave. Morrow 1955 282p o.p. 1970

Published in England with title: Requiem for a WREN

"After an absence of five years, during which he has been searching futilely for his dead brother's wartime fiancée, Alan Duncan returns to Australia to find his elderly parents bewildered and shocked by the inexplicable suicide of their exemplary parlormaid. Partial understanding comes with Alan's identification of the dead maid as the missing Janet; the rest of the tragic tale becomes clear as Janet's diary, and the facts gathered in Alan's search, gradually fill in the picture of a girl who was as much of a war casualty as if she had died in combat." Booklist

The checquer board. Large type ed. complete and unabridged. Watts, F. [1967 c1947] 380p $8.95

"A Keith Jennison book"
First published 1947 by Morrow

"Aware that, in all likelihood, he has not long to live, Mr Jackie Turner, a jaunty little Englishman with some shady business deals behind him, decides he doesn't want 'to pack up at the end and find he has done nothing but sell flour all his life.' Recalling the war, the hospital ward and the three men who, though in a mess of trouble themselves, had been good to him at the lowest point in his own checquered career, Mr Turner determines to find out how Fate has dealt with his vanished friends and to help them any way he can. This engrossing, realistic narrative brings out, through Mr Turner's far-reaching quest, the meaning of such episodes as the friendly acceptance of a lonely American Negro boy soldier as the husband of one of the girls in an English village and an R. A. F. pilot's decision to remain in Burma and marry a fine native girl." Bookmark

y The far country. Morrow 1952 343p o.p. 1970

"A love story, the scenes of which are present-day Australia, and England. A London doctor's daughter on a visit to cousins in Australia, meets a Czech surgeon, who is not yet an accredited doctor in his new country. The two become friends, and when Jennifer is summoned back to London, Carl finds a way to join her." Book Rev Digest

"Technical considerations will be of little moment to most readers of this sincere, generous, and clean tasting book. There are scenes in England as well as in Australia, and powerful contrasts are implied." Chicago Sunday Tribune

In the wet. Morrow 1953 339p o.p. 1970

"An attempt in novel form to forecast British Commonwealth relations (especially England and Australia) . . . [in 1983]. It pictures a strictly controlled, poverty-stricken Labor-ridden England, greatly reduced in population, in a constitutional crisis, threatening the Monarchy and hence the Commonwealth. The plot revolves around the present Queen Elizabeth and her Consort, with many descriptions of their travel by airplane from Dominion to Dominion. . . . A thrilling story; highly controversial politics." Library J

y The legacy; a novel. Morrow 1950 308p $4.95

"This story of Jean Paget, a London typist unknown to fame in her native country, falls into two parts, held together by the fact that an uncle had left her a fortune and the man who became her trustee became interested in her life before and after she received the legacy. First there is the story of Jean's experiences in Malaya during the war when she was an unwanted prisoner of the Japanese, and then comes the story of her return to Malaya and eventually to Australia, to pay her debt of gratitude to the Malayans and to the Australian soldier who had once befriended her." Book Rev Digest

Most secret. Morrow 1945 310p o.p. 1970

Story of an English-sponsored naval expedition, commanded by Free French officers, which was sent to an isolated Breton channel town to improve the morale of the Bretons and to wreak havoc on the German patrols guarding the fishing fleet

"Unusual and exceptionally skillful adventure-and-espionage story. . . . Probably as good a thing of its kind as you're likely to come across in some time." New Yorker

No highway; a novel. Morrow 1948 346p o.p. 1970

"Novel about Mr Honey, a shy little research worker in a British airplane testing station. Mr Honey is testing to find out what makes the planes of a great new transatlantic fleet subject to failure. One plane is wrecked in the wilderness of Labrador and Mr Honey is sent out to investigate in another plane of the same type. That plane gets across the ocean in safety and then the excitement begins." Book Rev Digest

y On the beach. Morrow 1957 320p $5.95

"In 1963 in Melbourne, Australia, people are gradually coming to accept the fact that they will die very soon. The results of an atomic war have wiped out all life in the Northern Hemisphere and the infection is moving southward. The story deals with the way these people face the inevitable end." Book Rev Digest

"I believe 'On the Beach' should be read by every thinking person. Nevil Shute has done an unusually able and imaginative job in depicting how people might act if there were a radioactive holocaust such as he envisages." N Y Her Trib Books

Trustee from the toolroom. Morrow 1960 311p boards $5

"A gently humorous, mildly adventurous story. . . . Its shy, middle-aged hero is Keith Stewart, a poorly educated ex-toolroom fitter who lives modestly and quietly in a London suburb, making miniature mechanical models and describing them in a small weekly magazine for an unknown but world-wide following of engineering hobbyists. Left sole trustee for his ten-year-old niece when her parents are drowned in a storm off Tahiti, Keith staunchly sets out, without money or worldly experience, to retrieve her legacy in jewels 12,000 miles away in the Pacific." Booklist

Sienkiewicz, Henryk

Nobel Prize in literature, 1905

Quo vadis; introduction by Allen Klots, Jr. With illustrations from the life of the author and the setting of the story. Dodd 1955 illus (Great illustrated classics) $4.50

First published 1896

A historical novel "dealing with the Rome of Nero and the early Christian martyrs. The Roman noble, Petronius, a worthy representative of the dying paganism, is perhaps the

Sienkiewicz, Henryk—*Continued*

most interesting figure, and the struggle between Christianity and paganism supplies the central plot, but the canvas is large. A succession of characters and episodes and, above all, the richly colorful, decadent life of ancient Rome give the novel its chief interest. The beautiful Christian Lygia is the object of unwelcome attentions from Vinicius, one of the Emperor's guards, and when she refuses to yield to his importunities, she is denounced and thrown to the wild beasts of the arena. She escapes and eventually marries Vinicius, whom Peter and Paul have converted to Christianity." Benét. The Reader's Encyclopedia

Sillanpää, F. E.

Nobel Prize in literature, 1939

The maid Silja; the history of the last offshoot of an old family tree; tr. from the Finnish by Alexander Matson. Macmillan (N Y) 1933 313p o.p. 1970

Published in England under title: Fallen asleep while young

"On a June morning Silja, a beautiful young country girl, maidservant on a farm in Finland dies of consumption. Her death is the end of a long chain of events beginning thirty years back, when her father inherited the prosperous Salmelus farm. In Kustaa's incapable hands, the once well-kept farm runs down and is finally lost. After her father's death Silja hires out as a milkmaid on various farms. Her sad story is told in this novel, a popular one in Finland." Book Rev Digest

"The novel is unusual and powerful in its utter simplicity and in its rarely beautiful expression." Boston Transcript

Siller, Hilda van. See Van Siller, Hilda

Sillitoe, Alan

Guzman, go home, and other stories. Doubleday 1969 192p $4.95

"Stories in this collection attempt to capture the dreams, frustrations, and despair of intelligent men trapped in the routines of middle-class British life." Library J

Contents: Revenge; Chicken; Canals; The road; The rope trick; Isaac Starbuck; Guzman, go home

The loneliness of the long-distance runner. Knopf 1960 [c1959] 176p boards $4.50

Analyzed in Short Story Index
First published in England 1959
Contents: The loneliness of the long-distance runner; Uncle Ernest; Mr Raynor the schoolteacher; The fishing-boat picture; Noah's ark; On Saturday afternoon; The match; The disgrace of Jim Scarfedale; The decline and fall of Frankie Buller

"He speaks, with a kind of nihilism, yet with a strange affirmation, of the native loneliness and rebellion of the pure animal self, the nodal center of life. . . . The title story in this volume is an extremely finished piece of work, a major study in rebellion. It is the work of a writer using all his controls. . . . The other stories in the volume are less substantial, but are full of observation and authority." N Y Times Bk R

The ragman's daughter, and other stories. Knopf 1964 [c1963] 189p $3.95

Analyzed in Short Story Index
First published 1963 in England
"Another collection of short stories about the British workingman today, by a writer who knows his people, their speech, attitudes and morality. Each brief story is filled with vitality and humor, qualities which enlist the reader's involvement." Cincinnati

Contents: The ragman's daughter; The other John Peel; The firebug; The magic box; The bike; To be collected; The good women

Saturday night and Sunday morning. Knopf 1959 [c1958] 239p $3.95

"Arthur Seaton, a restless, angry young man of present-day Nottingham, works in a bicycle factory, wins drinking contests at the local pub, and divides his amorous attention between two married women. Fate, in the form of one of the husbands, eventually ends Arthur's dual affair shortly after which he meets an attractive, unattached girl and, going against his principles, asks her to marry him." Booklist

"For the first time, English working-class life is treated . . . as a normal aspect of the human condition and as natural subject matter for a writer, and is written about by someone who understands it and its values. . . . The book describes with singular vividness [Arthur's] working through the phase of his youthful egotism and the collapse of his belief that he can live happily for himself. . . . Over the psychological depth of the story is strung a sharply observed and well-told net of incident that gives the true robust and earthly quality characteristic of English working-class life." New Yorker

Silone, Ignazio

Bread and wine. A new version tr. from the Italian by Harvey Fergusson II; with a new preface by the author. Atheneum Pubs. 1962 331p boards $5

First published in the United States 1937 by Harper

"Translated from the edition revised by the author to modify the political concepts of the original." Pub W

"The peasants in Italy under the Fascist dictatorship are shown to be crushed by fear, poverty, ignorance, and superstition. Pietro Spina, a young Socialist, secretly returns after fifteen years of exile to work for the liberty of his people. Disguised as a monk, he wanders over the countryside, but is forced to flee when the police discover his whereabouts. Social and philosophical in tone, this solid novel is vividly real and important, as an uncensored picture of modern Italy." Booklist

"This is a great and beautifully written novel by one of the most distinguished of modern writers. All libraries should obtain this revision and keep the original." Library J

Followed by: The seed beneath the snow

Fontamara; tr. from the Italian by Harvey Fergusson II; foreword by Malcolm Cowley. Atheneum Pubs. 1960 240p $4

The first American edition of this Italian novel, written in 1930, was published in 1934 by H. Smith. This 1960 American edition is a translation of the revised version published in Italy 1949. The new version represents a reshaping of the story to minimize its regional emphasis

The book "tells the story of Italian peasants, robbed of their source of water, and of one hero and martyr who goes to Rome to protest against Fascist greed and injustice." Bk Buyer's Guide

"'Fontamara' was effective when it first appeared, but it was then a story of a particular time and place, a document of Italian anti-Fascism. Silone has now liberated it from its particular reference and given it a tragic and classic grandeur as a story of universal application. A comparison of the two versions shows how much Silone has grown as a writer. . . . 'Fontamara' is one of those rare novels that really deserve to be called important." New Yorker

The fox and the camellias; tr. from the Italian by Eric Mosbacher. Harper 1961 139p o.p. 1970

First published in Italy 1960

"The setting is a Swiss farm near Brissago, where the novel's hero, Daniele, maintains a secret outpost for the Italian anti-Fascist underground. . . . The farm is really Daniele's first loyalty, and his teen-aged daughter Silvia is his chief joy. . . . A handsome young Fascist operative appears in the neighborhood. . . . A militant anti-Fascist friend of Daniele's beats the Fascist agent bloody. Unbeknownst to Daniele, the wounded agent is brought to the farm, and . . . nursing him, Silvia falls wildly in love with the stranger. He represents himself as a respectable accountant, and Silvia's mother is all for a wedding, but the story ends instead in an agony of divided loyalties, with each character losing what he loves." Time

Silone, Ignazio—*Continued*

A handful of blackberries; tr. by Darina Silone. Harper 1953 314p o.p. 1970

"The setting is a mountain village in the Naples region; and Silone's hero, the engineer Rocco, once an embattled Communist, has returned deeply disillusioned from a sojourn in Poland and Russia. After a harrowing struggle, Rocco decides to break with the Party, and the Party goes to work to shatter his life. It tricks the girl he loves, Stella, into providing evidence which can be used to disgrace Rocco, and which, at the same time, will make it appear that Stella has shamefully betrayed him." Atlantic

"It is a very simple story, but the clarity of its writing and the beauty of its images give it unusual strength and weight. While it is a far more mature work than either 'Fontamara' or 'The Seed Beneath the Snow,' it has all the freshness and bite of youth." New Yorker

The secret of Luca; tr. by Darina Silone. Harper 1958 183p o.p. 1970

First published 1956 in Italy

"Forty years before this book begins, a murder is committed and an Italian peasant imprisoned for it. When the real murderer confesses, Luca is released. Unable to comprehend why Luca refused to defend himself at his trial, Andrea, a revolutionary who comes from the same village, sets out to solve the mystery and makes a moving discovery about the loyalty of an apparently simple man." Cincinnati

"This quietly dramatic and very moving little novel is Silone's reply to the world's prejudices, his affirmation of the goodness and greatness to be found in unexpected places." Sat R

The seed beneath the snow; a new version tr. from the Italian by Harvey Fergusson II. Atheneum Pubs. 1965 464p $6.50

Sequel to: Bread and wine

First published 1942 in the United States by Harper

"Continues the story of Pietro Spina, begun in Bread and Wine [entered separately]. Pietro, an anti-Fascist is hiding in the home of his grandmother, Donna Maria Vincenza, the great lady of the little village of Colle in the Abruzzi. The time is during the period of the Ethiopian war. Pietro does not agree with his grandmother's attempts to win him a pardon, so he goes to another hideout. In the end he gives himself up to the authorities to save his friend, the half-idiot, deaf-mute Infante." Book Rev Digest

Silverberg, Robert

(ed.) Earthmen and strangers; nine stories of science fiction. Duell 1966 240p $3.95

Analyzed in Short Story Index

Contents: Dear Devil, by E. F. Russell; The best policy, by R. Garrett; Alaree, by R. Silverberg; Life cycle, by P. Anderson; The gentle vultures, by I. Asimov; Stranger Station, by D. Knight; Lower than angels, by A. Budrys; Blind lightning, by H. Ellison; Out of the sun, by A. C. Clarke

Hawksbill Station. Doubleday 1968 166p (Doubleday Science fiction) $3.95

"A barren, prison-like land is the setting to which malcontents and political revolutionaries are sent to live out their lives, with no hope of return, a billion years in the past." Chicago

"An orginal variation on the time machine gimmick, well carried out, this is much better than average science-fiction." Pub W

How it was when the past went away

In Three for tomorrow p 1-80

(ed.) Men and machines; 10 stories of science fiction. Meredith 1968 240p boards $4.95

Analyzed in Short Story Index

"The stories, all of which have to do with the relationship between man, the creator, and the machine which he has made, show man as both the master and the slave of the brain child he has brought into being." Pub W

Contents: Counter foil, by G. O. Smith; A bad day for sales, by F. Leiber; Without a thought, by F. Saberhagen; Solar plexus, by J. Blish; The Macauley circuit, by R. Silverberg; But who can replace a man, by B. W. Aldiss; Instinct,

by L. Del Rey; The Twonky, by L. Padgett; The hunting lodge, by R. Garrett; With folded hands, by J. Williamson

To live again. Doubleday 1969 231p (Doubleday Science fiction) $4.95

"This science fiction novel takes place sometime after the present century when the transplanting of 'personae' is common. The Scheffing Institute, a quasi-public corporation closely regulated by the government, maintains in its files the personalities and memories, that is personae, of the world's notables, some 80 million of whom died since the introduction of the Scheffing process. Individuals apply for transplants of the personae they believe it will be desirable to have as their own. The principal theme concerns who will receive the persona of Paul Kaufmann, 'one of the world's most powerful men, perhaps the most powerful of his age.' The story is a good one revealing the clash of personalities that often appears within one person after transplant has been achieved." Library J

(ed.) Tomorrow's worlds . . . Ten stories of science fiction. Meredith 1969 234p boards $4.95

This "anthology presents ten stories—one for each planet, one for the moon—written over the past thirty years by masters of science fiction." Book News

Contents: Sunrise on Mercury, by R. Silverberg; Before Eden, by A. C. Clarke; Seeds of the dusk, by R. Z. Gallun; The black pits of Luna, by R. A. Heinlein; Crucifixus etiam, by W. M. Miller; Desertion, by C. D. Simak; Pressure, by H. Harrison; The planet of Doubt, by S. G. Weinbaum; One Sunday in Neptune; by A. Panshin; Wait it out, by L. Niven

"The cast is an impressive one . . . [but] the authors have actually written far better stories than are presented here." Pub W

(ed.) Voyagers in time; twelve stories of science fiction. Meredith 1967 243p o.p. 1970

Analyzed in Short Story Index

Contents: The sands of time, by P. S. Miller; . . . and it comes out here, by L. Del Rey; Brooklyn project, by W. Tenn; The men who murdered Mohammed, by A. Bester; Time heals, by P. Anderson; Wrong-way street, by L. Niven; Flux, by M. Moorcock; Dominoes, by C. M. Kornbluth; A bulletin from the trustees, by W. Shore; Traveler's rest, by D. I. Mason; Absolutely inflexible, by R. Silverberg; The time machine [excerpts], by H. G. Wells

"These stories develop the situation, popular since H. G. Wells, of travelling backwards and forwards in time." Chicago

Simak, Clifford D.

All the traps of earth, and other stories. Doubleday 1962 287p o.p. 1970

Analyzed in Short Story Index

Contents: All the traps of earth; Good night, Mr James; Drop dead; No life of their own; The sitters; Crying jag; Installment plan; Condition of employment; Project mastodon

"These nine science fiction stories range in subject from a robot with 600 years of human experience to the problems arising when babysitters from another planet take charge of earthlings." McClurg. Book News

The big front yard

In Asimov, I. ed. The Hugo winners p171-226

City. Gnome Press 1952 244p o.p. 1970

Analyzed in Short Story Index

Contents: City; Huddling place; Census; Desertion; Paradise; Hobbies; Aesop; Simple way

The goblin reservation. Putnam 1968 192p $4.95

"A fanciful science-fiction tale of a world that has progressed beyond the imagination, where creatures from different ages—dinosaurs, goblins, great men like Shakespeare—coexist in time. This is the super-world to which Professor Peter Maxwell, specialist in Supernatural Phenomena, returns after he has accidentally stumbled upon a mysterious crystal planet whose treasury of information surpasses even the Earth's. In his attempt to convince those in power to seize the crystal planet, he is

Simak, Clifford D.—*Continued*

confronted by a still more mysterious discovery: that he has been ingeniously 'duplicated' and 'accidentally' murdered—and that no one will believe he is the real Maxwell." Publisher's note

Out of their minds. Putnam 1970 186p $4.95

"Horton Smith pooh-poohed the idea that nightmare creatures were emerging from the netherworld to claim the earth—until he hooked a sea monster and a werewolf pack attacked him at night." Bk Buyer's Guide

"A nice, light fantasy which deserves to be saved for a few light moments." Pub W

Ring around the sun; a story of tomorrow. Simon & Schuster 1953 242p o.p. 1970

"The world of 1977 is disturbed by the appearance of cars and light bulbs and houses and other objects that will wear forever, thus throwing the whole economic system out of joint. A writer hired to find out who is responsible for all this uncovers a strange truth about his own nature and the existence of a second world." Pub W

They walked like men. Doubleday 1962 234p o.p. 1970

Parker Graves, a newspaperman, watches as his entire city becomes a scene of strange happenings: buildings are bought up at a fantastic rate but people can't find places to live, leases aren't renewed and established businesses are closed. Parker investigates the situation and after adventures both hair-raising and humorous, uncovers the existence of an invasion by beings outside the earth who wish to end the human race. (Publisher)

"Fantastic but ingeniously plotted science-fiction tale." Booklist

Way Station. Doubleday 1963 210p (Doubleday Science fiction) o.p. 1970

Enoch Wallace managed Way Station 18327 where bizarre travelers from outer space told him strange tales. "Then the outside world threatened to destroy the Way Station, and with it, man's last hope of avoiding cataclysmic self-annihilation. The CIA suddenly became interested in [Wallace] a Civil War veteran who looked younger than thirty." Publisher's note

The werewolf principle. Putnam 1967 216p $4.95

"Found in a space capsule on a distant planet, Andrew Blake is brought back to an unfamiliar Earth. He soon meets a strange, tassel-eared creature who hints at the truth about Blake's origins. Slowly Blake becomes aware of the long hushed-up 'Werewolf Principle,' a scientific theory buried in the past, that holds the key to his own fate and the future of the human race." Huntting

Why call them back from heaven? Doubleday 1967 190p (Doubleday Science fiction) o.p. 1970

"Forever Center was dedicated to keeping humans alive forever—but there was no guarantee that either earth or space was big enough to hold all the dead called back from their frozen graves." McClurg. Book News

The worlds of Clifford Simak. Simon & Schuster 1960 378p o.p. 1970

Analyzed in Short Story Index

Contents: Dusty zebra; Honorable opponent; Carbon copy; Foundling father; Idiot's crusade; The big front yard; Operation Stinky; Jackpot; Death scene; Green thumb; Lulu; Neighbor

Simenon, Georges

The accomplices

In Simenon, G. The blue room [and] The accomplices p143-284

An American omnibus. . . . Harcourt 1967 500p $6.75

"A Helen and Kurt Wolff book"

Analyzed in Short Story Index

Contents: Belle; The brothers Rico; The hitchhiker; The watchmaker of Everton

The first three titles were originally published in France 1952, 1952 and 1953 respectively; the fourth, was included in a combined edition "The witnesses and The watchmaker," published 1955

"Simenon's psychological insight and his unique gift for creating a vivid atmosphere make these novels spellbinding reading." Publisher's note

At the Gai-Moulin

In Simenon, G. Maigret abroad p161-315

Belle

In Simenon, G. An American omnibus p3-125

The bells of Bicêtre. Harcourt [1964 c1963] 240p o.p. 1970

Original French edition 1963. First English translation published 1963 in England with title: The patient

"The poignant but astonishingly calm thoughts of a man who is in a hospital in Paris recovering from a stroke and, who for a long time cannot talk. He is a newspaper publisher, a very important person, but now merely existing in uncaring suspension. Almost completely helpless in his bed, but clear-minded, he bitterly reviews his life in the light of possible impending death." Pub W

"An admirable feat of writing and psychological probing. What could have been static and what would have been shorter from the pen of a less observant writer is here a vital, fascinating study. Ibsenesque in its subtle movements." Book Week

The blue room [and] The accomplices; two novels. Harcourt 1964 284p $4.95

The accomplices was first published in 1955 in France

The blue room is a murder story with "psychological probing of an apparently cold marriage, and a frenzied love affair. 'The Accomplices' is a . . . story of the crash of a bus filled with children and the reactions of the hit-run auto driver who caused the crash." Pub W

"The novels speak movingly and convincingly of the human condition at times of greatest testing." Book Week

The brothers Rico

In Simenon, G. An American omnibus p129-249

The cat; tr. from the French by Bernard Frechtman. Harcourt 1967 182p $4.50

"A Helen and Kurt Wolff book"

This is "an unusual novel which treats a relationship in which hate is as potent a tie as love. A 70-year-old couple, who have not spoken to each other for four years, communicate with each other via notes. Although they hate one another, they do not separate. In his treatment Simenon reveals the fibers that hold them together." McClurg. Book News

"It is with the publication of 'The Cat' that . . . [the author] shows himself to be a true master of the modern psychological novel." Library J

The confessional; tr. from the French by Jean Stewart. Harcourt [1968 c1967] 155p $4.50

"A Helen and Kurt Wolff book"

Original French edition 1966. This translation published 1967 in England

"André, a high school boy, comes to realize that his mother has a lover. He himself is the battlefield for his parents, each trying to win him over to his or her side. . . . [The father] is more discreet, more rational, more put upon than the strident, egocentric mother. The mother packs her bags and attempts to leave, but in the end a weary armistice is achieved, and the boy decides to try to hold on to his sanity, to keep his faith in love, to pass his exams, and to eventually begin his own life as a man." Am News of Bks

"The whole theme is delicately and effectively handled to make this another achievement in psychological understanding of the human condition." Best Sellers

Simenon, Georges—*Continued*

Crime in Holland
In Simenon, G. Maigret abroad p3-158

Five times Maigret. Harcourt 1964 525p $5.95

Analyzed in Short Story Index
Originally published 1962 in England with title: A Maigret omnibus
Contents: Maigret right and wrong (Maigret in Montmartre & Maigret's mistake); Maigret has scruples; Maigret and the reluctant witnesses; Maigret goes to school. English translations first published separately in England 1954, 1958, 1959 and 1957 respectively

The hitchhiker
In Simenon, G. An American omnibus p253-376

Inspector Maigret and the dead girl. Doubleday 1955 192p o.p. 1970

First published in England with title: Maigret and the young girl
"This expert and painstaking detection is well done. The dead girl, by far the most interesting person in the story, unfortunately but inevitably must be presented throughout at second hand." San Francisco Chronicle

The little man from Archangel
In Simenon, G. Sunday [and] The little man from Archangel p127-267

The little saint; tr. from the French by Bernard Frechtman. Harcourt 1965 186p $4.50
The author tells the story of a great 20th century French painter who "turns out impressionistic, dreamlike paintings about his early life and the market, Les Halles, where he worked for years as errand boy and pricemarker. His mother is a pushcart vendor. He has emerged from an incredibly sordid slum childhood which has not harmed his gentle, saint-like personality." Pub W

Madame Maigret's own case. Doubleday 1959 191p o.p. 1970
"When Inspector Maigret's wife agreed to look after the child of a harassed young woman, her kindness involved her in one of her husband's most baffling cases. Scene: Paris." McClurg. Book News

Maigret abroad; tr. from the French by Geoffrey Sainsbury. Harcourt 1940 315p o.p. 1970
In this "double-header, Inspector Maigret steps out of his own country to go sleuthing. The first novel, 'A Crime in Holland,' finds him crashing into the rigid decorum of smalltown Dutch society. In the second, 'At the Gai-Moulin,' his mystery solving involves a dancer called Adele; a corpse found in a wicker basket; and a spy ring. Both stories stress his talent for atmosphere and oddities of character, over and above the skillful puzzling." Huntting

Maigret and the Calame report; tr. from the French by Moura Budberg. . . . Harcourt 1969 183p $3.95
"A Helen and Kurt Wolff book"
Original French edition published 1954. "Originally published in England under the title 'Maigret and the Minister.'" Title page
"Maigret becomes involved in political intrigue, a world he dislikes, distrusts, and actually fears. A report highly compromising to the governing Cabinet and Party has disappeared from the private apartment of a Cabinet Minister. It concerns a construction scandal that has cost the lives of many children and set France in commotion. The Minister, facing utter ruin if the report is not found, turns to Maigret." Publisher's note
"Simenon fans will follow with much psychological satisfaction as Maigret, aided by Janvier, Lapointe and the C.I.D. and harassed by resentful concierges, goes about his business. . . . This newest Simenon has its full share of suspense." Book of the Month Club News

Maigret and the headless corpse; tr. from the French by Eileen Ellenbogen. Harcourt [1968 c1967] 183p $3.95
"A Helen and Kurt Wolff book"
First published 1955 in France; this translation published 1967 in England
"When legs, arms, torso, of a man's body, each part carefully wrapped and tied in newspapers, are found in a canal on the outskirts of Paris, Maigret determines that the secret of this murder lies in a small bistro nearby." Pub W
"As usual, Maigret's reluctance to draw the obvious conclusion is sound, based on his profound psychological insight and his marvelous eye for minute oddities in daily life—the very qualities that make Simenon mysteries a continuing delight." Book of the Month Club News

Maigret and the old lady
In Simenon, G. Maigret cinq p203-307

Maigret and the reluctant witnesses
In Simenon, G. Five times Maigret p323-421

Maigret and the young girl
In Simenon, G. Maigret cinq p7-105

Maigret cinq. Harcourt [1965] 523p $5.95
"A Helen and Kurt Wolff book"
First published 1964 in England with title: The second Maigret omnibus
Five cases featuring famed Chief Inspector of the Paris police, originally published 1951, 1955, 1957, 1958 and 1960 respectively
Contents: Maigret and the young girl; Maigret's little joke; Maigret and the old lady; Maigret's first case; Maigret takes a room

Maigret goes to school
In Simenon, G. Five times Maigret p425-525

Maigret has scruples
In Simenon, G. Five times Maigret p223-320

Maigret in Montmartre
In Simenon, G. Five times Maigret p9-116

Maigret in Vichy; tr. from the French by Eileen Ellenbogen. Harcourt 1969 177p $3.95
"A Helen and Kurt Wolff book"
Original French edition published 1968
Maigret and his wife visit Vichy where they notice "among the regulars an enigmatic woman who invariably dresses in lilac. Before very long the lady is strangled, her house ransacked, no one knows for what. Maigret, although he is on vacation, is drawn into helping . . . solve the crime." Pub W

Maigret takes a room
In Simenon, G. Maigret cinq p421-523

Maigret's dead man; tr. from the French by Jean Stewart. Doubleday 1964 192p o.p. 1970
First published 1948 in France
"The man had asked for Maigret's help, insisting that his life was in danger, that men were following him, but he didn't give his name. Then policemen recognized his body—stabbed. Maigret systematically set about identifying the man, discovering his background, and pinning down the killer." Bk Buyer's Guide

Maigret's first case
In Simenon, G. Maigret cinq p309-419

Maigret's little joke
In Simenon, G. Maigret cinq p107-202

Maigret's mistake
In Simenon, G. Five times Maigret p117-219

Maigret's pickpocket; tr. from the French by Nigel Ryan. Harcourt 1968 151p $3.95
"A Helen and Kurt Wolff book"
Original French edition, 1967
"'Inspector Maigret' is riding on the open platform of a Paris bus when, putting a hand to his pocket, he finds his wallet missing. Next

FICTION CATALOG
EIGHTH EDITION

Simenon, Georges—*Continued*

morning the wallet, its original contents intact, is returned by mail to Maigret's office, and soon afterward the pickpocket, a nervous young writer named François Ricain, gives himself into Maigret's custody, begging for protection against a larger charge—that of having murdered his wife, Sophie. So begins this newest Maigret story . . . which, from start to finish, is alive with keenly shared speculation on the reader's part as Maigret, trusting in Ricain's strong sense of human decency, begins his search for Sophie's actual murderer. Most of it takes place in a colorful café called Old Wine Press." Book of the Month Club News

The move; tr. from the French by Christopher Sinclair-Stevenson. Harcourt 1968 148p $4.50

"A Helen and Kurt Wolff book"
This translation first published in England 1968 with title: The neighbours
"Here is a crisp, perceptive study of the danger that success can bring to a little man. Emile Jovis reaches a point on the upward ladder that makes it possible for him to move with his drab wife, Blanche, and their son Alain from a dingy Paris apartment to a modern development outside the city. Through thin walls in the new bedroom he overhears nocturnal discussions about a strange and different life he cannot comprehend, but cannot ignore. . . . He feels compelled to follow the clues he collects through the wall, and is quickly carried from his sheltered existence into deeply troubled waters. Georges Simenon's particular brand of psychological suspense is expertly developed in the novel." Library J

No vacation for Maigret; tr. from the French Les vacances de Maigret, by Geoffrey Sainsbury. Doubleday 1953 191p o.p. 1970

First published in France. First English translation: Maigret on holiday, published in England 1950
"Monsieur and Mme. Maigret were on their vacation when Mme. Maigret was suddenly stricken with appendicitis. While visiting her at the hospital, Maigret learned of the rather mysterious death of a girl in Room 15. He started to do a little investigating and soon his vacation was forgotten when he found evidences of murder." Huntting

The old man dies; tr. from the French by Bernard Frechtman. Harcourt 1967 152p $4.50

"A Helen and Kurt Wolff book"
Original French edition published 1966
"Les Halles, that wonderful market in Paris where tourists go for onion soup at 4 a.m., is the setting for one of Simenon's superb character studies. The old man who dies is a restaurant owner whose life-long goal has been his estate. What happens to the legacy is less vital than what happens to his children." Cincinnati
"Georges Simenon is a kind of 20th-century Maupassant. His short, fluent novels make sad, quiet little comments, a sigh below even the level of irony. . . . [His] story exceeds its narrow limits. It is, simultaneously, a documentary on the restaurant business, a morality play about greed, and an essay on the change—generally, the corruption—of French middle-class values." Christian Science Monitor

The Premier [and] The train; two novels. Harcourt [1966 c1964] 248p $4.95

"A Helen and Kurt Wolff book"
Original French editions published 1958 and 1961 respectively
" 'The Premier,' is a tale of a very old ex-Premier of France, who is on his last legs. He has threatened to publish his memoirs, which could ruin a lot of important people. Or so he thinks. The other, 'The Train,' is a happy interlude of escape in a timid man's life, an interlude prefaced and followed by grim reality. The interlude is a love affair, set at the time of the German invasion of France." Pub W
"The two short novels included in this edition . . . are almost poles apart in substance, but oddly akin in their ability to open to the reader the inner life of two men. . . . Psychological studies, one may call these two short novels. . . . In their way, they are both small masterpieces." Best Sellers

The prison; tr. from the French by Lyn Moir. Harcourt 1969 182p $4.95

"A Helen and Kurt Wolff book"
Original French edition published 1968
"Alain Poitaud, 32 and already a fabulously successful Paris magazine publisher, arrives home one night to be told that his wife, Kitten, has shot her sister. This is the same Kitten he has taken for granted as being always at his side, who has listened without jealousy to his stories of sexual exploits with other women, and with whom, it occurs to him, he has seldom been alone during the years of their marriage. The fact that he had an affair with the murdered sister is irrelevant: it was broken off nearly a year earlier. Only when Kitten refuses to see him does Alain really begin to explore their life together." Pub W
"In the swift economical style that [Simenon] has developed, a style that is almost entirely dialogue, with precise backgrounds in and around Paris, this is a fast-paced but psychologically sound exploration of one man's psyche." Best Sellers

Short cases of Inspector Maigret. Doubleday 1959 188p o.p. 1970

Analyzed in Short Story Index
The stories in this volume made their initial appearance in "Ellery Queen's Mystery magazine"
Contents: Maigret's Christmas; Journey backward into time; Stan the killer; Old lady of Bayeux; Most obstinate man in Paris

Sunday [and] The little man from Archangel. Harcourt [1966 c1959] 267p $4.95

"A Helen and Kurt Wolff book"
Originally published in France, 1959 and 1956, respectively
" 'Sunday' is a psychological novel of a classic case of [marital] arsenic poisoning, French style, with an eerie twist at the very end. 'The Little Man from Archangel' enters into the suicidal feelings of a bookstore owner and stamp dealer, his despair at his wife's infidelity and his neighbors' hostility. . . . [In each] the crime is secondary to a skillful, merciless exposure of the emotions and ambitions of the characters. The translator of both these stories is Nigel Ryan." Pub W

The train
In Simenon, G. The Premier [and] The train p129-48

The watchmaker of Everton
In Simenon, G. An American omnibus p379-500

Simmel, Johannes Mario

Dear fatherland; tr. from the German by Richard and Clara Winston. Random House 1969 403p $6.95

"The setting is Berlin, East and West; the time, the recent past: the characters, an assortment of double agents, petty criminals, high government officials with questionable backgrounds, good-hearted prostitutes and idealists willing to sacrifice themselves for a cause. Bruno Knolle, sometime burglar, is the red threat of a plot centered around attempts to kidnap a financier of freedom tunnels from the East." Library J

Simon, Edith

The golden hand. Putnam 1952 501p o.p. 1970

"The society of fourteenth-century England, from the mighty lords to the craftsmen in the town and the peasants in the field, is pictured in this novel. It tells of the building of a cathedral, a mighty task in those days, on the spot where a miraculous hand of gold was found." Huntting
"The period, which covers the Black Death and the Peasants' revolt, emerges as though it were day before yesterday. This is historical romance at its best and should be widely read." Ontario Lib Rev

Simonov, Konstantin

Days and nights; tr. from the Russian by Joseph Barnes. Simon & Schuster 1945 421p illus o.p. 1970

"Novel about the Red Army. . . . Its setting is the Battle of Stalingrad—the main theme, the growth of a Soviet officer and a Red Army nurse—of their ideas about the war, their country, their future and their love for each other." Huntting

"The superb merit of the book is its series of portraits of men in battle. That they happen to be Russians is incidental; they are first of all human and after that brave." N Y Times Bk R

The living and the dead; tr. from the Russian by R. Ainsztein. Doubleday 1962 552p o.p. 1970

"The story of Sintsov, a Russian correspondent, who becomes flotsam on a sea of war and disorganization. During the fighting he is tossed from one unit to another, is wounded, captured, fights out of encirclement, and is decorated. To his hardship during this time is added, through no fault of his own, the loss of his papers. His anxiety about this shows that his danger from an inept bureaucracy is as great as from the enemy. A book that bears witness to Russian self-criticism." Booklist

"While the translation falters in places, it is successful in conveying the impact of some of the best-executed descriptions of human anguish, tenderness, and courage." Best Sellers

Simpson, Harriette Louisa. See Arnow, Harriette

Sinclair, Harold

The cavalryman. Harper 1958 342p map o.p. 1970

Sequel to: The horse soldiers
A "novel based on a campaign against the Sioux in 1864. General Jack Marlowe leads an undisciplined army against the Indians in their own homelands." The Bookseller

The horse soldiers. Harper 1956 336p maps lib. bdg. $5.11

Fictional account of Grierson's Cavalry Raid during the Civil War. "Colonel Jack Marlowe was assigned to lead two regiments of Illinois and one regiment of Iowa cavalry two hundred miles inside Confederate country. [This is the story of] the daring cavalry operations which took place during the seventeen-day raid." Huntting

"Mr. Sinclair treats an heroic episode without heroics. His narrative is simple and straightforward, and he wisely allows the drama which is innate in the exploit to come through without embellishment." N Y Her Trib Books
Followed by: The cavalryman

Sinclair, Jo

The changelings. McGraw 1955 323p o.p. 1970

"A tract—but also an appealing story—on race relations In a Midwest city, a Jewish street is pressed upon by the growing Negro population. The threat of riot broods over the families (four Jewish and one Italian) whose teenagers, the 'Changelings,' grope their way from incipient gangsterism to leading their own parents away from prejudice and toward realizing that groups can 'assimilate' and still preserve their best traditions." Library J

Sinclair, Upton

Between two worlds. Viking 1941 859p o.p. 1970

Sequel to: World's end
"The story of Lanny Budd through the period between Versailles and the stock market crash. By the device, made possible by Lanny's intricate relationships, of moving him about from place to place, the trend of events is shown: Mussolini coming into power in Italy; the

Nazis lifting their heads in Germany; the Future still 'working' in Russia. Lincoln Steffens appears in person, as in the first book; so does Isadora Duncan, and there are others. Lanny has two 'affairs' and at last takes a wife. With his heiress bride he is in New York when the 1929 crash occurs and there the story ends." Wis Lib Bul
Followed by: Dragon's teeth

Boston. Boni 1928 2v o.p. 1970

"Based on the Sacco-Vanzetti case [the story] is an indictment of Boston tradition and privilege. The novel, a vast pageant of the crime, is the story of Cornelia Thornwell, wife of a former governor, who leaves her life of ease to take a job in a factory. She befriends the two Italian workmen, witnesses the trials and the appeal and works vainly to save them." Haydn. Thesaurus of Book Digests

Dragon harvest. Viking 1945 703p o.p. 1970

Sequel to: Presidential agent
"Begins with Lanny Budd on the French Riviera and ends at Napoleon's tomb, after France has fallen to Hitler. Lanny Budd is once again an art agent, ostensibly, and in reality a secret agent for the President Roosevelt. As usual, he is on the scene wherever things happen: he visits Hitler at Berchtesgaden—he has a private audience with Chamberlain—and he takes part in the rescue at Dunkirk." Huntting
Followed by: A world to win

Dragon's teeth. Viking 1942 631p o.p. 1970

Pulitzer Prize, 1943
Sequel to: Between two worlds
"This third volume in the story of Lanny Budd, covers the years between 1930 and 1934. It describes the rich American playboy, who had spent much of his life abroad, living in Germany, where he met Hitler, Goering, and Goebbels; in Paris, where his feather-brained wife had established a salon; and on the yacht of the wealthy Jewish financier, who was a relative by marriage. When the Nazi terror broke out, Lanny moved by pity and friendship attempted to get his Jewish friend out of Dachau, and in consequence was imprisoned himself. The book closes with the release of Freddi Robin, broken in body and spirit." Book Rev Digest
Followed by: Wide is the gate

y The jungle. Viking 1946 343p o.p. 1970

First published 1906
"In this book the author has vividly portrayed life in the Chicago stockyards and his revelations are so shocking and revolting that one cannot read them without being filled with horror. . . . The central figure in the story is Jurgis Rudkus, a poor Slav immigrant, who comes to the new world to make his fortune. He is accompanied on his venture by his father, Ona Lukoszaite the girl to whom he is engaged, and her family. . . . Their experiences are harrowing in the extreme; they are cheated, abused and oppressed on every hand, suffer privations of every kind and find death a blessed release when it finally ends their sufferings. . . . Throughout the story the dominating influence of the trades' unions is strikingly illustrated and the futility of a workingman's struggle against them." Keller's Reader's Digest of Books

O shepherd, speak! Viking 1949 629p o.p. 1970

Sequel to: One clear call
"A segment of contemporary history with Lanny participating in the war trials and acting as Truman's representative in Moscow. The second part of the book deals with his effort to promote world peace as a result of a million dollar bequest left in his trust for this purpose." Ontario Lib Rev
Followed by: The return of Lanny Budd

Oil! A novel. Boni 1927 527p o.p. 1970

"The story from boyhood to marriage of Bunny Ross, son of an oil magnate. A far reaching story of oil, giving a clear idea of the production end in all its details. . . . Possibly the main character is not Bunny, but his much-admired friend Paul Watkins, who is sent during the war on the expeditionary force to Siberia and returns a communist. Sinclair is, however, fair; he brings out the good qualities of the oil magnates he detests and the squabbling and impracticability of the radicals. The scandals of the Harding regime come in but form only an incidental part of the story." Cleveland

Sinclair, Upton—*Continued*

One clear call. Viking 1948 629p o.p. 1970

Sequel to: Presidential mission
Again as President Roosevelt's secret agent [Lanny Budd] operates in Italy, France, Spain, and Germany where he poses as a friend of top Nazis until he is discovered. He serves in France before the invasion, as always the advisor on military and political moves. The story ends with Roosevelt's re-election in 1944
Followed by: O shepherd, speak!

Presidential agent. Viking 1944 655p o.p. 1970

Sequel to: Wide is the gate
Lanny Budd, socialite and art expert "assumes a new role—that of special secret agent to President Roosevelt. As an intimate of the great and the near-great in European diplomatic circles he can bring to the President first-hand information on the complicated political situation. The period covered is the crucial year between the summer of 1937 and the Munich agreement in 1938. In addition to his political activities he pursues his investigations of spiritualism and makes a futile search for Trudi, the fanatic anti-Nazi, whom he has secretly married." Book Rev Digest
Followed by: Dragon harvest

Presidential mission. Viking 1947 641p o.p. 1970

Sequel to: A world to win
This time, as President Roosevelt's secret agent, [Lanny Budd] operates in North Africa before the invasion, and inside Germany
Followed by: One clear call

The return of Lanny Budd. Viking 1953 555p o.p. 1970

Sequel to: O shepherd, speak!
As peace after World War II dissolves Lanny Budd emerges from retirement on call from Washington. He leaves his radio Peace Program to search out a ring of Nazis. In the events of the years 1946 to 1949, international crises alternate with crises in the Communist spy trial involving Lanny's sister. On his last trip to Berlin, he is kidnapped and tortured by the Russians. He escapes and thereafter abandons his pacific position

Wide is the gate. Viking 1943 751p o.p. 1970

Sequel to: Dragon's teeth
"Lanny Budd's anti-Nazi efforts while in Germany, supposedly as an art critic and personal friend of Hitler, Goering, Hess and others. Covers period from early 1938 to Spanish Civil War." Library J
Followed by: Presidential agent

A world to win. Viking 1946 627p o.p. 1970

Sequel to: Dragon harvest
Covers the war years 1940-1942. "Lanny Budd, still acting as confidential agent for President Roosevelt, makes another dangerous trip to Germany, visit Göring and other Nazis, and learns of their plans to attack Russia the following spring. Returning to report to the President he is assigned to a more hazardous mission—meeting a scientist in Germany to learn about the Nazis' atomic energy research. As a preparation Lanny is tutored by Einstein, but an airplane crash ends his mission and probably his career as a spy. A yacht cruise in the Pacific lands him in Hong Kong at the outbreak of war, but in the meantime he has made his choice of three women and is married again." Booklist
Followed by: Presidential mission

World's end. Viking 1940 740p o.p. 1970

The first of a series of novels in which the author uses the device of a single protagonist, Lanny Budd, to chronicle world events primarily as they concern the United States. Budd is the European born and reared illegitimate son of an American munitions manufacturer who draws him into the international intrigues of armament makers
"A novel of Europe in the period of the first World War . . . packed with characters and events, many of them actual. It is panoramic in setting, peopled by representatives of every race, social class and political opinion. The action turns upon the education-by-experience of an American boy in France, the son of a beautiful and impulsive woman and a powerful munitions-king. While his choice between their world and a world of his own provides the climax, beyond and above the story of Lanny Budd, it is the summation of an era." Huntting
Followed by: Between two worlds

Singer, I. J.

The brothers Ashkenazi; tr. from the Yiddish by Maurice Samuel. Knopf 1936 642p $5.95

"Deals with the rise and decay of the textile city of Lodz, Poland, and with the fortunes of the Polish-Jewish brothers, Max and Jacob Ashkenazi, whose personalities gradually come to dominate the life of the town. . . . What gives the book its significance is not the picture of nineteenth-century Jewish family life, and not the characterizations of the two brothers, but the clear exposition of the class struggle of which Max and Jacob form unconscious parts. . . . It is Lodz that is the real hero of the book. Lodz conceived not merely as a Polish-Jewish-German industrial town, but as the type of world-city whose growth is forced by an advancing capitalism and whose downfall is due to a retreating one." New Yorker

The family Carnovsky; tr. by Joseph Singer. Vanguard 1969 405p $6.95

Original Yiddish edition 1943
This "is the story of three generations of Jews—Orthodox David, who has left Poland for Berlin . . . his son Georg, who becomes a famous and fashionable doctor and marries a gentile; and their son . . . Jegor, a child pulled between his love of [Germany] and his own half Jewishness. . . . In America, to which they emigrate, they must face the reality of what they are . . . [and] come to terms with the terrible incompatibility of the Jewishness and Germanness." Publisher's note
"Singer writes with an old-fashioned flair for telling detail, lively dialogue, and sharp characterization. . . . [He] is at his best in his account of the dissensions within the Jewish community. It must be added, however, that Mr. Singer's own sympathies are not with the Jews from Germany. . . . [He] is more often generous and understanding than acerbic. . . . Despite its somber background, this is a thoroughly enjoyable book, a novel for people who read novels. And you don't have to be Jewish to like it." Sat R

Steel and iron; a novel; tr. from the Yiddish by Joseph Singer. Funk 1969 267p $6.95

"The scene is Poland and Russia in 1915; when fear, police, informers are everywhere and Jews live in terror. Benjamin Lerner, a deserter from the Imperial Russian Army, hides in Warsaw under a new name. When the Germans come, he gets a job in a labor camp, rebuilding a bridge across the Vistula. Religious, national and class hatreds flare as the men exert 'all their strength in the lunatic conflict of man against iron, stone and wood.' Lerner and a cohort lead a revolt among the workers on the bridge and escape. When revolution comes to Russia, however, Lerner is imprisoned by the Germans, then escapes again to breathe the heady air of the new times." Pub W
"The story is very readable, and the language is earthy. The characterization too is good. The only criticism is that the events are too kaleidoscopic." Library J

Yoshe Kalb; introduction by Isaac Bashevis Singer; tr. from the Yiddish by Maurice Samuel. Harper 1965 246p o.p. 1970

First English translation published in 1933 with title: The sinner
"The story concerns a young, sensitive, mystical student, brought by an arranged marriage into the emotional, bickering household and entourage of a rabbi of the Chassidic sect. Fleeing this world, to him uncouth and peasant-like, and his love for the youthful wife of his father-in-law, he becomes an insensate, withdrawn wanderer, seeking to expiate his sin by prayer, but bringing confusion and trouble into the households and communities he visits." Library J
"The reader, whether Jew or Gentile, will find 'Yoshe Kalb' filled with humor, pathos, and outstanding character portrayals." Best Sellers

Singer, Isaac Bashevis

The estate. Farrar, Straus 1969 374p $6.95

Sequel to: The manor

This novel covers the last years of the nineteenth century. It explores the lives of a Polish Jewish family who have emerged from the ghettos to seek a new life in a country that is itself struggling to emerge from a feudal past. "Calman Jacoby is now old; his wife Clara's young son, Sasha, has taken over the management of the estate. Clara herself is estranged from Calman. Count Lucian has been released from prison. Ezriel, Calman's enlightened son-in-law, has become a doctor and he has found that living life without religion is a questionable kind of intellectual freedom." Best Sellers

"Even in their manner of dying, Singer's characters seem to be literally swept away by storms of passion. Indeed, the only thing that keeps the book from disintegrating into an anthology of melodramatic episodes is Singer's unfaltering stylistic control. . . . There are no levels of allegory for the reader to assemble. . . . It is only as one approaches the end of 'The Estate' that the true dimensions of Singer's imaginative achievement becomes apparent." N Y Times Bk R

The family Moskat; tr. from the Yiddish by A. H. Gross. Farrar, Straus [1965 c1950] 611p illus $5.95

A reissue of a title first published 1950 by Knopf

"The complex chronicle of the family of Reb Meshulam Moskat who marries for the third time at 80; the young man who marries Meshulam's stepdaughter though he is in love with the granddaughter Hadassah; the changing fortunes of the family, which loses all its wealth over the years as the scene shifts from Warsaw to America and to Palestine. The time is the decade or so before 1914." Retail Bookseller

Gimpel the fool, and other stories. Farrar, Straus 205p $4.95

Analyzed in Short Story Index

A reprint of the title first published 1955 by Noonday

Translated from the Yiddish by Saul Bellow, Elaine Gottlieb, and others

Contains the following stories: By the light of memorial candles; Fire; From the diary of one not born; Gentleman from Cracow; Gimpel the fool; Joy; Little shoemakers; The mirror; Old man; The unseen; Wife killer

The magician of Lublin. Farrar, Straus 246p $4.95

A reprint of a title first published 1960 by Noonday

Translated from the Yiddish by Elaine Gottlieb and Joseph Singer

"Tale about Yasha Mazur, who makes his living in the circuses and theaters of 19th century Poland. He can skate on the high wire, eat fire . . . and, above all, charm any woman." Time

The manor. Farrar, Straus 1967 442p $6.95

"This novel portrays the epoch between the Polish insurrection of 1863 and the end of the nineteenth century. The title refers to the estate of Count Jampolski, which has been expropriated by the Russians and leased to Calman Jacoby, a pious Jewish grain merchant. Calman makes a fortune selling the timber on the land for railway ties. The impact of the modern era, as Poland emerged from the Middle Ages, on Calman and his four daughters forms the core of the story. This book was written between 1953 and 1955 and first serialized in Yiddish in the Jewish Daily Forward. The translation is the work of Joseph Singer and Elaine Gottlieb. This volume constitutes part one of the complete saga." Book Rev Digest

This "could be the breakthrough book to gain Singer the wider audience he deserves. Like all of his fiction . . . this work is a subtle form of autobiography, projecting the author's own sense of exile. . . . The central character is a kind of 'petit bourgeois' Job . . . who is condemned to watch his children depart, with brutal casualness and indifference, from their upbringing. . . . Yes, [Singer] seems to say, change is king. And yes, life goes on, about

as bad and as good and as endlessly fascinating as always. no other novelist today can balance this double truth so well." Time

Followed by: The estate

Satan in Goray. Farrar, Straus 239p $4.95

A reprint of a title first published 1955 by Noonday

Translated from the Yiddish by Jacob Sloan

"This black-mirror narrative of miracles and cabala, of a hamlet in seventeenth-century Poland and a false Messiah, is in the tradition of such classics as 'The Dybbuk' and 'The Golem.' Poetically conceived, it captures the fever of longing, the folk-frenzy for salvation, that possessed the Jewish population of central Europe after the dark decade of the Chmielnicki massacres, three centuries before Hitler." N Y Times Bk R

The séance, and other stories. Farrar, Straus 1968 276p $5.95

Analyzed in Short Story Index

Contents: The séance; The slaughterer; The dead fiddler; The lecture; Cockadoodledoo; The plagiarist; Zeitl and Rickel; The warehouse; Henne Fire; Getzel the monkey; Yanda; The needle; Two corpses go dancing; The parrot; The brooch; The letter writer

Singer's "subject is humanity in general, and the Jewish world of 1870 Poland in particular. Ghosts, demons, and spirits populate his tales of the Old World where justice is often long in coming, but appropriate when it finally does. His characters—the fool, the crone, the thief, the rabbi—are universals, recognizable in all of us." Library J

Selected short stories of Isaac Bashevis Singer; ed. and introduced by Irving Howe. Modern Lib. 1966 xxvi, 379p $2.95

Analyzed in Short Story Index

Contents: Gimpel the fool; The gentleman from Cracow; The wife killer; The mirror; The little shoemakers; The old man; The unseen; The Spinoza of Market Street; The black wedding; A tale of two liars; The beggar said so; The man who came back; In the poorhouse; Taibele and her demon; Blood; Esther Kreindel the second; The fast; The last demon; Alone; Three tales; Zeidlus the Pope; I place my reliance on no man; Short Friday

Short Friday, and other stories. Farrar, Straus 1964 243p boards $4.95

Analyzed in Short Story Index

"Characters steeped in the religion and superstition of European Judaism encounter real and imaginary spirits." Cincinnati

Contents: Taibele and her demon; Big and little; Blood; Alone; Esther Kreindel the second; Jachid and Jechidah; Under the knife; The fast; The last demon; Yentl the Yeshiva boy; Three tales; Zeidlus the Pope; A wedding in Brownsville; I place my reliance on no man; Cunegunde; Short Friday

The slave; a novel. Tr. from the Yiddish by the author and Cecil Hemley. Farrar, Straus 1962 311p boards $5.50

"The setting of the story is seventeenth-century Poland. . . . Jacob, a saintly young Jew, driven from his native town by a Cossack raid, has become a slave of a Polish peasant. He loves, and is loved by the peasant's daughter, Wanda. Polish and Jewish law forbid their marriage on pain of death, and the couple become wanderers, outcasts from both worlds. Yet, through the sufferings of their love they learn great wisdom and faith." Atlantic

"Singer is able, as few writers are, to transmute metaphysical ideas into pure emotion. What the novel really says is that one way or another we are all slaves. . . . Few writers since Shakespeare have been able to evoke so harrowingly the nightmare world of savage animals . . . and of man's kinship with them. . . . A brilliant portrayal of a tumultuous society and a poignant account of a man who in wrestling with God found his soul." Sat R

The Spinoza of Market Street. Farrar, Straus 1961 214p boards $3.95

Analyzed in Short Story Index

A "collection of stories about Polish Jews in Warsaw and various other towns, in the late nineteenth and early twentieth centuries. The background is . . . colorful, and many of the stories have the quality of folklore." Pub W

Singer, Isaac B.—*Continued*

Contents: The Spinoza of Market Street; The black wedding; A tale of two liars; The shadow of a crib; Shiddah and Kuziba; Caricature; The beggar said so; The man who came back; A piece of advice; In the poorhouse; The destruction of Kreshev

Singer, Israel Joshua. See Singer, I. J.

Singh, K. Natwar- See Natwar-Singh, K.

Sirin, Vl. See Nabokov, Vladimir

Sitwell, Osbert

Collected stories. Harper 1953 540p o.p. 1970

Analyzed in Short Story Index
Contents: Defeat: That flesh is heir to: Staggered holiday; The love-bird; Primavera: Shadow play; Machine breaks down; Dumb-animal; Glow-worm; His ship comes home; Charles and Charlemagne; Plague-cart before horse; Pompey and some peaches—I; Pompey and some peaches—II; Triple fugue; Idyll through the looking-glass; Champagne for the old lady; Lovers' meeting; Woman who hated flowers; Low tide; Man who drove Strindberg mad; Death of a God; Long journey; True lovers' knot; The messenger; Alive—alive oh; A place of one's own; Friendship's due; Touching wood; Dead heat; 'You can carry it, Mrs Parkin'; The greeting

Sjöwall, Maj

The laughing policeman [by] Maj Sjöwall and Per Wahlöö; tr. from the Swedish by Alan Blair. Pantheon Bks. 1970 211p boards $4.95

Original Swedish edition published 1968
"The rainy night a maniac gunned down eight people in a Stockholm city bus. Swedish detective Martin Beck seriously wondered what makes anyone want to be a policeman. One of the victims was a colleague of Beck's, and, unlike the criminals in some classic American cases of multiple murder, this culprit had got away without a trace. . . . In this . . . story of multiple murder, Maj. Sjöwall and Per Wahloo have re-created the seemingly random, complex, and ritualized violence that governs the mood of metropolitan life today." Publisher's note

The man on the balcony; the story of a crime [by] Maj Sjöwall and Per Wahlöö. Tr. from the Swedish by Alan Blair. Pantheon Bks. 1968 180p boards $4.50

Original Swedish edition published 1967
"A peaceful summer suddenly develops into a nightmare for Martin Beck, superintendent of the Stockholm Homicide Squad, when the city becomes the scene of a rash of brutal muggings and child sex-murders." McClurg. Book News
"First-rate detective fiction, highly recommended." Pub W

The man who went up in smoke, by Maj Sjöwall and Per Wahlöö; tr. from the Swedish by Joan Tate. Pantheon Bks. 1969 183p boards $4.50

Original Swedish edition 1966
Superintendent Martin has "to investigate the case of a missing Swedish journalist who has apparently disappeared on assignment in Budapest. The situation has sticky diplomatic overtones, the clues are almost nil. . . . The final solution lies back in Sweden after all, but it is the wonderfully rich, exotic and ultimately frightening sojourn in Budapest that the reader will enjoy most." Pub W

Roseanna [by] Maj Sjöwall and Per Wahlöö; tr. from the Swedish by Lois Roth. Pantheon Bks. 1967 212p $4.50

Originally published 1965 in Sweden
"A woman's body is scooped up by a dredge in the channel of an inland waterway in Sweden. . . . The investigation takes six months and nineteen days, involving a hundred people, several countries and daring police action before the murderer whose psychopathic image slowly builds, is trapped. . . . One is tempted to think this is based on fact, but no matter. Both cast and situation are intensely real." Book of the Month Club News

This "is a wonderfully tough and pleasantly chilling tale though told without a wasted word." Harper

Skinner, Burrhus F.

y Walden two. Macmillan (N Y) 320p $6.95

First published 1948
"A novel based on the life at a modern American Utopia. Two college professors, two ex-GI's, and their fiancées, visit the colony for a week, during the course of which the principles of the community are studied thoroughly." Book Rev Digest

Slaughter, Frank G.

Constantine: the miracle of the flaming cross. Doubleday 1965 430p $5.95

This novel about Constantine's life and conversion to Christianity portrays the Roman world of the third and fourth centuries
The author "takes few liberties with the facts as the standard histories present them to us but he makes them exceptionally interesting." Best Sellers

The curse of Jezebel; a novel of the Biblical Queen of Evil. Doubleday 1961 288p o.p. 1970

Based on the Old Testament story of the evil Queen Jezebel, this narrative "moves on two planes: the struggle of the Canaanite kings, led by Jezebel's husband, King Ahab of Israel, and the conflicts which arise because men cannot resist the tantalizing charms of Jezebel." Publisher's note

Daybreak. Doubleday 1958 320p o.p. 1970

The author, a doctor, has written this novel revolving "about the early use of the new tranquilizing drugs. His hero is a young neurosurgeon who experiments with the drugs on a schizophrenic girl with whom he is in love." Pub W
"An intriguing foundation of realism is given the novel by Dr. Slaughter's insights into the marriage of politics and medicine at a state hospital." Sat R

East Side General. Doubleday 1952 311p o.p. 1970

"Twenty-four hours in the life of the doctors, nurses and patients in a large city hospital. . . . There is an element of mystery which centers around a critically ill patient whose burns have been diagnosed as resulting from atomic radiation. The character of a brilliant surgeon, devoted to his mission of saving lives, is contrasted with that of a young, ambitious and unscrupulous doctor involved in activities in which the FBI becomes interested." Huntting

Epidemic! Doubleday 1961 286p o.p. 1970

This story "centers around a fictional epidemic of plague in New York City during the summer of 1965. Surgeon Robert Trent and Eric Stowe, world authority of the W.H.O., are in love with nurse Eve Bronson. The three unite their efforts with other key medical personnel and with city officials to control the spread of the disease. Interwoven is a complex municipal situation of gang warfare and organized violence." Library J

The Galileans; a novel of Mary Magdalene. Doubleday 1953 307p o.p. 1970

"The story of Mary Magdalene and Joseph of Galilee, nephew of Joseph of Arimathea. The story opens in the city of Tiberius where the young physician Joseph is studying Greek. Pilate is ruler, and Mary is dancing in the streets for money. It ends several years later when Mary learns that her beloved Master has risen from the dead." Huntting

God's warrior. Doubleday 1967 371p (The Pathway of faith ser) $5.95

"A novel based on the life of Saul of Tarsus, who at first persecuted the Christians but was converted by a miracle while he was on the way to Damascus to direct further persecutions and from that time on became the most zealous of the apostles." Bk Buyer's Guide
"Dr. Slaughter has fleshed out the familiar outlines of the biblical story with references to history, descriptions of the cities, countryside, daily life and trades. There is interesting material on the conflicts between the Jewish sects of the time as well as on the struggles of the early Christian church." Pub W

Slaugher, Frank G.—*Continued*

The road to Bithynia; a novel of Luke, the beloved physician. Doubleday 1951 330p $4.95

"The New Testament characters are given life-like interpretation in this popularized account of Luke's life after he attached himself to Christ's followers. Luke's first real awareness of Christ's influence came when he saw Stephen stoned and received from the dying martyr a scroll containing some of Christ's sayings. Paul is portrayed as Luke's friend in spite of differences over the meaning of Christ's teachings and in spite of the fact that Luke marries the woman whom Paul loves." Booklist

The song of Ruth; a love story from the Old Testament. Doubleday 1954 317p o.p. 1970

This narrative of the Book of Ruth tells of the marriage between Ruth, the Moabitess, and Mahlon, an Israelite, living in her country. It describes the war between Israel and Moab in which Mahlon is killed while helping Boaz, the leader of the Israelites, to escape. Then Ruth follows her mother-in-law, Naomi, to Bethlehem where she eventually marries Boaz

Surgeon's choice; a novel of medicine tomorrow. Doubleday 1969 345p $5.95

The author "describes a savage power struggle within the walls of a private medical center as a principled young doctor, hoping to perform the world's first heart and lung transplant, pushes for an advanced hospital building program. Professional jealousies, private intrigues, and 'transplant ethics' are all woven into this [story]." News of Bks

"Sophisticated readers will be able to tell exactly what's going to happen next every step of the way, but they aren't Dr. Slaughter's fans anyway. For the less demanding, the mixture of medicine, romance, behind-the-scenes financial maneuvering at a big hospital are expertly blended into a story centered on a highly dramatic experiment." Pub W

The thorn of Arimathea. Doubleday 1959 317p o.p. 1970

Based on the legends of St Veronica and the veil, and of the flowering thorn on the grave of Joseph of Arimathea on the Isle of Avalon

This book "tells the story of Quintus Volusianus, physician of the Emperor Tiberius, and his search for Jesus of Nazareth at the request of his royal patient. He finds Jesus crucified, but is deeply attracted and eventually converted by his many and various followers, falling in love with one of them, Veronica, a crippled girl healed by the veil that touched the Master's face." Ontario Lib Rev

Slonim, Marc

(ed.) Modern Italian short stories. Simon & Schuster 1954 429p o.p. 1970

Analyzed in Short Story Index

Contents: La Lupa, by G. Verga; The wake, by G. d'Annunzio; The bat, by L. Pirandello; This indolence of mine, by I. Svevo; The Sardinian fox, by G. Deledda; The mistress and the master speak, by A. Panzini; The mask factory, by G. Papini; The cloud maker, by G. Papini; Madmen's congress, by G. Papini; The Siracusan, by G. A. Borgese; The boy, by G. A. Borgese; Aquarium, by E. Cecchi; Visitors, by E. Cecchi; An Etruscan harvest, by R. Bacchelli; A day in Venice, by B. Tecchi; An indiscreet madrigal, by G. Manzini; Love letters, by A. Palazzeschi; Linaria, by M. Bontempelli; The sleeping beauty, by M. Bontempelli; Mario and fortune, by G. Comisso; The wedding journey, by C. Alvaro; Return to Fontamara, by I. Silone; The unfortunate lover, by A. Moravia; The massacre of Vallucciole, by C. Levi; His excellency, by I. Montanelli; The petition, by G. Guareschi; The flight to France, by F. Jovine; In a lane of Naples, by G. Marotta; The leather jacket, by C. Pavese; A mistress of twenty, by V. Pratolini; The cavaliere, by V. Brancati; Aunt Bess, in memoriam, by G. Berto; Piededeflco, by D. Rea; It's all a question of degree, by C. Bernari; A poor ghost, by G. B. Angioletti; Nora, by M. Soldati; Strange new friends, by D. Buzzati; One afternoon, Adam, by I. Calvino; Uncle Agrippa takes a train, by E. Vittorini

Smith, Betty

y Joy in the morning. Harper 1963 308p $6.95

A "story of an early marriage contracted joyously but with no money. . . . Miss Smith's new heroine, Annie McGairy, all of 18 years old, elopes with a 20-year-old law student, Carl Brown. Their first two years of marriage take place and their first baby comes while Carl works for his degree in a midwestern college town in the late 1920's. The two have no parental support, but a love that is cheerful, jealous, young and resilient. Annie is a charmer, a friendly soul with only an elementary education but great intelligence and a gift for writing. She is the center of the book." Pub W

"This human hearted song of joy is more than a pen sketch of human nature. The characterization is essentially dramatic and the dialogue is a marvel of accuracy. . . . As always in [Betty Smith's] writing this adroit naturalness and conciseness keeps the reader interested. The flashes of warm reality, of wit, and of truth, give universal interest to the simple tale." Best Sellers

Maggie-Now. Harper 1958 437p o.p. 1970

This story of Maggie-Now who grew up at the turn of the century among the immigrant Irish and Germans of Brooklyn "is really two stories, those of Maggie's father, an immigrant from Ireland . . . and of Maggie and her strange, unsatisfying marriage." Pub W

y A tree grows in Brooklyn; a novel; with drawings by Richard Bergere. Harper 1947 420p $6.95

First published 1943

"Poetically written novel about life in a slum section of Brooklyn—Williamsburg—during the first years of the twentieth century. It is a study of the childhood and youth of Francie Nolan, of her family and friends, and of all of the pain and beauty and mystery of a way of life as it appears to an exceptionally keen young girl." Book Rev Digest

"There is little story, or plot, as the reader encounters it in the average novel. This is rather a stringing together of memory's beads and the workmanship is extraordinarily good. . . . Above all, it is a faithful picture of a part of Brooklyn that was mostly slums and misery." N Y Times Bk R

Smith, Dodie

y I capture the castle. Little 1948 343p $4.95

"An Atlantic Monthly Press book"

The heroine, Cassandra Mortmain, in her girlish diary, unfolds the tale of her eccentric family living precariously in a ruined English castle. When two young American bachelors, who have inherited the castle arrive, romantic and humorous situations embroil the entire family

"The gayest and sweetest of modern novels. Skirting whimsy by a hair's breadth, Miss Smith saturates with blithe humor her story. . . . A quaint and old-fashioned story, as pure as it is pretty. But underneath this champagne-like surface of young romance and middle-aged confusion Miss Smith has fortified her novel with the strong alcoholic content of sound psychological principles." N Y Her Trib Books

It ends with revelations; a novel. Little 1967 280p boards $5.95

"The scene is an English spa town and London, the milieu the theatrical world, and the theme [is] love and loyalty. . . . To Miles Quentin, an actor of ability and kindness, Jill owes many years of care and friendship in a marriage unconsummated because of his homosexuality. When Jill falls in love with a Member of Parliament and her husband is threatened with blackmail she faces a crisis of honor that is deftly resolved by the author." Booklist

The new moon with the old; a novel. Little 1963 367p boards $5.95

"An Atlantic Monthly Press book"

Becoming a secretary-housekeeper, Jane Minton shares a pleasant country house with four young people. Then one day Rupert Carrington, the attractive, widowed father, tells

Smith, Dodie—*Continued*

Jane that he is quitting England to avoid prosecution for fraud. The young people must fend for themselves with Jane's willing help. (Publisher)

Smith, Dorothy Evelyn

Brief flower. Dutton 1966 224p boards $4.50

"Satisfying characterization of a young girl from the age of ten to her early teens and of the people around her who react to and effect her growing up. As the book opens Bunny, an illegitimate child, lives on a run-down farm in Yorkshire with two people who are not her parents. Although she wants to prolong the freedom and unconventionality of her childhood Bunny is faced with the decision of staying on the farm or living with her newly found, wealthy grandfather." Booklist

Smith, Dorothy Gladys. See Smith, Dodie

Smith, Lee

The last day the dogbushes bloomed. Harper 1968 180p boards $4.95

"A Southern girl named Susan on the verge of puberty tells about the summer which marked her realization of the sadness of life—the man who mows the lawn dies; her mother, the beautiful queen, leaves her family for another man; a precocious and repugnant city boy, Eugene, victimizes her in games which widen his first-hand sexual knowledge. Even the love of Elsie May, the maid with the tiny dancing feet, and the protection of Susan's secret hiding place behind the dogbushes cannot hide her from Little Arthur, the imaginary evil boy created by Eugene to control the others, as he assumes reality in her mind." Library J

"Lee Smith has been unusually successful in penetrating the private world of 9-year-old Susan Tobey. . . . Childhood is a country without maps; its passport is a fearlessness and lack of self-consciousness, a special grace given to children and, happily, on brief loan to the author, who manages here to avoid the pitfalls of cuteness." Book of the Month Club News

Smith, Lillian

One hour. Harcourt 1959 440p o.p. 1970

"David Landrum, an Episcopal minister in a Southern community, chronicles a series of tragic events set in motion when his closest friend, a brilliant scientist, is unjustly accused of molesting a small girl. This accusation not only drastically affects the lives of Mark Channing and his wife Grace but is responsible for the death of their teen-age son and David's belated realization of his love for Grace. A town in ferment and personal relationships in a period of emotional crisis are impressively created as are the philosophical undertones which give additional substance to a powerful novel." Booklist

Strange fruit; a novel. Harcourt 1944 371p $4.95

"Beautiful Nonnie Anderson, Negress college graduate, and white Tracy Deen, rootless young veteran of the last war, are lovers. From this fact the author has created a powerful, sustained drama of the deep South. Religion, social mores, family and townspeople all contribute to the final ironic tragedy. Written realistically, this novel is a sympathetic, authoritative portrayal of one of America's deep problems and is recommended both for its sociological value and its literary excellence." Library J

Smith, "Red"

(ed.) The Saturday Evening Post. The Saturday Evening Post Sports stories

Smith, Vian

The wind blows free. Doubleday 1968 [c1967] 301p $4.95

The story "set in early nineteenth-century England portrays the hopelessness of individuals struggling against inevitable change brought about by land enclosure. The Coldrick family and other commoners have eked out a living on the rugged Dartmoor moors for some 600 years, and now Parliament has allowed the purchase of 6,000 acres of moorland by Lord Cochrane who plans to enclose the land and promote modern methods of farming and animal husbandry. Unwilling to face exile or servitude Coldrick leads the commoners in a futile fight in which he loses his younger son and wife before giving up and emigrating to America with his older son and daughter-in-law." Booklist

Smith, Walter Wellesley. See Smith, "Red"

Smollett, Tobias

The expedition of Humphry Clinker

Some editions are:
Dutton (Everyman's lib) $2.95 Edited by Howard Mumford Jones
Oxford $4.80 Edited and with an introduction by Lewis M. Knapp
Oxford (World classics ed) $3

First published 1771

"A titular hero, Humphry Clinker, is a poor workhouse lad, put out by the parish as apprentice to a blacksmith, and afterwards employed as an ostler's assistant and extra postilion. When he is dismissed from the stables, he enters the service of Mr. Bramble, a fretful, grumpy, but kindhearted old gentleman, greatly troubled with gout. Here he falls in love with Winifred Jenkins. Miss Tabitha Bramble's maid, and turns out to be a natural son of Mr. Bramble. Though nominally the hero, Humphry plays a much less important part than the Brambles. The interest centers in the 'expedition' of the title, a family tour through England and Scotland." Benét. The Reader's Encyclopedia

"The sarcastic descriptions of towns and peoples are doubly comic from being in letters written by the different characters, with absurdly incompatible points of view. Parodies the language and manners of the Methodists. The Scottish portion is particularly familiar and racy, dealing with the scenes of Smollett's younger days." Baker's Best

Peregrine Pickle

Some editions are:
Dutton (Everyman's lib) 2v ea $2.95
Oxford $5.60 Edited by J. L. Clifford. Has title: The adventures of Peregrine Pickle

First published 1751

"Peregrine's schooling, his courtships (with most unsavoury interludes) his travels and amorous exploits on the Continent and in London, make a humorous but unedifying story. The realism is Hogarthian; the caricature, it has been said—but this is only a superficial impression—gives us comic beasts rather than men." Baker's Best

Roderick Random. Dutton xx, 428p (Everyman's lib) $2.95

First published 1784

"The career of an apprentice who goes out into the world to seek his fortune. He meets with many adventures, becoming in time a surgeon's assistant on a man-of-war. Here the story becomes autobiographical. The author's experiences as a surgeon in the attack on Carthagena is described, with satirical comments on the mismanagement of the expedition. Later, the hero enters the French army and fights at Dettingen. He returns to England, marries his sweetheart, finds his father whom he had supposed dead, and ends his life in prosperity. Various types of marriages are delineated in semi-caricature." Miller

Sneider, Vern

y The Teahouse of the August Moon. Putnam 1951 282p $5.95

This "novel centers around Captain Fisby, member of a Government Team in Okinawa, his colonel, and Plan B for the welfare of the natives. The plan would have gone according to schedule if Fisby hadn't received a gift of two geishas, and if Miss Higa Jiga and other maiden ladies hadn't felt they must compete on an equitable basis with the geishas. The chicanery of the ladies, and Fisby's coping with the situation make this a wonderfully humorous and satirical story." Library J

"In this gay little novel Mr. Sneider has entirely without preaching told us that our fault as occupiers is our tendency to think of Americanization only in terms of American institutions. . . . Everyone involved in such tasks both in Washington and overseas should read . . . [it]. A bitter but beneficial pill is not often so tastefully coated." Sat R

Snow, C. P.

The affair. Scribner 1960 374p (Strangers and brothers) $4.50

Eighth volume in the author's series: Strangers and brothers

Sequel to: The light and the dark

The Cambridge University, England "setting is the same as that of 'The masters,' [entered separately] and some of the same characters appear in it, though the time is 20 years later [1953-1954. Here] . . . Lewis Eliot, the hero is an observer rather than a doer. The 'affair' of the title concerns a Cambridge scientist falsely accused of scientific fraud." Pub W

"Like all this extraordinary writer's rich, adult and perceptive works, the present novel can be read separately from others in the series. Because it is something of a calm, conservative 'whodunit,' it may find a wider audience in this country than some of Snow's previous works. Brilliantly narrated and as readable as a novel by Maugham, it may also send many readers, as yet unfamiliar with them, back to Snow's other novels. This is a good idea. . . . In weighing the evidence, Snow's unhurried narrative becomes a novel of scientific ideas and an examination of college politics and ritual delivered with documentary fidelity. Snow's message, it seems to me, is that the search for truth is a moral responsibility as well as a scientific one. The manner in which this scientist and man of letters examines the problem at hand is a literary joy to behold." San Francisco Chronicle

The conscience of the rich. Scribner 1958 342p (Strangers and brothers) $4.95

Seventh volume in the author's series: Strangers and brothers

This novel deals less with Eliot than with his friend, Charles March

"As a result of his friendship with Charles March, Lewis Eliot is taken into the private world of one of England's wealthiest and most influential Jewish families and through his eyes the March drama is slowly unfolded; the close bond between Charles, his father, and his sister, Charles's marriage to a gentile Communist, and the ensuing political scandal which estranges father and son, brother and sister. . . . Set in London during the late 1920's and the 1930's." Booklist

Corridors of power. Scribner 1964 403p (Strangers and brothers) $5.95

Ninth volume in the author's series: Strangers and brothers

"The workings of inner power in the British government—with key administrators, politicians, and the wealthy manipulators, male and female—[are] traced in a novel of the period 1955-1958. . . . Since the power in this fictional case is concerned with the use of nuclear arms, the fate of the world can easily hang on the fate of one minister, Roger Quaife." Pub W

"We see the corridors of political power illuminated with a fine and discriminating light in what will become 'the' modern British political novel. But on the level of individual character we remain in the dark, knowing neither what moves Quaife to pursue his unconventional policy nor to stray from hearth and bed." Library J

Homecoming. Scribner 1956 399p (Strangers and brothers) $4.95

Sixth volume in the author's serise: Strangers and brothers

"An introspective, subtly shaded novel which again stars Lewis Eliot. . . . Eliot's unhappy marriage to a neurotic woman, her death, and his affair with and eventual marriage to a woman more worthy of his love comprise the chief incidents in a story that accents not the events themselves but their psychological effect upon the persons involved. Crisp, carefully fashioned prose; for the discriminating." Booklist

Period covered is 1938-1951

Last things. Scribner 1970 435p (Strangers and brothers) $7.95

This eleventh and concluding volume in the series Strangers and brothers "continues Sir Lewis Eliot's observations on the upper class English world around him into the mid-1960's. Plot is not stressed particularly in this volume. Lewis' father-in-law attempts suicide; Lewis himself undergoes an eye operation during which he suffers a terrifying cardiac arrest; his nephew is divorced by Muriel, the stepdaughter of his friend Sir Azik Schiff, who then lives with Lewis' son Charles; Lewis is offered a post in the government but, after some soul-searching, declines it; Charles and Muriel are involved in a student-mounted attack against government-sponsored research in biological warfare at the universities; and Charles decides to make his mark by becoming a foreign correspondent." Library J

This "is not a novel to be read at a sitting, or in isolation from the rest of this series; taken at full leisure, and with some background, it is a very fitting end to a remarkably fine series." Best Sellers

The light and the dark. Scribner [1961 c1947] 406p (Strangers and brothers) $4.95

First published 1947 in England

Second volume in the author's series: Strangers and brothers

This novel centers on "Roy Calvert, a Cambridge scholar with an international reputation at twenty-five and the close friend of Lewis Eliot, the central character in Snow's . . . series. Handsome, with great charm and gaiety, Calvert seems to do everything with elegance and ease. And yet the College rumors of his tormented private life are quite true; these are rumors of wild dissipation and self-destructive acts. Drawn close to Calvert partly because of his own personal despair, Lewis Eliot tries to help and shield his friend in crisis after crisis. And Eliot comes to understand what lies behind the profound division in Roy Calvert's nature; he gets to the source of the struggle between the light and the dark." Publisher's note

Period covered: 1935-1943. Followed chronologically by: The affair

The masters. Scribner 374p (Strangers and brothers) $4.95

First published in 1951 by Macmillan

Fourth volume in the author's series: Strangers and brothers

"Ambition leads to corruption even in the best of men, and this Mr. Snow proves in his extremely readable fifth novel in the Lewis Eliot series. The story is set in Cambridge [in 1937] where the Fellows of the college are shown intriguing to elect a new Master from among themselves. For a quiet novel of subtle characterization this one contains a surprising element of suspense." Ontario Lib Rev

The new men. Scribner 1954 311p (Strangers and brothers) $4.50

Fifth volume in the author's series: Strangers and brothers

The "novel deals with a small group of men, bureaucrats and scientists concerned with the research into nuclear fission in England during the war years. It's a dramatization of attitudes and moralities which produced the atom spies, and the discussions which are still going on." Publisher's note

Period covered is 1939-1946

The search. Bobbs 1935 375p o.p. 1970

First published in 1934 in England

"The story of a scientist, a well-known crystallographer, of his rise from indigence to eminence and of his decline from scientific eminence to hard-won matrimonial felicity." New Statesman & Nation

The sleep of reason. Scribner [1969 c1968] 483p (Strangers and brothers) $6.95

First published 1968 in England

"This is the tenth book in the Strangers and Brothers sequence. The time is 1963. Set chiefly in an English provincial town, and in London, the story begins calmly, dealing with Lewis Eliot's relationship with his father, his pride in his son, and his involvement with a university problem. Then, out of duty to his old friend George Passant, Eliot becomes involved in a particularly shocking murder case, in which two lesbians are charged with the torture and killing of an eight-year-old boy." Am News of Bks

This "can be read as a complete, isolated novel, and it brings its own sense of completeness and its own brand of enjoyment. This enjoyment is naturally somewhat richer for anybody who has read the first nine novels. . . . All the incidents are natural, easy; there is no artificial dragging up of discussion, no overt or even subtle didacticism—but the study of our times is real and fascinating." Best Sellers

Snow, C. P.—*Continued*

Strangers and brothers. Scribner [1960] 309p (Strangers and brothers) $4.50

First published 1940 in England
First volume in the author's series: Strangers and brothers

This is the first in a series of eleven novels set in England during the first half of the 20th century, depicting the life story of the narrator, Lewis Eliot, an English lawyer. This volume covers the years 1925-1933

George Passant, a solicitor in an English provincial town, exerts a crucial influence on his group of young protégés, Lewis Eliot among them. An idealist, courageous and high-principled Passant seems destined for great things yet the story ends in his trial for fraud. The reasons for this are revealed here. (Publisher)

"Essentially the tragedy of a good man defeated by the mediocrity of his world, the story of George Passant is completed in the novel 'Homecoming.' . . . Like all the novels in the series, 'Strangers and Brothers' is distinguished by virtue of its analysis of motive and character and its anatomization of a world in which a smooth mediocrity is the greatest virtue." Library J
Followed chronologically by: The conscience of the rich

Time of hope. Scribner [1961 c1949] 408p (Strangers and brothers) $4.95

First published 1950 by Macmillan
Third volume in the author's series: Strangers and brothers

"Here, as in 'Light and the Dark' (1948) Lewis Eliot is the main character that typifies middle class English life, and as in the earlier work, Mr. Snow shows the impact of spiritual values on individuals. The 1930s are the background here and the years are brilliantly drawn. Moral problems are vivid and the characters are varied in their reactions." Library J

Solberg, Gunard

Shelia. Houghton 1969 243p $4.95

"Wayne Divine is a sometime high school student, for he seldom attends school. He lives in suburban Chicago and thinks he is in love with Shelia, a Negro school friend whom he idealizes as a 'black priestess.' . . . He experiences with Shelia all the purples and blues of pushing drugs, wrecking a friend's car, and the inevitable attempt to escape from the middle-class morality of their parents by running away." Library J

"More of an adolescent love story than it is a racial recitative. But what ultimately makes Shelia valid as a character and as a book is Mr Solberg's expert probing of a confused young girl, not certain of her world, her love, or herself." Pub W

Soldati, Mario

The orange envelope; tr. by Bernard Wall. Harcourt 1969 251p $5.75

"A Helen and Kurt Wolff book"
Original Italian edition 1966

The author "gives a riveting picture of a mother-and-son relationship of the devouring and destructive sort. The protagonist, [Carlo] born into the rich Italian bourgeoise and brought up in a church school, ends up . . . as an insatiable consumer of women. When his affections eventually become fixed on one girl, whom he first meets at a brothel yet intends to marry, his mother, as her last act in life, frightens the girl away, throwing the son back into his old pattern and establishing her power even beyond the grave." Am News of Bks

"To say the story disappoints—because Carlo has no more resistance than peaked meringue—doesn't mean to miss it. . . . Soldati is superb in the seamless way he creates knowledgeable characters and leaves them unprotected." N Y Times Bk R

Solmssen, Arthur R. G.

Rittenhouse Square; a novel. Little 1968 313p boards $5.95

"This is a tale of a young man on his way up in an eminent Philadelphia law firm. His steady ascent is interrupted by a month of volunteer work as a public defender, an experience which shakes his smugness and ambition leading him to contemplate for a while a life of public service." Booklist

Mr Solmssen "certainly seems to have Philadelphia's legal world down pat and brings it vividly alive." Book of the Month Club News

Solzhenitsyn, Aleksandr I.

Nobel Prize in literature, 1970

The cancer ward

Some editions are:
Dial Press $8.50 Translated from the Russian by Rebecca Frank
Farrar, Straus $10 Translated from the Russian by Nicholas Bethell and David Burg
Original Russian edition published 1962; English translation, 1968

"The texts of the two editions are substantially the same. What may determine the relative success of the two editions is the translation. A comparison of the two reveals literal differences in almost every line. But the differences do not necessarily—or at all—reflect inaccuracy of translation in either version. Instead, they seem to reflect difference of interpretation and style. The Bethell-Burg translation is colloquial, almost breezy at times. The Frank translation is more literary and poetic. Readers will find both translations easy to read and free flowing." Pub W

This novel tells "the stories of the dozen or so patients who pass through the men's cancer ward, No. 13, between Pavel Rusanov's admission and discharge, in a hospital in a [Soviet] city in February and March, 1955. The hospital staff and the patients' relatives are as much parts of the novel as the sick men themselves." Book World

It "has universality and is a protest against senseless cruelty and the imprisonment of the spirit that follows physical confinement and yet is an affirmation of residual goodness that sometimes remains in the souls of victims of restraint." Booklist

"This is a work of crude but enormous power, and should further enhance Solzhenitsyn's position as one of the greatest of contemporary Russian writers." Library J

The first circle; tr. from the Russian by Thomas P. Whitney. Harper 1968 580p $10

The First Circle of Dante's Hell stands here as a metaphor for certain scientific research centers in Soviet Russia, operating within special prisons and staffed by political prisoners who are also scientists. Set in 1949, a period of political repression, this novel follows the fortunes of several different people who live in such a center. (Publisher)

This massive novel "escapes the danger of monotony and repetitiveness through the use of theoretical digressions, documentary chapters, and the introduction of historical personages, who then coexist with the fictitious heroes. . . . Belonging to the humanitarian tradition of great Russian novels, [this book] has most of their strengths and weaknesses. . . . Its construction is somewhat loose; the principal characters are occasionally verbose, and some of the discussions are mere intellectual gymnastics. Nevertheless, [it] is a splendid book." Sat R

One day in the life of Ivan Denisovich

Some editions are:
Dutton $4.95 With an introduction by Marvin L. Kalb; foreword by Alexander Tvardovsky. Translated from the Russian by Ralph Parker
Praeger $5.50 Translated by Max Hayward and Ronald Hingley; introduction by Max Hayward and Leopold Labedz
First Russian edition, 1962

A novel describing one day in the life of a Russian citizen imprisoned for a ten year sentence in a slave labor camp during the Stalin era. The chief character, an innocent man falsely accused, meets numerous people in prison, experiences brutality and constant struggles to survive. (Publisher)

Both the "authorized" (Dutton) and the "unauthorized" (Praeger) editions present "a bitter, unadorned documentary of that battle for survival. It is not, however, anti-Soviet, but simply anti-Stalinist. . . . It is also a moving human record. . . . Of the two competing translations, Mr. Parker's for all its niceties of accuracy, is blunted and smoothed. It misses the caustic directness of the original and the tough, spare quality of Solzhenitsyn's barracks prose. Hayward and Hingley, on the other hand, have conveyed the laconic speech

Solzhenitsyn, Aleksandr I.—*Continued*

of the camp inmates, with all its attendant
profanity, as well as any translators could.
The Dutton edition is enhanced by a lucid
and most enlightening critical introduction."
Library J

Somerlott, Robert

The inquisitor's house. Viking 1968 377p
boards $5.95

"When five people—an officer, a prostitute,
a rich lady, an American doctor, and a
medium—were all found dead after a white
fire destroyed a house in Mexico on the Day
of the Dead, the officials wanted to quiet
fears that these people had brought the
devil's wrath upon them. The novel traces the
lives of all five and two who escaped death."
Bk Buyer's Guide

The author "is a master of portraying personality. With each character he creates the
reader becomes intimately involved and has a
real understanding of the motives of each.
. . . The details of the conduct of spiritualism
are excellent and there is no doubt that the
author has researched and knows his subject
well. For a mystery fan this book is highly
recommended." Best Sellers

Sontag, Susan

Death kit. Farrar, Straus 1967 311p
boards $5.75

A stream-of-consciousness novel in which
the hero Dalton (called Diddy), works for a
microscope company, is a city-dweller, has a
love affair with a blind girl, and may have
committed murder on a train in a tunnel. On
the other hand, he may have been the one
who was murdered

"Miss Sontag's plot is a simple one, a recapitulation of Bierce's 'An Occurrence at Owl
Creek Bridge', but so embellished by philosophical comment and macabre phantasmagoria as to become new and startling. The incidents of this telling are an exteriorization
of a mild businessman's confrontation with
death, and the myths of train travel, tunnels,
blindness, violence, lust, and corpses that he
tells himself." Library J

Sorenson, Virginia

Kingdom come. Harcourt 1960 497p $5.75

"The love story of Hanne Dalsgaard, whose
parents own a great Jutland farm, and Svend
Madsen, one of her father's hired hands. The
Danish conflict with Prussia over Schleswig-
Holstein; the social unrest and spiritual ferment of the period; the arrival in Scandinavia
of Mormon missionaries—these are some of the
events that play a part in the destiny of
Hanne and Svend." Huntting

"The religious and social conflicts are
clearly defined, the many characters fully and
convincingly developed, and the background of
rural Danish life vividly drawn." Booklist

Many heavens; a new Mormon novel. Harcourt 1954 352p o.p. 1970

"A story of Mormon life around the turn of
the century soon after the official ending of
polygamy. Zina, a girl studying to be a nurse,
falls in love with the only doctor in their Utah
valley, a man already married to a crippled
wife. In the end she and the doctor decide
on a clandestine polygamous marriage with the
full approval of the first wife." Pub W

"This dubiously happy ending mars an
otherwise tender love story, filled with sympathetic character studies and fascinating
descriptions of Mormon life and customs."
Library J

The proper gods. Harcourt 1951 309p
o.p. 1970

The love story of a Yaqui Indian, Adan,
caught in the conflict between the traditions
of his tribe and the rootless existence of those
who have abandoned it

The author "has conjured up a fascinating
picture of the entire Yaqui way of life. The
temption to overburden her book with descriptive and expository matter must have been
strong, but she has nowhere succumbed to
it . . . . At once simple and close-textured,
this evocative prose has the quality of good
poetry." N Y Her Trib Books

Soseki, Natsume. See Natsume, Soseki

Spark, Muriel

The bachelors. Lippincott 1961 [c1960]
219p boards $3.95

First published 1960 in England

"Patrick Seton, a convicted fraud and trick-
ster, is charged with forging a letter to obtain
money from a rich widow, one of the members
of a spiritualist circle in which he acts as
medium. . . . The hero of the book, an epileptic
graphologist called Ronald [Bridges], is entangled on both sides; he is to appear as an
expert witness for his friend Martin, prosecuting counsel, but another friend, Matthew, is
deeply in love with Patrick's mistress, a beautiful coffee-bar waitress called Alice. To complicate the situation, Alice's friend Elsie is
being used by two crooks, Father Socket and
his homosexual medium friend, who are after
the forged letter." Times (London) Lit Sup

"Working with the oddest materials, she
manages a kind of grisly comedy of doom; with
exquisite tact and deftness she delivers a terrible judgment upon emblematic London, her
blighted contemporary city." Sat R

The ballad of Peckham Rye. Lippincott
1960 160p o.p. 1970

"Young Dougal Douglas, the Devil in contemporary clothing, has quite an impact on an industrial town adjacent to London since, among
other things, he is responsible for a groom
leaving his bride-to-be at the altar and the
nervous breakdown of a veteran employee in one
of the local factories." Booklist

"A fresh comic style does not appear every
day, and that is what Muriel Spark has developed in this expert fantasy. . . . The wack-
iness is cumulative, the style dead-pan and
blow-by-blow, and above all no overt attempt
is ever made to get a laugh." N Y Times
Bk R

also in Spark, M. Memento mori, and
The ballad of Peckham Rye

also in Spark, M. A Muriel Spark trio:
The comforters; The ballad of
Peckham Rye [and] Memento mori
p233-386

Collected stories: I. Knopf [1968 c1967]
359p $6.95

First published 1967 in England

This collection includes stories that appeared
in the earlier volumes, "The go-away bird, and
other stories," and "Voices at play," a collection of stories and plays, together with four
new stories she has written in the last few
years. (Publisher)

Contents: The Portobello Road; The curtain
blown by the breeze; The Black Madonna; Bang-
bang you're dead; The Seraph and the Zambesi;
The twins; The Playhouse called Remarkable;
The pawnbroker's wife; Miss Pinkerton's apocalypse; 'A sad tale's best for winter'; The leaf-
sweeper; Daisy Overend; You should have seen
the mess: Come along, Marjorie; The ormolu
clock; The dark glasses; A member of the
family; The house of the famous poet; The
fathers' daughters; Alice Long's dachshunds;
The go-away bird [novella]

"The settings of these stories are English
and African and Mrs. Spark evokes both backgrounds with ease and assurance. Her characters, as always gain one's confidence immediately. . . . But perhaps the author's
greatest skill is her ability to capture one's
complete attention quickly and to hold it unwaveringly until the very last word has been
said." Pub W

The comforters

In Spark, M. A Muriel Spark trio: The
comforters; The ballad of Peckham
Rye [and] Memento mori p13-228

The girls of slender means. Knopf 1963 176p
$3.95

This "novel shifts focus between a young
cynical poet (who, one finds out, is later to
die as a martyred missionary in Haiti) and
a group of girls with some of whom he is
vaguely in love. The girls live in a London
residence home for young women, just at the

Spark, Muriel—*Continued*

end of World War II when money is scarce,
food and ration coupons are precious, and
people are beginning to think of resuming their
normal lives." Pub W

The author "has been artful and splendidly
intelligent in seeing the deeply serious through
the slightly ridiculous. Her prose is always a
pleasure to read. . . . Her religious feeling is
free of cant. The quality of her achievement
is secure. What troubles one is the scale of her
undertaking; it is minor. Somehow one wants a
bigger book from a talent so considerable."
Book Week

The go-away bird
In Spark, M. Collected stories: I p302-59

The go-away bird, and other stories. Lippincott 1960 214p boards $3.75

Analyzed in Short Story Index
A novella and ten stories, the scenes of which
are either England or South Africa
Contents: The Black Madonna; The pawnbroker's wife; The twins; Miss Pinkerton's
apocalypse; 'A sad tale's best for winter'; The
go-away bird; Daisy Overend; You should have
seen the mess; Come along, Marjorie; The
Seraph and the Zambezi; The Portobello Road

The Mandelbaum Gate. Knopf 1965 369p
$5.95

"The changing shape of any identity, be it
of person or of situation, is the theme of this
novel, typified by the Mandelbaum Gate of the
title, 'hardly a gate at all, but a piece of street
between Jerusalem and Jerusalem'. . . . The
narrative goes and returns piecemeal between
the two parts of the Holy Land, focusing on
two English characters—Barbara Vaughan, a
spinster, half Jewish by birth and Roman
Catholic by conviction, come to Israel to be
near her archeologist finacé (and lover) in
Jordan and to make a pilgrimage to the Holy
sites; and Freddy Hamilton, proper foreign
officer, moved by an unexpected impulse to
change his personal pattern of responsibility and
by kindness to keep Barbara from the danger
of being apprehended by Jordan authorities
because of her background." Library J

"Humor, suspense, love and ethics are some
of the elements of this wholly enjoyable novel."
Cincinnati

Memento mori. Lippincott 1959 [c1958]
224p o.p. 1970

"A novel centering around the reactions of
a group of elderly people, including a celebrated
author, an unscrupulous housekeeper, an
octogenarian with an eye for women, and
the inhabitants of an old folks' home, when
they receive the message 'Remember you must
die.'" Pub W

"A very funny novel indeed about the ancient
and enterprising. . . . Miss Spark's technique
is to introduce her characters as they appear
in public and then to reveal what lurks behind
the facade. . . . Much of the fun of Memento
Mori lies in Miss Spark's style." Atlantic

also in Spark, M. A Muriel Spark trio:
The comforters; The ballad of
Peckham Rye [and] Memento mori
p398-608

Memento mori, and The ballad of Peckham
Rye. Modern Lib. 1966 376p $2.95

The two complete novels reprinted here were
first published 1958 and 1960 respectively and
are entered separately

A Muriel Spark trio: The comforters; The
ballad of Peckham Rye [and] Memento mori.
Lippincott 1962 608p boards $5.95

The three complete novels reprinted here were
first published 1957, 1960 and 1959 respectively. The first title is "a novel in experimental
form. It is a book within a book, in which many
of the characters are neurotics or oddities of
some sort. The most normal character is Louisa
Jepp, aged seventy-eight, whose experiments
with smuggling diamonds provide much of the
action. The scene is England, and Roman
Catholic life is part of the background." Book
Rev Digest

The second and third titles are entered
separately

The prime of Miss Jean Brodie. Lippincott
1962 [c1961] 187p $3.95

"Set in Edinburgh in the thirties, it is largely
a character sketch of a middle-aged school
teacher who has a tremendous influence over
a small group of girls attending the school in
which she teaches. Eventually, one of them
turns on her and brings about her dismissal."
Pub W

"It is a story that is funny, true, unpleasant,
and in the end, gloriously human—or ingloriously
human—both, actually. Along the way, there
are uncanny glimpses of the young, in all their
mercurial mystery, equally inclined to heroworship and treachery." N Y Her Trib Books

The public image. Knopf 1968 144p $4.50

Orginally published in England

"A young screen actress identifies with her
public image and is violently forced to become
herself again when her husband commits suicide and leaves diabolically destructive notes
calculated to destroy the false facade. A chiseled satire on the power of mass media."
Booklist

"It is certainly neither a light nor a shadow
book; for like all satirical treatments of human
behavior it carries a weight of implied corrective notions. . . . It is tightly, brightly written.
The prose is a joy to read for its very freshness. It seems to rise, not out of painstaking
self-conscious artistry but out of a natural sure
feeling for form, structure and phrase; it seems
spontaneously right." Book World

Spellman, Francis, Cardinal

The foundling. Scribner 1951 304p o.p. 1970

"The story of Peter Lane, abandoned when a
baby in St. Patrick's cathedral, New York City,
and his relationship to Paul Taggart, the
wounded and disillusioned soldier, who found
him there on his return from World War I.
Peter's growth and development, his interest in
farming and music, his love for Barbara Ross
and his own return from the wars, blinded and
dispirited, are simply, compassionately and
understandingly told. A knowledge of and a
love for the city of New York and its people
is shown." Ontario Lib Rev

Spencer, Elizabeth

The light in the piazza. McGraw 1960 110p
boards $3.95

"Margaret Johnson's persistent sorrow arises
from the fact that her daughter Clara, because
of an accident, has the mentality of a child of
ten, though she is in her twenties. A young
Italian named Fabrizio's begins to court Clara,
and she responds delightedly to his attentions.
Clara is an attractive girl, and Margaret . . .
temporizes. She takes Clara to Rome but the
girl is miserable. Margaret decides that Clara
should marry Fabrizio and that somehow, in
Italy, it is right for her to do so. She goes ahead
without telling her husband, who is at home in
America, and when Fabrizio's father raises the
price, she pays it." Sat R

"This is a very-well-told story, very lucid
and very smooth; although slight in treatment it
has a good deal of substance to it." New
Statesman

The voice at the back door. McGraw 1956
334p boards $5.95

An "attempt to reveal the emotional struggles churning the hearts of whites and Negroes
in a small Mississippi community where racial
integration is being bitterly resisted. The manyfaceted plot revolves around former football
hero Duncan Harper, who, after the death of
the local, tough sheriff, is chosen to carry on in
his stead until the next election, and follows
his high-principled fights for his unpopular
ideals." Library J

"There is some farce, some beautifully understated terror, much bitter satire, much tenderness. And there is always a compelling imagery,
whether of place or season or mood. But the
writing, like the characters and the plot, is
subservient to the central theme: the changing
pattern of race relations." N Y Her Trib Books

Spicer, Bart

Act of anger. Atheneum Pubs. 1962 505p
$5.95

"A record of a murder trial, presumably in
Arizona. An itinerant Mexican youth, a hitchhiker, is accused of killing a wealthy and no-

Spicer, Bart—*Continued*

torious Los Angeles homo-sexual during a journey across the Southwest desert. . . . Benson Kellogg reluctantly takes on the youth's defense. He attempts to investigate the background of his client's act of anger. But personal, family and State political pressures close in on Kellogg in an effort to soft-pedal his case during an election year in a community of strong Mexican-American voting strength. Striking back, the lawyer begins to take a deep moral interest in the case." San Francisco Chronicle

Brother to the enemy. Dodd 1958 308p o.p. 1970

"A novel based on the attempt to abduct the traitor, Benedict Arnold, from the British encampment in colonial New York and return him unharmed to his four comrades in Washington's Continental Army." McClurg. Book News
"'Brother to the Enemy' is most effective as a dual character study—of John Champion, a taciturn Hamlet, and of Benedict Arnold, the ruined idol of every Rebel soldier. It starts with a desperate assignment and closes with the gripping confrontation of the traitor and the spy." N Y Times Bk R

Kellogg Junction. Atheneum Pubs. 1969 430p $7.95

The setting of the novel "is a village near Rincon in an unidentified desert state. The Kellogg brothers are law partners in Rincon, Burr has political ambitions, and Ben is dedicated to the family ranch, La Canada, where he raises Palomino show horses. Problems begin when Ben decided to defend a former schoolmate, Bill Sarant, against a charge of murder in the death of a man at the Fiesta Motel. They increase as the gambling forces from Las Vegas start to move in." Library J
"At times, this colorful and suspenseful novel stops dead in its tracks while all concerned debate such arcane matters as the effect of artificial insemination on the economics of horse breeding, but all in all it is a superior, if sprawling, trial novel." Book of the Month Club News

Sprague de Camp, L. See De Camp, L. Sprague

Spring, Howard

The houses in between; a novel. Harper 1951 550p o.p. 1970

"A panorama of English and continental history told as the life story of Sarah Rainborough, an upper class English woman. As a child of three Sarah saw Queen Victoria open the Crystal Palace. After living thru four wars she died at ninety-nine in 1948." Book Rev Digest
"The novel is old-fashioned in style, it does miss something of life, truth, reality, but it has qualities of imagination and feeling." Spec

My son, my son! Viking 1938 649p o.p. 1970

Published in England under title: O Absalom!
"Told in the first person this is the story of William Essex and of his lifelong friend Dermot O'Riorden. Starting life in a Manchester slum both rise in the world, one becoming a wealthy furniture manufacturer, the other achieving fame as a novelist. Each has a son, extravagantly loved, and both sons come to a tragic end." Book Rev Digest
"A grim but vivid story of lives gone wrong with no apportionable blame. Scarcely one bright ray lights up the end, but vigour, unabated, keeps it vastly readable from first to last." Times (London) Lit Sup

Srivastava, Dhanpat Rai. See Premchand

Stafford, Jean

Bad characters. Farrar, Straus 1964 276p boards $4.95

Analyzed in Short Story-Index
Stories included are: Bad characters; The end of a career; A reasonable facsimile; In the zoo; Cops and robbers; The liberation; The captain's gift; A reading problem; Caveat emptor
The major piece in this collection is: A winter's tale, "a haunting and evocative novella set in Heidelberg just before the outbreak of the war." Publisher's note

The Catherine wheel; a novel. Harcourt 1952 281p o.p. 1970

"A modern novel with the scene laid in a small New England town near Boston. Katharine Congreve, the heroine, is the mistress of her ancestral home, Congreve House. Her cousin marries the man Katharine has secretly loved, and she becomes enmeshed in their lives. The Catherine wheel figures in a tragic scene in the novel." Huntting
"Miss Stafford has written a novel to compel the imagination and nurture the mind, she has also written one in which pity and terror combine to reach us in the secret, irrational places of the heart." Commonweal

Children are bored on Sunday. Farrar, Straus 1953 252p $3

Analyzed in Short Story Index
First published by Harcourt
Contents: The echo and the nemesis; A country love story; A summer day; The maiden; The home front; Between the porch and the altar; The bleeding heart; The interior castle; A modern proposal; Children are bored on Sunday
"Within its boundaries, Miss Stafford writes with certainty, understanding and beauty. Like her three novels, these stories, within their impeccable framework, are meaningful and complex." N Y Times Bk R

The collected stories of Jean Stafford. Farrar, Straus 1969 463p $10

Awarded the Pulitzer Prize, 1970
"These stories published over the period 1944 to 1968 include twelve not published in book form previously [and] are arranged geographically in four sections: The innocents abroad (Americans in Europe); The Bostonians, and other manifestations of the American scene; Cowboys and Indians, and magic mountains (The far West); and Manhattan Island." Book Rev Digest
Contents: Maggie Meriwether's rich experience; The children's game; The echo and the nemesis; The maiden; A modest proposal; Caveat emptor; Life is no abyss; The hope chest; Polite conversation; A country love story; The bleeding heart; The lippia lawn; The interior castle; The healthiest girl in town; The tea time of stouthearted ladies; The mountain day; The darkening moon; Bad characters; In the zoo; The liberation; A reading problem; A summer day; The philosophy lesson; Children are bored on Sunday; Beatrice Trueblood's story; Between the porch and the altar; I love someone; Cops and robbers; The captain's gift; The end of a career
"Readers of Stafford's short stories . . . should be delighted with this anthology of 30 of her best stories complete in one well organized, readably printed volume. . . . Excellent leisure readings, the stories may be chosen at random from the various sections. Recommended for literature students and the general reading public." Choice

A winter's tale
In Stafford, J. Bad characters p225-76

Starke, Roland

Lionel
In Starke, R. Something soft, and other stories p79-136

Something soft, and other stories. Doubleday 1969 [c1968] 213p $4.95

A collection of five long stories "running the gamut of human emotion and situation. Roland Starke, writes in the tradition of Roald Dahl and Paul Bowles, is a masterbuilder of suspense as he adroitly underplays the brutal characteristics of his subjects." Am News of Bks
Contents: Something soft; The day; Lionel [novelette]; The lights of Algeciras; To the cascade

Stead, Christina

The man who loved children; introduction by Randall Jarrell. Holt 1965 xli, 527p $5.95

First published 1940
"An analysis of family life as evidenced in one family, the Pollits, living near Washington, D.C. Sam Pollit, the father, a scientist,

FICTION CATALOG
EIGHTH EDITION

Stead, Christina—*Continued*

employed by the government; Henrietta, his second wife, a whiny neurotic always in debt; their five children; and Sam's oldest daughter, the only child of his first marriage, are the characters. Altho he thinks of himself as a great and good character, Sam, with his invented language, and his possessiveness almost amounting to incestuousness, is the chief contributor to the ultimate tragedy which overtakes the family." Book Rev Digest

"The author understands people, she can dissect them and lay bare all their strengths and weaknesses and show why they act as they do; but she has very little sympathy with them." Springf'd Republican

Steele, Max

Where she brushed her hair, and other stories. Harper 1968 215p boards $5.95

Analyzed in Short Story Index

Contents: The cat and the coffee drinkers; Captain of the white yacht; Big goat, little goat; The wanton troopers; The rescue; The glass-brick apartment; A caracole in Paris; Hereby hangs a tale; Hear the wind blow; From the French Quarter; Promiscuous unbound; The year of the lily-blight; What to do till the postman comes; Where she brushed her hair

"These tales are hard to describe and impossible to summarize adequately. There is bright fantasy in some, originality in all. They are sophisticated in the best sense." Sat R

Steen, Marguerite

The sun is my undoing; a novel. Viking 1941 1176p o.p. 1970

"A long, picaresque novel of eighteenth century life in England and the West Indies and at sea. The theme of the novel is the evils of slave trade and the work of the English abolitionists. The hero is Matthew Flood, who woos and wins the heart of a beautiful English girl. However, when he finds her an ardent abolitionist, he leaves England and enters the slave trade, takes a Negro mistress, and has many adventures culminating in his capture by Barbary pirates. After many years he returns home to face the results of his escapades." Book Rev Digest

"It has genuine epic sweep, in spite of its somewhat episodical development, and it is remarkably vivid and vital." Springf'd Republican

Followed by: Twilight on the Floods

Twilight on the Floods; a sequel to "The sun is my undoing." Doubleday 1949 782p o.p. 1970

Sequel to: The sun is my undoing

Saga of the remarkable Flood family against the background of Bristol, England, and the Gold Coast of Africa at the turn of the century. It is particularly the story of Johnny Flood, great grandson of old Matt Flood, the slave trader, and of Johnny's burning desire to expiate the sins of his forebears on the Gold Coast, and of his fight against the growing decadence in his family

Stegner, Wallace

All the little live things. Viking 1967 345p boards $5.75

"When Joseph Allston, 64, and his wife, Ruth, move West to their 'Prospero's island' (rural California, near San Francisco), the retirement days 'drip away like honey off a spoon.' They live quietly without involvement . . . hoping to erase scars caused by the death of their rebellious son. The press of life first intrudes on them when young Jim Peck, a bearded freethinker, camps on their property. . . . Then a young married couple, Marian and John Caitlin, arrive in the neighborhood, and the Allstons find themselves exposed to a depth of emotional involvement with others they had not wanted to experience ever again." Pub W

"Mr. Stegner's narrative skill and his talent for imaginative recreation is evident throughout the book. His choice of words, the turn of a phrase, evoking a scene, an emotion, or a personality are to be savored. His writing, leisurely as it may appear, can be dramatic and moving." Best Sellers

The Big Rock Candy Mountain. Duell 1943 515p o.p. 1970

The "story begins about 1906 and ends in 1942. [The] scene is in far western states and [Saskatchewan. The] principal characters are Bo Mason, his wife Elsa, and their two boys. Life is an almost continuous moving day because the next town, county, or state persistently beckons to Bo as the place where he will make his fortune." Library J

"A well-written study of a footloose family. . . . The life of the household is a misery of continual cruelty and often crushing poverty, alternating with occasional scenes of a simple family happiness which stand out beautifully and unforgettably." New Yorker

Joe Hill; a biographical novel. Doubleday [1969 c1950] 381p $6.95

First published 1950 with title: The preacher and the slave

A fictional biography of Joseph Hillstrom, the Joe Hill who as song writer and labor organizer became a martyr to labor's militant drive for organization, particularly of the cause of the Industrial Workers of the World

"A novel of astute insight and action. Though it is a convincing study of a complex human being, it is, as well, an exploration of the uses of violence and an inquiry into the meaning of justice. Time: 1910-1916." Huntting

Stein, Gertrude

Melanctha

In Blackmur, R. P. ed. American short novels p236-306

In Phillips, W. ed. Great American short novels p295-401

Three lives; stories of the good Anna, Melanctha, and the gentle Lena. Grafton Press 1909 279p o.p. 1970

"Three sympathetic character studies of woman in lowly circumstances. 'The Good Anna' deals with Anna Federner, a kindly, devoted housekeeper; 'The Gentle Lena' tells of the wretched married life of a German servant girl; 'Melanctha' is concerned with an intelligent, partially white Negro girl who finds only unhappiness among the Negroes with whom she grows up. The style in which 'Three lives' is written is extremely simple and concrete, suggesting the author's later experiments." Benét. The Reader's Encyclopedia

Steinbeck, John

Nobel Prize in literature, 1962

Cannery Row

Some editions are:

Viking $4

Watts, F. $8.95 Large type edition complete and unabridged. A Keith Jennison book

First published 1945

The "bravura sketch of the sardine-fishing foreshore of Monterey is not unlike Bret Harte's famous tales. . . . It is the wastrels, bums, loafers, and hard cases, the whorehouse madams or the the vacant-lot squatters, who are truly generous and relaxed and salt the earth with genuine romance. . . . [Its highlight is] the first party [the boys] planned for Doc. . . . The best of it is very acute comedy and strong feeling." Book of the Month Club News

"The story that John Steinbeck tells is suffused with warmth and understanding and a grasp of human values—and in it, he brings forth . . . a world of his own, with characters as universal as human nature." Huntting

Followed by: Sweet Thursday

also in Steinbeck, J. The short novels of John Steinbeck p355-469

Cup of gold; a life of Sir Henry Morgan, buccaneer, with occasional reference to history. Viking 1936 269p o.p. 1970

First published by R. M. McBride 1929

"Tells of Henry's boyhood in the Welsh glens, his sailing for the Indies at the age of fifteen, his slavery in Barbados and later triumphs on the Spanish Main, including the sack of Panama, the Cup of Gold, for love of

382

Steinbeck, John—*Continued*

the mysterious Ysobel, alias the Red Saint, and his respectable death years later as lieutenant governor of Jamaica." N Y Her Trib Books

East of Eden. Viking 1952 602p $7.95

"The saga of more than half a century in the lives of two American families—the Trasks, a mixture of gentleness and brutality doled out in unequal measure and the Hamiltons, Steinbecks' own forbears, a well adjusted, lovable group who provide a tranquil background for the turbulent careers of the Trasks. The scene is chiefly Salinas, California from the turn of the century through the first World War, and thanks to a great wealth of fascinating detail woven through the plot, we are given a complete and unforgettable picture of country and small town life during that period." Library J

"Through the exercise of a really rather remarkable freedom of his rights as a novelist, Mr. Steinbeck weaves in, and more particularly around, this story of prostitution a fantasia of history and of myth that results in a strange and original work of art." N Y Times Bk R

y The grapes of wrath

Some editions are:
Viking $7.50
Watts, F. $9.95 Large type edition complete and unabridged. A Keith Jennison book
Pulitzer Prize, 1940
First published 1939
"Saga of the small farmers and share croppers of the Southwest, driven out of their homes and moving westward with their families and a few household goods piled on a brokendown car. The fortunes of the Joad family, as related here, on their westward trek and after they reach California, symbolizes the whole movement." Book Rev Digest

"'The Grapes of Wrath' is worth all the talk, all the anticipation, all the enthusiasm. Here is the epitome of everything Steinbeck has so far given us. It has the humor and earthiness of 'Tortilla Flat,' the social consciousness of 'In Dubious Battle,' the passionate concern for the homeless and uprooted which made 'Of Mice and Men' memorable. These elements, together with a narrative that moves with excitement for its own sake, are not mixed but fused, to produce the unique quality of 'The Grapes of Wrath.' That quality is an understanding of courage." Sat R

In dubious battle. Viking 1936 349p $5

First published by Covici
"A proletarian novel with a real setting (the Californian fruit country) and flesh and blood characters. Told from the viewpoint of a radical sympathizer, Jim Nolan. It is the story of a strike among the fruit pickers. Jim comes to know the leaders—Mac, honest, capable, shrewd; the philosophical 'Doc' Burton; Joy; London, big, earthy, a born leader; and others. Why, and how, these migratory California workers turned to revolt is the theme of the story." Book Rev Digest

"'In Dubious Battle' cannot be dismissed as a 'propaganda' novel—it is another version of the eternal human fight against injustice. . . . It has a vigor of sheer story-telling that may sweep away many prejudices." New Repub

The long valley. Viking 1938 303p $5

Analyzed in Short Story Index
Contents: Chrysanthemums; White quail; Flight; Snake; Breakfast; Raid; Harness; Vigilante; Johnny Bear; Murder; St Katy the virgin; Red pony; Leader of the people

y The moon is down; a novel. Viking 1942 188p o.p. 1970

"Short, quietly written novel, describing the occupation of a small mining town, presumably in Norway, by an unidentified army, evidently German. The villagers resort to sabotage, they completely ignore the invaders whenever possible, and go on their way thwarting every move to the detriment of the morale of the invader. In the end the courageous village mayor is shot to bring the people to terms. The mayor goes to his death reciting Socrates' dying message, knowing full well that his people will understand his death, and will continue their resistance." Book Rev Digest

also in Steinbeck, J. The short novels of John Steinbeck p273-354

y Of mice and men

Some editions are:
Modern Lib. $2.95 With an introduction by Joseph Harry Jackson
Viking $4
Viking $6.50 A Viking Large type book
First published 1937 by Covici
"George and Lennie are two drifting ranch hands who dream, as rootless men do, of a piece of land of their own, where they will 'belong.' They have never been able to work up a stake because big, blundering, simple-witted [amazingly strong] Lennie keeps getting them into trouble. . . . George feels that Lennie has been given into his keeping. He controls him by talking about the rabbit farm they will have one day, where Lennie may look after the rabbits if he is good—for George too is webbed in the dream. They come to work in the Salinas Valley and it is there, among the people they meet at the ranch, that their story is worked out." New Repub

"The story is simple but superb in its understatements, its realisms which are used, not to illustrate behavior, but for character and situation. . . . Its style is right for its subject matter, and that subject matter is deeply felt, richly conceived, and perfectly ordered." Sat R

also in Steinbeck, J. The portable Steinbeck p227-323
also in Steinbeck, J. The short novels of John Steinbeck p201-72

y The pearl

Some editions are:
Viking $3.50 With drawings by José Clemente Orozco
Watts, F. $7.95 Large type edition. With drawings by José Clemente Orozco. A Keith Jennison book
First published 1947
Based on an old Mexican folk tale, this is the story of the great pearl, how it was found, the sorrow it caused, and how it was lost again. It is the story, too, of a family, the special solidarity of a man and a woman and their child: Kino, the fisherman, his wife, Juana, and the baby Coyotito

"One can take this as a parable or as an active and limpid narrative whose depth, like that of the tropical waters which Steinbeck so beautifully describes, is far more than one would suspect." Atlantic

also in Steinbeck, J. The short novels of John Steinbeck p471-527

The portable Steinbeck; selected by Pascal Covici; enl. ed. with an introduction by Lewis Gannett. Viking 1946 xxx, 609p (Viking Portable lib) $5.95

Partially analyzed in Short Story Index
First published 1943. The 1946 edition contains a new introduction; a complete novel "Of mice and men," selections from nine longer works, five letters and six short stories
Contents: Flight; The snake; The harness; The chrysanthemums; Origin of Tularecito; Molly Morgan; Pat Humbert's; Danny; Pilon; The pirate; Treasure hunt; Tortillas and beans; Future we can't foresee; Of mice and men; The gift; Great mountains; The promise; Leader of the people; Breakfast; The turtle; Burial of Grampa; Two-a-penny; Migrant people; Granma; Ma and Tom; The flood; The Birth; Old man of the sea; The hunt; Homing; Debt shall be paid; We're off to Berlin; How Edith McGillicuddy met R. L. S; Americans embark for war; Pvt. Big Train Mulligan; Battle scene; Why soldiers won't talk; Frog hunt

The red pony

In Steinbeck, J. The portable Steinbeck p327-415
In Steinbeck, J. The short novels of John Steinbeck p201-72

The short novels of John Steinbeck. . . . [New ed] With an introduction by Joseph Henry Jackson. Viking 1963 527p $6

First published 1953
An anthology of six of the 1962 literature Nobel Prize-winner's titles

Steinbeck, John—*Continued*

Contents: Tortilla Flat (1935); The red pony (1937); Of mice and men (1937); The moon is down (1942); Cannery Row (1945); The pearl (1947)

The short reign of Pippin IV; a fabrication; drawings by William Pène du Bois. Viking 1957 188p illus o.p. 1970

"A very engaging satire on French manners and politics which describes the havoc at Versailles when the people demand that the monarchy be revived and choose as their king an amiable amateur astronomer who happens to be a descendant of Charlemagne." Pub W

also in Costain, T. B. comp. Twelve short novels p703-98

Sweet Thursday. Viking 1954 273p o.p. 1970

Sequel to: Cannery Row
After World War II the "Palace Flophouse passed into new hands, the Bear Flag Café got a new madam named Fauna (nee Flora), and Doc lost his old pleasure in women, liturgical music, and the Western Biological Laboratories. Then Suzy came to Cannery Row . . . [and] egged on by the others, she brought Doc back to his prewar contentment." Booklist

"This is comedy—bawdy, sentimental, and in places implausible, as when Suzy takes to living in an abandoned boiler; but read in the spirit with which it is written, it is good fun." Atlantic

y Tortilla Flat

Some editions are:
Modern Lib. $2.95 With a foreword by the author. Illustrated by Ruth Gannett
Viking $4

First published 1935 by Covici
"Tortilla Flat was a tumble-down section of Monterey, California. The paisanos who lived there were a mixed race of Spanish, Indian, Mexican and Caucasian bloods. The central character is one of the paisanos, Danny, who came back from the [first] World War to discover that he had inherited two houses in Tortilla Fat. There he gathered his friends around him and they lived their carefree, unmoral lives with gay abandon until their beloved Danny died." Book Rev Digest

The characters "will make you laugh very hard—but as Jesus Maria says, 'there is another kind of laughing . . . when you open your mouth to laugh, something like a hand squeezes your heart.'" N Y Her Trib Books

also in Steinbeck, J. The short novels of John Steinbeck p 1-133

The wayward bus. Viking 1947 312p o.p. 1970

First published 1947 by Viking
The action of this story takes place within one day at a wayside cafe from which a short line bus operates. The characters are employees of the cafe, the bus driver, a mechanic, and some passengers, all of whom are drawn with emphasis on their weaknesses

"Very natural and funny, and at times very candid, is the talk. . . . But for all [the] animal magnetism and photographic reality, one ends by wondering if American life is actually so empty." Atlantic

The winter of our discontent. Viking 1961 311p $5

Ethan Allen Hawley, the impoverished heir to an upright New England tradition is the focus of this story. Ethan, under pressure from his restless wife and discontented children who want more of this world's goods than his grocery store job provides, decides to take a holiday from his scrupulous standards to achieve wealth and success. What happens as he compromises with his integrity makes up this story. (Publisher)

"The ethical problems involved in Ethan's successful attempt to gain ownership of the store lie at the heart of a story that explores with depth and perception an individual turning point and that has more than individual significance. The characters and the locale emerge with lifelike clarity, and each episode is meaningful to the story." Booklist

Stendhal

Chartreuse of Parma; tr. from the French by C. K. Scott-Moncrieff. Liveright 715p (Black and gold lib) $6.95

First published 1839; variant title: Charterhouse of Parma
"The scene is a little Italian Court, whither the young adventurer Fabrice has found his way, and in dramatic importance plays second fiddle to the fascinating Duchess Sanseverina and her jealous lover, Count Mosca, the astute minister. Count Mosca. The book opens with a famous narrative of the battle of Waterloo. It is a novel that set a standard of flawless technique, of the lucid unfolding of character and motive, of accurate comprehension of the inherent disorder of life, that has rarely been approached in dramatic narration." Baker's Best

The red and the black

Some editions are:
Heritage $7.50 Translated by C. K. Scott-Moncrieff; illustrated by Rafaello Busoni
Liveright (Black and gold lib) $6.95. Translated by C .K. Scott-Moncrieff
Modern Lib. $2.95
Original French edition published 1830
"The most celebrated novel of Stendhal, published in 1830. It deals with the rise to power of Julien Sorel, a handsome, cold, and intensely egotistical young man who uses his love affairs to serve his ambition and tries to murder his first mistress when she betrays him to her successor in his interest. The title refers to the colors of the military class, represented by Napoleon, the author's hero, and of the clergy, which Stendhal detested. The novel is noted for its psychological analysis and exposition of the character of Sorel." Benét. The Reader's Encyclopedia

Vanina Vanini
In Dupee, F. W. ed. Great French short novels p91-123

Stephens, Eve. See Anthony, Evelyn

Stephens, James

y The crock of gold; with eight illus. in colour and decorative headings and tailpieces by Thomas Mackenzie. Macmillan (N Y) 1940 227p $4.95

First published 1912
"This wise and aphoristic fairy tale for adults tells of the two philosophers who lived in the pine wood Coilla Doraca [in Ireland] of their quarrelsome old wives, of their respective offspring Seumas Beg and Brigid Beg, and of the strange consequences of a feud with the leprechauns." Haydn. Thesaurus of Book Digests

Stern, G. B.

A deputy was king
In Stern, G. B. The matriarch chronicles v2

The matriarch
In Stern, G. B. The matriarch chronicles v 1

The matriarch chronicles . . . with a new preface by the author. Knopf 1936 4v in 1 o.p. 1970

Contains four related novels previously published separately: The matriarch, 1925; A deputy was king, 1926; Mosaic, 1930; Shining and free, 1935

This tetralogy is the story, for 150 years, of the cosmopolitan Rakonitz family, Viennese Jews who spread over Europe. "The family went on ramifying thru successive generations, chiefly by intermarriage, and always yielding unquestioning loyalty to the clan and the family tradition. An enormous number of characters appear on the stage, but the virility of the family and the interest of the Digest

"The story begins [in England] with the fifteen-year old Babette, heroine of a Napoleonic legend. It is concentrated, in particular, in Anastasia Rakonitz, Babette's granddaughter,

Stern, G. B.—*Continued*

head of the London branch of the family. When she dies at eighty-nine, the matriarchy passes by tacit consent to the Toni of today, Anastasia's granddaughter

"A deputy was king" continues the adventures of the Rakonitz family, "with emphasis on those of Toni Rakonitz, Giles Goddard, her husband, and Loraine, a new cousin with a general capacity for making trouble and a special capacity for breaking up homes. . . . The events in 'A Deputy was King' include Toni's marriage to Giles, her surrender of responsibilities for home, children and a good time. . . . [Loraine's] temporary theft of Giles, the war between Cousin Val and Loraine over a Chinese coat; the prevention of a suicide, reconciliation between Giles and Toni, and a calm, graceful ascent into a life of peace in the Italian countryside." N Y World

"Mosaic" is an interwoven story of the Paris branch of the family. "It traces the colorful, the trivial, the pseudo-significant events in the lives of two sisters, Berthe and Letti Czelovar. The former—beautiful, self-centered, domineering—tries to rule the offspring of the family branch, until her two favorite nephews can bear it no more, and desert her. Then Letti, the self-effacing younger sister, comes to the rescue of the bitter and disappointed elder." Book Rev Digest

"Shining and free" is a sequel to The matriarch in that it "records the events of twenty-four hours in the life of Anastasia Rakonitz, now in her eighty-eighth year. The story begins with an account of a later evening at a restaurant and a subsequent quarrel with the matriarch's daughter, Truda; there follows an expedition to Brighton the next day; and a final reconciliation with Truda in the evening." Book Rev Digest

Mosaic
  In Stern, G. B. The matriarch chronicles v3

Shining and free
  In Stern, G. B. The matriarch chronicles v4

Stern, Gladys Bronwyn. See Stern, G. B.

Stern, James
  The stories of James Stern. Harcourt [1969 c1968] 270p $4.95

First published 1968 in England
"Widely differently settings, all drawn with authenticity, distinguish 16 short stories and three pieces of nonfiction previously published in earlier collections and in a periodical. Stern's art is paradoxical in that he can write of tragic and horrible events yet convey a feeling of deep humanity for his characters." Booklist
Stories included are: The man who was loved; The cloud; The force; Two men; Our father; The beginning and the end; Under the beech tree; Something wrong; The broken leg; On the Sabbath; Mister and Miss; Travellers' tears; The woman who was loved; Next door to death; Solitaire; The face behind the bar

Stern, Richard Martin
  Brood of eagles. World Pub. 1969 518p $7.95

"An NAL book"
This "is the intimate chronicle of the Dancer family [an aircraft dynasty]: the soarers like Tom and Grace, the builders like Ira and Ned . . . those who rejoice in the mission of the dynasty and those who reject the sacrifices it demands of them." Publisher's note

Sterne, Laurence
  A sentimental journey through France and Italy

Some editions are:
Oxford (English novels ser) $4.25 Edited by Ian Jack. Has title: Sentimental journey
Oxford (World classics) $2.25 Introduction by Virginia Woolf
Univ. of Calif. Press $10 Edited by Gardner D. Stout, Jr. Has title: Sentimental journey through France and Italy by Mr Yorick
First published 1768; in this edition, 1928
"The title of this unconventional mixture of autobiography, travel impressions, and fiction

is misleading. Sterne told of his travels through France, but he died of tuberculosis before he had written the Italian section of his narrative. Sentimental, as the title implies, outrageous and eccentric in its humorous effects, the novel entertains the reader with delightful accounts and observations of whatever came into the author's mind." Magill. Masterpieces

Tristram Shandy

Some editions are:
Harper (Harper Modern classics) $2.40
Modern Lib. $2.95
Oxford (World classics) $3 Has title: The life and opinions of Tristram Shandy, gentleman
First published 1759-1767. Full title: The life and opinions of Tristram Shandy
"A chaotic account by Tristram of his life from the time of his conception to the present. . . . In between are sandwiched his 'opinions,' longwinded and philosophical reflections on everything under the sun including his novel, and accounts of the lives of Yorick, his father Walter Shandy, his mother, and his Uncle Toby." Benét. The Reader's Encyclopedia

Stevenson, D. E.
  Gerald and Elizabeth. Holt 1969 245p boards $5.95

"Gerald Brown returns to his London home under a cloud. He lost his [engineering] job in a South African diamond mine, wrongly accused of stealing some rough stones. He goes to stay with his beautiful halfsister, Elizabeth Burleigh, now a successful actress. Elizabeth is afraid of her impending marriage because of insanity in her mother's family. Her fiancé hires Gerald to uncover the long lost secret of Elizabeth's birth. A ladylike blend of London theater atmosphere, mystery and love, with few surprises but pleasant diversion." Pub W

The house on the cliff. Holt 1966 282p $5.95

"Elfrida Thistlewood, a struggling young actress, inherited a large country house overlooking the English Channel. In spite of the arguments against it, she decided to live in the house. At first it was difficult to fit into the quiet country life but soon it became more exciting and more romantic." Bk Buyer's Guide
"Readers who demand a happy ending are sure of one more." Best Sellers

Miss Buncle; containing Miss Buncle's book and Miss Buncle married. Holt 1964 2v in 1 $5.95

A combination of two titles published 1937 by Farrar
In the first story, set in rural England, Miss Buncle antagonizes her neighbors by writing a book about them. In the second story which is in the nature of a sequel, the heroine, now wife of a publisher writes another book
"Long after serious novels of the mid-twentieth century will have become anachronisms, I predict that the works of D. E. Stevenson will be adorning bedside tables for reading and rereading, despite the fact that they are sentimental, foolish and virtually plotless." Best Sellers

Miss Buncle married
  In Stevenson, D. E. Miss Buncle v2

Miss Buncle's book
  In Stevenson, D. E. Miss Buncle v 1

Stevenson, Dorothy Emily. See Stevenson, D. E.

Stevenson, Janet
  Sisters and brothers; a novel. Crown 1966 278p o.p. 1970

"The sisters Angelina and Sarah Grimke, battlers for abolition of slavery and for women's rights, discover that they have a Negro nephew. The story goes back to the Civil War and forward again to show how the sisters react to their Negro 'sister' and how her two sons react to their white father." Bk Buyer's Guide

Stevenson, Janet—*Continued*

"The whole-hearted dedication of abolitionists is strikingly realistic. The whole is permeated with a rich realization of human values in both races. A powerful book, of great significance today." Library J

Stevenson, Robert Louis

The beach at Falesá

In Stevenson, R. L. The complete short stories of Robert Louis Stevenson p575-654

y The black arrow

Some editions are:

Dodd (Great illustrated classics) $4.50 With illustrations reproducing drawings for early editions and photographs of historical scenes together with an introductory biographical sketch of the author and anecdotal captions by Basil Davenport

Scribner (Scribner Illustrated classics) $6 Illustrated in color by N. C. Wyeth

First published 1888

"Set in the fifteenth century, the historical background of the plot deals with a minor battle of the Wars of the Roses and the appearance of the infamous Richard, Duke of Gloucester, as a young soldier. More interesting are the swift-paced adventures of Dick Shelton in his attempts to outwit his scheming guardian, Sir Daniel Brackley." Magill. Masterpieces

The complete short stories of Robert Louis Stevenson; with a selection of the best short novels. Ed. and with an introduction by Charles Neider. Doubleday 1969 xxx, 678p $10

"The 75th anniversary of Robert Louis Stevenson's death is the occasion for this first complete collection of his stories in one volume. Stevenson's talent was timeless—he is still greatly loved and admired by readers of all ages and the 24 stories in this collection clearly illustrate his genius." News of Bks

Contents: A lodging for the night; Story of the young man with the cream tarts; Story of the physician and the Saratoga trunk; The adventure of the hansom cab; Story of the bandbox; Story of the young man in holy orders; Story of the house with the green blinds; The adventure of Prince Florizel and a detective; Providence and the guitar; The Sire de Maletroit's door; Will o' the mill; The story of a lie [novelette]; Thrawn Janet; The merry men [novelette]; The body-snatcher; Markheim; Strange case of Dr Jekyll and Mr Hyde [novelette]; The bottle imp; The beach of Falesa [novelette]; The isle of voices

Dr Jekyll and Mr Hyde, The merry men & other tales. Dutton 244p (Everyman's lib) $2.95

Contents: The strange case of Dr Jekyll and Mr Hyde (1886); The merry men and other tales: The merry men; Will o' the mill; Markheim; Thrawn Janet; Olalla; The treasure of Franchard

y The master of Ballantrae; a winter's tale. Oxford 1957 301p $2.75

First published 1889

"The tale of a bitter hatred between two Scotch brothers. In the Stuart uprising of 1745 the elder brother, James, supports the Pretender, while the younger, Henry, is for King George. When James, the Master, does not come back, Alison Graeme, who has been betrothed to him, marries Henry instead. James, however, returns to subject Henry to persecutions of every imaginable sort. Eventually, after years of enmity, the end comes in a lonely American wilderness. The Master has been buried alive by Secundra Dass, his East Indian attendant, to deceive his foes, and Henry finds the Indian digging him up. James is only able to open his eyes, but at this dreadful portent Henry falls dead, and the two brothers are buried together. Much of the tale is told by the old steward of Ballantrae, John MacKellar." Benét. The Reader's Encyclopedia

The merry men

In Stevenson, R. L. The complete short stories of Robert Louis Stevenson p363-418

The story of a lie

In Stevenson, R. L. The complete short stories of Robert Louis Stevenson p287-348

The strange case of Dr Jekyll and Mr Hyde; illus. by Rick Schreiter. Watts, F. 1967 90p $3.95

Also available in a large type edition at $7.95

First published 1886

Depicts the dual nature of good and evil

also in Knight, D. ed. A century of great short science fiction novels p9-62

also in Stevenson, R. L. The complete short stories of Robert Louis Stevenson p463-538

y The strange case of Dr Jekyll and Mr Hyde, and other famous tales. With photographs of the author and his environment as well as illus. from early editions of the stories, together with an introduction by W. M. Hill. Dodd 1961 339p illus (Great illustrated classics) $4.50

Analyzed in Short Story Index

An edition of the fantastic title story depicting the dual nature of good and evil, and seven other "thrillers" including the three-part story "The suicide club"

Contents: The strange case of Dr Jekyll and Mr Hyde (1886); The pavilion on the links; A lodging for the night; Markheim; The Sire de Maletroit's door; The beach of Falesá; The suicide club: Story of the young man with the cream tarts; Story of the physician and the Saratoga trunk; The adventures of the hansom cab

Weir of Hermiston; an unfinished romance. Scribner 1896 266p o.p. 1970

"Weir of Hermiston" is "an unfinished novel which is often cited as Stevenson's masterpiece. It is written around the motive of deep antipathy between father and son. . . . Outlines a remarkable group of tragic personalities, hard, strong-natured Scotch folk, of the period of 1813-1814." Lenrow. Reader's Guide to Prose Fiction

The wrecker, by Robert Louis Stevenson and Lloyd Osbourne. Oxford 1950 457p (World classics) o.p. 1970

First published 1892

"One of the best of Stevenson's adventure stories, and full of exciting incident, quick action, and vivid characterization. The scene is modern, and shifts from land to sea. Preliminary chapters depict student life in Paris; but the main story begins in San Francisco, with the purchase of the wrecked ship Flying Scud by London Dodd and Jim Pinkerton, and with their voyage in quest of its supposed treasure. No treasure, but a ghastly tragedy, is revealed as the tale goes on. . . . So cunningly is the plot constructed that not until the very end is the key furnished." Keller's Reader's Digest of Books

Stewart, Fred Mustard

The Mephisto waltz; a novel. Coward-McCann 1969 256p $4.95

"An improbable but entertainingly suspenseful story of a contented young married couple's unfortunate meeting with a famous musician and his daughter. The young man, who has had a fiasco in a piano concert debut and has turned to journalism, interviews the eminent musician and a Faustian situation develops. The young wife comes too close to solving the change in her husband with dire but ironic results." Booklist

This "provides a reading experience which left my hackles in quivering agony. In theme and spirit, it recalls 'Rosemary's Baby.' . . . Mr. Stewart [weaves his] eerie plot, with diabolical skill." N Y Times Bk R

Stewart, George R.

y Earth abides. Random House 1949 373p o.p. 1970

"Plague devastates the United States. Ish, symbol of 'The Last American' tours the States, finding a survivor here, one there, but empty cities and country everywhere. Horrifying incidents threaten the tribe of survivors that have banded together under Ish's leadership. Civilization is in the formative process again, but life is meaningless, ambition and intellectual curiosity are negligible. As years roll on deterioration becomes more pronounced. Only the earth abides." Library J

Fire; a novel. Random House 1948 336p o.p. 1970

This novel "relates the life history of a forest fire, from its birth as the result of a lightning stroke, thru its obscure, puny infancy, to the days of its might and terror, and its final defeat. Against this story of the fire itself are set glimpses of the lives, hopes, fears and sorrows of the men and women who are called upon to fight it." Book Rev Digest

"Some years ago, 'Fire's' author wrote 'Storm,' a memorable account of the life and works of a tempest. In his new, taut story of the birth, rapacious existence and final slaughter of a forest fire, he has done a still better book, which is about as much praise as can be accorded any such volume." N Y Her Trib Books

y Storm; a novel; with a new introduction. Modern Lib. 349p $2.95

First published 1941 by Random House
"On the first day of the twelve covered by this novel a young meteorologist noted on his chart, a small storm center in the western Pacific, thousands of miles away from his San Francisco office. He dubbed the baby storm, Maria, and followed its course through the following days with an almost fatherly interest. 'Maria' grew with astounding swiftness, swept across the Pacific and over California, affecting the lives of millions, causing death and disaster and forcing men to perform almost impossible feats in many walks of life." Book Rev Digest

"A wealth of scientific data is accurately given in 'Storm,' and is most subtly related to mundane existence in what might be characterized as 'the' book for the layman who wishes to know how meteorology impinges upon human consciousness." Sci Bk Club R

Stewart, J. I. M.

Vanderlyn's kingdom. Norton [1968 c1967] 287p boards $4.95

Bernard Vanderlyn is a "rich American deeply concerned with the arts. He becomes a patron on a grand scale, buying an Aegean island and surrounding himself with . . . geniuses. In all but name he is lord of his island, prince of his own highly civilized court. Such hubris in such surroundings is doomed. But Vanderlyn disregards the lessons of Greek mythology." Christian Science Monitor

"A quiet novel, but an interesting one. Although the tone is a bit donnish for all but the most convinced Anglophiles, Mr. Stewart . . . builds his drama expertly and literately." Pub W

For another title by this author see Innes, Michael

Stewart, John Innes Mackintosh. See
Stewart, J. I. M.

Stewart, Mary

y Airs above the ground. Morrow 1965 286p boards $5.95

In this suspense novel, the author explores "the remote mountain villages of Austria, a small traveling circus, and a secret involving one of the famous Lippizaner white stallions. The heroine this time is . . . a young married Englishwoman on the track of an errant husband. Among the other characters are a charming German equestrienne, a 17-year-old English boy escaping an over-possessive mother [and] a sinister Hungarian high-wire performer, and a railroad train named 'Fiery Elijah.' " Pub W

"Its background is authentic, the action fast, the characterizations quite credible, the situations wonderfully adaptable to a film-thriller. And there is wonderful dash in the long case to the finish." Best Sellers

y The Gabriel hounds. Morrow 1967 320p boards $5.95

"This story is freely based on the accounts of the life of the Lady Hester Stanhope." Author's note
Christable and Charles, two young English cousins who are visiting Lebanon, plan to call on their eccentric Great Aunt Harriet, who lives in isolation with her dog and her servants in a palace at Dar Ibrahim. Word is sent that Charles will not be admitted. Christable succeeds in getting into the palace, and finds a strange Aunt Harriet and a strange situation. (Publisher)

"First-rate Mary Stewart thriller, complete with secret passages to a seraglio, jealous Arab servant girl, and quite the most exciting, action packed finale Miss Stewart has yet given us, with the palace burning down over our hero and heroine's heads." Pub W

y The ivy tree. Morrow 1961 320p boards $5.95

A story "about a Canadian girl visiting in northern England, who innocently becomes involved in a complex intrigue because she happens to look very much like an English heiress who has disappeared." Pub W

"The heroine of this cliff-hanger refers to her situation as a 'fantastic Oppenheim plot.' Actually this involved novel of impersonation and inheritance reads more like Daphne Du Maurier. . . . The author's easy narrative style, her vivid descriptions of the Northumberland countryside, the sharp delineation of her stock characters, her neat, contrived resolution, and her impeccable good taste guarantee satisfaction to fans of the genre." Library J

y Madam, will you talk? Morrow 1956 [c1955] 250p $4.95

First published 1955 in England
"France is the setting for this exciting tale of mystery and suspense. A lovely war widow, Charity Selborne, expects a quiet holiday but instead is involved in murder and a romance." Huntting

y The moon-spinners. Morrow 1963 [c1962] 303p boards $5.95

First published 1962 in England
"Nicola Ferris, an English girl on vacation in Crete, decides to walk the last mile over a rough track to the tiny village where she is expected the next day. She walks into a mystery. She stumbles upon a shepherd's hut guarded by a Greek who threatens to kill her if she makes a sound. Inside the hut, she finds a young Englishman seriously wounded and much upset by her intrusion. In her determination to help him, she is drawn into his dangerous situation." Horn Bk

"It is all very satisfying and leads up climactically to a splendid night struggle in the Aegean Sea. Besides weaving a fine story, Miss Stewart can create young people who are warmly and refreshingly their age." N Y Her Trib Books

y My brother Michael

Some editions are:
Morrow $5.95
Watts, F. $8.95 Large type edition complete and unabridged. A Keith Jennison Book

First published 1960
This suspense story has "a modern Greek setting enriched by classical antiquities and haunted by the shades of Hellenic tragedy. Camilla Haven, the heroine-narrator, is on her way to Delphi when she encounters Simon Lester, an English schoolmaster who has come to investigate the death of his brother Michael, supposedly killed fighting during World War II. A strange letter written just before his death leads Camilla, along with Simon, through a terrifying maze of danger and violence to an amazing discovery on the slopes of Mount Parnassus." Booklist

"Slightly sentimental overtones, but the Greek landscape and—much more subtle—the Greek character are splendidly done, in a long, charmingly written, highly evocative, imperative piece of required reading for an Hellenic cruise." Spec

Stewart, Mary—*Continued*

y Nine coaches waiting. Morrow 1959
[c1958] 342p boards $5.95

First published 1958 in England
"Intelligent, spirited Linda Martin comes to Valmy, an isolated château in the French Alps, as English governess to nine-year-old Philippe, the orphaned Comte de Valmy. After several frightening 'accidents' Linda discovers that her pupil is the object of a murder plot which apparently involves his crippled uncle and the latter's handsome son Raoul, with whom she is in love. This is another romantic suspense novel marked by a picturesque setting, genteel though sinister atmosphere, and literary flavor." Booklist

y This rough magic

Some editions are:
Morrow $5.95
Watts, F. $8.95 Large type edition complete and unabridged. A Keith Jennison book
First published 1964
A story "in which the heroine, an out-of-work young English actress, encounters high adventure on the Greek island of Corfu. She is visiting her sister, who is married to a wealthy Italian with an estate on the island. A distinguished, retired Shakespearian actor takes a hand in events. So does an amiable dolphin who plays with the heroine when she is in swimming. Also prominently present are a perfidious villain and a . . . romantic hero." Pub W
"Further to divulge the plot of this expertly written novel would be to jeopardize a reader's pleasure. But it can be and should be said that Mary Stewart is in the same category of excellence in fiction that has been, for many years, almost exclusively the domain of Helen MacInnes." Best Sellers

y Thunder on the right. Morrow 1958
[c1957] 284p $4.95

First published 1957 in England
"Jennifer goes to the convent in the French Pyrenees to dissuade her half-cousin, Gillian, from becoming a nun, only to be told she is dead. But with the help of Stephen Masefield she proves Gillian is still alive and discovers the reason for the lie." Retail Bookseller
"Romance, suspense, and adventure with a touch of violence constitute good recreational reading." Booklist

y Wildfire at midnight. Morrow 1961
[c1956] 214p boards $4.95

An American reissue of the title first published in England 1956
"Gianetta Brooke had come to the Isle of Skye to forget the husband she had painfully divorced. Then Gianetta learned that on the slopes of Blaven, murder had been done and the murderer struck again and again until he and Gianetta were face-to-face." McClurg. Book News

Stewart, Ramona
Casey. Little 1968 400p $6.95

The novel takes place in the nineteenth century in New York City. Beginning in the slums, among the Irish poor, Tom Casey climbs from gangfighter to vote repeater and strong-arm man, to alderman and the Board of Supervisors, and finally to Boss of the City. When his fight for power is over, however, he suffers a sense of the loss of his family and friends. (Publisher)
"The poignant choices between private power . . . and public morality that Tom Casey must make are especially well told. Often described in histories and memoirs of the period, this era becomes remarkably alive in this, one of the best fictional treatments given to the immigrant Irish city dwellers and 19th-century power politics." Choice

Stockton, Frank R.
Best short stories of Frank R. Stockton. Scribner 1957 128p $2.95

This selection first published 1895 with title: Chosen few, and is analyzed in Short Story Index

Contains the following short stories: A tale of negative gravity; Asaph; His wife's deceased sister; The lady, or the tiger; The remarkable wreck of the "Thomas Hyke"; Old pipes and the Dryad; The transferred ghost; "The philosophy of relative existence"; A piece of red calico

The casting away of Mrs Lecks and Mrs Aleshine
In Stockton, F. R. The storyteller's pack p275-351

y The storyteller's pack; a Frank R. Stockton reader; illus. by Bernarda Bryson. Scribner 1968 xxiv, 358p illus $5.95

Analyzed in Short Story Index
This collection of seventeen stories includes "ghost stories, sea yarns, romance, tall tales, and fairy tales, and 'The Casting Away of Mrs. Lecks and Mrs. Aleshine.' [first published 1886]." Publisher's note
Short stories included are: The bishop's ghost and the printer's baby; The Bee-man of Orn; The Queen's museum; Prince Hassak's march; The banished king; The Griffin and the Minor Canon; The accommodating circumstance; Old pipes and the Dryad; The philosophy of relative existences; The transferred ghost; Our story; The lady or the tiger; His wife's deceased sister; A tale of negative gravity; The remarkable wreck of the Thomas Hyke; The Water-devil

Stokely, Wilma Dykeman. See Dykeman, Wilma

Stoker, Bram
y Dracula

Some editions are:
Dodd (Great illustrated classics) $4.50 With illustrations of the author and the setting of the story, together with an introduction by James Nelson
Doubleday $3.95
Heritage $7.50 With an introduction by Anthony Boucher; illustrated with wood engravings by Felix Hoffmann
Modern Lib $2.95
First published 1897
"A very successful handling of horrible sensations in a realistic way. . . . A terrible baron in a Transylvanian castle is the chief of an army of human vampires that prey on mankind and pursue their ravages as far as London, demanding all the determination and resource of the hero and his friends to exterminate them." Baker's Best

Stone, Irving
Adversary in the house. Doubleday 1947 432p $5.95

Based on the life of "Eugene V. Debs, famous for his fanatic devotion to the cause of the working man. It's the tragic story of a man who married a woman who became his staunch adversary. She opposed him in his work until the end of his days, while the woman he lost remained unswervingly loyal to him." Literary Guild
"Accepting Stone's thesis [of Deb's marriage] as supportable, the novel is an interesting one, told with a sensitive humanism." N Y Times Bk R

y The agony and the ecstasy; a novel of Michelangelo. Doubleday 1961 664p $6.95

"Michelangelo's career is traced from his promising boyhood apprenticeships to the painter Ghirlandajo and the sculptor Bertoldo thru all the many years of his flowering genius. . . . Florence and Rome are the principal cities which serve as background for the development of the artist's life and work." Chicago Sunday Tribune
"There is much to admire in Mr. Stone's handling of materials the quantity of which could stagger any novelist, and the presentation of such themes as stone-quarrying and stone-cutting can be fascinating. On the other hand, he carries to unreasonable excess the literal descriptions of anatomical dissection; and the erotic filament he thrusts across the elaborate web of narrative tells us less about that titanic personage, Michelangelo, than about 20th century curiosity about passion and perversion." Christian Science Monitor

Stone, Irving—*Continued*

y Immortal wife; the biographical novel of Jessie Benton Fremont. Doubleday 1944 456p $5.95

"Jessie Benton Fremont, lovely, ambitious wife of a onetime candidate for President, is a colorful heroine for this long historical novel. The opening of California, political intrigue in Washington, the court martial of John Fremont, the western campaign in the Civil War, riches and poverty were experienced by this indomitable woman. Recommended as a novel of exciting historical events (accurately told), as a fine love story and as an excellent character study." Library J

y Love is eternal; a novel about Mary Todd and Abraham Lincoln. Doubleday 1954 468p $5.95

This novel presents a sympathetic portrait of Mary Todd Lincoln. The author absolves her from the shrewishness with which many historians have clothed her and pictures her marriage to Abraham Lincoln as a great love story

"Recommended in spite of the controversial nature of its interpretation of Mary Todd Lincoln for readers of the author's earlier biographical novels and as a possible steppingstone to the Sandburg biography." Booklist

y Lust for life; a novel of Vincent Van Gogh

Some editions are:
Doubleday $5.95 illustrated
Modern Lib. $2.95

First published 1934

"A novelized version of the career of Van Gogh, the mad genius. With apparent fidelity to the sources, but with imagined dialog, the author follows his whole tortured life, that ended at thirty-seven in suicide—his early apprenticeship as an art dealer, his agonizing years as a religious worker among the coal miners, his love for half a dozen women, some of them prostitutes, and his long, frenzied striving for a technique of painting. Almost too painful in parts, but probably true in essentials." Booklist

The passionate journey. Doubleday 1949 337p $3.95

"Biographical novel of John Noble, Kansas born artist, whose life and career spanned the years 1874-1934, took him to France, England, Provincetown, and New York, and brought him love, despair, rewards, and tragedy in his relentless search for beauty, for his own soul." Retail Bookseller

y The President's lady; a novel about Rachel and Andrew Jackson. Doubleday 1951 338p $5.95

The "story of Rachel and Andrew Jackson and of the vital part they played in [the country's] development. The story is one of continual failure and ultimate success; and of a woman's devotion to one of America's greatest men." Huntting

"The story moves . . . and is filled with the drama and the personalities of one of the most exciting periods of all American history." Sat R

y Those who love; a biographical novel of Abigail and John Adams. Doubleday 1965 662p $6.95

A novel portraying the love story of the second president of the United States and his wife against the background of the American Revolution

"Readers of historical novels will enjoy this one and libraries will find it a useful addition to the young adult shelves since history is accurate and romance is alluring enough, though definitely not the 20th century type." Library J

Story Magazine

Story jubilee; ed. by Whit and Hallie Burnett. Doubleday 1965 589p o.p. 1970

Analyzed in Short Story Index

This anthology "collects 50 of the best stories appearing in the magazine since its inception." Pub W

Contents: Two lovers, by S. Anderson; The ubiquitous wife, by M. Aymé: The crocus, by W. Beck; Inside, outside, by L. Bemelmans; Rest cure, by K. Boyle; Man gehorcht, by

L. A. Brownrigg; The calling cards, by I. Bunin; Heart is a masculine noun, by H. Burnett; Sherrel, by W. Burnett; Indian summer, by E. Caldwell; Rigmarole, by M. Callaghan; My side of the matter, by T. Capote; Homage to Shakespeare, by J. Cheever; Congo, by S. Cloete; The shadows behind the women, by E. Cohen; Pizzicato on the heartstrings, by P. Devries; Two bottles of relish, by Lord Dunsany; Artist at home, by W. Faulkner; Tom Wolfe slept here, by W. Fifield; The survivor, by B. Glanville; A chance for Mr Lever, by G. Greene; The strange thing, by E. Hahn; On the way home, by L. Hughes; The tourists, by E. Hunter; The trouper, by J. Iams; Fulvous yellow, by S. Kauffmann; At Mama's, by B. Kielty; Sam Small's tyke; by E. Knight; The greatest thing in the world, by N. Mailer; Wunderkind, by C. McCullers; Mr Nab, by F. Molnar; Exchange of men, by H. Nemerov; Michael's wife, by F. O'Connor; Kitty the Wren, by S. O'Faolain; Two lovely beasts, by L. O'Flaherty; My friend Flicka, by M. O'Hara; The sunken boat, by R. Payne; The captive, by L. Pirandello; Everything is a wife, by D. Powell; The flamingos, by F. Prokosch; The man who killed A. E. Housman, by N. W. Ross; The shepherd's daughter and other little moral tales, by W. Saroyan; Return of the Griffins, by A. E. Shandeling; God on Friday night, by I. Shaw; An underground episode, by E. W. Smith; Clothes make the man, by J. Stuart; The visitor, by H. Treece; Slipping beauty, by J. Weidman; The important thing by T. Williams; The night reveals, by C. Woolrich

Story: the yearbook of discovery, 1968; ed. by Whit and Hallie Burnett; the best creative work from the colleges of the United States and Canada as judged by J. Donald Adams [and others] cooperating in the Story college creative awards contest of 1967-1968. Four Winds 1968 351p $5.95

Short stories included are: The organizer, by M. Thelwell; The bill collector, by L. Logan; Monserrate, by C. Walker; The chicken, by E. Brawley; Chastain on the X-Axis, by M. Brannon; Barrell, by J. F. Hathaway; The slap, by C. Schupan; Madeleine, by D. Walton; A time for reason, by D. Harris

Story: the yearbook of discovery/1969; the best creative work from the universities and colleges of the United States & Canada as judged by Louise Bogan [and others] cooperating in the Story college creative awards contest of 1968-1969; ed. by Whit and Hallie Burnett. Four Winds 1969 416p $6.95

Short stories included are: The Nazi machine, by B. Steinberg; Barbara Ann, by K. Lance; Rats, by W. Joyce; Let fall no burning leaf, by B. P. James

Stout, Rex

All aces; a Nero Wolfe omnibus. Viking 1958 442p o.p. 1970

Includes: Some buried Caesar (1939); Too many women (1947) and, Trouble in triplicate (1949) which consists of three short stories: Before I die; Help wanted, male; Instead of evidence

Blood will tell

In Stout, R. Trio for blunt instruments p169-247

The cop-killer

In Stout, R. Kings full of aces p369-420

Counterfeit for murder

In Stout, R. Homicide trinity

Death of a demon

In Stout, R. Homicide trinity

Death of a doxy; a Nero Wolfe novel. Viking 1966 186p boards $3.75

Nero Wolfe and Archie are given some flamboyant assistance from a night club entertainer in this mystery. "When Isabel Kerr was murdered (she was a rich man's darling who had

Stout, Rex—*Continued*

unfortunately become pregnant), private detective Orrie Cather was jailed for it. Isabel's sugar-daddy wanted to avoid a scandal and so did her sister and brother-in-law. But Julie Jacquette . . . was willing to help [solve the crime]" Bk Buyer's Guide

Death of a dude; a Nero Wolfe novel. Viking 1969 181p boards $4.50

"When a friend of Archie Goodwin is accused of shooting a guest at Lily Rowan's Montana dude ranch, Archie refuses to leave without solving the case. So Nero Wolfe heaves himself out of his comfortable rut in New York and ventures into the wild West—and, of course, solves the case. Bk Buyer's Guide

"Even though Montana is the locale, all the familiar Wolfe-Goodwin habits of living and detecting are in full force to please their fans —but the case itself is not too much of a puzzler." Pub W

Die like a dog
In Stout, R. Royal flush p431-74

Door to death
In Stout, R. Five of a kind p399-441

The doorbell rang; a Nero Wolfe novel. Viking 1965 186p boards $3.50

Also available in a large type edition for $6.50

"A wealthy client demands that Wolfe protect her and her family from F.B.I. harrassment, and offers the largest fee Wolfe has ever seen. The fee is almost as improbable as the case but after careful consideration, and in spite of Archie's objections, they take it to the ultimate denouement, when Wolfe actually rises from his chair to see who is at the door." Library J

"The yarn has everything that Stout fans have been led to expect: good dialogue, wit, gourmet menus, Archie Goodwin, Saul Panzer, the dour Cramer and of course Fritz, the chef, who really shines. Nero Wolfe himself rises to new heights." Book of the Month Club News

Eeny meeny murder mo
In Stout, R. Homicide trinity

The father hunt; a Nero Wolfe novel. Viking 1968 183p $4.50

"Mysteries in which the detectives have no clues at all to work on are the best; this situation is exactly what is presented to Nero Wolfe and Archie Goodwin when a young girl asks them to find her father whom she has never known. Amy Denovo's mother, who never revealed the father's identity, has just been killed by a hit-and-run driver. She had blotted out her past up to Amy's birth. It is fascinating to watch Nero and Archie dig out the facts on a case which may be a murder case as well." Pub W

Fer-de-lance
In Stout, R. Royal flush p 1-180

Five of a kind; the third Nero Wolfe omnibus. Viking 1961 441p o.p. 1970

Partially analyzed in Short Story Index
Contains the complete text of: The rubber band, first published 1936 by Farrar & Rinehart; In the best families, and Three doors to death, both originally published 1950 by Viking. Included in the latter title are these three novelettes: Man alive; Omit flowers; and Door to death

Gambit; a Nero Wolfe novel. Viking 1962 188p o.p. 1970

"Nero Wolfe, with his usual witty, urbane conversational approach, looks into a case of arsenic poisoning in a Manhattan chess club. This is high-grade Wolfe, for his fans, but there is very little action in the story." Pub W

Home to roost
In Stout, R. Kings full of aces p325-68

Homicide trinity; a Nero Wolfe threesome. Viking 1962 182p $2.95

Contents: Eeny meeny murder mo; Death of a demon; Counterfeit for murder

"One ('Death of a Demon') is weakly plotted, unfair and illogical; but 'Eeny Meeny

Murder Mo' . . . is adroitly constructed. Moreover, landlady Hattie Annis (in 'Counterfeit for Murder') is the most entertaining client to visit West Thirty-fifth Street in some time." N Y Times Bk R

In the best families
In Stout, R. Five of a kind p155-303

Instead of evidence
In Haycraft, H. ed. A treasury of great mysteries v2 p209-44

Kill-now—pay later
In Stout, R. Trio for blunt instruments p 1-87

Kings full of aces; a Nero Wolfe omnibus. Viking [1969] 472p boards $4.50

Contains two full-length novels: Too many cooks, published 1938 and Plot it yourself, published 1959 together with three short novels: Home to roost; The cop-killer and The squirt and the monkey

Man alive
In Stout, R. Five of a kind p307-55

The mother hunt; a Nero Wolfe novel. Viking 1963 182p o.p. 1970

A mystery novel in which Nero Wolfe attempts to discover "who is guilty of the murders that follow Lucy Valdon's first visit to West 35th Street. It's a matter of maternity that brings her, and the trail that is blazed by a few handmade horsehair buttons has the rare effect of leading Nero out of his habitat and forcing him to set up shop outside." Publisher's note

Murder by the book
In Stout, R. Royal flush p181-333

Murder is corny
In Stout, R. Trio for blunt instruments p89-167

Murder is no joke
In Haycraft, H. ed. Three times three p551-86

The next witness
In Stout, R. Royal flush p337-84

Omit flowers
In Stout, R. Five of a kind p356-98

Plot it yourself
In Stout, R. Kings full of aces p189-322

Royal flush; the fourth Nero Wolfe omnibus. Viking 1965 474p $3.95

Contains the complete text of: Fer-de-lance, first published 1934 by Farrar & Rinehart; Murder by the book, and Three witnesses both published by Viking in 1951 and 1956, respectively. The latter title includes the three novelettes: The next witness; When a man murders and Die like a dog

The rubber band
In Stout, R. Five of a kind p 1-153

Some buried Caesar
In Stout, R. All aces p 1-153

The squirt and the monkey
In Stout, R. Kings full of aces p421-72

Three witnesses
In Stout, R. Royal flush p335-474

Too many clients; a Nero Wolfe novel. Viking 1960 183p $2.95

"When the big businessman, who lived in New York's fashionable East 60s but maintained an expensive love-nest in one of New York's worst neighborhoods, is murdered, Nero [Wolfe] is called in. In fact he is called in three times, the first two times by very wrong people. Hence before he can start to unravel the murder, he has to solve the unique problem of . . . the wrong clients." Publisher's note

Stout, Rex—*Continued*

Too many cooks
In Stout, R. Kings full of aces p 1-187

Too many women
In Stout, R. All aces p155-302

Trio for blunt instruments; a Nero Wolfe threesome. Viking 1964 247p $3.50
Contents: Kill now—pay later; Murder is corny; Blood will tell
"Three stories featuring Nero Wolfe and Archie Goodwin. They concern the defenestration of a businessman, the murder of a deliveryman, and a bloodstained tie sent to Archie from Greenwich Village." Pub W

Trouble in triplicate
In Stout, R. All aces p303-442

When a man murders
In Stout, R. Royal flush p385-430

Stowe, Harriet Beecher
y Uncle Tom's cabin
Some editions are:
Dodd (Great illustrated classics) $4.50 With sixteen full-page illustrations including reproductions from previous editions together with introductory remarks and captions by Langston Hughes
Dutton (Everyman's lib) $2.95
Harvard Univ. Press (The John Harvard lib) $5 Edited by Kenneth S. Lynn
Houghton (Riverside lib) $5.95
Modern Lib. $2.95 With an introduction by Raymond Weaver
First published in book form 1852
"The chief figure is the faithful old slave Uncle Tom. Sold by the Shelbys from his old home in Kentucky, where he leaves his wife Chloe, he lives for a time with the easy-going, good-tempered Augustine St. Clare, to whose gentle little daughter Eva he is devotedly attached. In the St. Clare household are also the Yankee old maid, Miss Ophelia, and the immortal Topsy, an amusing black 'limb of mischief.' After the death of Little Eva and her father, Uncle Tom is sold to the brutal Simon Legree, by whom he is treated with such harshness that when George Shelby, the son of his former master, finds him, he is dying. Among the slaves represented is Eliza, whose escape from the bloodhounds, with her boy Harry, by crossing the Ohio River on cakes of ice, is a familiar incident. Her husband, George Harris, follows her along the Underground Railway." Benét. The Reader's Encyclopedia

Stranger, Joyce
y Born to trouble. Viking [1969 c1968] 218p $4.95
First published 1968 in England with title: Casey
"Primarily the story of coal-black Casey, with the insatiable curiosity of all cats plus the strength and agility and raucous voice of his Siamese father. But, as in all the author's novels, there are people, too—the real kindly, grumbling farm-folk of England and especially Lew Martin, who could gentle 'owd bull' and other animals, and Liz Wayman, whose heart was big enough to hold animals, children, and her husband all at once." Bk Buyer's Guide
"An appealing animal story that does not anthropomorphize nor endow with super qualities its four-footed protagonists. . . . Well written, well paced, unsentimental." Library J

y The wind on the Dragon. Viking 1969 189p boards $4.95
"This is the story of a deer calf who was left an orphan when a forest fire set by careless tourists ravaged the Dragon, a mountain in the Scottish highlands. The calf was rescued by the gamekeeper and raised by his daughter. Like most animal stories, the book ends in tragedy when Rusty is shot by a young hunter with his first gun. This is a propaganda novel, but the moral does not interfere with the story." Library J

Street, Emmet. See Behan, Brendan

Street, James
Captain Little Ax. Lippincott 1956 377p $4.95
"Novel about a 15-year-old boy who organizes a company of boys to fight with the Confederate army in the Civil War. Despite the hostility of Confederate officers, the company inflicts considerable damage on the Union army until eventually all but the leader are killed in the Battle of Chickamauga." Pub W

The gauntlet. Doubleday 1945 311p o.p. 1970
"The story of London Wingo, young Missouri Baptist minister, in his first parish, where everything about him and his wife is criticized. The struggles of London and his wife Kathy to keep both their church and their spiritual integrity builds up to the climax
Followed by: The high calling

y Good-bye, my Lady. Lippincott 1954 222p $5.95
"The boy Skeeter living with old Uncle Jesse in a Mississippi swamp, finds a strange dog and the two become close friends. The time comes when Skeeter and Lady have to part, but thanks to Uncle Jesse's training the boy does what he has to do with dignity and integrity." Book Rev Digest

The high calling. Doubleday 1951 308p o.p. 1970
Sequel to: The gauntlet
"With twenty years of successful ministry behind him, London Wingo gives up an important city church to organize a new one in Linden, Missouri, scene of his first labors. . . . His rebellious daughter Paige marries a ministerial student and learns several hard lessons, the mousy girl who had hoped to marry Paige's husband dedicates herself to religion and sets off a revival, the town feels the impact of the father's and daughter's personalities in many other ways, and London at last finds a woman to take the place of his long-dead wife." Booklist

Mingo Dabney. Dial Press 1950 383p o.p. 1970
"A continuation of the story of the youngest Dabney [of Mississippi] who fell in love with Rafaela Gaban. . . . To the Cubans she was La Entorcha, symbol of freedom; to Mingo she was a fascinating woman. He followed her to Cuba where he became involved in the revolt against Spain . . . [and] imbued with the fervor which burned in the hearts of the Cuban patriots. Not historically accurate but a lusty adventure." Booklist

Oh, promised land. Dial Press 1940 816p $6.50
"A long historical novel based on the founding of Natchez [the battles of the Creek Indians] and the events leading to the War of 1812. The story centers about Sam and Honoria Dabney [a brother and sister] and their struggle to overcome their hereditary and environmental handicaps. Sam achieves his ends by hard work, perseverance and integrity—Honoria by deceit, lust and avarice. Though the language is often crude . . . the characters are well drawn and the author has evidently done an excellent job of research and reporting." Huntting
Followed by: Tap roots

Pride of possession [by] James Street and Don Tracy. Lippincott 1960 218p o.p. 1970
"This novel has been elaborated by Don Tracy from two of James Street's short stories —'Pud'n and Tayme' and 'Proud possessor.' . . . Set against an appropriate North Carolina background, it tells how thirteen-year-old Kiah McCable, with the help of his friends Puddin Tayme, and the Indian boy Hooty, trains a pair of runty hound pups and succeeds in fulfilling his pledge to track down the wild boar that killed his father. A patterned but nevertheless appealing regional boy and dog story." Booklist

Street, James—*Continued*

Tap roots. Dial Press 1942 593p o.p. 1970

Sequel to: Oh, promised land

Contiues the saga of the Dabney family begun in: Oh, promised land. The period covered is from 1858 to 1865, the scene the Dabney domain in southern Mississippi, where slavery-hating Southerners attempted to build a Free state of their own

"It is a swashbuckling tale, with a duelist who always got his man, a very noble Indian, and a beautiful hussy

The velvet doublet. Doubleday 1953 351p o.p. 1970

"A tale of fifteenth-century Spain, the first voyage of Columbus and life in Moorish Africa, recounted by Juan Bermejo, of Andalusia, more commonly known as Lepe the sailor, and in later life as Mudarra the Moor." N Y Her Trib Books

Streeter, Edward

Chairman of the bored. Harper 1961 274p o.p. 1970

This humorous novel centers around "the problems of the retired executive [who] finds himself at 65 facing a compulsory retirement rule he had instigated, when younger, for other people. He and his wife leave the city they love for a country cottage where they find life in retirement thoroughly tiresome." Pub W

"Having more of importance to say about retirement than many foreboding nonfiction works concerned with the subject, this urbane, most enjoyable novel should be included in all public library fiction collections." Library J

Father of the bride; illus. by Gluyas Williams. Simon & Schuster 1949 244p illus o.p. 1970

"From the day of her engagement to the end of the wedding day, the bride and her trousseau, her plans and her wedding, the in-laws and the guests, and especially the effect on his home life and his bank account are seen through the eyes of the Father of the Bride." Wis Lib Bul

also in Costain, T. B. comp. Twelve short novels p617-701

Mr Hobbs' vacation. Drawings by Dorothea Warren Fox. Harper 1954 248p illus o.p. 1970

"The story of the long-awaited vacation of Mr. Hobbs and family on an island off the coast of Massachusetts. Contributions by daughters, sons-in-law, grandchildren—and even Mrs. Hobbs—make it not quite what [Mr Hobbs] had expected." Pub W

Strindberg, August

The Cloister; ed. by C. G. Bjurström. Tr. and with a commentary and notes by Mary Sandbach. Hill & Wang [1969 c1966] 160p boards $5

Written in 1898. This translation first published 1966 in Sweden

"A translation of an uncompleted autobiographical novel which covers the short period after Strindberg's arrival in Berlin in 1892, his second marriage, the birth of a child, and separation from his wife. The story depicts a very somber stretch in Strindberg's life and is of value mainly because of that fact." Booklist

The natives of Hemso; tr. from the Swedish by Arvid Paulson; introduction by Richard B. Vowles. Eriksson 1965 202p $5

Written in 1887

Set against the background of Swedish rural folk who live on the skerries some distance from Stockholm. "Carlsson, the central character, takes his new job as overseer of the farm seriously, although he is a despicable person. His marriage with the widow-owner was for position and money and utterly without love, and though he comes to his tragic death without mourners life at 'Hemsö' will never be the same." Library J

The scapegoat; tr. from the Swedish by Arvid Paulson; introduction by Richard B. Vowles. Eriksson 1967 175p $4.50

"This is the first American edition of one of his most highly regarded novels, written in 1906. . . . When Edward Libotz set up law practice in a small Swedish village, he is greeted by almost universal dislike and distrust. Eventually, partly through the good offices of a local café proprietor, he acquires a substantial practice, if no real friends. The café proprietor, on the other hand, falls victim of his own excessive arrogance and ambition. His new, modern establishment fails, his wife dies, and he commits suicide. . . . When Libotz is again boycotted by the townspeople, he leaves unchanged to pursue his career elsewhere. And, although he has been persecuted and maligned by them, made to serve as a scapegoat for their own inadequacies and transgressions, he remains a largely unsympathetic figure: self-effacing but self-centered, a minor paragon of virtue, but terribly self-righteous." Pub W

Stroven, Carl

(jt. ed.) Day, A. G. ed. Best South Sea stories

Struther, Jan

Mrs Miniver. Harcourt 1942 298p $3.75

Analyzed in Short Story Index

First published in England 1939; in the United States 1940. This 1942 edition adds a new story: Mrs Miniver makes a list

A succession of episodes relating the daily occurrences over a period of two years in the life of the humorous, perceptive, contented Mrs Miniver

Contents: Mrs Miniver comes home; New car; Guy Fawkes' day; Eve of the shoot; Christmas shopping; Three stockings; New engagement book; Last day of the holidays; In search of a charwoman; First day of spring; On Hampstead Heath; Country house visit; Mrs Downce; Married couples; Drive to Scotland; Twelfth of August; At the games; Autumn flit; Gas masks; "Back to normal"; Badger and the echidna; Wild day; New Year's eve; Choosing a doll; At the dentist's; Pocketful of pebbles; Brambles and apple-trees; Khelim rug; On the river; Left and right; "Doing a mole"; New dimension; London in August; Back from abroad; At the hop-picking; "From needing danger. . ."; Mrs Miniver makes a list

Stuart, Jesse

Come gentle spring. McGraw 1969 282p $5.95

"A new collection of 20 short stories about Kentucky hill folk. . . . There is simplicity here and rusticity and a great deal of disingenuous charm harking back to the early part of the century when life was very different indeed. . . . This is writing far from the mainstream of most contemporary fiction, but it has its own homespun appeal." Pub W

Contents: Come gentle spring; Two worlds; The weakling; A Christmas present for Uncle Bob; The old law wasn't strong enough; Love in the spring; The water penalty; Our Wiff and Daniel Boone; Pa's a man's man all right; Mad Davids and a mechanical Goliath; The last round up; A land beyond the river; Powderday's red hen; Fast-Train Ike; Uncle Fonse laughed; Does the Army always get its man; Seventy-six days; The rainy day at Big Lost Creek; The war and Cousin Lum; King of the hills

Daughter of the legend. McGraw 1965 249p boards $5.95

"Dave Stoneking, a young lumberjack, tells of his love for Deutsia Huntoon, a tall, straight girl from Sanctuary Mountain, with blonde hair hanging to her knees. But the valley people in the Eastern Tennessee town considered the mountain people scrub stock, with Negro ancestry. Dave ignored them, married Deutsia, and found a brief happiness with her as a fellow outcast." Bk Buyer's Guide

Stuart, Jesse—*Continued*

My land has a voice. McGraw 1966 243p
boards $5.50

This collection by a genuinely American writer, depicts "the spirit and temper of the rural
American life in the Kentucky mountains."
McClurg. Book News
Contents: Corbie; Yoked for life; Beyond the
news in Still Hollow; Hand that fed him: He's
not our people; South America and Tiger Tom;
April; Red Mule and the changing world; A
mother's place is with her son; Lady; As a
man thinketh; Both barrels; Judge Ripper's
Day; The rightful owner; A stall for Uncle
Jeff; Remember the Sabbath Day and keep it
holy; Here; Nearly tickled to death; Uncle Jeff
and the family pride; Another Thanksgiving

Plowshare in heaven; stories. McGraw
1958 273p illus boards $5.50

Analyzed in Short Story Index
Contents. Zeke Hammertight; Walk in the
moon shadows; Land beyond the river; Rich
men; Sylvania is dead; Wind blew east; Sunday
afternoon hanging; The reaper and the flowers;
How sportsmanship came to Carver College;
Love in the spring; Settin'-up with Grandma;
Bird-neck; The chase of the skittish heifer;
Before the grand jury; The champions; Death
and decision; Alec's cabin; Old Dick; Grandpa;
The devil and the television; Plowshare in
heaven

Taps for Private Tussie; illus. by Thomas
Hart Benton. World Pub. [1969 c1943] 303p
illus boards $6.95

A reprint of a title first published 1943 by
Dutton
"A comic regional tale about the improvident
Tussies [Kentucky mountain folk, who] all
living happily on relief without any obligation
to work, come into money when Aunt Vittie
cashes in on [harddrinking, worthless] Kim's
war insurance. What this sudden wealth does
for them, while it lasts, is the theme of the
story." Wis Lib Bul
"Using the native speech of the Kentucky
mountaineers, Jesse Stuart has written a ro-
bustly hilarious folk tale, with overtones of
pathos and tragedy, and not a few sociological implications." Bookmark

Sturgeon, Theodore

It

In Hitchcock, A. ed. Alfred Hitchcock
presents: Stories that scared even
me p129-53

Some of your blood

In Hitchcock, A. ed. Alfred Hitchcock
presents: Stories my mother never
told me p305-401

Styron, William

The confessions of Nat Turner

Some editions are:
Modern Lib. $2.95
Random House $6.95
First published 1967
Pulitzer Prize, 1968
The author "tells the story of the short-
lived but bloody rebellion of slaves in South-
hampton, Virginia, in 1831, as seen through
the eyes of its instigator. Opening after Nat's
capture, as he dictates his confession to the
defense counsel, the story turns backward to
his youth as a prodigy in the household of an
opponent of slavery who had promised him his
freedom. Reverses of fortune force his master
to sell Nat, and the book describes in detail his
subsequent experiences under a number of masters as well as his phenomenal knowledge of
the Bible, his training as a carpenter, his complex emotions regarding the whites, and his
meticulously-planned campaign of extermination which was foredoomed to failure." Library J
"This represents a radical departure from
past writing about Negroes. . . . Styron thoroughly explores the Negro militant's hatred
of whites. . . . The position of the whites is
[also] thoroughly explored . . . without rancor
or even a hint of political 'parti pris' on the
author's part." N Y Rev of Books

"The book is more a psychological narrative
for 1967 than it is a social narrative of 1831. . . .
The real achievement of this beautiful, curious,
essentially dreamlike narrative is . . . [that Sty-
ron] has been able to create with his honest
sense of the tragic, a man whom the locked-up
force of daily, hourly, constant suppression has
turned into a Stranger—someone who remains
single, separate, wholly other from ourselves
and our notions. . . . What we have here is a
wonderfully evocative portrait of a gifted,
proud, long-suppressed human being who began to live only when he was sentenced to die."
Book World

Lie down in darkness. Modern Lib. [1964
c1951] 400p $2.95

A long novel, written in the stream of consciousness style, which traces "the development and dissolution of a Southern family. . . .
The story is a violent and sordid one in part.
. . . People, place and period are built up with
an intensity of feeling and purpose." Book
of the Month Club News
"Mr. Styron takes a marriage for the
framework of his story, the journey of a hearse
to the cemetery for his action, and the suicide
of a young woman for his impetus, his mood,
and his climax. The marriage is that of Milton
and Helen Loftis, a Virginia couple, and the
hearse, which they follow in separate limou-
sines, carries the remains of their daughter
Peyton, who is in death, as she was in life,
only a symbol of her parents' mutual hatred,
their despair, and their overpowering self-
pity." New Yorker

The long march. Random House [1968
c1952] 120p $3.95

First copyright 1952
"The story of a forced 36-mile march at a
Marine base in the Carolinas, it is essentially
a treatment of contrasts: the placid tenor of
civilian life against the brash authoritarian-
ism and occasional idiocy of the military; Captain Al Mannix, the eternal rebel, against Colonel 'Old Rocky' Templeton—both seen through
the eyes of Lieutenant Tom Culver, fledgling
lawyer, husband, father, and unwilling soldier.
Though these contrasts are pronounced, they
are the more disturbing because they are not
simply black against white but, as it were, a
struggle of grays." Library J

Set this house on fire. Random House 1960
507p $5.95

"On his way back to the States, Peter Leve-
rett stopped in Italy to see his old schoolmate
Mason Flagg in the little coastal town of
Sambuco. The following morning Mason was
found dead at the base of a cliff. . . . Peter
later realized that he had been witness to a
blaze of events which were ignited by a tragic
conflict between two men: one was Flagg himself; the other was Cass Kinsolving, a tortured,
self-destructive American painter who has settled in Sambuco after an alcoholic flight across
most of Europe. Mason, leading a hectic, pretentious, Don Juan life, found Cass his natural enemy and prey. Out of the enslavement,
the agony, the degradation of their relationship came the salvation of one man and the
destruction of the others." Publisher's note

Sue, Eugene

The Wandering Jew. Modern Lib. 1940
2v in 1 o.p. 1970

First English translation published by Harper
1846
Here "Ahasuerus [the Wandering Jew] and
his half-sister Herodias, both eternal wanderers, [since the time of Christ] find their
chief interest in guiding the affairs of their
descendants. The romance is episodic, but the
principal events take place in the Paris of 1832
and the plot centers about the struggle between the Protestants and Catholics to control a large sum of money invested for seven
heirs of Count Rennepont, a descendant of
Herodias. The Jesuits, led by a shrewd and
energetic little priest named Rodin, succeed in
bringing six of the seven heirs to disaster and
presenting the seventh. Gabriel Rennepont, a
young Jesuit priest, as the only claimant for
the inheritance, but their schemes are finally
thwarted." Benét. The Reader's Encyclopedia

Sue, Eugene—*Continued*

"Melodramatic in the extreme, and the style is often bombastic. . . . But when all abatement is made, 'The Wandering Jew' remains one of the famous books of the world, for its vigor, its illusion, its endless interest of plot and counterplot, and its atmosphere of romance." Keller's Reader's Digest of Books

Summerton, Margaret. See Roffman, Jan

Sumner, Cid Ricketts

Quality; a novel. Bobbs 1946 286p o.p. 1970

The "story of a girl born a Negro, but who has light hair and blue eyes. Pinkey Johnson through the efforts of her grandmother, a typical old-time southern negress, was sent to Boston for an education and became a graduate nurse. She is mistaken for a white person and never corrects the mistake in the North. But when a white doctor falls in love with her, she returns to Mississippi. Lost and heartsick she does not fit into the accepted social pattern of a southern town. Only after she solves her personal problem by aiding her own people through her nursing does she begin to lead a full and purposeful life." Booklist

Sutcliff, Rosemary

The flowers of Adonis. Coward-McCann 1970 [c1969] 383p $6.95

First published 1969 in England

The story of "Alkibiades, the godlike Athenian general of Peloponnesian War fame, is told . . . through the first-person reminiscences of a cast of characters consisting of citizens, soldiers, sailors, courtesans, and Spartans and Persians as well as Athenians." Horn Bk

"Affords a broad panorama of the internal and external politics of Athens and Sparta and their fluctuating alliances, as well as of their military and naval activities. The glamorous Alcibiades is plausibly portrayed as a keenly intelligent, arrogant, dynamic leader whose popularity with the Athenians created powerful enemies and was a strong factor in his betrayal and death. . . . Sutcliff has followed historians closely but has supplemented their accounts with her own interpretations where enigmas and gaps occurred." Booklist

Lady in waiting; a novel. Coward-McCann 1957 253p o.p. 1970

An historical novel which "portrays the life of Bess Throckmorton, who became the wife of Sir Walter Raleigh. Beginning with their first meeting, the richly descriptive narrative recounts Bess's romance and secret marriage and the turbulent years that followed. Raleigh's struggles to gain Queen Elizabeth's favor and establish an English empire in the New World, his imprisonment in the Tower as a victim of political intrigue [etc.] . . . are skillfully woven into the more intimate pattern of Bess's poignant story." Booklist

"A tale in which great charm and moving penetration are stirred up together, a book that deals with the past in a style of high romance, yet leaves the reader satisfied at a finale that is as tragic as it is inevitable." N Y Times Bk R

Rider on a white horse. Coward-McCann 1959 320p $5.50

"The tumultuous period of the English Civil War sets the scene. Until 1642 Sir Thomas Fairfax and his wife, Anne, had lived a quiet happy life at Nun Appleton. Then Tom went off to war and Anne followed, knowing that she would be needed to look after her husband. This is the story of the three years that followed and of a wife's steadfast devotion for her dedicated man." Huntting

"Distinguished by historical accuracy, rich period detail, and a depth of human feeling." Booklist

y Sword at sunset. Coward-McCann 1963 495p o.p. 1970

A novel based on historical facts about the legendary Arthur. "The time is the century after the last Roman legions leave Britain, and Arthur is desperately striving to hold Britain against the Saxons, Picts, and other invading savage tribes. [This is] the story of his tragic fate, his good times and bad." Pub W

The author "handles minute details meticulously. This is a very good book without being a great book. Critical readers will find it overly long, too full of campaigns and topography, and lacking in the psychological development of its characters, but none will deny the author's real artistry and technical skill. Warmly recommended for all libraries and all readers." Library J

Svevo, Italo

The confessions of Zeno; tr. from the Italian by Beryl de Zoete. Knopf 1930 406p o.p. 1970

Original Italian edition, 1923

"Confessions of Zeno is disguised as the story of [the author's] life as prepared by a psychoanalyst's patient for his doctor, and it is a masterpiece of sleepy wit and biting irony. Zeno is a foolish fellow. He is lazy, inquisitive, a master of indecision, always planning to give up his pet vices, always trying new careers, always expecting to do great things at something else, salving his conscience after each relapse and failure in the most mischievous, comic and natural ways. There is no describable plot to Zeno's confessions." Outlook

This is "a highly human story and its material is fundamentally as sound as its method. . . . The work of a man who wrote to please himself, it has an individuality and originality you cannot escape noticing, and it has, too, a fine and comprehensive knowledge of its character." N Y Times Bk R

A contract

In Svevo, I. Further confessions of Zeno p113-38

Further confessions of Zeno; tr. from the Italian by Ben Johnson and P. N. Furbank. Univ. of Calif. Press 1969 302p (Uniform edition of Svevo's works, v2) $5.95

This "volume contains the various surviving fragments and drafts of the sequel to 'The Confessions of Zeno.'" Bibliographical note

These five short sketches and play were originally published separately in Italian

Contents: The old old man [1959]; An old man's confessions [1957]; Umbertino [1957]; A contract [1957]; This indolence of mine [1957]; Regeneration: a comedy in three acts [play], [1960]

In "these delightful writings from Svevo's last years . . . the Chaplinesque Zeno, grown older, is now smoking his several-thousandth 'last cigarette,' comically overestimating his sexual powers, contributing generously to the universal generation gap, and earning anew our compassion by his innocent wisdom and his spirit of endurance." Library J

An old man's confessions

In Svevo, I. Further confessions of Zeno p27-67

The old old man

In Svevo, I. Further confessions of Zeno p11-23

This indolence of mine

In Svevo, I. Further confessions of Zeno p141-64

Umbertino

In Svevo, I. Further confessions of Zeno p71-109

Swanson, Neil H.

The Judas tree. Putnam 1933 360p o.p. 1970

"The long, agonizing siege, of Pittsburgh by Indian tribes during the Pontiac Conspiracy of 1763 is the event about which this romance centers . . . [an] adventure, with authentic historical background, a hero of incredible endurance and courage, and a heroine whose attractiveness is enhanced by the mystery surrounding her name and past." Booklist

Unconquered; a novel of the Pontiac Conspiracy. Doubleday 1947 440p o.p. 1970

A long adventure "story of the Pontiac Conspiracy, set for the most part in the Ohio River region of America in the 18th century and compounded of love, greed, courage, and tragedy." Retail Bookseller

Swarthout, Glendon

They came to Cordura. Random House 1958 213p $3.50

The "story of an Army major who leads five men, cited for heroism, and a woman, accused of treason, through dangerous country in Mexico to a rear base where the men are to receive their awards. The time is 1916 when a Mexican revolutionary force attacked an American border town." Pub W

"Primarily, it is a book about courage, an examination of its anatomy, a search for the mysterious factor that impels some men to live for a time beyond the edges of normal human conduct." N Y Her Trib Books

Swift, Jonathan

y Gulliver's travels

Some editions are:
Dodd (Great illustrated classics) $4.50 With illustrations reproducing drawings for early editions and photographs of historical scenes together with an introductory biographical sketch of the author and anecdotal captions by Allen Klots, Jr.
Dutton (The Children's illustrated classics) $3.50 Illustrated with 8 colour plates and line drawings by Arthur Rackham
Oxford (Worlds classics) $1.75
Watts, F. $4.95 A Watts ultratype edition. With a critical and biographical profile of Jonathan Swift by William T. Brewster

First published in 1726

"In the account of his four wonder-countries Swift satirizes contemporary manners and morals, art and politics—in fact the whole social scheme—from four different points of view. The huge Brobdingnagians reduce man to his natural insignificance, the little people of Lilliput parody Europe and its petty broils, in Laputa philosophers are ridiculed, and finally all Swift's hatred and contempt find their satisfaction in degrading humanity to a bestial condition." Baker's Best

Swinnerton, Frank

Nocturne; with a preface by the author. New ed. Dufour 1964 263p $3.95

First published 1917 by Doran
English edition has title: In the night
"An exceptionally authentic rendering of Cockney psychology and manners lifted by the sheer art of the author out of dinginess and pettiness on to the plane of beauty. The characters are Pa [a paralytic] his two very dissimilar daughters, and their 'blokes'; the action takes place in a single night." Cleveland

Sanctuary. Doubleday 1967 [c1966] 272p o.p. 1970

First published 1966 in England
Set in present-day London. "Eight elderly and indigent ladies are getting along beautifully in a Georgian home donated to them by Lady Horsham. The benevolent Miss Goodmayes is in charge. Then she gets sick and has to go into the hospital. Lady Horsham goes off to Australia, and the old dears are given over to the far from tender mercies of Annie Morgan. . . . Her attempt to run a tight ship brings the old ladies to a mild revolt but all works out well in the end, and Annie even acquires a little of the milk of kindness, herself. Enjoyable lending library fiction is the way we'd describe this." Pub W

Symons, Julian

The Belting inheritance. Harper 1965 210p o.p. 1970

"Lady Wainwright had lost both Hugh and David, her sons, in WW II. Now, as she lay awaiting death, with her family awaiting their share of her wealth, son David turned up—but was it really David? Lady Wainwright's grandnephew and his girl-friend believed David was a fake and followed his devious trail to Paris and danger." Bk Buyer's Guide

"These are not the characters you have so often met each one has the Symons individuality, and there's hugger-mugger in a lovely Paris before the unfathomable mysteries become no mysteries at all." Book Week

The color of murder. Harper 1957 184p o.p. 1970

"John Wilkins was an ineffectual fellow who worked in the complaints section of a big London department store, who was unhappily married, was given to daydreams and had occasional 'blackouts.' He built up a romantic fantasy about an attractive librarian and was, unfortunately, near the scene of crime when she was found murdered one night on Brighton Beach." Best Sellers

The man who killed himself. Harper 1967 186p boards $4.50

"Arthur Brownjohn was a little, henpecked man; Major Easonby Mellon was small, too, but quite a dashing gentleman—and when the Major met pretty Patricia Parker, who was looking for a husband, Arthur decided to murder Mrs. Brownjohn." Bk Buyer's Guide

The man whose dreams came true. Harper 1968 229p boards $4.95

"A Joan Kahn-Harper Novel of suspense"
"Tony was a weak but handsome rogue. He attempted forgery, he attempted blackmail, and he attempted to marry an heiress but failed at all three. He assumed various names. And at last he got into such trouble that only a wealthy widow was able to save him—at the price of satisfying her inordinate lust." Bk Buyer's Guide
Symons "does not quite succeed in presenting Tony, the non-hero, in a sympathetic light. Symons does, however, succeed in involving the reader. There is a certain inevitability about the outcome, still the author does manage to introduce a twist of sorts." Best Sellers

The progress of a crime. Harper 1960 211p o.p. 1970

"A gang of Teddy boys had been thrown out of a Far Wether dance; on Guy Fawkes Night they returned to Far Wether—and the man who had evicted them was stabbed to death. To the consternation of reporter Hugh Bennett, his girl friend's brother was one of the suspects. English setting." Bk Buyer's Guide

Szilard, Leo

The voice of the dolphins, and other stories. Simon & Schuster 1961 122p $3.95

Analyzed in Short Story Index
"These five stories by the famous atomic physicist express through satire his views on science and politics." Chicago
Contents: Nightmare for future reference [poem]; The voice of the dolphins; My trial as a war criminal. The Mark Gable Foundation; Calling all stars; Report on "Grand Central Terminal"

T

Taber, Gladys

One dozen and one; short stories. Lippincott 1966 239p boards $5.95

Analyzed in Short Story Index
"Quiet short stories about children, dogs, and family life." Pub W
Contents: Matchmakers; Impetuous wedding; Honey and the home front; Dear bachelor; Look homeward. Dusty; Money of her own; Letter to the Dean; Just a little havoc; When the wood grows dry; Portrait of a gentleman; The legend of Lavinia; Miss Fenella's story; Little Goat goes up

Tanizaki, Junichiro

Diary of a mad old man; tr. from the Japanese by Howard Hibbett. Knopf 1965 177p (UNESCO collection of representative works. Japanese ser) boards $3.95

"A seventy-seven-year-old Japanese writes in detail of his failing health and what the doctors are doing about it, his family, and especially about [his daughter-in-law] Satsuko, for whom he feels an entirely improper desire which she plays upon to win special favors." Bk Buyer's Guide

Tanizaki, Junichiro—*Continued*

"On one level the story may be read for its subtle characterization and at another as an allegory of a proud civilization in transition, seduced by the crassest qualities of the alien West." Booklist

The Makioka sisters; tr. from the Japanese by Edward G. Seidensticker. Knopf 1957 530p boards $6.95

"The four Makioka sisters represent the upper middle-class Japanese tradition and customs, though their circumstances leave them little substance to support this way of life. Two of the four sisters are unmarried. The elder, Yukiko, is retiring and highly conscious of her place in society. The younger, Taeko, is more susceptible to pernicious influences of a changing society. The conflict of personalities and environmental adjustments provide the motivating center for this novel." Library J

"The narrative is very quiet, very leisurely. At times it seems interminable, but it is like the pigment used by a Renaissance painter to build up his picture. It is done with utmost skill and results in a dignified masterpiece of great beauty and quality." Chicago Sunday Tribune

Tanner, Edward Everett. See Dennis, Patrick

Tapsell, R. F.

The year of the horsetails. Knopf 1967 310p $5.95

First published in England

"In ancient Asia the nomads swept westward—reckless and war like, they soon overpowered the peaceful inhabitants of agricultural communities. But, in this novel those bewildered and frightened people began to fight back in sheer desperation, led by one of their chieftains who taught them how to use the bow and how to meet the fierce Mongol charges." Bk Buyer's Guide

Tarassov, Lev. See Troyat, Henri

Tarkington, Booth

y Alice Adams; illus. by Arthur William Brown. Grosset 434p illus $2.50

Pulitzer Prize 1922

First published 1921 by Doubleday

"Alice Adams is a 'small town' girl of the Middle West. She has charm and ambition, but handicapped as she is by lack of money, background and ideals, her imagination can compass no higher career than struggling to keep up with her childhood friends whose fortunes have grown with the town. Alice is a pathetic figure, at once amusing, appealing and irritating, as are her self-sacrificing but one ideaed mother and her simple-minded, goaded father. A lightly handled albeit penetrating study." Cleveland

The gentleman from Indiana

Some editions are:
AMS Press $11.50
Reprint House International $14.50
Scholarly Press $14.50

First published 1899

"The hero is John Harkless, the young editor of a country newspaper in Indiana. His courageous struggles, particularly against the lawless White Caps, bring him enemies, and when he vanishes after an attack upon him, he is given up for dead. However, he reappears, and the novel ends with his marriage to the charming girl who has run his paper in his absence and so made possible his nomination to Congress." Benét. The Reader's Encyclopedia

The magnificent Ambersons. Smith, P. 1967 [c1918] 248p $3.75

Pulitzer Prize 1919

First published 1918 by Doubleday

"Follows the fortunes of a middle-western family risen to sudden wealth and local importance in the speculative days of the early '70s, and is especially concerned with the sole representative of the third generation, George Amberson Minifer, arrived at arrogant young manhood in the early days of the automobile." Cleveland

"Its achievement is not so much in pointed detail or penetrating phrase as in the exhaustive revelation of a thoroughly significant national type." New Repub

y Monsieur Beaucaire

Some editions are:
Doubleday $2.50 Introduction by Robert Cortes Holliday
Heritage $6.95 Illustrated and decorated by T. M. Cleland and with a preface by J. Donald Adams

First published 1900 by Doubleday

"The scene is laid in 18th-century Bath, and the hero is a cousin of Louis XV, Louis Philippe de Valois. Disguised as a barber, on adventure bent, he falls in love with Lady Mary Carlisle and forces his rival, the Duke of Winterset, whom he has caught cheating at cards, to present him as the Duke de Chateaurien. All goes well with his suit until Winterset announces that he is a mere barber, whereupon Lady Mary treats him with the utmost scorn. Shortly after, on an occasion of state, he is greeted as the Duke of Orleans, but her regret is of no avail." Benét. The Reader's Encyclopedia

"No one but a born romanticist could have written that dainty and consistent bit of artistry. Its best excuse was the blitheness of its mood, the symmetry of its form, the tingling vitality of it." F. T. Cooper

y Seventeen. Grosset 1916 249p $2.95

"A Thrushwood book"

"It's hero is William Sylvanus Baxter, known as 'Willie' at home and 'Silly Bill' at school. He is smitten by the charms of Lola Pratt, a stranger in town whose chief accomplishment is talking baby talk to her pet dog Flopit and to her numerous admirers. Willie calls upon Lola in his father's dress suit with awful but amusing consequences." Benét. The Reader's Encyclopedia

"This story of the first love experience of William Sylvanus Baxter shows an almost uncanny insight into the emotions and mental processes of the adolescent boy. It is full of humor and gentle sarcasm, but also understanding and sympathy for the tragedies and absurdities of youth." Wis Lib Bul

Tarr, Herbert

The conversion of Chaplain Cohen; a novel. Geis [distributed by Random House] 1963 341p o.p. 1970

A serio-comic novel "about the Air Force experiences of a young Jewish chaplain from Brooklyn who is yearning to get married, is completely unable to stop telling people unpleasant truths [is learning to make friends with non-Jews] and is desperately afraid of flying." Pub W

"It is quite clear, however, from the start, that this book is a gesture toward better understanding between Christians and Jews, and actually it succeeds quite well in attaining that aim. But midway a seriousness that is always implicit changes radically the book's emphasis so that humor gives way to pathos. . . . The humor persists but the laughter does not. Recommended not for the whole but for its many good moments." Best Sellers

Heaven help us! A novel. Random House 1968 277p $5.95

"A lighthearted tale of a young rabbi's struggle with his middle-class congregation. Devoted to learning, and the pursuit of the good, he finds himself in supernumerary roles involving rubber-stamping financial plans of his trustees, directing a play, and dodging marriage-minded girls." Booklist

"A fast, funny, slick treatment of a familiar theme—the plight of the young rabbi who finds out that his first congregation of wealthy suburbanites is more interested in the world and the flesh than the Word." Pub W

Tarsis, Valeriy

Ward 7; an autobiographical novel; tr. by Katya Brown. Dutton 1965 159p $3.95

"More a polemic than a novel this is a thinly fictionalized account of a writer's term in a mental hospital used as a place of incarceration

Tarsis, Valeriy—*Continued*

for political opponents of Russia's present regime. Tarsis was similarly imprisoned after foreign publication of a novel and his recitation of the injustices and hypocrisies behind his arrest and his sketches of his fellow prisoners is a diatribe against the Soviet regime." Booklist

Tate, Allen

(jt. ed.) Gordon, C. ed. The house of fiction

Tattersall, Jill

Lyonesse Abbey. Morrow 1968 248p boards $5.95

"Gothic suspense set in Cornwall in the mid-1800's. When the Hon. Richard Howard lost heavily at cards, in lieu of cash or land he offered the winner, Damon Tregaron, his youngest daughter. Thus it was that Tessa came to Lyonesse Abbey, a converted monastery perched half in ruins high above the sea. It was an eerie setting for a young and inexperienced girl, but one singularly suited to the mysterious events happening within it." Am News of Bks

"A typical undemanding but satisying historical Gothic romance with appeal for women readers." Booklist

Taylor, Anna

The gods are not mocked. Morrow [1969 c1968] 312p boards $5.95

First published 1968 in England

This novels "tells, in first-person narratives, of Lucius, a Roman soldier serving with Caesar in the invasion of Britain; Becca, the Druid priestess he takes as mistress; and Valeria, Lucius' older sister infatuated with another woman. . . . Interwoven with the stories of the main characters are those of their loved ones—Taskin, a member of a Kentish tribe captured by the Romans, whose life becomes irrevocably entwined with Becca's; Dechtine, Taskin's wife taken to Rome and sold as a slave; and Clodia, the infamous lady of Rome whose infatuation with men and her ties with Valeria lead to her downfall." Library J

Taylor, David

Farewell to Valley Forge. Lippincott 1955 378p $4.95

Set during the period of the American Revolution, the book 'describes General Charles Lee's plot to betray the colonial forces, the British evacuation of Philadelphia, and the decisive battle of Monmouth. Witness to and dangerously involved in these historic events are the dashing rebel captain Jonathan Kimball, who poses as a servant in occupied Philadelphia, and Elizabeth Ladd, spirited daughter of a patriot shipowner, who risks her life to help him secure military information for General Washington." Booklist

"'Farewell to Valley Forge' is solid historical fiction—the kind that tells a good story and manages to illuminate the past as well." N Y Times Bk R

Lights across the Delaware. Lippincott 1954 366p map $5.95

"Phoebe Runnels, a spirited farm girl, is torn between her devotion to the American revolutionists' struggle and her pacifist Quaker lover. The Christmas of 1776 brought little joy to the forlorn armies of Washington and less to Phoebe for though Wheeler sympathized with the rebels, he remained faithful to his religious convictions." McClurg. Book News

Mistress of the Forge. Lippincott 1964 350p $5.95

"A tale of romance, patriotism and adventure, based on fact. The setting is the troubled post-Revolutionary period; the hero is a young Philadelphian who is sent on a threefold mission to the Luken Furnace on the Susquehanna. Alexander Hamilton and Robert Morris play major parts in the story." Huntting

"It is good, passable entertainment of a light nature and gives an insight into the difficulties of the embryonic United States." Library J

Storm the last rampart. Lippincott 1960 384p boards $5.95

A story about the American Revolution which "covers the final months of the war. A lively fictional narrative follows the hazardous adventures of Bennett Paige, a captain in the colonial army and spy for Washington's intelligence staff, and Hannah Clements, a tavern girl posing as a Tory in British-held Tarrytown but also spying for the rebels. The well integrated, carefully detailed historical action begins with the treason of Benedict Arnold and reaches its conclusion with Cornwallis' surrender at Yorktown." Booklist

Taylor, Elizabeth

A dedicated man, and other stories. Viking 1965 223p boards $4.95

Analyzed in Short Story Index

12 short stories "all displaying Miss Taylor's flair for pinpointing oddities of personality and ironic turns of event contingent on them." Booklist

Contents: Girl reading; The prerogative of love; The Thames spread out; In a different light; The benefactress; A dedicated man; As if I should care; Mr Wharton; Mice and birds and boy; The voices; In the sun; Vron and Willie

In a summer season; a novel. Viking 1961 242p o.p. 1970

"How the insecurity of widowed Kate's marriage to charming Dermot 10 years her junior is heightened by the return of their neighbors in the country outside London forms the core of [this novel about] . . the conflict in generations when beguiling Araminta Thornton casts her spell on Kate's 22-year-old son and Dermot as well, bringing tragedy in her wake." Bookmark

The wedding group. Viking 1968 186p boards $4.50

"Eighteen-year-old Cressy's grandfather held court at Quayne and Cressy was very glad to escape, even into the household of a bachelor till now devoted to Midge, his charming mother, who soon began to rule David's new wife as well as David." Bk Buyer's Guide

"This quiet, very British character study which makes no bid for greatness is sheer delight and should provide entertainment for many feminine patrons of public libraries." Library J

Taylor, Kamala Purnaiya. See Markandaya, Kamala

Taylor, Peter

The collected stories of Peter Taylor. Farrar, Straus 1969 535p $10

"This collection of 21 of Peter Taylor's best stories over 30 years is high quality fare all the way. . . . Most of the stories are set against the dreamlike nostalgia of the vanishing borderline South—Tennessee and northern Alabama." Pub W

Contents: Dean of men; First heat; Reservations; The other times; At the drugstore; A spinster's tale; The fancy woman; Their losses; Two pilgrims; What you hear from 'em; A wife of Nashville; Cookie; Venus, Cupid, Folly and Time; 1939; There; The elect; Guests; Heads of houses; Mrs Billingsby's wine; Je suis perdu; Miss Leonora when last seen

Taylor, Robert Lewis

A journey to Matecumbe; with illus. by Joseph Papin. McGraw 1961 424p illus boards $5.95

Young Davy tells the story of a harrowing trek down the Mississippi from Kentucky to Key West, a decade after the Civil War. With Davy are his uncle Jim and a Negro servant, all escaping down the river, and pursued by the Ku Klux Klan. They travel by rowboat, houseboat, paddle-wheel steamer, horseback, canoe, pirate ship, and a few other conveyances, and meet an unusual assortment of people. (Publisher)

Taylor, Robert L.—*Continued*

"Those who read the author's prize-winning 'The Travels of Jaimie McPheeters' [entered below] will quickly recognize the Davey Burnie of this one as Jaimie's spiritual twin brother. They will anticipate with pleasure the fast-paced action, the wild escapades, the frontier horrors and humor, and the stock characters who, strangely enough, come to life through the vivid descriptions crammed with details of regional history and folklore." Library J

y The travels of Jaimie McPheeters. Doubleday 1958 544p $6.50

Pulitzer Prize 1959
"Fourteen-year old Jaimie McPheeters, the son of Sardius McPheeters, an unsuccessful, windy-minded doctor who is given to gambling and drink, sets out with his father from their Louisville home in the spring of 1849 for the California gold fields, and in the course of the next three years or so is kidnapped by outlaws; is captured by Indians; witnesses a lot of brutality, including a duel, fires, killings, and some startling Indian cruelty; suffers semi-starvation and degradation; and in the end, after his father's death, becomes part owner of a handsome California ranch, where he settles with his mother, his sisters, and his Indian sweetheart." New Yorker
"The piquant combination of solid historical content, satisfying adventure, good literary style, sophisticated wit and humor, will give this book wide appeal." Library J

Two roads to Guadalupé. Doubleday 1964 428p illus $5.95

"The Mexican War supplies the background for the story of Sam, a sixteen-year-old Missourian who runs off to join the army, and who, after many adventures, arrives at Chapultepec. Interwoven with Sam's account is the diary of his older brother, Blaine, who has accompanied the army as its literary historian." Huntting
"Humor and irony liberally season this story of . . . adventures, roughhousing, fighting, and narrow escapes." Pub W

Tchekhov, Anton. See Chekhov, Anton

Telfer, Dariel

The night of the comet. Doubleday 1969 297p $5.95

"A steel-mill town in midwest America early in the twentieth century is the setting. . . . Young widow Mary Frances Winthrop, who supports her four children through washing and ironing, is reluctant to decide upon either of her two suitors, the bachelor mill foreman or the rich widower. On the night of Halley's comet, the celestial phenomenon is overshadowed by the excitement surrounding the efforts of ten-year-old Boyd Winthrop in influencing his mother to marry the steel-mill worker." Booklist
"A good, old-time wholesome family novel, not for sophisticated readers, but just fine for the customer who is looking for this kind of story. The children are particularly sympathetic and well drawn." Pub W

Temple, Willard

The drip-dried tourist. Putnam 1969 219p $5.95

"How Ed and Claire Meadows of Montana decide (or rather Claire decides) to join another couple on a three-week tour of Europe—a sort of second honeymoon—and make the usual mistakes and have all sorts of wryly amusing adventures." Bk Buyer's Guide
This "never-a-dull-moment romp with apple pie Americans on tour see-saws amusingly through the all-too familiar trials and tribulations of innocents abroad." Pub W

Tenn, William

(ed.) Once against the law; ed. by William Tenn and Donald E. Westlake. Macmillan (N Y) 1968 330p $6.95

Partially analyzed in Short Story Index

"The world's greatest authors have written about crime, and mystery works by Dickens, Chaucer, Thurber, Steinbeck, Moravia, and Tolstoi, among others, are compiled here with introductory notes on each author and an introduction on what draws great writers to the study of crime." Bk Buyer's Guide
Contents: How Mr Hogan robbed a bank, by J. Steinbeck; The garden of Forking Paths, by J. Borges; The willow walk, by S. Lewis; The Pardoner's tale, by G. Chaucer; An illusion in red and white, by S. Crane; The fate of a hero, by J. Farrell; The two drovers, by Sir W. Scott; The flight of Sikes, by C. Dickens; The burglars and the boy, by H. Gold; The Succubus, by H. De Balzac; Incident on a street corner, by A. Maltz; Rendezvous, by R. Coates; God sees the truth but waits, by L. Tolstoy; The terror of Rome, by A. Moravia; The return of Imray, by R. Kipling; The sheep, by J. Cary; There are 43,200 seconds in a day, by P. Ustinov; The captive, by L. Pirandello

Tey, Josephine

y Brat Farrar. Macmillan (N Y) [1967 c1949] 219p $6.95

"A Macmillan Large print edition"
First published 1949
"Cleverly contrived and well-written story about a young English orphan who tried to pass himself off as the rightful heir in an enchantingly quaint horse-loving and horse-breeding family. The twenty-one year old Brat's regeneration and his unfolding of a murder mystery in the end are told with a refreshingly new twist." Library J
"There is much mystery, humor and real charm in a story which reaches its climax when Brat must disgrace either his new family or himself. Interesting psychology throughout the story." Wis Lib Bul

also in Tey, J. Three by Tey v3

y The daughter of time. Large type ed. Watts, F. [1966 c1951] 204p $7.95

"A Keith Jennison book"
First American publication 1952 by Macmillan (N Y). Original English publication 1951
"Alan Grant, injured policeman hospitalized and bored, is diverted by a photograph of Richard III, commonly conceded murderer of the princes in the Tower. With the invaluable assistance of a research student, Grant's convalescence becomes a lively pursuit of the truth as shown by records in Richard's time. Vindications of Richard had been proven in the 17th and 18th century, but are iconoclastic for 20th century readers." Library J
The author "not only reconstructs the probably historical truth, she re-creates the intense dramatic excitement of the scholarly research necessary to unveil it." N Y Times Bk R

also in Tey, J. Four, five and six by Tey v3

Four, five and six by Tey. . . . Macmillan (N Y) 1958 3v in 1 (Murder revisited ser) $6.95

Reprint in one volume of three complete Scotland Yard mysteries in which Inspector Alan Grant solves the crimes
Contents: The singing sands (1952); A shilling for candles (1936); The daughter of time (1951). All titles are entered separately

The Franchise affair. Macmillan (N Y) 1948 238p o.p. 1970

"A lawyer in an English country town answers an appeal for help from two women who, having only recently inherited a home, were still outsiders to the townspeople and, being independent, reserved, and unusual, were called witches. When a girl in another town accused them of imprisoning, starving, and beating her in their attic, they were helpless, for the circumstantial evidence seemed indisputable. Good characterization, good writing, and to the lawyer's surprise, an emotional involvement for him." Booklist

also in Haycraft, H. ed. Ten great mysteries p451-640

also in Tey, J. Three by Tey v2

Tey, Josephine—*Continued*

The man in the queue. Macmillan (N Y) 1953 [c1929] 213p (Murder revisited mystery novel) o.p. 1970

First published 1929 by Dutton under author's other pseudonym, Gordon Daviot
The author's first mystery in which "Inspector Grant finds the murder of a man standing in a queue for theatre tickets one of the most puzzling cases in his career." Huntting

Miss Pym disposes. Macmillan (N Y) 1948 [c1947] 213p o.p. 1970

First published 1947 in England
"An English woman psychologist goes to deliver a lecture at a physical training college. The year's term is about ended, so Miss Pym decides to stay a little longer. She becomes very friendly with some of the seniors, and eventually finds herself involved in an 'accident' which turns out to be a murder." Book Rev Digest

also in Tey, J. Three by Tey v 1

A shilling for candles. Macmillan (N Y) 1954 188p o.p. 1970

"A Cock Robin mystery"
Originally published in England 1936
"Christine Clay, famous British film star is strangled near her rented seashore cottage. Inspector Grant . . . is called in from Scotland Yard to solve the case, which he does after a few false starts." Library J

also in Tey, J. Four, five and six by Tey v2

The singing sands. Macmillan (N Y) 1953 [c1952] 221p o.p. 1970

First published 1952 in England
"The key to the murder of Bill Kenrick, a commercial pilot stationed in the Middle East, and traveling to Scotland under an assumed name, is in a little fragment of verse, and it takes all of Inspector Grant's great ingenuity to decipher its lines. The murder is found to be related to an even stranger mystery concerning the whereabouts of the ancient, fabled Arabian city of Wabar." McClurg. Book News

also in Tey, J. Four, five and six by Tey v 1

Three by Tey: Miss Pym disposes; The Franchise affair [and] Brat Farrar; with an introduction by James Sandoe. Macmillan (N Y) 1954 3v in 1 (Murder revisited ser) $6.95

"A Cock Robin mystery"
An omnibus volume of three titles entered separately
"If any one characteristic most distinguished Miss Tey's work it was her power to evoke character, atmosphere, mores by conversation. Her people talk as though speech comes natural to them. It is good talk as well as story propelling. Indeed it makes one nostalgic for the art of conversation." New Repub

To love and be wise. Macmillan (N Y) 1951 [c1950] 210p o.p. 1970

First published 1950 in England
"Although there is a detective—a very nice one—and a mystery, it involves a hoax, not murder. Leslie Searle, a too-handsome too-charming American photographer, wangles an invitation to the country, sets an artistic colony by the ears, and appears to be winning nice Liz Garrowby from her tiresome fiancé, Walter Whitcomb. When Leslie disappears, Walter is a likely murder suspect, but some intelligent police work [by Inspector Alan Grant] discovers what really happened and why." Booklist

Thackeray, William Makepeace

The history of Henry Esmond, esquire; with an introductory sketch of the author and with illustrations of characters and scenes belonging to the novel. Dodd 1945 434p illus (Great illustrated classics) $4.50

Written in 1852

"Written in the first person, supposedly by Henry Esmond. He is brought up by Francis Esmond, heir to the Castlewood estate with Francis' own children, Beatrix and Frank, and grows up in the belief that he is the illegitimate son of Thomas Esmond, the deceased viscount of Castlewood. On his deathbed Francis confesses to Harry that he is the lawful heir, but Harry keeps the information secret. He and Frank Esmond are ardent supporters of James the Pretender, who, however, falls in love with Beatrix and ruins his chances for the throne. Beatrix joins the Prince abroad, and Harry, who has been in love with her, renounces the Pretender, marries her mother Rachel, Lady Castlewood, instead, and takes her to America." Benét. The Reader's Encyclopedia

Followed by: The Virginians

The Newcomes. Dutton 2v (Everyman's lib) o.p. 1970

First published 1855; in this edition 1910
This novel deals "with three generations of Newcomes. Chief in interest and one of the most famous characters of all fiction is the lovable Colonel Thomas Newcome, a man of simple, unworldly tastes and the utmost honor. The Colonel's son, Clive, an artist, is in love with his cousin, Ethel Newcome, who, however, desires a more ambitious marriage. In this project Ethel is urged on by her selfish, cold-blooded brother, Barnes Newcome, but his true character is revealed to her when his mistreated wife, Lady Clara, elopes with her quondam lover, Jack Belsize, then Lord Highgate. Clive despairing of winning Ethel, marries Rosey Mackenzie, with whom he finds he is mismated. When his father, through a bank failure, loses their combined resources, the family live in poverty and the colonel finally becomes a brother at the Grey Friars to escape the bad temper of Clive's mother-in-law, Mrs. Mackenzie. Rosey dies in the course of time and Clive, who has fallen heir to some money, marries Ethel." Benét. The Reader's Encyclopedia

Pendennis. Dutton 2v (Everyman's lib) o.p. 1970

First published 1849-1850; in this edition 1910
A novel which is largely autobiographical. "The young hero, Arthur Pendennis, known as Pen for short, is spoiled by his mother and by Laura Bell, a distant relative of his own age with whom he grows up. He goes through the University, enters London society, writes a successful novel, becomes editor of the 'Pall Mall Gazette', and meantime is involved in love affairs of varying character with the actress Miss Fotheringay, with Fanny Bolton a London porter's daughter, and with Blanche Amory, daughter of Lady Clavering. He finally marries Laura, who has always loved him and whom he has grown to love. Pen's uncle, Mayor Arthur Pendennis, and his friend George Warrington play prominent roles." Benét. The Reader's Encyclopedia

y Vanity fair

Some editions are:
Dodd (Great illustrated classics) $5.50 with reproductions of the original illustrations by Thackeray and with an introductory biographical sketch of the author by Basil Davenport
Dutton (Everyman's lib) $3.25 Introduction by M. R. Ridley
Harcourt (Harcourt Lib. of English and American classics) $3.95

First published 1848
"A picture of society on a broad canvas, embracing a great variety of characters and interests, the object being to depict mankind with all its faults and meannesses, without idealization or romance. . . . The careers of Becky Sharp, the adventuress, and her husband, Rawdon Crawley, make an apt contrast to the humdrum loves of the good hero and heroine, Dobbin and Amelia. The nobility, fashionable people about town, the mercantile aristocracy and the needy classes below them are all portrayed in the most lifelike way. . . . Thackeray combines comment with narrative. . . . To many readers, indeed, his sarcastic dissertations are the chief intellectual delight." Baker's Best

The Virginians. Dutton 2v (Everyman's lib) ea $3.25

First published 1857; in this edition 1911
"A sequel to Henry Esmond, relating the story of George and Harry Warrington, the

Thackeray, William M.—*Continued*

twin grandsons of Colonel Esmond. The novel takes the two brothers, of differing tastes and temperaments, through boyhood in America, through various experiences in England, where they are favorites of their wicked old aunt, Baroness Bernstein (the Beatrix of 'Henry Esmond') and through the American Revolution, in which Harry fights on the side of his friend, George Washington, and George on the British side." Benét. The Reader's Encyclopedia

Thal, Herbert van. See Van Thal, Herbert

Thane, Elswyth

y Dawn's early light. Duell 1943 317p $4.95

"When, in May 1774, young fatherless Julian Day arrives in Virginia from London, he is uncertain of his next step, but the friendliness of St John Sprague impels him to stay on in Williamsburg as a teacher, and soon Julian, the Loyalist, is strangely interested in the activities of the Colonial government and in the personalities of men like Washington and Jefferson. His championship of the abused 11-year-old twin, Tibby Mawes, who displays an unusual bent for learning, wins him a place in the Southern community, while he is temporarily ensnared by Sprague's beautiful and flirtatious lady-love, Regina Gildersleeves. Authentic atmosphere and the vital spirit of the new republic are pleasantly conveyed in this historical romance, which leaves the once shy schoolmaster, Julian, a major in the Continental Army and confident of the future." Bookmark

Followed by: Yankee stranger

Ever after. Duell 1945 334p $6.95

Sequel to: Yankee stranger

Carries one generation further the evolution of a war correspondent—from Julian Day in "Dawn's early light" and Cabot Murray of "Yankee stranger" to Bracken Murray of the 1890's. The war with Spain takes Bracken Murray and his cousin to Cuba. The conditions under which the campaign was fought—the amateur invasion at Daiquiri, the advance of the Rough Riders up Kettle Hill before San Juan are described

"The author tells a good story, enlivened by colorful shifts of scene from Williamsburg to New York, London and Cuba." N Y Times Bk R

Followed by: The light heart

Homing. Duell 1957 272p $5.95

Sequel to: This was tomorrow

"The beginning of the war found many of the Williamsburg Spragues and Days in England; Jeff was a foreign correspondent; Evadne, new wife of Julian Sprague, had returned to London to serve as a warden; her husband was with a canteen; and her niece Mab, who looked like a reincarnation of Tibby, refused to be separated from Jeff, the apparent reincarnation of Tibby's husband, Julian." Retail Bookseller

Kissing kin. Duell 1948 374p $4.95

Sequel to: The light heart

The first World War and the confused, exotic years which followed it provide the time, and Williamsburg, London, and the continent provide the setting for this new novel. The Richmond twins, Calvert and Camilla, are central figures. Characters of the former Day family sagas reappear here

Followed by: This was tomorrow

y The light heart. Duell 1947 341p $5

Sequel to: Ever after

"The fourth volume in the author's series of historical novels about the Spragues and the Days of Williamsburg, Virginia. The heroine this time is Phoebe Sprague, who became engaged to her cousin Miles just before her departure for England to attend the coronation of Edward VII. There she met the man she really loved. The book closes after a raid on London during World War I." Book Rev Digest

Followed by: Kissing kin

y This was tomorrow. Duell 1951 319p $4.50

Sequel to: Kissing kin

The romance of two pairs of cousins; two of the cousins, from Virginia, who are dancers, take a show to London where they meet their English counterparts. The time is just before the Second World War. 1934-/1938

Followed by: Homing

y Tryst. Duell 256p $4.95

First published 1939 by Harcourt

"When Sabrina came to live in the gaunt stone house in the Wendip Hills which her father had rented because he wrote books about prehistoric Britain, she felt she had reached sanctuary at last from the London world which confused and frightened her. There was a closed room at the top of the house which they were not supposed to use, but Sabrina found a way and entered into enchantment. A ghost story, love story and a charming modern comedy." Ontario Lib Rev

y Yankee stranger. Meredith 1944 306p $5.95

Sequel to: Dawn's early light

"In Williamsburg, one gusty, stormy day just before the Civil War, a handsome, tall young Northerner, a newspaper correspondent, runs bang into lovely, 17-year-old Eden Day and, as suddenly, invades her heart. How Eden's remarkable 'Gran,' a beautiful old lady of 95 who had herself long ago fallen in love at first sight, aids and abets the lovers during the following terrible years is related in an attractive historical romance mingling events and effects of the war on human beings and clever characterization in a deftly contrived plot." Bookmark

Followed by: Ever after

Thirkell, Angela

The Brandons. Knopf 1939 358p o.p. 1970

"The characters are Mrs. Brandon, an attractive widow, her grown son and daughter, a wealthy, disagreeable spinster-relative, who may or may not leave her estate to Mrs. Brandon's son, a vicar and several other men, young and old, who are devoted to Mrs. Brandon. Most of the people are pleasant, comfortably settled, well and wittily characterized; they furnish good entertainment for readers who like the leisurely English setting." Booklist

Thomas, Dylan

Adventures in the skin trade, and other stories. New Directions 1955 275p o.p. 1970

Analyzed in Short Story Index

Contents: Adventures in the skin trade; After the fair; The enemies; The tree; The visitor; The lemon; The burning baby; The orchards; The mouse and the woman; The horse's ha; A prospect of the sea; The holy six; Prologue to an adventure; The map of love; In the direction of the beginning; An adventure from a work in progress; The school for witches; The dress; The vest; The true story; The followers

Rebecca's Daughters. Little [1966 c1965] 144p $4.50

First published 1965 in England

"Rebecca and Rebecca's daughters, dressed in traditional Welsh woman's costume and numbering more than three hundred, were in reality men. This is the legend of the revolt of the Welsh farmers against the hated tollgates of the Turnpike Trusts, told by Dylan Thomas in a new vein, delving deep into the history of his beloved Wales for a tale cast in the form of a screenplay and technically capable of being filmed without the slightest alteration, while remaining a fascinating adventure story." Am News of Bks

Thomas, Ross

The Singapore wink. Morrow 1969 253p $5.95

This mystery follows "Eddie Cauthorne, one-time movie stunt man, and Richard Trippet, retired British intelligence agent, . . . joint owners of Les Voitures Anciennes in Hollywood. . . . The problem is Cauthorne's repetitive hallucination that comes every evening at dusk when he sees the last wink of Angelo Sacchetti as he slides down a rope to drown in

Thomas, Ross—*Continued*

Singapore harbor. The hallucination makes him a sitting duck for the strange assignment from a Washington lawyer to go to Singapore and find Sacchetti." Library J

"Raw suspense overlaid with icings of humor: an exemplary combination." N Y Times Bk R

For another title by this author see Bleeck, Oliver

Thompson, Arthur Leonard Bill. See Clifford, Francis

Thompson, Morton

The cry and the covenant. Doubleday 1949 469p o.p. 1970

"A novel based on the life of a famous Hungarian obstetrician. Dr. Ignaz Semmelweis discovered that puerperal fever was caused by an infection. He devoted his life to an unsuccessful attempt to persuade all contemporary physicians of the necessity of disinfecting with a chlorine solution." Book Rev Digest

"This book is an event in literary history. To my knowledge it is the first novel truly to describe medical discovery and to tell truly the martyrdom of a discoverer, fighting to spread his life-saving truth against medical big shots who didn't care whether people lived or died." N Y Times Bk R

Not as a stranger. Scribner 1954 948p o.p. 1970

"Lucas Marsh has only one interest in life—the practice of medicine. The author has described all the things that make up a doctor's life from laboratory days, through graduation; then there is a small-town practice with its emergency cases, night calls, and a dreaded epidemic. His wife Kristina, whom he had married when he was in medical school when she was head operating nurse, perseveres in her efforts to make their marriage a success, although a long time elapses before he sees truly what she is." Huntting

"Years of research on the author's part made it possible for him, though he was not himself a doctor, to write with authenticity about disease, operations, treatments, techniques and routines. But the author's instinctive observations of the heart lift this long tale from the confines of the tract and make it a moving, wounding, absorbing human drama." N Y Her Trib Books

Thorp, Roderick

The detective. Dial Press 1966 598p $5.95

Private detective Joe Leland, "World War II hero and a former police officer, takes on a client, the young widow of an apparent suicide. She thinks her husband was murdered. What Leland discovers in his investigation affects his life, the life of his family, his client's life, and the lives of people at every level in his community." Am News of Bks

"Treating many of its characters in considerable depth, the novel may be too gamey for some palates; yet it has a certain force and fascination, and a gnawing suspense." Library J

Three for tomorrow; three original novellas of science fiction, by Robert Silverberg, Roger Zelazny [and] James Blish; with a foreword by Arthur C. Clarke. Meredith 1969 204p boards $5.95

Contents: How it was when the past went away, by R. Silverberg; The eve of Rumoko, by R. Zelazny; We all die naked, by J. Blish

These novelettes "dramatize a theme set forth by Arthur C. Clarke: With increasing technology goes increasing vulnerability. . . . In 'We All Die Naked,' James Blish makes a grim visit to Manhattan of the future, a city in which gas masks are normal apparel and atmospheric changes resulting from man's enterprises have wrought incredible consequences. 'The Eve of Rumoko,' by Roger Zelazny, considers the power, for good or evil, of a man

whose name does not appear in the Central Data Bank, who lives outside the computerized supervision of human activity. San Francisco, 2003 A.D., is the setting for Robert Silverberg's 'How It Was When the Past Went Away,' a story of the mass effect of a memory-destroying drug." Publisher's note

Thurber, James

y The 13 clocks; illus. by Mark Simont. Simon & Schuster 1950 124p illus $4.95

"A fairy tale not for children about a duke, so cold and cruel that time has frozen around him, who has imprisoned a beautiful princess in his castle, and about a prince who rescues her by performing a seemingly impossible task." New Yorker

"Mr. Thurber has done it again, though I don't know just what it is he has done this time—a fairy tale, a comment on human cruelty and human sweetness or a spell, an incantation compounded of poetry and logic and wit." N Y Her Trib Books

y The wonderful O; illus. by Marc Simont. Simon & Schuster 1957 72p illus boards $4.95

"A new adult fairy tale. . . . It involves a hidden treasure, a tyrannical villain named Black whose mother got stuck in a porthole, and Black's consequent attempts to ban everything spelled with the letter o from the peaceful island of Ooroo. Though the moral—Black's discovery that he cannot destroy hope, love, valor, and freedom—is obvious, details are ingeniously and subtly worked out, and the central device of deleting o's gives the reader a wonderful orthographic frolic through the English language." Booklist

"This is an elaborate adult fairy tale in the mode of Mr. Thurber's previous 'The Thirteen Clocks.' It is witty. It is extremely clever, sometimes to the point of seeming synthetically so. It has a moral. . . . On the whole Mr. Thurber manages to imbue his ingenious cipher-game with that kind of amazed freshness which is so characteristic of the Thurberian world." Christian Science Monitor

Tolkien, J. R. R.

y The fellowship of the ring; being the first part of The lord of the rings. Houghton 1954 423p illus maps $6.50

"Frodo, a home-loving young hobbit, inherits the magic ring which his uncle Bilbo brought back from the adventures described in the juvenile fantasy 'The hobbit,' This sequel, expressly addressed to adults, is the first of a three-part saga that tells of Frodo's valiant journey undertaken to prevent the ring from falling into the hands of the powers of darkness. Elves, dwarfs, hobbits, men, and sundry evil beings, each as real as the other, populate an allegorical tale that shows how power corrupts." Booklist

also in Tolkien, J. R. R. The lord of the rings v 1

y The hobbit; or, There and back again; illus. by the author. Houghton 1938 310p illus $3.95

"Hobbits are very small people, smaller than dwarfs but much larger than Lilliputians. The hero of this tale was a well-to-do hobbit who somehow found himself, accompanied by [a] wizard and dwarfs, off on a mad journey over the edge of the wilds to wrest from Smaug the dragon his hoard of long-forgotten gold." Huntting

"The background of the story is full of authentic bits of mythology and magic and the book has the rare quality of style. It is written with a quiet humor and the logical detail in which children take delight. . . . But this is a book with no age limits. All those, young or old, who love a finely imagined story, beautifully told, will take the Hobbit to their hearts." Horn Bk

y The lord of the rings. 2d ed. Houghton 1967 [c1966] 3v $18.50

Contents: v 1 The fellowship of the ring; v2 The two towers; v3 The return of the king, all entered separately

Tolkien, J. R. R.—*Continued*

y The return of the king; being the third part of The lord of the rings. Houghton 1956 416p $6.50

Third and final volume of the trilogy: The lord of the rings, which includes "The fellowship of the ring" and "The two towers"

This third volume "brings the War of the Rings to a close with the success of the forces for good in their fight against the Dark Lord of evil. It also carries Frodo and Sam, bearers of the Ring, to Mount Doom where the Ring is destroyed. Several lengthy appendixes add scholarly information on the past history of Middle Earth and its inhabitants— elves, dwarfs, men, and hobbits." Book Rev Digest

also in Tolkien, J. R. R. The lord of the rings v3

y Smith of Wootton Major; illus. by Pauline Baynes. Houghton 1967 61p illus $1.95

"Every 24 years, the Master Cook of Wootton Major bakes a great cake for the Feast of the Good Children. . . . A certain piece of the cake contains a tiny, magic star. It is swallowed by Smith, perhaps the least remarkable child in the village, and from that day on . . . his life becomes privileged. He travels deep into the world of Faery. . . . Then one day the time comes when Smith, now a grandfather, must give up his star and allow it to pass to another chosen child." N Y Times Bk R

y The two towers; being the second part of The lord of the rings. Houghton 1954 352p $6.50

Further adventures of the band of companions featured in "The fellowship of the ring"

"Here the Companions of the Ring, separated, meet Saruman the wizard, cross the Dead Marshes, and prepare for the Great War in which the power of the Ring will be undone." Library J

also in Tolkien, J. R. R. The lord of the rings v2

Tolkien, John Ronald Reuel. See Tolkien, J. R. R.

Tolstoǐ, Lev Nikolaevich, graf. See Tolstoy, Leo

Tolstoy, Alexis

The vampire

In Tolstoy, A. Vampires p9-91

Vampires; stories of the supernatural; tr. by Fedor Nikanov; ed. by Linda Kuehl; illus. by Mel Fowler. Hawthorn Bks. 1969 183p illus $4.95

"Originally published in Russia about a hundred years ago, this volume consists of four chilling adventures of men struggling against the supernatural." Book News

It includes a novella: The vampire, and the following short stories: The family of a Vourdalak; The reunion after three hundred years; Amena

Tolstoy, Leo

y Anna Karenina

Some editions are:

Dodd (Great illustrated classics: Titan eds) $5.50 Foreword by E. Hudson Long

Dutton (Everyman's lib) 2v ea $2.95 Translated by Rochelle S. Townsend. Introduction by Nikolay Andreyev

Modern Lib. $2.95 Edited and introduced by Leonard J. Kent and Nina Berberova. The Constance Garnett translation has been revised throughout by the editors

Norton (A Norton Critical ed) $8.97 The Maude translation, backgrounds and sources, essays in criticism. Edited by George Gibian

Oxford (The World classics) $2.50 Translated by Louise and Aylmer Maude

First published 1901 in English

"Gives a direct, truthful, unsentimentalized and unheightened transcript of life in all its multitudinous and complex phases. . . . The main action is profoundly tragic—a woman of fine nature forsakes husband for lover, and after a bitter experience rests in suicide." Baker's Best

"For its artistic qualities, Anna Karenina stands foremost among the many beautiful things Tolstoi has written. It is also a work of high moral import, for without sacrificing its value as a masterpiece of art Tolstoi demonstrates through its characters and events that a generous soul cannot live outside the moral law." Pratt Alcove

Childhood, Boyhood & Youth

Some editions are:

McGraw $6.95 Translated by Michael Scammell

Oxford (World classics) $3.50 Translated by Louise and Aylmer Maude

Originally published separately, 1852, 1854 and 1857 respectively

"A three-part novel autobiographical in source." Pub W

The Cossacks; tr. from the Russian by Vera Traill. Pantheon Bks. 1949 189p (Novel lib) o.p. 1970

Written in 1852, altho not published until 1862

"Written, at least in part, while he was serving in the army of the Caucasus, and rich in descriptions of that superb region. A story of the love of an educated Russian gentleman . . . for a beautiful savage. . . . The girl is a creature of instinct, and an insuperable barrier exists between her simple nature and the complex character of the man. So their lives go on as if they had never met." Baker's Best

also in Tolstoy, L. Short novels v 1 p279-455

The death of Ivan Ilyitch

In Neider, C. ed. Short novels of the masters p249-300

In Tolstoy, L. The death of Ivan Ilyitch, and other stories

In Tolstoy, L. Short novels v2 p3-62

The death of Ivan Ilyitch, and other stories; a new tr. from the Russian by Constance Garnett. Dodd 1927 362p o.p. 1970

Analyzed in Short Story Index

Contents: The death of Ivan Ilyitch; Family happiness; Polikushka; Two hussars; The snowstorm; Three deaths

The Devil

In Tolstoy, L. Short novels v2 p63-113

Family happiness

In Tolstoy, L. Short novels v 1 p127-213

Father Sergius

In Costain, T. B. comp. Twelve short novels p289-327

In Tolstoy, L. Short novels v2 p324-71

The forged coupon

In Tolstoy, L. Short novels v2 p503-75

Hadji Murád

In Tolstoy, L. Short novels v2 p372-502

The Kreutzer sonata

In Tolstoy, L. Short novels v2 p114-212

The Kreutzer sonata, The Devil, and other tales. Tr. of Family happiness, by J. D. Duff, and of other stories by Aylmer Maude. With an introduction by Aylmer Maude. Oxford [1957] xxi, 375p (World classics) o.p. 1970

Contents: Family happiness; The Kreutzer sonata; The Devil; Father Sergius; François; The porcelain doll

A landlord's morning

In Tolstoy, L. Short novels v 1 p71-126

Master and man

In Tolstoy, L. Russian stories and legends p163-224

In Tolstoy, L. Short novels v2 p272-323

Tolstoy, Leo—*Continued*

"Master and man," and other parables and tales. Dutton 320p (Everyman's lib) $2.95

Analyzed in Short Story Index
First published 1895 with title: Master and servant; in this edition 1910
The title story is "one of Tolstoy's later stories expressing his gospel of the divine charity latent in human hearts. Describes with his inimitable realism the sudden transformation of a callous and selfish master who in a momentary impulse sacrifices himself for a devoted servant perishing in a terrible blizzard on the steppe." Baker's Best

Contents: Master and man; How much land does a man require; That whereby men live; Elias; Children may be wiser than their elders; Labour, death, and disease; The grain that was like an egg; Where love is, there God is also; The two old men; The three old men; God sees the right, though he be slow to declare it; How the little Devil atoned for the crust of bread; The penitent sinner; The snowstorm; The raid; The candle; The godson; Croesus and Solon; Neglect a fire, and 'twill not be quenched

Polikúshka
In Tolstoy, L. Short novels v 1 p214-78

Resurrection

Some editions are:
Heritage $7.95 A novel in three parts. The translation by Leo Wiener, revised and edited for this edition by F. D. Reeve. With an introduction by Ernest J. Simmons and illustrated with wood engravings by Fritz Eichenberg
Oxford (The World classics) $2.25

First published in English 1900
"The young, noble and light-hearted hero, Nekhludov, is one of the jury to decide upon the case of a girl who has poisoned a merchant for his money. To his horror he recognizes Maslova, whom he has seduced on his aunt's estate years before. Tormented by a sense of responsibility that completely upsets his previous scheme of life, Nekhludov determines to follow her to Siberia and marry her. The novel deals with the working out of this strange undertaking. Maslova is also known as Katusha." Benét. The Reader's Encyclopedia

Russian stories and legends; illus. by Alexander Alexeieff. Pantheon Bks. [1967] 223p illus $3.95

Analyzed in Short Story Index
Translated from the Russian by Louise and Aylmer Maude, this is a reprint of a collection first published 1943 with title: What men live by
Contents: What men live by; How much land does a man need; The three hermits; Where love is, God is; Two old men; God sees the truth, but waits; The godson; Master and man

Short novels. . . . Selected and introduced by Ernest J. Simmons. Modern Lib. 1965-1966 2v ea $2.95

Analyzed in Short Story Index
v 1 "Stories of love, seduction and peasant life." v2 "Stories of God, sex and death." Title pages
Most of the stories have been translated by Louise and Aylmer Maude
Contents: v 1: Two hussars (1856); A landlords morning (1856); Family happiness (1859); Polikúshka (1863); The Cossacks: a tale of 1852 (1863)
v2: The death of Iván Ilyitch (1886); The Devil (1911); The Kreutzer sonata (1901); A talk among leisured people; an introduction to the story that follows; Walk in the light while there is light (1893); Master and man (1895); Father Sergius (1911); Hadji Murád (1911); The forged coupon (1911)

The short novels of Tolstoy; selection with an introduction by Philip Rahv; tr. by Aylmer Maude. Dial Press 1946 xx, 716p o.p. 1970

Analyzed in Short Story Index
Contents: Two Hussars; Family happiness; The Cossacks; Polikúshka; The death of Iván Ilyitch; The Devil; Master and man; Hadji Murád

Short stories; selected and introduced by Ernest J. Simmons. Modern Lib. 1964-1965 2v ea $2.95

Analyzed in Short Story Index
Contents: v 1; A history of yesterday; The raid; A billiard-marker's notes; The wood-felling; Sevastopol in December 1854; Sevastopol in May 1855; Sevastopol in August 1855; Meeting a Moscow acquaintance in the detachment; The snow storm. Lucerne; Albert; Three deaths; Strider; The porcelain doll
v2: God sees the truth, but waits; A prisoner in the Caucasus; The bearhunt; What men live by; A spark neglected burns the house; Two old men; Where love is, God is; Evil allures, but good endures; Little girls wiser than men; Elias; The story of Iván, the Fool; The repentant sinner; The three hermits; The imp and the crust; How much land does a man need; A grain as big as a hen's egg; The Godson; The empty drum; Esarhaddon, King of Assyria; Work death and sickness; Three questions; The memoirs of a madman; After the ball; Fëdor Kuzmích; Alyósha

Tolstoy's Tales of courage and conflict, by Count Leo N. Tolstoy; ed. with an introduction by Charles Neider. Hanover House 1958 574p o.p. 1970

Analyzed in Short Story Index
These are 36 stories of suspense, action, realism, and intense characterization. They reflect almost all periods and aspects of their author's long life of more than eighty years. (Publisher)
Contents: The invaders; Recollections of a billiard-marker; Sevastopol in December 1854; Sevastopol in May 1855; Sevastopol in August 1855; Wood-cutting expedition; Old acquaintance; Lost on the steppe; Lucerne; Albert; Three deaths; Desire stronger than necessity; Long exile; Prisoner in the Caucasus; What men live by; A candle; Devil's persistent, but God is resistant; Ilyas; Little girls wiser than their elders; Neglect a fire and it spreads; Skazka; Two brothers and gold; Two old men; Where love is, there God is also; Death of Ivan Ilyitch; The godson; How the little Devil earned a crust of bread; How much land does a man need; Kholstomer; Repentant sinner; A seed as big as a hen's egg; Three hermits; Kreutzer sonata; Story of Yemilyan and the empty drum; A dialogue among clever people; Walk in the light while there is light

Twenty-three tales; tr. by Louise and Aylmer Maude. Oxford 298p (World classics) $1.50

Analyzed in Short Story Index
First published in this edition 1906
Contents: God sees the truth, but waits; Prisoner in the Caucasus; The bear-hunt; What men live by; Spark neglected burns the house; Two old men; Where love is, God is; Story of Ivan the Fool; Evil allures, but good endures; Little girls wiser than men; Ilyás; Three hermits; Imp and the crust; How much land does a man need; A grain as big as a hen's egg; The godson; Repentant sinner; Empty drum; Coffee-house of Surat; Too dear; Esarhaddon, King of Assyria; Work, death and sickness; Three questions

Two hussars
In Tolstoy, L. Short novels v 1 p3-70

Walk in the light while there is light
In Tolstoy, L. Short novels v2 p218-71

y War and peace

Some editions are:
Dutton (Everyman's lib) 3v ea $2.95 Introduction by Vicomte de Vogué
Modern Lib. (Modern Lib. giants) $4.95
Oxford (The World classics) $5 Translated by Louise and Aylmer Maude

First published 1864-1869
"The most famous novel of Leo Tolstoi (1865-1872), dealing with Russia and France at the time of Napoleon Bonaparte, giving an epic picture of the invasion of Russia by Napoleon and his army, and presenting the author's theories of history." Benét. The Reader's Encyclopedia
"A multitude of characters are presented, officers and men, both French and Russian, the hostile emperors and their suites, gentry living quietly in Moscow or on their estates, great

Tolstoy, Leo—*Continued*

people of fashion, serfs, and all intermediate classes. The more important are portrayed from the inside, and the reader sees through their eyes, and coloured by their emotions, the entire life of the nation throughout this tremendous epoch. . . . Real personages occupy almost as much space as the fictitious, and are drawn with the same unerring insight." Baker's Best

Tomlinson, H. M.

(ed.) Great sea stories of all nations, by Giovanni Boccaccio [and others]; with many others from ancient Greece to modern Japan; ed. and with an introduction by H. M. Tomlinson. Doubleday 1930 xxiv, 1108p o.p. 1970

Analyzed in Short Story Index

Contents: How Odysseus made himself a raft and how Poseidon, shaker of the earth, overwhelmed him with a storm, by Homer; How the Greeks defeated the Persians off the isle of Salamis, by Æschylus; How the ship Argo passed between the clashing rocks, by Apollonius Rhodius; How Lucian of Samothrace voyaged to the moon and how he was afterward swallowed by a whale, by Lucian of Samothrace; Might of the whale, by Oppian; Dolphin—Lord of fishes, by Oppian; How Rome built her first ships and how C. Duilius Nepos defeated the Carthaginians therewith, by Polybius; How Æolus, king of the winds, sent forth a storm against Æneas, by Virgil; How Julius Caesar, taking fortune for his comrade, put out into the tumult of the sea, by Lucan; How Mark Anthony, following after Cleopatra, fled from the battle of Actium, by Plutarch; Gathering together of the waters, from Genesis: Waters of the flood, from Genesis; Jonah and the whale, from Jonah; Shipwreck of St Paul, from Acts of the apostles; First voyage of Es-Sindibád of the sea; Story of 'Abd-Allah of the land and 'Abd-Allah of the sea; Sailor and the pearl merchant; How Xerxes bridged the Hellespont, from Herodotus; Voyage of Maildun; Voyage of Saynt Brandon; How Scyld set forth upon his last voyage, from Beowulf; How Beowulf, for the space of five nights, abode in the sea, from Beowulf; How Richard Coeur de Lion, sailing to the Holy land, captured a Saracen ship, by G. de Vinsauf; Battle of Espagnois-sur-Mer, by Sir J. Froissart; How Sir Launcelot entered into the ship where Sir Percivale's sister lay dead: and how he met with Sir Galahad his son, by Sir T. Malory; Of the great sea fight between Sir Andrew Wood, knight, and Captain Stephen Bull, by R. Lindsay of Pitscottie; World encompassed by Sir Francis Drake, by R. Hakluyt; Death of Sir Humfrey Gilbert, by E. Hale; Last fight of the Revenge, by Sir W. Raleigh; True repertory of the wrackle and redemption of Sir Thomas Gates, Knight, by W. Strachey; Last voyage of Henry Hudson, by A. Pricket; Dangerous voyage of Captain Thomas James, told by himself, by T. James; Prince Rupert's exploits at sea, by V. Pyne; Some adventures of Crusoe, by D. Defoe; Gulliver at Lilliput and Brobdingnag, by J. Swift; How Commodore Anson came to Juan Fernandes, by R. Walter; Trafalgar, by R. Southey; Mr Midshipman Easy, by F. Marryat; Phantom ship, by F. Marryat; Whitby whalers, by E. Gaskell; In the steerage, by C. Dickens; How Gerard Amyas threw his sword into the sea, by C. Kingsley; Man with the belt of gold, by R. L. Stevenson; Abandoning ship, by J. Conrad; Lofty-minded mariner, by M. Roberts; In the abyss, by H. G. Wells; Derelict, by H. M. Tomlinson; Memory by J. Masefield; Davy Jones's gift, by J. Masefield; T'Wind'ard, by D. Bone; Voyage of the James Caird, by E. Shackleton; How the Cutty Sark raced the Thermopylae, by B. Lubbock; Ghost ship, by R. Middleton; Sealing of Zeebrugge, by A. Hurd; Five Wounds encounters a gale, by V. Hutchinson; Fruits of toil, by N. Duncan; Fourteen fathoms by Quetta rock, by R. Bedford; Voyage of the Mayflower, by W. Bradford; Phantom island, by W. Irving; Red Rover and the Royal Caroline, by J. F. Cooper; Descent into the maelstrom, by E. A. Poe; Chesapeake and the Shannon, by J. B. McMaster; Homeward bound, by R. H. Dana; Storm in the Pacific, by R. H. Dana; Moby Dick, by H. Melville; How Quintus Arrius defeated the pirates, by L. Wallace; Skipper and El Capitan, by F. R.

Stockton; High-water mark, by F. B. Harte; Devil at sea, by H. Van Dyke; How the gardener's son fought the Serapis, by W. Churchill; Merrimac and the Monitor, by M. Johnston; Bound for Rio Grande, by A. E. Dingle; Rounding Cape Horn, by F. Riesenberg; Yellow cat, by W. D. Steele; Way for a sailor, by B. Adams; How Pantagruel met with a great storm at sea and of what countenance Panurge and Friar John kept therein, by F. Rabelais; How Captain Jean Ribault came to Florida and of what befell the men he left there, by R. De Laudonnière; Telemachus in the island of Cyprus, by F. De La Mothe-Fénelon; Shipwreck of a modest young lady, by B. De Saint-Pierre; How malicious Gilliatt fought the tempest by V. Hugo; Gunner's fight with the carronade, by V. Hugo; How Dantès escaped from the château d'If, by A. Dumas; Whale of unknown species, by J. Verne; Atlantis, by J. Verne; Ocean Christ, by A. France; How St Mael voyaged to the island of the penguins, by A. France; Iceland fishermen, by P. Loti; Last voyage of Ulysses, by Dante Alighieri; Legend of St Mark and the fishermen of Venice, by A. Jameson; "Poetic tempest" by F. Petrarca; How Randolfo Ruffolo turned pirate, by G. Boccaccio; How Prince Gerbino fought the gallery of the king of Tunis, by G. Boccaccio; How the Galleon of Venice won glory at the battle of Prevesa, by J. De La Gravière; How Il Solitario escaped from Caprera, by G. Garibaldi; Ugly weather, by G. Verga; End, by G. Milanesi; How Don Pero Niño captured the Moorish galley—and how the sea fought for the English, by G. Diaz de Gomez; First voyage taken by the Admiral Don Cristobal Colon when he discovered the Indies, by C. Columbus; How Vasco Nuñez de Balboa discovered the Pacific, from Pinkerton's voyages; How Fernan de Magalhaes sailed into the southern sea—and the manner of his death, by A. Pigafetta; Battle of Lepanto, by W. H. Prescott; Captive's escape, by M. de Cervantes Saavedra; Beautiful Morisca, by M. de Cervantes Saavedra; Invincible armada, by J. A. Froude; Return, by J. A. Froude; Return of the fishing boats, by J. M. De Pereda; Trafalgar, by B. N. Perez Galdos; Fishermen of Rodillero, by A. Palacio Valdes; Triton, by V. Blasco Ibañez; Mare nostrum, by V. Blasco Ibañez; How the page of Prince Henry the Navigator brought home the ship, by G. Eannes de Zurara; Story of Gaspar and Miguel Corte Real, by D. de Goes. How Ferdinand Mendez Pinto sought fortune on the sea, and of some mischances that befell him there, by F. M. Pinto; How Vasco da Gama came to the land of Calicut, by L. De Camoës; How the São Thomé was wrecked off the Terra Dos Fumos, by D. Do Couto; How Alfonso Dalboquerque came to the end of his voyage, by B. Dalboquerque; Sea, by A. Karkavitsas; Beggars of Zealand, by C. De Coster; Flying Dutchman, by A. Jal; How William the Silent opened the gates of the sea, by J. L. Motley; Man who first rounded the Horn, by J. Callander; Dutch story of the four days' battle, from the life of Cornelius Van Tromp; Whaling voyage into Spitzbergen, by F. Martens; Baron Munchausen tells of pranks of a whale and of what happened on a voyage to the Indies, by R. E. Raspe; Rider on the white horse, by T. Storm; How the Black Galley took the Andrea Doria, by W. Raabe; How the sea saved Leyden, by G. Ebers; Of the company of the privateers, by J. G. Lockhart; Lighthouse keeper of Aspinwall, by H. Sienkiewicz; How Väinämöinen was born of the Mother of the sea, from the Kalevala; Smuggler, by A. Kallas; Onund Treefoot, from the saga of Grettir the Strong; How Ellidi the dragon-ship, at the command of Frithiof the bold, drove down upon the witches, from the saga of Frithiof the Bold; How Earl Eric Hakonson captured the Long Serpent, by S. Sturlason; How the Norsemen discovered America, by S. Sturlason; Cormorants of Andvaer, by J. Lie; Jack of Sjoholm and the Gan-Finn, by J. Lie; How Dammitall-with-the-limp saved the crew of the Seal, by J. Bojer; Outcast, by S. Lagerlöf; Ship, by V. von Heidenstam; Among the Swedish skerries, by V. von Heidenstam; How Leif son of Rodmar fought the sons of Atle, by G. Gunnarsson; Little mermaid, by H. C. Andersen; Cruise of the Wild Duck, by H. Drachmann; How the empress Jingo sailed unto the land called Chosen, from The Nihongi; How Hiko-hoho-demi-no Mikoto married the seaking's daughter from the Nihongi

Torday, Ursula. See Blackstock, Charity

Torres-Rioseco, Arturo

(ed.) Short stories of Latin America. Translators: Zoila Nelken [and] Rosalie Torres-Rioseco. Las Americas Pub. 1963 203p $2.50

Analyzed in Short Story Index
Contents: Tobias, by F. B. Rodriguez; That night, by L. N. Calvo: Justice, by H. Quiroga; The Last Supper, by F. Ayala; Biguu, by A. Henestrosa: The Zapotec Prometheus, by A. Henestrosa: The tree, by M. L. Bombal; Return to the seed, by A. Carpentier; The stone and the cross, by C. Alegria; The glass of milk, by M. Rojas; The moribund, by G. Dueñas; Alda or music discovered, by A. Yánez; Grubs, by A. P. Diez-Canseco; The funeral, by J. Marin; The Aleph, by J. L. Borges

Tournier, Michel

Friday; tr. by Norman Denny. Doubleday 1969 235p $4.95

Original French edition 1967
"A sly new twist on the legend of Robinson Crusoe, in which the hard-working Robinson almost succeeds in turning his tropical paradise into a 'tight little island,' until the appearance of Friday—irrepressible, 'noble savage,' who turns Robinson's neat Establishment inside out. This . . . entertaining [book] won the 1967 novel prize from the Academie Francaise." Am News of Bks
"A story of much more depth and sophistication than the original. Tournier's retelling is a satire on Western man's Puritanism and compulsion to organization and conquest." Booklist

Tracy, Don

(jt. auth.) Street, J. Pride of possession

Tracy, Honor

The first day of Friday; a novel. Random House 1963 246p $6.95

A humorous novel set in Ireland about a handsome young landowner and the trials and tribulations he faces in trying to manage his run-down estate. He is aided in his attempts by his slightly demented mother whose interests are burglars and television, his beautiful fiancée, the tormented parish priest, and an unusual servant girl. (Publisher)
The author "is very funny, but her fun is not a cozy fun. The comedy is the comedy of exacerbation and verges on the comedy of despair. One is never grateful for what one receives; and of this novel I felt, as I have of her earlier ones, that it ought to be better than it is. Miss Tracy has great gifts. She never stops being witty. . . . 'The First Day of Friday' is not so much a sustained whole as a novel of superb incidents." N Y Times Bk R

Settled in chambers; a novel. Random House [1968 c1967] 209p boards $6.95

Sir Toby Routh is a "High Court judge specializing in divorce. . . . Lady Routh is given to mild bouts with the bottle; their daughter has left home. Rectitude . . . has nagged his wife to drink, his daughter to illicit union with a coal miner's son. . . . [When he meets] Gerda, Baroness Trauenegg [an opera singer], . . . Sir Toby loses first his head, then his rectitude, and, for a time, even his sense of judgment." Christian Science Monitor
"Miss Tracy's people are all Platonic ideals of satiric subjects, and we miserable sinners can hope to achieve no more than dim approximations of their asininity, their malice and their folly. Her plot is a modest, efficient thing. . . . [Miss Tracy] manages to make the affair seem thoroughly plausible, so that the book takes off from farce into the blissful sphere of high comedy." Book World

The straight and narrow path. Random House 1956 245p o.p. 1970

"About the humorous confusion that results when a parish priest, an English scholar, two solicitors and a lord, all residents of a small Irish village, follow their separate versions of 'the straight and narrow path between right and wrong.' " Pub W

"Honor Tracy, for her first novel published in the U.S., has written the farce of the year. But Catholic readers, especially those of Irish descent, are warned that they will probably find it also highly scandalous." Time

Traven, B.

The cotton-pickers. Hill & Wang 1969 200p $5

Original German edition 1926; this translation published 1956 in England
"This novel follows the career of Gerard Gales, an itinerant worker in post-World War I Mexico. Gales works as a cotton picker, a baker's assistant, a carpenter, and finally drives a herd of cattle across 350 miles of tropical terrain." Library J
"Traven wrote [this] to expose the inhumanity of management, the injustice forced upon the Indian, the greed, paranoia and soul-suicide that money demands of men. . . . But he had not yet found a voice that would rouse a corresponding rage in the reader." Sat R

The death ship; the story of an American sailor. Knopf 1934 372p o.p. 1970

Original German edition 1926
"The narrator, a New Orleans sailor, begins his story in Antwerp where he was stranded without money, friends, or identification papers when his ship left port without him. The first third of the book tells the experiences of this man without country or identity, as he was shunted over Europe from one nation to another. Finally, he gets a ship—the Yorikke, which had been sent away by the owners to be sunk for its insurance. His experiences in the stokehold of this dreadful death ship make up the rest of the story." Book Rev Digest

The night visitor, and other stories; introduction by Charles Miller. Hill & Wang 1966 238p o.p. 1970

Analyzed in Short Story Index
This collection of ten "short stories mix humor with warm affection for the Mexican people." Chicago
Contents: The night visitor: Effective medicine; Assembly line; The cattle drive; When the priest is not at home; Midnight call; A new god was born; Friendship; Conversion of some Indians; Macario

The treasure of the Sierra Madre

Some editions are:
Hill & Wang $6.50
Modern Lib. $2.95

First published 1935
"Story of three American derelicts and their search for a lost gold mine in the Mexican wilderness." Book Rev Digest
The author "writes a good yarn; his talk and descriptions of behavior are not only convincing but illuminating . . . and his story is guided by an underlying theme and a slant on social behavior which if not original and at times exaggerated is sound in essence." N Y Times Bk R

Traver, Robert

Anatomy of a murder. St Martins 1958 437p boards $5.95

"Not the usual murder mystery but a review by the lawyer for the defense from the time he takes the case of an army lieutenant who admits to having killed the man who raped his wife, until the end of the trial. Much attention is given to establishing the fact of rape. Although the recital is wordy it maintains suspense in showing the legal and personal resources the lawyer calls on to build his defense and the way that rivalry between prosecution and defense shapes the trial." Booklist

Treat, Lawrence

(ed.) Mystery Writers of America. Murder in mind

Treece, Henry

The dark island; a novel. Random House 1953 [c1952] 312p map o.p. 1970

Sequel to: The golden strangers
First published 1952 in England

Treece, Henry—*Continued*

"Led by their brash young king, Caradoc, one of the several semibarbaric Celtic tribes of Britain attempted to repel the Roman invasion in the first century A.D.; Caradoc was captured and taken to Rome, and the conquerors set about Romanizing the tribesmen. This fictionized version of these events follows Caradoc, his bosom friend Gwyndoc, and the sycophantic brothers Morag and Beddyr from boyhood through the diastrous battle, then leaves Caradoc to history while it focuses on life in post-conquest Britain, particularly that part of it to be observed in Gwyndoc's shifting fortunes." Booklist
Followed by: Red queen, white queen

The golden strangers. Random House 1957 [c1956] 244p o.p. 1970

First published 1956 in England
"A novel of ancient Britain and the primitive inhabitants who fall to the might of the blond invaders who come across the northern sea to conquer and build Stonehenge." Ontario Lib Rev
Followed by: The dark island

Red queen, white queen. Random House 1958 243p o.p. 1970

Sequel to: The dark island
"The Roman occupation of Britain in the time of Nero provides the theme of this historical novel in which Queen Boadicea led Celtic England against the invaders." Chicago

Trevor, Elleston

The flight of the Phoenix. Harper 1964 242p $6.95

A "story of survival in a desert. Fourteen men in a plane from an oil town crashland in the Sahara, position unknown, radio out, almost no food, a meager supply of water. The clash of personalities, the increasing desperation of the situation, the triumph of brains and ingenuity that gives them a chance for survival make [up the story]." Pub W

"Some readers may feel there is rather too much aeronautical detail, but that makes us certain the story is authentic; some may find that the inevitable insistence on thirst becomes monotonous, but all survival has a special problem. The overall impression is vividly real, and, with all their unusual problems and conflicts, the characters are sympathetic. Recommended to those who like tales of danger and heroism in unknown lands." Book of the Month Club News

Gale force. Macmillan (N Y) 1957 [c1956] 246p o.p. 1970

First published 1956 in England
"The saga of a small British cargo vessel carrying grain and ten passengers from South America to England. When two hundred miles off Cornwall they are overtaken by a tremendous gale. The cargo shifts and the winds smash a hatch, so that the grain begins to swell. The great battle between a ship and the sea follows." Book Rev Digest

The killing-ground. Macmillan (N Y) 1957 [c1956] 266p o.p. 1970

This novel "traces the fortunes of a handful of tank men from D-Day to the fall of Falaise. The author covers not only the outward aspects of battle, but conveys its inward significance for the human beings engulfed in that battle." McClurg. Book News

The shoot; a novel. Doubleday 1966 234p o.p. 1970

"Around a British 'shoot' of a peaceful scientific missile from a Pacific island, Elleston Trevor has written a tense story of rocketry and of personalities, there is the head man, Dr. Chapel, a crack scientist and a fanatical pacifist; his lovely and sexually frustrated wife, Eve; Colonel Pyne, Army officer stationed on the island with an Army unit for a mysterious and dark purpose; and Security Officer Hurst, a snooper who is hated to the verge of murder. The troubles with the rocket, and the countdowns, are made enormously exciting, and Trevor's characters, worn and worried as the waiting goes by, play out a nerve-wracking human drama tied in with the 'shoot.' " Pub W

For other titles by this author see Hall, Adam

Trollope, Anthony

The American senator. Oxford 557p (The World's classics) $2.25

First published 1877
"A little-known but excellent story, with a more or less misleading title." Prolegomenon
Senator Elias Gotobed "represents the great Western State of Mickewa, and through him the author pokes good-natured fun both at the drabness of American culture, and at certain established English institutions, such as the purchase of livings, and the appointment thereto of younger sons of the nobility." Introduction

Barchester Towers

Some editions are:
Collins $1.95
Dutton (Everyman's lib) $3.25
Harcourt (The Harcourt Lib. of English and American classics) $3.95
Oxford (The World's classics) $1.75

Sequel to: The warden
First published 1857. Second of the Chronicles of Barsetshire
"Continues the picture of clerical society with its peculiar humors and foibles. The chief incidents are connected with the appointment of a new bishop, the troubles and disappointments this involves, and the intrigues and jealousies of the clergy: the henpecked bishop, the ambitious archdeacon, and the dean, canons, and others, with their wives. The picture of the eccentric Stanhope family is particularly delicious." Lenrow. Reader's Guide to Prose Fiction

Doctor Thorne

Some editions are:
Dutton (Everyman's lib) $3.25
Harcourt (The Harcourt Lib. of English and American classics) $3.95
Oxford (The World's classics) $2.25

First published 1858. Third of the Chronicles of Barsetshire
"A story of quiet country life; and the interest of the book lies in the character studies rather than in the plot. The scene is laid in the west of England about 1854. The heroine, Mary Thorne, is a sweet, modest girl, living with her kind uncle Doctor Thorne, in the village of Greshambury, where Frank Gresham, the young heir of Greshambury Park falls in love with her." Keller's Reader's Digest of Books

The Eustace diamonds. Oxford 726p (The World's classics) $2.50

First published 1872
"The story of the beautiful, mendacious Lady Elizabeth Eustace who tries to keep a valuable diamond necklace she had from her husband before he died. Since it is a family heirloom, the Eustace family tries to retrieve it. Lady Elizabeth fails in her attempt to keep it, is humiliated, and marries the dubious Mr. Emilius, an apparent bigamist." Benét. The Reader's Encyclopedia

Framley parsonage

Some editions are:
Dutton (Everyman's lib) $3.25
Harcourt (The Harcourt Lib. of English and American classics) $3.95
Oxford (The World's classics) $1.75

First published 1861. Fourth of the Chronicles of Barsetshire
"The vicar of Framley, a weak but honest young man, is led astray and into debt by a spendthrift M. P., and finds himself in a false position. The other branch of the story deals with his sister's chequered love affair and marriage to young Lord Lufton. A great crowd of characters are engaged in the social functions, the intrigues and the match making, the general effect of which is comic, though graver interest is never far off, and there are situations of deepest pathos." Baker's Best

Trollope, Anthony—*Continued*

The last chronicle of Barset

Some editions are:
Dutton (Everyman's lib) 2v ea $3.25
Harcourt (The Harcourt Lib. of English and American classics) $3.95
Oxford (The World's classics) $2.50

First published 1867. Sixth in the Chronicles of Barsetshire
"The ecclesiastical society of 'The Warden,' Mr Harding, Mrs Proudie, and the rest, make their last appearance. The dominant situation is one of intense anguish. A poor country clergyman, proud, learned, sternly conscientious is accused of a felony, and the pressure of family want makes his guilt seem only too probable." Baker's Best

Orley Farm. Oxford 1956 2v in 1 (The World's classics) $2.25

First published 1861-1862
"A lengthy chronicle of family life (two country houses supply most of the chief personages) events revolving round one figure, Lady Mason, a mixed character of guilt and innocence, weakness and strength, who forges a codicil in favour of her son and keeps the secret for twenty years. A chivalrous old baronet, his high-minded daughter-in-law, and a dry old lawyer, are all under the spell of Lady Mason's personality, and the drama of guilt and shame has a pathetic bearing on many lives. The legal case is complex and difficult." Baker's Best

The prime minister. Oxford 1951 2v in 1 (The World's classics) $3

First published 1876
"Chiefly devoted to the unhappy marriage of Emily Wharton and Ferdinand Lopez, a Portuguese adventurer, and to the affairs of the prime minister and his wife. The latter couple are known to readers of Trollope's earlier novels as Planty Paul and Lady Glencora, now Duke and Duchess of Omnium. The Duke is sensitive, proud, and shy, and feels the burden of his responsibility, while his wife is forever working for his advancement. He goes gladly out of office at last." Keller's Reader's Digest of Books

The small house at Allington

Some editions are:
Dutton (Everyman's lib) $3.25
Harcourt (The Harcourt Lib. of English and American classics) $3.95
Oxford (The World's classics) $2.25

First published 1864. Fifth in the "Chronicles of Barsetshire"
"Country life, its quiet, its pleasures and troubles, monotony and dullness, with digressions into boarding-house life in London and into high society. Many old friends appear in the usual concourse of characters, among whom stand out Mr Crosbie, a snobbish and cowardly trifler. . . . Lily Dale, the jilted maiden, amiable and weak Johnny Eames, and the aristocratic doll, Lady Dumbello; all closely copied from life." Bakers Best

The warden

Some editions are:
Collins $1.95
Dutton (Everyman's lib) $3.25
Oxford (The World's classics) $1.50

First published 1855. First of the Chronicles of Barsetshire
"The Warden, Mr. Harding, a gentle and innocent old cleric, living a quiet and contented life, is suddenly assailed by the newspapers for receiving the profits of a rich sinecure and, half in fear of the odium this created, half from conscientious scruples, resigns his income and accepts penury. The cathedral city with its ecclesiastical dignitaries was suggested by Salisbury." Baker's Best
Followed by: Barchester Towers

The way we live now. Oxford 2v in 1 (The World's classics) $2.50

First published 1875
"A study of aristocracy versus trade in the 1870's." Book Rev Digest
"Portrays many phases of English life, high society, country life, the genteel and the humble, journalists, commercial men and the world in general, with a keen eye for weak and flagitious motive. An exposure of the marriage market and the brutal indelicacy of the haggling between such people as the ruined family of patricians and the rascally millionaire, who is prepared to subsidize them with his daughter and his thousands. Even the honest young man is not altogether attractive." Baker's Best

Troy, Katherine

Roseheath. McKay 1969 252p $4.95
"Inheriting an old English estate, Roseheath, seems to be disastrous for Suzanna Wyncourt, who is confronted by two jealous cousins Oliver and Magda. The story that ensues includes the mysterious murder of Oliver and Suzanna's love for Magda's husband." Bk Buyers Guide

Troyat, Henri

Amelie and Pierre; a novel. Tr. from the French by Mary V. Dodge. Simon & Schuster 1957 338p (The Seed and the fruit v2) o.p. 1970

Sequel to: Amelie in love
Original French edition published 1955
"When Pierre is drafted into the army in 1914 Amelie efficiently manages their café in a working-class section of Paris and develops a business confidence that enables her to contract for a larger café even though Pierre's war injuries have left him apathetic as well as partially disabled. The somewhat prosaic events are made interesting by the very lifelike characterization of Amelie herself, her brother and father, and the people who frequent the café." Booklist
Followed by: Elizabeth

Amelie in love; a novel. Tr. from the French by Lily Duplaix. Simon & Schuster 1956 370p (The Seed and the fruit v 1) o.p. 1970

Original French edition published 1953
"The first of a series of novels dealing with the lives of a lower middle class French family during the first half of the present century. The present story covers roughly the years 1912 to 1915. During that time seventeen-year old Amelie breaks her engagement to one man and marries another. The book ends with the birth of their first child." Book Rev Digest
Followed by: Amelie and Pierre

The baroness; tr. from the French by Frances Frenaye. Simon & Schuster 1961 [c1960] 284p (The Light of the just v2) boards $4.50

Sequel to: The Brotherhood of the Red Poppy
Original French edition published 1960
"The present volume continues the story of the Russian officer, Nikolai Ozarev, and his French wife, Sophie. . . . Shortly after the death of their infant son in St. Petersburg, Nikolai and Sophie take up residence in his father's country house, Nikolai's father, an elderly but still vigorous baron, falls desperately in love with Sophie, while Nikolai gets involved in the activities of a secret political society and extra-marital love affairs. Sophie, on her part, remains loyal to her husband. Compassionate and just, she tries to improve the condition of her father-in-law's serfs. The action occurs between 1819 and 1825 up to Czar Alexander I's death." Booklist

The Brotherhood of the Red Poppy; tr. from the French by Elisabeth Abbott. Simon & Schuster 1961 281p (The Light of the just v 1) o.p. 1970

Original French edition 1959
This novel "tells the romantic story of Nikolai Mikhailovitch Ozeroff, lieutenant in the army of Czar Alexander, and Sophie de Champlitte, the young French widow he marries. The time covered is two years, 1814 and 1815. . . . [Sophie is] involved in politics, a member of an underground organization called, 'The Brotherhood of the Red Poppy,' whose slogan is 'Neither Napoleon, nor Bourbon, but the Republic!' " N Y Her Trib Books
Followed by: The baroness

Troyat, Henri—*Continued*

Elizabeth; a novel. Tr. from the French by Nicolas Monjo. Simon & Schuster 1959 407p (The Seed and the fruit v3) o.p. 1970

Sequel to: Amelie and Pierre

Original French edition published 1956
The "heroine of this novel is Elizabeth, Amelie's daughter, ten years old when the story opens. It takes her from boarding school to adolescence." Bk Buyer's Guide
"An everyday story about everyday preadolescence with the usual share of the unusual (has any other French girl ever attended a boys' school?). Good straightforward narrative told with humor and a solid understanding of people." Library J
Followed by: Tender and violent Elizabeth

The encounter; a novel. Tr. from the French by Gerard Hopkins. Simon & Schuster 1962 411p (The Seed and the fruit v5) o.p. 1970

Original French edition published 1958
This final volume of the chronicles portraying the past fifty years of French life finds Elizabeth "living alone in occupied Paris during the Hitler war, the proprietress of a small record shop. Here she meets, weds, and finds happiness with Boris, whose wife and child have been killed during a bombing. The story, ending with the liberation of France, reads smoothly but places more emphasis on romance than do Troyat's previous novels. It offers a good view of daily life in Paris during the occupation." Booklist

An extreme friendship; tr. by Eugene Paul. Phaedra Pubs. 1968 155p boards $4.95

Original French edition published 1963
"After 15 years of marriage Jean and Madeleine are happily taking a vacation at a French seashore when an old friend of Jean's, a worldly charmer who was most important in Jean's life before his marriage, intrudes in their idyllic situation." Booklist
This "book is never sentimental, and it is often funny in its dissection of human foibles. It is a book about 'ordinary' people, but an extraordinary one, and its savor lingers." Book of the Month Club News

The mountain; a novel. Tr. from the French by Constantine Fitz Gibbon. Simon & Schuster 1953 122p o.p. 1970

Original French edition published 1952
"Two brothers, Swiss mountaineers, set out to reach an airplane from Calcutta which has crashed on a nearby peak. One of them is driven by greed for gold which may be on the plane, the other, a retired guide, goes along to protect him in the dangerous ascent. When they reach the plane and find a seriously injured Indian woman in the wreckage the conflict between good and evil in their natures comes out into the open." Pub W

My father's house; a novel. Tr. from the French by David Hapgood. Duell 1951 692p (While the earth endures) o.p. 1970

Original French edition published 1947
"Russia from 1888 to 1914 and the author's own boyhood and family life provide the background for an epic novel of Michael Danov and his wife Tania, whom Michael has met through his dashing cousin, Volodia. In the end he loses her to Volodia and enlists for World War I. In the meantime there have been abortive plots against the Czar, the Russo-Japanese War, Polish pogroms, the cholera riots, etc." Retail Bookseller
"It is a simple straightforward tale that will enlighten the reader about events in Russia, and although the scene is large the family is small so the book is not crowded with people." Library J
Followed by: The red and the white

The red and the white; tr. from the French by Anthony Hinton. Crowell 1956 463p o.p. 1970

Sequel to: My father's house
Original French edition published 1948. This translation published in England with title: Sackcloth and ashes

The Russian Revolution furnishes the background for this novel about the death of an empire and the birth of Soviet Russia. Chief protagonists among the large cast of characters are Kisiakov, a Russian Mephistopheles; Volodia, a self-loving, self-pitying man; Liubov, an actress; Maria Ossipovna Danov, a proud white Russian dowager; and, Michael and Tania Danov, to whom the Revolution brought great suffering but a new maturity. (Publisher)
Followed by: Strangers on earth

Strangers on earth; tr. from the French by Anthony Hinton. Crowell 1958 328p o.p. 1970

Sequel to: The red and the white
Original French edition published 1950. This translation published in England with title: Strangers in the land
"Continues the story of the Michael Danov family . . . after they become exiles in Paris in the 1920's and 1930's. The proud Danovs are reluctantly reconciled to their new circumstances and the old grandmother believes until the day of her death that she is still in Moscow. In rebelling against family domination Serge, the older son, is led astray by a depraved woman to whom he has been introduced by the villainous Kisiakov; Boris, the younger, however, adjusts to French school and social life and eventually becomes a French citizen. There is more sympathy here for the characters as individuals than in the earlier book but less feeling of people caught up in events of the time." Booklist

Tender and violent Elizabeth; tr. from the French by Mildred Marmur. Simon & Schuster 1960 311p (The Seed and the fruit v4) o.p. 1970

Sequel to: Elizabeth
Original French edition published 1957
"Elizabeth was nineteen when she fell in love with a young man with lots of women and no intention of marrying any of them. So Elizabeth married a kind and gentle composer out of pique—and found she could not stay away from her lover." Bk Buyer's Guide

Tucker, Helen

The sound of summer voices. Stein & Day 1969 256p $5.95

SBN 8128-1258-1
"Patrick is a bright, likable, believable 10-year-old who decides one summer that his family has lied to him about his parentage, and then determines to find out the truth. He lives with relatives in a small southern town. His mother was supposedly the third sister, who ran away and got married. Patrick suspects that she never existed, however, and that one of his aunts is his real mother." Pub W
"Patrick is a sturdy character, but it is in the family conflict that the strength of the book lies. The writing is flowing and intimate." Sat R

Turgenev, Ivan

The Borzoi Turgenev; tr. from the Russian by Harry Stevens. Foreword by Serge Koussevitzky, introduction by Avrahm Yarmolinsky. Knopf 1950 xxiv, 801p o.p. 1970

An omnibus volume containing five novelettes and the following short stories: A quiet spot and The diary of a superfluous man
Novelettes included are: Smoke; Fathers and sons; First love; On the eve; Rudin

The district doctor, and other stories; illus. by Marvin Bileck. Story Classics 1951 206p illus o.p. 1970

Contents: The district doctor; Yermolai and the miller's wife; A strange story; Foma, the wolf; The counting-house; A living relic; A desperate character; Pyetushkov

Fathers and sons

Some editions are:
Dutton (Everyman's lib) $3.25 Translated by Avril Pyman; introduction by Nikolay Andreyev. Has title: Fathers and children
Modern Lib. $2.95 Newly translated from Russian by Bernard Guilbert Guerney. With the author's comments on his book and a foreword by the translator

Turgenev, Ivan—*Continued*

Norton (A Norton Critical ed) lib. bdg. $4.07
The author on the novel, contemporary reactions, essays in criticism. Edited, with a substantially new translation, by Ralph W. Matlaw

First published 1861
The book "is a description of the tendencies of Young Russia in the sixties, expressed through the hero Bazarov. These tendencies have since become widely known by the name of nihilism." Introduction
"The theme of this novel is the frequent conflict between the older and the younger generation, which the author has rendered particularly touching by his representation of 'the confused efforts of the father to understand his son's new ideas, and the young man's vain efforts to convert his father.'" Pratt Alcove

also in Turgenev, I. The Borzoi Turgenev p165-352

First love
In Turgenev, I. The Borzoi Turgenev p353-412
In Turgenev, I. A nest of gentlefolk, and other stories

The inn
In Turgenev, I. Three novellas: Punin and Baburin, The inn, The watch p87-148

Liza; tr. from the Russian by W. R. S. Ralston. Dutton 1914 231p (Everyman's lib) $3.25

Original Russian edition 1859. Also published with titles: A house of gentlefolk and A nest of gentlefolk, both o.p. 1970
This novel "tells the story of the tragic love affair between the hero Feodor Ivanovich Lavretzki and Liza Kalitina. Lavretzki is about to marry Liza when his first wife, whom he has believed dead, returns to him. Liza goes in to a convent, and Lavretzki is left to his bleak duty. The novel, which poetically evokes the peaceful atmosphere of the provincial Russian feudal estate, had a great success on its publication." Benét. The Reader's Encyclopedia

A nest of gentlefolk, and other stories; tr. from the Russian with an introduction by Jessie Coulson. Oxford 1959 461p o.p. 1970

Analyzed in Short Story Index
Contents: A nest of gentlefolk; A quiet backwater; First love [novelette]; A Lear of the steppes

On the eve
In Turgenev, I. The Borzoi Turgenev p413-558

Punin and Baburin
In Turgenev, I. Three novellas: Punin and Baburin, The inn, The watch p14-85

Rudin
In Turgenev, I. The Borzoi Turgenev p559-680

Smoke. Dutton 1949 242p (Everyman's lib) $2.95

First published 1867
"The unscrupulous heroine, Irene, cannot resist the temptation of reviving the smoldering fires in the heart of Litvinov, a former lover, whom she has refused and now sees betrothed to another. She succeeds in ruining his life, but wilfully draws back at the last minute from the very plan she has urged." Benét. The Reader's Encyclopedia

also in Turgenev, I. The Borzoi Turgenev p3-164

Three novellas: Punin and Baburin, The inn, The watch. Farrar, Straus [1969 c1968] 208p $5.95

This edition first published 1968 in England with title: Youth and age
Translated by Marion Mainwaring

"Three lesser known works by Turgenev, the 19th-century Russian novelist famous for his historically accurate portrayals of Russian aristocratic life. The three novellas chosen for translation here are representative of Turgenev's interest in the outcasts from that life. They show Turgenev's unerring sense of literary style." Choice

The torrents of spring. Farrar, Straus [1960 c1959] 188p o.p. 1970

First published 1871; translated from the Russian by David Magarshack
A translation of the popular Russian classic that is one of the greatest love stories. Sanin, a young Russian nobleman stopping off in Frankfort on his way home from Italy, meets and falls in love with a pure sweet young girl, Gemma. He plans to sell his estate in Russia to raise funds for their marriage. This plan involve him with the wife of a Russian friend, a wealthy, beautiful and sensuous woman. He forsakes the young girl for the older woman. In middle age, weary and bitter, he attempts to find Gemma. When he learns she married a merchant and is living in New York, he writes her. She replies, telling him of her happy marriage. Some of the events are based on similar circumstances in Turgenev's own life. In some scenes the author satirizes German mores, but the story is not complicated by social or political problems

Virgin soil; tr. from the Russian by R. S. Townsend. Dutton 1911 317p (Everyman's lib) $2.95

Original Russian edition published 1876
"A reply to 'The possessed' of Dostoevsky, which was itself called out by the Nihilist doctrines [of Turgenev] in 'Fathers and Children.' Both Turgenev and Dostoevsky deal with the same theme: the subterranean world of political agitation and conspiracy then threatening the peace of Russia. Like 'Smoke' (which also was written in exile from Russia), this is bitter in feeling and deeply pessimistic. The fainthearted Neshdanov, despairing of the cause of socialism, in which he and the girl he loves are workers, takes his own life. The official classes are painted in dark colours." Baker's Best

The watch
In Turgenev, I. Three novellas: Punin and Baburin, The inn, The watch p149-208

Turnbull, Agnes Sligh

y The Bishop's mantle. Macmillan (N Y) 1947 359p $6

"There is drama, humor, pathos, adventure in the daily round of Hilary Evans, young Episcopal rector and grandson of a bishop as he tries to live his faith, his idealism, and his enthusiasm for his chosen profession." Cleveland
"Arguments on topics ranging from the tenement situation of the city to the subject-matter of the Sunday sermon take up a goodly portion of the novel and give it a flavor of concrete reality that is so often missing from stories of professions. A flock of wonderful minor characters round out the pattern nicely." N Y Times Bk R

y The day must dawn. Macmillan (N Y) 1942 483p $6.95

A story of the pioneer experiences of a Scotch-Irish family in the back country of western Pennsylvania, against the background of the Revolutionary War
"Rich in color, written in a flexible style which shifts easily from such pure poetry as the race over the snow to the hard-bitten talk of the men at the tavern. More important still, the book is deeply American, both in matter and in spirit." N Y Times Bk R

The golden journey. Houghton 1955 303p o.p. 1970

"Anne Kirkland had been paralyzed; her father, who loved her, offered to make Paul Devereux a political power if he would marry Anne—and as soon as Paul saw the crippled girl he loved her." Retail Bookseller

Turnbull, Agnes S.—*Continued*

The gown of glory. Houghton 1952 403p $5.95

"A wholesome and sentimental story of a minister and his family in a small Pennsylvania town in the early part of this century. Though constantly hoping for larger opportunities, David Lyall and his wife, Mary, have created an enviable home and community life and their final happiness and fulfilment in these surroundings leaves the reader with a feeling of warm pleasure and a deep sense of peace" Ontario Lib Rev

The king's orchard. Houghton 1963 467p $6.95

"The fictionized life of James O'Hara, Irish born and French educated, who emigrated to America before the revolution, and, drawn to the frontier, settled at Fort Pitt, He served as an officer during the American Revolution, acted as an Indian agent, and as quartermaster general of the U.S., and made a fortune in land and industry. His courtship of and marriage to Mary Carson provide the romantic element in this wholesome historical novel." Booklist

y The rolling years. Macmillan (N Y) 1936 436p $5.95

"A chronicle of three generations of an American family living in a Scottish [Presbyterian] community in western Pennsylvania. The principal characters are Jeannie, born in 1852 and her daughter Connie. The time covered is from 1870-1910." Book Rev Digest
"Well told and interesting, and written with a sense of passing time and changing conditions. This is particularly noticeable with reference to the position of women and to religious observances." Cur Ref Bks

The wedding bargain. Houghton 1966 290p $4.95

"A gentle, old-fashioned story of a marriage of convenience between a coal-mining magnate and his secretary. Even the injection of a murder case (a murder of which the husband is unjustly accused) does not change the mood and atmosphere of this highly romantic tale. It is theoretically set in the 1930's but seems to belong to a much earlier period." Pub W

Turner, James

(ed.) Unlikely ghosts. Taplinger 1969 218p $4.95

SBN 8008-7940-6

"This collection of 12 ghost stories is built on the theme of humor, some of it black. The deadly dozen are of considerable high level." Pub W
Contents: The visitation of Aunt Clara, by K. Barlay; Everything a man needs, by R. Blythe; The eternal amateur, by D. G. Compton; Diary of a poltergeist, by R. Duncan; Salpingogram, by J. Hamilton-Paterson; The foot, by C. Brooke-Rose; My man Closters, by A. Rye; A tale in a club, by W. K. Seymour; Are you there, by J. Stubbs; The bridge, by P. Tabori; The ghostess with the mostest, by F. Urguhart; Shepard, show me, by R. Wade

Turton, Godfrey

My Lord of Canterbury. Doubleday 1967 316p o.p. 1970

"Thomas Cranmer, Archbishop of Canterbury, finishes his own story of his life and his beliefs as he waits for the morning on which he is to be burned alive as a heretic. He tells of his annulment of Henry VIII's marriage, of his support of the Reformed Religion in England, and at last of his misfortunes with the accession of Mary and the renewed power of Papacy." Bk Buyer's Guide
"The novel hardly dares to move away from the historical record, to develop the ironies latent in the contrast between Cranmer's express statements and his actions, or to venture upon any great scenes. . . . The book's most interesting moments come when it suggests that some of Anne Boleyn's curious behavior at the time of her death was the result of her belief in witchcraft." N Y Times Bk R

Tute, Warren

A matter of diplomacy. Coward-McCann [1970 c1969] 184p $4.95

First published 1969 in England
"Elissa Tarnham, whose husband had left his diplomatic post in Athens to go behind the Iron Curtain, arrives in Greece to stay at the home of a jet-set shipping magnate with her two children. Rupert, her husband's superior, immediately begins to pay her lots of attention, even though Tarnham's defection has wrecked Rupert's diplomatic career. Elissa finds something mysterious about it all." Bk Buyer's Guide

Twain, Mark

The adventures of Colonel Sellers. . . . Ed. and with an introduction and notes by Charles Neider. Doubleday 1965 xxxv, 244p o.p. 1970

"Being Mark Twain's share of 'The gilded age,' a novel which he wrote with Charles Dudley Warner [and entered separately]. Now published separately for the first time and comprising, in effect, a new work." Title page
"Satire of the Reconstruction Era, that boisterous time when Everyman's motto was 'get-rich-quicker,' and political chicanery ran rampant." Publisher's note
"The portions written by Warner are synopsized where necessary to carry along the narrative of this version of a joint production that was the first attempt at a novel for both authors. . . . Of main interest to students of American literature." Booklist

y The adventures of Huckleberry Finn
Some editions are:
Dodd (Great illustrated classics) $4.50 With sixteen full-page illustrations, descriptive captions and introductory remarks by Stanley T. Williams
Harper $4.50
Macmillan (N Y) $3.95
Watts, F. $4.95 Ultratype edition With a critical and biographical profile of Samuel L. Clemens by James M. Cox
Watts, F. $7.95 Large type edition. A Keith Jennison book
First published 1885, this has become the American classic of boy life; a companion volume to: The adventures of Tom Sawyer
"Famous story of boy life on the Mississippi. 'A combination of romance, realism, and humor, with a power in the delineation of character only attainable by a great genius.'" N Y Pub Lib

also in Twain, M. The complete novels of Mark Twain v 1 p731-969

y The adventures of Tom Sawyer
Some editions are:
Dial Press $7 Has title: Tom Sawyer
Dodd (Great illustrated classics) $4.50 Introduction by Louis Salomon. With 16 full-page illustrations
Harcourt (Harcourt Lib. of English and American classics) $3.95
Harper $4.50
Harper (Harper's Modern classics) $2
Macmillan (N Y) $2.95
Watts, F. $7.95 Large type edition. A Keith Jennison book
First published 1876, and still leads all other books for boys in popularity. "The adventures of Huckleberry Finn" is a companion volume
"Based on reminiscences of author's boyhood in Missouri; very full picture of life in the Southwest. Full of incident and fun." Baker's Best

also in Twain, M. The complete novels of Mark Twain v 1 p385-556

y Adventures of Tom Sawyer and Huckleberry Finn. Modern Lib. (Modern Lib. giants) $4.95

A combined edition of the titles listed separately

The American claimant
In Twain, M. The complete novels of Mark Twain v2 p263-416

Twain, Mark—*Continued*

American claimant, and other stories and sketches. Harper 397p front o.p. 1970

Analyzed in Short Story Index
First published 1892
Contents: American claimant; Private history of a campaign that failed; Luck; Curious experience; Mrs McWilliams and the lightning; Meisterschaft: in three acts; Playing courier

The complete novels of Mark Twain. Ed. with an introduction by Charles Neider. Doubleday 1964 2v (xxxiv, 1048p) o.p. 1970

Contents: v 1: The gilded age (1873); The adventures of Tom Sawyer (1876); The prince and the pauper (1881); Adventures of Huckleberry Finn (1884)
v2: A Connecticut Yankee in King Arthur's court (1889); The American claimant (1892); Tom Sawyer abroad (1894); Pudd'nhead Wilson (1894); Those extraordinary twins (1894); Personal recollections of Joan of Arc (1896); Tom Sawyer, Detective (1896)

y The complete short stories; now collected for the first time; ed. with an introduction by Charles Neider. Doubleday 1957 676p music $4.95

"Contains a total of sixty stories, thirteen of them gathered from works of non-fiction. They cover the entire span of Twain's writing life, from 1865 to 1916, six years after his death. . . . The stories are arranged chronologically according to the years of first publication, and alphabetically within a given year." Neider
Contents: The notorious jumping frog of Calaveras County; The story of the bad little boy; Cannibalism in the cars; A day at Niagara; Legend of the Capitoline Venus; Journalism in Tennessee; A curious dream; The facts in the great beef contract; How I edited an agricultural paper; A medieval romance; My watch; Political economy; Science vs. Luck; The story of the good little boy; Buck Fanshaw's funeral; The story of the Old Ram; Tom Quartz; A trial; The trials of Simon Erickson; A true story; Experience of the McWilliamses with membranous croup; Some learned fables for good old boys and girls; The canvasser's tale; The loves of Alonzo Fitz Clarence and Rosannah Ethelton; Edward Mills and George Benton: a tale; The man who put up at Gadsby's; Mrs McWilliams and the lightning; What stumped the Bluejays; A curious experience; The invalid's story; The McWilliamses and the burglar alarm; The stolen White Elephant; A burning brand; A dying man's confession; The professor's yarn; A ghost story; Luck; Playing courier; The Californian's tale; The diary of Adam and Eve; The Esquimau maiden's romance; Is he living or is he dead; The £1,000,000 bank-note; Cecil Rhodes and the shark; The joke that made Ed's fortune; A story without an end; The man that corrupted Hadleyburg; The death disk; Two little tales; The belated Russian passport; A double-barreled detective story; The five boons of life; Was it Heaven? or Hell; A dog's tale; The $30,000 bequest; A horse's tale; Hunting the deceitful turkey; Extract from Captain Stormfield's visit to Heaven; A fable; The mysterious stranger

y A Connecticut Yankee in King Arthur's court

Some editions are:
Dodd (Great illustrated classics) $4.50 Introduction by E. Hudson Long. With 16 full-page illustrations about the author and his work
Harcourt $3.95
Harper $4.50
Harper (Harper's Modern classics) $2.40
Heritage $7.50 Introduction by Carl Van Doren; illustrated by Honoré Guilbeau
First published 1889. Published in England with title: Yankee at the court of King Arthur
"Burlesque of the historical romance. A Yankee of the most arrant modern type is plumped down in the middle of King Arthur's England. The serious purpose, which is not obtruded, is to strip off the glamour and tinsel of chivalry . . . and show the evils . . . that actually underlay it." Baker's Best

also in Twain, M. The complete novels of Mark Twain v2 p 1-262

The gilded age [by] Mark Twain and C. D. Warner; ed. by Herbert Van Thal; with an introduction by Richard Church. Cassell [distributed by Dufour] 1967 xx, 427p $3.50

"The First novel library"
First published 1873
"Mark Twain and Dudley Warner were neighbours at Hartford, Conn, when they collaborated in this portrayal of their times; the bitter account of the Easterners is Warner's, the humorist drew the Westerners, scoffed at Washington and Congress, and created the mighty optimist Colonel Sellers." Baker's Best

also in Twain, M. The complete novels of Mark Twain v 1 p 1-383

y The jumping frog, and other stories and sketches; with an illus. from the hand of Donald McKay. Peter Pauper 1949 92p illus o.p. 1970

Contents: The jumping frog of Calaveras County; Journalism in Tennessee; Niagara; The killing of Julius Caesar "localized"; Cannibalism in the cars; Punch Brothers, punch; The invalid's story; How I edited an agricultural paper; Burlesque autobiography

The man that corrupted Hadleyburg
In Blackmur, R. P. ed. American short novels p68-96

The man that corrupted Hadleyburg, and other stories and essays. Harper 1900 364p front o.p. 1970

Partially analyzed in Short Story Index
Contents: The man that corrupted Hadleyburg; My début as a literary person; £1,000,000 bank-note; Esquimau maiden's romance; My first lie, and how I got out of it; Belated Russian passport; Two little tales; About playacting; Diplomatic pay and clothes; Is he living or is he dead; My boyhood dreams; Austrian Edison keeping school again; Death disk; Double-barreled detective story; Petition to the Queen of England

Mysterious stranger, and other stories. Harper 1922 324p illus $5.95

Analyzed in Short Story Index
Contents: Mysterious stranger; Horse's tale; Extract from Captain Stormfield's visit to heaven; Fable; My platonic sweetheart; Hunting the deceitful turkey; McWilliamses and the burglar alarm

y Personal recollections of Joan of Arc, by the Sieur Louis de Conte (her page and secretary) Illus. by G. B. Cutts. Harper 1926 596p illus $6.95

First published 1896
"De Conte, who tells the story in the first person, has been reared in the same village with its subject, has been her daily playmate there, and has followed her fortunes in later life, serving her to the end, his being the friendly hand that she touches last. After her death, he comes to understand her greatness; he calls hers "the most noble life that was ever born into this world save only One.' Begining with a scene in her childhood that shows her innate sense of justice, goodness of heart, and unselfishness, the story follows her throughout her stormy career. We have her audiences with the king; her marches with her army; her entry into Orleans; her fighting; her trial; her execution; all simply and naturally and yet vividly told. The historical facts are closely followed." Keller's Reader's Digest of Books

also in Twain, M. The complete novels of Mark Twain v2 p661-998

The prince and the pauper
In Twain, M. The complete novels of Mark Twain v 1 p559-730

Pudd'nhead Wilson
In Twain, M. The complete novels of Mark Twain v2 p491-608

Twain, Mark—*Continued*

y Pudd'nhead Wilson and Those extraordinary twins. Harper 295p illus o.p. 1970

Title story first published 1894

Pudd'nhead Wilson is "a story of a sober kind, picturing life in a little town of Missouri, half a century ago. . . . The principal incidents relate to a slave of mixed blood and her almost pure white son, whom she substitutes for her master's baby. The slave by birth grows up in wealth and luxury, but turns out a peculiarly mean scoundrel, and, perpetrating a crime, meets with due justice. The science of finger-prints is practically illustrated in detecting the fraud." Baker's Best

"Those extraordinary twins" tells of the problems of Luigi and Angelo, Siamese twins, two heads, four arms but only two legs. One was blond and the other brunette. Luigi liked to smoke a pipe which made Angelo cough, he also liked whiskey while Angelo could not endure intoxicants. When Luigi was trying to have a duel, Angelo became frightened and took their body soaring over the fence

$30,000 bequest, and other stories. Harper 1917 380p illus o.p. 1970

Partially analyzed in Short Story Index

Contents: $30,000 bequest; Dog's tale; Was it Heaven? or Hell; Cure for the blues; Enemy conquered; Californian's tale; Helpless situation; Telephonic conversation; Edward Mills and George Benton: a tale; Five boons of life; First writing-machines; Italian without a master; Italian with grammar; Burlesque biography; How to tell a story; General Washington's Negro body-servant; With inspirations of the "two-year-olds"; Entertaining article; Letter to the secretary of the treasury; Amended obituaries; Monument to Adam; Humane word from Satan; Introduction to "The new guide of the conversation in Portuguese and English"; Advice to little girls; Post-mortem poetry; Danger of lying in bed; Portrait of King William III; Does the race of man love a lord; Extracts from Adam's diary; Eve's diary

Those extraordinary twins
In Twain, M. The complete novels of Mark Twain v2 p609-60
In Twain, M. Pudd'nhead Wilson and Those extraordinary twins p205-95

Tom Sawyer abroad
In Twain, M. The complete novels of Mark Twain v2 p417-90

Tom Sawyer abroad, and other stories. Grosset 1924 217p o.p. 1970

Contents: Tom Sawyer abroad; The great revolution in Pitcairn; The canvasser's tale; An encounter with an interview; Paris notes; Legend of Sagenfeld, in Germany; Speech on the weather; Concerning the American language; Rogers; The loves of Alonzo Fitz Clarence and Rosannah Ethelton

Tom Sawyer, Detective
In Twain, M. The complete novels of Mark Twain v2 p999-1048

Tweedsmuir, Lord. See Buchan, John

U

Uhnak, Dorothy

The witness. Simon & Schuster [1969] 222p $4.95

SBN 671-20192-1

"An Inner samctum mystery"

"A woman detective is called upon to track down the real murderer of a young Negro law student supposedly shot by a cop during a violent civil rights demonstration that triggers a scandal of city-wide scope." Book News

Ullman, James R.

The sands of Karakorum. Lippincott 1953 254p o.p. 1970

"Frank Knight, a newspaper correspondent, sets out to find his old friends John and Eleanor Bickel, American missionaries who have vanished in Red China. The trail leads from Shanghai, through the interior of China and on to Central Asia. It ends in the 'desert of the black sands' at the ruins of Karakorum, the ancient capital of Genghis Khan." McClurg. Book News

The White Tower. Lippincott 1945 479p $6.95

"When Martin Ordway's plane crashed over Switzerland, he came down into a little valley in the Alps which he had known years before the war. Overshadowing the valley is the Weissturm, [White Tower] a high peak never climbed from that side. While he is waiting for an opportunity to get back home Martin succumbs to a long felt desire to try the climb and with five others he makes the attempt. The story combines the account of the adventure of climbing with the meditations and reminiscences of the various members of the group." Book Rev Digest

"'The White Tower' has a love-story in it and contains a lot of philosophizing about modern civilization and it presents a simplified picture of the opposition between the fascist and democratic views of life." Book of the Month Club News

Unamuno y Jugo, Miguel de

The Marquis of Lumbria
In Unamuno y Jugo, M. de. Three exemplary novels and a prologue

Nothing less than a man
In Unamuno y Jugo, M. de. Three exemplary novels and a prologue

Prologue
In Unamuno y Jugo, M. de. Three exemplary novels and a prologue

Three exemplary novels and a prologue. Tr. by Angel Flores. Boni 1930 227p o.p. 1970

Contents: Prologue; The Marquis of Lumbria; Two mothers; Nothing less than a man

Two mothers
In Unamuno y Jugo, M. de. Three exemplary novels and a prologue

Undset, Sigrid

Nobel Prize in literature, 1928

The axe
In Undset, S. The master of Hestviken v1

The bridal wreath
In Undset, S. Kristin Lavransdatter v1

The cross
In Undset, S. Kristin Lavransdatter v3

Four stories; tr. from the Norwegian by Naomi Walford. Knopf 1959 245p $4.95

Analyzed in Short Story Index

Norway, about fifty years ago is the setting for these "long, somber stories about the tragic lives of four who are unloved and no longer young." Chicago

Contents: Selma Brøter; Thjodolf; Miss Smith-Tellefsen; Simonsen

Each of the stories "is a tale of ordinary people at the mercy of one or another kind of frustrated love. Character and setting are skillfully indicated but the stories have a universal pathos which transcends their time and place." Booklist

In the wilderness
In Undset, S. The master of Hestviken v3

Undset, Sigrid—*Continued*

Kristin Lavransdatter; tr. from the Norwegian. Knopf 3v in 1 $7.95

Contains the novels originally published separately as follows: The bridal wreath, 1923; The mistress of Husaby, 1925; The cross, 1927
"From her happy childhood and later romance as wife and mother on a great estate, to her old age and loneliness, Kristin's experiences form one of the most realistic stories of a woman's life ever written. Despite the large number of characters and the complex psychological development of the main figures, the background of medieval Norway is vivid, true and amazingly alive." Enoch Pratt

The master of Hestviken; tr. from the Norwegian by Arthur G. Chater. Knopf 4v in 1 $8.95

Contains four volumes originally published separately as follows: The axe, 1928; The snake pit, 1929; In the wilderness, 1929; and The son avenger, 1930
"A rich picture of Norwegian life in the Middle ages [13th and 14th centuries], and resembles the 'Kristin Lavransdatter' trilogy in that it is concerned with the secret sin of a pair of young lovers, their suffering and final atonement." Cleveland
"No one . . . in the historical novel has given such realness to bygone days and such genius to the evocation of the past." N Y Her Trib Books

The Mistress of Husaby
In Undset, S. Kristin Lavransdatter v2

The snake pit
In Undset, S. The master of Hestviken v2

The son avenger
In Undset, S. The master of Hestviken v4

Updike, John

The centaur. Knopf 1963 302p boards $5.95

A retelling of the myth of Chiron the centaur "who, painfully wounded and yet unable to die, gave up his immortality on behalf of Prometheus. In the retelling, Olympus becomes Olinger High School, Chiron a teacher of general science there, and Prometheus his fifteen-year-old son. . . . The author alternates objective chapters with chapters told in retrospect by Chiron's son, and translates the agonized centaur's search for relief into the incidents and accidents of three winter days spent in Pennsylvania in 1947." Publisher's note
The author "is neither morbid nor sordid. He does not slobber. He is exquisitely sensitive, but his writing has dignity and nobility. It isn't his poetry, although his gift for that is a very great one, which moves you; it is his reticence. . . . This book is an achievement of writing excellence on every page: the interweaving of myth and modern narration; the superbly controlled dual-person point of view; the careful descriptions; and scene after scene of glittering technique." Critic

Couples. Knopf 1968 458p $6.95

"In the upperclass Boston suburb of Tarbox, Mass., live eight or ten couples, a close-knit group that plays together, parties together, sleeps around together. They are ritually obsessed with sex. infidelity is a way of life. . . . Mr. Updike couples and uncouples his players, focusing particularly on the fates of Piet Hanema, least successful businessman among the husbands, most successful in bed; Angela, his long-suffering, rather frigid wife; Foxy, the sly young mistress who traps Piet as none of the other Tarbox wives have been able to do." Pub W
The book can "be read simply as a fiendish compendium of exurban manners—to dinner party scenes, the protocol of adultery, the care and neglect of children. The games are described with loving horror. The incidents of wife-swapping are a nice blend of Noel Coward and Krafft-Ebing. As to that style—it is there in set-pieces, which can almost be read separately. . . . Updike's weakness is not too much beauty but too much precision; he tells you more than you want to know, in words as arcane and exact as old legal language." N Y Times Bk R

The music school; short stories. Knopf 1966 259p boards $4.95

Analyzed in Short Story Index
A collection of twenty short stories
"Most of them deal with marriage problems of one kind or another. They are set in New York, Rome, Antibes, Sofia, Charlotte Amalie, etc." Bk Buyer's Guide
Contents: In football season; The Indian; Giving blood; A madman; Leaves; The stare; Avec la bébé-sitter; Twin beds in Rome; Four sides of one story; The morning; At a bar in Charlotte Amalie; The Christian roommates; My lover has dirty fingernails; Harv is plowing now; The music school; The rescue; The dark; The Bulgarian poetess; The family meadow; The hermit
"These pieces show Updike at his best: his style is exquisitely crafted, his ear is sound, his eye is sharp, and the words dance like water over bright pebbles. If some of the stories fail, it is because they are echoes rather than original noises." Time

Of the farm. Knopf 1965 173p boards $4.50

"An advertising consultant employed in Manhattan describes the visit made by himself, his new second wife, and his 11-year-old stepson to [visit his mother on] the farm where he spent his childhood days. Set in southeastern Pennsylvania." Pub W
"It is difficult to be sure of [Updike's] purpose in writing 'Of the Farm'. Surely it must amount to more than a study in maternal possessiveness and on Oedipus fixation. On the other hand each scene, each tiny bit of dialogue is rendered with such psychological accuracy that, despite the vague sense of bafflement, one reads every page with fascination. . . . [The author] works small miracles of observation, delicate, highly nuanced. Somehow they reverberate in the memory." Book of the Month Club News

Pigeon feathers, and other stories. Knopf 1962 278p boards $4.95

Analyzed in Short Story Index
"These carefully polished stories of America today are filled with gentle humor and irony. Youth, marriage, and family life provide most of the themes." Cincinnati
Contents: Walter Briggs; The persistence of desire; Still life; Flight; Should wizard hit mommy; A sense of shelter; Dear Alexandros; Wife-wooing; Pigeon feathers; Home; Archangel; You'll never know, dear, how much I love you; The astronomer; A & P; The doctor's wife; Lifeguard; The crow in the woods; The blessed man of Boston, My grandmother's thimble, and Fanning Island; Packed dirt, churchgoing, a dying cat, a traded car

The poorhouse fair. Knopf 1959 [c1958] 185p o.p. 1970

This novel concerns the lives of a handful of marvelously eccentric and understandable people in a poorhouse on the undulating plains of central New Jersey. It begins on the morning of the annual Fair, an innovation of Conner, the new and very ambitious Prefect. Conner's struggle to institutionalize old age inevitably meets the stiff opposition of those who want to individualize it. (Publisher)
"This is a wise book with much to say on individualism and conformity, mechanization and craftsmanship, the 'welfare state' and the 'old days'—and, foremost, on 'death' as it is looked upon by the aged and the young. Updike's old people are memorable. . . . This is not a book that will appeal to all readers. For wherever there is a demand for a thoughtful, beautifully written novel, 'The Poorhouse Fair' is highly recommended." Library J

The poorhouse fair [and] Rabbit, run. Modern Lib. 1965 435p $2.95

A combination of two titles published by Knopf separately. 1958 and 1960 respectively, and entered separately

Rabbit, run. Knopf 1960 307p o.p. 1970

"Harry (Rabbit) Angstrom is twenty-six, an ex-basketball star who demonstrates kitchen gadgets in dime stores, and a man tired of his marriage and his pregnant wife. Leaving home suddenly. he begins a trip south but turns back to Pennsylvania and lives with a prostitute until the birth of his child brings him home

Updike, John—*Continued*

again. The baby's accidental death ends the marriage, and Rabbit again runs away from his wife, the prostitute, and his responsibilities." Booklist

"This is a book that is likely to cause something of a stir in the literary world, because of its frank love scenes and the philosophy of life, or lack of it, of the leading character." Pub W

also in Updike, J. The poorhouse fair [and] Rabbit, run p148-435

The same door; short stories. Knopf 1959 241p $4.95

Analyzed in Short Story Index

Contents: Ace in the hole; The alligators; Dentistry and doubt; Friends from Philadelphia; A gift from the city; His finest hour; Incest; Intercession; The kid's whistling; Snowing in Greenwich Village; Sunday teasing; Tomorrow and tomorrow and so forth; Toward evening; A trillon feet of gas; Who made yellow roses yellow

Upfield, Arthur W.

Death of a swagman. Published for the Crime Club by Doubleday 1945 221p o.p. 1970

"The murder of swagman in a sheep-hut near the little town of Merino was almost written off as an unsolved mystery until Bony saw a photograph of the hut in which the body was found. He asked to be sent to Merino and, once there, contrived to have himself arrested and put at the job of painting the police fence, where he picked up enough gossip to send him chasing a murderer across the dangerous sands of the lonely outback country. The local characters, the background and the feel of the Australian country are extremely well done." Huntting

The lure of the bush. Published for the Crime Club by Doubleday 1965 238p o.p. 1970

Originally published in Australia with title: The barrakee mystery

"Inspector Napoleon Bonaparte, surrounded by the lore and lure of the Australia bush country, relentlessly tracks the killer of an aborigine chieftain." McClurg. Book News

The will of the tribe. Published for the Crime Club by Doubleday 1962 216p o.p. 1970

Detective Inspector Napoleon Bonaparte's latest case is concerned with the finding of the body of a white man "in a meteor crater in the middle of an Australian desert, with no hint at how he had got there. The homesteading family with whom 'Bony' stayed were friendly enough—as was the lovely aborigine girl Tessa —but could nor or would not give him any real information." Publisher's note

Uris, Leon

Armageddon; a novel of Berlin. Doubleday 1964 632p $6.95

"Berlin from the close of World War II, to the end of the airlift is the setting of this novel. Sean O'Sullivan, an American captain responsible for the military government of the city of Rombaden, nurses a fierce hatred of the Germans, and is faced with a dilemma when he falls in love with a German girl." Book Rev Digest

"Once begun, this novel is hard to abandon; one feels impelled to read on, despite the author's penchant for frequent editorializing despite his inability to conceal his biases, and despite his lax attitude toward sexual dalliance. Squeamish readers are hereby warned that the dialogue tends to be gamy at times; former GI's will find it authentic." Best Sellers

Battle cry. Putnam 1953 505p $5.95

"The story of a battalion of the U.S. 6th Marines and of the particular platoon which came together from all over the country to go through Boot Camp Training before being shipped out in '42 to begin their island fighting at Guadalcanal." Am News of Bks

"This novel is balanced: not too many four-letter words, no exposés of corruption among the brass, and no long speeches. The marines seem real in their joys, sorrows, defeats, and victories." Wis Lib Bul

y Exodus. Doubleday 1958 626p maps boards $5.95

"A long novel about the fight of the dedicated Zionists against their enemies to establish the young nation of Israel. Scenes shift from the DP camps and ghettos which are the miserable sources of emigration and hope to the battles against active British restrictions of entry and against the Arabs' guerrilla warfare. Half a dozen leading characters include a young American gentile widow drawn actively into the fight as a nurse." Am News of Bks

Mila 18. Doubleday 1961 539p boards $5.50

The author has recreated the World War II story of the Warsaw Ghetto freedom fighters. For 42 days and nights in 1943 they fought off the German Army as it carried out the Nazis' plan for the systematic extermination of the Warsaw Jews. Headquarters were set up at Mila 18, where a brave band of men and women led a suicidal fight that lighted a flame of hope and ultimate victory for a handful of survivors. (Publisher)

"The novel is at its best in its nonfictional aspects: its historical passages, its descriptions of Ghetto life, its battle scenes. It is less successful, sometimes embarrassingly clumsy, in its love scenes and attempts at character delineation. Mr. Uris is a poor hand at realistic dialogue, and his grammar is appalling; yet a reader is likely to overlook these flaws as he is swept along by the force of the narrative and the momentousness of the events described." Book of the Month Club News

Topaz; a novel. McGraw 1967 341p $5.95

A Russian defector tells about Topaz, an espionage network operating inside the French government for the Soviet Union, and the existence of "Soviet offensive weapons in Cuba. The problem is to get the U.S. and France to believe what would rather not be believed, particularly by France. In the middle sits André Devereaux, a high-echelon French intrigue-diplomat loyal to America, but in love with France. The novel chronicles the attempt to get the French to believe in the existence of Topaz whose principal 'raison d'etre' is to discredit the Americans in the eyes of the rest of the world by supplying 'disinformation.' " Best Sellers

Ustinov, Peter

Add a dash of pity. Little 1959 245p boards $4.95

Analyzed in Short Story Index

Contents: The man who took it easy; The wingless Icarus; Add a dash of pity; The man in the moon; A word in the world's ear; There are 43,200 seconds in a day; A place in the shade; The aftertaste

The loser; a novel. Little 1960 308p boards $4.95

"An Atlantic Monthly Press book"

The "hero is a young German named Hans Winterschild, a product . . . of the Nazi generation. As a boy, Hans is convinced that smashing a Jewish sweet-shop has geo-political significance. As an adolescent, he struts happily off to conquer the world. . . . Late in the war, Hans is transferred to Italy where the German defenses, German discipline and the German character are beginning to crumble. Trying to deal with the new world rising up around him, he first wantonly massacres a Tuscan village, and then falls helplessly in love with a very young Florentine prostitute. Before either can save the other, the war is over. Shedding his uniform, Hans makes his way to the village he destroyed. . . . He is hired as an extra by an American film company making a gaudy movie of the town's martyrdom. Naturally there are avengers on his trail. In the end like Nazi Germany, Hans is the loser." N Y Times Bk R

V

Vance, Jack

Eight fantasms and magics; a science fiction adventure. Macmillan (N Y) 1969 288p $5.95

"Titillating tales of science fiction and the supernatural, superbly executed by a master of the genre, 'Jack Vance,' who has thrilled fans of all ages with his many works of the imagination." Publisher's note

Contents: The miracle workers; When the five moons rise; Telek; Noise; The new prime; Cil; Guyal of Sfere; The men return

Emphyrio. Doubleday 1969 261p (Doubleday Science fiction) $4.95

"The world of Ambroy, a totalitarian state, though existing thousands of years in the future, is famous for its handcrafts. Artisans guilty of machine duplication are severely punished or put to death. Ghyl Tavroke, the son of a wood-carver who has thus lost his life, is destined to be a master at the trade. His talents are great, but he is a rebel at heart. He flees to other planets to better his fortune and to try somehow and avenge his father's death." Library J

Vance, John Holbrook. See Vance, Jack

Van der Post, Laurens

A bar of shadow
In Van der Post, L. The seed and the sower p11-44

y Flamingo feather. Morrow 1955 341p o.p. 1970

"A novel of present-day life in Africa. Pierre de Beauvilliers goes on a search for his friend John Sandysse, when a messenger carrying a flamingo feather is killed. He goes to the great flamingo water, thru mountains and trackless jungles in his search. He is able in the end to stop a Communist-inspired plot to cause the rise of the natives against the whites." Book Rev Digest

"Author's understanding of methods used to create trouble in that area, and of the hold still maintained by superstition all come through with explanations in a good suspense tale that has more than its share of truth in it." Library J

The hunter and the whale; a tale of Africa. Morrow 1967 350p boards $5.95

"The time is just after World War I, and the hero is Peter, the young South African spotter, nicknamed 'Bright Eyes' because of his prowess. The novel follows him through four summers of whaling [in the area of Port Natal in the Indian Ocean, aboard the Norwegian ship] . . . the Kurt Hansen. Throughout these adventures, the Zulu stoker, 'Mlangeni . . . is an enlightening companion, but Peter is influenced in particular by his captain, Thor Larsen, a driven, dedicated man, respected but scarcely loved by his crew. And both in line of duty and as a result of his attachment to Laetitia, Peter is chief witness to the struggle for power between Larsen and her father, the great hunter of elephants, Herklaas de la Buschagne, that forms the climax." Publisher's note

'The drama of capturing the great blue and sperm whales is heightened by skillfull characterization of the crew . . . and by Van der Post's effective blending of suspense and adventure with African folklore and poetic descriptions of the sea." Booklist

The seed and the sower. Morrow 1963 256p $4.50

A trio of related stories all taking place on Christmas and loosely connected by having the same narrator and frame of reference. "The first episode, 'A Bar of Shadow,' [published separately] takes place in a Japanese prison camp with John Lawrence trying to do the best for his men, even to understanding and forgiving his captors. The next episode, "The Seed and the Sower' follows Jacques Celliers through his youth, his manhood, and into battle until the moment when he faces execution and then commits himself to an astonishing action. The third episode [The sword and the doll] tells a story of one night's love." Huntting

The sword and the doll
In Van der Post, L. The seed and the sower p191-256

Van der Zee, John

Blood brotherhood. Harcourt 1970 248p $5.95

"Joe Burke, president of a construction workers' union local, tells the story of Braxton Bragg. A militant leader, Bragg has tried to mold the San Francisco local he heads into a tough democratic group. His methods earn him the deadly hatred of both the contractors from whom he extracts better working contracts and the corrupt leadership of the national union, but they also win for him the fierce loyalty of the members of his local. Bragg is gunned down on a San Francisco Street, and Burke finds himself, to his own surprise, carrying on Bragg's battle, although his life too has been threatened." Library J

"A strong paean of praise for all those who in a society of compromise and corruption fight the establishment. The locale . . . is very well described, as are the union meetings and national conventions." Pub W

The plum explosion. Harcourt 1967 216p $4.75

Ray Moss, a law student who dreams of saving a California plum orchard from destruction by real estate developers, becomes a developer himself. Moss' dream is defeated, but through his defeat, he grows in understanding. (Publisher)

"It is one of the ironies of life that a man, through circumstances beyond his control, can eventually become the type of person he has always despised. It is also one of the ironies that a man's dreams, idealistic as they may be, can turn into a nightmare. . . . This is an exceptionally fine first novel, very well written, and with characters that the reader will identify with at once." Library J

Van de Water, Frederic F.

Catch a falling star. Duell 1949 362p o.p. 1970

Sequel, chronologically, to: Day of battle

"A historical novel, the scene of which is Vermont during the Revolution, when that state was practically a small independent republic. The theme of the book is a revaluation of the brothers Ethan and Ira Allen. The hero is Olin Royden, a follower of Ira, and his pursuit and final rescue of the beautiful young girl Faith Marshall, provides the love story." Book Rev Digest

Day of battle. Washburn 1958 365p $4.50

Sequel, chronologically, to: Wings of the morning

"Lieut. Jeremy Shaw of the Continental Army joins the Vermont cause and meets the beautiful ward of a Tory colonel in this novel of adventure and romance about Vermont's efforts in 1777 to secure its independence." Chicago

Followed, chronologically, by: Catch a falling star

Reluctant rebel. Duell 1948 442p o.p. 1970

"The years immediately prior to the outbreak of the American Revolution are covered in this novel—1771 to the first Continental Congress. Main action deals with quarrel between Ethan Allen's Green Mountain Boys and the royal governor of New York over the territory called 'The Grant's.' Central figures represent the various opinions and shades of loyalty that festered among the colonials at that period. Usual romance is threaded through the tale for added appeal." Library J

Followed, chronologically, by: Wings of the morning

Van de Water, Frederic F.—*Continued*

Wings of the morning. Washburn 1955 335p $3.95

Sequel, chronologically, to: Reluctnat rebel
In 1774 Quaker "Job Aldrich leaves Massachusetts to claim his dead brother's land in southern Vermont. He immediately becomes involved in eastern Vermont's dispute with York Province over the authority of its courts, and joins in the struggle for freedom. Job is also torn between his love for two women—beautiful Melissa Sprague and warm-hearted Silence Thayer." Huntting
Followed, chronologically, by: Day of battle

Van Doren, Mark

Collected stories v 1-3. Hill & Wang 1962-1968 3v boards ea $5.95

Analyzed in Short Story Index
Contents: v 1: If Lizzie tells; Big enough for a horse; The man who made people mad; April Fool; The uncertain glory; Nobody say a word; The bees; A good thing to know; The watchman; Only on rainy nights; Satan's best girl; Grandison and son; Not a natural man; Night at the Notch; The only bottomless thing; Dollar bill; Bad corner; The key; Father O'Connell; The strange girl; In what far country; So many years; The butterfly; I got a friend; One of the Garretsons; Still, still so; An episode at the Honeypot; The engine and the flare; Lucky Murdock; The pair; This other honor; Miss Hew; The prism; The valley of great wells; The pasture; Abide with me; The witch of Ramoth; A great deal of weather; The tall one; The three carpenters; The ballad singer

v2: Tregaskis horror; The man who had died a lot; Help for the senator; God has no wife; The birds; My son, my son; Mr Hasbrouck; A wild wet place; No thunder, no lightning; The miracle; Testimony after death; Sebastian; The dream; All us three; The imp of string; Me and Mac; Honeymoon; The facts about the hyacinthes, Maggie at the well; The brown cap; Twentieth floor; Rescue; Mandy's night; Plain and fancy; Fisk Fogle; The courage and the power; I Tobit; The sign; Birdie, come back; Skinny Melinda; The long shadow; The streamliner; Wild justice; Not like Tom; Consider courage; The little place; The lady over the wall; His waterfall

v3: Roberts and O'Hara; Stacey Bell; Memorial meeting; Not on the fancy side; Becky and Philander; Mrs Lancey; My mother was your wife; Home with Hazel; No laughing matter, maybe; The shelter; South Sea fruit; The little house; Wander's world; This terrible thing; Fifty-fifty; Some friend; The wild thing; McRuin; The quarry; Many are called; Man in hiding; Boy with sword; Crosstown chase; We had plans; In Springfield, Massachusetts; Nobody else's business. One of hers; Miss Swallow; The diary; Mortimer; The combination; How bad? How long; The tussle; Payment in full; The new girl; Like what; Rich, poor, and indifferent; Madam X and Madam Y; If only; The princess who couldn't say yes; The four brothers; The truth about Sylvanus

Van Dyke, Henry

Blood of strawberries. Farrar, Straus [1969 c1968] 277p $5.50

Sequel to: Ladies of the Rachmaninoff eyes
"Oliver, an intelligent and debonair black student at Cornell University narrates the story which occurs during a summer he spent in New York City with his patrons, Max and Tanja Rhode. . . . The plot revolves around a series of mysterious . . . events concurrent with the production of a Gertrude Stein play. Promoters of the drama are Max Rhode, an octogenarian 'littérateur,' and two ex-patriot English aristocrats, Clive and Margot Tibberton. The villain is Orson Valentine, Max's friendly enemy and director of the play." Best Sellers
"A macabre novel in which the ingredients are senility (with its accompanying distasteful physical deterioration, madness, obsession, theatrical and literary rivalries, transvestism, racism, murder." Pub W

Ladies of the Rachmaninoff eyes. Farrar, Straus 1965 214p boards $4.95

A story set in Michigan of the friendship "of two old ladies, Jewish Mrs. Klein and Negro Hatty Gibbs, who fuss and bicker at each other

like sisters. Oliver, Hatty's nephew, who is being put through college by Mrs. Klein, tells of the arrival of Maurice Le Fleur, who communes with the dead, and the dramatic consequences." Bk Buyer's Guide
"Scenes in the novel are ribald and hilarious, but the characters can also be pitiful or tragic." Pub W
Followed by: Blood of strawberries

Van Every, Dale

Bridal journey. Messner 1950 311p o.p. 1970

"On the day set for her wedding, Marah Blake is carried off by the Shawnees into a most unromantic and unpleasant captivity, which is described with extreme realism. Abner Gower, the half-Indian cousin of Marah's fiancé, agrees to undertake the girl's rescue only because it will give him an opportunity to serve his friend George Rogers Clark by spying on the Indians and British. In an exciting cross-country chase, Abner effects the rescue and wins Marah away from her more conventional cousin." Booklist

The scarlet feather. Holt 1959 315p o.p. 1970

Shortly after America's Revolutionary War, the Jordan family, Virginia gentry, traveled down the Ohio River to lay claim to a strip of land above Louisville. What they faced was more than a wilderness challenge, for the savage frontier was to invoke its own strange laws of survival. And a scarlet feather, once the talisman of an Indian girl, was to symbolize the final break with tradition. (Publisher)

Van Gulik, Robert. See Gulik, Robert van

Van Peebles, Melvin

A bear for the FBI. Trident Press 1968 157p $4.50

"The book opens with a [Negro] boy's first memories; it closes with his college graduation. But in the intervening pages is the story of a group of people, who in the sounds, the smells, the gestures, the silences of their densely knit family, love each other and, in this love, find sustenance and meaning for all their lives." Am News of Bks
The author "isn't uptight about anything, and that, as much as anything else, makes the novel engaging and delightful." Pub W

Van Siller, Hilda

The watchers. Published for the Crime Club by Doubleday 1969 192p $4.50

"A young woman struggles to prove her husband's sanity against seemingly overwhelming odds. The locale in New York and Connecticut." Am News of Bks
"A tense and moving story of murder and cruel deception." Book News

Van Thal, Herbert

(ed.) Great ghost stories; illus. by Edward Pagram. Hill & Wang 1960 239p illus $3.50

Analyzed in Short Story Index
Contents: Running Wolf, by A. Blackwood; The haunted and the haunters, by Lord Lytton; The spectre bridegroom, by W. Irving; Markheim, by R. L. Stevenson; The squire's story, by E. C. Gaskell; The story of Mary Ancel, by W. M. Thackeray; A terribly strange bed, by W. Collins; An account of some strange disturbances in Aungier Street, by J. S. Le Fanu; The phantom coach, by A. B. Edwards; The signal-man, by C. Dickens

Van Vechten, Carl

Nigger heaven. Knopf 1926 286p o.p. 1970

" 'Nigger heaven' tells a story of modern Negro life in the greatest Negro city in the world, the district of Harlem in New York City which is given over to this race. The characters who enter into the story are mostly Negroes of the wealthier and more educated class, the hero being a young graduate of the University of Pennsylvania who comes to New York with ambitions to become a writer but who has not developed sufficient stamina to

Van Vechten, Carl—*Continued*

withstand the vices to which he is introduced. His character gives way under the strain and he loses all self-respect. In the course of his brief downward career, the abnormal conditions under which the Negro is living in New York, his intellectual strivings, his opinions on race questions, the pleasures and vices of night life, his whole social background, are shown in detail." Book Rev Digest

Van Vogt, A. E.

The weapon makers. Greenberg 1952 220p o.p. 1970

Sequel to: the weapon shops of Isher
In this book "immortal Robert Hedrock, loved by the Empress Innelda, dared to pit himself against the powers of his own universe as well as against the aliens of outer space." Huntting

The weapon shops of Isher. Greenberg 1951 231p o.p. 1970

"It is the year 4784 and the Universe is contained within the empire of Isher, where the beautiful Empress Innelda rules with a firm but selfish hand, and where handsome Cayle Clark finally rescues her realm from cosmic crisis. Science-fiction romance." Retail Bookseller
Followed by: The weapon makers

Van Wijk, J. Louw

Tselane. Houghton 1961 282p o.p. 1970

"This novel, by a South African woman is based on an actual trial growing out of an attempted Basuto ritual murder. . . . A pregnant young wife, Tselane, was marked as a victim by a medicine man, who hoped that his medicine would bring a child to his chief's barren wife. Tselane hears of the plot and flees to a near-by mission for help. Her one desire is to reach her husband, working in one of the white man's towns. The terrified girl is placed on a train, where her ordeal brings on a premature birth. Convinced that she will be killed for her act, she throws the infant out of the train window, for which she is arrested and charged with murder." N Y Times Bk R
"Despite the latent horror of its theme, it is written in exquisite taste and reads easily." Best Sellers

Van Wyck Mason, F. See Mason, F. van Wyck

Vargas Llosa, Mario

The green house; tr. from the Spanish by Gregory Rabassa. Harper 1968 405p $6.95

Original Portuguese edition published 1965 in Spain
"Winner of the Romulo Gallegos Award in 1967. This vast novel concerns the nuns of the Mission of Santa Maria Nieva, the Aguaruna Indians, the city of Piura with the Green House, a brothel, right across the Amazon, a slum where the police do not venture, and an island in the Amazon where the Japanese smuggler lives. The story 'merges dream, memory and experience' with, sometimes, a bewildering if impressive effect." Bk Buyer's Guide

The time of the hero; tr. by Lysander Kemp. Grove 1966 409p $5.95

Original Spanish edition 1963
"A group of cadets led by the Jaguar rebel against the discipline and sadistic hazing at Leoncio Military Academy in Peru by smuggling cigarettes, running midnight poker games, selling answers to examinations, and distributing pornographic stories. By their third year (when the novel opens), these 'pranks' lead to murder and revenge, which places the whole military hierarchy in jeopardy." Bk Buyer's Guide
"The author, a young Peruvian, demonstrates talent by his use of sharp and graphic narration and he displays a striking, valid knowledge of life. The utter hopelessness of his vision, however, negates these assets. . . . [The cadets'] talk is strong and profane; their actions are reduced to an animalistic existence,

lacking the beauty of any philosophy, even of existentialism. This book has been burned in Peru and given an award in Spain—it merits neither action, in my opinion." Library J

Vasquez, Richard

Chicano. Doubleday 1970 376p $6.95

"In this novel, Vasquez traces the history of the Sandoval family through three generations: the first, which migrated to the U.S. during the Mexican Revolution; the second, which extended from the Depression through the post-war years; and the third, which lived in the last decade and which—exposed to prejudice in the public schools, an integrated neighborhood, and other social contacts—failed to fully adapt to either Anglo or Chicano culture. On occasion, the author's bitterness breaks through to ,add an emotional flavor to the book. While he does not fully develop the theme, Vasquez points to the gulf between well-to-do Chicanos [Mexican-Americans] and those less fortunate, and he succeeds in presenting the problems of the Chicano throughout the Southwest." Choice

Vassilikos, Vassilis

Z; tr. from the Greek by Marilyn Calmann. Farrar, Straus 1968 406p $6.95

Original Greek edition 1966
"A novel about the 1963 assassination of Greek Socialist deputy Gregory Lambrakis when he went to Salonika to address a pacifist meeting." Chicago
The author shows "considerable story telling and lyric powers. Designing a pattern as gracefully complex as an oriental carpet, he weaves fact with poetic fantasy, produces a texture peopled with dozens of characters, and knots them tightly one to the next." N Y Times Bk R

Vaughan, Carter A.

The Seneca hostage. Doubleday 1969 234p $4.95

Jonathan Lewis arrived in Philadelphia in 1753. "All he wanted from the New World was money; he planned to sell the land he had inherited from his cousin and return to London as soon as possible. But fate decreed he should stay. An unscrupulous innkeeper stole his money. A beautiful and kind woman stole his heart, and the Seneca Indians, his freedom. For he became their captive and was forced to undergo a series of bizarre rites and trials that taxed his body and his spirit to the limit. From this crucible, Jonathan emerged with a new life, a new love for America, and a new respect for himself, as well." Publisher's note

Vechten, Carl van. See Van Vechten, Carl

Veraldi, Gabriel

Spies of good intent; tr. from the French by Norman Denny. Atheneum Pubs. 1969 285p boards $5.95

"A secret international society of scientists, principally biologists and physicians based in Switzerland, is fighting by any means, including murder and terrorism, the development of mind-controlling devices in the modern world. Both this organization and the French security forces are concerned with a factory in upper New York state which is producing instruments for insertion in the human brain. The hero, a double agent for the French and the secret society, succeeds in disrupting the American company." Library J

Vercel, Roger

Tides of Mont St-Michel; tr. from the French by Warre Bradley Wells. Random House 1938 305p o.p. 1970

"Caught by the depression and having no alternative, a young Frenchman takes a job as guide at Mont St-Michel, and with him he takes his rebellious wife, shamed by his position, furious at him for dragging her down socially and determined to get him away, or go without him. How the Mount works its 'spell of peerless beauty' on André, until the

Vercel, Roger—_Continued_

last links with his treacherous wife are broken is skilfully woven into this brilliant evocation of the enchantment and inspiration of Mont St-Michel, while the life of the guardians, summer and winter, on duty or engaging in the activities of the permanent residents rounds out a unique and distinguished story." N Y Libraries

Verga, Giovanni

The house by the medlar tree; tr. from the Italian by Eric Mosbacher. Grove 1953 247p o.p. 1970

First Italian edition 1881; American edition 1890

"A realistic picture of peasant life in an Italian fishing hamlet. . . . It is the story of a grand old fisherman, whose god is financial integrity, and who exhausts his life and the life of his family in making reparation for debts incurred through misfortune." Baker's Best

Verissimo, Erico

Time and the wind; tr. by L. L. Barrett. Macmillan (N Y) 1951 624p o.p. 1970

Originally published in Portuguese

"The scene of this historical novel is the rough frontier country in the southern part of Brazil. It covers one hundred and fifty years, from the missionary settlements in 1745 to the Civil War in 1895, and portrays the drama of the times reflected in the fortunes of one family, the Terra-Cambaras. Bandits become respectable landowners; businessmen turn revolutionary; there are wars and murders, poverty and great wealth, stubborn defense of family pride." Huntting

"The novel is written with detail of setting and an understanding of character that enliven the narrative and prevent it from being a lifeless panorama." Booklist

Vermandel, Janet Gregory

So long at the fair. Dodd 1968 186p o.p. 1970

"Red badge mystery"

"A suspense novel about a young American career girl who meets peril and romance at the fair in Montreal, with interesting behind the scene pictures of how the exhibits are managed." McClurg. Book News

"Lightweight in plot and characterization, but agreeably spirited and amusing, with a nice blend of romance and action, [this book features] an interesting background of the turbulent days of preparation for Expo, and a clever crime-scheme which could happen only in Montreal in 1967." N Y Times Bk R

Verne, Jules

_y_ Around the world in eighty days

Some editions are:
Collins $1.95
Dodd (Great illustrated classics) $4.50 Translated by Geo. M. Towle; with biographical illustrations and drawings reproduced from early editions, together with an introduction and captions by Anthony Boucher
Dutton $3.50 Translated by Jacqueline and Robert Baldick; with four colour plates and line drawings in the text by W. F. Phillipps

First published 1873

"The hero, Phileas Fogg, undertakes his hasty world tour as the result of a bet made at his London club. He and his French valet Passepartout meet with some fantastic adventures, but these are overcome by the loyal servant, and the endlessly inventive Fogg. The feat they perform is incredible for its day; Fogg wins his bet, having circled the world in only 80 days." Benét. The Reader's Encyclopedia

also in Verne, J. The Jules Verne omnibus p297-485

Five weeks in a balloon. Associated Booksellers 1958 253p front (Fitzroy ed. by Jules Verne) $3

First published 1863

A description of five weeks of balloon travel, exploring the heart of Africa, visiting such strange places as the Cape, Zanzibar, The Nile and Timbuctoo

_y_ From the earth to the moon, and, Round the moon

Some editions are:
Dodd (Great illustrated classics) $4.50 With pictures of the author and his environment and illustrations of the setting of the book together with an introduction by Arthur C. Clarke
Lippincott $3.95 Has title: From the earth to the moon, and, A trip around it

The two books comprising this volume were first published 1865 and 1872 respectively

Two science fiction tales which relate the adventures of three men, accompanied by two dogs, who were shot to the moon in a specially constructed shell from an enormous gun

From the earth to the moon

_In_ Verne, J. The Jules Verne omnibus p545-667

_y_ A journey to the centre of the earth

Some editions are:
Associated Booksellers (Fitzroy edition of Jules Verne) $3
Dial Press $7.50 Illustrations by Edward A. Wilson; introduction by Isaac Asimov
Dodd (Great illustrated classics) $4.50 With 16 full-page illustrations of the author, his environment and the setting of the book, together with an introduction by Arthur C. Clarke

First published 1864. Variant title: A trip to the center of the earth

"A band of explorers go down the funnel of a volcano in Iceland, and are ejected near Stromboli in the Mediterranean, after journeying through the subterranean regions, where they find animal and vegetable productions akin to those of past geological periods." Baker's Best

_y_ The Jules Verne omnibus. Lippincott 1951 822p $4.95

"Three of the author's deservedly popular adventure stories: 'Twenty Thousand Leagues under the Sea,' 'Around the World in Eighty Days' and 'From the Earth to the Moon,' [including the sequel: Round the Moon] plus a less well-known, slighter work entitled 'The Blockade Runners.'" Library J

The first three titles are entered separately

_y_ Michael Strogoff; a courier of the Czar; illus. by N. C. Wyeth. Scribner 1927 397p illus (Scribner's Illustrated classics) $5

First French edition 1876

"The herculean Strogoff is sent by the Czar with a letter to a commandant in Irkutsk, beleaguered by hordes of Tartars. Traversing the vast extent of Siberia, accompanied by a beautiful girl, he encounters every conceivable kind of peril, but escapes, and executes his mission." Baker's Best

_y_ The mysterious island

Some editions are:
Dodd (Great illustrated classics) $4.50 With biographical illustrations and drawings reproduced from early editions together with an introduction and captions by Anthony Boucher
Scribner (The Scribner Illustrated classics) $6 Pictures by N. C. Wyeth

Sequel to: Twenty thousand leagues under the sea

First published 1874

A story of adventure in three parts: Dropped from the clouds; Abandoned; and The secret of the island

"Five men and a dog are carried out to sea in a balloon and drop from the clouds on the mysterious island. Their Crusoe-like resourcefulness and adventures are the theme of the book." Toronto

Round the moon

_In_ Verne, J. From the earth to the moon, and, Round the moon

_In_ Verne, J. The Jules Verne omnibus p671-822

Verne, Jules—*Continued*

y Twenty thousand leagues under the sea
Some editions are:
Associated Booksellers (Fitzroy edition of Jules Verne) $3
Collins $1.95
Dodd (Great illustrated classics) $4.50 With biographical illustrations and drawings reproduced from early editions, together with an introductory biographical sketch of the author and anecdotal captions by Allen Klots, Jr.
Dutton $3.50 With 4 colour plates and line drawings in the text by William McLaren
Dutton (Everyman's lib) $3.25
Macmillan (N Y) (The Macmillan classics) $4.95 Illustrated by Charles Molina. Afterword by Clifton Fadiman
Scribner (Scribner Illustrated classics) $6 Illustrated by W. J. Aylward
First published 1869
This romance is "remarkable for its prognostication of the invention of submarines. The central characters of the tale, in the process of exploring marine disturbances, are captured by the megalomaniacal Captain Nemo. An undersea tour in a strange craft and their ensuing escape conclude the work." Benét. The Reader's Encyclopedia
Followed by: The mysterious island

also in Verne, J. The Jules Verne omnibus p7-293

Vesaas, Tarjei
The birds; tr. from the Norwegian by Torbjørn Støverud and Michael Barnes. Morrow 1969 224p boards $5
Originally published 1957 in Norway. This translation published 1968 in England
"This novel tells the story of a relationship between a brother and sister, he the younger and mentally retarded, she his protector and provider, and at a time in her life when she very strongly questions her lonely and self-sacrificing existence. One day the brother brings a man into the house, and his sister finds that she must choose between her new lover and her dependent brother." Am News of Bks
The novel "is, without doubt, a volume that should be read for its superb technique and its penetrating portrayal of the human soul." Best Sellers

The great cycle. Det store spelet; tr. from the Norwegian by Elizabeth Rokkan; with an introduction by Harald S. Næss. Univ. of Wis. Press 1967 xxvi, 226p (The Nordic translation ser) $4.95
Originally published 1934 in Norway
"This deeply felt but quietly written paean to the enduring cycle of seasons, crops, men, and creatures is the work of a contemporary Norwegian steeped in the scenes and ways of rural Talemark. His realism, tempered by a gentle romanticism that admits but does not probe pain, follows the boyhood, adolescence, and growing up of Per Bufast on the Bufast farm. Per is often restive about the foregone conclusion that his destiny is linked with the farm, but his father's death finds him prepared to be caught up in its fate along with the girl he has chosen for life." Booklist

Palace of ice; tr. by Elizabeth Rokkan. Morrow 1968 [c1966] 176p (UNESCO collection of contemporary works) $4.50
Originally published 1963 in Norway. This translation published 1966 in England with title: The ice palace
This novel, which was awarded the Nordic Council Prize in 1963, "tells of the relationship between two 11-year-old girls: Siss [and Unn]. . . . [The latter] goes off alone to explore the ice palace, a gigantic frozen waterfall, and dies there. Siss is left with the problem of being true to her friend's memory . . . and for a time she assumes . . . [a] version of Unn's personality." New Statesman
This "is a novel without sexual conflict, violence or a sense of chaos. . . . The design of this novel is too simple, the allegory too obvious, the domestic scenes are too tame, but the vision of a wild, free landscape is wholly personal and exhilarating." Times (London) Lit Sup

Viaud, Louis Marie Julian. See Loti, Pierre

Vidal, Gore
Julian
Some editions are:
Little $6.95
Modern Lib. $2.95
First published 1964 by Little
A novel about Julian the Apostate who was brought up as a Christian but who tried to restore the old gods of Hellenism after he became emperor of Rome in 361 A.D. The author "imagines a correspondence between the great pagan orator Libanius and the philosopher Priscus, both of whom were old friends of Julian. Libanius, long after Julian's death, is proposing to write the life of his old friend, and Priscus fortunately has by him a journal written by Julian himself during the Persian campaign in which he lost his life. He sends this journal to Libanius together with his own comments." Book Week
The author displays "an easy and fluent gift for narrative; a theatrical sense of scene and dramatic occasion; and a revealing eye and ear for character delineation—to say nothing of wide reading. . . . For all its impressive narrative skill and immense readability, 'Julian' is, finally, metaphysical costume drama." Newsweek

Messiah. [Rev. ed] Little 1965 243p $5
First published 1954
Set in the future, this "is the story of the coming of a new Messiah, promoted and publicized by radio and television, who preaches the doctrine of the satisfaction of the death-wish in man." Book Rev Digest
"The book, boils down to an intellectual, satiric description of the kind of world this 'messiah' might create, a world quite without a spark of creativity or a hope of rebellion." Pub W

Viertel, Joseph
The last temptation. Simon & Schuster 1955 437p o.p. 1970
"Title from T. S. Eliot's definition of the 'last temptation': To do the right thing for the wrong reason. Debbie and Vic Marmorek, cultured young Viennese, and their son David find refuge in Jerusalem around the time of the British withdrawal and the war with the Arabs. Their intensely personal story, somewhat long-drawn-out, mounts credibly to the catastrophe of Vic's execution as a traitor for a fundamentally thoughtless act motivated by love of prestige, but an act which resulted in many deaths and the destruction of Haganah stores. Debbie fought successfully for vindication of his name, growing up herself in the struggle. Then she survived her 'last temptation'—to marry and become an American." Library J

Vigny, Alfred de
The Malacca cane
In Dupee, F. W. ed. Great French short novels p125-94

Vining, Elizabeth Gray
I, Roberta. Lippincott 1967 224p boards $4.95
"Roberta Dobson Morelli lives with her five-year-old son in a rundown house filled with ancestral pride and a few valuables. The time is 1895. Her husband, a handsome Italian handyman who married her because she was pregnant by him had deserted her three years before, taking all that was left of the Dobson money. Now he is dead and the woman he has married bigamously wants to adopt his son. She is generous and loving and she is wealthy. Roberta begins a painfully honest diary, which forms this novel. She is trying to make the most difficult decision of her life. . . . This is women's fiction but devoid of sentimentality or soapsuds. The people are real, the story well-plotted, the result is an absorbing character study." Pub W

Take heed of loving me. Lippincott 1964 [c1963] 352p boards $6.50
Set in Elizabethan and Jacobean England, this novel concerns "the great poet John Donne and Anne More, who defied her father and risked her inheritance to marry the man she loved." Publisher's note

Vining, Elizabeth G.—*Continued*

"To the reader's eyes, Donne becomes a very real, lustful, lyrical young man, then a loving fiancé and faithful husband though oppressed by poverty and lack of preferment, finally an eloquent churchman, in spite of his early worldly life. Donne's poetry winds through the story." Pub W

Vittorini, Elio

The dark and the light: Erica and La Garibaldina; two short novels; tr. with an introduction by Frances Keene. New Directions 1960 182p $4.75

"Erica is a young adolescent girl, abandoned by her mother and father. Supporting her brother and sisters, she turns, as a last resort, to prostitution. Life is dark for her, but at the same time she retains her dignity and courage. La Garibaldina is an ancient crone, once a camp follower in Garibaldi's army. She meets a young soldier on a train and forces the guards into letting him complete his journey across Sicily in her first-class carriage. Her bravado, her indomitable spirit, and her inexhaustible charm, expressed so well by Vittorini, represent a triumph of human optimism." Library J

Erica

In Vittorini, E. The dark and the light p 1-75

La Garibaldina

In Vittorini, E. The dark and the light p77-180

Vivante, Arturo

A goodly babe. Little 1966 178p boards $3.95

"A young doctor in Rome meets and falls in love with an attractive American tourist. . . . The two marry. The wife loses a malformed baby, and the young couple fear they will never be able to have a normal child. A move to America, another year, and they have a perfect little girl." Library J

"Cosimo, the hero, is quite fickle at first—he looks for love, finds it in Jessie, his wife, then looks for variety to other women, while remaining in love with his wife. A light novel, with appealing touches of local color." Pub W

Voelker, John Donaldson. See Traver, Robert

Vogt, A. E. van. See Van Vogt, A. E.

Volpe, Edmond L.

(jt. ed.) Hamalian, L ed. Great stories by Nobel Prize winners

Voltaire

Candide

In Voltaire. Voltaire's Candide, Zadig, and selected stories p3-101

Candide, and other writings; ed. with an introduction by Haskell M. Block. Modern Lib. 1956 576p $2.95

First French edition 1759

Candide was "written to satirize the optimistic creed that 'All is for the best in this best of all possible worlds.' Candide's tutor, the philosophic Dr. Pangloss, is the embodiment of this theory, maintaining it through thick and thin, in spite of the most blatant evidences to the contrary. He is considered to satirize the philosopher Leibnitz. Misadventures begin when the young Candide is kicked out of the castle of Thunder-tentronckh for making love to the baron's daughter, Cunagonde; and thereafter he and Pangloss and Cunagonde, sometimes together, more often apart, in various far quarters of the earth, endure a long succession of the most unfair and appalling calamities conceivable. Eventually they settle down together on a little farm. Candide marries Cunagonde, now alas grown ugly, and tells himself often. . . . 'We must cultivate our garden.' " Benét. The Reader's Encyclopedia

Voltaire's Candide, Zadig, and selected stories; tr. with an introduction by Donald M. Frame. Candide illustrations by Paul Klee. Ind. Univ. Press 1961 351p illus o.p. 1970

Contains 14 satiric tales in addition to Candide (1759) and Zadig (1748)

Contents: Candide; Zadig; Micromegas; The world as it is; Memnon; Bababec and the fakirs; History of Scarmentado's travels; Plato's dream; Account of the sickness, confession, death, and apparition of the Jesuit Berthier; Story of a good Brahman; Jeannot and Colin; An Indian adventure; Ingenuous; The one-eyed porter; Memory's adventure; Count Chesterfield's ears and Chaplain Goudman

Zadig

In Voltaire. Voltaire's Candide, Zadig, and selected stories p102-72

Zadig, and other romances; tr. by H. I. Woolf; with an introduction and notes. Dutton 320p (Broadway translations) o.p. 1970

Analyzed in Short Story Index

The title story, Zadig, "first published in France 1748, is a satire of unrealistic dogmas, demonstrating the difficulty of securing happiness by reason of the malice of one's neighbors. Zadig, a young Babylonian, tries to reform society, but finds human conventions and formulas invincible." Lenrow. Reader's Guide to Prose Fiction

Contains the following short stories: Micromegas; Story of a good Brahmin; The simple soul; Princess of Babylon

Von Doderer, Heimito. See Doderer, Heimito von

Von Goethe, Johann Wolfgang. See Goethe, Johann Wolfgang von

Von Hoffman, Nicholas

Two, three, many more; a novel. Quadrangle Bks. 1969 251p boards $5.95

This is an "account of an uprising at an anonymous university. The book presents the . . . characters and scenario for a campus explosion: the remote, authoritarian university president; the black students who seize a building to demand the firing of a racist professor; the whites who occupy other university halls to support them; and the impotent faculty members who search for a middle course to stave off the inevitable police bust." Newsweek

"What is happening to American universities seems more closely allied to fiction than to fact. . . . Perhaps that is why a novel like [this] best conveys the sense and the tone of a campus insurrection. . . . The only unresolved question is 'Why?' " N Y Times Bk R

Vonnegut, Kurt

Cat's cradle. Holt 1963 233p o.p. 1970

"A facetious, wildly satirical fantasy built up from Felix Hoenikker, father of the atomic bomb; his production of ice-mine, a seed-ice that could set off a chain reaction more deadly than that of nuclear fission; a dictator-ruled Carribean island, where the three Hoenikker children had taken their fatal ice-mine; and other unusual ingredients." Bk Buyer's Guide

"Vonnegut assaults the majority of our sacred cows, and most heartily the theory that scientific progression can be equated with progress. The central thesis of the book is essentially that the day the first atom bomb was dropped the world ended and Christianity ceased to be. Vonnegut sees man's historical progression not as factors of efficient continuity but as factors of efficient anti-continuity. That as man moves forward scientifically he moves backward humanistically in some ratio to what he calls his progress." Choice

Vonnegut, Kurt—*Continued*

God bless you, Mr Rosewater; or, Pearls before swine, by Kurt Vonnegut, Jr. Holt 1965 217p boards $4.95

"How unorthodox Eliot Rosewater maintains control of the 87-million dollars belonging to the Rosewater Foundation of Indiana despite the serious question of his sanity is the plot of this novel." McClurg. Book News

"A mad combination of humor, satire, political polemic, philosophy, and ribaldry." Bk Buyer's Guide

Mother night [by] Kurt Vonnegut, Jr. Harper 1966 202p o.p. 1970

This novel consists of the diary written in jail in Israel by a former Nazi radio broadcaster who is awaiting trial as a war criminal. It "presents Howard W. Campbell, Jr., 'a man who served evil too openly, and good too secretly, the crime of his times.' American by birth, Nazi by reputation, and former U.S. counter-intelligence agent, he was recruited in 1938 in a Berlin park by the man he called his blue fairy godmother." Library J

The plot gives free play to sardonic humor at the expense of the Nazis, the Russians, and American reactionary fringe movements." Pub W

Player piano, by Kurt Vonnegut, Jr. [New ed] Holt [1966 c1952] 295p boards $4.95

A reissue of the title first published 1952 by Scribner

"Unhappy in the age of machines, Dr. Paul Proteus, the 35-year-old manager of the vast Ilium Works, decides machines have taken away more than they have given. When his friend Ed Finnerty appears, Paul's ideas take shape and the revolt against machines is conceived." McClurg. Book News

"Mr. Vonnegut lacks the dark streak of personal horror that makes Orwell's work memorable; but he has, to compensate, a lively satirical humor that bubbles up, again and again, in fragments of fancy. 'Player Piano' is evidence of a probing mind and an observing eye." N Y Her Trib Books

Slaughterhouse-five; or, The children's crusade; a duty-dance with death, by Kurt Vonnegut, Jr. . . . Delacorte Press 1969 186p $5.95

"A Seymour Lawrence book"

A story of "a fourth-generation German-American now living in easy circumstances on Cape Cod [and smoking too much] who, as an American infantry scout 'Hors De Combat,' as a prisoner of war, witnessed the fire-bombing of Dresden, Germany, 'The Florence of the Elbe' a long time ago, and survived to tell the tale. This is a novel somewhat in the telegraphic schizophrenic manner of tales of the planet Tralfamadore, where the flying saucers come from. Peace." Title page

The hero of this novel "is one Billy Pilgrim, a successful optician from Ilium, New York, who goes to war, is captured by Germans and held in an old slaughterhouse in Dresden at the time of the Allied air raids and who later helps—as did Vonnegut—dig out the ash-filled city. But Billy Pilgrim also believes that he has been taken to the distant planet of Tralfamadore (where the flying saucers come from), where he is exhibited naked in the zoo with the beautiful film actress Montana Wildhack, his mate. Billy is able to fall in and out of time, and . . . is often able to know what is going to happen without being able to remember what already has happened. The novel is Billy's story, full of all the lackluster details of life in Ilium juxtaposed with the horror of Dresden and the exotica of Tralfamadore." Book of the Month Club News

The author "is now recognized by both readers and critics, so most libraries with representative fiction collections will buy this strongly autobiographical novel. It will not become a classic, but it contains some fine writing—like the image of the woman 'trying to construct a life that made sense from things she found in gift shops.' " Library J

Welcome to the monkey house; a collection of short works, by Kurt Vonnegut, Jr. Dial Press 1968 298p boards $5.95

"A Seymour Lawrence book"
Analyzed in Short Story Index

This collection "ranges in time from pieces written in 1950 to 1968 and in subject from observations on Barnstable Village on Cape Cod to a fictional exchange of letters between the fathers of deceased American and Soviet astronauts. In between, there's some semi-science fiction and even a fictional venture into cold war political psychology." Pub W

Contents: Where I live; Harrison Bergeron; Who am I this time; Welcome to the monkey house; Long walk to forever; The foster portfolio; Miss Temptation. All the king's horses; Tom Edison's shaggy dog; New dictionary; Next door; More stately mansions; The Hyannis Port story; D.P.; Report on the Barnhouse Effect; The euphio question; Go back to your precious wife and son; Deer in the works; The lie; Unready to wear; The kid nobody could handle; The manned missiles; EPICAC; Adam; Tomorrow and tomorrow and tomorrow

Vries, Peter de. See De Vries, Peter

W

Waddell, Helen

Peter Abelard; a novel. Drawings by Laszlo Matulay. Smith, P. 1959 277p illus $3.75

First published 1933 by Holt

"The famous story of those twelfth-century lovers, Heloise and Abelard . . . told . . . in romantic and distinguished style. Although the scholarly dissertations, religious discussions, songs, and stories of medieval days are present, the story is dominated by the compelling passion of the lovers and by the wise understanding of the gross, tender old Canon of Notre Dame, Gilles de Vannes. The book has dignity and beauty, but liveliness also, and the reader's interest does not wander." Booklist

Wagenknecht, Edward

(ed.) The fireside book of Christmas stories; illus. by Wallace Morgan. Grosset 677p illus $3.50

Original edition analyzed in Short Story Index

First published 1945 by Bobbs

Contents: Birth of Jesus Christ, from Saint Matthew; And it came to pass from Saint Luke; Even unto Bethlehem, by H. Van Dyke; Other wise man, by H. Van Dyke; Man at the gate of the world, by W. E. Cule; Husband of Mary, by E. Hart; Strange story of a traveler to Bethlehem, by J. Evans; Little hunchback Zia, by F. H. Burnett; Second Christmas, by F. K. Foraandh; How come Christmas, by R. Bradford; Visit from St Nicholas, by C. C. Moore; True story of Santy Claus, by J. Macy; When Father Christmas was young, by C. Dawson; Realm of midnight, by J. L. Allen; Marchpane for Christmas, by K. L. Bates; First Christmas tree, by H. Van Dyke; Santa Claus, by G. Bradford; Christmas with Sir Roger, by J. Addison; Christmas papers, by W. Irving; Christmas carol, by C. Dickens; Christmas at Dingley Dell, by C. Dickens; Christmas storms and sunshine, by Mrs Gaskell; Christmas, by A. Smith; Almond tree, by W. de la Mare; The prescription, by M. Bowen; White road, by E. F. Bozman; Oh, what a horrid tale, by P. S.; Christmas gift, by T. F. Powys; Happy Christmas, by D. du Maurier; Christmas at Orchard House, by L. M. Alcott; Birds' Christmas carol, by K. D. Wiggin; Mysterious chest, by H. Pyle; My first Christmas tree, by H. Garland; To Springvale for Christmas, by Z. Gale; "I gotta idee," by E. Singmaster; Christmas in our town by A. Van L. Carrick; Plantation Christmas, by A. Rutledge; Snow for Christmas, by V. Starrett; One Christmas Eve, by L. Hughes; Pasteboard star, by M. Carpenter; Little guest, by M. W. Bianco; Worst Christmas story, by C. Morley; Merry Christmas, by J. Falstaff; God rest you, merry gentlemen, by B. Adams

"The editor had combined old favorites with new, many of which have never been included in previous anthologies." Huntting

Wagenknecht, Edward—*Continued*

(ed.) The fireside book of ghost stories; with decorations by Warren Chappell. Bobbs 1947 xxiii, 593p illus. o.p. 1970

Analyzed in Short Story Index
41 supernatural tales by varied authors, from classics to the modern day
Contents: Witch of Endor, from Bible. Old Testament; House in Athens, by Pliny the Younger; The sandal, by Lucian; Murder will out, by G. Chaucer; Coverley ghost, by J. Addison; Southwest chamber, by M. E. W. Freeman; Room in the tower, by E. F. Benson; No. 252 Rue M. Le Prince, by R. A. Cram; Crown derby plate, by M. Bowen; Number 13, by M. R. James; Brickett bottom, by A. Northcote; Curate and the rake, by M. Irwin; Sheraton mirror, by A. Derleth; They found my grave, by J. Shearing; Strangers and pilgrims, by W. De La Mare; Corner shop, by C. Asquith; Unto salvation, by J. Forrest; Song in the house, by A. Bridge; Silver mirror, by Sir A. C. Doyle; Green scarf, by A. M. Burrage; The escort, by D. du Maurier; Dream woman, by W. Collins; Avenging of Leete, by M. Bowen; Jolly corner, by H. James; Ghost in the chamber, by E. Wagenknecht; Playmates, by A. M. Burrage; Courage, by F. Reid; How fear departed from the long gallery, by E. F. Benson; Madam Crowl's ghost, by J. S. Le Fanu; Spectre lovers, by J. S. Le Fanu; Let me go, by L. A. G. Strong; All souls', by E. Wharton; House in Half Moon Street, by H. Bolitho; The ghosts, by E. Daly; Unquiet grave, by F. M. Mayord; The creatures, by W. De La Mare; Added space, by M. Johnston; Woman in the way, by O. Onions; The past, by E. Glasgow; The riddle, by W. De La Mare; My platonic sweetheart, by M. Twain

(ed.) The fireside book of romance. Bobbs 1948 589p o.p. 1970

Analyzed in Short Story Index
Contents: Wife of Bath's tale, by G. Chaucer; How Sandro Botticelli saw Simonetta in the spring, by M. Hewlett; Story of a piebald horse, by W. H. Hudson; Blue roses, by L. Y. Tarleau; Thirty clocks strike the hour, by V. Sackville-West; Wandering Willie's tale, by Sir W. Scott; The cheerful tortoise, by J. N. Hall; Flying highway man, by L. De La Torre; Army of the shadows, by E. Ambler; Trail of the sandhill stag, by E. T. Seton; Mark on the wall, by V. Woolf; Doll's house, by K. Mansfield; The pardon, by M. K. Rawlings; The wharf, by W. De La Mare; Curious if true, by Mrs Gaskell; Wedding jest, by J. B. Cabell; Marriage of the puppets, by R. Nathan; Ann Mellor's lover, by M. Bowen; Three sleeping boys of Warwickshire, by W. De La Mare; Sire De Malétroit's door, by R. L. Stevenson; Tradition of eighteen hundred and four, by T. Hardy; Two sisters of Cologne; Scoured silk, by J. Shearing; Endicott and the Red Cross, by N. Hawthorne; Natchez, by J. Hergesheimer; Smoke on the prairie, by C. Richter; Bride comes to Yellow Sky, by S. Crane; Leader of the people, by J. Steinbeck; Coming of Pan, by J. Stephens; The lagoon, by J. Conrad; Faithful Jenny Dove, by E. Farjeon; Three fates, by S. V. Benét; Down Bayou Dubac, by B. Benefield; Sophistication, by S. Anderson; Sousa, by L. Y. Tarleau; Cherry tree, by A. E. Coppard; Municipal report, by O. Henry; Queen's twin, by S. O. Jewett; Dark in the forest, strange as time, by T. Wolfe; Half-holiday, by A. Huxley; Mr Know-all, by W. S. Maugham; Big man, by L. A. G. Strong

(ed.) A fireside book of Yuletide tales. Bobbs 1948 553p o.p. 1970

Companion volume to: The fireside book of Christmas stories, entered above
A selection of 51 stories reflecting many aspects of the essence of Christmas. There are old favorites by the masters and new ones by little-known writers
Contents: Stable of the inn, by T. N. Page; Frankincense and myrrh, by H. Broun; Inasmuch, by H. Broun; We, too, are bidden, by H. Broun; Sad shepherd, by H. Van Dyke; White shawl from Alexandria, by F. Mertz; To come unto Me, by R. Nathan; Midnight in the stable, by E. Goudge; On hanging a stocking at Christmas, by C. S. Brooks; The fir-tree, by H. C. Andersen; Christmas legend of Hamelin town, by C. Dawson; Legend of the Christmas rose, by S. Lagerlöf; Twinkle, by H. L. Bowman; Mrs Barber's Christmas, by M. Armstrong; State versus Santa Claus, by A. Stringer; Escape of Alice, by V. Starrett; Christmas dream, and how it came true, by L. M. Alcott; Empty purse, by S. O. Jewett; Gift of the Magi, by O. Henry; It happened at Wild Cat, by F. Landis; Cherished and shared of old, by S. Glaspell; Little Christmas tree, by S. Gibbons; David's star of Bethlehem, by C. W. Parmenter; Christmas every day, by W. D. Howells; Down pens, by Saki; Old folks' Christmas, by R. Lardner; Christmas card, by J. Bridie; Christmas carp, by V. Baum; Christmas formula, by S. Benson; Christmas in Maine, by R. P. T. Coffin; What Amelia wanted, by E. Singmaster; Mr Kaplan and the Magi, by L. Q. Ross; A little rain, by B. Gill; Christmas tree ship, by H. Hansen; Star in the east, by F. Ward; St Anthony's first Christmas, by W. T. Grenfell; Somerset Christmas, by L. Powys; Christmas day at Kirkby Cottage, by A. Trollope; Magic tree, by E. Neilson; Hallelujah chorus, by P. Van Paassen; Merry Christmas, by H. Melville; Seven poor travellers, by C. Dickens; Stranger knocked, by J. Shearing; Twilight of the wise, by J. Hilton; Christmas honeymoon, by H. Spring; What Christmas is as we grow older, by C. Dickens; Christmas in possession, by M. E. Braddon; Christmas Eve—Polchester winter piece, by H. Walpole; Pint of judgment, by E. Morrow; Country Christmas, by P. Hoffman; Once on Christmas, by D. Thompson

Wahl, Betty

Rafferty & Co.; a novel. Farrar, Straus 1969 293p $5.95

The hero is an Irish-American historian "who takes leave from his job at a mid-western college to go back to the old country and revive the . . . weaving of Irish tweed. . . . Rafferty leases a country house with a thirty-foot drawing room and a view of the Irish Sea for himself and his family and joins battle with the government bureaus to get his looms going and train his weavers. He fails. . . . His company goes bankrupt, his weavers scatter, his American drive breaks down. . . . We see him at the end, Rafferty at the Loom, going native. . . . And his wife, after some struggling with a primitive kitchen, seems as pleased as he is about the transformation of their lives." Commonweal

Wahlöö, Per

A necessary action; tr. from the Swedish by Joan Tate. Pantheon Bks. [1969 c1968] 275p $4.95

Original Swedish edition, 1962
"On one level this is a story of crime and passion involving a sexually free Norwegian couple, very much in love, their watchful German painter companion, and two smouldering Spanish fishermen who are consumed by lust for the young woman. On another level it is a graphic and grim depiction of secret police operations in Franco's Spain, the cruelty the tourist seldom sees. The young couple meet an ugly fate from men they believed were friends and the German, himself secretly in love with the woman, decides to take revenge. It is only then we learn the Spanish murderers are also key resistance fighters, and the German, a deliberately enigmatic character, is faced with the ultimate test about where his moral allegiance may lie." Pub W

(jt. auth.) Sjöwall, M. The laughing policeman

(jt. auth.) Sjöwall, M. The man on the balcony

(jt. auth.) Sjöwall, M. The man who went up in smoke

(jt. auth.) Sjöwall, M. Roseanna

Walker, David

Come back, Geordie. Houghton 1966 273p $4.95

Sequel to: Geordie
Geordie is now older, "married and the father of Charlie, a teen-age boy. Charlie's revolt against the near perfection of his father

Walker, David—*Continued*

and Geordie's reaction to this revolt create problems which are finally resolved with the aid of Geordie's patron, the wise but 'daft' laird of Drumtechan." Booklist

"The story of Charlie parallels that of Geordie, but with exciting variations. His romance is just as tumultuous. Like all Walker's Highland stories, written in lighter vein, the plot is ridiculous, but decidedly hilarious." Library J

Geordie. Houghton 1950 209p $4.95

"At fourteen Geordie MacTaggart was the smallest lad in his Highland village—even smaller than his friend, Jean, who was thirteen. But the boy grew into a great oak of a man, sandy-haired, lovable, quiet and slow. And the friendship between the young giant and Jean grew, too. Geordie's story—particularly of how he entered the shot-put in the Olympic games at Boston—is told with that tender and quiet humor which is part of the Highland spirit." Huntting

"It is a simple Scotch story with considerable charm, and a minimum of dialect. There is pleasant descriptive writing with a warm feeling for glens, woods, burns, birds and beasts. Unfortunately the tang of contest is lacking; the characters are good and inconsequential and the tale is almost elementary in its simplicity." N Y Her Trib Books

Followed by: Come back, Geordie

Walker, Margaret

y Jubilee. Houghton 1966 497p $6.95

A Houghton Mifflin Literary fellowship book "To Vyry, the heroine of Jubilee, a slave since her birth and the daughter of a slave, the first murmurings of freedom meant little. ...But as the murmurings became more insistent her mind began to fill with wishes, and dreams, and possibilities. Her wish was a home of her own—her dream, an education for her children. When the war ended and the Negroes were freed the possibility of her dream coming true seemed almost more remote than it had in the kitchen of the Big House. But Vyry fought, and was defeated and fought again, and in the end she won." Publisher's note

"Each of the fifty-eight chapters [of this novel] opens with lines from a spiritual or popular song of the day ... suggesting folk ways of thinking or folk wisdom. ... With a fidelity to fact and detail, [Margaret Walker] presents the little-known everyday life of the slaves, their modes of behavior, patterns and rhythms of speech, emotions, frustrations, and aspirations. Never done on such a scale before, this is the strength of her novel." Sat R

Walker, Mildred

y Winter wheat. Harcourt 1944 306p $3.50

"To Ellen Webb wheat-growing was a thing of pride and joy and deep satisfaction. But Gilbert Borden saw only bleak loneliness, her Russian mother's peasant stolidity, her New England father's frustration. He went away—afraid to marry her—and Ellen, seeing her parents through his eyes, lost her faith in the value of their life together. Only her own love of the land did not desert her—it helped her grow in understanding—and from this recognition of reality, hope came to her again." Huntting

"A simple, uncomplicated story, which though it lacks powerful action is full of moving incidents. In what is essentially a novel of character and place rather than plot, the creation of Ellen's mother, Anna Petrovna Webb, and the vivid sense of place and region are themselves major achievements." Sat R

Wallace, Irving

The man; a novel. Simon & Schuster 1964 766p o.p. 1970

"What would happen if a Negro became President of the U.S., in a time not very far away, and accidentally, not by election? That is the burning question Wallace explores in this fast-paced, exciting book, which begins when the Vice President dies, the President and the Speaker of the House are killed in an accident, and a Negro Senator, as President pro tempore of the Senate, is sworn in as President of the U.S. His foreign problems are bad enough; the domestic problems are dynamite;

and his personal life is bitter and frustrated. The portrayal of the Negro President as a man, an able, intelligent, politically moderate man who has never been to the fore but must take responsibility overnight, is excellent. With a huge cast of characters and one crisis after another in the plot, this makes an absorbing story." Pub W

The prize. Simon & Schuster 1962 768p $5.95

This novel is an "inquiry into the private lives of a batch of Nobel Prize winners. ... The prize winners are ... a French husband-and-wife team of chemists whose marriage is collapsing, a neurotic American heart surgeon broodingly resentful that he must share the award in medicine with an Italian doctor, a gentle German-born physicist from Atlanta who is being wooed by the Communists of East Germany, and an American novelist who is just coming out of a long alcoholic trance. Wallace ... assembles them all in Stockholm and embarks them on the frenzied series of public and private events that surround Nobel award week in the Swedish capital." N Y Her Trib Books

"The complex politics which sometimes decide the awards are carefully analyzed; mild historic scandals are disclosed; and the impressive pomp of the ceremonies is adequately conveyed. 'The Prize' is too long, too factual and occasionally descends to standard melodrama, but it is on the whole good entertainment and on occasion much more than that." Book of the Month Club News

Wallace, Lew

y Ben Hur

Some editions are:

Dodd (Great illustrated classics) $4.50 With 16 full-page illustrative and biographical pictures together with introductory remarks and captions by Basil Davenport

Harper lib. bdg. $5.79

First published 1880

"The hero, Judah Ben-Hur, head of a rich Jewish family, is sentenced to life at the galleys, after being accused by his former friend Messala of attempting to assassinate the new Governor of Jerusalem. His fortune is confiscated; his mother and young sister Tirzah are walled up in a forgotten prison cell, where they contract leprosy. The novel concerns Ben-Hur's escape, his revenge during an exciting chariot race, his search for his mother and sister and their miraculous cure by Christ, who (with His followers) is an important character. The family is converted to Christianity, and the crucifixtion on Calvary is graphically described." Haydn. Thesaurus of Book Digests

Wallant, Edward L.

The children at the gate. Harcourt 1964 184p $3.95

A hospital in a New England city is the setting for this novel. "Nineteen-year-old Angelo DeMarco, who regularly makes his rounds among the patients to take orders for the pharmacy where he works as a general handyman, shelters himself from life behind a barricade of toughness and arrogance. Sammy, the new orderly who suddenly emerges one night from the shadows of the children's ward, is a human being unlike anybody Angelo has previously known. The encounter between the contemptuous skeptic from a devout Catholic family and the Jew who seems at first no more than a wild, eccentric clown has profound consequences for them both." Publisher's note

"The novel is an artistic brief against those who accept the common belief that people are responsible for their lives. The world, it seems to say, is a vast hospital peopled by helpless victims of blind fate, disease, and brutality. No one is to blame for what he has become; it is senseless to seek sense or salvation in the web of kinetic idiocy surrounding us. ... The case is argued powerfully and relentlessly." Best Sellers

The human season. Harcourt 1960 192p o.p. 1970

"This short novel describes the plight of an ageing plumber in the months following the

Wallant, Edward L.—*Continued*

death of his beloved wife. It takes him from his initial despair at his loss to the time when he recovers his faith in God and man and is willing to go on living. The setting is New Haven, Connecticut." Pub W

"Quietly told, the story evokes the character of a good man with neither patronage nor sentimentality. . . . It is a moving and noteworthy addition to any collection." Library J

The pawnbroker. Harcourt 1961 279p o.p. 1970

The author creates a "portrait of Sol Nazerman, a Harlem pawnbroker who has led a death-in-life existence since his wife and children perished in a concentration camp. The nightmare of the past, the unsympathetic relatives with whom he lives, and the drabness of his job insulate Sol from those around him until his Negro assistant is killed in an attempt to protect his employer from a group of armed robbers." Booklist

"If 'The Pawnbroker' doesn't quite fulfill the heavy task the novelist has set for himself, it is consistently absorbing, highly serious, and often moving. . . . The pawnbroker's return to the emotionally-living is not entirely convincing, nor is the somewhat ambiguous sacrifice of his assistant. But there can be no gainsaying the power of this remorselessly honest book. And some of the portraits are triumphs of the imagination." Sat R

The tenants of Moonbloom. Harcourt 1963 245p o.p. 1970

Norman Moonbloom "who has failed in just about any line of human endeavour you could possibly think of has been reduced to working for his brother Irwin, who owns a number of down-at-the-heels apartment houses in New York City. Serving as agent and collector of rents for his unscrupulous brother, Norman, a humanist and man of deep sympathies, constantly violates the agent's code by showing interest in the apartment house tenants, and by attempting to make the repairs and the renovations so badly needed in the ramshackle flats from which Irwin extorts a considerable income. Norman's involvement with the cross section of the human race represented by the tenantry leads him into strange complications." Best Sellers

Wallop, Douglass

The good life. Atheneum Pubs. 1969 [c1968] 314p boards $5.95

"A business executive, Albert Miller, tired of the burdens of a suburban life, conceives the idea of selling his home and becoming with his wife that rarest of social phenomena, the live-in couple. The experiment works well until Albert overplays his needling of his employer Jake Dutton, who in turn decides to sell his home. Albert is hoist on his own petard. He has fallen in love with his employer's property and is forced into becoming an owner again; taking the Duttons in as boarders, he finds himself in turn the butt of Dutton's somewhat sadistic humor." Booklist

This novel "won't strain your intelligence; but it is good for laughs from the upper-middle and lower-upper class sets who know all too well what 'servant problems' mean." Pub W

The year the Yankees lost the pennant; a novel. Norton 1964 250p $4.50

First published 1954

"Joe Boyd, a middle-aged baseball fan, strikes a bargain with Mr. Applegate, a Mephistophelian apparition who offers him the opportunity to become the greatest outfielder of all time for his favorite team, the Washington Senators. Delighted with the prospect of beating the Yankees, Joe ignores certain devilish implications in the arrangement and accepts with the proviso that he may, if he so desires, cancel the bargain on a certain date. The sudden, phenomenal success of the Senators does not appease Joe's uneasy conscience, however, and his resistance to Mr. Applegate's determination that the bargain shall be permanent gives an unusual twist to an enjoyable, fast-paced, sports yarn." Booklist

Walpole, Horace

The castle of Otranto; a Gothic story. Ed. with an introduction by W. S. Lewis. Oxford 1964 110p front (Oxford English novels) $2.90

First published 1764

"A famous novel of the mystery and terror school. . . . After his son Conrad, who has been on the point of marrying Isabella, daughter of the Marquis of Vicenza, is found dead by mysterious means in the castle court, Manfred, prince of Otranto, decides to marry Isabella himself. His grandfather's portrait descends from the wall for an interview with Manfred, and meantime Isabella escapes, aided by the peasant Theodore [whom she later marries]. One supernatural horror now follows another." Benét. The Reader's Encyclopedia

"With its natural personages actuated by supernatural agencies . . . this wildly romantic tale, published in 1764, was enthusiastically received by the public." Keller's Reader's Digest of Books

Walpole, Hugh

The cathedral; a novel. St Martins 1949 531p $5

First published 1922 by Doran

"Pictures life in an English cathedral town (the 'Polchester' of Walpole's Jeremy); records an ecclesiastical intrigue reminiscent of Trollope; shows the transition from the magnificent conservatism of the late Victorian era to Modernism as it affected the Church of England; and tells a story in which the elements of tragedy and satirical comedy are nicely balanced. There are many vivid minor characters, but the central figure is Archdeacon Brandon, the autocrat of Polchester, a proud, domineering man of splendid physique and inflexible mind." Cleveland

Fortitude; being a true and faithful account of the education of an adventurer. Doran 1913 484p o.p. 1970

"Peter Wescott's childhood in Cornwall was grim and desolate, spent in a forbidding home where boyish offences were cruelly punished by a terrifying father. Even before he passed on to the brutalities of an inferior and disreputable school, he had gained the realization that what mattered in life was 'the courage you bring to it,' and throughout all the trials and disciplines of his later years he never lost sight of this as a goal." Lenrow. Reader's Guide to Prose Fiction

The fortress; a novel. St Martins 1952 811p (Herries chronicle v3) $5.50

Sequel to: Judith Paris

First published 1932 by Doubleday

"Third of the ample and leisurely Herries chronicles, crowded as usual with the family connections, but focusing in the deadly feud between the Fortress, home of Will Herries, and Fell House, from which Judith conducts the campaign, through half a lifetime. Judith's old age is portrayed with delightful understanding up to her hundredth birthday, when the clans assemble from far and near, old rancors forgotten to do her honor." N Y Libraries

"It forms a complete novel in itself, and is one of the best volumes in this chronicle of an English family, covering a period of English social life from 1825 to 1875." Ontario Lib Rev

Followed by: Vanessa

Judith Paris. St Martins 1952 802p (Herries chronicle v2) $7

Sequel to: Rogue Herries

First published 1931 by Doubleday

"The chronicle of the Herries family, begun in 'Rogue Herries' is continued, with its feuds and varying fortunes, in the story of Judith, the daughter of old Rogue Herries and his gipsy wife. She became the devoted wife of a genteel French scoundrel and tried all her life to escape from the Herries family." Booklist

Judith "is a vivid heroine for a lusty tale of Georgian England. The story is swift and dramatic." Cleveland

Followed by: The fortress

Walpole, Hugh—*Continued*

Rogue Herries; a novel. St Martins 1952 736p (Herries chronicle v 1) $6.50

First published 1930 by Doubleday

"To a decayed old family manor house in the English Lake District, Francis (Rogue) Herries, brings his timid wife, his two children and his mistress. The story follows the subsequent life of this eighteenth century gentleman, at once brilliant, charming, brutal and unstable, and devotes much attention to the trappings, superstitions, quaint and rude survivals of current customs and beautiful somber background of this (then) remote part of England." Open Shelf

"Rogue Herries's character with his wild, fantastic devotion to a vagabond girl is delineated and contrasted with that of his sturdy, steady son." N Y Libraries

Followed by: Judith Paris

Vanessa; a novel. St Martins 1952 851p (Herries chronicle v4) $5

Sequel to: The fortress

First published 1933 by Doubleday

This "final chronicle of the Herries series extends from the hundreth birthday of Judith Paris in 1874 to the present. The central theme is the steadfast and unquenchable love of her beautiful granddaughter, Vanessa, for Benjie, a charming scamp, true descendant of old Rogue Herries. The scene is laid in London and Cumberland." Book Rev Digest

Waltari, Mika

The Egyptian; a novel. Tr. by Naomi Walford. Putnam 1949 503p $6.95

"A story of Egypt, its religious, political, and everyday life [and the life of the then known world] a thousand years before Christ. The chief character and narrator is Sinuhe, the physician, whose fate it is to live amongst the lowly and the high born, to travel to far lands—Syria and Crete—to be the friend of Pharaohs and to end his days in exile." Book Rev Digest

"We see, feel, smell, and taste Waltari's Egypt. He writes in a pungent, easy style and it is obvious that he has been wonderfully served by his translator, Naomi Walford." Sat R

The Etruscan; tr. by Lily Leino. Putnam 1956 381p o.p. 1970

Set in the ancient Mediterranean world, this novel recounts "the life story of a wealthy Etruscan who, after a great many fantastic adventures, dies in the year 500 B.C. believing himself to be immortal. . . . Its plot [is filled] with narrow escapes, blighted love affairs and supernatural events." Pub W

" 'The Etruscan' is truly a remarkable novel, whether viewed as sheer adventure, or as mysticism with occult meaning." N Y Her Trib Books

The Roman; the memoirs of Minutus Launsus Manilianus, who has won the Insignia of a Triumph, who has the rank of Consul, who is chairman of the Priests' Collegium of the god Vespasian and a member of the Roman Senate; English version by Joan Tate. Putnam 1966 637p $6.95

Original Finnish edition published 1964. This is the final volume of the trilogy, the first being: The Egyptian, 1949, and the second, The Etruscan, 1956, both entered separately

The story "begins when Minutus of Antioch is fifteen and ends with his death. Meanwhile he has visited Jerusalem and England, has had several love affairs, has helped persecute both the Jews and the Christians, and at last has become a Christian himself." Bk Buyer's Guide

"Though Minutus is somewhat wooden, his adventures are astonishing. Waltari shuttles his hero around the empire, from Britain to Ephesus, in order to describe the growing decadence of Rome, the rise of Christianity, and the existence of other religions. Waltari's sense of humor and irony points up his pageant of Roman life." Pub W

Wang, Chi-chen

(tr.) Contemporary Chinese stories. Greenwood Press [1968 c1944] 242p $11.50

Analyzed in Short Story Index

First published 1944 by Columbia University Press

"This anthology covers the period from 1918 . . . to 1937." Preface

Contents: The road, by Chang T'ien-yi; The inside story, by Chang T'ien-yi; A country boy withdraws from school, by Lao Hsiang; Black Li and White Li, by Lao She; The glasses, by Lao She; Grandma takes charge, by Lao She; The philanthropist, by Lao She; Liu's court, by Lao She; The puppet dead, by Pa Chin; Night march, by Shen Ts'ungwen; Smile, by Chang T'ien-yi; Reunion, by Chang T'ien-yi; Little sister, by Feng Wen-ping; The helpmate, by Ling Shu-hua (Mrs Ch'en T'ung-po); Spring silkworms, by Mao Dun; "A true Chinese," by Mao Dun; Mrs Li's hair, by Yeh Shao-chün; Neighbors, by Yeh Shao-chün; What's the difference, by Lusin; Peking street scene, by Lusin; Yuchun, by Yang Chen-sheng

(tr.) Traditional Chinese tales. Greenwood Press [1968 c1944] 225p $10.75

Analyzed in Short Story Index

First published 1944 by Columbia University Press

"These 20 traditional Chinese stories include samples of both the classical and the vernacular." Pub W

Contents: Hsü Yen's strange enounter, by Wu Chün; The ancient mirror, by Wang Tu; The white monkey, by Ch'en Hsüan-yu; The disembodied soul, by Ch'en Hsüan-yu; The magic pillow, by Shen Chi-chi; Jenshih, by Shen Chi-chi; The dragon's daughter, by Li Ch'ao-wei; Huo Hsiaoyü, by Chiang Fang; Li Yahsien, a loyal courtesan, by Po Hsing-chien; The story of Ying Ying, by Yuan Chen; Hsieh Hsiaowo, by Li Kung-tso; The Kunlun slave, by P'ei Hsing; Yinniang the swordswoman, by P'ei Hsing; Predestined marriage, by Li Fu-yen; Tu Tzu-chun, by Li Fu-yen; The jade kuanyin; The judicial murder of Tsui Ning; The flower lover and the fairies; The oil peddler and the queen of flowers; The three brothers

Ward, Mary Jane

Counterclockwise. Regnery 1969 250p $5.95

"Susan Wood comes back from a mental illness to write a best-selling novel and achieve fame when the book is made into a hit movie. Despite her money and new fame, she devotes her life to working for a mental health foundation. . . . All the travel and work she does, however, gets to Susan eventually, and she has a recurrence of her illness that causes her to be hospitalized again, this time in as modern and well-equipped a private mental hospital as can be imagined. Her psychiatrist, her husband and all those around her are extremely competent and understanding, and 'Counterclockwise' becomes the story of Susan's fight to rise out of the fog of psychosis." Pub W

The snake pit. Random House 1946 278p o.p. 1970

Related in the first person, this tells of the experiences undergone by the patient, Virginia Cunningham, in a state mental hospital. It follows the course of her insanity from her commitment to her final release. It also takes the reader thru mental hospital routine in all its reality

"Chronicled so quietly and unemphatically, the horrors of asylum life become infinitely more poignant than they appear in the hands of grimmer writers who are out to shock. Obviously an incomplete picture, but an extraordinarily moving one." New Yorker

Waring, M. W.

The witnesses; a novel. Houghton 1967 695p $7.95

"In a story of Russia in the period 1903-1917 the characters both identified and disguised serve to illuminate the genesis and growth of the Russian Revolution. The charming world of great estates, the life of the peasants, and the fanatic self-sacrifice of the exiles who represent all shades of revolutionary thought are

Waring, M. W.—*Continued*

tellingly brought to life. Susie and Vladimir, an American girl and her princely consort, together with Vladimir's cousin, Max, who has the moral dilemma of being loyal and sympathetic to both his class and the revolutionists, are the center of a novel rich in atmosphere and effective detail." Booklist

Warner, C. D.

(jt. auth.) Twain, M. The gilded age

Warner, Douglas

Death on a warm wind. Published for the Crime Club by Doubleday 1969 [c1968] 157p $4.50

First published 1968 in England
"The story, told partly in flashback, depicts in minute-to-minute, 'you are there' fashion what happens when a devastating earthquake and tidal wave hit an English seaside resort with great loss of life. One man, scoffed at as a fool, had predicted the quake to the second and tried desperately to get someone to listen to him. Five years later, the story of his efforts, carefully hushed up, comes into the open—with a terrifying new immediacy as the same fatal warm wind that preceded the earlier earthquake sweeps down on London." Pub W

Warner, Lucy

Mirrors; stories. Knopf 1969 181p boards $4.95

A "first collection of short stories, particularly strong on characterization. . . . Here are human relationships in infinite variety: marriages fragmented and barely holding together, happy and tentatively beginning; parents and children eyeing each other with varying degrees of love, understanding, or animosity." Pub W

Contents: How sweet my daughter, how deep my anger; The minor repairs of life; A born homemaker; An insubstantial father; Breakthrough; The expectancy of my survival; The girl who liked Communists; Sky in winter; Every girl has a mother somewhere; Melissa Savage

Warner, Rex

Imperial Caesar. Little 1960 343p map $6.95

"An Atlantic Monthly Press book"
Sequel to: Young Caesar
"Covers the last fifteen years of Julius Caesar's life, the period of his great military conquests, his rise to power in the state, his affair with Cleopatra, and final reorganization of Rome. Set in the form of a fictional memoir by Caesar himself." Ontario Lib Rev

"An excellent recapitulation of history and dissection of character, but limited in interest to those who can appreciate these factors without the enlivenment of plot or romance." Booklist

Pericles the Athenian. Little 1963 240p $5.95

"An Atlantic Monthly Press book"
In this novel the author "seeks to take the literary measure of the most famous of all Greek rulers. The figure which appears is that of a man devoted to Athens first and then, by extension all of Greekdom, a man sincerely concerned with the welfare and interests of his fellow-citizens, an enthusiastic patron of the arts and of intellectual freedom and inquiry, and a man of brilliant intellect in his own right. . . . The tale of Pericles and his times is told by an Ionian Greek [Anaxagoras] who, a few years Pericles' senior, knew the great statesman from boyhood. This device permits the author to weave in much commentary on persons and times." Christian Science Monitor

"The real hero of Pericles the Athenian is Athens. Pericles himself turns out to be unimpeachable, gazing with the blank rectitude of a marble bust. . . . Anaxagoras' sonorities tend to crowd out Pericles." New Statesman

The young Caesar. Little 1958 353p $6.95

"An Atlantic Monthly Press book"
"Rome lives in the words of Caesar in this [fictional] biography. The narrative of his early life—told on the eve of his death—recreates his childhood, his discovery of strength, his plans for power, and the influential figures of the Rome of his day [up to his forty-third year]." Hunting

"With a poet's skill and style—and, most fortunately, with the caution of a sound historian—Warner pictures for us the emergence of Caesar into the sea of warring factions." Sat R

Followed by: Imperial Caesar

Warner, Sylvia Ashton- See Ashton-Warner, Sylvia

Warner, Sylvia Townsend

The corner that held them. Viking 1948 367p $3

"A novel relating the events, small and large, tragic and trivial, which were the history of the Convent of Oby in England during the period from the Black Death (1349) to the Peasant Uprising (1382)." Book Rev Digest

Lolly Willowes, and Mr Fortune's maggot; with wood engravings by Reynolds Stone. Viking 1966 310p illus $6

A combined edition of the titles first published 1926 and 1927 respectively
The first novel "is about an English spinster who sells her soul to the devil; the second is about a missionary who conspires in idolatry to save a South Sea island boy." Bk Buyer's Guide

Mr Fortune's maggot
In Warner, S. T. Lolly Willowes, and Mr Fortune's maggot p161-310

Swans on an autumn river; stories. Viking 1966 222p $4.50

Analyzed in Short Story Index
"Thirteen short stories of love, hate, loss, death, betrayal or simply disappointment." Pub W

Contents: A stranger with a bag; Johnnie Brewer; A jump ahead; Fenella; Healthy landscape with dormouse; Happiness; A love match; Swans on an autumn river; The view of Rome; An act of reparation; Their quiet lives; Total loss; A long night

Warren, Robert Penn

All the king's men

Some editions are:
Harcourt $7.50
Modern Lib. $2.95 With a new introduction by the author
Random House $4.50

First published 1946. Awarded Pulitzer Prize, 1947

A novel about a political boss, Willie Stark, as told by his publicity man. Stark, a young back-country Southern lawyer becomes a power in his state and then abuses his position

"The story of a corn-pone dictator, undoubtedly based on Huey Long. Remarkable not only for dramatic present-day scenes but also for its flashbacks written in ripe Victorian-type prose and telling about a mid-American journey before the Civil War." Good Reading

Band of angels. Random House 1955 375p $6.95

"A chronicle of the life of Amantha Starr, born and brought up on a Kentucky plantation before the Civil war. Summoned from her studies at Oberlin on her father's death 'Manty' is horrified to discover she is really a slave and is to be sold with the rest of the property. The long fight for freedom of body and soul she wages ends after years of marriage to a Union captain." Book Rev Digest

"The book carries numerous overtones on race relations and the history of Negro progress in the United States, but they are not permitted to slow up the fast and interesting story." Atlantic

Warren, Robert P.—*Continued*

The cave. Random House 1959 403p
o.p. 1970

"A novel about the furore in a small town of Tennessee as national attention is centered upon it when a young war veteran is believed trapped while exploring a newly found cave. His companion is sure he's dead, but exploits the publicity and commercial possibilities." Am News of Bks

Wilderness; a tale of the Civil War. Random House 1961 310p $7.95

In the summer of 1863 Adam Rosenzweig left a Bavarian ghetto and sailed for America to join the Union Army in order to fight for a cause he loved, freedom. But thwarted from actual combat by the discovery of a physical deformity, Adam had to seek another way to serve. How he found one is related here. (Publisher)
"An allegory of a man searching for the truth about himself and his father and the world. . . . To say that 'Wilderness' is not Mr. Warren's best book is not to say, however, that it is not a superior work of literature." Library J

World enough and time; a romantic novel. Random House 1950 512p $7.95

Based on a Kentucky murder and trial of the 1820's this is "the story of a young Kentucky lawyer . . . whose wife demanded that he kill her former lover. A dramatic story of romantic love and revenge, betrayal and murder. Like the author's earlier books, this novel is a serious and penetrating examination of human motives and aspirations." Hunting
"The turbulent politics of the period also enter the story and many tales of frontier characters . . . add to the background and atmosphere and make a full-bodied period novel of emotion and violence." Booklist

Wassermann, Jacob

The world's illusion; authorized translation by Ludwig Lewisohn. Harcourt 1930 2v in 1 o.p. 1970

Original German edition published 1919; this translation first published 1920
Contents: v 1 Eva; v2 Ruth
"This Viennese novelist paints a vivid picture of the feverishly brilliant society of pre-war Europe which Christian Wahnschaffe renounced in order to submerge himself among the lowest and most helpless classes in a search for truth and goodness in humanity. The force and mastery of a true artist are evident in Wassermann's writing, in his thought, and in the 'strange and sombre power' of this work." Enoch Pratt

Water, Frederic F. van de. See Van de Water, Frederic F.

Waterhouse, Keith

Everything must go. Putnam [1969 c1968] 188p $4.95

First published 1968 in England
"William is the owner of a second-rate antique shop, the husband of a wife he knows is quite as ordinary as his nine-year old daughter. He imagines himself as something of a Lothario but his 'affair' with Rosemary is frustrated by having no place to take her. Then at last he becomes the frightened 'lover' of a brazen actress." Bk Buyer's Guide

Watson, Colin

Lonelyheart 4122. Putnam 1967 191p o.p. 1970

"Red mask mystery"
Detective Inspector Purbright of the English village of Flaxborough becomes concerned about the disappearance of two respectable middle-aged women. The only thing they had in common was their interest in Handclasp House, a matrimonial agency. When elderly Miss Lucilla Teatime moves in and shows a similar interest, Sergeant Love is assigned to protect her from the still undiscovered danger. But Miss Teatime is more than a match for Sergeant Love, and is supremely confident of her ability to handle this or any other situation." Library J
"This is an engaging—and funny—mystery with a very neat twist at the end." Pub. W

Waugh, Alec

Island in the sun; a story of the 1950's set in the West Indies. Farrar, Straus 1955 538p o.p. 1970

A story of passion and murder and an analysis of self-government told through the "ideals and inhibitions of the colonial administrators, the feudal landowners, the educated colored lawyers, the slightly colored planters with chips on their shoulders, the ambitious but parochial politicians, the daughters of white planters who can find no suitable mates of their class and color, the ignorant, good-natured, easily inflamed proletariat—all the varied types who make their separate contribution to the turmoil under that hot sun of West Indian life." Publisher's note
"There is merit in Mr. Waugh's restraint in this work. Perhaps it is this restraint, however, which explains the absence of rewarding characterization. But in spite of this weakness, Island in the Sun is a good story, well told." Commonweal

Waugh, Evelyn

Black mischief. Little 1932 312p o.p. 1970

"The central figure of this satirical tale is Seth, a Negro educated at Oxford, who is determined to found a truly modern civilization in his native state of Azania, a small island off the coast of Africa. He is aided by Basil Seal, his English minister of modernization, who tries to put thru a grandiose one-year plan for improving and modernizing the empire." Book Rev Digest

Brideshead revisited; the sacred and profane memories of Captain Charles Ryder. Little 1946 351p o.p. 1970

"This book has much in common with the . . . novels of Aldous Huxley in its combination of extreme sophistication and religion. The story is told by Captain Charles Ryder, who in the course of troop movements, finds himself stationed at Brideshead, the great house with which he had had associations in his boyhood. In memory he turns back to those days, bringing to life the various members of a charming, eccentric family. Traditionally Catholic, three of the family's members have departed from the faith, but in the end all have returned. Contains good writing, especially in its earlier chapters." Wis Lib Bul

Decline and fall; an illustrated novelette. Doubleday 1929 293p illus o.p. 1970

"Paul Pennyfeather, a theological student at Oxford, is expelled as the result of a prank. His subsequent rococo adventures in a boy's school, in the smart set where he is the victim of a sophisticated seduction, and in prison, end with his return to the theological seminary." Book Rev Digest

The end of the battle. Little 1961 319p $4.95

Sequel to: Officers and gentlemen
Published in England with title: Unconditional surrender
The third volume in the author's series about the Crouchback family. The preceding volumes were: Men at arms; and, Officers and gentlemen, entered below
This story describes "the experiences of Guy Crouchback, scion of an old, English Catholic family, in World War II. In it, a war-weary Crouchback sees action in Yugoslavia, remarries his former wife and, after her death, nobly devotes himself to bringing up her illegitimate child." Pub W
"In contrast to the depth and seriousness of the religious theme, there is that old Waugh target—the Modern Age . . . the futility of secular life, again bludgeoned with the weapons of satire and farce. But here it must be said that there has been a definite falling off in his power to create wildly comic scenes and characters. The humor is there certainly . . . but it has lost much of its edge." Sat R

Waugh, Evelyn—*Continued*

The loved one; an Anglo-American tragedy. Little 1948 164p $4.95

A satirical story of a young British poet named Dennis Barlow, manager of a pet cemetery, and a young American crematorium cosmetician named Aimee Thanatogenos. Locale: Hollywood

Men at arms; a novel. Little 1952 342p $5.95

"An English Catholic gentleman brought up in Italy and no longer very young returns to his homeland in the hope of getting into the armed forces just before World War II. How he succeeds, his desires and ambitions, his adventures and mis-adventures with his comrades in the renowned Halberdier Regiment are told with inimitable skill and quiet restraint. It is a far more mellow Evelyn Waugh than has thus far appeared—less caustic and biting but none the less deadly in showing up the sins and foibles of army life." Library J
Followed by: Officers and gentlemen

Officers and gentlemen. Little 1955 339p $4.95

Sequel to: Men at arms
"As in 'Men at Arms' the central figure is Guy Crouchback whose military career in the early days of World War II is followed through to the catastrophic British defeat at Crete." McClurg, Book News
Followed by: The end of the battle

Put out more flags. Little 1942 286p o.p. 1970

"A satirical story of the opening days of the World war as it affected certain members of the English upper classes. Basil Seal, the idol of three women—his mother, his sister, and his mistress—has his own way of meeting the responsibilities devolving upon him, which tends to become a kind of blackmail. Eventually his better self comes to the fore." Book Rev Digest

Vile bodies. Cape [distributed by Farrar] 1930 321p o.p. 1970

A satire on the antics of London's bright young set of the 1920's with their mad whirl of extravagant parties and other pointlessly important social affairs

Waugh, Hillary

Run when I say go. Doubleday 1969 312p $5.95

This "novel features Peter Congdon, a private detective hired to bring back from Italy a Mafia leader's ex-mistress whose testimony is needed to crack a Senate Investigation of underworld crime. Peter finds himself racing across Europe with the beautiful girl in tow and the Mafia at his heels." Am News of Bks
"The deviousness of politics, and the violence of the Syndicate [are] portrayed with a light touch." Library J

(ed.) Mystery Writers of America. Merchants of menace

Webb, Jean Francis

Carnavaron's castle. Meredith 1969 314p $4.95

SBN 696-54880-1
The castle "is Tintagel, built by Charles Carnavaron out of an old fort on an island in Casco Bay, where his devoted widow and his mistress Kate Drummond still live. Jenny Stratton, publicity gal, believes the silver anniversary of the Carnavaron Awards, the 'Charlies' that are the final theatrical accolade and the ultimate symbol of stage quality, is the perfect time for her to persuade Miranda Carnavaron to talk about her late husband. When Jenny comes to Tintagel, she finds a haunted castle, and is determined to protect Miranda from the strange young man who seems determined to spoil her story." Library J

The Craigshaw curse; a novel. Meredith 1968 249p $4.95

"There is a different kind of ghost in . . . [this novel] a terror that haunts Constance Craigshaw in spite of her devotion to her important UN position and her fierce determination to put across the Mid-East settlement she has planned. But the rumor of the appearance of her former colleague, Ambassador Armstrong, in the vicinity of Flamingo, her stately family home in Florida, sends her scurrying there with her admiring secretary Jill Heaton." Library J
"The novel is Gothic in mood and setting. Each character's nature and motivation is left ambiguous until the end." Best Sellers

Webb, Mary

Precious bane; a novel. Dutton 1926 356p o.p. 1970

First published 1924 in England
"Set in the English county of Shropshire, it is a story of a harsh farming life, and fierce, morose country people. Prudence Sarn, the narrator, finds a husband who appreciates her in spite of her hare lip." Benét. The Reader's Encyclopedia

Webb, Robert Forrest. See Forrest, David

Weidman, Jerome

The center of the action. Random House 1969 367p $6.95

Ted Leff discovers a publishing company on Fourth Avenue in New York which is closing because the owners lack business sense. Through a series of clever maneuvers (such as originating the Twentieth Century Classics with no royalties to pay) Ted makes a fortune in the publishing industry. The final result of his ambitious venture occurs some years later. (Publisher)
The author "tells the story in his usual witty style, full of humor and wholesome philosophy, sprinkled generously with Yiddish jargon. It will be nostalgic reading, especially for native New Yorkers." Library J

The enemy camp; a novel. Random House 1958 561p $4.95

"Story about a New York Jew who has risen above his background in an East Side slum only to find his new position threatened with exposure of a sordid incident in his past, one which may well ruin him." Pub W
"This is a fascinating, well-paced novel spiced with deft satire and abounding in inimitable characters." Library J

I can get it for you wholesale

Some editions are:
Modern Lib. $2.95
Random House $5.50
First published 1937
"This novel, a realistic satire, tells the story of an ambitious and unscrupulous young Jew named Harry Bogen, who begins as a shipping clerk in the New York garment center and rapidly becomes a successful dress manufacturer with money to burn. In this process he double-crosses every friend he has, except the chorus girl whose sex appeal is his stimulus. A few compunctions, raised by associations with his mother and a childhood sweetheart, he stifles with a little vague discomfort. His only standard is to be smarter than the other fellow." Sat R

My father sits in the dark, and other selected stories. Random House 1961 xx, 521p $5.95

Analyzed in Short Story Index
"Dramatic, brief sequences in the lives of unimportant yet intriguing people who inhabit large cities like New York and Washington, so artfully constructed that the suspense they generate seems almost accidental." Booklist
Contents: And everything nice; My aunt from Twelfth Street; The bottom of the mountain; Briefing period; Chutzbach; The clean slate; Death in the family; A dime a throw; Dumb kid; Dummy run; An easy one; Everybody and his brother; Examination; The explorers; Eyewitness; Gallantry in action; Goodby forever; The great healer; The half-promised land; The hole card; Home by midnight; The horse that could whistle 'Dixie'; Houdini; I knew what I was doing; Invicta; I thought about this girl;

Weidman, Jerome—*Continued*

Joust; The kinnehórrah; Let me explain you something; A lodging for the night; Marriage broker; Monsoon; Movable feast; My father sits in the dark; The neat Mexicans; Off season; Old clothes for Poland; Pennants must have breezes; Philadelphia Express; The pleasure of the President; Portrait of a gentleman; Send four men to Hanoi; Shoe shine; The third alphabet; The tuxedos; Twice blest; The waiting game; Where the sun never sets; You and yours

The sound of Bow bells. Random House 1962 531p $7.95

A novel of the "world of Manhattan book and magazine publishing. . . . Sam Silver is a boy from the Lower East Side whose great ambition is to make it big and move uptown. Goaded by a strong and fiercely ambitious mother, abetted by an ingeniously scheming wife and encouraged by two understanding literary agents, he is at twenty already a success as a short story writer and novelist. . . . Sam's major problem is coming to terms as a writer with his Jewish background and instincts." N Y Her Trib Books

Weingarten, Violet

A loving wife. Knopf 1969 241p $5.95

This novel is " about a typical, comparatively well-to-do New York matron, whose husband is successful, but not the great scientist he might once have been, and whose grown son is shacking up with a girl friend and thinks his parents are hopelessly out of things. Molly Gilbert also has a career as a case worker for a social agency, which really involves her, and as we meet her, she is going through a wrenching love affair that she knows has no future." Pub W

"Molly is a prototype of a very familiar person to most middle-class people over thirty. She is portrayed with a clear and deft precision that takes a certain creative talent and Miss Weingarten has it. 'A Loving Wife' is a pleasant way to spend a few leisurely spare hours." Best Sellers

Mrs Beneker; a novel. Simon & Schuster [1968 c1967] 224p $4.50

"Enrolled in a class for the study of comparative religion, [the trim, middle-aged heroine] looks for the meaning of life while all around her life is running wild. Her son devotes his energies to civil rights marches instead of school, drags home one unsuitable girl after another, and conducts a low-grade war with his parents. Her daughter introduces a whole new concept of motherhood with such vitality and success that Mrs. B. feels like a relic. Her husband doesn't exactly wander, but his affection roves, and our heroine is forced to reexamine the modern institution of marriage. To top it off, her parents, of [a venerable age] are down in Miami swinging the circuit." America

"Mrs. Weingarten selects a veritable bouquet of middle-class hangups as the centerpiece of her novel, and arranges them with arresting freshness. . . . [She] doesn't attempt a diagnosis, but charts interesting symptoms of the 'mal de siecle,' the worst of which is an excess of tolerance." N Y Times Bk R

Weinreb, Nathaniel Norsen

The Babylonians. Doubleday 1953 381p o.p. 1970

"Beladar, physician and friend to Nebuchadnezzar, King of Babylon, is sent on a secret mission to Jerusalem to win over the prophet Jeremiah and persuade him to lead a rebellion against the King of Judah. Although his political conspiracy fails he himself is won over to another way of life through love of a Jewish woman and belief in Jeremiah's preaching." Pub W

"Foreshadowing the advent of Christianity, the book portrays the ancient world in all its splendor, poverty, barbarism, and misery, with its forces of corruption and its characters of integrity waging the age-old struggle for mastery." Booklist

Weiss, David

Naked came I; a novel of Rodin. Morrow 1963 660p $7.95

In this novel the sculptor "is first of all deeply passionate about his art and, second, a sensual lover of women. . . . The book is . . . full of intimate pictures of writers and painters in Paris at time of volcanic change in the arts." Pub W

"Rodin's long battle with the French Academy and his friendships and disagreements with Degas, Monet, Renoir, Zola, and Rilke will make this appealing to readers interested in nineteenth-century art and literature." Booklist

Sacred and profane; a novel of the life and times of Mozart. Morrow 1968 639p boards $7.95

"A sympathetic attempt to tell the truth about Mozart, the eighteenth century composer who made his first public appearance before he was six, produced an amazing number of operas, operettas, and concertos, but died sick and poor at the age of thirty-five and was buried in an unmarked grave." Bk Buyer's Guide

The author "has put down every harrowing detail from birth to death in his lengthy book, which is a 'novel' only to the extent that it dramatizes biographical material with a generous recreation of some rather poignant scenes and 'imagines' others where there are gaps in Mozart's known affairs." Pub W

Weiss, Peter

Exile; a novel. Translators: E. B. Garside, Alastair Hamilton [and] Christopher Levenson. Delacorte Press 1968 245p boards $5.95

"A Seymour Lawrence book"

In two parts entitled Leavetaking and Vanishing point. Originally both parts were published separately in Germany in 1961 and 1962 respectively. The first English translation of Leavetaking was published in 1962

This autobiographical novel "is the story of the inner conflicts of a man trying to come to grips with his own personality. The search starts with a childhood spent in four different countries (Germany, England, Sweden, Switzerland), between the two World Wars." Pub W

Leavetaking

In Weiss, P. Exile p3-88

Vanishing point

In Weiss, P. Exile p91-245

Wellman, Paul I.

The chain; a novel. Doubleday 1949 368p o.p. 1970

Sequel to: The walls of Jericho

This novel "tells the story of the Reverend John Carlisle who brings to the mid-Western town of Jericho an uncompromising conscience and a secret. His secret, which remains undiscovered until the end is the flagellant chain which he wears about his waist. Soon after his arrival the townspeople were arrayed in two groups—those who discovered in him new hope and faith and those who bitterly hated him for throwing open the doors of fashionable St Albans to Jericho's slum dwellers. A suave, polished novel which is more notable for fast-paced action than spiritual depth." Rel Bk Club Bul

Followed by: Jericho's daughters

The Comancheros. Doubleday 1952 286p o.p. 1970

"Driven from New Orleans following a duel with the son of an influential judge, Paul Regret, gentleman gambler, joins the Texas Rangers. On his first assignment he successfully tracks down and destroys a band of Comancheros who are leading the Indians in devastating raids on the white settlers along the Texas border." Booklist

Wellman, Paul I.—*Continued*

The iron mistress. Doubleday 1951 404p
o.p. 1970

"A super-Western or historical adventure
novel based on the life of James Bowie, inventor and deadly manipulator of the Bowie
knife. Beginning with Bowie's New Orleans
visit in 1817, it carries him through fights,
love affairs, slave dealing, the theft of private
Lafitte's mulatto mistress, making and gambling away fortunes, to his military triumphs
and heroic death at the Alamo." Retail Bookseller

Jericho's daughters; a novel. Doubleday
1956 380p $3.95

Sequel to: The chain
Another story of Jericho, Kansas, whose
various residents, now older, are the "daughters" of the title. Mary Agnes uses her husband's newspaper as a tool against his infidelity and the blackmail with which she is
threatened. Murder and numerous other events
are involved in this chronicle of the character
of a town and its inhabitants

Magnificent destiny; a novel about the
great secret adventure of Andrew Jackson
and Sam Houston. Doubleday 1962 479p
$7.50

A "novel about the life and times of Andrew Jackson and Sam Houston and the in-
tersections of their careers as soldiers, politicians and statesmen. Beginning in 1813 and
carrying through to the death of Jackson, it is
a . . . rendition of the two men's lives and
personalities." Pub W
"Although in novel form, this is history on
a grand scale. Jackson is a truly heroic figure,
worthy of the admiration of his countrymen for
all future ages. Sam Houston, a much more
enigmatic figure, is also impressive. Mr. Wellman is no feminist and seems to understand
women as little as his heroes. 'Magnificent
Destiny' is recommended to adult readers, especially those who like American history and
its heroes." Best Sellers

Ride the red earth; a novel. Doubleday
1958 448p o.p. 1970

A "historical novel of the Southwest and
Mexico in the early 1700's when France and
Spain were contending for supremacy in Texas.
The recklessly bold hero, Louis Juchereau de
St Denis, relates his own part in the strug-
gle. . . . The novel is good for its fast-paced
action and suspense. It also shows evidence of
careful research." Library J

The walls of Jericho. Lippincott 1947 423p
o.p. 1970

"Jericho, Kansas, is the scene as well as
one of the leading characters of this full-
bodied, satisfying novel. From the time David
Constable comes to Jericho in 1901 to his final
vindication, the [small] town motivates his
every action. Here is the story of a friendship broken by a scheming wife and the political turmoil that followed its rupture, here
is the story of a love born of youthful admiration dragged through the most cruel scandal,
triumphing in the courtroom. . . . [Here too]
is the hardy spirit of the mid-West." Literary
Guild
Followed by: The chain

Wells, H. G.

Best science fiction stories of H. G. Wells.
Dover [distributed by Smith, P.] 1966 303p
$3.75

Analyzed in Short Story Index
Includes The invisible man and the following
stories: The crystal egg; The man who could
work miracles; The Plattner story; The strange
orchid; The new accelerator; The diamond
maker; The apple; The purple pileus; A dream
of Armageddon; Aepyornis Island; In the abyss;
The star; The Lord of the Dynamos; The story
of Davidson's eyes; In the Avu observatory;
The sea raiders; Filmers

The first men in the moon
In Wells, H. G. Seven science fiction
novels p455-620

The food of the gods
In Wells, H. G. Seven science fiction
novels p621-815

In the days of the comet
In Wells, H. G. Seven science fiction
novels p817-1015

y The invisible man
Some editions are:
Collins $1.95
Dial Press $7.50 Illustrated by Charles Mozley;
the introduction by Bernard Bergonzi
First published by Harper 1897
"A scientist discovers a means to make himself invisible. The tremendous powers he thus
acquires are, however, counter-balanced by
unexpected disabilities. His first adventures
are absurdly comic; but the invisible man is
driven at length to become a terror to his
kind, and his last stage is a gruesome tragedy." Baker's Best

also in Knight, D. ed. A century of great
short science fiction novels p63-168
also in Wells, H. G. Best science fiction
stories of H. G. Wells p 1-108
also in Wells, H. G. Seven science fiction
novels p183-306

The island of Dr Moreau
In Wells, H. G. Seven science fiction
novels p77-182

Mr Britling sees it through. Macmillan
(N Y) 1916 443p o.p. 1970

Set in rural England, this story describes
"how the great war [of 1914-1918] affected an
English family, their German tutor and American guest, and especially Mr Britling himself."
N Y State Lib

y Seven science fiction novels. Dover 1950
[c1934] 1015p $5

This omnibus volume was first published
1934 by Knopf with title: Seven famous novels
Contents: The time machine (1895) [entered
separately]; The island of Dr Moreau (1896);
The invisible man (1897) [entered separately];
The war of the worlds (1898) [entered separ-
ately]; The first men in the moon (1901); The
food of the gods (1904); In the days of the
comet (1906)
"The stories are printed . . . curiously enough,
in the order of merit. 'The Time Machine' is
a strenuous and exciting vision. 'In the Days
of the Comet' is a sugar-water sermon. Between are gradually descending degrees of
narrative effectiveness. But all the first five
stories may be called excellent." N Y Times
Bk R

y The time machine; an invention. Holt
1895 216p o.p. 1970

The owner of the time machine can travel
into the past or future at will. "The Time
Traveler's description of the people of the
future, the weak Eloi and the predatory Mor-
locks, has its roots in some interesting scientific hypotheses. This speculative chronicle of
a space-time concept and a picture of life in
the world of the future is so exciting, however, that it may be read merely as an adventure story. The book is a mixture of fantasy and pseudo-scientific romance." Magill.
Masterpieces

also in Wells, H. G. Seven science fiction
novels p 1-76
also in Wells, H. G. The war of the
worlds, The time machine, and selected short stories p246-380

Tono-Bungay; with an intoduction by C.
M. Joad. Collins 1953 349p (Collins New
classics ser) $1.95

First published 1908
"Tono-Bungay is the name of a patent
medicine which is launched by a chemist in
a small town and so well advertised that the
inventor attains the eminence of principal
company promoter of his day. Mr. Wells, writing in the character of the inventor's nephew,
unfolds the story with much significant detail." Pittsburgh

Wells, H. G.—*Continued*

"A typical mixture of humorous realism, social criticism, and theory . . . [in which the nephew] states his views on education and different grades of schools, and the general lack of organization in capitalistic society." Baker's Best

28 science fiction stories. Dover 1952 915p $5

Partially analyzed in Short Story Index
Contents: Men like gods; Empire of the ants; Land ironclads; Country of the blind; Stolen bacillus; Strange orchid; In the Avu observatory; Story of the stone age; Aepyornis Island; Remarkable case; Plattner story; Argonauts of the air; Late Mr Elvesham; In the abyss; Star begotten; Under the knife; Sea raiders; Crystal egg; The star; Man who could work miracles; Filmer; Story of the days to come; Magic shop; Valley of spiders; Truth about Pyecraft; New accelerator; Stolen body; Dream of Armageddon

The war of the worlds. Harper 1898 290p o.p. 1970

"The inhabitants of Mars, a loathsome though highly organized race, invade England, and by their command of superior weapons subdue and prey on the people." Baker's Best

also in Wells, H. G. Seven science fiction novels p307-453

y The war of the worlds, The time machine, and selected short stories; special foreword by Kingsley Amis. Complete and unabridged. Platt 1963 514p (Platt & Munk Great writers collection) $2.95

Partially analyzed in Short Story Index
Includes two science fiction novels first published 1898 and 1895 respectively, entered separately, and the following short stories: The crystal egg; The story of the late Mr Elvesham; The red room; The valley of spiders; In the abyss; In the Avu observatory; The truth about Pyecraft

Welty, Eudora

The bride of the Innisfallen, and other stories. Harcourt 1955 207p $4.95

Analyzed in Short Story Index
Contents: No place for you, my love; The burning; The bride of the Innisfallen; Ladies in spring; Circe; Kin; Going to Naples

A curtain of green
In Welty, E. Selected stories v 1

Delta wedding; a novel. Harcourt 1946 247p $4.95

This novel "is, in effect, a family album of snap-shots as they impressed themselves upon the memory of nine-year-old Laura McRaven who came to visit the [Mississippi] delta plantation home of her numerous cousins in 1923 [as they prepared for a wedding]." Am News of Bks
"This book is, in its manner, a tour de force. It registers a mood. It presents the essence of the deep South and it does it with infinite finesse. . . . There isn't any plot. There isn't any action. There isn't any suspense or crisis or noticeable sex appeal. There is atmosphere only and in delicious gulps." Christian Science Monitor

The golden apples. Harcourt 1949 244p o.p. 1970

Analyzed in Short Story Index
"Seven short stories of varying length [and mood] reveal relationships as they changed during 40 years in a small Mississippi town and seem almost a continuous narrative. Written with artistry in the indirect characterization of people as they are seen by each other, and with some suggestion of folk quality." Booklist
Contents: Shower of gold; June recital; Sir Rabbit; Moon Lake; Whole wide world knows; Music from Spain; The wanderers

The Ponder heart; drawings by Joe Krush. Harcourt 1954 156p illus $4.50

"Edna Earle Ponder who runs a hotel in a Mississippi town tells the story of her beloved Uncle Daniel Ponder. Uncle Daniel was soft hearted and even softer headed but Edna Earle loved him and reveled in his erratic doings." Book Rev Digest
"This is an encompassing, heartfelt story, absurd, true, and pathetic by turns, memorably vivid in the big scenes in the courthouse and at the funeral, and informed from first to last with an intimacy that makes it live." Atlantic

The robber bridegroom. Harcourt [1948 c1942] 185p $4.95

First published 1942 by Doubleday
"Combination of fairy tale and ballad story about a bandit chief and Rosemond, the beautiful daughter of a Mississippi planter. Among the characters is one named simply Goat, because he could butt his way into and out of anything. There is Mike Fink, too, the Paul Bunyan of the rivermen; and there are Little Harp and Big Harp, a weird pair of brothers." Book Rev Digest

Selected stories; containing all of A curtain of green, and other stories, and The wide net, and other stories; with an introduction by Katherine Anne Porter. Modern Lib. 1954 2v in 1 $2.95

Analyzed in Short Story Index
First published as separate volumes by Doubleday 1941, and Harcourt 1943, respectively
Includes the following stories: v 1: Clytie; A curtain of green; Death of a traveling salesman; Flowers for Marjorie; The hitchhikers; Keela, the outcast Indian maiden; The key; Lily Daw and the three ladies; A memory; Old Mr Marblehall; Petrified man; Piece of news; Powerhouse; Visit of charity; The whistle; Why I live at the P.O.; Worn path
v2: The wide net; First love; A still moment; Asphodel; The winds; The purple hat; Livvie; At the landing

The wide net, and other stories
In Welty, E. Selected stories v2

Werfel, Franz

Embezzled heaven; tr. by Moray Firth. Viking 1940 427 o.p. 1970

Original German edition published 1939
First published in German, 1939
"The story of Teta, a shrewd but faithful peasant servant, who tries to guarantee her passage to heaven by educating a scapegrace nephew for the priesthood. The account of her schemings, her disillusionment, and her pilgrimage to Rome is set against the background of the doomed yet charming world of Viennese intellectual society in the days before the Anschluss. [The author] subtly contrasts Teta's strong but narrow faith with the broad but weak culture of her employer's world. A poignant and touching narrative." Huntting

The forty days of Musa Dagh. Viking 1934 824p o.p. 1970

Original German edition published 1933. English edition published with title: The forty days
"Gabriel Bagradian, a rich Armenian who had lived twenty-years in Paris and married a French wife, returned to his home in Syria in 1915, there to be caught in the Turkish campaign of extermination against the Armenians. The central episode of the story is the forty days' siege of Musa Dagh during which the inhabitants of seven villages, under the leadership of Bagradian, resisted the Turkish army until rescued by the French." Book Rev Digest

y The song of Bernadette; tr. by Ludwig Lewisohn. Viking 1942 575p o.p. 1970

Original German edition published 1941
"This lovely tale recounts the life of St. Bernadette of Lourdes. While it cannot be called a religious work, it is truly reverent in its approach to the inscrutable, the unfathomable, the divine. The conflict of the childishly naive, yet strong-willed and confident, Bernadette with the cynical rulers of her society

Werfel, Franz—*Continued*

is a compassionate and moving narrative. And into his story of the miracle, and the young girl through whom it was manifested, Werfel weaves an engrossing picture of emperor, bishops, priests, nuns, merchants and artisans —a fascinating and living pageant of the Second Empire in France." Huntting

Werner, Heinz

(jt. comp.) Fabricant, N. A treasury of doctor stories by the world's great authors

Wescott, Glenway

Apartment in Athens. Harper 1945 268p o.p. 1970

Set in occupied Athens, this is a story of the inhumanity of the Germans in their occupation of defeated countries. The author describes the influence upon a simple middle-class Greek family of a German officer who was quartered upon them
"A fine study of humiliation and nobility, and their culmination in tragedy and desperate resolve." N Y Times Bk R

The grandmothers; a family portrait; with an introduction by Fred B. Millett. Harper 1950 388p (Harper's Modern classics) $2

First published 1927
"To account for his own complex personality, Alwyn, the cosmopolitan grandson of Wisconsin farming folk, builds for himself, from keepsakes, daguerreotypes and tintypes, the story of his typically American clan which derives from and centers in the old home in Southern Wisconsin and epitomizes the growth of a civilization from pioneer days to the present. A series of fragmentary narratives, welded . . . into a moving chronicle, this story received the 1927-1928 Harper Prize Award." Open Shelf

The pilgrim hawk
In Phillips, W. ed. Great American short novels p625-82

West, Jessamyn

y Cress Delahanty; drawings by Joe Krush. Harcourt 1953 311p illus $4.95

"In story-sketches that reveal with touching humor an adolescent's real problems from her 12th to her 16th year, likable Cress grows up on a California ranch, making her mark at school, exploring the strange ways of 'boys,' and being always loved and cherished by her often bewildered parents." Bookmark
"Anyone who knows adolescence, and especially that of young girls, will love this book. It is beautifully written, with the most extraordinary insight and delicacy." Commonweal

y Except for me and thee; a companion to The friendly persuasion. Harcourt 1969 309p $5.95

This episodic narrative of the lives of Jess and Eliza Birdwell, the hero and heroine of The friendly persuasion, entered below, begins "at the time when Jess, 21 and experiencing his own brand of youthful rebellion against his parents and their Quaker teachings, finds himself engaged to three girls at the same time. Wisely, he marries Eliza. . . . The author describes how the Birdwells meet the challenges of their new home: facing the death of a young daughter . . . becoming involved with helping runaway slaves along the Underground Railway, finally seeing their lives affected by the onset of the Civil War." Pub W
This "book that has all the warmth, the sturdy affection, and the quiet humor of its predecessor. . . . In part the charm of the novel owes to the vibrant authenticity of its characters; in great part it is due to the practiced ease and resilience of style." Sat R

y The friendly persuasion. Harcourt 1945 214p $4.95

Analyzed in Short Story Index
Episodic chapters about the Birdwell family, nineteenth century Quakers living in Indiana during the period following the Civil War

Contents: Music on the Muscatatuck; Shivaree before breakfast; Pacing goose; Lead her like a pigeon; Battle of Finney's ford, Buried leaf; Likely exchange; First day finish; "Yes, we'll gather at the river"; Meeting house; The vase; The illumination; Pictures from a clapboard house; Homer and the lilies

Leafy Rivers. Harcourt 1967 310p $5.95

Set in Ohio of 1818
"Told in flashbacks as Leafy struggles to have her child. It is the story of Leafy's growing up, of her marriage to a handsome, unaggressive schoolteacher, Reno Rivers, and their efforts to make a home and a living in Whitewater Valley, of Leafy's brief, glorious affair with a drover, Cashie Wade, and her realization that she really does love her husband." Book of the Month Club News
"Jessamyn West's theme is meaningful and timeless. Gently and expertly told, the novel is never sentimental, never awkward. In fact, it seems so immediate, one forgets it's historical fiction. Miss West knows how to put her readers in touch with the realities of yesterday and today." Pub W

Love, death, and the ladies' drill team. Harcourt [1955] 248p o.p. 1970

Analyzed in Short Story Index
Contents: Time of learning; Mysteries of life in an orderly manner; Love, death, and the ladies' drill team; Home-coming; Battle of the suits; Tom Wolfe's my name; Learn to say goodby; Little collar for the monkey; Public-address system; Foot-shaped shoes; Horace Chooney, M.D.; Linden trees; Breach of promise; Singing lesson

West, Morris L.

The ambassador. Morrow 1965 275p boards $4.95

"A fictionalized facsimile of the U.S. dilemma in Vietnam uses the episode of the assassination of Ngo Dinh Diem as a pattern. The result is a timely dramatization of the failure of the Western mind to grasp the Eastern view of reality. The narrator, the American ambassador Amberley, in telling his own tragic involvement in the happenings shows the religious, political and national complexities of the situation and brings out American internecine disagreement. A polemic rather than a literary work." Booklist
"Mr. West manages to retain the reader's sympathy with 'Amberley' even as his disgust and horror mount; and there is a first-hand 'feel' of Saigon and spider-web intricacies of diplomatic and C.I.A. machinations that make the novel disturbingly realistic. . . . Its timeliness is searingly sardonic." Library J

Daughter of silence. Morrow 1961 275p boards $4.50

The setting is contemporary Italy in the upland valleys of Tuscany. The focal point of the novel is the trial of a young woman on a charge of murder and her defense by a fledgling lawyer. The trial is conducted under the classic Latin method of Inquisition and its revelations open up sixteen years of sinister history. (Publisher)
"Anna, the poignant young girl on trial; Carlo, her lawyer, a brilliant young man with a fatal flaw in his character; and Doctor Ascolini, celebrated old mountebank-advocateroué-philosopher: these are only three in a fascinating gallery of very real and fallible people. The story itself is as taut and demanding as the best of thrillers." Library J

The devil's advocate. Morrow 1959 319p boards $4.95

In this novel "the plot concerns a British Monsignor who investigates the petition for canonization of a man who died before a partisan firing squad in Calabria during World War II. As the investigation progresses, he learns a great deal about the man, his family, the village in which he lived and, especially, about himself." Pub W
"The characters all are firmly, brightly established. The writing, without fanciness or flourish, goes along with a fine, steady drive. There are no profound insights, no remarkable illuminations. But there is an engrossing story, expertly told, about a set of fascinating people whose lives are viewed as meaningful." Chicago Sunday Tribune

West, Morris L.—*Continued*

The shoes of the fisherman; a novel. Morrow 1963 374p boards $5.95

A "story about the problems of a newly elected Pope from the Ukraine who has spent many years as a prisoner of the Russians in Siberia. He knows, and has the grudging respect of Russia's Premier. . . . A subplot of a much more temporal nature is the story of an American newspaperman and a young Italian matron." Pub W

"This fantastic novel . . . is a whopper, a spellbinder, a cliff-hanger, an annoyance and a delight. Let those who disdain a story turn up their noses at this fine example of the craft of a notable spinner of tales. . . . Some of [the fictional pope's] supposed 'reforms' will strike many a reader, clerical or lay, as rather silly, but the underlying motivation is something with which no one can quarrel . . . . If there is no great spiritual profundity in his tale, at least it shows the Church as a mighty force in the world. And, come to think of it, the Church is pretty glamorous, too; so perhaps we can forgive West his penchant for seeing the sublime work of Christ's Mystical Body somewhat in terms of cloak and dagger." America

The tower of Babel; a novel. Morrow 1968 361p boards $5.95

"This novel begins with a mine explosion that kills an Israeli tractor operator, and comes to an end sometime in January, 1967. The rest of the book tells of a few days in the lives of five major characters as they create and react to the tensions of the Middle East during the period just before the six-day war. [They are] Jakov Baratz, Director of Israeli Military Intelligence; . . . Adom Ronen, Israel's man in Damascus; Safreddin, the Syrian director of security; . . . Nuri Chakry, a banker in Beirut; and . . . Idris Jarrah, a cynical but effective member of the [Palestine Liberation Front]." America

"The complexities of the economic, political, and even personal relationships in this novel cannot even be hinted at. A sparely written novel . . . there is action on every level of international intrigue, most plausibly asserted. . . . Mr. West has not written—those familiar with his work need no reassurance—merely a story of espionage and intrigue in the Middle East. He has written a novel that makes this time and place come alive." Best Sellers

West, Nathaniel

The complete works of Nathaniel West. Farrar, Straus 1957 xxii, 421p boards $6

"Included here are 'The Dream Life of Balso Snell' 1931, a surrealist sexual nightmare in prose, 'Miss Lonelyhearts,' 1933, [entered separately] a biting satire on modern man and his aspirations, 'A Cool Million,' 1934, melodramatic satire on the American dream of success, and 'The Day of the Locust,' 1939, a bitter tale of Hollywood and its hangers-on. There is a perceptive introduction by the British critic, Alan Ross." Library J

A cool million

In West, N. The complete works of Nathaniel West p143-256

The day of the locust

In West, N. The complete works of Nathaniel West p259-421

The dream life of Balso Snell

In West, N. The complete works of Nathaniel West p3-62

Miss Lonelyhearts. Liveright 1933 213p o.p. 1970

"The story of a man who writes an 'advice to the lovelorn' column, the theme of the book is the loneliness of the individual in modern society. The hero tries to live the role of omniscient counselor he has assumed for the paper, but his attempts to reach out to suffering humanity are twisted by circumstances, and he is finally murdered by a man he has tried to help." Benét. The Reader's Encyclopedia

also in West, N. The complete works of Nathaniel West p65-140

West, Rebecca

The birds fall down. Viking 1966 435p boards $5.95

"This is the world of turn-of-the-century Russian terrorists, fanatic idealists who would as soon hurl a bomb as pen a pamphlet. One of them accosts an aged Russian nobleman and his 18-year-old half-English granddaughter on a provincial French train. He unfolds a spellbinding tale of a double agent serving both the terrorists and the Tsar. The old man collapses from shock and dies, leaving his granddaughter, one of the most delightful heroines in many a day, at the mercy of the double agent whose identity she now knows. To save her life she enters into a fantastic alliance with the terrorist of the train." Pub W

"Based on true events and their participants . . . the Russian character as evinced by both anarchist and czarist and the reproduction of the social milieu are convincing, while the humor, tension, and tragedy make a full-bodied story." Booklist

The fountain overflows; a novel. Viking 1956 435p $5.95

A "story of a large London family of the Edwardian era, the talented children of a charming, wise mother and an improvident father." Pub W

"All of the best qualities of the superb writer are gathered together in this novel. . . . Wit, subtlety, and humour with a realistic approach to the problems of a family." Library J

West, Victoria Sackville- See Sackville-West, Victoria

Westcott, Jan

The white rose. Putnam 1969 448p $6.95

"The time is the turbulent reign of Edward IV and his queen, Elizabeth Woodville, whose family had been Edward's enemies in the bitter War of the Roses. It was inevitable that intrigue, murder and contests for the crown would follow. . . . Replete with details of customs of the time, the novel, even if it discloses no new insight into the politics of the time, is readable for its warmth, charm, solidity and clarity." Pub W

Western Writers of America

Frontiers West, by members of the Western Writers of America. Ed. and with an introduction by S. Omar Barker. Doubleday 1959 286p o.p. 1970

Partially analyzed in Short Story Index
Contents: Ghost town, by J. M. Myers; Spirit of Katyann, by V. Athanas; Bridegroom came late, by T. Ballard; First kill, by W. C. Brown; Decision, by W. R. Cox; Geranium house, by P. S. Curry; Herd law, by H. G. Evarts; Holecard, by B. Foster; Another man's boots, by N. A. Fox; Trial by jury, by B. Gulick; Therefore hog, by A. B. Guthrie, Jr; Lapwai winter, by W. Henry; Afternoon of a hero, by D. M. Johnson; Debt of Hardy Buckelew, by E. Kelton; Grandfather out of the past, by N. M. Loomis; Mean men are big, by W. D. Overholser; Silent ranch, by S. Payne; Bear-sign, by J. Prescott; Lady bandit and the blizzard, by F. C. Robertson; Blackie Gordon's corset, by W. O. Turner

Rawhide men, by members of the Western Writers of America; ed. by Kenneth Fowler. Doubleday 1965 215p o.p. 1970

Partially analyzed in Short Story Index
Ten "tales saluting the trailblazing scouts, cattle drivers and rugged pioneers that opened and settled the Old West." Publisher's note
Contents: Rawhide (verse), by S. O. Barker; Saddle or nothing, by S. O. Barker; Welcome from Broken Jaw, by T. W. Blackburn; A rose for Dan Robie, by A. R. Bosworth; Proud guidon, by W. Chamberlain; Caballero Alegre, by A. V. Elston; Deadline, by C. Farrell; The fitness of Sean O'Fallon, by N. A. Fox; Big Olaf paints for war, by B. Gulick; Crisis in the canyon, by E. Haycox; Winter harvest, by J. Prescott

Western Writers of America—*Continued*

Rivers to cross; a collection of stories by members of Western Writers of American; ed. by William R. Cox. Dodd 1966 208p o.p. 1970

Partially analyzed in Short Story Index
Contents: Los caballeros [poem] by S. O. Barker; Decision at the Rio Blanco, by N. S. Hall; One more river to cross, by W. R. Cox; Sacramento run, by T. W. Blackburn; Despatch to the general, by E. Haycox; Big Shad's bridge, by M. Evans; Dobbs Ferry, by L. B. Patten; The toll at Yaeger's Ferry, by B. Garfield; The cruise of the Prairie Queen, by D. D. Beauchamp; Goliad goes to war, by K. Fowler; Down by the banks of the Pecos [poem], by S. O. Barker

They opened the West; an anthology. Ed. by Tom W. Blackburn. Doubleday 1967 240p o.p. 1970

Partially analyzed in Short Story Index
Contents: High-water highway, by C. Farrell; The proud, by L. Moore; Where the wind blows free, by B. Gulick; Whistle on the river, by G. Cheshire; Riverboat fighter, by B. Garfield; Peaceful John, by K. Fowler; God help the Vigilantes, by F. C. Robertson; Mochila mail—epoch of courage; non-fiction, by G. Shirley; A place for Danny Thorpe, by R. Hogan; Rough road to Royal Gorge, by C. S. Park; The business of making money; non-fiction, by A. W. Spring; The homeseekers, by F. Grove; The windmill man, by A. R. Bosworth

A Western bonanza; eight short novels of the West by members of the Western Writers of Amrica; ed. by Todhunter Ballard. Doubleday 1969 419p $6.95

Contents: Hell command, by C. Adams; Marshall for Las Moras, by E. Barker; Mutiny on the Box Cross, by A. V. Elston; Westward—to blood and glory, by C. Farrell; The skinning of Black Coyote, by C. Fisher; The hexed rifle, by B. Gulick; Death trap for an iron horse rebel, by C. N. Heckelmann; Danger hole, by L. Short

Westheimer, David

My sweet Charlie. Doubleday 1965 255p o.p. 1970

"A story of the confrontation of an ignorant Southern young girl and a cultivated Northern Negro. They take refuge in a summer cottage on the Gulf of Mexico, he in flight after an accidental murder and she from shame of a pregnancy following seduction." Booklist
"The novel is a touching story of two people, thrown together by circumstance, who are brought to the realization that hate and prejudice are the products of ignorance and fear. Mr. Westheimer handles an explosive theme with delicacy and restraint." Library J

y Song of the young sentry. Little 1968 376p boards $6.95

"The hero, a soft, corpulent, and self-centered lieutenant, is imprisoned with his captain and another crew member in an Italian prison camp when their bomber falls in the water after a World War II attack on Naples. During his Italian incarceration and later in a German prison camp Lieutenant Long matures through the necessity of making the best of hardship." Booklist
"Concisely told, the narrative seems simple, but in the wealth of growing human relationships it becomes epic. The free-flowing narrative and dialogue style is replete with conscious endeavour, as the men rise above their conditions and mature into sensitory and sensible human beings. . . . The story has its funny moments and its poignant ones, interlaced with hairbreadth adventures, told with a fast direction that draws the reader on." Best Sellers

Von Ryan's Express. Doubleday 1964 327p $4.95

"A thousand British and American soldiers in a prisoner-of-war camp in Italy are augmented by one American colonel who outranks them all and whose strict discipline in bringing order into the camp earns him the Prussian title 'von.' When Italy surrenders and the Germans load the men in boxcars to be sent to Germany, Ryan with the assistance of his next in command with much derring-do plus commando tactics takes over the train and carries the men to Switzerland." Booklist
"There is a great deal of killing of the German guards on the train, necessary for the take-over, and readers with queasy stomachs will find some of it much too much for their sensitivities. But the suspense builds, with unforseen obstacles cropping up and nick-o'-time rescues and diversions about equal, so that it is safe to bet that most will not want to put the novel down until the end." Best Sellers

Westlake, Donald E.

The busy body. Random House 1966 176p o.p. 1970

"Aloysius Engel is a modern Syndicate man, who rarely soils his hands with the mechanics of crime, but helps his big boss direct overall operations on the financial level. But when an underling is inadvertently buried in a suit interlined with a quarter of a million dollars' worth of heroin, Engel is assigned to the job of digging up the body. When he finds the coffin empty, his troubles begin." Pub W
"The body keeps busy moving in this joyous comedy of peril, which some Runyonesque mobsters try to catch up with the remains of a dead confrere." Am News of Bks

The curious facts preceding my execution, and other fictions. Random House 1968 211p o.p. 1970

Analyzed in Short Story Index
"Contains 15 short stories, most of them concerned with the frustration of a criminal. . . . They are outstanding in inventiveness; their settings and characters marked by variety." Pub W
Contents: The curious facts preceding my execution; You put on some weight; Sniff; Good night, good night; Devilishly; Murder in outer space; No story; The sincerest form of flattery; Just one of those days; Never shake a family tree; Just the lady we're looking for; Domestic intrigue; One man on a desert island; The sweetest man in the world; The mother of invention is worth a pound of cure

The fugitive pigeon. Random House 1965 172p illus. o.p. 1970

"A Random House mystery"
A lazy, "inoffensive Brooklyn bartender with the bad luck to have an uncle in the criminal underground is slated for killing. . . . He keeps thinking there is a reasonable way out of his predicament, but with two thugs on his trail this doesn't seem likely, so he turns desperate and resourceful. The book becomes a riotous, hairbreadth escape chase through most of New York City." Pub W

God save the mark. Random House 1967 209p o.p. 1970

"Our hero is Fred Fitch, easy mark of every itinerant grifter, hipster, short-changer, and you-name-it artist to hit New York. When this instinctive sucker inherits $300,000, a sexy girl, and an unsolved murder, the situation means merry mayhem as only Westlake spells it." McClurg, Book News
"Entertaining and as mystifying to the reader as [the hero's] predicament is to the baffled victim." Pub W

The spy in the ointment. Random House 1966 200p o.p. 1970

"When the FBI learned that pacifist Gene Raxford and his girl friend, Angela, had by some mistake been invited to the meeting of a terrorist group headed by Angela's Communist brother, Tyrone, they persuaded Gene [Raxford, a dedicated Ban-the-Bomb advocate] to infiltrate the group—which led to wild adventure and danger." Bk Buyer's Guide

Up your banners; a novel. Macmillan (N Y) 1969 320p $5.95

" 'Racism!' cry the militant Blacks when a ghetto school hires a white teacher over a Negro. 'Nepotism!' cry the teachers upon discovering that the new man is the principal's son. Amidst ensuing hysterical calamities, the hapless young teacher complicates the crisis by falling in love with a fellow teacher who is both beautiful and black." News of Bks

Westlake, Donald E.—*Continued*

"This light compassionate and understanding view of secondary education in Brooklyn will be welcome wherever there is concern about integration and schools." Library J

Who stole Sassi Manoon? Random House 1969 178p boards $4.95

"Because Kelly Nicholas IV's education has left him 'unequipped for gainful labor,' this earnest young man decides to acquire, in one big criminal caper, enough money to live at ease the rest of his life. The crime—the kidnaping of the world's most highly-paid movie star—is entirely planned and directed by the computer Kelly has built on his cruiser, 'Nothing Ventured IV.' Kelly, with two companions selected by his computer, descends upon Montego Bay, where [actress] Sassi is to attend a film festival. Unknown to the computer, a few other characters are converging on Jamaica, bound to jam up Kelly's plan." Pub W

(jt. ed.) Tenn, W. ed. Once against the law

For other titles by this author see Coe, Tucker

Wharton, Edith

y The age of innocence; introduction by R. W. B. Lewis. Scribner 1968 361p $5.95

Pulitzer Prize 1921

First published by Appleton, 1920
"The novel gives an excellent picture of New York 'Society' in the 1870's, the age of propriety and inexorable convention, of clan spirit and tribal solidarity in support of prescribed amenities. The author lays bare the destructive powers of social codes when confronted by an exceptional person. A woman who has incurred scandal is loved by a man who has sufficient vision to penetrate the crust of conventionality but has not quite the courage to break with the conventions. . . . Later, when [this man's] children are full grown, he has the satisfaction of seeing them step out freely on the road that had been denied him." Lenrow. Reader's Guide to Prose Fiction

also In Wharton, E. An Edith Wharton treasury p3-232

The best short stories of Edith Wharton; ed. with an introduction by Wayne Andrews. Scribner 1958 292p o.p. 1970

Analyzed in Short Story Index
Contents: Roman fever; Xingu; The other two; Pomegranate seed; Souls belated; The angel at the grave; The last asset; After Holbein; Bunner sisters; Autres temps

Bunner sisters
In Wharton, E. An Edith Wharton treasury

Certain people
In Wharton, E. The collected short stories of Edith Wharton v2 p501-616

The collected short stories of Edith Wharton; ed. and with an introduction by R. W. B. Lewis. Scribner 1968 2v ea $8.95

Partially analyzed in Short Story Index
Contains ten collections of stories: The greater inclination (1899); Crucial instances (1901); The descent of man (1904); The hermit and the wild woman (1908); Tales of men and ghosts (1910); Xingu (1916); Here and beyond (1926); Certain people (1930); Human nature (1933); The world over (1936). Also included are thirteen miscellaneous stories, two dramatic sketches and some articles about the short story and ghost stories

Contents for the short stories included in the volumes are as follows:
The greater inclination: The muse's tragedy; A journey; The pelican; Souls belated; A coward; A cup of cold water; The portrait
Crucial instances: The Duchess at prayer; The angel at the grave; The recovery; The Rembrandt; The moving finger; The confessional

The descent of man: The descent of man; The mission of Jane; The other two; The quicksand; The dilettante; The reckoning; Expiation; The lady's maid's bell; A Venetian night's entertainment
The hermit and the wild woman: The hermit and the wild woman; The last asset; In trust; The pretext; The verdict; The potboiler; The best man
Tales of men and ghosts: The bolted door; His father's son; The daunt Diana; The debt; Full circle; The legend; The eyes; The blond beast; Afterward; The letters
Xingu: Xingu; Coming home; Autres temps . . . ; Kerfol; The long run; The triumph of night; The choice
Here and beyond: Miss Mary Pask; The young gentlemen; Bewitched; The seed of the faith; The temperate zone; Velvet ear pads
Certain people: Atrophy; A bottle of Perrier; After Holbein; Dieu d'amour; The refugees; Mr Jones
Human nature: Her son; The day of the funeral; A glimpse; Joy in the house; Diagnosis
The world over: Charm incorporated; Pomegranate seed; Permanent wave; Confession; Roman fever; The looking glass; Duration
Miscellaneous short stories: Mrs Manstey's views; The fullness of life; That good may come; The lamp of Psyche; April showers; Friends; The line of least resistance; The letter; The House of the Dead Hand; The introducers; Les metteurs en scène; Writing a war story; All souls'
"The collection is printed in a clear, virile type that is at once handsome and easy to read. As this will undoubtedly remain the standard edition of Edith Wharton's short stories in the foreseeable future, no library that collects fiction should be without it." Choice

Crucial instances
In Wharton, E. The collected short stories of Edith Wharton v 1 p227-343

The custom of the country. Scribner 1913 594p o.p. 1970

"This lengthy novel is almost a comprehensive treatise on the American problem of marriage and divorce. Undine, Mrs. Wharton's hard and empty adventuress, with no fortune but her face, is married and divorced with unblushing frequency and dispatch, and her vulgar ambitions meet with rebuffs in various social spheres. The lesson implied is that the American system of keeping the women as ornaments and luxuries with no interest in the business of life is what demoralizes them." Baker's Best

The descent of man
In Wharton, E. The collected short stories of Edith Wharton v 1 p345-490

An Edith Wharton treasury; ed. with an introduction by Arthur Hobson Quinn. Appleton 1950 xxxi, 581p o.p. 1970

Partially analyzed in Short Story Index
Includes the novel: The age of innocence, in entirety; three novelettes: The old maid, Madame de Treymes, Bunner sisters; and eight short stories: After Holbein, The other two, A bottle of Perrier, The lady's maid's bell, Roman fever, The moving finger, Xingu, and Autres temps

y Ethan Frome

Some editions are:
Scribner $4.50. With an introduction by Bernard de Voto
Watts, F. $7.95 Large type edition. A Keith Jennison book. With an introduction written for this edition
First published 1911
"A grim tale of retribution told in so masterly a manner that the story seems a transcription from real life. The three characters are a discouraged New England farmer, his hypochondriac wife, and a girl who still finds some joy in living." Booklist

False dawn
In Phillips, W. ed. Great American short novels p403-49
In Wharton, E. Old New York v 1

Wharton, Edith—*Continued*

The gods arrive. Scribner [1969 c1960] 439p $6.95

Sequel to: Hudson River bracketed
A reissue of a title first published 1932 by Appleton
"Picking up where 'Hudson River Bracketed' [entered separately] left off. Vance Weston and Halo Tarrant are reunited after his wife dies. Halo leaves her husband and she and Vance go to Europe where she hopes his writing career will flourish. Halo then faces a struggle with the emotional writer and with her own problem of being unable to obtain a divorce." Bk Buyer's Guide
"Mrs. Wharton satirizes the modernists in her own leisurely way, conceding not the fraction of an inch in either theory or practice to their literary claims. So the issue is fairly drawn; and the decision left to the reader." Books

The greater inclination
In Wharton, E. The collected short stories of Edith Wharton v 1 p65-185

Here and beyond
In Wharton, E. The collected short stories of Edith Wharton v2 p371-500

The hermit and the wild woman
In Wharton, E. The collected short stories of Edith Wharton v 1 p569-705

The house of mirth; with a foreword by Marcia Davenport. Scribner 1951 329p $5.95

First published 1905
"The title is ironical, in keeping with this book's implicit criticism of the garish life and shallow ethics of exclusive New York society. . . . Lily Bart, the orphaned child of a New York merchant, endowed with beauty, exquisite in physical charm, keen to seize advantages, alert in social crises, calmly prepares campaigns to marry for the power and luxury that money gives, despite the fact that she is impelled toward Lawrence Selden, a lawyer of moderate means, by everything fine in her nature. Relentlessly she is enmeshed in the toils of debt incurred at bridge; in scandal, the price of a trip upon a friend's yacht; and almost in a loveless marriage. . . . Unable to intrigue successfully and the victim of circumstances at every turn, Lily has no other way out save death." Lenrow. Reader's Guide to Prose Fiction

Hudson River bracketed. Scribner [1969 c1957] 536p $7.95

A reissue of a title first published 1929 by Appleton
"Vance Weston, a young writer, meets Halo Tarrant, who believes strongly in his talents and helps him as much as she can. Although she is in love with Vance, Halo marries a man she knew before and has to watch as Vance becomes disillusioned by the literary world of New York, and marries his ailing cousin." Bk Buyer's Guide
Followed by: The gods arrive

Human nature
In Wharton, E. The collected short stories of Edith Wharton v2 p617-740

Madame de Treymes
In Wharton, E. An Edith Wharton treasury

New Year's Day
In Wharton, E. Old New York v4

The old maid
In Costain, T. B. comp. Twelve short novels p235-88
In Wharton, E. An Edith Wharton treasury
In Wharton, E. Old New York v2

Old New York. Scribner 1952 306p $4.95

First published separately by Appleton 1924
Contents: False dawn; The old maid; The spark; New Year's Day
"Four stories of four successive decades in New York social life which together form an authentic social history of Old New York in the middle years of the last century. 'False dawn' is a picture of the city in the 'fabulous forties.'. . . 'The old maid' is an intense drama throbbing under the smooth surface of the complacent fifties—a story of mother-love revolving about the unacknowledged parentage of Tina Lovell. 'The spark' tells the story of Hayley Delane, apparently acquiescent to his frivolous wife and the petty social round in which he moves. . . . 'New Year's Day' is the story of Lizzie Hazeldean—another poignant tragedy unsuspected under the conventional surface of the seventies." Book Rev Digest

The reef. Scribner 1965 367p $5.95

First published 1912 by Appleton. The 1965 edition includes an introduction by Louis Auchincloss
Set in early twentieth-century France, this novel "concerns Anna's discovery that the man she is about to marry has had an affair with her daughter's governess whom her stepson wants to marry." Bk Buyer's Guide
According to Louis Auchincloss, this is Miss Wharton's most Jamesian novel

The spark
In Wharton, E. Old New York v3

Tales of men and ghosts
In Wharton, E. The collected short stories of Edith Wharton v2 p1-206

The world over
In Wharton, E. The collected short stories of Edith Wharton v2 p741-871

Xingu
In Wharton, E. The collected short stories of Edith Wharton v2 p207-356

Wheeler, Harvey
(jt. auth.) Burdick, E. Fail-safe

Wheeler, Keith
The last Mayday. Doubleday 1968 333p $5.95

"Kirov, former Soviet Government Chairman has decided to defect. Uzzumekis, once an American spy, has agreed to deliver him to the nuclear submarine 'Skate' in the Black Sea . . . [but] 'Skate' with Kirov aboard, is hit by a Russian torpedo and sinks, helpless in a trough on the ocean floor. Rescue of her more than 100-man crew is daringly undertaken by a small submarine. Scenes alternate between the sunken vessel, where air is rapidly diminishing, and the White House, with the President on the hot line to Moscow. Three times the rescue ship makes the trip to 'Skate,' taking off the men whom Captain Stephens must select for the chance to live. Finally, only Kirov, who has had a change of heart, and the Captain, under orders never to let 'Skate' be captured, are left." Pub W
"If you are looking for a good novel of 'international crises' for your male readers, don't overlook this one." Library J

Peaceable Lane. Simon & Schuster 1960 345p map boards $4.50

"A novel about a small Westchester community that learns to really known itself during the tense period when a Negro family is trying to buy a house. The main character, a kind of Everyman, knows the would-be buyer as a talented commercial artist and friend and business associate. The impact of unacknowledged racial fears on their friendship is also delineated." Pub W
"This novel is not a preachment on race relations, nor does it offer any panacea. It is effective, in fact rather terrifying, as a picture of something that might happen in a town one knows and of situations that it would take courage and integrity to face." N Y Her Trib Books

Whipple, Maurine

The giant Joshua. Houghton 1941 637p
o.p. 1970

"Mormon life is portrayed for the first time
from the woman's point of view. The story is
of a Mormon girl who learns to endure incredible hardships and to share her husband
with his other wives. The time is the 1860's,
and the scene, an outpost in the Utah desert."
Ontario Lib Rev

White, Alan

The long night's walk. Harcourt [1969
1968] 160p $4.50

First published 1968 in England
"In a fast-paced war adventure for men
four British commandos who parachute behind German lines in Holland have 36 hours
in which to upset the working of an entire
signal headquarters without being seen or doing
any damage that would cause the Germans to
suspect their presence. Plagued by a series of
misadventures and ferreted out by the Germans from whom they manage to escape, the
four realize they must rely only on themselves to effect a return to England." Booklist

White, Edward Lucas

The unwilling vestal; a tale of Rome
under the Cæsars. Dutton 1918 317p $5.95

"Rome, A.D. 161-191. A story dealing with
the time of Marcus Aurelius and his son.
Commodus: both figures appear prominently.
Illustrates especially the status of the Vestals.
The characters converse in modern familiar
language—the author insisting on this method
of presenting ancient life as fundamentally
truer and more illuminating than a more
strained or pedantic method." Nield

White, Helen C.

Bird of fire; a tale of St Francis of Assisi.
Macmillan (N Y) 1958 281p o.p. 1970

In this novel "St Francis himself springs
into life as he is shown as a high-spirited
Umbrian youth who became a humble man
and a great saint. The author portrays his
slow winning of the small world of Assisi,
and the gradual spread of his Franciscan
Order through a chaotic thirteenth century
world." Publisher's note

White, Nelia Gardner

The gift and the giver; a novel. Viking
1957 316p o.p. 1970

"A study of the character of Cornelia Boone,
'a big weather-beaten, middle-aged woman
with style,' who tells her own story in this
novel. Cornelia did not understand people,
least of all herself, but she inspired loyalties.
Her husband loved her, but left her to keep
his own integrity, and took their little daughter
with him. Cornelia was left with the house
she loved and the son she adored. Her story
traces her life and her son's and daughter's,
until they both married. Then there was nothing left but the house and one staunch friend,
and perhaps a better understanding of herself." Book Rev Digest

The thorn tree; a novel. Viking 1955
316p o.p. 1970

"When John Esker, the pianist, died, his
wife seemed to go into a strange form of
shock—not grief so much as withdrawal from
life. While her brother and sister, the talented
Doorns, wondered what had happened to Elspeth, Sebastian Esker flew over from Paris and
found out, because he loved her. An almost
Jamesian sort of story set partly in a New
England village, partly in New York." Retail
Bookseller

White, Patrick

The tree of man; a novel. Viking 1955
499p o.p. 1970

Set in Australia, this story "deals with a
young couple who, at the turn of the century,
pioneer in the wilderness, stake out a home,
prosper, rear a family, know vicissitudes of
content and despair and, in the end, face the
knowledge of frustration. The passing years

bring them substance and satisfaction, sickness, death, wavering loyalty and infidelity,
children of lax moral fiber and, at last, a passive relationship which recognizes the fact that
companionship has become more a habit than
a necessity." Book of the Month Club News

Voss; a novel. Viking 1957 442p o.p. 1970

"A long novel about Australia in mid-nineteenth century years. A German explorer, one
Voss, hopes to be the first to visit unexplored
parts of Australia, and for that purpose heads
an ill-fated expedition. He is unsuccessful in
his attempt and is lost to all except the faithful girl in Sydney who loved him and stayed
faithful to his memory." Book Rev Digest

White, Robin

Elephant Hill. Harper 1959 245p o.p. 1970

Beth Sumner, an American schoolteacher had
come to India to visit her sister, a medical
missionary's wife in Kasappur. There she met
Mr Alagarsami and his son, Mutthu who had
been adopted by Beth's sister and brother-in-
law. The story concerns itself with the gradual fusing of the cultures of East and West.
(Publisher)

White, Stewart Edward

The long rifle. Doubleday 1957 [c1932]
383p $4.95

A reissue of the title first published 1932
"The prologue to this long historical novel,
tells how young Daniel Boone won the first
long rifle at a shooting match in Western
Pennsylvania. The story itself relates the adventures of Andy Burnett, grandson of Boone's
friend, Gail Burnett. Andy inherits Boone's
long rifle, and, true to his clan and period,
moves further to the westward, joins the ranks
of the 'mountain men' who trapped and explored the Rockies in the 1820's, is captured by
Blackfeet Indians and is adopted into their
tribe." Book Rev Digest

Wild geese calling. Doubeday 1940 577p
o.p. 1970

"Sally Slocum and John Murdoch meet under
a cottonwood tree in Oregon and marry that
same day with little knowledge of each other,
but they soon find they have much in common,
in especial, the pioneering spirit. The leisurely, intimate story of this interesting pair and
the friends they make, takes them first to
Seattle where John works for a while in a
mill. From there they voyage in a small boat to
Klakan, Alaska, and here they settle down
while John and his friend Len get the machinery in order for a canning factory, but the
call of wild geese lures them still farther
north to the wilderness, the final fulfilment of
their dreams." Bookmark

White, T. H.

The candle in the wind
In White, T. H. The once and future
king p545-677

The ill-made knight; with decorations by
the author. Putnam 1940 291p illus. o.p.
1970

Sequel to: The witch in the wood
A humorous fantasy "with irreverent de-
bunking of heroic figures of the age of chivalry. It is a new version of the triangular affair
of King Arthur, Lancelot and Guenever (whom
Lancelot called Jenny), with the luckless Elaine
in the background." Booklist

also In White, T. H. The once and
future king p325-544

y Mistress Masham's repose; illus. by Fritz
Eichenberg. Putnam 1946 255p illus o.p. 1970

The heroine in this fantasy "is ten-year-
old Maria, who lives in a decaying English
castle called Mallaquet. Our hero is a whole
band of Lilliputians, descendants of those from
'Gulliver's Travels,' who live in a dome on an
island. Maria and the little people become fast
friends, and they side with her against her
wicked guardian, the Vicar, and evil Miss
Brown, Maria's governess." Literary Guild

White, T. H.—*Continued*

y The once and future king. Putnam 1958
677p $7.95

"The previously unpublished book 'The Candle in the Wind' completes the Arthurian series begun with 'The Sword in the Stone' and continued in 'The Witch in the Wood' (now called 'The Queen of Air and Darkness') and 'The Ill-made Knight.' All [entered separately] are contained in this omnibus edition as 'The Once and Future King.' A number of alterations have been made in the earlier books, especially in the second." Library J

"England's noblest tale, the composite memories of its golden age, have been put together by an expert medievalist who is also a brilliant storyteller, a wit, a master of romance and invention." Christian Science Monitor

The Queen of Air and Darkness
In White, T. H. The once and future king p215-323

y The sword in the stone; with decorations by the author and end papers by Robert Lawson. Putnam 1939 311p illus $5.95

An "account of everyday life in a great medieval manor, with two boys, Kay and the Wart (who turns out to be King Arthur) learning the code of being a gentleman, busy with hawking, jousting, sword play, and hunting. The whole trend of the story is how the boy Wart was made worthy to become a king. An unique book." Ontario Lib Rev

"Delightful, fantastic, satirical nonsense, for the reader with a background of Arthurian legend. With a mixture of modern life and medieval ways, it sells the story of the education of Arthur . . . under the tutorship of Merlin." Wis Lib Bul

Followed by: The witch in the wood

also In White, T. H. The once and future king p 1-213

The witch in the wood; with decorations by the author. Putnam 1939 269p illus o.p. 1970

In this sequel to: The sword in the stone, the boy, Wart, is now a mature King Arthur fighting against other kings for recognition. Merlin and other characters reappear in the fantasy but it is mainly the story of Queen Morgause (the witch in the wood) and her four sons. Set in the Land of Lothian and Orkney
Followed by: The ill-made knight

White, Terence Hanbury. See White, T. H.

White, Theodore H.

The mountain road. Sloane 1958 347p maps o.p. 1970

A story of World War II set in China. It unfolds the events of one week in 1944 when Major Philip Baldwin and his American demolition unit were caught between the Chinese blockade of the mountain roads and the Japanese push for one last victory. (Publisher)

"Although the book is alive with action and convincing characterizations it is the ethical problems posed by war, not physical warfare, that are important." Booklist

The view from the fortieth floor. Sloane 1960 468p o.p. 1970

John Ridgely Warren, the new, inexperienced but highly ambitious president of a publishing firm, came to New York to save the firm's two great but ailing magazines. Upon his efforts hung the fate of thousands of the firm's faithful employees, as well as the cold ambition of certain stockholders. These men saw in the firm's failure their opportunity for fortune at the expense of Warren's honor. Warren's struggles against impending disaster taught him some new values in responsibility." (Publisher)

This 'is not only a long, serious and informative novel. It is also a cautionary tale, for, while principally a record of a battle lost on the communications front, it carries more than a hint of how the battle might have been won." Book of the Month Club News

White, William Anthony Parker. See Boucher, Anthony

Whitehouse, Arch

Playboy squadron. Doubleday 1970 267p $5.95

"This is a fictionalized account of what happened to a group of American pilots who actually got 'lost in the shuffle' during World War I, were invited to join the Royal Flying Corps Camel squadron, and racked up a good record in combat. It is an all-action novel." Pub W

Whitehouse, Arthur George Joseph. See Whitehouse, Arch

Whitney, Phyllis A.

y Black amber. Appleton 1964 284p $4.95

A "suspense story in a Turkish setting, a villa on the water near Istanbul. The 23-year-old [American] heroine has come in the disguise of a secretary-researcher for an artist, to try to find out how her stepsister, the artist's wife, had died. She enters a mysterious household, full of rivalries and hatreds." Pub W

y Blue fire. Appleton 1961 312p boards $4.95

"Susan Hohenfield journeyed from Chicago to Africa, the scene of her childhood, with her new husband, Dirk. Soon after their arrival it became apparent that Africa was not the innocent place of early memories. As mystery and intrigue surrounded her, Susan found there was no one she could trust—not even her husband." McClurg. Book News

y Columbella. Doubleday 1966 306p $4.95

"A Virgin Island mystery-romance which pits two women against each other for a man, a child, and their very lives. One woman is a young, diffident teacher hired to tutor the 14-year-old daughter of an old family in Charlotte Amalie. The other woman is the child's mother, a selfish, venomous but very beautiful woman who is still loved by her daughter but not by her husband. A close-knit story with much suspense, exotic background, and good characterizations." Pub W

y Hunter's green. Doubleday 1968 252p $4.95

This story is "set in present-day England. Eve, young American wife of Justin North and narrator of the story, returns to her husband's English estate after a three-year separation from Justin who has now decided to divorce her and remarry. Eve determines to win back her husband's love, but a sinister turn of events seems to mark Eve for violent death." Booklist

y Sea Jade. Appleton [1965 c1964] 277p boards $4.95

"New England during the last days of the clipper ships is the setting for this novel about Miranda Heath. A murder, secret messages culled from old charts, violence and frustrated passion all surround her as she struggles to solve the mystery of the last voyage of the 'Sea Jade.'" McClurg. Book News

"The prose of Phillis Whitney is delicate yet strong, and her ability as a raconteur is first rate. The story is well-knit and fascinating without excessive recourse to contrivances." Best Sellers

y Seven tears for Apollo. Appleton 1963 305p boards $4.95

"After Gino, her husband, died, Dorcas went to Rhodes as a secretary to travel-writer Fern Farrar, but she was troubled by the interest Gino's lawless associates took in her, especially when she learned that somewhere she held the clue to the hiding place of a stolen marble head." Bk Buyer's Guide

y Silverhill. Doubleday 1967 244p $4.95

"An above-average, modern-day Gothic romance. . . . Set in an old New England house surrounded by ghostly white birch trees and occupied by a grandmother-dominated family with a curious past, the story centers on Mallie Rice, an unwelcome visitor to her ancestral

Whitney, Phyllis A.—*Continued*

home Silverhill. Determined to carry out her mother's dying request Mallie probes into the secrets of the house and unleashes ancient hatreds and fears." Booklist

"It's all very neat, professional, and especially skillfull in achieving a unity of time of under 36 hours—which may be a record for the romantic mystery." N Y Times Bk R

Skye Cameron. Appleon 1957 312p o.p. 1970

"The romance of Skye Cameron, daughter of a Scottish father and a Creole mother, in the New Orleans of the 1880's. Skye considers herself plain because of her red hair, but in time escapes the machinations of her beautiful black haired mother and her power-seeking uncle, and seems headed for a happy marriage." Book Rev Digest

y Thunder Heights. Appleton 1960 311p boards $4.95

"When the orphaned Camilla was summoned to her dying Grandfather's upstate mansion, she went with alacrity. What she found in the house where her own mother had died mysteriously was a strange family—and soon she was frightened by even stranger 'accidents.'" Bk Buyer's Guide

y The trembling hills. Appleton 1956 344p $4.95

"The unfolding of a skeleton-in-the-closet family history, several romances, and a young girl's emergence from adolescence to maturity provide the stock-in-trade elements of a novel set in San Francisco in the period of the 1906 earthquake." Booklist

y Window on the square. Appleton 1962 313p $4.95

"A psychological drama set in the opulent New York of the 1870's. Megan is a young woman who has been brought into a wealthy, important family to care for a disturbed boy who has shot and killed his father. Slowly she begins to realize that the boy did not kill his father—and that the real killer is another member of the household." Huntting

y The winter people. Doubleday 1969 285p $4.95

"Dina Blake, still bemused by a teenage love, is swept into marriage by sculptor Glen Chandler, and bundled off to the Chandler mansion. . . . There gather father Colton Chandler, famous portraitist, and Glen's twin sister Glynis. . . . It is quickly evident that the sister's psychological twinship with Glen is malevolently, preternaturally Siamese—and woe betide the wife who comes between them." N Y Times Bk R

In "this gothic romance the atmosphere, cleverly maintained, is truly eerie . . . [and] guaranteed to induce 'goosebumps' in the most jaded reader of mystery-and-suspense." Best Sellers

Wibberley, Leonard

Adventures of an elephant boy. Morrow 1968 160p boards $3.95

"When Dr. Pangloss became the President of the Best of All Possible Nations . . . he sent to Asia for an elephant boy—to be the President's personal guest and see for himself how every citizen of BAPN was able to pursue his own personal quest for life, liberty and happiness. So it was that Hari Ranjit Singh was torn from his quiet village life on a tributary of the Ganges and catapulted into horrendous adventures halfway around the world and back again, where he could rejoin his beloved elephant, Golden Lotus, on the banks of the peaceful river." Publisher's note

"Sharp political satire, amusing and horrifying at the same time. . . . Hari's experiences . . . enable Wibberley to prick many a sacred cow from politics to psychiatry to the war in Vietnam." Booklist

y Beware of the mouse; illus. by Ronald Wing. Putnam 1958 189p illus o.p. 1970

Story about the great crisis in the summer of 1450 in the little duchy of Grand Fenwick when Sir Roger Fenwick learns from an Irish knight, Sir Dermot of Ballycastle, that the French have a new instrument of warfare called a cannon. When the Irishman and the Englishman finally put their wits together, however, they manage a brilliant and decisive victory. (Publisher)

The centurion. Morrow 1966 251p boards $4.95

A "low-key retelling of the Christ story as a novel and in part from the point of view of a Roman centurion who, in the end, is put in charge of carrying out the crucifixion. This is bitterly ironic, since the centurion has been tolerant of the Jews and has admired Christ. As regards the story of Mary, the retelling is a Catholic version." Pub W

The story is told "with quiet dignity, straightforwardness and considerable emotional impact. There is, of course, the inescapable atmosphere of mystery, mysticism, miracles, omens and signs which must, perforce, surround this story and may deter the sceptic." Library J

y The hands of Cormac Joyce; illus. by Lydia Rosier. Morrow 1967 [c1960] 125p illus $3.75

First published 1960 by Putnam

When a serious storm threatened the islands off the coast of County Galway, Ireland, the Coast Guard offered to transport people to the safety of the mainland. Among those unwilling to leave their island homes was the family of Cormac Joyce. His son Jackie had always admired his father's strength, especially in his hands. But when the storm was at its worst the hands of young Jackie were also given the strength to make survival possible. (Publisher)

"If you love beautifully simple, lilting language describing a singularly moving story about genuine people, you will treasure this little gem of a book." Sat R

y The Island of the Angels. Morrow 1965 112p illus boards $4.50

"A hermit-like old fisherman living on an island off Baja California no longer thinks only of himself when a very sick boy is washed up on his island. To get help for the boy, the fisherman risks his life sailing through a fierce storm. His desperation galvanizes into action the people of a mainland village near his island." Pub W

"It is a short story, rather than a full length book, but it is a touching story, beautifully written, with such fine character delineation and accuracy of detail that it is much more than merely entertaining." Best Sellers

y The mouse on the moon. Morrow 1962 191p boards $4.95

"In this sequel to 'The Mouse That Roared' the Duchy of Grand Fenwick, the world's smallest nation, succeeds in a space exploit and, incidentally, picks up enough income to modernize the ducal castle's plumbing and buy a sable coat for the beautiful duchess." Pub W

"Fantastic, irreverent, cockeyed and funny; all of these and other adjectives describe this farce. There is considerable wisdom here too. But, one hardly knows what to do with it. Mr. Wibberley is a polished writer and this performance is no exception. . . . Once begun, it is irresistible." Library J

y The mouse on Wall Street. Morrow 1969 159p boards $4.95

"The Duchy of Grand Fenwick (five miles long by three miles wide) . . . is faced with a unique problem, too much money. The source of the Duchy's financial disaster-bonanza is Grand Pinot chewing gum, flavored with Grand Fenwick's vintage wine. Their windfall the first year is one million dollars; the second, ten million. Since all this cash could ruin the delicate balance of the Fenwickian economy and destroy incentive, Grand Fenwick decides to invest in stocks sold on Wall Street. . . . Mr. Wibberley is in fine form, romping with mergers and profits, brokerage houses and financial jackals with a wicked eye for the pitfalls and pratfalls of our tickertape age." Pub W

Wibberley, Leonard—*Continued*

y The mouse that roared. Little 1955 279p boards $4.95

The tiny Duchy of Grand Fenwick "undertakes to rehabilitate its national economy by declaring war on the U.S., since that nation takes tender care of its defeated enemies. This clever, amusing fantasy . . . tells how the Fenwickian invasion force of 23 longbowmen not only won the war, but seized the newly invented quadium bomb and by virtue of its possession compelled the cessation of the armament race." Booklist

"Along with his beautifully cockeyed humor, his lovely faculty for needle-sharp, ironic jabs delivered where they'll do the most good, and his nice talent for story-telling, Mr. Wibberley has serious things to suggest and he suggests them admirably." San Francisco Chronicle

Widdemer, Margaret

The Red Castle women. Doubleday 1968 273p $4.95

"The time is between the Mexican and Civil Wars. The hero served in the war against Mexico, and returns to the Red Castle on the Hudson. . . . The secret of the women who live in the Red Castle, the great Somerwell estate is a strange one. Into its mystery and a bit of danger is drawn Perdita, the young girl who does not know her ancestry and who is the ward of the river ferryman. Some of the action takes place in old New York City." Pub W

"There is much descriptive detail concerning dress, furnishings, and manners which were a part of living during this gilded age when servants were taken for granted even by the poor and these glimpses of elegance add to the reading pleasure and at the same time offer a bit of relaxation between horrors." Best Sellers

Wiesel, Elie

The accident; tr. from the French by Anne Borchardt. Hill & Wang 1962 120p $3.50

Original French edition, 1961

The author has chosen as his main character Eliezer, "a correspondent for an Israeli newspaper and a survivor of Auschwitz [who] is run over by a taxicab while crossing a New York street. For weeks Eliezer hovers between life and death. One of his frequent visitors in the hospital is Kathleen with whom he has long had an affair but without passion or commitment. In a number of . . . flashbacks the author sketches the history of this affair against the background of Eliezer's tragic fate at the hands of the Nazis. Only toward the end of his convalescence does [Eliezer] realize that his 'accident' was not an accident at all but a deliberate attempt to do away with himself." Library J

A beggar in Jerusalem; a novel. Tr. from the French by Lily Edelman and the author. Random House 1970 211p $5.95

Original French edition, 1969

This novel consists of the stories of the characters who have gathered at the Wailing Wall in Jerusalem. "A 'beggar' named David loiters and waits, in the aftermath of the Six-Day War in the company of . . . [a] crew of 'beggars.' . . . He is waiting—or passively searching—for his friend Katriel, who has died in the fighting, and for Katriel's widow, Malka. At the same time the 'beggar' is certainly no beggar; his name may not be David. . . . The war is not only the Six-Day War—it is every action in which the Jews have been threatened with destruction. And Katriel may not be dead at all." Book World

Reading Elie Wiesel is not an easy experience. It is certainly by no means an act of escape, the traditional function of literary entertainment. His works touch all of one's fibers. . . . After we have listened to what Wiesel has to say, other literature seems meaningless." Sat R

Dawn; tr. from the French by Frances Frenaye. Hill & Wang 1961 89p $3.50

Original French edition, 1960

"Elisha, an eighteen-year-old Jewish guerrilla in British-controlled Palestine, is ordered to shoot a captured British officer in reprisal for the execution of a Jewish prisoner. During the interminable night before the killing Elisha is haunted by persons from his past, many of whom died in German concentration camps. His horror at killing the Englishman deepens when, just before dawn, he spends some time with the condemned man and sees him not as an enemy but as a man who could be his friend. A very brief but telling indictment of war's tragedy." Booklist

The gates of the forest; tr. from the French by Frances Frenaye. Holt 1966 226p boards $4.95

Original French edition, 1964

An "allegorical restatement and exploration of the question of God's role or existence in man's cruelty and suffering. The story is carried by Gregor, orphaned by the Nazis, sheltering in a Transylvanian forest, and saved from discovery by the self-sacrifice of a Jew whose laughter in the face of misery pursues Gregor endlessly. Gregor's later disguise as a deaf mute fails when, cast in a pantomime role of Judas in a village play, he speaks out in Judas' behalf. Further flight, terror, love, torment, and survival follow." Booklist

The town beyond the wall; tr. from the French by Stephen Becker. [New ed] Holt [1967 c1964] 179p $4.95

First published 1964 in English by Atheneum Publishers

"Michael, a young Jew who has survived the Holocaust, decides to return to the [Hungarian] town behind the Iron Curtain from which he came, the town from which he and his family were deported, the town in which he seeks to solve the mystery of 'the face in the window'—that real and symbolic face of all those who stood by and never interfered while victims and executioners enacted their tragic roles." Publisher's note

"God-tormented, God-intoxicated, 'The Town beyond the Wall' is a fiction which refuses to be a novel in any usual sense. It is an exemplary tale such as people may in terror and in hope tell one another. It is a legend—archaic, modern, timeless; a legend of an ascent from purgatory to possibility." Newsweek

Wijk, J. Louw van. See Van Wijk, J. Louw

Wilchek, Stella

Judith. Harper 1969 592p map boards $6.95

"Based on the apochryphal Book of Judith, this is the story of the red-haired girl of Bethul, still a virgin but a widow, who saved her town from the Assyrians by going into the camp of Holofernes, seducing him by her beauty, and cut off his head while he lay in drunken sleep." Bk Buyer's Guide

"The author takes liberties with history and religion so students of these subjects might not be pleased with her rearrangement of events. However, the novel is an interesting portrait of those victims of history whose happenstance made them heroes or heroines. There is little in the way of religious overtones; rather we find skillful character studies which bring names and places long familiar to us in biblical history alive as in few novels in recent years." Library J

Wilde, Oscar

y The picture of Dorian Gray. Modern Lib. 248p $2.95

First published in England 1891

"The story concerns a beautiful youth, Dorian Gray, who has his portrait painted by Basil Hallward, an artist with a flair for the morbid. The portrait proves to have supernatural qualities, and becomes the mirror of its subject's inner life, so that whatever Dorian feels or thinks is reflected in the portrait, Dorian himself retaining his youth and beauty. Through Hallward, Dorian meets Lord Henry Wotten, a cynic and 'bon vivant,' who

Wilde, Oscar—*Continued*

has mastered all the secret vices. Under his influence he deteriorates rapidly. For a while he is fired with a pure love for a little Shakespearean actress, Sybil Vane, but he spurns her out of monstrous vanity, and she commits suicide. He degenerates still further, and his portrait mirrors all his hideous vices." Haydn. Thesaurus of Book Digests

Wilder, Robert

An affair of honor. Putnam 1969 383p $6.95

Set "in the Bahamas of the Twentieth Century it is the story of Max Hertog who regarded Nassau and the Out Islands as his by right, driving with heavy boots over those of the old, first families who would stand in his way It is also the story of Hertog's lovely and unconventional daughter, Jan, and of Royal Keating, the black man who walked among the whites in Nassau with the pride of a descendant of African kings." Publisher's note

The author "has a way of creating memorable characters. He also tells an intriguing, albeit unsavory tale in which honor is the principal's last concern. His title is ironic. And incidentally he tells us considerable about the Bahamas, setting of the novel, past and present." Best Sellers

Bright feather; a novel. Putnam 1948 408p o.p. 1970

"Against a background of Colonial Florida and the Seminole Wars, the author . . . has written [his] story. . . . The main characters are Clayfield Hammond . . . Clay, his orphaned grandson . . . and Asseola, a young Seminole. In the mounting climax of the Wars, Clay's path inevitably crosses that of his boyhood friend, and Old Clay comes to an end in keeping with his way of life . . . leaving his grandson to follow his own star." Huntting

Fruit of the poppy; a novel. Putnam 1965 317p o.p. 1970

"A novel of men of the United States Federal Bureau of Narcotics, of their counterparts in Mexico and the relentless war they wage against the forces of the underworld and the syndicates who constantly seek new ways to smuggle narcotics into the United States." Am News of Bks

"One runs into a number of old clichés . . . [but] the verisimilitude of the settings makes the book highly absorbing." Library J

Wind from the Carolinas. Putnam 1964 635p o.p. 1970

After the American Revolution, loyalist Ronald Cameron migrates to the Bahamas with his family to establish a plantation on an English land grant. This chronicle of the Cameron family encompasses the cotton failure, blockade running during the Civil War, and rum running during the Prohibition era. (Publisher)

"The author has done well with his characters, who are individuals of passion, fire, stubbornness and unexpected strength." Pub W

Wilder, Thornton

y The bridge of San Luis Rey. Harper [1967 c1927] 148p $3.95

Also available in a large type edition. $6.95 Pulitzer Prize. 1928

First published 1927 by Boni

"One midsummer day nearly two centuries ago an osier bridge built by the Incas collapsed and precipitated five Peruvian travellers into the abyss below. The story is supposed to be a retelling and interweaving of the minute inquiries into the secret lives of the five victims, made by the Franciscan Brother Juniper to prove that here was not a mere accident but rather the culmination of the finite pattern of each life, according to God's plan." Cleveland

also in Costain, T. B. ed. Stories to remember v2 p 1-67

also in Costain, T. B. comp. Twelve short novels p107-70

also in Wilder, T. A Thornton Wilder trio p149-243

The Cabala

In Wilder, T. A Thornton Wilder trio p21-147

The Cabala, and the woman of Andros. Harper [1968] 203p $5.95

The two short novels reprinted here were published by Boni, 1926 and 1930 respectively. The Cabala concerns a group of odd people at the top of the aristocratic society of Rome. The woman of Andros "is based upon the theme of the Andria, a comedy by Terence. The woman of Andros is Chrysis, a Greek hetaira, who has established herself on the island of Brynos and gathered about her the young men of the neighborhood, charming them all by her beauty and wisdom. The story turns on the love of Pamphilus, son of a merchant of the island, for Glycerium, sister of Chrysis, and the testing of that love thru bereavement." Book Rev Digest

The eighth day. Harper 1967 435p $6.95

Also available in a large type edition. $9.95 National Book Award 1968

A saga of two twentieth-century families in Coaltown, Illinois whose lives intertwine. The novel moves back and forth, beginning with John Ashley's trial for the murder of Breckenridge Lansing and Ashley's conviction and flight. It continues with the fortunes of the Ashley and the Lansing families, the solution of the murder, and concludes with descriptions of the children's children of the original families. (Publisher)

"Wilder's way of commenting on the characters does not diminish one's sense of their reality but enhances it. In fact, he seems more objective than the impersonal moderns, for he talks about these people as if they were real. . . . [He] offers the reader no certainty, but he does inspire a beautiful sense of human possibilities. He does not deny the existence of evil . . . but he believes that for some people in some places in some times life can be satisfying. . . . That is not exactly a robust faith, but it has sustained Wilder in a long and creative career and has inspired a novel that is as likely to survive, in part because it is unfashionable, as anything written in our time." Sat R

Heaven's my destination. Harper 1935 304p $5.95

A study of "young George Brush, a successful middle-west salesman of textbooks, one hundred per cent American and very religious, who insists upon being good and making everyone else good. This insistence gets him jailed, fooled in a house of prostitution, beaten by rowdies, deceived by women, disliked by everyone, but he is undaunted. Written in simple, direct, swiftmoving prose, the story evokes many chuckles, it is unusual. Apparently objective rather than satirical." Booklist

The ides of March. Harper 1948 246p $6.95

An "historical novel or fantasy which portrays the life of Julius Caesar and some other Romans during the months preceding Caesar's assassination. The narrative device consists of a series of imaginary documents: private letters; entries in journals; and reports of Caesar's secret police. Altho part of the events are historical the author has tampered with history to the extent of transposing some happenings of 62 B.C. to the year 45 B.C." Book Rev Digest

It is "a fascinating book, and while it owes some of its fascination to the period with which it deals, perhaps the most exciting of our history, a great deal of its charm is entirely the author's, who manages to depict with high effectiveness a number of vivid, glowing and powerful personalities." N Y Her Trib Books

A Thornton Wilder trio. Introduction by Malcolm Cowley. Criterion Bks. 1956 309p o.p. 1970

An omnibus of three novels formerly published separately: The Cabala (1926): The bridge of San Luis Rey (1927) entered separately; The woman of Andros (1930)

The woman of Andros

In Wilder, T. The Cabala, and The woman of Andros p135-203

In Wilder, T. A Thornton Wilder trio p245-309

Wilhelm, Kate

The downstairs room, and other specula-tive fiction. Doubleday 1968 215p $4.95

Analyzed in Short Story Index
Contents: Unbirthday party; Baby, you were great; When the moon was red; Sirloin and white wine; Perchance to dream; How many miles to Babylon; The downstairs room; Count-down; The plausible improbable; The feel of desperation; A time to keep; The most beauti-ful woman in the world; The planners; Wind-song

Let the fire fall. Doubleday 1969 228p (Doubleday Science fiction) $4.95

This story "begins with the birth here on earth of a child from an alien space ship. Star Child, it is christened. The destiny of this boy and that of two others, born about the same time, are intertwined as they grow up. In the end the reader is left guessing as to which is the real Star Child." Pub W
"This is a powerful, fire and brimstone—but often amusing—story about the eccentricities of mankind." Book News

Wilkinson, G. K.

Nick, the Click. Putnam 1968 189p board $4.50

"Red Mask mystery"
"When the famous London jewelry firm of Tassel and Leake installs the most foolproof alarm system ever, it provides the base for a happening that starts in New York's Central Park and winds up in an ancient luxury hotel in Geneva, Switzerland. Scotland Yard and Interpol pursue a parade of crooks, black-mailers and a journalist that stretches halfway across Europe. Gloria is the American expert who decides that Tassel and Leake can be taken: Nick the Click, who specializes in dirty photographs and Fanny, his model, just happen to take pictures of Gloria planning the crime with her English accomplices—the pictures that trigger a 1968 version of the old silent movie Keystone Cop chase. It's all fun and games, ending in confusion for the crooks and with the Click winding up with most of the loot." Pub W

Wilkinson, Sylvia

A killing frost; a novel. Houghton 1967 216p $4.95

"Thirteen-year-old Ramie, an orphan, tells about her life with her grandmother, Miss Liz, on a North Carolina farm. She pays touching tribute to Miss Liz, but she's also aware of her grandmother's superstitions, her stubborn streak, and her tendency to endless reminis-cences." Bk Buyer's Guide
"The writing is delicate and lyrical, and the book should have a special appeal to those who enjoy the work of Carson McCullers and Eudora Welty." Pub W

Moss on the north side. Houghton 1966 235p $3.95

"This is a novel about the illegitimate child of a Cherokee tenant farmer and a white woman of promiscuous habits—Cary, a half-Indian girl, who suffers the agonies of an adolescence devoid of middle-class salves. It is also the story of the indomitable spirit of a child." Am News of Bks

Williams, Ben Ames

Come spring. Houghton 1940 866p $5

A "long detailed novel of life in a Maine frontier village at the time of the Revolution. Although they are not far from the scene of war at times, the Indians and their own daily affairs are of more importance to these sturdy pioneers than are wars or rumors of wars. The story is based on the records of the Maine town of Union and the surrounding country." Book Rev Digest

House divided. Houghton 1947 1514p $10.95

"A long narrative about the American Civil War and its effect on the Currain family. As an old Virginia family with plantations in Virginia, and North and South Carolina, and houses in Richmond, the Currains were loyal to the Confederate cause and felt the full impact of the war. General James Longstreet is intro-duced as a friend of the Currains and his activities and the battles in which he took part are followed in considerable detail. An alleged relationship between the Currains and Abraham Lincoln adds . . . to a story that, in spite of its length, does not flag in interest." Booklist
Followed by: The unconquered

Leave her to heaven. Houghton 1944 429p o.p. 1970

A "psychological novel in which the char-acter of a despicable woman is the motivating force. Ellen Berent began her psychopathic possessiveness while she was still a baby. The object of her affection was her father. After his death she successfully pursued a man who re-sembled her father, married him, and proceeded to ruin his life. Even after her suicide, which she arranged to resemble a murder, her evil influence was not ended." Book Week

The unconquered. Houghton 1953 689p $7.95

Sequel to: House divided
"The saga of the many-branched Currain family, began in House Divided, is continued in setting of New Orleans and Louisiana pol-itics during the Reconstruction period (1865-1874). . . . Many historical characters, such as Gen. James Longstreet figure in the plot; un-forgettable scenes are portrayed as though by eye witnesses." Library J

Williams, Blanche Colton

(jt. ed.) Lieber, M. ed. Great stories of all nations

Williams, John A.

The man who cried I am; a novel. Little 1967 403p $6.95

"Max Reddich is an American Negro, a novel-ist, journalist, individualist. On leave from the magazine 'Century,' suffering from the painful ravages of rectal cancer, he has come to Am-sterdam to meet again his estranged white wife. Max must also meet Michelle, mistress of a fellow Negro expatriate, Harry Ames, another writer and a close friend, who has just died in Paris. When he does, he learns that Harry has willed him a letter and some explo-sive documents . . . [which] reveal a sinister plan held in readiness by the American govern-ment to stamp out minority (Negro) organiza-tions by force. Max manages to get this in-formation to Minister Q, a militant Negro activist in New York, but on the drive back to Amsterdam Max is murdered. Skillfully in-tertwined with the narrative of Max's last hours in Holland are a series of revealing flashbacks. They form yet another chronicle of Max, the man who cried 'I am:' his struggles in love, writing, career, identity. . . . It is a moving, disturbing, often frightening book, sure to arouse controversy." Pub W

Sons of darkness, sons of light; a novel of some probability. Little 1969 279p boards $5.95

"In New York one hot summer [in 1973] tensions run high after a white cop kills a Negro boy, an act predicated here as outright murder. A black worker with a civil rights group conceives the idea of revenge by arrang-ing secretly for the murder of the cop. To do this he seeks help from an old Mafia friend. A 'hit' is set up and carried out, but the Mafia Don passes it on to an outside operator, a former Irgun terrorist frdm Israel. Meanwhile, black militants have plans of their own. Over Labor Day weekend the black militants strike by blowing up bridges and tunnels around Manhattan." Pub W
"Williams' grasp of character, his rage and compassion, and his understanding of present racial strain outweigh his sometimes melo-dramatic stance." Booklist

Williams, Tennessee

The Roman spring of Mrs Stone. New Directions 1950 148p $4

"A wealthy widowed American ex-actress is the heroine of this short novel. At fifty Mrs Stone is losing her beauty, her stage career is ended, and she finds herself just 'drifting' thru

Williams, Tennessee—*Continued*

an aimless existence in Rome. When an un-scrupulous countess introduces a handsome young gigolo to Mrs Stone it is the beginning of the end." Book Rev Digest

"Mr. Williams evokes the Roman background with economy and vivid precision, and his prose has a pleasant undercurrent of quiet wit His novel is in sum, readable and admirably written, but in the final analysis rather pointless." N Y Times Bk R

Williams, Thomas

Whipple's castle. Random House [1969 c1968] 536p $6.95

"The time is the forties; the place is Leah, New Hampshire. Here live The Whip, Harvey Whipple, once an athlete and a winner but now condemned to a closed-in, wheelchair life; Mrs. Whipple; and the three brothers and Kate. Wood, eighteen when the story opens, goes off to war and is mutilated; Kate and David live normal lives, while Horace or Horse through his intensity of wanting to do the right thing often gets into trouble." Bk Buyer's Guide

"Mr. Williams' novel is a creditable example of a fictional form currently rather out of fashion: the family chronicle. . . . The minor characters, especially the compliant Susie Davis, are studied as conscientiously as is the Whipple family. There is no story line—merely a series of comic or tragic scenes played against a well-realized background of New England small-town life." Book of the Month Club News

Williams, Vinnie

Walk Egypt. Viking 1960 308p o.p. 1970

The story of Toy Crawford, "a young girl of the Georgia hills. . . . After her father's harsh death, she assumes responsibility for her brother and sister and demented mother, toiling unceasingly and again, after marriage, [she experiences] tragedy until peace comes with faith in God." Bookmark

"It is difficult to decide whether this is a stimulating novel adorned with an extra-ordinary treasure of North Georgia folksay, or a rich collection of rustic picture-language about a strong-willed woman who learned, almost too late, to love. Admirers of pithy folk talk may impute an immortality to this book that its plot alone could not justify. . . . 'Walk Egypt' is a rich storehouse for collectors of rural idiom." N Y Times Bk R

Williams, William Carlos

The great American novel

In Blackmur, R. P. ed. American short novels p307-43

Wilson, Angus

Anglo-Saxon attitudes; a novel. Viking 1956 410p o.p. 1970

"Gerald Middleton is the dominating figure in this story of men and women from all strata of present day English life. When the story opens, Middleton is a distinguished historian married to a sentimental Danish beauty. Although his marriage is based on pretense, he is unable to end it, just as he is incapable of investigating an archeological discovery which he knows is a farce. The results of his indecision are disastrous for his children. How he finally faces and overcomes his weakness forms the denouement." Huntting

Late call. Viking [1965 c1964] 316p o.p. 1970

First published 1964 in England

A story "of changing British social conditions as demonstrated in the case of a lady retired from small hotel management to one of the newly developed communities. She has a problem husband [widowed son] and even grandchildren." Am News of Bks

This "novel is a modest and intelligent work marred by long stretches of tedious social satire. . . . Optimistic without being sentimental, Late Call is a nineteenth-century kind of novel about self and society, commitment and blindness, textured with the barren stuff of contemporary English life. Yet for all its absorption with the surface of things, this is a book seriously concerned with the grace and mystery of the self." Sat R

The middle age of Mrs Eliot; a novel. Viking 1959 [c1958] 439p o.p. 1970

First published 1958 in England

The story tells how Mrs William Eliot, a wealthy and fashionable London matron, becomes an impoverished widow and learns to be a stenographer. More importantly it is the story of how this selfish and domineering woman becomes aware of what she is and finally devises a new life for herself that will not permit her to damage the people she values. (Publisher)

"There are colorful scenes to relieve the serious study of character that makes up the main body of the book, and there are occasional flashes of humor. It is an excellent job of writing." Pub W

No laughing matter. Viking 1967 496p boards $6.95

The story "opens in 1912 with the Matthews living a shabby genteel existence on the fringes of Bohemian London. Billy-Pop, the father, is an unsuccessful writer; Clara, the mother, nicknamed 'the Countess,' is a frustrated actress. . . . The farflung, varied fortunes of the children are followed over the next 50 years as they live out their lives against a background of events that are now history. A story told on many different levels." Pub W

"A brilliant, puzzling, always bemusing and sad tour de force. New and exciting in every sense (surprisingly so for Angus Wilson), but never loses touch with the old Anglo-Saxon attitudes. It is a massive comedy of mannered morals." Choice

Wilson, Dorothy Clarke

Prince of Egypt. Westminster Press 1949 423p o.p. 1970

A "novel based on the life of Moses, from the time of his youth spent in the Egyptian court, thru the days of his discovery of his true identity, and his three marriages, up to the time when he led the children of Israel out of Egypt." Book Rev Digest

"Out of the bare bones of the Exodus story, Miss Wilson has constructed a colorful and picturesque Egyptian background for her story of [Moses] a Hebrew youth who might have become Pharaoh if God had not chosen to set his feet on another path. After paying tribute to the skill with which Miss Wilson has sketched the background and portrayed the stages by which Moses arrives at his concept of the one, true God, it should be added that 'Prince of Egypt' takes liberties with Biblical narrative." Rel Bk Club Bul

Wilson, Gregory

The valley of time. Doubleday 1967 449p $5.95

"A convincing portrayal of a vanishing way of life. . . . Doug Emerson, fired from his teaching post for his unorthodox views, joins the new T. V. A. project, but becomes disillusioned with its 'progressive' ideas. When personal tragedy strikes his personal life, only his wife's support pulls him through." Cincinnati

"This novel, written by a Southern minister and laid in the TVA country of Tennessee from 1915 to 1965, is marked by an appealing candor, excitement and authenticity." Library J

Wilson, John Anthony Burgess. See Burgess, Anthony

Wilson, Neill C.

y The nine brides and Granny Hite. Morrow 1952 244p $4.95

"Awaiting the circuit-riding minister, the women of Cat Track Hollow have a quilting bee at lovable, independent Granny Hite's and each bride-to-be reveals the manner of her courtship in humorous, flavorful episodes in native speech." Bookmark

"The stories themselves are simple and refreshing, tightly written and plotted. A lot of readers will welcome this chance to enter a world in which people have time to be people, in their relationships with others and with themselves too." San Francisco Chronicle

Wilson, S. J.

To find a man. Viking 1969 185p boards $4.95

"When a young man of 18 tries to help out a childhood girl friend who's 'in trouble,' everyone naturally assumes that he's the prospective father. That is the fate of Andrew Z. Greenstone. . . . As Andrew sets out on his long quest to 'find a man' to help Rosalind Berk, what could have been a tasteless tale turns into a delight. Everything turns out all right. Rosalind is safely taken care of, and Andrew is a guest at her wedding." Pub W

"Although the book gives insight into Andrew and Rosalind as people, librarians with YA collections should read before purchase. The writing is poetic and good and the novel is recommended for modern fiction collections where the subject won't offend." Library J

Wilson, Sloan

The man in the gray flannel suit. Simon & Schuster 1955 304p o.p. 1970

"The man of the title is the ordinary, upper middle class New York business employee, who at five o'clock heads for his home, wife, and children in Connecticut. Thomas Rath is his name in this book. Tom joins a larger corporation, does an honest job, and is evidently headed for bigger money. As an undercurrent to his daily life Tom remembers his war service, the girl he met in Rome, and his illegitimate son." Book Rev Digest

"The Man in the Gray Flannel Suit most unsuitably mixes farce, satire, and humor, but most readers will not mind, for here is a book of pleasant wit and an unfailing charm." Cath World

Winterton, Paul. See Garve, Andrew

Winton, John

HMS Leviathan. Coward-McCann 1967 421p $5.95

"The story of a British jinx ship and of Commander Bob Markready, who has been given the thankless job of trying to subdue her. . . . Commander Markready, a man of little imagination and less tact, sets out to make a new ship out of the 'Leviathan,' and slowly he does begin to make headway, even though he sees his own ruin coming about in the process. This is essentially the story of the struggle for power between the old and new navy, of the war between the air crew officers and the sailors. The central character, the Commander, is British to the core, sometimes a bit too stiff-upper-lip for credibility. The minor characters, however, are excellent. They talk with Rabelaisian gusto. . . . All in all, good fare for men interested in naval action and in-service rivalries." Pub W

Wise, Herbert A.

(ed.) Great tales of terror and the supernatural; ed. by Herbert A. Wise and Phyllis Fraser. Random House 1944 1080p o.p. 1970

Analyzed in Short Story Index
Contents: La Grande Bretèche, by H. de Balzac; Black cat, by E. A. Poe; Facts in the case of M. Valdemar, by E. A. Poe; Terribly strange bed, by W. Collins; Boarded window, by A. Bierce; Three strangers, by T. Hardy; The interruption, by W. W. Jacobs; Pollock and the porroh man, by H. G. Wells; Sea raiders, by H. G. Wells; Sredni Vashtar, by Saki; Moonlight sonata, by A. Woollcott; Silent snow, secret snow, by C. Aiken; Suspicion, by D. L. Sayers; Most dangerous game, by R. Connell; Leiningen versus the ants, by C. Stephenson; Gentleman from America, by M. Arlen; Rose for Emily, by W. Faulkner; The killers, by E. Hemingway; Back for Christmas, by J. Collier; Taboo, by G. Household; The haunters and the haunted, by E. Bulwer-Lytton; Rappaccini's daughter, by N. Hawthorne; Trial for murder, by C. Collins and C. Dickens; Green tea, by J. S. Le Fanu; What was it, by F.-J. O'Brien; Sir Edmund Orme, by H. James; The Horla, by G. de Maupassant; Was it a dream, by G. de Maupassant; Screaming skull, by F. M. Crawford; Furnished room, by O. Henry; Casting the runes, by M. R. James; Oh, whistle, and I'll come to you my lad, by M. R. James;

Afterward, by E. Wharton; Monkey's paw, by W. W. Jacobs; Great god Pan, by A. Machen; How love came to Professor Guildea, by R. Hickens; Return of Imray, by R. Kipling; "They," by R. Kipling; Lukundoo, by E. L. White; Caterpillars, by E. F. Benson; Mrs Amworth, by E. F. Benson; Ancient sorceries, by A. Blackwood; Confession, by A. Blackwood; Open window, by Saki; Beckoning fair one, by O. Onions; Out of the deep, by W. de la Mare; Adam and Eve and Pinch Me, by A. E. Coppard; Celestial omnibus, by E. M. Forster; Ghost ship, by R. Middleton; Sailorboy's tale, by I. Dinesen; Rats in the walls, by H. P. Lovecraft; Dunwich horror, by H. P. Lovecraft

Wiseman, Thomas

The quick and the dead. Viking [1969 c1968] 442p boards $6.95

This is a novel about "Stefan Kazakh, a Viennese half-Jew who, by a combination of chance, courageous impertinence and near-compromise, escapes death in war-time Vienna and survives to return, a rich man, many years later. . . . His associate, the wealthy banker, Koeppler, is imprisoned after the Anschluss, and in negotiating vainly for his release, Stefan wins the respect and patronage of Nazi Gruppenführer Ludensheid. . . . Stefan thus stays alive through Nazi patronage, and the story largely centres on his fascination with [his childhood friends] the S.S. man Konrad Wirthof [and Wirthof's mistress, Leonie.]" Times (London) Lit Sup

Wodehouse, P. G.

The butler did it. Simon & Schuster 1957 214p o.p. 1970

"Eleven millionaires contribute $50,000 apiece to a pool to be won by the last to be married. The story [is] chiefly concerned with two embattled heirs, neck and neck for the grand prize —and, of course, Keggs, the butler." Retail Bookseller

The code of the Woosters. Simon & Schuster [1969 c1938] 222p $4.95

"A P.G. Wodehouse classic"
First published 1938 by Doubleday

"It was only the fact that Jeeves belonged to an exclusive club of gentlemen's personal gentlemen, where all the secrets in the lives of employers were filed for reference, that saved Bertie Wooster when the disappearance of an eighteenth-century silver cow-creamer threatened to land him in jail. Two rival collectors who coveted the piece of silver, and two pairs of bickering lovers, made Bertie's life a burden until Jeeves unearthed evidence that was a weapon." Booklist

"In no previous novel that we can recall has Mr. Wodehouse quoted and misquoted from the classics to better and more absurd effect than he does in his latest. The quality of the dialogue and of Wooster's monologues is so refined in its lunacy that, regarded as a whole, the book must be counted not only, as we have said, a masterpiece in its kind but equal with the best that Mr. Wodehouse has written." Times (London) Lit Sup

Fish preferred. Simon & Schuster [1969 c1929] 256p $4.95

"A P.G. Wodehouse classic"
First published 1929 by Doubleday

"Lady Constance Keeble's acid objection to the marriage of her niece Millicent with the blithe and careless Hugh, and of her nephew Ronnie Fish with a lovely chorister, are overcome by means of hilariously complicated doings at Blandings Castle." Book Rev Digest

How right you are, Jeeves. Simon & Schuster 1960 183p $3.50

"The world's most famous gentleman's gentleman [Jeeves] comes to the rescue after Bertie has managed to become inextricably tangled in his maneuvers to separate Phillis and an American playboy." Bk Buyer's Guide

The inimitable Jeeves. [Autograph ed] British Bk Centre 1956 192p $3.50

A reissue in a new format of the original English edition published 1924
The resourceful Jeeves again takes command of a typical Wodehouse situation

Wodehouse, P. G.—*Continued*

The most of P. G. Wodehouse. Simon & Schuster 1960 666p boards $7.95

Analyzed in Short Story Index
Thirty-two "tales out of the vast repertory of [the] Anglo-American humorist, P. G. Wodehouse. The book is divided into sections with these titles: 'The Drones Club,' 'Mr Mulliner,' 'Stanley Featherstone Ukridge,' 'Lord Emsworth,' 'The Gold Stories,' 'Jeeves,' and 'Quick Service,' a novel [published 1940] which contains none of the author's staple characters." Chicago Sunday Tribune
Contains the following short stories: Fate; Tried in the furnace; The amazing hat mystery; Noblesse oblige; Goodbye to all cats; All's well with Bingo; Uncle Fred flits by; The truth about George; A slice of life; Mulliner's Buck-U-Uppo; The reverent wooing of Archibald; The ordeal of Osbert Mulliner; Monkey business; The smile that wins; Strychnine in the soup; Ukridge's dog college; Ukridge's accident syndicate; A bit of luck for Mabel; Buttercup Day; Ukridge and the old stepper; "Pig-hoo-o-o-o-ey!"; The coming of Gowf; The awakening of Rollo Podmarsh; The clicking of Cuthbert; High stakes; The heel of Achilles; The purity of the turf; The great sermon handicap; The metropolitan touch; Jeeves and the Song of Songs; Jeeves and the impending doom

Quick service
In Wodehouse, P. G. The most of P. G. Wodehouse p519-666

Selected stories; introduction by John W. Aldridge. Modern Lib. 1958 382p $2.95

Analyzed in Short Story Index
Contents: Jeeves takes charge; The artistic career of Corky; Jeeves and the unbidden guest; The aunt and the sluggard; The rummy affair of old Biffy; Clustering around young Bingo; Bertie changes his mind; Jeeves and the impending doom; Jeeves and the Yuletide spirit; Jeeves and the Song of Songs; Episode of the dog McIntosh; Jeeves and the kid Clementina; The love that purifies; Jeeves and the old school chum; The ordeal of young Tuppy

Uncle Fred in the springtime. Simon & Schuster [1969 c1939] 220p $4.95

"A P.G. Wodehouse classic"
First published 1939 by Doubleday
"Another humorous and involved tale of the mad set at Blandings Castle, presided over by the Earl of Emsworth, and his sister Lady Constance. The mainspring of the action this time is the attempted kidnapping of the Earl's prize pig, the Empress of Blandings." Book Rev Digest
This novel has the author's "usual bubbling dialogue, the same jolly old set of characters, the same intricately improbable plot clicking along with the dizzy precision of a circus." Time

Very good, Jeeves. [Autograph ed] British Bk. Centre 1958 224p $3.50

1930 edition analyzed in Short Story Index
A reissue in a new format of the original English edition, published 1930
"Stories concerning the resourceful Jeeves, man servant to the irresponsible Bertie Wooster. In these tales Jeeves extricates Bertie from eleven overwhelming dilemmas." Book Rev Digest
Contains the following stories: Indian summer of an uncle; Inferiority complex of old Sippy; Jeeves and the dog McIntosh; Jeeves and the impending doom; Jeeves and the kid Clementina; Jeeves and the love that purifies; Jeeves and the old school chum; Jeeves and the Song of Songs; Jeeves and the spot of art; Jeeves and the Yuletide spirit; Tuppy changes his mind

Wohl, Louis de. *See* De Wohl, Louis

Woiwode, L.

y What I'm going to do, I think. Farrar, Straus 1969 309p $5.95

This first novel "centers on a honeymoon. Chris and Ellen get married (she is pregnant) after a year of estrangement. . . . They honeymoon in northern Michigan . . . [where they] make love and misunderstand one another and quarrel and make up. Chris buys a rifle and they both shoot endlessly at targets. . . . One day he shoots at a gull and in panic fears that he has hit his wife. His relief at finding her unharmed is intense. . . . A half-page coda reports her miscarriage in September, and an epilogue reveals them childless, listless, older." Book World
Woiwode "has written a touching, sometimes deeply moving novel about youth growing up to the pain of loss, the puzzle of love, and the sense of despair lying near the surface of modern consciousness. . . . The author has found the nearly perfect expression for the human condition he wants to arrest and examine within the boundaries of narrative. Form and content are so joined that one cannot imagine this novel stated any other way." N Y Times Bk R

Wolfe, Thomas

From death to morning. Scribner 1963 304p $4.50

First published 1935 and analyzed in Short Story Index. Copyright renewed 1963
These "stories" are sketches from life written between 1932 and 1935
Contents: No door; Death the proud brother; The face of the war; Only the dead know Brooklyn; Dark in the forest, strange as time; The four lost men; Gulliver; The bums at sunset; One of the girls in our party; The far and the near; In the park; The men of old Catawba; Circus at dawn; The web of earth

The hills beyond; with a note on Thomas Wolfe by Edward C. Aswell. Harper 1941 386p $6.95

Analyzed in Short Story Index
Contains one long story of the history of the Joyner family from the Revolutionary War until 1880, and ten short stories
Contents: Lost boy; No cure for it; Gentlemen of the press; Kinsman of his blood; Chickamauga; Return of the prodigal; On leprechauns; Portrait of a literary critic; Lion at morning; God's lonely man; The hills beyond [unfinished novel]

"I have a thing to tell you"
In Wolfe, T. The short novels of Thomas Wolfe p158-231

Look homeward, angel; a story of the buried life; with an introduction by Maxwell E. Perkins. Scribner 1957 522p $5.95

First published 1929
A novel autobiographical in character, "describes the childhood and youth of Eugene Gant in the town of Altamont, state of Catawba (said to be Asheville, North Carolina), as he grows up, becomes aware of the relations among his family, meets the eccentric people of the town, goes to college, discovers literature and ideas, has his first love affairs, and at last sets out alone on a mystic and romantic 'pilgrimage.'" Benét. The Reader's Encyclopedia
"There is such mammoth appreciation of experience and of living that the intention of the novel cannot be articulated. It comes through to you like fumes or like one supreme mood of courage that you can never forget, and with it all the awe, the defilement and grandeur of actual life." N Y Her Trib Books
Followed by: Of time and the river

No door
In Wolfe, T. The short novels of Thomas Wolfe p158-231

Of time and the river; a legend of man's hunger in his youth. Scribner 1935 912p $7.50

Sequel to: Look homeward, angel
"Eugene Gant, youngest son of the family made famous in 'Look homeward, Angel,' takes leave of his mother and sister and starts off for his three years at Harvard. The experiences here, the agonized waiting to hear whether or not his first play is accepted, the years of teaching, his sojourn in England and France, all these form the background against which are thrown all the varied personalities and experiences he encountered, written in equally varied style running the entire range from utter lack of taste to heights of sheer beauty. A work of genius." Wis Lib Bul

Wolfe, Thomas—*Continued*

"If you look for a plot, a story in the usual sense in 'Of Time and the River' you will not find it; but you will find a hundred stories and five years of life, richly experienced, deeply felt, minutely and lyrically recorded." N Y Her Trib Books

The party at Jack's
In Wolfe, T. The short novels of Thomas Wolfe p282-323

The portable Thomas Wolfe; ed. by Maxwell Geismar. Viking 1946 712p (Viking Portable lib) o.p. 1970

Partially analyzed in Short Story Index
Contains episodes from four novels; Look homeward, angel; Of time and the river; Web and the rock; You can't go home again. Also six short stories: Face of the war; Only the dead know Brooklyn; Dark in the forest, strange as time; Circus at dawn; In the park; Chickamauga. Also includes the complete work, Story of a novel

A portrait of Bascom Hawke
In Wolfe, T. The short novels of Thomas Wolfe p4-71

The short novels of Thomas Wolfe; ed. with an introduction and notes by C. Hugh Holman. Scribner 1961 xx, 323p $5.95

Analyzed in Short Story Index
"Five short novels—'A Portrait of Bascom Hawke,' 'The Web of Earth,' 'No Door,' 'I Have a Thing to Tell You' and 'The Party at Jack's'—originally published in magazines [between 1932 and 1939], with an introduction and notes by the editor. Several of these were modified later and woven in Wolfe's long novels." N Y Her Trib Books

The web and the rock. Harper 1939 695p $8.95

"This novel marks not only a turning away from the books I have written in the past, but a genuine spiritual and artistic change. It is the most objective novel that I have written. I have invented characters who are compacted from the whole amalgam and consonance of seeing, feeling, thinking, living, and knowing many people. I have sought, through free creation, a release of my inventive power." The Author

"In fictional form, but probably based on Wolfe's own life, it is the story of one George Webber—his youth in a Southern town, his college days, his teaching, trip abroad, and his unhappy love affair. Thru the whole book runs the account of George's unsuccessful quest for an understanding of the meaning of life." Book Rev Digest

Followed by: You can't go home again

The web of earth
In Wolfe, T. The short novels of Thomas Wolfe p76-154

You can't go home again. Harper 1940 743p $7.50

Sequel to: The web and the rock
A novel of life in America and Europe, which continues "the story of George Webber from the late nineteen twenties to the middle thirties. The book is divided into several sections, dealing respectively with Webber's experiences as a home-town visiting author, a traveler in England, and a sojourner in Germany during the early Nazi years there." Book Rev Digest

"Excellent characterizations; the book shows the same evidences of genius as are found in his other works." Booklist

Wolff, Ruth

y A crack in the sidewalk; a novel. Day 1965 281p boards $5.95

"As young Linsey Templeton narrates her story, the Templeton family comes to life—her tubercular, Bible-strict father, her mother who lives vicariously through the lives of others, her beautiful older sister, and the younger children including mentally retarded Pleas. Living on the second floor of a drab building surrounded by cement Linsey dreams of a better life and finds the means through her lovely voice by becoming a folk singer." Booklist

"It is not an important book, but it is pleasant and wholesome and honest, and it will bring enjoyment." Best Sellers

y I, Keturah; a novel. Day 1963 285p $5.95

"Keturah lives in a grim orphanage and dreams of being a lady. Life begins when she is taken in by a country couple to help around their farm. When they die, Keturah moves on to become governess to a silent, sickly little girl living on a fine estate occasionally visited by a moody man suffering some unrevealed sorrow who never goes near the child." Book Week

The author "has brought together a variety of people and portrayed them well, skillfully avoiding triteness and sentimentalism in this . . . appraisal of her own life, and the reader's interest is sustained throughout." Library J

A trace of footprints; a novel. Day 1968 252p $5.95

The author portrays a typical small American town "through the story of 82-year-old Sam Archer and his visiting grandson, Paul. Sam, the revered schoolteacher in Oakgrove for 52 years until his retirement, still plays the role of father confessor and knows most of the town's secrets. His grandson, Paul, recently estranged from his wife, visits his grandfather during the summer and discovers himself while rediscovering his town." Publisher's note

Wollaston, Nicholas

Pharaoh's chicken. Lippincott 1969 217p boards $4.95

"David Knapp is a young man who wants to contribute something worthwhile to life, so, encouraged by his wife, Liz, he goes off to India to expedite the work of the Famine Fund, the philanthropic organization for which she works. He immediately falls under the spell of the country and its people but his enchantment is mixed with exasperation, which does not make his struggle to alleviate the hunger and suffering any easier. David's involvement with the Indians—especially the gentle Hindu who is his assistant and Shashi, beautiful wife of an English-style Indian politician becomes deeper and more subjective." Am News of Bks

"Mr. Wollaston's sense of humor never deserts him in the telling of this somber and sardonic tale, and makes not only believable but thoroughly readable, the bitter lesson that must be learned. Required reading for anyone who thinks love alone can solve the ills of this world." Pub W

Wolpert, Stanley

Nine hours to Rama. Random House 1962 376p o.p. 1970

A novel about "the nine hours on that tragic January day immediately preceding the firing of the shots that killed Gandhi. . . . The central figure in the story is Naturam Vinayak Godse, the militant Hindu fanatic who fired them. . . . Flashbacks [tell] how the young Godse, snubbed by British officers in his attempt to join the Indian Army, first became involved in the revolutionary Hindu movement of Dhondo Kanetkar; how he found an outlet for his talents and his extremist feelings in journalism; how he and his fellow-Hindu fanatics came to look upon the saintly Gandhi as one of their greatest enemies; and how finally he was chosen by lot to murder him." Christian Science Monitor

"The book as a whole accomplishes a most difficult task: the conveying of an event, a moment in time, a fantastic episode in history, and a personality from so different a continent." N Y Times Bk R

Woodfin, Henry

Virginia's thing. Harper 1968 185p boards $4.95

"A Joan Kahn-Harper Novel of suspense"
"The main background [of this novel] is a university campus. . . . Virginia, who has disappeared, had been a student and an ardent civil rights worker, secretly married to a black power leader. (She is white.) Her father,

Woodfin, Henry—*Continued*

president of a formidable dock workers union, is concerned not only with his daughter's disappearance but also with the effect any scandal might have on his current union fight . . . [and hires detective John Foley] to find her." Pub W

"Foley is a welcome addition to the growing list of intelligent and sympathetic detectives who may one day bring the school of overstimulated, gunslinging heroes into better balance." Book World

Woodhouse, Martin

Tree Frog. Coward-McCann 1966 252p boards $4.95

This "novel of espionage re-introduces an element of puzzlement that is marvelous to find again in this type of fiction. A likable young aeronautical research scientist is sucked into working on Operation Tree Frog, supposedly a top-secret government project to perfect a pilotless reconnaissance plane. Not until the last few pages of the book does he (or the reader) learn what it is he is really being called upon to do. This is different, it is witty and it is good." Pub W

Woods, Sara

Enter certain murderers. Harper 1966 207p o.p. 1970

Barrister "Antony Maitland becomes involved in the murder of a restaurant-owner named Grainger only because of the pleading of his old friend, Meg Hamilton, a successful actress. In this intricate chase, Antony learns how dangerous friendship can be, not only to Meg, but to himself as well." Library J

Past praying for. Harper 1968 230p $4.95

"A Joan Kahn-Harper Novel of suspense"

"Camilla Barnard had served four years for manslaughter in the death of her first husband . . . and had married his cousin after her release. He died, and she was on trial again for her life." McClurg. Book News

"As always, Sara Woods gives her readers a good puzzle, close-ups of English legal procedure, and some interesting and entertaining characters." Pub W

Woolf, Virginia

Between the acts. Harcourt 1941 219p $4.75

"The action takes place on a summer day, and the characters are the members of an English county family, their guests, and the villagers who are giving a pageant. The scene is made manifest thru the thoughts and inner compulsions of the family. As the day wears on we see the family at luncheon; visitors are shown over the ancient house; people gather for the pageant; the pageant takes place—its lines given in italics; tea is served; the pageant ends; night falls and the family drifts off, each to his or her preoccupations." Book Rev Digest

"This short novel, by no means melancholy but often a humorously lively study of futility, was left by its author without final revision. Occasional compressions, jerking like Jingle, might have been eased out, but this is, in effect, finished work. It has the beauty, the elating beauty, of language of the assured matured Virginia Woolf." Manchester Guardian

also in Connolly, C. ed. Great English short novels p753-879

A haunted house, and other short stories. Harcourt 1944 148p $3.50

Analyzed in Short Story Index

Contents: A haunted house; Monday or Tuesday; An unwritten novel; The string quartet; Kew gardens; The mark on the wall; The new dress; The shooting party; Lappin and Lapinova; Solid objects; The lady in the looking-glass; The duchess and the jeweller; Moments of being; "Slater's pins have no points"; The man who loved his kind; The searchlight; The legacy; Together and part; A summing up

"In these tales, as in the sketches of a great painter, we can observe the [author's] characteristic method and the characteristic quality of perception. Together they show her brilliant fantasy, her subtle sense of humour and, above all, her compassionate understanding of men and women." New Statesman & Nation

Jacob's room. Harcourt 1923 303p o.p. 1970

"The brief career of Jacob Flanders, a silent lovable English youth, from boyhood, thru Cambridge University, to London, and finally to his death in Flanders, is seen thru a series of impressions." Book Rev Digest

"It is an amusingly clear and yet enchanted glass which she holds up to things; that is her quality. This stream of incidents, persons, and their momentary thoughts and feelings, which would be intolerable if it were just allowed to flow, is arrested and decanted, as it were, into little phials of crystal vividness." Times (London) Lit Sup

Mrs Dalloway. Harcourt 1949 296p (Harbrace Modern classics) $2.95

The novel deals with the events of a woman's single day—the day "upon which her central character meets after many years the old lover whom she did not marry, and in the course of the three hundred pages which record this day nothing happens except that the reader is brought into intimate contact with a group of people and made to participate in their consciousness." Nation

"The searchlight of Mrs. Woolf's suggestive art passes zigzag over the minds of men and women; illuminating those dark interiors with the light of an extraordinarily subtle vision." Sat R

Orlando; a biography. Harcourt 1928 333p illus o.p. 1970

"Mrs Woolf's hero-heroine is hundreds of years old. At the beginning of the book Orlando is a boy of 16, melancholy, indolent, loving solitude and given to writing poetry; the age is the Elizabethan; the book ends on the 11th of October 1928, and Orlando is a thoroughly modern matron of 36, who has published a successful book of poems and has evolved a hardearned philosophy of life." N Y Times Bk R

"The unusual merit and complete originality of 'Orlando' are due to Mrs. Woolf's daring choice of theme which involves the philosophy of literary history and the most acute and perceptive analysis of the English literary mind. The book must be read for this or it will not be truly read at all." Sat R

To the lighthouse. Harcourt 1949 310p (Harbrace Modern classics) $2.95

This story "has no plot, though it has a scheme and a motive. The first and longest part of the book is almost stationary, and describes a party of people gathered in the summer at a house on the Scottish coast. James, the youngest of the Ramsay children is thwarted of a visit to the lighthouse. In the next part, much briefer, sea-winds and caretakers are having their way with the house while one year follows another; Mrs. Ramsay and her eldest daughter have died, a son is killed in the war, and the place is forsaken. In the last part the house is alive again with the surviving Ramsays and two of the former guests. Mr Ramsay, the philosopher, grimly magnificent, heads an expedition to the lighthouse; and James, now sixteen, accomplishes his dream." Times (London) Lit Sup

Miss Woolf "once more proves herself to be a writer with astonishing intuition and mistress of a style that can make the obscurest processes of thought and emotion luminous. There are a dozen passages in which the secret reactions of men and women, especially women, to the apparently trifling events of life are rendered with a convincing and elaborate subtlety." Sat R

The voyage out. Harcourt 1920 375p o.p. 1970

First published 1915 in England

"In this kaleidoscopic picture of real life, people come and go with all their commonplace attributes. They are natural people and act naturally without any dramatic high lights to throw them into relief. To make the events transpire in a little world of their own a shipboard is chosen and a tourist's hotel on a South-American mountain side. Helen Ambrose, wife of a Greek scholar, is put in charge of a niece, twenty years her junior, who at the age of twenty-four is still a child in world wisdom and experience. Helen, with

Woolf, Virginia—*Continued*

rare insight and good sense, undertakes to initiate her into a larger life. In South America they meet the tourists—a variety of types compressed into a miniature world. Here Rachel unfolds and the greatest of experiences, love, comes her way, and there it all ends. Rachel falls a victim to the treacherous climate." Book Rev Digest

The waves. Harcourt 1931 297p $4.95

In this story "the substance of life, as we are accustomed to see it in fiction, is transposed and the form of the novel is transmuted to match it. The six characters, a band of friends—three of each sex—reveal themselves from childhood's spring to the autumn or winter of their lives; but all they feel or do is given to us from their own lips, each taking up the one before in a kind of tranced, yet impetuous soliloquy. Each is alone with himself and yet aware of the others; in the middle and again at the end we see them reunited as a group, and finally Bernard, the man of words and contacts, gathers up the whole perspective." Times (London) Lit Sup

"It is impossible to describe, impossible to do more than salute, the richness, the strangeness, the poetic illumination of this book. The characters are not analysed, as in a laboratory: they are entered into, intuited. In each soliloquy in this pattern of soliloquies we ourselves are at the centre. We are Bernard, we are Susan, but with this difference: that we have borrowed, for a moment, the lamp of genius, and by its light may read the secrets of our private universe." New Statesman and Nation

The years. Harcourt 1937 435p o.p. 1970

Taking the members of three interrelated English families as a basis, the author has woven together their stories to make a pattern of English upper middle-class life from 1880 to the present. "As in Tolstoy's War and Peace' and in Proust, the chief character is time itself. . . . A father leaves his club, goes to the City, returns home for tea, meets his children. A mother lies ill in a hushed house. A son worries about his career. A young girl goes in for good works. The generations grow up." Christian Science Monitor

"The writing throughout has a serene distinction; although there is little deliberate description of persons and places the whole book seems to breathe the very essence of English life." Manchester Guardian

Wouk, Herman

Aurora dawn; or, The true history of Andrew Reale, containing a faithful account of the great riot, together with the complete texts of Michael Wilde's oration and Father Stanfield's sermon. With drawings by Alajalov. Doubleday 1956 284p illus $5.95

First published 1947 by Simon & Schuster

A satire "dealing with the radio industry. The title is not the heroine's name, but the brand name of a soap. The antics of sponsors, account executives, network officials, and 'talent,' all come in for some gay spoofing. The hero is a salesman for one of the big networks." Book Rev Digest

y The Caine mutiny; a novel of World War II. Doubeday 1951 494p $5.95

Pulitzer Prize 1952

"One of the best naval yarns of World War II is this story of the old American destroyer 'Caine' and the men who sailed in her. The action shifts from the bridge to the wardroom and from scenes of petty tyranny to fierce action and heroism. From the time Ensign Willie Keith comes aboard, on through the mutiny and the trial of the paranoiac Captain Queeg it is a novel of action, character development and intrigue." Ontario Lib Rev

"There is a romance in his new novel that might fit in with some of his previous writing, but the Navy material is something else again. Mr. Wouk has a profound understanding of what Navy men should be, and against some who fell short of the mark he has fired a deadly broadside." N Y Times Bk R

City boy: the adventures of Herbie Bookbinder. 20th anniversary ed. Doubleday 1969 317p $5.95

First published 1948 by Scribner

"Story of an eleven-year-old boy plagued by the troubles of his age: bullies, first loves and frustrations, camp life, etc. The humor of the story is relieved by some sharp gibes at the adults who further complicate Herbie's life." Retail Bookseller

y Marjorie Morningstar. Doubleday 1955 565p $6.95

"A long, leisurely narrative, interesting mainly for the background detail on Jewish life, and for characters who are recognizable types. Marjorie Morgenstern, a nice, pretty young thing whose Broadway aspirations depend solely on youthful charm, is the rebellious daughter of immigrant parents who have achieved Central Park West and now live for the day when their daughter will become a modernized version of the traditional Jewish matron. At heart Marjorie has the same goal, but it takes years of thwarted ambition and a disillusioning love affair before she finds fulfillment in her middle-class fate." Booklist

Youngblood Hawke; a novel. Doubleday 1962 783p $2.49

A "story about an aspiring novelist named Arthur Youngblood Hawke. Hawke hails from the small coal-mining town of Hovey, Kentucky. From the age of 11, he has dreamed of the time when he will make his mark as a literary great. Upon leaving the Seabees, Hawke hikes to New York City with a completed war novel ready for market. The book is accepted by a successful publishing firm, and thus Artie Hawke's literary career pushes off to a fast start. It also marks the beginning of a lengthy passionate love affair with a wealthy mother of four children; a series of involved legal entanglements as a result of Hawke's obsession with money; and an unfulfilled romance with a pretty and intelligent young girl who edits Hawke's novels." Library J

Wren, Percival Christopher

Beau Geste; with illus. by Helen McKie. Lippincott 1927 579p illus $5.95

A mystery story, turning on the disappearance of a valuable gem, which eventually causes three English brothers to enlist in the Foreign Legion in Northern Africa. Follows adventures, mysteries, thrills in full measure, with vivid descriptions of life in the Foreign Legion

Wright, Austin Tappan

Islandia. Rinehart 1958 1018p o.p. 1970

A reissue of the title first published 1942 by Farrar

A "long novel describing in detail the life on an imaginary continent, called Islandia, situated in the South Pacific. Three million inhabitants, white, intelligent, and highly emotional, live on the island continent, separated by a high range of mountains from the savage black natives of the rest of the continent. Into this ideal country John Lang goes as American consul, and falls in love with its culture and its ways, and finally receives permission to spend the rest of his life there." Book Rev Digest

"The cards are stacked against the American way of life by the very origin of the book as a dream-compensation for personal lacks. But none the less it is a unique, brilliantly conceived and brilliantly executed book which one reads with avid excitement despite its great length." N Y Times Bk R

Wright, Richard

Eight men. World Pub. 1961 250p o.p. 1970

Analyzed in Short Story Index

"Published posthumously these stories, some of which are new, are about eight Negro men. Set in America, Europe and Africa, these stories show these men as they interact with their environment and situations. Simple, often stark style; realistic and sympathetic viewpoint." Cincinnati

Wright, Richard—*Continued*

Contents: The man who was almost a man; The man who lived underground; Big black good man; The man who saw the flood; Man of all work; Man, God ain't like that. . . ; The man who killed a shadow; The man who went to Chicago

Lawd today. Walker & Co. 1963 189p o.p. 1970

The novel is an "exposition of the life of a Negro worker in Chicago's post office, in the depression 1930's. Jake is no hero: he is a fat, bad-tempered wife-beater, ignorant, and prey to fake nostrums and foolish rumors. But . . . [the author] has compassion for him and for his three friends in the post office, revealing their sense of futility, as Negroes, in their sad and desultory conversation towards the end of a long day of mechanical work." Pub W

"The characterizations, especially that of Jake, are cruel and brilliant, but the basic implication, as in Wright's other novels, that Negroes are the victims of their environment and there is nothing they themselves can do about the situation, simply does not obtain today." Library J

Native son; with an introduction: "How 'Bigger' was born," by the author. Harper [1969 c1940] xxxiv, 392p $7.50

Reissue of title first published 1940
"In this story of a frustrated, inarticulate Chicago Negro whose bewildered resentment of life can only be expressed by violence and murder, there is a melodrama as well as stark realism, but above all there is unusual power, an understanding of Negro psychology, and compassion that never becomes special pleading. It is a disturbing book, and it will horrify many readers, not only by its frank brutalities, but by the menace that is implied in its revelation of Negro misery and degradation." Booklist

"As a Southerner I may be suspect, but I think this book is better as a headlong, hard-boiled narrative than as any preaching about race relations in America. North or South. Certainly no sensible Southerner will deny the authenticity of Mr. Wright's picture of the plight of his race. But not only Negro boys in pool rooms and slums in Chicago feel caught and find a distorted manhood in violence. The rules of an insensitive world may be more binding, more hope-denying among them. But every order creates its rats and rebels and every civilization—so far in existence—deserves them." Sat R

The outsider. Harper [1969 c1953] 440p $7.50

Reissue of title first published 1953
"Life has been a succession of traps for young Cross Damon, Chicago Negro and student of existentialism, who has always felt himself an outsider, even among outsiders. When a mangled body is mistaken for his in a subway accident he takes on a new identity, to escape from an unhappy marriage, a burden of debts, and a charge of rape. He kills four men and causes the suicide of the white girl with whom he has fallen in love before he learns that every man, white or black, must commit himself to some ethical system, that not even Cross Damon can live beyond good and evil. The novel proves most rewarding when it introspects the problems of man's isolation, freedom, and responsibility, less so when it relies on melodramatic excesses to pump up reader interest." Booklist

Uncle Tom's children. Harper [1969 c1938] 215p $5

Analyzed in Short Story Index
First published 1938. This is a reissue of the 1940 edition
Contents: The ethics of living Jim Crow; Big Boy leaves home; Down by the riverside; Long black song; Fire and cloud; Bright and morning star

Wright, Sarah E.

This child's gonna live. Delacorte Press 1969 276p $5.95

"A Seymour Lawrence book"
"Tangierneck is a Maryland black ghetto in the 1930's. Its residents are destitute and powerless to alter their fate. It is an environment of despair, hunger, disease, cold, and death, and Mariah Upshur, heroine of this novel, is determined to escape from it with her children. But her strong faith and years of work are futile; two of her children die, stricken horribly by disease, and her hopes are finally extinguished in guilt and despair." Library J

"Sarah Wright has a firm grasp of the idiom used by her people and recalls it with all the colorful remarks that make up the patois of a closed society. . . . The story is vividly told and gives a true picture of life among Negroes who live in a rural area without all the comforts of our civilized cities." Best Sellers

Wu Ch'êng-ên

Monkey; tr. from the Chinese by Arthur Waley. Grove [distributed by Smith, P.] [1958 c1943] 306p (UNESCO Collection of representative works—Chinese ser) $4.50

This translation was first published 1943 by Day

Selections from Hsi yu chi, a novel of the Ming Dynasty attributed to Wu Ch'êng-ên

"Describes the adventures of the priest Hsüan-tsang during his pilgrimage to India in search of the scriptures, accompanied by Monkey and other creatures. Humorous, satirical, and absurd, it has enjoyed continued popularity." Benét. The Reader's Encyclopedia

Wyckoff, Nicholas E.

The Braintree Mission; a fictional narrative of London and Boston, 1770-1771. Macmillan (N Y) 1957 184p o.p. 1970

An "historical novel about Boston in 1770.. The supposition is that the English government proposed to stop the trouble in the colonies by offering an earldom and a seat in Parliament to six outstanding colonists. The story is about the offering made to John Adams." Book Rev Digest

"Parallels between Pitt and Adams are made, particularly in their oratorical ability, and their good fortune in each having an understanding wife who plays no small part in her husband's affairs. Pleasing as a bit of conjecture and in its re-creation of the atmosphere of the time." Booklist

Wylie, Elinor

The Venetian glass nephew
In Blackmur, R. P. ed. American short novels p344-96

Wylie, Philip

The answer
In The Saturday Evening Post. The Post Reader of fantasy and science fiction p275-311

Tomorrow! Rinehart 1954 372p o.p. 1970

"The book is a dramatic appeal for the immediate organization of an effective program of civilian defense which will prepare the nation physically and mentally for the possible horrors of atomic attack. It tells of two neighboring American cities, one having an active civil defense program, the other scoffing at such 'nonsense,' and of their reactions when blitzed without warning by atomic weapons." Library J

"A novel that stuns and yet, paradoxically, alerts the reader, for tho it paints a staggering picture of what could happen in America it also is a warning for the present." Chicago Sunday Tribune

(jt. auth.) Balmer, E. When worlds collide

Wynd, Oswald. See Black, Gavin

Wyndham, John

The day of the triffids. Doubleday 1951 222p o.p. 1970

"A shower of atomic comets blinds most of the people of the world, making it possible for a species of walking plants to threaten inclinations—the totalitarian, socialistic, religextinction of human life. The few persons who can still see form groups according to personal ious, democratic—and set about reorganizing the earth." Booklist

Wyndham, John—*Continued*

"When British science fiction writers are good, they have a way of imparting a devastating reality to their inventions, and this is true of John Wyndham's first book." N Y Times Bk R

The Midwich cuckoos. Ballantine 1957 247p o.p. 1970

A fantasy set in the sleepy English village of Midwich which is isolated and immobilized for twenty-four hours. After their return to normal the people of Midwich can remember nothing about this "Dayout." Not until several weeks later does it become evident that every Midwich woman of childbearing age is unaccountably pregnant. And several months later the children born of this mass pregnancy are found to be slightly but ominously different. (Publisher)

"The impact of these infant invaders upon tiny Midwich, where nothing of importance has happened in all the previous centuries, is carried out not only with honesty and absolute credibility, but with humor, charm and a strong touch of terror, in one of the most inescapably readable of modern imaginative novels." N Y Her Trib Books

Out of the deeps

In Hitchcock, A. ed. Alfred Hitchcock presents: Stories that scared even me p309-463

Re-birth

In Boucher, A. ed. A treasury of great science fiction v 1 p9-135

Trouble with lichen. Walker & Co. [1969 c1960] 160p boards $4.95

First published 1960 in England

"At an English research corporation a lichen is discovered that will retard metabolism, extending a lifetime for hundreds of years. As the particular lichen grows only in a remote part of China, only a limited number of people will be able to benefit from it, and, of those, who would really want to live that long? As with all closely held secrets, time betrays what is going on and the public begins to learn that two at the institute, a man and a woman, hold the secret of eternal life. The characterizations are good, the dialog comes alive." Pub W

Y

Yáñez, Agustín

The edge of the storm (Al filo del agua); a novel; tr. by Ethel Brinton; illus. by Julio Prieto. Univ. of Tex. Press 1963 332p illus (The Texas Pan-American ser) $6.50

From "this story of a remote early twentieth-century Mexican village emanates the essence of Mexican character and history. Loving but exaggeratedly puritanic Father Martinez, the parish priest, and his Savonarolalike curate transfer their own fear of life to their flock, ignoring the affectionate warning of another curate, the open and forward-looking Father Reyes. They also close their ears to the distant thunder of the revolution and its winds of change. In the end Father Martínez has suffered the storm and faces the bitter knowledge that those he loved he has not loosed soon enough and all are lost to him." Booklist

The lean lands (Las tierras flacas); tr. by Ethel Brinton; illus. by Alberto Beltrán. Univ. of Tex. Press 1968 328p illus (The Texas Pan-American ser) $6.50

Original Spanish edition published 1962 in Mexico City

"This is a powerful story of tradition-bound farmers in an isolated region of Jalisco, Mexico, during the early 1920's who are confronted with the likelihood of change and progress. The countryside is dominated by an aging patriarchal cacique or chief whose numerous offspring are struggling for his power and wealth. Jacob, a rebellious son, has gained riches and

influence during the Revolution. He returns to the region introducing new ways and marvels such as electricity. Augustin Yáñez, an excellent craftman, evokes a sparse, harsh mood consonant with the relationship of the farmers to the land which gives reluctantly, if at all. Short interior monologues enhance the depth of characterization. Another technique, at times, is the use of hundreds of proverbs which reveal character and attitudes in a most concise way. The translation reads well." Library J

Yarmolinsky, Avrahm

(ed.) A treasury of great Russian short stories; Pushkin to Gorky. Macmillan (N Y) 1944 xxi, 1018p $9.75

Aanlyzed in Short Story Index

"The scope of the present collection . . . . opens with a story dated 1835 and closes with one first published in 1917. Soviet writing does not come within the purview of this book." Introduction

Contents: The undertaker, by A. Pushkin; Queen of spades, by A. Pushkin; Old-world landowners, by N. Gogol; The overcoat, by N. Gogol; The singers, by I. Turgenev; The tryst, by I. Turgenev; Moomoo, by I. Turgenev; Lear of the steppes, by I. Turgenev; Living relics, by I. Turgenev; Old portraits, by I. Turgenev; Honest thief, by F. Dostoevsky; Unpleasant predicament, by F. Dostoevsky; Notes from the underground, by F. Dostoevsky; Peasant Marey, by F. Dostoevsky; Chertogon, by N. Leskov; The sentry, by N. Leskov; Sevastopol in December, 1854, by L. Tolstoy; Three deaths, by L. Tolstoy; Polikushka, by L. Tolstoy; How much land does a man need, by L. Tolstoy; After the ball, by L. Tolstoy; Alyosha, by L. Tolstoy; Small fry, by A. Chekhov; The beggar, by A. Chekhov; Misery, by A. Chekhov; Vanka, by A. Chekhov; Easter eve, by A. Chekhov; Agafya, by A. Chekhov; The witch, by A. Chekhov; Volodya, by A. Chekhov; A father, by A. Chekhov; Happy ending, by A. Chekhov; Name-day party, by A. Chekhov; Gusev, by A. Chekhov; In exile, by A. Chekhov; The grasshopper, by A. Chekhov; Woman's kingdom, by A. Chekhov; "Anna on the neck," by A. Chekhov; The helpmate, by A. Chekhov; At home, by A. Chekhov; The schoolmistress, by A. Chekhov; Peasants, by A. Chekhov; Man in a case, by A. Chekhov; Gooseberries, by A. Chekhov; About love, by A. Chekhov; The darling, by A. Chekhov; On official duty, by A. Chekhov; Makar's dream, by V. Korolenko; Gambrinus, by A. Kuprin; Twenty-six men and a girl, by M. Gorky; Birth of a man, by M. Gorky; Going home, by M. Gorky; Lullaby, by M. Gorky

Yasunari Kawabata. See Kawabata, Yasunari

Yates, Richard

A special providence. Knopf 1969 340p $5.95

This novel describes "the maturation of Robert J. Prentice, an 18-year-old soldier who fights in the awful closing days of World War II in Europe. The major part of the book recounts his experiences in training camp and in the mud and debris of Belgium. . . . The central portion of the novel [is] concerned with Robert's childhood, and dominated by the . . . character of his mother Alice." Library J

". . . The author writes especially well of this curious, if not unfamiliar, mother and son—the straw-grasping girl-woman and the boy only becoming a man in the rough and tumble of war." Pub W

Yerby, Frank

The Foxes of Harrow. Dial Press 1946 534p $5.95

"Stephen Fox, tall and red-haired, arrived in New Orleans in 1825 on a pig boat, with a ten-dollar gold piece, a pearl stick-pin . . . and a dream. He saw his chance and took it from an indolent, slave-ridden, castebound people, with the skill and daring of the card-sharp he was. He gambled and won . . . and built 'Harrow' the greatest manor house and plantation in Louisiana. Two wives and a mistress supply the love interest. . . . Mr

Yerby, Frank—*Continued*

Yerby has overlooked none of the color and atmosphere of New Orleans through the troubled days between 1825 and the Civil War." Huntting

Yoshikawa, Eiji

The Heiké story; tr. from the Japanese by Fuki Wooyenaka Uramatsu; illus. by Kenkichi Sugimoto. Knopf 1956 626p illus map o.p. 1970

"A novel about the leader of the Heiké clan . . . which is engaged by the Japanese Emperor to quell civil uprisings. Their leader becomes the Emperor's Chief Councillor, succeeds in his mission, and rules for 10 years. The setting is 12th century Japan." Pub W

Young, Collier

The Todd dossier. Delacorte Press 1969 187p $4.95

"Hollis Todd is a flamboyant and dynamic billionaire who possesses everything—except a good heart. With death imminent, he is whisked to a transplant hospital, where soon afterwards the dying victim of an automobile accident is brought in. The victim is a former Olympic track star. His heart is successfully transplanted to Todd, and 'the heart of one of the world's great athletes beats on in the body of one of the world's richest men.' But to one member of the surgery team, there is something too fortuitous about the proceedings. Against stern warnings he delves deeper into the case, eventually exposing a masterly conceived plan to insure the longevity of Todd." Am News of Bks

Young, Stark

So red the rose. Scribner 1934 431p $5.95

"This novel of the South, just before and during the Civil War, portrays with beauty and understanding the life of the wealthy southern planter at its best. The story concerns the families of two plantations near Natchez, Mississippi, and the course of the war is described only as it touches these people. This is so skilfully done, however, that through brief episodes the whole panorama of the war is made clear." Booklist

"This novel is not 'sympathetic;' it is written out of the essence of a spirit of the South that survives today and that no doubt lived three score years ago." Boston Transcript

Yourcenar, Marguerite

Memoirs of Hadrian, and reflections on the composition of Memoirs of Hadrian; tr. from the French in collaboration with the author. Farrar, Straus 1963 347p $8.95

A reissue of the title first published 1954
"This fictitious autobiography recreates a segment of the second-century Roman world —its morals, philosophies and tastes, and brilliantly reveals the complex character of 'Hadrian.' As this over-civilized, introspective hedonist broods on life, death, love, pleasure and pain, determined to get the most in experience out of each, and as the conscientious ruler plans for the welfare of his people, the reader is moved to antipathy and admiration —which is stronger will depend on the reader's temperament. Homosexuality is accepted and the emotional climax is the suicide of the Emperor's boy-favorite. Hadrian's character fits known facts but is nevertheless fictional." Library J

Z

Zabel, Morton Dauwen

(ed.) Conrad, J. The portable Conrad
(ed.) Conrad, J. Tales of the East and West

Zangwill, Israel

The big bow mystery
In Santesson, H. S. ed. The locked room reader p127-225

Zee, John van der. See Van der Zee, John

Zelazny, Roger

The eve of Rumoko
In Three for tomorrow p81-152

(ed.) Nebula award stories, three. See Nebula award stories, three

Zilahy, Lajos

The Dukays; tr. from the Hungarian by John Pauker. Prentice-Hall 1949 795p o.p. 1970

Translation of Ararát, published in Hungary 1947
"An amazingly detailed and penetrating novel of an Hungarian family and the effect upon its members of two world wars. The Dukays had inherited tremendous wealth, prestige and power, but in a changing world order their feudal way of life suffered complete dislocation. The central characters are the daughters, Kristina and Zia, and the story of their lives involves most of the well-known European figures of the last fifty years. Here is romance and intrigue against a sumptuous background." Ontario Lib Rev

Zola, Émile

L'assommoir; tr. from the French; with an introduction by Havelock Ellis. Knopf 1924 437p o.p. 1970

First published in France 1877. Also published under titles: The dram-shop; Drunkard; Nana's mother. One of the Rougon-Macquart series
"This book first made Zola famous. The central idea is the ruinous effect, social and moral, of drinking [among the workmen of Paris]; and pathetic interest attaches to Gervaise [daughter of Antoine] the ill-used victim of circumstances, corrupted in her very infancy yet preserving the feminine traits of tenderness and modesty. The original is appallingly outspoken, and shocked the public with its terrible revelations of the social depravity due to drink. The grossness of the argot and of the incidents is, of course, much modified here." Baker's Best

Captain Burle
In Dupee, F. W. ed. Great French short novels p423-61

The debacle; introduction by Robert Baldick. Dufour 1969 499p $8.95

First published 1892 in France. One of the Rougon-Macquart series
Translated by John Hand
"Naturalistic account of the disastrous campaign that ended in Sedan as it was seen and endured by two private soldiers who were in the thick of the fight. Not only are the awful realities of modern warfare brought before the eye, but the intolerable fatigue of the marching, the agonies of the hospitals, and the degradation and misery experienced by prisoners of war are depicted with ruthless force. Still more tragic are the episodes of revolution and massacre inside beleaguered Paris." Baker's Best

Germinal; tr. with an introduction by Havelock Ellis. Dutton 1933 (Everyman's lib) 422p $2.95

First published in France 1885. One of the Rougon-Macquart series
"A study of life in the mines. The illegitimate son of Gervaise, Étienne Lanier, a socialist, is forced to work in the mines. Low wages and fines cause a strike, of which Lanier is one of the leaders. He counsels moderation; but hunger drives the miners to desperation, and force is met by force. Several are killed,

Zola, Émile—*Continued*

Lanier is deported, and the miners fall back into their old slavery." Keller's Reader's Digest of Books

"The greatest novel of the labor movement. one of the masterpieces of nineteenth century French literature and today, more than ever. a true model of the social novel." Matthew Josephson in Introduction [Knopf edition]

Nana

Some editions are:
Dufour $5.95 Translated by Victor Plarr, with an introduction by Alec Brown
Harper (Harper's Modern classics) $2.28
First published in France 1880. One of the Rougon-Macquart series

"A study of the life of a courtesan and actress. Nana is the daughter of Gervaise and the drunkard Coupeau. She grows up in the streets and disreputable haunts until she comes under the notice of a theatre manager. Her great physical beauty attracts men of all classes, and none resist her. . . . The greatest fortunes are dissipated by her, and yet at her door is heard the continual ring of the creditor. She contracts the black smallpox, and dies deserted and wretched." Keller's Reader's Digest of Books

Three faces of love; especially tr. for this volume by Roland Gant. Vanguard [1969 c1968] 151p $4.95

"Three little known stories about women in love." Bk Buyer's Guide
Contents: For one night of love; Round trip; Winkles for Monsieur Chabre

Zoshchenko, Mikhail

Scenes from the bathhouse, and other stories of Communist Russia; tr. with an introduction by Sidney Monas. Stories selected by Marc Slonim. Univ. of Mich. Press 1961 245p $5.95

Partially analyzed in Short Story Index
This selection "displays the development of the author's work from wry, man-in-the-street humor to bitter Orwellian satire and melancholia. . . . Both for its revelatory insight into Soviet life and psychology, and for the uniform excellence of the translation, this collection is highly recommended for all public and university libraries." Library J

Stories included are: Victoria Kazimirovna; A metropolitan deal; Confession; What good are relatives; The aristocrat; The bathhouse; The patient; Poverty; The overshoe; The actor; The crisis; The receipt; A weak container; Bathhouse and people; A romantic tale; Poor Liza; An amusing adventure; Liaisons dangereuses; Personal life; My professions; Love; On Pushkin's anniversary; Houses and people; Rose-Marie; The story of my illness; A happy game; A last unpleasantness; An instructive story; Kochergà (The poker); The photograph; The adventures of an ape; An extraordinary event; In the bathhouse; Before the sun rises

Zweig, Arnold

The case of Sergeant Grischa; tr. from the German by Eric Sutton. Stackpole Co. [1970 c1927] 449p (Great novels and memoirs of World War I) $6.95

Sequel to: Education before Verdun
A reissue of the title first published 1927 in Germany and 1928 by Viking in the United States
In 1917, "a poor little Russian soldier, longing for home is caught escaping from a German prison camp. Though he was erroneously condemned to death as a spy, the High Command decrees he must yet pay the penalty for political reasons and for the effect of discipline on the other men. Futile efforts are made in Grischa's behalf and the whole is a greatly moving, powerful tale, drawn with simple fidelity and pervaded with universal implications." N Y Libraries

Education before Verdun; tr. from the German by Eric Sutton. Viking 1936 447p o.p. 1970

Sequel to: Young woman of 1914
"While not of the same caliber as 'The case of Sergeant Grischa,' this novel of injustice within the German army is a powerful commentary on human nature under the stress of war, simply yet movingly written. How the life of Private Bertin becomes linked with the affairs of the Kroysing brothers, how he arouses one brother to avenge the death of the other, a victim of his superior officers' treachery, and how Bertin develops as a thinking man are the themes which stand out conspicuously against the dramatic recreation of the months before Verdun." N Y Libraries
Followed by: The case of Sergeant Grischa

Young woman of 1914; tr. from the German by Eric Sutton. Viking 1932 346p o.p. 1970

"The story of Werner Bertin. a gifted young writer who became a common soldier, and Lenore Wahl, who, for a year before the outbreak of the war, had been Bertin's mistress. Their forced separation, Lenore's resort to abortion because family opposition made marriage impossible, her resentment of Bertin's absorption in military life, and her changing attitude toward him, are handled in a masterly way, and the book, though lacking the intensity of 'The case of Sergeant Grischa,' is an impressive portrayal of people feeling the first impact of war, and of a girl groping toward a freer womanhood." Booklist
Followed by: Education before Verdun

Zweig, Stefan

Beware of pity; a novel; tr. from the German by Phyllis and Trevor Blewitt. Viking 1939 498p o.p. 1970

"'There are two kinds of pity,' says the author. and in this poignant story of Austria [in 1914] before the war, of a young officer and a crippled girl, and the men and women whose lives cross theirs, he shows what those two kinds may do for good or for evil." Huntting

TITLE AND SUBJECT INDEX

This is an index to the titles and subjects of the books listed in Part I. Full information for each book is given in Part I under the main entry.

Subject entries. The list of books under each subject indicates that a major portion of each book is on that subject.

Analytical entries. Title and occasionally subject analytical entries are made for novels and novelettes.

ADAMS, ABIGAIL (SMITH)
Stone, I. Those who love

ADAMS, JOHN, PRESIDENT U.S.
Stone, I. Those who love
Wyckoff, N. E. The Braintree Mission

Add a dash of pity. Ustinov, P.

Admiral Hornblower in the West Indies. Forester, C. S.
also in Forester, C. S. The indomitable Hornblower p415-640

ADMIRALS. See Great Britain. Navy—Officers; United States. Navy—Officers

ADOLESCENCE
Abaunza, V. Sundays from two to six
Agee, J. The morning watch
Anthony, M. Green days by the river
Arnow, H. S. The weedkiller's daughter
Bagnold, E. National Velvet
In Costain, T. B. ed. Stories to remember v2 p339-504
Barrett, B. L. Love in Atlantis
Bassani, G. The garden of the Finzi-Continis
Bedford, S. A compass error
Bennett, A. Clayhanger
Berto, G. The sky is red
Bowen, E. The death of the heart
Brunner, J. The devil's work
Bryher. Ruan
Canfield, D. The bent twig
Capote, T. Other voices, other rooms
Carpenter, D. The murder of the frogs
In Carpenter, D. The murder of the frogs, and other stories p79-130
Cocteau, J. The holy terrors
Colette. Claudine at school
Colette. Gigi
In Colette. Gigi. Julie de Carneilhan. Chance acquaintances p9-74
In Colette. 7 by Colette v 1 p 1-67
In Colette. Six novels p649-97
Colette. The ripening seed
Cronin, A. J. The green years
Davis, C. First family
Deal, B. The least one
Disney, D. M. Voice from the grave
Elliott, D. W. Listen to the silence
Farrell, J. T. Young Lonigan
Fast, H. April morning
Fielding, G. In the time of Greenbloom
Fitzgerald, F. S. This side of paradise
Fournier, A. The wanderer
Glyn, C. Don't knock the corners off
Godden, R. The river
Grass, G. Cat and mouse
Green, G. To Brooklyn with love
Hamner, E. Spencer's Mountain
Herlihy, J. L. All fall down
Hesse, H. Beneath the wheel
Hesse, H. Demian, the story of Emil Sinclair's youth
Holland, I. Cecily
Hunter, E. Last summer
Joyce, J. A portrait of the artist as a young man
Joyce, J. Stephen Hero
Kipling, R. The complete Stalky & Co.
Kirkwood, J. Good times/bad times
Knowles, J. A separate peace
Kops, B. The dissent of Dominick Shapiro
Lee, H. To kill a mockingbird
Lehmann, R. Invitation to the waltz
Macaulay, R. The world my wilderness
McCullers, C. Clock without hands
Maurois, A. The family circle
Meredith, G. The ordeal of Richard Feverel
Miller, W. The cool world
Murphy, R. A certain island
Murphy, R. The Pond
Nathan, R. Winter in April
Parks, G. The learning tree
Price, R. A generous man
Proust, M. Within a budding grove
Richter, C. The grandfathers
Robertson, D. The sum and total of now
Rolvaag, O. E. Peder Victorious
Rothberg, A. The song of David Freed
Salinger, J. D. The catcher in the rye
Sheed, W. The blacking factory
In Sheed, W. The blacking factory & Pennsylvania gothic p67-246
Shulman, M. I was a teen-age dwarf
Simenon, G. The confessional
Sinclair, J. The changelings
Smith, B. A tree grows in Brooklyn
Solberg, G. Shelia
Street, J. Captain Little Ax
Tarkington, B. Seventeen
Turgenev, I. The watch
In Turgenev, I. Three novellas: Punin and Baburin, The inn, The watch p149-208

Vittorini, E. Erica
In Vittorini, E. The dark and the light p 1-75
West, J. Cress Delahanty
Wilkinson, S. A killing frost
Wilkinson, S. Moss on the north side
Wilson, S. J. To find a man
Wolff, R. A crack in the sidewalk
Wouk, H. City boy: the adventures of Herbie Bookbinder
See also Boys; Girls; Youth

ADOLESCENTS. See Adolescence

ADOPTED CHILDREN. See Adoption; Foster children

ADOPTION
Banks, L. R. Children at the gate
De Vries, P. The tunnel of love
France, A. The crime of Sylvestre Bonnard
Lewis, R. Michel, Michel
Vining, E. G. I, Roberta
White, R. Elephant Hill
See also Foster children

ADULTERY. See Marriage problems

Advent. See Gunnarsson, G. The good shepherd

ADVENTURE
Abé, K. The ruined map
Albrand, M. Nightmare in Copenhagen
Aldridge, J. A captive in the land
Allen, H. Anthony Adverse
Ambler, E. Judgment on Deltchev
Ambler, E. A kind of anger
Ambler, E. The light of day
Arent, A. The laying on of hands
Asimov, I. Fantastic voyage
Bagley, D. The golden keel
Bagley, D. Landslide
Bagley, D. The spoilers
Bagley, D. The Vivero letter
Bagley, D. Wyatt's hurricane
Barry, J. Maximilian's gold
Bates, H. E. Fair stood the wind for France
Bengtsson, F. G. The long ships
Bleeck, O. The brass go-between
Brick, J. Rogues' kingdom
Bridge, A. Emergency in the Pyrenees
Bridge, A. The malady in Madeira
Bryher. Ruan
Buchan, J. Adventurers all
Buchan, J. Adventures of Richard Hannay
Buchan, J. Greenmantle
Buchan, J. Mountain meadow
Buchan, J. The thirty-nine steps
Caidin, M. Marooned
Carse, R. Great circle
Cervantes, M. de. Don Quixote de la Mancha
Cervantes, M. de. Don Quixote de la Mancha; abridged
In Cervantes, M. de. The portable Cervantes p39-702
Charques, D. The dark stranger
Churchill, W. Richard Carvel
Clarke, A. C. The deep range
Cleary, J. The long pursuit
Clifford, F. Another way of dying
Cloete, S. The fiercest heart
Cole, B. The funco file
Coles, M. Exploits of Tommy Hambledon
Collins, N. The Governor's lady
Conrad, J. The arrow of gold
Conrad, J. The Nigger of the Narcissus
Conrad, J. Nostromo
Conrad, J. The rescue
Conrad, J. The rover
Cooper, J. F. The Deerslayer
Cooper, J. F. The last of the Mohicans
Cooper, J. F. The Leatherstocking saga
Cooper, J. F. The Pathfinder
Cooper, J. F. The prairie
Costain, T. B. The black rose
Costain, T. B. For my great folly
Craig, P. Gate of ivory, Gate of Horn
Davidson, L. The Menorah men
Davidson, L. The rose of Tibet
Davis, H. L. Beulah Land
Defoe, D. The life, adventures & piracies of the famous Captain Singleton
Doyle, Sir A. C. The lost world
Doyle, Sir A. C. The Maracot Deep
Doyle, Sir A. C. Micah Clarke
Doyle, Sir A. C. The White Company
Dumas, A. The Count of Monte Cristo
Dumas, A. The three musketeers
Dumas, A. The Vicomte de Bragelonne
Du Maurier, D. Jamaica Inn
Dunnett, D. The disorderly knights
Dunnett, D. The game of kings
Dunnett, D. Pawn in frankincense
Eden, D. Waiting for Willa

ADVENTURE—*Continued*

Verne, J. A journey to the centre of the earth
Verne, J. The Jules Verne omnibus
Verne, J. Michael Strogoff
Verne, J. The mysterious island
Verne, J. Twenty thousand leagues under the sea
Wahlöö, P. A necessary action
Waltari, M. The Etruscan
Waugh, H. Run when I say go
Wellman, P. I. Ride the red earth
Westheimer, D. Von Ryan's Express
Westlake, D. E. The spy in the ointment
White, A. The long night's walk
White, S. E. The long rifle
White, S. E. Wild geese calling
Whitney, P. A. Black amber
Whitney, P. A. Seven tears for Apollo
Wren, P. C. Beau Geste

See also Escapes; International intrigue; Interplanetary voyages; Picaresque novels; Sea stories; Shipwrecks and castaways; The West

The adventurers. Hodge, J. A.

Adventurers all. Buchan, J.

Adventures and Memoirs of Sherlock Holmes. Doyle, Sir A. C.

Adventures in the skin trade, and other stories. Thomas, D.

Adventures of a young man. Dos Passos, J.
In Dos Passos, J. District of Columbia v 1

Adventures of an elephant boy. Wibberley, L.

The adventures of Augie March. Bellow, S.

The adventures of Baron Munchausen. Munchausen

The adventures of Colonel Sellers. Twain, M.

The adventures of Don Quixote de la Mancha. See Cervantes, M. de. Don Quixote de la Mancha

Adventures of Gil Blas of Santillane. Le Sage, A. R.

The adventures of Huckleberry Finn. Twain, M.
also in Twain, M. The complete novels of Mark Twain v 1 p731-969

The adventures of Joseph Andrews. See Fielding, H. The history of the adventures of Joseph Andrews and of his friend Mr Abraham Adams

The adventures of Menahem-Mendl. Aleichem, S.

The adventures of Mottel, the cantor's son. Aleichem, S.

The adventures of Oliver Twist. See Dickens, C. Oliver Twist

The adventures of Peregrine Pickle. See Smollett, T. Peregrine Pickle

Adventures of Richard Hannay. Buchan, J.

The adventures of Roderick Random. See Smollett, T. Roderick Random

Adventures of Sherlock Holmes. Doyle, Sir A. C.
also in Doyle, Sir A. C. Adventures and Memoirs of Sherlock Holmes
also in Doyle, Sir A. C. The complete Sherlock Holmes v 1 p177-380

The adventures of Tapiola. Nathan, R.

Adventures of the Scarlet Pimpernel. Orczy, B.

The adventures of Tom Sawyer. Twain, M.
also in Twain, M. The complete novels of Mark Twain v 1 p385-556

Adventures of Tom Sawyer and Huckleberry Finn. Twain, M.

Adversary in the house. Stone, I.

ADVERTISING
Beauvoir, S. de. Les belles images
Frankau, P. Slaves of the lamp
Green, G. The last angry man
Sayers, D. L. Murder must advertise
Wells, H. G. Tono-Bungay
Wouk, H. Aurora dawn

See also Business; Public relations; Salesmen and salesmanship

Advise and consent. Drury, A.

The advocate. Deal, B.

AERONAUTICS
Faulkner, W. Pylon
Gann, E. K. Blaze of noon
Shute, N. No highway
Stern, R. M. Brood of eagles

See also Flight

Flights
Gann, E. K. The high and the mighty
Saint Exupéry, A. de. Prisoner of the sand
In Costain, T. B. comp. Twelve short novels p457-90
Searls, H. The crowded sky

See also Pilots

AERONAUTICS, COMMERCIAL
Saint Exupéry, A. de. Night flight

AERONAUTICS, MILITARY
Gann, E. K. In the company of eagles
Heller, J. Catch-22
Malraux, A. Man's hope

The affair. Snow, C. P.

An affair of honor. Wilder, R.

AFGHANISTAN
Fraser, G. M. Flashman
Kessel, J. The horsemen
Michener, J. A. Caravans

AFRICA
Brunner, J. Stand on Zanzibar
Conrad, J. Heart of darkness
In Conrad, J. Great short works of Joseph Conrad p175-256
In Conrad, J. Stories and tales of Joseph Conrad
In Conrad, J. Tales of land and sea p33-104
In Conrad, J. Typhoon, and other tales of the sea p273-371
In Conrad, J. Youth, and two other stories
Greene, G. A burnt-out case
Lessing, D. African stories
Monsarrat, N. Richer than all his tribe
Monsarrat, N. The tribe that lost its head
Spark, M. The go-away bird, and other stories
Waugh, E. Black mischief

17th century
Defoe, D. The life, adventures & piracies of the famous Captain Singleton

18th century
Rabie, J. A man apart

19th century
Haggard, H. R. Five adventure novels of H. Rider Haggard
Haggard, H. R. King Solomon's mines
Haggard, H. R. She

20th century
Ferrars, E. X. The swaying pillars
Kayira, L. Jingala
Lessing, D. The golden notebook
Sherman, D. R. Into the noonday sun
Van der Post, L. The hunter and the whale

Communism
See Communism—Africa

Frontier and pioneer life
See Frontier and pioneer life—Africa

Hunting
See Hunting—Africa

Kings and rulers
Drury, A. A shade of difference

Native races
Abrahams, P. Mine boy
Abrahams, P. A wreath for Udomo
Becker, S. The outcasts
Bellow, S. Henderson the rain king
Bennett, J. Jamie
Cary, J. The African witch
Cary, J. Mister Johnson
Forester, C. S. The sky and the forest
Gary, R. The roots of heaven
Hulme, K. The nun's story
Kessel, J. The lion
Monsarrat, N. Richer than all his tribe
Monsarrat, N. The tribe that lost its head
Murray, A. A. The blanket
Rooke, D. Mittee
Ruark, R. Something of value
Ruark, R. Uhuru
Steen, M. Twilight on the Floods
Van der Post, L. Flamingo feather

See also Hottentots; Ibo tribe; Kafirs (African people); Zulus; etc.

Politics
See Politics—Africa

Race problems
See Race problems—Africa

ALABAMA
20th century
Calisher, H. False entry
Huie, W. B. The Klansman
Lee, H. To kill a mockingbird

ALAMANCE, BATTLE OF, 1771
Fletcher, I. The wind in the forest

Alas, Babylon. Frank, P.

ALASKA
See also Aleutian Islands
19th century
London, J. The call of the wild
White, S. E. Wild geese calling
20th century
Ferber, E. Ice Palace

Frontier and pioneer life
See Frontier and pioneer life—Alaska

ALBA, MARIA DEL PILAR TERESA CAYE-TANA DE SILVA ALVAREZ DE TOLEDO, 13, DUQUESA DE
Braider, D. Rage in silence

ALBANIA
Gilman, D. The unexpected Mrs Pollifax

ALBERT, CONSORT OF QUEEN VICTORIA
Anthony, E. Victoria and Albert

ALBIGENSES
Closs, H. Deep are the valleys
Closs, H. High are the mountains
Closs, H. The silent Tarn
Oldenbourg, Z. Cities of the flesh
Oldenbourg, Z. Destiny of fire

ALBUQUERQUE. See New Mexico—Albuquerque

ALCHEMY
O'Rourke, F. Instant gold

ALCIBIADES
Sutcliff, R. The flowers of Adonis

ALCOHOLICS. See Alcoholism

ALCOHOLISM
Brontë, A. The tenant of Wildfell Hall
Jackson, C. The lost weekend
Letton, J. Allegra's child
Lowry, M. Under the volcano
O'Hara, J. Appointment in Samarra
Schulberg, B. The disenchanted
Shaw, R. A card from Morocco
Styron, W. Set this house on fire
Zola, E. L'assommoir

ALEUTIAN ISLANDS
Marshall, J. V. A river ran out of Eden

ALEXANDER THE GREAT
Renault, M. Fire from heaven

ALEXANDRIA. See Egypt—Alexandria

The Alexandria quartet: Justine; Balthazar; Mountolive [and] Clea. Durrell, L.

Alfred Hitchcock presents: A month of mystery. Hitchcock, A. ed.
Alfred Hitchcock presents: My favorites in suspense. Hitchcock, A. ed.
Alfred Hitchcock presents: Stories for late at night. Hitchcock, A. ed.
Alfred Hitchcock presents: Stories my mother never told me. Hitchcock, A. ed.
Alfred Hitchock presents: Stories not for the nervous. Hitchcock, A. ed.
Alfred Hitchcock presents: Stories that scared even me. Hitchcock, A. ed.
Alfred Hitchcock presents: Stories they wouldn't let me do on TV. Hitchcock, A. ed.
Alfred Hitchcock's Fireside book of suspense. Hitchcock, A. ed.

ALGERIA
19th century
Daudet, A. Tartarin of Tarascon
Ouida. Under two flags
Oran
Camus, A. The plague

ALGERIANS IN FRANCE
Etcherelli, C. Elise
Knowles, J. Morning in Antibes

Alias Butch Cassidy. Henry, W.

Alias Uncle Hugo. Coles, M.
In Coles, M. The exploits of Tommy Hambledon p349-480

Alice Adams. Tarkington, B.

Alice's adventures in Wonderland. See Carroll, L. The annotated Alice

ALKIBIADES. See Alcibiades

All aces. Stout, R.
All fall down. Herlihy, J. L.
All green shall perish, and other novellas and stories. Mallea, E.
All honorable men. Karp, D.
All in the family. O'Connor, E.
All men are brothers. Shui hu chuan
All men are lonely now. Clifford, F.
All men are mortal. Beauvoir, S. de
All passion spent. Sackville-West, V.
All quiet on the western front. Remarque, E. M.
All the king's men. Warren, R. P.
All the little live things. Stegner, W.
All the living. Buckmaster, H.
All the Queen's men. Anthony, E.
All the traps of earth, and other stories. Simak, C. D.
All this, and heaven too. Field, R.

Allan Quatermain. Haggard, H. R.
In Haggard, H. R. Five adventure novels of H. Rider Haggard p417-636

Allan's wife. Haggard, H. R.
In Haggard, H. R. Five adventure novels of H. Rider Haggard p638-744

ALLEGORIES
Abé, K. The woman in the dunes
Agnon, S. Y. A guest for the night
Balzac, H. de. The wild ass's skin
Barth, J. Giles goat-boy
Beckford, W. Vathek
Bray, C. The scarecrow man
Bunyan, J. The Pilgrim's progress
Cabell, J. B. Jurgen: a comedy of justice
Camus, A. The fall
Chesterton, G. K. The man who was Thursday
Faulkner, W. A fable
Gallico, P. The Poseidon adventure
Gallico, P. Thomasina, the cat who thought she was God
Gary, R. The roots of heaven
Golding, W. The inheritors
Golding, W. Lord of the Flies
Golding, W. The spire
Hersey, J. Under the eye of the storm
Hesse, H. Narcissus and Goldmund
Hesse, H. Siddhartha
Jameson, S. The white crow
Johnson, S. The history of Rasselas, Prince of Abyssinia
Kafka, F. The castle
Kafka, F. Metamorphosis
In Pick, R. ed. German stories and tales p247-95
Kafka, F. The trial
Kazantzakis, N. The Greek passion
Laxalt, R. A man in the wheatfield
Lewis, C. S. Till we have faces
Melville, H. Billy Budd
In Blackmur, R. P. ed. American short novels p18-67
Murdoch, I. The unicorn
Nabokov, V. Invitation to a beheading
Nathan, R. The fair
O'Connor, F. The violent bear it away
Orwell, G. Animal farm
Porter, K. A. Ship of fools
Sarton, M. Miss Pickthorn and Mr Hare
Saxton, M. The Islar, a narrative of Lang III
Stevenson, R. L. The strange case of Dr Jekyll and Mr Hyde
Tolkien, J. R. R. The fellowship of the Rings
Tolkien, J. R. R. The return of the king
Tolkien, J. R. R. Smith of Wootton Major
Tolkien, J. R. R. The two towers
Twain, M. The man that corrupted Hadleyburg
In Blackmur, R. P. ed. American short novels p68-96
Van der Post, L. The seed and the sower
Wallant, E. L. The children at the gate
Wilde, O. The picture of Dorian Gray
Wu Ch'êng-ên. Monkey
See also Fantasies; Parables; Symbolism

Allegra's child. Letton, J.

ALLEN, ETHAN
Van de Water, F. F. Catch a falling star

The Arabian nights murder. Carr, J. D.
   In Carr, J. D. Three detective novels p3-195

ARABS
  Banks, L. R. Children at the gate
  Hempstone, S. In the midst of lions
  Spark, M. The Mandelbaum Gate
  West, M. L. The tower of Babel
    See also Jewish-Arab relations

ARABS IN BORNEO
  Conrad, J. Almayer's folly
    In Conrad, J. Tales of the East and West
    p 1-128

ARABS IN PALESTINE
  Douglas, L. C. The Big Fisherman
  Koestler, A. Thieves in the night
  Viertel, J. The last temptation

ARAN ISLANDS. See Ireland—Aran Islands

Arch of triumph. Remarque, E. M.

ARCHBISHOPS. See Bishops

ARCHEOLOGISTS AND ARCHEOLOGY
  Bagley, D. The Vivero letter
  Davidson, L. The Menorah men
  Flaubert, G. Salammbo
  Michener, J. A. The source
  O'Donnell, P. A taste for death
  Osborne, H. The yellow gold of Tiryns
  Wilson, A. Anglo-Saxon attitudes

ARCHEOLOGY. See Archeologists and archeology

Archer in Hollywood. Macdonald, R.

ARCHITECTS AND ARCHITECTURE
  Böll, H. Billiards at half-past nine
  Cadell, E. The golden collar
  Dickens, C. Martin Chuzzlewit
  Ferber, E. So Big
  Galsworthy, J. The man of property
    In Galsworthy, J. The Forsyte saga p3-309
    In Galsworthy, J. The Galsworthy reader p15-294
  Greene, G. A burnt-out case
  Hodgins, E. Mr Blandings builds his dream house
  MacInnes, H. Decision at Delphi
  Rand, A. The fountainhead

ARCHITECTURE. See Architects and architecture

ARCHITECTURE, ANCIENT
  De Camp, L. S. The bronze god of Rhodes

ARCTIC REGIONS
  Buchan, J. Mountain meadow
  MacLean, A. Ice Station Zebra
  Poyer, J. North Cape
    See also Greenland

ARDEN, ALICE
  Davidson, D. Feversham

ARGENTINE REPUBLIC
  Hudson, W. H. W. H. Hudson's Tales of the pampas
19th century
  Llewellyn, R. Up, into the singing mountain
20th century
  Blasco Ibáñez, V. The four horsemen of the Apocalypse
Buenos Aires
  Cortázar, J. Hopscotch

ARGENTINIANS IN EUROPE
  Blasco Ibáñez, V. The four horsemen of the Apocalypse

ARGONAUTS
  Graves, R. Hercules, my shipmate

ARISTOCRACY
    See also Society novels
England
  Amis, K. I want it now
  Berckman, E. The heir of Starvelings
  Christie, A. Lord Edgware dies
  Coward, N. Pomp and circumstance
  Du Maurier, D. Rebecca
  Ford, F. M. The fifth queen
  Galsworthy, J. The Forsyte saga
  Gary, R. Lady L.
  Heyer, G. Bath tangle
  Heyer, G. A civil contract
  Heyer, G. The convenient marriage
  Heyer, G. The Corinthian
  Heyer, G. Devil's cub
  Heyer, G. False colours
  Heyer, G. Faro's daughter
  Heyer, G. The foundling
  Heyer, G. Friday's child
  Heyer, G. The grand Sophy
  Heyer, G. Regency buck
  Heyer, G. Sprig muslin

James, H. A London life
Jameson, S. The early life of Stephen Hind
Kennedy, M. A night in Cold Harbor
Sackville-West, V. The Edwardians
Seton, A. Devil Water
Tarkington, B. Monsieur Beaucaire
Thackeray, W. M. The history of Henry Esmond, esquire
Wodehouse, P. G. The code of the Woosters
Wodehouse, P. G. Fish preferred
Wodehouse, P. G. Uncle Fred in the springtime

Europe
Komroff, M. Coronet
Wassermann, J. The world's illusion

France
Barnes, D. Nightwood
Chapman, H. W. Fear no more
Du Maurier, D. The scapegoat
Gerson, N. B. The anthem
Heyer, G. These old shades
Holt, V. The king of the castle
James, H. The American
Kenyon, F. W. That Spanish woman
Orczy, Baroness. Adventures of the Scarlet Pimpernel
Orczy, Baroness. The elusive Pimpernel
Orczy, Baroness. The Scarlet Pimpernel
Proust, M. Cities of the plain
Stendhal. The red and the black
Tarkington, B. Monsieur Beaucaire

Germany
Dinesen, I. Ehrengard
Goethe, J. W. von. Elective affinities

Hungary
Holland, C. Rakóssy
Zilahy, L. The Dukays

Italy
Bassani, G. The garden of the Finzi-Continis
Manzoni, A. The betrothed
Shellabarger, S. Lord Vanity
Stendhal. Chartreuse of Parma
Walpole, H. The castle of Otranto
Wilder, T. The Cabala
    In Wilder, T. The Cabala, and The woman of Andros p 1-134
    In Wilder, T. A Thornton Wilder trio p21-147

Japan
Mishima, Y. After the banquet

Portugal
Eça de Queiroz. The Maias

Rumania
Dumitriu, P. Family jewels
Dumitriu, P. The prodigals

Russia
Tolstoy, L. The Cossacks
Troyat, H. The baroness
West, R. The birds fall down

Scotland
Walker, D. Come back, Geordie

Sicily
Lampedusa, G. di. The Leopard

Turkey
Bridge, A. The dark moment

The aristocrat. Richter, C.

ARIZONA
19th century
Arnold, E. Blood brother
Henry, W. Mackenna's gold
Horgan, P. A distant trumpet

20th century
Burroway, J. The buzzards
Murphy, R. The mountain lion
Seton, A. Foxfire

The Arizona clan. Grey, Z.

ARKANSAS
19th century
Portis, C. True grit

20th century
Dutton, M. Thorpe
Pharr, R. D. The book of numbers

ARKANSAS TERRITORY. See Oklahoma—19th century

ATATURK, KEMAL
Bridge, A. The dark moment
ATHENS. See Greece—Athens; Greece, Modern—Athens
ATHLETES
Walker, D. Geordie
ATLANTA. See Georgia—Atlanta
ATLANTA CAMPAIGN, 1864
Brick, J. Jubilee
Atlantic fury. Innes, H.
ATLANTIS
Doyle, Sir A. C. The Maracot Deep
Atlas shrugged. Rand, A.
ATOMIC BOMB
Buchard, R. Thirty seconds over New York
Buck, P. S. Command the morning
Burdick, E. Fail-safe
Golding, W. Lord of the Flies
Masters, D. The accident
Frank, P. Alas, Babylon
Snow, C. P. The new men
Vonnegut, K. Cat's cradle
Wibberley, L. The mouse that roared
Wylie, P. Tomorrow!
See also Atomic warfare; War

Physiological effect
Bataille, M. The Christmas tree
Ibuse, M. Black rain
ATOMIC WAR. See Atomic warfare; War
ATOMIC WARFARE
Schoonover, L. Central passage
See also Atomic bomb
ATONEMENT
Lagerlof, S. The story of Gösta Berling
Shaw, R. The man in the glass booth
See also Conscience; Guilt
ATTACK ON PEARL HARBOR, 1941, See Pearl Harbor, Attack on, 1941
ATTACK TRANSPORTS. See Warships
ATTEMPTED MURDER. See Murder stories
ATTILA
Costain, T. B. The darkness and the dawn
ATTORNEYS. See Law and lawyers
Aucassin and Nicolette, and other mediaeval romances and legends. Aucassin et Nicolette
AUDUBON, JOHN JAMES
Kennedy, L. Mr Audubon's Lucy
AUDUBON, LUCY GREEN (BAKEWELL)
Kennedy, L. Mr Audubon's Lucy
AUGUSTUS, EMPEROR OF ROME
Duggan, A. Three's company
Graves, R. I, Claudius
AUK. See Great auk
Auntie Mame. Dennis, P.
AUNTS
Dennis, P. Around the world with Auntie Mame
Dennis, P. Auntie Mame
Dickens, C. David Copperfield
Greene, G. Travels with my aunt
Hale, N. Black summer
Heyer, G. Black sheep
Heyer, G. Cousin Kate
Heyer, G. Faro's daughter
James, H. Washington Square
In Blackmur, R. P. ed. American short novels p134-235
Locke Elliott, S. Careful, he might hear you
Macaulay, R. The towers of Trebizond
Perez Galdos, B. Doña Perfecta
Tucker, H. The sound of summer voices
Whitney, P. A. The trembling hills
AURELIUS, ANTONINUS MARCUS, EMPEROR OF ROME
White, E. L. The unwilling vestal
Aurora dawn. Wouk, H.
AUSTRALIA
18th century
Dark, E. The timeless land
19th century
Eden, D. The vines of Yarrabee
Maugham, R. The link
Richardson, H. H. The fortunes of Richard Mahony
White, P. Voss

20th century
Cleary, J. The sundowners
Keneally, T. Three cheers for the Paraclete
Locke Elliott, S. Careful, he might hear you
Locke Elliott, S. Edens lost
Shute, N. The breaking wave
Shute, N. The far country
Shute, N. In the wet
White, P. The tree of man
Army—Officers
Braddon, R. When the enemy is tired
Farm life
See Farm life—Australia
Frontier and pioneer life
See Frontier and pioneer life—Australia
Melbourne
Shute, N. On the beach
Native races
Dark, E. The timeless land
Marshall, J. V. A walk to the hills of the Dreamtime
Marshall, J. V. Walkabout
New South Wales
Dark, E. The timeless land
Eden, D. The vines of Yarrabee
Gaskin, C. Sara Dane
Nordhoff, C. Botany Bay
Queensland
Shute, N. The legacy
Sydney
Dark, E. The timeless land
White, P. Voss
AUSTRALIA, PROVINCIAL AND RURAL
Aldridge, J. My brother Tom
Australia Felix. Richardson, H. H.
In Richardson, H. H. The fortunes of Richard Mahony v 1
AUSTRALIAN ABORIGINES. See Australia—Native races
AUSTRALIANS IN AFRICA
Catto, M. Murphy's war
AUSTRALIANS IN ENGLAND
Francis, D. For kicks
Milne, A. A. Mr Pim
Priestley, J. B. It's an old country
AUSTRALIANS IN MALAYA
Braddon, R. When the enemy is tired
AUSTRIA
19th century
Hope, A. The prisoner of Zenda
20th century
MacInnes, H. The Salzburg connection
Zweig, S. Beware of pity
Army
Hasek, J. The good soldier: Schweik
Politics
See Politics—Austria
Salzburg
Behrman, S. N. The burning glass
Vienna
Doderer, H. von. The demons
Gainham, S. Night falls on the city
Gainham, S. A place in the country
Greene, G. The third man
Irving, J. Setting free the bears
Musil, R. The man without qualities
Stern, G. B. Mosaic
In Stein, G. B. The matriarch chronicles v3
Thompson, M. The cry and the covenant
Werfel, F. Embezzled heaven
Wiseman, T. The quick and the dead
AUSTRIA, PROVINCIAL AND RURAL
Stewart, M. Airs above the ground
AUSTRIAN ALPS. See Alps
AUSTRIANS IN ENGLAND
Goudge, E. The heart of the family
AUSTRIANS IN YUGOSLAVIA
Andrić, I. Bosnian chronicle

The beloved returns. Mann, T.

Below the salt. Costain, T. B.

The Belting inheritance. Symons, J.

Ben Hur. Wallace, L.

The bench of desolation. James, H.
In James, H. The portable Henry James p326-87

Beneath the wheel. Hesse, H.

BENEDICT, SAINT, ABBOT OF MONTE CASSINO
De Wohl, L. Citadel of God

BENGAL. See India—Bengal

Benito Cereno. Melville, H.
In Melville, H. Five tales p45-137
In Melville, H. Shorter novels of Herman Melville p 1-106
In Neider, C. ed. Short novels of the masters p52-124
In Phillips, W. ed. Great American short novels p 1-78

BENNINGTON, BATTLE OF, 1777
Van de Water, F. F. Day of battle

The bent twig. Canfield, D.

BEOWULF
Craig, P. Gate of ivory, Gate of Horn
Beowulf. Bryher

BERENGARIA, CONSORT OF RICHARD I, KING OF ENGLAND
Barnes, M. C. The passionate brood
Lofts, N. The lute player

BERKSHIRE MOUNTAINS. See Massachusetts—Berkshire Mountains

BERLIN
See also Germany—Berlin

Allied occupation—1945-
Deighton, L. Funeral in Berlin
Hall, A. The Quiller memorandum

BERLIN, BATTLE OF, 1945
Plievier, T. Berlin

Berlin. Plievier, T.

The Berlin stories. Isherwood, C.

BERMUDA ISLANDS
Mason, F. V. The Sea 'Venture

BERNADETTE, SAINT. See Soubirous, Bernadette, Saint

BERNADOTTE, JEAN BAPTISTE, MARSHAL OF FRANCE. See Karl XIV Johan, King of Sweden and Norway

Bernard Quesnay. Maurois, A.
In Maurois, A. Maurois reader

The Bess Streeter Aldrich reader. Aldrich, B. S.

A Bess Streeter Aldrich treasury. Aldrich, B. S.

The best American humorous short stories. Jessup, A.

The best American humorous short stories. Linscott, R. N. ed.

The Best American short stories, 1915-1969. Entered in Part I under title

Best British short stories, 1922-1940. Entered in Part I under title

Best cat stories. Joseph, M. ed.

Best detective stories of the year. See Bernkopf, J. F. comp. Boucher's choicest

Best detective stories of the year, 1946-1968. Entered in Part I under title

The Best from Fantasy and Science Fiction, 1st-18th ser. Entered in Part I under title

The best ghost stories

The best ghost stories. See Cerf, B. A. ed. Famous ghost stories

The best house in Stratford. Fisher, E.

The best is yet to be. Plagemann, B.

The best-known novels of George Eliot. Eliot, G.

The best known works of Anton Chekhov. Chekhov, A.

Best modern short stories. The Saturday Evening Post

The best novels and stories of Eugene Manlove Rhodes. Rhodes, E. M.

The best of Amazing. Amazing Stories

The best of Bret Harte. Harte, B.

The best of families. Berlin, E.

The best of Glencannon. Gilpatric, G.

The best of H. E. Bates. Bates, H. E.

The best of Hawthorne. Hawthorne, N.

Best of Runyon. Runyon, D.

The best of science fiction. Conklin, G. ed.

The best of Simple. Hughes, L.

Best of the Best American short stories, 1915-1950. Entered in Part I under title

Best of the Best detective stories. Entered in Part I under title

Best Russian short stories. Seltzer, T. comp.

Best SF: 1968. Entered in Part I under title

The Best science fiction stories and novels: 1949-1958. Entered in Part I under title

The best science-fiction stories of Brian W. Aldiss. See Aldiss, B. W. Who can replace a man?

Best science fiction stories of H. G. Wells. Wells, H. G.

Best short stories. Dickens, C.

Best short stories. London, J.

The best short stories by Negro writers. Hughes, L. ed.

Best short stories, 1915-1941. See The Best American short stories, 1915-1969

The best short stories of Bret Harte. Harte, B.

The best short stories of Dostoevsky. Dostoevsky, F.

The best short stories of Edith Wharton. Wharton, E.

Best short stories of Frank R. Stockton. Stockton, F. R.

The best short stories of O. Henry. Henry, O.

The best short stories of Ring Lardner. Lardner, R.

The best short stories of Rudyard Kipling. Kipling, R.

The best short stories of Theodore Dreiser. Dreiser, T.

The best short stories of W. Somerset Maugham. Maugham, W. S.

The best short stories of World War II. Fenton, C. A. ed.

Best South Sea stories. Day, A. G. ed.

Best stories, Charles Dickens'. See Dickens, C. Charles Dickens' Best stories

Best stories of Guy de Maupassant. Maupassant, G. de

The best stories of Sarah Orne Jewett. Jewett, S. O.

The best tales of Edgar Allan Poe. Poe, E. A.

Best world short stories: 1947. Cournos, J. ed.

Beti. Rooke, D.

BETROTHALS
Fowles, J. The French lieutenant's woman
Fremlin, C. Possession
Hardy, T. Under the greenwood tree
James, H. The American
Kauffmann, L. An honorable estate

Betrothed. Agnon, S. Y.
In Agnon, S. Y. Two tales p 1-139

The betrothed. Manzoni, A.

BETTING. See Gambling

Between day and dark. Angoff, C.

Between the acts. Woolf, V.
also in Connolly, C. ed. Great English short novels p753-879

Between two worlds. Sinclair, U.

Beulah Land. Davis, H. L.

Beware of pity. Zweig, S.

Beware of the mouse. Wibberley, L.

Beyond sing the woods. Gulbranssen, T.

Beyond this place. Cronin, A. J.

Beyond tomorrow. Knight, D. ed.

Bhowani Junction. Masters, J.

BIBLE
History of Biblical events
See Biblical stories

BIBLE. OLD TESTAMENT. See David, King of Israel

BIBLE. OLD TESTAMENT. KINGS
Israel, C. E. Rizpah

BRAZIL—*Continued*

Mato Grosso

Geld, E. B. The garlic tree

Minas Gerais

Rosa, J. G. The third bank of the river, and other stories

Politics

See Politics—Brazil

Rio de Janeiro

Machado de Assis. Esau and Jacob

Brazil. Marshall, P.
In Marshall, P. Soul clap hands and sing p131-77

Bread and wine. Silone, I.

Break for freedom. See Clark, E. Syla, the mink

Break of day. Colette

Breakfast at Tiffany's. Capote, T.

Breakfast with the Nikolides. Godden, R.

The breaking wave. Shute, N.

A breath of air. Godden, R.

A breath of French air. Bates, H. E.

BRETAGNE. See France, Provincial and rural—Brittany

BRIAN, BOROIMHE, KING OF IRELAND
Holland, C. The kings in winter

BRIAN BORU. See Brian, Boroimhe, King of Ireland

BRICKLAYERS
Di Donato, P. Christ in concrete

The bridal canopy. Agnon, S. Y.

Bridal journey. Van Every, D.

The bridal wreath. Undset, S.
In Undset, S. Kristin Lavransdatter v 1

The bride. Irwin, M.

Bride of fortune. Kane, H. T.

The bride of Lammermoor. Scott, Sir W.

The bride of Newgate. Carr, J. D.

Bride of Pendorric. Holt, V.

The bride of the Innisfallen, and other stories. Welty, E.

Brideshead revisited. Waugh, E.

The bridge of San Luis Rey. Wilder, T.
also in Costain, T. B. ed. Stories to remember v2 p 1-67
also in Costain, T. B. comp. Twelve short novels p 107-70
also in Wilder, T. A Thornton Wilder trio p149-243

The bridge on the Drina. Andrić, I.

The bridge over the River Kwai. Boulle, P.

BRIDGES
Andrić, I. The bridge on the Drina
Becker, S. The outcasts
Boulle, P. The bridge over the River Kwai
Garth, D. Watch on the bridge

The bridges at Toko-ri. Michener, J. A.

Brief flower. Smith, D. E.

Brief gaudy hour. Barnes, M. C.

The brigadier and the golf widow. Cheever, J.

BRIGANDS AND ROBBERS
Blackmore, R. D. Lorna Doone
Bridge, A. Peking picnic
Clifford, F. Another way of dying
Heyer, G. The Black Moth
Huffman, L. A house behind the mint
Kemal, Y. Memed, my hawk
Shui hu chuan. All men are brothers
See also Outlaws; Robberies

Bright feather. Wilder, R.

The bright feathers. Culp, J. H.

The bright morning. O'Rourke, F.

Bring me to the banqueting house. Biderman, S.

BRISTOL. See England—Bristol

Britannia Mews. Sharp, M.

BRITISH. See English

BRITISH AGENTS. See Spies

BRITISH ARMY. See Great Britain. Army

BRITISH COLUMBIA. See Canada—British Columbia

BRITISH GUIANA
Marshall, P. British Guiana
In Marshall, P. Soul clap hands and sing p67-127

BRITISH IN EGYPT. See English in Egypt

BRITISH IN GERMANY. See English in Germany

BRITISH IN HUNGARY. See English in Hungary

BRITISH IN INDIA. See English in India

BRITISH IN RUSSIA. See English in Russia

BRITISH IN THE UNITED STATES. See English in the United States

BRITISH IN YUGOSLAVIA. See English in Yugoslavia

The British Museum is falling down. Lodge, D.

BRITISH NAVAL OFFICERS. See Great Britain. Navy—Officers

BRITISH NAVY. See Great Britain. Navy

BRITISH SOLDIERS. See Soldiers, British

BRITISH WEST INDIES. See West Indies

BRITTANY. See France, Provincial and rural—Brittany

Broad and alien is the world. Alegría, C.

A Bromfield galaxy: The green bay tree. Early autumn. A good woman. Bromfield, L.

BRONTË, PATRICK BRANWELL
Brontë, A. The tenant of Wildfell Hall

BRONX. See New York (City)—Bronx

The bronze god of Rhodes. De Camp, L. S.

Brood of eagles. Stern, R. M.

BROOKLYN. See New York (City)—Brooklyn

Brooklyn. Marshal, P.
In Marshall, P. Soul clap hands and sing p31-64

Broome stages. Dane, C.

BROTHELS. See Prostitution

Brother to the enemy. Spicer, B.

BROTHERHOOD. See Brotherhoods; Brotherliness

The Brotherhood of the Red Poppy. Troyat, H.

BROTHERHOODS
Hawthorne, N. The Blithedale romance

BROTHERLINESS
Hesse, H. The journey to the East

BROTHERS
Aldridge, J. My brother Tom
Baldwin, J. Tell me how long the train's been gone
Brick, J. Rogues' kingdom
Caldwell, T. Testimony of two men
Davenport, M. My brother's keeper
De La Roche, M. Jalna
De La Roche, M. Whiteoak brothers: Jalna—1923
Dickinson, P. The old English peep show
Dostoevsky, F. The brothers Karamazov
Du Maurier, D. The flight of the falcon
Ford, F. M. The last post
In Ford, F. M. Parade's end p677-836
Gann, E. K. Blaze of noon
Ghose, Z. The murderer of Aziz Khan
Herlihy, J. L. All fall down
Heyer, G. False colours
Kerouac, J. Visions of Gerard
Kesey, K. Sometimes a great notion
Machado de Assis. Esau and Jacob
Macken, W. The scorching wind
Mann, T. Young Joseph
In Mann, T. Joseph and his brothers p261-444
Martin du Gard, R. Summer 1914
Martin du Gard, R. The Thibaults
Maupassant, G. de. Pierre and Jean
Moberg, V. A time on earth
Simenon, G. The old man dies
Singer, I. J. The brothers Ashkenazi
Stevenson, R. L. The master of Ballantrae
Taylor, R. L. Two roads to Guadalupé
Thackeray, W. M. The Virginians
Troyat, H. The mountain
Van der Post, L. The seed and the sower
Wallant, E. L. The tenants of Moonbloom
Wren, P. C. Beau Geste

C

C.I.A. See United States. Central Intelligence Agency; Secret service

The Cabala. Wilder, T.
In Wilder, T. A Thornton Wilder trio p21-147

The Cabala, and The woman of Andros. Wilder, T.

Cabbages and kings. Henry, O.
In Henry, O. The complete works of O. Henry p551-679

CABIN BOYS
Hartog, J. de. The lost sea
In Costain, T. B. comp. Twelve short novels p559-616
In Hartog, J. de. The call of the sea p3-85

CACAO
Amado, J. The violent land

The cactus and the crown. Gavin, C.

CAESAR, CAIUS JULIUS
Warner, R. Imperial Caesar
Warner, R. The young Caesar
Wilder, T. The ides of March

CAFÉS. See Restaurants, lunchrooms, etc.

CAGLIOSTRO, ALESSANDRO, CONTE DI, ASSUMED NAME OF GIUSEPPE BALSAMO
Dumas, A. The queen's necklace

Cain x 3. Cain, J. M.

The Caine mutiny. Wouk, H.

CAJUNS. See Acadians in Louisiana

Cakes and ale. Maugham, W. S.

Cakes and ale, and twelve short stories. Maugham, W. S.

CALABRIA. See Italy—Calabria

Calamity town. Queen, E.
In Queen, E. Wrightsville murders p7-204

Caleb, my son. Daniels, L.

CALIFORNIA
18th century
Lauritzen, J. The cross and the sword
1800-1846
Bristow, G. Jubilee Trail
Steinbeck, J. East of Eden
1846-1900
Bristow, G. Jubilee Trail
Harte, B. The Luck of Roaring Camp, and other sketches
Harte, B. Tales of the Argonauts
Norris, F. The octopus
Steinbeck, J. East of Eden
20th century
Barrett, B. L. Love in Atlantis
Bristow, G. Tomorrow is forever
Burdick, E. The ninth wave
Gores, J. A time of predators
Hitchens, D. A collection of strangers
Huxley, A. After many a summer dies the swan
Lasswell, M. Suds in your eye
Moberg, V. A time on earth
Nathan, R. The color of evening
Nathan, R. So love returns
Nathan, R. Stonecliff
Saroyan, W. The human comedy
Sinclair, U. Oil!
Stegner, W. All the little live things
Steinbeck, J. Cannery Row
In Steinbeck, J. The short novels of John Steinbeck p355-469
Steinbeck, J. East of Eden
Steinbeck, J. The grapes of wrath
Steinbeck, J. In dubious battle
Steinbeck, J. The long valley
Steinbeck, J. Of mice and men
Steinbeck, J. The red pony
In Steinbeck, J. The portable Steinbeck p327-415
In Steinbeck, J. The short novels of John Steinbeck p135-200
Steinbeck, J. The wayward bus
Stern, R. M. Brood of eagles
Van der Zee, J. The plum explosion.
West, J. Cress Delahanty
West, J. Love, death, and the ladies' drill team

Frontier and pioneer life
See Frontier and pioneer life—California
Glendale
Egan, L. The wine of violence
Hollywood
Behrman, S. N. The burning glass
Berckman, E. She asked for it
Fitzgerald, F. S. The last tycoon
Morris, W. Love among the cannibals
Schulberg, B. The disenchanted
Schulberg, B. What makes Sammy run?
Waugh, E. The loved one
West, N. Day of the locust
In West, N. Complete works p259-421
Los Angeles
Gerber, M. J. An antique man
Nathan, R. The wilderness-stone
Vasquez, R. Chicano
Monterey—20th century
Steinbeck, J. Cannery Row
Steinbeck, J. Sweet Thursday
Steinbeck, J. Tortilla Flat
Police
Ball, J. Johnny get your gun
Egan, L. The wine of violence
Huffman, L. A house behind the mint
Politics
See Politics—California
Ranch life
See Ranch life—California
San Diego
Lasswell, M. Let's go for broke
San Francisco
Busch, N. The San Franciscans
Carpenter, D. One of those big-city girls
In Carpenter, D. The murder of the frogs, and other stories p199-242
Huffman, L. A house behind the mint
Lee, C. Y. Flower drum song
Lipsky, E. The Devil's daughter
Norris, F. McTeague
Van der Zee, J. Blood brotherhood
Whitney, P. A. The trembling hills
Stockton
Gardner, L. Fat city

CALIFORNIA, LOWER. See Baja California

CALIGULA, EMPEROR OF ROME
Douglas, L. C. The robe

CALIPHS. See Arabia—Kings and rulers

Call for the dead. Le Carré, J.
In Le Carré, J. The incongrous spy v 1

A call from Austria. Albrand, M.

Call it sleep. Roth, H.

Call it treason. Howe, G.

The call of the sea. Hartog, J. de

The call of the wild. London, J.
also in Costain, T. B. ed. More Stories to remember v 1 p205-63

The call of the wild, and other stories. London, J.

CAMBRIDGE. UNIVERSITY
Snow, C. P. The affair
Snow, C. P. The light and the dark
Snow, C. P. The masters

Came a cavalier. Keyes, F. P.

The Camelot caper. Peters, E.

Camera obscura. See Nabokov, V. Laughter in the dark

Camille. Dumas, A.

Camp 7 last stop. See Kirst, H. H. Last stop Camp 7

CAMPAIGN MANAGEMENT
Barry, J. Grass roots

Campbell's kingdom. Innes, H.

CAMPUS LIFE. See College life; Students

Can such things be? Bierce, A.

CANADA
To 1763 (New France)
Cather, W. Shadows on the rock
Costain, T. B. High Towers

The captive. Proust, M.
  also in Proust, M. Remembrance of things past v2

A captive in the land. Aldridge, J.

Captive universe. Harrison, H.

CARACTACUS
  Treece, H. The dark island

CARADOC. See Caractacus

Caravan. Galsworthy, J.

Caravans. Michener, J. A.

A card from Morocco. Shaw, R.

The cardinal. Robinson, H. M.

The Cardinal and the queen. Anthony, E.

CARDINALS
  Druon, M. The royal succession
  Firbank, R. Concerning the eccentricities of Cardinal Pirelli
    In Firbank R. The complete Ronald Firbank p645-98
  Peyrefitte, R. Knights of Malta

CARDS
  Hodge, J. A. The adventurers

Cards of identity. Dennis, N.

Cards on the table. Christie, A.
  In Christie, A. Surprise endings by Hercule Poirot p275-405

CAREER STORIES. See names of occupations, professions, and vocations: e.g. Banks and bankers; Law and lawyers; Physicians; Scientists; Teachers; etc.

Careful, he might hear you. Locke Elliott, S.

Cargo of eagles. Allingham, M.

CARGO PLANES. See Transport planes

CARIBBEAN AREA
  Benchley, N. The wake of the Icarus
  See also Bahamas; West Indies

CARIBBEAN ISLANDS
  Bagley, D. Wyatt's hurricane
  Vonnegut, K. Cat's cradle
    See also specific islands in this area, e.g. Trinidad

A Caribbean mystery. Christie, A.

CARIBBEAN SEA
  Kent, A. To glory we steer

CARICATURE. See Satire

CARLOTA, EMPRESS OF MEXICO. See Charlotte, consort of Maximilian, Emperor of Mexico

Carmen. Merimée, P.

Carnavaron's castle. Webb, J. F.

CARNIVAL
  Bradbury, R. Something wicked this way comes
  Gold, H. The man who was not with it
  Read, Miss. Thrush Green

CAROLINE MATHILDE, CONSORT OF CHRISTIAN VII, KING OF DENMARK
  Lofts, N. The lost queen

CARPENTERS
  Eliot, G. Adam Bede
  Jennings, J. The Salem frigate

CARROLL, ANNA ELLA
  Noble, H. Woman with a sword

CARTHAGE
  Bryher. The coin of Carthage
  De Camp, L. S. The arrows of Hercules
  Flaubert, G. Salammbo

CARTHAGINIAN SOLDIERS. See Soldiers, Carthaginian

CARTHAGINIANS IN SPAIN
  Dolan, M. Hannibal of Carthage

CARTOGRAPHERS
  Basso, H. A touch of the dragon

Carwin the biloquist. See Brown, C. B. Wieland

CASANOVA DE SEINGALT, GIACOMO GIROLAMO
  Wylie. E. The Venetian glass nephew
  In Blackmur, R. P. ed. American short novels p344-96

Casanova's Chinese restaurant. Powell, A.
  In Powell, A. A dance to the music of time: second movement v2

The case against Carroll. Queen, E.
  In Queen, E. Queens full p117-73

The case book of Sherlock Holmes. Doyle, Sir A. C.
  In Doyle, Sir A. C. The complete Sherlock Holmes v2 p1160-1323

A case history. O'Hara, J.
  In O'Hara, J Assembly p382-429
  In O'Hara, J. 49 stories v 1 p382-429

A case of conscience. Blish, J.

The case of Jennie Brice. Rinehart, M. R.
  In Rinehart, M. R. Mary Roberts Rinehart's Mystery book p349-442

A case of need. Hudson, J.

The case of Sergeant Grischa. Zweig, A.

The case of the Baker Street Irregulars. Boucher, A.

The case of the constant suicides. Carr, J. D.
  In Carr, J. D. A John Dickson Carr trio p339-472

The case of the crimson kiss. Gardner, E. S.
  In Haycraft, H. ed. A treasury of great mysteries v 1 p147-87

The case of the deadly diamonds. Bush, C.

The case of the fabulous fake. Gardner, E. S.

The case of the innocent victims. Creasey, J.

The case of the worried waitress. Gardner, E. S.

The casebook of Solar Pons. Derleth, A.

Casey. Stewart, R.

Casey. See Stranger, J. Born to trouble

Cash McCall. Hawley, C.

Casino Royale. Fleming, I.
  also in Fleming, I. Gilt-edged Bonds v 1

The cask. Crofts, F. W.

Cass Timberlane. Lewis, S.

CASSIDY, BUTCH. See Parker, George Le Roy

Castaway. Cozzens, J. G.

CASTAWAYS. See Shipwrecks and castaways

The casting away of Mrs Lecks and Mrs Aleshine. Stockton, F. R.
  In Stockton, F. R. The storyteller's pack p275-351

The castle. Kafka, F.

Castle Dor. Quiller-Couch, A.

Castle keep. Eastlake, W.

The castle of Otranto. Walpole, H.

Castle Rackrent. Edgeworth, M.

Castle to castle. Céline, L. F.

CASTLES
  Eastlake, W. Castle keep
  Eden, D. The shadow wife
  Edgeworth, M. Castle Rackrent
  Holt, V. Bride of Pendorric
  Holt, V. The king of the castle
  Maybury, A. The Minerva stone
  Murdoch, I. The unicorn
  Radcliffe, A. The mysteries of Udolpho
  Smith, D. I capture the castle
  Stewart, M. Nine coaches waiting
  Walpole, H. The castle of Otranto
  Webb, J. F. Carnavarons castle
  White, T. H. Mistress Masham's repose
  Wodehouse, P. G. Fish preferred
  Wodehouse, P. G. Uncle Fred in the springtime

The cat. Colette
  In Colette. 7 by Colette v 1 p69-193

The cat. Simenon, G.

Cat and mouse. Grass, G.

The cat who ate Danish modern. Braun, L. J.

The cat who turned on and off. Braun, L. J.

The catalyst. Bell. J.

CATAPULT
  De Camp, L. S. The arrows of Hercules

Catch a brass canary. Hill, D.

Catch a falling star. Van de Water, F. F.

Catch-22. Heller, J.

The catcher in the rye. Salinger, J. D.

CATHARINE II, EMPRESS OF RUSSIA
  Anthony, E. Royal intrigue

CATHARINE HOWARD, CONSORT OF HENRY VIII, KING OF ENGLAND
  Ford, F. M. The fifth queen

CATHARINE OF ARAGON, CONSORT OF HENRY VIII, KING OF ENGLAND
  Lofts, N. The King's pleasure
  Macleod, A. The hireling

CATHARINE PARR, CONSORT OF HENRY VIII, KING OF ENGLAND
  Plaidy, J. The sixth wife

CATTLE
Guthrie, A. B. These thousand hills
See also Cattle drives

CATTLE DRIVES
Adams, A. Log of a cowboy
Barry, J. A shadow of eagles
Flynn, R. North to yesterday

Cause for alarm. Ambler, E.
In Ambler, E. Intrigue p295-465

The cavalryman. Sinclair, H.

The cave. Warren, R. P.

CAVES
Warren, R. P. The cave

The caves of steel. Asimov, I.
also in Asimov, I. The rest of the robots
p165-362

CECIL, WILLIAM, BARON BURGHLEY. See
Burghley, William Cecil, 1st Baron

Cecily. Holland, I.

Cefalù. See Durrell, L. The dark labyrinth

The celestial omnibus. See Forster, E. M. The
collected tales of E. M. Forster

Celia Garth. Bristow, G.

CELIBACY
Barrett, W. E. The wind and the music
Daley, R. A priest and a girl

The cell. Case, D.

CELTS
Treece, H. The dark island
Treece, H. Red queen, white queen
See also Picts

CEMETERIES
Beagle, P. S. A fine and private place

The centaur. Updike, J.

Centenary at Jalna. De La Roche, M.

CENTENNIAL EXPOSITION, 1876. See Philadelphia. Centennial Exposition, 1876

Centennial summer. Idell, A. E.

The center of the action. Weidman, J.

CENTRAL AFRICA. See Africa, Central

CENTRAL AMERICA
Asturias, M. A. Strong wind
Forester, C. S. Beat to quarters

CENTRAL INTELLIGENCE AGENCY. See
United States. Central Intelligence Agency

Central passage. Schoonover, L.

The centurion. Wibberley, L.

CENTURIONS. See Soldiers, Roman

A century of great short science fiction novels. Knight, D. ed.

A century of science fiction. Knight, D. ed.

CEREMONIES. See Rites and ceremonies

Ceremony in Lone Tree. Morris, W.

A certain island. Murphy, R.

Certain people. Wharton, E.
In Wharton, E. The collected short stories
of Edith Wharton v2 p501-616

A certain smile. Sagan, F.

César Birotteau. See Balzac H. de. The rise
and fall of César Birotteau

Chad Hanna. Edmonds, W. D.

The chain. Wellman, P. I.

The chains of love. Oldenbourg, Z.

Chairman of the bored. Streeter, E.

La chamade. Sagan, F.

CHAMPE, JOHN
Spicer, B. Brother to the enemy

CHANCE
Conrad, J. Chance

Chance acquaintances. Colette
In Colette. Gigi. Julie de Carneilhan. Chance
acquaintances p225-315
In Colette. 7 by Colette v3 p139-230

CHANCELLORSVILLE, BATTLE OF, 1863
Crane, S. The red badge of courage

A change of heir. Innes, M.

A change of season. Ehrenburg, I.

A change of skin. Fuentes, C.

The changelings. Sinclair, J.

CHANNEL ISLANDS
Christopher, J. The ragged edge
Goudge, E. Green Dolphin Street
Hugo, V. Toilers of the sea

CHANTRAINE, ANNE DE
Mallet-Joris, F. The witches

Chaos and night. Montherlant, H. de

CHARES OF LINDOS
De Camp, L. S. The bronze god of Rhodes

The charioteer. Renault, M.

CHARITIES. See Endowments

Charivari. Hawkes, J.
In Hawkes, J. Lunar landscapes p51-136

CHARLES I, KING OF GREAT BRITAIN
Anthony, E. Charles, the King
Barnes, M. C. Mary of Carisbrooke

CHARLES II, KING OF GREAT BRITAIN
Heyer, G. Royal escape

CHARLES VII, KING OF FRANCE
Costain, T. B. The moneyman

CHARLES XIV JOHN, KING OF SWEDEN.
See Karl XIV Johan, King of Sweden and
Norway

CHARLES STUART, KING OF ENGLAND.
See Charles I, King of Great Britain

**CHARLES THE BOLD, DUKE OF BURGUN-
DY**
Scott, Sir W. Quentin Durwood

Charles, Lincoln V.

Charles Dickens' Best stories. Dickens, C.

Charles, the King. Anthony, E.

CHARLESTON. See South Carolina—Charleston

Charley is my darling. Cary, J.

**CHARLOTTE, CONSORT OF MAXIMILIAN,
EMPEROR OF MEXICO**
Gavin, C. The cactus and the crown

Charlotte Lowenskold. Lagerlöf, S.

Charlotte Temple, a tale of truth. Rowson,
S. H.

A charmed life. McCarthy, M.

CHARMS. See Amulets

Charterhouse of Parma. See Stendhal. Chartreuse of Parma

CHARTISTS
Cordell, A. The rape of the fair country

Chartreuse of Parma. Stendhal

CHARWOMEN. See Servants—Charwomen

CHASIDISM. See Hasidism

The château. Maxwell, W.

CHATEAUX. See Castles

CHAUFFEURS. See Automobile drivers

CHAUTAUQUAS
Michener, J. A. The fires of spring

Chaves. Mallea, E.
In Mallea, E. All green shall perish, and
other novellas and stories p253-303

The checquer board. Shute, N.

CHEERFUL STORIES
Aldrich, B. S. A lantern in her hand
Aldrich, B. S. A white bird flying
Austen, J. The Watsons
Bagnold, E. National Velvet
In Costain, T. B. ed. Stories to remember
v2 p339-504
Barrett, B. L. Love in Atlantis
Barrie, J. M. Little minister
Bates, H. E. A breath of French air
Bennett, A. Buried alive
Cadell, E. The lark shall sing
Cadell, E. Six impossible things
Cockrell, M. The revolt of Sarah Perkins
Davies, V. It happens every spring
Davies, V. Miracle on 34th Street
Dick, R. A. The ghost and Mrs Muir
Durrell, G. Rosy is my relative
Goudge, E. A city of bells
Goudge, E. The Dean's watch
Goudge, E. Pilgrim's inn
Hanley, C. The red-haired bitch
Heyer, G. Bath tangle
Heyer, G. Black sheep
Heyer, G. A civil contract
Heyer, G. The convenient marriage
Heyer, G. The Corinthian
Heyer, G. Devil's cub
Heyer, G. False colours
Heyer, G. Faro's daughter
Heyer, G. The foundling
Heyer, G. Frederica
Heyer, G. Friday's child
Heyer, G. The grand Sophy
Heyer, G. The masqueraders
Heyer, G. The Nonesuch

Children of the wolf. Duggan, A.

Children of violence. Lessing, D.

Child's play. Christie, K.

CHINA
Eca de Queiroz. The mandarin
  In Eca de Queiroz. The mandarin, and oth-
  er stories p3-89
Lin, Yutang, ed. Famous Chinese short stor-
  ies
Wang, Chi-chen, tr. Traditional Chinese tales

Early to 1643
Byrne, D. Messer Marco Polo
Costain, T. B. The black rose
Eaton, E. Go ask the river
Gulik, R. van. The haunted monastery
Lin, Yutang, ed. Lady Wu

7th century
Gulik, R. van. The Chinese bell murders
Gulik, R. van. The emperor's pearl
Gulick R. van. The monkey and the tiger
Gulik, R. van. Murder in Canton
Gulik, R. van. The phantom of the temple
Gulik, R. van. The Red Pavilion
Gulik, R. van. The willow pattern

13th century
Shui hu chuan. All men are brothers

19th century
Buck, P. S. Imperial woman
Buck, P. S. Peony

War of 1840-1842
Clavell, J. Tai-Pan

1900-1949
Barrett, W. E. The left hand of God
Boulle, P. The executioner
Buck, P. S. Dragon seed
Buck, P. S. East wind: west wind
Buck, P. S. First wife, and other stories
Buck, P. S. The good earth
Buck, P. S. A house divided
Buck, P. S. The house of earth: The good
  earth; Sons: A house divided
Buck, P. S. Kinfolk
Buck, P. S. The mother
Buck, P. S. Pavilion of women
Buck, P. S. The promise
Buck, P. S. Sons
Cronin, A. J. The keys of the kingdom
Harris, J. The jade wind
Hersey, J. A single pebble
Hobart, A. T. Oil for the lamps of China
Lin, Yutang. Moment in Peking
Lin, Yutang. The vermilion gate
McKenna, R. The Sand Pebbles
Malraux, A. Man's fate
Wang, Chi-chen, tr. Contemporary Chinese
  stories
White, T. H. The mountain road

1949-date
Ullman, J. R. The sands of Karakorum

Army
Buck, P. S. Sons

Army—Officers
Braddon, R. When the enemy is tired
Buchard, R. Thirty seconds over New York

Canton
Clavell, J. Tai-Pan

Courts and courtiers
See Courts and courtiers—China

Farm life
See Farm life—China

Hongkong
Clavell, J. Tai-Pan
Eberhart, M. G. Message from Hong Kong
Gann, E. K. Soldier of fortune
Mason, R. The world of Suzie Wong

Kings and rulers
Buck, P. S. Imperial woman

Peasant life
See Peasant life—China

Peking
Bridge, A. Peking picnic
Buck P. S. God's men
Buck, P. S. Kinfolk

Politics
See Politics—China

Shanghai
Buck, P. S. The three daughters of Madame
  Liang
Malraux, A. Man's fate

China Court. Godden, R.

The china governess. Allingham, M.

The Chinese bell murders. Gulik, R. van

CHINESE IN BURMA
Buck, P. S. The promise
CHINESE IN INDIA
Wu Ch'êng-ên. Monkey
CHINESE IN MALAYA
Braddon, R. When the enemy is tired
CHINESE IN THE HAWAIIAN ISLANDS
Michener, J. A. Hawaii
CHINESE IN THE UNITED STATES
Buck, P. S. A house divided
Buck, P. S. Kinfolk
Hergesheimer, J. Java Head
Lee, C. Y. Flower drum song
Steinbeck, J. Cannery Row
CHINESE IN TIBET
Davidson, L. The rose of Tibet
CHINESE JUNKS. See Junks

The Chinese orange mystery. Queen, E.
  In Queen, E. The bizarre murders p175-327
CHINESE SOLDIERS. See Soldiers, Chinese
CHIPPEWA INDIANS
Fuller, I. The loon feather
CHIVALRY
Cervantes, M. de. Don Quixote de la Mancha
Cervantes, M. de. Don Quixote de la Mancha;
  abridged
  In Cervantes, M. de. The portable Cervantes
  p39-702
Doyle, Sir A. C. The White Company
Duggan, A. Lord Geoffrey's fancy
Scott, Sir W. The talisman
Twain, M. A Connecticut Yankee in King
  Arthur's court
White, T. H. The once and future king
Yoshikawa, E. The Heiké story
  See also Knights and knighthood; Middle
  ages

A choice of Kipling's prose. See Kipling, R.
  Maugham's choice of Kipling's best
CHORAL MUSIC
Bor, J. The Terezín Requiem

The chosen. Potok, C.

Chosen country. Dos Passos, J.

Chosen people. Rubens, B.

CHOUANS
Balzac, H. de. The Chouans

Christ in concrete. Di Donato, P.

Christ recrucified. See Kazantzakis, N. The
  Greek passion
CHRISTIAN VII, KING OF DENMARK
Lofts, N. The lost queen
CHRISTIAN ART AND SYMBOLISM. See Icons
CHRISTIAN LIFE
Bunyan, J. The Pilgrim's progress
Douglas, L. C. Doctor Hudson's secret jour-
  nal
CHRISTIAN MARTYRS. See Christians, Early
CHRISTIANITY
Asch, S. The Apostle
Asch, S. Mary
Asch, S. The Nazarene
Byrne, D. Messer Marco Polo
Costain, T. B. The silver chalice
De Wohl, L. The glorious folly
Flynn, R. In the house of the Lord
Kazantzakis, N. The fratricides
Lagerkvist, P. Pilgrim at sea
Merejkowski, D. The death of the gods
Oldenbourg, Z. The cornerstone
St Johns, A. R. Tell no man
Schoonover, L. The gentle infidel
Sienkiewicz, H. Quo vadis
Slaughter, F. G. Constantine: the miracle of
  the flaming cross
Vidal, G. Julian
  See also Catholic faith; Jesus Christ; Re-
  ligion; also names of Christian churches or
  sects

CLASS DISTINCTION
Braine, J. Life at the top
Braine, J. Room at the top
Bristow, G. The handsome road
Bristow, G. This side of glory
Crane, S. Active service
  In Crane, S. The complete novels of Stephen Crane p429-592
Crane, S. The third violet
  In Crane, S. The complete novels of Stephen Crane p349-428
Deeping, W. Sorrell and son
Dreiser, T. An American tragedy
Golding, W. The pyramid
Gulbranssen, T. Beyond sing the woods
Hardy, T. The woodlanders
Holt, V. The legend of the Seventh Virgin
Pavese, C. The Devil in the hills
  In Pavese, C. The selected works of Cesare Pavese p279-390
Pavese, C. The house on the hill
  In Pavese, C. The selected works of Cesare Pavese p59-171
Smith, V. The wind blows free
Tarkington, B. Alice Adams
Wellman, P. I. The chain
  See also Social classes

CLASS STRUGGLE
London, J. The iron heel

Claudia. Franken, R.

Claudine at school. Colette
  also in Colette. Six novels p 1-234

CLAUDIUS I, EMPEROR OF ROME
Graves, R. Claudius, the god and his wife Messalina
Graves, R. I, Claudius

Claudius, the god and his wife Messalina. Graves, R.

Clayhanger. Bennett, A.

Clea. Durrell, L.
  also in Durrell, L. The Alexandria quartet: Justine; Balthazar; Mountolive [and] Clea p653-884

CLÉMENCE, CONSORT OF LOUIS X, KING OF FRANCE
Druon, M. The poisoned crown

CLEOPATRA, QUEEN OF EGYPT
Davis, W. S. A friend of Caesar

CLERGY
Adams, S. H. Tenderloin
Andrew, P. A new creature
Andrézel, P. The angelic avengers
Auchincloss, L. The Rector of Justin
Baldwin, J. Go tell it on the mountain
Barrie, J. M. Little minister
Bjorn, T. F. Papa's daughter
Bjorn, T. F. Papa's wife
Bjorn, T. F. Papa's wife, Papa's daughter, Mama's way
Chase, M. E. The lovely ambition
Chute, B. J. Greenwillow
Cozzens, J. G. Men and brethren
Field, R. All this, and heaven too
Fielding, H. The history of the adventures of Joseph Andrews and of his friend Mr Abraham Adams
Flynn, R. In the house of the Lord
Frederic, H. The damnation of Theron Ware
Gide, A. The pastoral symphony
  In Gide, A. Two symphonies p139-233
Giles, J. H. Shady Grove
Gunnarsson, G. The black cliffs
Hartog, J. de. The little ark
Hawthorne, N. The scarlet letter
Kazantzakis, N. The fratricides
Kim, R. E. The martyred
Lewis, S. Elmer Gantry
Mercer, C. The minister
Orwell, G. A clergyman's daughter
Richter, C. A simple honorable man
St Johns, A. R. Tell no man
Street, J. The gauntlet
Street, J. The high calling
Turnbull, A. S. The gown of glory
Wilson, G. The valley of time
  See also Catholic priests; Monasticism and religious orders; Rabbis

CLERGY, ANGLICAN AND EPISCOPAL
Austen, J. Mansfield Park
Austen, J. Pride and prejudice
Austen, J. The Watsons
Brontë, C. Jane Eyre
Brontë, C. Shirley
Butler, S. The way of all flesh
Cronin, A. J. A thing of beauty
Eliot, G. Middlemarch

Goldsmith, O. The Vicar of Wakefield
Goudge, E. A city of bells
Goudge, E. The Dean's watch
Goudge, E. The rosemary tree
Lanning, G. Green corn moon
Macaulay, R. The towers of Trebizond
Mano, D. K. Horn
Paton, A. Cry, the beloved country
Smith, L. One hour
Trollope, A. Barchester Towers
Trollope, A. Framley parsonage
Trollope, A. The last chronicle of Barset
Trollope, A. The warden
Turnbull, A. S. The Bishop's mantle
Walpole, H. The cathedral
Wellman, P. I. The chain

CLERGY, CATHOLIC. See Catholic priests

CLERGY, ITINERANT
Eliot, G. Adam Bede

A clergyman's daughter. Orwell, G.

CLERGYMEN. See Clergy

CLERKS
Bodelsen, A. Think of a number
Camus, A. The stranger
Cary, J. Mister Johnson
Flaubert, G. Bouvard and Pécuchet
Kafka, F. The trial
  See also Civil service

CLEVELAND. See Ohio—Cleveland

CLIPPER SHIPS. See Sailing vessels

CLOCK AND WATCH MAKERS
Goudge, E. The Dean's watch

Clock without hands. McCullers, C.

The clocks. Christie, A.

CLOCKS AND WATCHES
Thurber, J. The 13 clocks
Turgenev, I. The watch
  In Turgenev, I. Three novellas: Punin and Baburin, The inn, The watch p149-208

A clockwork orange. Burgess, A.

A clockwork orange, and Honey for the bears. Burgess, A.

The Cloister. Strindberg, A.

The Cloister and the hearth. Reade, C.

CLONTARF, BATTLE OF, 1014
Holland, C. The kings in winter

Clothes of a king's son [series]
Frankau, P. Over the mountains
Frankau, P. Sing for your supper
Frankau, P. Slaves of the lamp

CLOTHING AND DRESS
Charteris, H. The coat
Gallico, P. Mrs 'Arris goes to Paris

CLOTHING INDUSTRY
Asch, S. East River
Moll, E. Seidman and son
Weidman, J. I can get it for you wholesale

A clouded star. Parrish, A.

The clown. Böll, H.

CLOWNS
Böll, H. The clown

CLUBS
Dennis, N. Cards of identity

Cluny Brown. Sharp, M.

Clutch of constables. Marsh, N.

A clutch of coppers. Ashe, G.

COACHING (ATHLETICS)
Glanville, B. The Olympian

COAL MINERS. See Coal mines and mining

COAL MINES AND MINING

England
Andrew, P. A new creature
Cronin, A. J. The stars look down

France
Zola, E. Germinal

Pennsylvania
Richter, C. The aristocrat
Richter, C. A simple honorable man

Wales
Llewellyn, R. How green was my valley

COAL TOWNS. See Coal mines and mining

The coat. Charteris, H.

COATES, JOHN
Austen, J. The Watsons

COATS. See Clothing and dress

COLUMNISTS. See Journalists

COMANCHE INDIANS
  Capps, B. The white man's road
  Capps, B. A woman of the people
  Culp, J. H. The restless land
  Prebble, J. The buffalo soldiers
  Wellman, P. I. The Comancheros

The Comancheros. Wellman, P. I.

Come along with me: part of a novel, sixteen stories, and three lectures. Jackson, S.

Come back, Geordie. Walker, D.

Come back if it doesn't get better. Gilliatt, P.

Come gentle spring. Stuart, J.

Come rack! Come rope! Benson, R. H.

Come spring. Williams, B. A.

Come to dust. Lathen, E.

Come to the bower. Bryan, J. Y.

Come with me home. Carroll, G. H.

The comedians. Greene, G.

COMEDY. See Humor; Satire

A comedy of terrors. Innes, M.
  In Innes, M. Appleby intervenes p 157-304

Comfort me with apples. De Vries, P.

The comforters. Spark, M.
  In Spark, M. A Muriel Spark trio: The comforters; The ballad of Peckham Rye [and] Memento Mori p13-228

The coming of rain. Marius, R.

Coming up for air. Orwell, G.

COMMANCHE INDIANS. See Comanche Indians

Command, and I will obey you. Moravia, A.

Command the morning. Buck, P. S.

COMMANDERS. See Great Britain. Navy—Officers

COMMENTATORS. See Journalists

COMMERCIAL AERONAUTICS. See Aeronautics, Commercial

Commodore Hornblower. Forester, C. S.
  also in Forester, C. S. The indomitable Hornblower p5-227

COMMODORES. See Great Britain. Navy—Officers

COMMODUS, LUCIUS AELIUS AURELIUS, EMPEROR OF ROME
  White, E. L. The unwilling vestal

The common heart. Horgan, P.
  In Horgan, P. Mountain standard time: Main line west, Far from Cibola [and] The common heart p279-595

COMMUNICATION
  Vidal, G. Messiah

COMMUNISM
  Sinclair, U. The return of Lanny Budd
  See also Totalitarianism

Africa
Van der Post, L. Flamingo feather

Africa, South
Lessing, D. Landlocked
  In Lessing, D. Children of violence v4
Lessing, D. A ripple from the storm
  In Lessing, D. Children of violence v3

China
Buck, P. S. The three daughters of Madame Liang
Davidson, L. The rose of Tibet
Gann, E. K. Soldier of fortune

Cuba
Uris, L. Topaz

Czechoslovak Republic
Beneš, J. Second breath
Kundera, M. The joke

England
Lessing, D. The golden notebook
Snow, C. P. The conscience of the rich

Europe
Ambler, E. Judgment on Deltchev

France
Koestler, A. The age of longing

Germany
Malraux, A. Days of wrath

Hungary
Aczel, T. The ice age
Bridge, A. The Portuguese escape
MacLean, A. The secret ways

Ireland
O'Flaherty, L. The informer

Italy
Guareschi, G. Comrade Don Camillo
Guareschi, G. Don Camillo and his flock
Guareschi, G. Don Camillo meets the flower children
Guareschi, G. Don Camillo takes the Devil by the tail
Guareschi, G. Don Camillo's dilemma
Guareschi, G. The little world of Don Camillo
MacInnes, H. North from Rome
Silone, I. A handful of blackberries

Korea
Kim, R. E. The martyred

Latin America
Schulberg, B. Sanctuary v

Poland
Hlasko, M. The eighth day of the week

Russia
Abramov, F. One day in the "new life"
Almedingen, E. M. Frossia
Bulgakov, M. The heart of a dog
Dudintsev, V. Not by bread alone
Ehrenburg, I. A change of season
Ehrenburg, I. The thaw
Koestler, A. Darkness at noon
Pasternak, B. Doctor Zhivago
Rand, A. We the living
Romains, J. The new day
Sholokhov, M. And quiet flows the Don
Sholokhov, M. The Don flows home to the sea
Sholokhov, M. Harvest on the Don
Sholokhov, M. Seeds of tomorrow
Sholokhov, M. Tales of the Don
Solzhenitsyn, A. I. The cancer ward
Tarsis, V. Ward 7
Waring, M. W. The witnesses

Spain
Del Castillo, M. The disinherited
Gironella, J. M. The cypresses believe in God
Herrick, W. ¡Hermanos!

United States
Dos Passos, J. Adventures of a young man
  In Dos Passos, J. District of Columbia v 1
Mankiewicz, D. M. Trial
Wright, R. The outsider

Vietnam
Greene, G. The quiet American

Yugoslavia
Durrell, L. White eagles over Serbia

COMMUNIST GERMANY. See Germany (Democratic Republic, 1949-)

COMMUTERS. See Suburban life

COMPANIONS. See Servants—Companions

Company K. March, W.
  In March, W. A William March omnibus p 1-132

Company of cowards. Schaefer, J.
  also in Schaefer, J. The short novels of Jack Schaefer p317-460

The company she keeps. McCarthy, M.

A compass error. Bedford, S.

COMPASSION. See Sympathy

The compleat werewolf, and other stories of fantasy and science fiction. Boucher, A.

The complete novels and selected tales of Nathaniel Hawthorne. Hawthorne, N.

The complete novels of Jane Austen. Austen, J.

The complete novels of Mark Twain. Twain, M.

The complete novels of Stephen Crane. Crane, S.

The complete prose tales of Alexandr Sergeyevitch Pushkin. Pushkin, A. S.

The complete Ronald Firbank. Firbank, R.

The complete Sherlock Homes. Doyle, Sir A. C.

The complete short stories. Lawrence, D. H.

Complete short stories. Maugham, W. S.

The complete short stories. Twain, M.

The complete short stories & sketches of St-phen Crane. Crane, S.

The complete short stories of Guy de Maupas-sant. Maupassant, G. de

Complete short stories of Nathaniel Hawthorne. Hawthorne, N.

The complete short stories of Robert Louis Stevenson. Stevenson, R. L.

The complete Stalky & Co. Kipling, R.

A complete state of death. Gardner, J.

Complete stories and poems of Edgar Allan Poe. Poe, E. A.

Complete stories of Erskine Caldwell. Caldwell, E.

The complete stories of Herman Melville. Mel-ville, H.

The complete tales and poems of Edgar Allan Poe. Poe, E. A.

The complete tales of Henry James. James, H.

Complete works. West, N.

The complete works of O. Henry. Henry, O.

COMPOSERS. See Musicians—Composers

Composition for four hands. Lawrence, D. H.
  In Hitchcock, A. ed. Alfred Hitchcock pre-sents: My favorites in suspense p130-227

Compulsion. Levin, M.

COMPUTERS. See Electronic computers

COMPUTERS, ELECTRONIC. See Electronic calculating-machines; Electronic computers

Comrade Don Camillo. Guareschi, G.

CONCENTRATION CAMPS
  Behn, N. The shadowboxer
  Charyn, J. American scrapbook
  Del Castillo, M. Child of our time
  Karmel, I. An estate of memory
  Levin, M. Eva
  Malraux, A. Days of wrath
  Wiesel, E. Dawn
    See also World War, 1939-1945—Prisoners and prisons; also names of camps, e.g. Tere-zín (Concentration camp)

Concerning .the eccentricities of Cardinal Pirelli. Firbank, R.
  In Firbank, R. The complete Ronald Fir-bank p645-98

The Concubine. Lofts, N.

CONDEMNED PRISONERS. See Prisoners, Condemned

CONDUCT OF LIFE. See Ethics

CONEY ISLAND. See New York (City)—Coney Island

CONFEDERACY. See Confederate States of America

CONFEDERATE AGENTS. See Spies

CONFEDERATE GENERALS. See Confeder-ate States of America—Army

CONFEDERATE SOLDIERS. See Veterans (Civil War)

CONFEDERATE STATES OF AMERICA
  Basso, H. The Light Infantry Ball
  De La Roche, M. Morning at Jalna
  Kane, H. T. Bride of fortune
  Kane, H. T. The smiling rebel
  Mason, F. V. Proud new flags

  Army
  Becker, S. When the War is over
  Borland, H. The amulet
  Boyd, J. Marching on
  Churchill, W. The crisis
  Kane, H. T. The gallant Mrs Stonewall
  Kane, H. T. The lady of Arlington
  Keyes, F. P. Madame Castel's lodger
  Street, J. Captain Little Ax

  Army—Prisons
  Kantor, M. Andersonville
  Lancaster, B. Night watch

  Navy
  Mason, F. V. Our valiant few

The confession. Rinehart, M. R.
  In Rinehart, M. R. Mary Roberts Rhine-hart Crime book p227-91

The confessional. Simenon, G.

The confessions of Arsène Lupin. Leblanc, M.

Confessions of Felix Krull, confidence man. Mann, T.

The confessions of Nat Turner. Styron, W.

The confessions of Zeno. Svevo, I.

The confidential agent. Greene, G.
  In Greene, G. 3: This gun for hire, The con-fidential agent, The ministry of fear v2

CONFLICT OF GENERATIONS
  Barnes, M. A. Years of grace
  Kayira, L. Jingala
  MacInnes, C. Absolute beginners
    In MacInnes, C. The London novels of Colin MacInnes p249-449
  Plagemann, B. A world of difference
  Snow, C. P. The sleep of reason

CONFORMITY
  Marquand, J. P. H. M. Pulham, esquire
  Powell, R. The Philadelphian
  Wilson, S. The man in the gray flannel suit
    See also Individualism

CONGO, BELGIAN
  Hulme, K. The nun's story
    See also Africa, Central

CONGREGATIONS. See Synagogues

CONGRESSES AND CONFERENCES

  Damascus
  Leasor, J. Passport for a pilgrim

  Évian
  Habe, H. The mission

CONGRESSMEN. See United States. Congress

CONNECTICUT
  Simenon, G. Belle
    In Simenon, G. An American omnibus p3-125

  20th century
  De Vries, P. Reuben, Reuben
  De Vries, P. The tents of wickedness
  De Vries, P. The tunnel of love
  Dolson, H. Heat lightning
  Franken, R. Claudia
  Hersey, J. The marmot drive
  Hobson, L. Z. Gentleman's agreement
  Knowles, J. Indian summer
  Savage, M. Parrish
  Shulman, M. Rally round the flag, boys!
  Streeter, E. Chairman of the bored
  Van Siller, H. The watchers

  New Haven
  Leggett, J. Who took the gold away
  Wallant, E. L. The human season

A Connecticut Yankee in King Arthur's court. Twain, M.
  also in Twain, M. The complete novels of Mark Twain v2 p 1-262

The conqueror. Atherton, G.

The Conqueror. Heyer, G.

The conquerors. Malraux, A.
  In Dupee, F. W. ed. Great French short novels p535-717

CONSCIENCE
  Asch, S. A passage in the night
  Camus, A. The fall
  Conrad, J. Lord Jim
  Dostoevsky, F. Crime and criminals
  Gide, A. The pastoral symphony
    In Gide, A. Two symphonies p139-233
  Hawthorne, N. The scarlet letter
  Kim, R. E. The martyred
    See also Ethics; Guilt; Responsibility

Conscience of the king. Duggan, A.

The conscience of the rich. Snow, C. P.

CONSCIENTIOUS OBJECTORS
  Renault, M. The charioteer

The constant nymph. Kennedy, M.

CONSTANTINE I, THE GREAT, EMPEROR OF ROME
  Slaughter, F. G. Constantine: the miracle of the flaming cross

Constantine: the miracle of the flaming cross. Slaughter, F. G.

CONSTANTINOPLE. See Turkey—Istanbul

CONSULS. See Diplomatic life

Contemporary Chinese stories. Wang, Chi-chen, tr.

A contract. Svevo, I.
  In Svevo, I. Further confessions of Zeno p113-38

TITLE AND SUBJECT INDEX
EIGHTH EDITION

COWBOYS
Adams, A. Log of a cowboy
Bass, M. R. Jory
Clark, W. V. The Ox-bow incident
Culp, J. H. The bright feathers
Culp, J. H. The restless land
Flynn, R. North to yesterday
James, W. The American cowboy
James, W. Sand
James, W. Will James' Book of cowboy stories
Schaefer, J. Monte Walsh
   See also Ranch life; The West; Western stories

COWHANDS. See Cowboys

COWS
Gallico, P. Ludmila
  In Gallico, P. Three legends: The snow goose; The small miracle; Ludmila p77-126

A crack in the sidewalk. Wolff, R.

The Craigshaw curse. Webb, J. F.

Cranford. Gaskell, E. C.

CRANMER, THOMAS, ABP. OF CANTERBURY
Turton, G. My Lord of Canterbury

CREE INDIANS
Bodsworth, F. The strange one

CREOLES
Bristow, G. Deep summer
Keyes, F. P. Madame Castel's lodger
Marshall, P. British Guiana
  In Marshall, P. Soul clap hands and sing p67-127
Whitney, P. A. Skye Cameron
Yerby, F. The Foxes of Harrow

Crescent carnival. Keyes, F. P.

Cress Delahanty. West, J.

CRETE
Ayrton, M. The maze maker
Durrell, L. The dark labyrinth
Renault, M. The king must die

        19th century
Kazantzakis, N. Freedom or death

        20th century
Kazantzakis, N. Zorba the Greek
Stewart, M. The moon-spinners

The cricket on the hearth. Dickens, C.
  also in Dickens, C. Best short stories p553-620
  also in Dickens, C. Charles Dickens' Best stories p206-70
  also in Dickens, C. Christmas tales p147-215

CRICKETS
Dickens, C. The cricket on the hearth

CRIME AND CRIMINALS
Airth, R. Snatch
Andreyev, L. The seven who were hanged
Asch, S. Mottke, the thief
Becker, S. A covenant with death
Behan, B. The Scarperer
Breslin, J. The gang that couldn't shoot straight
Burnett, W. R. The asphalt jungle
Burnett, W. R. Little Caesar
Camus, A. The plague
Chaze, E. Wettermark
Cuomo, G. Among thieves
Defoe, D. The fortunes and misfortunes of the famous Moll Flanders
Dickens, C. Great expectations
Dickens, C. Oliver Twist
Dostoevsky, F. The brothers Karamazov
Dostoevsky, F. Crime and criminals
Dostoevsky, F. The house of the dead
Dreiser, T. An American tragedy
Duerrenmatt, F. The pledge
Duerrenmatt, F. The quarry
Faulkner, W. Intruder in the dust
Fielding, G. In the time of Greenbloom
Fielding, H. Amelia
Gardner, J. A complete state of death
Garve, A. The long short cut
Gaskin, C. Sara Dane
Genêt, J. Our Lady of the Flowers
Genêt, J. The thief's journal
Graham, W. The walking stick
Gunnarsson, G. The black cliffs
Hemingway, E. To have and have not
Hugo, V. Les misérables
Kirst, H. H. Brothers in arms
Levin, M. Compulsion

MacInnes, C. Mr Love and justice
  In MacInnes, C. The London novels of Colin MacInnes p451-626
Markandaya, K. A handful of rice
Marric, J. J. Gideon's fire
Marric, J. J. Gideon's ride
Motley, W. Knock on any door
O'Rourke, F. The swift runner
Puzo, M. The godfather
Sanders, L. The Anderson tapes
Shannon, D. Schooled to kill
Spicer, B. Kellogg Junction
Tolstoy, L. Resurrection
Waugh, H. Run when I say go
Westlake, D. E. The fugitive pigeon
Wilder, R. Fruit of the poppy
Williams, J. A. Sons of darkness, sons of light
Woods, S. Past praying for
   See also Arson; Assassination; Brigands and robbers; Convicts. Escaped; Counterfeits and counterfeiting; Gangsters; Juvenile delinquency; Mafia; Murder stories; Mystery and detective stories; Punishment; Smuggling; Trials

Crime and Mr Campion. Allingham, M.

Crime and punishment. Dostoevsky, F.

Crime book, Mary Roberts Rinehart. Rinehart, M. R.

Crime in Holland. Simenon, G.
  In Simenon, G. Maigret abroad p3-158

CRIME OF PASSION. See Crime passionel

The crime of Sylvestre Bonnard. France, A.

Crime on their hands. Shannon, D.

CRIME PASSIONEL
Duras, M. Moderato cantabile
  In Duras, M. Four novels p73-140

Criminal conversation. Freeling, N.

CRIMINALLY INSANE. See Insane, Criminal and dangerous

CRIMINALS. See Crime and criminals

The crippled tanker. See Rayner, D. A. The long haul

CRIPPLES
Asch, S. East River
Ashton-Warner, S. Greenstone
Berckman, E. She asked for it
Bristow, G. Tomorrow is forever
Dickens, C. Our mutual friend
Graham, W. The walking stick
Hesse, H. Peter Camenzind
Heyward, Du B. Porgy
Maugham, W. S. Of human bondage
Ogilvie, E. Bellwood
Shute, N. The breaking wave
Stewart, M. Nine coaches waiting
Turnbull, A. S. The golden journey
West, N. Miss Lonelyhearts
  In West, N. Complete works p65-140
Williams, T. Whipple's castle
Zweig, S. Beware of pity
   See also Disabled; Paraplegics

The crisis. Churchill, W.

The crock of gold. Stephens, J.

Crome yellow. Huxley, A.

Cronopios and famas. Cortázar, J.

The crooked hinge. Carr, J. D.
  In Carr, J. D. A John Dickson Carr trio p175-338

The crooked shamrock. Gilford, C. B.

The cross. Undset, S
  In Undset, S. Kristin Lavransdatter v3

The cross and the sword. Lauritzen, J.

The cross of iron. Heinrich, W.

The crossbreed. Eckert, A. W.

The crossing. Churchill, W.

The crowded sky. Searls, H.

CROWNS
Komroff, M. Coronet

The Croxley master. Doyle, Sir A. C.
  In Costain, T. B. ed. More Stories to remember v2 p189-221

Crucial instances. Wharton, E.
  In Wharton, E. The collected short stories of Edith Wharton v 1 p227-343

CRUCIFIXION. See Jesus Christ—Crucifixion

The cruel sea. Monsarrat, N.

CRUELTY
Kantor, M. Andersonville
Kosinski, J. The painted bird
Plievier, T. Berlin
Plievier, T. Moscow
Rees, B. Sidney, oh Sidney
In Rees, B. Try another country p 1-53
CRUISES. See Ocean voyages
CRUSADES
Duggan, A. Lord Geoffrey's fancy
Holland, C. Antichrist
Oldenbourg, Z. The cornerstone
Oldenbourg, Z. The world is not enough
See also Knights and knighthood

Third, 1189-1192
Haycraft, M. C. My lord brother the Lion Heart
Scott, Sir W. The talisman

Later 13th, 14th and 15th centuries
De Wohl, L. The joyful beggar
De Wohl, L. The last crusader
The cry and the covenant. Thompson, M.
Cry, the beloved country. Paton, A.
The crying game. Braine, J.
CRYPTOZOIC! Aldiss, B. W.
CUBA

19th century
Thane, E. Ever after

19th century—Revolution, 1895-1898
Street, J. Mingo Dabney

20th century
Hemingway, E. The old man and the sea
In Hemingway, E. Three novels of Ernest Hemingway v3
Hemingway, E. To have and have not

Havana
Greene, G. Our man in Havana
Hemingway, E. The old man and the sea
Uris, L. Topaz
CULTURE CONFLICT
Courlander, H. The African
Sheed, W. The blacking factory
In Sheed, W. The blacking factory & Pennsylvania gothic p67-246
Sorensen, V. The proper gods
See also East and West
CUMBERLAND. See England, Provincial and rural—Cumberland
The cunning of the dove. Duggan, A.
Cup of gold. Steinbeck, J.
The cup, the blade or the gun. Eberhart, M. G.
CUPID
Lewis, C. S. Till we have faces
CURÉS. See Catholic priests
The curious facts preceding my execution, and other fictions. Westlake, D. E.
The currents of space. Asimov, I.
In Asimov, I. Triangle: The currents of space, Pebble in the sky, The stars, like dust p 1-172
Curse not the King. See Anthony, E. Royal intrigue
The curse of Jezebel. Slaughter, F. G.
CURSES, FAMILY
Chute, B. J. Greenwillow
Druon, M. The Iron King
Druon, M. The poisoned crown
Druon, M. The royal succession
Druon, M. The strangled queen
Hawthorne, N. The House of the Seven Gables
Holt, V. Bride of Pendorric
Lagerlöf, S. The general's ring
Webb, J. F. The Craigshaw curse
A curtain of green. Welty, E.
In Welty, E. Selected stories v 1
The curved saber. Lamb, H.
The custom of the country. Wharton, E.
CYCLING
Johnson, U. The third book about Achim
CYCLISTS. See Cycling
The cypresses believe in God. Gironella, J. M.
CYRUS, THE GREAT, KING OF PERSIA
Asch, S. The prophet
CZARIST RUSSIA. See Russia—1900-1917

CZECHOSLOVAK REPUBLIC
Beneš, J. Second breath
Kundera, M. The joke
Peters, E. The piper on the mountain

Communism
See Communism—Czechoslovak Republic

Prisons
See Prisons—Czechoslovak Republic
CZECHOSLOVAKIAN SOLDIERS. See Soldiers, Czechoslovakian
CZECHS IN THE UNITED STATES
Kafka, F. Amerika
See also Bohemians in the United States

D

DAEDALUS
Ayrton, M. The maze maker
DAHLGREN, ULRIC
Brick, J. The Richmond raid
The Dain curse. Hammett, D.
In Hammett, D. The novels of Dashiell Hammett p143-292
Daisy Miller. James, H.
also in James, H. The great short novels of Henry James p85-144
also in James, H. The Henry James reader p403-61
also in James, H. Short novels of Henry James p 1-58
also in James, H. Washington Square and, Daisy Miller p193-258
DAKOTA INDIANS
See also Wahpekute Indians

Wars, 1862-1865
Sinclair, H. The cavalryman
DALMATIA. See Yugoslavia—Dalmatia
DAMASCUS. See Syria—Damascus
The damnation of Theron Ware. Frederic, H.
DAMS
Markandaya, K. The coffer dams
The dance of Genghis Cohn.. Gary, R.
Dance of the dwarfs. Household, G.
A dance to the music of time. Powell, A.
A dance to the music of time: second movement. Powell, A.
DANCERS
Baum, V. Grand Hotel
Colette. The vagabond
In Colette. 7 by Colette v4 p 1-223
Cost, M. Jubilee of a ghost
Durrell, L. Justine
Godden, R. A candle for St Jude
Shellabarger, S. Lord Vanity
Dancers in mourning. Allingham, M.
In Allingham, M. Crime and Mr Campion p363-575
Dandelion wine. Bradbury, R.
DANES IN GREENLAND
Freuchen, P. White man
Danger. The Saturday Evening Post
Danger hole. Short, L.
In Western Writers of America. A Western bonanza p366-419
A dangerous innocence. Lincoln, V.
The dangerous islands. Bridge, A.
Dangling man. Bellow, S.
Daniel Deronda. Eliot, G.
DANZIG. See Poland—Danzig
The darfsteller. Miller, W. M.
In Asimov, I. ed. The Hugo winners p5-71
The daring young man on the flying trapeze, and other stories. See Saroyan, W. After thirty years: The daring young man on the flying trapeze
DARK AGES. See Middle Ages
The dark and the light. Vittorini, E.
Dark as the grave wherein my friend is laid. Lowry, M.
The dark island. Treece, H.
The dark labyrinth. Durrell, L.

Dark laughter. Anderson, S.
The dark moment. Bridge, A.
The dark side. Knight, D. ed.
The dark stranger. Charques, D.
Darkest hour. Nielsen, H.
Darkness and day. Compton-Burnett, I.
The darkness and the dawn. Costain, T. B.
Darkness at noon. Koestler, A.
Darkwater. Eden, D.
The darling, and other stories. Chekhov, A.
The darling buds of May. Bates, H. E.
D'ARTAGNAN. See Artagnan, Charles de Baatz de Castelmore, styling himself count d'
DARTMOOR. See England, Provincial and rural—Devonshire
DARTMOOR PRISON
Roberts, K. The Lively Lady
The daughter of Bugle Ann. Kantor, M.
Daughter of silence. West, M. L.
Daughter of the legend. Stuart, J.
The daughter of time. Tey, J.
  also in Tey, J. Four, five and six by Tey v3
DAUGHTERS. See Fathers and daughters; Mothers and daughters; Parent and child
DAUGHTERS-IN-LAW
Tanizaki, J. Diary of a mad old man
Daughters of Earth. Merril, J.
DAUPHINÉ. See France, Provincial and rural—Dauphiné
DAVID, KING OF ISRAEL
Schmitt, G. David the king
David Copperfield. Dickens, C.
David the king. Schmitt, G.
DA VINCI LEONARDO. See Leonardo da Vinci
DAVIS, JEFFERSON
Kane, H. T. Bride of fortune
DAVIS, VARINA (HOWELL)
Kane, H. T. Bride of fortune
Dawn. Wiesel, E.
Dawn's early light. Thane, E.
A day in Monte Carlo. Albrand, M.
The day must dawn. Turnbull, A. S.
Day of battle. Van de Water, F. F.
The day of the dolphin. Merle, R.
The day of the locust. West, N.
  In West, N. The complete works of Nathaniel West p259-421
The day of the scorpion. Scott, P.
The day of the triffids. Wyndham, J.
The day will come. See Feuchtwanger, L. Josephus and the Emperor
Daybreak. Slaughter, F. G.
Days and nights. Simonov, K.
Days of hope. See Malraux, A. Man's hope
Days of wrath. Malraux, A.
A daze of fears. Roffman, J.
The dead. Joyce, J.
  In Neider, C. ed. Short novels of the masters p499-536
Dead cert. Francis, D.
  In Francis, D. Three to show p3-216
Dead man's mirror. Christie, A.
  In Haycraft, H. ed. Three times three p479-543
Dead men don't ski. Moyes, P.
  In Moyes, P. Murder by 3's p3-288
DEAD SEA SCROLLS
Davidson, L. The Menorah men
Dead souls. Gogol, N.
Dead water. Marsh, N.
Dead woman of the year. Pentecost, H.
DEAF
Calisher, H. The New Yorkers
Field, R. And now tomorrow
McCullers, C. The heart is a lonely hunter
DEAN, JOHN
Roberts, K. Boon Island
DEANS. See Clergy, Anglican and Episcopal
The Dean's watch. Goudge, E.
DE ANZA, JUAN BAUTISTA. See Anza, Juan Bautista de
Dear and glorious physician. Caldwell, T.

Dear fatherland. Simmel, J. M.
Dear papa. Bjorn, T. F.
Dearly beloved. Lindbergh, A. M.
DEATH
Agee, J. A death in the family
Amis, K. The Anti-Death League
Andreyev, L. The seven who were hanged
Farrell, J. T. Judgement day
Gerber, M. J. An antique man
Gordon, N. The death committee
Le Clézio, J. M. G. The flood
Mann, T. Death in Venice
Murdoch, I. Bruno's dream
Power, R. The hungry grass
Sheed, W. Pennsylvania gothic
  In Sheed, W. The blacking factory & Pennsylvania gothic p3-63
Spark, M. Memento mori
Spark, M. Memento mori, and The ballad of Peckham Rye
Vidal, G. Messiah
  See also Murder; Suicide
DEATH, APPARENT
Frame, J. Yellow flowers in the antipodean room
Death and the lover. See Hesse, H. Narcissus and Goldmund
Death at the chase. Innes, M.
Death by water. Innes, M.
Death comes for the archbishop. Cather, W.
The death committee. Gordon, N.
The death dealers. See Asimov, I. A whiff of death
Death has two sons. Dayan, Y.
Death in diamonds. Giles, K.
A death in the family. Agee, J.
Death in Venice. Mann, T.
  also in Mann, T. The Thomas Mann reader
  also in Neider, C. ed. Short novels of the masters p439-98
  also in Pick, R. ed. German stories and tales p302-68
Death kit. Sontag, S.
Death of a demon. Stout, R.
  In Stout, R. Homicide trinity
Death of a doxy. Stout, R.
Death of a dude. Stout, R.
Death of a ghost. Allingham, M.
  In Allingham, M. Crime and Mr Campion p7-175
Death of a simple giant, and other modern Yugoslav stories. Lenski, B. ed.
Death of a swagman. Upfield, A. W.
The death of Ahasuerus. Lagerkvist, P.
The death of Artemio Cruz. Fuentes, C.
The death of Don Juan. Queen, E.
  In Queen, E. Queens full p 1-62
Death of Ivan Ilých. Tolstoy, L.
  In Neider, C. ed. Short novels of the masters p249-300
  In Tolstoy, L. Short novels v2 p3-62
The death of Ivan Ilyitch, and other stories. Tolstoy, L.
The death of the gods. Merejkowski, D.
The death of the heart. Bowen, E.
Death on a warm wind. Warner, D.
Death on the Nile. Christie, A.
  also in Christie, A. Perilous journeys of Hercule Poirot v2
Death shall overcome. Lathen, E.
The death ship. Traven, B.
Death trap for an iron horse. Heckelmann, C. N.
  In Western Writers of America. A Western bonanza p309-65
DEATHBED SCENES
Cullinan, E. House of gold
Fuentes, C. The death of Artemio Cruz
Murdoch, I. Bruno's dream
The debacle. Zola, E.
DEBS, EUGENE VICTOR
Stone, I. Adversary in the house
A decade of Fantasy and Science Fiction. Magazine of Fantasy and Science Fiction
DECADENCE. See Degeneration
The Decameron. Boccaccio, G.
DECEPTION. See Truthfulness and falsehood

DESTROYERS. See United States. Navy

Detection unlimited. Heyer, G.

The detective. Thorp, R.

DETECTIVE STORIES. See Mystery and detective stories

DETECTIVES
The following are characters prominent in solving the mysteries of specific authors

Adams, Hilda. See stories by Rinehart, M. R

Alleyn, Superintendent Roderick. See stories by Marsh, N.

Allwright, Superintendent Dudley. See stories by MacDonald, P.

Ames, Sergeant. See stories by Symons, J.

Appleby, Inspector John. See stories by Innes, M.

Archer, Lew. See stories by Macdonald, R.

Baley, Elijah. See stories by Asimov, I.

Barlach, Police Commissioner. See stories by Duerrenmatt, F.

Beaumont, Ned. See stories by Hammett, D.

Beck, Superintendent Martin. See stories by Sjöwall, M.

Bennett, Hugh. See stories by Symons, J.

Beresford, Tommy. See stories by Christie, A.

Beresford, Tuppence. See stories by Christie, A.

Blaise, Modesty. See stories by O'Donnell, P.

Boardman, Jane. See stories by Harrington, J.

Bonaparte, Inspector Napoleon. See stories by Upfield, A. W.

Bond, James. See stories by Fleming, I.

Brade, Professor Louis. See stories by Asimov, I.

Brightlaw, Doremus. See stories by Farris, J.

Broderick, Inspector. See stories by McLeish, D.

Brown, Father. See stories by Chesterton, G. K.

Bucket, Inspector. See stories by Dickens, C.

Campion, Albert. See stories by Allingham, M.

Carella, Lieutenant Steve. See stories by McBain, E.

Carver, Rex. See stories by Canning, V.

Chambers, Peter. See stories by Kane, H.

Chambrun, Pierre. See stories by Pentecost, H.

Charles, Nicholas. See stories by Hammett, D.

Cloverdale, Inspector. See stories by Symons, J.

Cockrill, Inspector. See stories by Brand, C.

Crook, Arthur. See stories by Gilbert, A.

Cuff, Sergeant. See stories by Collins, W.

Dawlish, Commissioner Patrick. See stories by Ashe, G.

Dee, Judge. See stories by Gulik, R. van

Drake, Simon. See stories by Nielsen, H.

Dupin, C. Auguste. See stories by Poe, E. A.

Easterbrook, Mark. See stories by Christie, A.

Falkinstein, Jesse. See stories by Egan, L.

Fansler, Kate. See stories by Cross, A.

Fell, Dr Gideon. See stories by Carr, J. D.

Felse, Detective Inspector George. See stories by Peters, E.

Foley, John. See stories by Woodfin, H.

Gamadge, Henry. See stories by Daly, E.

Ganimard, Chief Inspector. See stories by Leblanc, M.

Garvin, Willie. See stories by O'Donnell, P.

Gethryn, Colonel Anthony. See stories by MacDonald, P.

Ghote, Inspector Ganesh. See stories by Keating, H. R. F.

Gideon, Superintendent George. See stories by Marric, J. J.

Gillingham, Antony. See stories by Milne, A. A.

Gold, Lieutenant Paul. See stories by Greenbaum, L.

Goodwin, Archie. See stories by Stout, R.

Grant, Inspector Alan. See stories by Tey, J.

Hambledon, Tommy. See stories by Coles, M.

Hannay, Richard. See stories by Buchan, J.

Harding, Thomas. See stories by Aird, C.

Harrington, John. See stories by Cooper, B.

Harris, Paul. See stories by Black, G.

Heimrich, Captain. See stories by Lockridge, R.

Hemingway, Chief Inspector. See stories by Heyer, G.

Hero, Alexander. See stories by Gallico, P.

Holmes, Sherlock. See stories by Doyle, A. C.

Hoong, Sergeant. See stories by Gulik, R. van

Huish, Superintendent. See stories by Christie, A.

James, Inspector Harry. See stories by Giles, K.

Jamieson, Mr. See stories by Rinehart, M. R.

Jericho, John. See stories by Pentecost, H.

Kerrigan, Lieutenant. See stories by Harrington, J.

Killian, Francis. See stories by Peters, E.

Lane, Drury. See stories by Queen, E.

La Touche, Georges. See stories by Crofts, F. W.

Lee, Hannah. See stories by Nielsen, H.

Leland, Joe. See stories by Thorp, R.

Logan, Tom. See stories by Gruber, F.

Lonto, Detective Tony. See stories by Johnson, E. R.

Luke, Superintendent. See stories by Allingham, M.

McCaig, Chief Superintendent. See stories by Rae, H. C.

McGee, Travis. See stories by MacDonald, J. D.

McMahon, Father Joseph. See stories by Davis, D. S.

Maddox, Sergeant Ivor. See stories by Linington, E.

Maigret, Chief Inspector. See stories by Simenon, G.

Maitland, Anthony. See stories by Woods, S.

Malone, Sergeant Scobie. See stories by Cleary, J.

Marlowe, Philip. See stories by Chandler, R.

Marple, Miss Jane. See stories by Christie, A.

Martineau, Chief Inspector. See stories by Procter, M.

Mason, Perry. See stories by Gardner, E. S.

Mendoza, Lieutenant Luis. See stories by Shannon, D.

Midwinter, Julian. See stories by Davies, L. P.

Moto, T. A. See stories by Marquand, J. P.

Murdock, Kent. See stories by Coxe, G. H.

Neill, Henry F. See stories by Hammett, D.

O'Brien, Terrence. See stories by Rinehart, M. R.

Opara, Christie. See stories by Uhnak, D.

Parker, Chief Inspector Charles. See stories by Sayers, D. L.

Pearson, Detective Inspector. See stories by Davies, L. P.

Pibble, Superintendent Jimmy. See stories by Dickinson, P.

Poirot, Hercule. See stories by Christie, A.

Pons, Solar. See stories by Derleth, A.

Purbright, Detective Inspector. See stories by Watson, C.

Queen, Ellery. See stories by Queen, E.

Queen, Inspector Richard. See stories by Queen, E.

Qwilleran, Jim. See stories by Braun, L. J.

"The Saint." See stories by Charteris, L.

Sands, Inspector. See stories by Millar, M.

Seeton, Miss Emily. See stories by Carvic, H.

Selborne, Charity. See stories by Stewart, M.

Shapiro, Lieutenant Nathan. See stories by Lockridge, R.

Shomar, Shomri. See stories by Klinger, H.

Silva, Captain José da. See stories by Fish, R. L.

Silver, Jennifer. See stories by Stewart, M.

Silverman, Arthur. See stories by Graham, J. A.

Skragg, Police Chief Charlie T. See stories by Kamarck, L.

Sloan, Inspector. See stories by Aird, C.

Small, Rabbi David. See stories by Kemelman, H.

Spade, Sam. See stories by Hammett, D.

Templar, Simon. See stories by Charteris, L.

Thatcher, John Putnam. See stories by Lathen, E.

Tibbett, Inspector Henry. See stories by Moyes, P.

Tibbs, Virgil. See stories by Ball, J.

Tobin, Mitchell. See stories by Coe, T.

Torry, Detective Inspector Derek. See stories by Gardner, J.

Travers, Ludovic. See stories by Bush, C.

Trent, Inspector. See stories by Garve, A.

Trent, Philip Marsham. See stories by Bentley, E. C.

Van der Valk, Inspector. See stories by Freeling, N.

Vane, Harriet. See stories by Sayers, D. L.

Van Larsen, Max. See stories by Baxt, G.

Watson, Dr John H. See stories by Doyle, Sir A. C.

Welt, Nicky. See stories by Kemelman, H.

West, Superintendent Roger. See stories by Creasey, J.

Wimsey, Lord Peter. See stories by Sayers, D. L.

TITLE AND SUBJECT INDEX
EIGHTH EDITION

Doctor Martino, and other stories. See Faulkner, W. Collected stories of William Faulkner

Doctor No. Fleming, I.
  also in Fleming, I. Gilt-edged Bonds v3

Doctor stories. See Fabricant, N. comp. A treasury of doctor stories by the world's great authors

Doctor Thorne. Trollope, A.

Doctor Zhivago. Pasternak, B.

DOCTORS. See Physicians

DOCUMENTS. See Manuscripts

Dodsworth. Lewis, S.

Dog years. Grass, G.

DOGS
  Arnow, H. Hunter's horn
  Bulgakov, M. The heart of a dog
  Burnford, S. The incredible journey
  Cooper, P. ed. Famous dog stories
  Gipson, F. Hound-dog man
  Gipson, F. Old Yeller
  Gipson, F. Savage Sam
  Godden, J. A winter's tale
  Hartog, J. de. The artist
  Kantor, M. The daughter of Bugle Ann
  Kantor, M. The voice of Bugle Ann
  London, J. The call of the wild
  London, J. White Fang
  London, J. White Fang, and other stories
  Nathan, R. The adventures of Tapiola
  Shannon, D. Schooled to kill
  Street, J. Good-bye, my Lady
  Street, J. Pride of possession

The dollmaker. Arnow, H.

DOLPHINS
  Merle, R. The day of the dolphin
  Shadbolt, M. This summer's dolphin
  Sherman, D. R. Brothers of the sea

Dom Casmurro. Machado de Assis, J. M.

Dombey and son. Dickens, C.

DOMESTIC ANIMALS
  Stranger, J. Born to trouble

DOMESTIC RELATIONS. See Family life

The dominant fifth. Laski, A.

DOMINICANS
  De Wohl, L. Lay siege to heaven

DOMITIAN, TITUS FLAVIUS, EMPEROR OF ROME
  Feuchtwanger, L. Josephus and the Emperor

Don Camillo meets the flower children. Guareschi, G.

Don Camillo takes the Devil by the tail. Guareschi, G.

Don Camillo's dilemma. Guareschi, G.

The Don flows home to the sea. Sholokhov, M.
  also in Sholokhov, M. The silent Don v2

Don Quixote de la Mancha. Cervantes, M. de

Don Quixote de la Mancha; abridged. Cervantes, M. de
  In Cervantes, M. de. The portable Cervantes p39-702

Dona Flor and her two husbands. Amado, J.

Doña Perfecta. Perez Galdos, B.

DONKEYS. See Asses and mules

DONNE, JOHN, 1573-1631
  Vining, E. G. Take heed of loving me

DONNER PARTY
  Fisher, V. The mothers

DONS. See Teachers

Don't go near the water. Brinkley, W.

Don't knock the corners off. Glyn, C.

Don't rely on Gemini. Packer, V.

The doomed oasis. Innes, H.

The door. Rinehart, M. R.
  In Rinehart, M. R. Mary Roberts Rinehart Crime book p 1-226

A door fell shut. Albrand, M.

The door in the wall. La Farge, O.

The door into summer. Heinlein, R. A.

Door to death. Stout, R.
  In Stout, R. Five of a kind p399-441

The doorbell rang. Stout, R.

DOPE ADDICTS. See Narcotic habit

Dorothy L. Sayers omnibus. Sayers, D. L.

Dorothy Parker. Parker, D.

The Dorp. Arkin, F.

DORSET. See England, Provincial and rural—Dorset

The double. Dostoevsky, F.
  In Dostoevsky, F. The short novels of Dostoevsky p475-615

Double barrel. Freeling, N.

Double identity. Coxe, G. H.

The double image. MacInnes, H.

Double indemnity. Cain, J. M.
  In Cain, J. M. Cain x 3 p363-465

Double star. Heinlein, R. A.

DOUBLOONS
  Chandler, R. Farewell, my lovely
  In Chandler, R. The Raymond Chandler omnibus p141-315

Down among the dead men. Moyes, P.
  In Moyes, P. Murder by 3's p289-540

Down there on a visit. Isherwood, C.

The downfall. See Zola, E. The debacle

The downstairs room, and other speculative fiction. Wilhelm, K.

DOWRY
  Agnon, S. Y. The bridal canopy

DOYLE, SIR ARTHUR CONAN

Parodies, travesties, etc.
  Boucher, A. The case of the Baker Street Irregulars
  Derleth, A. The casebook of Solar Pons

Dracula. Stoker, B.

Dragon harvest. Sinclair, U.

Dragon seed. Buck, P. S.

Dragon's teeth. Sinclair, U.

Dragonwyck. Seton, A.

DRAKE, SIR FRANCIS
  Mason, F. V. Golden Admiral

The dram-shop. See Zola, E. L'assommoir

DRAMATISTS
  Ambler, E. Judgment on Deltchev
  Behrman, S. N. The burning glass
  Godden, R. A breath of air
  Johnson, P. H. Cork Street, next to the hatter's
  Kauffmann, L. An honorable estate
  Marquand, J. P. So little time
  Marquand, J. P. Women and Thomas Harrow
  Morris, W. The field of vision
  O'Hara, J. The instrument
  Plagemann, B. A world of difference
  Saroyan, W. One day in the afternoon of the world
  Weiss, P. Exile
  Wolfe, T. Of time and the river
  See also Amateur theatricals

The dream life of Balso Snell. West, N.
  In West, N. The complete works of Nathaniel West p3-62

Dream of fair woman. Armstrong, C.

A dream of kings. Petrakis, H. M.

The dreaming suburb. Delderfield, R. F.
  In Delderfield, R. F. The Avenue p13-446

DREAMS
  Davies, L. P. The Lampton dreamers
  Davies, L. P. Twilight journey
  Du Maurier, G. Peter Ibbetson
  Murdoch, I. Bruno's dream
  West, N. The dream life of Balso Snell
  In West, N. Complete works p3-62

DRESDEN. See Germany—Dresden

The Dresden Green. Freeling, N.

DRESS. See Clothing and dress

DRESSMAKERS
  Bristow, G. Celia Garth
  Stern, G. B. A deputy was king
  In Stern, G. B. The matriarch chronicles v2

DREYFUS, ALFRED
  France, A. Penguin Island

Drink to yesterday. Coles, M.
  also in Coles, M. Exploits of Tommy Hambledon p7-162

The drip-dried tourist. Temple, W.

Droll stories. Balzac, H. de

A drop of patience. Kelley, W. M.

DROPOUTS. See School attendance

DROUGHTS
  Johnson, J. W. Now in November
  Marius, R. The coming of rain

DROWNING
  Cather, W. Lucy Gayheart
DRUG ADDICTION. See Narcotic habit
DRUGGISTS. See Pharmacists
DRUGS
  Du Maurier, D. The house on the strand
  Slaughter, F. G. Daybreak
    See also Narcotics, Control of; and names
  of drugs, e.g. Lysergic acid diethylamide
DRUIDS AND DRUIDISM
  Treece, H. The dark island
Drumbeat. Pope, D.
Drums. Boyd, J.
Drums along the Mohawk. Edmonds, W. D.
Drums of destiny. Bourne, P.
DRUNKARDS. See Alcoholism
DRUNKENESS. See Alcoholism
DUAL PERSONALITY
  This subject is used for novels describing a
  condition in which one individual shows in
  alternation two very different characters. For
  novels dealing with individuals who assume
  or act the character of another, see the sub-
  ject; Impersonations
  Hesse, H. Steppenwolf
  Nabokov, V. Despair
  Stevenson, R. L. The strange case of Dr Jekyll
    and Mr Hyde
DUBLIN. See Ireland—Dublin
Dubliners. Joyce, J.
  also in Joyce, J. The portable James Joyce
    p17-242
DUDLEY, AMY (ROBSART) LADY
  Scott, Sir W. Kenilworth
DUDLEY, LADY JANE. See Grey, Lady Jane
DUDLEY, ROBERT, EARL OF LEICESTER.
  See Leicester, Robert Dudley, earl of
The duel. Conrad, J.
  In Conrad, J. Tales of land and sea
    p441-504
  In Costain, T. B. comp. Twelve short novels
    p171-234
The duel, and other stories. Chekhov, A.
DUELING
  Conrad, J. The duel
  In Costain, T. B. comp. Twelve short novels
    p171-234
DUELS. See Dueling
The Dukays. Zilahy, L.
DUMAS, ALEXANDRE, 1802-1870
  Endore, G. King of Paris
DUMAS, ALEXANDRE, 1824-1895
  Endore, G. King of Paris
DUMB (DEAFMUTES) See Deaf
Dunbar's Cove. Deal, B.
Dune. Herbert, F.
Dune messiah. Herbert, F.
DUNKIRK, BATTLE OF, 1940
  Gallico, P. The snow goose
The Dunwich horror, and others. Lovecraft,
  H. P.
Duplicate death. Heyer, G.
DÜSSELDORF. See Germany—Düsseldorf
Dusty answer. Lehmann, R.
DUTCH EAST INDIES
  Titles listed here are for the period prior
  to the formation of the Republic of Indonesia,
  1949; for novels since 1949, see Indonesia
        17th century
  Lofts, N. Scent of cloves
  Lofts, N. Silver nutmeg
        20th century
  Hartog, J. de The spiral road
        Molucca Islands
  Dermoût M. The ten thousand things
        Native races
  Hartog, J. de. The spiral road
DUTCH IN AFRICA, SOUTH
  Cloete, S. The fiercest heart
  Cloete, S. Rags of glory
  Cloete, S. The turning wheels
  Rooke, D. Mittee
DUTCH IN BORNEO
  Conrad, J. Almayer's folly

DUTCH IN INDONESIA
  Van der Post, L. The sword and the doll
  In Van der Post, L. The seed and the sower
    p191-256
DUTY
  Santayana, G. The last Puritan
DWARFS
  De La Mare, C. Memoirs of a midget
  Grass, G. The tin drum
  Household, G. Dance of the dwarfs
  Swift, J. Gulliver's travels
DWELLINGS. See Houses
DYGARTSBUSH. See New York (State)—Dy-
  gartsbush
The dying man. Knight, D.
  In Knight, D. Three novels p151-89
DYNASTY of death. Caldwell, T.

E

E for effort. Sherred, T. L.
  In Knight, D. ed. A century of great short
    science fiction novels p295-341
EQMM annual. 1946-1968. Entered in Part I
  under title
ESP. See Extrasensory perception
Eagle in the air. Robinson, R.
Eagle in the sky. Mason, F. V.
The eagles gather. Caldwell, T.
Early autumn. Bromfield, L.
  In Bromfield, L. Bromfield galaxy: The
    green bay tree, Early autumn, A good
    woman p217-403
EARLY CHRISTIANS. See Christians, Early;
  Church history—Primitive and early church
The early life of Stephen Hind. Jameson, S.
Early stories of Willa Cather. Cather, W.
Earth abides. Stewart, G. R.
The earth trembles. Romains, J.
Earthlight. Clarke, A. C.
  also in Clarke, A. C. Across the sea of
    stars p435-584
Earthmen and strangers. Silverberg, R. ed.
EARTHQUAKES
  Christopher, J. The ragged edge
  Warner, D. Death on a warm wind
  Whitney, P. A. The trembling hills
    See also Disasters
EAST (FAR EAST)
  Hesse, H. The journey to the East
    See also Asia, Southeastern; also names
  of individual countries of this region, e.g.
  China; Japan; etc.
EAST AND WEST
  For novels about culture conflict between
  Occidental and Oriental civilizations
  Ashton-Warner, S. Greenstone
  Buck, P. S. East wind: west wind
  Buck, P. S. Kinfolk
  Buck, P. S. Letter from Peking
  Hersey, J. A single pebble
  Hobart, A. T. Oil for the lamps of China
  Markandaya, K. Some inner fury
  Menen, A. The prevalence of witches
  Moll, E. Mr Seidman and the geisha
  Narayan, R. K. The vendor of sweets
  Raja Rao. The serpent and the rope
  Rama Rau, S. Remember the house
  Scott, P. The jewel in the crown
  Sneider, V. The Teahouse of the August
    Moon
  West, M. L. The ambassador
  West, M. L. The shoes of the fisherman
  White, R. Elephant Hill
    See also Culture conflict
East and West. Maugham, W. S.
  In Maugham, W. S. Complete short stories
    v 1
EAST ANGLIA. See England, Provincial and
  rural—East Anglia
East of desolation. Higgins, J.
East of Eden. Steinbeck, J.
East River. Asch, S.

ELIZABETH, CONSORT OF EDWARD IV, KING OF ENGLAND
Westcott, J. The white rose
ELIZABETH, CONSORT OF HENRY VII, KING OF ENGLAND
Barnes, M. C. The Tudor rose
Elizabeth. Troyat, H.
Elizabeth and the Prince of Spain. Irwin, M.
Elizabeth Appleton. O'Hara, J.
Elizabeth, captive princess. Irwin, M.
An Elizabeth Daly Mystery omnibus. Daly, E.
Elizabeth; or, Demonic love. See Mallet-Joris, F. The witches
ELIZABETHAN ENGLAND. See England— 16th century
Ellery Queen's All-star lineup. See EQMM annual, 1946-1969
Ellery Queen's annual. See EQMM annual, 1946-1969
Ellery Queen's awards. See EQMM annual, 1946-1969
Ellery Queen's Crime carousel. See EQMM annual, 1946-1969
Ellery Queen's Double dozen. See EQMM annual, 1946-1969
Ellery Queen's minimysteries. Queen, E. ed.
Ellery Queen's Murder menu. See EQMM annual, 1946-1969
Ellery Queen's Mystery annual. See EQMM annual, 1946-1969
Ellery Queen's Mystery mix. See EQMM annual, 1946-1969
Ellery Queen's Mystery parade. See EQMM annual, 1946-1969
Ellery Queen's 20th anniversary annual. See EQMM annual, 1946-1969
Elmer Gantry. Lewis, S.
The elusive Pimpernel. Orczy, Baroness
Embezzled heaven. Werfel, F.
EMBEZZLEMENT
Auchincloss, L. The embezzler
Dreiser, T. The financier
The embezzler. Auchincloss, L.
EMDEN (CRUISER)
Jennings, J. The raider
Emergency in the Pyrenees. Bridge, A.
The emigrants. Bojer, J.
The emigrants. Moberg, V.
EMIGRÉS. See Refugees
Emma. Austen, J.
also in Austen, J. The complete novels of Jane Austen
EMOTIONALLY DISTURBED CHILDREN. See Problem children
The emperor of ice-cream. Moore, B.
The emperor's pearl. Gulik, R. van
Emphyrio. Vance, J.
The empty hours: an 87th Precinct mystery. McBain, E.
In Haycraft, H. ed. Three times three p233-88
The Encantadas. Melville, H.
In Melville, H. Shorter novels of Herman Melville p157-225
The enchanted cup. Roberts, D. J.
The enchanted voyage. Nathan, R.
The enchanted wanderer. Leskov, N.
In Leskov, N. Selected tales p51-211
The encounter. Troyat, H.
Encounters with aliens. Earley, G. W. ed.
End of a mission. Böll, H.
The end of my life. Bourjaily, V.
The end of the affair. Greene, G.
The end of the battle. Waugh, E.
End of the chapter. Galsworthy, J.
End of the game, and other stories. Cortázar, J.
The end of the road. Barth, J.
The end of the tether. Conrad, J.
In Conrad, J. Tales of land and sea p505-610
In Conrad, J. Youth, and two other stories

END OF THE WORLD
Jackson, S. The sundial
Rand, A. Atlas shrugged
Shute, N. On the beach
Wyndham, J. The day of the triffids
Enderby. Burgess, A.
Endless night. Christie, A.
ENDOWMENTS
Karp, D. All honorable men
Vonnegut, K. God bless you, Mr Rosewater
Wollaston, N. Pharaoh's chicken
The enemy camp. Weidman, J.
Enemy in the house. Eberhart, M. G.
Enfants terrible. See Cocteau, J. The holy terrors
ENGAGEMENTS. See Betrothals
ENGINEERING. See Engineers
ENGINEERS
Ambler, E. State of siege
In Ambler, E. The intriguers p169-290
Becker, S. The outcasts
Bojer, J. The great hunger
Deal, B. Dunbar's Cove
De Camp, L. S. The arrows of Hercules
Dudintsev, V. Not by bread alone
Hersey, J. A single pebble
Household, G. The courtesy of death
Markandaya, K. The coffer dams
Shute, N. Trustee from the toolroom
Stevenson, D. E. Gerald and Elizabeth
Vonnegut, K. Player piano
ENGINEERS, MARINE
Gilpatric, G. The best of Glencannon
Gilpatric, G. The Glencannon omnibus
McFee, W. The harbourmaster
ENGLAND
Christopher, J. The ragged edge
Davies, L. P. The artificial man
Saki. The short stories of Saki
Spark, M. The go-away bird, and other stories
Woolf, V. Orlando

To 55 B.C.
Treece, H. The golden strangers

Roman period, 55 B.C.-449 A.D.
Duggan, A. Conscience of the king
Graves, R. Claudius, the god and his wife Messalina
Shipway, G. The Imperial Governor
Slaughter, F. G. The thorn of Arimathea
Taylor, A. The gods are not mocked
Treece, H. The dark island
Treece, H. Red queen, white queen

449 to 1066
Bryher. The fourteenth of October
Bryher. Ruan
Duggan, A. Conscience of the king
Duggan, A. The cunning of the dove
Muntz, H. The golden warrior
Nathan, R. The fair
Seton, A. Avalon
Sutcliff, R. Sword at sunset
Twain, M. A Connecticut Yankee in King Arthur's court

11th century
Bryher. This January tale
Heyer, G. The Conqueror

12th century
Barnes, M. C. The passionate brood
Costain, T. B. Below the salt
Duggan, A. My life for my sheep
Haycraft, M. C. My lord brother the Lion Heart
Lofts, N. The lute player
Mydans, S. Thomas

13th century
Costain, T. B. The black rose
White, T. H. The ill-made knight
White, T. H. The once and future king
White, T. H. The sword in the stone
White, T. H. The witch in the wood

14th century
Anderson, P. The high crusade
Barnes, M. C. Isabel the Fair
Druon, M. The Lily and the Lion
Druon, M. The She-Wolf of France
Haycraft, M. C. The Lady Royal
Lofts, N. The town house
Seton, A. Katherine
Simon, E. The golden hand
Warner, S. T. The corner that held them

ENGLAND—20th century—_Continued_
Caldwell, T. Grandmother and the priests
Campbell, M. Lord dismiss us
Cary, J. First trilogy
Cary, J. Herself surprised
Cary, J. Not honour more
Charteris, H. The coat
Clifford, F. All men are lonely now
Compton-Burnett, I. Mother and son
Cost, M. Jubilee of a ghost
Cronin, A. J. Beyond this place
Cronin, A. J. A thing of beauty
Davies, L. P. The white room
Deeping, W. Sorrell and son
Delderfield, R. F. The green gauntlet
Delderfield, R. F. A horseman riding by
Dick, R. A. The ghost and Mrs Muir
Dickens, M. The landlord's daughter
Dickinson, P. The old English peep show
Durrell, G. Rosy is my relative
Ford, F. M. The last post
  _In_ Ford, F. M. Parade's end p677-836
Forster, E. M. A room with a view
Forster, M. Miss Owen-Owen
Forster, M. The travels of Maudie Tipstaff
Fowles, J. The collector
Francis, D. Forfeit
Francis, D. Nerve
Francis, D. Three to show
Frankau, P. Colonel Blessington
Fremlin, C. Possession
Galsworthy, J. End of the chapter
Garve, A. The long short cut
Gloag, J. A sentence of life
Godden, R. In this house of Brede
Godden, R. Take three tenses
Hilton, J. So well remembered
Holland, I. Cecily
Household, G. The courtesy of death
Howard, E. J. Something in disguise
Hughes, R. The fox in the attic
Huxley, A. Antic hay
Huxley, A. Antic hay, and The Gioconda smile
Kops, B. The dissent of Dominick Shapiro
Le Carré, J. A murder of quality
  _In_ Le Carré, J. The incongruous spy v2
Lehmann, R. Dusty answer
Lehmann, R. Invitation to the waltz
Lessing, D. The golden notebook
Mortimer, P. The pumpkin eater
Murdoch, I. The bell
Murdoch, I. An unofficial rose
Powell, A. The acceptance world
  _In_ Powell, A. A dance to the music of time v3
Powell, A. A buyer's market
  _In_ Powell, A. A dance to the music of time v2
Powell, A. A dance to the music of time
Powell, A. A dance to the music of time: second movement
Powell, A. A question of upbringing
  _In_ Powell, A. A dance to the music of time v1
Powell, A. The soldier's art
Powell, A. The valley of bones
Powell, A. What's become of Waring
Priestley, J. B. The image men
Priestley, J. B. It's an old country
Priestley, J. B. Lost Empires
Read, Miss. Fresh from the country
Renault, M. The charioteer
Rendell, R. The secret house of death
Sharp, M. In pious memory
Shute, N. No highway
Sillitoe, A. Guzman, go home, and other stories
Sillitoe, A. The loneliness of the long-distance runner
Sillitoe, A. The ragman's daughter, and other stories
Smith, D. I capture the castle
Snow, C. P. Corridors of power
Snow, C. P. Last things
Snow, C. P. The new men
Snow, C. P. Time of hope
Spark, M. The comforters
  _In_ Spark, M. A Muriel Spark trio: The comforters; The ballad of Peckham Rye [and] Memento mori p13-228
Spark, M. Memento mori
Spark, M. Memento mori, and The ballad of Peckham Rye
Spring, H. The houses in between
Spring, H. My son, my son!
Troy, K. Roseheath
Walpole, H. Vanessa
Waterhouse, K. Everything must go
Waugh, E. Brideshead revisited
Waugh, E. Decline and fall
Wells, H. G. Mr Britling sees it through

Wells, H. G. Tono-Bungay
Whitney, P. A. Hunter's green
Wilson, A. Anglo-Saxon attitudes
Wilson, A. Late call
Wodehouse, P. G. The code of the Woosters
Wodehouse, P. G. Fish preferred
Wodehouse, P. G. The inimitable Jeeves
Wodehouse, P. G. Uncle Fred in the springtime
Woods, S. Past praying for
Woolf, V. Jacob's room
Woolf, V. The years

Aristocracy
See Aristocracy—England

Barsetshire
See England, Provincial and rural—Barsetshire

Bath
See England, Provincial and rural—Bath

Bristol
Andrew, P. A new creature
Steen, M. The sun is my undoing
Steen, M. Twilight on the Floods

Buckinghamshire
See England, Provincial and rural—Buckinghamshire

Cheshire
See England, Provincial and rural—Cheshire

Church and state
See Church and state—England

Civil War
See England—17th century

Coal mines and mining
See Coal mines and mining—England

College life
See College life—England

Cornwall
See England, Provincial and rural—Cornwall

Courts
See Courts—England

Courts and courtiers
See Courts and courtiers—England

Cumberland
See England, Provincial and rural—Cumberland

Derbyshire
See England, Provincial and rural—Derbyshire

Devon
See England, Provincial and rural—Devon

Devonshire
See England, Provincial and rural—Devonshire

Dorset
See England, Provincial and rural—Dorset

East Anglia
See England, Provincial and rural—East Anglia

Essex
See England, Provincial and rural—Essex

Exeter
See England, Provincial and rural—Exeter

Farm life
See Farm life—England

Hampshire
See England, Provincial and rural—Hampshire

Kent
See England, Provincial and rural—Kent

Kings and rulers
Ford, F. M. The fifth queen
Shute, N. In the wet

Labor and laboring classes
See Labor and laboring classes—England

Lancashire
See England, Provincial and rural—Lancashire

ENGLAND—*Continued*

Oxfordshire
See England, Provincial and rural—Oxfordshire

Politics
See Politics—England

Prisons
See Prisons—England

School life
See School life—England

Secret service
See Secret service—England

Shropshire
See England, Provincial and rural—Shropshire

Somerset
See England, Provincial and rural—Somerset

Somersetshire
See England, Provincial and rural—Somersetshire

Staffordshire
See England, Provincial and rural—Staffordshire

Suffolk
See England, Provincial and rural—Suffolk

Surrey
See England, Provincial and rural—Surrey

Sussex
See England, Provincial and rural—Sussex

Warwickshire
See England, Provincial and rural—Warwickshire

Wiltshire
See England, Provincial and rural—Wiltshire

Yorkshire
See England, Provincial and rural—Yorkshire

ENGLAND, PROVINCIAL AND RURAL
Titles listed here are located in rural parts of England, but of undetermined locality

Allingham, M. Cargo of eagles
Amis, K. The Anti-Death League
Andrew, P. A new creature
Austen, J. Emma
Austen, J. Pride and prejudice
Austen, J. Sense and sensibility
Bagnold, E. National Velvet
  In Costain, T. B. ed. Stories to remember v2 p339-504
Bates, H. E. The darling buds of May
Bawden, N. A little love, a little learning
Berckman, E. The heir of Starvelings
Butler, S. The way of all flesh
Cadell, E. The lark shall sing
Cadell, E. Six impossible things
Calder-Marshall, A. The Scarlet boy
Cary, J. Charley is my darling
Cary, J. Herself surprised
Cary, J. To be a pilgrim
Christie, K. Child's play
Chute, B. J. Greenwillow
Compton-Burnett, I. Darkness and day
Davies, L. P. The Lampton dreamers
Davies, L. P. Stranger to town
De La Mare, C. Memoirs of a midget
Dickens, C. David Copperfield
Dickens, C. Nicholas Nickleby
Eden, D. Ravenscroft
Eliot, G. Adam Bede
Eliot, G. The mill on the Floss
Fletcher, I. Roanoke hundred
Forster, E. M. Howards End
Frankau, P. Sing for your supper
Godden, J. A winter's tale
Golding, W. The pyramid
Goldsmith, O. The Vicar of Wakefield
Goudge, E. A city of bells
Goudge, E. The Dean's watch
Goudge, E. The white witch
Hardy, T. The woodlanders
Heyer, G. The Black Moth
Heyer, G. The Corinthian
Heyer, G. Cousin Kate
Household, G. Run from the hangman
  In The Saturday Evening Post. Danger p296-368
Hutchinson, R. C. The stepmother

Lawrence, D. H. Sons and lovers
Lawrence, D. H. The white peacock
Lindop, A. E. I start counting
Meredith, G. The egoist
Moore, J. The waters under the earth
Murdoch, I. The Italian girl
Murdoch, I. The unicorn
Orwell, G. A clergyman's daughter
Orwell, G. Coming up for air
Pearson, D. The marigold field
Peters, E. The Camelot caper
Priestley, J. B. The good companions
Pritchett, V. S. The key to my heart
Read, Miss. The Fairacre Festival
Read, Miss. The Howards of Caxley
Read, Miss. The market square
Read, Miss. Miss Clare remembers
Read, Miss. Over the gate
Read, Miss. Thrush Green
Read, Miss. Village Christmas
Read, Miss. Winter in Thrush Green
Richardson, H. H. The way home
  In Richardson, H. H. The fortunes of Richard Mahony v2
Sackville-West, V. The Edwardians
Scott, Sir W. Kenilworth
Sharp, M. Something light
Smith, D. It ends with revelations
Snow, C. P. The sleep of reason
Snow, C. P. Strangers and brothers
Stevenson, D. E. Miss Buncle
Struther, J. Mrs Miniver
Taylor, E. In a summer season
Taylor, E. The wedding group
Thane, E. Tryst
Thirkell, A. The Brandons
Trollope, A. The American senator
Trollope, A. Orley Farm
Walpole, H. The cathedral
Warner, S. T. Lolly Willowes
  In Warner, S. T. Lolly Willowes, and Mr Fortune's maggot p3-158
White, T. H. Mistress Masham's repose
Wodehouse, P. G. How right you are, Jeeves
Wodehouse, P. G. Very good, Jeeves
Woolf, V. Between the acts

Barsetshire
Golding, W. The spire

Bath
Austen, J. Persuasion
Dickens, C. The posthumous papers of the Pickwick Club
Heyer, G. Bath tangle
Heyer, G. Black sheep
Heyer, G. The foundling
Tarkington, B. Monsieur Beaucaire

Buckinghamshire
Milne, A. A. Mr Pim

Cheshire
Gaskell, E. C. Cranford
Stranger, J. Born to trouble

Cornwall
Bryher. Ruan
Du Maurier, D. Frenchman's Creek
Du Maurier, D. The house on the strand
Du Maurier, D. Jamaica Inn
Du Maurier, D. The King's general
Du Maurier, D. My cousin Rachel
Du Maurier, D. Rebecca
Du Maurier, D. Three romantic novels of Cornwall: Rebecca, Frenchman's Creek and Jamaica Inn
Godden, R. China Court
Graham, W. The grove of eagles
Hardy, T. A pair of blue eyes
Holt, V. Bride of Pendorric
Holt, V. The legend of the Seventh Virgin
Holt, V. Menfreya in the morning
Holt, V. Mistress of Mellyn
Quiller-Couch, A. Castle Dor
Roberts, D. J. The enchanted cup
Tattersall, J. Lyonesse Abbey
Walpole, H. Fortitude

Cumberland
Walpole, H. The fortress
Walpole, H. Judith Paris
Walpole, H. Rogue Herries
Walpole, H. Vanessa

Derbyshire
Benson, R. H. Come rack! Come rope!
Heyer, G. The toll-gate
Lawrence, D. H. Lady Chatterley's lover

ENGLISH IN CANADA
MacLennan, H. Return of the sphinx
MacLennan, H. Two solitudes

ENGLISH IN CHINA
Bridge, A. Peking picnic
Harris, J. The jade wind

ENGLISH IN CORFU
Stewart, M. This rough magic

ENGLISH IN CRETE
Stewart, M. The moon-spinners

ENGLISH IN DENMARK
Kelly, M. Assault

ENGLISH IN EGYPT
Aldridge, J. The last exile
Durrell, L. Mountolive
Newby, P. H. Something to answer for

ENGLISH IN EUROPE
Ambler, E. Judgment on Deltchev
In Ambler, E. The intriguers p433-592
MacInnes, H. Above suspicion

ENGLISH IN FRANCE
Andrézel, P. The angelic avengers
Bates, H. E. A breath of French air
Du Maurier, D. The scapegoat
Ellis, A. E. The rack
Gaie, J. The family man
Godden, R. The greengage summer
Haycraft, M. C. The Lady Royal
Hemingway, E. The sun also rises
Holt, V. The king of the castle
Jameson, S. The blind heart
Mitford, N. The blessing
Orczy, Baroness. Adventures of the Scarlet
    Pimpernel
Orczy, Baroness. The elusive Pimpernel
Orczy, Baroness. The Scarlet Pimpernel
Sharp, M. The nutmeg tree
Shellabarger, S. The King's cavalier
Stewart, M. Nine coaches waiting

ENGLISH IN GERMANY
Anthony, E. The legend
Clifford, F. The naked runner
Coles, M. Exploits of Tommy Hambledon
Coles, M. A toast to tomorrow
Hall, A. The Quiller memorandum
Hughes, R. The fox in the attic
Isherwood, C. The last of Mr Norris
In Isherwood, C. The Berlin stories v 1
Le Carré, J. A small town in Germany
Le Carré, J. The spy who came in from the
    cold
MacLean, A. Where eagles dare

ENGLISH IN GREECE
Firbank, R. Inclinations
In Firbank, R. The complete Ronald Fir-
    bank p223-317
Fowles, J. The magus
Osborne, H. The yellow gold of Tiryns
Tute, W. A matter of diplomacy

ENGLISH IN HONGKONG
Mason, R. The world of Suzie Wong

ENGLISH IN HUNGARY
Bridge, A. The tightening string

ENGLISH IN INDIA
Cleeve, R. The last, long journey
Forster, E. M. A passage to India
Fraser, G. M. Flashman
Godden, R. Black Narcissus
Godden, R. Breakfast with the Nikolides
Godden, R. The river
Markandaya, K. The coffer dams
Markandaya, K. Possession
Markandaya, K. Some inner fury
Masters, J. Bhowani Junction
Masters, J. Far, far the mountain peak
Masters, J. Nightrunners of Bengal
Masters, J. To the coral strand
Menen, A. The prevalence of witches
Scott, P. The day of the scorpion
Scott, P. The jewel in the crown
Sherman, D. R. Old Mali and the boy
Wollaston, N. Pharaoh's chicken

ENGLISH IN INDONESIA
Ambler, E. State of siege
In Ambler, E. The intriguers p169-290
Van der Post, L. The sword and the doll
In Van der Post, L. The seed and the sow-
    er p191-256

ENGLISH IN IRELAND
Ballinger, W. A. The men that God made mad
Green, H. Loving
Tracy, H. The straight and narrow path

ENGLISH IN ISLANDS OF THE PACIFIC
Trevor, E. The shoot

ENGLISH IN ISRAEL
Davidson, L. The Menorah men
Spark, M. The Mandelbaum Gate

ENGLISH IN ITALY
Forster, E. M. A room with a view
Godden, R. The battle of the Villa Fiorita
Macleod, A. City of light
Rees, B. Mrs Wall, Mrs Wall
In Rees, B. Try another country p55-120
Spark, M. The public image
West, M. L. The devil's advocate

ENGLISH IN JAPAN
Fleming, I. You only live twice

ENGLISH IN LATIN AMERICA
Marshall, B. Father Hilary's holiday

ENGLISH IN LEBANON
Stewart, M. The Gabriel hounds

ENGLISH IN MEXICO
Bagley, D. The Vivero letter
Lowry, M. Under the volcano

ENGLISH IN MOROCCO
Bawden, N. A woman of my age

ENGLISH IN NEW ZEALAND
Ashton-Warner, S. Greenstone
Frame, J. Yellow flowers in the antipodean
    room

ENGLISH IN NIGERIA
Achebe, C. Arrow of God
Cary, J. The African witch
Cary, J. Mister Johnson

ENGLISH IN PALESTINE
Viertel, J. The last temptation
Wiesel, E. Dawn

ENGLISH IN PORTUGAL
Bridge, A. The Portuguese escape

ENGLISH IN RHODES
Whitney, P. A. Seven tears for Apollo

ENGLISH IN RUSSIA
Aldridge, J. A captive in the land
Burgess, A. Honey for the bears
Burgess, A. Tremor of intent
Garve, A. The ashes of Loda
Lambert, D. Angels in the snow

ENGLISH IN SICILY
Clifford, F. Another way of dying

ENGLISH IN SPAIN
Godden, J. In the sun
Hemingway, E. The sun also rises
Shaw, R. A card from Morocco

ENGLISH IN SWEDEN
Eden, D. Waiting for Willa

ENGLISH IN SWITZERLAND
Macleod, A. City of light

ENGLISH IN THAILAND
Boulle, P. The bridge over the River Kwai

ENGLISH IN THE DUTCH EAST INDIES
Lofts, N. Scent of cloves

ENGLISH IN THE NEAR EAST
Bagley, D. The spoilers
Innes, H. The doomed oasis

ENGLISH IN THE UNITED STATES
Balchin, N. Kings of infinite space
Bristow, G. Celia Garth
Chase, M. E. The lovely ambition
Fletcher, I. Roanoke hundred
Fletcher, I. The wind in the forest
Johnson, P. H. Night and silence, who is
    here?
Michaels, B. Prince of darkness
Raddall, T. H. The Governor's lady
Twain, M. The American claimant
In Twain, M. The complete novels of Mark
    Twain v2 p263-416
Waugh, E. The loved one
Wyckoff, N. E. The Braintree Mission

ENGLISH IN THE WEST INDIES
Waugh, A. Island in the sun

ENGLISH IN TIBET
Davidson, L. The rose of Tibet

ENGLISH IN TURKEY
Bridge, A. The dark moment
Macaulay, R. The towers of Trebizond

ENGLISH IN URUGUAY
Hudson, H. W. The purple land

ENGLISH IN VIETNAM
Greene, G. The quiet American

ENGLISH IN YUGOSLAVIA
Bridge, A. Illyrian spring
Durrell, L. White eagles over Serbia
MacLean, A. Force 10 from Navarone

ENOCH ARDEN STORIES
Bristow, G. Tomorrow is forever

TITLE AND SUBJECT INDEX
EIGHTH EDITION

507

EUROPE—20th century—*Continued*
Sinclair, U. The return of Lanny Budd
Sinclair, U. Wide is the gate
Sinclair, U. A world to win
Sinclair, U. World's end
Weiss, P. Exile
West, R. The birds fall down
Wharton, E. The gods arrive
Zilahy, L. The Dukays

Aristocracy
See Aristocracy—Europe

Communism
See Communism—Europe

Politics
See Politics—Europe

EUROPE, CENTRAL
Costain, T. B. The darkness and the dawn

EUROPE, EASTERN

13th century
Holland, C. Until the sun falls

EUROPEAN WAR, 1914-1918
Bromfield, L. The green bay tree
  In Bromfield, L. Bromfield galaxy: The green bay tree, Early autumn, A good woman p5-216
Buchan, J. Greenmantle
Canfield, D. The deepening stream
Cather, W. One of ours
Ford, F. M. The last post
  In Ford, F. M. Parade's end p677-836
Ford, F. M. A man could stand up
  In Ford, F. M. Parade's end p503-674
Ford, F. M. Parade's end
Hasek, J. The good soldier: Schweik
March, W. Company K
  In March, W. A William March omnibus p 1-132
Mason, F. ed. American men at arms
Remarque, E. M. The road back
Sholokhov, M. And quiet flows the Don
Sholokhov, M. The silent Don
Sinclair, U. World's end
Thane, E. Kissing kin

Aerial operations
Gann, E. K. In the company of eagles
Nordhoff, C. Falcons of France
Whitehouse, A. Playboy squadron

Africa
Forester, C. S. The African Queen
Oppenheim, E. P. The great impersonation

England
Hilton, J. Random harvest
Wells, H. G. Mr Britling sees it through

France
Barbusse, H. Under fire
Blasco-Ibáñez, V. The four horsemen of the Apocalypse
Celine, L. F. Journey to the end of the night
Cocteau, J. The imposter
Colette. Mitsou
  In Colette. Six novels p339-410
Faulkner, W. A fable
Ford, F. M. No more parades
  In Ford, F. M. Parade's end p291-500
Hunter, E. Sons
Keyes, F. P. Came a cavalier
Remarque, E. M. All quiet on the western front
Romains, J. Verdun
Troyat, H. Amelie and Pierre

Germany
Zweig, A. The case of Sergeant Grischa
Zweig, A. Education before Verdun
Zweig, A. Young woman of 1914

Ireland
Macken, W. The scorching wind

Italy
Hemingway, E. A farewell to arms

Naval operations
Jennings, J. The raider
Reeman, D. H.M.S. Saracen

Naval operations—Submarine
Blasco Ibáñez, V. Mare nostrum

Near East
Werfel, F. The forty days of Musa Dagh

Netherlands
Morgan, C. The fountain

Poland
Singer, I. J. Steel and iron

Prisoners and prisons
Cummings, E. E. The enormous room

Russia
Singer, I. J. Steel and iron

Secret service
Coles, M. Drink to yesterday
Maugham, W. S. Ashenden

Turkey
Bridge, A. The dark moment

United States
Bristow, G. This side of glory
Dos Passos, J. Manhattan transfer
Dos Passos, J. 1919
Dos Passos, J. Three soldiers

EUROPEAN WAR, 1939-1945. See World War, 1939-1945

The Europeans. James, H.
  In James, H. The American novels and stories of Henry James p37-161

EUROPEANS IN INDIA
Bromfield, L. The rains came
Jhabvala, R. P. A stronger climate

The Eustace diamonds. Trollope, A.

EUTHANASIA
Boulle, P. The executioner

Eva. Levin, M.

Eva Trout. Bowen, E.

EVANGELISTS
Lewis, S. Elmer Gantry
Vidal, G. Messiah

  See also Missionaries

The eve of Rumoko, Silverberg, R.
  In Three for tomorrow p81-152

Evelina. Burney, F.

Ever after. Thane, E.

Everything must go. Waterhouse, K.

Everything that rises must converge. O'Connor, F.

Everything to live for. Horgan, P.

Evidence of things seen. Daly, E.
  In Daly, E. An Elizabeth Daly Mystery omnibus v2

EVIL. See Good and evil

Except for me and thee. West, J.

Except the Lord. Cary, J.

EXCHANGE OF PERSONALITIES. See Impersonations

EX-CONVICTS
Dark, E. The timeless land
Grubb, D. Fools' parade
Heinlein, R. A. The moon is a harsh mistress
The executioner. Boulle, P.

EXECUTIONERS. See Executions and executioners

The executioners. Creasey, J.

EXECUTIONS AND EXECUTIONERS
Becker, S. When the War is over
Boulle, P. The executioner

Executive suite. Hawley, C.

EXECUTIVES
Cozzens, J. G. Morning, noon, and night
Hawley, C. The hurricane years
White, T. H. The view from the fortieth floor
Exercise Hoodwink. Procter, M.

EXETER. See England, Provincial and rural—Exeter

EX-HUSBANDS. See Divorce

Exile. Weiss, P.

Exile and the kingdom. Camus, A.
  also in Camus, A. The fall & Exile and the kingdom p149-361

EXILES
Costain, T. B. The last love
Del Castillo, M. Child of our time
Dumitriu, P. The extreme Occident
Gellhorn, M. The lowest trees have tops
Goytisolo, J. Marks of identity
Horia, V. God was born in exile
Montherlant, H. de. Chaos and night
  See also Refugees

FAMILY CHRONICLES—*Continued*
Bristow, G. This side of glory
Bromfield, L. The green bay tree
Buck, P. S. The house of earth: The good earth; Sons; A house divided
Buck, P. S. The living reed
Butler, S. The way of all flesh
Caldwell, T. Dynasty of death
Caldwell, T. The eagles gather
Caldwell, T. The final hour
Chase, M. E. Silas Crockett
Chase, M. E. Windswept
Cheever, J. The Wapshot chronicle
Cheever, J. The Wapshot scandal
Condon, R. Mile high
Costain, T. B. The tontine
Dane, C. Broome stages
Davenport, M. The valley of decision
Davis, P. The seasons of heroes
De La Roche, M. The building of Jalna
De La Roche, M. Centenary at Jalna
De La Roche, M. Finch's fortune
De La Roche, M. Jalna
De La Roche, M. Mary Wakefield
De La Roche, M. The master of Jalna
De La Roche, M. Morning at Jalna
De La Roche, M. Renny's daughter
De La Roche, M. Return to Jalna
De La Roche, M. Variable winds at Jalna
De La Roche, M. Wakefield's course
De La Roche, M. Whiteoak brothers: Jalna—1923
De La Roche, M. Whiteoak harvest
De La Roche, M. Whiteoak heritage
De La Roche, M. Whiteoaks of Jalna
De La Roche, M. Young Renny (Jalna-1906)
Delderfield, R. F. The green gauntlet
Delderfield, R. F. A horseman riding by
Dermoût, M. The ten thousand things
Dos Passos, J. District of Columbia
Du Maurier, D. Hungry hill
Dumitriu, P. Family jewels
Dykeman, W. The far family
Farrell, J. T. A world I never made
Faulkner, W. Sartoris
Ferber, E. Ice Palace
Ferber, E. Show boat
Field, R. Time out of mind
Galsworthy, J. End of the chapter
Galsworthy, J. The Forsyte saga
Galsworthy, J. The man of property
Galsworthy, J. A modern comedy
Gerson, N. B. The anthem
Glasgow, E. Vein of iron
Godden, R. China Court
Godden, R. Take three tenses
Gulbranssen, T. Beyond sing the woods
Gulbranssen, T. The wind from the mountains
Hamsun, K. Growth of the soil
Hawthorne, N. The House of the Seven Gables
Hergesheimer, J. The three black Pennys
Humphrey, W. The Ordways
Hunter, E. Sons
Ikor, R. The sons of Avrom
Jacobson, D. The beginners
Keyes, F. P. Crescent carnival
Keyes, F. P. Steamboat Gothic
Lawrence, D. H. The rainbow
Lehmann, R. The ballad and the source
Lewisohn, L. The island within
Lofts, N. Bless this house
Lofts, N. The house at Old Vine
Lofts, N. The town house
Mann, T. Buddenbrooks
Marquand, J. P. The late George Apley
Marquand, J. P. Wickford Point
Moore, R. Speak to the winds
Nabokov, V. Ada
O'Faolain, S. A nest of simple folk
O'Hara, J. Ten North Frederick
Oldenbourg, Z. The cornerstone
Page, E. The tree of liberty
Powell, R. The Philadelphian
Rawlings, M. K. The sojourner
Rolland, R. Jean-Christophe
Sarton, M. The birth of a grandfather
Schoonover, L. Key of gold
Scott, Sir W. The bride of Lammermoor
Seton, A. The Hearth and Eagle
Sharp, M. Britannia Mews
Sharp, M. Rosa
Shellabarger, S. Tolbecken
Singer, I. J. The family Carnovsky
Spring, H. The houses in between
Steen, M. Twilight on the Floods
Stern, G. B. The matriarch chronicles
Stern, R. M. Brood of eagles
Stevenson, R. L. The master of Ballantrae

Thackeray, W. M. The Newcomes
Thane, E. This was tomorrow
Troyat, H. Amelie and Pierre
Troyat, H. Amelie in love
Troyat, H. Elizabeth
Troyat, H. The encounter
Turnbull, A. S. The rolling years
Undset, S. Kristin Lavransdatter
Undset, S. The master of Hestviken
Vasquez, R. Chicano
Verissimo, D. Time and the wind
Walpole, H. The fortress
Walpole, H. Judith Paris
Walpole, H. Vanessa
Wescott, G. The grandmothers
Wilder, R. Wind from the Carolinas
Williams, T. Whipple's castle
Wilson, A. No laughing matter
Woolf, V. The years
Zilahy, L. The Dukays
  See also Family life

The family circle. Maurois, A.

FAMILY CURSES. See Curses, Family

Family happiness. Tolstoy, L.
  In Tolstoy, L. Short novels v 1 p127-213

Family jewels. Dumitriu, P.

FAMILY LIFE
Abaunza, V. Sundays from two to six
Agee, J. A death in the family
Aldrich, B. S. A lantern in her hand
Aldrich, B. S. Spring came on forever
Aldrich, B. S. A white bird flying
Amado, J. The violent land
Ames, F. H. That Callahan spunk!
Anderson, S. Tar: a midwest childhood
Angoff, C. Between day and dark
Angoff, C. The bitter spring
Angoff, C. In the morning light
Angoff, C. Journey to the dawn
Angoff, C. Summer storm
Angoff, C. The sun at noon
Angoff, C. Winter twilight
Arnow, H. Hunter's horn
Arnow, H. The weedkiller's daughter
Asch, S. East River
Asch, S. The mother
Asch, S. Three cities
Ashton-Warner, S. Greenstone
Auchincloss, L. The house of five talents
Auchincloss, L. Portrait in brownstone
Auchincloss, L. A world of profit
Austen, J. Emma
Austen, J. Mansfield Park
Austen, J. Northanger Abbey
Austen, J. Sense and sensibility
Austen, J. The Watsons
Azuela, M. The trials of a respectable family
  In Azuela, M. Two novels of the Mexican Revolution: The trials of a respectable family, and The underdogs p 1-59
Bagnold, E. National Velvet
  In Costain, T. B. ed. Stories to remember v2 p339-504
Baldwin, J. Go tell it on the mountain
Balzac, H. de. Cousin Bette
Barnes, M. A. Years of grace
Barry, J. A shadow of eagles
Basso, H. The Light Infantry Ball
Basso, H. The view from Pompey' Head
Bates, H. E. A breath of French air
Bates, H. E. The darling buds of May
Bawden, N. A little love, a little learning
Bawden, N. Tortoise by candlelight
Beauvoir, S. de. Les belles images
Bellow, S. Henderson the rain king
Bellow, S. Mr Sammler's planet
Bennett, A. The old wives' tale
Berlin, E. The best of families
Bjorn, T. F. Dear papa
Bjorn, T. F. Papa's daughter
Bjorn, T. F. Papa's wife
Bjorn, T. F. Papa's wife, Papa's daughter, Mama's way
Blais, M. C. A season in the life of Emmanuel
Bottome, P. The mortal storm
Bowen, E. The death of the heart
Bradbury, R. Dandelion wine
Bradford, R. Red sky at morning
Braine, J. Life at the top
Bristow, G. Deep summer
Bristow, G. Tomorrow is forever
Bromfield, L. Early autumn
  In Bromfield, L. Bromfield galaxy: The green bay tree, Early autumn, A good woman p217-403
Bromfield, L. Mrs Parkington
Buck, P. S. Dragon seed
Buck, P. S. God's men

FAMILY LIFE—*Continued*

Oates, J. C. Expensive people
Oates, J. C. Them
O'Connor, E. All in the family
O'Connor, E. The edge of sadness
O'Flaherty, L. Famine
Ogilvie, E. Waters on a starry night
O'Hara, J. The Lockwood concern
Pasinetti, P. M. Venetian red
Paton, A. Too late the phalarope
Plagemann, B. The best is yet to be
Plagemann, B. Father to the man
Plagemann, B. A world of difference
Popkin, Z. Herman had two daughters
Powell, R. Pioneer, go home!
Price, R. A generous man
Priestley, J. B. Angel Pavement
Puzo, M. The fortunate pilgrim
Rama Rau. S. Remember the house
Rawlings, M. K. The sojourner
Read, Miss. The Howards of Caxley
Richter, C. The fields
Richter, C. The grandfathers
Richter, C. The town
Richter, C. The trees
Rolvaag, O. E. Giants in the earth
Rolvaag, O. E. Peder Victorious
Romains, J. The proud, and The meek
Rosten, N. Under the boardwalk
Roth, H. Call it sleep
Roy, G. Street of riches
Roy, G. The tin flute
Rubens, B. Chosen people
Salinger, J. D. Franny and Zooey
Salinger, J. D. Raise high the roof beam,
   carpenters, and Seymour: an introduction
Saroyan, W. The human comedy
Simenon, G. The confessional
Simenon, G. The little saint
Singer, I. B. The estate
Singer, I. B. The family Moskat
Singer, I. B. The manor
Singer, I. J. The family Carnovsky
Smith, B. Maggie-Now
Smith, B. A tree grows in Brooklyn
Smith, D. I capture the castle
Smith, L. The last day the dogbushes
   bloomed
Snow, C. P. The conscience of the rich
Snow, C. P. Last things
Snow, C. P. Time of hope
Stead, C. The man who loved children
Stegner, W. The Big Rock Candy Mountain
Steinbeck, J. East of Eden
Steinbeck, J. The grapes of wrath
Steinbeck, J. The pearl
Stern, G. B. A deputy was king
   In Stern, G. B. The matriarch chronicles v2
Stern, G. B. Mosaic
   In Stern, G. B. The matriarch chronicles v3
Stern, G. B. Shining and free
   In Stern, G. B. The matriarch chronicles v4
Stone, I. Those who love
Street, J. Tap roots
Streeter, E. Mr Hobbs' vacation
Struther, J. Mrs Miniver
Stuart, J. Taps for Private Tussie
Styron, W. Lie down in darkness
Tanizaki, J. The Makioka sisters
Tarkington, B. Alice Adams
Tarkington, B. The magnificent Ambersons
Tarkington, B. Seventeen
Taylor, E. In a summer season
Taylor, E. The wedding group
Telfer, D. The night of the comet
Thackeray, W. M. The Virginians
Thane, E. Ever after
Thane, E. Homing
Thane, E. Kissing kin
Thane, E. The light heart
Thane, E. Yankee stranger
Thirkell, A. The Brandons
Trollope, A. Orley Farm
Troyat, H. The baroness
Troyat, H. The red and the white
Troyat, H. Strangers on earth
Turnbull, A. S. The gown of glory
Turnbull, A. S. The rolling years
Twain, M. The adventures of Huckleberry
   Finn
Twain, M. The adventures of Tom Sawyer
Updike, J. Of the farm
Van Peebles, M. A bear for the FBI
Verga, G. The house by the medlar tree
Vesaas, T. The great cycle
Wallant, E. L. The human season
Walpole, H. Rogue Herries
Warner, S. T. Lolly Willowes
   In Warner, S. T. Lolly Willowes, and Mr
   Fortune's maggot p3-158

Weidman, J. I can get it for you wholesale
Weingarten, V. Mrs Beneker
Welty, E. Delta wedding
Wescott, G. Apartment in Athens
West, J. Cress Delahanty
West, J. Except for me and thee
West, J. The friendly persuasion
West, R. The fountain overflows
White, N. G. The thorn tree
White, P. The tree of man
White, R. Elephant Hill
Whitney, P. A. Skye Cameron
Whitney, P. A. The trembling hill
Wibberley, L. The hands of Cormac Joyce
Wilder, T. The eighth day
Williams, B. A. House divided
Williams, T. Whipple's castle
Williams, V. Walk Egypt
Wilson, A. Late call
Wilson, A. No laughing matter
Wolfe, T. Look homeward, angel
Wolff, R. A crack in the sidewalk
Woolf, V. To the lighthouse
Wouk, H. Marjorie Morningstar
Wylie, P. Tomorrow!
Young, S. So red the rose
   See also Brothers; Brothers and sisters;
   Family chronicles; Fathers and daughters;
   Fathers and sons; Marriage problems;
   Mothers and daughters; Mothers and sons;
   Parent and child; Sisters

The family man. Gale, J.

The family Moskat. Singer, I. B.

The family on vendetta street. Longo, L.

Famine. O'Flaherty, L.

FAMINES

Buck, P. S. The good earth
Macken, W. The silent people
O'Flaherty, L. Famine

Famous Chinese short stories. Lin, Yutang, ed.

Famous dog stories. Cooper, P. ed.

Famous ghost stories. Cerf, B. A. ed.

Famous monster tales. Davenport, B. comp.

Famous science fiction stories. Healy, R. J. ed.

Famous tales of Sherlock Holmes. Doyle, Sir
A C.

Fancies and goodnights. Collier, J.

Fanshawe. Hawthorne, N.
   In Hawthorne, N. The complete novels and
   selected tales of Nathaniel Hawthorne
   p3-80

FANTASIES

Asimov, I. Fantastic voyage
Asturias, M. A. Mulata
Beagle, P. S. A fine and private place
Beagle, P. S. The last unicorn
Beauvoir, S. de. All men are mortal
Beckford, W. Vathek
Beerbohm, M. Zuleika Dobson
Bellairs, J. The face in the frost
Bellamy, E. Looking backward: 2000-1888
Bemelmans, L. The Blue Danube
Bernanos, M. The other side of the mountain
Boucher, A. The compleat werewolf, and oth-
   er stories of fantasy and science fiction
Bradbury, R. Fahrenheit 451
Bradbury, R. Twice twenty-two: The golden
   apples of the sun; A medicine for melan-
   choly
Bradbury, R. The Vintage Bradbury
Bulgakov, M. The heart of a dog
Bulgakov, M. The Master and Margarita
Cabell, J. B. Jurgen: a comedy of justice
Calvino, I. Cosmicomics
Capote, T. The grass harp
Carroll, L. The annotated Alice
Chesterton, G. K. The man who was Thurs-
   day
Cole, B. The funco file
Collier, J. Fancies and goodnights
Cortázar, J. End of the game, and other sto-
   ries
Davidson, A. The phoenix and the mirror
Davies, L. P. Twilight journey
Davies, V. It happens every spring
Davies, V. Miracle on 34th Street
Dick, R. A. The ghost and Mrs Muir
Dickens, C. The cricket on the hearth
Dinesen, I. Ehrengard
Du Maurier, G. Peter Ibbetson
Ely, D. Seconds
Fast, H. The general zapped an angel
France, A. Penguin Island
France, A. The revolt of the angels

FARM LIFE—*Continued*

Nebraska
Aldrich, B. S. Spring came on forever
Cather, W. O pioneers!
Cather, W. One of ours

New England
Wharton, E. Ethan Frome

New Hampshire
Benét, S. V. The Devil and Daniel Webster

New York (State)
Edmonds, W. D. The Boyds of Black River
Rawlings, M. K. The sojourner

North Dakota
Bojer, J. The emigrants
Hudson, L. P. The bones of plenty

Norway
Gulbranssen, T. Beyond sing the woods
Hamsun, K. Growth of the soil
Undset, S. Kristin Lavransdatter
Undset, S. The master of Hestviken
Vesaas, T. The great cycle

Pakistan
Ghose, Z. The murder of Aziz Khan

Pennsylvania
Mannix, D. P. The killers
Updike, J. Of the farm

Poland
Reymont, L. The peasants

Russia
Abramov, F. One day in the "new life"
Sholokhov, M. Harvest on the Don
Sholokhov, M. Seeds of tomorrow
Sholokhov, M. Tales of the Don

South Dakota
Rolvaag, O. E. Giants in the earth
Rolvaag, O. E. Peder Victorious

Southern States
Deal, B. The least one
Wilkinson, S. A killing frost

Sweden
Budd, L. April snow
Moberg, V. The emigrants
Strindberg, A. The natives of Hemso

Tennessee
Deal, B. Dunbar's Cove

Vermont
Mather, M. One summer in between
Van de Water, F. F. Wings of the morning

The West
Stegner, W. The Big Rock Candy Mountain

FARM TENANCY
Deal, B. The least one
Delderfield, R. F. A horseman riding by
Faulkner, W. The mansion
Hudson, L. P. The bones of plenty
Macken, W. The silent people

FARMERS. See Farms life

FARMHOUSES. See Houses

Faro's daughter. Heyer, G.

The farthest reaches. Elder, J. ed.

FASCISM
See also Communism; National socialism; Totalitarianism
Germany
See National socialism
Italy
Bassani, G. The garden of the Finzi-Continis
Gadda, C. E. Acquainted with grief
Silone, I. Bread and wine
Silone, I. Fontamara
Silone, I. The fox and the camellias
Silone, I. The seed beneath the snow
United States
Lewis, S. It can't happen here

The fashion in shrouds. Allingham, M.
In Allingham, M. Three cases for Mr Campion p9-255

Fat city. Gardner, L.

FATE AND FATALISM
Hugo, V. Ninety-three
Wilder, T. The bridge of San Luis Rey
See also Chance

Father Brown mystery stories. Chesterton, G. K.

The Father Brown omnibus. Chesterton, G. K.

Father Hilary's holiday. Marshall, B.

The father hunt. Stout, R.

Father of the bride. Streeter, E.
also in Costain, T. B. comp. Twelve short novels p617-701

Father Sergius. Tolstoy, L.
In Costain, T. B. comp. Twelve short novels p289-327
In Tolstoy, L. Short novels v 2 p324-71

Father to the man. Plagemann, B.

FATHERS
Glasgow, E. In this our life
Troyat, H. The baroness

Fathers. Gold, H.

Fathers and children. See Turgenev, I. Fathers and sons

FATHERS AND DAUGHTERS
Bellow, S. Mr Sammler's planet
Conrad, J. Almayer's folly
In Conrad, J. Tales of the East and West p 1-128
Cronin, A. J. Hatter's castle
De Vries, P. The blood of the lamb
Duras, M. The afternoon of Mr Andesmas
In Duras, M. Four novels p241-303
Edelman, M. The Prime Minister's daughter
Freeling, N. This is the castle
Galsworthy, J. The silver spoon
In Galsworthy, J. A modern comedy p295-504
Godden, R. Breakfast with the Nikolides
Godden, R. A breath of air
Grubb, D. Shadow of my brother
Hutchinson, R. C. A child possessed
James, H. The golden bowl
James, H. Washington Square
Marquand, J. P. B. F.'s daughter
Orwell, G. A clergyman's daughter
Priestley, J. B. Angel Pavement
Sagan, F. Bonjour tristesse
Segal, E. W. Love story
Street, J. The high calling
Streeter, E. Father of the bride
Swinnerton, F. Nocturne
Turnbull, A. S. The golden journey
Wilkinson, S. Moss on the north side
See also Family life; Mothers and daughters; Parent and child

FATHERS AND SONS
Bataille, M. The Christmas tree
Bennett, A. Clayhanger
Boll, H. End of a mission
Buechner, F. The entrance to Porlock
Butler, S. The way of all flesh
Cronin, A. J. Beyond this place
Daniels, L. Caleb, my son
Dayan, Y. Death has two sons
Deeping, W. Sorrell and son
De Vries, P. Let me count the ways
Dickens, C. Dombey and son
Gold, H. Fathers
Gold, H. The man who was not with it
Green, G. To Brooklyn with love
Gulbranssen, T. The wind from the mountains
Hesse, H. Rosshalde
Humphrey, W. Home from the hill
Hunter, E. Sons
Hutchinson, R. C. The stepmother
Ikor, R. The sons of Avrom
Kayira, L. Jingala
Kessel, J. The horsemen
Lee, C. Y. Flower drum song
MacLennan, H. Return of the sphinx
Macleod, A. City of light
Marquand, J. P. So little time
Martin du Gard, R. The Thibaults
Mauriac, F. The desert of love
In Mauriac, F. A Mauriac reader p133-269
Meredith, G. The ordeal of Richard Feverel
Merejkowski, D. Peter and Alexis
Murphy, R. A certain island
Narayan, R. K. The vendor of sweet
Neugeboren, J. Corky's brother [novelette]
In Neugeboren, J. Corky's brother p213-61
O'Connor, E. I was dancing
Petrakis, H. M. A dream of kings
Potok, C. The chosen
Potok, C. The promise
Priestley, J. B. It's an old country

Fireside book of suspense, Alfred Hitchcock's. Hitchcock, A. ed.

A fireside book of Yuletide tales. Wagenknecht, E. ed.

First blood. Schaefer, J.
In Schaefer, J. The short novels of Jack Schaefer p113-220

The first circle. Solzhenitsyn, A. I.

The first day of Friday. Tracy, H.

First family. Davis, C.

First love. Turgenev, I.
In Turgenev, I. The Borzoi Turgenov p353-412
In Turgenev, I. A nest of gentlefolk, and other stories

The first men in the moon. Wells, H. G.
In Wells, H. G. Seven science fiction novels p455-620

First papers. Hobson, L. Z.

First-prize stories, 1919-1966: from the O. Henry Memorial Awards. Entered in Part I under title

The first Saint omnibus. Charteris, L.

The [first]-tenth Galaxy reader. Galaxy Magazine

First trilogy. Cary, J.

First wife, and other stories. Buck, P. S.

Fish preferred. Wodehouse, P. G.

FISHERMEN
Chase, M. E. The edge of darkness
Grau, S. A. The hard blue sky
Hemingway, E. The old man and the sea
In Hemingway, E. Three novels of Ernest Hemingway v3
Loti, P. Iceland fisherman
Macken, W. Rain on the wind
Mishima, Y. The sound of waves
Moore, R. Candlemas Bay
Moore, R. The Sea Flower
Moore, R. Spoonhandle
Sherman, D. R. Brothers of the sea
Verga, G. The house by the medlar tree
Wibberley, L. The Island of the Angels

FISHING
Grau, S. A. The hard blue sky
Hemingway, E. The old man and the sea
Powell, R. Pioneer, go home!
See also Fishermen; Pearl-fishing

The Fitzgerald reader. Fitzgerald, F. S.

Five adventure novels of H. Rider Haggard. Haggard, H. R.

FIVE CIVILIZED TRIBES
Culp, H. The bright feathers

Five of a kind. Stout, R.

The five red herrings (Suspicious characters) Sayers, D. L.

Five smooth stones. Fairbairn, A.

Five spy novels. Haycraft, H. ed.

Five tales. Melville, H.

Five times Maigret. Simenon, G.

Five weeks in a balloon. Verne, J.

The fixer. Malamud, B.

Flamingo feather. Van der Post, L.

FLANNIGAN, KATHERINE MARY (O'FALLON)
Freedman, B. Mrs Mike

Flashman. Fraser, G. M.

FLIERS. See Air pilots

FLIGHT
Ríos, T. The fifteenth pelican
See also Aeronautics

The flight from the enchanter. Murdoch, I.

The flight of the falcon. Du Maurier, D.

The flight of the Phoenix. Trevor, E.

The floating opera. Barth, J.

The flood. Le Clézio, J. M. G.

Flood warning. Romains, J.
In Romains, J. The earth trembles

FLOODS
Hartog, J. de. The little ark
See also Disasters

FLORENCE. See Italy—Florence

FLORIDA
Frank, P. Alas, Babylon

19th century
Taylor, R. L. A journey to Matecumbe
Wilder, R. Bright feather

20th century
Cozzens, J. G. Guard of honor
Ford, J. H. The feast of Saint Barnabas
MacLean, A. Fear is the key
Merle, R. The day of the dolphin
Rawlings, M. K. South moon under
Webb, J. F. The Craigshaw curse

Key West
Hemingway, E. To have and have not

FLORIDA CRACKERS. See Florida—20th century

FLOUR MILLS
Bacchelli, R. The mill on the Po

The flower beneath the foot. Firbank, R.
In Firbank, R. The complete Ronald Firbank p499-592

FLOWER CHILDREN. See Youth

Flower drum song. Lee, C. Y.

Flowering Judas, and other stories. Porter, K. A.
also in Porter, K. A. The collected stories of Katherine Anne Porter p3-170

Flowering wilderness. Galsworthy, J.
In Galsworthy, J. End of the chapter p331-592

Flowers. Keyes, D.

Flowers for Algernon, Keyes, D.
In Asimov, I. ed. The Hugo winners p245-73

Flowers for the judge. Allingham, M.
In Allingham, M. Crime and Mr Campion p177-362

The flowers of Adonis. Sutcliff, R.

The flowers of Hiroshima. Morris, E.

The fly. Langelaan, G.
In Hitchcock, A. ed. Alfred Hitchcock presents: Stories for late at night p225-55

FLYING. See Flight

Flying colours. Forester, C. S.
also in Forester, C. S. Captain Horatio Hornblower p459-662

Flying finish. Francis, D.

FLYING SAUCERS
Caidin, M. The Mendelov conspiracy
Earley, G. W. ed. Encounters with aliens
Heinlein, R. A. The puppet masters

FOLK SINGERS. See Musicians—Singers

FOLK TALES. See Legends and folk tales

FOLKLORE. See Legends and folk tales

Follow me down. Foote, S.
In Foote, S. Three novels v 1

Fontamara. Silone, I.

The food of the gods. Wells, H. G.
In Wells, H. G. Seven science fiction novels p621-815

FOOD POISONING
Lathen, E. Murder to go

FOOLS AND JESTERS
Barnes, M. C. King's fool

Fools' parade. Grubb, D.

For kicks. Francis, D.

For my great folly. Costain, T. B.

For whom the bell tolls. Hemingway, E.

For your eyes only. Fleming, I.
In Fleming, I. Bonded Fleming p189-328

For your eyes only [novelette]. Fleming, I.
In Fleming, I. Bonded Fleming p214-47

Forbidden colors. Mishima, Y.

Forbush and the penguins. Billing, G.

Force 10 from Navarone. MacLean, A.

FORCED LABOR
Solzhenitsyn, A. One day in the life of Ivan Denisovich

FOREIGN CORRESPONDENTS. See Journalists

FOREIGN LEGION (FRENCH ARMY) See France. Army—Foreign Legion

FOREIGN SERVICE. See Diplomatic life

The forerunner. See Merejkowski, D. The romance of Leonardo da Vinci

The forest and the fort. Allen, H.

The forest and the fort [abridged]. Allen, H.
In Allen, H. The city in the dawn p 1-223

TITLE AND SUBJECT INDEX
EIGHTH EDITION

FOREST FIRES
Stewart, G. R. Fire
The forest path to the spring. Lowry, M.
In Lowry, M. Hear us O Lord from heaven
thy dwelling place p215-83
Forever free. Morrow, H. W.
Forfeit. Francis, D.
The forged coupon. Tolstoy, L.
In Tolstoy, L. Short novels v2 p503-75
FORGERY OF WORKS OF ART
Marsh, N. Clutch of constables
FORGIVENESS
Murdoch, I. Bruno's dream
Form line of battle! Kent, A.
The Forsyte saga. Galsworthy, J.
Fortitude. Walpole, H.
The fortress. Walpole, H.
The fortunate mistress. See Defoe, D. Roxana,
the fortunate mistress
The fortunate pilgrim. Puzo, M.
FORTUNES. See Wealth
The fortunes and misfortunes of the famous
Moll Flanders. Defoe, D.
The fortunes of Richard Mahony. Richardson,
H. H.
The forty days of Musa Dagh. Werfel, F.
44 Irish short stories. Garrity, D. A. ed.
49 stories. O'Hara, J.
The 42nd parallel. Dos Passos, J.
also in Dos Passos, J. U.S.A. v 1
Forward, Gunner Asch! Kirst, H. H.
FOSSILS
Doyle, Sir A. C. The lost world
FOSTER CHILDREN
Austen, J. Mansfield Park
Eliot, G. Silas Marner
Hartog, J. de. The little ark
March, W. The bad seed
Smith, D. E. Brief flower
See also Adoption; Orphans
Foundation, Asimov, I.
Foundation and empire. See Asimov, I.
FOUNDATIONS (ENDOWMENTS) See Endowments
FOUNDATIONS, EDUCATIONAL. See Endowments
The foundling. Heyer, G.
The foundling. Spellman, F. Cardinal
FOUNDLINGS. See Orphans
The fountain. Morgan, C.
The fountain overflows. West, R.
The fountainhead. Rand, A.
Four came back. Caidin, M.
The four-chambered heart. Nin, A.
Four feathers. Mason, A. E. W.
Four, five and six by Tey. Tey, J.
The four-gated city. Lessing, D.
In Lessing, D. Children of violence v5
The four horsemen of the Apocalypse. Blasco
Ibáñez, V.
The four million. Henry, O.
also in Henry, O. The complete works of
O. Henry p 1-108
Four novels. Duras, M.
Four stories. Undset, S.
Fourteen great detective stories. Haycraft, H.
ed.
Fourteen stories. Buck, P. S.
The fourteenth of October. Bryher
FOURTH DIMENSION See Time, Travels in
FOURTH OF JULY CELEBRATIONS
Dolson, H. Heat lightning
Lockridge, R. Raintree County
Shulman, M. Rally round the flag, boys!
The fourth side of the triangle. Queen, E.
The fox. Lawrence, D. H.
In Neider, C. ed. Short novels of the masters p580-643
The fox and the camellias. Silone, I.
FOX HUNTING
Arnow, H. Hunter's horn
Kantor, M. The daughter of Bugle Ann
Kantor, M. The voice of Bugle Ann
Moore, J. The waters under the earth

The fox in the attic. Hughes, R.
The fox of Maulen. See Kirst, H. H. The
wolves
FOXES
Garnett, D. Lady into fox
The Foxes of Harrow. Yerby, F.
Foxfire. Seton, A.
Fragments. Armah, A. K.
Framley parsonage. Trollope, A.
FRANCE
Gerson, N. B. The anthem
Maupassant, G. de. Best stories of Guy de
Maupassant
11th century
Heyer, G. The Conqueror
12th century
Oldenbourg, Z. Cities of the flesh
Oldenbourg, Z. The world is not enough
Waddell, H. Peter Abelard
13th century
Closs, H. Deep are the valleys
Closs, H. High are the mountains
Closs, H. The silent Tarn
Oldenbourg, Z. The cornerstone
Oldenbourg, Z. Destiny of fire
14th century
Druon, M. The Iron King
Druon, M. The Lily and the Lion
Druon, M. The poisoned crown
Druon, M. The royal succession
Druon, M. The She-Wolf of France
Druon, M. The strangled queen
15th century
Costain, T. B. The moneyman
Maughan, A. M. Harry of Monmouth
Schoonover, L. The burnished blade
Schoonover, L. The Spider King
Scott, Sir W. Quentin Durward
Twain, M. Personal recollections of Joan of
Arc
Westcott, J. The white rose
16th century
Dumas, A. Marguerite de Valois
Haycraft, M. C. The reluctant queen
Mann, H. Henry, King of France
Mann, H. Young Henry of Navarre
Shellabarger, S. The King's cavalier
17th century
Anthony, E. The Cardinal and the Queen
Dumas, A. The man in the iron mask
Dumas, A. The three musketeers
Dumas, A. Twenty years after
Dumas, A. The Vicomte de Bragelonne
Irwin, M. Royal flush
Lafayette, Mme de. The Princess of Cleves
Mallet-Joris, F. The favourite
Sanders, J. Baneful sorceries
18th century
Dumas, A. The queen's necklace
Heyer, G. These old shades
Holt, V. The Queen's confession
Kent, A. Form line of battle!
Selinko, A. Desiree
Sterne, L. A sentimental journey through
France and Italy
18th century—To 1789
Martin, S. I, Madame Tussaud
18th century—1789-1799
Chapman, H. W. Fear no more
Dickens, C. A tale of two cities
Du Maurier, D. The glass-blowers
Feuchtwanger, L. Proud destiny
Forester, C. S. Lord Hornblower
Hugo, V. Ninety-three
Kenyon, F. W. Marie Antoinette
Orczy, Baroness. Adventures of the Scarlet
Pimpernel
Orczy, Baroness. The elusive Pimpernel
Orczy, Baroness. The Scarlet Pimpernel
Sabatini, R. Scaramouche, the king-maker
19th century
Aragon, L. Holy Week
Colette. Claudine at school
Du Maurier, G. Peter Ibbetson
Flaubert, G. Bouvard and Pécuchet
Flaubert, G. Sentimental education

517

FRANCE—19th century—*Continued*
Gautier, T. Mademoiselle de Maupin
Hugo, V. Les misérables
Maupassant, G. de. Bel-Ami
Maupassant, G. de. A woman's life
 In Maupassant, G. de. The portable Maupassant p377-631
Poldermans, J. Vincent
Proust, M. Jean Santeuil
Selinko, A. Desiree
Zola, E. The debacle

1800-1815
Balzac, H. de. The Chouans
Conrad, J. The rover
Forester, C. S. Lord Hornblower

1815-1848
Field, R. All this, and heaven too
Stendhal. The red and the black

1848-1870
Werfel, F. The song of Bernadette

1870-1940
Celine, L. F. Journey to the end of the night
Conrad, J. The arrow of gold
Faulkner, W. A fable
Ford, F. M. No more parades
 In Ford, F. M. Parade's end p291-500

20th century
Bataille, M. The Christmas tree
Bedford, S. A compass error
Colette. Music-hall sidelights
 In Colette. Six novels p237-337
Colette. The ripening seed
Cronin, A. J. A thing of beauty
Freeling, N. Valparaiso
Gide, A. The counterfeiters
Hemingway, E. The sun also rises
Hutchinson, R. C. A child possessed
James, H. The ambassadors
Lewis, R. Michel, Michel
Mauriac, F. Thérèse
Montherlant, H. de. The girls
Nin, A. The four-chambered heart
Proust, M. Remembrance of things past
Romains, J. Aftermath
Romains, J. The depths and the heights
Romains, J. The earth trembles
Romains, J. Escape in passion
Romains, J. The seventh of October
Romains, J. The wind is rising
Romains, J. Work and play
Sartre, J. P. The reprieve
Sartre, J. P. The troubled sleep
Simenon, G. The Premier [and] The train
Troyat, H. An extreme friendship
Veraldi, G. Spies of good intent
Wharton, E. The reef

1940-1945
Bates, H. E. Fair stood the wind for France
Genet, J. Funeral rites

Aristocracy
 See Aristocracy—France

Army
Barbusse, H. Under fire
Tolstoy, L. War and peace

Army—Air Force
Gann, E. K. In the company of eagles

Army—Officers
Conrad, J. The duel
 In Costain, T. B. comp. Twelve short novels p171-234

Army. Foreign Legion
Ouida. Under two flags
Wren, P. C. Beau Geste

Army. Lafayette Flying Corps
Nordhoff, C. Falcons of France

Bordeaux
Mauriac, F. Questions of precedence

Brittany
 See France, Provincial and rural—Brittany

Cannes
 See France, Provincial and rural—Cannes

Courts and courtiers
 See Courts and courtiers—France

Dauphiné
 See France—Provincial and rural—Dauphiné

Évian
Habe, H. The mission

Gascony
 See France, Provincial and rural—Gascony

German occupation, 1940-1945
 See France—1940-1945

Guyenne
 See France, Provincial and rural—Guyenne

Kings and rulers
Anthony, E. The Cardinal and the Queen
Chapman, H. W. Fear no more
Druon, M. The Iron King
Druon, M. The poisoned crown
Druon, M. The royal succession
Druon, M. The strangled queen
Feuchtwanger, L. Proud destiny
Steinbeck, J. The short reign of Pippin IV

Marseille
Hutchinson, R. C. A child possessed

Nice
Le Clézio, J. M. G. The flood
 See also Riviera

Normandy
 See France, Provincial and rural—Normandy

Paris—12th century
Moore, G. Heloise and Abelard

Paris—15th century
Hugo, V. The hunchback of Notre Dame

Paris—17th century
Anthony, E. The Cardinal and the Queen

Paris—18th century
Chapman, H. W. Fear no more
Dickens, C. A tale of two cities
Hugo, V. Ninety-three
Romains, J. The world from below
Sabatini, R. Scaramouche, the king-maker

Paris—19th century
Balzac, H. de. Cousin Bette
Balzac, H. de. Cousin Pons
Balzac, H. de. Lost illusions
Cost, M. I. Rachel
Dumas, A. Camille
Dumas, A. The Count of Monte Cristo
Du Maurier, G. Trilby
Endore, G. King of Paris
France, A. The crime of Sylvestre Bonnard
Heyer, G. Devil's cub
James, H. The American
Keyes, F. P. The chess players
Stern, G. B. Mosaic
 In Stern, G. B. The matriarch chronicles v3
Sue, E. The Wandering Jew
Troyat, H. The Brotherhood of the Red Poppy
Weiss, D. Naked came I
Zola, E. L'assommoir
Zola, E. Nana

Paris—20th century
Baldwin, J. Giovanni's room
Barnes, D. Nightwood
Beauvoir, S. de. Les belles images
Beauvoir, S. de. The mandarins
Bromfield, L. The green bay tree
Canfield, D. The deepening stream
Cocteau, J. The holy terrors
Colette. Break of day
Colette. Chance acquaintances
 In Colette. Gigi. Julio de Carneilhan. Chance acquaintances p225-315
 In Colette. 7 by Colette v3 p139-230
Colette. Gigi
 In Colette. Gigi. Julie de Carneilhan. Chance acquaintances p9-74
 In Colette. 7 by Colette v 1 p 1-67
 In Colette. Six novels p649-97
Colette. Julie de Carneilhan
 In Colette. Gigi Julie de Carneilhan. Chance acquaintances p77-222
Colette. Mitsou
 In Colette. Six novels p339-410
Cortázar, J. Hopscotch
Deighton, L. An expensive place to die
Dutourd, J. The horrors of love

FRENCH ARISTOCRATS. See Aristocracy—
France

FRENCH CANADIANS
Blais, M. C. A season in the life of Emmanuel
Buchan, J. Mountain meadow
Fuller, I. The loon feather
MacLennan, H. Two solitudes
Roy, G. Street of riches
Roy, G. The tin flute

FRENCH COUNTRY LIFE. See France, Provincial and rural

FRENCH FOREIGN LEGION. See France.
Army. Foreign Legion

FRENCH IN AFRICA
Daudet, A. Tartarin of Tarascon
Ousmane, S. God's bits of wood

FRENCH IN ALGERIA
Camus, A. The stranger

FRENCH IN CANADA
Cather, W. Shadows on the rock
MacLennan, H. Return of the sphinx

FRENCH IN ENGLAND
Barnes, M. C. Isabel the Fair
Tarkington, B. Monsieur Beaucaire

FRENCH IN GERMANY
Céline, L. F. Castle to castle

FRENCH IN HAITI
Bourne, P. Drums of destiny

FRENCH IN INDOCHINA, FRENCH
Duras, M. The sea wall

FRENCH IN MEXICO
Gavin, C. The cactus and the crown

FRENCH IN RUSSIA
Troyat, H. The baroness

FRENCH IN THE CARIBBEAN AREA
Benchley, N. The wake of the Icarus

FRENCH IN THE UNITED STATES
Field, R. All this, and heaven too
Mason, F. V. Young titan

FRENCH IN YUGOSLAVIA
Andrić, I. Bosnian chronicle

FRENCH INDOCHINA. See Indochina, French

The French lieutenant's woman. Fowles, J.

FRENCH RESISTANCE MOVEMENT. See
World War, 1939-1945—France

FRENCH REVOLUTION. See France—18th century—1789-1799

FRENCH RIVIERA. See Riviera

FRENCH SOLDIERS. See Soldiers, French

French stories and tales. Geist, S. ed.

FRENCH WEST AFRICA. See Africa, West

Frenchman's Creek. Du Maurier, D.
also in Du Maurier, D. Three romantic novels of Cornwall: Rebecca, Frenchman's Creek and Jamaica Inn p317-495

Fresh from the country. Read, Miss

FRIARS. See Franciscans; Monasticism and religious orders

Friday. Tournier, M.

Friday the rabbi slept late. Kemelman, H.

Friday's child. Heyer, G.

FRIEDRICH II, EMPEROR OF GERMANY.
See Frederick II, Emperor of Germany

A friend in power. Baker, C.

A friend of Caesar. Davis, W. S.

The friend of the family. Dostoevsky, F.
also in Dostoevsky, F. The short novels of Dostoevsky p617-811

The friendly persuasion. West, J.

FRIENDS. See Friendship

FRIENDS, SOCIETY OF
Dreiser, T. The bulwark
Fletcher, I. The wind in the forest
Giles, J. H. The land beyond the mountains
Renault, M. The charioteer
Taylor, D. Lights across the Delaware
Van de Water, F. F. Wings of the morning
West, J. Except for me and thee
West, J. The friendly persuasion

Friends at court. Cecil, H.

FRIENDSHIP
Balzac, H. de. Cousin Pons
Bawden, N. The grain of truth
Crumley, J. One to count cadence
Del Castillo, M. The seminarian
Fournier, A. The wanderer

Hesse, H. Beneath the wheel
Hesse, H. Rosshalde
Kipling, R. The light that failed
Leggett, J. Who took the gold away
Machado de Assis, J. M. Dom Casmurro
Potok, C. The chosen
Potok, C. The promise
Powell, A. A question of upbringing
In Powell, A. A dance to the music of time v 1
Read, Miss. The market square
Remarque, E. M. Three comrades
Shaw, R. A card from Morocco
Spring, H. My son, my son!
Steinbeck, J. Of mice and men
Steinbeck, J. Tortilla Flat
Van Dyke, H. Ladies of the Rachmaninoff eyes
Vesaas, T. Palace of ice
Wellman, P. I. The walls of Jericho

From a view to kill. Fleming, I.
In Fleming, I. Bonded Fleming p191-213

From death to morning. Wolfe, T.

From here to eternity. Jones, J.

From Russia, with love. Fleming, I.
also in Fleming, I. Gilt-edged Bonds v2

From the earth to the moon. Verne, J.
In Verne, J. The Jules Verne omnibus p545-667

From the earth to the moon, and, Round the moon. Verne, J.

From the ocean, from the stars. Clarke, A. C.

From the terrace. O'Hara, J.

FRONTENAC, LOUIS DE BUADE, COMTE DE
Cather, W. Shadows on the rock

FRONTIER AND PIONEER LIFE
Davis, H. L. Beulah Land
Erdman, L. G. The far journey
Giles, J. H. Voyage to Santa Fe
Page, E. The tree of liberty
Page, E. Wilderness adventure
Richter, C. The light in the forest
Taylor, R. L. A journey to Matecumbe

Africa
Cloete, S. The turning wheels

Alaska
Ferber, E. Ice Palace
White, S. E. Wild geese calling

Australia
Dark, E. The timeless land
Eden, D. The vines of Yarrabee
Gaskin, C. Sara Dane
Nordhoff, C. Botany Bay
White, P. The tree of man

California
Bristow, G. Jubilee Trail

Canada
Freedman, B. Mrs Mike

Colorado
Cockrell, M. The revolt of Sarah Perkins

Georgia
Miller, C. Lamb in his bosom

Indiana
Eggleston, E. The Hoosier school-boy
Eggleston, E. The Hoosier schoolmaster

Iowa
Aldrich, B. S. Song of years
Kantor, M. Spirit Lake

Kentucky
Giles, J. H. The believers
Giles, J. H. Hannah Fowler
Giles, J. H. The land beyond the mountains
Van Every, D. The scarlet feather

Louisiana
Bristow, G. Deep summer
Keyes, F. P. Blue camellia

Maine
Williams, B. A. Come spring

Middle West
Churchill, W. The crossing
Cooper, J. F. The prairie

Minnesota
Moberg, V. The last letter home
Moberg, V. Unto a good land

FUTURE, NOVELS OF THE—*Continued*
Frayn, M. A very private life
Heinlein, R. A. The moon is a harsh mistress
Heiniem, R. A. Waldo and Magic, inc.
Herbert, F. Dune
Herbert, F. Dune messiah
Hesse, H. The glass bead game (Magister Ludi)
Huxley, A. Brave new world
Knebel, F. Seven days in May
Knebel, F. Trespass
Lessing, D. The four-gated city
  In Lessing, D. Children of violence v5
London, J. The iron heel
Mannes, M. They
Mano, D. K. Horn
Miller, W. M. A canticle for Leibowitz
Orwell, G. Nineteen eighty-four
Pohl, F. The age of the pussyfoot
Pohl, F. The space merchants
Schoonover, L. Central passage
Serling, R. J. The President's plane is missing
Shute, N. In the wet
Shute, N. On the beach
Simak, C. D. The goblin reservation
Simak, C. D. Ring around the sun
Simak, C. D. Why call them back from heaven?
Stewart, G. R. Earth abides
Three for tomorrow
Vidal, G. Messiah
Vonnegut, K. Cat's cradle
Williams, J. A. Sons of darkness, sons of light
Wylie, P. Tomorrow!
  See also Science fiction
Fuzz. McBain, E.

G

The Gabriel hounds. Stewart, M.
Gabriela, clove and cinnamon. Amado, J.
Gale force. Trevor, E.
GALES. See Storms
GALICIA. See Poland—Galicia
The Galileans. Slaughter, F. G.
GALILEI, GALILEO
  Harsányi, Z. de. The star-gazer
The gallant Mrs Stonewall. Kane, H. T.
The gallery. Burns, J. H.
Gallery of modern fiction. The Kenyon Review
The Galsworthy reader. Galsworthy, J.
GALWAY. See Ireland, Provincial and rural—Galway
Gambit. Stout, R.
The gambler. Dostoevsky, F.
  In Dostoevsky, F. The short novels of Dostoevsky p 1-126
The gambler, and other stories. Dostoevsky, F.
GAMBLERS. See Gambling
GAMBLING
  Amado, J. Dona Flor and her two husbands
  Edmonds, W. D. The wedding journey
  Ferber, E. Show boat
  Fleming, I. Casino Royale
  Francis, D. Forfeit
  Heyer, G. Faro's daughter
  Keyes, F. P. Steamboat Gothic
  Leiber, F. Gonna roll the bones
    In Nebula award stories, three p89-120
  Pharr, R. D. The book of numbers
  Wilder, R. An affair of honor
    See also Lotteries
GAME HUNTING. See Hunting
The game of kings. Dunnett, D.
GAME PROTECTION
  Kessel, J. The lion
GAME WARDENS. See Game protection
GAMEKEEPERS
  Lawrence, D. H. Lady Chatterley's lover
GAMES, OLYMPIC. See Olympic games
GANDHI, MOHANDAS KARAMCHAND
  Narayan, R. K. Waiting for the Mahatma
  Wolpert, S. Nine hours to Rama

The gang that couldn't shoot straight. Breslin, J.
GANGS. See Crime and criminals; Juvenile delinquency
GANGSTERS
  Burnett, W. R. The asphalt jungle
  Burnett, W. R. Little Caesar
  Loraine, P. A Mafia kiss
  Powell, R. Pioneer, go home!
  Schulberg, B. Waterfront
  Simenon, G. The brothers Rico
    In Simenon, G. An American omnibus p129-249
  Westlake, D. E. The busy body
    See also Crime and criminals; Mafia
A garden of earthly delights. Oates, J. C.
The garden of the Finzi-Continis. Bassani, G.
Garden on the moon. Boulle, P.
The garden party, and other stories. Mansfield, K.
GARDENERS
  Anderson, S. Dark laughter
  Pearson, D. The marigold field
  Sherman, D. R. Old Mali and the boy
GARDENS AND GARDENING
  Godden, R. An episode of sparrows
La Garibaldina. Vittorini, E.
  In Vittorini, E. The dark and the light p77-180
The garlic tree. Geld, E. B.
GARMENT INDUSTRY. See Clothing industry
The Garretson chronicle. Brace, G. W.
GASCONY. See France, Provincial and rural—Gascony
Gate of ivory, Gate of Horn. Craig, P.
Gate to the sea. Bryher
The gates of the forest. Wiesel, E.
The gathering of the gangs. Romains, J.
  In Romains, J. The wind is rising
GAUCHOS
  Hudson, W. H. Tales of the gauchos
Gaudy Night. Sayers, D. L.
GAUGUIN, PAUL
  Maugham, W. S. The moon and sixpence
GAUL
                    To 58 B.C.
  Warner, R. Imperial Caesar
The gauntlet. Street, J.
The Gay Galliard. Irwin, M.
GEESE
  Bodsworth, F. The strange one
  Gallico, P. The snow goose
GEISHAS
  Kawabata, Y. Snow country
    In Kawabata, Y. Snow country and Thousand cranes v 1 p 1-175
  Moll, E. Seidman and the geisha
The general zapped an angel. Fast, H.
GENERALS, AMERICAN. See names of countries with subheads Army—Officers; e.g. United States. Army—Officers; Germany. Army—Officers; etc.
The general's ring. Lagerlöf, S.
  also in Costain, T. B. ed. Stories to remember v 1 p 1-64
GENERATION GAP. See Conflict of generations
Generation without farewell. Boyle, K.
A generous man. Price, R.
GENETICS. See Heredity and environment
Genetrix. Mauriac, F.
  In Mauriac. F. A Mauriac reader p63-130
GENEVA. See Switzerland—Geneva
Genevieve. Gide, A.
  In Gide, A. The school for wives, Robert, Genevieve p145-241
GENIUS
  Hersey, J. The child buyer
  Kennedy, M. The constant nymph
  Mann, T. The beloved returns
  Rand, A. The fountainhead
  Rolland, R. Jean-Christophe
Gentian Hill. Goudge, E.
The gentle grafter. Henry, O.
  In Henry, O. The complete works of O. Henry p267-354

GERMANY—Army—Officers—*Continued*
Kirst, H. H. The night of the generals
Kirst, H. H. The officer factory
Kirst, H. H. Return of Gunner Asch
Kirst, H. H. Revolt of Gunner Asch
Kirst, H. H. Soldiers' revolt

Bavaria
MacLean, A. Where eagles dare

Berlin
Albrand, M. A door fell shut
Baum, V. Grand Hotel
Deighton, L. Funeral in Berlin
Hall, A. The Quiller memorandum
Isherwood, C. The Berlin stories
Johnson, U. The third book about Achim
Nabokov, V. The gift
Nabokov, V. King, queen, knave
Nabokov, V. Laughter in the dark
Plievier, T. Berlin
Simmel, J. M. Dear fatherland
Singer, I. J. The family Carnovsky
Strindberg, A. The Cloister
Uris, L. Armageddon

Bonn
Böll, H. The clown
Le Carré, J. A small town in Germany

Cologne
Albrand, M. Rhine replica

Communism
See Communism—Germany

Courts and courtiers
See Courts and courtiers—Germany

Crime and criminals
See Crime and criminals—Germany

Dresden
Vonnegut, K. Slaughterhouse-five

Düsseldorf
Mann, T. The black swan

Heidelberg
Stafford, J. A winter's tale
In Stafford, J. Bad characters p225-76

Navy
Ott, W. Sharks and little fish

Navy—Officers
Catto, M. Murphy's war
Reeman, D. With blood and iron

Peasant life
See Peasant life—Germany

Politics
See Politics—Germany

Remagen
Garth, D. Watch on the bridge

Weimar
Mann, T. The beloved returns

GERMANY (DEMOCRATIC REPUBLIC, 1949-)
Johnson, U. The third book about Achim

GERMANY (FEDERAL REPUBLIC, 1949-)
Johnson, U. The third book about Achim

GERMANY, EASTERN. See Germany (Democratic Republic, 1949-)

GERMANY, PROVINCIAL AND RURAL
Böll, H. End of a mission
Goethe, J. W. von. Elective affinities
Kirst, H. H. What became of Gunner Asch
Kirst, H. H. The wolves
Remarque, E. M. The black obelisk

Germinal. Zola, E.

GERMS. See Microorganisms

GERONA. See Spain—Gerona

Gertrude. Hesse, H.

Gervaise. See Zola, E. L'assommoir

GESTAPO. See National socialism

GETTYSBURG. See Pennsylvania—Gettysburg

GETTYSBURG, BATTLE OF, 1863
Kantor, M. Long remember

GETTYSBURG ADDRESS
Andrews, M. R. S. The perfect tribute

GHANA
20th century
Armah, A. K. The beautiful ones are not yet born
Armah, A. K. Fragments

Politics
See Politics—Ghana

GHETTOS. See Jews—Segregation

The ghost and Mrs Muir. Dick, R. A.

GHOST STORIES
Asquith, C. ed. A book of modern ghosts
Beagle, P. S. A fine and private place
Benchley, N. The visitors
Blackstock, C. A house possessed
Blackwood, A. In the realm of terror
Blackwood, A. Tales of the uncanny and supernatural
Butler, W. The house at Akiya
Calder-Marshall, A. The Scarlet boy
Cerf, B. A. ed. Famous ghost stories
Davenport, B. ed. Ghostly tales to be told
Davenport, B. ed. Tales to be told in the dark
Davies, L. P. The reluctant medium
De La Mare, C. comp. They walk again
Dick, R. A. The ghost and Mrs Muir
Dickens, C. A Christmas carol
Dickens, M. The room upstairs
Eyre, K. W. The lute and the glove
Gallico, P. Too many ghosts
Jackson, S. The haunting of Hill House
James, H. The ghostly tales of Henry James
James, H. The turn of the screw
    In Costain, T. B. comp. Twelve short novels p329-412
    In James, H. The Henry James reader p255-356
    In James, H. Short novels of Henry James p407-530
Leiber, F. Gonna roll the bones
    In Nebula award stories, three p89-120
Macardle, D. The uninvited
Manley, S. ed. Shapes of the supernatural
Margolies, J. A. ed. Strange and fantastic stories
Michaels, B. Ammie, come home
Randall, F. E. The place of sapphires
Tattersall, J. Lyonesse Abbey
Thane, E. Tryst
Turner, J. ed. Unlikely ghosts
Van Thal, H. ed. Great ghost stories
Wagenknecht, E. ed. The fireside book of ghost stories
Wise, H. A. ed. Great tales of terror and the supernatural
    See also Horror stories; Supernatural phenomena

GHOST WRITERS. See Authors

The ghostly tales of Henry James. James, H.

Ghostly tales to be told. Davenport, B. ed.

The ghosts' high noon. Carr, J. D.

Giant. Ferber, E.

The giant Joshua. Whipple, M.

GIANTS
Swift, J. Gulliver's travels
Wells, H. G. The food of the gods
    In Wells, H. G. Seven science fiction novels p621-815

Giants in the earth. Rolvaag, O. E.

Giants unleashed. Conklin, G. ed.

Gideon's day. Marric, J. J.

Gideon's fire. Marric, J. J.

Gideon's power. Marric, J. J.

Gideon's ride. Marric, J. J.

Gideon's river. Marric, J. J.

Gideon's wrath. Marric, J. J.

The gift. Nabokov, V.

The gift and the giver. White, N. G.

The gift of a cow. Premchand

The gift shop. Armstrong, C.

GIFTED CHILDREN. See Children, Gifted

Gigi. Colette
    In Colette. Gigi. Julie de Carneilhan. Chance acquaintances p9-74
    In Colette. 7 by Colette v 1 p 1-67
    In Colette. Six novels p649-97

Gigi. Julie de Carneilhan. Chance acquaintances. Colette

Gil Blas. See Le Sage, A. R. Adventures of Gil Blas of Santillane

The gilded age. Twain, M.
  also in Twain, M. The complete novels of Mark Twain v 1 p 1-383
The gilded age [another version] See Twain, M. The adventures of Colonel Sellers
The gilded nightmare. Pentecost, H.
Giles goat-boy. Barth, J.
Gilligan's last elephant. Hanley, G.
Gilt-edged Bonds. Fleming, I.
Gimpel the fool, and other stories. Singer, I. B.
The ginger man. Donleavy, J. P.
The Gioconda smile. Huxley, A.
  In Huxley, A. Antic hay, and The Gioconda smile
Giovanni's room. Baldwin, J.

GIPSIES
  Barrie, J. M. Little minister
  Goudge, E. The white witch
  Hugo, V. The hunchback of Nortre Dame
  Lofts, N. The town house
  Merimée, P. Carmen
The girl in Melanie Klein. Harwood, R.
Girl on a high wire. Foley, R.
The girl on the baggage truck. O'Hara, J.
  In O'Hara, J. Sermons and soda water v 1
The girl on the Via Flaminia. Hayes, A.
Girl watcher's funeral. Pentecost, H.

GIRLS
  Bawden, N. Devil by the sea
  Bowen, E. The little girls
  Colette. Claudine at school
  Dickens, C. The old curiosity shop
  Garnett, D. Two by two
  Godden, R. The river
  Goudge, E. The rosemary tree
  Kessel, J. The lion
  Lehmann, R. Invitation to the waltz
  March, W. The bad seed
  Saroyan, W. Mama, I love you
  Smith, L. The last day the dogbushes bloomed
  Tarkington, B. Alice Adams
  Troyat, H. Elizabeth
  Vesaas, T. Palace of ice
  West, J. Cress Delahanty
  Westheimer, D. My sweet Charlie
  See also Adolescence; Children
The girls. Montherlant, H. de
The girls of slender means. Spark, M.
Give me liberty. Gerson, N. B.

GLADIATORS
  Bryher. Roman wall
  Bulwer-Lytton, Sir E. The last days of Pompeii
  Koestler, A. The gladiators
  Sienkiewicz, H. Quo vadis
The gladiators. Koestler, A.

GLASGOW. See Scotland—Glasgow

GLASS
  Gaskin, C. Edge of glass
The glass bead game. Hesse, H.
The glass-blowers. Du Maurier, D.
The glass key. Hammett, D.
  also in Hammett, D. The novels of Dashiell Hammett p441-588

GLASS MANUFACTURE
  Du Maurier, D. The glass-blowers
  Jordan, M. One red rose forever
The glass-sided ants' nest. Dickinson, P.
The glass triangle. Coxe, G. H.
  In Coxe, G. H. Triple exposure p3-161
The Glencannon omnibus. Gilpatric, G.

GLENDALE. See California—Glendale

The glorious folly. De Wohl, L.
Glory Road. Heinlein, R. A.
The glory tent. Barrett, W. E.

GLOUCESTER. See Massachusetts—Gloucester

Go ask the river. Eaton, E.
The go-away bird. Spark, M.
  In Spark, M. Collected stories: I p302-59
The go-away bird, and other stories. Spark, M.
Go down, Moses, and other stories. Faulkner, W.
Go tell it on the mountain. Baldwin, J.
The goblin reservation. Simak, C. D.

GOD
  Wiesel, E. The gates of the forest
  See also Religion
God bless you, Mr Rosewater. Vonnegut, K.
God save the mark. Westlake, D. E.
God was born in exile. Horia, V.
The godfather. Puzo, M.
God's angry man. Ehrlich, L.
The gods are not mocked. Taylor, A.
The gods arrive. Wharton, E.
God's bits of wood. Ousmane, S.
God's little acre. Caldwell, E.
God's men. Buck, P. S.
God's pauper. See Kazantzakis, N. Saint Francis
God's warrior. Slaughter, F. G.

GOETHE, JOHANN WOLFGANG VON
  Mann, T. The beloved returns

GOGH, THEO VAN
  Poldermans, J. Vincent

GOGH, VINCENT VAN
  Poldermans, J. Vincent
  Stone, I. Lust for life
Going to Jerusalem. Charyn, J.
Going to meet the man. Baldwin, J.

GOLD
  Fleming, I. Goldfinger
  O'Rourke, F. Instant gold
The gold and silver hooks. Moore, R.

GOLD MINES AND MINING
  Abrahams, P. Mine boy
  Caldwell, E. God's little acre
  Harte, B. The Luck of Roaring Camp, and other sketches
  Henry, W. Mackenna's gold
  Richardson, H. H. The fortunes of Richard Mahony
  Traven, B. The treasure of the Sierra Madre
Golden Admiral. Mason, F. V.
The golden apples. Welty, E.
The golden apples of the sun. Bradbury, R.
  also in Bradbury, R. Twice twenty-two: The golden apples of the sun; A medicine for melancholy p7-209
The golden bowl. James, H.
The golden calf. Ilf
  In Ilf. Ilf & Petrov's The complete adventures of Ostap Bender v 1
The golden collar. Cadell, E.
The golden fruits. Sarraute, N.
The golden hand. Simon, E.
The golden journey. Turnbull, A. S.
The golden keel. Bagley, D.
The golden notebook. Lessing, D.
The golden princess. Baron, A.
The golden rendezvous. MacLean, A.
The golden strangers. Treece, H.
The golden trap. Pentecost, H.
The golden warrior. Muntz, H.
Goldfinger. Fleming, I.
Goldmund. See Hesse, H. Narcissus and Goldmund
Gone. Godden, R.
Gone with the wind. Mitchell, M.
Gonna roll the bones. Leiber, F.
  In Nebula award stories, three p89-120

GOOD AND EVIL
  Bellairs, J. The face in the frost
  Bernanos, G. Under the sun of Satan
  Brunner, J. The devil's work
  Gloag, J. Our mother's house
  Herlihy, J. L. All fall down
  James, H. The turn of the screw
    also in Costain, T. B. comp. Twelve short novels p329-412
    also in James, H. The great short novels of Henry James p621-748
    also in James, H. The Henry James reader p255-356
    also in James, H. Short novels of Henry James p407-530
  Jameson, S. The white crow
  Laxalt, R. A man in the wheatfield
  Lewis, C. S. Out of fthe silent planet
  Lewis, C. S. Perelandra
  Lewis, C. S. That hideous strength
  Lewis, C. S. Till we have faces
  Linney, R. Slowly, by thy hand unfurled

GOOD AND EVIL—*Continued*
Melville, H. Billy Budd, foretopman
Murdoch, I. The nice and the good
Murdoch, I. The unicorn
Rawlings, M. K. The sojourner
Salamanca, J. R. Lilith
Steinbeck, J. East of Eden
Stevenson, R. L. Strange case of Dr Jekyll and Mr Hyde
  In Knight, D. ed. A century of great short science fiction novels p9-62
Styron, W. Set this house on fire
Troyat, H. The mountain
Twain, M. The man that corrupted Hadley-burg
  In Blackmur, R. P. ed. American short novels p68-96
Vargas Llosa, M. The green house
Wilder, T. Heaven's my destination
Wright, R. The outsider
    See also Devil; Ethics

The good companions. Priestley, J. B.

The good deed, and other stories of Asia, past and present. Buck, P. S.

The good earth. Buck, P. S.
  also in Buck, P. S. The house of earth: The good earth; Sons; A house divided v 1

GOOD FRIDAY
Agee, J. The morning watch

The good life. Wallop, D.

The good light. Bjarnhof, K.

A good man is hard to find, and other stories. O'Connor, F.

Good men and true. Rhodes, E. M.
  In Rhodes, E. M. The best novels and stories of Eugene Manlove Rhodes p45-104

Good morning, Miss Dove. Patton, F. G.
  also in Costain, T. B. ed. More Stories to remember v2 p 1-95

The good shepherd. Forester, C. S.

The good shepherd. Gunnarsson, G.

The good soldier: Schweik. Hasek, J.

Good times/bad times. Kirkwood, J.

A good woman. Bromfield, L.
  In Bromfield, L. Bromfield galaxy: The green bay tree, Early autumn, A good woman p405-639

Goodbye, Aunt Elva. Fenwick, E.

Goodbye, Columbus, and five short stories. Roth, P.

The goodbye look. Macdonald, R.

Good-bye Mr Chips. Hilton, J.
  also in Costain, T. B. comp. Twelve short novels p417-55

Good-bye, my Lady. Street, J.

Goodbye to Berlin. Isherwood, C.
  In Isherwood, C. The Berlin stories v2

A goodly babe. Vivante, A.

GOOSE. See Geese

The goose on the grave. Hawkes, J.
  In Hawkes, J. Lunar landscapes p200-75

GORDON RIOTS, 1870
Dickens, C. Barnaby Rudge

GOSSIP
Smith, L. One hour

GOTHIC NOVELS. See Gothic romances

GOTHIC ROMANCES
Andrézel, P. The angelic avengers
Berckman, E. The heir of Starvelings
Brown, C. B. Wieland
Dale, C. Act of love
Disney, D. M. At some forgotten door
Eden, D. The shadow wife
Heyer, G. Cousin Kate
Hodge, J. A. Maulever Hall
Hodge, J. A. The winding stair
Holt, V. Bride of Pendorric
Holt, V. The king of the castle
Holt, V. The legend of the Seventh Virgin
Holt, V. Menfreya in the morning
Holt, V. Mistress of Mellyn
Holt, V. The shivering sands
Letton, J. Allegra's child
Lindop, A. E. Sight unseen
Maybury, A. The Minerva stone
Ogilvie, E. Bellwood
Peters, E. The Camelot caper
Peters, E. The Jackal's head
Radcliffe, A. The mysteries of Udolpho
Randall, F. E. The place of sapphires

Sanders, J. Baneful sorceries
Sheed, W. Pennsylvania gothic
  In Sheed, W. The blacking factory & Pennsylvania gothic p3-63
Shelley, M. W. Frankenstein
Stoker, B. Dracula
Tattersall, J. Lyonesse Abbey
Thomas, D. Rebecca's Daughters
Troy, K. Roseheath
Walpole, H. The castle of Otranto
Webb, J. F. The Craigshaw curse
Whitney, P. The winter people
    See also Horror stories

GOTHS
De Wohl, L. Citadel of God

GOULD, HORACE BUNCH
Price, E. New moon rising

GOVERNESSES
Allingham, M. The china governess
Berckman, E. The heir of Starvelings
Brontë, A. Agnes Grey
Brontë, C. Jane Eyre
De La Roche, M. Mary Wakefield
Eden, D. Lady of Mallow
Field, R. All this, and heaven too
Hodge, J. A. The adventurers
Holt, V. Menfreya in the morning
James, H. The turn of the screw
  also in Costain, T. B. comp. Twelve short novels p329-412
  also in James, H. The great short novels of Henry James p621-748
  also in James, H. The Henry James reader p255-356
  also in James, H. Short novels of Henry James p407-530
Seton, A. Dragonwyck
Stewart, M. Nine coaches waiting
Wharton, E. The reef
Whitney, P. A. Window on the square
    See also Servants—Housekeepers

GOVERNMENTAL INVESTIGATIONS
United States
Hersey, J. The child buyer

The Governor's lady. Collins, N.

The Governor's lady. Raddall, T. H.

The gown of glory. Turnbull, A. S.

GOYA Y LUCIENTES, FRANCISCO JOSÉ DE
Braider, D. Rage in silence

GRAFT IN POLITICS. See Corruption (in politics)

GRAIL
Costain, T. B. The silver chalice
Roberts, D. J. Kinsmen of the Grail
Roberts, D. J. Launcelot, my brother

The grain of truth. Bawden, N.

The grand design. Dos Passos, J.
  also in Dos Passos, J. District of Columbia v3

Grand Hotel. Baum, V.

The grand Sophy. Heyer, G.

GRANDCHILDREN
Wilson, A. Late call

GRANDFATHERS
Beerbohm, M. Zuleika Dobson
Buechner, F. The entrance to Porlock
Cronin, A. J. The green years
Dickens, C. The old curiosity shop
Ferber, E. Ice Palace
Fleming, J. No bones about it
Humphrey, W. The Ordways
Nathan, R. Winter in April
Smith, D. E. Brief flower
Streeter, E. Mr Hobbs' vacation
Wolff, R. A trace of footprints

The grandfathers. Richter, C.

Grandmother and the priests. Caldwell, T.

GRANDMOTHERS
Armah, A. K. Fragments
Bedford, S. A favourite of the gods
Blais, M. C. A season in the life of Emmanuel
Bromfield, L. Mrs Parkington
Caldwell, T. Grandmother and the priests
Colette. Gigi
  In Colette. Gigi. Julie de Carneilhan. Chance acquaintances p9-74
  In Colette. 7 by Colette v 1 p 1-67
  In Colette. Six novels p649-97
Davenport, M. My brother's keeper
De La Roche, M. Jalna
Dermoût, M. The ten thousand things
Dickens, M. The room upstairs

GRECO, EL. See Theotocopuli, Dominico, known as El Greco

GREECE
Novels given this subject deal with Greece before 323 A.D. For periods following this date, see Greece, Modern
Bryher. Gate to the sea
Graves, R. Hercules, my shipmate
Renault, M. The bull from the sea
Renault, M. Fire from heaven
Renault, M. The last of the wine
Renault, M. The mask of Apollo
Schmitt, G. Electra
Wilder, T. The woman of Andros
In Wilder, T. The Cabala, and The woman of Andros p135-203
In Wilder, T. A Thornton Wilder trio p245-309

Athens
Douglas, L. C. The robe
Renault, M. The king must die
Renault, M. The last of the wine
Sutcliff, R. The flowers of Adonis
Warner, R. Pericles the Athenian

Peloponnesian War, 431-404 B.C.
Sutcliff, R. The flowers of Adonis

GREECE, MODERN
Crane, S. Active service
In Crane, S. The complete novels of Stephen Crane p429-592
See also Rhodes—20th century

13th century
Duggan, A. Lord Geoffrey's fancy

20th century
Ambler, E. A coffin for Dimitrios
Amis, K. I want it now
Fowles, J. The magus
Kazantzakis, N. The fratricides
MacInnes, H. Decision at Delphi
Osborne, H. The yellow gold of Tiryns
Sarton, M. Joanna and Ulysses
Vassilikos, V. Z
Wescott, G. Apartment in Athens

Athens
Durrell, L. Tunc
Tute, W. A matter of diplomacy
Wescott, G. Apartment in Athens

Mykonos
MacInnes, H. The double image

Politics
See Politics—Greece, Modern

Salonika
Vassilikos, V. Z

GREECE, MODERN, PROVINCIAL AND RURAL
Kazantzakis, N. The fratricides
Stewart, J. I. M. Vanderlyn's kingdom

GREED. See Avarice

GREEK CHURCH. See Orthodox Eastern Church

GREEK CIVIL WAR, 1944-1949. See Greece, Modern—20th century

GREEK ISLANDS. See Greece, Modern

The **Greek** passion. Kazantzakis, N.

GREEK SOLDIERS. See Soldiers, Greek

GREEK TEMPLES. See Temples, Greek

GREEKS IN CARTHAGE
Bryher. The coin of Carthage

GREEKS IN CHINA
Kazantzakis, N. The rock garden

GREEKS IN FRANCE
Jameson, S. The blind heart

GREEKS IN JAPAN
Kazantzakis, N. The rock garden

GREEKS IN ROME
Bryher. The coin of Carthage

GREEKS IN THE UNITED STATES
Petrakis, H. M. A dream of kings
Petrakis, H. M. The waves of night, and other stories

GREEKS IN TURKEY
Kazan, E. America, America
Kazantzakis, N. The Greek passion

The **green** bay tree. Bromfield, L.
also in Bromfield, L. Bromfield galaxy: The green bay tree, Early autumn, A good woman p5-216

The **green** berets. Moore, R.

Green corn moon. Lanning, G.
Green days by the river. Anthony, M.
Green Dolphin Street. Goudge, E.
The green gauntlet. Delderfield, R. F.
The green hills of earth. Heinlein, R. A.
The green house. Vargas Llosa, M.
Green mansions. Hudson, W. H.
The green years. Cronin, A. J.

GREENE, NATHANAEL
Boyd, J. Drums

The greengage summer. Godden, R.

GREENLAND
Freuchen, P. Eskimo
Freuchen, P. White man
Higgins, J. East of desolation
MacLean, A. Night without end

Greenmantle. Buchan, J.
also in Buchan, J. Adventures of Richard Hannay v2
also in Haycraft, H. ed. Five spy novels p163-342

Greenmask! Linington, E.
Greenstone. Ashton-Warner, S.
Greenwillow. Chute, B. J.

GRENVILLE, SIR RICHARD
Du Maurier, D. The King's general
Fletcher, I. Roanoke hundred

GREY, LADY JANE
Harwood, A. The lily and the leopards
Irwin, M. Elizabeth, captive princess

GREY, KATHERYN. See Hertford, Catherine (Grey) Seymour, Countess of

GREY, MARY. See Keys, Lady Mary (Grey)

The Grey Horse legacy. Hunt, J.

GRIERSON'S CAVALRY RAID, 1863
Sinclair, H. The horse soldiers
See also United States—19th century—Civil War—Campaigns and battles

GROCERS
Ainsworth, W. H. Old Saint Paul's
Malamud, B. The assistant
Spencer, E. The voice at the back door
Steinbeck, J. The winter of our discontent

GROTESQUE
Lind, J. Landscape in concrete

GROUNDHOGS. See Marmots

The group. McCarthy, M.
The grove of eagles. Graham, W.
The groves of Academe. McCarthy, M.
Growth of the soil. Hamsun, K.

GUADALAJARA. See Mexico—Guadalajara

GUADALCANAL CAMPAIGN. See World War, 1939-1945—Solomon Islands

Guard of honor. Cozzens, J. G.

GUARDIAN AND WARD
Heyer, G. Regency buck

GUATEMALA
Asturias, M. A. Mulata

GUENEVERE, QUEEN
White, T. H. The candle in the wind
In White, T. H. The once and future king p545-677
White, T. H. The ill-made knight

The Guermantes way. Proust, M.
also in Proust, M. Remembrance of things past v 1

GUERNSEY. See Channel Islands

GUERRILLAS
Becker, S. When the War is over
Hemingway, E. For whom the bell tolls
Kazantzakis, N. The fratricides
Kazantzakis, N. Freedom or death
MacLean, A. Force 10 from Navarone
Moore, R. The green berets
Nathanson, E. M. The dirty dozen

A guest for the night. Agnon, S. Y.

The guide. Narayan, R. K.

GUIDED MISSILES
Shulman, M. Rally round the flag, boys!
Trevor, E. The shoot

GUILT
Elman, R. M. The 28th day of Elul
Hutchinson, R. C. Johanna at daybreak
Johnson, P. H. An error of judgement
Peters, E. The house of green turf
Shaw, R. The man in the glass booth
See also Conscience; Responsibility

GUINEA PIGS
  Butler, E. P. Pigs is pigs
GUITARISTS. See Musicians—Guitarists
Gulf. Heinlein, R. A.
  In Knight, D. ed. A century of great short
    science fiction novels p231-93
GULF STREAM
  Hemingway, E. The old man and the sea
Gulliver's travels. Swift, J.
GUNBOATS. See Warships
GUNGA DIN. See Mirdrekvandi Gunga Din, Ali
Gunner Asch goes to war. See Kirst, H. H.
    Forward, Gunner Asch!
GUNS. See Munitions
Guns of Burgoyne. Lancaster, B.
The guns of Navarone. MacLean, A.
GUYENNE. See France, Provincial and rural
  —Guyenne
Guys and dolls. Runyon, D.
Guzman, go home, and other stories. Silli-
  toe, A.
Gwen Bristow's Plantation trilogy. Bristow, G.
GYPSIES. See Gipsies
The Gyrth Chalice mystery. Allingham, M.
  In Allingham, M. Three cases for Mr Cam-
    pion p421-604

H

H. M. Pulham, esquire. Marquand, J. P.
HMS Leviathan. Winton, J.
H.M.S. Saracen. Reeman, D.
H.M.S. Ulysses. MacLean, A.
The hack. Sheed, W.
Hadji Murád. Tolstoy, L.
  In Tolstoy, L. Short novels v2 p372-502
HADRIAN, EMPEROR OF ROME
  Yourcenar, M. Memoirs of Hadrian, and re-
    flections on the composition of Memoirs of
    Hadrian
Haircut, and other stories. Lardner, R.
HAITI
            18th century
  Bourne, P. Drums of destiny
  Carpentier, A. The kingdom of this world
      18th century—Revolution, 1791-1804
  Roberts, K. Lydia Bailey
            20th century
  Greene, G. The comedians
HALF-BROTHERS
  Nabokov, V. The real life of Sebastian
    Knight
HALF-CASTES
  Masters, J. Bhowani Junction
Half-seas over. Gilpatric, G.
  In Gilpatric, G. The Glencannon omnibus
    v2
HALF-SISTERS
  Scott, Sir W. The heart of Midlothian
The hallelujah trail. Gulick, B.
Hallelujah train. See Gulick, B. The hallelujah
  trail
HALLET, ELIZABETH (FONES) WINTHROP
    FEAKE
  Seton, A. The Winthrop woman
Hallowe'en party. Christie, A.
HALLUCINATIONS AND ILLUSIONS
  Armstrong, C. The witch's house
  Van Siller, H. The watchers
    See also Mental illness
HALLUCINATORY DRUGS. See Drugs
HAMILTON, ALEXANDER
  Atherton, G. The conqueror
  Taylor, D. Mistress of the Forge
The hamlet. Faulkner, W.
HAMPSHIRE. See England, Provincial and ru-
  ral—Hampshire

Hand in glove. Marsh, N.
The hand of Mary Constable. Gallico, P.
A handful of blackberries. Silone, I.
A handful of rice. Markandaya, K.
The hands of Cormac Joyce. Wibberley, L.
The handsome road. Bristow, G.
  also in Bristow, G. Gwen Bristow's Plan-
    tation trilogy p263-530
HANDYMEN. See Servants—Hired men
Hanger Stout, awake! Matthews, J.
Hanging by a thread. Kahn, J. ed.
The hanging tree. Johnson, D. M.
Hannah Fowler. Giles, J. H.
HANNIBAL
  Dolan, M. Hannibal of Carthage
Hannibal of Carthage. Dolan, M.
HAPPINESS
  Hesse, H. The journey to the East
  Hesse, H. Siddhartha
Happiness in crime. D'Aurevilly, J. B.
  In Dupee, F. W. ed. Great French short
    novels p341-90
Happy stories just to laugh at. Leacock, S.
HARBORS
            Brazil
  Amado, J. Shepherds of the night
The harbourmaster. McFee, W.
The hard blue sky. Grau. S. A.
Hard times. Dickens, C.
Hard times for these times. See Dickens, C.
  Hard times
HARELIP. See Face—Abnormities and deformi-
  ties
HARLEM. See New York (City)—Harlem
HARLOTS. See Prostitutes
Harm's way. Bassett, J.
HAROLD, KING OF ENGLAND
  Muntz, H. The golden warrior
HARPER'S FERRY, W. VA.
            John Brown raid, 1859
  Ehrlich, L. God's angry man
Harpoon in Eden. Mason, F. V.
Harry of Monmouth. Maughan, A. M.
HARVARD UNIVERSITY
  Kaufmann, M. S. Remember me to God
  Wolfe, T. Of time and the river
A harvest of stories. Canfield, D.
Harvest on the Don. Sholokhov, M.
HARWILLIERS, JEANNE
  Mallet-Joris, F. The witches
HASIDISM
  Agnon, S. Y. The bridal canopy
  Agnon, S. Y. In the heart of the seas
  Potok, C. The chosen
  Potok, C. The promise
  Singer, I. J. Yoshe Kalb
HASTINGS, BATTLE OF, 1066
  Heyer, G. The Conqueror
  Muntz, H. The golden warrior
The hat on the bed. O'Hara, J.
HATE
  Simenon, G. The cat
Hatter's castle. Cronin, A .J.
The haunted bookshop. Morley, C.
A haunted house, and other short stories.
  Woolf, V.
HAUNTED HOUSES. See Ghost stories
Haunted lady. Rinehart, M. R.
  In Rinehart, M. R. Miss Pinkerton p249-403
The haunted monastery. Gulik, R. van
The haunting of Hill House. Jackson, S.
HAVANA. See Cuba—Havana
Have his carcase. Sayers, D. L.
HAWAII
  Eyre, K. W. The sandalwood fan
  Jones, J. From here to eternity
  Jones, J. The pistol
  London, J. Stories of Hawaii
  Michener, J. A. Hawaii
HAWAIIAN ISLANDS. See Hawaii
HAWKS
  Mannix, D. P. The killers
  Murphy, R. The peregrine falcon

Hawksbill Station. Silverberg, R.

Hawthorne's Short stories. Hawthorne, N.

A hazard of new fortunes. Howells, W. D.

HEADMASTERS. See Teachers

HEADMISTRESSES. See School superintendents and principals

Hear us O Lord from heaven thy dwelling place. Lowry, M.

HEART

Diseases
Hawley, C. The hurricane years
Marttin, P. Heartsblood

A heart for the gods of Mexico. Aiken, C.
  In Aiken, C. The collected novels of Conrad Aiken p415-72

The heart is a lonely hunter. McCullers, C.
  also in McCullers, C. The ballad of the sad café p141-498

The heart of a dog. Bulgakov, M.

The heart of a Russian. See Lermontov, M. Y. A hero of our own times

Heart of darkness. Conrad, J.
  In Conrad, J. Great short works of Joseph Conrad p175-256
  In Conrad, J. The portable Conrad p490-603
  In Conrad, J. Stories and tales of Joseph Conrad
  In Conrad, J. Tales of land and sea p33-104
  In Conrad, J. Typhoon, and other tales of the sea p273-371
  In Conrad, J. Youth, and two other stories

The heart of Midlothian. Scott, Sir W.

The heart of the family. Goudge, E.

The heart of the matter. Greene, G.

Heart of the West. Henry, O.
  In Henry, O. The complete works of O. Henry p109-266

HEART TRANSPLANT. See Transplantation of organs, tissues, etc.

Heart troubles. Birmingham, S.

The Hearth and Eagle. Seton, A.

Heartsblood. Marttin, P.

Heat lightning. Dolson, H.

The heat of the day. Bowen, E

The heat of the sun. O'Faolain, S.

Heather Mary. Scott, J. M.

HEAVEN
Mirdrekvandi Gunga Din, A. No heaven for Gunga Din

Heaven has no favorites. Remarque, E. M.

Heaven help us! Tarr, H.

Heaven's my destination. Wilder, T.

HEBREWS. See Jews

HEBRIDES
Bridge, A. The dangerous islands
Innes, H. Atlantic fury
Mackenzie, C. Whisky galore
Woolf, V. To the lighthouse

HEDONISM
Kazantzakis, N. Zorba the Greek
Sagan, F. La chamade

HEIDELBERG. See Germany—Heidelberg

The Heiké story. Yoshikawa, E.

The heir of Starvelings. Berckman, E.

HEIRESSES. See Wealth

HEIRLOOMS. See Rings

HEIRS. See Inheritance and succession

Hell command. Adams, C.
  In Western Writers of America. A Western bonanza p 1-65

HÉLOÏSE
Moore, G. Heloise and Abelard
Waddell, H. Peter Abelard

Heloise and Abelard. Moore, G.

HELVETIA. See Switzerland

Hemingway. Hemingway, E.

The Hemingway reader. Hemingway, E.

Henderson the rain king. Bellow, S.

HENRIETTA MARIA, CONSORT OF CHARLES I
Anthony, E. Charles, the King

Henrietta who? Aird, C.

HENRY II, KING OF ENGLAND
Barnes, M. C. The passionate brood
Duggan, A. My life for my sheep
Mydans, S. Thomas

HENRY V, KING OF ENGLAND
Jackson, D. V. S. Walk with peril
Maughan, A. M. Harry of Monmouth

HENRY VII, KING OF ENGLAND
Barnes, M. C. The King's bed
Barnes, M. C. The Tudor rose

HENRY VIII, KING OF ENGLAND
Anthony, E. Anne Boleyn
Barnes, M. C. Brief gaudy hour
Barnes, M. C. King's fool
Barnes, M. C. My lady of Cleves
Brady, C. A. Stage of fools
Ford, F. M. The fifth queen
Haycraft, M. C. The reluctant queen
Lofts, N. The Concubine
Lofts, N. The King's pleasure
Macleod, A. The heretic
Macleod, A. The hireling
Plaidy, J. The sixth wife
Turton, G. My Lord of Canterbury

HENRY IV, KING OF FRANCE
Dumas, A. Marguerite de Valois
Mann, H. Henry, King of France
Mann, H. Young Henry of Navarre

HENRY OF NAVARRE. See Henry IV, King of France

HENRY, PATRICK
Gerson, N. B. Give me liberty

The Henry James reader. James, H.

Henry, King of France. Mann, H.

Henry quatre, King of France. See Mann, H. Henry, King of France

The Herb of Grace. See Goudge, E. Pilgrim's inn

Hercules, my shipmate. Graves, R.

Here and beyond. Wharton, E.
  In Wharton, E. The collected short stories of Edith Wharton v2 p371-500

Here lies. Disney, D. M.

Here lies. See Parker, D. The collected stories of Dorothy Parker

HEREDITY AND ENVIRONMENT
Herbert, F. Dune
Herbert, F. Dune messiah
Hergesheimer, J. The three black Pennys
March, W. The bad seed
Marquand, J. P. H. M. Pulham, esquire
Walpole, H. Fortitude

The heretic. Macleod, A.

The heretics. See Macleod, A. The heretic

The heritage. Keyes, F. P.

Herman had two daughters. Popkin, Z.

¡Hermanos! Herrick, W.

The hermit and the wild woman. Wharton, E.
  In Wharton, E. The collected short stories of Edith Wharton v 1 p569-705

HERMITS
France, A. Thaïs
Wibberley, L. The Island of the Angels

A hero of our own times. Lermontov, M. Y.

A hero of our time. See Lermontov, M. Y. A hero of our own times

The hero ship. Searls, H.

HEROD I, THE GREAT, KING OF JUDEA
Caldwell, T. Dear and glorious physician
Lagerkvist, P. Herod and Mariamne

Herod and Mariamne. Lagerkvist, P.

HEROISM
Robertson, D. The greatest thing since sliced bread
  See also Courage

Herries chronicle [series]
Walpole, H. The fortress
Walpole, H. Judith Paris
Walpole, H. Rogue Herries
Walpole, H. Vanessa

Herself surprised. Cary, J.
  also in Cary, J. First trilogy v 1

HERTFORD, CATHERINE (GREY) SEYMOUR, COUNTESS OF
Harwood, A. So merciful a queen, so cruel a woman

Herzog. Bellow, S.

HESSIAN MERCENARIES
Lancaster, B. Guns of Burgoyne

The hexed rifle. Gulick, B.
  In Western Writers of America. A Western bonanza p270-308

HOMOSEXUALITY—*Continued*
  O'Hara, J. A few trips and some poetry
    In O'Hara, J. And other stories p42-165
  O'Hara, J. Lovey Childs: a Philadelphian's story
  Pavese, C. Among women only
    In Pavese, C. The selected works of Cesare Pavese p175-275
  Renault, M. The charioteer
  Renault, M. The mask of Apollo
  Smith, D. It ends with revelations
  Snow, C. P. The sleep of reason
  Taylor, A. The gods are not mocked
  West, M. L. The devil's advocate
    See also Sex problems

HOMOSEXUALS. See Homosexuality

An honest thief, and other stories. Dostoevsky, F.

Honey. Jenkins, E.

Honey for the bears. Burgess, A.
  also in Burgess, A. A clockwork orange, and Honey for the bears p187-436

Honey in the horn. Davis, H. L.

HONGKONG. See China—Hongkong

An honorable estate. Kauffmann, L.

The Hoosier school-boy. Eggleston, E.

The Hoosier schoolmaster. Eggleston, E.

Hopscotch. Cortázar, J.

Horizon. MacInnes, H.
  In MacInnes, H. Assignment: suspense p195-313

Horn. Mano, D. K.

Hornblower and the Atropos. Forester, C. S.
  also in Forester, C. S. Young Hornblower p431-672

Hornblower and the Hotspur. Forester, C. S.

Hornblower during the crisis, and two stories: Hornblower's temptation and The last encounter. Forester, C. S.

HORROR STORIES
  Aiken, C. King Coffin
    In Aiken, C. The collected novels of Conrad Aiken p297-414
  Andrézel, P. The angelic avengers
  Blackburn, J. Children of the night
  Blackwood, A. In the realm of terror
  Blackwood, A. Tales of the uncanny and supernatural
  Bradbury, R. The October country
  Bradbury, R. Something wicked this way comes
  Brontë, E. Wuthering Heights
  Caird, J. The Loch
  Canning, J. ed. 50 great horror stories
  Case, D. The cell
  Christie, K. Child's play
  Christopher, J. The little people
  Christopher, J. Pendulum
  Cozzens, J. G. Castaway
  Davenport, B. comp. Famous monster tales
  Davies, L. P. A grave matter
  Davies, L. P. The paper dolls
  Davies, L. P. Twilight journey
  Disney, D. M. At some forgotten door
  Duerrenmatt, F. The quarry
  Du Maurier, D. Kiss me again, stranger
  Fowles, J. The collector
  Frankau, P. Colonel Blessington
  Fremlin, C. Possession
  Gilbert, S. Ratman's notebooks
  Gloag, J. Our mother's house
  Hamilton, A. ed. Splinters
  Hintze, N. A. You'll like my mother
  Hitchcock, A. ed. Alfred Hitchcock presents: Stories for late at night
  Hitchcock, A. ed. Alfred Hitchcock presents: Stories my mother never told me
  Hitchcock, A. ed. Alfred Hitchcock presents: Stories not for the nervous
  Hitchcock, A. ed. Alfred Hitchcock presents: Stories that scared even me
  Hitchcock, A. ed. Alfred Hitchcock presents: Stories they wouldn't let me do on TV
  Hitchcock, A. ed. Alfred Hitchcock's Fireside book of suspense
  Household, G. The courtesy of death
  Household, G. Dance of the dwarfs
  Jackson, S. The lottery
  Jackson, S. We have always lived in the castle

James, H. The turn of the screw
    also in Costain, T. B. comp. Twelve short novels p329-412
    also in James, H. The great short novels of Henry James p621-748
    also in James, H. The Henry James reader p255-356
    also in James, H. Short novels of Henry James p407-530
  Knight, D. ed. The dark side
  Langelaan, G. The fly
    In Hitchcock, A. ed. Alfred Hitchcock presents: Stories for late at night p225-55
  Levin, I. Rosemary's baby
  Machen, A. Tales of horror and the supernatural
  March, W. The bad seed
  Margolies, J. A. ed. Strange and fantastic stories
  Millar, M. The iron gates
    In Hitchcock, A. ed. Alfred Hitchcock presents: Stories for late at night p315-469
  Oates, J. C. Expensive people
  Playboy. The Playboy Book of horror and the supernatural
  Protter, E. ed. Monster festival
  Radcliffe, A. The mysteries of Udolpho
  Scott, J. M. Heather Mary
  Sheed, W. Pennsylvania gothic
    In Sheed, W. The blacking factory & Pennsylvania gothic p3-63
  Shelley, M. W. Frankenstein
  Sontag, S. Death kit
  Stevenson, R. L. The strange case of Dr Jekyll and Mr Hyde
  Stoker, B. Dracula
  Sturgeon, T. It
    In Hitchcock, A. ed. Alfred Hitchcock presents: Stories that scared even me p129-53
  Tolstoy, A. Vampires
  Walpole, H. The castle of Otranto
  Whitney, P. A. Hunter's green
  Whitney, P. A. Silverhill
  Whitney, P. A. The winter people
  Widdemer, M. The Red Castle women
    See also Gothic romances

The horrors of love. Dutourd, J.

A horse and two goats. Narayan, R. K.

Horse in the moon. Pirandello, L.

The horse knows the way. O'Hara, J.

HORSE RACING
  Bagnold, E. National Velvet
    In Costain, T. B. ed. Stories to remember v2 p339-504
  Edmonds, W. D. The Boyds of Black River
  Francis, D. For kicks
  Francis, D. Forfeit
  Francis, D. Nerve
  Francis, D. Three to show
  Moore, G. Esther Waters
    See also Jockeys

The horse soldiers. Sinclair, H.

HORSE THIEVES
  O'Rourke, F. The swift runner

A horseman riding by. Delderfield, R. F.

The horsemen. Kessel, J.

HORSES
  Bagnold, E. National Velvet
    In Costain, T. B. ed. Stories to remember v2 p339-504
  Cooper, P. ed. Great horse stories
  Francis, D. Flying finish
  James, W. Sand
  Kessel, J. The horsemen
  Steinbeck, J. The red pony
    In Steinbeck, J. The portable Steinbeck p327-415
    In Steinbeck, J. The short novels of John Steinbeck p135-200
    See also Lippizaner horses

The horse's mouth. Cary, J.
  also in Cary, J. First trilogy v3

HOSPITAL SHIPS
  Hartog, J. de. The little ark

HOSPITALS AND SANITORIUMS
  Aczel, T. The ice age
  Baldwin, F. The velvet hammer
  Bottome, P. Private worlds
  Brand, M. The outward room
  Brand, M. Savage sleep
  Cronin, A. J. A pocketful of rye
  Cronin, A. J. Shannon's way

The Human predicament [series]
Hughes, R. The fox in the attic

The human season. Wallant, E. L.

HUMOR
Ade, G. The America of George Ade (1866-1944)
Airth, R. Snatch
Alarcón, P. A. Ce. The three-cornered that
Aleichem, S. The adventures of Menahem-Mendl
Aleichem, S. The adventures of Mottel, the cantor's son
Amis, K. Lucky Jim
Bates, H. E. A breath of French air
Bates, H. E. The darling buds of May
Beagle, P. S. A fine and private place
Beerbohm, M. Zuleika Dobson
Behan, B. The Scarperer
Bellow, S. Henderson the rain king
Bellow, S. Mr Sammler's planet
Benchley, N. The off-islanders
Benchley, N. The visitors
Benchley, N. A winter's tale
Bennett, A. Buried alive
Berger, T. Little Big Man
Bradford, R. Ol' man Adam an' his chillun
Bradford, R. Red sky at morning
Breslin, J. The gang that couldn't shoot straight
Brinkley, W. The ninety and nine
Brinkley, W. Don't go near the water
Burgess, A. Honey for the bears
  In Burgess, A. A clockwork orange, and Honey for the bears p187-436
Butler, E. P. Pigs is pigs
Cadell, E. The lark shall sing
Capote, T. The grass harp
Cary, J. First trilogy
Cary, J. Herself surprised
Cary, J. The horse's mouth
Cecil, H. Friends at court
Cheever, J. The Wapshot chronicle
Cheever, J. The Wapshot scandal
Chekhov, A. St Peter's Day, and other tales
Chesterton, G. K. The man who was Thursday
Compton-Burnett, I. Mother and son
Connell, E. S. Mr Bridge
Coward, N. Pomp and circumstance
Craig, P. Gate of ivory, Gate of Horn
Crichton, R. The secret of Santa Vittoria
Cunningham, E. V. Penelope
Davies, V. It happens every spring
Davies, V. Miracle on 34th Street
Dennis, P. Around the world with Auntie Mame
Dennis, P. Auntie Mame
De Vries, P. The cat's pajamas & Witches milk
De Vries, P. Comfort me with apples
De Vries, P. The tunnel of love
De Vries, P. The vale of laughter
Dick, R. A. The ghost and Mrs Muir
Dickens, C. The posthumous papers of the Pickwick Club
Donleavy, J. P. The beastly beatitudes of Balthazar B
Durrell, G. Rosy is my relative
Faulkner, W. The reivers
Fish, R. L. The murder league
Fleming, J. No bones about it
Forrest, D. And to my nephew Albert I leave the island what I won off Fatty Hagan in a poker game
Franken, R. Claudia
Fraser, G. M. Flashman
Giles, J. H. Shady Grove
Gilford, C. B. The crooked shamrock
Gilpatric, G. The best of Glencannon
Gilpatric, G. The Glencannon omnibus
Greene, G. Travels with my aunt
Guareschi, G. Comrade Don Camillo
Guareschi, G. Don Camillo and his flock
Guareschi, G. Don Camillo meets the flower children
Guareschi, G. Don Camillo takes the Devil by the tail
Guareschi, G. Don Camillo's dilemma
Guareschi, G. The little world of Don Camillo
Gulick, B. Liveliest town in the West
Hanley, C. The red-haired bitch
Hasek, J. The good soldier: Schweik
Heller, J. Catch-22
Heyer, G. A civil contract
Heyer, G. False colours
Heyer, G. Sprig muslin
Hodgins, E. Mr Blandings builds his dream house

Hooker, R. MASH
Housepian, M. A houseful of love
Hughes, L. The best of Simple
Hughes, L. Simple speaks his mind
Hughes, L. Simple stakes a claim
Hughes, L. Simple takes a wife
Hughes, L. Simple's Uncle Sam
Hyman, M. No time for sergeants
Ilf. Ilf & Petrov's The complete adventures of Ostap Bender
Jerome, J. K. Three men in a boat
Jessup, A. The best American humorous short stories
Jhabvala, R. P. The householder
Johnson, P. H. Night and silence, who is here?
Kafka, F. Amerika
Kirst, H. H. Forward, Gunner Asch!
Kirst, H. H. Revolt of Gunner Asch
Kirst, H. H. The wolves
Lanning, G. Green corn moon
Lardner, R. You know me, Al
Lasswell, M. High time
Lasswell, M. Let's go for broke
Lasswell, M. One on the house
Lasswell, M. Suds in your eyes
Lasswell, M. Tooner Schooner
Lasswell, M. Wait for the wagon
Laumer, K. Retief and the warlords
Leacock, S. Happy stories just to laugh at
Lindop, A. E. I start counting
Linscott, R. N. ed. The best American humorous short stories
Lodge, D. The British Museum is falling down
Mackenzie, C. Whisky galore
Marshall, B. Father Hilary's holiday
Moll, E. Mr Seidman and the geisha
Moll, E. Seidman and son
Molloy, P. A pennant for the Kremlin
Morris, W. Love among the cannibals
Morris, W. What a way to go
Munchausen. The adventures of Baron Munchausen
Murdoch, I. Bruno's dream
Murdoch, I. The flight from the enchanter
Murdoch, I. The nice and the good
Murdoch, I. The sandcastle
Murdoch, I. A severed head
Nabokov, V. Lolita
Nabokov, V. Pnin
Narayan, R. K. The guide
Nathan, R. The devil with love
Natsume, S. Botchan
O'Rourke, F. The swift runner
Portis, C. Norwood
Portis, C. True grit
Powell, A. What's become of Waring
Powell, R. Pioneer, go home!
Pritchett, V. S. The key to my heart
Purdy, J. Malcolm
Richter, C. The grandfathers
Rosten, L. Captain Newman, M.D.
Roth, P. Portnoy's complaint
Runyon, D. Best of Runyon
Runyon, D. Guys and dolls
Saroyan, W. My name is Aram
Sarton, M. The fur person
Sharp, M. In pious memory
Sharp, M. The nutmeg tree
Sharp, M. Rosa
Sharp, M. Something light
Shulman, M. Anyone got a match?
Shulman, M. I was a teen-age dwarf
Shulman, M. The many loves of Dobie Gillis
Shulman, M. Rally round the flag, boys!
Smollett, T. The expedition of Humphry Clinker
Smollett, T. Peregrine Pickle
Sneider, V. The Teahouse of the August Moon
Spark, M. The comforters
  In Spark, M. A Muriel Spark trio: The comforters; The ballad of Peckham Rye [and] Memento mori p13-228
Spark, M. The prime of Miss Jean Brodie
Steinbeck, J. Cannery Row
Steinbeck, J. Sweet Thursday
Sterne, L. A sentimental journey through France and Italy
Stockton, F. R. The storyteller's pack
Streeter, E. Chairman of the bored
Streeter, E. Father of the bride
Streeter, E. Mr Hobbs' vacation
Struther, J. Mrs Miniver
Stuart, J. Taps for Private Tussie
Svevo, I. The confessions of Zeno
Tarkington, B. Seventeen
Tarr, H. The conversion of Chaplain Cohen
Taylor, R. L. A journey to Matecumbe
Temple, W. The drip-dried tourist

HUMOR—*Continued*
Thurber, J. The 13 clocks
Tracy, H. The first day of Friday
Tracy, H. The straight and narrow path
Twain, M. The adventures of Huckleberry Finn
Twain, M. The adventures of Tom Sawyer
Twain, M. Those extraordinary twins
In Twain, M. Pudd'nhead Wilson and Those extraordinary twins p205-95
Wahl, B. Rafferty & Co.
Walker, D. Geordie
Wallop, D. The good life
Wallop, D. The year the Yankee lost the pennant
Waugh, E. Decline and fall
Waugh, E. The loved one
Waugh E. Men at arms
Waugh, E. Officers and gentlemen
Weidman, J. The center of the action
Welty, E. The Ponder heart
West, J. Cress Delahanty
West, J. Except for me and thee
West, J. The friendly persuasion
West, N. Cool million
In West, N. Complete works p143-256
Westlake, D. E. The busy body
Westlake, D. E. The fugitive pigeon
Westlake, D. E. God save the mark
Westlake, D. E. The spy in the ointment
Westlake, D. E. Who stole Sassi Manoon?
Whitehouse, A. Playboy squadron
Wibberley, L. Beware of the mouse
Wibberley, L. The mouse on the moon
Wibberley, L. The mouse on Wall Street
Wibberley, L. The mouse that roared
Wilson, N. C. The nine brides and Granny Hite
Wodehouse, P. G. The butler did it
Wodehouse, P. G. The code of the Woosters
Wodehouse, P. G. Fish preferred
Wodehouse, P. G. How right you are, Jeeves
Wodehouse, P. G. The inimitable Jeeves
Wodehouse, P. G. The most of P. G. Wodehouse
Wodehouse, P. G. Selected stories
Wodehouse, P. G. Uncle Fred in the springtime
Wodehouse, P. G. Very good, Jeeves
Wouk, H. City boy: the adventures of Herbie Bookbinder
See also Cheerful stories; Parodies; Satire

Practical jokes
Kundera, M. The joke

Humphry Clinker, The expedition of. Smollett, T.

The hunchback of Notre Dame. Hugo, V.

HUNCHBACKS
Hugo, V. The hunchback of Notre Dame
Lofts, N. The lute player
See also Cripples

HUNDRED YEARS' WAR, 1339-1453
Doyle, Sir A. C. The White Company
Haycraft, M. C. The Lady Royal

HUNGARIANS. See Magyars

HUNGARIANS IN AUSTRIA
Thompson, M. The cry and the covenant

HUNGARIANS IN BELGIUM
Albrand, M. Meet me tonight

HUNGARIANS IN PORTUGAL
Bridge, A. The Portuguese escape

HUNGARY
16th century
Holland, C. Rakóssy
19th century
Zilahy, L. The Dukays
20th century
Aczel, T. The ice age
Blackstock, C. The knock at midnight
Bridge, A. The tightening string
Elman, R. M. Lilo's diary
Elman, R. M. The reckoning
MacLean, A. The secret ways
Zilahy, L. The Dukays
Aristocracy
See Aristocracy—Hungary
Budapest
Aczel, R. The ice age
Bridge, A. The tightening string
Sjöwall, M. The man who went up in smoke

Communism
See Communism—Hungary

Hunger. Hamsun, K.
The hungry grass. Power, R.
Hungry hill. Du Maurier, D.
The hunter and the whale. Van der Post, L.
Hunter, come home. McKenna, R.
In Knight, D. ed. A century of great short science fiction novels p343-79

HUNTERS. See Hunting
Hunter's green. Whitney, P. A.
Hunter's horn. Arnow, H.

HUNTING
Bodsworth, F. The sparrow's fall
Cooper, J. F. The pioneers
Faulkner, W. Big woods
Gipson, F. Hound-dog man
Guthrie, A. B. The big sky
Hersey, J. The marmot drive
Household, G. Rogue male
Humphrey, W. Home from the hill
Lott, M. The last hunt
Marshall, J. V. A river ran out of Eden
Prebble, J. The buffalo soldiers
Rawlings, M. K. South moon under
See also Fox hunting; Trappers and trapping
Africa
Hanley, G. Gilligan's last elephant
Ruark, R. Something of value
Sherman, D. R. Into the noonday sun
India
Scott, J. D. Elephant grass
Sherman, D. R. Old Mali and the boy
Norway
Hamsun, K. Pan

Huntingtower. Buchan, J.
In Buchan, J. Adventurers all v 1
The hurricane. Nordhoff, C.
The hurricane years. Hawley, C.

HURRICANES
Bagley, D. Wyatt's hurricane
La Farge, C. The sudden guest
Moore, R. The Sea Flower
Nordhoff, C. The hurricane

HUSBAND, HARMON
Fletcher, I. The wind in the forest

HUSBANDS AND WIVES. See Marriage problem

Hushed were the hills. McWhirter, M.

HYDROGEN BOMB. See Atomic bomb

HYPNOTISM
Davies, L. P. The white room
Du Maurier, G. Trilby
Stoker, B. Dracula

I

I.W.W. See Industrial Workers of the World
I am Mary Dunne. Moore, B.
I can get it for you wholesale. Weidman, J.
I capture the castle. Smith, D.
I, Claudius. Graves, R.
I don't need you any more. Miller, A.
I, Eugenia. See Kenyon, F. W. That Spanish woman
"I have a thing to tell you." Wolfe, T.
In Wolfe, T. The short novels of Thomas Wolfe p158-231
I, Keturah. Wolff, R.
I loved Tiberius. Dored, E.
I, Madame Tussaud. Martin, S.
I never promised you a rose garden. Green, H.
I, Rachel. Cost, M.
I remember! I remember! O'Faolain, S.
I, Roberta. Vining, E. G.
I, robot. Asimov, I.
"I!" said the demon. Baxt, G.
I sing the Body Electric! Bradbury, R.

I start counting. Lindop, A. E.

I, the King. Keyes, F. P.

I want it now. Amis, K.

I was a teen-age dwarf. Shulman, M.

I was dancing. O'Connor, E.

IBO TRIBE
Achebe, C. Arrow of God
Achebe, C. Things fall apart

The ice age. Aczel, T.

The ice-cream headache, and other stories. Jones, J.

Ice Palace. Ferber, E.

The ice palace. See Vesaas, T. Palace of ice

Ice Station Zebra. MacLean, A.

ICELAND
Gunnarsson, G. The good shepherd
Seton, A. Avalon

10th century
Roberts, D. J. Fire in the ice

19th century
Gunnarsson, G. The black cliffs
Laxness, H. Paradise reclaimed

20th century
Laxness, H. Independent people
Laxness, H. World light

Farm life
See Farm life—Iceland

Iceland fisherman. Loti, P.

ICELANDERS IN THE UNITED STATES
Laxness, H. Paradise reclaimed

ICONS
Godden, R. The kitchen Madonna

IDEALISM
Morrison, T. The stones of the house
Van der Zee, J. The plum explosion
Wilder, T. Heaven's my destination

IDENTITY, PERSONAL. See Personality

The ides of March. Wilder, T.

IDIOCY
Lofts, N. Scent of cloves

The idiot. Dostoevsky, F.

IDIOTS. See Idiocy

Idiots first. Malamud, B.

The idol of the flies. Rice, J.
In Hitchcock, A. ed. Alfred Hitchcock presents: Stories my mother never told me p207-28

If Israel lost the war. Chesnoff, R. Z.

The If Reader of science fiction. If

Ilf & Petrov's The complete adventures of Ostap Bender. Ilf

The ill-made knight. White, T. H.
also in White, T. H. The once and future king p325-544

ILLEGITIMACY
Allen, H. Anthony Adverse
Buck, P. S. The new year
Cheever, J. Bullet Park
Compton-Burnett, I. Darkness and day
Compton-Burnett, I. Mother and son
Defoe, D. Roxana, the fortunate mistress
De Wohl, L. The last crusader
Dreiser T. Jennie Gerhardt
Endore, G. King of Paris
Graham, W. The grove of eagles
Hawthorne, N. The scarlet letter
Hutchinson, R. C. The inheritor
Macleod, A. City of light
Maupassant, G. de. Pierre and Jean
Moore, G. Esther Waters
Moore, R. Second growth
Oates, J. C. A garden of earthly delights
Peterkin, J. Scarlet Sister Mary
Sharp, M. Rosa
Smith, D. E. Brief flower
Wharton, E. The old maid
In Wharton, E. An Edith Wharton treasury
In Wharton, E. Old New York v2
Wilkinson, S. Moss on the north side

ILLINOIS
19th century
Dickens, C. Martin Chuzzlewit

20th century
Bradbury, R. Dandelion wine
Cather, W. My mortal enemy
Maxwell, W. They came like swallows
Wilder, T. The eighth day

Chicago
Algren, N. The man with the golden arm
Barnes, M. A. Years of grace
Bellow, S. The adventures of Augie March
Bellow, S. Dangling man
Brooks, G. Maud Martha
Budd, L. April harvest
Burnett, W. R. Little Caesar
De Vries, P. The blood of the lamb
Dos Passos, J. Chosen country
Dreiser, T. Jennie Gerhardt
Dreiser, T. Sister Carrie
Dreiser, T. The titan
Farrell, J. T. Judgement day
Farrell, J. T. Studs Lonigan
Farrell, J. T. A world I never made
Farrell, J. T. Young Lonigan
Farrell, J. T. The young manhood of Studs Lonigan
Greenlee, S. The spook who sat by the door
Hailey, A. Airport
Levin, M. The old bunch
Motley, W. Knock on any door
Motley, W. Let no man write my epitaph
Norris, F. The pit
Petrakis, H. M. A dream of kings
Sinclair, U. The jungle
Solberg, G. Shelia
Wright, R. Lawd today
Wright, R. Native son
Wright, R. The outsider

Farm life
See Farm life—Illinois

ILLNESS
James, H. The wings of the dove
Tanizaki, J. Diary of a mad old man
See also name of particular illness or disease, e.g. Leukemia

The illustrated man. Bradbury, R.

Illyrian spring. Bridge, A.

The image men. Priestley, J. B.

The image of Chekhov. Chekhov, A.

Image of my father. See Hutchinson, R. C. The inheritor

Imaginary friends. Lurie, A.

IMAGINARY KINGDOMS
Cabell, J. B. Jurgen: a comedy of justice
Hope, A. The prisoner of Zenda
Swift, J. Gulliver's travels
Thurber, J. The 13 clocks

Imagine kissing Pete. O'Hara, J.
In O'Hara, J. Sermons and soda water v2

IMMIGRANTS
Asch, S. The mother
Bojer, J. The emigrants
Cather, W. My Antonia
Levin, M. My father's house
See also names of nationals in other countries: e.g. Italians in the United States; Swedes in the United States

The immoralist. Gide, A.

Immortal queen. Byrd, E.

Immortal wife. Stone, I.

IMMORTALITY
Beauvoir, S. de. All men are mortal

Imperial Caesar. Warner, R.

The Imperial Governor. Shipway, G.

Imperial Palace. Bennett, A.

IMPERIAL ROME. See Rome—510-30 B.C.

Imperial woman. Buck, P. S.

IMPERIALISM
Abrahams, P. A wreath for Udomo
Scott, P. The jewel in the crown

IMPERSONATIONS
This subject is used for novels dealing with individuals who assume or act the character of another. For novels describing a condition in which one individual shows in alternation two very different characters, see subject: Dual personality
Albrand, M. Reunion with terror
In The Saturday Evening Post. Danger p 1-106
Barrett, W. E. The left hand of God
Barrie, J. M. Little minister
Behn, N. The shadowboxer
Bennett, A. Buried alive
Collins, W. The woman in white
Coxe, G. H. The candid impostor

INDIA—*Continued*
Race problems
See Race problems—India
INDIA, PROVINCIAL AND RURAL
Banerji, B. Pather Panchali: Song of the road
Markandaya, K. The coffer dams
Markandaya, K. Nectar in a sieve
Narayan, R. K. The man-eater of Malgudi
Premchand. The gift of a cow
INDIAN SOLDIERS. See Soldiers, Indian
Indian summer. Howells, W. D.

Indian summer. Knowles, J.

Indian summer of a Forsyte. Galsworthy, J.
In Galsworthy, J. The Galsworthy reader p543-86
INDIANA
Jones, J. The ice cream headache
In Jones, J. The ice-cream headache, and other stories p213-38
19th century
Eggleston, E. The Hoosier school-boy
Eggleston, E. The Hoosier schoolmaster
Lockridge, R. Raintree County
Tarkington, B. The gentleman from Indiana
Tarkington, B. The magnificent Ambersons
West, J. Except for me and thee
West, J. The friendly persuasion
20th century
Anderson, S. Dark laughter
De Vries, P. Let me count the ways
Morris, W. In orbit
Tarkington, B. Alice Adams
Vonnegut, K. God bless you, Mr Rosewater
Frontier and pioneer life
See Frontier and pioneer life—Indiana
Indianapolis
Hayes, J. The desperate hours
Politics
See Politics—Indiana
Terre Haute
Stone, I. Adversary in the house
INDIANAPOLIS. See Indiana—Indianapolis
INDIANS OF GUATEMALA. See Mayas
INDIANS OF MEXICO
Baron, A. The golden princess
Olsen, P. The Virgin of San Gil
Traven, B. The cotton-pickers
See also Aztecs
INDIANS OF NORTH AMERICA
Allen, T. D. Doctor in buckskin
Cooper, J. F. The pioneers
Culp, J. H. The bright feathers
Davis, H. L. Beulah Land
Giles, J. H. Johnny Osage
Grey, Z. The vanishing American
Gulick, B. The hallelujah trail
Guthrie, A. B. The big sky
Guthrie, A. B. The way west
Johnston, M. To have and to hold
Mason, F. V. Young titan
Momaday, N. S. House made of dawn
Roberts, K. Northwest Passage
Schaefer, J. The canyon
In Schaefer, J. The short novels of Jack Schaefer p221-316
Van Every, D. The scarlet feather
See also Cheyenne Indians; Comanche Indians; Cree Indians; Five Civilized Tribes; Navaho Indians; Ojibway Indians; Sauk Indians; Seneca Indians; Ute Indians; Wahpekute Indians
California
Lauritzen, J. The cross and the sword
Canada
Bodsworth, F. The sparrow's fall
Captivities
Allen, H. The forest and the fort
Berger, T. Little Big Man
Capps, B. A woman of the people
Edmonds, W. D. In the hands of the Senecas
Giles, J. H. Hannah Fowler
Richter, C. A country of strangers
Richter, C. The light in the forest
Van Every, D. Bridal journey
Vaughan, C. A. The Seneca hostage

New Mexico
Cather, W. Death comes for the archbishop
Northwest, Pacific
Berry, D. Trask
Rites and ceremonies
Sorensen, V. The proper gods
Wars
Allen, H. Bedford Village
Arnold, E. Blood brother
Capps, B. The white man's road
Churchill, W. The crossing
Cooper, J. F. The Deerslayer
Cooper, J. F. The last of the Mohicans
Cooper, J. F. The Leatherstocking saga
Cooper, J. F. The Pathfinder
Cooper, J. F. The prairie
Edmonds, W. D. Drums along the Mohawk
Giles, J. H. Six-horse hitch
Wilder, R. Bright feather
See also names of Indian wars, e.g. Black Hawk War, 1832
The West
Fisher, V. Mountain man
INDIANS OF SOUTH AMERICA
Caillou, A. Bichu the jaguar
Hudson, W. H. Green mansions
Matthiessen, P. At play in the fields of the Lord
Peru
Alegría, C. Broad and alien is the world
INDIVIDUALISM
Knowles, J. Indian summer
Orwell, G. Nineteen eighty-four
Pasternak, B. Doctor Zhivago
Rand, A. Anthem
Rand, A. Atlas shrugged
Rand, A. The fountainhead
See also Conformity
INDIVIDUALITY
Dennis, N. Cards of identity
Green, G. The last angry man
See also Personality
INDOCHINA, FRENCH
Duras, M. The sea wall
Farm life
See Farm life—Indochina, French
The indomitable Hornblower. Forester, C. S.
INDONESIA
Ambler, E. Passage of arms
Ambler, E. State of siege
In Ambler, E. The intriguers p169-290
See also Dutch East Indies
INDONESIANS IN THE NETHERLANDS
Hartog, J. de. The little ark
INDUSTRIAL CONDITIONS
Bennett, A. Clayhanger
Bennett, A. The old wives' tale
Dickens, C. Hard times
Durrell, L. Tunc
Hergesheimer, J. The three black Pennys
Markandaya, K. Nectar in a sieve
Romains, J. The earth trembles
INDUSTRIAL WORKERS OF THE WORLD
Stegner, W. Joe Hill
Stegner, W. The preacher and the slave
INDUSTRIALISTS. See Capitalists and financiers
INDUSTRIALIZATION. See Industrial conditions
INDUSTRY AND STATE
Rand, A. Atlas shrugged
An infamous army. Heyer, G.
INFANTRYMEN. See Soldiers, American; Soldiers, German; etc.
INFIDELITY, MARITAL. See Marriage problems
INFLATION
Remarque, E. M. The black obelisk
The informer. O'Flaherty, L.
INFORMERS. See Treason
The ingenious gentleman, Don Quixote de la Mancha. See Cervantes, M. de. Don Quixote de la Mancha
INHERITANCE (BIOLOGY) See Heredity and environment
Inheritance. Bentley, P.

The Islar, a narrative of Lang III. Saxton, M.

ISLE OF SKYE. See Scotland—Isle of Skye

ISLE OF WIGHT
Barnes, M. C. Mary of Carisbrooke

ISOLDE
Roberts, D. J. The enchanted cup

ISRAEL
Banks, L. R. Children at the gate
Blocker, J. ed. Israeli stories
Davidson, L. The Menorah men
Dayan, Y. Death has two sons
Jacobson, D. The beginners
Michener, J. A. The source
Nathan, R. A star in the wind
Shaw, R. The man in the glass booth
Uris, L. Exodus
Viertel, J. The last temptation
Vonnegut, K. Mother night
West, M. L. The tower of Babel
    See also Palestine

Jerusalem
Kaniuk, Y. Himmo, King of Jerusalem
Spark, M. The Mandelbaum Gate

ISRAEL-ARAB WAR, 1948-1949
Kaniuk, Y. Himmo, King of Jerusalem
Nathan, R. A star in the wind

ISRAEL-ARAB WAR, 1967-
Chesnoff, R. Z. If Israel lost the war
Cleary, J. Season of doubt
Hempstone, S. In the midst of lions
West, M. L. The tower of Babel
Wiesel, E. A beggar in Jerusalem

Israel Potter: his fifty years of exile. Melville, H.

ISRAELI SOLDIERS. See Soldiers, Israeli

Israeli stories. Blocker, J. ed.

ISRAELITES. See Jews; Jews in Egypt; Jews in Palestine, Ancient

ISTANBUL. See Turkey—Istanbul

It. Sturgeon, T.
    In Hitchcock, A. ed. Alfred Hitchcock presents: Stories that scared even me p129-53

It can't happen here. Lewis, S.

It ends with revelations. Smith, D.

It happened in Boston? Greenan, R. H.

It happens every spring. Davies, V.

The Italian girl. Murdoch, I.

ITALIAN REFUGEES. See Refugees, Italian

ITALIANS IN NEW YORK (CITY)
Puzo, M. The fortunate pilgrim

ITALIANS IN RUSSIA
Guareschi, G. Comrade Don Camillo

ITALIANS IN SOUTH AMERICA
Conrad, J. Nostromo

ITALIANS IN SWITZERLAND
Silone, I. The fox and the camellias

ITALIANS IN THE UNITED STATES
Breslin, J. The gang that couldn't shoot straight
Charles-Roux, E. To forget Palermo
Di Donato, P. Christ in concrete
Laxalt, R. A man in the wheatfield
Longo, L. The family on vendetta street
Malamud, B. The assistant
    In Malamud, B. A Malamud reader p75-305
Shulman, M. Rally round the flag, boys!
Sinclair, J. The changelings
Wallant, E. L. The children at the gate

ITALY
Dolan, M. Hannibal of Carthage
Pirandello, L. Horse in the moon
Vittorini, E. Erica
    In Vittorini, E. The dark and the light p 1-75

13th century
De Wohl, L. The joyful beggar
De Wohl, L. The quiet light
Kazantzakis, N. Saint Francis

14th century
De Wohl, L. Lay siege to heaven

15th century
Eliot, G. Romola
Jensen, J. V. Christopher Columbus
    In Jensen, J. V. The long journey p491-677
Merejkowski, D. The romance of Leonardo da Vinci
Stone, I. The agony and the ecstasy

16th century
Harsányi, Z. de. The star-gazer
Maugham, W. S. Then and now
Peyrefitte, R. The prince's person
Radcliffe, A. The mysteries of Udolpho
Stone, I. The agony and the ecstasy

17th century
Cervantes, M. de. Man of glass
    In Cervantes, M. de. The portable Cervantes p760-96
    In Cervantes, M. de. Three exemplary novels p75-121
Manzoni, A. The betrothed

18th century
Stendhal. Chartreuse of Parma

19th century
Bacchelli, R. The mill on the Po
Lampedusa, G. di. The Leopard

20th century
Ambler, E. Cause for alarm
    In Ambler, E. Intrigue p295-465
Bassani, G. The garden of the Finzi-Continis
Berto, G. The sky is red
Gadda, C. E. Acquainted with grief
Godden, R. The battle of the Villa Fiorita
Guareschi, G. Don Camillo and his flock
Guareschi, G. Don Camillo meets the flower children
Guareschi, G. Don Camillo takes the Devil by the tail
Guareschi, G. Don Camillo's dilemma
Guareschi, G. The little world of Don Camillo
Heller, J. Catch-22
Moravia, A. Command, and I will obey you
Pasinetti, P. M. Venetian red
Plagemann, B. The best is yet to be
Rees, B. Mrs Wall, Mrs Wall
    In Rees, B. Try another country p55-120
Silone, I. Bread and wine
Silone, I. A handful of blackberries
Silone, I. The seed beneath the snow
Slonim, M. ed. Modern Italian short stories
Soldati, M. The orange envelope
Svevo, I. Further confessions of Zeno
West, M. L. Daughter of silence

Aristocracy
See Aristocracy—Italy

Assisi
De Wohl, L. The joyful beggar
Gallico, P. The small miracle

Calabria
West, M. L. The devil's advocate

Courts and courtiers
See Courts and courtiers—Italy

Fascism
See Fascism—Italy

Ferrara
Bassani, G. The garden of the Finzi-Continis

Florence
Du Maurier, D. My cousin Rachel
Eliot, G. Romola
Forster, E. M. A room with a view
Howells, W. D. Indian summer
Huxley, A. Time must have a stop
Lawrence, D. H. Aaron's rod
Maugham, W. S. Then and now
Spencer, E. The light in the piazza
Stone, I. The agony and the ecstasy

Milan
Manzoni, A. The betrothed

Naples
Burns, J. H. The gallery
Griffin, G. A last lamp burning

Parma
Stendhal. Chartreuse of Parma

Peasant life
See Peasant life—Italy

Politics
See Politics—Italy

Pompeii
Bulwer-Lytton, Sir E. The last days of Pompeii

JAPAN—*Continued*

Farm life
See Farm life—Japan

Hiroshima
Ibuse, M. Black rain
Morris, E. The flowers of Hiroshima

Rites and ceremonies
See Rites and ceremonies—Japan

Tokyo
Abé, K. The ruined map
Mishima, Y. After the banquet
Mishima, Y. Forbidden colors
Roberts, J. H. The Q document

Yokahama
Mishima, Y. The sailor who fell from grace with the sea

JAPAN, PROVINCIAL AND RURAL
Abé, K. The woman in the dunes
Natsume, S. Botchan

JAPANESE-AMERICANS
Charyn, J. American scrapbook

JAPANESE IN HAWAII
Michener, J. A. Hawaii

JAPANESE IN THE PHILIPPINE ISLANDS
Mydans, S. S. The open city

JAPANESE IN THE UNITED STATES
Buck, P. S. The hidden flower

Japanese short stories. Akutagawa, R.

Java Head. Hergesheimer, J.

JAZZ ORCHESTRAS
Baker, D. Young man with a horn
Kelley, W. M. A drop of patience

JEALOUSY
Balzac, H. de. Cousin Bette
Caldwell, T. The eagles gather
Caldwell, T. This side of innocence
Cather, W. Sapphira and the slave girl
Colette. The cat
In Colette. 7 by Colette v 1 p69-193
Eliot, G. Middlemarch
Godden, J. A winter's tale
Machado de Assis, J. M. Dom Casmurro
Mann, T. Young Joseph
In Mann, T. Joseph and his brothers p261-444
Pirandello, L. The outcast
Proust, M. The captive
Williams, B. A. Leave her to heaven

Jean-Christophe. Rolland, R.

Jean Santeuil. Proust, M.

JEANNE D'ARC. See Joan of Arc, Saint

Jeanne; or, Revolt. See Mallet-Joris, F. The witches

JEFFERSON, THOMAS, PRESIDENT U.S.
Page, E. The tree of liberty

JEFFERSON. See Mississippi—Jefferson

JEFFREYS, GEORGE JEFFREYS, 1st BARON
Doyle, Sir A. C. Micah Clarke

Jennie Gerhardt. Dreiser, T.

JEREMIAH, THE PROPHET
Weinreb, N. N. The Babylonians

Jericho's daughters. Wellman, P. I.

JERUSALEM
See also Israel—Jerusalem; Palestine—Jerusalem

Siege, 70 A.D.
Feuchtwanger, L. Josephus

A jest of God. Laurence, M.

JESTERS. See Fools and jesters

JESUITS
Benson, R. H. Come rack! Come rope!
Del Castillo, M. Child of our time
De Wohl, L. Set all afire
Sue, E. The Wandering Jew
See also Monasticism and religious orders

JESUS CHRIST
Asch, S. Mary
Asch, S. The Nazarene
Bekessy, E. Barabbas
Douglas, L. C. The Big Fisherman
Douglas, L. C. The robe
Kazantzakis, N. The last temptation of Christ
Lofts, N. How far to Bethlehem?
Rayner, W. The last days
Wallace, L. Ben Hur
See also Christianity

Crucifixion
Bulgakov, M. The Master and Margarita
De Wohl, L. The spear
Moorcock, M. Behold the man
In Nebula award stories, three p121-92
Wibberley, L. The centurion

Drama
Kazantzakis, N. The Greek passion

Holy coat
See Holy coat

JET PLANES. See Aeronautics

The Jew of Rome. Feuchtwanger, L.

The Jewel in the crown. Scott, P.

JEWEL ROBBERIES. See Robbery

JEWEL THIEVES. See Robbery

JEWELRY
Borland, H. The amulet
Charteris, H. The coat
Christie, A. The mystery of the blue train
In Christie, A. Perilous journeys of Hercule Poirot v 1
Collins, W. The moonstone
Dumas, A. The queen's necklace
Trollope, A. The Eustace diamonds
See also Rings

JEWELS. See Jewelry

JEWISH-ARAB RELATIONS
Davidson, L. The Menorah men

The Jewish caravan. Schwarz, L. W. ed.

JEWISH REFUGEES. See Refugees, Jewish

JEWISH SECTS. See Pharisees

JEWS
Agnon, S. Y. In the heart of the seas
Agnon, S. Y. Two tales
Aleichem, S. Selected stories of Sholom Aleichem
Aleichem, S. Some laughter, some tears
Asch, S. Tales of my people
Blocker, J. ed. Israeli stories
Bor, J. The Terezin Requiem
Charles, G. ed. Modern Jewish stories
Gary, R. The dance of Genghis Cohn
Hempstone, S. In the midst of lions
Howe, I. ed. A treasury of Yiddish stories
Koestler, A. Thieves in the night
Malamud, B. Idiots first
Malamud, B. The magic barrel
Meisels, A. Son of a star
Nathan, R. Road of ages
Nathan, R. A star in the wind
Schwarz, L. W. ed. The Jewish caravan
Singer, I. B. Selected short stories of Isaac Bashevis Singer
Singer, I. B. Short Friday, and other stories
Slaughter, F. G. The song of Ruth
Spark, M. The Mandelbaum Gate
Wiesel, E. A beggar in Jerusalem
See also Antisemitism; Hasidism; Israel; Judaism; Zealots (Jewish Party)

Antiquities
Davidson, L. The Menorah men

Persecutions
Elman, R. M. The reckoning
Elman, R. M. The 28th day of Elul
Ettinger, E. Kindergarten
Fuks, L. Mr Theodore Mundstock
Kuznetsov, A. Babi Yar
Levin, M. Eva
Malamud, B. The fixer
Schoonover, L. Key of gold
Schwarz-Bart, A. The last of the Just
Uris, L. Exodus
Viertel, J. The last temptation
Wiesel, E. The town beyond the wall

Religion
See Judaism

Segregation
Hersey, J. The wall
Uris, L. Mila 18

JEWS AS SOLDIERS
Singer, I. J. Steel and iron

JEWS IN AFGHANISTAN
Michener, J. A. Caravans

JEWS IN AFRICA, SOUTH
Gordimer, N. The lying days
Jacobson, D. The beginners
Jacobson, D. Through the wilderness, and other stories

JEWS IN THE UNITED STATES—*Continued*

New York (City)

Aleichem, S. The adventures of Mottel, the cantor's son
Aleichem, S. Wandering star
Asch, S. East River
Asch, S. The mother
Auchincloss, L. A world of profit
Beagle, P. S. A fine and private place
Bellow, S. Mr Sammler's planet
Bellow, S. The victim
Calisher, H. The New Yorkers
Friedman, B. J. A mother's kisses
Green, G. The last angry man
Hudson, H. Meyer, Meyer
Lewisohn, L. The island within
Malamud, B. The assistant
Marshall, P. Brooklyn
  In Marshall, P. Soul clap hands and sing p31-64
Moll, E. Seidman and son
Potok, C. The chosen
Potok, C. The promise
Rees, B. Sidney, oh Sidney
  In Rees, B. Try another country p 1-53
Rosten, N. Under the boardwalk
Roth, H. Call it sleep
Rothberg, A. The song of David Freed
Schoonover, L. Key of gold
Singer, I. J. The family Carnovsky
Wallant, E. L. The tenants of Moonbloom
Weidman, J. The center of the action
Weidman, J. I can get it for you wholesale
Weidman, J. The sound of Bow bells
Wiesel, E. The accident

JEZEBEL, WIFE OF AHAB, KING OF ISRAEL
Slaughter, F. G. The curse of Jezebel

Jingala. Kayira, L.

JOAN OF ARC, SAINT
Twain, M. Personal recollections of Joan of Arc

JOAN, QUEEN OF SICILY
Haycraft, M. C. My lord brother the Lion Heart

JOANNA, QUEEN OF CASTILE
Schoonover, L. The prisoner of Tordesillas

Joanna and Ulysses. Sarton, M.

JOCKEYS
Francis, D. Flying finish
Francis, D. Nerve
Francis, D. Odds against
Francis, D. Three to show

Joe Hill [variant title: The preacher and the slave] Stegner, W.

Johanna at daybreak. Hutchinson, R. C.

JOHANNESBURG. See Africa, South—Johannesburg

JOHN, SAINT, APOSTLE
Caldwell, T. Dear and glorious physician

JOHN, KING OF ENGLAND
Costain, T. B. Below the salt

JOHN OF AUSTRIA
De Wohl, L. The last crusader

JOHN OF GAUNT, DUKE OF LANCASTER
Seton, A. Katherine

A John Dickson Carr trio. Carr, J. D.

John Macnab. Buchan, J.
  In Buchan, J. Adventurers all v2

Johnny get your gun. Ball, J.

Johnny Osage. Giles, J. H.

JOHNSON, ANDREW, PRESIDENT U.S.
Gerson, N. B. The Yankee from Tennessee

The Joke. Kundera, M.

JONES, JOHN PAUL
Boyd, J. Drums
Churchill, W. Richard Carvel
Cooper, J. F. The pilot
Ellsberg, E. Captain Paul
Schoonover, L. The revolutionary

JORDAN
Spark, M. The Mandelbaum Gate

Jordan County. Foote, S.
  In Foote, S. Three novels v2

Jory. Bass, M. R.

JOSEPH, SAINT
Lofts, N. How far to Bethlehem?

JOSEPH, THE PATRIARCH
Mann, T. Joseph and his brothers

JOSEPH OF ARIMATHEA
Slaughter, F. G. The thorn of Arimathea

Joseph and his brothers. Mann, T.

Joseph Andrews. See Fielding, H. The history of the adventures of Joseph Andrews and of his friend Mr Abraham Adams

Joseph in Egypt. Mann, T.
  In Mann, T. Joseph and his brothers p447-840

Joseph the provider. Mann, T.
  In Mann, T. Joseph and his brothers p843-1207

JOSEPHUS, FLAVIUS
Feuchtwanger, L. The Jew of Rome
Feuchtwanger, L. Josephus
Feuchtwanger, L. Josephus and the Emperor

Josephus. Feuchtwanger, L.

Josephus and the Emperor. Feuchtwanger, L.

Journal of The counterfeiters. See Gide, A. The counterfeiters

JOURNALISTS
Adams, S. H. Tenderloin
Albrand, M. Rhine replica
Ambler, E. A kind of anger
Anderson, S. Dark laughter
Angoff, C. Summer storm
Angoff, C. Winter twilight
Basso, H. The Light Infantry Ball
Blair, C. The board room
Boucher, A. We print the truth
  In Boucher, A. The compleat werewolf, and other stories of fantasy and science fiction p170-239
Boulle, P. Planet of the Apes
Boyle, K. Generation without farewell
Braine, J. The crying game
Bridge, A. The Portuguese escape
Brinkley, W. Don't go near the water
Buck, P. S. God's men
Caidin, M. The Mendelov conspiracy
Caird, J. In a glass darkly
Camus, A. The plague
Chaze, E. Wettermark
Coxe, G. H. The candid impostor
Coxe, G. H. An easy way to go
Cuomo, G. Among thieves
De Vries, P. Comfort me with apples
De Vries, P. The tents of wickedness
Drury, A. Capable of honor
Fearing, K. The big clock
Ferber, E. Cimarron
Francis, D. Forfeit
Freeling, N. This is the castle
Gale, J. The family man
Garth, D. Watch on the bridge
Garve, A. The ashes of Loda
Gissing, G. New Grub Street
Greene, G. The quiet American
Gulick, B. Liveliest town in the West
Hempstone, S. In the midst of lions
Hobson, L. Z. First papers
Hobson, L. Z. Gentleman's agreement
Howells, W. D. A hazard of new fortunes
Howells, W. D. A modern instance
Huxley, A. Island
Johnson, U. The third book about Achim
Kipling, R. The light that failed
Lancaster, B. Roll Shenandoah
Land, M. Quicksand
Linington, E. The long watch
MacInnes, H. The Venetian affair
Maupassant, G. de. Bel-Ami
Naipaul, V. S. A house for Mr Biswas
Nathan, R. A star in the wind
Romains, J. Aftermath
Sheed, W. Office politics
Simak, C. D. They walked like men
Stewart, F. M. The Mephisto waltz
Symons, J. The progress of a crime
Tarkington, B. The gentleman from Indiana
Taylor, E. The wedding group
Thane, E. Ever after
Thane, E. Yankee stranger
Ullman, J. R. The sands of Karakorum
Wellman, P. I. Jericho's daughters
West, N. Miss Lonelyhearts
Wiesel, E. The accident
  See also Authors; War correspondents; Women as journalists

JOURNALS. See Diaries

Journey into Christmas, and other stories. Aldrich, B. S.

Journey into fear. Ambler, E.
  In Ambler, E. Intrigue p 1-145
  In Haycraft, H. ed. A treasury of great mysteries v 1 p437-576

KENTUCKY—*Continued*

20th century

Arnow, H. The dollmaker
Arnow, H. Hunter's horn
Giles, J. H. Shady Grove
Marshall, C. Christy

Farm life

See Farm life—Kentucky

Frankfort

Giles, J. H. The land beyond the mountains

Frontier and pioneer life

See Frontier and pioneer life—Kentucky

Lexington

Francis, D. Blood sport

KENTUCKY MOUNTAINS
Stuart, J. Come gentle spring
Stuart, J. My land has a voice
Stuart, J. Taps for Private Tussie

KENYA
Hanley, G. Gilligan's last elephant

KENYA COLONY AND PROTECTORATE
Dinesen, I. Shadows on the grass
Kessel, J. The lion
Ruark, R. Something of value
Ruark, R. Uhuru

Farm life

See Farm life—Kenya Colony and Protectorate

KESTNER, CHARLOTTE (BUFF)
Mann, T. The beloved returns

Key of gold. Schoonover, L.

The key to my heart. Pritchett, V. S.

KEY WEST. See Florida—Key West

KEYS, LADY MARY (GREY)
Harwood, A. So merciful a queen, so cruel a woman

The keys of the kingdom. Cronin, A. J.

KHRUSHCHEV, NIKITA SERGEEVICH
Burdick, E. Fail-safe

A kid for two farthings. Mankowitz, W.

KIDNAPPING
Airth, R. Snatch
Benchley, N. Welcome to Xanadu
Clifford, F. Another way of dying
Ferrars, E. X. The swaying pillars
Fish, R. L. The Xavier affair
Fowles, J. The collector
France, A. The crime of Sylvestre Bonnard
Gilford, C. B. The crooked shamrock
The Gordons. Night before the wedding
Levin, M. Compulsion
Marric, J. J. Gideon's river
Westlake, D. E. Who stole Sassi Manoon?

KIEV. See Russia—Kiev

Kill now—pay later. Stout, R.
In Stout, R. Trio for blunt instruments p 1-87

Kill with kindness. Shannon, D.

KILLAMOOK INDIANS. See Indians of North America—Northwest Pacific

KILLDEER MOUNTAIN, BATTLE OF, 1864
Sinclair, H. The cavalryman

Killer dolphin. Marsh, N.

The killers. Mannix, D. P.

KILLIGREW FAMILY
Graham, W. The grove of eagles

A killing frost. Wilkinson, S.

The killing-ground. Trevor, E.

KILPATRICK, HUGH JUDSON
Brick, J. The Richmond raid

KILPATRICK-DAHLGREN RAID, 1864
Brick, J. The Richmond raid

A kind of anger. Ambler, E.

Kindergarten. Ettinger, E.

The kindly ones. Powell, A.
In Powell, A. A dance to the music of time: second movement v3

Kinfolk. Buck, P. S.

KING ARTHUR. See Arthur, King

King coffin. Aiken, C.
In Aiken, C. The collected novels of Conrad Aiken p297-414

The king must die. Renault, M.

King of Paris. Endore, G.

The king of the castle. Holt, V.

King, queen, knave. Nabokov, V.

King Rat. Clavell, J.

King Solomon's mines. Haggard, H. R.
also in Haggard, H. R. Five adventure novels of H. Rider Haggard p240-415

King Wren. See Mann, H. Young Henry of Navarre

Kingdom come. Sorenson, V.

The kingdom of this world. Carpentier, A.

KINGS AND RULERS. See Courts and courtiers; names of kings and rulers, e.g. Louis XVI, King of France; also subdivision Kings and rulers, under specific countries, e.g. China—Kings and rulers

The King's bed. Barnes, M. C.

The King's cavalier. Shellabarger, S.

King's fool. Barnes, M. C.

Kings full of aces. Stout, R.

The King's general. Du Maurier, D.

Kings go forth. Brown, J. D.

The kings in winter. Holland, C.

Kings of infinite space. Balchin, N.

The king's orchard. Turnbull, A. S.

The King's pleasure. Lofts, N.

Kings Row. Bellamann, H.

Kingsblood royal. Lewis, S.

Kinsmen of the Grail. Roberts, D. J.

KIOWA INDIANS
Le May, A. The unforgiven

Kirkland Revels. Holt, V.

A kiss before dying. Levin, I.

A kiss for the leper. Mauriac, F.
In Mauriac, F. A Mauriac reader p3-60

Kiss, kiss. Dahl, R.
also in Dahl, R. Selected stories of Roald Dahl

Kiss me again, stranger. Du Maurier, D.

Kissing kin. Thane, E.

The kitchen Madonna. Godden, R.

KITTENS. See Cats

Kitty Foyle. Morley, C.

The Klansman. Huie, W. B.

KLONDIKE
London, J. The call of the wild

KNIGHTS AND KNIGHTHOOD
Anderson, P. The high crusade
Cervantes, M. de. Don Quixote de la Mancha
Costain, T. B. Below the salt
Doyle, Sir A. C. The White Company
Duggan, A. Lord Geoffrey's fancy
Dunnett, D. The disorderly knights
Holland, C. The firedrake
Oldenbourg, Z. Cities of the flesh
Oldenbourg, Z. The cornerstone
Oldenbourg, Z. The world is not enough
Prescott, H. F. M. Son of dust
Roberts, D. J. Kinsmen of the Grail
Roberts, D. J. Launcelot, my brother
Scott, Sir W. The talisman
White, T. H. The once and future king
See also Chivalry; Crusades; Knights of Malta; Middle ages

Knight's gambit. Faulkner, W.

KNIGHTS OF MALTA
Peyrefitte, R. Knights of Malta
See also Knights and knighthood

Knights of Malta. Peyrefitte, R.

The knock at midnight. Blackstock, C.

Knock on any door. Motley, W.

The knot of vipers [variant title: Vipers' tangle] Mauriac, F.
In Mauriac, F. A Mauriac reader p273-430

KNOXVILLE. See Tennessee—Knoxville

KOREA
Buck, P. S. The living reed

20th century

Bryan, C. D. B. P. S. Wilkinson

KOREAN SOLDIERS. See Soldiers, Korean

KOREAN WAR, 1950-1953
Kim, R. E. The martyred
Mason, F. V. ed. American men at arms
Michener, J. A. The bridges at Toko-ri

LAPLAND
Bjorn, T. F. Papa's daughter
Bjorn, T. F. Papa's wife
Frison-Roche, R. The raid

LAPPS. See Lapland

Large economy size, Max Shulman's. Shulman, M.

LARGE TYPE BOOKS
Arnow, H. The dollmaker
Austen, J. Pride and prejudice
Boulle, P. The bridge over the River Kwai
Braddon, R. When the enemy is tired
Brontë, C. Jane Eyre
Brontë, E. Wuthering Heights
Buck, P. S. The good earth
Burnford, S. The incredible journey
Cannon, L. Look to the mountain
Carroll, G. H. As the earth turns
Cather, W. My Antonia
Cather, W. O pioneers!
Collins, W. The moonstone
Conrad, J. Lord Jim
Cooper, J. F. The last of the Mohicans
Crane, S. The red badge of courage
Crane, S. The red badge of courage, and other stories
Deighton, L. Funeral in Berlin
Dickens, C. A Christmas carol
Dickens, C. Great expectations
Dickens, C. A tale of two cities
Dostoevsky, F. Crime and punishment
Doyle, Sir A. C. Sherlock Holmes' greatest cases
Eliot, G. Silas Marner
Fast, H. April morning
Flaubert, G. Madame Bovary
Forester, C. S. Lord Hornblower
Garve, A. The ashes of Loda
Gipson, F. Old Yeller
Greene, G. The comedians
Greene, G. The power and the glory
Grey, Z. The Arizona clan
Guthrie, A. B. The big sky
Guthrie, A. B. The way west
Hardy, T. The return of the native
Hawthorne, N. The House of the Seven Gables
Heggen, T. Mister Roberts
Heller, J. Catch-22
Hersey, J. A bell for Adano
Hilton, J. Good-bye Mr Chips
Hudson, W. H. Green mansions
Hughes, L. Simple's Uncle Sam
Hughes, R. A high wind in Jamaica
Hulme, K. The nun's story
Jackson, S. The haunting of Hill House
Jackson, S. We have always lived in the castle
James, H. The turn of the screw
Jerome, J. K. Three men in a boat
Jewett, S. O. The country of the pointed firs
Joyce, J. A portrait of the artist as a young man
Kantor, M. The voice of Bugle Ann
Kemelman, H. Sunday the rabbi stayed home
Knebel, F. Seven days in May
Knowles, J. A separate peace
Lane, R. W. Let the hurricane roar
Le Carré, J. A small town in Germany
Le Carré, J. The spy who came in from the cold
Lee, H. To kill a mockingbird
Lewis, C. S. Out of the silent planet
London, J. The call of the wild
London, J. The Sea-Wolf
London, J. White Fang
MacInnes, H. Decision at Delphi
Maupassant, G. de. Selected short stories
Melville, H. Billy Budd, foretopman
Melville, H. Moby Dick
Michener, J. A. Tales of the South Pacific
Mitchell, M. Gone with the wind
Narayan, R. K. The vendor of sweets
Nathan, R. One more spring
Nathan, R. Portrait of Jennie
Nordhoff, C. Mutiny on the Bounty
Paton, A. Cry, the beloved country
Poe, E. A. Selected stories and poems
Poe, E. A. Short stories
Portis, C. True grit
Potok, C. The chosen
Richter, C. The sea of grass
Richter, C. The trees
Salinger, J. D. The catcher in the rye
Sayers, D. L. Strong poison
Shute, N. The checquer board
Steinbeck, J. Cannery Row
Steinbeck, J. The grapes of wrath
Steinbeck, J. Of mice and men
Steinbeck, J. The pearl
Stevenson, R. L. Strange case of Dr Jekyll and Mr Hyde

Stewart, M. My brother Michael
Stewart, M. This rough magic
Stout, R. The doorbell rang
Swift, J. Gulliver's travels
Tey, J. Brat Farrar
Tey, J. The daughter of time
Twain, M. The adventures of Huckleberry Finn
Twain, M. The adventures of Tom Sawyer
Wharton, E. Ethan Frome
Wilder, T. The bridge of San Luis Rey
Wilder, T. The eighth day

The lark shall sing. Cadell, E.

The last angry man. Green, G.

The last chronicle of Barset. Trollope, A.

The last circle. Benét, S. V.

The last crusader. De Wohl, L.

The last day the dogbushes bloomed. Smith, L.

The last days. Rayner, W.

The last days of Pompeii. Bulwer-Lytton, Sir E.

The last doorbell. Harrington, J.

The last exile. Aldridge, J.

The last full measure. Morrow, H. W.

The last hunt. Lott, M.

The last hurrah. O'Connor, E.

A last lamp burning. Griffin, G.

The last letter home. Moberg, V.

The last, long journey. Cleeve, B.

The last love. Costain, T. B.

The last Mayday. Wheeler, K.

The last nine days of the Bismarck. Forester, C. S.

The last of Chéri. Colette
In Colette. Chéri, and The last of Chéri p155-296
also in Colette. 7 by Colette v2 p155-296
also in Colette. Six novels p535-648

The last of Mr Norris. Isherwood, C.
In Isherwood, C. The Berlin stories v 1

The last of the Just. Schwarz-Bart, A.

The last of the Mohicans. Cooper, J. F.

The last of the Mohicans [abridged]. Cooper, J. F.
In Cooper, J. F. The Leatherstocking saga p275-462

The last of the wine. Renault, M.

The last post. Ford, F. M.
In Ford, F. M. Parade's end p677-836

The last Puritan. Santayana, G.

Last stop Camp 7. Kirst, H. H.

Last summer. Hunter, E.

Last tales. Dinesen, I.

The last temptation. Viertel, J.

The last temptation of Christ. Kazantzakis, N.

Last things. Snow, C. P.

The last tycoon. Fitzgerald, F. S.

The last unicorn. Beagle, P. S.

The last warpath. Henry, W.

Late-blooming flowers, and other stories. Chekhov, A.

Late call. Wilson, A.

The late George Apley. Marquand, J. P.

The late Mattia Pascal. Pirandello, L.

The later adventures of Sherlock Holmes. Doyle, Sir A. C.

LATIN AMERICA
Garcia Marquez, G. One hundred years of solitude
Prize stories from Latin America
Torres-Rioseco, A. ed. Short stories of Latin America
20th century
Marshall, B. Father Hilary's holiday
Schulberg, B. Sanctuary V

LATTER-DAY SAINTS. See Mormons and Mormonism

Laughing Boy. La Farge, O.

The laughing policeman. Sjöwall, M.

Laughing to keep from crying. Hughes, L.

Laughter in the dark. Nabokov, V.

Launcelot, my brother. Roberts, D. J.

LA VALLIÉRE, LOUISE FRANÇOISE DE LA BAUME LE BLANC, DUCHESSE DE
Dumas, A. The Vicomte de Bragelonne

The little world of Don Camillo. Guareschi, G.
Live and let die. Fleming, I
   In Fleming, I. More Gilt-edged Bonds p 1-218
Liveliest town in the West. Gulick, B.
The Lively Lady. Roberts, K.
LIVIA DRUSILLA, EMPRESS OF ROME
   Graves, R. I, Claudius
The living and the dead. Simonov, K.
The living reed. Buck, P. S.
Liza [variant title: A nest of gentlefolk] Turgenev, I.
The Loch. Caird, J.
The locked room reader. Santesson, H. S. ed.
LOCKETS. See Jewelry
LOCKOUTS. See Strikes and lockouts
The Lockwood concern. O'Hara, J.
LODGERS. See Boarding houses
LODZ. See Poland—Lodz
LOEB, RICHARD A.
   Levin, M. Compulsion
Log of a cowboy. Adams, A.
LOGGING. See Lumber industry
Lolita. Nabokov, V.
LOLLARDS
   Jackson, D. V. S. Walk with peril
Lolly Willowes, and Mr Fortune's maggot. Warner, S. T.
LONDON
   See also England—London

      Fire, 1666
   Ainsworth, W. H. Old Saint Paul's

      Police
   Allingham, M. The mind readers
   Ashe, G. A clutch of coppers
   Christie, A. The pale horse
   Gardner, J. A complete state of death
   MacInnes, C. Mr Love and justice
     In MacInnes, C. The London novels of Colin MacInnes p451-626
   MacLean, A. Puppet on a chain
   Marric, J. J. Gideon's day
   Marric, J. J. Gideon's fire
   Marric, J. J. Gideon's power
   Marric, J. J. Gideon's ride
   Marric, J. J. Gideon's river
   Marric, J. J. Gideon's wrath
   Rendell, R. The secret house of death
LONDON BLITZ. See World War, 1939-1945—England
London End. See Priestley, J. B. The image men
A London life. James, H.
The London novels of Colin MacInnes. MacInnes, C.
LONELINESS
   Billing, G. Forbush and the penguins
   Bowen, E. The death of the heart
   Carpenter, D. One of those big-city girls
     In Carpenter, D. The murder of the frogs, and other stories p199-242
   Hudson, H. Meyer, Meyer
   Moore, B. The lonely passion of Judith Hearne
   Wallant, E. L. The human season
The loneliness of the long-distance runner. Sillitoe, A.
The lonely. Romains, J.
   In Romains, J. The world from below
The lonely passion of Judith Hearne. Moore, B.
Lonelyheart 4122. Watson, C.
The loners. Schulman, L. M. ed.
The lonesome traveler, and other stories. Corrington, J. W.
A long and happy life. Price, R.
The long goodbye. Chandler, R.
The long haul. Rayner, D. A.
LONG ISLAND. See New York (State)—Long Island
The long journey. Jensen, J. V.
The long march. Styron, W.
The long night's walk. White, A.
The long pursuit. Cleary, J.
Long remember. Kantor, M.

The long rifle. White, S. E.
The long ships. Bengtsson, F. G.
The long short cut. Garve, A.
The long twilight. Laumer, K.
The long valley. Steinbeck, J.
The long watch. Linington, E.
The longest voyage. Anderson, P.
   In Asimov, I. ed. The Hugo winners p279-310
LONGEVITY
   Huxley, A. After many a summer dies the swan
LONGSHOREMEN
   Schulberg, B. Waterfront
LONGSTREET, JAMES
   Williams, B. A. The unconquered
Look away, look away. Haas, B.
Look homeward, angel. Wolfe, T.
Look to the mountain. Cannon, L.
Look to the river. Owens, W. A.
Looking backward: 2000-1888. Bellamy, E.
The looking glass murder. Gilbert, A.
The looking glass war. Le Carré, J.
LOOKOUT MOUNTAIN, BATTLE OF, 1863
   Brick, J. Jubilee
The loon feather. Fuller, I.
Lord dismiss us. Campbell, M.
Lord Edgware dies. Christie, A.
Lord Geoffrey's fancy. Duggan, A.
Lord Hornblower. Forester, C. S.
   also in Forester, C. S. The indomitable Hornblower p229-413
Lord Jim. Conrad, J.
Lord of the Flies. Golding, W.
The lord of the rings. Tolkien, J. R. R.
Lord Vanity. Shellabarger, S.
Lorna Doone. Blackmore, R. D.
LOS ALAMOS. See New Mexico—Los Alamos
LOS ANGELES
   See also California—Los Angeles

      Police
   The Gordons. Night before the wedding
   Linington, E. Greenmask!
   Linington, E. Policeman's lot
   Shannon, D. Crime on their hands
   Shannon, D. Schooled to kill
The loser. Ustinov, P.
Lost Empires. Priestley, J. B.
Lost horizon. Hilton, J.
   also in Costain, T. B. ed. More Stories to remember v1 p 1-119
Lost illusions. Balzac, H. de
Lost in the funhouse. Barth, J.
A lost lady. Cather, W.
The lost queen. Lofts, N.
The lost queen of Egypt. Morrison, L.
The lost sea. Hartog, J. de
   In Costain, T. B. comp. Twelve short novels p559-616
   In Hartog, J. de. The call of the sea p3-85
The lost wagon. Kjelgaard, J.
The lost weekend. Jackson, C.
The lost world. Doyle, Sir A. C.
Lotte in Weimar. See Mann, T. The beloved returns
LOTTERIES
   Costain, T. B. The tontine
   Wodehouse, P. G. The butler did it
The lottery. Jackson, S.
LOUIS X, KING OF FRANCE
   Druon, M. The poisoned crown
   Druon, M. The strangled queen
LOUIS XI, KING OF FRANCE
   Schoonover, L. The Spider King
   Scott, Sir, W. Quentin Durward
LOUIS XIII, KING OF FRANCE
   Anthony, E. The Cardinal and the Queen
   Mallet-Joris, F. The favourite
LOUIS XIV, KING OF FRANCE
   Dumas, A. The man in the iron mask
   Dumas, A. The Vicomte de Bragelonne

LOUIS XVI, KING OF FRANCE
  Chapman, H. W. Fear no more
  Feuchtwanger, L. Proud destiny
  Holt, V. The Queen's confession
  Kenyon, F. W. Marie Antoinette

LOUIS XVII, KING OF FRANCE
  Chapman, H. W. Fear no more

LOUIS XVIII, KING OF FRANCE
  Aragon, L. Holy Week

LOUISBURG
            Siege, 1758
  Mason, F. V. Young titan

LOUISE HOLLANDINE, COUNTESS PAL-
    ATINE, ABBESS OF MAUBUISSON
  Irwin, M. The bride

Louise de la Valliere. See Dumas, A. The
  Vicomte de Bragelonne

LOUISIANA
            18th century
  Bristow, G. Deep summer
  Costain, T. B. High Towers
  Wellman, P. I. Ride the red earth

            19th century
  Bristow, G. The handsome road
  Keyes, F. P. Blue camellia
  Keyes, F. P. Steamboat Gothic
  Williams, B. A. The unconquered

            20th century
  Bristow, G. This side of glory
  Capote, T. Other voices, other rooms
  Grau, S. A. The black prince, and other sto-
    ries
  Grau, S. A. The hard blue sky
  Keyes, F. P. The River Road
  Langley, A. L. A lion is in the streets

        Frontier and pioneer life
  See Frontier and pioneer life—Louisiana

            New Orleans
  Algren, N. A walk on the wild side
  Bryan, J. Y. Come to the bower
  Carr, J. D. Papa Là-bas
  Costain, T. B. High Towers
  Ferber, E. Saratoga trunk
  Hailey, A. Hotel
  Keyes, F. P. The chess players
  Keyes, F. P. Crescent carnival
  Keyes, F. P. Dinner at Antoine's
  Keyes, F. P. Madame Castel's lodger
  Percy, W. The moviegoer
  Warren, R. P. Brand of angels
  Whitney, P. A. Skye Cameron
  Williams, B. A. The unconquered
  Yerby, F. The Foxes of Harrow

            Plantation life
  See Plantation life—Louisiana

LOVE
  Murdoch, I. Bruno's dream

LOVE AFFAIRS
  Bowen, E. The heat of the day
  Boyle, K. Generation without farewell
  Calisher, H. False entry
  Colette. Chéri
    In Colette. 7 by Colette v2 p 1-154
    In Colette. Six novels p411-534
  Colette. Chéri, and The last of Chéri
  Colette. The last of Chéri
    In Colette. 7 by Colette v 2 p155-296
    In Colette. Six novels p535-648
  Cowley, J. Nest in a falling tree
  Daley, R. A priest and a girl
  Harris, M. Trepleff
  Hayes, A. The girl on the Via Flaminia
  Hemingway, E. A farewell to arms
  Howard, E. J. Something in disguise
  Kawabata, Y. Snow country
    In Kawabata, Y. Snow country and Thou-
      sand cranes v 1 p 1-175
  Kawabata, Y. Thousand cranes
  Kerouac, J. The subterraneans
  Morgan, C. The fountain
  Morley, C. Kitty Foyle
  Morris, W. Love among the cannibals
  Murdoch, I. The nice and the good
  Murdoch, I. A severed head
  Murdoch, I. The unicorn
  Nabokov, V. Ada
  Nin, A. The four-chambered heart
  O'Hara, J. Elizabeth Appleton
  O'Hara, J. From the terrace

  Sagan, F. A certain smile
  Sillitoe, A. Saturday night and Sunday morn-
    ing
  Turgenev, I. Smoke
    See also Love stories; Marriage problems

Love among the cannibals. Morris, W.

Love, death, and the ladies' drill team. West, J.

Love in a dry season. Foote, S.
  In Foote, S. Three novels v3

Love in Atlantis. Barrett, B. L.

Love is a bridge. Flood, C. B.

Love is eternal. Stone, I.

The love letters. L'Engle, M.

Love on a dark street, and other stories.
  Shaw, I.

LOVE STORIES
  Aldrich, B. S. The lieutenant's lady
  Aldrich, B. S. Song of years
  Aldridge, J. My brother Tom
  Amis, K. I want it now
  Baldwin, F. The velvet hammer
  Barrie, J. M. Little minister
  Bates, H. E. Fair stood the wind for France
  Birmingham, S. Heart troubles
  Bodsworth, F. The strange one
  Bridge, A. The dangerous islands
  Budd, L. April harvest
  Cadell, E. Canary yellow
  Cadell, E. The golden collar
  Cadell, E. Six impossible things
  Cadell, E. The yellow brick road
  Cather, W. Lucy Gayheart
  Chekhov, A. Late-blooming flowers, and
    other stories
  Conrad, J. The arrow of gold
  Conrad, J. Chance
  Costain, T. B. The darkness and the dawn
  Crane, S. Active service
    In Crane, S. The complete novels of Ste-
      phen Crane p429-592
  Crane, S. The third violet
    In Crane, S. The complete novels of Ste-
      phen Crane p349-428
  Eden, D. Darkwater
  Elgin, M. Highland masquerade
  Elgin, M. A man from the mist
  Ellis, A. E. The rack
  Field, R. And now tomorrow
  Fletcher, I. Toil of the brave
  Fuller, I. The loon feather
  Garth, D. Watch on the bridge
  Gautier, T. Mademoiselle de Maupin
  Gide, A. Strait is the gate
  Goudge, E. Gentian Hill
  Goudge, E. Green Dolphin Street
  Hamsun, K. Pan
  Hamsun, K. Victoria
  Han, S. The mountain is young
  Hardy, T. A pair of blue eyes
  Hardy, T. Two on a tower
  Harwood, A. Merchant of the ruby
  Heyer, G. Beauvallet
  Heyer, G. Black sheep
  Heyer, G. The convenient marriage
  Heyer, G. The Corinthian
  Heyer, G. Devil's cub
  Heyer, G. False colours
  Heyer, G. Faro's daughter
  Heyer, G. The foundling
  Heyer, G. Frederica
  Heyer, G. Friday's child
  Heyer, G. The grand Sophy
  Heyer, G. An infamous army
  Heyer, G. The masqueraders
  Heyer, G. The Nonesuch
  Heyer, G. Powder and patch
  Heyer, G. Regency buck
  Heyer, G. The Spanish bride
  Heyer, G. Sprig muslin
  Heyer, G. The talisman ring
  Heyer, G. These old shades
  Heyer, G. The toll-gate
  Hilton, J. Random harvest
  Hodge, J. A. Mary in haste
  Jackson, D. V. S. Walk with peril
  Jennings, J. The tall ships
  Keyes, F. P. Crescent carnival
  Knight, E. This above all
  Lagerlöf, S. Charlotte Lowenskold
  L'Engle, M. The love letters
  Lin, Yutang. The vermilion gate
  Major, C. When knighthood was in flower
  Masters, H. An American marriage
  Michener, J. A. Sayonara
  Mishima, Y. The sound of waves
  Moore, G. Heloise and Abelard
  Mosley, N. Impossible object

Magic, inc. Heinlein, R. A.
In Heinlein, R. A. Three by Heinlein p327-426
In Heinlein, R. A. Waldo and Magic, inc.

The magic mountain. Mann, T.

Magic skin. See Balzac, H. de. The wild ass's skin

The magician of Lubin. Singer, I. B.

MAGICIANS
Beerbohm, M. Zuleika Dobson
Bellairs, J. The face in the frost
Priestley, J. B. Lost Empires
White, T. H. The sword in the stone

Magister Ludi. See Hesse, H. The glass bead game (Magister Ludi)

The magnificent Ambersons. Tarkington, B.

Magnificent destiny. Wellman, P. I.

Magnificient obsession. Douglas, L. C.

MAGNÚSSON, MAGNUS HJALTASON
Laxness, H. World light

The magus. Fowles, J.

MAGYARS
Holland, C. Rakóssy

The Maias. Eça de Queiroz

Maid in waiting. Galsworthy, J.
In Galsworthy, J. End of the chapter p 1-330

The maid Silja. Sillanpää, F. E.

MAIDS. See Servants—Maids

Maigret abroad. Simenon, G.

Maigret and the Calame report. Simenon, G.

Maigret and the headless corpse. Simenon, G.

Maigret and the minister. See Simenon, G. Maigret and the Calame report

Maigret and the old lady. Simenon, G.
In Simenon, G. Maigret cinq p203-307

Maigret and the reluctant witnesses. Simenon, G.
In Simenon, G. Five times Maigret p323-421

Maigret and the young girl. Simenon, G.
In Simenon, G. Maigret cinq p7-105

Maigret cinq. Simenon, G.

Maigret goes to school. Simenon, G.
In Simenon, G. Five times Maigret p424-525

Maigret has scruples. Simenon, G.
In Simenon, G. Five times Maigret p223-320

Maigret in Montmartre. Simenon, G.
In Simenon, G. Five times Maigret p9-116

Maigret in Vichy. Simenon, G.

Maigret on holiday. See Simenon, G. No vacation for Maigret

Maigret takes a room. Simenon, G.
In Simenon, G. Maigret cinq p421-523

Maigret's dead man. Simenon, G.

Maigret's first case. Simenon, G.
In Simenon, G. Maigret cinq p309-419

Maigret's little joke. Simenon, G.
In Simenon, G. Maigret cinq -107-202

Maigret's mistake. Simenon, G.
In Simenon, G. Maigret sinq p107-202

Maigret's pickpocket. Simenon, G.

Main line west. Horgan, P.
In Horgan, P. Mountain standard time: Main line west, Far from Cibola [and] The common heart p 1-201

Main Street. Lewis, S.

Main-travelled roads. Garland, H.

MAINE
Chase, M. E. Silas Crockett
Chase, M. E. Windswept

18th century
Williams, B. A. Come spring

19th century
Chase, M. E. Mary Peters
Field, R. Time out of mind
Jewett, S. O. The country of the pointed firs
also in Jewett, S. O. The best stories of Sarah Orne Jewett v 1
Jewett, S. O. The country of the pointed firs, and other stories
Moore, R. Speak to the winds

20th century
Beckham, B. My main mother
Carroll, G. H. As the earth turns
Carroll, G. H. Come with me home
Chase, M. E. The edge of darkness
Chase, M. E. The lovely ambition
Disney, D. M. Voice from the grave
Moore, R. Candlemas Bay
Moore, R. The Sea Flower
Moore, R. Second growth
Moore, R. Speak to the winds
Moore, R. Spoonhandle
Ogilvie, E. Bellwood
Ogilvie, E. The seasons hereafter
Ogilvie, E. Waters on a starry night
Stafford, J. The Catherine wheel
Webb, J. F. Carnavaron's castle

Farm life
See Farm life—Maine

Frontier and pioneer life
See Frontier and pioneer life—Maine

Negroes
See Negroes—Maine

Maiwa's revenge. Haggard, H. R.
In Haggard, H. R. Five adventure novels of H. Rider Haggard p746-819

MAJORS. See subdivision: Army—Officers under name of country

Make mine murder! Christie, A.

The Makioka sisters. Tanizaki, J.

The Malacca cane. De Vigny, A.
In Dupee, F. W. ed. Great French short novels p125-94

MALADJUSTED CHILDREN. See Problem children

The malady in Madeira. Bridge, A.

A Malamud reader. Malamud, B.

MALAWI, PROVINCIAL AND RURAL
Kayira, L. Jingala

MALAY RACE. See Malayans

MALAYA
Braddon, R. When the enemy is tired
Shute, N. The legacy

MALAYANS
Conrad, J. Almayer's folly
Conrad, J. The rescue

Malcolm. Purdy, J.

MALDIVE ISLANDS
Innes, H. The Strode venturer

Malone dies. Beckett, S.
In Beckett, S. Molloy, Malone dies, and The unnamable p241-398

MALTA
Dunnett, D. The disorderly knights

MALTA, KNIGHTS OF. See Knights of Malta

The Maltese falcon. Hammett, D.
also in Hammett, D. The novels of Dashiell Hammett p293-440
also in Haycraft, H. ed. Ten great mysteries p11-159

Mama, I love you. Saroyan, W.

Mama's way. Bjorn, T. F.
also in Bjorn, T. F. Papa's wife, Papa's daughter, Mama's way v3

Mamba's daughters. Heyward, Du B.

MAN, PREHISTORIC. See Prehistoric times

The man. Wallace, I.

Man alive. Stout, R.
In Stout, R. Five of a kind p307-55

A man and two women. Lessing, D.

A man apart. Rabie, J.

A man could stand up. Ford, F. M.
In Ford, F. M. Parade's end p503-674

The man-eater of Malgudi. Narayan, R. K.

Man from Mt Vernon. Boyce, B.

A man from the mist. Elgin, M.

The man in lower ten. Rinehart, M. R.
In Rinehart, M. R. Mary Roberts Rinehart's Mystery book p181-345

The man in the glass booth. Shaw, R.

The man in the gray flannel suit. Wilson, S.

MAN IN THE IRON MASK
Dumas, A. The Vicomte de Bragelonne

TITLE AND SUBJECT INDEX
EIGHTH EDITION

The man in the iron mask. Dumas, A.
The man in the queue. Tey, J.
A man in the wheatfield. Laxalt, R.
The man in the yellow raft. Forester, C. S.
Man of glass. Cervantes, M. de
  In Cervantes, M. de. The portable Cervantes p760-96
  In Cervantes, M. de. Three exemplary novels p75-121
The man of property. Galsworthy, J.
  also in Galsworthy, J. The Forsyte saga p3-309
  also in Galsworthy, J. The Galsworthy reader p15-294
The man on a donkey. Prescott, H. F. M.
The man on the balcony. Sjöwall, M.
The man on the Raffles verandah. Kirk, L.
The man that corrupted Hadleyburg. Twain, M.
  In Blackmur, R. P. ed. American short novels p68-96
The man that corrupted Hadleyburg, and other stories and essays. Twain, M.
The man who cried I am. Williams, J. A.
The man who killed himself. Symons, J.
The man who loved children. Stead, C.
The man who was not with it. Gold, H.
The man who was Thursday. Chesterton, G. K.
The man who went up in smoke. Sjöwall, M.
The man whose dreams came true. Symons, J.
The man with the golden arm. Algren, N.
The man with the golden gun. Fleming, I.
The man without a country. Hale, E. E.
The man without qualities. Musil, R.
MANCHURIA
  Hobart, A. T. Oil for the lamps of China
The mandarin, and other stories. Eca de Queiroz
The mandarins. Beauvoir, S. de
The Mandelbaum Gate. Spark, M.
MANHATTAN. See New York (City)—Manhattan
Manhattan transfer. Dos Passos, J.
MANHUNTS. See Adventure
MANILA. See Philippine Islands—Manila
Manila Galleon. Mason, F. V.
MANITOBA. See Canada—Manitoba
Manon Lescaut. Prévost, A.
The manor. Singer, I. B.
MANORS. See Houses
Man's fate. Malraux, A.
Man's hope. Malraux, A.
Mansfield Park. Austen, J.
  also in Austen, J. The complete novels of Jane Austen
The mansion. Faulkner, W.
MANSIONS. See Houses
MANUSCRIPTS
  Durrell, L. Balthazar
  Roberts, J. H. The Q document
Many heavens. Sorensen, V.
The many loves of Dobie Gillis. Shulman, M.
MAORIS
  Ashton-Warner, S. Greenstone
  Ashton-Warner, S. Spinster
Maracaibo mission. Mason, V.
The Maracot Deep. Doyle, Sir A. C.
The Marble Faun. Hawthorne, N.
  also n Hawthorne, N. The complete novels and selected tales of Nathaniel Hawthorne p589-858
MARBLEHEAD. See Massachusetts—Marblehead
Marching on. Boyd, J.
MARDI GRAS
  Faulkner, W. Pylon
  Keyes, F. P. Crescent carnival
Mare nostrum. Blasco Ibáñez, V.
Margin for doubt. Borgenicht, M.
MARGUERITE DE BOURGOGNE, CONSORT OF LOUIS X, KING OF FRANCE
  Druon, M. The strangled queen

MARGUERITE DE VALOIS, CONSORT OF HENRY IV, KING OF FRANCE
  Dumas, A. Marguerite de Valois
Marguerite de Valois. Dumas, A.
MARIA DE JESUS DE AGREDA, MOTHER
  Keyes, F. P. I, the King
MARIAMNE, WIFE OF HEROD I, KING OF JUDEA
  Lagerkvist, P. Herod and Mariamne
MARIANA OF AUSTRIA, CONSORT OF PHILIP IV, KING OF SPAIN
  Keyes, F. P. I, the King
MARIE ANTOINETTE, CONSORT OF LOUIS XVI, KING OF FRANCE
  Chapman, H. W. Fear no more
  Dumas, A. The queen's necklace
  Feuchtwanger, L. Proud destiny
  Holt, V. The Queen's confession
  Kenyon, F. W. Marie Antoinette
Marie Antoinette. Kenyon, F. W.
The marigold field. Pearson, D.
MARINA
  Baron, A. The golden princess
MARINE ANIMALS
  Clarke, A. C. The deep range
MARINE BIOLOGISTS. See Biologists
MARINE BIOLOGY. See Marine animals
MARINE ENGINEERS. See Engineers, Marine
MARINE FAUNA. See Marine animals
MARINES. See United States. Marine Corps
Marius the Epicurean. Pater, W.
Marjorie Morningstar. Wouk, H.
The Marjorie Rawlings reader. Rawlings, M. K.
The market square. Read, Miss
Marks of identity. Goytisolo, J.
The marmot drive. Hersey, J.
MARMOTS
  Hersey, J. The marmot drive
Marooned. Caidin, M.
MARQUESAS ISLANDS
  Melville, H. Omoo
  Melville, H. Typee
The Marquis of Lumbria. Unamuno y Jugo, M. de
  In Unamuno y Jugo, M. de. Three exemplary novels and a prologue
MARRIAGE
  Auchincloss, L. The house of five talents
  Connell, E. S. Mr Bridge
  Connell, E. S. Mrs Bridge
  Hersey, J. Under the eye of the storm
  Heyer, G. The convenient marriage
  Holt, V. The legend of the Seventh Virgin
  Howells, W. D. Indian summer
  James, H. The spoils of Poynton
  James, H. Washington Square
  In Blackmur, R. P. ed. American short novels p134-235
  James, H. The wings of the dove
  Kauffmann, L. An honorable estate
  Lindbergh, A. M. Dearly beloved
  Masters, H. An American marriage
  Peyrefitte, R. The prince's person
  Turnbull, A. S. The wedding bargain
  See also Celibacy; Divorce; Family life; International marriages; Inter-racial marriages; Marriage problems; Weddings
MARRIAGE, INTERNATIONAL. See International marriages
MARRIAGE, INTER-RACIAL. See Inter-racial marriage
MARRIAGE, MIXED
  Asch, S. East River
  Barker, S. Strange wives
  Bottome, P. The mortal storm
  Gordon, N. The rabbi
  Lewisohn, L. The island within
  Roth, P. Letting go
  Singer, I. B. The slave
  Singer, I. J. The family Carnovsky
  Weidman, J. The enemy camp
  See also Marriage problems
MARRIAGE BROKERS
  Watson, C. Lonelyheart 4122
MARRIAGE PROBLEMS
  Aiken, C. Conversation
  In Aiken, C. The collected novels of Conrad Aiken p473-575

557

MASSACHUSETTS—20th century—*Continued*
Dickens, M. The room upstairs
Marquand, J. P. Point of no return
Marquand, J. P. Sincerely, Willis Wayde
Updike, J. Couples

Berkshire Mountains
Cross, A. The James Joyce murder

Boston—17th century
Hawthorne, N. The scarlet letter

Boston—18th century
Wyckoff, N. E. The Braintree Mission

Boston—19th century
Caldwell, T. A prologue to love
Howells, W. D. The rise of Silas Lapham
James, H. The Bostonians
Marquand, J. P. The late George Apley

Boston—20th century
Angoff, C. Between day and dark
Angoff, C. In the morning light
Angoff, C. Journey to the dawn
Angoff, C. The sun at noon
Brace, G. W. The department
Coxe, G. H. An easy way to go
Fenwick, E. Goodbye, Aunt Elva
Flood, C. B. Love is a bridge
Gordon, N. The death committee
Greenan, R. H. It happened in Boston?
Herron, S. Miro
Hudson, J. A case of need
Kaufmann, M. S. Remember me to God
Keyes, F. P. Joy Street
Marquand, J. P. H. M. Pulham, esquire
Marquand, J. P. The late George Apley
Moynahan, J. Pairing off
O'Connor, E. The edge of sadness
Sarton, M. The birth of a grandfather
Sinclair, U. Boston

Cape Cod
Benchley, N. The off-islanders
Nathan, R. The sea-gull cry

Gloucester
Graham, J. A. Arthur

Lexington
Fast, H. April morning

Marblehead
Seton, A. The Hearth and Eagle

Nantucket
Benchley, N. A winter's tale
Mason, F. V. Harpoon in Eden

Plymouth
Gerson, N. B. The land is bright

Salem
Barker, S. Peace, my daughters
Forbes, E. The running of the tide
Hawthorne, N. The House of the Seven
  Gables
Hergesheimer, J. Java Head
Jennings, J. The Salem frigate
Lincoln, V. A dangerous innocence

MASSACRES
Cloete, S. The turning wheels
  See also Spirit Lake, Iowa—Massacre,
  1857

MASSAI (AFRICAN TRIBE) See Masai (African tribe)

Master and commander. O'Brian, P.

Master and man. Tolstoy, L.
  In Tolstoy, L. Russian stories and legends
  p163-224
  In Tolstoy, L. Short novels v2 p272-323

"Master and man," and other parables and
tales. Tolstoy, L.

The Master and Margarita. Bulgakov, M.

The master key. Anderson, P.
  In Anderson, P. Trader to the stars p127-
  76

The master of Ballantrae. Stevenson, R. L.

The master of Hestviken. Undset, S.

The master of Jalna. De La Roche, M.

Master of this vessel. Griffin, G.

Masterpieces of science fiction. Moskowitz, S.
ed.

The masters. Snow, C. P.
Masters of mayhem. Mystery Writers of America
MASTERS OF SHIPS. See Shipmasters
Masters of the modern short story. Havighurst,
  W. ed.
Matador. Conrad, B.
MATO GROSSO. See Brazil—Mato Grosso
The matriarch. Stern, G. B.
  In Stern, G. B. The matriarch chronicles
  v 1
The matriarch chronicles. Stern, G. B.
A matter of diplomacy. Tute, W.
MAU MAU
Ruark, R. Something of value
Maud Martha. Brooks, G.
Maugham's choice of Kipling's best. Kipling,
  R.
Maulever Hall. Hodge, J. A.
A Mauriac reader. Mauriac, F.
Maurois reader. Maurois, A.
Max Brand's Best stories. See Brand, M.
Max Shulman's Large economy size. Shulman,
  M.
MAXIMILIAN, EMPEROR OF MEXICO
Gavin, C. The cactus and the crown
Maximilian's gold. Barry, J.
MAY DAY
Read, Miss. Thrush Green
May Day. Fitzgerald, F. S.
  In Fitzgerald, F. S. The Fitzgerald reader
  p3-53
MAYAS
Asturias, M. A. Mulata
Bagley, D. The Vivero letter
The mayor of Casterbridge. Hardy, T.
MAYORS
Alarcón, P. A. de. The three-cornered hat
Crichton, R. The secret of Santa Vittoria
Guareschi, G. Comrade Don Camillo
Guareschi, G. Don Camillo and his flock
Guareschi, G. Don Camillo meets the flower
  children
Guareschi, G. Don Camillo takes the Devil
  by the tail
Guareschi, G. Don Camillo's dilemma
Guareschi, G. The little world of Don Camillo
Kirst, H. H. What became of Gunner Asch
MAZARIN, JULES, CARDINAL
Dumas, A. The Vicomte de Bragelonne
The maze maker. Ayrton, M.
MEAT INDUSTRY AND TRADE
Sinclair, U. The jungle
MECHANICAL BRAINS. See Electronic computers
MEDICAL ETHICS
Bawden, N. A little love, a little learning
Green, G. The last angry man
MEDICAL LIFE. See Physicians
MEDICAL MISSIONARIES. See Missionaries,
  Medical
MEDICAL RESEARCH. See Medicine, Experimental
MEDICAL SCHOOLS. See Medicine—Study and
  teaching
MEDICI, LORENZO DE' KNOWN AS IL MAGNIFICO
Eliot, G. Romola
MEDICINE
Caldwell, T. Testimony of two men
  See also Physicians

Study and teaching
Baroja y Nessi, P. The tree of knowledge
MEDICINE, EXPERIMENTAL
Christopher, J. The little people
Cronin, A. J. Shannon's way
Slaughter, F. G. Surgeon's choice
MEDICINE, PRACTICE OF. See Physicians
A medicine for melancholy. Bradbury, R.
  also in Bradbury, R. Twice twenty-two:
    The golden apples of the sun; A medicine for melancholy p213-406
MEDICINE MEN. See Religion, Primitive

Metamorphosis. Kafka, F.
    also in Kafka, F. The penal colony
    also in Kafka, F. Selected short stories
    also in Neider, C. ed. Short novels of the
      masters p537-79
    also in Pick, R. ed. German stories and
      tales p247-95
METAPHYSICS
  Murdoch, I. The flight from the enchanter
METEOROLOGISTS
  Aldridge, J. A captive in the land
  Bagley, D. Wyatt's hurricane
  Stewart, G. R. Storm
METHODISM
  Andrew, P. A new creature
METHODIST CHURCH. See Methodism
METHODIST MINISTERS. See Clergy
MEXICAN REVOLUTION. See Mexico—20th
  century
MEXICANS IN BAJA CALIFORNIA
  Steinbeck, J. The pearl
MEXICANS IN THE UNITED STATES
  Barry, J. A shadow of eagles
  Bryan, J. Y. Come to the bower
  Mankiewicz, D. M. Trial
  Vasquez, R. Chicano
MEXICO
  Olsen, P. The Virgin of San Gil
  Traven, B. The night visitor, and other sto-
    ries
    See also Baja California
       16th century
  Baron, A. The golden princess
  Shellabarger, S. Captain from Castile
       18th century
  Wellman, P. I. Ride the red earth
       19th century
  Fuentes, C. The death of Artemio Cruz
  Gavin, C. The cactus and the crown
  Lea, T. The wonderful country
  Maugham, R. The link
  Somerlott, R. The inquisitor's house
       20th century
  Azuela, M. Two novels of the Mexican Revo-
    lution: The trials of a respectable family,
    and The underdogs
  Fuentes, C. A change of skin
  Greene, G. The power and the glory
  Hobart, A. T. The peacock sheds his tail
  Lawrence, D. H. The plumed serpent
  Lea, T. The brave bulls
  Lowry, M. Dark as the grave wherein my
    friend is laid
  Lowry, M. Under the volcano
  Sorensen, V. The proper gods
  Swarthout, G. They came to Cordura
  Traven, B. The cotton-pickers
  Wilder, R. Fruit of the poppy
  Yáñez, A. The edge of the storm
  Yáñez, A. The lean lands
       Acapulco
  Morris, W. Love among the cannibals
       Farm life
    See Farm life—Mexico
       Guadalajara
  Yáñez, A. The edge of the storm
       Mexico City
  Fuentes, C. Where the air is clear
  Gilman, D. The unexpected Mrs Pollifax
  Morris, W. The field of vision
       Sierra Madre
  Traven, B. The treasure of the Sierra Madre
MEXICO, PROVINCIAL AND RURAL
  Bagley, D. The Vivero letter
  Gellhorn, M. The lowest trees have tops
  Yáñez, A. The lean lands
MEXICO CITY. See Mexico—Mexico City
Meyer, Meyer. Hudson, H.
Micah Clarke. Doyle, Sir A. C.
Michael Strogoff. Verne, J.
Michel, Michel. Lewis, R.
MICHELANGELO BUONARROTI
  Stone, I. The agony and the ecstasy
MICHIGAN
       20th century
  Traver, R. Anatomy of a murder
  Van Dyke, H. Ladies of the Rachmaninoff
    eyes
  Woiwode, L. What I'm going to do, I think

       Detroit
Arnow, H. The dollmaker
Arnow, H. S. The weedkiller's daughter
Douglas, L. C. Magnificent obsession
Lathen, E. Murder makes the wheels go
  'round
Oates, J. C. Them
       Milton
Greenbaum, L. Out of shape
MICROBES. See Microorganisms
MICROORGANISMS
  Crichton, M. The Andromeda strain
Midcentury. Dos Passos, J.
MIDDLE AGE
  Beauvoir, S. de. The woman destroyed
  Benedetti, M. The truce
  Bridge, A. Illyrian spring
  Cather, W. The professor's house
  Colette. Chéri
    In Colette. Chéri, and The last of Chéri
    In Colette. 7 by Colette v2 p 1-154
    In Colette. Six novels p411-534
  Connell, E. S. Mr Bridge
  Connell, E. S. Mrs Bridge
  Gordon, N. The rabbi
  Goudge, E. The scent of water
  Howells, W. D. Indian summer
  Hudson, H. Meyer, Meyer
  Lewis, S. Cass Timberlane
  Lewis, S. Dodsworth
  Mann, T. The black swan
  Marquand, J. P. Melville Goodwin, USA
  Mishima, Y. After the banquet
  Murdoch, I. The sandcastle
  Orwell, G. Coming up for air
  Shaw, R. A card from Morocco
  Troyat, H. An extreme friendship
  Weingarten, V. A loving wife
  Weingarten, V. Mrs Beneker
  West, N. Day of the locust
    In West, N. Complete works p259-421
  White, N. G. The gift and the giver
  Williams, T. The Roman spring of Mrs Stone
  Wilson, A. The middle age of Mrs Eliot
    See also Old age
The middle age of Mrs Eliot. Wilson, A.
MIDDLE AGES
  Aucassin et Nicolette. Aucassin and Nicolette,
    and other mediaeval romances and legends
  Barnes, M. C. Isabel the Fair
  Byrne, D. Messer Marco Polo
  Closs, H. Deep are the valleys
  Closs, H. High are the mountains
  Closs, H. The silent Tarn
  Costain, T. B. Below the salt
  Costain, T. B. The black rose
  Doyle, Sir A. C. The White Company
  Druon, M. The Iron King
  Druon, M. The Lily and the Lion
  Druon, M. The poisoned crown
  Druon, M. The royal succession
  Druon, M. The strangled queen
  Duggan, A. Lord Geoffrey's fancy
  Hesse, H. Narcissus and Goldmund
  Holland, C. Antichrist
  Holland, C. The firedrake
  Lofts, N. The town house
  Mydans, S. Thomas
  Oldenbourg, Z. Cities of the flesh
  Oldenbourg, Z. The cornerstone
  Oldenbourg, Z. Destiny of fire
  Oldenbourg, Z. The world is not enough
  Prescott, H. F. M. Son of dust
  Reade, C. The cloister and the hearth
  Roberts, D. J. The enchanted cup
  Roberts, D. J. Launcelot, my brother
  Scott, Sir W. Quentin Durward
  Twain, M. Personal recollections of Joan of
    Arc
  Undset, S. Kristin Lavransdatter
  White, H. C. Bird of fire: a tale of St Francis
    of Assisi
  White, T. H. The ill-made knight
  White, T. H. The once and future king
  White, T. H. The sword in the stone
  White, T. H. The witch in the wood
  Wibberley, L. Beware of the mouse
    See also names of countries during this
    period, e.g. England—14th century; France
    —Paris—15th century; also Feudalism;
    Knights and knighthood

Miro. Herron, S.

The mirror crack'd. Christie, A.

The mirror crack'd from side to side. See Christie, A. The mirror crack'd

Mirrors. Warner, L.

MISCEGNATION. See Inter-racial marriages

Les misérables. Hugo, V.

MISERS
  Andric, I. The woman from Sarajevo
  Eliot, G. Silas Marner

Miss Bishop. Aldrich, B. S.
  also in Aldrich, B. S. A Bess Streeter Aldrich treasury p211-379

Miss Buncle. Stevenson, D. E.

Miss Buncle married. Stevenson, D. E.
  In Stevenson, D. E. Miss Buncle v2

Miss Buncle's book. Stevenson, D. E.
  In Stevenson, D. E. Miss Buncle v 1

Miss Clare remembers. Read, Miss

Miss Lonelyhearts. West, N.
  also in West, N. The complete works of Nathaniel West p65-140

Miss Lulu Bett. Gale, Z.

Miss Morissa, doctor of the gold trail. Sandoz, M.

Miss Owen-Owen. Forster, M.

Miss Pickthorn and Mr Hare. Sarton, M.

Miss Pinkerton. Rinehart, M. R.

Miss Pinkerton [novelette]. Rinehart, M. R.
  In Rinehart, M. R. Miss Pinkerton p95-245

Miss Pym disposes. Tey, J.
  also in Tey, J. Three by Tey v 1

Miss Seeton draws the line. Carvic, H.

Missing from her home. Gilbert, A.

The missing Matisse. Levy, B.

The mission. Habe, H.

A mission for Betty Smith. See Cooper, B. Monsoon murder

Mission to Rome. Romains, J.
  In Romains, J. Death of a world

MISSIONARIES
  Achebe, C. Things fall apart
  Allen, T. D. Doctor in buckskin
  Barrett, W. E. The left hand of God
  Bromfield, L. A good woman
    In Bromfield, L. Bromfield galaxy: The green bay tree, Early autumn, A good woman p405-639
  Buck, P. S. Pavilion of women
  Cather, W. Death comes for the archbishop
  Cronin, A. J. The keys of the kingdom
  De Wohl, L. Set all afire
  Forester, C. S. The African Queen
  Giles, J. H. Johnny Osage
  Matthiessen, P. At play in the fields of the Lord
  Melville, H. Omoo
  Michener, J. A. Hawaii
  Sorensen, V. Kingdom come
  Warner, S. T. Mr Fortune's maggot
    In Warner, S. T. Lolly Willowes, and Mr Fortune's maggot p161-310
  White, R. Elephant Hill

MISSIONARIES, MEDICAL
  Hartog, J. de. The spiral road

MISSIONS. See Missionaries

MISSISSIPPI
  Faulkner, W. Knight's gambit
  Faulkner, W. The portable Faulkner
  Faulkner, W. Sanctuary
  Foote, S. Follow me down
    In Foote, S. Three novels v 1
  Foote, S. Jordan County
    In Foote, S. Three novels v2

19th century
  Eberhart, M. G. The cup, the blade or the gun
  Faulkner, W. Absalom, Absalom!
  Faulkner, W. The hamlet
  Faulkner, W. The unvanquished
  Street, J. Tap roots
  Young, S. So red the rose

20th century
  Chaze, E. Wettermark
  Deal, B. The advocate
  Faulkner, W. Light in August
  Foote, S. Love in a dry season
    In Foote, S. Three novels v3
  Mahoney, W. Black Jacob

Spencer, E. The voice at the back door

Street, J. Good-bye, my Lady

Sumner, C. R. Quality

Welty, E. Delta wedding

Welty, E. The golden apples

Welty, E. The Ponder heart

Jefferson
Faulkner, W. Go down, Moses, and other stories
Faulkner, W. Intruder in the dust
Faulkner, W. The mansion
Faulkner, W. Requiem for a nun
Faulkner, W. Sartoris
Faulkner, W. The town

Natchez
Street, J. Oh, promised land

MISSISSIPPI RIVER
  Ferber, E. Show boat
  Taylor, R. L. A journey to Matecumbe
  Twain, M. The adventures of Huckleberry Finn
  Twain, M. The adventures of Tom Sawyer

MISSISSIPPI VALLEY
  Churchill, W. The crossing
  Keyes, F. P. Steamboat Gothic
  Welty, E. The robber bridegroom

MISSOURI
19th century
  Borland, H. The amulet
  Erdman, L. G. Another spring
  Erdman, L. G. The far journey
  Twain, M. The adventures of Tom Sawyer
  Twain, M. Pudd'nhead Wilson and Those extraordinary twins

20th century
  Barrett, W. E. The glory tent
  Carleton, J. The moonflower vine
  Kantor, M. The daughter of Bugle Ann
  Kantor, M. The voice of Bugle Ann
  Street, J. The gauntlet
  Street, J. The high calling

Farm life
See Farm life—Missouri

Kansas City
Connell, E. S. Mr Bridge
Connell, E. S. Mrs Bridge

St Louis
Churchill, W. The crisis

MISSOURI RIVER
  Aldrich, B. S. The lieutenant's lady

MISTAKEN IDENTITY
  Clifford, F. Another way of dying
  Coxe, G. H. Double identity
  Gilford, C. B. The crooked shamrock
  MacInnes, H. North from Rome
  Milne, A. A. The red house mystery
  Stewart, M. The ivy tree
  See also Impersonations

Mr and Mrs Bo Jo Jones. Head, A.

Mr Audubon's Lucy. Kennedy, L.

Mr Blandings builds his dream house. Hodgins, E.

Mr Bridge. Connell, E. S.

Mr Britling ses it through. Wells, H. G.

Mr Campion's farthing. Carter, Y.

Mr Fairlie's final journey. Derleth, A.

Mr Fortune's maggot. Warner, S. T.
  In Warner, S. T. Lolly Willowes, and Mr Fortune's maggot p161-310

Mr Hobbs' vacation. Streeter, E.

Mister Johnson. Cary, J.

Mr Lincoln's wife. Colver, A.

Mr Love and justice. MacInnes, C.
  In MacInnes, C. The London novels of Colin MacInnes p451-626

Mr Midshipman Easy. Marryat, F.

Mr Midshipman Hornblower. Forester, C. S.
  also in Forester, C. S. Young Hornblower p9-208

Mr Moto is so sorry. Marquand, J. P.
  In Marquand, J. P. Mr Moto's three aces p291-447

Mr Moto's three aces. Marquand, J. P.

Mr Pim. Milne, A. A.

Mister Roberts. Heggen, T.

The mountain lion. Murphy, R.
MOUNTAIN LIONS. See Pumas
Mountain man. Fisher, V.
Mountain meadow. Buchan, J.
MOUNTAIN MEN. See Trappers and trapping
The mountain road. White, T. H.
Mountain standard time: Main line west, Far from Cibola [and] The common heart. Horgan, P.
MOUNTAIN WHITES. See Mountain life—Southern States
MOUNTAIN WHITES (SOUTHERN STATES) DIALECT. See Dialect stories—Mountain whites (Southern States)
MOUNTAINEERING
 Daudet, A. Tartarin on the Alps
  In Daudet, A. Tartarin of Tarascon
 Garve, A. The ascent of D-13
 Masters, J. Far, far the mountain peak
 Troyat, H. The mountain
 Ullman, J. R. The White Tower
MOUNTED POLICE. See Canada. Royal Canadian Mounted Police
Mountolive. Durrell, L.
 also in Durrell, L. The Alexandria quartet: Justine; Balthazar, Mountolive [and] Clea p391-652
The mouse on the moon. Wibberley, L.
The mouse on Wall Street. Wibberley, L.
The mouse that roared. Wibberley, L.
The mousetrap [play] See Christie, A. Three blind mice
The move. Simenon, G.
The moviegoer. Percy, W.
The moving finger. Christie, A.
 In Christie, A. Murder in our midst p319-444
MOVINNG PICTURE ACTRESSES. See Actresses; Moving pictures
MOVING PICTURE PLAYS
 Thomas, D. Rebecca's Daughters
MOVING PICTURE STARS. See Actresses
MOVING PICTURES
 Boucher, A. The case of the Baker Street Irregulars
 Fitzgerald, F. S. The last tycoon
 O'Hara, J. The girl on the baggage truck
  In O'Hara, J. Sermons and soda water v 1
 Schulberg, B. What makes Sammy run?
The moving target. Macdonald, R.
 In Macdonald, R. Archer in Hollywood p3-169
MOZART, JOHANN CHRYSOSTOM WOLFGANG AMADEUS
 Weiss, D. Sacred and profance
The mudlark. Bonnet, T.
Mulata. Asturias, M. A.
MULATTOES
 Cather, W. Sapphira and the slave girl
 Warren, R. P. Band of angels
MULTIPLE PERSONALITY. See Personality, Disorders of
Mum is the word. Queen, E.
 In Queen, E. Q.E.D. Queen's experiments in detection p3-63
MUNITIONS
 Ambler, E. Passage of arms
 Benchley, N. The wake of Icarus
 Caldwell, T. Dynasty of death
 Cleary, J. Season of doubt
 Garner, W. The us or them war
 Sinclair, U. World's end
MUNITIONS INDUSTRY
 Caldwell, T. The eagles gather
 Caldwell, T. The final hour
 Van Vogt, A. E. The weapon makers
 Van Vogt, A. E. The weapon shops of Isher
MUNITIONS TRADE. See Munitions
Murder against the grain. Lathen, E.
Murder among children. Coe, T.
The murder at the vicarage. Christie, A.
 In Christie, A. Murder in our midst p131-317
Murder by the book. Stout, R.
 In Stout, R. Royal flush p181-333
Murder by 3's. Moyes, P.

Murder for art's sake. Lockridge, E.
Murder in Canton. Gulik, R. van
Murder in Mesopotamia. Christie, A.
 In Christie, A. Perilous journeys of Hercule Poirot v3
Murder in mind. Mystery Writers of America
Murder in our midst. Christie, A.
Murder in the Calais coach. Christie, A.
 In Haycraft, H. ed. A treasury of great mysteries v 1 p9-146
Murder in three acts. Christie, A.
 In Christie, A. Surprise endings by Hercule Poirot p139-272
Murder is corny. Stout, R.
 In Stout. R. Trio for blunt instruments p89-167
Murder is no joke. Stout, R.
 In Haycraft, H. ed. Three times three p551-86
The murder league. Fish, R. L.
Murder, London-Australia. Creasey, J.
Murder, London-Miami. Creasey, J.
Murder, London-South Africa. Creasey, J.
Murder makes the wheels go 'round. Lathen, E.
Murder must advertise. Sayers, D. L.
The murder of Aziz Khan. Ghose, Z.
A murder of quality. Le Carré, J.
 In Le Carré J. The incongruous spy v2
The murder of Roger Ackroyd. Christie, A.
 also In Christie, A. Christie classics p 1-167
 also In Costain, T. B. ed. More Stories to remember v2 p281-438
The murder of the frogs, and other stories. Carpenter, D.
Murder Off-Broadway. Klinger, H.
 In Klinger, H. The three cases of Shomri Shomar p157-303
Murder on the Orient Express [variant title: Murder in the Calais coach] Christie, A.
Murder reflected. See Caird, J. In a glass darkly
MURDER STORIES
 Bagley, D. The Vivero letter
 Beckham, B. My main mother
 Behan, B. The Scarperer
 Bell. J. The upfold witch
 Berckman, E. Stalemate
 Black, G. The cold jungle
 Blackburn, J. Children of the night
 Boulle, P. Face of a hero
 Buchan, J. The thirty-nine steps
 Burnett, W. R. Little Caesar
 Cain, J. M. Double indemnity
  In Cain, J. M. Cain x 3 p363-465
 Caird, J. In a glass darkly
 Camus, A. The stranger
 Canning, V. The melting man
 Carr, J. D. Papa Là-bas
 Christie, A. And then there were none
 Christie, A. Endless night
 Collins, N. The Governor's lady
 Coxe, G. H. The candid impostor
 Coxe, G. H. An easy way to go
 Cross, A. The James Joyce murder
 Davenport, B. ed. 13 ways to kill a man
 Davidson, D. Feversham
 Davies, L. P. A grave matter
 Dickinson, P. The old English peep show
 Disney, D. M. Voice from the grave
 Dostoevsky, F. The brothers Karamazov
 Dostoevsky, F. Crime and punishment
 Dreiser, T. An American tragedy
 Du Maurier, D. The flight of the falcon
 Du Maurier, D. Rebecca
 Eberhart, M. G. The cup, the blade or the gun
 Eberhart, M. G. Message from Hong Kong
 Edwards, A. The survivors
 Ellin, S. The Valentine estate
 Faulkner, W. Requiem for a nun
 Faulkner, W. Sanctuary
 Fenwick, E. Goodbye, Aunt Elva
 Ferrars, E. X. The swaying pillars
 Field, R. All this, and heaven too
 Foote, S. Follow me down
  In Foote, S. Three novels v 1
 Frankau, P. Colonel Blessington
 Garve, A. The far sands
 Gary, R. The dance of Genghis Cohn
 Gaskin, C. Edge of glass
 Gide, A. Lafcadio's adventures
 Gilbert, S. Ratman's notebooks
 Gloag, J. A sentence of life
 Gores, J. A time of predators

MYSTERY AND DETECTIVE STORIES—England—*Continued*

Christie, A. Surprise endings by Hercule Poirot
Christie, A. They do it with mirrors
Christie, A. Third girl
Christie, A. 13 clues for Miss Marple
Christie, A. What Mrs McGillicuddy saw!
Cleary, J. The High Commissioner
Collins, W. The moonstone
Collins, W. The woman in white
Conrad, J. Secret agent
In Conrad, J. Tales of the East and West p353-544
Creasey, J. The case of the innocent victims
Creasey, J. The executioners
Creasey, J. Murder, London-Miami
Creasey, J. Murder, London-South Africa
Crofts, F. W. The cask
Davies, L. P. The reluctant medium
Derleth, A. The casebook of Solar Pons
Derleth, A. Mr Fairlie's final journey
Dickens, C. Bleak House
Dickens, C. The mystery of Edwin Drood
Dickinson, P. The glass-sided ants' nest
Doyle, A. C. Exploits of Sherlock Holmes
Doyle, Sir A. C. Adventures and Memoirs of Sherlock Holmes
Doyle, Sir A. C. Adventures of Sherlock Holmes
Doyle, Sir A. C. The Croxley master
In Costain, T. B. ed. More Stories to remember v2 p189-221
Doyle, Sir A. C. Famous tales of Sherlock Holmes
Doyle, Sir A C. The hound of the Baskervilles
Doyle, Sir A. C. The later adventures of Sherlock Holmes
Doyle, Sir A. C. The memoirs of Sherlock Holmes
Doyle, Sir A C. Sherlock Holmes: detective
Doyle, Sir A. C. Sherlock Holmes' greatest cases
Doyle, Sir A. C. Tales of Sherlock Holmes
Fish, R. L. The murder league
Francis, D. Odds against
Gallico, P. Too many ghosts
Garve, A. A very quiet place
Gilbert, A. The looking glass murder
Gilbert, A. Missing from her home
Gilbert, A. The visitor
Giles, K. Death in diamonds
Heyer, G. Detection unlimited
Heyer, G. Duplicate death
Heyer, G. Envious Casca
Heyer, G. The talisman ring
Heyer, G. The toll-gate
Hichens, R. The Paradine case
Holt, V. Kirkland Revels
Hubbard, P. M. A hive of glass
Innes, M. Appleby intervenes
Innes, M. The bloody wood
Innes, M. Death at the chase
Innes, M. Death by water
Innes, M. Picture of guilt
Keating, H. R. F. Inspector Ghote hunts the peacock
MacDonald, P. The list of Adrian Messenger
Marric, J. J. Gideon's day
Marsh, N. Clutch of constables
Marsh, N. Dead water
Marsh, N. False scent
Marsh, N. Hand in glove
Marsh, N. Killer dolphin
Marsh, N. Scales of justice
Marsh, N. Singing in the shrouds
Marsh, N. Three-act special
Milne, A. A. The red house mystery
Peters, E. The grass-widow's tale
Peters, E. Who lies here?
Procter, M. Exercise Hoodwink
Roffman, J. A daze of fears
Sayers, D. L. Busman's honeymoon
Sayers, D. L. Dorothy L. Sayers omnibus
Sayers, D. L. Gaudy Night
Sayers, D. L. Have his carcase
Sayers, D. L. Murder must advertise
Sayers, D. L. The nine tailors
Sayers, D. L. The unpleasantness at the Bellona Club
Symons, J. The Belting inheritance
Symons, J. The color of murder
Symons, J. The man who killed himself
Symons, J. The progress of a crime
Tey, J. Brat Farrar
Tey, J. The daughter of time
Tey, J. Four, five and six by Tey
Tey, J. The Franchise affair
Tey, J. The man in the queue
Tey, J. Miss Pym disposes

Tey, J. A shilling for candles
Tey, J. Three by Tey
Tey, J. To love and be wise
Watson, C. Lonelyheart 4122
Woods, S, Enter certain murderers

Europe
Christie, A. Murder on the Orient Express

France
Leblanc, M. Extraordinary adventures of Arsène Lupin, gentleman burglar
Marsh, N. Spinsters in jeopardy
Poe, E. A. The purloined letter [and] The murders in the Rue Morgue
Simenon, G. Five times Maigret
Simenon, G. Madame Maigret's own case
Simenon, G. Maigret and the Calame report
Simenon, G. Maigret and the headless corpse
Simenon, G. Maigret cinq
Simenon, G. Maigret in Vichy
Simenon, G. Maigret's dead man
Simenon, G. Maigret's pickpocket
Simenon, G. No vacation for Maigret
Simenon, G. Short cases of Inspector Maigret
Stewart, M. Madam, will you talk?
Stewart, M. Thunder on the right

Greece
Bell, J. The catalyst
Lathen, E. When in Greece

India
Cooper, B. Monsoon murder
Keating, H. R. F. Inspector Ghote caught in meshes

Israel
Klinger, H. The three cases of Shomri Shomar

Italy
Gruber, F. The Etruscan bull

Mexico
Chandler, R. The long goodbye

Netherlands
Freeling, N. Criminal conversation
Freeling, N. Double barrel
Freeling, N. Tsing-boom!
Simenon, G. Maigret abroad

New Zealand
Marsh, N. Colour scheme

Palestine
Christie, A. Appointment with death
In Christie, A. Make mine murder! p9-155

Scotland
Rae, H. C. The house at Balnesmoor
Sayers, D. L. The five red herrings (Suspicious characters)
Sayers, D. L. Strong poison
Tey, J. The singing sands

Sweden
Sjöwall, M. The laughing policeman
Sjöwall, M. The man on the balcony
Sjöwall, M. Roseanna

Switzerland
Duerrenmatt, F. The judge and his hangman

United States
Armstrong, C. Dream of fair woman
Armstrong, C. The gift shop
Armstrong, C. The protégé
Asimov, I. A whiff of death
Ball, J. In the heat of the night
Baxt, G. "I!" said the demon
Biggers, E. D. Seven keys to Baldpate
Borgenicht, M. Margin for doubt
Boucher, A. The case of the Baker Street Irregulars
Braun, L. J. The cat who ate Danish modern
Braun, L. J. The cat who turned on and off
Carr, J. D. The ghosts' high noon
Chandler, R. The big sleep
Chandler, R. The lady in the lake
Chandler, R. The Raymond Chandler omnibus
Chandler, R. The simple art of murder
Charteris, L. The second Saint omnibus
Christie, A. Christie classics
Coe, T. Murder among children
Coe, T. Wax apple
Coxe, G. H. Triple exposure
Creasey, J. Murder, London-Miami
Cross, A. The James Joyce murder

NATCHEZ. See Mississippi—Natchez

NATIONAL AERONAUTICS AND SPACE AD-
MINISTRATION. See United States. National Aeronautics and Space administration

NATIONAL SOCIALISM
Albrand, M Rhine replica
Arent, A. The laying on of hands
Behn, N. The shadowboxer
Behrman, S. N. The burning glass
Bemelmans, L. The Blue Danube
Blackstock, C. The knock at midnight
Bor, J. The Terezin Requiem
Bottome, P. The mortal storm
Coles, M. A toast to tomorrow
Gainham, S. Night falls on the city
Gary, R. The dance of Genghis Cohn
Gheorghiu, C. V. The twenty-fifth hour
Giovannitti, L. The prisoners of Combine D
Grass, G. Dog years
Hall, A. The Quiller memorandum
Hall, A. The Striker portfolio
Kirst, H. H. Forward, Gunner Asch!
Kirst, H. H. The officer factory
Kirst, H. H. The wolves
Levin, M. Eva
MacInnes, H. Above suspicion
Malraux, A. Days of wrath
Shaw, I. The young lions
Shaw, R. The man in the glass booth
Sinclair, U. Dragon's teeth
Sinclair, U. Wide is the gate
Singer, I. J. The family Carnovsky
Ustinov, P. The loser
Wiseman, T. The quick and the dead
    See also Germany—1918-1945
National Velvet. Bagnold, E.
    In Costain, T. B. ed. Stories to remember
    v2 p339-504

NATIONALISM
Abrahams, P. A wreath for Udomo
Macken, W. The scorching wind
Monsarrat, N. The tribe that lost its head
Ullman, J. R. The White Tower
Werfel, F. The forty days of Musa Dagh

NATIONALITY. See Nationalism

NATIVE RACES. See names of countries with
subdivision Native races, e.g. Africa—Native races; New Guinea—Native races; etc.

Native son. Wright, R.

The natives of Hemso. Strindberg, A.

The natural. Malamud, B.

Natural state. Knight, D.
    In Knight, D. Three novels p82-150

NATURALISTS
Husdon, W. H. Green mansions
    See also Ornithologists

NATURE
Bodsworth, F. The sparrow's fall
Bodsworth, F. The strange one
Clarkson, E. Syla, the mink
Eckert, A. W. The great auk
Frison-Roche, R. The raid
Hudson, W. H. Green mansions
Hudson, W. H. The purple land
Mannix, D. P. The killers
Murphy, R. A certain island
Murphy, R. The mountain lion
Murphy, R. The Pond
Rawlings, M. K. South moon under

Nausea. Sartre, J. P.

NAVAHO INDIANS
Eastlake, W. Portrait of an artist with twen-
ty-six horses
La Farge, O. Laughing Boy

NAVAJO INDIANS. See Navaho Indians

NAVAL BATTLES
Cooper, J. F. The Red Rover
Fletcher, I. Roanoke hundred
Forester, C. S. Beat to quarters
Forester, C. S. Commodore Hornblower
Forester, C. S. Hornblower and the Atropos
Forester, C. S. The last nine days of the Bis-
marck
Forester, C. S. The ship
Forester, C. S. Ship of the line
Kent, A. Form line of battle!
Kent, A. To glory we steer
Pope, D. Drumbeat
Reeman, D. H.M.S. Saracen
    See also Sea stories; also names of
    wars with subdivision Naval operations,
    e.g. United States—18th century—Revolu-
    tion—Naval operations

NAVAL LIEUTENANTS. See names of countries with subhead: Navy—Officers, e.g.
United States. Navy—Officers

NAVAL LIFE, BRITISH. See Great Britain.
Navy

NAVAL LIFE, ENGLISH. See Great Britain.
Navy

NAVAL OFFICERS. See names of countries
with subhead: Navy—Officers

NAVY. See names of countries with subdivision: Navy; e.g. Great Britain. Navy

NAVY LIFE. See names of countries with
subdivision: Navy, e.g. United States.
Navy

The Nazarene. Asch, S.

NAZI MOVEMENT. See National socialism

NAZIS. See Germany—1918-1945; National socialism

NAZISM. See National socialism

NEANDERTHAL PEOPLE. See Prehistoric
times

NEAR EAST
Ambler, E. The light of day
Bagley, D. The spoilers
Hempstone, S. In the midst of lions
Llewellyn, R. White horse to Banbury Cross
West, M. L. The tower of Babel
    See also specific countries in the region

Politics
    See Politics—Near East

NEBRASKA
19th century
Aldrich, B. S. A lantern in her hand
Aldrich, B. S. Spring came on forever
Cather, W. Early stories of Willa Cather
Cather, W. Lucy Gayheart
Cather, W. My Antonia
Cather, W. O pioneers!
Sandoz, M. Miss Morissa, doctor of the gold
trail

20th century
Aldrich, B. S. A white bird flying
Cather, W. A lost lady
Cather, W. One of ours
Morris, W. Ceremony in Lone Tree

Farm life
    See Farm life—Nebraska

Frontier and pioneer life
    See Frontier and pioneer life—Nebraska

NEBUCHADNEZZAR
Weinreb, N. N. The Babylonians

Nebula award stories, 1965 [1]-4. Entered in
Part I under title

A necessary action. Wahlöö, P.

NECKLACES. See Jewelry

Nectar in a sieve. Markandaya, K.

NEGRO DIALECT. See Dialect stories—Negro

NEGRO LIFE. See Negroes

NEGRO MUSICIANS
Kelley, W. M. A drop of patience

NEGROES
Anderson, S. Dark laughter
Baker, D. Young man with a horn
Baldwin, J. Another country
Baldwin, J. Go tell it on the mountain
Baldwin, J. Going to meet the man
Baldwin, J. Tell me how long the train's
been gone
Ball, J. In the heat of the night
Ball, J. Johnny get your gun
Barrett, W. E. The glory tent
Barrett, W. E. The lilies of the field
Bourne, P. Drums of destiny
Bristow, G. Deep summer
Brooks, G. Maud Martha
Carpentier, A. The kingdom of this world
Clarke, J. E. ed. American Negro short sto-
ries
Conrad, J. The Nigger of the Narcisus
Corley, E. Siege
Courlander, H. The African
Cozzens, J. G. Guard of honor
Daniels, L. Caleb, my son
Davis, C. First family
Drury, A. A shade of difference
Dunbar, P. L. The strength of Gideon, and
other stories

NEVADA

19th century

Clark, W. V. The Ox-bow incident

20th century

Clark, W. V. The track of the cat

Ranch life

See Ranch life—Nevada

NEW AMSTERDAM. See New York (City)—17th century

A new creature. Andrew, P.

The new day. Romains, J.

NEW DELHI. See India—New Delhi

NEW ENGLAND

Bjorn, T. F. Papa's wife
Cozzens, J. G. Morning, noon, and night
Hawthorne, N. Twice-told tales
Jackson, S. The bird's nest
Jackson, S. We have always lived in the castle
Jewett, S. O. The best stories of Sarah Orne Jewett
Potts, J. The little lie
Santayana, G. The last Puritan
Wallant, E. L. The children at the gate
See also names of individual New England States

17th century

Seton, A. The Winthrop woman

18th century

Mason, F. V. Young titan
Stone, I. Those who love

19th century

Brace, G. W. The Garretson chronicle
Disney, D. M. At some forgotten door
Wharton, E. Ethan Frome
Whitney, P. A. Sea Jade

20th century

Auchincloss, L. The Rector of Justin
Baldwin, F. The velvet hammer
Benchley, N. The visitors
Bjorn, T. F. Papa's daughter
Buechner, F. The entrance to Porlock
Cheever, J. The Wapshot chronicle
Cheever, J. The Wapshot scandal
Cozzens, J. G. By love possessed
Field, R. And now tomorrow
Kemelman, H. Friday the rabbi slept late
Kemelman, H. Saturday the rabbi went hungry
Kirkwood, J. Good times/bad times
Knowles, J. A separate peace
Lurie, A. Real people
McCarthy, M. A charmed life
Marquand, J. P. Wickford Point
Marquand, J. P. Women and Thomas Harrow
Moore, R. The gold and silver hooks
Morley, C. Parnassus on wheels
Morrison, T. The stones of the house
Randall, F. E. The place of sapphires
Sarton, M. Miss Pickthorn and Mr Hare
Sarton, M. The small room
Steinbeck, J. The winter of our discontent
Streeter, E. Mr Hobbs' vacation
White, N. G. The gift and the giver
White, N. G. The thorn tree

Farm life

See Farm life—New England

Frontier and pioneer life

See Frontier and pioneer life—New England

NEW ENGLAND DIALECT. See Dialect stories—New England

NEW FRANCE. See Canada—To 1763 (New France)

New Grub Street. Gissing, G.

NEW GUINEA

20th century

Cleary, J. North from Thursday

Native races

Cleary, J. North from Thursday
Dickinson, P. The glass-sided ants' nest

NEW HAMPSHIRE

18th century

Cannon, L. Look to the mountain
Raddall, T. H. The Governor's lady

19th century

Benét, S. V. The Devil and Daniel Webster

20th century

Goudge, E. The bird in the tree
Johnson, P. H. Night and silence, who is here?
Sarton, M. The poet and the donkey
Whitney, P. A. Silverhill
Williams, T. Whipple's castle

Farm life

See Farm life—New Hampshire

Frontier and pioneer life

See Frontier and pioneer life—New Hampshire

NEW HAVEN. See Connecticut—New Haven

NEW JERSEY

19th century

Vining, E. G. I, Roberta

20th century

Hawley, C. The Lincoln Lords
Sheed, W. The hack
Sheed, W. Square's progress
Updike, J. The poorhouse fair
Whitney, P. A. The winter people

Trenton

Taylor, D. Lights across the Delaware

A new life. Malamud, B.

The new men. Snow, C. P.

NEW MEXICO

Schaefer, J. Monte Walsh

19th century

Arnold, E. Blood brother
Bean, A. Time for outrage
Cather, W. Death comes for the archbishop
O'Rourke, F. The far mountains
Richter, C. The lady

20th century

Benchley, N. Welcome to Xanadu
Bradford, R. Red sky at morning
Eastlake, W. Portrait of an artist with twenty-six horses

Albuquerque

Horgan, P. The common heart
In Horgan, P. Mountain standard time: Main line west, Far from Cibola [and] The common heart p279-595

Frontier and pioneer life

See Frontier and pioneer life—New Mexico

Los Alamos

Masters, D. The accident

Taos

O'Rourke, F. The far mountains

New moon rising. Price, E.

The new moon with the old. Smith, D.

NEW ORLEANS. See Louisiana—New Orleans

NEW SOUTH WALES. See Australia—New South Wales

NEW SOUTHWEST. See Southwest, New

The new year. Buck, P. S.

New Year's Day. Wharton, E.
In Wharton, E. Old New York v4

NEW YORK (CITY)

Asimov, I. The caves of steel

17th century

Schoonover, L. Key of gold

18th century

Atherton, G. The conqueror
Linington, E. The long watch

19th century

Adams, S. H. Tenderloin
Auchincloss, L. The house of five talents
Bromfield, L. Mrs Parkington
Edmonds, W. D. Young Ames
Field, R. All this, and heaven too
Henry, O. The four million
Howells, W. D. A hazard of new fortunes
James, H. Washington Square
Stewart, R. Casey
Wharton, E. The age of innocence
Wharton, E. Bunner sisters
In Wharton, E. An Edith Wharton treasury
Wharton, E. Old New York
Whitney, P. A. Window on the square

NEW YORK (STATE)—*Continued*
20th century
Arkin, F. The Dorp
Auchincloss, L. The embezzler
Baker, E. The penny wars
Cheever, J. Bullet Park
Dreiser, T. An American tragedy
Edmonds, W. D. The boyds of Black River
Hale, N. Black summer
Horgan, P. Things as they are
Puzo, M. The godfather
Whitney, P. A. Thunder Heights

Cooperstown
Cooper, J. F. The pioneers

Dygartsbush
Edmonds, W. D. In the hands of the Senecas

Farm life
See Farm life—New York (State)

Frontier and pioneer life
See Frontier and pioneer life—New York (State)

Long Island
Fitzgerald, F. S. The Great Gatsby
Hobson, L. Z. First papers
Lancaster, B. The secret road
O'Hara, J. The girl on the baggage truck
In O'Hara, J. Sermons and soda water v 1

Mohawk Valley
Edmonds, W. D. Chad Hanna
Edmonds, W. D. Drums along the Mohawk

Saratoga Springs
Ferber, E. Saratoga trunk

Westchester County
Weingarten, V. Mrs Beneker
Wheeler, K. Peaceable Lane
NEW YORK. BASEBALL CLUB (AMERICAN LEAGUE)
Wallop, D. The year the Yankees lost the pennant

The New Yorkers. Calisher, H.

NEW ZEALAND
19th century
Goudge, E. Green Dolphin Street
Mason, F. V. Harpoon in Eden

20th century
Ashton-Warner, S. Bell call
Ashton-Warner, S. Greenstone
Ashton-Warner, S. Spinster
Cowley, J. Nest in a falling tree
Frame, J. Faces in the water
Frame, J. Yellow flowers in the antipodean room
Marsh, N. Colour scheme

Frontier and pioneer life
See Frontier and pioneer life—New Zealand

The Newcomes. Thackeray, W. M.

NEWGATE PRISON, LONDON
Carr, J. D. The bride of Newgate

NEWPORT. See Rhode Island—Newport

NEWSPAPER PUBLISHERS. See Publishers and publishing

NEWSPAPERMEN. See Journalists

NEWSPAPERS
Ambler, E. The Intercom conspiracy
Boucher, A. We print the truth
In Boucher, A. The compleat werewolf, and other stories of fantasy and science fiction p170-239
The next witness. Stout, R.
In Stout, R. Royal flush p337-84

NICE. See France—Nice

The nice and the good. Murdoch, I.

Nicholas Nickleby. Dickens, C.

Nick, the Click. Wilkinson, G. K.

NIECES
Anthony, E. The legend
Ibuse, M. Black rain

NIGERIA
Achebe, C. Arrow of God
Achebe, C. Things fall apart
Cary, J. The African witch
Cary, J. Mister Johnson

NIGERIANS IN ENGLAND
Blackstock, C. The lemmings
NIGGER heaven. Van Vechten, C.
The Nigger of the Narcissus. Conrad, J.
also in Conrad, J. Great short works of Joseph Conrad p21-140
also in Conrad, J. The portable Conrad p292-453
also in Conrad, J. Tales of land and sea p106-210
also in Conrad, J. Typhoon, and other tales of the sea p91-236
Night and silence, who is here? Johnson, P. H.
Night at the Vulcan. Marsh, N.
In Haycraft, H. ed. Three times three p639-830
In Marsh, N. Three-act special p381-541
Night before the wedding. The Gordons
The night-comers. See Ambler, E. State of siege
Night falls on the city. Gainham, S.
Night flight. Saint Exupéry, A. de
A night in Cold Harbor. Kennedy, M.
The night in Lisbon. Remarque, E. M.
Night journey. Graham, W.
Night march. Lancaster, B.
Night of Camp David. Knebel, F.
The night of the comet. Telfer, D.
The night of the generals. Kirst, H. H.
The night of the hunter. Grubb, D.
The night of the tiger. Gulik, R. van
In Gulik, R. van. The monkey and the tiger p71-141
A night of watching. Arnold, E.
The night visitor, and other stories. Traven, B.
Night without end. MacLean, A.
Nightfall, and other stories. Asimov, I.
Nightmare in Copenhagen. Albrand, M.
Nightmare in pink. MacDonald, J. D.
In MacDonald, J. D. Three for McGee p5-148
Nightrunners of Bengal. Masters, J.
Nightwood. Barnes, D.
NIHILISM
Dostoevsky, F. The possessed
Dumitriu, P. The extreme Occident
Pynchon, T. V
Styron, W. Set this house on fire
Tolstoy, L. War and peace
Turgenev, I. Fathers and sons
Turgenev, I. Virgin soil
The nine billion names of God. Clarke, A. C.
The nine brides and Granny Hite. Wilson, N. C.
Nine by Laumer. Laumer, K.
Nine coaches waiting. Stewart, M.
Nine hours to Rama. Wolpert, S.
The nine mile walk. Kemelman, H.
Nine stories. Salinger, J. D.
The nine tailors. Sayers, D. L.
Nine tomorrows. Asimov, I.
Nineteen eighty-four. Orwell, G.
1919. Dos Passos, J.
also in Dos Passos, J. U.S.A. v2
Nineteen stories. See Greene, G. 21 stories
The ninety and nine. Brinkley, W.
Ninety-three. Hugo, V.
The 9th directive. Hall, A.
The ninth wave. Burdick, E.
NISEI. See Japanese-Americans
No bones about it. Fleming, J.
No bugles tonight. See Lancaster, B.
No door. Wolfe, T.
In Wolfe, T. The short novels of Thomas Wolfe p158-231
No entry. Coles, M.
In Haycraft, H. ed. Five spy novels p615-758
No heaven for Gunga Din. Mirdrekvanki Gunga Din, Ali
No hiding place. Foley, R.
No highway. Shute, N.

The past recaptured. Proust, M.
    also in Proust, M. Remembrance of things past v2
The past through tomorrow. Heinlein, R. A.
The pastoral symphony. Gide, A.
    In Gide, A. Two symphonies p139-223
PASTORS. See Clergy
The Pat Hobby stories. Fitzgerald, F. S.
PATAGONIA
19th century
Llewellyn, R. Up, into the singing mountain
Pather Panchali: Song of the road. Banerji, B.
The Pathfinder. Cooper, J. F.
The Pathfinder [abridged]. Cooper, J. F.
    In Cooper, J. F. The Leatherstocking saga p463-613
PATHOLOGISTS
    Hailey, A. The final diagnosis
    See also Physicians
PATRIOTISM
    Forester, C. S. The last nine days of the Bismarck
    Hale, E. E. The man without a country
    Knight, E. This above all
    Taylor, D. Lights across the Delaware
    See also Loyalty
PATTERSON, BETSY. See Bonaparte, Elizabeth (Patterson)
PAUL, SAINT, APOSTLE
    Asch, S. The Apostle
    Caldwell, T. Dear and glorious physician
    De Wohl, L. The glorious folly
    Slaughter, F. G. God's warrior
PAUL OF TARSUS. See Paul, Saint, Apostle
PAUL I, EMPEROR OF RUSSIA
    Anthony, E. Royal intrigue
PAULINUS, GAIUS SUETONIUS
    Shipway, G. The Imperial Governor
Pavilion of women. Buck, P. S.
Pawn in frankincense. Dunnett, D.
The pawnbroker. Wallant, E. L.
PAWNBROKERS
    Wallant, E. L. The pawnbroker
PEACE
    Buckmaster, H. The lion in the stone
    Sinclair, U. O shepherd, speak!
Peace after war. Gironella, J. M.
PEACE CORPS. See United States. Peace Corps
Peace, my daughters. Barker, S.
The peaceable kingdom. Kennelly, A.
Peaceable Lane. Wheeler, K.
The peach stone. Horgan, P.
The peacock sheds his tail. Hobart, A. T.
The pearl. Steinbeck, J.
    also in Steinbeck, J. The short novels of John Steinbeck p471-527
PEARL-FISHING
    Steinbeck, J. The pearl
PEARL HARBOR, ATTACK ON, 1941
    Jones, J. The pistol
PEARLS
    Steinbeck, J. The pearl
Pearls before swine. See Vonnegut, K. God bless you, Mr Rosewater
PEASANT LIFE
    See also Farm life
China
Buck, P. S. Dragon seed
Buck, P. S. The good earth
Buck, P. S. The house of earth: The good earth; Sons; A house divided
Buck, P. S. The mother
Buck, P. S. The promise
Finland
Sillanpää, F. E. The maid Silja
France
Berri, C. The two of us
Germany
Werfel, F. Embezzled heaven
India
Banerji, B. Pather Panchali; Song of the road
Markandaya, K. Nectar in a sieve

Iran
Mirdrekvandi Gunga Din, A. No heaven for Gunga Din
Ireland
O'Flaherty, L. Famine
Italy
Gadda, C. E. Acquainted with grief
Silone, I. Bread and wine
Silone, I. Fontamara
Norway
Hamsun, K. Growth of the soil
Poland
Reymont, L. The peasants
Rumania
Dumitriu, P. Family jewels
Russia
Abramov, F. One day in the "new life"
Gogol, N. Dead souls
Sholokhov, M. Harvest on the Don
Sholokhov, M. Seeds of tomorrow
Sholokhov, M. Tales of the Don
Tolstoy, L. The Cossacks
Tolstoy, L. The Cossacks: a tale of 1852
    In Tolstoy, L. Short novels v 1 p279-455
Sicily
Verga, G. The house by the medlar tree
Spain
Bates, R. The olive field
Sweden
Budd, L. April snow
Turkey
Kazantzakis, N. The Greek passion
Kemal, Y. Anatolian tales
Kemal, Y. Memed, my hawk
PEASANTRY. See Peasant life
The peasants. Reymont, L.
PEASANT'S REVOLT. See England—14th century
Pebble in the sky. Asimov, I.
    In Asimov, I. Triangle: The currents of space, Pebble in the sky, The stars, like dust p173-346
Peder Victorious. Rolvaag, O. E.
Pedlock & Sons. Longstreet, S.
Pedlock saint, Pedlock sinner. Longstreet, S.
PEIPING. See China—Peking
PEKING. See China—Peking
Peking picnic. Bridge, A.
Pelle the conqueror. Nexo, M. A.
Pelle the conqueror: Apprenticeship. Nexo, M. A.
    In Nexo, M. A. Pelle the conqueror v2
Pelle the conqueror: Boyhood. Nexo, M. A.
    In Nexo, M. A. Pelle the conqueror v 1
Pelle the conqueror: Day break. Nexo, M. A.
    In Nexo, M. A. Pelle the conqueror v4
Pelle the conqueror: The great struggle. Nexo, M. A.
    In Nexo, M. A. Pelle the conqueror v3
PELOPONNESIAN WAR, 431-404 B.C. See Greece—Peloponnesian War, 431-404 B.C.
PENAL COLONIES
    Gaskin, C. Sara Dane
The penal colony. Kafka, F.
Pendennis. Thackeray. W. M.
Pendulum. Christopher, J.
Penelope. Cunningham. E. V.
Penguin Island. France, A.
PENGUINS
    Billing, G. Forbush and the penguins
PENINSULAR WAR, 1807-1814
    Conrad, J. The rover
    Forester, C. S. Captain Horatio Hornblower
    Forester, C. S. Commodore Hornblower
    Forester, C. S. Hornblower and the Hotspur
    Forester, C. S. Lieutenant Hornblower
    Forester, C. S. Ship of the line
    Heyer, G. The Spanish bride
    Marryat, F. Mr Midshipman Easy
    O'Brian, P. Master and commander
    Pope, D. Ramage

The phantom of the temple. Gulik, R. van

PHARAOHS. See Egypt—Kings and rulers

Pharaoh's chicken. Wollaston, N.

PHARISEES
Asch, S. The Nazarene

PHARMACISTS
Amado, J. Dona Flor and her two husbands
Beagle, P. S. A fine and private place
Cather, W. Shadows on the rock
McCullers, C. Clock without hands
    See also Medicines, Patent, proprietary, etc.

PHARSALUS, BATTLE OF, 48 B.C.
Davis, W. S. A friend of Caesar

PHILADELPHIA. See Pennsylvania—Philadelphia

PHILADELPHIA. CENTENNIAL EXPOSITION, 1876
Idell, A. E. Centennial summer

The Philadelphian. Powell, R.

PHILANTHROPISTS
Stewart, J. I. M. Vanderlyn's kingdom

PHILANTHROPY. See Endowments; Philanthropists

PHILATELY. See Booksellers and bookselling

PHILIP II, KING OF MACEDONIA
Renault, M. Fire from heaven

PHILIP II, KING OF SPAIN
De Wohl, L. The last crusader
Irwin, M. Elizabeth and the Prince of Spain

PHILIP IV, KING OF SPAIN
Keyes, F. P. I, the King

PHILIPPE IV, LE BEL, KING OF FRANCE
Druon, M. The Iron King

PHILIPPE VI, DE VALOIS, KING OF FRANCE
Druon, M. The Lily and the Lion

PHILIPPINE ISLANDS
Crumley, J. One to count cadence

Manila
Mydans, S. S. The open city

PHILLIP, ARTHUR
Dark, E. The timeless land

PHILOSOPHERS
Stephens, J. The crock of gold

PHILOSOPHERS, GREEK
Warner, R. Pericles the Athenian

PHILOSOPHICAL NOVELS
Andrić, I. The bridge on the Drina
Balzac, H. de. The wild ass's skin
Baroja y Nessi, P. The tree of knowledge
Beauvoir, S. de. All men are mortal
Beauvoir, S. de. The mandarins
Beckett, S. Molloy, Malone dies, and The unnamable
Beckett, S. Murphy
Beckford, W. Vathek
Bellow, S. Henderson the rain king
Bellow, S. Herzog
Bellow, S. Mr Sammler's planet
Bellow, S. The victim
Bourjaily, V. The end of my life
Buchan, J. Mountain meadow
Camus, A. The fall
Cervantes, M. de. The colloquy of the dogs
    In Cervantes, M. de. Three exemplary novels p125-217
Cervantes, M. de. Man of glass
    In Cervantes, M. de. The portable Cervantes p760-96
Eliot, G. Middlemarch
Golding, W. The inheritors
Huxley, A. Eyeless in Gaza
Le Clézio, J. M. G. Terra Amata
Mann, T. The magic mountain
Mannes, M. They
Mishima, Y. The temple of the golden pavilion
Moberg, V. A time on earth
Sartre, J. P. Nausea
Wilder, T. The woman of Andros
    In Wilder, T. The Cabala, and The woman of Andros p135-203

Phineas. Knowles, J.

The phoenix and the mirror. Davidson, A.

PHOTOGRAPHERS
Gann, E. K. Soldier of fortune
Garve, A. A very quiet place
Sharp, M. Something light
Wilkinson, G. K. Nick, the Click

PHYSICALLY HANDICAPPED. See Cripples

PHYSICIANS
Aczel, T. The ice age
Adams, S. H. Canal town
Allen, T. D. Doctor in buckskin
Bagley, D. The spoilers
Baldwin, F. The velvet hammer
Balzac, H. de. The country doctor
Barnes, D. Nightwood
Baroja y Nessi, P. The tree of knowledge
Baum, V. Grand Hotel
Bawden, N. A little love, a little learning
Bell, J. The upfold witch
Bellamann, H. Kings Row
Bottome, P. The mortal storm
Bottome, P. Private worlds
Bourne, P. Drums of destiny
Buck, P. S. East wind: west wind
Buck, P. S. Kinfolk
Caldwell, T. Dear and glorious physician
Caldwell, T. Testimony of two men
Camus, A. The plague
Céline, L. F. Castle to castle
Céline, L. F. Journey to the end of the night
Cronin, A. J. The citadel
Cronin, A. J. A pocketful of rye
Cronin, A. J. Shannon's way
Deeping, W. Sorrell and son
Dickens, C. A tale of two cities
Douglas, L. C. Doctor Hudson's secret journal
Douglas, L. C. Magnificent obsession
Duerrenmatt, F. The quarry
Eliot, G. Middlemarch
Ellis, A. E. The rack
Fabricant, N. comp. A treasury of doctor stories by the world's great authors
Flaubert, G. Madame Bovary
Frederic, H. The damnation of Theron Ware
Gavin, C. The cactus and the crown
Gordon, N. The death committee
Green, G. The last angry man
Hailey, A. The final diagnosis
Hartog, J. de. The spiral road
Hay, J. Autopsy for a cosmonaut
Hersey, J. Under the eye of the storm
Hooker, R. MASH
Horgan, P. The common heart
    In Horgan, P. Mountain standard time: Main line west, Far from Cibola [and] The common heart p279-595
Hudson, J. A case of need
Huxley, A. After many a summer dies the swan
Huxley, A. Eyeless in Gaza
Jennings, J. The Salem frigate
Johnson, P. H. An error of judgement
Leasor, J. Passport for a pilgrim
Lewis, S. Arrowsmith
MacLean, A. Ice Station Zebra
Macleod, A. City of light
Mahoney, W. Black Jacob
Marttin, P. Heartsblood
Mason, F. V. Eagle in the sky
Maugham, W. S. Of human bondage
Mauriac, F. The desert of love
    In Mauriac, F. A Mauriac reader p133-269
Nathan, R. The devil with love
Pasternak, B. Doctor Zhivago
Read, Miss. Thrush Green
Remarque, E. M. Arch of triumph
Richardson, H. H. The fortunes of Richard Mahony
Rosten, L. Captain Newman, M.D.
Sabatini, R. Captain Blood
Sandoz, M. Miss Morissa, doctor of the gold trail
Schoonover, L. Key of gold
Shute, N. The far country
Singer, I. J. The family Carnovsky
Slaughter, F. G. Daybreak
Slaughter, F. G. East Side General
Slaughter, F. G. Epidemic!
Slaughter, F. G. The road to Bithynia
Slaughter, F. G. Surgeon's choice
Slaughter, F. G. The thorn of Arimathea
Stevenson, R. L. The strange case of Dr Jekyll and Mr Hyde
Taylor, R. L. The travels of Jaimie McPheeters
Thompson, M. The cry and the covenant
Thompson, M. Not as a stranger
Trollope, A. Doctor Thorne
Vassilikos, V. Z
Vivante, A. A goodly babe
Wallace, I. The prize
Waltari, M. The Egyptian
West, M. L. The devil's advocate
Young, C. The Todd dossier
    See also Psychiatrists; Surgeons; Women as physicians

FICTION CATALOG
EIGHTH EDITION

A place in the country. Gainham, S.
The place of sapphires. Randall, F. E.
PLAGUE
  Ainsworth, W. H. Old Saint Paul's
  Caidin, M. Four came back
  Camus, A. The plague
  Mann, T. Death in Venice
  Manzoni, A. The betrothed
  Simon, E. The golden hand
  Slaughter, F. G. Epidemic!
  Stewart, G. R. Earth abides
    See also Disasters
The plague. Camus, A.
Plain tales from the hills. Kipling, R.
Planet of the Apes. Boulle, P.
PLANTATION LIFE
  Amado, J. The violent land
  Asturias, M. A. Strong wind
  Basso, H. The Light Infantry Ball
  Boyd, J. Marching on
  Bristow, G. Deep summer
  Bristow, G. The handsome road
  Bristow, G. This side of glory
  Courlander, H. The African
  Eberhart, M. G. The cup, the blade or the gun
  Faulkner, W. Absalom, Absalom!
  Fletcher, I. Raleigh's Eden
  Keyes, F. P. Blue camellia
  Keyes, F. P. Madame Castel's lodger
  Keyes, F. P. The River Road
  Keyes, F. P. Steamboat Gothic
  Mitchell, M. Gone with the wind
  Parrish, A. A clouded star
  Spark, M. The go-away bird
   In Spark, M. Collected stories: I p302-59
  Stowe, H. B. Uncle Tom's cabin
  Walker, M. Jubilee
  Wilder, R. Bright feather
  Yerby, F. The Foxes of Harrow
  Young, S. So red the rose

    Dutch East Indies
Lofts, N. Scent of cloves
Plantation trilogy, Gwen Bristow's. Bristow, G.
PLASTIC SURGERY. See Surgery, Plastic
Platero and I. Jiménez, J. R.
PLAY PRODUCTION (THEATER). See Theater—Production and direction
The Playboy Book of horror and the supernatural. Playboy
The Playboy Book of science fiction and fantasy. Playboy
Playboy squadron. Whitehouse, A.
Player piano. Vonnegut, K.
The player's boy. Bryher
PLAYING CARDS. See Cards
PLAYWRIGHTS. See Dramatists
The pleasant comedy of young Fortunatus. See Cozzens, J. G. Ask me tomorrow
PLEASURE. See Hedonism
The pledge. Duerrenmatt, F.
Plot it yourself. Stout, R.
  In Stout, R. Kings full of aces p189-322
PLOWSHARE in heaven. Stuart, J.
PLUM
  Van der Zee, J. The plum explosion
The plum explosion. Van der Zee, J.
The plum tree. Chase, M. E.
PLUM TREES. See Plum
PLUMBERS
  Wallant, E. L. The human season
The plumed serpent. Lawrence, D. H.
PLYMOUTH. See Massachusetts—Plymouth
Pnin. Nabokov, V.
PO RIVER
  Bacchelli, R. The mill on the Po
A pocketful of rye. Cronin, A. J.
Poe's Tales of mystery and imagination. See Poe, E. A. Tales
The poet and the donkey. Sarton, M.
POETS
  Baker, E. A fine madness
  Balzac, H. de. Lost illusions
  Burgess, A. Enderby
  De Vries, P. Reuben, Reuben
  De Vries, P. The tents of wickedness

Eaton, E. Go ask the river
Hesse, H. Beneath the wheel
Huxley, A. Crome yellow
Jiménez, J. R. Platero and I
Laxness, H. World light
Nabokov, V. The gift
Orwell, G. Keep the aspidistra flying
Salinger, J. D. Raise high the roof beam, carpenters, and Seymour: an introduction
Sarton, M. The poet and the donkey
Spark, M. The girls of slender means
Waugh, E. The loved one
POGROMS. See Jews—Persecution
Point counter point. Huxley, A.
Point of no return. Marquand, J. P.
  also in Marquand, J. P. So little time, and Point of no return p403-792
The point of the game. Cox, M. E.
The point of view. James, H.
  In James, H. Lady Barbarina, The siege of London, An international episode, and other tales p535-[607]
POISON
  Simenon, G. Sunday
   In Simenon, G. Sunday [and] The little man from Archangel
The poisoned crown. Druon, M.
The poisoned stream. Habe, H.
POLAND
    1572-1763
  Gogol, N. Taras Bulba, a tale of the Cossacks
  Singer, I. B. Satan in Goray
  Singer, I. B. The slave
    19th century
  Agnon, S. Y. The bridal canopy
  Asch, S. Salvation
  Singer, I. B. The estate
  Singer, I. B. The magician of Lublin
  Singer, I. B. The manor
  Singer, I. B. The séance, and other stories
  Singer, I. J. Yoshe Kalb
    20th century
  Asch, S. The little town
   In Asch, S. Tales of my people
  Kosinski, J. The painted bird
  Kuniczak, W. S. The thousand hour day
  Singer, I. J. Steel and iron
    Army—Officers
  Kuniczak, W. S. The thousand hour day
    Communism
  See Communism—Poland
    Danzig
  Grass, G. Cat and mouse
  Grass, G. Dog years
  Grass, G. The tin drum
    Farm life
  See Farm life—Poland
    Galicia
  Agnon, S. Y. The bridal canopy
  Agnon, S. Y. A guest for the night
    Lodz
  Singer, I. J. The brothers Ashkenazi
    Peasant life
  See Peasant life—Poland
    Warsaw
  Asch, S. Mottke, the thief
  Asch, S. Three cities
  Hersey, J. The wall
  Kirst, H. H. The night of the generals
  Singer, I. B. The family Moskat
  Uris, L. Mila 18
    Warsaw—20th century
  Hlasko, M. The eighth day of the week
POLAND, PROVINCIAL AND RURAL
  Reymont, L. The peasants
  Singer, I. B. The estate
  Singer, I. B. The manor
  Singer, I. B. Satan in Goray
POLES IN ENGLAND
  Sharp, M. Cluny Brown
POLES IN THE UNITED STATES
  De Vries, P. Let me count the ways
  Janney, R. The miracle of the bells
  Nathan, R. The sea-gull cry

TITLE AND SUBJECT INDEX
EIGHTH EDITION

POLITICS—*Continued*

Louisiana

Keyes, F. P. Crescent carnival
Keyes, F. P. The River Road
Langley, A. L. A lion is in the streets
Williams, B. A. The unconquered

Mexico

Fuentes, C. Where the air is clear
Gavin, C. The cactus and the crown

Near East

Chesnoff, R. Z. If Israel lost the war

New York (City)

Charles-Roux, E. To forget Palermo

Oklahoma

Ferber, E. Cimarron

Palestine

Koestler, A. Thieves in the night

Pennsylvania

Dreiser, T. The financier

Rome

Caldwell, T. A pillar of iron
De Wohl, L. Citadel of God
Duggan, A. Three's company
Waltari, M. The Roman

Russia

Anthony, E. Royal intrigue
Conrad, J. Under Western eyes
Koestler, A. Darkness at noon
Pasternak, B. Doctor Zhivago
Tarsis, V. Ward 7
Troyat, H. The baroness
Turgenev, I. Virgin soil
Waring, M. W. The witnesses

Scotland

Dunnett, D. The game of kings
Dunnett, D. Queen's play
Kenyon, F. W. Mary of Scotland
Oliver, J. Candleshine no more

South America

Conrad, J. Nostromo

South Carolina

Fast, H. Freedom road

Southern States

Basso, H. The Light Infantry Ball
Warren, R. P. All the king's men

Spain

Bates, R. The olive field
Braider, D. Rage in silence
Del Castillo, M. The disinherited
Gironella, J. M. The cypresses believe in God
Gironella, J. M. One million dead
Gironella, J. M. Peace after war
Herrick, W. ¡Hermanos!
Schoonover, L. The prisoner of Tordesillas
Schoonover, L. The Queen's cross

Switzerland

Bryher. The colors of Vaud

Turkey

Bridge, A. The dark moment

United States

Lewis, S. It can't happen here
Merle, R. The day of the dolphin

United States—To 1900

Adams, H. Democracy
Boyce, B. Man from Mt Vernon
Churchill, W. The crisis
Gerson, N. B. The slender reed
Gerson, N. B. The Yankee from Tennessee
Kane, H. T. Bride of fortune
Lockridge, R. Raintree County
Morrow, H. W. Forever free
Morrow, H. W. The last full measure
Morrow, H. W. With malice toward none
Stewart, R. Casey
Stone, I. Immortal wife
Stone, I. Love is eternal
Stone, I. The President's lady
Twain, M. The gilded age
Wellman, P. I. Magnificent destiny

United States—1900-date

Barry, J. Grass roots
Buck, P. S. The new year
Buechner, F. The return of Ansel Gibbs
Burroway, J. The buzzards
Dos Passos, J. District of Columbia
Dos Passos, J. Grand design
Drury, A. Advise and consent
Drury, A. Capable of honor
Drury, A. Preserve and protect
Drury, A. A shade of difference
Galbraith, J. K. The triumph
Greenlee, S. The spook who sat by the door
Haas, B. Look away, look away
Hailey, A. In high places
Karp, D. All honorable men
Knebel, F. Night of Camp David
Knebel, F. Seven days in May
Knebel, F. Vanished
Mahoney, W. Black Jacob
O'Connor, E. All in the family
O'Connor, E. The last hurrah
Pearson, D. The senator
Sandburg, C. Remembrance Rock
Wallace, I. The man
West, N. Cool million
    In West, N. Complete works p143-256

Vermont

Van de Water, F. F. Wings of the morning

Vietnam

West, M. L. The ambassador

Virginia

Gerson, N. B. Give me liberty

West Indies

Waugh, A. Island in the sun

POLK, JAMES KNOX, PRESIDENT U.S.
Gerson, N. B. The slender reed

POLO, MARCO
Byrne, D. Messer Marco Polo

POLYGAMY. See Mormons and Mormonism

POLYNESIANS
Michener, J. A. Hawaii
Nordhoff, C. The hurricane
Nordhoff, C. Pitcairn's Island

Pomp and circumstance. Coward, N.

POMPEII. See Italy—Pompeii

The Pond. Murphy, R.

The Ponder heart. Welty, E.

PONTIAC'S CONSPIRACY, 1763-1765
Swanson, N. H. The Judas tree
Swanson, N. H. Unconquered

PONTIC TRIBUNALS. See Pilate, Acts of

POOR. See Poverty

Poor Margaret. Rees, B.
    In Rees, B. Try another country p121-78

POOR PRIESTS. See Lollards

POOR RELIEF. See Public welfare

Poor white. Anderson, S.

The poorhouse fair. Updike, J.

The poorhouse fair [and] Rabbit, run. Updike, J.

POPES
De Wohl, L. Lay siege to heaven
West, M. L. The shoes of the fisherman

Porgy. Heyward, Du B.

PORPOISES. See Dolphins

PORT SAID. See Egypt—Port Said

The portable Cervantes. Cervantes, M. de

The portable Conrad. Conrad, J.

The portable F. Scott Fitzgerald. Fitzgerald, F. S.

The portable Faulkner. Faulkner, W.

The portable Hawthorne. Hawthorne, N.

The portable Henry James. James, H.

The portable James Joyce. Joyce, J.

The portable Maupassant. Maupassant, G. de

The portable Steinbeck. Steinbeck, J.

The portable Stephen Crane. Crane, S.

The portable Thomas Wolfe. Wolfe, T.

Portnoy's complaint. Roth, P.

Portrait in brownstone. Auchincloss, L.

The portrait of a lady. James, H.

The portrait of an artist with twenty-six horses. Eastlake, W.

TITLE AND SUBJECT INDEX
EIGHTH EDITION

A portrait of Bascom Hawke. Wolfe, T.
  In Wolfe, T. The short novels of Thomas Wolfe p4-71

Portrait of Jennie. Nathan, R.
  also in Costain, T. B. ed. Stories to remember v 1 p229-96
  also in Costain, T. B. comp. Twelve short novels p491-558

A portrait of the artist as a young man. Joyce, J.
  also in Joyce, J. The portable James Joyce p243-526

PORTS. See Harbors

PORTUGAL
19th century
Eca de Queiroz. The Maias
Hodge, J. A. Marry in haste
Hodge, J. A. The winding stair
20th century
Cadell, E. The golden collar
Lisbon
Bridge, A. The Portuguese escape
Eca de Queiroz. Cousin Bazilio
Eca de Queiroz. The Maias

PORTUGAL, PROVINCIAL AND RURAL
Bridge, A. The episode at Toledo
L'Engle, M. The love letters

The Portuguese escape. Bridge, A.

PORTUGUESE IN ENGLAND
Jameson, S. The white crow

The Poseidon adventure. Gallico, P.

The possessed. Dostoevsky, F.

Possession. Fremlin, C.

Possession. Markandaya, K.

Possible worlds of science fiction. Conklin, G. ed.

The Post Reader of Civil War stories. The Saturday Evening Post

The Post Reader of fantasy and science fiction. The Saturday Evening Post

POSTAGE STAMPS
Simenon, G. The little man from Archangel
  In Simenon G. Sunday [and] The little man from Archangel p127-267

POSTAL CLERKS. See United States. Post Office

POSTAL SERVICE. See United States. Post Office

The posthumous papers of the Pickwick Club. Dickens, C.

The postman always rings twice. Cain, J. M.
  In Cain, J. M. Cain x 3 p 1-101

POTATO FAMINES. See Famines

POTTER, ISRAEL RALPH
Melville, H. Israel Potter: his fifty years of exile

POVERTY
Amado, J. Shepherds of the night
Balzac, H. de. Cousin Pons
Baroja y Nessi, P. The tree of knowledge
Bermant, C. Diary of an old man
Berto, G. The sky is red
Bjarnhof, K. The stars grow pale
Blais, M. C. A season in the life of Emmanuel
Caldwell, E. Tobacco road
Deal, B. The least one
Dickens, C. Little Dorrit
Di Donato, P. Christ in concrete
Duras, M. The sea wall
Edgeworth, M. Castle Rackrent
Fallada, H. Little man, what now?
García Márquez, G. No one writes to the colonel
  In García Márquez, G. No one writes to the colonel, and other stories p3-62
Gissing, G. New Grub Street
Hugo, V. Les misérables
Johnson, J. W. Now in November
Killens, J. O. Youngblood
McCullers, C. The heart is a lonely hunter
Macken, W. Rain on the wind
Markandaya, K. A handful of rice
Markandaya, K. Nectar in a sieve
Norris, F. McTeague
Oates, J. C. A garden of earthly delights
Oates, J. C. Them
Ogilvie, E. Waters on a starry night
Richter, C. A simple honorable man
Roy, G. The tin flute

Silone, I. Fontamara
Sinclair, U. The jungle
Solmssen, A. R. G. Rittenhouse Square
Traven, B. The cotton-pickers
Vittorini, E. Erica
  In Vittorini, E. The dark and the light p 1-75
West, R. The fountain overflows
Wolfe, T. The web and the rock
Wright, R. Native son
Wright, S. E. This child's gonna live
Yáñez, A. The lean lands
  See also Social problems

Powder and patch. Heyer, G.

POWER (SOCIAL SCIENCES)
Armah, A. K. The beautiful ones are not yet born
Rand, A. Atlas shrugged
Simenon, G. The Premier
  In Simenon, G. The Premier [and] The train p3-125
  See also Political ethics

The power and the glory. Greene, G.

Powers of attorney. Auchincloss, L.

The powers that be. Romains, J.
  In Romains, J. The earth trembles

PRACTICAL JOKES. See Humor—Practical jokes

The prairie. Cooper, J. F.

The prairie [abridged]. Cooper, J. F.
  In Cooper, J. F. The Leatherstocking saga p763-829

PRAIRIE LIFE
Aldrich, B. S. A lantern in her hand
Aldrich, B. S. Song of years
Aldrich, B. S. Spring came on forever
Cather, W. O pioneers!

Prancing nigger. Firbank, R.
  In Firbank, R. The complete Ronald Firbank p593-643

Pray for a brave heart. MacInnes, H.

The preacher and the slave. [variant title: Jo Hill] Stegner, W.

PREACHERS. See Clergy

Precious bane. Webb, M.

PREDESTINATION
Wilder, T. The bridge of San Luis Rey

PREGNANCY
Hintze, N. A. You'll like my mother
Vivante, A. A goodly babe
Westheimer, D. My sweet Charlie
Wyndham, J. The Midwich cuckoos

PREHISTORIC ANIMALS. See Fossils

PREHISTORIC MAN. See Prehistoric times

PREHISTORIC TIMES
Golding, W. The inheritors
Jensen, J. V. The Cimbrians
  In Jensen, J. V. The long journey p227-487
Jensen, J. V. Fire and ice
  In Jensen, J. V. The long journey p3-224

PREJUDICES AND ANTIPATHIES
Aldridge, J. My brother Tom
Barker, S. Strange wives
Bawden, N. Under the skin
Blackstock, C. The lemmings
Buck, P. S. The hidden flower
Davis, C. First family
Dutton, M. Thorpe
Grau, S. A. The keepers of the house
Grubb, D. Shadow of my brother
Hersey, J. The marmot drive
Hill, D. Catch a brass canary
Knebel, F. Trespass
Perez Galdos, B. Doña Perfecta
Silone, I. The secret of Luca
Sinclair, J. The changelings
Stuart, J. Daughter of the legend
Weidman, J. The enemy camp
  See also Antisemitism; Race problems

The prelude. Romains, J.
  In Romains, J. Verdun

Prelude to Mars. Clarke, A. C.

Prelude to space. Clarke, A. C.
  also in Clarke, A. C. Prelude to Mars p 1-143

The Premier [and] The train. Simenon, G.

Preserve and protect. Drury, A.

Presidential agent. Sinclair, U.

Presidential mission. Sinclair, U.

591

PRESIDENTS
Election
Drury, A. Preserve and protect
United States
Burdick, E. Fail-safe
Drury, A. Preserve and protect
Knebel, F. Night of Camp David
Serling, R. J. The President's plane is missing
Wallace, I. The man
The President's lady. Stone, I.
The President's plane is missing. Serling, R. J.
Press censorship. See Liberty of the press
The prevalence of witches. Menen, A.
Pride and prejudice. Austen, J.
also in Austen, J. The complete novels of Jane Austen
The pride and the anguish. Reeman, D.
Pride of possession. Street, J.
A priest and a girl. Daley, R.

PRIESTS. See Catholic priests; Clergy; Clergy, Anglican and Episcopal

PRIESTS, CATHOLIC. See Catholic priests

The prime minister. Trollope, A.
PRIME MINISTERS
Abrahams, P. A wreath for Udomo
Anthony, E. Victoria and Albert
Edelman, M. The Prime Minister's daughter
Hailey, A. In high places
Monsarrat, N. Richer than all his tribe
Simenon, G. The Premier
In Simenon, G. The Premier [and] The train p3-125
The Prime Minister's daughter. Edelman, M.
The Prime Minister's wife. Leslie, D.
The prime of Miss Jean Brodie. Spark, M.
PRIMITIVE CHRISTIANITY. See Church history—Primitive and early church
PRIMITIVE RELIGION. See Religion, Primitive
The prince and the pauper. Twain, M.
In Twain, M. The complete novels of Mark Twain v 1 p559-730
Prince of darkness. Michaels, B.
Prince of Darkness, and other stories. Powers, J. F.
Prince of Egypt. Wilson, D. C.
Prince of foxes. Shellabarger, S.
Princes
Gilford, C. B. The crooked shamrock
The prince's person. Peyrefitte, R.
The Princess Casamassima. James, H.
The Princess of Cleves. Lafayette, Mme de
PRINTERS
Narayan, R. K. The man-eater of Malgudi
PRIORESS. See Nuns
The prison. Simenon, J.
PRISON CAMPS. See World War, 1939-1945—Prisoners and prisons
PRISON ESCAPES. See Escapes
Prison life in Siberia. See Dostoevsky, F. The house of the dead
PRISON SHIPS
Roberts, K. Captain Caution
PRISON WARDENS
Cuomo, G. Among thieves
Prisoner of grace. Cary, J.
Prisoner of the sand. Saint Exupéry, A. de
In Costain, T. B. comp. Twelve short novels p457-90
The prisoner of Tordesillas. Schoonover, L.
The prisoner of Zenda. Hope, A.
PRISONERS, CONDEMNED
Carr, J. D. The bride of Newgate
PRISONERS, POLITICAL
Barnes, M. C. Mary of Carisbrooke
Braddon, R. When the enemy is tired
Karmel, I. An estate of memory
Kirst, H. H. Last stop Camp 7
Schoonover, L. The prisoner of Tordesillas
Solzhenitsyn, A. I. The first circle
Tarsis, V. Ward

PRISONERS AND PRISONS
Behn, N. The shadowboxer
See also names of wars with subdivision Prisoners and prisons, e.g. World War, 1939-1945—Prisoners and prisons
The prisoners of Combine D. Giovannitti, L.
The prisoners of Quai Dong. Kolpacoff, V.
PRISONERS OF WAR
Behn, N. The shadowboxer
Boyd, J. Marching on
Céline, L. F. Castle to castle
Giovannitti, L. The prisoners of Combine D
Howe, G. Call it treason
Kantor, M. Andersonville
Kolpacoff, V. The prisoners of Quai Dong
Morgan, C. The fountain
Roberts, K. Captain Caution
Van der Post, L. A bar of shadow
In Van der Post, L. The seed and the sower p11-44
Vonnegut, K. Slaughterhouse-five
Westheimer, D. Song of the young sentry
Zweig, A. The case of Sergeant Grischa
See also Concentration camps; also names of wars with subdivision Prisoners and prisons
PRISONS
Czechoslovak Republic
Benes, J. Second breath
Denmark
Freuchen, P. White man
England
Carr, J. D. The bride of Newgate
Cronin, A. J. Beyond this place
Defoe, D. The fortunes and misfortunes of the famous Moll Flanders
Dickens, C. Little Dorrit
Dickens, C. The posthumous papers of the Pickwick Club
Fielding, H. Amelia
See also Dartmoor Prison
France
Cummings, E. E. The enormous room
Dumas, A. The Count of Monte Cristo
Germany
See Concentration camps
Ireland
Behan, B. The Scarperer
Russia
Andreyev, L. The seven who were hanged
Koestler, A. Darkness at noon
Solzhenitsyn, A. I. The first circle
Scotland
Scott, Sir W. The heart of Midlothian
Siberia
Dostoevsky, F. The house of the dead
Dudintsev, V. Not by bread alone
United States
Cuomo, G. Among thieves
Lewis, S. Ann Vickers
PRIVATE DETECTIVES. See Detectives, Private
PRIVATE SCHOOLS. See School life
Private worlds. Bottome, P.
PRIVATEERING
Boyd, J. Drums
Jennings, J. The sea eagles
Jennings, J. The tall ships
Mason, F. V. Stars on the sea
Pope, D. The Triton brig
Roberts, K. The Lively Lady
Privy Seal. Ford, F. M.
In Ford, F. M. The fifth queen p237-413
The prize. Wallace, I.
Prize stories from Latin America. Entered in Part I under title
Prize stories, 1919-1970: The O. Henry Awards. Entered in Part I under title
PROBLEM CHILDREN
Berckman, E. The heir of Starvelings
Potok, C. The promise
The problem of the wire cage. Carr, J. D.
In Carr, J. D. Three detective novels p357-508

The prodigals. Dumitriu, P.
PRODIGIES. See Children, Gifted
The professor. Brontë C.
The Professor Challenger stories. Doyle, Sir A. C.
PROFESSORS. See Teachers
The professor's house. Cather, W.
The progress of a crime. Symons, J.
PROHIBITION
 Condon, R. Mile high
PROJECT MERCURY
 Caidin, M. Marooned
Project Nursemaid. Merril, J.
 In Merril, J. Daughters of Earth p7-96
PROLETARIAN NOVELS
 Alegría, C. Broad and alien is the world
 Bates, R. The olive field
 Gorky, M. Mother
 Nexo, M. A. Pelle the conqueror
 Ousmane, S. God's bits of wood
 Stegner, W. Joe Hill
 Stegner, W. The preacher and the slave
 Steinbeck, J. In dubious battle
 Traven, B. The cotton-pickers
 Zola, E. Germinal
Prologue. Unamuno y Jugo, M. de
 In Unamuno y Jugo, M. de. Three exemplary novels and a prologue
A prologue to love. Caldwell, T.
The promise. Buck, P. S.
The promise. Potok, C.
Promise of dawn. Romains, J.
 In Romains, J. The new day
The proper gods. Sorensen, V.
A proper marriage. Lessing, D.
 In Lessing, D. Children of violence v2
The prophet. Asch, S.
PROSTITUTES
 Andrić, I. Anika's times
 In Andrić, I. The vizier's elephant p55-130
 Crane, S. Maggie: a girl of the streets
 In Blackmur, R. P. ed. American short novels p97-133
 In Crane, S. The complete novels of Stephen Crane p99-154
 In Crane, S. The portable Stephen Crane p3-74
 Defoe, D. The fortunes and misfortunes of the famous Moll Flanders
 Dumas, A. Camille
 Faulkner, W. Sanctuary
 Gary, R. Lady L.
 Lagerkvist, P. The death of Ahasuerus
 Mason, R. The world of Suzie Wong
 Nathan, R. One more spring
 Vittorini, E. Erica
 In Vittorini, E. The dark and the light p 1-75
PROSTITUTION
 Adams, S. H. Tenderloin
 Andrézel, P. The angelic avengers
 Vargas Llosa, M. The green house
 Wharton, E. New Year's Day
 In Wharton, E. Old New York v4
The protégé. Armstrong, C.
PROTESTANT REFORMATION. See Reformation
PROTESTANTISM
 Flynn, R. In the house of the Lord
 Gerson, N. B. The anthem
 Macleod, A. City of light
 Macleod, A. The heretic
The proud, and The meek. Romains, J.
Proud destiny. Feuchtwanger, L.
Proud new flags. Mason, F. V
PROVENCE. See France, Provincial and rural—Provence
PROVINCIAL AND RURAL CANADA. See Canada, Provincial and rural
PROVINCIAL AND RURAL ENGLAND. See England, Provincial and rural
PROVINCIAL AND RURAL FRANCE. See France, Provincial and rural
PROVINCIAL AND RURAL GERMANY. See Germany, Provincial and rural
PROVINCIAL AND RURAL IRELAND. See Ireland, Provincial and rural
PROVINCIAL AND RURAL ITALY. See Italy, Provincial and rural

PROVINCIAL AND RURAL NORWAY. See Norway, Provincial and rural
PROVINCIAL AND RURAL POLAND. See Poland, Provincial and rural
PROVINCIAL AND RURAL PORTUGAL. See Portugal, Provincial and rural
PROVINCIAL AND RURAL RUSSIA. See Russia, Provincial and rural
PROVINCIAL AND RURAL SCOTLAND. See Scotland, Provincial and rural
PROVINCIAL AND RURAL SPAIN. See Spain, Provincial and rural
PROVINCIAL AND RURAL TURKEY. See Turkey, Provincial and rural
PROVINCIAL AND RURAL WALES. See Wales, Provincial and rural
Provincial interlude. Romains, J.
 In Romains, J. The world from below
PSEUDO-SCIENCE. See Science fiction
PSYCHE (GODDESS)
 Lewis, C. S. Till we have faces
PSYCHIATRISTS
 Armah, A. K. Fragments
 Baker, E. A fine madness
 Bottome, P. Private worlds
 Brand, M. Savage sleep
 Dighton, L. An expensive place to die
 Fitzgerald, F. S. Tender is the night
 Green, H. I never promised you a rose garden
 Harris M. Trepleff
 Harwood, R. The girl in Melanie Klein
 Hawley, C. The hurricane years
 Jackson, S. The bird's nest
 Lewisohn, L. The island within
 Morris, W. The field of vision
 Potok, C. The promise
 Rosten, L. Captain Newman, M.D.
 Slaughter, F. G. Daybreak
 West, M. L. Daughter of silence
 See also Mentally ill—Care and treatment; Physicians; Psychoanalysis
PSYCHIC PHENOMENA. See Spiritualism; Supernatural phenomena
PSYCHICAL RESEARCH. See Extrasensory perception
PSYCHOANALYSIS
 Amis, K. The Anti-Death League
 Koestler, A. Arrival and departure
 Murdoch, I. A severed head
 Roth, P. Portnoy's complaint
PSYCHOLOGICAL NOVELS
 Abé, K. The ruined map
 Aiken, C. The blue voyage
 In Aiken, C. The collected novels of Conrad Aiken p15-166
 Aiken, C. Great circle
 In Aiken, C. The collected novels of Conrad Aiken p167-295
 Aiken, C. King Coffin
 In Aiken, C. The collected novels of Conrad Aiken p297-414
 Anderson, S. Dark laughter
 Andreyev, L. The seven who were hanged
 Armstrong, C. The balloon man
 Barnes, D. Nightwood
 Barrie, J. M. Sentimental Tommy
 Bassing, E. Home before dark
 Bawden, N. Devil by the sea
 Bawden, N. The grain of truth
 Bellow, S. Dangling man
 Bellow, S. The victim
 Bennett, A. Clayhanger
 Berckman, E. She asked for it
 Bodelsen, A. Think of a number
 Borgenicht, M. The tomorrow trap
 Bottome, P. Private worlds
 Bowen, E. The death of the heart
 Bowen, E. Eva Trout
 Bowen, E. The little girls
 Bowles, J. Two serious ladies
 In Bowles, J. The collected works of Jane Bowles p 1-201
 Brand, M. The outward room
 Bridge, A. Illyrian spring
 Bromfield, L. A good woman
 In Bromfield, L. Bromfield galaxy: The green bay tree, Early autumn, A good woman p405-639
 Bromfield, L. The green bay tree
 Brown, H. A walk in the sun
 Chaze, E. Wettermark
 Christie, A. Endless night
 Christie, K. Child's play
 Christopher, J. The little people

RACE PROBLEMS—*Continued*
Grey, Z. The vanishing American
Killens, J. O. And then we heard the thunder
Lockridge, R. With option to die
Mankiewicz, D. M. Trial
Masters, J. Bhowani Junction
Monsarrat, N. The tribe that lost its head
Murray, A. A. The blanket
Rooke, D. Mittee
Ruark, R. Something of value
Sinclair, J. The changelings
Smith, L. Strange fruit
Van Vechten, C. Nigger heaven
Vasquez, R. Chicano
Wheeler, K. Peaceable Lane
Wright, R. Native son
See also Africa—Native races; Negroes; Prejudices and antipathies; Social problems

Africa
Van der Post, L. Flamingo feather

Africa, South
Abrahams, P. Mine boy
Gordimer, N. The lying days
Gordimer, N. Occasion for loving
Paton, A. Cry, the beloved country
Paton, A. Too late the phalarope
Rabie, J. A man apart

Bahamas
Wilder, R. An affair of honor

Canada
Bodsworth, F. The strange one

France
Etcherelli, C. Elise

India
Forster, E. M. A passage to India

Rhodesia, Southern
Burgess, A The word of love

United States
Baldwin, J. Another country
Corley, E. Siege
Drury, A. A shade of difference
Dutton, M. Thorpe
Dykeman, W. The far family
Fairbairn, A. Five smooth stones
Faulkner, W. Light in August
Ford, J. H. The feast of Saint Barnabas
Grau, S. A. The keepers of the house
Greenlee, S. The spook who sat by the door
Grubb, D. Shadow of my brother
Haas, B. Lock away, look away
Hughes, L. Not without laughter
Hughes, L. Simple speaks his mind
Hughes, L. Simple stakes a claim
Hughes, L. Simple takes a wife
Huie, W. B. The Klansman
Kelley, W. M. A different drummer
Killens, J. O. Youngblood
Knebel, F. Trespass
Lee, H. To kill a mockingbird
Lewis, S. Kingsblood royal
McCullers, C. Clock without hands
Mahoney, W. Black Jacob
Mano, D. K. Horn
Mather, M. One summer in between
Parks, G. The learning tree
Prebble, J. The buffalo soldiers
Robinson, R. Eagle in the air
Spencer, E. The voice at the back door
Styron, W. The confessions of Nat Turner
Sumner, C. R. Quality
Wallace, I. The man
Warren, R. P. Band of angels
Westlake, L. E. Up your banners
Williams, J. A. The man who cried I am
Williams, J. A. Sons of darkness, sons of light

West Indies
Waugh, A. Island in the sun

RACHEL, ORIGINALLY ELISA FELIX. See Felix, Elisa Rachel

RACIAL INTERMARRIAGE. See Inter-racial marriages

The rack, Ellis, A. E.

RACKETEERS. See Crime and criminals; Gangsters

RACKETS. See Gambling

RADCLIFFE, CHARLES
Seton, A. Devil Water

RADIATION
Physiological effect
Masters, D. The accident
Morris, E. The flowers of Hiroshima

RADICALS AND RADICALISM. See Anarchism and anarchists

RADIOACTIVITY
Physiological effect
Shute, N. On the beach

Rafferty & Co. Wahl, B.

Rage in silence. Braider, D.

A rage to live. O'Hara, J.

The ragged edge. Christopher, J.

The ragman's daughter, and other stories Sillitoe, A.

Rags of glory. Cloete, S.

The raid. Frison-Roche, R.

The raider. Jennings, J.

RAILROADS
Cather, W. A lost lady
Ferber, E. Saratoga trunk
Norris, F. The octopus
Ousmane, S. God's bits of wood

Travel
Simenon, G. The train
In Simenon, G. The Premier [and] The train p129-48
Vittorini, E. La Garibaldina
In Vittorini, E. The dark and the light p77-180
West, R. The birds fall down

Rain on the wind. Macken, W.

The rainbow. Lawrence, D. H.

The rains came. Bromfield, L.

Raintree County. Lockridge, R.

Raise high the roof beam, carpenters, and Seymour: an introduction. Salinger, J. D.

Rakóssy. Holland, C.

RALEIGH, ELIZABETH (THROCKMORTON) LADY
Sutcliff, R. Lady in waiting

RALEIGH, SIR WALTER
Graham, W. The grove of eagles
Sutcliff, R. Lady in waiting

Raleigh's Eden. Fletcher, I.

Rally round the flag, boys! Shulman, M.

Ramage. Pope, D.

Rameau's nephew. Diderot, D.
In Dupee, F. W. ed. Great French short novels p 1-90

RANCH LIFE
Barry, J. A shadow of eagles
Bass, M. R. Jory
Clark, W. V. The track of the cat
Culp, J. H. The restless land
Ferber, E. Giant
James, W. The American cowboy
MacInnes, H. Rest and Be Thankful
Norris, F. The octopus
Richter, C. The lady
In Costain, T. B. ed. More Stories to remember v 1 p364-440
Richter, C. The sea of grass
Schaefer, J. Monte Walsh
Schaefer, J. Shane
Spicer, B. Kellogg Junction
Steinbeck, J. Of mice and men
Steinbeck, J. The red pony
In Steinbeck, J. The portable Steinbeck p327-415
Walker, M. Winter wheat

Random harvest. Hilton, J.

RANFAING, ÉLISABETH DE
Mallet-Joris, F. The witches

RANSOM
Habe, H. The mission

RAPE
Burgess, A. The word for love
Gores, J. A time of predators
Scott, P. The jewel in the crown

The rape of the fair country. Cordell, A.

RAPISTS. See Crime and criminals

Rashomon, and other stories. Akutagawa, R.

Rasselas. See Johnson, S. The history of Rasselas, Prince of Abyssinia

Ratman's notebooks. Gilbert, S.
RATS
  Gilbert, S. Ratman's notebooks
Ravenscroft. Eden, D.
A raw youth. Dostoevsky, F.
Rawhide men. Western Writers of America
The Raymond Chandler omnibus. Chandler, R.
The razor's edge. Maugham, W. S.
REAL ESTATE
  Auchincloss, L. A world of profit
The real life of Sebastian Knight. Nabokov, V.
Real people. Lurie, A.
Rebecca. Du Maurier, D.
  also in Du Maurier, D. Three romantic novels of Cornwall: Rebecca, Frenchman's Creek and Jamaica Inn p7-316
  also in Haycraft, H. ed. A treasury of great mysteries v2 p301-576
REBECCA RIOTS, 1839-1844
  Cordell, A. Robe of honour
REBECCAS. See Secret societies
Rebecca's Daughters. Thomas, D.
Rebellion. See Ballinger, W. A. The men that God made mad
Re-birth. Wyndham, J.
  In Boucher, A. ed. A treasury of great science fiction v 1 p9-135
The reckoning. Elman, R. M.
RECLUSES
  Nathan, R. Stonecliff
  O'Hara, J. Ourselves to know
  See also Hermits
RECONSTRUCTION
  Bristow, G. The handsome road
  Fast, H. Freedom road
  Mitchell, M. Gone with the wind
  Morrow, H. W. The last full measure
  Twain, M. The adventures of Colonel Sellers
  Williams, B. A. The unconquered
    See also United States—19th century—1865-1898
RECONSTRUCTION (1939-1951)

Sicily
  Hersey, J. A bell for Adano
The Rector of Justin. Auchincloss, L.
RECTORS. See Clergy
The red and the black. Stendhal
The red and the green. Murdoch, I.
The red and the white. Troyat, H.
The red badge of courage. Crane, S.
  also in Crane, S. The complete novels of Stephen Crane p197-299
The red badge of courage, and other stories. (Oxford) Crane, S.
The red badge of courage, and other stories. (Watts, F. Ultratype ed) Crane, S.
The Red Castle women. Widdemer, M.
Red cavalry. Babel, I.
  In Babel, I. The collected stories p41-20
RED CROSS
  Keyes, F. P. Came a cavalier
The red-haired bitch. Hanley, C.
Red harvest. Hammett, D.
  In Hammett, D. The novels of Dashiell Hammett p 1-142
The red house mystery. Milne, A. A.
The red lamp. Rinehart, M. R.
  In Rinehart, M. R. Mary Roberts Rinehart Crime book p293-505
Red Orm. See Bengtsson, F. G. The long ships
The Red Pavilion. Gulik, R. van
The red pony. Steinbeck, J.
  In Steinbeck, J. The portable Steinbeck p327-415
  In Steinbeck, J. The short novels of John Steinbeck p135-200
Red queen, white queen. Treece, H.
The Red Rover. Cooper, J. F.
Red sky at morning. Bradford, R.
REDEMPTION. See Atonement
REDEMPTIONERS
  Edmonds, W. D. Erie water
  Swanson, N. H. Unconquered
The reef. Wharton, E.

Reflections in a golden eye. McCullers, C.
  also in McCullers, C. The ballad of the sad café p499-567
REFORMATION
  Anthony, E. Anne Boleyn
  Macleod, A. City of light
    See also Europe—16th century
The refugee. See Melville, H. Israel Potter
REFUGEES
  Bristow, G. Tomorrow is forever
  Koestler, A. Arrival and departure
  Kosinski, J. The painted bird
  Nabokov, V. The defense
  Nabokov, V. The gift
  Nabokov, V. The real life of Sebastian Knight
  Oldenbourg, Z. The chains of love
  Remarque, E. M. The night in Lisbon
  Uris, L. Exodus
  Viertel, J. The last temptation
REFUGEES, AUSTRIAN
  Goudge, E. The heart of the family
  Graham, W. Night journey
REFUGEES, BELGIAN
  Simenon, G. The train
    In Simenon, G. The Premier [and] The train p129-48
REFUGEES, GERMAN
  Hutchinson, R. C. Johanna at daybreak
  Remarque, E. M. Arch of triumph
REFUGEES, ITALIAN
  Pope, D. Ramage
REFUGEES, JEWISH
  Bellow, S. Mr Sammler's planet
  Habe, H. The mission
  Levin, M. My father's house
  Oldenbourg, Z. The awakened
  Simenon, G. The train
    In Simenon, G. The Premier [and] The train p 129-48
  Wallant, E. L. The pawnbroker
  Wiesel, E. The accident
  Wiesel, E. The gates of the forest
REFUGEES, LATIN AMERICAN
  Schulberg, B. Sanctuary v
REFUGEES, POLISH
  Nathan, R. The sea-gull cry
  Sharp, M. Cluny Brown
REFUGEES, RUSSIAN
  Nabokov, V. Pnin
  Troyat, H. Strangers on earth
Regency buck. Heyer, G.
REGENCY ENGLAND. See England—19th century
REGULATOR INSURRECTION, 1766-1771
  Fletcher, I. The wind in the forest
REHABILITATION
  Greenberg, J. The Monday voices
REINCARNATION
  Costain, T. B. Below the salt
  Davies, L. P. Stranger to town
  London, J. The star rover
  Shute, N. In the wet
REINDEER
  Frison-Roche, R. The raid
The reivers. Faulkner, W.
REJUVENATION
  Haggard, H. R. She
RELATIVES. See Family life
RELIEF, PUBLIC. See Public welfare
RELIGION
  Baldwin, J. Go tell it on the mountain
  Barrie, J. M. Little minister
  Bernanos, G. The diary of a country priest
  Bjorn, T. F. Mama's way
  Bjorn, T. F. Papa's daughter
    In Bjorn, T. F. Papa's wife, Papa's daughter, Mama's way v2
  Bojer, J. The great hunger
  Brady, C. A. Stage of fools
  Bray, C. The scarecrow man
  Bunyan, J. The Pilgrim's progress
  Caldwell, T. Dear and glorious physician
  Cary, J. Except the Lord
  Charques, D. The nunnery
  Closs, H. Deep are the valleys
  Closs, H. High are the mountains
  Closs, H. The silent Tarn
  Cozzens, J. G. Men and brethren
  Del Castillo, M. The seminarian
  De Vries, P. The blood of the lamb
  De Vries, P. Let me count the ways
  De Wohl, L. Citadel of God
  Dreiser, T. The bulwark

RELIGION—*Continued*
Eliot, G. Romola
Flynn, R. In the house of the Lord
Frederic, H. The damnation of Theron Ware
Grass, G. Cat and mouse
Greene, G. A burnt-out case
Hesse, H. The journey to the East
Horia, V. God was born in exile
Huxley, A. Time must have a stop
Jackson, D. V. S. Walk with peril
Kazantzakis, N. The Greek passion
Kazantzakis, N. Saint Francis
Kenyon, F. W. Mary of Scotland
Lagerkvist, P. The Holy Land
Lagerkvist, P. The sibyl
Lawrence, D. H. The plumed serpent
Laxness, H. Paradise reclaimed
Lewis, S. Elmer Gantry
MacLennan, H. Two solitudes
Mano, D. K. Bishop's progress
Marshall, C. Christy
Mauriac, F. The mask of innocence
Mauriac, F. Woman of the Pharisees
Merejkowski, D. The death of the gods
Michener, J. A. The source
Mishima, Y. The temple of the golden pavilion
Murdoch, I. The bell
O'Connor, F. Wise blood
Oldenbourg, Z. Cities of the flesh
Oldenbourg, Z. Destiny of fire
Olsen, P. The Virgin of San Gil
Perez Galdos, B. Doña Perfecta
Prescott, H. F. M. Son of dust
Raja Rao. The serpent and the rope
Salinger, J. D. Franny and Zooey
Slaughter, F. G. The thorn of Arimathea
Spark, M. The Mandelbaum Gate
Turnbull, A. S. The rolling years
Turton, G. My Lord of Canterbury
Vidal, G. Messiah
West, M. L. The devil's advocate
Wiesel, E. The town beyond the wall
Wilder, T. The Cabala
In Wilder, T. The Cabala, and The woman of Andros p 1-134
Williams, V. Walk Egypt
Yáñez, A. The edge of the storm
See also Biblical stories; Catholic faith; Catholic priests; Christianity; Christians, Early; Clergy; Evangelists; God; Judaism; Religion, Primitive; also names of denominations, e.g. Methodism

RELIGION, PRIMITIVE
Achebe, C. Arrow of God
Bodsworth, F. The sparrow's fall
Hartog, J. de. The spiral road
Jensen, J. V. The Cimbrians
In Jensen, J. V. The long journey p227-487
Treece, H. The golden strangers
Van Wijk, J. L. Tselane
See also Paganism

RELIGION AND SCIENCE
Mano, D. K. Bishop's progress

The religious body. Aird, C.

RELIGIOUS CONVERSION. See Conversion

RELIGIOUS LIBERTY
Barker, S. Strange wives
Gerson, N. B. The anthem
Macleod, A. The heretic
See also Persecution

RELIGIOUS LIFE. See Convents and nunneries; Monasticism and religious orders

RELIGIOUS ORDERS. See Monasticism and religious orders

RELIGIOUS PERSECUTION. See Persecution

RELIGIOUS PSYCHOLOGY
Fisher, V. Children of God

RELIGIOUS STORIES. See Religion

The reluctant medium. Davies, L. P.

The reluctant queen. Haycraft, M. C.

Reluctant rebel. Van de Water, F. F.

REMAGEN. See Germany—Remagen

REMBRANDT HERMANSZOON VAN RIJN
Schmitt, G. Rembrandt

Rembrandt. Schmitt, G.

Remember me to God. Kaufmann, M. S.

Remember the house. Rama Rau, S.

Remembrance of things past. Proust, M.

Remembrance Rock. Sandburg, C.

REMUS
Duggan, A. Children of the wolf

RENAISSANCE
Komroff, M. Coronet
Merejkowski, D. The romance of Leonardo da Vinci
Reade, C. The cloister and the hearth
See also Italy—15th century; Italy—Rome (City)

Renny's daughter. De La Roche, M.

REPORTERS. See Journalists

The reprieve. Sartre, J. P.

REPUBLIC OF ROME. See Rome—510-30 B.C.

REPUBLICAN PARTY
Barry, J. Grass roots

Requiem for a nun. Faulkner, W.

Requiem for a WREN. See Shute, N. The breaking wave

The rescue. Conrad, J.

RESCUE OPERATIONS. See Search and rescue operations

RESCUES. See Search and rescue operations

RESEARCH
Buck, P. S. Command the morning
Hersey, J. The child buyer
Snow, C. P. the search
Wyndham, J. Trouble with lichen

RESORTS, See Hotels, taverns, etc.; Summer resorts

RESPONSIBLITY
Gloag, J. A sentence of life

Rest and Be Thankful. MacInnes, H.

The rest of the robots. Asimov, I.

RESTAURANTS, LUNCH ROOMS, ETC.
Bryher. Beowulf
Buck, P. S. The three daughters of Madame Liang
Cain, J. M. The postman always rings twice
In Cain, J. M. Cain x 3 p 1-101
Jameson, S. The blind heart
Jameson, S. The white crow
Powell, A. Casanova's Chinese restaurant
In Powell, A. A dance to the music of time: second movement v2
Simenon, G. The old man dies
Steinbeck, J. Sweet Thursday
Steinbeck, J. The wayward bus
Troyat, H. Amelie and Pierre
Troyat, H. Elizabeth

The restless land. Culp, J. H.

RESTORATION ENGLAND. See England—17th century

RESURRECTION
Amado, J. Dona Flor and her two husbands
Pohl, F. The age of the pussyfoot

Resurrection. Tolstoy, L.

The resurrection of the gods. See Merejkowski, D. The romance of Leonardo da Vinci

RETARDED CHILDREN. See Slow learning children

Retief and the warlords. Laumer, K.

RETIREMENT
Cary, J. To be a pilgrim
Stegner, W. All the little live things
Streeter, E. Chairman of the bored
Wilson, A. Late call
See also Old age

The return of Ansel Gibbs. Buechner, F.

Return of Gunner Asch. Kirst, H. H.

The return of Lanny Budd. Sinclair, U.

The return of Sherlock Holmes. Doyle, Sir A. C.
In Doyle, Sir A. C. The complete Sherlock Holmes v2 p559-780
In Doyle, Sir A. C. The later adventures of Sherlock Holmes p767-1069

The return of the king. Tolkien, J. R. R.

The return of the native. Hardy, T.

The return of the ring. Tolkien, J. R. R.
In Tolkien, J. R. R. The lord of the rings v3

Return of the sphinx. MacLennan, H.

Return to Glenshael. See Elgin, M. Highland masquerade

Return to Jalna. De La Roche, M.

Reuben, Reuben. De Vries, P.

Reunion with terror. Albrand, M.
In The Saturday Evening Post. Danger p 1-106

Roads of destiny. Henry, O.
  In Henry, O. The complete works of O.
    Henry p355-550
The Roads to freedom [series]
  Sartre, J. The age of reason
  Sartre, J. P. The reprieve
  Sartre, J. P. Troubled sleep
Roanoke hundred. Fletcher, I.
ROANOKE ISLAND
  Fletcher, I. Roanoke hundred
ROB ROY. See Macgregor, Robert, called Rob
  Roy
Rob Roy. Scott, Sir W.
ROBBER BARONS. See Capitalists and finan-
  ciers
The robber bridegroom. Welty, E.
ROBBERS. See Brigands and robbers
ROBBERY
  Burnett, W. R. The asphalt jungle
  Garve, A. A very quiet place
  Malamud, B. The assistant
  Queen, E. Cop out
  Sanders, L. The Anderson tapes
  Wilkinson, G. K. Nick, the Click
    See also Bank robbers
The robe. Douglas, L. C.
Robe of honour. Cordell, A.
Robert. Gide, A.
  In Gide, A. The school for wives, Robert,
    Geneviève p95-143
ROBIN HOOD
  Barnes, M. C. The passionate brood
ROBOTS. See Automata
ROBSART, AMY. See Dudley, Amy (Robsart)
  Lady
The rock garden. Kazantzakis, N.
ROCKETS (AERONAUTICS)
  Boulle, P. Garden on the moon
  Wibberley, L. The mouse on the moon
RODEOS
  Borland, H. When the legends die
Roderick Hudson. James, H.
Roderick Random. Smollett, T.
RODIN, AUGUSTE
  Weiss, D. Naked came I
ROGERS, ROBERT
  Roberts, K. Northwest Passage
ROGERS RANGERS. See Rogers, Robert
Rogue Herries. Walpole, H.
Rogue male. Household, G.
  also in Haycraft, H. ed. Three times three
    p295-419
ROGUES AND VAGABONDS
  Brick, J. Rogues' kingdom
  Ilf. Ilf & Petrov's The complete adventures
    of Ostap Bender
  Kerouac, J. The Dharma bums
  Kerouac, J. On the road
  Kerouac, J. The subterraneans
  Le Sage, A. R. Adventures of Gil Blas of
    Santillane
  Mann, T. Confessions of Felix Krull, confi-
    dence man
  Steinbeck, J. Cannery Row
  Steinbeck, J. Sweet Thursday
  Steinbeck, J. Tortilla Flat
  Walpole, H. Rogue Herries
  Walople, H. Vanessa
Rogues' kingdom. Brick, J.
Roll Shenandoah. Lancaster, B.
Rolling stones. Henry, O.
  In Henry, O. The complete works of O.
    Henry p941-1060
The rolling years. Turnbull, A. S.
The Roman. Waltari, M.
ROMAN BRITAIN. See England—Roman pe-
  riod, 55 B.C.-449 A.D.
ROMAN CATHOLIC CHURCH. See Catholic
  faith
ROMAN CATHOLIC RELIGION. See Catholic
  faith
ROMAN EMPERORS. See names of emperors,
  e.g. Hadrian, Emperor of Rome
ROMAN REPUBLIC. See Rome—510-30 B.C.
ROMAN SOLDIERS. See Soldiers, Roman
The Roman spring of Mrs Stone. Williams, T.

ROMAN STATESMEN. See Statesmen, Roman
Roman tales. Moravia, A.
Roman tales, More. Moravia, A.
Roman wall. Bryher
The romance of Leonardo da Vinci. Merejkow-
  ski, D.
ROMANIA. See Rumania
ROMANS IN BRITAIN. See England—Roman
  period, 55 B.C.-449 A.D.
ROMANS IN ENGLAND. See England—Roman
  period, 55 B.C.-449 A.D.
ROMANS IN PALESTINE, ANCIENT
  Bekessy, E. Barabbas
  Meisels, A. Son of a star
  Rayner, W. The last days
  Slaughter, F. G. God's warrior
  Wibberley, L. The centurion
ROME
  Used for ancient Rome and its empire to
  476 A.D. The modern city of Rome is en-
  tered under Italy—Rome (city)

510-30 B.C.
  Bryher. The coin of Carthage
  Caldwell, T. A pillar of iron
  Davidson, A. The phoenix and the mirror
  Davis, W. S. A friend of Caesar
  Duggan, A. Three's company
  Jensen, J. V. The Cimbrians
    In Jensen, J. V. The long journey p227-487
  Koestler, A. The gladiators
  Taylor, A. The gods are not mocked
  Warner, R. Imperial Caesar
  Warner, R. The young Caesar
  Wilder, T. The ides of March

30 B.C.-476 A.D.
  Asch, S. The Nazarene
  Bulwer-Lytton, Sir E. The last days of Pom-
    peii
  Caldwell, T. Dear and glorious physician
  Costain, T. B. The darkness and the dawn
  Costain, T. B. The silver chalice
  De Wohl, L. The glorious folly
  De Wohl, L. The spear
  Dored, E. I loved Tiberius
  Douglas, L. C. The robe
  Feuchtwanger, L. The Jew of Rome
  Feuchtwanger, L. Josephus
  Feuchtwanger, L. Josephus and the Emperor
  Graves, R. Claudius, the god and his wife
    Messalina
  Graves, R. I, Claudius
  Horia, V. God was born in exile
  Merejkowski, D. The death of the gods
  Pater, W. Marius the Epicurean
  Shipway, G. The Imperial Governor
  Sienkiewicz, H. Quo vadis
  Slaughter, F. G. Constantine: the miracle of
    the flaming cross
  Vidal, G. Julian
  Wallace, L. Ben Hur
  Waltari, M. The Roman
  White, E. L. The unwilling vestal
  Yourcenar, M. Memoirs of Hadrian, and re-
    flections on the composition of Memoirs
    of Hadrian

6th century
  De Wohl, L. Citadel of God

Aristocracy
  See Aristocracy—Rome

Kings and rulers
  De Wohl, L. The glorious folly
  Duggan, A. Children of the wolf
ROME (CITY) See Italy—Rome (City)
Rome haul. Edmonds, W. D.
Romola. Eliot, G.
  also in Eliot, G. The best-known novels of
    George Eliot p925-1350
ROMULUS, KING OF ROME
  Duggan, A. Children of the wolf
Room at the top. Braine, J.
The room upstairs. Dickens, M.
A room with a view. Forster, E. M.
ROOSTERS
  García Márquez, G. No one writes to the
    colonel
    In García Márquez, G. No one writes to the
      colonel, and other stories p3-62
  Mannix, D. P. The killers
The roots of heaven. Gary, R.
Rosa. Sharp, M.

SATIRE—_Continued_

Guareschi, G. Don Camillo's dilemma
Guareschi, G. The little world of Don Camillo
Harwood, R. The girl in Melanie Klein
Hasek, J. The good soldier: Schweik
Hazzard, S. People in glass houses
Heinlein, R. A. The moon is a harsh mistress
Hemingway, E. The torrents of spring
 _In_ Hemingway, E. The Hemingway reader
  p25-86
Hersey, J. The child buyer
Hersey, J. Too far to walk
Hesse, H. The glass bead game (Magister Ludi)
Hodgins, E. Mr Blandings builds his dream house
Hoyle, F. Fifth planet
Huxley, A. After many a summer dies the swan
Huxley, A. Antic hay
Huxley, A. Brave new world
Huxley, A. Crome yellow
Huxley, A. Point counter point
Huxley, A. Time must have a stop
James, H. The Bostonians
Jarrell, R. Pictures from an institution
Johnson, P. H. Cork Street, next to the hatter's
Johnson, P. H. The unspeakable Skipton
Kafka, F. Amerika
Kafka, F. Metamorphosis
 _In_ Pick, R. ed. German stories and tales
  p247-95
Kaufman, B. Up the down staircase
Kirst, H. H. The night of the generals
Kirst, H. H. Return of Gunner Asch
Kirst, H. H. Revolt of Gunner Asch
Kirst, H. H. What became of Gunner Asch
Kops, B. The dissent of Dominick Shapiro
Lewis, C. S. That hideous strength
Lewis, S. Babbitt
Lewis, S. Cass Timberlane
Lewis, S. Dodsworth
Lewis, S. Elmer Gantry
Lewis, S. It can't happen here
Lewis, S. Main Street
Lodge, D. The British Museum is falling down
Lurie, A. Imaginary friends
Lurie, A. Real people
McCarthy, M. The group
McCarthy, M. The groves of Academe
Machado de Assis. Epitaph of a small winner
MacInnes, C. Westward to Laughter
Malamud, B. A new life
Marquand, J. P. B. F.'s daughter
Marquand, J. P. H. M. Pulham, esquire
Marquand, J. P. The late George Apley
Marquand, J. P. Point of no return
Marquand, J. P. Sincerely, Willis Wayde
Marquand, J. P. So little time
Marquand, J. P. Wickford Point
Marryat, F. Mr Midshipman Easy
Maugham, W. S. Cakes and ale
Mauriac, F. Questions of precedence
Menen, A. The prevalence of witches
Meredith, G. The egoist
Merle, R. The day of the dolphin
Mirdrekvandi, G. D. Ali. No heaven for Gunga Din
Mitford, N. The blessing
Montherlant, H. de. The girls
Morris, W. In orbit
Morris, W. What a way to go
Moynahan, J. Pairing off
Murdoch, I. A fairly honourable defeat
Murdoch, I. A severed head
Nabokov, V. Despair
Nabokov, V. Lolita
Nabokov, V. Pale fire
Nabokov, V. Pnin
Naipaul, V. S. A house for Mr Biswas
Narayan, R. K. The guide
Narayan, R. K. The man-eater of Malgudi
Narayan, R. K. The vendor of sweets
Nathan, R. The devil with love
Nathan, R. One more spring
Natsume, S. Botchan
O'Rourke, F. Instant gold
Orwell, G. Animal farm
Orwell, G. A clergyman's daughter
Orwell, G. Coming up for air
Orwell, G. Keep the aspidistra flying
Orwell, G. Nineteen eighty-four
Perez Galdos, B. The spendthrifts
Peyrefitte, R. Knights of Malta
Pirandello, L. The late Mattia Pascal
Powell, A. The acceptance world
 _In_ Powell, A. A dance to the music of time
  v3

Powell, A. A buyer's market
 _In_ Powell, A. A dance to the music of time
  v2
Powell, A. A dance to the music of time
Powell, A. A dance to the music of time: second movement
Powell, A. The military philosophers
Powell, A. A question of upbringing
 _In_ Powell, A. A dance to the music of time
  v
Powell, R. Pioneer, go home!
Powers, J. F. Morte d'Urban
Priestley, J. B. The image men
Remarque, E. M. The black obelisk
Santayana, G. The last Puritan
Sarraute, N. The golden fruits
Sayers, D. L. Murder must advertise
Sharp, M. Britannia Mews
Sharp, M. In pious memory
Sharp, M. Rosa
Sheed, W. The hack
Sheed, W. Office politics
Sheed, W. Square's progress
Shulman, M. Anyone got a match?
Shulman, M. I was a teen-age dwarf
Shulman, M. Max Shulman's Large economy size
Shulman, M. Rally round the flag, boys!
Smollett, T. Peregrine Pickle
Smollett, T. Roderick Random
Sneider, V. The Teahouse of the August Moon
Spark, M. The bachelors
Spark, M. The ballad of Peckham Rye
Spark, M. The girls of slender means
Spark, M. Memento mori
Spark, M. The public image
Steinbeck, J. The short reign of Pippin IV
Sterne, L. Tristram Shandy
Svevo, I. The confessions of Zeno
Swift, J. Gulliver's travels
Tarr, H. Heaven help us!
Thackeray, W. M. Pendennis
Tolkien, J. R. R. The fellowship of the ring
Tolkien, J. R. R. The return of the king
Tolkien, J. R. R. The two towers
Tracy, H. The first day of Friday
Tracy, H. Settled in chambers
Twain, M. The adventures of Colonel Sellers
Twain, M. A Connecticut Yankee in King Arthur's court
Ustinov, P. Add a dash of pity
Ustinov, P. The loser
Van der Zee, J. The plum explosion
Vidal, G. Messiah
Voltaire, F. M. A. de. Candide, and other writings
Voltaire. Voltaire's Candide, Zadig, and selected stories
Voltaire. Zadig, and other romances
Vonnegut, K. Cat's cradle
Vonnegut, K. God bless you, Mr Rosewater
Vonnegut, K. Mother night
Vonnegut, K. Player piano
Vonnegut, K. Slaughterhouse-five
Wallop, D. The good life
Waterhouse, K. Everything must go
Waugh, E. Black mischief
Waugh, E. Brideshead revisited
Waugh, E. Decline and fall
Waugh, E. The end of the battle
Waugh, E. The loved one
Waugh, E. Men at arms
Waugh, E. Officers and gentlemen
Waugh, E. Put out more flags
Waugh, E. Vile bodies
Weidman, J. I can get it for you wholesale
Weidman, J. The sound of Bow bells
Wells, H. G. Tono-Bungay
West, N. Complete works
West, N. Miss Lonelyhearts
White, T. H. The ill-made knight
White, T. H. Mistress Masham's repose
White, T. H. The sword in the stone
White, T. H. The witch in the wood
Wibberley, L. Adventures of an elephant boy
Wibberley, L. Beware of the mouse
Wibberley, L. The mouse on the moon
Wibberley, L. The mouse on Wall Street
Wibberley, L. The mouse that roared
Wilder, T. The Cabala
 _In_ Wilder, T. The Cabala, and The woman of Andros p 1-134
 _In_ Wilder, T. A Thornton Wilder trio p21-147
Wilson, A. Late call
Wollaston, N. Pharaoh's chicken
Wouk, H. Aurora dawn
 See also Grotesque; Humor

The **Saturday** Evening Post Reader of sea stories. The Saturday Evening Post

The **Saturday** Evening Post Reader of western stories. The Saturday Evening Post

The **Saturday** Evening Post Sports stories. The Saturday Evening Post

Saturday night and Sunday morning. Sillitoe, A.

Saturday the rabbi went hungry. Kemelman, H.

Saturn over the water. Priestley, J. B.

SAUK INDIANS
Fuller, I. The shining trail

SAUL OF TARSUS. See Paul, Saint, apostle

SAUL, KING OF ISRAEL
Israel, C. E. Rizpah

Savage Sam. Gipson, F.

Savage sleep. Brand, M.

Savanna. Giles, J. H.

SAVANNAH
See also Georgia—Savannah
Siege, 1779
Mason, F. V. Rivers of glory

Saving face. See Boulle, P. Face of a hero

SAVONAROLA, GIROLAMO MARIA FRANCESCO MATTEO
Eliot, G. Romola
Merejkowski, D. The romance of Leonardo da Vinci

SAXONS. See Anglo-Saxons

Sayonara. Michener, J. A.

SCALDS
Jensen, J. V. The Cimbrians
In Jensen, J. V. The long journey p227-487

Scales of justice. Marsh, N.
also in Marsh, N. Another Three-act special p177-368

Scandal at High Chimneys. Carr, J. D.

The **scandal** of Father Brown. Chesterton, G. K.
In Chesterton, G. K. The Father Brown omnibus p815-974

SCANDINAVIANS IN THE UNITED STATES
Kennelly, A. The peaceable kingdom

The **scapegoat.** Du Maurier, D.

The **scapegoat.** Strindberg, A.

Scaramouche, the king-maker. Sabatini, R.

The **scarecrow** man. Bray, C.

The **Scarlet** boy. Calder-Marshall, A.

The **scarlet** feather. Van Every, D.

The **scarlet** letter. Hawthorne, N.
also In Hawthorne, N. The best of Hawthorne p182-392
also in Hawthorne, N. The complete novels and selected tales of Nathaniel Hawthorne p85-240
also in Hawthorne, N. The portable Hawthorne p269-489

The **Scarlet** Pimpernel. Orczy, Baroness

Scarlet Sister Mary. Peterkin, J.

The **Scarperer.** Behan, B.

SCENARIOS. See Moving picture plays

Scenes from the bathhouse, and other stories of Communist Russia. Zoshchenko, M.

Scent of cloves. Lofts, N.

The **scent** of water. Goudge, E.

SCHÄCHTER, RAPHAEL
Bor, J. The Terezin Requiem

The **Schirmer** inheritance. Ambler, E.
also in Ambler, E. The intriguers p291-432

SCHIZOPHRENIA. See Mental illness

SCHOLARS
Bellow, S. Herzog
Hesse, H. The glass bead game (Magister Ludi)
Johnson, P. H. Night and silence, who is here?
MacInnes, H. The double image
Roberts, J. H. The Q document
Snow, C. P. The light and the dark
Wilson, A. Anglo-Saxon attitudes

SCHOOL ATTENDANCE
Morris, W. In orbit

The **school** for wives. Robert, Geneviève. Gide, A.

SCHOOL GIRLS. See Girls

SCHOOL LIFE
Kirkwood, J. Good times/bad times
See also College life; Education; Student; Teachers
Belgium
Brontë, C. Villette
Edinburgh
Spark, M. The prime of Miss Jean Brodie
England
Campbell, M. Lord dismiss us
Davies, L. P. The paper dolls
Dickens, C. David Copperfield
Dickens, C. Nicholas Nickleby
Donleavy, J. P. The beastly beatitudes of Balthazar B
Fielding, G. In the time of Greenbloom
Forster, M. Miss Owen-Owen
Glyn, C. Don't knock the corners off
Goudge, E. The rosemary tree
Hilton, J. Good-bye Mr Chips
Holland, I. Cecily
Kipling, R. The complete Stalky & Co.
Le Carré J. A murder of quality
In Le Carré, J. The incongruous spy v2
Maugham, W. S. Of human bondage
Murdoch, I. The sandcastle
Orwell, G. A clergyman's daughter
Read, Miss. Fresh from the country
Sheed, W. The blacking factory
In Sheed, W. The blacking factory & Pennsylvania gothic p67-246
France
Colette. Claudine at school
Flaubert, G. Sentimental education
Fournier, A. The wanderer
Troyat, H. Elizabeth
Germany
Hesse, H. Beneath the wheel
Maugham, W. S. Of human bondage
Peru
Vargas Llosa, M. The time of the hero
United States
Auchincloss, L. The Rector of Justin
Eggleston, E. The Hoosier school-boy
Farrell, J. T. A world I never made
Hunter, E. The blackboard jungle
Kaufman, B. Up the down staircase
Knowles, J. A separate peace
Patton, F. G. Good morning, Miss Dove
Solberg, G. Shelia
Von Hoffman, N. Two, three, many more

SCHOOL STORIES. See School life

SCHOOL SUPERINTENDENTS AND PRINCIPALS
Forster, M. Miss Owen-Owen

SCHOOL TEACHERS. See Teachers

Schooled to kill. Shannon, D.

The **schoolmaster.** Lovelace, E.

SCHOOLMASTERS. See Teachers

SCIENCE
Fiction
See Science fiction

SCIENCE AND RELIGION. See Religion and science

SCIENCE FICTION
Aldiss, B. W. Cryptozoic!
Aldiss, B. W. Who can replace a man?
Allingham, M. The mind readers
Amazing Stories. The best of Amazing
Amis, K. ed. Spectrum [1]-V
Analog 1-7
Anderson, P. Brain wave
Anderson, P. The corridors of time
Anderson, P. The high crusade
Anderson, P. Satan's world
Anderson, P. Seven conquests
Anderson, P. Trader to the stars
Asimov, I. Asimov's mysteries
Asimov, I. The caves of steel
Asimov, I. Foundation
Asimov, I. Foundation and empire
Asimov, I. ed. The Hugo winners
Asimov, I. I, robot
Asimov, I. The naked sun
Asimov, I. Nightfall, and other stories
Asimov, I. Nine tomorrows

SCIENCE FICTION—*Continued*
Asimov, I. The rest of the robots
Asimov, I. Second Foundation
Asimov, I. Triangle: The currents of space, Pebble in the sky, The stars, like dust
Balmer, E. When worlds collide
The Best from Fantasy and Science Fiction; 1st-18th ser.
Best SF: 1968
The Best science fiction stories and novels: 1949-1958
Blish, J. A case of conscience
Boucher, A. The compleat werewolf, and other stories of fantasy and science fiction
Boucher, A. ed. A treasury of great science fiction
Bradbury, R. I sing the Body Electric!
Bradbury, R. The illustrated man
Bradbury, R. The Martian chronicles
Bradbury, R. Twice twenty-two: The golden apples of the sun; A medicine for melancholy
Caidin, M. Marooned
Caidin, M. The Mendelov conspiracy
Carr, T. ed. Science fiction for people who hate science fiction
Clarke, A. C. Across the sea of stars
Clarke, A. C. Childhood's end
Clarke, A. C. The city and the stars
Clarke, A. C. The deep range
Clarke, A. C. Earthlight
Clarke, A. C. Expedition to earth
Clarke, A. C. A fall of moondust
Clarke, A. C. From the ocean, from the stars
Clarke, A. C. The lion of Comarre & Against the fall of night
Clarke, A. C. The nine billion names of God
Clarke, A. C. The other side of the sky
Clarke, A. C. Prelude to Mars
Clarke, A. C. Prelude to space
Clarke, A. C. The sands of Mars
Clarke, A. C. Tales of ten worlds
Clarke, A. C. ed. Time probe: the sciences in science fiction
Clarke, A. C. 2001: a space odyssey
Cole, B. The funco file
Conklin, G. ed. The best of science fiction
Conklin, G. ed. Giants unleashed
Conklin, G. ed. Invaders of Earth
Conklin, G. ed. Possible worlds of science fiction
Conklin, G. ed. Science-fiction adventures in dimension
Conklin, G. ed. Science-fiction thinking machines: robots, androids, computers
Davies, L. P. The artificial man
Davies, L. P. The Lampton dreamers
Davies, L. P. The paper dolls
Derleth, A. ed. The other side of the moon
Derleth, A. ed. Strange ports of call
Dickson, G. R. None but man
Doyle, Sir A. C. The lost world
Doyle, Sir A. C. The Maracot Deep
Earley, G. W. ed. Encounters with aliens
Elder, J. ed. The farthest reaches
Fast, H. The general zapped an angel
Galaxy Magazine. The [first]-tenth Galaxy reader
Harrison, H. Captive universe
Harrison, H. ed. Nova I
Hay, J. Autopsy for a cosmonaut
Healy, R. J. ed. Famous science fiction stories
Heinlein, R. A. The door into summer
Heinlein, R. A. Double star
Heinlein, R. A. Glory road
Heinlein, R. A. The green hills of earth
Heinlein, R. A. The menace from earth
Heinlein, R. A. The moon is a harsh mistress
Heinlein, R. A. The past through tomorrow
Heinlein, R. A. The puppet masters
Heinlein, R. A. Three by Heinlein
Heinlein, R. A. Waldo and Magic, inc.
Henderson, Z. The people: no different flesh
Hoyle, F. A for Andromeda
Hoyle, F. Andromeda breakthrough
Hoyle, F. Fifth planet
Hoyle, F. October the first is too late
Hoyle, F. Ossian's ride
If. The If Reader of science fiction
Keyes, D. Flowers for Algernon
Knight, D. ed. Beyond tomorrow
Knight, D. ed. A century of great short science fiction novels
Knight, D. ed. A century of science fiction
Knight, D. ed. Cities of wonder
Knight, D. ed. The dark side
Knight, D. ed. One hundred years of science fiction

Knight, D. Three novels
Knight, D. ed. Toward infinity
Laumer, K. The long twilight
Laumer, K. Nine by Laumer
Laumer, K. Retief and the warlords
Lewis, C. S. Out of the silent planet
Lewis, C. S. Perelandra
London, J. The star rover
Magazine of Fantasy and Science Fiction. A decade of Fantasy and Science Fiction
Magidoff, R. ed. Russian science fiction, 1968-1969
Merle, R. The day of the dolphin
Merril, J. Daughters of Earth
Merril, J. ed. SF: best of the best
Merril, J. ed. The 6th-12th annual of the year's best SF
Miller, W. M. A canticle for Leibowitz
Moore, C. L. The vintage season
  In Hitchcock, A. ed. Alfred Hitchcock presents: Stories for late at night p100-40
Moskowitz, S. ed. Masterpieces of science fiction
Moskowitz, S. ed. Modern masterpieces of science fiction
Nebula award stories, 1965 [1]-4
Orbit 1-6
Playboy. The Playboy Book of science fiction and fantasy
Pohl, F. The age of the pussyfoot
The Saturday Evening Post. The Post Reader of fantasy and science fiction
Shelley, M. W. Frankenstein
Silverberg, R. ed. Earthmen and strangers
Silverberg, R. Hawksbill Station
Silverberg, R. ed. Men and machines
Silverberg, R. To live again
Silverberg, R. ed. Tomorrow's worlds
Silverberg, R. ed. Voyagers in time
Simak, C. D. All the traps of earth, and other stories
Simak, C. D. City
Simak, C. D. The goblin reservation
Simak, C. D. Out of their minds
Simak, C. D. Ring around the sun
Simak, C. D. They walked like men
Simak, C. D. Way Station
Simak, C. D. The werewolf principle
Simak, C. D. Why call them back from heaven?
Simak, C. D. The worlds of Clifford Simak
Stewart, G. R. Earth abides
Szilard, L. The voice of the dolphins, and other stories
Three for tomorrow
Vance, J. Eight fantasms and magics
Vance, J. Emphyrio
Van Vogt, A. E. The weapon makers
Van Vogt, A. E. The weapon shops of Isher
Verne, J. From the earth to the moon, and, Round the moon
Verne, J. A journey to the centre of the earth
Vonnegut, K. Cat's cradle
Vonnegut, K. Slaughterhouse-five
Wells, H. G. Best science fiction stories of H. G. Wells
Wells, H. G. The invisible man
Wells, H. G. Seven science fiction novels
Wells, H. G. The time machine
Wells, H. G. 28 science fiction stories
Wells, H. G. The war of the worlds, The time machine, and selected short stories
Wilhelm, K. Let the fire fall
Wyndham, J. The day of the triffids
Wyndham, J. The Midwich cuckoos
Wyndham, J. Out of the deeps
  In Hitchcock, A. ed. Alfred Hitchcock presents: Stories that scared even me p309-463
Wyndham, J. Trouble with lichen
  See also Fantasies; Fantastic fiction; Future, Novels of the; Horror stories; Mars (Planet); Flight; Space flight to the moon; Space probes; Time, Travels in

Science-fiction adventures in dimension. Conklin, G. ed.

Science fiction for people who hate science fiction. Carr, T. ed.

Science-fiction thinking machines: robots, androids, computers. Conklin, G. ed.

SCIENTIFIC DISCOVERY. See Research

SCIENTIFIC RESEARCH. See Research

SCIENTISTS
Albrand, M. Nightmare in Copenhagen
Asimov, I. Fantastic voyage
Boulle, P. Garden on the moon
Buck, P. S. Command the morning
Carter, Y. Mr Campion's farthing
Crichton, M. The Andromeda strain

SELFISHNESS
Balzac, H. de. Père Goriot
Glasgow, E. In this our life
Meredith, G. The egoist

The seminarian. Del Castillo, M.

SEMINOLE INDIANS
Wilder, R. Bright feather

SEMINOLE WAR, 2D, 1835-1842
Wilder, R. Bright feather

SEMMELWEIS, IGNAC FÜLÖP
Thompson, M. The cry and the covenant

The Sempinski affair. Kuniczak, W. S.

SENATE. See United States. Congress. Senate

The senator. Pearson, D.

SENATORS. See United States. Congress. Senate

The Seneca hostage. Vaughan, C. A.

SENECA INDIANS
Edmonds, W. D. In the hands of the Senecas
Vaughan, C. A. The Seneca hostage

SENILITY. See Old age

Sense and sensibility. Austen, J.
    also in Austen, J. The complete novels of
    Jane Austen

The sense of the past. James, H.

A sentence of life. Gloat, J.

Sentimental education. Flaubert, G.

Sentimental journey. See Sterne, L. A senti-
    mental journey through France and Italy

A sentimental journey through France and It-
    aly. Sterne, L.

Sentimental journey through France and Italy
    by Mr Yorick. See Sterne, L. A. sentimental
    journey through France and Italy

Sentimental Tommy. Barrie, J. M.

A separate peace. Knowles, J.

SEPOY REBELLION. See India—British oc-
    cupation, 1765-1947

SEPULCHERS. See Tombs

SERBIA. See Yugoslavia

SERFDOM
                    Russia
Gogol, N. Dead souls

SERFS AND SERFDOM. See Serfdom

A serious investigation. Egan, L.

Sermons and soda water. O'Hara, J.

The serpent and the rope. Raja Rao

SERRA, JUNIPERO
Lauritzen, J. The cross and the sword

SERVANTS
Buck, P. S. Peony
Dourado, A. A hidden life
Faulkner, W. Requiem for a nun
Godden, J. A winter's tale
Green, H. Loving
Greene, G. A burnt-out case
Mather, M. One summer in between
Mishima, Y. Thirst for love
Moore, G. Esther Waters
Murdoch, I. The unicorn
Osborne, H. The yellow gold of Tiryns
Petry, A. The street
Pushkin, A. The captain's daughter, and
    other stories
Richardson, S. Pamela
Scott, Sir W. The bride of Lammermoor
Tolstoy, L. Master and man
    In Tolstoy, L. Russian stories and legends
    p163-224
Tolstoy, L. "Master and man," and other
    parables and tales
Wallop, D. The good life
    See also Governesses; Indentured ser-
    vants
                    Butlers
Wodehouse, P. G. The butler did it
                  Charwomen
Gallico, P. Mrs 'Arris goes to Paris
Gallico, P. Mrs 'Arris goes to Parliament
                  Companions
Dickens, M. The room upstairs
Ogilvie, E. Bellwood

Cooks
Amado, J. Gabriela, clove and cinnamon
Bernanos, M. The other side of the mountain
Cary, J. Herself surprised
McCullers, C. The member of the wedding
Werfel, F. Embezzled heaven
    See also Chefs

Hired men
Hubbard, P. M. Cold waters
Malamud, B. The fixer

Housekeepers
Balzac, H. de. The bachelor's house
Cary, J. Herself surprised
Chase, M. E. The lovely ambition
Eden, D. The vines of Yarrabee
Frankau, P. Sing for your supper
Murdoch, I. The Italian girl
Smith, D. The new moon with the old
Stein, G. Three lives
Van Dyke, H. Ladies of the Rachmaninoff
    eyes

Maids
Bjorn, T. F. Papa's wife
Davenport, M. The valley of decision
Defoe, D. Roxana, the fortunate mistress
Godden, R. The kitchen Madonna
Macleod, A. The heretic
Pearson, D. The marigold field
Rooke, D. Mittee
Sharp, M. Cluny Brown
Shute, N. The breaking wave
Sillanpää, F. E. The maid Silja
Tracy, H. The first day of Friday

Nursemaids
Duras, M. The square
    In Duras, M. Four novels p 1-72

Stewards
Stevenson, R. L. The master of Ballantrae

Valets
Bennett, A. Buried alive
Verne, J. Around the world in eighty days
Wodehouse, P. G. The code of the Woosters
Wodehouse, P. G. How right you are, Jeeves
Wodehouse, P. G. The inimitable Jeeves
Wodehouse, P. G. Very good, Jeeves

Set all afire. De Wohl, L.

A set of variations. O'Connor, F.

Set this house on fire. Styron, W.

Setting free the bears. Irving, J.

Settled in chambers. Tracy, H.

7 1/2 cents. Bissell, R.

7 by Colette. Colette

Seven by five. See Bates, H. E. The best of
    H. E. Bates

Seven conquests. Anderson, P.

Seven days in May. Knebel, F.

Seven famous novels. See Wells, H. G. Seven
    science fiction novels

Seven Gothic tales. Dinesen, I.

Seven keys to Baldpate. Biggers, E. D.

Seven science fiction novels. Wells, H. G.

Seven seats to the moon. Armstrong, C.

Seven tears for Apollo. Whitney, P. A.

The seven who were hanged. Andreyev, L.

SEVEN WONDERS OF THE WORLD. See Co-
    lossus of Rhodes

Seventeen. Tarkington, B.

Seventeen lost stories. Maugham, W. S.

The seventh of October. Romains, J.

A severed head. Murdoch, I.

SEVILLE. See Spain—Seville

SEX
Anderson, S. Poor white
Donleavy, J. P. The beastly beatitudes of
    Balthazar B
Lodge, D. The British Museum is falling
    down
Mishima, Y. Thirst for love
Simenon, G. The blue room [and] The ac-
    complices

SEX CRIMES. See Rape

The shoes of the fisherman. West, M. L.

The shoot. Trevor, E.

SHOPKEEPERS. See Merchants

Short cases of Inspector Maigret. Simenon, G.

Short fiction of the masters. Hamalian, L. ed.

Short Friday, and other stories. Singer, I. B.

Short novels. Tolstoy, L.

The short novels of Balzac. Balzac, H. de

The short novels of Dostoevsky. Dostoevsky, F.

Short novels of Henry James. James, H.

The short novels of Jack Schaefer. Schaefer, J.

The short novels of John Steinbeck, Steinbeck, J.

Short novels of the masters. Neider, C. ed.

The short novels of Thomas Wolfe. Wolfe, T.

The short novels of Tolstoy. Tolstoy, L.

The short reign of Pippin IV. Steinbeck, J.
  also in Costain, T. B. comp. Twelve short novels p703-98

SHORT STORIES

Ade, G. The America of George Ade (1866-1944)

Aiken, C. The collected short stories of Conrad Aiken

Akutagawa, R. Exotic Japanese stories, the beautiful and the grotesque

Akutagawa, R. Japanese short stories

Akutagawa, R. Rashomon, and other stories

Aldiss, B. W. Who can replace a man?

Aldrich, B. S. The Bess Streeter Aldrich reader

Aldrich, B. S. A Bess Streeter Aldrich treasury

Aldrich, B. S. Journey into Christmas, and other stories

Aleichem, S. Inside Kasrilevke

Aleichem, S. The old country

Aleichem, S. Old country tales

Aleichem, S. Selected stories of Sholom Aleichem

Aleichem, S. Some laughter, some tears

Aleichem, S. Stories and satires

Aleichem, S. Tevye's daughters

Allingham, M. The Allingham Case-book

Amazing Stories. The best of Amazing

Ambler, E. ed. To catch a spy

American short stories of the nineteenth century

Amis, K. ed. Spectrum [I]-V

Anderson, P. Seven conquests

Anderson, S. Sherwood Anderson: Short stories

Anderson, S. Winesburg, Ohio

Andrić, I. The Pasha's concubine, and other tales

Angoff, C. ed. Stories from The Literary Review

Asch, S. Tales of my people

Asimov, I. Asimov's mysteries

Asimov, I. ed. The Hugo winners

Asimov, I. I, robot

Asimov, I. Nightfall, and other stories

Asimov, I. Nine tomorrows

Asimov, I. The rest of the robots

Asquith, C. ed. A book of modern ghosts

Aucassin et Nicolette. Aucassin and Nicolette, and other mediaeval romances and legends

Auchincloss, L. Powers of attorney

Auchincloss, L. Tales of Manhattan

Babel, I. The collected stories

Babel, I. You must know everything

Baldwin, J. Going to meet the man

Balzac, H. de. Droll stories

Barth, J. Lost in the funhouse

Barthelme, D. Unspeakable practices, unnatural acts

Barzun, J. ed. The delights of detection

Bates, H. E. The best of H. E. Bates

Beckett, S. Stories & Texts for nothing

Beerbohm, M. A Christmas garland

Bellow, S. Mosby's memoirs, and other stories

Bellow, S. Seize the day

Benét, S. V. The last circle

Benét, S. V. Selected works. Volume two: Prose

Benét, S. V. Thirteen o'clock

Benét, S. V. Twenty-five short stories

Bentley, E. C. Trent intervenes
  In Bentley, E. C. Trent's case book v3

Bernkopf, J. F. comp. Boucher's choicest

The Best American short stories, 1915-1969

Best British short stories, 1922-1940

Best detective stories of the year, 1946-1959/1961-1968

The Best from Fantasy and Science Fiction; 1st-18th ser.

Best of the Best American short stories, 1915-1950

Best of the Best detective stories

Best SF: 1968

The Best science fiction stories and novels: 1949-1958

Bierce, A. Can such things be?

Bierce, A. In the midst of life

Birmingham, S. Heart troubles

Blacker, I. R. ed. The Old West in fiction

Blackwood, A. In the realm of terror

Blackwood, A. Tales of the uncanny and supernatural

Blocker, J. ed. Israeli stories

Boccaccio, G. The Decameron

Böll, H. Children are civilians too

Böll, H. 18 stories

Borges, J. L. Ficciones

Boucher, A. The compleat werewolf, and other stories of fantasy and science fiction

Boucher, A. ed. A treasury of great science fiction

Bowles, J. The collected works of Jane Bowles

Boyle, P. At night all cats are grey, and other stories

Bradbury, R. Fahrenheit 451

Bradbury, R. The golden apples of the sun

Bradbury, R. I sing the Body Electric!

Bradbury, R. The illustrated man

Bradbury, R. The machineries of joy

Bradbury, R. The Martian chronicles

Bradbury, R. A medicine for melancholy

Bradbury, R. The October country

Bradbury, R. Twice twenty-two: The golden apples of the sun; A medicine for melancholy

Bradbury, R. The Vintage Bradbury

Bradford, R. Ol' man Adam an' his chillun

Brand, M. Max Brand's Best stories

Brennan, M. In and out of never-never land

Buck, P. S. First wife, and other stories

Buck, P. S. Fourteen stories

Buck, P. S. The good deed, and other stories of Asia, past and present

Bunin, I. The gentleman from San Francisco

Burnett, W. ed. The modern short story in the making

Burrell, A. ed. An anthology of famous American stories

Caldwell, E. Complete stories of Erskine Caldwell

Calisher, H. Extreme magic

Calvino, I. Cosmicomics

Camus, A. Exile and the kingdom

Canby, H. S. ed. The book of the short story

Canfield, D. A harvest of stories

Canning, J. ed. 50 great horror stories

Capote, T. Breakfast at Tiffany's

Capote, T. A tree of night, and other stories

Carpenter, D. The murder of the frogs, and other stories

Carr, T. ed. Science fiction for people who hate science fiction

Case, D. The cell

Cather, W. Early stories of Willa Cather

Cather, W. Obscure destinies

Cather, W. The old beauty, and others

Cather, W. Willa Cather's Collected short fiction, 1892-1912

Cather, W. Youth and the bright Medusa

Cerf, B. ed. An anthology of famous British stories

Cerf, B. A. ed. Famous ghost stories

Cerf, B. A. ed. Great German short novels and stories

Cerf, B. A. ed. Great modern short stories

Chandler, R. The simple art of murder

Charles, G. ed. Modern Jewish stories

Charteris, L. The first Saint omnibus

Charteris, L. The second Saint omnibus

Charyn, J. ed. The single voice

Cheever, J. The brigadier and the golf widow

Cheever, J. The housebreaker of Shady Hill, and other stories

Chekhov, A. The best known works of Anton Chekhov

Chekhov, A. The darling, and other stories

Chekhov, A. The duel, and other stories

Chekhov, A. The image of Chekhov

Chekhov, A. Late-blooming flowers, and other stories

Chekhov, A. The Oxford Chekhov v8

Chekhov, A. St Peter's Day, and other tales

Chekhov, A. Select tales of Tchekhov

Chekhov, A. The stories of Anton Tchekov

Chekhov, A. The unknown Chekhov

Chesterton, G. K. Father Brown mystery stories

SHORT STORIES—*Continued*

Chesterton, G. K. The Father Brown omnibus

Christie, A. 13 clues for Miss Marple

Clark, B. H. comp. Great short novels of the world

Clark, B. H. comp. Great short stories of the world

Clarke, A. C. Across the sea of stars

Clarke, A. C. Expedition to earth

Clarke, A. C. From the ocean, from the stars

Clarke, A. C. The nine billion names of God

Clarke, A. C. The other side of the sky

Clarke, A. C. Prelude to Mars

Clarke, A. C. Tales of ten worlds

Clarke, A. C. ed. Time probe: the sciences in science fiction

Clarke, J. H. ed. American Negro short stories

Collier, J. Fancies and goodnights

Collins, W. Short stories

Conklin, G. ed. The best of science fiction

Conklin, G. ed. Giants unleashed

Conklin, G. ed. Invaders of Earth

Conklin, G. ed. Possible worlds of science fiction

Conklin, G. ed. Science-fiction adventures in dimension

Conklin, G. ed. Science-fiction thinking machines: robots, androids, computers

Conrad, J. Great short works of Joseph Conrad

Conrad, J. The portable Conrad

Conrad, J. Stories and tales of Joseph Conrad

Conrad, J. Tales of land and sea

Conrad, J .Tales of the East and West

Conrad, J. Typhoon, and other tales of the sea

Conrad, J. Youth, and two other stories

Cooper, P. ed. Famous dog stories

Cooper, P. ed. Great horse stories

Coppard, A. E. The collected tales of A. E. Coppard

Corrington, J. W. The lonesome traveler, and other stories

Cortázar, J. End of the game, and other stories

Costain, T. B. ed. More Stories to remember

Costain, T. B. ed. Stories to remember

Costain, T. B. comp. Twelve short novels

Cournos, J. ed. Best world short stories: 1947

Coward, N. Bon voyage

Cozzens, J. G. Children and others

Crane, S. The complete short stories & sketches of Stephen Crane

Crane, S. Maggie, together with George's mother and The blue hotel

Crane, S. The portable Stephen Crane

Crane, S. The red badge of courage, and other stories (Oxford)

Crane, S. The red badge of courage, and other stories (Watts, F. Ultratype ed)

Dahl, R. Kiss, kiss

Dahl, R. Selected stories of Roald Dahl

Daniel, Y. This is Moscow speaking, and other stories

Davenport, B. comp. Famous monster tales

Davenport, B. ed. Ghostly tales to be told

Davenport, B. ed. Tales to be told in the dark

Davenport, B. ed. 13 ways to dispose of a body

Davenport, B. ed. 13 ways to kill a man

Day, A. G. ed. Best South Sea stories

Day, A. G. ed. Greatest American short stories

De La Mare, C. comp. They walk again

De La Mare, W. Collected tales

De Onis, H. ed. Spanish stories and tales

Derleth, A. The casebook of Solar Pons

Derleth, A. ed. The other side of the moon

Derleth, A. ed. Strange ports of call

Dickens, C. Best short stories

Dickens, C. Charles Dickens' Best stories

Dickens, C. Christmas stories

Dickens, C. Christmas tales

Dickens, C. Sketches by Boz

Dinesen, I. Last tales

Dinesen, I. Seven Gothic tales

Dinesen, I. Shadows on the grass

Dinesen, I. Winter's tales

Dostoevsky, F. The best short stories of Dostoevsky

Dostoevsky, F. The eternal husband, and other stories

Dostoevsky, F. The gambler, and other stories

Dostoevsky, F. An honest thief, and other stories

Dostoevsky, F. The short stories of Dostoevsky

Doyle, A. C. Exploits of Sherlock Holmes

Doyle, Sir A. C. Adventures and Memoirs of Sherlock Holmes

Doyle, Sir A. C. Adventures of Sherlock Holmes

Doyle, Sir A. C. The complete Sherlock Holmes

Doyle, Sir A. C. Famous tales of Sherlock Holmes

Doyle, Sir A. C. The later adventures of Sherlock Holmes

Doyle, Sir A. C. The memoirs of Sherlock Holmes

Doyle, Sir A. C. The Professor Challenger stories

Doyle, Sir A. C. Sherlock Holmes: detective

Doyle, Sir A. C. Sherlock Holmes' greatest cases

Doyle, Sir A. C. Tales of Sherlock Holmes

Dreiser, T. The best short stories of Theodore Dreiser

Dulles, A. ed. Great spy stories from fiction

Dumas, A. Short stories

Du Maurier, D. Kiss me again, stranger

Dunbar, P. L. The strength of Gideon, and other stories

EQMM annual, 1947-1968

Earley, G. W. ed. Encounters with aliens

Eca de Queiroz. The mandarin, and other stories

Elder, J. ed. The farthest reaches

Ellery Queen's Mystery Magazine. The quintessence of Queen

Ellin, S. The Blessington Method, and other strange tales

Ely, D. Time out

Fabricant, N. comp. A treasury of doctor stories by the world's great authors

Farrell, J. T. An omnibus of short stories

Fast, H. The general zapped an angel

Faulkner, W. Big woods

Faulkner, W. Collected stories of William Faulkner

Faulkner, W. The Faulkner reader

Faulkner, W. Go down, Moses, and other stories

Faulkner, W. Knight's gambit

Faulkner, W. The portable Faulkner

Faulkner, W. Selected short stories

Faulkner, W. The unvanquished

Fenton, C. A. ed. The best short stories of World War II

Ferber, E. One basket

Fiedler, L. A. Nude croquet

First-prize stories, 1919-1966

Fitzgerald, F. S. Babylon revisited, and other stories

Fitzgerald, F. S. The Fitzgerald reader

Fitzgerald, F. S. The Pat Hobby stories

Fitzgerald, F. S. The portable F. Scott Fitzgerald

Fitzgerald, F. S. Six tales of the jazz age, and other stories

Fitzgerald, F. S. The stories of F. Scott Fitzgerald

Fitzgerald, F. S. Taps at reveille

Fleming, I. Bonded Fleming

Flores, A. ed. Great Spanish stories

Foley, M. ed. Fifty best American short stories, 1915-1965

Foley, M. ed. U.S. stories

Forester, C. S. The man in the yellow raft

Forester, C. S. Mr Midshipman Hornblower

Forster, E. M. The collected tales of E. M. Forster

Friedman, B. J. Black angels

Friedman, B. J. Far from the city of class, and other stories

Gaines, E. J. Bloodline

Galaxy Magazine. The [first]-tenth Galaxy reader

Galsworthy, J. Caravan

Galsworthy, J. The Galsworthy reader

García Márquez, G. No one writes to the Colonel, and other stories

Garland, H. Main-travelled roads

Garrity, D. A. ed. 44 Irish short stories

Gass, W. H. In the heart of the heart of the country

Geist, S. ed. French stories and tales

Gilliatt, P. Come back if it doesn't get better

Gilpatric, G. The best of Glencannon

Gilpatric, G. The Glencannon omnibus

Glasgow, E. The collected stories of Ellen Glasgow

Godden, R. Gone

Gogol, N. The overcoat, and other stories

Gold, H. ed. Fiction of the fifties

Gordimer, N. Not for publication, and other stories

SHORT STORIES—*Continued*

Gordon, C. ed. The house of fiction
Gorky, M. A book of short stories
Gorky, M. Selected short stories
Gorky, M. Through Russia
Graham, S. ed. Great Russian short stories
Grau, S. A. The black prince, and other stories
Graves, R. Collected short stories
Greene, G. 21 stories
Hamalian, L. ed. Great stories by Nobel Prize winners
Hamalian, L. ed. Short fiction of the masters
Hamilton, A. ed. Splinters
Hammett, D. The big knockover
Hardy, T. Wessex tales
Harrison, H. ed. Nova I
Harte, B. The best of Bret Harte
Harte, B. The best short stories of Bret Harte
Harte, B. The Luck of Roaring Camp, and other sketches
Harte, B. The Luck of Roaring Camp, and other tales
Harte, B. Tales of the Argonauts
Harte, B. Tales of the gold rush
Havighurst, W. ed. Masters of the modern short story
Hawkes, J. Lunar landscapes
Hawthorne, N. The best of Hawthorne
Hawthorne, N. The complete novels and selected tales of Nathaniel Hawthorne
Hawthorne, N. Complete short stories of Nathaniel Hawthorne
Hawthorne, N. The Great Stone Face, and other tales of the White Mountains
Hawthorne, N. Hawthorne's Short stories
Hawthorne, N. Mosses from an old manse
Hawthorne, N. The portable Hawthorne
Hawthorne, N. Twice-told tales
Haycraft, H. ed. Fourteen great detective stories
Haycraft, H. ed. Ten great mysteries
Haycraft, H. ed. Three times three
Haycraft, H. ed. A treasury of great mysteries
Haydn, H. ed. A world of great stories
Healy, R. J. ed. Famous science fiction stories
Hecht, B. The collected stories of Ben Hecht
Heinlein, R. A. The green hills of earth
Heinlein, R. A. The menace from earth
Heinlein, R. A. The past through tomorrow
Heinlein, R. A. Waldo and Magic, inc.
Hemingway, E. Hemingway
Hemingway, E. The Hemingway reader
Hemingway, E. In our time
Hemingway, E. ed. Men at war
Hemingway, E. Men without women
Hemingway, E. The short stories of Ernest Hemingway
Hemingway, E. The snows of Kilimanjaro, and other stories
Hemingway, E. Winner take nothing
Henderson, Z. The people: no different flesh
Henry, O. The best short stories of O. Henry
Henry, O. The complete works of O. Henry
Henry, O. The four million
Henry, O. Tales of O. Henry
Hitchcock, A. ed. Alfred Hitchcock presents: A month of mystery
Hitchcock, A. ed. Alfred Hitchcock presents: My favorites in suspense
Hitchcock, A. ed. Alfred Hitchcock presents: Stories for late at night
Hitchcock, A. ed. Alfred Hitchcock presents: Stories my mother never told me
Hitchcock, A. ed. Alfred Hitchcock presents: Stories not for the nervous
Hitchcock, A. ed. Alfred Hitchcock presents: Stories that scared even me
Hitchcock, A. ed. Alfred Hitchcock presents: Stories they wouldn't let me do on TV
Hitchcock, A. ed. Alfred Hitchcock's Fireside book of suspense
Horgan, P. The peach stone
Howe, I. ed. A treasury of Yiddish stories
Hudson, W. H. Tales of the gauchos
Hudson, W. H. W. H. Hudson's Tales of the pampas
Hughes, L. The best of Simple
Hughes, L. ed. The best short stories by Negro writers
Hughes, L. Laughing to keep from crying
Hughes, L. Simple's Uncle Sam
Humphrey, W. A time and a place
Huxley, A. Collected short stories

If. The If Reader of science fiction
Inoue, Y. The counterfeiter, and other stories
Irving, W. Tales
Isherwood, C. Goodbye to Berlin
In Isherwood, C. The Berlin stories v2
Jackson, S. Come along with me: part of a novel, sixteen stories, and three lectures
Jackson, S. The lottery
Jacobs, H. The egg of the Glak, and other stories
Jacobson, D. Through the wilderness, and other stories
James, H. The American novels and stories of Henry James
James, H. The complete tales of Henry James
James, H. The ghostly tales of Henry James
James, H. The great short novels of Henry James
James, H. The short stories of Henry James
James, W. Will James' Book of cowboy stories
Jessup, A. The best American humorous short stories
Jewett, S. O. The best stories of Sarah Orne Jewett
Jewett, S. O. The country of the pointed firs, and other stories
Jhabvala, R. P. A stronger climate
Johnson, D. M. The hanging tree
Jones, J. The ice-cream headache, and other stories
Jones, L. Tales
Joseph, M. ed. Best cat stories
Joyce, J. Dubliners
Kafka, F. The penal colony
Kafka, F. Selected short stories
Kantor, M. Story teller
Kawabata, Y. House of the sleeping beauties, and other stories
Kemal, Y. Anatolian tales
Kemelman, H. The nine mile walk
The Kenyon Review. Gallery of modern fiction
Kielty, B. ed. Treasury of short stories
Kipling, R. The best short stories of Rudyard Kipling
Kipling, R. The complete Stalky & Co.
Kipling, R. Maugham's choice of Kipling's best
Kipling, R. Plain tales from the hills
Kipling, R. Puck of Pook's Hill
Knight, D. ed. Beyond tomorrow
Knight, D. ed. A century of science fiction
Knight, D. ed. Cities of wonder
Knight, D. ed. The dark side
Knight, D. ed. One hundred years of science fiction
Knight, D. Three novels
Knight, D. ed. Toward infinity
Knowles, J. Phineas
La Farge, O. The door in the wall
Lagerkvist, P. The eternal smile, and other stories
Lardner, R. The best short stories of Ring Lardner
Lardner, R. Haircut, and other stories
Laumer, K. Nine by Laumer
Laurence, M. A bird in the house
Laurence, M. The tomorrow-tamer
Lavin, M. In the middle of the fields, and other stories
Lawrence, D. H. The complete short stories
Lawrence, D. H. The woman who rode away, and other stories
Leacock, S. Happy stories just to laugh at
Leblanc, M. The confessions of Arsène Lupin
Lederer, W. J. The ugly American
Lenski, B. ed. Death of a simple giant, and other modern Yugoslav stories
Leskov, N. Selected tales
Lessing, D. African stories
Lessing, D. A man and two women
Lieber, M. ed. Great stories of all nations
Lin, Yutang, ed. Famous Chinese short stories
Linscott, R. N. ed. The best American humorous short stories
London, J. Best short stories
London, J. The call of the wild, and other stories
London, J. Jack London: short stories
London, J. Jack London's Tales of adventure
London, J. South sea tales
London, J. Stories of Hawaii
Lovecraft, H. P. The Dunwich horror, and others
Lowry, M. Hear us O Lord from heaven thy dwelling place

SHORT STORIES—*Continued*

McCullers, C. The ballad of the sad café

McFee, W. ed. Great sea stories of modern times

McFee, W. ed. World's great tales of the sea

Machen, A. Tales of horror and the supernatural

McPherson, J. A. Hue and cry

Magazine of Fantasy and Science Fiction. A decade of Fantasy and Science Fiction

Magidoff, R. ed. Russian science fiction, 1968-1969

Malamud, B. Idiots first

Malamud, B. The magic barrel

Malamud, B. A Malamud reader

Malamud, B. Pictures of Fidelman

Mallea, E. All green shall perish, and other novellas and stories

Manley, S. ed. Shapes of the supernatural

Mann, T. Stories of three decades

Mansfield, K. Bliss, and other stories

Mansfield, K. The garden party, and other stories

Mansfield, K. The short stories of Katherine Mansfield

March, W. A William March omnibus

Margolies, J. A. ed. Strange and fantastic stories

Maugham, W. S. Ashenden

Maugham, W. S. The best short stories of W. Somerset Maugham

Maugham, W. S. Cakes and ale, and twelve short stories

Maugham, W. S. Complete short stories

Maugham, W. S. Quartet

Maugham, W. S. Seventeen lost stories

Maugham, W. S. ed. Tellers of tales

Maugham, W. S. The trembling of a leaf

Maugham, W. S. Trio

Maupassant, G. de. Best stories of Guy de Maupassant

Maupassant, G. de. The complete short stories of Guy de Maupassant

Maupassant, G. de. The portable Maupassant

Maupassant, G. de. Selected short stories

Maupassant, G. de. Tales of Guy de Maupassant

Maurois, A. The collected stories of André Maurois

Maurois, A. Maurois reader

Melville, H. The complete stories of Herman Melville

Melville, H. Five tales

Melville, H. Piazza tales

Melville, H. Selected writings of Herman Melville

Merril, J. Daughters of Earth

Merril, J. ed. SF: best of the best

Merril, J. ed. The 6th-12th annual of the year's best SF

Michener, J. A. Tales of the South Pacific

Miller, A. I don't need you any more

Moore, R. The green berets

Moravia, A. Command, and I will obey you

Moravia, A. More Roman tales

Moravia, A. Roman tales

Morris, I. ed. Modern Japanese stories

Moskowitz, S. ed. Masterpieces of science fiction

Moskowitz, S. ed. Modern masterpieces of science fiction

Mystery Writers of America. Masters of Mayhem

Mystery Writers of America. Merchants of menace

Mystery Writers of America. Murder in mind

Mystery Writers of America. Sleuths and consequences

Mystery Writers of America. With malice toward all

Nabokov, V. Nabokov's dozen

Nabokov, V. Nabokov's quartet

Narayan, R. K. A horse and two goats

Natwar-Singh, K. ed. Tales from modern India

The New Yorker. 55 short stories from The New Yorker

The New Yorker. Short stories from The New Yorker

The New Yorker. Stories from The New Yorker, 1950-1960

Nebula award stories, [1]-4

Neider, C. ed. Great short stories from the world's literature

Neugeboren, J. Corky's brother

Oates, J. C. Upon the sweeping flood

O'Brien, E. J. ed. The great modern English stories

O'Connor, F. Everything that rises must converge

O'Connor, F. A good man is hard to find, and other stories

O'Connor, F. More stories

O'Connor, F. A set of variations

O'Connor, F. The stories of Frank O'Connor

O'Faolain, S. The finest stories of Sean O'Faolain

O'Faolain, S. The heat of the sun

O'Faolain, S. I remember! I remember!

O'Flaherty, L. The stories of Liam O'Flaherty

O'Hara, J. And other stories

O'Hara, J. Assembly

O'Hara, J. The Cape Cod lighter

O'Hara, J. 49 stories

O'Hara, J. The hat on the bed

O'Hara, J. The horse knows the way

O'Hara, J. The O'Hara generation

O'Hara, J. Selected short stories of John O'Hara

O'Hara, J. Waiting for winter

Orbit 1-6

Paley, G. The little disturbances of man

Parker, D. The collected stories of Dorothy Parker

Parker, D. Dorothy Parker

Paton, A. Tales from a troubled land

Patton, F. G. Twenty-eight stories

Petrakis, H. M. The waves of night, and other stories

Phillips, W. ed. Great American short novels

Pick, R. ed. German stories and tales

Pirandello, L. Horse in the moon

Pirandello, L. Short stories

Playboy. The Playboy Book of horror and the supernatural

Playboy. The Playboy Book of science fiction and fantasy

Poe, E. A. The best tales of Edgar Allen Poe

Poe, E. A. Complete stories and poems of Edgar Allan Poe

Poe, E. A. The complete tales and poems of Edgar Allan Poe

Poe, E. A. Edgar Allan Poe

Poe, E. A. Selected stories and poems

Poe, E. A. Short stories

Poe, E. A. Tales

Poe, E. A. Tales and poems of Edgar Allan Poe

Poe, E. A. Tales of mystery and imagination

Porter, K. A. The collected stories of Katherine Anne Porter

Porter, K. A. Flowering Judas, and other stories

Porter, K. A. The leaning tower, and other stories

Porter, K. A. Pale horse, pale rider

Potter, N. A. J. We have seen the best of our times

Powers, J. F. Prince of Darkness, and other stories

Price, R. The names and faces of heroes

Pritchett, V. S. Blind love, and other stories

Prize stories from Latin America

Prize stories, 1919-1970: The O. Henry Awards

Protter, E. ed. Monster festival

Pushkin, A. The captain's daughter, and other stories

Pushkin, A. The complete prose tales of Alexandr Sergeyevitch Pushkin

Queen, E. ed. Ellery Queen's Minimysteries

Queen, E. ed. 101 years' entertainment

Queen, E. Q.E.D. Queen's experiments in detection

Queen, E. Queen's Bureau of Investigation

Rahv, P. ed. Great Russian short novels

Rawlings, M. K. The Marjorie Rawlings reader

Rhodes, E. M. The best novels and stories of Eugene Manlove Rhodes

Ribalow, H. U. ed. Treasury of American Jewish stories

Rosa, J. G. The third bank of the river, and other stories

Roth, P. Goodbye, Columbus, and five short stories

Runyon, D. Best of Runyon

Runyon, D. Guys and dolls

Runyon, D. Runyon first and last

Saki. The short stories of Saki

Salinger, J. D. Nine stories

Sansom, W. The stories of William Sansom

Santesson, H. S. ed. The locked room reader

Saroyan, W. After thirty years: The daring young man on the flying trapeze

Saroyan, W. My name is Aram

Saroyan, W. The Saroyan special

Sartre, J. P. Intimacy, and other stories

The Saturday Evening Post. Best modern short stories

The Saturday Evening Post. Danger

SHORT STORIES—*Continued*

The Saturday Evening Post. The Post Reader of Civil War stories
The Saturday Evening Post. The Post Reader of fantasy and science fiction
The Saturday Evening Post. The Saturday Evening Post Reader of sea stories
The Saturday Evening Post. The Saturday Evening Post Reader of western stories
The Saturday Evening Post. The Saturday Evening Post Sports stories
Schaefer, J. The collected stories of Jack Schaefer
Schaefer, J. The Kean land, and other stories
Schaefer, J. ed. Out West
Schorer, M. ed. The story
Schulman, L. M. ed. The loners
Schwarz, L. W. ed. The Jewish caravan
Seltzer, T. comp. Best Russian short stories
Shaw, I. Love on a dark street, and other stories
Shaw, I. Selected short stories
Sholokhov, M. Fierce and gentle warriors
Sholokhov, M. Tales of the Don
Shulman, M. The many loves of Dobie Gillis
Sillitoe, A. Guzman, go home, and other stories
Sillitoe, A. The loneliness of the long-distance runner
Sillitoe, A. The ragman's daughter, and other stories
Silverberg, R. ed. Earthmen and strangers
Silverberg, R. ed. Men and machines
Silverberg, R. ed. Tomorrow's worlds
Silverberg, R. ed. Voyagers in time
Simak, C. D. All the traps of earth, and other stories
Simak, C. D. City
Simak, C. D. The worlds of Clifford Simak
Simenon, G. An American omnibus
Simenon, G. Short cases of Inspector Maigret
Singer, I. B. Gimpel the fool, and other stories
Singer, I. B. The séance, and other stories
Singer, I. B. Selected short stories of Isaac Bashevis Singer
Singer, I. B. Short Friday, and other stories
Singer, I. B. The Spinoza of Market Street
Sitwell, O. Collected stories
Slonim, M. ed. Modern Italian short stories
Spark, M. Collected stories: I
Spark, M. The go-away bird, and other stories
Stafford, J. Bad characters
Stafford, J. Children are bored on Sunday
Stafford, J. The collected stories of Jean Stafford
Starke, R. Something soft, and other stories
Steele, M. Where she brushed her hair, and other stories
Steinbeck, J. The long valley
Steinbeck, J. The portable Steinbeck
Stern, J. The stories of James Stern
Stevenson, R. L. The complete short stories of Robert Louis Stevenson
Stevenson, R. L. Dr Jekyll and Mr Hyde, The merry men & other tales
Stevenson, R. L. The strange case of Dr Jekyll and Mr Hyde, and other famous tales
Stockton, F. R. Best short stories of Frank R. Stockton
Stockton, F. R. The storyteller's pack
Story Magazine. Story jubilee
Story: the yearbook of discovery, 1968-1969
Struther, J. Mrs Miniver
Stuart, J. Come gentle spring
Stuart, J. My land has a voice
Stuart, J. Plowshare in heaven
Szilard, L. The voice of the dolphins, and other stories
Taber, G. One dozen and one
Taylor, E. A dedicated man, and other stories
Taylor, P. The collected stories of Peter Taylor
Tenn, W. ed. Once against the law
Thomas, D. Adventures in the skin trade, and other stories
Tolstoy, A. Vampires
Tolstoy, L. The death of Ivan Ilyitch, and other stories
Tolstoy, L. "Master and man," and other parables and tales
Tolstoy, L. Russian stories and legends
Tolstoy, L. Short stories
Tolstoy, L. Tolstoy's Tales of courage and conflict
Tolstoy, L. Twenty-three tales
Tomlinson, H. M. ed. Great sea stories of all nations

Torres-Rioseco, A. ed. Short stories of Latin America
Traven, B. The night visitor, and other stories
Turgenev, I. The district doctor, and other stories
Turgenev, I. A nest of gentlefolk, and other stories
Turner, J. ed. Unlikely ghosts
Twain, M. American claimant, and other stories and sketches
Twain, M. The complete short stories
Twain, M. The jumping frog, and other stories and sketches
Twain, M. The man that corrupted Hadleyburg, and other stories and essays
Twain, M. Mysterious stranger, and other stories
Twain, M. $30,000 bequest, and other stories
Twain, M. Tom Sawyer abroad, and other stories
Undset, S. Four stories
Updike, J. The music school
Updike, J. Pigeon feathers, and other stories
Updike, J. The same door
Ustinov, P. Add a dash of pity
Vance, J. Eight fantasms and magics
Van Doren, M. Collected stories v 1-3
Van Thal, H. ed. Great ghost stories
Voltaire. Voltaire's Candide, Zadig, and selected stories
Voltaire. Zadig, and other romances
Wagenknecht, E. ed. The fireside book of Christmas stories
Wagenknecht, E. ed. The fireside book of ghost stories
Wagenknecht, E. ed. The fireside book of romance
Wagenknecht, E. ed. A fireside book of Yuletide tales
Wang, Chi-chen, tr. Contemporary Chinese stories
Wang, Chi-chen, tr. Traditional Chinese tales
Warner, L. Mirrors
Warner, S. T. Swans on an autumn river
Weidman, J. My father sits in the dark, and other selected stories
Wells, H. G. Best science fiction stories of H. G. Wells
Wells, H. G. 28 science fiction stories
Wells, H. G. The war of the worlds, The time machine, and selected short stories
Welty, E. The bride of the Innisfallen, and other stories
Welty, E. The golden apples
Welty, E. Selected stories
West, J. The friendly persuasion
West, J. Love, death, and the ladies' drill team
Western Writers of America. Frontiers West
Western Writers of America. Rawhide men
Western Writers of America. Rivers to cross
Western Writers of America. They opened the West
Westlake, D. E. The curious facts preceding my execution, and other fictions
Wharton, E. The best short stories of Edith Wharton
Wharton, E. The collected short stories of Edith Wharton
Wharton, E. An Edith Wharton treasury
Wilhelm, K. The downstairs room, and other speculative fiction
Wise, H. A. ed. Great tales of terror and the supernatural
Wodehouse, P. G. The most of P. G. Wodehouse
Wodehouse, P. G. Selected stories
Wodehouse, P. G. Very good, Jeeves
Wolfe, T. From death to morning
Wolfe, T. The hills beyond
Wolfe, T. The portable Thomas Wolfe
Woolf, V. A haunted house, and other short stories
Wright, R. Eight men
Wright, R. Uncle Tom's children
Yarmolinsky, A. ed. A treasury of great Russian short stories
Zola, E. Three faces of love
Zoshchenko, M. Scenes from the bathhouse, and other stories of Communist Russia
  See also Novelettes

Short stories. Collins, W.

Short stories. Dumas, A.

Short stories. Poe, E. A.

Short stories. Tolstoy, L.

Short stories from The New Yorker, The New Yorker

The short stories of Dostoevsky. Dostoevsky, F.

The short stories of Ernest Hemingway. Hemingway, E.

The short stories of Henry James. James, H.

The short stories of T. Katherine Mansfield. Mansfield, K.

Short stories of Latin America. Torres-Rioseco, A. ed.

The short stories of Saki. Saki

A shorter Finnegans wake. Joyce, J.

Shorter novels of Herman Melville. Melville, H.

SHOT-PUTTING. See Athletes

Shotgun. McBain, E.

Show boat. Ferber, E.

SHOW BOATS
Ferber, E. Show boat

SHROPSHIRE. See England, Provincial and rural—Shropshire

SHROPSHIRE DIALECT. See Dialect stories—English—Shropshire

SIAMESE CATS. See Cats

The Siamese twin mystery. Queen, E.
In Queen, E. The bizarre murders p7-173

SIAMESE TWINS
Twain, M. Those extraordinary twins
In Twain, M. The complete novels of Mark Twain v2 p609-60
In Twain, M. Pudd'nhead Wilson and Those extraordinary twins p205-95

SIBERIA
Dostoevsky, F. The house of the dead
Pasternak, B. Doctor Zhivago
Verne, J. Michael Strogoff

The sibyl. Lagerkvist, P.

SICILY
Lampedusa, G. di. Two stories and a memory
Pirandello, L. The outcast
Vittorini, E. La Garibaldina
In Vittorini, E. The dark and the light p77-180

13th century
De Wohl, L. The joyful begger

19th century
Lampedusa, G. di. The Leopard
Verga, G. The house by the medlar tree

20th century
Clifford, F. Another way of dying
Hersey, J. A bell for Adano
Loraine, P. A Mafia kiss

Palermo
Charles-Roux, E. To forget Palermo

Sick heart river. See Buchan, J. Mountain meadow

Siddhartha. Hesse, H.

Sidney, oh Sidney. Rees, B.
In Rees, B. Try another country p 1-53

Siege. Corley, E.

The siege of London. James, H.
In James, H. Lady Barbarina, The siege of London, An international episode, and other tales p143-271

SIENA. See Italy—Siena

SIERRA MADRE. See Mexico—Sierra Madre

SIERRA NEVADA MOUNTAINS
Lofts, N. Winter harvest
Stewart, G. R. Fire

SIGHT SAVING BOOKS. See Large type books

Sight unseen. Lindop, A. E.

The sign of the four. Doyle, Sir A. C.
In Doyle, Sir A. C. The complete Sherlock Holmes v 1 p91-173
In Doyle, Sir A. C. Famous tales of Sherlock Holmes p187-311
In Doyle, Sir A. C. Tales of Sherlock Holmes p131-255

Silas Crockett. Chase, M. E.

Silas Marner. Eliot, G.
also in Eliot, G. The best-known novels of George Eliot p787-917

The silence of Colonel Bramble. Maurois, A.
In Maurois, A. Maurois reader

A silence of desire. Markandaya, K.

The silent Don. Sholokhov, M.

The silent people. Macken, W.

The silent sky. Eckert, A. W.

The silent Tarn. Closs, H.

The silver chalice. Costain, T. B.

SILVER MINES AND MINING
Conrad, J. Nostromo

Silver nutmeg. Lofts, N.

The silver spoon. Galsworthy, J.
In Galsworthy, J. A modern comedy p295-504

Silverhill. Whitney, P. A.

SILVERSMITHS
Costain, T. B. The silver chalice

SIMON CALLED PETER. See Peter, Saint, apostle

SIMON BAR KOCHBA. See Bar Kokba

The simple art of murder. Chandler, R.

Simple heart. Flaubert, G.
In Neider, C. ed. Short novels of the masters p220-48

A simple honorable man. Richter, C.

SIMPLE MINDED. See Feeble-minded

Simple speaks his mind. Hughes, L.

Simple stakes a claim. Hughes, L.

Simple takes a wife. Hughes, L.

Simple's Uncle Sam. Hughes, L.

SIN
Bernanos, G. Under the sun of Satan

SINAI CAMPAIGN, 1956. See Egypt—20th century—Intervention, 1956

Sincerely, Willis Wayde. Marquand, J. P.

Sing for your supper. Frankau, P.

SINGAPORE
Boulle, P. The bridge over the River Kwai
Kirk, L. The man on the Raffles verandah

Siege, 1942
Reeman, D. The pride and the anguish

The Singapore wink. Thomas, R.

SINGERS. See Musicians—Singers

Singing in the shrouds. Marsh, N.
also in Marsh, N. Another Three-act special p369-541

The singing sands. Tey, J.
also in Tey, J. Four, five and six by Tey v 1

A single pebble. Hersey, J.

The single voice. Charyn, J. ed.

SINGLE WOMEN
Aldrich, B. S. Miss Bishop
Andrić, I. The woman from Sarajevo
Ashton-Warner, S. Spinster
Auchincloss, L. The house of five talents
Balzac, H. de. Cousin Bette
Blackstock, C. The knock at midnight
Bryher. Beowulf
Capote, T. The grass harp
Carroll, G. H. Come with me home
Cowley, J. Nest in a falling tree
Faulkner, W. Intruder in the dust
Firbank, R. Inclinations
In Firbank, R. The complete Ronald Firbank p223-317
Forester, C. S. The African Queen
Gale, Z. Miss Lulu Bett
Gaskell, E. C. Cranford
Godden, J. In the sun
La Farge, C. The sudden guest
Laurence, M. A jest of God
Moore, B. The lonely passion of Judith Hearne
Morley, C. Parnasssus on wheels
Orwell, G. A clergyman's daughter
Patton, F. G. Good morning, Miss Dove
Read, Miss. Village Christmas
Rees, B. Poor Margaret
In Rees, B. Try another country p121-78
Richter, C. The aristocrat
Sarton, M. Joanna and Ulysses
Simenon, G. Maigret in Vichy
Warner, S. T. Lolly Willowes
In Warner, S. T. Lolly Willowes, and Mr Fortune's maggot p3-158
Wharton, E. The old maid
In Costain, T. B. comp. Twelve short novels p235-88
In Wharton, E. An Edith Wharton treasury
In Wharton, E. Old New York v2
White, R. Elephant Hill

A singular man. Donleavy, J. P.

SINN FEIN REBELLION, 1916. See Ireland—20th century—Sinn Fein Rebellion, 1916

SINUHE. See Sanehet

SIOUX INDIANS. See Dakota Indians

Sister Carrie. Dreiser, T.

SISTERS
Aldrich, B. S. Song of years
Austen, J. Pride and prejudice
Austen, J. Sense and sensibility
Bennett, A. The old wives' tale
Berlin, E. The best of families
Bromfield, L. The green bay tree
Capote, T. The grass harp
Chute, B. J. The moon and the thorn
Eden, D. Ravenscroft
Goudge, E. Green Dolphin Street
Halévy, L. Abbé Constantin
Harwood, A. So merciful a queen, so cruel a woman
Heyer, G. The convenient marriage
Heyer, G. Frederica
Jackson, S. We have always lived in the castle
Lin, Yutang. Moment in Peking
McKay, A. The women at Pine Creek
Randall, F. E. The place of sapphires
Read, Miss. Village Christmas
Stern, G. B. Mosaic
In Stern, G. B. The matriarch chronicles v3
Stevenson, J. Sisters and brothers
Swinnerton, F. Nocturne
Tanizaki, J. The Makioka sisters
Wharton, E. Bunner sisters
In Wharton, E. An Edith Wharton treasury
See also Brothers and sisters; Half-sisters

SISTERS (IN RELIGION) See Nuns

SISTERS AND BROTHERS. See Brothers and sisters

Sisters and brothers. Stevenson, J.

SIX-DAY WAR. See Israel—Arab War, 1967

Six-horse hitch. Giles, J. H.

Six impossible things. Cadell, E.

Six novels. Colette

Six tales of the jazz age, and other stories. Fitzgerald, F. S.

Sixes and sevens. Henry, O.
In Henry, O. The complete works of O. Henry p811-940

SIXTEENTH CENTURY
Braider, D. Color from a light within
See also subdivision: 16th century, under names of regions, countries, or states

The sixth of October. Romains, J.
In Romains, J. Men of good will

The 6th-12th annual of the year's best SF. Merril, J.

The sixth wife. Plaidy, J.

SKERRIES. See Islands

Sketches by Boz (Oxford) Dickens, C.

Sketches by Boz (St Martins) Dickens, C.

SKI RESORTS. See Hotels, taverns, etc

The skinning of Black Coyote. Fisher, C.
In Western Writers of America. A Western bonanza p247-69

SKIPPERS. See Seamen

SKIS AND SKIING
Troyat, H. Tender and violent Elizabeth

The sky and the forest. Forester, C. S.

The sky is red. Berto, G.

SKYE, ISLE OF. See Scotland—Isle of Skye

Skye Cameron. Whitney, P. A.

Slaughterhouse-five. Vonnegut, K.

SLAVE TRADE
Andrew, P. A new creature
Forester, C. S. The sky and the forest
Schoonover, L. The revolutionary
Steen, M. The sun is my undoing

SLAVERY
Bourne, P. Drums of destiny
Bristow, G. Deep summer
Bristow, G. The handsome road
Bryher. Gate to the sea
Cather, W. Sapphira and the slave girl
Courlander, H. The African
Dolan, M. Hannibal of Carthage
Koestler, A. The gladiators
Lofts, N. Silver nutmeg
MacInnes, C. Westward to Laughter
Stevenson, J. Sisters and brothers
Stowe, H. B. Uncle Tom's cabin
Styron, W. The confessions of Nat Turner

Twain, M. Pudd'nhead Wilson
In Twain, M. The complete novels of Mark Twain v2 p491-608
In Twain, M. Pudd'nhead Wilson and Those extraordinary twins p 1-204
Twain, M. Pudd'nhead Wilson and Those extraordinary twins
Walker, M. Jubilee
Warren, R. P. Band of angels
See also Abolitionists; Negroes; Slave trade

Fugitive slaves
Parrish, A. A clouded star

SLAVES. See Slavery

Slaves of the lamp. Frankau, P.

SLEEP
Heinlein, R. A. The door into summer

The sleep of reason. Snow, C. P.

SLEEP WALKING. See Somnambulism

The slender reed. Gerson, N. B.

Sleuths and consequences. Mystery Writers of America

SLOW LEARNING CHILDREN
Hutchinson, R. C. A child possessed
Wolff, R. A crack in the sidewalk

Slowly, by thy hand unfurled. Linney, R.

SLUM LIFE
Abrahams, P. Mine boy
Algren, N. A walk on the wild side
Bellow, S. The adventures of Augie March
Charteris, H. The coat
Crane, S. George's mother
In Crane, S. The complete novels of Stephen Crane p301-47
Crane, S. Maggie: a girl of the streets
In Blackmur, R. P. ed. American short novels p97-133
In Crane, S. The complete novels of Stephen Crane p99-154
In Crane, S. The portable Stephen Crane p3-74
Dickens, C. Oliver Twist
Farrell, J. T. Studs Lonigan
Green, G. The last angry man
Griffin, G. A last lamp burning
Llewellyn, R. None but the lonely heart
Mankowitz, W. A kid for two farthings
Motley, W. Knock on any door
Motley, W. Let no man write my epitaph
Nexo, M. A. Pelle the conqueror: The great struggle
In Nexo, M. A. Pelle the conqueror v3
Oates, J. C. Them
Petry, A. The street
Plunkett, J. Strumpet city
Sharp, M. Britannia Mews
Sillitoe, A. The ragman's daughter, and other stories
Simenon, G. The little saint
Smith, B. A tree grows in Brooklyn
Vargas Llosa, M. The green house
Vittorini, E. Erica
In Vittorini, E. The dark and the light p1-75
Wallant, E. L. The tenants of Moonbloom
Wright, R. Native son
See also Social problems

SLUMS. See Slum life

The small house at Allington. Trollope, A.

The small miracle. Gallico, P.
also in Gallico, P. Three legends: The snow goose; The small miracle; Ludmila p47-75

The small room. Sarton, M.

A small town in Germany. Le Carré, J.

SMALL TOWN LIFE
Aldrich, B. S. A white bird flying
Anderson, S. Poor white
Anderson, S. Tar: a midwest childhood
Anderson, S. Winesburg, Ohio
Arkin, F. The Dorp
Baker, E. The penny wars
Basso, H. The view from Pompey's Head
Beckham, B. My main mother
Bellamann, H. Kings Row
Bittle, C. R. A Sunday world
Bradbury, R. Dandelion wine
Caldwell, T. Testimony of two men
Calisher, H. False entry
Capote, T. The grass harp
Carroll, G. H. Come with me home
Chase, M. E. The edge of darkness
Chase, M. E. The lovely ambition
Chase, M. E. Mary Peters

SMALL TOWN LIFE—*Continued*

Chaze, E. Wettermark
Cheever, J. The Wapshot chronicle
Cheever, J. The Wapshot scandal
Chute, B. J. The moon and the thorn
Cockrell, M. The revolt of Sarah Perkins
Cozzens, J. G. By love possessed
Cozzens, J. G. The just and the unjust
Deal, B. The advocate
Dostoevsky, F. The friend of the family
Eckert, A. W. The crossbreed
Faulkner, W. Soldiers pay
Faulkner, W. The town
Foote, S. Love in a dry season
  In Foote, S. Three novels v3
Gale, Z. Miss Lulu Bett
Gass, W. H. Omensetter's luck
Giles, J. H. Shady Grove
Hammer, E. Spencer's Mountain
Hersey, J. The marmot drive
Humphrey, W. Home from the hill
Jackson, S. We have always lived in the castle
Jewett, S. O. The country of the pointed firs
  also in Jewett, S. O. The best stories of Sarah Orne Jewett v 1
  also in Jewett, S. O. The country of the pointed firs, and other stories p 1-226
Laxalt, R. A man in the wheatfield
Lee, H. To kill a mockingbird
Lewis, S. Main Street
Lockridge, R. Raintree County
McCullers, C. Clock without hands
McCullers, C. The heart is a lonely hunter
McWhirter, M. Hushed were the hills
Marius, R. The coming of rain
Marquand, J. P. Point of no return
Matthews, J. Hanger Stout, awake!
Moore, R. Second growth
Moore, R. Speak to the winds
Moore, R. Spoonhandle
Nathan, R. The devil with love
Ogilvie, E. The seasons hereafter
O'Hara, J. The instrument
O'Rourke, F. The bright morning
Parks, G. The learning tree
Patton, F. G. Good morning, Miss Dove
Price, R. A generous man
Price, R. A long and happy life
Queen, E. Cop out
Roth, P. When she was good
Saroyan, W. The human comedy
Smith, L. One hour
Steinbeck, J. East of Eden
Street, J. The gauntlet
Street, J. The high calling
Streeter, E. Chairman of the bored
Tarkington, B. Alice Adams
Tarkington, B. The gentleman from Indiana
Tarkington, B. Seventeen
Telfer, D. The night of the comet
Thompson, M. Not as a stranger
Tucker, H. The sound of summer voices
Turnbull, A. S. The gown of glory
Twain, M. Pudd'nhead Wilson
  In Twain, M. Pudd'nhead Wilson and Those extraordinary twins p 1-204
Warren, R. P. The cave
Wellman, P. I. The chain
Wellman, P. I. Jericho's daughters
Wellman, P. I. The walls of Jericho
Welty, E. The golden apples
White, N. G. The thorn tree
Williams, T. Whipple's castle
Wolfe, T. Look homeward, angel
Wolff, R. A trace of footprints
  See also subdivision: Provincial and rural, under names of foreign countries

The smiling rebel. Kane, H. T.

SMITH, SIR HARRY GEORGE WAKELYN, BART.
Heyer, G. The Spanish bride

SMITH, JOSEPH
Fisher, V. Children of God

SMITH, JUANA MARIA DE LOS DELORES DE LEON, LADY
Heyer, G. The Spanish bride

Smith of Wootton Major. Tolkien, J. R. R.

Smoke. Turgenev, I.
  also in Turgenev, I. The Borzoi Turgenev p3-164

Smoke over the prairie. Richter, C.
  In The Saturday Evening Post. The Saturday Evening Post Reader of western stories p333-58

SMUGGLERS. See Smuggling

SMUGGLING
Bagley, D. The golden keel
Coxe, G. H. The candid imposter
Creasey, J. Murder, London-South Africa
Du Maurier, D. Jamaica Inn
Eberhart, M. G. Message from Hong Kong
Fleming, I. Diamonds are forever
Hemingway, E. To have and have not
Kane, H. The narrowing list
  In Santesson, H. S. ed. The locked room reader p331-464
Marric, J. J. Gideon's river
Spark, M. The comforters
  In Spark, M. A Muriel Spark trio: The comforters; The ballad of Peckham Rye [and] Memento mori p13-228
Vargas Llosa, M. The green house
Wilder, R. Fruit of the poppy

The snake pit. Undset, S.
  In Undset, S. The master of Hestviken v2

The snake pit. Ward, M. J.

SNAKES
Laxalt, R. A man in the wheatfield

Snatch. Airth, R.

Snopes, v 1. See Faulkner, W. The hamlet

Snow country and Thousand cranes. Kawabata, Y.

The snow goose. Gallico, P.
  also in Gallico, P. Three legends: The snow goose; The small miracle; Ludmila p21-45

SNOW STORMS. See Blizzards; Storms

The snows of Kilimanjaro, and other stories. Hemingway, E.

So Big. Ferber, E.

So little time. Marquand, J. P.

So little time, and Point of no return. Marquand, J. P.

So long at the fair. Vermandel, J. G.

So love returns. Nathan, R.

So merciful a queen, so cruel a woman. Harwood, A.

So red the rose. Young, S.

So well remembered. Hilton, J.

SOCIAL CLASSES
Bellow, S. The adventures of Augie March
Griffin, G. A last lamp burning
James, H. A London life
James, H. The portrait of a lady
James, H. The Princess Casamassima
Morley, C. Kitty Foyle
O'Hara, J. Ourselves to know
O'Hara, J. A rage to live
O'Hara, J. Ten North Frederick
Popkin, Z. Herman had two daughters
Sorensen, V. Kingdom come
Waugh, E. Decline and fall
  See also Class distinction; Society novels

SOCIAL CONDITIONS. See Social problems

SOCIAL CONFORMITY. See Conformity

SOCIAL PROBLEMS
Abrahams, P. Mine boy
Alegría, C. Broad and alien is the world
Bellamy, E. Looking backward: 2000-1888
Bittle, C. R. A Sunday world
Buck, P. S. Command the morning
Caldwell, T. Dynasty of death
Caldwell, T. The final hour
Cronin, A. J. The citadel
Cronin, A. J. The stars look down
Cuomo, G. Among thieves
Dickens, C. Little Dorrit
Dos Passos, J. District of Columbia
Dos Passos, J. The 42nd parallel
Dos Passos, J. Manhattan transfer
Dos Passos, J. 1919
Dos Passos, J. U.S.A.
Dreiser, T. An American tragedy
Dreiser, T. Jennie Gerhardt
Farrell, J. T. Young Lonigan
Farrell, J. T. The young manhood of Studs Lonigan
Forster, E. M. A passage to India
Fuentes, C. Where the air is clear
Gironella, J. M. The cypresses believe in God
Godden, R. An episode of sparrows
Green, G. The last angry man
Greenberg, J. The Monday voices
Hlasko, M. The eighth day of the week
Hugo, V. Les misérables
Ikor, R. The sons of Avrom
Lewis, S. Ann Vickers
Llewellyn, R. None but the lonely heart
London, J. The iron heel

SOUTH AMERICA
Conrad, J. Nostromo
Doyle, Sir A. C. The lost world
Household, G. Dance of the dwarfs
Hudson, W. H. Tales of the gauchos
Hudson, W. H. W. H. Hudson's Tales of the pampas
Mallea, E. All green shall perish, and other novellas and stories
Matthiessen, P. At play in the fields of the Lord
Woolf, V. The voyage out
South by Java Head. MacLean, A.

SOUTH CAROLINA
Peterkin, J. Scarlet Sister Mary

18th century
Wilder, R. Wind from the Carolinas

19th century
Basso, H. The Light Infantry Ball
Fast, H. Freedom road

20th century
Basso, H. The view from Pompey's Head

Charleston
Bristow, G. Celia Garth
Heyward, Du B. Mamba's daughters
Heyward, Du B. Porgy
Mason, F. V. Our valiant few

SOUTH DAKOTA

19th century
Rolvaag, O. E. Giants in the earth
Rolvaag, O. E. Peder Victorious

Farm life
See Farm life—South Dakota

Frontier and pioneer life
See Frontier and pioneer life—South Dakota

South moon under. Rawlings, M. K.
also in Rawlings, M. K. The Marjorie Rawlings reader p3-270

SOUTH PACIFIC. See Islands of the Pacific

SOUTH SEA ISLANDS. See Islands of the Pacific

South sea tales. London, J.

SOUTH SEAS. See Islands of the Pacific

SOUTHAMPTON INSURRECTION, 1831
Styron, W. The confessions of Nat Turner

SOUTHEAST ASIA. See Asia, Southeastern

SOUTHEASTERN ASIA. See Asia, Southeastern

SOUTHERN DIALECT. See Dialect stories—Southern

SOUTHERN STATES
Capote, T. The grass harp
Corrington, J. W. The lonesome traveler, and other stories
O'Connor, F. Everything that rises must converge
O'Connor, F. A good man is hard to find, and other stories
See also Appalachian Mountains; Confederate States of America; Reconstruction; and names of individual states in this region

19th century
Courlander, H. The African
Ferber, E. Show boat
Lancaster, B. Night march
Mitchell, M. Gone with the wind
Walker, M. Jubilee
Wellman, P. I. The iron mistress
Yerby, F. The Foxes of Harrow
Young, S. So red the rose

20th century
Amis, K. I want it now
Ball, J. In the heat of the night
Bittle, C. R. A Sunday world
Daniels, L. Caleb, my son
Deal, B. The least one
Faulkner, W. As I lay dying
Faulkner, W. Pylon
Faulkner, W. The sound and the fury
Gaines, E. J. Bloodline
Grau, S. A. The keepers of the house
Grubb, D. Shadow of my brother
Haas, B. Look away, look away

Jarrell, R. Pictures from an institution
McCullers, C. Clock without hands
McCullers, C. The heart is a lonely hunter
McCullers, C. Reflections in a golden eye
Pharr, R. D. The book of numbers
Smith, L. One hour
Tucker, H. The sound of summer voices
Westheimer, D. My sweet Charlie

Farm life
See Farm life—Southern States

Frontier and pioneer life
See Frontier and pioneer life—Southern States

Mountain life
See Mountain life—Southern States

Politics
See Politics—Southern States
The southpaw. Harris, M.

SOUTHWEST
Humphrey, W. A time and a place
Rhodes, E. M. The best novels and stories of Eugene Manlove Rhodes
Richter, C. The sea of grass
Wellman, P. I. Ride the red earth

Frontier and pioneer life
See Frontier and pioneer life—Southwest

SOUTHWEST, NEW
Barrett, W. E. The lilies of the field
Becker, S. A covenant with death
Fergusson, H. Grant of kingdom
In Blacker, I. R. ed. The Old West in fiction p3-198
Horgan, P. A distant trumpet
Horgan, P. Far from Cibola
In Horgan, P. Mountain standard time: Main line west, Far from Cibola [and] The common heart p203-78
Laxalt, R. A man in the wheatfield
O'Rourke, F. The far mountains
Spicer, B. Kellogg Junction
See also New Mexico

Frontier and pioneer life
See Frontier and pioneer life—Southwest, New

SOVIET RUSSIA. See Russia

SPACE FLIGHT
Balchin, N. Kings of infinite space
Caidin, M. Four came back
Caidin, M. Marooned
See also Rockets (Aeronautics); Science fiction

SPACE FLIGHT TO THE MOON
Boulle, P. Garden on the moon
The space merchants. Pohl, F.

SPACE PROBES
Crichton, M. The Andromeda strain
Trevor, E. The shoot

SPACE SHIPS
Balmer, E. When worlds collide
Harrison, H. Captive universe

SPACE VEHICLES. See Space probes

SPAIN
Blasco Ibáñez, V. Blood and sand
Dolan, M. Hannibal of Carthage
Firbank, R. Concerning the eccentricities of Cardinal Pirelli
In Firbank, R. The complete Ronald Firbank p645-98
Merimée, P. Carmen

15th century
Schoonover, L. Key of gold
Schoonover, L. The prisoner of Tordesillas
Schoonover, L. The Queen's cross
Street, J. The velvet doublet

16th century
Cervantes, M. de. Don Quixote de la Mancha
Cervantes, M. de. Don Quixote de la Mancha; abridged
In Cervantes, M. de. The portable Cervantes p39-702
De Wohl, L. The last crusader
Heyer, G. Beauvallet
Shellabarger, S. Captain from Castile

17th century
Cervantes, M. de. The colloquy of the dogs
In Cervantes, M. de. Three exemplary novels p125-217

SPIES—*Continued*
Hall, A. The 9th directive
Hall, A. The Quiller memorandum
Hall, A. The Striker portfolio
Haycraft, H. ed. Five spy novels
Hodge, J. A. The winding stair
Howe, G. Call it treason
Kane, H. T. The smiling rebel
Kelly, M. Assault
Keyes, F. P. The chess players
Kirk, L. The man on the Raffles verandah
Lancaster, B. No bugles tonight
Lancaster, B. The secret road
Lathen, E. Murder against the grain
Le Carré, J. Call for the dead
In Le Carré, J. The incongruous spy v 1
Le Carré, J. The looking glass war
Le Carré, J. A small town in Germany
Le Carré, J. The spy who came in from the cold
Llewellyn, R. White horse to Banbury Cross
MacInnes, H. The double image
MacInnes, H. Pray for a brave heart
MacInnes, H. The Salzburg connection
MacLean, A. Ice Station Zebra
MacLean, A. The secret ways
MacLean, A. Where eagles dare
Macleod, A. The hireling
Mason, V. Maracaibo mission
Pentecost, H. The golden trap
Peters, E. The piper on the mountain
Poyer, J. North Cape
Priestley, J. B. Saturn over the water
Rosten, L. A most private intrigue
Shellabarger, S. The King's cavalier
Silone, I. The fox and the camellias
Simmel, J. M. Dear fatherland
Sinclair, U. Dragon harvest
Sinclair, U. One clear call
Sinclair, U. Presidential agent
Sinclair, U. Presidential mission
Sinclair, U. The return of Lanny Budd
Sinclair, U. A world to win
Spicer, B. Brother to the enemy
Stewart, M. Airs above the ground
Taylor, D. Farewell to Valley Forge
Taylor, D. Storm the last rampart
Uris, L. Topaz
Vonnegut, K. Mother night
West, M. L. The tower of Babel
West, R. The birds fall down
Westlake, D. E. The spy in the ointment
Woodhouse, M. Tree Frog
See also International intrigue; Secret service; World War, 1939-1945—Underground movements

Spies of good intent. Veraldi, G.

The Spinoza of Market Street. Singer, I. B.

Spinster. Ashton-Warner, S.

SPINSTERS. See Single women

Spinsters in jeopardy. Marsh, N.
also in Marsh, N. Three-act special p193-380

The spiral road. Hartog, J. de.

The spire. Golding, W.

SPIRIT LAKE, IOWA

Massacre, 1857
Kantor, M. Spirit Lake
Spirit Lake. Kantor, M.

SPIRITUALISM
Egan, L. A serious investigation
Gallico, P. The hand of Mary Constable
Jackson, S. The haunting of Hill House
Lurie, A. Imaginary friends
Michaels, B. Ammie, come home
Michaels, B. Prince of darkness
Somerlott, R. The inquisitor's house
Spark, M. The bachelors
Van Dyke, H. Ladies of the Rachmaninoff eyes

Splinters. Hamilton, A. ed.

SPLIT PERSONALITY. See Personality, Disorders of

The spoilers. Bagley, D.

The spoils of Poynton. James, H.

The spook who sat by the door. Greenlee, S.

Spoonhandle. Moore, R.

SPORTS
The Saturday Evening Post. The Saturday Evening Post Sports stories
See also names of sports, e.g. Boxing; Track athletics

Sports stories, The Saturday Evening Post. The Saturday Evening Post

The spring. Ehrenburg, I.
In Ehrenburg, I. A change of season p157-299

Spring came on forever. Aldrich, B. S.

The spring madness of Mr Sermon. See Delderfield, R. F. Mr Sermon

Spring muslin. Heyer, G.

The spy. Cooper, J. F.

A spy in the house of love. Nin, A.

The spy in the ointment. Westlake, D. E.

The spy who came in from the cold. Le Carré, J.

The spy who loved me. Fleming, I.
In Fleming, I. Bonded Fleming p329-439

The square. Duras, M.
In Duras, M. Four novels p 1-72

Square's progress. Sheed, W.

The squirt and the monkey. Stout, R.
In Stout, R. Kings full of aces p421-72

STAFFORDSHIRE. See England, Provincial and rural—Staffordshire

STAFFORDSHIRE DIALECT. See Dialect stories—England—Staffordshire

STAGE-COACH DRIVERS. See Stage-coach lines

STAGE-COACH LINES
Giles, J. H. Six-horse hitch

STAGE LIFE. See Theater and stage life

Stage of fools. Brady, C. A.

Stalemate. Berckman, E.

STALINGRAD. See Russia—Stalingrad

STALINGRAD, BATTLE OF, 1942-1943
Plievier, T. Stalingrad

Stalingrad. Plievier, T.

Stalky & Co., The complete. Kipling, R.

Stand on Zanzibar. Brunner, J.

STANHOPE, LADY HESTER LUCY
Stewart, M. The Gabriel hounds

The star-gazer. Harsányi, Z. de

A star in the wind. Nathan, R.

The star of Satan. See Bernanos, G. Under the sun of Satan

The star rover. London, J.

The stars grow pale. Bjarnhof, K.

The stars, like dust. Asimov, I.
In Asimov, I. Triangle: The currents of space, Pebble in the sky, The stars, like dust p347-516

The stars look down. Cronin, A. J.

Stars on the sea. Mason, F. V.

STARVATION
Hamsun, K. Hunger

STATE DEPARTMENT. See United States. Department of State

State of siege. Ambler, E.
In Ambler, E. The intriguers p169-290

STATESMEN. See Prime ministers

STATESMEN, ROMAN
Caldwell, T. A pillar of iron

STATUES
Gruber, F. The Etruscan bull
Olsen, P. The Virgin of San Gil

Steamboat Gothic. Keyes, F. P.

STEAMBOATS
Forester, C. S. The African Queen
Keyes, F. P. Steamboat Gothic

Steel and iron. Singer, I. J.

STEEL INDUSTRY
Bromfield, L. A good woman
In Bromfield, L. Bromfield galaxy: The green bay tree, Early autumn, A good woman p405-639
Davenport, M. The valley of decision
Hergesheimer, J. The three black Pennys

STEEPLECHASING. See Horse racing

STEPCHILDREN
Bottome, P. The mortal storm
Heyer, G. Bath tangle
Hutchinson, R. C. The stepmother
Updike, J. Of the farm
Wharton, E. The reef

STREAM OF CONSCIOUSNESS—*Continued*
Godden, R. Breakfast with the Nikolides
Grubb, D. The night of the hunter
Hamsun, K. Hunger
Hartog, J. de. The spiral road
Jones, L. Tales
Joyce, J. Finnegans wake
Joyce, J. A shorter Finnegans wake
Joyce, J. Ulysses
Lessing, D. The golden notebook
Lowry, M. Under the volcano
Morris, W. The field of vision
Proust, M. The captive
Proust, M. Cities of the plain
Proust, M. The Guermantes way
Proust, M. Jean Santeuil
Proust, M. The past recaptured
Proust, M. Remembrance of things past
Proust, M. Swann's way
Proust, M. The sweet cheat gone
Proust, M. Within a budding grove
Sarraute, N. The golden fruits
Sontag, S. Death kit
Styron, W. Lie down in darkness
Williams, W. C. The great American **novels**
In Blackmur, R. P. ed. American short
novels p307-43
Woolf, V. Jacob's room
Woolf, V. Mrs Dalloway
Woolf, V. To the lighthouse
Woolf, V. The waves
Woolf, V. The years

The street. Petry, A.

Street of riches. Roy, G.

The strength of Gideon, and others stories.
Dunbar, P. L.

Strictly business. Henry, O.
In Henry, O. The complete works of O.
Henry p1484-1631

The Striker portfolio. Hall, A.

STRIKES AND LOCKOUTS
Bissell, R. 7 1/2 cents
Bromfield, L. A good woman
In Bromfield, L. Bromfield galaxy: The
green bay tree, Early autumn, A good
woman p405-639
Cary, J. Not honour more
Galsworthy, J. Swan song
In Galsworthy, J. A modern comedy p578-
889
Howells, W. D. A hazard of new fortunes
Nexo, M. A. Pelle the conqueror: The great
struggle
In Nexo, M. A. Pelle the conqueror v3
Ousmane, S. God's bits of wood
Steinbeck, J. In dubious battle
Traven, B. The cotton-pickers
See also Labor unions

The Strode venturer. Innes, H.

STROKE. See Apoplexy

STROLLING PLAYERS
Dickens, C. The old curiosity shop
Goethe, J. W. von. Wilhelm Meister's appren-
ticeship
Priestley, J. B. The good companions
Sabatini, R. Scaramouche, the king-maker
Strong poison. Sayers, D. L.

Strong wind. Asturias, M. A.

A stronger climate. Jhabvala, R. P.

Strumpet city. Plunkett, J.

Students. See College life; School life

Studs Lonigan. Farrell, J. T.

A study in scarlet. Doyle, Sir A. C.
also in Doyle, Sir A. C. The complete Sherlock Holmes v 1 p3-88
also in Doyle, Sir A. C. Famous tales of
Sherlock Holmes p 1-131
also in Doyle, Sir A. C. Tales of Sherlock
Holmes p 1-129

SUBMARINE DIVING. See Diving, Submarine

SUBMARINE WARFARE. See Submarines;
also names of wars with subdivision Naval operations—Submarine, e.g. European
War, 1914-1918—Naval operations—Submarine; World War, 1939-1945—Naval operations—Submarine

SUBMARINES
Asimov, I. Fantastic voyage
Beach, E. L. Run silent, run deep
Benchley, N. The off-islanders
Catto, M. Murphy's war
Griffin, G. An operational necessity
Hardy, W. M. U.S.S. Mudskipper

MacLean, A. Ice Station Zebra
Rascovich, M. The Bedford incident
Reeman, D. The deep silence
Verne, J. Twenty thousand leagues under the
sea
Wheeler, K. The last Mayday

The subterraneans. Kerouac, J.

SUBURBAN LIFE
Arnow, H. S. The weedkiller's daughter
Braine, J. Life at the top
Cheever, J. Bullet Park
Cheever, J. The housebreaker of Shady Hill,
and other stories
Connell, E. S. Mr Bridge
Davis, C. First family
De Vries, P. Comfort me with apples
De Vries, P. Reuben, Reuben
De Vries, P. The tunnel of love
Dolson, H. Heat lightning
Franken, R. Claudia
Oates, J. C. Expensive people
Sheed, W. Square's progress
Shulman, M. Rally round the flag, boys!
Stead, C. The man who loved children
Updike, J. Couples
Wallop, D. The good life
Weingarten, V. Mrs Beneker
Wheeler, K. Peaceable Lane
Wilson, A. Late call
Wilson, S. The man in the gray flannel suit

SUBURBS. See Suburban life

SUBVERSIVE ACTIVITIES. See Terrorism

SUBWAY
Dreiser, T. The stoic

SUCCESS
Edmonds, W. D. Young Ames
Marquand, J. P. Sincerely, Willis Wade
O'Hara, J. Ten North Frederick
West, N. Cool million
In West, N. Complete works p143-256
See also Self-made men

SUCCESSION. See Inheritance and succession

SUDAN
Mason, A. E. W. Four feathers
See also Africa, West; Egypt

The sudden guest. La Farge, C.

Suds in your eye. Lasswell, M.

The sufferings of young Werther. Goethe, J. W.
von

SUFFOLK. See England, Provincial and rural—
Suffolk

SUGAR CANE PLANTATIONS
Keyes, F. P. The River Road

SUICIDE
Baroja y Nessi, P. The tree of knowledge
Barth, J. The floating opera
Brown, J. D. Kings go forth
Butler, W. The house at Akiya
Flaubert, G. Madame Bovary
Harrison, W. In a wild sanctuary
Pavese, C. Among women only
In Pavese, C. The selected works of Cesare
Pavese p175-275
Sheed, W. Pennsylvania gothic
In Sheed, W. The blacking factory & Penn-
sylvania gothic p3-63
Shute, N. The breaking wave
Styron, W. Lie down in darkness

SULTANS. See Arabia—Kings and rulers

The sum and total of now. Robertson, D.

SUMATRA
Cleary, J. The long pursuit

SUMMER
Bradbury, R. Dandelion wine
Grau, S. A. The hard blue sky
Smith, L. The last day the dogbushes bloomed

Summer 1914. Martin du Gard, R.

SUMMER RESORTS
Barrett, B. L. Love in Atlantis
Bawden, N. Devil by the sea
Carpenter, D. The murder of the frogs
In Carpenter, D. The murder of the frogs,
and other stories p79-130
Hunter, E. Last summer

Summer storm. Angoff, C.

SUMMER VACATIONS. See Vacations

SUMNER, CHARLES
Morrow, H. W. With malice toward none

SWITZERLAND
Daudet, A. Tartarin on the Alps
In Daudet, A. Tartarin of Tarascon
Edwards, A. The survivors

3d century
Bryher. Roman wall

18th century
Bryther. The colors of Vaud
Ramuz, C. F. When the mountain fell

19th century
James, H. Daisy Miller

20th century
Cronin, A. J. A pocketful of rye
Duerrenmatt, F. The judge and his hangman
Silone, I. The fox and the camellias
Ullman, J. R. The White Tower

Geneva
Ambler, E. The Intercom conspiracy
Macleod, A. City of light

Police
Duerrenmatt, F. The pledge
Duerrenmatt, F. The quarry

Politics
See Politics—Switzerland

SWITZERLAND, PROVINCIAL AND RURAL
Hesse, H. Peter Camenzind
The sword and the doll. Van der Post, L.
In Van der Post, L. The seed and the sower
p191-256
Sword at sunset. Sutcliff, R.
The sword in the stone. White, T. H.
also in White, T. H. The once and future
king p 1-213

SWYNFORD, KATHERINE. See Katherine,
Duchess of Lancaster

SYDNEY. See Australia—Sydney

Syla, the mink. Clarkson, E.

SYMBOLICAL NOVELS. See Symbolism

SYMBOLISM
Abé, K. The woman in the dunes
Agnon, S. Y. A guest for the night
Agnon, S. Y. Two tales
Balzac, H. de. The wild ass's skin
Barth, J. Giles goat-boy
Bellow, S. Henderson the rain king
Bernanos, M. The other side of the mountain
Bodsworth, F. The strange one
Böll, H. Billiards at half-past nine
Cela, C. J. Mrs Caldwell speaks to her son
Clark, W. V. The track of the cat
Conrad, J. The Nigger of the Narcissus
Durrell, L. The dark labyrinth
Faulkner, W. A fable
Fowles, J. The magus
Frederic, H. The damnation of Theron Ware
Gary, R. The dance of Genghis Cohn
Grass, G. Cat and mouse
Grass, G. Dog years
Grass, G. The tin drum
Hersey, J. The marmot drive
Hesse, H. Demian, the story of Emil Sin-
clair's youth
Hesse, H. The glass bead game (Magister
Ludi)
Hesse, H. The journey to the East
Hesse, H. Narcissus and Goldmund
Hesse, H. Steppenwolf
Jensen, J. V. Christopher Columbus
In Jensen, J. V. The long journey p491-677
Jensen, J. V. The Cimbrians
In Jensen, J. V. The long journey p227-487
Jensen, J. V. Fire and ice
In Jensen, J. V. The long journey p3-224
Joyce, J. Ulysses
Kafka, F. The castle
Kafka, F. The trial
Kafka, F. Metamorphosis
Kawabata, Y. Thousand cranes
Kazantzakis, N. The rock garden
Lawrence, D. H. The plumed serpent
Lind, J. Landscape in concrete
Mann, T. The black swan
Mann, T. Death in Venice
Mann, T. The magic mountain
Melville, H. Billy Budd, foretopman
Melville, H. Moby Dick
Morris, W. The field of vision
Murdoch, I. The unicorn
Murdoch, I. An unofficial rose
Nabokov, V. Ada
Nabokov, V. Pale fire
Nathan, R. Road of ages

Poe, E. A. The narrative of Arthur Gordon
Pym
Porter, K. A. Ship of fools
Pynchon, T. V
Rand, A. Atlas shrugged
Richter, C. The waters of Kronos
Shadbolt, M. This summer's dolphin
Sontag, S. Death kit
Spark, M. The go-away bird
In Spark, M. The go-away bird, and other
stories p74-137
Vesaas, T. The birds
Vesaas, T. Palace of ice
Wiesel, E. A beggar in Jerusalem
Woiwode, L. What I'm going to do, I think
Woolf, V. Between the acts
Woolf, V. The waves
See also Allegories; Parables

SYMPATHY
Zweig, S. Beware of pity

SYNAGOGUES
Tarr, H. Heaven help us!

SYRACUSE, SICILY
De Camp, L. S. The arrows of Hercules
Renault, M. The mask of Apollo

SYRIA
20th century
Werfel, F. The forty days of Musa Dagh

Antioch
Caldwell, T. Dear and glorious physician

Damascus
Leasor, J. Passport for a pilgrim

SYRIANS IN AFRICA, WEST
Greene, G. The heart of the matter

SYRIANS IN BRAZIL
Amado, J. Gabriela, clove and cinnamon

T

TVA. See Tennessee Valley Authority

TAHITI
Maugham, W. S. The moon and sixpence
Melville, H. Omoo

TAILORS
Asimov, I. Pebble in the sky
In Asimov, I. Triangle; The currents of
space, Pebble in the sky, The stars, like
dust p173-346
Mankowitz, W. A kid for two farthings
Markandaya, K. A handful of rice

Tai-Pan. Clavell, J.

Take heed of loving me. Vining, E. G.

Take three tenses. Godden, R.

The tale of Genji. Murasaki, L.

A tale of two cities. Dickens, C.

Tales. Irving, W.

Tales. Jones, L.

Tales. Poe, E. A.

Tales and poems of Edgar Allen Poe. Poe, E. A.

Tales before midnight. Benét, S. V.
In Benét, S. V. Twenty-five short stories
v2

Tales from a troubled land. Paton, A.

Tales from modern India. Natwar-Singh, K. ed.

Tales of adventure, Jack London's. London, J.

Tales of courage and conflict, Tolstoy's. Tolstoy, L.

Tales of Guy de Maupassant. Maupassant, G. de

Tales of horror and the supernatural. Machen,
A.

The tales of Jacob. Mann, T.
In Mann, T. Joseph and his brothers p3-258

Tales of land and sea. Conrad, J.

Tales of Manhattan. Auchincloss, L.

Tales of men and ghosts. Wharton, E.
In Wharton, E. The collected short stories
of Edith Wharton v2 p 1-206

Tales of my people. Asch, S.

Tales of mystery and imagination. Poe, E. A.

TEACHERS—*Continued*
Wahl, B. Rafferty & Co.
West, J. Leafy Rivers
Westlake, D. E. Up your banners
White, R. Elephant Hill
Whitney, P. A. Columbella
Wilson, A. Anglo-Saxon attitudes
Wolff, R. A trace of footprints
    See also College life; School life; Tutors

The Teahouse of the August Moon. Sneider; V.

TECHNOLOGY AND CIVILIZATION
Anderson, S. Poor white
Burdick, E. Fail-safe
Durrell, L. Tunc
Frayn, M. A very private life
Vonnegut, K. Cat's cradle
Vonnegut, K. Player piano
Yáñez, A. The lean lands

TEEN-AGERS. See Adolescence; Youth

TELEGRAPHERS
James, H. In the cage
    In James, H. The complete tales of Henry
    James v10 p139-242
Saroyan, W. The human comedy

TELEVISION
Buechner, F. The return of Ansel Gibbs
Green, G. The last angry man
Shulman, M. Anyone got a match?

TELEVISION PROGRAMS
Amis, K. I want it now

Tell me how long the train's been gone. Baldwin, J.

Tell me that you love me, Junie Moon. Kellogg, M.

Tell no man. St Johns, A. R.

Tellers of tales. Maugham, W. S. ed.

TEMPERANCE
Gulick, B. The hallelujah trail

The temple of the golden pavilion. Mishima, Y.

TEMPLES, BUDDHIST
Bridge, A. Peking picnic

TEMPLES, GREEK
Bryher. Gate to the sea

Ten days' wonder. Queen, E.
    In Queen, E. Wrightsville murders p379-575

Ten great mysteries. Haycraft, H. ed.

Ten little niggers. See Christie, A. And then
there were none

Ten North Frederick. O'Hara, J.

Ten-thirty on a summer night. Duras, M.
    In Duras, M. Four novels p141-239

The ten thousand things. Dermoût, M.

Ten years later. See Dumas, A. The Vicomte de
Bragelonne

TENANT FARMERS. See Farm tenancy

TENANT FARMING. See Farm tenancy

The tenant of Wildfell Hall. Brontë, A.

TENANTS. See Landlordism

The tenants of Moonbloom. Wallant, E. L.

Tender and violent Elizabeth. Troyat, H.

Tender is the night. Fitzgerald, F. S.
    also in Fitzgerald, F. S. The portable F.
    Scott Fitzgerald p169-545
    also in Fitzgerald, F. S. Three novels of
    F. Scott Fitzgerald v2

Tenderloin. Adams, S. H.

TENNESSEE
18th century
Mason, F. V. Wild horizon
19th century
Gerson, N. B. The Yankee from Tennessee
Lancaster, B. No bugles tonight
Marius, R. The coming of rain
20th century
Deal, B. Dunbar's Cove
Ford, J. H. The liberation of Lord Byron
Jones
McWhirter, N. Hushed were the hills
O'Connor, F. The violent bear it away
O'Connor, F. Wise blood
Stuart, J. Daughter of the legend
Warren, R. P. The cave
Wilson, G. The valley of time
Farm life
See Farm life—Tennessee

Frontier and pioneer life
See Frontier and pioneer life—Tennessee
Knoxville
Agee, J. A death in the family
Memphis
Faulkner, W. The reivers
Faulkner, W. Sanctuary

TENNESSEE VALLEY AUTHORITY
Deal, B. Dunbar's Cove
Wilson, G. The valley of time

The tents of wickedness. De Vries, P.

TEREZÍN (CONCENTRATION CAMP)
Bor, J. The Terezín Requiem

The Terezín Requiem. Bor, J.

Terra amata. Le Clézio, J. M. G.

TERRE HAUTE. See Indiana—Terre Haute

Territory. Anderson, P.
    In Anderson, P. Trader to the stars p55-124

TERRORISM
Albrand, M. Reunion with terror
    In The Saturday Evening Post. Danger
    p 1-106
Drury, A. Preserve and protect
Greenbaum, L. Out of shape
Kemal, Y. Memed, my hawk
Queen, E. Cop out
Schulberg, B. Waterfront
West, R. The birds fall down
Westlake, D. E. The spy in the ointment
Williams, J. A. Sons of darkness, sons of light

Tess of the D'Urbervilles. Hardy, T.

Testimony of two men. Caldwell, T.

Tevye's daughters. Aleichem, S.

TEXAS
Humphrey, W. The Ordways
18th century
Wellman, P. I. Ride the red earth
19th century
Barry, J. A shadow of eagles
Bass, M. R. Jory
Culp, J. H. The restless land
Erdman, L. G. The edge of time
Erdman, L. G. The far journey
Gipson, F. Old Yeller
Gipson, F. Savage Sam
Lea, T. The wonderful country
Le May, A. The unforgiven
Wellman, P. I. The Comancheros
19th century—Revolution, 1835-1836
Bryan, J. Y. Come to the bower
20th century
Ferber, E. Giant
Humphrey, W. Home from the hill
Owens, W. A. Look to the river
Frontier and pioneer life
See Frontier and pioneer life—Texas
Houston
Balchin, N. Kings of infinite space

TEXAS RANGERS
Wellman, P. I. The Comancheros

TEXTILE INDUSTRY
Bentley, P. Inheritance
Field, R. And now tomorrow
Singer, I. J. The brothers Ashkenazi
    See also Weavers

Textures of life. Calisher, H.

THAILAND
Bangkok
Hall, A. The 9th directive

Thaïs. France, A.

THAMES RIVER
Marric, J. J. Gideon's river

Thank you, Mr Moto. Marquand, J. P.
    In Marquand, J. P. Mr Moto's three aces
    p7-147

THANKSGIVING DAY
Capote, T. The Thanksgiving visitor

The Thanksgiving visitor. Capote, T.

That Callahan spunk! Ames, F. H.

That hideous strength. Lewis, C. S.

That Spanish woman. Kenyon, F. W.

Three-act special, Another. Marsh, N.

The three black Pennys. Hergesheimer, J.

Three blind mice. Christie, A.
  In Christie, A. Christie classics p357-410

Three by Heinlein. Heinlein, R. A.

Three by Tey. Tey, J.

Three cases for Mr Campion. Allingham, M.

The three cases of Shomri Shomar. Klinger, H.

Three cheers for the Paraclete. Keneally, T.

Three cities. Asch, S.

The three coffins. Carr, J. D.
  In Carr, J. D. A John Dickson Carr trio p 1-173

Three comrades. Remarque, E. M.

The three-cornered hat. Alarcón, P. A. de

The three daughters of Madame Liang. Buck, P. S.

Three detective novels. Carr, J. D.

Three exemplary novels. Cervantes, M. ed

Three exemplary novels and a prologue. Unamuno y Jugo, M. de

Three faces of love. Zola, E.

Three for McGee. MacDonald, J. D.

Three for tomorrow. Entered in Part I under title

The three guardsmen. See Dumas, A. The three musketeers

Three harbours. Mason, F. V.

The three hostages. Buchan, J.
  In Buchan, J. Adventurers all v3

Three legends: The snow goose; The small miracle; Ludmila. Gallico, P.

Three lives. Stein, G.

Three men in a boat. Jerome, J. K.

The three musketeers. Dumas, A.

Three novellas: Punin and Baburin, The inn, The watch. Turgenev, I.

Three novels. Foote, S.

Three novels. Knight, D.

Three novels of Ernest Hemingway. Hemingway, E.

Three novels of F. Scott Fitzgerald. Fitzgerald F. S.

Three romantic novels of Cornwall; Rebecca, Frenchman's Creek and Jamaica Inn. Du Maurier, D.

Three sheets in the wind. Gilpatric, G.
  In Gilpatric, G. The Glencannon omnibus v3

Three soldiers. Dos Passos, J.

3: This gun for hire, The confidential agent, The ministry of fear. Greene, G.

Three times three. Haycraft, H. ed

Three to show. Francis, D.

Three witnesses. Stout, R.
  In Stout, R. Royal flush p335-474

Threepenny novel. Brecht, B.

Three's company. Duggan, A.

Through Russia. Gorky, M.

Through the looking glass. Carroll, L.
  In Carroll, L. The annotated Alice p175-352

Through the Panama. Lowry, M.
  In Lowry, M. Hear us O Lord from heaven thy dwelling place p29-98

Through the wilderness, and other stories. Jacobson, D.

Thrush Green. Read, Miss

Thunder Heights. Whitney, P. A.

Thunder Moon. Brand, M.

Thunder on the right. Stewart, M.

Thunderball. Fleming, I.
  In Fleming, I. Bonded Fleming p 1-188

Thy tears might cease. Farrell, M.

TIBERIUS, EMPEROR OF ROME
  Dored, E. I loved Tiberius
  Douglas, L. C. The robe

TIBET
  Davidson, L. The rose of Tibet
  Hilton, J. Lost horizon

Tides of Mont St-Michel. Vercel, R.

Tight little island. See Mackenzie, C. Whisky galore

The tightening string. Bridge, A.

Till we have faces. Lewis, C. S.

TIME
  Hoyle, F. October the first is too late
  Nabokov, V. Ada

TIME, TRAVELS IN
  Anderson, P. The corridors of time
  Conklin, G. ed. Science-fiction adventures in dimension
  Davies, L. P. The white room
  Du Maurier, D. The house on the strand
  James, H. The sense of the past
  Moorcock, M. Behold the man
    In Nebula award stories, three pJ21-92
  Silverberg, R. ed. Voyagers in time
  Wells, H. G. The time machine

A time and a place. Humphrey, W.

Time and the wind. Verissimo, E.

Time for outrage. Bean, A.

The time machine. Wells, H. G.
  also in Wells, H. G. Seven science fiction novels p 1-76
  also in Wells, H. G. The war of the worlds, The time machine, and selected short stories p246-380

Time must have a stop. Huxley, A.

Time of hope. Snow, C. P.

A time of predators. Gores, J.

The time of the hero. Vargas Llosa, M.

A time on earth. Moberg, V.

Time out. Ely, D.

Time out of mind. Field, R.

Time probe: the sciences in science fiction Clarke, A. C. ed.

Time regained. See Proust, M. The past recaptured

A time to love and a time to die. Remarque, E. M.

The timeless land. Dark, E.

The tin drum. Grass, G.

The tin flute. Roy, G.

'Tis sixty years since. See Scott, Sir W. Waverley

The titan. Dreiser, T.

To be a pilgrim. Cary, J.
  also in Cary, J. First trilogy v2

To be read before midnight. See EQMM annual, 1946-1969

To Brooklyn with love. Green, G.

To catch a spy. Ambler, E. ed.

To find a man. Wilson, S. J.

To forget Palermo. Charles-Roux, E.

To glory we steer. Kent, A.

To have and have not. Hemingway, E.

To have and to hold. Johnston, M.

To kill a mockingbird. Lee, H.

To let. Galsworthy, J.
  In Galsworthy, J. The Forsyte saga p665-921

To live again. Silverberg, R.

To love and be wise. Tey, J.

To the coral strand. Masters, J.

To the gutter. Romains, J.
  In Romains, J. The depths and the heights

To the Indies. Forester, C. S.

To the lighthouse. Woolf, V.

To the stars. Romains, J.
  In Romains, J. The depths and the heights

To whom it may concern. Farrell, J. T.
  In Farrell, J. T. An omnibus of short stories v2

A toast to tomorrow. Coles, M.
  also in Coles, M. The exploits of Tommy Hambledon p163-347

TOBACCO
  Savage, M. Parrish

Tobacco road. Caldwell, E.

TODD, MARY. See Lincoln, Mary (Todd)

The Todd dossier. Young, C.

Toil of the brave. Fletcher, I.

Toilers of the sea. Hugo, V.

TOKYO. See Japan—Tokyo

Tolbecken. Shellabarger, S.

UNITED STATES—20th century—*Continued*
Deal, B. H. High lonesome world
Dos Passos, J. Chosen country
Dos Passos, J. District of Columbia
Dos Passos, J. The 42nd parallel
Dos Passos, J. Grand design
Dos Passos, J. Midcentury
Dos Passos, J. 1919
Dos Passos, J. U.S.A.
Dreiser, T. The bulwark
Fitzgerald, F. S. The beautiful and damned
Fitzgerald, F. S. The Great Gatsby
Hawley, C. The hurricane years
Hersey, J. The child buyer
Hunter, E. Last summer
Hunter, E. Sons
Kerouac, J. The Dharma bums
Kerouac, J. On the road
Knebel, F. Night of Camp David
Knebel, F. Trespass
Marquand, J. P. So little time
Masters, H. An American marriage
Mercer, C. The minister
St Johns, A. R. Tell no man
Sinclair, U. Between two worlds
Sinclair, U. Dragon's teeth
Sinclair, U. The return of Lanny Budd
Sinclair, U. World's end
Stern, R. M. Brood of eagles
Wallop, D. The good life

Air Force
Rosten, L. Captain Newman, M.D.
Tarr, H. The conversion of Chaplain Cohen

Air Force—Officers
Westheimer, D. Song of the young sentry
Westheimer, D. Von Ryan's Express

Armed Forces
Boyle, K. Generation without farewell
Knebel, F. Seven days in May

Army
Crumley, J. One to count cadence
Henry, W. The last warpath
Hooker, R. MASH
Jones, J. From here to eternity
Killens, J. O. And then we heard the thunder
McCullers, C. Reflections in a golden eye
Marquand, J. P. Melville Goodwin, USA
Myrer, A. Once an eagle
Ríos, T. The fifteenth pelican
Sinclair, H. The cavalryman
Sinclair, H. The horse soldiers
Taylor, D. Farewell to Valley Forge

Army—Officers
Aldrich, B. S. The lieutenant's lady
Brown, J. D. Kings go forth
Ford, N. R. The black, the gray, and the gold
Gulick, B. The hallelujah trail
Halberstam, D. One very hot day
Hemingway, E. Across the river and into the trees
Hersey, J. A bell for Adano
Hooker, R. MASH
Horgan, P. A distant trumpet
Jones, J. The thin red line
Keefe, F. L. The investigating officer
Kolpacoff, V. The prisoners of Quai Dong
Lancaster, B. Night march
Marquand, J. P. Melville Goodwin, USA
Mirdrekvandi Gunga Din, A. No heaven for Gunga Din
Myrer, A. Once an eagle
Nathanson, E. M. The dirty dozen
Prebble, J. The buffalo soldiers
Schaefer, J. Company of cowards
Shulman, M. Rally round the flag, boys!
Sneider, V. The Teahouse of the August Moon
Swarthout, G. They came to Cordura
Traver, R. Anatomy of a murder
Uris, L. Armageddon

Army. Special Forces
Moore, R. The green berets

Army Air Forces
Heller, J. Catch-22

Biography
Dos Passos, J. Midcentury

Bureau of Narcotics
Wilder, R. Fruit of the poppy

Central Intelligence Agency
Knebel, F. Vanished

Civilian defense
Wylie, P. Tomorrow!

Civilization
See United States—20th century

College life
See College life—United States

Communism
See Communism—United States

Congress
Land, M. Quicksand

Congress. Senate
Buechner, F. The return of Ansel Gibbs
Burroway, J. The buzzards
Carr, J. D. Papa Là-bas
Costain, T. B. Below the salt
Drury, A. Advise and consent
Dykeman, W. The far family
Knebel, F. Night of Camp David
Lipsky, E. The Devil's daughter
Pearson, D. The senator
Waugh, H. Run when I say go

Defenses
Shulman, M. Rally round the flag, boys!

Department of State
Galbraith, J. K. The triumph

Federal Bureau of Investigation
Stout, R. The doorbell rang

Labor and laboring classes
See Labor and laboring classes—United States

Marine Corps
Forrest, D. And to my nephew Albert I leave the island what I won off Fatty Hagan in a poker game
Uris, L. Battle cry

Marine Corps—Officers
Corley, E. Siege
Styron, W. The long march

Military Academy, West Point
Ford, N. R. The black, the gray, and the gold

National Aeronautics and Space Administration
Balchin, N. Kings of infinite space

Navy
Brinkley, W. The ninety and nine
Dodson, K. Away all boats
Forester, C. S. The man in the yellow raft
Heggen, T. Mister Roberts
Jennings, J. The Salem frigate
Jennings, J. The sea eagles
Jennings, J. The tall ships
McKenna, R. The Sand Pebbles
Mason, F. V. Rivers of glory
Melville, H. White-jacket
Michener, J. A. The bridges at Toko-ri
Rascovich, M. The Bedford incident
Schoonover, L. The revolutionary
Wouk, H. The Caine mutiny

Navy—Officers
Bassett, J. Harm's way
Beach, E. Run silent, run deep
Benchley, N. The wake of the Icarus
Brinkley, W. Don't go near the water
Brinkley, W. The ninety and nine
Forester, C. S. The good shepherd
Hardy, W. M. U.S.S. Mudskipper
Mandel, P. The Black Ship
Searls, H. The hero ship
Wouk, H. The Caine mutiny

Peace Corps
Knebel, F. The Zinzin Road

Politics
See Politics—United States

Post Office
Wright, R. Lawd today

Prisons
See Prisons—United States

Race problems
See Race problems—United States

VENUS (PLANET)
Lewis, C. S. Perelandra
VERDI, GIUSEPPE

Requiem
Bor, J. The Terezín Requiem
VERDUN, BATTLE OF, 1916
Romains, J. Verdun
Zweig, A. Education before Verdun
Verdun. Romains, J.
VERGILIUS MARO, PUBLIUS. See Virgil

The vermilion gate. Lin, Yutang
VERMONT

18th century
Van de Water, F. F. Catch a falling star
Van de Water, F. F. Day of battle
Van de Water, F. F. Wings of the morning

20th century
Buck, P. S. Letter from Peking
Mather, M. One summer in between
O'Hara, J. The instrument

Farm life
See Farm life—Vermont

Politics
See Politics—Vermont
VERMOUTH. See Wine and wine making
VERONICA, SAINT
Slaughter, F. G. The thorn of Arimathea
VERSAILLES. See France—Versailles

Very good, Jeeves. Wodehouse, P. G.

A very private life. Frayn, M.

A very quiet place. Garve, A.

VESSELS (SHIPS) See Ships

VESTALS
White, E. L. The unwilling vestal
VETERANS (BOER WAR)
Delderfield, R. F. A horseman riding by
VETERANS (CIVIL WAR)
Barry, J. Maximilian's gold
Redgate, J. Barlow's kingdom
VETERANS (EUROPEAN WAR, 1914-1918)
Deeping, W. Sorrell and son
Delderfield, R. F. The Avenue
Faulkner, W. Soldiers pay
Ford, F. M. The last post
In Ford, F. M. Parade's end p677-836
Remarque, E. M. Three comrades
Spellman, F. Cardinal. The foundling
VETERANS (KOREAN WAR, 1950-1953)
Moll, E. Seidman and son
Percy, W. The moviegoer
Warren, R. P. The cave
VETERANS (WORLD WAR, 1939-1945)
Algren, N. The man with the golden arm
Barrett, W. E. The glory tent
Böll, H. Absent without leave: two novellas
Böll, H. Enter and exit
In Böll H. Absent without leave: two novellas p91-148
Godden, R. The river
Haas, B. Look away, look away
Hutchinson, R. C. The inheritor
Hutchinson, R. C. The stepmother
Kerouac, J. On the road
Kirst, H. H. Brothers in arms
Knowles, J. Indian summer
Portis, C. Norwood
Shute, N. The breaking wave
Shute, N. The chequer board
Sorensen, V. The proper gods
Ustinov, P. The loser
Wilson, S. The man in the gray flannel suit
VETERANS DAY
Ford, F. M. A man could stand up
In Ford, F. M. Parade's end p503-674
VETERINARIANS
Gallico, P. Thomasina, the cat who thought she was God
Stewart, M. Airs above the ground
The Vicar of Wakefield. Goldsmith, O.

The Vicomte de Bragelonne [variant title: Man in the iron mask] Dumas, A.

The victim. Bellow, S.

VICTORIA, QUEEN OF GREAT BRITAIN
Anthony, E. Victoria and Albert
Bonnet, T. The mudlark
Victoria. Hamsun, K.

Victoria and Albert. Anthony, E.
VICTORIAN ENGLAND. See England—19th century
Victory. Conrad, J.
VIENNA. See Austria—Vienna
VIETNAM
Kolpacoff, V. The prisoners of Quai Dong
Moore, R. The green berets
West, M. L. The ambassador

Army—Officers
Halberstam, D. One very hot day

Saigon
Greene, G. The quiet American
West, M. L. The ambassador
VIETNAMESE CONFLICT, 1961-
Crumley, J. One to count cadence
Halberstam, D. One very hot day
Hunter, E. Sons
Kolpacoff, V. The prisoners of Quai Dong
The view from Pompey's Head. Basso, H.
The view from the fortieth floor. White, T. H.
VIKINGS
Bengtsson, F. G. The long ships
Seton, A. Avalon
Vile bodies. Waugh, E.
Village Christmas. Read, Miss
VILLAGE LIFE. See phrase: Provincial and rural, after names of foreign countries, e.g. England, Provincial and rural. For the United States, see Small town life
Villette. Brontë, C.
Vincent. Poldermans, J.
VINCENZO I GONZAGA, DUKE OF MANTUA
Peyrefitte, R. The prince's person
VINCI, LEONARDO DA. See Leonardo da Vinci
The vines of Yarrabee. Eden, D.
VINEYARDS. See Viticulture
The Vintage Bradbury. Bradbury, R.
The vintage season. Moore, C. L.
In Hitchcock, A. ed. Alfred Hitchcock presents: Stories for late at night p100-40
VIOLENCE
Monsarrat, N. Richer than all his tribe
See also Murder stories; Terrorism
The violent bear it away. O'Connor, F.

The violent land. Amado, J.

VIOLINISTS. See Musicians—Violinists
Vipers' tangle. Mauriac, F.
VIRGIL
Davidson, A. The phoenix and the mirror
VIRGIN ISLANDS. See St Thomas
VIRGIN MARY. See Mary, Virgin
The Virgin of San Gil. Olsen, P.
Virgin soil. Turgenev, I.
Virgin soil upturned. See Sholokhov, M. Seeds of tomorrow
VIRGINIA

To 1800
Gerson, N. B. Give me liberty
Johnston, M. To have and to hold
Page E. The tree of liberty
Page, E. Wilderness adventure
Settle, M. L. O Beulah Land
Thackeray, W. M. The Virginians

17th century
Defoe, D. The fortunes and misfortunes of the famous Moll Flanders

18th century
Seton, A. Devil Water

19th century
Cather, W. Sapphira and the slave girl
Davis, P. The seasons of heroes
Kane, H. T. The lady of Arlington
Styron, W. The confessions of Nat Turner
Williams, B. A. House divided

20th century
Davis, P. The seasons of heroes
Glasgow, E. In this our life
Glasgow, E. Vein of iron
Hamner, E. Spencer's Mountain
Murphy, R. The Pond
Styron, W. Lie down in darkness

WAR—*Continued*
De Camp, L. S. The arrows of Hercules
Faulkner, W. A fable
Frank, P. Alas, Babylon
Hemingway, E. ed. Men at war
Macken, W. Seek the fair land
Marquand, J. P. So little time
Merle, R. The day of the dolphin
Moravia, A. Two women
Myrer, A. Once an eagle
Rosa, J. G. The devil to pay in the Backlands
Sholokhov, M. And quiet flows the Don
Sholokhov, M. The Don flows home to th
sea
Tapsell, R. F. The year of the horsetails
Wibberley, L. Beware of the mouse
Zola, E. The debacle
Zweig, A. The case of Sergeant Grischa
Zweig, A. Education before Verdum
Zweig, A. Young woman of 1914
See also Battles; also names of wars and
battles, e.g. Lexington, Battle of, 1775;
World War, 1939-1945; also Indians of North
America—Wars
War and peace. Tolstoy, L.

WAR CORRESPONDENTS. See Journalists

WAR CRIME TRIALS
Shaw, R. The man in the glass booth
Nuremburg, 1946-1949
Sinclair, U. O shepherd, speak!

WAR CRIMINALS
Marlowe, S. The search for Bruno Heidler
The war lover. Hersey, J.

WAR OF 1812. See United States—19th century
War of 1812

WAR OF THE ROSES. See England—15th century

The war of the worlds. Wells, H. G.
also in Wells, H. G. Seven science fiction
novels p307-453
The war of the worlds, The time machine, and
selected short stories. Wells, H. G.

WAR PRISONERS. See Prisoners of war

WAR WITH MEXICO, 1845-1848. See United
States—19th century—War with Mexico,
1845-1848

WARBECK, PERKIN
Harwood, A. Merchant of the ruby

WARD, JOHN
Costain, T. B. For my great folly
Ward no. 6. Chekhov, A. P.
In Neider, C. ed. Short novels of the master
p386-438
Ward 7. Tarsis, V.

The warden. Trollope, A.

WARDENS, PRISON. See Prison wardens

WARDS. See Guardian and ward

WARFARE. See War

Warlock. Hall, O.

Warrant for X. MacDonald, P.
In MacDonald, P. Triple jeopardy p5-204
WARSAW. See Poland—Warsaw

WARSHIPS
Dodson, K. Away all boats
Forester, C. S. The ship
McKenna, R. The Sand Pebbles
Reeman, D. H.M.S. Saracen
Reeman, D. The pride and the anguish

WARWICKSHIRE. See England, Provincial
and rural—Warwickshire

WASHINGTON, GEORGE, PRESIDENT U.S.
Boyce, B. Man from Mt Vernon
Ford, P. L. Janice Meredith

WASHINGTON, MARTHA (DANDRIDGE)
CUSTI
Boyce, B. Man from Mt Vernon

WASHINGTON FAMILY
Boyce, B. Man from Mt Vernon

WASHINGTON (STATE)
McKay, A. They came to a river
McKay, A. The women at Pine Creek
White, S. E. Wild geese calling
Frontier and pioneer life
See Frontier and pioneer life—Washington
(State)

WASHINGTON, D. C.
19th century
Adams, H. Democracy
Kane, H. T. Bride of fortune
20th century
Blair, C. The board room
Dos Passos, J. Grand design
Drury, A. Advise and consent
Drury, A. Capable of honor
Knebel, F. Vanished
Marquand, J. P. B. F.'s daughter
Pearson, D. The senator
Serling, R. J. The President's plane is missing
Stead, C. The man who loved children
Washington Square. James, H.
also in Blackmur, R. P. ed. American short
novels p134-235
also in James, H. The American novels and
stories of Henry James p162-295
also in James, H. The Henry James reader
p 1-163
also in James, H. Short novels of Henry
James p59-256
also in Phillips, W. ed. Great American
short novels p79-236
Washington Square, and Daisy Miller, James,
H.
The watch. Turgenev, I.
In Turgenev, I. Three novellas: Punin and
Baburin, The inn, The watch p149-208
Watch on the bridge. Garth, D.
Watcher in the shadows. Household, G.
The watchers. Van Siller, H.
WATCHES. See Clocks and watches
The watchmaker of Everton. Simenon, G.
In Simenon, G. An American omnibus
p379-500
The waterfall. Drabble, M.
Waterfront. Schulberg, B.
WATERLOO, BATTLE OF, 1815
Heyer, G. An infamous army
The waters of Kronos. Richter, C.
Waters on a starry night. Ogilvie, E.
The waters under the earth. Moore, J.
The Watsons. Austen, J.
Waverley. Scott, Sir W.
The waves. Woolf, V.
The waves of night, and other stories. Petrakis, H. M.
Wax apple. Coe, T.
WAX WORKS
Martin, S. I, Madame Tussaud
The way home. Richardson, H. H.
In Richardson, H. H. The fortunes of
Richard Mahony v2
The way of all flesh. Butler, S.
The way some people die. Macdonald, R.
In Macdonald, R. Archer in Hollywood
p347-528
Way Station. Simak, C. D.
The way we live now. Trollope, A.
The way west. Guthrie, A. B.
The wayward bus. Steinbeck, J.
We all die naked. Silverberg, R.
In Three for tomorrow p153-204
We have always lived in the castle. Jackson, S.
We have seen the best of our times. Potter,
N. A. J.
We print the truth. Boucher, A.
In Boucher, A. The compleat werewolf, and
other stories of fantasy and science fiction p170-239
We the living. Rand, A.
WEALTH
Amis, K. I want it now
Auchincloss, L. The house of five talents
Auchincloss, L. A world of profit
Balzac, H. de. Eugénie Grandet
Basso, H. A touch of the dragon
Caldwell, T. A prologue to love
Costain, T. B. The tontine
Cunningham, E. V. Penelope
Donleavy, J. P. A singular man
Dostoevsky, F. A raw youth
Dumitriu, P. The extreme Occident

WEALTH—*Continued*
Eca de Queiroz. The mandarin
  In Eca de Queiroz. The mandarin, and other stories p3-89
Fitzgerald, F. S. The beautiful and damned
Fitzgerald, F. S. The Great Gatsby
Fitzgerald, F. S. The rich boy
  In Fitzgerald, F. S. The Fitzgerald reader p239-75
Fitzgerald, F. S. Tender is the night
Horgan, P. Everything to live for
Knowles, J. Indian summer
Marquand, J. P.   B. F.'s daughter
O'Hara, J. From the terrace
O'Hara, J. The Lockwood concern
Pavese, C. Among women only
  In Pavese, C. The selected works of Cesare Pavese p175-275
Pritchett, V. S. The key to my heart
Symons, J. The man whose dreams came true
Vonnegut, K. God bless you, Mr Rosewater
  See also Capitalists and financiers; Millionaires

The weapon makers. Van Vogt, A. E.
The weapon shops of Isher. Van Vogt, A. E.
WEAPONS. See Munitions
WEATHER
Stewart, G. R. Storm
  See also Hurricanes; Storms
WEAVERS
Eastlake, W. Portrait of an artist with twenty-six horses
Eliot, G. Silas Marner
Singer, I. J. The brothers Ashkenazi
Wahl, B. Rafferty & Co.
The web and the rock. Wolfe, T.
The web of earth. Wolfe, T.
  In Wolfe, T. The short novels of Thomas Wolfe p76-154
WEBSTER, DANIEL
Benét, S. V. The Devil and Daniel Webster
The wedding bargain. Turnbull, A. S.
The wedding group. Taylor, E.
The wedding journey. Edmonds, W. D.
WEDDINGS
Jensen, J. V. The Cimbrians
  In Jensen, J. V. The long journey p227-487
Kauffmann, L. An honorable estate
Lindbergh, A. M. Dearly beloved
Streeter, E. Father of the bride
Welty, E. Delta wedding
  See also Marriage
The weedkiller's daughter. Arnow, H. S.
The weigher of souls. Maurois, A.
  In Maurois, A. Maurois reader
WEIMAR. See Germany—Weimar
Weir of Hermiston. Stevenson, R. L.
Welcome to the monkey house. Vonnegut, K.
Welcome to Xanadu. Benchley, N.
WELFARE. See War
WELFARE STATE. See Industry and state
The well-beloved. Hardy, T.
The well of loneliness. Hall, R.
WELLINGTON, ARTHUR WELLESLEY, 1ST DUKE OF
Heyer, G. An infamous army
WELSH DIALECT. See Dialect stories—Welsh
WELSH IN SOUTH AMERICA
Llewellyn, R. Up, into the singing mountain
WELSH IN THE NEAR EAST
Innes, H. The doomed oasis
WENTWORTH, FRANCES (WENTWORTH) LADY
Raddall, T. H. The Governor's lady
WENTWORTH, SIR JOHN
Raddall, T. H. The Governor's lady
We're friends again. O'Hara, J.
  In O'Hara, J. Sermons and soda water v3
The werewolf principle. Simak, C. D.
WERWOLVES
Boucher, A. The compleat werewolf
  In Boucher, A. The compleat werewolf, and other stories of fantasy and science fiction p7-62
WESLEY, JOHN
Andrew, P. A new creature
Wessex tales. Hardy, T.

THE WEST
Blacker, I. R. ed. The Old West in fiction
Henry, W. Alias Butch Cassidy
  See also Adventure; Cowboys; Frontier and pioneer life—The West; Ranch life; Western stories; also names of states in this region
19th century
Guthrie, A. B. The big sky
Farm life
See Farm life—The West
Frontier and pioneer life
See Frontier and pioneer life—The West
WEST AFRICA. See Africa, West
WEST INDIANS
Anthony, M. Green days by the river
WEST INDIES
Atherton, G. The conqueror
Firbank, R. Prancing nigger
  In Firbank, R. The complete Ronald Firbank p593-643
Forester, C. S. Admiral Hornblower in the West Indies
Forester, C. S. The captain from Connecticut
MacInnes, C. Westward to Laughter
Pope, D. The Triton brig
Steinbeck, J. Cup of gold
Waugh, A. Island in the sun
Wilder, R. Wind from the Carolinas
  See also Bahamas; Caribbean Islands; Trinidad
WEST POINT MILITARY ACADEMY. See United States. Military Academy, West Point
WEST VIRGINIA
Grubb, D. Fools' parade
Grubb, D. The night of the hunter
WESTCHESTER COUNTY. See New York (State)—Westchester County
A Western bonanza. Western Writers of America
WESTERN CIVILIZATION. See Civilization, Occidental
WESTERN STORIES
Adams, A. Log of a cowboy
Adams, C. Tragg's choice
Barry, J. Maximilian's gold
Bass, M. R. Jory
Bean, A. Time for outrage
Berger, T. Little Big Man
Blacker, I. R. ed. The Old West in fiction
Brand, M. The Stingaree
Brand, M. Thunder Moon
Cheshire, G. Ambush at Bedrock
Clark, W. V. The Ox-bow incident
Culp, J. H. The bright feathers
Flynn, R. North to yesterday
Giles, J. H. Six-horse hitch
Grey, Z. The Arizona clan
Grey, Z. Riders of the purple sage
Grey, Z. The vanishing American
Gulick, B. The hallelujah trail
Gulick, B. Liveliest town in the West
Guthrie, A. B. The way west
Hall, O. Warlock
Henderson, Z. The people: no different flesh
Henry, W. The last warpath
Henry, W. Mackenna's gold
Horgan, P. Main line west
  In Horgan, P. Mountain standard time: Main line west, Far from Cibola [and] The common heart p 1-201
Hough, E. The covered wagon
Huffman, L. A house behind the mint
Hunt, J. The Grey Horse legacy
James, W. The American cowboy
James, W. Sand
James, W. Will James' Book of cowboy stories
Johnson, D. M. The hanging tree
Lea, T. The wonderful country
Le May, A. The unforgiven
Lott, M. The last hunt
O'Rourke, F. The swift runner
Portis, C. True grit
The Saturday Evening Post. The Saturday Evening Post Reader of western stories
Schaefer, J. The canyon
  In Schaefer, J. The short novels of Jack Schaefer p221-316
Schaefer, J. The collected stories of Jack Schaefer
Schaefer, J. Company of cowards

WESTERN STORIES—*Continued*
Schaefer, J. First blood
  In Schaefer, J. The short novels of Jack Schaefer p113-220
Schaefer, J. The Kean land
  In Schaefer, J. The short novels of Jack Schaefer p461-525
Schaefer, J. The Kean land, and other stories
Schaefer, J. Monte Walsh
Schaefer, J. ed. Out West
Schaefer, J. Shane
Schaefer, J. The short novels of Jack Schaefer
Wellman, P. I. The Comancheros
Western Writers of America. Frontiers West
Western Writers of America. Rawhide men
Western Writers of America. Rivers to cross
Western Writers of America. They opened the West
Western Writers of America. A Western bonanza
White, S. E. The long rifle
  See also Cowboys; Frontier and pioneer life—The West; Ranch life; The West; also names of states in this region
Westward ho! Kingsley, C.
Westward—to blood and glory. Farrell, C.
  In Western Writers of America. A Western bonanza p190-246
Westward to Laughter. MacInnes, C.
Wettermark. Chaze, E.

WHALES
Clarke, A. C. The deep range
Melville, H. Moby Dick

WHALING
Carse, R. Great circle
Mason, F. V. Harpoon in Eden
Melville, H. Moby Dick
Van der Post, L. The hunter and the whale
What a way to go. Morris, W.
What became of Gunner Asch. Kirst, H. H.
What Maisie knew, In the cage, The pupil. James, H.
What makes Sammy run? Schulberg, B.
What men live by. See Tolstoy, L. Russian stories and legends
What Mrs McGillicuddy saw! Christie, A.
What's become of Waring. Powell, A.

WHEAT
Norris, F. The octopus
Norris, F. The pit
When a man murders. Stout, R.
  In Stout, R. Royal flush p385-430
When eight bells toll. MacLean, A.
When in Greece. Lathen, E.
When knighthood was in flower. Major, C.
When Michael calls. Farris, J.
When rain clouds gather. Head, B.
When she was good. Roth, P.
When the enemy is tired. Braddon, R.
When the legends die. Borland, H.
When the mountain fell. Ramuz, C. F.
When the War is over. Becker, S.
When worlds collide. Balmer, E.
Where eagles dare. MacLean, A.
Where she brushed her hair, and other stories. Steele, M.
Where the air is clear. Fuentes, C.
A whiff of death. Asimov, I.
Whipple's castle. Williams, T.
Whirligigs. Henry, O.
  In Henry, O. The complete works of O. Henry p1094-1252

WHISKEY
Mackenzie C. Whisky galore
Whisky galore. Mackenzie, C.
A white bird flying. Aldrich, B. S.
  also in Aldrich, B. S. The Bess Streeter Aldrich reader p211-392
The white boar. Palmer, M.
The White Company. Doyle, Sir A. C.
The white crow. Jameson, S.
White eagles over Serbia. Durrell, L.
White Fang. London, J.
White Fang, and other stories. London, J.
White horse to Banbury Cross. Llewellyn, R.

White-jacket. Melville, H.
White man. Freuchen, P.
The white man's road. Capps, B.
The white monkey. Galsworthy, J.
  In Galsworthy, J. A modern comedy p3-248
The white peacock. Lawrence, D. H.
The white room. Davies L. P.
The white rose. Westcott, J.

WHITE SLAVERY. See Prostitution
The White Tower. Ullman, J. R.
The white witch. Goudge, E.
Whiteoak brothers: Jalna—1923. De La Roche, M.
Whiteoak harvest. De La Roche, M.
Whiteoak heritage. De La Roche, M.
Whiteoaks of Jalna. De La Roche, M.

WHITMAN, MARCUS
Allen, T. D. Doctor in buckskin

WHITMAN, NARCISSA (PRENTISS)
Allen, T. D. Doctor in buckskin

WHITTLING. See Wood carving
Who can replace a man? Aldiss, B. W.
Who lies here? Peters, E.
Who stole Sassi Manoon? Westlake, D. E.
Who took the gold away. Leggett, J.
Whose body? Sayers, D. L.
  In Sayers D. L. Dorothy L. Sayers omnibus v 1
Why call them back from heaven? Simak, C. D.
Wickford Point. Marquand, J. P.
Wide is the gate. Sinclair, U.
The wide net, and other stories. Welty, E.
  In Welty, E. Selected stories v2

WIDOWERS
Benedetti, M. The truce
Nathan, R. So love returns
Sagan, F. Bonjour tristesse
Street, J. The high calling
White, R. Elephant Hill
Wilson, A. Late call

WIDOWS
Abé, K. The woman in the dunes
Baldwin, F. The velvet hammer
Beagle, P. S. A fine and private place
Bjorn, T. F. Dear papa
Bowen, E. The heat of the day
Bridge, A. The malady in Madeira
Busch, N. The San Franciscans
Cela, C. J. Mrs Caldwell speaks to her son
Dick, R. A. The ghost and Mrs Muir
Du Maurier, D. My cousin Rachel
Duras, M. The sea wall
Elgin, M. A man from the mist
Faulkner, W. Soldiers pay
Gadda, C. E. Acquainted with grief
Giles, J. H. Savanna
Gilman, D. The amazing Mrs Pollifax
Gilman, D. The unexpected Mrs Pollifax
Harris, M. Trepleff
Heyer, G. Bath tangle
Hintze, N. A. You'll like my mother
Holt, V. The shivering sands
Howells, W. D. Indian summer
Mann, T. The black swan
Mauriac, F. Genetrix
  In Mauriac, F. A Mauriac reader p63-130
Michaels, B. Ammie, come home
Mishima, Y. Thirst for love
Moore, R. Candlemas Bay
Newby, P. H. Something to answer for
Priestley, J. B. The image men
Sharp, M. In pious memory
Sharp, M. The nutmeg tree
Sharp, M. Rosa
Stockton, F. R. The casting away of Mrs Lecks and Mrs Aleshine
  In Stockton, F. R. The storyteller's pack p275-351
Telfer, D. The night of the comet
Thirkell, A. The Brandons
Vining, E. G. I, Roberta
Wharton, E. The reef
White, N. G. The thorn tree
Williams, T. The Roman spring of Mrs Stone
Wilson, A. The middle age of Mrs Eliot
Wieland. Brown, C. B.
The wild ass's skin. Balzac, H. de.

WOMAN—Social and moral questions—*Cont.*
O'Hara, J. A rage to live
Richardson, S. Clarissa Harlowe
Richardson, S. Pamela
Stein, G. Three lives
Wharton, E. The custom of the country
Wharton E. The house of mirth
Whipple, M. The giant Joshua
Wilder, T. The woman of Andros
In Wilder, T. The Cabala, and The woman of Andros p135-203
In Wilder, T. A Thornton Wilder trio p245-309
Zola, E. L'assommoir
Zola, E. Nana
Zweig, A. Young woman of 1914

The woman destroyed. Beauvoir, S. de

The woman destroyed [novelette] Beauvoir, S. de
In Beauvoir, S. de. The woman destroyed p121-254

The woman from Sarajevo. Andric, I.

Woman in black. See Bentley, E. C. Trent's last case

The woman in the dunes. Abé, K.

The woman in white. Collins, W.

The woman of Andros. Wilder, T.
In Wilder, T. The Cabala, and The woman of Andros p135-203
In Wilder, T. A Thornton Wilder trio p245-309

A woman of my age. Bawden, N.

A woman of the people. Capps, B.

Woman of the Pharisees. Mauriac, F.
also in Mauriac, F. A Mauriac reader p433-610

Woman on the roof. Eberhart, M. G.

The woman who rode away, and other stories. Lawrence, D. H.

Woman with a sword. Noble, H.

A woman's life. Maupassant, G. de
In Maupassant, G. de. The portable Maupassant p377-631

Women and Thomas Harrow. Marquand, J. P.

WOMEN AS AUTHORS
Lurie, A. Real people

WOMEN AS JOURNALISTS
Charles-Roux, E. To forget Palermo
See also Journalists; Women as authors

WOMEN AS MINISTERS
West, J. Except for me and thee

WOMEN AS PHYSICIANS
Bottome, P. Private worlds
Sandoz, M. Miss Morissa, doctor of the gold trail

The women at Pine Creek. McKay, A.

WOMEN IN BUSINESS
Beauvoir, S. de. Les belles images
Bristow, G. This side of glory
Morley, C. Kitty Foyle
Stern, G. B. A deputy was king
In Stern, G. B. The matriarch chronicles v2

Women in love. Lawrence, D. H.

WOMEN IN POLITICS
Ferber, E. Cimarron
Noble, H. Woman with a sword

WOMEN'S CLUBS
Spark, M. The girls of slender means

The wonderful country. Lea, T.

The wonderful O. Thurber, J.

WOOD CARVING
Arnow, H. The dollmaker

WOODCHUCKS. See Marmots

The woodlanders. Hardy T.

The word for love. Burgess, A.

Work and play. Romains, J.
also in Romains, J. Work and play

The works of love. Morris, W.
In Morris, W. Wright Morris: a reader p53-192

World enough and time. Warren, R. P.

The world from below. Romains, J.

A world I never made. Farrell, J. T.

The world is not enough. Oldenbourg, Z.

The world is your adventure. Romains, J.
In Romains, J. The new day

World light. Laxness, H.

The world my wilderness. Macaulay, R.

A world of difference. Plagemann, B.

A world of great stories. Haydn, H. ed.

A world of profit. Auchincloss, L.

The world of Suzie Wong. Mason, R.

World over. Maugham, W. S.
In Maugham, W. S. Complete short stories v2

The world over. Wharton, E.
In Wharton, E. The collected short stories of Edith Wharton v2 p741-871

WORLD POLITICS
Habe, H. The mission
See also Politics

The world, the flesh, and Father Smith. Marshall, B.

A world to win. Sinclair, U.

WORLD WAR, 1914-1918. See European War, 1914-1918

WORLD WAR I. See European War, 1914-1918

WORLD WAR, 1939-1945
Böll, H. Enter and exit
In Böll, H. Absent without leave: two novellas p91-148
Bourjaily, V. The end of my life
Céline. L. F. Castle to castle
Eastlake, W. Castle keep
Fenton, C. A. ed. The best short stories of World War II
Frankau, P. Over the mountains
Garth, D. Watch on the bridge
Killens, J. O. And then we heard the thunder
Lind, J. Landscape in concrete
MacInnes, H. Assignment: suspense
Mason, F. V. ed. American men at arms
Myrer, A. Once an eagle
Nathanson, E. M. The dirty dozen
Plievier, T. Stalingrad
Sinclair, U. Dragon harvest
Sinclair, U. O shepherd, speak!
Sinclair, U. One clear call
Sinclair, U. Presidential mission
Sinclair, U. A world to win
Steinbeck, J. The moon is down
Van der Post, L. The seed and the sower
Vonnegut, K. Mother night
Waugh, E. The end of the battle
Waugh, E. Men at arms
Waugh, E. Officers and gentlemen
Westheimer, D. Song of the young sentry
Wiseman, T. The quick and the dead
Yates, R. A special providence

Aerial operations
Heller, J. Catch-22
Hersey, J. The war lover
Vonnegut, K. Slaughterhouse-five

Africa, South
Lessing, D. Landlocked
In Lessing, D. Children of violence v4
Lessing, D. A ripple from the storm
In Lessing, D. Children of violence v3

Africa, West
Catto, M. Murphy's war

Atlantic Ocean
Forester, C. S. The good shepherd
MacLean, A. H.M.S. Ulysses
Monsarrat, N. The cruel sea

Atrocities
Hersey, J. The wall
Kuznetsov, A. Babi Yar
Wiesel, E. The town beyond the wall

Belgium
Hulme, K. The nun's story

Children
Berto, G. The sky is red

China
Buck, P. S. The promise
White, T. H. The mountain road

Czechoslovak Republic
Fuks, L. Mr Theodore Mundstock

Denmark
Arnold, E. A night of watching

WORLD WAR, 1939-1945—*Continued*

Submarine operations
See World War, 1939-1945—Naval operations—Submarine

Sumatra
Cleary, J. The long pursuit

Underground movements
Arnold, E. A night of watching
Kelly, M. Assault
Kirst, H. H. Soldiers' revolt
Mandel, P. The Black Ship

United States
Caldwell, T. The final hour
Charyn, J. American scrapbook
Cozzens, J. G. Guard of honor
Kaufmann, M. S. Remember me to God

Vienna
Gainham, S. Night falls on the city

Yugoslavia
Andrić, I. Zeko
In Andrić, I. The vizier's elephant p131-247
MacLean, A. Force 10 from Navarone

WORLD WAR II. See World War, 1939-1945
World's end. Sinclair, U.
World's end [series] See Lanny Budd [series]
World's great tales of the sea. McFee, W. ed.
The world's illusion. Wassermann, J.
The worlds of Clifford Simak. Simak, C. D.
A wreath for Rivera. Marsh, N.
In Marsh, N. Three-act special p5-192
A wreath for Udomo. Abrahams, P.
The wreck of the Mary Deare. Innes, H.
The wrecker. Stevenson, R. L.
Wright Morris: a reader. Morris, W.
The Wrightsville heirs. Queen, E.
In Queen, E. Queens full p73-105
Wrightsville murders. Queen, E.
WRITERS. See Authors
WRITERS' WORKSHOPS. See Authors' conferences
WU HOU, DOWAGER EMPRESS OF CHINA
Lin, Yutang, ed. Lady Wu
Wuthering Heights. Brontë, E.
Wyatt's hurricane. Bagley, D.
WYCLIFITES. See Lollards
WYNDHAM, SIR RICHARD
Heyer, G. The Corinthian
WYOMING

19th century
Gulick, B. Liveliest town in the West
Schaefer, J. Shane

20th century
James, W. Sand
MacInnes, H. Rest and Be Thankful

X

The XYZ murders. Queen, E.
XAVIER, SAINT FRANCIS. See Francis Xavier, Saint
The Xavier affair. Fish, R. L.
XHOSA. See Africa—Native races
Xingu. Wharton, E.
In Wharton, E. The collected short stories of Edith Wharton v2 p207-356

Y

YACHTS AND YACHTING. See Sailing vessels
YALE UNIVERSITY
Leggett, J. Who took the gold away
YANGTZE RIVER
Hersey, J. A single pebble

YANKEE BASEBALL TEAM. See New York. Baseball Club (American League)
The Yankee from Tennessee. Gerson, N. B.
Yankee stranger. Thane, E.
YAQUI INDIANS
Sorensen, V. The proper gods
The year of the horsetails. Tapsell, R. F.
The year the Yankees lost the pennant. Wallop, D.
The years. Woolf, V.
Years of grace. Barnes, M. A.
The yellow brick road. Cadell, E.
Yellow flowers in the antipodean room. Frame, J.
The yellow gold of Tiryns. Osborne, H.
YOKAHAMA. See Japan—Yokahama
YORKSHIRE. See England, Provincial and rural—Yorkshire
YORKSHIRE DIALECT. See Dialect stories—English—Yorkshire
Yoshe Kalb. Singer, I. J.
You can't go home again. Wolfe, T.
You know me, Al. Lardner, R.
You must know everything. Babel, I.
You only live twice. Fleming, I.
You'll like my mother. Hintze, N. A.
YOUNG, BRIGHAM
Fisher, V. Children of God
Young Ames. Edmonds, W. D.
Young Bess. Irwin, M.
The young Caesar. Warner, R.
The young Elizabeth. Letton, J.
Young Henry of Navarre. Mann, H.
Young Hornblower. Forester, C. S.
Young Joseph. Mann, T.
In Costain, T. B. comp. Twelve short novels p 1-105
In Mann, T. Joseph and his brothers p261-444
The young lions. Shaw, I.
Young Lonigan. Farrell, J. T.
also in Farrell, J. T. Studs Lonigan v 1
Young man with a horn. Baker, D.
The young manhood of Studs Lonigan. Farrell, J. T.
also in Farrell, J. T. Studs Lonigan v2
YOUNG MEN. See Youth
Young Renny (Jalna-1906) De La Roche, M.
Young titan. Mason, F. V.
Young woman of 1914. Zweig, A.
Youngblood. Killens, J. O.
Youngblood Hawke. Wouk, H.
YOUNGER GENERATION. See Youth
YOUTH
Baker, E. The penny wars
Bradford, R. Red sky at morning
Christopher, J. Pendulum
Colette. Chéri
In Colette. Chéri, and The last of Chéri
In Colette. 7 by Colette v2 p 1-154
In Colette. Six novels p411-534
Colette. The ripening seed
Cronin, A. J. A song of sixpence
Donleavy, J. P. The beastly beatitudes of Balthazar B
Dostoevsky, F. A raw youth
Fitzgerald, F. S. The beautiful and damned
Fitzgerald, F. S. This side of paradise
Galsworthy, J. The white monkey
In Galsworthy, J. A modern comedy p3-248
Guareschi, G. Don Camillo meets the flower children
Head, A. Mr and Mrs Bo Jo Jones
Hesse, H. Demian, the story of Emil Sinclair's youth
Irving, J. Setting free the bears
Knowles, J. Phineas
Lehmann, R. Dusty answer
Mannes, M. They
Mauriac, F. A kiss for the leper
In Mauriac, F. A Mauriac reader p3-60
Mishima, Y. The sound of waves
Nichols, J. The sterile cuckoo
Robinson, R. Eagle in the air

DIRECTORY OF PUBLISHERS AND DISTRIBUTORS

AMS Press. AMS Press, 56 E 13th St, New York, N.Y. 10003
Abelard-Schuman. Abelard-Schuman, 6 W 57th St, New York, N.Y. 10019
Abingdon. Abingdon Press, Hdqrs, 201 8th Av, S, Nashville, Tenn. 37203
Appleton. Appleton-Century-Crofts, 440 Park Av, S, New York, N.Y. 10016
Arkham House. Arkham House, Sauk City, Wis. 53583
Arno Press. Arno Press, Inc, 330 Madison Av, New York, N.Y. 10017
Associated Booksellers. Associated Booksellers, 1582 Post Rd, Westport, Conn. 06880
Astor-Honor. Astor-Honor, Inc, 26 E 42d St, New York, N.Y. 10017
Atheneum Pubs. Atheneum Publishers, 122 E 42d St, New York, N.Y. 10017

Ballantine. Ballantine Books, Inc, 101 5th Av, New York, N.Y. 10003
Barnes, A.S. A. S. Barnes & Company, Box 421, Cranbury, N.J. 08512
Barnes & Noble. Barnes & Noble, Inc, 105 5th Av, New York, N.Y. 10003
Bentley. Robert Bentley, Inc, 872 Massachusetts Av, Cambridge, Mass. 02139
Berg. Norman S. Berg, Sallanraa, Dunwoody, Ga. 30338
Binfords. Binfords & Mort, Publishers, 2505 S.E. 11th Av, Portland, Ore. 97202
Black. Walter J. Black, Inc, Flower Hill, Roslyn, N.Y. 11576
Blue Ribbon Bks. (N Y) See Garden City Bks.
Bobbs. Bobbs-Merrill Company, Inc, 4300 W 62d St, Indianapolis, Ind. 46206
Boni. Albert & Charles Boni, Inc, 5 Union Sq, New York, N.Y. 10011
Boni & Liveright. See Liveright
Bramhall House. See Potter, C.N.
Braziller. George Braziller, Inc, 1 Park Av, New York, N.Y. 10016
Brentano's. Brentano's Inc, 586 5th Av, New York, N.Y. 10019
British Bk. Centre. The British Book Centre, Inc, 996 Lexington Av, New York, N.Y. 10017
Burt. See Random House

Capricorn Bks. See Putnam
Caxton Ptrs. Caxton Printers, Ltd, Caldwell, Idaho 83605
Century. See Appleton
Chilton Bks. See Chilton Co.
Chilton Co. Chilton Book Company (Chilton Books) 401 Walnut St, Philadelphia, Pa. 19106
Collier Bks. Collier Books, 60 5th Av, New York, N.Y. 10011
Collins. William Collins Sons & Company, Ltd. (Collins Clear-Type Press) 215 Park Av, S, New York, N.Y. 10003
Cooper Sq. Cooper Square Publishers, Inc, 59 4th Av, New York, N.Y. 10003
Cornell Univ. Press. Cornell University Press, 124 Roberts Pl, Ithaca, N.Y. 14850
Covici. See Crown
Coward-McCann. Coward-McCann, Inc, 200 Madison Av, New York, N.Y. 10016
Creative Age. See Farrar, Straus
Criterion Bks. Criterion Books, Inc, 6 W 57th St, New York, N.Y. 10019
Crowell. Thomas Y. Crowell Company, 201 Park Av, S, New York, N.Y. 10003
Crown. Crown Publishers, Inc, 419 Park Av, S, New York, N.Y. 10016

Day. The John Day Company, 62 W 45th St, New York, N.Y. 10036
Delacorte Press. See Dial Press
Devin-Adair. Devin-Adair Company, 23 E 26th St, New York, N.Y. 10010
Dial Press. The Dial Press, Inc. 750 3d Av, New York, N.Y. 10017
Dodd. Dodd, Mead & Company, Inc, 79 Madison Av, New York, N.Y. 10016
Donohue. M. A. Donohue & Company, 711 S Dearborn St, Chicago, Ill. 60605
Doran. See Doubleday

Doubleday. Doubleday & Company, Inc, 277 Park Av, New York, N.Y. 10017
Dover. Dover Publications, Inc, 180 Varick St, New York, N.Y. 10014
Duell. Duell, Sloan & Pearce, Inc, 60 E 42d St, New York, N.Y. 10017
Dufour. Dufour Editions, Chester Springs, Pa. 19425
Dutton. E. P. Dutton & Company, Inc, 201 Park Av, S, New York, N.Y. 10003

Eriksson. Paul S. Eriksson, Inc, 119 W 57th St, New York, N.Y. 10019
Evans, M.&Co. M. Evans & Company, Inc, 216 E 49th St, New York, N.Y. 10017

Fairleigh Dickinson Univ. Press. Fairleigh Dickinson University Press, Box 421, Cranbury, N.J. 08512
Farrar. See Holt
Farrar, Straus. Farrar, Straus & Giroux, Inc, 19 Union Sq, W, New York, N.Y. 10003
Fell. Frederick Fell, Inc, 386 Park Av, S, New York, N.Y. 10016
Four Winds. The Four Winds Press, 50 W 44th St, New York, N.Y. 10036
Frommer, A. Arthur Frommer, Inc, 70 5th Av, New York, N.Y. 10011
Frommer-Pasmantier. See Frommer, A.
Funk. Funk & Wagnalls Company, Inc, 380 Madison Av, New York, N.Y. 10017

Garden City Bks. Garden City Books, 277 Park Av, New York, N.Y. 10017
Garden City Pub. Co. See Garden City Bks.
Gnome Press. Gnome Press, Box 161, Hicksville, New York, N.Y. 11802
Greenberg. See Chilton Co.
Greenwood Press. Greenwood Press, Inc, 51 Riverside Av, Westport, Conn. 06880
Gregg Press, Inc. The Gregg Press, Inc, 121 Pleasant Av, Upper Saddle River, N.J. 07458
Grosset. Grosset & Dunlap, Inc, 51 Madison Av, New York, N.Y. 10010
Grove. Grove Press, Inc, 214 Mercer St, New York, N.Y. 10012

Hanover House. See Doubleday
Harcourt. Harcourt Brace Jovanovich, Inc, 757 3d Av, New York, N.Y. 10017
Harper. Harper & Row, Publishers, 49 E 33d St, New York, N.Y. 10016
Harvard Univ. Press. Harvard University Press, Publishing Department (Belknap Press) Kittredge Hall, 79 Garden St, Cambridge, Mass. 02138
Hawthorn Bks. Hawthorn Books, Inc, 70 5th Av, New York, N.Y. 10011
Hendricks House. Hendricks House, Inc, 103 Park Av, New York, N.Y. 10017
Heritage. Heritage Press, 207 W 25th St, New York, N.Y. 10001
Hill & Wang. Hill & Wang, Inc, 72 5th Av, New York, N.Y. 10011
Holt. Holt, Rinehart & Winston, Inc, 383 Madison Av, New York, N.Y. 10017
Houghton. Houghton Mifflin Company (Riverside Press, Cambridge) 2 Park St, Boston, Mass. 02107
Huebsch, B.W. See Viking

Ind. Univ. Press. Indiana University Press, 10th & Morton Sts, Bloomington, Ind. 47401
Int. Publications. International Publications Service, 303 Park Av, S, New York, N.Y. 10010

Jewish Pub. Jewish Publication Society of America, 222 N 15th St, Philadelphia, Pa. 19102

Kenedy. P. J. Kenedy & Sons, Publishers, 866 3d Av, New York, N.Y. 10022
Knopf. Alfred A. Knopf, Inc, 201 E 50th St, New York, N.Y. 10022
Kodansha. Kodansha International/USA, Ltd, 577 College Av, Palo Alto, Calif. 94306

Lane. See Dodd
Lanewood Press. Lanewood Press, Inc, 739 Boylston St, Boston, Mass. 02116
La. State Univ. Press. Louisiana State University Press, University Station, Baton Rouge, La. 70803
Lippincott. J. B. Lippincott Company, E Washington Sq, Philadelphia, Pa. 19105
Literature House. See Gregg Press, Inc.
Little. Little, Brown & Company, 34 Beacon St, Boston, Mass. 02106
Liveright. Liveright Publishing Corporation, 386 Park Av, S, New York, N.Y. 10016

McDowell, Obolensky. See Astor-Honor
McGraw. McGraw-Hill Book Company, Inc, 330 W 42d St, New York, N.Y. 10036
McKay. David McKay Company, Inc, Publishers, 750 3d Av, New York, N.Y. 10017
Macmillan (N Y) The Macmillan Company, Publishers, 866 3d Av, New York, N.Y. 10022
Macrae Smith Co. Macrae Smith Company, Lewis Tower Bldg, 225 S 15th St, Philadelphia, Pa. 19102
Meredith. Meredith Press, 1716 Locust St, Des Moines, Iowa 50303
Messner. See Simon & Schuster
Mich. State Univ. Press. The Michigan State University Press, Box 550, East Lansing, Mich. 48823
Mill. M. S. Mill Company, Inc, 105 Madison Av, New York, N.Y. 10016
Modern Lib. Modern Library, Inc, 201 E 50th St, New York, N.Y. 10022
Moffat. See Dodd
Morrow. William Morrow & Company, Inc, Publishers, 105 Madison Av, New York, N.Y. 10016
Mycroft & Moran. See Arkham House

N.Y. Graphic. New York Graphic Society Publishers, Ltd, 140 Greenwich Av, Greenwich, Conn. 06830
N.Y. Univ. Press. New York University Press, Washington Sq, New York, N.Y. 10003
Nelson. Thomas Nelson & Sons, Copewood & Davis Sts, Camden, N.J. 08103
New Am. Lib. The New American Library of World Literature, Inc, 1301 Av. of the Americas, New York, N.Y. 10019
New Directions. New Directions, 333 Av. of the Americas, New York, N.Y. 10014
Noonday. The Noonday Press, 19 Union Sq, W, New York, N.Y. 10003
Northwestern Univ. Press, Northwestern University Press, 1735 Benson Av, Evanston, Ill. 60201
Norton. W. W. Norton & Company, Inc, Publishers, 55 5th Av, New York, N.Y. 10003

Obolensky. See Astor-Honor
Ohio Univ. Press. Ohio University Press, Athens, Ohio 45701
Orion. Orion Press, Inc, 150 E 35th St, New York, N.Y. 10016
Osgood, J.R. See Houghton
Oxford. Oxford University Press, Inc, 200 Madison Av, New York, N.Y. 10016

Pantheon Bks. Pantheon Books, Inc, 201 E 50th St, New York, N.Y. 10022
Pellegrini & Cudahy. See Farrar, Straus
Peter Pauper. Peter Pauper Press, 629 N McQuesten Pkwy, Mt Vernon, N.Y. 10552
Phaedra Pubs. Phaedra Publishers, Inc, 156 5th Av, New York, N.Y. 10010
Phillips. S. G. Phillips, Inc, 305 W 86th St, New York, N.Y. 10024
Platt. The Platt & Munk Company, Inc, 1055 Bronx River Av, Bronx, N.Y. 10472

Playboy Press. Playboy Press, 919 N Michigan Av, Chicago, Ill. 60611
Potter, C.N. Clarkson N. Potter, Inc, Publisher, 419 Park Av, S, New York, N.Y. 10016
Praeger. Frederick A. Praeger, Inc, Publishers, 111 4th Av, New York, N.Y. 10003
Prentice-Hall. Prentice-Hall, Inc, Route 9W, Englewood Cliffs, N.J. 07632
Press of Case Western Reserve Univ. The Press of Case Western Reserve University, Frank Adgate Quail Bldg, Cleveland, Ohio 44106
Principia Press of Trinity Univ. See Trinity Univ. Press
Putnam. G. P. Putnam's Sons, 200 Madison Av, New York, N.Y. 10016

Quadrangle Bks. Quadrangle Books, Inc, 180 N Wacker Dr, Chicago, Ill. 60606

Random House. Random House, Inc, 201 E 50th St, New York, N.Y. 10022
Regnery. Henry Regnery Company, 114 W Illinois St, Chicago, Ill. 60610
Reprint House International. Reprint House International, 200 Park Av, Suite 303 E, New York, N.Y. 10017
Reynal. See Harcourt
Reynal & Co. See Morrow
Richard W. Baron Pub. Co. Richard W. Baron Publishing Company, Inc, 243A E 49th St, New York, N.Y. 10017
Rinehart. See Holt
Ronald. The Ronald Publishing Company, 79 Madison Av, New York, N.Y. 10016
Rutgers Univ. Press. Rutgers University Press, 30 College Av, New Brunswick, N.J. 08903

Salem Press. Salem Press, Inc, 475 5th Av, New York, N.Y. 10017
Schocken. Schocken Books, Inc, 67 Park Av, New York, N.Y. 10016
Scholarly Press. Scholarly Press, Inc, 22929 Industrial Dr, E, St. Clair Shores, Mich. 48080
Scribner. Charles Scribner's Sons, 597 5th Av, New York, N.Y. 10017
Seltzer, T. See Boni
Shasta Pubs. Shasta Publishers, 5525 S Blackstone St, Chicago, Ill. 60637
Sheed. Sheed & Ward, Inc, 64 University Pl, New York, N.Y. 10003
Sherbourne. Sherbourne Press, 1640 S La Cienega Blvd, Los Angeles, Calif. 90035
Simon & Schuster. Simon & Schuster, Inc. Publishers, 630 5th Av, New York, N.Y. 10020
Sloane. William Sloane Associates, Inc. 425 Park Av, S, New York, N.Y. 10016
Smith, H. See Random House
Smith, P. Peter Smith, 6 Lexington Av, Magnolia, Mass. 01930
Southern Ill. Univ. Press. Southern Illinois University Press, Carbondale, Ill. 62901
St Martins. St Martin's Press, Inc, 175 5th Av, New York, N.Y. 10010
Stackpole Co. Stackpole company (Stackpole Bks) Cameron & Kelker Sts, Harrisburg, Pa. 17105
Stein & Day. Stein & Day Publishers, 7 E 48th St, New York, N.Y. 10017
Stokes. See Lippincott
Swallow Press. Swallow Press, Inc, 1138 S Wabash Av, Chicago, Ill. 60605

Taplinger. Taplinger Publishing Company, Inc, 29 E 10th St, New York, N.Y. 10003
Ticknor, See Houghton
Transatlantic. Transatlantic Arts, Inc, 565 5th Av, New York, N.Y. 10017
Translation Pub. Translation Publishing Company, Inc, P.O. Box 34, Eastchester, N.Y. 10709
Trident Press. See Simon & Schuster
Trinity Univ. Press. Trinity University Press, Trinity Episcopal Church, 708 Bethlehem Pike, Ambler, Pa. 19002
Tuttle. Charles E. Tuttle Company, Inc, 28-30 Main St, Rutland, Vt. 05701

Ungar. Frederick Ungar Publishing Company, 250 Park Av. S, New York, N.Y. 10003
Univ. of Calif. Press. University of California Press, 2223 Fulton St, Berkeley, Calif, 94720
Univ. of Mich. Press. Universiy of Michigan Press, 615 E University Av, Ann Arbor, Mich. 48106
Univ. of Neb. Press. University of Nebraska Press, 901 N 17th St, Lincoln, Neb. 68508
Univ. of Tex. Press. University of Texas Press, Box 7819, Austin, Tex. 78712
Univ. of Wis. Press. The University of Wisconsin Press, Box 1379, Madison, Wis. 53701

Vanguard. The Vanguard Press, Inc, 424 Madison Av, New York, N.Y. 10017
Van Nostrand. See Van Nostrand-Reinhold
Van Nostrand-Reinhold. Van Nostrand-Reinhold Company, 450 W 33d St, New York, N.Y. 10001
Viking. The Viking Press, Inc, 625 Madison Av, New York, N.Y. 10022
Vintage. Vintage Books, Inc, 201 E 50th St, New York, N.Y. 10022

Walker & Co. Walker & Company, 720 5th Av, New York, N.Y. 10019
Warne. Frederick Warne & Company, Inc, 101 5th Av, New York, N.Y. 10003
Washburn. Ives Washburn, Inc, 750 3d Av, New York, N.Y. 10017
Washington Sq. Press. See Simon & Schuster
Watts, F. Franklin Watts, Inc, 575 Lexington Av, New York, N.Y. 10022
Westminster Press. Westminster Press (Westminster Bk. Stores) Room 908, Witherspoon Bldg, Walnut & Juniper Sts, Philadelphia, Pa. 19107
Winston. See Holt
World Pub. The World Publishing Company, 2231 W 110th St, Cleveland, Ohio 44102

Yoseloff. Thomas Yoseloff, Inc, Publishers, Box 421, Cranbury, N.J. 08512

Ziff-Davis. Ziff-Davis Publishing Co, 1 Park Av, New York, N.Y. 10016
Zondervan. Zondervan Publishing House, 1415 Lake Dr, S.E. Grand Rapids, Mich. 49506

5699